Twenty-Third Edition
Blue Book
of Gun Values™
by S.P. Fjestad

$34.95
Publisher's Softcover
Suggested List Price

Publisher's Limited
Edition Hardcover
Suggested List Price - $49.95

Twenty-Third Edition
Blue Book of Gun Values ™

Publisher's Note:

This book is the result of nonstop and continuos firearms research obtained by attending and/or participating in trade shows, gun shows, auctions, and also communicating with contributing editors, gun dealers, collectors, company historians, and other knowledgeable industry professionals worldwide each year. This book represents an analysis of prices for which collectible firearms have actually been selling during that period at an average retail level. Although every reasonable effort has been made to compile an accurate and reliable guide, gun prices may vary significantly (especially auction prices) depending on such factors as the locality of the sale, the number of sales we were able to consider, and economic conditions. Accordingly, no representation can be made that the guns listed may be bought or sold at prices indicated, nor shall the author or publisher be responsible for any error made in compiling and recording such prices and related information.

Blue Book Publications, Inc.
8009 34th Avenue South, Suite 175
Minneapolis, MN 55425 U.S.A.

Orders Only: 800-877-4867
Phone No.: 952-854-5229
Fax No.: 952-853-1486
Email: bluebook@bluebookinc.com
Website/homepage: http://www.bluebookinc.com

Published and printed in the United States of America

ISBN No. 1-886768-31-5

Library of Congress ISSN number - 1524-6043

TABLE OF CONTENTS

ABOUT THE COVER

This year's cover features two of America's finest shotguns, a pre-WWII Parker Brothers Invincible Grade (top) and a recently manufactured A. Galazan O/U.

In 1930, the beginning of the Great Depression, Parker Brothers offered the Invincible Grade for sale at $1,250, and claimed it to be the finest, and most expensive shotgun ever manufactured and sold in America. This was at the same time a plain Jane Winchester Model 12 retailed for under $40. Note the extremely tight scroll engraving, single gold inlay (per side), scalloped shoulders, and elaborate stock carving and checkering. Only three were special ordered and custom built, and all three are well preserved today. These surviving specimens are truly the Stradivarius' of this golden age of classic shotgun building. Robert E. Petersen owns two of the Parker Invincibles (including the one of the cover), and the third belongs to Anthony Galazan. This cover Parker can currently be seen at the National Firearms Museum, located in Fairfax, VA.

Anthony Galazan, owner of Connecticut Shotgun Manufacturing Company, located New Britain, CT, manufactures best quality shotguns, in both SxS and O/U configurations. The cover gun (bottom) features an extremely low profile, with best mechanical design and English type metal forearm reinforcement. Each gun requires over 1,000 man hours to complete, and the base price starts at $38,000, including English style rose and scroll engraving. They are available in all gauges, and frames are individually sized for each gauge. With optional engraving coverage like the cover gun, the final price can easily hit $90,000+.

This exquisite A. Galazan O/U was elegantly engraved by renowned Italian engraving firm G.S. Pedretti, and elaborately inlaid with 24 Kt. gold cattails, each of which took 20 minutes. Note the realistic Bulino style, razor sharp hunting images, in addition to the delicate Italian filigree engraving on the front of the frame and forearm. The G.S. Pedretti firm consists of Giancarlo (father), who engraved for both Pietro Beretta and Abbiatico, his son Stefano Pedretti, in addition to several other in-house engravers. These 3-4 people typically engrave 11-12 guns annually, mostly by arranged contracts, and a few knives. Clients include James Purdey & Sons, David McKay Brown, Piotti, Fabbri, and A. Galazan.

Additionally, many of Robert E. Petersen's personal effects also share the cover, including hunting pictures, licenses and stamps, NRA Life membership card, and several older photos of Robert and his wife Margie. Note the 1984 Olympics pin on the bottom left - Petersen was very influential for the U.S. shooting venue, and turned a near disaster around into a huge success. Two of Petersen's most successful magazines, *Guns & Ammo* and *Sports Afield* are also pictured, which continue to inform outdoor enthusiasts worldwide.

Cover design and layout – Thomas D. Heller & S.P. Fjestad
Production Manager – Thomas D. Heller
Cover photography – Anthony Galazan, props courtesy of Robert E. Petersen
Cover printing – LeHigh Press located in Pennsauken, New Jersey
Text printing – Sandy Rehmert & crew at Von Hoffman Graphics, located in Owensville, MO

23rd Edition credits:
Manuscript Production – Cassandra Faulkner
Art Dept. – Thomas D. Heller & Clint Schmidt
Research & Contribution Coordinator – Associate Editor, John Allen
Proofing - John Allen, Heather Mohr, Cassandra Faulkner, Rachel Klinger, and David Kosowski
IGH Messenger Delivery Service - Beth Marthaler & the Taurus Turnaround

GENERAL INFORMATION

While many of you have probably dealt with our company for years, it may be helpful for you to know a little bit more about our operation, including information on how to contact us regarding our various titles, software programs, and other informational services.

Blue Book Publications, Inc. contact information:
Mailing Address:
Blue Book Publications, Inc.
8009 34th Avenue South, Suite 175
Minneapolis, MN 55425   U.S.A.
Phone No. 952-854-5229 • Orders Only (domestic and Canada): 800-877-4867
Fax No. 952-853-1486 (available 24 hours a day)
Website: http://www.bluebookinc.com
E-Mail: bluebook@bluebookinc.com - we check our email at 9am, 12pm, and 3:30pm M-F
(excluding major U.S. holidays). Please refer to individual email addresses listed below with phone extension numbers.

To find out the latest information on our products (including availability and pricing) and related consumer services, and up-to-date industry information (trade show recaps with photos/captions, upcoming events, feature articles, etc.), please check our web site, as it is updated on a regular basis. Surf us - you'll have fun!

Since our phone system is equipped with voice mail, you may also wish to know extension numbers which have been provided below:

Ext. No.: 11 - Tom Stock (toms@bluebookinc.com)
Ext. No.: 12 - Zach Fjestad (zachf@bluebookinc.com)
Ext. No.: 13 - S.P. Fjestad (stevef@bluebookinc.com)
Ext. No.: 14 - Honored Guest
Ext. No.: 15 - Thomas D. Heller (tomh@bluebookinc.com)
Ext. No.: 16 - John Allen (johna@bluebookinc.com)
Ext. No.: 17 - Honored Guest
Ext. No.: 18 - Katie Sandin (katies@bluebookinc.com)
Ext. No.: 19 - Cassandra Faulkner (cassandraf@bluebookinc.com)
Ext. No.: 20 - Clint Schmidt (clints@bluebookinc.com)
Ext. No.: 22 - Heather Mohr (heatherm@bluebookinc.com)
Ext. No.: 25 - Beth Marthaler (bethm@bluebookinc.com)

Office hours are: 8:30am - 5:00pm CST, Monday - Friday.

Additionally, an after hours answering service is available for ordering. All orders are processed within 24 hours of receiving them, assuming payment and order information is correct. Depending on the product, we typically ship either UPS, 4th Class, or Priority Mail. Expedited shipping services are also available both domestically and internationally for an additional charge. Please contact us directly for an expedited shipping quotation, especially overseas.

All correspondence regarding technical information/values on guns or guitars, and is answered in a FIFO (first in, first out) system. That means that letters, faxes, and email are answered in the order in which they are received, even though some people think that their emails take preference over everything else. Please refer to our Gun Questions/PCS Program on pages 52-53 for more information on telephone questions regarding firearms.

GENERAL INFORMATION

As this edition goes to press, the following titles/products are currently available, unless otherwise specified:
Online subscriptions and individual downloading services for the *Blue Book of Gun Values*, *Blue Book of Modern Black Powder Values*, *Blue Book of Airguns*, *Blue Book of Electric Guitars*, and *Blue Book of Acoustic Guitars*.
Blue Book of Gun Values, 23rd Edition by S.P. Fjestad (ISBN No. 1-886768-31-5 1,680 pages)
Colt Black Powder Reproductions & Replicas by Dennis Adler (ISBN: 1-886768-11-0)
2nd Ed. *Blue Book of Modern Black Powder Values* by Dennis Adler (ISBN: 1-886768-32-3)
2nd Ed. *Blue Book of Airguns* by Dr. Robert Beeman & John Allen (ISBN 1-886768-30-7, available May, 2002)
Blue Book of Electric Guitars, 7th Edition, edited by S.P. Fjestad (ISBN 1-886768-26-9)
Blue Book of Acoustic Guitars, 7th Edition, edited by S.P. Fjestad (ISBN 1-886768-25-0)
Blue Book of Guitars **CD-ROM** (ISBN: 1-886768-27-7)
Blue Book of Pool Cues, 2nd Edition, by Brad Simpson, edited by Victor Stein and Paul Rubino (ISBN: 1-886768-12-9)

Tear-out order forms have also been provided for the our online e-commerce services, as well as the *Blue Book of Gun Values*, *Blue Book of Airguns*, and *Blue Book of Modern Black Powder Values*. If you would like to get more information about any of the above publications/products, simply check our web site.

We would like to thank all of you for your business in the past - you are the reason(s) we are successful. Our goal remains the same - to give you the best products, the most accurate and up-to-date information for the money, and the highest level of customer service available in today's marketplace. If something's right, tell the world over time. If something's wrong, please tell us immediately - we'll make it right.

FACES BEHIND THE PHONE

Many of you may want to know what the person on the other end of the telephone/fax/email looks like, so here are the faces that go with the voices.

S.P. Fjestad – Author, Editor & Publisher

John Allen – Author, Associate Editor & Firearms Researcher

Cassandra Faulkner – Executive Assistant Editor

FACES BEHIND THE PHONE

Tom Stock - CFO

Tom Heller – Art Director

Beth Marthaler – Operations Manager

Zach Fjestad – Author & Guitar Researcher

Katie Sandin - Operations

Heather Mohr - Operations

Clint Schmidt – Assistant Art Director

David Kosowski, Favorite Part-Time Underpaid Spearchucker!

ACKNOWLEDGEMENTS

Undoubtedly, one of the most frequently asked questions received over the years is, "How do you come up with the prices for the book?". A simple question, and a difficult answer. Almost all the currently manufactured firearms values and information are researched by John Allen & myself. On many collectible antique and discontinued guns, the professionals listed below typically specialize within a certain company/trademark/configuration, and their expertise and knowledge obtained and shared within these specific areas has helped this publication tremendously over the years. These people are truly experts within their field(s) and deserve much of the credit on older makes/models. Despite using a PC since 1982 in writing each new manuscript, this scribe is proud to say that not once has a computer set a price in this text. Each new *Blue Book of Gun Values*™ is pretty much a fresh batch of cookies. While the publishing recipe stays the same, each year the ingredients get better. Very few other resources are used, since there seems to be nothing else that's as up-to-date or useful. Every new entry/revision is put in knowing that the courtroom could be the final stop if it's wrong. Once again, the people listed below are to be thanked for their contributions, and more importantly, sharing their knowledge. Without them, this new 23rd Edition would have been a lot thinner, and you wouldn't be as informed.

Leonardo M. Antaris, M.D.
J.L. Spinks
Steve Engleson
LeRoy Merz
Earl Sheehan, Jr.
David Kosowski
James W. Whitcomb
Richard Spurzem
Don "Duck" Combs
Robert Rayburn
Jim Supica
Lynn Oliver
Jim King
Glen Jenson & Chip Hewlett of Browning
Anthony Vanderlinden & the Browning Collectors Association
Kevin Cherry
Gurney Brown
Carol and the late Don Wilkerson
Charles Layson
Bertram O'Neill, Jr.
Bob Ball
Dr. Robert & Toshika Beeman (Honorary)
Lowell Pauli
Dennis Adler
John Kopec
Joe Gillenwater
John T. Callahan
Charles E. Carder
Charlie Price
Fred Sweeney
Jack Heath - Remington historian
James A. Buelow
John Lacy
Richard Machniak

Roy Marcot
Randy Shuman
David Avery, D.D.S.
John Gyde
J.B. Wood
William Drollinger
Dwight Van Brunt from Kimber
Karl Lippard - First National Gun Banque
Kathleen Hoyt - Colt historian
R.L. Wilson
Brad Taylor
Roy Jinks - S&W historian
Joyce Gentilo from Beretta
Robert (Doc) Adelman a.k.a., the "mad" rocket scientist
Daniel Sheil, Jr.
Paul Warden from America Remembers
Doug Turnbull
Jim Spacek
Joe Prather from Griffin & Howe
Edmund Goldshinsky of Marlin Firearms
Stephen Lamboy from Ithaca Classic Doubles
Pierangelo Pedersoli
Luciano & Paolo Amadi
Tullio Fabbri
The Pietta family
Suzanne Webb & Giacomo of Uberti
Elena Micheli
Creative Art
William R. Mook
T. Rees Day
Thad Scott
Larry "Iron" Orr
Jon Vander Bloomen

Mims Reed
Bill Allen
George C. Carlson
Dave Wills
Charles Semmer
Thomas Mintner
Phil Schreier III from the NFM
Mike Weatherby
Major Mark Rendina
David M. Rachwal
Buck Dickinson
Rick Crosier
W.H. Fluitt
Alvin Olson
Roger Morris
Jim Jasken
Robert Greenleaf
Harrison Carroll
Hal Hamilton
John Stimson, Jr.
W. R. Powell
Richard Rohal
Don Anderson
James Goergen
Tor Karstenson
Woody Woodall
Byron Price, Karen Gibbons, Waddy Culvert,
Simeon Stoddard, Paul Fees, & crew at the
Buffalo Bill Historical Center in Cody, WY
F.E. "Pete" Wall
David Noll

Dean Rinehart
Eric M. Larson
Val Sr. & Val Forgett III of Navy Arms
A.O. Salvo
Jack McNearney
Don Criswell
Sal Raimondi
Dr. Lance Christiansen
Steve Barnett
Larry Baer
Dr. Joseph Eisenlauer
John Dougan
Rodney Herrmann
Jim Lutes
Morris Hallowell IV
Rick Maples
George Fram
Jim Foral
Jef Pesel
Jim Ellis
Richard Skeuse of Parker Reproductions
Bruce Canfield
Lewis Yearout
Norm Carroso
Robert White
Ruger Collectors Association (RCA)
Colt Collectors Association (CCA)
Remington Society of America
Marlin Firearms Collectors Association, Ltd.

In Remembrance

It's never easy to put names in this box, but the following people are to be remembered for their significant contributions in this publication, as well as helping others.

Don Wilkerson started collecting Colt Single Actions in the 1970s, and by the time he passed away last Spring, he had written over a half dozen titles on Colt revolvers. Don and his wife Carol were truly a team, and our condolences go out to her, their friends and family.

F.R. "Rudy" Etchen of Remington, was one of the all time great trap shooters, and just as important, a real nice guy. Every year at the Antique Arms Show, Rudy & I would go downstairs to the deli in the Riviera, have a sandwich, and review Remington & Parker prices. Missed you this year Rudy - hope we can share some corned beef again.

Pat Redmond made significant contributions in the Trench/Riot guns section, and attended the OGCA gun shows regularly. His dream was always to get a book out on the subject, but we're all glad that he took the time to share some of his knowledge in the *Blue Book of Gun Values*.

FOREWORD

What a 12 month period! It began routinely, and ended with us being at war with terrorism. Looking back, we started out with the economy in good shape, witnessed many cities lose their frivolous anti-gun lawsuits, slid into the normal summer dormancy period, and then had our lives changed forever on Sept. 11th. Afterwards came a general recession for many industries (not the firearms industry, however), a major change in public perception and attitude, and a slow but sure return to normalcy. Patriotism and pride in our country, our armed forces, fire fighters, and police are the highest they have been since WWII. It hasn't been all bad, and for the vast majority of lawful gun owners, protecting our freedoms with vigilance is something we have always taken seriously.

Now if we could only get the remaining terrorists residing in the U.S. to live in caves and tunnels, appearing only occasionally (like they do in Afghanistan), we could treat them like prairie dogs, and make this a similar shooting sport taken to higher levels!

Our Commitment to You

Many of you have indicated that you would like to know more about how each edition of the *Blue Book of Gun Values* gets published. It's an honest question, but a more difficult answer. Hopefully, this will shed some light on the process.

Every year it starts out the same. In late November, we send out to contributing editors their respective section(s) for their review. This is a huge job unto itself, as there are nearly 150 scattered throughout the United States. Each one gets the information pertaining to their area(s) of expertise, and most send it back for review. These knowledgeable collectors and dealers, (please see Acknowledgements) are responsible for updating most of the values and information on many of the collectible firearms listed in this publication. They deserve our gratitude, and we can't thank them enough for their important contributions over the years.

Stage 2 begins the first week in December. Every manufacturer, importer, distributor, historian, and factory authorized repair center in this book gets a current copy of their section(s), along with a letter asking them to send us a current catalog and retail price list, as well as any changes in their address, phone number, email, etc. This is the monster job, as there are over 700 sections that get sent out all over the world. Additionally, we contact the conservation and firearms organizations to get their current information as well.

Many companies/organizations oblige us by sending in their information in time for publication, especially the international companies. Others need to be chased down, called, cajoled, and finally chastised into sending us their current information. All we want to do is get their information listed correctly, for no charge. It's an uphill battle we fight annually on your behalf.

Additionally, Blue Book Publications, Inc. attends 5 major industry trade shows annually, both domestic and international, and talks with firearms industry professionals and personnel, collecting information from sellers, dealers, contributing editors, and manufacturers on both new and used firearms. Our staff also interfaces with people all year long, helping them with information or advice, and sometimes getting useful information in return. We make notes, collect and file the information alphabetically, which are then included in the next edition of the *Blue Book of Gun Values*.

Part of the reason the *Blue Book of Gun Values* is so popular is because we listen to the people who use our books. If you feel that you can contribute to the new edition, please feel free to contact us. We've never pretended to be an ivory tower that throws books out to the masses. There's two-way traffic on our street.

After compiling this valuable information, we organize it and enter it into the new edition's manuscript, with many review processes in between. This year, we had accumulated over 3 linear feet (read that 60+ lbs.) of information before we even started. The grind begins right after Thanksgiving, and Cassandra Faulkner & myself gear up for working 7 days a week for over 4 months (except for Christmas).

Spring arrives and the new edition takes form - we publish proof copies, review our information, and finally end up with a printed book. What actually happens within the last sentence is a mountain of work for 5-6 people. This year, once we got the format finalized (now there's a story!), got all the machinery interfaced and running properly (read that a half dozen computers hooked up to a network being fed by modem information coming from multiple phone lines and high speed Internet cable connection), had plenty of coffee on hand, we were able to publish over 1,500 pages in 2 days! Some readers this year will be looking at information and pricing that is less than 2 weeks old! 15 years ago, it took 2 months just to set the type, and we were lucky to get a book out in May or

June. Nothing has been spared to make this publication the most up-to-date and accurate it can possibly be.

What's New & Exciting This Year?

Online subscriptions through our new e-commerce web site! It is now possible to get information during the year that may not be contained within these pages. Now we can update our database all year long, not just over a 4-month period. Please visit our web site, www.bluebookinc.com, to learn more about our exciting new online *Blue Book of Gun Values* subscription service, in addition to the other books we publish. We also offer individual downloads and online subscriptions for airguns, modern black powder, and guitars.

You're probably also wondering about gun values overall. It's safe to say that after the economy slowed down after 9/11, most collectible firearms have not set any new records in terms of price. On the other hand, they also haven't fallen substantially, like the stock market and many other investments. Good solid guns from major trademarks in excellent original condition continue to lead the firearms pack in terms of desirability and price appreciation. Some average guns may have slipped a little in value, but overall, the secondary marketplace within the firearms industry is still strong and healthy.

In terms of new guns, if the recent SHOT Show was any indication, most new gun manufacturers are very bullish and optimistic about the next 12 months. Demand for new products remains steady, and distributors are also pleased what's being shipped now compared to a year ago. Inventory is no longer a bad word - now it now typically represents something they're out of.

Make sure that you read all the editorial in this year's 23rd Edition. We are fortunate to have an interview with publishing icon Robert E. Petersen, and both he and his guns are featured on this year's cover. Additionally, a special NRA limited edition of the *Blue Book of Gun Values* is available - all proceeds will benefit the National Firearms Museum Endowment. Please check our web site for more information - www.bluebookinc.com.

This year marks the end of an era. Robert Delfay, President of the National Shooting Sports Foundation (NSSF) and longtime advocate for the fight to preserve hunting and shooting rights, has provided us with an exclusive interview. Bob is stepping down after 16 years as President, and 33 years with the NSSF, and we wish him the best. A special NSSF limited edition of the *Blue Book of Gun Values* is available as well - all proceeds will benefit the NSSF Shooting & Hunting Heritage Fund. Please check our web site for more information - www.bluebookinc.com.

Since this year's cover features shotguns, you can't afford to miss John Taylor's definitive article on shot - it is the most informative treatise I've ever read. Not only does it include all of the most recent non-toxic shot alternatives, but he also provides a detailed history of the shotshell and its development, including powder. If you've been confused about non-toxic shot in the past, this will clear it up.

And if you have some extra time, don't forget to check out the auction article by yours truly, and long time contributor & auctioneer Jim Supica. Things have changed in this business, and you should be aware of the changes.

In closing, thanks again for all your help & support over the years. Keeping this publication up-to-date and fresh is an overwhelming job that still must be considered a labor of love, even though the stakes have been raised every year. A lot of people think that once you've reached the top, it gets easier and requires less work - maybe even coast occasionally. It hasn't - this project is not an annuity. Every edition is an all out attempt to better the previous one, and nothing gets taken for granted. Our satisfaction comes from knowing that we have put together the most up-to-date and accurate firearms pricing guide available in the marketplace today.

Sincerely,

S.P. Fjestad
Author & Publisher
Blue Book Publications, Inc.

HOW TO USE

The prices listed in this 23rd Edition of the *Blue Book of Gun Values* are based on national average retail prices for both antique and modern firearms, and some accessories/acoutrements. **This is not a firearms wholesale pricing guide. More importantly, do not expect to walk into a gun/pawn shop or gun show and think that the proprietor/dealer should pay you the retail price listed within this text for your gun**(s). Resale offers on most models could be anywhere from near retail to 20%-50% less than the values listed, depending upon locality, desirability, dealer inventory, and profitability.

In other words, if you want to receive 100% of the price (retail value), then you have to do 100% of the work (become the retailer, which also includes assuming 100% of the risk).

Percentages of original condition (with corresponding prices) are listed between 10%-100% for most antiques (unless configuration, rarity, and age preclude upper conditions), and 60%-100% on modern firearms since condition below 60% is seldom encountered (or purchased). Please consult our revised, 48-page, Photo Percentage Grading System™ located on pages 65-112 to learn more about the condition of your firearm(s). Since condition is the overriding factor in price evaluation, study these photos and captions carefully to learn more about the condition of your specimen(s).

Please refer to the Abbreviations Section (page 1,609) for a complete listing of abbreviations used within this text. Also, the Glossary is now located on pages 1,610-1,615. Updated ATF regional information also is provided in this edition - see page 1,663. You may also want to check out the Store Brand Cross-Over List on pages 1,624-1,629, hundreds of models are referenced.

Since the 23rd Edition is now 1,680 pages, it may be easier to zero in on a particular manufacturer model by referring to the updated Index on pages 1,665 -1,679. On trademarks/companies with more than one configuration of firearms, individual category names are listed alphabetically. Hopefully, the alphabetical tabs on page sides will also assist you in finding your section(s) faster. As in previous editions, the NRA condition standards and grading criteria have been included to make the conversion to percentages easier (see page 63). This will especially be helpful when evaluating antiques.

To find a model in this text, first look under the name of the manufacturer, trademark, brand name, and in some cases, the importer (please consult the Index if necessary). Next, find the correct category name(s) (Pistols, Rifles, Shotguns, etc.). When applicable, antiques will appear before modern guns and are subdivided like modern firearms.

Once you find the correct model or sub-model under its respective subheading, determine the specimen's percentage of original condition (see the Photo Percentage Grading System™ on pages 65-112) and find the corresponding percentage column showing the price. Commemoratives or special/limited editions will generally appear last under a manufacturer's heading. For those of you who would like to make notes within this publication, there may be a Notes Page at the end of each alphabetical section allowing you room for notes and miscellaneous observations. For the sake of simplicity, the following organizational framework has been adopted throughout this publication.

1. Alphabetical names are located on the top of right-facing, odd-numbered pages and appear as follows:

M SECTION

2. Trademark, manufacturer, brand name, importer, or organization is listed in bold face type alphabetically, i.e.,

BROWNING, DPMS, HIGH STANDARD, SAKO

3. Manufacturer information is listed directly beneath the trademark heading, i.e.

   Current manufacturer located in Brescia, Italy, 1526-present and Accokeek, MD, 1978 to date. Beretta U.S.A. Corp. was formed in 1977 and is located in Accokeek, MD. Beretta U.S.A. Corp. has been importing Beretta Firearms exclusively since 1980.

4. Manufacturer notes may appear next under individual heading descriptions and can be differentiated by the following typeface,

   Purdey guns have long been regarded as among the finest in the world. They have typically been made to customer specifications, and as such, should be appraised individually for purposes of evaluation. Values vary with gauge, barrel length, chamber length and age. Listed are the modern models and approximate values for reference purposes.

5. Next classification is the category name (normally, in alphabetical sequence) in upper case (inside a screened gray box) referring mostly to a firearm's configuration, i.e.,

CARBINES, PISTOLS, REPRODUCTIONS, REVOLVERS, RIFLES, SHOTGUNS

6. A further sub-classification may appear under a category name in both upper and lower case, as depicted below. These are sub-categories of a major category name, and again, appear in alphabetical order whenever possible.

Lugers: KDF, Interarms, Stoeger & Recent Import

7. Following a category or sub-category name, a category note may follow to help explain the category, and/or provide limited information on models and values. They appear as follows:

   Note: Post-WWII Lugers have been manufactured by Mauser Werke in Oberndorf, W. Germany during the 1970s, and by both Stoeger Industries and Mitchell Arms (see separate listing under Mitchell Arms) in recent years.

8. Model names appear flush left, are bold faced, and capitalized either in chronological order (normally) or alphabetical order (sometimes, the previous model name and/or close sub-variation will appear at the end in parenthesis) and are listed under the individual category names, examples include:

CE GRADE, AIRCREW MODEL, DAYTONA SL, SINGLE ACTION ARMY

9. Model descriptions are denoted by the following typeface and usually include information, i.e.,

   -calibers, gauges/bore, action type, barrel lengths, finishes, weight, and other descriptive data are further categorized adjacent to model names in this typeface. This is where most of the information is listed for each specific model including identifiable features and possibly some production data (including weight, quantity, circa of manufacture, discontinuance date, if known).

10. Variations within a model appear as sub-models - they are differentiated from model names by an artistic icon ✳ prefix, are indented, and are in upper and lower case type, i.e., cont.

   ✳ *Etched Panel 44-40 SAA, Victor 10X, Stepped Barrel Variation*

   and are usually followed by a short description of that sub-model. These sub-model descriptions have the same typeface as the model descriptions, i.e.,

   -additional sub-model information that could include finishes, calibers, barrel lengths, special order features, and other production data specific for that sub-model.

11. Also included is yet another layer of model/information nomenclature differentiating sub-models from variations of sub-models or a lower hierarchy of sub-model information.

   These items are indented in from the sub-models, have the icon graphic ✧ and are in upper/lower case, i.e.,

   ✧Cattleman Millenium, Earlier Mfg. w/o Invector Choking.

   A description for this level of submodel information may appear next to the subentry, and uses the same typeface as model and submodel descriptions shown above.

12. Manufacturer and other notes/information appear in smaller type, and should be read since they contain both important and other critical, up-to-date information, i.e.,

    Since P series Superposed were disc. in 1985, collector interest has increased substantially. Interestingly, the P Series models are rarer than most of the pre-1976 high grade Superposed models.

13. Extra cost features/special value orders and other value added/subtracted features are placed directly under individual price lines or in some cases, category names. These individual lines appear bolder than other descriptive typeface, i.e.,

    Add 10%-25% for Superlight Models, depending on condition.
    Subtract $700 for fiberglass stock.

    On many guns less than 16 years old, these add/subtract items will be the last factory price for that option.

14. On many discontinued models/variations after 1985, a line may appear under the price line, indicating the last manufacturer's suggested retail price flush right on the page, i.e.,

    Last MSR was $675.

15. Grading lines normally appear at the top of each page and in the middle if pricing lines change. If you are uncertain as to how to properly grade a particular firearm, please refer to the Photo Percentage Grading System™ on pages 65-112 for more assistance. The most commonly encountered grading line (shown with typical price line) in this text is from 100%-60%, i.e.,

Grading		100%	98%	95%	90%	80%	70%	60%
MSR	$1,225	$1,100	$975	$875	$775	$675	$575	$495

Antique grading lines have additional values listed for 100%-10% and 80%-10%, N/A (Not Applicable) indicates this particular model is not encountered enough in either 98% or 100% original condition to warrant pricing. Examples (with pricing lines) are as follows:

100%	98%	95%	90%	80%	70%	60%	50%	40%	30%	20%	10%
$1,250	$1,125	$975	$900	$825	$750	$675	$575	$475	$425	$375	$335
N/A	N/A	$9,950	$9,100	$8,500	$7,950	$7,450	$6,850	$6,250	$5,600	$5,000	$4,350

Commemorative/limited edition grading and pricing lines will appear as follows:

Grading	100%	Issue Price	Qty. Made
	$475	$395	1,250

In some cases, an organization's or company's listing (i.e. Ducks Unlimited, the National Wild Turkey Federation, etc.) of guns will appear as follows:

Manufacturer	Model	Quantity	Year	Issue Price
Winchester	Model 12 12 ga.	800	1975	N/A

16. Price line format is as follows - when the price line shown below (with proper grading line) is encountered,

Grading		100%	98%	95%	90%	80%	70%	60%
MSR	$975	$850	$775	$695	$625	$550	$475	$395

it automatically indicates the gun is currently manufactured and the MSR is shown left of the 100% column. Following are the 100%-60% values. **This 100% price is the national average price a consumer will typically expect to pay for that model in NIB unfired condition.** 100% specimens without boxes, warranties, etc., that are currently manufactured must be discounted slightly (5%-20%, depending on the desirability of make and model). **This 100% price on currently manufactured guns also assumes not previously sold at retail. In a few cases, a N/A(s) may appear for both the MSR and 100% values. This indicates that NIB and 100% pricing is not predictable in this model.**

Grading	100%	98%	95%	90%	80%	70%	60%

17. A currently manufactured gun without a retail price published by the manufacturer/ importer will appear as follows:

	100%	98%	95%	90%	80%	70%	60%
No MSR	$1,300	$1,150	$925	$800	$675	$595	$500

Obviously, the 100% price is the national average price a consumer will pay for a gun in new condition. Again, on currently manufactured guns, this assumes NIB condition, and not previously sold at retail.

18. When a currently manufactured stainless steel or limited mfg./special edition firearm with or without retail pricing is encountered, it will not have prices listed from 90%-60%, as these lower condition factors are seldom encountered below 90%. The price lines will appear as follows:

	100%	98%	95%
MSR $475	$395	$325	$250
No MSR	$2,300	$1,900	$1,450

19. A price line with 7 values listed and represented below indicates a discontinued, out of production model with values shown for 100%-60% conditions. Values are normally not listed for 50%-10% condition factors, since these lower conditions are seldom encountered on recently discontinued models. Examples include:

100%	98%	95%	90%	80%	70%	60%
$625	$575	$500	$450	$400	$350	$300
N/A	$1,125	$975	$850	$725	$650	$550

Values for condition under 60% will typically be no less than 66% (2/3) of the last price, unless the gun has been shot to a point where the action may be loose or questionable. Obviously, no "MSR" will appear in the left margin, but a last manufacturer's suggested retail price may appear flush right below the price line, automatically indicating a discontinued gun, i.e.,

Last MSR was $850.

20. Early Winchester lever action grading and price lines incorporate price ranges on certain Winchester models which are most frequently encountered in 50% or less condition. These grading and price range lines appear as follows:

Above Average	Average	Below Average
$800 - $1,000	$600 - $800	$450 - $600

An explanation of what to look for in these three condition ranges will precede this information in that section. The 23rd Edition also includes a grading/price line that represents percentages and respective values for guns above 50% condition. This grading/value line appears as follows:

95% = $2,250	70% = $1,500	50% = $1,100

Since this publication is now 1,680 pages, you may want to take advantage of our new expanded Index (pages 1,665-1,679) as a speedy alternative to going through the pages.

Enlarged in the 23rd Edition are sections on Trademark Index (pages 1,573-1,608), Model Serialization breakdown of major trademarks (pages 1,630-1,656), and a Store Brand Cross-Over List (pages 1,624-1,629). When using the expanded Model Serialization section, make sure your model is listed and find the serial number within the yearly range listings.

REVOLVER

SEMI-AUTO

1. Muzzle	10. Takedown Lever	19. Rear Grip Strap
2. Front Sight	11. Slide Release Lever	20. Hammer
3. Barrel	12. Magazine Release Button	21. Rear Sight
4. Gas Ports	13. Cylinder Release Latch	22. Safety Lever
5. Ventilated Rib	14. Extractor Rod	23. Lanyard Loop
6. Frame	15. Magazine	24. Crane
7. Slide	16. Cylinder	25. Top Strap
8. Trigger Guard	17. Front Grip Strap	26. Cylinder Flute
9. Trigger	18. Grip	27. Full Length Barrel Shroud

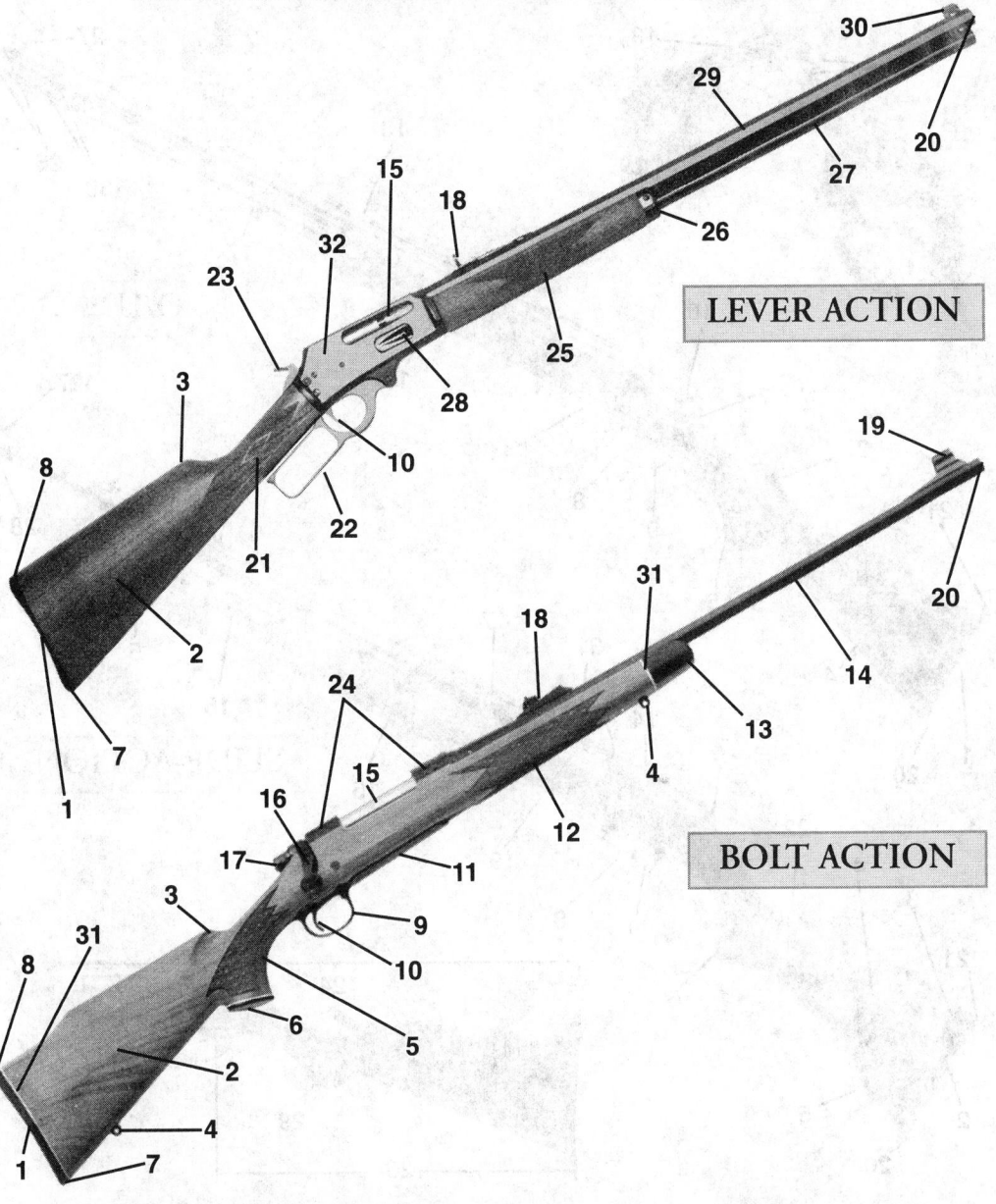

LEVER ACTION

BOLT ACTION

1. Buttplate	12. Forend	22. Lever
2. Buttstock	13. Forend Cap	23. Hammer
3. Comb	14. Barrel	24. Receiver
4. Sling Swivel Stud	15. Bolt	25. Forearm
5. Semi-Pistol Grip	16. Bolt Handle	26. Forearm Cap
6. Pistol Grip Cap	17. Safety Button	27. Magazine Tube
7. Toe	18. Rear Sight	28. Loading Port
8. Heel	19. Hooded-Ramp Front Sight	29. Octagon Barrel
9. Trigger Guard	20. Muzzle	30. Blade Front Sight
10. Trigger	21. Straight Grip	31. Spacer
11. Floor Plate		32. Frame

ANATOMY OF A SHOTGUN

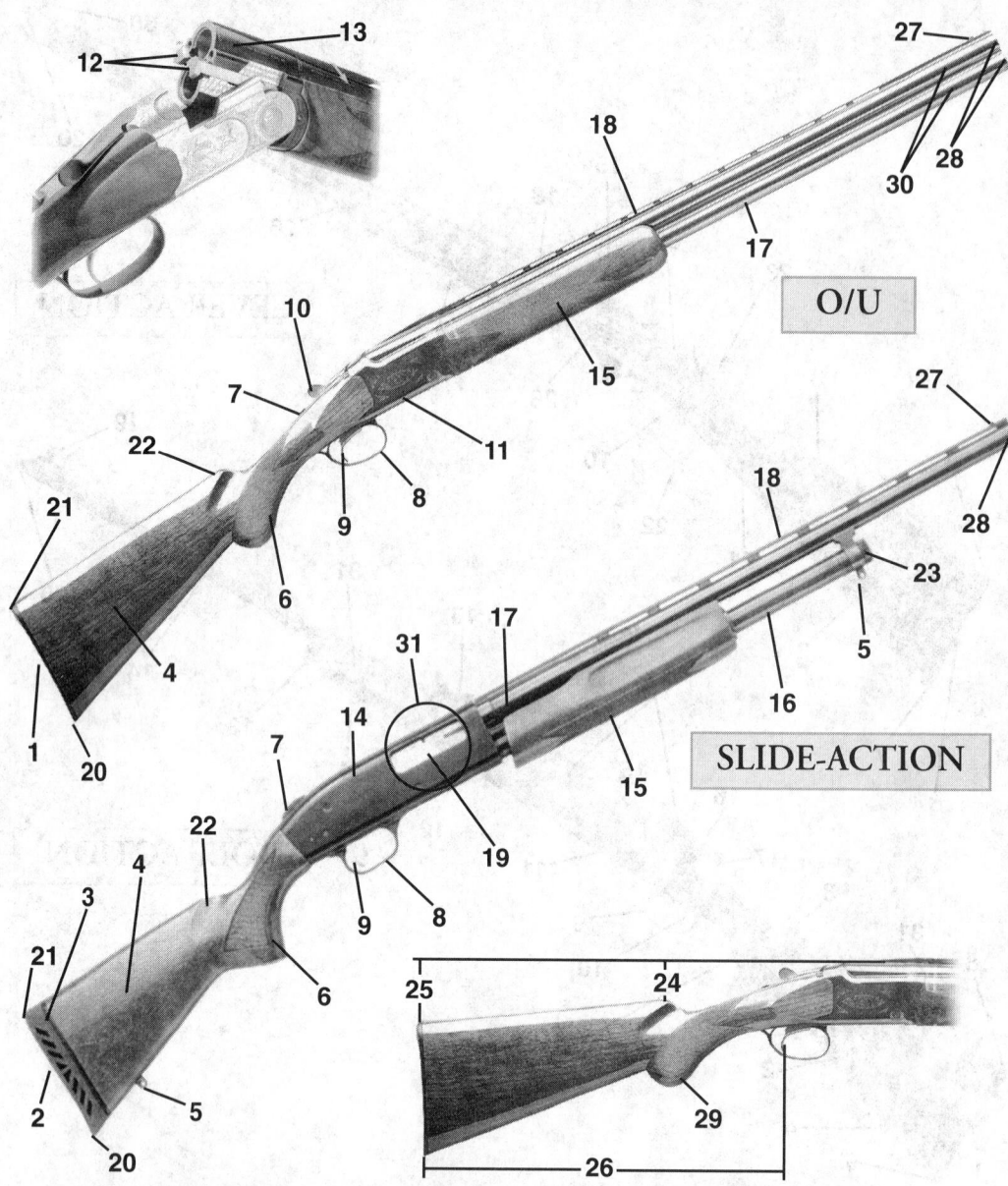

O/U

SLIDE-ACTION

1. Buttplate	12. Ejectors or Extractors	23. Magazine Tube Cap
2. Ventilated Recoil Pad	13. Breech/Chamber	24. Drop at Comb
3. Spacer	14. Receiver	25. Drop at Heel
4. Buttstock	15. Forearm	26. Length of Pull (LOP)
5. Sling Swivel Stud	16. Magazine Tube	27. Front Sight Bead
6. Semi-Pistol Grip	17. Barrel(s)	28. Muzzle
7. Safety Button	18. Ventilated Rib	29. Rounded Pistol Grip
8. Trigger Guard	19. Breech Block	(Browning Style)
9. Trigger	20. Toe	30. Porting
10. Top Lever	21. Heel	31. Ejection Port
11. Frame	22. Comb (fluted)	

An Interview

with
Robert E. Petersen
by S.P. Fjestad

Robert E. Petersen is to the magazine industry what William Ruger Sr. is to the firearms industry - a living icon. He was born on Sept. 10th, 1926, in Los Angeles, CA. The son of a Danish immigrant father, his mother died of tuberculosis when he was 10. Some of his fondest memories were going out into the California desert shooting with his dad, Einar. The following questions and answers will give you a much clearer picture of this publishing mogul, pro-gun supporter, and conservation philanthropist.

During this recent lengthy telephone interview, Mr. Petersen mentioned that he likes Lazzeroni's new .308 Warbird, Anschütz Mannlicher rifles in .22 Hornet, Jarrett's "Beanfield" rifles, duck hunting with .410 bore shotguns ("you have to be on them"), and Galazan's mini-double rifle in .22 Mag. cal., among others. It's very obvious that

Throughout his lifetime, Robert E. Petersen has never been too busy to pursue his favorite pastime, both shooting and hunting. Regardless if it's a handgun, rifle, shotgun, or even black powder (pictured), he pulls the trigger on a regular basis, all over the world.

"Pete", as his friends call him, is very active in shooting, hunting, and conservation. If there's been a recent firearms development, he's not only heard about it, he's probably shooting it already!

The National Firearms Museum (NFM), located in Fairfax, VA, one of Mr. Petersen's favorite non-profit projects, has recently received on loan a grouping of some of America's most important and historic shotguns from Mr. Petersen's extensive collection, including the Parker Invincible on the cover. To support this unique firearms museum, a special NRA Foundation *Blue Book of Gun Values*, signed by Robert E. Petersen and author & publisher S.P. Fjestad, is now available. All proceeds from this special limited edition will go to the National Firearms Museum Endowment.

How did you get started collecting guns?

When I was young, I lived with my dad in every place in the desert so he could work on the Boulder Dam power lines to bring power up from there to Los Angeles. And so, I lived in very little towns from Victorville to Yermo, Barstow, and so on, all the way up to Nevada. I lived in the desert where I hunted everyday. Having my own guns and getting to go out on my own when we were young was very influential, and I had a great time. After that, I started *Guns and Ammo* magazine with Tom Siatos as my publisher. Tom kept coming into my office and saying, "This is the greatest gun I've ever seen. You should have one of these." Before long, I started collecting and I've been doing it ever since.

So, you got your love of hunting and the outdoors from your father?

My dad liked to go shooting and he always had different .22 plinkers, and so on. He liked to go out and just shoot and have a good time.

Where did you spend your formative years? After graduating from high school, what did you do?

Well, I graduated from high school and went to a college for a short time until I ran out of money. Then I went to work at MGM as a messenger, followed by working in the publicity department, where I was a guide. I gave tours there for VIPs, and then became a publicist. I went in the service for a couple years and was trained in the air corps as a photographer. I was supposed to become a pilot on P38 photo missions. They trained me to be both an air and ground photographer. They were about to send me into flight training and then the war ended. So, I went back to MGM. While there, I did many different things. I worked all around the studio with different jobs, including the assistant to the head photographer Clarence Bull. I worked as a junior publicist, writing stories and columns. And then, they fired me.

And then you started *Hot Rod* magazine?

First I started a company with some other people called Hollywood Publicity Associates. We had all kinds of accounts, from a soccer team, KFWB Radio, to Mad Man Muntz. And gradually, we wound up doing a Hot Rod Show, which was supposed to be a P.R. job for Mad Man Muntz. He kind of left the scene, but we continued, did the first Hot Rod show, and then started Hot Rod Magazine at the same time.

During your tenure with Petersen Publishing, what would you say would be the most frustrating or difficult thing that you've ever dealt with?

Getting computerized. I've also had more problems with bad advisors. I hate bad advisors.

Consultants, they're called.

Yeah, they're called consultants. That's someone who can't get a job, but can tell you what to do.

If you were to start another magazine now, what do you think it would be? What niche would you follow?

Well, of course, I have started a magazine. I'm running one now.

Sports Afield?

Sports Afield, yes.

But, if you were to start another one from the ground up, what do you think it would be?

I don't know. I think in the business world, to start a new magazine, things have never been tougher. When we started magazines, we made money selling copies on a newsstand. Now even the best magazines, if they can sell 50% of the newsstand copies, they would be very happy. It's just really hard to sell anything on newsstands.

All of the corner drug stores are now gone and the magazines go to a few big distribution organizations who don't have a care for how the little guy did on the newsstand. That's all changed in the past few years.

Now, if you were to reverse any professional decision that you've made. What would that be?

I don't know. I don't think I've ever done anything wrong.

No regrets? Okay.

I'm lying, of course.

Of course. It's all right.

We started a lot of magazines that didn't make it. I guess I'd have to say that for a long time we started magazines that the public wasn't ready for.

Can you tell us about your involvement in the '84 Summer Olympics?

During the '84 Olympics the committee had a person who was in charge of the shooting sports who was a doctor that had some problems getting the whole thing together. Peter Ueberroth called me and said, "I need

An older picture of Robert & Margie Petersen, taken on an African safari. He proposed to her on their first date, and they have been lifelong partners on a lot of things, including hunting and shooting, ever since. "Margie is a fine shot," says Petersen, who has hunting in Africa over 15 times.

you to be the commissioner of shooting sports, because you know everybody and you're the only guy that can do it," which shot my ego up a little bit. While challenging, it turned out to be a tremendous job, and a very popular Olympic venue.

The timeline was early January when I got the call, and we had our first international shooting in April. Since the venue was being built specifically for the 1984 Olympics, it had to be proven before the Olympics with the 1984 Inaugural Championships of the Olympic shooting range competition at Prado Park in Chino, CA. All the international shooting teams, including the Russians, attended this international shooting competition. My job was to try and get the Russians to come back for the summer games. I couldn't keep them for the Olympics. They came for the pre-game shoot, but they wouldn't come for the Olympics.

Because we had boycotted the 1980 Moscow Olympics four years before?

That's right, the Russians boycotted the '84 shooting sports. Regardless, our shooting sports venue turned out to be quite a deal, drawing record crowds. We also did a gun show out there at the same time.

I had Ken Elliott running that for me. And so, between that we had a really nice venue, before, during, and after the Olympics, we ran the shooting arena for quite a while afterwards. Recently, we turned it over to some other people who are now running it. It's nice to have a place in California where international meets can be held.

Talking about the Olympics and the other things I was involved in, I have to give credit to Margie and GiGi both. They were the two that were, day and night, working on it and they have been very instrumental in the final results. I have to give them credit, because I don't want to take all the credit myself.

You have hunted extensively around the world. Is there a favorite place that you have for hunting waterfowl?

The best waterfowl hunting I've ever done has been in Argentina. That's because there's so many ducks and geese there. But, mostly, I have my own ranch that I go to and enjoy. I belong to the Venice Island Duck Club and alternate between the ranch and the club, which is fun, since they're two different kinds of hunting. I just came back from a hunt in Arkansas, and shot at some different clubs. And so, I do get out of my own area.

Do you have a favorite story that you'd like to share from the multiple hunting trips that you've taken?

All of my hunting trips have been very calm.

Chris Dorsey's *Ducks Unlimited* article mentioned a bull elephant that charged you. Is that the most dangerous and closest call you've ever had?

On that trip, I had shot an elephant and nothing happened to him. I couldn't figure out what was wrong, so we went into the forest afterwards, and he came out and charged me. I shot him in the face about four times and nothing happened. My

Robert E., "on location", duck hunting with one of his favorite shotguns, the venerable Browning A-5. "I like the people associated with hunting. Waterfowling especially is a social occasion, where the actual hunting is an incidental experience." states this seasoned waterfowler.

Scotland together. Some places have been rough, including India. We've done that.

How active is she in shooting sports nowadays? Does she shoot at all?

She does. She likes to shoot trap, mostly, and wins an occasional medal at that and embarrasses me. Since she's very fast, she shoots trap very well and she shoots skeet and sporting clays.

Hunter Backup shot him with a .460 Weatherby and dropped him. We couldn't figure out what I was doing wrong, so we went up to the elephant and discovered that my bullets were blowing apart upon hitting the elephants face, right between the eyes. The cartridge company had tried to save some money and changed the design of the solid bullet. The new ones didn't work and I happened to find out the hard way.

Not exactly a time you want the cartridge to fail.

It did fail. I couldn't figure it out, because I thought I was doing everything right. I've had this happen before, so even though it wasn't my first time, it was kind of scary hunting dangerous game.

Do you have a favorite shotgun that you use for hunting?

I use everybody's shotguns. I shoot a .410 Purdey over and under that I had made for me. If I'm really serious, I shoot an A-5 Browning, 12 gauge.

Have you and Margie always been a hunting team?

She does quite a bit, but I also go on my own frequently. When it's kind of rough, of course, I don't take her. She's been to Uganda and other places in the Africas, in addition to going to Spain and

Speaking of talented women, can you tell us a little about your extremely capable executive assistant, GiGi Carleton? She never gets mentioned in anything about you and she's worked with you for a very long time.

Yeah, she's been with me for many years and was married once and went away to live in Hawaii, but she came back thankfully. We've fought a lot of battles together for many years and without her help, I don't think we could have done the Olympics and the auto museum, in addition to all the things that we're still doing. She's been very great at all of this.

You were the first to pioneer the idea of nontoxic shot. How do you feel about today's variety of nontoxic shot for hunting?

Yes, Bismuth shot pioneered the field, and developed it to the point where the government finally had to approve it. Of course, first it was steel. We spend millions of dollars because the government made us test it, retest it, and then retest it again. We spent a tremendous amount of money, and finally got it approved after a long government fight. After we got the final approval, everybody else who walked up to the platform was OK'd in five minutes. I sort of regret that part - it wasn't too good. I don't think the government wanted anybody to shoot anything but steel, because they were able to tell if it was a steel load by using magnets. Their attitude was, "we just don't want you there,

The good old days! Petersen Publishing is working out of its trailer at a car show. He started *Hot Rod* magazine in 1948, and says "The secret is recognizing a trend and getting in early. A magazine has to have a soul, and is only as good as its editor, who must know the subject."

because we have no way to tell what kind of load someone's shooting." It's all over now, as far as hunters shooting all kinds of different concoctions.

What about the high price of nontoxic shock? Do you think that forces hunters to shoot steel?

When you get down to what it costs to go duck hunting compared to your ammunition costs, it's a very small part of a hunter's budget. Besides that, when you start looking at ammunition, the cost of Bismuth is four times the cost of lead. Every nontoxic load that is made now is very expensive. They're all made with some kind of synthetic material. After you've joined a duck club, and spent a couple hundred thousand dollars a year, why worry about another $50.00 for ammo. I don't think that's too big a deal. For the person that doesn't belong to a club, and still shoots on a ditch bank or rented property, how many shells do you shoot in a day? And how much does that cost, versus being

able to actually get ducks. We know that we can kill more ducks per box than you can kill with steel.

Since steel shot was initially rushed into production without adequate time for alternative developments, do you think that this was a big setback for the shotgun industry?

Well, I don't know. I think a lot of people shot it, but it still not really efficient. If you're shooting at a close range it works okay, but when you're out to forty yards or so, it starts to fall off rapidly. So I think it depends on where someone's shooting. I think the government had to do something, but they over-reacted. They had to do something, because we know that lead does kill ducks if they ingest it. I don't think more than 3% of the ducks die because of lead ingestion, but that was enough to turn the corner for an alternative shot.

Steel shot was forced on people without any really viable alternatives to lead. A lot of older hunters had very few options, since damage could occur to their Model 12s and their Browning Superposed.

That did happen. Guns that were damaged by shooting a lot of steel shot in fixed, tight chokes could have experienced a bulbous blowout at the end of the barrel. But, all in all, most duck hunters shoot kind of basic guns and there wasn't, I don't think, that much damage to guns. I don't think as many ducks died because of lead poisoning as from other problems. If they would've taken that same effort and put it into eliminating predators, they could have saved a lot more ducks than getting rid of the lead.

Recently, you loaned some of America's finest shotguns to the National Firearms Museum in Fairfax, VA. How important is it that people see these fine firearms?

I think that it's wonderful for people to get to see some of the artwork and the craftsmanship of these guns, and these Parker Invincibles are supposedly the finest shotguns made in America. That, of course, can be disputed by everybody. My two Parker Invincibles are on display in the National

Firearms Museum in Fairfax, VA. Tony Galazan owns the third one, and I am trying to get him to display his there too. Only three of them are known. Annie Oakley's gun is something that anyone can enjoy.

Is there a particular philanthropic project that you are proud of funding? You do fund a lot of things, but is there one in particular that you're very proud of?

We've been into a lot of things, I think our business project has been something that has helped a lot. You know we've backed a lot of different organizations, from elk, to antelope, to quail, etc. We've tried to help everyone that we could, and we like to spread it around.

So you'd pick conservation, then, above anything else?

Well, I think we have to do that, or else we won't have a sport. Everyone's pretty much into that now, since it's a very popular issue.

Since you live in California, land of "no smoking" and rolling black outs, how do you feel about the future of pro-gunners in California? Also, do you feel that the trickle down effect from your state laws are impacting the rest of us who live elsewhere? The fact that the laws that are passed in California regarding gun ownership are effecting the rest of us who live elsewhere, how do you feel about that?

Many of the gun laws do start here in California, we have not had the best political climate. It's a problem and we have to face it all the time.

Now, as the current publisher of *Sports Afield* magazine, how much more sophisticated is the anti-gun press now than when you started *Guns and Ammo*?

Well, they're a tough adversary and they play on emotion and they are pretty good at what they do.

While Ken Elliot (l), Petersen's long time right hand man, John Risdall and Jim Skildum (r) from Magnum Research appear to be shooting the bull, Mr. Petersen obviously prefers shooting something else - in this case, the BFR revolver from Magnum Research. Of Petersen, Elliot states, "Sometimes, he's like trying to corral smoke!"

GiGi Carleton is Mr. Petersen's extremely capable executive assistant and longtime employee, with many decades of experience. Petersen states, "We've fought a lot of battles together for many years, and without her help, I don't think we could have done the Olympics and the auto museum, in addition to all the things that we're still doing."

I think that the public attitude has not been in the state of panic that it was in at one time when the antis were driving everyone wild and telling stories. So, I don't think that they have as many people "dancing to the tune" now, as they did during the previous administration.

In regards to the individual city lawsuits - a lot of those lawsuits have been dropped or the decisions have been reversed in favor of the gun industry. What do you think made the difference in helping that? Was that due to the NSSF and the NRA?

There's a lot of good work that's been done and the lawsuits were frivolous at best. Yet it was just another ploy by the anti-gun people, who try and get at gun owners and cause a lot of problems.

Now, do you think the Brady Bill and anti-gun legislation has reduced criminal use of guns at all? Especially in California?

I don't really think so. No, I think it's all a lot of political pandering and it might make people feel better, but it's the type of stuff that doesn't really do much.

Now, are there any big projects that you have on the burner that you can talk to us about?

Big projects? Nothing that exciting. I think one thing I didn't mention that's helped the pro-gun movement has been all the magazines. Because I think our magazines, while we preach to the choir, we have them disseminating the true story on what's happening on these gun laws and on the frivolous suits. And I think there is a pretty strong group of people that read all of these magazines or some of them and I think that has helped a great deal. But, all of the magazines have done, I think, a very good job of that.

Now, given the success of the Petersen Automotive Museum, is a Petersen Firearms Museum anywhere in the future?

I have kicked it around, but I just can't figure out how to do it.

Where would you locate this?

I don't know. The problems of doing it to get safe storage is pretty tough. And we're thinking about it, but I just don't know how to do it this time.

Still an idea then, an idea in the works.

It's a good idea. The car museum, of course, is really great. We're getting ready to do an expansion and a refinished job on a building and that's doing very well. It's great, but it could be a lot better. We just don't have room for all the cars that we own and that we can get, but a gun museum, it's just harder than a car museum, because [with] a car museum, you have all the people to help you. We've had such tremendous help from car buffs, or gearheads, or whatever you want to call them and while there are a lot of gun people, it's not the same kind of a thing. It's a different kind of group. We're just kind of playing at what the answers could be. The NRA has done a very nice job, because they have a spot to do it, where they're kind of away from everything.

Can you give us your thoughts on how you see the current state of shooting sports today?

I think it's much better, because this administration is so much friendlier than the past administration. We had all of those liberals trying to muck everything up there for so long. So, it kind of feels good not to have everybody on your back.

Along those same lines, if we were to change administrations, what do you think is the most important thing that an average American can do to insure hunting and shooting sports for the future?

I think Americans should be vigilant about whom they elect. People need to know who's good and who's bad.

We're very lucky to have Wayne LaPierre and James Jay Baker running the NRA/ILA and doing the good things they're doing. And Delfay at the NSSF doing such a great job with shooting sports. I think between all of it, we have a much more powerful group there protecting us.

How do you feel about the American Firearms industry today? Is there anything that you think we can all do to help?

I think it's gone through some tough times, with all the mergers and takeovers, yet I kind of see a lot of new fresh thinking coming in. I think that there's a lot of new stability. I was just at the SHOT Show, and visited with the heads of the various companies there. Everybody had great optimism, from Ruger, Smith & Wesson, to the people making Kimbers. And they all seemed to be having pretty good sales.

Thanks for taking this time for this interview. Finally, are there any public misconceptions about you that you would like to clear up?

No, none that I know of. I don't know what anybody says, they won't tell me. God only knows what people think.

Mr. Petersen is a life member of the NRA, as well as a Golden Eagle member, a life member of the Safari Club International (SCI), lifetime member of the Foundation for North American Wild Sheep (FNAWS), life member of the Rocky Mountain Elk Foundation, founding honorary member of the Arizona Mule Deer Association, member and major benefactor of Ducks Unlimited, and a member of the International Order of St. Hubertus.

Mr. Petersen, along with his wife Margie, are the founding benefactors of the non-profit charity the Petersen Automotive Museum Foundation, and have contributed to a number of charities, including the Operation Children adoption program for minority children, are active supporters of Los Angeles music and art communities, and are longtime benefactors of the Boys & Girls Club of Hollywood.

The publisher wishes to thank Ms. GiGi Carleton for coordinating this interview, and Chris Dorsey and Ducks Unlimited for contributing some of the information that appears in this article, originally published in the March/April 1997 issue of Ducks Unlimited magazine.

Petersen is as noted for his automobiles as he is for his guns. This picture of wife Margie, noted automotive & firearms photojournalist Dennis Adler, and Petersen was taken at an art gallery during the recent 50th anniversary of the Pebble Beach Concours d' Elegance. Don't miss the Petersen Automotive Museum if you are in Los Angeles.

SHOT
Yesterday, Today, and Tomorrow

by John M. Taylor

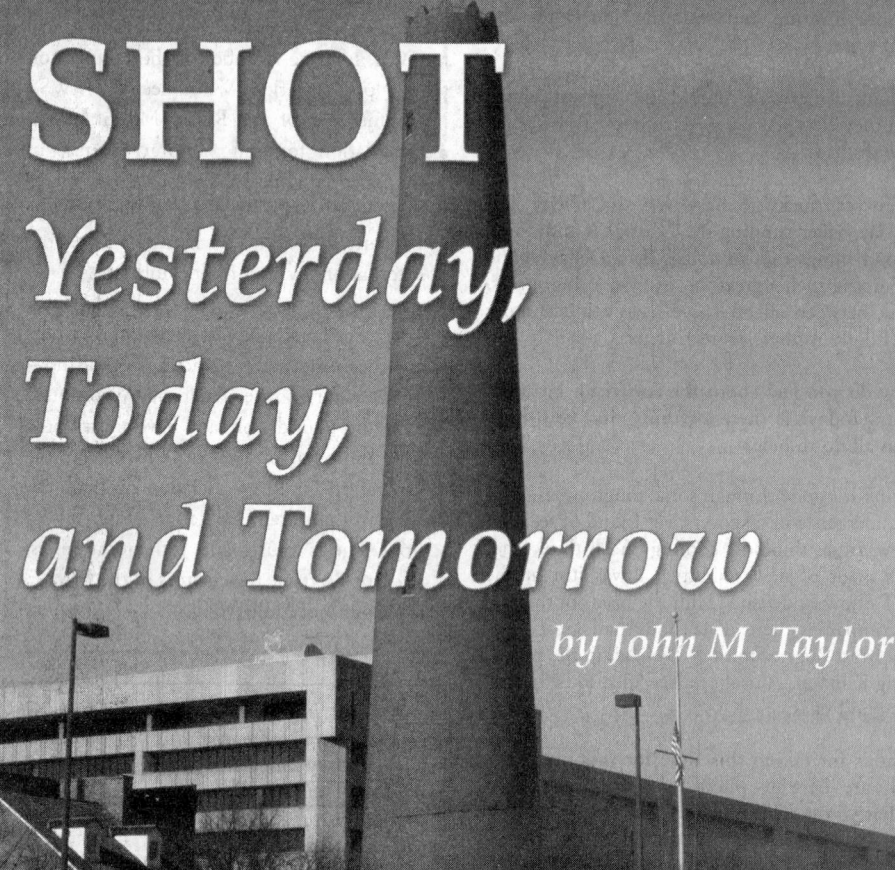

The historic shot tower in downtown Baltimore, Maryland. Built in 1828, current manufacturing of shot is little changed today. Although ammunition manufacturers, such as Federal Cartridge, use the German Bleimeister process to make their shot, Winchester, Remington, and others still use shot towers, albeit now mechanized, very similar to this one in Baltimore.

When firearms replaced bows, arrows and spears, gentlemen began to hunt and shoot game with their match and flintlock firearms. Using those primitive guns, they shot birds and other quary on the ground as they stood still. Early paintings show these 18th Century hunters peering over cover at stationary birds trying to get a shot. When the shotgun took form at the hands of Joseph Manton (1766 - 1835) and others, these gentlemen sportsmen began shooting flying and moving targets both for sport and the pot. Still, it was difficult. Black powder, that held sway into the 20th Century, produced clouds of thick smoke that made seeing the bird for a second shot difficult if not impossible, and shot and barrel boring techniques that we take for granted were still on the horizon.

The 40-year period between 1880 and 1920 has rightly been called the "Golden Age" of shotgunning. It was then that the breechloading side-by-side was perfected, Winchester's John Browning designed Model 1893 and 1897 pumps came to fruition and Browning's own recoil-operated semi-automatic Auto-5 came into being. It was also during this period that the substance that propelled the shot charge underwent drastic change.

Black powder is made of 75% potassium nitrate,15%charcoal and 10% sulphur. When fired, great clouds of smoke are generated, obscuring the target. Not only is black powder very dirty to shoot, it was also greatly affected by moisture. "Keep your powder dry," may be a cute line today, but it was a deadly serious line during the days of black powder.

Although Alfred Nobel discovered nitroglycerin, it was the Germans that developed nitrocellulose for use as gunpowder. Called by its German inventors "Schultze", it was the first of the smokeless powders. Early shooters didn't call this new powder "smokeless," but rather "wood" or "white" powder, and in the 1880s, it was hard to find and expensive. Soon followed E.C., Dittmar, and other brands. As smokeless powders made inroads into black powder-as with any change, there was great controversy that was hotly debated in the sporting press-there appeared a powder that made loading easier. Called "bulk powder," this smokeless powder was loaded bulk for bulk the

same as black powder. Essentially, all of these early smokeless powders were quite fast burning, much like the powders used in today's target loads. Building their pressures very quickly, fast burning powders launch lighter charges of shot at moderate velocities. It was left to John Olin and his ballisticians at the Western Cartridge Company to develop a slower burning, progressive powder that led to the high velocity, heavier payload Super-X cartridge in 1922.

Although smokeless powder revolutionized shotshells, when introduced, it was not without its apparent drawbacks. Black powder does not burn, it explodes. However, the explosion generates relatively low pressures; below 6,000 LUP (Lead Units of Pressure, a means of measuring pressure that has been largely superceded by PSI, Pounds per Square Inch, but black powder data is still stated in LUP). While black powder explodes, smokeless powders burn, and because they continue to produce an ever-expanding volume of gas until completely burned or the ejecta exits the muzzle, relieving the pressure, smokeless powder pressures are considerably higher with LUP pressures beginning at about 8,000 LUP and reaching 10,000 LUP and higher. Hence, many Damascus, laminated, and twist barrels failed under the higher pressures, promulgating the notice on shell boxes that still exists, warning users not to fire smokeless-powder cartridges in these barrels.

Many of the refinements we take for granted today were yet to come, yet these early shotgunners persisted, and today, shotgun-

Today, shotgunners can select from shot made from several materials. Although lead shot is the time honored standard, when the use of nontoxic shock was mandated for waterfowl hunting, several alternative, nontoxic material are now in use. (L. to R.) Lead, steel, bismuth, Tungsten/Matrix, and Hevi-Shot.

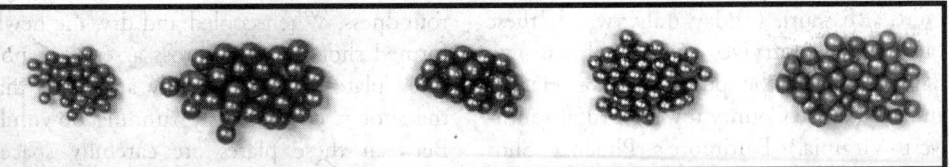

ning has become as exacting and every bit as much of an art and science as any other firearm discipline.

In the almost prehistoric days of shotgunning, those primitive wing shots used any projectile that was small and could be crammed down the muzzle of their gun. Pebbles were popular, as were stubs of nails, and other iron "findings." Finally, better technology prevailed in the form of round, sized shot, and despite its crude beginnings, shot is little changed today. Certainly the making of shot has benefitted from science and advanced metallurgy, but the basics remain unchanged.

Even in the 18th Century, it had been determined that lead was the metal of choice for making all projectiles. Rifle bullets and balls were cast commercially and equally at the hearthside, and while shot could be home-made, commercial production provided better and more round pellets.

According to W. W. Greener in his landmark book The Gun and its Development, the first commercially produced shot was made in Germany, and then in England by Messrs. Lampen and Roberts, late directors of the Newcastle Chilled Shot Company. Due to a lack of start-up capital, Lampen initially used an abandoned coal-mine shaft until he had sufficient money to erect a proper shot tower. By the mid-19th Century, shot towers dotted the landscape across Great Britain, Europe, and America. In the United States there were two shot towers in New York, and one each in Baltimore, Maryland, Wythe County, Virginia; Philadelphia, Pennsylvania; and St. Louis, Missouri. (Today only two of these early towers survive, one in downtown Baltimore near the popular Inner Harbor and the Wythe County tower in rural southwest Virginia.) Baltimore's Phoenix Shot

> **...wing shots used any projectile that was small and could be crammed down the muzzle of their gun. Pebbles were popular, as were stubs of nails, and other iron "findings."...**

Tower was begun on June 2, 1828, when the corner stone was laid by one of my ancestors, Charles Carroll of Carrollton, who was, at that time, the last living signer of the Declaration Of Independence. Of all brick construction-built without scaffolding-the Phoenix Shot Tower was completed on November 25, 1828. The Phoenix Shot Tower, also called the Merchants Shot Tower, has a diameter of 40 feet at the bottom, tapering to 20 feet at the top, and rises to 243 feet three inches, and was at the time, and perhaps still is, the tallest shot tower in the world. The Phoenix Shot Tower and every other shot tower contains four essential elements, a hoist or elevator to lift heavy lead ingots to the top, a furnace to melt the lead, a sieve with appropriate holes to the shot size being made through which the molten lead was poured and a pool of water at the bottom to cool the hot pellets. Today's shot towers, now owned by Olin/Winchester, Remington, Lawrence, and others still produce shot using these tall towers.

Another technology, the German Belimeister process, is also used to make lead and nontoxic bismuth shot. This machine replicates the shot tower in miniature. The shot material is still melted and poured through a sieve, but instead of dropping 100 feet or more, it drops only about three feet into hot water. Easily contained in a conventional warehouse, Federal Cartridge Company produces all of their shot using the Bleimeister method, as does Bismuth Cartridge Company to make their shot.

Once shot is formed, it is then tested for roundness. When cooled and dry, the newly formed shot is rolled across a series of polished plates that are slightly angled so that the shot is continuously running downhill. Between these plates are carefully spaced gaps. Round pellets will roll at a predictable velocity, but misshaped, flattened, and out-of-round pellets will roll at a slower rate, and will then drop through the gaps between the plates. Although it's an ancient process, the uniformity of today's lead pellets is excellent. Certainly, some shot that's imported from Mexico, Italy and elsewhere can and often is inferior to standard American shot, but the better shot is remarkably uniform in both size and sphericity.

Lead shot was the first, and still remains the standard. Sizes run from very large pellets, buckshot, for use on big game and in warfare, to near dust for gallery and exhibition shooting. Early performers like the late Annie Oakley, whose exhibition shooting in shows like Buffalo Bill's Wild West Show was legend, used dust shot so as to not injure the audience. Although at one time there were many sizes of shot commercially produced and loaded, shot sizes have condensed over the decades, although some variations between European, British, and American sizes still persist. With the increased importation of shotshells from Europe to the U. S., those shot sizes have gradually come into line with shot most commonly found in America.

Nearly as important as shot size is the hardness of the shot. Initially, lead shot was just that, lead. It was soft and easily deformed. It is doubtful that shotgunners of the early 1800s analyzed their patterns, but as shotgun making became more sophisticated, so came gun trials sponsored by sporting magazines. Gunmakers quickly found that their guns did not fare very well using soft lead. Early shot came in two varieties, dropped and chilled. German shot makers found that if cold air were blown across the falling shot, it formed more uniform pellets and also harder pellets. Southern quail hunters preferred dropped shot, because the soft, malleable pellets easily deformed and gave them extra-

28-gauge Peters High Velocity
Peters, a popular brand, was absorbed by Remington in May, 1934. This box tells the buyer that these Peters shells are primed with a non-corrosive "Rustless" primer, and as their premium hunting shell, loaded with good-quality shot.

wide patterns for short-range bobwhites. On the other hand, duck hunters wanted something harder that wouldn't deform and hence keep the greatest number of spherical pellets in the pattern out to their target at 35, 40, and 45 yards.

It was soon learned that the addition of antimony provided increased hardness. Now routinely added to all shot, antimony certainly helped lead shot to perform better. Today, antimony is alloyed with lead in amounts between one-half to six percent, depending on the intended use of the shot. A trace of arsenic is added to very large shot and buckshot to act as a surfactant. Surfactant is a $100-word that means arsenic causes increased surface tension and helps these large pellets to form as perfect spheres. Low-priced loads that are found in the various marts, and called promotions loads by the gun trade, are loaded with shot containing only one-half-percent antimony. Top-of-the-line waterfowl, turkey, premium upland,

This 1920 era salesman's cutaway shell, a Western Super-X, shows the construction of a modern shotshell. Progressive-burning powder lies beneath a card and two felt filler wads-subsequently superceded by plastic wads that both seal the powder chamber and protect the shot column- and the shot column lying below the rolled up crimp common th shotshells of that era.

routinely exposed to the extremely hot gasses produced by the burning powder that seeped past the wads. With only a card and felt filler wads separating these gasses from the shot charge, many pellets were fused before the shot charge left the barrel. In 1926, Western-Winchester was granted a patent for their Lubaloy shot. Lubaloy shot was simply hard shot that was copper plated. The copper plating, although it provided a harder surface to the pellets, was intended to protect the pellets from the hot propellent gasses. So too does nickel plating. Copper plating has also been used to coat nontoxic steel shot, but in that instance it is used as a rust preventative.

Nickel plated shot remains the shot most preferred by live pigeon shooters where hundreds and even thousands of dollars can ride on a single bird. For these loads, extra-hard, six-percent antimony shot is coated with hard, slippery nickel in an effort to keep the majority of pellets round and undeformed and in the very tight pattern.

Briefly, deformed shot reacts in the atmosphere much differently than round pellets. Certainly, spherical pellets are not the most aerodynamic of projectiles, but in a shotgun they work the best. Any deformation, intentional or unintentional, caused these pellets to sail away from the remainder of the shot column. In an effort to make tightly choked shotguns shoot wide, short-range patterns, pellets have been purposely flattened into plomb disco, or formed as cubes, whose flat sides cause them to widely disperse. Those are intentionally deformed pellets, but far more frequent are those pellets we don't want deformed. Pellets deform at four points during firing. The first is called setback. When the propellent gasses begin to thrust the shot up the bore the rearmost pellets are set in motion, yet the forward-most pellets are still stationary. The result is that the rear pellets are crushed against those not yet in motion. Buffering with ground polyethylene and other powdered plastic materials helps prevent setback deformation, and keeps more pellets round. Next, as the pellets are

and target loads generally carry the maximum of six-percent antimony, and a price tag commensurate with the premium shot. Even though these loads carry a sometimes hefty price tag, they also provide the very best performance, and well worth the additional cost.

In addition to the hardness of lead shot, coatings have been added to further enhance performance. Common lead shot is routinely coated with graphite to provide lubricity that allows the pellets to slip and slide against each other as they make their violent trip through the bore.

Prior to the advent of the plastic shot cup and bore-sealing over powder wads, shot was thrust into the forcing cone, the transition between the cylindrical chamber and the smaller bore, those pellets on the outside of the shot column are compressed and subject to deformation, as are other pellets in the shot column that are compressed. As the shot charge is flung up the bore, pellets on the exterior of the shot column are subject to scrubbing along the entire length of the barrel. Finally, the shot charge is further compressed in all but a true cylinder bore by the choke and the choke forcing cone. Prior to protective plastic shot cups, it's a wonder any shot exited the muzzle undeformed. And while these shot cups, that have become standard with nearly every load, do a good job of protecting the shot, there is still some deformation.

One interesting aspect of all the add-ons to lead shot is that regardless of plating, buffering, shot cups, and anything else, shot, just like any other moving object, is subject to the laws of physics. A perfectly round pellet fired at a given velocity flies to the target in a predictable manner, slows or loses velocity at a predictable rate, and strikes the target with predictable force. All the extras applied to shot are purely to prevent deformation or other problems such as rusting and consequent balling of steel shot, and while they definitely enhance and improve shotshell performance, they cannot make pellets hit harder than prescribed by their initial velocity, nor can they make a poor marksman

a Dead-Eye Dick.

Nontoxic Shot

Prior to the 1970s, lead shot was it. The choices were what size you preferred and what velocity, normally dictated by the height of the brass on the shell head. High and low brass does not indicate relative pressure, as so many incorrectly believe. The amount of brass or metal in the shell head had solely to do with the height of the internal base wad. Those shells with high base wads needed less support than those with lower base wads, but brass height does not dictate pressure. Be that as it may, as early as the late 1940s, scientists and biologists, such as Frank Bellrose of the Illinois Natural History Survey, had diagnosed lead poisoning in waterfowl. Mainly evident in mallard ducks that fed on corn, then picked up grit

Winchester Super-Speed

Winchester's Model 12 magnum duck gun is marked "For Super-Speed," the name given Western-Winchester's early magnum loads. Loaded with their best lead shot, it is not, however, W-W's premium copper-plated Lubaloy shot.

and spent lead pellets prevalent in shallow and heavily hunted waters. When fluoroscoped, these ducks showed pellets in their crops and digestive systems. As these pellets dissolved along the ducks' digestive tract, lead entered their systems. The results varied from death, to the inability to reproduce to deformed offspring that had no chance of survival.

Initially, the plan was to initiate nontoxic shot in areas the U. S. Fish and Wildlife Service (USFWS) designated as hot spots. These were primarily found along the Illinois River, Maryland's Eastern Shore, areas near Stuttgart, Arkansas, California's Sacramento River Valley and elsewhere where hunting pressure was high and large amounts of lead shot was deposited in shallow water where ducks gathered grit and collaterally lead pellets.

Because of the shooting characteristics of steel shot, which no one fully understood at the time, hunters' resistance to steel shot was universal and strong. States wrangled with the federal agencies until finally, the National Wildlife Federation brought a law suit against the USFWS, stating that bald eagles were suffering the same debilitating affects from lead poisoning as were ducks, because they allegedly ate lead-tainted ducks. Rather than fight a protracted suit, the USFWS settled the suit by mandating the use of nontoxic shot nationwide for the hunting of all waterfowl.

At the time of the mandate for nontoxic shot, the only proven and approved material was steel, which is really soft iron. Many times harder than lead, high-antimony lead shot measures 12 on the Brinell hardness scale, bismuth shot measures 18, common steel shot goes 96, while tungsten-iron blends tip the scale at 260. Hunters were immediately confronted with several problems. These new hard pellets presented definite hazards to shotgun barrels not designed for this hard shot. An unprotected pellet could score the barrel from forcing cone to muzzle, firing steel shot in a full-choked shotgun caused muzzles to bulge and side-by-side and over/under shotgun barrels could be forced apart by their bulging chokes. On the plus side, steel shot is so hard that deformation is not a problem. Guns aside, many hunters stated that steel would not kill, but the facts were that steel shot provided

Winchester Xpert steel
In order to make less expensive steel shot available to hunters, Winchester's Xpert line of steel loads are not buffered and the shot is not plated, yet the performance is excellent.
In 1991, lead shot was banned by USFWS, and only nontoxic shot could be used to take waterfowl.

such tight patterns that hunters were no longer scratching down ducks and geese with the wide fringe of their lead-shot pattern. No longer were tight chokes needed, rather open chokes that allowed the pellets to follow their own course.

The major ballistic problem with steel shot is that it is only about 60 percent as heavy as lead shot. Returning to physics, a lighter pellet will lose velocity and momentum faster than a heavier pellet of the same size. Hence the range at which steel shot could be used was significantly reduced compared to lead. On the positive side of the ledger, the absolute nonsense of 60- and 70-yard kills that prevailed during the lead-shot era went into a cocked hat. Ducks shot over tall trees were consistently called 60-yard shots. A tall oak tree can be 100-feet high, and that's a tall tree. The last time I looked, 100 feet is 33 yards. So the long-range thinking had to end. So did traditional shot sizes.

> ...larger pellets were needed to anchor large Canada geese. No longer was it possible to shoot the traditional lead goose pellets...

Early on, it was determined that because steel was significantly lighter than equivalent size lead shot, larger pellets needed to be used in order to provide sufficient downrange energy to ensure proper kills. The rule became selecting steel pellets one or two sizes larger than traditional lead shot, depending on how you count. I always considered No. 2 shot to be one size larger than No. 4 shot, but some count that as two sizes larger; take your pick. However you count it, if you liked No. 6 for ducks, No. 4 would seem to be the choice, but therein was a problem. Early in the steel shot debate, the late John Olin, then president of Winchester-Western, ordered a series of tests using tethered mallards run down a track with the shotgun fired with the optimum lead to ensure the duck was centered in the pattern. It was discovered that, although on paper No. 4 steel should be the equal of No. 6 lead, it wasn't, and in fact was responsible for most of the test ducks being crippled and not killed.

As time went on, it was found that increasingly larger pellets were needed to anchor large Canada geese. No longer was it possible to shoot the traditional lead goose pellets, No. 2s and BBs, but instead large steel pellets of BBB, T and even F, which is .22-caliber, were becoming more and more common in goose hunters' shell bags. In order to shoot these really big pellets, the 10 gauge that was all but moribund, saw an enormous upswing in popularity. Even though steel pellets are very hard and don't deform, these large pellets needed a larger bore to function and pattern efficiently. In addition, the 10 gauge offered increased case capacity for these large pellets.

Steel shot is made by snipping off precise lengths of given diameters of iron wire that relate to the size of pellet being made. The billets are then cold rolled into round pellets, and finally annealed to draw as much of the hardness as possible. Most are then plated with copper, zinc or other rust preventative, and then are graphited to add some lubricity. One of the early problems with steel shot was that unless it was kept in the driest of conditions, rusting was a constant problem. Not that a rusty pellet wouldn't work, it's that as they rusted, the pellets formed clumps. It was not unusual for an entire payload of shot to form one solid slug. Only through the greatest stroke of luck would such a projectile strike the target, and the potential for barrel damage was increased several fold. Today, with the application of rust inhibitors, such stories are rare, and when they occur, it's almost always with old ammunition that's gotten wet.

As steel shot evolved, the constant quest was to increase its downrange ballistic performance. Compared to lead, steel shot is about one-third lighter, therefore either pellets had to be made heavier or fly faster. A pellet that starts faster sheds its velocity a little slower, thereby enhancing its downrange performance. Today, we have high-velocity steel loads that were unheard of 20 years ago. By blending new propellents that provide higher velocity, yet retain safe chamber pressures, steel pellets are going faster and faster, but the increase in lethal range is marginal.

Federal Tungsten/Iron
In order to make steel shot more ballistically viable, Federal Cartridge Company developed a pellet that combined tungsten and iron, producing a heavier pellet that would perform more like lead.

Adding weight or density is the other way to enhance steel shot's performance. Federal Cartridge Company began blending tungsten with its steel shot to increase the weight and density. Powdered tungsten and iron are blended then sintered under high pressure and high heat, creating a molded pellet that is ballistically more efficient than steel without the heavy tungsten additive.

Shotshells are a continuing evolution, and it's doubtful that we will, thankfully, ever arrive at the perfect shell that needs no further development. In no other element of shooting has evolution been more evident than with nontoxic shot. Metallurgist Darrel Amick working with familiar metals blended iron, tungsten, and nickel into a pellet he calls Hevi-Shot. Hevi-Shot is indeed heavy; its heavier and denser than lead shot. It's hard like steel shot, but does produce excellent downrange ballistics, and more importantly, downrange lethality. I've shot some large Canada geese with Hevi-Shot, and unlike ordinary steel shot, they did not require the customary coup de grace generally necessary with steel. I do, however, discount the somewhat outrageous claims of extreme long-range kills under impossible weather conditions. Regardless of the pellet,

marksmanship is still the major part of clean kills and some semblance of reason must enter the equation. Ranges frequently stretch in the eye of the shooter, sometimes into the land of dreams. In late 2001, Remington began loading Hevi-Shot as part of its product line.

One facet of shot performance is the aspect of stringing. When any shotshell is fired, and once the shot leaves the muzzle it does not fly in a flat pancake, it flies more like a sausage shaped cloud. Called "shot string" or "stringing," the shot charge has both length and width. A shot charge that flies as a pancake would deliver most of its shot to the target in one dense, but flat pattern. However, this pancake would not allow for any variance in lead. If you shoot behind a moving target, there is no remedy. However, if you're a bit ahead, the length of the shot string will compensate. At one time, lead shot shells were advertised as having a "short shot string," with steel shot, stringing is less of an issue, but still one that needs consideration. Shells loaded with very long shot columns tend to string, regardless of the pellet, and large steel pellets string badly in smaller bores, hence the 10-gauge became, and still is, the gauge of choice for many goose hunters. One reason for the absolutely abysmal performance of the three-inch .410-bore cartridge is the puny shot charge that is strung out for many feet. Commonly thought to be a "beginner's shotgun," the .410 isn't an expert's gun, because of its poor downrange performance.

Nontoxic shot is now considered to have been a good move that benefitted waterfowl populations, although habitat and good weather on the breeding grounds remain the primary stabilizing factors of waterfowl. Still, those who wished to hunt with their favorite pre-steel shotgun, remained morose. Hunters had an amazing array of steel-shot designed and manufactured shotguns, including doubled and over/unders, yet older hunters yearned to use their favorite shotguns, or an heirloom given to them or willed by an ancestor.

Canadian carpenter and inventor John Brown sought a better form of nontoxic shot; something heavier; something more like lead. Looking at the periodic table of the elements-the big chart over the science teacher's desk-right next to lead is bismuth. Bismuth is a by-product of metal refining, and occurs by itself in mineable quantities. In addition, it is the key ingredient in patent stomach remedies, i.e. Pepto-Bismol. In the 1980s, Brown began hand casting pellets and testing them. He found that although bismuth is lighter than lead, its performance on ducks was similar. At the time Brown was doing his work, Canada had not mandated nontoxic shot, something that happened only in the past few years.

Brown struggled along on a meager budget until publishing magnate and avid hunter Robert Petersen took up the cause. With Petersen's resources and deep pockets, bismuth took wing. Initially, USFWS was cool

Remington Hevi-Shot
A blend of tungsten, iron and nickel, Hevi-Shot pellets are actually more dense than lead, and offer excellent downrange performance. In 2001, Remington entered into an agreement to be the exclusive loader of Hevi-Shot.

Bismiuth No-Tox
The first alternative to steel shot, this blend of bismuth and tin enabled hunters to shoot shotguns rendered obsolete by steel shot. Because of its heavier density, its performance is more like lead.

to the idea, and made Petersen's people negotiate a no man's land of obstacles, but Petersen is a persistent man, and they kept at it until USFWS had to admit the obvious, that bismuth shot was, indeed, nontoxic, and gave it unconditional approval.

At the time this occurred, 1991 and 1992,

I was associate editor of NRA's American Hunter, and in order to fully test bismuth shot, I traveled to Mexico, who also had no nontoxic regulations. There it was found that bismuth shot did kill with authority, and because I was a child of the lead-shot era, I could make a good comparison. Because bismuth shot is so much softer than steel, it is completely compatible with older shotguns that were made exclusively to shoot lead shot. Bismuth is a relatively brittle metal, and there are pellets that are lost to shattering, but as recently as last week, I killed two big Canada geese stone dead at 30 yards with No. 2 bismuth shot, and that's as good as it needs to be.

Although bismuth shot has proved to be a wonderful alternative to steel shot, some sought something that could be closer to the density of lead, yet, like lead and bismuth, be compatible with any safe shotgun, i.e. A. H. Foxes, Parkers, Winchester 21s, Purdeys, Hollands, etc. A group of Canadian investors became intrigued with a British Royal Ordinance patent that blended micro-fine, powdered tungsten with a polymer, then formed into pellets. This shot made a brief appearance as Molyshot, and was loaded for a very, very short time by Eley Hawk. The problem with Molyshot was that the tungsten would settle in one place, rather than being uniformly distributed throughout the pellet. Like a ball that was too heavy on one side, these lopsided pellets quickly looped their way out of the pattern. Taking the bull by the horns, the Canadians bought Kent Cartridge in Hull, England, who was making and loading Molyshot pellets, took the pellet formula to a polymer scientist at

Since the mandate for nontoxic shot in the late 1970s, great strides have been made from the early steel shot loads. Using Kent's Impact Tungsten/Matrix in a nitro-proofed William Evans shotgun built in the late 19th century, the author took his limit of teal on a bright autumn afternoon.

Pennsylvania State University, and said, "Here, fix it." And he did. It was determined that the polymer Eley had been using was too thin, and in the words of Kent officials, what was needed was a thick "goo" that would keep the powdered tungsten in uniform suspension until the pellets could be formed. How the pellets are made is a closely kept secret, but it's not cheap, nor particularly fast, but the resulting pellets have the density and malleability of lead, and work like a charm. I've shot lots of them from Uruguay to Alberta in a variety of shotguns including a 1926 Parker and 1924 A. H. Fox HE-the Super Fox-and never wanted for a better duck or goose pellet.

Shot is the final connection between the hunter and clay shooter and his target. Shot has come a long way since our ancestors stuffed rocks and "findings" down the barrel of his shotgun. As hunting and clay shooting continues to evolve and as environmentalists, liberals, and other extremists continue to batter away against our American culture and way of life, there is little to convince one that nontoxic shot will continue to be more important as these ill-informed, anti-American forces attempt to stifle our dearly held traditions. Hunters and shooters continue to carry the burden of wildlife conservation efforts, and have always been ready to assume the mantle of conservators and protectors in order to perpetuate species that are hunted and those that are not, and that add so much to the quality of the daily lives of all. To be sure, there are exciting developments at every turn, and shot is constantly at the forefront of these developments. Still, today's shotgunned has an extensive array of shotshells from which to choose, and each contains just the right shot for the need. It's an exciting time.

Shotshell - Game Chart

Game	Shot Type	Shot Size	Choke	Gauge
Geese	Steel	T, BBB, BB	I. Mod. Mod.	10, 12
	Bismuth, Tungsten/Polymer	BB, 2	Mod., I. Mod. Full	10, 12
Ducks	Steel	1, 2, 3	I.C., Mod.	10, 12, 20
	Bismuth, Tungsten/Polymer	2, 4, 5, 6	I.C., Mod.	12, 16, 20
Turkey	Lead	4, 5, 6	Full, Extra-Full	10, 12
	Bismuth, Tungsten/Polymer	4, 5, 6	Full, Extra Full	10, 12
Pheasant	Lead	4, 5, 6, 7½	I.C., Mod. I. Mod.	12, 16, 20
	Bismuth, Tungsten/Polymer	4, 5, 6	I.C., Mod. I. Mod.	12, 16,20
Grouse	Lead	5, 6, 7½, 8	I.C., Mod.	12, 16, 20, 28
	Bismuth, Tungsten/Polymer	5, 6, 7½, 8	I.C., Mod.	12, 16, 20, 28
Partridge	Lead	5, 6, 7½, 8	I.C., Mod.	12, 16, 20, 28
	Bismuth, Tungsten/Polymer	5, 6, 7½, 8	I.C., Mod.	12, 16, 20, 28
Woodcock	Lead	6, 7½, 8	I.C., Mod.	12, 16, 20, 28
	Bismuth, Tungsten/Polymer	6, 7½, 8	I.C., Mod.	2, 16, 20, 28
Snipe/Rail	Lead	7½, 8	I.C., Mod.	12, 16, 20, 28
	Bismuth, Tungsten/Polymer	7½, 8	I.C., Mod.	12, 16, 20, 28
Quail	Lead	7½, 8	I.C., Mod.	12, 16, 20, 28
	Bismuth, Tungsten/Polymer	7½, 8	I.C., Mod.	12, 16, 20, 28
Dove	Lead	7½, 8	I.C., Mod., I. Mod.	12, 16, 20, 28
	Bismuth, Tungsten/Polymer	7½, 8	I.C., Mod., I. Mod.	12, 16, 20, 28
Rabbit	Lead	4, 5, 6, 7½	I.C., Mod.	12, 16, 20, 28
	Bismuth, Tungsten/Polymer	4, 5, 6, 7½	I.C., Mod.	12, 16, 20, 28*
Squirrel	Lead	4, 5, 6	Mod., I. Mod., Full	12, 16, 20, 28*
	Bismuth, Tungsten/Polymer	4, 5, 6	Mod., I. Mod., Full	12, 16, 20, 28*

* In some instances, the .410-bore can be used for rabbits and squirrels. However, because of the .410's very light shot load and propensity for poor patterns, its use can only be suggested on very close game, and then only with backup by a hunter shooting a larger-bore shotgun.
Choke abbreviations: I.C. = Improved Cylinder; Mod. = Modified; I. Mod.= Improved Modified. Actual choke constrictions vary by gauge and individual manufacturers' standards.

TODAY'S AUCTION MARKETPLACE
TRUTH & CONSEQUENCES

by S.P. Fjestad, with last minute
professional air brushing
by Jim Supica.

This isn't going to read like you thought it would. The auction business has changed, maybe a lot more than you think. Here's the 2K2 update.

Back in the 80s and early 90s, the few auction companies around were selling virtually anything at higher than normal prices compared to the bulk of private sales and dealer to consumer transactions. Almost anything brought a premium, and as a result, many price records were established not only on top shelf items, but also on the few average condition, major trademarks. The Butterfield & Butterfield auction of the John Woods Winchester collection in Oct., 1991, is a classic example of the headiness and unpredictable auction pricing at the time. One Winchester Deluxe Model 94 takedown with factory engraving was estimated at $40,000 - $60,000. When the gavel finally hammered, the price was $126,500, plus the 10% auction commission! This seemed like a win/win situation - the consignor in most cases got more than he/she wanted, the auction company got their cut, and the buyers fought for what they wanted, even though the price(s) may have been a "little high".

With the advent of more competitive auction houses throughout the 1990s, the exclusivity of a few auction houses dominating the marketplace was over. Following the birth of the Internet and more sophisticated auction services, many auction companies actively competed for top guns and large/important collections. As a result, many gun collections, including the standard and even substandard guns, were auctioned off, with average gavel prices resulting on those average items. This created a situation where out of 1,000 guns; an auction may have had less than 50 prime specimens that really qualified for a potential auction premium price.

At this point, with so many more average guns being sold at auction per year, many dealers started buying these at the auctions for their inventory, rather than trying to find them at gun shows, gun shops, pawn shops, etc. Currently, on any one given auction, there are typically less than 2 dozen dealers who buy the majority of the common and average merchandise (sweeping up the floor, as it's called). Most of the guns they buy are average condition major trademarks, which typically auction off between minimum bid and low estimate. Because of this, many of today's auction prices realized are actually under current values, since these dealers are marking up their auction purchases to a price where being profitable and not holding the item for a long time (i.e., fast sale) are the keys. Several dealers have told me that they buy almost all their guns through auction now, since it saves the expense, hassle, and time of going to gun shows/shops to try to find resellable inventory. One dealer interviewed has purchased over $500,000 worth of inventory at 2 major auctions recently, and never left his couch!

Another trend worth noting is the guns that go from one auction house to another (again, most interesting w/ high end guns). Sometimes this is a legit purchase at the first auction, and a quick resale by the buyer at the next. Other times, it's a bit like "forum-shopping" -- when the gun doesn't bring it's reserve at one auction, the consignor just ships it to another.

Because of this significant change on what gets sold and who participates in today's auctions, it has never been more important to follow a few cardinal rules regarding auctions.

Tips to Make You a Better Auction Buyer

The first rule is to look at the auction catalog (some are online now) and pick out only the items you actually want to buy first, then mark the stuff you're interested in at a ceiling price. That means flagging the pages/items, knowing the condition and other important information, and if you have any questions, have

consider
the following guidelines.

them answered before the auction starts. On mixed lots, check to see if there's maybe a gold nugget in the pan of washed gravel.

The second rule is to determine the highest price you'll pay for it before the auction starts, and not go over that amount. This price also must include an auction buyer's premium (if any), S/H charges, sales tax (if any), credit card processing charges, and any other hidden expenses. While the rule is simple - don't go over your ceiling (maximum bid) on any item - it can be very hard to follow unless you exercise discipline. Once you go past your maximum purchase price, the auction house is making you perform, not the other way around. No matter how badly you want something, if you don't subscribe to the ceiling rule, you may never feel as comfortable with the purchase (this is called buyer's remorse, another term for the guilt of overpaying). On the other end, don't be scared to jump in & bid when a gun is going at a bargain price. There are at least as many "I-can't-believe-it-sold-so-cheap, I-wish-I'd-bid-on-it" stories after an auction as there are "What-was-I-thinking-to-bid-so-much" tales of woe.

The third rule is to not get distracted or annoyed during the auction, especially if you are attending. Stay focused and alert. Once while midway through a boring auction, an item came up that sold for almost twice its high estimate. While having a good chuckle with the guy next to me about the buyer who appeared to be spending money like a recent lottery winner, the following item I was interested in gaveled off fast at just over minimum bid. While not paying attention for 30 seconds, I lost out, and the joke was really on me. As a buyer, who cares how high it sells for if you're not interested? Your job is to concentrate on the items you want, and pay as little as possible.

The fourth rule is to physically inspect your item(s) carefully (if possible), before the auction starts. Read an auction's policy before you bid. Look carefully before you buy. That also means keeping any auction paperwork and/or provenance that may have been supplied. Buying a bogus item from an auction house is possible, and as a buyer, getting your money back may not be an option.

Tips for Potential Auction Consignors

If you have a gun(s) or a collection that you are thinking about consigning to an auction house, please

The first rule is to have an accurate and up-to-date inventory listing of what you want to put up for auction, with realistic prices. It is not the auction company's job to perform an appraisal for you - that's your part of the homework assignment. This may involve getting someone to independently appraise the item(s) at fair market values, if they can be determined. Once this is completed, you can send it to the auction company for a preliminary review, to see if it is a good fit for both parties. Do your research here, as auctions have become more specialized, and your comfort level with the auction house is everything.

The second rule is to negotiate the pricing with the auction house, and see if it is agreeable to you. That means figuring out if you can establish a minimum reserve (difficult on low and medium end items) to ensure that you will at least get a specified minimum for the item(s). Which also means paying attention to the minimum bid(s) and estimates, both high and low. In the words of one dealer interviewed for this article, his auction advice was simple. "If you have a kick ass gun, you'll probably get a kick ass price. If you have an average gun, you're probably going to get your ass kicked!" Another dealer relishes a story about an older customer who decided to go the auction route on 6 guns he had purchased from the dealer years before. The dealer had made him a good cash offer, but the lure of the potential high prices from the auction house won the customer over. During the auction, the dealer ended up buying all 6 guns at 20% less than what his original cash offer was 6 months earlier. Hmm.....

The third rule is to know and accept the fact that if you consign to an auction house; it's going to be awhile to before you get your money. And it might not be as much as you were expecting, especially if there are no reserves. Most auction houses need approx. 2-7 months to liquidate items and pay the consignors after the buyer's inspection period is over.

Not all sellers considering auction will necessarily do best with a national level auction house.

These rules and guidelines will serve you well at any auction, and you'll also feel better about your sales and purchases if you follow them religiously. These are the only ways that you can make an auction house go to work for you, rather than you working for the auction house.

THE NSSF AND ROBERT DELFAY

OVER 3 DECADES OF FIREARMS INDUSTRY LEADERSHIP!

Robert Delfay was born on November 18, 1947, in Tarrytown, New York, and grew up in the upstate Brewster, New York, graduating from Brewster High School in 1965. In these formative years, his interests were mostly those of a typical high school teenager: sports, cars and, in Bob's case, hunting. Bob spent most of his weekends and summers working on the dairy farm of a friend, which he considers one of the most educational experiences of his life.

It's rumored that Bob may have made a "mistake" on his first hunting license application that allowed him to hunt one year earlier than fish-and-game regulations permitted.

Bob attended Western Connecticut State University in nearby Danbury, Connecticut, and worked full-time in the evenings to pay tuition and to help his single-parent mom with family expenses. He graduated in 1969 with a BS in biology and English. In college, his fondest memories revolved around the successful completion of each semester. Upon graduating, he worked for a few months as a newspaper sports reporter until he heard about an opening for a writer at the National Shooting Sports Foundation. He applied for the job and started work at NSSF in November of 1969, 8 years after the NSSF was founded.

Bob and his family currently reside in Southbury, Connecticut, some 15 miles from the NSSF offices in Newtown. Bob and his wife, Kay, spend most of their free time restoring and maintaining a 260-year old historic residence. Bob's 33-year-old son and 26-year-old daughter both live within an hour, and gather frequently.

Bob admits that his work at NSSF is a very major part of his life and often goes weeks without taking a day off. "In part, I spend a lot of time in the office and on the road because there are so many challenges and opportunities facing our industry and NSSF," Delfay said. "But in part, it's also because I get to work with so many talented and dedicated people, and the work is totally enjoyable."

Those who have worked with Bob describe him as being very media savvy without being slick. He chooses his words

and messages carefully, always gets his homework done, usually listens before carefully speaking and, most importantly, never shoots from the hip. "I once overheard my father-in-law telling someone that 'Bob is not the smartest person I've ever known but he's one of the hardest workers.' I always thought that was a fair description," Delfay said.

During his 33 years with the NSSF, including the last 16 years as president, Delfay has provided successful leadership by successfully dealing with scores of personal agendas, huge egos, short-term

Over the years, all of us have become so used to seeing Robert in a suit and tie, that's it's always a pleasure to see him enjoying the shooting sports, which he has helped to preserve with his diligent efforts and signal contributions through the NSSF over the past 33 years.

thinking, naïve new ideas and old opinions, and lots of other firearms industry baggage the anti-gun press can smell and easily hose down a mile away. Perhaps his greatest asset is never deliberately putting a bull's-eye target on his chest while on the front lines of the pro-gun battlefields. He learned a long time ago that those who do usually end up as press fodder and early casualties, never getting the opportunity to go on to another bigger fight.

Delfay is not afraid to enter the enemy's own turf in his efforts to dispel myths about the firearms industry. He has spoken before strongly anti-gun crowds and has attended anti-gun conferences held by the American Medical Association with good success, earning respect for himself and for the firearms industry from many leaders in the medical community.

Of Delfay's many notable NSSF achievements, his real shining moment came in 1999 and 2000, in leading the industry's response to nearly 30 individual municipal lawsuits from cities such as Atlanta, Chicago and New Orleans. When many thought that the firearms industry would roll over (much like the tobacco industry) because

of the overwhelming job of defending so many lawsuits, the industry hung tough thanks to the leadership of the National Shooting Sports Foundation and the Hunting and Shooting Sports Heritage Fund Board of Governors. While Bob insists the industry's early success in fighting these lawsuits was very much a team effort, many acknowledge Delfay's quiet leadership as a key influence. After conducting polls within months of the first lawsuits, the NSSF found out that 75%-78% of the public said the lawsuits were wrong. The American public embraced the idea that you can't hold manufacturers responsible for what a criminal does with a firearm. Kind of like automobiles, drunk drivers and vehicular homicides. Nobody blames the Lincoln. This isn't rocket science, just good solid Constitutional thinking, doing your homework, and never firing an angry shot in vain.

With the firearms industry's annual SHOT (Shooting, Hunting, Outdoor Trade) SHOW scheduled to be in the New Orleans Convention Center in January of 2001, Bob Delfay and the NSSF played their cards well. While some in the firearms industry knee-jerked at the idea of spending their hard-earned convention dollars in a city with a vocal anti-gun mayor and a lawsuit on the books, Delfay insisted that it would be wrong to let this anti-gun politician dictate where the industry would hold its convention and refused to incur perhaps millions of dollars in losses by attempting to relocate or reschedule the show. The 2001 SHOT SHOW went off without a hitch and was positively covered by the media, while tens of thousands New Orleans residents learned that the firearms industry was not the evil empire that was portrayed by their mayor.

Rodeo director, urban cowboy, or maybe even a Jim Carmichel wannabe? This earlier photo of Delfay with trademark beard and 10 gallon Stetson shows us that continuous big city politicking doesn't have to mean that the Western wear has to go away.

Shortly after the SHOT SHOW, the Louisiana Supreme Court ruled the New Orleans suit was ". . . an indirect attempt to regulate [at the local level] the lawful design, manufacture, marketing and sale of firearms." The Court said the [Louisiana] preemption law was passed "in the interest of the public" and that state regulation of firearms "is of vital interest to the citizens of Louisiana" which "preserves the public safety and welfare." The Court noted that municipal suits that attempt to regulate the firearms industry would result in haphazard and inconsistent rules that would threaten public safety.

Robert seems pleased holding his Joe Foss autographed 22nd Ed. cover while in the Blue Book Publications, Inc. booth during the recent New Orleans SHOT Show. He's probably asking the author S.P. Fjestad (l) "When are you going to join the NSSF Shooting Sports Heritage Fund?" The answer came last fall in Phoenix.

"We are pleased that the Louisiana Supreme Court has a greater respect for the authority of the state legislature and the constitutionally prescribed legislative process than does the Mayor of New Orleans and his Handgun Control, Inc. allies," said Delfay.

Delfay attributes the industry's early success to a carefully laid out strategy that was backed with the considerable revenue generated through the new Hunting and Shooting Sports Heritage Fund. Heritage Fund membership dues began as 1% of a company's gross revenue and were recently reduced to ½% as a result of an increase in the number of companies supporting the Heritage Fund and to significant non-industry revenue, including a $1 million grant from the National Wild Turkey Federation (NWTF.)

Unlike the fate of the tobacco industry, which leveraged itself into a big settlement, the firearms industry stood firm, and was proactive in its aggressive response. "That's been an absolute shock to the cities that filed the suits," Delfay says. "They figured the industry would just roll over. What they didn't figure was that an optics manufacturer would pledge 1% of its sales to fight these lawsuits, that the NWTF would join the battle, and that individual sportsmen would send e-mails to the NSSF that they wanted to contribute."

Since the 1998 New Orleans suit, some 27 states have passed preemptive legislation that expressly bars municipalities from filing politically motivated lawsuits against the firearms industry, and several other state legislatures are currently considering passage of such laws. Delfay publicly credits the National Rifle Association of America with making the passage of these laws possible. "While these lawsuits threaten firearms manufacturers, it is our customers, through the NRA, that have come to the defense of the industry," Delfay said.

Throughout 2001, lawsuit after lawsuit in city after city were being dismissed in favor of the firearms industry. New Orleans joined Atlanta, Chicago, Philadelphia, Miami, Cincinnati, Gary, Indiana, Bridgeport, Connecticut, Camden County, New Jersey, and the State of New York in having their cases against the firearms industry dismissed.

While the NRA has over 4 million members in its boat, most of which have their oars in the water and pull on command, the NSSF has 1,900 skilled oarsmen who are experienced in rowing their streamlined boat and know how get to their destination quickly. Their helmsman, Bob Delfay, also never compromises their direction, and always knows their exact location.

Delfay lists the first Shooting Sports Summit among his personal triumphs. It positioned the NSSF as the organization that was trying to plan for the future of the industry.

"Certainly, my small role in the SHOT SHOW has been gratifying. When you spend an entire career in a nonprofit sector, you take great pride if you've been lucky enough to build a few things," says Delfay. Once again, Bob's inclination to carefully orchestrate from the sidelines has enabled him to almost achieve "stealth status" on both pro and anti-gun radar screens. Of this, he is the master, never jeopardizing his profile or the NSSF.

His plan after he steps down from the NSSF? "I have no idea, and I have a hundred ideas," he says. After 33 years with the same company, it's hard to imagine that he won't continue his involvement on some level. He's certainly earned a prime spot in the pasture, if that's where he wants to graze.

Regardless, every person who likes guns and believes in the 2nd Amendment is indebted to Robert Delfay and the NSSF for their signal accomplishments within the firearms industry. While attending the NASGW (National Association of Sporting Goods Wholesalers) Show last November in Phoenix, I walked by the NSSF booth. Bob looked at me and said, "Why haven't you joined the Heritage Foundation yet?" His tone was friendly but clearly expressed disappointment that Blue Book Publications had not added their support to the Heritage Foundation. Backpedaling with some lame excuses, we quickly got down to business. Within several minutes, Blue Book Publications, Inc., became a sponsor of the Hunting and Shooting Sports Heritage Foundation. It was the most significant thing that I accomplished at the show, and looking back, wonder why we didn't make the move earlier. Any company or individual who derives revenue from the firearms industry needs to belong to this organization.

In that behalf, Blue Book Publications, Inc. is offering a limited Special Hunting and Shooting Sports Heritage Foundation 23rd Edition. One hundred percent of the proceeds go directly to the Hunting and Shooting Sports Heritage Foundation. It's money well spent, is signed by Bob himself, and is available directly from Blue Book Publications, Inc.-so order yours today.

Blue Book Publications, Inc. thanks Bob Delfay for his hard work and quiet professionalism in support of our hunting and shooting sports traditions and our firearms freedoms, and we are proud to be able to play a small role in supporting the organizations and programs Bob has helped develop over his successful career. If it's true that Bob "made a mistake" in beginning his hunting career a year early, we hope Bob enjoys many more hunting seasons in his retirement.

We were fortunate enough to catch up with Rapid Robert after his final SHOT Show as NSSF President recently in Las Vegas, a resounding success with overall attendance just 200 short of the 1997 record.

The following questions and answers will give you insights on how important his and the NSSF's contributions have been within the firearms industry. With over 1,900 member companies all pledging a part of their annual revenue, the NSSF is well positioned and funded to continue our fight to preserve America's gun rights well into the future.

Since you came from a PR background, how important do you think this has been in the development of the NSSF?

It has certainly been essential. Throughout its history, the NSSF has primarily been a communications organization. It seems that everything we do starts with a blank sheet of paper. Whether it's the original proposal to the Board of Governors for a new program, the brochure to announce that program to the industry or communications with the media, communications and public relations skills are critically important.

What does the Heritage Fund do and why is it so important to become a member?

The Heritage Fund accomplishes many things for our industry but probably none is more important than the unity it has brought. Firearms manufacturers, ammunition makers, optic suppliers, retailers, distributors and individuals have come together in support of common industry efforts. Perhaps the best-known program is the defense of the politically motivated lawsuits against our industry. But there are many other very important Heritage Fund activities such as providing the media and the American public with a better understanding of the firearms industry, the people who make and sell firearms and those of us who use them recreationally.

No stranger to the lectern, Robert Delfay addresses a standing room only crowd on the State of the Shooting Sports Industry at the recent Las Vegas SHOT Show. Bob's successor, the new President of the NSSF, Doug Painter, is seated on the right.

What's been your greatest accomplishment?

Some say not getting fired in 33 years is my greatest accomplishment. Other than that, I probably take the greatest professional pride in the organization and tremendous success of the first Shooting Sports Summit and in the three follow up Summits. These activities clearly focused the challenges and the opportunities facing our industry and positioned NSSF as the logical organization to lead these efforts. Working closely with the other highly effective organizations in our business from the National Rifle Association of America to the National Wild Turkey Federation, NSSF has been able to launch, expand and assist with a number of essential programs. Actually, the creation of the highly successful Hunting and Shooting Sports Heritage Foundation was also an outcome of one of the early Shooting Sports Summits.

When things unraveled with the individual cities initiating manufacturer liability lawsuits, many people thought that the firearms industry would lie down like the tobacco industry. What do you think made the difference in the reversal in so many of these lawsuits?

There can be no question that our early success in fighting the city lawsuits has been a result of the leadership that came from many industry executives in the firearms industry and the focus which NSSF was able to bring to this leadership.

If you had to characterize anti-gun people (there are limited flavors), what's the one element that they all seem to have in common?

Clearly, one thing that they had in common was they all voted for Bill Clinton and would vote for Hillary Clinton if they had a chance today. These are people who feel that the answer to all of our country's problems is more government and more government interference in our personal lives. They put more faith in government than they do in individual responsibility. That having been said, some of the people who don't support individual firearms ownership and who would like to see much stricter limitations on firearms in our nation are well intentioned. They are, however, misinformed and, perhaps, naïve but they are well intentioned. Others are simply mean-spirited. They have come to hate firearms and they will never consider the possibility that firearms might have a valuable and appropriate place in our society. For some reason, when a criminal uses a firearm in the commission of a crime their response is to regulate the firearm and not the criminal.

If your average American told you "Bob, I have $150 a year to spend to support firearms issues and never-ending political battles", how would you tell him/her how to spend it?

That's a good question. Assuming they would not want to contribute to the Bob Delfay Retirement Fund, I think my first recommendation would be support of the National Rifle Association of America. Beyond that, they should, obviously, take a look at their special interests and support related organizations which might be the National Wild Turkey Federation, the Amateur Trapshooting Association or the Hunting and Shooting Sports Heritage Foundation. They might also want to consider support for the United States Olympic Shooting Team or the United States Biathlon Association.

What do see for the future of the NSSF?

I think the future of the NSSF is huge. It has grown very rapidly over the past several years with the budget tripling in less than 10 years. I believe similar growth can be accomplished in the next 10 years and I am confident that it will. It is immensely gratifying to me that the NSSF has so much respect from other organizations in our industry. They view NSSF as not trying to interfere with the activities of any other organization but merely trying to assist wherever possible. That is how we view ourselves and we are proud that we have been able to establish so many partnerships. Going forward, I am particularly pleased and excited that the NSSF Board of Governors has named Doug Painter as the new NSSF President. Doug has tremendous creativity and visibility, and is as dedicated to the future of the hunting and shooting sports as anyone I know.

After you step down as President of the NSSF, what are your plans?

At this point I am not sure whether I will become a professional tennis player, NASCAR driver or rock star. Maybe I'll do all three. In the meantime, I need to paint my house and repair the roof on the barn.

Did your job evolve into being a lot more difficult and hazardous than you originally expected it to be? If so, why?

It sure did. It became much more political and much more public. There were days in 1999 and 2000 where we would receive upwards of 10 requests in one day to do newspaper, radio or television appearances. We responded to as many as we could but simply couldn't respond to all.

How do you feel about the state of the American firearms industry today? And how can all of us continue to help?

I have said on many occasions that I believe our industry is as strong as it has ever been. This is because I think we are probably more unified than ever. There can be no better example of this than the Hunting and Shooting Sports Heritage Fund and its role in our successful efforts to coordinate a defense of the politically motivated lawsuits against our industry. While those city lawsuits were aimed primarily at handgun manufacturers, a broad-range of industry companies, from accessory to optics manufacturers, committed significant dollars to fight those lawsuits. While we are on the subject of supporters, I cannot thank Steve Fjestad and Blue Book Publications enough for their tremendous support of the NSSF and the Hunting and Shooting Sports Heritage Fund.

What are your favorite shooting sports, and do you go hunting? Any safaris?

I truly enjoy all of the shooting sports. I probably do more shotgun shooting than anything else but that's largely because is more accessible in Connecticut than rifle shooting.

One of the most enjoyable days of shooting that I can remember was an afternoon of plinking with a .22 target rifle with a good friend of mine and former member of U.S. Biathlon Team, Lyle Nelson. We started by throwing a soda can out in front of us. First Lyle had to hit it then I had to hit it and the contest was to see who would miss first. I remember that we ended up shooting at a piece of aluminum the size of a quarter and I have no doubt that I was the first to miss.

I like all forms of hunting. I have been fortunate enough to have taken several elk trips to Montana (a few of them successful). I took my first safari in 2001. Also successful. Probably my favorite form of hunting today is South Dakota pheasant.

Decades earlier, Bob was at the forefront of the fight to preserve hunting and shooting sports. While the color of his hair may have changed, his passionate dedication and devotion to conservation and preservation of the 2nd Amendment has never wavered.

What are your favorite guns to shoot?

Again, this is very hard to answer. On the safari I just mentioned, I took a Griffin & Howe sporterized 30-06 Springfield that was given to me by my father-in-law in 1969. I am very glad I did that. It meant a lot to me to bring that rifle and to be successful with it.

Did you personally blow the duck call at 4pm at the end of each SHOT SHOW? How did that tradition start?

Heavens no! I may not be the best duck caller in the world but I'm not that bad. This tradition was started by Jerry Van Dyke, the original SHOT SHOW manager and he continued it over the years. Jerry is now retired and for the first time did not blow the call at the last show.

Explain to the readers how the NSSF originally got started and how it's become what it is today.

I find it very interesting that the NSSF was formed in 1961 following a strategic conference on the hunting and shooting sports-not unlike the Shooting Sports Summit that we first organized in 1996. The NSSF grew slowly but steadily over its first decade. Our growth really took off in 1979 with the launch of the SHOT SHOW. There was another major period of growth in 1996 following the first Shooting Sports Summit and then again in 1999-2000 with the response to the politically motivated lawsuits against our industry.

If you could give the inimitable Jim Carmichel one last parting shot - what would it be?

Who is Jim Carmichel?

What's the most frustrating and/or difficult thing that you've ever dealt with during your tenure at the NSSF?

Without question, it's been dealing with negative people within our industry who are not members

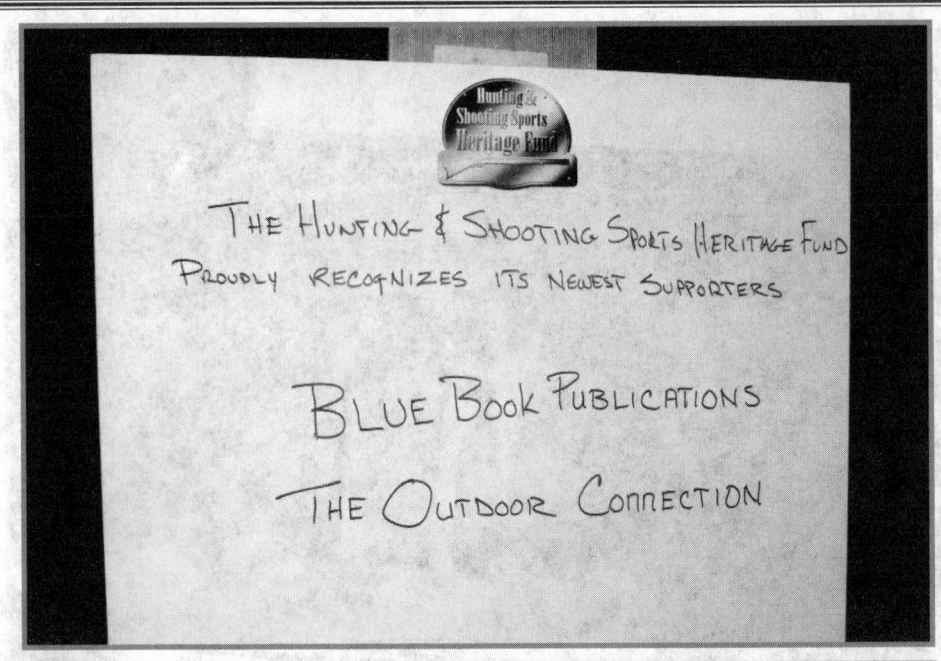

Blue Book Publications, Inc. became a proud sponsor of the NSSF Shooting Sports Heritage Fund at the 2001 NASGW Show in Phoenix, after a quick 5-minute chat with Robert Delfay. Member companies pledge their financial support to help keep the tradition and heritage of shooting sports alive and well.

of our industry organizations and view their role in life as criticizing what everyone else does. One specific example is a letter circulated by one of these individuals to every single SHOT SHOW exhibitor a few years ago telling them that they should not support the SHOT SHOW and they should not support the NSSF because we were going to hold the show in Atlanta even though that Mayor was threatening a lawsuit against our industry. That was an extraordinarily irresponsible thing to do. Our options were to take the show to Atlanta or to cancel the SHOT SHOW and send a message that an anti-gun politician could dictate where our show would be held. Dealing with these people has been frustrating but fortunately for every one of these negative types, there are 100 people who are dedicated to our industry and are all pulling in the same direction.

How much more sophisticated is the anti-gun press today than when you started at the NSSF? How do you think both the NSSF and the NRA have risen to the task of defending America's constitutional right to keep and bear arms?

I'm not sure that our adversaries are anymore

sophisticated today than they were 20 years ago and I am not sure that they are any more sophisticated than we. The advantage they have over us is that they can work full-time attacking us and what we stand for.

Organizations like NSSF have to divide our resources between responding to attacks by our adversaries at the same time that we pursue our own strategic goals to impact hunter recruitment and retention, promotion of the recreational target shooting sports, issues of public visibility and voter education. Our adversaries would like nothing better than if we spent all our time attempting to stamp out brush fires that they ignite. We have not done that and we never will.

Interested in buying or selling a particular firearm(s)? Depending on what you are interested in, a referral can be made that will enable you to be sure that you are getting a fair price. This service is designed to help all those people who are worried or scared about purchasing a potentially "bad gun" or getting "ripped off" when selling.

Remember, Blue Book Publications is a publisher, not a gun dealer, so we have no vested interest in trying to buy/sell your firearms. Our established international network of reliable dealers and collectors allows your particular buy/sell request to be referred to the right company/individual, based on both your region and area of collectibility. There is no charge for this referral service (a thank you would be nice) - we are simply connecting you with the best person(s)/company possible ensuring that you get a fair deal. All replies are treated strictly confidentially. Correspondence/replies should be directed to:

Blue Book Publications, Inc.
Attn: John Allen
8009 34th Ave. So., Ste. 175 • Minneapolis, MN 55425 USA
Phone No.: 952-854-5229 • Fax No.: 952-853-1486
johna@bluebookinc.com

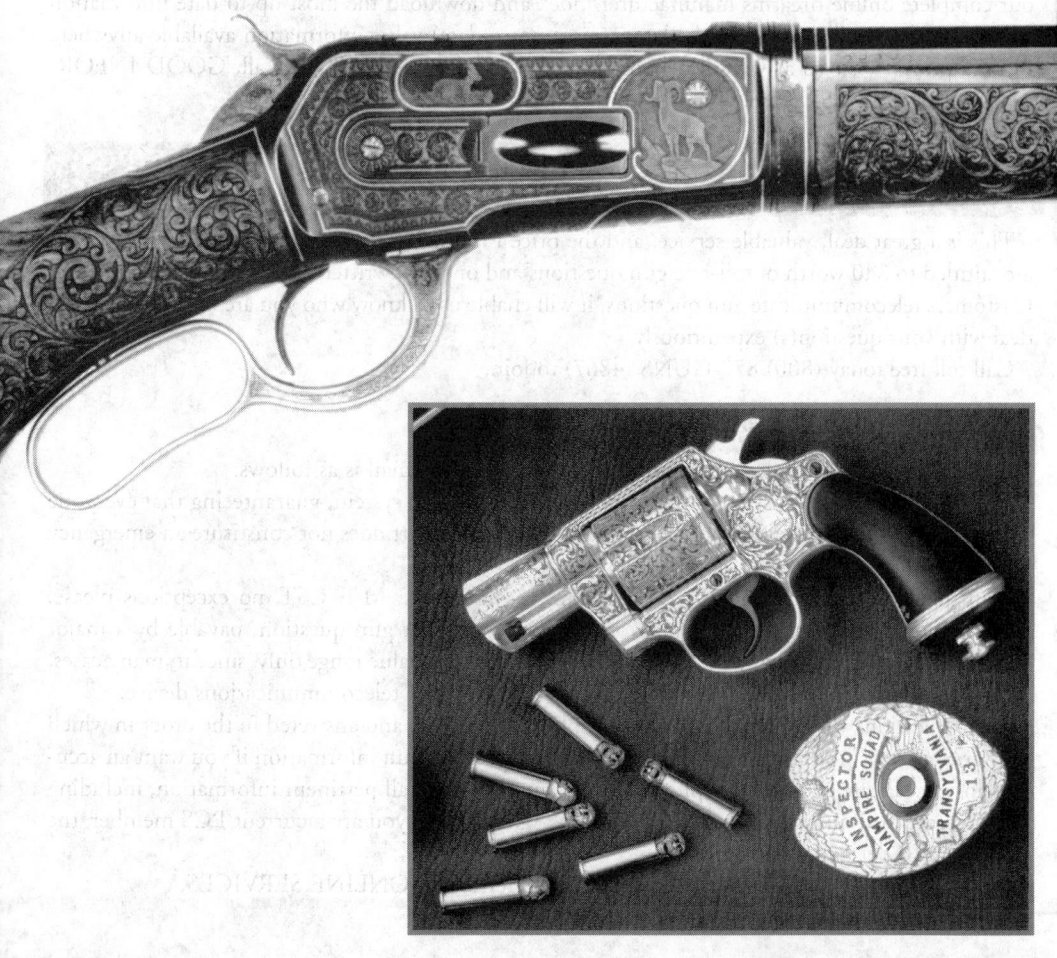

GUN QUESTIONS/APPRAISALS POLICY & PREFERRED CUSTOMER SERVICE (PCS)

W e certainly never asked for this - it just happened. Whether we wanted it or not, Blue Book Publications, Inc. has ended up in the driver's seat as the clearing-house for gun information. While somewhat manageable for the past 18 years, a change of policy has been implemented to better serve our customers. Because the volume of gun questions now requires full-time attention, we have developed a Preferred Customer Service (PCS) program that will enable us to provide you with the service you have come to expect from Blue Book Publications, Inc. To that end, we have extended all of these services to our state-of-the-art web site (www.bluebookinc.com).

To ensure that the Research Dept. can answer every gun question with an equal degree of thoroughness, a $100,000 firearms library is maintained and constantly updated. Additionally, hundreds of both new and old factory brochures, price sheets, and dealer inventory listings are kept on file to help assist in answering the thousands of gun-related questions that are received annually. For those questions that require further "digging," we are fortunate enough to have many of the leading experts only a phone call/fax/email away. It's a huge job, and we answer every question like we could go to court on it.

ONLINE SERVICES

You now have the ability to submit an online Firearms Inquiry, request a written Appraisal, browse our complete online firearms manufacturer index and download the most up-to-date information available, or subscribe online to the latest (most up-to-date) value information available anywhere for any price. Visit us at www.bluebookinc.com - you'll be amazed! After all, GOOD INFORMATION NEVER SLEEPS!™

JOIN OUR NEW PREFERRED CUSTOMER SERVICE PROGRAM (PCS) for GUN QUESTIONS & APPRAISALS answered by industry professionals

This is a great deal, valuable service, and the price is only $25 per year. As a PCS member, you are entitled to $40 worth of toll-free gun questions and one $20 written appraisal! When Preferred Customers telecommunicate gun questions, it will enable us to know who you are immediately, and deal with your question(s) expeditiously.

Call toll free today (800) 877-GUNS (4867) to join.

POLICY FOR GUN QUESTIONS

Our policy for answering gun questions by phone, fax, or email is as follows:

All gun questions are answered in a FIFO (first in, first out) system, guaranteeing that everyone will be treated equally. Remember - poor planning on your part does not constitute an emergency for us.

Gun question telephone hours are 9:00 a.m. to 4:00 p.m., M-F, CST, no exceptions please. Unless you are a current PCS member, the charge is $10 per gun question, payable by a major credit card. Telephone pricing requests will be given within a value range only, since in many cases, a condition factor cannot be accurately represented through a telecommunications device.

Faxed questions will be treated similarly to phone questions, and answered in the order in which they are received. You must provide us with all the necessary gun information if you want an accurate answer. Please enclose your phone and fax numbers, and all pertinent information, including major credit card number and expiration date. Again, unless you are a current PCS member, the charge is $10 per gun question.

For email questions (Firearms Inquiries) please refer to our ONLINE SERVICES, www.bluebookinc.com.

Online "Firearms Inquiries" will be put in the FIFO system. We have noticed a sense of urgency in some email requests. When you submit an online request, please be as thorough as possible. Also include your major credit card number and expiration date. Again, unless you are a current PCS member, the charge is $10 per gun question.

Letter questions (preferred, with photos) will also be answered in the order of arrival. Good quality photos would certainly help, especially if a written appraisal is required. Make sure you include the proper return address and phone number. Again, unless you are a current PCS member, the charge is $10 per gun question.

APPRAISAL INFORMATION

Written appraisals will be performed only if the following criteria are met:

If you wish to have a gun(s) appraised accurately based on the correct condition factor(s), we must have good quality photos with a complete description, including manufacturer's name, model, gauge/caliber, barrel length. On some firearms (depending on the Trademark and Model) a factory letter may be necessary. Our charge for a written appraisal is $20 per gun, up to 5 guns. At 6 guns, the charge is normally $15 per gun. If you are a current PCS member, you are entitled to one free appraisal per year. Larger collections may be discounted somewhat, depending on the complexity and the size of the collection. Unfortunately, we cannot appraise emailed requests with images, as the condition factor cannot be accurately ascertained. Please allow 2-3 weeks response time per appraisal request.

ADDITIONAL SERVICES

Individuals requesting a photocopy of a particular page or section from any edition for insurance or reference purposes will be billed at $5 per page, up to 5 pages, and $3.50 per page thereafter. Simply let us know what you would like copied, including which edition and how you would like it sent to you (mail or fax only).

TURNAROUND TIME

Our goal is to answer most telephone, mail, email, or faxed gun questions in no longer than 3 business days - unless we're away attending trade/gun shows. This also assumes that all information needed to process the question(s) is initially provided, otherwise delays may occur. In instances where additional time is required to properly research your request, you will be notified within the first week.

We hope that you can appreciate this new policy regarding gun questions and/or appraisals. Just as millions of computer users are now paying for reliable and speedy hardware/software support, it is time to take a similar service approach, ensuring that the most accurate and up-to-date gun information is provided to you on a professional and reliable basis.

Please direct all gun questions and appraisals to the following:
Blue Book Publications, Inc.
Attn: Research Dept.
8009 34th Ave. S., Suite 175
Minneapolis, MN 55425 USA
Phone: 800-877-4867 (Toll-free in U.S. & Canada)
Fax: 952-853-1486 • www.bluebookinc.com

DEFENDING **YOUR** SECOND AMENDMENT RIGHT TO OWN GUNS, HUNT, SHOOT, PROTECT YOURSELF AND SO MUCH MORE...

For nearly 130 years the National Rifle Association has been the leader in defending our Second Amendment right to keep and bear arms as well as protecting our hunting rights and traditions. We're fighting the gun banners and animal rights fanatics on all fronts. By joining the NRA, or renewing your existing membership, you will help to keep our unique American traditions alive.

When you join NRA you will receive these great benefits:

- NRA Black and Gold Shooters Cap
- A no-annual-fee NRA Visa card (for qualified individuals)
- Your choice of NRA monthly publications, *America's 1st Freedom, American Hunter* or *American Rifleman*

- $10,000 Personal Accident Insurance
- $1,000 in ArmsCare Firearm Insurance
- Hotel, Car Rental and Interstate Moving Discounts
- Discounts at local Gun Stores and other Retail Outlets

And much, much, more…

NATIONAL RIFLE ASSOCIATION

☐ 1 Year Regular……… $35   ☐ 3 Year Regular……… $85
☐ 5 Year Regular……… $125   Date_____   NRA Recruiter #X012415

If renewal, give ID# ☐☐☐☐☐☐☐☐   Payment Information:

Mr./Mrs./Ms. _____   ☐ Check/Money Order

Street: _____ Apt.#: _____   Charge to: ☐ MC   ☐ VISA   ☐ Amex

City: _____ State: _____ Zip _____   ☐ Discover   Expiration Date ☐☐☐☐

Daytime Phone: (_____)_____   Credit Card#

Choose ONE Magazine: ☐ America's 1st Freedom   ☐☐☐☐☐☐☐☐☐☐☐☐☐☐☐☐

☐ American Rifleman   ☐ American Hunter   Member Signature _____

Contributions gifts or membership dues made or paid to the National Rifle Association of America are not refundable or transferable and are not deductible as charitable contributions for Federal Income Tax purposes.
Mail with payment to: NRA, 11250 Waples Mill Rd., Fairfax, VA 22030

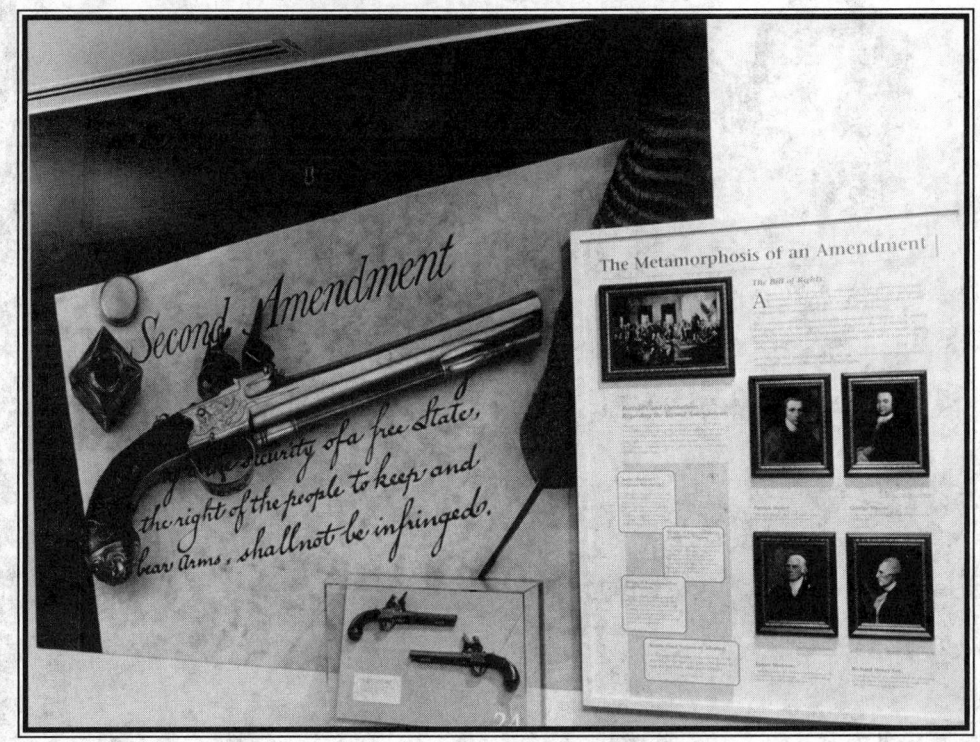

National Firearms Museum

The only museum dedicated to telling our story of freedom
and the American experience through firearms…the
NATIONAL FIREARMS MUSEUM

As a firearms owner, the National Firearms Museum accurately tells
your story through 85 educational exhibits displaying over 2,000
historic and rare firearms.

Your TAX-DEDUCTIBLE GIFT to the NATIONAL FIREARMS
MUSEUM ENDOWMENT will help guarantee that future generations
will be able to learn of America's constitutional rights and firearms heritage.

For further information on how you can help permanently endow the National
Firearms Museum's future contact: The NRA Foundation
11250 Waples Mill Road, Fairfax, VA 22030
or call 703-267-1121 or 1-800-423-6894

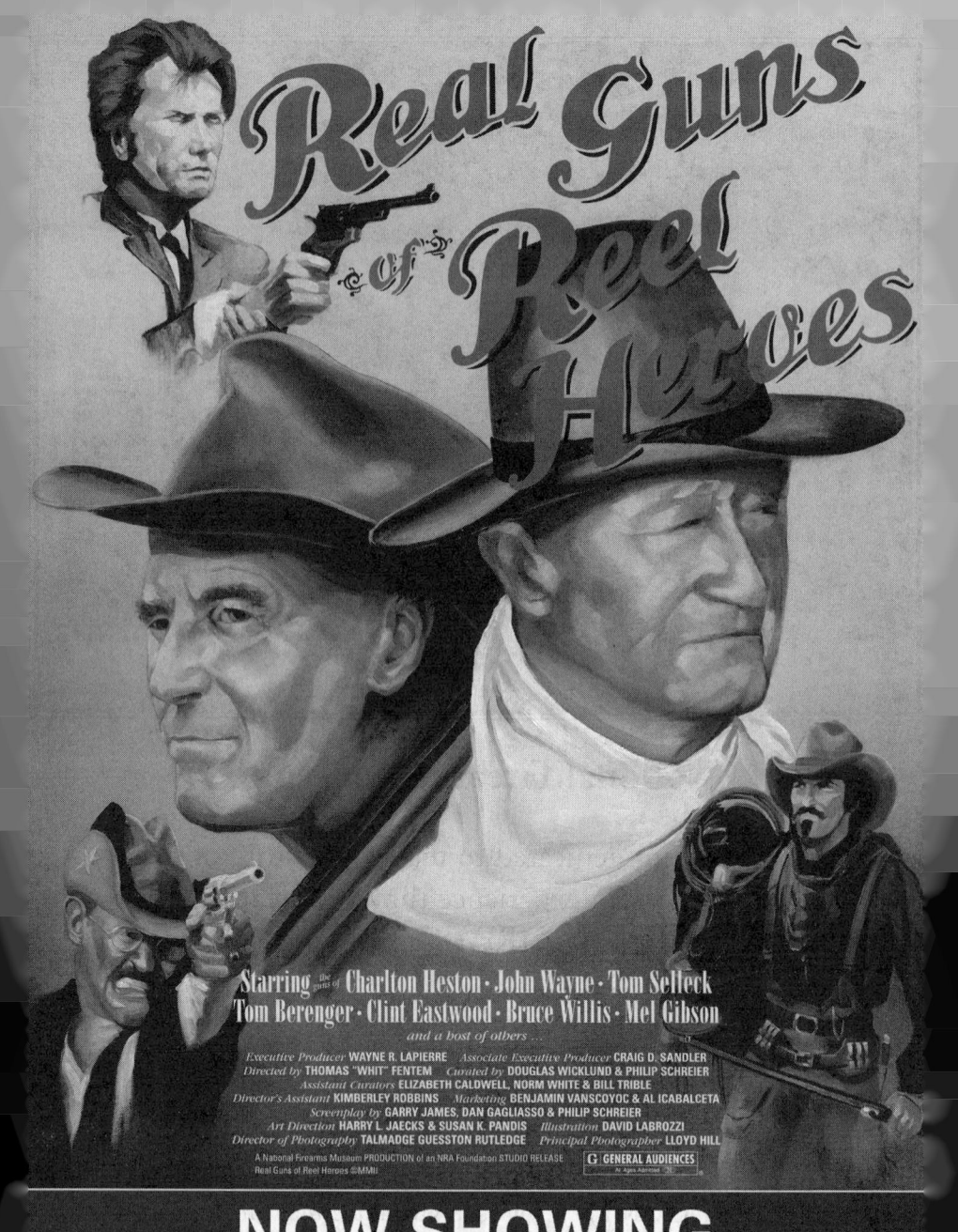

Starring the guns of **Charlton Heston · John Wayne · Tom Selleck
Tom Berenger · Clint Eastwood · Bruce Willis · Mel Gibson**
and a host of others ...

Executive Producer **WAYNE R. LAPIERRE**   *Associate Executive Producer* **CRAIG D. SANDLER**
Directed by **THOMAS "WHIT" FENTEM**   *Curated by* **DOUGLAS WICKLUND & PHILIP SCHREIER**
Assistant Curators **ELIZABETH CALDWELL, NORM WHITE & BILL TRIBLE**
Director's Assistant **KIMBERLEY ROBBINS**   *Marketing* **BENJAMIN VANSCOYOC & AL ICABALCETA**
Screenplay by **GARRY JAMES, DAN GAGLIASSO & PHILIP SCHREIER**
Art Direction **HARRY L. JAECKS & SUSAN K. PANDIS**   *Illustration* **DAVID LABROZZI**
Director of Photography **TALMADGE GUESSTON RUTLEDGE**   *Principal Photographer* **LLOYD HILL**

A National Firearms Museum PRODUCTION of an NRA Foundation STUDIO RELEASE
Real Guns of Reel Heroes ©MMII

G | GENERAL AUDIENCES
At Ages Admitted

NOW SHOWING
at the National Firearms Museum through December 31, 2002

The National Firearms Museum
Open to the public from 10 a.m. to 4 p.m. every day except major holidays
Address: 11250 Waples Mill Road, Fairfax, Virginia 22030
For additional information, call (703)267-1600
www.nrahq.org/shooting/museum

PASS ON
THE TRADITION

Designate your valuable guns to the Hunting and Shooting Sports Heritage Trust

If you'd like to assure the heritage and tradition of the shooting sports is here for the next generation to enjoy, donate your valuable firearms to the Hunting and Shooting Sports Heritage Trust. Upon the settlement of your estate, your collection will help the HSSHT generate much-needed income to ensure the shooting sports live on. What better way to make a lasting impression.

For more information on the Hunting and Shooting Sports Heritage Trust, and the tax advantages of "willing" your valuable collection, call 203-426-1320. Do it today...for the good of tomorrow.

Hunting & Shooting Sports Heritage Trust

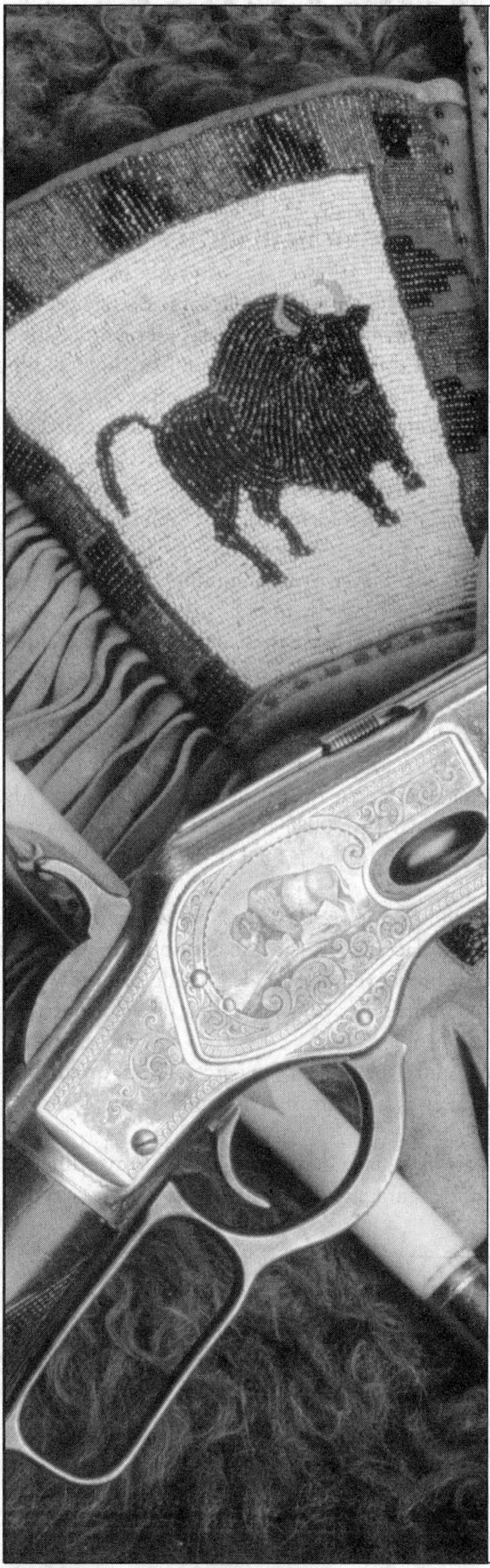

GRADING CRITERIA

The old, NRA method of firearms grading - relying upon adjectives such as "Excellent" or "Fair" - has served the firearms community for a many years. Today's dealers/collectors, especially those who deal in modern guns, have turned away from the older subjective system. There is too much variance within some of the older subjective grades, therefore making accurate grading difficult.

Most dealers and collectors are now utilizing what is essentially an objective method for deciding the condition of a gun: THE PERCENTAGE OF ORIGINAL FACTORY FINISH(ES) REMAINING ON THE GUN. After looking critically at a variety of firearms and carefully studying the **Photo Percentage Grading System™** (pages 65-112), it will soon become evident whether a gun has 98%, 90%, 70% or less finish remaining. Remember, sometimes an older gun described as NIB can actually be 98% or less condition, simply because of the wear accumulated by taking it in and out of the box and being handled too many times (commemoratives are especially prone to this problem). Of course, factors such as quality of finish(es), engraving (and other embellishments), special orders/features, historical significance and/or provenance, etc. can and do affect prices immensely. Also, it seems that every year bore condition becomes more important in the overall grading factor (and price) of collectible, major trademarks like Winchester levers, Schuetzens, older Springfields & Sharps, etc. Because of this, bore condition must be listed separately for those guns where it makes a difference in value. Never pay a premium for condition that isn't there. Remember, original condition still beats everything else to the bank.

Every gun's unique condition factor - and therefore the price - is best determined by the percentage of original finish(es) remaining, with the key consideration being the overall frame/receiver finish. The key word here is "original," for if anyone other than the factory has refinished the gun, its value as a collector's item has been diminished, with the exception of rare and historical pieces that have been properly restored. Every year, top quality restorations have become more accepted, and prices have gone up proportionately with the quality of the workmanship. Also popular now are antique finishes, and the question is, what is 100% antique finish on new reproductions? Answer - a gun that started out as new, and then has been aged to a lower condition factor to duplicate natural wear and tear.

Carefully study the photographs and read the captions on pages 65-112. Note where the finishes of a firearm typically wear off first. These are usually places where the gun accumulates wear from holster/case rubbing, and contact with the hands or body over an extended period of time. A variety of firearms have been shown in four-color to guarantee that your "sampling rate" for observing finishes with their correct colors is as diversified as possible.

It should be noted that the older a collectible firearm is, the smaller the percentage of original finish one can expect to find. Some very old and/or very rare firearms are acceptable to collectors in almost any condition!

For your convenience, NRA Condition Standards are listed next door on page 63. Converting from this grading system to percentages can now be done accurately. **Remember, the price is wrong if the condition factor isn't right!**

CONVERTING TO NRA MODERN STANDARDS

When converting from NRA Modern Standards, the following rules generally apply:

New/Perfect - 100% with or without box. Not mint - new (i.e., no excuses). 100% on currently manufactured firearms assumes NIB condition and not sold previously at retail.

Excellent - 95%+ - 99% (typically).

Very Good - 80% - 95% (should be all original).

Good - 60% - 80% (should be all original).

Fair - 20% - 60% (may or may not be original, but must function properly and shoot).

Poor - under 20% (shooting not a factor).

The NRA conditions listed below have been provided as guidelines to assist the reader in converting and comparing condition factors to the Photo Percentage Grading System™ (see pages 65-112). In order to use this book correctly, the reader is urged to consult these condition standards when converting to percentages of condition. Once the gun's condition has been accurately assessed, only then can the correct values be ascertained.

NRA MODERN CONDITION DESCRIPTIONS

New - not previously sold at retail, in same condition as current factory production.

Perfect - in new condition in every respect.

Excellent - new condition, used but little, no noticeable marring of wood or metal, bluing near perfect (except at muzzle or sharp edges).

Very Good - in perfect working condition, no appreciable wear on working surfaces, no corrosion or pitting, only minor surface dents or scratches.

Good - in safe working condition, minor wear on working surfaces, no broken parts, no corrosion or pitting that will interfere with proper functioning.

Fair - in safe working condition, but well worn, perhaps requiring replacement of minor parts or adjustments which should be indicated in advertisement, no rust, but may have corrosion pits which do not render article unsafe or inoperable.

NRA ANTIQUE CONDITION DESCRIPTIONS

Factory New - all original parts; 100% original finish; in perfect condition in every respect, inside and out.

Excellent - all original parts; over 80% original finish; sharp lettering, numerals and design on metal and wood; unmarred wood; fine bore.

Fine - all original parts; over 30% original finish; sharp lettering, numerals and design on metal and wood; minor marks in wood; good bore.

Very Good - all original parts; none to 30% original finish; original metal surfaces smooth with all edges sharp; clear lettering, numerals and design on metal; wood slightly scratched or bruised; bore disregarded for collectors firearms.

Good - some minor replacement parts; metal smoothly rusted or lightly pitted in places, cleaned or reblued; principal lettering, numerals and design on metal legible; wood refinished, scratched, bruised or minor cracks repaired; in good working order.

Fair - some major parts replaced; minor replacement parts may be required; metal rusted, may be lightly pitted all over, vigorously cleaned or reblued; rounded edges of metal and wood; principal lettering, numerals and design on metal partly obliterated; wood scratched, bruised, cracked or repaired where broken; in fair working order or can be easily repaired and placed in working order.

Poor - major and minor parts replaced; major replacement parts required and extensive restoration needed; metal deeply pitted; principal lettering, numerals and design obliterated, wood badly scratched, bruised, cracked or broken; mechanically inoperative, generally undesirable as a collector's firearm.

Grading in 2K2
The Price is Wrong if the Condition Isn't Right

This 23rd Edition's color Photo Percentage Grading System™ (PPGS) marks its 13th anniversary as a pictorial solution for accurately grading firearms. As in the past, 3 primary categories of firearms have been visually included: Handguns, Rifles, and Shotguns. Please study the photos and captions to better understand the various condition percentages. The 23rd Edition also retains the "PPGS-o-meters" whenever possible, so you can get a quick fix on condition factors.

More than ever, it still takes a well-trained person's eyes, ears, touch, and nose properly hooked up to the most powerful computer ever built, a trained brain, to accurately fingerprint a gun's correct condition factor. More than anything else, a gun's overall condition must "add up" (i.e., a Winchester lever action with 90% bright blue remaining should not have a pitted bore, and a Colt SAA with little frame finish remaining should not have excellent grips, etc.).

Computer savvy readers will be pleased to know that this updated 23rd Edition PPGS is also included free of charge on our new e-commerce web site: www.bluebookinc.com. Sections of the *Blue Book of Gun Values*™ are now available online for downloading, anytime, anywhere.

Condition factors pictured (indicated by PPGS-o-meters), unless otherwise noted, are for a gun's approximate blue, case colors, nickel, or other type of original finish remaining on the frame/receiver. On older guns, describing the receiver/frame finish accurately is absolutely critical for providing a gun with a reliable and accurate grade(s). Typically, a long gun with 80% frame finish will have at least 95% barrel blue remaining, due to the way these parts wear differently.

Additional percentages of condition may be used to describe other specific parts of a gun (i.e. barrel, wood finish, plating, mag. tube, etc.). Percentages of patina/brown or other finish discoloration factors must also be explained separately when necessary, and likewise be interpolated accurately. **With antiques, the overall percentage within this text is NOT an average of the various condition factors, but again, refers to the overall original condition of the frame/receiver.** Remember, the price is wrong if the condition factor isn't right.

The trend for professionally restored firearms with correct antique finishes continues. Restoration people are mentioning that some of their clients are requesting a 95%-98% restoration. This is accomplished by restoring an older gun to 100%, then "backing off" the condition accordingly by polishing, tumbling, grinding, chemical treatment(s), etc. Remember, even though a metal finish/polish can be almost perfectly duplicated today, the original wood is another matter, since it is nearly impossible to restore without telling (especially if it was in poor condition to begin with). Being able to spot original condition has never been more important, especially when the prices get into 4, 5, and 6 digits.

More and more collectors and shooters (especially cowboy action shooters) don't want their new guns to look like fresh paint. In other words, some new reproductions are now being skillfully aged, and the antiqued (aged) finish is done so well that it can even fool some experts. Fortunately, the difference in serialization on these new reproductions and replicas precludes them for being mistakenly identified as originals.

While this latest Photo Percentage Grading System™ certainly isn't meant to be the Last Testament on firearms grading, it hopefully goes further than anything else published on the subject. Once you get good at grading guns accurately, a 10 second "cat scan" is usually all the time needed to zone in on each gun's unique condition factor.

S.P. Fjestad
Author & Publisher - *Blue Book of Gun Values*™

P.S. Special thankx go out to Merz Antique Guns, Lynn Oliver, Keith Rolf, Jeff Sundvall of J&S Custom Guns located in Lakeville, MN, and Vern Berning. All Photo Percentage Grading System™ photography by ASAP Studios, S.P. Fjestad, Dennis Adler, Cable Photo Systems, Dr. Leonardo Antaris and James Perron.

Photos 1 & 2 = Colt SAA, .357 Mag. cal., 5 ½ in. barrel, ser. no. 30,301SA, mint except for rear grip strap polishing, (see photo at right). Fittingly, this all-new **Photo Percentage Grading System** section starts out with the world's most famous and enduring revolver, the Colt Single Action Army. Having been collectible for over a century, Colt SAAs, at today's prices, can literally range from $450-$300,000! Before he died, Keith Cochran, author of *The Colt Peacemaker Encyclopedia, Vol. II,* guesstimated ½ of all pre-WW II revolvers were no longer factory original. So on 1st generation SAAs through ser. no. 343,000, know what you're doing, get a factory letter (if possible), and always be in close proximity to a high output ATM machine. This 2nd generation specimen was manufactured approximately the same time John F. Kennedy was elected during 1960. Note the shininess of the rear grip strap, indicative of after factory polishing. Could be the result of a perfectionist SAA collector, when upon discovering some light freckling (i.e. rust) due to improper storage, decided to make it "perfect" again by polishing the problem areas first, then realizing he had to do the whole grip strap to make it look it consistent. This "perfectionist" mistake cost someone $400-$500. More importantly, he/she had to get rid of it, because with the owner's 100% or nothing attitude, it could never be good enough again.

Photo 3 = Colt SAA, .357 Mag. cal., 5 ½ in. barrel, ser. no. 356,593, approx. 75%-80% frame case colors and 95% overall bluing. Note the slight wear at the end of the barrel and around cylinder flutes on this revolver as compared to Photo 1. Manufactured around Christmas, 1939, 525 SAAs were built in .357 Mag. cal. pre-WWII, making this gun relatively rare.

Photo 4 = Colt SAA, .45 LC, 4 ¾ in. barrel, ser. no. 356,169, approx. 80% frame case colors with light perimeter frame freckling and 85%-90% overall bluing. While this specimen has slightly more case colors than the gun pictured above, note the additional wear at the end of the barrel and between the cylinder lock-up notches.   Light pitting must be evaluated per individual gun when determining value.

Photo 5 = Colt SAA, .38 Colt cal., 5 ½ in. barrel, ser. no. 348,684, approx. 30%-40% frame case colors and 70% overall bluing. Another post-WW I – pre-WW II SAA, this example was made in 1926. Close observation will reveal checkering wear on the bottom of the grips. Nice strong patent legend and "non-boogered" frame screws are always a plus on any Colt SAA.

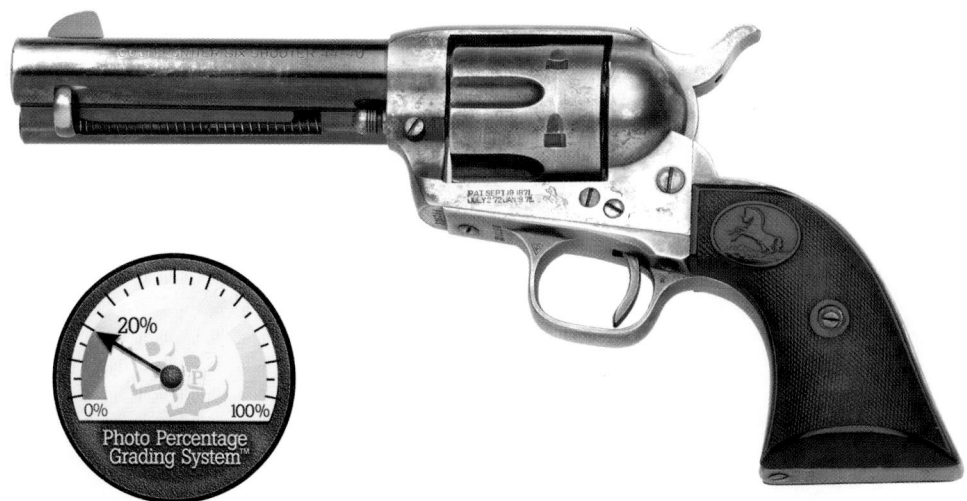

Photo 6 = Colt SAA, .44-40 cal., 4 ¾ in. barrel, ser. no. 336,296, approx. 15%-20% case colors, frame mostly shiny, and approx. 50% overall bluing. Manufactured late during WWI, any condition on a Colt Frontier Six Shooter .44-40 is still collectible. Front frame screw has probably been replaced. Overall wear is consistent, with no one major part being noticeably different than another.

Photo 7 = Colt SAA, .41 Colt, 4 ¾ in. barrel, ser. no. 303,805, finish mostly turned a greyish/brown patina – approx. 15% overall. Again, all wear on this gun seems to "add up" for its overall condition factor. In some areas, the grip checkering is almost gone, and note smooth prancing stallion. In this condition factor, barrel bore wear adversely affects the price tag more than a 90%+ SAA, since the shooting performance is of greater importance to this type of buyer.

Photo 8 = Colt SAA, .45 Colt, 4 ¾ in. barrel, ser. no. 172,433, original finish mostly turned to brown patina, with discolored, badly worn, hard rubber grips. This revolver would fall under the 10%-15% condition factors in this text. While appearing very worn, the original condition factor of this SAA is actually close to average when comparing it with other specimens from this era. This smokeless powder model celebrated its 100th anniversary last year.

Photo 9 = **Colt SAA Frontier Six Shooter**, .44-40 cal., 4 ¾ in. barrel, ser. no. 161,423, most of the finish has been worn off, and now has a shiny appearance – approx. 5%-10% overall. A black powder frame specimen (note front of frame does not have the horizontal cylinder pin latch as compared to Photos 3-8). This gun was manufactured during the first year of Browning's new Winchester Model 1895. Grips are not original and 7½ in. barrel has been cut down to 4 ¾ in – sight placement on barrel is also wrong.

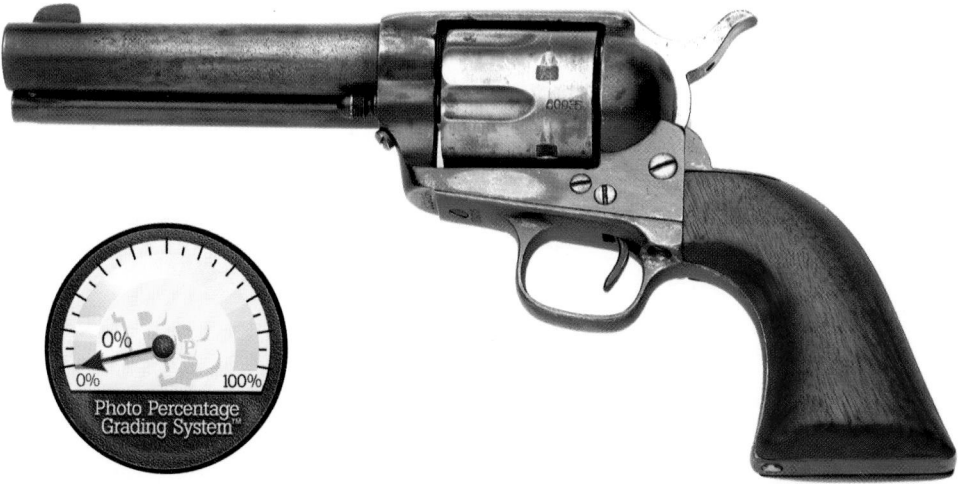

Photo 10 = **Colt SAA**, .45 cal, 4 ¾ in. barrel, ser. no. 60,935, condition isn't really a factor on this multiple "organ transplant" example. If you can't see anything wrong with this Colt Revolver, you'd better put a one-year moratorium on your SAA purchases until you bone up on what to look for. This is living proof that gun collecting became more difficult after Eli Whitney came up with interchangeable parts. Believe it or not, if you add up the parts total, this SAA is still worth $1000!

Photo 11 = Hawes Western Marshal Model SAA manufactured by J.P. Sauer & Sohn, .357 Mag., 6 in. barrel, ser. no. 192,413. 95%+ overall – would be near mint without hammer wear and major scratching on frame shoulder. Typical fine German quality with all-steel construction, no hammer-block safety indicates older mfg. While not very collectible, these guns make great shooters, especially since they are usually seen priced between $130-$250.

Photo 12 = Ruger Super Single Six Revolver, .22 LR, 6 ½ in. barrel, ser. no. 535,367, approx. 90% overall. Typical example of a meat & potatos Ruger Single Six Revolver – note the plum-colored bluing on the anodized aluminum ejector rod housing, indicating the metallurgy change between the rest of the gun and this component. 1/8 inch sized serial number indicates post-1962-pre-GCA of 1968 manufacture. This era of production had a "XR3 RED" indicating a redesign cast into the grip frame.

Photo 13 = Ruger Single Six Revolver, .22 LR, 5 ½ in. barrel, ser. no. 146,035, approx. 80% overall condition. Smaller sized serial numbers (1/16 in.) such as this one were produced 1953-1961. Note XR3 frame, steel ejector housing, and black paint missing from inside of Ruger grip medallion (compared to Photos 12 & 14). Another "Old Model", this variation can be denoted by 3 frame screws as opposed to 2 pins found on "New Models" mfg. beginning 1973.

Photo 14 = Ruger Single Six Revolver, .22 LR, 5 ½ in. barrel, ser. no. 107,263, approx. 70%+ overall condition. Ruger Single Six collectors will immediately note this "Heinz 57" has the wrong ejector rod housing (should be steel, not aluminum) and the grip frame has been replaced with XR3 RED type – should be XR3 type. Despite this revolver's non-originality and condition factors, it still makes a good shooter in the $125-$150 price range. Additional wear will not decrease its shooting value any more.

Photo 15 = Colt New Service, .45 LC, ser. no. 342,839, NIB condition. Colt double action collectors can't get enough of these. This specimen was manufactured during 1937, and was never used or fired. Carefully observe the box wear, especially by the end of the barrel and hammer. Due to its age, it's common to see box wear in these areas. Also note quality of metal polishing and finish, in addition to the sharp prancing stallion logo on rear of frame.

Photo 16 = Colt Officer's Model, .38 LC cal., ser. no. 248,197, 95% overall, checkered grips. Nice original specimen, showing minor freckling on barrel end and cylinder. Fire bluing on trigger and grip screw was standard. Observe upper portion of frame Colt logo as compared to Photo 15 – while appearing to have been partially polished away, "weak" logo die hits, barrel address information, and other markings did occur at the factory, are original and not a tell-tale sign of rebluing.

Photo 17 = Colt Police Positive Target, .22 LR, ser. no. 41,601, approx. 90%+ overall. Compare this gun to Photo 16, and observe the cylinder wear on flutes and between lock-up notches. Bottoms of grips also show slight wear and adjustable sights are indicative of a target model. Colt started using wood grips circa 1924 (this gun was mfg. 1936), and DA collectors will note the wider butt of this specimen compared to the earlier round butt variation.

Photo 18 = Colt Model 1878 DA "Colt Frontier Six Shooter" Revolver, .44-40 cal., ser. no. 39,189, nice original early gun with approx. 85%-90% condition. Currently celebrating its 100th anniversary, the fit and finish on these early double action Colts were perfect. This model's barrel and ejector rod housing interchanges with the SAA. The owner spotted this revolver from across the room at a local gun show after a potential buyer held it up in good light, suspecting refinishing.

Photo 19 = Colt Model 1917, .45 ACP, ser. no. 95,419, approx. 80% original thinning brushed blue finish. As with many military wartime handguns, polishing and commercial finishing tend to be overlooked in favor of increased production. Note the rough circular polishing marks on the back of frame and where they meet the horizontal frame polishing below the cylinder. While exterior finish is rough, the inner mechanism is equivalent to any similar commercial model.

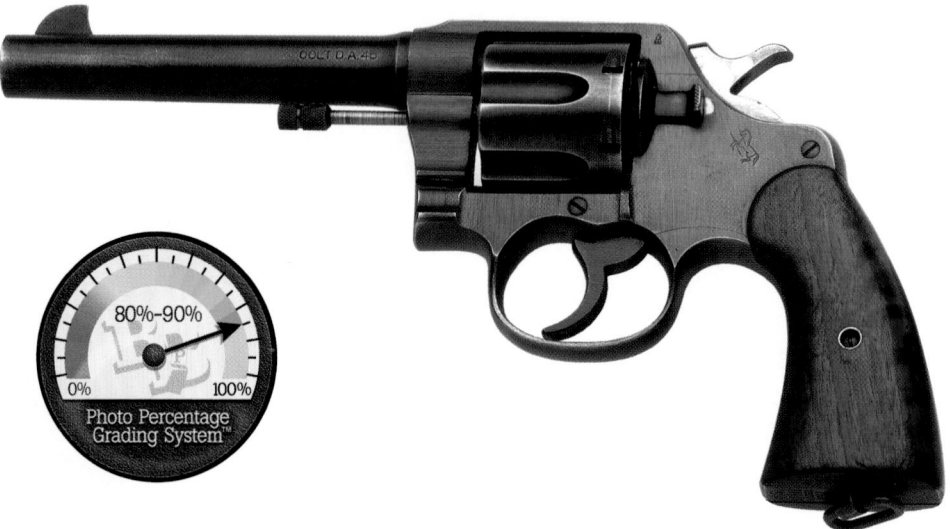

Photo 20 = Colt Model 1917, .45 LC, ser. no. 95,419 (left side of Photo 19), 80%-85% original thinning brushed blue finish. The left side of this gun appears to be in slightly better condition than the right side pictured above, and rear frame polishing is more vertical. Interestingly, don't be surprised to see one of these with a crooked front sight, since this military model was sighted in horizontally by using a wooden mallet to bend the front sight!

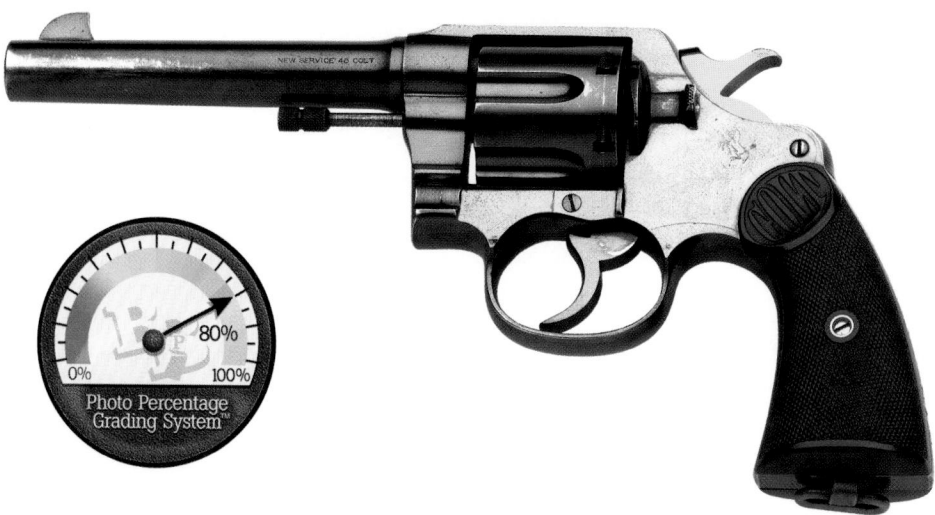

Photo 21 = Colt New Service, .45 LC, ser. no. 145,386, approx. 80% overall, hard rubber grips. Examine this commercial finish compared to Photo 20. Observe the bolstered barrel where it meets the frame (compare to Photo 24). This revolver is crudely stamped "RCMP 2212", so condition and holster wear is appropriate for use in the Royal Canadian Mounted Police. While its ser. no. indicates 1917 mfg., it was not shipped until Oct. 24th, 1919, due to wartime military considerations.

Photo 22 = Colt New Service, .45 LC, ser. no. 353,244, approx. 75%-80% overall. While the barrel and grips on this gun are near mint, frame and cylinder pitting lower this gun's overall condition factor. Many collectors would rather own a clean, 80%-90% gun than a 95%-98% similar model with this kind of pitting. This type of metal finish condition usually indicates improper storage, where moisture was allowed to oxidize the bluing over a period of time.

Photo 23 = Colt Marshal, .38 Spl., ser. no. 838,365, approx. 70% overall. Typical major wear patterns are exhibited on this specimen, including barrel, cylinder and grips. This variation was basically an Official Police with a rounded butt. Less than 2,500 were manufactured between 1954-1956. While a mint gun might command $800 today, this condition factor is usually priced in the $300-$350 range.

Photo 24 = Colt New Service, .455 Eley cal., ser. no. 61,867, approx. 50%-60% original finish, hard rubber grips. Unless a revolver is ultra-rare due to its configuration (barrel length, caliber, finish, features, etc.), most guns in this condition are shooters, with no collector premiums. Note brownish metal discoloration on straight, untapered barrel and frame. This New Service is poorly stamped R.N.W.M.P.9.3.5 on rear grip strap, another Canadian contract variation of the gun pictured in Photo 21.

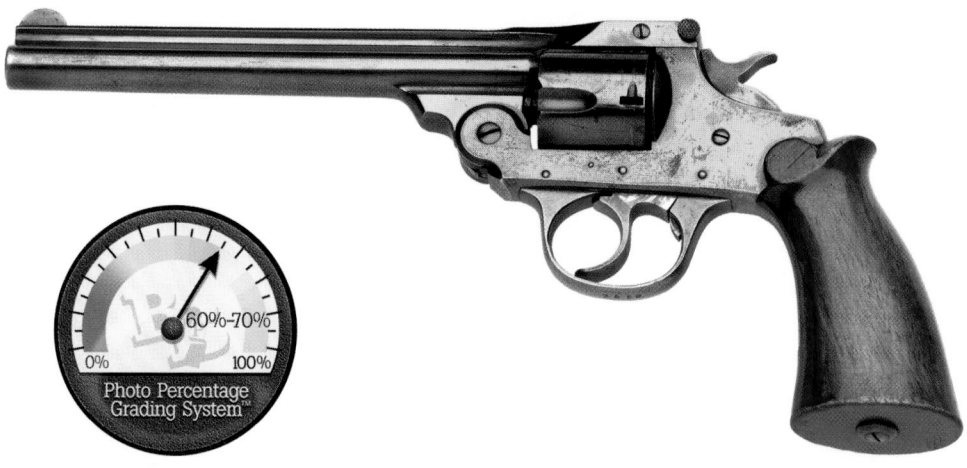

Photo 25 = Iver Johnson Top-break Revolver, .38 cal., ser. no. 3,690, approx. 60%-70% overall, shooter status only. If condition is worse than this, it still doesn't make much difference on the price tag. On this type of bottom shelf price point, don't be surprised if an unknown gun shop owner asks you for 4 or 5 forms of I.D. Typically seen priced between $25-$75, and don't bring your American Express card. To maintain respect, leave in safe when having friends over.

Photo 26 = Colt Police Positive, .38 New Police cal., ser. no. 20,553, approx. 40%-50% overall, with pitting. Close observation reveals this is a transition gun, with the New Police frame marking and older Police Positive stamped barrel. Manufactured during 1908, this revolver still maintains a $100-$125 price as a reliable shooter. When purchasing a shooter in a lower price range, always concentrate on how good it is mechanically, rather than quality of exterior finish and other potentially rare features.

Photo 27 = Colt Official Police, .38 Spl., ser. no. 615,076, approx. 80%-85% original nickel finish. This is a good example of what nickel finish looks like once it has flaked off or started to corrode. Nickel finishes are rapidly becoming a thing of the past, as many current manufacturers cannot afford today's hazardous waste costs incurred by the production of such a finish. Butt is marked "P&W No. 24" (perhaps Pratt & Whitney security revolver).

Photo 28 = H&R Top-break, .22 LR, ser. no. 8,908, approx. 70%+ overall. On nickel finished guns, once the nickel has worn or flaked off, only the dark metal remains visible, giving it the appearance of being in worse condition than it is. Indeed, in many cases, an 80% gun with bluing will appear in better condition than a 95% nickel finished variation. Since nickel plating produces a soft finish, surface scratching is more prevalent than on blue finish.

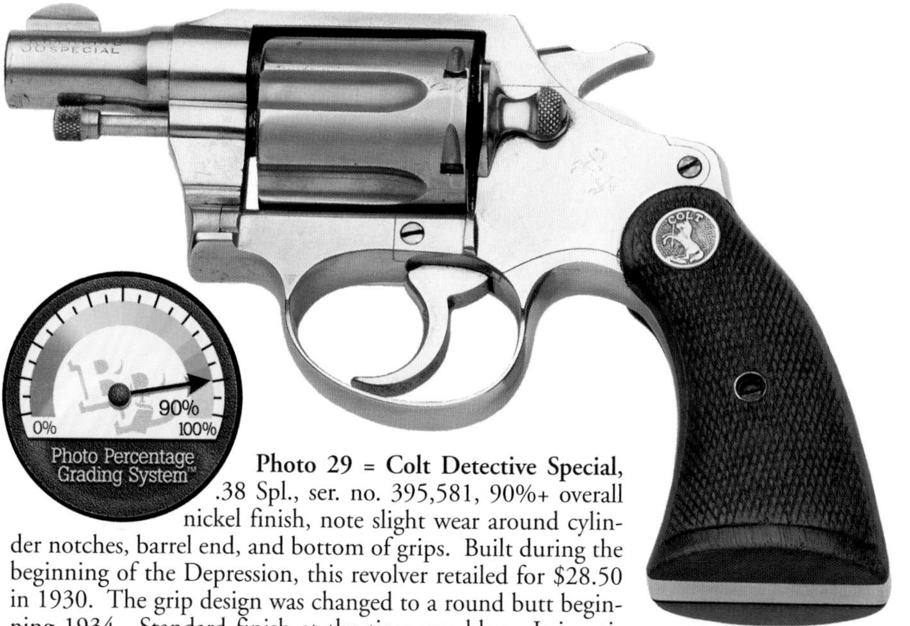

Photo 29 = Colt Detective Special, .38 Spl., ser. no. 395,581, 90%+ overall nickel finish, note slight wear around cylinder notches, barrel end, and bottom of grips. Built during the beginning of the Depression, this revolver retailed for $28.50 in 1930. The grip design was changed to a round butt beginning 1934. Standard finish at the time was blue. It is estimated that approx. 5% of all Colt revolver production was nickel finished. While rarer, most collectors still prefer blue.

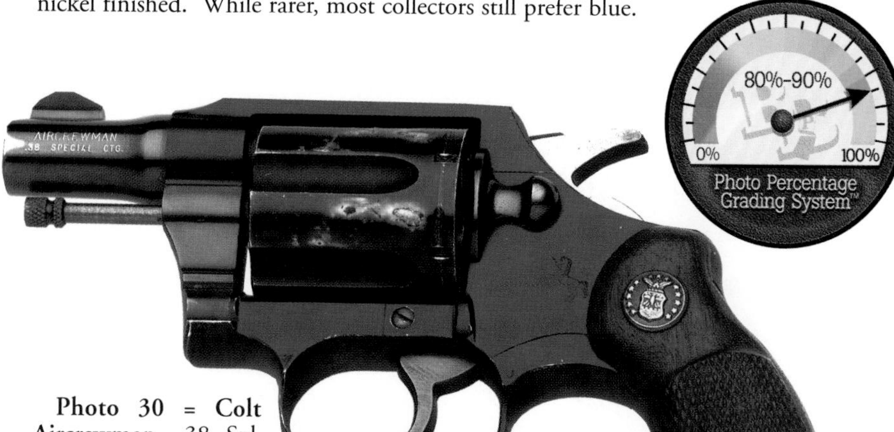

Photo 30 = Colt Aircrewman, .38 Spl., ser. no. 3,478LW, 80%-85% overall (cylinder oxidation lowers the condition factor 10%). Originally designed as a lightweight, survival throwaway revolver for the Air Force, this model featured a unique aluminum frame and cylinder. Tests, however, revealed the cylinder could not withstand some .38 Special loads, and the Pentagon, circa 1961, ordered the entire run destroyed – approx. only 2 dozen survived. Cylinder wear is due to intense heat generated when fired (not recommended!).

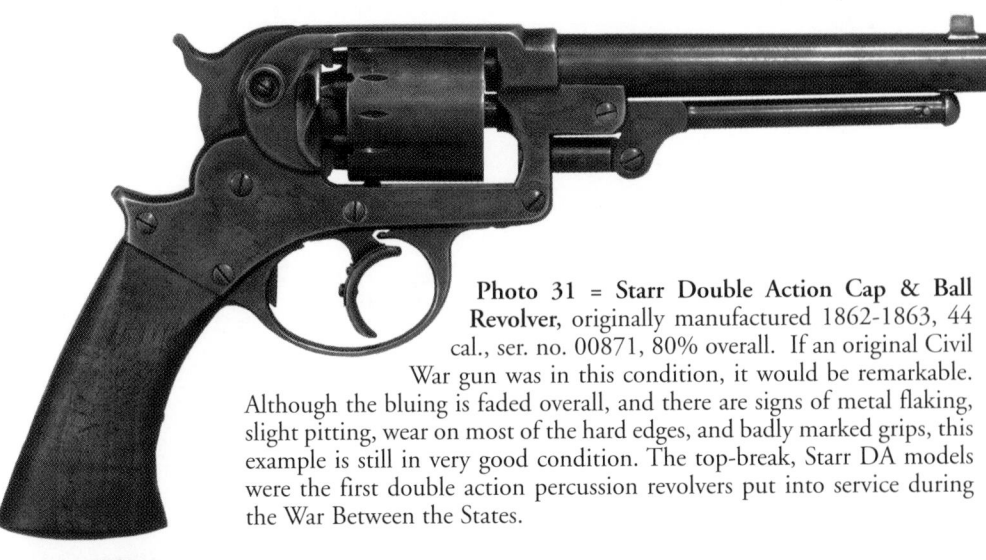

Photo 31 = Starr Double Action Cap & Ball Revolver, originally manufactured 1862-1863, 44 cal., ser. no. 00871, 80% overall. If an original Civil War gun was in this condition, it would be remarkable. Although the bluing is faded overall, and there are signs of metal flaking, slight pitting, wear on most of the hard edges, and badly marked grips, this example is still in very good condition. The top-break, Starr DA models were the first double action percussion revolvers put into service during the War Between the States.

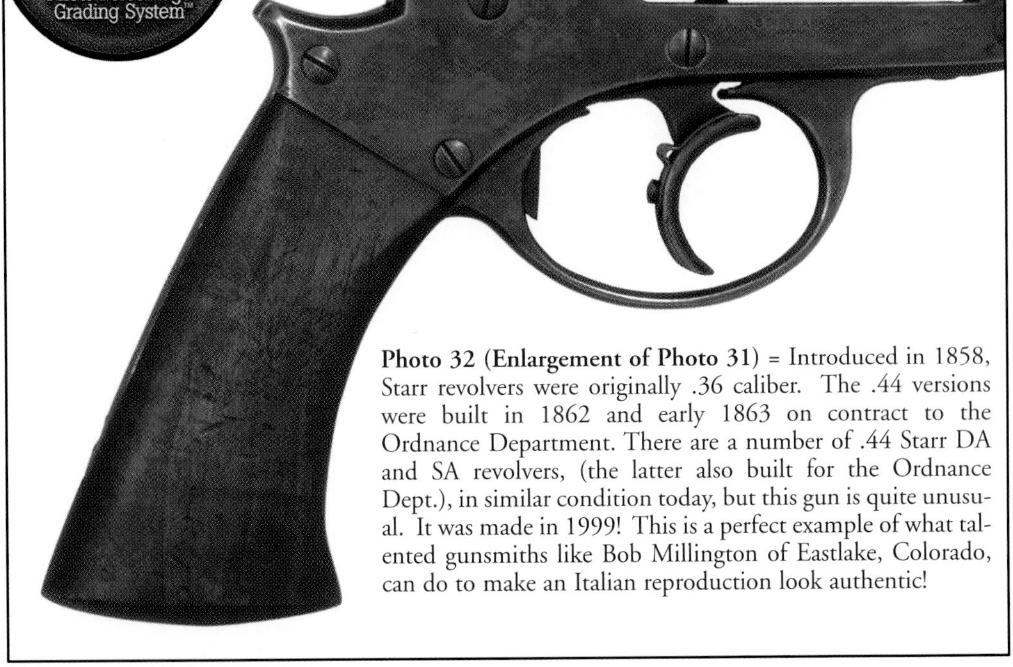

Photo 32 (Enlargement of Photo 31) = Introduced in 1858, Starr revolvers were originally .36 caliber. The .44 versions were built in 1862 and early 1863 on contract to the Ordnance Department. There are a number of .44 Starr DA and SA revolvers, (the latter also built for the Ordnance Dept.), in similar condition today, but this gun is quite unusual. It was made in 1999! This is a perfect example of what talented gunsmiths like Bob Millington of Eastlake, Colorado, can do to make an Italian reproduction look authentic!

Photo 33 = Colt Gold Cup National Match, .38 Special Mid Range, ser. no. 8591-MR, NIB condition. Slide legend indicates that this is a pre-Series 70 National Match. First offered in 1957 in .45 ACP only, the .38 mid-range or wad-cutter cal. was introduced during 1961. Redesigned in 1962, the result was the so-called Mark III Gold Cup 38 Special. This Colt semi-auto has the Elliason adj. rear sight, mfg. 1972 (parts cleanup). Note top of slide and front frame non-glare matte finish.

Photo 34 = Remington Rand Model 1911A1, .45 ACP, ser. no. 1,322,815, 95% overall, original parkerized military finish. Without frame edge wear, this gun would jump up to 98% in a hurry. Brown plastic grips are mint, and magazine bottom is very clean. Color of parkerized frame and slide is typical for this period of military manufacture. Some enthusiasts seem to think this model is rare – not so, Remington made almost 900,000 of these between 1941-1945, using mostly Colt parts.

Photo 35 = Colt Model 1911A1 U.S. Military, .45 ACP, ser. no. 2,302,708, 75%-80% overall. Nice original military model with mostly holster edge wear. Rear of frame next to grip safety shows some abuse – hopefully, a wartime story could justify this. Grips are near perfect, but screws show holster wear. Observe lack of wear on front grip strap, another indication this gun probably went in and out of the holster more often than it was shot.

Photo 36 = Colt Model 1911A1 Commercial, .45 ACP, ser. no. C177,027, approx. 70% overall. Again, note the holster wear on the frame and slide edges – front grip strap shows more wear than Photo 35. The fit and finish on these commercial models were far superior to military production. While this condition factor today isn't worth the big bucks, the shootability is excellent, because of the crisp trigger pull and overall production tolerances are not as sloppy as most military 1911A1s.

Photo 37= **Colt Model 1908 Pocket**, .380 ACP, ser. no. 64,984, 80%-85% overall. Typical freckling and bluing discoloration are evident on this semi-auto. Also observe nice, strong rampant Colt logo on rear of slide and slight wear on grips. A John Browning design, over 138,000 of this model were made during its 37 years of production – including this 1923 specimen. Outselling its .32 ACP counterpart by over 400%, this model gained rapid consumer acceptance – John Dillinger even preferred it!

Photo 38 = Browning Model 1905-FN (Vest Pocket), second variation, .25 ACP, ser. no. 388,888, 75%-80% overall. Compare the wear on this gun to Photo 37, observe how the front of slide and butt has suffered serious abuse. Not rare, over one million (both variations) were manufactured by Browning between 1906-1959. This Browning model and its configuration became a yardstick for other manufacturers - over 200 different companies manufactured copies of this model! Typically priced in the $120-$150 range in today's shooter marketplace.

Photo 39 = Ruger Standard Model Semi-Auto, .22 LR, ser. no. 410,587, 98%+ overall. Slight frame wear in front of ser. no. knocks this gun out of mint condition. 1/8 in. high ser. no. indicates 1962-1968 mfg. After the GCA of 1968, Sturm Ruger started putting a prefix in front of the serial number. Certainly nothing rare here, simply a nice, original gun with box and papers. Every year, there are a few less specimens in this condition factor, due to normal use and abuse.

Photo 40 = Luger 1920 Commercial Model with grip safety, 7.65 Luger cal., ser. no. 4,089N, 97%-98% overall. One of the more collectible German handguns, there is a Luger for almost everyone's particular preference and budget. Prices can range from $175 to $1,000,000! Original condition is polar north for Luger collectors, and sometimes, the price difference between even 98% and mint can be over double. Observe slight wear at end of barrel, side plate, safety pivot, and grip safety.

Photo 41 = Walther Model PP, .380 ACP (9mm kurz) ser. no. 32,807A, 98% overall, includes cardboard "alligator" box and 15 meter test target. Note very light frame pitting next to finger extension magazine. This pistol is marked "Interarms" on right side. Quantities of used West German Police PPs (mostly in .32 ACP) have been recently imported into the U.S., affecting the normal supply/demand economics for this model. For this reason, earlier guns without recent import markings are currently more desirable.

Photo 42 = Walther Model PPK (Eagle N proofed), .32 ACP (7.65 mm), ser. no. 280,446 K, 95% overall. Standard WW II German commercial pistol - wear on front of slide is indicative of holster use. Note slight wear on magazine release button, it appears that the fire-blued safety lever on this specimen has had the color "touched up". Slight mill marks on frame are typical for this period of manufacture (after April, 1940). Finger extension mag is original.

Photo 43 = WW II P.38, byf-44 (code for Mauser production during 1944), 9mm Para., ser. no. 6,431R, 95% overall. WW II P.38s were made by Mauser, Walther, and Spreewerke, resulting in a variety of manufacturing quality. Early wartime production retained the quality of pre-war commercial models, while late-war guns were inconsistent in finish quality. Condition below 95% on common wartime P.38s loses collectibility in a hurry, as many premium condition pistols survived the war.

Photo 44 = Walther Model PPK (Eagle C Nazi proofed), .32 ACP (7.65 mm), ser. no. 409,844 K, 65%-70% overall. An original wartime Nazi Police issue, this gun has accumulated some serious pitting and rust. Examine circular rough milling on frame (indicative during this period of late war mfg.), in addition to serious pitting on slide grips, and trigger guard. Pin protruding in front of hammer is loaded chamber indicator – obviously, this pistol is ready to fire.

Photo 45 = Walther Olympia Sport Model, .22 LR, ser. no. 53,640, 80%+ overall. Even though this commercial model (mfg. 1936-1940) shows considerable exterior finish wear, its capabilities as a shooter have certainly not been diminished. Equipped with a glass-like mechanism while combining a hot, butter-like trigger pull, this 60 year old gun, in the right hands, will shoot as well or better than anything manufactured today. Seldom seen in today's marketplace, don't underestimate this model's quality and shooting value.

Photo 46 = Magnum Research Stainless Desert Eagle .44 Mag. Pistol? Notta! Becoming ever more popular, this Japanese "air-soft" replica utilizes a working, blowback action supplied by compressed air stored in the magazine to fire plastic pellets. The warning tag attached to the trigger guard lets you know that pointing this type of realistic toy at somebody without their suspecting it originally sent David Horowitz into a tailspin on national television. While a conversation piece, treat it like a real gun!

Photos 47 & 48 = Gastinne Renette (Paris) Parlour Pistol, 6mm rimfire, w/o ser. no., engraved, 95%+ overall. Probably made for a well-to-do pre WW I European who wanted a top-quality rimfire pistol to shoot inside during the winter. If you're looking for Old World quality and craftsmanship, this type of gun offers both at minimal cost. Elaborate wood carving & checkering, platinum & gold inlays on the staggered fluted barrel, extensive engraving, and ultra-smooth rolling block action would cost thousands to replace today. Most of these pistols are in this condition or better, since they were never misused and probably treated as well as the owner's children.

Photo Percentage Grading System

0% 95% 100%

Photo Percentage Grading System

Gold damascened Astra Model 902, serial #22,486. The vast majority of these impressive pistols, with their integral 20 shot magazines and booted shoulder stocks, were selective fire guns. It is estimated that fewer than 100 were manufactured as strict semiautomatics, and of these, only two are known to have been gold damascened.

This extraordinary pistol was manufactured in 1932 and damascened by Adolfo Santos of Eibar, Spain, purportedly to fill a request from Egypt's King Farouk. As befitting a monarch, the pistol was richly embellished with exquisite geometric patterns, Arabic inscriptions, and elegant views from the terrace of the Alhambra Palace in Granada, Spain.

Where there can be no doubt that this Model 902 stands as one of the finest semiautomatic pistols to ever emerge from Spain, its historic associations coupled with rarity, charisma, and condition support its position as one of the world's most desireable guns. Collection: Leonardo M. Antaris MD

2002 — Twenty-Third Edition — 2002
Blue Book of Gun Values™

APRIL
S						S
	1	2	3	4	5	6
7	8	9	10	11	12	13
14	15	16	17	18	19	20
21	22	23	24	25	26	27
28	29	30				

MAY
S						S
		1	2	3	4	
5	6	7	8	9	10	11
12	13	14	15	16	17	18
19	20	21	22	23	24	25
26	27	28	29	30	31	

JUNE
S						S
						1
2	3	4	5	6	7	8
9	10	11	12	13	14	15
16	17	18	19	20	21	22
23	24	25	26	27	28	29
30						

JULY
S						S
	1	2	3	4	5	6
7	8	9	10	11	12	13
14	15	16	17	18	19	20
21	22	23	24	25	26	27
28	29	30	31			

AUGUST
S						S
				1	2	3
4	5	6	7	8	9	10
11	12	13	14	15	16	17
18	19	20	21	22	23	24
25	26	27	28	29	30	31

SEPTEMBER
S						S
1	2	3	4	5	6	7
8	9	10	11	12	13	14
15	16	17	18	19	20	21
22	23	24	25	26	27	28
29	30					

OCTOBER
S						S
	1	2	3	4	5	
6	7	8	9	10	11	12
13	14	15	16	17	18	19
20	21	22	23	24	25	26
27	28	29	30	31		

NOVEMBER
S						S
					1	2
3	4	5	6	7	8	9
10	11	12	13	14	15	16
17	18	19	20	21	22	23
24	25	26	27	28	29	30

DECEMBER
S						S
1	2	3	4	5	6	7
8	9	10	11	12	13	14
15	16	17	18	19	20	21
22	23	24	25	26	27	28
29	30	31				

2003 — Twenty-Third Edition — 2003
Blue Book of Gun Values™

JANUARY
S						S
		1	2	3	4	
5	6	7	8	9	10	11
12	13	14	15	16	17	18
19	20	21	22	23	24	25
26	27	28	29	30	31	

FEBRUARY
S						S
						1
2	3	4	5	6	7	8
9	10	11	12	13	14	15
16	17	18	19	20	21	22
23	24	25	26	27	28	

MARCH
S						S
						1
2	3	4	5	6	7	8
9	10	11	12	13	14	15
16	17	18	19	20	21	22
23	24	25	26	27	28	29
30	31					

Photo 51 = Left side of Marlin Model 94 in Photo 50 – probably 95%+ case colors. If you like strong original case colors, it doesn't get much better than this! This side of the rifle has more vivid case colors than shown above. Colors, mottling, and swirl patterns are indicative of typical Marlin case colors. A Marlin lever action with this amount of original case colors, bluing, and stock/forearm finish is encountered in approximately only 1 out of 500 rifles.

95%

0% 100%

Photo Percentage
Grading System™

Photo 50 = Marlin Model 94, .25-20 cal., ser. no. 447,669, 95% overall case colors on frame and lever, 98% bluing on barrel and magazine tube. Marlin & Winchester collectors will always reach a little deeper into their wallets when encountering case colors and overall condition like this. Careful observation will reveal light flaking on sliding breech bolt, minimal hammer wear, and slightly oversized stock and forearm wood (normal for this serial range).

Photo 52 = Marlin Model 1893, .32-40 cal., ser. no. 329,262, 98% vivid case colors. Observe the original case colors on the sliding breech block of this gun compared to the flaked bluing depicted in Photo 50. Also, the stock and forearm condition (note the light dings, nicks and scratches) are not as pristine as pictured above. When this type of superior receiver condition is encountered, barrel and magazine tube bluing should always be 90% or greater.

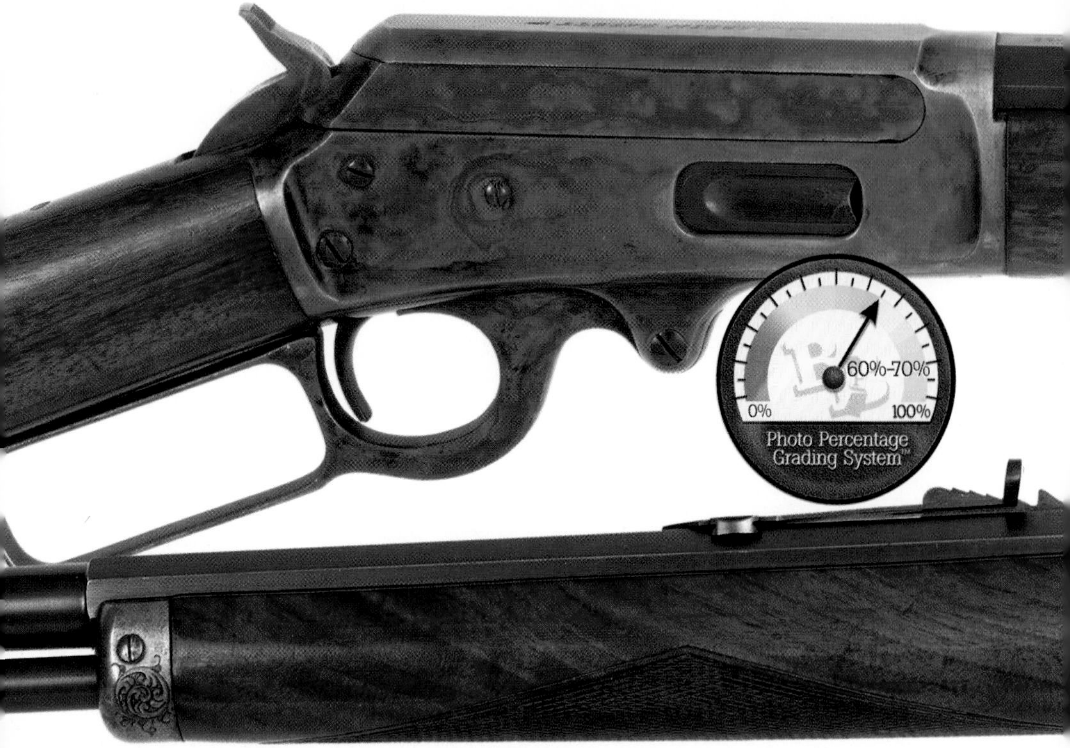

Photo 54 = Left side of engraved Marlin Model 97 pictured below. Engraved No. 2 oval panel scene with perimeter scrollwork depicts a good-sized buck making tracks in a hurry. Marlin's factory engraving patterns included Nos. 1, 2, 3, 5, (four different styles), 10, and 15. This gun has seen very little use as evident by the lack of handling nicks, scratches, and normal dings. Also, almost all the original stock and forearm varnish remains in addition to checkering being sharp.

Photo 53 = Marlin Model 1893, .30-30 cal., ser. no. 235,827, approx. 60% case colors, 95% barrel bluing. This standard rifle features a full octagon barrel and buckhorn rear sight. Overall excellent wood, retaining most of the original stock and forearm varnish. The condition factor of this Marlin Model 1893 is still considerably above the average specimen collectors may encounter at a typical gun show.

Photo 55 = Marlin engraved Model 97, .22 LR cal., ser. no. 417,509, 20%-30% receiver case colors with 95%+ barrel (½ round, ½ octagon) and mag tube bluing. This Deluxe Model 97 features a standard No. 2 Marlin engraving pattern, including forearm cap. Case colors on engraved guns are usually less prominent than a similar model without engraving. Examine the figure in the checkered walnut forearm, always a sign of top-quality American crotch walnut.

Photo 56 = Marlin Model 94, .32-20 cal., ser. no. 377,920, approx. 20% fading receiver case colors with minor freckling and 90% barrel and mag tube bluing. Note condition of stock as compared to Photo 57. This round barreled rifle is still in better condition than an average gun. Most collectors would consider this Marlin a nice, "no problem" gun – how much would you take for it?

Photo 57 = Marlin Model 1889, .32-20 cal., ser. no. 95,404, plum colored receiver with traces of bluing left in protected areas only, approx. 75% browning barrel blue. Compare the color of this gun's receiver to Photo 56. Notice normal oil soaking in stock and forearm where they meet frame. Careful observation also shows that bolt and frame use different metals, as color of bluing is different.

Photo 58 = Marlin Model 1893, .32-20 cal., ser. no. 336,107, overall receiver finish has turned to a smooth plum-brown patina, devoid of any bluing, but note that frame metal surface is fairly clean with minor surface oxidation. Marlin lever action aficionados have probably already spotted that the front end of this rifle (i.e. barrel, mag. tube, and forearm) is not original and has been replaced by similar parts from a later Model 336 with beavertail forearm.

Photo 59 = **Remington Rolling Block Baby Carbine**, .44-40 cal., no ser. no., approx. 95% overall original nickel finish. Original early Remington nickel finish sometimes looks questionable to the untrained eye, but everything on this Carbine is original. Nicely figured walnut stock and forearm are in excellent condition, except for the gouge on right side of upper tang. Nickel finish in this model is rare, and this specimen's condition factor makes it even more scarce.

Photo 60 =
**Colt Lightning
Saddle Ring Baby Carbine**, .44-40 cal., ser. no. 28,454, approx. 20% nickel finish, with receiver mostly dark. This photo proves that a badly worn nickel finish in most cases will look worse than an equally worn blue finish. Yet this specimen rates about average condition when sampling nickel-finished Colt Lightnings. Observe traces of barrel finish around the perimeter of forearm and lack of wood varnish.

Photo 61 = **Marlin Model 1894, Saddle Ring Carbine**, .44-40 cal., ser. no. 185,126, approx. 50% overall, with factory nickel finish. While this gun's condition does not appear too pleasing, it is an average example of a worn nickel finish from this bygone era. Observe light crack in stock. Very few nickel Marlin Model 1894s are known to exist, so this gun's condition factor takes a back seat due to rarity.

Photo Percentage Grading System™ 98%
0% 100%

Photo Percentage Grading System™ 80%
0% 100%

Photo Percentage Grading System™ 50%
0% 100%

Photo 62 = Marlin Model 27-S, .32-20 cal., ser. no. 2,134, 98% bright blue overall - a very crisp specimen with no problems, observe slight wear on back of hammer and overall sharpness of frame edges and octagon barrel. Whenever condition looks this good, be somewhat cautious, as refinishing could explain the superior condition factor. Overpolishing when refinishing sometimes makes these crisp edges look soft, even round. Examine the light wood color, free of oil soaking.

Photo 63 = Marlin Model 27-S, .25 cal. (changeable firing pin allows converting from rimfire to centerfire), ser. no. 150, approx. 80%+ bright blue overall. Compare this gun's overall condition factor to the one pictured in Photo 62. The additional wear explains metal and wood coloration differences. The takedown lever is also down on this photo, revealing a thin, circular line of frame wear created when pivoting. Still, a much better than average condition specimen.

Photo 64 = Marlin Model 20-A, .22 cal., no ser. no., approx. 50% receiver and barrel bluing, starting to turn a brownish patina. This rifle has good-looking original wood with some wear to varnish. Close scrutiny will reveal the middle screw on top of frame is missing – a minor problem. Since most guns like this were used rather heavily, the condition factor is appropriate for this gun's utilitarian nature.

Photo Percentage Grading System™

Photo Percentage Grading System™

Photo 65 = Marlin Model 1891(rare side-loader variation), .22 cal., ser. no. 47,791, Plum brown-dark patina finish on receiver and octagon barrel. Typical nicely worn and smooth wood to metal fit, with normal oil soaking evident on average wood - this is an average condition factor for this model. It is important to remember that when this gun was first purchased, it could have literally been used everyday for years, something that happens very rarely in today's firearms marketplace.

Photo 66 = Winchester Model 1906 slide action, .22 LR, no ser. no. Traces of bluing left in protected areas with balance of metal finish turning a plum brown patina. Originally priced in 1906 with gumwood stock at $10.50, this model's price appeared inexpensive to the older Model 1890 priced at $16. This type of bread and butter shooter is almost impossible to find today in better than 80% original condition, despite Winchester having made almost 850,000 of this model alone.

Photo 67 = Winchester Model 1892 Short Rifle, .44-40 cal., ser. no. 414,816. Mostly greyish patina overall, and apparent nickel finish are explained by the metal becoming shiny with age and wear. Special order 14 in. octagon barrel (very rare), was probably sold to South America originally, as this barrel length was banned due to the 1928 Machine Gun Act, making anything less than 16 in. barrels illegal. Would you believe $2,250 for this rusty dug-up? Moral – Winchester + rarity = BUCK$.

Photo 68 = Army & Navy Sidelock Model, 12 ga., ser. no. 21,488, approx. 10% receiver case colors, mostly in protected areas, 95% barrel bluing, Purdey-style tight scroll and rose engraving, note engraved scalloped shoulders, probably manufactured by W.J. Jeffery for London's Army & Navy store pre-WW I. Many quality English side-by-sides have had their barrels refinished (including this one) – value is not affected that much, however.

Photo Percentage Grading System™

Photo 69 = Winchester Model 21, 16 ga., ser. no. 28,721, 95%+ overall, boxlock action, Winchester's best quality, relatively low production side-by-side has always been collectible, especially in the smaller gauges. On this model, always inspect the receiver bottom carefully, as this area is usually the first to accumulate wear, especially flaking. Checkering is still in excellent condition, with only slight point wear in front of forearm.

Photo Percentage Grading System™

Photo 70 = Browning Superposed Skeet Model, .410 bore, ser. no. 669J3, 99% overall. A rounded pistol grip indicates pre-1966 mfg., in addition to the light-colored walnut. A good way to tell if a Superposed has been shot a lot, is to notice if the barrel assembly opens almost automatically when the opening lever has been engaged. Another tell-tale sign is when the opening lever has worn its way left of center on the upper tang.

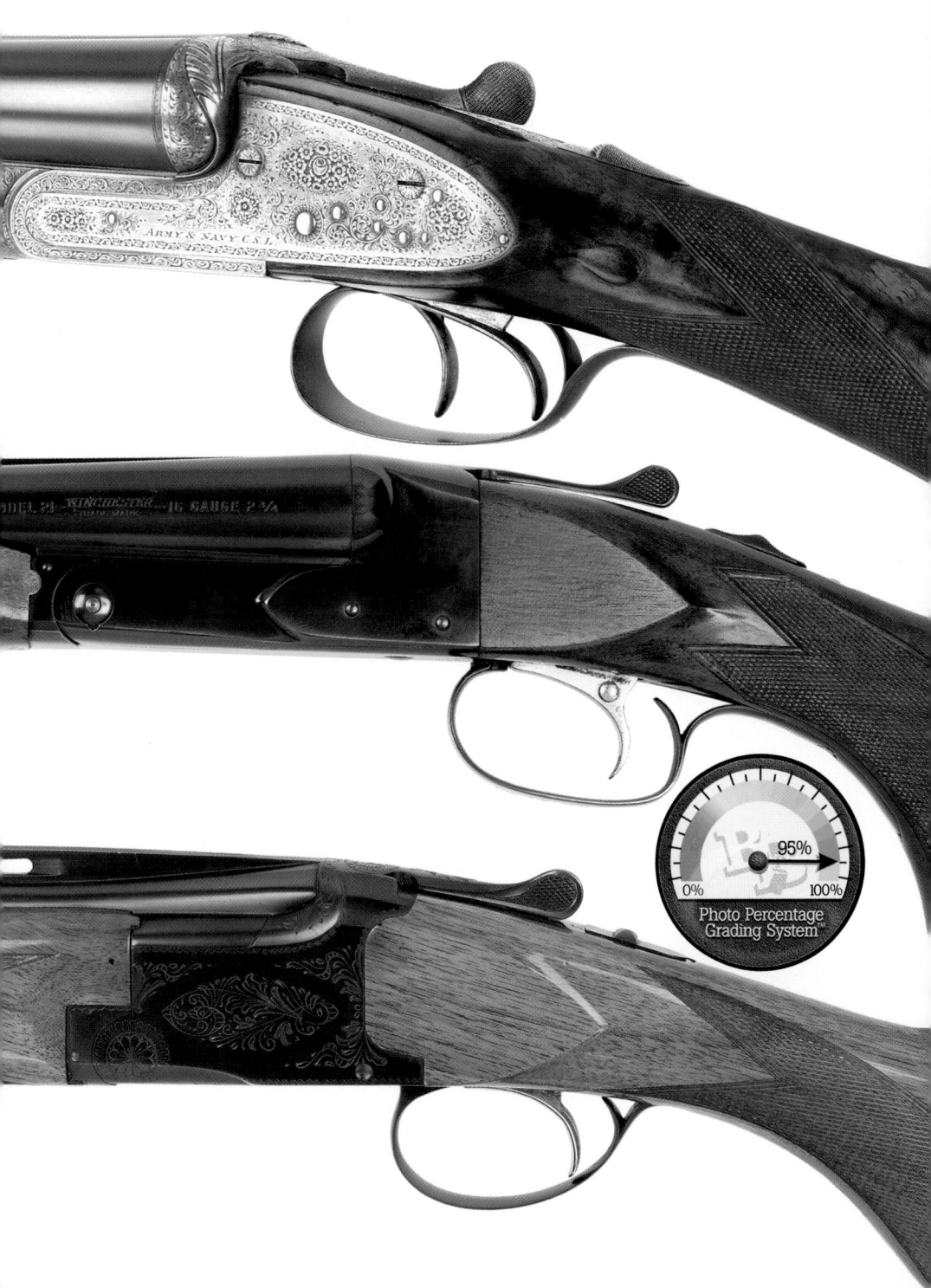

Photo 71 = **Remington Damascus Model 1900,** 12 ga., ser. no. 316,534, NRA Poor Condition, note poorly installed screw in the chipped stock by frame. Barrels have been cleaned starting halfway up the forearm - observe how the damascus patterning is much more vivid after the layers of surface oxidation, dirt/grime, and dried gun oil have been removed. Thousands of similar condition, under $125 shotguns could also be dramatically improved with a little oil & elbow grease!

Photo 73 = **Parker Damascus GH Model,** 12 ga., ser. no. 113,550, 100% professionally refurbished, a good example of what kind of results you can get from the right gun refurbished by the right people. Owner originally paid $350 for this shiny, no problem damascus Parker. After another $450, it looked like this! Professional restorations can actually enhance a worn-out gun's value, but you **must** have the **right combination** of gun and refurbishing expertise.

Photo 72 = Remington Damascus Model 1894, 12 ga., ser. no. 126, 715, approx. 50% case colors with 80% damascus barrel patterns and wood finish, compare condition to Photo 71. The wide range of damascus steel barrel patterns is also evident looking at the shotguns on these pages. Note how tight these patterns are compared to the Model 1900 pictured above. Older SxSs in this original condition factor or better are becoming more popular every year.

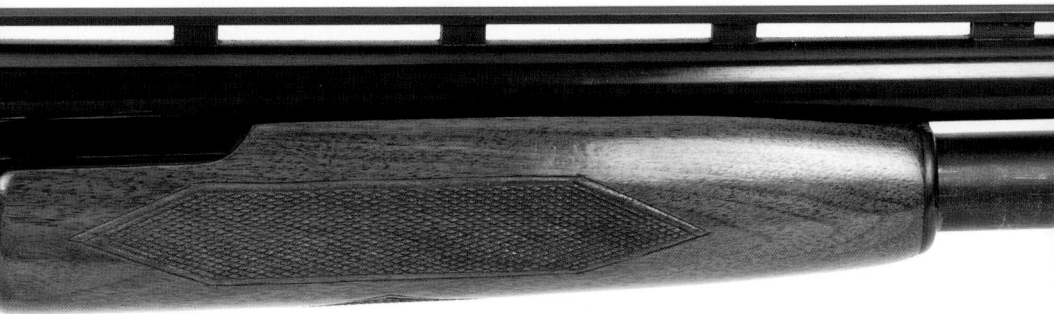

Photo 74 = Winchester Model 12 Trap Model, 12 ga., ser. no. 1,921,515, 98% overall. A nice straight Model 12 that has been shot very little. Notice the lack of wear on magazine tube compared to Photos 76 & 78. No visible wear on checkering and the breech block is still shiny with no horizontal striations, which would indicate frequent use (see Photo 78). Also examine sharp edges and lines on this shotgun's frame.

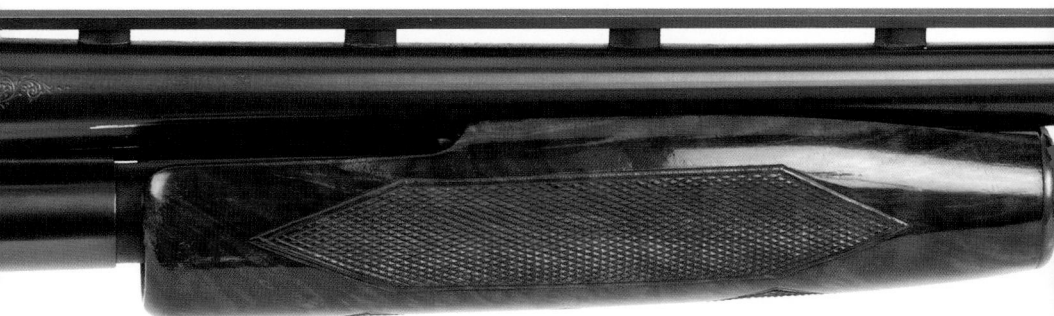

Photo 75 = Winchester Model 12 Pigeon Grade with No. 5 factory engraving, 16 ga., ser. no. 1,844,108, 95%+ overall. Manufactured early in 1960, the engine-turned breech block is tell-tale sign of a Pigeon Grade. The No. 5 engraving pattern was Winchester's most elaborate engraving option at the time, and included light scroll-work on barrel assembly as well. While a plain Jane Model 12 retailed for $109.15, this Pigeon Grade with engraving tipped the scales at almost $450!

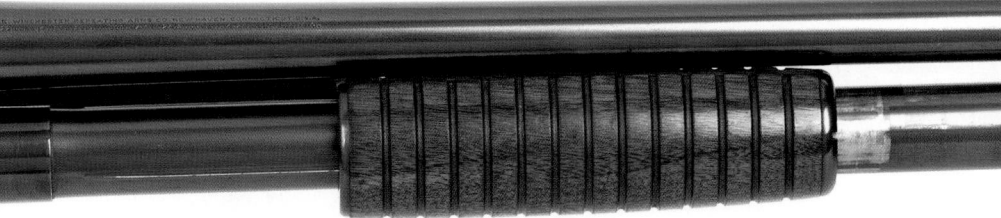

Photo 76 = Winchester Model 1912, 20 ga., ser. no. 2,011, 90% overall, full choke. This Model 1912 was built during the first year of manufacture – always a plus for Winchester collectors. Note the original thin-grip stock configuration, mag. tube wear (important on any Model 12), and perfect wood to metal fit. While open choke (cylinder & improved cylinder) Model 12s are currently more desirable than full choke, this first year gun will still command a front row position in a Model 12 collection.

Photo Percentage Grading System™

Photo 77 = **Winchester Model 25,** 12 ga., ser. no. 47,808, approx. 85% overall. The Model 12's red-headed cousin, the Model 25 was manufactured 1949-1954 as a non-takedown version of the Model 12. Close inspection reveals major pitting on barrel and magazine hanger bracket. Receiver and slide edge wear are typical for this condition factor. The shooting value of this specimen largely determines its value.

Photo 79 = **Winchester Model 25,** 12 ga., ser. no. 4,936, approx. 75% overall, modified choke. Another Model 25 with more visible wear on the barrel, slide rail, and bottom of magazine tube. Even though this specimen does not have the condition of gun pictured in Photo 77, it also doesn't have any pitting. As a result, many potential buyers would rather own this gun than the one in Photo 77.

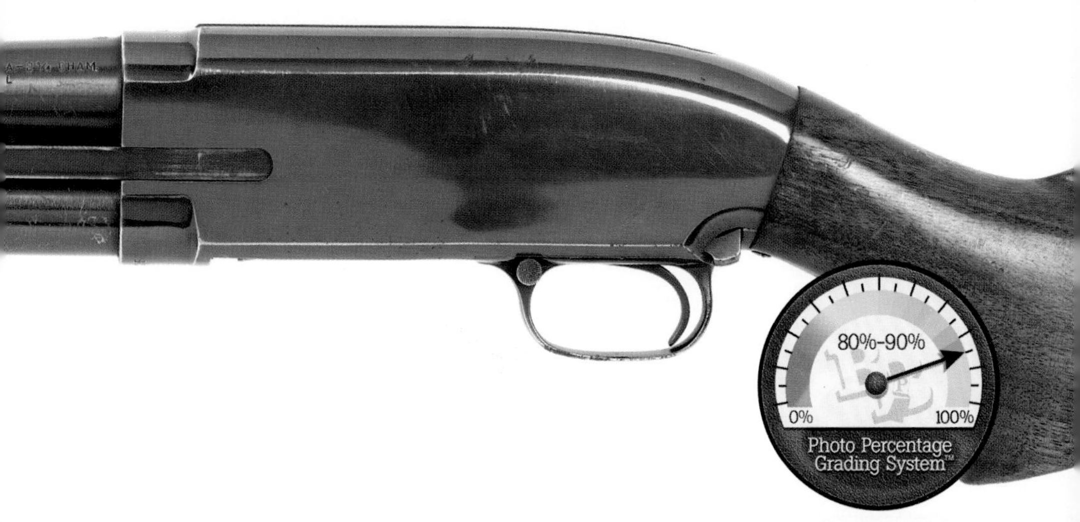

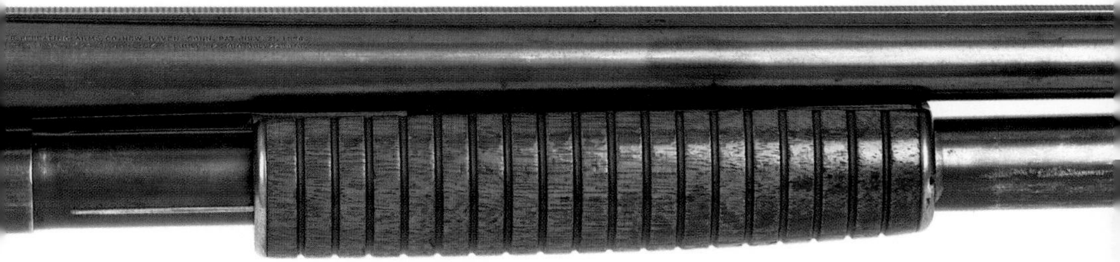

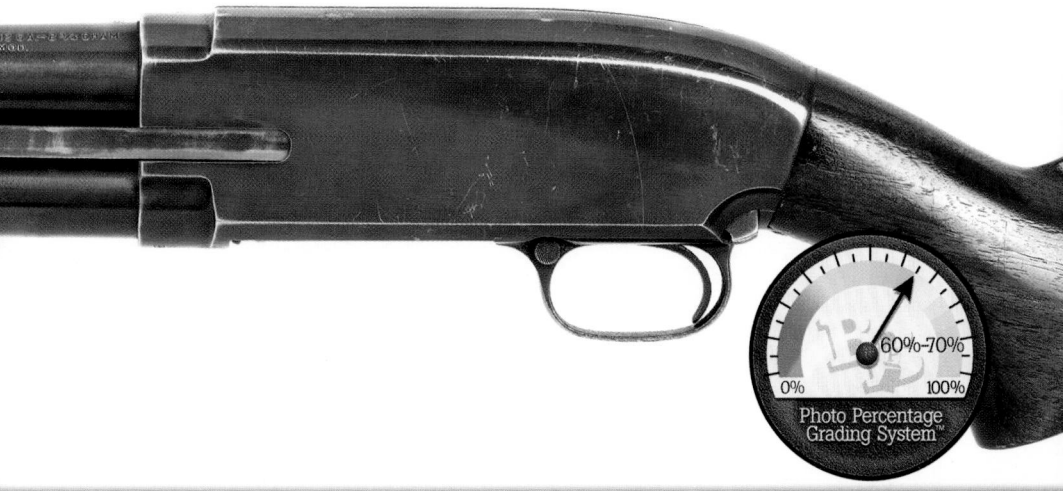

Photo 78 = Winchester Model 12, 12 ga. Mag., ser. no. 667,728, 60%-70% over-all. Appears to have had the receiver cold-blued at an earlier date (note the color difference between frame and barrel), factory solid rib with cut-off barrel, observe replacement unfinished checkered stock. For most shotguns with this many problems, either figure out what the parts are worth or what you want to pay for it as a shooter and don't spend a penny more.

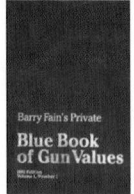

1st Edition (Vol. I, No. I)
1981

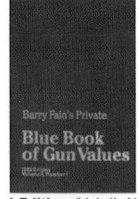

2nd Edition (Vol. II, No. I)
1982

3rd Edition (Vol. II, No. II)
1982

4th Edition
1983

5th Edition
1984

6th Edition
1985

7th Edition
1986

8th Edition
1987

9th Edition
1988

10th Edition
1989

11th Edition
1990

12th Edition
1991

13th Edition
1992

14th Edition
1993

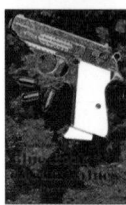

15th Edition
1994

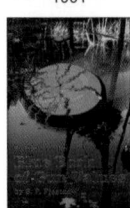

16th Edition
1995

17th Edition
1996

18th Edition
1997

19th Edition
1998

20th Edition
1999

21st Edition
2000

22nd Edition
2001

For more information on these older editions, please contact us at:

Blue Book Publications, Inc.
1-800-877-4867
www.bluebookinc.com

A SECTION

A.A.

Previously manufactured by Azanza & Arrizabalaga located in Eibar, Spain.

Grading	100%	98%	95%	90%	80%	70%	60%

PISTOLS: SEMI-AUTO

A.A. - 7.65mm cal., semi-auto pistol, slide marked Azanza & Arrizabalaga Model 1916, A.A. in oval on frame.

$235	$200	$165	$135	$115	$85	$75

REIMS - 6.35mm or 7.65mm cal., semi-auto pistol, copies of M1906 Browning, marked 1914 Model.

$185	$150	$130	$110	$90	$70	$50

A.A.A.

Previously manufactured by Aldazabal located in Spain.

PISTOLS: SEMI-AUTO

M1919 - 7.65mm cal., semi-auto pistol.

$110	$100	$85	$70	$65	$60	$55

A.A. ARMS INC.

Previous manufacturer located in Monroe, NC until 1999. Distributor, dealer, and direct consumer sales.

CARBINES: SEMI-AUTO

AR9 CARBINE - similar action to AP9, except has carbine length barrel and side-folding metal stock. Banned 1994.

$750	$625	$550	$475	$400	$350	$300

PISTOLS: SEMI-AUTO

AP9 MINI-SERIES PISTOL - 9mm Para. cal., semi-auto blowback paramilitary design, phosphate/blue or nickel finish, 2 barrel lengths, 10 (C/B 1994) or 20* shot mag. Disc. 1999, parts cleanup during 2000.

$210	$185	$165	$150	$135	$125	$115

Last MSR was $245.

Add $20 for nickel finish.
Add $200 for AP9 long barrel Target Model (banned 1994).

A & B HIGH PERFORMANCE FIREARMS

Previous competition pistol manufacturer located in Arvin, CA.

PISTOLS: SEMI-AUTO

LIMITED CLASS - 9mm Para. or .38 Super cal., single action, competition M1911-styled action, STI frame, Ultimatch bull barrel, Caspian slide, Bo-Mar adj. rear sight, blue or chrome finish.

$1,875	$1,600	$1,375	$1,150	$925	$700	$550

Last MSR was $1,875.

Grading	100%	98%	95%	90%	80%	70%	60%

OPEN CLASS - 9mm Para. or .38 Super cal., single action, competition M1911-styled action, STI frame, Ultimatch or Hybrid compensated barrel, Caspian slide, C-More scope, blue or chrome finish.

	100%	98%	95%	90%	80%	70%	60%
	$2,800	$2,300	$1,875	$1,600	$1,375	$1,000	$750

Last MSR was $2,800.

A & R SALES

Previous manufacturer located in South El Monte, CA.

PISTOLS: SEMI-AUTO

HANDGUN - .45 ACP cal., semi-auto patterned after Colt Model 1911 Govt., less weight than normal Colt .45.

	$225	$205	$175	$155	$145	$135	$125

RIFLES: SEMI-AUTO

RIFLE: MARK IV SPORTER - .308 Win. cal., semi-auto, M-14 style action, clip-fed, adj. sights.

	$295	$260	$225	$200	$175	$155	$140

ADC

Current pistol manufacturer and customizer located in Gardone, Italy. Consumer direct sales.

ADC manufactures high quality custom pistols, mainly M1911 design. ADC also provides a complete range of customizing and gunsmithing services. Please contact the company directly for more information (see Trademark Index).

AFC

Previously manufactured by Auguste Francotte located in Liege, Belgium, 1912-1914.

PISTOLS: SEMI-AUTO

SEMI-AUTO PISTOL - 6.35mm cal., 6 shot mag., frame marked "Francotte Liege".

	$275	$250	$220	$165	$140	$110	$85

A. J. ORDNANCE

Previous manufacturer located in Covina, CA.

PISTOLS: SEMI-AUTO

THOMAS - .45 ACP cal., semi-auto, double action only, 6 shot, 3½ in. barrel, fixed sights, checkered plastic grips, delayed blowback action, stainless steel barrel. Disc. mid-1970s.

	$600	$525	$450	$400	$350	$300	$250

Add 50% for chrome or stainless steel.

A K S (AK-47, AK-74, & AKM Copies)

Select fire paramilitary design rifle originally designed in Russia (initials refer to Avtomat Kalashnikova, 1947). Russian mfg. select fire AK-47s have not been mfg. since the mid 1950s. Semi-auto AK-47 and AKM clones are currently manufactured by several arsenals in China including Norinco and Poly Technologies, Inc. (illegal to currently import), in addition to other countries including the Czech Republic, Bulgaria, Russia, Egypt and Hungary. On April 6th, 1998, recent "sporterized" variations (imported 1994-1998) with thumbhole stocks were banned by presidential order. Beginning 2000, AK-47s are bring assembled in the U.S., using both new mfg. and

Grading	100%	98%	95%	90%	80%	70%	60%

older original military parts/components.

AK-47s are not rare - over 700 million have been manufactured in China alone since WW II.

AK/AK-47/AKM HISTORY & RECENT IMPORTATION

Since the early 1950s, the AK/AK-47/AKM series of select fire rifles has been the standard issue military rifle of the former Soviet Union and its satellites. It continues to fulfill that role reliably today. The AK series of rifles, from the early variants of the AK-47 through the AKM and AK-74, is undoubtedly the most widely used military small arms design in the world. Developed by Mikhail Kalashnikov (the AK stands for Avtomat Kalashnikova) in 1946, the AK went into full production in 1947 in Izhevsk, Russia. Since then, variants of the original AK-47 have been manufactured by almost every former Soviet bloc country and some free world nations, including Egypt. Even the Israeli Galil borrows design characteristics from the Kalashnikov. The AK action is the basis for numerous other weapons, including the RPK (Ruchnoy Pulemyot Kalashnikova). The basic AK design was changed in the mid-1950s to the AKM and incorporates more efficient production methods, using stamped rather than milled receivers. The AKM's modifications also incorporated numerous internal design changes to improve reliability and ease of maintenance.

The AK was designed to be, and always has been, a "peasant-proof" military weapon. It is a robust firearm, both in design and function. Its record on the battlefields around the world is impressive, rivaled only by the great M1 Garand of the U.S. or bolt rifles such as the English Mark III Enfield. The original AK-47 prototypes are on display in the Red Army Museum in Moscow.

All of the current semi-auto AK "clones" are copies of the AKM's basic receiver design and internal components minus the full-auto parts. The Saiga rifle, manufactured by the Izhevsk Machining Plant, in Izhevsk, Russia, is the sole Russian entry in this market. It is available in the standard 7.62X39mm, 5.45X39mm and in .410 bore. Other European manufacturers include companies in the Czech Republic, Bulgaria, as well as the former Yugoslavia. The Egyptian-made Maadhi AK clones were also available in the U.S. market.

Value for almost all of the imported AK clones is based solely on their use as sporting or target rifles. Fit and finish varies by country and importer. Most fall on the "low" side. Interest peaked prior to the passage of the 1994 Crime Bill and both AK clones and their "high capacity" magazines were bringing a premium for a short period of time in 1993 and 1994. However, interest waned during 1995-97, and the reduced demand lowered prices. In November of 1997, the Clinton Administration instituted an "administrative suspension" on all import licenses for these types of firearms in order to do a study on their use as "sporting firearms".

On April 6th, 1998, the Clinton Administration, in the political wake of the Jonesboro tragedy, banned the further import of 58 "assault-type" rifles, claiming that these semi-autos could not be classified as sporting weapons - the AK-47 and most related configurations were included. During 1997, firearms importers obtained permits to import almost 600,000 reconfigured rifles - approximately only 20,000 had entered the country when this bill took effect. When the ban occurred, applications were pending to import an additional 1,000,000 guns. Previously, thumbhole- stocked AK Sporters were still legal for import, and recent exporters included the Czech Republic, Russia, and Egypt.

RIFLES: SEMI-AUTO, AK-47, AK-74, & AKM MODELS

Also refer to separate listings under Poly Technologies, Inc., Norinco, Federal Ordnance, B-West, K.B.I., Sentinel Arms, American Arms, Inc., and others who have recently imported this configuration.

With the Bush administration now in power, it remains to be seen if future political windmilling will once again affect the supply/demand economics of this paramilitary configuration.

AK-47 (AKM) RECENT IMPORTS - 7.62x39mm (most common cal., former Russian M43 military), 5.45x39mm (Romanian mfg. or Saiga/MAK - recent mfg. only), or .223 Rem. cal., semi-auto Kalashnikov action, stamped (most common) or milled receiver, typically 16½ in. barrel, 5, 10, or 30* (C/B 1994) shot mag., wood or synthetic stock and forearm except

Grading	100%	98%	95%	90%	80%	70%	60%

on folding stock model, recent importation (1994-early 1998) mostly had newer "sporter-ized" fixed stocks with thumbholes, may be supplied with bayonet, sling, cleaning kit, pat-terned after former military production rifle of China and Russia.

AK-47 technically designates the original select fire (semi or full-auto), Russian made military rifle with milled receiver. Recent semi-auto "clones" normally have stamped receivers and are techni-cally designated AKMs. Recent mfg. AK-47 clones refer to rifles with milled receivers. Chinese importation stopped during late 1990.

Add 10-15% for 5.45x39mm cal. on Eastern European mfg. (non-recent import).
Add 20% for older folding stock variations.

	100%	98%	95%	90%	80%	70%	60%
Chinese mfg. (usually poor quality)	$225	$195	$175	$150	$135	$120	$110
Egyptian mfg. (recent import)	$295	$265	$225	$195	$175	$150	$125
Romanian mfg. (recent import)	$335	$285	$260	$240	$220	$200	$180
Yugoslavian mfg.	$450	$375	$315	$275	$240	$220	$200
Hungarian mfg.	$450	$375	$315	$275	$240	$220	$200
Czech mfg.	$450	$375	$315	$275	$240	$220	$200
Bulgarian mfg.	$450	$375	$315	$275	$240	$220	$200
Recent U.S. assembly	$495	$425	$325	$295	$250	$230	$210

Recent U.S. assembly refers to an original stamped European (mostly FEG) or milled receiver with U.S. assembly, using either new parts or matched, older unused original Eastern European mfg. parts (BATF 922.R compliant). This newest generation of AK-47s is high quality overall, and can-not be sold in California. Check city and state laws regarding high capacity magazine compli-ance.

AK-74- 5.45x39mm cal., semi-auto action based on the AKM, imported from Bulgaria and other previous Eastern bloc countries, in addition to current assembly in the U.S., using FEG receivers, Bulgarian parts sets, and additional U.S. made components.

	100%	98%	95%	90%	80%	70%	60%
Bulgarian mfg.	$450	$375	$315	$275	$240	$220	$200
Recent U.S. assembly	$495	$425	$325	$295	$250	$230	$210

A M A C

See Iver Johnson section in this text. AMAC stands for American Military Arms Cor-poration manufactured in Jacksonville, AR. AMAC ceased operations early 1993.

AMP TECHNICAL SERVICE GmbH

Current manufacturer located in Puchheim, Germany. Currently imported and dis-tributed exclusively beginning 2001 by CQB Products, located in Tustin, CA. Dealer and consumer direct sales.

RIFLES: BOLT ACTION

DSR-1 - .300 Win. Mag., .308 Win., or .338 Lapua cal., bolt action, bull pup design with in-line stock, receiver is made from aluminum, titanium, and polymers, internal parts are stainless steel, two-stage adj. trigger, 4 or 5 shot mag., 25.6 Lothar Walther fluted barrel with muzzl-ebrake and vent. shroud, includes bi-pod, ambidextrous 3 position safety, 13 lbs. Importa-tion began 2002.

MSR	$7,795		$7,295	$6,300	$5,200	$4,100	$3,000	$2,500	$2,000

Add $100 for .300 Win. Mag. cal.
Add $300 for .338 Lapua cal.

Grading	100%	98%	95%	90%	80%	70%	60%

A M T

Previous trademark manufactured by Galena Industries Inc. located in Sturgis, SD, 1999-Jan., 2001. Previously located in Irwindale, CA until 1998. From 1998-2001, all AMTs manufactured by Galena Industries Inc. had a lifetime warranty, which is now void. Also see Irwindale Arms, Inc. and Auto-Mag for older discontinued models.

Galena Industries phased out the use of the AMT name, but continued to use individual model nomenclature until 2001.

PISTOLS: SEMI-AUTO

From 1999-2001, AMT began using Millett sights exclusively. Between 1993-98, AMT changed from white outline Millett adj. sights to an adj. 3 dot (white) system mfg. by LPA in Italy.
Early production pistols were made in El Monte, CA, and are marked "El Monte".

LIGHTNING - .22 LR cal., semi-auto, stainless steel only, 5 (bull only), 6½, 8½, 10½, or 12½ (disc. 1987) in. bull or tapered barrels, adj. sights and trigger, pistol based on semi- auto Ruger action, tapered barrels. 23,903 were mfg. 1984-87.

$350 $200 $150

Last MSR was $289.

This model featured a frame grooved for scope mounts, Clark trigger, Millett sights, and either Pachmayr rubber or Wayland wood grips as standard equipment.

* ***Bull's Eye Regulation Target*** - similar to 6½ in. Lightning with bull barrel, except has vent. rib, wood grips, extended rear sight. Mfg. 1986 only.

$425 $350 $285

Last MSR was $436.

BABY AUTOMAG - .22 LR cal., semi-auto, stainless steel only, 8½ in. vent. rib barrel, Millett adj. sights, smooth walnut grips, 1,001 mfg.

$750 $650 $550

AUTOMAG II - .22 Mag. cal., stainless steel only, 3 3/8 (Compact Model), 4½, or 6 in. barrel, gas assisted action, white outline Millett adj. sights, grooved Lexan grips, 7 (Compact) or 9 shot mag., 24-32 oz. Mfg. 1987-2001.

$345 $255 $200

Last MSR was $459.

AUTOMAG III - .30 Carbine or 9mm Win. Mag. (mfg. 1993 only) cal., stainless steel, 6 3/ 8 in. barrel, patterned after Colt Govt. Model, white outline Millett adj. sights, grooved Lexan grips, 8 shot mag., 43 oz. Mfg. 1992-2001.

$530 $445 $335

Last MSR was $549.

AUTOMAG IV - 10mm (disc. 1993) or .45 Win. Mag. cal., 6½ (.45 Win. Mag. only) or 8 5/8 (disc. 1993) in. barrel, 7/8 shot mag., Millett adj. sights, stainless steel, 46 oz. Mfg. 1992-2001.

$530 $445 $325

Last MSR was $649.

AUTOMAG V - .50 AE cal., stainless steel, 6½ in. barrel, gas venting system reduces recoil, 5 shot mag., 46 oz. Mfg. 1993-95.

$815 $700 $625

Last MSR was $900.

A

Grading	100%	98%	95%	90%	80%	70%	60%

AUTOMAG 440 - .440 Cor-Bon cal., special order only. Mfg. 1999-2001.

	$775	$650	$550

Last MSR was $899.

JAVELINA - 10mm cal., semi-auto, 7 in. barrel, 8 shot mag., Millett adj. sights, wraparound Neoprene grips, wide adj. trigger, long grip safety, 48 oz. Mfg. 1992 only.

	$560	$460	$360

Last MSR was $676.

BACKUP PISTOL - .22 LR (disc. 1987), .357 Sig. (new 1996), .380 ACP, .38 Super (new 1995), 9mm Para. (new 1995), .40 S&W (new 1995), .400 Cor-Bon (new 1997), or .45 ACP (new 1995) cal., semi- auto, choice of traditional double action (disc. 1992) or double action only (new 1992), 2½ (.22 LR or .380 ACP) or 3 in. barrel, stainless steel, Lexan grips, 5 (.380 ACP or .40 S&W), 6, or 8 (.22 LR) shot mag., 18 (.380 ACP only) or 23 oz. Older disc. walnut grip models are worth a slight premium.

* *.22 LR cal.* - .22 LR cal., limited production.

	$300	$185	$140

* *.380 ACP cal.* - disc. 2000.

	$225	$175	$135

Last MSR was $319.

* *9mm Para., .40 S&W, or .45 ACP cal.*

	$250	$190	$145

Last MSR was $349.

* *.357 Sig., .38 Super, or .400 Cor-Bon cal.*

	$275	$200	$155

Last MSR was $389.

In 1992, AMT re-engineered this model and removed all external levers.

BACKUP PISTOL II - .380 ACP cal., single action, semi-auto, stainless steel, 2½ in. barrel, 5 shot finger extension mag., black carbon fiber grips, 18 oz. Mfg. 1993-1998.

	$260	$190	$150

Last MSR was $369.

.45 ACP STANDARD GOVERNMENT MODEL - .45 ACP cal., similar to Colt semi- auto Govt. model, stainless steel, 5 in. barrel, fixed rear sight, loaded chamber indicator, adj. trigger, wraparound neoprene grips, 38 oz. Disc. 1999.

	$325	$275	$225

Last MSR was $399.

HARDBALLER II - .45 ACP cal., similar to Colt Gold Cup Model, stainless steel, 5 in. barrel, adj. Millett rear sight, serrated rib, loaded chamber indicator, adj. trigger, wraparound neoprene grips, 38 oz. Disc. 2001.

	$400	$325	$250

Last MSR was $499.

Add $280 for 7 in. Hardballer conversion kit (disc. 1997).

* *Hardballer Longslide* - similar to Hardballer, except 7 in. barrel, longer slide assembly, and also available in .400 Cor-Bon (named .400 Accelerator, new 1998), 46 oz. Disc. 2001.

	$425	$320	$250

Last MSR was $549.

Add $50 for .400 Cor-Bon (.400 Accelerator) cal.
Add $300 for 5 in. Longslide conversion kit (disc. 1997).

Grading	100%	98%	95%	90%	80%	70%	60%

COMMANDO - .40 S&W cal., 4 in. barrel. Mfg. 1998-2001.

	$400	**$325**	**$250**

Last MSR was $499.

SKIPPER - .45 ACP cal., re-released in 1991 with choice of .40 S&W or .45 ACP cal., similar to Hardballer, except approx. 1 in. shorter slide on pre-'84 mfg, 4¼ in. barrel, checkered walnut grips, matte finish stainless steel, Millett adj. rear sight, 7 shot mag., 33 oz. Disc. 1991.

	$350	**$285**	**$250**

Last MSR was $450.

COMBAT SKIPPER - similar to Skipper, only with fixed sights. Disc. 1984.

	$375	**$330**	**$295**

BULL'S EYE TARGET MODEL - .40 S&W cal., similar to Hardballer with 5 in. barrel, 8 shot mag., adj. Millett sights, wraparound neoprene grips, 38 oz. Mfg. 1991 only.

	$400	**$340**	**$295**

Last MSR was $500.

"ON DUTY" DOUBLE ACTION - 9mm Para., .40 S&W, or .45 ACP (new late 1994) cal., stainless steel slide and barrel, 4½ in. barrel, 10 (C/B 1994), 15* (9mm Para.), 11* (.40 S&W), or 9 (.45 ACP) shot mag., 3-dot sighting system, anodized aluminum frame, trigger disconnect safety with inertia firing pin, carbon fiber grips, 32 oz. Mfg. 1991-94.

	$385	**$295**	**$250**

Last MSR was $470.

Add $60 for .45 ACP cal.

In 1992, this model became available with either traditional double action with decocking lever or double action only with safety.

RIFLES: BOLT ACTION

All AMT rifles were discontinued in 1998.

BOLT ACTION STANDARD SINGLE SHOT - 11 various cals., post-64 push-feed action, pre-64 3-position side safety, cone breech, composite stock, cryogenic treated stainless steel barrel w/o sights, 8½ lbs. Mfg. 1996-97.

	$825	**$650**	**$450**

Last MSR was $1,500.

✳ *Bolt Action Deluxe Single Shot* - 11 various cals., Mauser type controlled feeding, short, medium, or long right-hand or left-hand action, pre-64 3-position side safety and claw type extractor, cryogenic treated stainless steel barrel w/o sights, custom Kevlar stock, approx. 8½ lbs. Mfg. 1996 only.

	$995	**$800**	**$600**

Last MSR was $2,400.

BOLT ACTION STANDARD REPEATER - 21 various cals., post-64 push-feed action, Mauser type mag., pre-64 3-position side safety, Model 70 type trigger, composite stock, cryogenic treated stainless steel barrel w/o sights. 8½ lbs. Mfg. 1996 only.

	$800	**$625**	**$500**

Last MSR was $1,110.

✳ *Bolt Action Deluxe Repeater* - similar features to Bolt Action Deluxe Single Shot, except has Mauser type mag. Mfg. 1996 only.

	$1,000	**$800**	**$650**

Last MSR was $1,596.

Grading	100%	98%	95%	90%	80%	70%	60%

RIFLES:SEMI-AUTO

LIGHTNING (25/22) - .22 LR cal., semi-auto based on Ruger 10-22 action, stainless steel, 30 shot mag., 17½ in. bull or tapered barrel, nylon pistol grip handle and forearm, folding stock with recoil pad or youth stock, fixed sights, 6 lbs. Mfg. 1986-1993.

$220   **$175**   **$150**

Last MSR was $296.

SMALL GAME HUNTER (SGH) - .22 LR cal., same mechanical action as Lightning, except has matte black nylon stock with checkered forearm and grip, 22 in. barrel, 10 shot mag., no sights, removable recoil pad allows storage in stock, 6 lbs. Mfg. 1986- 1993.

$230   **$190**   **$160**

Last MSR was $300.

SMALL GAME HUNTER II - similar to Small Game Hunter, except has match grade 22 in. heavyweight full-floating barrel, 10 shot rotary mag., black fiberglass nylon stock, no sights, 6 lbs. Mfg. 1993 only.

$230   **$190**   **$160**

Last MSR was $300.

Add $70 for 17½ in. stainless steel barrel.
Add $150 for 22½ in. stainless steel match grade barrel.

CHALLENGE EDITION (I, II, III) - .22 LR cal., semi-auto target variation featuring McMillan fiberglass stock, 16¼ (choice of 6 in. barrel weight extension or 3 in. muzzle brake, new 1997), 18, 20 (mfg. 1994-96), or 22 (mfg. 1994-96) in. floating stainless steel bull barrel, custom designed or Jewell (new 1997) trigger, custom order through AMT's Custom Shop. Mfg. 1994-98.

$800   **$600**   **$450**

Last MSR was $1,296.

Subtract $200 without Jewell trigger.
Add $144 for 16¼ barrel with 3 in. muzzle brake (Challenge Edition II, new 1997).
Add $85 for 16¼ barrel with 6 in. barrel extension (Challenge Edition III).

✱ ***Challenge Edition Elite With Bloop Tube*** - features 16¼ in. barrel with a 6 in. bloop tube extension enabling increased bullet velocity with muzzle heavy characteristics, McMillan fiberglass STC stock. Mfg. 1996-98.

$925   **$700**   **$550**

Last MSR was $1,498.

Subtract $255 if without compensator.

SPORTER EDITION - .22 LR cal., 16½, 18, 20, or 22 in. tapered sporter barrel, McMillan fiberglass sporter stock. Mfg. 1996 only.

$650   **$525**   **$400**

Last MSR was $900.

HUNTER EDITION I - .22 LR cal., 18, 20, or 22 in. regular barrel with injection molded sporter stock. Mfg. 1996 only (replaced with Hunter Edition II).

$550   **$425**   **$300**

Last MSR was $800.

Hunter Edition II - .22 LR cal., 22 in. tapered sporter barrel with 2 lb. Jewell trigger, McMillan synthetic sporter stock. Mfg. 1997-98.

$750   **$575**   **$425**

Last MSR was $1,354.

FLY SWATTER I - .22 LR cal., 16½ in. regular barrel with injection molded (1996 only) or Hogue over-molded (new 1997) sporter stock. Mfg. 1996-97.

$575 $450 $325

Last MSR was $822.

❋ *Fly Swatter II* - similar to Fly Swatter I, except has 3 in. muzzle brake. Mfg. 1997 only.

$675 $475 $350

Last MSR was $936.

BR-50 ACCELERATOR EDITION - .22 LR cal., features 16¼ (new 1998) or 16½ (disc. 1997) in. bull barrel with 3 in. muzzle brake (new 1998), McMillan bench rest stock, Hoehn barrel tuner (disc. 1997), and Jewell trigger. Mfg. 1997-98.

$795 $600 $450

Last MSR was $1,440.

ACCULITE EDITION RIFLE - .22 LR cal., features 18 in. Magnum Research graphite barrel with muzzle brake, thumbhole sporter stock, adj. Jewell trigger, 4¾ lbs. Mfg. 1998 only.

$750 $575 $425

Last MSR was $1,321.

INTIMIDATOR EDITION RIFLE - .22 LR cal., 16¼ Shilen select match grade barrel with 6 in. bloop tube, adj. Jewell trigger, 6¼ lbs. Mfg. 1998 only.

$875 $625 $475

Last MSR was $1,581.

MAGNUM HUNTER - .22 Mag. cal., semi-auto, 20 in. free-floating barrel, stainless steel, 10 shot straight stacked mag., w/o sights, drilled and tapped for Weaver 87-A scope base, black synthetic stock, 6 lbs. Mfg. 1995-98.

$375 $295 $225

Last MSR was $459.

TARGET RIFLE SEMI-AUTO - .22 LR cal., button rifled Cryogenic treated barrel with target crown, choice of Fajen laminate or Hogue composite stock, 10 shot mag., 1-piece receiver with integral Weaver mount, 7½ lbs. Mfg. 1997-98.

$425 $350 $275

Last MSR was $549.

Add $50 for Fajen laminate stock.

AR-7 INDUSTRIES, LLC

Current manufacturer established 1998, and located in Meriden, CT. Dealer and distributor sales.

RIFLES: BOLT ACTION

AR-7 TAKEDOWN - .22 LR cal., bolt action variation of the AR-7 Explorer rifle, similar takedown/storage configuration, 2½ lbs. New 2002.

As this edition went to press, prices had yet to be established on this model.

Grading	100%	98%	95%	90%	80%	70%	60%

RIFLES: SEMI-AUTO

AR-7 EXPLORER RIFLE - .22 LR cal., takedown barrelled action stores in synthetic stock which floats, 8 shot mag., aperture rear sight, 16 in. barrel (synthetic barrel with steel liner), black matte finish on AR-7, silvertone on AR-7S (disc. 2000), camouflage finish on AR-7C, two-tone (silver receiver with black stock and barrel) on AR-7T (disc. 2000), walnut finish on AR-W (new 2001), stowed length 16½ in., 2½ lbs. New late 1998.

	MSR	$150		$125	$100	$85	$75	$65	$55	$50

Add $15 for camo or walnut finish.

This model was also previously manufactured by Survival Arms, Inc. and Charter Arms - see individual listings for information. Current production still utilizes the original tooling, with improvements.

AR-7 SPORTER (AR-20) - .22 LR cal., 16½ in. steel barrel with vent. aluminum shroud, metal skeleton fixed stock with pistol grip, 8 (new 2001) or 16 shot "flip clip" (optional) mag., 3.85 lbs. New late 1998.

	MSR	$200		$170	$145	$120	$105	$95	$80	$70

Add $100 for sporter conversion kit (includes aluminum shrouded barrel, pistol grip stock, and 16 shot flip clip).

This model was also previously manufactured by Survival Arms, Inc. - see individual listing for information.

AR-7 TARGET - .22 LR cal., 16 in. bullbarrel with cantilever scope, tube stock, 8 shot mag., includes 3x9x40mm compact rubber armored scope, 5.65 lbs. New 2002.

As this edition went to press, prices had yet to be established on this model.

ASAI AG (ADVANCED SMALL ARMS INDUSTRIES)

Current manufacturer located in Solothurn, Switzerland since 1994. No current importation. Previously imported until 2000 by Magnum Research, Inc. located in Minneapolis, MN.

PISTOLS:SEMI-AUTO

ONE PRO.45 - 9mm Para. (limited mfg. in Europe, never imported into the U.S.), .40 S&W (limited mfg. in Europe, never imported into the U.S.), .400 Cor-Bon (conversion only), or .45 ACP cal., SA or DA, 3 (disc. 1998) or 3¾ in. barrel with polygonal rifling, steel or alloy (not imported into U.S.) frame, black contoured synthetic grips, black or two-tone (less than 10 mfg.) finish, 10 shot mag., includes plastic case, extra 10 shot mag., and cleaning kit, 25 or 31 oz. Imported mid- 1997-2000.

	$595	$485	$410	$360	$330	$300	$275

Last MSR was $699.

Add $209 for .400 Cor-Bon conversion kit without compensator.
Add $249 for .45 ACP or .400 Cor-Bon conversion kit with extended barrel, compensator, and recoil spring guide.

Grading	100%	98%	95%	90%	80%	70%	60%

A-SQUARE COMPANY

Current firearms and ammunition manufacturer located in Bedford, KY beginning 2001. A-Square Company is a wholly owned subsidiary of JISTA, LLC. Previously located in Louisville, KY until 2000, and in Madison, IN until 1991.

A-SQUARE

A-Square also offers different grades of walnut, different metal finishes, and various sights/scope rings as special orders. Custom calibers are also available upon special order.

RIFLES: BOLT ACTION

Add $325 for A-Grade walnut, add $625 for AAA-Grade fancy walnut, add $500 for English walnut (disc.), add $100 for accent package (disc.), add $550 for black synthetic stock, add $600 for weather-impervious package (disc.), add $325 for 3-leaf steel express sights, add $300 for royal high gloss blue finish (disc. 1995), add $150 for high gloss polymer wood finish (disc. 1993).

HANNIBAL MODEL - most cals. available, bolt action built on a P-17 Enfield receiver, 22-26 in. barrel, deluxe oil finished walnut with pistol grip and recoil pad, Teflon coated metal, choice of barrel length and LOP, 9 - 11¼ lbs. New 1986.

MSR	$3,625		$3,400	$2,850	$2,400	$2,100	$1,875	$1,725	$1,575

HAMILCAR MODEL - various cals. available, smaller variation of the Hannibal model featuring slimmer design gained by not needing the reinforcement for heavy Mag. cals., 4-7 shot mag., cocks on opening, 8 - 8½ lbs. New 1994.

MSR	$3,625		$3,400	$2,850	$2,400	$2,100	$1,875	$1,725	$1,575

CAESAR MODEL - most cals. available, bolt action built on a Remington M-700 receiver until 1993, Sako L-V actions were utilized beginning 1993, 22-26 in. barrel, select walnut with pistol grip and recoil pad, primarily a left-handed action with right-hand a special order, 9 - 10¾ lbs. New 1986.

MSR	$3,625		$3,400	$2,850	$2,400	$2,100	$1,875	$1,725	$1,575

GENGHIS KHAN MODEL - .22-250 Rem., .243 Win., .25-06, or 6mm Rem. cal., features Winchester pre-64 Model 70 action, heavy tapered barrel, Coil-Chek stock helps reduce recoil, designed for varmint hunting. New 1995.

MSR	$3,625		$3,400	$2,850	$2,400	$2,100	$1,875	$1,725	$1,575

A T C S A

Previously manufactured by Armas De Tiro Y Casa located in Spain.

REVOLVERS

COLT POCKET PISTOL COPY - revolver, .38 cal., 6 shot.

	$155	$140	$110	$100	$90	$75	$65

SINGLE SHOT REVOLVER - target pistol.

	$195	$165	$145	$110	$100	$90	$75

Grading	100%	98%	95%	90%	80%	70%	60%

AYA (AGUIRRE Y ARANZABAL)

Current manufacturer established in 1917, and located in Eibar, Spain. Currently imported and distributed by Fieldsport, located in Traverse City, MI, New England Custom Gun Service, Ltd. (NECG), located in Plainfield, NH, John F. Rowe, located in Enid, OK. Previously imported by William Larkin Moore 1969-1978 (with Agoura, CA import marking) and 1978-1986 (with West Lake, CA import marking). Diarm also manufactured AYAs circa 1986-88 in Eibar, Spain. Retail and dealer sales by importer and AYA select distributors.

AYA manufactured shotguns can be denoted by serialization. Serial numbers over 600,001 with barrel flats marked Arms de Chasse or Scotia Group are post-1988 AYA manufactured while specimens under 600,000 may have been manufactured by Diarm - Diarm manufacture is not covered by the AYA warranty, nor is the resale the same as values listed below.

SHOTGUNS: O/U

Additionally, AYA manufactures a Coral boxlock, both in standard and deluxe configurations, the Excelsior sidelock model is also available. The MD2 and MD6 models complete their European line. Please contact the factory directly for more information on these guns.

Add 5% for gauges smaller than 12 ga.
Add 5% for magnum chambers.

AUGUSTA - 12 ga. only, deluxe O/U sidelock, arabesque engraving in deep relief, select walnut.

This model has been imported off and on over the years and the importers should be contacted directly for current pricing information and availability.

CORAL "A" - 12 or 16 ga., boxlock action with Kersten cross bolt, vent. rib, ejectors, double triggers. Disc. 1985.

$1,275	$1,050	$875	$775	$695	$625	$560

Last MSR was $2,195.

CORAL "B" - similar to Coral A, except for coin-wash engraved receiver. Disc. 1985.

$1,395	$1,100	$925	$820	$720	$650	$595

Last MSR was $2,450.

MODEL 37 SUPER - 12, 16, or 20 ga., various barrel lengths and chokes, vent. rib, sidelock, auto ejector, elaborate engraving, high grade wood. Merkel style action. Prices below reflect older models. Disc.

12 ga.	$2,600	$2,350	$2,100	$1,900	$1,700	$1,500	$1,250
16 ga.	$2,550	$2,200	$2,000	$1,700	$1,500	$1,350	$1,150
20 ga.	$3,000	$2,500	$2,200	$1,900	$1,700	$1,600	$1,475

✳ **New Model 37 A/B/C** - game scene engraved, detachable sidelock action, nickel steel receiver. This model has been imported off and on over the years.

Please contact the importer directly for pricing information and availability on this model.

MODEL 77 - 12 ga. only, Merkel style O/U sidelock with Greener crossbolt, deluxe engraving checkering. Disc. 1985.

$3,100	$2,750	$2,500	$2,255	$2,030	$1,805	$1,600

Last MSR was $4,100.

MODEL 79 "A" - 12 ga. only, boxlock with double locking lugs, sel. trigger, ejectors. Disc. 1985.

$1,275	$1,075	$965	$880	$790	$705	$640

Last MSR was $1,595.

Grading	100%	98%	95%	90%	80%	70%	60%

MODEL 79 "B" - similar to Model 79 "A", only more elaborate engraving. Disc. 1985.

	$1,395	$1,200	$1,085	$990	$890	$790	$695

Last MSR was $1,795.

MODEL 79 "C" - similar to Model 79 "B", only more elaborate engraving, double triggers on request. Disc. 1985.

	$2,050	$1,825	$1,605	$1,460	$1,315	$1,165	$1,000

Last MSR was $2,650.

SHOTGUNS: SxS

Current retail values on the AYA shotguns listed below could vary somewhat from importer to importer.

On current models listed below, add 5% to values if other than 12 ga.

BILL HANUS BIRDGUN - 16, 20, or 28 ga., similar wood, fit, checkering, and finish as the No. 53 sidelock, except is Anson & Deeley boxlock, individual frames proportionate to ga., 27 in. barrels with concave rib choked Sk. 1 & 2, case colored receiver with moderate engraving, SST, ejectors, includes leather covered handguard, splinter forearm and straight grip, 5 lbs., 4 oz. (28 ga.) - 6 lbs., 5 oz. (16 ga.). Importation began 1997.

MSR	$2,495	$2,225	$1,850	$850	$575	$475	$410	$365

Subtract $300 for DT.

This model is available only through Bill Hanus Birdguns LLC.

BOLERO - similar to Matador, with non-selective single trigger and extractors. Disc. 1984.

	$440	$360	$330	$305	$275	$250	$220

COUNTRYMAN GAME GUN - 12 or 20 ga. New 1998.

MSR	$2,295	$2,050	$1,650	$675	$525	$450	$410	$365

IBERIA - 12 or 20 ga., 3 in., boxlock, double triggers, plain walnut. Disc. 1984.

	$566	$440	$370	$315	$285	$255	$230

IBERIA II - 12 or 16 ga., 28 in. barrels, 2¾ in. chamber only, double triggers, plain walnut. Mfg. 1984-1985 only.

	$515	$430	$370	$315	$285	$255	$230

Last MSR was $570.

MATADOR - 10, 12, 16, 20, 28 ga., or .410 bore, 26, 28, or 30 in. barrel, various chokes, Anson & Deeley boxlock, auto ejectors, beavertail forearm, SST, checkered pistol grip stock. Mfg. 1955-1963.

	$475	$375	$325	$275	$225	$200	$180

Add 20% for .410 bore or 28 ga.

MATADOR NO. 2 - similar to Matador, with vent. rib, 12 or 20 ga. only. Disc.

	$525	$425	$360	$315	$265	$225	$200

MATADOR NO. 3A - 12 or 20 ga., 3 in. chamber in 20 ga. only, boxlock, vent. rib, ejectors, SST. Disc. 1985.

	$750	$650	$550	$495	$440	$385	$335

Last MSR was $1,235.

SENIOR - 12 ga. only, self-opener, engraved sidelock action, select walnut. Top-of-the-line quality, made to special order only. Lighter up-land version also available. Disc. 1987.

	$15,500	$12,000	$10,000	$8,000	$6,500	$5,500	$4,500

Last MSR was $21,000.

Grading	100%	98%	95%	90%	80%	70%	60%

NO. 1 - 12, 16, 20, 28 ga. or .410 bore, full sidelock action, straight grip, ejectors, DTs, elaborate fine scroll engraving. Importation disc. 1987, resumed in 1991.

MSR	$7,170		$6,325	$2,925	$2,250	$1,800	$1,500	$1,200	$950

Add approx. $100 for rounded action.
Add approx. $2,640 for extra set of barrels.

✱ *No. 1 DeLuxe* - features bold folliate engraving.

MSR	$8,870		$7,825	$3,500	$2,700	$2,100	$1,800	$1,400	$1,150

Add $100 for rounded action.
Add approx. $2,640 for extra set of barrels.

✱ *No. 1 de Luxe English* - exhibition quality wood and engraved by Geoff Moore, English metal finish, custom order only.

This shotgun is specifically made for A.S.I., and is sold exclusively in the U.K. marketplace. Please contact A.S.I. for more information, including availability and prices.

NO. 2 - 12, 16, 20, 28 ga., or .410 bore, 3 in. chambers, English-style sidelock, ejector, cocking indicators, DTs. Importation disc. 1987, resumed 1991.

MSR	$3,375		$2,975	$1,350	$950	$750	$600	$500	$425

Add $100 for rounded action.
Add approx. $1,454 for extra set of barrels.

✱ *Bill Hanus Super No. 2 Sidelock* - features Boss rounded action and No. 1 grade wood. Limited importation 2000 only.

	$3,495	$2,975	$1,350	$950	$750	$600	$500

Last MSR was $3,895.

This model was only available from Bill Hanus Birdguns LLC.

NO. 3-A - 12, 16, 20, 28 ga., or .410 bore, boxlock, extractors, double triggers. Disc. 1985.

	$640	$540	$495	$450	$400	$375	$350

Last MSR was $850.

Add 25%-35% for 28 ga. or .410 bore.

NO. 4 & NO. 4/53 - 12, 16, 20, 28 ga., or .410 bore, 3 in. chambers, English-style straight stock, boxlock action, ejectors, double trigger, straight grip stock, No. 4 has standard wood, No. 4/53 has No. 53 wood upgrade. Importation disc. 1987, resumed 1991.

MSR	$1,845		$1,650	$675	$525	$450	$410	$365	$325

Add $877 for extra set of barrels.
Add approx. $180 for No. 4/53S (includes wood upgrade, NSST, and round knob pistol grip).

NO. 4 DELUXE - English-style, boxlock, ejector, stock, forearm, trigger to order. Importation disc. 1985, resumed 1991.

MSR	$3,045		$2,700	$1,300	$975	$875	$800	$740	$680

Add $962 for extra set of barrels.

XXV BOXLOCK (BL) - 12 or 20 ga. only, similar to No. 4 Deluxe, except 25 in. barrels, Churchill rib. Importation disc. 1986, resumed 1991.

MSR	$2,920		$2,675	$1,225	$975	$875	$800	$740	$680

Add approx. $1,509 for extra set of barrels.

XXV SIDELOCK (SL) - 12, 16, 20 (disc. 1997), 28 (disc. 1997) ga., or .410 bore (disc. 1997), sidelock ejector, 25 in. barrels, Churchill rib. Stock, forearm, trigger to order. Importation disc. 1986, resumed 1991.

✱ *12, 16, or 20 ga.*

MSR	$4,080		$3,600	$1,750	$1,350	$975	$850	$750	$650

Add approx. $1,720 for extra set of barrels.
Add 15% for 28 ga. or .410 bore.

Grading	100%	98%	95%	90%	80%	70%	60%

NO. 53 - 12, 16 (disc. 1997), or 20 ga., engraved sidelock ejector, sideclips, third lock. Stock, forearm, trigger to order. Importation disc. 1986, resumed 1991.

MSR	$4,745		$4,425	$2,050	$1,525	$1,100	$950	$850	$750

Add $1,733 for extra set of barrels.

NO. 56 - 12, 16 (disc. 1997), or 20 (disc. 1999) ga., sidelock action-engraved, ejectors, sel. trigger. Importation disc. 1985, resumed 1991.

MSR	$7,870		$7,150	$3,375	$2,700	$2,300	$1,950	$1,650	$1,400

Add $2,640 for extra set of barrels.

NO. 106 - 12, 16, or 20 ga., English-style boxlock, double trigger, pistol grip, 28 in. barrels. Disc. 1985.

	$530	$440	$400	$360	$320	$300	$275

Last MSR was $585.

107-LI - 12 or 16 ga., English-style boxlock, double trigger, straight grip, light English scroll engraving. Disc. 1985.

	$675	$560	$520	$480	$425	$400	$360

Last MSR was $745.

MODEL 116 - 12, 16, or 20 ga., 27-30 in. barrels, any choke, hand detachable H&H sidelocks, double triggers, engraved, select checkered walnut pistol grip stock. Disc. 1985.

	$1,000	$845	$795	$750	$675	$600	$500

Last MSR was $1,125.

MODEL 117 - 10, 12, 16 or 20 ga., 3 in. chambers, 26-30 in. barrels, any choke, hand detachable H&H sidelocks, ejectors, SST, engraved, select checkered walnut pistol grip stock. Disc. 1986.

	$835	$715	$660	$620	$585	$545	$500

Last MSR was $1,075.

QUAIL UNLIMITED MODEL 117 - 12 ga. only, 26 in. barrels choked IC/M with 3 in. chambers, upgraded wood and checkering, high gloss bluing, gold colored ST, engraved by Baron Technologies in PA, only 42 mfg. for Quail Unlimited of North America.

	$1,650	$1,400	$1,150	$975	$875	$800	$725

This model had a retail price of $1,700 but was made available to Quail Unlimited members for approx. $1,200.

MODEL 210 - 12 or 16 ga., boxlock, exposed hammers, double triggers, plain walnut, light engraving. Disc. 1985.

	$795	$675	$550	$475	$435	$395	$350

Last MSR was $900.

711 BOXLOCK - 12 ga. only, boxlock, selective trigger, ejectors, vent. rib. Disc. 1984.

	$880	$680	$575	$490	$445	$395	$350

✳ **711 *Sidelock*** - sidelock action. Mfg. 1985 only.

	$995	$850	$775	$695	$625	$550	$475

Last MSR was $1,250.

ABADIE

Previous trademark of Portuguese military revolvers manufactured by several Belgian makers.

Grading	100%	98%	95%	90%	80%	70%	60%

REVOLVERS

MODEL 1878 (OFFICER'S MODEL) - 9.1mm cal., solid frame revolver, 6 shot, ejector rod, officer's issue A.

$220	$195	$165	$130	$120	$110	$100

MODEL 1886 (TROOPER'S MODEL) - similar to 1878, but larger, trooper issue A.

$195	$175	$160	$120	$110	$100	$90

ABBEY, GEORGE T.

Previous manufacturer of percussion and breechloading firearms located in Utica, NY from 1845-1852, and Chicago, IL from 1852-1874.

100%	98%	95%	90%	80%	70%	60%	50%	40%	30%	20%	10%

RIFLES: PERCUSSION

PERCUSSION RIFLE

✳ **.44 cal.** - 32 in. octagon barrel.

100%	98%	95%	90%	80%	70%	60%	50%	40%	30%	20%	10%
$605	$550	$470	$415	$370	$340	$305	$275	$250	$220	$195	$165

✳ **.44 cal.** - octagon barrel, brass trimmed.

$770	$735	$695	$605	$550	$485	$450	$405	$365	$330	$275	$220

✳ **.44 cal.** - 31 in. side-by-side barrels.

$1,210	$1,100	$880	$770	$715	$650	$595	$550	$515	$475	$430	$360

✳ **.44 cal.** - O/U, brass trimmed.

$1,485	$1,295	$1,130	$990	$910	$855	$770	$715	$660	$605	$495	$330

ABBEY, F.J. & COMPANY

Previous manufacturer located in Chicago, IL, 1858-1878. Muzzle and breechloading shotguns and rifles.

RIFLES: PERCUSSION

PERCUSSION RIFLE - several variations.

$605	$550	$470	$415	$360	$305	$275	$250	$210	$175	$145	$110

SHOTGUNS: PERCUSSION

PERCUSSION SHOTGUN - several variations.

$800	$715	$635	$550	$470	$415	$360	$320	$285	$250	$210	$155

ABBIATICO & SALVINELLI (FAMARS)

Please refer to the Famars di Abbiatico & Salvinelli srl listing.

ACCU-MATCH INTERNATIONAL INC.

Previous handgun and pistol parts manufacturer located in Mesa, AZ circa 1996.

Grading	100%	98%	95%	90%	80%	70%	60%

PISTOLS: SEMI-AUTO

ACCU-MATCH PISTOL - .45 ACP cal., patterned after the Colt Govt. 1911, competition pistol features stainless steel construction with 5½ in. match grade barrel with 3 ports, recoil reduction system, 8 shot mag., 3 dot sight system. Approx. 160 mfg. 1996 only.

		$795	$700	$625	$550	$450	$375	$325

Last MSR was $840.

ACCU-TEK

Current trademark manufactured by Excel Industries, Inc., located in Chino, CA. Distributor and dealer direct sales.

PISTOLS: SEMI-AUTO

MODEL AT-25 - .25 ACP cal., single action, 2½ in. barrel, 7 shot mag. with finger extension, similar design to AT-32, stainless steel, aluminum, or alloy construction with choice of stainless, satin aluminum, or black finish, 11 (Model AT-25AL) or 18 (Model AT-25B, disc.) oz. Mfg. 1992-95.

		$150	$125	$105	$90	$80	$70	$60

Last MSR was $182.

This model was available in satin aluminum (Model AT-25AL) or black (Model AT-25SSB) finish.

MODEL AT-32SS - .32 ACP cal., single action design, 2½ in. barrel, 5 shot mag. with finger extension, alloy (disc. 1991) or stainless steel (new 1992) construction, black synthetic grips, manual safety with firing pin block and trigger disconnect, side mag. release, exposed hammer, satin aluminum (disc. 1991) finish , 16 oz. Mfg. in U.S. New 1990.

MSR	$239		$190	$155	$120	$100	$80	$70	$60

Add $5 for black finish (Model AT-32SSB).

MODEL AT-380SS - .380 ACP cal., similar to Model AT-32, except has 2¾ in. barrel, alloy (disc. 1991) or stainless steel construction, 20 oz. New 1990.

MSR	$239		$190	$155	$120	$100	$90	$80	$70

Add $5 for black finish (Model AT-380SSB, disc. 1999).

BL-380 - .380 ACP cal., double action only, carbon steel, black finish, compact size, two 5 shot mags., lockable case. Mfg. 1997-99.

		$165	$140	$120	$100	$90	$80	$70

Last MSR was $199.

MODEL HC-380SS - .380 ACP cal., single action semi-auto, stainless steel, 2½ in. barrel, 10 (C/B 1994) or 13* shot mag., manual safety with firing pin block and trigger disconnect, exposed hammer, 26 oz. New 1993.

MSR	$249		$210	$155	$120

Add $5 for black finish (Model HC-380B, mfg. 1995-99).

MODEL AT-9SS - 9mm Para. cal., double action only, stainless steel, 3.2 in. barrel, 8 shot mag., firing pin block with no external safety, black or brushed stainless finish, 3 dot sights adj. for windage, 28 oz. Mfg. 1995-96 only.

		$260	$205	$165

Last MSR was $317.

BL-9 - 9mm Para. cal., double action only, carbon steel, black finish, ultra compact size, includes two 5 shot mags., and lockable case. Mfg. 1997-2002.

		$195	$150	$120	$100	$90	$80	$70

Last MSR was $232.

Grading	100%	98%	95%	90%	80%	70%	60%

CP-9SS - 9mm Para. cal., double action only, stainless steel, black finish, compact size, 8 shot mag. Mfg. 1997-99.

	$220	$165	$125

Last MSR was $265.

MODEL XL-9SS - 9mm Para. cal, double action only, stainless steel, 3 in. barrel, 5 shot mag., black pebble finished grips, 3 dot adj. sights, 24 oz. New 1999.

MSR $267	$215	$170	$125

MODEL AT-40SS - .40 S&W cal., double action only, 3.2 in. barrel, 7 shot mag., firing pin block with no external safety, black or brushed stainless finish, 3 dot sights adj. for windage, 28 oz. Mfg. 1995-96 only.

	$260	$205	$165

Last MSR was $317.

CP-40SS - .40 S&W cal., 7 shot mag., otherwise similar to CP-9SS. Mfg. 1997-99.

	$220	$165	$125

Last MSR was $265.

MODEL AT-45SS - .45 ACP cal., similar to Model AT-40SS, except has 6 shot mag., stainless only, 28 oz. Mfg. 1996 only.

	$265	$210	$165

Last MSR was $327.

CP-45SS - .45 ACP cal., 6 shot mag., otherwise similar to CP-40SS. Mfg. 1997-99.

	$220	$165	$125

Last MSR was $265.

ACCURACY INTERNATIONAL LTD.

Current rifle manufacturer located in Hampshire, England since 1982. Currently imported and distributed by Accuracy International North America Inc., located in Oak Ridge, TN. Previously imported until 1998 by Gunsite Training Center, located in Paulden, AZ.

RIFLES: BOLT ACTION

In addition to the models listed below, Accuracy International also makes military and law enforcement rifles, including the SR98 Austrian ($10,839), G22 German ($13,483), and the Dutch SLA ($9,166).

AW MODEL - .243 Win. (new 2000) or .308 Win. cal., precision bolt action featuring 26 in. 1:12 twist stainless steel barrel with muzzle brake, 3 lug bolt, 10 shot detachable mag., synthetic thumbhole adj. stock, Parker-Hale bipod, 14 lbs. Importation began 1995.

MSR $5,224	$4,850	$3,600	$2,750	$2,200	$1,800	$1,500	$1,300

Add $376 for AW-F Model.

AWP MODEL - similar to AW Model, except has 24 in. barrel w/o muzzle brake, 15 lbs. Importation began 1995.

MSR $4,972	$4,525	$3,400	$2,650	$2,200	$1,800	$1,500	$1,300

Add $310 for AWP-F Model.
Subtract $639 if w/o bipod.

AWM MODEL (SUPER MAGNUM) - .300 Win. Mag. or .338 Lapua cal., 6 lug bolt, 26 or 27 in. 1:9/1:10 twist stainless steel barrel with muzzle brake, Parker-Hale bipod, 5 shot mag., 15½ lbs. Importation began 1995.

MSR $5,626	$5,200	$3,875	$3,000	$2,500	$2,000	$1,750	$1,500

Add $324 for AWM-F Model.
Subtract $641 if w/o bipod.

Grading	100%	98%	95%	90%	80%	70%	60%

PALMAMASTER - .308 Win. cal., available with either NRA prone or UIT style stock, 30 in. stainless steel fluted barrel, designed for competition shooting, laminate stock.

	MSR	$2,850	$2,600	$2,350	$2,100	$1,900	$1,700	$1,500	$1,250

CISMMASTER - .22 BR, 6 BR, .243 Win., .308 Win., 6.5x55mm, or 7.5x55mm cal., designed for slow and rapid fire international and military shooting competition, 10 shot mag., 2 stage trigger.

	MSR	$3,480	$3,175	$2,850	$2,600	$2,350	$2,100	$1,900	$1,700

VARMINT RIFLE - .22 Middlested, .22 BR, .22-250 Rem., .223 Rem., 6mm BR, .243 Win., .308 Win., or 7mm-08 Rem. cal., features 26 in. fluted stainless steel barrel. New 1997.

	MSR	$3,650	$3,200	$2,725	$2,350	$1,950	$1,675	$1,475	$1,300

AW50 - .50 BMG, advanced ergonomic design, features built-in anti-recoil system, adj. third supporting leg, folding stock, 35 lbs. New 1998.

	MSR	$10,950	$10,250	$8,750	$7,500	$6,250	$4,950	$3,750	$2,900

ACHA

Previous manufacturer located in Eibar, Spain until 1936.

PISTOLS: SEMI-AUTO

MODEL 1916 - 6.35mm cal., semi-auto pistol, 7 shot mag., 1905 Browning copy.

$250	$185	$130	$90	$80	$70	$60

ATLAS - 6.35mm cal., semi-auto pistol, 6 shot mag., slide marked ATLAS, 1905 Browning copy.

$200	$165	$125	$95	$75	$65	$50

LOOKING GLASS - 6.35mm cal., semi-auto pistol, 6 shot mag., blued or nickel, 1905 Browning copy, slide marked "Looking Glass", many variations.

$235	$170	$130	$100	$85	$70	$55

Add 50% for extended grip.

LOOKING GLASS - 7.65mm cal., semi-auto pistol.

$245	$175	$140	$105	$90	$75	$65

ACME

Previous trade name of Davenport Arms Company Shotguns, Maltby Henley & Co. Revolvers, and Merwin Hulbert & Co. Owl Head Revolvers.

100%	98%	95%	90%	80%	70%	60%	50%	40%	30%	20%	10%

REVOLVERS

SEVEN SHOT REVOLVER - .22 Short rimfire cal., single action.

$360	$310	$240	$185	$165	$150	$120	$110	$100	$90	$65	$55

FIVE SHOT REVOLVER - .32 Short rimfire cal., single action.

$360	$320	$255	$200	$175	$160	$120	$110	$100	$90	$65	$55

ACME ARMS

Previous trade name for Cornwall Hardware Co., NY.

100%	98%	95%	90%	80%	70%	60%	50%	40%	30%	20%	10%

REVOLVERS

SEVEN SHOT - .22 Short rimfire cal., single action.

$275	$250	$210	$185	$165	$155	$140	$125	$110	$90	$85	$75

FIVE SHOT - .32 Short Rimfire cal., single action.

$285	$255	$215	$195	$175	$165	$145	$120	$100	$90	$85	$75

SHOTGUNS: SxS

SIDE-BY-SIDE - 12 ga., damascus barrel.

$275	$240	$195	$165	$145	$125	$110	$95	$65	$60	$50	$45

ACME HAMMERLESS

Previously manufactured by Hopkins & Allen, for Hulbert Brothers, 1893.

REVOLVERS

FIVE SHOT - .32 centerfire cal., double action, top break, non-ejecting.

$145	$125	$100	$90	$80	$70	$60	$50	$40	$30	$20	$15

Also known as Forehand Model 1891, can be hammer or hammerless.

FIVE SHOT - .38 centerfire cal., double action, top break, non-ejecting.

$145	$125	$100	$90	$80	$70	$60	$50	$40	$30	$20	$15

Also known as Forehand Model 1891, can be hammer or hammerless.

ACTION (M.S.)

Previously manufactured by Modesto Santos, located in Eibar, Spain.

Grading	100%	98%	95%	90%	80%	70%	60%

PISTOLS: SEMI-AUTO

MODEL 1915 - 7.65mm cal., semi-auto pistol (French Military).

	$245	$175	$140	$105	$90	$75	$65

MODEL 1920 - 6.35mm cal., semi-auto pistol, slide marked "Action".

	$195	$150	$110	$85	$65	$45	$40

ACTION ARMS LTD.

Previous firearms importer and distributor until 1994, located in Philadelphia, PA.

Only Action Arms Models AT84S, AT88S, and the Model B Sporter will be listed under this heading. Galil, Timberwolf, and Uzi trademarks can be located in their respective sections.

CARBINES: SEMI-AUTO

MODEL B SPORTER - 9mm Para. cal., patterned after the original Uzi Model B Sporter, 16.1 in. barrel, closed breech, thumbhole stock with recoil pad, 10 shot mag., adj. rear sight, 8.8 lbs. Limited importation from China 1994 only.

	$545	$475	$435	$385	$335	$295	$275

Last MSR was $595.

Grading	100%	98%	95%	90%	80%	70%	60%

PISTOLS: SEMI-AUTO

AT-84S - 9mm Para. cal., selective double action design, patterned after the CZ-75, 4.8 in. barrel, 15 shot mag., originally introduced in 1985.

		100%	98%	95%	90%	80%	70%	60%
		$470	$415	$385	$360	$330	$275	$220

> The AT-84S Series was mfg. in Switzerland by Industrial Technology & Machines A.G. and was sold by Action Arms between June of 1987 and 1989. Serial number range is 01201- 06000. No P or H models were ever mfg. in this series (2 or 3 prototypes only).

AT-88S - 9mm or .41 Action Express (available early 1990) cal., selective double action design patterned after CZ-75, 4.8 in. barrel, 15 shot (9mm) or 10 shot (.41 AE) mag., can be "cocked and locked", fixed sights, blued metal, walnut grips, 35.3 oz. Introduced in 1987 with limited production samples imported in 1989.

$500	$450	$395	$360	$330	$275	$220

> A very small quantity of AT-88Ss (various configurations) were made by I.T.M. of Switzerland and finishes included all blue, all chrome, or 2-tone. These pistols may exhibit both I.T.M. and A.A.L. markings. More recent manufacture was performed by Sphinx-Muller of Switzerland. These pistols were mfg. by Sphinx-Muller, renamed the AT-2000 Series and previously imported by Sile Distributors.

RIFLES: SLIDE ACTION

TIMBERWOLF - see separate listing in T section.

ADAMS

Previously manufactured by Deane, Adams, & Deane, located in London, England.

100%	98%	95%	90%	80%	70%	60%	50%	40%	30%	20%	10%

REVOLVERS: PERCUSSION

MODEL 1851 - .38 cal., double action, 4½ in. barrel.

$1,375	$1,265	$1,100	$990	$855	$745	$690	$605	$550	$440	$385	$330

MODEL 1851 - .44 cal., double action, 6 in. barrel.

$935	$880	$800	$690	$550	$495	$440	$395	$340	$305	$275	$255

MODEL 1851 - .50 cal., Dragoon, double action, 8 in. barrel.

$1,375	$1,265	$1,100	$990	$855	$715	$690	$605	$550	$385	$360	$340

MODEL 1851 - .38 cal., cased with accessories.

$1,760	$1,595	$1,375	$1,100	$990	$910	$825	$745	$660	$605	$550	$525

MODEL 1851 - .44 cal., cased with accessories.

$1,295	$1,155	$990	$880	$770	$690	$635	$550	$440	$385	$360	$330

MODEL 1851 - .50 cal., Dragoon, cased with accessories.

$1,680	$1,485	$1,210	$1,185	$990	$880	$800	$715	$635	$550	$495	$470

ADAMS, JOSEPH

Previous manufacturer located in Birmingham, England.

PISTOLS: FLINTLOCK

OFFICER MODEL - .65 cal., flintlock pistol, Brown Bess.

$2,850	$2,500	$2,250	$2,000	$1,800	$1,600	$1,400	$1,100	$900	$825	$725	$600

Grading	100%	98%	95%	90%	80%	70%	60%

ADAMY, GEBR. JAGDWAFFEN

Current manufacturer established circa 1921 and located in Suhl, Germany. Currently imported by New England Custom Guns, Ltd., located in Plainfield, NH. The Adamy gunmaking tradition goes back to 1820, and sixth and seventh generation descendants are currently building guns.

Adamy Jadgwaffen currently specializes in custom made break open rifles, drillings, and combination guns, SxS and O/U shotguns, and double rifles featuring an Anson & Deeley boxlock action or H&H type sidelocks. Since all guns are made to custom order, please contact New England Custom Gun Service (current importer) directly for more information.

ADCO SALES INC.

Current firearms importer and accessory manufacturer established circa 1981, and currently located in Woburn, MA. Distributor sales.

SHOTGUNS: SEMI-AUTO

All semi-auto shotguns are mfg. in Turkey.

GOLD SERIES - 12 ga., 3 in. chamber, gas operated, 24 (slug gun, non-rifled, includes open sights) or 28 in. VR barrel with 3 choke tubes, semi-humpback style, annodized alloy frame with gold etching, rotary bolt, grey trigger guard, choice of black synthetic or checkered Turkish walnut stock with recoil pad, and forearm. Importation began 2001.

MSR	$549		$450	$375	$325	$295	$270	$235	$200

Subtract $50 for black synthetic stock and forearm.

DIAMOND ELITE SERIES - 12 ga., 3 in. chamber, gas operated, similar to Gold Series, except has engraved receiver with choice of 22 (slug), 24, 26, or 28 in. VR barrel with 3 choke tubes, deluxe checkered walnut stock and forearm. Importation began 2001.

MSR	$449		$375	$330	$295	$260	$230	$200	$175

DIAMOND PANTHER SERIES - 12 ga., 3 in. chamber, gas operated, similar to Diamond Elite Series, except has black synthetic stock and forearm, 20 (slug), 20 regular, or 28 in. barrel with 3 choke tubes. Importation began 2002.

MSR	$419			$350	$300	$275	$250	$225	$200	$175

Subtract $20 for 20 in. slug variation.

MARINER SILVER SERIES - 12 ga., 3 in. chamber, gas operated, 22 in. VR barrel, annodized alloy frame receiver with high strength satin silver metal finish, checkered walnut stock and forearm. Importation began 2002.

MSR	$499		$425	$350	$300	$250	$225	$200	$175

SHOTGUNS: SLIDE ACTION

All Adco slide action shotguns are mfg. in Turkey.

GOLD ELITE SERIES - 12 ga., 3 in. chamber, 24 (slug gun, non-rifled, includes open sights) or 28 in. VR barrel with 3 choke tubes, semi-humpback style, annodized alloy frame, choice of black synthetic or checkered Turkish walnut stock with recoil pad, and forearm, 7 lbs. Importation began 2001.

MSR	$399		$315	$275	$240	$200	$175	$160	$145

Subtract $20 for black synthetic stock and forearm.
Subtract $20 for slug gun.

Grading	100%	98%	95%	90%	80%	70%	60%

DIAMOND ELITE SERIES - 12 ga., 3 in. chamber, similar to Gold Elite Series, except has engraved receiver with choice of 20 (slug), regular 20, 24, or 28 in. VR barrel with 3 choke tubes, deluxe checkered walnut stock and forearm. Importation began 2001.

	MSR $259		$210	$190	$170	$150	$135	$120	$105

DIAMOND PANTHER SERIES - 12 ga., 3 in. chamber, similar to Diamond Elite Series, except has black synthetic stock and forearm, 18½ (slug), 20, or 28 in. barrel with 3 choke tubes. Importation began 2001.

	MSR $219		$175	$160	$145	$130	$120	$110	$100

Subtract $30 for 18½ in. slug variation.

ADIRONDACK ARMS COMPANY

Previous manufacturer located in Plattsburgh, NY, 1870-1874.

Magazine loaded repeating rifle, .44 cal., brass or iron frame, later model, may also be marked A.S. Babbitt, Plattsburgh, N.Y., absorbed by Winchester in 1874, then disc.

This rifle was designed in 1870 and patented by Orvill M. Robinson in Upper Jay, NY. It was available in .38 and .44 cal. rimfire versions without a wood forend and had a high cyclic rate of fire. Original models were made in Plattsburgh, NY, at which time A.S. Babbitt became one of several additional partners. In 1872, Robinson was granted a patent for a second model rifle. It was similar to the Model 1870, except a wood forend was added and the operating mechanism was changed considerably. Following these improvements, Mr. Oliver Winchester contacted Mr. Robinson and purchased the entire Robinson company, discontinuing manufacture.

100%	98%	95%	90%	80%	70%	60%	50%	40%	30%	20%	10%

RIFLES

EARLY MODEL - finger holds on hammer.

$2,400	$2,100	$1,750	$1,450	$1,325	$1,200	$1,075	$975	$875	$775	$675	$600

LATE MODEL - action worked by buttons top of receiver mid-section.

$2,200	$1,950	$1,675	$1,300	$1,200	$1,100	$975	$875	$775	$675	$550	$495

ADLER

Previously manufactured by Engelbrecht & Wolff located in Blasii, Germany, 1905-1907.

Grading	100%	98%	95%	90%	80%	70%	60%

PISTOLS: SEMI-AUTO

SEMI-AUTO PISTOL - 7mm Adler cal., 8 shot mag., cocking lever on top of frame.

		$4,500	$3,500	$2,500	$1,950	$1,750	$1,495	$1,100

ADVANTAGE ARMS USA, INC.

Previous manufacturer located in St. Paul, MN. Advantage Arms USA, Inc. was distributed by Wildfire Sports, Inc. also located in St. Paul, MN.

Grading	100%	98%	95%	90%	80%	70%	60%

DERRINGERS

MODEL 422 - .22 LR or 22 Mag. cal., 4 barrel double action derringer, rotating firing pin, this model is patterned after the Mossberg "Brownie", 2½ in. barrel, high grade alloy frame and barrel, 4 shot, available in blue, nickel, or QPQ (heat treated but appears blued) finish, 15 oz. Mfg. 1986-87 only.

	100%	98%	95%	90%	80%	70%	60%
	$150	$135	$115	$105	$95	$85	$75

Last MSR was $166.

Add $10 for .22 Mag. cal.
Add $6 for nickel finish.
Add $11 for QPQ finish.

AETNA

Previous trademark manufactured by Harrington & Richardson located in Worchester, MA.

Type: single action revolvers, all of the same general size and configuration, solid frame, spur trigger, so-called "Suicide Specials" during their day.

100%	98%	95%	90%	80%	70%	60%	50%	40%	30%	20%	10%

REVOLVERS

AETNA NO. 2 - .32 rimfire cal., 5 shot.

100%	98%	95%	90%	80%	70%	60%	50%	40%	30%	20%	10%
$330	$275	$215	$185	$170	$155	$145	$120	$100	$85	$75	$55

AETNA NO. 2½ - .32 rimfire cal., 5 shot.

100%	98%	95%	90%	80%	70%	60%	50%	40%	30%	20%	10%
$330	$275	$215	$185	$170	$155	$145	$120	$100	$85	$75	$55

MODEL 1876 - .22 rimfire cal., 7 shot.

100%	98%	95%	90%	80%	70%	60%	50%	40%	30%	20%	10%
$330	$275	$210	$195	$175	$165	$155	$130	$110	$95	$90	$65

MODEL 1876 - .32 rimfire cal., 5 shot.

100%	98%	95%	90%	80%	70%	60%	50%	40%	30%	20%	10%
$330	$275	$210	$175	$165	$155	$145	$120	$105	$90	$75	$55

MODEL 1876 - .38 rimfire cal., 5 shot.

100%	98%	95%	90%	80%	70%	60%	50%	40%	30%	20%	10%
$330	$275	$220	$205	$195	$175	$165	$145	$120	$105	$95	$85

AETNA ARMS COMPANY

Previous manufacturer located in New York, 1869-1883.

Single action pocket revolver, blued or nickel, birdshead grip, copy of S&W models 1-3, models marked ALLING are worth a slight premium.

REVOLVERS

SEVEN SHOT - .22 rimfire cal.

100%	98%	95%	90%	80%	70%	60%	50%	40%	30%	20%	10%
$250	$235	$210	$195	$175	$165	$155	$130	$110	$95	$90	$65

FIVE SHOT - .32 rimfire cal.

100%	98%	95%	90%	80%	70%	60%	50%	40%	30%	20%	10%
$230	$220	$205	$175	$165	$155	$145	$120	$105	$90	$75	$55

AGNER

Previous trademark manufactured by Saxhoj Products Inc. in Denmark. Imported until 1986 by Beeman Arms, Inc. located in Santa Rosa, CA.

Grading	100%	98%	95%	90%	80%	70%	60%

PISTOL: SEMI-AUTO

MODEL M 80 - .22 LR cal. only, stainless steel, semi-auto target pistol, new design features unique security key safety feature, adj. French walnut grips, dry fire mechanism, 5.9 in. barrel, 5 shot mag., limited production, 2.4 lbs. Imported 1981-1986.

$1,125 $1,040 $950

Last MSR was $1,295.

Add $100 for left-hand action.

AIR MATCH

Previously imported by Kendall International, located in Paris, KY.

PISTOLS: SINGLE SHOT

AIR MATCH 500 - .22 LR cal. match single shot pistol, target grips, adj. front counterweight, 10½ in. barrel. Imported 1984-86.

$550 $495 $450 $425 $395 $360 $330

Last MSR was $788.

AJAX ARMY

Previously distributed by E.C. Meacham Co., maker unknown, circa 1880s.

100%	98%	95%	90%	80%	70%	60%	50%	40%	30%	20%	10%

REVOLVERS

SINGLE ACTION - .44 rimfire cal., spur trigger, solid frame.

$550	$440	$360	$315	$275	$255	$230	$210	$185	$170	$155	$140

AKRILL, E.

Previously manufactured in France, c. mid-1800s.

RIFLES: FLINTLOCK

FLINTLOCK RIFLE - .69 cal., breech loaded, damascus octagon barrel.

$3,300	$2,750	$2,200	$1,980	$1,460	$1,320	$1,240	$1,075	$935	$800	$745	$660

ALAMO RANGER

Previous manufacturer located in Spain.

Grading	100%	98%	95%	90%	80%	70%	60%

REVOLVERS

REVOLVER - .38 Spl. cal., Spanish copy of Colt Model 1929.

$140 $120 $110 $100 $90 $85 $75

ALASKA

Previous trademark manufactured by Hood Firearms Company, Norwich, CT, 1873-1884.

These inexpensive utilitarian revolvers were dubbed "Suicide Specials" in their day.

100%	98%	95%	90%	80%	70%	60%	50%	40%	30%	20%	10%

REVOLVERS

SINGLE ACTION - .22 rimfire cal, 7 shot, spur trigger, solid frame.

$275	$220	$195	$145	$140	$125	$110	$100	$90	$75	$70	$65

FIVE SHOT - .32 Short rimfire cal.

$220	$195	$160	$155	$150	$140	$125	$105	$95	$85	$75	$70

ALASKAN COMMEMORATIVES

The following is a complete chronological listing of Alaskan special and limited editions.

Grading	100%	Issue Price	Qty. Made

COMMEMORATIVES, SPECIAL EDITIONS, & LIMITED MFG.

1967 ALASKAN PURCHASE CENTENNIAL WINCHESTER 94 CARBINE - see listing under Winchester Commemoratives.

1967 ALASKA PURCHASE CENTENNIAL CONTENDER - .22 Hornet and .357 Mag. cal., Thompson Contender with 2 barrels, Ser. no. range beginning with C0001.

    Issue price is unknown and rarity precludes accurate secondary market pricing.

1976 ALASKA PIPELINE COMMEMORATIVE - .45 LC cal., Colt SAA, cased with Kershaw knife.

	$1,495	$800	801

1981 ALASKA STATE TROOPER 40TH ANNIVERSARY - .357 Mag. cal., Smith & Wesson Model 19-5, 4 in. barrel, cased with belt buckle and patch.

	$850	$500	250

1984 STATE OF ALASKA SILVER ANNIVERSARY EDITION - .44 Mag. cal., Smith & Wesson Model 29-3, 6 in. barrel, cased with bronze brown bear and ivory grips with scrimshaw AK state seal and silver engraving.

	$12,250	$10,000	10

1984 ALASKA SILVER ANNIVERSARY - .44 Mag. cal., Smith & Wesson Model 29-3, 6 in. barrel, cased with gold engraving.

	$1,500	$1,195	300

1984 ALASKA STATEHOOD 25TH ANNIVERSARY - .338 Win. Mag. cal., Winchester Model 70XTR, sterling silver engraving.

	$1,100	$1,080	500

1984 ALASKA 25TH ANNIVERSARY - .357 Mag. cal., Colt Python, 6 in. barrel, engraved brown bear with gold lettering and numbers, cased.

	$1,000	$500	200

1988 IDITAROD "1 OF 1,000" - .44 Mag. cal., Smith & Wesson Model 629-1, 6 in. barrel, cased with laser-etched box, while a thousand were planned, only 500 were mfg.

	$995	$775	500

1988 ALASKA SERIES "TOKLAT" SPECIAL - .45 Win. Mag. cal., LAR mfg. Grizzly Mag., mfg. for Great Northern Guns in Anchorage, AK, cased with plaque.

	$1,800	$1,195	20

Grading	100%	Issue Price	Qty. Made

1990 ALASKA "GUIDE" SERIES - .454 Casull cal., Freedom Arms mfg. for Great Northern Guns in Anchorage, AK, 5½ in. barrel, Custom Field Grade, engraved handle.

| | $1,900 | $1,300 | 25 |

1991 ALASKA "MASTER GUIDE" SERIES - .454 Casull cal., Freedom Arms mfg. for Great Northern Guns in Anchorage, AK, 5½ in. barrel, Custom Premier Grade, engraved handle.

| | $2,200 | $1,600 | 26 |

1997 ALASKA IDITAROD TRAPPER SILVER ANNIVERSARY EDITION - .45 LC cal., Win. Mod. 94 Trapper rifle, 24Kt. gold engraving, extensive laser carved stock and forearm with musher and dog team, cased.

| | $4,950 | $2,495 | 149 |

1997 ALASKA IDITAROD SINGLE ACTION SILVER ANNIVERSARY EDITION - .45 LC cal., Colt SAA, 24Kt. gold engraving with Iditarod logo and trail scenes, cased.

| | $4,950 | $2,495 | 149 |

1998 ALASKA "KLONDIKE" COMMEMORATIVE GRADE I - .30-30 Win. cal., Winchester Model 94, 24 in. round barrel, roll engraved with Klondike scene on receiver, sponsored by the Alaskan Gun Collectors Association.

| | $550 | $550 | 450 |

✳ *1998 Alaska "Klondike" Commemorative Hi-Grade* - similar to Grade I, except has gold plated receiver.

| | $1,000 | $1,000 | 100 |

1998 ALASKA GOLD RUSH (1898-1998) CENTENNIAL - .38-55 WCF cal., Winchester Model 94 rifle, featuring 24Kt. gold engraving, serial numbered, silver medallion inlayed in stock, and extensive laser carving on stock and forearm, cased. New 1998.

| | $6,500 | $2,795 | 25 |

2000 ALASKA AMERICAN BALD EAGLE LIMITED EDITION - .45-70 Govt., Marlin Model 1895SS lever action rifle, 24Kt. gold etching of American eagle, extensive laser etched stock and forearm with Alaska and eagle scenes, includes special glass display case and leather carrying case.

| | N/A | $2,750 | 10 per state |

2000 ALASKA MILLENNIUM RIFLE - .45LC cal., Winchester Model 1866 Sporting Rifle mfg. by Uberti, cased with silver and gold presentation numbered buckle, features 24Kt. gold engraving with symbols representing events in U.S. history.

| | N/A | $2,495 | 10 per state |

2000 ALASKA MILLENNIUM REVOLVER - .44 cal., Colt Model 1860 mfg. by Colt, cased, 24 Kt. gold engraved with Statue of Freedom, "Don't Tread On Me", "One Nation, Under God, Indivisible with Liberty and Justice for All".

| | N/A | $1,895 | 10 per state |

2001 JOE REDDINGTON SR. "FATHER OF THE IDITAROD" - .45 LC cal., Winchester Model 1866 lever action carbine mfg. by Uberti, 24 Kt. gold engraved map of the 1,049 mile Iditarod Trail, "Last Great Race".

| | N/A | $2,750 | 82 |

Grading	100%	Issue Price	Qty. Made

2001 80th ANNIVERSARY ACHORAGE POLICE DEPARTMENT - 12 ga., Remington Model 870 in riot configuration, mfg. by Remington, special combat sights, extended mag., 24 Kt. gold engraved receiver, cased with officer's badge, personalized for owner officer, honors the fallen officers of the Anchorage Police Dept. from 1921-2001.

	N/A	$1,895	100

ALCHEMY ARMS COMPANY

Current manufacturer established during 1999, and located in Auburn, WA. Dealer sales.

Grading	100%	98%	95%	90%	80%	70%	60%

PISTOLS: SEMI-AUTO

SPECTRE STANDARD ISSUE (SI) - 9mm Para., .40 S&W, or .45 ACP cal., single action full size design, hammerless firing mechanism, linear action trigger, keyed internal locking device, aluminum receiver with 4½ in. match grade stainless steel barrel and slide, tactical rail, various silver/black finishes, lowered ejection port, 10 shot double column mag, 32 oz. New 2000.

MSR	$749		$675	$585	$525	$465	$415	$350	$300

SPECTRE SERVICE GRADE (SG & SGC) - similar to Spectre Standard Issue, except does not have tactical rail and rounded trigger guard, SGC is Commander style with 4 in. barrel and weighs 27 oz. New 2000, SGC new 2001.

MSR	$749		$675	$585	$525	$465	$415	$350	$300

SPECTRE TITANIUM EDITION (TI/TIC) - similar to Spectre Series, except features a titanium slide with aluminum receiver, 22 (TIC is Commander style) or 24 oz. New 2000.

MSR	$999		$895	$775	$675	$575	$500	$450	$395

ALDAZABAL

Previously manufactured by Aldazabal, Leturiondo & Cia., located in Spain.

PISTOLS: SEMI-AUTO

SEMI-AUTOMATIC PISTOL - 7.65mm cal., 7 shot, Eibar style.

	$195	$165	$110	$100	$90	$75	$65

ALERT

Previous trademark manufactured by Hood Firearms Company, Norwich, CT, 1873-1881.

These revolvers were dubbed "Suicide Specials" in their day.

100%	98%	95%	90%	80%	70%	60%	50%	40%	30%	20%	10%

REVOLVERS

SINGLE ACTION - .22 rimfire cal., 7 shot, spur trigger, solid frame.

100%	98%	95%	90%	80%	70%	60%	50%	40%	30%	20%	10%
$220	$195	$165	$145	$130	$125	$110	$100	$90	$75	$70	$65

FIVE SHOT - .32 Short rimfire cal..

100%	98%	95%	90%	80%	70%	60%	50%	40%	30%	20%	10%
$170	$165	$160	$155	$150	$140	$125	$105	$95	$85	$75	$70

100%	98%	95%	90%	80%	70%	60%	50%	40%	30%	20%	10%

ALESSANDRI, LOU, AND SON

Previous custom rifle manufacturer located in Rehoboth, MA 1975-circa 1998.

Lou Alessandri and Son were noted for their top-quality custom rifles (bolt action and side-by-side). Double rifles started at $18,500, while Express bolt actions started at $5,600. All guns were custom built per individual specifications and a wide variety of special order options were available. In addition to building custom rifles, Lou Alessandri and Son also offered a complete line of high-quality cleaning kits and related accessories. To determine the used value of a Lou Alessandri & Son rifle, the configuration has to be evaluated carefully (caliber, grade of wood, embellishments, and overall desirability).

ALEXIA

Previous trademark manufactured by Hopkins & Allen, located in Norwich, CT, 1867-1915.

Also known as: Blue Jacket, Captain Jack, Chichester, Defender, Dictator, Monarch, Mountain Eagle, Hopkins & Allen, Towers Police Safety, and Universal.

REVOLVERS

The revolvers listed below are single action design, solid frame, spur trigger - they were an inexpensive vest pocket pistol issued under numerous names for private companies, octagon barrel.

.22 RIMFIRE - 7 shot.

$165	$160	$155	$145	$130	$125	$110	$100	$90	$75	$70	$65

.32 SHORT RIMFIRE - 5 shot.

$170	$165	$160	$155	$150	$140	$125	$105	$95	$85	$75	$70

SINGLE ACTION .38 SHORT RIMFIRE - 5 shot.

$195	$180	$170	$165	$160	$145	$140	$120	$110	$100	$90	$85

.41 SHORT RIMFIRE - 5 shot.

$220	$210	$205	$195	$180	$170	$160	$145	$125	$110	$100	$90

ALFA

Previous trademark manufactured by Armero Especialistas Reunidas, located in Eibar, Spain, circa 1920.

All revolvers are marked Alfa on grips.

Grading	100%	98%	95%	90%	80%	70%	60%

REVOLVERS

EARLY MODEL - .32, .38, or .44 cal., copies of S&W No. 2 by O. Hermanos.

	$145	$130	$120	$110	$105	$95	$75

Add 50% for .44 cal.

LATE MODEL - .22 LR, .32 S&W, or .38 S&W cal., copies of Colt Police Positive and S&W Military and Police.

	$160	$150	$130	$120	$110	$100	$90

ALFA PROJ

Current handgun and starter revolver manufacturer located in Brno, Czech Republic. No current U.S. importation.

Alfa Proj marked handguns are of good quality and utilitarian manufacture, and are currently available in both Double Action revolvers and semi-auto pistols.

Grading	100%	98%	95%	90%	80%	70%	60%

ALKARTASUNA FABRICA DE ARMAS, S.A.

Previous manufacturer located in Guernica, Spain.

PISTOLS: SEMI-AUTO

ALKARTASUNA CARTRIDGE COUNTER - 6.35mm cal., 7 shot, left grip panel cartridge counter, loaded indicator, grip safety.

$450	$350	$275	$225	$175	$150	$125

ALKARTASUNA RUBY AUTOMATIC - 7.65mm cal., 2 variations - more common is the "Ruby" type, 9 shot, 3 5/8 in. barrel, blue, fixed sights, checkered wood or hard rubber grips, used by French Army in WWI and WWII. Mfg. 1917-1922.

$265	$195	$165	$110	$65	$55	$45

Add 10% for extended barrel.

ALLEN & THURBER

Previous manufacturer/trademark originally located in Grafton, Mass. Ethan Allen started many plants to keep up with expanding business after 1832. Listed below is a chronological order of the firms constituting the family dynasty founded by Ethan Allen.

E. Allen - Grafton, Mass. 1832-1837

Allen & Thurber - Grafton, Mass. 1837-1842

Allen & Thurber - Norwich, Conn. 1842-1847

Allen & Thurber - Worcester, Mass. 1847-1854

Allen, Thurber, & Co. - Worcester, Mass. 1854-1856

Allen & Wheelock - Worcester, Mass. 1856-1865

E. Allen & Co. - Worcester, Mass. 1865-1871

Forehand & Wadsworth - Worcester, Mass. 1871-1890

Forehand Arms Co. - Worcester, Mass. 1890-1902

No other 19th-century American firm produced a wider variety of firearms than did Ethan Allen & subsidiaries.

ALLEN FIREARMS

Previous importer located in Santa Fe, NM importing A. Uberti Firearms until early in 1987. After Allen Firearms closed, Cimarron F.A. Mfg. Co. located in Houston, TX purchased the remaining inventory (in addition to ordering new products under their name).

Allen Firearms was formerly called Western Arms and manufactured both modern and black powder reproduction firearms and accessories patterned after famous older models. Only modern cartridge guns will be shown in this section.

Rather than provide a complete listing of Allen Firearms models, the following rules usually apply. Since Allen Firearms imported A. Uberti firearms, the Uberti section in this text should be referenced for current values regarding models with similar configurations. Collectibility to date has been limited on most Allen Firearms models, and as a rule, up-to-date values on this trademark are established by current importation prices of Uberti firearms. A complete listing of older Allen Firearms models can be found in Blue Book editions Eleven and Twelve. The models listed below are provided since Uberti is not currently manufacturing them.

Grading	100%	98%	95%	90%	80%	70%	60%

RIFLES: REPRODUCTIONS

SHARPS/GEMMER SPORTING RIFLE - .45-70 Govt. cal. only, copy of the famous Sharps rifle. Introduced 1985.

	100%	98%	95%	90%	80%	70%	60%
	$575	$515	$430	$375	$320	$295	$270

Last MSR was $599.

Grading		100%	Issue Price	Qty. Made

1979 JUSTIN CENTENNIAL COMMEMORATIVE - includes specially engraved 1866 sporting rifle and 1873 single action revolver (7½ in. barrel) with gold plated parts and inlay. Both guns are chambered for .44-40 cal. Also includes special hand signed pair of Justin boots, serial numbered belt buckle and presentation oak case. All serial numbers are matching.

MODEL 1873 1 of 1,000 - .44-40 cal, special wood, only 1,000 manufactured. Disc. 1985.

	100%	Issue Price	Qty. Made
	$1,350	$1,500	1,000

ALPHA ARMS INC.

Previous manufacturer located in Flower Mound, TX from 1983-87.

Retail price included custom hard case.

Grading		100%	98%	95%	90%	80%	70%	60%

RIFLES: BOLT ACTION

Many special order options including an octagonal barrel, various finishes, special sights, and deluxe wood were available at extra cost on the models listed below. These options, while not listed separately by price, will add value to the prices shown below. All Alpha Arms rifles were manufactured under stringent quality control.

ALPHA CUSTOM - available in most calibers from .222 Rem. through .338 Win. Mag., many other calibers available on special order, 3 position Model 70 type safety, 60 degree bolt, 20 to 24 in. Douglas barrel, limited production, right-hand or left-hand, deluxe checkered Claro walnut standard, approx. 6 lbs. Mfg. 1984-1987.

	100%	98%	95%	90%	80%	70%	60%
	$1,525	$1,200	$975	$850	$725	$640	$560

Last MSR was $1,735.

ALPHA GRAND SLAM - same general specifications as the Alpha Custom, except comes standard with laminated wood stock, fluted bolt and non-glare matte finished metal parts, right-hand or left-hand, approx. 6½ lbs. Mfg. 1985-1987.

	100%	98%	95%	90%	80%	70%	60%
	$1,200	$950	$875	$750	$650	$600	$525

Last MSR was $1,465.

ALPHA ALASKAN - .308 Win., .350 Rem. Mag., .358 Win., or .458 Win. Mag. cal., action is similar to Alpha Grand Slam, except barrel, receiver, bolt and safety are stainless steel, right-hand or left-hand, Nitex coated small parts, approx. 6¾ - 7½ lbs. Mfg. 1985- 1987.

	100%	98%	95%	90%	80%	70%	60%
	$1,525	$1,200	$975	$850	$725	$640	$560

Last MSR was $1,735.

ALPHA BIG-FIVE - .300 H&H thru .375 H&H or .458 Win. Mag. cal., reinforced stock and decelerator recoil pad. Mfg. 1987 only.

	100%	98%	95%	90%	80%	70%	60%
	$1,575	$1,250	$1,050	$895	$750	$640	$560

Last MSR was $1,795.

Manufacturer	Model	Edition Limit	Official Issue Price

AMERICA REMEMBERS

Current organization located in Ashland, VA, that privately commissions historical, limited/special editions in conjunction with various manufacturers. Previously located in Mechanicsville, VA until 1999.

America Remembers is a private non-governmental organization dedicated to the remembrance of notable Americans and important historical American events. Along with its affiliates, the Armed Forces Commemorative Society®, American Heroes and Legends®, and the United States Society of Arms and Armour™, the company produces special issue limited edition firearms. America Remembers purchased the antique arms division of the U.S. Historical Society on April 1, 1994. Older U.S.H.S. firearms can be located in the U section of this text.

LIMITED/SPECIAL EDITIONS

Values listed below reflect America Remembers most recent issue prices. These do not necessarily represent secondary marketplace prices. No other values are listed since America Remembers limited edition firearms do not appear that frequently in the secondary marketplace. This is because America Remembers typically sells to consumers directly, without involving normal gun dealers and distributors. Because of this consumer direct sales program, many gun dealers do not have a working knowledge about what America Remembers firearms are currently selling for. The publisher suggests that those people owning America Remembers Limited/Special Editions contact America Remembers (See Trademark Index) for current information, including secondary marketplace liquidity.

Please refer to the 2nd Ed. *Blue Book of Modern Black Powder Values* by Dennis Adler (now online also) for more information and prices on America Remembers black powder models.

HANDGUNS

While not specifically mentioned, the handguns listed below all have various degrees of ornamentation and other embellishments (including some inscriptions).

REVOLVERS: SINGLE ACTION

Manufacturer	Model	Edition Limit	Official Issue Price
Uberti	American Indian Tribute SAA.45 LC	300	$1,795
Uberti	Buffalo Bill Sesquicentennial SAA .45 LC	500	$1,500
Uberti	Doc Holliday SAA .45 LC	200	$1,795
Colt	Interpol SAA .45 LC	154	$4,500
Uberti	Gene Autry Cowboy Edition SAA	1,000	$1,520
Colt	Gene Autry Premier Colt SAA	100	$5,250
Uberti	George Jones SA .45 LC	950	$1,675
Uberti	Herb Jeffries Tribute .45 LC	500	$1,695
Uberti	Hopalong Cassidy Cowboy SAA	950	$1,550
Colt	Hopalong Cassidy Premier Colt SAA	100	$4,500
Colt	James Arness Colt Cowboy SA Revolver	250	$1,895
Colt	Roy Rogers & Dale Evans SAA	250	$3,195
Uberti	Seventh Cavalry SAA Tribute	500	$1,695
Uberti	Sitting Bull Colt Cowboy SA Revolver .45 Colt	300	$1,995
Uberti	Tom Mix Tribute SAA .45 LC	200	$1,395
Colt	Tom Mix Premier Edition .45 LC	50	$2,595
Uberti	Travis Tritt SAA .45 LC	500	$1,695
Ruger	Ruger and His Guns Classic .44 Magnum	400	$1,995
Ruger	Ruger and His Guns Classic .44 Magnum	100	$3,595
Uberti	Clayton Moore SAA .45 LC	500	$1,695
Colt	Geronimo Colt Cowboy SA .45 LC	100	$1,995

Manufacturer	Model	Edition Limit	Official Issue Price
Colt	Heroic Indian Leaders SAA .44 Spl.	50	$3,195
Navy Arms	Frank & Jesse James Tribute .45 LC Schofield Cavalry Model	100	$1,695

SEMI-AUTOS: .45 ACP

Manufacturer	Model	Edition Limit	Official Issue Price
Colt	Army Air Corp. Tribute M-1911A1	300	$1,795
Colt	American Eagle Tribute M-1911A1	2,500	$1,995
Colt	American Patriot Tribute M-1911A1	N/A	$1,695
Colt	Army Air Forces Tribute M-1911A1	500	$1,500
Colt	Audie Murphy Tribute M-1911A1	1,000	$1,795
Colt	Chuck Yeager Tribute M-1911A1	1,000	$1,750
Colt	Ernie Irvan Tribute M-1911A1	250	$1,895
Colt	Leatherneck Tribute Pistol M-1911A1	300	$1,795
Colt	Navajo Code Talkers M-1911A1	300 (w/knife)	$3,000
Auto-Ordnance	Pacific Naval Tribute M-1911A1	500	$1,500
Colt	Pearl Harbor Tribute Pistol M-1911A1	500	$1,795
Colt	Purple Heart Tribute Pistol M-1911A1	250	$1,485
Colt	VJ-Day Tribute M-1911A1	250	$1,495
Colt	West Point Tribute M-1911A1	300	$1,995
Colt	West Point WWII Tribute Pistol M-1911A1	500	$1,995
Colt	Wings of Freedom-USAF 50th Anniversary Tribute M-1911A1	250	$1,695
Colt	20th Century Salute to the Military/VFW 100th	500	$1,695
Colt	Special Operations Associations Tribute M-1991A1	250	$1,695
Colt	Spirit of America Tribute Pistol M-1911A1	911	$1,495
Colt	Berlin Airlift Golden Anniversary Tribute M-1991A1	250	$1,595
Colt	Elvis Tribute Pistol M-1991A1	300	$1,895
Colt	VFW Korean War Tribute M-1991A1	300	$1,695

RIFLES

Manufacturer	Model	Edition Limit	Official Issue Price
Winchester	Model 94 (.22 LR) King Richard Tribute	200	$1,495
Winchester	Model 94 (.30-30) American Eagle Tribute	500	$1,595
Winchester	Model 94 (.30-30) American Wildlife Tribute	300	$1,495
Winchester	Model 94 (.30-30)B. Bill Sesqui. Tribute	300	$1,850
Winchester	Model 94 (.30-30) Babe Ruth Tribute	300	$1,850
Winchester	Model 94 (.30-30) Bruce Boxleitner Tribute	100	$1,895
Winchester	Model 94 (.30-30) California Sesquicentennial	150	$1,495
Winchester	Model 94 (.30-30) C.M. Russell Tribute	300	$1,850
Winchester	Model 94 (.30-30) Cherokee Trail of Tears Tribute	300	$1,795
Winchester	Model 94 (.30-30) Cochise Tribute Rifle	300	$1,695
Winchester	Model 94 (.30-30) Dale Berry Tribute	300	$1,850
Winchester	Model 94 (.30-30) Davey Allison Tribute	500	$1,695
Winchester	Model 94 (.30-30) Deer Hunter Tribute	300	$1,795
Winchester	Model 94 (.30-30) Dennis Weaver Tribute	100	$1,895
Winchester	Model 94 (.30-30) Elvis and Graceland Tribute	1,000	$1,895
Winchester	Model 94 (.30-30) Field & Stream Tribute	300	$1,595
Winchester	Model 94 (.30-30) Wrangler Ft. Worth Tribute	300	$1,895

Manufacturer	Model	Edition Limit	Official Issue Price
Winchester	Model 94 (.30-30) Gene Autry Tribute	300	$2,100
Winchester	Model 94 (.30-30) George Jones Tribute	300	$1,595
Winchester	Model 94 (.30-30) Great North American Rodeo	500	$1,595
Winchester	Model 94 (.30-30) Heroic Indian Leaders Tribute	300	$1,650
Winchester	Model 94 (.30-30) Hopalong Cassidy Tribute	500	$1,850
Winchester	Model 94 (.30-30) Leatherneck Sportsman Tribute	300	$1,895
Winchester	Model 94 (.30-30) Roy Rogers Tribute	300	$2,100
Winchester	Model 94 (.30-30) Roy Rogers & Gabby Hayes	300	$1,850
Winchester	Model 94 (.30-30) Rusty Wallace Tribute	1,000	$1,850
Winchester	Model 94 (.30-30) Tennessee Ernie Ford Tribute	100	$1,895
Winchester	Model 94 (.30-30) Terry Labonte Tribute	1,000	$1,850
Winchester	Model 94 (.30-30) Texas Motor Speedway	500	$1,795
Winchester	Model 94 (.30-30) Ty Murray Tribute	500	$1,695
Winchester	Model 94 (.30-30) U.S. Cavalry Association Tribute	300	$1,850
Winchester	Model 94 (.30-30) Tribute to Yellowstone National Park	125	$1,695
Marlin	Model 336CS (.30-30) Whitetail Trophy	500	$1,595
Marlin	Model 336CS (.30-30) Whitetail Hunter Tribute	300	$1,395
Marlin	Model 336CS (.30-30) Whitetail Deer Trophy	300	$1,595
Marlin	Model 1894 (.45 LC) White Buffalo Spirit Tribute	300	$2,100
Winchester	Model 94 (.45 LC) American Cowboy Tribute	200	$3,195
Winchester	Model 94 (.45 LC) American Indian Tribute	300	$1,250
Winchester	Model 94 (.45 LC) Citation Bass Tribute	300	$1,695
Winchester	Model 94 (.45 LC) Darrell Waltrip 25th Anniversary	750	$1,795
Winchester	Model 94 (.45 LC) Monte Hale Tribute	300	$1,850
Winchester	Model 94 (.45 LC) Rex Allen Tribute	500	$1,595
Winchester	Model 94 (.45 LC) Clint Walker Tribute	300	$1,850
Winchester	Model 94 (.45 LC) Lawmen & Outlaws of the Wild West	300	$1,850
Marlin	Model 336CS (.30-30) American Hunter Tribute	300	$1,695
Uberti	Model 1873 (.44-40) Buffalo Bill's Wild West Tribute	300	$1,995
Uberti	Model 1873 (.44-40) Scouts of the Western Frontier	300	$1,995
Uberti	Model 1873 (.44-40) Wild West Exhibition Shooters Tribute	300	$1,795
Uberti	Model 1873 (.44-40) Wild West Frontier Tribute	125	$1,695
Winchester	Model 94 (.30-30) Wrangler Gene Autry, Smiley Burnette, & Pat Buttram Tribute	300	$1,895
Winchester	Model 94 (.30-30) Iron Eyes Cody Tribute	300	$1,795
Winchester	Mode 94 (.30-30) James Arness Tribute	250	$1,895
Winchester	Model 94 (.30-30) NRA Tribute	300	$1,850
Winchester	Model 94 (.30-30) Nolan Ryan Tribute	324	$1,850
Winchester	Model 94 (.30-30) Tribute to the Rough Riders	300	$1,595
Winchester	Model 94 (.30-30) Richard Boone Tribute	250	$1,895
Winchester	Modle 94 (.30-30) Richard Farnsworth	100	$1,895

A

Manufacturer	Model	Edition Limit	Official Issue Price
Winchester	Model 94 (.30-30) Texas Ranger 175th Anniversary Tribute	300	$1,950
Winchester	Mode 94 (.30-30) Texas Trophy Hunters	250	$1,695
Uberti	Henry (.44-40) A Nation Reunited: Civil War Tribute	300	$1,895
Uberti	Henry (.44-40) West Point Civil War Tribute	300	$1,995
Uberti	Model 1873 (.45 LC) Wyatt Earp Sesquicentennial Tribute	300	$1,895
Marlin	Model 1894 (.45 LC) Cowboy Limited Roy Rogers/Dale Evans & Dusty Rogers Tribute	300	$1,850
Winchester	Model 94 Audie Murphy Tribute	250	$1,895
Winchester	Model 94 Frederic Remington Art Museum Tribute	300	$1,695
Winchester	Model 94 National Cowboy Hall of Fame	300	$1,895
Winchester	Model 94 Travis Tritt Tribute	300	$1,850
Winchester	Model 94 101 Ranch Western Tribute	300	$1,850
Uberti	Model 1873 Heroes of Texas Tribute	300	$2,195
Uberti	Model 1866 Yellow Boy American Buffalo Tribute	300	$1,995
Uberti	Henry Civil War Cavalry Leaders Tribute	300	$2,195
Uberti	Henry Mort Künstler Civil War Tribute	300	$2,195
Uberti	Henry Quanah Parker Red River War Tribute	300	$2,195
Uberti	Henry Sons of Confederate Veterans	300	$2,295
Uberti	Henry (.44-40) West Point Civil War Tribute	300	$1,995
Uberti	Henry (.44-40) West Point Civil War Union Leaders	500	$2,295
Uberti	Henry (.44-40) West Point Civil War Confederate Leader	500	$2,295

SHOTGUNS

Manufacturer	Model	Edition Limit	Official Issue Price
Browning	BAR Semi-Auto (.30-06) Rocky Mt. Elk Tribute	300	$2,195
Remington	Model 870 Wingmaster (12 ga.) Ned & Dale Jarrett	750	$1,595
SIACE	Law & Order (12 ga.) double-hammered shotgun	100	$3,000
Remington	Model 870 (12 ga.) Deer Hunter Tribute	300	$1,495
Remington	Model 870 (12 ga.) Waterfowl Tribute	300	$1,795
Browning	Model BPS (12 ga.) Texas Sportsman Tribute	250	$1,495
Remington	Model 870 Wingmaster Ducks Unlimited Tribute	300	$1,795

AMERICAN ARMS

Previous manufacturer located in Garden Grove, CA.

Grading	100%	98%	95%	90%	80%	70%	60%

PISTOLS: SEMI-AUTO

EAGLE 380 - .380 ACP cal. only, stainless steel semi-auto, copy of Walther PPK/S, 6 shot mag., 3¼ in. barrel, limited production, 20 oz.

	100%	98%	95%
	$400	$250	$215

Last MSR was $289.

Add $25 for case.
Add $50 for case and belt buckle.
Add $25 for black teflon finish (disc. 1985).

AMERICAN ARMS CO.

Previous manufacturer located in Boston, MA from 1870-1901 and Milwaukee, WI. from 1893-1904. American Arms Co. was acquired by Marlin in 1901.

100%	98%	95%	90%	80%	70%	60%	50%	40%	30%	20%	10%

DERRINGERS

O/U DESIGN - .22 Short R.F., .32 Short R.F., or .41 Short R.F. cal., Wheeler Pat. Action, brass frame, spur trigger.

$800	$750	$700	$650	$575	$500	$420	$360	$300	$225	$160	$110

SHOTGUNS: SxS

HAMMERLESS MODEL - 12 ga., semi-hammerless.

$600	$550	$500	$450	$350	$275	$225	$175	$150	$125	$100	$75

WHITMORE PATENT - 10 or 12 ga., hammerless, checkering, SxS.

$685	$625	$575	$520	$460	$400	$340	$270	$200	$150	$125	$100

Add 10% for 10 ga. (2 7/ 8 in. chambers)

SINGLESHOT - 12 ga., semi-hammerless, damascus barrel.

$260	$225	$200	$175	$150	$125	$90	$70	$50	$40	$30	$20

AMERICAN ARMS, INC.

Previous importer and manufacturer located in North Kansas City, MO until 2000. American Arms imported various Spanish shotguns (Indesal, Lanber, Norica, and Zabala Hermanos), Italian shotguns including F. Stefano, several European pistols and rifles, and Sites handguns (1990-2000) mfg. in Torino, Italy. This company also manufactured several pistols in North Kansas City, MO. For more information and pricing on Norica airguns previously imported by American Arms, please refer to the 2nd Edition *Blue Book of Airguns* by Dr. Robert Beeman & John Allen (now online also).

In late 2000, TriStar Sporting Arms, Ltd. acquired the parts inventory for some models previously imported by American Arms, Inc. Original warranties from American Arms do not apply to TriStar Sporting Arms, Ltd.

Grading	100%	98%	95%	90%	80%	70%	60%

COMBINATION GUNS

RS COMBO - choice of .222 Rem. or .308 Win. rifle barrel under 12 ga. barrel, engraved box-lock frame with antique silver finish, DTs, 24 in. VR barrels with shotgun choke tubes, rifle sights, grooved for scope mounting, Monte Carlo stock, 7 lbs. 14 oz. Imported 1989 only.

$675	$595	$550	$495	$450	$420	$385

Last MSR was $749.

PISTOLS: SEMI-AUTO

MODEL TT-9MM TOKAREV - 9mm Para. cal., semi-auto single action, 4½ in. barrel, 9 shot mag., hammer block external safety, 31 oz. Imported 1988-89 only.

$250	$230	$210	$195	$180	$170	$160

Last MSR was $289.

This model is patterned after the Tokarev action and was made from machined steel parts in Yugoslavia.

MODEL EP-380 - .380 ACP cal., semi-auto double action, stainless steel, 3½ in. barrel, 7 shot mag., wood checkered grips, adj. rear sight, 25 oz. Imported 1988-90 only.

$375	$325	$250

Last MSR was $449.

This model was made in West Germany.

MODEL PK-22 CLASSIC - .22 LR cal., semi-auto double action, styled after Govt. .45 ACP, 3 1/3 in. barrel, 8 shot finger extension mag., black polymer grips, 22 oz. Mfg. 1988-96.

$165	$140	$115	$100	$90	$80	$70

Last MSR was $199.

This model was made in North Kansas City, MO. It has patented safety features such as external hammer block and internal blocking of the firing pin until the trigger is pulled.

MODEL CX-22 CLASSIC - .22 LR cal., style patterned after Walther PPK, 3 1/3 in. barrel, 8 shot finger extension mag., 22 oz. Mfg. 1990-95.

$175	$145	$125	$110	$100	$90	$80

Last MSR was $213.

This model was made in North Kansas City, MO. It has patented safety features such as external hammer block and internal blocking of the firing pin until the trigger is pulled.

✴ **CXC-22** - similar to CX-22 Classic, except has chrome slide. Mfg. in 1990 only.

$170	$150	$125	$110	$100	$90	$80

Last MSR was $189.

MODEL PX-22/25 CLASSIC - .22 LR or .25 ACP (mfg. 1991 only) cal., compact variation of the Model CX-22, 2¾ in. barrel, 7 shot finger extension mag., 15 oz. New 1989, PX-25 was mfg. 1991 only, PX-22 was disc. 1995.

$175	$145	$125	$110	$100	$90	$80

Last MSR was $206.

This model was made in North Kansas City, MO. It has patented safety features such as external hammer block and internal blocking of the firing pin until the trigger is pulled.

MODEL P-98 CLASSIC - .22 LR cal., semi-auto double action patterned after Walther P.38, 5 in. barrel, 8 shot mag., blue/black finish, grooved wraparound grips, 26 oz. Mfg. 1990-96.

$170	$145	$125	$110	$100	$90	$80

Last MSR was $209.

Grading	100%	98%	95%	90%	80%	70%	60%

ESCORT - .380 ACP cal., double action only, 3 3/8 in. barrel, 7 shot mag., unique thin profile, matte stainless steel, soft polymer grips, polygonal rifling, 19 oz. Mfg. 1995-97.

	$285	$230	$200	$185	$170	$160	$150

Last MSR was $349.

SABRE - while this model was advertised, it was never mfg.

SPECTRE - 9mm Para., .40 S&W (mfg. 1991 only), or .45 ACP (new 1993) cal., semi- auto double action, 6 in. barrel with polygonal rifling, 30 shot mag., ambidextrous safety, decocking lever, adj. sights, 4½ lbs., mfg. in Italy by Sites. Imported 1990-1993.

	$500	$325	$275	$240	$200	$185	$170

Last MSR was $429.

Add $28 for .45 ACP cal.

This model was previously imported by F.I.E. located in Hialeah, FL (1989-1990).

AUSSIE SEMI-AUTO - 9mm Para. or .40 S&W cal., semi-auto double action, polymer frame with nickeled steel slide and 4¾ in. barrel, 10 shot mag., features 5 safeties, open slide after last shot, 23 oz. Limited importation from Spain 1996 only.

	$350	$250	$225	$200	$185	$170	$160

Last MSR was $425.

REVOLVERS: SAA

REGULATOR MODEL - .357 Mag., .44-40, or .45 LC cal., 4¾, 5½ (new 1993), or 7½ in. barrel, reproduction of the Colt Peacemaker, featuring brass trigger guard and back strap, fixed sights, half-cock and hammer block safeties, blade front, grooved rear sights, color case hardened frame and blued barrel/cylinder or nickel finish (imported 1999 only in .45 LC cal.), walnut grips, 35 oz. Mfg. by Uberti. Imported 1992-2000.

	$270	$230	$200	$185	$170	$160	$150

Last MSR was $320.

Add $55 for nickel finish (disc. 1999).
Add $40 for dual cylinder set (.44-40/.44 Spl. or .45 LC/.45 ACP). Disc. 1998.

✳ *Regulator Deluxe* - similar to Regulator Model, except .45 LC cal. only, all blue charcoal finish (mfg. 1996-97) or color case hardened frame (new 1998), case hardened (pre-1993) or blued (post- 1993) steel trigger guard and back strap. Importation disc. 1992, resumed 1994-2000.

	$315	$260	$215	$190	$170	$160	$150

Last MSR was $365.

Add $70 for dual cylinder set (.44-40/.44 Spl. or .45 LC/.45 ACP). Disc. 1992.

✳ *Buckhorn* - .44 Mag cal., 4¾, 6, or 7½ in. barrel, otherwise similar to Regulator Model, 44 oz. Imported 1993-96.

	$305	$255	$205	$185	$170	$160	$150

Last MSR was $379.

Add $10 for Target variation (flat top and adj. rear sight). Imported 1994 only.

✳ *Storekeeper* - .44-40 WCF or .45 LC cal., 4 in. barrel, smooth walnut curved grips, nickel or B/H nickel finish, 31 oz. Imported 1999 only.

	$320	$265	$215	$190	$170	$160	$150

Last MSR was $375.

Add $44 for B/H nickel finish.

UBERTI BISLEY - .45 LC cal., patterned after the Colt Bisley, case hardened steel frame, 4¾, 5½, or 7½ in. barrel with fixed sights, hammer block safety. Imported 1997-98 only.

	$425	$340	$275	$215	$190	$170	$160

Last MSR was $475.

Grading	100%	98%	95%	90%	80%	70%	60%

UBERTI .454 SAA - .454 cal., 6 SR or 7½ in. top-ported barrel, hammer block safety, satin nickel finish, custom hardwood grips, wide trigger, adj. rear sight. Imported 1996- 97 only.

	$750	$625	$550	$495	$465	$435	$375

Last MSR was $869.

SILVERADO - .357 Mag., .44 Mag., or .45 LC cal., 4¾, 5½, or 7½ barrel, brushed nickel finish, unfluted cylinder, laminated charcoal grips. Mfg. by Uberti, imported 1999- 2000.

	$345	$285	$220	$195	$170	$160	$150

Last MSR was $409.

RIFLES: O/U

SILVER EXPRESS - 8x57JRS or 9.3x74R cal., O/U boxlock design, gold SNT, monoblock 28 in. separated barrels, manual safety, silver finished receiver with light engraving, skipline checkered walnut stock and forearm, approx. 7¾ lbs. Limited importation 1999-2000.

	$1,800	$1,625	$1,500	$1,375	$1,250	$1,125	$1,000

Last MSR was $1,949.

RIFLES: REPRODUCTIONS

MODEL 1860 HENRY REPLICA - .44-40 WCF or .45 LC cal., 24¼ in. blued or white finish (new 1999) barrel, 9 1/4 lbs. Mfg. by Uberti, importation disc. 2000.

	$835	$625	$525	$425	$360	$320	$260

Last MSR was $940.

Add $50 for white barrel finish.

❋ *Henry Trapper* - similar to the Henry Replica, except has 18½ in. barrel, 8 lbs. Imported 1999-2000.

	$835	$625	$525	$425	$360	$320	$260

Last MSR was $940.

Add $50 for white barrel finish.

MODEL 1866 WINCHESTER REPLICA - .44-40 WCF or .45 LC cal., 19 (Carbine) or 24¼ (Rifle) in. barrel, approx. 8 lbs. Mfg. by Uberti, importation disc. 2000.

	$650	$550	$460	$375	$300	$250	$200

Last MSR was $730.

Subtract $20 for Carbine variation (Yellowboy).

MODEL 1873 WINCHESTER REPLICA - .44-40 WCF or .45 LC cal., 24¼ or 30 (new 1999) in. octagon barrel, case colored receiver, approx. 8¼ lbs. Mfg. by Uberti, importation disc. 2000.

	$775	$625	$525	$425	$360	$320	$260

Last MSR was $860.

Add $80 for 30 in. barrel.

❋ *Model 1873 Deluxe Winchester Replica* - similar to Model 1873 Winchester Replica, except has better quality checkered pistol grip stock and forearm. Disc. 1997.

	$1,100	$775	$625	$500	$425	$350	$275

Last MSR was $1,299.

MODEL 1885 SINGLE SHOT HIGH WALL - .45-70 Govt. cal., 28 in. round barrel, color case hardened frame, 8.82 lbs. Mfg. by Uberti, imported 1998-2000.

	$700	$575	$495	$395	$350	$300	$260

Last MSR was $810.

Grading	100%	98%	95%	90%	80%	70%	60%

SHARPS CAVALRY CARBINE - .45-70 Govt. cal., 22 in. heavy round barrel, case colored action, blued barrel with adj. rear ladder sight, DST, uncheckered walnut stock and forearm, 8 lbs. 3 oz. Imported 1999-2000.

	$625	$525	$450	$400	$360	$330	$300

Last MSR was $660.

SHARPS FRONTIER CARBINE - similar to Cavalry Carbine, except has regular barrel with barrel band and single trigger, 7 lbs. 13 oz. Imported 1999-2000.

	$615	$535	$450	$400	$360	$330	$300

Last MSR was $675.

SHARPS 1874 SPORTING RIFLE - .45-70 Govt. or .45-120 black powder cartridge, 28 in. octagon barrel, checkered walnut stock and forearm, DST, 9 lbs. 3 oz. Imported 1999-2000.

	$635	$535	$450	$400	$360	$330	$300

Last MSR was $685.

⁕ *Sharps 1874 Deluxe Sporting Rifle* - similar to Sharps 1874 Sporting Rifle, except has brown barrel finish. Imported 1999-2000.

	$650	$545	$460	$410	$360	$330	$300

Last MSR was $705.

RIFLES: SEMI-AUTO

MODEL ZCY 308 - .308 Win. cal., gas operated semi-auto AK-47 type action, Yugoslavian mfg. Imported 1988 only.

	$775	$650	$550	$450	$400	$375	$350

Last MSR was $825.

MODEL AKY 39 - 7.62x39mm cal., gas operated semi-auto AK-47 type action, teakwood fixed stock and grip, flip up Tritium night front sight and rear, Yugoslavian mfg. Imported 1988-89 only.

	$550	$495	$440	$395	$350	$300	$270

Last MSR was $559.

This model was supplied with sling and cleaning kit.

⁕ *Model AKF 39 Folding Stock* - 7.62x39mm cal., folding stock variation of the Model AKY-39. Imported 1988-89 only.

	$575	$500	$450	$400	$350	$300	$270

Last MSR was $589.

EXP-64 SURVIVAL RIFLE - .22 LR cal., semi-auto, takedown rifle stores in oversize synthetic stock compartment, 21 in. barrel, 10 shot mag., open sights, receiver grooved for scope mounting, cross bolt safety, 40 in. overall length, 7 lbs. Imported 1989-90 only.

	$150	$135	$125	$115	$105	$95	$85

Last MSR was $169.

MINI-MAX - .22 LR cal., semi-auto, 18¾ in. barrel, wood or black synthetic stock, 10 shot mag., adj. rear sight, 4 1/3 lbs. Imported in 1990 only.

	$85	$75	$65	$55	$45	$40	$35

Last MSR was $99.

Add $6 for wood stock.

SM 64 TD SPORTER - .22 LR cal., semi-auto, takedown barrel, 21 in. barrel, checkered walnut finished hardwood stock and forend, hooded front sight and adj. rear sight, 7 lbs. Imported 1989-90 only.

	$130	$115	$105	$95	$85	$75	$65

Last MSR was $149.

Grading	100%	98%	95%	90%	80%	70%	60%

SHOTGUNS: O/U

American Arms imported Spanish shotguns manufactured by Zabala Hermanos, Lanber, and Indesal. Italian shotguns were also imported and mfg. by Stefano Fausti (Models Silver, Waterfowl, and Turkey Special). American Arms also imported Franchi Black Magic semi-auto and O/U shotguns until 1998. These shotguns will appear under the Franchi section in this text. Older Diarm models have been listed below.

LINCE - 12 or 20 ga., 3 in. chambers, boxlock with Greener crossbolt, various barrel lengths and chokings, available in either blue or shiny chrome finish, SST, VR, ejectors. Imported 1986 only.

	$510	$400	$380	$360	$340	$320	$300

Last MSR was $610.

Add $70 for choke tubes.

SILVER MODEL - 12 or 20 ga. only, similar to Lince Model, except has brushed aluminum finished receiver, no engraving. Imported 1986-87 only.

	$495	$450	$390	$360	$330	$300	$285

Last MSR was $545.

Add $50 for multi-chokes.

SILVER I - similar to Silver Model, except also available in 28 ga. or .410 bore (both new 1988), single selective trigger became standard in 1988, extractors, engraved frame, fixed chokes, recoil pad. Imported 1986-2000.

	$535	$430	$350	$300	$285	$270	$255

Last MSR was $649.

Add $30 for 28 ga. or .410 bore.
Engraved frame became standard in 1987.

SILVER II - similar to Silver I, except is supplied with choke tubes, deluxe walnut, and ejectors, 16 ga. new 1999. Imported 1987-2000.

	$660	$560	$475	$400	$360	$330	$300

Last MSR was $769.

Add $46 for 28 ga. or .410 bore (fixed chokes only).

✴ ***Silver II Lite (Silver Upland Lite)*** - 12, 20, or 28 ga. (disc. 1995), 3 in. chambers (except for 28 ga.), 26 in. VR barrels, with Franchoke tubes (except for 28 ga.), SST, ejectors, engraved frame with antique silver finish, checkered walnut stock and forearm, 5¾-6¼ lbs. Imported 1994-98.

	$800	$660	$550	$485	$440	$400	$360

Last MSR was $925.

✴ ***Small Gauge Combo*** - includes either 20/28 ga. (new 1997) or 28 ga./.410 bore barrels. Imported 1989-2000.

	$1,080	$925	$750	$625	$550	$495	$450

Last MSR was $1,239.

SILVER LITE - 12 or 20 ga., 2¾ in. chambers, boxlock action, 26 in. vent. barrels with VR and choke tubes, blued alloy receiver, SST, ejectors, gold trigger, checkered walnut stock and forearm, 5 lbs. 14 oz. or 6 (12 ga.) lbs., mfg. by Lanber. Imported 1990-92.

	$625	$535	$460	$400	$360	$330	$300

Last MSR was $749.

Grading	100%	98%	95%	90%	80%	70%	60%

SILVER HUNTER - 12 or 20 ga., steel boxlock action, SST, extractors, monoblock VR 26 or 28 (12 ga. only) in. barrels with 2 choke tubes, checkered walnut stock and forearm. Imported 1999 only.

	$550	$450	$375	$315	$285	$270	$255

Last MSR was $629.

SILVER SPORTING - 12 ga. or 20 ga. (new 1996), Sporting Clay model, boxlock action, 28, 29 (new 1999), or 30 (new 1993) in. ported vent. barrels with channelled broadway VR, choke tubes, and elongated forcing cones, nickel finished engraved receiver, SST, ejectors, figured walnut stock and forearm with handcut checkering, 7 lbs. 6 oz. Mfg. by Lanber, imported 1990-2000. 1993 manufacture by Pedersoli.

	$835	$680	$550	$485	$440	$400	$360

Last MSR was $965.

SILVER SKEET - 12 ga. only, similar appearance to Silver Sporting, 26 or 28 (new 1993) in. ported vent. barrels with raised VR, 4 choke tubes, recoil pad, 7 lbs. 6 oz. Imported 1992-1993 only.

	$790	$685	$575	$495	$450	$400	$360

Last MSR was $899.

SILVER TRAP - similar appearance to Silver Sporting, 30 in. ported barrels with raised VR, 4 choke tubes, recoil pad, trap stock dimensions, 7¾ lbs. Imported 1992-1993 only.

	$790	$685	$575	$495	$450	$400	$360

Last MSR was $899.

STERLING/BRISTOL - 12 or 20 ga., 3 in. chambers, boxlock with Greener crossbolt and false side plates, various barrel lengths and choke tubes, chrome finished receiver with moderate game scene engraving, SST, VR, ejectors. Imported 1986-89.

	$695	$550	$495	$450	$400	$375	$350

Last MSR was $825.

Until 1989, this model was designated the Bristol. In 1988, the engraving pattern was changed from game scene to elaborate scroll type.

SIR - 12 or 20 ga., 3 in. chambers, sidelock with Greener crossbolt, various barrel lengths and chokings, chrome finished receiver with game scene engraving, ST, VR, ejectors, deluxe checkered pistol grip stock and forearm. Imported 1986 only.

	$900	$725	$660	$610	$565	$520	$485

Last MSR was $1,090.

Add $75 for choke tubes.

ROYAL - 12 or 20 ga., 3 in. chambers, sidelock with Greener crossbolt, various barrel lengths and chokings, chrome finished receiver with elaborate scroll engraving, ST, VR, ejectors, oil finished deluxe checkered pistol grip and forearm. Imported 1986-87 only.

	$1,595	$1,310	$1,080	$960	$850	$750	$675

Last MSR was $1,730.

Add $65 for choke tubes.

EXCELSIOR - 12 or 20 ga., 3 in. chambers, sidelock with Greener crossbolt, various barrel lengths and chokings, chrome finished receiver with elaborate deep relief engraving and multiple gold inlays, ST, VR, ejectors, oil finished deluxe checkered pistol grip and forearm. Imported 1986-87 only.

	$1,775	$1,510	$1,250	$1,100	$975	$885	$780

Last MSR was $1,925.

Add $70 for choke tubes.

Grading	100%	98%	95%	90%	80%	70%	60%

WS/WT - O/U (SILVER) 12 WATERFOWL/TURKEY SPECIAL

12 ga. only, Mag. chambers (3½ in. was added in 1989), 24 (Turkey - disc. 1996), 26 (Turkey) or 28 (Waterfowl) in. barrels with choke tubes, SST, ejectors, parkerized metal finish, matte finished stock and forearm, Mossy Oak Breakup camo pattern began 1997 for Turkey Special, sling swivels, recoil pad, approx. 7 lbs. Imported 1987-2000.

	$650	$550	$460	$395	$360	$330	$300

Last MSR was $799.

Add $86 for Camo Turkey Model (WT/OU Camo 12, Breakup camo pattern, new 1997).

✳ *10 ga. Waterfowl* - 10 ga. Mag., double triggers, extractors, matte finishes similar to 12 ga. Waterfowl, beavertail forearm. Imported 1988-89 only.

	$750	$625	$550	$495	$450	$390	$360

Last MSR was $829.

WT-O/U10 TURKEY SPECIAL

10 ga., 3½ in. Mag., 26 in. barrels with choke tubes, SST (became standard in 1990), extractors, recoil pad, non-glare metal finish, 9 lbs. 10 oz. Imported 1988-2000.

	$865	$695	$550	$500	$450	$390	$360

Last MSR was $995.

F.S. 200

12 ga., trap or skeet model, 26 or 32 in. separated barrels only, SST, ejectors, boxlock with Greener crossbolt, black or chromed receiver, checkered walnut stock and forearm. Imported 1986-87 only.

	$690	$560	$500	$450	$410	$375	$350

Last MSR was $835.

F.S. 300

12 ga., trap or skeet model, 26, 30, or 32 in. separated barrels only, SST, ejectors, boxlock with Greener crossbolt and false side plates lightly engraved, chromed receiver, checkered walnut stock and forearm. Imported 1986 only.

	$825	$675	$610	$555	$510	$470	$440

Last MSR was $995.

F.S. 400

12 ga., trap or skeet model, 26, 30, or 32 in. separated barrels only, ST, ejectors, sidelock with Greener crossbolt, lightly engraved chromed receiver, checkered walnut stock and forearm. Imported 1986 only.

	$1,145	$945	$860	$800	$740	$680	$620

Last MSR was $1,360.

F.S. 500

same specifications as F.S. 400. Importation disc. 1985.

	$1,175	$950	$860	$795	$730	$660	$595

Last MSR was $1,360.

SHOTGUNS: SxS

American Arms imported Spanish shotguns manufactured by Zabala Hermanos and Grulla. Older discontinued Diarm models will also be shown in this section.

GENTRY/YORK - 12, 16 (disc. 1990), 20, 28 ga., or .410 bore, 3 in. chambers, boxlock, ejectors (extractors after 1986), double or SST (became standard in 1992), chromed receiver features fine scroll engraving, fixed chokes, pistol grip stock with recoil pad and beavertail forearm. Imported 1986-2000.

	$625	$475	$375	$300	$280	$260	$240

Last MSR was $750.

Add $45 for 28 ga. or .410 bore.

Before 1988 this model was designated York (case coloring began 1988, silver finish began 1993). DTs were supplied with 28 ga. or .410 bore 1990-2000.

Grading	100%	98%	95%	90%	80%	70%	60%

BRITTANY - 12 or 20 ga., boxlock action, 25 (20 ga. only, disc. 1996), 26, or 27 (12 ga. only, disc. 1996) in. barrels, SST, ejectors, matted solid rib, choke tubes, engraved case colored frame, checkered walnut straight grip stock with recoil pad and semi-beavertail forearm, 6½ or 7 lbs. Imported 1989-2000.

	$725	$575	$485	$435	$400	$375	$350

Last MSR was $885.

The wood finish was changed in this model from oil to semi-gloss in 1991.

SHOGUN - 10 ga., 3½ in. chambers, boxlock, ejectors, double triggers, chromed receiver features fine scroll engraving. Imported 1986 only.

	$440	$350	$325	$300	$280	$260	$240

Last MSR was $525.

DERBY - 12, 20, 28 (disc. 1991) ga., or .410 bore (disc. 1991) ga., 3 in. chambers, sidelock, ejectors, double (disc. 1989) or SNT, chromed receiver features fine scroll engraving, fixed chokes, straight grip walnut stock and forearm. Imported 1986-94.

	$880	$750	$625	$500	$425	$385	$350

Last MSR was $1,039.

Add 10% for 28 ga. or .410 bore (disc. 1991).
Subtract 10% for DT.
Add approx. 50%-60% for 2-barrel set (20 and 28 ga. - approx. 300 sets mfg.) - disc. 1990.

This model featured a case-colored receiver between 1988-90 and was changed to coin finish in late 1991. At the same time, the wood finish was changed from oil to semi-gloss.

GRULLA NO. 2 - 12, 20, 28 ga., or .410 bore, hand fitted sidelock action, 26 or 28 in. barrels, DTs, ejectors, fixed chokes, concave rib, case colored receiver with elaborate engraving, deluxe English style straight stock and splinter forearm (checkered and hand rubbed), between 5¾ - 6¼ lbs. Imported 1989-2000.

This model was individually handcrafted with less than 800 mfg. each year. Before going to a special order basis, this model retailed for $3,099 (1994).

✳ Small Gauge Set - includes choice of 20/28 ga. or 28 ga./.410 bore barrel combination (26 in. fixed choke barrels). Imported 1989-95.

	$3,600	$3,000	$2,375	$2,000	$1,650	$1,325	$1,150

Before going to a special order basis, this combination last retailed for $4,219 (1994/5).

WS/SS 10 WATERFOWL SPECIAL - 10 ga. only, 3½ in. chambers, 32 in. barrels, DTs, parkerized finish, sling swivels and camouflaged sling, extractors, fixed chokes, recoil pad, 11 lbs. 3 oz. Imported 1987-1993.

	$560	$500	$440	$400	$375	$350	$325

Last MSR was $639.

WT/SS 10 - 10 ga. only, 3½ in. chambers, similar to TS/SS 12, except as 28 in. barrels with multi-chokes. Imported 1998-2000.

	$775	$650	$550	$450	$400	$375	$350

Last MSR was $860.

TS/SS 10/12 TURKEY SPECIAL - 10 (disc. 1995) or 12 ga., 3 or 3½ in. chambers (3½ in. 12 ga. introduced in 1989), 26 in. barrels only, double triggers, parkerized finish, dull finish stock and forearm, sling swivels, recoil pad, choke tubes, 7 lbs. 6 oz. or 10 lbs. 13 oz. (10 ga.). Imported 1987-2000.

	$665	$550	$450	$400	$375	$350	$325

Last MSR was $799.

This model in 12 ga. was supplied with a SST.

Grading	100%	98%	95%	90%	80%	70%	60%

SHOTGUNS: SEMI-AUTO

PHANTOM FIELD - 12 ga. only, 3 in. chamber, gas operated, 24, 26, or 28 in. VR barrel with 3 choke tubes, black synthetic or checkered walnut stock and forearm, blue finish. Imported 1999-2000.

	$395	$360	$330	$275	$250	$225	$200

Last MSR was $439.

✳ **Phantom HP** - similar to Phantom synthetic, except has 19 in. threaded barrels for external choke tubes, swivel studs, and extended mag. Imported 1999-2000.

	$400	$365	$330	$275	$250	$225	$200

Last MSR was $449.

SHOTGUNS: SINGLE SHOT

SINGLE SHOT MODEL - 12, 20 ga., or .410 bore, 3 in. chamber non-exposed hammer, pistol grip stock, non-reflective finish. Imported 1988-89 only.

	$90	$80	$70	$60	$55	$50	$45

Last MSR was $99.

✳ **Camper Special** - 12, 20 ga., or .410 bore, 3 in. chamber folding design, 21 in. barrel, pistol grip. Imported 1988-89 only.

	$95	$80	$70	$60	$55	$50	$45

Last MSR was $107.

✳ **Slugger** - 12 or 20 ga., 24 in. Slug shotgun barrel with adj. rear sight and blade front, recoil pad. Imported 1989 only.

	$100	$85	$75	$65	$55	$50	$45

Last MSR was $115.

✳ **Youth** - 20 ga. or .410 bore, 26 in. barrel, 12½ in. stock dimensions, recoil pad. Imported 1989 only.

	$100	$85	$75	$65	$55	$50	$45

Last MSR was $115.

✳ **Combo** - interchangeable rifle and shotgun barrels, choice of .22 Hornet/12 ga. with 28 in. barrel or .22 LR/20 ga. with 26 in. barrel, includes fitted hard case. Imported 1989 only.

	$195	$165	$130	$115	$100	$90	$80

Last MSR was $235.

✳ **10 Ga. Model** - 10 ga. only, 3½ in. chambers, 26 in. multi-choke or 32 in. full fixed choke barrel, non-exposed hammer, non-reflective finish. Imported 1988-89 only.

	$135	$115	$95	$80	$70	$60	$55

Last MSR was $149.

Add $30 for multi-chokes (26 in. barrel).

AMERICAN BARLOCK WONDER

Previous trademark manufactured by Crescent Arms for Sears Roebuck & Co.

SHOTGUNS: SxS

SIDE-BY-SIDE - various gauges, hammerless or outside hammer, damascus or steel barrels.

	$240	$225	$200	$175	$140	$100	$75

Add 15% for steel barrels, smaller gauges.

SINGLE SHOT - various gauges, hammer, steel barrel.

	$125	$115	$100	$90	$75	$60	$50

Add 35% for smaller gauges.

Grading	100%	98%	95%	90%	80%	70%	60%

AMERICAN DERRINGER CORPORATION

Current manufacturer located in Waco, TX 1980-present. Distributor and dealer sales.

DERRINGERS: STAINLESS STEEL

MODEL 1 - available in over 55 cals. including .22 LR through .45-70 Govt., also 2½ in. .410 shot shell, O/U stainless steel derringer, satin or high polish finish, 3 in. barrels, automatic barrel selection, hammer block type safety, 15 oz., spur trigger, rosewood grips. New 1980.

* *Regular Cals.* - most cals. between .22 LR and .40 S&W.

MSR	$325		$250	$190	$140

  Add $25 for high polish finish.
  Add approx. $140 for .22 Hornet (disc. 1989).
  Add $165 for .223 Rem. or $135 for .30-30 Win. cal.

* *Larger Cals.* - typically .357 Mag.-.45 Mag. cal.

MSR	$335		$255	$200	$150

  Add $25 for high polish finish.
  Add $63-$145 for larger Mag. cals.

  This model can be ordered with special ser. nos. and other custom features at additional cost(s).

* *Model 1 Engraved* - limited mfg., mostly special ordered.

  Please contact the factory regarding a price quotation for this special order model.

* *Model 1 Millennium 2000 Series* - .45 LC/.410 shotshell only, 3 in. barrel, 15,000 mfg. beginning 1998 in various configurations including Gambler and Cowboy.

MSR	$450		$355	$285	$230

* *Model 1 United We Stand Commemorative* - .45 LC/.410 shotshell only, 3 in. barrel, choice of custom grips, includes red, white and blue presentation case. Limited mfg. beginning 2002.

MSR	$450		$355	$285	$230

  American Derringer Corporation will donate a portion of the proceeds from this commemorative to the recovery effort.

LADY DERRINGER - available in various cals. between .22 LR - .45 LC, and .45 LC/.410 shotshell cal., O/U top break action, 3 in. barrel, high polish stainless steel, spur trigger, scrimshawed synthetic ivory grips, handfitted action allowing easy cocking, with French styled leatherette display case, 15½ oz. New 1990.

MSR	$360		$300	$225	$175

Add $15 for .32 Mag., $45 for .357 Mag., and $75 for .45 LC or .45 LC/.410 shotshell.

* *Deluxe Engraved* - similar to Deluxe Grade, except hand engraved with circa 1880 patterns. Disc. 1994.

	$650	$515	$400

  Last MSR was $750.

  Mother-of-pearl grips and personalized engraving were available as extra cost options on this model.

* *14 KT. Gold Engraved* - entire Derringer manufactured out of a 14 KT. gold bar (contains approx. 20 oz. of 14 KT. gold and 3 oz. of stainless steel), custom engraved with diamond sights, special order only until late 1993.

	N/A	N/A	N/A

  Last MSR was $100,000.

* *Millenium Lady Derringer* - similar to Model 1 Millenium 2000 Series.

MSR	$450		$375	$280	$200

Grading	100%	98%	95%	90%	80%	70%	60%

LADY DERRINGER II - .22 LR (disc.), .32 ACP (disc.), .38 Spl., or .22 Mag. (disc.) cal., O/U pivot design with double action, aluminum frame, trigger guard stops at trigger bottom, 8 oz. New 1999.

MSR	$460		$380	$280	$200

Grading	100%	Issue Price	Qty. Made

MODEL 1 TEXAS COMMEMORATIVE - .38 Spl., .44-40, or .45 LC cal., similar to Model 1 except has brass frame, stainless steel barrel, and stag grips.

	100%	Issue Price	Qty. Made
.44-40 cal.	$385	$420	N/A
.45 cal.	$400	$450	N/A
Add $25 for special serial number.			
.32 Mag.	$205	$255	500+
.38 Spl.	$325	$365	N/A
.22 LR (mfg. 1991-92)	$200	$238	500
.41 Rimfire (not shootable)	$235	$295	500
Fully engraved model	$695	$750	limited

125TH ANNIVERSARY - special edition 125th anniversary variation with pistol case. Disc. 1993.

	100%	Issue Price	Qty. Made
.44-40 or .45 cal.	$285	$320	500
.38 Spl.	$185	$225	500
Deluxe engraved model	$650	$750	limited

Grading	100%	98%	95%	90%	80%	70%	60%

MODEL 3 - .32 Mag. (new 1990 - limited availability) or .38 Spl. cal., single shot, 2½ in. barrel, 8½ oz., spur trigger, rosewood grips. Disc. 1994.

	$95	$70	$55

Last MSR was $120.

MODEL 4 - .357 Mag., .357 Max., .44 Mag., .45 ACP, .45-70 Govt., or .45 LC cal. on upper barrel, 3 in. .410 shotshell lower barrel, O/U derringer combination pistol, 4 1/10 in. barrel, rosewood grips, 16½ oz. New 1985.

MSR	$410		$360	$280	$215

Add $55 for oversized grips.
Add $105 for .44 Mag. cal. (oversized grips became standard 1997).
Add $150 for .45-70 Govt. cal. in both barrels.

This model was also available on special order in either .50-70 or .50 Saunders cal. (new 1989 - single shot only). Retail was $395.

✸ **Model 4 Engraved** - .45 LC/.410 shotshell cal., allow 12 weeks for delivery. New 1997.
Please contact the factory directly for a price quotation on this special order model.

✸ **Alaskan Survival Model** - similar to Model 4, except .45-70 Govt. cal. top barrel, and choice of .44 Mag. (disc.), .45 LC, or .45 LC/.410 shotshell lower barrel.

MSR	$475		$400	$325	$280

Add $25 for high polish finish.

Grading	100%	98%	95%	90%	80%	70%	60%

MODEL 6 - .22 Mag., .357 Mag., .45 LC, .45 ACP, or .45 LC/.410 shotshell cal., O/U, 6 in. barrel, 21 oz. Available in high polish, satin, or grey matte finish (standard). New 1986.

MSR	$440	$340	$240	$195

Add $10 for either .45 LC or .45 LC/.410 shotshell.
Add $13 for satin finish (disc. 1994).
Add $33 for high polish finish.
Add $50 for oversized grips (disc. 1994, reinstated 1998-99).

✳ *Model 6 Engraved* - .45 LC/.410 shotshell cal., allow 12 weeks for delivery. New 1997.
Please contact the factory directly for a price quotation on this special order model.

MODEL 7 - .22 LR, .22 Mag. (new 1992), .32 H&R Mag., .38 Spl., .38 S&W (disc. 1989), .380 ACP, or .44 Spl. cal., O/U, same basic specifications as Model 1, except ultra lightweight (7½ oz.).

MSR	$325	$260	$175	$135

✳ *.44 Special Cal.* - .44 Spl. cal. only.

MSR	$565	$490	$435	$365

MODEL 8 - .45 LC/.410 shotshell cal., O/U, 8 in. barrel, nickel finish, grooved grips, 24 oz. New 1997.

MSR	$510	$425	$340	$285

✳ *Model 8 Engraved* - .45 LC/.410 shotshell cal. Limited mfg. 1997-98 only.

	$1,675	$1,300	$975

Last MSR was $1,917.

MODEL 10 - .38 Spl. (new 1995), .45 ACP, .45 LC, or .45 LC/.410 shotshell (disc. 1997), O/U, 3 in. stainless barrels, aluminum frame and barrel, matte grey finish, 7.5 oz. New 1988.

MSR	$305	$255	$195	$155

Add $80 for .45 LC cal.
Add $25 for .45 ACP cal.

MODEL 11 - .22 LR (new 1995), .22 Mag. (new 1995), .32 H&R Mag. (new 1995), .380 ACP (new 1995), or .38 Spl. cal., same basic specifications as Model 1, matte grey finish, only 11 oz.

MSR	$310	$245	$185	$140

RIMFIRE DOUBLE ACTION - .22 LR or .22 Mag. cal., 3½ in. O/U barrels, double action trigger, dual extraction, hammerless, blue finish with black synthetic grips, 11 oz. Mfg. 1990-95.

	$145	$115	$95

Last MSR was $170.

This O/U Derringer was patterned after the original High Standard design.

DS .22 MAG. - .22 Mag. cal., 3 in. barrel, stainless steel with blue finish, 11 oz. Special order beginning 1998.

MSR	$355	$305	$235	$180

DA 38 DOUBLE ACTION - .22 LR (new 1996), .357 Mag. (new 1991), .38 Spl., 9mm Para., or .40 S&W (new 1993) cal., 3 in. O/U barrels, satin stainless steel with aluminum grip frame, double action trigger design, hammerblock thumb safety, choice of checkered rosewood, walnut, or other hardwood grips, 14.5 oz. New 1990.

MSR	$435	$345	$245	$185

Add $10 for 9mm Para., $15 for .357 Mag., or $40 for .40 S&W cal.
Add $15 for Lady Derringer Model (scrimshawed synthetic ivory grips, .38 Spl. only. Mfg. 1992-94.)

Grading	100%	98%	95%	90%	80%	70%	60%

MINI-COP - .22 Mag. cal., 4 shot double action design, stainless steel construction, patterned after the original Mini-Cop mfg. in Torrance, CA. Mfg. 1990-94.

	$250	$220	$185

Last MSR was $313.

4-BARREL DERRINGER - .22 LR, .38 Spl., or .357 Mag. cal., double action, similar design to Mini-Cop, semi-matte finish, 28 oz. While advertised beginning 1991 at $425, only a few prototypes were manufactured during 1997.

CUSTOM TARGET MODELS - .38 Spl. Wadcutter or 9mm Federal (disc.) cal., mfg. for End of Trail Derringer Match, limited production. Mfg. 1990-92.

	$695	$575	$475

Last MSR was $750.

4 BARREL DERRINGER - while advertised, this model never went into production.

PISTOLS: PEN DESIGN

MODEL 2 PEN PISTOL - .22 LR, .25 ACP, or .32 ACP cal., unique hinged action allows pen to be converted into a legal pistol within two seconds, folding design, 2 in. barrel, cocks on opening action, firing pin block grip safety, brushed stainless finish, 5 oz. Mfg. 1993-1994.

	$145	$120	$100

Last MSR was $203.

Add $24 for .32 ACP cal.

PISTOLS: SEMI-AUTO

STANDARD MODEL

✳ ***.25 Mag. Cal.*** - .25 Mag., semi-auto single action, less than 100 manufactured in stainless steel only.

	$500	$400	$300

✳ ***.25 ACP Cal.*** - .25 ACP, semi-auto single action, less than 400 manufactured in stainless steel, less than 50 in blued steel.

Stainless	$400	$300	$250
Blue	$550	$400	$325

LM-5 - .25 ACP, .32 Mag. (disc. 1997), or .380 ACP (mfg. 1998-99) cal., compact stainless semi-auto, single action, 2¼ in. barrel, hammerless, wood grips, 4 (.32 Mag. or .380 ACP) or 5 (.25 ACP) shot mag., 15 oz. Limited mfg. beginning 1997.

MSR	$333	$275	$205	$165

Add $27 for .32 Mag. cal. (disc. 1997).

✳ ***LM-5 .380 ACP*** - limited mfg., disc. 1999.

	$365	$295	$215

Last MSR was $425.

PISTOLS: SLIDE-ACTION

LM-4 (SEMMERLING) - .45 ACP cal., 2 in. barrel, super compact, thumb activated slide mechanism, blue finish, 4 shot mag., 24 oz., limited manufacture beginning 1998.

MSR	$2,635	$2,375	$2,035	$1,875	$1,700	$1,550	$1,450	$1,375

Grading	100%	98%	95%	90%	80%	70%	60%

AMERICAN FIREARMS MANUFACTURING CO., INC.

Previous manufacturer located in San Antonio, TX between 1972-1974.

DERRINGERS

AMERICAN .38 SPL. - .38 Spl. cal., O/U configuration, approx. 3,000-4,000 mfg. between 1972-74.

$200	$165	$135	

AMERICAN .380 AUTOMATIC - .380 ACP cal., 8 shot, 3½ in. barrel, stainless steel, smooth walnut grips, approx. 10 mfg. 1972-1974.

$700	$500	$300	

PISTOLS: SEMI-AUTO

AMERICAN .25 AUTOMATIC - .25 ACP cal., 8 shot, 2 1/10 in. barrel, smooth walnut grips. Mfg. 1966-74.

	100%	98%	95%	90%	80%	70%	60%
Stainless	$195	$180	$165				
Blue	$165	$150	$140	$120	$100	$90	$85

AMERICAN FRONTIER FIREARMS MFG., INC.

Previous manufacturer located in Aguanga, CA 1995-2000.

American Frontier Firearms Mfg., Inc. manufactured a line of older replica metallic cartridge firing revolvers (black powder or smokeless). These revolvers were manufactured, fit, and finished in the U.S. Modern smokeless cals. including .22 LR, .32 Spl., .38 Spl., .44 Russian, or .45 LC. During 2000, AFF developed a new cartridge, a .44 A.F.F. It can be used in revolvers firing .44-40 WCF, .44 Russian, .44 Spl., and .44 Mag. It also meets current S.A.S.S. specifications.

Please refer to the 2nd Ed. *Blue Book of Modern Black Powder Values* by Dennis Adler (now online also) for more information and pricing on American Frontier Firearms Mfg., Inc.'s previously manufactured black powder models.

REVOLVERS: REPRODUCTIONS

Production on these models was mid-1997-2000. Revolvers were supplied with standard finish high polish blued steel parts, color case hardened hammer and/or trigger, silver-plated or blued backstrap and trigger guard, and varnished walnut grips. Special orders were also available featuring simulated ivory grips, special finishes, and engraving options. Some models and variations had very limited production, due to problems procuring parts.

RICHARDS 1851 NAVY CONVERSION STANDARD MODEL - .38 Spl. or .44 Spl. cal., non-rebated cyl., 4¾, 5½ or 7½ in. barrel, w/o ejector rod assembly.

$695	$550	$375	$325	$295	$265	$235

Last MSR was $795.

RICHARDS & MASON CONVERSION 1851 NAVY STANDARD MODEL - .38 Spl. or .44 Spl. cal., features Mason ejector rod assembly and non-rebated cyl., otherwise similar to Richards 1851 Navy Conversion.

$695	$550	$375	$325	$295	$265	$235

Last MSR was $795.

RICHARDS 1860 ARMY CONVERSION STANDARD MODEL - .38 Spl. or .44 Spl. cal., rebated cyl., with or w/o ejector assembly, 4¾, 5½ or 7½ in. barrel.

$695	$550	$375	$325	$295	$265	$235

Last MSR was $795.

Grading	100%	98%	95%	90%	80%	70%	60%

RICHARDS 1861 NAVY CONVERSION - similar to Richards 1860 Army Conversion, except has non-rebated cylinder and Navy sized grips.

	$695	$550	$375	$325	$295	$265	$235

Last MSR was $795.

1871-72 OPEN-TOP STANDARD MODEL - .38 Spl. or .44 Spl. cal., 7½ or 8 in. round barrel, non-rebated cyl.

	$695	$550	$375	$325	$295	$265	$235

Last MSR was $795.

* *1871-72 Open-Top Tiffany Model* - similar to 1871-72 Standard Model, except has engraved gold/silver finished Tiffany grips and also available with 4¾ in. barrel. Mfg. 2001.

	$995	$895	$700	$525	$450	$395	$350

Last MSR was $1,200.

AMERICAN GUN CO.

Previous trademark manufactured by Crescent Firearms Co. and distributed by H. & D. Folsom Co.

REVOLVERS

REVOLVER - .32 S&W cal., 5 shot, double action, top break-open action.

	$175	$160	$140	$120	$95	$65	$50

SHOTGUNS: SxS

SxS - various gauges, hammer or hammerless, damascus or steel barrels.

	$240	$225	$200	$175	$140	$100	$75

Add 15% for small gauges or steel barrels.

AMERICAN HISTORICAL FOUNDATION, THE

Current organization which privately commissions historical commemoratives in conjunction with leading manufacturers and craftsmen around the world. The Foundation is located in Richmond, VA. Direct to collector sales only, via phone, correspondence or personal visit to their headquarters and museums. Delivery to local FFL holder.

The Foundation's limited/special edition models are not all manufactured at one time. Rather, guns are fabricated as demand dictates. Limited editions include guns by Colt, Winchester, Browning, Dan Wesson, Auto-Ordnance/Thompson, Sturm Ruger, Holland & Holland, Walther, Smith & Wesson, Mauser, and Beretta.

LIMITED/SPECIAL EDITIONS

AHF consumers include members, history buffs, veterans, museums, and other interested parties who normally keep these items for a considerable time period, and very few are sold in the secondary marketplace annually. Because of this consumer direct sales program, many non-AHF consumers and gun dealers do not have a working knowledge on current pricing for AHF firearms.

The publisher suggests that those people who want more information about American Historical Foundation's Commemorative Issue firearms contact AHF directly (see Trademark Index).

Grading	100%	98%	95%	90%	80%	70%	60%

AMERICAN HUNTING RIFLES, INC. (AHR)

Current rifle manufacturer established in 1998 and located in Hamilton, MT.

RIFLES: BOLT ACTION

CZ-550 actions are also available individually. Prices range from $450-$575.

CLASSIC 550 - standard and various Howell proprietary cals., CZ 550 double square bridge standard action, controlled feed claw extractor, 25 in. chrome- moly sporter barrel, also available in optional stainless steel, blue finish, black fiberglass or optional walnut stock with Decelerator recoil pad. New 1999.

MSR	$1,495		$1,325	$1,050	$900	$775	$650	$550	$495

Add $75 for stainless steel barrel.
Add $150 for integral and removable muzzle brake, with protective cap.

VARMINT 550 PRO - .220 Howell, .220 Swift, .22-250 Rem., .30-06, or .308 Win. cal., CZ 550 double square bridge standard action, 26 in. stainless heavy barrel, SST, black fiberglass stock with Decelerator recoil pad. New 2001.

MSR	$1,795		$1,625	$1,250	$1,050	$900	$725	$650	$500

SAFARI 550 - various Mag. cals., similar to Classic 550, except has Magnum action with integral scope mounts, oil finished fancy walnut stock, trigger guard safety. New 2001.

MSR	$2,995		$2,675	$2,075	$1,725	$1,450	$1,175	$950	$825

SAFARI 550 DGR - various standard Mag. cals. from .404 Jeffery - .500 AHR, excluding special orders, similar to Safari 550, except has 3 position safety, extra fancy wood, and banded front sling attachment. New 2001.

MSR	$3,495		$3,050	$2,550	$2,075	$1,625	$1,400	$1,125	$875

585 DGR - .585 AHR cal., otherwise similar to Safari 550 DGR. New 2002.

Please contact the factory directly for current pricing and availability.

AMERICAN INDUSTRIES

Please refer to the Calico section in this text.

AMERICAN INTERNATIONAL CORP.

Previous manufacturer and importer located in Salt Lake City, UT, c. 1972-1984. American International was a wholly owned subsidiary of ARDCO (American Research & Development). ARDCO's previous name was American Mining & Development. American International imported firearms from Voere, located in Kufstein, Austria. American Arms International (AAI) was another subsidiary of ARDCO.

In 1979, after American International Corp. had dissolved, AAI resumed production using mostly Voere parts. After running out of Voere parts, late production featured U.S. mfg. receivers (can be recognized by not having a pivoting barrel retainer slotted on the bottom of the receiver). American Arms International declared bankruptcy in 1984.

Grading	100%	98%	95%	90%	80%	70%	60%

CARBINES: SEMI-AUTO

AMERICAN 180 AUTO CARBINE (M-1) - .22 LR cal., a specialized design for paramilitary use, 177 round drum mag., 16½ in. barrel, aperture sight, high impact plastic stock and forearm, aluminum alloy reciever with black finish. Semi-auto variation mfg. 1979-c.1984. Total Voere production (denoted by A prefix serial number) between 1972-1979 was 2,300 carbines (includes both full and semi-auto versions). Later mfg. was marked either M-1 (semi-auto) or M-2 (fully auto). B ser. no. prefix was introduced in 1980, and barrel markings were changed to "Amer Arms Intl, SLC, UT".

	$660	$550	$440	$360	$330	$305	$275

Add $550 for Laser Lok System – first commercially available laser sighting system.
Add approx. $300 for extra drum mag. and winder (fragile and subject to breakage).

AMERICAN LEGENDS

Current trademark of some handguns manufactured by IAI. Please refer to the IAI section in this text.

AMERICAN SPIRIT ARMS CORP.

Current rifle and components manufacturer established in 1998, and located in Scottsdale, AZ. Dealer and direct sales.

RIFLES: SEMI-AUTO

Add $25 for green furniture, $65 for black barrel finish, $75 for fluted barrel, $125 for porting, $119 for two-stage match trigger, and $55 for National Match sights on .223 Cal. models listed below.

ASA 24 IN. BULL BARREL FLATTOP RIFLE - .223 Rem. cal., patterned after AR-15, forged steel lower receiver, forged aluminum flattop upper receiver, 24 in. stainless steel bull barrel, free floating aluminum handguard, includes Harris bipod. New 1999.

MSR	$950	$850	$700	$625	$550	$500	$450	$400

ASA 24 IN. BULL BARREL A2 RIFLE - similar to ASA Bull Barrel Flattop, except features A2 upper receiver with carrying handle and sights. New 1999.

MSR	$980	$875	$725	$650	$565	$500	$450	$400

OPEN MATCH RIFLE - .223 Rem. cal., 16 in. fluted and ported stainless steel match barrel with round shroud, flattop without sights, forged upper and lower receiver, two-stage match trigger, upgraded pistol grip, individually tested, USPSA/IPSC open class legal. New 2001.

MSR	$1,500	$1,350	$1,100	$950	$825	$725	$650	$525

LIMITED MATCH RIFLE - .223 Rem. cal., 16 in. fluted stainless steel match barrel with round shroud with staggered hand grip, National Match front and rear sights, two-stage match trigger, upgraded pistol grip, individually tested, USPSA/IPSC open class legal. New 2001.

MSR	$1,300	$1,175	$975	$825	$725	$650	$525	$475

DCM SERVICE RIFLE - .223 Rem. cal., 20 in. stainless steel match barrel with ribbed free floating shroud, National Match front and rear sights, two-stage match trigger, pistol grip, individually tested. New 2001.

MSR	$1,300	$1,175	$975	$825	$725	$650	$525	$475

ASA 16 IN. M4 RIFLE - .223 Rem. cal., features non-collapsible stock and M4 handguard, 16 in. barrel with muzzlebrake, aluminum flattop upper receiver. New 2002.

MSR	$850	$790	$665	$595	$500	$450	$400	$350

A

Grading	100%	98%	95%	90%	80%	70%	60%

ASA 20 IN. A2 RIFLE - .223 Rem. cal., features A2 receiver and 20 in. National Match barrel. New 1999.

MSR	$820		$765	$640	$565	$500	$450	$400	$350

ASA CARBINE WITH SIDE CHARGING RECEIVER - .223 Rem. cal., features aluminum side charging flattop upper receiver, M4 handguard, 16 in. NM barrel with slotted muzzlebrake. New 2002.

MSR	$970		$865	$750	$650	$565	$500	$450	$400

C.A.R. POST-BAN 16 IN. CARBINE - .223 Rem. cal., non-collapsible stock, Wilson 16 in. National Match barrel. New 1999.

MSR	$830		$775	$650	$575	$500	$450	$400	$350

ASA 16 IN. BULL BARREL A2 INVADER - .223 Rem. cal., similar to ASA 24 in. Bull Barrel rifle, except has 16 in. stainless steel barrel. New 1999.

MSR	$955		$860	$725	$630	$550	$500	$450	$400

ASA 9MM A2 CAR CARBINE - 9mm Para. cal., forged upper and lower reciever, non-collapsible CAR stock, 16 in. Wilson heavy barrel w/o muzzlebrake, with birdcage flash hider (pre-ban) or muzzlebrake (post-ban), includes 9mm conversion block, 25 shot modified Uzi mag. New 2002.

MSR	$950		$860	$725	$630	$550	$500	$450	$400

Add $550 per extra 25 shot mag.

ASA 9MM FLATTOP CAR RIFLE - 9mm Para. cal., similar to A2 CAR Rifle, except has is flattop w/o sights. New 2002.

MSR	$950		$860	$725	$630	$550	$500	$450	$400

ASA 16 IN. TACTICAL RIFLE — .308 Win. cal., 16 in. stainless steel air gauged regular or match barrel, side charging handle, Hogue pistol grip, guaranteed ½ in. MOA, individually tested, 8¾ lbs. New 2002.

MSR	$1,675		$1,475	$1,200	$995	$850	$750	$650	$525

Add $515 for Match Rifle (includes fluted and ported barrel, 2 stage trigger, and hard chromed bolt and carrier).

ASA 24 IN. MATCH RIFLE - .308 Win. cal., 24 in. stainless steel air gauged match barrel with or w/o fluting/porting, side charging handle, Hogue pistol grip, guaranteed ½ in. MOA, individually tested, approx. 12 lbs. New 2002.

MSR	$1,675		$1,475	$1,200	$995	$850	$750	$650	$525

Add $515 for Match Rifle (includes fluted and ported barrel, 2 stage trigger, and hard chromed bolt and carrier).

AMERICAN WESTERN ARMS, INC.

Current trademark and importer established during 1999, and located in Delray Beach, FL. SAA revolver components are currently manufactured in the former Armi San Marco factory in Italy (now AWA International, Inc.), and assembled in the U.S. This plant was thoroughly updated during 2000 with all new tooling, stringent quality control, and now has bone colored case hardening in house. Dealer sales.

AWA International Inc. purchased American Western Arms, Inc. in 2000, along with Classic Old West Styles (COWS) and Millenium Leather.

Please refer to the 2nd Ed. *Blue Book of Modern Black Powder Values* by Dennis Adler (now online also) for more information and prices on American Western Arms' lineup of modern black powder models.

Grading	100%	98%	95%	90%	80%	70%	60%

REVOLVERS: SINGLE ACTION

PEACEKEEPER (MODEL 1) - .32-20 WCF (special order), .38-40 WCF (special order), .357 Mag., .44 Spl. (special order), .44-40 WCF, or .45 LC cal., 3, 3½ (Sheriff), 4, 4¾, 5½, 7½, 10 (Buntline), or 12 (Buntline) in. barrel, charcoal case colored receiver, blue finish, black powder or cross-pin frame, beveled cylinder, original hammer design w/o transfer bar safety, 2-line patent dates, 1st Generation Colt style hard rubber grips, assembled in America. While original prototypes were developed in 2000, actual importation began late 2000.

MSR	$835	$725	$600	$550	$500	$460	$430	$400

Add $35 for Sheriff, Thunderer, Birdshead, or Cavalry/Artillery configurations.
Add $165 for bright nickel finish.
Add $1,450 for grade A (25% coverage), $1,750 for grade B (50% coverage), $1,920 for grade C (75% coverage), or $2,240 for grade D (100% coverage) engraving – nickel finish only.
Add $90 for dual cylinder.

LONGHORN - .357 Mag., .44-40 WCF, or .45 LC cal., 3½ (Sheriff), 4¾, 5½, or 7½ in. barrel, case colored receiver, blue finish, one-piece walnut grips, 2 line address, transfer bar safety, assembled in America. Importation began 2001.

MSR	$495	$435	$375	$340	$315	$285	$260	$230

Add $30 for Sheriff or Birdshead/Thunderer model.
Add $100 for nickel finish.

RIFLES: LEVER ACTION

1892 CARBINE/RIFLE - .357 Mag., .44-40 WCF, or .45 LC cal., 20 (short rifle - octagon, carbine - round) or 24½ octagon barrel, blue finish, uncheckered walnut stock and forearm. Limited importation from Italy late 2000 only.

	$625	$525	$450	$395	$350	$300	$250

Last MSR was $695.

SHOTGUNS: SXS

HAMMERLESS COACHGUN - while initially advertised during 2000, this model was never manufactured.

AMTEC 2000, INC.

Previous trademark incorporating Erma Werke (German) and H & R 1871 (U.S.) companies located in Gardner, MA until 1999. Amtec 2000, Inc. Previously imported the Erma SR 100 rifle (see listing in Erma Suhl section).

REVOLVERS

5 SHOT REVOLVER - .38 S&W cal., 5 shot double action, swing-out cylinder, 2 or 3 in. barrel, transfer bar safety, Pachmayr composition grips, high polish blue, matte electroless nickel, or stainless steel construction, fixed sights, approx. 25 oz., 200 mfg. 1996-99, all were distributed and sold in Europe only (no U.S. pricing).

ANCIENS ETABLISSEMENTS PIEPER

Please refer to the Bayard section in this text for Bayard Models 1908, 1923, and 1930. In addition, Bergmann-Bayard Models 1908 and 1910 mfg. in Gaggenau, Germany will appear under the Bergman heading.

Grading	100%	98%	95%	90%	80%	70%	60%

ANGEL ARMS INC.
Previous manufacturer located in Hayward, CA, 1998-2001.

PISTOLS: SEMI-AUTO

The pistols listed below were designed to shoot a unique integrated case projectile (ICP). These projectiles were hollow, contained the powder charge, and since the case was the projectile, there was no ejection.

MODEL 1000 SE GUN ONE - .45 ICP (Integrated Case Projectile) cal., unique semi-auto design, mag tube is located on top of 6 in. fixed barrel.

While advertised, this model never went into production. $1,900 was the projected MSR.

MODEL QT 427 ZMR - .427 ICP (Integrated Case Projectile) cal., break open action, 5 shot tube or 10 shot staggered mag, 3½ in. barrel, located underneath clear mag tube, 5 oz., compact size.

While advertised, this model never went into production. $900 was the projected MSR.

ANSCHÜTZ

Current manufacturer (J. G. Anschütz, GmbH & Co. KG) established in 1856 and currently located in Ulm, Germany. Sporting and certain models of target rifles are currently distributed by AcuSport since 1996, headquartered in Billings, MT, Zanders Sporting Goods (1997) located in Baldwin, IL, and Ellett Brothers, located in Chapin, SC, beginning 2000. Target rifles are imported by various distributors (please see Trademark Index for current listing). Sporting rifles are currently imported exclusively beginning in 1996 by Tristar Sporting Arms. Ltd., located in N. Kansas City, MO. Previously distributed until 2000 by Go Sportsmen's Supply, located in Billings, MT. Previously imported and distributed through 1995 in the U.S. by Precision Sales International Inc., located in Westfield, MA.

DIE MEISTER MACHER

For more information and current pricing on both new and used Anschütz airguns, please refer to the 2nd Ed. Blue Book of Airguns by Dr. Robert Beeman & John Allen (now online also).

PISTOLS: BOLT ACTION

Anschütz also manufactured an MSP Pistol Series with ergonomic stock for the silhouette shooters. This series was designed for target shooting. All currently produced Anschütz pistols are delivered with a keyed security gun lock.

MODEL 1416P/1451P (EXEMPLAR) - .22 LR cal., bolt action, Match 64 left-hand action (for right-hand shooters), approx. 7 (original Silhouette Model, mfg. 1994-95) or 10 in. barrel, single shot (Model 1451P, new 1997) or repeater with 5 shot mag. (Model 1416P), two-stage trigger, adj. rear sight, receiver grooved for scope, contoured grip and forestock stippled, 3 1/3 lbs., also available for left-hand shooters. Mfg. 1987-1997.

	$395	$345	$295	$250	$225	$200	$180

Last MSR was $470.

Add $17 for single shot (Model 1451P).
Add $110 for right-hand action (for left-hand shooters).
This model was previously designated the Exemplar until 1996.

✳ *Exemplar Magnum* - while advertised in 1987, only one .22 Mag. was manufactured.

A

Grading	100%	98%	95%	90%	80%	70%	60%

✻ *Exemplar XIV* - .22 LR cal., similar to Exemplar, except has 14 in. barrel, 4.15 lbs. Imported 1988-95.

	$450	$370	$300	$250	$225	$200	$180

Last MSR was $562.

✻ *Exemplar Hornet* - .22 Hornet cal., 5 shot mag., Match 54 left-hand action, 10 in. barrel, grooved and tapped w/o sights, 4.35 lbs. Imported 1988-95.

	$835	$685	$575	$525	$475	$415	$365

Last MSR was $995.

✻ *Model 1416 MSPR/MSPE* - .22 LR cal., silhouette variation of the Exemplar pistol, MSPR designates repeater, MSPE designates single shot. Mfg. 1997 only.

	$1,100	$875	$750	$625	$525	$450	$375

Last MSR was $1,260.

MODEL 64P - .22 LR or .22 Mag. (disc. 2001) cal., right-hand bolt action, 10 in. barrel drilled and tapped (sights not included), weather proof "Choate" Rynite stock with stippling, 2 stage trigger, 4 (.22 Mag.) or 5 shot mag., 3½ lbs. New 1998.

MSR	$474		$400	$355	$300	$255	$225	$200	$180

Add $34 for .22 Mag. cal. (Model 64P Mag., disc. 2001).
Add $73 for accessory sight set.

RIFLES: BOLT ACTION, DISC.

Sile Distributors located in NY acted as an import agent during the early 1960s which can be identified by Sile barrel markings. Savage imported Anschütz rifles were available from 1963-1981 and also have Savage/Anschütz barrel markings. While some of those models might not be listed below, refer to models of similar caliber and quality that are listed to ascertain values.

During the period when Savage was importing Anschütz rifles, certain models in the Anschütz line were designated either "Savage-Anschütz" or "Anschütz-Savage" for sales by Savage in the U.S. Conversely, certain models manufactured by Savage were designated "Anschütz-Savage" for sale by Anschütz in Europe. Some of these models did not have any modifications but others were restocked, supplied with different sights, and had other different features from their original counterparts. In most cases, the original model numbers were used.

Some "Anschütz-Savage" rifles have made their way into the U.S. While somewhat rare, these rifles are typically based on the Savage Model 110 action. They are not as desirable as those "Savage-Anschütz" marked rifles utilizing the superior Anschütz actions. Anschütz also manufactured between 1,000-2,000 rifles utilizing SAKO actions in .222 Rem. cal. in the late 50s-early 60s. These guns will approximate values shown on the discontinued centerfire models listed below.

Currently, Anschütz offers 3 different actions. The 1451 action is Anschütz's entry level action, which is lightweight in design, utilizes cam cocking, and has a lateral sliding safety. The 1451 action is currently used in the Models 1416, 1418, and 1451. The Match 64 utilizes a cam cocking system with claw extractor and ejector, grooved receiver, and sliding safety on the right side behind the bolt. The Model 64 match action is used on the Model 1416 and variations, 1418, 64MPR, 1516, and the Model 64 Target pistol. The Match 54 is Anschütz's top-of-the-line action, and features dual locking lugs on the bolt which are seated eccentricaly in the receiver, allowing more support for improved stock bedding. It also features a cam cocking bolt, 2 position pivot rear safety, and is drilled and tapped. The Match 54 action is currently utilized on the 1710 series, 1712D (disc.), 1717, 1730 series, 1733, and 1740 models.

The models below have been listed in numerical sequence.

MARK 10 TARGET RIFLE - .22 LR cal., single shot. 26 in. heavy barrel, adj. sights, globe front, target stock with full pistol grip, adj. palm stop. Mfg. 1963-1981.

	$350	$320	$290	$260	$230	$210	$195

Grading	100%	98%	95%	90%	80%	70%	60%

MODEL 54 SPORTER - .22 LR cal., Match 54 action, 5 shot mag., 24 in. round tapered barrel, Monte Carlo roll-over cheekpiece, folding leaf sight, checkered pistol grip. Mfg. 1963-1981.

	$695	$625	$525	$450	$400	$360	$330

MODEL 54M - similar to Model 54 Sporter, except .22 Mag. cal.

	$750	$675	$575	$500	$435	$395	$360

MODEL MATCH 64 - .22 LR cal., Match 64 action, single shot, 26 in. barrel, hardwood stock with stipled ergonomic pistol grip, adj. pad, grooved receiver, approx. 8 lbs. Disc.

	$500	$450	$400	$350	$295	$250	$195

Subtract $150 if w/o correct Anschütz micrometer sights (front and rear).

MODEL 141 - .22 LR cal., 5 shot mag., 23 in. round tapered barrel, Monte Carlo stock, folding leaf sight. Disc.

	$350	$280	$240	$200	$180	$160	$140

✳ *Model 141M (Mag.)* - similar to Model 141, except .22 Mag. cal.

	$400	$365	$300	$265	$225	$200	$180

MODEL 153 - .222 Rem. cal., 24 in. barrel, folding leaf rear sight, French walnut stock, rosewood forend tip and pistol grip cap. Mfg. 1963-1981.

	$625	$550	$475	$400	$375	$350	$300

MODEL 153-S - similar to Model 153, 24 in. barrel, double set triggers.

	$700	$600	$525	$450	$425	$385	$330

MODEL 164 - .22 LR cal., 5 shot mag., 23 in. round tapered barrel, Monte Carlo stock, folding leaf sight. Mfg. 1963-1981.

	$395	$375	$325	$300	$250	$200	$160

MODEL 164M - similar to 164, except .22 Mag. cal.

	$450	$425	$375	$325	$275	$210	$180

MODEL 184 - .22 LR cal., 21½ in. barrel, Monte Carlo combination, checkered pistol grip, Schnabel forend, folding leaf sight. Mfg. 1963-1981.

	$450	$425	$375	$325	$275	$210	$180

MODEL 1400 - .22 LR cal., regular barrel, with sights. Disc.

	$350	$320	$290	$260	$230	$210	$195

MODEL 1407 I.S.U. MATCH 54 - .22 LR cal., heavy barrel, match two-stage trigger, stippled walnut stock and forearm with aluminum rail, aperture sights. Disc.

	$550	$475	$400	$350	$300	$260	$230

Last MSR was approx. $530.

MODEL 1408 - .22 LR cal., heavy barrel, no sights. Disc.

	$400	$350	$300	$260	$230	$210	$195

Add $150 for 1408 ED Model.

MODEL 1411 MATCH 54 - .22 LR cal., prone position target model, heavy barrel, aperture sights, side safety, fast lock time, adj. cheekpiece. Disc.

	$400	$350	$290	$260	$230	$210	$195

Last MSR was approx. $575.

Subtract $150 if w/o correct Anschütz micrometer sights (front and rear).

MODEL 1413 SUPER MATCH 54 - .22 LR cal., top-of-the-line free style international target rifle, adj. cheekpiece and curved buttplate, heavy target barrel with aperture sights. Disc.

	$725	$650	$550	$475	$420	$375	$325

Last MSR was approx. $875.

Subtract $150 if w/o correct Anschütz micrometer sights (front and rear).

MODEL 1418 - .22 LR cal., sporter variation, previous importation by Savage Arms.

	100%	98%	95%	90%	80%	70%	60%
	$300	$260	$225	$200	$175	$150	$125

MODEL 1418 MANNLICHER - .22 LR cal., hunting model, fine checkering, 5 shot mag.

	$650	$575	$500	$450	$365	$315	$275

MODEL 1450 - .22 LR cal., Sporter, 5 shot mag.

	$350	$300	$260	$225	$200	$175	$150

MODEL 1518 MANNLICHER - deluxe model of Model 1418.

	$725	$625	$550	$485	$430	$375	$325

MODEL 1574 SPORTER - .22 Mag., .222 Rem., .22-250 Rem., .223 Rem., .243 Win., or .308 Win. cal. Mfg. by Krico (Kriegeskorte) located at Stuttgart and distributed by Anschütz, approx. 1,000 imported during 1970-73.

	$795	$695	$595	$540	$485	$430	$375

MODEL 1807 - .22 LR cal., replacement for the Model 1407 Match 54, for I.S.U. and NRA shooting, 26 in. barrel, Match 54 action, 10 lbs. Disc.

	$425	$365	$315	$275	$230	$210	$195

RIFLES: BOLT ACTION SPORTER, .22 LR - RECENT MFG.

All currently produced Anschütz rifles are delivered with a keyed security gun lock.

Current manufactured Anschütz rifles use the following abbreviations when describing factory options. G = threaded barrel, KL = folding leaf sight, KV = heavy tangent sight, and ST = double set trigger.

KADETT - .22 LR cal., bolt action, youth dimensions, 22 in. barrel, 5 shot clip mag., folding leaf rear sight, single stage trigger, grooved receiver, checkered hard-wood stock, 5½ lbs. Mfg. 1987 only.

	$235	$200	$180	$165	$150	$135	$120

Last MSR was $265.

ACHIEVER - .22 LR cal., bolt action, 19½ in. barrel, single shot, folding leaf rear sight, two stage trigger, grooved receiver, stippled hard-wood stock with vented forearm and adj. length of pull, 5¼ lbs. Mfg. 1987-95.

	$340	$280	$230	$205	$185	$165	$150

Last MSR was $399.

❋ *Achiever ST* - .22 LR cal., 2000 MK single shot action, slide safety, two stage trigger, adj. length of pull stock, target sights, approx. 6½ lbs. Mfg. 1994-95.

	$415	$360	$315	$260	$230	$205	$185

Last MSR was $485.

❋ *Model Woodchucker* - .22 LR cal., similar to Model 1449D Youth, sold exclusively by R.S.R. Wholesale.

	$210	$185	$165	$150	$135	$120	$110

MODEL 1416D CUSTOM (LUXUS) - .22 LR cal., Match 64 action, 22½ in. barrel, 5 or 10 shot mag., cam cocking system on recent mfg., checkered Monte Carlo walnut stock, folding leaf sight, 6 lbs. 2 oz.

MSR	$684		$610	$500	$430	$365	$295	$240	$225

This model utilizes the Match 64 action, similar to the Anschütz Model 1403 Target.

Grading	100%	98%	95%	90%	80%	70%	60%

✳ Model 1416D Fiberglass - similar to Model 1416D Custom, except has McMillan fiberglass stock in hunter brown color and includes roll-over cheekpiece and checkered Wundhammer swell pistol grip, 5¼ lbs. Imported 1991 only.

	$755	**$650**	**$575**	**$525**	**$475**	**$415**	**$365**

Last MSR was $842.

✳ 1416D Classic - same specifications as 1416D Custom, except straight hardwood stock.

MSR	**$599**	**$510**	**$460**	**$400**	**$350**	**$295**	**$240**	**$225**

Add $70 for left-hand action (Model 1416LD).

✳ 1416D Heavy Barrel - similar to Model 1416D Classic, except has heavy barrel and no sights. Mfg. 2000-2001.

	$500	**$425**	**$360**	**$295**	**$240**	**$225**	**$200**

Last MSR was $580.

MODEL 1418D - .22 LR cal., Match 64 action, Mannlicher full stock, skipline checkering, 19¾ in. barrel, same action as Model 1416D, 5 lbs. 5 oz. Importation disc. 1995, resumed 1998.

MSR	**$983**	**$895**	**$785**	**$675**	**$550**	**$495**	**$425**	**$360**

Add $40 for set trigger (mfg. 1985-89).

MODEL 1448D - .22 Clay Bird cal., 1451 action, 22½ in. smooth bore barrel w/o sights, repeater, 5 shot mag., checkered walnut stained stock and forend. Imported 1999-2001.

	$295	**$265**	**$240**	**$220**	**$200**	**$185**	**$170**

Last MSR was $349.

MODEL 1449D YOUTH - .22 LR cal., bolt action design, youth dimensions, 16¼ in. tapered barrel with adj. rear sight, receiver is grooved for scope mounting, 5 shot mag. with single shot adapter available, European hardwood stock, 12¼ in. trigger pull, 3½ lbs. Imported 1990-91 only.

	$210	**$185**	**$165**	**$150**	**$135**	**$120**	**$110**

Last MSR was $249.

MODEL 1451 E/R SPORTER/TARGET - .22 LR cal., single shot (Model 1451E) or 5 shot repeater (Model 1451R), 1451 action, sporter target model w/o front sight, 22 (new 1998) or 22¾ (disc. 1997) in. barrel w/o sights, stippled pistol grip wood stock and vent. forend (with or w/o beavertail), 6½ lbs. Mfg. 1996-2001.

	$435	**$395**	**$360**	**$330**	**$300**	**$280**	**$260**

Last MSR was $485.

Subtract approx. $100 for Model 1451E (single shot).
Add $110 for Model 1451 Junior Super Target (single shot only).

✳ Model 1451R Sporter Target Prisma - .22 LR cal., 5 shot repeater, entry level cam cocking, claw extractor, and recessed bolt face, sliding safety, fully adj. stipled hardwood stock, 22 in. target barrel, grooved receiver, optional micrometer sights, 6.3 lbs. Importation began 2001.

MSR	**$499**	**$445**	**$410**	**$380**	**$350**	**$325**	**$300**	**$275**

✳ Model 1451ST-R - .22 LR cal., repeater, 5 shot mag., drilled and tapped 22 in. barrel w/o sights, cam cocking system, 2 stage trigger, uncheckered walnut stained hardwood stock. Imported 1999-2001.

	$435	**$395**	**$360**	**$330**	**$300**	**$280**	**$260**

Last MSR was $485.

✳ Model 1451D Custom - similar to Model 1451D Classic, except has walnut stock with Monte Carlo cheekpiece, Schnabel forend, and sling swivels, 5 lbs. Mfg. 1998-2001.

	$430	**$395**	**$360**	**$330**	**$300**	**$280**	**$260**

Last MSR was $480.

Grading	100%	98%	95%	90%	80%	70%	60%

❊ *Model 1451D Classic (Super)* - .22 LR cal., 5 shot, 22¾ in. barrel with front sights, grooved receiver, walnut finished straight hardwood stock, 5 lbs. Mfg. 1996-2001.

	$335	$280	$245	$210	$175	$160	$150

Last MSR was $398.

This model was designated the 1451 Super during 1996-97.

MODEL 1466D REPEATER - .22 LR cal., 24 in. conically tapered barrel with open sights, grooved receiver, checkered Monte Carlo walnut stock and forend. Imported 1996 only.

	$660	$525	$435	$375	$315	$260	$235

Last MSR was $766.

MODEL 1710D CUSTOM (1700D) - .22 LR - .22 LR cal., bolt action, Match 54 action, 5 shot mag., 23¾ (new 1998) or 24 (disc. 1997) in. regular (new 1998) or heavy (disc. 1997) barrel, folding iron rear sight (KL), Monte Carlo stock with roll-over cheekpiece and skipline checkering, 6½-7¼ lbs.

MSR	$1,116	$1,000	$825	$685	$580	$475	$375	$325

Add $177 for Meistergrade (select walnut and gold etched trigger guard - disc. 1996, resumed 1998 w/o gold trigger guard).

This model was designated 1422D until 1989 when it was changed to the Model 1700D with some modifications. In 1996, model nomenclature changed from Model 1700D Custom to the Model 1710D Custom. The Model 1400D Meistergrade was disc. 1987 - the last advertised retail price was $930.

The Model 1700D Custom employs the Anschütz Match 54 action.

❊ *1700D Graphite* - similar to Model 1700D Custom, except has McMillan black graphite reinforced stock with Monte Carlo roll-over cheekpiece, includes sling and swivels, 22 in. barrel, 7¼ lbs. Imported 1991-95.

	$1,130	$885	$760	$650	$550	$450	$375

Last MSR was $1,299.

❊ *1710D Classic (1700D)* - same general specifications as 1700D/1710D Custom, regular straight stock, choice of regular, heavy (new 1999), or heavy stainless (new 2000) barrel, open sights (disc. 1994), 7.3-8 lbs. Disc. 1994. Importation resumed 1998.

MSR	$1,030	$915	$835	$725	$650	$550	$450	$375

Add $78 for heavy stainless barrel.

Add $181 for Meistergrade (select walnut and gold etched trigger guard, disc. 1994, reintroduced 2000).

This model is also available as a 2000 Signature Series - includes high polish bluing, select American black walnut, "1 of 200" and "Dieter Anschütz 2000" signature in 24Kt. gold on bottom of trigger guard, aluminum case, and dated certificate at no extra charge.

This model was designated 1422DCL Classic until 1989 when it was changed to the Model 1700D Classic with some modifications. The Model 1422DCL Classic Meistergrade was disc. 1987 - the last advertised retail price was $875. In 1998, this model was reintroduced as the Model 1710D Classic.

1700D FEATHERWEIGHT (FWT) - similar to Model 1700D Custom, except has matte black McMillan fiberglass stock configured like the Custom Model, 22 in. barrel, no sights, 6¼ lbs. Imported 1989-95.

	$1,075	$895	$775	$650	$550	$450	$375

Last MSR was $1,230.

❊ *1700D Featherweight Deluxe* - similar specification to the 1700D Featherweight, except has skip-line checkered Fibergrain synthetic stock with realistic wood grain. Imported 1990-95.

	$1,235	$1,050	$875	$775	$650	$550	$450

Last MSR was $1,460.

Grading	100%	98%	95%	90%	80%	70%	60%

MODEL 1700D BAVARIAN - .22 LR cal., 24 in. barrel, 5 shot mag., checkered European style stock with European Monte Carlo cheekpiece and schnabel forend, 7½ lbs. Mfg. 1988-95.

| | $1,165 | $935 | $775 | $650 | $550 | $450 | $375 |

Last MSR was $1,364.

Add $199 for Meistergrade variation (select walnut).

MODEL 1712D - .22 LR cal., current top-of-the-line sporter rifle with deluxe walnut. Imported 1997-98 only.

| | $1,300 | $1,100 | $895 | $775 | $650 | $550 | $450 |

Last MSR was $1,495.

MODEL 1717D CLASSIC - .17 HMR cal., 4 shot mag., regular or heavy barrel, otherwise similar to Model 1710D Classic. New 2002.

| MSR | $1,051 | $930 | $845 | $735 | $650 | $575 | $500 | $450 |

Add $178 for Meistergrade (select walnut and gold etched trigger guard).

DIE MEISTERMACHER - .22 LR cal., Match 54 action, top-of-the-line model, limited edition of 25 guns, select wood, extra polish on metal parts, hand-lapped barrel, with numerous gold inlays including Olympic wreath. Mfg. 1985.

| | $2,500 | $2,000 | $1,600 |

Last MSR was $2,475.

This variation sold out in late 1988.

RIFLES: BOLT ACTION SPORTER, .22 MAG. - RECENT MFG.

All currently produced Anschütz rifles are delivered with a keyed security gun lock.

Current manufactured Anschütz rifles use the following abbreviations when describing factory options. G = threaded barrel, KL = folding leaf sight, KV = heavy tangent signt, and ST = double set trigger.

MODEL 1516D CUSTOM (LUXUS) - similar to Model 1416D, except .22 Mag. cal., 4 shot mag., 6 lbs. 2 oz.

| MSR | $704 | $620 | $525 | $465 | $385 | $335 | $275 | $250 |

This model utilizes the Match 64 action, similar to the Anschütz Model 1403 Target. In 1996, model nomenclature changed from the Model 1516D Custom to 1516D Luxus and during 1998, it changed back to 1516D Custom.

✴ *1516D/DCL Classic* - same specifications as 1516DL Custom, except regular hardwood stained stock, regular or heavy (new 2000) barrel.

| MSR | $619 | $555 | $485 | $430 | $355 | $300 | $240 | $225 |

MODEL 1518D (LUXUS) - .22 Mag. cal., otherwise similar to Model 1418D (Mannlicher stock), 4 shot mag., 5½ lbs. Importation disc. 1995, reintroduced 1997, nomenclature was changed to Model 1518D in 1997, disc. 2001.

| | $895 | $795 | $675 | $550 | $440 | $375 | $325 |

Last MSR was $987.

Add $50 for set trigger (disc. 1995).

MODEL 1720D CUSTOM (1700D) - .22 MAG. - .22 Mag. cal., bolt action, 5 shot mag., 23¾ (new 1998) or 24 (disc. 1991) in. regular (new 1998) or heavy (disc. 1991) barrel, iron sights, Monte Carlo stock with skipline checkering, 6 lbs. 10 oz - 7¼ lbs. Importation disc. 1991, resumed 1998, disc. 2001.

| | $995 | $875 | $750 | $650 | $550 | $450 | $375 |

Last MSR was $1,104 for the Model 1720D Custom.
Last MSR was $1,229 for the Model 1700D.

Add $174 for Meistergrade variation (select walnut).

This model was designated 1522D until 1989 and then reintroduced as the Model 1700D with

Grading	100%	98%	95%	90%	80%	70%	60%

some modifications. The Model 1522D Custom Meistergrade was disc. 1985 - last advertised retail price was $678. In 1998, this model was reintroduced as the 1720D Custom.

✴ *1700D/1720D Classic* - same general specifications as 1700D Custom, straight regular stock, choice of heavy (new 1999), or regular diameter barrel. Importation disc. 1991, resumed 1998, disc. 2001.

$900	$795	$700	$625	$525	$425	$350

Last MSR was $1,021 for the Model 1720D Classic.
Last MSR was $1,199 for the Model 1700D Classic.

Add $174 for Meistergrade variation (select walnut).

This model was designated 1522DCL until 1989 and then reintroduced as the Model 1700D with some modifications. In 1998, this model was reintroduced as the 1720D Classic. The Model 1522DCL Classic Meistergrade was disc. 1985 - the last advertised retail price was $660.

MODEL 1700D BAVARIAN - .22 Mag. cal., 24 in. barrel, clip mag., checkered European style stock with European Monte Carlo cheekpiece and schnabel forend, 7½ lbs. Mfg. 1988-95.

$1,165	$935	$775	$650	$550	$450	$375

Last MSR was $1,364.

Add $199 for Meistergrade variation (select walnut).

RIFLES: BOLT ACTION SPORTER, CENTERFIRE - RECENT MFG.

All currently produced Anschütz rifles are delivered with a keyed security gun lock.

Current manufactured Anschütz rifles use the following abbreviations when describing factory options. G = threaded barrel, KL = folding leaf sight, KV = heavy tangent signt, and ST = double set trigger.

MODEL 1433D - .22 Hornet cal., special order only, Match 54 target action, Mannlicher full stock, 4 shot mag. Disc. 1986.

$995	$840	$740	$640	$525	$425	$350

Last MSR was $826.

Add 5% for set trigger (new 1985).

MODEL 1730D CUSTOM (1700D) - .22 HORNET - .22 Hornet cal., 24 in. barrel, folding leaf sight, Monte Carlo stock with skipline checkering and rosewood grip cap, 4 shot mag., 7¾ lbs. Model 1432D was disc. 1987, and the Model 1700D was introduced 1989.

MSR	$1,244						
		$1,100	$940	$810	$700	$600	$500	$400

Add $181 for Meistergrade variation (select walnut).

This model was designated 1432D until 1987 and then reintroduced 1989 as the Model 1700D with some modifications. In 1996, model nomenclature changed from the Model 1700D Custom to the Model 1730D Custom. The Model 1432D Custom Meistergrade was disc. 1986 - the last advertised retail price was $770.

The 1700D Custom comes standard with the Anschütz Match 54 action.

✴ *1700D Graphite* - similar to Model 1700D Custom, except has McMillan black graphite reinforced stock with Monte Carlo roll-over cheekpiece, includes sling and swivels, 22 in. barrel, 7¼ lbs. Imported 1995 only.

$1,235	$1,025	$840	$725	$625	$525	$425

Last MSR was $1,478.

✴ *Model 1730D Classic (1700D)* - same general specifications as 1700D Custom, except regular stock and 23½ (1432DCL), 5 shot, 23¾ regular, heavy (new 1999) - 1730D, or heavy stainless (new 2001), or 24 (1700D) in. barrel. Disc. 1994, reintroduced 1998.

MSR	$1,159						
		$1,025	$895	$785	$680	$550	$450	$400

Last MSR was $1,395 on the Model 1700D Classic.

Add $181 for Meistergrade variation (select walnut).
Add $77 for heavy stainless barrel.

This model was designated 1432D until 1987 and then reintroduced 1989 as the Model 1700D

with some modifications. In 1998, this model was reintroduced as the Model 1730D Classic. This model comes standard with the Anschütz Match 54 action.

MODEL 1700D BAVARIAN - .22 Hornet or .222 Rem. cal., 24 in. barrel, 5 shot mag., checkered European style stock with European Monte Carlo cheekpiece and schnabel forend, 7½ lbs. Mfg. 1988-95.

	$1,325	$1,050	$900	$775	$650	$550	$425

Last MSR was $1,364.

Add approx. $200 for Meistergrade variation (select walnut).

MODEL 1733D - .22 Hornet cal., Mannlicher full stock featuring skipline checkering, European walnut, and rosewood Schnabel tip, 19¾ in. barrel with hooded front sight, 6 lbs. 6 oz. Imported 1993-95, reintroduced 1998.

MSR	$1,416	$1,255	$1,025	$895	$760	$625	$500	$400

MODEL 1740D CUSTOM (1700D) - .222 REM. - .222 Rem. cal., 3 shot, otherwise similar to Model 1700D Custom, except is also available with 23¾ in. barrel.

MSR	$1,244	$1,100	$940	$840	$740	$615	$500	$400

Last MSR was $909 on the Model 1532D.

Add $181 for Meistergrade variation (select walnut).

This model was designated 1532D until 1987 and then reintroduced 1989 as the Model 1700D with some modifications. In 1996, model nomenclature changed from the Model 1700D Custom to the Model 1740D Custom. The Model 1532D MG Custom Meistergrade was disc. 1986 - the last advertised retail price was $770.

＊ ***1740D Classic (1700D)*** - similar to Model 1700D Custom, except regular stock. Disc. 1994, reintroduced 1998.

MSR	$1,159	$1,025	$875	$785	$700	$600	$500	$400

Last MSR was $849 on the Model 1532DCL.
Last MSR was $1,395 on the Model 1700D Classic.

Add $181 for Meistergrade variation (select walnut).
Add $77 for heavy stainless barrel.

This model was designated 1532DCL until 1987 and then reintroduced 1989 as the Model 1700D with some modifications. In 1998, this model was reintroduced as the 1740D Classic.

MODEL 1743D - .222 Rem. cal., Mannlicher full stock variation of the Model 1740D, 6.8 lbs. Imported 1997-2001.

	$1,225	$1,000	$850	$750	$625	$500	$400

Last MSR was $1,373.

MODEL 1533 - .222 Rem. cal., open sights, checkered walnut stock. Disc. 1994.

	$795	$725	$660	$600	$550	$475	$400

RIFLES: BOLT ACTION, SILHOUETTE

Currently imported Anschütz silhouette rifles can vary somewhat in price, depending on the distributor and inventory. All currently produced Anschütz rifles are delivered with a keyed security gun lock.

MODEL 2013 SUPER-MATCH FREE RIFLE (BR-50) - .22 LR cal., single shot, 20 in. heavy barrel, no sights, black synthetic stock with adj. cheekpiece and widened forend ("ANSCHÜTZ BR-50" is stenciled on sides), 15.4 lbs. Limited importation 1994-98.

	$2,225	$1,750	$1,375	$1,050	$900	$725	$625

Last MSR was $2,880.

Add $300 for color laminate stock (mfg. 1997-98 only).

Model nomenclature changed from the BR-50 to the Model 2013 in 1997.

Grading	100%	98%	95%	90%	80%	70%	60%

MODEL 64S RIFLE - .22 LR cal., single shot, 26 in. round barrel, beavertail forearm, adj. single stage trigger, aperture sights, target stock with Wundhammer grip and adj. butt plate, checkered pistol grip. Mfg. 1963-1981.

	$475	$425	$375	$325	$285	$240	$220

Subtract 15% if without sights (Model 64).

This model was available in left-hand or right-hand action.

MODEL 64MS R - .22 LR cal., single shot (Model 64MS, disc. 1996) or 5 shot repeater (Model 64MS R), silhouette target model, 21¼ in. barrel, no sights, Wundhammer swell stippled pistol grip beechwood stock, adj. trigger, 8 lbs.

MSR	$884	$775	$675	$575	$475	$400	$350	$325

Add $50 for left-hand action (disc.).

This variation employs a Match 64 action. R suffix nomenclature started 1997.

MODEL 64MP - .22 LR cal., repeater, 5 shot mag., 21.2 in. drilled and tapped heavy steel or stainless steel (new 2000) barrel, 2 stage trigger, uncheckered walnut stained stock and beavertail forend, adj. rubber buttplate. Importation began 1999.

MSR	$729	$650	$550	$450	$365	$300	$240	$225

Add $76 for stainless steel barrel.
Subtract approx. $75 if w/o swivel rail.

* ***Model 64MS - FWT*** - similar to Model 64MS, except single stage trigger, 6¼ lbs. Disc. 1988.

	$550	$475	$425	$350	$325	$260	$230

Last MSR was $596.

MODEL 54.18MS - .22 LR cal., silhouette target model, 22 in. barrel, Match 54 single shot action, walnut Wundhammer stock is stippled on pistol grip and entire forearm, no sights, 8 lbs. 6 oz. Disc. 1997.

	$1,295	$1,075	$895	$760	$650	$550	$475

Last MSR was $1,579.

Add $96 for left-hand action.

This model employs the Super Match 54 action.

* ***Model 54.18MS ED*** - same action as Model 54.18MS, except has 19¼ in. barrel 7/8 in. diameter) with 14¼ in. extension tube, 3 removable muzzle weights. Disc. 1988.

	$1,075	$900	$775	$675	$575	$485	$410

Last MSR was $1,215.

Add $100 for left-hand action.

MODEL 54.18MS REP - similar to Model 54.18MS, except has repeating action, 5 shot mag., thumbhole wood stock with vented forestock, 7¾ lbs. This model was introduced in 1989 with a wood stock and a retail price of $1,650. In 1990, the stock was changed to a synthetic McMillan fiberglass finished in grey.

MSR	$1,735	$1,525	$1,175	$995	$875	$750	$625	$550

Add 10% for wood stock (1989 mfg. only).

This model features a Super Match 54 action with clip mag.

* ***Model 54.18MS REP Deluxe*** - Deluxe version of the Model 54.18MS REP featuring Fibergrain McMillan stock with advanced thumbhole design and stippled checkering. Imported 1990- 97.

	$2,035	$1,600	$1,275	$1,025	$915	$785	$695

Last MSR was $2,450.

Grading	100%	98%	95%	90%	80%	70%	60%

RIFLES: BOLT ACTION MATCH, RECENT MFG.

All currently manufactured Anschütz match/target and biathlon rifles listed in the following sections are imported by Champion's Choice, Inc., Champions Shooter's Supply, Gunsmithing, Inc., and International Shooters Service, unless otherwise noted. These match/target models may vary somewhat in price, depending on the distributor and inventory. All currently produced Anschütz match rifles are delivered with a keyed security gun lock.

MODEL 2000 MK - .22 LR cal., single shot match, 26 in. barrel, aperture sights, 7½ lbs. Disc. 1988.

$340	$290	$250	$210	$180	$160	$145

Last MSR was $400.

MODEL 1403D - .22 LR cal., improved Model 64S match rifle, single shot, no sights, adj. trigger, 8 lbs. 6 oz. Importation disc. in 1990.

$600	$525	$450	$360	$300	$260	$225

Last MSR was $700.

Add $50 for left-hand action (disc. 1988).

MODEL 1803D - .22 LR cal., Match 64 action, 25½ in. target barrel, single stage adj. trigger, blond finished wood with dark stippling on pistol grip and forearm, adj. cheekpiece and butt plate, 8.6 lbs. Imported 1987-1993.

$850	$725	$625	$525	$430	$365	$310

Last MSR was $1,012.

Add $70 for left-hand action (disc. 1989).

MODEL 1808D RT/1808MS R (RUNNING TARGET) - .22 LR cal., single shot running target model, 19 (w/o barrel weights) - 32½ in. barrel, adj. stock, cheekpiece, trigger, heavy beavertail forend, no sights, muzzle barrel weights, 9¼ lbs. Importation disc. 1998.

$1,850	$1,400	$1,075	$950	$800	$695	$595

Last MSR was $2,220.

Add $50 for left-hand action (disc. 1991).
Subtract 20% for earlier models (Model 1808D RT and Model 1808 ED-Super).

This model was previously designated Model 1808D RT from 1991-96, and also the Model 1808 ED-Super during 1990 and earlier mfg.

MODEL 1808MS R - .22 LR cal., 5 shot repeater designed for metallic silhouette shooting, 19.2 in. barrel w/o sights, thumbhole Monte Carlo stock with grooved forearm featuring "ANSCHÜTZ" in panel scene, approx. 8 lbs. Importation began 1998.

MSR	$1,916		$1,695	$1,450	$1,175	$1,025	$900	$800	$700

This sporting model is distributed by Acusport Corp., Zander's Sporting Goods, Inc., and Ellett Brothers.

MODEL 1813 SUPER MATCH - .22 LR cal., top-of-the-line competition model with sophisticated adj. cheekpiece, buttplate, trigger, pistol grip, and palm rest, Super Match 54 action, stippled walnut stock with thumbhole grip, 15.4 lbs. Mfg. 1979-1988.

$1,850	$1,600	$1,400	$1,200	$975	$875	$775

This model previously held all the Olympic and world records. The model nomenclature was changed to Model 1913 Super Match in 1988.

MODEL 1903D - .22 LR cal., similar specifications to the Model 1803D, except has new improved target stock and adj. cheekpiece made from walnut finished European hardwood, color laminated stock mfg. 1995-98, full length stippled checkering on forend and contoured pistol grip, fully adj. new style buttplate, 9.9 lbs. New 1990.

MSR	N/A		$670	$570	$525	$485	$445	$400	$365

Add $35 for left-hand action.
Add $130 for color laminated stock (disc. 1998).

Grading	100%	98%	95%	90%	80%	70%	60%

MODEL 1907 ISJF - .22 LR cal., single shot match "I.S.U." model, 26 in. button-rifled barrel, prone and position shooting, removable cheekpiece, adj. buttplate, hand stippled stock with ventilated forearm and choice of beechwood (new 1997) walnut, blond laminated (disc.), or color laminated (mfg. 1995-96) wood stock, 10½ lbs.

MSR	**N/A**	$1,435	$1,250	$1,075	$875	$725	$600	$550

Add $70 for left-hand action.
Add $130 for stainless steel barrel.
Add $125 for quick adj. cheekpiece (disc.).
Add $125 for color laminated stock (disc.).

This model is also available with an Anschütz stock no. 2213 blue laminate (Alu Color), featuring the most recent technology in stock innovation – MSR is $2,012.

This variation was designated Model 1807 before 1989.

MODEL 1909 - target variation of the Model 1910 Super Match II, limited importation 1997-98 only.

$2,050	$1,550	$1,225	$1,025	$895	$785	$695

Last MSR was $2,480.

MODEL 1910 SUPER MATCH II - .22 LR cal., single shot, 27¼ in. barrel, diopter sights, thumbhole stock is fully adj., 12 lbs., model down from 1813 (or 1913), special order only - limited quantities imported until 1998.

$2,415	$1,925	$1,475	$1,100	$900	$725	$625

Last MSR was $2,967.

Add $149 for left-hand action.
Subtract 20% for Model 1810.

This variation was designated as Model 1810 before 1988.

MODEL 1911 PRONE MATCH - .22 LR cal., single shot match prone rifle, 27¼ in. barrel, beechwood stock with adj. cheekpiece, buttplate, no sights, 11.9 lbs.

MSR	**N/A**	$1,680	$1,475	$1,175	$995	$925	$825	$700

Add $80 for stainless steel barrel.
Add $100 for left-hand action (disc. 1993).
Subtract 20% for Model 1811.

This variation was designated Model 1811 before 1988.

MODEL 1912 LADIES SPORT RIFLE - .22 LR cal., designed for new ladies I.S.S.F. standards, features 1907 barreled action w/o sights, walnut stock with shorter dimensions, 11.4 lbs. Importation began 1999.

MSR	**N/A**	$1,690	$1,485	$1,325	$1,100	$975	$825	$700

Add $85 for left-hand action.
Add $306 for aluminum stock (disc.).
Add $554 for left-handed aluminum stock (disc.).

MODEL 1913 SUPER MATCH FREE RIFLE - .22 LR cal., single shot, top-of-the-line match rifle, every possible refinement, international diopter sights, 27¼ in. button rifled barrel, hand and palm rest, wood or blue aluminum Alu Color (new 2000) stock, 15.5 lbs.

MSR	**N/A**	$2,120	$1,800	$1,525	$1,200	$1,050	$925	$785

Add $105 for left-hand action.
Add $130 for stainless steel barrel.

This variation was designated Model 1813 before 1988 (see separate listing).

Grading	100%	98%	95%	90%	80%	70%	60%

MODEL 2007 ISSF STANDARD - .22 LR cal., ISSF model, featuring 19¾ in. standard or heavy (new 2001) barrel with 8 in. detachable front tube allowing for different sights and counter-weights (total barrel length with tube is 27¼ in.), adj. cheekpiece and rubber butt plate, grooved and vented forearm, choice of blond (disc. 2000), walnut, or blue aluminum Alu Color (new 2001) stock, Match 54 action, 12 lbs. New 1992.

MSR	N/A	$1,635	$1,550	$1,325	$1,100	$965	$800	$695

Add $215 for left-hand action (new 1993).
Add $135 for stainless steel barrel.
Add $725 for Alu Color aluminum stock.

This model underwent significant engineering changes during 1994, including a heavier receiver.

MODEL 2012 LADIES SPORT RIFLE - .22 LR cal., utilizes 2007 rectangular receiver barreled action designed for new ladies ISSF rules, smaller dimensions, walnut stock, 11.4 lbs. Importation began 1999.

MSR	N/A	$2,040	$1,775	$1,500	$1,200	$1,025	$950	$785

Add $100 for left-hand action (new 2000).

MODEL 2013 SUPER MATCH "SPECIAL" - .22 LR cal., top-of-the-line international target rifle featuring 19¾ in. standard or heavy (new 2001) barrel with 8 in. detachable front tube allowing for different sights and counter-weights (total barrel length with tube is 27¼ in.), top grain walnut or color laminate stock with adj. hand rest, palm rest, cheekpiece, and elaborate metal butt plate, Match 54 action, 15.4 lbs. New 1992.

MSR	N/A	$2,350	$2,025	$1,600	$1,250	$1,025	$895	$785

Add $120 for left-hand action.
Add $135 for stainless steel barrel.
Add $135 for Acu Color aluminum stock.

This model underwent significant engineering changes during 1994.

✷ Model 2013 BR-50 (Benchrest) - .22 LR cal., developed especially for benchrest competition, trigger can be adjusted for either light single or two-stage action, 19.6 in. barrel, uncheckered walnut stock with wide forend, 10.3 lbs. Importation began 1999.

MSR	N/A	$1,635	$1,475	$1,250	$1,050	$900	$800	$700

RIFLES: BOLT ACTION, BIATHLON

MODEL 1450B - .22 LR cal., 2000 MK action, 19½ in. barrel, European hardwood with vent. forearm and adj. butt plate, aperture sights, 5 lbs. Mfg. 1993 only.

		$650	$550	$450	$375	$300	$260	$230

Last MSR was $765.

MODEL 1403B - .22 LR cal., Match 64 action, 21½ in. barrel, blonde finished European hardwood with stippled pistol grip, Biathlon design allows 4 mags. to be stored in a housing attached to the forend on right side, entry level Biathlon gun, 8½ lbs. Mfg. 1990-92.

		$850	$730	$660	$525	$450	$375	$335

Last MSR was $998.

MODEL 1827B - .22 LR cal., biathlon rifle, carries four 5 shot mags. in stock, special biathlon features, 21½ in. barrel, limited mfg.

		$1,875	$1,550	$1,225	$1,025	$895	$785	$695

Last MSR was $2,457.

Add $120 for left-hand action (disc. 1989).

In 1990, the stock design was changed permitting 8 mags. to be stored in two housings attached to both the stock and forend on right side.

Grading	100%	98%	95%	90%	80%	70%	60%

✷ *Model 1827BT Fortner* - same general specifications as Model 1827B, except has Fortner straight pull-through bolt action, color laminated stock became available 1995, blued or stainless barrel, 8.8 lbs. New 1986.

	MSR N/A	$2,050	$1,775	$1,475	$1,175	$995	$875	$775

Add $105 for left-hand action.
Add $140 for stainless steel barrel.

In 1990, the stock design was changed permitting 8 mags. to be stored in two housings attached to both the stock and forend on right side.

RIFLES: SEMI-AUTO

MODEL 520/61 - .22 LR cal., semi-auto, 24 in. barrel, 10 shot mag., Monte Carlo stock, 6½ lbs. Disc. 1983.

	$260	$205	$185	$155	$145	$130	$120

MARK 525 SPORTER RIFLE - .22 LR cal., semi-auto, 24 in. barrel, 10 shot mag., adj. rear sight, Monte Carlo stock, 6½ lbs. Imported 1984-95.

	$460	$395	$350	$295	$250	$215	$175

Last MSR was $547.

✷ *Mark 525 Carbine* - similar to Mark 525 Rifle, except has 20 in. barrel. Importation disc. 1986.

	$400	$315	$265	$225	$200	$180	$160

SHOTGUNS: O/U

Anschütz marked O/U shotguns were manufactured by Miroku of Japan and distributed in Germany only. Several grades of these shotguns were manufactured and while rarely seen in the U.S., values approximate other Miroku O/Us of similar quality and features ($650-$1,000 assuming 95% or better condition).

ANZIO IRONWORKS CORP.

Current manufacturer established during 2000, and located in St. Petersburg, FL. Anzio Ironworks has been making gun parts and accessories since 1994. Dealer sales.

RIFLES: SINGLE SHOT

.50 BMG TAKEDOWN MODEL - .50 BMG cal., modified bullpup configuration, tube stock with 2 in. buttpad, 17 in. barrel with match or military chambering and muzzle brake, automatic ambidextrous safety and decocking mechanism, takedown action allowing disassembly in under 25 seconds, adj. target trigger, inclined mounting rail, cased, 25 lbs. New 2000.

	MSR $2,500	$2,350	$2,000	$1,800	$1600	$1,400	$1,200	$1,000

Add $150 for 29 in. barrel or $1,050 for 29 in. barrel assembly.

.50 BMG TITANIUM TAKEDOWN MODEL - .50 BMG cal., modified bullpup configuration, tube stock, 16 in. barrel with match or military chambering and muzzlebrake, automatic ambidextrous safety and decocking mechanism, interrupted thread lockup, takedown action allowing disassembly in under 12 seconds, adj. target trigger, picatinny rail mount, cased, 11 lbs. New 2002.

	MSR $3,200	$2,995	$2,600	$2,350	$2,000	$1,800	$1600	$1,400

Add $250 for 29 in. barrel, $350 for custom barrel length to 45 in., or $1,050 for 29 in. barrel assembly.

Grading	100%	98%	95%	90%	80%	70%	60%

.50 BMG BOLT ACTION MODEL - .50 BMG cal., laminated wood stock, butter knife bolt handle, bolt complete with ejector and extractor, parkerized finish, inclined mounting rail, 17 in. barrel with match or military chambering and muzzlebrake, 21 lbs. New 2002.

	MSR	$2,750		$2,500	$2,200	$1,950	$1,675	$1,400	$1,200	$1,000

Add $150 for 29 in. barrel or $250 for custom barrel length to 45 in.

APACHE

Previous trademark manufactured by Ojanguren Y Vidosa located in Eibar, Spain.

PISTOLS: SEMI-AUTO

SEMI-AUTO - 6.35mm cal., clip fed.

	$190	$175	$160	$140	$120	$95	$75

ARCUS CO.

Previous trademark of handguns manufactured in Bulgaria and imported until 2000 by Miltex, Inc., located in Waldorf, MD.

PISTOLS: SEMI-AUTO

ARCUS-94 - 9 mm Para. cal., semi-auto, SA or DA, 5¼ in. barrel, 10 shot mag., choice of blue, two-tone, or silver matte metal finish, molded synthetic grips, 32 oz. Imported 1998-2000.

	$275	$250	$225	$200	$180	$160	$140

Last MSR was $300.

ARLINGTON ORDNANCE

Previous importer located in Westport, CT until 1996. Formerly located in Weston, CT.

CARBINES & RIFLES: SEMI-AUTO

M1 GARAND RIFLE - .30-06 cal., these Garands were imported from Korea in used condition, various manufacturers, with import stamp. Imported 1991-96.

	$325	$285	$250	$200	$180	$160	$140

Add $40 for stock upgrade (better wood).

✱ *Arsenal Restored M1 Garand Rifle* - .30-06 or .308 Win. cal., featured new barrel, rebuilt gas system, and reinspected components. Mfg. 1994-96.

	$475	$385	$325	$285	$250	$200	$180

Add 5% for .308 Win. cal.

TROPHY GARAND - .308 Win. cal. only, action was original mil-spec., included new barrel and checkered walnut stock and forend, recoil pad. Mfg. 1994-96.

	$625	$525	$375	$325	$275	$225	$200

Last MSR was $695.

T26 TANKER - .30-06 or .308 Win. cal., included new barrel and other key components, updated stock finish. Mfg. 1994-96.

	$550	$415	$340	$295	$265	$200	$180

.30 CAL. CARBINE - .30 Carbine cal., 18 in. barrel, imported from Korea in used condition, various manufacturers, with import stamp. Imported 1991-1996.

	$225	$185	$160	$140	$125	$115	$100

Add approximately $55 for stock upgrade (better wood).

MODEL FIVE CARBINE - while advertised, this model was never produced.

Grading	100%	98%	95%	90%	80%	70%	60%

ARMALITE

Previous manufacturer located in Costa Mesa, CA, approx. 1959-1973.

RIFLES: SEMI-AUTO

AR-7 EXPLORER - .22 LR cal., 16 in. aluminum barrel with steel liner, aperture sight, take down action and barrel stores in hollow plastic stock, gun will float, designed by Gene Stoner, mfg. 1959-1973 by Armalite, 1973- 1990 by Charter Arms, 1990-1997 by Survival Arms located in Cocoa, FL and currently mfg. beginning 1997 by Henry Repeating Arms Co. located in Brooklyn, NY, and AR-7 Industries, LLC, located in Meriden, CT, starting 1998.

$135	$110	$90	$80	$65	$55	$50

Some unusual early Costa Mesa AR-7 variations have been observed with ported barrels, extendable wire stock, hooded front sight, and hollow pistol grip containing cleaning kit, perhaps indicating a special military contract survival weapon.

AR-7 CUSTOM - similar to AR-7 Explorer, only with custom walnut stock including cheekpiece, pistol grip. Mfg. 1964-1970.

$185	$150	$125	$100	$90	$80	$70

AR-180 - .223 Rem. cal., semi-auto, gas operated, 18¼ in. barrel, folding stock. Manufactured by Armalite in Costa Mesa, CA, 1969-1972, Howa Machinery Ltd., Nagoya, Japan 1972 and 1973. Since 1976 the AR-180 has been made by Sterling Armament Co. Ltd., Dagenham, Essex, England.

Sterling Mfg.	$850	$775	$695	$625	$550	$495	$450
Costa Mesa Mfg.	$995	$875	$750	$675	$600	$550	$500
Howa Mfg.	$1,350	$1,110	$995	$875	$795	$725	$650

SHOTGUNS: SEMI-AUTO

AR-17 - 12 ga., semi-auto, 24 in. barrel, interchangeable choke tubes, gas operated, high strength aluminum barrel and receiver, plastic stock and forearm, either gold anodized or black finish. Only 2,000 mfg. 1964-1965.

$575	$460	$420	$360	$310	$260	$220

ARMALITE, INC.

Current manufacturer located in Geneseo, IL. New manufacture began in 1995 after Eagle Arms, Inc. purchased the Armalite trademarks. The Armalite trademark was originally used by Armalite (no relation to Armalite, Inc.) during mfg. in Costa Mesa, CA, approx. 1959-1973 (see Armalite listing above). Dealer direct sales.

RIFLES: BOLT ACTION

AR-30M - .300 Win. Mag. or .338 Lapua cal., scaled down AR-50, repeater, w/o muzzle brake, detachable mag. While advertising during 2001, this model has yet to make it into production.

Grading	100%	98%	95%	90%	80%	70%	60%

AR-50 - .50 BMG cal., single shot bolt action with octagonal receiver integrated into a skeletonized aluminum stock with adj. cheekpiece and recoil pad, 31 in. tapered barrel w/o sights and sophisticated muzzle brake (reduces felt recoil to approx. .243 Win. cal.), removable buttstock, single stage trigger, 33.2 lbs. New 1999.

	MSR	$2,615		$2,300	$1,950	$1,750	$1,575	$1,400	$1,225	$1,100

Plans are underway to develop a true left-hand action in this model.

RIFLES: SEMI-AUTO

All Armalite semi-auto rifles have a limited lifetime warranty.

Add $100 for stainless steel barrel on those AR-10 models which are available with that option.

Add $100 for black stock, forearm, and pistol grip where applicable.

AR-10 SERIES - .243 Win. (new 1998) or .308 Win. cal., semi-auto paramilitary design, various configurations, with or w/o sights and carry handle, choice of green or black (new 1999) finish, supplied with two 10 shot mags. New late 1995.

* ✷ *AR-10B Rifle* - .308 Win. cal., patterned after the early Armalite AR-10 rifle, featuring tapered M16 handguards, pistol grip, shortened buttstock, distinctive charging bolt on top inside of carry handle (cannot be scoped), original brown color, 20 in. barrel, 9½ lbs. New 1999.

	MSR	$1,635		$1,450	$1,200	$1,050	$950	$875	$750	$675

Add $100 for NM trigger.

* ✷ *AR-10T Rifle* - .243 Win. or .308 Win. cal., features 24 in. chrome-moly 1:11.25 twist heavy barrel, two-stage NM trigger, smooth fiberglass handguard tube, Picatinny rail, w/o sights or carry handle, 10.4 lbs.

	MSR	$2,080		$1,825	$1,525	$1,275	$1,075	$995	$875	$750

* ✷ *AR-10T Carbine* - .308 Win. cal., similar to AR-10T Rifle, except has 16 in. standard barrel and match trigger, 8½ lbs.

	MSR	$2,080		$1,825	$1,525	$1,275	$1,075	$995	$875	$750

* ✷ *AR-10A4 SPR (Special Purpose Rifle)* - .243 Win. or .308 Win. cal., features 20 in. chrome-lined 1:12 twist H-Bar barrel, removable front sight, Picatinny rail, w/o carry handle, approx. 9 lbs.

	MSR	$1,383		$1,225	$995	$850	$775	$675	$595	$525

* ✷ *AR-10A4 Carbine* - .308 Win. cal., similar to AR-10A4 Rifle, except has 16 in. barrel, 8.4 lbs.

	MSR	$1,383		$1,225	$995	$850	$775	$675	$595	$525

* ✷ *AR-10A2 Infantry Model Rifle* - .243 Win. or .308 Win. cal., features 20 in. chrome-lined 1:12 twist H-Bar barrel, includes fixed sights and carry handle, 9.4 lbs.

	MSR	$1,435		$1,175	$995	$850	$750	$675	$595	$525

* ✷ *AR-10A2 Carbine* - .308 Win. cal., similar to AR-10A2 Rifle, except has 16 in. barrel, 8.7 lbs.

	MSR	$1,435		$1,175	$995	$850	$750	$675	$595	$525

M15 RIFLE/CARBINE VARIATIONS - .223 Rem. cal., various configurations, barrel lengths, sights, and other features.

* ✷ *M15A2 National Match Rifle* - features 20 in. stainless steel NM sleeved 1:8 twist barrel with National Match sights and NM two-stage trigger, grooved barrel shroud, 9 lbs.

	MSR	$1,435		$1,225	$1,025	$850	$750	$675	$595	$525

This model is also available with black stock, forearm, and pistol grip at no extra charge.

Grading	100%	98%	95%	90%	80%	70%	60%

✹ M15A2 Golden Eagle - similiar to M15A2 National Match Rifle, except has 20 in. heavy barrel, 9.4 lbs. Limited mfg. 1998 only.

	$1,200	$975	$850	$750	$675	$595	$525

Last MSR was $1,350.

✹ M15A2 Service Rifle - includes 20 in. chrome-lined 1:9 twist barrel, fixed sights and carrying handle, grooved barrel shroud, 8.2 lbs.

MSR	$935		$825	$700	$625	$550	$500	$450	$415

✹ M15A2 Carbine - similar to M15A2 Service Rifle, except has 16 in. barrel, 7 lbs.

MSR	$935		$825	$700	$625	$550	$500	$450	$415

✹ M15A4 SPR (Special Purpose Rifle) - includes 20 in. chrome-lined H-Bar 1:9 twist barrel with National Match sights, Picatinny rail, detachable carry handle, grooved barrel shroud, 7.9 lbs.

MSR	$900		$815	$695	$635	$575	$500	$450	$415

✹ M15A4 Carbine - similar to M15A4 Special Purpose Rifle, except has 16 in. barrel, 7 lbs.

MSR	$900		$815	$695	$635	$575	$500	$450	$415

✹ M4A1C Carbine - features 16 in. chrome-lined 1:9 twist heavy barrel with National Match sights and detachable carrying handle, grooved barrel shroud, 7 lbs. Disc. 1997.

	$840	$725	$640	$560	$500	$450	$415

Last MSR was $935.

✹ M4C Carbine - similar to M4A1C Carbine, except has non-removable carrying handle and fixed sights, 7 lbs. Disc. 1997.

	$785	$675	$600	$550	$500	$450	$415

Last MSR was $870.

✹ M15A4T Rifle (Eagle Eye) - 24 in. stainless steel 1:8 twist heavy barrel, two-stage trigger, smooth fiberglass hand guard, Picatinny front sight rail but w/o sights and carrying handle, 9.2 lbs.

MSR	$1,383		$1,225	$995	$850	$775	$675	$595	$525

✹ M15A4T Carbine (Eagle Eye) - features 16 in. stainless steel 1:9 twist heavy barrel, Picatinny rail, smooth fiberglass handguard tube, two-stage trigger, 7.1 lbs. New 1997.

MSR	$1,383		$1,225	$995	$850	$775	$675	$595	$525

✹ M15A4 Predator - similar to M15A4T Eagle Eye, except has 1:12 twist barrel. Disc. 1996.

	$1,215	$985	$850	$750	$675	$595	$525

Last MSR was $1,350.

✹ M15A4 Action Master - includes 20 in. stainless steel 1:9 twist barrel, two-stage trigger, muzzle brake, Picatinny flat top design w/o sights or carrying handle, 9 lbs. Disc. 1997.

	$1,050	$900	$800	$700	$625	$565	$500

Last MSR was $1,175.

✴ AR-180B - .223 Rem. cal., incorporates the best features of the M15 (lower group with trigger and mag. well) and early AR-180 (gas system allowing operating gases to be kept outside the receiver) rifles, barrel has Armalite's new integral muzzle brake. While advertising during 2001, this model has yet to go into production.

Grading	100%	98%	95%	90%	80%	70%	60%

ARMAMENT TECHNOLOGY

Current manufacturer located in Halifax, Nova Scotia, Canada since 1988. Direct consumer sales.

A⊤rmament Technology

RIFLES: BOLT-ACTION

AT1-C24 TACTICAL RIFLE - .308 Win. or .300 Win. Mag. (disc. 2000) cal., similar to AT1-M24, except has detachable mag., adj. cheekpiece and buttstock for LOP, includes 3.5-10X 30mm tactical scope and Mil-Spec shipping case, ½" MOA guaranteed, 14.9 lbs. New 1998.

MSR	$4,195		$4,095	$3,650	$2,775	$2,250	$1,825	$1,500	$1,275

AT1-C24B TACTICAL RIFLE - .308 Win. cal., similar to AT1-C24, except is not available in left-hand, 15.9 lbs. New 2001.

MSR	$4,695		$4,250	$3,750	$2,850	$2,300	$1,850	$1,525	$1,300

AT1-M24 TACTICAL RIFLE - .223 Rem. (new 1998), .308 Win., or .300 Win. Mag. (disc. 2000) cal., bolt action, tactical rifle with competition tuned right-hand or left-hand Rem. 700 action, stainless steel barrel, Kevlar reinforced fiberglass stock, Harris bipod, matte black finish, competition trigger, ½" MOA guaranteed, 14.9 lbs.

MSR	$4,495		$4,350	$3,850	$2,850	$2,350	$1,900	$1,600	$1,350

ARMAMENT TECHNOLOGY CORP.

Previous manufacturer located in Las Vegas, NV between 1972-1978.

RIFLES: SEMI-AUTO

In addition to the models listed below, ATC also manufactured a select fire pistol named "Firefly II".

MODEL 4 POCKET RIFLE - .22 LR cal., semi-auto action (supplied by Mossberg), 5 in. barrel, shortened rifle (18½ in. overall length) with cut stock, 7 shot mag., approx. 450 mfg., approx. 3 lbs.

			$350	$295	$260	$230	$195	$175	$150

MODEL 6 - full length variation of the Model 4, Mossberg Model 453-T with ATC trademarks, approx. 12 mfg., approx. 5½ lbs.

			$125	$100	$85	$75	$65	$55	$45

M-2 FIREFLY - 9mm Para. cal., featured a unique gas delayed blowback action, paramilitary configuration, collapsible stock, very limited mfg., 4¾ lbs.

			$695	$625	$550	$475	$395	$350	$295

ARMAS AZOR, S.A.

Previous manufacturer of double rifles located in Eibar, Spain. Previously imported 1994-97 by Armes De Chasse located in Hertford, NC.

RIFLES: SxS, SIDELOCK

The models listed below are English styled sidelock double rifles. Gold inlay and custom engraving prices were quoted per individual request.

AFRICA MARK I - available in most cals. between 9.3 X 74R and .375 H&H, nominal engraving and select grade wood.

Previous retail prices ranged between $8,000-$10,000.

Grading	100%	98%	95%	90%	80%	70%	60%

AFRICA MARK II - available in most cals. between 9.3 X 74R and .375 H&H, African game scene engraving and superior grade wood.

  Previous retail prices ranged between $10,000-$12,000.

AFRICA MARK III - available in most cals. between 9.3 X 74R and .470 NE Mag., intricate scroll engraving, cartridge trap, top tang, and superior quality grade wood.

  Previous retail prices ranged between $13,000-$18,000.

SHOTGUNS: SxS, SIDELOCK

SIDELOCK MODEL - 12 ga.-.410 bore, English style sidelock game gun.

	$3,275	$2,700	$2,200	$1,750	$1,500	$1,250	$995

Last MSR was $3,500.

ARMES DE CHASSE LLC

Current importer and distributor located in Hertford, NC.

SHOTGUNS: SxS

ALBEMARLE GAME GUN - 12, 16 (special order only), 20, 28 ga., or .410 bore (new 2001), H&H style detachable sidelock action, Purdey style bolt, DT with articulated front trigger, 26, 27, or 28 in. barrels with concave solid rib, ejectors, checkered English stock and forearm (base price includes custom stock dimensions), extensive lockplate engraving, 5¾ (20 ga.) or 6 7/8 (12 ga.) lbs. Allow 5-6 months for delivery. Spanish importation began late 1999.

MSR	$2,195	$2,050	$1,800	$1,500	$1,200	$995	$875	$775

  Add $1,050 for extra set of barrels.
  Add $630 for Grade A option.
  Add $1,330 for Grade A black and gold option (new 2000).

ARMES PIERRE ARTISAN ETS.

Current manufacturer located in St. Bonnet Le Chateau, France.

  Armes Pierre Artisan manufactures high quality double rifles and shotguns on a custom order basis. Please contact the factory directly for more information, including a price quotation, delivery time, and available options.

ARMINEX LTD.

Previous manufacturer located in Scottsdale, AZ.

PISTOLS: SEMI-AUTO

TRI-FIRE - .45 ACP cal., single action auto, interchangeable barrels allow caliber conversion. Available in 5, 6, or 7 (disc. 1984) in. stainless barrel lengths, no grip safety, steel frame construction, ambidextrous thumb safety (on Target and Presentation only), smooth walnut grips, 38 oz. Approx. 400 mfg. between 1981-85.

	$750	$650	$475	$400	$375	$350	$325

Last MSR was $396.

  Add $50 if presentation cased.
  Add approx. $130/conversion unit.

* *Target Model* - same specifications as Tri-Fire, except has 6 or 7 (disc. 1984) in. barrel. Very limited mfg.

	$850	$725	$550	$450	$400	$360	$330

Last MSR was $448.

Grading	100%	98%	95%	90%	80%	70%	60%

ARMINIUS

Current trademark of revolvers manufactured by Weihrach, located in Mellrickstadt, Germany. No current U.S. importation. Previously manufactured in Zella-Mehlis, Germany beginning c. 1922-mid 1970s.

PISTOLS: SINGLE SHOT

MODEL 1 - .22 LR cal., target model, adj. sights.

	100%	98%	95%	90%	80%	70%	60%
	$275	$210	$195	$165	$155	$140	$110

MODEL 2 - similar to Model 1, except has set trigger.

	100%	98%	95%	90%	80%	70%	60%
	$340	$255	$225	$190	$170	$155	$140

REVOLVERS

Currently manufactured Arminius revolvers are not individually listed, since they are not currently imported into the U.S. There are however, many models, including combat, sport, and target variations. Calibers include .22 LR. .22 Mag., .32 S&W Wadcutter, .357 Mag., and .38 Spl.

MODEL 3 - .25 ACP cal., folding trigger, hammerless.

	100%	98%	95%	90%	80%	70%	60%
	$175	$135	$125	$105	$100	$90	$80

MODEL 8 - .320 Revolver cal., folding trigger, hammerless.

	100%	98%	95%	90%	80%	70%	60%
	$175	$135	$125	$105	$100	$90	$80

MODEL 9 - .32 ACP cal.

	100%	98%	95%	90%	80%	70%	60%
	$185	$140	$130	$115	$105	$95	$85

MODEL 10 - .32 ACP cal., hammerless.

	100%	98%	95%	90%	80%	70%	60%
	$165	$125	$120	$100	$95	$85	$75

TARGET - .22 LR cal.

	100%	98%	95%	90%	80%	70%	60%
	$90	$70	$65	$55	$50	$45	$45

ARMITAGE INTERNATIONAL, LTD.

Previous manufacturer until 1990 located in Seneca, SC.

PISTOLS: SEMI-AUTO

SCARAB SKORPION - 9mm Para. Cal., paramilitary design patterned after the Czech Model 61, direct blow back action, 4.63 in. barrel, matte black finish, 12 shot (standard) or 32 shot (optional) mag., 3.5 lbs. Mfg. in U.S. 1989-90 only.

	100%	98%	95%	90%	80%	70%	60%
	$550	$475	$400	$350	$300	$260	$230

Last MSR was $400.

Add $45 for threaded flash hider or imitation suppressor.

Only 602 Scarab Skorpions were manufactured during 1989-90.

ARMS CORPORATION OF THE PHILIPPINES

Please refer to the Armscor listing in this section.

ARMS MORAVIA LTD.

Current European importer/exporter of firearms and accessories located in Ostrava, Czech Republic. Previously imported into the United States by Anderson & Richardson Arms Co., located in Ft. Worth, TX until 2001.

Arms Moravia Ltd. exports a wide variety of European trademarks, including their own (PS 97 & Z-75 semi-auto pistols).

ARMS RESEARCH ASSOCIATES

Previous manufacturer until 1991, located in Stone Park, IL.

CARBINES: SEMI-AUTO

KF SYSTEM - 9mm Para. cal., paramilitary design carbine, 18½ in. barrel, vent. barrel shroud, 20 or 36 shot mag., matte black finish, 7½ lbs., select fire-class III transferable only.

| | $395 | $350 | $300 | $275 | $250 | $230 | $210 |

Last MSR was $379.

ARMS TECH LTD.

Previous manufacturer located in Phoenix, AZ 1987-1998.

RIFLES: SEMI-AUTO

SUPER MATCH INTERDICTION POLICE MODEL - .243 Win., .300 Win. Mag., or .308 Win. (standard) cal., features 22 in. free floating Schnieder or Douglas air gauged stainless steel barrel, gas operation, McMillan stock, updated trigger group, detachable box mag., 13¼ lbs. Limited mfg. 1996-98.

| | $4,550 | $4,050 | $3,675 | $3,300 | $3,000 | $2,500 | $2,000 |

Last MSR was $4,800.

ARMSCOR

Current trademark of firearms manufactured by Arms Corporation of the Philippines (manufacturing began 1952) established in 1995. Currently imported and distributed by Armscor Precision International (full line), located in Las Vegas, NV beginning 2001, and by K.B.I., Inc. (paramilitary style rifles only) located in Harrisburg, PA beginning 1995. Previously imported by Ruko located in Buffalo, NY until 1995 and by Armscorp Precision Inc. located in San Mateo, CA until 1991.

In 1991, the importation of Arms Corporation of the Philippines firearms was changed to Ruko Products, Inc., located in Buffalo, NY. Barrel markings on firearms imported by Ruko Products, Inc. state "Ruko-Armscor" instead of the older "Armscorp Precision" barrel markings. All Armscorp Precision, Inc. models were discontinued in 1991.

The models listed below also provide cross-referencing for older Armscorp Precision and Ruko imported models.

PISTOLS: SEMI-AUTO

M-1911-A1 STANDARD - .45 ACP cal., patterned after the Colt Govt. Model, 7 shot mag. (2 provided), 5 in. barrel, parkerized (disc. 2001), blued (new 2002), two-tone (new 2002), or stainless steel (new 2002), skeletonized combat hammer and trigger, front and rear slide serrations, hard rubber grips, 38 oz. Imported 1996-97, reintroduced 2001.

| MSR | $399 | | $350 | $300 | $280 | $260 | $240 | $220 | $200 |

Add $31 for two-tone finish.
Add $75 for stainless steel.

This model is also available in a high capacity configuration (Model 1911-A2 HC, 12 shot mag., $519 MSR) for law enforcement only.

Grading	100%	98%	95%	90%	80%	70%	60%

M-1911-A1 COMMANDER - .45 ACP cal., Commander configuration with 4 in. barrel, otherwise similar to M-1911 A1 Standard, rear slide serrations only. Importation began 2001.

MSR	$408	$360	$300	$280	$260	$240	$220	$200

Add $37 for two-tone finish.
Add $90 for stainless steel.

M-1911-A1 CS COMBAT - .45 ACP cal., Combat configuration with 3½ in. barrel, checkered hardwood grips, 2.16 lbs. Importation began 2002.

MSR	$423	$370	$310	$285	$265	$245	$220	$200

Add $52 for two-tone finish.
Add $105 for stainless steel.

M-1911-A1 MEDALLION SERIES - 9mm Para., .40 S&W, or .45 ACP cal., 5 in. barrel, customized model including many shooting enhancements, match barrel, hand fitted slide and frame, choice of checkered wood or Pachmayr grips, available in either Standard or Tactical variation, blue finish standard. Importation began 2002.

MSR	$539	$445	$350	$310	$285	$260	$240	$220

Add $129 for Tactical Model, add $198 for Tactical Model two-tone, or $203 for Tactical Model chrome.

REVOLVERS

MODEL 200 (DC) REVOLVER - .38 Spl. cal., 6 shot, double action, 2½ (importation disc.), 4 (new 1998) or 6 (new 1998, importation disc.) in. barrel with shroud, transfer bar safety, combat style rubber grips, blue finish only, fixed rear sight, 26 oz. Imported 1996-99, reintroduced 2001.

MSR	$166	$145	$125	$105	$90	$75	$65	$60

Add approx. $6 for 4 in. barrel or $16 for 6 in. barrel.

MODEL 202 REVOLVER - similar to Model 200, except does not have barrel shroud. Importation began 2001.

MSR	$156	$135	$115	$100	$85	$75	$65	$60

MODEL 206 REVOLVER - similar to Model 200, except has 2 7/8 in. barrel, 24 oz. Importation began 2001.

MSR	$180	$160	$125	$105	$90	$75	$65	$60

MODEL 210 REVOLVER - similar to Model 200, except has 4 in. VR barrel, and adj. rear sight, 28 oz. Importation began 2001.

MSR	$196	$175	$150	$125	$105	$90	$75	$65

RIFLES: BOLT ACTION

M12Y/12-TY - .22 LR cal., bolt action, single shot, youth model with 18 3/8 in. barrel. Imported 1997 only, reintroduced during 2001.

	$95	$80	$70	$60	$50	$40	$35

Last MSR was $109.

M-14P - .22 LR cal., bolt action, 10 shot mag., 23 in. barrel, open sights, 6 lbs. Disc. 1997.

	$95	$75	$60	$50	$45	$40	$35

Last MSR was $129.

A youth model was also available with shorter dimensions at no extra charge (M-14Y).

* **M14-D** - .22 LR cal., bolt action, similar to M-14P, except has adj. rear sight and checkered mahogany stock. Importation disc. 1995.

	$105	$85	$70	$60	$50	$45	$40

Last MSR was $139.

Grading	100%	98%	95%	90%	80%	70%	60%

M-20 - .22 LR cal., 10 shot mag., deluxe checkered hardwood stock and forend, blue or stainless steel. Importation began 2002.

	MSR	$245		$205	$155	$110	$85	$70	$60	$55

Add $15 for stainless steel construction (new 2002).

M-1400LW - .22 LR cal., similar action to M-14P, except has checkered stock and Schnabel forend, 10 shot mag., hard rubber pad, 6 lbs. Imported 1990-92.

	$185	$165	$150	$135	$120	$105	$95

Last MSR was $219.

✳ **M-1400S** - .22 LR cal., similar to M-1500(S), except has 10 shot mag., 6.7 lbs. Imported 1996-97.

	$175	$125	$100	$75	$65	$55	$50

Last MSR was $224.

✳ **M-1400 (SC-Super Classic)** - .22 LR cal., otherwise similar to M-1500SC, except has 10 shot mag. and 23 in. barrel, 6 lbs. Imported 1990-97, reintroduced 2001.

MSR	$242		$200	$150	$110	$85	$70	$60	$55

Add $18 for stainless steel construction (new 2002).

M-1500S - .22 Mag. cal., deluxe bolt action, 5 shot mag., 21½ or 22 5/8 in. barrel, checkered mahogany stock, open sights, 7 lbs. Disc. 1997, reintroduced 2001.

	$145	$125	$110	$95	$85	$75	$65

Last MSR was $160.

✳ **Model 1500LW (Lightweight)** - similar to Model M-1500, except has lightweight classic European styled stock made of checkered American Walnut, with buttpad. Imported 1990-92.

	$190	$170	$150	$135	$120	$105	$95

Last MSR was $229.

✳ **M-1500 (SC-Super Classic)** - checkered American Walnut stock with hard rubber pad and Monte Carlo cheekpiece, hardwood forend tip, engine turned bolt, 7 lbs. Imported 1990-97, reintroduced 2001.

MSR	$260		$215	$165	$120	$100	$85	$70	$60

Subtract $3 for stainless steel.

M-1800S (CLASSIC) - .22 Hornet cal., 5 shot mag., double locking lugs, checkered hardwood stock, adj. rear sight, 6.6 lbs. Imported 1996-97.

	$250	$225	$200	$180	$165	$150	$135

Last MSR was $358.

✳ **M-1800SC (Super Classic)** - similar to M-1800S, except has checkered walnut stock with forend tip, and high polish bluing, 7¼ lbs. Imported 1996-97, reintroduced during 2001.

	$285	$260	$240	$220	$200	$185	$170

Last MSR was $323.

RIFLES: SEMI-AUTO

M-1600 - .22 LR cal., semi-auto, 10 or 15 (disc.) shot mag., 18 in. barrel, copy of the Armalite M16, ebony stock, 5¼ lbs.

MSR	$205		$170	$130	$100	$80	$65	$55	$50

✳ **M-1600R** - similar to M-1600, except has stainless steel retractable buttstock and vent. barrel hood, 7¼ lbs. Importation disc. 1995.

	$155	$115	$95	$75	$65	$55	$50

Last MSR was $199.

Grading	100%	98%	95%	90%	80%	70%	60%

M-20P - .22 LR cal., semi-auto, 15 shot mag., 20¾ in. barrel, open sights, 5½ lbs. Disc. 1997, reintroduced during 2001

	$100	$80	$60	$50	$45	$40	$35

Last MSR was $120.

✴ *M-20C* - similar to Model M-20P, except has carbine style stock, barrel band, and curved steel buttplate, 16½ in. barrel, 5¼ lbs. Previously available from K.B.I. only, disc. 2001.

	$130	$100	$80	$60	$50	$45	$40

Last MSR was $159.

✴ *M-20D* - .22 LR cal., 21 in. barrel, 10 or 15 shot mag., checkered hardwood stock and forend, 6½ lbs. Importation began 2002.

MSR	$245	$205	$155	$110	$85	$70	$60	$55

Add $15 for stainless steel construction (new 2002).

M-2000(S) - same specifications as M-20P, except has checkered mahogany stock and adj. rear sight. Disc. 1997.

	$140	$120	$95	$75	$60	$55	$50

Last MSR was $213.

✴ *M-2000SC (Super Classic)* - similar to M-2000, except has checkered American Walnut stock with cheekpiece and hardwood forend tip, engine turned bolt, 6 lbs. Imported 1990-97.

	$270	$215	$175	$140	$110	$95	$85

Last MSR was $340.

MODEL M-50S - .22 LR cal., semi-auto design, 16½ in. shrouded barrel, 25 or 30 shot mag., uncheckered mahogany stock, 6½ lbs. Disc. 1995.

	$155	$115	$95	$75	$65	$50	$45

Last MSR was $209.

M-AK22(S) - .22 LR cal., semi-auto, copy of the famous Russian Kalashnikov AK-47 rifle, 18½ in. barrel, 10 or 15 (disc.) shot mag., mahogany stock and forearm, 7 lbs.

MSR	$224	$185	$165	$145	$120	$95	$85	$80

✴ *M-AK22(F)* - similar to M-AK22, except has metal folding stock, and 30 shot mag. Disc. 1995.

	$275	$225	$185	$150	$115	$95	$80

Last MSR was $299.

SHOTGUNS: SLIDE ACTION

MODEL M30 F (INTERCHANGEABLE CHOKES) - 12 ga. only, 28 in. plain barrel with 3 choke tubes, 5 shot mag., uncheckered stock and forearm. Disc. 1999.

	$225	$190	$160	$140	$120	$95	$85

Last MSR was $269.

✴ *Model M30 D/IC (Deluxe)* - similar to Model M30 IC, except has checkered walnut stock and forearm with recoil pad. Importation reintroduced during 2001 only.

	$180	$155	$125	$110	$95	$85	$75

Last MSR was $208.

M-30 DG (DEER GUN) - 12 ga. only, law enforcement version of Model M30, 20 in. plain barrel, iron sights, 7 shot mag., approx. 7 lbs. Disc. 1999, reintroduced during 2001.

	$165	$140	$120	$100	$85	$75	$70

Last MSR was $195.

Grading	100%	98%	95%	90%	80%	70%	60%

M-30SAS1 - 12 ga. only, riot configuration with 20 in. barrel and vent. barrel shroud, and speedfeed 4 shot (disc.) or regular synthetic buttstock and forearm, 6 shot mag., matte finish, 8 lbs. Mfg. 1996-99, reintroduced 2001.

	MSR	$211	$180	$155	$130	$110	$95	$85	$75

Add $56 for Speedfeed stock (new 2002).

M-30F/FS - 12 ga. only, 28 in. barrel, fixed mod. choke. Disc. 1999, reintroduced 2001.

	MSR	$211	$180	$155	$130	$110	$95	$85	$75

M-30 R6/R8 (RIOT) - 12 ga. only, similar to Model M30DG, except has front bead sight only, 5 or 7 shot mag., cyl. bore. Disc. 1999, reintroduced 2001.

	MSR	$181	$155	$135	$110	$90	$80	$75	$70

Add $7 for 7 shot mag.

MODEL M30 C (COMBO) - 12 ga., 20 in. barrel, 5 shot mag., unique detachable black synthetic buttstock that separates, allowing pistol grip only operation. Disc. 1995.

$210	$175	$145	$120	$100	$90	$80

Last MSR was $289.

MODEL M30 RP (COMBO) - 12 ga. only, same action as M-30 DG, interchangeable black pistol grip, 18¼ in. plain barrel w/front bead sight, 6¼ lbs. Disc. 1995.

$210	$175	$145	$120	$100	$90	$80

Last MSR was $289.

ARMSCORP USA, INC.

Current manufacturer and importer located in Baltimore, MD. Dealer direct sales only.

PISTOLS: SEMI-AUTO

HI POWER - 9mm Para. cal., patterned after Browning design, 4 2/3 in. barrel, military finish, 13 shot mag., synthetic checkered grips, spur hammer, 2 lbs. mfg. in Argentina, imported 1989-90 only,

$395	$350	$295	$275	$250	$225	$200

Last MSR was $450.

Add $15 for round hammer.
Add $50 for hard chrome finish w/combat grips (disc. 1989).

* ***Compact Detective HP*** - similar to Hi Power, except has 3½ in. barrel, 1.9 lbs. Mfg. 1989 only.

$395	$350	$295	$275	$250	$225	$200

Last MSR was $475.

SD-9 - 9mm Para. cal., double action only, blowback mechanism, 3.07 in. barrel, 6 shot mag., frame is fabricated mostly of heavy gauge sheet metal stampings, chamber indicator, limited Israeli mfg., 1½ lbs. Imported 1989-90 only.

$350	$250	$230	$210	$195	$180	$170

Last MSR was $350.

This pistol has also been manufactured by Sirkis Industries - refer to their section in this text.

P22 - .22 LR cal., patterned after the Colt Woodsman, 4 or 6 in. barrel, 10 shot mag., checkered wood grips, mfg. in Argentina. Imported 1989-90 only.

$190	$150	$130	$115	$100	$95	$85

Last MSR was $225.

Grading	100%	98%	95%	90%	80%	70%	60%

RIFLES: SEMI-AUTO

M-14 RIFLE (NORINCO PARTS) - .308 Win. cal., 20 shot mag., newly mfg. M-14 using Norinco parts, wood stock. Mfg. 1991-92 only.

	$875	$800	$725	$650	$550	$450	$375

Last MSR was $688.

M-14R RIFLE (USGI PARTS) - .308 Win. cal., 10 (C/B 1994) or 20* shot mag., newly manufactured M-14 using original excellent condition forged G.I. parts including USGI fiberglass stock with rubber recoil pad. New 1986.

MSR	$1,695	$1,475	$1,275	$1,075	$950	$825	$700	$550

Add $100 for medium weight National Match walnut stock (M-14RNS).
Add $25 for G.I. buttplate (disc.).
Add $45 for USGI birch stock (Model M-14RNSB, disc.).

M-14 BEGINNING NATIONAL MATCH - .308 Win. cal., mfg. from hand selected older USGI parts, except for new receiver and new USGI air gauged premium barrel, guaranteed to shoot 1¼ in. group at 100 yards. Mfg. 1993-96.

	$1,750	$1,350	$1,050	$925	$825	$725	$625

Last MSR was $1,950.

M-14 NMR (NATIONAL MATCH) - .308 Win. cal., built in accordance with A.M.T.U. mil. specs., 3 different barrel weights to choose from, NM rear sight system, calibrated mag., leather sling, guaranteed 1" MOA. New 1987.

MSR	$2,795	$2,400	$1,850	$1,500	$1,150	$950	$825	$700

M-21 MATCH RIFLE - .308 Win. cal., NM rear lugged receiver, choice of McMillan fiberglass or laminated wood stock, guaranteed 1" MOA.

MSR	$3,395	$3,075	$2,450	$1,925	$1,650	$1,300	$995	$825

T-48 FAL ISRAELI PATTERN RIFLE - .308 Win. cal., mfg. in the U.S. to precise original metric dimensions (parts are interchangeable with original Belgium FAL), forged receiver, hammer forged chrome lined mil-spec. 21 in. barrel (standard or heavy) with flash suppressor, adj. front sight, aperture rear sight, 10 lbs. Imported 1990-92.

	$1,225	$1,050	$925	$775	$625	$525	$465

Last MSR was $1,244.

This model was guaranteed to shoot within 2.5 MOA with match ammunition.

　❊ *T-48 FAL L1A1 Pattern* - .308 Win. cal., fully enclosed forend with vents, 10 lbs. Imported 1992 only.

	$1,225	$1,050	$925	$775	$625	$525	$465

Last MSR was $1,181.

Add $122 for wood handguard sporter model (limited supply).

T-48 BUSH MODEL - similar to T-48 FAL, except has 18 in. barrel, 9¾ lbs. Mfg. 1990 only.

	$1,225	$1,050	$925	$775	$625	$525	$465

Last MSR was $1,250.

FRHB - .308 Win. cal., Israeli mfg. with heavy barrel and bipod. Imported 1990 only.

	$1,725	$1,450	$1,150	$975	$875	$795	$725

Last MSR was $1,895.

Grading	100%	98%	95%	90%	80%	70%	60%

FAL - .308 Win. cal., Armscorp forged receiver, 21 in. Argentinian rebuilt barrel, manufactured to military specs., supplied with one military 20 shot mag., aperture rear sight, 10 lbs. Mfg. 1987-89.

| | $1,225 | $1,050 | $925 | $775 | $625 | $525 | $465 |

Last MSR was $875.

Subtract $55 if without flash hider.
Add $75 for heavy barrel with bipod (14 lbs.).
Add $400 (last retail) for .22 LR conversion kit.
This model was guaranteed to shoot within 2.5 MOA with match ammunition.

* **FAL Bush Model** - similar to FAL, except has 18 in. barrel with flash suppressor, 9¾ lbs. Mfg. 1989 only.

| | $2,100 | $1,900 | $1,800 | $1,700 | $1,500 | $1,250 | $1,000 |

Last MSR was $900.

* **FAL Para Model** - similar to FAL Bush Model, except has metal folding stock, leaf rear sight. Mfg. 1989 only.

| | $2,450 | $2,150 | $1,950 | $1,800 | $1,600 | $1,475 | $1,250 |

Last MSR was $930.

* **FAL Factory Rebuilt** - factory (Argentine) rebuilt FAL without flash suppressor in excellent condition with Armscorp forged receiver, 9 lbs. 10 oz. Disc. 1989.

| | $1,475 | $1,250 | $995 | $825 | $750 | $575 | $495 |

Last MSR was $675.

Add 20% for heavy barrel variation manufactured in Argentina under license from F.N.

M36 ISRAELI SNIPER RIFLE - .308 Win. cal., gas operated semi-auto, Bullpup configuration, 22 in. free floating barrel, Armscorp M14 receiver, 20 shot mag., includes flash suppressor and bipod, 10 lbs. Civilian offering 1989 only.

| | $2,900 | $2,500 | $2,275 | $2,050 | $1,900 | $1,775 | $1,600 |

Last MSR was $3,000.

EXPERT MODEL - .22 LR cal., semi-auto, 20.9 in. barrel, 10 shot mag., wood stock with one-screw takedown, iron sights with grooved receiver, 5.1 lbs. New 1989.

| | $195 | $150 | $125 | $115 | $105 | $95 | $85 |

Last MSR was $225.

ARMSPORT, INC.

Previous importer and distributor located in Miami, FL. Armsport imported shotguns (various configurations, mfg by Sarsilmaz of Turkey) until 2000. Armsport, Inc. imported a revolver and offered a complete line of accessories (snap caps, scope rings, and cleaning kits).

For a complete listing of older Armsport, Inc. models, please refer to the 20th - 21st Editions of the Blue Book of Gun Values. This older information is also available online at www.bluebookinc.com.

REVOLVERS

4540 - .38 Spl. cal., single or double action, 6 shot, 4 in. VR barrel with fixed sight, blued finish, checkered grips, approx. 32 oz. Imported 1999-2000.

| | $125 | $95 | $85 | $75 | $70 | $65 | $60 |

Last MSR was $140.

Grading	100%	98%	95%	90%	80%	70%	60%

ARNOLD ARMS CO., INC.

Previous rifle manufacturer located in Arlington, WA 1994-2001.

In addition to making a series of accurate rifles built on their own Apollo action, Arnold Arms Co. also built rifles on Remington, Ruger, Sako, or Winchester actions. All Arnold Arms rifles had a written guarantee on accuracy (½ in. group or less at 100 yards with handloads), and a 5 year limited warranty. Any Arnold Arms warranty is now void. The company also made proprietary cartridges in 6mm Arnold, .257 Arnold, .270 Arnold, .300 Arnold, .338 Arnold, or .458 Arnold.

RIFLES: BOLT ACTION

Arnold Arms Co., Inc. made a wide variety of quality bolt action rifles, including the African Trophy, Grand African Rifle, Alaskan Series, Classic Hunter Series, Neutralizer Series, Varminter Series, and the Strike Viper Series. For more information and pricing on these custom rifles, please visit www.bluebookinc.com.

ARRIETA, S.L.

Current manufacturer located in Elgoibar, Spain. Currently imported by several importers including New England Arms Corp., Wingshooting Adventures, Quality Arms, Griffin & Howe, and Orvis (see separate listing).

More information can be obtained on the Arrieta models listed below by contacting the importers listed above.

RIFLES: SxS

R-1 - 7x65R, 8x57JRS, or 9.3x74R cal., true sidelock, ejectors, quarter rib barrel with express rear sight.

MSR	$10,170		$9,350	$7,400	$6,200	$5,250	$4,700	$4,000	$3,450

R-2 - similar to R-1, except has more elaborate H&H style engraving, elongated tangs, and choice of English or reinforced pistol grip with metal cap, ejectors.

MSR	$14,490		$12,900	$10,450	$9,250	$7,950	$6,850	$5,900	$4,950

R-3 - similar to R-1, except includes .375 H&H or .470 NE cal.

MSR	$16,500		$14,750	$12,500	$9,950	$8,950	$7,850	$6,850	$5,900

SHOTGUNS: SxS

The models listed below are essentially custom ordered per individual specifications - delivery time is approx. 10-14 months.

All Arrieta shotguns have frames scaled to individual gauges. Standard gauges are 12 & 16. Many factory upgrades and custom options/special orders are available from the individual importers – please contact them directly for availability and current pricing on these special orders.

On the models listed below, there are 4 different types of sidelock actions. One is used on the Model 550. Another is used on Models 557, 578, and 871. A third is used on Models 590 and 595 (designed for heavy use). Finally, the best quality is used on Models 600-903, except for Model 900 (557 action), and Model 871. All Arrieta actions are assisted opening, except the Models 557, 570, 578, and 871.

Additionally, some special order, non-cataloged models, including Ligera, 590 Regina, 595 Principe, 871 Extra Finish, and Renaissance models are available directly from New England Arms. Please contact them directly for more information and current prices.

Grading	100%	98%	95%	90%	80%	70%	60%

ADD THE FOLLOWING AMOUNTS FOR CURRENTLY MANUFACTURED SHOTGUNS.
Add 5% for small gauges (20, 24, 28, 32 ga., or .410 bore).
Add approx. $750 for single trigger depending on action.
Add 5% for matched pair.
Add 10% for rounded action on standard models.
Extra barrels are priced from $1,295-$1,750/set depending on model.

557 - 12, 16, or 20 ga., Demi-Bloc steel barrels, detachable engraved sidelocks, double triggers, ejectors.

	MSR	$3,250		$2,850	$2,000	$1,500	$1,100	$900	$750	$640

570 - 12, 16, or 20 ga., similar to 560 (non-standard model), except has non- detachable sidelocks.

	MSR	$3,950		$3,475	$2,450	$1,825	$1,375	$1,075	$850	$750

578 - 12, 16, or 20 ga., similar to 570, except is fine English scrollwork engraved.

	MSR	$4,350		$3,975	$2,750	$1,950	$1,450	$1,125	$925	$850

600 - 12, 16, or 20 ga., top-of-the-line self-opening action, very ornate engraving throughout.

	MSR	$6,050		$5,275	$4,150	$3,300	$2,600	$2,150	$1,775	$1,350

601 - all gauges, sidelock action with nickel plating, ejectors, SST, self- opening action, border engraving.

	MSR	$6,925		$6,250	$5,175	$4,300	$3,450	$2,975	$2,500	$2,000

801 - all gauges, Holland-style detachable sidelocks, self-opening action standard, ejectors, coin- wash finish, finest Churchill style engraving.

	MSR	$9,145		$8,175	$7,200	$6,325	$5,275	$4,750	$4,000	$3,450

802 - 12, 16, or 20 ga., similar to 801 only non-detachable sidelocks, finest Holland-style engraving.

	MSR	$9,135		$8,175	$7,200	$6,300	$5,275	$4,750	$4,000	$3,450

"BOSS" ROUND BODY - all gauges, Boss pattern best quality engraving, includes $1,500 wood upgrade, imported exclusively by New England Arms.

	MSR	$9,750		$9,375	$8,250	$7,150	$5,950	$5,200	$4,400	$3,600

803 - all gauges, similar to 801, finest Purdey-style engraving.

	MSR	$6,930		$6,175	$5,300	$4,175	$3,500	$2,950	$2,500	$2,000

871 - all gauges, rounded frame sidelock action with Demi-Bloc barrels, scroll engraved, ejectors, DTs.

	MSR	$5,060		$4,400	$3,425	$2,750	$2,200	$1,750	$1,450	$1,275

872 - all gauges, rounded frame sidelock action with Demi-Bloc barrels, elaborate scroll engraving with third lever fastener.

	MSR	$12,375		$10,940	$9,500	$8,200	$6,350	$5,400	$4,500	$3,600

873 - all gauges, sidelock action with Demi-Bloc barrels, game scene engraving, ejectors, SST.

	MSR	$8,200		$7,450	$5,450	$4,300	$3,550	$3,000	$2,500	$2,000

874 - all gauges, sidelock action with Demi-Bloc barrels, action is gold line engraved.

	MSR	$9,250		$8,225	$7,200	$6,200	$5,250	$4,650	$4,000	$3,450

875 - all gauges, top-of-the-line quality, built to individual customer specs. only, elaborate engraving with gold inlays.

	MSR	$14,900		$13,000	$10,650	$9,450	$8,100	$7,100	$6,000	$5,000

931 - all gauges, self-opening action, elaborate engraving, H&H selective ejectors.

	MSR	$16,480		$14,250	$11,000	$9,500	$8,300	$7,150	$6,000	$5,000

Grading	100%	98%	95%	90%	80%	70%	60%

ARRIZABALAGA, PEDRO

Current manufacturer located in Eibar, Spain since 1940. Currently imported and distributed by Harry Marx Hi-Grade Imports located in Gilroy, CA, and by New England Arms Corp. located in Kittery Point, ME. Previously imported until 2000 by Lion Country Supply located in Port Matilda, PA.

Arrizabalaga manufactures best quality guns only, carefully made to individual customer specifications. Shotguns listed below have demi-bloc, chopper lump barrels and self-opening hand- detachable locks as standard features. The models listed below are essentially custom ordered per individual specifications - delivery time is approx. 12 months.

ADD THE FOLLOWING AMOUNTS ON ARRIZABALAGA SHOTGUNS:

Add 10% for matched pair.
Add $3,500 per extra barrels.
Add 10% for 28 ga.
Add 12% for .410 bore.
Add $1,000 for single non-selective trigger.
Add $300 for pistol grip stock.

SHOTGUNS: SxS

HEAVY SCROLL MODEL - all gauges, sidelock action, elaborate engraving, deluxe oil finished stock and forearm.

MSR	$11,950	$10,800	$7,350	$5,750	$5,000	$4,350	$3,850	$3,325

ENGLISH SCROLL MODEL - all gauges, sidelock action, English scroll engraving, deluxe oil finished walnut stock and forearm.

MSR	$12,500	$11,650	$7,850	$6,000	$5,000	$4,500	$4,000	$3,450

MODEL DELUXE - all gauges, limited importation.

MSR	$12,850	$11,700	$9,000	$7,500	$6,000	$5,250	$4,500	$4,000

BOSS STYLE ROUND ACTION MODEL - all gauges, features English Boss style scroll engraving.

MSR	$12,850	$11,700	$9,000	$7,500	$6,000	$5,250	$4,500	$4,000

Add $450 for Luxe engraving.

This model is imported exclusively by New England Arms Corp.

SPECIAL MODEL - all gauges, sidelock top-of-the-line model, best quality wood and engraving.

MSR	$16,500	$15,000	$10,150	$9,000	$8,000	$7,000	$6,000	$5,000

ARSENAL, BULGARIA

Current manufacturer located in Bulgaria. Previously imported exclusively 1994-96 by Sentinel Arms located in Detroit, MI.

PISTOLS: SEMI-AUTO

MAKAROV MODEL - 9mm Makarov cal., 3 2/3 in. barrel, 8 shot mag., black synthetic grips, blued finish. Disc. 1996.

	$185	$165	$125	$115	$105	$95	$85

RIFLES: SEMI-AUTO

BULGARIAN SA-93 - 7.62x39mm cal., Kalashnikov milled action with hardwood thumbhole stock, 16.3 in. barrel, 5 shot detachable mag., 9 lbs. Disc. 1996.

	$335	$295	$250	$215	$190	$180	$170

Grading	100%	98%	95%	90%	80%	70%	60%

✳ *Bulgarian SA-93L* - 7.62x39mm cal., similar to Bulgarian SA-93 except has 20 in. barrel, with or without optics, 9 lbs. Disc. 1996.

		$595	$525	$450	$395	$350	$295	$250

Add $145 with optics.

BULGARIAN SS-94 - 7.62x39mm cal., Kalashnikov action featuring single shot operation, thumbhole hardwood stock, 5 shot detachable mag., 9 lbs. Disc. 1996.

		$425	$360	$315	$260	$215	$190	$180

ARSENAL INC.

Current manufacturer established during 2001 and located in Las Vegas, NV. Dealer and distributor sales.

RIFLES: SEMI-AUTO

Arsenal Inc. manufactures AK style/design rifles in various configurations, all in 7.62x39mm cal. All models feature forged and milled receivers, hammer forged barrels, and will accept dohble stack magazines. Models include the SAM-7 (black polymer, 16 in. barrel - $750 MSR), SAM-7S (similar to SAM-7, except has scope rail - $825 MSR), SAM-7 Classic (limited edition, blonde wood, $875 MSR), and the SA RPK-7 (23 in. barrel, bi-pod, blonde wood - $975 MSR). Please contact the company directly for availability.

ARSENAL USA LLC

Current manufacturer established during 2000, and located in Houston, TX.

RIFLES: SEMI-AUTO

Arsenal USA, LLC produces a variety of AK-47/AK-74 semi-auto rifles, utilizing mostly Bulgarian, Hungarian and Polish made parts, including stocks. Some components are made in the U.S., in compliance with the BATF. These guns are assembled and parkerized in the U.S., and overall quality contol is very good. Current models include: SSR-47, SSR-47S, SSR-74, SSR-74S, SSR-85B, SSR-85C, and the AMD-63. Most of these models are currently priced in the $500-$550 range. Quantities are limited, as permits are no longer available for many of the parts needed to build these rifles.

Please contact the company directly for information and model availability.

ART MANIFATTURA ARMI

Current longarm manufacturer located in Gardone, Italy. No current U.S. importation. Art Manifacttura Armi manufactures high quality custom long guns, including rifles and shotguns. Please contact the factory directly for more information, including availability and pricing.

ASP

Previously manufactured customized variation of a S&W Model 39-2 semi-auto pistol (or related variations) mfg. by Armament Systems and Procedures located in Appleton, WI.

PISTOLS: SEMI-AUTO

ASP - 9mm Para. cal., compact double action semi-auto, features see-through grips with cutaway mag. making cartridges visible, Teflon coated, re-contoured lightened slide, combat trigger guard, spurless hammer, and mostly painted Guttersnipe rear sight (no front sight), supplied with 3 mags., 24 oz. loaded. Approx. 3,000 mfg. until 1981.

	$1,500	$1,275	$1,050	$875	$775	$695	$625

Add $200 for Tritium filled Guttersnipe.

Grading	100%	98%	95%	90%	80%	70%	60%

This pistol is marked ASP on the magazine extension.

✳ *ASP Quest For Excellence* - special edition, marked "Quest for Excellence", included buffalo horn grips, presentation book case and letter opener. Approx. 100 mfg.

	$3,150	$2,700	$2,400	$2,050	$1,775	$1,525	$1,275

REVOLVERS

ASP REVOLVER - .44 Spl. cal., conversion from a Ruger Speed or Security Six, 5 shot. Less than 100 mfg., unmarked.

	$1,275	$1,075	$950	$875	$775	$700	$650

ASPREY, WILLIAM R.

Current manufacturer located in London, England. While established in 1781, Asprey has been manufacturing high quality shotguns and rifles since 1990. During 1998, the name was changed to Asprey & Garrard. In 2000, the name changed again to William R. Asprey, Esq. Consumer direct sales only.

Prices indicated below for manufacturer's suggested retail and 100% condition factors are listed in English pounds. All new prices do not include English VAT. Values for used guns in 98%-60% condition factors are priced in U.S. dollars.

RIFLES: BOLT ACTION

BOLT ACTION MAGAZINE RIFLE – standard cals. include .243 Win., .270 Win., .308 Win., or .375 H&H, Mauser or Mannlicher action, ¾ rib with standard and two-folding leaf rear sight, best quality pistol grip walnut stock with traditional cheekpiece, custom order only - prices below reflect base model, with leather case and accessories. Magnum or Kurtz action and scopes are priced upon individual quotation only.

MSR	£10,500	£10,500	£12,000	$9,500	$8,000	$7,200	$6,500	$5,750

RIFLES: SxS, SIDELOCK

SxS DOUBLE RIFLE - various cals. up to .700, sidelock ejector with engraved reinforced action, pinless lockplates, best quality walnut, folding leaf rear sight on ¾ rib, custom order only - prices below reflect base models, and include leather case with accessories. Limited mfg.

Add £2,250 for detachable scope mounts.

✳ *Cals. up to .300*

MSR	£45,000	£45,000	$57,500	$47,500	$42,500	$36,500	$29,500	$25,000

✳ *Cals. up to .470*

MSR	£50,000	£50,000	$62,500	$50,000	$45,000	$38,500	$32,000	$26,500

✳ *Cals. up to .577*

MSR	£55,000	£55,000	$67,000	$52,500	$47,500	$40,000	$33,500	$27,500

✳ *.600 and .700 Bore* - prices start at £60,000 and £70,000, respectively.

SHOTGUNS: O/U

SIDELOCK MODEL - 20 ga. currently (other gauges to follow), best quality sidelock ejector model, features pinless lockplates, DTs, best quality checkered walnut, custom order only - prices below reflect base model, and include leather case with accessories.

MSR	£32,500	£32,500	$39,750	$34,250	$30,000	$26,500	$21,050	$17,000

Add £250 for pistol grip stock.
Add £1,700 for ST.
Add £5,000 for game scene engraving.

Grading	100%	98%	95%	90%	80%	70%	60%

SHOTGUNS: SxS, SIDELOCK

SIDELOCK MODEL - available in 12 ga. - .410 bore, best quality sidelock ejector model, features pinless lockplates, DTs, best quality checkered walnut, custom order only - prices below reflect base model, and include leather case with accessories.

MSR	£27,500		£27,500	$34,250	$30,000	$26,500	$21,050	$17,000	$13,750

Add £1,700 for ST.
Add £5,000 for game scene engraving.

ASTRA

Previous manufacturer located in Guernica, Spain. Astra was one of the oldest and most widely recognized trademarks in Spain, with a history dating back to 1908. Though arms were manufactured for many years by UNCETA y COMPANIA., S.A., located in Guernica, Spain, corporate reorganization resulted in renaming the same firm ASTRA SPORT, S.A. (1995-1997), and ASTRA SPORT GUERNIQUESA de MECANIZADO TRATAMIENTO y MONTAJE de ARMAS, S.A. (1997-1998).

Although ASTRA had hoped to acquire STAR patents and relocate to a smaller facility, these efforts were not successful. Foreclosure sealed the factory doors in July, 1998, and all inventory, including the "factory collection," was released for sale in 1999.

PISTOLS: SEMI-AUTO

MODEL 1911 - .25 ACP or .32 ACP cal., semi-auto, may have external or internal hammer.

	$365	$265	$175	$135	$115	$100	$85

Add 50% if with external hammer.

MODEL 1915/1916 - .32 ACP cal., semi-auto.

	$350	$265	$175	$135	$115	$100	$85

Note: Models 1915/1916 were later referred to as Model 100 Special.

CAMPO GIRO 1913 - mfg. 1913-14. Ser. No. range 1-1,300.

	$3,500	$2,650	$1,850	$1,350	$925	$700	$500

Add 10% for matching magazine.

CAMPO GIRO 1913-1916 - mfg. 1915-19. Ser. No. range 1-13,625.

	$2,000	$1,800	$1,200	$800	$600	$500	$400

Add 10% if fit with horn logo grips.
Add 10% for matching magazine.

MODEL 200 FIRECAT AUTOMATIC PISTOL - .25 ACP cal., 2¼ in. barrel, 6 shot, blue, plastic grips. Mfg. 1920-1968.

	$240	$190	$165	$145	$125	$110	$100

100% prices assume N.I.B. condition.
Add 50% for engraved M-200.

MODEL 300 - .32 ACP or .380 ACP cal., semi-auto.

	$600	$500	$300	$240	$210	$180	$150

Add 20% if Nazi-proofed.
Add 200% for engraved M-300.

Grading	100%	98%	95%	90%	80%	70%	60%

MODEL 400 AUTOMATIC PISTOL - 9mm Bayard Long cal., 9 shot, 6 in. barrel, blue, fixed sights, plastic grips. Mfg. 1921-1945.

	$400	$325	$230	$200	$170	$135	$100

Add 200% for Navy variation.

Add 100% for Nazi accepted specimens.

Approx. serial range of Nazi accepted specimens (no markings) is S/N 92,851 - 98,850.

This particular model in "reworked" configuration has recently been imported in large quantities.

✴ **"F. Ascaso" Marked Model 400 Copies** - close copy of the Astra Model 400, produced by the Spanish Republican forces during the later part of the Spanish Civil War, F. Ascaso marked (un-numbered) mags., salt blued, estimated production is approx. 8,000, has identifying logo on slide and grip panels, and base of magazine.

	$600	$475	$325	$250	$200	$175	$150

✴ **R.E. (Republica Espagnola) Marked Model 400 Copies** - ser. range to approx. 15,000, has identifying logo on forward slide and grip panels.

	$475	$400	$295	$240	$210	$170	$125

Add $200 if pistol is fit with wood serrated grips having brass RE medallion.

MODEL 600 MOD. AUTOMATIC - 9mm Para. cal., 8 shot, 5¼ in. barrel, blue, fixed sights, wood or plastic grips. Mfg. 1944-1945.

	$395	$325	$250	$175	$155	$140	$130

Add 100% for Nazi Waffenamt proofing (serial range 1 - 10,500).

MODEL 700 SPECIAL - .32 ACP cal., semi-auto.

	$600	$500	$425	$350	$275	$215	$170

MODEL 800 CONDOR AUTOMATIC - 9mm Para. cal., similar to 600, except has exposed hammer. Mfg. 1958-1965.

	$1,250	$1,100	$950	$800	$700	$550	$500

Add 20% if NIB with accessories.

MODEL 900 - 7.63 Mauser cal., Broomhandle copy, parts non-interchangeable with Mauser. Mfg. from 1928-1936.

	$2,500	$1,850	$1,350	$850	$700	$525	$425

Add $500 for non-matching shoulder stock.

Add $750 for matching stock.

Add 50% for early Bolo grip variation.

Add 20% for specimens with Japanese characters.

MODEL 902 - 7.63 Mauser cal., semi-auto, similar to 900 except 20 shot mag. Beware of fakes - usually created by welding up selective fire pistols.

	$15,000	$12,000	$9,500	$6,500	$3,500	$3,000	$2,500

Add $1,500 for original "booted" stock.

Subtract 60% for selective fire version.

MACHINE PISTOLS - class III, transferrable only, 10 or 20 shot detachable mag., several variations.

	$4,000	$3,000	$2,000	$1,750	$1,500	$1,200	$1,000

MODEL 3000 POCKET AUTOMATIC - .32 ACP or .380 ACP cal., 4 in. barrel, fixed sights, blue, plastic grips. Mfg. 1947-1956.

	$550	$395	$305	$250	$205	$175	$145

Add 100% for engraved M3000.

MODEL 1000 OR 1000 SPECIAL - .32 ACP cal., semi-auto, extended frame to hold 12 shot mag.

	$695	$550	$400	$310	$280	$255	$225

Grading	100%	98%	95%	90%	80%	70%	60%

MODEL 2000 CUB - .22 Short or .25 ACP cal., 2¼ in. barrel, fixed sights, blue, plastic grips, also chrome finish, mfg. 1954-1998, U.S. importation stopped by GCA 68. Astra also made 2000 Cubs for Colt called Jr. Model {see Colt section}.

	$250	$190	$140	$115	$95	$85	$75

Add 25% for chrome finish.
Add 50% for engraved M-2000.

MODEL 2000 CAMPER - .22 Short cal. only, similar to Cub, with 4 in. barrel. Mfg. 1955- 1960.

	$350	$275	$200	$160	$125	$90	$70

Add 10% if in original box.

CONSTABLE - .22 LR (10 shot, disc. in 1990.), .32 ACP (8 shot, disc. 1984), or .380 ACP (7 shot) cal., double action, exposed hammer, 3½ in. barrel, fixed sight, blue or chrome (disc.) finish, plastic grips. Imported 1965-91.

	$295	$250	$210	$180	$165	$150	$135

Last MSR was $380.

Add $10 for chrome finish or wood grips (disc. in 1990).

* ***Constable Stainless*** - .380 ACP cal. only, stainless version of the Constable. Mfg. 1986 only.

	$350	$300	$240				

Last MSR was $345.

* ***Constable Sport*** - similar to Constable, except has 6 in. barrel, blue finish only, 35 oz. Mfg. 1986-87 only.

	$325	$245	$210	$180	$165	$150	$135

Last MSR was $330.

* ***Blue Engraved Constable*** - blue engraved. Importation disc. 1987.

	$395	$295	$250				

Last MSR was $375.

Add $20 for .22 LR or checkered wood grips.

* ***Chrome Engraved Constable*** - chrome engraved. Importation disc. 1987.

	$350	$295	$250				

Last MSR was $390.

Add $20 for .22 LR or checkered wood grips.

CONSTABLE A-60 - .380 ACP cal., double action, 3½ in. barrel, 13 shot mag., ambidextrous safety, adj. rear sight, blue finish only. Imported 1986-91.

	$395	$325	$280	$245	$220	$185	$160

Last MSR was $475.

MODEL A-70 - 9mm Para. or .40 S&W cal., single action, 3½ in. barrel, steel frame and slide, 7 (.40 S&W) or 8 (9mm Para.) shot mag., compact design, dual safeties, 3-dot sights, matte blue or nickel (new 1993) finish, 25¾ oz. Imported 1991-1996.

	$275	$250	$225	$200	$185	$170	$160

Last MSR was $358.

Add $29 for nickel finish.

* ***Model A-70 Stainless*** - stainless steel variation of the A-70. Mfg. 1994 only.

	$365	$325	$275				

Last MSR was $435.

MODEL A-75 - 9mm Para., .40 S&W, or .45 ACP (new 1994) cal., action similar to Model A-70, except has selective double action with a decocking lever, steel or aluminum (9mm Para. only) frame. Importation began 1993.

✳ ***9mm Para or .40 S&W.*** - choice of blue or nickel steel frame or lightweight aluminum frame (23½ oz.), 7 (.40 S&W) or 8 (9mm Para.) shot mag. Disc. 1998.

	$275	$250	$225	$200	$185	$170	$160

Last MSR was $303.

Add $17 for nickel finish.
Add $20 for lightweight model (aluminum frame).

✳ ***.45 ACP*** - blue or nickel finish, 7 shot mag. Disc. 1998.

	$310	$250	$225	$200	$175	$160	$150

Last MSR was $358.

Add $23 for nickel finish.

✳ ***Model A-75 Stainless*** - stainless steel variation of the A-75. Mfg. 1994 only.

	$375	$325	$295				

Last MSR was $485.

MODEL A-80 - 9mm Para, .38 Super (disc.), or .45 ACP cal., double action, semi-auto, 15 shot mag. (9 for .45 ACP), 3¾ in. barrel. Imported 1982-89.

	$370	$320	$285	$265	$240	$210	$185

Last MSR was $425.

Add $35 for chrome finish (disc.).
.38 Super cal. in chrome finish will command a premium (10%-20%).

MODEL A-90 - 9mm Para. or .45 ACP cal., 1986 designation for Model A-80 with updated slide mounted safety and pushbutton mag. release, 3¾ in. barrel, 14 shot mag. (9mm), or 8 shot (.45 ACP), blue only, approx. 48 oz. Imported 1986-90, replaced by Model A-100.

	$375	$325	$295	$275	$245	$225	$200

Last MSR was $500.

MODEL A-100 - 9mm Para., .40 S&W, or .45 ACP cal., replaced the Model A-90 in 1990, with similar specifications, blue or nickel finish, re-engineered 1993 incorporating increased mag. capacity, 10 (C/B 1994), 17*/9mm, 12*/.40 S&W, or 9 shot/.45 ACP, approx. 29 oz. Imported 1990-97.

	$375	$325	$295	$275	$245	$225	$175

Last MSR was $351.

Add $22 for nickel finish.
A small number of pistols with an extended slide were made for the Turkish police - add 50%.

MODEL 4000 FALCON - .22 LR, .32 ACP, or .380 ACP cal., 4 in. barrel, fixed sights, blue, plastic grips, exposed hammer. Mfg. 1956-1986.

	$500	$400	$330	$260	$235	$200	$150

Last MSR was $340.

Add 50% for .22 cal.
Add 10% for .380 ACP.
Add 100% for engraved M-4000.

✳ ***Model 4000 Tri-cal. Kit*** - includes frame and 3 barrels (.22 LR, .32 ACP, and .380 ACP cals.), may have rust blued, salt blued, or chromed (rare) finish, less than 200 mfg.

	$1,250	$950	$750	$650	$575	$500	$450

Subtract 15% if not in factory box.

REVOLVERS

CADIX DOUBLE ACTION REVOLVER - .22 LR cal., 9 shot, .38 Spl., 5 shot, 4 or 6 in. barrel, adj. sights, blue, plastic grips. Mfg. 1960-1968.

	$195	$165	$140	$120	$110	$85	$55

Grading	100%	98%	95%	90%	80%	70%	60%

.357 D/A REVOLVER - .357 Mag. cal., 6 shot, 3, 4, 6, or 8½ in. barrel (add $10), adj. sights, blue, checkered wood grips. Mfg. 1972-1988.

	$250	$215	$185	$170	$155	$140	$125

Last MSR was $295.

Add 50% for 8 ½ in. barrel.

✳ *Stainless Steel* - 4 in. barrel only. Disc. 1987.

	$285	$245	$205

Last MSR was $330.

LARGE CAL. D/A REVOLVER - .41 Mag. (disc. 1985), .44 Mag., or .45 LC (disc. 1987) cal., 6 shot, 6 or 8½ in. (.44 Mag. only) barrels. Mfg. 1980-87.

	$280	$235	$210	$190	$180	$170	$160

Last MSR was $315.

✳ *Stainless Steel* - .44 Mag. cal. only, 6 in. barrel only, 2½ lbs. Importation disc. 1993.

	$370	$300	$265

Last MSR was $450.

CONVERTIBLE REVOLVER - 9mm Para. cal. with extra .357 Mag. cal. cylinder, 6 shot, 3 in. barrel, blue only, checkered walnut grips, 2¼ lbs. Imported 1986-1993.

	$335	$275	$250	$225	$200	$180	$160

Last MSR was $395.

TERMINATOR - .44 Mag. or .44 Spl. (disc.) cal., 6 shot, adj. rear sight, Roberts rubber grips, 2¾ in. shrouded barrel only. Inventories were depleted in 1989.

Blue finish	$250	$225	$190	$175	$160	$150	$140

Last MSR was $250.

Stainless steel	$275	$235	$190

Last MSR was $275.

These models were distributed by Sile Distributors, Inc. located in New York, NY.

ATKIN, HENRY

Current trademark manufactured by Atkin, Grant & Lang, established in 1821 and located in Hertfordshire, England. No current U.S. importation.

Atkin, Grant & Lang provide a useful historical research service on older Henry Atkin shotguns and rifles. The charge for this service is £25 per gun, and the company will give you all pertinent factory information regarding the history.

SHOTGUNS: SxS

Prices below do not include VAT or importation costs. Values for used guns in 98%-60% condition factors are priced in U.S. dollars.

Add 10% for matched pairs.

BOXLOCK MODEL - 28 (2 mfg.) or 20 (3 mfg.) ga., very limited Millenium Edition.

Rarity precludes accurate pricing evaluation on this model – 2000 MSR was £14,000.

SIDELOCK MODEL - 12, 20 ga., or .410 bore, best quality sidelock ejector model with opening assist.

MSR	N/A		N/A	$12,000	$9,900	$8,700	$7,500	$6,250	$5,000

Add 20% for 20 ga., 30% for .410 bore.

AUSTRALIAN AUTOMATIC ARMS PTY. LTD.

Previous manufacturer located in Tasmania, Australia. Previously imported and distributed by California Armory, Inc. located in San Bruno, CA.

Grading	100%	98%	95%	90%	80%	70%	60%

PISTOLS: SEMI-AUTO

SAP - .223 Rem. cal., semi-auto paramilitary design pistol, 10½ in. barrel, 20 shot mag., fiberglass stock and forearm, 5.9 lbs. Imported 1986-1993.

	$725	$650	$575	$525	$495	$475	$450

Last MSR was $799.

RIFLES: SEMI-AUTO

SAR - .223 Rem. cal., semi-auto paramilitary design rifle, 16¼ or 20 in. (new 1989) barrel, 5 or 20 shot M-16 style mag., fiberglass stock and forearm, 7½ lbs. Imported 1986-89.

	$725	$625	$550	$510	$465	$410	$370

Last MSR was $663.

Add $25 for 20 in. barrel.
This model was also available in fully auto version (AR).

SAC - .223 Rem. cal., semi-auto paramilitary design carbine, 10½ in. barrel, 20 shot mag., fiberglass stock and forearm, 6.9 lbs. New 1986.

This model was available to class III dealers and law enforcement agencies only.

SP - .223 Rem. cal., semi-auto, sporting configuration, 16¼ or 20 in. barrel, wood stock and forearm, 5 or 20 shot M-16 style mag., 7.5 lbs. Imported late 1991-1993.

	$795	$675	$575	$525	$495	$475	$450

Last MSR was $879.

Add $40 for wood stock.

AUSTRALIAN INTERNATIONAL ARMS

Current exporter located in Brisbane, Australia. Australian Interntaional Arms works in cooperation with ADI Limited Lithgow, formerly Small Arms Factory, known for its SMLE No. I MKIII and L1A1 rifles. Currently imported and distributed by Tristar Sporting Arms, Ltd., located in N. Kansas City, MO.

RIFLES: BOLT ACTION

M10 ENFIELD - .223 Rem., .308 Win., or 7.62x39mm cal., features L42A1 improved action, all new components, teak stock with steel buttplate, 16.1 (short carbine), 20 (carbine or sporter), or 25.2 (.308 Win. cal. only) in. barrel, two-stage trigger, CNC milled receiver. Importation began 2002.

As this edition went to press, prices had yet to be established on this model.

SHOTGUNS: LEVER ACTION

MODEL 1887 - 12 ga., 2¾ in. chamber, reproduction of the Winchester Model 1887, uncheckered oil finished walnut stock and forearm, blue finish, steel buttplate, 5 shot, exposed hammer with half cock, 22 in. barrel, 8¾ lbs. Importation began 2002.

MSR	$1,195		$995	$850	$750	$650	$600	$550	$500

AUTAUGA RIFLES, INC.

Current manufacturer established in 1996, and located in Prattville, AL. In 2000, Autauga Arms, Inc. changed their name to Autauga Rifles, Inc. Dealer and consumer sales.

Grading	100%	98%	95%	90%	80%	70%	60%

PISTOLS: SEMI-AUTO

AUTAUGA MKII 32 - .32 ACP cal., double action only, 2 in. barrel, hammerless, blow- back type action, 6 shot mag., stainless steel, black polymer grips, 12 oz. 3,200 mfg. 1996-2000.

$325 $225 $185

Early guns did not have the MKII designation.

Last MSR was $399.

RIFLES: BOLT ACTION

Autauga Rifles, Inc. manufactures a complete line of precision bolt action rifles that are special ordered per individual customer specifications. Configurations include hunting, long range competition, law enforcement and military tactical rifles. Complete packages include rifle, optics, hardware, and cleaning equipment. Standard rifle prices vary from $2,500-$3,500, depending on options. Rifles are supplied with a Pelican 1750 case. Please contact the factory directly to find out more information and pricing on these rifles.

AUTO MAG

Previously manufactured (circa 1971-1982) by Auto Mag. Corp. and TDE Corp. Recent manufacture (Harry Sanford Commemorative) was produced by Galena Industries, located in Sturgis, SD.

Less than 9,000 Auto Mags were produced by all manufacturers. All pistols originally had all stainless steel mags.

Short recoil rotary bolt system made entirely of stainless steel. Most pistols were sold in .44 AMP cal., although .357 AMP was also a popular factory option.

A unique handgun, the Auto Mag was never a commercial success due to high manufacturing costs and initial functioning problems (mostly attributed to hand loading all the ammo - once factory ammo became available, reliability improved significantly). Initial reaction to Dirty Harry's use of this weapon in the movie "Sudden Impact" (1983) made prices escalate considerably, but most values appear to have stabilized since 1986. Be aware of fakes - especially of the XP variety (re-serialized, re- stamped, location of markings, etc.). Also, the ease of barrel swapping should be considered when deciding on a potential purchase. Auto Mags were never magna ported from the factory (only The Custom 100 Series). Non-original magna porting actually detracts from the values listed below, since it is a non-factory alteration.

Serial number ranges for the various models are as follows: Pasadena mfg. - A0000 through A03700. TDE North Hollywood - mostly A02500 through A05015, although some were marked with very low ser. no.'s. TDE El Monte mfg. - A05016 through A08300. High Standard guns were originally marked with "H" prefix serial numbers (only 132 made), after which they carried standard "A0" prefix serial numbers. The "H" prefix guns remain a collectors item and command a 25% premium over values listed below. TDE/OMC marked pistols - B00001 through B00370 are known as the "B" series or solid bolt models (only 370 manufactured). This "B" series also commands collector premiums.

AMT manufactured the last two lots of Auto Mags; the first was the "C" series and was basically the same as the "B" except that only 50 guns were fabricated. The last Auto Mags made by AMT were appropriately serial numbered LAST 1 through LAST 50. These guns had the reputation of being the poorest quality but do carry collector premiums. One interesting variation is the North Hollywood "two-line" model. Also, the first .357 cal. pistols manufactured did not have the words AUTO MAG appearing on the gun. These are also collectors items.

In addition to the above calibers, a very few non-factory .22, .25 and .30 LMP (Lomont Magnum Pistols) cal. prototypes were fabricated by Kent Lomont. These specimens will usually demand a premium over the values listed below. Also, some barrels and pistols were made in Covina, CA.

Grading	100%	98%	95%	90%	80%	70%	60%

PISTOLS: SEMI-AUTO

ORIGINAL PASADENA - .44 AMP cal. only, 6½ in. VR barrel, ser. no. A0001 – A3,300.

$2,500 $2,300 $1,995

This model is generally regarded as having the most quality, as all components were milled from Carpenter 455 stainless steel stock.

TDE NORTH HOLLYWOOD - ser. no. range A3,400 – A05015.

✳ *.44 AMP* - 6½ in. VR barrel, initial guns were mfg. from existing Pasadena parts, later mfg. required new components made by TDE.

$2,275 $1,850 $1,700

Quality on this model goes down in later mfg. (some small parts are not stainless). Because of this, higher serial numbered guns in this model are less desirable.

✳ *.357 AMP* - two line address, there are no factory records verifying this caliber, and most were assembled with spare barrels.

$1,850 $1,600 $1,450

TDE EL MONTE - ser. no. range A05016 – A08300.

✳ *.44 AMP* - 6½ VR, 8½ , or 10½ in. tapered barrel.

$2,000 $1,700 $1,600

✳ *.357 AMP* - 6½ VR, 8½ , or 10½ in. tapered barrel.

$1,750 $1,600 $1,450

HIGH STANDARD - "H" prefixed serial numbers, approx. 132 mfg. by TDE with High Standard markings.

$2,250 $2,100 $1,850

LEE JURRAS STANDARD MODELS - see listings below, custom features would vary from presentation grade polishing of barrel and frame to exotic wood or micarta grips.

✳ *LEJ Standard Automag* - .357 AMP or .44 AMP cal., 6½ w/VR, 8½, or 10½ in. non-rib barrel, TDE markings, lion's head logo. 1,100 – 1,200 mfg. 1974-76 by Lee Jurras & Associates.

$2,225 $2,050 $1,775

Lee Jurras added his Lion's head logo (1974-1976) on TDE manufactured guns. There were also a very limited quantity of original shoulder stocks (less than 12), and were available for the International and Alaskan models only - extreme rarity precludes accurate price evaluation.

Several other calibers and variations were marketed through Lee Jurras including one-of-a-kind exotics like a .30 cal. Cougar with 12 in. barrel and highly polished metal.

LEE JURRAS CUSTOM MODELS - Lee Jurras Custom Models included the 100 (listed below), 200 International (12 mfg.), 300 Alaskan (9 mfg.), 400 Backpacker (5 mfg.), 500 Grizzly (5 mfg.), 600 Condor (2 mfg.), and Metallic Silouhette (2 mfg.). Because of the rarity factor, these models with 12 or less mfg. are difficult to price accurately, and must be evaluated and appraised individually.

✳ *LEJ Custom Model 100* - .357 AMP, .41 JMP (Jurras Magnum Pistol), or .44 AMP cal., 6½ in. VR or 8½ non-rib (only 10 mfg. in each cal.) polished magna-ported barrel, custom laminated wood grips, special carrying case. 100 mfg. in each cal.

$3,150 $2,850 $2,350

TDE/OMC "B" SERIES - 6½ VR or 10 in. barrel, ser. no. range B00001 – B00370.

$2,250 $2,100 $1,850

Grading	100%	98%	95%	90%	80%	70%	60%

AMT "C" SERIES - 6½ VR or 10 in. barrel, designated by "C" no. prefix.

| | | **$2,250** | **$2,100** | **$1,850** | | | |

Note: guns were cased (plastic attache style) with accessories. Original Auto-Mag ammo (only original mfg. by CDM in Mexico and Norma in Sweden) is currently selling for approx. $75-$95 a box. Starline now has .44 AMP brass, and Cor-bon loaded .44 AMP ammo also – new 2001.

HARRY SANFORD COMMEMORATIVE AUTO MAG - .44 AMP cal., Automag, Inc. commemorative reissue, "STURGIS, SD" barrel address with Harry Sanford signature on left rear of slide, cased. 1,000 pistols mfg. by Galena Industries 1999-2000.

| | | **$2,750** | **$2,300** | **$1,995** | | | |

Last MSR was $2,750.

AUTO-ORDNANCE CORP.

Current manufacturer with facilities located in Worcester, MA, and corporate offices in Blauvelt, NY. Auto-Ordnance Corp. became a division of Kahr Arms in 1999. Auto-Ordnance Corp. was a division of Gun Parts Corp. until 1999. Previously located in West Hurley, NY. Consumer, dealer and distributor sales.

Auto-Ordnance Corp. manufactures an exact reproduction of the original 1927 Thompson machine gun. They are currently available from Kahr Arms in semi-auto only since production ceased on fully automatic variations (Model 1928 and M1) in 1986 (mfg. 1975- 1986 including 609 M1s). All guns currently manufactured utilize the Thompson trademark, are manufactured in the U.S. and come with a lifetime warranty.

PISTOLS: SEMI-AUTO

During 1997, Auto Ordnance discontinued all calibers on the pistols listed below, except for .45 ACP cal. or 9mm Para. slide kits were available for $179. Also, conversion units (converting .45 ACP to .38 Super or 9mm Para.) were available for $195.

All current Auto Ordnance 1911 Models include a spent case, plastic case, and cable lock.

1911 A1 STANDARD/COMPACT STANDARD - .38 Super (disc. 1996), 9mm Para. (disc. 1996), .40 S&W (mfg. 1991-93), 10mm (mfg. 1991-96), or .45 ACP cal., 4¼ (.45 ACP only, Compact Standard Model), 4½ (.40 S&W cal. only) or 5 (Standard Model) in. barrel, 7 shot mag., single action, parts interchange with the original Colt Govt. Model, blue or nickel finish, checkered plastic grips, 39 oz.

| MSR | **$447** | **$360** | **$295** | **$255** | **$235** | **$225** | **$215** | **$200** |

Add $28 for satin nickel (mfg. 1990-96) or $37 for duo-tone (mfg. 1992-96) finish (.45 ACP only).

* *1911 A1 Deluxe* - .38 Super (disc. 1996), 9mm Para. (disc. 1996), or .45 ACP cal., 5 in. barrel, 3 dot sights, wraparound grips, 39 oz. New 1991.

| MSR | **$455** | **$375** | **$320** | **$260** | **$235** | **$225** | **$215** | **$200** |

* *1911 A1 General* - .38 Super (mfg. 1996 only) or .45 ACP cal., 4½ in. barrel with full length recoil guide system, 7 shot mag., blued finish, 3 dot fixed Millett sights, black rubber wraparound grips, Commander styling, 37 oz. Mfg. 1992-98.

| | **$385** | **$315** | **$255** | **$235** | **$225** | **$215** | **$200** |

Last MSR was $465.

* *1911 A1 Custom High Polish* - .45 ACP cal., 8 shot mag., 5 in. barrel, custom combat hammer, beavertail grip safety, rosewood grips with medallions, 3-dot sights, flat mainspring housing, Videcki speed trigger, 39 oz. Mfg. 1997-99.

| | **$485** | **$395** | **$325** | **$265** | **$235** | **$225** | **$215** |

Last MSR was $585.

Grading	100%	98%	95%	90%	80%	70%	60%

* **WWII Parkerized 1911 A1** - .45 ACP cal., no frills variation of the Model 1911 A1, military parkerizing, G.I. detailing with military style roll stamp, plastic or checkered walnut (disc. 2001) grips, and lanyard loop. New 1992.

MSR	$462		$375	$295	$265	$245	$230	$215	$200

* **Competition 1911** - .38 Super (1996 only) or .45 ACP cal., competition features include compensated barrel, commander hammer, flat mainspring housing, white 3- dot sighting system, beavertail grip safety, black textured wraparound grips. Mfg. 1993-96.

			$530	$415	$375	$330	$300	$285	$270

Last MSR was $636.

Add $10 for .38 Super cal.

MODEL ZG-51 "PIT BULL" - .45 ACP cal. only, compact variation of the 1911 A1, 3 5/8 in. standard (disc. 1996) or 4 3/8 in. compensated (new 1997) barrel, 7 shot mag., 36 oz. Mfg. 1988-1999.

			$385	$310	$255	$235	$225	$215	$200

Last MSR was $470.

RIFLES: SEMI-AUTO

Until the Crime Bill was passed in 1994, the Auto-Ordnance Thompson replicas listed below were supplied with either 15, 20, or 30 shot mags. Tommy Guns are not currently legal in CA or CT.

Thompson®
Auto-Ordnance Corporation

1927 A-1 STANDARD - .45 ACP cal., 16 in. plain barrel, solid steel construction, standard military sight, walnut stock and horizontal forearm. Disc. 1986.

		$570	$490	$430	$360	$315	$290	$270

Last MSR was $575.

1927 A-1 DELUXE CARBINE - 10mm (mfg. 1991-93) or .45 ACP cal., 16½ in. finned barrel with compensator, includes one 30 shot original surplus mag., current mfg. accepts drum mags., solid steel construction, matte black finish, adj. rear sight, walnut stock, pistol grip, and finger grooved forearm grip, 13 lbs.

MSR	$950		$775	$600	$475	$385	$325	$295	$275

Add $55 for current mfg. 30 shot stick mag.
Add $119 for current mfg. 10 shot X-drum mag. (they resemble the older 50 shot L-type drum) – new 1994.
Add $190 for 50* shot drum mag. or $350 for 100* shot drum mag. (mfg. 1990-93) on this model and other 1927 variations.
Add $113 for factory violin case or $124 for hard case.

* **1927 A-1C Lightweight Deluxe** - .45 ACP cal., similar to 1927 A-1 Deluxe, except receiver made of a lightweight alloy, current mfg. accepts drum mags., 9½ lbs. New 1984.

MSR	$950		$775	$600	$475	$385	$325	$295	$275

* **1927 A-1 Deluxe .22 LR Cal.** - .22 LR cal., very limited mfg., 30 shot mag. standard.

		$1,100	$995	$925	$800	$700	$650	$575

1927 A-1 COMMANDO - .45 ACP cal., 16½ in. finned barrel with compensator, 30 shot mag., black finished stock and forearm, parkerized metal, black nylon sling, 13 lbs. New 1997.

MSR	$950		$775	$600	$475	$385	$325	$295	$275

Add $119 each for current mfg. 10 shot X-drum mags. (they resemble the older 50 shot L-type drums) – new 1994.

Grading	100%	98%	95%	90%	80%	70%	60%

M1 CARBINE - .45 ACP cal., combat model, 16½ in. smooth barrel w/o compensator, 30 shot original surplus mag., side-cocking lever, matte black finish, walnut stock, pistol grip, and grooved horizontal forearm, current mfg. will not accept drum mags., 11½ lbs. New 1986.

	MSR	$850		$695	$575	$475	$385	$325	$295	$275

✳ **1927 M1-C Lightweight** - similar to M1 Carbine, except receiver is made of a lightweight alloy, current mfg. accepts drum mags., 9½ lbs. New 2001.

	MSR	$850		$695	$575	$475	$385	$325	$295	$275

1927 A5 PISTOL/CARBINE - .45 ACP cal., 13 in. finned barrel, alloy construction, overall length 26 in., 10 (C/B 1994) shot mag., 7 lbs. Mfg. disc. 1994.

	$625	$515	$440	$360	$305	$280	$260

Last MSR was $765.

1927 A3 - .22 CAL. - .22 LR cal., 16 in. finned barrel, alloy frame and receiver, walnut stock, pistol grip, and forearm pistol grip, 7 lbs. Mfg. disc. 1994.

	$650	$550	$475	$400	$360	$330	$300

Last MSR was $510.

AUTO-POINTER

Previous trademark manufactured by Yamamoto Co. Formerly imported by Sloans.

SHOTGUNS: SEMI-AUTO

SEMI-AUTO SHOTGUN - 12 or 20 ga., gas operated. Disc.

	$275	$240	$220	$195	$180	$160	$145

AXTELL RIFLE CO.

Current rifle manufacturer located in Sheridan, MT. Distributed by The Riflesmith Inc., located in Sheridan, MT. Consumer direct sales.

RIFLES: REPRODUCTIONS

New Model 1877 Sharps reproductions are available for both long-range and sporting rifles listed below in the following black powder calibers: .40-50, .40-70, .40-90, .45- 70 Govt., .45-90, and .45-100 cal. The Riflesmith Inc. should be contacted directly for accessories and/or engraving options.
    Add $275 for bull hide rifle case.

NUMBER ONE CREEDMOOR - features 34 in. Rigby style barrel, choice of high-grade black or English checkered walnut stock and forearm with ebony inlays. Long range sights. 10 lbs.

	MSR	$4,700		$4,700	$3,950	$3,500	$3,025	$2,500	$2,000	$1,575

C-EXPRESS - top-of-the-line model with double set triggers, 32 or 34 in. ½ round, ½ octagon barrel, select walnut checkered stock, deluxe front and rear sights, approx. 13 lbs.

	MSR	$5,200		$5,200	$4,300	$3,750	$3,150	$2,600	$2,100	$1,650

NUMBER TWO LONG RANGE - choice of 30-34 in. Rigby style barrel, select black or English checkered walnut stock and forearm. Long range sights.

	MSR	$3,900		$3,900	$3,150	$3,000	$2,525	$2,000	$1,650	$1,300

OVERBAUGH SCHUETZEN - features 26-30 in. octagon barrel, double-set triggers, Schuetzen buttplate with cheekpiece, palm rest, short-range sights, 11-14 lbs.

	MSR	$4,500		$4,500	$3,650	$3,350	$2,675	$2,125	$1,700	$1,300

LOWER SPORTER - 28 or 30 in. octagon barrel, double-set triggers, steel buttplate with straight grip, standard rifle weight of 9 lbs.

	MSR	$2,600		$2,600	$2,000	$1,625	$1,300	$995	$825	$700

Grading	100%	98%	95%	90%	80%	70%	60%

LOWER BUSINESS - 28 in. contoured round barrel, double-set triggers, black walnut stock has steel shotgun buttplate with straight grip, hunter tang, blade front sights, approx. 8½ lbs.

	MSR	$2,600		$2,600	$1,950	$1,675	$1,300	$975	$800	$700

Die Meistermacher himself! What better way to start out the 23rd Edition than with Dieter Anschütz holding the Anschütz Olympic biathlon rifle which swept the recent 2002 Winter Olympics biathlon competition in Salt Lake City, thanks to Ole the Norwegian! For everything else, there's MasterCard.

B SECTION

BSA GUNS LIMITED

Current airgun manufacturer established in 1861 and located in Birmingham, England. BSA (Birmingham Small Arms) currently manufactures airguns only. Firearms were imported until 1985 by Precision Sports, from Ithaca, NY and 1986 by BSA Guns Ltd., located in Grand Prairie, TX. Imported and distributed until 1989 by Samco Global Arms, Inc., located in Miami, FL. For more information and current pricing on both new and used BSA airguns, please refer to the 2nd Ed. Blue Book of Airguns by Dr. Robert Beeman & John Allen (now online also).

Grading	100%	98%	95%	90%	80%	70%	60%

RIFLES: BOLT ACTION

Importation of all BSA rimfire and centerfire rifles was disc. 1987.

MAJESTIC FEATHERWEIGHT DELUXE - .243 Win., .270 Win., .308 Win., or .30-06 cal., bolt action, 22 in. barrel, folding sight, checkered European style stock, mfg. 1959- 1965.

	100%	98%	95%	90%	80%	70%	60%
	$330	$250	$220	$195	$180	$165	$145
.458 Mag.	$445	$375	$305	$275	$220	$210	$200

MAJESTIC DELUXE - .222 Rem., .22 Hornet, .243 Win., 7x57mm, .308 Win., or .30- 06 cal., heavier barrel.

	100%	98%	95%	90%	80%	70%	60%
	$330	$250	$220	$195	$180	$165	$145

MONARCH DELUXE - similar to Majestic Deluxe, but American design stock, mfg. 1965-1974.

100%	98%	95%	90%	80%	70%	60%
$350	$275	$250	$220	$195	$180	$165

MONARCH DELUXE VARMINT - similar to Monarch Deluxe, except .222 Rem. or .243 Win. cal., 24 in. heavy barrel. Disc.

100%	98%	95%	90%	80%	70%	60%
$370	$305	$275	$250	$210	$195	$180

MARTINI ISU MATCH .22 - single shot, bolt action, .22 LR cal. only, similar to CFT Model. Disc. 1985.

100%	98%	95%	90%	80%	70%	60%
$825	$700	$600	$530	$475	$435	$400

Last MSR was $1,000.

Add $100 for Mk. V.H.B. Model.

CF-2 ACTION - .222 Rem., .22-250 Rem., .243 Win., 6.5x55mm, 7x57mm, 7x64mm, 7mm Rem. Mag., .270 Win., .308 Win., .30-06, or .300 Win. Mag. cal., bolt action, barrel length 23-26 in., 7½-8 lbs. CF-2 nomenclature designates an action rather than a model. The following are CF-2 actioned models.

Add $70 for double set trigger option on the following models.

* ***Sporter/Classic*** - same cals. as above, checkered oil finished walnut stock. Imported 1986-87.

100%	98%	95%	90%	80%	70%	60%
$325	$275	$250	$225	$210	$195	$180

Last MSR was $360.

Sporter Model features Monte Carlo stock, rosewood capped forearm and pistol grip stock, and swivels.

* ***Classic Varminter*** - .222 Rem. - .243 Win. cals. only, heavy barrel, matte finish, with swivels. Imported 1986 only.

100%	98%	95%	90%	80%	70%	60%
$325	$275	$250	$225	$210	$190	$175

Last MSR was $345.

Grading	100%	98%	95%	90%	80%	70%	60%

✳ Heavy Barrel Model - .222 Rem., .22-250 Rem., or .243 Win. cal., approx. 9 lbs., no sights.

	$375	$300	$260	$240	$225	$210	$180

Last MSR was $410.

✳ Carbine Mode - 20 in. barrel. Disc. 1985.

	$495	$375	$300	$270	$250	$225	$200

Last MSR was $480.

✳ Stutzen Rifle - Mannlicher style full length stock, same general specifications as Sporter/Classic, 20½ in. barrel. Not available in 7mm Rem. Mag. or .300 Win. Mag. cal.

	$595	$400	$325	$300	$275	$250	$225

Last MSR was $385.

✳ Regal Custom - similar to Sporter Model, except has slim classic European style stock with Schnabel forend, deluxe walnut with extra checkering, ebony forend cap, engraved action and floorplate. Limited importation (1986 only).

	$875	$795	$685	$590	$550	$500	$450

Last MSR was $950.

This model was custom made by special order only.

CFT TARGET RIFLE - 7.62mm cal., single shot, bolt action, globe front and aperture rear sights, 26½ in. barrel, 11 lbs. Disc. 1987.

	$675	$590	$550	$500	$450	$400	$360

Last MSR was $780.

RIFLES: SINGLE SHOT

NO. 12 MARTINI - .22 LR cal., 29 in. barrel, target sights, straight stock, pre-WWII.

	$595	$495	$375	$300	$250	$200	$175

MILITARY MARTINI HENRY - various cals., pre-WWII mfg. many configurations and barrel lengths. Pricing takes into consideration most commonly encountered types with no engraving or special orders.

	$900	$700	$500	$450	$400	$365	$335

MARTINI CADET - various cals., mostly military issue, many thousands previously imported into the U.S. from England, many have been sporterized or modified.

	$600	$450	$400	$350	$300	$275	$250

MODEL 15 - similar to No. 12 Martini, except pistol grip stock, better grade target sights, pre-WWII.

	$595	$495	$375	$300	$250	$200	$175

CENTURION MATCH RIFLE - similar to Model 15, except Centurion guarantee - 1½ in. grouping at 100 yards, 24 in. barrel, pre-WWII.

	$440	$385	$330	$275	$240	$220	$175

MATCH 12/15 - similar to Model 15, except made after WWII.

	$595	$495	$375	$300	$250	$200	$175

MODEL 12/15 - heavy barrel.

	$595	$495	$375	$300	$250	$200	$175

MODEL 13 - lighter version of No. 12 Martini.

	$595	$495	$375	$300	$250	$200	$175

MODEL 13 SPORTER - similar to Model 13, except has sport sights.

	$595	$495	$375	$300	$250	$200	$175
.22 Hornet	$795	$700	$575	$450	$375	$325	$275

Grading	100%	98%	95%	90%	80%	70%	60%

MARTINI INTERNATIONAL MATCH - .22 LR cal., 29 in. heavy barrel, international sights, mfg. 1950-1953.

	$695	$600	$475	$400	$350	$325	$300

INTERNATIONAL LIGHT - 26 in. lightweight barrel.

	$600	$500	$450	$400	$350	$325	$300

INTERNATIONAL MKII - improved trigger, ejectors and stock design, mfg. 1953-1959.

	$700	$600	$550	$500	$450	$400	$350

INTERNATIONAL MKIII - longer action, floating barrel, mfg. 1959-1967.

	$800	$700	$650	$600	$550	$500	$450

INTERNATIONAL ISU - modeled to meet ISU standards, 28 in. barrel, mfg. 1968-disc.

	$800	$700	$650	$600	$550	$500	$450

INTERNATIONAL MARK V - similar to ISU, but heavier barrel, mfg. 1976-disc.

	$800	$700	$650	$600	$550	$500	$450

SHOTGUNS: SxS

BSA also manufactured SxS boxlock shotguns in various grades. Normally encountered in 12 ga. with DTs and extractors, these shotguns are of good quality and are typically encountered in the secondary market in the $250-$500 range, assuming standard grade.

B-WEST

Previous importer/distributor located in Tucson, AZ, until 1997.

B-West previously imported rifles (including AK-47 clones, the Saiga, Dragunov, etc.), the IJ series .380 ACP Makarov pistol, and the Daewoo DP-51 semi-auto pistol.

LES BAER CUSTOM, INC.

Please refer to the L section of this text.

BAFORD ARMS, INC.

Previous manufacturer located in Bristol, TN. Previously distributed by C.L. Reedy & Associates, Inc. located in Melbourne, FL.

DERRINGERS

THUNDER DERRINGER - .44 Spl. cal./.410 shotshell, single shot, tip-up action, 3 in. barrel, blue finish steel finish, spur trigger, wood grips. Introduced late 1988 with limited mfg. until 1991, when production permanently ceased.

	$130	$110	$95	$90	$85	$80	$75

Last MSR was $130.

Add $90 for interchangeable barrel kit.

Interchangeable pistol barrels are chambered in various calibers between .22 Short and 9mm Para. There are two types: one fits flush while the other facilitates a scope mounting.

PISTOLS: SEMI-AUTO

MODEL 35 FIRE POWER - 9mm Para. cal., semi-auto single action, patterned after the Browning Hi-Power, total stainless steel construction, 4¾ in. barrel, combat hammer and safety, Pachmayr grips, removable barrel bushing, Millett Mk. II sights, 14 shot mag., 32 oz. Introduced late 1988 with limited mfg. until 1993.

	$500	$425	$350

Last MSR was $550.

B BAIKAL

Current trademark of products manufactured by the Russian State Unitary Plant "Izhevsky Mechanichesky Zavod" (SUP IMZ). Many Baikal SxS and O/U hunting guns (including air guns) are currently being imported and distributed exclusively beginning late 1998 by European American Armory Corp., located in Sharpes, FL. Previously imported 1993-96 by Big Bear, located in Dallas, Tx. Please contact the EAA Corp. for more information on current Baikal models and retail prices.

Baikal (name of the lake in Siberia) was one of the first state-run holdovers from the former Soviet Union to market firearms, ammunition, optics and other sporting goods from a variety of plants within Russia. Now Baikal is the state licenced trademark of the Izhevsky Mechanichesky Zavod, a government owned plant in Izhevsk, Russia.

The company was founded in 1942 as part of the Russian National Defense Industry. At that time, the plant produced world renowned Tokarev TT pistols. Upon conclusion of WWII, the company expanded its operation to include non-military weapons (O/U, SxS, and single barrel shotguns). Today, the SUP IMZ is one of the world's largest manufacturers of military and non-military weapons. The products range from various smoothbore, rifled and combination guns, including slide action and self-loading guns, air pistols and rifles, to a full array of sporting, civil and combat pistols, including the internationally famous Makarov pistol. Today, the SUP IMZ features the efficient manufacturing capacity and unique intellectual potential of qualified engineers-and-technicians' staff.

The SUP IMZ is also undertaking the task of reintroducing the world to the "Russian Custom Gunsmith". A section of the factory area has been set aside for custom, one-of-a-kind hand engraved shotguns and rifles. The guns produced by the custom shop are top quality by any standards and rival many of the custom guns elsewhere. The custom shop also serves as the birthplace for many of the innovations being introduced by the SUP IMZ.

In the past, Baikal shotguns have had limited importation into the U.S. 1993 marked the first year that Baikals were officially (and legally) imported into the U.S., because of Russia's previous export restrictions domestically. In prior years, however, a few O/Us have been seen for sale and have no doubt been imported into this country one at a time. Currently produced Baikals are noted for their high quality at low-level costs.

COMBINATION GUNS

IZH-94 O/U - 12 or 20 (new 2001) ga. over various cals. (domestic and metric), 3 in. chamber, boxlock action, 24 in. separated barrels with express sights, DT, extractors, choke tube (shotgun barrel), checkered walnut stock and forearm, approx. 7¼ lbs.

MSR	$549	$460	$385	$300	$275	$250	$235	$220

PISTOLS: SEMI-AUTO

IZH-35M - 22 LR cal., semi-auto target pistol featuring fully adj. walnut target grip, 6 in. hammer forged barrel, adj. trigger assembly, integral grip safety, 5 shot mag., cocking indicator and detachable scope mount, 2.3 lbs. Importation began 2000.

MSR	$539	$480	$425	$385	$335	$300	$275	$250

IJ-70 - .380 ACP or 9x18 Makarov cal., double action semi-auto, all steel blue construction, 4 in. barrel, slide mounted safety with decocking, fully adj. target sights, choice of two 8 shot (IJ- 70), two 10 (C/B 1994, Model IJ-70-HC), or two 12* shot mag., holster and cleaning rod, checkered plastic grips, 25 oz. Disc. 1996.

		$175	$150	$135	$120	$105	$95	$85

Last MSR was $199.

Add $40 for IJ-70-HC (High Capacity).
Add $50 for .380 ACP cal.
Add $10 for nickel finish (disc.).

Grading	100%	98%	95%	90%	80%	70%	60%

RIFLES: O/U

IZH-94 - .222 Rem., .223 Rem., .30-06, .308 Win., 6.5x55mm, or 7.62x39mm cal., DT, extractors, mono bloc construction, 24 in. barrels with express sights, checkered walnut stock and forearm, 8.3 lbs. Importation began 2001.

	MSR	$629		$525	$425	$365	$335	$295	$280	$265

SHOTGUNS: O/U, RECENT IMPORTATION

IJ-27 FIELD MODEL - 12 or 20 (new 1992) ga., double triggers, extractors, 26 or 28 in. barrels. Disc. 1996.

	$330	$275	$250	$225	$195	$180	$165

Last MSR was $399.

Add $40 for single trigger and automatic ejectors (Model IJ-27EIC).

IZH-27 - 12, 16 (new 2000), 20, 28 ga., or .410 bore, 3 in. chambers (2¾ in. on 28 ga.) boxlock action, 26 or 28 in. VR barrels with (standard on 12 and 20 ga.) or w/o chokes, monobloc receiver, walnut checkered stock (with or w/o Monte Carlo) and forearm, extractors (disc.) or ejectors, blue or nickel finish (new 2001), SST. Importation began 1999.

MSR	$509		$420	$350	$295	$265	$225	$200	$190

Add $60 for 28 ga. or .410 bore.
Add $110 for 20 ga. 2 barrel set.
Add $30 for nickel finish (12 or 20 ga. only, new 2001).
Add $80 for nickel finish with barrel porting (12 ga. only).

IZH-MP 233 SPORTING - 12 ga. only, 3 in. chambers, 26, 28, or 29½ in. unported (disc.) or ported barrels with multi-chokes and wide VR, removable trigger group, SST, ejectors, checkered walnut stock and forearm, includes carrying case, 7.2 lbs. Importation began 1999.

MSR	$939		$795	$650	$575	$500	$460	$430	$395

SHOTGUNS: SxS, RECENT IMPORTATION

The following Bounty Hunters are available in either 12 or 20 ga., include 3 in. chambers, are designed for cowboy action shooting, with choice of hammers or hammerless action, SST, DT (disc.), or double selective triggers, 20 in. barrels with or w/o choke tubes, hardwood or walnut stock and forearm, engraved receiver, extractors, and weigh approx. 7 lbs.

IJ-43 FIELD MODEL - 12 or 20 ga., double triggers, extractors, 20, 26 (disc.), or 28 in. barrels. Disc. 1996.

	$235	$200	$160	$130	$105	$95	$75

Last MSR was $299.

Add $20 for 20 in. barrels bored C/C.

IZH-43 TRADITIONAL HUNTING MODEL - 12, 16 (new 2000), 20, 28 ga., or .410 bore, 3 in. chambers only on .410 bore, Anson & Deeley style boxlock action with monobloc, SST, 24, 26, or 28 in. barrels with or w/o (28 ga. and .410 bore) choke tubes, checkered walnut stock and forearm, approx. 7 lbs. Importation began 1999.

MSR	$389		$330	$285	$235	$215	$185	$165	$150

Add $50 for 16, 20, 28 ga., or .410 bore.

❋ *IZH-43 2 Barrel Set* - includes both 20 and 28 ga. barrels. Importation began 2000.

MSR	$629		$535	$465	$415	$375	$345	$315	$290

Grading	100%	98%	95%	90%	80%	70%	60%

B

✴ *IZH-43 Traditional Bounty Hunter* -12, 20 ga., or .410 bore (new 2001), 2¾ in. chambers, hammerless, 20 in. barrels with choice of cyl./cyl. bore or multichokes, DT or double selective triggers (walnut only), hardwood or walnut stock. Importation began 2000.

MSR $299	$260	$225	$200	$185	$165	$150	$145

Add $10 for 20 ga.
Add $60 for walnut stock and forearm.
Add $60 for double selective triggers on 12 ga., $50 for 20 ga.
Add $159 for .45-70 cal. barrel inserts (only if shotgun is 12 ga., has 2¾ in. chambers, and 20 in. barrels with choke tubes).

IZH-43K EXTERNAL HAMMER -12 or 20 (disc.) ga., similar to IZH-43 Hunting Model, except has engraved sideplates and external cocking hammers, approx. 7¼ lbs. Importation began 2000.

MSR $439	$365	$300	$260	$235	$215	$200	$195

Subtract $60 for cyl./cyl. fixed chokes (20 ga. only).

✴ *IZH-43K External Hammer 2 Barrel Set* - includes both 20 and 28 ga. barrels. Imported 2000 only.

$550	$500	$460	$420	$395	$360	$330

Last MSR was $639.

✴ *IZH-43K Bounty Hunter Traditional* - 12 or 20 ga., 20 in. barrels with choice of cyl./cyl. bore or multichokes. Importation began 2000.

MSR $379	$335	$295	$260	$225	$200	$180	$165

Add $50 for multichokes.
Add $10 for external firing pins and traditional sideplates.
Add $159 for .45-70 cal. barrel inserts (only if shotgun is 12 ga., has 2 ¾ in. chambers, and 20 in. barrels with choke tubes).

IZH MP-213 - 12 ga. only, 3 in. chambers, hammerless, SST (disc. 2000) or double selective triggers, ejectors, removable trigger assembly, 20 (Coach Gun), 24, 26, or 28 in. monobloc barrels with choke tubes, checkered walnut stock and forearm, includes carrying case, approx. 7 lbs. Importation began 1999.

MSR $939	$795	$675	$595	$525	$450	$400	$360

Add $159 for .45-70 cal. barrel inserts (only if shotgun is 12 ga., has 2 ¾ in. chambers, and 20 in. barrels with choke tubes).

SHOTGUNS: SEMI-AUTO, RECENT IMPORTATION

MP-151 - 12 ga., 3 in. chamber, 26 or 28 in. plain barrel with 2 choke tubes, black synthetic or checkered walnut Monte Carlo stock, tube or detachable box (available late 1999) mag., approx. 7.8 lbs. Imported 1999 only.

$275	$235	$215	$195	$180	$165	$150

Last MSR was $310.

MP-153 - 12 ga. only, 3½ in. chamber, 24 (new 2001), 26 or 28 in. VR barrel with choke tubes, black synthetic or walnut stock and forearm, approx. 8 lbs. Importation began 2000.

MSR $509	$445	$375	$320	$285	$235	$200	$190

Add $30 for MC-4 choke tubes (24 in. barrel only).
Subtract $90 for black synthetic stock and forearm.

SHOTGUNS: SINGLE SHOT, RECENT IMPORTATION

IJ-18M - 12, 16, 20 ga., or .410 bore, 26 or 28 in. barrel. Disc. 1996.

$60	$50	$40	$35	$30	$30	$25

Last MSR was $74.

Grading	100%	98%	95%	90%	80%	70%	60%

IZH-18 - 12, 16 (new 2000), 20 ga., or .410 bore, only .410 bore has 3 in. chamber, hammerless, 26 or 28 in. barrel with fixed or multichokes (12 or 20 ga. only, new 2001), ejector, blue or nickel (new 2001) finish, decocking/cocking lever on rear of triggerguard, cocking indicator, hardwood or walnut (new 2001) stock and forearm, trigger block safety, approx. 5½ lbs. Importation began 1998.

	MSR	$95	$80	$65	$55	$45	$35	$30	$30

Add $14 for Youth Model (20 ga. or .410 bore only).
Add $94 for .410 bore with nickel receiver and walnut stock and forearm.
Add $74 for nickel finished receiver (IZH-18 Max) with MC-3 multichokes and walnut stock and forearm (12 or 20 ga. only).

✱ **IZH-18 Sport** - 12 ga. only, 29½ in. VR barrel with porting, rubber butt pad. Importation begain 2002.

	MSR	$219	$185	$160	$135	$110	$95	$80	$65

SHOTGUNS: SLIDE ACTION, RECENT IMPORTATION

IZH-81 - 12 ga. only, 3 in. chamber, 5 shot box mag., 20, 26, or 28 in. plain or VR barrel with (26 or 28 in. barrel only) or w/o choke tubes, hardwood or walnut (disc. 1999) stock and corncob style forearm, blue finish. Imported 1999-2000.

	$235	$190	$170	$160	$145	$135	$125

Last MSR was $269.

Add $17 for walnut stock (disc.1999).
Add $68 for VR barrel (walnut stock only).

IZH MP-133 - 12 ga., 3½ in. chamber, 20, 24 (new 2001), 26, or 28 in. VR barrel with choke tubes (not available with 20 in. barrel), walnut stock and forearm, approx. 7 lbs. Importation began 2000.

	MSR	$329	$275	$215	$185	$175	$155	$145	$135

BAILONS GUNMAKERS LIMITED

Previous manufacturer located in Birmingham, England until 1993, when operations ceased. Inquiries regarding this trademark (including repairs) should be directed to Guthrie Consulting (see Trademark Index for listing).

RIFLES: BOLT ACTION

HUNTING RIFLE - various cals., modified Mauser bolt action, barrel length to suit from 18 to 30 in., set triggers or match, Habicht Telescope sight (magnification and reticle to suit), engraving, and types of finishes are at optional cost, prices below reflect standard rifle with no options. Imported 1986-1993.

	$2,495	$2,250	$1,995	$1,775	$1,625	$1,450	$1,300

Last MSR was $2,750.

BAKER, W.H. & CO.

Previous manufacturer located in Syracuse, NY circa 1878-1883.

Originally started by William H. and Ellis L. Baker circa 1878. During this time, Leroy H. and Lyman C. Smith financed the new company, W.H. Baker & Co. Circa 1880, L.C. Smith bought the interest from the two Baker partners and continued production with markings reading "L. C. Smith and Co., Maker of the Baker Gun" on the rib, "Baker Pat." on the locks. Smith decided to drop the Baker name in 1883, but continued to manufacture this gun and a shotgun/rifle combination gun in Syracuse, NY until 1888. At this point, the company was sold to the Hunter Brothers and this new company, Baker Gun & Forging Co., began making both the New Baker shotguns (see separate listing below) in addition to the Ithaca gun. The company was sold to the Hunter Brothers circa 1888, and the Hunter Arms Company made

Grading	100%	98%	95%	90%	80%	70%	60%

B

L.C. Smith shotguns for approximately 60 years at which point the Marlin Firearms Company bought the business during the early 1940s.

Baker guns were originally 10 or 12 ga., and unusual in that the opening mechanism was operated by pressing forward on the front trigger. While relatively rare, most original Baker guns (including the shotgun/rifle) do not have a lot of original finish remaining. Most specimens are priced in the $400-$850 range, assuming finish is less than 10%. If condition is better than 40%, guns have to be evaluated individually for accurate pricing.

BAKER GUN & FORGING CO.
Previous manufacturer located in Batavia, NY circa 1889-1933.

SHOTGUNS: SxS

Note: Original damascus guns in 80% or better condition with bright case colors will approach the values of steel barrel counterparts. Average original condition (0%-30%) receiver finish models are typically priced in the $275-$400 range, if working. Check for short chambers and chokes to make sure barrels haven't been shortened.

THE NEW BAKER - 10 or 12 ga., exposed hammers, damascus barrels, extractors.

	100%	98%	95%	90%	80%	70%	60%
	$350	$300	$260	$225	$195	$175	$150

BATAVIA SPECIAL - 12, 16, or 20 ga., 26, 28, 30, or 32 in. barrels, any standard choke, checkered pistol grip stock, sidelock, extractors.

	$385	$305	$275	$260	$250	$220	$200

BATAVIA LEADER - similar to Special, except has deluxe finish.

	$440	$360	$335	$305	$285	$265	$220
Auto ejectors	$525	$440	$415	$385	$370	$330	$305

BLACK BEAUTY - similar to Batavia Special with light engraving.

	$500	$440	$360	$335	$305	$285	$265

BLACK BEAUTY SPECIAL - similar to Leader, except has engraved, select wood.

	$745	$650	$615	$590	$550	$525	$495
Auto ejectors	$855	$760	$725	$700	$660	$635	$605

BATAVIA EJECTOR - similar to Leader, but finer finish.

	$880	$770	$745	$715	$690	$660	$635
Damascus barrels	$440	$330	$305	$275	$250	$220	$165

BAKER S GRADE - similar to Leader, but finer finish, better grade wood.

	$880	$775	$745	$715	$690	$650	$635
Auto ejectors	$1,100	$990	$965	$935	$910	$880	$745

BAKER R GRADE - similar to Leader, except scroll and game scene engraved, Krupp barrels, fancy wood.

	$1,100	$990	$965	$935	$910	$880	$745
Auto ejectors	$1,320	$1,210	$1,155	$1,100	$1,075	$1,045	$965
Damascus barrel	$550	$415	$385	$360	$330	$275	$230

PARAGON GRADE - custom order only to customer specifications.

	$1,650	$1,430	$1,320	$1,210	$1,155	$1,045	$770
Auto ejectors	$1,815	$1,595	$1,485	$1,375	$1,210	$1,100	$990

EXPERT GRADE - auto ejectors standard, overall finer grade wood and engraving.

	$2,500	$2,100	$1,850	$1,500	$1,250	$1,000	$750

DELUXE GRADE - best quality.

	$3,750	$3,250	$2,950	$2,650	$2,300	$2,000	$1,600

Add $200 for single trigger.

Grading	100%	98%	95%	90%	80%	70%	60%

SHOTGUNS: SINGLE BARREL TRAP

Baker single barrel trap guns, although more rare than their side-by-side counterparts, are not as desirable as those models listed. Typically, values will be 50%-75% less for a side-by-side model of equal grade.

BALLARD RIFLE, LLC

Current rifle manufacturer located in Cody, WY, since 1996. Dealer and consumer direct sales.

RIFLES: SINGLE SHOT

All Ballard rifles feature receivers milled from solid stock, hand polished barrels, and authentic "packed" case hardening. Many custom features are also available - contact the factory directly for availability and pricing. In addition to the standard models listed (up to 12 months delivery time), special order models include No. 1 ($2,200 MSR), No. 2 Sporting ($1,850 MSR), No. 4 Perfection ($2,250 MSR), No. 5½ Montana ($2,725 MSR), No. 6 Offhand ($3,250 MSR), No. 8 Union Hill ($2,500 MSR), No. 3F Gallery ($2,050 MSR), and No. 3F Fine Gallery ($2,300 MSR). Allow up to 12 months for delivery.

BALLARD 1½ HUNTER'S RIFLE - available in 7 cals. between .22 LR - .50-70, single trigger, unchecked stock and forearm, S style lever action, approx. 10½ lbs. 9¾ - 10½ lbs.

	MSR	$2,050		$1,875	$1,575	$1,325	$1,075	$925	$850	$725

BALLARD 1¾ FAR WEST RIFLE - available in 8 cals. between .32-40 WCF-.50-90 SS, patterned after the original Ballard Far West Model, 30 or 32 in. standard or heavyweight octagon barrel, double set triggers, ring style lever, 9¾ - 10½ lbs.

	MSR	$2,250		$2,075	$1,750	$1,425	$1,150	$975	$875	$750

BALLARD NO. 5 PACIFIC - available in 9 cals. between .32-40 WCF-.50-90 SS, includes under-barrel wiping rod, otherwise similar to No. 1¾ Far West Rifle.

	MSR	$2,575		$2,325	$2,000	$1,625	$1,325	$1,050	$925	$795

BALLARD NO. 4½ MID RANGE - available in 5 cals. between .32-40 WCF-.45-110, configured for black powder cartridge silhouette, half-round, half-octagon 30 or 32 in. standard or heavyweight barrel, single or double set triggers, pistol grip stock, full loop lever, hard rubber Ballard buttplate, Vernier tang sight. 10¾-11½ lbs.

	MSR	$2,250		$2,075	$1,750	$1,425	$1,150	$975	$875	$750

BALLARD NO. 7 LONG RANGE - available in 5 cals. between .40-65 Win.- .45-110, designed for long range shooting, half- round, half-octagon 32 or 34 in. standard or heavyweight barrel, other features similar to Ballard No. 4½ Mid Range.

	MSR	$2,250		$2,075	$1,750	$1,425	$1,150	$975	$875	$750

WINCHESTER MODEL 1885 HIGH WALL - various cals., exact copy of original Winchester Model 1885 (parts interchange), 30 or 32 in. octagon barrel, ST with small lever, case colored receiver, unchecked straight grip walnut stock and forearm, approx. 9 lbs. New 2001.

	MSR	$2,050		$1,875	$1,575	$1,325	$1,075	$925	$850	$725

Add $200 for Special Sporting Model.
Add $325 for Helm Schuetzen Model.

＊ **Winchester Model 1885 High Wall Deluxe** - similar to Model 1885 High Wall, except has deluxe checkered pistol grip stock with shotgun buttplate and forearm, double set triggers, 32 in. No. 4 barrel, aperture sights, 11 lbs. new 2001.

	MSR	$3,815		$3,475	$2,950	$2,650	$2,225	$1,975	$1,575	$1,375

Grading	100%	98%	95%	90%	80%	70%	60%

BALTIMORE ARMS COMPANY

Previous manufacturer of SxS shotguns located in Baltimore, MD circa 1895-1902.

SHOTGUNS: SxS

STYLE 1 - mfg. 1895-1900, this variation does not have the improved Hollenbeck barrel locking mechanism characterized by the eye-shaped hole in the top rib extension.

> There are 4 grades of Baltimore Arms Company shotguns: Field, Grade A, Grade B, and Grade C. Prices generally range from $295-$1,500 depending on condition and grade.

STYLE 2 - mfg. 1900-1902, this variation has the improved barrel locking mechanism and is patent date marked "FEB. 13, 1900" on the water table.

> There are 4 grades of Baltimore Arms Company shotguns: Field, Grade A, Grade B, and Grade C. Prices generally range from $295-$2,000 depending on condition and grade.

BANSNER'S ULTIMATE RIFLES, L.L.C.

Current custom rifle manufacturer established during 1981 and located in Adamstown, PA. In 2000, the company name changed from Bansner's Gunsmithing Specialities to Bansner's Ultimate Rifles, L.L.C. Consumer direct sales.

RIFLES: BOLT ACTION

All Bansner's UR rifles up to approx. June 1, 1999 have either Remington 700 or Winchester post-64 claw extractor actions. After this approx. date, Bansner's started using their own proprietary action. Bansner's also continues to manufacture several models utilizing a customer's Rem. 700 or Win. 70 action. Prices range from $2,395 (Ultimate Rifle, w/o action) to $3,295 (Sheep Hunter, lightweight, w/o Rem. 700 action).

The 100% value does not include federal excise tax.

ULTIMATE ONE - various cals. and configurations including different metal finishes and special orders, Rem. 700 (disc. 1999), Win. post-64 Model 70 (disc. 1999), exclusive action mfg. by McMillan Bros. Rifle Co., Inc. (steel or stainless steel, new 2001), Douglas premium air gauged (disc.) or Lilja fluted barrel with M-50 muzzle brake, large extractor, plunger ejector, 3 lbs. custom tuned trigger, custom color synthetic stock with Pachmayr decelerator pad, includes Talley custom scope bases and rings, various weights.

MSR	$3,995		$3,675	$3,000	$2,500	$2,150	$1,950	$1,700	$1,450

Add $250 for 3 position Model 70 style safety or Lazzeroni calibers.

HIGH TECH SERIES - various cals., Howa 1500 steel or stainless steel action with factory barrel and Bansner's synthetic stock with Pachmayr decelerator pad. New 1997.

MSR	$1,030		$950	$825	$725	$625	$575	$500	$450

Add $90 for all stainless steel.

BARRETT FIREARMS MANUFACTURING, INC.   BARRETT

Current manufacturer located in Murfreesboro, TN. Dealer direct sales.

Grading	100%	98%	95%	90%	80%	70%	60%

RIFLES: BOLT ACTION

MODEL 90 - .50 BMG cal., bolt action design, 29 in. match grade barrel with muzzle brake, 5 shot detachable box mag., includes extendible bi-pod legs, scope optional, 22 lbs. Mfg. 1990-95.

	$3,450	$2,950	$2,400	$2,150	$1,875	$1,600	$1,500

Last MSR was $3,650.

Add $1,150 for Swarovski 10X scope and rings.

MODEL 95 - .50 BMG cal., bolt action design, 29 in. match grade barrel with high efficiency muzzle brake, 5 shot detachable box mag., includes extendible bi-pod legs, scope optional, 22.5 lbs. New 1995.

MSR	$5,100	$4,475	$3,450	$2,700	$2,325	$1,875	$1,600	$1,500

MODEL 99 - .50 BMG cal., single shot bolt action, 33 in. barrel with muzzle brake, straight through design with pistol grip and bi-pod, black or silver finish, 25 lbs. New 1999.

MSR	$3,100	$2,725	$2,300	$1,825	$1,625	$1,475	$1,350	$1,225

Add $200 for fluted barrel.

RIFLES: SEMI-AUTO

MODEL 82 RIFLE - .50 BMG cal., semi-auto recoil operation, 33-37 in. barrel, 11 shot mag., 2,850 FPS muzzle velocity, scope sight only, parkerized finish, 35 lbs. Mfg. 1985- 87.

	$4,350	$3,950	$3,450	$2,700	$2,150	$1,800	$1,500

Last MSR for consumers was $3,180 in 1985.

This model underwent design changes since initial production. Only 115 were mfg. starting with ser. no. 100.

MODEL 82A1 - .50 BMG cal., paramilitary design, variant of the original Model 82, back-up iron sights provided, 2 mags., and fitted hard case, 29 (new late 1989) or 33 (disc. 1989) in. barrel, 10 shot detachable mag., 32½ lbs. for 1989 and older mfg., 28½ lbs. for 1990 mfg. and newer. Current mfg. includes watertight case and cleaning kit.

MSR	$7,300	$6,750	$5,200	$4,375	$3,700	$3,150	$2,650	$2,200

Add $300 for pack-mat backpack case (new 1999).
Add $275 for camo backpack carrying case (disc.)
Add $1,325 for Swarovski 10X scope and rings.

This model boasts official U.S. rifle status following government procurement during Operation Desert Storm. In 1992, a new "arrowhead" shaped muzzle brake was introduced to reduce recoil.

MODEL 98 - .338 Lapua Mag. cal., 10 shot box mag., 24 in. match grade barrel with muzzle brake, bi- pod, 15½ lbs.

While advertised during mid-1999, this model was never produced.

BAR-STO

Previous manufacturer located in 29 Palms, CA. Bar-Sto still manufactures barrels and firearms related accessories.

PISTOLS: SEMI-AUTO

BAR-STO .25 ACP PISTOL - .25 ACP cal., patterned after the Baby Browning, brushed stainless steel finish, walnut grips, approx. 250 manufactured in circa 1974.

	$195	$165	$125

Grading	100%	98%	95%	90%	80%	70%	60%

B BATTAGLIA, MAURO

Current manufacturer established in 1992 and located in Ravenna, Italy. No current U.S. importation.

Mauro Battaglia manufactures custom order high quality SxS shotguns. He also manufactures a sidelock action with new, unique design. Please contact the factory directly for more information.

BAUER FIREARMS CORPORATION

Previous manufacturer located in Fraser, MI circa 1971-1984.

DERRINGERS

THE RABBIT - .22 LR cal. and .410 bore, combination gun, all metal construction, O/U configuration. Mfg. 1982-1984.

	$125	$100	$90	$80	$70	$60	$50

PISTOLS: SEMI-AUTO

BAUER .25 ACP - .25 ACP cal., 2½ in. barrel, 6 shot, fixed sights, checkered walnut or pearlite grips, mfg. 1972-1984.

	$150	$130	$110

Note: These guns are identical to the Baby Browning, except stainless steel.

* ***Bauer .25 ACP Bicentennial Model*** - .25 ACP cal., engraved with buckle in display case.

	$300	$200	$150

BAYARD

Previously manufactured by Anciens Etablissements Pieper located in Herstal, Belgium.

Even though Bayard Models 1908, both 1923s, and 1930 were manufactured only by Anciens Etablissements Pieper of Herstal, Belgium, these pistols are listed under this heading as they are most commonly referred to by this trademark designation.

PISTOLS: SEMI-AUTO

.25 ACP and .380 ACP cals. are more rare than the .32 ACP, and will command a 20%+ premium above values listed unless indicated differently.

MODEL 1908 POCKET AUTOMATIC - .25 ACP, .32 ACP, or .380 ACP cal., 6 shot, 2¼ in. barrel, fixed sights, blue, hard rubber grips.

	$350	$250	$165	$100	$85	$70	$55

Add 10% for .25 ACP cal.
Add 25% if marked with Imperial Eagle.

MODEL 1923 POCKET AUTOMATIC - .25 ACP cal., 2½ in. barrel, blue, fixed sights, checkered hard rubber grips.

	$350	$295	$225	$170	$140	$125	$95

BAYARD 1923 POCKET AUTOMATIC - .32 ACP or .380 ACP cal., 6 shot, 3 5/16 in. barrel, fixed sights, blue, checkered hard rubber grips.

	$350	$295	$225	$170	$140	$125	$95

Add 100% for .380 ACP cal.

BAYARD 1930 POCKET AUTOMATIC - slight modification of 1923.

	$350	$250	$200	$170	$145	$120	$95

Grading	100%	98%	95%	90%	80%	70%	60%

B

BEEMAN OUTDOOR SPORTS

Previous importer and distributor located in Santa Rosa, CA.

On April 1, 1993, Beeman Precision Arms, Inc. was split into two independent companies: Beeman Precision Airguns, division of S/R Industries (Maryland Corp.), located in Huntington Beach, CA retains worldwide distribution of Beeman airguns and accessories. Beeman Outdoor Sports, a Division of Robert's Precision Arms, Inc., located in Santa Rosa, CA distributed Feinwerkbau firearms until 1995.

Beeman Precision Arms, Inc. was a large importer, primarily specializing in high quality European air rifles and pistols. Firearms trademarks previously distributed in the U.S. include the following trademarks: Agner (disc. 1986), Erma (disc. 1985), FAS (disc. 1987), Fabarm (disc. 1985), Feinwerkbau, Korth (disc. 1990), Krico (disc. 1988), Unique (disc. 1991), and Weihrauch (disc.). These trademarks appear under their respective alphabetical headings.

For more information and current pricing on both new and used Beeman Precision Airguns, please refer to the 2nd Ed. Blue Book of Airguns by Dr. Robert Beeman & John Allen (now online also).

The following firearms were manufactured to Beeman specifications, and are therefore listed under the Beeman Outdoor Sports heading.

PISTOLS: SEMI-AUTO

BEEMAN MP-08 - .380 ACP cal., Luger type toggle action, 3½ in. barrel, 6 shot mag., blue, 1.4 lbs. Mfg. 1968-1990.

$395	$335	$275	$240	$185	$145	$115

Last MSR was $390.

In 1988, Beeman took over importation of these two models (MP-08 and P-08). These revised models have new Luger style checkered walnut grips and 3½ in. barrel. Previous variations had plastic grips.

BEEMAN P-08 - .22 LR cal., Luger type toggle action, 8 shot mag., 3.8 in. barrel, blue, checkered walnut grips, 1.9 lbs. Mfg. 1969-1990.

$395	$335	$275	$240	$185	$145	$115

Last MSR was $390.

PISTOLS: SINGLE SHOT

MODEL SP/SPX - .22 LR cal., designed for silhouette shooting, 10 in. heavy bull barrel, blue metal parts, birchwood stocks and forearm, aperture sights, 3.9 lbs. Disc. 1994.

$625	$550	$475	$425	$375	$330	$295

Last MSR was $700.

Only a few of these models were actually delivered.

✳ **Model SPX Deluxe** - similar to Model SPX, except has matte chrome metal finish, hand stippled walnut grips, and Anschütz rear sight. Limited mfg. 1993-94.

$800	$725	$650	$575	$500	$425	$350

Last MSR was $900.

SP STANDARD - .22 LR cal., sidelever action, 8, 10, 12, or 15 in. barrel, adj. sights and walnut grips, single shot. Made in W. Germany. Imported 1985-86 only.

$250	$220	$180	$170	$160	$150	$140

Last MSR was $250.

Add $10 or $30 for 12 or 15 in. barrel respectively.

SP DELUXE - similar to SP Standard, except has forearm, about 3½ lbs. Made in W. Germany. Imported 1985-86 only.

$275	$240	$200	$185	$170	$155	$145

Last MSR was $300.

Add $10 or $30 for 12 or 15 in. barrel respectively.

Grading	100%	98%	95%	90%	80%	70%	60%

B BEHOLLA PISTOL

Previously manufactured by Becker & Hollander located in Suhl, Germany.

PISTOLS: SEMI-AUTO

BEHOLLA POCKET AUTOMATIC - .32 ACP cal., 7 shot, 2.9 in. barrel, blue, serrated wood or rubber grips, mfg. 1915-1920, from 1920-1925 the same gun was mfg. by Stenda-Werke.

| | $225 | $170 | $150 | $135 | $120 | $100 | $90 |

BENELLI

Current manufacturer located in Urbino, Italy. Benelli USA, was formed during late 1997, and is currently importing all Benelli shotguns. Benellis pistols were discontinued during 2002. Company headquarters are located in Accokeek, MD. Shotguns were previously imported 1983-1997 by Heckler & Koch, Inc., located in Sterling, VA. Handguns were previously imported until 1997 by European American Armory, located in Sharpes, FL, in addition to Sile Distributors, Inc., until 1995, located in New York, NY, and Saco, located in Arlington, VA.

PISTOLS: SEMI-AUTO

Models B-77, B-80, and MP3S were previously imported by Sile Distributors. Models MP90S and MP95E Atlanta were imported by Benelli USA until 2002.

MODEL B-76 - 9mm Para. cal., selective double action, all steel, 4¼ in. barrel, 8 shot mag., 34 oz. Importation disc. in 1990.

| | $400 | $375 | $335 | $295 | $245 | $225 | $210 |

Last MSR was $428.

MODEL B-76S TARGET - 9mm Para. cal., similar to B-76, except has 5½ in. barrel, target grips, and adj. rear sights. Importation disc. 1990.

| | $550 | $475 | $425 | $395 | $350 | $325 | $300 |

Last MSR was $595.

MODEL B-77 - .32 ACP cal., selective double action, all steel, 4¼ in. barrel, 8 shot mag. Importation disc. 1995.

| | $395 | $350 | $295 | $255 | $225 | $200 | $180 |

Last MSR was $385.

MODEL B-80 - .30 Luger cal., selective double action, all steel, 4¼ in. barrel, 8 shot mag., 34 oz. Importation disc. 1995.

| | $395 | $350 | $295 | $255 | $225 | $200 | $180 |

Last MSR was $385.

MODEL B-80S TARGET - similar to B-80, except has 5½ in. barrel, target grips, and adj. rear sights. Importation disc. 1995.

| | $500 | $450 | $375 | $325 | $295 | $275 | $250 |

Last MSR was $572.

MODEL MP3S - .32 S&W Long Wadcutter cal., target variation with 5½ in. barrel, high gloss bluing, target grips, and adj. rear sights. Importation disc. 1995.

| | $550 | $450 | $375 | $325 | $295 | $275 | $250 |

Last MSR was $785.

Grading	100%	98%	95%	90%	80%	70%	60%

MODEL MP90S WORLD CUP - .22 S (disc.), .22 LR, or .32 S&W Wadcutter (disc. 1999) cal., 4.4 in. barrel, blue finish, target pistol featuring forward assisted breech bolt mechanism, anatomic grips, and adj. weight, 5 (disc.), 6 or 9 (optional) shot mag., 2.5 lbs. Imported 1992-2002.

	$1,230	$1,050	$850	$725	$650	$600	$550

Last MSR was $1,465.

Add 10% for .32 S&W Wadcutter cal.

Conversion kits were previously available for this model at an extra charge.

MODEL MP95E ATLANTA - .22 LR or .32 S&W Wadcutter (disc. 1999) cal., 4.4 in. barrel, features inertial recoiling mass system, integral Weaver style base mount, 5 (disc.), 6 or 9 (optional) shot mag., adj. trigger assembly, fully adj. sight, modular firing system, blue or matte chrome finish, smooth laminate (chrome finish only) or choice of checkered adj. (disc.) or non-adj. walnut grips, 2.5 lbs. Mfg. late 1994-2002.

	$700	$575	$495	$450	$400	$375	$350

Last MSR was $815.

Add $85 for chrome finish.
Add 10% for .32 S&W Wadcutter cal.

This model was originally designated the Model MP95.

RIFLES: SEMI-AUTO

ARGO - .30-06 or .300 Win. Mag. cal., features rotating bolt head and unique gas design, 20 in. barrel with cryogenic treatment and interchangeable rear rib, fixed two or detachable (optional) four shot mag., forearm is fixed to the alloy receiver, available in black or nickel plated receiver finish, checkered walnut stock and forearm, recoil pad is cut into the stock (adj., with shims), ambidextrous safety. approx. 7 1/8 lbs. New 2002.

As this edition went to press, U.S. availability and pricing had yet to be established on this model. Argo is an abbreviation for auto-regulating gas operated.

SHOTGUNS: SEMI-AUTO, 1985-OLDER

Benelli semi-auto 3rd generation (inertia recoil) shotguns were imported starting in the late 1960s. The receivers were mfg. of light aluminum alloy - the SL-80 Model 121 had a semi-gloss, anodized black finish, the Model 123 had an ornate photo-engraved receiver, the Model Special 80 had a brushed, white nickel-plated receiver, and the Model 121 M1 had a matte finish receiver, barrel, and stock. All 12 ga. SL-80 Series shotguns will accept 2 ¾ or 3 in. shells, and all SL-80 Series 12 ga. Models have interchangeable barrels (except the 121 M1) with 4 different model receivers (121, 121 M1, 123, or Special 80). All 4 models had fixed choke barrels.

The SL-80 Series shotguns were disc. during 1985, and H&K and Benelli USA do not have parts for these guns. There may be stocks, forearms, used barrels (CDNN only), and other misc. parts still available for the 12 ga. from CDNN (800-588-9500), and Gun Parts Corp. (see Trademark Index for more information). Approx. 50,000 SL-80 series shotguns were mfg. before discontinuance - choke markings (located on side or underneath barrel) are as follows: * full choke, ** imp. mod., *** mod., **** imp. cyl. SL-80 series guns used the same action (much different than current mfg.) and all had the split receiver design. Be aware of possible wood cracking where the barrel rests on the thin area of the forend and also on the underside of the buttstock behind trigger guard. When buying or selling a SL-80 Series shotgun, be aware that when comparing the SL-80 Series with the newer action Benellis (post 1985), there is a big difference between the action, design changes, and actual selling prices in today's marketplace. Just because the prices on new Benellis have gone up considerably, it doesn't mean that the SL-80 Series prices will follow suit.

Interest and sales in the older SL-80 Series Benelli shotguns have fallen sharply in recent years, since in the semi-auto shotgun marketplace, newer is always better. Also, buyers are reluctant to

Grading	100%	98%	95%	90%	80%	70%	60%

purchase a gun that may have a parts availability problem.

100% values within this section assume NIB condition.

Subtract 5% for "SACO" importation (Saco was located in Arlington, VA).

SL-80 SERIES MODEL SL-121V - 12 ga., field grade, 26, or 28 in. fixed choke VR barrel, anodized and black semi-gloss finish on lower receiver. Disc. 1985.

	$365	$325	$275	$225	$200	$185	$160

Last MSR was $397.

SL-80 SERIES MODEL SL-121/SL-122 SLUG - 12 ga., features Monte Carlo stock and flat bottom Trap Grade beavertail forearm, 21 1/16 cyl. bore barrel, fixed open ring rear iron sights and fixed front ramp, 5 shot mag., recoil pad, 7 lbs. 3 oz. Disc. 1985.

	$350	$300	$250	$225	$200	$185	$160

Last MSR was $434.

SL-80 SERIES MODEL SL-123V - 12 ga., stylish field grade, receiver Ergal special aluminum alloy with photo engraving, 26 or 28 in. VR barrel with various chokes, approx. 6 lbs. 13 oz. Disc. 1985.

	$425	$365	$315	$265	$225	$200	$185

Last MSR was $464.

Add $20 for trap stock, $10 for beavertail forearm and $25 for skeet barrel.

The only difference between the SL-123V and SL-121V is the photo engraved receiver. The SL-123V was at times referred to as the deluxe model when comparing it with the SL-121V. Both models were field grade shotguns.

EX-L - 12 ga., similar in appearance to the Model SL123V, except has hand-engraved receiver, very limited mfg. with unpredictable premiums over Model SL123V.

SL-80 SERIES MODEL 121 M1 POLICE/MILITARY - 12 ga. only, similar in appearance to the Super 90 M1, hardwood stock, 7 shot mag., matte metal and wood finish, most stocks had adj. lateral sling attachment inside of buttstock, 18¾ in. barrel. Disc. 1985.

	$445	$385	$325	$285	$250	$225	$195

Since many of this model were sold to the police and military, used specimens should be checked carefully for excessive wear and/or possible damage.

MODEL 80 SPECIAL SKEET/TRAP - 12 ga. only, 28 in. VR with mod. choke and phosphorescent bead sight, has trap/skeet Monte Carlo grade/style wood stock with recoil pad, lower receiver is nickel plated, 7 lbs. 10 oz. Disc. 1986.

	$450	$395	$350	$295	$250	$225	$195

Last MSR was $531.

Trap guns should have high comb trap stock and trap grade forearm (not field grade/style wood). Trap guns should also be inspected carefully for internal wear before buying/selling.

SL-80 SERIES MODEL SL201 - 20 ga., 26 in. VR barrel bored mod., black anodized lower receiver, approx. 5 lbs. 10 oz., mfg. in France for Benelli. Disc. 1985.

	$350	$300	$265	$235	$210	$185	$165

Last MSR was $399.

BRI-BENELLI SL-80 123 SLUG GUN - 12 ga. only, custom designed, premium slug gun featuring SL-80 Series action and drilled and tapped rifle bored barrel by E. R. Shaw Barrel Co., assembled by BRI in the U.S., Monte Carlo stock with beavertail forend, approx. 25 guns total mfg. 1986-1987.

	$1,895	$1,275	$1,025	$875	$750	$625	$525

Original issue price on this model was $750-$850. These specimens are marked "BRI- Benelli" on barrel. No warranties exist on this model.

Grading	100%	98%	95%	90%	80%	70%	60%

B

SHOTGUNS: SEMI-AUTO, 1986-NEWER

Extra barrels (non-slug)for the currently manufactured models are typically priced in the $305-$385 range, depending on the model. Unless indicated otherwise, all currently manufactured Benelli shotguns utilize a red bar front sight, and are equipped with a patented Benelli keyed chamber lock.

M1 FIELD (SUPER 90) - 12 or 20 (new 2001) ga., 3 in. chamber, inertia recoil operating system, alloy receiver, 21 (new 1990, 12 ga. only), 24 (new 1990), 26, or 28 in. vent. rib barrel and 3-shot mag., includes 5 screw in choke tubes, satin walnut (new 1994), black polymer, 100% Realtree X-tra Brown (mfg. 1997-2001) or Advantage Timber HD (new 2001, 20 ga. only) camo coverage, approx. 5.8 (20 ga.) or 7.2 (12 ga.) lbs.

MSR	$970		$780	$665	$575	$445	$375	$335	$300

Add $10 for satin walnut stock (26 or 28 in. barrel only).
Add $100 for Advantage Timber HD camo finish.
Add $95 for Realtree Xtra Brown camo finish (disc. 2001).
Add $42 for 11 oz. mercury recoil reducer (synthetic stock only).
Add $20 for left-hand action (new 2000, available in synthetic and camo, 12 ga. only).
During 2000, Benelli improved this model with a stepped VR and oversized safety.
This model was available with an extended magazine tube (26 or 28 in. barrel only).

M1 SLUG (SUPER 90) - 12 ga. only, 3 in. mag., incorporates improvements on the Benelli action, including rotating Montefeltro bolt system, 19¾ cyl. bore (disc. 1997) or 24 (new 1998) in. rifled barrel with iron sights (disc. 1997, reintroduced 2001), drilled and tapped beginning 1998, 3 (new 1998) or 7 (disc. 1997) shot mag., Realtree Xtra Brown camo (mfg. 2000-2001), Advantage Timber HD (new 2002) camo, or black fiberglass stock and forearm, 6.7 - 7.6 lbs. New 1986.

MSR	$1,040		$850	$675	$595	$450	$375	$335	$300

Add $110 for Advantage Timber HD camo finish.
Add $105 for Realtree Xtra brown camo finish (disc. 2001).
Subtract 15% for 19¾ cyl. bore barrel with iron sights.

M1 DEFENSE (SUPER 90) - similar to Super 90 Slug, except has pistol grip stock, 7.1 lbs. Disc. 1998.

$685	$525	$395	$325	$300	$270	$250

Last MSR was $851.

Add $41 for ghost-ring sighting system.

M1 PRACTICAL (SUPER 90) - 12 ga. only, 3 in. chamber, 26 in. plain barrel with muzzle brake, designed for IPSC events, extended 8 shot mag. tube, oversized safety, speed loader, larger bolt handle, Milspec adj. ghost-ring sight and Picatinny rail, black regular synthetic stock and forearm, matte metal finish, includes 3 choke tubes, 7.6 lbs. New 1998.

MSR	$1,255		$1,035	$850	$725	$600	$525	$450	$400

M1 TACTICAL (SUPER 90) - 12 ga. only, 3 in. chamber, 18½ in. barrel, fixed rifle or ghost-ring sighting system, available with synthetic pistol grip or standard buttstock, includes 3 choke tubes, 5 shot mag., 6.7 - 7 lbs. New 1993.

MSR	$950		$790	$660	$580	$445	$375	$335	$300

Add $50 for ghost-ring sighting system.
Add $15 for pistol grip stock.

✳ *M1 Tactical M* - similar to M1 Tactical, except has military ghost-ring sights and standard synthetic stock, 7.1 lbs. Mfg. 1999-2000.

$795	$595	$435	$375	$315	$275	$250

Last MSR was $960.

Add $10 for pistol grip stock.

Grading	100%	98%	95%	90%	80%	70%	60%

B

M1 ENTRY (SUPER 90) - 12 ga. only, includes 14 in. barrel, choice of synthetic pistol grip or standard stock, choice of rifle or ghost-ring sights, 5 shot mag. (2 shot extension), approx. 6.7 lbs. New 1992.

MSR	$970	$800	$670	$585	$450	$395	$340	$310

Add $15 for synthetic pistol grip stock.
Add $65 for ghost-ring sighting system.

This model requires special licensing (special tax stamp) for consumers, and is also available to law enforcement.

M1 SPORTING SPECIAL (SUPER 90) - 12 ga., 18½ in. barrel, black matte finish, includes ghost ring sighting system, 6½ lbs. Mfg. 1993-97.

	$750	$650	$550	$450	$395	$340	$310

Last MSR was $924.

M3 SUPER 90 - 12 ga. only, defense configuration incorporating convertible (fingertip activated) pump or semi-auto action, 19¾ in. cyl. bore barrel with ghost ring or rifle sights, 5 shot mag., choice of standard black polymer stock or integral pistol grip (disc. 1996, reintroduced 1999), approx. 7.3 lbs. New 1989.

MSR	$1,110	$920	$725	$625	$525	$450	$375	$325

Add $10 for pistol grip stock.
Add $45 for ghost-ring sighting system.
Add $110 for folding stock (mfg. 1990-disc.) - only available as a complete gun.
Add $340 for Model 200 Laser Sight System with bracket (disc.).

MONTEFELTRO STANDARD HUNTER (SUPER 90) - 12 or 20 (new 1993) ga., 3 in. chamber, aluminum alloy receiver, rotary bolt, 21 (disc. 1997), 24, 26, or 28 (12 ga. only) in. VR barrel with 5 choke tubes, matte black metal or 100% Realtree camo (20 ga. only, mfg. 1998-2000) finish, checkered walnut stock and forearm with choice of high gloss (disc. 1997) or satin finish, 4 shot mag., approx. 5.3 (20 ga.) or 7.1 lbs. New 1988.

MSR	$980	$820	$680	$585	$450	$395	$340	$310

Add $100 for 100% Realtree camo finish on 20 ga. only (disc.).
Add $15 for left-hand action (12 ga., 26 or 28 in. barrel only).
Add $35 for shortened stock with 12½ in. LOP, approx. 5.3 lbs. (20 ga. only, new 1999).

* *Montefeltro Limited Edition (Super 90)* - 20 ga. only, nickel plated lower receiver with etched gold highlights, 26 in. VR barrel. Limited mfg. 1995-96.

	$1,825	$1,525	$1,225	$995	$875	$750	$625

Last MSR was $2,080.

* *Montefeltro Turkey Gun* - similar to Montefeltro Standard Hunter except has 24 in. VR barrel with 3 choke tubes, satin finish wood only, 7 lbs. Imported 1989 only.

	$650	$575	$500	$450	$415	$365	$310

Last MSR was $675.

* *Montefeltro Uplander* - similar to Montefeltro Turkey Gun except has 21 or 24 in. VR barrel with 3 choke tubes, satin finish wood only, 7 lbs. Mfg. 1989-92.

	$650	$575	$500	$450	$415	$365	$310

Last MSR was $799.

* *Montefeltro Slug Gun* - deer gun configuration with 19¾ in. slug barrel. Disc. 1992.

	$650	$500	$475	$425	$400	$350	$310

Last MSR was $799.

SPORT MODEL - 12 ga., 3 in. chamber, one piece alloy receiver, 26 (disc. 1999, reintroduced during 2001 only) or 28 in. barrel with 5 choke tubes and 2 removable and interchangable carbon fiber vent. ribs, 4 shot mag., adj. butt pad and butt stock, satin finished select checkered walnut stock and forearm, "Benelli" outlined in red on matte finished receiver side, approx. 7.1 lbs. New 1997.

MSR	$1,375	$1,125	$895	$750	$575	$500	$450	$400

Grading	100%	98%	95%	90%	80%	70%	60%

LEGACY MODEL - 12 or 20 (new 1999) ga., 3 in. chamber, 24 (20 ga. only), 26 or 28 (12 ga. only) in. VR barrel with 5 choke tubes and red bar front sight with bead mid-sight, 4 shot mag., engraved nickel finished alloy lower or all alloy (20 ga. only) receiver, cartridge drop lever, select checkered walnut stock with vent. recoil pad and forearm, stock shim kit provided, mfg. to commemorate the 30th Anniversary of Benelli shotgun manufacturing, approx. 5.8 lbs. or 7.5 lbs. New 1998.

MSR $1,390	$1,125	$900	$750	$575	$500	$450	$400

* **Legacy Limited Edition** - 12 or 20 ga., features acid etched engraving with gold filled game scenes, only 250 of each ga. mfg. for the new millennium only, deluxe checkered walnut stock and forearm. Limited mfg. 2000 only.

$1,750	$1,475	$850	$675	$600	$500	$450

Last MSR was $1,600.

Add 20% to individual prices for a 2 gun set with matching serial numbers (NIB only).

EXECUTIVE SERIES - 12 ga. only, 3 in. chamber, features engraved all-steel greyed lower receiver by Giovanelli, mid-rib barrel bead, high polish upper receiver and barrel bluing, extra select grade walnut, 5 choke tubes, and other accessories, choice of 21 (disc.), 24 (disc.), 26, or 28 in. VR barrel, aprrox. 7¾ lbs. Special order only beginning 1996.

* **Grade/Type I**

MSR $5,200	$4,625	$3,650	$2,500

* **Grade/Type II**

MSR $5,870	$5,175	$4,050	$3,025

* **Grade/Type III**

MSR $6,800	$6,050	$4,500	$3,425

BLACK EAGLE - 12 ga., 3 in. chamber, Montefeltro action, similar to Montefeltro Super 90 Standard Hunter except has black synthetic regular or pistol grip stock and forearm, 21 (disc. 1990), 24 (disc. 1990), 26, or 28 (new 1990) in. VR barrel with 3 choke tubes, right hand only. Originally imported 1989-90, resumed 1997 only.

$825	$675	$550	$450	$375	$315	$285

Last MSR was $992.

This configuration changed to competition in 1991 (see Black Eagle Competition Model).

* **Black Eagle Competition Model** - 12 ga. only, designed for competition shooting with action adj. for lighter loads, silver finished etched lower receiver, 26 or 28 in. VR barrel with 5 choke tubes and wrench provided, includes buttstock drop adjustment kit. Mfg. 1991-97.

$1,025	$795	$675	$550	$475	$375	$300

Last MSR was $1,229.

* **Black Eagle 1994 Limited Edition** - 12 ga. only, features 26 in. VR barrel with extra fancy grade checkered walnut and gold inlays on receiver sides, 1,000 mfg. 1994-95 only with special serialization.

$1,775	$1,500	$1,225	$995	$875	$750	$625

Last MSR was $2,000.

* **Black Eagle Slug Gun** - 12 ga., 24 in. rifled barrel with receiver scope mount. Imported 1990-91 only.

$735	$625	$500	$425	$365	$315	$285

Last MSR was $859.

Grading	100%	98%	95%	90%	80%	70%	60%

B **SUPER BLACK EAGLE** - 12 ga. only, 3½ in. chamber, updated Montefeltro action accepts all 12 ga. loads, right or left hand (new 1999) action, upper steel/lower alloy receiver, 24, 26, or 28 in. VR barrel with 5 choke tubes and wrench provided, 3 shot mag., choice of matte finish and satin wood stock, blue finish and high gloss wood finish (26 or 28 in. barrel only), or 100% coverage Advantage Timber HD (new 2002) or Realtree X-tra Brown camo. finish (mfg. 1997-2001) on polymer stock and forearm, black synthetic stock and forearm with matte metal finish was introduced in 1993, vent. recoil pad, includes buttstock drop adjustment kit, approx. 7.4 lbs. New 1991.

MSR	$1,260	$1,040	$880	$750	$625	$525	$475	$425

Add $100 for Advantage Timber HD camo finish.
Add $95 for 100% coverage Realtree camo wood/metal finish (disc. 2001).
Add $15 for satin wood stock and forearm (26 or 28 in. barrel only).
Add $42 for 11 oz. mercury recoil reducer (synthetic stock only).
Add $50 for left hand action for either black synthetic stock/forearm or full coverage camo finish.

* ***Super Black Eagle Limited Edition*** - 12 ga. only, features 26 in. VR barrel with extra fancy grade checkered walnut and gold inlays on nickel plated receiver sides, 1,000 mfg. beginning 1997 with special serialization, 7.4 lbs. Disc. 1999.

		$1,825	$1,500	$1,225	$995	$875	$750	$625

Last MSR was $2,095.

* ***Super Black Eagle Slug Gun*** – 12 ga., 3 in. chamber, includes 24 in. rifled barrel with adj. rifle sights, drilled and tapped receiver, choice of matte or camo metal finish, choice of black polymer (new 1993), satin finished wood, or 100% Advantage Timber HD (new 2002) or Realtree X-tra Brown camo (mfg. 2000-2001), 7.6 lbs. New 1992.

MSR	$1,320	$1,100	$900	$775	$650	$575	$475	$425

Add $15 for wood stock.
Add $130 for Advantage Timber HD camo finish.
Add $100 for Realtree X-tra Brown camo finish (disc. 2001).

SHOTGUNS: SLIDE-ACTION

All currently manufactured Benelli shotguns are equipped with a patented Benelli keyed chamber lock.

NOVA - 12 or 20 (new 2001) ga., 3 (20 ga. only) or 3½ in. chamber, unique design allows stock and internal metal receiver "shell" to be molded in one unit, utilizing a glass polymer matrix, Montefeltro rotating bolt, double action bars, 24, 26, or 28 in. VR barrel with 3 choke tubes and red bar front sight, 3 (3½ in. shells) or 4 shot mag., matte metal finish, choice of black synthetic, full coverage Realtree X-tra brown or Advantage Timber HD (new 2001, 20 ga. only) camo stock and forearm with grooved hand ribs, mag. stop button in forearm, approx. 6.5 (20 ga.) or 8 lbs. New 1999.

MSR	$405	$350	$315	$285	$250	$235	$220	$215

Add $45 for 20 ga.
Add $65 for Realtree X-tra Brown full camo finish (12 ga. only).
Add $85 for 20 ga. with Advantage Timber HD full camo coverage.
Add $55 for 2 or 4 (disc.) shot magazine extension.
Add $42 for recoil reducer - 10 oz. (disc.) or 14 oz. Mercury, installed in stock with reduction tube operation.

* ***Nova Special Purpose Smooth Bore*** - similar action to Nova, features 18½ in. cyl. bore barrel with choice of rifle or ghost ring (new 2000) sights, black synthetic stock and forearm only, 7.2 lbs. New 1999.

MSR	$355		$300	$265	$245	$225	$210	$200	$195

Add $40 for ghost ring sights.

Grading	100%	98%	95%	90%	80%	70%	60%

* ***Nova Slug Rifled Bore*** - 12 ga. only, features 24 in. rifled bore drilled and tapped barrel with open rifle sights, black synthetic stock and forearm, 8.1 lbs. New 2000.

| MSR | $575 | | $495 | $440 | $385 | $330 | $300 | $280 | $260 |

BENSON FIREARMS LTD.

Previous importer for guns manufactured by Aldo Uberti in Italy. Previously imported and distributed from 1987-1989 by Benson Firearms Ltd. located in Seattle, WA. Benson Firearms Ltd. combined with A. Uberti USA Inc. in early 1989 and discontinued importation.

Benson Firearms can be differentiated from other A. Uberti imports by the "Benson Firearms Seattle, WA" barrel marking.

Rather than provide a complete listing of Benson Firearms models, the following rules usually apply. Since Benson Firearms imported A. Uberti firearms, the Uberti section in this text should be referenced for current values regarding models with similar configurations. Collectibility to date has been limited on most Benson Fireams models, and as a rule, up-to-date values on this trademark are established by current importation prices of Uberti firearms. A complete listing of older Benson Firearms models can be found in the 11th & 12th Editions of the Blue Book of Gun Values.

BENTON & BROWN FIREARMS, INC.

Previous manufacturer located in Fort Worth, TX and Delhi, LA circa 1993-1996.

RIFLES: BOLT ACTION

MODEL 93 - available in 15 cals. between .243 Win. and .375 H&H Mag., patterned after the Model R-84 Blaser, takedown, free floating 22 or 24 in. barrels, right or left-hand action, checkered walnut stock and forearm, 7-8½ lbs. New 1993.

| | $1,875 | $1,550 | $1,225 | $1,100 | $995 | $875 | $750 |

Last MSR was $2,075.

Subtract $200 for fiberglass stock.
Add $450 per interchangeable barrel.

BERETTA, DR. FRANCO

Previous manufacturer located in Concesio (Brescia), Italy until 1994.

SHOTGUNS: O/U, BLACK DIAMOND SERIES

Black Diamond target guns were imported exclusively by Double M Shooting Sports until 1988.

FIELD MODEL - 12, 16, 20, 28 ga., or .410 bore, variety of chokes, coin finish receiver.

| | $595 | $550 | $495 | $450 | $395 | $365 | $335 |

Last MSR was $960.

GRADE ONE - 12, 16, 20, 28 ga., or .410 bore, variety of chokes, coin finish receiver with acid etched engraving, French walnut. Trap or skeet model also available, except in 16 ga.

| | $1,020 | $900 | $810 | $720 | $630 | $570 | $525 |

Last MSR was $1,440.

GRADE TWO - 12, 16, 20, 28 ga., or .410 bore, variety of chokes, coin finish receiver with moderate engraving, French walnut. Trap or skeet model also available, except in 16 ga.

| | $1,475 | $1,320 | $1,200 | $1,080 | $930 | $815 | $750 |

Last MSR was $2,040.

GRADE THREE - 12, 16, 20, 28 ga., or .410 bore, variety of chokes, coin finish receiver with scrollwork engraving, French walnut. Trap or skeet model also available, except in 16 ga.

| | $2,100 | $1,920 | $1,775 | $1,560 | $1,410 | $1,200 | $1,035 |

Last MSR was $3,000.

Grading	100%	98%	95%	90%	80%	70%	60%

B **GRADE FOUR** - 12, 16, 20, 28 ga., or .410 bore, variety of chokes, coin finish receiver with elaborate engraving, French walnut. Trap or skeet model also available, except in 16 ga.

	100%	98%	95%	90%	80%	70%	60%
	$2,500	$2,250	$1,950	$1,650	$1,375	$1,125	$995

Last MSR was $3,960.

SKEET SET - includes 12, 20, 28 ga., and .410 bore barrels, available in Grades One through Four.

Multiply values on Grades One - Four by 275% for 4 ga. Skeet sets.

SHOTGUNS: O/U, SxS, & SINGLE BARREL, RECENT MFG.

GAMMA STANDARD O & U - 12, 16, or 20 ga., 26 or 28 in. barrels, coin finish receiver with extensive engraving, Italian walnut. Imported 1984-1988.

	$400	$360	$330	$300	$275	$260	$240

Last MSR was $445.

Add $83 with single trigger and ejectors.

* *Gamma Standard* - with interchangeable choke tubes. Importation disc. 1993.

	$825	$695	$525	$425	$325	$250	$195

Last MSR was $1,000.

Add 20% for auto ejectors.
Add $100 for single trigger.
Add 36% for Gamma Trap or Skeet variation (ST).

GAMMA DELUXE O & U - 12, 16, or 20 ga., 26 or 28 in. barrels, coin finish receiver with extensive engraving, Italian walnut. Imported 1984-1988.

	$445	$405	$370	$350	$325	$300	$275

Last MSR was $480.

Add $84 with single trigger and ejectors.

* *Gamma Deluxe* - with interchangeable choke tubes. Importation disc. 1988.

	$635	$570	$530	$490	$450	$420	$390

Last MSR was $685.

GAMMA TARGET O & U - 12 ga. only, SST, ejectors, Wundhammer swell pistol grip, English walnut stock and beavertail forearm. Imported 1986-1988.

	$550	$505	$455	$410	$370	$350	$325

Last MSR was $595.

ALPHA STANDARD O & U - 12, 16, or 20 ga., 26 or 28 in. barrels, coin finish receiver with extensive engraving, Italian walnut. Imported 1984-1988, resumed 1993.

	$720	$650	$525	$450	$375	$300	$250

Last MSR was $780.

Add 18% for auto ejectors.
Add $100 for single trigger.

ALPHA DELUXE O & U - 12, 16, or 20 ga., 26 or 28 in. barrels, coin finish receiver with extensive engraving, sling swivels, Italian walnut. Imported 1984-1988.

	$395	$355	$330	$300	$275	$250	$230

Last MSR was $435.

Add $75 with single trigger and ejectors.
Add $80 for interchangeable choke tubes (disc. 1985).

AMERICA STANDARD O & U - .410 bore only, 26 or 28 in. barrels, coin finish receiver with extensive engraving, Italian walnut. Imported 1984-1988.

	$305	$280	$265	$240	$215	$205	$190

Last MSR was $335.

Add $85 for Deluxe model.

Grading	100%	98%	95%	90%	80%	70%	60%

EUROPA O & U - .410 bore only, 26 in. barrels, coin finish receiver with some engraving, Italian walnut. Imported 1984-1988.

	$275	$250	$235	$220	$210	$200	$185

Last MSR was $295.

Add $95 for Deluxe model (disc. 1985).

FRANCIA STANDARD SxS - .410 bore only, double triggers, extractors, checkered walnut. Imported 1986-1988.

	$235	$220	$210	$200	$185	$175	$160

Last MSR was $255.

Add $19 for Deluxe Model.

OMEGA STANDARD SxS - 12, 16, or 20 ga., 26 or 28 in. barrels, coin finish receiver with extensive engraving, Italian walnut. Imported 1984-93.

	$780	$695	$550	$450	$375	$300	$250

Last MSR was $880.

Add 32% for auto ejectors.
Add 10% for single trigger (disc. 1985).

MILANO O/U - 9mm Flobert, folding design. Imported 1993 only.

	$380	$330	$295	$250	$210	$180	$150

Last MSR was $420.

VERONA/BERGAMO SxS - 9mm Flobert, folding design, Bergamo model has hammers, Verona model is hammerless. Imported 1993 only.

	$270	$225	$180	$140	$115	$95	$75

Last MSR was $300.

BRESCIA SINGLE BARREL - 9mm Flobert, folding design. Imported 1993 only.

	$175	$150	$130	$110	$90	$70	$55

Last MSR was $200.

BETA SINGLE BARREL - 12, 16, 20, 24, 28, 32 ga., or .410 bore, single barrel field gun, VR, chrome finish receiver, folding design. Imported 1985-93.

	$215	$185	$160	$145	$135	$125	$115

Last MSR was $240.

Add 10% for VR.

SHOTGUNS: SEMI-AUTO

ARIETE STANDARD - 12 ga. only, gas operated, 2¾ or 3 in. chamber, various barrel lengths, with or without choke tubes, aluminum receiver, checkered stock and forearm, approx. 6.9 lbs. Imported 1993 only.

	$995	$795	$525	$425	$325	$250	$195

Last MSR was $1,180.

Add $20 for 3 in. mag. variation.

SHOTGUNS: SLIDE ACTION

ARIETE - 12 ga. only, 3 in. chamber, various barrel lengths without VR, twin action bars, matte finish, recoil pad. Imported 1993 only.

	$780	$695	$550	$450	$375	$300	$250

Last MSR was $880.

Grading	100%	98%	95%	90%	80%	70%	60%

BERETTA, PIETRO

Current manufacturer located in Brescia, Italy, 1526-present and Accokeek, MD, 1978 to date. Beretta U.S.A. Corp. was formed in 1977 and is located in Accokeek, MD. Beretta U.S.A. Corp. has been importing Beretta Firearms exclusively since 1980. 1970-1977 manufacture was imported exclusively by Garcia. Distributor and dealer direct sales.

Beretta is one of the world's oldest family owned industrial firms, having started business in 1526. In addition to Beretta owning Benelli & Franchi, the company also purchased Sako and Tikka Companies in late 1999, and Aldo Uberti & Co. in 2000. Beretta continues to be a continual leader in firearms development and safety, and shooters attest to the reliability of their weapons worldwide.

For more information and current pricing on both new and used Beretta precision airguns, please refer to the 2nd Edition Blue Book of Airguns by Dr. Robert Beeman & John Allen (now online also).

PISTOLS: SEMI-AUTO, PRE-WWII MFG.

MODEL 1915 - .32 or 9mm Glisenti cal., Beretta's first military pistol, exaggerated slide stop, safety on rear of tang, checkered wood grips, 7 shot mag., serial range 1-16,000.

$950	$700	$550	$400	$325	$275	$225

9mm Para. cal. is not interchangeable and potentially dangerous if interchanged with 9mm Glisenti cal.

MODEL 1915-1917 - later 7.65mm cal. variation, 8 shot mag., exaggerated slide stops, wood grips, sold commercially and to the military. A few marked "RM" were issued to the Italian Navy, ser. no. range 16,000-72,000. Mfg. 1917-1921.

$550	$475	$400	$300	$250	$200	$165

Add 100% if Navy issue.

MODEL 1922 - successor to the Model 1915-1917, mfg. with more open slide and modern slide stop, wood or pressed metal grips, ser. no. range 200,000-243,000. Mfg. 1922- 1932.

$500	$425	$375	$275	$235	$195	$160

Add 100% if Navy issue.

MODEL 1923 - 9mm Glisenti cal., 8 shot, 4 in. barrel, fixed sights, usually with pressed steel grips, less frequently smooth wood with PB emblem, occasionally slotted for shoulder stock. Most were purchased by the Italian Army and marked "RE", ser. no. range 300,000-310,400. Mfg. 1923-1926.

$1,000	$850	$550	$400	$325	$275	$250

Add 25% if slotted for shoulder stock.

MODEL 1919 - .25 ACP cal., SA, 8 shot mag., offered in several variations. First type in serial range 100,000-156,000, subsequent improvement involved changing the disconnector and left panel in the range 156,000-185,000.

$375	$325	$275	$225	$195	$165	$135

MODEL 1926 - similar to Model 1919, except fit with wood panels bearing an encircled PB. Approx. 11,000 pistols were mfg. in ser. no. range 187,000-198,000.

$350	$315	$270	$220	$190	$160	$130

Grading	100%	98%	95%	90%	80%	70%	60%

MODEL 1926-31 - similar to Model 1926, except has small modifications in the slide, grips are no longer impressed with the PB monogram, interrupted serial range from 198,000-200,000 and 600,000-601,000.

	$325	$310	$265	$215	$190	$160	$125

MODEL 318 - .25 ACP cal., 2½ in. barrel, fixed sights, blue, modifications in the slide legend, grip configuration, and magazine floor plate. Limited production during 1936-37, in ser. no. range 609,000-615,000.

	$275	$240	$215	$180	$160	$140	$120

Add 50%-100% for engraved and plated variations if in 98%+ original condition.

Embellished variations of the Model 318 included the Model 319 (engraved/blue), Model 320 (engraved/nickel plated) and Model 321 (engraved/gold plated).

MODEL 418 - .25 ACP cal., fixed sights, similar to Model 318, but with loaded indicator and grip safety (early type is semi-circular, late type is curved), occasionally was made with an alloy frame, popular pistol mfg. 1937-1961 with minor modifications. Later guns are suffixed with the letters A, B, and C, 178,000 mfg.

	$250	$225	$200	$175	$155	$135	$120

Add 50%-100% for engraved and plated variations if in 98%+ original condition.

Embellished variations of the Model 418 included the Model 419 (engraved blue), Model 420 (engraved nickel), and Model 421 (engraved gold plated).

MODEL 1932 - 7.65mm cal., two variations including straight and curved rear grip strap, smooth wood grips bearing PB monogram (commercial) or RM monogram (Italian Navy). 8,000 mfg. in ser. no. range 400,000-408,000.

	$1,400	$1,100	$750	$550	$400	$350	$300

MODEL 1934 - .380 ACP cal., (9mm Kurz cal.), 3 3/8 in. barrel, fixed sights, blue, plastic grips, Italy's service weapon in WWII, one of the most common Beretta pistols - over one million manufactured between 1934-1980, many of the military pistols have a parkerized finish, usually fit with metal-backed grips, later guns have an alphabetical prefix. Post war production (1946) serial numbers start with C00001.

	$375	$325	$275	$225	$195	$165	$135

Add 10% for high polish, unless post-war production.
Add 20% for Italian Air Force.
Add 300% for post-war commercial deluxe pistols which were engraved, gold plated, and cased with a spare mag. and cleaning brush.

MODEL 1935 - similar to the Model 1934, except 7.65mm cal., 3½ in. barrel, fixed sights, blue, plastic grips, the wartime model had poor finish, a small number were fit with an experimental slide safety in the ser. no. range 500,xxx, military issue was often parkerized. 525,000 mfg. 1935-1967.

	$350	$315	$270	$220	$190	$160	$130

Add 10% for high polish, unless post-war production.
Add 300% for post-war commercial deluxe pistols which were engraved, gold plated, and cased with a spare mag. and cleaning brush.

PISTOLS: SEMI-AUTO, POST WWII MFG.

100% values on below listed models assume NIB condition.

MODEL 948 - .22 LR cal., 3½ or 6 in. barrel, fixed sights, hammer.

	$175	$150	$125	$100	$75	$60	$50

Grading	100%	98%	95%	90%	80%	70%	60%

MODEL 949 OLYMPIC TARGET - .22 S or LR cal., 8¾ in. barrel, target sights, adj. barrel weights, blue, muzzle brake, checkered wood grips with thumbrest, limited mfg. 1959-1964.

	$660	$550	$495	$385	$305	$250	$195

MODEL 950CC MINX M2 - .22 Short cal., hinged 2 3/8 in. barrel, fixed sights, blue, plastic grips. Mfg. 1955-disc.

	$135	$115	$105	$95	$85	$75	$70

MODEL 950CC SPECIAL MINX M4 - similar to M2, with 4 in. barrel.

	$135	$115	$105	$95	$85	$75	$70

MODEL 950B JETFIRE - similar to M2, in .25 ACP cal..

	$150	$120	$105	$95	$85	$75	$70

MODEL 951 BRIGADIER - 9mm Para. cal., 4½ in. barrel, fixed sights, blue, plastic grips, current Italian service pistol and immediate predecessor to the M92 Series. Mfg. 1952- disc.

	$285	$235	$195	$175	$150	$130	$115

    Add $350 for "Egyptian" (denoted by EC prefix) or "Israeli" Model.

MODEL 20 - .25 ACP cal., double action, alloy frame, 9 shot, 2½ in. barrel, plastic or walnut grips, 10.9 oz. Disc. 1985.

	$160	$140	$125	$115	$95	$85	$75

        Last MSR was $214.

MODEL 70 PUMA OR COUGAR - .32 ACP or .380 ACP cal., 3½ in. barrel, fixed or adj. sights, blue, plastic grips, .32 Puma alloy frame, .380 Cougar steel frame. Disc.

	$215	$180	$165	$150	$130	$110	$90

    Add 10% for .380 ACP cal.

MODEL 70T - .32 ACP cal., similar to Model 70, target sights. Disc.

	$275	$250	$220	$195	$165	$150	$140

MODEL 70S - .22 LR or .380 ACP cal., single action, 3½ in. barrel, 9 shot, blue finish, plastic grips, weight .22 cal. - 18 oz., .380 ACP - 23 oz., steel frame, .22 LR has adj. rear sight. Disc. 1985.

	$240	$210	$185	$170	$155	$140	$125

        Last MSR was $295.

MODEL 71 JAGUAR - .22 LR cal., version of Model 70, alloy frame. Disc.

	$220	$195	$180	$160	$150	$140	$110

MODEL 72 JAGUAR - similar to 71, with 6 in. barrel. Disc.

	$220	$195	$180	$160	$150	$140	$110

MODEL 76P-76W TARGET PISTOL - .22 LR cal., single action, 11 shot, steel frame, 6 in. barrel, adj. sights, blue finish, thumbrest plastic grips (76-P). Disc. 1985.

	$345	$300	$275	$245	$220	$195	$170

        Last MSR was $395.

    Add $40 for thumbrest wood grips (Model 76-W).

MODEL 80 - .22 Short cal., target pistol with limited importation into the U.S.

	$750	$675	$595	$550	$495	$450	$395

MODEL 81P-81W - .32 ACP cal., double action, 13 shot, 3.8 in. barrel, fixed sights, blue. Imported 1976- 1984.

	$300	$250	$225	$195	$175	$155	$135

    Add $90 for nickel finish.
    Add $20 for wood grips (W Suffix).

Grading	100%	98%	95%	90%	80%	70%	60%

MODEL 82W - .32 ACP cal., double action, more compact than Model 81, 10 shot, walnut grips, 17 oz. Importation disc. 1984.

| | $295 | $250 | $225 | $195 | $175 | $155 | $135 |

  Add $75 for nickel finish.

MODEL 84B - .380 ACP cal., double action, brown wood or plastic grips, 13 shot mag., blue finish, fixed sights. Disc.

| | $295 | $250 | $225 | $195 | $175 | $155 | $135 |

MODEL 84W-EL - similar to Model 84 only specially engraved, select walnut grips. Presentation case. Disc. 1984.

| | $1,025 | $770 | $720 | $615 | $565 | $520 | $460 |

MODEL 86P-86W - .380 ACP cal. only, double action, tip-up 4 1/3 in. barrel, 8 shot mag., plastic or walnut grips, 23 oz. While this model was advertised, it was never released.

  MSR was $480 in 1986, walnut grips were $80 extra (86-W).

MODEL 90 DOUBLE ACTION AUTOMATIC - .32 ACP cal., 3 5/8 in. barrel, fixed sights, blue, plastic grips. Mfg. 1969-1983.

| | $275 | $195 | $175 | $155 | $130 | $110 | $95 |

  Add 25% if without external slide latch.

MODEL 100 - .32 ACP cal., fixed sights. Disc.

| | $250 | $220 | $195 | $165 | $150 | $140 | $130 |

MODEL 101 - similar to Model 70T, except in .22 LR. Disc.

| | $250 | $220 | $195 | $165 | $150 | $140 | $130 |

MODEL 102 - .22 LR cal., target pistol, single action, steel/alloy construction, plastic grips, 10 shot mag. with finger extension, adj. rear sight. Disc.

| | $325 | $250 | $220 | $195 | $165 | $150 | $140 |

PISTOLS: SEMI-AUTO, RECENT AND CURRENT MFG.

On Beretta's large frame pistols, alphabetical suffixes refer to the following: F Model - double/single action system with external safety decocking lever, G Model - double/single action system with external decocking only lever, D Model - double action only without safety lever, DS Model - double action only with external safety lever.

The models in this section appear in numerical sequence.

MODEL 21(A)-W BOBCAT - .22 LR or .25 ACP cal., double action, alloy frame, 7 (.22 LR) or 8 (.25 ACP) shot mag., 2.4 in. barrel, plastic or walnut (EL Model, disc. 2000) grips, 11½ oz.

* **Blue Finish**

| MSR $285 | | $225 | $180 | $140 | $130 | $115 | $95 | $85 |

  Add approx. $75 for engraving and wood grips (EL Model, disc. 2000).

* **Nickel Finish** - disc. 2000.

| | $255 | $215 | $165 | $140 | $130 | $115 | $95 |

  Last MSR was $322.

* **Matte Finish** - matte finished metal, plastic grips. New 1992.

| MSR $252 | | $200 | $165 | $135 | $115 | $95 | $85 | $80 |

  This model is manufactured by Beretta U.S.A. Corp. in Accokeek, MD.

* **Stainless Steel (Inox)** - similar to Model 21 Bobcat, except is .22 LR only, stainless steel with plastic grips, approx. 11.5 oz. New 2000.

| MSR $307 | | $245 | $205 | $160 | | | | |

Grading	100%	98%	95%	90%	80%	70%	60%

✳ Lady Beretta - .22 LR cal. only, similar to Model 21-W, except is specially serial numbered and has gold etching on top of frame and slide sides. Supplied with a blue velvet drawstring bag. 1990 issue.

	$245	$185	$160	$140	$130	$115	$100

Last MSR was $285.

This model was sold exclusively by Lew Horton Distributing Co.

MODEL U22 NEOS - .22 LR cal., single action, unique design features modular construction and modern styling, matte black finish, 10 shot mag., 4½ or 6 in. barrel with sights incorporated into integral full length sight rail, plastic interchangeable grip panels, 31.5 or 34 oz. New 2002.

MSR	$256		$215	$185	$160	$140	$120	$100	$90

✳ Model U22 Neos Inox - similar to Model U22 Neos, except slide and barrel are stainless steel. New 2002.

MSR	$299		$250	$210	$185

MODEL 71 - .22 LR cal., single action, 8 shot, 6 in. barrel, plastic grips with thumbrest, finger extension mag. Imported 1987 only.

	$190	$160	$140	$130	$115	$95	$85

Last MSR was $215.

MODEL 84P-84W CHEETAH - .380 ACP cal., single/double action semi-auto, 3.82 in. barrel, alloy frame, steel slide, 10 (C/B 1994) or 13* shot staggered mag., firing pin block, ambidextrous manual safety (also used as a decocking lever), low profile 3 dot sights, curved trigger guard, plastic or wood (available with nickel finish 2001 only) grips, blue (disc.), Bruniton, or nickel (disc. 2001) finish, 23 oz.

MSR	$589		$455	$360	$315	$275	$240	$210	$190

Add $30 for wood grips (Model 84W, disc. 2001).
Add $76 for nickel finish (includes checkered wood grips, disc. 2001).

✳ Model 84F - similar specifications to the Model 84P-84W, except patterned after the Model 92F Govt. Model, matte black Bruniton finish, squared off trigger guard, plastic or wood grips, 23 oz. Mfg. 1990 only.

	$395	$330	$300	$270	$240	$210	$190

Last MSR was $479.

MODEL 85P-85W CHEETAH - .380 ACP cal., same general specifications as the Model 84, except slimmer profile because of 8 shot straight line mag., Model 85P has plastic grips, 22 oz.

MSR	$556		$435	$340	$290	$240	$210	$190	$175

Add $64 for nickel finish (includes wood grips, disc. 2001).
Add $33 for wood grips with blue finish (Model 85W – disc. 2000).

Model 85F - similar specifications to the Model 85P-85W, except patterned after the Model 92F Govt. Model, matte black Bruniton finish, squared off trigger guard, plastic or wood grips, 21.8 oz. Mfg. in 1990 only.

	$375	$300	$270	$240	$210	$190	$175

Last MSR was $440.

Add $25 for wood grips.

MODEL 86 CHEETAH - .380 ACP cal., single/double action semi-auto with 4.4 in. tip-up barrel, 8 shot mag., checkered walnut grips, matte Bruniton finish, fixed sights, gold trigger, 23.3 oz. Importation began 1991.

MSR	$591		$485	$380	$310	$250	$225	$190	$175

Grading	100%	98%	95%	90%	80%	70%	60%

MODEL 87 CHEETAH - .22 LR cal., single/double action semi-auto, 7 shot mag., 3.82 or 6 in. target barrel with counterweight (disc. 1994), blue finish, wood grips, 20 oz. (3.82 in. barrel). Importation began 1986.

MSR	$589	$485	$380	$310	$250	$225	$190	$175

✳ *Model 87 Target* - single action only target variation of the Model 87 with 6 in. barrel, 10 shot mag., 23.3 (older mfg.) or 41 (new mfg.) oz. Disc. 1994, reintroduced 2000.

MSR	$669	$570	$375	$305	$250	$220	$195	$175

This model was reintroduced in 2000, and now features adj. rear target sight, integral scope base rail that is machined on the aluminum barrel sleeve, and Bruniton finish with anodized aluminum frame.

MODEL 89 GOLD STANDARD - .22 LR cal., single action target semi-auto, matte Bruniton black finish on metal parts, 6 in. barrel, 10 shot mag., anatomical wood grips, adj. sights, 41 oz. Imported 1988- 2000.

		$630	$510	$410	$360	$310	$275	$250

Last MSR was $802.

MODEL 950 JETFIRE (BS) - .22 Short (disc. 1992) or .25 ACP cal., single action, alloy frame, 8 shot (.25 cal. only) or 6 shot mag., tip-up 2½ and 4 in. (.22 S only) barrel, plastic grips, thumb safety, matte (new 1992, plastic grips only), blue or nickel finish, 9.9 oz.

MSR	$226	$180	$140	$115	$100	$90	$80	$70

Add $22 for blue finish (disc. 1999).
Add $80 for nickel finish (disc. 1999).

This model is manufactured by Beretta U.S.A. Corp. in Accokeek, MD.

✳ *Model 950 Jetfire Stainless (Inox)* - similar to Model 950 BS, except is stainless steel. New 2000.

MSR	$267	$210	$150	$120				

✳ *Model 950 EL* - same general specifications as Model 950 BS, only with wood grips and gold plated parts. Disc. 1999.

		$275	$230	$200	$180	$165	$150	$135

Last MSR was $337.

MODEL 3032 TOMCAT - .32 ACP cal., similar to Model 21 Bobcat, except has 2.45 in. barrel, 7 shot mag., choice of matte or blue finish, plastic grips, regular or Tritium AO Big Dot Express (new 2002) sights, approx. 14½ oz. New 1996.

MSR	$340	$265	$200	$160	$135	$115	$95	$85

Add $30 for blue finish.
Add $72 for Alley Cat package – includes Tritium AO Big Dot Express sights and in-the-pants Alcantara synthetic holster.

✳ *Model 3032 Tomcat Stainless (Inox)* - similar to Model 3032 Tomcat, except has stainless steel slide and barrel, grey anodized alloy frame, 15.8 oz. New 2000.

MSR	$418	$325	$245	$195				

✳ *Model 3032 Tomcat Titanium* - similar to Model 3032 Tomcat, except has titanium frame, blue finish only, 16.9 oz. New 2001.

MSR	$572	$460	$360	$310				

MODEL 8000 COUGAR D/F - 9mm Para. cal., single/double (Model 8000 Cougar F) or DA (Model 8000 Cougar D, disc. 2000) only, short recoil system with 3.6 in. rotating barrel, 10 shot mag., fixed sights, anodized aluminum alloy frame, black plastic grips, Bruniton matte black finish, 32.6 oz. New 1995.

MSR	$709	$600	$545	$415	$375	$330	$300	$275

Grading	100%	98%	95%	90%	80%	70%	60%

✳ *Model 8000 Mini Cougar* - similar to Model 8000 Cougar, except overall height has been reduced to 4½ in. and weight is 27.6 oz. New 1998.

MSR	$709	$600	$545	$415	$375	$330	$300	$275

MODEL 8040 COUGAR D/F - .40 S&W cal., single/double (Model 8040 Cougar F) or DA (Model 8040 Cougar D, disc. 2000) only, short recoil system with 3.6 in. rotating barrel, 10 shot mag., fixed sights, anodized aluminum alloy frame, Bruniton matte black finish, 32.4 oz. New 1995.

MSR	$709	$600	$545	$415	$375	$330	$300	$275

✳ *Model 8040 Mini Cougar* - similar to Model 8040 Cougar, except overall height has been reduced to 4 ½ in. and weight is 27.6 oz., supplied with 8 and extended 10 shot mag. New 1998.

MSR	$709	$600	$545	$415	$375	$330	$300	$275

MODEL 8045 COUGAR D/F - .45 ACP cal., 8 shot mag., otherwise similar to Models 8000 and 8040, 32 oz. New 1998.

MSR	$739	$620	$490	$425	$380	$335	$300	$275

Add $25 for single/double action (Model 8045 Cougar F).

✳ *Model 8045 Mini Cougar D/F* - similar to Model 8045 Cougar, except overall height has been reduced to 4½ in. and weight is 27.6 oz, supplied with 6 shot mag. Importation began 1999.

MSR	$739	$620	$490	$425	$380	$335	$300	$275

Add $25 for single/double action (Model 8045 Mini Cougar F).

MODEL 8357 COUGAR F - .357 Sig cal., single/double action, 5½ in. barrel, blue finish with plastic grips, 10 shot mag., 32.4 oz. New 2001.

MSR	$709	$600	$545	$415	$375	$330	$300	$275

MODEL 9000S TYPE D/F - 9mm Para. or .40 S&W cal., single/double (Model 9000S Type F) or DA only (Model 9000S Type D), 3½ in. tilt barrel, 10 shot mag., spurless (Type D only) or external (Type F) hammer, ambidextrous safety with hammer decocking, sub-compact pistol utilizing state of the art ergonomic design by Giugiaro Design, matte black techno-polymer frame, overmolded rubber grip, cased, approx. 26½ oz. New 2000.

MSR	$551	$445	$350	$300	$280	$260	$240	$220

Pistols: Semi-Auto, Model 92 & Variations - 4.9 in. barrel

MODEL 92 (FIRST SERIES) - 4.9 in. barrel, early production Model 92s had a flat slide, frame mounted safety, and mag. release button at base of pistol grip. Production of the M92 was approx. 5,000 pistols. Originally mfg. 1976. Disc.

		$650	$550	$400	$300	$255	$240	$220

MODEL 92S (SECOND SERIES) - similar to Model 92, except has a slide mounted firing pin safety. Disc.

		$550	$475	$375	$300	$250	$240	$220

MODEL 92SB-P (THIRD SERIES) - 9mm Luger cal., double action, 15 shot mag., 4.9 in. barrel, fixed sights, alloy frame, high-polish blue finish, plastic grips (Model 92SB- P), conventionally located push button magazine release, ambidextrous safety, 34½ oz. Mfg. 1980-1985.

		$475	$425	$385	$345	$310	$285	$260

Last MSR was $600.

✳ *Model 92SB-W* - similar to above, only with wood grips. Disc. 1985.

		$495	$430	$390	$355	$330	$290	$260

Last MSR was $620.

Grading	100%	98%	95%	90%	80%	70%	60%

MODEL 92D - 9mm Para. cal., double action only, otherwise similar to Model 92F, except does not have a manual safety lever, includes black plastic grips, 3 dot sights, 33.8 oz. Introduced 1992 - disc. 1998.

	$460	$360	$300	$250	$210	$190	$175

Last MSR was $586.

Add $90 for Tritium (new 1994) sight system.
Add 10% for Trijicon (disc.) sights.

MODEL 92F & 92FS - 9mm Para. cal., official U.S. military variation of 92 Series, 4.9 in. barrel, alloy frame, steel slide, 10 (C/B 1994) or 15* shot mag., chamber loaded indicator, matte black Bruniton finish, squared off trigger guard to facilitate two-hand shooting, extended mag. base, choice of regular or 3 dot sights (new 1991), approx 34 ½ oz. Model 92F-P has plastic grips. Model 92F-W has wood grips. New 1984.

MSR	$676	$570	$460	$415	$370	$330	$300	$275

Add $335 for .22 LR conversion kit (includes slide, barrel, spring, follower, and .22 LR mag., new 2002).
Add approx. $20 for checkered wood grips (Model 92F-W, disc. 1998).
Add approx. $80 for Tritium sight system (mfg. 1994-98).
Add 10% for Trijicon (disc.) sights.
Add approx. $175 for gold engraving/accenting (Model EL-3, 92F-W only, disc. 1998).
Add $395 for 9mm Competition Conversion Kit (mfg. 1992-98).

The Model 92FS incorporates a slide retaining pin engineering change not included in the Model 92F.

The U.S. military on January 15, 1985 announced that the M9 military variation of the commercial Model 92F would replace the Colt Govt. Model .45 ACP as the standard government issue sidearm. Because of domestic political pressures, Congress requested that a new sidearm competition be conducted again in 1988. The result of this second trial was that the Department of the Army announced on May 22, 1989 that Beretta had won again. This military contract with Beretta U.S.A. Corp. initially involved over 320,000 Model M9s (military designation for the commercial Model 92F) manufactured for U.S. military consumption in the 1990s. Actual delivery of commercial Model 92s began in January of 1986, while M9 delivery to U.S. Armed Forces exceeded 430,000 units, and was completed in 1999.

✱ Model 92F & 92FS Stainless (Inox) - similar to Model 92F/92FS, except is mfg. from stainless steel, satin finish with plastic grips, 3 dot sights, initially released to law enforcement agencies only, this model is now commercially manufactured in quantity.

MSR	$734	$610	$485	$390

Add approx. $20 for wood grips (disc. 1998).
Add approx. $90 for Trijicon (1993 only) or Tritium (mfg. 1994-98) sight system.

MODEL 92FS BRIGADIER - similar to the Model 92FS, except has heavier slide to reduce felt recoil, wraparound rubber grips, and 3 dot sights, 35.3 oz. New 1999.

MSR	$731	$620	$490	$425	$380	$335	$300	$275

✱ Model 92FS Brigadier Stainless (Inox) - similar to Model 92FS Brigadier, except is stainless steel, 35.3 oz. New 2000.

MSR	$771	$645	$545	$465

MODEL 92FS B.A.T.S. - 9mm Para. cal., 4.9 in. barrel, features black matte Bruniton finish and textured rubber wraparound grips with finger grooves, package includes both 10 and 15 shot mags., Airlight knife, aluminum carrying case, 34.4 oz. Limited mfg. late 2000 only.

	$665	$550	$465	$415	$360	$300	$275

Last MSR was $785.

Grading	100%	98%	95%	90%	80%	70%	60%

B

MODEL 92FS VERTEC - 9mm Para. cal., single/double action, features vertical grip design, special short reach trigger, thin dual textured grip panels, and integral accessory rail on lower frame, removable front sight, beveled 10 shot mag., Bruniton finish, 32.2 oz. New 2002.

MSR $712	$605	$475	$425	$380	$340	$300	$275

* *Model 92FS Vertec Stainless (Inox)* - stainless variation of the Model 92FS Vertec. New 2002.

MSR $762	$630	$500	$415				

MODEL 92 BLACK INOX - 9mm Para. cal., single/double action, features black stainless slide and stipled, finger groove plastic grips. Limited mfg. beginning 2002.

MSR $734	$610	$485	$390				

MODEL 92 BILLENIUM - 9mm Para. cal., single action only, frame mounted safety, contoured steel frame with checkered grip straps and contoured carbon fiber grips, interchangeable sights, oversize mag. release button, unique slide serrations and Billenium engraving, nickel alloy surface treatment finish, includes deluxe lockable carrying case. Limited mfg. of 2,000 beginning 2002.

MSR $1,357	$1,050	$875	$725	$650	$575	$500	$425

MODEL 92FS YEAR 2000 - 9mm Para. cal., 4.9 in. barrel, matte black Bruniton finish, features rosewood laminate grips with Beretta "trident" logo on brass medallions. 2,000 mfg. during 2000 only.

	$615	$500	$450	$400	$350	$300	$275

Last MSR was $726.

MODEL 92F-ELS - deluxe variation of the Model 92F featuring high polish stainless steel finish with gold highlights on trim, frame etchings, and small parts, plastic grips. Mfg. 1992-94.

	$685	$550	$425				

Last MSR was $790.

MODEL 92F "UNITED WE STAND" LIMITED EDITION - 9mm Para. cal., features laser etched gold American flag and "United We Stand" slide lettering, Bruniton finish, black plastic grips. Mfg. limited to 2001 pistols beginning late 2001.

MSR $734	$625	$560	$485	$425	$375	$300	$275

Beretta USA will make a donation from the proceeds of this model to the NYPD Foundation and the Survivor's Fund of the National Capitol Region.

MODEL 92FS 470th ANNIVERSARY LIMITED EDITION - features stainless steel construction with mirror polished finish, smooth select walnut grips with inlaid gold plated medallions, gold filled engraving with Dr. Ugo Gussalli-Beretta's signature, 470th Anniversary logos, only 470 mfg. (with "1 of 470" gold filled on each gun) beginning 1999, lockable walnut case.

MSR $2,082	$1,835	$1,495	$1,075				

MODEL 92F DELUXE - deluxe model featuring gold or silver plating and elaborate engraving. Importation began 1993.

MSR $5,750	$4,950	$3,750	$2,500				

This model is available at the Beretta Galleries or select Beretta Premium dealers only.

MODEL 92G - 9mm Para. cal., identical to the Model 92F, except features a spring loaded decocking lever that safely lowers the hammer allowing fire-ready when unholstering the pistol. New 1990.

The Model 92G is sold to law enforcement agencies only and prices are slightly higher than the standard Model 92FS. This pistol has been used by French Gendarmes since 1987.

Grading	100%	98%	95%	90%	80%	70%	60%

MODEL 92F WITH U.S. M9 MARKED SLIDE/FRAME - 9mm Para. cal., approx. 2,000 mfg. with special serial no. range, "BER" prefix, government assembly numbers on frame, slide, hammer, mag. etc. Mfg. for the Armed Forces Reserve shooters, identical to military M9, except for serial number.

	$1,000	$900	$800	$725	$650	$575	$500

M9 LIMITED STANDARD EDITION - commercial limited edition of the U.S. Govt. M9 military pistol, features gold inscribed slide legend "The First Decade 1985-1995", Air Force or Marine Corps emblems on right slide side, 10,000 mfg. during 1995-97.

	$600	$475	$425				

Last MSR was $643.

* ✱ *M9 Limited Deluxe Edition* - features checkered walnut grips, gold-plated hammer, grip screws, and mag. release button. Disc. 1997.

	$695	$525	$475				

Last MSR was $750.

M9 SPECIAL EDITION - patterned after the U.S. Armed Forces M9, special M9- XXXX ser. no. range, one 15 shot mag. (pre-1994 mfg.), dot and post sight system, M9 military packaging including Army operator's manual, Bianchi M12 holster, mag. pouch, and web pistol belt. Mfg. 1998-2000.

	$850	$700	$550				

Last MSR was $861.

Pistols: Semi-Auto, Model 92 & Variations - 4.7 in. barrel

MODEL 92FS INOX TACTICAL - 9mm Para. cal., 4.7 in. barrel, features satin matte finished stainless steel slide and alloy frame, rubber grips, Tritium sights. Mfg. 1999-2000.

	$695	$560	$480	$425	$375	$325	$295

Last MSR was $822.

MODEL 92FS BORDER MARSHAL - 9mm Para. cal., commercial equivalent of the I.N.S. (Immigration & Naturalization Service) government contract, 4.7 in. barrel, heavy duty steel slide, Tritium sights, Border Marshal engraving on the slide. Mfg. 1999- 2000.

	$670	$560	$480	$425	$375	$325	$295

Last MSR was $802.

MODEL 92G ELITE IA (BRIGADIER) - 9mm Para. cal., similar to Model 92FS Brigadier, except has 4.7 in. stainless barrel and many standard I.D.P.A. competition features including front and rear serrated slide, skeletonized hammer, and removable 3 dot sighting system, plastic grips, includes Elite engraving on slide. New 1999.

MSR	$812		$685	$550	$475	$410	$360	$300	$275

* ✱ *Model 92G Elite II (Brigadier)* - similar to Model 92G Elite, except has stainless steel slide with black "Elite II" markings, target barrel crown, extended mag. release, optimized trigger mechanism, front and back strap checkering, low profile Novak rear sight, 35 oz. New mid-2000.

MSR	$912		$765	$600	$510	$440	$385	$325	$295

Pistols: Semi-Auto, Model 92 & Variations - 4.3 in. barrel

MODEL 92D CENTURION - 9mm Para. cal., compact variation with 4.3 in. barrel, plastic grips only, without safety, choice of 3 dot or Tritium sights. Mfg. 1994-98.

	$460	$360	$300	$250	$210	$190	$175

Last MSR was $586.

Add $90 for Tritium sights.

Grading	100%	98%	95%	90%	80%	70%	60%

MODEL 92SB-P COMPACT - similar to Model 92SB, except has 4.3 in. barrel, 14 shot, plastic grips (Model 92SB-P), rarer when frontstrap has curved lip, 31 oz. Disc. 1985.

	$500	$440	$385	$345	$310	$285	$260

Last MSR was $620.

Add $60 for nickel finish.

✴ *Model 92SB-W Compact* - similar to above only with wood grips. Disc. 1985.

	$525	$465	$395	$355	$335	$300	$280

Last MSR was $635.

MODEL 92F COMPACT - similar to Model 92F, except has 4.3 in. barrel and 13 shot mag., plastic or wood grips, 31½ oz. While temporarily suspended in 1986, production was resumed 1989-1993.

	$550	$450	$415	$375	$335	$300	$275

Last MSR was $625.

Add $20 for checkered walnut grips (Model 92F Wood).
Add $65 for Trijicon sight system.

✴ *Model 92F Compact "M"* - similar to Model 92F Compact, except has 8 shot straight line mag., plastic grips only. Imported 1990-93.

	$550	$450	$415	$375	$335	$300	$275

Last MSR was $625.

Add $65 for Trijicon sight system.
Approx. 1,200 92SBM Models were imported in the 1980s.

MODEL 92F & 92FS CENTURION - similar to Model 92F, except has compact barrel slide unit with full size frame, 4.3 in. barrel, choice of plastic or wood grips, 3 dot sight system, same length as Model 92F Compact, 10 (C/B 1994) or 15* shot mag., 33.2 oz. Mfg. 1992-98.

	$525	$435	$395	$365	$335	$300	$275

Last MSR was $613.

Add approx. $20 for checkered walnut grips (Model 92F Wood).
Add $90 for Tritium sight system (mfg. 1994-98).
Add 10% for Trijicon sights (disc).

MODEL 92FS COMPACT - 9mm Para. cal., similar to Model 92 Compact L Type M, except has 10 shot staggered mag., 32 oz. New 1999.

MSR	$676		$565	$460	$410	$365	$335	$300	$275

✴ *Model 92FS Compact Stainless (Inox)* - similar to Model 92FS Compact, except is stainless steel. New 2000.

MSR	$734		$610	$485	$395

✴ *Model 92FS Custom Carry* - 9mm Para. cal., 4.3 in. barrel, shortened grip, low profile control levers, left side only safety lever, blue only, 10 shot staggered mag., plastic grips. Mfg. 1999-2000.

	$550	$450	$400	$365	$335	$300	$275

Last MSR was $655.

✴ *Model 92FS Custom Carry II (Type M)* - 9mm Para. cal., similar dimensions as Custom Carry, except is stainless steel construction with black components and black slide markings, Novak low profile 3-dot sights, 8 shot single stack mag., 30.9 oz. Mfg. 2000.

	$560	$455	$410

Last MSR was $669.

MODEL 92 TYPE M COMPACT - same features as the Model 92FS, except has 4.3 in. barrel, overall height is 5.3 in., Bruniton matte finish, choice of single/double or double action only (disc. 1998), plastic grips, single column 8 shot mag., 30.9 oz. New 1998.

MSR	$676		$565	$460	$415	$370	$335	$300	$275

Add approx. $90 for Tritium sight system (disc. 1998).
Subtract approx. $25 for double action only (disc. 1998).

Grading	100%	98%	95%	90%	80%	70%	60%

B

* **Model 92 Type M Compact Stainless (Inox)** - similar to Model 92 Type M, except is stainless steel. New 2000.

MSR	$721		$600	$465	$390		

Pistols: Semi-Auto, Model 96 & Variations, Recent Mfg.

The models in this section appear in approximate chronological sequence.

MODEL 96D - .40 S&W cal., 4.9 in. barrel, double action only variation of the Model 96F, no safety, 3 dot sight system, 33.8 oz. Introduced 1992 - disc. 1998.

			$460	$360	$300	$250	$210	$190	$175

Last MSR was $586.

Add $90 for Tritium sight system (new 1994).
Add $65 for Trijicon sights (disc.).

* **Model 96D Centurion** - similar to Model 96D, except is compact variation with 4.3 in. barrel, 3 dot sights. Mfg. 1994-98.

			$460	$360	$300	$250	$210	$190	$175

Last MSR was $586.

Add $90 for Tritium sight system.

MODEL 96F & 96FS - .40 S&W cal., similar to Model 92F, 4.9 in. barrel, plastic grips only, flared grip with grip strap serrations, Bruniton matte black finish, 3 dot sight system, 10 shot mag., 34.4 oz. Introduced 1992.

MSR	$676		$570	$460	$410	$370	$335	$300	$275

Add $91 for Tritium sight system (mfg. 1994-99).
Add 10% for Trijicon sights (disc.).

* **Model 96F Compact** - 4.3 in. barrel, 10 shot mag., 3 dot sights, plastic grips, approx. 32 oz. New 2000.

MSR	$676		$570	$460	$410	$370	$335	$300	$275

While advertised during the 1990s, this gun finally went into production during 2000.

* **Model 96F Compact Stainless (Inox)** - similar to Model 96F Compact, except is stainless steel. New 2000.

MSR	$734		$610	$495	$410			

* **Model 96F Centurion** - similar to Model 96F, except has 4.3 in. barrel, 33.2 oz. Mfg. 1992-99.

			$525	$435	$395	$365	$335	$300	$275

Last MSR was $613.

Add $91 for Tritium sight system (new 1994).

* **Model 96FS Stainless (Inox)** - stainless variation of the Model 96FS, rubber grips, 34.4 oz. Importation began 1999.

MSR	$734		$610	$495	$410			

* **Model 96FS B.A.T.S.** - .40 S&W cal., 4.9 in. barrel, features black matte Bruniton finish and textured rubber wraparound grips with finger grooves, package includes both 10 and 11 shot mags., Airlight knife, aluminum carrying case, 34.4 oz. Limited mfg. mid-2000 only.

			$665	$550	$465	$415	$360	$300	$275

Last MSR was $785.

* **Model 96G Elite IA (Brigadier)** - .40 S&W cal., similar to Model 96 Brigadier, except has 4.7 in. stainless barrel and many standard I.D.P.A. competition features including front and rear serrated slide, skeletonized hammer, and removable 3 dot sighting system, plastic grips, includes Elite engraving on slide. New 1999.

MSR	$812		$680	$550	$465	$410	$350	$300	$275

Grading	100%	98%	95%	90%	80%	70%	60%

✴ Model 96G Elite II (Brigadier) - similar to Model 96G Elite, except has stainless steel slide with black "Elite II" markings, target barrel crown, extended mag. release, optimized trigger mechanism, front and back strap checkering, low profile Novak rear sight, 35 oz. New mid-2000.

MSR	$912	$765	$600	$510	$440	$385	$325	$295

MODEL 96 COMBAT - .40 S&W cal., single action only, similar to Model 96 Stock, except has factory tuned trigger, 4.9 (new 1998) or 5.9 in. barrel with weight and fully adj. rear target sight, aluminum or plastic grips. Mfg. 1997-2001.

	$1,350	$1,060	$900	$775	$625	$550	$495

Last MSR was $1,735.

Add approx. $250 for 5.9 in. barrel (previously available as a Combat Combo).

MODEL 96 VERTEC - .40 S&W cal., single/double action, 4.9 in. barrel, features vertical grip design, special short reach trigger, thin dual textured grip panels, and integral accessory rail on lower frame, removable front sight, beveled 10 shot mag., Bruniton finish, 32.2 oz. New 2002.

MSR	$712	$605	$475	$425	$380	$340	$300	$275

✴ Model 96 Vertec Stainless (Inox) - stainless variation of the Model 96 Vertec. New 2002.

MSR	$762	$630	$500	$415

MODEL 96 BLACK INOX - .40 S&W cal., single/double action, features black stainless slide and stipled, finger groove plastic grips. Limited mfg. beginning 2002.

MSR	$734	$610	$485	$390

MODEL 96 BORDER MARSHAL - .40 S&W cal., commercial equivalent of the I.N.S. (Immigration & Naturalization Service) government contract, 4.7 in. barrel, heavy duty steel slide, Tritium sights, Border Marshal engraving on the slide. Mfg. 1999-2000.

	$670	$560	$480	$425	$375	$325	$295

Last MSR was $802.

MODEL 96 BRIGADIER - similar to Model 96FS, except has heavier slide to reduce felt recoil, wraparound rubber grips, and 3 dot sights, 35.3 oz. New 1999.

MSR	$731	$620	$485	$425	$380	$335	$300	$275

✴ Model 96 Brigadier Stainless (Inox) - similar to Model 96 Brigadier, except is stainless steel. New 2000.

MSR	$771	$625	$500	$400

MODEL 96 CUSTOM CARRY - .40 S&W cal., 4.3 in. barrel, shortened grip, low profile control levers, left side only safety lever, blue only, 10 shot staggered mag., plastic grips. Mfg. 1999-2000.

	$550	$450	$400	$365	$335	$300	$275

Last MSR was $655.

MODEL 96 STOCK - .40 S&W cal., designed for practical shooting competition, includes accurized barrel bushing, 4.9 in. barrel, competition frame mounted ambidextrous safety, 3 interchangeable front sights, checkered front and back grip straps, aluminum grips, beveled mag. well, cased with two mags. and tool kit, 35 oz. Mfg. 1997-99, limited quantities remained into 2000.

	$1,200	$995	$865	$725	$600	$550	$495

Last MSR was $1,407.

Grading	100%	98%	95%	90%	80%	70%	60%

RIFLES: BOLT ACTION, RECENT MFG.

MODEL 500 CUSTOM - .222 Rem., .223 Rem., .243 Win., .270 Win., .30-06, or .308 Win. cal., 3 action lengths, 24 in. barrel, iron sights, checkered walnut stock with recoil pad. Importation was resumed 1988 only.

| | $595 | $530 | $450 | $395 | $350 | $315 | $275 |

Last MSR was $725.

Add 10%-15% for .223 Rem. cal.

* *Model 500 S* - similar to Model 500, except is equipped with iron sights. Imported 1986 only.

| | $615 | $560 | $460 | $400 | $350 | $315 | $275 |

Last MSR was $700.

* *Model 500 DL* - same specifications as Model 500, only better walnut and light engraving. Disc. 1986.

| | $1,395 | $1,260 | $1,000 | $875 | $795 | $725 | $650 |

Last MSR was $1,595.

Add 10%-15% for .223 Rem. cal.

* *Model 500 DLS* - similar to Model 500 DL, except is equipped with iron sights. Imported 1986 only.

| | $1,420 | $1,285 | $1,020 | $875 | $795 | $725 | $650 |

Last MSR was $1,625.

* *Model 500 EELL* - same specifications as Model 500 DL, only select walnut and more engraving. Disc. 1986.

| | $1,550 | $1,260 | $1,150 | $1,000 | $875 | $800 | $725 |

Last MSR was $1,745.

Add 10%-15% for .223 Rem. cal.

* *Model 500 EELL*S - similar to Model 500 EELL, except is equipped with iron sights. Imported 1986 only.

| | $1,575 | $1,425 | $1,200 | $1,120 | $875 | $800 | $725 |

Last MSR was $1,785.

MODEL 501 - .243 Win. or .308 Win. cal., medium bolt action, 6 shot, 23 in. barrel, no sights, checkered walnut stock. Disc. 1986.

| | $595 | $530 | $465 | $395 | $350 | $315 | $275 |

Last MSR was $665.

* *Model 501 S* - similar to Model 501, except is equipped with iron sights. Imported 1986 only.

| | $615 | $560 | $460 | $400 | $350 | $315 | $275 |

Last MSR was $700.

* *Model 501 DL* - same specifications as Model 501, only better walnut and light engraving. Disc. 1986.

| | $1,395 | $1,260 | $1,000 | $875 | $795 | $725 | $650 |

Last MSR was $1,575.

* *Model 501 DLS* - similar to Model 501 DL, except is equipped with iron sights. Imported 1986 only.

| | $1,420 | $1,285 | $1,020 | $875 | $795 | $725 | $650 |

Last MSR was $1,625.

* *Model 501 EELL* - same specifications as Model 501 DL, only select walnut and more engraving. Disc. 1986.

| | $1,550 | $1,260 | $1,150 | $1,000 | $875 | $800 | $725 |

Last MSR was $1,745.

B

Grading	100%	98%	95%	90%	80%	70%	60%

✳ ***Model 501 EELLS*** - similar to Model 501 EELL, except is equipped with iron sights. Imported 1986 only.

	$1,575	$1,425	$1,200	$1,120	$875	$800	$725

Last MSR was $1,785.

MODEL 502 - .30-06, .270 or 7mm Rem. Mag. cal., long bolt action, 5 or 6 shot, 24 in. barrel, no sights, checkered walnut stock. Disc. 1986.

	$625	$565	$490	$440	$395	$360	$330

Last MSR was $710.

✳ ***Model 502 S*** - similar to Model 502, except is equipped with iron sights. Imported 1986 only.

	$650	$595	$525	$460	$395	$360	$330

Last MSR was $745.

✳ ***Model 502 DL*** - same specifications as Model 502, only better walnut and light engraving. Also available in .375 H&H Mag. Disc. 1986.

	$1,495	$1,310	$1,175	$1,025	$900	$775	$695

Last MSR was $1,640.

✳ ***Model 502 DLS*** - similar to Model 502, except is equipped with iron sights. Imported 1986 only.

	$1,410	$1,325	$1,175	$1,025	$900	$775	$695

Last MSR was $1,660.

✳ ***Model 502 EELL*** - same specifications as Model 502 DL, only select walnut and more engraving. Also available in .375 H&H Mag. Disc. 1986.

	$1,575	$1,425	$1,200	$1,120	$875	$800	$725

Last MSR was $1,785.

✳ ***Model 502 EELLS*** - similar to Model 502 EELL, except is equipped with iron sights. Imported 1986 only.

	$1,575	$1,425	$1,200	$1,120	$875	$800	$725

Last MSR was $1,785.

MATO SYNTHETIC - .270 Win., .280 Rem., .30-06, .300 Win. Mag., .338 Win. Mag., .375 H&H, or 7mm Rem. Mag. cal., 23.6 in. barrel, composite black synthetic stock with integral bedding block, Mauser style 98 action with controlled round feeding, 3 position safety, ergonomic bolt handle, 3 or 4 shot detachable box mag., adj. trigger, black satin metal finish, mfg. in the U.S., 8 lbs. New 1997.

MSR	$1,117		$975	$825	$750	$675	$575	$495	$400

Add $357 for .375 H&H cal. (includes muzzle brake and iron sights).

✳ ***Mato Deluxe*** - same cals. as the standard model, features deluxe checkered walnut with ebony forend tip, cased, 7.9 lbs. New 1997.

MSR	$2,470		$2,025	$1,575	$1,150	$995	$825	$675	$600

Add $325 for .375 H&H cal. (includes muzzle brake and iron sights).

✳ ***Mato Deluxe Safari Grade*** - .375 H&H cal. only, elaborately hand engraved with best quality wood. Available through Beretta Premium dealers only.

MSR	$16,500		$14,750	$12,500	$10,250	$8,000	$6,750	$5,500	$4,350

RIFLES: SEMI-AUTO, RECENT MFG.

BM-59 M-1 GARAND - with original Beretta M1 receiver, only 200 imported into the U.S.

	$1,850	$1,475	$1,250	$1,000	$895	$850	$800

Last MSR was $2,080.

BM-62 - similar to BM-59, except has flash suppressor and is Italian marked.

	$1,850	$1,475	$1,250	$1,000	$895	$850	$800

Grading	100%	98%	95%	90%	80%	70%	60%

AR-70 - .222 Rem. or .223 Rem. cal., semi-auto paramilitary design rifle, 5, 8, or 30 shot mag., diopter sights, epoxy finish, 17.72 in. barrel, 8.3 lbs.

	100%	98%	95%	90%	80%	70%	60%
	$1,850	$1,625	$1,350	$1,100	$995	$850	$750

Last MSR was $1,065.

1989 Federal legislation banned the importation of this model into U.S.

RIFLES: O/U, CUSTOM

Current high grade Beretta O/U and SxS rifles are sold only by premium grade franchised Beretta dealers. For a listing of these dealers, contact a Beretta Gallery (see Trademark Index).

MODEL S686/S689 SILVER SABLE - .30-06, 9.3x74R, or .444 cal. (disc. 1995), boxlock action, single or double (special order only) triggers. Importation began 1995.

MSR	$4,200	$3,500	$3,000	$2,700	$2,200	$2,000	$1,800	$1,550

Add $500 for 9.3x74R cal.

MODEL S689 GOLD SABLE - 9.3x74R or 30-06 cal., boxlock action, nickel (disc. 1985) or case hardened (new 1986) receiver, double triggers, 23 in. barrels, auto ejectors, sling swivels, 7.7 lbs.

MSR	$5,950	$4,875	$4,250	$3,750	$2,950	$2,350	$1,900	$1,600

Add $500 for 9.3x74R cal.
Add approx. $2,000 for scope and quick detachable claw mounts.

MODEL S686/S689 EELL DIAMOND SABLE - .30-06, 9.3x74R, or .444 Marlin cal., moderate engraving. New 1995.

MSR	$12,750	$10,500	$8,750	$7,750	$6,750	$5,975	$5,325	$4,700

Add $1,250 for an extra set of 20 ga. barrels with forearm.
Add approx. $2,000 for scope and quick detachable claw mounts.

SSO EXPRESS - .375 H&H or .458 Win. Mag. cal., sidelock action, case hardened receiver, double triggers, 23 in. barrels, auto ejectors, 11 lbs., cased. Importation disc. 1989.

	$12,500	$9,500	$8,250	$6,950	$6,100	$5,600	$4,875

Last MSR was $17,533.

Add $425 for claw mounts.

SSO5 EXPRESS - similar to SSO Express except has more elaborate engraving and better walnut.

	$14,250	$11,750	$8,750	$7,500	$6,750	$6,100	$5,600

Last MSR was $19,600.

SSO6 EXPRESS CUSTOM SIDELOCK - 9.3x74R, .375 H&H, or .458 Win. Mag. cal., next to top-of-the-line sidelock double rifle, individually built to the customer's specifications, cased. New 1990.

MSR	$41,225	$33,950	$19,750	$16,000	$12,250	$9,750	$8,750	$7,000

Add $6,750 for extra set of barrels.
Add approx. $600 for Cookleigh scope mounts or $1,400 for Zeiss 4x32mm scope.

* *SSO6 EELL Gold Custom* - same cals. as SSO6 Express, features multiple gold inlays and best quality wood.

MSR	$48,300	$39,750	$25,000	$18,500	$14,000	$11,500	$9,000	$7,500

Add $6,750 for extra set of barrels.
Add approx. $25,000-$45,000 for upgraded master engraving.
Add approx. $600 for Cookleigh scope mounts or $1,400 for Zeiss 4Xx32mm scope.

Grading	100%	98%	95%	90%	80%	70%	60%

B

RIFLES: SxS, CUSTOM

MODEL 455 SIDE-BY-SIDE - .375 H&H, .416 Rigby, .458 Win. Mag., .470 NE, or .500 3 in. NE cal., top of the line sidelock double rifle, individually built to the customer's specifications, cased. New 1990.

MSR	$55,650	$46,250	$36,500	$28,500	$24,000	$19,250	$16,000	$13,000

Add approx. $600 for Cookleigh scope mounts or $1,400 for Zeiss 4Xx32mm scope.

* **Model 455 EELL** - similar cals. as Model 455 SxS, top-of-the-line custom sidelock double rifle featuring every refinement of the gunmaker's art, cased.

MSR	$75,000	$65,000	$45,000	$38,500	$31,000	$25,000	$21,750	$18,000

Add approx. $13,000-$28,000 for upgraded master engraving.
Add approx. $600 for Cookleigh scope mounts or $1,400 for Zeiss 4Xx32mm scope.

SHOTGUNS: O/U, DISC.

BL-1 - 12 ga., 26, 28, or 30 in. barrels, various chokes, boxlock, extractors, double triggers, checkered pistol grip stock. Mfg. 1968-1973.

	$385	$330	$275	$220	$190	$175	$160

BL-2 - similar to BL-1, with single selective trigger, more engraving.

	$420	$385	$360	$305	$265	$225	$185

BL-2 STAKE-OUT - riot configuration with 18 in. barrels, DT, blue finish, approx. 6,000 mfg.

	$400	$340	$275	$220	$190	$175	$160

BL-2/S - similar to BL-2, with vent. rib and speed trigger. Mfg. 1974-1976.

	$440	$385	$330	$305	$265	$225	$185

BL-3 - also available in 20 ga., similar to BL-2, with more engraving, vent. rib, and ejectors. Mfg. 1968-1976.

	$595	$550	$525	$470	$440	$385	$350

Add 15% for 20 ga., if original condition is 90%+.

BL-3 SKEET

	$660	$605	$580	$525	$470	$415	$370

BL-3 TRAP

	$580	$520	$495	$450	$415	$375	$335

BL-4 - 12, 20, or 28 ga., deluxe version of BL-3, more engraving, better wood, and ejectors.

	$895	$825	$775	$700	$600	$550	$475

Add 25% for 20 ga.
Add 100% for 28 ga.

BL-4 SKEET

	$850	$745	$675	$635	$550	$495	$450

BL-4 TRAP

	$625	$575	$525	$475	$425	$360	$325

BL-5 - higher grade version of BL-4.

	$1,195	$995	$900	$800	$750	$700	$650

Add 50% for 20 ga.
Add 100% for 28 ga.

BL-5 SKEET

	$1,100	$960	$875	$795	$725	$650	$595

Grading	100%	98%	95%	90%	80%	70%	60%

BL-5 TRAP

| | $850 | $775 | $695 | $595 | $525 | $465 | $400 |

BL-6 - boxlock with scroll engraved sideplates, ejectors, SST.

| | $1,450 | $1,250 | $1,025 | $935 | $850 | $765 | $680 |

Add 50% for 20 ga.
Add 100% for 28 ga.

BL-6 SKEET

| | $1,525 | $1,300 | $1,075 | $975 | $915 | $825 | $715 |

BL-6 TRAP

| | $1,100 | $950 | $885 | $810 | $715 | $650 | $575 |

MODEL S55 B - 12 or 20 ga., 26, 28, or 30 in. barrels, various chokes, boxlock, extractors, selective trigger, checkered pistol grip stock. Disc.

| | $600 | $550 | $495 | $440 | $385 | $330 | $300 |

Add 25% for 20 ga.

MODEL S56 E - similar to S55B, with engraved receiver and auto ejectors. Disc.

| | $850 | $775 | $700 | $650 | $600 | $550 | $500 |

MODEL S58 SKEET - similar to S56E, with 26 in. Bohler steel barrels, skeet bore, wide vent. rib, skeet.

| | $800 | $725 | $650 | $550 | $495 | $445 | $395 |

MODEL S58 TRAP - similar to S58 Skeet, with 30 in. barrels, imp. mod. and full choke, Monte Carlo stock with pad.

| | $650 | $575 | $525 | $495 | $450 | $410 | $365 |

SILVER SNIPE - 12, 20 or 28 ga., 26, 28, or 30 in. barrels, boxlock, extractors, trigger optional, checkered pistol grip stock. Mfg. 1955-1967.

| | $725 | $650 | $595 | $550 | $475 | $425 | $395 |

Add 50% for 20 ga.
Add 100% for 28 ga.

* *Silver Snipe SST* - with vent. rib and SST.

| | $775 | $695 | $650 | $595 | $550 | $495 | $450 |

Add 20% for 20 ga.
Add 25% for ejectors.
Add 100% for 28 ga.

GOLDEN SNIPE - similar to Silver Snipe, with auto ejectors and vent. rib standard.

| | $995 | $875 | $775 | $700 | $650 | $600 | $550 |

Add 50% for 20 ga.
Add 100% for 28 ga.

* *Golden Snipe SST* - with SST.

| | $995 | $875 | $775 | $700 | $650 | $600 | $550 |

Add 50% for 20 ga.
Add 100% for 28 ga.

MODEL (S)57 E - higher quality version of Golden Snipe. Mfg. 1955-1967.

| | $825 | $770 | $660 | $635 | $550 | $495 | $450 |

Add 50% for 20 ga.
Add 100% for 28 ga.

* *Model (S)57 E SST* - with single selective trigger.

| | $1,050 | $950 | $825 | $750 | $650 | $550 | $495 |

Add 50% for 20 ga.
Add 100% for 28 ga.

Grading	100%	98%	95%	90%	80%	70%	60%

ASE MODEL - 12 or 20 ga., light border scroll engraving, mfg. approx. 1947-1964.

	100%	98%	95%	90%	80%	70%	60%
12 ga.	$1,875	$1,600	$1,425	$1,175	$895	$750	$625
20 ga.	$2,600	$2,200	$1,875	$1,500	$1,250	$1,050	$675

ASEL MODEL - 12 or 20 ga., 26, 28, or 30 in. barrels, various chokes, single trigger, receiver moderately engraved, checkered pistol grip stock, auto ejectors. Mfg. 1947- 1964.

12 ga.	$2,750	$2,375	$1,975	$1,600	$1,375	$1,050	$875
20 ga.	$4,450	$3,750	$3,300	$2,850	$2,475	$2,050	$1,675

ASEELL MODEL - 12 or 20 ga., full coverage engraving, very limited mfg.

12 ga.	$4,500	$3,950	$3,350	$2,825	$2,350	$2,100	$1,900
20 ga.	$7,950	$7,350	$6,350	$5,500	$4,875	$4,250	$3,500

GRADE 100 - 12 ga., 26, 28, or 30 in. barrels, any choke, sidelock, double trigger, auto ejectors, checkered pistol grip or straight stock.

	$1,820	$1,550	$1,300	$1,100	$900	$775	$695

MODEL 200 - similar to 100, with chrome lined bores and action parts, higher quality engraving.

	$2,310	$2,000	$1,870	$1,650	$1,375	$1,100	$875

MODEL 680 - 12 ga. only, competition trap and skeet model, boxlock, various chokes. Mono-trap model available. Silver finish receiver, hand engraved, premium walnut. Disc.

	$1,215	$1,030	$870	$790	$715	$635	$550

Add approx. $300 for 2 barrel combo. package.

SHOTGUNS: O/U, FIELD - RECENT MFG.

All models listed in this category are field grade configuration regardless of model nomenclature.

BERETTA CHOKES AND THEIR CODES (ON REAR LEFT-SIDE OF BARREL)

* designates full choke (F).

** designates improved modified choke (IM).

*** designates modified choke (M).

**** designates improved cylinder choke (IC).

FK designates skeet (SK).

***** designates cylinder bore (CYL).

MODEL 685 - 12 or 20 ga. 2¾ or 3 in. chambers, matte chromed receiver, extractors, single trigger. Disc. 1986.

	$595	$525	$460	$420	$360	$320	$295

Last MSR was $875.

MODEL 686 ONYX - 12 or 20 ga., 3 in. chambers, boxlock action, 26 or 28 in. barrels with multi-chokes, matte finish on metal parts, choice of standard pistol grip or English straight (disc. 1999) stock with gloss (new 1999) or matte wood finish, single trigger, ejectors, approx. 6.2 or 6.8 lbs. New 1988.

MSR $1,583		$1,285	$955	$765	$615	$550	$480	$425

Add $154 for deluxe wood upgrade (new 2001, includes case).

❋ *Onyx Waterfowler Magnum* - 12 ga. only, similar to Model S686 Onyx, except has 3½ in. chambers, 28 in. barrels only, matte wood and metal finish. Mfg. 1993, reintroduced 1996.

MSR $1,648		$1,330	$975	$800	$675	$600	$550	$495

Grading	100%	98%	95%	90%	80%	70%	60%

B

* **Ultralight (Onyx)** - 12 ga. only, 2¾ in. chambers, Ergal alloy receiver reinforced with titanium plate, electroless nickel finish receiver with game scene engraving (new 1998, restyled 2002 with several gold inlays) or matte black finish on receiver (disc. 1997) and 26 (disc. 2001) or 28 in. VR barrels, choice of English (new 2001) straight or pistol grip checkered walnut stock and forearm, matte (new 2001, restyled) or gloss wood finish, choke tubes, gilded lettering and logo (disc. 1997), gold SST, ejectors, very light weight, 5 lbs. 11 oz. Importation began 1992.

MSR	$1,931		$1,565	$1,135	$865	$760	$650	$575	$525

Add approx. $150 for deluxe wood upgrade (includes case, mfg. 2001 only).
Subtract approx. 10%-15% if with matte black finish, depending on condition.

* **Ultralight Deluxe (Onyx)** - 12 ga. only, 2¾ in. chambers, similiar to 1998 Model 686 Ultralight, except has gold game scene engraving and select walnut stock and forearm. Mfg. began 1998.

MSR	$2,323		$1,825	$1,500	$1,225	$965	$885	$800	$695

* **Model 686 Essential** - 12 ga. only, 3 in. chambers, 26 or 28 in. VR separated barrels with choke tubes, checkered high-gloss walnut stock and forearm, matte finished metal, 6.7 lbs. Mfg. 1994- 96.

			$1,075	$950	$800	$650	$550	$500	$450

Last MSR was $1,186.

* **Model S686 Silver Essential** - 12 ga. only, 3 in. chambers, 26 or 28 in. VR separated barrels with choke tubes, checkered matte finished walnut stock and forearm, matte chrome finished receiver, 6.7 lbs. Imported 1997-98 only.

			$1,075	$950	$800	$650	$550	$500	$450

Last MSR was $1,070.

* **Whitewing** - 12 or 20 ga., 3 in. chambers, 26 or 28 in. separated VR barrels and MC3 choke tubes, similar to Model 686 Silver Essential, except has checkered gloss finish walnut stock and silver polished receiver with game scene engraving, 6.7 lbs. New 1999.

MSR	$1,298		$1,130	$985	$860	$750	$650	$525	$400

* **Blackwing** - similar to Whitewing, except has matte black receiver finish, lower stock dimensions, and Schnabel forearm. New 2002.

MSR	$1,398		$1,200	$1,000	$875	$750	$650	$525	$400

* **Onyx Model 686 Quail Unlimited Covey Limited Edition** - 12 or 20 ga., similar to Model 686 Onyx, except includes 6 quail inlays in 24 Kt. gold on receiver sides and Quail Unlimited logo on bottom of receiver, marked "1 of 750," deluxe checkered stock and forearm, 750 of each ga. mfg. beginning 2002.

MSR	$1,947		$1,600	$1,175	$975	$800	$700	$600	$550

This model is available through Beretta Showcase Dealers only.

* **Onyx Model 686 Silver Pigeon & Silver Pigeon S (Silver Perdiz)** - 12, 20, or 28 (mfg. 1995-2001) ga., 3 in. chambers (except for 28 ga.), 26 or 28 in. VR barrels with choke tubes, choice of polished (new 1999) or regular nickel finished receiver with scroll engraving, gold trigger, gloss finish checkered pistol grip or straight grip (disc. 1999) walnut stock and forearm, 6.8 lbs. New 1992.

MSR	$1,869		$1,525	$1,115	$925	$765	$650	$575	$525

Subtract $55 for English straight grip stock (20 ga. only, disc. 1999).
Add $153 for deluxe wood upgrade (Silver Pigeon only, 12 or 20 ga. only, includes case, new 2001).
Add $48 for Silver Pigeon S Model (includes carrying case with 5 choke tubes, recoil pad, and sling swivels).
During 1996, the model nomenclature was changed from the Silver Perdiz to the Silver Pigeon.

B

Grading	100%	98%	95%	90%	80%	70%	60%

✳ *Onyx Model 686 Silver Pigeon (Silver Perdiz) and 686 Silver Pigeon S Combo* - similar to Model 686 Onyx, except is supplied with 1 set each of 20 ga. (28 in.) and 28 ga. (26 in.) barrels, polished receiver became standard 1999. Introduced 1986.

MSR $2,587	$2,050	$1,525	$1,275	$985	$875	$820	$775

Add $47 for Model Silver Pigeon S (includes carrying case, 5 choke tubes, recoil pad, and sling swivels).

MODEL 686(L) SILVER PERDIZ - 12 (disc. 1990), 20 (disc. 1990), or 28 ga., field model, boxlock action, various barrels/ chokes, ejectors, single trigger, engraved silver finished receiver, special walnut, pistol or straight grip stock, fixed chokes disc. 1987. Importation disc. 1994.

$1,100	$850	$650	$575	$525	$460	$415

Last MSR was $1,355.

Subtract 10% with fixed chokes (disc.).
Add 20% for 28 ga.

MODEL S686 EL GOLD PERDIZ - 12 or 20 ga., 3 in. chambers, boxlock action with floral scroll engraved sideplates, silver receiver finish, 26 or 28 (20 ga. only beginning 1997) VR in. barrels with choke tubes, gold SST, checkered walnut stock and forearm, cased, approx. 6.8 lbs. Mfg. 1992-97.

$1,600	$1,350	$1,150	$950	$875	$800	$695

Last MSR was $1,930.

MODEL S687(L) SILVER PIGEON - 12 (disc. 1999) or 20 ga., 3 in. chambers, boxlock, various barrels/chokes, ejectors, game scene engraved nickel finished receiver, gloss finished select walnut stock and forearm, approx. 6.8 lbs., fitted case was optional. Disc. 2000.

$1,825	$1,450	$1,215	$975	$875	$800	$695

Last MSR was $2,255.

Subtract 10% without multi-chokes (disc.).
The "L" suffix model nomenclature was disc. 1996.

SILVER PIGEON II S687 - 12 or 20 ga., similar to Model S687 Silver Pigeon, except has deep relief engraved game scenes on receiver sides and oil finished (matte) walnut stock and forearm, 26 or 28 in. VR barrels with MC3 choke tubes. New 1999.

MSR $2,196	$1,785	$1,425	$1,175	$965	$860	$750	$650

MODEL 687 DU - 12 (1990 release) or 20 ga., mfg. for DU dinner gun auctions and membership, prices may vary significantly from region to region.

$1,950	$1,700	$1,450	$1,175	$895	$725	$575

Add 10% for 20 ga., 15% for 28 ga. or .410 bore.

MODEL 687 L ONYX - 12 or 20 ga., 3 in. chambers, same game scene engraving as standard Model 687 L, except has Onyx blackened receiver, multi-chokes standard. Mfg. 1990 only.

$1,375	$1,100	$900	$750	$650	$575	$525

Last MSR was $1,590.

MODEL 687 GOLDEN ONYX - 12 or 20 ga., 3 in. chambers, similar to Model 686 Onyx, except has more engraving, better walnut, and several gold inlays. Imported 1988-89 only.

$1,525	$1,275	$995	$825	$700	$650	$575

Last MSR was $1,800.

Add 15% for 20 ga.

MODEL S687 EL GOLD PIGEON - same general specifications as Model 687L, except also available in 28 ga. (new 1990) or .410 (new 1990) bore, 20 ga. disc. 2001, 2¾ or 3 in. chambers, boxlock with gold inlaid game scene on sideplates, highly figured walnut, and more engraving, oval nameplate, approx. 6.8 lbs, cased.

MSR $4,099	$3,335	$2,475	$1,950	$1,575	$1,350	$1,150	$1,000

Add $174 for 28 ga. or .410 bore.

Grading	100%	98%	95%	90%	80%	70%	60%

✳ *Model 687 EL DU* - 28 ga. or .410 bore, small frame, released 1992 for DU auctions and membership.

	$2,850	$2,200	$1,800	$1,550	$1,400	$1,200	$1,050

MODEL S687 EL GOLD PIGEON II - 12, 20, 28 ga., or .410 bore, similar to EL Gold Pigeon, except features deep relief engraving on sideplates, 6.8 lbs., cased. New 2001.

MSR	$4,513	$3,650	$2,650	$2,100	$1,650	$1,400	$1,150	$1,000

MODEL 687 EL ONYX - 12 or 20 ga., 3 in. chambers, simulated sidelock plates with classic scroll engraving. Mfg. 1990 only.

	$2,295	$2,000	$1,725	$1,500	$1,350	$1,150	$1,000

Last MSR was $2,660.

MODEL S687 EELL DIAMOND PIGEON - 12, 20, or 28 ga., boxlock action, silver receiver with full sideplates and hand engraved game scenes, 26 or 28 in. VR barrels, 3 (except 28 ga.) in. chambers and gold plated trigger, cased, multi-chokes introduced 1988, 6.8 lbs.

MSR	$5,630	$4,420	$3,350	$2,650	$2,050	$1,725	$1,500	$1,250

Subtract 10% if without multi-chokes.

This model is also available with a straight grip English stock at no extra charge (20 ga. only).

✳ *Model S687 EELL Combo* - includes one set of 20 and 28 ga. multi-choke 26 or 28 in. barrels, cased. Limited importation.

MSR	$6,279	$5,145	$3,825	$2,875	$2,200	$1,750	$1,500	$1,250

Subtract 10% for fixed chokes.

Multi-chokes became standard in 1991.

✳ *Model S687 EELL Gallery Edition* - 12, 20, 28 ga., or .410 bore, available as a pair (optional) or 2 barrel sets, featuring special engraving and upgraded wood with oil finish. New 2000.

Prices range from $7,250 -$8,750 for single guns and 2 barrel sets, depending on ga. and options. Pairs start at $16,675. Available at Beretta Galleries only.

MODEL S687 EXTRA - 12, 20, 28 ga., or .410 bore, available in pairs or 2 barrel sets (special order only), features special engraving and upgraded wood with oil finish. New 2001.

Prices range from $7,250 -$8,750 for single guns and 2 barrel sets, depending on ga. and options. Pairs start at $16,675. Available at Beretta Premium dealers only.

MODEL ASE 90 PIGEON - 12 ga. only, 28 in. fixed choke (IM/F) vent. barrels with VR, new design features nickel- chromium-molybdenum receiver with special hardening and cross bolt engaging 2 monobloc lugs, detachable trigger grouping, V-shaped main springs, cold hammered barrels, choice of silver or blue receiver with gold etching and no engraving, top quality checkered walnut stock and forearm with vent. recoil pad, choke tubes, 7 lbs. 13 oz., cased. Imported 1992-94.

	$5,500	$4,850	$3,950	$3,300	$2,850	$2,500	$2,150

Last MSR was $8,070.

SHOTGUNS: O/U, SKEET - RECENT MFG.

Full descriptions for the following models may be found under the corresponding model numbers in the Field Shotguns category.

MODEL S682 GOLD SKEET - 12, 20 (disc. 1991), 28 ga. (disc. 1988), or .410 bore (disc. 1988), competition skeet model, 26 (disc.) or 28 in. barrels, boxlock, skeet chokes, silver finish (disc.) or Greystone (titanium nitrate) receiver, hand engraved, premium walnut, cased. Mfg. 1984-1999.

	$2,100	$1,650	$1,275	$1,025	$900	$800	$700

Last MSR was $2,850.

Grading	100%	98%	95%	90%	80%	70%	60%

✳ *Model S682 Gold Skeet With Adj. Stock* - similar to Model S682 Gold Skeet, except has fully adj. stock, allowing the comb, drop, and cast to be adjusted per shooter. Imported 1999-2000.

	$2,650	$2,275	$1,950	$1,700	$1,350	$1,075	$950

Last MSR was $3,515.

✳ *Model S682 Gold E Skeet* - 12 ga. only, 28 or 30 in. VR barrels with Optima-Bore and Optima-Choke, adj. stock with memory system, dual color finished receiver with engraved merging circular lines and gold highlights, including trigger, deluxe wide checkered stock and Schnabel forearm with gloss wood finish, 7.6 lbs. New 2001.

MSR	$4,320		$3,500	$2,525	$2,000	$1,600	$1,350	$1,150	$1,000

✳ *Model 682 Super Skeet* - 12 ga. only, 28 in. VR barrels bored SK/SK featuring factory porting, stock has separate adj. comb cheekpiece. Mfg. 1991-95.

	$2,275	$1,850	$1,575	$1,250	$1,050	$900	$800

Last MSR was $3,006.

✳ *Model 682 Skeet Deluxe* - similar to Model 682, except deluxe walnut and elaborate engraving. Disc. 1986.

	$2,275	$1,850	$1,575	$1,250	$1,050	$900	$800

Last MSR was $3,000.

✳ *Model 682 2-Barrel Skeet Set* - 12 ga. only, two barrel set bored for skeet and sporting clays competition. Imported 1988 only.

	$4,500	$3,600	$3,100	$2,750	$2,450	$2,100	$1,875

Last MSR was $6,650.

✳ *Model 682 4-Ga. Skeet Set* - four barrel skeet set comes with interchangeable barrels (28 in.) in 12, 20, 28 ga.'s, and .410 bore. Imported 1985-95.

	$5,000	$3,995	$3,300	$2,850	$2,500	$2,175	$1,900

Last MSR was $6,037.

MODEL S686 SKEET SILVER PERDIZ/SILVER PIGEON - 12 ga. only, 28 in. VR barrels bored SK/SK, checkered walnut stock and forearm, Silver Perdiz was disc. 1996 and featured silver finish, while Silver Pigeon nomenclature began 1997 and features nickel finish, 7.6 lbs. Imported 1994-98.

	$1,425	$1,295	$900	$675	$595	$550	$480

Last MSR was $1,795.

MODEL S687 EELL SKEET DIAMOND PIGEON - 12 ga. only, fixed chokes, 28 in. barrels, elaborate game scene engraving on sideplates, cased.

MSR	$4,984		$4,155	$3,075	$2,550	$2,000	$1,800	$1,500	$1,250

✳ *Model S687 EELL Skeet Diamond Pigeon With Adj. Stock* - similar to Model S687 EELL Skeet Diamond Pigeon, except has fully adj. stock, allowing the comb, drop, and cast to be adjusted per shooter. Importation began 1999.

MSR	$6,050		$5,295	$4,675	$4,125	$3,350	$2,500	$2,000	$1,600

✳ *Model S687 EELL 4-Ga. Skeet Set* - four ga. skeet set, cased. Imported 1988-1998.

	$7,200	$6,150	$4,750	$3,900	$3,400	$3,000	$2,700

Last MSR was $8,405.

DT10 TRIDENT SKEET - 12 ga. only, 3 in. chambers, 28 or 30 in. vent. barrels with target VR, specially designed skeet gun featuring removable adj. trigger group, massive crossbolt locking system, Optima- choke competition choke tubes, Optima-Bore internal barrel configuration, specific point of impact, and unique distribution of mass that helps target acquisition and eliminate muzzle rise, adj. walnut stock with memory system, carbon reinforced frame, 7.9 lbs. New 2000.

MSR	$8,030		$7,200	$6,500	$5,200	$4,100	$3,300	$2,800	$2,500

Grading	100%	98%	95%	90%	80%	70%	60%

MODEL ASE 90 GOLD SKEET - 12 ga. only, 28 in. fixed choke vent. barrels with VR, similar action and specifications as the Model ASE 90 Pigeon, except has more elaborate hand scroll engraving and extra fine wood, 7.6 lbs., cased. Mfg. 1992-99.

	$6,950	$6,150	$5,150	$4,150	$3,300	$2,850	$2,500

Last MSR was $12,060.

SHOTGUNS: O/U, SPORTING CLAYS - RECENT MFG.

These variations have been specifically designed for sporting clay target shooting. All of the following models have 3 in. chambers, unless specified otherwise. Full descriptions for the following models may be found under the corresponding model numbers in the Field Shotguns category. Sporting Clays models with 30 in. barrels are currently more desireable than either 26 or 28 in., and premiums of 5%-10% are being asked.

MODEL S682 CONTINENTAL COURSE - 12 ga. only, 2¾ in. chambers, 28 or 30 (disc. 1995) in. VR barrels with multi-chokes, designed for English Sporting Clays courses, previously was Model Super Sport with tapered rib, cased. Mfg. 1993-97.

	$1,695	$1,450	$1,225	$975	$875	$775	$675

Last MSR was $2,345.

MODEL S682 GOLD SPORTING - 12 or 20 (mfg. 1992-94) ga., similar specifications to Model 682 Skeet, 2¾ in. chambers, 28, 30 (new 1989), or 31 (new 1997) in. unported or ported (new 1995) VR barrels, except over-field stock dimensions and hand engraved silver (disc.) or Greystone (titanium nitrate) finished receiver, cased, 7.6 lbs. Multi-chokes are standard. Disc. 2000.

	$2,275	$1,850	$1,400	$1,075	$950	$875	$800

Last MSR was $3,100.

Add $130 for ported barrels (28 or 30 in. only).
Add $865 for extra set of 12 ga. barrels (combo. package - mfg. 1990-94).

✳ *Model S682 Gold E Sporting* - 12 ga. only, 28, 30, or 32 in. VR barrels with Optima-Bore and Optima-Choke, adj. stock with memory system, dual color finished receiver with engraved merging circular lines and gold highlights, including trigger, select wide checkered stock and Schnabel forearm with gloss wood finish, approx. 7.6 lbs. New 2001.

MSR	$3,850	$3,250	$2,500	$2,100	$1,650	$1,400	$1,200	$1,000

MODEL 682 SUPER SPORTING - 12 ga. only, 2¾ in. chambers, 28 or 30 in. VR ported (new 1993) barrels with multi- chokes and tapered rib, otherwise similar to Model 682 Sporting, cased, 7.6 lbs. Imported 1989-95.

	$2,275	$1,850	$1,400	$1,075	$950	$875	$800

Last MSR was $3,017.

Beginning 1993, this model featured a special fully adj. stock and LOP.

MODEL 686 SPORTING/SPECIAL SPORTING - 12 ga. only, 3 in. chambers, deluxe checkered walnut stock and forearm with over-field dimensions, 28 or 30 (new 1991) in. barrels only, multi-chokes standard. Mfg. 1987-92.

	$1,475	$1,100	$950	$825	$675	$625	$550

Last MSR was $1,940.

The Model 686 Special Sporting is marked "Model S686 Special," and the barrels are marked "Sporting."

Grading	100%	98%	95%	90%	80%	70%	60%

✳ *Model S686 Silver Pigeon (Silver Perdiz) Sporting* - 12 or 20 (disc. 2000) ga., 28 or 30 in. VR barrels with multi-chokes, 7.7 lbs. New 1993.

MSR $1,931	$1,550	$1,175	$995	$850	$725	$650	$575

Add $139 for deluxe wood upgrade (includes case, new 2001).

Until 1994, this model was named the Model 686 Hunter Sport. Between 1994-95, this model was named the S686 Silver Perdiz, and beginning 1996, this model was again renamed to the 686 Silver Pigeon Sporting.

✳ *Model 686 E Sporting* - 12 or 20 ga., 3 in. chambers, 28 (20 ga. only) or 30 in. VR barrels with 5 chokes, improved styling, oil finished walnut stock and Schnabel forearm, includes accessories, 5 choke tubes, and carrying case, 7.7 lbs. New 2001.

MSR $2,008	$1,675	$1,250	$1,050	$875	$750	$675	$600

✳ *Model 686 Silver Perdiz/S686 Silver Pigeon Sporting Combo* - 12 ga., includes extra set of 30 in. barrels. Model 686 Silver Perdiz was manufactured 1991-95, Model S686 Silver Pigeon was manufactured 1997-99.

$1,925	$1,700	$1,475	$1,250	$1,025	$900	$800

Last MSR was $2,210.
Last MSR was $2,687 for the 686 Silver Perdiz Combo.

MODEL 686 COLLECTION SPORT - 12 ga. only, features multi-colored checkered wood stock and forearm, 28 in. VR barrels, 7.7 lbs. Mfg. 1996 only.

$1,225	$900	$695	$575	$525	$460	$415

Last MSR was $1,499.

MODEL 686 ONYX SPORTING - 12 ga. only, 28 or 30 in. vent. fixed choke barrels with VR, high luster blue finish with gold lettering on receiver sides. Mfg. 1992 only.

$1,600	$1,300	$1,050	$925	$875	$775	$695

Last MSR was $1,940.

✳ *Model 686 Onyx Sporting w/Multi-chokes* - 12 ga. only, 28 or 30 in. VR barrels with multi-chokes, matte wood finish, choice of semi-matte black (disc. 1998) or polished black receiver with "P. Beretta" engraved in gold, 7.7 lbs. New 1993.

MSR $1,639	$1,325	$985	$775	$595	$525	$460	$415

Add $139 for deluxe wood upgrade (includes case, new 2001).

✳ *Model 686 English Course* - 12 ga. only, features 28 in. VR barrels and special reverse tapered VR with special sighting plane designed for English courses. Mfg. 1991-92.

$1,675	$1,350	$1,050	$925	$875	$775	$695

Last MSR was $2,015.

MODEL S687(L) SILVER PIGEON (SILVER PERDIZ) SPORTING - 12 or 20 ga. only, deluxe checkered walnut stock and forearm with over-field dimensions, 28 or 30 (12 ga. only) in. barrels, multi-chokes standard. Mfg. 1987-2001.

$1,995	$1,535	$1,215	$975	$875	$775	$675

Last MSR was $2,363.

✳ *Model 687 Silver Pigeon Sporting Combo* - 12 ga., includes set of 28 and 30 in. barrels. New 2002.

MSR $3,151	$2,650	$2,250	$2,000	$1,850	$1,600	$1,400	$1,200

✳ *Model 687 English Course* - 12 ga. only, features 28 in. VR barrels and special reverse tapered VR with special sighting plane designed for English courses. Mfg. 1991-92.

$2,225	$1,750	$1,325	$1,050	$950	$895	$800

Last MSR was $2,630.

Grading	100%	98%	95%	90%	80%	70%	60%

❋ **Model S687 Silver Pigeon II Sporting** - 12, 20 (new 2002), or 28 ga. (new 2002), features deep relief game scene engraving on receiver sides, matte oil finished select walnut stock and forearm, 28, 30, or 32 (12 ga. only, new 2002) in. barrels with choke tube, 7.7 lbs. Importation began 1999.

MSR $2,196	$1,865	$1,435	$1,165	$950	$850	$775	$675

MODEL S687 EL GOLD PIGEON SPORTING - 12 ga. only, 28 or 30 in. VR barrels with multi-chokes, 7.7 lbs. Mfg. 1993-2001.

	$3,700	$3,125	$2,625	$2,200	$1,850	$1,500	$1,250

Last MSR was $4,182.

MODEL S687 EL GOLD PIGEON II SPORTING - similar to Model S687 Gold Pigeon Sporting, except features deep relief engraving on sideplates, also available in 28 ga. and 32 in. barrels beginning 2002. New 2001.

MSR $4,595	$4,000	$3,275	$2,725	$2,250	$1,975	$1,500	$1,250

❋ **Model 687 Gold Pigeon II Sporting Combo** - 28 ga. or .410 bore, includes set of 30 in. barrels. New 2002.

MSR $5,244	$4,550	$3,900	$3,325	$2,800	$2,325	$1,975	$1,625

MODEL S687 EELL DIAMOND PIGEON SPORTING - 12 or 20 (disc. 1992) ga. only, deluxe checkered walnut stock and forearm with over-field dimensions, 28, 30 (new 1995), or 32 (new 2002) in. barrels only, multi-chokes standard, cased, 7.6 lbs. New 1987.

MSR $5,737	$4,735	$3,525	$2,675	$2,075	$1,725	$1,500	$1,250

Subtract $735 for 2¾ in. chambers (28 in. barrels only, disc. 1999).
Add $875 for extra set of barrels (combo. package - 1990 mfg. only).

DT10 TRIDENT SPORTING - 12 ga. only, 3 in. chambers, 28, 30, or 32 in. vent. barrels with target VR, specially designed sporting gun featuring removable adj. trigger group, massive crossbolt locking system, Optima-choke competition choke tubes, Optima-Bore internal barrel configuration, specific point of impact, and unique distribution of mass that helps target acquisition and eliminate muzzle rise, deluxe checkered walnut stock and Schnabel forearm, carbon reinforced frame, cased, approx. 8 lbs. New 2000.

MSR $7,850	$6,850	$5,650	$4,950	$4,250	$3,750	$3,250	$2,750

MODEL ASE 90 GOLD SPORTING CLAYS - 12 ga. only, 28, 30, or 31 (new 1997) in. vent. barrels with VR, similar action and specifications to Model ASE 90 Pigeon, 7.5 lbs., cased. Mfg. 1992-99.

	$7,500	$6,500	$5,250	$4,150	$3,300	$2,850	$2,500

Last MSR was $12,145.

SHOTGUNS: O/U, TRAP - RECENT MFG.

Full descriptions for the following models may be found under the corresponding model numbers in the Field Shotguns category.

MODEL S682 GOLD TRAP (GOLD X) - 12 ga. only, competition trap model, Greystone (titanium nitrate) or Bruniton finish (matte black, disc.), 30 or 32 in. barrels with or w/o choke tubes (became standard 1996), adj. trigger, supplied with case, 8.8 lbs. Mfg. 1985-2000.

	$2,150	$1,650	$1,325	$1,050	$900	$775	$650

Last MSR was $3,100.

Subtract 10% if without multi-chokes.

B

✴ *Model S682 Mono/Top Combo (Gold X)* - 12 ga. only, supplied with mono under or upper single barrel and O/U barrel sets, multi-chokes became standard 1996. Otherwise same specifications as Model S682 Gold Trap. Cased. Disc. 2000.

	$2,950	$2,350	$1,900	$1,600	$1,400	$1,200	$1,000

Last MSR was $4,085.

Add $115 for combo package (includes extra set of 34 in. barrels, disc. 1999).
Subtract 5% if without multi-chokes.

✴ *Model S682 Gold Trap Adjustable Stock* - 12 ga. only, features Monte Carlo style stock with adj. comb, stock drop and cast may also be adjusted, 30 or 32 in. barrels, 8.8 lbs. Mfg. 1998-2000.

	$2,700	$2,200	$1,800	$1,475	$1,250	$1,050	$895

Last MSR was $3,625.

Add $985 for combo package (includes extra set of 34 in. barrels).

✴ *Model 682 Mono* - single under-barrel trap model, high post vent. rib, 32 or 34 in. barrel. Imported 1985-1988.

	$1,395	$1,200	$1,025	$925	$875	$775	$675

Last MSR was $1,890.

✴ *Model S682 Gold Live Bird (Pigeon Trap)* - 12 ga. only, includes features for international style pigeon and competition shooters including international style stock, standard or flat (new 1995) VR, and mid-rib sights, Greystone (new 1991) or matte black (disc.) metal finish, semi-gloss American walnut stock, light scroll engraving, sliding trigger, includes multi-chokes, cased, 8.8 lbs. Imported 1990-98.

	$2,000	$1,625	$1,325	$1,175	$950	$895	$800

Last MSR was $2,910.

Add $71 for tapered flat rib (disc. 1995).

✴ *Model 682 Gold X Trap Mono (Top Single)* - 12 ga. only, single over-barrel trap model, 32 or 34 in. barrel. Imported 1986-95.

	$1,975	$1,600	$1,300	$1,150	$925	$875	$775

Last MSR was $2,734.

Subtract 5% if without multi-chokes.
Multi-chokes became standard in 1989.

✴ *Model 682 Unsingle* - 12 ga. only, single under barrel trap model with 32 in. high post VR, choke tubes. Imported 1992-94.

	$1,950	$1,575	$1,275	$1,125	$925	$875	$775

Last MSR was $2,650.

MODEL S682 (GOLD X) SUPER TRAP - 12 ga. only, competition trap model, 30 in. barrels, step tapered rib, factory porting, LOP, and separate stock cheekpiece are adjustable, cased. Imported 1991-95.

	$2,100	$1,700	$1,375	$1,050	$900	$800	$700

Last MSR was $2,907.

Add $69 for multi-chokes.

✴ *Model S682 Top Mono Super Trap (Gold X)* - 12 ga. only, single over-barrel trap model, 32 or 34 in. barrel with choice of fixed or multi-chokes. Imported 1991-95.

	$2,150	$1,700	$1,375	$1,050	$900	$800	$700

Last MSR was $3,083.

Add $73 for multi-chokes (32 in. barrels only) or 34 in. barrels.

✴ *Model S682 Gold Super Trap Top Combo (Gold X)* - 12 ga. only, supplied with upper single barrel and O/U barrel sets. Otherwise same specifications as Model 682 Super Trap, multi-chokes became standard 1996, cased. Imported 1991-97.

	$2,950	$2,350	$1,900	$1,600	$1,375	$1,125	$895

Last MSR was $4,040.

Grading	100%	98%	95%	90%	80%	70%	60%

MODEL S682 GOLD E TRAP - 12 ga. only, 30 or 32 in. VR barrel with Optima-Bore and Optima-Choke, adj. stock with memory system, dual color finished receiver with engraved merging circular lines and gold highlights, including trigger, deluxe wide checkered stock and Schnabel forearm with gloss wood finish, 7.6 lbs. New 2001.

	MSR	$4,320	$3,500	$2,525	$2,000	$1,600	$1,350	$1,150	$1,000

✹ *Model S682 Gold E Trap Combo Top* - 12 ga. only, includes 30 (disc. 2001), 32 (disc. 2002) or 34 (new 2002) in. mono top barrel and choice of 30 or 32 in. O/U barrels, cased. New 2001.

	MSR	$5,305	$4,400	$3,500	$2,675	$2,075	$1,725	$1,500	$1,250

MODEL S686 SILVER PIGEON TRAP - 12 ga. only, low-profile action, 30 in. VR barrels with 3/8 in. flat rib, matte wood finish, nickel finished receiver with scroll engraving, 7.7 lbs. Mfg. 1997-99.

$1,425	$1,000	$725	$600	$525	$460	$415

Last MSR was $1,795.

✹ *Model S686 Silver Pigeon Trap Top Mono* - 12 ga. only, single over-barrel trap model, 32 or 34 in. barrel with multi-chokes, gloss wood finish, 8.14 lbs. New 1998.

MSR	$1,869	$1,475	$1,035	$735	$600	$525	$460	$415

MODEL 686 INTERNATIONAL - 12 ga. only, 30 in. VR barrels bored IM/F, checkered walnut stock and forearm. Imported 1994 only.

$1,250	$1,075	$800	$625	$550	$500	$460

Last MSR was $1,300.

MODEL S687 EELL DIAMOND PIGEON (X TRAP) - 12 ga. only, boxlock action with engraved black (new 1992) or silver (disc. 1991) finished side plates, Monte Carlo stock with recoil pad, 30 in. barrels with choke tubes, cased, 8.8 lbs. Disc. 1999.

$3,850	$3,175	$2,475	$2,050	$1,725	$1,500	$1,250

Last MSR was $4,815.

✹ *Model S687 EELL Diamond Pigeon Trap Top Mono* - 12 ga. only, single over-barrel trap model, 32 or 34 in. barrel, fixed chokes standard. Imported 1988-92, resumed 1996, disc. 1999.

$3,250	$2,850	$2,550	$2,250	$1,950	$1,725	$1,475

Last MSR was $5,060.

Add 5% for multi-chokes.

✹ *Model S687 EELL Diamond Pigeon X Bottom Mono Trap Combo* - 12 ga. only, supplied with 30 or 32 in. O/U barrels and a mono trap bottom barrel. Imported 1986-1988, resumed 1994-95.

$4,250	$3,300	$3,400	$3,000	$2,775	$2,550	$2,250

Last MSR was $4,984.

Add 5% for multi-chokes.

✹ *Model S687 EELL Diamond Pigeon X Top Mono Trap Combo* - 12 ga. only, supplied with 30 or 32 in. O/U barrels and a mono trap upper barrel, multi-chokes became standard 1995. Mfg. 1988-1997.

$4,750	$4,025	$3,300	$2,875	$2,500	$2,175	$1,900

Last MSR was $6,070.

Subtract 5% if without multi-chokes.

Grading			100%	98%	95%	90%	80%	70%	60%

MODEL ASE 90 GOLD TRAP - 12 ga. only, 30 in. vent. barrels with VR, similar action and specifications to Model ASE 90 Pigeon, 8.2 lbs., cased with extra trigger group, multi- chokes became standard 1995. Mfg. 1992-99.

		$5,750	$4,500	$3,750	$3,250	$2,750	$2,450	$2,250

Last MSR was $12,145.

Subtract 5% if without multi-chokes.
Add $3,910 for Trap Combo package.

DT10 TRIDENT TRAP - 12 ga. only, 3 in. chambers, 30 or 32 in. vent. barrels with target VR, specially designed trap gun featuring removable adj. trigger group, massive crossbolt locking system, Optima- choke competition choke tubes, Optima-Bore internal barrel configuration, specific point of impact, and unique distribution of mass that helps target acquisition and eliminate muzzle rise, adj. walnut stock with memory system, carbon reinforced frame, 8.8 lbs., cased. New 2000.

MSR	$8,500	$7,550	$6,500	$5,750	$5,000	$4,250	$3,450	$2,750

* **DT10 Trident Trap Top Single** - includes 34 in. top single barrel, cased. New 2000.

MSR	$8,500	$7,550	$6,500	$5,750	$5,000	$4,250	$3,450	$2,750

* **DT10 Trident Trap Combo** - includes choice of 30 or 32 in. O/U barrels and a 34 in. top single barrel, cased. New 2000.

MSR	$10,790	$9,250	$7,750	$6,500	$5,500	$4,750	$4,000	$3,250

* **DT10 Trident Trap Bottom Single Combo** - includes 34 in. bottom single barrel and choice of 30 or 32 in. O/U barrels, rib on bottom single barrel is adj. for point of impact, cased. New 2001.

MSR	$11,040	$9,500	$7,875	$6,600	$5,500	$4,750	$4,000	$3,250

SHOTGUNS: O/U, CUSTOM GRADE - RECENT MFG.

Current high grade Beretta O/U and SxS shotguns are sold only by premium grade franchised Beretta dealers. For a listing of these dealers, contact a Beretta Gallery (see Trademark Index).

Where applicable, Beretta's new SST, with selector switch built into safety, is more desirable than older manufacture utilizing the disc. single, non-selective trigger.
Add $1,200 per extra set of barrels.
Subtract 10%-15% for older style non-selective single trigger.

JUBILEE - 12, 20, 28 ga., or .410 bore, choice of Field or Sporting Clays configuration, signed scroll or game scene engraving, upgraded wood, tru-oil finish, and hand polished details throughout, cased. New 1998.

MSR	$13,750	$11,600	$7,750	$5,950	$4,650	$3,100	$2,780	$2,500

* **Jubilee Matched Pair** - available with consecutive serial numbers, made to special order, cased. New 2002.

MSR	$31,650	$25,000	$20,000	$15,000	$11,750	$7,000	$6,500	$5,000

SO-2 - 12 ga., 26-30 in. barrels, sidelock, any chokes, vent. rib, auto ejectors, SST, checkered stock in various configurations (field, skeet, or trap), grades differ in wood, engraving, and finish, cased. SO series mfg. 1948-disc.

MSR	$4,750	$3,995	$2,950	$2,350	$1,950	$1,675	$1,475	$1,250

SO-3 - 2nd grade of the SO series.

MSR	$6,250	$4,500	$3,550	$3,200	$2,800	$2,400	$2,100	$1,850

SO-3 EL - grade-up from SO-3 with better wood and engraving.

MSR	$7,750	$6,250	$4,250	$3,600	$3,050	$2,500	$2,200	$1,950

SO-3 EELL - best quality model, custom specifications, choice of engraving motifs.

MSR	$11,995	$10,250	$8,000	$6,850	$5,850	$5,100	$4,250	$3,600

Add $2,000 for master engraving.

SO-4 - 12 ga., sidelock, available in field, skeet, or trap configurations, custom specs., fluorescent sights, wide rib, cased. Disc. 1987, reintroduced 2001.

MSR $5,950	$5,250	$4,550	$4,100	$3,550	$3,200	$2,800	$2,400

ASE GOLD - see individual models with descriptions under Skeet, Sporting Clays, and Trap category names.

ASE 90 DE LUXE - 12 ga. only, specifications furnished by customer, deep scroll engraving signed by the engraver, upgraded wood, Sporting or Field Model, cased. New 1996.

MSR $24,500	$20,500	$15,000	$10,750	$8,750	$7,250	$6,000	$5,000

SO-5 COMPETITION - best quality O/U, extensively engraved, top quality checkered walnut stock (semi-pistol grip) and forearm, available in either Trap, Skeet, or Sporting configurations, limited importation, leather cased.

MSR $17,490	$15,500	$9,500	$7,750	$6,750	$5,750	$5,200	$4,500

Add $5,900 for extra set of barrels.
Add $3,500 for Trap Combo set (disc.).

SO-5 EELL - next to top-of-the-line model, available in either Trap, Skeet, or Sporting Clays configuration, custom built to customer dimensions.

MSR $15,000	$13,750	$9,250	$7,750	$6,250	$5,250	$4,750	$3,950

SO-6 COMPETITION - 12 ga. only high quality O/U, extensively scroll engraved, top quality checkered walnut stock (semi-pistol grip) and forearm, choice of Field (reintroduced during 1998), Trap, Skeet, or Sporting Clays configuration, built to customer specifications, limited importation, leather cased.

MSR $23,900	$16,650	$13,500	$10,750	$8,500	$7,450	$6,350	$5,100

Add $6,250 for extra set of barrels.

SO-6 EELL - 12 ga., current next to top-of-the-line model, field dimensions, custom built to customer specifications, leather cased.

MSR $34,900	$27,500	$21,500	$16,750	$12,750	$10,750	$9,500	$8,500

Add $6,250 for extra set of barrels.

SO-6 EESS - 12 ga., features green enamel sideplates with diamond inlays. New 1998.

MSR $84,000	$77,500	$65,000	$52,000	$45,000	$39,000	$32,000	$26,500

✳ **SO-6 EESS w/o Diamonds** - features red or blue enamel sideplates, w/o diamonds. New 1998.

MSR $34,900	$27,500	$21,500	$16,750	$12,750	$10,750	$9,500	$8,500

SO-9 - 12, 20, 28 ga., or .410 bore, top-of-the-line sidelock model, 1990 was the first time the SO series was offered in smaller gauges, 28 ga. or .410 bore models have smaller proportionate frames. New 1990.

MSR $46,725	$35,000	$27,500	$20,500	$16,000	$12,000	$9,200	$7,000

Add $6,275 for extra set of barrels.
Subtract 10% for 12 ga. on used specimens.

✳ **SO-9 EELL Special** - top-of-the-line O/U model, retail prices range from $55,000-$110,000, depending on individual custom order engraving options.

SHOTGUNS: SxS, RECENT MFG.

MODEL 409 PB - 12, 16, 20, or 28 ga., 27, 28, and 30 in. barrels, various chokes, double triggers, plain extractors, checkered pistol grip stock. Mfg. 1934-1964.

	$770	$660	$605	$550	$495	$440	$385

Add 20% for 20 ga.
Add 100% for 28 ga.

Grading	100%	98%	95%	90%	80%	70%	60%

MODEL 410 E - higher quality, auto ejector version of 409 PB.

12 ga.	$1,275	$1,000	$895	$775	$675	$575	$475
20 ga.	$1,750	$1,550	$1,275	$1,000	$895	$775	$675
28 ga.	$3,775	$3,300	$2,800	$2,275	$1,800	$1,450	$1,100

MODEL 410 - similar to 410 E, except 10 ga. Mag., 32 in. barrel, full choke, heavier construction, mfg. 1934-1981.

	100%	98%	95%	90%	80%	70%	60%
	$1,200	$995	$880	$795	$700	$625	$550

MODEL 411 E - similar to 409 PB, with false sideplates and finer finishing. Mfg. 1934- 1964.

12 ga.	$2,000	$1,750	$1,350	$1,050	$895	$775	$675
20 ga.	$2,750	$2,325	$1,750	$1,300	$1,000	$895	$775
28 ga.	$4,250	$3,775	$3,300	$2,800	$2,275	$1,800	$1,450

MODEL 424-426 - 12 and 20 ga. (Model 426 only), 26 and 28 in. barrels, various chokes, box-lock, extractors, double triggers, light engraving, checkered straight stock.

	100%	98%	95%	90%	80%	70%	60%
	$1,395	$1,125	$950	$800	$675	$600	$550

Add $115 for Model 426.
Add 25% for 20 ga.

MODEL 426 E - similar to 424, with auto ejectors, SST, select wood and more intricate engraving, silver pigeon inlay. Disc. 1983.

	100%	98%	95%	90%	80%	70%	60%
	$1,850	$1,575	$1,250	$1,025	$875	$700	$625

MODEL 625 - 12 or 20 ga., 26-30 in. barrels, various chokes, boxlock, extractors, DTs or SST, light engraving, checkered straight stock. Imported 1984-1986.

	100%	98%	95%	90%	80%	70%	60%
	$995	$900	$800	$700	$600	$550	$500

Last MSR was $835.

Add 25% for 20 ga.
Add 15% for SST.

MODEL GR-2 - 12 and 20 ga.'s, 26 and 28 in. barrels, various chokes, boxlock, extractors, double triggers, checkered pistol grip stock. Mfg. 1968-1976.

	100%	98%	95%	90%	80%	70%	60%
	$660	$605	$550	$495	$385	$330	$275

Add 25% for 20 ga.

MODEL GR-3 - similar to GR-2, with select wood and more engraving. Mfg. 1968-1976.

	100%	98%	95%	90%	80%	70%	60%
	$770	$715	$640	$560	$475	$425	$375

Add 25% for 20 ga.

MODEL GR-4 - similar to GR-3, with auto ejectors. Mfg. 1968-1976.

	100%	98%	95%	90%	80%	70%	60%
	$1,500	$1,275	$1,075	$900	$775	$675	$600

Add 25% for 20 ga.

SILVER HAWK - 12 ga. Mag. (3 in. chambers) & 10 ga. Mag. (3½ chambers) with double triggers and extractors. Disc. 1967.

	100%	98%	95%	90%	80%	70%	60%
	$595	$495	$400	$350	$300	$275	$250

Add $100 for 10 ga.

SILVER HAWK FEATHERWEIGHT - 12, 16, 20, or 28 ga., 26-32 in. barrels, high solid rib, various chokes, single or double triggers, checkered pistol grip stock, beavertail forearm. Disc. 1967.

	100%	98%	95%	90%	80%	70%	60%
	$495	$440	$415	$385	$360	$330	$275
Single trigger	$550	$495	$440	$415	$385	$360	$330

Add 50% for 20 ga.
Add 100% for 28 ga.

Grading	100%	98%	95%	90%	80%	70%	60%

MODEL 470 SILVER HAWK (CURRENT MFG.)

- 12 or 20 ga., 3 in. chambers, 26 or 28 in. barrels with choice of fixed or multi-chokes (new 1999), satin chrome receiver finish, selector lever on forearm allows either automatic ejection or mechanical extraction, straight grip stock with matte finish, 5.9 or 6.5 lbs. New 1998.

MSR	$2,596	$1,950	$1,700	$1,475	$1,300	$1,050	$900	$750

Add $130 for multi-chokes (new 1999).

MODEL 470 EL

- 12 or 20 ga., 3 in. chambers, 26 (20 ga. only) or 28 in. barrels with Optima-Chokes (12 ga. only) or MC3 multichokes, case colored boxlock receiver with 4 gold inlays (doves and ducks) on sideplates, selector lever on forearm allows either automatic ejection or mechanical extraction, deluxe straight grip stock and splinter forearm with oil finish, 5.9 or 6.5 lbs. New 2002.

MSR	$5,980	$5,265	$4,550	$4,100	$3,550	$3,200	$2,800	$2,400

MODEL 626 FIELD

- 12 or 20 (disc. 1987) ga., 2¾ in. chambers, 26 and 28 in. barrels, various chokes, boxlock, ejectors, single trigger, moderate engraving, pistol grip or straight checkered stock. Imported 1984-1988.

	$1,450	$1,050	$875	$725	$625	$550	$495

Last MSR was $995.

Add 35% for 20 ga.

MODEL 626 ONYX

- 12 or 20 ga., 3 in. chambers, 26 or 28 (new 1990) in. VR barrels with multi-chokes, matte finished metal parts, select checkered walnut stock and forearm. Imported 1988-1993.

	$1,650	$1,250	$1,000	$850	$750	$685	$595

Last MSR was $1,870.

* *Model 626 Onyx Magnum* - 12 ga. only, 3½ in. chambers. Mfg. 1990-92.

	$1,700	$1,300	$1,050	$850	$750	$600	$550

Last MSR was $1,870.

Add 50% for 20 ga.

MODEL 627 EL FIELD

- 12 and 20 (disc. 1987) ga., 2¾ (disc. 1990) or 3 in. (became standard in 1991) chambers, 26 and 28 in. barrels, various chokes, boxlock, ejectors, single trigger, extensive engraving, pistol grip or straight checkered stock, cased. Imported 1985-1993.

	$2,550	$2,150	$1,850	$1,500	$1,350	$1,150	$1,000

Last MSR was $3,270.

Subtract 5% for fixed chokes and 2¾ in. chambers.
Add 25% for 20 ga.

* *Model 627 EL Sport* - similar to Model 627 EL Field, except 12 ga. only, knurled rib, sporting clays dimensions. Importation disc. 1988.

	$2,750	$2,350	$1,925	$1,625	$1,475	$1,150	$1,000

Last MSR was $1,995.

Add 25% for 20 ga.

MODEL 627 EELL

- 12 or 20 (disc. 1987) ga., 2¾ (disc.) or 3 (12 ga. only) in. chambers, 26 or 28 in. barrels, various chokes, boxlock, ejectors, single trigger, elaborate engraving, pistol grip or straight English checkered stock, cased. Imported 1985-1993.

	$4,300	$3,675	$3,150	$2,800	$2,500	$2,175	$1,900

Last MSR was $5,405.

Add 20% for 20 ga.
Subtract 5% if fixed chokes only.
Multi-chokes became standard in 1991.

Grading	100%	98%	95%	90%	80%	70%	60%

B

SHOTGUNS: SxS, CUSTOM GRADE

Current Custom grade Beretta O/U and SxS shotguns are sold only by premium grade franchised Beretta dealers. For a listing of these dealers, contact a Beretta Gallery (see Trademark Index).

Where applicable, Beretta's new SST, with selector switch built into safety, is more desirable than older manufacture utilizing the disc. single, non-selective trigger.

MODEL 450 SERIES - 12 ga. only, built to individual customer order, various levels of engraving. Disc.

✳ *Model 450 EL* - incorporates H&H type sidelocks.

	100%	98%	95%	90%	80%	70%	60%
	$7,500	$6,950	$5,750	$5,250	$4,700	$4,200	$3,600

✳ *Model 450 EELL* - features third fastener with H&H type sidelocks.

	$8,000	$7,500	$6,000	$5,500	$4,850	$4,300	$3,750

SO-6 - same general specifications and embellishments as the SO series O/U guns, but SxS. Mfg. 1948-1982.

	$7,250	$6,500	$5,925	$5,300	$4,700	$4,250	$3,850

SO-7 - top of the line SxS, finest quality wood, more elaborate engraving. Disc.

	$8,950	$7,950	$6,875	$6,000	$5,250	$4,600	$4,000

MODEL 451 SERIES - 12 ga., totally hand-made, sidelock action, ejectors, scroll engraving. Custom made to order with fitted luggage case, various grades have increasing embellishments in EL Models.

✳ *Model 451* - disc. 1987.

	$6,250	$5,500	$4,875	$4,600	$4,300	$3,995	$3,600

Last MSR was $12,375.

✳ *Model 451 E* - 12 ga. only, double triggers, specifications furnished by individual customer. Limited importation since 1989.

MSR	$7,250	$6,750	$6,200	$5,500	$4,750	$4,000	$3,500	$2,750

Add approx. 40% for extra set of barrels.
Add $750 for SST (disc.).

✳ *Model 451 EL* - limited importation, temporarily disc. 1984.

MSR	$15,250	$14,500	$7,750	$6,750	$5,600	$5,000	$4,500	$4,100

✳ *Model 451 EELL* - top-of-the-line for Model 451, choice of engraving motifs per customer specifications. Disc. 1987, reintroduced 1989.

MSR	$18,500	$16,750	$8,500	$7,500	$6,500	$5,750	$5,150	$4,600

MODEL 452 CUSTOM - 12 ga. only, next to top-of-the-line side-by side shotgun featuring H&H style detachable locks, built to customer's specifications, leather cased. New 1990.

MSR	$35,000	$28,750	$20,500	$15,750	$11,750	$8,750	$6,650	$5,500

Add $6,275 for extra set of barrels.

✳ *Model 452 EELL Custom* - 12 ga. only, top-of-the-line custom sidelock model featuring every refinement, built to customer's specifications, leather cased. Importation began 1992.

MSR	$46,500	$38,950	$27,750	$21,000	$15,750	$11,750	$9,000	$6,750

Add $6,275 for extra set of barrels.
Add approx. $8,500-$43,500 for special master engraving options.

MODEL 470 EL CUSTOM - 12 or 20 ga., mfg. by Beretta's custom shop per individual order, custom case hardened frame with 24 Kt. bird inlays, upgraded wood with oil finish. New 1999.

MSR	$6,500	$5,225	$3,775	$2,825	$2,200	$1,725	$1,500	$1,200

Grading	100%	98%	95%	90%	80%	70%	60%

MODEL JUBILEE II (MODEL 470 EELL) - 12 or 20 ga., scroll or game scene engraving signed by the engraver, select SO quality wood with Tru-oil finish, includes suede case, also available in pairs. New 1999.

	MSR $13,750	$11,725	$7,825	$5,900	$4,650	$3,150	$2,780	$2,500

This model was designated the Model 470 EELL through 1999.

SHOTGUNS: SINGLE BARREL, DISC.

MARK II TRAP - 12 ga., 32 or 34 in. wide vent. rib, full choke, boxlock with auto ejector, Monte Carlo stock, recoil pad. Mfg. 1972-1976.

	$550	$450	$400	$360	$330	$295	$260

MODEL FS-1 SINGLE BARREL - 12, 16, 20, 28 ga., or .410 bore, 26 or 28 in. barrels, full choke, checkered semi-pistol grip, under lever break open, folds to length of barrel (also known as Companion).

	$175	$150	$125	$110	$100	$90	$80

TR-1 TRAP - 12 ga., 32 in. full choke barrel, under lever break open, Monte Carlo pistol grip stock with pad, engraved. Mfg. 1968-1971.

	$275	$250	$220	$195	$140	$110	$100

TR-2 TRAP - similar to TR-1, with high rib, mfg. 1969-1973.

	$290	$260	$230	$205	$150	$120	$110

MODEL 412 - 12, 20, 28 ga., or .410 bore, monobloc construction, folding action, sling swivels, checkered walnut stock and forearm, 5 lbs. Importation disc. 1988.

	$190	$170	$125	$100	$85	$70	$60

Last MSR was $215.

SHOTGUNS: SLIDE ACTION, DISC.

MODEL SL-2 - 12 ga., 26, 28, or 30 in. barrels, various chokes, vent. rib, checkered pistol grip stock. Mfg. 1968-1971.

	$300	$275	$250	$220	$195	$165	$140

SILVER PIGEON - 12 ga., various chokes, light engraving.

	$250	$200	$175	$160	$150	$140	$130

GOLD PIGEON - 12 ga., various chokes, vent. rib, engraved.

	$475	$375	$310	$275	$240	$215	$195

Add $200 for deluxe models.

RUBY PIGEON - 12 ga., various chokes, vent. rib, elaborately engraved, special deluxe walnut.

	$600	$475	$395	$350	$295	$260	$230

SHOTGUNS: SEMI-AUTO, DISC.

SILVER LARK - 12 ga., various chokes.

	$295	$260	$240	$220	$200	$185	$170

GOLD LARK - 12 ga., vent. rib, light scroll engraving, select walnut.

	$480	$400	$325	$260	$230	$210	$195

RUBY LARK - 12 ga., vent. rib, heavy engraving, deluxe walnut.

	$675	$550	$475	$395	$350	$295	$260

MODEL AL-1 - 12 and 20 ga., semi-auto gas operated, 26, 28, and 30 in. plain barrel, various chokes, checkered pistol grip stock. Mfg. 1971-1973.

	$385	$360	$330	$305	$250	$195	$165

Beretta

Grading	100%	98%	95%	90%	80%	70%	60%

MODEL AL-2 - 12 or 20 ga., 26, 28, or 30 in. barrels, vent. rib, various chokes, gas operated, checkered pistol grip stock. Mfg. 1973-1975.

	$330	$305	$275	$250	$220	$195	$165

MODEL AL-2 SKEET - similar to AL-2, with 26 in. wide rib skeet bored barrel, mfg. 1973-1975.

	$395	$360	$320	$275	$220	$200	$185

MODEL AL-2 TRAP - similar to AL-2, with 30 in. full choke barrel, wide rib, Monte Carlo stock, with recoil pad. Mfg. 1973-1975.

	$375	$345	$315	$285	$250	$195	$165

MODEL AL-2 MAGNUM - 12 or 20 ga., 3 in. chamber, heavier action bar, 28 and 30 in. mod. or full choke. Mfg. 1973-1975.

	$415	$385	$330	$275	$250	$230	$210

MODEL AL-3 - continuation of the AL-2 series. Mfg. 1975-1976.

	100%	98%	95%	90%	80%	70%	60%
Field grade	$395	$360	$330	$260	$240	$220	$190
Magnum grade	$425	$385	$330	$275	$250	$230	$210
Skeet grade	$400	$360	$330	$260	$240	$220	$190
Trap grade	$385	$350	$295	$250	$225	$210	$185

MODEL AL-3 DELUXE TRAP - similar to AL-3, with fully engraved receiver, premium grade wood. Mfg. 1975-1976.

	$770	$715	$660	$605	$550	$495	$440

SHOTGUNS: SEMI-AUTO, RECENT MFG.

It is possible on some of the following models to have production variances occur including different engraving motifs, stock configurations and specifications, finishes, etc. These have occurred when Beretta changed from production of one model to another. Also, some European and English distributors have sold their excess inventory through Beretta U.S.A., creating additional variations/configurations that are not normally imported domestically. While sometimes rare, these specimens typically do not command premiums over Beretta's domestic models.

The following Beretta semi-auto models have been listed in numerical sequence, if possible, disregarding any alphbetical suffix or prefix.

BERETTA CHOKES AND THEIR CODES (ON REAR LEFT-SIDE OF BARREL)

* designates full choke (F).

** designates improved modified choke (IM).

*** designates modified choke (M).

**** designates improved cylinder choke (IC).

FK designates skeet (SK).

***** designates cylinder bore (CYL).

MODEL ES100 PINTAIL (VICTORIA) - 12 ga., 3 in. chamber, uses Montefeltro short action, 24, 26, or 28 (new 1999) in. VR barrel, choice of matte finished wood (disc. 1998), camouflage (new 2001), or black synthetic stock and forearm (new 1999), includes sling swivels, 7.3 lbs. Mfg. 1993-2001.

	$625	$425	$375	$335	$280	$250	$230

Last MSR was $757.

In 1999, this model was renamed the ES 100 Pintail (with synthetic stock).

Grading	100%	98%	95%	90%	80%	70%	60%

B

✸ *ES100 Rifled Slug (Pintail Rifled Slug)* - 12 ga., 3 in. chamber, 24 in. rifled barrel with drilled and tapped upper receiver, barrel and upper receiver are permanently joined, anti-glare matte black metal finish, choice of matte finished wood (disc. 1998) or black synthetic (new 1999) stock and forearm, includes swivels, 7 lbs. Mfg. 1998-2001.

| | $750 | $550 | $450 | $400 | $325 | $280 | $250 |

Last MSR was $899.

Add $148 for combo package (includes extra 28 in. smooth bore barrel with MC3 choke, new 2001).

In 1999, the model nomenclature changed from Pintail Rifled Slug to ES100 Rifled Slug.

✸ *Pintail Slug (Victoria)* - 12 ga. only, 24 in. slug barrel, includes rifle sights and rifle choke tubes, 7 lbs. Imported 1993-95.

| | $595 | $425 | $360 | $325 | $280 | $250 | $230 |

Last MSR was $700.

✸ *Model ES100 Camouflage* - 12 ga. only, features 100% Advantage Wetlands camo coverage, 28 in. VR barrel only, 7.3 lbs. New 2000.

| MSR | $766 | $635 | $430 | $375 | $335 | $280 | $250 | $230 |

✸ *Model ES100 NWTF Special Camouflage (Pintail)* - 12 ga. only, 24 in. VR barrel with 3 dot TruGlo fiber optic sight system, includes Briley extended extra-full choke tube and 3 standard Mobilchoke tubes, features Mossy Oak Break-up treatment on synthetic stock and forearm, black matte anti-glare finish on metal components, includes nylon sling. Limited mfg. 1999, reintroduced 2002 (limited mfg.).

| MSR | $966 | $795 | $600 | $475 | $375 | $325 | $290 | $265 |

MODEL 300/301 - continuation of the AL-3 series, scroll engraved receiver. Mfg. 1977- 1982.

	100%	98%	95%	90%	80%	70%	60%
Field grade	$395	$360	$330	$260	$240	$220	$190
Magnum grade	$425	$385	$330	$275	$250	$230	$210
Skeet grade	$400	$360	$330	$260	$240	$220	$190
Trap grade	$385	$350	$295	$250	$225	$210	$185

Beretta changed model nomenclature rapidly during the Model 300 Series. In approx. 10 months, the evolution of this model had progressed from the 300 to 303 Series. Beginning with the Model 303, all receivers were milled with a 3 in. ejection port window.

MODEL 301 SLUG GUN - 22 in. barrel, with sights. Disc.

| | $395 | $360 | $330 | $305 | $265 | $230 | $190 |

MODEL 302 - 12 or 20 ga., self-compensating gas operation semi-auto, designed for both 2¾ and 3 in. shells, available with interchangeable chokes, slug barrel, trap and skeet models (disc.), VR, mag. cut-off. Mfg. 1982-1987. This model was superceded by the Model 303.

| | $395 | $365 | $340 | $310 | $280 | $255 | $225 |

Last MSR was $480.

Add $30 for multi-choke set.

✸ *Model 302 Super Lusso* - same specifications as Model A302, but includes hand engraved receiver, many gold plated parts, and stock and forearm made from presentation grade walnut. Disc. 1986.

| | $2,150 | $1,950 | $1,750 | $1,550 | $1,300 | $1,050 | $895 |

Last MSR was $2,500.

Grading	100%	98%	95%	90%	80%	70%	60%

MODEL A-303 FIELD - 12 (disc. 1993) or 20 ga., 2¾ or 3 in. chambers, same gas operation as the Model 302, 26 or 28 in. VR barrel, high-strength alloy receiver, select wood with choice pistol grip or straight English stock, beavertail forearm, multi-chokes became standard 1987. Disc. 1996.

	$655	$465	$380	$335	$300	$270	$240

Last MSR was $799.

Subtract 10% without multi-chokes.
Subtract $20 for straight grip English stock.

✳ *A-303 Upland* - 12 (disc. 1993) or 20 ga., 2¾ or 3 in. chamber, 24 in. VR barrel with multi- chokes, English style straight stock, approx. 7 lbs. Importation began 1989. Disc. 1996.

	$640	$465	$380	$335	$300	$270	$240

Last MSR was $772.

✳ *A-303 Waterfowl/Turkey* - 12 ga. only, 3 in. chamber, choice of 24, 26, 28, or 30 in. VR barrel, matte finished wood and metal, multi-chokes are standard. Imported 1991 only.

	$540	$450	$395	$350	$300	$270	$240

Last MSR was $665.

✳ *A-303 Sporting* - 12 (disc. 1994) or 20 (new 1991) ga. only, 2¾ in. chambers, sporting clay dimensions, 28 or 30 (12 ga. only) in. VR barrel with multi-chokes. Mfg. 1988-96.

	$685	$510	$445	$375	$325	$300	$275

Last MSR was $822.

✳ *A-303 Skeet* - 12 (disc. 1994) or 20 ga., 26 in. VR barrel with fixed skeet choking. Importation disc. 1995.

	$615	$440	$375	$335	$300	$270	$240

Last MSR was $736.

✳ *A-303 Super Skeet* - 12 ga. only, 28 in. VR fixed choke barrel, features factory porting, adj. LOP, and adj. separate cheekpiece on stock. Mfg. 1991-92.

	$975	$750	$625	$500	$425	$365	$300

Last MSR was $1,160.

✳ *A-303 Trap* - 12 ga. only, 30 or 32 in. VR barrel with fixed choking or multi-chokes. Importation disc. 1994.

	$615	$425	$360	$325	$280	$250	$220

Last MSR was $735.

Add $40 for multi-chokes (with Monte Carlo stock).

✳ *A-303 Super Trap* - 12 ga. only, 30 or 32 in. VR multi-choke barrel with step tapered rib, features factory porting, adj. LOP, and adj. separate cheekpiece on stock. Mfg. 1991-92.

	$1,025	$775	$625	$500	$425	$365	$300

Last MSR was $1,210.

✳ *A-303 Slug* - 12 or 20 ga., 3 in. chamber (12 ga. only), 22 in. cylinder bore barrel, iron sights. Importation disc. 1991.

	$540	$425	$360	$325	$295	$265	$240

Last MSR was $665.

✳ *A-303 Youth* - 20 ga. only, 2¾ or 3 (disc.) in. chamber, 24 in. VR barrel with multi- chokes, shortened stock, approx. 6 lbs. Mfg. 1988-96.

	$640	$450	$375	$330	$300	$270	$240

Last MSR was $772.

Grading	100%	98%	95%	90%	80%	70%	60%

MODEL AL390 FIELD SILVER MALLARD - 12 or 20 (new 1997) ga. only, 3 in. chamber, features new gas system that will accept all 2¾ and 3 in. shotshells, single stainless steel piston with self regulating valve, mag. cut-off on left side of receiver, 22 slug (12 ga. only, new 1994), 24, 26, 28, or 30 (12 ga. only) in. VR barrel with Mobilchoke system, choice of gloss or matte (includes sling swivels) wood finish on lightly engraved receiver, adj. checkered walnut stock, gold trigger, 6.4 (20 ga.) or 7.2 (12 ga.) lbs. Mfg. 1992-99.

	$700	$525	$415	$350	$300	$270	$240

Last MSR was $860.

Add $25 for 20 ga.
Add $25 for 26, 28, or 30 in. barrel (12 ga. only).
Beginning 1997, Beretta introduced the "AL" Series of the 390, which is the lightweight variation of the 390. Prior to 1997, this model was designated the A390 Series.

* ***Model AL390 Field Deluxe Gold Mallard*** - similar to Model 390 Field, except has gold accents on receiver frame, including a gold inlaid snipe, setter, and P. Beretta signature, deluxe walnut, 7.2 lbs. Mfg. 1993-99.

	$850	$575	$460	$400	$360	$320	$285

Last MSR was $1,025.

Add $30 for 20 ga.
Add $30 for 26, 28, or 30 in. barrel (12 ga. only).

* ***Model AL390 Lioness Limited Edition*** - 12 ga. only, 28 in. VR barrel with MC3 choke tubes, deluxe checkered walnut stock and forearm. Limited mfg. beginning 2002.

MSR	$2,969	$2,450	$1,950	$1,600

* ***Model AL390 Silver Mallard Synthetic*** - 12 ga. only, 3 in. chamber, 24, 26, 28, or 30 in. barrel with multi-choke, black synthetic stock and forearm with sling swivels, matte finish, approx. 7.2 lbs. Mfg. 1996- 99.

	$715	$535	$425	$350	$300	$270	$240

Last MSR was $885.

* ***Model AL390 Silver Mallard Camouflage*** - 12 ga. only, 3 in. chamber, Advantage camo finish on entire gun, 24 or 28 in. VR barrel with choke tubes, synthetic stock and forearm, 7.2 lbs. Mfg. 1997-99.

	$825	$600	$450	$375	$300	$270	$240

Last MSR was $1,020.

* ***Model AL390 Silver Mallard Slug*** - 12 ga. only, 3 in. chamber, 22 in. barrel with slug choke, gloss wood finish, adj. rear sight, approx. 6.8 or 7.4 (Model A390) lbs. Mfg. 1995-97.

	$700	$525	$415	$350	$300	$270	$240

Last MSR was $860.

* ***Model AL390 Silver Mallard Youth*** - 20 ga. only, 3 in. chamber, gloss wood finish, 24 in. VR barrel only with choke tubes, features youth stock dimensions, 6.4 lbs. Mfg. 1997-99.

	$715	$550	$425	$350	$300	$270	$240

Last MSR was $885.

* ***Model AL390 NWTF Special Camouflage*** - 12 ga. only, 3 in. chamber, 24 in. VR barrel with 3 dot TruGlo fiber optic sight system, includes Briley extended extra-full choke tube and 3 standard Mobilchoke tubes, full Realtree X-tra brown camo treatment (including synthetic stock and forearm), includes camo nylon sling. Special Edition released during 1999 only.

	$895	$700	$575	$525	$495	$460	$425

Last MSR was $1,105.

✧ **Model AL390 NWTF Special Synthetic** - similar to NWTF Special Camouflage, except has matte black anti-glare finish. Mfg. 1999 only.

	$795	$575	$450	$365	$315	$275	$240

Last MSR was $970.

❋ *Model AL390 NWTF Special Youth* - 20 ga. only, 3 in. chamber, 24 in. barrel, shorter stock dimensions with 13½ LOP, matte finished wood stock and forearm, matte black metal anti-glare finish. Mfg. 1999 only.

	$760	$535	$425	$350	$300	$270	$240

Last MSR was $910.

MODEL AL390 SPORT SPORTING
- 12 or 20 (new 1997) ga., 3 in. chamber, designed for sporting clays competition, similar to Model 390 Sport Skeet, 28 or 30 (12 ga. only) in. VR ported or unported barrel with choke tube, 6.8 (20 ga.) or 7.6 (12 ga.) lbs. Imported 1995-99.

	$775	$540	$425	$350	$300	$270	$240

Last MSR was $925.

Add $70 for ported barrel.

❋ *Model AL390 Sport Sporting Collection* - 12 or 20 (Youth Model) ga., 3 in. chamber, 26 (20 ga. only), 28 in. VR barrel with multi-choke, features multi-colored, gloss finished stock and forearm, 6.7 (20 ga.) or 7.6 (12 ga.) lbs. Mfg. 1998-99.

	$795	$575	$450	$365	$315	$275	$240

Last MSR was $965.

The 20 ga. in this model is a youth model with 13½ LOP.

❋ *Model AL390 Sport Gold Sporting* - 12 ga. only, 28 or 30 in. VR barrel with multi- chokes, gloss finished wood, gold engraved receiver, 7.6 lbs. Mfg. 1997-99.

	$925	$725	$575	$525	$495	$460	$425

Last MSR was $1,145.

❋ *Model AL390 Sport Diamond Sporting* - 12 ga. only, 3 in. chamber, silver sided receiver with multiple gold inlays, EELL quality stock and forearm with oil finish, matte 28 or 30 in. barrel with multi-chokes, oval nameplate on stock, 7.6 lbs. Mfg. 1998-99.

	$2,750	$2,400	$2,050	$1,800	$1,600	$1,400	$1,175

Last MSR was $3,075.

❋ *Model AL390 Sport Sporting Youth* - 20 ga. only, 3 in. chamber, matte finished checkered stock and forearm, 26 in. VR barrel only with choke tubes, features youth stock dimensions (13½ LOP), 6.7 lbs. Imported 1997-98 only.

	$755	$525	$400	$350	$300	$270	$240

Last MSR was $900.

MODEL AL390 SPORT SKEET
- 12 ga. only, 3 in. chamber, 26 (disc.) or 28 in. SK bored VR barrel, matte finish on wood and metal, black rubber recoil pad, 7.6 lbs. Imported 1995-99.

	$745	$525	$415	$350	$300	$270	$240

Last MSR was $890.

Add $105 for ported barrel (28 in. only).

❋ *Model AL390 Sport Super Skeet* - 12 ga. only, 28 in. skeet choke VR ported barrels, includes adj. stock comb and LOP (using 3 different recoil pads) approx. 8.1 lbs. Mfg. 1993-99.

	$965	$750	$565	$525	$475	$440	$400

Last MSR was $1,160.

Grading	100%	98%	95%	90%	80%	70%	60%

MODEL AL390 SPORT TRAP - 12 ga. only, 3 in. chamber, 30 or 32 in. VR barrel, matte finish on wood and metal, black rubber recoil pad, 7.8 or 8¼ (A390) lbs. Imported 1995- 99.

	$740	$525	$415	$360	$300	$270	$240

Last MSR was $890.

Add $35 for multi-choke barrel (30 in. only).
Add approx. $105 for ported barrel (fixed 30 in. or multi-choke).

✳ *Model AL390 Sport Super Trap* - 12 ga. only, 30 or 32 in. VR multi-choke ported barrels, adj. stock comb and LOP, approx. 8 lbs. Mfg. 1993-97.

	$995	$775	$600	$550	$495	$460	$425

Last MSR was $1,215.

MODEL AL391 URIKA - 12 or 20 ga., 3 in. chamber, features new self-compensating gas valve and receiver recoil absorber for internal shock reduction, satin finished checkered walnut stock and forearm, gas valve is located on the front bottom of the forearm, alloy receiver with thin design, cold hammer forged barrel, black anodized metal surfaces, gold trigger, molded synthetic case included, 6.3-7.3 lbs. New 2000.

✳ *Model AL391 Urika Standard* - 12 or 20 ga., 24 (20 ga. only), 26, 28, or 30 (12 ga. only) in. VR barrel, approx. 5.95 (20 ga.) or 7¼ lbs. New 2000.

MSR	$984	$810	$585	$460	$375	$335	$300	$275

✳ *Model AL391 Urika Synthetic* - 12 ga. only, 24, 26, 28, or 30 in. VR barrel with matte finish, features black synthetic stock with oversized grip area for a secure grip and recoil absorption and forearm, approx. 7¼ lbs. New 2000.

MSR	$984	$810	$585	$460	$375	$335	$300	$275

✳ *Model AL391 Urika Camouflage* - 12 ga. only, choice of 100% RealTree Hardwoods (24 in. barrel only, turkey configuration) or Advantage Wetlands camo (28 in. barrel only, waterfowl configuration) finish, with oversized stock grip, approx. 7¼ lbs. New 2000.

MSR	$1,090	$900	$640	$485	$400	$350	$325	$295

✳ *Model AL391 Urika Youth* - 20 ga. only, 24 in. VR barrel only, shortened walnut stock and regular forearm, 5.95 lbs. New 2000.

MSR	$984	$810	$585	$460	$375	$335	$300	$275

✳ *Model AL391 Urika Gold* - 12 or 20 ga., similar to Model AL391 Urika Standard, except has deluxe checkered walnut stock and forearm, choice of black (standard) or partial silver (lightweight configuration, 12 ga. only) receiver finish, multiple gold receiver inlays, 26 or 28 in. VR barrel, jewelled bolt, 5.9 (20 ga.), 6.6 (12 ga. lightweight), or approx. 7¼ lbs. New 2000.

MSR	$1,213	$995	$700	$540	$430	$395	$375	$350

Add $41 for lightweight model (12 ga. only with partial silver receiver).

MODEL AL391 XTREMA 3.5 - 12 ga. only 3½ in. chamber, features Gel-Tek recoil pad, spring mass and bolt travel recoil reducers lower felt recoil up to 20%, 24, 26, or 28 in. VR barrel with Optima-Choke Plus, gas operating system with rotating locking bolt, black synthetic stock and forearm with rubber inserts for firm control instead of traditional checkering, grooved receiver, removable trigger grip, includes carrying case, 7.8 lbs. New 2002.

MSR	$1,129	$915	$750	$625	$550	$475	$425	$365

✳ *Model AL391 Xtrema Camouflage* - 12 ga. only, similar operating system to Model AL391 Xtrema 3.5, choice of 100% RealTree Hardwoods HD (24 in. barrel only, turkey configuration), Advantage Timber HD camo (26 in. barrel only) or Advantage Wetlands (26 or 28 in. barrel) finish, 7.8 lbs. New 2002.

MSR	$1,241	$1,025	$775	$650	$575	$500	$450	$395

Grading	100%	98%	95%	90%	80%	70%	60%

MODEL AL391 URIKA SPORTING - 12 or 20 ga., 3 in. chamber, gas operating system the same as Model Al391 Urika Standard, 28 or 30 in. wide VR barrel with 2 beads, features special competition checkered walnut sporting stock with rounded solid rubber recoil pad, satin black receiver with silver markings, gold trigger, Mobilchoke tubes are standard, molded synthetic case included, 5.95 or 7.3 lbs. New 2000.

	MSR	$1,027		$845	$625	$500	$425	$365	$335	$300

* ✳ *Model AL391 Urika Gold Sporting* - similar to Model AL391 Urika Gold, except has deluxe walnut stock and forearm, with choice of black or silver receiver and gold accents. New 2000.

	MSR	$1,254		$1,025	$725	$565	$450	$415	$395	$365

Add $42 for lightweight model (12 ga. only with partial silver receiver).

* ✳ *Model AL391 Diamond Sporting* - 12 ga. only, 3 in. chamber, silver sided receiver with multiple gold inlays, EELL quality stock and forearm with oil finish, matte 28 in. barrel with MC4 multi-chokes, oval nameplate on stock, 7.6 lbs. New 2002.

MSR	$3,139		$2,675	$2,200	$1,850	$1,525	$1,200	$995	$775

MODEL AL391 URIKA TRAP - 12 ga. only, 30 or 32 in. wide VR barrel with 2 beads, Monte Carlo stock with special trap recoil pad, satin black receiver with glossy side panels and silver markings, gold trigger, molded synthetic case included, 7¼ lbs. New 2000.

MSR	$1,027		$845	$625	$500	$425	$365	$335	$300

* ✳ *Model AL391 Urika Gold Trap* - similar to Model AL391 Urika Trap, except has black receiver with gold filled Beretta logo and P. Beretta signature, jewelled bolt and carrier, 7¼ lbs. New 2000.

MSR	$1,254		$1,025	$725	$565	$450	$415	$395	$365

MODEL AL391 URIKA PARALLEL TARGET RL/SL - 12 ga. only, similar to Model AL391 Urika Trap, except features a Monte Carlo stock with parallel comb and reduced grip radius, RL suffix designates shorter LOP and slimmer grip, molded synthetic case included, 7¼ lbs. New 2000.

MSR	$1,027		$845	$625	$500	$425	$365	$335	$300

MODEL 1200 FIELD - 12 ga., inertia recoil system, 28 in. VR barrels with multi- chokes, checkered European walnut stock and forearm (pre-1989), matte black polymer stock and forearm (starting 1989), recoil pad, 4 shot mag., approx. 8 lbs. Imported 1984- 1989.

			$475	$415	$350	$295	$250	$225	$200

Last MSR was $580.

* ✳ *Model 1200 Riot* - 12 ga. only, 2¾ or 3 in. chamber, 20 in. cyl. bore barrel with iron sights, extended mag. Imported 1989-90 only.

			$525	$425	$350	$295	$250	$225	$200

Last MSR was $660.

MODEL 1201 FIELD MAGNUM - 12 ga., 3 in. chamber, 24, 26, or 28 in. VR barrel with multi-chokes (2), matte black polymer stock and forearm. Imported 1989-94.

			$500	$395	$340	$285	$250	$225	$200

Last MSR was $625.

The Model 1201 can be differentiated from the Model 1200 by stock spacers to adjust length.

Grading	100%	98%	95%	90%	80%	70%	60%

B

✳ Model 1201 FP (Riot) - 12 ga., riot configuration featuring 18 (new 1997) or 20 (disc. 1996) in. cylinder bore barrel, 5 shot mag, choice of adj. rifle sights (disc.), Tritium sights (disc. 1998) or ghost ring (new 1999, Tritium front sight insert) sights, matte wood (disc.) or black synthetic stock and forearm, matte metal finish (disc.), 6.3 lbs. New 1991.

MSR	$890		$695	$515	$385	$325	$265	$225	$200

Add $80 for Tritium sights (mfg. 1997-98).
Add $45 for pistol grip configuration (Model 1201 FPG3 - mfg. 1994 only).

MODEL AL3901 - 12 ga. only, 3 in. chamber, 28 in. VR barrel with MC3 multi-chokes, features charcoal grey synthetic checkered stock and forearm, gold trigger, matte metal finish, reversible crossbolt safety. New 2002.

MSR	$749		$615	$425	$375	$335	$280	$250	$230

This model is available through Beretta Showcase Dealers only.

COMMEMORATIVES

MODEL A-303 DUCKS UNLIMITED - 12 or 20 ga., D.U. serialization, 5,500 mfg. in 12 ga. 1986-87, 3,500 mfg. in 20 ga. 1987-88.

12 ga.	$575	$450	$350
20 ga.	$675	$475	$375

These D.U. Models had no retail pricing from Beretta. Rather, they were auctioned off at D.U. dinners, and as a result, prices could vary substantially from region to region.

MODEL 687 O/U SHOTGUN TERCENTENNIAL - 12 ga., SST and ejectors. Limited production, only 300 manufactured.

$2,500	$1,950	$1,400

MODEL 84 PISTOL TERCENTENNIAL - commemorative, only 300 manufactured. Fully engraved with gold inlays. Presentation case. Only 100 imported to U.S.

$1,450	$1,100	$850

BERGMANN

Previous manufacturer located in Gaggenau, Germany circa 1892-1944. Re-established in 1931 under Bergmann Erben.

100%	98%	95%	90%	80%	70%	60%	50%	40%	30%	20%	10%

PISTOLS: SEMI-AUTO

Prices established are for original guns with matching parts.

MODEL 1894 (ANTIQUE) - 8mm "Bergmann Schmeisser" cal. Extremely rare.

N/A	N/A	$18,500	$16,000	$12,000	$8,000	$7,500	$7,000	$6,500	$6,000	$5,500	$5,000

MODEL 1896-NO. 2 - 5mm cal., smaller type frame.

$2,400	$1,900	$1,600	$1,300	$1,100	$895	$715	$660	$610	$565	$515	$450

Add 50% for "folding trigger" version.

MODEL 1896-NO. 3 - 6.5mm - 80mm cal. barrel.

$3,250	$2,750	$2,250	$1,800	$1,450	$925	$750	$700	$665	$630	$600	$565

Add 10% for early pistols without extractors and narrow grips.
Add 20% if hexagonal chamber.
Add 100% for target variation.

MODEL 1896-NO. 4 - 8mm cal., military contract. Rarely seen.

$4,950	$4,250	$3,500	$3,000	$2,200	$1,500	$900	$725	$665	$630	$600	$565

100%	98%	95%	90%	80%	70%	60%	50%	40%	30%	20%	10%

B

MODEL 1897-NO. 5 - 7.8mm cal., commercial manufacture. May be fit with shoulder stock.

| $6,000 | $4,750 | $3,500 | $3,000 | $2,200 | $1,500 | $925 | $750 | $700 | $665 | $630 | $600 |

Add 200% for long barrel carbine version.
Add 100% if fit with shoulder stock, add another 20% to total if matching stock.

BERGMANN MARS MODEL 1903 - .30 or 9mm Bergmann cal.

| $4,500 | $3,750 | $3,000 | $2,500 | $2,000 | $1,750 | $1,500 | $1,250 | $1,000 | $750 | $600 | $500 |

Add 100% if fit with shoulder stock.
Add 25% if .30 caliber (first 100 pistols).

MODEL 2 - .25 cal., small frame.

| $350 | $295 | $260 | $240 | $215 | $180 | $160 | $135 | $115 | $95 | $80 | $65 |

Add $100 for Model 2A.

MODEL 3 - .25 cal., small frame.

| $350 | $295 | $260 | $240 | $215 | $180 | $160 | $135 | $115 | $95 | $80 | $65 |

Add $100 for Model 3A.

ERBEN - .25 cal., Models I, II, and Special (.32 cal.).

| $335 | $300 | $285 | $260 | $240 | $215 | $180 | $160 | $135 | $115 | $95 | $80 |

PISTOLS: SEMI-AUTO - BERGMANN-BAYARD

Even though the below listed Bergmann-Bayard models were manufactured only by Anciens Etablissements Pieper of Herstal, Belgium, these pistols are listed under this heading as they are most commonly referred to by this trademark designation.

MODEL 1908 STANDARD COMMERCIAL - 9mm Bergmann/Bayard cal., identified by a mounted knight on the left magazine housing and is without finger cuts at base of magazine housing.

| $1,900 | $1,500 | $1,100 | $800 | $625 | $500 | $400 | $360 | $335 | $310 | $285 | $260 |

Add 25% if backstrap is slotted for shoulder stock.
Add $3,000 for excellent original leather/wood shoulder stock.

MODEL 1908 SPANISH CONTRACT - 9mm Bergmann/Bayard cal., total contract was for 3,000 pistols, can be identified from standard commercial pistols by the Spanish military acceptance stamp struck on the receiver.

| $1,750 | $1,400 | $1,000 | $750 | $600 | $450 | $400 | $360 | $335 | $310 | $285 | $260 |

MODEL 1910 STANDARD COMMERCIAL - 9mm Bergmann/Bayard cal., mechanically similar to Model 1908 Standard Commercial except has finger cuts in bottom of magazine housing, circular grooves are present on each side of magazine base.

| $1,300 | $1,000 | $700 | $600 | $500 | $400 | $350 | $315 | $280 | $265 | $245 | $225 |

MODEL 1910 DANISH GOVERNMENT CONTRACT - 9mm Bergmann/ Bayard cal., Trolit grips were used for the original conversion, followed later by wood replacements, total contract was for 4,840 pistols with delivery mfg. 1911- 1914. This variation can be identified from the usual commercial pistols by the Danish proof mark on the left receiver side and Danish inventory number on right side of receiver.

| $1,450 | $1,150 | $900 | $750 | $600 | $450 | $400 | $360 | $335 | $310 | $285 | $260 |

Subtract 20% if converted and overstamped M.1910/21.

MODEL 1910/21 TOJHUS - 9mm Bergmann/Bayard cal., these pistols are marked "Haerens Tojhus" and are numbered from 1-900, original grips were black Trolit, replacement grips are either all smooth or with checkered circles above and below grip screw.

| $1,950 | $1,650 | $1,250 | $950 | $600 | $500 | $400 | $360 | $335 | $310 | $285 | $260 |

This contract was manufactured by the Danish Royal Arsenal located in Copenhagen.

| 100% | 98% | 95% | 90% | 80% | 70% | 60% | 50% | 40% | 30% | 20% | 10% |

MODEL 1910/21 RUSTKAMMER - 9mm Bergmann/Bayard cal., pistols are marked "Haerens Rustkammer", and numbered 901-2204, grip replacements are the same as noted for Haerens Tojhus.

| $1,750 | $1,500 | $1,100 | $900 | $600 | $450 | $400 | $360 | $335 | $310 | $285 | $260 |

This contract was manufactured by the Danish Royal Arsenal located in Copenhagen.

WAYNE BERGQUIST CUSTOM PISTOLS

Current custom pistolsmith located in Naples, FL. The company should be contacted directly (see Trademark Index for current information) regarding its Bullseye, IPSC Tactical, and Defense/Carry models.

BERNARDELLI, VINCENZO

Current trademark manufactured in Brescia, Italy beginning mid-2002. Previously manufactured from 1721 to August, 1997. Previously imported and distributed until 1997 by Armsport, Inc. located in Miami, FL. Previously imported and distributed by Magnum Research, Inc. located in Minneapolis, MN (1989-92), Quality Arms, Inc. located in Houston, TX, Armes De Chasse located in Chadds Ford, PA, Stoeger located in New York, NY, and Action Arms, Ltd. located in Philadelphia, PA.

There is some confusion on the Bernardelli trademark as there have been three different companies (Pietro Bernardelli, Vincenzo Bernardelli, and Santini Bernardelli) that have produced firearms. During the late 1980s, there were quite a lot of Pietro Bernardellis that were "dumped" in the American marketplace - these guns do not have the quality of Vincenzo Bernardelli and are not covered within the scope of this text.

The Vincenzo Bernardelli trademark was purchased in early 2002, and plans are under way to begin manufacture again shortly. Please contact the company directly for more information, including model availability, pricing, and importation.

| Grading | 100% | 98% | 95% | 90% | 80% | 70% | 60% |

COMBINATION GUNS

MODEL 190 - 12, 16, or 20 ga. under .243 Win., .30-06, or .308 Win. cal., combination rifle/shotgun, boxlock action, DTs, extractors. Imported 1989 only.

| | | | $1,295 | $1,025 | $895 | $800 | $700 | $600 | $525 |

Last MSR was $1,393.

Add $700 for extra set of 12 ga. O/U barrels.

MODEL COMB 2000 - 12, 16, or 20 ga. under choice of rifle cals., ejectors, set trigger. Imported 1990-97.

| | | | $2,300 | $1,550 | $1,075 | $875 | $750 | $675 | $575 |

Last MSR was $2,920.

Add $621 for extra set of O/U shotgun barrels (Model COMB 2000S - disc.).

MODEL 120 - 12 ga. over choice of 12 cals., deluxe checkered walnut stock and forearm, iron sights, double triggers, vent. recoil pad, coin washed receiver with light engraving.

| | | | $1,950 | $1,585 | $1,300 | $1,050 | $850 | $760 | $650 |

Last MSR was $2,411.

Add $130 for extra set of shotgun barrels.

Grading	100%	98%	95%	90%	80%	70%	60%

PISTOLS: SEMI-AUTO

VEST POCKET MODEL - .25 ACP cal., 2 1/8 in. barrel, fixed sights, blue, bakelite grips. Mfg. 1945-1948.

	$250	$195	$165	$140	$110	$90	$65

BABY SEMI-AUTO - .22 S or L cal., 2 1/8 in. barrel, fixed sights, blue, bakelite grips. Mfg. 1949-1968.

	$250	$175	$150	$130	$100	$90	$80

SPORTER MODEL - .22 LR cal., 6, 8, or 10 in. barrels, target sights, blue, wood grips. Mfg. 1949-1968.

	$305	$275	$220	$165	$140	$110	$85

MODEL 60 - .22 LR cal., .32 ACP, or .380 ACP cal., 3½ in. barrel, fixed sights, blue, bakelite grips. Mfg. 1959-disc.

	$220	$195	$180	$165	$155	$135	$120

This model was not imported domestically.

MODEL 68 - .22 Short or .22 LR cal., vest pocket model, 6 shot, bakelite grips, 8½ oz. Disc.

	$140	$120	$110	$100	$90	$80	$70

This model was not imported domestically.

MODEL 80 - .22 LR or .380 ACP cal., 3½ in. barrel, adj. sights, blue, thumbrest plastic grips. Imported 1968-1988.

	$185	$160	$150	$140	$130	$115	$100

Add $5 for .380 ACP.

Note: This model was produced to conform to import regulations of GCA 1968. Importation of this model was disc. 1988.

MODEL USA - .22 LR, .32 ACP (disc.), or .380 ACP. cal., semi-auto, single action, steel frame, loaded chamber indicator, adj. sights, target bakelite grips, 7 shot (.380 ACP) or 10 shot (.22 LR) mag. Disc. 1997.

	$380	$295	$250	$215	$185	$165	$145

Last MSR was $425.

Add $60 for chrome finish.

This model has the same technical specifications as the Model 60.

MODEL AMR - .22 LR, .32 ACP (disc.), or .380 ACP cal., similar action to USA Model except has 6 in. barrel and adj. rear sight. Disc. 1994.

	$395	$325	$275	$225	$185	$165	$145

Last MSR was $445.

MODEL 90 SPORT TARGET - .32 ACP or .22 LR cal., similar to Model 80, with 6 in. barrel. Imported 1968-1988.

	$210	$185	$170	$155	$140	$120	$110

Last MSR was $245.

MODEL 69 TARGET - .22 LR cal., target semi-auto, single action, 5.9 in. heavy barrel, 10 shot mag., wraparound checkered wood grips, 38 oz.

	$575	$475	$400	$350	$275	$225	$185

Last MSR was $660.

This model was previously designated Model 100.

MODEL 100 TARGET - .22 LR cal., 5.9 in. barrel, adj. sight, blue, checkered wood, thumbrest grips, cased. Imported 1968-1988.

	$395	$325	$295	$260	$225	$190	$175

Last MSR was $360.

Grading	100%	98%	95%	90%	80%	70%	60%

B

P-ONE - 9mm Para. or .40 S&W cal., double action, 10 shot mag., choice of matte black or chrome finish. Imported 1993-97.

	$580	$495	$400	$360	$330	$295	$265

Last MSR was $684.

Add $36 for chrome finish.
Add $36 for wood grips.

✳ *P-One Compact* - compact variation of the P-One. Disc. 1997.

	$595	$500	$400	$360	$330	$295	$265

Last MSR was $702.

Add $48 for chrome finish.
Add $48 for wood grips.

MODEL P010 TARGET - .22 LR cal., single action, 5.9 in. barrel, adj. sights and trigger, matte black finish, large anatomic walnut stippled grips with thumbrest, 10 shot mag., 40.5 oz. Imported 1989-92, re-introduced 1995-97.

	$675	$575	$495	$425	$375	$325	$275

Last MSR was $768.

Add $132 for wood case and two sets of weights.

MODEL P018 - 7.65mm (disc. 1988), .380 ACP (mfg. 1993-94), or 9mm Para. cal., double action, semi- auto, steel construction, 4 7/8 in. barrel, 10 (C/B 1994) or 16* shot mag., black plastic (standard) or walnut checkered (disc. 1992) grips, blue (disc.), black (new 1994), or chrome finish, 36 oz. Imported 1985-96.

	$485	$400	$350	$300	$275	$250	$230

Last MSR was $560.

Add $40 for walnut grips (disc. 1992).
Add $60 for chrome finish.
Add $30 for carrying case w/combination lock (disc. 1989).

This model was extensively redesigned in 1989 and included a "cocked and locked" feature, thumb mag. release, loaded chamber indicator, as well as other improvements.

✳ *P018 Compact* - .380 ACP or 9mm Para. cal., similar to Model P018 except has 4 in. barrel and 10 (C/ B 1994) or 14* shot mag., approx. 2 lbs. Imported 1989-96.

	$545	$430	$375	$310	$275	$250	$230

Last MSR was $610.

Add $55 for chrome finish.

This model was also redesigned in 1989 to incorporate the same features as the Model P018.

PRACTICAL VB - 9x21mm cal., comp. gun built for IPSC competition, various configurations, black or matte chrome finish, 2, 4, or 6 port compensating system. Mfg. 1993-97.

	$1,100	$925	$775	$675	$575	$475	$400

Last MSR was $1,260.

Add $60 for 4 port compensator.
Add $60 for chrome finish.

✳ *Practical VB Customized* - state-of-the-art competition pistol featuring 4+2 port compensating system. Mfg. 1993-97.

	$1,775	$1,325	$1,100	$975	$850	$725	$600

Last MSR was $1,920.

Add $60 for chrome finish.

Grading	100%	98%	95%	90%	80%	70%	60%

RIFLES: DOUBLE

EXPRESS VB - various cals., side-by-side sidelock action, ejectors, single or double triggers. Imported 1990-97.

	$5,475	$4,100	$3,400	$2,725	$2,275	$1,900	$1,600

Last MSR was $6,000.

Add $1,000 for Deluxe Model (double triggers).

EXPRESS 2000 - .30-06, 7x65R, 8x57JRS, or 9.3x74R cal., O/U boxlock design, single or double trigger, extractors, checkered walnut stock and forearm. Imported 1994-97.

	$2,600	$1,995	$1,600	$1,275	$1,100	$975	$875

Last MSR was $3,192.

Add $130 for single trigger.

MINERVA EXPRESS - various cals., exposed hammers, extractors, double triggers, moderate engraving. Imported 1995-97.

	$4,975	$3,850	$3,250	$2,725	$2,275	$1,900	$1,600

Last MSR was $5,850.

RIFLES: SEMI-AUTO

CARBINA .22 - .22 LR cal., blow back action. Imported 1990-97.

	$575	$375	$295	$210	$170	$150	$135

Last MSR was $720.

SHOTGUNS: FOLDING MODELS

SINGLE BARREL - 12, 16, 20, 24, 28, 32 ga., or .410 bore, gun folds in half. Importation disc. 1990.

	$230	$185	$150	$135	$125	$115	$100

Last MSR was $265.

DOUBLE BARREL - 12 and 16 ga., gun folds in half, double triggers. Previously available in Europe only.

	$570	$430	$370	$315	$285	$260	$230

SHOTGUNS: O/U

MODEL 115 HUNTING - 12 ga. only, boxlock action, monobloc frame, inclined plane lockings, blue receiver, single trigger, ejectors. Importation disc. 1989.

	$1,770	$1,425	$1,225	$1,000	$895	$750	$650

Last MSR was $1,915.

* **Model 115S** - similar to 115, except moderate engraving.

	$2,150	$1,925	$1,745	$1,500	$1,250	$1,025	$950

Last MSR was $2,500.

* **Model 115L** - similar to 115S, except extensive scroll engraving on silver finish receiver.

	$2,600	$2,375	$2,050	$1,750	$1,450	$1,100	$850

Last MSR was $3,170.

* **Model 115E** - sideplate, boxlock action, ejector, bulino game scene engraving.

	$4,650	$4,125	$3,600	$3,100	$2,650	$2,200	$1,800

Last MSR was $5,200.

MODEL 115 TARGET - 12 ga. only, same specifications as Model 115, except trap dimensions. Importation disc. 1989.

	$1,800	$1,595	$1,375	$1,175	$1,000	$895	$750

Last MSR was $2,160.

Grading	100%	98%	95%	90%	80%	70%	60%

B

* **Model 115S** - same specifications as 115 Target, except light engraving. Importation disc. 1992.

| | $3,275 | $2,425 | $1,825 | $1,500 | $1,250 | $1,025 | $895 |

Last MSR was $3,920.

This model was available in either Pigeon, Skeet, Sporting Clays, or Trap configuration.

* **Model 115L** - similar to 115S, except extensive scroll engraving on silver finish receiver. Importation disc. 1990.

| | $3,700 | $2,995 | $2,600 | $2,375 | $2,050 | $1,750 | $1,450 |

Last MSR was $4,201.

* **Model 115E** - same specifications as 115S, except with extensively engraved sideplates. Importation disc. 1990.

| | $5,950 | $4,800 | $4,125 | $3,600 | $3,100 | $2,650 | $2,200 |

Last MSR was $6,827.

* **Model 115S Trap/Skeet** - 12 ga. only, available in Trap or Skeet configuration, ejectors, single trigger. Disc. 1997.

| | $3,250 | $2,450 | $1,825 | $1,425 | $995 | $875 | $725 |

Last MSR was $3,780.

* **Model 115S Sporting Clays** - 12 ga. only, SST, ejectors, choke tubes. Imported 1995-97.

| | $3,875 | $3,350 | $2,775 | $2,100 | $1,750 | $1,500 | $1,350 |

Last MSR was $4,200.

MODEL 190 TARGET - 12 ga, SST, ejectors, engraved silver receiver, select checkered walnut stock and forearm. Imported 1986-1989.

| | $1,425 | $1,095 | $925 | $800 | $700 | $600 | $525 |

Last MSR was $1,572.

* **Model 190 MC** - similar to Model 190 Target except has Monte Carlo stock. Imported 1989 only.

| | $1,000 | $825 | $700 | $600 | $525 | $475 | $450 |

Last MSR was $1,155.

* **Model 190 Special** - 12 ga. only, similar to Model 190 Target, except has better walnut and engraving. Imported 1988-1989.

| | $1,335 | $1,000 | $895 | $800 | $700 | $600 | $525 |

Last MSR was $1,456.

Add $75 for single trigger (Model 190 Special MS).

These variations are hunting models.

MODEL 192 FIELD - 12 ga. only, single or double triggers, ejectors, choke tubes optional. Imported 1995-97.

| | $1,175 | $895 | $750 | $650 | $550 | $450 | $375 |

Last MSR was $1,425.

Add $65 for single trigger.
Add $200 for choke tubes.
Add $350 for 192 Special (includes double triggers, ejectors).

MODEL 192 MS COMPETITION - 12 ga. only, ejectors, selective or non-selective triggers, multichokes standard on Sporting Clays Model. Mfg. 1990-97.

| | $1,725 | $1,475 | $1,150 | $925 | $775 | $675 | $575 |

Last MSR was $1,930.

Add $120 for SST.
Add $200 for choke tubes.
Add $485 for Special Sport.

This model was available in either Pigeon, Skeet, Sporting Clays, Special Sport, or Trap configuration.

Grading	100%	98%	95%	90%	80%	70%	60%

MODEL 192 MS-MC HUNTING - 12 ga. only, boxlock action with engraved coin finished receiver, 3 in. chambers, ejectors, SST, 26¾ or 28 in. VR barrels with choke tubes, steel shot compatible. Imported 1990- 1992.

| | $1,400 | $995 | $825 | $700 | $600 | $525 | $475 |

Last MSR was $1,833.

✷ Model 192 MS-MC-WF - waterfowler variation which includes 3½ in. chambers, 3 choke tubes, and SST. Imported 1990 only.

| | $1,275 | $950 | $875 | $775 | $675 | $575 | $500 |

Last MSR was $1,444.

MODEL 200 LIGHTWEIGHT MS - 12 ga. only, silver grey finished receiver with game scene engraving, ejectors, DTs. Imported 1988-1989, resumed 1993-97.

| | $1,325 | $975 | $850 | $725 | $650 | $550 | $450 |

Last MSR was $1,525.

MODEL 220 MS HUNTING - 12 or 20 ga., silver grey finished receiver with engraving. Mfg. 1988-1997.

| | $1,350 | $995 | $850 | $725 | $650 | $550 | $450 |

Last MSR was $1,560.

Add $75 for SST.
Add $180 for 12 ga. slug variation with DTs (new 1994).
Add $700 for extra set of 12 ga. barrels (disc. 1990).

This model was available with either a pistol grip or English grip (straight) stock.

MODEL LUCK - 12 ga., ejectors, boxlock action, choice of double or single trigger. Imported 1994-97.

| | $1,450 | $995 | $725 | $650 | $550 | $450 | $375 |

Last MSR was $1,795.

Add $275 for single trigger.

SATURNO MS-MC COMPETITION - 12 ga. only, sporter configuration, boxlock action with lightly engraved side plates, ejectors, DTs. Imported 1991-97.

| | $2,325 | $1,725 | $1,150 | $925 | $775 | $675 | $575 |

Last MSR was $2,760.

This model was available in either Pigeon, Skeet, Sporting Clays, or Trap configuration.

SATURNO MS-MC HUNTING - 12 ga. only, boxlock action with lightly engraved side plates, ejectors, SST, includes multi- chokes. Imported 1991-1992.

| | $2,275 | $1,525 | $1,050 | $875 | $750 | $695 | $600 |

Last MSR was $2,609.

ORIONE S - 12 ga., double Purdey lock, VR, ejectors, engraved nickel finish receiver. Importation disc. 1989.

| | $1,175 | $1,025 | $860 | $760 | $650 | $560 | $510 |

Last MSR was $1,425.

ORIONE L - similar to Orione S, single trigger, finer engraving, English or pistol type select walnut stock. Importation disc. 1989.

| | $1,285 | $1,125 | $950 | $840 | $750 | $650 | $550 |

Last MSR was $1,550.

ORIONE E - top-of-the-line, deep relief engraving. Importation disc. 1989.

| | $1,375 | $1,200 | $1,020 | $900 | $820 | $710 | $650 |

Last MSR was $1,660.

Grading	100%	98%	95%	90%	80%	70%	60%

SHOTGUNS: SxS

Bernardelli side-by-side shotguns were manufactured with straight grip, English style stocks with pistol grip available as a special order. Importation of Bernardelli shotguns was inconsistent over the years.

A wide variety of special order options was available on these shotguns.

> Barrel choke markings for V. Bernardelli shotguns are as follows; Full: *, Impr. Mod: **, Mod: ***, Impr. Cyl: ****, Cylinder: CL.

MODEL 110 - 12 ga., trap or skeet model, separated barrels, high post rib.

$2,000	$1,500	$1,300	$1,100	$1,000	$900	$800

MODEL 110 EXTRAO - similar to Model 110, except engraved.

$3,021	$2,265	$1,970	$1,665	$1,510	$1,360	$1,210

S. UBERTO 1 GAMECOCK - 12, 16, 20, or 28 ga., 25¾ in. imp. cyl. and mod., 27½ in. full and mod., hammerless, boxlock, extractors, two triggers, English style stock, checkered.

$853	$635	$605	$550	$495	$440	$415

Add 20% for ejectors.

BRESCIA HAMMER DOUBLE BARREL - 12, 16, or 20 ga., 25¾, 27½ and 29½ in. mod. and full, 12 ga., 25½ in. imp. cyl. and mod., sidelock, extractors, two triggers, straight English stock, splinter forearm, checkered. Importation disc.

$2,050	$795	$600	$450	$425	$395	$350

Last MSR was $2,482.

ITALIA HAMMER DOUBLE BARREL - similar to Brescia, except higher grade engraving and wood. Importation disc.

$2,275	$1,200	$900	$735	$650	$600	$550

Last MSR was $2,844.

ITALIA EXTRA HAMMER - 12, 16, or 20 ga., hammer double. Top-of-the-line hammer model. Importation disc.

$6,400	$3,150	$2,200	$1,650	$1,375	$1,050	$800

Last MSR was $7,861.

MODEL 112 - 12 ga., entry-level model with extractors and DTs. Imported 1989 only.

$850	$750	$675	$625	$550	$495	$450

Last MSR was $998.

Add $65 for single trigger (Model 112 M - disc.).

MODEL 112 E - 12 ga., Anson & Deeley action, light engraving. Importation disc. 1989.

$995	$850	$775	$695	$625	$550	$495

Last MSR was $1,108.

MODEL 112 SI/S (EM) - similar to Model 112E, except has single or double triggers. Disc. 1997.

$1,795	$1,000	$825	$725	$650	$550	$450

Last MSR was $2,100.

Add $174 for ejectors.
Add $138 for ST.
Add $420 for choke tubes.

* ***Model 112 EM - MC*** - similar to Model 112 EM, except has 3 in. chambers and 5 choke tubes. Imported 1990-1992.

$1,600	$1,000	$850	$775	$675	$575	$495

Last MSR was $1,971.

B

Grading	100%	98%	95%	90%	80%	70%	60%

❋ *Model 112 EM-MC-WF* - includes 3½ in. chambers, waterfowl model with matte finish, single trigger and 3 choke tubes. Importation disc. 1990.

	$1,275	$975	$850	$775	$675	$575	$495

Last MSR was $1,444.

S. UBERTO 1 - 12, 16, 20, or 28 ga., Anson & Deeley action, Purdey locks, light engraving, case hardened receiver, double triggers, extractors.

	$1,050	$900	$800	$700	$625	$550	$495

Last MSR was $1,164.

Add $65 for single trigger (Model S. Uberto 1M).

❋ *S. Uberto 1E* - similar to S. Uberto 1, except with ejectors. Importation disc. 1990.

	$1,175	$950	$850	$740	$650	$565	$495

Last MSR was $1,357.

Add $65 for single trigger (Model S. Uberto 1EM).

S. UBERTO 2 - 12, 16, 20, and 28 ga.'s, Anson & Deeley action, Purdey locks, light scroll engraving, silver finished receiver, double triggers, extractors. Importation disc. 1989, resumed 1993 -97.

	$1,375	$1,150	$875	$725	$650	$550	$450

Last MSR was $1,580.

Add $35 for single trigger (Model S. Uberto 2M - disc.).

❋ *S. Uberto 2E* - similar to S. Uberto 2, except with ejectors. Disc. 1997.

	$1,525	$1,300	$1,050	$875	$725	$650	$550

Last MSR was $1,710.

Add $80 for single trigger (Model S. Uberto 2EM - disc.).

S. UBERTO FS - 12, 16, 20, or 28 ga., Purdey locks, relief engraved with hunting scenes on silver finished receiver, double triggers, extractors. Importation disc. 1989, resumed 1993-97.

	$1,695	$1,450	$1,125	$895	$750	$675	$575

Last MSR was $1,915.

Add $65 for single trigger (Model S. Uberto FSM - disc. 1989).

❋ *S. Uberto FSE* - similar to S. Uberto FS, except with ejectors. Importation disc. 1989.

	$1,375	$1,100	$975	$850	$750	$625	$550

Last MSR was $1,537.

Add $65 for single trigger (Model S. Uberto FSEM).

ROMA 3 - similar to S. Uberto, double triggers, extractors, false sideplates, case hardened receiver. Importation disc. 1989, resumed 1993-97.

	$1,425	$1,200	$895	$775	$675	$575	$475

Last MSR was $1,625.

Add $65 for single trigger (Model Roma 3M - disc.).

❋ *Roma 3E* - similar to Roma 3, except with ejectors. Disc. 1997.

	$1,550	$1,325	$1,050	$875	$725	$650	$550

Last MSR was $1,770.

Add $80 for single trigger (Model Roma 3EM - disc.).

ROMA 4 - more deluxe model than Roma 3, false sideplates, scroll engraved, silver finished receiver. Importation disc. 1989.

	$1,250	$1,025	$900	$800	$700	$625	$550

Last MSR was $1,439.

Add $65 for single trigger (Model Roma 4M).

❋ *Roma 4E* - similar to Roma 4, except with ejectors. Disc. 1997.

	$1,775	$1,475	$1,150	$925	$775	$675	$575

Last MSR was $2,000.

Add $80 for single trigger (Model Roma 4EM - disc.).

Grading	100%	98%	95%	90%	80%	70%	60%

ROMA 6 - 12, 16, 20, or 28 ga., fully engraved sideplates with hunting scenes, Purdey locks, silver finish receiver, single trigger, finely figured English walnut. Importation disc. 1989.

| | $1,395 | $1,150 | $975 | $875 | $775 | $675 | $600 |

Last MSR was $1,619.

Add $175 for single trigger (Model Roma 6M).

❋ *Roma 6E* - similar to Roma 6, except with ejectors, 16 ga. was disc. 1989. Disc. 1997.

| | $2,400 | $1,825 | $1,475 | $1,150 | $925 | $775 | $675 |

Last MSR was $2,880.

Add $180 for single trigger (Model Roma 6EM).

ROMA 7 - 12 ga., ejectors, grade up from the Roma 6. Imported 1994-97.

| | $3,200 | $2,200 | $1,675 | $1,375 | $995 | $875 | $750 |

Last MSR was $3,840.

ROMA 8 - 12 ga., ejectors, grade up from the Roma 7. Imported 1994-97.

| | $3,700 | $2,700 | $1,950 | $1,675 | $1,375 | $995 | $875 |

Last MSR was $4,740.

ROMA 9 - 12 ga., ejectors, grade up from the Roma 8. Imported 1994-97.

| | $4,550 | $3,200 | $2,500 | $1,950 | $1,675 | $1,375 | $995 |

Last MSR was $5,520.

ELIO - 12 ga. only, lightweight, extractors, fine English style scroll engraving on silver finish receiver. Importation disc. 1989.

| | $1,125 | $925 | $850 | $740 | $650 | $565 | $475 |

Last MSR was $1,238.

Add $65 for single trigger (Model Elio M).

❋ *Elio E* - similar to Elio, except with ejectors. Importation disc. 1989.

| | $1,200 | $1,000 | $895 | $795 | $695 | $595 | $500 |

Last MSR was $1,353.

Add $65 for single trigger (Model Elio EM).

SLUG GUN - 12 ga. only, 23¾ in. slug bored barrels, extractors, Anson & Deeley action, Purdey locks, lightly engraved, silver finish receiver. Importation disc. 1990.

| | $1,325 | $1,000 | $895 | $795 | $695 | $595 | $500 |

Last MSR was $1,575.

Add $65 for single trigger (Model Slug M).

SLUG LUSSO - 12 ga. only, 23¾ in. slug bored barrels, sideplates, with extensive engraving featuring hunting scenes, cheekpiece, ejectors, silver finished receiver. Importation disc. 1992.

| | $2,325 | $1,550 | $1,200 | $995 | $875 | $750 | $650 |

Last MSR was $2,793.

Add $80 for single trigger (Model Slug Lusso M).

This model was previously designated Slug Deluxe (1988 or earlier).

HEMINGWAY - 12, 20, or 28 (new 1992) ga., boxlock action, coin finished receiver with game scene engraving, 23½ in. barrels, DTs, deluxe checkered walnut stock and forearm, 6¼ lbs. Disc. 1997.

| | $2,050 | $1,500 | $1,050 | $875 | $750 | $675 | $575 |

Last MSR was $2,520.

Add $70 for single trigger.
Add $120 for single selective trigger.

HEMINGWAY DE LUXE - similar to Hemingway, except is also available in 16 ga. and has sideplates, better wood, and more engraving. Disc. 1997.

| | $2,350 | $1,750 | $1,150 | $925 | $775 | $675 | $575 |

Last MSR was $2,874.

Add $126 for single trigger (Model Hemingway De Luxe M).

Grading	100%	98%	95%	90%	80%	70%	60%

B

LAS PALOMAS PIGEON - 12 ga. live pigeon gun, single trigger, special dimensions for live pigeon shooting. Disc. 1997.

		$3,125	$2,550	$2,000	$1,700	$1,375	$995	$875

Last MSR was $3,700.

Add $750 for Pigeon Model (includes single trigger).

HOLLAND V.B. LISCIO - 12 ga. only, Holland type sidelocks, light engraving, silver finish receiver, single trigger, ejectors, select walnut. Disc. 1997.

	$10,350	$5,300	$4,450	$3,900	$3,350	$2,850	$2,400

Last MSR was $12,600.

HOLLAND V.B. INCISO - 12 ga. only, H&H sidelock action, Purdey locks, various barrel lengths, single trigger, ejectors, straight or pistol grip stock, 100% engraved on coin finished receiver. Importation disc. 1992.

	$10,700	$7,000	$5,500	$4,700	$4,200	$3,500	$3,000

Last MSR was $12,929.

HOLLAND V.B. LUSSO - 12 ga. only, H&H sidelock action, Purdey locks, various barrel lengths, single trigger, ejectors, straight or pistol grip stock, same features as Holland V.B. Inciso, only extra select wood and game scene engraving. Importation disc. 1992.

	$8,900	$7,900	$6,500	$5,200	$4,750	$4,000	$3,450

Last MSR was $14,377.

HOLLAND V.B. EXTRA - 12 ga. only, H&H style action, any barrel length and choke, double triggers, auto ejectors, straight or pistol grip stock, 100% engraved on coin finished receiver. Prices are completely dependent upon individual customer specifications. Values are for engraving pattern No. 3. Importation disc. 1992.

	$13,250	$9,700	$7,450	$6,150	$5,200	$4,600	$3,950

Last MSR was $16,549.

Add $1,034 for engraving pattern No. 4.
Add $4,551 for engraving pattern No. 12.
Add $8,895 for engraving pattern No. 20.
Add $621 for single trigger.

Older specimens ordered before 1992 could have values considerably lower than those listed.

HOLLAND V.B. GOLD - top-of-the-line model, made to individual order. Very limited production and ultra-rare. Importation disc. 1992.

	$47,500	$32,500	$24,000	$18,500	$13,000	$11,500	$9,950

Last MSR was $57,922.

Older specimens ordered before 1992 could have values considerably lower than those listed.

SHOTGUNS: SEMI-AUTO

MODEL 9MM FLOBERT - 9mm Flobert cal. (rimfire shot cartridge), 24.4 in. smooth bore barrel, 3 shot mag., steel receiver, walnut stock and forearm with sling and swivels, 5 lbs. 3 oz. Disc. 1997.

	$385	$265	$175	$150	$125	$105	$95

Last MSR was $474.

BERSA

Current manufacturer located in Argentina. Currently distributed exclusively by Eagle Imports, Inc. located in Wanamassa, NJ. Previously imported and distributed before 1988 by Rock Island Armory located in Geneseo, IL, Outdoor Sports Headquarters, Inc. located in Dayton, OH, and R.S.A. Enterprises, Inc. located in Ocean, NJ. Distributor sales only.

B

Grading	100%	98%	95%	90%	80%	70%	60%

PISTOLS: SEMI-AUTO

THUNDER 9 - 9mm Para. cal., double action semi-auto, 3½ in. barrel, 10 (C/B 1994) or 14* shot mag., ambidextrous manual safety and decocking lever, automatic firing pin safety, 3-dot sights, aluminum frame, wraparound matte black polymer grips, link-free locked breech design, non-glare matte blue, satin nickel (new 1995), or duo-tone (new 1995) finish. Imported 1993-95.

	$400	$335	$295	$265	$235	$210	$190

Last MSR was $475.

Add $17 for duo-tone finish.
Add $50 for satin nickel finish.

THUNDER 22 (MODEL 23) - .22 LR cal., double action semi-auto, 9 shot mag., 3½ in. barrel, black polymer (new 1997) or walnut (disc. 1996) grips, 24½ oz. Imported 1988- 1998.

	$230	$195	$155	$125	$115	$105	$95

Last MSR was $265.

Add $17 for satin nickel finish.

THUNDER 380 - .380 ACP cal., double action, 3½ in. barrel, fixed sights, 7 shot mag., deep blue, satin nickel, or duo-tone (disc. 1995) finish, rubber grips, 25¾ oz. Imported 1995-98.

	$235	$195	$155	$125	$115	$105	$95

Last MSR was $275.

Add $16 for satin nickel finish.
Add $16 for duo-tone finish.

❋ *Thunder 380 Deluxe* - .380 ACP cal., 9 shot mag., black polymer grips, extended slide release and mag. bottom, polished blue, 3 dot sights, 23 oz. New 1997.

MSR	$292	$245	$205	$165	$125	$115	$105	$95

❋ *Thunder 380 Plus* - similar to Thunder 380, except has 10 shot mag. Mfg. 1995-97.

	$265	$210	$165	$130	$115	$105	$95

Last MSR was $316.

Add $32 for satin nickel finish.
Add $17 for duo-tone finish.

THUNDER SERIES (95) - .380 ACP cal., double action, 3½ in. barrel, fixed sights, 7 shot mag., matte blue, satin nickel, or duotone (3,000 mfg. 2001 only) finish, black polymer grips, 23 oz. New 1995.

MSR	$257	$215	$175	$145	$125	$115	$105	$95

Add $17 for satin nickel finish.

MODEL 83 - .380 ACP cal., double action semi-auto, 3½ in. barrel, blue or satin nickel finish, custom walnut grips, 6 shot mag., 24½ oz. Imported 1988-94.

	$235	$180	$150	$125	$115	$105	$95

Last MSR was $288.

Add $34 for satin nickel finish.

MODEL 85 - .380 ACP cal., similar specifications to Model 83 except has 12 or 13 shot mag., 30½ oz. Imported 1988-94.

	$285	$245	$220	$195	$170	$150	$130

Last MSR was $340.

Add $47 for satin nickel finish.

MODEL 86 - .380 ACP cal., blue matte or nickel finish, undercover model, wraparound rubber grips, 12 shot mag. Imported 1991-94.

	$315	$265	$225	$200	$170	$150	$130

Last MSR was $375.

Add $29 for nickel finish.

Grading	100%	98%	95%	90%	80%	70%	60%

B

MODEL 90 - 9mm Para. cal., single action, semi-auto, steel frame, checkered walnut grips, 13 shot mag., deep blue finish. Imported 1990-91 only.

	$325	$280	$250	$220	$195	$170	$150

Last MSR was $384.

MODEL 223 - .22 LR cal., single action semi-auto, 10 shot mag., 3½ in. barrel, blue finish, squared- off trigger guard, nylon grips. Importation disc. 1987.

	$200	$170	$150	$125	$115	$105	$95

Last MSR was $239.

MODEL 224 - similar to Model 223, except has 4 in. barrel. Imported 1987 only.

	$200	$170	$150	$125	$115	$105	$95

Last MSR was $239.

MODEL 225 - similar to Model 223, except has 5 in. barrel and 10 shot mag. Disc. 1987.

	$155	$135	$125	$115	$105	$95	$85

Last MSR was $170.

MODEL 226 - similar to Model 225, except has 6 in. barrel. Importation disc. 1987.

	$200	$170	$150	$125	$115	$105	$95

Last MSR was $239.

MODEL 323 - .32 ACP cal., single action semi-auto, 8 shot mag., thumbrest plastic grips, 25 oz. Disc. 1987.

	$105	$95	$85	$75	$65	$55	$45

Last MSR was $125.

MODEL 383 - .380 ACP cal., single or double action semi-auto, 3½ in. barrel, blue finish, nylon grips, 7 shot mag. Importation disc. 1988.

	$120	$95	$90	$80	$70	$60	$50

Last MSR was $188 for single action.
Last MSR was $239 for double action.

Add $15 for double action.

BERTUZZI

Current manufacturer located in Brescia, Italy since 1886. Imported and distributed exclusively by New England Arms Corp. located in Kittery Point, ME.

Bertuzzi makes only best quality sidelock O/U and SxS shotguns, both with and w/o external hammers.. Only 40-50 guns are mfg. annually, and all are custom ordered per individual specifications.

SHOTGUNS: O/U

ZEUS - 12 ga., sidelock, auto ejector, deluxe engraving, deluxe wood checkering, SST. This model is available on special order only - contact the distributor for availability, prices, and options. Importation disc. 1994. Retail prices generally ranged from $18,500-$27,500.

ZEUS EXTRA LUSSO - 12, 16, or 20 ga., sidelock, auto ejector, deluxe wood, deluxe checkering and engraving, SST. This model is available on special order only - contact the distributor for availability, prices, and options. Prices generally range $35,000+.

ZEUS BOSS SYSTEM - 12 or 20 ga., features Boss locking system. Importation began 1995. Prices start at $45,000.

SHOTGUNS: SxS

MODEL ORIONE - 12 , 16, 20, or 28 ga., round boxlock action, SST, ejectors, base price includes full coverage engraving, deluxe Turkish walnut, and custom stock dimensions. Prices start at $18,950.

Grading	100%	98%	95%	90%	80%	70%	60%

B

VENERE BEST QUALITY SIDELOCK - various gauges, best quality sidelock model with extensive engraving. Prices start at $18,500.

ARIETE HAMMER GUN - all gauges, upper tang safety, double triggers, fine quality engraving. Prices start at $17,500. The self-cocking, auto-ejector mechanism is popular in this model and prices can vary between $20,000-$40,000.

BESCHI, MARIO

Previous manufacturer until circa 1983 located in Italy.

SHOTGUNS: O/U

BOXLOCK MODEL - 12 or 20 ga., standard model with light engraving.

$3,000	$2,600	$2,300	$1,950	$1,600	$1,300	$995

SHOTGUNS: SxS

EXTRA LUSSO SIDELOCK - 12 or 20 ga., elaborate game scene engraving.

12 ga.	$12,000	$10,750	$9,250	$8,000	$6,750	$5,500	$4,250
20 ga.	$12,000	$10,750	$9,250	$8,000	$6,750	$5,500	$4,250

BOXLOCK MODEL - prices assume moderate engraving.

$1,650	$1,475	$1,300	$1,050	$850	$650	$500

BETTINSOLI, TARCISIO, Srl

Current manufacturer located in Brescia, Italy. No current U.S. importation.

Bettinsoli manufactures fine quality O/U shotguns, express rifles, and combination guns. Please contact the factory directly for more information.

BIG BEAR ARMS & SPORTING GOODS INC.

Previous firearms importer located in Carrollton, TX 1992-99, specializing in the importation of both Russian military surplus and new firearms. Limited inventories remained through 2000.

PISTOLS: SEMI-AUTO

IZH-70 MAKAROV - .380 ACP or 9mm Makarov cal., 8 shot mag., current mfg. from Russia. Imported 1994- 99.

$265	$185	$155	$135	$115	$100	$90

Last MSR was $325.

RIFLES: SEMI-AUTO

SAIGA SPORTER RIFLE - 7.62x39mm cal., semi-auto with improved Kalashnikov design, checkered hardwood (disc.) or synthetic stock and forearm, 5 or 10 (disc.) shot mag. Imported 1996-99.

$575	$400	$325	$250	$225	$200	$175

Last MSR was $750.

Add $169 for 3.5X scope and mount.

SHOTGUNS

SAIGA SEMI-AUTO - .410 bore, 3 in. chamber, paramilitary configuration. Imported 1996- 99.

$425	$350	$295	$250	$200	$180	$165

Last MSR was $499.

Grading	100%	98%	95%	90%	80%	70%	60%

IJ-27 O/U - 12 ga., 2¾ in. chambers. Imported 1995-99.

	100%	98%	95%	90%	80%	70%	60%
	$425	$350	$295	$250	$200	$180	$165

Last MSR was $499.

IJ-39E O/U - 12 ga., 2¾ in. chambers. Imported 1995-99.

	100%	98%	95%	90%	80%	70%	60%
	$760	$600	$495	$400	$360	$330	$295

Last MSR was $895.

IJ-43 SxS - 12 ga., 2¾ in. chambers. Imported 1995-99.

	100%	98%	95%	90%	80%	70%	60%
	$325	$250	$200	$175	$155	$145	$135

Last MSR was $399.

BIG HORN ARMS CORP.
Previous manufacturer located in Watertown, SD.

PISTOLS: SINGLE SHOT

TARGET PISTOL - .22 Short cal. only, unique action permitting auto. ejection, ambidextrous stock made of molded Tufflex with carvings, 26 oz. Approx. 1,200 mfg. Disc. in the late '60s.

	100%	98%	95%	90%	80%	70%	60%
	$175	$150	$135	$125	$115	$105	$95

SHOTGUNS: SINGLE SHOT

LIL' MAGNUM SHOTGUN - .410 diameter reloadable shot cartridge, single shot open bolt operation, included reloading equipment, approx. 2,000 mfg. in the late '60s.

	100%	98%	95%	90%	80%	70%	60%
	$125	$100	$75	$65	$55	$50	$45

BIGHORN RIFLE CO.
Previous manufacturer located in Orem, UT.

PISTOLS: BOLT ACTION

BIGHORN PISTOL.22 LR cal., bolt action design.
Lack of information on this pistol precludes accurate pricing.

RIFLES: BOLT ACTION

BIGHORN RIFLE - Mauser action, choice of calibers, custom made bolt action of high quality, interchangeable barrels (gun is supplied with 2 barrels), adj. trigger, deluxe walnut stock, many custom options. Mfg. 1984 only.

	100%	98%	95%	90%	80%	70%	60%
	$2,100	$1,800	$1,600	$1,400	$1,200	$1,000	$850

BILL HANUS BIRDGUNS LLC
Current dealer located in Newport, OR. Bill Hanus currently sells a private label model from AYA (see listing under AYA), and previously had his own model manufactured by Armas Ugartechea (see separate listing) located in Eibar, Spain until 1997.

BINGHAM, LTD.
Previous manufacturer located in Norcross, GA circa 1976-1985.

RIFLES: BOLT ACTION

BANTAM - .22 LR or 22 Mag. cal., bolt action single shot, 18½ in. barrel. Disc. 1985.

	100%	98%	95%	90%	80%	70%	60%
	$110	$90	$75	$65	$55	$45	$40

Last MSR was $120.

Grading	100%	98%	95%	90%	80%	70%	60%

B

RIFLES: SEMI-AUTO

PPS 50 - .22 LR cal. only, blowback action, 50 round drum mag., standard model has Beechwood stock. Disc. 1985.

$250	$225	$195	$180	$145	$135	$125

Last MSR was $230.

Add 15% for deluxe model with walnut stock.
Add 20% for Duramil model with chrome finish and walnut stock.
This model was styled after the Soviet WWII Model PPSh Sub Machine Gun.

AK-22 - .22 LR cal. only, blowback action, styled after AK-47, 15 shot mag. standard, 29 shot mag. available. Standard model has beechwood stock. Disc. 1985.

$250	$225	$195	$180	$145	$135	$125

Last MSR was $230.

Add $20 for Deluxe model with walnut stock.

GALIL-22 - .22 LR cal. only, patterned after Galil semi-auto paramilitary design rifle. Disc.

$250	$225	$195	$180	$145	$135	$125

FG-9 - 9mm Para. cal., blowback action, semi-auto paramilitary design carbine, 20½ in. barrel. While advertised during 1984, this gun was never manufactured.

BITTNER

Previously manufactured by Gustav Bittner located in Vieprty, Bohemia (Austria, Hungary), circa 1893.

PISTOLS

BITTNER MODEL 1893 - 7.7mm Bittner cal., pistol with hand activated repeater mechanism, box magazine, checkered grips, limited manufacture in circa 1893.

$5,500	$4,500	$3,500	$2,700	$2,300	$1,900	$1,500

BLAND, THOMAS & SONS GUNMAKERS LTD.

Current English manufacturer located in England since 1840. This firm was purchased in 1990 by Woodcock Hill located in Benton, PA. Manufacturer direct sales only.

Woodcock Hill should be contacted directly (address listed in Trademark Index) for more information (including current models and prices) regarding Thomas Bland & Sons firearms. Prices will vary depending on the exchange rate between the pound/dollar.

Record checks by serial number on all Thomas Bland & Sons rifles and shotguns are also available .

RIFLES: CUSTOM

Double rifles are available in almost all calibers and specifications. Prices vary between $14,000 - $45,000 depending upon configuration, finish, and accessories. Bolt action rifles are available in any type of action, most popular calibers, and other special options. The bolt action models are not manufactured in England. Prices begin at $1,500.

SHOTGUNS: CUSTOM

Both boxlock and sidelock best quality shotguns are available in all gauges with prices ranging between $12,000 - $40,000 depending upon configuration, finish, and accessories.

B BLASER

Currently manufactured by Blaser Jagd-waffen GmbH in Isny im Allgäu, Germany. Currently imported and distributed by SIG Arms located in Exeter, NH. Previously distributed until 1998 by Autumn Sales Inc. located in Fort Worth, TX. Dealer sales.

Blaser

The Blaser Company was founded in 1963 by Horst Blaser. In 1986, the company was taken over by Gerhard Blenk. During 1997, the company was sold to SIG. In late 2000, SIG Arms AG, the firearms portion of SIG, was purchased by SAN Swiss Arms AG, a newly formed company whose investors have a background in textiles. This new group includes 6 independently operational companies – Blaser Jadgwaffen GmbH, Hämmerli AG, Mauser, J.P. Sauer & Sohn GmbH, SIG-Sauer, and SAN Swiss Arms AG. The restructured Blaser group now includes the primary factories of Blaser (Germany) and SIG-Blaser (Switzerland), in addition to much outsourcing in the smaller Blaser operations located in Lichtenstein, Ungarn (Hungary), and Bulgaria. Blaser currently makes approx. 20,000 rifles annually, with most bring sold in Europe to France, Austria, Italy, Spain, and Norway/Sweden. Current SAN Swiss Arms AG trademarks include: Blaser, Hämmerli, Mauser (pistols & rifles), Sauer rifles, and Sig-Sauer pistols. All trademarks are currently imported by SIG Arms, located in Exeter, NH. Please refer to these individual listings for current information and pricing.

Blaser Jagdwaffen manufactures a large variety of rifles, drillings, and combination guns for the European market that are not imported domestically.

RIFLES: BOLT ACTION

Add approx. $155 for left-hand action available on most of the currently manufactured rifles.

R-84 - .22-250 Rem. (disc. 1993), .243 Win., 6mm Rem., .25- 06 Rem., .270 Win., .280 Rem., or .30-06 standard cals., .257 Wby. Mag., .264 Win. Mag., 7mm Rem. Mag., .300 Win. Mag., .300 Wby. Mag., .338 Win. Mag., or .375 H&H cal., 23 or 24 (Mag. cals. only) in. interchangeable barrel, scroll engraving on receiver, short bolt action with 60 degree rotation, checkered Turkish walnut stock and forearm, approx. 7 lbs. Mfg. 1988-94.

$2,100	$1,575	$1,275	$1,050	$950	$850	$775

Last MSR was $2,300.

Add $50 for left-hand action.
Add $600 per interchangeable barrel (w/scope mounts).

This model has the scope mounted directly to the barrel (and not the receiver). Since the scope mounts are on the barrel extension, this takedown rifle is unique in that it does not require re- zeroing when the rifle is reassembled, regardless of caliber change.

✷ *R-84 Deluxe* - features a better grade of Turkish walnut with a North American game scene engraved on receiver, silver pistol grip cap with animal scene engraving.

$2,375	$2,025	$1,650	$1,200	$1,000	$925	$825

Last MSR was $2,600.

Add $50 for left hand action.

✷ *R-84 Super Deluxe* - best grade Turkish walnut with receiver featuring African game scene engraving (animals are in gold and silver), and silver pistol grip cap with gold animal engraving.

$2,675	$2,225	$1,775	$1,300	$1,100	$975	$895

Last MSR was $2,950.

Add $50 for left hand action.

R-93 CLASSIC - available in various domestic (.22-250 Rem. - .416 Rem. Mag.) and European (6.5x55mm and 7x57mm currently) calibers, 22, 24 (Mag. cals.), or 27½ (disc.) in. barrel, unique patented rifle features straight pull bolt action (0 degree bolt lift), 360 degree radial locking system eliminates bolt rotation, unique safety offering cartridge in chamber

Grading	100%	98%	95%	90%	80%	70%	60%

capability, 3 shot mag, features interchangeable barrel system and newly designed bolt, searfree trigger mechanism, matte finished nickel receiver with engraving, non-glare "black velvet" barrel finish, integrated low scope mounts standard (1994-97 only), custom gun case with combination lock became standard 1998, 6½ - 7 lbs. Importation began 1994, R-93 Classic introduced 1998, disc. May, 2002.

MSR	$2,950		$2,600	$2,200	$1,850	$1,675	$1,500	$1,375	$1,250

Add $595 per interchangeable barrel (w/o mounts).

During 1998, this model's nomenclature changed to the R-93 Classic. Scope mounts are no longer included. Between 1994-97, this model retailed for approx. $2,800 and a Deluxe Grade was available for $3,100, while the Super Deluxe Grade retailed for $3,500.

* **Model R-93 Classic Safari** - .416 Rem. Mag. cal., features 24 in. heavy barrel, open sights, large forearm, 9½ lbs., this model was renamed the R-93 Classic in 1998. Imported 1994-2002.

	$3,575	$3,100	$2,650	$2,275	$1,825	$1,350	$1,150

Last MSR was $4,140.

R-93 LUXUS - available in 20 calibers from .222 Rem. - .375 H&H., similar to the R-93 Classic, except has higher quality walnut and ebony forend tip, available in right or left hand action, case not included. New 2002.

MSR	$3,050		$2,695	$2,275	$1,900	$1,700	$1,500	$1,350	$1,200

* **R-93 Luxus Safari** .416 Rem Mag. cal., similar to R-93 Classic Safari, except has higher quality walnut and ebony forend tip, available in right or left hand action, case not included. New 2002.

MSR	$3,350		$2,950	$2,425	$2,000	$1,800	$1,600	$1,500	$1,400

R-93 ATTACHE - various cals., features premium walnut stock and forearm with receiver wood panel inserts, wood bolt knob, ebony forearm tip, fluted barrel, includes case, approx. 6½ lbs. New 1998.

MSR	$4,150		$3,600	$3,200	$2,850	$2,400	$1,950	$1,675	$1,325

Add $968 per interchangeable barrel (w/o mounts).

R-93 GRAND LUXE - various cals., deluxe model with high grade checkered walnut stock and forearm, fully hand engraved receiver, 3 shot mag, 6½ - 7 lbs. New 1999.

MSR	$5,160		$4,350	$3,675	$2,800	$2,350	$1,850	$1,350	$1,150

R-93 LONG RANGE SPORTER 2 - .22-250 Rem., .223 Rem., .308 Win., .300 Win. Mag. (new 2000), or .338 Lapua (new 2000) cal., competition styled long range sporter with adj. trigger and stock, 5 or 10 (disc. 1999) shot removable box mag, free floating fluted barrel, many competition features, 10.4 lbs. New 1999.

MSR	$2,480		$2,075	$1,750	$1,450	$1,225	$1,025	$875	$795

Add $870 for .338 Lapua cal.

Add $1,035 per interchangeable barrel (w/o mounts).

Add $1,000 for Leupold Vari-XIII scope, mounts, muzzle brake, bi-pod, and hard carry case (Long Range Sporter 2 Tactical Package).

R-93 SYNTHETIC - available in 21 cals. between .22-250 Rem. - .416 Rem. Mag., also available by special order in the same European cals. as the Model R-93 Repeater, features one-piece conventional black synthetic stock, 22 or 26 in. barrel, without scope mounts and rings, 6½ - 7 lbs. New 1998.

MSR	$1,695		$1,475	$1,200	$1,025	$900	$775	$695	$625

Add $235 for Safari Model in .416 Rem. Mag.

Add $595 per interchangeable barrel (w/o mounts).

Grading	100%	98%	95%	90%	80%	70%	60%

R-93 LX - similar cals. as Model R-93 Synthetic, features checkered walnut stock and forearm, coin finished stippled receiver sides, without scope mounts and rings, 6½ - 7 lbs. New 1998.

| | MSR | $1,990 | | $1,750 | $1,425 | $1,195 | $1,000 | $875 | $795 | $695 |

Add $275 for Safari LX Model in .416 Rem. Mag. cal.
Add $595 per interchangeable barrel (w/o mounts).

R-93 PRESTIGE - similar to R-93 LX, except receiver has fine scroll engraving, and higher grade walnut, case not included. New 2002.

| | MSR | $2,100 | | $1,825 | $1,525 | $1,250 | $1,050 | $900 | $800 | $700 |

Add $265 for Prestige Safari Model in .416 Rem. Mag. cal.

MODEL K77 A SINGLE SHOT - .22-250 Rem., .243 Win., 6.5x55mm, .270 Win., 7x57R, 7x65R, or .30-06 standard cals., 7mm Rem. Mag., .300 Win. Mag. or .300 Wby. Mag. cal., break open action, 23 or 24 in. barrel, 3 piece take down, upper tang safety, checkered walnut stock and forearm, engraved silver finished receiver, sling swivels, 5½ lbs. Imported 1988-90.

| | | | | $2,000 | $1,675 | $1,475 | $1,300 | $1,100 | $925 | $800 |

Last MSR was $2,280.

Add $50 for Mag. calibers.
Add $730-$778 per interchangeable barrel.

K95 PRESTIGE SINGLE SHOT - .222 Rem. (disc.), .243 Win., .270 Win., .308 Win., .30-06, 7mm Rem. Mag., .300 Win. Mag., or .300 Wby. Mag. cal., break open action, 22 (standard cals.) or 25 (Mag. cal.s) in. barrel, upper tang safety/cocking lever, 3 piece takedown, checkered walnut stock and forearm, scroll engraved sideplates, sling swivels. Importation began 2000.

| | MSR | $2,895 | | $2,550 | $2,175 | $1,825 | $1,675 | $1,500 | $1,375 | $1,250 |

Add $700 per interchangeable barrel.

K95 LUXUS SINGLE SHOT - similar to Prestige, except has high grade checkered stock and forearm, engraved sideplates and receiver. Importation began 2000.

| | MSR | $3,395 | | $2,950 | $2,475 | $2,025 | $1,775 | $1,600 | $1,475 | $1,350 |

Add $700 per interchangeable barrel.

ULTIMATE BOLT ACTION - .22-250 Rem., .243 Win., .25-06 Rem., .270 Win., .308 Win., .30-06, 7x57mm, 7x64mm, .264 Win. Mag., 7mm Rem. Mag., .300 Win. Mag., .338 Win. Mag., or .375 H&H cal., unique bolt action design with 60 degree bolt throw, interchangeable barrel capability, 3 locking lugs, safety lever cocks and uncocks the firing pin spring, exposed hammer, aluminum receiver, 22 or 24 in. barrel, single set trigger, silver finished receiver has light engraving, select checkered walnut stock and forearm, 6¾ lbs. Extra interchangeable barrels were $545 each, extra bolt heads were $175 each. Mfg. 1985-1989.

| | | | | $1,350 | $1,100 | $975 | $925 | $825 | $750 | $675 |

Last MSR was $1,495.

All models were available in left-hand version at no extra charge.

ULTIMATE BOLT ACTION - SPECIAL ORDER - all of the following models may have been ordered with a buttstock cartridge trap - add $250-$500 depending on model. Mfg. was disc. 1989 on all models. Please contact SIG Arms for more information regarding Blaser's current extensive listing of special order rifles.

✳ *Ultimate Deluxe* - similar to Ultimate, except better wood and game scene engraving.

| | | | | $1,425 | $1,175 | $1,000 | $950 | $850 | $775 | $700 |

Last MSR was $1,595.

Grading	100%	98%	95%	90%	80%	70%	60%

* **Ultimate Deluxe Carbine** - .243 Win. or .308 Win. cal. only, 19½ in. barrel with full length forearm. New 1986.

| | $1,600 | $1,375 | $1,150 | $1,000 | $900 | $825 | $750 |

Last MSR was $1,800.

* **Ultimate Super Deluxe** - similar to Ultimate Deluxe, except features better wood and game scene engraving. New 1986.

| | $3,750 | $3,250 | $2,900 | $2,600 | $2,300 | $2,100 | $1,850 |

Last MSR was $4,030.

* **Ultimate Exclusive** - similar to Ultimate Super Deluxe, except features better wood and game scene engraving. New 1986.

| | $4,850 | $4,300 | $3,500 | $2,975 | $2,600 | $2,275 | $1,975 |

Last MSR was $5,655.

Add $700 per interchangeable barrel.

* **Ultimate Super Exclusive** - similar to Ultimate Exclusive, except features better wood and game scene engraving. New 1986.

| | $7,700 | $6,800 | $5,750 | $4,700 | $3,950 | $3,450 | $2,950 |

Last MSR was $8,905.

Add $950 per interchangeable barrel.

* **Ultimate Royal** - best quality Ultimate, featuring Bavarian cheekpiece and checkering/ carving on stock and forearm, elaborate game scene engraving, gold plated hammer. New 1986.

| | $9,000 | $7,500 | $6,750 | $6,000 | $5,375 | $4,600 | $4,000 |

Last MSR was $11,500.

Add $1,200 per interchangeable barrel.

BLEIKER, HEINRICH

Current rifle manufacturer located in Buetschwil, Switzerland.

RIFLES: BOLT ACTION

Please contact the factory directly for more information, including current U.S. pricing and availability (see Trademark Index).

CHALLENGER - .22 LR cal., Bleiker action featuring minimum firing pin resonance and precise head space clearance, super match trigger, match barrel, many options available. New 2002.

| MSR | $2,900 | | $2,750 | $2,250 | $1,775 | $1,400 | $1,100 | $875 | $725 |

MATCH RIFLE - 6mm BR, .308 Win., or 7.5x55mm Swiss cal., Bleiker alloy action featuring titanium hardening/coating, integrated magazine, super match trigger, match barrel, many options available, including different colors. New 2002.

| MSR | $2,900 | | $2,750 | $2,250 | $1,775 | $1,400 | $1,100 | $875 | $725 |

BOHICA

Previous manufacturer and customizer located in Sedalia, CO circa 1993-94.

RIFLES: SEMI-AUTO

M16-SA - .223 Rem., .50 AE, or various custom cals., AR-15 style, 16 or 20 in. barrel, A-2 sights, standard handguard, approx. 950 were mfg. through September, 1994.

| | $1,375 | $1,225 | $1,000 | $850 | $725 | $600 | $525 |

Add $100 for flat-top receiver with scope rail.
Add $65 for two-piece, free floating handguard.

In addition to the rifles listed, Bohica also manufactured a M16-SA Match variation (retail was

Grading	100%	98%	95%	90%	80%	70%	60%

B

$2,295, approx. 10 mfg.), a pistol version of the M16-SA in both 7 and 10 in. barrel (retail was $1,995, approx. 50 mfg.), and a limited run of M16-SA in .50 AE cal. (retail was $1,695, approx. 25 mfg.).

BOITO

Previous manufacturer located in Brazil. Previously imported by F.I.E. Corp. located in Hialeah, FL.

Boito shotguns were inexpensive, utilitarian shotguns that are shootable, but not collectible. Because of this, prices typically range between $75 - $175, depending on the gauge and condition.

BOND ARMS, INC.

Current manufacturer located in Granbury, Texas beginning 1998.

DERRINGERS: O/U

A key entry internal safety locking device was introduced for all Defender models beginning in 2000. This device locks the preexisting crossbolt safety in the on-safe position.

TEXAS DEFENDER - 9mm Para., .32 H&R Mag., .357 Mag., .357 Max, .40 S&W, .44 Mag., .45 ACP, or .45 LC/.410 shot shell cals., O/U design, 3 in. barrels with spring loaded extractors, stainless steel, removable trigger guard, rebounding hammer, crossbolt safety, spring loaded cammed locking lever, 21 oz. New 1998.

	MSR	$359		$295	$240	$195

Add $129 per extra set of barrels.
Add $15 for left-hand model.

CENTURY 2000 DEFENDER (C2K) - .410 bore/.45 LC cal. with 2½ in. chambers and 3 in. barrels, or .410 bore with 3 in. chambers and 3½ in. barrels. New 1999.

	MSR	$379		$310	$255	$195

Add $15 for left-hand model.

COWBOY DEFENDER - similar cals. as Texas Defender, designed specifically for cowboy action shooting, w/o trigger guard. New 2000.

	MSR	$359		$295	$240	$195

Add $15 for left-hand model.

BORCHARDT

Previous pistol design originating in Germany circa 1894-1897.

PISTOLS: SEMI-AUTO

Prices below assume matching parts and original condition.

MODEL 1893 - 7.65mm Borchardt cal., original Luger design, 6½ in. barrel, blue finish with fire-blue small parts, checkered walnut grips, 8 shot mag., distinguished by elongated spring mechanism housing located behind the toggle assembly, may include accessories (mags., holster, stock) and/ or case.

   ✳ *Ludwig Loewe Mfg.* - serial numbered 1-1104.

	$12,000	$10,500	$9,000	$7,500	$6,250	$4,950	$3,750

Original stocks (with attached leather holster) are priced starting at $3,500.

    ◇**Cased With Accessories** - original cased gun was supplied with matching shoulder stock, detachable cheekpiece, leather holster, 3 regular mags. and a hold-open mag.

	$23,500	$18,000	$12,500	$10,000	$8,000	$6,500	$5,000

Grading	100%	98%	95%	90%	80%	70%	60%

※ DWM Mfg. - starting approx. 1895, serial numbered 1105-3000.

	$11,250	$9,995	$8,500	$7,000	$5,750	$4,350	$3,250

Original stocks (with attached leather holster) are priced starting at $3,500.

◇**Cased With Accessories** - original cased gun was supplied with unnumbered shoulder stock, detachable cheekpiece, leather holster, 3 regular mags. and a hold-open mag.

	$22,500	$18,000	$12,500	$10,000	$8,000	$6,500	$5,000

BOSIS, LUCIANO

Current manufacturer located in Travagliato, Italy. Currently imported beginning 2000 by New England Arms, located in Kittery Point, ME. Previously imported by William Larkin Moore & Co., located in Scottsdale, AZ.

All Luciano Bosis guns are manufactured on a custom order only basis. Annual production is approx. 25 best quality guns. Please contact the importer directly for current availability and pricing.

SHOTGUNS

Add 20% for 28 ga. or .410 bore, $1,250 for single trigger.

MICHAELANGELO O/U - 12, 16, 20, 28 ga., or .410 bore, Boss style sidelock action, 28 in. chopper lump barrels. Prices reflect base value w/o engraving options.

Prices start in the $35,000 range and go up according to special orders.

HAMMER GUN SxS - 12 ga., sidelock action.

Prices start in the $11,500 range and go up according to special orders.

QUEEN SxS - 12, 16, 20, 28 ga., or .410 bore, H&H type sidelock action, 27 in. chopper lump barrels, fine and elaborate engraving.

Prices start in the $25,000 range and go up according to special orders.

COUNTRY SxS - 12, 16, 20, 28 ga., or .410 bore, Anson & Deeley type scalloped boxlock action, 27 in. chopper lump barrels, DT, checkered deluxe English straight grip stock and forearm.

Prices start in the $15,000 range and go up according to special orders.

BOSS & CO., LTD.

Current manufacturer located in London, England 1812 to date. Direct sales from the manufacturer only.

Boss manufactures some of the world's finest shotguns and rifles (best quality guns only). Their shotguns and rifles have always been custom built per individual order. Approximately 10,000 have been manufactured to date. The following are basic models (does not include special orders, optional engraving patterns, and other possible options). Prices indicated below for manufacturer's suggested retail and 100% condition factors are listed in English pounds. All new prices do not include English VAT. Delivery time for new guns is approx. 3 years. Values for used guns in 98%-60% condition factors are priced in U.S. dollars.

RIFLES: BOLT ACTION

BOSS BOLT ACTION - .270 Win. or .275 Rigby (disc.) cal., Mauser action with Walther premium sporter barrel, Win. Model 70 three position side safety, box mag., includes mounts and Zeiss scope.

MSR	N/A		N/A	$13,000	$11,500	$7,750	$6,500	$5,500	$4,500

This model has very limited manufacture, and Boss should be contacted directly for a firm price quotation.

Grading	100%	98%	95%	90%	80%	70%	60%

RIFLES: O/U & SxS, CUSTOM

Boss Express O/U double rifles are quoted per individual request only. Current pricing for the .470 NE or .500 NE cal. starts at £150,000 (w/o VAT). Approx. 12½ lbs. Older double rifles must be appraised individually. The Boss SxS rifle starts at £85,000 (w/o VAT). These models have had very limited manufacture.

SHOTGUNS: CUSTOM

BOSS O/U - 12, 16, 20, 28 ga., or .410 bore standard, barrel lengths and chokes to specifications, shell-framed sidelock, auto ejectors, double triggers or single non-selective, English straight stock standard to specifications, VR or pistol grip stock optional, best English bouquet & scroll fine engraving, limited production.

MSR	£70,000	£70,000	$72,000	$55,500	$38,750	$32,500	$27,500	$22,500

Add £5,000 for 16 or 20 ga.
Add £10,000 for 28 ga. or .410 bore.

Note: above values represent base gun only. Any additional engraving (tight bouquet and scroll is the traditional standard) and/or special orders will add considerably to the above prices.

BOSS SxS - all gauges, barrel lengths and chokes to specifications, bar-action sidelock, easy open/close action (not self-opening), square or rounded action, checkered stock, pistol grip (optional) or straight grip stock, single (patented 3 pull system) or double triggers, splinter or beavertail (optional) forearm, best English bouquet & scroll engraving, limited production.

MSR	£40,000	£40,000	$35,000	$27,750	$21,500	$18,000	$15,000	$13,000

Add £5,000 for 16 or 20 ga.
Add £10,000 for 28 ga. or .410 bore.

Note: above values represent base gun only. Any additional engraving (tight rose and scroll is the traditional standard) and/or special orders will add considerably to the above prices.

BOSWELL, CHARLES

Previous trademark manufactured in London, England and Charlotte, NC.

In 1988, Charles Boswell was purchased by U.S. interests and Cape Horn International (previously Cape Horn Outfitters) located in Charlotte, NC, was retained to sell and manufacture the Boswell Guns in the U.S. In addition to acquiring their entire inventory of English manufactured firearms, Charles Boswell fabricated new shotguns and double rifles in the U.S. using the best materials including English lock mechanisms and retained the Charles Boswell Co. trademark. Every gun was custom ordered to an individual client's requirements/specifications. Previously imported by Saxon Arms, Ltd., located in Clearwater, FL.

RIFLES: SxS

BOXLOCK RIFLE - .300 Express, .375 H&H, .458 Win. Mag., or .500 NE cal., made to individual order, choice of game scene engraving, Anson & Deeley boxlock actions, select European hybrid walnut, double triggers, leather cased. Disc. 1996.

		$17,500	$14,750	$11,750	$9,500	$8,500	$7,500	$6,500

Last MSR was $35,000.

* **.600 Nitro Express**

This model was priced by quotation only. A .600 NE sold for $123,000 in 1991. Disc. 1996.

SIDELOCK RIFLE - .300 Express, .375 H&H, or .458 Win. Mag. cal., made to individual order, choice of game scene engraving, H&H sidelock action, select European hybrid walnut, double triggers, leather cased. Disc. 1996.

		$35,000	$29,500	$25,000	$20,000	$16,500	$13,250	$10,750

Last MSR was $65,000.

Grading	100%	98%	95%	90%	80%	70%	60%

❋ **.600 Nitro Express**

	$65,000	$55,000	$45,000	$37,500	$30,000	$25,000	$19,950

Last MSR was $125,000.

SHOTGUNS: SxS

BOXLOCK MODEL - previously made to individual order, choice of engraving - including game scenes with gold, Anson & Deeley boxlock actions, select European hybrid walnut, double triggers, leather cased. While each shotgun was priced per individual special order, the below listed prices represented standard features and embellishments. Disc. 1996.

❋ *Best Quality*

	$5,500	$4,750	$4,150	$3,550	$3,150	$2,650	$2,000

Last MSR was $9,500.

❋ *Deluxe Grade* - game scene engraved.

	$6,750	$5,250	$4,500	$4,000	$3,550	$3,000	$2,500

Last MSR was $10,500.

Add $900 for single trigger.
Add $2,800 for extra set of barrels.
Add $2,200 for smaller gauges.

FEATHERWEIGHT MONARCH GRADE - lavishly engraved with gold game scenes, lightweight model, specifications per individual customer special order. Mfg. 1989- 1996.

❋ *Boxlock Model*

	$9,750	$7,350	$6,000	$5,000	$4,400	$3,750	$3,150

Last MSR was $12,500.

❋ *Sidelock Model*

	$16,500	$14,000	$12,000	$9,750	$8,500	$7,250	$6,250

Last MSR was $25,000.

SIDELOCK MODEL - previously made to individual order, choice of game scene engraving, H&H sidelock action, select European hybrid walnut, double triggers, leather cased, while each shotgun was priced per individual special order, the below listed values represented standard features and embellishments.

	$11,750	$9,450	$8,250	$7,000	$6,000	$5,000	$4,000

Last MSR was $17,500.

Add $4,000 for smaller gauges except .410 bore - add $5,000.
Add $2,800 for extra set of barrels.
Add $2,800 for extra set of .410 bore barrels.

BOWEN, BRUCE & COMPANY

Current shotgun manufacturer established 2001 and located in Sturgis, SD. Consumer direct sales only. Bruce Bowen & Company is a division of NIP Manufacturing, Inc.

SHOTGUNS: SINGLE SHOT

BOWEN TRAP GUN 12 ga. only, unique break open action, 32, 33, 34, or 35 in. fixed full choke barrel with adj. rib allowing for different point of impact, both release and pull triggers included, deluxe checkered walnut with either regular or Monte Carlo stock, individually made per customer's specifications, 9 lbs.

The base price for the Bowen Trap Gun is $16,500. Please contact the factory directly for a firm price quotation with various options and a delivery date.

Grading		100%	98%	95%	90%	80%	70%	60%

B BREDA MECCANICA BRESCIANA

Current manufacturer located in Brescia, Italy. Previous company name was Ernesto Breda. Currently imported beginning 2002 by Tristar, located in No. Kansas City, MO. Previously imported 2000-2001 by Gryphon International, located in Kansas City, MO, and by Diana Imports Co., located in San Francisco, CA.

SHOTGUNS: O/U

VEGA SPECIAL - 12 or 20 ga., boxlock action, 26 or 28 in. barrels, single trigger, ejectors, blue only.

	$575	$495	$460	$440	$400	$375	$350

Last MSR was $650.

VEGA SPECIAL TRAP - 12 ga. only, boxlock action, triggers and locks designed for competition shooting, 30 or 32 in. barrels, single trigger, ejectors, blue only.

	$885	$820	$760	$720	$675	$635	$575

Last MSR was $1,114.

VEGA LUSSO - 12 ga. only, 3 in. chambers, scalloped boxlock action, SST, ejectors, 26 or 28 in. VR barrels, coin finished receiver with light perimeter engraving, deluxe checkered Circassian walnut stock and forearm. Importation began 2001.

MSR	$1,858	$1,695	$1,375	$1,100	$975	$850	$725	$600

SIRIO STANDARD - 12 or 20 ga., boxlock action, 26 or 28 in. barrels, single trigger, ejectors, blue only, action extensively engraved. Also available in skeet model (28 in. barrels).

	$2,000	$1,850	$1,630	$1,480	$1,320	$1,200	$1,050

Last MSR was $2,225.

PEGASO - 12 or 20 ga., 3 in. chambers, 26 or 28 (12 ga. only) in. VR barrels with 5 interchageable chokes, engraved steel action, inertia SST, oil finished deluxe walnut stock and forearm, approx. 6 1/4 (20 ga.) or 6 3/4 lbs. Importation began 2002.

As this edition went to press, prices had yet to be established on this model.

SHOTGUNS: SxS

ANDROMEDA SPECIAL - 12 ga. only, single trigger, ejectors, select checkered walnut, satin finish receiver with elaborate engraving.

	$640	$550	$480	$420	$365	$300	$250

Last MSR was $685.

SHOTGUNS: SEMI-AUTO

Add approx. 5% for vent. rib on those discontinued models below where applicable.
Add approx. 10% for choke tubes on discontinued models.

GOLD SERIES - 12 or 20 (lightweight) ga., 2¾ in. chamber, 25 or 27 in. barrels, recoil operated, interchangeable choke tubes on recent mfg., vent. rib is standard.

❋ *Antares Standard* - all steel construction. Importation disc. 1988.

	$440	$375	$340	$310	$285	$260	$240

Last MSR was $495.

❋ *Argus* - lightweight standard, weighs only 6.6 lbs. Importation disc. 1988.

	$450	$380	$340	$310	$285	$260	$240

Last MSR was $510.

B

Grading	100%	98%	95%	90%	80%	70%	60%

✳ *Aries* - Magnum, 3 in. chambers, 7.9 lbs. Importation disc. 1988.

	$460	$395	$350	$320	$295	$270	$250

Last MSR was $525.

STANDARD - 12 ga., 2¾ in. chamber, recoil operated, 25 or 27 in. barrel, lightly engraved, interchangeable choke tubes on recent mfg. Disc.

	$300	$275	$255	$230	$215	$200	$180

GRADE 1 - 12 ga., similar to standard, except with fancier wood and engraving.

	$575	$530	$485	$440	$410	$380	$350

GRADE 2 - 12 ga., exceeds Grade 1 on embellishments.

	$685	$620	$560	$500	$460	$420	$375

GRADE 3 - 12 ga., top-of-the-line semi-auto.

	$850	$790	$700	$640	$590	$540	$480

MAGNUM MODEL - 12 ga. only, chambered for 3 in. shells.

	$470	$415	$380	$350	$315	$290	$265

ALTAIR SPECIAL - 12 ga., 2¾ in. chamber, gas operated, 25 or 27 in. barrel, alloy construction, interchangeable choke tubes on recent mfg., vent. rib is standard, choice of blue or chromed receiver.

	$440	$375	$340	$310	$285	$260	$240

Last MSR was $495.

ASTRO - 12 or 20 ga., 3 in. chamber, inertia movement action, 22 (slug), 24, 26, 28, or 30 in. VR barrel with choke tube, choice of black synthetic, Advantage camo, or Circassian walnut stock (recoil pad on 20 ga. only) and forearm. Importation began 2001.

MSR	$995	$895	$725	$575	$525	$475	$425	$375

Add $39 for 20 ga.
Add $100 for Advantage camo coverage.

ASTROLUX - similar to Astro, except has two-tone receiver with engraving and deluxe checkered Circassian walnut stock and forearm. Importation began 2001.

MSR	$1,665	$1,475	$1,200	$995	$875	$750	$625	$550

ERMES 2000/2000 L - 12 ga., 3 in. chamber, inertia recoil operating system, aluminum alloy receiver, nickel plated or blue (lower receiver only) finish, 24, 26, or 28 in. barrel with choke tube, deluxe chckered Circassian walnut stock and forearm. Importation began 2001.

MSR	$1,134	$975	$850	$750	$650	$550	$475	$395

Add $364 for Ermes 2000 L with nickel finished receiver.

✳ *Ermes Silver* - similar to Ermes 2000, except has engraved nickel plated silver finish on lower receiver. Importation began 2002.

MSR	$1,536	$1,325	$1,025	$900	$775	$650	$550	$495

✳ *Ermes Gold* - similar to Ermes 2000, except has nickel plated silver finish with engraving and 24 Kt. animal gold inlays on lower receiver. Importation began 2002.

MSR	$1,756	$1,400	$1,150	$975	$800	$700	$600	$550

MIRA - 12 ga. only, 3 in. chamber, gas operated, Ergal aluminum alloy receiver, choice of annodized black metal or Advantage camo finish, 22 (slug), 24, 26, 28, or 30 in. VR barrel with choke tube, Circassian walnut or black synthetic stock and forearm. Importation began 2001.

MSR	$751	$675	$600	$550	$475	$395	$350	$295

Add $25 for walnut stock.
Add $58 for Advantage camo coverage.
Add $67 for Sporting Clays configuration.

Grading	100%	98%	95%	90%	80%	70%	60%

ARIES 2 - 12 ga. only, 2¾ in. chamber, gas operated, engraved two-tone receiver, 28 or 30 in. VR barrel, deluxe checkered Circassian walnut stock and forearm. Limited importation 2001 only.

| | $815 | $725 | $595 | $550 | $495 | $445 | $395 |

Last MSR was $925.

BREN 10

Previous trademark manufactured 1983-86 by Dornaus & Dixon Ent., Inc., located in Huntington Beach, CA.

Bren 10 magazines played an important part in the failure of these pistols to be accepted by consumers. Originally, Bren magazines were not shipped in some cases until a year after the customer received his gun. The complications arising around manufacturing a reliable magazine domestically led to the downfall of this company. For this reason, original Bren 10 magazines are currently selling for $125- $150 if new (watch for fakes).

PISTOLS: SEMI-AUTO

Note: the Bren 10 shoots a Norma factory loaded 10mm auto. cartridge. Ballistically, it is very close to a .41 Mag. Bren pistols also have unique power seal rifling, with five lands and grooves. While in production, Bren pistols underwent (4) engineering changes, the most important probably being re-designing the floorplate of the magazine, thus preventing mag. shifting while undergoing recoil.

100% values in this section assume NIB condition. Subtract 10% without box/manual.

BREN 10 STANDARD MODEL - 10mm cal. only, semi-auto selective double action design, blue slide/silver frame finish, 5 in. barrel, 11 shot, stainless steel frame, usually supplied with two mags. although early mfg. did not include a mag. because of design problems, "83SM" ser. no. prefix. Mfg. 1984-86.

| | $1,575 | $1,275 | $750 | $650 | $550 | $475 | $395 |

Last MSR was $500.

Add $600 for .45 conversion unit.

Be wary of Standard Models with wooden cases and conversion kits – they are fakes!

BREN 10 MILITARY/POLICE MODEL - 10mm cal. only, identical to standard model, except has all black finish, "83MP" ser. no. prefix. Mfg. 1984-86.

| | $1,575 | $1,275 | $750 | $650 | $550 | $475 | $395 |

Last MSR was $550.

BREN 10 SPECIAL FORCES MODEL - 10mm cal. only, commercial version of the military pistol submitted to the U.S. gov't. Model D has dark finish. Model L has light finish, "SFD" ser. no. prefix on Model D, "SFL" ser. no. prefix on Model L. Disc. 1986.

| Dark finish - Model D | $1,595 | $1,275 | $750 | $650 | $550 | $475 | $395 |
| Light finish - Model L | $1,895 | $1,575 | $995 | $825 | $700 | $575 | $475 |

Last MSR was $600.

BREN 10 DUAL-MASTER PRESENTATION MODEL - 10mm and .45 ACP cal., supplied with extra slide and barrel (numbered to gun) to accommodate the .45 ACP, same mags. (two) for both cals., extra fine finish, light scroll engraving, with wood presentation case, "83DM" ser. no. prefix, less than 50 mfg. Disc. 1986.

| | $3,900 | $3,000 | $2,000 | $1,500 | | | |

Last MSR was $800.

BREN 10 JEFF COOPER COMMEMORATIVE - 10mm cal. only, while 2,000 were annnounced for mfg., sources believe that approx. 13 were actually made, 22Kt. gold plated detailing, laser engraved stocks, special presentation chest. Disc. 1986.

| | $4,800 | $4,500 | $3,200 | $2,950 | | | |

Last MSR was $2,000.

Grading	100%	98%	95%	90%	80%	70%	60%

MARKSMAN MODEL - .45 ACP cal., 250 mfg. (in its own ser. range) for a retail shop in Chicago called "The Marksman", action similar to Bren 10 Standard Model, "MSM" ser. no. prefix.

		$1,200	$895	$695	$500	

Add $750 for 10mm conversion unit.
Add $100 for original nylon carrying case marked "Marksman".

BRETTON

Current manufacturer located in Saint-Etienne, France. Previously imported and distributed by Mandall Shooting Supplies, Inc. located in Scottsdale, AZ.

SHOTGUNS: O/U

All Bretton shotguns are extremely lightweight and well balanced because of their unique design (permitting total disassembly including barrels) and use of various composition alloys.

BABY STANDARD (SPRINT MODEL) - 12 or 20 ga. only, sliding breech action allows barrels to move straight forward, 27½ in. separated barrels, double triggers, side opening lever, blue action and barrels, recoil pad, checkered walnut stock and forearm, 4.8 lbs. Importation disc.

	$995	$885	$700	$625	$575	$475	$430

Prices reflect most recent importation information.

SPRINT DELUXE - 12, 16 (disc.), or 20 ga., action similar to Baby Standard, engraved coin finished receiver, 27½ in. separated barrels, deluxe checkered walnut stock and forearm, extremely lightweight, 4.8 lbs. Importation disc. 1994.

	$895	$725	$625	$575	$475	$430	$395

Last MSR was $975.

FAIR PLAY MODEL - 12 or 20 ga., differs from Sprint Models in that action pivots like normal O/U, 27½ in. separated barrels, lightweight construction, 4.8 lbs. Importation disc.

	$966	$850	$675	$625	$575	$475	$430

Add $64 for Fair Play Limited Model.

BRILEY

Current trademark manufactured by Briley Manufacturing Inc., and located in Houston, TX. Briley produces both pistols and rifles, in addition to manufacturing a complete line of top quality shotgun barrel tubes and chokes since 1976 - please contact the factory directly (see Trademark Index) for more information on these shotgun accessories.

PISTOLS: SEMI-AUTO

FANTOM - 9mm Para., .38 Super, .40 S&W, or .45 ACP cal., features Caspian aluminum wide body frame, Briley match barrel, and many competition features, hot blue slide finish and armor coated frame, 8 or 10 shot mag, black synthetic grips, approx. 22-24 oz. New 1998.

MSR	$1,895	$1,675	$1,300	$1,075	$875	$750	$625	$575

Add $95 for hard chrome finish.
Add $75 for night sights.
Add $350 for 2 port barrel compensator.

ADVANTAGE - 9mm Para., .40 S&W, or .45 ACP cal., features 5 in. Briley match barrel, checkered walnut grips and front grip strap, hot blue finish. New 1998.

MSR	$1,650	$1,495	$1,250	$1,050	$875	$750	$625	$575

Add $175 for hard chrome finish.
Add $100 for stainless steel (new 2000).

Grading	100%	98%	95%	90%	80%	70%	60%

VERSATILITY PLUS - 9mm Para., .40 S&W, or .45 ACP cal., features steel or stainless steel (new 2000) 1911 Govt. length modular or Caspian frame, 5 in. barrel, checkered black synthetic grips and front grip strap, squared off trigger guard, hot blue finish. New 1998.

	MSR	$1,850		$1,625	$1,300	$1,050	$875	$725	$600	$550

Add $175 for hard chrome finish.
Add $175 for stainles steel (new 2000)

SIGNATURE SERIES - .40 S&W cal. only, similar to Versatility Plus. New 1998.

	MSR	$2,250		$1,975	$1,650	$1,325	$1,125	$900	$775	$625

Add $175 for hard chrome finish.

PLATE MASTER - 9mm Para. or .38 Super cal., features 1911 Govt. length frame, Briley TCII titanium barrel compensator, Briley scope mount, and other competition features, hot blue finish. New 1998.

	MSR	$1,895		$1,675	$1,325	$1,075	$895	$775	$625	$575

Add $175 for hard chrome finish.

EL PRESIDENTE - 9mm Para. or .38 Super cal., top-of-the-line competition model with Briley quad compensator with side ports, checkered synthetic grips and front grip strap, squared off trigger guard. New 1998.

	MSR	$2,550		$2,250	$1,925	$1,625	$1,325	$1,075	$875	$750

Add $175 for hard chrome finish.

RIFLES: BOLT ACTION

TRANS PECOS - .22-250 Rem., .243 Win., .260 Rem., .308 Win., or 7mm-08 Rem. cal., solid aluminum frame fits metal to metal with barreled action, bench rest grade Jewell trigger, match grade L. Walther barrel, 3 lug 45 degree one-piece bolt, choice of black synthetic (single shot) or checkered high gloss stock and forearm (repeater). New 1998.

	MSR	$3,495		$3,200	$2,750	$2,275	$1,950	$1,775	$1,525	$1,250

Subtract $500 for single shot action.
This model is guaranteed to shoot ½ in. groups at 100 yards with factory ammo.

RIFLES: SEMI-AUTO

HUNTER - .22 LR cal., utilizes Ruger 10/22 action, 21½ in. tapered match stainless steel barrel with crown, Hogue rubber or wood stock, 10 shot mag., includes Briley integral scope mount, approx. 6¼ - 6 5/8 lbs.

	MSR	$600		$550	$475	$395	$360	$330	$300	$285

Add $250 for wood stock.
Add $100 for fluted barrel.

✳ **Hunter Magnum** - .22 Mag. cal., similar to Hunter, except is 9 shot mag. and 21 ½ in. bull barrel.

	MSR	$850		$750	$575	$475	$425	$375	$325	$295

Add $250 for walnut or laminate stock.
Add $100 for fluted barrel.

SPORTER - .22 LR cal., similar to Hunter, except has 18½ or 21½ in. match stainless steel bull barrel with crown, Hogue rubber, brown laminate, or uncheckered walnut sporter stock, 10 shot mag., approx. 6½ lbs.

	MSR	$600		$550	$475	$395	$360	$330	$300	$285

Add $250 for laminate or sporter style walnut stock.
Add $100 for fluted barrel.

Grading	100%	98%	95%	90%	80%	70%	60%

BMG - .22 LR cal., 17 in. match stainless steel bull barrel with target crown, includes 3½ lbs. adj. match barrel weights, choice of Hogue rubber, brown laminate sporter, or walnut sporter stock, 10 shot mag., designed for match grade ammunition only.

MSR	$750		$675	$600	$525	$465	$425	$385	$350

Add $250 for laminate or sporter style walnut stock.

BRITARMS

Previous trademark manufactured by Berdan Gunmakers Ltd. located in England. Previously imported and distributed until 1994 by Mandall Shooting Supplies, Inc. located in Scottsdale, AZ. Previously by Action Arms Ltd. (1982-83) located in Philadelphia, PA.

Britarms Target Pistols had very limited importation into the U.S. While Britarms manufactured other models, only the Model 2000 is listed since it was formally imported through U.S. firms.

PISTOLS: SEMI-AUTO

MODEL 2000 (MK II) - .22 LR cal., standard fire target semi-auto pistol, adj. trigger and rear sight, anatomical adj. grips, 5.82 in. barrel, 5 shot mag., 3 lbs., limited importation, including approx. 2000 through Action Arms Ltd.

	$995	$825	$700	$625	$550	$495	$450

Last MSR was $1,295.

This model features a bolt hold-open mechanism which serves as a manual safety to allow importation.

BRNO ARMS (ZBROJOVKA BRNO)

Currently manufactured by Zbrojovka Brno located in Brno, Czech Republic (formerly Czechoslovakia) since 1918. Brno 98 bolt action rifles and actions are currently imported by EAA Corp, located in Sharpes, FL. Imported and distributed by Euro-Imports, previously located in El Cajon, CA until 2001. Previously imported by Bohemia Arms located in Fountain Valley, CA until 1997. Brno rifles, shotguns, and combination guns produced at the Brno factory were previously imported and distributed by Magnum Research Inc. located in Minneapolis, MN (c. 1994-96). In the early '50s, Brno rifles were imported by Continental Arms Corp. located in New York City. Pragotrade located in Ontario, Canada also imports this trademark for Canada currently (and exclusively). Previously imported by T.D. Arms located in New Baltimore, MI.

As more history is becoming available on this important European trademark, the following biographical sketch will provide some information. Circa 1918, some military personnel took over the controlling interest of the Austro-Hungarian armament shop in Brno, Czechoslovakia, renaming it The State Armament and Engineering Works. Approximately a year later, the name was changed to Czechoslovak State Armament Works. The former provinces of Bohemia and Moravia had long been firearms manufacturing centers within their regions. Prior to 1924, this firm was involved mainly with Mauser Model 98 type rifles (both assembly and mfg.).

Pistol manufacture was tranferred from Brno to Ceská Zbrojovka, located in Strakonice, Czechoslovakia, circa 1923. During 1964-1966, the Czech government transferred the production of long guns from Zbrojovka Brno to Ceská Zbrojovka Uhersky Brod. During the

1970s & 1980s, the arms production of Zbrojovka Brno accounted for less than 3% of its total capacity. The activities of this company were deverted into the production of typewriters, diesel motors, and automatic machine tools. While many firearm designs originated in Brno, Zbrojovka Brno was not the manufacturer. Because of this, the long guns manufactured in the mid-1960s, including the ZKK 600 - 602 series and ZKM rimfires, were manufactured in CZ Uhersky Brod. Because of the Czech government's decision to merge manufacture within both companies, the Brno trademark was also used by Ceská Zbrojovka Uhersky Brod.

This relationship was terminated in 1983, when both companies became part of the Agrozet conglomerate. While confusing, the arms utlizing the Brno trademark were not produced in Brno during this time. All firearms exported from Czechoslovakia at the time carried the Brno logo, and most of them were manufactured by Ceská Zbrojovka Uhersky Brod.

CZ PISTOLS & RIFLES

See separate listing under CZ in this text.

PISTOLS: SEMI-AUTO

MODEL ZBP-99 - 9mm Para. or .40 S&W cal., double action, while advertised in 1998, this gun was never manufactured.

REVOLVERS

ZKR 551 - .32 S&W Long or .38 Spl. cal., double action, fixed access 6 shot cylinder, adj. sights, checkered wood grips with thumb rest, 6 in. barrel, approx. 2 lbs. Importation began 1999.

MSR	$1,556	$1,375	$1,100	$978	$875	$775	$675	$600

RIFLES: BOLT ACTION

The Brno Lightweight Sporter was introduced in the late 1930s. A small quantity was manufactured during pre-war and WWII. Most production occured between 1946-1955. Total production of this model was approx. 40,000+ units. A design change was implemented at approximately serial number 23,000, at which time the receiver was changed to a double square bridge dovetailed to accept scope mounts.

Earlier mfg. had a rounded receiver and some had claw type scope mounts installed. These guns were referenced as Models 21 and 22 domestically, but no model designation appears on the gun. Available cals. were 6.5x57mm, 7x57mm, 7x64mm, 8x57mm, or 8x60mm. Configuration was small ring Mauser 98 receiver with double set trigger(s), butterknife bolt, checkered walnut pistol grip stock (half or full length), with cheekpiece and sling swivels, late production incorporated four variations and two barrel lengths (20.5 or 23.6 in.).

All currently manufactured Brno firearms have a 3 year guarantee.

BRNO RIFLES MAY BE DATED BY THE 2-DIGIT DATE BESIDE THEIR PROOFMARKS.

HORNET SPORTER (MODEL ZKW 465) - .22 Hornet cal., miniature Mauser action, 22¾ in. barrel, 5 shot clip mag., 3-leaf express sight, double set trigger(s), checkered pistol grip stock, also called Z-B Mauser, serial range noted is 02,901-37,393, approx. 40,000 mfg. between 1949- 1973.

$1,200	$925	$750	$625	$500	$400	$295

There are few examples in .218 Bee and .222 Rem. cal. - premiums can be added.

This model was redesigned with a subsequent designation of ZKB 680 Fox in approx. 1975.

Grading	100%	98%	95%	90%	80%	70%	60%

MODEL ZG-47 - .270 Win., .30-06, 7x57mm, 7x64mm, 8x64S, 8x57mm, 9.3x62mm, or 10.75x68mm cal., large ring Mauser 98 action with 20mm dovetails on receiver ring and bridge, single trigger, hinged floorplate, rollover type safety and bolt handle designed for low scope mounting, 23½ in. barrel, checkered pistol grip walnut stock with sling swivels and Schnabel forend, approx. serial range is 0-20,000, mfg. and exported world-wide between 1956- 1962 (approx.).

	$1,125	$895	$725	$600	$495	$395	$295

Early specimens of this model are marked "BRNO MADE IN CZECHOSLOVAKIA". This model is generally regarded as being one of the finest rifles that Brno has manufactured.

MODEL G 33-40 - 8mm cal., mfg. between 1940-42, prices below assume sporterized condition.

	$350	$295	$260	$230	$200	$175	$150

MODEL 21H - 6.5x57mm, 7x57mm, 7x64mm (scarce), 8x57mm, or 8x60mm cal., featherweight style design of the small ring Mauser type action, with (post-1949) or without 20mm dovetails on receiver ring and bridge, 20½ or 23 in. barrel, butterknife style bolt handle, double set triggers, 2-leaf rear sight, checkered pistol grip walnut stock with cheekpiece and plastic buttplate/grip cap, small Schnabel forend, sling swivels included, noted serialization is 14,410-40,098, mfg. approx. 1946-1955.

	$1,200	$925	$750	$625	$500	$400	$295

This model was available in 4 different variations: short barrel/short stock, short barrel/full length stock, long barrel/short stock, long barrel/full length stock. The left receiver rail on these models is marked "ZBROJOVKA BRNO, NARODNI PODNIK".

MODEL 22F - similar to 21H, with full length stock. Disc.

	$1,400	$1,100	$925	$800	$675	$550	$475

MODEL 1 - .22 LR cal., 22¾ in. barrel, 3-leaf sight, 5 shot clip mag., checkered pistol, 6 lbs. Mfg. 1946-1957.

	$595	$540	$485	$405	$375	$320	$265

MODEL 2 - similar to Model 1, with checkered deluxe walnut stock.

	$635	$570	$515	$430	$405	$350	$295

MODEL 3 - .22 LR cal., target rifle model with 27½ in. heavy barrel, adj. click target sights, 5 shot clip mag., plain target style stock with large swivels, 9½ lbs. Mfg. 1949- 1956.

	$635	$570	$515	$430	$405	$350	$295

MODEL 4 - similar to Model 3, except has improved trigger design and safety. Mfg. 1957-1962.

	$700	$635	$570	$515	$430	$405	$350

MODEL 5 - similar to Model 1, except has improved trigger design and safety. Mfg. 1957-1973.

	$650	$570	$515	$430	$405	$350	$295

BRNO 98 STANDARD - .243 Win., .270 Win., .30-06, .308 Win., .300 Win. Mag., 7mm Rem. Mag. (new 2000), 7x64mm, or 9.3x62mm cal., Mauser 98 style action, 23.6 in. barrel with or without iron sights, checkered walnut stock with Bavarian cheekpiece, or synthetic stock and forearms (new 2002) single or set trigger, 7¼ lbs. Importation began 1998.

MSR	$339		$295	$275	$260	$240	$225	$210	$195

Add approx. $150 for checkered walnut stock with Bavarian cheekpiece.
Add $48 for Mag. cals.
Add $117 for single set trigger.

Grading	100%	98%	95%	90%	80%	70%	60%

✳ Brno 98 Mannlicher - similar to Brno 98 Standard, except has full length stock. New 1998.

| MSR | $791 | $675 | $540 | $475 | $385 | $350 | $315 | $295 |

Add $46 for Mag. cals.

✳ MODEL ZKB-110 SINGLE SHOT - .22 Hornet, .222 Rem., 5.6x52R, 5.6x50R Mag., 6.5x57R (disc. 1999), 7x57R (disc. 1999), or 8x57JRS (disc. 1999) cal., single shot break open rifle/shotgun, top lever opening, 23.6 in. barrel, uncheckered (Standard Model) or checkered walnut stock with Bavarian cheekpiece and forearm (Lux Model), includes sling swivels, 6 lbs. Importation began 1998.

| MSR | $263 | $225 | $185 | $160 | $140 | $120 | $110 | $100 |

Add $77 for ZKB-110 Lux Model.
Add $205 for ZKB-110 Super Lux Model (new 2000).
Add $48 for 7x57R or 8x57JRS cal. (disc. 1999).
Add $132 (standard) or $142 (Lux) for an interchangeable 12 ga. shotgun barrel.

MODEL ZOM-451 - .22 LR cal., straight pull bolt action, while advertised in 1998, this model was never manufactured.

MODEL ZKM-451 - .22 LR cal. Importation began 1995.

| MSR | $251 | $215 | $200 | $185 | $170 | $155 | $140 | $125 |

Add $62 for Lux Model (deluxe checkered wood).

MODEL ZKM-452 - please refer to the CZ listing in this text for current information (current mfg. is by CZ).

MODEL ZKM-456 LUX SPORTER - .22 LR cal., bolt action, 5 or 10 shot mag., 24.4 in. barrel, folding rear sight, blue finish, beechwood stock with pistol grip, 6.8 lbs. Imported 1992-98.

| | | $315 | $260 | $215 | $175 | $155 | $135 | $120 |

Last MSR was $370.

Add $18 for micrometer rear sight (ZKM-456 MI).

✳ Model 456 L/LK Target - .22 LR cal., Target variation of the ZKM-456 Lux featuring 25 or 28 in. barrel with adj. front and rear sights, 10.1 lbs. Imported 1992-98.

| | | $305 | $250 | $210 | $170 | $150 | $130 | $115 |

Last MSR was $358.

Add $7 for 25 in. barrel.

✳ Model 456 Match Single Shot - .22 LR cal., designed for UIT competition at 50 M, features 27½ in. barrel, adj. cheekpiece and buttplate, aperture sights, 9.9 lbs. Imported 1992-98.

| | | $375 | $335 | $280 | $250 | $215 | $175 | $155 |

Last MSR was $459.

ZKK 600 - please refer to the CZ listing in this text for current information (recent mfg. is by CZ).

ZKK 601 - please refer to the CZ listing in this text for current information (recent mfg. was by CZ).

ZKK 602 - please refer to the CZ listing in this text for current information (current mfg. is by CZ).

ZKB 680 (FOX II) - .22 Hornet or .222 Rem. (disc.) cal., 23½ in. barrel, 5 shot mag., set triggers, 5 lbs. 12 oz. Importation disc. 1991.

| | | $445 | $380 | $340 | $295 | $255 | $230 | $200 |

Last MSR was $499.

RIFLES: O/U

Grading	100%	98%	95%	90%	80%	70%	60%

ZH-344, 348, & 349 - 7x57R (Model ZH-344), 7x65R (Model ZH-348), or 8x57JRS (Model ZH-349) cal., 23.6 in. VR barrels, double triggers, skip line checkering, sling swivels, approx. 7½ lbs. Importation began 1998.

	MSR	**$1,297**			$1,100	$978	$875	$775	$675	$600	$550

Add $324-$357 per additional set of shotgun barrels, $418 per additional rifle barrel, and $829 for additional Mag. cal. rifle barrels.

SUPER EXPRESS - 7x65R, 9.3x74R, .375 H&H, or .458 Win. Mag. (disc.) cal., sidelock action with Kersten breech crossbolt, hand engraved, skipline checkering, approx. 9 lbs. Importation disc. 1992.

	$3,450	**$2,875**	**$2,300**	**$1,875**	**$1,600**	**$1,375**	**$1,200**

Last MSR was $3,900.

This model previously could be ordered with 6 different types of engraving options. They were: Grade I - add $2,060, Grade II - add $1,030, Grade III - add $1,545, Grade IV - add $1,030, Grade V - add $620, Grade VI - add $660.

SUPER SAFARI - 7x64R, .375 H&H Mag., or 9.3x74R cal., action derived from the Super Express, sidelock, DT with set trigger built in, adj. point of impact, 23.6 in. barrels with open sights, deluxe skipline checkered walnut stock and forearm with vent. recoil pad, approx. 9 lbs. Imported 1992-disc.

	$2,375	**$1,975**	**$1,675**	**$1,450**	**$1,225**	**$1,000**	**$900**

RIFLES: SEMI-AUTO

ZKM-611 - .22 Mag. cal., 20½ in. barrel, 6, 10 (C/B 1994), or 12* shot mag., black metal finish, beechwood (new 1996) or checkered walnut stock and forend, grooved receiver, 6.2 lbs. Importation began 1992.

	MSR	**$459**			$395	$350	$300	$265	$230	$200	$185

Add $70 for walnut stock (disc. 1999).

MODEL 581 - .22 LR cal., semi-auto, select walnut stock, adj. sights, 5 shot mag. Disc.

	$600	**$540**	**$495**	**$440**	**$395**	**$350**	**$295**

RIFLES: SINGLE SHOT

ZK 99 - various cals., break open action with top lever, quarter rib on barrel, checkered walnut stock with cheekpiece and Schnabel forearm, includes swivels and slings, 5¾ lbs. Importation began 2000.

	MSR	**$940**			$875	$725	$625	$550	$500	$450	$400

SHOTGUNS/COMBINATIONS GUNS: O/U

The following current models are being imported and distributed by Euro-Imports, located in El Cajon, CA.

ZH-300 SHOTGUN - 12 ga. only, double triggers with rear trigger doubling as single trigger, 27½ in. barrels, 7 lbs. Imported 1986-92.

	$530	**$430**	**$395**	**$360**	**$330**	**$300**	**$275**

Last MSR was $599.

This model was available in skeet, trap, or field configuration.

ZH-301 FIELD SHOTGUN - 12 or 16 ga. field, 27½ in. barrels, optional Monte Carlo stock (disc.).

	MSR	**$677**			$600	$475	$375	$315	$240	$200	$180

Add $20 for Monte Carlo stock.

ZH-302 SKEET SHOTGUN - 12 ga., skeet model, 26 in. barrels, optional Monte Carlo stock

Grading	100%	98%	95%	90%	80%	70%	60%
(disc.).							
MSR $710	$650	$515	$375	$300	$250	$225	$195

Add $20 for Monte Carlo stock.

ZH-303 TRAP SHOTGUN - 12 ga., trap model, 30 in. barrels, optional Monte Carlo stock (disc.).

MSR $710	$650	$515	$375	$300	$250	$225	$195

Add $20 for Monte Carlo stock.

ZH-300 SERIES COMBINATION GUNS - 7x57R x 12 ga. (ZH-304), 6x52R x 12 ga. (ZH-305), 6x50R Mag. x 12 ga. (ZH-306), .22 Hornet x 12 ga. (ZH-307), 7x65R x 12 ga. (ZH-308), 8x57JRS x 12 ga. (ZH-309), 7x57R x 16 ga. (ZH-324), 7x65R x 16 ga. (ZH-328), combination rifle/shotgun, optional adj. trigger and Monte Carlo stock. Importation disc. 1994 - reintroduced 1999.

MSR $821	$695	$575	$425	$350	$300	$250	$195

Add $73 for cheekpiece and set trigger.
Add $35 for adj. trigger (disc.).
Add $20 for Monte Carlo stock (disc.).

ZH 300 Series over and unders are unique in that they permit 8 different interchangeable barrels including rifle and shotgun sets, interrupter on double trigger, blue action, engraved, diamond checkered walnut.

MODEL ZH-300 COMBO SET - Model ZH-300 style engraving and features, equipped with 8 interchangeable barrels that include various O/U configurations including shotgun/shotgun and shotgun/rifle configurations in various ga.'s and cals. Imported 1986-91.

$2,950	$2,600	$2,250	$2,000	$1,800	$1,600	$1,450

Last MSR was $3,500.

MODEL 500/501 SHOTGUN - 12 ga. only, 28 in. VR barrels, double or single (disc. 1999) trigger.

MSR $975	$845	$725	$625	$525	$425	$350	$295

Add $50 for single trigger (disc. 1999).

✳ Model 500 Combo Set - shotgun/rifle set comprised of 4 barrels including 12 ga. over barrels with choice of 5.6x52R (disc.), 7x57R, 7x65R, or 12 ga. under barrels (in either field, skeet, or trap chokings), sling swivels, set trigger on rifle/shotgun combo, chemically engraved, about 7½ lbs. Imported 1987-91.

$1,925	$1,625	$1,400	$1,200	$1,075	$950	$825

Last MSR was $2,169.

This model was available in limited quanitity.

MODEL 502 SERIES COMBINATION GUN - 12 ga. only, ejectors, combination shotgun/rifle available in .222 Rem., .243 Win., .30-06, .308 Win., and 4 metric cals., fixed choke, acid etched engraving, skipline checkering and cheekpiece. New 1986.

MSR $1,174	$1,050	$850	$695	$600	$525	$425	$350

Add $699 for interchangeable 12 ga. shotgun barrels (new 1998).

BS-571/572 SHOTGUN/COMBINATION GUN - 12 ga. only, boxlock action with ejectors, 6x65R (disc.) or 7x65R rifle cal. only. Limited importation 1992-95.

$825	$700	$600	$550	$475	$425	$375

Last MSR was $995.

Add approx. $115 for rifle/shotgun (12 ga. only) combination (Model 572).

MODEL 571 SUPER SERIES - 12 ga. field, skeet, and trap configuration as well as combination

Grading	100%	98%	95%	90%	80%	70%	60%

shotgun/rifle in 12 ga. x 7x57R or 7x65R cal. Importation disc. 1991.

	$800	$700	$640	$590	$550	$515	$475

Last MSR was $899.

Add $70 for single trigger or trap/skeet configuration (disc.).
Add $700 for extra set of 12 ga. field barrels.
Add $1,101 for hand engraving.

* ✳ ***Super Combo*** - 3 barrel set including 12 ga., 7x57R, and 7x65R barrels. Imported 1987-90.

	$1,925	$1,640	$1,425	$1,250	$1,100	$1,000	$925

Last MSR was $2,169.

SHOTGUNS: SxS

ZP-49 - 12 ga. only, ejectors, double triggers, true sidelock, Purdey-type top bolt, cocking indicators, walnut stock, swivels. Imported 1986-91.

	$535	$460	$420	$385	$350	$320	$290

Last MSR was $589.

Add $20 for engraving.

ZP-149 - similar to ZP-49, except has game scene engraving on sideplates, choice of English or pistol grip stock. Imported 1986-1998.

	$575	$495	$425	$350	$300	$250	$225

Last MSR was $676.

Add $23 for pistol grip stock.

ZP-349 - 12 ga. only, extractors, double triggers, true sidelock, Purdey-type top bolt, cocking indicators, walnut stock with cheek piece, beavertail forearm, swivels, 7.3 lbs. Imported 1986 only.

	$450	$390	$360	$325	$300	$270	$250

Last MSR was $520.

Add $20 for engraving.

SHOTGUNS: SINGLE SHOT

ZBK 100 - 12 or 20 ga., 3 in. chamber, walnut stock and forearm. Importation began 1999.

MSR	$203		$180	$160	$140	$120	$105	$95	$85

BROCKMAN'S CUSTOM GUNSMITHING

Current custom rifle manufacturer and gunsmith established in 1986, and located in Gooding, Idaho. Consumer direct sales only.

Brockman's Custom Gunsmithing manufactures a wide variety of custom bolt action rifles typically based on Win. Model 70, Rem. Model 700, Dakota, or Nesika action. Please contact the company directly to find out more about their wide variety of custom rifles and gunsmithing services.

RIFLES: BOLT ACTION

Specific models and/or configurations include the Universal Hunter (complete gun base price $2,625), Dangerous Game (last MSR $2,450, disc. 2001), Premier Practical (base price $3,295), Model 70 Classic Practical (base price $2,695), Ladies rifles (base price was $2,100-$2,895 – disc. 2000), and Scout rifles (last MSR $1,995 – disc. 2000), and other handcrafted custom bolt action rifles.

RIFLES: LEVER ACTION

Grading	100%	98%	95%	90%	80%	70%	60%

B

Brockman's modifies general purpose lever action rifles based on the Marlin 1895G/SS actions, including the Beast (base price $2,195), and the SOB (last MSR $1,995 – disc. 2001, is based on shorter and lighter Beast), Master Guide Package (base price $1,062).

BROLIN ARMS, INC.

Previous importer of handguns (FEG mfg.), rifles (older Mauser military, see Mauser listing), shotguns (Chinese mfg.), and airguns from 1995-1999. Previously located in Pomona, CA, until 1999, and in La Verne, CA until 1997.

PISTOLS: SEMI-AUTO, SINGLE ACTION

LEGEND SERIES MODEL L45 - .45 ACP cal., patterned after the Colt 1911 Government Model, features include throated match 5 in. barrel, polished feed ramp, flared ejection port, beveled mag. well, flat top slide, flat mainspring housing, front strap high relief cut, aluminum lightweight extended trigger, high visibility sights, 7 shot mag., commander style hammer and checkered walnut grips, 38 oz. Mfg. 1995-98.

$425	$365	$325	$295	$275	$250	$225

Last MSR was $500.

* ***Legend Series Model L45C (Compact)*** - similar to Model L45, except has 4 in. barrel, 35 oz. Mfg. 1995-98.

$440	$380	$330	$295	$275	$250	$225

Last MSR was $520.

* ***Legend Series Model L45T*** - features standard frame with compact slide, 4 in. barrel, 36 oz. Mfg. 1997-98.

$440	$380	$330	$295	$275	$250	$225

Last MSR was $520.

PATRIOT SERIES MODEL P45 COMP - .45 ACP cal., similar to Legend Series Model L45, except has one-piece match 4 in. barrel with integral dual port compensator, 7 shot mag., Millett or Novak combat sights (new 1997), test target provided, choice of blue or satin (frame only) finish, 38 oz. Mfg. 1996-97 only.

$585	$475	$415	$365	$325	$285	$250

Last MSR was $649.

Add $70 for Novak combat sights (new 1997).
Add $20 for T-tone finish (frame only).

* ***Patriot Series Model P45C (Compact)*** - .45 ACP cal., similar to Model P45 Comp, except has 3¼ in. barrel with integral conical lock-up system, 34.5 oz. Mfg. 1996-97.

$610	$495	$425	$375	$325	$285	$250

Last MSR was $689.

Add $70 for Novak combat sights.
Add $20 for T-tone finish (frame only).

* ***Patriot Series Model P45T*** - features standard frame with compact slide, 3.25 in. barrel, 35.5 oz. Mfg. 1997 only.

$620	$500	$425	$375	$325	$285	$250

Last MSR was $699.

Add $60 for Novak combat sights (new 1997).
Add $10 for T-tone finish (frame only).

PRO STOCK MODEL COMPETITION PISTOL - .45 ACP cal., competition pistol featuring most state-of-the-art competitive improvements, 5 in. barrel, 8 shot mag., blue or satin (frame

Grading	100%	98%	95%	90%	80%	70%	60%

only) finish, signature wood grips, 40 oz. Mfg. 1996-97.

	$685	$550	$475	$415	$360	$295	$260

Last MSR was $779.

Add $20 for T-tone finish (frame only).

✳ *Pro Comp Model Competition Pistol* - similar to Pro Stock Model, except has 4 in. dual port compensated heavy match barrel, blue or satin (frame only) finish, 40 oz. Mfg. 1996-97.

	$800	$650	$525	$435	$375	$325	$295

Last MSR was $919.

Add $10 for T-tone finish (frame only).

TAC 11 - .45 ACP cal., 5 in. conical barrel w/o bushing, beavertail grip safety, 8 shot mag., T-tone or blue finish, Novak low profile combat or Tritium sights, black rubber contour grips, 37 oz. Mfg. 1997-98.

	$595	$485	$425	$365	$325	$285	$250

Last MSR was $670.

Add $90 for Tritium sights (disc. 1997).

✳ *Tac 11 Compact* - similar to Tac 11, except has shorter barrel. Mfg. 1998 only.

	$610	$495	$435	$365	$325	$285	$250

Last MSR was $690.

Add $60 for hard-chrome finish.

GOLD SERIES - .45 ACP cal., 5 in. barrel w/o barrel bushing and supported chamber, IPSC configuration with many features, adj. aluminum trigger, front and rear slide serations, stainless steel construction with choice of natural stainless or blue stainless finish. Limited mfg. 1998 only.

	$715	$625	$525

Last MSR was $800.

PISTOLS: SEMI-AUTO, DOUBLE ACTION

The following models had limited manufacture 1998 only.

TAC SERIES SERVICE MODEL - .45 ACP cal., full sized double action service pistol, single/double action, 8 shot single column mag., front and rear slide serations, combat style trigger guard, royal or satin blue finish, low profile 3-dot sights. Mfg. 1998 only.

	$360	$315	$285	$260	$240	$220	$200

Last MSR was $400.

Add $20 for royal blue finish.

TAC SERIES FULL SIZE MODEL - 9mm Para., .40 S&W, or .45 ACP cal., similar to Tac Series Service Model, except longer barrel, checkered walnut or plastic grips, 8 (.45 ACP only) or 10 shot mag. Mfg. 1998 only.

	$360	$315	$285	$260	$240	$220	$200

Last MSR was $400.

Add $20 for royal blue finish.

TAC SERIES COMPACT MODEL - 9mm Para. or .40 S&W cal., shortened barrel/slide with full size frame, 10 shot mag. Mfg. 1998 only.

	$360	$315	$285	$260	$240	$220	$200

Last MSR was $400.

Add $20 for royal blue finish.

TAC SERIES BANTAM MODEL - 9mm Para. or .40 S&W cal., super compact size, single/dou-

Grading	100%	98%	95%	90%	80%	70%	60%

ble action with concealed hammer, all steel construction, 3-dot sights. Mfg. 1998 only.

	100%	98%	95%	90%	80%	70%	60%
	$360	$315	$285	$260	$240	$220	$200

Last MSR was $399.

BANTAM MODEL - 9mm Para. or .40 S&W cal., single or double action, super compact size, concealed hammer, all steel construction, 3-dot sights, royal blue or matte finish. Limited mfg. by FEG 1999 only.

	$360	$315	$285	$260	$240	$220	$200

Last MSR was $399.

PISTOLS: CUSTOM

Brolin Arms manufactured a small quantity of high performance M1911 based custom combat and competition pistols during 1998 only. The Formula Z Model Custom Combat Model retail price range was $1,300-$1,600, the Formula One RS Limited Class Competition Model was priced at $2,000-$2,300, and the Formula One RZ Competition Race Gun Model topped the line at $2,450-$2,750.

SHOTGUNS: SEMI-AUTO

MODEL BL-12 - 12 ga. only, 3 in. chamber, 18½ (security) or 28 (field) in. VR barrel with 3 choke tubes (Beretta compatible), satin blue finish, choice of wood or synthetic stock and forearm. Mfg. 1998 only.

	$375	$325	$300	$280	$260	$240	$220

Last MSR was $430.

MODEL SAS-12 - 12 ga. only, 2¾ in. chamber, 24 in. barrel with IC choke tube, 3 (standard) or 5 shot (disc. late 1998) detachable box mag., synthetic stock and forearm, gas operated. Mfg. 1998-99.

	$445	$385	$335	$300	$280	$260	$240

Last MSR was $499.

Add $39 for extra 3 or 5 (disc.) shot mag.

SHOTGUNS: SLIDE ACTION

Brolin shotguns were manufactured by Hawk Industries.

FIELD SERIES - 12 ga. only, 3 in. chamber, 24, 26, 28, or 30 in. VR barrel with mod. choke tube, steel receiver and aluminum trigger guard, choice of black synthetic or wood stock, bead sights, 5 shot mag., matte finish, 7.3 lbs. Mfg. 1997-98.

	$195	$170	$155	$140	$130	$120	$110

Last MSR was $240.

✳ *Field Combo* - includes choice of extra 12 ga. 18½ or 22 in. barrel, choice of regular or pistol grip stock. Mfg. 1997-98.

	$230	$195	$175	$155	$140	$130	$120

Last MSR was $270.

Add approx. $25 for rifled deer barrel.

LAWMAN MODEL - 12 ga. only, 3 in. chamber, action patterned after the Rem. Model 870 (disc. 1998) or the Ithaca Model 37 (new 1999) 18½ in. barrel, choice of bead, rifle (disc. 1998), or ghost ring (disc. 1998) sights, matte (disc. 1998), nickel (disc. 1997), royal blue (new 1998), satin blue (new 1998) or hard chrome finish, black synthetic or hardwood stock and forearm, 7 lbs. Mfg. in China 1997-99.

	$165	$155	$145	$135	$125	$115	$105

Last MSR was $189.

Add $20 for nickel finish (disc. 1997).
Add $20 for hard chrome finish.

Grading	100%	98%	95%	90%	80%	70%	60%

Add $20 for ghost ring sights.

SLUG SPECIAL - 12 ga. only, 3 in. chamber, choice of 18½ or 22 in. barrel with either rifle sights, ghost ring, or cantilevered scope mount, wood or synthetic stock, choice of fixed IC choke, 4 in. extended rifled choke, or fully rifled barrel, 5 shot mag. Mfg. 1998 only.

	$230	$180	$165	$150	$140	$130	$120

Last MSR was $270.

Add $10 for rifled barrel.
Add $20 for cantilevered scope mount.

SLUGMASTER - 12 ga. only, 3 in. chamber, action patterned after the Model 37 Ithaca, bottom ejection, choice of royal blue metal finish with wood stock or satin blue metal with synthetic stock, rifle sights, mfg. in China. Limited importation 1999 only.

	$165	$155	$145	$135	$125	$115	$105

Last MSR was $189.

TURKEY SPECIAL - 12 ga. only, 3 in. chamber, 22 in. VR barrel with extra-full extended turkey choke, choice of wood or synthetic stock. Mfg. 1998 only.

	$215	$165	$155	$145	$135	$125	$115

Last MSR was $250.

BRONCO

Previous trademark manufactured by Echave Y Arizmendi, located in Eibar, Spain.

PISTOLS: SEMI-AUTO

MODEL 1918 POCKET AUTOMATIC - 7.65mm cal., 6 shot, 2½ in. barrel, fixed sights, blue, hard rubber grips. Mfg. 1918-1925.

	$175	$150	$100	$80	$70	$60	$50

VEST POCKET AUTOMATIC - 6.35mm cal., small frame. Disc.

	$160	$125	$110	$95	$80	$60	$40

DAVID MCKAY BROWN (GUNMAKERS) LTD.

Current long gun manufacturer established in 1967 and located in Bothwell, Glasgow, Scotland. Makers of Scottish Round Action SxS and O/U shotguns and rifles (approx. 30 guns mfg. annually). David McKay Brown apprenticed with Alex Martin Ltd. and John Dickson & Son before establishing his own gunmaking company. All guns made to customer order on round actions. Delivery approximately 20-24 months, depending on the configuration. Available through U.S. agent, Griffin & Howe, New York City and Bernardsville, NJ or the manufacturer directly.

Prices indicated below for manufacturer's suggested retail and 100% condition factors are listed in English pounds. Values for used guns in 98%-60% condition factors are priced in U.S. dollars.

RIFLES: CUSTOM, SxS

David Mckay Brown should be contacted directly for a firm quotation on a SxS double rifle.

SHOTGUNS: CUSTOM

Add £250 for Pistol/Prince of Wales grip.

SxS SHOTGUN - 12, 16, 20, 28 ga., or .410 bore, features rounded case colored action, double

Grading		100%	98%	95%	90%	80%	70%	60%

triggers, full scroll engraving, custom order only.

> **MSR   £26,000**   £26,000 $29,650 $24,000 $19,250 $15,750 $13,000 $11,000
> Add £1,000 for .410 bore.
> Add £750 for single trigger.

O/U SHOTGUN - 12, 16, 20, 28 ga., or .410 bore, features rounded case colored action, double triggers, full scroll engraving, custom order only.

> **MSR   £32,000**   £32,000 $38,000 $32,000 $27,500 $22,500 $18,500 $14,750
> Add £1,000 for .410 bore.
> Add £750 for single trigger.

ED BROWN CUSTOM, INC.

Current rifle manufacturer located in Perry, MO. Direct sales only.

RIFLES: BOLT ACTION

The following MSRs represent each model's base price, with many options available at additional charge.

MODEL 702 BUSHVELD - .338 Win. Mag., .375 H&H, .416 Rem. Mag., or .458 Win. Mag. cal., dangerous game rifle utilizing Ed Brown custom action, match grade 24 in. medium or heavyweight barrel, fiberglass stock with cheekpiece and recoil pad, approx. 8¼ lbs.

> **MSR $2,900** $2,900 $2,400 $1,850 $1,550 $1,250 $995 $750

MODEL 702 SAVANNA - various long and short action cals., hunting rifle utilizing Ed Brown Model 702 custom action, fiberglass stock with steel trigger guard and floor plate, Talley rings and bases, 24 or 26 in. match grade barrel, approx. 8 lbs.

> **MSR $2,800** $2,800 $2,300 $1,775 $1,500 $1,200 $975 $725

MODEL 702 DENALI - various short and long action cals., designed as lightweight mountain hunting rifle, 22 or 23 in. lightweight barrel, glass bedded McMillian sporter stock with checkering and recoil pad, 3 position safety,. 7¾ lbs. New 2002.

> **MSR $2,800** $2,800 $2,300 $1,775 $1,500 $1,200 $975 $725

MODEL 702 OZARK - various cals., lightweight hunting rifle utilizing Ed Brown custom short action, steel trigger guard and floorplate, 3 position safety, checkered lightweight fiberglass stock, match grade, hand lapped 21 in. barrel, approx. 6½ lbs.

> **MSR $2,800** $2,800 $2,300 $1,775 $1,500 $1,200 $975 $725

MODEL 702 VARMINT - various varmint cals., features Ed Brown short single shot action with steel trigger guard and adj. trigger., match grade 24 or 26 (optional) barrel, hand bedded McMillian fiberglass stock and recoil pad, approx. 9 lbs.

> **MSR $2,500** $2,500 $2,150 $1,625 $1,300 $1,050 $825 $700

MODEL 702 LIGHT TACTICAL - .223 Rem. or .308 Win. cal., features Ed Brown short repeater action, aluminum trigger guard and floorplate, 21 in. match grade barrel, includes Talley scope mounts, approx. 8¾ lbs.

> **MSR $2,800** $2,800 $2,300 $1,775 $1,500 $1,200 $975 $775

MODEL 702 TACTICAL - .308 Win. or .300 Win. Mag. cal., top-of-the-line sniper weapon, 26 in. heavyweight match grade hand lapped barrel, McMillian fiberglass A-3 tactical stock, includes Leupold Mark IV scope mounts, 11¼ lbs.

> **MSR $2,900** $2,900 $2,375 $1,825 $1,525 $1,225 $975 $775

MODEL 702 M40A2 MARINE SNIPER - .30-06 or .308 Win. cal., 24 in. match grade barrel, spe-

Grading	100%	98%	95%	90%	80%	70%	60%

cial McMillian GP fiberglass tactical stock with recoil pad, Woodlands camo is molded into stock, this model is a duplicate of the original McMillian Marine Sniper rifle used in Vietnam, except for the Ed Brown action, with Leupold Mark IV scope mounts, 9¼ lbs. New 2002.

MSR $2,900	$2,900	$2,375	$1,825	$1,525	$1,225	$975	$775

ED BROWN PRODUCTS, INC.

Current pistol manufacturer located in Perry, MO. Direct sales only.

PISTOLS: SEMI-AUTO

Add $100 for stainless steel frame and lower parts and $100 for stainless steel slide (new 2002, .45 ACP cal. only) on the following models.

CLASSIC CUSTOM - .45 ACP cal., M1911 style SA, top-of-the-line model with highest level of cosmetic finishing, 5 in. barrel, incorporates all custom Ed Brown features, including slide and frame, all blue or stainless steel frame, Hogue exotic wood checkered grips, adj. Bo-Mar rear sight, custom made per individual order, 39 oz.

MSR $2,895	$2,750	$2,250	$1,725	$1,475	$1,175	$950	$725

CLASS A LIMITED – available in 8 cals., basic custom pistol and features all custom Ed Brown accessories, including slide and frame, 7 shot mag., 4¼ (Commander) or 5 in. barrel length, Hogue exotic grips, 34 or 39 oz.

MSR $2,250	$2,250	$1,900	$1,550	$1,300	$1,050	$825	$700

Add $100 for stainless steel frame and all lower parts.
Add $100 for Novak night sights.

COMMANDER BOBTAIL – various cals., carry configuration, features round butt variation of the Class A Limited frame, incorporating frame and grip modifications, including a special housing w/o checkering, 4¼ in. barrel, Hogue exotic wood grips, 34 oz.

MSR $2,300	$2,300	$1,900	$1,550	$1,325	$1,075	$850	$725

KOBRA – .45 ACP cal., 7 shot, 5 in. barrel, features metal "snakeskin" treatment on frame, mainspring housing and slide, fixed Novak low mount night sights, Hogue exotic wood grips, 39 oz. New 2002.

MSR $1,795	$1,795	$1,500	$1,250	$1,000	$900	$750	$600

KOBRA CARRY – .45 ACP cal., 4¼ in. barrel, features round butt (Bobtail) and metal "snakeskin" treatment on frame, mainspring housing and slide, fixed Novak low mount night sights, 34 oz. New 2002.

MSR $1,995	$1,995	$1,650	$1,300	$1,025	$900	$750	$600

BROWN PRECISION, INC.

Current manufacturer established in 1968, and located in Los Molinos, CA. Previously manufactured in San Jose, CA. Consumer direct sales.

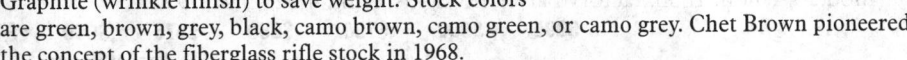

Brown Precision Inc. manufactures rifles primarily using Remington or Winchester actions and restocks them using a combination of Kevlar, Fiberglass and Graphite (wrinkle finish) to save weight. Stock colors are green, brown, grey, black, camo brown, camo green, or camo grey. Chet Brown pioneered the concept of the fiberglass rifle stock in 1968.

Brown Precision is also offering custom hand loaded ammunition for all rifles manufactured by Trophy Ammo of Chico, CA.

PISTOLS: BOLT ACTION

Grading	100%	98%	95%	90%	80%	70%	60%

B

CUSTOM XP-100 HIGH COUNTRY - various cals., includes highly tuned XP-100 single shot action with Shilen stainless match grade barrel, electroless nickel or Teflon finish, fiberglass stock. Limited mfg. 1993-96.

	$1,550	$1,375	$1,150	$950	$775	$650	$525

Last MSR was $1,690.

RIFLES: BOLT ACTION

Brown Precision also manufactures a High Country Rifle from a customer supplied action. This conversion includes a Brown Precision stock, custom glass bedding, recoil pad, stock finish, etc. Prices range from $795-$895.

STANDARD HIGH COUNTRY - various cals. within those factory barreled actions, choice of Rem. 700 ADL/BDL, Model 7, Ruger 77 (disc.), or Win. Model 70 push feed (disc.) or Winchester Model 70 Classic with controlled round feeding action and custom trigger guard, brown fiberglass/Kevlar stock (various colors), electroless nickel or Teflon metal finish, sling swivels and pad. Mfg. 1975-present.

MSR	$2,895	$2,575	$2,000	$1,500	$1,300	$1,075	$950	$775

Add $100 for Rem. 700 BDL or Model 7 action.
Add $300 for stainless steel Rem. 700 BDL action.
Add $400 for Win. Model 70 Classic action with controlled round feeding.
Add $200 for left-hand action.
Subtract $600 if action is supplied by customer.

✳ *Custom High Country ES II* - similar to High Country, except includes cryogenic barrel treatment and speed lock firing pin spring, includes 60 rounds of custom ammo.

MSR	$3,995	$3,400	$2,650	$2,100	$1,725	$1,400	$1,125	$995

Add $100 for Rem. 700 BDL or Model 7 action.
Add $300 for stainless steel Rem. 700 BDL action.
Add $500 for Win. Model 70 Classic action with controlled round feeding.
Add $300 for left-hand action.
Subtract $700 if action is supplied by customer.

HIGH COUNTRY YOUTH RIFLE - various cals., choice of Rem. Model 7 or 700 factory barreled action, fiberglass stock. Mfg. 1993-2000.

	$1,250	$1,050	$825	$700	$550	$495	$440

Last MSR was $1,435.

Add $145 for lengthening stock.

BROWN PRECISION WINCHESTER 70 - .270 Win. or .30-06 cal., 22 in. featherweight barrel, camo stock in four colors with black recoil pad, 6¼ lbs. Mfg. 1989-92.

	$650	$575	$475	$425	$385	$325	$300

Last MSR was $750.

Add $20 for 7mm Rem. Mag. (24 in. sporter barrel).

BLASER BOLT ACTION RIFLE - standard Camex Blaser cals. and action, fiberglass stock and nickel plated barrel. Disc. 1989.

	$1,395	$1,150	$995	$875	$750	$675	$600

Last MSR was $1,395.

MODEL 7 SUPER LIGHT - .223 Rem., .243 Win., 6mm Rem., 7mm-08 Rem., or .308 Win. cal., Model 7 action, 18 in. factory barrel, no sights, 5 lbs. 4 oz. Disc. 1992.

	$995	$900	$750	$650	$575	$500	$450

Last MSR was $1,059.

This model could have been special ordered with similar options from the Custom High Country Model, with the exception of left-hand action.

LAW ENFORCEMENT SELECTIVE TARGET - .308 Win. cal., Model 700 Varmint action with 20,

Grading	100%	98%	95%	90%	80%	70%	60%

22, or 24 in. factory barrel, O.D. green camouflage treatment. Disc. 1992.

$995	**$900**	**$750**	**$650**	**$575**	**$500**	**$450**

Last MSR was $1,086.

This model could have been special ordered with similar options from the Custom High Country Model, with the exception of left-hand action.

TACTICAL ELITE - various cals. and custom features, customized per individual order. New 1997.

MSR	$3,395	$2,925	$2,250	$1,775	$1,500	$1,250	$995	$825

Add $545 for 3 way adj. buttplate.
Subtract $600 if action is supplied by customer.

PRO VARMINTER - various cals., includes custom tuned Rem. Model 700 ADL action, Shilen match stainless steel barrel. New 1993.

MSR	$2,595	$2,275	$1,750	$1,375	$1,075	$850	$750	$650

Add $300 for left-hand action.
Add $700 for optional Rem. Model 40-XB action with target trigger.
Subtract $600 if action is supplied by customer.

PRO HUNTER - available in over 25 cals., Model 700 ADL action is standard, match grade stainless steel barrel, dull electroless nickel, blue, or teflon finish, express sights, synthetic stock (four different colors). New 1988.

MSR	$3,595	$3,050	$2,350	$1,825	$1,525	$1,275	$1,075	$875

Add $300 for left-hand action.
Subtract $600 if action is supplied by customer.

✱ *Pro Hunter Elite* - various cals., custom tuned Winchester Model 70 Super Grade action with controlled feed claw extractor, includes many custom order features. New 1993.

MSR	$4,595	$4,075	$3,400	$2,700	$2,250	$1,875	$1,650	$1,350

Add $695 for drop box trigger guard (allows additonal round in mag.).
Subtract $600 if action is supplied by customer.

In late 1991, improvements were made including decelerator recoil pad, barrel band swivel, and speed lock firing pin spring.

THE UNIT - .270 Win., .300 Win. Mag., .300 Wby. Mag., .338 Win. Mag., 7mm-08 Rem., 7mm Rem. Mag., or 7mm STW cal., Rem. 700 BDL or Win. Mod. 70 controlled feed action, various lengths match grade stainless steel barrel with cryogenic treatment, Teflon or electroless nickel finish, Brown Precision Kevlar or graphite reinforced fiberglass stock, include 60 rounds of custom ammo. Limited mfg. 2001 only.

$3,225	**$2,500**	**$2,000**	**$1,650**	**$1,350**	**$1,125**	**$995**

Last MSR was $3,795.

Add $500 for Win. Model 70 Super Grade action with controlled round feeding.
Add $200 for left-hand action.
Subtract $600 if action is supplied by customer.

SUPER BOLT RIMFIRE - .22 LR or .22 Mag. cal., modified Ruger 77/22 action, 20 in. heavy Shilen match grade steel or stainless steel barrel, extended mag. release, choice of lightweight fiberglass or Kevlar stock, blue or silver metal finish, 6½ lbs.

MSR	$1,795	$1,525	$1,150	$900	$800	$675	$600	$550

Add $100 for stainless steel barrel.
Add $200 for stainless steel action & barrel.

RIFLES: SEMI-AUTO

Grading	100%	98%	95%	90%	80%	70%	60%

B CUSTOM TEAM CHALLENGER - .22 LR cal., modified Ruger 10/22 action, 20 in. heavy Shilen match grade steel or stainless steel barrel, extended mag. release, choice of lightweight fiberglass or Kevlar stock, blue or silver metal finish.

MSR	$1,495		$1,275	$1,025	$800	$650	$525	$440	$400

Add $100 for stainless steel barrel.
Add $200 for stainless steel barrel & action.

BROWNING

Current manufacturer with headquarters located in Morgan, UT. Browning guns originally were manufactured in Ogden, UT, circa 1880. Browning firearms are manufactured by Fabrique Nationale in Herstal and Liege, Belgium. Since 1976, Browning has also contracted Miroku of Japan and A.T.I. in Salt Lake City, UT to manufacture both long arms and handguns. In 1992, Browning (including F.N.) was acquired by GIAT of France. During late 1997, the French government received $82 million for the sale of F.N. Herstal from the Walloon business region surrounding Fabrique Nationale in Belgium.

The category names within the Browning section have been arranged in an alphabetical format: - PISTOLS (& variations), RIFLES (& variations), SHOTGUNS (& variations), SPECIAL EDITIONS, COMMEMORATIVES & LIMITED MFG.

The author would like to express his sincere thanks to the Browning Collector's Association, including members Anthony Vanderlinden, Richard Spurzem, Jim King, Bert O'Neill, Jr., and Rodney Herrmann for continuing to make their important contributions to the Browning section.

BROWNING HISTORY

The Browning firm, first known as J.M. Browning & Bro., was established in Ogden, Utah about 1880. Later known as Browning Brothers and Browning Arms Company (BAC), the firm actually manufactured only one gun - the Model 1878 Single Shot which was John M.'s first patent. Winchester bought the production and distribution rights to this gun in 1883, bringing it out as the Winchester M1885. From that time until 1900, Mr. Browning sold Winchester the exclusive rights to 31 rifles and 13 shotguns, of which Winchester produced only 7 rifles (M1885SS: the lever actions M1886, 1892, 1894 and 1895: and the slide action .22s M1890 and 1906) and 3 shotguns (M1887, M1893 and M1897). The other models were bought from Browning simply to keep them out of the hands of other arms makers.

John M. Browning, perhaps the greatest firearms inventor the world has ever known, was directly responsible for an estimated 80 separate firearms that evolved from his 128 patents. During his most prolific period from 1894 to 1910, Browning sold the rights to his rifles, semi-auto pistols, shotguns and machine guns to Winchester, Remington, Colt and Stevens in this country and to Fabrique Nationale (Belgium) for sale outside the U.S. Every Colt and F.N. semi-auto pistol is based on a Browning patent. In 1902, Browning broke off relations with Winchester when the company refused to negotiate a royalty arrangement for his new semi-auto shotgun(A-5). Browning took the prototype to F.N. where it became the most commercially successful of all his inventions. F.N. has produced numerous automatic pistols, 3 rifles and 2 shotguns designed by John M. Browning and is still a major producer of arms sold by Browning in the U.S. and by F.N. distributors worldwide.

Our American military was armed for many years with Browning designed weaponry, not the least of which is the venerable "Old Slabside" 1911 Govt. Model .45 ACP. Today, the firm that bears the Browning name still stands at the forefront with the other makers of fine sporting firearms.

BROWNING

Grading	100%	98%	95%	90%	80%	70%	60%

BROWNING FACTS

Note: Between 1966-1971 Browning used a salt-curing process to speed the drying time needed for their walnut stock blanks. Unfortunately, the salt would be released from the wood and oxidize the metal surface(s) after a period of time. These guns, especially bolt action rifles in all grades, some BARs, Superposed shotguns, and T-bolt models should be examined carefully around the edges of the wood for signs of freckling and rust. Discount values on guns which show tell-tale characteristics of salt corrosion 15%-50%, depending on how bad rusting has occurred. Check screws and wood under butt plate as well. Original Superposed owners of salt wood guns who still have their warranty card are still eligible for Browning factory refurbishing of affected parts only without charge. Otherwise, Browning has a standardized charge for each model.

Since the inception and standardization of steel shot for hunting purposes, the desirability factor of shotguns has changed considerably. On newer manufacture, choke tubes have become very desirable, and specimens without choke tubes (especially guns with longer barrels) must be discounted somewhat. Browning does not recommend using steel shot in any Superposed (B-25) or older Belgian Auto-5 barrels.

BROWNING VALUES INFORMATION

Editor's Note: It is important to note the differences in values of Browning firearms manufactured in Belgium by F.N. and those made recently in Japan by Miroku. We feel that these values are somewhat higher because of collector interest in Belgian guns, and not as the result of any inferiority of the quality of Browning guns made anywhere else.

AS A FINAL NOTE: Most post-war Brownings are collectible only if in 95% or better condition as most models have relatively high mfg. and are not that old. Condition under 95% is normally very shootable, but not as collectible and values for 95% or less condition could be lower than shown in some areas.

All add-ons or deductions on Browning's currently manufactured models reflect retail pricing without any discounting. On higher grade Browning firearms that are engraved, signed specimens by FN's master engravers Funken, J. Baerten, Vrancken, and Watrin will command premiums over the values listed.

BROWNING SERIALIZATION

In addition to the Browning serialization listed in the back of this text, the following codes will determine the year and origin of those guns made from 1975 to date. The 2 letters in the middle of the serial number are the code designations for year of manufacture. They represent the following: RV - 1975, RT - 1976, RR - 1977, RP - 1978, RN - 1979, PM - 1980, PZ - 1981, PY - 1982, PX - 1983, PW - 1984, PV - 1985, PT -1986, PR - 1987, PP - 1988, PN - 1989, NM - 1990, NZ - 1991, NY - 1992, NX - 1993, NW - 1994, NV - 1995, NT - 1996, NR - 1997, NP - 1998, NN - 1999, MM - 2000, MZ - 2001, MY - 2002, MX - 2003.

Since most Brownings use a 3-digit model identification code (appearing first on European or U.S. mfg. guns and last on Japanese mfg.), both where and when the specimen was made can easily be determined (i.e. Ser. No. 611RP2785 would be a Model B-2000 made in Belgium, and assembled in Portugal during 1978 with 2785 being the Ser. No.- Ser. No. 01479PX368 indicates a BSS 20 ga. mfg. in Japan in 1983).

BROWNING CUSTOM SHOP

Browning's Custom Shop in Herstal, Belgium, continues to make a wide variety of firearms, a number of which have limited importation into the U.S. Current Custom Shop Superposed prices and model information have been provided in the Superposed section. For more information on the Browning Custom Shop's additional offerings (including the A-5, BMS bolt action, BMM, SxSs, BARs, semi-auto .22, and the G.P., please contact Browning directly (see Trademark Index).

PISTOLS: SEMI-AUTO, F.N. PRODUCTION UNLESS OTHERWISE NOTED

Grading	100%	98%	95%	90%	80%	70%	60%

B

MODEL 1899-FN - 7.65mm cal., first Belgian Browning, 4 in. barrel, similar to later M- 1900 but w/o safety markings or lanyard rings, serial range 1-10,000, 10,000 mfg. 1899- 1901.

	$695	$645	$600	$500	$450	$400	$350

Add 15% for guns manufactured in 1899 (ser. nos. 1-3900).
Add 50% for factory nickel finish (nickel finish with blue trigger and blue safety lever) – if 95% condition or better.
Add $400 for factory presentation case with accessories.

MODEL 1900-FN - 7.65mm cal., 4 in. barrel. 724,500 mfg. 1900-1914.

	$450	$375	$300	$250	$175	$125	$100

Add 50% for factory nickel finish (nickel finish with blue trigger and safety lever) – if 95% condition or better.
Add $400 for factory presentation case with accessories.
Add $500 for Imperial Russian contract (crossed rifles marking on blue or nickel guns).
Add $100 for Imperial German contracts with German safety markings (Feuer & Sicher).
Add $100 minimum for special contract markings.

MODEL 1903-FN - 9mm Browning Long cal., 5 in. barrel. 58,400 mfg. 1903-1927.

	$600	$500	$425	$375	$325	$275	$225

Add 50% if slotted to accept shoulder stock - beware of fakes.
Add $150 minimum for special contract markings.

This variation was also manufactured with a detachable shoulder stock. This accessory is rare and can add $1,000-$1,250 (shoulder stock w/o extended magazine) or $1,650-$1,850 (shoulder stock with extended magazine) to the values listed.

MODEL 1903-SWEDISH CONTRACT - 9mm Browning Long cal., manufactured by Husqvarna, many were imported into U.S. and converted to .380 ACP from original Browning 9mm Long.

	$350	$300	$240	$220	$195	$175	$150

Add 40% for factory blue finish.
Subtract 30% for .380 ACP conversion.

MODEL 1905-FN (VEST POCKET) - 6.35mm cal. (.25 ACP), dubbed "Vest Pocket" model, 2 in. barrel, manufactured by Fabrique Nationale, Herstal, Belgium. 1,086,133, mfg. 1906-1959.

✳ *First Variation* - no slide lock/safety lever.

	$475	$425	$375	$325	$275	$225	$175

Add 50% for factory nickel finish (nickel finish with blue trigger and blue safety lever) – if 95% condition or better.
Add $200 for factory presentation case.
Add $500 for Imperial Russian contract (crossed rifles marking on blue or nickel guns).

✳ *Second Variation* - post 1908, with slide lock/safety lever.

	$395	$325	$275	$225	$175	$125	$100

Add 50% for factory nickel finish (nickel finish with blue trigger and blue safety lever) – if 95% condition or better.
Add $200 for factory presentation case.
Add $500 for Imperial Russian contract (crossed rifles marking on blue or nickel guns).
Add $100 minimum for special contract markings.

MODEL 1910-FN (MODEL 1955) - 7.65mm (.32 ACP) or Browning 9mm short (.380 ACP) cal., 4 in. barrel. FN manufacture. 701,266 mfg. 1912-1980.

	$350	$325	$300	$275	$250	$195	$150

Add 20% if BAC marked and 7.65mm cal., or if FN marked and .380 ACP cal.
Add $100 minimum for special contract markings.

This model is also referred to as the Model 1910/55. BAC marked pistols were imported 1954-1968. Importation ceased after the 1968 GCA.

Grading	100%	98%	95%	90%	80%	70%	60%

MODEL 1922 OR 10/22 FN - 7.65mm (.32 ACP) or .380 ACP cal., modified Model 1910 with 4½ in. barrel, longer grip frame and mag., made for commercial sale as well as military and police contracts. Several hundred thousand made by Nazis during the occupation of Liege, Belgium 1940-1944. Mfg. between 1922-1983.

	$275	$250	$200	$175	$150	$125	$110

Add 150% if .380 ACP Waffenamt proofed.
Add 15% for A prefix serial number.
Add $100 minimum for special contract markings.

The Model 10/22 and M1922 are the same pistol. The Model 1910 was modified by FN technicians for sale to Serbian armed forces in 1923. Also sold to France, Holland, Germany, Greece, Turkey, and other countries.

FN "BABY" MODEL - 6.35mm (.25 ACP) cal., 2 in. barrel, lighter, smaller modification of Browning Model 1905 Vest Pocket, w/o grip safety or separate slide lock lever, imported under BAC trademark from 1954-1968+ in standard blue finish, lightweight nickel and alumnium frame, and engraved Renaissance models. Over 510,000 mfg. 1931- 1983.

* *FN Marked* - slide marked Fabrique Nationale, blue finish standard.

	$500	$440	$375	$295	$225	$200	$150

Add $100 for original cardboard or plastic box with extras.

* *BAC Marked* - slide marked Browning Arms Co., blue finish standard.

	$325	$275	$225	$195	$180	$165	$150

Add 20% if coin finished.
Add $50-$100 for original box or manual, or $25-$50 for original BAC pouch and manual.

* *Lightweight Model* - nickel or aluminum (introduced 1954) frame, with pearl grips.

	$450	$365	$325	$280	$245	$225	$200

* *Renaissance Model* - engraved, satin grey finish.

	$975	$750	$550				

FN/BROWNING MODEL 10/71 - .380 ACP cal., 4½ in. barrel, modified version of Model 1922 (10/22)in .380 ACP cal., grip safety, includes target sights and grips in addition to incorporating a magazine finger tip extension designed to comply with GCA of 1968. Sold in U.S. by BAC 1970-1974 as the "Standard .380", still mfg. by FN as Model 125.

	$395	$300	$250	$220	$205	$190	$160

* *Renaissance Model*

	$975	$775	$625				

MODEL 1935 HI-POWER - 9mm Para. cal., 13 shot mag., 4 21/32 in. barrel, Browning's last pistol design, over one million mfg. 1935 to date in variations for commercial, military, and police use in over 68 countries, first imported under BAC trademark in 1954.

Please refer to the Fabrique Nationale section of this book for pre-1954 variations (including pre-WWII, WWII, and earlier commercial models), as well as contemporary production of those variations not imported by BAC.

HI-POWER: POST-1954 MFG. - 9mm Para. or .40 S&W (new 1995) cal., similar to FN model 1935, has BAC slide marking, 10 (C/B 1994) or 13* shot mag., 4¾ in. barrel, polished blue finish, checkered walnut grips, fixed sights, molded grips were introduced in 1986 (disc. in 2000), ambidextrous safety was added to all models in 1989, approx. 32 (9mm Para.) or 35 (.40 S&W) oz., mfg. by FN in Belgium, imported 1954-2000, reintroduced 2002.

* *Polished Blue Finish* - includes fixed sights

MSR $694		$560	$440	$375	$325	$300	$275	$250

Grading	100%	98%	95%	90%	80%	70%	60%

Subtract $30 for molded grips (disc. 1990).
Add 25% for ring hammer and internal extractor.
Add 10% for ring hammer and external (more recent) extractor.

Major identifying factors of the Hi-Power are as follows: the "Thumb-Print" feature was mfg. from the beginning (including FN mfg.) through 1958. Old style internal extractor was mfg. from the beginning (including FN mfg.) through 1962, the "T" SN prefix (T-Series start visible extractor) was mfg. 1963-mid-1970s for all U.S. imports by BAC, 69C through 77C SN prefixes were mfg. 1969-1977. Rounded type Ring Hammers with new external extractor were mfg. from 1962-1972 (for U.S. imports by BAC, much later on FN marked pistols). Spur Hammers are mfg. 1972-present, and the "245" SN prefix has been mfg. 1977-present. Some "215" ser. no. prefixes are scarce, and seldom encountered.

Older specimens in original black, maroon, or red/black plastic boxes were mfg. 1954-1965 and are very scarce - add $100+ in value. Black pouches (circa 1965-1968, especially with gold metal zipper) will also command a $25-$50 premium, depending on condition.

＊ *Adj. sights*

MSR	$745	$590	$450	$385	$345	$310	$290	$265

＊ *Mark III Matte Blue Finish* - 9mm Para. or .40 S&W (mfg. 1994-2000) cal., non-glare matte finish, ambidextrous safety, tapered dovetail rear fixed sight, two-piece molded grips, Mark III designation became standard in 1994, approx. 35 oz. Imported 1985-2000, reintroduced 2002.

MSR	$675	$540	$395	$340	$290	$270	$250	$230

This model's finish may be confused with some recent imports which have a "black" finish. These black finish guns are painted rather than blue, and some parties have been selling them as original military FNs. Do not confuse these painted specimens for original pistols and remember, original guns will be worth more than refinished pistols. Also, beware of 9mm Para. cal. pistols manufactured in Argentina under F.N. license.

＊ *Silver Chrome Finish* - 9mm Para. or .40 S&W (new 1995) cal., entire gun finished in silver chrome, includes adj. sights and Pachmayr rubber grips, 36 (9mm Para.) or 39 (.40 S&W) oz. Assembled in Portugal, and imported 1991-2000.

		$570	$435	$370	$330	$300	$280	$255

Add 50% for circa 1980 Belgian model marked "Made in Belgium".

Last MSR was $718.

＊ *Practical Model* - 9mm Para. or .40 S&W (new 1995) cal., features blue slide, silver-chromed frame finish, wraparound Pachmayr rubber grips, round style serrated hammer, and choice of adj. sights (new 1993) or removable front sight, 36 (9mm Para.) or 39 (.40 S&W) oz. Imported 1990-2000, reintroduced 2002.

MSR	$731	$570	$435	$375	$340	$310	$290	$265

Add $58 for adj. sights (disc. 2000).

＊ *Nickel/Silver Chrome finish* - not to be confused with stainless steel (never offered in the Hi-Power), this nickel/silver chrome finish is different from the silver chrome finish released in 1991. Disc. 1985.

		$695	$550	$425	$375	$360	$340	$315

Add 50% for circa 1980 Belgian model marked "Made in Belgium".

Last MSR was $525.

＊ *.30 Luger Hi-Power* - .30 Luger cal., mfg. for European sales (most are marked BAC on slide), approx. 1,500 imported late 1986-89, similar specifications as 9mm Para. model.

		$675	$575	$450	$400	$365	$345	$315

This model was never cataloged for sale by BAC in the U.S. A few earlier specimens have been noted with F.N. markings and ring hammer.

＊ *GP Competition* - 9mm Para. cal., competition model with 6 in. barrel, detent adj. rear sight, rubber wraparound grips, front counterweight, improved barrel bushing,

Grading	100%	98%	95%	90%	80%	70%	60%

decreased trigger pull, approx. 36½ oz.

| | $950 | $850 | $650 | $500 | $425 | $375 | $325 |

The original GP Competition came in a black plastic case w/accesories and is more desirable than later imported specimens which were computer serial numbered and came in a styrofoam box. Above prices are for older models - subtract 10% if newer model (computer serial numbered). This model was never cataloged for sale by BAC in the U.S., and it is not serviced by Browning.

* ***Tangent Rear Sight*** - 9mm Para. cal., manufactured from 1965-1978. Adj. rear sight to 500 meters. A total of approx. 7,000 were imported by Browning Arms Co. Early pistols are designated by "T" prefix and were mfg. 1964-69, later pistols mfg. 1972-76 had spur hammers and followed the 69C-76C ser. no. prefixes.

| | $775 | $650 | $550 | $450 | $400 | $370 | $340 |

Add $100 for "T" prefix.
Add $50 for original pouch and instruction manual.

* ***Tangent Capitan Polished Blue Finish*** - 9mm Para. cal., features 50-500 meter tangent rear sight, blue finish with walnut grips, 32 oz. Imported 1993-2000.

| | $610 | $500 | $400 | $350 | $300 | $280 | $260 |

Last MSR was $764.

* ***Tangent Rear Sight & Slotted*** - 9mm Para. cal., variation with grip strap slotted to accommodate shoulder stock. Early pistols had "T" prefixes. Later pistols had spur hammers and are in the serial range 73CXXXX-74CXXXX.

| | $1,250 | $975 | $775 | $650 | $525 | $440 | $400 |

Add $150 if with "T" prefix.
Add $50 for original pouch and instruction booklet.

This variation will command a premium; beware of fakes, however (carefully examine slot milling and look for ser. no. in 3 places).

BCA EDITION HI-POWER - 9mm Para. cal., limited edition made specifically for the Browning Collectors Association in 1980, approx. 100 were delivered.

| | $700 | $575 | $475 |

GOLD LINE HI-POWER - 9mm Para. cal., blue finish with gold line perimeter engraving.

| | $5,000 | $3,500 | $2,500 |

Add 10% for Ring Hammer - check carefully for factory originality.

RENAISSANCE HI-POWER - 9mm Para. cal., extensive scroll engraving on grey silver receiver, synthetic pearl grips, gold plated trigger. Disc. approx. 1978.

| Round Hammer/fixed sights | $1,425 | $1,025 | $825 |
| Spur Hammer/fixed sights | $1,300 | $950 | $775 |

Add $200 for internal extractor.
Add $100 for "Thumb Print".
Add $50-$100 for original pouch and booklet.
Add $500 for older individual blue leatherette European case.
Add $300-$500 for coin finish, depending on condition.

Target sights do not affect the value of this model significantly.

CASED GRADE I (BLUE) SET - one pistol each in .25 ACP, .380 ACP, and 9mm Para. cal., Hi-Power Grade I Models in walnut or black vinyl case, serial numbers not related to other calibers.

| | $1,500 | $1,250 | $895 |

Add $100 for walnut presentation case.

All original Grade I blue cased sets had a Ring Hammer 9mm Para. Hi-Power.

CASED RENAISSANCE SET - one pistol each in .25 ACP, .380 ACP, and 9mm Para. cal., Hi-Power Renaissance models in walnut or black vinyl case, serial numbers not related to

Grading	100%	98%	95%	90%	80%	70%	60%

other calibers. Offered 1954- 1969.

	$3,750	$3,100	$2,250

Add 20% for coin finish in early walnut case.

All original Renaissance cased sets had a Ring Hammer 9mm Para. Hi-Power.

CENTENNIAL MODEL HI-POWER - similar to fixed sight Hi-Power, chrome plated with inscription "Browning Centennial/ 1878-1978", engraved on side, cased, 3,500 mfg. in 1978. Original issue price was $495.

	$825	$650	$450

CENTENAIRRE MODEL HI-POWER 1 OF 100 - 9mm Para. cal., unique pattern chemically etched, checkered walnut grips with border. 100 mfg. during 1989 – approx. half were sold in U.S., the other half in Europe.

	$3,500	$2,750	$2,000

LOUIS XVI MODEL - 9mm Para., chemically etched throughout in leaf scroll patterns, satin finish, checkered grips, walnut case. Disc. 1984.

	$995	$850	$625

Add 5% for adj. sights.

CLASSIC HI-POWER SERIES - 9mm Para. cal., less than 2,500 manufactured in Classic model and under 350 manufactured in Gold Classic. Both editions feature multiple engraved scenes, and a special silver grey finish, presentation grips, cased. Mfg. 1984-86.

	$950	$675	$495

Last MSR was $1,000.

* ***Gold Classic Hi-Power*** - 5 gold inlays, select walnut grips are both checkered and carved. Less than 500 mfg. 1984- 86.

	$1,850	$1,500	$1,150

Last MSR was $2,000.

BROWNING DOUBLE ACTION - this model was first listed in the Browning catalog in 1985 but was never imported commercially. The advertised 1985 retail price was $494.

BDM/BPM/BRM SINGLE/DOUBLE ACTION - 9mm Para. cal., double mode design featuring slide selector allowing choice between pistol (true double action operation) or revolver mode (full hammer decocking after each shot), available in double mode, single mode (BPM-D decocker, mfg. 1997), or double action only (BRM-DAO, mfg. 1997), dual purpose decocking lever/safety, 4.73 in. barrel, 10 (C/B 1994) or 15* shot mag., matte blue finish, black molded wraparound grips, unique breech block allows visible cartridge inspection, adj. rear sight, 31 oz, mfg. in U.S. 1991-97.

$465	$395	$365	$330	$300	$280	$260

Last MSR was $551.

This model features hammer block and firing pin block safeties.

* ***BDM Practical*** - similar to Standard BDM, except has matte blue slide and silver chrome frame. Mfg. 1997-98.

$480	$400	$365	$330	$300	$280	$260

Last MSR was $571.

* ***BDM Silver Chrome*** - similar to Standard BDM, except has silver chrome finish. Only 119 mfg. in 1997 only.

$480	$400	$365	$330	$300	$280	$260

Last MSR was $571.

FN DA 9 - 9mm Para. cal., choice of double action or double action only, 4 5/8 in. barrel, molded rubber grips, 10 shot mag., 31 oz. Mfg. by FN. While advertised in 1996, this

Grading	100%	98%	95%	90%	80%	70%	60%

model was never imported commercially - the retail price was listed at $613.

BDA-380 - .380 ACP cal., double action, 10 (C/B 1994) or 14* shot, 3 13/16 in. barrel, fixed sights, smooth walnut grips, 23 oz., introduced 1978 - recent production was by Beretta. Disc. 1997.

	100%	98%	95%	90%	80%	70%	60%
	$450	$345	$260	$220	$175	$150	$125
					Last MSR was $564.		
Nickel finish	$480	$360	$275	$230	$180	$150	$125
					Last MSR was $607.		

BDA MODEL - 9mm Para. (9 shot, 2,740 mfg.), .38 Super (752 mfg.), or .45 ACP (7 shot) cal., mfg. from 1977-1980 by Sig-Sauer of W. Germany (same as Sig-Sauer 220).

	100%	98%	95%	90%	80%	70%	60%
9mm Para.	$550	$450	$375	$295	$250	$225	$200
.38 Super	$650	$575	$495	$450	$390	$350	$300
.45 ACP	$550	$450	$375	$295	$250	$225	$200

NOMAD MODEL - .22 LR cal., 10 shot, 4½ and 6¾ in. barrels, steel or alloy frame, adj. sights, blue finish, black plastic grips. Mfg. 1962-1974 by FN.

	100%	98%	95%	90%	80%	70%	60%
	$295	$245	$185	$140	$125	$100	$85

Add 10% for alloy frame.

CHALLENGER MODEL - .22 LR cal., 10 shot, 4½ and 6¾ in. barrels, steel frame, adj. sights, checkered walnut or plastic (mfg. 1974 only) wraparound grips, gold plated trigger. Mfg. 1962-1975 by FN.

	100%	98%	95%	90%	80%	70%	60%
	$375	$315	$265	$215	$190	$170	$155

Add 10% for late production plastic grips.

✳ *Renaissance* - engraved satin nickel finish.

	100%	98%	95%
	$1,450	$1,250	$850

✳ *Gold Line* - blue finish, gold lining on perimeter of frame surfaces.

	100%	98%	95%
	$1,450	$1,250	$850

CHALLENGER II - .22 LR cal., Salt Lake City mfg., 6 ¾ in. barrel, steel frame, plastic impregnated hardwood grips, 38 oz. Mfg. 1975-1982.

	100%	98%	95%	90%	80%	70%	60%
	$230	$180	$170	$145	$135	$120	$110

✳ *Challenger II BCA Commemorative* - .22 LR cal., mfg. to commemorate BCA's fourth anniversary.

	100%	98%	95%
	$295	$240	$175

CHALLENGER III - .22 LR cal., Salt Lake City mfg., 5½ in. bull barrel, 11 shot, alloy frame, adj. sights, 35 oz. Mfg. 1982-1985.

	100%	98%	95%	90%	80%	70%	60%
	$220	$190	$170	$145	$135	$120	$110
					Last MSR was $240.		

CHALLENGER III SPORTER - similar to Challenger III, except 6¾ in. round barrel, wide trigger, 29 oz. Mfg. 1982-85.

	100%	98%	95%	90%	80%	70%	60%
	$220	$190	$170	$145	$135	$120	$110
					Last MSR was $240.		

MEDALIST MODEL - .22 LR cal., 6¾ in. barrel, vent. rib, adj. target sights and barrel weights (3 supplied), blue finish, target walnut grips with thumbrest, dry-fire mechanism, 46 oz.,

Grading	100%	98%	95%	90%	80%	70%	60%

cased. Mfg. 1964-1975 by FN.

	$850	$700	$595	$500	$425	$375	$325

Subtract 15% if without case and accessories.

Gold Line (407 mfg. 1963)	$1,950	$1,400	$950				
Renaissance Model	$2,350	$1,750	$1,250				

A total of 337 were mfg. by FN 1964-82.

BAC Edition

Engraved (60 mfg.)	$2,450	$1,900	$1,400				

INTERNATIONAL MEDALIST - target variation model manufactured 1977-80, 5.9 in. barrel, only 681 made with BAC markings and blue finish. Currently manufactured by FN in the parkerized international configuration.

	$615	$535	$475	$410	$350	$300	$275
Early Model	$795	$625	$550	$425	$360	$330	$280

BUCK MARK STANDARD .22 - .22 LR cal., 11 shot, 5½ in. bull barrel, composite grips with skipline checkering (disc. 1990) or molded rubber grips (new 1991), adj. sights, gold trigger, matte blue finish, 34- 36 oz. New 1985.

MSR	**$292**	$215	$175	$150	$125	$110	$100	$90

Add $53 for nickel finish (new 1991).

Buck Mark models are manufactured in Salt Lake City, UT.

* ***Buck Mark Micro Standard*** - similar to Buck Mark Standard, except has 4 in. barrel, choice of standard or nickel finish, 32 oz. New 1992.

MSR	**$292**	$215	$175	$150	$125	$110	$100	$90

Add $53 for nickel finish.

* ***Buck Mark Micro Plus*** - similar to Micro Buck Mark, except has ambidextrous contoured laminated wood grips, nickel (new 1996) or blue finish. Disc. 2001.

	$265	$210	$155	$135	$120	$110	$100

Last MSR was $350.

Add $33 for nickel finish.

* ***Buck Mark Challenge*** - features smaller grip circumference for smaller hands, smooth walnut grips with medallions, matte blue finish, 5½ in. lightweight barrel, Pro-Target sights, 25 oz. New 1999.

MSR	**$326**	$245	$190	$150	$120	$110	$100	$90

* ***Buck Mark Micro Challenge*** - similar to Buck Mark Challenge, except has 4 in. barrel. 23 oz. Mfg. 1999-2000.

	$230	$180	$140	$120	$110	$100	$90

Last MSR was $311.

* ***Buck Mark Camper*** - features 5½ in. heavy barrel, ambidextrous molded black composite grips, matte blue or satin nickel finish, Pro-Target sights, 34 oz. New 1999.

MSR	**$263**	$205	$165	$135	$115	$100	$95	$85

Add $30 for satin nickel finish.

* ***Buck Mark Plus*** - similar to Buck Mark Standard, except has uncheckered laminated wood grips, Tru- Glo Marble front sight (new 2002), and choice of high polish blue or nickel (new 1996), 34 oz. New 1987.

MSR	**$357**	$270	$210	$160	$135	$120	$110	$100

Add $34 for nickel finish.

* ***Buck Mark Classic Plus*** - similar to Buck Mark Plus, except has rosewood grips and Tru-

Grading	100%	98%	95%	90%	80%	70%	60%

Glo Marble front sight. New 2002.

| | MSR | $357 | $270 | $210 | $160 | $135 | $120 | $110 | $100 |

This model is available from Full-Line dealers only.

* **Buck Mark Bullseye Standard** - similar to Buck Mark Bullseye Target, except has molded composite ambidextrous grips, 36 oz. New 1996.

| | MSR | $428 | | $325 | $265 | $210 | $170 | $150 | $135 | $120 |

* **Buck Mark Bullseye Target** - Bullseye model featuring 16 click per turn Pro-Target rear sight, 7¼ in. fluted barrel, matte blue finish, adj. trigger pull, contoured rosewood target or wraparound finger groove (disc.) grips, 10 shot mag., 36 oz. New 1996.

| | MSR | $552 | | $400 | $300 | $240 | $190 | $165 | $140 | $125 |

* **Buck Mark 5.5 Field** - same action and barrel as the Target 5.5, except sights are designed for field use, anodized blue finish, contoured walnut grips, choice of contoured walnut or walnut wraparound finger groove grips (new 1992-disc.), 35½ oz. New 1991.

| | MSR | $468 | | $350 | $280 | $230 | $190 | $160 | $140 | $125 |

* **Buck Mark 5.5 Target** - same action as Buck Mark, 5½ in. barrel with serrated top rib allowing adj. sight positioning, target sights, matte blue finish, choice of contoured walnut or walnut wraparound finger groove grips (new 1992-disc.), 35 oz. New 1990.

| | MSR | $468 | | $350 | $280 | $230 | $190 | $160 | $140 | $125 |

Add $54 for nickel finish (mfg. 1994-2000).

* **Buck Mark 5.5 Gold Target** - similar to 5.5 Target, except has gold anodized frame and top rib. Mfg. 1991-99.

| | | | $355 | $275 | $220 | $180 | $160 | $140 | $125 |

Last MSR was $477.

* **Buck Mark Commemorative** - features 6¾ in. Challenger style tapered barrel, white bonded ivory grips with scrimshaw style patterning including "1 of 1,000 Commemorative Model" on sides, matte blue finish, gold trigger, 30 ½ oz. 1,000 mfg. 2001 only.

| | | | $335 | $275 | $225 | | | | |

Last MSR was $437.

* **Buck Mark Varmint** - same action as Buck Mark, 9 7/8 in. barrel with serrated top rib allowing adj. sight positioning, laminated wood grips, choice of contoured walnut or walnut wraparound finger groove grips (new 1992), optional detachable forearm, matte blue, 48 oz. Mfg. 1987-1999.

| | | | $315 | $255 | $200 | $175 | $155 | $135 | $120 |

Last MSR was $403.

* **Buck Mark Silhouette** - silhouette variation of the Buck Mark, 9 7/8 in. bull barrel with serrated top rib allowing adj. sight positioning, hooded target sights, laminated wood stocks and forearm, choice of contoured walnut or walnut wraparound finger groove grips (new 1992), matte blue, 53 oz. Mfg. 1987-1999.

| | | | $360 | $285 | $230 | $195 | $170 | $150 | $135 |

Last MSR was $448.

* **Buck Mark Unlimited Silhouette (Match)** - similar to Silhouette Model featuring 14 in. barrel with set back front sight, choice of contoured walnut or walnut wraparound finger groove grips (new 1992), 64 oz. Mfg. 1991-99.

| | | | $425 | $330 | $270 | $230 | $195 | $170 | $150 |

Last MSR was $536.

RIFLES: BOLT ACTION

Grading	100%	98%	95%	90%	80%	70%	60%

B

MODEL 52 LIMITED EDITION - .22 LR cal., virtually identical to the original Winchester Model 52C Sporter, except for minor safety enhancements, bolt action, 24 in. drilled and tapped barrel, 5 shot detachable mag., pistol grip walnut stock with oil style finish, deep blue finish, adj. trigger, two position safety, 7 lbs. 5,000 mfg. 1991-92.

	$525	$450	$395				

Last MSR was $500.

MODEL BBR - .25-06 Rem., .270 Win., .30-06, 7mm Mag., .300 Win. Mag. or .338 Win. Mag. cal., short action available in .22-250 Rem., 243 Win., 257 Roberts, 7mm- 08 Rem., or 308 Win. cal., 24 in. standard or heavy barrel, 60 degree throw, fluted bolt, adj. trigger, hidden detachable mag., no sights, checkered pistol grip, Monte Carlo stock. Mfg. 1978-1984 by Miroku.

$500	$375	$335	$310	$250	$220	$200

Some rare production calibers will add premiums to the values listed (i.e., add 50% for .243 Win. cal.).

BBR RIFLE ELK ISSUE - 7mm Rem. Mag. cal., bolt action rifle, 1,000 manufactured, deeply blue receiver which has multiple animals gold inlaid, high grade walnut stock and forearm feature skipline checkering. Disc. 1986.

$1,275	$950	$795				

Last MSR was $1,395.

T-BOLT T-1 - .22 LR cal., straight pull bolt action, 5 shot mag., 22 in. barrel, adj. rear sight, 5½ lbs., plain pistol grip stock. Mfg. 1965-1974 by FN.

$425	$350	$295	$255	$210	$180	$160

Add 10%-15% for left-hand model (mfg. 1967-74 only).

An aperture rear sight was standard for the first nine years of production.

T-BOLT T-2 - similar to T-1, only with select checkered walnut stock (lacquer finished), pinned front sight blade, 24 in. barrel, 6 lbs.

$600	$450	$350	$295	$240	$200	$180

Add 10%-15% for left-hand model (mfg. 1969-74 only).

* *Late production T-2* - features oil finished stock, press fit plastic front sight, and Browning computerized serialization.

$425	$350	$295	$255	$190	$175	$150

FN HIGH-POWER BOLT ACTION MODEL - .222 Rem. (Sako action), .222 Rem. Mag. (Sako action), .22-250 Rem. (Sako action), .243 Win., .257 Roberts, .264 Win. Mag., .270 Win., .284 Win. (Sako action), .30-06, .308 Win., 7mm Mag., .300 Win. Mag., .308 Norma Mag., .300 H&H, .338 Win. Mag., .375 H&H, or .458 Win. Mag. cal., standard Mauser type action with either short or long (more desirable) extractor, 22 or 24 in. (heavy available) barrel, folding leaf sight, checkered pistol grip stock. Mfg. 1959- 1974 by FN.

The .243 Win. and .308 Win. cals. were built on the small ring Mauser action prior to using the Sako medium action.

Note: Grades differ in engraving, finish, checkering, and grade of wood. It should be noted that the salt wood problem is more common in these high powered models. Guns should be checked carefully for rust below wood surfaces.

* *Safari Grade* - basic model with blue finish.

	100%	98%	95%	90%	80%	70%	60%
Standard cals.	$795	$675	$550	$450	$400	$350	$325
Mag. cals.	$900	$750	$650	$595	$525	$450	$400

Grading	100%	98%	95%	90%	80%	70%	60%
.257 Roberts	$1,295	$1,050	$825	$700	$600	$525	$450
.284 Win.	$1,550	$1,200	$950	$800	$700	$600	$500
.308 Norma Mag.	$1,050	$850	$700	$600	$525	$450	$400
.338 Win. Mag.	$1,150	$950	$850	$735	$650	$595	$525
.375 H&H	$1,300	$1,000	$800	$700	$600	$525	$450
.458 Win. Mag.	$1,095	$995	$895	$750	$625	$525	$450

Add 15% for Magnum long extractor models.

Between 1963 and 1974, Browning also offered short and medium barrelled actions in the Safari, Medallion and Olympian Grades. These models have Sako barrelled actions and were stocked by FN. Medium weight barrels could also be ordered.

✳ *Safari Grade* - Short Sako Action - short action, .222 Rem. or .222 Rem. Mag. cal.

$800	$675	$550	$450	$400	$350	$325

✳ *Safari Grade* - Medium Sako Action - medium action, .22-250 Rem., .243 Win., .284 Win. or .308 Win. cal.

$800	$675	$550	$450	$400	$350	$325

Add 100% for .284 Win. cal. (mfg. 1965-1976).

In .284 Win. cal., only 162 rifles were mfg. in Safari Grade, 20 in Medallion Grade, and 10 in Olympian Grade.

✳ *Medallion Grade* - features select figured walnut with skipline checkering, rosewood grip and forearm caps, blue/black lustre bluing, receiver and barrel portion scroll engraved, ram's head engraved on floor plate.

$1,250	$995	$895	$795	$700	$600	$500

Add 10%-50% for rare calibers.
Add 15% for Mag. cals. with long extractor.

Caliber rarity is as follows: .264 Win. Mag. (least rare), .300 H&H, .375 H&H long extractor, .222 Rem./.222 Rem. Mag., .284 Win. (rarest).

This model was also available with a Sako short or medium action - cals. are the same as listed for the Sako Safari.

✳ *Olympian Grade* - top-of-the-line model featuring highly figured walnut stock that is both checkered and carved. Receiver, floor plate, and trigger guard are chrome plated in a satin finish that has deep relief animal scenes engraved, as well as deep scroll work on other metal parts.

$2,750	$2,350	$1,925	$1,700	$1,550	$1,350	$1,175

Add 10%-50% for rare calibers.
Add 15% for Mag. cals. with long extractor.

Caliber rarity is as follows: .264 Win. Mag. (least rare), .300 H&H, .375 H&H long extractor, .222 Rem./.222 Rem. Mag., .284 Win. (rarest).

This model was also available with a Sako short or medium action - cals. are the same as listed for the Sako Safari.

ACERA MODEL - .30-06 or .300 Win. Mag. cal., features straight pull action, Teflon coated breech block face, 7 lug bolt, 22 or 24 (.300 Win. Mag.) in. barrel, available w/o sights, with sights (disc. 1999), or with BOSS, detachable box mag., checkered walnut stock, gloss metal finish, 7 lbs. 3 oz. – 7 lbs. 9 oz. Mfg. 1999-2000, reintroduced 2002.

MSR	$896		$820	$745	$660	$600	$550	$495	$450

Add $34 for .300 Win. Mag. cal.
Add $24 for iron sights (disc. 1999).
Add $80 for barrel BOSS (.30-06 cal. only beginning 2002).

Grading	100%	98%	95%	90%	80%	70%	60%

RIFLES: BOLT ACTION, CENTERFIRE A-BOLT SERIES

A-BOLT HUNTER MODEL - available in .25-06 Rem., .270 Win., .280 Rem. (new 1988), .30-06, 7mm Rem. Mag., .300 Win. Mag., or .338 Win. Mag. cal. in long action, short action available in .223 Rem. (new 1988), .22-250 Rem., .243 Win., .257 Roberts, .284 Win. (new 1989), 7mm-08 Rem., or .308 Win. cal., 3 or 4 shot mag., matte blue finish, 3 lug rotary bolt locking, 22 (short action only), 24 in. (disc. 1987), or 26 in. barrel (new 1988 - long action Mag. cals. only), 60 degree bolt throw, adj. trigger, hidden detachable mag., with or without sights, top tang thumb safety, checkered pistol grip stock, 6 lbs. 3 oz. - 7 lbs. 11oz. Mfg. 1985- 1993 by Miroku. Replaced by A-Bolt Model II in 1994.

$415	$340	$295	$265	$240	$225	$210

Last MSR was $510.

Add $65 for open sights.

❋ *Medallion Model* - same A-Bolt specifications, except also available in .375 H&H cal., features better grade walnut stock with rosewood pistol grip and forend cap, synthetic floor plate, high lustre bluing, no sights. Disc. 1993. Replaced by A-Bolt Medallion Model II in 1994.

$475	$385	$330	$290	$265	$250	$235

Last MSR was $597.

Add $25 for left-hand action (avail. in long action cals. only).
Add $100 for .375 H&H cal. (open sights only).
Left hand action available in .25-06 Rem., .270 Win., .280 Rem., .30-06, 7mm Rem. Mag., .300 Win. Mag., .338 Win. Mag., or .375 H&H cal.

❋ *Micro Medallion Model* - .223 Rem. (new 1988), .22-250 Rem., .243 Win., .257 Roberts, .284 Win., .308 Win., or 7mm-08 Rem. cal., scaled down variation of the A-Bolt Hunter Model, 20 in. barrel, short action only, 13 5/16 in. LOP, 3 shot mag., no sights, 6 lbs. 3 oz. for short action. Mfg. 1988-1993. Replaced by A-Bolt Micro Medallion Model II in 1994.

$475	$385	$330	$290	$265	$250	$235

Last MSR was $597.

❋ *Gold Medallion Model* - .270 Win., .30-06, .300 Win. Mag. (new 1993), or 7mm Rem. Mag. cal., similar to Medallion Model, except has extra select walnut stock with continental style cheekpiece, gold lettering and light engraving, no sights. Mfg. 1988- 1993. Replaced by A- Bolt Gold Medallion Model II in 1994.

$670	$535	$430	$360	$330	$300	$265

Last MSR was $810.

❋ *Euro-Bolt* - .22-250 Rem., .243 Win., .270 Win., .30-06, .308 Win., or 7mm Rem. Mag. cal., features European styling including Schnabel style forearm, rounded rear receiver, Mannlicher style bolt, European cheekpiece on satin finished checkered stock, low- lustre bluing, hinged floor plate with removable mag., cocking indicator, upper tang thumb activated safety, 6 lbs. 14 oz. - 7 lbs. 6 oz. (Mag.). Mfg. 1993-96.

$600	$475	$395	$350	$300	$265	$250

Last MSR was $700.

❋ *Stainless Stalker* - .22-250 Rem. (left-hand only, new 1993), .25-06 Rem., .270 Win., .280 Rem., .30- 06, 7mm Rem. Mag., .300 Win. Mag., .338 Win. Mag. or .375 H&H (new 1990) cal., action and barrel are stainless steel, matte black graphite fiberglass composite stock, dull stainless finish, no sights, 6 lbs. 11 oz. - 7 lbs. 3 oz. Mfg. 1987-1993. Replaced by Stainless Stalker II in 1994.

$575	$430	$350

Last MSR was $665.

Grading	100%	98%	95%	90%	80%	70%	60%

Add $100 for .375 H&H cal.
Add $20 for left hand action.
Originally, this model was offered in .270 Win., .30-06, or 7mm Rem. Mag. cal. only.

* ✱ ***Camo Stalker*** - .270 Win., .30-06, or 7mm Rem. Mag. cal., laminated black and green wood stock, matte finish on metal parts, no sights. Mfg. 1987-1989.

	$400	$340	$310	$285	$250	$230	$215

Last MSR was $483.

* ✱ ***Composite Stalker*** - .25-06 Rem., .270 Win., .280 Rem., .30-06, 7mm Rem. Mag., .300 Win. Mag., or .338 Win. Mag. cal., black graphite fiberglass composite stock, matte non-glare metal finish, 6 lbs. 11 oz. - 7 lbs. 3 oz. Mfg. 1988-1993. Replaced by Composite Stalker II in 1994.

	$410	$340	$295	$265	$240	$225	$210

Last MSR was $525.

A-BOLT BIGHORN SHEEP ISSUE - .270 Win. cal. only, 22 in. barrel, high grade walnut stock with gloss finish and skipline checkering, deep relief engraving on receiver barrel, floorplate, and trigger guard, two 24Kt. inlays depicting bighorn sheep. 600 mfg. 1986-87 only.

	$975	$750	$625

Last MSR was $1,365.

A-BOLT PRONGHORN ISSUE - .243 Win. cal., presentation grade walnut with skipline checkering and pearl borders, receiver and barrel engraving, multiple gold inlays on receiver top and floor plate. 500 mfg. 1987 only.

	$925	$725	$600

Last MSR was $1,302.

RIFLES: BOLT ACTION, CENTERFIRE A-BOLT II SERIES

The A-Bolt II Series was introduced in 1994, and differs from the original A-Bolt variations (disc. 1993) in that a new anti-bind bolt featuring a non-rotating bolt sleeve has been incorporated in addition to an improved trigger system. Consumers also may have their name/inscription engraved on the flat bolt-face on any A- Bolt II Series variation for an additional $25. Browning introduced the BOSS (ballistic optimizing shooting system) in 1994 as an option on A-Bolt rifles, except Micro- Medallion models and the .375 H&H caliber. It is available with ported BOSS (results in approx. 30% less recoil) or unported (designated BOSS-CR, for conventional recoil) muzzle brake.

A-BOLT HUNTER MODEL II - available in various cals. between .22-250 Rem. - .338 Win. Mag., .300 WSM cal. (new 2001), .270 WSM and 7mm WSM cals. (new 2002), 22, 23 (.300 WSM cal. only) or 26 in. barrel with or w/o open sights, 6 lbs. 7 oz. – 7 lbs. 3 oz.

MSR	$639		$495	$400	$335	$280	$240	$225	$210

Add $26 for Mag. cals.
Add approx. $60 for open sights (available in 8 cals., disc. 1998).

* ✱ ***Hunter Model II with BOSS*** - same cals. as Hunter Model II until 1999, available only in .22- 250 Rem., .243 Win., .270 Win., .280 Rem., .30-06, or .308 Win. cal. during 1999, features 22 or 26 (Mag. cals. only, disc. 1998) in. barrel with BOSS. Mfg. 1994-99.

	$510	$455	$400	$350	$300	$275	$250

Last MSR was $617.

A-BOLT CLASSIC HUNTER - .270 Win. (disc. 2001), .270 WSM (new 2002), .30-06 (disc. 2001), .300 Win. Mag. (disc. 2001), .300 WSM (new 2002), 7mm Rem. Mag. (disc. 2001), or 7mm WSM (new 2002) cal., 22 (disc. 2001), 23 (new 2002, WSM cals. only), or 26 (disc. 2001) in. barrel, 4 or 5 shot mag., features low-lustre bluing and select checkered Monte Carlo walnut stock and forend, approx. 6 ½ - 7¼ lbs. New 1999.

MSR	$746		$610	$500	$425	$365	$310	$275	$250

This model is available to Full-line and Medallion dealers only.

Grading	100%	98%	95%	90%	80%	70%	60%

A-BOLT MICRO HUNTER - .22 Hornet, .22-250 Rem., .223 Rem. (new 2000), .243 Win., .260 Rem. (disc. 2001), .308 Win., or 7mm-08 Rem. cal., features shorter LOP and 20 or 22 (.22 Hornet only) in. barrel w/o sights, checkered walnut stock and forend, approx. 6 ¼ lbs. New 1999.

MSR $632	$485	$410	$330	$280	$245	$225	$210

A-BOLT MEDALLION MODEL II - available in various cals. between .22-250 Rem. - .375 H&H, .260 Rem. new 1999, .223 Rem. disc. 2000, .300 WSM, .300 Rem. Ultra Mag., and .338 Rem. Ultra Mag. (new 2001), .270 WSM and 7mm WSM (new 2002), similar to Medallion Model with A-Bolt II improvements, without sights, except for .375 H&H cal. (open sights standard), 6 lbs. 7 oz. – 7 lbs. 1 oz. New 1994.

MSR $752	$605	$510	$430	$360	$300	$275	$250

Add $27 for all Mag. cals.

Add $29 for left-hand action w/o sights.

Left hand action available in .25-06 Rem. (disc. 1998), .270 Win., .280 Rem. (disc. 1997),.30- 06, 7mm Rem. Mag., .300 Win. Mag., .338 Win. Mag. (disc. 1998), or .375 H&H (disc. 1997) cal.

* *Medallion Model II with BOSS* - similar to Medallion Model II, .25-06 Rem., .260 Rem., .280 Rem., and .308 Win. cals. were disc. 1999, 22, 23 (new 2002, .300 WSM cal. only) or 26 in. BOSS barrel. New 1994.

MSR $832	$680	$560	$450	$395	$325	$295	$265

Add $27 for all Mag. cals.

Add $29 for left-hand action.

Left hand action available in .270 Win., .280 Rem. (disc. 1998),.30-06, 7mm Rem. Mag., .300 Win. Mag., or .375 H&H (disc. 1998) cal.

* *Micro Medallion Model II* - .22 Hornet, .22-250 Rem., .223 Rem., .243 Win., 7mm-08 Rem., .284 Win. (disc. 1997), or .308 Win. cal., similar to Micro Medallion Model with A-Bolt II improvements, 20 or 22 (.22 Hornet only) in. barrel without sights, 6 lbs. Mfg. 1994-98.

	$525	$465	$400	$350	$300	$275	$250

Last MSR was $636.

A-BOLT CUSTOM TROPHY - .270 Win., .30-06, .300 Win. Mag., or 7mm Rem. Mag. cal., features 24 or 26 (Mag. cals. only) in. octagon barrel with gold band at muzzle, no sights, gold outlines on barrel and receiver, checkered select American walnut stock with shadowline cheekpiece and skeleton pistol grip, approx. 7½ lbs. Mfg. 1998-2000.

	$1,150	$925	$800	$660	$525	$450	$375

Last MSR was $1,428.

A-BOLT GOLD MEDALLION MODEL II - .270 Win., .30-06, .300 Win. Mag. or 7mm Rem. Mag. cal., similar to Gold Medallion Model, except has A-Bolt II improvements, 22 or 26 in. barrel, approx. 7½ lbs. Mfg. 1994- 98.

	$695	$595	$450	$375	$335	$300	$265

Last MSR was $855.

* *Gold Medallion Model II with BOSS* - mfg. 1994-97.

	$750	$625	$525	$450	$375	$325	$285

Last MSR was $916.

A-BOLT WHITE GOLD MEDALLION - .270 Win., .30-06, .300 Win. Mag., or 7mm Rem. Mag. cal., stainless steel receiver and barrel, gold engraving, checkered high gloss walnut stock with cheekpiece and rosewood forend cap, 7 lbs. 3 oz. - 7 lbs. 11 oz. New 1999.

MSR $1,077	$875	$690	$560	

Add $27 for Mag. cals.

Grading	100%	98%	95%	90%	80%	70%	60%

* **White Gold Medallion with BOSS** - similar to White Gold Medallion, except has barrel with BOSS.

| | MSR | $1,157 | | $925 | $730 | $590 | | | |

Add $27 for Mag. cals.

A-BOLT ECLIPSE HUNTER WITH BOSS - .22-250 Rem. (disc. 1999), .243 Win. (disc. 1997), .270 Win., .30-06, .308 Win. (disc. 2000), or 7mm Rem. Mag. cal., features laminated thumbhole wood stock with cheekpiece, long action, 22 or 26 (7mm Rem. Mag. only) in. barrel with BOSS, approx. 7½ lbs. New 1996.

| MSR | $1,048 | | $840 | $695 | $560 | $465 | $375 | $325 | $285 |

Add $26 for Mag. cals.

* **Eclipse Varmint with BOSS** - .22-250 Rem., .223 Rem., or .308 Win. cal., 24 in. heavy barrel with BOSS, 4 shot mag., otherwise similar to Eclipse Model, approx. 9 lbs. Mfg. 1996-99.

| | | $810 | $655 | $535 | $455 | $375 | $325 | $285 |

Last MSR was $969.

* **Eclipse M-1000 with BOSS** - .300 Win. Mag. cal., features special 26 in. heavy target barrel, refined trigger system, 9 lbs. 13 oz.

| MSR | $1,079 | | $880 | $695 | $560 | $460 | $375 | $325 | $285 |

A-BOLT VARMINT II WITH BOSS - .22-250 Rem., .223 Rem., or .308 Win. (new 1995) cal., features A-Bolt II improvements, 22 in. heavy barrel with BOSS, blue/gloss or satin/ matte (new 1995, .223 Rem. disc. 1999) finish, black laminated wood stock with checkering, palm swell, and solid recoil pad, without sights, 9 lbs. Mfg. 1994- 2000.

| | | $715 | $600 | $465 | $380 | $335 | $300 | $265 |

Last MSR was $879.

A-BOLT EURO-BOLT II - .243 Win., .270 Win., .30-06, .308 Win., or 7mm Rem. Mag. cal., similar to Euro-Bolt with A-Bolt II improvements, 22 or 26 (7mm Rem. Mag. only) in. barrel w/o sights, 6 lbs. 7 oz. - 7 lbs. 3 oz. (Mag.). Mfg. 1994-96.

| | | $625 | $510 | $410 | $355 | $300 | $265 | $250 |

Last MSR was $824.

* **Euro-Bolt II with BOSS** - .243 Win., .270 Win., or .308 Win. cal., 22 in. barrel with BOSS, 6 lbs. 7 oz.

| | | $725 | $600 | $500 | $425 | $350 | $325 | $295 |

Last MSR was $922.

A-BOLT STAINLESS STALKER II - similar to Stainless Stalker with A-Bolt improvements, also available in .22-250 Rem. (mfg. 1995-99), .223 Rem. (mfg. 1995-2000), .243 Win. (new 1994), .260 Rem. (new 1999), 7mm-08 Rem. (new 1995), .308 Win. (new 1995), .300 WSM (new 2001), .300 Rem. Ultra Mag. (new 2001), .338 Rem. Ultra Mag. (new 2001) cal., .270 WSM and 7mm WSM cals. (new 2002), w/o sights, 6 lbs. 4 oz. - 7 lbs. 3 oz. New 1994.

| MSR | $837 | | $695 | $510 | $380 | | | | |

Add $27 for all Mag. cals.
Add $26 for left-hand action.

Left-hand action cals. include .270 Win., .280 Rem. (disc. 1998), .30-06, .300 Win. Mag., .338 Win. Mag., .375 H&H, or 7mm Rem. Mag.

Grading	100%	98%	95%	90%	80%	70%	60%

✳ *Stainless Stalker II with BOSS* - .223 Rem. (disc. 2000), .22-250 Rem. (disc. 2000), .243 Win. (disc. 2000), .308 Win. (disc. 1999), .25-06 Rem. (disc. 1999), 7mm-08 Rem., .270 Win., .280 Rem. (disc. 1999), .30-06, 7mm Rem. Mag., .300 Win. Mag., .300 WSM (new 2002), .338 Win. Mag., or .375 H&H cal., 22, 23 (new 2002, .300 WSM cal. only), 24 (.375 H&H cal. only) 26 (Mag. cals. only) in. barrel with BOSS.

MSR	$914		$760	$560	$450		

Add $27 for all Mag. cals.
Add $26 for left-hand action.
Left-hand action cals. include .25-06 Rem. (disc. 1998), .270 Win., .280 Rem. (disc. 1998), .30-06, .300 Win. Mag., .338 Win. Mag., .375 H&H, or 7mm Rem. Mag.

A-BOLT CARBON FIBER STAINLESS STALKER - .22-250 Rem. or .300 Win. Mag. cal., features Christensen lightweight 22 or 26 in. carbon fiber barrel with steel liner, stainless steel action, black synthetic stock, 4 or 5 shot mag., approx. 6¼ or 7¼ lbs. Mfg. 2000-2001.

			$1,475	$1,225	$975		

Last MSR was $1,750.

A-BOLT COMPOSITE STALKER II - similar to Composite Stalker with A-Bolt II improvements, also available in .223 Rem., .22-250 Rem., .243 Win., .260 Rem. (mfg. 1999 only), .270 WSM (new 2002), 7mm-08 Rem., .308 Win., .300 WSM (new 2001), or 7mm WSM (new 2002) cal., 22, 23 (.300 WSM cal. only), or 26 (Mag. cals. only) in. barrel without sights, 6 lbs. 4 oz. - 7 lbs. 3 oz. New 1994.

MSR	$658		$495	$395	$325	$275	$240	$225	$210

Add $27 for all Mag. cals.

✳ *Composite Stalker II with BOSS* - .22-250 Rem. (disc. 1997), .223 Rem. (disc. 1999), .243 Win. (disc. 2001), .25-06 Rem., .260 Rem. (disc. 1999), 7mm-08 Rem. (disc. 1999), .270 Win., .280 Rem. (disc. 1999), .30-06, .308 Win. (disc. 2001), 7mm Rem. Mag., .300 Win. Mag., .300 WSM (new 2002), .338 Win. Mag., 22 or 26 (Mag. cals. only) in. barrel with BOSS.

MSR	$738		$595	$495	$395	$335	$285	$250	$225

Add $27 for Mag. cals.

✳ *Varmint Stalker* - .22-250 Rem. or .223 Rem. cal., 24 or 26 (.22-250 Rem. cal. only) in. heavy barrel, features Dura-Touch armor coated composite stock with slight palm swell, matte blue metal, 4 or 6 shot mag., approx. 8-8¼ lbs. New 2002.

MSR	$772		$620	$510	$410	$345	$290	$255	$230

A-BOLT GREYWOLF - .25-06 Rem., .270 Win., .280 Rem., .30-06, .300 Win. Mag., .338 Win. Mag., or 7mm Rem. Mag. cal., stainless steel, classic sporter with select walnut stock. Limited mfg. during 1994 only.

			$850	$675	$595		

Last MSR was $935.

RIFLES: BOLT ACTION, RIMFIRE A-BOLT SERIES

A-BOLT GRADE I RIMFIRE - .22 LR or .22 Mag. (new 1989) cal., 60 degree bolt throw, 22 in. barrel, checkered walnut stock and forearm or laminated stock (scarce - approx. 1,500 mfg., 390 had no sights), 5 or 15 (optional) shot mag., adj. trigger, available with or without open sights, 5 lbs. 9 oz. Mfg. 1986-96.

✳ *.22 LR cal.*

			$320	$255	$195	$175	$160	$145	$130

Last MSR was $425.

Add $14 for open sights.
A 15 shot mag. is also available for this model at $45 retail.

Grading	100%	98%	95%	90%	80%	70%	60%

* .22 Win. Mag. cal.

| | $375 | $295 | $225 | $195 | $175 | $160 | $150 |

Last MSR was 493.

Add $21 for open sights.

A-BOLT GOLD MEDALLION RIMFIRE - .22 LR cal. only, similar to A-Bolt, except has high grade select walnut stock checkered 22 lines per inch, rosewood pistol and forend cap, high gloss finish, gold filled lettering and moderate engraving, solid recoil pad. Mfg. 1988-96.

| | $455 | $365 | $310 | $270 | $240 | $225 | $210 |

Last MSR was $567.

RIFLES: LEVER ACTION

BL-22 GRADE I - .22 S, L, and LR cal., 20 in. barrel, short throw (33 degree) lever, folding leaf sight, 15 shot (LR) mag., blue finish, exposed hammer, Western style gloss finished uncheckered stock and forearm, 5 lbs. Mfg. 1970-present by Miroku.

| MSR | $423 | | $330 | $240 | $195 | $150 | $125 | $110 | $100 |

* *BL-22 Classic* - similar to BL-22 Grade I, except has satin finished stock and forearm. New 1999, mfg. by Miroku.

| MSR | $423 | | $330 | $240 | $195 | $150 | $125 | $110 | $100 |

This model is available through Full-Line and Medallion dealers only.

BL-22 GRADE II - same general specifications as BL-22, except scroll engraved blue receiver and deluxe high gloss checkered walnut stock and forearm.

| MSR | $480 | | $375 | $290 | $220 | $175 | $140 | $125 | $115 |

* *BL-22 Grade II Classic* - similar to BL-22 Grade II, except has satin finished stock and forearm. New 1999, mfg. by Miroku.

| MSR | $480 | | $375 | $290 | $220 | $175 | $140 | $125 | $115 |

MODEL 53 DELUXE LIMITED EDITION - .32-20 WCF cal. (round nose or hollow point bullets only), patterned after the original Winchester Model 53 (redesigned Model 1892), 7 shot tube mag., high polished blue metal, open sights, 22 in. tapered barrel, high grade checkered walnut stock featuring full pistol grip cap and shotgun style metal butt plate, 6½ lbs. Only 5,000 mfg. in 1990.

| | $795 | $525 | $425 | | | | |

Last MSR was $675.

MODEL 65 GRADE I LIMITED EDITION - .218 Bee cal., patterned after the Winchester Model 65, round tapered 24 in. barrel, open sights (hooded front), blue metal finish, 7 shot tube mag., uncheckered pistol grip stock and semi-beavertail forearm, metal butt plate, 6¾ lbs. 3,500 total mfg. for Grade I in 1989 only, inventory depleted in 1990.

| | $550 | $425 | $375 | | | | |

Last MSR was $550.

* *Model 65 High Grade* - greyed receiver (and lever) with scroll engraving and gold plated animals, gold plated trigger, deluxe checkered walnut stock and semi-beavertail forearm. 1,500 total mfg. in 1989, inventory depleted in 1990.

| | $850 | $775 | $700 | | | | |

Last MSR was $850.

MODEL 71 LIMITED EDITION CARBINE - .348 Win. cal., reproduction of the Winchester Model 71 Carbine, 20 in. barrel, open sights, 4 shot mag., 8 lbs. New 1987 with inventory depleted in 1990.

Grading	100%	98%	95%	90%	80%	70%	60%

B

✳ *Grade I* - uncheckered satin finished walnut stock and forearm. 4,000 mfg. 1986-87 only.

	$600	$475	$400	$350	$325	$300	$275

Last MSR was $600.

✳ *High Grade* - deluxe checkered walnut stock and forearm with high gloss finish, scroll engraved- grey receiver with gold inlays and trigger. 3,000 mfg. 1986-87 only.

	$825	$625	$500

Last MSR was $980.

MODEL 71 LIMITED EDITION RIFLE - .348 Win. cal., reproduction of the Winchester Model 71 Rifle, 24 in. barrel, open sights, 4 shot mag., 8 lbs. 2 oz. Mfg. 1986-87 only with inventory depleted in 1990.

✳ *Grade I* - uncheckered satin finished walnut stock and forearm. 3,000 mfg. 1986-87 only.

	$675	$525	$425	$375	$350	$300	$275

Last MSR was $600.

✳ *High Grade* - deluxe checkered walnut stock and forearm with high gloss finish, scroll engraved- grey receiver with gold inlays and trigger. 3,000 mfg. 1986-87 only.

	$895	$675	$525

Last MSR was $980.

MODEL 81/BLR SHORT ACTION - .22-250 Rem., .222 Rem. (disc. 1989), .223 Rem., .243 Win., .257 Roberts (disc. 1992), 7mm-08 Rem., .284 Win. (disc. 1994), .308 Win., or .358 Win. (disc. 1992) cal., steel receiver, rotary bolt locking lugs, 20 in. barrel with band, 3 (.284 Win. only) or 4 shot detachable mag., adj. rear sight, checkered straight grip stock, recoil pad, approx. 7 lbs, no sights optional 1988-89.

.243 Win., .308 Win. and 7mm-08 Rem. cals. are the most popular in this model.

✳ *Model BLR USA* - .243 Win. or .308 Win. cal., this model was originally scheduled to be manufactured by TRW in Cleveland, OH for Browning. Originally assembled in 1966, these rifles are considered prototypes as they were never sold through regular channels and at one time were scheduled to be destroyed. Approx. 50-250 of these rifles exist, some still NIB.

	$995	$895	$750	$600	$550	$500	$450

This variation has a 2-line legend on the right side marked "MADE IN USA" and "PATENT PENDING".

✳ *Model BLR Belgian* - .243 Win. or .308 Win. cal., mfg. was moved to F.N. in Belgium with original assembly beginning 1969 and concluding in 1973. This F.N. model included a number of small dimensioning and engraving changes.

	$525	$450	$400	$370	$345	$315	$275

✳ *Model BLR Japan* - cals. as noted above, mfg. was moved to Miroku in Japan 1974- 1980. Early guns during 1974 had stocks with impressed checkering. By 1975, cut checkering and gloss wood finish was used on stocks and forearms.

	$450	$365	$300	$265	$225	$195	$165

Last MSR was $550.

Add $40 without sights (scarce).

✳ *Model BLR 81 Short Action* - cals. as noted above, mfg. 1981-1995 by Miroku in Japan.

	100%	98%	95%	90%	80%	70%	60%
.257 Roberts	$595	$525	$400	$295	$250	$200	$165
Standard cals.	$450	$375	$300	$265	$225	$195	$165
.284 Win./.358 Win.	$650	$550	$450	$325	$300	$250	$225
.222 Rem.	$795	$695	$550	$495	$425	$350	$300

Last MSR was $550.

Grading	100%	98%	95%	90%	80%	70%	60%

MODEL BLR 81 LONG ACTION - .270 Win., .30-06, or 7mm Rem Mag. cal., incorporates distinct design changes, 22 or 24 in. barrel, approx. 8½ lbs. Mfg. 1991-95 by Miroku.

	$450	$365	$300	$265	$230	$200	$170

Last MSR was $580.

NEW MODEL LIGHTNING BLR (SHORT ACTION) - .22-250 Rem., .223 Rem. (disc. 1998), .243 Win., 7mm-08 Rem., or .308 Win. cal., rotary bolt locking lugs, 20 in. barrel w/o barrel band, similar action as the BLR 81, but features aluminum alloy receiver, checkered pistol grip stock and forearm, rack and pinion geared slide, fold down hammer, trigger travels with lever, 3-5 shot detachable mag., adj. rear sight, approx. 6½ lbs. Mfg. by Miroku beginning late 1995.

MSR	$681		$515	$390	$315	$270	$220	$195	$165

NEW MODEL LIGHTNING BLR (LONG ACTION) - .270 Win., .30-06, .300 Win. Mag. (new 1997), or 7mm Rem. Mag. cal., 22 or 24 (Mag. cals.) in. barrel, approx. 7¼ - 7¾ lbs. Mfg. by Miroku beginning 1995.

MSR	$721		$550	$415	$335	$280	$230	$200	$170

MODEL 1886 LIMITED EDITION GRADE I RIFLE - .45-70 Govt. cal. only, patterned after the Winchester Model 1886, blue receiver, 26 in. octagon barrel, full mag., crescent butt plate, open sights. 7,000 mfg. 1986 only.

			$1,225	$950	$750				

Last MSR was $578.

❋ **Model 1886 Limited Edition High Grade Rifle** - same general specifications as Model 1886, except has checkered high grade walnut stock and forearm, greyed steel receiver, with game scene engraving including elk and American Bison, gold accenting with "1 of 3,000" engraved on top of barrel. 3,000 mfg. 1986 only.

		$1,795	$1,350	$995			

Last MSR was $935.

❋ **Model 1886 Montana Centennial Rifle** - similar to Model 1886 High Grade. 2,000 mfg. 1986 only to commemorate Montana Centennial.

		$1,795	$1,350	$995			

Last MSR was $935.

MODEL 1886 LIMITED EDITION GRADE I CARBINE - .45-70 Govt. cal. only, saddle ring carbine, patterned after the Winchester Model 1886 Carbine, blue receiver, 22 in. round barrel, 8 shot full mag., crescent butt plate, open sights. 7,000 total mfg. 1992- 1993.

		$750	$575	$450			

Last MSR was $750.

❋ **Model 1886 Limited Edition High Grade Carbine** - same general specifications as Model 1886, except has checkered high grade walnut stock and forearm, greyed steel receiver, with game scene engraving including bear and elk, gold accenting, 3,000 total mfg. 1992-1993.

		$1,250	$925	$675			

Last MSR was $1,175.

B-92 CARBINE - .357 Mag. or .44 Rem. Mag. cal., 20 in. barrel, patterned after the Winchester Model 92, 11 shot mag. (tubular), blue finish. Disc. 1986.

		$475	$375	$295	$200	$175	$160	$150

Last MSR was $342.

❋ **B-92 Centennial** - .44 Mag. cal., 6,000 mfg. in 1978.

		$495	$395	$350			

Last MSR was $220.

Grading	100%	98%	95%	90%	80%	70%	60%

❋ ***B-92 BCA Commemorative*** - mfg. to commemorate BCA's third anniversary.

	$495	**$395**	**$350**				

MODEL 1895 LIMITED EDITION GRADE I

- .30/40 Krag or .30-06 cal. only, patterned after the Winchester Model 1895, blue receiver, 24 in. barrel, 4 shot mag.(box type), select walnut, rear buckhorn sight, 8 lbs. Mfg. 1984 only.

.30/40 Krag	**$550**	**$475**	**$375**	**$325**	**$300**	**$280**	**$260**
.30-06	**$600**	**$525**	**$400**	**$350**	**$325**	**$300**	**$280**

Production totaled 6,000 in the .30-06 cal. and 2,000 in .30/40 Krag for this model.

❋ ***Model 1895 Limited Edition High Grade*** - same general specifications as Model 1895, except gold plated game scenes on satin finish receiver, gold trigger, and finely checkered select French walnut.

	$1,200	**$975**	**$850**				

Production totaled 1,000 in the .30-06 cal. and 1,000 in .30/40 Krag for this model.

RIFLES: O/U

EXPRESS RIFLE - .270 Win., .30-06 cal., or 9.3x74R cal., Superposed style action. 24 in. barrels, auto ejectors, Fleur-de-lis engraving, single trigger, folding leaf rear sight, 6 lbs. 14 oz., cased. Disc. 1986.

	$2,800	**$2,400**	**$1,950**	**$1,650**	**$1,450**	**$1,250**	**$1,000**

Last MSR was $3,125.

GRADE I CONTINENTAL SET - includes .30-06 O/U rifle barrels with extra set of 20 ga. O/U shotgun barrels (26½ in.), rifle barrels are 24 in., 20 ga. frame, SST, ejectors, blue receiver with scroll engraving, supplied with 2 barrel takedown case. Mfg. 1978-1986.

	$3,495	**$2,995**	**$2,495**	**$1,795**	**$1,495**	**$1,295**	**$1,050**

RIFLES: SEMI-AUTO, .22 LR

AUTO RIFLE GRADES I - VI - .22 LR or .22 Short (disc.) cal., takedown design, 11 shot (16 for .22 Short) tube mag. in buttstock, 19¼ in. barrel in LR, 22¼ in. barrel in short (rare), checkered pistol grip stock, semi-beavertail forearm, stock has hole machined halfway to allow partial filling of tube mag., adj. folding rear sight, grades differ in finish, amount of engraving, and grade of wood, 4¾-5¾ lbs. Mfg. 1914-1976 by FN, 1976-present by Miroku in Japan.

❋ ***Grade I - FN***

	$575	**$475**	**$375**	**$300**	**$250**	**$225**	**$200**

Add 25% for "Shorts only" or thumb wheel rear sight older models if in 95% or better condition.

FN Grade Is have a lightly engraved blue steel receiver, checkered walnut, blue trigger, and a variety of rear sights.

❋ ***Grade I - Miroku***

MSR	**$489**	**$375**	**$285**	**$235**	**$200**	**$160**	**$150**	**$140**

Miroku manufactured .22s can be determined by year of manufacture in the following manner: RV suffix - 1975, RT - 1976, RR - 1977, RP - 1978, RN - 1979, PM - 1980, PZ - 1981, PY - 1982, PX - 1983, PW - 1984, PV - 1985, PT - 1986, PR - 1987, PP - 1988, PN - 1989, NM - 1990, NZ - 1991, NY - 1992, NX - 1993, NW - 1994, NV - 1995, NT - 1996, NR - 1997, NP - 1998, NN - 1999, MM - 2000, MZ - 2001, MY - 2002, MX - 2003.

❋ ***Grade II - FN***

	$1,095	**$850**	**$650**	**$450**	**$375**	**$350**	**$300**

FN Grade IIs have grey chromed receiver, deluxe wood with finer checkering, gold plated trigger, and engraving depicting two squirrels and two prairie dogs. Signed or unsigned by engraver.

Grading	100%	98%	95%	90%	80%	70%	60%

* Grade II - Miroku - disc. 1984.

	$450	$375	$295	$225	$200	$180	$160

* Grade III - FN

	$2,450	$1,950	$1,500	$850	$770	$715	$605

FN Grade IIIs have coin finish or grey chromed receiver, extra deluxe walnut with skipline checkering, gold plated trigger, and more elaborate game scene engraving usually featuring a dog flushing ducks or upland game. Signed or unsigned by engraver (Funken, J. Baerten, Vrancken, and Watrin will command premiums over values listed). A few were also special ordered with blue finish and special engraving - these command an extra premium.

* Grade III - Miroku - disc. 1983.

	$850	$650	$550	$495	$475	$425	$395

* Grade VI - Miroku - game scene engraved with gold plating, choice of blue or greyed receiver, deluxe walnut. New 1987.

MSR	$1,049	$860	$620	$465	$380	$335	$295	$260

BAR-22 - .22 LR cal., 20¼ in. barrel, 15 shot tube mag., folding leaf sight, high polish alloy receiver, checkered pistol grip stock, 5 lbs. 13 oz. Mfg. 1977-1985 by Miroku.

	$275	$225	$185	$170	$155	$140	$125

Last MSR was $245.

BAR-22 GRADE II - engraved model of BAR-22 featuring game scenes on silver greyed alloy receiver, select French walnut. Disc. 1985.

	$450	$350	$295	$250	$195	$175	$160

Last MSR was $350.

BUCK MARK RIFLE - .22 LR cal., Buck Mark pistol blowback action, 18 in. tapered barrel with Hi-Viz fiber optic sights (Sporter Rifle) or heavy barrel w/o sights (Target Rifle), unique wood or grey laminate (new 2002, no sights, Classic Target Rifle) Monte Carlo stock that attaches to non-detachable, one-piece skeletonized and enclosed rear grip assembly, 4 lbs. 6 oz. or 5 lbs. 6 oz. New 2001.

MSR	$528	$415	$305	$260	$230	$200	$160	$150

Subtract $8 for Buck Mark Classic Target Rifle (new 2002).

The Buck Mark Classic Target Rifle is available through Full-Line and Medallion dealers only.

RIFLES: SEMI-AUTO, BAR SERIES

BROWNING PATENT 1900 - .35 Rem. cal. only, features matted rib barrel and checkered stock and forearm, similar to Remington Model 8 auto-loading rifle, 4,913 mfg. 1910-1931 by FN.

	$875	$750	$650	$600	$550	$500	$450

BAR SEMI-AUTO - .243 Win., .270 Win., .280 Rem. (new 1990), .308 Win., or .30-06 cal. available in standard model, Mag. cals. include 7mm Rem., .300 Win., and .338 Win. Mag. (reintroduced 1990), gas operated, blue receiver, 22 or 24 (Mag. only) in. barrel, rotary bolt with seven lugs, folding leaf sight, walnut stock. Grades differ in engraving, finish, and grade of wood, in 1993, to celebrate the 25th Anniversary of the BAR, Browning introduced the BAR MK II Safari (see model listing), approx. 7 lbs. 6 oz. Mfg. 1967-present (includes BAR MK II).

Add 20% for FN mfg. and assembled BARs (marked "Made in Belgium").
Add 10% for .338 Win. Mag. cal. (FN mfg. only).

Note: Original .338s were limited production, mostly seen in the deluxe Grade II only. During the last year of FN .338 production, several were delivered in a Grade I by FN. Although being rarer than the Grade II, it is not as desirable. The following prices are for Portugese assembled guns, manufactured by FN, and are so stamped on the barrel.

Grading	100%	98%	95%	90%	80%	70%	60%

✸ *Grade I* - standard grade without engraving, blue finish. Ordering this model without sights became an option in 1988. Disc. 1992.

	$550	$475	$400	$350	$325	$300	$280

Last MSR was $633.

Subtract $16 without sights.

FN mfg. and assembled Grade Is can be denoted by light scroll engraving on the receiver.

✸ *Grade I Magnum* - standard grade without engraving, with recoil pad, 8 lbs. 6 oz. Disc. 1992.

	$575	$495	$425	$375	$350	$330	$310

Last MSR was $680.

Subtract $16 without sights.

Ordering this gun without sights became an option in 1988.

✸ *Grade II* - blue receiver, engraved with big game heads. Mfg. 1967-1974.

	$695	$625	$575	$525	$470	$440	$415

This model was previously designated Deluxe.

✸ *Grade II Magnum* - magnum version of Grade II. Mfg. 1967-1974.

	$750	$675	$625	$550	$510	$475	$450

✸ *Grade III* - features elk and sheep game scenes etched on greyed steel receiver, select checkered stock and forearm. Disc. 1984.

	$925	$800	$675	$625	$595	$550	$525

✸ *Grade III Magnum* - magnum version of Grade III. Disc. 1984.

	$1,025	$850	$700	$660	$620	$595	$580

✸ *Grade IV* - engraved satin finish greyed receiver depicts big game animal scenes and trigger guard, carved borders on checkering. Disc. 1989.

	$1,475	$1,300	$1,150	$1,000	$900	$825	$750

Last MSR was $1,670.

✸ *Grade IV Magnum* - magnum version of Grade IV. Disc. 1984.

	$1,675	$1,495	$1,225	$1,050	$950	$850	$775

Last MSR was $1,720.

✸ *Grade V* - more elaborate engraving than Grade IV, with gold inlays. Mfg. 1971- 1974.

	$3,000	$2,600	$2,250	$1,850	$1,600	$1,450	$1,250

✸ *Grade V Magnum* - magnum version of Grade V.

	$3,650	$2,900	$2,400	$1,950	$1,700	$1,595	$1,400

BAR NORTH AMERICAN DEER RIFLE ISSUE - .30-06 cal. only, BAR style action with silver grey finish and engraved action, 600 total production, walnut cased with accessories. Disc. 1983 but were sold through 1989.

	$2,950	$2,300	$1,850				

Last MSR was $3,550.

BAR MK II SAFARI - .22-250 Rem. (mfg. 1997 only), .25-06 Rem. (new 1997), .243 Win., .270 Win., .30-06, .308 Win., .270 Wby. Mag. (mfg. 1996-2000), 7mm Rem. Mag., .300 Win. Mag., or .338 Win. Mag. cal., improved BAR action featuring redesigned bolt release, new gas operating system, and reduced recoil, removable trigger assembly, 22 or 24 (Mag. cals. only) in. barrel with (adj. for windage and elevation) or without sights, BOSS became optional 1994, and is available with ported BOSS, which results in approx. 30% less recoil, or unported (designated BOSS-CR, for conventional recoil) muzzle brake, blue finish with

Grading	100%	98%	95%	90%	80%	70%	60%

engraved receiver, checkered walnut stock and forearm, gold trigger, detachable 3 (.300 WSM cal. only), 4 (Mag. cals. only) or 5 shot box mag., approx. 7 lbs. 6 oz. except for Mag. cals. (8 lbs. 6 oz.). Mfg. by F.N. in Belgium. New 1993.

MSR	$815		$675	$530	$450	$385	$360	$330	$310

Add $76 for Mag. cals.
Add $18 for open sights (not available in .270 Wby. Mag.).

The new BAR MK II Safari does not have interchangable magazine capability with the older pre-1993 BARs.

✳ ***BAR Classic Mark II Safari*** - .270 Win. (disc. 2001), .30-06 (disc. 2001), 7mm Rem. Mag., (disc. 2001), .300 Win. Mag. (disc. 2001), or .300 WSM (new 2002) cal., similar to BAR Mark II Safari, except has satin finished checkered stock and forearm, 7 lbs. 6 oz. or 8 lbs. 6 oz. New 1999.

MSR	$890		$770	$600	$510	$425	$375	$335	$310

Subtract $75 for standard cals. in 95%+ condition.
Add $17 for open sights (disc. 2000).

This model is available to Full-line and Medallion dealers only.

✳ ***BAR Mark II Safari with BOSS*** - .243 Win. (disc. 1999), .308 Win. (disc. 1999), .270 Win., .30-06, 7mm Rem. Mag., .300 Win. Mag., .338 Win. Mag. cal., similar to BAR MK II Safari, with BOSS (ballistic optimizing shooting system) accurizing adj. assembly on barrel end, no sights, 7½ or 8½ lbs. New 1994.

MSR	$895		$770	$600	$510	$425	$375	$335	$310

Add $75 for Mag. cals.

✳ ***BAR Mark II Lightweight*** - .243 Win., .270 Win., .30-06, .308 Win., 7mm Rem. Mag. (new 1999), .300 Win. Mag. (new 1999), or .338 Win. Mag. (new 1999) cal., features alloy receiver and 20 or 24 (Mag. cals. only) in. barrel, matte wood and barrel finish, open sights, 7 lbs. 2 oz. or 7 lbs. 12 oz. New 1997.

MSR	$833		$695	$530	$445	$385	$350	$330	$310

Add $76 for Mag. cals. (new 1999).

✳ ***BAR MK II Lightweight with BOSS*** - 7mm Rem. Mag., .300 Win. Mag., or .338 Win. Mag. (disc. 1999) cal., similar to BAR Mark II Lightweight, except has 24 in. barrel with BOSS, 8 lbs., 6 oz. Mfg. 1999-2000.

			$800	$625	$525	$445	$385	$350	$310

Last MSR was $939.

✳ ***BAR MK II Lightweight Stalker*** - .243 Win., .270 Win., .30-06, .308 Win., 7mm Rem. Mag., .300 Win. Mag., .300 WSM (new 2002), or .338 Win. Mag. cal., similar to BAR Mark II Safari, except has aluminum alloy receiver and checkered black synthetic stock and forearm, matte metal finish, 20, 22, 23 (new 2002, .300 WSM cal. only), or 24 (Mag. cals. only) in. barrel with open sights, 7 lbs. 2 oz. – 7 lbs. 12 oz. New 2001.

MSR	$809		$675	$530	$450	$385	$360	$330	$310

Add $74 for Mag. cals.

✧***BAR MK II Lightweight Stalker with BOSS*** - 7mm Rem. Mag., .300 Win. Mag., .300 WSM (new 2002), or .338 Win. Mag. cal., similar to BAR Mark II Stalker, except has 23 (new 2002, .300 WSM cal. only) or 24 in. barrel with BOSS, approx. 7¾ lbs. New 2001.

MSR	$944		$805	$625	$525	$435	$380	$335	$310

✳ ***BAR MK II High Grade*** - .270 Win., .30-06, .300 Win. Mag., or 7mm Rem. Mag. cal., satin finished receiver with either whitetail/mule deer or moose/elk etched game scenes and gold border, checkered high grade gloss finished walnut stock and forearm, 7 lbs. 6 oz. or 8 lbs. 6 oz. New 2001.

MSR	$1,820		$1,450	$995	$775	$650	$550	$450	$400

Add $56 for Mag. cals.

Grading	100%	98%	95%	90%	80%	70%	60%

❊ BAR MK II Grade III - features Grade III engraving pattern. Mfg. by the FN custom shop 1996- 99.

	$3,100	$1,875	$1,375	$1,000	$775	$675	$575

Last MSR was $3,754.

❊ BAR MK II Grade IV - features Grade IV engraving pattern. Mfg. by the FN custom shop beginning 1996.

	$3,180	$1,930	$1,400	$1,025	$795	$675	$575

Last MSR was $3,859.

RIFLES: SEMI-AUTO, FAL SERIES

The following semi-auto FALs were imported by BAC in limited numbers. Current production FALs can be found under the Fabrique Nationale heading.

FAL G SERIES STANDARD - 7.62mm cal., paramilitary design rifle, wood buttstock, wood or nylon forearm, milled receiver.

	$3,200	$2,850	$2,300	$1,950	$1,650	$1,350	$1,040

❊ G Series Heavy Barrel - wood furniture, milled receiver with special bipod.

	$6,000	$5,250	$4,700	$4,160	$3,600	$3,100	$2,650

❊ G Series Lightweight - lightweight variation of the FAL.

	$4,000	$3,500	$3,000	$2,500	$2,100	$1,875	$1,600

The Lightweight Model had the trigger frame, magazine, and return spring tube made out of aluminum.

❊ Browning Arms Co. Import - milled receiver, wood or nylon furniture.

	$2,400	$2,000	$1,700	$1,550	$1,400	$1,275	$1,150

❊ CAL Prototype - originally imported in 1980, prototype to the current FN FNC, at first declared illegal but later given amnesty, only 20 imported.

	$6,000	$5,250	$4,700	$4,160	$3,600	$3,100	$2,650

G series FALs were imported between 1959-1962 by Browning Arms Co. This rifle was declared illegal by the GCA of 1968 and was exempted 5 years later. Total numbers exempted are: Standard model-1822, Heavy Barrel model-21, Paratrooper model-5.

Above Average	Average	Below Average

RIFLES: SINGLE SHOT

MODEL 1878 STANDARD - various cals., J.M. Browning's first patent, fewer than 600 made (highest known ser. no. is 542) by Browning Brothers in Ogden, Utah between 1878-1883, octagon barrel marked "Browning Bros. Ogden, Utah USA" plain wood stock and forearm with and without pistol grips, crescent steel buttplate, with or without ramrod, several receiver configurations, a very few were made in the deluxe model, seldom found in better than average used condition, with or w/o serial number. Approx. only 100 have survived – Browning Arms Co. & the Winchester Museum have no factory records on this model.

$14,000 - $19,000	$11,000 - $14,000	$7,700 - $11,000

Add 50% for Deluxe Rifle (checkered stock and forearm), 10% for Early Rifle with Sharps Borchardt type lever, 40% for Early Rifle stamped "Ogden, U.T.", 20% for any caliber other than .40-70 SS or .45-70 Govt., 25% for Late Model with rammer rod under barrel held by two thimbles (known as "Montana Model").

Subtract 20% if the original sights have been removed or replaced incorrectly.

Calibers in this model are listed from rarest to most commonly encountered: .50-70 Govt., .45 Sharps, .44 Rem., .40-90 Sharps, .44-77 Sharps, .45-70 Govt., and .40-70 Sharps Straight.

This model is rare since approx. only 550 were mfg. (approx. ser. range 1-550). This patent was sold to Winchester, which became their Model 1885 single shot. To date, less than 100 original Model 1878s have been encountered indicating a high mortality rate (most remaining specimens

Grading	100%	98%	95%	90%	80%	70%	60%

are in poor original condition). An inherent weakness of the original design was the way the stock attached to the action - Winchester later corrected this design flaw. A few remaining examples are not serial numbered. Barter guns are rifles that have Browning stamped actions and barrels of an older gunsmith's identity.

MODEL B-78 - .22-250 Rem., 6mm Rem., .243 Win., .25-06 Rem., 7mm Mag., .30-06, or .45-70 Govt. cal., 24 or 26 in. round or octagon barrel, lever activated falling block, no sights except .45- 70 Govt., checkered walnut stock, approx. 24,000 mfg. 1973-1982.

	$695	$595	$465	$325	$295	$275	$250
.45-70 Govt. cal.	$795	$650	$475	$325	$295	$275	$250

The Model B-78 was reintroduced as the Model 1885 in 1985.

MODEL 1885 HIGH WALL - .22-250 Rem., .223 Rem. (disc. 1994), .270 Win., .30-06, 7mm Rem. Mag., .45-70 Govt., or .454 Casull (new 1998) cal., falling block action, sear safety, 28 in. octagonal barrel, adj. trigger, no sights, checkered walnut stock and Schnabel forearm, exposed hammer, gold trigger, approx. 8¾ lbs. Mfg. 1985-2001.

$775	$585	$455	$365	$330	$295	$275

Last MSR was $1,027.

This model is equipped with open sights in .45-70 Govt. and .454 Casull cals.

MODEL 1885 LOW WALL - .22 Hornet, .223 Rem. (disc. 2000), .243 Win. (disc. 2000), or .260 Rem. (new 1999) cal., action patterned after the Winchester Low Wall receiver, 24 in. barrel, adj. trigger, features thinner 24 in. barrel, 6¼ lbs. Mfg. 1995-2001.

$755	$575	$450	$360	$330	$295	$275

Last MSR was $997.

MODEL 1885 HIGH WALL TRADITIONAL HUNTER - .30-30 Win., .38-55 WCF or .45-70 Govt. cal., High-Wall action, 30 in. octagon barrel with ejector, blue receiver, rear tang aperture sight, crescent buttplate, checkered stock and forearm, approx. 9 lbs. Mfg. 1997-2000.

$1,075	$780	$585	$450	$360	$330	$295

Last MSR was $1,220.

MODEL 1885 LOW WALL TRADITIONAL HUNTER - .357 Mag., .44 Mag., or .45 LC cal., 24 in. half-round, half-octagon barrel, case colored receiver and buttplate, gold bead front, semi-buckhorn rear, and upper tang aperture sights, 6½ lbs. Mfg. 1998-2001.

$1,130	$800	$615	$450	$375	$330	$295

Last MSR was $1,289.

MODEL 1885 BPCR (BLACK POWDER CARTRIDGE) - .40-65 Win. (black powder only) or .45-70 Govt. (black powder or smokeless) cal., case colored high wall action, 30 in. half-round, half-octagon barrel, checkered pistol grip stock with shotgun butt, w/o ejector system and shell deflector, vernier tang rear sight and globe front sight with spirit level, approx. 11 lbs. Mfg. 1996-2001.

$1,595	$1,275	$1,085	$925	$800	$700	$600

Last MSR was $1,766.

✴ ***Model 1885 BPCR Creedmoor*** - .45-90 cal., blue receiver, 34 in. half-round, half- octagon barrel with globe front and aperture rear tang sights, 11¾ lbs. Mfg. 1998-99.

$1,595	$1,285	$1,090	$925	$800	$700	$600

Last MSR was $1,764.

Grading	100%	98%	95%	90%	80%	70%	60%

RIFLES: SLIDE ACTION

BPR - .243 Win., .270 Win., .30-06, .308 Win., .300 Win. Mag., or 7mm Rem. Mag. cal., 7 lug rotary bolt, blue alloy receiver, 22 or 24 (Mag. cals. only) in. barrel with open sights, features downward camming slide action assembly, checkered walnut stock and forend, cross-bolt safety, 3 or 4 shot mag., approx. 7 lbs. 3 oz. New 1997.

	MSR $725	$635	$565	$510	$455	$400	$360	$330

Add $55 for Mag. cals.

BPR-22 - .22 LR or .22 Mag. cal., short-stroke action, 20¼ in. barrel, 11 shot tube mag., mfg. 1977-1982.

	$275	$195	$170	$160	$140	$130	$100

✳ **BPR-22 Grade II** - similar to BPR-22, only engraved action, select walnut.

	$450	$350	$295	$260	$230	$200	$175

Add 10% for .22 Mag. cal.

TROMBONE MODEL - .22 LR cal. only, slide action with tube mag., fixed sights, takedown, 24 in. barrel, hammerless, similar to Win. Model 61, with either F.N. or U.S. (rare) barrel address.

✳ **FN Barrel Address**

	$695	$595	$450	$375	$295	$260	$225

✳ **BAC Barrel Markings**

	$850	$695	$525	$450	$350	$295	$250

Over 150,000 "Trombones" were mfg. by FN from 1922-1974. About 3,200 were imported by BAC in late 1960s. Very rare with factory engraving.

BCA GRADE III FN TROMBONE - only 60 manufactured for the Browning Collectors Association 1985-86, silver engraved frame with deluxe walnut.

	$2,500	$2,100	$1,650

SHOTGUNS: BOLT ACTION, A-BOLT SERIES

A-BOLT MODEL - 12 ga. only, 3 in. chamber, 2 shot mag., same bolt system as A-Bolt II Rifle, 22 or 23 in. barrel (rifled or Invector with rifled tube), available in Stalker Model with graphite fiberglass composite stock or Hunter Model with select satin finished walnut stock, dull matte finished barrel and receiver, top tang safety, choice of no sights (new 1996) or adj. rear sight, drilled and tapped receiver, approx. 7 lbs. Mfg. by Miroku 1995-98.

✳ **Stalker Model**

	$435	$335	$300	$275	$260	$240	$220

Last MSR was $720.

Add $25 for open sights.
Add $100 for rifled barrel.

✳ **Hunter Model**

	$425	$325	$295	$275	$260	$240	$220

Last MSR was $805.

Add $24 for open sights.
Add $100 for rifled barrel.

SHOTGUNS: O/U, CITORI HUNTING SERIES

All Citori shotguns which incorporate the Invector choke tube system may be used with steel shot. Invector Plus choke tubes are designed for backbored barrels. DO NOT USE Standard Invector choke tubes in barrels marked for the Invector Plus choking system.

Grading	100%	98%	95%	90%	80%	70%	60%

CITORI HUNTING MODELS - 12, 16 (mfg. 1986-89), 20, 28 ga. (disc. 1994) or .410 bore (disc. 1994), 26, 28, or 30 in. barrels, various chokes, boxlock, auto ejectors, SST, vent. rib, features checkered semi-pistol grip stock with grooved semi-beavertail forearm, grades differ in amount of engraving, finish, and wood. Invector chokes became standard in 1988, Invector Plus chokes became standard 1995 on 12 or 20 ga., 6 lbs. 9 oz. - 8 lbs. 5 oz. Mfg. 1973-2001 by Miroku.

❋ *Grade I 12 or 20 ga.* - blue finish with light scroll engraving.

◇**Earlier Mfg. without Invector Choking**

$750	$675	$575	$525	$475	$425	$395

Add 15% for 16 ga. if in 90%+ original condition.

◇**Grade I Hunter Model** - current Mfg. with Invector Choking - 12 or 20 ga., 3 in. chambers, 20 ga. available with Standard Invector or Invector Plus (new 1994) choking system, Invector Plus choking standard on recently mfg. 12 and 20 ga., 6 lbs. 9 oz. - 8 lbs. 5 oz. Disc. 2001.

$1,110	$795	$675	$525	$465	$395	$350

Last MSR was $1,486.

❋ *Grade I Smaller Gauges*

◇**28 ga. or .410 bore** - without Invector choking. Disc. 1994.

$850	$700	$575	$495	$450	$395	$350

Last MSR was $1,097.

❋ *Grade II* - 12, 20, 28 ga., or .410 bore. Disc. 1983.

$995	$810	$740	$685	$610	$570	$540

❋ *Grade III* - 12, 16 (mfg. 1986-89), 20, 28 ga. (disc. 1994), or .410 bore (disc. 1994), greyed steel receiver with engraved game scenes featuring grouse (20 ga.) and ducks (12 ga.), Invector chokes standard, Invector Plus became standard in 12 ga. in 1994. Mfg. 1985-95.

$1,425	$1,025	$835	$725	$625	$585	$550

Last MSR was $1,875.

Add 15% for 16 ga. if in 90%+ original condition.
Add 15%-25% for 28 ga. or .410 bore (both disc. 1989).

❋ *Grade V* - 12, 20, 28 ga., or .410 bore, extensive deep relief engraving with game scenes on satin grey receiver. Disc. 1984.

$1,550	$1,265	$1,100	$990	$880	$795	$695

❋ *Grade VI* - 12, 16 (mfg. 1986-89), 20, 28 ga. (disc. 1992), or .410 bore (disc. 1989), blue or greyed receiver with extensive engraving including multiple gold inlays, Standard Invector (12 ga. disc. 1993) or Invector Plus chokes. Mfg. 1985-95.

$2,100	$1,500	$1,225	$1,000	$895	$795	$695

Last MSR was $2,715.

Add 15% for 16 ga. if in 90%+ original condition.
Add 15%-25% for 28 ga.

❋ *3½ in. Magnum Model* - 12 ga., 3½ in. chambers, 28 or 30 in. VR barrels with back-bored Invector plus choke tubes, with recoil pad, approx. 8½ lbs. 9 oz. Mfg. 1989-2000.

$1,250	$950	$825	$695	$600	$550	$495

Last MSR was $1,563.

Grading	100%	98%	95%	90%	80%	70%	60%

✳ *Sporting Hunter* - 12 or 20 ga., 3 or 3½ (12 ga. only) in. chambers, 26, 28, or 30 (12 ga. only) in. barrels with Invector Plus choking, configured for both hunting and sporting clays shooting, Superposed style forearm, contoured recoil pad, front and center bead sights, gloss or satin (3½ in. only) wood finish, 6 lbs. 9 oz. - 8 lbs. 9 oz. Mfg. 1998-2001.

| | **$1,250** | **$895** | **$725** | **$585** | **$475** | **$425** | **$375** |

Last MSR was $1,607.

Add $102 for 3½ in. Mag. (wood satin finish only).

✳ *Satin Hunter* - 12 ga. only, 3 or 3½ (disc. 2000) in. chambers, 26, 28, or 30 (3½ in. Mag. only, disc. 1998) in. VR backbored barrels with Invector Plus choking, features satin wood finish, approx. 8¼ lbs. Mfg. 1998-2001.

| | **$1,150** | **$825** | **$650** | **$535** | **$445** | **$400** | **$350** |

Last MSR was $1,535.

✳ *Upland Special* - 12, 16 (mfg. 1989 only), or 20 ga. (2¾ in. chambers), shortened checkered straight grip walnut stock (14 in. LOP) and Schnabel forearm, 24 in. barrels, blue finish, Invector (12 ga. disc. 1993) or Invector Plus choking, 6-6¾ lbs. Mfg. 1984-2000.

| | **$1,125** | **$850** | **$660** | **$550** | **$450** | **$425** | **$395** |

Last MSR was $1,514.

Add 15% for 16 ga. if in 90%+ original condition.
Subtract $125 for Invector choking.

✳ *White Upland Special* - 12 or 20 ga., 2¾ in. chambers, similar to Upland Special, except features silver nitride finished receiver, 6 1/8 or 6½ lbs. Mfg. 2000-2001.

| | **$1,185** | **$885** | **$785** | **$575** | **$465** | **$440** | **$400** |

Last MSR was $1,583.

CITORI SUPERLIGHT MODELS - 12, 16, 20, 28 ga., or .410 bore, 2¾ in. chambers except for .410 bore, English stock, oil finish, Invector chokes became standard in 1988, Invector Plus became standard 1995 for 12 or 20 ga., approx. 6 lbs.-6¾ lbs. Mfg. 1983- present.

✳ *Grade I 12, 16, or 20 ga.*

◇**Earlier Mfg. without Invector Choking**

| | **$795** | **$700** | **$600** | **$550** | **$495** | **$445** | **$395** |

◇**Grade I** - Current Mfg. with Invector Choking - 12 or 20 ga., 20 ga. available with Standard Invector or Invector Plus (new 1994, became standard 1995) choking system, Invector Plus choking standard on recently mfg. 12 ga.

| **MSR** | **$1,590** | | **$1,175** | **$875** | **$675** | **$575** | **$475** | **$425** | **$395** |

Subtract $125 for Standard Invector choking in 20 ga.

✳ *Grade I Smaller Gauges*

◇**28 ga. or .410 bore** - without Invector choking until 1993, Invector choking became an option in 1994 and standard in 1995.

| **MSR** | **$1,666** | | **$1,295** | **$925** | **$775** | **$675** | **$550** | **$495** | **$450** |

Subtract 10% if without Invector choke tubes.

✳ *Superlight Feather* - 12 or 20 (new 2002) ga., greyed alloy receiver, 26 in. Invector choked VR barrels, straight grip English stock and scaled down Schnabel forearm, 5¾ or 6¼ lbs. New 1999.

| **MSR** | **$1,809** | | **$1,385** | **$995** | **$785** | **$635** | **$535** | **$460** | **$425** |

✳ *Grade III* - same gauges as Grade I, Standard Invector on 12 or 20 (disc.) ga. or Invector Plus (standard in 12 ga. beginning 1994) chokes. New 1986.

| **MSR** | **$2,300** | | **$1,750** | **$1,275** | **$975** | **$825** | **$675** | **$600** | **$550** |

Add $270 for 28 ga. or .410 bore (disc. 1997).
Subtract 10% if without Invector choke tubes.

Grading	100%	98%	95%	90%	80%	70%	60%

✳ ***Grade V*** - sideplate available. Disc. 1984.

	$1,550	$1,265	$1,100	$990	$880	$795	$695

✳ ***Grade VI*** - older mfg. has Invector chokes standard (option on 28 ga. or .410 bore beginning 1994) or Invector Plus (standard and available in 12 or 20 ga. only) chokes, choice of blue or grey (new 1996) receiver finish. New 1983.

MSR $3,510	$2,625	$1,875	$1,425	$1,250	$1,025	$850	$700

Subtract 10% for 28 ga. or .410 bore without choke tubes.
Add $270 for 28 ga. or .410 bore with Standard Invector choking.

✳ ***Grade VI Sideplate*** - 20 ga. only. Disc.

	$2,950	$2,250	$1,950	$1,775	$1,650	$1,400	$1,175

CITORI SPORTER MODELS - similar to Citori Superlight, except with 3 in. chambers, 26 in. barrels, various chokes, straight grip stock, Schnabel forearm. Disc. 1983.

	$875	$740	$600	$550	$495	$440	$385

Add $50 for 28 ga. or .410 bore.

✳ ***Sporter Grade II*** - 12, 20, 28 ga., or .410 bore.

	$1,250	$1,075	$1,020	$965	$880	$770	$715

✳ ***Sporter Grade V*** - 12, 20, 28 ga., or .410 bore.

	$1,575	$1,395	$1,225	$1,100	$990	$880	$825

CITORI LIGHTNING MODELS - 12, 16 (disc. 1989), 20, 28 ga., or .410 bore, 2 ¾ (28 ga. only), or 3 in. (standard on 12 ga., 20 ga., and .410 bore) chamber, 26, 28, or 30 (disc.) in. barrels, Invector chokes standard on newer mfg. smaller ga.'s, Invector Plus became standard 1995 for 12 or 20 ga., boxlock, auto ejectors, SST, vent. rib, features checkered round knob pistol grip stock and slimmer forearm, grades differ in amount of engraving, finish, and quality of wood, approx. 6½-8 lbs. Introduced 1988.

✳ ***Grade I 12, 16 or 20 ga.***

◇**Earlier Mfg.** - without Invector Choking.

	$795	$700	$600	$550	$495	$445	$395

Add 15% for 16 ga.

◇**Grade I** - current mfg. with Invector Choking - 12 or 20 ga., Invector (disc. 1994) or Invector Plus choking (became standard on 12 ga. in 1994, 20 ga. in 1995).

MSR $1,534	$1,135	$855	$685	$600	$550	$500	$460

Subtract 10% for Standard Invector choking.

✳ ***Grade I Smaller Gauges***

◇**28 ga. or .410 bore** - without Invector choking until 1993, Invector choking became an option in 1994, standard in 1995.

MSR $1,594	$1,225	$895	$750	$650	$595	$550	$500

Subtract 10% if without Standard Invector choking.

✳ ***Grade III*** - 12, 16 (disc. 1989), 20, 28 ga., or .410 bore, greyed steel receiver with engraved game scenes, older mfg. may or may not have Invector choking, Invector Plus choking is now standard on 12 or 20 ga. New 1988.

MSR $2,346	$1,785	$1,295	$995	$835	$675	$600	$550

Add $275 for 28 ga. or .410 bore.
Subtract 10% if without Invector choking.
Add 15% for 16 ga. (disc. 1989).

Grading	100%	98%	95%	90%	80%	70%	60%

✴ **Grade VI** - 12, 16 (disc. 1989), 20, 28 ga., or .410 bore, blue or greyed receiver with extensive engraving including 7 gold inlays.

MSR	$3,615	$2,700	$1,925	$1,450	$1,250	$1,025	$850	$700

Add $278 for 28 ga. or .410 bore.
Add 15% for 16 ga. (disc. 1989).

CITORI MODEL 525 - 12 or 20 ga., 3 in. chambers, silver nitride receiver, 26 or 28 in. unported barrels featuring VR with forward angled posts, pronounced walnut pistol grip stock with European comb, flush fit Invector Plus choke tubes, European checkered stock with vent recoil pad, Schnabel forearm, 6 lbs. 6 oz. – 8 lbs. New 2002.

MSR	$1,777	$1,385	$995	$780	$640	$525	$475	$450

CITORI ESPRIT - 12 ga. only, 3 in. chambers, 28 in. barrels with VR and 3 choke tubes, features removable and interchangeable sideplates on the back of greyed receiver, choice of scroll or pointer engraving scenes, gold enhancements are optional, 8¼ lbs. New 2002.

MSR	$2,453	$1,900	$1,400	$1,050	$875	$725	$625	$575

CITORI PRIVILEGE - 12 or 20 (new 2001) ga., 3 in. chambers, boxlock with extensively hand engraved sideplates, silver finished receiver, 26 or 28 in. barrels with 5/16 in. VR and Invector Plus choking, approx. 8 lbs. New 2000.

MSR	$5,376	$4,650	$3,975	$3,400	$2,850	$2,475	$2,025	$1,750

CITORI LIGHTNING FEATHER - 12 or 20 (new 2000) ga., 3 in. chambers, greyed alloy receiver, 26 or 28 in. Invector choked VR barrels, select checkered walnut stock and forearm, approx. 7 lbs. New 1999.

MSR	$1,744	$1,360	$985	$775	$640	$525	$475	$450

✴ **Citori Lightning Feather Combo** - includes set of 27 in. 20 ga. (3 in. chambers) and 28 ga. barrels with Invector Plus (20 ga.) and standard Invector (28 ga.) chokes, cased. New 2000.

MSR	$2,834	$2,435	$2,000	$1,825	$1,600	$1,375	$1,175	$995

CITORI GRAN LIGHTNING (GL) MODEL - 12, 20, 28 ga. (new 1994), or .410 bore (new 1994) only, 2 ¾ (28 ga. only) or 3 in. chambers, similar to Lightning Model, except has higher grade walnut stock and forearm with satin/oil finish, includes recoil pad, 26 or 28 in. barrels, Invector chokes standard on newer mfg. smaller ga.'s, Invector Plus became standard 1995 for 12 or 20 ga., 6½ - 8 lbs. New 1990.

MSR	$2,228	$1,760	$1,250	$1,035	$900	$775	$675	$575

Add $120 for 28 ga. or .410 bore.

CITORI WHITE LIGHTNING - 12, 20, 28 (new 2000) ga., or .410 bore (new 2000), 3 in. chambers, silver nitride receiver with scroll and rosette engraving, satin wood finish with round pistol grip stock and vent recoil pad, 26 or 28 in. VR barrels with Invector Plus choking, 6 lbs. 7 oz - 8 lbs. 2 oz. New 1998.

MSR	$1,583	$1,245	$940	$785	$650	$600	$550	$500

Add $71 for .28 ga. or .410 bore (new 2000).

CITORI MICRO LIGHTNING - 20 ga. only, 2¾ in. chambers, 24 in. VR barrels, Invector (disc. 1993) or Invector Plus (new 1994) choking, 13¾ LOP (½ in. shorter), 6 lbs. 3 oz. Mfg. 1991-2001.

✴ **Grade I**

	$1,250	$945	$785	$650	$600	$550	$500

Last MSR was $1,591.

Subtract 10% for standard Invector choking.

Grading	100%	98%	95%	90%	80%	70%	60%

✳ Grade III - Invector (disc. 1993) or Invector Plus choking. Mfg. 1993-94.

	$1,415	$1,050	$850	$750	$625	$585	$550

Last MSR was $1,850.

✳ Grade VI - Mfg. 1993-94.

	$2,025	$1,575	$1,225	$1,025	$895	$795	$695

Last MSR was $2,680.

Subtract $267 for standard Invector choking.

SHOTGUNS: O/U, CITORI SKEET

CITORI SKEET/SPECIAL SKEET MODELS - 12, 20, 28 ga., or .410 bore, same action as Citori Field, only with high post target rib (standard 1985), 26 and 28 in. skeet barrels, recoil pad, Invector chokes became standard in 1990 in 12 and 20 ga., Invector Plus chokes with ported barrels were an option during 1992 and became standard on the 12 ga. in 1994, new Special Skeet models were introduced during 1995 with decreased weight (¼ lb. lighter) and better swing/balance characteristics.

✳ Grade I

◇**12 or 20 Ga.** - Invector Plus choking, high-post target rib, and ported barrels became standard in 1994, 7¼ - 8 lbs. Disc. 2000.

	$1,395	$995	$800	$700	$625	$575	$500

Last MSR was $1,742.

Add $210 for adj. comb (mfg. 1995-98).
Subtract 10% if without Invector chokes.
Earlier mfg. skeet guns had a low profile, wide VR.

◇ **Smaller Guages**- 28 ga. or .410 bore, 6 lbs. 15 oz. Disc. 1999.

	$1,300	$950	$775	$650	$550	$500	$450

Last MSR was $1,627.

Subtract 10% if without Invector chokes.

✳ Grade II - 12, 20, 28 ga., or .410 bore, high rib. Disc. 1983.

	$1,000	$850	$800	$740	$690	$650	$600

✳ Grade III - 12, 20, 28 ga., or .410 bore, Invector chokes originally in 12 and 20 ga. and became an option on 28 ga. and .410 bore in 1994. Mfg. 1986-1999.

◇**12 or 20 Ga.** - Invector Plus choking, high-post target rib, and ported barrels became standard in 1994. Disc. 1999.

	$1,775	$1,300	$975	$795	$650	$550	$495

Last MSR was $2,310.

Add $210 for adj. comb (mfg. 1995-98).

◇ **Smaller Gauges**- 28 ga. or .410 bore. Disc. 1999.

	$1,795	$1,325	$975	$825	$675	$595	$550

Last MSR was $2,316.

Subtract 10% if without standard Invector choking (new 1994).

✳ Grade V - 12, 20, 28 ga., or .410 bore, high rib. Disc. 1984.

	$1,495	$1,265	$1,100	$990	$880	$795	$650

✳ Grade VI - Skeet gauges, choice of blue or grey finished receiver with multi gold inlays, deluxe walnut. Disc. 1995.

◇**12 Ga** - Invector Plus choking, high-post target rib, and ported barrels became standard in 1994.

	$2,025	$1,600	$1,325	$1,100	$960	$875	$825

Last MSR was $2,555.

Grading	100%	98%	95%	90%	80%	70%	60%

◇**Smaller Gauges** - 20, 28 ga., or .410 bore, 20 ga. available with standard Invector choking, 28 ga. and .410 bore are choked SK/SK.

	$2,000	**$1,600**	**$1,325**	**$1,100**	**$960**	**$875**	**$825**

Last MSR was $2,518.

❋ *Skeet Golden Clays (GC)* - 12, 20, 28 ga., or .410 bore, 26 or 28 in. ported VR barrels, Invector Plus choking, Skeet features, satin grey receiver with Grade VI level of engraving and gold inlays depicting a transitional hunting to clay pigeon scene. Disc. 1993-99.

◇ **12 or 20 Ga.** - Invector (disc. 1995) or Invector Plus choking, high-post target rib, and ported barrels (12 ga. only).

	$2,800	**$2,025**	**$1,625**	**$1,250**	**$1,050**	**$900**	**$825**

Last MSR was $3,434.

Add $210 for adj. comb (mfg. 1995-98).
Subtract approx. 10% if without Invector Plus choking.

◇ **Smaller Gauges** - 28 ga. or .410 bore, standard Invector or fixed SK/SK choking.

	$2,725	**$2,050**	**$1,675**	**$1,300**	**$1,075**	**$950**	**$850**

Last MSR was $3,356.

Subtract approx. 10% with fixed choking.

CITORI XS SKEET - 12 or 20 (new 2001) ga., 28 or 30 in. vent. barrels with 5/16 in. VR and Invector Plus choking, checkered walnut stock available with or without adj. comb, features similar to the Ultra XS Sporting Model, approx. 7 lbs., 14 oz. New 2000.

MSR	**$2,227**	**$1,775**	**$1,325**	**$1,000**	**$895**	**$775**	**$675**	**$575**

Add $224 for adj. comb.

This model's nomenclature was changed from Ultra XS Skeet to Citori XS Skeet in 2002.

CITORI 3 GAUGE SKEET SETS - supplied with one 20 ga. frame, 1 removable forearm, and 3 barrels consisting of 20, 28 ga. and .410 bore, cased. Mfg. 1987-96.

❋ *Grade I* - with high post target rib, standard Invector choking became standard 1994.

	$2,525	**$2,075**	**$1,675**	**$1,450**	**$1,275**	**$1,050**	**$975**

Last MSR was $3,100.

❋ *Grade III* - with high post target rib, available with standard Invector choking (new 1994) or fixed SK/SK chokes.

	$3,100	**$2,350**	**$1,875**	**$1,550**	**$1,395**	**$1,250**	**$1,125**

Last MSR was $3,900.

Subtract 10% for fixed SK/SK chokes.

❋ *Grade VI* - with high post target rib, fixed SK/SK chokes only. Disc. 1994.

	$3,250	**$2,500**	**$2,000**	**$1,775**	**$1,600**	**$1,400**	**$1,275**

Last MSR was $3,990.

❋ *Golden Clays* - features Golden Clays accents and engraving, standard Invector choking. Mfg. 1994-95 only.

	$4,250	**$3,075**	**$2,600**	**$2,100**	**$1,900**	**$1,750**	**$1,600**

Last MSR was $5,100.

CITORI 4 GAUGE SKEET SETS - supplied with one 12 ga. frame, 1 removable forearm, and 4 barrels consisting of 12, 20, 28 ga., and .410 bore, cased. Imported 1985 only.

❋ *Grade I* - with high post target rib, choice of standard Invector (new 1994) or fixed SK/SK choking.

	$3,750	**$2,850**	**$2,400**	**$1,975**	**$1,800**	**$1,775**	**$1,600**

Last MSR was $4,450.

Subtract 10% for fixed SK/SK choking.

Grading	100%	98%	95%	90%	80%	70%	60%

* **Grade III** - with high post target rib, choice of standard Invector (new 1994) or fixed SK/ SK choking.

	$4,575	$3,250	$2,700	$2,250	$1,950	$1,800	$1,700

Last MSR was $5,450.

Subtract 10% for fixed SK/SK choking.

* **Grade VI** - with high post target rib, fixed SK/SK choking only. Disc. 1994.

	$4,600	$3,350	$2,775	$2,300	$2,100	$2,000	$1,900

Last MSR was $5,225.

* **Golden Clays** - features Golden Clays accents and engraving, standard Invector choking. Mfg. 1994 only.

	$5,650	$4,100	$3,300	$2,600	$2,350	$2,100	$1,975

Last MSR was $6,750.

SHOTGUNS: O/U, CITORI SPORTING CLAYS

All sporting clays models mfg. after 1994 have the Triple Trigger System which includes 3 interchangeable trigger shoes.

MODEL 325 - 12 or 20 ga., 28, 30, or 32 (12 ga. only) in. 10mm VR barrels with Invector Plus choking, 12 ga. has ported barrels, European styling featuring checkered walnut stock and Schnabel forearm, greyed nitrous finished receiver, top tang safety, SST, ejectors, 6 lbs. 12 oz. - 7 lbs. 15 oz. Mfg. 1993-94.

	$1,395	$975	$850	$715	$575	$495	$450

Last MSR was $1,625.

* **Model 325 Golden Clays** - 12 or 20 ga., 28, 30, or 32 in. ported (12 ga. only) or unported (20 ga. only) VR barrels, Invector Plus choking, Model 325 Grade II features, satin grey receiver with engraving and gold inlays depicting a transitional hunting to clay pigeon scene. Mfg. 1994 only.

	$2,425	$1,850	$1,450	$1,150	$975	$875	$825

Last MSR was $3,030.

MODEL 425 SPORTING CLAYS GRADE I - 12 or 20 ga., 28, 30, or 32 (disc. 2000 - 12 ga. only, adj. comb) in. 10mm VR barrels with Invector Plus choking, 12 ga. has ported barrels, with or without adj. comb (disc. 2000), European styling featuring checkered walnut stock and Schnabel forearm, mono-bloc action with greyed nitrous finished receiver, top tang safety, SST, ejectors, solid pad, approx. 6¾ - 8 lbs. Mfg. 1995-2001.

	$1,665	$1,150	$935	$825	$725	$625	$525

Last MSR was $2,006.

Add $231 for adj. comb.

* **Model 425 Golden Clays (GC)** - 12 or 20 ga., 28, 30, or 32 (disc. 1999) in. ported (12 ga. only) or unported (20 ga. only) VR barrels, with (disc. 1998) or without adj. comb, Invector Plus choking, Model 325 Grade II features, satin grey receiver with engraving and gold inlays depicting a transitional hunting to clay pigeon scene, 6 lbs., 13 oz. - 7 lbs., 14 oz. Mfg. 1995-2001.

	$3,150	$2,275	$1,675	$1,325	$1,100	$995	$875

Last MSR was $3,977.

Add $210 for adj. comb (disc. 1998).

* **Model 425 WSSF** - 12 ga. only, special dimensions for Women's Shooting Sports Foundation, features painted turquoise finish with WSSF logo on stock or natural walnut finish (new 1997), 7¼ lbs. Mfg. 1995-99.

	$1,550	$1,075	$895	$725	$575	$495	$450

Last MSR was $1,855.

Grading	100%	98%	95%	90%	80%	70%	60%

B

MODEL 525 SPORTING - 12 or 20 ga., 2¾ in. chambers, 28 or 30 in. vent. barrels with 8-11 mm (12 ga. only) or 10 mm (20 ga. only) width VR and porting, redesigned stock, includes full set of Midas Grade Invector Plus choke tubes, European style checkered walnut stock and forearm, 7–8 ¼ lbs. New 2002.

MSR	$2,493		$1,950	$1,600	$1,300	$1,000	$895	$775	$675

MODEL 525 GOLDEN CLAYS - 12 or 20 ga., similar features to the Model 525 Sporting, except has oil finished high grade walnut stock and forearm, engraving pattern that depicts the transistion of a game bird into a clay bird in 24Kt. gold, 7-8½ lbs. New 2002.

MSR	$3,993		$3,165	$2,275	$1,675	$1,325	$1,100	$995	$875

XS GOLDEN CLAYS - similar to Model 525 Golden Clays, except has traditional checkering pattern and ½ - 3/ 8 in. width VR. New 2002.

MSR	$4,080		$3,225	$2,300	$1,675	$1,325	$1,100	$995	$875

MODEL 802 EXTENDED SWING (ES) SPORTING - 12 ga. only, 2¾ in. chambers, features 28 in. ventilated ported VR barrels (low post, 6.2mm wide) which accept either Invector Plus 2 or 4 stainless steel extension tubes (extends barrels to 30 or 32 in.), adj. pull trigger, slimmer checkered and Schnabel forearm, 7 lbs. 5 oz. Mfg. 1996-2001.

			$1,700	$1,175	$975	$800	$700	$600	$550

Last MSR was $2,063.

GTI GRADE I - 12 ga. only, 28 or 30 in. barrel with 13mm vent. rib and barrels, red lettering on receiver during 1989 only - changed to gold lettering and borders with Browning logo in 1990, checkered stock and semi-beavertail forearm, ported barrels were introduced 1990 and became standard 1992, Invector chokes standard, back-bored Invector plus chokes became standard in 1990, approx. 8 lbs. Mfg. 1989-94.

			$1,225	$885	$700	$600	$525	$495	$450

Last MSR was $1,450.

Subtract $75 without ported barrels (disc. 1992).
Add $35 for Signature Painted Model.

The Signature Painted Model includes special paint treatment on stock and forearm featuring Browning logos and trademark - new 1993.

✳ ***GTI Golden Clays*** - 12 ga. only, 28, 30, or 32 in. ported VR barrels, Invector Plus choking, GTI features, satin grey receiver with Grade VI level of engraving and gold inlays depicting a transitional hunting to clay pigeon scene. Mfg. 1993-94.

		$2,350	$1,800	$1,450	$1,150	$975	$875	$825

Last MSR was $2,930.

GRADE I SPECIAL SPORTING - 12 ga. only, 2¾ in. chambers, target dimensions, high-post tapered rib, 28, 30, or 32 in. barrels, full pistol grip with palm swell, adj. comb became optional in 1994, approx. 8 lbs. 3 oz. Mfg. 1989-1999.

			$1,300	$925	$775	$635	$525	$495	$450

Last MSR was $1,636.

Add $220 for adj. comb.
Add $35 for Signature Painted Model (disc. 1994).
Subtract $75 without ported barrels (disc. 1992).
Add $800 for 2 barrel set (28 and 30 in. barrels), disc. 1990.

The Signature Painted Model includes special paint treatment on stock and forearm featuring Browning logos and trademark - mfg. 1993-94.

Ported barrels were new in 1990 and became standard in 1992.

In 1990, the Grade I designation was added to this model. Changes include back-bored barrels with Invector plus choke tubes.

Grading	100%	98%	95%	90%	80%	70%	60%

✳ *Special Sporting Golden Clays (GC)* - 12 ga. only, 28, 30, or 32 in. ported barrels with high-post VR, Invector Plus choking, Special Sporting features, satin grey receiver with Grade VI level of engraving and gold inlays depicting a transitional hunting to clay pigeon scene. Mfg. 1993-98.

	$2,575	$1,925	$1,500	$1,175	$995	$875	$825

Last MSR was $3,203.

Add $210 for adj. comb.

GRADE I SPECIAL SPORTING PIGEON GRADE - 12 ga. only, Vector Plus choking and ported barrels, higher grade of Special Sporting model featuring higher grade walnut and gold line receiver accents. Mfg. 1993-94.

	$1,400	$975	$850	$700	$575	$495	$450

Last MSR was $1,630.

ULTRA SPORTER - 12 ga. only, 28, 30, or 32 in. barrels with vent rib separating barrels, low tapered 13- 10mm VR, blue or grey (new 1996) receiver with gold accents, satin finished checkered pistol grip stock and forearm, Invector Plus choking, 7 lbs. 10 oz. - 8 lbs. 4 oz. Mfg. 1995-99.

	$1,525	$1,050	$875	$750	$575	$495	$450

Last MSR was $1,800.

Add $210 for adj. comb (disc. 1998).
This model was designated GTI until 1995.

✳ *Ultra Sporter Golden Clays (GC)* - 12 ga. only, features better wood and satin finished engraved receiver with gold inlays clay target scene. Mfg. 1995-99.

	$2,750	$2,025	$1,575	$1,200	$1,000	$875	$825

Last MSR was $3,396.

Add $210 for adj. comb (disc. 1997).

CITORI FEATHER XS SPORTING - 12, 20, 28 ga., or .410 bore, 2¾ in. chambers (3 in. standard on .410 bore), 28 or 30 in. vent. barrels with tapered VR (12 ga. only) and Invector Plus choking on 12 and 20 ga. (standard Invector on 28 ga. and .410 bore, 28 in. barrels), alloy receiver with dovetailed steel breechface and hinge pin, Schnabel forearm, Hi-Viz comp. sighting system (includes 8 interchangeable colored light pipes), Nitex receiver finish, includes triple trigger system (3 interchangeable trigger shoes), 6 lbs. (28 ga. or .410 bore) - approx. 7 lbs. (12 ga., 30 in. barrels). New 2000.

MSR	$2,311		$1,800	$1,375	$1,150	$995	$875	$775	$675

Add $74 for 28 ga. or .410 bore.

CITORI XS SPORTING (ULTRA) - 12, 20, 28 ga. or .410 bore, greyed steel receiver with silver Nitrex finish, 24 Kt. gold accents and light engraving, with or w/o (30 in. barrels only) barrel porting on 12 ga., 12 ga. features Invector Plus choking and right hand palm swell, select checkered walnut stock and and Schnabel forearm, 6 lbs. 5 oz. – 7 lbs. 14 oz. New 1999.

MSR	$2,262		$1,770	$1,325	$1,125	$975	$850	$750	$650

Add $74 for 28 ga. or .410 bore.

CITORI LIGHTNING SPORTING (GRADE I) - 12 ga. only, features 3 in. chambers, rounded pistol grip, Lightning style forearm, choice of high or low post VR, standard or adj. (new 1995) comb stock, "Lightning Sporting Clays Edition" inscribed and gold-filled on receiver, 28 in. ported or 30 in. ported or unported (disc.) barrels, approx. 8½ lbs. New 1989.

MSR	$1,691		$1,385	$995	$865	$750	$650	$550	$495

Add $210 for adj. comb (disc. 1998).
Add $79 for high-post rib.
Subtract 10% if with unported barrels.

B

The Signature Painted Model includes special paint treatment on stock and forearm featuring Browning logos and trademark - mfg. 1993-94.

Ported barrels were new in 1990 and became standard in 1992.

Between 1990-2000, the Grade I designation was added to this model. Changes include back-bored barrels with Invector plus choke tubes.

＊ *Lightning Sporting Golden Clays (GC)* - 12 ga. only, 28, 30, or 32 (disc.) in. ported barrels with choice of low or high-post VR, standard or adj. (new 1995) comb stock, Invector Plus choking, Lightning Sporting features, satin grey receiver with Grade VI level of engraving and gold inlays depicting a transitional hunting to clay birds scene, approx. 8½ lbs. Mfg. 1993-98.

$2,495	$1,850	$1,475	$1,150	$995	$875	$825

Last MSR was $3,092.

Add $210 for adj. comb.
Add $111 for high-post VR.

GRADE I LIGHTNING SPORTING PIGEON GRADE - 12 ga. only, higher grade model featuring higher grade walnut and gold line receiver accents. Mfg. 1993-94.

$1,350	$950	$850	$700	$575	$495	$450

Last MSR was $1,566.

Add $64 for high-post VR.

SPORTING HUNTER - please refer to description and pricing under Shotguns: O/U Citori Hunting Series category.

SHOTGUNS: O/U, CITORI TRAP

CITORI TRAP MODELS - 12 ga., similar to Standard Citori, 30 or 32 in. barrels, trap chokes, Monte Carlo stock, recoil pad. Invector chokes became standard in 1988, Invector Plus chokes with ported barrels became an option in 1992, and were made standard in 1993, new Special Trap models were introduced during 1995 with decreased weight (¼ lb. lighter) and better swing/balance characteristics.

＊ *Grade I Special Trap* - approx. 8½ lbs. Mfg. 1995-99.

$1,340	$975	$795	$650	$525	$495	$450

Last MSR was $1,658.

Add $220 for adj. comb.
Subtract 10% without Invector chokes or high rib.

＊ *Trap Combination Set* - Grade I only, 32 in. O/U and 34 in. single barrel, cased. Disc.

$1,395	$1,100	$975	$900	$825	$775	$725

＊ *Grade I Plus Trap* - features adj. rib and stock, back-bored barrels, Invector Plus choke system. Mfg. 1990-94.

$1,560	$1,200	$940	$800	$700	$600	$500

Last MSR was $2,005.

Add 5% for ported barrels.

In 1991 this model included a travel vault gun case at no extra charge. Subtract $50 for older mfg. without travel case.

＊ *Grade I Plus Trap Combo* - includes ported barrels with Invector Plus choking and extra standard single ported barrel, luggage case. Mfg. 1992-94.

$2,850	$2,425	$2,100	$1,900	$1,700	$1,500	$1,250

Last MSR was $3,435.

Grading	100%	98%	95%	90%	80%	70%	60%

B

❋ *Plus Trap Golden Clays* - 12 ga. only, 30 or 32 in. ported VR barrels, Invector Plus choking, Trap features, satin grey receiver with Grade VI level of engraving and gold inlays depicting a transitional hunting to clay birds scene. Mfg. 1993-94.

	$2,850	$2,275	$1,900	$1,600	$1,400	$1,200	$995

Last MSR was $3,435.

❋ *Plus Trap Golden Clays Combo* - includes O/U ported barrels with Invector Plus choking and extra standard single ported barrel, luggage case. Mfg. 1993-94.

	$4,425	$3,300	$2,775	$2,250	$1,925	$1,800	$1,700

Last MSR was $5,200.

❋ *Citori XT Trap* - 12 ga. only, features greyed receiver with 24 Kt. gold accents and light engraving, triple trigger system (includes 3 interchangeable triggers for 1/8 in. adj. on LOP), 30 or 32 in. vent. backbored barrels with high-post VR, checkered high gloss Monte Carlo walnut stock and forearm, waffle-style recoil pad, approx. approx. 8 3/8 lbs. New 1999.

MSR $2,083		$1,650	$1,200	$915	$775	$650	$550	$500

Add $250 for adj. comb.

❋ *Pigeon Grade* - 12 ga. only, features extra deluxe walnut, Invector Plus ported barrels, and receiver gold accents. Mfg. 1993-94.

	$1,715	$1,250	$950	$800	$700	$600	$500

Last MSR was $2,225.

❋ *Signature Painted* - 12 ga. only, features painted red/black stock with Browning logos on stock and forearm, Invector Plus ported barrels. Mfg. 1993-94.

	$1,595	$1,200	$940	$800	$700	$600	$500

Last MSR was $2,065.

❋ *Grade II* - high post rib. Disc. 1983.

	$1,000	$850	$800	$740	$690	$650	$600

❋ *Grade III* - 12 ga. only, high post rib, Invector Plus choking and ported barrels became standard in 1994. Mfg. 1986-1999.

	$1,795	$1,250	$950	$795	$625	$550	$495

Last MSR was $2,310.

Add $220 for adj. comb.
Subtract 10% if without Invector Plus chokes or ported barrels.

❋ *Grade V* - high post rib. Disc. 1984.

	$1,475	$1,150	$990	$880	$795	$710	$620

❋ *Grade VI* - 12 ga. only, Invector chokes became standard in 1985, Invector Plus chokes became standard in 1994. Disc. 1994.

	$1,925	$1,525	$1,225	$1,100	$960	$875	$825

Last MSR was $2,555.

Subtract $150 if without Invector Plus chokes or ported barrels.

❋ *Trap Golden Clays (GC)* - 12 ga. only, 30 or 32 in. ported VR barrels, Invector Plus choking, Trap features, Monte Carlo or regular stock, satin grey receiver with Grade VI level of engraving and gold inlays depicting a transitional hunting to clay pigeon scene. Mfg. 1993-99.

	$2,800	$2,025	$1,625	$1,250	$1,050	$900	$825

Last MSR was $3,434.

Add $220 for adj. comb (new 1995).

Grading	100%	98%	95%	90%	80%	70%	60%

B **CITORI XS PRO-COMP** - 12 ga. only, 2¾ in. chambers, 28 or 30 in. vent. and ported VR barrels with spreader chokes, adj. comb, beavertail forearm, GraCoil recoil reduction system, right hand palm swell, triple trigger system, features removable tungsten alloy forearm weight which approximates the same weight as barrel tubes, also has removable/removable front barrel weight to adj. the swing through, approx. 9 lbs. New 2002.

MSR	$3,796	$3,200	$2,300	$1,700	$1,400	$1,100	$975	$850

SHOTGUNS: O/U, SUPERPOSED GENERAL INFO & CHOKE CODES

SUPERPOSED MODEL - 12, 20 (introduced circa 1948-49), 28 ga. (introduced 1960) or .410 bore (introduced 1960), 26½, 28, 30, or 32 in. barrels, various chokes, boxlock, auto ejectors, various trigger combinations (single & double), checkered pistol grip stock, mfg. 1931-1940 and 1948- 1976 by FN, grades differ in amount of engraving, inlays, general quality of workmanship and wood.

NOTE: The use of steel shot is NOT recommended in any Superposed Series manufactured in Belgium (B-25 variations).

BROWNING CHOKES AND THEIR CODES (MARKED NEXT TO EJECTORS)

* designates full choke (F).

*- designates improved modified choke (IM).

** designates modified choke (M).

**- designates improved cylinder choke (IC).

**$ designates skeet (SK).

*** designates cylinder bore (CYL).

SKEET MODELS were available in every ga. and grade.

TRAP MODELS were available in every grade in 12 ga. only.

BROADWAY TRAP MODELS (mfg. 1961-1975) featured a 5/8 in. wide vent. rib and were also available in every grade.

Please refer to the new expanded Browning Superposed serialization section in this text for determining year of manufacture.

SUPERPOSED: 1931-1940 MFG. (PRE-WWII)

Early pre-war guns had long slender forearms with a metal plate at the front called a horseshoe plate. Approx. circa 1936, the forearm was changed to the one used post war – smaller with a transverse bolt to hold the forearm on. The earlier forearm had a long bolt that ran from front to back through the metal plate to hold the forearm on. The earlier transverse bolts were recessed into the sides of the forearms. Later the head and fastener on the other side of the forearm were flush with the wood.

Pre-war cases were manufactured in black or brown, with a textured surface called elephant hide, in leather or tex leather. Insides were lined with grey or blue cloth, and the Browning brass label was on the inside top of the case, not the outside. Depending on original condition, these cases sell in the $200-$400 range – single barrel cases are more common than multi-barrel ones.

Extra barrels (same ga. only) could be ordered with the original gun, and were supplied in a Browning hard case.

Very few pre-war Pigeon, Diana, and Midas Grades were signed by the engraver.

Add approx. 35%-50% per extra set of barrels (same ga. only), depending on condition.

Subtract 10%-25% for recoil pad (depending on originality, deterioration, and condition).

STANDARD GRADE/GRADE I/LIGHTNING - 12 ga. only, boxlock action, blue w/border receiver engraving until 1938, when a simple small center rosette engraving pattern was introduced, 4 trigger options until 1938, when the barrel selector was moved to the top tang, trigger options included: double normal, selective single with the selector on the bottom next to the trigger, twin single, and non- selective single, Standard model nomenclature was changed to Grade I during 1938, in addition to changing the trigger to SST with the barrel selector on the top tang, raised hollow or ventilated rib, Lightning Model introduced during 1936 in Standard grade with striped barrels – ribs were extra cost. Original buttplates featured intertwined twin circles and were made of horn.

12 ga.	N/A	$1,850	$1,500	$1,275	$995	$875	$825

Original buttplates with unaltered (uncut) stock are very important to collectors for this period of Superposed manufacture.

First year production Superposed will command a premium (approx. ser. no. range 1-2,000). The twin single trigger is also very desirable for collectors.

Recoil pads were an extra option during this time, and even though they might be factory installed, they are not desirable to collectors, and as a result, prices could be reduced substantially based on pad deterioration. Pad makers included: Jostam, Hawkins, Noshoc, D&W, and Black Diamond – these pads were $5 options pre-WWII.

PIGEON GRADE - grey receiver with 2 pigeons on either side, these earlier guns had larger engraved pigeons than later production (1960 and later). Mfg. 1931-1940.

12 ga.	N/A	$4,000	$3,400	$2,150	$1,850	$1,600	$1,400

The Pigeon Grade style of engraving is the only pre-war style that was continued after WWII.

DIANA GRADE - grey receiver with lighter style, delicate European style engraving, boars and stags were pictured in the 1931 catalog, but dogs and birds could also be special ordered at no additional cost until 1936, after which it became extra cost, dogs and birds engraving are more common than boars and stag. Mfg. 1931-1940.

12 ga.	N/A	$4,950	$4,250	$3,750	$3,250	$2,650	$2,000

The Diana Grade was changed dramatically in post-WWII production.

MIDAS GRADE - featured gold inlaid pigeons with outstretched wings on blue frame sides and bottom plus trigger guard. This Germanic syle engraving also exhibited multiple gold escutcheons and gold lining, ejector trip rods, ejector hammers and firing pins are also 18 Kt. gold plated, finest checkered walnut.

12 ga.	N/A	$6,950	$6,000	$4,950	$3,500	$3,000	$2,450

The Midas Grade was changed dramatically in post-WWII production.

SUPERPOSED: 1948-1960 MFG. (POST-WWII)

Model nomenclature was changed from pre-war designations to Grades I-VI. During this period, extra barrels could only be ordered in the same gauge as the original gun. Hardshell cases from this era are referred to as Tolex cases – they have blue velvet lining, and a brass Browning label on the outside top.

Engraved guns signed by Browning's top engravers (Funken, Vrancken, Watrin, Doyen, Müeller, & Magis) will command a premium over unsigned guns. Felix Funken retired in 1960, and died in 1966.

Add approx. 35%-50% per extra set of barrels (same ga. only), depending on condition.
Add $200-$300 for correct Tolex hardshell case with paperwork.
Subtract $500 for recoil pads on Grade I models.
Subtract $750 for recoil pads on the higher grades.
Special order Superposed with non-standard factory engraving, checkered buttstocks, 3 piece forearms, and other special orders will command premiums over standard configurations.

On most Superposed with added recoil pads, the stock has usually been cut to keep the LOP the same. The correct LOP on a Superosed is 14¼ inches, with or w/o a recoil pad.

The twin circle buttplate was always horn, and was used on very early post war guns until 1949-1950.

Grading	100%	98%	95%	90%	80%	70%	60%

B

GRADE I STANDARD WEIGHT - 12 or 20 ga. (3 in. chambers were introduced in the 12 ga. during 1955, and in 20 ga. during 1957), otherwise similar to pre-war mfg., blue finish and triggers until 1955, gold trigger(s) became standard in 1955, raised (standard until 1959) or vent. rib only beginning in 1959, round knob long tang (RKLT) stock configuration, this earlier period of mfg. also featured smaller, narrower forearms and thinner pistol grip stock with horn buttplate (can be determined by the rounded "g" in Browning, not square), early post-war production had similar pre-WWII minimal engraving until circa 1952-53, more standard engraving continued through 1955, when Grade I models featured considerably more engraving, post-war 12 ga. serialization began at approx. 17,100, and with 200 on 20 ga. Mfg. 1948-1960.

	100%	98%	95%	90%	80%	70%	60%
12 ga.	$1,850	$1,450	$1,050	$900	$825	$750	$700
20 ga.	$3,000	$2,750	$2,100	$1,550	$1,275	$1,100	$995

Grade I models had 3 levels of standard engraving coverage.

* *Grade I Lightning Hunting Model* - 12 or 20 ga., 6 oz. lighter than Standard Weight. Introduced in all Grades beginning 1956.

	100%	98%	95%	90%	80%	70%	60%
12 ga.	$1,850	$1,450	$1,050	$900	$825	$750	$700
20 ga.	$3,000	$2,750	$2,100	$1,550	$1,275	$1,100	$995

* *Grade I Magnum* - 12 ga. only, 3 in. chambers, 28, 30, or 32 in. barrels with raised or vent. rib, recoil pad standard, introduced in all Grades in 1955.

	100%	98%	95%	90%	80%	70%	60%
12 ga.	$1,850	$1,500	$1,200	$1,000	$825	$775	$725

This model with 30 in. barrels is now popular again, as Sporting Clays shooters like this desirable configuration.

* *Grade I Trap Standard Weight Model* - 12 ga. only, various configurations, Introduced 1952.

	100%	98%	95%	90%	80%	70%	60%
	$1,850	$1,500	$1,200	$1,000	$825	$750	$700

Pre-war trap guns and those manufactured post-war until approx. 1955 were virtually indistinguishable from field guns as they had field style forearms, round knob (semi-pistol grip) and long tangs. The only way to tell the difference is they had a longer LOP (14½ in.) and a shorter drop at the heel – 1¾ in. vs. 2½ in. for field stocks. These early trap guns did not come with recoil pads. Between 1956-1960, trap guns had the forearm changed to semi- beavertail. These late guns with semi-beavertail forearms are very desirable today due to their rarity and overall desirability.

GRADE II - featured pre-war Pigeon Grade engraving with large pigeons, some early post- war mfg. were signed by Funken.

	100%	98%	95%	90%	80%	70%	60%
12 ga.	$3,500	$3,000	$2,500	$1,850	$1,650	$1,550	$1,450
20 ga.	$5,000	$4,000	$3,250	$2,550	$2,250	$1,950	$1,750

GRADE III - 12 or 20 ga., European style engraving, commonly referred to as "fighting cocks", pheasants on right side, fighting cocks on left, most were signed by the engraver.

	100%	98%	95%	90%	80%	70%	60%
12 ga.	$4,000	$3,250	$2,500	$1,950	$1,750	$1,650	$1,550
20 ga.	$6,500	$5,250	$4,000	$3,250	$2,500	$2,175	$1,850

GRADE IV - 12 or 20 ga., features deeper European style engraving with dogs and foxes, most were signed by the engraver.

	100%	98%	95%	90%	80%	70%	60%
12 ga.	$6,500	$5,750	$4,750	$3,000	$1,850	$1,700	$1,625
20 ga.	$8,500	$7,000	$6,000	$5,000	$3,750	$2,950	$2,450

GRADE V - 12 or 20 ga., features deeper engraving than pre-war Diana Grade, pheasants and ducks on reciever, most were signed by the engraver – Doyen was prevalant on this model.

	100%	98%	95%	90%	80%	70%	60%
12 ga.	$6,500	$5,750	$4,750	$3,500	$2,500	$1,800	$1,700
20 ga.	$8,500	$7,000	$6,000	$4,500	$3,750	$2,950	$2,450

Grading	100%	98%	95%	90%	80%	70%	60%

GRADE VI - 12 or 20 ga., engraving pattern similar to later production Midas Grade, almost all of these were signed by Müller. Introduced in July, 1957, changed in 1960, limited production, and rarest of the 6 grades.

	100%	98%	95%	90%	80%	70%	60%
12 ga.	$7,000	$5,650	$3,650	$3,000	$2,600	$2,300	$1,950
20 ga.	$9,500	$7,250	$6,000	$5,000	$4,500	$3,950	$3,600

SUPERPOSED:1960-1976 MFG.

In early 1960, a major change was made in the manner in which the various grades of Superposed were designated. The Roman numerals used in the 1950s were dropped, and Browning once again returned to names. The Pigeon, Diana, and Midas names used for pre-war designations were brought back and replaced the Grade II, Grade V, and Grade VI respectively. Grades III & IV were dropped and replaced by the Pointer. The Grade I remained unchanged.

The Broadway Trap Model was introduced in 1961. Browning's lifetime Superposed warranty began in 1963. During 1965, the Hydro Coil stock (1 year only) and barrel Super Tubes were introduced. During 1966, a major change was implemented to save money when Browning switched from a long tang to short tang. During 1970-71, the stock configuration was once again changed to a full pistol grip (referred to as flat knob), and the long tang was brought back. Also at this time, mechanical triggers were implemented vs. the older inertial design, and silver solder vent. ribs vs. tin solder. As a result, this period of Superposed manufacture was mechanically better and more reliable. The Superlight Model was introduced in 12 ga. during 1967, 20 ga. during 1969, and became available in all Grades beginning in 1971. All gauge Skeet sets became available in all Grades during 1972.

During late 1966, Browning's salt wood problems began to emerge, and continued until 1972. Most experts have never seen a long tang salt gun, and therefore believe that almost 100% of the salt guns had short tangs. Depending on the damage (it can vary a lot), values for salt damaged guns can be reduced as much as 50% (heavy pitting and original salt wood). Those salt guns that have been restocked by Browning are accepted by the shooting fraternity, and can command as much as 90% of the value of non-salt original guns. To determine if a Superposed has salt damage, examine carefully any gun where the serial number is within the 1966- 1971 production range (please refer to the Browning Superposed serialization section), and carefully inspect the wood around the buttplate, forearm, and where the wood joins the receiver metal for any telltale rusting or pitting.

Engraved guns signed by Browning's top engravers (Funken, Vrancken, Watrin, Magis, Müeller, and J. Baerten) will command a premium over unsigned guns. Also, more and more Superposed models are appearing with Angelo Bee's signature (while non-factory, Mr. Bee's work is universally recognized. He engraved in Belgium at FN from 1951-1974).). Louis Vrancken & Watrin took over as heads of the engraving department in 1960.

> Subtract approx. 15%-50% for salt wood (depending on extent of damage).
> Subtract 10% for new style Skeet configuration on models.
> Subtract $500 for recoil pads on Grade I models.
> Subtract $750 for recoil pads on the higher grades.
> Special order Superposed with non-standard factory engraving, checkered buttstocks, 3 piece forearms, and other special orders will command premiums over standard configurations.
>
> On most Superposed with added recoil pads, the stock has usually been cut to keep the LOP the same. The correct LOP on a Superposed is 14¼ inches (14½ in. on Trap & New Style Skeet), with or w/o a factory recoil pad, unless special ordered from the factory.

The following values are for 1960-1976 Superposed production non-salt damaged guns. Most desirable period of mfg. is 1960-66 (round knob, long tang, pre-salt). Guns made during 1970-76 (FKLT) are worth more than RKST, but probably less than RKLT. Lowest values are for 1966-1971 mfg. (round/flat knob, short tang and potential salt problems).

Grading	100%	98%	95%	90%	80%	70%	60%

B

Superposed with Extra Barrel(s) or Super-Tubes

The Superposed could be special ordered from the factory in the following combinations: 12 or 20 ga. with one extra set of barrels in same ga., 12 ga. with one extra set in 20 ga., 12 or 20 ga. with two extra barrel sets of same ga., 20 ga. with one extra set in either 28 ga. or .410 bore, 20 ga. with both 28 ga. and .410 bore barrel sets, and 28 ga. with extra set of .410 bore barrels. Super-Tubes were adaptable on 12 ga. guns only; came from the factory cased with accessories, 16½ in. long, factory installation.

Add 40-50% of the gun's value for each Grade I extra barrel set(s). For higher grades, add approx. $1,000-$2,500 per barrel set, depending on grade.

Add $250 for Super-Tubes - available for 12 ga. only.

Add $400 for Super-Tube Set - 3 ga. set (20, 28 ga., and .410 bore).

Superposed Variations

GRADE I STANDARD WEIGHT & LIGHTNING - 12, 20, 28 ga., or .410 bore (the 28 ga. & .410 bore were not cataloged until 1960), 28 ga. and .410 bore were built on a 20 ga. frame, the buttplate was changed from horn to plastic during 1961, 12 and 20 ga. Lightning Models were approx. 6 oz. lighter than Standard Weight.

	100%	98%	95%	90%	80%	70%	60%
12 ga.	$1,850	$1,450	$1,050	$900	$825	$750	$700
20 ga.	$3,000	$2,500	$2,100	$1,550	$1,275	$1,100	$995
28 ga.	$4,500	$4,000	$3,500	$3,000	$2,500	$2,250	$2,100
.410 Bore	$3,500	$3,000	$2,500	$2,000	$1,475	$1,225	$1,100

Subtract 10%-15% for Grade I Standardweight (12 ga. only).

Add 20%-25% for round knob, long tang stock variations (pre-1966), unless Skeet choked.

Subtract 10%-15% for newer Skeet style model with beavertail forearm and recoil pad.

✹ *Grade I Magnum* - 12 ga. only, 3 in. chambers, 28, 30, or 32 in. barrels with vent. rib, recoil pad standard.

	100%	98%	95%	90%	80%	70%	60%
12 ga.	$1,850	$1,500	$1,100	$1,000	$825	$775	$725

This model with 30 in. barrels is now popular again, as Sporting Clays shooters like this desirable configuration.

✹ *Grade I Superlight* - 12 (mfg. 1967-1976), 20 (1969-1976), 28 (very rare) ga. or .410 bore (mfg. 1970-76) features lightweight construction and straight grip stock. During 1971, the Superlight was offered in all Grades.

Add 10%-30% over Standardweight and Lightning values, depending on condition and overall desirability.

A Quail Unlimited limited edition was also available in the Superlight Series, add 10%-15% if in 98%+ original condition.

✹ *Grade I Trap Model (Lightning and Broadway)* - 12 ga. only, FKLT, Trap dimension stock with recoil pad, semi-beavertail forearm, 30 or 32 in. barrels with either standard 5/16 in. VR (Lightning) or 5/8 in. Broadway VR, first cataloged in 1961, this new Lightning Model Trap was approx. 6 oz. lighter than previous mfg., front and center ivory bead sights standard, 14 3/8 in. LOP, Broadway is approx. 1 lbs. heavier than Lightning with same length barrels.

	100%	98%	95%	90%	80%	70%	60%
	$1,850	$1,500	$1,100	$1,000	$825	$750	$700

PIGEON GRADE -12, 20, 28 ga. or .410 bore, features a silver grey receiver with 2 smaller flying pigeons surrounded by fine scroll engraving on each side of the frame, receiver bottom and tangs also exhibit fine scroll work. Disc. 1974.

	100%	98%	95%	90%	80%	70%	60%
12 ga.	$3,500	$3,000	$2,500	$1,825	$1,650	$1,570	$1,485
20 ga.	$4,500	$4,000	$3,500	$3,000	$2,150	$1,995	$1,850

Grading	100%	98%	95%	90%	80%	70%	60%
28 ga.	$6,000	$5,500	$4,500	$4,000	$3,500	$2,500	$2,250
.410 bore	$4,500	$4,000	$3,500	$3,000	$2,450	$2,150	$1,900

Add 20%-25% for round knob, long tang stock variations (pre-1966), unless Skeet choked.
Subtract 20% for newer Skeet style model with beavertail forearm and recoil pad.
Between 1948-1960, this model was designated the Grade II.

* ✱ ***Pigeon Grade Superlight*** - 12 (mfg. 1967-1976), 20 (1969-1976), 28 (very rare) ga. or .410 bore (mfg. 1970-76) features lightweight construction and straight grip stock. During 1971, the Superlight was offered in all Grades.

  Add 15%-30% over standard Pigeon Grade values, depending on condition and overall desirability.

POINTER GRADE - features engraved silver grey receiver with a pointer on one side, and a setter on the other, select checkered walnut, early production was engraved by Funken, while the final design was executed by Vrancken. Mfg. 1959-Disc. 1966, except for special orders.

Grading	100%	98%	95%	90%	80%	70%	60%
12 ga.	$6,000	$5,000	$4,250	$3,750	$2,500	$2,000	$1,625
20 ga.	$8,000	$6,500	$6,000	$5,000	$4,000	$3,200	$2,700
28 ga. (rare)	$12,500	$10,000	$8,000	$6,000	$4,150	$3,500	$3,150
.410 bore (rare)	$9,500	$8,000	$7,000	$5,000	$4,000	$3,100	$2,850

Add 20%-25% for round knob, long tang stock variations (pre-1966), unless Skeet choked.
Subtract 20% for newer Skeet style model with beavertail forearm and recoil pad.

DIANA GRADE - deeper engraving with duck and pheasant game scenes - similar to 1948-1960 mfg. Grade V. Disc. 1976.

Grading	100%	98%	95%	90%	80%	70%	60%
12 ga.	$6,000	$4,750	$2,850	$2,150	$1,900	$1,800	$1,700
20 ga.	$7,000	$5,900	$4,500	$3,750	$3,500	$3,150	$2,800
28 ga.	$9,500	$7,500	$6,500	$6,000	$5,000	$4,000	$3,650
.410 bore	$7,000	$6,200	$4,750	$4,000	$3,650	$3,250	$2,950

Add 25% for round knob, long tang stock variations (pre-1966).
Subtract 20% for newer Skeet style model with beavertail forearm and recoil pad.
Between 1948-1960, this model was designated the Grade V.

* ✱ ***Diana Grade Superlight*** - 12 (mfg. 1967-1976), 20 (1969-1976), 28 (very rare) ga. or .410 bore (mfg. 1970-76) features lightweight construction and straight grip stock. During 1971, the Superlight was offered in all Grades.

  Add 20%-30% over standard Diana Grade values, depending on condition and overall desirability.

MIDAS GRADE - features new design by Vrancken with deep relief scroll engraving with gold inlaid ducks and pheasants on frame sides and a quail on the bottom, ejector trip rods, ejector hammers, and firing pins are also 18 Kt. gold plated, best quality walnut with fine checkering. Disc. 1976.

Grading	100%	98%	95%	90%	80%	70%	60%
12 ga.	$7,000	$6,000	$5,000	$4,250	$3,750	$3,250	$2,500
20 ga.	$9,000	$7,500	$6,500	$6,000	$4,500	$4,000	$3,650
28 ga.	$12,500	$9,995	$8,500	$6,500	$5,500	$5,000	$4,650
.410 bore	$9,000	$7,000	$6,000	$5,000	$4,000	$3,500	$3,150

Add 25% for round knob, long tang stock variations (pre-1966), unless Skeet choked.
Subtract 20% for newer Skeet style model with beavertail forearm and recoil pad.
Between 1948-1960, this model was designated the Grade VI.

* ✱ ***Midas Grade Superlight*** - 12 (mfg. 1967-1976), 20 (1969-1976), 28 (very rare) ga. or .410 bore (mfg. 1970-76) features lightweight construction and straight grip stock. During 1971, the Superlight was offered in all Grades.

  Add 20%-30% over standard Midas Grade values, depending on condition and overall desirability.

Grading	100%	98%	95%	90%	80%	70%	60%

BICENTENNIAL SUPERPOSED SUPERLIGHT - specially engraved limited edition Model, 51 mfg. - one for each state and Washington, D.C. Left side has U.S. Flag, bald eagle and state emblem inlaid in gold. Right side has gold inlaid hunter and turkey. Blue receiver, fancy checkered English stock, Schnabel forend, velvet lined wood case. Made 1976 by FN.

$10,500   **$7,950**   **$6,950**

EXPOSITION/EXHIBITION MODEL - this specially manufactured Superposed saw limited production from pre-WWII through 1976. There are true exhibition models and a "C" series. Most "C" series did not have carved stocks, and were a special BAC sale of FN guns which did not sell well in Europe. True exhibition guns had gold lettering on the barrels in most cases, and many also had carved stocks. These guns were made for a very special reason, purpose, or person. Prices usually start in the 5 digit level – the C Series is typically priced between $17,500 - $25,000, and true Exhibition guns can get much more expensive, depending on how elaborate the embellishments are.

SUPERPOSED PRESENTATION MODELS (P1-P4) - custom made versions of the Lightning Field, Super Light, Trap, and Skeet guns, specifications the same as Standard models, with differences in finish, engraving and inlay(s), and grade of wood and checkering. These guns were introduced by FN in 1977 and were disc. after 1984. Gauge premiums below refer to Models P1-P3.

> **Add 30% for 20 ga.**
> **Add 70% for 28 ga.**
> **Add 30% for .410 bore.**
> **Add $1,000 of the gun's value for each P1 extra barrel set(s). For higher grades, add approx. $1,000-$2,500 per barrel set, depending on grade.**
> **Subtract 25% for P Series Trap Models.**
> **Subtract 25% for P Series Broadway Trap Models.**
> **Subtract 20% for P Series Skeet 12 and 20 ga. guns.**

Since P Series Superposed were disc. in 1985, collector interest has increased substantially. Interestingly, the P series models are rarer than most of the pre-1976 high grade Superposed models.

✳ *Presentation 1* - silver grey or blue receiver, oak leaf and fine scroll engraved, choice of 6 different animal scenes.

	100%	98%	95%	90%	80%	70%	60%
	$3,300	$2,500	$2,100	$1,850	$1,500	$1,250	$1,000

✳ *Presentation 1 w/gold inlays* - similar to Presentation 1, only with gold inlays.

	$4,200	$3,200	$2,800	$2,100	$1,825	$1,700	$1,500

✳ *Presentation 2* - silver grey or blue receiver, high relief engraving, choice of 3 different sets of game scenes.

	$4,800	$4,000	$2,750	$2,050	$1,825	$1,700	$1,500

✳ *Presentation 2 w/gold inlays* - similar to Presentation 2, only with gold inlays.

	$6,500	$5,500	$3,700	$2,150	$1,925	$1,750	$1,550

✳ *Presentation 3* - silver grey or blue receiver, more elaborate high relief engraving with choice of partridges, mallards, or geese depicted on frame sides in 18 Kt. gold.

	$8,000	$6,500	$4,800	$3,600	$3,200	$2,875	$2,300

✳ *Presentation 4* - features engraved side plates in either silver grey or blue finish, engraved game scenes include waterfowl on right frame side, 5 pheasants on left frame side, 2 quail on receiver bottom, and a retriever's head on trigger guard. Extra figure walnut stock and forearm.

	$7,600	$6,500	$4,950	$3,825	$3,350	$2,950	$2,375

Add 30% for 20 ga., 70% for 28 ga., or 25% for .410 bore.

Grading	100%	98%	95%	90%	80%	70%	60%

✳ *Presentation 4 w/gold inlays* - similar to Presentation 4, only with game scenes inlaid in 18Kt. gold.

	$10,500	$9,000	$7,500	$6,000	$4,250	$3,650	$2,950

Add 30% for 20 ga., 70% for 28 ga., or 25% for .410 bore.

P SERIES SUPERLIGHT - available in various configurations including multi-barrel sets.

Add approx. 20%-25% for special orders (checkered buttstock, oil finish, 3 piece forend, etc.).

Add 25% for J. Baerten engraving with signature (rare).

Subtract $500-$750 for non-factory recoil pad.

LIEGE - 12 ga., 26½, 28 or 30 in. barrels, various chokes, boxlock, auto ejectors, non- selective single trigger, vent. rib, checkered pistol grip stock. Approx. 10,000 mfg. 1973- 1975 by FN.

	$850	$700	$600	$500	$425	$400	$375

This model is also known as the B-26.

GRAND LIEGE - similar to Liege, except has deluxe checkered walnut stock and forearm, and engraved receiver. Disc.

	$1,150	$875	$750	$675	$600	$550	$495

B-26 - with BAC markings. Mfg. 1973-75.

	$750	$625	$575	$500	$425	$400	$375

B-27 - F.N. manufactured modified B-26, imported into the U.S. in 1984, same action as Liege (B 26), blue or satin finished receiver with light engraving, no BAC markings and never cataloged.

✳ *Standard Game* - 28 in. barrels, 9/32 in. vent. rib, pistol grip stock, Schnabel forearm, SST, blue receiver, choking M/F only.

	$825	$700	$550	$475	$425	$400	$375

Also available in Skeet model with gold "Browning" logo on blue receiver. Prices are the same.

✳ *Deluxe Game (Grade II)* - similar to Standard Grade, except has 30 in. barrels, better wood and English scroll engraved satin finished receiver, choking M/F only.

	$875	$725	$625	$575	$510	$475	$445

✳ *Grand Deluxe Game* - 28 in. IC/IM & M/F choked barrels, game scene engraved, signed by the engraver, 90% receiver coverage.

	$1,100	$850	$775	$700	$640	$580	$520

This model was also available in a Trap configuration - values are about the same as above.

✳ *Deluxe Skeet* - similar to Deluxe Game (Grade II), except is designed for skeet shooting.

	$850	$725	$625	$575	$510	$475	$445

International Skeet is also available at same price; hand fit pistol grip with stippling and International Type recoil pad.

✳ *Deluxe Trap* - similar to Deluxe Game (Grade II), except is configured for trap shooting.

	$750	$650	$560	$530	$500	$475	$445

✳ *City of Liege Commemorative* - limited edition of 250 units manufactured to commemorate the 1,000th anniversary of the city of Liege, cased. Only 29 imported into the U.S.

	$1,125	$975	$910	$850	$775	$700	$600

ST-100 - 12 ga., Belgian mfg., O/U trap configuration with separated barrels and adj. point of impact, manufactured 1979-1981 for European sale mostly, floating VR, ST, deluxe checkered walnut stock and forearm, non-BAC model.

	$3,500	$2,750	$2,000	$1,850	$1,200	$975	$825

Grading	100%	98%	95%	90%	80%	70%	60%

B

WATERFOWL SUPERPOSED SHOTGUN SERIES - 12 ga., 500 made of each issue, 7 gold inlays with extensive engraving on French Grey receiver, lightning action, 28 in. barrels, checkered buttstock, full-length walnut case, factory inventories were depleted on Mallard, Pintail, and Black Duck Issues in 1989.

Add 20% for 3 gun set with same serial number.

❋ *1981 Mallard Issue*

$6,500 $4,750 $3,750

Last MSR was $7,000.

This issue was sold out in 1988.

❋ *1982 Pintail Issue*

$6,500 $4,750 $3,750

Last MSR was $7,000.

❋ *1983 Black Duck Issue*

$6,500 $4,750 $3,750

Last MSR was $8,800.

SUPERPOSED SHOTGUN: 1983-86 MFG. - 12 or 20 ga. In 1983, Browning announced renewed production of the famous Belgian "Superposed" O/U in Grade I only. Available in Lightning or Superlight models, 3 in. chambers in Lightning 20 ga., 26½ or 28 in. barrels. Belgian manufactured from 1983-86.

❋ *Grade I* - limited mfg., not compatible with steel shot.

Lightning	$2,500	$1,975	$1,450	$950	$800	$675	$550
Superlight	$3,300	$2,750	$1,850	$1,400	$1,000	$850	$675

Last MSR was $1,995.

Add 25% for 20 ga.

OVER/UNDER CLASSIC SERIES SHOTGUN - 20 ga. only, 26 in. barrels, less than 2,500 manufactured in Classic model and under 350 manufactured in Gold Classic. Both editions feature multiple engraved scenes and a special silver grey finish. Select American walnut featuring oil finish. Available 1986 only.

$2,750 $2,200 $1,800

Last MSR was $2,000.

❋ *Gold Classic* - 8 gold inlays, select walnut forearm and stock are both checkered and carved, many were shipped back to Belgium due to poor sales domestically. Available 1986 only.

$5,995 $4,150 $3,150

Last MSR was $6,000.

SHOTGUNS: O/U, SUPERPOSED HIGH GRADES: 1985-PRESENT

Browning, in 1985, resumed production of the Superposed in Pigeon, Pointer, Diana, and Midas grades. They were available in 12 and 20 ga. only, in either a Lightning or Superlight configuration. These higher grades were custom ordered from the factory with delivery ranging from 8 to more than 12 months. Custom options could be special ordered on each grade with corresponding prices being higher than shown below. B-25 engraving patterns on these various grades will nearly duplicate those styles manufactured before 1976. Skeet models were not available.

Superposed: Custom Shop Current Pricing & Models

In 2000, Browning changed the nomenclature of their B-25 Series. These new boxlock grades include: Special Woodcock $8,665, Special Duck $8,796, Special Pigeon $9,695, Evolution 2 $10,098, Gold 25 $9,105, Diana UK $12,950, and Grades B11 - $9,590, B12 - $9,680, B2G - $9,733, C11 - $11,950, C12 - $12,520, C2G - $12,595, C2S $17,850, D11 - $17,590, D12 - $17,299, D4G

Grading	100%	98%	95%	90%	80%	70%	60%

$20,580, D5G - $20,650.

Grade I Traditional, Pigeon Grade, Pointer Grade, Diana Grade, and Midas Grade are listed separately under the B-25 model listing.

Additionally, Browning also offers the following grades with engraved sideplates: Grade II - $23,234, Grade E1 - $25,410, Grade F1 - $25,995, Grade I1 - $26,680, Grade M1 - $27,495, and Grade M2 - $26,090. These new grades are special order only through the Browning Custom Shop.

    Add 20% for 20 ga. on previously owned models.
    Add approx. $1,250 for a previously owned extra set of barrels.

B-25 - 12 or 20 ga. only, original Superposed Model manufactured entirely from parts fabricated in Herstal, Belgium. Also available in Superlight configuration. This older nomenclature series was discontinued domestically in 1999, but the Custom Shop is still producing these grades.

✳ *Grade I Traditional*

	100%	98%	95%	90%	80%	70%	60%
MSR $9,030	$7,750	$2,500	$2,100	$1,700	$1,100	$800	$650

✳ *Pigeon Grade*

	100%	98%	95%	90%	80%	70%	60%
MSR $9,655	$8,000	$3,400	$2,750	$2,150	$1,700	$1,450	$1,275

    Add approx. $1,250 for an extra set of barrels.

✳ *Pointer Grade*

	100%	98%	95%	90%	80%	70%	60%
MSR $10,880	$9,250	$3,700	$2,950	$2,350	$1,800	$1,500	$1,300

    Add approx. $1,250 for an extra set of barrels.

✳ *Diana Grade*

	100%	98%	95%	90%	80%	70%	60%
MSR $11,315	$9,550	$4,000	$3,250	$2,500	$1,950	$1,650	$1,350

    Add approx. $1,500 for an extra set of barrels.

✳ *Midas Grade*

	100%	98%	95%	90%	80%	70%	60%
MSR $15,120	$12,750	$6,500	$5,950	$4,000	$3,150	$2,600	$2,250

    Add approx. $1,500 for an extra set of barrels.

B-125 - 12 or 20 ga. only, retains all the features of the original Superposed, except parts are subcontracted worldwide to decrease production costs and are assembled "in the white" at Herstal's Custom Gun Shop in Belgium, choice of three different engraving styles and two receiver finishes. Introduced 1988.

✳ *Hunting Model* - available in either Hunting Lightning or Superlight configuration.

  ◆**"A" Style Engraving** - blue receiver with border engraving featuring Browning logo engraved on each side.

	100%	98%	95%	90%	80%	70%	60%
MSR $3,925	$3,400	$2,750	$2,150	$1,700	$1,450	$1,275	$1,050

  ◆**"B" Style Engraving** - coin finished receiver with smaller game scene engravings.

	100%	98%	95%	90%	80%	70%	60%
MSR $4,360	$3,700	$3,100	$2,250	$1,800	$1,500	$1,300	$1,100

  ◆**"C" Style Engraving** - coin finished receiver with elaborate scroll work and game scene engraving.

	100%	98%	95%	90%	80%	70%	60%
MSR $4,903	$4,100	$3,475	$2,450	$1,900	$1,600	$1,400	$1,200

✳ *Sporting Clays Model* - 12 ga. only, designed for sporting clays competition and includes Invector plus choke tube system.

  ◆ **"A" Style Engraving**- blue receiver with border engraving featuring Browning logo engraved on each side.

	100%	98%	95%	90%	80%	70%	60%
MSR $3,925	$3,400	$2,750	$2,150	$1,700	$1,450	$1,275	$1,050

  ◆**"B" Style Engraving** - coin finished receiver with smaller game scene engravings.

	100%	98%	95%	90%	80%	70%	60%
MSR $4,360	$3,700	$3,100	$2,250	$1,800	$1,500	$1,300	$1,100

Grading	100%	98%	95%	90%	80%	70%	60%

◇ **"C" Style Engraving** - coin finished receiver with elaborate scroll work and game scene engraving.

MSR	$4,903	$4,100	$3,475	$2,450	$1,900	$1,600	$1,400	$1,200

※ **Trap Model** - standard F-1 style engraving.

MSR	$5,452	$4,950	$3,550	$2,325	$1,750	$1,450	$1,275	$1,050

SHOTGUNS: SxS, DISC.

B-SS - 12 or 20 ga., 26, 28, or 30 in. barrels, various chokes, engraved boxlock action, auto ejectors, checkered pistol grip walnut stock, beavertail forearm, SST. Mfg. 1971- 1988 by Miroku.

$895	$675	$475	$400	$365	$330	$300

Last MSR was $775.

Add 10%-15% for 20 ga.

Early guns had a single non-selective trigger (silver plated) - subtract 10%.

※ **Grade II** - satin greyed steel receiver featuring an engraved pheasant, duck, quail, and dogs. Disc. 1983.

$1,400	$1,100	$900	$750	$600	$525	$450

B-SS SPORTER - has straight grip stock and slim forearm, oil finish, 26 or 28 in. barrels. Disc. 1988.

$1,000	$850	$575	$500	$445	$410	$370

Last MSR was $775.

Add 10%-15% for 20 ga.

※ **B-SS Sporter Grade II** - satin greyed steel receiver featuring an engraved pheasant, duck, quail and dogs. Disc. 1983.

$1,550	$1,250	$995	$750	$625	$500	$425

Add 10%-15% for 20 ga.

B-SS SIDELOCK - 12 or 20 ga., engraved sidelock action in satin grey finish, ST, 26 or 28 in. barrels, English select walnut stock, splinter forend. Mfg. 1983-1988 in Miroku in Japan.

12 ga.	$2,300	$1,650	$1,250	$1,050	$850	$750	$675
20 ga.	$2,800	$2,100	$1,575	$1,350	$1,000	$875	$775

Last MSR was $2,000.

SHOTGUNS: SEMI-AUTO, DISC.

BROWNING CHOKES AND THEIR CODES (ON REAR LEFT-SIDE OF BARREL)

* designates full choke (F).

*- designates improved modified choke (IM).

** designates modified choke (M).

**- designates improved cylinder choke (IC).

**$ designates skeet (SK).

*** designates cylinder bore (CYL).

INV. designates barrel is threaded for Browning Invector choke tube system.

INV. PLUS designates back-bored barrels.

Add $145-$295 per additional barrel, depending on the condition and configuration.

AUTO-5 STANDARD - 1903-1939 MFG. - 12 or 16 ga.(introduced in U.S. in 1903-1904), 26-32 in. barrel, recoil operated, 4 shot mag. with cut-off, various chokes, checkered pistol grip stock, mfg. 1903- 1939 and limited post-war mfg. by FN, grades differ in engraving, inlays, and grade of wood. Approx. ser. range 1-229,000 (12ga.), 1-128,000 (16 ga.).

Grade 1	$675	$575	$475	$375	$325	$285	$250

Grading	100%	98%	95%	90%	80%	70%	60%
Solid matte rib	$750	$675	$575	$475	$375	$325	$285
With vent. rib	$825	$725	$650	$575	$465	$375	$325
Grade 2 (disc.1940)	$1,350	$1,100	$925	$825	$725	$650	$575
Solid matte rib	$1,525	$1,350	$1,100	$925	$760	$685	$625
With vent. rib	$1,695	$1,500	$1,250	$1,025	$825	$775	$675
Grade 3 (disc. 1940)	$2,625	$2,350	$2,100	$1,900	$1,600	$1,375	$1,095
Solid matte rib	$2,800	$2,500	$2,250	$2,050	$1,750	$1,500	$1,195
With vent. rib	$3,195	$2,795	$2,475	$2,225	$2,000	$1,700	$1,350
Grade 4 (disc. 1940)	$3,995	$3,655	$3,300	$2,995	$2,550	$2,050	$1,650
Solid matte rib	$4,350	$3,995	$3,655	$3,300	$2,975	$2,350	$2,050

Early models with safety mounted in front of trigger guard are not as desirable as there are potential safety problems inherent in the design.

Pre-WWII 16 ga. A-5s could be chambered for 2 9/16 in. shells. These shotguns are considerably less desirable than 16 ga. A-5s chambered for 2¾ in. modern shotshells. Since some guns have been modified to 2¾ in., careful inspection is advised before purchasing or shooting. The 2 9/16 chambered guns can be modified by the Browning Service Dept. to accept 2¾ in. shells if so desired.

AUTO-5 POLICE CONTRACT - 12 ga. only, 5 or 8 (factory extended) shot mag., black enamel finish on receiver and barrel, can be recognized by the European "POL" police markings below serial number, 24 in. barrel. Imported in limited quantities during 1999.

5 shot mag.	$N/A	$550	$525	$495	$450	$400	$375
8 shot mag.	$N/A	$1,100	$995	$895	$795	$750	$650

"AMERICAN BROWNING" AUTO-5 - 12, 16, or 20 ga., Remington-produced model of the Auto-5, very similar to the Remington Model 11, except with Browning logo, mag. cut-off, and different engraving, over 38,000 mfg. in 12 ga. (ser. no. range B5000- B43129), over 14,000 in 16 ga. (ser. no. range A5000-A19450), and 11,000 in 20 ga. (ser. no. range C5000-C16152), stocks have Remington style round knob pistol grip. Mfg. 1940-1949.

$495	$395	$350	$325	$295	$250	$225

Add 10% for vent. rib and/or 20 ga.

An easy way to identify this configuration is to look for the "A", "B", or "C" prefix on the left side of receiver.

SHOTGUNS: SEMI-AUTO, RECENT MFG.

BROWNING CHOKES AND THEIR CODES (ON REAR LEFT-SIDE OF BARREL)

* designates full choke (F).

*- designates improved modified choke (IM).

** designates modified choke (M).

**- designates improved cylinder choke (IC).

**$ designates skeet (SK).

*** designates cylinder bore (CYL).

INV. designates barrel is threaded for Browning Invector choke tube system.

INV. PLUS designates back-bored barrels.

Miroku manufactured A-5s can be determined by year of manufacture in the following manner: RV suffix - 1975, RT - 1976, RR - 1977, RP - 1978, RN - 1979, PM - 1980, PZ - 1981, PY - 1982, PX - 1983, PW - 1984, PV - 1985, PT - 1986, PR - 1987, PP - 1988, PN - 1989, NM - 1990, NZ - 1991, NY - 1992, NX - 1993, NW - 1994, NV - 1995, NT - 1996, NR - 1997, NP - 1998, NN - 1999, MM - 2000, MZ - 2001, MY - 2002, MX - 2003.

On November 26, 1997, Browning announced that the venerable Auto-5 would finally be discontinued. Final shipments were made in February, 1998.

NOTE: Barrels are interchangeable between older Belgian A-5 models and recent Japanese A-5s

Grading	100%	98%	95%	90%	80%	70%	60%

mfg. by Miroku. A different barrel ring design might necessitate some minor sanding of the inner forearm on the older model, but otherwise, these barrels are fully interchangeable.

NOTE: The use of steel shot is recommended ONLY in those recent models manufactured in Japan incorporating the Invector choke system - NOT in the older Belgian variations.

Add 10-15% for the round knob (rounded pistol grip knob on stock) variation on FN models only. Add $195-$375 per additional barrel, depending on the condition and configuration.

AUTO-5 STANDARDWEIGHT - 12, 20, or 16 ga., recoil operation, 26-32 in. barrels, standard production gun mfg. circa 1947-1969, various chokes, checkered walnut stock and forearm, synthetic Browning marked butt plate, lacquer (until approx. 1966) or polyurethane finish, buttstock has either round knob pistol grip (1952-1976) or flat knob (introduced 1967), watch for cracked forearms on all A-5s (due to barrel recoil), between 7 1/3-8 lbs.

	100%	98%	95%	90%	80%	70%	60%
Plain barrel	$495	$425	$375	$325	$295	$270	$240
Matted rib	$650	$550	$450	$400	$350	$300	$275
Vent rib	$795	$650	$550	$500	$450	$400	$375

Add 20% for NIB condition.
Add 10% for round knob.

Barrel addresses appeared as follows: circa 1947-1958 "St. Louis, M.O." (earliest BAC markings) or "St. Louis, Missouri", 1959-1968 "St. Louis, Missouri and Montreal P.Q.", 1969-1975 "Morgan, Utah and Montreal, P.Q.". Make sure barrel address date matches year of mfg. (see listings in the back of this text). Standardweight models had H or M prefixes.

AUTO-5 LIGHTWEIGHT (LIGHT 12) - 12 or 20 ga., recoil operated, 26, 28, and 30 in. barrels, various chokes, scroll engraved receiver, checkered pistol grip stock, approx. 10 oz. lighter than Standardweight, mfg. 1952- 1976 by FN and 1976-1998 by Miroku in Japan. Over 2,750,000 A-5s were mfg. by FN in all configurations between 1902- 1976.

	100%	98%	95%	90%	80%	70%	60%
FN model	$650	$550	$450	$400	$375	$350	$325
FN-vent. rib	$850	$725	$645	$575	$465	$435	$395

Add 10% for NIB condition.
Add 10% for 20 ga. with VR.

❊ *Light 12 Miroku* - 12 ga. only, 22, 26, 28, or 30 in. VR (became standard 1986) barrel with Invector choke system, approx. 8-8½ lbs. Mfg. 1976-Feb., 1998.

	100%	98%	95%	90%	80%	70%	60%
	$775	$595	$525	$465	$415	$365	$315

Last MSR was $840.

Subtract 10% without Invector chokes.

❊ *Light 20 Miroku* - 20 ga. only, 2¾ in. chamber, similar to original Belgian Light 20, VR, 22 (new 1995), 26, or 28 in. barrel, Invector chokes standard until 1993, Invector Plus choking became standard 1994, 6 lbs. 12 oz - 7 lbs. 2 oz. Mfg. 1987-1997.

	100%	98%	95%	90%	80%	70%	60%
	$825	$625	$550	$495	$435	$385	$335

Last MSR was $840.

AUTO-5 MAGNUM - 12 or 20 ga., 3 in. chamber, 26, 28, 30, or 32 in. barrels, various chokes, VR, similar to Standard, 8½ - 9 lbs. Mfg. 1958-1976 by FN, 1976-Feb., 1998 by Miroku.

	100%	98%	95%	90%	80%	70%	60%
FN model.	$725	$650	$550	$450	$400	$375	$350
FN-vent. rib.	$925	$795	$695	$645	$575	$465	$415

Add 10% for NIB condition.
Add 15% for 20 ga. with VR if NIB.

Between 1976-1985 approx. 2,000 Belgian 12 ga. A-5 Mags. were imported into the U.S. These late models can be differentiated by serialization - also, slight premiums may be asked. The 20 ga. Mag. was not introduced until 1967.

Grading	100%	98%	95%	90%	80%	70%	60%

✻ *A-5 Mag. Miroku* - 12 or 20 ga., VR barrel with Invector choke system until 1993, Invector Plus choking became standard 1994, 8½ - 9 lbs. Disc. 1997.

| | $825 | $650 | $595 | $525 | $465 | $400 | $350 |

Last MSR was $866.

Subtract $87 for 20 ga. Mag.
Subtract 10% without Invector chokes.

AUTO-5 STALKER - 12 ga. only, 2¾ (Light-12) or 3 (Mag. Stalker) in. chamber, 22 (Light-12 only), 26, 28, or 30, or 32 (Mag. only) in. VR barrel with Invector chokes, black matte finish graphite-fiberglass stock and forearm, matte finished metal, recoil pad, 8 lbs. 1 oz. - 8 lbs. 13 oz. Mfg. 1992-97.

| | $775 | $595 | $525 | $465 | $415 | $365 | $315 |

Last MSR was $840.

Add $26 for Mag. Stalker.

AUTO-5 LIGHT 12 BUCK SPECIAL - similar to Standard only with 24 in. barrel, slug bore, adj. sight, mfg. 1958-1976 by FN, mfg. 1976-1984 and 1989 again by Miroku, includes slings and one inch leather carrying strap, 8 lbs. 6 oz. Between 1985-1988, Buck Special barrels were available at extra cost.

✻ *FN Mfg.*

| | $850 | $665 | $625 | $575 | $465 | $415 | $365 |

This model was made in Light 12, Standard 12, 3 in. Mag. 12, Sweet 16, Standard 16, and Lightweight 20 configurations.

✻ *Miroku model* - mfg. 1989-1997.

| | $725 | $575 | $525 | $475 | $395 | $355 | $315 |

Last MSR was $829.

Add $35 for Buck Special on 3 in. Mag. receiver.

AUTO-5 SKEET - similar to Standard Light, only with 26 or 28 in. skeet bored, vent. rib barrel. Pre-1976 mfg. by FN, 1976-1983 mfg. by Miroku.

✻ *FN Mfg.*

| | $725 | $575 | $495 | $445 | $375 | $325 | $285 |

Add 20% for vent. rib.

✻ *Standard Miroku*

| | $775 | $595 | $525 | $465 | $415 | $365 | $315 |

AUTO-5 TRAP MODEL - 12 ga. only, similar to Standard, 30 in. full vent. rib barrel, 8½ lbs., mfg. by FN until 1971.

| | $850 | $665 | $625 | $575 | $465 | $415 | $365 |

AUTO-5 SWEET 16 - 16 ga. (2¾ in. chamber) only and approx. 10 oz. lighter, similar to Standardweight Model, gold plated trigger. Mfg. 1950-1976 by Fabrique Nationale.

Plain Barrel	$850	$665	$625	$575	$465	$415	$365
Solid Matte Rib	$1,295	$995	$825	$775	$650	$575	$475
Vent. Rib	$1,495	$1,195	$950	$825	$700	$625	$550

✻ *Sweet 16 Miroku* - 16 ga. only, similar to original Belgian Sweet 16, VR, Invector choke standard. Mfg. 1987-92.

| | $1,095 | $925 | $850 | $725 | $625 | $525 | $450 |

Last MSR was $720.

AUTO-5 TWO MILLIONTH COMMEMORATIVE - 12 ga., 2,500 mfg., 1971-74 mfg., special walnut, engraving, high-lustre bluing, cased with Browning book. Issue price was $550- $700, serial range 2,000,000-1 to 2,000,000- 2,500.

| | $1,395 | $1,095 | $950 |

Grading	100%	98%	95%	90%	80%	70%	60%

A-5 CLASSIC SERIES SHOTGUN - 12 ga., 5,000 mfg. in Classic model, 500 mfg. in Gold Classic. Both editions feature game scenes, John M. Browning's profile, and other inscriptions, special silver grey finished receiver. Introduced 1984.

✴ *Classic Model* - no inlays. Factory inventories were depleted in 1987.

	100%	98%	95%
	$1,095	$895	$725

Last MSR was $1,260.

✴ *Gold Classic Model* - features 5 inlays depicting duck hunting scenes. Mfg. 1986 with inventory depleted 1989.

	100%	98%	95%
	$3,895	$3,195	$2,395

Last MSR was $6,500.

A-5 BCA COMMEMORATIVE - 12 ga., 3 in. Mag., round knob, Belgian mfg., issue price was $595.

	100%	98%	95%
	$850	$725	$650

A-5 DU 50TH ANNIVERSARY

✴ *A-5 DU Light 12* - 12 ga. only, 5,500 mfg. in 1987 only for Ducks Unlimited chapters throughout North America. Prices will fluctuate greatly from chapter to chapter as these guns were auctioned to the highest bidder. Receiver is specially engraved and has "Fiftieth Year" depicted on right side of receiver, deluxe checkered stock and forearm, high gloss blue.

	100%	98%	95%
	$950	$750	$650

✴ *A-5 DU Sweet 16* - 16 ga. only, companion 1988-89 DU auction gun, 4500 mfg. 1988 only.

	100%	98%	95%
	$1,395	$1,150	$850

✴ *A-5 DU Light 20* - 20 ga. only, companion 1990 DU auction gun, 4500 mfg. 1990 only.

	100%	98%	95%
	$1,095	$900	$800

A-5 FINAL TRIBUTE - 12 ga. only, limited edition of 1,000 guns, features elaborate engraving on white receiver, the last of the A-5 semi-autos. Mfg. 1999 only, sellout occurred during 2000.

	100%	98%	95%	90%	80%	70%	60%
	$1,595	$1,295	$1,095	$950	$825	$700	$575

Last MSR was $1,330.

STANDARD DOUBLE AUTO - 12 ga. only, short recoil action, 2 shot, 26, 28, or 30 in. barrel, various chokes, checkered pistol grip stock, blue steel receiver was disc. approx. 1960, frame engraving is gold foil filled (and can flake). Mfg. 1952- 1971.

	100%	98%	95%	90%	80%	70%	60%
	$650	$525	$450	$400	$350	$300	$260
w/vent. rib	$750	$650	$575	$525	$475	$425	$350

TWELVETTE DOUBLE AUTO - similar to Double Auto, except hiduminum (aircraft alloy) frame and color anodized in royal or light blue, satin grey, maroon red, light brown, several shades of green, gold, jet, and dragon black, approx. 7 lbs. without rib. Approx. 67,000 (all variations) mfg. 1952-1971.

	100%	98%	95%	90%	80%	70%	60%
	$650	$525	$450	$400	$350	$300	$260
w/vent. rib	$750	$650	$575	$525	$475	$425	$350

Add 20-25% for brown or gold colored receiver.
Add 50%+ for maroon red or royal blue receiver (rare, only a few mfg.).

TWENTYWEIGHT DOUBLE AUTO - similar to Twelvette, but ¾ pound lighter, jet black finish with engraving accented with gold foil, 26½ in. barrel only. Mfg. 1952-1971.

	100%	98%	95%	90%	80%	70%	60%
	$650	$525	$450	$400	$350	$300	$260
w/vent. rib	$825	$725	$625	$575	$525	$475	$395

Grading	100%	98%	95%	90%	80%	70%	60%

B/2000 STANDARD - 12 or 20 ga., 26, 28, or 30 in. barrel, various chokes, vent. rib, gas operated, checkered pistol grip stock, Belgian manufactured but assembled in Portugal, approx. 115,000 imported into the U.S. between 1974-1983.

	$380	$345	$315	$295	$265	$240	$210

B/2000 MAGNUM - similar to B/2000 Auto Shotgun, except with 3 in. chambered barrel (all receivers were the same), recoil pad, vent. rib.

	$410	$360	$330	$305	$275	$250	$220

B/2000 SKEET - similar to Standard, with 26 in. skeet bored barrel, floating vent. rib, skeet stock, pad.

	$400	$345	$315	$295	$265	$240	$210

B/2000 TRAP - similar to Standard, with 30 or 32 in. barrel bored F or IM, floating rib, Monte Carlo trap stock.

	$400	$345	$315	$295	$265	$240	$210

B/2000 BUCK SPECIAL - 12 or 20 ga., barrel sights on 24 in. barrel.

	$400	$345	$315	$295	$265	$240	$210

1976 CANADIAN OLYMPICS B2000 - 12 ga., 100 manufactured in 1976 for Canadian sales only, high polish blue with multiple gold inlays including Olympic crest, 30 in. barrel, cased. Issue price was $1,295.

	$1,395	$995	$695

MODEL B-80 - 12 or 20 ga., 3 in. capability by changing barrel, gas operation, 4 shot, hunting models use choice of steel or aluminum receiver, anodized aluminum was used in the Superlight (12 ga. mfg. 1984 only), 6 to 8 lbs. 1 oz. Buck special disc. 1984. Components manufactured by Beretta of Italy and finished and assembled FN's plant in Portugal. Mfg. 1981-late 1988, final inventory was sold in 1991. Invector chokes became standard in 1985.

	$450	$375	$325	$295	$275	$250	$230

Last MSR was $562.

Steel frames were reintroduced into production again in 1988.

* ***Model B-80 Upland Special*** - 12 or 20 ga., 2¾ in. chamber, 22 in. vent. rib barrel, straight grip stock, Invector chokes. Mfg. 1986-1988.

	$475	$390	$340	$305	$280	$260	$240

Last MSR was $562.

MODEL B 80 DU COMMEMORATIVE - mfg. for American DU Chapters (The Plains and others), price fluctuates greatly as collector support is sometimes limited. Unless new, this model's values approximate those of the regular Model B-80. If NIB, values recently have been in the $700-$995 range.

A-500 (R) HUNTING - 12 ga. only, 3 in. chamber, new design utilizing short recoil system with a four- lug rotary bolt design, capable of shooting all 12 gauge loads interchangeably, magazine cut-off, 26, 28, or 30 in. VR barrel with Invector chokes standard, 24 in. barrel on Buck Special (fixed choke), high polished blue finish with red accents on receiver sides, gold trigger, checkered semi-pistol grip walnut stock with vent. recoil pad, 7 lbs. 11 oz. - 8 lbs. 1 oz. Mfg. 1987- 1993.

	$475	$425	$375	$325	$295	$275	$250

Last MSR was $560.

Add $33 for Buck Special variation (Invector chokes).

This model features fewer moving parts than many other semi-auto shotguns due to the short recoil operating system. From 1987-1990, this model was the Model A-500 – R suffix was added in 1991.

Grading	100%	98%	95%	90%	80%	70%	60%

B

A-500G HUNTING - similar to A-500, except is gas operated, distinguishable by "A- 500G" in gold accents on receiver, capable of shooting all 2¾ or 3 in. shells interchangeably, approx. 8 lbs. Mfg. 1990-1993.

	$555	$425	$375	$325	$295	$275	$250

Last MSR was $653.

A Buck Special variation was mfg. until 1992. No premiums currently exist.

✳ **A-500G Sporting Clays** - 12 ga. only, Sporting Clays variation with 30 in. VR barrel, 8 lbs. 2 oz. Mfg. 1992- 1993.

	$555	$425	$375	$325	$295	$275	$250

Last MSR was $653.

GOLD HUNTER - 12 or 20 ga., 3 in. chamber, self-cleaning piston rod gas action with self-regulation, alloy receiver with non-glare black finish and "Gold Hunter" on receiver side, 26, 28, or 30 (12 ga. only, disc. 2001) in. VR Invector Plus (12 ga. only) or Invector (20 ga. only) choked barrel with high polish bluing, cross-bolt safety, checkered walnut stock and forearm with recoil pad (vent on 12 ga.), 6 lbs. 12 oz. - 7 lbs. 10 oz. Parts mfg. in Belgium and final assembly in Portugal. New 1994.

MSR	$894		$735	$525	$415	$360	$295	$275	$250

Do not use 12 ga. 3½ in. chambered barrels on a either 2¾ or 3 in. receiver, or vice versa.

GOLD CLASSIC HUNTER - similar to Gold Hunter, except has semi-hump back receiver design, magazine cutoff, adj. comb, and satin finished wood, 26 or 28 in. VR barrel. New 1999.

MSR	$894		$735	$525	$415	$360	$295	$275	$250

This model is available through Full-line and Medallion dealers only.

✳ **Gold Classic High Grade Hunter** - 12 (disc. 2001) or 20 ga. (new 2002), similar to Gold Classic Hunter, except has nickel finished receiver featuring multiple gold inlays (ducks and dogs) and light scroll engraving, deluxe checkered walnut stock and forearm, 28 in. barrel only, 6 lbs. 14 oz. New 1999.

MSR	$1,716		$1,485	$1,165	$1,000	$875	$725	$625	$550

This model is available through Full-line and Medallion dealers only.

◇**Gold Upland Special** - 12 or 20 ga., 3 in. chamber, 24 or 26 in. VR barrel, checkered high gloss straight grip stock, 6¾ (20 ga.) or 7 lbs. New 2001.

MSR	$894		$735	$525	$415	$360	$295	$275	$250

◇**Gold Micro** - 20 ga. only, 3 in. chamber, 24 (new 2002) or 26 in. VR barrel, features shorter stock (13 7/ 8 LOP) and lighter weight, 6 lbs., 10 oz. New 2001.

MSR	$894		$735	$525	$415	$360	$295	$275	$250

✳ **Gold Turkey/Waterfowl Hunter Camo** - similar to Gold Hunter, full coverage (including barrel) Mossy Oak Breakup camo finish, 24 in. VR barrel with Hi-Viz sights and extra full choke tube, 7 lbs. Mfg. 1999- 2000.

	$715	$500	$400	$350	$295	$275	$250

Last MSR was $867.

✳ **Gold Mossy Oak Break-up/Shadow Grass** - similar to Gold Hunter, choice of full coverage (including barrel) Mossy Oak Breakup or Shadow Grass camo finish, 24 (Mossy Oak Breakup only), 26 (Mossy Oak Shadow Grass only), or 28 (Mossy Oak Shadow Grass only) in. VR back-bored barrel with Invector Plus choke tubes, approx. 7 ¼ lbs. New 1999.

MSR	$967		$795	$565	$450	$375	$310	$285	$250

Grading	100%	98%	95%	90%	80%	70%	60%

✳ *Gold NWTF Mossy Oak Break-Up* - 12 ga. only, 3 in. chamber, 24 in. VR barrel with 4 chokes tubes and Hi-Viz sight, full coverage Mossy Oak Breakup camo pattern, 7 lbs. New 2001.

	MSR	$1,018		$830	$585	$470	$385	$325	$285	$250

GOLD DEER HUNTER - 12 or 20 (new 2001) ga., 3 in. chamber, 22 in. barrel with choice of 5 in. rifled Invector choke (disc. 1998) or rifled plain barrel, cantilevered scope mount, sling swivels, 6¾ (20 ga.) or 7¾ lbs. New 1997.

	MSR	$987		$815	$575	$450	$375	$310	$285	$250

Subtract approx. $40 for rifled choke tube (disc. 1998).

✳ *Gold Deer Hunter with Mossy Oak Breakup Camo* - similar to Gold Deer Hunter, except has full Mossy Oak Breakup camo coverage. New 1999.

	MSR	$1,046		$875	$695	$585	$500	$425	$365	$335

GOLD 3½ IN. HUNTER - 12 ga., 3½ in. chamber, 24 (new 2002), 26, 28, or 30 in. VR barrel with Invector Plus choking, otherwise similar to Gold Hunter, 3-4 shot mag., approx. 7¼ - 7¾ lbs. New 1998.

	MSR	$1,038		$875	$695	$600	$500	$425	$375	$335

✳ *Gold 3½ In. Turkey/Waterfowl Hunter* - similar to Gold 3½ in. Hunter, full coverage (including barrel) Mossy Oak Breakup camo finish, 24 in. VR barrel with extra full choke tube, 7¼ lbs. Mfg. 1999-2000.

			$875	$695	$600	$500	$425	$375	$335

Last MSR was $1,038.

✳ *Gold 3½ In. Mossy Oak Breakup/Shadow Grass* - similar to Gold 3½ in. Hunter, choice of full coverage (including barrel) Mossy Oak Breakup or Shadow Grass camo finish, 24 (Mossy Oak Breakup only, disc. 2001), 26 (Mossy Oak Shadow Grass only), or 28 (Mossy Oak Shadow Grass only) in. VR back-bored barrel with Invector Plus choke tubes, approx. 7½ lbs. New 1999.

	MSR	$1,146		$965	$750	$635	$525	$435	$385	$335

✳ *Gold 3 ½ In. NWTF Mossy Oak Breakup* - 12 ga. only, 3 ½ in. chamber, 24 in. VR barrel with 4 chokes tubes and Hi-Viz sight, full coverage Mossy Oak Breakup camo pattern, 7 ¼ lbs. New 2001.

	MSR	$1,221		$1,025	$800	$660	$545	$450	$385	$335

GOLD STALKER - similar to Gold Hunter (3 in. chamber), except has checkered black composite stock and forearm, approx. 7 3/8 lbs. New 1998.

	MSR	$856		$715	$525	$425	$350	$295	$275	$250

✳ *Gold Stalker Classic* - similar to Gold Stalker, except has semi-hump back receiver design, magazine cutoff and adj. comb, 26 or 28 in. VR barrel. New 1999.

	MSR	$856		$715	$525	$425	$350	$295	$275	$250

This model is available through Full-line and Medallion dealers only.

✳ *Gold Turkey/Waterfowl Stalker* - similar to Gold Stalker, except has 24 in. VR barrel with extra full choke tube, Hi-Viz sights, matte non-glare wood and finish, 7 lbs. Mfg. 1999-2000.

			$710	$525	$425	$350	$300	$275	$250

Last MSR was $850.

✳ *Gold NWTF Stalker* - 12 ga. only, 3 in. chamber, 24 in. VR barrel with 3 chokes tubes and Hi-Viz sight, 7 lbs. New 2001.

	MSR	$744		$635	$475	$415	$350	$295	$275	$250

Grading	100%	98%	95%	90%	80%	70%	60%

B **GOLD 3½ IN. STALKER** - 12 ga., 3½ in. chamber, 26, 28, or 30 in. VR barrel with Invector Plus choking, otherwise similar to Gold Stalker, 3-4 shot mag., approx. 7 lbs. 10 oz. New 1998.

	MSR	$1,002	$850	$675	$585	$495	$415	$375	$335

* *Gold 3½ Turkey/Waterfowl Stalker* - similar to Gold 3½ Stalker, except has 24 in. VR barrel with extra full choke tube, matte non-glare wood and finish, 7¼ lbs. Mfg. 1999-2000.

			$860	$685	$595	$500	$420	$375	$335

Last MSR was $1,022.

* *Gold Rifled Deer Stalker* - 12 ga. only, 22 in. rifled barrel, cantilevered scope mount, sling swivels, 7¾ lbs. New 1997.

	MSR	$948	$780	$550	$450	$375	$325	$285	$265

GOLD SPORTING CLAYS - similar specs as the Gold Hunter, except has 2¾ in. chamber, 28 or 30 in. ported barrel with Invector Plus choking, approx. 7½ lbs. New 1996.

	MSR	$965	$780	$545	$445	$365	$315	$285	$260

* *Gold Sporting Ladies/Youth* - similar to Gold Sporting Clays, except has shorter 13 ½ in. LOP stock, 28 in. barrel only, 7 lbs. 9 oz. New 1999.

	MSR	$902	$735	$525	$440	$365	$325	$295	$275

* *Gold Fusion* - 12 or 20 (new 2002) ga., 26, 28, or 20 (12 ga. only, new 2002) in. VR barrel with 5 chokes and Hi-Viz pro-comp sight system, checkered satin finished wood with adj. comb system, 6 3/8 - 7 lbs. New 2001.

	MSR	$985	$795	$550	$450	$375	$325	$285	$260

* *Gold Golden Clays* - 12 ga. only, 2 ¾ in. chamber, nickel finished engraved receiver with gold accents and game birds, deluxe checkered walnut stock and forearm, 28 or 30 in. VR ported barrel, approx. 7½ lbs. New 1999.

	MSR	$1,490	$1,195	$975	$815	$700	$550	$450	$375

BSA 10 - while advertised, this gun had its model nomenclature changed to the Gold 10 Ga. before mfg. started.

GOLD LIGHT 10 GA. HUNTER/STALKER - 10 ga. Mag., 3½ in. chamber, short stroke self-cleaning gas action, 4 shot mag., steel (disc. 2000) or aluminum (new 2001) receiver, choice of high polish (Hunter Model, disc. 2000), dull finish (Stalker Model, disc. 1999, reintroduced 2000) bluing, 24 (NWTF Model only with Breakup, new 2001), 26, 28, or 30 (disc. 2001) in. VR standard Invector choke barrel, available with either high-gloss checkered walnut (Hunter) stock/forearm, matte black fiberglass (Stalker, disc. 1998, reintroduced 2000) stock/forearm, or choice of 100% camo treatment in Shadow Grass or Breakup (new 2001), vent recoil pad, approx. 9½ lbs. (aluminum reciever) or 10 lbs. 10 oz. (steel receiver), mfg. by Miroku, Japan. New 1994.

	MSR	$1,184	$995	$785	$675	$550	$475	$425	$395

Add $71 for Breakup or Shadow Grass finish.
Add $19 for the NWTF Model with Mossy Oak Break-Up.
Subtract 10% for steel receiver.
Subtract approx. $175 if w/o extra barrel.
Beginning 1999, this model was packaged to include an extra 24 in. Turkey barrel.

Grading	100%	98%	95%	90%	80%	70%	60%

SHOTGUNS: SINGLE BARREL, BT-99 & BT-100

BT-99 STANDARD TRAP GUN - 12 ga., 32 or 34 in. vent. rib barrel, mod., imp. mod., or full choke, boxlock, auto ejector, checkered pistol grip with Monte Carlo or conventional style stock, beavertail forearm. Invector chokes became standard in 1986 and ported barrel with Invector Plus chokes became standard in 1992, back boring became standard in 1993. Values below assume Invector Plus choking with ported barrel. Mfg. 1968-94 by Miroku.

	$895	$700	$550	$460	$400	$360	$330

Last MSR was $1,288.

Subtract $125 without Invector chokes or ported barrels.

* **BT-99 2 Barrel Set** - without Invector choking or barrel porting. Disc. 1983.

	$1,050	$850	$750	$700	$650	$600	$550

* **BT-99 Stainless** - features all stainless construction with Invector Plus ported 32 or 34 in. black VR barrel. Mfg. 1993-94.

	$1,325	$995	$850	$700	$575	$495	$450

Last MSR was $1,738.

* **Current Mfg. BT-99** – choice of 32 or 34 in. back bored barrel with 11/32 in. high post rib and one full Invector Plus choke tube, conventional or adj. comb stock, beavertail forearm, ejector only, 8 lbs. 10 oz. New 2001.

MSR $1,240	$1,040	$810	$685	$555	$475	$425	$395

Add $238 for adj. comb stock.

* **Pigeon Grade** - features higher grade walnut and gold receiver accents, Invector chokes and ported barrels. Mfg. 1993-94.

	$1,225	$895	$715	$600	$525	$495	$450

Last MSR was $1,505.

Older pre-1985 mfg.	$1,275	$950	$775	$650	$575	$525	$475

Older Pigeon Grade guns featured a satin grey receiver with deep relief, engraved pigeons in a fleur-de-lis background.

* **Signature Painted** - features painted red/black stock with Browning logos on stock and forearm, Invector Plus ported barrels. Mfg. 1993-94.

	$1,015	$715	$550	$460	$400	$360	$330

Last MSR was $1,323.

* **BT-99 Golden Clays** - features high-grade wood and gold outline receiver and inlays depicting a transitional hunting to clay pigeon scene. Mfg. 1994 only.

	$2,300	$1,750	$1,450	$1,125	$975	$875	$795

Last MSR was $2,800.

GRADE I BT-99 PLUS - similar to BT-99, except has adj. rib to control point of impact and new recoil reduction system that reduces felt recoil by 50%, stock has adj. comb and butt plate (recoil pad), back-bored barrel, Invector chokes, 8¾ lbs. Mfg. 1989-94.

	$1,200	$1,000	$875	$775	$675	$595	$550

Last MSR was $1,835.

Add 5% for ported barrel.

In 1990, the Grade I designation was added to this model. Changes include back-bored barrels with Invector plus choke tubes. In 1991, this model was supplied with a travel vault gun case as standard equipment. Older mfg. will not have these cases as an original accessory.

Beginning 1991, a Micro Plus Model was introduced that incorporates smaller dimensions (shorter stock and choice of shorter barrel). Values are the same as listed.

Grading	100%	98%	95%	90%	80%	70%	60%

❋ *BT-99 Plus Stainless* - features all stainless construction with Invector Plus ported 32 or 34 in. black VR barrel. Mfg. 1993-94.

| | $1,710 | $1,245 | $975 | | | | |

Last MSR was $2,240.

Beginning 1991, a Micro Plus Model was introduced that incorporates smaller dimensions (shorter stock and choice of shorter barrel). Values are the same as listed.

❋ *BT-99 Plus Pigeon Grade* - features higher grade walnut and gold receiver accents, Invector chokes and ported barrels. Mfg. 1993-disc.

| | $1,595 | $1,200 | $925 | $800 | $700 | $600 | $500 |

Last MSR was $2,065.

Beginning 1991, a Micro Plus Model was introduced that incorporates smaller dimensions (shorter stock and choice of shorter barrel). Values are the same.

❋ *BT-99 Plus Signature Painted* - features painted red/black stock with Browning logos on stock and forearm, Invector Plus ported barrels. Mfg. 1993-94.

| | $1,500 | $1,150 | $915 | $800 | $700 | $600 | $500 |

Last MSR was $1,890.

Beginning 1991, a Micro Plus Model was introduced that incorporates smaller dimensions (shorter stock and choice of shorter barrel). Values are the same.

❋ *BT-99 Plus Golden Clays* - features high-grade wood and gold outline receiver and inlays depicting a transitional hunting to clay pigeon scene. Mfg. 1994 only.

| | $2,700 | $2,350 | $2,050 | $1,850 | $1,700 | $1,550 | $1,395 |

Last MSR was $3,205.

Beginning 1991, a Micro Plus Model was introduced that incorporates smaller dimensions (shorter stock and choice of shorter barrel). Values are the same.

BT-99 MAX - 12 ga. only, choice of blue steel with engraving or stainless steel barrel, receiver, and trigger guard, 32 or 34 in. high post VR ported barrel, thin forearm with finger grooves, select walnut pistol grip stock (regular or Monte Carlo) with high gloss finish, ejector/ extractor selector, no safety, approx. 8 lbs. 10 oz. Mfg. 1995-96.

| | $1,250 | $925 | $725 | $600 | $525 | $495 | $450 |

Last MSR was $1,496.

Add $400 for stainless steel.

BT-100 STANDARD TRAP GUN - 12 ga. only, 32 or 34 in. steel high-post ported Invector Plus or fixed choked (F) barrel, without safety, choice of blue or stainless steel receiver, removable trigger assembly, ejector selector (either ejects or extracts) adj. comb and thumbhole stock (disc. 1999) are optional, approx. 8 lbs. 10 oz. New 1995.

| MSR | $2,266 | | $1,835 | $1,225 | $985 | $780 | $575 | $495 | $450 |

Subtract approx. 10% for fixed choke.
Add $238 for adj. comb.
Add $289 for thumbhole stock (mfg. 1995-99).
Add $558 for replacement trigger assembly (blue or stainless).

❋ *Stainless BT-100* - features stainless steel barrel, receiver, trigger guard and top lever.

| MSR | $2,742 | | $2,310 | $1,475 | $1,125 |

Subtract approx. 10% for fixed choke.
Add $239 for adj. comb.
Add $289 for thumbhole stock (mfg. 1995-99).
Add $558 for replacement trigger assembly (blue or stainless).

BT-100 SATIN (LOW LUSTRE) - features 32 or 34 in. Invector Plus barrel, satin/ low lustre metal/wood finish, conventional type stock without Monte Carlo, quick removable trigger with adj. trigger pull, 8 lbs. 10 oz. Mfg. 1998-2000.

| | $1,365 | $1,100 | $935 | $750 | $650 | $575 | $495 |

Last MSR was $1,684.

Grading	100%	98%	95%	90%	80%	70%	60%

SHOTGUNS: SINGLE BARREL, RECOILLESS TRAP

RECOILLESS SINGLE BARREL TRAP - 12 ga., special bolt action design that eliminates 72% of felt recoil, 27 (also available in Micro Model) or 30 in. high-post vent. rib Invector Plus choked back-bored barrel, rib adjusts for 3 points of impact (3, 6 or 9 in.), stock has adj. pull (2 sizes) and comb height, anodized receiver, no safety, approx. 8½ lbs. Mfg. 1994-96.

	$825	$725	$650	$575	$500	$450	$400

Last MSR was $1,995.

The Micro Model features a 27 in. barrel and shorter length of pull.

* **Signature Painted** - features painted red/black stock with Browning logos on stock and forearm, Invector Plus ported barrels. Mfg. 1994 only.

$1,580	$1,050	$895	$725	$575	$495	$450

Last MSR was $1,900.

SHOTGUNS: SLIDE ACTION

BPS Models are available in 12, 20, 28 (new 1994) ga., or .410 bore (new 2000), 3 in. chamber, except for 28 ga. Invector option (standard for 1985) allows 6 screw-in choke tubes to be interchanged, Invector Plus chokes became standard in 1993 (except 28 ga.), bottom ejection, double action bars, top tang safety, 5 shot capacity, vent. rib, all steel receiver with variety of finishes, receiver engraving became standard 1991 and was disc. during 1998, 20 and 28 ga. are approx. ½ lb. lighter than 12 ga. Field Models. Mfg. by Miroku 1977-to-date.

Do not use BPS 3½ in. barrels on a BPS 3 in. receiver or vice versa.

BPS FIELD/HUNTING MODEL - 12, 20, or 28 (new 1994) ga. or .410 bore (new 2000), 2¾ (28 ga. only) or 3 in. chamber, Invector or Invector Plus (new 1994 in 20 ga.) choking, various barrel lengths, Invector Plus choking became standard 1995 (except 28 ga.), 6¾ lbs. - 8 lbs. 3 oz.

MSR	$473		$385	$300	$260	$225	$200	$185	$170

Add $32 for 28 ga. or .410 bore.
Subtract 10% if without Invector Plus choke tubes.

* **Stalker Model** - 12 ga. only, 3 in. chamber, all metal parts have a dull matte finish, non-glare black synthetic composite stock and forearm, 24 (mfg. 1999-2000), 26, 28, or 30 in. VR barrel, approx. 7 lbs. 9 oz. New 1987.

MSR	$457		$370	$295	$255	$225	$200	$185	$170

Add approx. $20 for 24 in. barrel (disc. 2000).

* **BPS Camouflage** - 12 ga. only, 3 in. chamber, features Mossy Oak Shadow Grass or Mossy Oak Break-Up (new 2000) full camo treatment, 24 (standard model disc., or NWTF Model with Mossy Oak Break-Up camo – new 2001), 26, or 28 in. barrel, approx. 8 lbs. New 1999.

MSR	$540		$435	$370	$330	$300	$275	$245	$215

Add $20 for 24 in. barrel with Mossy Oak Break-Up camo treatment.

* **Pigeon Grade** - 12 ga. only, 3 in. chamber, features high grade walnut and gold trimmed receiver, 26 or 28 in. VR barrel with Invector chokes, 7 lbs. 10 oz. Mfg. 1992-98.

$500	$465	$395	$350	$310	$290	$275

Last MSR was $603.

* **Upland Special** - 12 or 20 ga., 3 in. chamber, 22 in. VR barrel, straight grip stock with Schnabel forearm, Invector (pre-1994) or Invector Plus (new 1994, standard 1995) choking, 6¾ - 7½ lbs. Mfg. 1985-current.

MSR	$473		$385	$300	$260	$225	$200	$185	$170

Subtract 10% if without Invector Plus choke tubes.

Grading	100%	98%	95%	90%	80%	70%	60%

✴ *Turkey Special* - 12 ga. only, 3 in. chamber, 20½ in. lightened barrel, non-glare walnut stock, matte finished barrel and receiver, receiver is drilled and tapped for scope base, rifle-style stock dimensions, sling swivels, new extra-full Invector choke tube, 7 lbs. 8 oz. Mfg. 1992-2001.

	$400	$340	$275	$240	$215	$190	$175

Last MSR was $500.

✴ *Micro Model* - 20 ga. only, 22 in. vent. rib barrel, pistol grip stock (13¼ LOP), Invector Plus choking (includes 3 chokes), 6¾ lbs. New 2001.

MSR	$473	$385	$300	$260	$225	$200	$185	$170

✴ *Micro - Youth and Ladies Model* - 20 ga. only, 22 in. vent. rib barrel, straight grip shortened stock (13¼ LOP), Invector (pre-1994) or Invector Plus (new 1994, standard 1995) choking, 6¾ lbs. Mfg. beginning 1986.

MSR	$473	$385	$300	$260	$225	$200	$185	$170

Subtract 10% if without Invector Plus choke tubes.

✴ *Deer Hunter/Special (DG, DS or DH)* - 12 ga. only, 3 in. chamber, 20½ (disc. 2000) or 22 in. barrel with 5 in. rifled choke tube or rifled barrel (DH, cantilever scope mount with satin finish only, new 1997), iron sights, scope mount base, choice of gloss (DG, disc. 1997) or satin (DS, disc. 2000) finish checkered stock with recoil pad and forearm, sling swivels, polished or matte finished metal, approx. 7½ lbs. New 1992.

MSR	$579	$450	$380	$300	$255	$220	$195	$175

Subtract approx. 10% for rifled choke tube.

✴ *Buck Special* - 12 or 20 (disc. 1984) ga., 3 in. chamber, 24 in. cyl. bore barrel, iron sights, 7 lbs. 10 oz. Reintroduced 1988-disc. 1998.

	$335	$275	$230	$200	$185	$175	$160

Last MSR was $409.

BPS MAGNUM HUNTER OR STALKER 3½ IN. - 10 (disc. 2001) or 12 ga., 3½ in. chamber, 12 ga. 3½ in. chamber was new 1989, 24 (disc. 1997, reintroduced 1999-2000 - Stalker only), 26, 28, or 30 (disc. 1997) in. barrel with Invector chokes and vent. rib, 4 shot mag., 7¾ - 10¾ lbs., depending on ga./configuration.

MSR	$537	$435	$375	$330	$315	$275	$245	$215

Add $15 for Hunter Model or approx. $20 for 24 in. barrel on Stalker Model.

In 1990, the back-bored Invector plus choke tube system became standard in 12 ga. 3½ in. chamber only.

✴ *Camo Magnum Hunter 3½ In.* - similar to Magnum Hunter or Stalker, features Mossy Oak Shadow Grass or Mossy Oak Break-Up (new 2000) full camo treatment, 24 (standard model disc., or NWTF Model with Mossy Oak Break-Up camo – new 2001), 26, or 28 in. VR barrel, approx. 7¾ - 9¼ lbs. New 1999.

MSR	$617	$515	$475	$395	$350	$310	$290	$275

Add $33 for NWTF Model with 24 in. barrel (available in Mossy Oak Break-Up only beginning 2000).

✴ *Magnum Hunting Waterfowl* - 10 ga., 3½ in. Mag. with choice of 28 or 30 in. matte finished VR barrel with standard Invector choking, features higher grade walnut and gold trimmed receiver with Waterfowl outlined, approx. 9 lbs. 6 oz. Mfg. 1993-98.

	$615	$525	$450	$400	$350	$315	$285

Last MSR was $750.

✴ *3½ In. Buck Special* - 10 or 12 (disc. 1994) ga., 3½ in. chambers, 24 in. cyl. bore barrel, 7 lbs. 10 oz. Mfg. 1990-97.

	$570	$460	$410	$370	$335	$310	$290

Last MSR was $677.

Grading	100%	98%	95%	90%	80%	70%	60%

BPS TRAP MODEL - 12 ga., 30 in. barrel. Disc. 1984 but trap barrels were available separately for several years.

| | $360 | $300 | $270 | $230 | $210 | $190 | $170 |

BPS WILD TURKEY FEDERATION COMMEMORATIVE - only 500 manufactured. Disc. 1991.

| | $495 | $395 | $325 |

BPS PACIFIC EDITION DU - limited mfg., DU serialization, cased.

| | $595 | $475 | $350 |

BPS COASTAL DU - limited mfg., DU serialization, cased.

| | $595 | $475 | $350 |

BPS WATERFOWL DELUXE - 12 ga. Mag., gold trigger and etching, Invector chokes, limited mfg.

| | $625 | $525 | $450 |

MODEL 12 LIMITED EDITION SERIES

* **Grade I 20 Ga.** - 20 ga. only, 2¾ in. chamber only, reproduction of the famous Winchester Model 12 with slight design improvements, 26 in. VR barrel bored modified, 5 shot mag., high post floating rib, walnut stock and forearm with semi-gloss finish, take down, serialization format similar to 28 ga., 7 lbs. 1 oz. 8,000 mfg. in 1988 with inventory depleted 1990.

| | $450 | $400 | $300 |

Last MSR was $735.

* **Grade V 20 Ga.** - similar specifications to Grade I, except has select walnut checkered 22 lines per inch with high gloss finish, extensive game scene engraving including multiple gold inlays serialization format similar to 28 ga. Mfg. 1988 only.

| | $795 | $695 | $575 |

Last MSR was $1,187.

Browning Arms Company limited manufacture to 4,000 Grade V 20 Ga.'s.

* **Grade I 28 Ga.** - 28 ga. only, similar to Grade I 20 Ga., except in 28 ga., 26 in. VR modified choke barrel, 5 digit ser. no. with NM872 suffix. 7,000 mfg. 1991-92.

| | $450 | $400 | $300 |

Last MSR was $772.

* **Grade V 28 ga.** - 28 ga. only, similar to Grade V 20 ga., except in 28 ga., 26 in. VR modified choke barrel, 5 digit ser. no. with NM972 suffix. 5,000 mfg. 1991-92.

| | $795 | $695 | $575 |

Last MSR was $1,246.

MODEL 42 LIMITED EDITION

* **Model 42 Grade I** - .410 bore, 3 in. chamber, reproduction of the Winchester Model 42 with slight design improvements, 26 in. VR full choke barrel, select walnut stock, 5 digit ser. no. with NZ882 suffix, 6 lbs. 12 oz. 6,000 mfg. late 1991-1993.

| | $495 | $400 | $300 |

Last MSR was $800.

* **Model 42 Grade V** - .410 bore, engraving and embellishments similar to the Model 12 Grade V, 5 digit ser. no. with NZ982 suffix, 6,000 mfg. late 1991-1993.

| | $795 | $695 | $575 |

Last MSR was $1,360.

B

SPECIAL EDITIONS, COMMEMORATIVES, & LIMITED MFG.

Please refer to the Blue Book of Modern Black Powder Values by Dennis Adler (now online also) for more information and prices on Browning black powder rifles.

BICENTENNIAL 1876-1976 SET - .45-70 Govt. cal., Model 78 rifle with specially engraved receiver, silver finish, fancy wood, cased, with engraved knife and medallion, 1,000 sets mfg. in 1976. Issue price - $1,500.

$1,750   **$1,300**   **$850**

CENTENNIAL O/U RIFLE/SHOTGUN - 20 ga. O/U shotgun w/extra set of .30-06 O/U rifle barrels. Shotgun barrels are 26½ in., rifle barrels are 24 in., SST, ejectors, elaborate scroll engraved receiver with 2 gold inlays, special oil finish walnut, deluxe walnut full- length case. 500 mfg. 1978 only.

$4,450   **$3,900**   **$3,150**   **$2,550**   **$2,100**   **$1,850**   **$1,650**

Last MSR was $7,000.

CENTENNIAL SET - complete Browning set mfg. in 1978, includes the Centennial O/U Rifle/ Shotgun, 9mm Hi-Power, B92 .44 Mag., Mountain Rifle, and a set of three knives.

$6,250   **$5,000**   **$3,950**

1 OF 50 BICENTENNIAL RIFLE - .30-06 cal., Model 78 single shot with 26 in. octagon barrel, includes special engraving by Neil Hartliep (non-factory), extra fine walnut, 4X wide angle scope, special luggage case. 50 mfg. (one for each state) during 1976 only and sold by silent mail order bidding (minimum bid was $3,100 in 1976).

As very few specimens are bought or sold each year, pricing is rather unpredictable. A few specimens have been sold in the $5,000 range recently. Remember, the work on this gun was subcontracted by Centennial Guns (division of Frigon Guns located in Clay Center, KS).

BUCK MARK COMMEMORATIVE PISTOL - features 6¾ in. Challenger style tapered barrel, white bonded ivory grips with scrimshaw style patterning including "1 of 1,000 Commemorative Model" on sides, matte blue finish, gold trigger, 30½ oz. 1,000 mfg. beginning 2001.

MSR   **$437**   **$335**   **$275**   **$225**

BRUCHET

Current manufacturer located in Saint Etienne, France. Distributed exclusively from 1982- 1989 by Wes Gilpin located in Dallas, TX. In 1989, Bruchet was able to get permission to use the older Darne trademark and all new manufacture will be entered under the Darne listing.

Paul Bruchet has been manufacturing his shotguns patterned after the Darne action since 1981, following his tenure at Darne as line foreman until 1979 (at which time the Darne plant closed). These new Bruchet Models were designated "A" or "B". All shotguns were totally hand made with approx. 50 guns being mfg. each year.

Since Paul Bruchet was able to retain the Darne trademark in 1989, please refer to the Darne section in this text for current manufacture.

SHOTGUNS: SxS

MODEL A - 12, 16, 20, 28 ga., or .410 bore, small key opening, ejectors, double triggers only, basically 4 variations (1, 1A, 2, and 2A), wide assortment of customer specified special orders.

Retail values were as follows: Model 1A started at under $2,000, the Model 2 started at $3,000, and the Model 2A started at $3,500. Each additional grade represented more embellishments and better grade of walnut. Magnum chambers could be ordered at a small surcharge. Importation began 1982, values represent the last published retail prices from 1989.

Grading	100%	98%	95%	90%	80%	70%	60%

B

MODEL B - 12, 16, 20, 28 ga., or .410 bore, large key opening, self-opening (assisted) action, ejectors, double triggers only, basically special ordered to individual customer specifications.

> Retail values were as follows: Model B starts at $5,800 and included deluxe carrying case. Each additional upgrade represented more embellishments and a better grade of walnut. Magnum chambers could be ordered at a small surcharge. Importation began 1982, values represent the last published retail prices from 1989.

BRYCO ARMS

Current manufacturer located in Irvine, CA. Distributed by Jennings Firearms, Inc. located in Carson City, NV. Distributor sales only.

PISTOLS: SEMI-AUTO, SINGLE ACTION

MODEL T-22 - while advertised during 1997 at a retail price of $179, this model was never produced.

MODEL J-25 - .25 ACP cal., aluminum alloy frame, 2.5 in. barrel, single action, synthetic ivory, walnut, or black combat grips, positive safety, 11 oz. Mfg. 1988-95, reintroduced 1999.

	MSR	$79		$65	$55	$45	$40	$35	$30	$30

> This model is available in either satin nickel, bright chrome, or black teflon finish.

MODEL M-32/M-38 - .22 LR (disc.), .32 ACP, or .380 ACP cal., semi-auto single action, 2.8 in. barrel, pressure cast fabrication using non-ferrous alloy, chrome or blue finish, black combat grips, 16 oz. New 1991.

	MSR	$79		$65	$50	$40	$35	$30	$30	$30

Add $20 for .380 ACP cal.

MODEL M-48 - .22 LR, .32 ACP, or .380 ACP cal., semi-auto single action, 4 in. barrel, larger frame variation of the M-38, chrome or blue finish, black combat grips, 24 oz. Mfg. 1991-95.

$85	$75	$65	$55	$50	$45	$40

Last MSR was $96.

MODEL M-5 - .380 ACP or 9mm Para. cal., 3¼ in. barrel, 10 or 12 shot mag., blue or nickel finish, black synthetic grips, 36 oz. Disc. 1995.

$85	$75	$65	$55	$50	$45	$40

Last MSR was $100 for the .380 ACP, $119 for 9mm Para.

Add $15 for 9mm Para. cal.

MODEL M-59 - .380 ACP or 9mm Para. cal., 4 in. barrel, 10 shot mag., blue or nickel finish, black synthetic grips, 36 oz. Disc. 1995.

$95	$85	$75	$70	$65	$60	$55

Last MSR was $119.

Add $15 for 9mm Para. cal.

JENNINGS NINE - 9mm Para. cal., single action, redesigned model 59, frame mounted ejector, contour grips, loaded chamber indicator, 30 oz. New 1997.

	MSR	$145		$120	$100	$85	$75	$65	$55	$50

Grading	100%	98%	95%	90%	80%	70%	60%

B BUDISCHOWSKY
Previous manufacturer located in Mt. Clemens, MI.

PISTOLS: SEMI-AUTO

TP-70 - .22 LR cal., double action, 2½ in. barrel, stainless steel, fixed sights, plastic grips. Mfg. 1973-1977.

	$440	$385	$330				

TP-70 - similar to TP-70, except .25 ACP cal. Mfg. 1973-1977.

	$330	$275	$220				

> Note: In 1977, Norton Arms marketed this pistol. Quality of workmanship is not on par with the early Budischowsky and values are approx. 35% less.

SEMI-AUTO PISTOL - .223 Rem. cal., 11 5/8 in. barrel, 20 or 30 shot mag., fixed sights, a novel paramilitary designed type pistol.

	100%	98%	95%	90%	80%	70%	60%
	$470	$415	$385	$360	$305	$250	$220

RIFLES: SEMI-AUTO

PARAMILITARY DESIGN RIFLE - .223 Rem. cal., semi-auto, 18 in. barrel, wood paramilitary stock.

	100%	98%	95%	90%	80%	70%	60%
	$505	$440	$415	$385	$330	$275	$250

PARAMILITARY DESIGN RIFLE W/FOLDING STOCK

	100%	98%	95%	90%	80%	70%	60%
	$575	$500	$450	$425	$395	$360	$330

BULLARD ARMS
Previous manufacturer located in Springfield, MA, circa 1880s. Designed by prolific inventor James Bullard, the design, quality, and workmanship of Bullard rifles rivaled those of any competitor during the 1880s. Bullard made two basic rifles: a lever action repeater and a single shot. The repeater was made in two frame styles: large and small. The single shot was also made in two basic styles; solid frame and detachable-interchangeable barrel model.

100%	98%	95%	90%	80%	70%	60%	50%	40%	30%	20%	10%

RIFLES: LEVER ACTION

LEVER ACTION REPEATER - rack and pinion style lever activated mechanism, mag. mounted under barrel, loaded through underside of action while lever was opened, blue finish with various parts (including receiver) sometimes case hardened.

* ***Large Frame*** - .40-60, .45-60, .45-70 Govt., .45-75, .50-95 and .40-70 Bullard, .40- 90 Bullard, .45- 85 Bullard or .50-115 Bullard cal., 26 or 28 in. round, octagon, or part round barrel, crescent steel or hard rubber buttplates with elk motif, ser. no. range 1-1,500 and 2,000-3,000.

100%	98%	95%	90%	80%	70%	60%	50%	40%	30%	20%	10%
N/A	N/A	$2,800	$2,450	$1,950	$1,750	$1,625	$1,450	$1,275	$1,150	$975	$850

Add 25% for .40-90 Bullard, .50-95, or .50-115 Bullard cal.
Add 25% for deluxe checkered wood with pistol grip.

> Various military and experimental models are found in this frame size and will command significant premiums.

* ***Small Frame*** - .32-40 Bullard or .38-45 Bullard cal., (other calibers cataloged, but essentially unknown), 24, 26, or 28 in. round, octagon or part round barrel, crescent steel or hard rubber buttplates with turkey motif, ser. no. range 1,500-2,000.

100%	98%	95%	90%	80%	70%	60%	50%	40%	30%	20%	10%
N/A	N/A	$2,400	$2,000	$1,750	$1,550	$1,375	$1,175	$1,025	$900	$825	$750

Add 25% for deluxe checkered wood with pistol grip.
Add 40% for any caliber other than .32-40 and .38-45.

Although the small frame saw less production and is scarcer than the large frame repeater, it was not as popular, and is typically priced less than a large frame model.

RIFLES: SINGLE SHOT

SINGLE SHOT MODEL - thin receiver with full lever, similar in appearance to small frame repeater action, except shorter (several parts including lever will interchange), 26, 28, or 30 in. round, octagon, or part round barrel, blue finish with various parts sometimes case hardened (including receiver), crescent steel or hard rubber buttplates, ser. no. range 3,500-4,100.

❋ **Solid Frame** - wide variety of cals. from .22 rimfire to .50 cal., (.22 and .32-40 are most common), essentially one frame size, except the .22 was somewhat smaller.

N/A	N/A	$2,500	$2,200	$1,850	$1,575	$1,450	$1,375	$1,250	$1,125	$995	$900

❋ **Detachable-Interchangeable Barrel Model** - same cals. as small frame model with two frame sizes - small (.38 cal. and smaller) and large (.40 cal. and larger), interchangeable barrels could not be switched between the two frame sizes, barrel and breech detach from action.

N/A	N/A	$2,500	$2,200	$1,850	$1,575	$1,450	$1,375	$1,250	$1,125	$995	$900

Add 20% for large frame.
Add 30% for .50 cals.
Add 30% for extra barrel with forend (numbers matching).
Add 30% for Schuetzen model.
Add 25% for deluxe checkered wood with pistol grip.

BUL TRANSMARK LTD.

Current manufacturer located in Tel Aviv, Israel. Currently imported and distributed in North America beginning 2002 by EAA Corp., located in Sharpes, FL. Previously imported and distributed 1997-2001 by International Security Academy (ISA) located in Los Angeles, CA, and from 1996-97 by All America Sales, Inc. located in Memphis, TN. Dealer sales only.

Grading	100%	98%	95%	90%	80%	70%	60%

PISTOLS: SEMI-AUTO

M-5 frame kits were previously available at $399 retail.

BUL IMPACT - while advertised during 1999, this model was never produced.

BUL STORM & COMPACT - while advertised during 1999, this model was never produced.

BUL 1911 GOVERNMENT (M-5 STANDARD) - .38 Super (disc.), 9mm Para. (disc.), .40 S&W (disc.), or .45 ACP cal., single action, 5 in. barrel, polymer double column frame, steel slide, aluminum speed trigger, checkered front and rear grip straps, blue or chrome (new 2000) finished slide, 10 shot staggered mag., 31-33 oz. Imported 1995-2000, reintroduced 2002.

MSR	$559		$495	$425	$375	$325	$295	$275	$250

Add 10% for .38 Super or .40 S&W cal.
Add $40 for chrome finished slide.

Grading	100%	98%	95%	90%	80%	70%	60%

✳ **Bul Commander (M-5 Standard)** - similar to Bul 1911 Government, except has 3.8 or 4¼ (disc.) in. barrel, 29-30 oz. Imported 1998-2000, reintroduced 2002.

MSR	$559	$495	$425	$375	$325	$295	$275	$250

Add 10% for .38 Super or .40 S&W cal.

Add $40 for matte chrome finished slide.

✳ **Bul Stinger** - similar to Bul 1911 Government, except has 10 shot mag., 3 in. barrel, 24 oz. Importation began 2002.

MSR	$559	$495	$425	$375	$325	$295	$275	$250

✳ **Bul M-5 Standard Street Comp.** - similar to M-5 Standard Commander, except has single port compensated 4¼ in. barrel, 32 oz. Imported 1998-99.

		$960	$825	$700	$600	$500	$450	$375

Last MSR was $1,060.

Add $28 for .38 Super or .40 S&W cal.

✳ **Bul M-5 Multi Caliber** - similar cals. as the M-5 Standard Government, includes 3 upper-ends including Commander length, another with adj. sights, and a third with a single port compensator, cased. Imported 1999-2000.

	$1,575	$1,275	$1,050	$850	$725	$625	$525

Last MSR was $1,768.

BUL M-5 STANDARD IPSC - .38 Super, 9mm Para., .40 S&W, or .45 ACP cal., configured for IPSC competition, with custom slide to frame fit and match grade barrel bushing. Imported 1998-2001.

	$695	$625	$575	$525	$475	$425	$375

Last MSR was $852.

Add $111 for .38 Super or .40 S&W cal.

Add $70 for chrome finish (new 2000).

BUL M-5 STANDARD MATCH - IPSC custom race gun, includes multi-port compensator system. Imported 1998-99.

	$1,200	$1,000	$825	$700	$600	$500	$425

Last MSR was $1,655.

Add $24 for .38 Super or .40 S&W cal.

BUL M-5 JET - same cals. as the M-5 Standard IPSC, features Commander length with 4¼ in. barrel and 4 port compensator on top of barrel, 31 oz. Imported 1999-2000.

	$875	$725	$625	$525	$475	$400	$350

Last MSR was $1,158.

Add $51 for .38 Super or .40 S&W cal.

BUL M-5 MODIFIED - 9mm Para., .38 Super, .40 S&W, or .45 ACP cal., designed for Modified class competition, features new Optima 2000 optical sight fitted to slide, 5 port compensation on top of barrel, includes carrying case, 38 oz. Imported 1998-2001.

	$1,075	$925	$800	$675	$550	$500	$450

Last MSR was $1,430.

BUL M-5 TARGET - same cals. as the M-5 Modified, features 6 in. slide and barrel, choice of sights, and match grade oversize barrel bushing, includes 3 mags and carrying case, 38 oz. Imported 1999-2001.

	$895	$775	$700	$600	$500	$450	$400

Last MSR was $1,196.

Add $315 for Aristocrat Tri-state sights.

Grading	100%	98%	95%	90%	80%	70%	60%

BUL M-5 ULTIMATE RACER - top-level IPSC competition gun, includes 3 mags. and carrying case, 38 oz. Imported 1998-2001.

$1,050	$925	$800	$700	$600	$525	$450

Last MSR was $1,573.

Add $306 for fitted C-more optical sight.

BUSHMASTER FIREARMS

Currently manufactured by Bushmaster Firearms/Quality Parts Company located in Windham, ME. Older mfg. was by Gwinn Arms Co. located in Winston-Salem, NC 1972-1974. The Quality Parts Co. gained control in 1986. Distributor, dealer, or consumer direct sales.

Bushmaster®

PISTOLS: SEMI-AUTO

BUSHMASTER PISTOL - .223 Rem. cal., top bolt (older models with aluminum receivers) or side bolt (most recent mfg.) operation, steel frame (current mfg.), 11½ in. barrel, parkerized finish, adj. sights, wood stock, 5¼ lbs.

$500	$425	$350	$280	$250	$225	$180

Last MSR was $375.

Add $40 for electroless nickel finish (disc. 1988).

This model uses a 30 shot M-16 mag. and the AK-47 gas system.

RIFLES: SEMI-AUTO

All currently manufactured Bushmaster rifles are shipped with a hard plastic lockable case.

BUSHMASTER RIFLE - .223 Rem. cal., semi-auto., top bolt (older models with aluminum receivers) or side bolt (current mfg.) operation, steel frame (current mfg.), 18½ in. barrel, parkerized finish, adj. sights, wood stock, 6¼ lbs., base values are for folding stock model.

$425	$325	$280	$250	$225	$180	$140

Last MSR was $350.

Add $40 for electroless nickel finish (disc. 1988).
Add $65 for fixed rock maple wood stock.

This model uses a 30 shot M-16 mag. and the AK-47 gas system.

* ***Rifle Combination System*** - includes rifle with both metal folding stock and wood stock with pistol grip.

$400	$360	$330	$300	$275	$250	$230

Last MSR was $450.

XM15-E2S/A-3 TARGET RIFLE - .223 Rem. cal., semi-auto patterned after the Colt AR-15, 20, 24, or 26 in. Govt. spec. match grade chrome lined barrel, manganese phosphate barrel finish, rear sight adj. for windage and elevation, cage flash suppressor (disc. 1994), approx. 8.3 lbs. Mfg. began 1989 in U.S.

MSR	$960						
		$825	$700	$650	$595	$535	$475	$425

Add $70 for fluted barrel.
Add $15 for 24 in. or $25 for 26 in. barrel.
Add $75 for A-3 removable carry handle.

* ***XM15-E2S/A-3 Shorty Carbine*** - similar to above, except with telescoping buttstock and 11½ (disc. 1995), 14 (disc. 1994), or 16 in. barrel with (disc. 1994) or w/o suppressor, approx. 7.4 lbs. Mfg. began 1989.

MSR	$945						
		$800	$695	$645	$585	$525	$465	$415

Add $70 for fluted barrel.
Add $15 for dissipator models (features lengthened handguard).

This model does not have the target rear sight system of the XM15-E2S rifle.

B

Grading	100%	98%	95%	90%	80%	70%	60%

❊ *E2 Carbine* - .223 Rem. cal., features 16 in. match chrome barrel with new M16A2 hand-guard and short suppressor, choice of A1 or E2 sights. Mfg. 1994-95.

		$895	$825	$725	$650	$600	$550	$500

Add approx. $50 for E2 sighting system.

V-MATCH COMPETITION RIFLE - .223 Rem. cal., top-of-the line match/competition rifle, flat-top receiver with extended aluminum barrel shroud, choice of 20, 24, or 26 in. barrel, 8.3 lbs. New 1994.

MSR	$1,025		$935	$850	$725	$650	$575	$515	$465

Add $70 for fluted barrel.
Add $15 for 24 in. or $25 for 26 in. barrel.
Add $75 for A-3 removeable carry handle.

❊ *V-Match Commando Carbine* - similar to V-Match Competition Rifle, except has 16 in. barrel. New 1997.

MSR	$1,015		$925	$840	$715	$650	$575	$515	$465

Add $70 for fluted barrel.
Add $75 for A-3 removeable carry handle.

VARMINTER - .223 Rem. cal., includes DCM 24 in. extra heavy fluted varmint barrel, competition trigger, rubberized pistol grip, flattop receiver with mini-risers (add ½ in. height for scope mounting), free floating vented tube forearm, 5 shot mag, controlled ejection path. New 2002.

MSR	$1,200		$995	$875	$750	$675	$600	$550	$500

DCM COMPETITION RIFLE - .223 Rem. cal., includes DCM competition features such as modified A2 rear sight, 20 in. extra heavy 1 in. diameter competition barrel, custom trigger job, and free-floating hand guard. New 1998.

MSR	$1,525		$1,395	$1,125	$975	$875	$800	$725	$650

M17S BULLPUP - .223 Rem. cal., semi-auto bullpup configuration featuring gas operated rotating bolt, 10 (C/B 1994) or 30* shot mag., 21½ plain or 22 (disc.) in. barrel with flash-hider (disc.), glass composites and aluminum materials, phosphate coating, 8.2 lbs. New 1992.

MSR	$765		$700	$650	$525	$475	$425	$400	$385

C SECTION

CETME

Previous manufacturer located in Madrid, Spain. CETME is an abbreviation for Centro Estudios Technicos de Materiales Especiales.

RIFLES: SEMI-AUTO

AUTOLOADING RIFLE - .308 Win. cal., 17¾ in. barrel, gas operated, roller cam action, similar to HK-91 in appearance, wood military style stock, aperture rear sight.

$2,950	$2,650	$2,350	$2,000	$1,725	$1,500	$1,350

C Z (CESKÁ ZBROJOVKA)

Current manufacturer located in Uhersky Brod, Czech Republic, 1936- current. Previous manufacture was in Strakonice, Czechoslovakia circa 1923-late 1950s. Newly manufactured CZ firearms are currently imported exclusively by CZ USA located in Kansas City, KS. Previously imported by Magnum Research, Inc. located in Minneapolis, MN until mid-1994. Previously imported before 1994 by Action Arms Ltd. located in Philadelphia, PA. Dealer and distributor sales.

Ceská Zbrojovka simply means Czech weapons factory. CZ's full name is Ceská Zbrojovka a.s. Uhersky Brod, often abbreviated to CZUB a.s., meaning joint stock company. Uhersky Brod is the town the factory is located in. Zbrojovka Brno means weapons or arms factory located in Brno.

Zbrojovka Brno was built in 1916-1918, as a subsidiary of the Vienna Arsenal. After WWI, this factory was given the responsibility of providing the newly formed Czechoslovakian military with infantry weapons - specifically rifles and light machine guns. Circa 1923, pistol manufacture was transferred from Brno to Ceská Zbrojovka, located in the town of Strakonice, southwest of Bohemia. Since the location change, Zbrojovka Brno has never produced pistols on any great scale (please refer to the Brno section in this text for more information).

Ceská Zbrojovka Strakonice began developing many innovative and revolutionary pistol designs. These models, including the CZ-24, CZ-27, and CZ-52 are certainly well-known throughout the world. During the mid-1950s, CZ's facilities were converted to making motorcycles and precision engineering products.

Ceská Zbrojovka, located in the town of Uhersky Brod, was founded in 1936, as a subsidiary of Ceská Zbrojovka Strakonice, in a government decision designed to move firearms production further away from the German border, and out of the reach of German bombers. Uhersky Brod is located approx. 60 miles east of Brno. Before WWII, the factory produced aircraft machine guns (LK-30), the military pistol (CZ-38 in 9mm Para.), in addition to rifle Models Z242-Z247. During WWII, the factory was taken over by the Germans, and the facilities were used for the production of aircraft machine guns (German designed MG 17s) and related components for other models of military weapons.

Shortly after WWII, Ceská Zbrojovka Uhersky Brod resumed production of firearms for the civilian marketplace, including the CZ 241 semi-auto shotgun, and some O/U shotguns. The production of pistols commenced during the mid-1950s, with the introduction of the Model CZ-50 and other small pistol models named DUO in 6.35mm cal. Up to this point, the main pistol producer in Czechoslovakia was CZ Strakonice as stated above. The CZ-52 pistol was the last model they produced. Since the end of the 1950s, Ceská Zbrojovka Uhersky Brod has become the sole producer of pistols.

After WWII, the Ceská Zbrojovka Uhersky Brod became massively involved in other types of production besides sporting and hunting firearms. Production reached a high during the 1980s, when hunting/sporting firearms manufacture resulted in approx. 30% of total production. The balance of manufacture was devoted to the production of power hydraulics for tractors, while gears and accessory drive boxes for speed reduction in turbo prop airplane engines made up the rest.

During 1964-1966, the Czech government transferred the production of long guns from Zbrojovka Brno to Ceská Zbrojovka Uhersky Brod. During the 1970s & 1980s, the arms production of Zbrojovka Brno accounted for less than 3% of its total capacity. The activities of this company were diverted into the production of typewriters, diesel motors, and automatic machine tools. While many firearm designs originated in Brno, Zbrojovka Brno was not the manufacturer. Because of this, the long guns manufactured in the mid-1960s, including the ZKK 600 - 602 series and ZKM rimfires, were manufactured in CZ Uhersky Brod. Because of the Czech government's decision to merge manufacture within both companies, the Brno trademark was also used by Ceská Zbrojovka Uhersky Brod.

This relationship was terminated in 1983, when both companies became part of the Agrozet conglomerate. While confusing, the arms utlizing the Brno trademark were not produced in Brno during this time. All firearms exported from Czechoslovakia at the time carried the Brno logo, and most of them were manufactured by Ceská Zbrojovka Uhersky Brod.

During 1975, Ceská Zbrojovka Uhersky Brod designed and began manufacture of the famous CZ-75 pistol. Production in quantity began in 1977. To date, over 700,000 CZ-75s have been produced. This semi-auto has been made in many variations and/or modifications to suit the many military and commercial contracts. During the mid-1980s, the CZ factory released the CZ-85, basically a CZ-75 with ambidextrous safety and slide stop. In the mid-1990s, production of the CZ-100 began - this new model featured a polymer frame. The CZ 550 line of rifles was also introduced at this same time.

For more information and current pricing on both new and used CZ airguns, please refer to the 2nd Ed. *Blue Book of Airguns* by Dr. Robert Beeman & John Allen (now online also).

Grading	100%	98%	95%	90%	80%	70%	60%

COMBINATION GUNS

CZ 584 SOLO - 12 ga. over choice of 7x57mm Mauser (importation disc. 1999), 7x57R, 7x65R, .222 Rem. (importation disc. 1999), .223 Rem. (imported 1994-99), .243 Win. (imported 1994-99), .30-06 (new 1994), 7mm Mauser (imported 1994-99), and .308 Win. (importation disc. 1999) cals. also available, 24½ in. barrels, similar action to CZ 581 O/U shotgun, extractors or ejectors, rifle sights, approx. 7.4 lbs. Importation disc. 1986, resumed 1994 -disc. 1995, importation resumed 1999.

MSR	$889	$755	$640	$585	$510	$450	$385	$350

Add 20% for ejectors.

PISTOLS: SEMI-AUTO, DISC.

The models listed below were made in Ceská Zbrojovka Strakonice, with the exception of some models manufactured in Ceská Zbrojovka Prague during the Nazi occupation of Czechoslovakia. The VZ38 was also produced in Uhersky Brod.

"DUO" POCKET AUTOMATIC - .25 ACP cal., 6 shot, 2 1/8 in. barrel, fixed sights, blue or nickel, plastic grips. Mfg. 1926-present (current Z pistol by Brno).

	$225	$190	$170	$150	$125	$100	$75

Add 40% for WWII years.

This model was manufactured by Dushek and is similar to the Z pistol equivalent by Brno.

CZ 22 - .380 ACP cal., derived from Mauser variation and manufactured under license from Mauser. Mfg. 1923 only.

	$400	$350	$320	$300	$275	$235	$200

Grading	100%	98%	95%	90%	80%	70%	60%

CZ 24 - .380 ACP cal.

✳ Standard Frame - 8 shot mag. Over 175,000 mfg. 1924-38. Over half issued to Czech Army. Same general design as CZ 22 except no gap between trigger and frame. Production continued to 1941.

	$350	$320	$290	$260	$230	$195	$150

Add $50 if Nazi proofed.

Add 200% if Kriegsmarine proofed (scarce, be wary of counterfeit markings).

✳ Long Frame - 9 shot mag.

	$1,500	$1,250	$1,000	$900	$800	$700	$600

Add $750 if fit with stock slot (either standard frame or long frame).

CZ 27 - .32 ACP cal.

✳ "CESKA" Slide Legend Variation - slanted slide grooves, high polish, available as Prewar Commercial, DR proofed, or Nazi proofed. Ser. range 16,000-21,500.

	$550	$450	$350	$300	$250	$200	$150

✳ "BÖHMISCHE" Slide Legend Variation - vertical slide grooves, high or medium polish, Nazi Police pistols dated 1941, 1942, or 1943 marked with Eagle/K on left trigger guard web, ser. no. range 21,500-261,000.

	$265	$225	$185	$150	$135	$120	$110

Add 125% if 1941 dated.

Add 100% if 1942 or 1943 dated.

Add 200% if Kriegsmarine proofed (beware of counterfeit markings).

✳ "fnh" Slide Legend Variation - Medium polish or phosphate. Ser. range 261,000- 476,000.

	$250	$195	$150	$125	$100	$85	$70

Add 50% for late phosphate war finish.

✳ Sound Suppressor Barrel Variation - a small number of phosphate pistols were fitted with an extended barrel for suppressor attachment. Usually in 450,000- 460,000 ser. range.

	$1,000	$900	$800	$700	$600	$500	$400

✳ Post WWII mfg. - dated 1945, 1946, 1947, 1948, 1949, 1950, 1951. These models will have the "NARODNI PODNIK" inscription on slide.

Currently, these variations average $250 in 95%+ condition while reworks (very common) average under $200.

VZ 38 DOUBLE ACTION AUTOMATIC - .380 ACP cal., 9 shot, double action only, 4 5/8 in. barrel, fixed sights, blue, plastic grips. Mfg. 1938-1939.

	$425	$335	$275	$225	$170	$140	$125

For Waffenampt proofed (E/WaA76 on barrel and left frame), usually phosphate finished and either unnumbered or in B291,000-B293,000 ser. range - add $1,000.

Changed to Model 39T after 1939.

VZ 38 "BULGARIAN CONTRACT" - .380 ACP cal., 9 shot, single or double action, prominent safety on left frame. Usually in 420,000-423,000 ser. range.

	$2,500	$1,800	$1,400	$1,000	$800	$600	$500

MODEL 1945 DOUBLE ACTION AUTOMATIC - .25 ACP cal., 8 shot, 2½ in. barrel, fixed sights, blue, plastic grips. Double action only. Mfg. between 1945-1952.

	$250	$200	$165	$150	$140	$130	$120

PISTOLS: SEMI-AUTO, RECENT MFG.

The CZ-52 was manufactured in Strakonice.

Grading	100%	98%	95%	90%	80%	70%	60%

CZ-40 -.40 S&W cal. only, CZ-75B operating mechanism in alloy M1911 style frame, single/ double action, black polycoat finish, 10 shot double column mag., fixed sights, firing pin block safety. New 2002.

	MSR	$494		$420	$350	$315	$290	$275	$250	$225

CZ-50/70 - .32 ACP cal., double action, blowback action, 3¾ in. barrel, loaded chamber indicator, 8 shot mag.

				$150	$125	$110	$100	$90	$80	$70

Used models are currently imported by Century International Arms, Inc. located in St. Albans, VT.

CZ-52 - 7.62 Tokarev or 9mm Para. cal., single action semi-auto, roller locking breech system, 4.9 in. barrel, 8 shot mag.

				$180	$150	$135	$125	$95	$85	$75

Add $40 for extra 9mm Para. barrel.

Used models are currently imported by Century International Arms, Inc. located in St. Albans, VT.

CZ-70 - 7.65mm/.32 ACP cal., double action, similar to Walther PP, 8 shot mag., 1 lb. 9 oz. Disc.

				$400	$350	$300	$275	$250	$225	$200

A very limited quantity of this model was imported.

CZ-75, CZ-75 B, CZ-75 BD - 9mm Para. or .40 S&W (disc. 1997, reintroduced 1999) cal., Poldi steel, selective double action, double action only, or single action only, frame safety, 4¾ in. barrel, 10 (C/B 1994) or 15* shot mag., currently available in black polycoat/polymer (standard, DA and SA only), matte blue (disc. 1994), high polish (disc. 1994), glossy blue (new 1999), dual tone (new 1998), or satin nickel (new 1994) finish, black plastic grips, non-suffix early guns did not have a firing pin block safety, reversible mag. release, ambidextrous safety, and were usually shipped with two mags., B suffix model nomenclature was added 1998, and designated some internal mechanism changes, BD suffix indicates decocker mechanism, 34.3 oz.

	MSR	$480		$410	$345	$295	$265	$225	$210	$195

Add $14 for .40 S&W cal.
Add $9 for Model CZ-75 BD (decocker).
Add approx. $14 for glossy blue, dual tone, or satin nickel finish.
Add $282 for CZ Kadet .22 LR adapter (includes .22 LR upper slide assembly and mag., new 1998).
Subtract $15 for double action only (black polymer frame), add $9 for single action only (black polymer frame).

"First Model" variations, mostly imported by Pragotrade of Canada, are identifiable by short slide rails, no half-cock feature, and were mostly available in high polish blue only. These early pistols sell for $1,000 if NIB condition, chrome engraved $1,500 (NIB), factory competition $1,350 (NIB).

✱ **CZ-75 B Military** - 9mm Para. cal. Importation began 2000.

	MSR	$429		$365	$315	$270	$250	$225	$210	$195

✱ **CZ-75 Semi-Compact** - 9mm Para. cal. only, 13 shot mag., choice of black polymer, matte, or high polish blue finish. Imported 1994 only.

				$350	$300	$275	$250	$230	$250	$200

Last MSR was $519.

Add $20 for matte blue finish.
Add $40 for high polish blue finish.

Grading	100%	98%	95%	90%	80%	70%	60%

✶ CZ-75 Compact - 9mm Para. cal. only, otherwise similiar to CZ-75, full-size frame, except has 3.9 in. barrel, 10 (C/B 1994) or 13* shot mag., checkered walnut grips, 32 oz. New 1993.

MSR	$508		$420	$360	$335	$290	$255	$230	$210

Add $15 for glossy blue, dual tone, or stain nickel finish.
Add $282 for CZ Kadet .22 LR adapter (includes .22 LR upper slide assembly and mag., new 1998).

✶ CZ-75 PCR Compact - 9mm Para. cal., similar to CZ-75 Compact, except has black polymer frame, decocker, 1.7 lbs. Importation began 2000.

MSR	$523		$425	$370	$325	$295	$265	$235	$210

✶ CZ-75 Kadet - .22 LR cal., black polymer finish, 10 shot mag, 4.88 in. barrel. New 1999.

MSR	$477		$390	$335	$300	$275	$255	$235	$215

✶ CZ-75 25th Anniversary - 9mm Para. cal., features include 25th Anniversary markings. Limited mfg. 2000 only.

			$625	$450	$375				

Last MSR was $699.

✶ CZ-75 Champion - 9mm Para. (new 2000) or .40 S&W cal., dual tone finish, IPSC competition features including 2 port compensator, finger grooved synthetic grips, target trigger and sights, 4½ in. barrel, approx. 2.2 lbs. Importation began 1999.

MSR	$1,551		$1,375	$1,125	$995	$865	$725	$600	$500

✶ CZ-75 Standard IPSC - .40 S&W cal., IPSC features, dual tone finish. New 1999.

MSR	$1,086		$960	$875	$735	$610	$530	$450	$350

✶ CZ-75 Modified - similar to Standard, except has dual port compensator and red dot reflex sight, approx. 2.8 lbs. Importation began 2001.

MSR	$1,567		$1,385	$1,135	$1,000	$875	$735	$600	$500

✶ Model CZ-75 Special Editions - 9mm Para. cal., similar to CZ-75, except has optional special edition finishes including all matte nickel, bright nickel frame, matte chrome, all brushed chrome, bright chrome, or gold frame, choice of matching finish slide, master blue slide, gold small parts, or master blue slide with gold small parts, price line refers to all matte nickel finish. Imported 1993-94 by Action Arms only.

			$525	$465	$415	$375	$335	$310	$285

Last MSR was $699.

Add approx. $120 for matte nickel frame with master blue small parts.
Add approx. $180 for matte nickel with gold small parts, matte nickel frame with master blue slide and gold small parts, master blue with gold small parts, or gold frame with master blue slide.

CZ-82 - 9x18mm Makarov cal., current Czech military sidearm, most recent exportation was to W. Germany in Makarov chambering.

This model is similar to the CZ-83 except for cal. Prices are similar to the model CZ-83.

CZ-83 - .32 ACP (disc. 1994, reintroduced 1999) or .380 ACP (new 1986), or 9mm Makarov (mfg. 1999-2001) cal., modern design, 3 dot sights, 3.8 in. barrel, choice of carry modes, blue (disc. 1994), glossy blue (new 1998), satin nickel (new 1999, not available in .32 ACP), or black polymer (disc. 1997) finish, black synthetic grips, 10 (C/B 1994), 12* (.380 ACP) or 15* (.32 ACP) shot mag., 26.2 oz. Mfg. began 1985, but U.S. importation started in 1992.

MSR	$397		$330	$260	$225	$195	$180	$170	$160

Grading	100%	98%	95%	90%	80%	70%	60%

* **CZ-83 Special Editions** - .380 ACP cal. only, similar to CZ-83, has optional special edition finishes including all matte nickel, master high polish blue, bright nickel frame, matte chrome, all brushed chrome, bright chrome, or gold frame, choice of matching finish slide, master blue slide, gold small parts, or master blue slide with gold small parts, price line refers to all matte nickel or high polish blue finish. Importation disc. 1994.

| | $425 | $375 | $335 | $295 | $250 | $225 | $200 |

Last MSR was $569.

Add approx. $90 for matte nickel frame with master blue small parts.
Add approx. $175 for matte nickel with gold small parts, matte nickel frame with master blue slide and gold small parts, master blue with gold small parts, or gold frame with master blue slide.

CZ-85, CZ-85 B - 9mm Para. or 9x21mm (imported 1993-94 only) cal., variation of the CZ-75 with ambidextrous controls, new plastic grip design, sight rib, available in black polymer, matte blue (disc. 1994), glossy blue (mfg. 2001 only), or high-gloss blue (9mm Para. only, disc. 1994) finish, includes firing pin block and finger rest trigger, plastic grips, B suffix model nomenclature was added during 1998, approx. 2.2 lbs.

| MSR | $504 | $425 | $355 | $315 | $285 | $255 | $230 | $210 |

Add $282 for CZ Kadet .22 LR adapter (includes .22 LR upper slide assembly and mag., mfg. 1998 only).

* **CZ-85 Combat** - similar to CZ-85B, except has fully adj. rear sight, available in black polymer, matte blue (disc. 1994), glossy blue (new 2001), dual-tone, satin nickel, or high-gloss blue finish, walnut (disc. 1994) or black plastic (new 1994) grips, extended mag. release, and free dropping mag. Importation began 1992.

| MSR | $566 | $455 | $395 | $355 | $325 | $295 | $265 | $240 |

Add $20 for glossy blue, satin nickel, or duo-tone finish.
Add $282 for CZ Kadet .22 LR adapter (includes .22 LR upper slide assembly and mag., mfg. 1998 only).

* **CZ-85 Champion** - .40 S&W or 9x21mm cal., similar to CZ-75 Champion, except has 3 port compensator. Imported 1999 only.

| | $1,325 | $1,100 | $975 | $850 | $725 | $600 | $500 |

Last MSR was $1,484.

* **Model CZ-85 Special Editions** - 9mm Para. cal., similar to CZ-85, has optional special edition finishes including all matte nickel, bright nickel frame, matte chrome, all brushed chrome, bright chrome, or gold frame, choice of matching finish slide, master blue slide, gold small parts, or master blue slide with gold small parts, price line refers to all matte nickel finish. Imported 1993-94 only.

| | $575 | $495 | $450 | $395 | $350 | $325 | $285 |

Last MSR was $749.

Subtract $60 for matte nickel frame with master blue slide.
Add $130 for matte nickel frame with master blue small parts, matte nickel with gold small parts, matte nickel frame with master blue slide and gold small parts, master blue with gold small parts or gold frame with master blue slide.

* **Model CZ-85 Combat Special Editions** - 9mm Para. cal., similar finishes to Model CZ-85 Special Editions, price line refers to all matte nickel finish. Limited importation 1994-95.

| | $775 | $725 | $650 | $595 | $525 | $450 | $375 |

Last MSR was $1,049.

Subtract $125 for matte nickel frame with master blue small parts.
Add $245 for matte nickel with gold small parts, matte nickel frame with master blue slide and gold small parts, master blue with gold small parts, or gold frame with master blue slide.

Grading	100%	98%	95%	90%	80%	70%	60%

CZ-97 B - .45 ACP cal., single or double action, manual safety with firing pin block safety, 4.84 in. barrel with short recoil system, black polymer or glossy blue finish, checkered wood grips, double column 10 shot mag., last shot hold open slide, 40 oz. New 1998.

MSR $625		$525	$460	$390	$335	$295	$260	$240

Add $16 for glossy blue finish.

CZ-100 - 9mm Para. or .40 S&W cal., double action only with firing pin block and locked breech, w/o external manual safety, black polymer finish, 3 dot sights, high impact plastic frame, 10 shot mag., 3¾ in. barrel, approx. 24 oz. New 1996.

MSR $424			$365	$310	$265	$235	$210	$195	$180

CZ-122 B SPORT - .22 LR cal., semi-auto, single action only, 6 in. solid ribbed barrel with adj. rear sight, manual and firing pin block safety, last shot hold open slide, steel frame and slide with two-tone finish, ribbed black polymer grips, 10 shot mag., 30 oz. Limited mfg. 1998 only.

		$225	$190	$175	$160	$150	$140	$135

Last MSR was $259.

RIFLES: BOLT ACTION, COMMERCIAL MFG.

Ceská Zbrojovka began manufacturing rifles circa 1936. Long gun production was discontinued between 1948-1964, with the exception of the massive military contracts during that time period.

CZ 513 HUNTER - .22 LR cal., entry level bolt action, 5 shot detachable mag., beechwood stock. Imported 1994 only.

		$195	$175	$150	$125	$95	$80	$65

Last MSR was $225.

Add $30 for Farmer Model.

This model was imported exclusively by Action Arms.

CZ 527 (LUX) - .22 Hornet, .222 Rem., .223 Rem. cal., Mauser style bolt action with silent safety, 21.9 in. barrel with open sights, 5 shot detachable mag., hardwood or checkered walnut stock and forearm (CZ-527 FS), 6.2 lbs. Importation began 1995.

MSR $566			$480	$410	$375	$340	$300	$275	$250

Add $84 for Model CZ-527 FS with checkered walnut stock and forearm.

* *CZ 527 Prestige* - similar to CZ 527 Lux, except has deluxe checkered walnut stock and forend, no sights, scope rings included. Importation began 2001.

MSR $829			$725	$500	$400	$375	$325	$285	$260

* *CZ 527 American Classic* - similar to CZ 527 Lux, scope rings included. New 1999.

MSR $566			$480	$410	$375	$340	$300	$275	$250

* *CZ 527 Varmint* - .223 Rem. cal. only, varmint configuration with heavy barrel and no sights, choice of wood (mfg. 2001 only), laminated (new 2002), or H-S Precision Kevlar (new 2002) black stock, approx. 8 lbs. Importation began 2001.

MSR $658			$550	$450	$400	$350	$310	$285	$250

Add $95 for H-S Precision Kevlar stock.

Subtract approx. $60 for plain wood stock.

* *CZ 527 M Carbine* - .223 Rem. (new 2001) or 7.62x39mm cal., carbine configuration with shorter barrel, 6 lbs. New 1999.

MSR $566			$480	$410	$375	$340	$300	$275	$250

Grading	100%	98%	95%	90%	80%	70%	60%

CZ 537 - .243 Win., .270 Win., .30-06, .308 Win., or 7x57mm cal., detachable 4 shot (.243 Win. and .308 Win. cals. only) or 5 shot fixed mag., choice of regular or Mannlicher (.30-06 or .308 Win. cal. only) stock, hooded ramp front sight, 7¼ lbs. Importation 1995 only.

	$495	$425	$370	$330	$300	$275	$250

Last MSR was $649.

Add $100 for Mannlicher style stock.

* **CZ 537 Mountain Carbine** - .243 Win. only, 19 in. barrel, 5 shot detachable mag., includes ring mounts, 7.1 lbs. Imported 1994 only.

	$525	$450	$375	$330	$300	$275	$250

Last MSR was $669.

CZ 550 STANDARD - various cals. have been imported to date, 4 shot detachable mag. (.243 Win. or .308 Win. only) or internal 5 shot, 23.6 in. barrel, receiver drilled and tapped for Remington 700 style scope base, no sights, checkered walnut stock and forearm, 7 ¼ lbs. Imported 1995-2000.

	$475	$395	$340	$310	$285	$260	$240

Last MSR was $561.

Add $21 for .243 Win. or .308 Win. cal. with detachable mag.

* **CZ 550 Lux** - various cals., similar to CZ 550 Standard, except has deluxe checkered walnut stock with Bavarian style cheekpiece and vent. recoil pad. New 1998.

MSR	$566	$480	$405	$345	$315	$285	$260	$240

Add $20 for detachable mag. (.22-250 Rem., .243 Win., or .308 Win. cal.)

◇**CZ 550 Battue Lux**- similar to CZ 550 Lux, except has 20½ in. barrel with integral barrel fixed rear sight. Limited mfg. 1998 only.

	$450	$375	$330	$300	$280	$260	$240

Last MSR was $519.

Add $30 for .243 Win. or .308 Win. cal. with removable mag.

* **CZ 550 Magnum Standard** - .300 Win. Mag., .375 H&H, .416 Rem. Mag. (disc. 1998), .416 Rigby, .458 Win. Mag., or 7mm Rem. Mag. (importation disc. 1997) cal., 3-5 shot fixed mag., 25 in. barrel with express rear sight, checkered hardwood stock, 9¼ lbs. Limited mfg. 1998 only.

	$525	$475	$440	$400	$375	$350	$335

Last MSR was $595.

Add $40 for .416 Rem. Mag., .416 Rigby, or .458 Win. Mag. cal.

◇**CZ 550 Magnum Standard Lux** - similar to CZ 550 Magnum, except has select checkered walnut. New 1998.

MSR	$650	$570	$485	$430	$390	$350	$335	$300

Add $159 for .300 Win. Mag., .375 H&H., .416 Rigby, or .458 Win. Mag. cal.

* **CZ 550 Prestige-** .270 Win. or .30-06 cal., similar to CZ 550 Lux, except has deluxe checkered walnut stock and forend, no sights, scope rings included. Imported 2001 only.

	$525	$425	$385	$350	$310	$285	$260

Last MSR was $621.

* **CZ 550 American Classic** - .22-250 Rem., .243 Win., .270 Win., .30-06, .308 Win., 6.5x55mm (new 2001), 7x57mm, or 9.3x62mm cal., features American style walnut stock, fixed or detachable mag., scope rings included, approx. 7½ lbs. New mid-1999.

MSR	$566	$480	$405	$345	$315	$285	$260	$240

Add $20 for detachable 4-5 shot mag. (.22-250 Rem., .243 Win. and .308 Win. only).

Grading	100%	98%	95%	90%	80%	70%	60%

* **CZ 550 Varmint** - .22-250 Rem. (new 2002) or .308 Win. cal., 25.6 in. barrel w/o sights, 4 shot detachable mag., checkered walnut (.308 Win. cal. only) or laminated (new 2002) stock with vent. recoil pad, 9.3 lbs. Importation began 2000.

MSR	$615	$510	$420	$365	$320	$285	$260	$240

Add $91 for laminated stock (new 2002).

* **CZ 550 FS Mannlicher** - similar to CZ 550 American Classic, except has Mannlicher stock and 20½ in. barrel, fixed 5 shot or 4 shot detachable mag. (.243 Win. or .308 Win. cal. only), 7¼ lbs. Imported 1996-98, reintroduced 2001.

MSR	$663	$545	$480	$425	$385	$355	$335	$300

Add $22 for 4 shot detachable mag.

* **CZ 550 Battue FS Mannlicher** - similar to CZ 550 FS Mannlicher, except has integral barrel fixed rear sight. Limited mfg. 1998 only.

	$525	$465	$425	$395	$360	$330	$300
						Last MSR was $609.	

Add $30 for .243 Win. or .308 Win. cal. with removable mag.

* **CZ 550 Minnesota** - similar to CZ 550 Lux, except has select walnut stock w/o cheekpiece, and barrel has no sights. Limited mfg. 1998 only.

	$445	$375	$330	$300	$280	$260	$240
						Last MSR was $505.	

Add $30 for .243 Win. or .308 Win. cal. with removable mag.

CZ-700 SNIPER - .308 Win. cal., sniper design features forged billet receiver with permanently attached Weaver rail, 25.6 in. heavy barrel w/o sights, 10 shot detachable mag., laminated thumbhole stock with adj. cheekpiece and buttplate, large bolt handle, fully adj. trigger, 11.9 lbs. Limited importation 2001 only.

	$1,875	$1,575	$1,250	$1,025	$895	$775	$650
						Last MSR was $2,097.	

MODEL CZ-452 (ZKM-452) - .22 LR or .22 Win. Mag. (disc. 1998) cal., bolt action, 5, 6 (.22 Mag. only), or 10 shot mag., 24.8 in. barrel, choice of black synthetic stock and matte nickel metal finish (new 1999) or uncheckered hardwood stock with Schnabel forend and blue metal finish (disc. 1998), adj. rear sight, 6.6 lbs. Importation began 1995 from CZ, earlier mfg. was by Brno.

MSR	$368	$300	$245	$205	$175	$150	$135	$120

Add $50 for .22 Win. Mag. cal. (disc. 1998).

* **Model CZ-452D Deluxe/Lux (ZKM-452D)** - similar to ZKM-452 only with checkered walnut stock. Importation began 1995.

MSR	$368	$300	$250	$210	$175	$150	$135	$120

Add $26 for .22 Win. Mag. cal.

* **Model CZ-452 American Classic (ZKM-452)** - .22 LR or .22 Win. Mag. cal., 5 shot mag., American style walnut stock. Importation began 1999.

MSR	$368	$300	$250	$210	$175	$150	$135	$120

Add $26 for .22 Win. Mag. cal.

* **Model CZ-452 Scout (ZKM-452)** - .22 LR cal. only, youth configuration with shorter 16.2 in. barrel and uncheckered hardwood stock, 5 shot mag., 4 lbs. Importation began 2000.

MSR	$191	$165	$145	$125	$105	$85	$70	$60

* **Model CZ-452 Training Rifle** - .22 LR cal., military training rifle configuration with beechwood stock and 5 shot mag. New 2002.

MSR	$233	$185	$150	$135	$115	$95	$75	$65

* **Model CZ-452 Varmint (ZKM-452)** - .22 LR cal. only, similar to Model ZKM-452D, except

Grading	100%	98%	95%	90%	80%	70%	60%

has longer barrel and no sights. Importation began 1998.

	MSR	$394	$325	$270	$230	$190	$170	$150	$140

ZKK 600 - .270 Win., .30-06, or 7x57mm cal., improved Mauser type action, 23½ in. barrel, checkered walnut stock, 5 shot internal mag., thumb safety, 7.2 lbs. Importation disc. 1995.

			$500	$425	$370	$330	$300	$275	$250

Last MSR was $589.

ZKK 601 - .243 Win. or .308 Win. cal., otherwise similar to ZKK 600. Importation disc. 1995.

			$500	$425	$370	$330	$300	$275	$250

Last MSR was $589.

ZKK 602 - .300 Win. Mag. (disc.), .375 H&H, .416 Rigby (new 1996), .416 Rem. (new 1996), 8x68mm (disc.), or .458 Win. Mag. cal., similar to ZKK 600, except has 25.2 in. barrel and 3 leaf express rear sight, 9.3 lbs. Disc. 1997.

			$675	$575	$495	$450	$395	$350	$310

Last MSR was $799.

RIFLES: O/U

CZ-589 STOPPER - .458 Win. Mag. cal. only, Kersten style boxlock action with Blitz type trigger, checkered Turkish walnut stock and forearm, fixed iron sights, includes sling swivels, 9.3 lbs. Imported 2001 only.

			$2,695	$2,300	$2,000	$1,750	$1,500	$1,250	$1,050

Last MSR was $2,999.

Add $1,000 for sideplates and special engraving/checkering.

RIFLES: SEMI-AUTO

CZ-M52 (1952) - 7.62x45mm Czech cal., semi-auto, 20 2/3 in. barrel, 10 shot detachable mag., tangent rear sight, this model was also imported briefly by Samco Global Arms, Inc. located in Miami, FL.

			$350	$295	$260	$230	$200	$175	$150

CZ-M52/57 (1957) - 7.62x39mm cal., later variation of the CZ-M52.

			$250	$215	$185	$160	$140	$125	$110

CZ-511 - .22 LR cal., blowback action, 22.2 in. barrel, uncheckered beechwood stock, flip-up rear sight, receiver top slotted for scope mounts, 8 shot mag., approx. 5½ lbs. Previously disc. 1986, importation resumed 1998-2001.

			$295	$245	$210	$190	$175	$160	$150

Last MSR was $351.

SHOTGUNS: O/U

CZ 581 SOLO - 12 ga., 2¾ in. chambers, boxlock action with Kersten upper locking mechanism, ejectors, checkered walnut stock and forearm, approx. 7.4 lbs. Importation disc. 1995, resumed during 1999.

	MSR	$846		$725	$615	$565	$485	$425	$385	$350

Add 10% for single trigger (disc.).

CABANAS

Grading	100%	98%	95%	90%	80%	70%	60%

Previous trademark manufactured by Industrias Cabanas, S.A. in Aguilas, Mexico 1949-1999. Previously imported and retailed by Mandall Shooting Supplies, Inc. located in Scottsdale, AZ.

Cabanas manufactured a unique single shot bolt action rifle which shot oversized .177 pellets/BBs powered by .22 blanks at 1,150 feet per second. There were at least 8 variations, and secondary market prices today for 95%+ original condition ranges from approx. $65- $120. Transfer requires FFL. This trademark had limited U.S. importation.

CABELA'S INC.

Current sporting goods dealer and catalog company headquartered in Sidney, NE. Consumer direct (store or mail order catalog) sales only.

In addition to the models listed below, Cabela's also imports black powder cartridge Sharps replicas, revolvers, and other reproductions, mostly manufactured in Italy by A. Uberti, Pedersoli, and Pietta (please see individual sections for more info).

Cabela's also has a wide variety of black powder muzzleloading rifles and pistols, in addition to replicas of popular older Colt and Winchester firearms.

Please refer to the *Colt Blackpowder Reproductions & Replicas* and the 2nd Edition *Blue Book of Modern Black Powder Values* (now online also) by Dennis Adler for more information and prices on Cabela's lineup of modern black powder models.

Cabela's should be contacted directly (see Trademark Index) to receive the most recent information on their complete firearms and black powder line-ups, including related accessories.

SHOTGUNS: SxS

HEMINGWAY MODEL - mfg. for Cabela's by V. Bernardelli located in Italy, ST, ejectors. Disc. 1994.

$925	$775	$700	$640	$575	$525	$465

Last MSR was $975.

AYA GRADE II CUSTOM - mfg. for Cabela's by AYA located in Eibar, Spain, ST, ejectors, similar to AYA Model II with Model 53 engraving and trim. Disc. and sold out.

$1,295	$,1,150	$895	$775	$700	$640	$575

CAEM, RENATO

Current manufacturer of small gauge, SxS shotguns located in Marcheno Val Trompia, Italy. Currently imported and distributed by S.R. Lamboy & Co., Inc. located in Victor, NY. Consumer direct sales.

Renato Caem manufactures approx. 5 best quality scalloped boxlock SxS shotguns annually, only in 20 ga., 28 ga., or .410 bore. Please contact the importer directly for more information regarding specifications, delivery, and current prices (see Trademark Index).

CAESAR GUERINI, s.r.l.

Current manufacturer located in Marcheno, Italy. No current U.S. importation.

Caesar Guerini manufactures good quality 12 ga. O/U and semi-auto shotguns, in either boxlock or sidelock action, and with or w/o sideplates. Please contact the company directly for more information. See Trademark Index.

Grading	100%	98%	95%	90%	80%	70%	60%

CALICO LIGHT WEAPONS SYSTEMS

Previous manufacturer established during 1986, and located in Sparks, NV 1998-2001. Previously located in Bakersfield, CA.

A complete line of accessories was available for all Calico carbines and pistols.

CARBINES

LIBERTY 50-100 - 9mm Para. cal., 16.1 in. barrel, downward ejection, aluminum alloy receiver, synthetic stock with pistol grip (some early post-ban specimens had full wood stocks with thumbhole cutouts), 50 or 100 shot helical feed mag., ambidextrous safety, 7 lbs. Mfg. 1995-2001.

$750	$625	$525	$450	$395	$350	$300

Last MSR was $860.

Add $65 for 100 shot helical feed mag.

M-100 - .22 LR cal., semi-auto carbine, paramilitary design with folding buttstock, 100 shot helical feed mag., alloy frame, ambidextrous safety, 16.1 in. shrouded barrel with flash suppressor/muzzle brake, 4.2 lbs. empty. Mfg. 1986-94.

$625	$550	$450	$400	$350	$300	$275

Last MSR was $308.

❋ **M-100 FS** - similar to M-100, except has solid stock and barrel does not have flash suppressor. Mfg. 1996-2001.

$550	$450	$400	$360	$315	$275	$250

Last MSR was $650.

M-101 - while advertised, this model was never mfg.

M-105 SPORTER - similar to M-100, except has walnut distinctively styled buttstock and forend, 4¾ lbs. empty. Mfg. 1989-94.

$280	$235	$200	$175	$160	$150	$140

Last MSR was $335.

M-106 - while advertised, this model was never mfg.

M-900 - 9mm Para. cal., retarded blowback action, paramilitary design with collapsible buttstock, cast aluminum receiver with stainless steel bolt, static cocking handle, 16 in. barrel, fixed rear sight with adj. post front, 50 (standard) or 100 shot helical feed mag., ambidextrous safety, black polymer pistol grip and forend, 3.7 lbs. empty. Mfg. 1989- 1990, reintroduced 1992-1993.

$560	$475	$350	$300	$285	$270	$255

Last MSR was $618.

❋ **M-900S** - similar to M-900, except has non-collapsible shoulder stock. Disc. 1993.

$575	$485	$360	$300	$285	$270	$255

Last MSR was $632.

❋ **M-901 Canada Carbine** - 9mm Para. cal., similar to M-900, except has 18½ in. barrel and sliding stock. Disc. 1992.

$575	$475	$350	$300	$285	$270	$255

Last MSR was $643.

This model was also available with solid fixed stock (Model 901S).

M-951 TACTICAL CARBINE - 9mm Para. cal., 16.1 in. barrel, similar appearance to M-900 Carbine, except has muzzle brake and extra pistol grip on front of forearm, 4¾ lbs. Mfg. 1990-94.

$475	$395	$350	$300	$275	$250	$225

Last MSR was $556.

Grading	100%	98%	95%	90%	80%	70%	60%

✳ M-951S - similar to M-951, except has synthetic buttstock. Mfg. 1991-94.

	$485	$400	$350	$300	$275	$250	$225

Last MSR was $567.

PISTOLS: SEMI-AUTO

M-110 - .22 LR cal., same action as M-100 Carbine, 6 in. barrel with muzzle brake, 100 round helical feed mag., includes notched rear sight and adj. windage front sight, 10½ in. sight radius, ambidextrous safety, pistol grip storage compartment, 2.21 lbs. empty. Mfg. 1989-2001.

	$475	$395	$315	$260	$230	$200	$180

Last MSR was $570.

M-950 - 9mm Para. cal., same operating mechanism as the M-900 Carbine, 6 in. barrel, 50 (standard) or 100 shot helical feed mag., 2¼ lbs. empty. Mfg. 1989-94.

	$450	$375	$325	$285	$260	$240	$225

Last MSR was $518.

Many accessories were also available for this model.

CAMEX-BLASER USA, INC.

Previous importer/distributor of Blaser Jagdwaffen Gmbh rifles.

Previously imported Camex-Blaser rifles can be located in the Blaser section in this text.

CAPRINUS

Previous shotgun manufacturer located in Varberg, Sweden.

SHOTGUNS: O/U

CAPRINUS SWEDEN - 12 ga., boxlock action, ejectors, ST, stainless steel receiver, unique design incorporates breaking down without forearm disassembly, 29½ in. barrels with choke tubes, limited mfg. during early 1980s.

	$3,750	$3,250	$2,850	$2,400	$2,000	$1,600	$1,200

Last MSR was approx. $5,955.

CARL GUSTAF

Previous manufacturer located in Eskilstuna, Sweden. No current importation. Previously imported by Hansen & Co. located in Southport, CT during 1994-95, and by Precision Sales International located in Westfield, MA during 1991-93.

RIFLES: BOLT ACTION

MODEL CG 2000 STANDARD GRADE - 6.5x55mm, 7x64mm, 9.3x62mm, .243 Win., .270 Win., .30-06, .308 Win., 7mm Rem. Mag., or .300 Win. Mag. cal., bolt action, Monte Carlo walnut stock with checkering and Wundhammer grip, 24 in. barrel, detachable 3 or 4 shot mag., with or without sights, cold-swaged barrel and receiver, 60 degree bolt, 3-way slide safety, 7½ lbs. Imported began 1991-95.

	$1,325	$1,050	$875	$725	$575	$475	$375

Last MSR was $1,535.

Add $540 for Mag. cals.

This model was supplied with individual 80 meter signed test targets. This model was also been imported as the Fairfax 2000 series.

Grading	100%	98%	95%	90%	80%	70%	60%

✳ *Model 2000 Luxe Grade* - .270 Win., .30-06, .308 Win., or 6.5x55mm cal., features choice of regular or Mannlicher deluxe walnut stock. Imported 1995 only.

| | $1,695 | $1,400 | $1,200 | $975 | $825 | $650 | $475 |

Last MSR was $1,935.

A Model 2000 Super-Luxe was also available in 6.5x55mm or .30-06 cal. - retail was $4,250.

MODEL 3000 - various cals., features Sauer action with non-rotating bolt. Previously imported by Aimpoint.

| | $675 | $575 | $475 | $400 | $375 | $350 | $325 |

STANDARD BOLT ACTION RIFLE - 6.5x55mm, 7x64mm, .270 Win., 7mm Rem. Mag., .308 Win., .30-06, or 9.3x62mm cal., 24 in. barrel, folding rear sight, checkered classic style stock. Mfg. 1970-1977.

| | $375 | $325 | $300 | $275 | $250 | $225 | $200 |

✳ *Monte Carlo stock*

| | $450 | $395 | $350 | $300 | $275 | $250 | $225 |

GRADE II - similar to Monte Carlo Standard, in .22-250 Rem., .25-06 Rem., 6.5x55mm, .270 Win., 7mm Rem. Mag., .308 Win., .30-06, or .300 Win. Mag. cal., select stock and rosewood pistol grip cap, and forearm tip.

| | $500 | $425 | $375 | $325 | $295 | $275 | $250 |

GRADE III - similar to Grade II, except fancy wood, deluxe high gloss finish.

| | $575 | $475 | $425 | $350 | $325 | $300 | $275 |

DELUXE - similar to Grade III, except engraved floorplate and trigger guard, Deluxe French walnut, and jeweled bolt.

| | $675 | $575 | $475 | $400 | $375 | $350 | $325 |

VARMINT TARGET MODEL - .222 Rem., .22-250 Rem., .243 Win., bolt action, fast lock time, or 6.5x55mm cal., 27 in. barrel, no sights, large bakelite bolt knob, target type stock. Mfg. 1970. Disc.

| | $550 | $495 | $440 | $385 | $360 | $320 | $290 |

GRAND PRIX SINGLE SHOT TARGET - .22 LR cal., fastest lock time bolt action, 27 in. heavy barrel with adj. weight, no sights, target stock, adj. butt plate. Mfg. 1970. Disc.

| | $550 | $495 | $440 | $385 | $360 | $320 | $290 |

CASARTELLI, CARLO

Previous manufacturer located in Brescia, Italy until 2000. Previously imported and distributed until 1999 by New England Arms Corp. located in Kittery Point, ME.

Casartelli rifles and shotguns were available through special order only. Virtually any custom gun configuration could be manufactured to the customer's exact specifications and requirements.

RIFLES

AFRICA MODEL - BOLT ACTION - various heavy and Mag. cals., action is square bridge type Mauser, full coverage game scene engraving appropriate to caliber, takedown, limited production.

| | $10,200 | $7,500 | $5,900 | $5,300 | $4,700 | $4,100 | $3,600 |

Last MSR was $12,000.

SAFARI MODEL - BOLT ACTION - standard cals., regular Mauser action, full coverage game scene engraving, limited production.

| | $6,250 | $5,900 | $5,250 | $4,950 | $4,150 | $3,650 | $3,150 |

Last MSR was $8,250.

Grading	100%	98%	95%	90%	80%	70%	60%

KENYA - DOUBLE RIFLE - most standard and Mag. cals., sidelock action, elaborate game scene and/or scroll engraving, limited production.

	$24,250	$21,500	$17,750	$14,750	$12,000	$9,950	$8,250

Last MSR was $35,000.

SHOTGUNS: SxS

SIDELOCK MODEL - various ga.'s, elaborate game scene and/or scroll engraving, limited production.

$13,000	$9,750	$7,900	$6,500	$5,200	$4,250	$3,750

Last MSR was $17,000.

CASPIAN ARMS, LTD.

Current parts manufacturer located in Hardwick, VT. Dealer direct sales only.

Caspian Arms currently fabricates high quality steel, stainless steel, titanium (new 2002), and alloy frames for the Colt Government Model 1911/A1, both in standard and high capacity frames. Frame sizes include the Government, Commander, and Officer's. Caspian Arms Ltd. also manufactures slides, including a damascus variation ($525), and related small parts, in addition to having many special order machine operations available. Please contact them directly for current information on their extensive line of pistol-related components.

PISTOLS: SEMI-AUTO

VIETNAM COMMEMORATIVE - .45 ACP, total production was 1,000, hand engraved by J.J. Adams, nickel plated, branch service medallion installed in grips. Limited mfg. 1986-93.

$1,450	$995	$795

Last MSR was $1,500.

Add $350 for gold plating.
Add $200 for serial numbers below RVN100.

This Vietnam Commemorative was also available in 24Kt. gold hand inlay edition for $14,000 - very limited production.

CASULL ARMS CORPORATION

Current manufacturer and distributor located in Afton, WY, since 1996. Consumer direct and dealer sales.

PISTOLS: SEMI-AUTO

CA-3800 - .38 Casull cal., single action, 6 in. match barrel, 8 shot mag., blue or stainless finish, checkered exotic wood grips, 2 piece guide rod, fully adj. rear sight and Casull mfg. adj. front sight, hand fitted slide to frame, slide features Dick Casull signature on left side, includes locking aluminum carrying case and 2 mags., 40 oz. New 2001.

MSR	$2,495		$2,395	$2,150	$1,975	$1,825	$1,675	$1,550	$1,425

Add $300 for 6 in. .45 ACP barrel.
Add $400 for all stainless model.
Add $100 for either stainless steel frame and blue slide or vice versa.
Add $900 for both cals. with custom fitted extra slides.
Add $400 for compensator.

Grading	100%	98%	95%	90%	80%	70%	60%

REVOLVERS

CA2000 MINI-FRAME REVOLVER - .22 LR or .32 ACP cal., double-action, fold up trigger, hammerless, manual safety, hardwood grips. New 1997.

MSR	$398	$350	$295	$250	$225	$200	$185	$170

CA3000 SMALL FRAME REVOLVER - while advertised during 1997 (MSR - $1,495), this model was never manufactured.

CA4000 LARGE FRAME REVOLVER - while advertised during 1997 (MSR - $1,995), this model was never manufactured.

RIFLES: BOLT ACTION

CAC5000 CONVENTIONAL - standard cals. include .270 Win., .300 Win. Mag., .375 H&H, .458 Win. Mag., or 7mm Rem. Mag. cal., features improved bolt action with conventional extraction, box mag. Limited mfg. 1997-99.

	$2,275	$1,950	$1,600

Last MSR was $2,495.

CRS7000 CASULL RIFLE SYSTEM - .30 Casull or 6.5 Casull cal., patented bolt and extraction system, features new, all-metal bedding system allowing take-down and reassembly without affecting accuracy, box mag., stainless barrel without sights, uncheckered walnut stock, sporter or benchrest configuration. Limited mfg. 1997-99.

	$2,700	$2,350	$2,000

Last MSR was $2,995.

CENTURION ORDNANCE, INC.

Current manufacturer and importer located in Helotes, TX. Centurion Ordnance also imports Aguila ammunition, in addition to customizing a Ruger M-77 .22 cal. action.

SHOTGUNS: SLIDE ACTION

POSEIDON - 12 ga., 1¾ in. chamber (shoots "mini-shells" and slugs), 18¼ in. smoothbore barrel, 13 in. LOP, black synthetic stock and forearm, 6 shot mag., adj. rear sight, 5 lbs., 5 oz. New 2001.

MSR	N/A	$285	$250	$225	$200	$185	$170	$155

Mini-shells currently retail for $12.60 for a box of 20 (shot sizes include 7, #4 & #1 buckshot).

CENTURY ARMS

Previous manufacturer circa 1996-1998 located in Balwyn, Victoria, Australia.

RIFLES: SINGLE SHOT

REWA RIFLE - 4 bore ball, break open action, massive single shot with case colored and engraved action, deluxe checkered stock and forearm with ebony tip, iron sights, production limited to a few prototypes only (a convertible shotgun barrel was also planned).
Extreme rarity precludes accurate pricing on this model.

Grading	100%	98%	95%	90%	80%	70%	60%

CENTURY INTERNATIONAL ARMS, INC.

Current importer and distributor with offices located in Boca Raton, FL, beginning 1997. Century International Arms, Inc. was previously headquartered in St. Albans, VT until 1997.

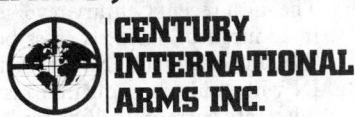

CENTURY INTERNATIONAL ARMS INC.

Century International Arms, Inc. has imported a wide variety of used military rifles and pistols, including various Mauser rifle contract models, French Lebels and MAS models, Mannlichers, F.N. Model 49s, Lee Enfields, Hakims, Mosin-Nagants, Egyptian Rashids, Swedish Ljungman Model 42Bs, Eastern Bloc M-44s, Chinese and Russian SKSs, and M-1 Carbines/ Garands. Imported pistols include various WWI and WWII used military pistols including Mauser Broomhandles, Lugers, P.38s, Argentine mfg. M1911s, French PA 35s, and recently, models from both FEG and Republic Arms, located in South Africa. Additionally, some shotguns have also been imported (including Chinese O/Us and Turkish slide actions and semi-autos), in addition to a wide range of accessories, including bayonettes, holsters, stocks, grips, mounts, scopes, etc. Because most of these items range in the $125-$550 price range, individual listings are not listed in this text. Most of these models are in good to new condition overall. In addition, surplus and currently manufactured ammunition is available at very competitive prices. Generally, these models offer good values to the shooter and some may be collectible. Because importation of Eastern Bloc military rifles has changed so dramatically over the past several years, Century International Arms, Inc. should be contacted directly (see Trademark Index) for a copy of their most recent catalog, or check their web site for current offerings.

PISTOLS: SEMI-AUTO

BLUE THUNDER - .45 ACP cal., patterned after the Colt Govt. Model 1911, choice of 4 ¼ (Commodore Blue Thunder) or 5 (Blue Thunder) ported or unported barrel, 7 shot mag., various configurations and finishes, many target features are standard. Importation from Phillipines began 2001.

No MSR	$375	$325	$295	$275	$250	$225	$200

RIFLES: SEMI-AUTO

G-3 SPORTER - .308 Win. cal., mfg. from genuine G3 parts, and American made receiver with integrated scope rail, pistol grip stock, matte black finish, refinished condition only. New 1999.

No MSR	$600	$500	$450	$425	$395	$375	$350

CENTURY MFG., INC.

Current manufacturer located in Knightstown, IN, beginning Feb., 2002. Previously manufactured in Evansville and Greenfield, IN 1973-circa 1999. Consumer direct and dealer sales.

This revolver design was originally manufactured in 1972 by Russell Wilson, who sandcasted the bronze frame (cloned from the Colt SAA configuration) in Evansville, IN. Gene Phelps purchased the manufacturing rights for this gun and formed a partnership with Earl Keller to produce a redesigned frame, also using sandcast bronze.

The original Century revolver was made in Evansville, IN beginning in 1973 (1973 was the 100th anniversary of the .45-70 Govt. cartridge - hence the term Century) and production was halted in 1976 at ser. no. 524. In late 1976, Phelps and Keller (the 2 original partners on the venture) dissolved their partnership and each began manufacturing their own version of the .45-70 revolver. Gene Phelps completely redesigned the gun's interior and began manufacturing the Heritage I, with an investment-cast steel frame, and without the Century's novel cross-bolt safety. Keller's Century Manufacturing, Inc. continued to produce the original Century, with some design refinements, and in 1985 the company was purchased by Dr.

Grading	100%	98%	95%	90%	80%	70%	60%

Paul Majors, who died in Dec. of 2001.

The most recent Century revolver featured a manganese bronze frame and other components in addition to having a cross-bolt safety. They were produced in .45-70 and various other cals., in Greenfield, IN. Earl Keller died in 1986. The second series was made in Greenfield, IN with limited production resuming in 1986. Earlier handmade "Evansville" Model 100s (disc.) are currently selling for between $2,500-$3,500, depending on the region.

In Feb., 2002, Century Mfg. was purchased by Dale Lukens & Jeff Yelton and moved to Knightstown, IN. New production guns are scheduled for delivery in April, 2002, and will also include a revolving rifle built on the Model 100 frame. These new production guns will carry a limited lifetime guarantee. Additionally, older Century Mfg. revolvers can also be serviced (non-warranty).

REVOLVERS

Less than 1,300 Model 100s were manufactured 1976-2001. The following values below are for .45-70 Govt. cal. Other calibers are priced from $2,000 on up.

MODEL 100 - .30-30 Win. (new 1987), .375 Win. (new 1986), .444 Marlin (new 1986), .45-70 Govt., .50-70 Govt. (new 1987), or .50-110 cal., single action 6 shot, manganese bronze frame, steel cylinder, 6½, 8, 10, or 12 (disc.) in. round or octagon barrel, unique crossbolt safety that locks the hammer, adj. sights, walnut grips, 5 lbs. 14 oz. Disc. 2000, to be resumed 2002.

$2,000	$1,750	$1,500	$1,350	$1,100	$995	$850

Last MSR was $2,000.

Add $750 for .50-70 Govt. cal.
Add $110 for normal octagon barrel.
Add $200 for stainless steel fabrication.

As this edition went to press, 2002 retail prices had yet to be established.

CHAMPLIN FIREARMS, INC.

Current custom manufacturer, gunsmith, and importer located in Enid, OK. Champlin Firearms was established in 1966. Direct sales only.

Champlin Firearms, Inc. manufactures handcrafted rifles built around a patented bolt action of their own design and manufacture. Most guns are built per individual customer order and specifications. Values will vary greatly depending on the configuration, desirability, and special order specifications. All Champlin rifles are built along classic lines with best quality wood and exemplary workmanship. They have been used successfully on safaris and have shot dangerous game throughout the world.

Champlin Firearms, Inc. also inventories a wide selection of high grade, top quality shotguns and rifles (especially top trademark doubles and bolt actions). Contact George Caswell (owner) directly for a current listing (please refer to Trademark Index). Additional services include a complete gunsmithing service for all grades of English double rifles and shotguns. Custom stocks are also built to individual customer specifications. All double rifles are test fired and checked thoroughly upon completion of manufacture or repair. Again, Champlin Firearms should be contacted for consultation and quotation regarding this additional work.

RIFLES: BOLT ACTION

BOLT ACTION RIFLE - various cals., round or octagon barrel, adj. trigger, each rifle is built to customer specifications. Values below represent base gun with standard wood, no options, and no engraving.

MSR	$8,500		$8,500	$8,000	$7,000	$6,750	$6,000	$5,250	$4,500

Many additional special order options are available on this model and Champlin Firearms should be contacted directly for price quotations.

Grading	100%	98%	95%	90%	80%	70%	60%

CHAPUIS ARMES

Current manufacturer located in St. Bonnet Le Chateau, France. Currently, Chapuis Armes is exclusively imported by Chadick's, Ltd. located in Terrell, TX. Previously imported by GSI, Inc. located in Trussville, AL until 1995 and Armes De Chasse located in Chadds Ford, PA until 1993.

Chapuis rifles and shotguns are manufactured on a limited basis. Most of their emphasis is on high quality double rifles and shotguns. For further information regarding this respected French trademark, please contact the importer.

RIFLES: O/U

SUPER ORION C15 MODEL - .300 Win. Mag. or .375 H&H cal., notched boxlock action with ejectors, coin finish only, 23.6 in. barrels with quarter rib, engraved action, approx. 8 lbs. Imported 1995-96.

$8,250	$7,150	$6,250	$5,400	$4,200	$3,500	$3,150

Last MSR was $9,195.

Add $2,900 for .375 H&H cal.

RIFLES: SxS

RGEX EXPRESS MODEL - .30-06, .300 Win. Mag., 7x65R, 8x57JRS, or 9.3x74R cal., double rifle, ejectors, boxlock action, 23.6 in. barrels, deluxe checkered walnut stock with cheekpiece, full line of options are available, 7 lbs. 6 oz. Imported 1989-1998.

Values below assume metric or .30-06 cal.

$7,675	$5,850	$4,925	$4,250	$3,650	$2,995	$2,450

Last MSR was $8,500.

Add approx. $700 for .300 Win. Mag. cal.
Add approx. 60% for HGEX Express Supreme Model (engraved, not avail. in .300 Win. Mag. cal.).
Add 110% for HGEX Express Imperial Model (scroll engraved, not avail. in .300 Win. Mag. cal.).

UGEX UTILITY GRADE EXPRESS - similar to RGEX, except has select walnut. New 1998.

MSR	$5,000		$4,500	$3,950	$3,500	$2,950	$2,550	$2,100	$1,700

Add $500 for .300 Win. Mag. cal.

AFRICAN P.H. (PROFESSIONAL HUNTER) GRADE I - .30-06, .300 Win. Mag., .375 H&H, .416 Rigby, 9.3x74R, or .470 NE cal., notched boxlock action with English scroll border engraving, case colored receiver, selective ejectors, deluxe walnut stock with English cheekpiece.

Values below are for .375 H&H cal.

MSR	$8,500		$7,925	$6,500	$5,650	$4,600	$4,000	$3,500	$2,950

Add $3,000 for .470 NE cal.
Add $4,000 for .416 Rigby cal.
Subtract $1,500 for .30-06 or 9.3x74R.
Subtract $1,000 for .300 Win. Mag. cal.

This model was previously designated Express Agex Brousse.

Grading	100%	98%	95%	90%	80%	70%	60%

✳ *African PH Grade II* - similar to Grade I, except has master signed scroll engraving with game scene on bottom of coin finished receiver.

Values below are for .375 H&H cal.

MSR	$10,500		$9,745	$8,750	$7,650	$6,350	$5,500	$4,750	$3,900

Add $2,000 for .470 NE cal.
Add $3,500 for .416 Rigby cal.
Subtract $1,500 for .30-06 or 9.3x74R.
Subtract $1,000 for .300 Win. Mag. cal.

BROUSSE MODEL - .375 H&H, .416 Rigby, or .470 NE cal., similar to Grade I Professional Hunter, except has full rose and scroll engraving coverage on coin finished receiver. New 1998.

MSR	$7,500		$6,800	$5,750	$4,850	$4,150	$3,500	$2,900	$2,450

Add $3,000 for .416 Rigby cal.
Add $2,000 for .470 NE cal.

SAVANA MODEL - .30-06, .300 Win. Mag., .375 H&H, .416 R Chapuis (disc.), .416 Rigby, .470 NE, or 9.3x74R cal., deluxe version of the Agex Jungle, except has hand- engraved game scenes on action sides and Cape Buffalo head on floorplate of action, case colored (disc.) or coin finish.

Values below are for .375 H&H cal.

MSR	$23,000		$20,250	$17,350	$15,300	$13,000	$10,500	$8,750	$7,500

Add $2,000 for .470 NE cal.
Add $3,000 for .416 Rigby cal.
Subtract $2,500 for .30-06 or 9.3x74R.
Subtract $2,000 for .300 Win. Mag. cal.

JUNGLE MODEL - .30-06, .300 Win. Mag., .375 H&H, .416 R Chapuis (mfg. 1993- 96), .470 NE (new 1992), or 9.3x74R cal., boxlock action, case colored (disc.) or coin finish, special reinforced receiver with double underbites, 25 5/8 in. barrels, fine English scroll engraving with 3 African animals, ejectors, select French walnut with compartment in pistol grip cap.

Values below are for .375 H&H cal.

MSR	$13,500		$11,850	$9,950	$8,150	$7,200	$6,250	$5,400	$4,350

Add $2,500 for .470 NE cal.
Add $3,500 for .416 Rigby cal.
Subtract $2,000 for .30-06 or 9.3x74R.
Subtract $1,000 for .300 Win. Mag. cal.

✳ *Jungle Second Grade* - features elaborate engraving and best quality wood. Disc. 1996.

$26,000	$22,500	$19,000	$16,000	$13,000	$10,000	$8,750

Last MSR was $29,395.

Add $3,900 for .470 NE cal.

EXPRESS AGEX AFRICA - same cals. as AGEX Jungle, notched boxlock action, master signed scroll engraving and African game scenes, selective ejectors, cased. Importation disc. 1994.

$19,250	$17,750	$15,250	$13,500	$11,250	$10,000	$9,000

Last MSR was $20,954.

Add $2,896 for .470 NE cal.
Add $5,626 for .416 R Chapuis cal.

EXPRESS AGEX SAFARI - similar to AGEX Africa, except has top-of-the-line engraving and wood. Importation disc. 1994.

$29,000	$26,550	$22,350	$19,150	$16,950	$14,000	$12,000

Last MSR was $30,375.

Add $2,040 for .470 NE cal.
Add $5,134 for .416 R Chapuis cal.

Grading	100%	98%	95%	90%	80%	70%	60%

RIFLES: SINGLE SHOT

OURAL EXEL MODEL - .270 Win., .300 Win. Mag., 7mm Rem. Mag. cal., notched boxlock action, English scroll engraving, extractors, 23 5/8 in. barrel, fitted and engraved scope mounts. Importation disc. 1994, reintroduced 1999, current pricing is POR.

MSR	N/A	$4,875	$4,200	$3,775	$3,250	$2,800	$2,400	$1,775

Add approx. 20% for Oural Luxe Model (features better engraving and wood).
Add approx. 58% for Oural Elite Model (features game scene engraving and presentation walnut).

SHOTGUNS

SPORTING CLAYS MODEL O/U - 12 or 20 (3 in. Mag.) ga., scalloped boxlock action, 27½ or 30 in. VR barrels, ST, case colored receiver with English scroll engraving. Limited importation 1997-98.

		$3,675	$3,300	$2,900	$2,500	$2,100	$1,675	$1,300

Last MSR was $3,995.

ST. BONETT MODEL SxS - 12, 16, or 20 (3 in. Mag.) ga., boxlock with case colored (disc.) or coin finished sideplates featuring fine English scroll (disc.) or game scene engraving, 27½ in. monobloc barrels, DT's, ejectors, checkered straight grip walnut stock and forearm, hardshell case. Limited importation began 1997.

MSR	N/A	$2,675	$2,300	$2,000	$1,675	$1,300	$1,000	$850

CHAPUIS, P. ETS

Current manufacturer located in Saint-Bonnet le Chateau, France.

P. Chapuis specializes in custom order rifles and shotguns. Recently, this company has developed a process to color the receiver sideplates while using traditional engraving techniques - this results in a unique 3-D scene. Currently, this manufacturer has no U.S. importation and should be contacted directly (see Trademark Index) for more model information and current pricing. This is a different company than Chapuis Armes.

CHARLES DALY

See Daly, Charles.

CHARLIN ARMS

Previous manufacturer located in St. Etienne, France.

Charlin Arms previously made shotguns which were patterned after Darne firearms. Typically, they are very high quality and values seem to approximate the Darne guns. Once you have determined the comparable model in Darne, please refer to the Darne section in this book.

CHARTER 2000, INC.

Current manufacturer located in Shelton, CT established during 1998.

Charter 2000, Inc. acquired the rights to reproduce the original Charter Arms Undercover Model. Otherwise, it is not affiliated with Charter Arms in any way, nor is it responsible for repair or service on older Charter Arms handguns.

DERRINGERS

DIXIE DERRINGER - .22 LR or .22 Mag. cal., 5 shot, 1 1/8 in. barrel, stainless construction, spur trigger, hardwood grips, 5 oz. New 2002.

MSR	$154	$135	$110	$100

Add $16 for .22 Mag. cal.

Grading	100%	98%	95%	90%	80%	70%	60%

REVOLVERS

BULLDOG - .44 Spl. cal., 5 shot, 2½ in. barrel, steel or stainless steel construction, hammer block safety, choice of standard or pocket hammer, round butt with finger groove grips, 21 oz. New late 1999.

MSR	$314		$265	$230	$210	$185	$170	$150	$130

Add $23 for stainless steel.

POLICE BULLDOG - .38 Spl. cal., 5 shot, large frame, 4 in. tapered or bull barrel, exposed ejector rod, full rubber grips, approx. 23 oz. New 2002.

MSR	$284		$245	$210	$185	$170	$150	$135	$115

UNDERCOVER - .38 Spl. cal., regular double action or DAO, 5 shot, 2 in. barrel, steel or stainless steel construction, checkered compact round butt (standard hammer) or super compact (concealed hammer) synthetic grips (full rubber of boot compact) with finger grooves, 18 oz. New late 1998.

MSR	$276		$240	$205	$180	$165	$145	$135	$115

Add $26 for stainless steel.

OFF DUTY - .38 Spl. cal., DAO, 5 shot, 2 in. barrel, aluminum frame, hammerless, combat synthetic grips, 12 oz. New 2002.

MSR	$353		$295	$260	$225	$200	$185	$160	$140

MAG. PUG - ..357 Mag./.38 Spl., 5 shot, 2.2 in. ported barrel, blue or stainless steel, full rubber grips, 24 oz. New 2001.

MSR	$307		$260	$220	$195	$175	$160	$145	$130

Add $15 for stainless steel.

PATHFINDER - .22 LR or .22 Mag. cal., 6 shot, 2 in. barrel, stainless construction, checkered walnut grips, approx. 18 oz. New 2002.

MSR	$277		$240	$205	$180				

RIFLES: BOLT ACTION

FIELD KING - .243 Win. (disc. 2000), .25-06 Rem., .270 Win., or .30-06 cal., blue or stainless Mauser long action, 4 shot mag., blue or stainless 22 in. E.R. Shaw barrel, checkered black fiberglass reinforced stock with recoil pad, 6¾ lbs. New 2000.

MSR	$345		$300	$250	$215				

Subtract $46 for non-stainless standard blue rifle.

✳ *Field King Carbine* - .308 Win. only, similar to Field King, except is available in 18 in. barrel with compensator only, blue finish or stainless steel. New 2000.

MSR	$345		$300	$250	$215	$200	$185	$175	$165

CHARTER ARMS

Previously manufactured by Charco, Inc. located in Ansonia, CT 1992-96. Previously manufactured by Charter Arms located in Stratford, CT 1991- earlier.

PISTOLS: SEMI-AUTO

MODEL 40 - .22 LR cal. only, double action semi-auto., 3.3 in. barrel, 8 shot mag., 21½ oz., fixed sights, stainless steel. Mfg. 1984-86.

			$265	$240	$220				

Last MSR was $319.

Grading	100%	98%	95%	90%	80%	70%	60%

MODEL 79K - .32 or .380 ACP cal., double action semi-auto., 3.6 in. barrel, 7 shot mag., 24½ oz., fixed sights, stainless steel. Mfg. 1984-86.

| | $325 | $300 | $280 | | | | |

Last MSR was $390.

EXPLORER II & S II PISTOL - .22 LR cal., semi-auto survival pistol, barrel unscrews, 8 shot mag., black, gold (disc.), silvertone, or camouflage finish, 6, 8, or 10 in. barrels, simulated walnut grips. Disc. 1986.

| | $90 | $80 | $70 | $60 | $55 | $50 | $45 |

Last MSR was $109.

This model uses a modified AR-7 action.

Manufacture of this model was by Survival Arms located in Cocoa, FL.

MODEL 42T (COMPETITION II TARGET) - .22 LR cal. only, single action, 5.9 in. barrel, target model with checkered walnut grips, adj. sights, blue finish only. Mfg. 1984- 1985 only.

| | $490 | $450 | $395 | $350 | $300 | $260 | $220 |

Last MSR was $599.

REVOLVERS: DOUBLE ACTION

All Charter Arms revolvers had a hammer block safety system, 8 groove rifling, unbreakable beryllium copper firing pin, triple safety features, no sideplate, steel frames, and lifetime warranty to the original owner.

BONNIE & CLYDE SET - .32 H&R Mag. (Bonnie) and .38 Spl. (Clyde) cal., matched pair, 6 shot, 2½ in. fully shrouded barrel, wood laminate grips (color coordinated), blue finish, pistols individually marked Bonnie or Clyde on barrels, supplied with gun rugs. Mfg. 1989-91.

| | $425 | $365 | $335 | $295 | $260 | $240 | $220 |

LADY ON DUTY - .32 S&W or .38 Spl. cal., 5 (.38 Spl.) or 6 shot, 2 in. shrouded barrel, fixed sights, rose neoprene grips, cased. Mfg. 1995-96.

| | $195 | $165 | $145 | $130 | $115 | $100 | $85 |

Last MSR was $219.

PATHFINDER - .22 LR or .22 Mag. (disc. 1989) cal., 6 shot, 2, 3, or 6 (disc. 1985) in. barrels, round butt, adj. sights, walnut grips, wide trigger and spur hammer. Disc. 1990.

| | $185 | $150 | $125 | $110 | $90 | $70 | $50 |

* ***Pathfinder - Square Butt*** - .22 LR or .22 Mag. (disc. 1989) cal., 6 in. barrel, square butt, otherwise similar to Pathfinder. Disc. 1990.

| | $190 | $155 | $125 | $110 | $90 | $70 | $50 |

* ***Pathfinder Stainless*** - .22 LR or .22 Mag. (disc. 1989) cal., stainless variation, 3½ in. shrouded barrel. Disc. 1990.

| | $185 | $150 | $130 | | | | |

UNDERCOVER - .32 S&W (disc. 1989) or .38 Spl. cal., 5 shot in .38 Spl., 6 shot in .32 S&W, 2 (.38 Spl.) or 3 in. barrel, wide trigger and spur hammer, fixed sights, .38 Spl. can also be ordered with pocket hammer. Disc. 1991.

| | $175 | $145 | $115 | $100 | $90 | $85 | $80 |

* ***Undercover Stainless*** - 2 in. shrouded barrel only. Disc. 1994.

| | $260 | $195 | $140 | | | | |

Last MSR was $304.

Grading	100%	98%	95%	90%	80%	70%	60%

UNDERCOVERETTE - .32 S&W Long cal., similar to Undercover, 6 shot, 2 in. barrel, blue. Disc.

	$155	$140	$110	$100	$90	$70	$55

BULLDOG - .44 Spl. cal., 5 shot, 2½ or 3 (disc. 1988) in. barrels, wide trigger and spur or pocket hammer, checkered bulldog grips (walnut or neoprene), blue or electroless nickel finish. Disc. 1991, reinstated 1994-disc.1996.

	$225	$195	$155	$125	$110	$90	$70

Last MSR was $268.

Add $22 for electroless nickel finish.

* *Bulldog Stainless* - 2½ in. bull or 3 (disc. 1989) in. regular barrel. Disc. 1991.

	$195	$155	$125

* *Target Bulldog* - .357 Mag. or .44 Spl. cal., 5 shot, 4 in. shrouded barrel, adj. sights, square butt only, blue finish. Mfg. 1980-1988.

	$225	$150	$125	$110	$100	$90	$80

Last MSR was $255.

Subtract $10 for .357 Mag. cal.

* *Target Bulldog Stainless* - 9mm Federal, .357 Mag. or .44 Spl. cal., 5 shot, 5½ in. shrouded VR barrel, adj. sights, square butt target grips only, matte finished, 28 oz. Mfg. 1989-91.

	$250	$175	$125

BULLDOG PUG - .44 Spl. cal., 5 shot, 2½ in. shrouded barrel, fixed sights, walnut or neoprene grips. Mfg. 1986-1993.

	$240	$195	$160	$130	$110	$100	$90

Last MSR was $279.

* *Bulldog Pug Stainless* - 2½ in. shrouded barrel. Mfg. 1987-1993.

	$300	$235	$175

Last MSR was $334.

BULLDOG TRACKER - .357 Mag. (.38 Spl.) cal., 5 shot, 2 ½, 4 (disc. 1989), and 6 (disc. 1989) in. bull barrels, adj. sights, blue only, checkered bulldog grips, square butt on 4 or 6 in. barrel only. Disc. 1986, - reintroduced 1989-91.

	$185	$150	$125	$110	$100	$90	$80

MAGNUM PUG - .357 Mag. cal., 5 shot, fixed sights, 2.2 in. shrouded barrel, blue finish. Mfg. 1995-96.

	$225	$195	$155	$125	$110	$90	$70

Last MSR was $268.

POLICE BULLDOG - .32 H&R Mag., .38 Spl. or .44 Spl. cal., 5 (.44 Spl. only) or 6 shot, fixed sights, blue only, 3½ or 4 in. barrel, Neoprene grips or square butt (.44 Spl. only). Disc. 1991.

	$175	$140	$120	$105	$95	$85	$75

Add $20 for either .44 Spl. cal or 3½ in. shrouded barrel.

* *Stainless Police Bulldog* - .32 Mag., .357 Mag. (new 1989), .38 Spl. (disc. 1988 - reintroduced 1990) or .44 Spl. (new 1989) cal., 5 (.357 Mag. or .44 Spl.) or 6 (.32 Mag. or .38 Spl.) shot, square butt, 3½ or 4 in. shrouded barrel. Mfg. 1987-91.

	$195	$160	$150	$140

Add $20 for .357 Mag. or .44 Special cal.

Neoprene grips are standard on these models except for the .357 Mag. (square butt).

Grading	100%	98%	95%	90%	80%	70%	60%

POLICE UNDERCOVER - .32 H&R Mag. or .38 Spl. cal., 6 shot, spur or pocket hammer, 2.2 in. shrouded barrel, checkered walnut grips, fixed sights, blue or electroless nickel (new 1994) finish. Disc. 1996.

		$205	$175	$145	$120	$100	$85	$75

Last MSR was $238.

Add $14 for electroless nickel finish.

✳ *Stainless Police Undercover* - similar to Police Undercover. Disc. 1993.

$240 $185 $150

Last MSR was $276.

OFF DUTY - .22 LR (new 1993), .22 Mag. (new 1994), or .38 Spl. cal., 5 (.38 Spl.) or 6 (.22 LR) shot, 2 in. barrel, fixed sights, conventional or DA only, blue, matte black (disc.), or electroless nickel (new 1994) finish. Disc. 1996.

$170 $145 $120 $105 $90 $85 $80

Last MSR was $200.

Add $39 for electroless nickel finish.
Add $7 for double action only.

✳ *Stainless Off Duty* - similar to Off Duty. Disc. 1993.

$235 $180 $145

Last MSR was $268.

PIT BULL - 9mm Federal (rare), .357 Mag. (disc. 1989), or .38 Spl. (disc. 1989) cal., 5 shot, 2½, 3½, or 4 (disc. 1989) in. full shrouded barrel, Neoprene grips, approx. 26 oz. Mfg. 1989-91.

$230 $180 $150 $125 $115 $100 $90

✳ *Stainless Pit Bull* - 2½ or 3½ in. shrouded barrel. Disc. 1991.

$240 $190 $155

RIFLES: SEMI-AUTO

AR-7 EXPLORER RIFLE - .22 LR cal., takedown, barreled action stores in Cycolac synthetic stock, 8 shot mag., adj. sights, 16 in. barrel, black finish on AR-7, silvertone on AR-7S. Camouflage finish new 1986 (AR-7C). Mfg. until 1990.

$125 $100 $85 $75 $65 $55 $50

Last MSR was $146.

In 1990, the manufacturing of this model was taken over by Survival Arms located in Cocoa, FL. Current mfg. AR-7 rifles will be found under the Henry Repeating Arms Company and AR-7 Industries.

CHIPMUNK RIFLES

Current trademark manufactured by Rogue Rifle Co., Inc., located in Lewiston, ID, beginning 2001. Previously located in Prospect, OR from 1997-2001. Previously manufactured by Oregon Arms, Inc. located in Prospect, OR 1988-1996. Previously manufactured by Chipmunk Manufacturing located in Medford, OR until 1988.

PISTOLS: SINGLE SHOT

SILHOUETTE PISTOL - .22 LR cal., bolt action design with 14 7/8 in. barrel, iron sights, rear grip walnut stock. Mfg. 1984-88.

$135 $115 $95 $80 $70 $60 $50

Last MSR was $150.

Grading	100%	98%	95%	90%	80%	70%	60%

RIFLES: BOLT ACTION, SINGLE SHOT

C **CHIPMUNK RIFLE** - .17 HMR (new 2002), .22 LR or .22 Win. Mag. (disc. 1987, reintroduced 1999) cal., manually cocked single shot, youth model with 16 1/8 in. barrel and 11½ LOP, choice of black or brown laminate (new 1999), camo (new 2002), or uncheckered Monte Carlo walnut stock, iron sights (adj. aperture rear), 30 in. overall length, 2½ (standard barrel) or 4 (bull barrel) lbs.

MSR $195	$160	$125	$100	$90	$80	$70	$60

Add $15 for .22 Win. Mag. cal.
Add $15 for laminate or camo stock.
Subtract approx. 10% for black coated wood stock.

✳ *Bull Barrel Model* - similar to Chipmunk Single Shot rifle, features 18 1/8 in. bull barrel, 4 lbs. New 1999.

MSR $210	$175	$135	$100	$90	$80	$70	$60

Add $16 for .22 Win. Mag. cal.
Add $15 for laminate or camo stock.

✳ *Deluxe Rifle* - similar to standard rifle, except has deluxe hand checkered Monte Carlo walnut stock. New 1987.

MSR $247	$200	$170	$145	$110	$90	$75	$65

Add $16 for .22 Win. Mag. cal.

✳ *Target Rifle* - similar to Chipmunk rifle, except has 18 in. heavy barrel, micrometer target sights, target stock with adj. accessory rail and buttplate, 5 lbs. New mid-2002.

MSR $330	$285	$245	$215	$185	$165	$150	$135

✳ *Chipmunk Special Edition* - similar to Deluxe Model, except has hand engraving. Please contact the company directly for pricing and availability on this model.

SHOTGUNS: SINGLE SHOT

CHIPMUNK .410 SHOTGUN- .410 bore, 18¼ in. smoothbore barrel, single shot, manual cocking, blue only, 11½ in. LOP, walnut stock, approx. 3¼ lbs. New mid-2002.

MSR $226	$185	$160	$145	$130	$120	$110	$100

CHRISTENSEN ARMS

Current rifle manufacturer established in 1995, and currently located in Fayette, UT. Previously located in St. George, UT during 1995-99. Direct sales only.

Christensen Arms

PISTOL

CARBON ONE PISTOL - various cals., graphite barrel lengths up to 14 in., uses Thompson Center Encore or Contender pistol frame, less than 1 in. grouping for 3 shots at 100 yards, satin nickel receiver, approx. 2½-3 lbs. New 1999.

This model is basically a special order, and prices range from $749-$849.

RIFLES: BOLT ACTION

In addition to the models listed below, Christensen Arms also offers the Carbon One Custom barrel installed on a customer action (any caliber) for $950 ($775 if short chambered by compentent gunsmith), as well as providing a Carbon Wrap conversion to an existing steel barrel ($500).

Grading	100%	98%	95%	90%	80%	70%	60%

Add $325 for Remington titanium action, $185 for titanium muzzle brake, $150 for Jewel trigger, $135 for Teflon coated action, and $75 for lightened action on the models listed below.

CARBON ONE CUSTOM - most popular cals., features Remington 700 BDL short action or Winchester Model 70 action, barrel (up to 28 in. long) features a match grade Shilen/ Christensen precision 416R stainless steel barrel liner inside a larger diameter graphite/ epoxy barrel casing with crown, black synthetic stock, Shilen trigger, 5½-6½ lbs. New 1996.

MSR	$2,950		$2,675	$2,325	$1,975	$1,650	$1,425	$1,225	$1,000

Variations include the Carbon Lite (5 lbs.), Carbon King (6-7 lbs., .25-.308 cal.), Carbon Cannon (includes muzzle brake, 6½-7½ lbs., Magnum series), or Carbon Tactical (includes muzzle brake, 6½ lbs., new 1997), or Carbon Conquest (new 1998).

CARBON ONE HUNTER - various popular cals., features Remington M700 (regular or stainless) or Winchester Model 70 stainless action, available with HS Precision or synthetic stock, large diameter graphite barrel with stainless steel barrel liner, 6½-7¼ lbs. New 1999.

MSR	$1,499		$1,325	$1,150	$925	$800	$700	$600	$500

CARBON RANGER CONQUEST - .50 BMG cal., single shot or repeater (5 shot), McMillian stainless steel bolt action, max barrel length is 32 in. with muzzle brake, Christensen composite stock with bipod, approx. 16 (single shot) -20 lbs. New 2001.

MSR	$4,999		$4,550	$3,800	$3,300	$2,925	$2,575	$2,200	$1,900

Subtract $1,049 if single shot.

CARBON RANGER - .50 BMG cal., large diameter graphite barrel casing (up to 36 in. long), no stock or forearm, twin rails extending from frame sides are attached to recoil pad, Omni Wind Runner action, bipod and choice of scope are included, 25-32 lbs. Limited mfg. 1998-2000 only.

			$9,950	$8,900	$8,000	$7,100	$6,200	$5,300	$4,400

Last MSR was $10,625.

RIFLES: SEMI-AUTO

Christensen Arms also offers a Carbon One Challenge drop-in barrel (16 oz.) for the Ruger Model 10/22. MSR for the .22 LR is $399, $430 for .22 Mag.

CARBON ONE CHALLENGE (CUSTOM) - .22 LR or .22 Mag. cal., features Ruger 10/22 Model 1103 action with modified bolt release, synthetic bull barrel with precision stainless steel liner, 2 lb. Volquartsen trigger, Fajen brown laminated wood (disc.) or black synthetic stock with thumbhole, approx. 3½ -4 lbs. New 1996.

MSR	$999		$895	$750	$600	$525	$475	$400	$350

✱ *Carbon One Challenge* - .22 LR cal., non custom shop variation, 4 lbs. New 1999.

			$550	$495	$440	$400	$365	$330	$295

Last MSR was $599.

CARBON CHALLENGE II - similar to Carbon Challenge I, except has AMT stainless receiver and trigger, black synthetic stock, approx. 4½ lbs. Limited 1997-98 only.

			$1,150	$975	$875	$800	$725	$650	$525

Last MSR was $1,299.

Grading	100%	98%	95%	90%	80%	70%	60%

E.J. CHURCHILL GUNMAKERS

Current manufacturer established in 1891, and located in High Wycombe, England since 1996. Previously imported until 2001 by Aspen Outfitters, located in Aspen, CO. Previously manufactured in London, England. This company underwent various trading forms until Churchill, Atkin, Grant & Lang Ltd. closed in 1981. Currently, Churchill Gunmakers' rifles and shotguns are manufactured in High Wycombe, England.

Churchill Guns are very fine quality, and can be ordered with many custom features. We will list both discontinued and current models and approximate values, but strongly urge competent appraisal if purchase or sale is contemplated.

Prices indicated below for manufacturer's suggested retail and 100% condition factors are listed in English pounds. All new prices do not include English VAT. Values for used guns in 98%-60% condition factors are priced in U.S. dollars.

RIFLES: BOLT ACTION

"ONE OF ONE THOUSAND RIFLE" - .270 Win., 7mm Rem. Mag., .308 Win., .30-06, .300 Win. Mag., .375 H&H, or .458 Win. Mag. cal., Mauser type bolt action, 5 shot standard, 3 shot mag. Magnum, 24 in. barrel, classic French walnut stock, swivel recoil pad with trap, trap pistol grip cap. Mfg. 1973 for Interarms 20th Anniversary, only 100 mfg.

	100%	98%	95%	90%	80%	70%	60%
	$3,500	$2,950	$2,500	$2,000	$1,650	$1,350	$1,000

Add 50% for .375 H&H or .458 Win. Mag. cal.

BARONET RIFLE - .30-06 or .375 H&H cal., standard Mauser 98 action with swept bolt handle, fully adj. trigger and 3 position side safety, border engraving, deluxe checkered European walnut stock and forearm, custom order only, allow 8-10 month for delivery, approx. 8½ - 9 lbs. New 2001.

	MSR	£7,550					
		£7,550	$7,250	$6,500	$5,500	$4,500	$3,750	$3,000

Add £2,500 for Magnum Mauser action.
Add £1,350 for detachable scope mounts.

RIFLES: SxS

PREMIERE MODEL - various cals. up to .600 NE, pinless sidelock ejector mechanism with cocking indicators, 24 or 26 in. chopper lump barrels, double triggers, extended top tang, square or rounded body, full traditional fine scroll engraving, color case hardened action, allow 18-24 months for delivery, 9½-12½ lbs. Mfg. resumed 1998.

	MSR	£37,000					
		£37,000	$34,500	$29,250	$26,000	$22,500	$18,750	$15,500

Add £500 for hand detachable sidelocks.
Add £2,500 for .300 - .500 NE cals. (Cals. over .500 NE are P.O.R.)

SHOTGUNS: O/U

PREMIERE MODEL - 12, 16 (limited mfg.), 20, or 28 ga., 2¾ in. chambers, similar barrels and bores as Premiere SxS Model engraved, pinless sidelock ejector with cocking indicators, choice of monobloc (disc.) or chopper lump barrels, mechanical ST, auto ejectors, checkered pistol grip or straight stock, allow 18-24 months for delivery, 6½ (20 ga.) or 7 (12 ga.) lbs.

	MSR	£32,000					
		£32,000	$22,500	$18,000	$15,000	$12,000	$10,000	$9,000

Add £2,000 for 28 ga.
Add £6,350 for extra set of barrels.
Add approx. 10% for ordering pair of matched guns.
Subtract approx. £1,500 for DT. (disc.).

Grading	100%	98%	95%	90%	80%	70%	60%

SHOTGUNS: SxS

All models below were built or finished to customer specifications pertaining to choking, chambers, barrel lengths, stock measurements, weight, engraving patterns. Standardized patterns did exist, however, for each model. The "XXV" designation referred to the 25 in. barrel length, which was a Churchill specialty and was also a registered trademark.

PREMIERE MODEL - most ga.'s, 2¾ in. chambers, best quality, easy opening or standard opening, 25 (XXV), 28, 30, or 32 (disc.) in. chopper lump barrels, any choke, sidelock, pinless sidelock ejector with cocking indicators, double triggers standard, engraved, color case hardened action, checkered, straight or pistol grip stock, allow 18-24 months for delivery, 5 lbs. 14 oz. (20 ga.) or 6 lbs. 6 oz. (12 ga.).

	MSR	£26,000	£26,000	£19,750	£16,000	£12,500	£10,000	£9,000	£8,000

Add £2,000 for 28 ga.
Add £4,950 for extra set of barrels.
Add £1,550 for ST.
Add approx. 10% for ordering pair of matched guns.

IMPERIAL MODEL - most ga.'s, most barrel lengths, second quality sidelock model, ejectors, mostly standard opening, a few made as easy opening. Also mfg. in some double rifles. Disc.

$13,500	$11,500	$9,500	$7,500	$6,500	$5,250	$4,000

Add 20% for 20 ga., 40% for 28 ga., and $1,000 for SST, or 35% for double rifle.
Subtract 10% for 16 ga.

FIELD MODEL - 12 ga. only, most barrel lengths, third quality sidelock model. Disc.

$9,000	$8,000	$7,000	$6,000	$5,000	$4,500	$3,500

HERCULES MODEL - most ga.'s, 25-30 in. barrels, best quality boxlock model, ejectors, easy opening or standard opening. Also made in some double rifles in .22 Hornet and similar cals.

$9,000	$8,000	$7,000	$6,000	$5,000	$4,500	$3,500

Add 20% for 20 ga., 40% for 28 ga., $1,000 for SST, and 35% double rifle.
Subtract 10% for 16 ga.

UTILITY MODEL - all ga.'s (mostly encountered in 12 ga.), 25-30 in. barrels, second quality boxlock model, ejectors, checkered straight or pistol grip stock. Disc.

$6,250	$4,500	$3,500	$3,000	$2,500	$2,000	$1,800

Add 20% for 20 ga., 40% for 28 ga., 60% for .410 bore, and $500 for SST.
Subtract 10% for 16 ga.

CROWN MODEL - 12, 16, 20 ga., or .410 (rare) bore, third quality boxlock model, various barrel lengths. Disc.

$4,500	$3,500	$3,000	$2,500	$2,000	$1,600	$1,200

Add 20% for 20 ga., 40% for 28 ga., 60% for .410 bore, and $500 for SST.
Subtract 10% for 16 ga.

REGAL MODEL - 12, 16, 20, 28 ga., or .410 bore, second quality boxlock model introduced after WWII, released after Utility Model was disc. Premium for 28 ga. or .410 bore.

$6,000	$4,300	$3,750	$3,100	$2,500	$2,000	$1,800

Add 20% for 20 ga., 40% for 28 ga., 60% for .410 bore, and $500 for SST.
Subtract 10% for 16 ga.

✱ *Regal Grade* - 12, 20, 28 ga., or .410 bore, best quality boxlock model, ejectors, standard opening, limited production.

$4,800	$4,000	$3,500	$3,000	$2,500	$2,000	$1,800

Last MSR was $5,625.

Grading	100%	98%	95%	90%	80%	70%	60%

CHURCHILL

Previous trademark imported and distributed by Ellett Brothers located in Chapin, SC until 1993. Previously imported (until 1988) by Kassnar Imports, Inc. located in Harrisburg, PA. Not affiliated with E.J. Churchill Gunmakers, Ltd.

In late 1988, the Churchill trademark was sold to Ellett Brothers located in Chapin, SC.

RIFLES: BOLT ACTION

HIGHLANDER - .25-06 Rem., .243 Win., .270 Win., .308 Win., .30-06, 7mm Rem. Mag., or .300 Win. Mag. cal., bolt action, 22 in. barrel, thumb safety, no sights, 3 or 4 shot mag., checkered walnut stock, 7½ lbs. Importation disc. 1991.

	$395	$350	$330	$300	$270	$240	$215

Last MSR was $460.

Add $30 for iron sights (disc).

REGENT - same cals. as Highlander, deluxe checkered walnut with Monte Carlo comb and cheekpiece. Last imported by Kassnar in 1988.

	$555	$455	$385	$340	$300	$280	$260

Last MSR was $610.

Add $30 for iron sights.

RIFLES: SEMI-AUTO

ROTARY 22 - .22 LR cal, beginners rifle, bolt hold-open device, adj. rear sight, 10 shot rotary mag. Imported 1989 only.

	$120	$105	$95	$85	$75	$65	$55

Last MSR was $130.

SHOTGUNS: O/U

MONARCH - 12, 20, 28 (disc.) ga., or .410 (disc.) bore, 25 (disc.), 26, or 28 in. vent. rib barrels, SST, extractors, boxlock action, DT, silver finish receiver with fine scroll engraving, checkered European walnut stock and forearm, 6½-7½ lbs.

	$460	$370	$340	$300	$250	$230	$210

Last MSR was $520.

Add $67 for .410 bore with 26 in. barrels (disc.).
Subtract $40 without SST.

* **Monarch Turkey Gun** - 12 ga. only, 24 in. barrels with matte finish. Imported 1990-1991 only.

	$460	$370	$340	$300	$250	$230	$210

Last MSR was $529.

SPORTING CLAYS MODEL - 12 ga. only, designed for sporting clays competition with 28 in. VR ported barrels with choke tubes, ejectors, raised target style VR, checkered high gloss finish stock and forearm, 7 lbs. 6 oz. Imported 1992 only.

	$800	$725	$650	$575	$500	$450	$395

Last MSR was $900.

WINDSOR III - 12, 20 ga., or .410 bore (disc.), 27 or 30 in. barrels, double bottom lock, antique silver finish receiver with fine scroll engraving, extractors, SST, vent. rib, checkered pistol grip and forend. Importation disc. 1991.

	$550	$495	$450	$380	$340	$300	$280

Last MSR was $625.

Add $140 for Flyweight Model or choke tubes (disc.).
Add $75 for .410 bore.

Grading	100%	98%	95%	90%	80%	70%	60%

NEW WINDSOR IV - 12 or 20 ga., 3 in. chambers, boxlock action, silver receiver with full scroll engraving, 26 or 28 (12 ga. only) VR barrels with choke tubes, ejectors, SST, checkered walnut pistol grip stock with black rubber vent. recoil pad, finger grooved forearm, gloss finish, gold trigger, 5 year warranty. Mfg. 1992 only.

	$625	$525	$450	$375	$325	$295	$275

Last MSR was $690.

WINDSOR IV - DISC. - 12, 20, 28 ga., or .410 bore, 26-30 in. barrels, double bottom lock, antique silver finish receiver with fine scroll engraving, ejectors, SST, vent. rib, checkered pistol grip and forend. Interchangeable chokes became standard in 1989. Importation disc. 1991.

	$725	$640	$530	$470	$430	$395	$360

Last MSR was $852.

Subtract $52 for 28 ga. or .410 bore.
Subtract $100 if without choke tubes.

REGENT V - 12 or 20 ga., 27 in. barrels, double bottom lock, antique silver finish receiver with extra fine scroll engraving, ejectors, single trigger, vent. rib, checkered pistol grip and forend. Interchangeable choke tubes standard. Disc. 1986, reintroduced 1990-disc. 1993.

	$895	$795	$700	$620	$560	$510	$470

Last MSR was $1,100.

This model was previously designated Regent VII until 1989 when it changed to the Regent V.

REGENT TRAP AND SKEET - 12 or 20 ga., 26 or 30 in. barrels, double bottom lock, antique silver finish receiver with sideplates engraved in fine scroll, ejectors, SST, vent. rib, checkered pistol grip and forend. Importation disc. 1991.

	$795	$650	$575	$540	$485	$440	$390

Last MSR was $963.

Add $40 for trap variation.

REGENT GRADE SHOTGUN/RIFLE COMBINATION - 12 ga. over either .222 Rem., .223 Rem., .243 Win. (disc.), .270 Win., .30-06, or .308 Win. cal., 25 in. barrels, double bottom lock, antique silver finish receiver with extra fine scroll engraving, ejectors, single trigger, vent. rib, checkered pistol grip and forend. Importation disc. 1991.

	$800	$700	$635	$560	$510	$475	$440

Last MSR was $927.

SHOTGUNS: SxS

WINDSOR I - 10 (disc. 1988), 12, 16, 20, 28 ga., or .410 bore, double barrel, 23-32 in. barrels, Anson and Deeley boxlock, antique silver finish receiver with fine scroll engraving, extractors, double triggers, checkered pistol grip and forend. Importation disc. 1991.

	$550	$465	$450	$385	$300	$250	$230

Last MSR was $653.

Add $150 for 10 ga.
Add $55 for 28 ga. or .410 bore.
Add $30 for Flyweight Models (25 in. barrels - disc. 1988).

WINDSOR II - 12 or 20 ga., 26-30 in. barrels, Anson and Deeley boxlock, antique silver finish receiver with fine scroll engraving, ejectors, double triggers, checkered pistol grip and forend. Add $100 for 10 ga. (disc.). Importation disc. 1987.

	$595	$485	$415	$350	$315	$270	$240

Last MSR was $638.

Grading	100%	98%	95%	90%	80%	70%	60%

WINDSOR VI - 12 or 20 (disc.) ga., 25 or 28 in. barrels, sidelock, antique silver finish receiver with fine scroll engraving, ejectors, double triggers, checkered pistol grip and forend. Disc. 1987.

	$840	$700	$600	$550	$510	$460	$420

Last MSR was $900.

ROYAL - 10, 12, 20, 28 ga., or .410 bore, DTs, extractors, checkered walnut stock and forearm, case hardened receiver. Imported late 1988-1991.

	$485	$405	$370	$310	$275	$250	$230

Last MSR was $540.

Add $20 for 28 ga.
Add $74 for .410 bore.

SHOTGUNS: SEMI-AUTO

STANDARD MODEL - 12 ga. only, gas operated and shoots different loads interchangeably without alterations, 24, 26, 28 in. VR barrel, magazine cut-off, hand checkered walnut with satin finish, matte metal finish, includes ICT choke tubes. New 1990.

	$495	$415	$375	$310	$275	$250	$230

Last MSR was $550.

❋ *Turkey Model* - similar to Standard Model, except has 24 in. barrel only. New 1990.

	$510	$425	$380	$315	$275	$250	$230

Last MSR was $570.

WINDSOR GRADE - 12 ga. only, 26, 28, or 30 in. barrels, gas operation, anodized alloy receiver, vent. rib, checkered pistol grip and forend, 7½ lbs. Deluxe model includes polished receiver with etching.

	$380	$320	$300	$275	$250	$225	$200

Last MSR was $420.

Add $35 for choke tubes.
Add $55 for Deluxe model.

REGENT GRADE - 12 ga. only, 26, 28, or 30 in. barrels, gas operation, anodized alloy receiver, vent. rib, checkered pistol grip and forend, 7½ lbs. Deluxe model includes polished receiver with etching. Disc. 1986.

	$440	$365	$340	$320	$300	$285	$270

Last MSR was $495.

Add $35 for choke tubes.
Add $55 for Deluxe model.

SHOTGUNS: SLIDE ACTION

WINDSOR GRADE - 12 ga. only, 26, 27, 28, or 30 in. barrels, double slides, anodized alloy receiver, vent. rib, checkered pistol grip and forend, 7½ lbs. Disc. 1986.

	$385	$330	$310	$275	$250	$225	$200

Last MSR was $430.

CIMARRON F.A. CO.

Current importer/distributor/retailer located in Fredricksburg, TX. Cimarron is currently importing Aldo Uberti and D. Pedersoli firearms, in addition to black powder reproductions/replicas. Previously named Old-West Guns Co. Dealer sales only.

Grading	100%	98%	95%	90%	80%	70%	60%

Please refer to the 2nd Edition *Blue Book of Modern Black Powder Values* by Dennis Adler (now online also) for more information and prices on Cimarron's lineup of modern black powder models.

C

REVOLVERS: REPRODUCTIONS, COLT

The Cimarron Arms reproductions of the 1873 Colt Peacemaker, mostly mfg. by Uberti, with the exception of previous limited production by Armi San Marco, are available in two configurations listed below. These pistols are extremely accurate reproductions of the original Colt pre-war Peacemaker and are marked (and machined) the same as the originals, including serial numbers on frames, backstrap, trigger guard, and cylinder. Barrels are radiused and cylinders are beveled. Frames are color case hardened, stocks are walnut - choice of 4¾, 5½, or 7½ in. barrel. All Cimarron SAAs are currently barrel marked "- CIMARRON F.A. MFG. Co. FREDERICKSBURG, TX. U.S.A. -".

The "Old Model" configuration has the older style black powder frame, screw in cylinder pin retainer, and circular "bullseye" ejector head. The Standard Model includes the post-1890 style frame with spring loaded cross-pin cylinder retainer and "half-moon" ejector head. Only the Old Model is available in the authentic old style "charcoal blue" finish (sometimes referred to as fire-bluing).

During 1998, Cimarron introduced an Original Finish (antiqued) that resembles the older, worn finish seen on many of the well-used, original Colt SAAs. This distressed finish is a greyish-brown patina color, and certain areas of these guns (end of barrel, grip straps, frame/cylinder edges, and grips) have been artifically aged to give them an authentic "been carried and used for 100 years" appearance.

Add $40 for Original Finish on SAAs listed below (disc. 2002). Add $40 for charcoal blue finish on SAAs listed below (disc. 2002). Add $150 for antique custom nickel or custom nickel finish. Add $350 for silver plating. Add $250 for U.S. Armory finish utilizing bone-meal case coloring. Add $45 for hand checkered walnut grips. Add $595 for ivory grips. Add $250 for mother-of-pearl grips. Add $600 for "A" style engraving (30% coverage) on SAAs listed below. Add $750 for "B" style engraving (50% coverage) on SAAs listed below. Add $1,100 for "C" style engraving (70% coverage) on SAAs listed below. Add $1,475 for "Texas Cattle Brands" or full (100% coverage) engraving pattern.

1871-72 OPEN TOP - .38 Long Colt, .38 S&W Spl., .44-40 WCF, .44 Russian, or .45 Schofield cal., 5½ (Navy size grips) or 7½ (Army size grips) in. barrel, patterned after the Colt 1871-1872 Open Top, Navy grip frame is available in brass or silver plated. Mfg. by A. Uberti beginning 1999.

MSR	$469	$395	$300	$250	$220	$195	$175	$160

Add $30 for charcoal blue finish.
Add $40 for original finish.

FRONTIER SIX SHOOTER - .22 LR (disc. 1995), .22 Mag. (disc.), .357 Mag., .38 Spl.(disc.), .38-40 WCF, .44 Spl. (new 1998), .44-40 WCF, or .45 LC cal., 4¾, 5½, and 7½ in. barrel lengths, steel backstraps and trigger guard. Importation disc. 1999.

* *Standard or Old Model*

	$395	$300	$250	$220	$195	$175	$160

Last MSR was $469.

Add $30 for convertible .45 ACP cylinder.

* *Sheriff's Model* - .44-40 WCF or .45 LC cal., w/o ejector, 3 or 4 (disc. 1992) in. barrel, steel backstraps and trigger guard. Disc. 1998, reintroduced 2000-2001.

	$395	$300	$250	$220	$195	$175	$160

Last MSR was $469.

Grading			100%	98%	95%	90%	80%	70%	60%

✴ *New Sheriff Model* - .357 Mag., .44-40 WCF, .44 Spl., or .45 LC cal., 3½ in. barrel with ejector, Old Model frame only. Importation began 1995.

MSR	$469	$395	$300	$250	$220	$195	$175	$160

Add $30 for charcoal blue finish.
Add $35 for checkered walnut grips.

✴ *Target Model* - similar to Standard Model, except has fully adj. target rear sight, brass or steel backstrap. Importation disc. 1991.

$355	$280	$255	$220	$195	$175	$160

Last MSR was $400.

Add $40 for .357 Mag. cal.

This variation is available in the Standard Model configuration only and with standard finish.

MODEL P SAA - .32-20 WCF, .38-40 WCF, .357 Mag., .44-40 WCF, .44 Spl., or .45 LC cal., features either pinched frame (.45 LC cal. with 7½ in. barrel only) or pre-war configuration, standard finish or charcoal blue, 4¾, 5½, or 7½ in. barrel. Importation began 1996.

MSR	$469	$395	$295	$250	$220	$195	$175	$160

Add $30 for convertible .45 ACP cylinder.
Add $40 for original finish.
Add $25 for charcoal blue finish.
Add $10 for target model with adj. sights and flattop frame (7½ in. barrel with .45 LC or .44-40 WCF cal. only)

✴ *Model P Jr. SAA* - .38 Colt and S&W Spl. cal., features smaller size frame (20% less) proportioned from the SAA, but with standard single action grip frame, 3½, 4¾, or 5½ in. barrel. Mfg. by A. Uberti 2000-2001.

$325	$285	$260	$240	$220	$180	$160

Last MSR was $389.

Add $30 for charcoal blue.
Add $30 for checkered walnut grips.

WYATT EARP LIMITED EDITION BUNTLINE - .45 LC cal., only, 10 in. barrel, sterling silver plaque inlaid into wood grips, case colored receiver. Importation began 2002.

MSR	$569	$480	$400	$360	$330	$300	$275	$250

Add $40 for original finish.

BISLEY SAA - .357 Mag., .44 Spl., .44-40 WCF, or .45 LC cal., 4¾, 5½, or 7½ in. barrel, Bisley configured grips, case colored receiver, smooth walnut grips, flattop target model available with 7½ in. barrel in .44-40 WCF or .45 LC cal. only. Importation began 2002.

MSR	$499	$430	$365	$315	$280	$260	$240	$220

EL PISTOLERO - .357 Mag. or .45 LC cal., similar to the Model P, except has brass backstrap and trigger guard, 4¾, 5½, or 7½ in. barrel, case hardened frame with blue barrel and cylinder. Mfg. 1997 only.

$320	$275	$250	$225	$210	$195	$180

Last MSR was $359.

BUNTLINE MODEL - .357 Mag., .44-40 WCF, or .45 LC cal., 18 in. barrel, brass or steel backstrap cut for shoulder stock. Disc. 1989.

$355	$280	$255	$220	$195	$175	$160

Last MSR was $400.

Add $10 for target sights.

Grading	100%	98%	95%	90%	80%	70%	60%

BUNTLINE CARBINE - similar cals. to Buntline Model, except also includes .22 LR/.22 Mag. (convertible cylinders), 18 in. barrel, includes non-detachable shoulder stock with brass hardware and finger extension trigger guard. Importation disc. 1991.

| | $380 | $295 | $260 | $225 | $195 | $175 | $160 |

Last MSR was $440.

Add $20 for target sights.
Add $20 for .22 LR/.22 Mag. combo.

BUCKHORN - .44 Spl. or .44 Mag. cal., reinforced variation of the Cimarron SAA designed for more powerful cartridges, 4¾, 6 or 7½ in. barrel, brass or steel backstrap. Disc. 1993.

| | $355 | $285 | $260 | $220 | $195 | $175 | $160 |

Last MSR was $400.

* *Buckhorn Convertible Model* - .44 Mag./.44-40 WCF cylinders are included, 4¾, 6 or 7½ in. barrel. Disc. 1989.

| | $375 | $295 | $265 | $220 | $195 | $175 | $160 |

Last MSR was $427.

Add $12 for target sights.

* *Buckhorn Target Model* - .44 Spl. or .44 Mag. cal., 4¾, 6 or 7½ in. barrel, adj. rear sight. Importation disc. 1991.

| | $370 | $290 | $265 | $225 | $195 | $175 | $160 |

Last MSR was $420.

* *Buckhorn Buntline* - .44-40 WCF, .44 Spl., or .44 Mag. cal., 18 in. barrel, fixed or target sights. Disc. 1989.

| | $370 | $285 | $265 | $220 | $195 | $175 | $160 |

Last MSR was $419.

Add $30 for target sights.

* *Buckhorn Carbine* - .44-40 WCF, .44 Spl., or .44 Mag. cal., 18 in. barrel, includes non-detachable shoulder stock with brass hardware and lanyard ring. Disc. 1990.

| | $375 | $290 | $265 | $220 | $195 | $175 | $160 |

Last MSR was $429.

Add $30 for target sights.

THUNDERER - .357 Mag., .44 Spl., .44-40 WCF or .45 LC cal., patterned after Colt's Thunderer Model, 3½, 4¾, or 5½ (new 2000) in. barrel with full ejector rod housing, birdshead grips, choice of case colored or nickel finish. Importation began 1994.

| MSR $489 | $410 | $310 | $260 | $220 | $195 | $175 | $160 |

Add $35 for checkered walnut grips.
Add $40 for convertible .45 ACP cylinder (4¾ in. only until 1999).

* *Thunderer Long Tom* - .357 Mag., .44-40 WCF or .45 LC cal., 7½ in. barrel. New 1997.

| MSR $529 | $440 | $325 | $275 | $225 | $200 | $175 | $160 |

Add $35 for checkered walnut grips.

U.S. 7TH CAVALRY CUSTER MODEL - authentic reproduction of original Colt military cavalry contract, 7½ in. barrel, marked U.S. on lower left frame, one piece walnut grips with military cartouche.

| MSR $499 | $430 | $365 | $315 | $280 | $260 | $240 | $220 |

Add $30 for charcoal blue finish.
Add $40 for original finish.

U.S. CAVALRY MODEL P (A.P. CASEY) - .45 LC cal. only, 7½ in. barrel, Old Model frame. Mfg. 1996-97.

| | $430 | $365 | $315 | $280 | $260 | $240 | $220 |

Last MSR was $499.

Grading	100%	98%	95%	90%	80%	70%	60%

U.S. ARTILLERY MODEL - Renaldo A. Carr 1895 U.S. Artillery Model Commemorative, 5½ in. barrel, limited mfg.

	$430	$365	$315	$280	$260	$240	$220

Last MSR was $499.

U.S. ARTILLERY ROUGH RIDER - .45 LC cal. only, 5 ½ in. barrel, Old Model frame. New 1996.

MSR $499 $430 $365 $315 $280 $260 $240 $220

Add $30 for charcoal blue finish.
Add $40 for original finish.

7TH CAVALRY CASED SET - U.S. Cavalry Model in case with accessories. Disc. 1990.

	$695	$625	$550	$500	$460	$420	$385

Last MSR was $780.

WILD BILL ELLIOT TEXAS CATTLEBRAND - .45 LC cal. Mfg. 1994-96.

	$1,225	$1,025	$875	$750	$625	$550	$475

Last MSR was $1,395.

JUDGE ROY BEAN COMMEMORATIVE - mfg. to commemorate Judge Roy Bean's Texas cattle-brand. Disc. 1996.

	$1,500	$1,175	$995	$875	$750	$625	$550

Last MSR was $1,695.

LIGHTNING - .38 Colt and .38 S&W Spl. cal., patterned after the original Colt Lightning, 3½, 4¾ or 5½ in. barrel, birdshead grips. Mfg. by A. Uberti 1999-2001.

	$325	$285	$260	$240	$220	$180	$160

Last MSR was $389.

Add $30 for charcoal blue.
Add $30 for checkered walnut grips.

REVOLVERS: REPRODUCTIONS, REMINGTON

These guns are reproductions of the Models 1875 and 1890.
Add $90 for nickel plating, $10 for charcoal blue finish on models listed below.

MODEL 1875 - .357 Mag., .44-40 WCF, or .45 LC cal., 7½ barrel. Disc. 1993.

	$340	$250	$200	$170	$155	$140	$120

Last MSR was $390.

✳ *Model 1875 Carbine* - same cals. as Model 1875, 18 in. barrel, includes non- detachable shoulder stock with brass hardware and lanyard ring. Importation disc. 1990.

	$410	$340	$300	$265	$230	$200	$180

Last MSR was $460.

MODEL 1890 - .357 Mag., .44-40 WCF, or .45 LC cal., 5½ or 7½ in. barrel. Disc. 1993.

	$340	$250	$210	$175	$160	$145	$125

Last MSR was $390.

1871 ROLLING BLOCK TARGET PISTOL - .22 LR, .22 Hornet (new 1990), .22 Mag., or .357 Mag. cal., 9½ in. barrel. Importation disc. 1990.

	$250	$200	$180	$160	$140	$125	$110

Last MSR was $280.

✳ *1871 Rolling Block Baby Carbine* - same cals. as Target Pistol, has 22 in. barrel and walnut stock and forearm, brass trigger guard and butt plate. Importation disc. 1990.

	$310	$245	$205	$170	$155	$140	$120

Last MSR was $340.

Grading	100%	98%	95%	90%	80%	70%	60%

REVOLVERS: REPRODUCTIONS, SMITH & WESSON

SCHOFIELD MODEL NUMBER THREE - .38 Spl. (disc. 1997), .38-40 WCF (disc. 1997), .44 Russian/Spl., .44-40 WCF, .45 Schofield, .45 ACP (disc.), or .45 LC cal., available in 7 (Civilian or Military) or 5 (Wells Fargo only) in. barrel. Mfg. by Armi San Marco 1996-99.

	$730	$640	$570	$515	$450	$400	$360

Last MSR was $849.

Add $100 for nickel finish.
Add $150 for custom nickel finish.

This model was also available as a "Little Big Horn" variation with sub-inspector markings and "SBL" cartouche.

RIFLES: REPRODUCTIONS, REMINGTON ROLLING BLOCK

Add $150 for AA select wood, $250 for AAA premium select wood.

ROLLING BLOCK SPORTING RIFLE - .45-70 cal., 30 in. barrel, walnut stock and forearm. Imported 1989-1990 only.

	$625	$565	$430	$395	$350	$320	$300

Last MSR was $620.

✳ **Deluxe Rolling Block Sporting Rifle** - similar to standard model, except has select wood. Importation disc. 1990.

	$725	$640	$485	$450	$375	$340	$320

Last MSR was $720.

REMINGTON ROLLING BLOCK LONG RANGE CREEDMOOR - .45-70 Govt. cal., 30 in. tapered octagon barrel, deluxe checkered walnut stock. Importation began 1997.

	$1,125	$825	$700	$625	$550	$500	$450

Last MSR was $1,295.

RIFLES: REPRODUCTIONS, SHARPS

Add $150 for AA select wood, $250 for AAA premium select wood.

SPORTING #1 RIFLE - .40-65 Win. or .45-70 Govt. cal., 32 in. octagon barrel, pistol grip stock. Importation began 2000.

MSR	$1,095	$975	$800	$675	$600	$525	$475	$375

BILLY DIXON MODEL 1874 SPORTING RIFLE - .45-70 Govt. or .45-90 Win. cal., 32 in. barrel, nickel silver front blade and forearm cap, checkered deluxe walnut stock, double set triggers. Importation began 1997.

MSR	$1,295	$1,125	$825	$700	$625	$550	$500	$450

QUIGLEY MODEL 1874 SPORTING RIFLE - .45-70 Govt., .45-90 Win., or .45-120 Sharps cal., 34 in. octagon barrel with storage compartment in stock. Importation began 2000.

MSR	$1,495	$1,350	$1,175	$975	$825	$700	$625	$550

RIFLES: REPRODUCTIONS, WINCHESTER

Add $150 for AA select wood, $250 for AAA premium select wood.

Grading	100%	98%	95%	90%	80%	70%	60%

HENRY RIFLE/CARBINE - .44-40 WCF, .44 Spl. (mfg. 1993-95), or .45 LC (new 1993) cal., brass or case colored steel (.44-40 WCF and .45 LC cal. only, new 2002) frame, 24¼ in. barrel on rifle, 22 (disc. 1995, .44-40 WCF cal. only) in. barrel on carbine.

MSR	$1,029	$875	$650	$550	$475	$400	$325	$295

Add $40 for charcoal blue or in-the-white finish.
Add $50 for original finish.
Add $20 for steel frame model.
Add $700 for standard engraving.
Add $1,495 for Lincoln Presentation engraving.
Previous to 1997, this model could also be special ordered with Grade A engraving ($450 extra), Grade B engraving ($550 extra), and Grade C engraving ($725 extra).

CIVIL WAR HENRY RIFLE - .44-40 WCF or .45 LC (new 1998) cal., 24 in. barrel, patterned after the U.S. issue original inspected by Chas. G. Chapman (C.G.C.) with military inspector's marks and cartouche, military sling swivels became standard in 1996. Importation began 1993.

MSR	$1,069	$910	$685	$575	$500	$425	$350	$315

Add $80 for charcoal blue or in-the-white finish.
Add $30 for original finish.

1866 SPORTING RIFLE (YELLOWBOY) - .22 LR (disc. 1993), .22 Mag. (disc. 1993), .32-20 WCF (new 2002), .38 Spl. (new 1995), .38-40 WCF (new 2002), .44-40 WCF, or .45 LC (new 1993) cal., brass receiver, 20 (new 2000, Short Rifle) or 24 in. octagon barrel.

MSR	$839	$725	$550	$440	$375	$285	$240	$200

Add $50 for charcoal blue finish (new 1997).
Add $700 for standard engraving (new 1997).
Add $1,495 for Mexican Eagle engraving (new 1997).
Add $500 (retail) for A engraving, $650 for B engraving, $1,175 for C engraving. Disc. 1996.

1866 YELLOWBOY CARBINE - .38 Spl., .44 Spl., .44-40 WCF, or .45 LC cal., similar to Model 1866 Sporting Rifle, except has 19 in. round barrel with 2 bands, saddle ring, uncheckered walnut stock and forearm.

MSR	$829	$715	$550	$440	$375	$285	$240	$200

Add $40 for charcoal blue finish (new 1997).
Add $50 for original finish (available in .44-40 WCF or .45 LC cal.)
Add $25 for saddle ring.

* **1866 Trapper Carbine** - .38 Spl. (new 2002), or .44-40 WCF cal., 16 in. round barrel. Importation disc. 1990, reintroduced 2002.

MSR	$829	$715	$550	$440	$375	$285	$240	$200

* **1866 Yellowboy Indian Carbine** - .22 LR, .22 Mag., .38 Spl., or .44-40 WCF cal., 19 in. round barrel. Disc. 1989.

		$575	$475	$400	$350	$300	$260	$220

Last MSR was $649.

This model had a photo engraved frame and brass tacks in stock and forearm.

* **Red Cloud Commemorative Carbine** - same cals. as Yellowboy Indian Carbine, includes special engraving representing Oglalla Indian tribe symbols, brass tacks in forearm and stock. Disc. 1989.

		$575	$475	$400	$350	$300	$260	$220

Last MSR was $649.

Grading	100%	98%	95%	90%	80%	70%	60%

1873 SPORTING RIFLE - .22 LR (disc. 1993), .22 Mag. (disc. 1993), .32-20 WCF (new 2002), .357 Mag., .38-40 WCF (new 2002), .44 Spl. (new 2002), .44-40 WCF, or .45 LC cal., 24¼ in. octagon barrel, case hardened receiver, full mag., iron sights.

MSR	$949		$815	$625	$525	$450	$375	$325	$295

Add $40 for charcoal blue finish (new 1997, not available in .32-20 WCF or .38-40 WCF cal.).
Add $50 for original finish (.44-40 WCF or 45 LC cal. only).
Add $140 for Deluxe Model with pistol grip.
Add $1,250 for 1 of 1,000 engraving.
Add $500 (retail) for A engraving, $650 for B engraving, $1,075 for C engraving.

✳ *1873 Short Rifle* - .32-20 WCF (new 2002), .357 Mag. (new 2000), .38-40 WCF (new 2002), .44 Spl. (new 2002), .44-40 WCF or .45 LC cal., features 20 in. octagon barrel, case hardened receiver, iron sights. Importation began 1990.

MSR	$949		$815	$625	$525	$450	$375	$325	$295

Add $40 for charcoal blue finish (not available in .32-20 WCF or .44 Spl cal.).
Add $50 for original finish (.44-40 WCF or .45 LC only).
Add $140 for Deluxe Model with pistol grip.

✳ *1873 Long Range Rifle* - .44-40 WCF or .45 LC cal., includes 30 in. octagon barrel with full mag., case hardened receiver, iron sights. New 1990.

MSR	$999		$850	$650	$550	$475	$385	$330	$295

Add $50 for charcoal blue finish (new 1997).
Add $150 for Deluxe Model with pistol grip.
Add $1,250 for 1 of 1,000 engraving.

✳ *1873 Saddle Ring Carbine* - .22 LR (disc. 1993), .22 Mag. (disc. 1993), .32-20 WCF (new 2002), .357 Mag., .38-40 WCF (new 2002), .44 Spl. (new 2002), .44-40 WCF, or .45 LC cal., blue steel receiver, with or w/o saddle ring, 19 in. round barrel.

MSR	$949		$815	$625	$525	$450	$375	$325	$295

Add $25 for saddle ring.
Add $50 for charcoal blue finish (new 1997).
Add $50 for original finish (.44-40 WCf or 45 LC cal. only).
Add $90 for nickel plating (disc.).

✳ *1873 Trapper Carbine* - .357 Mag. (new 1990), .44-40 WCF, or .45 LC (new 1990) cal., 16 in. barrel, blue finish only. Importation disc. 1990.

			$575	$475	$400	$350	$300	$260	$220

Last MSR was $650.

1885 HI-WALL RIFLE - .38-55 WCF (new 2000), .40-65 WCF, .45-70 Govt., .45-90 WCF (new 2000), .45-120 WCF (new 2002) cal., 28 (disc.) or 30 in. octagon barrel, case hardened finish on frame, iron sights (standard) or optional apeture rear and globe front sight (new 2002). New 1998.

MSR	$995		$850	$675	$575	$475	$375	$325	$295

Add $180 for engraved reciever and adj. sights (new 2002).
Add $795 for standard engraving, $1,150 for deluxe engraving, or $1,895 for deluxe gold line engraving.

CLARIDGE HI-TEC INC.

Previous manufacturer located in Northridge, CA 1990-1993. In 1990, Claridge Hi-Tec, Inc. was created and took over Goncz Armament, Inc.

All Claridge Hi-Tec firearms utilized match barrels mfg. in-house that were button-rifled. The Claridge action is an original design and does not copy other actions. Claridge Hi-Tec models can be altered (Law Enforcement Companion Series) to accept Beretta 92F or Sig Model 226 magazines.

Grading	100%	98%	95%	90%	80%	70%	60%

PISTOLS

Add $40 for polished stainless steel frame construction.

L-9 PISTOL - 9mm Para., .40 S&W, or .45 ACP cal., semi-auto paramilitary design, 7½ (new 1992) or 9½ (disc. 1991) in. shrouded barrel, aluminum receiver, choice of black matte, matte silver, or polished silver finish, one piece grip, safety locks firing pin in place, 10 (disc.), 17, or 30 shot double row mag., adj. sights, 3¾ lbs. Mfg. 1991-1993.

	$525	$375	$300	$265	$225	$200	$175

Last MSR was $598.

Add $395 for a trigger activated laser sighting scope was available in Models M, L, C, and T new mfg.

S-9 PISTOL - similar to L-9, except has 5 in. non-shrouded threaded barrel, 3 lbs. 9 oz. Disc. 1993.

	$475	$350	$280	$250	$225	$200	$175

Last MSR was $535.

T-9 PISTOL - similar to L-9, except has 9½ in. barrel. Mfg. 1992-1993.

	$525	$375	$300	$265	$225	$200	$175

Last MSR was $598.

M PISTOL - similar to L Model, except has 7½ in. barrel, 3 lbs. Disc. 1991.

	$500	$375	$300	$265	$225	$200	$175

Last MSR was $720.

RIFLES: CARBINES

C-9 CARBINE - same cals. as L and S Model pistols, 16.1 in. shrouded barrel, choice of composite or uncheckered walnut stock and forearm, 5 lbs. 12 oz. Mfg. 1991-1993.

	$595	$525	$450	$395	$350	$300	$275

Last MSR was $675.

Add $74 for black graphite composite stock.
Add $474 for integral laser model (with graphite stock).

This model was available with either gloss walnut, dull walnut, or black graphite composite stock.

LAW ENFORCEMENT COMPANION (LEC) - 9mm Para., .40 S&W, or .45 ACP cal., 16¼ button rifled barrel, black graphite composition buttstock and foregrip, buttstock also provides space for an extra mag., available in either aluminum or stainless steel frame, matte black finish, available with full integral laser sighting system. Limited mfg. 1992-93.

	$650	$575	$495	$425	$375	$325	$295

Last MSR was $749.

Add $400 for integral laser sighting system.

CLARK CUSTOM GUNS, INC.

Current custom gun maker and gunsmith located in Princeton, LA. Clark Custom Guns, Inc. has been customizing various configurations of handguns, rifles, and shotguns since 1950. It would be impossible to list within the confines of this text the many conversions this company has performed. It is recommended to contact this company directly (see Trademark Index) for an up-to-date price sheet and catalog on their extensive line-up of high quality competition pistols and related components. Custom revolvers, rifles, and shotguns are also available in addition to various handgun competition parts, related gunsmithing services, and a firearms training facility called The Shootout.

The legendary James E. Clark, Sr. passed away during 2000. In 1958, he became the first and only full-time civilian to win the National Pistol Championships.

Grading	100%	98%	95%	90%	80%	70%	60%

PISTOLS: SEMI-AUTO

Clark Custom Guns currently manufactures a wide variety of M1911 style handguns, including the Bullseye Pistols (MSR $1,420-$2,065), the Custom Combat (MSR $1,560-$2,260), the Meltdown (MSR $1,380-$1,680), Millennium Meltdown (features damascus slide, only 50 mfg. during 2000 - MSR was $3,795), and the Unlimited (MSR $2,020-$2,405). Clark will also build the above configurations on a customer supplied gun – prices are less, please contact the company directly regarding more information on these pistol conversions.

CLASSIC DOUBLES

Previous trademark manufactured in Tochigi City, Japan until 1987. Previously imported and distributed by Classic Doubles International, Inc. located in St. Louis, MO.

The factory closed in 1987, and all Classic Doubles remaining in inventory were sold to GU Wholesalers located in Omaha, NE in 1990. To date, there has been little collectibility in the Classic Doubles trademark. As a result, values are determined by the shooting value each model has to offer against other competing models in the same configuration. Also, in some regions of the country, 98% condition or less specimens may be priced lower than values shown in this section.

In late 1987, Winchester/Olin discontinued importation of their Japanese shotgun models (Models 101 and 23). At that point, Classic Doubles International, Inc. became the sole importer of these shotguns. There were very few changes made during this changeover of importation. The late manufacture Classic Double shotguns (Models 101 and 201) do not have the Winchester trademark or definitive Winchester proofmark stamped on the barrels. The Model 201 was a new model designation.

SHOTGUNS: O/U, MODEL 101 - FIELD MODELS

The late manufacture Classic Doubles have an interchangeable choke tube system compatible with the older Winchester manufactured models. Prices listed include a luggage style carrying case.

Values listed below for the Classic Doubles Shotguns assume NIB condition - subtract 10%-15% if without box, warranty card, and original shipping container (with packing materials).

CLASSIC FIELD GRADE I - 12 or 20 ga., 3 in. chambers, vent. rib, 25½ or 28 in. vent. barrels with choke tubes, blue receiver with moderate scroll engraving, ejectors, checkered pistol grip or English stock and forearm, 6¼ - 7 lbs.

	$1,400	$1,250	$1,100	$1,000	$900	$825	$750

Last MSR was $1,905.

WATERFOWL MODEL - 12 ga. only, 3 in. chambers, 30 in. barrels with vent. rib and choke tubes, matte blue receiver with moderate engraving, low gloss walnut stock with vent. recoil pad, 7¾ lbs.

	$1,150	$995	$895	$800	$700	$600	$500

Last MSR was $1,520.

CLASSIC SPORTER - 12 ga. only, made for Sporting Clays competition, 28 or 30 in. vent. barrels and rib with choke tubes, quick detachable stock system, border engraved coin finished receiver with non-reflective matte surface on top frame and lever, checkered walnut stock and forearm, 7¾ lbs.

	$1,995	$1,500	$1,295	$1,150	$1,000	$900	$775

Last MSR was $1,980.

Add $965 for extra barrel.

Grading	100%	98%	95%	90%	80%	70%	60%

CLASSIC FIELD GRADE II - 12, 20, 28 ga., or .410 bore, 28 in. VR barrels with choke tubes, deluxe walnut with round knob pistol grip stock and forearm with fine fleur-de-lis checkering, coin finished receiver (different sizes) with game scene engraving featuring hunting motifs on receiver sides and bottom, .410 bore bored M/F only, 6¼ - 7 lbs.

	$1,795	$1,475	$1,275	$1,100	$1,000	$900	$795

Last MSR was $2,190.

Add 15% for .410 bore (baby frame).
Add 50% for 28 ga. (baby frame).

The lack of supply of the Winchester/Olin Model 101 28 ga. small frame has caused a significant in demand for the .410 bore or 28 ga. The Grade II .410 bore is the only round knob pistol grip produced in both Winchester and Classic Doubles manufacture.

CLASSIC FIELD GRADE II TWO BARREL SET - 12 and 20 ga. barrels, both with Winchokes, 26 in. barrels - 20 ga., 28 in. barrels - 12 ga., coin finished receiver with game scene engraving and borders, 6½ (20 ga.) or 7 (12 ga.) lbs.

	$2,695	$2,175	$1,825	$1,550	$1,375	$1,200	$1,075

Last MSR was $3,420.

SHOTGUNS: O/U, MODEL 101 - TARGET MODELS

CLASSIC TRAP SINGLE - 12 ga. only, over single 32 or 34 in. VR barrel with choke tubes, blue receiver with light engraving, choice of Monte Carlo or regular stock, recoil pad, 8½ lbs.

	$1,425	$1,250	$1,100	$1,000	$900	$825	$750

Last MSR was $2,070.

CLASSIC TRAP - 12 ga. only, 30 or 32 in. vent. barrels and rib with choke tubes, finish and engraving similar to Classic Trap Single, choice of Monte Carlo or standard stock with recoil pad, 8¾ or 9 lbs.

	$1,300	$1,125	$1,000	$900	$825	$750	$675

Last MSR was $1,905.

CLASSIC TRAP COMBO - includes one set of O/U barrels (30 or 32 in.) and one over single barrel (32 or 34 in.), choke tubes, choice of Monte Carlo or standard stock, 8¾ or 9 lbs.

	$2,125	$1,875	$1,600	$1,475	$1,300	$1,175	$995

Last MSR was $2,825.

CLASSIC SKEET - 12 or 20 ga., 27 ½ in. vent. barrels and rib, choke tubes on 12 ga. only, smaller ga.'s are bored SK/SK, similar metal finish to Classic Trap models, 7¼ or 7¾ lbs.

	$1,695	$1,375	$1,175	$1,025	$900	$825	$750

Last MSR was $1,905.

✷ *Classic Skeet 4 ga. Set* - similar to Classic Skeet except has 4 barrels (12, 20, 28 ga., or .410 bore), 12 ga. has choke tubes, smaller ga.'s are bored SK/SK.

	$3,900	$3,500	$3,100	$2,875	$2,600	$2,300	$1,995

Last MSR was $4,765.

Grading	100%	98%	95%	90%	80%	70%	60%

SHOTGUNS: SxS

MODEL 201 CLASSIC - 12 or 20 ga., 3 in. chambers, forged steel monobloc with improved lug design, 26 in. choke tube barrels with vent. rib, high lustre bluing, no engraving, SST, ejectors, premium walnut stock and beavertail forearm with fancy checkering pattern, solid red rubber recoil pad, 6¾ - 7 lbs.

$1,400	$1,200	$995	$775	$650	$575	$495

Last MSR was $2,190.

Add $120 for 20 ga.

The 12 ga. could be ordered with choke tubes at no extra charge. Only 63 were mfg. with choke tubes and slight premiums are being asked.

✱ ***Model 201 Classic Small Bore Set*** - 28 ga. and .410 bore two barrel set, similar to Model 201 Classic except has smaller frame and overall dimensions, 28 in. VR barrels only bored IC/M on 28 ga. and M/F on .410 bore, very limited importation, 6 or 6 ½ lbs.

$4,250	$3,650	$3,250	$2,800	$2,400	$1,950	$1,475

Last MSR was $3,675.

CLERKE ARMS, LTD.

Previous manufacturer located in Raton, New Mexico 1997-2001.

PISTOLS: SINGLE SHOT

COMPETITOR PISTOL - available in 16 centerfire and 2 rimfire cals., 10, 12, 14, 16, or 20 (.410 bore only) in. barrel, features new uplifting C Breech gun system, Xtender slide can be fitted to all Colt .45 ACPs and replicas with no frame modification, matte finish, checkered wood grips. Mfg. 1998-2001.

$300	$285	$265	$240	$220	$200	$185

Last MSR was $325.

Add $135-$155 per interchangeable barrel, depending on length.

CLERKE PRODUCTS

Previous manufacturer located in Santa Monica, CA.

REVOLVERS: DOUBLE ACTION

DOUBLE ACTION REVOLVER - .22 S, L, LR, or .32 S&W Long cal., inexpensive double action revolvers that sold to dealers for $15 in 1971.

RIFLES: SINGLE SHOT

HI-WALL - single shot rifle, falling block replica of Winchester 1885 High Wall, lever operated, case hardened receiver, 26 in. barrel, available in most modern calibers, no sights, checkered walnut pistol grip stock, Schnabel forearm. Mfg. 1972-1974.

$250	$225	$185	$175	$150	$140	$125

DELUXE HI-WALL - similar to Hi-Wall, except half octagon barrel, select wood and recoil pad.

$300	$275	$235	$210	$180	$160	$145

CLIFTON ARMS

Previous manufacturer of custom rifles from 1992-1997 located in Medina, TX. Clifton Arms specialized in composite stocks (with or without integral, retractable bipod).

Clifton Arms manufactured composite, hand laminated stocks that were patterned after the Dakota 76 stock configuration.

Grading	100%	98%	95%	90%	80%	70%	60%

RIFLES: BOLT ACTION

CLIFTON SCOUT RIFLE - .243 Win. (disc. 1993), .30-06, .308 Win., .350 Rem. Mag., .35 Whelen, 7mm-08 Rem. (disc. 1993), or .416 Rem. Mag. cal., choice of Dakota 76, pre-64 Winchester Model 70, or Ruger 77 MK II (standard) stainless action with bolt face altered to controlled round feeding, Shilen stainless premium match grade barrel, Clifton synthetic stock with bipod, many other special orders were available, mfg. 1992- 97.

$3,000 $2,350 $1,650

This model was available as a Standard Scout (.308 Win. cal. with 19 in. barrel), Pseudo Scout (.30-06 cal. with 19 ½ in. barrel), Super Scout (.35 Whelen or .350 Rem. Mag. with 20 in. barrel), or African Scout (.416 Rem. Mag. with 22 in. barrel).

COACH GUNS

A coach gun is a SxS shotgun with short barrels, and was used extensively in the American West for the protection of horse-drawn coach passengers, hence the name. They were also called guard guns, as they were used for guard duty and other security purposes.

SHOTGUNS: SxS, COACH/GUARD GUNS

The author wishes to express his thanks to Jon Vander Bloomen for compiling much of the following information.

Extensive research indicates that three American gun companies made coach guns in the late 1800s and early 1900s – Colt, Parker, and Ithaca. Remington & Whitney may also have produced some, but there are no factory records to prove it. W.W. Greener of Birmingham, England may have made some short double barrel shotguns for guard use, but no one has seen any factory documentation to support this.

An "original" coach gun, properly called a guard gun, is a double barrel (SxS) shotgun that was made with short barrels, not a long barreled sporting gun that was cut off (see muzzle diagram). However, the muzzles of an original coach gun and a gun whose barrels have been cut off look the same. On both, there is a gap between the muzzles that is filled in with lead. The reason for this is because shotgun barrels are tapered. In order for the muzzles to touch on a 26 inch or shorter gun, the barrel walls would need to be thicker at the muzzle to eliminate the gap.

Some original coach guns may also have original factory markings, identification letters/numerals on the stock and other distinquishing features that indicate that the gun was originally made and marked to identify it as company property. However, don't think that there's "safety in numbers." There are a lot more Wells Fargo marked guns today than there were 85 years ago.

The real question is, how can you tell an original coach gun from a sporting arm whose barrels have been cut down to potentially "enhance" its desirability factor? Hopefully, by obtaining factory documentation. To find out if a coach gun is an original or a "cut" gun, it is recommended that you contact the factory for documentation (if possible), giving the serial number of the gun and asking for the proper barrel length at the time the gun left the factory. Unfortunately, no Remington records exist. Parker records can be found in Vols. I & II of *The Parker Story*. W.W. Greener is still in business, and will look up a serial number, but it will take some time.

Colt records show that several double barrel shotguns left the factory with short barrels. Most of them were the Model 1878 hammer guns with 18 inch barrels. There where only 3 Model 1883 hammerless, boxlock guns made with short barrels; the lengths are as follows, 18, 22, and 24 inches. All of the Colt Damascus barrels were made in Belgium and shipped to the Colt factory in an unfinished state, they were just Damascus tubes. Therefore when Colt got an order for a coach/ guard gun, the barrels were custom made to length just as the longer barreled guns. These short barreled Colts are "original coach/guard guns". The extreme rarity of a Colt factory coach gun precludes accurate pricing evaluation.

Parker records show that several guns were made with short barrels. Not all short Parkers were made for guard use however, since some hunters preferred short barrels for in the field (fast upland birds). Parker purchased different grades of steel tubes and made their own barrels. When Parker received an order for a guard gun, the barrels were custom made to length. It would have been more costly for Parker to cut a long barreled choked gun, except in the case of used sporting arms that were cut for guard use. It is likely that the lower grade 10 and 12 ga. guns that left the Parker factory with short barrels are "original" coach/guard guns. The extreme rarity factor of a Parker factory coach gun precludes accurate pricing evaluation.

Ithaca records show that 750 hammer doubles were made for Wells Fargo between 1909 and 1917. The first 200 guns had 26 in. barrels, and the remaining 550 had 24 in. barrels. Wells Fargo, as well as other express companies, used various makes of shotguns, mostly used lower grade models that were cut to a shorter length. There is no proof that any company other than Ithaca made guard guns for Wells Fargo. It is recommended that a buyer get original documentation when considering a purchase of a Wells Fargo coach gun or any other gun that is claimed to have been used by a famous person. Average condition Wells Fargo coach guns are typically priced in the $4,000 range, regardless if they are manufactured by Ithaca or are another trademark that had barrels cut. What's important to the buyer is that the gun is a documented Wells Fargo gun.

What's important to remember is that if there is no original documentation, there's no proof. And if there's no proof, the shotgun may or may not be an original coach gun. It is recommended that when buying, selling, or trading coach guns, the price tag should be proportional to the gun's originality and provenance. Anything less could result in an unwarranted premium for a tired out, "reconfigured" SxS plain Jane shotgun, with some added non-original markings/carvings.

Older sawed off double barrel shotguns with no documentation as being an express company gun, or a gun used by a famous person are valued in the $200 to $2,000 range, depending on trademark and condition; condition being most important. A good guide for pricing sawed off doubles is to check the value of the same gun that has not been cut and then deduct 5 % to 50 %. If no price guide is available for that particular make, then consider availability. For example tens of thousands of Belgian doubles were made in the 1800's. Because of the increase in collect ability of American western artifacts, original coach guns and all express company guns are highly prized and sought after, but the buyer must always be wary.

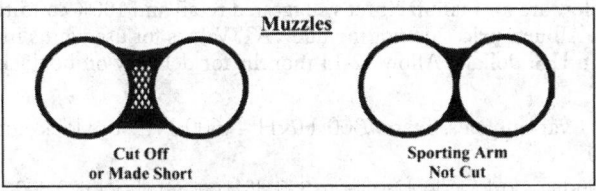

COBRA ENTERPRISES

Current pistol manufacturer established in 2001, and located in Montana with headquarters in Salt Lake City, UT.

DERRINGERS

COBRA DERRINGER - .22 LR, .22 Win Mag., .25 ACP, or .32 ACP cal., 2.4 (Standard Series), 2¾ (Big Bore Series) or 3½ (Long Bore Series) in. barrel, tip-up action, spur trigger, internal hammer block safety, pearl or laminated wood grips, chrome, black teflon, or satin chrome finish, 9.5 oz.

MSR	$89		$75	$60	$50	$45	$40	$35	$35

Add $21 for .22 Mag., .32 H&R Mag., .38 Spl., or 9mm Para cal. with 2¾ in. barrel.
Add $21 for .22 Mag., .38 Spl., or 9mm Para cal. with 3½ in. barrel.

PISTOLS: SEMI-AUTO

COBRA SERIES - .32 ACP or 380 ACP cal., blowback single action, 2.8 in. barrel, 5 or 6 shot mag., chrome, black teflon, or satin chrome finish, 22 oz.

MSR	$96		$80	$65	$55	$50	$45	$40	$35

Grading	100%	98%	95%	90%	80%	70%	60%

PATRIOT SERIES- .380 ACP or 9mm Para. cal., DAO, 3.3 in. barrel, polymer frame, 10 shot mag., loaded indicator, 20.5 oz.

MSR	$131	$110	$95	$85	$80	$75	$70	$65

Add $19 for 9mm Para cal.

* *Patriot 45* - .45 ACP cal., DAO, black polymer frame with stainless steel slide, 3 in. barrel, 6 shot mag., 20 oz.

MSR	$266	$225	$195	$175	$150	$135	$120	$110

COBRAY INDUSTRIES
See listing under S.W.D. in the S section of this text.

COGSWELL & HARRISON (GUNMAKERS), LTD.

Current manufacturer established durng 1770, and located in London, England. Previously imported by British Game Guns, located in Kent, WA.

In 1993, Cogswell & Harrison came under new management and have concentrated on building best quality guns utilizing Beesley or Purdey type sidelocks, Woodward styled O/Us, and a round action boxlock. The company also provides a serialization service (free of charge), that provides the exact date of manufacture. A Certificate of Origin is also available for $60 per gun, and specifies the original specifications and configuration – weights, dimensions, materials, points of choke, and original owner (including price paid). Cogswell & Harrison also offers a full repair and restoration service.

RIFLES: SxS

Prices indicated below are for manufacturer's suggested retail and 100% condition factors are listed in English pounds. All new prices do not include VAT. Values for used guns in 98%-60% condition factors are priced in U.S. dollars. Allow 12-14 months for delivery on boxlocks, 18-24 months on sidelocks.

BOXLOCK MODEL - various cals. from .300 H&H - .600 NE, boxlock action, custom order only. New 1999.

> Currently, a standard boxlock double rifle in .300 H&H cal. retails for £20,800, and £30,500 for .600 NE, with standard fine engraving, and w/o case.

SIDELOCK MODEL - standard cals. include .300 H&H, .375 H&H, .465, .470 NE, .577, and .600 NE, Beesley or Purdey type action standard, also available with H&H type system, individually made per customer specifications, 8 lbs. 10 oz. - 14 lbs. 6 oz., depending on caliber. New 1999.

MSR	£40,800	£40,800	$50,000	$42,000	$36,000	$30,000	$24,000	$18,000

Add £1,100 for .375 H&H cal.
Add £3,100 for .465 or .470 NE cal.

* *Cals. .577 & .600 NE*

MSR	£50,500	£50,500	$60,000	$50,000	$42,000	$36,000	$30,000	$24,000

SHOTGUNS: O/U, SIDELOCK

WOODWARD TYPE - Woodward style action, finest materials, each gun custom built for individual specifications, delivery time approx. 18-23 months.

MSR	£31,770	£31,770	$47,250	$41,000	$36,000	$29,500	$22,350	$16,750

Add £1,250 for 20 ga.
Add £3,500 for 28 ga.

Grading	100%	98%	95%	90%	80%	70%	60%

SHOTGUNS: SxS, OLDER MFG.

REGENCY - 12, 16, or 20 ga., 26, 28, or 30 in. barrels, any choke combination, hammerless Anson & Deeley system, boxlock, double triggers, auto ejectors, straight English stock.

$4,275	$3,750	$3,450	$3,125	$2,750	$2,500	$2,250

Last MSR was $3,200.

AMBASSADOR MODEL - same gauges and barrels as Regency, boxlock with ornamental strengthening sideplates, auto ejectors, double triggers, engraved game scene or scroll rose motif, English stock.

$5,500	$4,950	$4,450	$3,950	$3,500	$3,100	$2,850

Last MSR was $4,000.

MARKOR - 12, 16, or 20 ga., 27½ or 30 in. barrel and choke, boxlock, double trigger, English stock. Disc.

$1,675	$1,475	$1,300	$1,050	$975	$825	$700

Add 20% for auto ejectors.

HUNTIC MODEL - 12, 16, or 20 ga., 25, 27, or 30 in. barrels, any choke, sidelock, auto ejectors, English style stock. Disc.

$3,900	$3,500	$3,200	$3,000	$2,800	$2,500	$2,175

Add $400 for SST.

AVANT TOUT SERIES - 12, 16, or 20 ga., 25, 27½, or 30 in. barrels, boxlock, ornamental strengthening sideplates, straight English stock, auto ejectors, series disc.

$2,550	$2,250	$1,925	$1,700	$1,495	$1,350	$1,200

REX OR AVANT TOUT III - no sideplates.

$2,150	$1,800	$1,650	$1,500	$1,350	$1,200	$1,075

SANDHURST OR AVANT TOUT II

$2,800	$2,500	$2,300	$2,150	$2,000	$1,750	$1,500

KONOR OR AVANT TOUT I

$3,275	$2,850	$2,500	$2,250	$2,000	$1,750	$1,500

Add $400 for SST.
Add 20% for 20 ga.
Subtract 10% for 16 ga.

BEST QUALITY - 12, 16, or 20 ga.'s, 25, 26, 28, or 30 in. barrels, any choke, hand detachable sidelock, auto ejectors, double triggers standard, English stock.

* *Primic Model* - disc.

$6,200	$5,750	$4,650	$4,150	$3,650	$3,050	$2,500

* *Victor Model*

$9,250	$8,500	$7,250	$6,250	$5,000	$4,350	$3,740

Add $400 for SST.
Add 20% for 20 ga.

Note: Degree of engraving and grade of wood are the basic differences among models.

SHOTGUNS: SxS, BOXLOCK & SIDELOCK - CURRENT MFG.

Prices indicated below are for manufacturer's suggested retail and 100% condition factors are listed in English pounds. All new prices do not include VAT. Values for used guns in 98%-60% condition factors are priced in U.S. dollars. Allow 9-12 months for delivery on boxlocks, 18-23 months on sidelocks.

All models below are available in 12, 20, or 28 ga.

Grading	100%	98%	95%	90%	80%	70%	60%

REGENCY - scalloped boxlock action, DT's, 100% large scroll engraving coverage on receiver and tangs, light barrel engraving, checkered straight grip stock with teardrop. Introduced 1970 to commemmorate C&H's bicentennial.

	MSR	£9,760	£9,760	$14,750	$12,250	$10,000	$8,000	$6,500	$4,950

Add £310 for 20 ga.
Add £510 for 28 ga.

VICTORIA - features scalloped round body boxlock action with 100% medium scroll engraving coverage on receiver and tangs, moderate barrel engraving, select checkered stock and forearm.

	MSR	£11,770	£11,770	$16,950	$14,500	$12,250	$10,000	$7,800	$6,100

Add £360 for 20 ga.
Add £585 for 28 ga.

EXTRA QUALITY VICTORIA - similar to Victoria Model, except has better quality wood and more engraving.

	MSR	£13,180	£13,180	$18,750	$16,250	$14,000	$11,750	$8,900	$7,350

Add £440 for 20 ga.
Add £890 for 28 ga.

EXTRA QUALITY (SPECIAL) VICTORIA - top-of-the-line round boxlock action with best quality walnut and chopperlump barrels, removable crosspin, and other refinements.

	MSR	£15,180	£15,180	$22,350	$19,450	$16,350	$13,150	$10,250	$8,400

Add £440 for 20 ga.
Add £810 for 28 ga.

SELF-OPENING SLE SxS - sidelock action, best quality Beesley action and engraving, each gun custom built per individual specifications, delivery time approx. 18-23 months.

	MSR	£27,170	£27,170	$41,000	$36,000	$29,500	$22,350	$16,750	$12,500

Add £1,250 for 20 ga.
Add £3,500 for 28 ga.

COLT'S MANUFACTURING COMPANY, INC.

Current manufacturer with headquarters located in West Hartford, CT.

Manufactured from 1836-1841 in Paterson, NJ; 1847 to 1848 in Whitneyville, CT; 1854 to 1864 in London, England; and from 1848 to date in Hartford, CT. Colt Firearms became a division of Colt Industries in 1964. In March, 1990, the Colt Firearms Division was sold to C.F. Holding Corp. located in Hartford, CT, and the new company is called Colt's Manufacturing Company, Inc. The original Hartford plant was closed during 1994, the same year the company was sold again to a new investor group headed by Zilkha Co., located in New York, NY.

In late 1999, Colt discontinued many of their consumer handguns. Values for those discontinued models have remained relatively stable, except for those rare and desirable production for variances which collectors will pay a premium. The semi-auto pistols remaining in production are now referred to as Model "O".

For more information and current pricing on both new and used Colt airguns, please refer to the 2nd Ed. *Blue Book of Airguns* by Dr. Robert Beeman & John Allen (now online also).

REVOLVERS: PERCUSSION

Prices shown for percussion Colts are for guns only. Original cased guns with accessories will bring a healthy premium over non-cased models (200-350% over a gun only is common). Be very careful

100%	98%	95%	90%	80%	70%	60%	50%	40%	30%	20%	10%

when buying an "original" cased gun, as many fake cases have shown up in recent years.

If possible, it is advisable to procure a factory letter (available only within the following ser. no. ranges) before buying, selling, or trading Models 1851 Navy (ser. range 98,000-132,000), 1860 Army (ser. range 2,000-130,000), or 1861 Navy (ser. range 1-10,000). These watermarked letters are available by writing Colt Firearms in Hartford, CT, with a charge of $300 per serial number (if they can research it). Include your name and address, Colt model name, serial number, and check to: COLT HISTORIAN, P.O. Box 1868, Hartford, CT 06144. Please allow 4-6 weeks for a response.

Prices shown on the following pages for extremely rare Colt's firearms might not include values in the 90%, 95%, 98%, and 100% condition columns. Prices are very hard to establish since these excellent to mint specimens are seldomly seen or sold.

Revolvers: Percussion, Paterson Variations

POCKET MODEL PATERSON NO. 1 - also known as "Baby Paterson", .28 cal., 5 shot, 2½ in. to 4¾ in. octagon barrels, blue metal, varnished walnut grips. Serial range 1 to approx. 500. Standard bbl. marking "Patent Arms M'g Co. Paterson N.J.-Colt's Pt.". Centaur scene with four horse head trademark and "COLT" on 1 1/16 in. cylinder of round or square type. Mfg. 1837-1838.

> This and all other Paterson models have 5 shot cylinders and serial numbers are not commonly in evidence externally. Disassembly of the arm is usually necessary to determine the serial number.
>
> The Pocket Model Paterson No. 1 (Baby Paterson) is the first production made handgun in Colt's Paterson, N.J. facility. It is very small in size, almost appearing as a toy or miniature.

* ***Standard Production Model*** - without attached loading lever.

N/A	N/A	$35,700	$28,350	$21,840	$19,050	$15,300	$13,250	$11,750	$10,250	$9,000	$8,000

* ***Late Production Ehlers Model*** - with attached loading lever, 31/32 round back cylinder and recoil shield milled for ease of capping. Barrel marked "Patent Arms Paterson N.J.-Colt's Pt.". Approx. 500 mfg. including the Ehlers Model under Belt Model No. 2 Mfg. 1840-1843.

N/A	N/A	$39,650	$31,500	$23,925	$19,575	$15,825	$13,750	$12,250	$10,750	$9,500	$8,500

BELT MODEL PATERSON NO. 2 - .31 or .34 cal., 5 shot, 2½ in. to 5½ in. octagon barrels, blue metal, varnished walnut grips. Serial range 1- approx. 850 which includes the Belt Model No. 3. All standard production Belt Models No. 2 have straight bottom style grips. Standard bbl. markings "Patent Arms M'g Co. Paterson N-J. Colt's Pt.". Centaur scene with four horse head trademark and "COLT" on cylinder of round or square backed type. Mfg 1837-1840. Somewhat heavier than the Pocket No. 1 revolver.

* ***Standard Production Model*** - without attached loading lever.

N/A	N/A	$35,700	$28,350	$21,840	$19,050	$15,300	$13,250	$11,750	$10,250	$9,000	$8,000

* ***Ehlers Model*** - with attached loading lever, 1 1/16 in. round back cylinder, recoil shield milled for ease of capping. Barrel marked "Patent Arms Paterson N-J. Colt's Pt.". Approx. 500 mfg. including the Ehlers Model under Pocket Model No. 1. Mfg. 1840-1843.

N/A	N/A	$43,575	$34,650	$27,050	$23,175	$19,380	$15,500	$13,500	$12,000	$10,600	$9,500

BELT MODEL PATERSON NO. 3 - .31 or .34 cal., 5 shot, 3½ in. to 5½ in. octagon barrels, blue metal, a few having case hardened hammers. Varnished walnut grips. Serial range 1- approx. 850 which includes the Belt Model No. 2. All standard production Belt Models No. 3 have the flared bottom style grips. Standard barrel markings "Patent Arms M'g Co. Paterson N-J. Colt's Pt." The square backed cylinder is seen less often than the more common round back, both bearing the Centaur scene with four horse head trademark and "COLT". With both Belt Models, revolvers exhibiting attached loading levers are less common than those without a lever. Mfg. 1837-1840.

100%	98%	95%	90%	80%	70%	60%	50%	40%	30%	20%	10%

✴ Standard Model w/o Lever - without attached loading lever.

100%	98%	95%	90%	80%	70%	60%	50%	40%	30%	20%	10%
N/A	N/A	$35,700	$30,200	$23,925	$20,075	$17,340	$15,000	$13,500	$11,750	$10,500	$9,250

✴ Standard Model With Lever - with attached loading lever and recoil shield milled for ease of capping (scarce).

N/A	N/A	$39,275	$32,550	$26,525	$23,175	$20,150	$17,500	$15,250	$13,500	$12,000	$10,750

HOLSTER MODEL NO. 5 - also known as "Texas Paterson" - .36 cal., 5 shot, 4 in. to 12 in. octagon barrels, blue metal with case hardened frame and hammer. All cylinders bear the stage coach hold-up scene. Varnished walnut grips of flared bottom style. Serial range 1 to approx. 1,000. As with all models of Patersons, the serial number usually cannot be seen without disassembly of the revolver. Very large and heavy compared to the other Paterson models. Enjoys more popularity with collectors because of its military and frontier use. Mfg. 1838-1840.

Many specimens encountered in this variation show extreme use. Consequently, fine to mint specimens are quite rare and highly prized by collectors. Values are given for non-military marked specimens. Any specimen bearing an authenticated martial marking is truly a rarity and should be appraised individually. NOTE: Watch for fakes here. There are now many times more faked martial markings, often times on non-original Patersons, than there are originals.

✴ Standard Production Model w/o Lever - without attached loading lever, round or square backed cylinder.

N/A	N/A	$147,000	110,250	$85,800	$68,500	$58,150	$49,000	$42,000	$37,000	$32,500	$28,000

✴ Standard Production Model With Lever - with attached loading lever, round backed cylinder and recoil shield milled for ease of capping.

N/A	N/A	$159,500	116,000	$91,000	$75,700	$64,775	$55,000	$47,500	$41,500	$37,000	$32,500

Revolvers: Percussion, Walker Model

WALKER MODEL REVOLVER - .44 cal., 6 shot, 9 in. part round, part octagon barrel, blue metal with case hardened frame, lever and hammer. Cylinder left without finish, brass trigger guard. One piece walnut grips. Mfg. 1847; total production approx. 1,100. Ser. numbers beginning with no. 1 were applied for each of five different military companies (A,B,C,D, & E). The total for the military issue Walkers was approx. 1,000 revolvers; the remaining approx. 100 revolvers were produced for civilian distribution. Barrels marked "Address SamL Colt New-York City". Found on right side of barrel lug is "US" over "1847". Cylinder bears Texas Ranger/Indian fight scene. Various metal parts and walnut grips stamped with Govt. Inspectors' marks.

Because of these arms being subjected to great extremes of use, they will exhibit high degrees of wear, often to the extent that most or all markings will be worn off. Replaced parts are common and many badly worn and damaged specimens have been extensively rebuilt and restored. NOTE: Use great caution when contemplating the purchase of a Walker. A multitude of out-and-out fakes and "antiqued" reproduction Walkers have been fed into the market over the past few decades. Some of these are old enough (and have aged enough naturally) to almost resemble an authentic specimen. Enlist the services of a qualified expert before your dollars are spent. Only 10-12% of the original production of approx. 1,100 specimens have been accounted for. The acquisition of an authenticated Walker revolver is the ultimate goal of serious Colt collectors.

✴ Standard Military Issue Model

N/A	N/A	N/A	$262,500	187,200	154,500	132,600	87,500	77,500	$67,500	$57,500	$52,500

✴ Limited Civilian Issue Model - serial range 1001 to approx. 1100. Similar to military model except Govt. inspectors' marks were not applied. Pricing is difficult on the civilian issue arms. They tend to be in considerably better condition than the much more common military specimens. The factors of scarcity and condition will often bring higher prices from the advanced collector of means, especially in the finer grades of condition. On

100%	98%	95%	90%	80%	70%	60%	50%	40%	30%	20%	10%

the other hand, the collector appreciating military usage will pay more for military marked examples. This publication tries to reflect the latest trends on purchase of civilian models.

100%	98%	95%	90%	80%	70%	60%	50%	40%	30%	20%	10%
N/A	N/A	N/A	$257,250	$187,200	$147,900	$127,500	$90,000	$75,000	$65,000	$55,000	$50,000

Revolvers: Percussion, Dragoon Series

WHITNEYVILLE HARTFORD DRAGOON - .44 cal., 6 shot, 7½ in. part octagon, part round barrel, some of the left-over Walker parts were used in Dragoons, blue metal with casehardened frame, lever, hammer, brass trigger guard and steel cylinder bears Texas Ranger and Indian battle scene. Mfg. 1847. Total production approx. 240. Serial range approx. 1,100 to 1,340 in sequence following civilian Walkers.

* *Rear frame cut out for grips*

| N/A | N/A | $141,750 | $112,350 | $89,500 | $73,950 | $61,200 | $53,000 | $47,000 | $42,000 | $38,000 | $35,000 |

* *Straight rear frame*

| N/A | N/A | $104,475 | $77,700 | $55,640 | $47,895 | $37,230 | $30,000 | $25,000 | $22,000 | $20,000 | $18,500 |

FIRST MODEL DRAGOON - .44 cal., 6 shot, 7½ in. round and octagon barrel, blue metal with case hardened frame, lever, hammer, brass grip straps, silvered straps for civilian market, serial range numbered after Hartford Dragoon, 1341 to around 8000. Mfg. 1848-1850. Total production approx. 7,000. Oval cyl. slots, square back trigger guard, Texas Ranger and Indian fight scene on cylinder.

* *Military Model*

| N/A | N/A | $50,400 | $40,425 | $28,600 | $21,630 | $17,075 | $14,250 | $11,000 | $9,000 | $8,000 | $7,000 |

* *Civilian Model*

| N/A | N/A | $42,000 | $27,300 | $22,875 | $17,500 | $13,260 | $10,500 | $8,000 | $6,500 | $6,000 | $5,500 |

FLUCK MODEL DRAGOON - basically a First Model Dragoon, with 7½ in. altered Walker barrels and fully martially marked, should be extensively checked over, used to replace defective Walkers. Mfg. 1848. Total production 300. Serial range approx. 2,216 to 2,515.

| N/A | N/A | $47,250 | $36,750 | $31,200 | $23,700 | $19,375 | $17,000 | $15,000 | $11,000 | $10,000 | $9,500 |

SECOND MODEL DRAGOON - .44 cal., 6 shot, 7½ in. round and octagon barrel, serial range following the First Model Dragoon 8000-10,700. Mfg. 1850-1851. Texas Ranger and Indian fight scene on cylinder.

* *Military Model*

| N/A | N/A | $40,950 | $32,025 | $24,450 | $18,550 | $15,050 | $12,000 | $10,000 | $8,500 | $7,500 | $6,500 |

* *Civilian Model*

| N/A | N/A | $36,225 | $27,050 | $20,800 | $17,250 | $13,500 | $11,500 | $9,500 | $7,750 | $6,500 | $5,500 |

* *New Hampshire or Massachusetts* - notice state markings on front portion of trigger guard.

| N/A | N/A | $44,625 | $33,350 | $25,750 | $20,075 | $16,075 | $13,250 | $11,250 | $9,500 | $8,500 | $7,750 |

THIRD MODEL DRAGOON - .44 cal., 6 shot, 7½ in. round or octagon barrel, same basic features as earlier models, but with round trigger guard and rectangular cylinder slots, serial range approx. 10,200-19,600, some overlapping of numbers, with approx. 10,500 mfg. from 1851-1861. Texas Ranger and Indian fight scene on cylinder.

* *Third Model Dragoon*

| N/A | N/A | $34,125 | $23,100 | $15,075 | $12,375 | $10,450 | $8,900 | $7,800 | $6,900 | $6,250 | $5,750 |

* *Martially marked U.S.*

| N/A | N/A | $36,750 | $26,250 | $20,275 | $15,195 | $13,000 | $11,000 | $9,500 | $8,250 | $7,250 | $6,500 |

* *Third Model* - 8 in. barrel.

| N/A | N/A | $38,850 | $31,500 | $28,080 | $23,700 | $19,900 | $16,500 | $14,000 | $11,500 | $9,500 | $8,000 |

100%	98%	95%	90%	80%	70%	60%	50%	40%	30%	20%	10%

✳ *First and Second Variation* - shoulder stock model.

| N/A | N/A | $39,375 | $30,450 | $23,925 | $19,575 | $16,675 | $14,000 | $11,750 | $9,750 | $8,250 | $7,250 |

✳ *Third Variation*

| N/A | N/A | $37,800 | $29,925 | $22,625 | $19,055 | $16,075 | $13,250 | $11,000 | $9,000 | $7,500 | $6,500 |

✳ *C.L. Dragoon*

| N/A | N/A | $50,925 | $38,600 | $29,125 | $24,650 | $20,860 | $17,250 | $14,750 | $12,500 | $10,500 | $8,500 |

ENGLISH HARTFORD DRAGOON - basically a Third Model Dragoon, assembled at Colt's London factory, with unique serial range 1-700, some were assembled from earlier parts inventories, easy to spot with British proofs of crown over V and crown over GP, the blue was of the English type, many were engraved.

| N/A | N/A | $33,075 | $23,100 | $16,650 | $13,400 | $10,975 | $9,300 | $8,200 | $7,300 | $6,600 | $6,000 |

1848 BABY DRAGOONS - .31 cal., 5 shot, 3, 4, 5, or 6 in. octagon barrels, most without loading lever, serial range 1-15,500, a scaled down version of the .44 caliber Dragoons, early ones with Texas Ranger scene and later ones with the holdup scene.

✳ *Type I* - left hand barrel stamping, Texas Ranger and Indian scene, approx. serial range 1-150.

| N/A | N/A | $15,750 | $12,350 | $10,250 | $8,900 | $7,650 | $6,500 | $5,750 | $5,250 | $4,850 | $4,350 |

✳ *Type II* - with Texas Ranger and Indian scene, 11,600 serial range, without loading lever.

| N/A | N/A | $12,075 | $8,675 | $7,375 | $5,925 | $4,850 | $3,950 | $3,300 | $3,000 | $2,800 | $2,600 |

✳ *Type III* - with Stagecoach scene and oval cylinder slots, serial range 10,400-12,000.

| N/A | N/A | $12,075 | $8,875 | $7,075 | $5,625 | $4,600 | $3,800 | $3,200 | $2,800 | $2,500 | $2,200 |

✳ *Type IV* - with Stagecoach holdup scene, rectangle cylinder slots, serial range 11,000-12,500.

| N/A | N/A | $12,000 | $9,000 | $7,250 | $5,900 | $5,000 | $4,250 | $3,600 | $3,250 | $3,000 | $2,750 |

✳ *Type V* - with Stagecoach holdup scene, rectangle cylinder slots and loading lever, serial range 11,600-15,500.

| N/A | N/A | $12,600 | $8,875 | $7,075 | $5,600 | $4,600 | $3,800 | $3,200 | $2,850 | $2,550 | 2,250 |

Revolvers: Percussion, Models 1849, 1851, 1855, 1860, 1861, & 1862

1849 POCKET MODEL - .31 cal., 5 or 6 shot, 3, 4, 5, and 6 in. octagon barrels, most with loading levers, blue metal with case hardened frame, lever and hammer, grip straps of brass (silver plated), or steel (silver plated or blue), stagecoach hold-up scene on cylinder, serial range 12,000 to 340,000. Mfg. 1850-1873.

✳ *First Type* - 4, 5, or 6 in. barrel, loading lever and small or large brass trigger guard.

| N/A | N/A | $3,550 | $2,750 | $2,125 | $1,700 | $1,375 | $1,000 | $750 | $600 | $550 | $475 |

✳ *Second Type* - 4, 5, or 6 in. barrel, loading lever and steel grip straps.

| N/A | N/A | $4,275 | $3,350 | $2,550 | $2,000 | $1,675 | $1,150 | $850 | $700 | $650 | $575 |

✳ *Wells Fargo Model* - 3 in. barrel, without loading lever and with small round trigger guard.

| N/A | N/A | $11,275 | $8,025 | $5,565 | $3,875 | $2,700 | $2,000 | $1,700 | $1,525 | $1,375 | $1,150 |

1849 LONDON POCKET MODEL - London pistols were of the same general configuration, but of better finish, serial range 1-11,000. Mfg. 1853-1857.

✳ *Early Type* - serial numbered under 1500, with small trigger guard and brass grip straps.

| N/A | N/A | $5,725 | $4,675 | $3,800 | $3,025 | $2,400 | $1,850 | $1,450 | $1,150 | $1,000 | $875 |

✳ *Late Type* - oval trigger guard and steel grip straps.

| N/A | N/A | $3,675 | $2,900 | $2,350 | $1,900 | $1,500 | $1,175 | $950 | $825 | $725 | $625 |

1851 NAVY - .36 cal., 6 shot, 7½ in. octagon barrel and loading lever, blue metal with case-

100%	98%	95%	90%	80%	70%	60%	50%	40%	30%	20%	10%

hardened frame, lever and hammer, one piece walnut finished grips, cylinder scene of Texas Navy battle with Mexico, serial range 1-highest recorded number was 215,348, three barrel addresses 1-74,000 (ADDRESS SAML COLT, NEW YORK CITY), 74,000-101,000 (ADDRESS SAML COLT, HARTFORD, CT.) 101,000-215,348 (ADDRESS COL. SAML COLT, NEW YORK, U.S. AMERICA). Mfg. 1850-1873.

* **First Model** - square back trigger guard, bottom wedge screw, serial range 1-1,250.

| N/A | N/A | $22,575 | $18,475 | $14,875 | $12,375 | $9,385 | $7,700 | $6,300 | $5,200 | $4,400 | $3,400 |

* **Second Model** - square back trigger guard, top wedge screw, serial range 1,250- 4,000.

| N/A | N/A | $14,700 | $10,250 | $8,000 | $6,650 | $5,560 | $4,600 | $3,900 | $3,300 | $2,800 | $2,300 |

* **Third Model** - small round brass trigger guard, serial range 4,200-85,000.

| N/A | N/A | $6,925 | $5,525 | $4,275 | $3,500 | $2,850 | $2,300 | $1,900 | $1,550 | $1,250 | $995 |

* **Fourth Model** - large round brass trigger guard, serial range 85,000-215,348.

| N/A | N/A | $6,175 | $5,025 | $4,135 | $3,275 | $2,650 | $2,125 | $1,750 | $1,425 | $1,175 | $900 |

* **Iron Gripstrap Model** - most often seen in fourth model.

| N/A | N/A | $7,775 | $6,300 | $5,125 | $4,300 | $3,500 | $2,750 | $2,200 | $1,750 | $1,425 | $1,125 |

* **Martially Marked U.S. Navys** - brass or iron gripstrap.

| N/A | N/A | $11,300 | $7,875 | $6,250 | $4,900 | $3,825 | $2,900 | $2,325 | $1,875 | $1,500 | $1,200 |

* **Cut for shoulder stock** - first and second type (like third model Dragoon).

| N/A | N/A | $14,175 | $9,450 | $7,275 | $5,675 | $4,600 | $3,750 | $3,000 | $2,450 | $1,950 | $1,475 |

* **Third Type** - four screw frame.

| N/A | N/A | $9,075 | $7,600 | $6,250 | $5,000 | $3,925 | $3,100 | $2,500 | $2,000 | $1,650 | $1,325 |

51 NAVY LONDON MODEL - basically the same gun as the Hartford piece with London barrel address, with British proof marks in serial range 1-42,000. Mfg. 1853-1857.

* **Early First Model** - serial range below 2000, brass grip straps and small trigger guard.

| N/A | N/A | $7,875 | $6,300 | $5,225 | $4,350 | $3,550 | $2,800 | $2,250 | $1,800 | $1,475 | $1,175 |

* **Late Second Model** - balance of production, large round trigger guard, steel grip straps, all London parts.

| N/A | N/A | $7,275 | $5,900 | $4,925 | $4,100 | $3,350 | $2,575 | $2,000 | $1,650 | $1,375 | $1,100 |

1855 SIDEHAMMER POCKET MODEL (ROOT MODEL) - .28 cal., had 3½ in. octagon barrel, .31 cal. usually had 3½ in. or 4½ in. round barrel. Blue with case hardened lever and hammer, one piece wraparound style walnut grips.

Commonly called the "Root" Model by collectors, manufactured 1855 through 1870. The .28 cal. model serial numbered 1 through approx. 30,000. The .31 cal. round barrel model serial numbered 1 through approx. 14,000. Total production approx. 44,000.

Easily recognizable by its side mounted hammer and cylinder rotation ratchet at rear of frame.

* **Model 1 and 1A** - .28 cal., 3 7/16 in. octagonal bbl., oct. load lever, Indian/cabin cyl. scene, Hartford barrel address. Serial range 1 to 384.

| N/A | N/A | $6,050 | $3,885 | $3,225 | $2,775 | $2,350 | $2,000 | $1,825 | $1,650 | $1,400 | $1,100 |

* **Model 2** - .28 cal., 3½ in. oct. bbl., Indian/cabin cyl. scene, Hartford barrel address with pointed hand. Serial range 476 to 25,000.

| N/A | N/A | $2,250 | $1,400 | $1,075 | $900 | $775 | $665 | $595 | $535 | $485 | $425 |

* **Model 3** - .28 cal., 3½ in. oct. bbl., full fluted cylinder, Hartford barrel address with pointed hand. Serial range 25,001 to 30,000.

| N/A | N/A | $2,275 | $1,450 | $1,100 | $950 | $850 | $750 | $650 | $585 | $535 | $485 |

* **Model 3A** - .31 cal., 3½ in. oct. bbl., full fluted cylinder, Hartford barrel address. Serial range 1 to 1,350.

| N/A | N/A | $2,325 | $1,375 | $1,150 | $995 | $895 | $775 | $675 | $595 | $535 | $485 |

* **Model 4** - .31 cal., 3½ in. oct. bbl., full fluted cylinder, Hartford barrel address. Serial

100%	98%	95%	90%	80%	70%	60%	50%	40%	30%	20%	10%

range 1,351 to 2,400.

| N/A | N/A | $2,325 | $1,375 | $1,150 | $995 | $895 | $775 | $675 | $595 | $535 | $485 |

✳ **Model 5** - .31 cal., 3½ in. round bbl., full fluted cylinder, "COL. COLT NEW- YORK" barrel address. Serial range 2,401 to 8,000.

| N/A | N/A | $2,325 | $1,375 | $1,150 | $995 | $895 | $775 | $675 | $595 | $535 | $485 |

✳ **Model 5A** - .31 cal., 4½ in. round bbl., included in same serial range as Model 5.

| N/A | N/A | $3,675 | $2,200 | $1,825 | $1,400 | $1,225 | $1,075 | $975 | $875 | $775 | $695 |

✳ **Model 6** - .31 cal., 3½ in. round bbl., stage coach hold-up cylinder scene, "COL. COLT NEW- YORK" barrel address. Serial range 8,001 through 11,074.

| N/A | N/A | $2,325 | $1,375 | $1,150 | $995 | $895 | $775 | $675 | $595 | $535 | $485 |

✳ **Model 6A** - .31 cal., 4½ in. round bbl., included in same serial range as Model 6.

| N/A | N/A | $2,325 | $1,375 | $1,150 | $995 | $895 | $775 | $675 | $595 | $535 | $485 |

✳ **Model 7** - .31 cal., 3½ in. round bbl., stage coach hold-up cylinder scene, "COL. COLT NEW- YORK" barrel address. Cylinder pin retained by screw-in cylinder. Serial range 11,075 through 14,000.

| N/A | N/A | $3,375 | $1,925 | $1,400 | $1,225 | $1,125 | $995 | $900 | $800 | $725 | $650 |

✳ **Model 7A** - .31 cal., 4½ in. round bbl., including same cylinder scene, barrel address and serial range as Model 7.

| N/A | N/A | $4,225 | $2,600 | $1,825 | $1,400 | $1,275 | $1,150 | $1,025 | $925 | $825 | $750 |

1860 MODEL ARMY - .44 cal., 6 shot, 7½ and 8 in. round barrels with loading lever, blue metal with case hardened frame, lever and hammer, one piece walnut grips, normally blue steel back strap and brass trigger guard, barrel markings were (ADDRESS SAM COLT, HART-FORD, CT.) on early productions and (ADDRESS COL. SAM COLT, NEW YORK, U.S. AMERICA) on balance, serial range 1-about 200,500, Texas Navy scene on round cylinder model. Mfg. 1860-1873.

✳ **Fluted Cylinder Model** - Fluted Cylinder Model, full length cylinder flutes and no cylinder scene, 7½ or 8 in. barrel, grips of Navy (very rare) or Army size, usually 4 screw frames.

| N/A | N/A | $13,650 | $10,400 | $8,075 | $6,650 | $5,500 | $4,550 | $3,850 | $3,250 | $2,750 | $2,350 |

✳ **Round Cylinder Model** - roll engraved Texas Navy scene, some with early Hartford address, Army grips, four screw frame to about 50,000 range, most were sold to the U.S. Government and will be martially marked.

| N/A | N/A | $10,175 | $7,625 | $6,250 | $5,000 | $3,925 | $3,100 | $2,500 | $2,000 | $1,650 | $1,375 |

✳ **Civilian Model** - same general configurations as Round Cylinder Model, but with 3 screw frame, no shoulder stock cuts and better blue finish than military pieces, late New York barrel address.

| N/A | N/A | $9,975 | $6,950 | $5,600 | $4,525 | $3,600 | $2,825 | $2,275 | $1,850 | $1,500 | $1,225 |

1861 MODEL NAVY - .36 cal., 6 shot, 7½ in. round barrel with loading lever, blue metal with case hardened frame, lever and hammer, silver plated brass grip straps, the barrel address was (ADDRESS COL. SAM COLT, NEW YORK, U.S. AMERICA), serial range 1 - 38,843, cylinder scene of Texas Navy and Mexico Battle, mfg. 1861- 1873.

✳ **Fluted Cylinder Navy** - in serial range 1-100, with fluted cylinder and without rolled cylinder scene.

| N/A | N/A | $28,100 | $20,750 | $16,900 | $13,650 | $10,975 | $8,750 | $7,250 | $6,250 | $5,550 | $4,875 |

✳ **Regular production model**

| N/A | N/A | $11,550 | $8,725 | $6,350 | $5,100 | $4,000 | $3,275 | $2,600 | $2,150 | $1,725 | $1,475 |

✳ **Martially Marked Navys** - will bear the U.S. stamp and inspector's marks, those marked U.S.N. on butt were of a 650 piece order for the Navy.

| N/A | N/A | $13,125 | $9,025 | $6,875 | $5,100 | $4,125 | $3,350 | $2,775 | $2,300 | $1,900 | $1,550 |

✳ **London Marked Navy** - with (ADDRESS COL. COLT, LONDON), for barrel address.

100%	98%	95%	90%	80%	70%	60%	50%	40%	30%	20%	10%
N/A	N/A	$9,925	$7,900	$6,175	$4,925	$3,975	$3,225	$2,675	$2,225	$1,850	$1,475

✳ Shoulder Stock Cut Navy - 4 screw frames in serial range 11,000-14,000, made for third style stock (see Dragoon stocks).

N/A	N/A	$17,325	$11,025	$8,320	$6,700	$5,600	$4,650	$3,950	$3,350	$2,850	$2,375

1862 POLICE MODEL - .36 cal., 5 shot half fluted and rebated cylinder, 4½, 5½, and 6½ in. round barrels (also 3½ in. bbl. but quite rare) and loading lever. Mfg. 1861 to 1873. Serial numbered with Model 1862 Pocket Navy, approx. 28,000 1862 Police Models were produced. Blue with case hardened frame, lever and hammer, grip straps silver plated, one piece walnut grips. Serial range 1 through approx. 47,000. Standard barrel marking "ADDRESS COL. SAML COLT NEW-YORK U.S. AMERICA". "COLTS/PATENT" on left side of frame, "PAT SEPT. 10TH 1850" stamped in cyl. flute.

Many Model 1862 Police and 1862 Pocket Navy revolvers were converted to cartridge with the advent of the metallic cartridge. Consequently these models in their original cap and ball chambering are quite desirable to collectors.

✳ Early Model - "ADDRESS SAM COLT/HARTFORD CT" barrel address, silvered iron grip straps.

N/A	N/A	$10,175	$6,825	$5,300	$4,375	$3,525	$2,750	$2,200	$1,750	$1,375	$1,075

✳ Early Model - same but silvered brass grip straps.

N/A	N/A	$9,450	$6,450	$4,950	$3,975	$3,075	$2,300	$1,875	$1,535	$1,235	$1,000

✳ Standard Production Model - with New York barrel address.

N/A	N/A	$8,400	$4,425	$3,225	$2,475	$2,025	$1,675	$1,400	$1,175	$925	$775

✳ Export Production Model - with "L" below serial numbers (for export to England), steel grip straps. Most often but not always bearing British proofs.

N/A	N/A	$8,925	$4,700	$3,450	$2,675	$2,175	$1,810	$1,525	$1,275	$1,050	$875

✳ London Marked Model - similar to above, except with "ADDRESS, COL. COLT/LONDON" address on barrel.

N/A	N/A	$12,075	$8,925	$6,750	$5,250	$4,125	$3,250	$2,750	$2,400	$2,150	$1,800

1862 POCKET MODEL NAVY - .36 cal., 5 shot rebated cylinder, 4½ in., 5½ in., and 6½ in. octagonal barrels with loading lever. Mfg. 1861 to 1873. Serial numbered with Model 1862 Police Model, approx. 19,000 Model 1862 Pocket Navy Revolvers produced. Blue with case hardened frame, lever and hammer, grip straps silver plated brass, one piece walnut grips. Serial range 1 through approx. 47,000. Standard barrel markings "ADDRESS COL. SAML COLT NEW-YORK U.S. AMERICA". "COLTS/ PATENT" on left side of frame, stage coach hold-up scene on cylinder.

Known to collectors for many years as the Model 1853, this model has finally been correctly identified through diligent combing of factory ledgers.

Because of being produced during the advent of the metallic cartridge, the number remaining in the original cap and ball configuration is rather few; scarce with any serial number, but particularly so in numbers over approx. 19,800.

✳ Standard Model - 4½, 5½ and 6½ barrel lengths.

N/A	N/A	$8,925	$6,475	$4,950	$3,975	$3,075	$2,300	$1,875	$1,535	$1,235	$1,000

✳ Export Production Model - with "L" below serial numbers (for export to England), steel grip straps. Often found with British proofs.

N/A	N/A	$9,450	$7,875	$6,250	$4,900	$3,850	$3,025	$2,475	$2,000	$1,650	$1,375

✳ London Marked Model - similar to above but "ADDRESS COL. COLT/LONDON" address on barrel.

N/A	N/A	$14,900	$11,200	$8,575	$6,750	$5,625	$4,650	$3,950	$3,350	$2,850	$2,375

REVOLVERS: PERCUSSION CONVERSIONS

100%	98%	95%	90%	80%	70%	60%	50%	40%	30%	20%	10%

Colt Thuer Conversions

COLT THUER CONVERSIONS (c. 1868-1872)- less than 5,000 produced in all models. This was Colt's first commercial attempt at converting percussion revolvers to fire fixed ammo. Standard features: usually threaded inside rammer for a Thuer loading tool, a hardened flat face on hammer, deepened loading cutout on right side of lug, Thuer ring and back of cylinder have matching assembly numbers. Beware of fakes! Only non-experimental Colt models are listed. Rarity by barrel length will not be considered here. Serial numbers are often missing on cylinder. .31, .36 and .44 CF cal.

Prices for Colt Conversions reflect values for blue and case hardened examples. Nickel plated specimens are rarely seen, but typically sell for 20%-40% less than blue finish.

Any defects, excessive wear, or dulled blue will affect value. Nickeled conversions that have lost their translucence (become cloudy) should be discounted more than usual 20%-40% from blue and case hardened examples- especially on near mint to mint specimens.

* *1849 Pocket*

$25,000 $22,500 $17,500 $15,000 $13,000 $11,000 $9,500 $8,500 $7,500 $6,750 $6,000 $5,000

* *1851 Navy*

$23,000 $21,000 $16,000 $14,000 $12,000 $10,000 $8,500 $7,750 $7,000 $6,500 $5,750 $4,750

* *1860 Army* - the most common Thuer, but popular because it's a large frame model.

$27,000 $24,000 $19,000 $16,000 $14,000 $12,000 $11,000 $10,000 $9,500 $8,500 $7,500 $6,500

* *1861 Navy*

$25,000 $22,500 $19,000 $16,000 $14,000 $11,000 $9,500 $8,500 $7,500 $6,700 $6,000 $5,000

* *1862 Police*

$20,000 $18,000 $15,000 $13,000 $11,000 $8,500 $7,500 $6,750 $6,000 $5,500 $5,000 $4,500

* *1862 Pocket Navy*

$20,000 $18,000 $15,000 $13,000 $11,000 $8,500 $7,500 $6,750 $6,000 $5,500 $5,000 $4,500

Richards Conversions: All Variations

RICHARDS CONVERSION, COLT 1860 ARMY REVOLVER - .44 CF cal., produced c. 1870s, special machining to barrel and breech of cylinder for conversion to a cartridge weapon. Produced in two serial ranges: one numbered under 10,000 and a separate group generally in the 190,000 to 200,000 range.

* *1860 Army First Model Richards* - quick ID: integral rear sight on breech plate. Floating firing pin in breechplate. Front edge of barrel lug is same as 1860 percussion Army. Breechplate extends over rear edge of cylinder.

$24,000 $20,000 $16,000 $13,000 $9,000 $7,000 $6,000 $5,250 $4,500 $4,000 $3,500 $3,000

* *1860 Army Second Model Richards* - quick ID: standard Richards type barrel. A space between face of conversion ring and rear of cylinder when viewed from the side. No integral sight on breechplate, cut away at top allowing hammer to directly strike the cartridge.

$24,000 $22,000 $17,000 $14,500 $9,500 $7,500 $6,500 $6,000 $5,250 $4,500 $4,000 $3,500

* *1860 Army Twelve Stop Cylinder Variation Richards* - quick ID: generally the same as standard model Richards except cylinder has extra "safety" notches between the locking notches. This variation was usually produced in the 100-300, 1000-1700 and 200,000 serial ranges. Cylinder locking notches over chambers often broken through. Watch for alterations.

$27,500 $24,000 $19,000 $15,000 $12,500 $8,500 $7,000 $6,500 $6,000 $5,500 $5,000 $4,500

* *1860 Army U.S. Marked Richards* - quick ID: generally the same as 1st Model Richards (many minor differences). Has "U.S." stamped on left barrel lug and "A" (Ainsworth) inspector marks in several places. They are converted 1860 percussion Armys, so origi-

100%	98%	95%	90%	80%	70%	60%	50%	40%	30%	20%	10%

nal numbers are typically in 23,000-144,000 range plus a second set of assembly numbers. Oiled grips, military soft blue finish.

| $30,000 | $27,000 | $22,500 | $17,500 | $13,000 | $9,500 | $7,750 | $7,000 | $6,500 | $6,000 | $5,500 | $4,500 |

Richards-Mason Conversions: All Variations

1860 ARMY RICHARDS-MASON - .44 CF cal., overall, much rarer than Richards Army Conversions. C. 1870s, approximately 2100 produced. A rare variation has an 1860 Army rebated cylinder and a barrel with a lug shaped similar to 1861 Navy Conversion.

* ✳ *1860 Army Richards-Mason* - quick ID: breechplate without integral rear sight, cutout at top so hammer can strike primer directly. A space can be seen between breechplate and rear of cylinder. Rear of lug is a vertical line instead of the bullet shape cutout seen on Richards models.

| $25,000 | $20,000 | $15,000 | $12,500 | $9,000 | $8,000 | $7,500 | $7,000 | $6,250 | $5,500 | $4,500 | $3,750 |

1851 NAVY RICHARDS-MASON - .38 CF and RF cal., c. 1870s. Produced in two different serial ranges. Has improved Richards-Mason breechplate that is flush with diameter of recoil shield. Difficult to locate in prime condition.

* ✳ *1851 Navy Civilian Model Richards-Mason* - quick ID: Richards-Mason breechplate which is same diameter as recoil shield, octagon barrel, mirrored civilian blue. Nickel finish commonly seen.

| $11,000 | $10,000 | $7,500 | $6,500 | $5,500 | $4,500 | $4,000 | $3,500 | $3,000 | $2,500 | $2,000 | $1,500 |

* ✳ *1851 U.S. Navy Richards-Mason* - quick ID: Richards-Mason breechplate, oiled grips, soft blue military finish, produced in US. percussion range of 40,000-90,000 ranges. Inconsistent "U.S.N." and other inspector markings. Iron straps, "U.S." on frame.

| $15,000 | $13,000 | $10,000 | $7,500 | $6,000 | $5,000 | $4,500 | $4,000 | $3,500 | $3,000 | $2,250 | $1,750 |

1861 NAVY RICHARDS-MASON - produced in civilian and military versions. C. 1870s, made in RF and CF cal. in two serial ranges. Round 7½ in. barrel.

* ✳ *1861 Navy Civilian Model Richards-Mason* - quick ID: Richards-Mason breechplate, round 7½ in. barrel with attached ejector housing, unrebated cylinder. When blue, has a commercial high gloss finish.

| $13,000 | $11,000 | $8,500 | $6,500 | $4,750 | $4,250 | $3,750 | $3,400 | $3,000 | $2,400 | $2,000 | $1,500 |

* ✳ *1861 Navy U.S. Navy Richards-Mason* - soft military blue finish, oiled grips, converted from percussion U.S. Navy revolvers, inconsistent military markings, centerfire, set of extra serial numbers often seen on cylinder.

| $17,500 | $15,000 | $11,000 | $8,500 | $5,500 | $5,000 | $4,500 | $4,000 | $3,500 | $3,000 | $2,500 | $2,000 |

COLT 1862 POLICE & POCKET NAVY RICHARDS-MASON CONVERSIONS (c. 1870s) - .38 RF and CF cal., parts for 1862 Police, 1862 Pocket Navy, as well as 1849 Pockets are often intermixed. As parts bins were depleted, Colt used whatever components that would fit, resulting in a tremendous amount of minor variations. Some barrels were converted from percussion models while others were newly made as cartridge barrels without rammer plugs and loading slots in the lug. There are three different serial ranges (1849, 1862 Police/Pocket Navy, Conversion). 3½ to 6½ in. barrels, again not all features available on all models.

Nickel plated conversions will bring 20%- 40% less than blue and case hardened specimens.

* ✳ *4½ in. Octagon Barrel Model* - quick ID: 4½ in. octagon barrel without ejector. Rebated Pocket Navy Cylinder.

| $7,000 | $6,000 | $5,000 | $4,000 | $3,000 | $2,500 | $1,750 | $1,350 | $1,150 | $950 | $750 | $650 |

* ✳ *Round (Percussion) Barrel Pocket Navy with Ejector* - quick ID: plug in rammer slot; ejector housing, loading cutout in right side of lug, barrel remachined from Pocket Navy percussion barrel, Pocket Navy rebated cylinder. Similar appearance to cartridge barrel

100%	98%	95%	90%	80%	70%	60%	50%	40%	30%	20%	10%

variation.

$7,250 $6,250 $5,250 $4,250 $3,000 $2,500 $2,000 $1,750 $1,500 $1,200 $1,000 $850

1862 POLICE AND POCKET NAVY CONVERSION - 4½, 5½, or 6½ in. barrels with 1862 Police percussion profile and added ejector housing. Has rebated Pocket Navy cylinder or rarer half fluted 1862 Police cylinder. 6½ in. barrel will bring a premium.

* ***1862 Police/Pocket Navy with Rebated Pocket Navy Cylinder***- quick ID: 1862 Police profile barrel with ejector housing and rebated 1862 Pocket Navy cylinder.

$7,500 $6,500 $4,500 $4,000 $2,750 $2,250 $1,750 $1,400 $1,100 $900 $650 $550

* ***1862 Police/Pocket Navy with Half Fluted Cylinder***- quick ID: 1862 Police profile barrel with ejector housing and ½ fluted Police cylinder.

$9,000 $7,500 $5,000 $4,500 $3,250 $2,750 $2,000 $1,600 $1,300 $1,100 $850 $700

Conversions with Round Cartridge Barrel

ROUND CARTRIDGE BARREL WITH EJECTOR - .38 RF and CF cal. 4½, 5½, or 6½ in. barrels produced as a cartridge component without rammer slots and lug cutouts inherent to a percussion barrel.

* ***1862 Pocket Navy Round Cartridge Barrel***- quick ID: much shorter lug area than similar model converted from percussion barrel. No slots or loading cutouts on barrel. With ejector housing and Pocket Navy rebated cylinder. Often called the "Baby Open Top". Very scarce.

$9,500 $7,250 $5,750 $5,000 $4,250 $3,250 $2,800 $2,500 $2,000 $1,750 $1,450 $1,250

3½ IN. ROUND CARTRIDGE BARREL CONVERSION - .38 RF or CF cal., sometimes seen with serial numbers that are from 1849 Pocket Model (300,000 range). Barrel newly made for cartridges, not converted from a percussion barrel.

* ***3½ in. Round Cartridge Barrel*** - quick ID: only type conversion with 3½ in. barrel. No ejector, no loading lever slot or loading cutout in lug area. Pocket Navy rebated cylinder.

$5,000 $4,000 $2,400 $1,800 $1,400 $1,100 $975 $875 $800 $700 $600 $500

REVOLVERS: "OPEN TOP" MODELS

If possible, it is advisable to procure a factory letter before buying/selling this Open Top Revolver. These watermarked letters are available by writing Colt Firearms in Hartford, CT, with a charge of $200 per serial number (if they can research it). Include your name and address, Colt model name, serial number, and check to: COLT HISTORIAN, P.O. Box 1868, Hartford, CT 06101. Please allow 4-6 weeks for a response.

1871-72 OPEN TOP MODEL RIMFIRE - .44 cal. rimfire, 6 shot, 7½ in. barrel, without frame topstrap, blue metal with casehardened hammer, serial range 1-approx. 7000, barrel address (ADDRESS COL. SAM COLT, NEW YORK, U.S. AMERICA), forerunner of the single action Army, quite desirable. Mfg. 1871-1872.

Add 20% for blue finish on models listed below.

* ***Regular Production Model*** - 7½ in. barrel, New York address, Navy grips.

N/A N/A $27,500 $22,750 $18,500 $15,000 $12,750 $8,750 $6,750 $6,000 $5,300 $4,850

* ***Regular Production*** - with Army grips.

N/A N/A $24,000 $18,750 $15,000 $12,500 $10,250 $7,000 $5,750 $5,000 $4,450 $4,250

* ***Late Production*** - with address (COLT PT. F. A. MANUFACTURING CO., HARTFORD, CT., U.S.A.).

N/A N/A $21,000 $16,000 $13,000 $10,750 $7,500 $6,000 $5,200 $4,650 $4,150 $3,700

100%	98%	95%	90%	80%	70%	60%	50%	40%	30%	20%	10%

Add 40% for models with 8 in. barrel or COLTS/PATENT frame markings.

REVOLVERS: PERCUSSION, 2ND & 3RD GENERATION BLACK POWDER SERIES

To learn more about the 2nd & 3rd Generation Percussion Black Powder Series, it is recommended to purchase *Colt Black Powder Reproductions & Replicas - A Collector's & Shooter's Guide* and the 2nd Edition *Blue Book of Modern Black Powder Values* by Dennis A. Adler. This new 2nd Edition contains more information on the Colt 2nd Generation Black Powder Series than anything else previously published. These definitive books are available from Blue Book Publications, Inc. To order, please call, fax, email, or use the insert order card located in this book.

DERRINGERS

FIRST MODEL DERRINGER - .41 rimfire cal., single shot, 2½ in. barrel, scroll engraving standard, blue, nickel, or silver plated barrel, downward pivoting barrel, no grips, serial numbered 1-6,500. Mfg. approx. 1870-1890.

$3,325	$2,500	$2,150	$1,925	$1,700	$1,450	$1,275	$1,075	$875	$750	$675	$650

SECOND MODEL DERRINGER - .41 rimfire or centerfire cal., single shot, 2½ in. barrel, scroll engraving standard, blue, nickel, or silver plated barrel, downward pivoting barrel, checkered and varnished walnut grips, "No 2" marked on top of barrel, serial numbered 1-9,000. Mfg. approx. 1870-1890.

$1,775	$1,475	$1,275	$1,100	$950	$850	$750	$650	$585	$535	$500	$475

Add 100% for .41 centerfire cal.

THIRD MODEL DERRINGER (THUER MODEL) - .41 rimfire or centerfire (rare) cal., single shot, side pivoting 2½ in. barrel, varnished walnut grips, blue barrels, bronze frames were either nickel or silver plated, engraving optional, Colt-barrel address, spur trigger, serial numbered approx. 1-45,000. Mfg. approx. 1875-1910.

$1,500	$1,275	$950	$825	$725	$625	$550	$495	$450	$415	$385	$360

Add 30% - 50% for .41 centerfire cal. Early models are worth considerably more.

Grading	100%	98%	95%	90%	80%	70%	60%

FOURTH MODEL DERRINGER (FIRING) - .22 Short cal., single shot similar in appearance to the 3rd Model, 2½ in. barrel, approx. 112,000 mfg. between 1959-1963 with either D or N suffix. A few were put in books (sometimes as pairs), picture frames, penholders, bookends, etc. (these will command premiums).

	100%	98%	95%
Gun only	$100	$85	$65
Gun w/accessories	$375	$275	$175

✳ *Fourth Model Derringer (non-firing)* - this variation was normally used for decoration and is normally encountered in books, picture frames, penholders, bookends, etc. Values below assume all factory materials intact - if not, prices are reduced to $50-$75 for gun only.

	100%	98%	95%
	$375	$250	$150

Non-firing guns usually do not have the barrel notch, thus preventing the hammer from striking the cartridge.

LORD DERRINGER - .22 Short cal. only, side pivoting Thuer action, gold plated with black chrome barrel and walnut grips. Mfg. approx. 1959-1963 by Colt, cased.

	100%	98%	95%
	$175	$140	$100

LADY DERRINGER - .22 Short cal. only, side pivoting Thuer action, full gold plated finish with pearlite grips. Mfg. approx. 1959-1963 by Colt, cased.

	100%	98%	95%
	$175	$140	$100

Grading	100%	98%	95%	90%	80%	70%	60%

LORD & LADY CASED SET - one each of the Lord & Lady derringers or combinations, consecutive serial numbers.

	$495	$375	$275

LADY CASED SET - cased pair of Lady Derringers.

	$495	$375	$275

LORD CASED SET - cased pair of Lord Derringers.

	$495	$375	$275

BOOKCASE DERRINGER PAIR - .22 Short cal., consecutively numbered derringers with synthetic ivory grips and nickel finish, cased inside unique hard cover "Colt Derringers" labeled book with red velvet lining, limited mfg. in early '60s.

	$350	$275	$200

100%	98%	95%	90%	80%	70%	60%	50%	40%	30%	20%	10%

REVOLVERS: POCKET MODELS

If possible, it is advisable to procure a factory letter before buying/selling this variation (open top only). These water marked letters are available by writing Colt Firearms in Hartford, CT, with a charge of $100 per serial number (if they can research it). Include your name and address, Colt model name, serial number, and check to: COLT HISTORIAN, P.O. Box 1868, Hartford, CT 06101. Please allow 4- 6 weeks for a response.

CLOVERLEAF HOUSE PISTOL - .41 Short or L rimfire cal., cloverleaf configured 4 shot cylinder, spur trigger, 1½ or 3 in. barrel, blue or nickel plated, approx. 7,500 mfg. in ser. no. range 1-8,300 during 1871-1876.

$2,550	$2,300	$1,850	$1,600	$1,400	$1,200	$1,100	$925	$825	$725	$650	$600

Add 30% for blue finish.

Add 80% for 1½ in. barrel.

This model is sometimes referred to as the Jim Fisk model, as he was murdered by Edward Stokes with a Cloverleaf.

٭ 5-shot Cloverleaf - similar to 4-shot model, except has round 5-shot cylinder and 2 5/8 in. barrel only, approx. 2,500 mfg. in ser. no. range 6,160-9,950 during 1871- 1876.

$2,175	$1,900	$1,600	$1,325	$1,150	$975	$850	$750	$650	$600	$550	$500

OPEN TOP REVOLVER (OLD LINE) - .22 Short or L rimfire cal., 2 3/8 or 2 7/8 in. barrel, without topstrap on frame, with or without integral ejector, blue or nickel plated, varnished walnut grips, approx. 114,200 mfg. 1871-1877.

$1,450	$1,250	$1,150	$950	$850	$750	$700	$600	$550	$450	$375	$325

Add 30% for blue finish.

Add 120% for Early Model with ejector and high hammer spur.

REVOLVERS: NEW LINE SERIES & VARIATIONS

If possible, it is advisable to procure a factory letter before buying/selling New Line Revolvers. These water marked letters are available by writing Colt Firearms in Hartford, CT, with a charge of $100 per serial number (if they can research it). Include your name and address, Colt model name, serial number, and check to: COLT HISTORIAN, P.O. Box 1868, Hartford, CT 06101. Please allow 4-6 weeks for a response.

Add 30% for blue finish on models listed below.

1ST MODEL - .22, .30, .32, .38, or .41 cal. rim and centerfire, mfg. 1873-1876, 7 (.22 cal. only) or 5 shot, short cylinder flutes, cylinder stop slots cut on exterior of cylinder, 1¾, 2¼, or 4 in. barrel, full nickel or blue/case hardened finish, spur trigger, many thousands mfg. 1873-1884.

100%	98%	95%	90%	80%	70%	60%	50%	40%	30%	20%	10%
$1,250	$1,050	$925	$825	$750	$675	$600	$550	$450	$350	$300	$250

2ND MODEL - similar to 1st Model, except has longer cylinder flutes and cylinder stop slots are on the back of cylinder, may or may not have loading gate. Mfg. 1876-1884.

$1,125	$995	$875	$800	$725	$650	$575	$500	$400	$325	$275	$235

Caliber rarity on both models from highest mfg. to lowest is: .22, .32, .30, .41, and .38.

NEW HOUSE MODEL - .38 or .41 cal. centerfire, 5 shot, 2¼ in. barrel, spur trigger, checkered hard rubber grips. Approx. 4,000 mfg. 1880-1886 starting at ser. no. 10,300.

$1,475	$1,150	$1,000	$875	$775	$675	$600	$485	$425	$360	$325	$310

NEW POLICE MODEL - .32, .38, or .41 cal. centerfire, 5 shot, 2¼, 4½, 5, or 6 in. barrel, spur trigger, with or without ejector, stamped or etched "NEW POLICE" on barrel. Approx. 4,000 mfg. 1882-1886.

$1,800	$1,525	$1,275	$1,100	$925	$800	$725	$650	$600	$550	$525	$495

REVOLVERS: SAA, 1873-1940 MFG. (SER. NOS. 1 - 357,000)

The author wishes to express thanks to Charles Layson for making the following information available and reformatting the Colt 1st Generation SAA section.

The Colt SAA was produced in 36 calibers with many special order features or combinations available directly from the Colt factory. These factory special order features can greatly enhance the value of the revolver. The Single Action Colt, or "Peacemaker", as it is often called, is undoubtedly the most collectible handgun in the world, and as such, can command very high prices.

It is prudent to secure several professional opinions as to originality when contemplating an expensive purchase, since many SAAs have been altered or "improved" over the decades. Before he died, Keith Cochran, author of the *Colt Peacemaker Encyclopedia, Vol. II*, guesstimated that over ½ of all pre-WWII revolvers were no longer factory original. Because of this, it is advisable to procure a factory letter when buying or selling older or recently manufactured Colt Single Actions (hence guaranteeing original configuration and value credibility). These watermarked letters are based on the original factory handwritten shipping ledgers and are available by writing Colt Firearms in Hartford, CT, with a charge of $100 per serial number. While not totally infallible, these letters are normally very accurate. If Colt cannot provide you with proper documentation after conducting research, they will issue a $50 refund. The charge is $200+ per custom engraved gun - see the Trademark Index for the address. Include your name and address, Colt model name, serial number, and check to: COLT HISTORIAN, P.O. BOX 1868, HARTFORD, CT 06144-1868. Please allow 12-15 weeks for proper response. In addition, phone service SAA configuration validation is also provided on a premium basis on first generation SAAs ONLY (ser. no. range 354,000 - 357,859 cannot be researched) to assist in possible purchases of a critical nature. Fees for this phone service are $150 per gun ($25 for date of manufacture only) for 1st Generation SAA pistols, payable by Visa or MasterCard - letter is included for this price. The phone number is 860-244-1343 and ask for the Historical Dept. between the hours of 1-4 P.M. EST.

Values shown below are for guns without special order features. Factory engraving, ivory grips, very rare special order barrel lengths, and special finishes would add considerably to the values shown below. One final word on single action Colts: Black Powder Colts (pre 165,000 serial range) should be scrutinized carefully for potential problems, including refinishing (including aging), replacement parts, restamped serial numbers, and added, non-factory special order features. This makes a major difference in pricing the SAA, as a genuine, original SAA's price tag will vary immensely from a non-original, made-up "parts gun".

SAA - 1ST GENERATION CIVILIAN/COMMERCIAL (MFG. 1873-1940)

SINGLE ACTION ARMY - STANDARD MFG. - over 30 cals., six shot single action revolver, 4¾, 5½, or 7½ in. standard barrel lengths – 5½ and 7½ have the one-line barrel address, 4¾ has a two-line barrel address, blue with color case hardened frame or full nickel finish stan-

100%	98%	95%	90%	80%	70%	60%	50%	40%	30%	20%	10%

dard, one-piece, varnished walnut grips standard until 1882, when black, gutta percha (hard rubber) grips were introduced with eagle motif. Eagle-less grips became standard circa 1893. One-piece wood available upon request until approx. 1903. Rarely seen, two-piece, oil finished, walnut available thereafter. Mfg. 1873-1940.

* **Pinch Frame SAA (ser. no. range 1-160)** - .45 LC cal., 7½ in. barrel, frame pinched to form rear sight. Mfg. 1873.

N/A	N/A	N/A	$65,000	$60,000	$55,000	$47,500	$42,000	$37,000	$32,000	$26,000	$20,000

Be aware! There are many counterfeits in this variation.

* **Early Black Powder SAA (ser. no. range 160-22,000)** - .45 LC cal., 7½ in. barrel standard, blue or nickel finish, distinctive italic script style lettering used in barrel address, 5½ in. barrels introduced in 1875, ser. nos. shared with early martial production. Mfg. 1873-1876.

N/A	$35,000	$32,000	$28,000	$22,000	$16,000	$14,000	$12,000	$10,000	$8,000	$6,000	$4,000

Subtract 40% for nickel finish.

* **Intermediate Black Powder SAA (ser. no. range 22,000-130,000)** - .44-40 WCF (.44 WCF) cal. introduced in ser. no. range 41,000 (1878) as a companion to the Winchester 1873 rifle, other calibers follow, 4¾ or 5½ in. barrel became popular during this era, at appox. 60,000 ser. no. range the round ejector head was changed to an oval shape. During this same time period, Colt gradually abandoned the practice of placing the ser. nos. on the cylinders and barrels of civilian revolvers. Cylinders are often found unnumbered after ser. no. 80,000, especially on nickel plated guns, and barrels are seldom numbered after ser. no. 100,000. Mfg. 1876-1890.

N/A	$30,000	$25,000	$22,000	$18,000	$16,000	$12,000	$10,000	$8,000	$6,000	$4,000	$2,800

Subtract 30% for nickel finish.
Add 25% for original box.
Add 10% for 4¾ in. barrel.

* **Late Black Powder SAA (ser. no. range 130,000-165,000)** - three line patent date format changes to two line, circled rampant colt stamped on frame. Mfg. 1890- 1896.

N/A	$22,000	$19,000	$15,000	$11,000	$9,000	$7,500	$6,700	$6,000	$4,500	$3,500	$2,200

Subtract 20% for nickel finish.
Add 25% for original box.
Add 10% for 4¾ in. barrel.
Add 20% for one-piece wood or eagle grips.

* **Early Smokeless Powder SAA (Ser. no. range 165,000-300,000)** - several important physical characteristics were changed during this transition period. Most notably, in 1896 the vertical screw retaining the cylinder pin was eliminated in favor of the horizontal latch. This was similar to what had already been used on the double action models since 1877. The knurling pattern on the hammer spur began a two step revision in 1906. Although Colt advertised their improved smokeless powder single action as early as 1897, they did not add the "VP" proofmark (verified proof, Colt's guarantee for smokeless powder use) to the trigger guard until 1904. Also, the company continued to use black powder rifling (wide grooves and narrow lands) and black powder front sights (small and low) until approx. 1911, when inventories were depleted. While the highest production figures were reached during this period, quality did not suffer. Many collectors feel that the polish, fit, and finish work performed during this 12 year span was at least as good, if not better, than before or since this period. Mfg. 1896-1908.

N/A	$12,000	$9,000	$7,000	$5,700	$4,900	$4,200	$3,700	$3,200	$2,500	$2,000	$1,600

Subtract 10% for nickel finish.

100%	98%	95%	90%	80%	70%	60%	50%	40%	30%	20%	10%

Add 20% for original box.
Add 25% for checkered walnut grips w/o medallions.
Add 20% for pre-1900 period mfg.

* ***Intermediate Smokeless Powder SAA (ser. no. range 300,000-339,000)*** - transitional changes to front sight and rifling were completed by 1914, the Bisley model was discontinued, the first Colt medallions were found in pearl and ivory grips starting in 1909, the new .44 Special caliber was introduced, the method of bluing was changed, WWI comes and goes, and SAA sales began to decline. 1920 is significant to Colt SAA collectors since this was the year the company completed the relocation of the serial numbers. Those on the trigger guard and backstrap were moved under the grips beginning in the late 338,000 ser. no. range (1919), leaving only the ser. no. on the frame visible. This brought to a close the original ser. no. stamping location which began with the percussion revolvers. Many collectors regard this as the end of the "cowboy" period. Mfg. 1908-1920.

N/A	$9,000	$7,500	$5,700	$4,500	$3,800	$3,200	$2,700	$2,200	$1,900	$1,600	$1,400

Add 15% for original box.
Add 15% for smooth, two-piece walnut grips.
Add 25% for checkered, varnished walnut grips with deep set medallions.

* ***Late Smokeless Powder SAA (ser. no. range 339,000-357,000)*** - complete ser. no. visible only on frame, many cylinders are stamped at rear with the last two digits of ser. no., caliber marking on side of barrel was changed in 1928 to "Colt Single Action Army", followed by caliber, finish on hammer was changed from case hardening to blue with polished sides in 1935, and "V" notch rear sight was replaced with square groove to match wider front sight configuration during 1930. Mfg. 1920-1940.

$7,800	$6,700	$5,500	$4,200	$3,700	$3,200	$2,700	$2,200	$1,800	$1,600	$1,400	$1,200

Add 15% for original box.
Add 20% for checkered, oil finished grips with flush medallions, post-1923.
Add 25% for checkered, varnished grips, pre-1924.

SAA 1ST GENERATION COMMERCIAL, NON-STANDARD MFG.

SINGLE ACTION ARMY, NON-STANDARD MFG. - throughout the 1873-1940 period of production, Colt manufactured several distinct types or configurations of SAAs that varied from the standard and therefore, have special significance to the collector.

* ***.22 Rimfire SAA*** - 5½ or 7½ in. barrel, both blue and nickel finishes, mfg. in two distinct runs, slightly less than 100 converted from unsold .44 rimfire revolvers on hand in the late 1880s, and in 1891, approx. 20 were mfg. as new guns.

N/A	N/A	$25,000	$18,000	$16,000	$14,500	$12,500	$11,000	$10,000	$8,500	$7,500	$6,500

Subtract 10% for those converted from .44 rimfire.

* ***.44 Rimfire SAA*** - .44 Henry rimfire cal., 7½ in. barrel, most were shipped to Mexico and saw hard use, rare with any condition remaining, serial numbered in their own range, 1-1,863. Mfg. 1875-1880.

N/A	N/A	N/A	$30,000	$25,000	$18,000	$15,000	$13,500	$12,500	$11,000	$9,500	$8,000

Beware! Many have been found with cut and/or stretched barrels.

* ***Buntline Special Model SAA*** - .45 LC cal., 12 or 16 in. non-standard barrel, rear adj. sight, long hammer screw for attachment of shoulder stock, very rare.

N/A	N/A	$135,000	$120,000	$100,000	$85,000	$75,000	$60,000	$50,000	$42,000	$35,000	$28,000

It is believed only 28 were produced in the 28,800 ser. no. range. Although other standard frame SAAs were mfg. with barrels over 7 ½ in. long, and these will command higher than normal prices.

100%	98%	95%	90%	80%	70%	60%	50%	40%	30%	20%	10%

✳ Etched Panel .44-40 SAA - during 1878, soon after Colt began offering the .44 WCF cal., the new model nomenclature was changed to "Frontier Model". This may have been changed due to some persuasion from one of Colt's largest wholesalers, B. Kittredge & Co., of Cincinatti, OH. Kittredge had already begun advertising the .45 as the "Peacemaker" in 1876. Starting in the 41,000 ser. no. range, an acid etching process was used to mark the barrels "COLT FRONTIER SIX SHOOTER". Barrels so marked were continued until approx. the 129,000 ser. no. range (circa 1890).

	100%	98%	95%	90%	80%	70%	60%	50%	40%	30%	20%
N/A	$35,000	$28,000	$21,000	$16,000	$13,500	$11,000	$9,000	$7,500	$6,200	$5,000	$4,000

Subtract 40% for nickel finish.

This variation continues to be very sought after amongst Colt SAA collectors. Beware of re-etched barrel logos.

✳ Sheriff's Model SAA1 - .44-40 WCF or .45 LC cal., 2½, 3, 4, 4¾ (rare) or 7½ (rare) in. barrel, configuration denotes barrel w/o ejector rod housing. Mfg. throughout production until 1927.

	100%	98%	95%	90%	80%	70%	60%	50%	40%	30%	20%
N/A	$40,000	$35,000	$28,000	$23,000	$18,000	$16,000	$14,000	$12,000	$10,000	$8,000	$7,000

Beware of fakes!

✳ Flat-top Target Model SAA - various cals. from .22 to .476 Eley, 7½ in. barrel, all blue finish, two-piece smooth walnut or rubber grips standard, occasionally with checkered walnut. Approx. 925 mfg. 1888-1896.

	100%	98%	95%	90%	80%	70%	60%	50%	40%	30%	20%
N/A	$20,000	$18,000	$15,000	$12,000	$10,000	$8,000	$7,000	$6,000	$5,000	$4,000	$3,000

While rare, this model has limited collector appeal.

✳ Long Flute Series SAA - .32 WCF, .38 WCF, .41 LC, .44 S&W Spl., or .45 LC cal., during 1913, Colt decided to make use of approx. 1,500 DA model cylinders remaining in inventory. Since it was necessary to add a bolt lock notch and lead-in on these longer flute cylinders, they looked ahead of current production and blocked off ser. nos. 330,000-331,480 for this special treatment. Shipped 1913-1915.

According to Hull & Radcliffe, whose survey includes 114 long flutes, no .44 WCF long flutes have been found. Quite possibly, the true number of long flutes mfg. slightly exceeds 1,500, and while rare, sell for only 5%-10% more than other SAAs of this period.

✳ Pre-war parts/Post-war Mfg. SAAs - .30 Carbine, .357 Mag., .38 Spl., .44 Spl., .44-40 WCF, or .45 LC cal., 5½ in. barrel is the most common, as is blue barrel with case colors on frame, nickel finish is rare, many given as gifts to dignitaries and retiring Colt employees, shipping cartons were both brown and black, 338 SAAs were assembled from pre-war parts and shipped 1947-1961.

Subtract 10%-20% from Late Smokeless Powder SAA values.

These SAAs shipped post-war are usually encountered in 95%+ condition.

✳ Factory Engraved SAAs - slightly less than 1% (approx. 3,200) SAAs are thought to have been engraved at the factory or elsewhere by authority from Colt 1873-1940. Colt offered 3 basic grades of engraving and since many of these guns carried special inscriptions, initials, grips, etc., the value ranges are very wide. Factory engraved black powder SAAs typically sell in the $2,500 - $50,000 range, while factory engraved smokeless powder models usually peak in the $25,000 range. Very special or one-of-a-kind pieces, such as the 5 known "panel" engraved guns may bring upward of $300,000, depending on conditions and particulars. The Colt Historical Dept. can document most factory work.

✳ Non-factory Engraved SAAs - value depends upon when and where the engraving was done. Early "New York" or "dealer" engraved guns done outside the factory were usually shipped from Colt in the "soft" or w/o finish. The majority of these were done in the early 1880s, and condition being equal, are generally priced at 50%-75% of factory

100%	98%	95%	90%	80%	70%	60%	50%	40%	30%	20%	10%

original specimens. Later guns, well done by a known contemporary artist, are usually priced by adding the values of the gun and the cost of engraving. Poor execution may actually lower the value of a plain, but original gun, as much as refinishing would. Here again, a factory letter can make a big difference. The notation of "soft" in the finish column is almost as desirable as the word "engraved", since the large wholesalers in the northeast used many of the same engravers as Colt.

* ❋ ***Bisley Model SAA***- features more curved and longer grip strap, smaller hammer raked backward, this model was designed with the target shooter in mind, and named after Bisley, England, location of the international shooting matches during the late 19th and early 20th century. Approx. 45,000 were mfg. 1894-1913.

N/A	$7,500	$6,000	$4,500	$3,200	$2,800	$2,300	$2,000	$1,800	$1,500	$1,200	$1,000

* ❋ ***Flat-top Target Bisley SAA***- all standard SAA cals., similar to the Flat-top SAA, usually found with 7½ in. barrel with all blue finish, two-piece walnut or rubber grips. 976 mfg. 1894-1913.

N/A	$11,250	$9,000	$6,750	$4,800	$4,200	$3,450	$3,000	$2,700	$2,250	$1,800	$1,500

SAA U.S. MILITARY, MFG. 1873 - 1903

Since many of the military models listed below are frequently encountered with no original finish remaining, prices for original no condition specimens will be approx. one half of the 10% prices listed below. With original specimens getting harder and harder to come by, many guns are now observed with major parts replacements, including barrels, cylinders, grips, etc.

Beware of restorations that are purported to be original! One expert believes that as many as 90% of Colt SAA Cavalry & Artillery models currently offered for sale, especially at gun shows, have been intentionally faked, or "enhanced" in some way. Many have been done in the last 40 years in all inspector serial ranges. Some have now been skillfully "aged" to look more original. When making a substantial purchase, a letter of authentication from a reliable source is suggested in addition to a factory historical letter. Also ask for a guarantee of originality in writing from the seller. No factory information is available on U.S. Cavalry revolvers below ser. no. 30,600.

Blue Book Publications, Inc. would be happy to refer you to a credible source for authenticating the military revolvers listed below (very important). While a factory letter (if possible) verifies the configuration, it does not verify originality and/or authenticity. All inquiries are treated confidentially.

SINGLE ACTION ARMY (CAVALRY) - U.S. MILITARY CONTRACT - the Colt SAA was the primary sidearm of the U.S. military forces between 1873 and 1892, carried by all commissioned officers and mounted troops. While sometimes identified as the "Cavalry" model, this revolver was issued to all branches of service and state militia units. A total of 37,063 were purchased by the U.S government at an average cost of $12.50. Specifications called for 7½ in. barrel, .45 LC cal., blue & color case hardened finish, one-piece, oil finished walnut grips. Each gun was stamped with the initial(s) of a U.S. ordnance principal sub-inspector and finally, with the letters "U.S." on the frame after being approved for delivery to the National Armory at Springfield, MA.

* ❋ ***Early U.S. Model SAA*** - principal sub-inspectors of this early period of military mfg. were O.W. Ainsworth (A), S.B. Lewis (L), A.P. Casey (C), and W.W. Johnson (J), examples with ser. nos. below 20,000 are most desirable and command premium prices, these guns are marked with only the single letter of the last name and were mfg. before 1876,

100%	98%	95%	90%	80%	70%	60%	50%	40%	30%	20%	10%

ser. nos. are mixed with civilian sales up to ser. no. 20,000. There are no known sales to the U.S. government between the 20,000-30,000 ser. no. range.

| N/A | N/A | $47,000 | $42,000 | $35,000 | $25,000 | $18,000 | $16,000 | $14,000 | $13,000 | $12,000 | $10,000 |

Of this group, early Ainsworth inspected guns are the most valuable.

✳ Mid-Range U.S. Model SAA - the primary ordnance sub-inspectors of this group were John T. Cleveland (J.T.C.), Henry Nettleton (H.N.), and David F. Clark (D.F.C.), these guns fall between ser. nos. 30,693-121,147. Mfg. 1876-1887.

| N/A | N/A | $37,000 | $32,000 | $25,000 | $18,000 | $15,000 | $14,000 | $13,000 | $12,000 | $10,000 | $8,000 |

✳ Late U.S. Model SAA - all inspected by Rinaldo A. Carr (R.A.C.) from 1890-1891, ser. no range 131,208-140,361. The last SAA purchased by the U.S. government was shipped from the factory on April 29, 1891.

| N/A | N/A | $20,000 | $18,000 | $15,000 | $13,000 | $12,000 | $10,000 | $9,000 | $8,000 | $6,000 | $5,000 |

✳ Artillery Model SAAs - refers to U.S. government model SAA revolvers with 5½ in. barrels and mis-matched numbered parts. In 1896, it was decided that the barrels of all 15,000+ SAAs in storage should be shortened by 2 inches and re-issued into service at the outbreak of the Spanish-American War. At the same time, Colt replaced worn parts and refurbished all guns to new condition. Between 1900-1903, these guns were returned to Colt a second time for refurbishing, and were reassembled without regard to matching component serial numbers. This shortcut minimized time and cost for the refurbishing process. Only rarely will one be found with all the matching serial numbers, indicating that it escaped the last refinish - these guns will bring a premium price.

| N/A | N/A | $7,500 | $6,500 | $5,400 | $4,500 | $4,000 | $3,750 | $3,500 | $3,000 | $2,750 | $2,500 |

✳ New York State Militia SAA - in 1895, before work began on the artillery models, Colt refurbished 800 SA revolvers supplied by Springfield Armory to honor a request from the state of New York. These guns retained their 7½ in. barrels and all original parts wherever possible (replacement parts were serial numbered to match). All were stamped on the bottom of the grips with the initials of Rinaldo A. Carr (R.A.C.). They were given a high polish blue and case hardened civilian finish with blue hammers. Since all other cavalry models in the government's possession were cut to 5½ in. shortly thereafter, these 800 are quite possibly the only quantity of original 7½ in. guns remaining that could actually have seen service on the frontier. All other 7½ in. cavalry models that are seen today were most likely originally issued to state militias rather than to U.S. government miltary forces. These 800 revolvers therefore occupy a very significant position in the history of Colt firearms.

| N/A | N/A | $15,250 | $13,750 | $10,000 | $9,000 | $8,000 | $7,200 | $6,500 | $5,000 | $4,500 | $4,000 |

REVOLVERS: SAA, 2ND GENERATION: 1956-1975 MFG.

The author wishes to express his thanks to Charles Layson, Carol & the late Don Wilkerson for their generous contributions and helping to reformat the 2nd & 3rd Generation Colt SAA information.

Popular demand brought back the Single Action Army in 1956 with minor modifications, most not detectable except to experts. Serial numbers began at 0001SA, and continued to 73,000SA before the "New Model" was introduced in 1976 (ser. no. 80,000SA). Premiums are paid for rare production variances in NIB condition. It should be noted "premium niches" exist in this model as collectors are establishing premiums paid for rarer production variances (the interrelation of barrel length, caliber, frame type, finish quality, year of manufacture, and other special features).

The order of desirability on standard 2nd Generation SAAs is as follows: 4¾ in. barrels are the most desirable, followed by 7½ in., and then 5½ in. Caliber desirability is as follows: .45 LC has the most demand, followed by .44 Spl., .38 Spl., and then .357 Mag. It follows that desirable calibers found with desirable barrel lengths will command healthy premiums - especially if production was unusually low for a particular combination. Reference books specifically on the post-war SAA are a

Grading	100%	98%	95%	90%	80%	70%	60%

must when determining the rarity factors on these multiple production combinations. Buntlines, Sheriff's Models, and special orders through the Custom Gun Shop are in a class by themselves, and have to be evaluated one at a time.

It is advisable to procure a factory letter when buying or selling older or recently manufactured Colt single actions (hence, guaranteeing authenticity and value credibility). The watermarked letters are available to: Colt's Manufacturing Company, Inc., located in Hartford, CT. The charge is $100 per serial number - if Colt cannot provide you with proper documentation after conducting research, they will refund you $50. Please include your name, address, Colt model name, serial number, and payment to: COLT HISTORIAN, P.O. 1868, Hartford, CT, 06144. Please allow adequate time for proper response.

In addition, phone service for 2ND Generation SAA configuration validation is also provided on a premium basis (ser. no. range 0001SA – 73,205SA). Fees for this phone service are $200 per gun ($25 for date of manufacture only) for 2nd Generation SAA pistols, payable by Visa or MasterCard - letter is included for this price. The phone number is 860-244-1343 and ask for the Historical Dept. between the hours of 1-4 P.M. EST.

SINGLE ACTION ARMY (2ND GENERATION) - .357 Mag., .38 Spl., .44 Spl., or .45 LC cal., denoted by SA suffix, 3 (Sheriff's Model), 4¾, 5½, 7½, or 12 (Buntline) in. barrel length – 5½, 7½, and 12 in. barrels have the one-line barrel address, 4¾ has a two-line barrel address, all blue, blue/case hardened, or nickel finish. 2nd Generation SAAs have been grouped into the following 3 categories.

✳ *Early 2nd Generation* - ser. no. range 0001SA to approx. 39,000SA, shipped in one-piece black box similar to pre-war box. Mfg. from 1956-1965.

.45 LC cal.	$2,350	$1,875	$1,500	$1,200	$1,000	$900	$800
.44 Spl. cal.	$2,100	$1,750	$1,350	$1,050	$900	$800	$700
.38 Spl. cal.	$1,995	$1,600	$1,200	$900	$800	$700	$600
.357 Mag. cal.	$1,795	$1,350	$1,000	$800	$700	$600	$500

Add 30% for original black box in good condition.
Add 20% for original nickel finish.
Add 15% for original 4¾ in. barrel.

✳ *Mid-range 2nd Generation* - ser. no. range 39,000SA to 70,055SA, shipped in a red and white, two-piece, stagecoach box. Mfg. from 1965-1973.

.45 LC cal.	$1,625	$1,350	$1,100	$1,000	$900	$800	$700
.44 Spl. cal.	$1,500	$1,225	$1,000	$900	$800	$700	$600
.357 Mag. cal.	$1,295	$975	$800	$700	$600	$550	$450

Add 30% for original stagecoach box.
Add 10% for original nickel finish.
Add 15% for original 4 ¾ in. barrel.

✳ *Late 2nd Generation* - ser. no. range 70,055SA to 73,205SA, shipped in a brown, wood grain cardboard shell with 2 styrofoam inserts. Mfg. from 1973-1976.

.45 LC cal.	$1,395	$1,150	$1,000	$900	$800	$700	$600
.357 Mag. cal.	$1,195	$950	$800	$750	$700	$650	$600

Add 15% for original brown/styrofoam box.
Add 10% for original nickel finish.
Add 10% for original 4¾ in. barrel.

2nd Generation SAAs in stagecoach box w/o eagle black grips (ser. numbered under approx. 52,000SA) are more desirable than those with eagle. Also, flat-top hammers are more desirable than round top hammers found between ser. no. range 27,012SA-61,575SA (mfg. mid- 1959-1972).

SHERIFF'S MODEL (1961 MODEL) - .45 LC cal., distinctive configuration with 3 in. barrel and no ejector rod housing, ser. no. followed by SM suffix, 503 were mfg. for Centennial Arms

Grading	100%	98%	95%	90%	80%	70%	60%

Corp. - 478 had a blue/case hardened finish and 25 were done in nickel.

	$1,895	$1,600	$1,400	$1,200	$1,000	$800	$700

Add 25% for original two-piece box.
Add 200% for original nickel finish.

BUNTLINE SPECIAL - .45 LC cal. only, 12 in. barrel, blue/case hardened finish, rubber (early mfg.) or walnut grips. Over 3,900 mfg. between 1957-1975.

	$1,695	$1,275	$1,000	$900	$850	$800	$750

Add 100% for original nickel finish (rare, watch for refinishing).
Add 30% for original black box in good condition.

NEW FRONTIER - .357 Mag., .38 Spl. (rare), .44 Spl., or .45 LC cal., denoted by flat- top frame, adj. rear sight, and "NF" after the serial number, 4 ¾ (scarce), 5 ½ (scarce), or 7 ½ (most common) in. barrel, case hardened frame/blue finish and smooth walnut grips were standard. Approx. 4,200 mfg. 1961-1975.

	$1,250	$950	$900	$850	$800	$750	$700

Add 15% for later brown/styrofoam box.
Add 20% for stagecoach or black box (must be in correct ser. no. range).
Add 35% for early black and gold box.
Add 50% for 4¾ in. barrel.
Add 25% for 5½ in. barrel.
Add 200% for .38 Spl. cal. with 5½ in. barrel, 600% for 7½ in. barrel.

NEW FRONTIER BUNTLINE - .45 LC cal. only, 12 in. barrel, flat-top frame and adj. rear sight. Approx. 72 mfg. 1962-1967.

	$2,500	$2,150	$1,650	$1,400	$1,200	$1,100	$1,000

Add 50% for original black or tan box (must be serial numbered to the gun).

FACTORY ENGRAVED 2ND GENERATION SAAs - approx. 350 revolvers were factory engraved with 90% being in .45 LC cal. Values range from 75%-100% higher than non- engraved specimens, with additional premiums paid for rare styles and configurations and/or for the notoriety of the engraver. Those SAAs done by Albert Herbert, A.A. White, Robert Burt, Leonard Francolini, and Dennis Kiesler are probably the highest priced examples. Always check authenticity when buying, selling, or trading engraved 2nd Generation SAAs with the Colt Historical Dept. The charge for a factory letter per engraved gun is $150, $50 will be refunded if Colt cannot provide historical documentation.

Factory engraved 2nd Generation SAAs are at least 10 times rarer than engraved 3rd Generation pistols.

REVOLVERS: SAA, 3RD GENERATION: 1976-CURRENT MFG.

After a short break in production, Colt Firearms announced the resumption of full scale production of the Single Action on Feb. 4th, 1976, at the N.S.G.A. (National Sporting Goods Association) Bi- Centennial show in Chicago.

The "New Model Colt Single Action Army" or the "Colt Post-War Single Action Army - New Model", as it was commonly referred to at the time, is known today to collectors as the "3rd Generation Colt Single Action Army". Minor changes include a modified, thin front sight contour, and the elimination of the cylinder pin bushing, plus a few other "minor, modern manufacturing techniques that have not change the appearance, feel, action, or performance of this historic handgun...", according to Colt's press release at the time.

Production began with ser. no. 80,000SA, and reached 99,999SA in 1978. At this point, the SA suffix changed to a prefix beginning with SA01001. Serialization reached SA99,999 during 1993, and began over, this time separating the letters SA, and starting with S02001A. As this edition went to press, serial numbers had reached S34800A (excludes custom serial numbers). For whatever reasons, a few writers have erroneously referred to this current production run as "4th Generation Single Actions". This is an incorrect description, as these revolvers are mechanically identical to those

Grading	100%	98%	95%	90%	80%	70%	60%

produced since 1976, and should still be considered 3rd Generation guns.

For a listing of Colt's "P-Codes" (referring to the factory's model number designations specifing frame type, caliber, finish, and barrel length), please refer to the Colt Single Action Model Numbers section in the back of this book (located in Colt Serialization).

As with 1st and 2nd Generation Single Actions, a factory letter authenticating configuration and shipping destination can be obtained for $100 by writing to: COLT HISTORIAN, P.O. Box 1868, Hartford, CT, 06144. If Colt cannot provide proper documentation after conducting research, they will issue a refund of $50. Please allow 60-90 days for proper response.

POPULAR SAA CUSTOM SHOP SPECIAL ORDER OPTIONS

Add $175 for special barrel length or cal., add $125 for custom-tuned action, add $228 (available in .45 LC only beginning 2000) for extra regular fluted or unfluted cylinder, add $308 for extra long fluted cylinder, add $65 for beveled front of cylinder, add $200 for mirror brite finish (disc.), add $425 for gold or silver plating, add $80 for black eagle grips, add $15 for grip medallions, add $85 for smooth walnut grips, add $345 for North American elkhorn grips, add $225 for buffalo horn grips, add $425 for mother of pearl grips, add $760 for plain ivory grips, $345 for imitation ivory, approx. 10% for grip checkering, add $155 for scrimshaw engraving (3 initials only), add $115 for consecutive serial numbers (pair), add $310 for individual unique serial number, add $105 to modify and shorten ejector housing, add $155 (per set) for heat blue small parts, add $255 for birdshead and $390 for extended butt frame, $350 for screwless frame. While a very few screwless frame SAAs have been mfg. to date, the Custom Shop now lists this option as a standard custom order feature.

Please contact the Colt Custom Shop for a written quotation ($25) regarding a custom built SAA with special options/features. Their address is: Colt Manufacturing Company, Inc. P.O. Box 1868, Hartford, CT 06101, ATTN: Custom Shop.

STANDARD/CUSTOM SINGLE ACTION ARMY (3RD GENERATION) - .357 Mag. (disc. approx. 1983), .38 Spl. (disc.), .38-40 WCF (disc.), .44 Spl. (disc. approx. 1983), .44-40 WCF, or .45 LC cal., 4 (disc. 1988), 4¾, 5 (disc. 1987), 5½, or 7½ (limited production since 1992) in. barrel – 5½ and 7½ in. barrels have the one-line barrel address, 4¾ has a two-line barrel address, standard finishes include color case hardened/blue or nickel, plastic black eagle or walnut grips (used mostly during 1991-92) standard, most recent mfg. has blue shipping box with white slip cover. Mfg. 1976 to date. Original 1976 issue price was approx. $242.

MSR	$1,530	$1,495	$995	$800	$700	$650	$600	$550

Subtract $50 for .357 Mag. cal.
Add 10% for original .38-40 WCF cal.
Add 25% for original .38 Spl. cal.
Add 20% for black powder frame (disc. 1995).
Add $700 for original two-piece ivory grips with screw.
Add $700 for original one-piece ivory grips w/o screw.
Add 5% for original brown box with styrofoam inserts (mfg. 1976-1993).

Through 2001, Colt offered the SAA as both Standard and Custom Models. The difference is that single actions that are further customized with engraving, special barrel lengths, stocks, etc., are packaged more eloquently because of the added value of the customizing.

Beginning 2001, all orders for SAA models are processed through the Colt Custom Shop. The 2001 Custom Shop MSR for the Custom SAA was $2,100.

Various custom order barrel lengths have been available on this model for some time.

The .357 Mag. and .44 Spl. cals. were mostly discontinued by 1983.

To reference factory coding for the various Standard Model P (SAA) configurations, please refer to the Colt Single Action Model Numbers within the Colt Serialization section in the back of this text.

COLT COWBOY SINGLE ACTION ARMY - .45 LC cal., 4¾ (disc. 1999), 5½, or 7½ (disc. 1999) in. barrel marked "COLT COWBOY .45 COLT" on left side, transfer bar safety, all steel construction, frame assembly done in the U.S., charcoal case colors on frame with blue

Grading	100%	98%	95%	90%	80%	70%	60%

metal parts, rampant Colt black competition grips similar in design to those used on 1st generation SAAs, 40 oz. While advertised beginning 1998, this model was not manufactured until 1999.

MSR	**$670**	$575	$475	$450	$400	$375	$350	$335

★ **Cowboy Collection Set** - includes SAA in .45 LC cal., with 5½ in. barrel, stag (very limited) or imitation ivory (more common) grips, blue/color case hardened finish, accesories includes collector's Bowie knife, silver medallion and collector's case. Limited mfg. 2000 only.

		$1,250	$750	$625	$500	$425	$400	$400

Last MSR was approx. $1,600.

SHERIFF'S MODEL (3RD GENERATION) - .44-40 WCF or .45 LC cal., 3 in. barrel w/o ejector rod, blue/case colored, nickel, or royal blue finish. Approx. 4,560 guns mfg. 1980-85.

.45 LC cal. (blue/CH)	$1,395	$1,150	$900	$850	$800	$750	$700

Add 10% for extra convertible cylinder.
Add 10% for original nickel finish.
Add $400 for original ivory grips.
Subtract 20% for .44-40 WCF cal. or all blue finish.

BUNTLINE MODEL (3RD GENERATION) - .44-40 WCF or .45 LC cal. only, 12 in. barrel, blue/case hardened finish, walnut grips.

	$1,395	$995	$800	$750	$700	$650	$600

Add 10% for original nickel finish.
Add $400 for original ivory grips.

NEW FRONTIER (3RD GENERATION) - .357 Mag., .44-40 WCF (rare), .44 Spl., or .45 LC cal., denoted by "NF" serial suffix, 4¾, 5½, or 7½ in. barrel, blue/case hardened finish, flat-top frame, adj. rear sight, plain two-piece walnut grips. Mfg. 1978- 1981.

.44-40 WCF/.45 LC cal.	$1,050	$900	$800	$750	$700	$650	$600
.44 Spl. cal.	$795	$650	$500	$450	$425	$400	$400
.357 Mag. cal./7 ½ in. nickel	$1,050	$900	$800	$750	$700	$650	$600

Subtract 10% for 5 ½ in. barrel.
Subtract 15% for 7 ½ in. barrel.
Add 5% for original brown box with styrofoam inserts.

Serial numbers on the New Frontier started at 01001NF, but during 1980, a few New Frontiers with 5½ in. barrels were produced in the 7,000NF serial range, where 2nd Generation New Frontiers left off. Therefore, a 3rd Generation New Frontier will either have a ser. no. starting with "O" or will have a higher number than 7288NF with no "O" prefix.

NEW FRONTIER BUNTLINE SPECIAL (3RD GENERATION)- .45 LC cal. only, 12 in. barrel, flat-top frame, adj. rear sight, limited mfg. as the New Buntline Commemorative during 1979. Please refer to the Colt Commemorative section for value information.

STOREKEEPER'S MODEL (3RD GENERATION) - .45 LC cal. only, black powder frame, 4 in. barrel w/o ejector rod, full nickel or royal blue/case hardened finish, ivory grips. Approx. 280 mfg. 1984-1985.

	$1,700	$1,450	$1,300	$1,100	$900	$800	$750

Add 10% for original nickel finish.

FACTORY ENGRAVED SAAs (3RD GENERATION) - the rarity of the SAA configuration in addition to the notability of the engraver will make the difference on the premiums commanded. 3rd Generation factory engraved SAAs were produced in much greater numbers

Grading	100%	98%	95%	90%	80%	70%	60%

than were 2nd Generation SAAs. Over 80% of engraved 3rd Generation SAAs are .45 LC caliber, the majority have 7½ in. barrels, and some variation of blue finish. Grade "C" (41% of engraved mfg.) and Grade "D" (24% of engraved mfg.) dominate production.

During 1978-79, Colt engraved as many as 300-500 guns on a single factory order. Unfortunately, the quality on many SAAs during this period was substandard, and as a result, these guns usually cap at approx. $2,000. If the level of quality is similar to today's SAAs, the price will also be similar. Today's Custom Shop is once again producing excellent quality engraved SAAs, and Class C engraved revolvers (with ivory grips) are currently priced in the $3,750 range.

* *Class "A" Engraved (25% coverage)*

	100%	98%	95%	90%	80%	70%	60%
	$1,550	$1,200	$1,050	$900	$800	$700	$600

* *Class "B" Engraved (50% coverage)*

	$1,850	$1,400	$1,250	$1,100	$1,000	$900	$800

* *Class "C" Engraved (75% coverage)*

	$2,300	$1,750	$1,400	$1,300	$1,200	$1,100	$1,000

* *Class "D" Engraved (100% coverage)*

	$2,800	$2,200	$1,800	$1,400	$1,300	$1,200	$1,100

Add 10% for original nickel finish.
Add 25% for 4¾ in. barrel.
Add 15% for 5½ in. barrel.
Add 10% for calibers other than .45 LC.
Add 30% for factory ivory grips.
Add 10% for original blue cardboard or plastic box.

CUSTOM & SPECIAL ENGRAVED EDITIONS (3RD GENERATION)
- beginning in 1976, with the introduction of the "New Model" SAA (3rd Generation), the Colt Custom Shop produced many custom and special edition engraved Single Army Action revolvers. According to Mr. Don Wilkerson, author of The Post-War Single Action Revolver 1976-1986, "the term custom edition is defined as a group of identical revolvers assembled under the direction of the Custom Gun Shop at Colt's and sold through the normal distribution system. A custom edition differs from a special edition in that special editions are a group of revolvers made up to a customer's unique specifications, and sold as a group to one purchaser...". While the exact number is not known, it is thought that approx. 3,500 SAAs have been engraved since 1976. Since each edition is unique, values vary widely, depending upon the notability of the engraver, the amount and type of coverage, and the number produced. Models listed below are recent Colt Custom Editions.

* *Engraved European Model* - 9mm Para. cal., nickel finish only, 4¾, 5½, or 7½ in. barrel, rosewood grips with silver medallions, 40-43 oz. Mfg. 1991-92 only.

	$1,395	$1,195	$995

Last MSR was $1,990.

* *Engraved U.S. Model* - .45 ACP cal., royal blue finish only, 4¾, 5½, or 7½ in. barrel, walnut grips, 40-43 oz. Mfg. 1991-92 only.

	$1,295	$1,095	$875

Last MSR was $1,960.

* *Old World Engravers Sampler* - .45 LC cal., 5½ in. barrel, nickel finish, buffalo horn grips, includes four unique styles of engraving. Mfg. 1997-98, reintroduced 2001.

MSR	$3,445		$2,975	$2,450	$2,000

* *Legend Rodeo II SAA* - disc. 1998.

	$1,950	$1,500	$1,250

Last MSR was $2,450.

* *125th Anniversary Edition* - 2 line frame address, "45 COLT" barrel address marked bar-

Grading	100%	98%	95%	90%	80%	70%	60%

rel, beveled cylinder, oven blue finish. 1,000 mfg. beginning 1997.

MSR	**$2,070**	**$1,600**	**$1,150**	**$825**

SAA CUSTOM SHOP ENGRAVING PRICES - PRE-1997 - values below represent 1995 published SAA Custom Shop A-D engraving options, before the company started separate Standard, Expert, and Master level pricing during 1997. For current Colt Custom Shop engraving prices, please refer to the "Colt Custom Shop Engraving - Current Mfg." listed below.

> **Add $1,163 for Class "A" engraving (25% metal coverage).**
> **Add $2,324 for Class "B" engraving (50% metal coverage).**
> **Add $3,487 for Class "C" engraving (75% metal coverage).**
> **Add $4,647 for Class "D" engraving (100% metal coverage).**
> **Add an additional 13% (approx.) for buntline engraving.**
>
> Standard Engraving was performed mostly by standard level factory engravers and engraving options generally include A-D style coverage. Typically, gold work was not performed by these engravers and specimens are mostly unsigned. Expert Engravers executed classic American style scroll, no gold, and may be signed.

COLT CUSTOM SHOP ENGRAVING - CURRENT MFG.

The chart below indicates current Custom Shop engraving prices for the various frame sizes, amount of engraving coverage, and the three levels of engraving execution (i.e., Standard, Expert, and Master levels). SAAs are considered large frame, revolvers and full-size Government Models are considered medium frame, and Government Model 380s are considered small frame.

Most buyers of engraved Colt SAAs today are very knowledgeable, and many of them are no longer satisfied with Standard types of patterns and styles. As a result, those engraved guns with the rarest production variances coupled with unique engraving done at an Expert or better level are currently more desireable than their counterparts with Standard engraving patterns. Colt currently employs three full-time engravers at the factory, in addition to several outside sources (at all engraving levels).

The name of the engraver is available only when ordering either Expert or Master level of engraving. Most collectors would rather have the Expert level of engraving currently.

LARGE FRAME SIZE

ENGRAVING COVERAGE	STANDARD LEVEL	EXPERT LEVEL	MASTER LEVEL
A	$800	$900 (disc.)	$1,200 (disc.)
B	$900	$1,700	$3,150
C	$1,200	$2,500	$4,580
D	$1,600	$3,600	$6,300

Other Custom Shop options are priced on request, including a wide variety of gold/silver inlays, panel scenes, color enamel inlays, gold/silver frame outlines, etc.

MEDIUM FRAME SIZE

A	$900	N/A	N/A
B	$1,000	$1,200	$1,600
C	$1,200	$1,600	$2,400
D	$1,600	$2,400	$3,200

C

SMALL FRAME SIZE

Factory small frame engraving was disc. 1998.

ENGRAVING COVERAGE	STANDARD LEVEL	EXPERT LEVEL	MASTER LEVEL
A	$400	$600	$800
B	$600	$800	$1,000
C	$800	$1,100	$1,500
D	$1,100	$1,300	$1,900

Add 20% to large frame pricing for Buntline Models.
Subtract 20% from small frame pricing for Mustang Models.

Grading	100%	98%	95%	90%	80%	70%	60%

REVOLVERS: SAA, SCOUT MODEL

100% values below assume NIB condition. Subtract 10% without box.

FRONTIER SCOUT (Q or F SUFFIX) - .22 LR or .22 Mag. (introduced after 1960) cal., "Q" or "F" suffix, blue with bright alloy frame, all blue, or duotone ("Q" models only) finish (rare), 4¾ or 9½ (Buntline) barrel, available with interchangeable cylinders after 1964, black composition or walnut grips, approx. 246,000 mfg. 1957-1970.

$450	$375	$275	$225	$175	$150	$140

Add 10% for extra cylinder.
Add 20% for Buntline model.
Add 25% for "Q" suffix with duo-tone finish (mfg. 1957-58 only).
Add 10% for original box.

FRONTIER SCOUT (K SUFFIX) - Zamac alloy frame version of "Q" Model with "K" suffix, blue or nickel finish with walnut stocks, approx. 44,000 mfg. 1960-1970.

$450	$375	$225	$225	$175	$150	$140

Add 100% for double cased Scout set.
Add 150% for double cased Scout Buntline set.
Add 10% for original box.

This model used the alloy Zamac for manufacture (as opposed to aluminum in the "Q" and "F" suffix models), and specimens are 6 oz. heavier as a result.

FRONTIER SCOUT '62 (P SUFFIX) - blue finish version of "K" Model, except has "P" suffix, staglite grips, approx. 68,000 mfg. 1962-1970.

$475	$400	$325	$250	$200	$150	$140

Add 20% for Buntline.
Add 10% for original box.
Add 50% with extra cylinders.
Add 100% for double cased Scout set.
Add 150% for double cased Scout Buntline set.

PEACEMAKER - .22 LR/.22 Mag. cal., color casehardened steel frame, 4.4, 4¾, 6, or 7½ (nicknamed Buntline Model but may be marked Peacemaker or Buntline) in. barrel, black composition grips, furnished with interchangeable .22 LR/.22 Mag. cylinders, approx. 190,000 mfg. 1970-1977.

$500	$350	$275	$225	$175	$150	$140

Add 20% for 4.4 in. barrel.
Add 30% for 4¾ in. barrel.
Add 10% for original box.
Subtract 10% if without extra cylinder.

This model can be denoted by a "G" or "L" prefix.

Grading	100%	98%	95%	90%	80%	70%	60%

NEW FRONTIER - similar features as Peacemaker Model, except with flat top frame, ramp front and adj. rear sight, mfg. 1970-1977. Reintroduced in 1982 without convertible .22 Mag. cylinder and added cross bolt safety, available in Coltguard finish, all blue finish became standard in 1985, mfg. disc. 1986.

	$325	$275	$215	$185	$155	$140	$130

Last MSR was $181.

Add 15% for Buntline model or 4 ¾ in. barrel.

PISTOLS: SEMI-AUTO, DISC.

Most of the semi-auto pistol models listed in the various pistol categories can have their original configuration confirmed with a Colt factory letter. To receive a letter, write: COLT HISTORIAN, P.O. Box 1868, Hartford, CT, 06144. The research fee for these pistols is typically either $75 or $100, depending on the model. If they cannot obtain additional information on the variation you request, they will refund $50.

Until several years ago, the Single Action Army revolver commanded the most attention among Colt handgun collectors. Since 1987, Colt Semi-Autos have been in tremendous demand and have out-accelerated many other areas of Colt collecting. Because condition and originality play such a key role in determining Colt Semi- Auto prices, many variations have had their values pushed upward to the point where it is difficult to accurately determine a realistic price - especially on those models in 98% original condition or better. As a result, some of the rarer models seldomly encountered in true 100% original condition have had their values deleted since extreme rarity precludes accurate price evaluation in this 100% condition category. As always, the hardest prices to ascertain when firearms market conditions are bullish are the 98-100% values.

Somewhere between serial number 2200 and 2450, Colt began altering the sights to fixed sights in the production process, shipping both types. By approx. serial number 3300, most guns shipped were altered during production. Guns altered during production are not refinished. Altered guns below serial number 2200 were refinished, or at least had the slides refinished.

MODEL 1900 - .38 ACP cal., 6 in. barrel, blue, plain walnut grips - checkered hard rubber grips after S/N 2,450, high spur hammer, sight safety. Mfg. 1900-1903.

	N/A	$6,500	$4,650	$3,150	$2,000	$1,700	$1,350

Add 60%+ for USN marked.
Add 50% for US marked with inspector initials.
Subtract 30%-50% for sight safety altered (factory refinished).
This model is serial numbered approx. between 1-4,274.

MODEL 1902 SPORTING - .38 ACP, 6 in. barrel, blue, fixed sights, checkered hard rubber grips, no safety, high spur hammer and round hammer. Mfg. 1902-1908.

	N/A	$3,500	$2,250	$1,500	$950	$850	$700

This model is serial numbered approx. 4,275-11,000 and 30,000-30,190.

MODEL 1902 MILITARY - .38 ACP cal., 6 in. barrel, blue, similar to 1902 Sporting, hammer changed to spur type in 1908, checkered black hard rubber grips, lanyard swivel on bottom rear of left grip. Mfg. 1902-1929.

	N/A	$2,300	$1,550	$950	$750	$625	$500

Add 30% for front slide checkering.
Add 20% with original box and instructions.
This model is serial numbered approx. 11,000-16,000 and 30,200-43,266.

MODEL 1902 MILITARY-U.S. ARMY MARKED - similar specifications to 1902 Military, only serial number range 15,001-15,200.

	N/A	$8,500	$6,500	$5,500	$4,250	$3,250	$2,500

Grading	100%	98%	95%	90%	80%	70%	60%

MODEL 1903 POCKET (38 ACP) - .38 ACP cal., 3¾ or 4½ in. barrel, blue finish standard, checkered black hard rubber grips, similar to 1902 Sporting, but 4½ in. barrel, 7½ in. overall. Mfg. 1903-1929.

$1,450	$1,150	$850	$700	$525	$475	$425

Add 30% for early round hammer.
Add 20% with original box and instructions.
This model is serial numbered approx. 16,000-47,226.

MODEL 1903 POCKET (MODEL M 32 ACP) - .32 ACP cal., 4 in. barrel, charcoal blue, checkered hard rubber grips, hammerless, slide lock and grip safety, barrel lock bushing. Mfg. 1903-1946.

$600	$450	$350	$300	$275	$250	$200

Add 20% for nickel finish (mostly w/pearl grips).
Add 60% for first model (Type I) mfg. 1903-1911 if in 100%-98% condition. If lower than 98%, add 20%.
Add 30% for Type II if in 100%-98% condition.
Add 10% with original box and instructions.

Type I - 32 ACPs have a 4 in. barrel, barrel bushing, no magazine safety, and are serial numbered 1-71,999.

Type II - 32 ACPs still retain their barrel bushing but have a 3 ¾ in. barrel and were mfg. from 1908-1910. They are serial numbered 72,000-105,050.

Type III - 32 ACPs do not have a barrel bushing and were mfg. from 1910-1926. They are serial numbered 105,051-468,096.

Type IV - 32 ACPs have the added magazine safety (of which there are both the commercial and "U.S. Property" variations). They are serial numbered 468,097-554,446.

✳ *Model 1903 Parkerized* - U.S. Property, 3¼ in. barrel, no barrel bushing, magazine safety, serial numbered 554,447-572,214.

$950	$775	$625	$475	$375	$320	$275

Add 50% for blue U.S. Property S/N 554,447 - approx. 562,000.
Add 20% with original box and instructions.
The 100% value on this model assumes NIB condition.

✳ *Model 1903 General Officer's Pistol* - .32 ACP cal., blue (mfg. until 1942) or parkerized (mfg. started 1942) finish.

	100%	98%	95%	90%	80%	70%	60%
Parkerized	N/A	$1,550	$1,275	$1,100	$975	$875	$775
Blue Finish	N/A	$2,250	$1,975	$1,725	$1,500	$1,300	$1,100

Values above assume issue to a General, and there must be paperwork to link up the gun to the recipient. Otherwise, these values do not apply - see U.S. Property above for applicable values.

MODEL 1905 - .45 ACP cal., 5 in. barrel, blue, fixed sights, checkered walnut stocks, similar to 1902 .38 ACP. Mfg. 1905-1911.

	100%	98%	95%	90%	80%	70%	60%
	N/A	$5,500	$3,250	$2,150	$1,750	$1,425	$1,100

Add 50% for factory slotted specimens (500 manufactured).
Add 250% for 1907 U.S. Military Contract variation (205 manufactured).
The shoulder stock option for this pistol is exceedingly rare. Depending on the condition, this accessory can add $7,500-$10,000 to the price of the gun.

Grading	100%	98%	95%	90%	80%	70%	60%

MODEL 1908 POCKET (MODEL M 380 ACP)

- .380 ACP cal., first issue, 3¾ in. barrel only, similar to Pocket Model .32 ACP (32 ACP), except chambered for .380 ACP. Mfg. 1908-1940.

	100%	98%	95%	90%	80%	70%	60%
	$850	$650	$450	$350	$300	$250	$225

Add 15% for Type I (see explanation below).
Add $100 for nickel finish.
Add 15% for pearl grips.

100% values assume NIB condition. Subtract 15% if without cardboard box. Pearl grips are normally encountered with nickel finish on this model.

Type I - 380 ACPs with barrel bushing and were mfg. 1908-1910 (6,251 mfg.). They are serial numbered 1-6,251.

Type II - 380 ACPs do not have a barrel bushing and were mfg. 1910-1926. They are serial numbered 6,252-92,893.

Type III - 380 ACPs have the added magazine safety (of which there are both the commercial and "U.S. Property" variations). They are serial numbered 92,894-134,499.

✴ ***Model 1908 "U.S. Property"*** - blue finish only, U.S. Property. Serial numbered 134,500-138,000.

	100%	98%	95%	90%	80%	70%	60%
	$2,250	$1,650	$925	$750	$650	$500	$350

✴ ***Model 1908 General Officer's Pistol*** - .380 ACP cal., blue finish only.

	100%	98%	95%	90%	80%	70%	60%
	$2,950	$2,400	$2,100	$1,850	$1,600	$1,400	$1,200

Values above assume issue to a General, and there must be paperwork to link up the gun to the recipient. Otherwise, these values do not apply - see U.S. Property above for applicable values.

VEST POCKET MODEL 1908-HAMMERLESS

- .25 ACP cal., 2 in. barrel, fixed sights, checkered hard rubber grips on early models, walnut on later, magazine disconnect added on guns made after 1916. Mfg. 1908-1946.

	100%	98%	95%	90%	80%	70%	60%
Blue finish	$575	$425	$325	$275	$225	$200	$155
Nickel finish	$695	$475	$335	$285	$240	$215	$175

Add 15% for pearl grips.

100% values assume NIB condition. Subtract 15% if without cardboard box in 95% or better condition only. This model was also supplied with a suede purse - add $100-$150, depending on condition.

Add 200% if "U.S. Property" marked.

MODEL 1909

- .45 ACP cal., straight handle design, 5 in. barrel, checkered walnut grips, approx. 22 mfg., ultra rare.

Extreme rarity factor precludes accurate price evaluation by individual condition factors. Specimens that are original and over 90% have sold for over $35,000 recently.

MODEL 1910

- .45 ACP cal., while not a production model, this gun is probably the most desirable semi-auto Colt pistol. A nice specimen at a recent auction was gavelled down at $195,000.

GENERAL OFFICER'S PISTOL

- issued not only to Generals, but many were also issued to the OSS, U.S. Navy, and other government agencies, .32 ACP cal. U.S. Properties were blue until 1942, after which the parkerized finish became standard (most went to England and exhibit British proofmarks), .380 cal. U.S. Properties were always blue, 1911A1 WWII specimens have standard military finish, and the Rock Island Arsenal .45s were all issued to Generals - see listing below.

	100%	98%	95%	90%	80%	70%	60%
M15 (RIA mfg.)	$5,750	$4,750	$3,750	$2,900	$2,500	$1,850	$1,500

Please refer to separate Model 1903, Model 1908, and Model 1911A1 Military General Officer's Model listings.

Grading	100%	98%	95%	90%	80%	70%	60%

PISTOLS: SEMI-AUTO, GOVT. MODEL 1911 COMMERCIAL VARIATIONS

MODEL 1911 - .45 ACP cal., 5 in. barrel, fixed sights, 7 shot mag., flat main spring housing, polished blue finish only (commercial and original military), checkered walnut grips. Colt licensed other companies to manufacture under government contracts, 39 oz. Mfg. 1912-1925.

Most M1911 variations listed below are not as collectible if under 60% original condition. However, they are still very desirable as shooters and values (if in original condition) will approximate the 60% prices if in good mechanical condition.

Colt Model 1911s continue to enjoy high demand as of this writing and prices continue to be strong in the 95%-100% condition factors. Be careful on the 98%+ condition specimens, especially the rarer variations. Some collectors are now requiring a potential high-dollar Model 1911 to pass a metallurgical X-ray examination before purchasing.

✳ ***Model 1911 Commercial*** - denoted by "C" preceding serial number, approx. ser. number range C1-C138,532. Watch for fakes.

◇**Model 1911 High Polish Blue** - mfg. 1912 through ser. no. 4,500.

	100%	98%	95%	90%	80%	70%	60%
	$6,750	$5,000	$4,000	$2,500	$1,500	$800	$600

◇**Model 1911 Regular Finish** - pistols mfg. after ser. no. 4,500.

	100%	98%	95%	90%	80%	70%	60%
	$2,750	$1,750	$1,200	$900	$700	$575	$450

Subtract 15% if without cardboard box in 100% condition only.

Approx. 138,532 were mfg. between 1912-1925.

100% values assume NIB condition.

PISTOLS: SEMI-AUTO, GOVT. MODEL 1911 MILITARY VARIATIONS

All pistols in this section are .45 ACP (11.25mm) cal., unless so noted.

COLT MFG. MODEL 1911 MILITARY - right side of slide marked "MODEL OF 1911 U.S. ARMY", blue finish only (NOT parkerized unless reworked).

	100%	98%	95%	90%	80%	70%	60%
1912-1913 mfg.	$2,900	$1,995	$1,325	$925	$550	$475	$400

Add 100% for the first 114 pistols with oversize "United States Property" marking.
Add 75% for pistols in the ser. no. range 115-2,400.

	100%	98%	95%	90%	80%	70%	60%
1914-1925 mfg.	$2,300	$1,600	$975	$625	$525	$425	$375

Over 2,550,000 M1911 pistols were ordered for WWI and WWII by U.S. Government but approx. 650,000 were mfg. between 1911-1925. Those pistols with a parkerized finish will indicate post-WWI reworking, usually marked with an arsenal code (ie. AA-AUGUSTA ARSENAL, SA-SPRINGFIELD ARSENAL, etc.). These reworks do not have the same values as original, unaltered specimens and prices generally are in the $325-$550 range.

NORTH AMERICAN ARMS COMPANY - less than 100 mfg. in Quebec, Ontario during 1918 only, blue finish. Be very wary of fakes, as this variation is perhaps this most desirable Colt WWI Govt. semi-auto.

	100%	98%	95%	90%	80%	70%	60%
	N/A	$24,000	$18,500	$15,000	$11,500	$10,000	$8,500

Most mint/100% specimens encountered in this model have been refinished - be careful.

REMINGTON - UMC - over 21,500 mfg. (ser. numbered 1-21,676) in 1918-1919 only, blue finish.

	100%	98%	95%	90%	80%	70%	60%
	N/A	$2,500	$1,675	$950	$700	$575	$525

Most mint/100% specimens encountered in this model have been refinished - be careful.

SPRINGFIELD ARMORY - approx. 30,000 mfg. between 1914-1915, blue finish.

	100%	98%	95%	90%	80%	70%	60%
	N/A	$2,575	$1,525	$975	$725	$600	$550

Serialization is 72,751-83,855, 102,597-107,596, 113,497-120,566, and 125,567-133,186.

Most mint/100% specimens encountered in this model have been refinished - be careful.

Grading	100%	98%	95%	90%	80%	70%	60%

U.S. NAVY - over 31,000 mfg. for U.S. Navy contract between 1911-1914 in defined serial ranges, blue finish. Marked "MODEL OF 1911 U.S. NAVY" on right slide side.

	$4,450	$2,800	$1,950	$1,700	$1,375	$995	$750

Add 100% for specimens under serial no. 3,500.

U.S. Navy specimens are seldomly found in over 80% original condition because of the corrosive factor encountered while at sea.

U.S. MARINE CORPS. - approx. 13,500 mfg. between 1911-1913 and 1916-1918 in defined serial ranges, blue finish, right side of slide marked "MODEL OF 1911 U.S. ARMY".

	$3,200	$2,675	$2,025	$1,725	$1,275	$1,050	$750

WWI BRITISH SERIES - .455 cal., serialized W19,000-W110,695, marked "CALIBRE 455", blue finish, proofed with broad arrow British Ordnance punch. Mfg. 1915-1919.

	$2,750	$2,150	$1,400	$975	$775	$650	$550

Many WWI British-series M1911s were exported back to the U.S. following WWI and were converted to .45 ACP. Usually, a "5" has been crossed-out of the original cal. designation.

BRITISH RAF REWORK - this variation is the WWI British series re-issued to RAF officers in the early 1920s, blue finish, differentiated by hand-stamped "RAF" or "R.A.F." on left side of frame.

	$1,250	$1,050	$825	$675	$575	$495	$460

A.J. SAVAGE MUNITIONS CO. - mfg. slides only, blue finish, marked in middle on left side of slide with flaming ordnance bomb with "S" in center.

	$1,425	$1,125	$875	$725	$625	$550	$495

NORWEGIAN TRIAL MODEL 1911 COLT - 11.25mm cal., approx. 300 mfg. with "C" prefix in 1913-14 only, usually encountered in 90% or less condition.

	$1,875	$1,325	$995	$875	$775	$625	$525

These guns were ordered for Norwegian service evaluation and were mfg. by Colt in Hartford, CT.

NORWEGIAN MODEL 1912 11.25MM - 11.25mm cal., mfg. under license from Colt's during 1917, "M1912" slide designation, approx. 95 mfg.

	$3,950	$3,500	$3,000	$2,500	$2,100	$1,825	$1,475

NORWEGIAN 1914 11.25MM - This model has a distinctive extended slide release, all parts should be serial numbered and have numerous matching numbers, approx. 32,750 mfg. between 1918-1947, mostly military contract, commercial production was very limited.

	$1,000	$825	$695	$525	$475	$425	$375

Add 150% for Waffenamt Nazi mfg. (mfg. 1945 only).

Serial ranges with corresponding year of manufacture on this model are as follows: 96-600 - 1918, 601-1,150 - 1919, 1,151-1,650 (Naval Artillery) - 1920, 1,651-2,200 - 1921, 2,201- 2,950 - 1922, 2,951-4,610 - 1923, 4,611-6,700 - 1924, 6,701-8,940 - 1925, 8,941-11,820 - 1926, 11,821- 15,900 - 1927, 15,901-20,100 - 1928, 20,101-21,440 - 1929, 21,441-21,940 - 1932, 21,941-22,040 - 1933, 22,041-22,141 - 1934, 22,142-22,211 - 1936, 22,212-22,311 - 1939, 22,312-22,361 - 1940, 22,362-26,460 - 1941, 26,461-29,614 - 1942, 29,615-32,335 (Waffenamt Nazi proofed) - 1945, 32,336-32,854 - (last original production) 1947.

Nazi production of the M1914 began in 1941. Between 1941-42, approx. 7,000 pistols were mfg. without Waffenamt stampings. Nazi proofed guns (all 1945 dated) began in the mid- 29,000 serial range, and 920 were mfg. with the Nazi Eagle.

ARGENTINE CONTRACT MODEL 1916 - identified by the Argentine seal on top of slide, 1,000 mfg. in ser. range C20,001-C21,000, mfg. 1916.

	$1,400	$1,000	$725	$575	$450	$410	$350

Most specimens of this model have been refinished.

Grading	100%	98%	95%	90%	80%	70%	60%

RUSSIAN CONTRACT - approx. 50,000 mfg. with frame marked "ANGLO ZAKAZIVAT", blue finish. Mfg. 1915-1917.

| | $3,500 | $2,900 | $2,500 | $1,800 | $1,250 | $1,100 | $1,000 |

Several years ago, a European distributor imported a quantity of this Russian contract variation with a C prefix, but marked "ANGLO ZAKAZIVAT". This contract is seldolmly encountered - beware of fakes.

PISTOLS: SEMI-AUTO, GOVT. MODEL 1911A1 COMMERCIAL VARIATIONS

All pistols in this section are .45 ACP cal., unless so noted.

MODEL 1911A1 - blue or parkerized, checkered walnut grips, plastic on later military guns, checkered arched mainspring housing and longer grip safety spur. As in the Model 1911, Colt licensed other companies to produce under govt. contract during WWII. Mfg. 1925-1970.

Inspect carefully for arsenal reworks (so marked by proofing, normally on left side of frame above or behind trigger), and reparkerizing.

Most M1911A1 variations listed below are not as collectible if under 60% original condition. However, they are still very desirable as shooters and values (if in original condition) will approximate the 60% prices if in good mechanical condition.

MODEL 1911A1 PRE-WWII COLT COMMERCIAL - "C" preceding serial number, mfg. 1925-1942. Approx. ser. no. range C138,533-C215,000.

| | $2,500 | $1,950 | $1,225 | $850 | $695 | $550 | $425 |

Add 50% for nickel finish.
Add 20% with original box and instructions.

MODEL 1911A1 1946-1969 COLT COMMERCIAL - 5 in. barrel, fixed sights, "C" prefix until 1950 when changed to "C" suffix. approx. 196,000 mfg. 1946-1970.

❋ *1946-1950 Mfg.* - C-Prefix with serial numbers C221,000 - C240,227.

| | $1,450 | $1,175 | $900 | $750 | $675 | $550 | $475 |

❋ *1950-1970 Mfg.* - C-Suffix with serial numbers 240,228C - 336,169C.

| | $850 | $745 | $675 | $550 | $475 | $425 | $400 |

Add 10% for nickel finish.

SUPER .38 AUTOMATIC PISTOL - identical to Govt. Model .45, except chambered for .38 Super automatic, blue or nickel finish. Mfg. 1928-1970.

	100%	98%	95%	90%	80%	70%	60%
Pre-War	$3,700	$2,375	$1,750	$1,250	$1,000	$875	$750
2nd Model	$1,450	$1,100	$875	$725	$660	$550	$475
3rd Model	$1,200	$875	$725	$660	$575	$500	$435
4th Model	$1,100	$775	$675	$575	$500	$435	$385
CS Prefix	$1,100	$745	$675	$550	$475	$415	$375

Add approx. 50% for nickel finish.
Pre-war variations are serialized below approx. 37,000.
The 2nd Model may be differentiated by noticing the heavier barrel and Rampant Colt on right side. The 3rd Model has a fat barrel with Rampant Colt on left side. The 4th Model has a thin barrel and Rampant Colt on left side.

SUPER MATCH .38 - similar to Super .38, but hand honed action, match grade barrel. Mfg. 1935-1946. Examine carefully for fakes.

| Fixed sights | $4,950 | $4,150 | $3,450 | $2,350 | $1,575 | $1,275 | $1,050 |

Add 35% for adj. sights (be cautious of fixed sight Super Matches converted to adj. sights).
A Colt historical letter is available for this model at $100 each.

Grading	100%	98%	95%	90%	80%	70%	60%

MATCH .38 AMU - .38 rimless Spl. cal. (cartridges were mfg. by Win.), this variation was mfg. by Colt from a .38 Super frame (and has .38 Super serialization) with a .38 AMU conversion kit slide, the Army took .45 frames and assembled their guns using .38 AMU kits, blue finish.

Colt mfg. (unmodified)	$2,500	$2,200	$1,900	$1,675	$1,400	$1,175	$975
Army modified	$1,400	$1,200	$995	$800	$650	$550	$495
AMU kit only	$550	$475	$425	$385	$350	$325	$295

On this configuration, the barrel, slide, and mag. were marked ".38 AMU".

SUPER MATCH .38 MS - .38 Super cal., 1961 mfg., serial numbered 101MS - 855MS, 754 total manufactured, same configuration as the .38 Midrange.

	$3,750	$2,950	$1,850	$1,495	$1,375	$1,175	$1,000

1968-1969 BB TRANSITIONAL - denoted by BB prefix on serial number.

	$995	$850	$625	$550	$495	$425	$375

.45 ACP TO .22 LR CONVERSION UNIT - consists of slide assembly, barrel, bushing, floating chamber, ejector, recoil spring and guide, fitted with Stevens adj. rear sight, mfg. 1938 to 1947. Colt Master adj. sight 1947-54.

	$450	$400	$325	$250	$215	$150	$125

Add 100% for prewar mfg. (U-prefix S/N on top of slide).
Add 200% for pre-war documented Marine Corp units.

.22 LR TO .45 ACP CONVERSION UNIT - converted service Ace .22 to .45 ACP cal. Mfg. 1938-1942. Very rare - 112 mfg.

	$3,500	$2,500	$1,750	$1,000	$800	$700	$600

Add 50% for original box and instructions.

These units have "U" prefixed serial numbers on top of slide.

PISTOLS: SEMI-AUTO, GOVT. MODEL 1911A1 MILITARY VARIATIONS

All pistols in this section are .45 ACP (11.25mm) cal., unless so noted.

COLT MFG. MODEL 1911A1 MILITARY - approx. 1,643,068 mfg. between 1924- 1945, ser. nos. 700,000 - on up, right side of frame marked "M1911A1 U.S. ARMY", bright blue finish up to approx. ser. no. 780,000, parkerized finish after that.

	$1,150	$895	$625	$485	$385	$350	$325

Add 50% for 1937-38 mfg.
Add 50% for 1939 Navy variation (S/N 713,646 - 717,281).
Add 20% for 1942 Navy ser. no. range.
Add 150% for on early 1911A1 military models with bright blue finish, if in 95%+ original condition.

A large grouping of over 7,000 Commercial 1911A1s was transferred to the U.S. government - these pistols had their commercial serial numbers crudely removed (in ser. range 860,000 - 866,000) and renumbered with a new military serial number. Some of these guns are unusual as the frames and slides have been cut for the Schwartz safety. This variation is rare, and a 20%- 30% premium exists depending on the condition.

✳ **Model 1911A1 General Officer's Pistol** - standard military finish.
(WWII mfg.)

	$2,000	$1,750	$1,500	$1,000	$800	$675	$595

Values above assume issue to a General, and there must be paperwork to link up the gun to the recipient.

DRAKE NATIONAL MATCH - Drake made slides only for use by U.S. Army Marksmanship Unit to allow assembly of match guns.

	$1,275	$1,075	$850	$700	$585	$510	$450

Grading	100%	98%	95%	90%	80%	70%	60%

GOVERNMENT NATIONAL MATCH REWORKS - assembled by government armorers, all parts marked "NM", parkerized finish. Most will be S.A. marked.

	$1,275	$1,075	$850	$675	$585	$510	$450

Add 25% for Air Force pistols marked "AFPG" on slide.

These pistols were made specifically for the U.S. shooting team at Camp Perry.

ITHACA - approx. 369,129 mfg. 1943-1945 in Ithaca, NY, ser. no. ranges 856,405 - 916,404, 1,208,674 - 1,279,673, 1,441,431 - 1,471,430, 1,743,847 - 1,890,503, 2,075,104 - 2,134,403, and 2,619,014 - 2,693,613. Parkerized finish.

	$800	$600	$500	$450	$375	$350	$325

Add 20% with original shipping carton.

UNION SWITCH AND SIGNAL - approx. 55,000 mfg. 1943 only in Swissvale, PA, ser. no. range 1,041,405 - 1,096,404. Sandblast and blue finish.

	$1,495	$1,150	$900	$600	$500	$450	$425

REMINGTON RAND - approx. 1,086,624 mfg. 1943-1945 in Syracuse, NY, ser. no. ranges 916,405 - 1,041,404, 1,279,649 - 1,441,430, 1,471,431 - 1,609,528, 1,743,847 - 1,816,641, 1,890,504 - 2,075,103, 2,134,404 - 2,244,803, and 2,380,014 - 2,619,013. Parkerized finish.

	$795	$625	$525	$425	$375	$350	$325

Add 20% with original shipping carton.

SINGER MFG. CO. - 500 mfg. 1942 in Elizabeth, NJ, ser. no. range S800,001 - S800,500. Blue finish with plastic grips.

	N/A	$24,000	$18,500	$15,000	$11,500	$10,000	$8,500

The Singer 1911A1 variation is one of the most sought after Colt models. In recent years, values have increased significantly and as a result, many fakes have emerged. Most specimens are now recognized by ser. no. and be very cautious when contemplating a purchase. Some collectors unsure of authenticity are now requiring X-ray testing to determine originality (slide restampings, ser. no. changes, etc.).

MEXICAN CONTRACT - mfg. approx. 1921-1927 with "C" prefix ser. nos., frames marked "EJERCITO MEXICANO", most surviving examples show much use.

	$2,650	$1,975	$1,525	$1,250	$975	$775	$575

BRAZILIAN CONTRACT

	$2,600	$1,950	$1,500	$1,250	$975	$775	$575

ARGENTINE CONTRACT MODEL 1927 - serial numbered 1-10,000 under the mainspring housing and on the top of slide (should be matching), must have Argentine crest and "Model 1927" on right side of slide, external serial number applied to top of slide by the Argentine Arsenal, most have been Arsenal refinished.

	$1,150	$950	$750	$625	$550	$495	$450

ARGENTINE MFG.- in 1927, the Argentina Arsenal "DGFM-FMAP" began manufacturing the Model 1911A1. The slide marking is two lines and reads "EJERCITO ARGENTINO SIST.COLT.CAL. 11.25mm MOD.1927".

	$750	$650	$500	$450	$400	$350	$325

Add 20% for Argentine Navy "ARMADA NACIONAL" (small shipments between 1912-1948). Markings vary on different types.

This variation is not to be confused with the Ballester Molina/Rigaud Models (sold by Hispano Argentino Fabrica de Automoviles SA, Buenos Aires, Argentina - also known as the HAFDASA). Please refer to the Hispano Argentino Fabrica de Automovilas SA section of this text.

Grading	100%	98%	95%	90%	80%	70%	60%

ARGENTINE SERVICE MODEL ACE - .22 LR cal., conversion of the 1927 Argentine Contract Model, bottom right side of slide is marked "TRANSE A CAL .22 POR EST. VENTURINI S.A.". Originally imported during 1996, this model was arsenal refinished and most pistols were in the 70%-95% condition range.

	$575	$525	$475	$425	$400	$375	$350

PISTOLS: SEMI-AUTO, ACE MODELS - PRE-WWII

COMMERCIAL ACE - .22 LR cal., similar to Government .45 ACP, but in .22LR cal., 4¾ in. barrel, blue, adj. sights, checkered walnut grips, almost 11,000 mfg. (ser. no. range 1-10,935) 1931- 1941 and 1947.

		$2,750	$2,000	$1,300	$975	$775	$600	$500

Add 20% with original box and instructions.

SERVICE MODEL ACE - .22 LR cal., 5 in. barrel, blue or parkerized finish, similar to .45 ACP National Match except for caliber, has floating chamber to simulate .45 ACP recoil, limited mfg. 1935-1945.

	$3,000	$2,400	$2,000	$1,500	$1,000	$700	$575

Add 20% with original box and instructions.
Subtract 10% for parkerized finish.

This variation is marked "SERVICE MODEL" on left frame, serial numbers have "SM" prefix and have ranges to approx. 13,800. Other markings such as "USCG", "U.S. PROP'Y" or "R.S." (inspectors marks) have also been observed on this model, and can add a premium, if original condition is 95% or more.

PISTOLS: SEMI-AUTO, NATIONAL MATCH MODELS - PRE-WWII

NATIONAL MATCH - .45 ACP cal., similar to Government Model, except has hand honed action, match grade barrel, blue. Mfg. 1933-1941 within ser. no. range C164,800 - C215,000.

Add 10% with original box and instructions.

✳ *Fixed sights*

	$2,750	$2,150	$1,350	$925	$625	$550	$500

✳ *Adj. sights*

	$3,650	$2,950	$1,975	$1,625	$1,275	$1,075	$850

PISTOLS: SEMI-AUTO, NATIONAL MATCH MODELS – WWII & POST-WWII

Add 10% for NIB condition on models listed below.

GOLD CUP NATIONAL MATCH - .45 ACP cal., match grade barrel, new design bushing, flat or arched (mfg. approx. 1959-1964) mainspring housing, long adj. stop trigger, hand fitted slide with enlarged ejection port, adj. target sights, gold medallions in grips, "NM" suffix. Mfg. 1957-1970.

	$1,095	$900	$650	$500	$450	$425	$400

Note: This model was the first Gold Cup National Match Model manufactured following WW II.

GOLD CUP MKIII NATIONAL MATCH - .38 Spl. cal., similar to Gold Cup National Match, except chambered for .38 Spl., mid-range wadcutter, NMR or MR suffix. Mfg. 1961-1974.

	$1,100	$895	$775	$675	$625	$525	$475

Grading	100%	98%	95%	90%	80%	70%	60%

MKIV/SERIES 70 GOLD CUP NATIONAL MATCH- .45 ACP cal., flat mainspring housing, accurizer barrel and bushing, adj. trigger, target hammer, solid rib, Colt-Elliason sight. Mfg. 1970-1983.

	$1,150	$895	$650	$495	$450	$395	$375

MKIV/SERIES 70 GOLD CUP 75TH ANNIVERSARY NATIONAL MATCH - similar to Gold Cup, except was mfg. for commemorative aspect of Camp Perry, 1978, 200 mfg. 1978 only.

	$1,250	$995	$750	$650	$550	$450	$425

GOLD CUP MKIV SERIES 80 NATIONAL MATCH- .45 ACP cal., 5 in. barrel, 7 or 8 (new 1992) shot mag., 39 oz., Colt-Elliason adj. rear sight, wide grooved adj. target trigger, under cut front sight, flat mainspring housing, critical internal parts are hand honed. Mfg. 1983-1996.

	$900	$725	$550	$425	$400	$350	$325

Last MSR was $937.

In 1992, this model was updated to accept an 8 shot mag.

* ***Stainless Gold Cup National Match***- similar to Gold Cup, only manufactured from stainless steel, matte finish, mfg. late 1986-1996.

	$900	$725	$550

Last MSR was $1,003.

Add $70 for "Ultimate" bright stainless steel finish.

* ***.38 Super Elite National Match*** - two-tone gun (stainless slide and blue frame), special edition by Accu-Sports.

	$1,150	$925	$700

* ***Bullseye National Match*** - .45 ACP cal., hand built, tuned, and adjusted by Colt's custom gunsmiths for precise match accuracy, includes factory installed Bo- Mar sights, equipped with carrying case and 2 extra mags. Mfg. 1991-92.

	$1,325	$1,075	$895	$800	$725	$650	$600

Last MSR was $1,500.

Presentation Gold Cup - .45 ACP cal., similar to regular Gold Cup Series 80 National Match, except has a deep blue-mirror bright finish accented by custom jeweled hammer, trigger, and barrel hood. Supplied with oak and velvet custom case. Mfg. 1991-92.

	$1,075	$895	$800	$725	$650	$600	$550

Last MSR was $1,195.

PISTOLS: SEMI-AUTO, SINGLE ACTION - RECENT MFG.

SEMI-AUTO CUSTOM SHOP ENGRAVING PRICING - PRE-1991

Values below represent pre-1991 factory semi-auto Custom Shop A-D engraving options, before they started separate Standard, Expert, and Master level pricing (1997). It should also be understood that, in most cases, the quality of the engraving and notoriety of the engraver can be as important as the amount of coverage.

Small Frame Engraving Options

includes Mustang, .380 ACP Government, Detective Special, and Diamondback models.

Add $776 for Class "A" Engraving (¼ Metal Coverage).
Add $959 for Class "B" Engraving (½ Metal Coverage).
Add $1,426 for Class "C" Engraving (¾ Metal Coverage).
Add $1,814 for Class "D" Engraving (Full Metal Coverage).

Medium Frame Engraving Options includes .45 ACP Gold Cup, Government Model, Officer's ACP, Python, Combat Commander, King Cobra, Trooper MKV, Lawman MKV, and Delta Elite models.

Add $969 for Class "A" Engraving (¼ Metal Coverage).
Add $1,199 for Class "B" Engraving (½ Metal Coverage).

Grading	100%	98%	95%	90%	80%	70%	60%

Add $1,783 for Class "C" Engraving (¾ Metal Coverage).

Add $2,289 for Class "D" Engraving (Full Metal Coverage).

Add 7% for 6 in. barrel, 14% for 8 in. barrel, or 25% for stainless steel construction.

Special engraving/options include inlays, seals, custom grips, lettering, prices were quoted upon request. Smooth ivory grips were $215 extra (1990 retail).

Beginning in 1991, Colt began shipping all models in a distinctive blue plastic carrying case/ shipping container.

SEMI-AUTO CURRENT CUSTOM SHOP ENGRAVING PRICING

Please refer to the "Colt Custom Shop Engraving - Current Mfg." listing earlier in this section for current semi-auto engraving options and pricing. Semi-auto custom order quotations from Colt are available at $25 each (deductible from work order).

JUNIOR POCKET MODEL - .22 S or .25 ACP cal., 2¼ in. barrel, blue, checkered walnut grips, made by Astra in Spain from 1958-1968.

	100%	98%	95%	90%	80%	70%	60%
.22 Short	$320	$280	$240	$210	$180	$160	$140
.25 ACP	$260	$235	$195	$180	$150	$140	$130

Add 10% for nickel finish.

A very few conversion kits were offered for this model. They are rare and asking prices are $250-$325 if in mint condition.

COLT AUTOMATIC CALIBER .25 - .25 ACP cal., mfg. by Firearms International for Colt between 1970-1973.

100%	98%	95%	90%	80%	70%	60%
$300	$275	$225	$185	$150	$140	$130

COMMANDER (PRE-70 SERIES) - 9mm Para., .38 Super, or .45 ACP cal., 4¼ in. barrel, full size grips, alloy (Lightweight Model) variations. Mfg. 1950-1976.

	100%	98%	95%	90%	80%	70%	60%
9mm Para.	$650	$550	$475	$395	$365	$325	$295
.38 Super/.45 ACP	$750	$650	$550	$450	$395	$350	$300

Add 50% for Springfield Armory test pistols.

This model has a "LW" suffix.

GOVERNMENT MODEL MKIV/SERIES 70 - .45 ACP, .38 Super, 9mm Para., or 9mm Steyr cal., 5 in. barrel, checkered walnut grips/medallion, Series 70 models were serial numbered with "SM" prefixes (approx. 3,000 mfg.), "70G" prefixes 1970-1976, "70L" and "70S" prefixes also (see Serialization section for more information), "G70" suffixes 1976-1980, "B70" suffixes 1979-1981, and "70B" prefixes 1981-1983. Mfg. 1970-1983.

	100%	98%	95%	90%	80%	70%	60%
Blue finish	$925	$700	$525	$425	$350	$315	$285
Nickel finish	$1,000	$750	$550	$450	$350	$315	$285

Add 10% if in NIB condition, 20% for NIB with early two-piece box.

9mm Steyr was made for European exportation only. However, a few specimens have found their way into the United States. Prices for NIB specimens are in the $750 range.

✱ Series 70 Combat Govt. -.45 ACP cal., bluish-black metal finish, features modifications for combat shooting, forerunner to the Combat Elite.

100%	98%	95%	90%	80%	70%	60%
$875	$750	$650	$550	$475	$395	$335

Add 10% for NIB condition.

✱ Series 70 Lightweight Commander - 7.65mm (.30 Luger), 9mm Para, .38 Super, or .45 ACP cal., 4¼ in. barrel, full size grips, this model is denoted by a "CLW" prefix. Mfg. 1970-1983.

	100%	98%	95%	90%	80%	70%	60%
9mm Para.	$850	$700	$625	$525	$450	$375	$315
.38 Super/.45 ACP	$900	$750	$650	$550	$450	$375	$315
7.65mm	$2,500	$2,000	$1,575	$1,250	$995	$875	$750

Add 10% for NIB condition.

500 Lightweight Commanders were mfg. in 7.65mm cal. during 1971. While most of these were mfg. for export trade, 5 were sold in the U.S.

Grading	100%	98%	95%	90%	80%	70%	60%

❊ Series 70 Combat Commander

	$875	$725	$625	$525	$450	$375	$300

Add 10% for NIB condition.

This model was also available in satin nickel finish (scarce).

❊ Conversion Unit - converts .45 ACP to .22 LR, mfg. 1954-84 with either Accro adj. rear sight or fixed sight.

Adj. Sight	$450	$400	$275	$220	$195	$165	$140
Fixed Sight	$500	$450	$275	$225	$190	$165	$140

Add 50% for conversion units in bright nickel finish (very scarce).

GOVERNMENT MODEL SERIES 70 MODEL O - .45 ACP cal., new release from the custom shop beginning 2002, available in either blue finish or as a WWII replica. New 2002.

MSR $940	$825	$750	$650	$575	$495	$400	$300

Add $50 for WWII replica variation.

POST-WAR ACE SERVICE MODEL - .22 LR cal., similar specifications to previous Pre-WWII manufacture, blue (most common) or electroless nickel from Custom Shop finish, "SM" prefix (most common) or "B 70" suffix, approx. 30,000 mfg. between 1978-1982.

	$950	$795	$675	$575	$525	$450	$425

Add 10% for NIB condition.

This model is serial numbered approx. SM14,001-SM43,830.

GOVERNMENT MODEL MKIV/SERIES 80 - .38 Super, 9mm Para. (disc. 1992), or .45 ACP (disc. 1996) cal., single action, 5 in. barrel, 7 or 8 (new 1992) shot mag. in .45 ACP, approx. 38 oz., action has firing pin safety, checkered walnut (pre-1991 mfg.) or rubber combat style grips with medallion (new 1991). Production started in 1983 with ser. no. FG01000.

❊ Blue Finish - this finish was disc. in 1997.

	$725	$600	$475	$375	$325	$285	$260

Last MSR was $600.

Add 5% for 9mm Para. (disc. 1992) cal.
Add 10% for NIB condition.

❊ Nickel Finish - .45 ACP (disc. 1986) or .38 Super (disc. in 1987) cal.

	$775	$625	$500	$395	$335	$295	$275

Last MSR was $735.

Add 10% for NIB condition.

❊ Satin Nickel/Blue - is supplied with Colt-Pachmayr grips. Disc. 1986.

	$725	$600	$475	$375	$325	$285	$260

Last MSR was $557.

Add 10% for NIB condition.

❊ Stainless Steel - 9mm Para. (mfg. 1991-92), .38 Super (new 1990), .40 S&W (new 1992) or .45 ACP cal. Disc. 1998.

	$725	$600	$475

Last MSR was $813.

Add 5% for 9mm Para. (disc. 1992) cal.
Add 10% for NIB condition.

❊ "Ultimate" Bright Stainless Steel - .38 Super (new 1991) or .45 ACP cal., high polish stainless finish. Mfg. 1986-96.

	$750	$625	$495

Last MSR was $863.

Add 10% for NIB condition.

Grading	100%	98%	95%	90%	80%	70%	60%

* **Limited Class Model .45 ACP** - .45 ACP cal., designed for tactical competition, includes parkerized matte finish, lightweight composite trigger, ambidextrous safety, upswept grip safety, beveled mag. well, accurized, includes signed target. Mfg. 1994- 97.

	$725	$575	$450	$400	$350	$325	$300

Last MSR was $936.

* **Custom Compensated Model .45 ACP** - .45 ACP cal., designed for serious competitive shooting, blue slide with full profile BAT Compensator, Bo-Mar rear sight, flared funnel mag. well. Mfg. by Custom Shop 1994-98.

	$1,900	$1,500	$1,250	$1,000	$875	$750	$625

Last MSR was $2,428.

MODEL M1911A1 CUSTOM TACTICAL GOV'T - LEVEL I

- .45 ACP cal., designed for tactical competition, Commander style hammer, beveled/contoured mag. well, nylon flat mainspring housing, ambidextrous safety, long nylon trigger with over-travel stop, available in Officer's or Commmander's length. Mfg. 1998-2001.

	$640	$560	$495	$450	$400	$360	$330

Last MSR was $730.

In late 1999, this model was redesignated the Model O Custom Tactical Gov't.

* **Custom Tactical Gov't. Model - Level II** - similar to Level I, except has Videcki long aluminum trigger with over-travel stop, Heine fixed combat sights, Colt match grade barrel bushing, high-ride grip safety with palm swell, double diamond stocks. Mfg. 1998-2001.

	$825	$750	$650	$575	$495	$400	$300

Last MSR was $935.

* **Custom Tactical Gov't. Model - Level III** - similar to Level II, except has Bo-Mar adj. rear sight, super match hammer. Mfg. 1998-2001.

	$1,150	$1,025	$875	$750	$650	$575	$495

Last MSR was $1,350.

COMBAT GOVERNMENT SERIES 80

- .45 ACP cal., dark matte metal finish, features modifications for combat shooting, successor to the Series 70 Combat Govt. Disc.

	$650	$550	$475	$400	$345	$310	$280

Add 10% for NIB condition.

* **Special Combat Government Competition Model** - .45 ACP cal., competition model featuring skeletonized trigger, custom tuning, polished ramp, throated barrel, flared ejection port, and cut-out hammer. Supplied with two 8 shot mags., hard chrome slide and receiver, Bo-Mar rear and Clark dovetail front sight, flared mag. well, shipped with certified target. New 1992.

MSR	$1,640		$1,350	$1,050	$925	$800	$650	$575	$495

* **Special Combat Government (Carry Model)** - similar to Special Combat Government, except has royal blue finish, bar-dot night sights, and ambidextrous safety. Mfg. 1992-2000.

	$1,125	$925	$750	$650	$575	$495	$400

Last MSR was $1,365.

* **Combat Elite** - .38 Super or .45 ACP cal., similar to Gold Cup, only with wraparound rubber grips, beveled magazine well, stainless steel receiver with carbon steel slide, and Accro adj. sighting system. Disc. 1996.

	$730	$620	$455	$400	$360	$330	$300

Last MSR was $895.

Grading	100%	98%	95%	90%	80%	70%	60%

* *Conversion Unit - Series 80* - converts Series 80 Govt. Model only to .22 LR or 9mm Para., mfg. 1984-86, 1995, and 1998, with Accro adj. rear sight.

9mm Para.	$675	$550	$450	$375	$325	$250	$200
.22 LR (mfg. 1984-86)	$675	$550	$450	$375	$325	$250	$200

Last MSR was $305.

.22 LR(mfg. 1995 only, rare)	$675	$550	$450	$375	$325	$250	$200

◇**Colt Ace II Conversion Unit** - similar to above, except features an aluminum slide and barrel w/o floating chamber, does not have hold open feature. Mfg. 1998.

	$350	$295	$275	$225	$190	$175	$150

COMBAT TARGET MODEL SERIES 80 - .45 ACP cal. only, 5 in. barrel, adj. sights, matte finish. Mfg. 1997 only.

	$615	$495	$400	$350	$320	$300	$280

Last MSR was $768.

* *Combat Target Model Stainless* - similar to Combat Target Model, except stainless steel finish. Mfg. 1997 only.

	$745	$625	$500

Last MSR was $820.

COMMANDER LIGHTWEIGHT SERIES 80 - .45 ACP cal., 4¼ in. barrel, similar to Government Model, except shorter and lighter alloy frame, fixed sights, round spur hammer, 27½ oz. Mfg. 1983-1997.

	$595	$485	$395	$345	$320	$300	$280

Last MSR was $735.

Add 10% for .38 Super or 9mm Para. (disc.) cals.

COMBAT COMMANDER SERIES 80 - .38 Super (disc.), 9mm Para. (disc. 1992), or .45 ACP cal., similar to Lightweight, except has steel frame.

* *Blue Finish* - disc. 1996.

	$575	$475	$385	$340	$315	$295	$275

Last MSR was $735.

Add $20 for 9mm Para. (disc.) or .38 Super (disc.) cal.

* *Blue Slide/Stainless Steel Receiver* - .45 ACP cal., two-tone matte finish, upswept grip safety, lightweight perforated trigger, black Hogue grips, 8 shot mag., 35 oz. Mfg. 1998 only.

	$650	$525	$450	$410	$380	$350	$325

Last MSR was $813.

* *Stainless Steel* - .38 Super (mfg. 1992-97) or .45 ACP cal. Mfg. 1990-98.

	$640	$520	$430

Last MSR was $813.

* *Satin Nickel* - disc. 1986.

	$575	$475	$410	$365	$310	$275	$250

Last MSR was $550.

* *Gold Cup Commander* - .45 ACP cal., features custom shop alterations including heavy duty adj. target sights, beveled mag. well, serrated front strap, checkered mainspring housing, wide grip safety, and Palo Alto wood grips. Mfg. 1991-1993.

	$865	$715	$595	$550	$495	$440	$395

Last MSR was $936.

* *Gold Cup Commander Stainless* - stainless variation of the Gold Cup Commander. Mfg. 1992 - disc.

	$870	$715	$595

Last MSR was $949.

Grading	100%	98%	95%	90%	80%	70%	60%

OFFICER'S MODEL SERIES 80 - .45 ACP cal. only, 3½ in. barrel, 34 oz., 6 shot mag., short version of the Government Model. Mfg. 1985 - disc.

* ✹ *Blue Finish* - disc. 1996.

	$575	$475	$385	$340	$315	$295	$275

Last MSR was $735.

* ✹ *Matte Blue Finish*

	$525	$440	$370	$330	$280	$250	$225

Last MSR was $625 (disc. 1991).

* ✹ *Officer's Stainless Steel* - matte stainless steel finish. Mfg. 1986-1997.

	$640	$520	$430

Last MSR was $813.

Add $74 for "Ultimate" bright stainless steel finish (mfg. 1987-96).

* ✹ *Officer's Lightweight* - similar to Officer's ACP, except has alloy frame and weighs 24 oz. Mfg. 1986-1997.

	$575	$475	$385	$340	$315	$295	$275

Last MSR was $735.

* ✹ *Concealed Carry Officer* - .45 ACP cal., features matte stainless steel slide with matte blue aluminum alloy receiver, 7 shot mag., black contoured Hogue grips, upswept grip safety, lightweight perforated trigger, 26 oz. Mfg. 1998 only.

	$650	$525	$450	$410	$380	$350	$325

Last MSR was $813.

* ✹ *Officer's Satin Nickel* - disc. 1985.

	$575	$475	$450	$375	$295	$260	$235

Last MSR was $513.

* ✹ *General Officer's Model* - bright stainless steel with rosewood grips, special edition. Disc. 1996.

	$650	$550	$450

Last MSR was $750.

COLT Z 40 - .40 S&W cal., DAO, alloy frame, double column mag., firing pin safety, 3 dot sights, blue finish with black checkered synthetic grips and silver trigger, straight backstrap, marked "Colt Z40" on top of slide, while approx. 750-800 pieces were mfg. 1998-99 by CZ for a Colt subcontract, they were never shipped, and as a result, very few have made it into the U.S. to date from the Czech Republic.

	$595	$525	$475	$425	$400	$375	$350

DEFENDER MODEL O - .40 S&W (mfg. 1999 only) or .45 ACP cal., 3 in. barrel with 3 dot sights, 7 shot mag., rubber wrap-around grips with finger grooves, lightweight perforated trigger, steel slide with aluminum frame finished in matte stainless, firing pin safety, 22½ oz. New 1998.

MSR	$842		$695	$575	$475

* ✹ *Defender Plus* - .45 ACP cal., as this edition went to press, information was not available on this model. New 2002.

MSR	$876		$715	$600	$500

XSE SERIES MODEL O - .45 ACP cal., 4 or 5 (Govt. Model only) in. barrel, stainless brushed finish, front and rear slide serrations, checkered double diamond rosewood grips, 3 dot sights, new roll marking and enhanced tolerances, extended ambidextrous thumb safeties. New 2000.

* ✹ *Government* - 5 in. barrel, blue (new 2002) or stainless brushed (SS Model) finish, 8 shot mag.

MSR	$950		$800	$650	$500

Grading	100%	98%	95%	90%	80%	70%	60%

✳ *Concealed Carry Officers SS* - features lightweight aluminum alloy frame, 4¼ in. barrel and 7 shot mag. Limited mfg. 2000 only.

	$650	$550	$450				

Last MSR was $750.

✳ *Commander SS* - features 4¼ in. barrel and 8 shot mag.

MSR	$950	$800	$650	$500			

✳ *Lightweight Commander SS* - features lightweight aluminum alloy frame, 4¼ in. barrel and 8 shot mag.

MSR	$950	$800	$650	$500			

GOLD CUP NATIONAL MATCH MKIV/SERIES 80 - .45 ACP cal., flat mainspring housing, 8 shot mag., accurizer barrel and bushing, adj. trigger, target hammer, solid rib, Colt-Elliason sight. Mfg. 1983-1996.

	$875	$700	$550	$425	$395	$350	$325

Last MSR was $937.

Add 10% for NIB condition.

In 1992, this model was updated to accept an 8 shot mag. During 1997, this updated model was designated the Colt Gold Cup Trophy.

✳ *Elite IX Gold Cup National Match* - 9mm Para. cal., stainless steel and blue, marked "GCNM" on right side, and "ELITE IX – 9mm Luger" on left side, IX prefix in ser. no.

	$895	$725	$575	$450	$400	$365	$335

Add 10% for NIB condition.

✳ *Stainless Gold Cup National Match* - similar to Gold Cup, only manufactured from stainless steel, matte finish. Mfg. late 1986-1996.

	$895	$725	$575				

Last MSR was $1,003.

Add $70 for "Ultimate" brite stainless steel finish.
Add 10% for NIB condition.

GOLD CUP TROPHY (MODEL O) - .45 ACP cal., flat mainspring housing, 7 (disc.) or 8 shot mag., accurizer barrel and bushing, round top slide, adj. aluminum trigger, target hammer, Bo-Mar Elliason style rear sight, checkered black wrap-around rubber grips, shipped with test target, 39 oz. New 1997.

MSR	$1,050	$975	$700	$550	$425	$395	$350	$325

This model replaced the MKIV/Series 80 Gold Cup National Match in 1997, and is only available from the Colt Custom Shop.

✳ *Stainless Gold Cup Trophy* - similar to Gold Cup Trophy, only manufactured from stainless steel, matte finish, 39 oz. New 1997.

MSR	$1,116	$895	$650	$525			

1991 SERIES MODEL O (MKIV SERIES 80) - 9mm Para. (disc. 2001) or .45 ACP cal., similar to original WWII issue pistols with government issue parkerized matte finish, fixed sights, and black composite grips, 5 in. barrel, 7 shot mag., 38 oz., includes brown molded case. New 1991.

MSR	$699	$565	$450	$385	$325	$295	$275	$250

This model is serialized consecutively with the last batch of Govt. models manufactured during 1945.

✳ *Model 1991 Stainless Steel* - features matte stainless steel frame and slide. New 1996.

MSR	$800	$650	$525	$400			

Grading	100%	98%	95%	90%	80%	70%	60%

✳ ***Model 1991 Commander*** - .45 ACP cal., 4¼ in. barrel, full size grip, 7 shot mag., parkerized finish, 36 oz. New 1993.

    MSR   **$699**   **$565**   **$450**   **$385**   **$325**   **$295**   **$275**   **$250**

✳ ***Model 1991 Officer's Compact*** - similar to Model M1991 A1, except has 3½ in. barrel, 6 shot mag., 34 oz. Mfg. 1992-99.

                  $460   **$375**   **$335**   **$295**   **$275**   **$250**   **$225**

        Last MSR was $556.

◇**Model 1991 Officer's Stainless Compact** - similar to Model M1991 A1 Officer's Compact, except is stainless steel. Mfg. 1999 only.

                  $510   **$440**   **$355**

        Last MSR was $610.

◇**Model 1991 Commander SS** - similar to Model M1991 A1 Commander, except is stainless steel. New 1999.

    MSR   **$800**   **$650**   **$525**   **$400**

DELTA ELITE - 10mm cal., 5 in. barrel, black neoprene grips, high profile 3 dot sights, blue finish, 8 shot mag., 38 oz. Mfg. 1987-96.

                  $700   **$515**   **$450**   **$375**   **$335**   **$300**   **$275**

        Last MSR was $807.

The first 500 guns of this model (mfg. 1985) were called the Delta Elite First Edition, and featured laser engraving with gold-fill, smooth wood grips, and were furnished with presentation cases. Current pricing is in the $795-$995 range.

✳ ***Stainless Steel*** - matte stainless steel finish. Mfg. 1989-96.

                  $750   **$550**   **$455**

        Last MSR was $860.

Add $78 for "Ultimate" brite stainless steel finish (disc. 1993).

The first 1,000 guns of this model (mfg. 1988) were called the Delta Elite First Edition, and featured stamped lettering on slide, ebony grips, and did not have display cases. Current pricing is in the $795-$850 range.

DELTA GOLD CUP STAINLESS - 10mm cal., target variation, includes Accro adj. rear sight and trigger (serrated also), wraparound combat grips. Mfg. 1989-1993, re-released 1995-96.

                  $900   **$650**   **$525**

        Last MSR was $1,027.

✳ ***Delta Gold Cup Blue*** - similar to Delta Gold Cup Stainless, except has blue finish. Mfg. 1991 only.

                  $775   **$600**   **$500**   **$450**   **$400**   **$360**   **$330**

        Last MSR was $870.

.380 GOVERNMENT MODEL SERIES 80 - .380 ACP cal. only, single action, 3¼ in. barrel, 7 shot mag., fixed sights, composition stocks, 21¾ oz. New 1985.

✳ ***Blue Finish*** - finish disc. in 1997.

                  $395   **$325**   **$250**   **$215**   **$200**   **$190**   **$180**

        Last MSR was $474.

✳ ***Nickel Finish*** - bright polish nickel finish with white composite grips. Disc. 1994.

                  $450   **$350**   **$265**   **$225**   **$200**   **$190**   **$180**

        Last MSR was $504.

✳ ***Coltguard Finish*** - employs a high strength electroless matte nickel finish. Mfg. 1986-1989.

                  $395   **$325**   **$250**   **$215**   **$200**   **$190**   **$180**

        Last MSR was $406.

Grading	100%	98%	95%	90%	80%	70%	60%

✳ Stainless Steel - mfg. 1989-1997.

        $425 $335 $270

Last MSR was $508.

GOVT. POCKETLITE L.W. - similar to .380 Series 80 Govt. Model, except frame is mfg. with alloy, blue or nickel/stainless (mfg. 1992-1993) finish only, black composition grips, 14 ¾ oz. Mfg. 1991-97.

        $375 $315 $250 $215 $200 $190 $180

Last MSR was $462.

    Add $30 for nickel/stainless finish (disc. 1993).

✳ Govt. Pocketlite Teflon Nickel/Stainless - similar to Govt. Pocketlite L.W., except has combination of Teflon nickel, stainless steel finish. Mfg. 1997-98.

        $425 $350 $270

Last MSR was $508.

MUSTANG - similar to .380 Series Govt., except has 2¾ in. barrel, single action, 5 or 6 (new 1992) shot mag., blue finish only, 18½ oz. Mfg. 1986-1997.

        $375 $300 $250 $215 $200 $190 $180

Last MSR was $462.

✳ Nickel finish - bright polish nickel finish with white composite grips. Mfg. 1987- 94.

        $415 $330 $270 $240 $220 $210 $200

Last MSR was $504.

✳ Stainless Steel - stainless steel variation of the Mustang. Mfg. 1990-97.

        $425 $350 $275

Last MSR was $508.

✳ Coltguard finish - employs a high strength electroless matte nickel finish. Mfg. 1987.

        $335 $300 $260 $235 $210 $200 $185

Last MSR was $406.

MUSTANG PLUS II - .380 ACP cal. only, 2¾ in. barrel, blue finish, black composition grips, 7 shot mag., 20 oz. Mfg. 1988-96.

        $370 $300 $250 $215 $200 $190 $180

Last MSR was $462.

    This model has the full grip length of the .380 Government Model.

✳ Stainless Steel - stainless steel variation of the Mustang Plus II. Mfg. 1990-97.

        $395 $335 $270

Last MSR was $508.

MUSTANG POCKETLITE L.W. - similar to Mustang, except has aluminum alloy receiver and stainless slide, blue (disc. 1997) or nickel/stainless finish, black composite grips, 12½ oz. Introduced 1987.

        $370 $300 $250 $215 $200 $190 $180

Last MSR was $462.

✳ Nickel/Stainless Steel Finish - similar to Mustang Pocketlite, except has nickel finish frame and stainless steel slide. Mfg. 1991-96.

        $385 $330 $270 $230 $200 $190 $180

Last MSR was $493.

✳ Mustang Pocketlite Teflon Nickel/Stainless - similar to Mustang Pocketlite L.W., except has combination of Teflon nickel, stainless steel finish. Mfg. 1997-99.

        $395 $335 $270

Last MSR was $508.

Grading	100%	98%	95%	90%	80%	70%	60%

✳ **Lady Elite** - features hard chrome receiver, blue slide with silver painted rollmark, finger extension mag., soft carrying case, limited mfg. 1995-96.

	$525	$450	$325	$250	$225	$200	$185

Last MSR was $612.

✳ **Nite Lite .380** - .380 ACP cal., features bar-dot glowing night sight, Teflon coated alloy receiver with stainless slide, finger extension mag., includes carrying case. Mfg. 1994 only.

	$495	$425	$325	$250	$225	$200	$185

Last MSR was $577.

PISTOLS: SEMI-AUTO, DOUBLE ACTION - RECENT MFG.

DOUBLE EAGLE SERIES 90 I & II - 9mm Para. (mfg. 1991 only), .38 Super (mfg. 1991 only), .45 ACP, or 10mm (disc. 1993) cal., double action semi-auto that operates on the Browning/ Colt short recoil, link pivot locking system used by the Govt. Model, 5 in. barrel, matte stainless steel only, 3 dot sighting system or Accro adj. rear sight (disc. 1994), checkered synthetic Xenoy grips, 8 shot mag. (9 shot in 9mm Para. or .38 Super cal.), decocking lever, squared off combat trigger guard, 39 oz. Mfg. 1990-96.

	$850	$650	$500

Last MSR was $727.

Add $50 for 9mm Para. or .38 Super cal.
Add $20 for 10mm cal.
Add 10% for NIB condition.

The first edition (1,000 mfg. in 1989) on this model did not have a decocking lever - retail was $916.

✳ **Double Eagle Combat Commander** - .40 S&W (new 1992) or .45 ACP cal., 4¼ in. barrel, 8 shot mag., white dot sights, 36 oz. Mfg. 1991-96.

	$850	$650	$500

Last MSR was $727.

✳ **Officer's Model** - .45 ACP cal., 3½ in. barrel, 8 shot mag., 35 oz. Mfg. 1991-disc.

	$850	$650	$500

Last MSR was $727.

✳ **Officer's Lightweight Model** - .45 ACP cal. only, 3½ in. barrel, alloy frame with blue finish only, white dot sights, 25 oz. Mfg. 1991-1993.

	$900	$700	$500	$400	$365	$330	$295

Last MSR was $696.

ALL AMERICAN MODEL 2000 - 9mm Para. cal. only, double action semi-auto, new design features roller-bearing mounted trigger allowing double action only trigger pull every shot, utilizes a recoil operated rotary action featuring integral locking lugs similar to the military M-16 rifle, hammerless, 4½ in. barrel, matte finished steel slide and polymer receiver, 15 shot mag., 3-dot sighting system, ambidextrous mag. release, black synthetic checkered grips, internal striker block safety, checkered trigger guard and front grip strap, 29 oz. Manufacturing difficulty forced discontinuance and design and tooling were returned to Reed Knight. Mfg. 1991-1993.

✳ **Model 2000 - Polymer Frame**

	$750	$650	$525	$450	$375	$325	$275

Last MSR was $575.

Add 10% for NIB condition.

This model could also be converted to a shorter version using a 3¾ in. barrel/bushing kit (no tools or other components were needed - $75 retail during 1993 only).

Grading	100%	98%	95%	90%	80%	70%	60%

✷ **Model 2000 - Aluminum Frame** - similar to polymer Model 2000, except frame is aluminum, serial numbered RK00001-RK03000 to commemorate the designer (Reed Knight), mfg. 1993.

| | $850 | $700 | $550 | $465 | $375 | $325 | $275 |

Last MSR was $575.

Add 10% for NIB condition.

PONY SERIES 90 - .380 ACP cal., double action only, 2³⁄₄ in. barrel, bobbed hammer, 6 shot mag., stainless construction, brushed finish, fixed sights, black composition grips, 19 oz. Mfg. 1997 only.

| | $425 | $350 | $295 |

Last MSR was $529.

✷ **Pony Pocketlite Lightweight** - .380 ACP cal., similar to Pony Series 90, except utilizes aluminum and stainless steel construction, brushed finish, 13 oz. Mfg. 1997- 99.

| | $425 | $350 | $295 |

Last MSR was $529.

POCKET NINE - 9mm Para. cal., double action only, 2³⁄₄ in. barrel, aluminum frame, ultra slim profile, 6 shot mag, matte/brushed stainless steel, wraparound rubber grips, 3- dot sights, 17 oz. Mfg. 1999 only.

| | $500 | $425 | $350 |

Last MSR was $615.

PISTOLS: SEMI-AUTO, .22 CAL. - WOODSMAN SERIES

The publisher wishes to once again express his thanks to Major (ret.) Robert J. Rayburn for his continued generous contributions of information regarding the Colt Woodsman Series.

The Colt Woodsman was made for 62 years, and included a multitude of variations/options in models, sights, barrels, grips, markings, etc. Many of the variations are quite scarce and desirable, but generally known only to specialized collectors. The following price guidelines are for standard production models, and only for those specimens in unmodified, factory original condition.

Over 690,000 Woodsmans with variations were mfg. between 1915-1977.

Factory engraved and special order Woodsmans are relatively rare and very desirable. Prices can fluctuate greatly, and auctions can sometimes be the only source of supply for these seldomly encountered pistols.

Note: All 100% condition Woodsmans with the original serial numbered box, test target, instruction folder, hang tag, and screw driver typically command a 10-25% premium, depending on the model's age and rarity.

PRE-WOODSMAN - .22 LR cal., 6 5/8 in. barrel. 10 shot mag., blue only, bottom mag. release, checkered wood grips, adj. front and rear sights. Mfg. 1915-1927, production totaled about 54,000, this model was officially named "Colt Automatic Pistol, Caliber .22 Target Model", magazine base has 2-line legend "CAL .22" "COLT". Standard velocity ammo. only.

| | $1,295 | $995 | $575 | $475 | $375 | $300 | $275 |

This model was manufactured to use standard velocity ammunition only (not high speed). Colt did offer a conversion kit for high velocity ammo. after the transition to high velocity in 1931.

Woodsmans mfg. between 1915-1922 had a lightweight pencil barrel (approx. serial range 1-31,000). The medium barrel was introduced in 1922 and was retained until the 90,000 serial range (approx. mfg. 1922-1934).

Grading	100%	98%	95%	90%	80%	70%	60%

WOODSMAN 1ST SERIES - .22 LR cal., 10 shot mag., blue only, bottom mag. release, checkered wood grips, marked "The Woodsman" on receiver, adj. sights, mfg. from 1927-1947, total production was approx. 112,000.

> Note: Guns made prior to 1931 were designed for standard velocity .22 LR ammunition only. The new style main spring housing, designed for high velocity ammunition, began appearing at approx. ser. no. 80,000 and was completely phased in by approx. ser. no. 85,000. Later guns, INCLUDING ALL PISTOLS MADE AFTER WWII, were designed for high velocity ammunition.
>
> Between 1934 and 1947 a tapered barrel was standard production (approx. ser. range 90,000-187,423).

✳ *Sport Model* - 4½ in. barrel, this model was introduced in 1933.

	$1,295	$995	$650	$550	$450	$395	$350

Add 10% for adj. front sight (available beginning 1937).
Add 50% for medium weight barrel (1933-34 mfg. only), and an additional 50% for semi-circular "half moon" front sight (1933 mfg. only).

> Approx. serial range on this variation is 86,105 - 187,423 from 1933 to 1947.

✳ *Target Model* - 6 5/8 in. barrel.

	$1,150	$850	$550	$400	$325	$275	$250

> Note: Colt discontinued the 1st series in 1947. These guns are quite different from the 2nd series started later in 1947.

WOODSMAN 1ST SERIES MATCH TARGET - .22 LR cal. only, 6 5/8 in. heavy barrel, commonly called "Bullseye" Match Target, mfg. 1938-1944, production totaled around 16,000. Difficult to find in mint condition. Values listed assume original one- piece extended walnut grips.

	$2,395	$1,595	$995	$750	$650	$550	$500

> The correct magazine on this model has a 3-line legend "COLT WOODSMAN", "CAL. 22 L.R.", and "MATCH TARGET MOD.".

✳ *"U.S. Property" Marked* - approx. 4,000 Match Target Woodsmans were sold to the U.S. Army and U.S. Navy during WWII. Most have serial numbers above MT12500, although some were shipped out of sequence with lower numbers. The wartime guns had elongated plastic stocks and standard blue finish, although some of them are now parkerized as the result of arsenal refinishing or other non-factory modifications. They are marked with either "US PROPERTY" or the ordnance wheel with crossed cannon, as well as the initials of the govt. inspector. Some also have additional markings.

	$2,495	$1,995	$1,425	$1,150	$925	$750	$575

> Check parkerized finish carefully for originality on this variation, as some "recent parkerizing" has been observed.

WOODSMAN 2ND SERIES - .22 LR cal. only, slide stop and hold open, push button mag. release on this model is located on the left side of frame, Coltwood plastic grips (mfg. 1947-1950) or brown plastic grips (mfg. 1950-1955), total production on all 2nd Series was (not including the Challenger) approx. 146,000, serialization has S suffix. Mfg. 1947-1955.

✳ *Sport Model* - 4½ in. barrel.

	$895	$695	$495	$395	$350	$295	$250

✳ *Target Model* - 6 in. barrel.

	$795	$595	$450	$350	$325	$275	$225

✳ *Match Target Model* - 4½ in. heavy barrel. This variation will command a premium over the 6 in. barrel.

	$1,195	$895	$595	$450	$425	$400	$375

✳ *Match Target Model* - 6 in. heavy barrel.

	$995	$795	$500	$400	$350	$325	$300

WOODSMAN 3RD SERIES - .22 LR cal. only, slide stop and hold open, mfg. between 1955-1977, black plastic grips (mfg. 1955-1960) or walnut grips (1960-1977), 3rd Models can be differentiated from 2nd Models by their bottom mag. release. Total production of all 3rd series Woodsman models (not including the Huntsman or Targetsman) exceeded 100,000, serialization has S suffix.

* **Sport Model** - 4½ in. barrel.

	100%	98%	95%	90%	80%	70%	60%
	$650	$550	$395	$325	$300	$275	$250

* **Target Model** - 6 in. barrel.

	$595	$495	$350	$275	$250	$235	$225

* **Match Target Model** - 4½ or 6 in. heavy barrel.

	$795	$695	$495	$400	$350	$325	$295

Add $100 4 ½ in. barrel if condition is 95% or better.

CHALLENGER MODEL - similar to Woodsman 2nd Series, only with fixed sights, without hold open, and bottom mag. release, 4½ and 6 in. barrels, mfg. between 1950-1955 with total production reaching approx. 77,000. Plastic grips.

	$495	$395	$275	$250	$225	$210	$180

HUNTSMAN MODEL - .22 LR cal. only, fixed sights and no hold open, 4½ and 6 in. barrels, black plastic grips to serial number 141094-C - walnut grips after that cutoff. Mfg. between 1955- 1977 with total production reaching over 100,000.

	$450	$350	$250	$225	$200	$180	$160

The Huntsman is very similar to the Challenger Model, except is built on a 3rd series frame.

* **Huntsman Model S Master Series** - approx. 400 Model S Masters were sold in 1983. This was a parts clean up by Colt, using Huntsman frames left over from the last days of production. They were equipped with automatic slide stop and Elliason rear sight, gold etching on the slide, and a French fitted walnut case marked "1 of 400". Approx. 285 had straight, non-tapered Huntsman barrel, while the remainder had the tapered Woodsman Sport barrel with pinned front sight.

	100%	98%	95%	90%	80%	70%	60%
Huntsman barrel	$1,095	$895	$500	$425	$350	$325	$295
Woodsman barrel	$1,195	$800	$600	$500	$425	$350	$325

Above values assume original walnut case included. Values for this model in 98%-60% original condition are hard to compute, as most are mint or new.

TARGETSMAN MODEL - similar to the Huntsman, except has adj. rear sight and thumbrest on left grip, 6 in. barrel only, approx. 65,000 mfg. 1959-1977.

	$495	$395	$295	$260	$240	$220	$200

CADET - .22 LR cal., 4½ in. barrel, stainless steel, 10 shot mag., predecessor to the Colt 22 Model, originally introduced in 1994, fixed sights, this model was disc. by 1995 because of litigation involving the trademarked model name, 33½ oz.

	$395	$295	$250

COLT 22 - .22 LR cal., 4½ in. VR barrel, stainless steel, fixed sights, 10 shot mag., one- piece black Pachmayr rubber grips, 33½ oz. Mfg. 1994-98.

	$295	$250	$225

Last MSR was $248.

* **Colt 22 Target** - .22 LR cal., 6 in. VR barrel with full length grooved sight rib, adj. rear sight, 40½ oz. Mfg. 1995-99.

	$295	$250	$225

Last MSR was $377.

100%	98%	95%	90%	80%	70%	60%	50%	40%	30%	20%	10%

REVOLVERS: DOUBLE ACTION

Most of these double action revolvers listed can have their original configuration confirmed with a Colt factory letter. To receive a letter, write: COLT HISTORIAN, P.O. Box 1868, Hartford, CT, 06144. The research fee for these revolvers is typically either $75 or $100, depending on the model. If they cannot obtain additional information on the variation you request, they will refund $50.

In Oct. of 1999, Colt announced that all double action revolvers would be discontinued, including any custom shop manufacture. After over 120 years of continuous production, the series of swing out double action revolvers finally ended. As a result, interest and prices for this discontinued revolver configuration have already increased, even on recently discontinued models/configurations. After discontinuance, many dealers reported that they were able to finally sell their Colt DAs for retail, as opposed to them being slow movers previously. As in any situation where the supply becomes fixed and demand goes up, prices will also increase. Values below represent the current marketplace as this edition went to press.

By the end of 2001, Colt resumed shipping a few double action revolvers to some dealers in limited quantity via the Custom Shop. Whether this represents a continued commitment or just a parts "clean-up", combined with targets of opportunity remains to be seen.

MODEL 1877 LIGHTNING - .38 Colt or .32 Colt (very rare) cal., 2, 2½, 3½, 4½, or 6 in. barrels without ejector, 4½, 5, 6, 7, or 7½ in. barrels with ejector, 6 shot double action, long cylinder fluting, blue finish with case hardened frame and hammer, full nickel plating also available. Over 166,000 mfg. from 1877-1910.

$1,775	$1,500	$1,200	$950	$875	$775	$700	$650	$575	$475	$350	$295

MODEL 1877 THUNDERER - .41 Colt cal. only, otherwise same general specifications as Model 1877 Lightning.

$1,800	$1,600	$1,150	$975	$875	$775	$675	$600	$525	$450	$325	$285

MODEL 1878 DA - .22 LR (very rare), .32-20 WCF (scarce), .38 Colt, .38-40 WCF (scarce, approx. 1,600 mfg.), .41 LC (scarce), .44 Russian, .44 German, .44 S&W, .44- 40 WCF (Colt Frontier Six Shooter), .45 LC, .450 Eley, .455 Eley, or .476 Eley cal., 2½ (scarce), 3½, or 4 in. barrels without ejector, 4¾, 5½, or 7½ in. with ejector, 6 in. is 1902 U.S. Revolver (Alaskan/Phillipines Models), 6 shot cylinder with long flutes, pinched frame, removable trigger guard, early guns have checkered walnut stocks, later guns have hard black rubber. Mfg. 1878-1905. Over 51,000 made.

$5,250	$4,750	$3,750	$3,000	$2,500	$1,750	$1,500	$950	$850	$750	$625	$500

This model in .44-40 WCF was called the Colt Frontier Six Shooter, and this inscription is either etched or roll marked on the barrel.

This model is commonly encountered with a broken mechanism. Since original parts are scarce, at least $500 must be deducted for a non-working action.

Many original 1878 barrels have "found their way" on the front end of a SAA frame, since the barrels are interchangable. Because of this, many "original" Model 1878 DAs may have an incorrect and/or later SAA Colt barrel attached. Watch yourself here!

MODEL 1889 "NAVY" (NEW NAVY DA, MODEL OF 1889) - .38 Short and Long Colt, and .41 Short and Long Colt cal., 3, 4½, and 6 in. barrel, blue (military and civilian) or nickel (civilian only) finish, wood (military) or hard rubber (civilian) grips, the first solid frame, swing out cylinder with no visible locking latches (rotates counter-clockwise), sideplate is also on the right-hand side of frame, Colt produced approx. 31,000 mfg. 1889-1894, 1st 5,000 were ordered by U.S. Navy, with some additional orders later in production - hence name.

$1,750	$1,550	$1,350	$1,150	$950	$750	$650	$575	$500	$425	$350	$300

Add 40% for 3 in. barrel.

Add 35% for .38 Short or Long Colt cal.

Add 65%-100% for U.S. Navy Contract (S.N. 1-5,000), U.S.N. on butt (.38 LC cal. only), depending on condition.

100%	98%	95%	90%	80%	70%	60%	50%	40%	30%	20%	10%

MODEL 1892 "NEW ARMY & NAVY" (2ND ISSUE) - similar to 1889 Navy, but double cylinder notches, double locking bolt, and shorter flutes, square cyl. release thumb catch, hard rubber (commercial models) or plain uncheckered wood (military models) grips, .32-20 WCF cal. (uncommon) added in 1905, mfg. 1892-1907.

$1,350	$1,100	$900	$700	$500	$400	$300	$250	$225	$210	$195	$180

Add $100-$750 for U.S.N. markings, depending on condition.
Add 25% for 3 in. barrel.

* *Models 1892, 1894, 1895, 1896, 1901, 1903* - these were variations of the Model 1892, military model (.38 Long Colt only) values will approximate those shown above, while civilian models will be approx. 10%-25% less, depending on condition.

OFFICER'S MODEL TARGET (FIRST ISSUE) - .38 Spl. or .38 Long Colt cal., 6 in. barrel, cylinder rotates counter-clockwise and sideplate is on right-hand side of frame, adj. front - adj. rear type sights, high luster blue, flat-top. Mfg. 1904-1908.

$1,350	$1,100	$900	$750	$625	$550	$495	$395	$295	$275	$250	$225

OFFICER'S MODEL TARGET (SECOND ISSUE) - .32 Colt or .38 Spl. cal., 4, 4½, 5, 6, or 7½ in. barrel, cylinder rotates clockwise, high luster blue through 1916, adj. front - adj. rear type sights, checkered walnut grips, deep set medallions in grips were standard from 1913-1923. Mfg. 1908-1926. Last patent date July 4, 1905.

$1,150	$1,000	$850	$515	$450	$395	$330	$290	$250	$225	$210	$195

Add 60% for .32 Colt cal.
Add 60% for 4, 4½, or 5 in. barrel.

OFFICER'S MODEL TARGET (THIRD ISSUE) - similar design to the Second Issue, .22 cal. was added beginning 1930, heavy barrel was introduced in 1935. Mfg. 1927- 1949. Last patent date Oct. 5, 1926.

$725	$675	$600	$500	$450	$375	$325	$295	$265	$245	$225	$205

Add 10% for .22 LR cal. (mfg. started 1930).

MODEL 1905 MARINE CORPS - .38 Short or Long, similar to New Navy Second Issue, except has a round butt, checkered wood grips w/o medallion, and 6 in. barrel only. Mfg. 1905-1909 in approx. ser. no. range 10,001- 10,926, about 926 mfg.

$2,650	$2,350	$2,050	$1,750	$1,625	$1,425	$1,250	$1,000	$895	$795	$695	$595

Add 30% for Military issue marked "USMC" on butt.

ARMY SPECIAL MODEL - .32-20 WCF, .38 (various), and .41 Colt cals., 4, 4½, 5, and 6 in. barrels, hard rubber grips standard through 1923 - checkered wood with medallions beginning about 1924, blue finish, fixed sights, rounded checkered cylinder release thumb catch, smooth trigger, has heavier frame than New Navy, approx. ser. no. range 291,000-540,000, last patent date on barrel was July 4, 1905. Mfg. 1908-1927.

$725	$650	$500	$400	$325	$295	$275	$250	$225	$200	$185	$175

Add 15% for nickel finish.

NEW SERVICE MODEL - .38 Spl., .357 Mag., .38-40 WCF, .44-40 WCF, .44 Russian, .44 Spl., .45 ACP, .45 LC, .450 Eley, .455 Eley, or .476 Eley cals., 4, 5, or 6 in. barrels in .357 Mag. and .38 Spl., 4½, 5½, and 7½ in. barrel in all others, blue or nickel finish, bright blue finish was used through circa 1916, originally hard rubber (until approx. late '20s), with later guns having walnut grips with medallions. Mfg. 1898-1942. Rare cals. (.450 and .476 Eley cals.) and 4 in. barrels will command premiums over values listed below.

New Service Models marked "NEW SERVICE 45 COLT" in .45 ACP cal. with shorter cylinder for rimmed cartridge are rare. Early models (first type) have flat latches. Later models (second type) have rounded cylinder latches.

* *Commercial*

$1,500	$1,375	$1,175	$1,000	$925	$850	$775	$650	$500	$425	$375	$295

Nickel finish will command a slight premium, particularly in short barrel lengths.

100%	98%	95%	90%	80%	70%	60%	50%	40%	30%	20%	10%

✳ 1909 Army Model

100%	98%	95%	90%	80%	70%	60%	50%	40%	30%	20%	10%
$1,795	$1,275	$1,125	$1,000	$925	$850	$775	$680	$590	$510	$435	$375

✳ 1909 Navy Model - shortest production run of the Model 1909 variations.

$2,950	$2,500	$2,100	$1,500	$1,150	$1,000	$895	$775	$725	$650	$525	$500

✳ 1909 - USMC

$3,100	$2,400	$2,100	$1,775	$1,500	$1,250	$975	$850	$775	$675	$550	$500

✳ 1917 Army

$1,300	$995	$875	$700	$610	$525	$455	$390	$335	$295	$250	$200

✳ 1917 Civilian/Commercial (1917 C/CM)

.45 ACP cal., 5½ in. barrel only, last patent date is OCT 5, 1926, checkered walnut grips with medallions, left side of barrel marked "Colt Model 1917 Auto Ctge." approx. 1,000 mfg. during 1932, serialized 335,000-336,000.

$1,500	$1,275	$1,050	$850	$650	$525	$450	$415	$385	$350	$325	$295

✳ 1917 Civilian/Commercial (Piece Parts Model)

.38-40 WCF, .44-40 WCF, or .45 LC cal., 4½ or 5½ in. barrel, hard rubber grips, or checkered walnut with medallions, last patent date is July 4, 1905, approx. 1,000 mfg. serialized 336,450- 337,500.

$1,200	$995	$900	$800	$625	$495	$415	$380	$360	$330	$300	$275

✳ New Service Target

similar to New Service Model, flat-top frame, hand-honed action and adj. front - adj. rear type sights, 6 (scarce) or 7½ in. barrel, square butt, round butt available after 1930, checkered grip straps, checkered walnut grips with medallion after 1913, blue or nickel (scarce) finish. Mfg. 1900-1940.

$3,000	$2,650	$2,100	$1,750	$1,500	$1,250	$900	$750	$635	$550	$460	$400

Add 40% - 60% for 6 in. barrel, depending on original condition.

✳ Shooting Master

various cals. from 38 Spl. through .45 LC, 6 in. barrel, checkered walnut grips with Colt Medallion, machined grip straps, trigger, hammer, and ejector rod head, round or square butt, approx. ser. no. range 333,000 - 350,000.

✳ Regular cals.

$1,250	$1,100	$975	$900	$825	$755	$665	$575	$500	$435	$395	$375

Add 35% for .357 Mag.

✳ .45 ACP or .45 LC cals.

N/A	N/A	$3,600	$3,300	$3,000	$2,500	$2,050	$1,675	$1,350	$1,000	$750	$600

✳ .44 Spl. cal.

N/A	N/A	$4,400	$3,950	$3,500	$3,000	$2,500	$2,000	$1,575	$1,250	$1,000	$850

The Shooting Master could be ordered with a square butt after 1933.

OFFICIAL POLICE PRE-WAR

.32-20 WCF (disc. 1942), .38-200 (British), .41 long (disc. 1930), .38 Spl., or .22 LR (introduced 1930 - 4 or 6 in. barrel only, 4 in. scarce) cal., blue finish, 6 shot, round (very scarce) or square butt, 4, 5, or 6 in. barrels, 2 in. barrel (scarce) in .38 Spl., checkered walnut grips, fixed sights, last patent date on barrel was Oct. 5, 1926. Mfg. 1927-1946.

$550	$495	$425	$350	$325	$300	$275	$250	$210	$185	$165	$145

Add 15% for nickel finish.
Add 15% for .22 LR cal.

OFFICIAL POLICE POST-WAR

.22 LR or .38 Spl. cal., 2, 4, 5, or 6 in. barrel, Coltwood plastic grips 1947-1954 - checkered walnut thereafter, fixed sights, no patent dates on barrel. Mfg. 1947-1969.

$475	$395	$325	$295	$265	$235	$210	$185	$165	$145	$135	$125

Add 15% for nickel finish.
Add 15% for .22 cal.

On this model, the 2 in. barrel in .38 Spl. cal. is scarce. .22 cal. was available with 4 or 6 in. barrel only.

100%	98%	95%	90%	80%	70%	60%	50%	40%	30%	20%	10%

MARSHAL MODEL - .38 Spl. cal., 2 (less common) or 4 in. barrel, round butt, differentiated by "M" suffix and "COLT MARSHAL" on barrel, about 2,500 mfg. 1954-1956 in approx. ser. no. range 833350-M through 845320-M.

| $875 | $775 | $675 | $500 | $395 | $335 | $305 | $275 | $245 | $215 | $180 | $160 |

Add 60% for 2 in. barrel.

COMMANDO MODEL - .38 Spl. cal., 2 in. (less common), 4 in. (common), or 6 in. (rare) barrel, should have plastic grips, parkerized finish, about 50,000 mfg. between 1942-1945, 32 oz., marked "COLT COMMANDO" on barrel, last patent date on barrel was Oct. 5, 1926.

| $550 | $450 | $400 | $375 | $350 | $315 | $280 | $260 | $240 | $220 | $195 | $180 |

Add 15% for 2 in. barrel.

OFFICIAL POLICE MKIII - .38 Spl. cal., 4, 5, or 6 in. barrels, no patent dates on barrel. Mfg. 1969-1975.

✱ *Blue finish*

| $375 | $295 | $200 | $150 | $135 | $125 | $115 | $105 | $100 | $95 | $90 | $85 |

✱ *Nickel finish*

| $350 | $295 | $200 | $175 | $165 | $155 | $145 | $135 | $125 | $115 | $105 | $100 |

METROPOLITAN MK III - .38 Spl. cal., similar to Official Police, except heavier and 4 in. heavy barrel only, blue finish. Mfg. 1969-1972.

| $495 | $395 | $300 | $250 | $200 | $180 | $160 | $140 | $120 | $110 | $100 | $90 |

OFFICER'S MODEL SPECIAL (FOURTH ISSUE) - .22 LR or .38 Spl. cal., 6 in. barrel, blue, similar to Third Issue, only heavier non-tapered barrel, new style hammer and "Coltmaster Sight", checkered plastic grips, no patent dates on barrel. Mfg. 1949-1952.

| $700 | $575 | $500 | $375 | $325 | $295 | $265 | $245 | $225 | $205 | $190 | $175 |

Add $75 for .22 LR cal.

OFFICER'S MODEL MATCH (FIFTH ISSUE) - .22 LR, .22 Mag, or .38 Spl. cal., 6 in. barrel, single (rare) or double action, tapered heavy barrel, wide spur hammer, Accro sight, large target grips (walnut). Mfg. 1953-1969.

| $575 | $525 | $425 | $325 | $300 | $275 | $250 | $225 | $200 | $185 | $170 | $155 |

Add $75 for .22 LR cal.
Add 100% for .22 Mag. cal. (approx. 850 mfg.).

✱ *Officer's Model Match Single Action only* - limited mfg.

| $1,325 | $1,200 | $995 | $925 | $850 | $775 | $700 | $650 | $600 | $550 | $475 | $425 |

OFFICER'S MODEL MATCH MK III (SIXTH ISSUE) - .38 Spl. cal. only, 6 in. shrouded VR barrel, wide spur hammer, Accro sights, target grips, 496 mfg. 1969-70 only.

| $1,325 | $1,200 | $995 | $925 | $850 | $775 | $700 | $650 | $600 | $550 | $475 | $425 |

NEW POCKET - .32 Short and LC, or .32 Colt New Police cal., 2½, 3½, 5, or 6 in. barrel, rubber grips, blue or nickel finish, last patent date on barrel was Nov. 6, 1888. Mfg. 1895-1905.

| $650 | $550 | $440 | $350 | $300 | $275 | $250 | $215 | $190 | $170 | $150 | $140 |

Subtract $25-$50 for chipped hard rubber grips (commonly found on this model).

POCKET POSITIVE (FIRST ISSUE) - similar to New Pocket, except has positive lock feature, also chambered for .32 Colt, .32 S&W, and .32 Colt New Police cals., last patent date on barrel was July 4, 1905. Mfg. 1905-1927.

| $525 | $465 | $385 | $350 | $325 | $295 | $265 | $235 | $210 | $185 | $165 | $145 |

Add 15%-20% for nickel finish.
Add 15% for 90%+ condition early transitional guns that are double marked with "NEW POCKET" on frame.
Subtract $25-$50 for chipped hard rubber grips (commonly found on this model).

100%	98%	95%	90%	80%	70%	60%	50%	40%	30%	20%	10%

POCKET POSITIVE (SECOND ISSUE) - similar to Pocket Positive First Issue, except has stippled and matted top strap, last patent date on barrel was Oct. 5, 1926. Mfg. 1927-1940.

| $525 | $465 | $385 | $350 | $325 | $295 | $265 | $235 | $210 | $185 | $165 | $145 |

Add 15%-20% for nickel finish.

Subtract $25-$50 for chipped hard rubber grips (commonly found on this model).

NEW POLICE - .32 Colt and .32 Colt New Police cal., 2½, 4, and 6 in. barrels, fixed sights, same frame as New Pocket, except larger grips, rubber grips, last patent date on barrel was Nov. 6, 1888. Mfg. 1896-1907.

| $650 | $550 | $475 | $375 | $325 | $275 | $215 | $185 | $170 | $160 | $150 | $145 |

Add 25% for nickel finish.

Subtract $25-$50 for chipped hard rubber grips (commonly found on this model).

NEW POLICE TARGET - .32 Colt cal., 6 in. barrel, blue, last patent date on barrel was Nov. 6, 1888, approx. 5,000 mfg. 1897-1907.

| $1,350 | $1,200 | $950 | $900 | $475 | $395 | $350 | $300 | $275 | $250 | $225 | $200 |

POLICE POSITIVE (FIRST ISSUE) - .32 Colt, .32 New Police, .38 New Police, or .38 S&W cals., 2½ in. (.32 only), 4, 5, or 6 in. barrels, improved "positive lock" version of the New Police, hard rubber grips standard through 1923, checkered walnut grips became standard 1924, denoted by 1905 last patent date and smooth top strap. Mfg. 1907-1927.

| $450 | $395 | $335 | $295 | $275 | $250 | $225 | $205 | $185 | $170 | $160 | $150 |

Add 15% for nickel finish.

Add 10% for 90%+ condition early transitional guns that are double marked with "NEW POLICE" on frame.

POLICE POSITIVE (SECOND ISSUE) - similar to Police Positive First Issue, except has 1926 last patent date, serrated top strap, and slightly heavier frame, walnut grips standard. Mfg. 1928-1947.

| $450 | $395 | $335 | $295 | $275 | $250 | $225 | $205 | $185 | $170 | $160 | $150 |

Add 15% for nickel finish.

POLICE POSITIVE TARGET MODEL (FIRST ISSUE, MODEL "G") - .22 LR, .22 WRF, .32 Colt, or .32 New Police cals., 6 in. barrel, blue, adj. sight, hard rubber grips standard through 1923, checkered walnut grips thereafter, last patent date on barrel was July 4, 1905, 22 oz. Mfg. 1907-1925.

| $750 | $625 | $575 | $525 | $475 | $425 | $390 | $360 | $325 | $285 | $250 | $210 |

Add 40% for .32 cal.

POLICE POSITIVE TARGET MODEL (SECOND ISSUE, MODEL "C") - similar to First Issue, except has slightly heavier frame and a last patent date of Oct. 5, 1926, 26 oz. Mfg. 1926-1941.

| $750 | $625 | $575 | $525 | $475 | $425 | $390 | $360 | $325 | $285 | $250 | $210 |

Add 40% for .32 cal.

POLICE POSITIVE SPECIAL (FIRST ISSUE) - .32-20 WCF, .32 New Police, .38 New Police, or .38 Spl. cals., 4, 5, or 6 in. barrels, fixed sights, frame longer to permit longer cylinder, denoted by 1905 last patent date on top of barrel, longer frame and smooth top strap, rubber grips. Mfg. 1907-1927.

| $495 | $450 | $395 | $325 | $300 | $275 | $250 | $225 | $200 | $185 | $170 | $155 |

POLICE POSITIVE SPECIAL (SECOND ISSUE) - similar to Police Positive Special (First Issue), except has 1926 last patent date on top of barrel, wood grips only, smooth (early mfg.) or checkered (later mfg.) trigger, and serrated top strap. Mfg. 1928-1946.

| $495 | $450 | $395 | $325 | $300 | $275 | $250 | $225 | $200 | $185 | $170 | $155 |

100%	98%	95%	90%	80%	70%	60%	50%	40%	30%	20%	10%

CAMP PERRY MODEL - .22 LR cal., 8 in. (less common) or 10 in., Officer's Model frame modified to accept a flat single shot chamber. The model name was stamped on the left side of the chamber, the only single shot Colt on a revolver frame, last patent date on barrel was Oct. 5, 1926. 2,488 mfg. between 1926-1941.

| $1,795 | $1,400 | $1,150 | $950 | $875 | $775 | $715 | $645 | $575 | $495 | $425 | $365 |

Add 25% for 8 in. barrel.

BANKER'S SPECIAL - 2 in. barrel, blue, square butt standard through 1933, round butt standard 1934-1940, last patent date on barrel was Oct. 5, 1926. Mfg. 1926-1940.

* *.38 cal.* - available in .38 Colt Police Positive (New Police) or .38 S&W cal.

| $1,150 | $975 | $750 | $595 | $495 | $395 | $325 | $275 | $235 | $205 | $185 | $165 |

Add 45% for nickel finish.

* *.22 LR cal.*

| $2,000 | $1,750 | $1,450 | $1,100 | $750 | $650 | $550 | $475 | $425 | $385 | $355 | $325 |

Add 30%-50% for nickel finish, depending on original condition.

COURIER - .22 S, L, & LR. or .32 New Police cals., double action, 6 shot, 3 in. barrel, approx. 3,053 mfg. 1953-1956.

| $825 | $750 | $700 | $550 | $475 | $425 | $395 | $350 | $325 | $295 | $260 | $230 |

Add 10% for .22 cal.

Even though fewer .22 cal. Couriers were mfg. than Banker's Specials, the Banker's Specials are still more desirable, as they are less frequently encountered in 95-100% condition.

Some .32 New Police cal. models can be found with alloy or steel cylinders.

AIRCREWMAN SPECIAL - .38 Spl. cal., double action, aluminum frame and cylinder, 2 in. barrel, 11 oz., fixed sights, checkered walnut grips overlapping at top of frame, inset with silver Air Force buttons, mfg. 1951 mostly.

| $4,000 | $3,500 | $2,750 | $2,100 | $1,700 | $1,350 | $1,075 | $950 | $850 | $750 | $675 | $595 |

Approx. 1,200 mfg. within ser. no. range 2,900LW - 7,775LW. Most were ordered destroyed. Perhaps less than 25 have survived.

BORDER PATROL (FIRST ISSUE) - .38 Spl. cal., double action, 6 shot, 4 in. heavy barrel, should have plastic grips, 400 mfg. during 1952 only in 823,000 ser. no. range.

| $3,500 | $3,000 | $2,500 | $1,400 | $1,125 | $995 | $875 | $775 | $675 | $595 | $525 | $475 |

This model is built on the Official Police Model frame.

DETECTIVE SPECIAL PRE-WAR (FIRST ISSUE) - .38 Spl. cal., 2 in. barrel, blue, wood grips, square butt standard through 1933, round butt standard 1934-1936, last patent date on barrel was Oct. 5, 1926. Mfg. 1927-1946.

| $795 | $695 | $550 | $450 | $375 | $325 | $275 | $250 | $225 | $205 | $190 | $175 |

Add 15% for nickel finish.
Add 20% for square butt.

DETECTIVE SPECIAL POST-WAR (SECOND ISSUE) - .32 New Police, .38 New Police, or .38 Spl. cal., 2 or 3 (scarce) in. barrel, plastic grips 1947-1954 - wood grips thereafter, wrap-under wood grips started in 1966. Mfg. 1947-1972.

| $475 | $395 | $325 | $275 | $250 | $200 | $185 | $170 | $160 | $150 | $140 | $120 |

Add 15% for nickel finish.
Add 15% for 3 in. barrel.

100%	98%	95%	90%	80%	70%	60%	50%	40%	30%	20%	10%

COBRA (FIRST ISSUE) - .22 LR, .32 Colt NP, .38 Colt NP, or .38 Spl. cal., first issue, 2, 3, or 4 (square butt on early model, later models had round butt) in. barrel, blue or nickel finish, similar to Detective Special, only alloy frame and available in .22 LR, very early guns had plastic grips with silver medallions, changed to plastic w/ o medallions, and finally changed to wood grips. Mfg. 1950-1972.

| $445 | $385 | $325 | $250 | $225 | $200 | $185 | $170 | $160 | $150 | $140 | $120 |

Add 20% for .22 LR cal.
Add 15% for nickel finish.
Add 15% for .38 cal. with 3 in. barrel.

The .22 LR cal. is available in 3 in. barrel only.

AGENT (FIRST ISSUE) - .38 Spl. cal., similar to Cobra first issue, except shorter grip frame. Mfg. 1955-1972.

| $425 | $375 | $325 | $275 | $235 | $180 | $160 | $145 | $130 | $120 | $110 | $100 |

AGENT L.W. (SECOND ISSUE) - .38 Spl. cal., similar to First Issue, except shrouded ejector rod, alloy frame, matte finish since 1982. Mfg. 1973-86.

| $375 | $325 | $275 | $215 | $195 | $175 | $150 | $135 | $125 | $115 | $105 | $100 |

Last MSR was $260.

COBRA (SECOND ISSUE) - .38 Spl. cal., similar to Cobra first issue, except shrouded ejector rod, some were shipped with factory installed hammer shroud. Mfg. 1973-1981.

| $395 | $365 | $275 | $250 | $225 | $200 | $190 | $175 | $160 | $150 | $140 | $120 |

DETECTIVE SPECIAL (THIRD ISSUE) - .38 Spl. cal., similar to Second Issue, shrouded ejector rod, 2 or 3 (scarce) in. barrel, fixed sights, wraparound wood grips. Mfg. 1973-86.

| $425 | $395 | $375 | $300 | $260 | $230 | $200 | $185 | $175 | $160 | $150 | $140 |

Last MSR was $429.

Add $50 for nickel.
Add 15% for 3 in. barrel.

Also available with class A engraving - add $590 if in 98% condition or better.

COMMANDO SPECIAL - .38 Spl. cal., similar to Detective Special with steel frame, shrouded ejector rod, 2 in. barrel, matte parkerized finish, rubber grips. Mfg. 1984-86.

| $425 | $325 | $265 | $225 | $195 | $185 | $155 | $140 | $125 | $115 | $105 | $100 |

Last MSR was $260.

POLICE POSITIVE SPECIAL (THIRD ISSUE) - .38 Spl. cal., similar to Detective Special Second Issue, except 4, 5 or 6 in. barrel. Mfg. 1947-76.

| $395 | $350 | $300 | $225 | $195 | $185 | $165 | $140 | $125 | $115 | $105 | $100 |

POLICE POSITIVE SPECIAL (FOURTH ISSUE) - .38 Spl. cal., shrouded ejector rod housing only, steel frame, blue or nickel finish. Mfg. 1977-78 and 1994-95.

| $395 | $350 | $300 | $220 | $195 | $175 | $165 | $135 | $125 | $115 | $105 | $100 |

Last MSR was $400.

Add 10% for nickel finish.

VIPER MODEL - .38 Spl. cal., similar to Police Positive Special (Fourth Issue), alloy frame, 4 in. ejector rod housing only. Mfg. 1977 only.

| $425 | $375 | $325 | $250 | $225 | $200 | $190 | $175 | $160 | $150 | $140 | $120 |

Add 30% for nickel finish.

DIAMONDBACK - .22 LR, .22 Mag. (limited mfg.), or .38 Spl. cal., 2½ (scarce in .22 LR), 4, or 6 in. VR barrel, adj. sights, steel frame, checkered walnut grips. Mfg. 1966- 86.

| $650 | $550 | $475 | $425 | $350 | $285 | $260 | $230 | $210 | $190 | $175 | $160 |

Last MSR was $461.

Add 20% for nickel finish.
Add 20% for .22 LR cal.
Add 30% for .22 LR cal. with 2½ in. barrel or .22 Mag. cal.

Note: Approx. 2,200 Diamondbacks were made with 6 in. barrels and nickel finish in .22 cal. - made 1979. Add additional $150 for 95+% specimens.

100%	98%	95%	90%	80%	70%	60%	50%	40%	30%	20%	10%

COLT .357 MAG - 4 in. or 6 in. barrel, heavy frame, Accro sight, blue or nickel finish, checkered walnut grips. Mfg. 1953-1961.

* **Standard hammer**

100%	98%	95%	90%	80%	70%	60%	50%	40%	30%	20%	10%
$575	$475	$425	$295	$275	$265	$255	$245	$230	$220	$210	$200

* **Wide hammer w/target grips**

100%	98%	95%	90%	80%	70%	60%	50%	40%	30%	20%	10%
$600	$525	$450	$300	$285	$265	$255	$245	$235	$225	$215	$205

Add 15% for nickel finish.

In 1962, this model was absorbed into the Trooper line.

TROOPER - .22 LR (4 in. only, scarce), .357 Mag., or .38 Spl. cal., 4 or 6 in. barrel, blue or nickel finish, quick draw ramp front sight, adj. rear sight, checkered walnut grips. Mfg. 1953-1969.

* **Standard hammer**

100%	98%	95%	90%	80%	70%	60%	50%	40%	30%	20%	10%
$495	$425	$325	$210	$200	$190	$180	$170	$165	$160	$155	$150

* **Wide hammer and target grips**

100%	98%	95%	90%	80%	70%	60%	50%	40%	30%	20%	
$525	$450	$375	$225	$210	$200	$190	$180	$170	$165	$160	$155

Add $75-$125 for .22 LR cal. (4 in. barrel only), depending on condition.
Add 15% for nickel finish.

Grading	100%	98%	95%	90%	80%	70%	60%

TROOPER MK III - .22 LR, .22 Mag., .357 Mag., or .38 Spl. cal., 4, 6, or 8 in. solid rib barrel, adj. sights, walnut target grips, redesigned lock work to reduce amount of hand fitting needed on earlier predecessors. Mfg. 1969-1983.

	100%	98%	95%	90%	80%	70%	60%
Blue finish	$395	$325	$225	$180	$170	$160	$150
Nickel finish	$440	$350	$250	$200	$185	$170	$160

TROOPER MK V - .357 Mag. cal. only, 4, 6, or 8 in. barrel, adj. sights, walnut target grips, improved version of Mark III action, vent. rib barrel, redesigned 1982. Disc. 1986.

	100%	98%	95%	90%	80%	70%	60%
Blue finish	$425	$350	$275	$215	$185	$170	$160

Last MSR was $362.

	100%	98%	95%	90%	80%	70%	60%
Nickel finish	$475	$400	$300	$235	$200	$185	$170

Last MSR was $396.

LAWMAN SKY MARSHALL - .38 Spl. cal., 2 in. barrel, experimental revolver with a replaceable plastic cylinder preloaded with plastic bullets, blue finish, checkered walnut grips, this model was designed to be carried on airliners by Federal Marshals during the 1970s.

	100%	98%	95%	90%	80%	70%	60%
	$925	$850	$775	$700	$625	$550	$475

LAWMAN MK III - .357 Mag. cal., 2 in. and 4 in. barrel, unshrouded or shrouded ejector rod for 2 in. barrel, fixed sights, checkered walnut grips. Mfg. 1969-1983.

	100%	98%	95%	90%	80%	70%	60%
Blue finish	$375	$275	$225	$180	$170	$160	$150
Nickel finish	$395	$295	$250	$200	$180	$170	$160

LAWMAN MK V - .357 Mag. cal., 2 or 4 in. barrel, shrouded ejector rod for 2 in. barrel, fixed sights, checkered walnut grips, improved version of MK III action. Mfg. 1984 and 1985 only.

	100%	98%	95%	90%	80%	70%	60%
Blue finish	$375	$275	$225	$180	$165	$150	$140

Last MSR was $309.

	100%	98%	95%	90%	80%	70%	60%
Nickel finish	$395	$295	$250	$200	$180	$170	$160

Last MSR was $328.

Grading	100%	98%	95%	90%	80%	70%	60%

BORDER PATROL (SECOND ISSUE) - .357 Mag. cal., 4 in. heavy barrel, similar to Trooper Mark III frame, less polishing to frame, limited mfg. 1970-75.

* *Blue Finish* - 5,356 mfg.

$625	$495	$375	$275	$235	$200	$180

* *Nickel Finish* - 1,152 mfg.

$725	$625	$500	$400	$325	$275	$235

PEACEKEEPER - .357 Mag. cal. only, similar to Trooper MK V, 4 or 6 in. barrel, matte blue finish, rubber combat grips, adj. rear sight, about 42 oz. Mfg. 1985-1987.

$395	$325	$275	$225	$195	$180	$165

Last MSR was $330.

BOA - .357 Mag. cal., deep blue polish, full length ejector shroud with Mark V action, 600 each mfg. in 4 and 6 in. barrel lengths. Entire production run was purchased by Lew Horton Distributing Co., Inc. located in Southboro, MA. 1985 retail was $525.

$675	$575	$475	$425	$375	$350	$325

* *Boa Set* - 100 sets mfg. including 4 and 6 in. barrels with fully shrouded ejector rod housing, consecutive serial numbers, cases were supplied by Lew Horton. 1985 retail was $1,200.

$1,495	$1,100	$875

POLICE POSITIVE MARK MK V (FIFTH ISSUE) - .38 Spl. cal., full shrouded 4 in. barrel, steel frame, blue or nickel finish, rubber grips. Mfg. 1994-95.

$425	$350	$295	$250	$195	$180	$165

Add 10% for nickel finish.

DETECTIVE SPECIAL (FOURTH ISSUE) - .38 Spl. cal., 6 shot, 2 in. barrel, alloy frame, blue finish, black composition grips with gold medallions, 21 oz. Reintroduced 1993, disc. 1995.

$425	$350	$295	$250	$195	$180	$165

Last MSR was $400.

* *Bobbed Detective Special* - .38 Spl. cal., double action only with bobbed hammer, night front sight, honed action, choice of hard chrome or standard blue finish. Mfg. 1994-95.

$595	$500	$375	$300	$250	$200	$175

Last MSR was $599.

Add $30 for hard chrome finish.

COLT .38 SF-VI - .38 Spl. cal., 6 shot, 2 or 4 in. barrel, transfer bar safety, choice of matte (2 in.), bright polished (4 in.), or black (4 in.) finish, stainless steel, regular or bobbed (4 in. barrel only) hammer, fixed sights, black composition combat grips, 21 oz. Mfg. 1995-96.

$425	$350	$295

Last MSR was $408.

* *Colt Special Lady* - while advertised during 1996, this model had very limited mfg.

COLT .38 DSII - .357 Mag. (new 1998) or .38 Spl. cal., 6 shot, 2 in. barrel, stainless steel, service hammer, rubber combat style checkered grips, 21 oz. Mfg. 1997-98.

$450	$365	$300

Last MSR was $435.

This model features a redesigned trigger grouping and is capable of shooting .38+P ammo.

COLT MAGNUM CARRY - .357 Mag. cal., 6 shot, 2 in. barrel, transfer bar safety, satin stainless steel, wraparound rubber grips with finger grooves, ramp front sight, 21 oz. Mfg. 1999 only.

$440	$360	$295

Last MSR was $460.

Grading	100%	98%	95%	90%	80%	70%	60%

COMBAT COBRA - .357 Mag. cal., 2½ in. barrel, special edition for Lew Horton with CC prefix and stainless steel construction.

$575	$475	$400	

KING COBRA - .357 Mag. cal., blue metal, black neoprene round butt grips, 2½ (new 1990), 4 or 6 in. solid rib barrel only, outline sights, approx. 42 oz. (4 in. barrel). Mfg. 1988-92.

	$400	$350	$300	$250	$210	$200	$185

Last MSR was $410.

KING COBRA STAINLESS - .357 Mag. cal., stainless steel construction, black neoprene round butt grips, 2 (mfg. 1988-94), 4, 6, or 8 (mfg. 1990-94) in. solid rib barrel, white outline sights, approx. 36 oz. (2½ in. barrel). Mfg. late 1987-92, production resumed 1994, disc. 1998.

$495	$425	$325

Last MSR was $485.

✳ *King Cobra "Ultimate" Bright Stainless* - similar to King Cobra, except for bright stainless steel, 2 ½ (new 1990), 4, 6, or 8 (new 1991) in. barrel. Mfg. 1988- 92.

$475	$400	$300

Last MSR was $470.

PYTHON - .357 Mag. cal., 2 ½ (disc. 1994), 3 (disc., very scarce), 4, 6, or 8 in. barrel with vent rib, Royal Blue finish, full shrouded ejector rod, adj. rear sight, checkered walnut grips (prior to 1991), rubber Hogue monogrips (2½ or 4 in. barrel), or rubber target (6 or 8 in. barrel) grips, 38-48 oz. Mfg. 1955-1996.

✳ *Blue or royal blue finish*

$895	$775	$650	$575	$475	$395	$350

Add 10% for NIB condition.
Add 50% for early production with high polish finish.

Last MSR was $815.

The standard Python was disc. during 1996, and 1997-1999 production was through the Colt Custom Shop by special order only.

During 2001, Colt shipped some Pythons with 6 in. barrels to dealers – with prices at the $1,100 - $1,200 level. These guns had a slightly different (rougher) line checkering pattern on the cylinder release and hammer parts. Whether these guns reflect a long terms production commitment, or simply a "parts clean-up", combined with a target piece of opportunity, remains to be seen.

Early 2½, 4 or 6 in. Pythons without letter prefix before ser. no. will bring a small premium if in 100% condition or NIB, as well as the disc. 3 in. barrel. There were also a few Pythons mfg. in .256 Win. Mag. (circa 1961), .38 Spl., .41 Mag., and .44 Spl. cals. While the .22 LR and the .22 WMR (.22 Mag.) were advertised in earlier factory catalogs, they were never manufactured - only a few prototypes exist. The amount of premium on these cals. depends on how serious (and deep-pocketed) the Python collector is.

A California distributor special ordered a quantity of 3 in. barreled Pythons, which at the time were not available. Colt probably utilized made-up 8 in. guns and either had them modified or re-barreled, with the distributors name part of the barrel marking. These guns are an unusual variant (sometimes referred to as a Combat Python), and are priced similarly to factory 3 in. barrel Pythons.

✳ *Nickel finish* - available in polished or satin nickel, disc. 1985.

$995	$825	$675	$575	$475	$395	$300

Last MSR was $693.

Add 10% for NIB condition.
Add 10% for satin nickel finish.

Satin nickel finish is so designated on original boxes as "Royal Coatguard" or "E NICK" (electroless nickel).

Grading	100%	98%	95%	90%	80%	70%	60%

* **Stainless Steel** - stainless steel construction, matte finish, neoprene target or combat stocks, 2½ (disc. 1994), 4, 6 or 8 (new 1989) in. barrel. Mfg. 1983-1996.

　　　　　　　$925 $775 $600

Last MSR was $904.

Add 10% for NIB condition.

The 6 in. barrel includes neoprene target stocks.

* **"Ultimate" Bright Stainless Steel** - deluxe, highly polished stainless model, 2½ (disc.), 4, 6, or 8 in. VR barrel. Mfg. 1985-disc.

　　　　　　　$950 $775 $600

Last MSR was $935.

Add 10% for NIB condition.

PYTHON ELITE
- .357 Mag. cal., 4 or 6 in. VR barrel, choice of Royal Blue (mfg. 1997 only) or stainless steel, Colt-Elliason adj. rear sight, rubber service style grips, 38 or 43½ oz. New 1997, disc. 1998, reintroduced 1999, again during 2002.

MSR	**$1,150**		**$995**	**$850**	**$725**	**$650**	**$550**	**$475**	**$395**

This model is available by custom order only through the Colt Custom Shop.

* **Python Elite Stainless** - similar to Python Elite, except is stainless steel. Mfg. 1997-99, again in 2002.

MSR	**$1,150**		**$995**	**$850**	**$725**

This model is available by custom order only through the Colt Custom Shop.

ULTIMATE PYTHON
- .357 Mag. cal., specially tuned by the custom gun shop, supplied with both Colt-Elliason target and Accro white outline sighting systems, walnut and rubber grips also included, choice of Colt Royal Blue or Ultimate Stainless finish, 6 in. barrel only. Mfg. 1991-1993.

　　$1,150 $925 $795 $695 $595 $495 $450

Last MSR was $1,140.

Add $120 for Ultimate Stainless Model.

PYTHON HUNTER
- .357 Mag. cal., 8 in. barrel, includes Leupold 2X scope, Halliburton aluminum case and accessories. Mfg. 1981 only.

　　$1,395 $1,225 $1,050 $775 $650 $575 $525

Last MSR was $995.

Add 10% for NIB condition.

PYTHON SILHOUETTE
- .357 Mag. cal., 8 in. barrel, includes Leupold 2X scope, similar to Python Hunter, except barrel is roll marked with Silhouette name and scope position has been moved rearward, black luggage type case. Mfg. circa 1983.

　　$1,450 $1,275 $1,050 $775 $650 $575 $525

Add 10% for NIB condition.

PYTHON .38 SPECIAL
- 8 in. barrel, blue or nickel finish. Disc.

　　$825 $725 $625 $525 $475 $395 $350

Add 10% for NIB condition.

GRIZZLY
- .357 Mag. cal., 6 in. barrel, matte stainless finish, approx. 500 mfg.

　　$800 $675 $575 $550 $525 $375 $350

Add 10% for NIB condition.

This model was mfg. by the Colt Custom Shop.

WHITETAILER
- .357 Mag. cal., 8 in. barrel, matte stainless finish, aluminum hard shell cased with 2X scope.

　　$1,095 $950 $750

Add 10% for NIB condition.

Grading	100%	98%	95%	90%	80%	70%	60%

* ***Whitetailer II*** - similar to Whitetailer, except has high polish finish.

	$1,050	$875	$750				

Add 10% for NIB condition.

ANACONDA - .44 Mag. or .45 LC (6 in. only, mfg. 1992-99) cal., double action, 4 (.44 Mag. only, new 1991, 6-11 also mfg. in .45 LC - rare), 6, or 8 in. VR barrel, transfer bar safety system, 6 shot, choice of matte or Realtree Grey camo (.44 Mag. with 8 in. barrel only, mfg. 1996 only) metal finish, stainless steel only, black neoprene combat grips with Colt medallion, red ramp front sight, full length ejector rod housing, white outline rear adj. sight, approx. 47-59 oz. Mfg. 1990-99, reintroduced 2002.

* ***Anaconda Current Mfg.*** - beginning 2002, the Anaconda is only available through the Colt Custom Shop.

MSR	$1,000	$850	$475	$400			

* ***Anaconda 1990-99 Mfg.*** - standard production, this period of production was not manufactured by the Colt Custom Shop.

	$650	$495	$395				

* ***Anaconda with scope*** - .44 Mag. cal. only, 8 in. barrel, Realtree Grey camo finish on gun and scope. Mfg. 1996 only.

	$795	$625	$475				

Last MSR was $999.

* ***Anaconda Hunter*** - .44 Mag. cal., supplied with Leupold 2X scope, carrying case, cleaning accessories, and both walnut and rubber grips, 8 in. barrel only. Mfg. 1991- 1993.

	$1,095	$895	$725				

Last MSR was $1,200.

* ***Custom Ported Anaconda*** - .44 Mag. cal., features 6 (disc.) or 8 in. Magna-ported barrel and Colt-Elliason rear sight, contoured trigger, and Pachmayr rubber grips, brushed stainless steel. Mfg. 1992-1993, re-released 1995-96, again in 2002.

MSR	$1,050	$875	$600	$495			

* ***Anaconda 1st Edition*** - .44 Mag. cal., Ultimate Stainless finish, special rollmark on left side of barrel reads "Colt Anaconda First Edition", with aluminum carrying case, ser. no. range MM00001-MM01000, 1,000 mfg. 1990 only.

	$950	$750	$625				

100%	98%	95%	90%	80%	70%	60%	50%	40%	30%	20%	10%

RIFLES: PRE-1904

A Colt letter of provenance for the Lightning models listed below is $100/each for the large frame and $75/each for the small/medium frames. Colt-Burgess model factory letters are also available at $100/each.

FIRST MODEL RING LEVER - .34, .36, .38, .40, or .44 cal., 8 or 10 shot revolving cylinder, 32 in. octagon barrel, walnut stock, no forend, 200 mfg., Percussion. Mfg. 1837- 1838.

* ***Standard Model***

N/A	N/A	N/A	$37,500	$28,000	$21,500	$16,500	$13,500	$11,000	$9,000	$7,500	$6,500

* ***Improved Model*** - attached loading lever.

N/A	N/A	N/A	$41,000	$29,650	$22,750	$17,500	$14,500	$12,000	$10,000	$8,500	$7,500

SECOND MODEL RING LEVER - similar to First Model, without top strap over cylinder, .44 caliber only, Percussion, 5000 mfg., 1838-1841.

* ***Standard Model***

N/A	N/A	N/A	$33,500	$24,500	$17,000	$13,000	$11,000	$8,780	$7,200	$6,300	$5,650

100%	98%	95%	90%	80%	70%	60%	50%	40%	30%	20%	10%

* Improved Model

| N/A | N/A | N/A | $34,750 | $26,000 | $17,750 | $13,300 | $11,200 | $8,900 | $7,325 | $6,390 | $5,725 |

MODEL 1839 CARBINE - .52 smooth bore cal., 6 shot cylinder, 24 in. barrel, exposed hammer for cocking, blue, walnut stock, percussion, approx. 950 mfg., 1838-1841.

* Early Model

| N/A | N/A | N/A | $38,500 | $29,000 | $22,000 | $17,500 | $14,750 | $11,500 | $9,350 | $7,750 | $6,750 |

* Standard Model - no loading lever.

| N/A | N/A | N/A | $31,000 | $22,500 | $17,000 | $13,500 | $11,250 | $9,000 | $7,500 | $6,600 | $6,000 |

MODEL 1855 REVOLVING - .36, .44, or .56 cal., various barrel lengths and stock styles, 5 or 6 shot cylinder, blue with walnut buttstock, no forend, percussion. Mfg. 1856- 1864.

* ½ Stock Sporter - 24, 27, or 30 in. barrel, approx. 1500 mfg.

| N/A | N/A | N/A | $11,500 | $9,000 | $7,850 | $7,000 | $6,500 | $6,000 | $5,500 | $5,100 | $4,750 |

* Full Stock Sporter - 21, 24, 27, 30, or 31 in. barrel, approx. 2000 mfg.

| N/A | N/A | N/A | $13,500 | $11,275 | $9,150 | $8,250 | $7,500 | $6,950 | $6,500 | $6,100 | $5,750 |

* Military Model, U.S. - marked, 21-37 in. barrel, 9310 mfg.

| N/A | N/A | N/A | $17,500 | $14,650 | $11,900 | $10,500 | $9,800 | $9,050 | $8,450 | $7,900 | $7,475 |

* .36 Caliber Carbine Model - 15, 18, or 21 in. barrel, 4400 mfg.

| N/A | N/A | N/A | $17,150 | $14,350 | $11,660 | $10,525 | $9,600 | $8,875 | $8,275 | $7,750 | $7,300 |

* .56 Caliber Artillery Carbine - 5 shot, 21 in. barrel with bayonet lug and forestock, approx. 64 mfg.

| N/A | N/A | N/A | $19,000 | $16,500 | $13,500 | $10,875 | $9,850 | $9,100 | $8,400 | $7,950 | $7,500 |

* Shotgun Model - .60 or .75 cal., smooth bore, 27, 30, 33, or 36 in. barrels, 1100 mfg.

| N/A | N/A | N/A | $12,750 | $11,000 | $9,000 | $8,000 | $7,250 | $6,750 | $6,300 | $6,000 | $5,600 |

BERDAN - .42 bottle-necked CF cal., approx. 30,000 mfg. 1866-circa 1870. Scarce since most were sent to Russia and have Russian barrel markings, approx. 50-100 are Hartford marked.

* Berdan Rifle - .32½ in. barrel, approx. 10 lbs.

| N/A | N/A | N/A | $3,250 | $2,750 | $2,250 | $1,850 | $1,650 | $1,450 | $1,325 | $1,250 | $1,175 |

* Berdan Carbine - half stock, 18¼ in. barrel, approx. 50 mfg., both Russian and Hartford marked.

| N/A | N/A | N/A | $8,300 | $7,600 | $6,725 | $6,100 | $5,500 | $4,750 | $3,950 | $3,275 | $2,750 |

MODEL 1861 MUSKET - .58 cal., percussion, muzzle loader, 40 in. barrel, with 3 bands, metal parts, white walnut stock, 75,000 mfg., 1861-1865.

| N/A | N/A | N/A | $1,895 | $1,750 | $1,650 | $1,500 | $1,350 | $1,250 | $1,150 | $1,000 | $850 |

COLT-BURGESS LEVER ACTION - .44-40 WCF cal., 25½ in. barrel, 15 shot tube mag., blue with case hardened lever and hammer, walnut stock, 6400 mfg., 1883-1885.

| N/A | N/A | N/A | $5,500 | $4,900 | $4,465 | $4,170 | $3,930 | $3,700 | $3,525 | $3,350 | $3,100 |

COLT-BURGESS CARBINE - similar to Rifle, with 20 in. barrel.

| N/A | N/A | N/A | $7,900 | $7,300 | $6,725 | $6,250 | $5,850 | $5,500 | $5,200 | $4,950 | $4,750 |

COLT-BURGESS BABY CARBINE - similar to Carbine, with lightened frame.

| N/A | N/A | N/A | $9,720 | $8,975 | $8,275 | $7,695 | $7,200 | $6,765 | $6,395 | $6,100 | $5,850 |

LIGHTNING SLIDE ACTION - SMALL FRAME - .22 cal., 24 in. barrel, open sights, walnut straight stock, round or octagon barrel, 90,000 mfg. Mfg. 1887-1904.

| N/A | N/A | N/A | $1,000 | $795 | $650 | $575 | $535 | $495 | $450 | $400 | $375 |

LIGHTNING SLIDE ACTION - MEDIUM FRAME - in .32-20 WCF, .38-40 WCF, or .44-40 WCF cal., similar to small frame, except with 26 in. barrel and larger frame.

| N/A | N/A | N/A | $1,775 | $1,475 | $1,175 | $950 | $775 | $650 | $550 | $495 | $450 |

100%	98%	95%	90%	80%	70%	60%	50%	40%	30%	20%	10%

LIGHTNING SLIDE ACTION - LARGE FRAME - .38-56 WCF, .40-60 WCF, .45- 60 WCF, .45-65 WCF, .45-85 WCF, or .50-95 Express cal., large version of previously described Lightnings, 6,500 mfg. 1887-1894.

| N/A | N/A | N/A | $3,250 | $2,750 | $2,250 | $1,850 | $1,650 | $1,450 | $1,325 | $1,250 | $1,175 |

    Add 25% for .50-95 Express cal.

LIGHTNING CARBINE MEDIUM FRAME - similar to Rifle, with 20 in. barrel.

| N/A | N/A | N/A | $2,850 | $2,450 | $2,150 | $1,950 | $1,750 | $1,450 | $1,175 | $1,050 | $950 |

LIGHTNING CARBINE LARGE FRAME - 22 in. barrel.

| N/A | N/A | N/A | $6,250 | $5,350 | $4,850 | $4,375 | $3,925 | $3,625 | $3,375 | $3,150 | $2,975 |

LIGHTNING BABY CARBINE MEDIUM FRAME - lightened version of Carbine.

| N/A | N/A | N/A | $4,000 | $3,450 | $2,950 | $2,450 | $2,100 | $1,850 | $1,650 | $1,425 | $1,350 |

LIGHTNING BABY CARBINE LARGE FRAME - lightened version.

| N/A | N/A | N/A | $8,500 | $7,750 | $6,850 | $6,300 | $5,825 | $5,425 | $5,075 | $4,775 | $4,350 |

    Add 50% for .50-95 Express cal.

Grading	100%	98%	95%	90%	80%	70%	60%

DOUBLE RIFLE SxS - various cals. in the .45 range, hammers, very limited production between 1878-1880. Most guns were owned by friends of Caldwell Colt - Sam Colt's son, the original designer. Colt Double Rifles are extremely rare and desirable, and should be examined carefully. Prices typically range between $15,000-$25,000, if all original.

COLTEER 1-22 - .22 LR or .22 Mag. cal., single shot bolt action, 20, 22, or 24 (.22 Mag. only, w/o sights) in. round barrel, adj. rear sight (20 or 22 in. barrel), plain walnut stock. Approx. 50,000 mfg. 1957-1966.

| | | | $275 | $215 | $175 | $140 | $110 | $95 | $80 |

    Add 10% for .22 Mag. cal.

STAGECOACH - .22 LR cal., semi-auto, 16½ in. barrel, 13 shot mag., deluxe walnut, saddle ring w/leather thong, roll-engraved hold-up scene. Over 25,000 mfg. 1965-mid '70s.

| | | | $325 | $275 | $215 | $175 | $140 | $110 | $90 |

COLTEER - .22 LR cal., similar to Stagecoach, except 19 3/8 in. barrel, 15 shot mag., no engraving and plain walnut. Over 25,000 mfg. 1965-mid '70s.

| | | | $275 | $215 | $175 | $140 | $110 | $95 | $80 |

COURIER - similar to Colteer semi-auto, except pistol-grip stock and enlarged forearm. Mfg. 1970-mid '70s.

| | | | $275 | $215 | $175 | $140 | $110 | $95 | $80 |

RIFLES: BOLT ACTION, CENTERFIRE

COLT "57" - .243 Win. or .30-06 cal., FN Mauser action, mfg. by Jefferson Mfg. Co. in N. Haven, CT during 1957, approx. 5,000 mfg. starting at ser. no. 1, checkered American Monte Carlo walnut stock, rear apeture and wraparound front sight, drilled and tapped for scope.

| | | | $595 | $550 | $500 | $450 | $400 | $350 | $325 |

    This model was also available in a deluxe version with deluxe hand checkered walnut stock - add 15%.

COLTSMAN STANDARD RIFLE - .223 Rem., .243 Win., .264 Win. Mag., .30-06, .300 Win. Mag., or .308 Win. cal., mfg. by Kodiak, Mauser or Sako-action, 22 in. or 24 in.(.300 Win. Mag.), 5 or 6 shot mag. Approx. 10,000 (both models) mfg. 1958-1966.

| | | | $495 | $450 | $425 | $400 | $350 | $325 | $300 |

Grading	100%	98%	95%	90%	80%	70%	60%

COLTSMAN CUSTOM RIFLE - deluxe variation including deluxe walnut with skipline checkering and rosewood forearm cap.

	$695	$650	$600	$550	$500	$450	$400

COLT SAUER RIFLE (STANDARD ACTION) - .25-06 Rem., .270 Win. or .30-06 cal., non-rotating bolt action, manufactured in Germany by J. P. Sauer & Sohn, 24 in. barrel, 4 round mag., no sights, checkered walnut stock with rosewood forend tip and pistol grip cap, recoil pad. Mfg. 1974-1985.

	$1,150	$975	$800	$700	$660	$620	$575

Last MSR was $1,257.

This model was also available in a Grade IV with silver receiver. Each caliber featured a different engraved animal. Add 50%-70%, depending on condition and caliber desirabilty.

COLT SAUER SHORT ACTION - similar to the standard except in .22-250 Rem., .243 Win. cal. or .308 Win. cal. Mfg. 1976-1985.

	$1,200	$975	$800	$700	$660	$620	$575

Last MSR was $1,257.

COLT SAUER MAGNUM - similar to the standard except in 7mm Rem. Mag., 300 Win. Mag., or 300 Weatherby Mag. cal. Mfg. 1974-1985.

	$1,250	$1,000	$800	$700	$660	$620	$575

Last MSR was $1,300.

COLT SAUER GRAND ALASKAN - heavier version in .375 H&H cal., adj. sights. Mfg. 1978-1985.

	$1,375	$1,125	$995	$900	$820	$740	$690

COLT SAUER GRAND AFRICAN - .458 Win. Mag. cal., 4 round capacity, 9 lb. 12 oz. Mfg. 1974-1985.

	$1,450	$1,150	$995	$900	$820	$740	$690

Last MSR was $1,400.

COLT LIGHT RIFLE - .243 Win., .260 Rem., .270 Win., .280 Rem., .25-06 Rem., .30- 06, .308 Win., 7x57mm, .300 Win. Mag., 7mm-08, or 7mm Rem. Mag. cal., short or long action, matte black synthetic stock, matte metal finish, adj. trigger, 3 position side safety, approx. 5.4 lbs. in short action, manufactured by Saco Defense in the U.S. New 2000.

MSR	$779		$675	$550	$500	$450	$400	$350	$295

RIFLES: SINGLE SHOT, CENTERFIRE

COLT-SHARPS RIFLE - .17 Bee, .22-250 Rem., .243 Win., .25-06 Rem., 7mm Rem. Mag., .30-06, or .375 H&H cal., Sharps falling block action, high-gloss bluing, deluxe checkered walnut stock and forearm. Approx. 500 mfg. 1970-1977.

	$2,295	$1,950	$1,650	$1,200	$1,000	$800	$650

DRILLINGS

COLT SAUER DRILLING - 12 ga./.30-06 or .243 Win. cal., 25 in. barrels, engraved receiver, 8 lbs. Disc. 1985.

	$2,950	$2,500	$2,100	$1,800	$1,500	$1,250	$1,000

Last MSR was $4,228.

RIFLES: SEMI-AUTO, AR-15 & VARIATIONS

Prices of currently manufactured models listed below automatically refer to post- ban (if any) configurations. Because of the increased consumer/collector interest in the M-16 and variations (full

Grading	100%	98%	95%	90%	80%	70%	60%

auto), many pre-ban AR-15 values have recently gone up as a result.

Rifling twists on the Colt AR-15 have changed throughout the years. They started with a 1:12 in. twist, changed to a 1:7 in. twist (to match with the new, longer .223 Rem./5.56mm SS109-type bullet), and finally changed to a 1:9 in. twist in combination with 1:7 in. twist models as a compromise for bullets in the 50-68 grain range. Current mfg. AR-15s/Match Targets have rifling twists/turns incorporated into the model descriptions.

Add $368 for Colt Scout C-More Sight on current mfg.

Add $444 for Colt Tactical C-More Sight on current mfg.

Older mfg. with green boxes will command a premium.

SP-1 - .223 Rem. cal., original Colt paramilitary configuration without forward bolt assist, finishes included parkerizing and electroless nickel. Mfg. 1963-84.

	$1,250	$1,050	$925	$850	$775	$700	$650

SPORTER II (R6500) - .223 Rem. cal., various configurations, disc.

	$1,150	$995	$875	$750	$675	$595	$525

MATCH TARGET LIGHTWEIGHT (R/MT6430, R/MT6530, or R/MT6830)- .223 Rem. (6530, 1 turn in 7 in.), 7.62x39mm (6830, new 1992, disc. 1996, 1 turn in 12 in.), or 9mm Para. (6430, new 1992, disc. 1996, 1 turn in 10 in.) cals., features 16 in. barrel (non-threaded per C/B 1994), initially shorter stock and handguard, adj. rear sight for windage and elevation, includes 2 detachable 5, 8, or 9 (new 1999) shot mags., approx. 7 lbs. New 1991.

MSR $1,111	$925	$795	$725	$665	$600	$550	$495
Pre-ban	$1,450	$1,300	$1,100	$975	$875	$800	$750

Add $200 for .22 LR conversion kit (disc. 1994).

TARGET GOVT. MODEL RIFLE (R6550/R or MT6551) - .223 Rem. cal., semi-auto version of the M-16 rifle with forward bolt assist, gas operated, 20 in. barrel (1 turn in 7 in.), straight line black nylon stock, aperture rear, post front sight, 5, 8, 9 (new 1999), 20 (disc.), or 30 (disc.) shot detachable box mag., Model 6550 was disc. 1990, 7½ lbs.

MSR $1,144	$950	$825	$750	$675	$600	$550	$495
Pre-ban	$1,495	$1,325	$1,150	$995	$875	$800	$750

Add $200 for .22 LR conversion kit (mfg. 1990-94).

Subtract $70 for older field-style rear sight assembly (pre-1987).

In 1987, Colt replaced the AR-15A2 Sporter II Rifle with the AR-15A2 Govt. Model. This new model has the 800 meter rear sighting system housed in the receiver's carrying handle (similar to the M-16 A2).

MATCH TARGET M4 RIFLE (MT6400C) - 223 Rem. cal. As this edition went to press, further information was not available. New 2002.

MSR $1,220		$1,025	$895	$825	$750	$650	$575	$525

MATCH TARGET COMPETITION H-BAR RIFLE (R or MT6700) - .223 Rem. cal., features flat top upper receiver for scope mounting, 20 in. barrel (1 turn in 9 in.), quick detachable carry handle which incorporates a 600-meter rear sighting system, counterbored muzzle, dovetailed upper receiver is grooved to accept Weaver style scope rings, supplied with two 5, 8, or 9 (new 1999) shot mags., cleaning kit, and sling, matte black finish, 8½ lbs. New 1992.

MSR $1,199		$995	$875	$800	$725	$650	$575	$525

Add $61 for compensator (MT6700C, new 1999).

Pre-ban	$1,650	$1,450	$1,250	$1,025	$900	$800	$700

COMPETITION H-BAR RIFLE RANGE SELECTED (R6700CH) - similar to Sporter Competition I, except has been range selected for optimal accuracy, includes Cordura nylon case, 3-9X rubber armored variable scope, and cleaning kit, 10½ lbs. Limited mfg. 1992 only.

Pre-ban	$1,575	$1,350	$1,200	$995	$875	$750	$675

Last MSR was $1,527.

Grading	100%	98%	95%	90%	80%	70%	60%

MATCH TARGET H-BAR (R6600/R or MT6601) - similar to AR-15A2 Govt. Model Rifle, except has heavy 20 in. barrel (1 turn in 7 in.), Model 6600 was disc. 1993, 8 lbs. New 1986.

	MSR	$1,194	$990	$875	$800	$725	$650	$575	$525

Add $71 for compensator (MT6601C, new 1999).

	Pre-ban		$1,625	$1,395	$1,200	$995	$875	$750	$675

Add $200 for .22 LR conversion kit (mfg. 1990-94).

* *Match Delta H-Bar (M6600DH/6601DH)* - similar to AR-15A2 H-Bar, except has 3-9X rubber armored variable scope, removable cheekpiece, adj. scope mount, and leather sling, range selected, aluminum cased, pre-ban mfg. Mfg. 1987-1991.

$1,625	$1,395	$1,200	$995	$875	$750	$675

Last MSR was $1,460.

Add $160 for .22 LR conversion kit (mfg. 1990-91).

COLT ACCURIZED RIFLE (CR6724) - .223 Rem. cal., 24 in. stainless match barrel, matte finish, accurized AR-15, 8 (disc. 1998) or 9 (new 1999) shot mag., 9.41 lbs. New 1997.

	MSR	$1,424	$1,150	$995	$850	$795	$725	$650	$575

MATCH TARGET COMPETITION H-BAR II (MT6731) - .223 Rem. cal., 16.1 in. barrel (1 turn in 9 in.), matte finish, 7.1 lbs. New 1995.

	MSR	$1,172	$975	$895	$825	$725	$625	$575	$525

AR-15A2 SPORTER II - .223 Rem., standard 20 in. barrel, rear sight adj. for windage only, 7½ lbs. Disc. 1989.

$995	$900	$800	$700	$600	$525	$470

Last MSR was $740.

AR-15A2 CARBINE - similar to older AR-15A2 Sporter II Rifle, except has collapsible buttstock, field sights, 16 in. barrel, shortened forearm, 5 lbs. 13 oz. Disc. 1988.

$2,125	$1,800	$1,550	$1,325	$1,100	$975	$850

Last MSR was $770.

AR-15A3 TACTICAL CARBINE (R-6721) - .223 Rem. cal., M4 flattop with 16 in. heavy barrel, pre-ban configuration with flash hider, bayonet lug, and collapsible stock, removable carry handle, approx. 135 were sold commercially in the U.S. Mfg. 1994.

$4,950	$4,250	$3,600	$3,100	$2,750	$2,400	$2,125

AR-15A2 GOVT. MODEL CARBINE (R6520) - similar to AR-15A2 Govt. Model Rifle, except has collapsible buttstock, 800 meter adj. rear sight, 16 in. barrel, 5 lbs. 13 oz., shortened forearm. Mfg. 1988-1994 (civilian sales disc. because of Federal/State regulations).

$1,675	$1,495	$1,275	$1,050	$925	$825	$725

Last MSR was $880.

* *AR-15 9mm Para. Carbine (R6450)* - similar to AR-15A2 Carbine, except 9mm Para. cal. with 20 shot mag., 6 lbs. 5 oz. Mfg. 1985-86 only.

$1,625	$1,475	$1,250	$1,025	$925	$850	$750

Last MSR was $696.

AR-15 SCOPE (3X/4X) AND MOUNT - initially offered with 3X scope, then switched to 4X. Disc.

$250	$200	$165

Last MSR was $344.

SHOTGUNS: O/U

ARMSMEAR - 12 ga. only, 2¾ in. chambers, a few prototypes were mfg. by Worshipful Co. Gunmakers of London, boxlock action with engraved sideplates, checkered high-grade European walnut stock and forearm, 28 (HE) or 30 (LE) in. VR barrels with screw-in chokes, choice of light (Armsmear 12 LE) or heavy (Armsmear 12 HE) engraving, 7½ lbs. This model was originally advertised in 1995.

While advertised, this model was never manufactured.

100%	98%	95%	90%	80%	70%	60%	50%	40%	30%	20%	10%

SHOTGUNS: SxS, DISC.

Strong, original case colors and vivid damascus barrel patterning will make the difference when determining values on the Models 1878 and 1883. Remember, the models listed below were designed to shoot black powder loads only, not smokeless powder.

MODEL 1878 HAMMER SHOTGUN - 10 or 12 ga., 28-32 in. blue or browned damascus barrels, double triggers, sideplates, case hardened breech, extractors, semi-pistol grip stock, 22,683 mfg. between 1878-1889. Many of these guns were ordered with special features - these original guns command premiums above the prices listed below.

$3,750	$3,250	$2,950	$2,675	$2,200	$1,925	$1,650	$1,485	$1,100	$990	$880	$725

MODEL 1883 HAMMERLESS - 8, 10 or 12 ga., 28-32 in. damascus barrels, many deluxe custom orders occur in this model. Mfg. from 1883-1895. Approx. serial range is No. 1-3,050 and 4,055-8,365. Seldom encountered in mint condition.

$4,250	$3,750	$3,350	$2,995	$2,675	$2,200	$1,925	$1,650	$1,485	$1,100	$990	$875

Add 200% for 8 ga.

This model was generally a custom order gun with no standard grades being designated. Quality was extremely high, and the high cost of manufacture is a large reason why the gun never sold in large numbers commercially. The Model 1883 was discontinued after only 12 years of manufacture (it was one of the most expensive shotguns during its day). Values above assume moderate engraving and above average walnut.

Grading	100%	98%	95%	90%	80%	70%	60%

SxS SHOTGUN MFG. 1961-62 - 12 ga. or 16 ga., various barrel lengths, DTs, checkered stock and forearm, mfg. in France 1961-62 by Fabrication Mechanique, estimated total between 25-50 guns in serial range 467,000-469,000.

	$675	$595	$525	$450	$400	$360	$320

SHOTGUNS: SEMI-AUTO

STANDARD AUTO SHOTGUN - 12 or 20 ga. (also available in Mags.), mfg. by Franchi of Italy, aluminum frame, 26, 28, 30, or 32 in. plain or VR barrel almost 5,300 mfg. (both models) 1962-1966.

	$375	$350	$325	$295	$260	$230	$200

Add $50 for VR barrel.

CUSTOM AUTO SHOTGUN - similar to Standard Model, except deluxe walnut, hand engraved receiver. Mfg. 1962-1966.

	$475	$425	$375	$350	$325	$295	$260

SHOTGUNS: SLIDE ACTION

COLTSMAN PUMP SHOTGUN - 12, 16, or 20 ga., Franchi frame assembled by both Kodiak and Montgomery Wards, 26 or 28 in. plain barrel, aluminum frame. Approx. 2,000 mfg. 1961-1965.

	$325	$295	$260	$230	$200	$180	$165

COMMEMORATIVES, SPECIAL EDITIONS, & LIMITED MFG.

During the course of a year, we receive many phone calls and letters on Colt special editions and limited editions that do not appear in this section. It should be noted that a factory commemorative issue is a gun that has been manufactured, marketed, and sold through the auspices of the specific trademark (in this case Colt). There have literally been hundreds of special and limited editions which, although mostly made by Colt (some were subcontracted), were not marketed or retailed by Colt. These guns are NOT Colt commemoratives and, for the most part, do not have the desirability factor that the factory commemoratives have. Your best alternative to find out more information about the multitude of these special/limited editions is to write: COLT HISTORIAN, P.O. Box 1868, Hartford, CT, 06144. If anyone could have any information, it will be the factory. Their research fee starts at $100 per gun, and if they cannot obtain additional information on the variation you request, they will refund $50. Unfortunately, in some cases, a special/limited edition may not be researchable. In situations like this, do not confuse rarity with desirability.

Typically, special and limited editions are made for distributors. These sub-contracts seem to be mostly made to signify/commemorate an organization, state, special event or occasion, personality, etc. These are typically marketed and sold through a distributor to dealers, or a company/individual to those people who want to purchase them. These special editions may or may not have a retail price and often times, since demand is regional, values decrease rapidly in other areas of the country. In some cases, if the distributor/wholesaler who ordered the initial special/limited edition is known (and still in business), you may be able to find more information by contacting them directly. Desirability is the key to determining values on these editions.

Until recently, the over-production of many factory commemoratives had created a "softness" in the commemorative marketplace. Over a decade ago, Colt decided to cut down on commemorative manufacture after perhaps too many years of over- production. Many commemorative consumers were starting to think that these "limited manufacture" guns had become more of a company marketing tool and sales gimmick rather than a legitimate vehicle for investment potential and collector support. During the end of this period of commemorative "over-production", both distributors and retailers finally saw their commemorative inventory levels gradually reach zero - perhaps the first time in over two decades that they were sold out of factory commemoratives. In other words, the commemorative "blow-out" sales were over. As this transition from distributor/dealer inventory to consumer purchases occurred, the commemorative marketplace became stronger and prices began to rise.

Because the commemorative consumer is now more in charge (consumers now own most of the guns since distributor/dealer inventories are depleted) than during the 1980s, commemorative firearms are possibly as strong as they have ever been. When the supply side of commemorative economics has to be purchased from knowledgable collectors or savvy dealers and demand stays the same or increases slightly, prices have no choice but to go up. If and when the manufacturers crank up the commemorative production runs again (and it won't be like the good old days), the old marketplace characteristics may reappear. Until then, however, the commemorative marketplace remains strong, with values becoming more predictable.

As a reminder on commemoratives, I would like to repeat a few facts, especially for the beginning collector, but applicable to all manufacturers of commemoratives. Commemoratives are current production guns designed as a reproduction of an historically famous gun model, or as a tie-in with historically famous persons or events. They are generally of very excellent quality and often embellished with select woods and finishes such as silver, nickel, or gold plating. Obviously, they are manufactured to be instant collectibles and to be pleasing to the eye. As with firearms in general, not all commemorative models have achieved collector status, although most enjoy an active market - especially recently. Consecutive-numbered pairs as well as collections based on the same serial number will bring a premium. Remember that handguns usually are in some type of wood presentation case, and that rifles may be cased or in packaging with graphics styled to the particular theme of the collectible. The original factory packaging and papers should always accompany the firearm, as they are necessary to realize full value at the time of sale.

All commemorative firearms should be absolutely new, unfired, and as issued, since any obvious use or wear removes it from collector status and lowers its value significantly. Many owners have allowed their commemoratives to sit in their boxes while encased in plastic wrappers for years without inspecting them for corrosion or oxidation damage. This is risky, especially if stored inside

Grading	100%	Issue Price	Qty. Made

a plastic wrapper for long periods of time, since any accumulated moisture cannot escape. Periodic inspection should be implemented to ensure no damage occurs - this is important, since even light "freckling" created from touching the metal surfaces can reduce values significantly. A fired gun with obvious wear or without its original packaging can lose as much as 50% of its normal value - many used commemoratives get sold as "fancy shooters" with little, if any, premiums being asked. A final note on commemoratives: One of the characteristics of commemoratives/ special editions is that over the years of ownership, most of the original amount manufactured stays in the same NIB condition. Thus, if supply always is constant and in one condition, demand has to increase before price appreciation can occur. After 40 years of commemorative/special edition production, many models' performance records can be accurately analyzed and the appreciation (or depreciation) can be compared against other purchases of equal vintage. You be the judge.

1961 GENESEO, ILLINOIS 125TH ANNIVERSARY DERRINGER
$650 $28 104

1961 SHERIFF'S MODEL - blue and case hardened, 3 in. barrel, SM suffix.
$1,995 $130 478

1961 SHERIFF'S MODEL - nickel, 3 in. barrel, SM suffix.
$5,500 $140 25

1961 125TH ANNIVERSARY MODEL SAA
$1,395 $150 7,390

1961 KANSAS STATEHOOD SCOUT
$450 $75 6,201

1961 PONY EXPRESS CENTENNIAL SCOUT
$475 $80 1,007

1961 CIVIL WAR CENTENNIAL PISTOL .22 SHORT
$175 $33 24,114

1962 ROCK ISLAND ARSENAL CENTENNIAL SCOUT
$250 $39 550

1962 COLUMBUS, OHIO SESQUICENTENNIAL SCOUT
$550 $100 200

1962 FORT FINDLAY, OHIO SESQUICENTENNIAL SCOUT
$650 $90 110

1962 FORT FINDLAY CASE PAIR - .22 LR and .22 Mag. cals.
$2,500 $185 20

1962 NEW MEXICO GOLDEN ANNIVERSARY SCOUT
$450 $80 1,000

1962 FORT MCPHERSON, NEBRASKA CENTENNIAL DERRINGER
$395 $29 300

1962 WEST VIRGINIA STATEHOOD CENTENNIAL SCOUT
$450 $75 3,452

1963 WEST VIRGINIA STATEHOOD CENTENNIAL SAA .45
$1,395 $150 600

Grading	100%	Issue Price	Qty. Made
1963 ARIZONA TERRITORIAL CENTENNIAL SCOUT			
	$450	$75	5,355
1963 ARIZONA TERRITORIAL CENTENNIAL SAA .45			
	$1,395	$150	1,280
1963 CAROLINA CHARTER TERCENTENARY SCOUT			
	$450	$75	300
1963 CAROLINA CHARTER TERCENTENARY 22/45 COMBO			
	$1,795	$240	251
1963 H. COOK "1 TO 100" 22/45 COMBO			
	$1,895	$275	100
1963 FORT STEPHENSON, OHIO SESQUICENTENNIAL SCOUT			
	$550	$75	200
1963 BATTLE OF GETTYSBURG CENTENNIAL SCOUT			
	$450	$90	1,019
1963 IDAHO TERRITORIAL CENTENNIAL SCOUT			
	$450	$75	902
1963 GEN. JOHN HUNT MORGAN INDIANA RAID SCOUT			
	$650	$75	100
1964 CHERRY'S SPORTING GOODS 35TH ANNIVERSARY 22/45 COMBO			
	$1,895	$275	100
1964 NEVADA STATEHOOD CENTENNIAL SCOUT			
	$450	$75	3,984
1964 NEVADA STATEHOOD CENTENNIAL SAA .45			
	$1,795	$150	1,688
1964 NEVADA STATEHOOD CENTENNIAL 22/45 COMBO			
	$1,595	$240	189
1964 NEVADA ST. CENT. 22/45 COMBO W/EXTRA ENGR. CYLS.			
	$1,895	$350	577
1964 NEVADA "BATTLE BORN" SCOUT			
	$450	$85	981
1964 NEVADA "BATTLE BORN" SAA .45			
	$1,395	$175	80
1964 NEVADA "BATTLE BORN" 22/45 COMBO			
	$2,595	$265	20
1964 MONTANA TERRITORIAL CENTENNIAL SCOUT			
	$450	$75	2,300
1964 MONTANA TERRITORIAL CENTENNIAL SAA .45			
	$1,395	$150	851

Approx. 100-200 sets (including the Scout) were sold with matching ser. numbers.

Grading	100%	Issue Price	Qty. Made

1964 WYOMING DIAMOND JUBILEE SCOUT

| | $450 | $75 | 2,357 |

1964 GENERAL HOOD CENTENNIAL SCOUT

| | $450 | $75 | 1,503 |

1964 NEW JERSEY TERCENTENARY SCOUT

| | $450 | $75 | 1,001 |

1964 NEW JERSEY TERCENTENARY SAA .45

| | $1,395 | $150 | 250 |

1964 ST. LOUIS BICENTENNIAL SCOUT

| | $450 | $75 | 802 |

1964 ST. LOUIS BICENTENNIAL SAA .45

| | $1,395 | $150 | 200 |

1964 ST. LOUIS BICENTENNIAL 22/45 COMBO

| | $1,795 | $240 | 250 |

1964 CALIFORNIA GOLD RUSH SCOUT

| | $475 | $80 | 500 |

1964 PONY EXPRESS PRESENTATION SAA .45

| | $1,495 | $250 | 1,004 |

1964 CHAMIZAL TREATY SCOUT

| | $450 | $85 | 450 |

1964 CHAMIZAL TREATY SAA .45

| | $1,395 | $170 | 50 |

1964 CHAMIZAL TREATY 22/45 COMBO

| | $1,995 | $280 | 50 |

1964 COL. SAM COLT SESQUI. PRESENTATION SAA .45

| | $1,495 | $225 | 4,750 |

1964 COL. SAM COLT SESQUI. DELUXE PRES. SAA .45

| | $2,500 | $500 | 200 |

1964 COL. SAM COLT SESQUI. SPEC. DELUXE PRES. SAA .45

| | $4,000 | $1,000 | 50 |

1964 WYATT EARP BUNTLINE SAA .45

| | $2,500 | $250 | 150 |

1965 OREGON TRAIL SCOUT

| | $450 | $75 | 1,995 |

1965 JOAQUIN MURIETTA 22/45 COMBO

| | $1,795 | $350 | 100 |

1965 FORTY-NINER MINER SCOUT

| | $450 | $85 | 500 |

Grading	100%	Issue Price	Qty. Made
1965 OLD FT. DES MOINES RECONSTRUCTION SCOUT			
	$475	$90	700
1965 OLD FT. DES MOINES RECONSTRUCTION SAA .45			
	$1,395	$170	100
1965 OLD FT. DES MOINES RECONSTRUCTION 22/45 COMBO			
	$1,895	$290	100
1965 APPOMATTOX CENTENNIAL SCOUT			
	$450	$75	1,001
1965 APPOMATTOX CENTENNIAL SAA .45			
	$1,395	$150	250
1965 APPOMATTOX CENTENNIAL 22/45 COMBO			
	$1,795	$240	250
1965 GENERAL MEADE CAMPAIGN SCOUT			
	$450	$75	1,197
1965 ST. AUGUSTINE QUADRACENTENNIAL SCOUT			
	$475	$85	500
1965 KANSAS COWTOWN SERIES - Wichita Scout.			
	$450	$85	500
1966 KANSAS COWTOWN SERIES - Dodge City Scout.			
	$450	$85	500
1966 COLORADO GOLD RUSH SCOUT			
	$475	$85	1,350
1966 OKLAHOMA DIAMOND JUBILEE			
	$450	$85	1,343
1966 DAKOTA TERRITORY SCOUT			
	$450	$85	1,000
1966 GENERAL MEADE SAA .45			
	$1,395	$165	200
1966 ABERCROMBIE & FITCH "TRAILBLAZER" - New York.			
	$1,295	$275	200
1966 KANSAS COWTOWN SERIES - Abilene Scout.			
	$450	$95	500
1966 INDIANA SESQUICENTENNIAL SCOUT			
	$450	$85	1,500
1966 PONY EXPRESS .45 SAA 4-SQUARE SET (4 GUNS)			
	$5,995	$1,400	unknown
1966 CALIFORNIA GOLD RUSH SAA .45			
	$1,495	$175	130

Grading	100%	Issue Price	Qty. Made

1966 ABERCROMBIE & FITCH "TRAILBLAZER" - Chicago.

$1,295 — $275 — 100

1966 ABERCROMBIE & FITCH "TRAILBLAZER" - San Francisco.

$1,295 — $275 — 100

1967 LAWMAN SERIES - Bat Masterson Scout.

$475 — $90 — 3,000

1967 LAWMAN SERIES - Bat Masterson SAA .45.

$1,500 — $180 — 500

1967 ALAMO SCOUT

$450 — $85 — 4,250

1967 ALAMO SAA .45

$1,395 — $165 — 750

1967 ALAMO 22/45 COMBO

$1,795 — $265 — 250

1967 KANSAS COWTOWN SERIES - Coffeyville Scout.

$450 — $95 — 500

1967 KANSAS TRAIL SERIES - Chisolm Trail Scout.

$450 — $100 — 500

1967 WWI SERIES - .45 ACP cal., Chateau Thierry.

$795 — $200 — 7,400

1967 WWI SERIES - Chateau Thierry Deluxe.

$1,350 — $500 — 75

1967 WWI SERIES - Chateau Thierry Spec. Deluxe.

$2,750 — $1,000 — 25

1968 NEBRASKA CENTENNIAL SCOUT

$450 — $100 — 7,001

1968 KANSAS TRAIL SERIES - Pawnee Trail Scout.

$450 — $110 — 501

1968 WWI SERIES - .45 ACP cal., Belleau Wood.

$795 — $200 — 7,400

1968 WWI SERIES - Belleau Wood Deluxe.

$1,350 — $500 — 75

1968 WWI SERIES - Belleau Wood Special Deluxe.

$2,750 — $1,000 — 25

1968 LAWMAN SERIES - Pat Garrett Scout.

$475 — $110 — 3,000

1968 LAWMAN SERIES - Pat Garrett .45 SAA.

$1,495 — $220 — 500

Grading	100%	Issue Price	Qty. Made

1969 GEN. NATHAN BEDFORD FORREST SCOUT

| | $450 | $110 | 3,000 |

1969 KANSAS TRAIL SERIES - Santa Fe Trail Scout.

| | $450 | $120 | 501 |

1969 WWI SERIES - .45 ACP cal., 2nd Battle of the Marne.

| | $795 | $220 | 7,400 |

1969 WWI SERIES - 2nd Battle of the Marne Deluxe.

| | $1,350 | $500 | 75 |

1969 WWI SERIES - 2nd Battle of the Marne Spec. Deluxe.

| | $2,750 | $1,000 | 25 |

1969 ALABAMA SESQUICENTENNIAL SCOUT

| | $450 | $110 | 3,001 |

1969 ALABAMA SESQUICENTENNIAL .45 SAA

| | $15,000 | unknown | 1 |

1969 GOLDEN SPIKE SCOUT

| | $475 | $135 | 11,000 |

1969 KANSAS TRAIL SERIES - Shawnee Trail Scout.

| | $450 | $120 | 501 |

1969 WWI SERIES - .45 ACP cal., Meuse-Argonne.

| | $795 | $220 | 7,400 |

1969 WWI SERIES - Meuse-Argonne Deluxe.

| | $1,350 | $500 | 75 |

1969 WWI SERIES - Meuse-Argonne Spec. Deluxe.

| | $2,750 | $1,000 | 25 |

1969 ARKANSAS TERRITORIAL SESQUICENTENNIAL SCOUT

| | $450 | $110 | 3,500 |

1969 LAWMAN SERIES - .45 SAA Wild Bill Hickok.

| | $1,495 | $220 | 500 |

1969 LAWMAN SERIES - Wild Bill Hickok Scout.

| | $475 | $117 | 3,000 |

1969 CALIFORNIA BICENTENNIAL SCOUT

| | $450 | $135 | 5,000 |

1970 KANSAS FORT SERIES - Ft. Larned Scout.

| | $450 | $120 | 500 |

1970 WWII SERIES - European Theatre.

| | $795 | $250 | 11,500 |

Grading	100%	Issue Price	Qty. Made

1970 WWII SERIES - Pacific Theatre.

	$795	$250	11,500

Note: A complete set of the WWI and WWII Series standard grade models (6 guns) with matching serial numbers in NIB condition is currently selling in the $4,500 range.

1970 TEXAS RANGER SAA .45

	$2,250	$650	1,000

1970 TEXAS RANGER GRADE I (95% ENGRAVING COVERAGE)

	$6,000	N/A	90

1970 TEXAS RANGER GRADE II (75% ENGRAVING COVERAGE)

	$5,500	$2,250	80

1970 TEXAS RANGER GRADE III (50% ENGRAVING COVERAGE)

	$5,000	$2,950	90

1970 KANSAS FORTS - Ft. Hays Scout.

	$450	$130	500

1970 MAINE SESQUICENTENNIAL SCOUT

	$450	$120	3,000

1970 MISSOURI SESQUICENTENNIAL SCOUT

	$450	$125	3,000

1970 MISSOURI SESQUICENTENNIAL .45 SAA

	$1,395	$220	900

1970 KANSAS FORTS - Ft. Riley Scout.

	$450	$130	500

1970 LAWMAN SERIES - Wyatt Earp Scout.

	$495	$125	3,000

1970 LAWMAN SERIES - Wyatt Earp .45 SAA.

	$2,500	$395	500

1971 NRA CENTENNIAL .45 SAA

	$1,495	$250	5,000

1971 NRA CENTENNIAL .357 SAA

	$1,395	$250	5,000

1971 NRA CENTENNIAL GOLD CUP .45 ACP

	$1,295	$250	2,500

1971 1851 NAVY - U.S. Grant.

	$595	$250	4,750

1971 1851 NAVY - Robert E. Lee.

	$595	$250	4,750

1971 1851 NAVY - Lee-Grant Set.

	$1,350	$500	250

1971 KANSAS SERIES - Ft. Scott Scout.

	$450	$130	500

Grading	100%	Issue Price	Qty. Made

1972 FLORIDA TERRITORY SESQUICENTENNIAL SCOUT

	$450	$125	2,001

1972 ARIZONA RANGER SCOUT

	$450	$135	3,001

1975 PEACEMAKER CENTENNIAL .45

	$1,495	$300	1,500

1975 PEACEMAKER CENTENNIAL 44.40

	$1,495	$300	1,500

1975 PEACEMAKER CENT. CASED PAIR

	$2,995	$625	500

USS TEXAS BATTLESHIP SPECIAL EDITION (1975) - .45 ACP cal., Model 1911A1 with special embellishments, nickel finish, this model is not a factory commemorative.

	$995	unknown	500

USS ARIZONA BATTLESHIP SPECIAL EDITION (1975) - .45 ACP cal., Model 1911A1 with special embellishments, nickel finish, this model is not a factory commemorative.

	$995	unknown	500

1976 U.S. BICENTENNIAL SET - includes SAA .45, Python .357 Mag., and black powder Dragoon in walnut display case with drawers.

	$2,995	$1,695	1,776

1976 BICENTENNIAL SAA FREEDOM COLTS - consisted of A, B, and C sets, set As were engraved, Bs had gold work and accessories, Cs were similar to Bs, but had shoulder stock. Set A prices averaged $1,500-$3,000 in 1976, set B prices varied between $3,500- $20,000, and set C prices started at $5,000. Total mfg. was 4 set As, 6 set Bs, and 1 set C. These sets in today's marketplace are too rare to accurately evaluate and pricing is literally "what the market will bear".

These guns were all engraved by Dwain Wright located in Applegate, OR.

1977 2ND AMENDMENT .22

	$450	$195	3,020

1977 U.S. CAVALRY 200TH ANNIVERSARY SET

	$1,250	$995	3,000

1978 STATEHOOD 3RD MODEL DRAGOON

	$6,995	$12,500	52

1979 NED BUNTLINE .45 SAA

	$1,295	$895	3,000

OHIO PRESIDENT'S SPECIAL EDITION (1979) - .45 ACP cal., Model 1911A1 with special Ohio embellishments, this is not a factory commemorative.

	$995	unknown	250

1979 TOMBSTONE CENTENNIAL .45 SAA - .45 LC cal., 7½ in. barrel, nickel finish, two-piece walnut stocks, P-1876 Model, etched with scroll engraving and Western scenes. 300 mfg. (200 singles and 50 pairs).

	$1,495	$995	300

This model was not sold retail through the auspices of Colt.

Grading	100%	Issue Price	Qty. Made

1980 DRUG ENFORCEMENT AGENCY (DEA) .45 AUTO

	$1,100	$550	910

This model was not sold retail through the auspices of Colt.

1980 OLYMPICS ACE MODEL SPECIAL EDITION

	$1,195	$1,000	200

This model was not sold retail through the auspices of Colt.

1980 HERITAGE-WALKER .44 PERCUSSION

	$950	$1,475	1,847

1981 "JOHN M. BROWNING" .45 ACP SEMI-AUTO

	$995	$1,100	3,000

1980-81 .45 ACP GOVT. SIGNATURE SERIES - .45 ACP cal., blue finished Govt. slide with gold auroplated slide or nickel finish. 250 mfg. in both finishes.

	$995	$833	250

Add $50 for blue finish.

1980-81 ACE SIGNATURE SERIES - .22 LR cal., featured Cocobolo grips with medallions, blue finish with photo engraving, cased. 1,000 mfg.

	$1,195	$955	1,000

1981 BUFFALO BILL SPECIAL EDITION - .44-40 WCF cal., 7½ in. barrel, gold and silver plating, Class C engraved, scrimshaw ivory grips featuring Buffalo Bill and his TE Wyoming Ranch brand, leather cased, 250 mfg. serialized 1BB- 250BB.

	$4,975	$4,200	250

This model was a special edition (not commemorative) that was made specifically for the Buffalo Bill Historical Center.

1982 JOHN WAYNE SAA STANDARD

	$1,995	$2,995	3,100

While advertising literature indicated 3,100 were mfg., 3,041 were sold.

1982 JOHN WAYNE SAA DELUXE

	$7,500	$10,000	500

While advertising literature indicated 500 were mfg., only 90 were sold.

1982 JOHN WAYNE SAA PRESENTATION

	$12,000	$20,000	100

While advertising literature indicated 100 were mfg., only 47 were sold.

Note: Each grade of the above John Wayne commemoratives has its own serial number range.

1983 BUFFALO BILL WILD WEST SHOW CENTENNIAL SAA .45

	$1,595	$1,350	500

1983 CCA LIMITED EDITION SAA - .44-40 WCF cal., 4¾ in. barrel, nickel finish, fleur-de-lis checkered wood grips, 250 mfg. in 1983 to commemorate Colt Collector's Assn.

	$1,595	$825	250

This model was not sold retail through the auspices of Colt.

Grading	100%	Issue Price	Qty. Made

1983 "ARMORY MODEL" SAA .45 ACP - this model had limited production, and should not be confused as being a commemorative. So called because it was shipped with extra .45 long Colt cylinder and the "Colt Armory Edition" book by E. Grant, presentation cased.

	$1,795	$1,125	500

Armory model commemoratives available with class A engraving - $2,595, B engraving - $2,995, C engraving - $3,250, D engraving - $3,500. 20 total available.

1983 PYTHON SILVER SNAKE SPECIAL EDITION - .357 Mag. cal., 6 in. barrel, black chrome stainless steel, Pachmayr grips with custom shop pewter medallions, etched engraving, includes custom gun pouch.

	$1,495	$1,150	250

1984 1ST EDITION GOVT. MODEL .380 ACP

	$550	$425	1,000

Serial range RC00000-01000.

1984 JOHN WAYNE "DUKE" FRONTIER .22

	$550	$475	5,000

1984 COLT/WINCHESTER SET - 1 ea. of the Model 1894 Winchester carbine and Colt Peacemaker, serial numbered 1WC-4440WC, .44-40 WCF cal., elaborate gold etching, cased. Pistol became available for sale individually in 1986 - see individual listing below for values.

Please refer to 1984 Winchester/Colt Set in the Winchester Commemorative section in this text.

WINCHESTER/COLT SAA - .44-40 WCF cal., 7½ in. barrel, gold etching, this commemorative was originally made as part of the 1984 Winchester/Colt rifle-pistol set, but was later able to be purchased individually. Originally mfg. 1984.

	$1,495	N/A	4,000

1984 USA EDITION SAA - .44-40 WCF cal., 7½ in. barrel, old style black powder frame, bullseye ejector rod head, 3 line patent date, high polished blue with gold line engraving. 100 guns total mfg. - 1 for each state and its capitol.

	$5,000	$4,995	100

1984 KIT CARSON .22 NEW FRONTIER - 6 in. barrel, color case hardened frame, gold artwork, serial numbered KCC0001-KCC1000, cased.

	$450	$550	1,000

1984 SECOND EDITION GOVT. MODEL .380 ACP - serial numbered 00000- 01000RC.

	$550	$525	1,000

1984 OFFICER'S COMMENCEMENT ISSUE - Officer's ACP with Marine Corps emblem, rosewood grips, silver plated oak leaf scroll, cased.

	$995	$700	1,000

This model was not sold retail through the auspices of Colt.

1984 THEODORE ROOSEVELT COMMEMORATIVE SAA - .44-40 WCF cal., 7½ in. barrel, black powder frame, case colored receiver, factory "B" hand engraving, ivory stocks, cased.

	$1,995	$1,695	500

Grading	100%	Issue Price	Qty. Made

1984 NORTH AMERICAN OILMEN SAA BUNTLINE - .45 LC cal., 12 in. barrel, non-fluted cylinder, elaborate gold etching, ebony grips with ivory inlays, stand-up glass case, ser. nos. 1-100 mfg. for Canada, 101-200 for the U.S.

	$3,250	$3,900	200

This model was not sold retail through the auspices of Colt.

1985 TEXAS 150th SESQUICENTENNIAL SAA - .45 cal., Sheriff's model, 4¾ in. barrel, mirror bright blue, gold etching, 24 Kt. gold plated backstrap and trigger guard, smooth ivory grips, French fit oak presentation case. Mfg. 1985 only.

✳ *Standard Model* - 1,000 mfg.

	$1,495	$1,836	1,000

✳ *Premier Model* - elaborate engraving, 75 mfg.

	$4,995	$7,995	75

1986 150th ANNIVERSARY SAA - .45 LC cal., 10 in. barrel, 50% engraved, royal blue finish, Goncalo Alves smooth grips, 150th anniversary logo in stocks, cherrywood case. 490 mfg. 1986 only.

	$1,995	$1,595	490

1986 150th ANNIVERSARY ENGRAVING SAMPLER SAA - various cals., 4 different engraving styles on metal surfaces, 75% coverage, ivory grips, signed by the engraver, available with either blue or nickel finish. New 1986.

	$2,995	$1,613	unknown

1986 150th ANNIVERSARY ENGRAVING SAMPLER .45 M1911A1 - .45 ACP cal., 4 different engraving styles on metal surfaces, 75% coverage, ivory grips, signed by the engraver, available with either blue or nickel finish. New 1986.

	$1,495	$1,155	unknown

Add $60 for nickel.

1986 MUSTANG FIRST EDITION - .380 ACP cal., 1,000 manufactured serialized MU00001-MU01000 (the first thousand of production), rosewood stocks, walnut presentation case. Mfg. 1986 only.

	$495	$475	1,000

OFFICER'S ACP HEIRLOOM EDITION - .45 ACP cal., personalized with individual's choice for serial number (ie. John Smith 1), mirror brite bluing, jeweled barrel, hammer, and trigger, ivory grips, with historical letter and mahogany case. New 1986.

	$1,550	$1,643	open

1986 DOUBLE DIAMOND SET - set is comprised of a Python Ultimate .357 Mag. revolver and Officer's Model .45 ACP, both guns in stainless steel, smooth rosewood grips, presentation cased. 1,000 sets mfg. 1986 only, serial numbered 1-1,000 (matched).

	$1,695	$1,575	1,000

DELTA MATCH H-BAR RIFLE - AR-15 A2 H-Bar rifle selectively chosen and equipped with 3x9 variable power rubber armored scope, leather sling, shoulder stock cheekpiece, cased. Mfg. 1987.

	$1,500	$1,425	open

Grading	100%	Issue Price	Qty. Made

12TH MAN-'SPIRIT OF AGGIELAND' - .45 ACP cal., mfg. to commemorate Texas A & M University, serial numbered TAM001-TAM999, 24Kt gold plating including wreaths on left frame and inscription on right, cherrywood glass top presentation case, includes personalized class graduation inscription. Available 1987 only.

	$950	$950	999

This model was not sold retail through the auspices of Colt.

KLAY-COLT 1851 NAVY - .36 cal., cased reproduction of the 3rd Model 1851 Navy, special fabrication insuring old world quality, charcoal bluing, heat treated screws and accessories, cased. Introduced 1986.

※ *Standard Edition* - no engraving.

	$1,850	$1,850	150

※ *Engraved Edition* - choice of engraving.

	$3,150	$3,150	50

Optional engraving patterns with or without gold inlays available at extra cost.

COMBAT ELITE CUSTOM EDITION - .45 ACP cal., with ambidextrous thumb safety, wide grip safety, hand honed action, and carrying case, ser. numbered CG00001 - CG00500. Mfg. 1987.

	$1,095	$900	500

1987 SHERIFF'S EDITION - set of 5 SAA Sheriff's configuration pistols in .45 LC cal., barrel lengths include 2, 2½, 3, 4, and 5½ in., royal blue finish, smooth rosewood grips with medallions, supplied with glass top display case which displays the revolvers in a circle around a brass sheriff's badge. Serialization has 3 numeral prefix (which is the same in each set), followed by the letters "SE", followed by 1 or 2 numerals (indicating barrel length) - i.e. serial number 002SE25 indicates the second set built, Sheriff's Edition (SE), and a barrel length of 2½ inches.

	$4,500	$7,500	100 sets

1989 SNAKE EYES LIMITED EDITION - includes two Python revolvers (2½ in. barrels), one finished in brite stainless steel and the other in Royal Blue finish, grips are ivory-like with scrimshaw "snake eyes" dice on left side and royal flush poker hand on right, includes chips and playing cards, 500 sets only of consecutive serial numbers. New 1989.

	$1,950	$2,950	500

1990 SAA HEIRLOOM II EDITION - .45 LC cal., 7½ in. barrel, color case hardened frame and hammer, balance of metal finished in Colt Royal Blue, one piece American Walnut grips with cartouche on lower left side, personalized inscription on backstrap, walnut cased. Available 1990 only.

	$1,595	$1,600	open

1990 JOE FOSS LIMITED EDITION .45 ACP GOVT. MODEL - .45 ACP cal., first limited edition in Colt's All American Hero Series, commemorates Joe Foss, famous American WWII Marine Fighter Pilot, gun features gold etched scenes on slide sides, smooth walnut grips, while 2,500 were advertised, only 300+ were mfg. serial numbered beginning with JF 0001. French fitted walnut presentation case, 38 oz. Mfg. 1990 only.

	$1,450	$1,375	300+

Grading	100%	Issue Price	Qty. Made

1911A1 50th ANNIVERSARY BATTLE OF THE BULGE - .45 ACP cal., special edition commemorating the Battle of the Bulge, silver plated with gold inlays, 300 mfg. serialized BB001-BB300.

	$1,495	$1,250	300

Add $150 for deluxe presentation case.

This special edition is sold exclusively by Cherry's located in Greensboro, NC.

COMANCHE

Current trademark manufactured in South America beginning 2001. Currently imported and distributed beginning 2002 by SGS Importers, located in Wanamassa, NJ. Distributor and dealer sales.

Grading	100%	98%	95%	90%	80%	70%	60%

PISTOLS: SINGLE SHOT

SUPER COMANCHE - .45 LC cal./.410 bore, 10 in. rifled barrel, blue finish, adj. sights. New 2002.

MSR	$168	$140	$120	$100	$85	$70	$60	$50

REVOLVERS

COMANCHE I - .22 LR cal., 6 in. barrel, 9 shot, blue or stainless, adj. sights, rubber grips. New 2002.

MSR	$232	$195	$175	$160	$145	$130	$120	$110

Add $17 for stainless steel construction.

COMANCHE II - .38 Spl. +P cal., 4 in. barrel, 6 shot, blue or stainless, adj. sights. New 2002.

MSR	$215	$180	$165	$150	$135	$120	$110	$95

Add $17 for stainless steel construction.

COMANCHE III - .357 Mag. cal., 3, 4, or 6 in. barrel, 6 shot, blue or stainless, adj. sights. New 2002.

MSR	$249	$215	$180	$165	$150	$140	$130	$100

Add $16 for stainless steel construction.

COMMANDO ARMS

Previous manufacturer located in Knoxville, TN.

Commando Arms became the new name for Volunteer Enterprises in the late 1970s.

RIFLES: CARBINES

MARK 45 - .45 ACP cal., carbine styled after the Thompson sub-machine gun, 16½ in. barrel.

	$495	$425	$350	$315	$280	$225	$195

COMPETITOR CORPORATION

Current manufacturer established in 1988 and located in Jaffrey, NH. Previously located in New Ipswich, NH until 2001, and in West Groton, MA from 1988-1995. Dealer direct or distributor sales.

Grading	100%	98%	95%	90%	80%	70%	60%

PISTOLS: SINGLE SHOT

C COMPETITOR - available in over 400 cals. from .17 LR - .50 AE, ranging from small rimfire to large belted Magnums, 14 in. barrel standard, rotary cannon action, cocks on opening, dual sliding thumb and trigger safety, rotary style ejector, click adj. sights, matte blue or optional electroless nickel finish, choice of synthetic, laminated, or natural wood grips (ambidextrous), extractor or ejector, approx. 59-73 oz. New 1988.

MSR	$460		$395	$340	$295	$265	$230	$200	$185

    Add $20 for laminated wood stock.
    Add approx. $50 for walnut grips.
    Add $60 for electroless nickel finish (barreled action only).
    Add $175 for extra 14 in. standard cal. barrel with sights.
    Add $210 for 10½ - 16 in. standard cal. barrel with sights.
    Add $240 for 17-23 in. barrel.
    Add $60 for factory installed muzzle brake.

CONNECTICUT SHOTGUN MANUFACTURING CO.

Current shotgun manufacturer established during 1995, and located in New Britain, CT.

SHOTGUNS: O/U, SIDELOCK

A. GALAZAN MODEL - 12, 16, 20, 28 ga., or .410 bore, features strong, low profile sidelock action with Boss-style metal reinforced forearm, top-of-the-line model utilizing best quality materials and U.S. workmanship, wide choice of custom features and engraving options. Each gun is custom-built to the customer's exact specifications and prices start at $38,000 without engraving.

SHOTGUNS: SxS

Connecticut Shotgun Manufacturing Company will also be manufacturing the Winchester Model 21 shotgun again shortly, using all new parts. Please contact the company directly for more information.

CONNECTICUT VALLEY CLASSICS, INC.

Previous trademark manufactured by Cooper Arms, located in Stevensville, MT 1996-1998.

CVC, Inc. was a division of CVC Sports, Inc. Previous sales and marketing offices were located in Holyoke, MA until 1996 and in Westport, CT 1993-95.

SHOTGUNS: O/U

The models listed below have receiver dimensions built to the exact specifications of the original Classic Doubles Model 101. The only difference is that the tang spacer has been made an integral part of the frame.

    Add $1,350 for each additional barrel set.

CLASSIC 101 SPORTER - 12 ga. only, boxlock action, monoblock, 28, 30, or 32 in. VR barrels with multi-chokes, SST, ejectors, nickel finished receiver with light engraving, checkered American black walnut stock and forearm with low luster finish, approx. 7¾ lbs.

	$1,875	$1,550	$1,225	$1,000	$825	$700	$600

Last MSR was $2,195.

Grading	100%	98%	95%	90%	80%	70%	60%

CLASSIC SPORTER SB - 12 ga. only, boxlock action, entry level sporter model. Mfg. 1997-98.

	$2,250	$1,875	$1,575	$1,175	$950	$775	$650

Last MSR was $2,495.

GRADE I CLASSIC SPORTER - 12 ga. only, boxlock action, monoblock, 28, 30, or 32 in. vented barrels with VR, lengthened forcing cones, and 2 3/8 in. multi-chokes, SST, ejectors, stainless steel receiver with light engraving, checkered 20 LPI AA American black walnut stock and forearm with low luster finish, approx. 7¾ lbs. Disc. 1998.

	$2,695	$2,100	$1,675	$1,250	$1,000	$825	$700

Last MSR was $2,995.

✳ *Women's Classic Sporter* - similar to Grade I Classic Sporter, except has smaller stock dimensions and 28 in. barrels only, 7½ lbs. Mfg. 1996-98.

	$2,695	$2,100	$1,675	$1,250	$1,000	$825	$700

Last MSR was $2,995.

This model was also available in Grade II or Grade III Woman's Classic Sporter.

✳ *Grade II Classic Sporter* - similar to Grade I Classic Sporter, except has AAA American or Claro walnut with 22 LPI hand-checkering, 30 in. barrels only.

	$3,100	$2,350	$1,800	$1,325	$1,050	$850	$725

Last MSR was $3,595.

✳ *Grade III Classsic Sporter* - similar to Grade II Classic Sporter, except has Fleur- de-lis checkering patterns and gold accents. Disc. 1998.

	$3,600	$2,750	$1,975	$1,450	$1,175	$925	$750

Last MSR was $4,195.

GRADE I CLASSIC FIELD - 12 ga. only, similar to Grade I Classic Sporter, except has solid rib and standard flush-mounted choke-tubes, 27½ in. barrels, 7½ lbs. Mfg. 1996- 98.

	$2,695	$2,100	$1,675	$1,250	$1,000	$825	$700

Last MSR was $2,995.

✳ *Classic Waterfowler* - 12 ga. only, 30 or 32 (disc. 1995) in. VR barrels, non- reflective surfaces, bird scene engraving, overbored barrels with lengthened forcing cones and four standard CVC chokes, 8 lbs. Mfg. 1993-98.

	$2,495	$2,000	$1,575	$1,175	$950	$775	$650

Last MSR was $2,795.

✳ *Grade II Classic Field* - similar to Grade I Classic Field, except has AAA American or Claro walnut with 22 LPI hand-checkering.

	$3,025	$2,250	$1,750	$1,300	$1,050	$850	$725

Last MSR was $3,495.

✳ *Grade III Classic/English Field* - similar to Grade II Classic Field, except has Fleur-de-lis checkering patterns and gold accents, choice of straight English (25½ in. VR barrels only) or pistol grip stock. Disc. 1998.

	$3,575	$2,850	$2,025	$1,500	$1,200	$925	$750

Last MSR was $4,195.

Add $100 for straight English stock.

✳ *Classic Skeet* - 12 ga. only, 29 in. vented barrels with 9mm VR, otherwise similar to Grade I Classic Sporter, 7½ lbs. Mfg. 1996-98.

	$2,695	$2,100	$1,675	$1,250	$1,000	$825	$700

Last MSR was $2,995.

✳ *Classic Flyer* - 12 ga. only, live bird gun featuring AAA walnut and 22 LPI checkering, oil finish, 30 in. vented overbored barrels with 11mm tapered top rib and lengthened forcing cones, scroll engraving with pigeon scene on bottom, 8 lbs. Mfg. 1996-98.

	$3,100	$2,350	$1,800	$1,325	$1,050	$850	$725

Last MSR was $3,595.

Grading	100%	98%	95%	90%	80%	70%	60%

CONQUEST

Current trademark of guns manufactured by various companies in Spain, Turkey, Germany, and Italy. No current U.S. importation.

The Conquest trademark currently includes shotguns in O/U, SxS, slide action, and semi-auto configuration. Please contact the company directly for more information.

CONTENTO/VENTURA

Previously imported by Ventura Imports in Seal Beach, CA. Ventura also imported Bertuzzi and Piotti.

SHOTGUNS: O/U

CONTENTO O/U - 12 ga., 32 in. barrels, boxlock, optional screw in choke tubes, high vent. rib, SST, auto ejectors, hand checkered Monte Carlo trap stock.

	100%	98%	95%	90%	80%	70%	60%
	$1,045	$990	$935	$880	$770	$690	$635

MK 2 - includes O/U barrels, with extra single barrel.

	$1,375	$1,320	$1,265	$1,210	$1,100	$1,020	$965

MK 2 - leather cased, combination set.

	$1,705	$1,650	$1,595	$1,540	$1,430	$1,350	$1,295

MK 3 - engraved, O/U.

	$1,650	$1,570	$1,485	$1,375	$1,295	$1,185	$1,100

MK 3 - includes O/U barrels, with extra single barrel.

	$2,200	$2,035	$1,925	$1,815	$1,650	$1,595	$1,515

MK 3 - leather cased, combination set.

	$2,750	$2,420	$2,200	$2,090	$1,955	$1,815	$1,760

SHOTGUNS: SxS

MODEL 51 - 12, 16, 20, 28 ga., or .410 bore, 26-32 in. barrels, various chokes, extractors, boxlock, double triggers, checkered straight stock.

	$385	$360	$330	$305	$250	$220	$165
Auto ejectors	$495	$440	$385	$360	$305	$275	$220

MODEL 52 - 10 ga., double triggers only, otherwise similar to Model 51.

	$525	$495	$470	$415	$360	$305	$250

MODEL 53 - deluxe version of Model 51, scalloped frame, auto ejectors.

	$470	$440	$415	$385	$330	$275	$220
SST	$605	$550	$525	$495	$440	$385	$330

MODEL 61 - 12 or 20 ga., 26, 27, 28, or 30 in. barrels, H&H sidelocks, various chokes, floral engraved, hand detachable locks, cocking indicators, select walnut pistol grip stock, auto ejectors.

	$880	$825	$770	$745	$690	$605	$550
SST	$1,020	$965	$910	$855	$800	$715	$660

MODEL 65 - similar to Model 61, with elaborate engraving and quality hand finishing.

	$1,100	$1,045	$990	$965	$880	$825	$770

Grading	100%	98%	95%	90%	80%	70%	60%

CONTINENTAL ARMS CORPORATION

Previous importer that imported high quality shotguns and rifles (usually Belgian), circa mid '50s - mid '70s.

RIFLES

BOLT ACTION - mostly large cals., typically custom Mauser action, makers include Defourney and Dumoulin.

> Specimens should be evaluated individually due to the many configurations and embellishments encountered. This model is rarely seen in today's marketplace.

DOUBLE RIFLE - .270 Win., .303 British, .30-40 Krag, .348 Win., .30-06, .375 H&H, .400 Jeffreys, .470, .475, .500, or .600 Nitro Express cal., 24 or 26 in. barrels, Anson & Deeley boxlock system, although some sidelocks were mfg., double triggers, checkered stock.

$5,500	$4,620	$3,850	$3,300	$2,970	$2,750	$2,420

Add 10% for boxlock with sideplates.
Add 15% for ejectors.
Add 25% for .375 H&H and larger cals.

SHOTGUNS: O/U

Add 20% for .410 bore.
Add 30% for 28 ga.
Add 10% for Defourney mfg.

CENTAURE BOXLOCK - 12, 20, 28 ga., or .410 bore, ejectors, light engraving, chopper lump barrels with cross-bolt double underlocks, SST, 3-piece forearm.

$2,000	$1,675	$1,500	$1,250	$1,025	$875	$750

CENTAURE LIEGE ROYAL CROWN GRADE - similar to Centaure Boxlock, except has game scene engraving, better figured wood and silver crown inlay.

$3,150	$2,850	$2,600	$2,250	$1,900	$1,600	$1,400

CENTAURE IMPERIAL CROWN GRADE - similar to Royal Crown Grade, except has higher grade wood, extensive game scene engraving, oak leaf engraving on barrels, and gold inlay on top lever.

$4,500	$4,150	$3,750	$3,500	$3,200	$2,900	$2,700

SHOTGUNS: SxS

Add 20% for .410 bore.
Add 30% for 28 ga.
Add 10% for Defourney mfg.

CENTAURE - all gauges, basic boxlock action with double triggers and extractors.

$1,050	$950	$895	$850	$700	$500	$400

Add 35% for ejectors.

CENTAURE ROYAL CROWN GRADE - all gauges, single trigger, ejectors, checkered stock and forearm, game scene engraving, can be identified by silver crown inlaid on top lever.

$3,400	$3,150	$2,800	$2,600	$2,325	$2,100	$1,950

CENTAURE IMPERIAL CROWN GRADE - similar to Royal Crown, except gold inlay on top lever, extensive game scene engraving on receiver and barrels.

$4,275	$3,850	$3,500	$3,150	$2,850	$2,575	$2,300

Grading	100%	98%	95%	90%	80%	70%	60%

COOEY MACHINE & ARMS CO. LTD.

Previous manufacturer located in Cobourg, Ontario - Canada 1903-1961. During 1961, Cooey was sold to the Olin Corporation and placed under the supervision of the Winchester Western Division. At that point, the manufacture of Winchesters (primarily for Winchester Canada) began and continued through the mid-'70s.

Models manufactured by Cooey pre-1961 include various repeating .22 rifles, single shot shotguns (Models 84 and 840), and maybe a few others. There is limited information available on the variety of shotguns and rifles manufactured by this company (most distribution occurred in Canada). To date, there is limited collector demand for most models in this trademark and values should be based on the shooting utility rather than collector premiums due to rarity. Most values will range between $75- $150.

RIFLES: BOLT ACTION

COOEY .22 RIFLE- .22 LR cal., post-WWI mfg., bolt action, open sights.

$150	$130	$110	$95	$80	$70	$60

COONAN ARMS

Previously manufactured by K & B Custom 1996-late 1999, and distributed by JS Worldwide Distribution Co. located in Maplewood, MN. Previously located in St. Paul, MN, approx. 1983-1996.

PISTOLS: SEMI-AUTO

COONAN .357 MAG. MODEL B - .357 Mag. cal. only, stainless steel and alloy construction, single action, semi-auto, design based on the Colt Model 1911, 7 shot mag., 5 or 6 (new 1989) in. barrel, smooth or checkered (new 1996) walnut grips, Teflon finish options new 1996, 42 oz. Mfg. 1983-1999.

$685	$535	$425

Last MSR was $735.

Add $40 for checkered walnut grips.
Add $33 for 6 in. barrel (new 1989).
Add $140 for Millett adj. rear sight.
Add $165 for Bo-Mar sight.
Add $45 for .38 Spl. conversion kit (new 1986).

This model could be differentiated from the Model A in that it had an extended grip safety lever, linkless barrel system, trigger bar slot is enclosed, and recontoured rear grip strap. This model became standard in 1985.

✳ *Coonan .357 Cadet Model* - similar to .357 Mag. Model B, except is compact variation with 3.9 in. barrel and 6 shot mag., 39 oz. Mfg. 1993-99.

$785	$630	$500

Last MSR was $855.

Options were similar to those listed for the Model B.

✳ *Coonan .357 Cadet II* - features standard grip with 7/8 shot mag. Mfg. 1996-99.

$785	$630	$500

Last MSR was $855.

Options were similar to those listed for the Model B.

✳ *Model B Compensated*- 6 in. barrel with compensator. Mfg. 1990-99.

$900	$795	$650

Last MSR was $1,015.

Options were similar to those listed for the Model B.

Grading	100%	98%	95%	90%	80%	70%	60%

* **Model Classic Compensated** - features 5 in. barrel with integral compensator, Millett white/orange outline sights, checkered black walnut grips, Teflon black and matte stainless two- tone finish, 42 oz. Mfg. 1996-99.

	$1,275	$1,025	$825	$675	$595	$525	$450

Last MSR was $1,400.

COONAN .357 MAG. MODEL A - original model without above listed improvements, special order only, inventory depleted in 1991. Serialization is under 2,000 for this model (less than 1,200 were mfg.).

	$1,150	$775	$550

Last MSR was $625.

Add approx. $350 for early variations with engraved slide.

This variation will also shoot .38+P loads. The first 25 Model A's were engraved on both sides of slide.

COONAN .41 MAGNUM - .41 Mag. cal., 5 in. barrel, smooth or checkered walnut grips. Mfg. 1997-99.

	$760	$625	$500

Last MSR was $825.

Options were similar to those listed for the .357 Mag.

COOPER FIREARMS OF MONTANA, INC.

Current manufacturer located in Stevensville, MT since 1991. Available through Cooper Arms registered dealers only.

RIFLES: BOLT ACTION

Approx. 10,000 Cooper rifles have been manufactured in over 50 calibers to date.

Add $150 for left hand action (custom order only) on the models listed below.

MODEL 21 SINGLE SHOT - various medium size cals., 3 front locking lugs. New 1998.

* **Model 21 Classic** - various cals., single shot, 20 in. chrome moly match grade barrel, stock is AA Claro walnut with 20 LPI hand checkering and hand rubbed oil finish, machined aluminum trigger guard, matte metal finish, approx. 7-7¼ lbs. New 1999.

MSR	$1,100	$950	$800	$650	$550	$495	$450	$400

* **Model 21 Custom Classic** - includes Brownell No. 1 checkering pattern, ebony forend tip, and steel grip cap.

MSR	$1,995		$1,725	$1,300	$975	$750	$650	$550	$475

* **Model 21 Western Classic** - various cals., features octagon barrel and case hardened action and bolt. New 1997.

MSR	$2,595		$2,250	$1,800	$1,550	$1,275	$995	$875	$750

* **Model 21 Varminter** - various cals., 24 in. stainless steel match grade barrel, stock is AA Claro walnut with 20 LPI hand checkering and hand rubbed oil finish, machined aluminum trigger guard, approx. 7-7¼ lbs. New 1999.

MSR	$995		$875	$750	$625	$550	$495	$450	$400

* **Model 21 Varmint Extreme** - various cals. between .17 Rem.-.223 Rem. (including metric cals.), features heavy Varmint stainless barrel, checkered stock. New 1994.

MSR	$1,995		$1,725	$1,300	$975	$750	$650	$550	$475

Add $465 for Benchrest Model with Jewell trigger (mfg. 1995-96).

* **Model 21 Montana Varminter-** various cals. New 2000.

MSR	$1,295		$1,150	$975	$825	$650	$550	$475	$425

Grading	100%	98%	95%	90%	80%	70%	60%

MODEL 22 - various mid-action cals., larger scale action of the Model 21.

* *Model 22 Classic* - various mid-action cals., 20 in. chrome moly match grade barrel, stock is AA Claro walnut with 20 LPI hand checkering and hand rubbed oil finish, machined aluminum trigger guard, matte metal finish, approx. 7-7¼ lbs. New 1999.

| MSR | $1,295 | | $1,150 | $975 | $825 | $650 | $550 | $475 | $425 |

* *Model 22 Custom Classic* - includes Brownell No. 1 checkering pattern, ebony forend tip, and steel grip cap.

| MSR | $2,195 | | $1,900 | $1,400 | $1,050 | $775 | $675 | $575 | $475 |

* *Model 22 Western Classic* - various cals., features octagon barrel and case hardened action and bolt, only 2 have been mfg. to date. New 1997.

| MSR | $2,795 | | $2,375 | $1,950 | $1,675 | $1,375 | $1,050 | $925 | $825 |

* *Model 22 Varminter* - various cals., otherwise similar to the Model 21 Varminter. New 2000.

| MSR | $1,199 | | $1,025 | $850 | $700 | $600 | $525 | $450 | $400 |

* *Model 22 Montana Varminter* - various cals. New 2000.

| MSR | $1,495 | | $1,300 | $1,075 | $900 | $700 | $600 | $500 | $425 |

* *Model 22 Pro-Varmint Extreme* - .220 Swift, .22 BR (new 1996), .22-250 Rem., .243 Win., .25- 06 Rem., .308 Win., 6mm PPC, 6.5x55mm (new 1996) or 7.62x39mm (new 1996) cal., available in either Pro-Varmint, Benchrest, or Black Jack (black synthetic stock) configuration. New 1995.

| MSR | $2,195 | | $1,850 | $1,375 | $1,025 | $800 | $650 | $550 | $475 |

Add $400 for Benchrest Model.

MODEL 22 CLASSIC REPEATER - .22-250 Rem., .243 Win., .308 Win., or 7mm-08 Rem. cal., 3 shot mag. While advertised during 1996 only at $2,400 retail, this model was never mfg.

MODEL CUSTOM CLASSIC - .22 LR, .22 Mag., .22 Hornet or .222 Rem. cal., features Anschutz Match 54 action with deluxe walnut stock with American features and smaller trigger guard. Mfg. 1996-99.

| | | | $1,750 | $1,375 | $1,075 | $900 | $725 | $600 | $500 |

Last MSR was $1,995.

MODEL CUSTOM MANNLICHER - .22 LR, .22 Mag., .22 Hornet, or .222 Rem. cal., features newest Anschutz Match 54 action with deluxe Mannlicher walnut stock and other special features. Mfg. 1996-99.

| | | | $1,975 | $1,625 | $1,425 | $1,225 | $975 | $850 | $700 |

Last MSR was $2,195.

MODEL 36 SPORTSMAN - .22 LR, .17 CCM, or .22 Hornet cal., without Shilen barrel, standard wood with rubber recoil pad. Mfg. 1994 only.

| | | | $675 | $575 | $495 | $450 | $400 | $350 | $295 |

Last MSR was $750.

MODEL 36 MARKSMAN - .22 LR, .17 CCM, or .22 Hornet cal., 4 shot mag., 23 in. chrome moly barrel, AA Claro walnut with 22 LPI checkering, 45 degree bolt, sling swivels, hand rubbed oil finish, 7 lbs. Mfg. 1992-94.

| | | | $975 | $750 | $625 | $550 | $495 | $450 | $400 |

Last MSR was $1,125.

* *Model 36 Montana Trail Blazer* - .22 LR cal. only, lightweight field gun with sporter barrel. Mfg. 1996 only.

| | | | $1,300 | $1,025 | $775 | $650 | $575 | $475 | $425 |

Last MSR was $1,475.

Grading	100%	98%	95%	90%	80%	70%	60%

✹ **Model 36 Classic** - .22 LR cal. only, features choice of AAA Claro or AA French walnut with Monte Carlo cheekpiece. Disc. 1996.

	$1,500	$1,175	$875	$700	$625	$525	$450

Last MSR was $1,695.

✹ **Model 36 Varmint Extreme** - various cals., heavy Varmint stainless barrel, checkered stock. Mfg. 1997 only.

	$1,525	$1,175	$875	$700	$625	$525	$450

Last MSR was $1,695.

✹ **Model 36 Western Classic** - various cals., features octagon barrel and case hardened action and bolt. Mfg. 1997-99.

	$1,900	$1,400	$1,000	$775	$650	$550	$475

Last MSR was $2,195.

✹ **Model 36 Custom Classic** - includes Brownell No. 1 checkering pattern, ebony forend tip, and steel grip cap. Disc. 1999.

	$1,625	$1,325	$1,050	$825	$700	$600	$50

Last MSR was $1,850.

✹ **Model 36 TRP-1** - target variation of the Model 36 with ISU synthetic stock and adj. cheekpiece, 23 in. Wiseman/McMillan stainless steel or chrome moly barrel, single shot, fully adj. single stage trigger, vent. forearm. Mfg. 1992-1993.

	$950	$795	$625	$525	$475	$425	$375

Last MSR was $1,095.

✹ **Model MS-36 (TRP-1S)** - silhouette variation of the Model 36 TRP-1, clear epoxy finish, silhouette style stock, Pachmayr buttpad. Mfg. 1992-1993.

	$895	$725	$625	$550	$495	$450	$400

Last MSR was $995.

✹ **Model 36 BR-50** - .22 LR cal., benchrest variation featuring black synthetic stock and heavy stainless barrel, Jewell trigger. Mfg. 1993-99.

	$1,675	$1,250	$950	$750	$650	$550	$475

Last MSR was $1,950.

✹ **Model 36 IR-50/50** - .22 LR cal. only, lightweight sporter style competition rifle with heavy 20 in. barrel. Mfg. 1996-99.

	$1,675	$1,250	$950	$750	$650	$550	$475

Last MSR was $1,950.

✹ **Model 36 Featherweight** - .17 CCM, .22 LR, or .22 Hornet cal., features matte black synthetic stock and metal, Jewell trigger. Mfg. 1994-99.

	$1,600	$1,225	$900	$700	$625	$525	$450

Last MSR was $1,795.

MODEL 38 SPORTER - .17 CCM, or .22 CCM cal., 3 shot mag., 24 in. chrome moly barrel, AA Claro walnut with 22 LPI checkering, 45 degree bolt, sling swivels, hand rubbed oil finish, 8 lbs. Mfg. 1992-1993.

	$965	$750	$625	$550	$495	$450	$400

Last MSR was $1,095.

Add $100 for Standard Grade (AA Claro walnut).
Add $200 for Custom Grade.
Add $300 for Custom Classic Grade.

The custom grade includes choice of AAA Claro or AA French walnut with Monte Carlo cheekpiece.

The .17 CCM and .22 CCM cartridges designate Cooper Centerfire Magnum. Basically, the .22 CCM is a centerfire derivative of the .22 Mag. cal., and the .17 CCM is simply a necked down variation.

Grading	100%	98%	95%	90%	80%	70%	60%

* **Model 38 Repeater (Deluxe)** - deluxe variation of the Model 38 Sporter, 650 mfg. 1992-1994.

| | | $1,750 | $1,400 | $1,000 | $775 | $650 | $550 | $475 |

MODEL 38 SINGLE SHOT - small, mostly rimmed cals., 3 front locking lugs. New 1998.

* **Model 38 Classic** - various cals., single shot, 20 in. chrome moly match grade barrel, stock is AA Claro walnut with 20 LPI hand checkering and hand rubbed oil finish, machined aluminum trigger guard, matte metal finish, approx. 7-7¼ lbs. New 1999.

| MSR | $1,100 | $950 | $800 | $650 | $550 | $495 | $450 | $400 |

* **Model 38 Custom Classic** - includes Brownell No. 1 checkering pattern, ebony forend tip, and steel grip cap.

| MSR | $1,995 | $1,735 | $1,325 | $975 | $750 | $650 | $550 | $475 |

* **Model 38 Western Classic** - various cals., features octagon barrel and case hardened action and bolt. New 1997.

| MSR | $2,595 | $2,250 | $1,800 | $1,550 | $1,275 | $995 | $875 | $750 |

* **Model 38 Varminter** - various cals., single shot, 24 in. stainless steel match grade barrel, stock is AA Claro walnut with 20 LPI hand checkering and hand rubbed oil finish, machined aluminum trigger guard, approx. 7-7¼ lbs. New 1999.

| MSR | $995 | $875 | $750 | $625 | $550 | $495 | $450 | $400 |

* **Model 38 Varmint Extreme** - various cals. including the new .19-223, heavy stainless steel barrel w/o sights, checkered stock. New 1997.

| MSR | $1,995 | $1,725 | $1,300 | $975 | $750 | $650 | $550 | $475 |

* **Model 38 Montana Varminter** - various cals. New 2000.

| MSR | $1,295 | $1,150 | $975 | $825 | $650 | $550 | $475 | $425 |

MODEL 40 - .17 CCM (disc. 1995), .17 Ackley Hornet, .22 CCM (disc. 1995), .22 Hornet, or .22 K Hornet cal., 3 lug action, incorporates Anschütz mag., choice of Classic, Custom Classic, or Classic Varminter configuration. Mfg. 1995-96.

| | | $1,600 | $1,200 | $950 | $750 | $650 | $550 | $475 |

Last MSR was $1,825.

Add $200 for Custom Classic or Classic Varminter (disc.) Model.

MODEL 57 CLASSIC - .17 HRM (new 2002), .22 LR or .22 Mag. (new 2001) cal., 3 rear locking lugs, various configurations, barrel lengths, and features. New 2000.

Add approx. $100 for .17 HRM or .22 Mag. cal. on the following models.

| MSR | $1,100 | $940 | $795 | $665 | $550 | $495 | $450 | $400 |

* **Model 57 Custom Classic** - new 2000.

| MSR | $1,895 | $1,650 | $1,275 | $900 | $725 | $625 | $525 | $450 |

* **Model 57 Western Classic** - new 2000.

| MSR | $2,495 | $2,250 | $1,650 | $1,175 | $825 | $725 | $650 | $575 |

* **Model 57 Light Varmint Target** - new 2000.

| MSR | $1,295 | $1,150 | $975 | $825 | $650 | $550 | $475 | $425 |

MODEL 72 MONTANA PLAINSMAN - various cals., single shot featuring case colored Win. Model 1885 action with heavy octagon barrel, double set triggers, deluxe checkered straight grip stock and forearm, no sights. While advertising during 1997 at a retail price of $2,195, this model was never mfg.

Grading	100%	98%	95%	90%	80%	70%	60%

RIFLES: SINGLE SHOT

MODEL 7 PEREGRINE FALLING BLOCK - various cals., falling block action with under lever, choice of varmint extreme or custom sporter configuration, 24 in. barrel, deluxe checkered walnut stock, tang mounted safety, approx. 6 lbs. Limited production 2001 only.

	$1,750	$1,400	$1,100	$925	$800	$675	$550

Last MSR was $1,995.

Add $300 for custom sporter variation.

COP

Previous Derringer manufacturer located in Torrance, CA.

DERRINGERS

COP DERRINGER - .357 Mag. cal., 4 shot, 3 in. barrel, stainless steel mfg., double action, wood grips, 28 oz. COP stands for Compact Off-Duty Police. Disc.

$350	$325	$285

COSMI, AMERICO & FIGLIO

Current semi-auto shotgun manufacturer established during 1930, and located in Ancona, Italy. Currently imported beginning 2001 by Autumn Sales, Inc., located in Fort Worth, TX. Please contact the importer for more information and model availability (see Trademark Index).

Approximately 7,100 Cosmi shotguns have been manufactured since 1930 (the design dates back to 1925). They are known for their unique mechanism and high-quality fabrication techniques. Since each gun's parts are made separately (and individually serial numbered), most components are not interchangeable from one gun to another.

SHOTGUNS: SEMI-AUTO

STANDARD MODEL - 12, 16, or 20 ga., (a 28 ga. and .410 bore will be available shortly), 2¾ (16 ga. only) or 3 in. chamber, semi-auto, unique pivoting break open action loads cartridges into stock chamber from inside of receiver, 8 shot mag. with 3 shot option reducer, steel, alloy, or titanium frame, Boehler Antinit steel barrel (moves when shooting) available with or without choke tubes, all internal parts are mfg. from special chrome-nickel steel or titanium (new 1990), custom order gun only with dimensions specified by individual customer (approx. 6 month delivery time on 12 and 20 ga.).

* ***Standard Grade*** - barrel and attached receiver assembly are blue, frame is chromed-nickel steel or aluminum, w/o engraving.

	MSR	$9,940		$9,475	$8,300	$7,300	$6,400	$5,500	$4,600	$3,800

Add $1,600 for extra barrel.

* ***Model De Luxe*** - features 3 different levels of engraving and select walnut.

◇**Model De Luxe with No. 1 or No. 2 Engraving Pattern**

	MSR	$14,200		$13,175	$10,800	$9,400	$8,250	$7,300	$6,400	$5,500

Add $690 for No. 1 engraving pattern.

◇**Model De Luxe with No. 3 Engraving Pattern**

	MSR	$11,360		$10,125	$9,350	$8,250	$7,300	$6,400	$5,500	$4,600

* ***Model Extra De Luxe*** - choice of No. 4 or No. 5 engraving.

	MSR	$15,620		$14,300	$11,200	$9,650	$8,500	$7,500	$6,500	$5,500

Add $1,420 for No. 5 engraving pattern.

Grading	100%	98%	95%	90%	80%	70%	60%

* **Model Prestige** - top-of-the-line model with 3 engraving options, standard is B.

  MSR $25,560 $23,000 $19,350 $15,620 $14,300 $11,200 $9,650 $8,500

  Add $4,260 for C engraving option.

  ◇**Model Prestige with A Engraving Pattern**

  MSR $38,340 $35,000 $30,000 $25,560 $23,000 $19,350 $15,620 $12,750

* **Titanium Model** - 12 or 20 ga., receiver made out of machined titanium, approx. 6.8 lbs. in 12 ga., approx. 5.7 lbs. in 20 ga. New 1990.

  MSR $14,200 $13,150 $10,800 $9,400 $8,250 $7,300 $6,400 $5,500

  This model is also available with optional engraving styles 1-5. Engraving prices vary between $1,420-$11,360.

COUNTY, S.A.L.

Previous shotgun manufacturer located in Eibar, Spain.

SHOTGUNS: O/U

County manufactured a wide variety of both boxlock and sidelock O/Us, which had very limited U.S. importation.

CRESCENT FIRE ARMS CO.
& CRESCENT-DAVIS ARMS CO.

Previous manufacturers and trademarks manufactured circa 1888-1931 in Norwich, CT.

In 1888, George W. Cilley bought out the defuct Bacon Arms Co. of Norwich, CT. He then formed an alliance with Frank Foster, and borrowed enough money to form the Crescent Fire Arms Company. Cilley and Foster each held several firearms patents, and both were highly qualified in firearms design and manufacture. Production began with single shot tip-up shotguns that had an external side hammer. Double barrel shotgun production was started in 1891. In 1893, they began making bicycle chains, and that same year, H&D Folsom took over the company's financial control. Early in the 1890s, Crescent built a rifle that resembled the Remington No. 4. A very rare Crescent was the .410 bore shotgun pistol, which was introduced in the 1920s. In 1929, N.R. Davis Firearms Co., then owned by Warner Arms Corp., merged with Cresent to become Crescent-Davis Arms Co. Because of financial crisis, business continued to decline, and they were forced to sell out. Savage Arms Co. acquired Davis-Cresent in 1931, assembled guns from the remaining parts, and these guns were sold under the Crescent name only. In 1932, the city of Norwich, CT, took over the Crescent property for non-payment of back taxes. After the Norwich facility was closed, manufacture was moved to Chicopee Falls.

It is unknown whether or not Crescent did any high grade or custom work. However, a very well engraved SxS, with the Crescent logo, is known to exist in a private collection.

Crescent Firearms Company remains best known as a manufacturer of "house brand" shotguns (i.e., Crescent private labeled guns for retailers, distributors, mail-order houses, etc.). Over 100 different trademarks have been observed to date, manufactured by Crescent - almost all the remaining specimens today are priced as shooters, and have no collector value.

SHOTGUNS

SINGLE SHOT MODEL - 12, 16, 20, 28 ga., or .410 bore, exposed hammer, various barrel lengths, walnut stock and forearm. Disc.

$125 $100 $85 $70 $60 $45 $30

Add 15% for 16 or 20 ga., 50% for 28 ga. or .410 bore.

Grading	100%	98%	95%	90%	80%	70%	60%

SxS MODEL - values below assume standard models with double triggers, extractors, original finish, and 100% working order. Sidelock actions were also available and will command premiums from prices listed below. Shotguns with exposed hammers can equal their hammerless counterparts if condition is 80% or better.

	100%	98%	95%	90%	80%	70%	60%
12 ga.	$195	$175	$150	$125	$100	$85	$65
16 ga.	$195	$175	$150	$125	$100	$85	$65
20 ga.	$295	$265	$230	$200	$170	$150	$125
28 ga.	$375	$325	$280	$250	$200	$150	$100
.410 bore	$400	$350	$300	$250	$200	$150	$100

KNICKERBOCKER - 20 ga., 14 in. nickel-plated barrels, case-hardened receiver, pistol grip, mfg. circa 1900s.

Extreme rarity factor precludes accurate pricing information.

VICTOR EJECTOR - .410 bore, 12 in. single barrel, total production unknown, possibly prototype for Crescent Certified Shotgun.

Extreme rarity factor precludes accurate pricing information.

NEW EMPIRE - hammerless .410 smooth bore or 20 ga., 12¼ in. barrels, extremely rare firearm whose total production and years of manufacture are unknown at this time (only known documentation is mentioned as an "Auto Burglar Gun" in an advertisement by "Saul Ruben, The Gun Store, 68 E. Long St., Columbus, OH" of the October 1932 issue of Hunter-Trader-Trapper, which lists a $14.75 retail price). The receiver is marked New Empire. At this time, 5 specimens are known in .410 smooth bore, with ser. nos. scattered throughout the S-1 to S-19 range. The ser. no. appears on the metal under the forearm. The Crescent Auto & Burglar Gun may have been distributed by the H.&D. Folsom Arms Co. of New York City through its manufacturing division, the Crescent Firearms Co., Norwich, CT. Crescent's sellers included the Belknap Hardware Co., Louisville, KY and Hibbard- Spencer-Bartlett Co., Chicago, IL.

$1,200	$1,000	$900	$800	$700	$600	$500

CRESCENT CERTIFIED SHOTGUN - .410 smooth bore, 12½ in. barrel, approx. 4,000 mfg. from approx. 1930-32 by the Crescent-Davis Arms Corp., and possibly thereafter until 1934 by the J. Stevens Arms Co., left receiver side is stamped "Crescent Certified Shotgun/Crescent-Davis Arms Corp./Norwich, Conn. U.S.A.", also termed the "Ever- Ready" Model 200 and advertised with a blue frame, but specimens with "tiger stripe" and regular case coloring have been observed, guns not currently registered with ATF cannot be legally owned and are subject to seizure.

$1,200	$1,000	$900	$800	$700	$600	$500

Add $100-$300 for original cardboard box.

CRICKET RIFLE

Please refer to the Keystone Sporting Arms, Inc. section in this text.

Grading	100%	98%	95%	90%	80%	70%	60%

CROSSFIRE LLC

Previous manufacturer located in La Grange, GA 1998-2001.

COMBINATION GUNS

CROSSFIRE MK-I - 12 ga. (3 in. chamber) over .223 Rem. cal., unique slide action O/U design allows stacked shotgun/rifle configuration, 18¾ in. shotgun barrel with invector chokes over 16¼ in. rifle barrel, detachable 4 (shotgun) and 5 (rifle) shot mags., open sights, Picatinny style rail scope mount, synthetic stock and forearm, choice of black (MK- I) or Real-Tree 100% camo (MK-1RT) finish, single trigger with ambidextrous fire control lever, 8.6 lbs. Mfg. mid-1998-2001.

$1,750	$1,550	$1,350	$1,175	$995	$895	$825

Last MSR was $1,895.

Add $100 for camo finish.

CUMBERLAND MOUNTAIN ARMS, INC.

Previous manufacturer located in Winchester, TN early 1993-99.

RIFLES: SINGLE SHOT

PLATEAU RIFLE - .40-65 or .45-70 Govt. cal., patterned after the Browning Hi-wall single shot, various barrel lengths up to 32 in., manual safety, blue receiver and barrel, Marble's style buckhorn rear sight, receiver drilled for scope mounts. Mfg. 1993-99.

$1,075	$825	$675	$575	$500	$450	$400

Last MSR was $1,295.

Add approx. $200-$350 for deluxe wood.

CUSTOM GUN GUILD

Previous manufacturer located in Doraville, GA.

WOOD'S MODEL IV SINGLE SHOT - various cals., custom manufactured, falling block type single shot, lightweight, only 5½ lbs. Mfg. 1984 only.

$2,975	$2,500	$2,000	$1,850	$1,700	$1,500	1,250

Kathleen Hoyt, Colt Historian and Joseph Canali from the Colt Custom Shop, taking a break at a recent Las Vegas Antique Arms Show.

D SECTION

DGS, INC.

Current custom rifle gunsmith located in Casper, WY.

Custom gunsmith Dale A. Storey manufactures a variety of bolt action rifles built per individual customer order only. They include the Storey Custom, Storey Lightweight, as well as other variations. Please contact the company directly for more information and current prices on these quality custom rifles.

CUSTOM GUNSMITHING

DPMS, INC.

Current manufacturer established in 1986 and located in Becker, MN. DPMS (Defense Procurement Manufacturing Services, Inc.) manufactures high quality AR-15 style rifles, barrel assemblies (including a new conversion for .22 cal.), related parts and components. Distributor, dealer, and consumer direct sales.

Grading	100%	98%	95%	90%	80%	70%	60%

PISTOLS: SEMI-AUTO

DPMS .45 - .45 ACP cal., patterned after the Colt M1911A-1, 7 shot mag., 5 in. barrel, 38 oz. Limited mfg. 2001 only.

	100%	98%	95%	90%	80%	70%	60%
	$475	$425	$360	$330	$300	$275	$250

Last MSR was $519.

PISTOLS: SLIDE ACTION

PANTHER PUMP PISTOL - .223 Rem. cal., slide action paramilitary design, 10½ in. threaded heavy barrel, aluminum handguard incorporates slide action mechanism, pistol grip only (no stock), carrying handle with sights, 5 lbs.

	MSR	$1,595					
			$1,475	$1,200	$1,025	$925	$825	$700	$575

RIFLES: BOLT ACTION

PHANTOM II - various cals., trued and blue printed custom Evolution repeater action, match stainless steel barrel, Timney match trigger, McMillian A2 or A3 tactical stock, matte black metal, 11½ lbs. Mfg. by Evolution. New 2001.

	MSR	$3,200					
			$3,200	$2,725	$2,350	$2,025	$1,650	$1,325	$1,050

PHANTOM III - .50 BMG cal., single shot, 28 in. contoured barrel with muzzle brake, larger but similar to the contour and specs of the Phantom II, 22 lbs. Mfg. by Evolution. New 2001.

	MSR	$4,400					
			$4,400	$3,625	$3,100	$2,750	$2,350	$2,000	$1,650

COYOTE II - various cals., trued Remington M700 action and customized trigger, matte black metal parts, HS Precision Kevlar graphite tactical stock with aluminumn and fiberglass reinforced bedding. Mfg. by Evolution. New 2001.

	MSR	$1,965					
			$1,965	$1,750	$1,495	$1,225	$1,000	$875	$775

Grading	100%	98%	95%	90%	80%	70%	60%

BOLT ACTION SNIPER/VARMINT SERIES - various cals., 3 different configurations included Sniper, Informal Target Varmint, and Field Grade Varmint, featured match barrel, action, and tuned trigger. Prices for the Sniper rifle started at approx. $3,000 while the Varmint guns started at approx. $2,000. Disc. 2000.

RIFLES: SEMI-AUTO

Each new DPMS rifle/carbine comes equipped with two 10 shot mags., a nylon web sling, and a cleaning kit.

PANTHER AR-15 SERIES - .223 Rem. or 7.62x39mm Russian (new 2000) cal., semi- auto or slide action, paramilitary design, various barrel lengths and configurations, 10 shot mag., black synthetic stock and forearm, various weights. Introduced 1993.

* **Panther Classic** - 20 in. heavy barrel, ribbed barrel shroud, includes carrying handle with sights, 8 lbs.

MSR	$799	$725	$625	$550	$475	$425	$375	$335

Add $76 for left-hand variation (Southpaw Panther).

* **Panther Bulldog** - 20 in. stainless fluted bull barrel, flat-top, adj. buttstock, vented free float handguard, 11 lbs.

$1,150	$835	$725	$625	$550	$475	$425

Last MSR was $1,219.

* **Panther 7.62x39mm** - 7.62x39mm Russian cal., 20 in. heavy barrel, black Zytel buttstock with trapdoor. New 2000.

MSR	$849	$765	$650	$575	$495	$440	$385	$335

* **Panther DCM** - 20 in. stainless steel heavy barrel, adj. sights, black Zytel composition buttstock, 9 lbs. New 1998.

MSR	$1,099	$975	$795	$675	$595	$525	$460	$415

* **Panther Lite 16** - 16 in. 1x9 twist post-ban chrome moly barrel, non-collapsible fiberite CAR stock, forged A1 upper with forward bolt assist, black Teflon finish, 5¾ lbs. New 2002.

MSR	$699	$650	$595	$550	$475	$425	$375	$335

* **Panther Classic Sixteen** - 16 in. heavy barrel, adj. sights, black Zytel composition buttstock, 6½ lbs. New 1998.

MSR	$789	$715	$630	$550	$475	$425	$375	$335

Add $55 for Panther Free Float Sixteen with free floating barrel and vent. handguard.

* **Panther Lo-Pro Classic** - 16 in. bull barrel, features flatop lo-pro upper receiver with push pin. New 2002.

MSR	$699	$650	$595	$550	$475	$425	$375	$335

* **Panther Tuber** - features 16 in. post-ban heavy barrel with full length 2 inch aluminum free float handguard, adj. A2 rear sights. New 2002.

MSR	$749	$675	$625	$565	$485	$435	$375	$335

* **Panther Carbine** - 16 in. heavy barrel, collapsible stock, includes carrying handle, 6½ lbs. This model is available for law enforcement only.

* **Prairie Panther** - 20 in. heavy fluted barrel, flat-top, vented free float handguard, 8¾ lbs. Disc. 1999.

$875	$750	$635	$550	$475	$425	$375

Last MSR was $959.

* **Arctic Panther** - similar to Panther Bull, except has white powder coat finish on receiver and handguard, 10 lbs. New 1997.

MSR	$1,099	$995	$795	$675	$595	$525	$460	$415

Grading	100%	98%	95%	90%	80%	70%	60%

❋ *Panther Bull* - features 16, 20 (standard), or 24 in. stainless free floating bull barrel, flat-top, aluminum forearm, 10 lbs.

MSR	$915	$835	$725	$600	$525	$450	$400	$360

Subtract $30 for 16 in. barrel (Panther Bull Sweet Sixteen).
Add $30 for 24 in. barrel (Panther Bull Twenty-Four).

❋ *Panther Bull Classic* - features 20 in. long, 1 in. bull barrel, adj. sights, 10 lbs. New 1998.

MSR	$905	$825	$725	$600	$525	$450	$400	$360

Add $200 for SST lower.

❋ *Panther Deluxe Bull Twenty-Four Special* - features 24 in. stainless fluted barrel, adj. A2 buttstock with sniper pistol grip. New 1998.

MSR	$1,189	$1,075	$825	$700	$600	$525	$460	$415

❋ *Panther Super Bull* - 16, 20, or 24 in. extra heavy bull barrel, flat-top receiver, free float handguard, approx. 11 lbs. Mfg. 1997-98.

	$925	$835	$725	$600	$525	$450	$400

Last MSR was $1,005.

❋ *Panther Extreme Super Bull* - features 24 in. extra heavy stainless steel bull barrel (1 1/8 in. diameter barrel), flat-top, hi-rider upper receiver, skeletonized A2 buttstock, 11¾ lbs. New 1999.

MSR	$1,199	$1,075	$835	$715	$600	$525	$460	$415

❋ *Panther Race Gun* - .223 Rem. cal., 24 in. stainless steel barrel with Hot Rod hand guard, IronStone steel and aluminum stock with rubber buttplate and brass weights, 16 lbs. New 2001.

MSR	$1,699	$1,550	$1,250	$1,050	$950	$850	$725	$600

PANTHER SINGLE SHOT - single shot only w/o magazine.

MSR	$814	$725	$640	$560	$485	$435	$375	$335

RIFLES: SLIDE ACTION

❋ *Panther Pump* - .223 Rem. cal., paramilitary design, 20 in. threaded heavy barrel with flash hider, aluminum handguard incorporates slide action mechanism, carrying handle with sights, bayonet lug, designed by Les Branson, 8½ lbs.

MSR	$1,695	$1,525	$1,275	$1,050	$925	$775	$650	$575

DSA INC.

Current manufacturer, importer, and distributor of semi-auto rifles and related components located in Barrington, IL. Previously located in Round Lake and Grayslake, IL.

DSA Inc. is a manufacturer that sells FAL/SA58 .308 Win. cal. rifles for both civilian and law enforcement purposes (L.E. certificates must be filled out for L.E. purchases). Until recently, DSA, Inc. also imported a sporterized Sig 550 rifle.

RIFLES: SEMI-AUTO

SA58 STANDARD RIFLE - .308 Win. cal., FAL design using high precision CNC machinery, 21 (standard or bull) or 24 in. (bull only) steel or stainless steel cyrogenically treated barrel, black synthetic stock, pistol grip (standard 2001) attached to frame, 8¾ -11½ lbs.

MSR	$1,595	$1,425	$1,200	$1,025	$900	$775	$650	$575

Add $200 for stainless steel 21 or 24 in. bull barrel.
Add $150 for bull barrel.

Grading	100%	98%	95%	90%	80%	70%	60%

* **SA58 Standard Carbine** - similar to SA58 Standard Rifle, except has 16¼ in. barrel, 8¼ lbs. New 1999.

MSR $1,595	$1,425	$1,200	$1,025	$900	$775	$650	$575

Add $200 for SA58 Lightweight Carbine with aluminum receiver components.
Add $500 for SA58 Stainless Steel Carbine (included scope mount, disc. 2000).

* **SA58 T48 Replica** - .308 Win. cal., 10 or 20 shot fixed mag., stripper clip top cover, cryogenic barrel, wood furniture, replica Browning flash hider. Importation began 2002.

MSR $1,795	$1,595	$1,350	$1,150	$950	$800	$675	$575

DWM

Previous manufacturer located in Berlin, Germany circa 1900-1930. DWM (Deutsche Waffen und Munitions Fabriken) manufactured Lugers are listed in the Luger section.

PISTOLS: SEMI-AUTO

POCKET AUTOMATIC - 7.65mm cal., 3½ in. barrel, blue, hard rubber grips. Mfg. 1921-1931.

	$700	$630	$580	$500	$420	$380	$330

DAEWOO

Current manufacturer located in Korea. No current U.S. importation. Previous importation included Kimber of America, Inc. until 1997, Daewoo Precision Industries, Ltd., until mid-1996, located in Southampton, PA, and previously distributed by Nationwide Sports Distributors 1993-96. Previously imported by KBI, Inc. and Firstshot, Inc., both located in Harrisburg, PA, and B-West located in Tucson, AZ.

Daewoo makes a variety of firearms, most of which are not imported into the U.S.

PISTOLS: SEMI-AUTO

DH380 - .380 ACP cal., double action design. Imported 1995-96.

	$330	$285	$260	$235	$210	$185	$165

Last MSR was $375.

DH40 - .40 S&W cal., otherwise similar to DP51. Imported 1995-96.

	$385	$325	$295	$250	$225	$200	$180

Last MSR was $450.

DP51 STANDARD (S), COMPACT ©, OR (B) - 9mm Para. cal., double action enabling lowering hammer w/o depressing trigger, 3½ (DP51 C or S) or 4 (DP51 B) in. barrel, 10 (C/B 1994), 12* (.40 S&W), or 13* (9mm Para.) shot mag., 3-dot sighting, tri-action mechanism, ambidextrous controls, alloy receiver, polished or sand-blasted black finish, 28 or 32 oz., includes lockable carrying case with accessories. Imported 1991-96.

	$350	$295	$270	$250	$225	$200	$180

Last MSR was $400.

Add $45 for DP51 Compact.

DP52 - .22 LR cal., double action, 3.8 in. barrel, alloy receiver, 10 shot mag., blue finish, 23 oz. Imported 1994-96.

	$320	$275	$225	$200	$180	$165	$150

Last MSR was $380.

Grading	100%	98%	95%	90%	80%	70%	60%

D

RIFLES: SEMI-AUTO

MAX II (K2) - .223 Rem. cal., paramilitary design rifle, 18 in. barrel, gas operated rotating bolt, folding fiberglass stock, interchangeable mags. with the Colt M16, 7 lbs. Importation disc. 1986.

	$950	$875	$800	$725	$625	$550	$475

Last MSR was $609.

✳ MAX I (K1A1) - similar to above, except has retractable stock. Importation disc. 1986.

	$1,050	$925	$850	$750	$650	$575	$500

Last MSR was $592.

DR200 - .223 Rem. cal., paramilitary configuration with sporterized stock, 10 shot mag. Imported 1995-96.

	$650	$550	$475	$425	$395	$375	$350

Last MSR was $535.

DR300 - 7.62x39mm cal., paramilitary configuration with or w/o thumbhole stock. Importation disc.

	$550	$475	$425	$395	$375	$350	$325

DAISY

Current airgun manufacturer with headquarters located in Rogers, AR.

For more information and current pricing on both new and used Daisy airguns, please refer to the 2nd Ed. *Blue Book of Airguns* by Dr. Robert Beeman & John Allen (now online also).

RIFLES: SINGLE SHOT, DISC.

As the V/L ammunition availability diminishes, values listed below may fluctuate.

V/L STANDARD RIFLE - .22 V/L cal. (caseless air ignited cartridge), 1,100 FPS, 18 in. barrel, plastic stock, not particularly accurate, approx. 19,000 mfg. 1968-1969.

	$200	$175	$150	$125	$95	$80	$65

V/L PRESENTATION - similar to Collector's Kit, except does not have owner's name inscribed on butt plate, walnut stock, 4,000 mfg. for dealers.

	$235	$195	$160	$130	$100	$85	$70

Last MSR was $125.

V/L COLLECTOR'S KIT - comes with case, gun cradles, 300 rounds of ammo, and a gold plated brass butt plate with owner's name and serial number of gun, approx. 4,000 mfg., available only by direct factory order.

	$350	$250	$200	$165	$125	$100	$85

Last MSR was $125.

Note: The Daisy .22 V/L was discontinued because the BATF ruled that the gun constituted a firearm, and since Daisy was federally licensed to manufacture air weapons only, the factory decided to discontinue manufacture.

RIFLES: BOLT ACTION, DISC.

All Legacy models have a removable trigger, slings and swivels, takedown barrel, dovetail receiver for scope mounting, rifled inner steel barrel with 12 lands and grooves, and an adj. rear sight. Weight is between 6½-7 lbs.

Grading	100%	98%	95%	90%	80%	70%	60%

MODEL 8 - .22 S or LR cal., single shot, 16 in. barrel, black synthetic stock, 30,000 mfg. for Wal-mart only 1987-88.

	$175	$150	$125	$95	$80	$70	$55

During 1987, Daisy assembled this model using left-over Iver Johnson parts.

LEGACY MODELS 2201/2211 - .22 LR cal., single shot, bolt action, plastic (2201) or walnut finished hardwood (2211) stock, models vary in features, prices range from $150-$175. Mfg. 1988-91.

LEGACY MODELS 2202/2212 - .22 LR cal., bolt action repeater, 10 shot rotary mag., plastic (2202) or walnut finished hardwood (2212) stock, models vary in features, prices range from $150-$175. Mfg. 1988-91.

Model 2202 has copolymer stock with adj. butt plate.

RIFLES: SEMI-AUTO

LEGACY MODELS 2203/2213 - .22 LR cal., 7 shot box mag., models vary in features, prices range from $165-$190. Mfg. 1988-91.

Model 2203 has copolymer stock with adj. butt plate. Model 2213 has American hardwood stock.

DAKIN GUN CO.

Previous importer located in San Francisco, CA circa 1960s.

SHOTGUNS: O/U

MODEL 170 - 12, 16, 20 ga., or .410 bore, boxlock, light engraving, double triggers, vent rib.

	$495	$400	$325	$275	$245	$220	$195

SHOTGUNS: SxS

MODEL 100 - 12 or 20 ga., boxlock, engraved, double trigger.

	$425	$350	$275	$240	$205	$190	$170

MODEL 147 - 12 or 20 ga., boxlock, engraved, vent. rib, double trigger.

	$495	$385	$300	$265	$235	$215	$195

MODEL 160 - 12 or 20 ga., boxlock, single trigger, ejectors, vent. rib.

	$825	$700	$595	$495	$450	$395	$360

MODEL 215 - 12 or 20 ga., sidelock, heavy engraving, special walnut, single trigger, ejectors, vent. rib.

	$2,250	$1,900	$1,675	$1,300	$1,100	$925	$775

DAKOTA ARMS, INC.

Current manufacturer and importer established in 1987, located in Sturgis, SD. Dealer and direct sales through manufacturer only. This company is not affiliated with Dakota Single Action Revolvers.

Dakota Arms models listed below are also available with many custom options - please contact the factory directly for availability and pricing. Left-hand rifles are also available at no extra charge on all models. Actions (barreled or unbarreled) may also be purchased separately. Please contact the manufacturer directly for individual quotations.

Grading	100%	98%	95%	90%	80%	70%	60%

D

RIFLES: BOLT ACTION

DAKOTA .22 RIFLE - .22 LR or .22 Hornet (disc.) cal., combines features of the Win. Model 52 Sporter and Dakota 76, full sized receiver, trigger and striker block safety similar to Dakota 76, 5 shot mag., 22 in. chrome moly barrel, checkered walnut stock, no sights, 6½ lbs. Mfg. 1992-98.

	$1,550	$1,150	$900	$800	$695	$625	$550

Last MSR was $1,995.

DAKOTA 76 TRAVELER - various cals. between .25-06 Rem. - .450 Dakota, in addition to Dakota proprietary calibers, almost seamless take down rifle based on the Dakota 76 design, threadless disassembly ensuring scope stability and accuracy, in addition to no possibility of increasing the head space during repeated disassembly, wood stock, right or left-hand action. New 1999.

MSR	$4,495	$4,050	$3,550	$2,950	$2,575	$2,150	$1,750	$1,450

Add $1,000 for Safari Traveler.
Add $1,500 for African Traveler.
Add $1,650 (standard cals.) or $1,950 (Safari cals.) per interchangable barrel.

DAKOTA 76 CLASSIC GRADE - available in various cals. (short, standard, or long action), custom frame incorporating many Win. Model 70 features, 21 or 23 in. barrel, Mauser type extractor, checkered X English walnut stock, 7½ lbs. Left-hand action available at no extra charge. New 1987.

MSR	$3,595	$3,175	$2,675	$2,250	$1,900	$1,625	$1,350	$1,125

This Model is also available with a composite stock at no extra charge.

DAKOTA 76 VARMINT GRADE - available in 9 cals. between .17 Rem. and 6mm PPC, single shot bolt-action, heavy barrel. Mfg. 1994-97.

	$2,275	$1,775	$1,425	$1,175	$990	$880	$770

Last MSR was $2,500.

DAKOTA 76 SAFARI GRADE - available in various cals., 23 in. barrel, one-piece drop trigger guard assembly with hinged floor plate, checkered XXX English walnut stock with ebony forearm tip. Left-hand action available at no extra charge, 8½ lbs. New 1987.

MSR	$4,595	$4,125	$3,625	$3,075	$2,600	$2,200	$1,800	$1,500

Subtract $400 (retail) if ordered with composite stock (disc.).

DAKOTA 76 AFRICAN GRADE - .404 Jeffery, .416 Dakota, .416 Rigby, or .450 Dakota cal., 4 shot mag., select wood with cross bolts in the stock, other features similar to Safari Grade Model, 24 in. barrel,"R" prefix on serial number, 9½ lbs. New 1989.

MSR	$4,995	$4,500	$3,750	$3,250	$2,800	$2,400	$1,900	$1,625

DAKOTA 76 ALPINE GRADE - .22-250 Rem., .243 Win., 6mm Rem., .250-3000 Savage, 7mm-08 Rem., .308 Win., or .358 Win. cal., short action variation of the Classic Grade, 21 or 23 in. barrel, lighter weight model featuring a blind 4 shot mag., checkered X English walnut slimmer stock and barrel, serial numbered with a "K" prefix, 6½ lbs. Mfg. 1989-92.

	$1,850	$1,495	$1,300	$1,075	$925	$800	$700

Last MSR was $1,995.

Other calibers were available on a special order basis.

DAKOTA LONGBOW TACTICAL E.R. (T-76) - .300 Dakota Mag., .330 Dakota Mag., or .338 Lapua Mag. cal., 28 in. stainless barrel, tactical designed for long range, black synthetic stock with adj. comb, includes Picatinny optical rail, Model 70 style trigger, matte finish metal, controlled round feeding, includes deployment kit, 13.7 lbs. New 1997.

MSR	$4,250	$3,850	$3,350	$2,800	$2,450	$2,050	$1,675	$1,375

Grading	100%	98%	95%	90%	80%	70%	60%

DAKOTA MODEL 97 LIGHTWEIGHT HUNTER - available in most popular cals. between .22-250 Rem. and .308 Win., features fiberglass stock with black recoil pad, right hand only, 6 lbs. New 1998.

	MSR	$1,995		$1,775	$1,495	$1,200	$975	$875	$750	$650

Add $500 for Wood Hunter 97 (includes semi-fancy wood and blind mag.).
Add $1,000 for Deluxe Hunter 97 (includes semi-fancy wood and point panel checkering with floorplate).

DAKOTA MODEL 97 LONG RANGE HUNTER - available in 13 popular cals. between .25-06 Rem. and .375 Dakota Mag., composite black H-S Precision stock, 24 or 26 in. barrel, adj. match trigger, Model 76 ejector system, approx. 7.7 lbs. New 1997.

	MSR	$1,995		$1,775	$1,495	$1,200	$975	$875	$750	$650

Add $500 for Wood Hunter 97 (includes semi-fancy wood and blind mag.).
Add $1,000 for Deluxe Hunter 97 (includes semi-fancy wood and point panel checkering with floorplate).

RIFLES: SxS

DOUBLE RIFLE - .470 NE or .500 NE cal., round boxlock action similar to Dakota shotgun, 25 in. chopper lump barrels, selective ejectors, supplied with Americase. New 2001.

	MSR	$25,000		$22,750	$18,000	$16,000	$13,000	$11,000	$9,250	$7,850

RIFLES: SINGLE SHOT

DAKOTA MODEL 10 - available in most rimmed and rimless commercially loaded standard and Mag. cals., standard or enlarged Magnum (new 1994) action, 23 in. round barrel, top tang safety, deluxe checkered XX English walnut stock and forearm, 6 lbs. New 1990.

	MSR	$3,595		$3,175	$2,750	$2,425	$2,150	$1,625	$1,350	$1,150

DAKOTA MODEL 97 VARMINT HUNTER - various varmint cals., rounded short action, 24 in. chrome-moly barrel, adj. trigger, black fiberglass stock standard, right hand only, approx. 8 lbs. New 1998.

			$1,600	$1,375	$1,100	$950	$750	$650	$550

Last MSR was $1,795.

Add $700 for Wood Varmint Hunter 97 (includes semi-fancy wood and blind mag.).
Add $1,200 for Deluxe Varmint Hunter 97 (includes semi-fancy wood and point panel checkering with floorplate).

SHOTGUNS: SxS

CLASSIC GRADE - 20 ga. only, case colored round boxlock action, 27 in. barrels with fixed chokes, DTs, straight grip checkered English walnut stock and splinter forearm, no engraving, 6 lbs. Mfg. 1996-98.

			$7,450	$6,750	$6,000	$5,400	$4,800	$4,200	$3,450

Last MSR was $7,950.

PREMIER GRADE - 20, 28 ga. (new 2000), or .410 bore (new 2000), similar to Dakota Classic Field Grade, 27 in. barrels, exhibition grade English walnut, French grey metal finish, 50% engraving coverage, straight grip, splinter forend, DT, hand-rubbed oil finish stock, game rib with gold bead, ejectors, choice of chokes.

	MSR	$13,950		$13,950	$10,250	$8,300	$6,950	$5,650	$4,850	$4,000

Add 10% for 28 ga. or .410 bore.

Grading	100%	98%	95%	90%	80%	70%	60%

DAKOTA AMERICAN LEGEND - 20, 28 ga., or .410 bore, fully scroll-engraved coin finish round boxlock action with gold inlays, French grey metal finish, special select English walnut mfg. to customer dimensions, 27 in. barrels with game rib and gold bead, straight grip, DT, round action, ejectors, choice of chokes, oak and leather trunk case, 6 lbs. New 1996.

MSR	$18,000	$16,000	$13,000	$11,000	$9,250	$7,500	$6,250	$5,000

Add 10% for 28 ga. or .410 bore.

Only 100 guns are scheduled to be mfg. Also offered in a 12 ga. and .410 bore/28 ga. set.

DAKOTA SINGLE ACTION REVOLVERS

Dakota revolvers are currently manufactured in Italy by Uberti, imported and distributed by E.M.F. Co., Inc. located in Santa Ana, CA. Dealer direct sales only.

Other firearms imported by E.M.F. Co., Inc. will be found in the E section of this book.

REVOLVERS: REPRODUCTIONS

Until 2000, most Dakota SAAs were manufactured by Armi San Marco. Beginning 2001, all current SAAs are manufactured by Uberti.

OLD MODEL SAA - .22 LR, .32-20 WCF, .357 Mag., .38-40 WCF, .44 Spl., .44-40 WCF, or .45 LC cal., copy of the Colt SAA, 4 5/8, 5½, or 7½ in. barrels, blue finish, case hardened frame, 1-piece walnut grips, solid brass backstrap and trigger guard. Importation disc. 1991.

			$325	$250	$200	$175	$150	$135	$120

Last MSR was $600.

Add $100 for nickel finish (disc.).
Add $110 for convertible cylinders.

* ***Engraved Old Model*** - .32-20 WCF, .357 Mag., .38-40 WCF, .44-40 WCF, or .45 cal., 4¾, 5½, or 7½ in. barrel. Disc. 1993, reintroduced 1996, disc. 1998.

			$695	$500	$425	$350	$325	$300	$275

Last MSR was $840.

Add $160 for nickel finish (disc).

* ***Cattlebrand Engraved*** - .44-40 WCF or .45 LC cal., 5½ or 7½ in. barrel, patterned after the famous Colt Cattlebrand variation (features various cattlebrands engraved on the barrel, frame and cylinder). Imported 1992-1993, reintroduced 1996, disc. 1998.

			$695	$500	$425	$350	$325	$300	$275

Last MSR was $840.

Add $140 for silver-plating.

PREMIER CUSTOM - various cals., case colored frame, choice of black Colt style or stag grips. Importation began 1999.

MSR	$500		$400	$350	$325	$300	$285	$275	$265

Add $115 for stag grips (disc.).

NEW DAKOTA MODEL SAA - .357 Mag., .44-40 WCF, or .45 LC cal., features forged steel frame, black nickel backstrap and trigger guard, 4 (.45 LC cal. with standard grips), 4¾, 5½, or 7½ in. barrel, choice of case hardened or nickel frame, one piece walnut grips, original Colt type hammer (without transfer bar safety). Importation began 1991.

MSR	$300		$260	$230	$175	$150	$135	$120	$105

Add $85 for combo. cylinder.
Add $125 for nickel finish (bright or satin).

Grading	100%	98%	95%	90%	80%	70%	60%

✻ Sheriff Model - cals. similar to New Model, 3½ in. barrel. Imported 1997-99.

	$340	$285	$230	$175	$150	$135	$120

Last MSR was $435.

DAKOTA PREMIER SAA - .45 LC cal., black powder frame, initial mfg. was with 4 5/8 or 5½ in. barrel, set screw cylinder pin release, steel backstrap and trigger guard, one-piece grips. This model was the predecessor to the New Hartford Model.

	$375	$295	$250	$190	$170	$160	$150

Last MSR was $520.

NEW HARTFORD MODEL SAA - .22 LR (disc. 1992), .32-20 WCF, .357 Mag., .38-40 WCF, .44-40 WCF, .44 Spl., or .45 LC cal., features forged steel frame, backstrap, and trigger guard, exact reproduction of Colt's 1st or 2nd generation SAA, choice of black powder (with base pin frame set screw) or 2nd generation (push button cylinder pin release) frame, case hardened frame, original Colt markings, 4 (.45 LC cal. with standard grips), 4 ¾, 5 ½ or 7 ½ in. barrel. Importation began 1991.

MSR	$365	$330	$295	$260	$225	$175	$150	$125

Add $85 for combo. cylinder (.45 ACP/.44 Spl.).
Add $10 for Old Model frame (cals. .32-20 WCF, .38-40 WCF, .44-40 WCF, or. 45 LC).
Add $125 for nickel finish (bright or satin).

✻ Antique Finish - .45 LC cal. only, 4¾ in. barrel, black powder frame, finish has been aged for older appearance. New 2001.

MSR	$425	$375	$325	$285	$240	$190	$165	$145

✻ Pinkerton Model - .357 Mag., .38-40 WCF (disc. 1999), or .45 LC cal., birdshead grips, 4 in. barrel. New 1994.

MSR	$375	$340	$300	$265	$225	$175	$150	$125

✻ Deputy Model - .45 LC cal., 4 in. barrel with full length ejector shroud, standard SAA grips. Imported 2000 only.

	$330	$295	$260	$225	$175	$150	$125

Last MSR was $365.

✻ Express Model - .45 LC cal., features "Lightning" grips, 4 or 4¾ in. barrel, New Model. Imported 1999-2000.

	$340	$300	$265	$225	$175	$150	$125

Last MSR was $375.

✻ Cavalry Model - .45 LC cal., 7½ in. barrel, faithful reproduction of the original Colt Cavalry Model, one-piece walnut grips with inspector cartouche, case hardened frame and hammer. Importation began 1991.

MSR	$390	$355	$310	$275	$230	$180	$155	$130

✻ Artillery Model - .45 LC cal., similar to Cavalry Model, except has 5½ in. barrel. Importation began 1991.

MSR	$390	$355	$310	$275	$230	$180	$155	$130

✻ Texas Sesquicentennial - .45 LC cal., 4¾ in. barrel, 50 mfg. for Texas Sesquicentennial with special engraving, includes numbered belt buckle and presentation case. Disc. 1991.

	$1,200	$925	$725

Original list price was $4,550.

✻ Target Model - .357 Mag., .44-40 WCF, or .45 LC cal., 5½ or 7½ in. barrel, case hardened frame, brass backstrap. Imported 1987-90.

	$325	$240	$185	$150	$140	$130	$120

Last MSR was $500.

Grading	100%	98%	95%	90%	80%	70%	60%

✴ *Buntline Model* - .357 Mag. (disc.), .44-40 WCF (disc.), or .45 LC cal., blue only, 10 (new 1997) or 12 in. barrel. Importation disc. 1990, reintroduced 1997.

MSR	$450	$400	$350	$300	$250	$215	$195	$175

✴ *Buckhorn Model* - 16¼ in. barrel, otherwise similar to Buntline. Importation disc. 1987.

		$295	$250	$180	$170	$160	$150	$140

Last MSR was $495.

D

SHERIFF'S OLD/NEW MODEL SAA - .32-20 WCF (disc.), .357 Mag., .38-40 WCF (disc.), .44 Spl. (disc.), .44-40 WCF, or .45 LC cal., 3½ in. barrel only. Importation disc. 1991, resumed 1994-2000.

	$330	$295	$260	$225	$175	$150	$125

Last MSR was $365.

U.S. ARMY SAA - variety of cals., premium quality construction. Disc. 1985.

	$300	$205	$180	$165	$155	$145	$135

Last MSR was $395.

✴ *U.S. Army Commemorative* - .45 LC cal., 7½ in. barrel, serial numbered 1-500, blue finish, case hardened frame, steel backstrap and trigger guard, 1-piece walnut grips. Importation disc. 1987.

	$350	$265	$185	$170	$160	$150	$135

Last MSR was $495.

CONVERTIBLE MODEL SAA - available with .22 LR/.22 Mag., .32-20 WCF/.32 H&R Mag., .357 Mag./9mm Para., .44-40 WCF/.44 Spl. cal., or .45 LC/.45 ACP double cylinders. Imported 1986-90.

	$380	$310	$260	$220	$195	$170	$150

Last MSR was $580.

FAST DRAW MODEL SAA - .22 LR, .22 Mag., .32-20 WCF, .32 H&R Mag., .357 Mag., .38-40 WCF, 9mm Para., .44 Spl., .44-40 WCF, .45 ACP, or .45 LC cal., case hardened frame, 4 5/8 in. barrel. Importation disc. 1990.

	$340	$295	$225	$165	$150	$135	$125

Last MSR was $480.

BISLEY MODEL SAA - .22 LR (disc.), .22 Mag.(disc.), .32-20 WCF (disc.), .32 H&R Mag. (disc.), .38-40 WCF, .357 Mag. (disc. 1999), 9mm Para. (disc.), .44 Spl. (disc.), .44-40 WCF, .45 ACP (disc.), or .45 LC (current mfg.) cal., 4¾ (disc. 1994, reintroduced 2001 in .44-40 WCF cal. only), 5½, or 7½ in. barrel lengths. Imported 1986-91, reintroduced 1993-disc. 1995, reintroduced 1997.

MSR	$400	$365	$350	$280	$230	$180	$155	$130

Add $125 for bright or satin (disc.) nickel finish.
Add $112 for combo. cylinder (.45 ACP - disc.).

✴ *Engraved Bisley* - .32-20 WCF, .38-40 WCF, .357 Mag., .44-40 WCF, or .45 LC cal. (disc. 1990), 4¾, 5½ or 7½ in. barrel, action engraved throughout. Imported 1987-91.

	$425	$350	$275	$250	$225	$200	$180

Last MSR was $570.

Add $100 for nickel finish.

1873 FRONTIER MODEL SAA - .22 LR cal., 4¾ in. barrel, case colored frame, black nickel backstrap and trigger guard. Mfg. by IAR, importation began 1999.

MSR	$315	$275	$250	$225	$175	$150	$135	$120

Add $125 for bright nickel finish.

Grading	100%	98%	95%	90%	80%	70%	60%

DALVAR OF USA

Current importer of recently manufactured Radom pistols located in Henderson NV. Please refer to the Radom listing in this text.

DALY, CHARLES: PRUSSIAN MFG.

Previous trademark manufactured in Prussia, England, Belgium, and the U.S. circa 1875-pre- WWII.

Charles Daly was a gentleman (not a company) whose goal was to give the U.S. shotgun consumer a European manufactured gun of similar quality to the premier American shotguns of the same era. In that behalf, he had various European firms fabricate shotguns with American shooting features and preferences. Many "Prussian" Dalys were built by various firms in Suhl, Germany. Importation ceased prior to WWII. These Prussian Charles Dalys utilized the finest materials and best workmanship of their time.

In 1865, Charles Daly was one of two partners who founded the sporting goods business named Schoverling & Daly. They were importers and dealers located in New York City. In 1873, the company reorganized to include a third parter, and the corporate name was changed Schoverling, Daly & Gates.

Marking the Charles Daly name on firearms began some time around 1875. Daly's name was chosen because it had an appealing sound and would likely influence potential buyers to choose their firearms. Schoverling, Daly & Gates established their lofty reputation by dealing in top quality merchandise. Because they were known for their high standard of excellence, the Charles Daly brand garnered much esteem.

Schoverling, Daly & Gates made every effort to select only the finest quality firearms for sale in the United States. Initially, manufacturers in Prussia were selected for their suberbly constructed shotguns - makers such as Schiller and Lindner, and later Heym and Sauer of Germany. Early manufacturers also included J&W Tolley of England, Newmann of Belgium, and even Lefever Arms of New York.

Schoverling, Daly & Gates changed ownership several times throughout the years. Eventually, the company's primary asset was the Charles Daly trademark. In 1910, Henry Modell bought the company, and controlled it for several years. In the 1920s, he sold out to the Walzer family, owners of Sloan's Sporting Goods of Ridgefield, CT. The Walzers established a branch of Sloan's in New York known as Charles Daly & Company. Sloan's imported quality shotguns from many companies, including Italian gun makers Beretta and Vincenzo Bernardelli, Miroku of Japan, and Garbi of Spain.

DRILLINGS

DRILLING MODEL - 12, 16, or 20 ga.'s and .25-20 WCF, .25-35 WCF, or .30-30 WCF cal., 3 barrel combination gun, extractors, double triggers, engraved action, select walnut, mfg. by both Linder and Sauer. Linder mfg. guns are extremely rare - very few specimens are to be found domestically. Sauer guns were not marked for grade, but rather had three levels of engraving which determined the grade. Most Sauer guns had a tang mounted aperture rear sight and a separate rifle cock and were sidelocks. Disc. 1933.

* *Superior Quality* - borderline engraving only.

Sauer mfg.	$3,000	$2,600	$2,300	$2,000	$1,700	$1,500	$1,200

* *Diamond Quality* - full scroll engraving.

Sauer mfg.	$5,500	$4,800	$4,400	$4,000	$3,500	$3,000	$2,200

* *Regent Diamond Quality* - top-of-the-line model featuring full game scene coverage.

Linder mfg.	$12,000	$11,000	$10,000	$9,000	$7,000	$6,000	$5,000
Sauer mfg.	$8,000	$7,000	$6,700	$6,000	$5,000	$4,000	$3,000

Grading	100%	98%	95%	90%	80%	70%	60%

RIFLES

BOLT ACTION GRADE I - .22 Hornet cal., mfg. by F. Jaeger & Co. of Suhl, Germany, 5 shot mag., 24 in. barrel, miniature Mauser bolt action, deluxe walnut. Disc.

	100%	98%	95%	90%	80%	70%	60%
	$820	$615	$535	$455	$410	$370	$330

SHOTGUNS

In the higher grade Prussian Daly variations, there is quite a bit of difference in their manufacture, including engraving options, levels of wood embellishment, and other extra cost features at the time. H. A. Linder produced approx. 2,500 guns (ser. numbered accordingly), and many of the higher grades show a noticeable difference in the amount of engraving (from minimal to considerable game scene engraving), can be either case colored only or have gold inlaid birds and animals (the number of which can also vary), barrels can have various levels of engraving on both the breech and muzzle ends - all of these factors have considerable impact on the overall value of a particular specimen. It is estimated that it took three craftsmen one year to produce a single Diamond Regent gun.

COMMANIDER O&U - 12, 16, 20, 28 ga., or .410 bore, Anson & Deeley boxlock action, single or double triggers, ejectors. Mfg. in Belgium circa 1939.

* *Model 100*

	100%	98%	95%	90%	80%	70%	60%
	$500	$375	$325	$275	$250	$225	$200

  Add $100 for single trigger.

* *Model 200* - similar to Model 100, except has deluxe walnut.

	100%	98%	95%	90%	80%	70%	60%
	$650	$490	$425	$360	$325	$300	$260

  Add 10%-30% for 28 ga. and .410 bore.

EMPIRE O&U - 12, 16, or 20 ga., various barrel lengths, Anson & Deeley boxlock, ejectors and double triggers, fine engraving, deluxe walnut. Disc. 1933.

	100%	98%	95%	90%	80%	70%	60%
	$4,000	$3,400	$2,750	$2,375	$2,000	$1,825	$1,625

DIAMOND O&U - similar to Empire model, only finer workmanship and materials.

	100%	98%	95%	90%	80%	70%	60%
	$5,000	$4,300	$3,475	$3,000	$2,600	$2,300	$2,000

SUPERIOR SxS - 10, 12, 20, 28 ga., or .410 bore, Anson & Deeley boxlock, various barrel lengths, extractors. Disc. 1933.

	100%	98%	95%	90%	80%	70%	60%
	$1,050	$790	$690	$580	$525	$475	$420

EMPIRE SxS - similar to Superior, only more engraving and better wood.

	100%	98%	95%	90%	80%	70%	60%
Linder mfg.	$5,000	$4,400	$3,900	$3,500	$2,800	$2,200	$1,500
Sauer mfg.	$4,200	$3,500	$3,100	$2,800	$2,200	$1,800	$1,400

DIAMOND SxS - similar to Empire model, only more elaborate and with gold inlays.

	100%	98%	95%	90%	80%	70%	60%
Linder mfg.	$10,000	$9,000	$8,500	$8,000	$7,000	$6,000	$4,500
Sauer mfg.	$7,000	$6,200	$5,500	$5,000	$4,000	$3,000	$2,000

  Subtract 20%-25% if without gold inlays.

DIAMOND REGENT SxS - top-of-the-line Prussian side-by-side and with gold inlays.

	100%	98%	95%	90%	80%	70%	60%
Linder mfg.	$16,000	$13,500	$12,000	$11,000	$8,500	$7,000	$5,000
Sauer mfg.	$8,500	$7,700	$7,000	$6,500	$5,000	$4,000	$3,000

EMPIRE SINGLE BARREL TRAP - 12 ga., 30-34 in. barrel, Anson & Deeley boxlock, ejector, vent. rib, finely engraved with select walnut, chopper lump extension, top quality. Disc. 1933.

	100%	98%	95%	90%	80%	70%	60%
Linder mfg.	$3,995	$3,500	$3,100	$2,800	$2,200	$1,800	$1,400
Sauer mfg.	$2,150	$1,675	$1,475	$1,100	$960	$850	$750

Grading	100%	98%	95%	90%	80%	70%	60%

SEXTUPLE SINGLE BARREL TRAP - 12 ga., 30-34 in. barrel, six locking bolts, ejector, vent. rib, elaborately engraved and checkered. Regent Diamond Model has better engraving and wood.

✳ Empire Quality

Linder mfg.	$4,600	$4,150	$3,650	$3,100	$2,800	$2,200	$1,800
Sauer mfg.	$2,600	$2,100	$1,700	$1,400	$1,100	$900	$750

✳ Regent Diamond Quality

Linder mfg.	$5,000	$4,400	$3,900	$3,500	$2,800	$2,200	$1,500
Sauer mfg.	$3,300	$2,850	$2,400	$1,950	$1,650	$1,350	$995

DALY, CHARLES: JAPANESE MFG.

Previously manufactured by B.C. Miroku, located in Kochi, Japan until 1976.

SHOTGUNS: O/U

In the early sixties, C. Daly guns were manufactured by the firm of B.C. Miroku in Kochi, Japan. This Japanese gun manufacturing company has produced guns for many companies, Browning being the biggest current customer. Miroku guns are high quality with excellent fit and finish. Many of them are highly engraved and are fine examples of the gunmaker's art. Charles Daly Miroku Guns are becoming quite collectible in some areas (smaller gauges with open chokes). Their production ceased in 1976.

O/U MODELS - 12, 20, 28 ga., or .410 bore, 26, 28, or 30 in. vent. rib barrels, various chokes, boxlock, auto ejectors, SST, select walnut checkered pistol grip stock, Superior and Diamond Grade Trap have Monte Carlo stocks, the grades differ in amount of engraving and wood. Mfg. 1963-1976 by Miroku.

Approx. 1,000 28 ga. Lightweight guns were manufactured. All 28 ga. Lightweights (approx. observed ser. range 230185-230998) have barrel spacing ¾ in. center to center, while the normal 28 ga. has a measurement of 7/8 in. After the Charles Daly line of O/Us were mechanically redesigned, both the 28 ga. and .410 bore were made on only the new 20 ga. frame. To date, no one has observed a .410 bore Lightweight Charles Daly.

Add 20% for 20 ga. on models listed below.
Add 50% for 28 ga. on models listed below.
Add 60% for .410 bore on models listed below.
Add 200% for original 28 ga. Lightweight models in 98%+ condition (rare).

✳ Field Grade - 12 or 20 ga., light engraving.

	100%	98%	95%	90%	80%	70%	60%
	$795	$750	$650	$595	$550	$475	$400

✳ Venture Grade - all gauges, moderate engraving.

	$675	$600	$550	$500	$450	$400	$350

✳ Venture Skeet - 26 in. barrels choked skeet and skeet.

	$700	$625	$575	$525	$475	$425	$375

✳ Venture Trap - 30 in. imp. mod. and full.

	$625	$550	$500	$475	$425	$375	$350

✳ Superior Grade - all gauges, select checkered walnut stock with round knob, scroll engraving similar to Grade I Browning Superposed.

	$995	$875	$775	$700	$650	$600	$550

✳ Superior Trap

	$775	$650	$575	$550	$500	$440	$390

This model had an optional selective ejection system enabling the shooter to deactivate the ejectors.

Grading	100%	98%	95%	90%	80%	70%	60%

✻ *Diamond Grade* - all gauges, extensive engraving with better quality wood.

	$1,475	$1,275	$1,100	$995	$895	$775	$700

✻ *Diamond Grade Skeet*

	$1,525	$1,325	$1,125	$1,000	$900	$775	$700

✻ *Diamond Grade Trap*

	$1,100	$975	$850	$775	$700	$625	$550

✻ *Wide Rib Diamond Grade Flat-Top Trap*

	$1,100	$975	$850	$775	$700	$625	$550

✻ *Diamond Regent Grade*

- mostly 12 ga., extensive frame engraving with gold inlays, rare.

	$3,150	$2,750	$2,250	$1,950	$1,750	$1,500	$1,250

SHOTGUNS: SxS

EMPIRE SHOTGUN - 12, 16, or 20 ga., 26, 28, or 30 in. barrels, various chokes, boxlock, extractors, single trigger, checkered pistol grip stock. Mfg. 1968-1971.

	$545	$495	$470	$415	$360	$305	$250
Vent. rib	$595	$535	$500	$450	$400	$350	$300

Add 50% for 20 ga.

1974 WILDLIFE COMMEMORATIVE - duck scene engraved, Diamond Grade, Trap, or Skeet, limited to 500 guns. Mfg. 1974 only.

	$1,800	$1,625	$1,425	$1,250	$995	$875	$775

SHOTGUNS: SINGLE BARREL, TRAP

SUPERIOR GRADE SINGLE BARREL TRAP - 12 ga., 32 or 34 in. vent. rib, full choke barrel, auto ejector, Monte Carlo stock with recoil pad. Mfg. 1968-1976.

	$600	$550	$525	$495	$440	$385	$330

DALY, CHARLES: 1976 TO PRESENT

Currently manufactured trademark imported since late 1996 by KBI, Inc. located in Harrisburg, PA. Previously imported by Outdoor Sports Headquarters, Inc. located in Dayton, OH until 1995.

In 1976, Sloan's Sporting Goods sold the Daly division to Outdoor Sports Headquarters, Inc., a sporting goods wholesaler located in Dayton, OH. OSHI contined the importation of high grade Daly shotguns, primarily from Italy and Spain. By the mid-1980s, the Charles Daly brand was transformed into a broad consumer line of excellent firearms and hunting accessories.

In 1996, OSHI was sold to Jerry's Sports Center, Inc. of Forest City, PA, a major wholesaler of firearms and hunting supplies. Within a few months of Jerry's acquisition of OSHI, K.B.I., Inc. of Harrisburg, PA, purchased the Charles Daly trademark from JSC. As it turned out, Michael Kassnar, president of K.B.I., Inc., had produced almost all of the Charles Daly products for OSHI from 1976-1985, in his capacity of president of Kassnar Imports, Inc. KB.I., Inc. resurrected the complete line of O/U and SxS shotguns in early 1997.

In 1998, the line expanded to include rimfire rifles, and the first pistol produced under the Daly name, a Model 1911-A1 in .45 ACP cal.. In 1999, semi-auto and slide action shotguns were also reintroduced. In 2000, the additions included 3½ in. slide actions and semi-autos, Country Squire .410 bore shotguns, bolt action centerfire rifles, and the DDA 10-45, the first double action pistol produced under the Charles Daly name.

Grading	100%	98%	95%	90%	80%	70%	60%

D

COMBINATION GUNS

SUPERIOR COMBINATION MODEL - 12 ga. (multi-chokes became standard in 2001) over choice of .22 Hornet, .22-250 Rem. (disc. 1998), .223 Rem., .243 Win. (disc. 1998), .270 Win. (disc. 1998), .30-06, or .308 Win. (disc. 1998) cal., boxlock action with dovetailed receiver (accepts scope mounts and iron sights), 23½ in. barrels with iron sights, approx. 7 5/8 lbs. Importation began 1997.

	MSR	$1,359		$1,175	$975	$850	$725	$625	$525	$450

EMPIRE COMBINATION MODEL - 12 ga. (multi-chokes became standard in 2001) over choice of .22 Hornet, .22-250 Rem. (disc. 1998), .223 Rem., .243 Win. (disc. 1998) , .270 Win. (disc. 1998), .30-06, or .308 Win. (disc. 1998) cal., boxlock action, 23½ in. barrels, engraved with choice checkered walnut stock and forearm. Importation began 1997.

	MSR	$1,799		$1,600	$1,350	$1,125	$950	$800	$700	$600

PISTOLS: SEMI-AUTO

During 2001, the nomenclature on these 1911 models was changed to a new E prefix. The new E stands for enhanced, and features include extended high-rise beavertail grip safety, combat trigger, combat hammer, beveled magwell, flared and lowered ejection port, dovetailed front and low profile rear sights, and hand checkered double diamond grips.

GOVERNMENT 1911-A1 FIELD EFS/FS - .45 ACP cal., steel frame, single action, skeletonized combat hammer and trigger, ambidextrous safety, 8 or 10 shot mag., extended slide release and beavertail grip safety, oversized and lowered ejection port, 5 in. barrel with solid barrel bushing, matte blue (Field FS), stainless slide/blue frame (Superior FS, new 1999), or all stainless (Empire FS, new 1999) finish, includes two 8 or 10 shot mags. and lockable carrying case. New 1998.

	MSR	$499		$435	$375	$340	$315	$300	$280	$250

Add $50 for Superior EFS Model.
Add $100 for Empire EFS Model.
Add $199 for .22 LR conversion kit with adj. sight (disc. 1999).

GOVERNMENT 1911-A1 TARGET EFST/FST - similar to Government 1911- A1 Field FS, except has target sights. Importation began 2000.

	MSR	$599		$525	$425	$385	$350	$320	$295	$260

Add $40 for Superior FST Model (disc. 2000).
Add $65 for Empire FST Model (disc. 2000)

✱ **Stainless Empire EFST** – similar to Target EFST, except is stainless steel. New 2001.

	MSR	$699		$595	$475	$400				

✱ **Field EFSTC** – .45 ACP cal., 5¾ in. compensated barrel with 3 ports, blue or stainless steel, 44.5 oz. Limited importation 2001 only.

				$550	$450	$395	$360	$330	$300	$265

Last MSR was $679.

Add $100 for stainless steel (Empire EFSTC).

EMPIRE ECMT CUSTOM MATCH - .45 ACP cal., match features, high polish stainless steel, 38½ oz. Importation began 2001.

	MSR	$749		$625	$550	$475	$400	$350	$325	$295

COMMANDER 1911-A1 FIELD EMS/MS - similar to Government 1911-A1, except has 4 in. Commander barrel and features. Importation began 1999.

	MSR	$499		$435	$375	$340	$315	$300	$280	$255

Add $40 for Superior MS Model (includes stainless steel slide and blue frame, disc. 2000).
Add $100 for Empire EMS Model (full stainless steel construction).

Grading	100%	98%	95%	90%	80%	70%	60%

* Field EMSCC - carry comp., similar to Commander Field EMS, except has single port compensator, blue or stainless. Imported 2001 only.

	$540	$435	$395	$360	$325	$295	$260

Last MSR was $619.

OFFICER'S 1911-A1 FIELD ECS/CS - similar to Commander, except has 3½ in. barrel and Officer's Model features. Importation began 1999.

MSR	$499	$435	$375	$340	$315	$300	$280	$255

Add $40 for Superior CS Model (includes stainless steel slide and blue frame, disc. 2000).
Add $100 for Empire ECS Model (full stainless steel construction).

* Field ECSCC - carry comp., similar to Officer's Field ECS, except has single port compensator, blue or stainless. Importation began 2001.

	$540	$435	$395	$360	$325	$295	$260

Last MSR was $619.

Add $100 for Empire ECS Model (full stainless steel construction).

COMMANDER 1911-A1 POLYMER FRAME PC - .45 ACP only, features polymer frame, 4 in. barrel, available in matte blue (Field PC) or stainless slide/blue frame (Superior PC). Imported 1999-2000.

	$460	$400	$360	$330	$295	$280	$260

Last MSR was $530.

Add $25 for Superior PC Model (includes stainless steel slide and blue frame).

MODEL DDA 10-45 FS (DOUBLE ACTION) - .40 S&W (disc. 2001) or .45 ACP cal., single or double action, 4 3/8 in. barrel, polymer frame with checkering, double stacked 10 shot mag. with interchangeable base plate (allowing for extra grip length), matte black or two-tone (new 2001) finish, 28½ oz. Importation began 2000.

MSR	$519	$450	$395	$360	$325	$300	$280	$260

Add $40 for two-tone finish.

* Model DDA 10-45 CS - similar to Model DDA 10-45 FS, except has 3 5/8 in. barrel, 26 oz. Importation began 2000.

MSR	$519	$450	$395	$360	$325	$300	$280	$260

Add approx. $10 for colored frame (yellow, OD green, or fuschia, new 2001) and compensated barrel.

RIFLES: BOLT ACTION

MAUSER 98 - various cals., Mauser 98 action, 22 (new 2001) or 23 (disc.) in. barrel, 3-5 shot, hinged floorplate, fiberglass/graphite composite (Field Grade) or checkered European walnut (Superior grade) stock, open sights, drilled and tapped receiver, side safety. Importation began 1998, and resumed during 2001.

* Field Grade - features fiberglass/graphite composite stock, matte blue finish or matte stainless steel.

MSR	$449	$395	$345	$310	$285	$255	$225	$200

Add $40 for stainless steel.
Add $30 for current Mag. cals. (.330 Win. Mag. or 7mm Rem. Mag.).
Add 50% for .375 H&H or .458 Win. Mag. cal. (disc.).

* Superior Grade - features checkered European walnut stock and high polish blue finish.

MSR	$529	$565	$400	$350	$325	$295	$275	$250

Add $200 for .375 H&H or .458 Win. Mag. cal.
Add $30 for current Mag. cals. (.330 Win. Mag. or 7mm Rem. Mag.).
Add $30 for left hand action (.30-06 cal. only).

Grading	100%	98%	95%	90%	80%	70%	60%

D

MINI-MAUSER 98 - .22 Hornet, .22-250 Rem. (disc.), .223 Rem., or 7.62x39mm (disc.) cal., similar to Mauser 98, except has 18.1 (new 2001) or 19¼ (disc.) in. barrel, 5 shot.

* **Field Grade** - features fiberglass/graphite composite stock.

	$345	$295	$265	$230	$200	$185	$170

Last MSR was $399.

* **Superior Grade** - features checkered European walnut stock.

MSR $529	$465	$375	$340	$300	$275	$250	$225

Add $30 for left hand action (.223 Rem. cal. only).

FIELD HUNTER - .22 Hornet, .223 Rem., .243 Win., .270 Win., .30-06, .308 Win., .300 Rem. Ultra Mag., .330 Win. Mag., .338 Win. Mag., or 7mm Rem. Mag. cal., 22 or 24 (Mag. cals. only) barrel w/o sights, detachable mag. on short action cals. (.22 Hornet, .223 Rem., or .243 Win.), high polish bluing, checkered walnut stock and forend, right or left-hand action, gold trigger, approx. 7 1/3 lbs. Imported 2000 only.

	$475	$425	$375	$350	$325	$280	$240

Last MSR was $565.

Add approx. $31 for left-hand action (.223 Rem., .243 Win., .270 Win., .30-06, .300 Rem. Ultra Mag., or 7mm Rem. Mag.).

* **Field Hunter Stainless/Polymer** - similar to Field Hunter, except has stainless steel barrel and action, black polymer stock with checkering. Imported 2000 only.

	$495	$450	$395				

Last MSR was $580.

FIELD GRADE - .22 LR cal., 16¼ (True Youth Standard), 17½ (Youth), or 22 5/8 (Standard) in. barrel, single shot (True Youth Standard) or 6 shot mag., all steel shrouded action, grooved receiver, walnut finished hardwood stock. Importation began 1998.

MSR $135	$110	$95	$80	$70	$60	$55	$50

Add $14 for repeater Youth Model (6 shot, new 2000).
Add $20 for single shot True Youth Standard with shortened dimensions.

* **Field Grade Polymer/Hardwood** - similar to Field Grade, except has stainless steel action and barrel with black polymer (disc.) or hardwood (new 2001) checkered stock, 6 1/3 lbs. Importation began 2000.

MSR $149	$120	$100	$85	$70	$60	$55	$50.

* **Superior Grade** - .22 LR (disc. 2001), .22 Mag., or .22 Hornet cal., 22 5/8 in. barrel, 5 or 6 shot mag., features checkered walnut finished stock with adj. rear sight. Importation began 1998.

MSR $209	$175	$135	$105	$90	$80	$70	$60

Add $160 for .22 Hornet cal.
Subtract $20 for .22 LR cal. (disc. 2001).

* **Empire Grade** - similar to Superior Grade, except has checkered California walnut stock with rosewood grip and forend caps, high polish bluing and damascened bolt. Imported 1998-2001.

	$290	$260	$230	$215	$195	$180	$170

Last MSR was $349.

Add $20 for .22 Mag. cal.
Add $130 for .22 Hornet cal.

RIFLES: O/U

SUPERIOR EXPRESS - .30-06 cal., 23½ in. barrels with quarter rib and leaf sights, dovetailed receiver for scope mounting, silver finished boxlock receiver, gold SST, checkered walnut stock and forearm, 7¾ lbs. Importation began 2000.

MSR $1,879	$1,675	$1,425	$1,250	$1,075	$950	$875	$775

Grading	100%	98%	95%	90%	80%	70%	60%

EMPIRE EXPRESS - .30-06 cal., 23½ in. barrels with quarter rib and leaf sights, dovetailed receiver for scope mounting, silver finished boxlock receiver with shoulders, gold SST, checkered European style walnut stock with Bavarian cheekpiece and forearm, 7¾ lbs. Importation began 2000.

MSR $2,219	$1,995	$1,675	$1,450	$1,250	$1,075	$950	$875

RIFLES: SEMI-AUTO

SEMI-AUTO RIFLE - .22 LR cal., steel receiver, 20¾ in. barrel with adj. rear sight, 10 shot mag. New 1998.

✳ *Field Grade* - features uncheckered walnut finished hardwood stock.

MSR $135	$110	$95	$80	$70	$60	$55	$50

✳ *Field Grade Polymer/Hardwood* - similar to Field Grade, except has stainless steel action and barrel with black polymer (disc.) or hardwood checkered stock, 6 1/8 lbs. New 2000.

MSR $149	$120	$100	$85

✳ *Superior Grade* - features checkered walnut finished stock. Disc. 2001.

$175	$130	$100	$90	$80	$70	$60

Last MSR was $209.

✳ *Empire Grade* - features checkered California walnut stock. Disc. 2001.

$275	$245	$220	$195	$180	$170	$160

Last MSR was $334.

RIFLES: SINGLE SHOT

FIELD GRADE - .22 Hornet, .223 Rem., .243 Win., or .270 Win. cal., single shot break open action, 22 in. barrel with mount base, drilled and tapped, adj. or no sights, checkered hardwood stock and forearm. Limited importation 2001 only.

$165	$140	$110	$95	$80	$70	$60

Last MSR was $189.

Add $10 for adj. sights.

This model is also available in a Youth configuration at no extra charge.

SHOTGUNS: O/U

Current O/U production is from Italy.

PRESENTATION MODEL - 12 or 20 ga., with choke tubes, Purdey double underlug locking action with decorative engraved sideplates, French walnut, single trigger, ejectors. Disc. 1986.

$995	$840	$750	$670	$615	$560	$520

Last MSR was $1,165.

COUNTRY SQUIRE MODEL - .410 bore only, 3 in. chambers, case colored boxlock action, gold DT, 25½ in. vent. barrels with VR and F/F chokes, checkered straight grip stock and Schnabel forearm, approx. 6 lbs.

MSR $715	$640	$575	$525	$475	$425	$375	$350

FIELD II HUNTER - 12, 16 (new 2001), 20, 28 ga., or .410 bore, similar to DeLuxe Model except has fixed chokes, extractors, machine stock checkering, and blued receiver, 5½ - 7 lbs., depending on ga./barrel lengths. New 1989.

MSR $789	$665	$470	$395	$335	$295	$275	$260

Add $60 for 28 ga. or $106 for .410 bore.

Grading	100%	98%	95%	90%	80%	70%	60%

* **Field Hunter with Ejectors** - similar to Field II Hunter, except has ejectors and multi-chokes (not available on 28 ga. or .410 bore), Monte Carlo stock. Importation began 1997.

	MSR **$999**		**$865**	**$745**	**$640**	**$560**	**$475**	**$395**	**$350**

* **Field Hunter Ultra-Light** - 12 or 20 ga., alloy frame, 26 in. VR barrels only with fixed IC/M (disc. 2000) or multi-chokes (new 2001), thin forearm, approx. 5½ lbs. Importation began 1999.

	MSR **$899**		**$745**	**$520**	**$435**	**$380**	**$325**	**$295**	**$275**

DELUXE MODEL - 12, 20, 28 ga. (disc. 1995), or .410 bore (disc. 1995), boxlock with self adj. crossbolt, 26 or 28 in. chrome lined VR barrels with internal choke tubes, SST, ejectors, antique silver finish on receiver, deluxe hand checkered walnut stock and forearm. Imported 1989-96.

			$650	**$525**	**$475**	**$425**	**$400**	**$375**	**$350**

Last MSR was $770.

SPORTING CLAYS MODEL - 12 ga. only, SST, ejectors, silver engraved receiver, checkered walnut stock and forearm, screw-in chokes, 28 (disc.) or 30 (new 1996) in. VR ported barrels. Imported 1995-96.

			$775	**$700**	**$625**	**$550**	**$475**	**$395**	**$350**

Last MSR was $895.

SUPERIOR II - 12 or 20 ga., various chokes, boxlock action, single trigger, ejectors, engraved. Disc. 1988.

			$675	**$575**	**$475**	**$425**	**$395**	**$375**	**$350**

Last MSR was $875.

Add $35 for 12 ga. Mag. (disc. 1987).

FIELD III - 12 or 20 ga., various chokes, boxlock action, single trigger. Disc. 1989.

			$395	**$370**	**$340**	**$315**	**$285**	**$260**	**$230**

Last MSR was $450.

SUPERIOR II HUNTER - 12, 20, 28 ga. (new 1998), or .410 bore, 3 in. chambers (except 28 ga.), boxlock action, ejectors, 26, 28, or 30 in. VR barrels with multi-chokes (except 28 ga. and .410 bore), barrel porting became standard during 2000, select checkered walnut stock and forearm, 6 1/8 – 7 lbs. Importation began 1997.

	MSR **$1,199**		**$1,095**	**$965**	**$790**	**$660**	**$550**	**$475**	**$395**

Subtract $90 for 28 ga. or $44 for .410 bore.

* **Superior II Sporting** - 12 or 20 ga. (disc. 1998), 26 (disc. 1998), 28, or 30 (12 ga. only) in. 10mm VR barrels with multi-chokes and ported barrels. Importation began 1997.

	MSR **$1,279**		**$1,125**	**$950**	**$790**	**$660**	**$550**	**$475**	**$395**

* **Superior II Trap** - 12 ga. only, 30 or 32 (disc. 2001) in. VR barrels with choice of fixed chokes or multi-chokes, regular or Monte Carlo stock. Importation began 1997.

	MSR **$1,325**		**$1,150**	**$985**	**$815**	**$665**	**$550**	**$475**	**$395**

Subtract 10% if w/o multi-chokes with Monte Carlo stock.

* **Superior Skeet** - 12 or 20 ga., 26 in. VR barrels with choice of Skeet fixed chokes or multi- chokes, regular or Monte Carlo stock. Imported 1997-98.

			$935	**$800**	**$700**	**$600**	**$500**	**$450**	**$375**

Last MSR was $1,039.

Add $120 for multi-chokes with Monte Carlo stock.

Grading	100%	98%	95%	90%	80%	70%	60%

EMPIRE DL HUNTER - 12, 20, 28 ga., or .410 bore, boxlock action, silver receiver with game scene engraving, ejectors, SST, 26 or 28 (12 or 20 ga. only) in. VR barrels with multi-chokes (except 28 ga. and .410 bore). Imported 1997-98.

	$1,025	$875	$750	$650	$550	$475	$395

Last MSR was $1,159.

Add $65 for 28 ga. or $110 for .410 bore.

EMPIRE II EDL HUNTER - similar to Empire DL Hunter, except has engraved sideplates featuring game scenes. New 1998.

MSR	$1,619	$1,350	$1,065	$875	$730	$625	$500	$450

Subtract $40 for 28 ga.
Add $10 for .410 bore.

❋ *Empire II Sporting* - 12 or 20 ga. (disc. 1999), 26 (disc. 1999), 28, or 30 (12 ga. only) in. VR barrels with multi-chokes. Importation began 1997.

MSR	$1,519	$1,295	$1,025	$865	$725	$625	$500	$450

❋ *Empire II Trap* - 12 ga. only, 30 or 32 (disc. 2000) in. VR barrels with choice of fixed chokes (32 in. barrel only) or multi-chokes, regular (disc. 1998) or Monte Carlo stock. Importation began 1997.

MSR	$1,559	$1,325	$975	$840	$700	$600	$475	$425

Subtract 10% if w/o multi-chokes.

❋ *Empire II Mono Trap* - features 30 or 32 in. single top barrel, standard or adj. Monte Carlo stock. Importation began 1999.

MSR	$1,589	$1,355	$980	$845	$710	$600	$475	$425

Add $660 for adj. Monte Carlo stock.

❋ *Empire II Trap Combo* - includes mono 32 in. barrel and extra set of 30 in. O/U barrels, standard or adj. Monte Carlo stock. Importation began 1999.

MSR	$2,399	$2,115	$1,760	$1,510	$1,250	$975	$850	$675

Add $600 for adj. Monte Carlo stock.

❋ *Empire Skeet* - 12 or 20 ga., 26 in. VR barrels with choice of Skeet fixed chokes or multi-chokes, regular or Monte Carlo stock. Imported 1997-98.

	$1,050	$875	$750	$650	$550	$475	$395

Last MSR was $1,189.

Add $125 for multi-chokes with Monte Carlo stock.

DIAMOND FIELD - 12 or 20 ga. (disc. 1986) Mag., with choke tubes. Same action as Presentation Model without sideplates, engraved, select walnut, single trigger, ejectors. Disc. 1986.

	$695	$600	$550	$510	$460	$420	$380

Last MSR was $895.

❋ *Diamond Trap or Skeet* - 12 ga. only, 26 or 30 in. barrels only. Disc. 1986.

	$850	$700	$550	$500	$475	$450	$425

Last MSR was $1,050.

Subtract $50 for Skeet Model.

DIAMOND GTX DL HUNTER - 12, 20, 28 ga., or .410 bore, sidelock action, ejectors, SST, elaborate engraving with select checkered walnut stock and forearm, 26, 28 (12 or 20 ga. only), or 30 (12 ga. only) in. VR barrels with multi-chokes (except 28 ga. and .410 bore). Imported 1997 only.

	$11,250	$9,000	$7,000	$5,700	$4,900	$4,200	$3,750

Last MSR was $12,399.

❋ *Diamond GTX EDL Hunter* - more elaborate variation of the Diamond GTX DL Hunter. Imported 1997 only.

	$13,750	$11,250	$9,000	$7,000	$5,700	$4,900	$4,200

Last MSR was $15,999.

Grading	100%	98%	95%	90%	80%	70%	60%

DIAMOND GTX SPORTING - 12 or 20 (disc. 1998) ga., boxlock Boss action with light perimeter engraving, 28 or 30 (12 ga. only) in. VR barrels with multi-chokes and porting. Imported 1997-2001.

	$5,260	$4,750	$4,275	$3,675	$3,150	$2,750	$2,175

Last MSR was $5,849.

DIAMOND GTX TRAP - 12 ga. only, boxlock Boss action with light perimeter engraving, 30 in. VR barrels with choice of fixed (disc. 1999) or multi-chokes with barrel porting, regular or adj. (new 1999) Monte Carlo stock. Imported 1997-2001.

	$5,865	$4,900	$4,400	$3,825	$3,175	$2,750	$2,175

Last MSR was $6,699.

Subtract 10% w/o fixed chokes.

DIAMOND GTX MONO TRAP - features single top barrel, adj. Monte Carlo stock. Imported 1999-2001.

	$5,795	$4,850	$4,400	$3,825	$3,150	$2,750	$2,175

Last MSR was $6,619.

✳ Diamond GTX Trap Combo - includes 32 in. mono barrel and extra set of 30 in. O/U barrels, adj. Monte Carlo stock. Imported 1999-2001.

	$6,775	$5,775	$4,825	$4,325	$3,775	$3,150	$2,750

Last MSR was $7,419.

DIAMOND GTX SKEET - 12 or 20 ga., 26 or 28 (20 ga. only with Monte Carlo stock) in. VR barrels with choice of Skeet fixed chokes or multi-chokes, regular or Monte Carlo stock. Imported 1997-98.

	$4,700	$4,100	$3,800	$3,400	$2,975	$2,700	$2,100

Last MSR was $5,149.

Add $140 for multi-chokes with Monte Carlo stock.

DIAMOND REGENT GTX DL HUNTER - 12, 20, 28 ga., or .410 bore, sidelock action, ejectors, SST, best quality engraving with premium checkered walnut stock and forearm, 26, 28 (12 or 20 ga. only), or 30 (12 ga. only) in. VR barrels with multi-chokes (except 28 ga. and .410 bore). Imported 1997 only.

	$19,750	$16,250	$13,750	$11,250	$9,000	$7,000	$5,700

Last MSR was $22,299.

✳ Diamond Regent GTX EDL Hunter - top-of-the-line model incorporating best quality engraving and premium walnut. Imported 1997 only.

	$23,000	$19,500	$16,000	$13,750	$10,500	$8,750	$7,700

Last MSR was $26,429.

SHOTGUNS: SxS

FIELD III - 12 or 20 ga., various chokes, boxlock action, single trigger. Disc.

	$350	$315	$285	$260	$230	$210	$195

COUNTRY SQUIRE MODEL - .28 ga. or .410 bore, 3 in. chambers, case colored boxlock action, gold DT, 26 in. barrels with fixed chokes, checkered stock and splinter forearm, approx. 6 lbs. Disc. 2000.

	$600	$550	$500	$450	$400	$360	$330

Last MSR was $680.

Grading	100%	98%	95%	90%	80%	70%	60%

FIELD II HUNTER MODEL - 10, 12, 20, 28 ga., or .410 bore, boxlock action, 26, 28, 30 (12 ga. only), or 32 (10 ga. only) in. barrels, fixed (disc. 2000) or multi-chokes, 6 – 7 3/ 8 lbs., or 11¼ (10 ga.) lbs. Importation began 1997.

	MSR	$759		$635	$450	$395	$340	$295	$275	$260

Subtract $70 for 28 ga. or .410 bore (extractors only).
Add $30 for 10 ga.
Subtract approx. 15% if w/o ejectors and multi-chokes (not available in 28 ga. or .410 bore).

SUPERIOR - 12 or 20 ga., boxlock action, various chokes, single trigger. Disc. 1985.

$550	$470	$405	$345	$315	$280	$250

Last MSR was $624.

SUPERIOR HUNTER - 12 ,20, or 28 (new 1999) ga. or .410 bore (new 2000), 26 or 28 in. barrels with fixed (disc. 2000) or multi-chokes (new 2001) chokes, 5 7/8 – 6¾ lbs. Importation began 1997.

MSR	$1,059	$890	$775	$650	$560	$475	$395	$350

Subtract $30 for 28 ga. or .410 bore.

LUXE MODEL - 12 (disc. 1991) or 20 ga., boxlock action, SST, ejectors, 26 in. barrels with choke tubes, checkered pistol grip walnut stock with semi-beavertail forearm, recoil pad. Imported 1990-94.

$575	$450	$395	$350	$315	$285	$260

Last MSR was $650.

This model was manufactured by Hermanos located in Spain.

EMPIRE HUNTER - 12, 20, or 28 (disc. 1998) ga., 26 or 28 in. barrels with fixed or multi-chokes (new 2001), 6-6 7/8 lbs. Importation began 1997.

MSR	$1,349	$1,165	$975	$790	$675	$575	$475	$425

DIAMOND DL - 12, 20, 28 ga., or .410 bore, case colored sidelock action with 3rd lever fastener, scroll engraving, select checkered walnut stock and splinter forearm, 26 or 28 in. barrels with fixed chokes. Importation began 1997.

$6,060	$4,950	$4,375	$3,775	$3,200	$2,750	$2,175

Last MSR was $6,999.

DIAMOND REGENT DL - 12, 20, 28 ga., or .410 bore, sidelock action with best quality engraving and premium checkered walnut stock and forearm, 26 or 28 in. barrels with fixed chokes. Imported 1997 only.

$18,950	$15,750	$13,250	$10,750	$8,900	$6,900	$5,600

Last MSR was $21,659.

SHOTGUNS: SEMI-AUTO

The Charles Daly "Novamatic" shotguns were produced in 1968 by Breda in Italy. The Novamatic series was not imported by Outdoor Sport Headquarters, Inc.

NOVAMATIC LIGHTWEIGHT MODEL - 12 ga., 26 or 28 in. barrel, various chokes, available with quick choke interchangeable tubes, checkered pistol grip stock, similar to the Breda shotgun. Mfg. 1968 only.

$305	$275	$250	$220	$195	$165	$140

Add $25 for vent. rib.
Add $15 for quick choke.

Grading	100%	98%	95%	90%	80%	70%	60%

NOVAMATIC SUPER LIGHTWEIGHT - 12 or 20 ga., similar to Lightweight, except approx. ½ lb. lighter.

	$330	$305	$275	$250	$220	$195	$165

Add $25 for vent. rib.
Add $15 for quick choke.

NOVAMATIC MAGNUM - 12 or 20 ga. with 3 in. chambers, similar to Lightweight, 28 or 30 in. vent rib barrel, full choke.

	$330	$305	$275	$250	$220	$195	$165

NOVAMATIC TRAP - similar to Lightweight, with 30 in. full vent. rib barrel, Monte Carlo stock.

	$360	$330	$305	$275	$250	$220	$195

CHARLES DALY AUTOMATIC - 12 ga., 2¾ or 3 in. chambers, gas operation, alloy frame, pistol grip (high gloss) or English stock, vent. rib, 5 shot mag. Also available as slug gun with iron sights. Invector chokes became standard in 1986. Disc. 1988.

	$320	$275	$235	$205	$190	$170	$150

Last MSR was $365.

Add $15 for oil finished English stock.

MULTI-XII - 12 ga. only, 3 in. chamber, 27 in. VR multichoke barrel, self adjusting gas operation, deluxe checkered walnut stock with recoil pad and forearm. Imported 1987- 88 only.

	$425	$360	$320	$285	$250	$225	$195

Last MSR was $498.

FIELD HUNTER - 12, 20 (new 2002), or 28 (new 2002) ga., 3 in. chamber (12 or 20 ga.), gas operated, aluminum receiver, 22 (Youth), 24, 26, 28, or 30 in. VR barrel with multi-chokes, choice of standard wood/metal or 100% Advantage (disc. 2001), Advantage Timber HD (new 2002), Realtree (disc. 2001), Realtree Hardwoods HD, Advantage Wetlands (new 2001), or Advantage Classic (disc. 2001) camo coverage, synthetic stock and forearm, 6 7/8 - 7 1/8 lbs. Importation began 1999.

MSR	$399	$350	$315	$290	$275	$250	$225	$200

Add $90 for 100% camo coverage.
Add $50 for 28 ga.

✳ ***Field Hunter Maxi-Mag*** - 12 ga. only, 3½ in. chamber, 24, 26 (new 2001), or 28 in. VR barrel with multi-choke, 7mm VR rib, choice of wood/metal or 100% camo coverage similar to Field Hunter, 6 7/8 - 7 1/8 lbs. Importation began 2000.

MSR	$579	$510	$440	$400	$365	$330	$300	$275

Add $100 for 100% camo coverage.

A camo Turkey Model is also available at no extra charge with Hi-Viz fiber optic sights and XX full ported turkey choke tube – also includes sling and sling swivels (new 2002).

✳ ***Field Slug*** - 12 ga. only, 22 in. cyl. bore barrel with adj. sights, black synthetic stock and forearm, nickel or black chrome finish, adj. open sights. Importation began 1999.

MSR	$399	$350	$315	$290	$275	$250	$225	$200

Add $20 for satin nickel finish.
Add $37 for fully rifled barrel with adj. sights (new 2002).

SUPERIOR II HUNTER - similar to Field Hunter, except has 20 LPI checkered Turkish walnut stock and forearm, gold highlights and trigger. Importation began 1999.

MSR	$529	$465	$415	$370	$330	$295	$275	$250

Add $60 for 28 ga.

✳ ***Superior II Sporting*** - 12 ga. only, similar to Superior Hunter, except has 28 or 30 in. ported 10mm VR barrels. Importation began 1999.

MSR	$559	$495	$435	$385	$340	$300	$275	$250

Grading	100%	98%	95%	90%	80%	70%	60%

* ***Superior II Trap*** - 12 ga. only, 30 or 32 in. ported barrel with front and mid bead sights. Importation began 1999.

	MSR	$569	$500	$395	$350	$320	$295	$275	$250

SHOTGUNS: SLIDE ACTION

FIELD HUNTER - 12 or 20 (new 2001) ga., 3 in. chamber, 22 (Youth, 20 ga. only), 24, 26, 28, or 30 in. VR barrel with multi-choke, synthetic stock and forearm, choice of standard wood/metal or 100% Advantage Timber HD (new 2002), Realtree Hardwoods HD 12 ga. only, (new 2002) or Advantage Classic (disc. 2001) camo coverage, 5 5/8 - 6 7/8 lbs. Importation began 1999.

	MSR	$269	$230	$200	$185	$165	$155	$145	$135

Add $90 for Advantage Classic camo coverage.

* ***Field Hunter Maxi-Mag.*** - 12 ga. only, 3½ in. chamber, 24, 26 (new 2001), or 28 in. VR barrel with multi-choke, 7mm VR rib, choice of wood/metal or 100% camo coverage similar to Field Hunter, approx. 6¾ lbs. Importation began 2000.

	MSR	$329	$290	$265	$245	$225	$210	$200	$190

Add $100 for 100% camo finish.
Add $150 for camo Turkey Model with Hi-Viz fiber optic sights and XX full ported turkey choke tube – also includes sling and sling swivels (new 2002).

* ***Field Slug*** - 12 ga. only, 18½ in. cyl. bore or 22 in. fully rifled (new 2002) barrel with adj. sights, black synthetic stock and forearm, black chrome or dull nickel finish. Importation began 1999.

	MSR	$264	$235	$200	$185	$165	$150	$135	$125

Add $21 for fully rifled barrel (Field FRB).
Subtract $20 for blue finish (disc. 2001).

* ***Field Tactical*** - 12 ga. only, 18½ in. cyl. bore barrel with front sight, black synthetic stock and forearm, matte blue metal finish, 6 lbs.. Importation began 2000.

	MSR	$239	$215	$195	$180	$165	$150	$135	$125

DAN ARMS OF AMERICA

Previous trademark of shotguns manufactured in Italy by Silma. Previously imported by Dan Arms of America located in Allentown, PA and by Dan Arms of North America (previously called Sportsman's Emporium Ltd.) located in Fort Washington, PA.

All shotguns listed below were discontinued in early 1988.

SHOTGUNS: O/U

LUX GRADE I - 12 or 20 ga., 3 in. Mag. chambers, 26, 28, or 30 in. barrels, vent. rib, extractors, pistol grip, double trigger, European walnut.

	$280	$220	$210	$200	$190	$180	$170

Last MSR was $350.

LUX GRADE II - 12 ga. only, 3 in. Mag. chambers, 26, 28, or 30 in. barrels, vent. rib, extractors, pistol grip, single trigger, European walnut.

	$320	$250	$240	$230	$215	$200	$190

Last MSR was $395.

LUX GRADE II I - 12 or 20 ga., 3 in. Mag. chambers, 26, 28, or 30 in. barrels, vent. rib, ejectors, pistol grip, single trigger, checkered European walnut.

	$375	$300	$285	$270	$255	$240	$220

Last MSR was $450.

Grading	100%	98%	95%	90%	80%	70%	60%

LUX GRADE IV - 12 ga. only, 3 in. Mag. chambers, 28 in. barrels, vent. rib, ejectors, pistol grip, single trigger, checkered European walnut, multi-choked with 5 tubes.

	$460	$390	$350	$310	$285	$265	$245

Last MSR was $550.

SKEET MODEL - 12 ga. only, 26½ in. barrels, 10mm vent. rib, anatomical pistol grip.

	$550	$450	$400	$355	$320	$300	$285

Last MSR was $650.

TRAP MODEL - 12 ga. only, 30 in. barrels, 10mm vent. rib, anatomical pistol grip.

	$550	$450	$400	$355	$320	$300	$285

Last MSR was $650.

SILVERSNIPE - 12 or 20 ga., made to customer specifications, sideplates, select high grade walnut, name engraving upon request.

	$1,300	$1,200	$1,050	$900	$800	$700	$600

Last MSR was $1,475.

SHOTGUNS: SxS

FIELD MODEL - 12, 16, 20, 28 ga., or .410 bore, double triggers, extractors, 26 or 28 in. barrels.

	$285	$220	$210	$200	$190	$180	$170

Last MSR was $350.

DELUXE FIELD MODEL - 12 or 20 ga., single triggers, ejectors, 26 or 28 in. barrels.

	$440	$375	$340	$310	$290	$260	$230

Last MSR was $500

DARDICK
Previous manufacturer located in Hamden, CT.

CARBINES

DARDICK CARBINE CONVERSION - .22 or .38 Dardick Tround cal., 23 in. barrel (interchangeable), walnut stock, limited mfg.

	$1,275	$1,075	$900	$825	$750	$700	$650

PISTOLS: SEMI-AUTO

SERIES 1100 - .38 Dardick Tround cal., double action, 10 shot mag.

	$560	$420	$365	$310	$255	$225	$200

Dardick ammunition in itself is collectible - currently, individual "Trounds" are selling in the $5- $10 range.

SERIES 1500 - .22, .30, or .38 Dardick Tround cal., double action.

	$875	$660	$570	$490	$440	$395	$350

Subtract 40% for .30 cal.
Add $175-$400 for the carbine conversion unit (.22 or .38 cal).

DARNE S.A.
Current manufacturer producing shotguns 1881-1979 and 1990 to date in Saint Etienne, France. Darne also began making double rifles circa 1996. Currently imported by The Drumming Stump, Inc. located in Circle Pines, MN beginning 1996. Previously

Grading	100%	98%	95%	90%	80%	70%	60%

imported by Wes Gilpin located in Dallas, TX until 1992.

For F. Darne Fils Aîné please refer to the F Section. Also, please refer to the Bruchet section for 1982-1990 mfg. utilizing the Darne action.

RIFLES: DOUBLE

MODEL R EXPRESS SxS - 8x57 JRS or 9.3x74R cal., double rifle version of the Darne Model R Series shotgun, many options available, including style of rib, sights, stock configuration, etc. Importation began 1996.

MSR $13,995	$12,250	$9,750	$8,100	$7,000	$6,000	$5,000	$4,000

EXPRESS SUPERPOSEÉ - .30-06, 8x57 JRS, or 9.3.74R cal., double rifle version of the Darne O/U shotgun, boxlock with false sideplates, straight grip stock, many options available. Importation began 1996.

MSR $7,200	$5,625	$5,300	$4,500	$3,800	$3,300	$2,900	$2,650

SHOTGUNS: SxS, PRE-1980 MFG.

DARNE SLIDING BREECH SHOTGUN - 12, 16, 20, or 28 ga., SxS, unique action utilizes sliding breech lock-up, high quality mfg., 27½ in. barrel standard with other lengths available, any choke combination, either straight grip or pistol grip stock, checkered, models differ in amount of engraving and grade of wood.

* **Bird Hunter Model R11**

	$1,500	$1,350	$1,100	$950	$825	$700	$600

* **Pheasant Hunter Model R15**

	$2,250	$2,000	$1,800	$1,625	$1,500	$1,425	$1,300

* **Magnum Model R16**

	$3,500	$3,150	$2,650	$2,300	$2,000	$1,750	$1,500

* **Quail Hunter Model V19**

	$4,500	$4,150	$3,700	$3,350	$2,850	$2,400	$1,950

* **Model V22**

	$5,750	$5,300	$4,600	$4,150	$3,650	$3,000	$2,500

* **Hors Series No. 1 Model V**

	$6,350	$5,750	$5,250	$4,500	$3,850	$3,150	$2,600

SHOTGUNS: 1989-CURRENT MFG.

In 1990, Paul Bruchet (the old Darne plant superintendent) obtained permission to once again use the Darne trademark. Hence, all 1990 and later mfg. has been produced by Paul Bruchet.

All new mfg. Darnes can be choked to the customer's choice. All models listed below have automatic ejectors, are oil finished by hand, and may be barreled to any length (except for Models R 11, 12, and 13). All prices are subject to change without notice.

O/U Models

SB1 - similar to SB3, traditional European O/U, DT, extractors, straight or semi-pistol grip stock. Importation began 1998.

MSR $2,700	$2,475	$2,000	$1,650	$1,450	$1,100	$950	$825

SB2 - similar to SB3, except has scroll engraving, wood upgrade, and 28 in. barrels. Importation began 1996.

MSR $3,500	$3,100	$2,400	$1,975	$1,625	$1,250	$1,000	$875

Grading	100%	98%	95%	90%	80%	70%	60%

SB3 - 12 or 20 ga., scalloped boxlock action, extractors, 26 in. barrels, DTs, choice of English straight grip stock or semi-pistol grip. Importation began 1996.

	MSR	$4,600		$4,175	$2,900	$2,300	$1,925	$1,800	$1,650	$1,375

SxS Sliding Breech Models

D

R 11 - 12 or 16 ga., half pistol grip stock, light engraving. Disc. 1999.

	$4,000	$2,825	$2,275	$1,925	$1,775	$1,650	$1,375

Last MSR was $4,500.

Add 10% for R 11 Slug (includes duck bill rib).

R 12 - similar to R 11, except with better engraving.

MSR	$6,000	$5,350	$3,625	$2,775	$2,250	$1,925	$1,775	$1,650

R 13 - 12, 16, or 20 ga., straight or pistol grip stock, traditional action with bouquet engraving and obturator discs.

MSR	$6,500	$5,950	$4,250	$3,375	$2,675	$2,250	$1,950	$1,760

R 14 - 12, 16, or 20 ga., slug gun, choice of forearms, light engraving, and optional cheek rest pistol grip stock is also available.

MSR	$6,600	$6,025	$4,300	$3,400	$2,675	$2,250	$1,950	$1,760

R 15 - 12, 16, 20, 24, 28 ga., or .410 bore, select walnut stock and forearm with fine checkering, large scroll engraving, obturator disks.

MSR	$7,600	$6,775	$4,500	$3,550	$2,850	$2,400	$1,975	$1,825

R 16 - same as R 15, except has 3 in. chambers.

MSR	$7,800	$6,950	$4,600	$3,625	$2,900	$2,450	$1,975	$1,825

R 17 - 12 (including Mag.), 16, 20, 24, 28 ga., or .410 bore., Magnum model (3 in. chambers), customer's choice engraving patterns, superior quality wood finish.

MSR	$8,900	$8,100	$6,900	$5,900	$4,950	$3,625	$2,950	$2,575

V 19 - all gauges, easy opening large key action, top quality walnut and checkering, full coverage rose and scroll engraving with chiseled fences.

MSR	$10,995	$9,925	$8,500	$7,300	$6,100	$5,150	$4,200	$3,150

V 20 - similar to V 19, except has deep relief rosace engraving and chiseled fences.

MSR	$12,300	$10,975	$8,950	$7,600	$6,275	$5,350	$4,200	$3,150

V 21 - similar to V 19, except has 100% coverage English rose and scroll engraving and chiseled fences.

MSR	$14,400	$12,750	$10,250	$8,650	$7,425	$6,150	$5,250	$4,200

V 22 - similar to V 21, except has 100% engraving coverage featuring bouquet patterns and deeply chiseled fences, sculpted shoulders, best quality walnut.

MSR	$18,900	$16,750	$13,500	$11,000	$9,775	$8,500	$7,225	$6,000

VHS - all gauges, top-of-the-line model incorporating customers choice of engraving style, type of inlays, and checkering pattern, best quality wood. Due to the unique nature of this model, each specimen must be appraised individually. New guns are priced per individual customer order.

DAVID MILLER CO.

Current custom rifle manufacturer located in Tucson, AZ since 1973.

The David Miller Co. is a custom rifle maker fabricating best quality bolt action rifles only. All guns are essentially built per individual custom order and the company should be contacted directly for more information and price quotations. Currently manufactured D. Miller rifles feature the new Winchester Model 70 Super Grade action. Used rifles have to be

Grading	100%	98%	95%	90%	80%	70%	60%

appraised one-at-a-time to ascertain up-to-date values. Please contact the David Miller company directly for a quotation - almost any feature(s) can be special ordered to produce a truly one-of-a-kind firearm.

DAVIDSON FIREARMS

Previously manufactured by Fabrica De Armas, located in Eibar, Spain.

SHOTGUNS: SxS

MODEL 63B - 12, 16, 20, 28 ga., or .410 bore, 25, 26, 28, or 30 in. barrels, Anson & Deeley boxlock, engraved and nickel plated frame, various chokes, walnut checkered stock. Mfg. 1963-disc.

	$275	$260	$220	$200	$175	$165	$155

✳ *Model 63B Magnum* - similar to 63B, except 10 ga. Mag., 12, or 20 ga. Mag., 32 in. barrel.

12 or 20 ga.	$360	$340	$310	$275	$230	$195	$165
10 ga.	$385	$370	$340	$305	$250	$220	$195

MODEL 69SL - 12 or 20 ga., true detachable sidelock action, engraved nickel plated action, 26 in. and 28 in. barrels, imp. cyl. and mod., mod. and full, checkered walnut stock. Mfg. 1963-1976.

	$415	$395	$375	$340	$320	$290	$260

MODEL 73 STAGECOACH - 12 or 20 ga., detachable sidelock exposed hammers, 3 in. chambers, 20 in. mod. and full barrels, checkered walnut stock. Mfg. 1976-disc.

	$275	$260	$220	$200	$175	$165	$155

DAVIS N.R.

Please refer to the Crescent Fire Arms Co. listing.

DAVIS INDUSTRIES

Previous manufacturer located in Chino, CA 1995-2001. Previously located in Mira Loma, CA until 1995. Distributor sales only.

Davis Industries provided a lifetime warranty on all products, which is now void.

DERRINGERS

D-SERIES DERRINGER - .22 LR, .22 Mag., .25 ACP, .32 ACP, .32 H&R Mag. (new 1995), .38 Spl. (new 1992), or 9mm Para. cal., O/U steel construction, 2.4 or 2¾ (.38 Spl. only) in. vent. rib barrel, 9½ or 11½ oz., black Teflon or chrome finish. Disc. 2001.

	$65	$55	$45	$40	$35	$30	$30

Last MSR was $75.

Add $23 for Big-Bore series (larger frame) in .22 Mag., .32 H&R Mag., .38 Spl., or 9mm Para. cal.

Add $29 for Long-Bore cals. (.22 Mag., .32 H&R Mag. - disc., .38 Spl., or 9mm Para.).

In this series, the .25 ACP cal. is the Model D-25 and the .32 ACP cal. is the Model D-32.

LONG BORE DERRINGER - .22 Mag., .32 H&R Mag. (disc. 1998), .38 Spl., or 9mm Para. cal., similar to D Series, except has 3¾ in. barrel, 13 oz. Mfg. 1995-2001.

	$90	$75	$65	$55	$45	$40	$35

Last MSR was $104.

Grading	100%	98%	95%	90%	80%	70%	60%

PISTOLS: SEMI-AUTO

P-32 - .32 ACP cal., single action, 6 shot mag., 2.8 in. barrel, black Teflon or chrome finish, laminated wood grips, 22 oz. Mfg. 1987-2001.

	$75	$65	$55	$50	$45	$35	$35

Last MSR was $88.

P-380 - .380 ACP cal., single action, similar to P-32, 5 shot mag., 2.8 in. barrel, bright chrome or black Teflon finish, internal shock resister for recoil, wood (disc.) or black synthetic grips, 22 oz. Mfg. 1989-2001.

	$85	$75	$65	$55	$45	$35	$35

Last MSR was $98.

DEFOURNEY

Current long gun manufacturer located in Belgium. No current U.S. importation.

Defourney specializes in both quality sidelock and boxlock (with or w/o sideplates) shotguns. Prices range from $750-$3,250 for boxlock shotguns and start in the $2,500 range for sidelock models, assuming 80% or better original condition.

DEMAS, ETS

Current manufacturer located in St. Etienne, France since 1967. Currently imported by The Drumming Stump, located in Circle Pines, MN.

Demas manufactures a full line of quality O/U and SxS rifles and shotguns. Prices vary according to configuration, engraving options, and quality of wood. Please contact The Drumming Stump directly for current information and domestic prices.

DEMRO

Previous manufacturer located in Manchester, CT.

RIFLES: SEMI-AUTO

T.A.C. MODEL 1 RIFLE - .45 ACP or 9mm Luger cal., blow back operation, 16 7/8 in. barrel, open bolt fire combination, lock-in receiver must be set to fire, also available in carbine model and fully auto.

	$595	$525	$475	$425	$395	$360	$330

XF-7 WASP CARBINE - .45 ACP or 9mm Luger cal., blow back operation, 16 7/8 in. barrel, also available in fully auto.

	$595	$525	$475	$425	$395	$360	$330

Add $45 for case.

DEPAR

Previous manufacturer located in Istanbul, Turkey.

Depar manufactured both semi-auto and O/U shotguns.

SHOTGUNS

ATAK O/U - 12 ga. only, 2¾ in. chambers, ejectors, SST.

	$350	$295	$250	$225	$200	$185	$170

Last MSR was $350.

Add approx. 30% with scroll engraving and walnut stock and forearm.

Grading	100%	98%	95%	90%	80%	70%	60%

ATILGAN SEMI-AUTO - 12 ga. only, 3 in. chamber, gas operated, includes multichokes.

| | $170 | $150 | $135 | $125 | $115 | $105 | $95 |

Last MSR was $195.

❋ *Atilgan Semi-Auto De Luxe* - similar to Atilgan Semi-Auto, except has engraved receiver and deluxe walnut stock and forearm.

| | $350 | $295 | $250 | $225 | $200 | $185 | $170 |

Last MSR was $350.

SAFARI SLIDE ACTION - 12 ga. only, 3 in. chamber, synthetic stock standard.

| | $170 | $150 | $135 | $125 | $115 | $105 | $95 |

Last MSR was $170.

Add 10% for walnut stock and forearm.
Add approx. 50% for nickel chrome receiver finish and light scroll engraving.

DESERT INDUSTRIES, INC.

Previous manufacturer located in Las Vegas, NV 1991-96. See listing under Steel City Arms, Inc. for older models.

In 1990, Desert Industries, Inc. was created - this new company took over Steel City Arms, Inc. More recently manufactured guns will have the Las Vegas slide address.

PISTOLS: SEMI-AUTO

THE DOUBLE DEUCE - .22 LR cal., double action, 2½ in. barrel, matte stainless steel construction, 6 shot mag., rosewood grips, 15 oz. Mfg. 1991-96.

| | 350 | $295 | $275 |

Last MSR was $400.

TWO BIT SPECIAL - .25 ACP cal., double action, 2½ in. barrel, similar to Double Deuce, except has 5 shot mag., 15 oz. Mfg. 1991-96.

| | $350 | $295 | $275 |

Last MSR was $400.

DETONICS FIREARMS INDUSTRIES

Previous manufacturer located in Bellevue, WA 1976-1988. Detonics was sold in early 1988 to the New Detonics Manufacturing Corporation, a wholly owned subsidiary of "1045 Investors Group Limited".

Please refer to the New Detonics Manufacturing Corporation in the "N" section of this text for complete model listings of both companies.

DIAMOND SHOTGUNS

Please refer to the Adco Sales Inc. listing.

DIARM S.A.

Previous manufacturing conglomerate (25 companies) located in Deba, Spain 1986-1989. Previously imported and distributed by American Arms, Inc. located in North Kansas City, MO. Older Diarm models can be found under the American Arms, Inc. heading in this publication.

DIAWA

Previous U.S. firearms importer and distributor.

Diawa imported various firearms circa 1960s-early 1970s. Configurations included semi-auto shotguns mfg. by Singer Nikko, Ltd. of Japan, and bolt action rifles. Values are based on the current utilitarian value, since there is little collectibility on these guns.

DICKSON & MACNAUGHTON

Current trading company established in 1996, and located in Edinburgh, Soctland.

During 1999, the directors of James MacNaughton & Sons acquired the whole share capital of John Dickson & Son, from whom they purchased the MacNaughton manufacturing rights in 1996. The two companies now trade under the name of Dickson & MacNaughton, and trademarks currently owned are: John Dickson & Son, Dan'l Fraser, Alex Henry, James Mac-Naughton & Sons, Alex Martin, and Thomas Mortimer.

JOHN DICKSON & SON

Current trademark purchased during 1999 by James MacNaughton & Sons, located in Edinburgh, Scotland. Both trademarks are currently traded under the name Dickson & MacNaughton.

Please contact the company directly for more information on this trademark (see Trademark Index).

DLASK ARMS CORP.

Current manufacturer located in British Columbia, Canada. Sales offices are located in Blaine, WA. Direct sales.

PISTOLS: SEMI-AUTO

Dlask Arms Corp. manufactures custom M-1911 style custom guns for all levels of competition. Current models include the TC Tactical Carry at $1,200 MSR, Gold Team at $2,000 MSR, Silver Team L/S at $1,700 MSR, and the Master Class at $3,500 MSR. In addition, Dlask also manufactures a wide variety of custom parts for the M-1911. For more information, please contact the company directly (see Trademark Index).

DOMINGO ACHA

Previous manufacturer located in Spain.

PISTOLS: SEMI-AUTO

LOOKING GLASS - .25 and .32 cal. auto pistol.

$150	$125	$105	$85	$75	$60	$50

DOMINO, IGI

Previous Italian company absorbed during 1990 by FAS (see separate listing in F section). Previously imported by Mandall Shooting Supplies located in Scottsdale, AZ.

PISTOLS: SEMI-AUTO

MODEL OP 601 MATCH PISTOL - .22 Short cal., 5 shot, 5.6 in. barrel, match sights, full target grips, vent barrel and slide to reduce recoil, adj. and removable trigger.

$1,300	$1,000	$715	$635	$550	$495	$440

Last MSR was $1,495.

MODEL SP 602 MATCH PISTOL - .22 LR cal., 5½ in. barrel, similar to 601, but .22 LR and slightly different trigger.

$1,300	$1,100	$800	$700	$600	$550	$495

Last MSR was $1,495.

Grading	100%	98%	95%	90%	80%	70%	60%

DOWNSIZER CORPORATION

Current pistol manufacturer established in 1994, and located in Santee, CA. Dealer sales only.

DERRINGERS

MODEL WSP (WORLD'S SMALLEST PISTOL) - 9mm Para. (disc. 1999), .357 Mag., .357 Sig. (disc. 1999), .40 S&W (disc. 1999), or .45 ACP cal., single shot pistol, tip-up 2.1 in. barrel with push button release, internal firing pin block, double action only, synthetic grips, stainless steel, overall size is smaller than a playing card, 11 oz. New 1997.

D

MSR $499	$415	$300	$235

DREYSE PISTOL

Previously manufactured by Rheinische Metallwaren and Machinenfabrik, located in Sommerda, Germany.

PISTOLS: SEMI-AUTO

MODEL 1907 AUTOMATIC - 7.65mm/.32 ACP cal., 8 shot, 3½ in. barrel, blue, fixed sights, hard rubber grips. Mfg. 1907-1914.

$250	$185	$150	$120	$95	$75	$50

MODEL 1910 - 9mm Para. cal., mfg. 1912-1915. Production estimated at 1,000 pistols, usually found in the 12xx - 13xx ser. no. range. Seldom encountered.

$6,500	$5,500	$4,500	$3,500	$2,500	$2,000	$1,500

VEST POCKET AUTOMATIC - .25 ACP cal., 6 shot, 2 in. barrel, blue, fixed sights, hard rubber grips. Mfg. 1912-1915.

$325	$235	$150	$130	$100	$75	$65

DRILLINGS

A Drilling is a three-barrel combination gun (two shotgun barrels and a rifle barrel, vice versa, or three shotgun barrels). Normally, two triggers fire the shotgun barrels and one of them activates the rifle barrel when the barrel selector is moved forward (usually located on the upper tang). Most well made Drillings in above average condition are surprisingly accurate when using the rifle barrel(s), because the stiffness gained with 3 barrels fixed together.

DRILLINGS

Drilling Configurations & Explanations

Please refer to illustrations below depicting the most commonly encountered Drilling configurations.

D

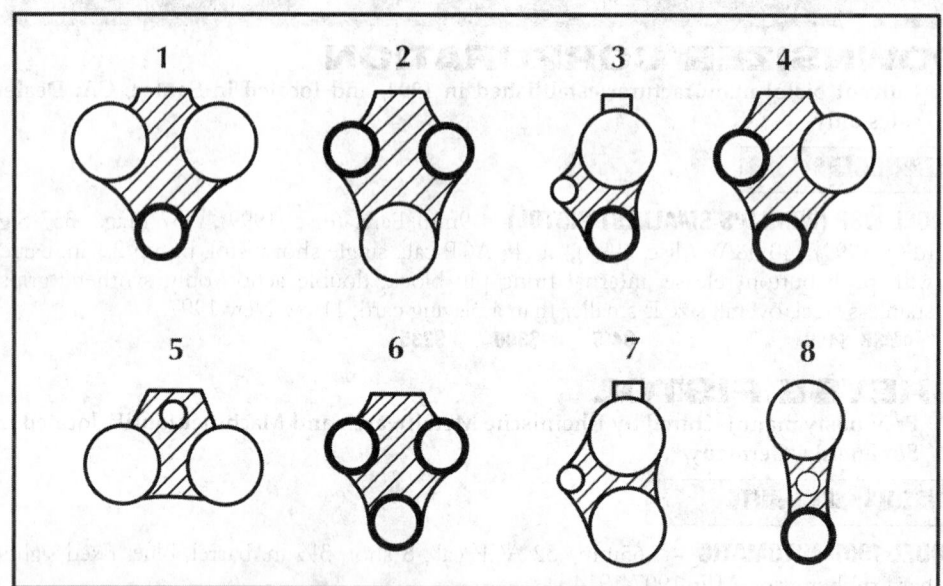

Illustration No. 1 - Normal Drilling configuration with 2 shotgun barrels over a rimmed, centerfire rifle (most are 16 ga. x 16 ga. by either 9.3x72R or 8x57JR cal.).

Illustration No. 2 - Two rifle barrels over a shotgun. This configuration will normally command twice the price as No. 1. German designation is "Doppelbüchsdrilling".

Illustration No. 3 - Three barrels with no two being the same gauge or caliber. This configuration is very collectible, especially if the smallest caliber is .22 LR. Again, price will be double of No. 1.

Illustration No. 4 - Sometimes called a Bock Drilling with one shotgun and two rifle barrels. This variation brings a good premium over No. 1.

Illustration No. 5 - Rib Drilling with rifle caliber generally small (.22LR or .22 Hornet). German designation is "Schienendrilling".

Illustration No. 6 - Three shotgun barrels with the same gauge or three rifle barrels with different calibers. This configuration is quite rare and healthy premiums are charged over No. 1.

Illustration No. 7 - A variation of No. 3, this configuration features shotgun O/U barrels with a rifle barrel on the side. German designation is "Bock-Doppelflinte mit seitlichem Kleinkaliberlauf".

Illustration No. 8 - Very unusual - a 3-barrel drilling in vertical design - 2 rifle barrels under a shotgun barrel. This configuration is seldomly encountered.

The following German nomenclatures apply as follows: single barrel rifle = Büchse; SxS double rifle = Doppelbüchse; O/U double rifle = Bock-Doppelbüchse; SxS double shotgun = Doppelflinte; O/U double shotgun = Bock-Doppelflinte; SxS double shotgun, rifle bbl. under = Drilling; SxS double shotgun, rifle bbl. on top = Schienendrilling; single shotgun, rifle bbl. under = Bock-Büchsflinte; single shotgun, rifle bbl. at side = Büchsflinte; single shotgun, rifle bbl. under and at side = Bock-Drilling; double rifle, shot bbl. under = Doppelbüchsdrilling; O/U double shotgun, rifle bbl. at side = Bock-Doppelflinte mit seitlichem Kleinkaliberlauf; SxS double shotgun, plus two rifle bbls. = Vierling.

Drilling History

For over 140 years Drillings have been the classic hunting gun of many European countries, especially Germany and Austria. Because a single hunting trip may require shooting both wildfowl and animals (often times within several hours), Europeans have long favored a single long-arm that could afford both rifle and shotgun shooting, be reliable, and not wear the hunter out while transporting it in the field. Americans, on the other hand, have not placed as much emphasis on this combination gun principle, and more often than not have chosen to buy both a rifle and shotgun for each specific hunting application. Since Drillings are becoming more popular, collectibility has improved in this country for those collectors who see the utility and functionality of these mostly hand assembled weapons. Very few Drillings manufactured before WWII are alike today in configuration and condition.

Drilling Calibers

Some people may be confused as to how the European metric calibers compare to domestic cartridges in terms of overall performance. This comparison has been added to assist you when contemplating what type of field performance, velocity, and killing power you can expect in these European calibers: 9.3x74 is similar to .375 Win. Mag., 9.3x72R is similar to .44 Mag. or .44-40 WCF, 8x57JRS is similar to .30-06, .30-30 Win. is 7.62x51R, 8x57JR is similar to .30-06, 7x65R is similar to .280 Rem., 7x57R is similar to .257 Roberts, 6.5x57R is similar to .243 Win., 5.6x52R is a .22 Savage Hi-Power, 5.6x34R is similar to .22 Hornet. Drillings can also be encountered in American calibers such as .270 Win., .30-06, .30-30 Win., .38-55 WCF, or .32-20 WCF.

Drilling Values and Condition Factors

Rather than list the various manufacturers of Drillings (there are hundreds), it should be noted that guns with major trademarks and established provenances (i.e. Charles Daly, Colt Sauer, Ferlach addressed, Heym, Krieghoff, J.P. Sauer, Berlin (rare) and Suhl addressed, etc.) will usually be more collectible than other lesser known brands - even if the quality of workmanship is similar. The overall quality, condition, engraving, wood type/fanciness, and carving all have to be taken into consideration when evaluating a Drilling. Some Drillings were assembled from manufactured parts by skilled and crafted gunsmiths and are sometimes better quality than factory specimens. Pre-war specimens are generally more desirable to collectors (even though less expensive than post-war variations) and to date, have outperformed post-war specimens in price appreciation. Many older pre-war specimens were designed for rimmed cartridges with lower breech pressures and should not be re-bored or reloaded for the "hotter" cartridges/loads available today. It should be noted that since Drillings are more complex than a typical shotgun, most of the manufacture has been done by hand - some guns have taken individual craftsmen over a year to fabricate! Ordering a new Drilling today would be a very expensive proposition, and buying a good used specimen will save you thousands of dollars (and maybe a year wait). For these reasons, many collectors feel Drillings today are under-priced since they can be purchased at a fraction of the cost for a new one (and may well be better quality also).

Condition is another major consideration - a gun that shows much use and is not operationally intact/correct may bring several thousand dollars less than another similar specimen showing little wear and excellent original finish (including the case colors or coin finish).

Most above average condition boxlock Drillings in the above mentioned trademarks start in the $1,750 range and can go to $10,000 and higher if the configuration, features, and condition are all desirable. Average Drillings usually sell in the $1,500 - $2,500 range assuming worn condition, metric calibers and few features. For these reasons, Drillings have to be evaluated one at a time and a COMPETENT appraisal/evaluation should be procured before buying or selling a specimen.

Drillings with original claw-mounted scopes (rail-mount or swing-off) are worth 30-40% premiums.

Features That Add Value To Drillings

Drillings with American calibers and smaller gauges will sometimes be more desirable (depending on engraving, case colors, or coin finish) than the European metric calibers (i.e. a gun configured 20 ga. x 20 ga. by .243 Win. will sell for more than a similar gun in 16 ga. x 16 ga. by 9.3 x 72R cal.). The most commonly encountered gauges and calibers are 16 ga. (most pre-war guns are chambered for 2 9/16 in.). In addition, a sidelock action will be more desirable than a boxlock, and a lot more expensive if the locks are also detachable.

Drilling aficionados will mention there are four main things to look for when contemplating a drilling purchase - beauty, condition, quality, and features. Features and embellishments become very critical in ascertaining Drilling values also - a gun with deep relief engraving, carved stock, claw mounts w/scope, buffalo horn trigger guard and butt plate, cocking indicators, two position front sight (i.e. night sight), middle set of express sights, adj. trigger, concealed upper tang peep sight, a non-Greener safety system, lightweight (under 6½ lbs.), separate rifle cocking, shotgun barrel inserts in .22LR or .22 Mag. cal. (approx. 8 or 11 in. long), cartridge trap, etc. is going to be A LOT more collectible than a plain-Jane hammer model with a loose action.

Grading	100%	98%	95%	90%	80%	70%	60%

Features That Detract Value From Drillings

If it isn't beautiful, it probably won't sell. Beauty sells.

Observations On Drilling Collectibility

Condition determines whether a Nitro-proofed Drilling's value is comparable to its black powder or damascus barrel counterparts.

DRULOV

Previous handgun manufacturer located in north Bohemia.

PISTOLS: SINGLE SHOT

PAV - .22 LR cal., single shot, 9¾ in. barrel, all steel construction. Imported 1986 only.

$95	$85	$75	$65	$60	$55	$50

Last MSR was $105.

DRULOV 70 - .22 LR cal., single shot. Add $30 for set trigger. Disc. 1986.

$105	$95	$85	$75	$70	$65	$60

Last MSR was $115.

DRULOV 75 - .22 LR cal., single shot with set trigger & micrometer sights. Also available in left-hand. Importation disc. 1991.

$300	$250	$215	$185	$155	$140	$120

Last MSR was $349.

DRULOV 78 - .22 LR cal., similar to Drulov 75. Imported 1986 only.

$275	$240	$200	$175	$150	$130	$110

Last MSR was $180.

DUBIEL ARMS COMPANY

Previous manufacturer located in Sherman, TX. Dubiel Arms made custom bolt action rifles from 1973-approx. 1990.

RIFLES: BOLT ACTION

BOLT ACTION RIFLE - .22-250 Rem.-.458 Win. Mag. cals., custom made bolt action, barrel length and weight to order, no sights, Canjar trigger, all steel parts, custom made rifle stocks available in five styles. Disc.

$2,000	$1,750	$1,500	$1,275	$1,125	$975	$825

Last MSR was $2,500.

DUCKS UNLIMITED, INC.

National wildlife organization with headquarters located in Memphis, TN.

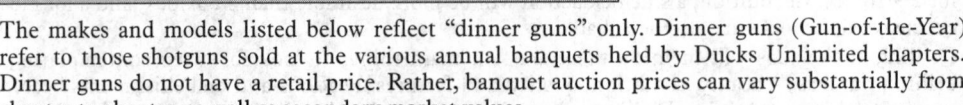

DUCKS UNLIMITED INC.

SHOTGUNS: DINNER GUNS (GUN-OF-THE-YEAR)

The makes and models listed below reflect "dinner guns" only. Dinner guns (Gun-of-the-Year) refer to those shotguns sold at the various annual banquets held by Ducks Unlimited chapters. Dinner guns do not have a retail price. Rather, banquet auction prices can vary substantially from chapter to chapter, as well as secondary market values.

Manufacturer	Model	Quantity	Year
Remington	Model 1100 12 ga.	500	1973

Manufacturer	Model	Quantity	Year
Remington	Model 870 12 ga.	600	1974
Winchester	Model 12 12 ga.	800	1975
Winchester	Model Super X-1 12 ga.	900	1976
Ithaca	Model 37 12 ga. (40th Ann'y)	1,125	1977
Ithaca	Model 51 12 ga.	1,250	1978
Weatherby	Model Patrician 12 ga.	1,600	1979
Weatherby	Model Centurion 12 ga.	2,000	1980
Remington	Model 1100 12 ga. Mag.	2,400	1981
Remington	Model 870 12 ga. Mag.	3,000	1982
Browning	Model B-80 12 ga.	3,400	1983
Browning	Model BPS 12 ga.	3,800	1984
Remington	Model 1100 12 ga.	4,500	1985
Beretta	Model A303 12 ga.	5,500	1986
Beretta	Model A303 20 ga.	3,500	1987
Browning	Model A5 12 ga. (50th Ann'y)	5,000	1987
Browning	Model A5 16 ga.	4,500	1988
Browning	Model A500 12 ga.	4,500	1989
Browning	Model A5 20 ga.	4,500	1990
Beretta	Model A390 12 ga.	4,200	1991
Franchi	Model Semi-Auto 12 ga.	4,200	1992
Winchester	Model 12 20 ga.	3,800	1993
Browning	Model A500R 12 ga.	3,300	1994
Browning	Model 12 Repro. 28 ga.	1,000	1995
Browning	Model BPS 12 ga.	3,500	1996
Browning	Model Gold Hunter	2,500	1997

This model commemorates DU's 60th anniversary.

Manufacturer	Model	Quantity	Year
Remington	Model 11-87 12 ga.	3,500	1998
Browning	Model BPS 20 ga.	3,500	1999
Beretta	Model AL390 12 ga.	3,500	2000

This dinner gun is the Gold Mallard variation of the Model Al390.

Manufacturer	Model	Quantity	Year
Fabarm	Model Red Lion 12 ga.	3,600	2001
Browning	Model BPS 28 ga.	3,500	2002

DUMOULIN, ERNEST S.P.R.L.

Current manufacturer located in Herstal, Belgium. No current U.S. importation. Previously imported 1998-2000 by Armes De Chasse LLC, located in Hertford, NC. Previously imported and retailed on a very limited basis by Midwest Gun Sport located in Zebulon, NC until 1990 (formerly from Ellisville, MO.). Older importation was by Abercrombie & Fitch located in New York, NY.

Most Ernest Dumoulin (son of Henri) drillings, rifles, and shotguns are essentially custom ordered firearms with a long list of options available which, in some cases, can easily double the values of models shown below. Because of this, these options are not listed individually. Please contact the factory directly for more information regarding current models and pricing.

Grading	100%	98%	95%	90%	80%	70%	60%

D

COMBINATION GUNS

EAGLE MODEL - O/U configuration (shotgun barrel on bottom), 12 or 20 ga., .22 Hornet, .222 Rem., .222 Rem. Mag., 6mm Rem., .243 Win., .25-06 Rem., .30-06, 6.5x57R, 7x57R, 8x57JRS, or 9.3x74R cal., boxlock action. 1989-disc.

	$2,700	$2,400	$2,175	$1,850	$1,595	$1,400	$1,195

Last MSR was $2,700.

RIFLES: BOLT ACTION

E. Dumoulin has had very limited importation since 1989. Beginning in 1998, some bolt action models have been imported into the U.S.

BAVARIA DELUXE - .243 Win. through .458 Win. cals., 21½, 24, or 25½ in. octagonal barrel, French walnut stock with rosewood forend tip and pistol grip cap, no sights, custom made essentially with Sako (disc.) or Mauser action. Many engraving options available from $510-$1,900. Disc. 1985.

Series I	$995	$890	$775	$650	$575	$530	$460

Last MSR was $1,080.

Add 15% for .375 H&H or .458 Win. Mag. cal.

RIFLE MOUSQUETON - .243 Win. through .338 Win. cals., 20 in. barrel, Mannlicher style, French walnut stock and pistol grip cap, no sights, custom made essentially with Sako or Mauser action. Many engraving options available from $510 - $1,900. Disc.

	$720	$620	$560	$510	$470	$420	$360

CENTURION MODEL - .270 Win. through .458 Win. cals., 21½, 24, or 25½ in. barrels, French walnut stock with rosewood forearm tip and pistol grip cap, no sights, custom made essentially with Sako or Mauser action. Many engraving options available from $510 - $1,900. Importation disc. 1986.

	$660	$590	$535	$480	$425	$390	$360

Last MSR was $740.

CENTURION CLASSIC - standard cals. only, similar to Centurion, Mauser 98 action only and has better wood.

	$1,525	$1,375	$1,175	$975	$800	$700	$600

Last MSR was $1,525.

These models were also available in Mag. cals. that are divided into 4 groups - 1, 2, 3, and 4 Mag. Series. These options retailed in the $50 - $300 price range.

* *Diane* - grade up from Centurion Classic, 22 in. barrel, Mauser 98 action, M-70 safety, adj. steel trigger.

	$1,450	$1,250	$1,000	$825	$700	$600	$500

Last MSR was $1,450.

* *Amazone* - grade up from Diane, 20 in. barrel, full stock.

	$1,750	$1,525	$1,325	$1,075	$865	$750	$600

Last MSR was $1,750.

* *Bavaria Deluxe* - .243 Win. through .458 Win. cals., 21½, 24, or 25½ in. octagonal barrel, French walnut stock with rosewood forend tip and pistol grip cap, no sights, custom made essentially with Sako (disc.) or Mauser action. Many engraving options available from $510 - $1,900.

	$1,900	$1,675	$1,450	$1,200	$995	$775	$650

Last MSR was $1,900.

Grading	100%	98%	95%	90%	80%	70%	60%

* *Safari* - Mag. cals. only.

	$2,350	$1,775	$1,475	$1,200	$995	$775	$650

Last MSR was $2,350.

MANNLICHER MODEL - various cals., Mauser type bolt action, full stocked. Disc. 1985.

	$730	$660	$580	$520	$470	$430	$395

Last MSR was $825.

* *Mannlicher Classic* - similar to basic Mannlicher, except has better walnut. Disc. 1985.

	$995	$890	$775	$650	$575	$530	$460

Last MSR was $1,065.

MATCH MODEL - match target rifle, adj. sights and stock. Disc. 1985.

	$1,640	$1,490	$1,300	$1,050	$900	$800	$700

Last MSR was $1,860.

* *Match NATO* - 7.62 cal. match rifle. Disc. 1985.

	$2,640	$2,400	$2,175	$1,850	$1,595	$1,400	$1,195

Last MSR was $3,000.

ST. HUBERT MODEL - Sako action, various cals. and barrel lengths. Disc. 1985.

	$1,900	$1,700	$1,495	$1,300	$1,150	$995	$850

Last MSR was $2,125.

SAFARI SPORTSMAN - .416 Rigby, .375 H&H, .505 Gibbs, or .404 Jeffreys cal., Mauser 98 action, 4 shot mag., limited availability in 1986.

	4,000	$3,550	$3,250	$2,800	$2,400	$2,000	$1,750

Last MSR was $4,000.

Add $300 for .505 Gibbs cal.

SAFARI PROFESSIONAL - various Mag. cals., prices below reflect rifle w/o engraving. Limited importation.

MSR	N/A	$9,100	$8,150	$7,400	$6,500	$5,500	$4,500	$3,750

AFRICAN PRO - similar to Safari Sportsman except has ebony or buffalo horn forend tip, tilting hood for the front sight, multiple folding rear sight.

	$4,800	$4,000	$3,550	$3,250	$2,800	$2,400	$2,000

Last MSR was $4,800.

GRAND CLASSIC - various cals., prices below reflect rifle w/o engraving. Limited importation.

MSR	N/A	$7,300	$6,500	$5,500	$4,500	$3,750	$3,000	$2,500

RIFLES: SxS

EUROPA I - .22 Hornet, .222 Rem., .222 Rem. Mag., 6mm Rem., .243 Win., .25-06 Rem., .30-06, 6.5x57R, 7x57R, 8x57JRS, or 9.3x74R cal., Anson & Deeley boxlock action, moderate engraving. 1989- disc.

	$4,800	$4,200	$3,800	$3,500	$3,250	$2,995	$2,700

Last MSR was $4,800.

CONTINENTAL I - same calibers as Europa I, sidelock action, 12 engraving options to choose from, many options available on special order. 1989-disc.

	$8,600	$7,700	$6,995	$6,400	$5,600	$4,750	$4,150

Last MSR was $8,600.

"PIONNIER" EXPRESS MODEL - assorted cals. from .22 Hornet through .600 Nitro Express, SxS configuration, heavily engraved, select walnut. Limited production, Anson & Deeley triple lock action, sideplates available at extra charge.

Grading	100%	98%	95%	90%	80%	70%	60%

✳ P-I and P-II - English style scroll or bouquet (P-II) engraving.

| | $7,850 | $6,500 | $5,825 | $5,200 | $4,650 | $4,160 | $3,700 |

Last MSR was $7,850.

Add $400 for P-II engraving.

✳ P III - English style lace engraving (tapestry style).

| | $8,640 | $7,750 | $7,000 | $6,400 | $5,600 | $4,750 | $4,150 |

Last MSR was $8,640.

✳ P-IV through P-VIII - various styles of royal engraving with or without hunting scenes.

| | $9,100 | $7,995 | $7,450 | $6,800 | $6,000 | $5,000 | $4,350 |

Last MSR was $9,100.

Add $400 for gold inlays.

✳ P-IX through P-XII - Louis XVI style engraving.

| | $9,540 | $8,600 | $7,800 | $7,250 | $6,400 | $5,250 | $4,500 |

Last MSR was $9,540.

✳ Pionnier Magnum - .338 Win. Mag., .375 H&H, .416 Rigby, .416 Hoffman, .458 Win. Mag., .577 Nitro Express, or .600 Nitro Express cal.. Boxlock action with Greener crossbolt.

| | $10,900 | $9,400 | $8,650 | $7,800 | $7,000 | $6,450 | $5,825 |

Last MSR was $10,900.

PIONNIER RECENT IMPORTATION - .300 H&H, .300 Win. Mag., .338 Win. Mag., .375 H&H, .416 Rigby, .458 Win. Mag., or .470 NE cal., similar action as described above, prices below reflect rifle w/o engraving. Limited importation.

| MSR | N/A | $15,000 | $12,250 | $9,975 | $8,200 | $7,000 | $6,000 | $5,000 |

ARISTOCRATE MODEL - available in all cals. up to .375 H&H (also in 20 ga.), single shot action with low profile, exhibition oil finished walnut stock and forearm. Values below assume standard model (12 engraving options available). Imported 1987-1988 only.

| | $9,100 | $8,450 | $7,775 | $7,000 | $6,450 | $5,825 | $5,275 |

Last MSR was $10,400.

PRESTIGE SIDELOCK - similar cals. as the Pionnier Model, best quality sidelock, triple locking, 10 different presentation options available, values below reflect standard model without options. Custom order only, 1 year waiting period. Mfg. began 1986, limited importation.

| MSR | N/A | $29,000 | $25,000 | $21,750 | $19,250 | $16,250 | $13,750 | $11,000 |

FLEURON SIDELOCK - 6.5x57R, 7x57R, 7x65R, .30 Blaser, 8x57 JRS, 8x57 RS, or 9.3x74R cal., made per individual customer specifications. Limited importation.

| MSR | N/A | $26,000 | $21,750 | $19,250 | $16,750 | $14,000 | $11,750 | $9,975 |

SHOTGUNS: O/U

BOSS ROYAL SUPERPOSED - 12, 20 or 28 ga., full sidelock, exhibition grade walnut, double triggers, top-of-the-line quality, built to special order. Values listed assume standard gun (12 engraving options available). 1987-disc.

| | $18,500 | $16,000 | $13,750 | $11,000 | $9,775 | $8,000 | $6,950 |

Last MSR was $18,500.

Add 6% for 28 ga.

SUPERPOSED EXPRESS "INTERNATIONAL" - O/U shotgun, includes extra set of rifle barrels, 20 ga., 7 choices of rifle cals., deluxe walnut. Elaborate engraving patterns available at extra charge, limited production. Disc. 1985.

| | 2,400 | $2,000 | $1,800 | $1,575 | $1,400 | $1,200 | $1,050 |

Last MSR was $2,490.

Grading	100%	98%	95%	90%	80%	70%	60%

SHOTGUNS: SxS

EUROPA MODEL - 12, 20, 28 ga., or .410 bore, Anson & Deeley boxlock action, single or double trigger, moderately engraved, oil finished stock and forearm, choice of 6 engraving options. 1989- disc.

	$3,300	$2,750	$2,350	$2,000	$1,800	$1,575	$1,400

Last MSR was $3,300.

LIEGE MODEL - 12, 16 (disc. 1986), 20, or 28 ga., Anson & Deeley locking action, elaborate engraving, deluxe walnut. 1986-disc.

* **Luxe Model**

	$5,300	$4,600	$3,900	$3,300	$2,900	$2,600	$2,300

Last MSR was $5,900 (disc. 1988).

* **Grand Luxe**

	$6,900	$6,000	$5,000	$4,300	$3,600	$3,200	$2,875

Last MSR was $6,900.

Add 15% for 28 ga.
Add 15% for sideplates.

Many engraving options and other special order features can be added to the above models.

CONTINENTAL MODEL - 12, 20, 28 ga., or .410 bore, sidelock action, double or single trigger, deluxe oil finished walnut stock, choice of 6 engraving options. 1989-disc.

	$7,400	$6,250	$5,200	$4,400	$3,700	$3,200	$2,875

Last MSR was $7,400.

ETENDARD MODEL - 12, 20, 28 ga., or .410 bore, full sidelock, exhibition grade walnut, double triggers, top-of-the-line quality, built to special order. Values listed assume standard gun (many engraving options available). Mfg. began 1987, limited importation.

MSR	**N/A**	$25,750	$21,750	$19,250	$16,750	$14,000	$11,750	$9,975

Add $890 for 20, 28 ga. or .410 bore.

DUMOULIN, HENRI & FILS

Current manufacturer located in Herstal, Belgium. Currently imported and distributed by New England Arms Corp. located in Kittery Point, ME.

H. Dumoulin has manufactured quality firearms in Liege/Herstal, Belgium since 1947. They specialize in big-bore, high quality bolt action rifles, generally built on Mauser 98 or commercial Mauser actions. The improved Imperial Magnum action was developed and introduced in 1987.

RIFLES: BOLT ACTION

GRAND LUXE BOLT ACTION - .300 Wby. Mag., .338 Win. Mag., .375 H&H, .378 Wby. Mag., .404 Jeffrey, .416 Rigby, .460 Wby. Mag., or .505 Gibbs cal., 24, 25.6, or 26 in. barrel, European walnut stock with ebony forend tip and pistol grip cap, folding leaf sights with hooded front, custom made on the Dumoulin Imperial Magnum double square bridge action. Many engraving options available.

MSR	**$7,995**	$7,525	$6,700	$5,750	$5,100	$4,400	$3,650	$3,250

Add $750 for left-hand action.
Add $1,150 for extended top and bottom tang.
Add $1,000 for claw mounts.
Add $1,000 for .505 Gibbs cal.

SOVEREIGN - available in same cals. as Grand Luxe Bolt Action, except with a higher quality finish, knurled bolt handles, gold inlayed lettering. Many engraving options available.

Grading	100%	98%	95%	90%	80%	70%	60%

Pricing on this model depends on engraving, wood and other options. Imperial Magnum is also available in various stages of completion, barreled actions, actions in the white, etc. Please contact New England Arms, Co. directly for quotation.

RIFLES: SxS CUSTOM

BOXLOCK RIFLE - boxlock action, best quality double rifle, highly figured European walnut, finely hand checkered with standard scroll engraving. Custom ordered to customer's dimensions. Prices start at $12,000.

SIDELOCK RIFLE - sidelock action, best quality hand detachable locks, top quality European walnut, finely hand checkered with standard scroll engraving. Additional engraving or deluxe wood quoted on request. Prices start at $15,000.

SHOTGUNS: SxS, CUSTOM

BOXLOCK MODEL - available in most ga.'s, individually built per customer special order. The importer should be contacted directly for more information and a price quotation.

SIDELOCK MODEL - available in most ga.'s, individually built per customer special order. The importer should be contacted directly for more information and a price quotation.

DUMOULIN HERSTAL S.A.

Current manufacturer established in 1997 and located in Herstal, Belgium. This manufacturer's sister company is Ernest Dumoulin S.P.R.L. Previously imported by Arms De Chasse, LLC, located in Hertford, NC.

Dumoulin Herstal manufactures a complete line of quality bolt action rifles in many configurations and calibers. They also produce their own A2000 LM (Long Magnum) action, based on the 1930s Mauser Oberndorf design, which is available separately. Dumoulin manufactures 100-150 guns annually. Please contact the factory directly regarding current information, including model availability and prices.

RIFLES: BOLT ACTION

The following models employ the A2000 Dumoulin action featuring forged flat top receiver, 3 locking lugs with claw extractors, and one-piece bolt, handle, and knob.

ADVENTURER SERIES - various cals. from .25-06 Rem. - .458 Win. Mag., configurations include Euro 2000 and Euroforest. Limited importation began 1999.

Depending on variation and caliber, prices for this series range from $1,510 - $1,936.

GENTLEMAN HUNTER SERIES (LIEGE MODEL) - various cals. from .25- 06 Rem. - .458 Win. Mag., including some additional Safari cals., configurations include Liege, Liege Safari, Liege Full Stock (Mannlicher), or Liege Thumbhole. Limited importation began 1999.

Depending on variation and caliber, prices for this series range from $2,368 - $3,268.

TRADITIONAL LIEGE CRAFTSMAN SERIES (HERSTAL MODEL) - various cals. from .25-06 Rem. - .458 Win. Mag., including many Safari cals., configurations include Herstal, Herstal Full Stock (Mannlicher), or Herstal Safari (5 shot mag.). Limited importation began 1999.

Depending on variation and caliber, prices for this series range from $3,232 - $5,053.

MODEL WHITE HUNTER SAFARI SPECIAL - .375 H&H, .416 Rigby, .416 Wby. Mag., .500 Jeffery, or .505 Gibbs cal., other cals. available upon request, this model features the proprietary Dumoulin Herstal A2000/LM (Long Magnum) action, hinged floorplate, express sights, deluxe checkered walnut stock with ebony forend. Limited importation began 1999.

Prices for this model start at $7,902.

E SECTION

E.D.M. ARMS

Current manufacturer located in Redlands, CA. Dealer and consumer direct sales.

Grading	100%	98%	95%	90%	80%	70%	60%

RIFLES: BOLT ACTION

WINDRUNNER (XM107) - .338 Lapua (new 2002) or .50 BMG cal., takedown repeater action, EDM machined receiver, fully adj. stock, match grade 28 in. barrel that removes within seconds, allowing exact head space every time the barrel is reinstalled, includes two 5 (.50 BMG cal.) or 8 (.338 Lapua) shot mags., Picatinny rail, and bipod, 24 (Lightweight Tactical Takedown) or 36 lbs.

	MSR	$7,250		$7,250	$6,700	$6,200	$5,500	$5,000	$4,500	$4,000

Subtract $1,000 for .338 Lapua cal.

✳ *Windrunner SA99* – similar to Windrunner, except is single shot, w/o mag., includes bipod and sling, 32 lbs. New 2002.

	MSR	$5,250		$5,250	$4,750	$4,250	$3,750	$3,250	$2,850	$2,450

INTERVENTION .408 CHEYENNE TACTICAL - .408 CheyTac cal., takedown repeater, tactical bolt action configuration, 5 shot mag., 30 in. fluted barrel with supressor, desert camo finish, retractable stock, effective range is 2,500+ yards, 27 lbs. New 2002.

	MSR	$7,100		$7,100	$6,600	$6,100	$5,400	$4,950	$4,450	$3,950

This model is sold exclusively by Theis, LLC, located in Grosse Pointe Woods, MI.

E.M.F. CO., INC.

Current importer and distributor located in Santa Ana, CA. Distributor and dealer sales.

Please refer to the 2nd Ed. *Blue Book of Modern Black Powder Values* by Dennis Adler (now online also) for more information and prices on E.M.F.'s lineup of modern black powder models.

DERRINGERS: REPRODUCTIONS

STANDARD MODEL - .22 Short cal., copy of Colt Model Lord or Lady Derringer, blue, gold (disc.), or silver gold finish. Importation disc. 1992.

				$95	$80	$70	$60	$55	$50	$45

Last MSR was $125.

PISTOLS: REPRODUCTIONS

REMINGTON ROLLING BLOCK PISTOL - .357 Mag. cal., rolling block design. Disc. 1992.

				$300	$225	$185	$165	$155	$145	$135

Last MSR was $395.

1875 REMINGTON OUTLAW - .357 Mag., .44-40 WCF, or .45 LC cal., copy of the Rem. Model 1875 SA, 5½ (disc.) or 7½ in. barrel only, case hardened frame, walnut grips, blue only. Mfg. by A. Uberti.

	MSR	$575		$395	$295	$200	$165	$155	$145	$135

Add $15 for steel trigger guard.
Add $160 for bright or satin (disc. 2000) nickel plating.
Add $250 for engraving (disc.).
Add $85 for convertible cylinder (.45 LC/.45 ACP).

Grading	100%	98%	95%	90%	80%	70%	60%

1890 REMINGTON POLICE SINGLE ACTION - .357 Mag., .44-40 WCF, or .45 LC cal., 5½ in. barrel, lanyard ring in buttstock, blue frame, walnut grips, mfg. by A. Uberti. New 1986.

MSR	$590		$410	$300	$215	$175	$155	$145	$135

    Add $10 for steel trigger guard.
    Add $160 for bright or satin (disc. 2000) nickel plating.
    Add $85 for convertible cylinder (.45 LC/.45 ACP).
    Add $260 for engraving.

SCHOFIELD MODEL - .45 LC cal., replica of the original S&W Schofield, choice of 3½ (Hideout), 5 (Wells Fargo) or 7 in. (Civilian/Cavalry) barrel, blue finish. Mfg. by Uberti. Importation began 1999.

MSR	$625		$575	$500	$450	$415	$385	$360	$340

RIFLES: SEMI-AUTO, REPRODUCTIONS

These models are authentic shooting reproductions previously mfg. in Italy.

AP 74 - .22 LR or .32 ACP cal., copy of the Colt AR-15, 15 shot mag., 20 in. barrel, 6¾ lbs. Importation disc. 1989.

	$295	$250	$200	$175	$155	$145	$135

Last MSR was $295.

    Add $25 for .32 cal.

✳ *Sporter Carbine* - .22 LR cal. only, wood sporter stock. Importation disc. 1989.

	$320	$275	$225	$195	$175	$160	$140

Last MSR was $320.

✳ *Paramilitary Paratrooper Carbine* - .22 LR cal. only, folding wire stock, black nylon on paramilitary design model. Importation disc. 1987.

	$260	$190	$175	$165	$155	$145	$135

Last MSR was $325.

    Add $10 for wood folding stock.

✳ *"Dressed" Military Model* - with Cyclops scope, Colt bayonet, sling, and bipod. Disc. 1986.

	$330	$265	$240	$220	$200	$185	$170

Last MSR was $450.

GALIL - .22 LR cal. only, reproduction of the Israeli Galil. Importation disc. 1989.

	$295	$250	$200	$175	$155	$145	$135

Last MSR was $295.

KALASHNIKOV AK-47 - .22 LR cal. only, reproduction of the Russian AK-47, semi- auto. Importation disc. 1989.

	$295	$250	$200	$175	$155	$145	$135

Last MSR was $295.

FRENCH M.A.S. - .22 LR cal. only, reproduction of the French Bull-Pup Combat Rifle, with carrying handle, 29 shot mag. Importation disc. 1989.

	$320	$265	$240	$220	$200	$185	$170

Last MSR was $320.

M1 CARBINE - .30 cal. only, copy of the U.S. Military M1 Carbine. Disc. 1985.

	$175	$150	$140	$130	$120	$110	$100

Last MSR was $205.

    Add $43 for Paratrooper variation.

Grading	100%	98%	95%	90%	80%	70%	60%

RIFLES: REMINGTON REPRODUCTIONS

ROLLING BLOCK RIFLE - .45-70 Govt. cal., authentic reproduction of the Remington Rolling Block Rifle, 30 in. octagon barrel. Mfg. by Pedersoli, importation began 1991.

MSR $750	$675	$600	$550	$500	$450	$425	$400

✳ *Deluxe Rolling Block Rifle* - .45-70 Govt. cal., similar to Rolling Block Rifle, except has 32 in. barrel, checkered pistol grip stock, and German silver forearm cap. Importation began 2000.

MSR $1,125	$900	$700	$500	$450	$400	$365	$330

QUIGLEY MODEL 1874 SPORTING RIFLE - .45-70, or .45-120 cal., 34 in. octagon barrel with storage compartment in stock. Importation began 2000.

MSR $1,500	$1,350	$1,175	$975	$825	$700	$625	$550

BABY ROLLING BLOCK CARBINE - .357 Mag. cal. Mfg. 1992 only.

$395	$300	$260	$220	$185	$160	$140

Last MSR was $490.

REVOLVING CARBINE - .357 Mag. (disc.), .44-40 WCF (disc.), or .45 LC cal., 18 in. barrel, Model 1875 Army Single Action design, 5 lbs. Importation disc. 1995.

$720	$550	$445	$325	$295	$260	$230

Last MSR was $960.

TEXAS CARBINE (1858 REMINGTON) - .22 LR cal., action patterned after Remington revolving carbine, 21 in. octagon barrel, wood stock and forearm, brass frame. Also available with extra .22 Mag. cylinder. Importation disc. 1998.

$295	$225	$175	$150	$135	$125	$110

Last MSR was $400.

RIFLES: SHARPS REPRODUCTIONS

These reproductions are mfg. by Pedretti & Sons.

SHARPS SPORTING OR MILITARY RIFLE - .45-70 Govt. cal., copy of the Sharps Single Shot, 28 in. octagonal barrel, case hardened frame, single or double set triggers. Importation disc. 1999.

$525	$460	$420	$380	$340	$315	$290

Last MSR was $870.

✳ *1874 Deluxe Rifle* - .45-70 Govt. or .45-120 cal., blued or brown finish Deluxe rifle with double set triggers.

MSR $750	$665	$595	$545	$495	$450	$425	$400

Add $25 for checkered stock.
Add $50 for in-the-white (no metal finish) or ½ round, ½ octagon barrel.
Add $25 for .45-120 cal.
Add $25 for brown finish.
Subtract $50 for 1874 Business Rifle configuration.
An engraved version of this model is also available for $1,750.

✳ *1874 Military Carbine* - saddle ring carbine with 22 in. round barrel, single trigger.

MSR $650	$575	$525	$425	$325	$295	$260	$230

Grading	100%	98%	95%	90%	80%	70%	60%

RIFLES: SPRINGFIELD REPRODUCTIONS

SPRINGFIELD 1873 TRAPDOOR CARBINE/RIFLE - .45-70 Govt. cal., trapdoor single shot action, 22 (carbine), 26 (Officer's Model), or 32 (Rifle) in. barrel, blued action, walnut stock. Mfg. by Pedersoli.

	MSR	$875	$795	$725	$650	$575	$495	$425	$350

Add $125 for Officer's Model, or $225 for Rifle.

RIFLES: WINCHESTER REPRODUCTIONS

DELUXE 1860 HENRY RIFLE - .44-40 WCF or .45 LC cal. only, brass or steel frame, deluxe walnut, reproduction of New Haven Arms Co.'s Henry Rifle, 24 in. blued or white barrel. New 1987.

	MSR	$850	$775	$600	$450	$330	$295	$260	$230

Add $25 for in-the-white barrel.
Add $100 for steel frame (.45 LC cal. only).

* *Engraved Henry Rifle* - similar to deluxe Henry Rifle except has hand engraved receiver. Imported 1987-90.

$1,350	$975	$700	$525	$400	$340	$295

Last MSR was $1,598.

1866 YELLOWBOY CARBINE - .22 LR, .22 Mag. (new 2000), .32-20 WCF (new 2000), .38 Spl., .38-40 WCF (new 2000), .44-40 WCF, or .45 LC (new 1993) cal., 19 in. barrel, brass frame, saddle ring carbine.

	MSR	$675	$575	$425	$335	$250	$235	$220	$200

* *1866 Rifle* - same cals. as 1866 Yellowboy Carbine, 20 (short rifle, new 1999) or 24 ¼ in. barrel.

	MSR	$690	$595	$435	$340	$255	$235	$220	$200

Add $35 for in-the-white barrel.
Add $35 for short rifle (.45 LC cal. only).

* *Engraved Yellowboy Carbine* - .38 Spl. or .44-40 WCF cal. Importation disc. 1990.

$875	$575	$440	$330	$295	$260	$230

Last MSR was $1,080.

1873 CARBINE - .22 Mag. (disc.), .32-20 WCF (mfg. 1999-2000), .357 Mag. (disc. 2000), .38-40 WCF (mfg. 2000 only), .44 Spl. (mfg. 2000 only), .44-40 WCF (disc. 2000), or .45 LC cal., 19 in. barrel, copy of the Winchester Model 1873, blued (disc. 2000) or case hardened steel receiver.

	MSR	$865	$750	$600	$450	$330	$295	$260	$230

* *1873 Rifle* - .32-20 WCF (new 1999), .357 Mag., .38-40 WCF (new 2000), .44 Spl. (new 2000), .44-40 WCF, or .45 LC cal., 20 (short rifle, new 1999, .45 LC cal. only), 24¼, or 30 (limited importation 2000 only) in. barrel, case hardened receiver.

	MSR	$865	$750	$600	$450	$330	$295	$260	$230

Add $50 for 30 in. barrel (disc.).
Add $135 for Deluxe model with checkered pistol grip stock (.45 LC cal. only).

* *1873 "Young Boy" Carbine/Rifle* - .22 LR cal., blued steel, 19 or 24¼ in. barrel. Imported 1995-96.

$800	$600	$450	$330	$295	$260	$230

Last MSR was $1,050.

Add $50 for rifle barrel.

Grading	100%	98%	95%	90%	80%	70%	60%

* **Engraved Rifle** - .357 Mag. or .44-40 WCF cal. only. Importation disc. 1987.

	$895	$635	$500	$450	$400	$360	$325

Last MSR was $850.

PREMIER 1873 CARBINE & RIFLE - .45 LC cal., case hardened frame, uncheckered walnut stock and forearm, full mag., rifle has 24¼ in. barrel, carbine has 19 in. barrel. Imported 1988-1989 only.

	$850	$595	$450	$330	$295	$260	$230

Last MSR was $1,160.

1885 HIGH WALL RIFLE - .38-55 WCF (new 2000) or .45-70 Govt. cal., action patterned after the Winchester Model 1885 High Wall, 30 in. barrel, checkered walnut stock. Mfg. by Uberti. Importation began 1998.

MSR	$825	$750	$650	$550	$450	$375	$325	$295

Add $50 for checkered stock and forearm.

1892 RIFLE - .44-40 WCF or .45 LC cal., action patterned after the Winchester Model 1892, case hardened receiver, 24 in. octagon barrel with buckhorn sights, standard stock with crescent buttplate and forearm. Importation began 1998.

MSR	$590	$525	$450	$420	$375	$340	$325	$295

SHOTGUNS: SxS

HARTFORD MODEL COWBOY SHOTGUN - 12 ga., exposed hammers, 20 in. barrels, checkered walnut stock and forearm, mfg. by in Spain by Aral. Importation began 2001.

MSR	$625	$550	$495	$450	$420	$375	$340	$325

STAGECOACH MODEL - 12 ga. only, features exposed hammers and 20 in. brown barrels, mfg. by S.I.A.C.E. Importation began 2000.

MSR	$1,375	$1,175	$900	$700	$500	$450	$400	$365

84 GUN CO.

Previous manufacturer located in Eighty Four, PA. Circa early 1970s.

RIFLES: BOLT ACTION

CLASSIC RIFLE - various calibers. Grades 1-4.

	100%	98%	95%	90%	80%	70%	60%
Grade 1	$420	$315	$275	$235	$210	$190	$170
Grade 2	$780	$585	$512	$430	$390	$355	$315
Grade 3	$860	$645	$560	$475	$430	$390	$345
Grade 4	$1,580	$1,185	$1,030	$870	$790	$715	$640

LOBO RIFLE - various calibers. Grades standard, 1-4.

	100%	98%	95%	90%	80%	70%	60%
Standard	$415	$315	$270	$230	$210	$190	$170
Grade 1	$540	$405	$355	$300	$270	$245	$220
Grade 2	$795	$600	$520	$440	$400	$360	$320
Grade 3	$1,600	$1,200	$1,040	$880	$800	$720	$640
Grade 4	$2,350	$1,765	$1,530	$1,295	$1,175	$1,060	$940

PENNSYLVANIA RIFLE - various calibers. Grades standard, 1-4.

	100%	98%	95%	90%	80%	70%	60%
Standard	$420	$315	$275	$235	$210	$190	$170
Grade 1	$540	$405	$355	$300	$270	$245	$220
Grade 2	$795	$600	$520	$440	$400	$360	$320
Grade 3	$1,600	$1,200	$1,040	$880	$800	$720	$640
Grade 4	$2,350	$1,765	$1,530	$1,295	$1,175	$1,060	$940

Grading	100%	98%	95%	90%	80%	70%	60%

EAGLE ARMS, INC.

Current division of ArmaLite, Inc., located in Geneseo, IL. During 1995, Eagle Arms, Inc. became a division of ArmaLite, Inc. Manufacture of pre-1995 Eagle Arms rifles was in Coal Valley, IL.

During 1995, Eagle Arms, Inc. reintroduced the ArmaLite trademark. The new company was organized under the ArmaLite name and Eagle Arms is now a division of ArmaLite.

RIFLES: SEMI-AUTO, RECENT MFG.

On the following M-15 models manufactured 1995 and earlier, A2 accessories included a collapsible carbine type buttstock (disc. per 1994 C/B) and forward bolt assist mechanism, accessories are similar, except also have national match sights. The A2 suffix indicates rifle is supplied with carrying handle, A4 designates a flat-top receiver, some are equipped with a detachable carrying handle.

AR-10 - .308 Win. cal., very similar to the Armalite AR-10 A4 rifle, 20 or 24 (Match rifle) in. chrome moly barrel, A2 (Service rifle) or A4 style flattop upper receiver (no sights), black stock with pistol grip and forearm, 10 shot mag., 9.6 lbs. New 2001.

MSR	$1,000	$925	$850	$775	$700	$650	$600	$550

Add $55 for Service rifle.
Add $480 for Match rifle.

MODEL M15 A2/A4 RIFLE (EA-15 E-1) - .223 Rem. cal., patterned after the Colt AR-15A2, 20 in. barrel, A2 sights or A4 flat-top, with (pre 1993) or w/o forward bolt assist, 7 lbs. Mfg. 1990-1993, reintroduced 2002.

MSR	$795	$725	$600	$525	$450	$400	$375	$350

Add $40 for flat-top (Model E15A4B).

* **M15 A2/A4 Carbine (EA9025C/EA9027C)** - features collapsible (disc. per C/B 1994) or fixed (new 1994) buttstock and 16 in. barrel, 5 lbs. 14 oz. Mfg. 1990-95, reintroduced 2002.

MSR	$795	$725	$600	$525	$450	$400	$375	$350

Add $40 for flat-top (Model E15A4CB).

1997 retail for the pre-ban models was $1,100 (EA9396).

Beginning 1993, the A2 accessory kit became standard on this model.

* **M15 A2 H-BAR Rifle (EA9040C)** - features heavy Target barrel, 8 lbs. 14 oz., includes E-2 accessories. Mfg. 1990-95.

	$825	$725	$600	$525	$450	$400	$375

Last MSR was $895.

1997 retail for this pre-ban model was $1,100 (EA9200).

* **M15 A4 Eagle Spirit (EA9055S)** - includes 16 in. premium air gauged national match barrel, fixed stock, full length tubular aluminum hand guard, designed for IPSC shooting, includes match grade accessories, 8 lbs. 6 oz. Mfg. 1993-95, reintroduced 2002.

MSR	$850	$725	$650	$550	$500	$450	$395	$350

The 1995 pre-ban variation of this model retailed at $1,475 (EA9603).

* **M15 A2 Golden Eagle (EA9049S)** - similar to M15 A2 H-BAR, except has (N.M.) National Match accessories and two-stage trigger, 20 in. extra heavy barrel, 12 lbs. 12 oz. Mfg 1991-95, reintroduced 2002.

MSR	$1,125	$995	$850	$725	$650	$550	$500	$450

The 1997 pre-ban variation of this model retailed at $1,300 (EA9500).

Grading	100%	98%	95%	90%	80%	70%	60%

* **M15 A4 Eagle Eye (EA9901)** - includes 24 in. free floating 1 in. barrel with tubular aluminum hand guard, weighted buttstock, designed for silhouette matches, 14 lbs. Mfg. 1993-95.

	$1,325	$1,075	$875	$725	$600	$525	$450

Last MSR was $1,495.

* **M15 Action Master (EA9052S)** - match rifle, flat-top, solid aluminum handguard tube that allows for free floating 20 in. barrel with compensator, N.M. accessories, fixed stock, 8 lbs. 5 oz. Mfg. 1992- 95, reintroduced 2002.

MSR	$850		$725	$650	$550	$500	$450	$395	$350

The 1995 pre-ban variation of this model retailed at $1,475 (EA5600).

* **M15 A4 Special Purpose Rifle (EA9042C)** - 20 in. barrel, flat-top (A4) or detachable handle receiver. Disc. 1995.

	$850	$725	$600	$525	$450	$400	$375

Last MSR was $955.

The 1995 pre-ban variation of this model retailed at $1,165 (EA9204).

* **M15 A4 Predator (EA9902)** - post-ban only, 18 in. barrel, National Match trigger, flat-top (A4) or detachable handle receiver. Mfg. 1995 only.

	$1,125	$895	$725	$600	$525	$450	$400

Last MSR was $1,350.

EFFEBI SNC

Current manufacturer located in Concesio, Italy since 1994. No current U.S. importation. Previously named Dr. Franco Beretta until 1994. Also refer to the Dr. Franco Beretta listing.

To date, Effebi snc di F. Beretta & C. has had limited importation into the U.S. The manufacturer should be contacted directly (see Trademark Index) for more information regarding current pricing and shotgun model availability.

EGO ARMAS, S.A.

Current manufacturer located in Eibar, Spain. No current U.S. importation.

Ego Armas manufactures high quality sidelock double rifles ranging in price from $4,000-$14,000. Calibers include .375 H&H and .416 Rigby in their high quality deluxe models. Mounted scopes are also available. Boxlock and sidelock shotguns are also available ranging in price from $400-$4,000. More information, including current models and approximate U.S. pricing, can be obtained by contacting this manufacturer directly (see Trademark Index).

ENFIELDS

Previously manufactured by the Royal Small Arms Factory, located in Middlesex, England.

REVOLVERS

NO. 2 MK. I REVOLVER - .380 British Service (based on .38 S&W with a 200 grain bullet) cal., double action, 6 shot, 5 in. barrel, fixed sights, blue, composition grips, top break, issued to British army 1932.

	$235	$195	$175	$140	$130	$120	$110

Grading	100%	98%	95%	90%	80%	70%	60%

RIFLES: BOLT ACTION

SMLE stands for Short, Magazine, Lee-Enfield. The SMLE rifles served the British Military from 1903-1954.

LEE ENFIELD MK. I - .303 British cal., bolt action, 10 shot attached mag., 30 in. barrel, military sights. Mfg. 1895-1899.

	$650	$575	$525	$475	$425	$400	$375

NO. 1 MK. III* SMLE - .303 British cal., bolt action, 10 shot mag., 25.2 in. barrel, open sights, long range volley sights, magazine cut-off, adopted by British Army in 1907.

	$335	$285	$225	$185	$150	$135	$110

NO. 1 MK. III SMLE - a simplified rifle adopted by the British during WWI, volley sights and magazine cut-off deleted, the most common variation of SMLE.

	$225	$190	$150	$125	$100	$90	$75

NO. 2 MK. IV* - .22 LR cal., single shot, recently imported from Australia.

	$495	$425	$375	$315	$260	$215	$160

NO. 2 (PATTERN 14 RIFLE) - .22 LR cal., single shot military training model.

	$350	$300	$275	$250	$225	$200	$175

NO. 3 MK. I (PATTERN 14 RIFLE) - .303 British cal., modified Mauser type bolt action, issued as substitute standard by British Army during WWI, manufactured in U.S. (the later U.S. 1917 Enfield is identical except for caliber and sights).

	$225	$190	$150	$125	$100	$90	$75

NO. 4 MK. I AND I* - an improved SMLE with aperture rear sight, stronger receiver and more easily manufactured parts, adopted in 1939 by the British Army.

	$215	$185	$145	$120	$95	$75	$55

This model was manufactured during WWII in Canada, England, and the U.S. To determine which armory manufactured this model, the following information should be studied. Savage- Stevens mfg. is denoted by "US Property S" with a C in ser. no., Canadian mfg. (Long Branch, Ontario) is indicated by "Long Branch" - no code, British mfg. was by B.S.A., Shirley and marked "M.47C"., Royal Ordnance Factory (near Liverpool) marked "ROF(F)", or Royal Ordnance Factory (near Sheffield) marked "ROFM" or "RM" or "M".

✳ *No. 4 Mark I T Sniper Model* - with or w/o scope, with or w/o case.

		100%	98%	95%	90%	80%	70%	60%
Gun w/o scope		$575	$495	$450	$385	$315	$285	$260
Gun with scope		$1,425	$1,275	$1,075	$950	$875	$825	$750

Add $175-$225 for case, depending on condition.

NO. 4 MK. II - post-war No. 4 with hung trigger, converted to No. 4 MK. I and I*.

	$300	$250	$175	$125	$115	$90	$85

NO. 5 MK. I JUNGLE CARBINE - .303 British cal., a shorter, lighter version of the No. 4 MK. I with a 20.5 in. barrel, flash hider, recoil pad and shortened forend and hand guard, 7.2 lbs., developed during WWII.

	$350	$275	$200	$150	$125	$100	$85

NO. 7 MK. I - .22 LR cal., training rifle, U.K. and Canadian conversions.

	$750	$675	$575	$525	$475	$425	$400

Grading	100%	98%	95%	90%	80%	70%	60%

ENFIELD AMERICA, INC.

Previous manufacturer located in Atlanta, GA.

PISTOLS: SEMI-AUTO

MP-9 - 9mm Para. cal., paramilitary design, similar to MP-45. Mfg. 1985.

	$550	$475	$425	$350	$295	$260	$240

    Add $150 for carbine kit.

MP-45 - .45 ACP cal., paramilitary design, 4½, 6, 8, 10, or 18½ in. shrouded barrel, parkerized finish, 10, 30, 40, or 50 shot mag., 6 lbs. Mfg. 1985 only.

	$550	$475	$425	$350	$295	$260	$240

    Last MSR was $350.

ENTRÉPRISE ARMS INC.

Current manufacturer located in Irwindale, CA, since 1996. Dealer sales only.

PISTOLS: SEMI-AUTO

The models listed below are patterned after the Colt M1911, but have "Widebody" frames.

ELITE SERIES - .45 ACP cal., 3¼ in. barrel, features steel 1911 Widebody frame, flat mainspring housing, flared ejection port, 10 shot mag., bead blasted black oxide finish, tactical sights, 36 oz. New 1997.

* **Elite P325**

MSR	$700	$625	$565	$500	$450	$400	$360	$330

* **Elite P425** - similar to Elite P325, except has 4¼ in. barrel, 38 oz. New 1997.

MSR	$700	$625	$565	$500	$450	$400	$360	$330

* **Elite P500** - similar to Elite P325, except has 5 in. barrel, 40 oz. New 1997.

MSR	$700	$625	$565	$500	$450	$400	$360	$330

TACTICAL SERIES - .45 ACP cal., 3¼ in. barrel, features Tactical Widebody with "Dehorned" slide and frame allowing snag-free carry, narrow ambidextrous thumb safety, 10 shot mag., low profile Novak or ghost ring sights, squared trigger guard, flat main spring housing, matte black oxide finish, 36 oz. New 1997.

* **Tactical P325**

MSR	$979	$875	$750	$650	$575	$500	$450	$395

Tactical P325 Plus - similar to P325, except has short officer's length slide/barrel fitted onto a full government frame, designed as concealed carry pistol. New 1998.

MSR	$1,049	$925	$825	$725	$650	$575	$500	$450

* **Tactical P425** - similar to Tactical P325, except has 4¼ in. barrel, 38 oz. New 1997.

MSR	$979	$875	$750	$650	$575	$500	$450	$395

* **Tactical P500** - similar to Tactical P325, except has 5 in. barrel, 40 oz. New 1997.

MSR	$979	$875	$750	$650	$575	$500	$450	$395

MEDALIST SERIES (TITLEIST, P500 NATIONAL MATCH) - .40 S&W or .45 ACP cal., 5 in. barrel, features tighter tolerances and numerous custom features, 10 shot mag., front and rear slide serrations, blued slide, includes Bo-Mar low mount rear adj. sight, 40 oz. New 1997.

MSR	$979	$875	$750	$675	$575	$525	$475	$425

    Add $120 for .40 S&W cal.

During 1999, this model's nomenclature changed from the Titleist Series to the Medalist Series.

Grading	100%	98%	95%	90%	80%	70%	60%

BOXER SERIES - similar to Titleist Series, except has fully machined "high mass" and flat-top slide. New 1998.

	MSR	$1,399	$1,200	$995	$850	$750	$625	$550	$500

Add $100 for .40 S&W cal.

TOURNAMENT SHOOTER MODEL (TSM I-III) - .40 S&W or .45 ACP cal., 5, 5½ (TSM III only), or 6 (.45 ACP only) in. barrel, blued finish, designed for IPSC competition, 10 shot mag., TSM II is standard, 40-44 oz. New 1997.

	MSR	$2,000	$1,800	$1,550	$1,325	$1,100	$950	$875	$750

Add $300 for TSM I.
Add $700 for TSM III.

RIFLES: CARBINES, SEMI-AUTO

STG58C CARBINE - .308 Win. cal., paramilitary design, 16½ in. barrel with muzzle brake, synthetic pistol grip stock, last shot bolt hold open, adj. gas system, mil-spec black oxide finish, 20 shot mag., 200-600 meter apeture sights, supplied with black nylon sling, various configurations, approx. 9 lbs. New 2000.

* **STG58C Scout Carbine** - Entreprise Type 03 receiver, integral bipod, includes carry handle. New 2000.

	MSR	$1,199	$1,075	$875	$750	$625	$575	$500	$450

* **STG58C Carbine** - Entreprise Type 01 receiver, machined aluminum free-floating handguards, carry handle. New 2000.

	MSR	$1,399	$1,200	$995	$850	$750	$625	$550	$500

RIFLES: SEMI-AUTO

STG58C RIFLE - .308 Win. cal., paramilitary design, choice of 16½, 21, or 24 in. barrel with muzzle brake, synthetic pistol grip stock, last shot bolt hold open, adj. gas system, mil-spec black oxide finish, 20 shot mag., 200-600 meter apeture sights, supplied with black nylon sling, various configurations, 8½ - 13 lbs. New 2000.

* **STG58C Lightweight Model** - 16½ in. barrel, Entreprise Type 03 receiver, 8½ lbs. New 2000.

	MSR	$1,199	$1,050	$900	$800	$725	$650	$600	$550

* **STG58C Standard Model** - 21 in. barrel, Entreprise Type 03 receiver, integral bipod, 9.8 lbs. New 2000.

	MSR	$999	$895	$775	$675	$575	$525	$475	$425

* **STG58C Government Model** - 21 in. barrel, Entreprise Type 01 receiver, integral bipod, 9.5 lbs. New 2000.

	MSR	$1,199	$1,050	$900	$800	$725	$650	$600	$550

* **STG58C Target Model** - 21 in. barrel, Entreprise Type 01 receiver, with aluminum free-floating handguards, 11½ lbs. New 2000.

	MSR	$1,399	$1,200	$995	$850	$750	$625	$550	$500

* **STG58C Match Target Model** - 24 in. match heavy barrel, Entreprise Type 01 receiver, with aluminum fee-floating handguards, 13 lbs. New 2000.

	MSR	$1,999	$1,825	$1,650	$1,475	$1,200	$1,000	$850	$750

Grading	100%	98%	95%	90%	80%	70%	60%

ERA

Previous manufacturer located in Brazil.

SHOTGUNS

ERA O/U - 12 or 20 ga., 28 in. vent. rib barrel, full and mod., double triggers, extractors, checkered hardwood stock.

	100%	98%	95%	90%	80%	70%	60%
	$275	$250	$225	$200	$170	$150	$125
Trap version	$300	$275	$250	$225	$200	$175	$150
Skeet version	$300	$275	$250	$225	$200	$175	$150

ERA SxS - 12, 20 ga., or .410 bore, 26, 28, or 30 in. barrels, various chokes, double triggers, extractors, checkered pistol grip stock.

$165	$150	$135	$125	$110	$100	$85

ERA RIOT SxS - 12 or 20 ga., 18 in. barrels.

$185	$175	$150	$140	$125	$110	$95

ERA QUAIL SxS - 12 or 20 ga., 20 in. barrels.

$185	$175	$150	$140	$125	$110	$95

ERMA SUHL, GmbH

Current manufacturer located in Suhl, Germany, since January 1998. No current U.S. importation. Erma Suhl purchased the remaining assets from Erma-Werke, and production was once again resumed.

RIFLES: BOLT ACTION

SR100 SNIPER RIFLE - .300 Win. Mag., .308 Win., or .338 Lapua Mag. cal., bolt action, tactical rifle featuring brown laminated wood stock with thumbhole, adj. buttplate/cheekpiece, and vent. forend, forged aluminum receiver, 25½ or 29½ in. barrel, muzzle brake, adj. match trigger, approx. 15 lbs. Limited importation 1997-98 only.

$6,500	$5,750	$5,000	$4,350	$3,750	$3,000	$2,350

Last MSR was $8,600.

This model was imported exclusively by Amtec 2000, Inc., located in Gardner, MA.

Most recent importation was in .300 Win. Mag., and included a Steyr scope mount.

ERMA-WERKE

Previous manufacturer located in Dachau, Germany (Erma-Werke production) until bankruptcy occured in October of 1997. Pistols were previously imported and distributed by Precision Sales International, Inc. located in Westfield, MA, Nygord Precision Products located in Prescott, AZ and Mandall's Shooting Supplies, Inc. located in Scottsdale, AZ. Previously distributed by Excam located in Hialeah, FL.

Erma-Werke also manufactured private label handguns for American Arms Inc. (refer to their section for listings).

PISTOLS: SEMI-AUTO

MODEL LA 22 - .22 LR cal., action patterned after the Luger, mfg. 1964-1967.

$395	$335	$275	$240	$200	$175	$140

Grading	100%	98%	95%	90%	80%	70%	60%

ERMA KGP68A/BEEMAN MP-08 - .32 ACP or .380 ACP cal., Luger type toggle action, 3½ (Beeman) or 4 in. barrel, 6 shot mag., blue, 1.4 lbs. Mfg. 1968-disc.

	$450	$400	$335	$275	$240	$185	$145

Last MSR was $500.

This model was imported exclusively by Mandall's Shooting Supplies, Inc. located in Scottsdale, AZ. From 1988-90, Beeman took over importation of this model in .380 ACP cal. only with new Luger style checkered walnut grips and 3½ in. barrel. Previous models had plastic grips.

ERMA KGP69/BEEMAN P-08 - .22 LR cal., Luger type toggle action, 8 shot mag., 3¾ in. barrel, blue, plastic (disc.) or checkered walnut grips. Mfg. 1969-disc.

	$335	$275	$240	$185	$145	$115	$95

Last MSR was $390.

Beeman was the sole importer of this model between 1988-90.

MODEL ESP 85A SPORT/MATCH PISTOL - .22 LR or .32 S&W Long Wadcutter cal., blow back semi-auto, 6 in. barrel, 5 or 8 (.32 S&W only) shot mag., choice of sporting or adj. stippled match grips with thumbrest, fully adj. and interchangeable sights, gun is supplied with 1 extra weight, extra mag., sights, disassembly tools, and attache style case ($134 option) with foam rubber cut-outs, 2½ lbs. Imported 1989- 1997.

	$1,225	$925	$800	$650	$550	$495	$450

Last MSR was $1,785.

Subtract $315 for Junior Model.
Add $215 for .32 S&W cal.
Add $110 for Match Model (with anatomical grips).
Add $980-$1,390 for conversion unit.
Add approx. $215 for chrome finish.
Add $24 for left-hand action (Match Model only - disc. 1994).
ESP 85 refers to Junior Model (new 1995). The ESP 85 series was distributed by Precision Sales International, Inc. and Mandall Shooting Supplies, Inc.

✸ ***Model ESP 85A Complete Set*** - includes both .22 LR and .32 S&W Long Wadcutter barrels and mags., cased with accessories, complete set was disc. 1991.

	$1,525	$1,350	$1,125	$950	$825	$750	$625

Last MSR was $1,995.

EP-22 - similar to Model LA 22.

	$395	$335	$275	$240	$200	$175	$140

ET-22 LUGER CARBINE - .22 LR cal., 11¾ in. barrel, blue rear ramp sight, checkered walnut grips and uncheckered forearm, adj. artillery type rear sight, rarely seen.

	$425	$365	$330	$275	$240	$200	$175

Add 20% for leatherette case.

REVOLVERS: DOUBLE ACTION

These models were distributed by Precision Sales International, Inc. only.

ER-772 STANDARD/MATCH - .22 LR cal., standard or match gun with special adj. contoured grips with stippling, 6 in. barrel, action similar to ER-777, fully adj. and extended rear sight, interchangeable front sight, 3 lbs. Imported 1990-94.

	$1,100	$875	$725	$625	$550	$495	$450

Last MSR was $1,371.

ER-773 STANDARD/MATCH - .32 S&W Long Wadcutter cal., otherwise similar to ER- 772 Match, 2.9 lbs. Imported 1990-95.

	$925	$825	$695	$525	$475	$425	$385

Last MSR was $1,068.

Grading	100%	98%	95%	90%	80%	70%	60%

ER-777 STANDARD - .357 Mag. cal., 6 shot, 4 or 5½ in. barrel, solid rib and full barrel shroud, adj. target rear sight, blued steel, checkered sport grips, 2¾ lbs. Imported 1990-95.

	$875	$775	$650	$475	$425	$385	$350

Last MSR was $1,019.

RIFLES

Models listed below were available from Mandall Shooting Supplies, unless otherwise noted.

EM-1 .22 CARBINE - .22 LR cal., M1 copy, 10 or 15 shot mag., 18 in. barrel, rear adj. aperature sight, 5.6 lbs. Mfg. 1966-1997.

	$365	$295	$250	$215	$190	$175	$160

Last MSR was $400.

EGM-1 - similar to EM-1 except for unslotted buttstock, 5 shot mag.

	$260	$230	$195	$175	$150	$125	$100

Last MSR was $295.

EG-72 PUMP - .22 LR cal., outside hammer, 15 shot mag., 18½ in. barrel. Mfg. 1970- 1976.

	$125	$95	$90	$75	$70	$65	$60

EG-712 LEVER-ACTION - .22 LR cal., Win. Model 94 copy, tube mag., 18½ in. barrel. Mfg. 1976-1997.

	$260	$230	$195	$175	$150	$125	$100

Last MSR was $295.

EG-73 - .22 Mag. cal., similar to EG-712 12 shot mag. Mfg. 1973-1997.

	$265	$230	$195	$175	$150	$125	$100

Last MSR was $300.

ESCORT

Current trademark of semi-auto shotguns manaufactured by Hatsan Arms Co., located in Izmir, Turkey, and imported beginning 2002 by Legacy Sports International, located in Alexandria, VA.

SHOTGUNS: SEMI-AUTO

ESCORT – 12 ga. only, 3 in. chamber, gas operated action with 2 position adj. screw, 28 in. VR barrel with 3 multi-chokes, blue finish, vent recoil pad, gold trigger, checkered walnut (Model AS) or polymer (Model PS) stock and forearm, 7 lbs. Importation began 2002.

MSR	$382		$335	$300	$285	$260	$245	$230	$215

EUROARMS OF AMERICA

Current black powder importer and distributor located in Winchester, VA. Manufactured by Euroarms – Armi San Paolo, established circa late 1950s, and located in Concesio, Italy.

Euroarms imported a variety of firearms, including revolvers and rifles, mfg. by Armi San Paolo between 1970-1996. Values are currently in the $135-$835 range, depending on configuration and condition.

Please refer to the 2nd Edition *Blue Book of Modern Black Powder Values* by Dennis Adler (now online also) for more information and prices on Euroarms of America's quality lineup of modern black powder reproductions and replicas.

Grading	100%	98%	95%	90%	80%	70%	60%

EUROPEAN AMERICAN ARMORY CORP.

Current importer and distributor located in Sharpes, FL beginning late 1990. Distributor and dealer sales.

EAA currently imports their handguns from Tanfoglio, located in Italy, and from H. Weihrauch, located in Germany. All guns are covered by EAA's lifetime limited warranty.

PISTOLS: SEMI-AUTO, EUROPEAN SERIES

MODEL EA220 - .22 LR cal., 3.88 in. barrel, 10 shot mag., single action, steel frame, 26 oz., blue, chrome or blue/chrome, wood grips. Importation disc. 1992.

$185	$150	$120	$100	$95	$85	$75

Last MSR was $225.

Add approx. $20 for chrome or blue/chrome finish.

MODEL EA22-T - .22 LR cal., 6 in. barrel, cocking indicator and grip safety, 5 or 12 shot mag., adj. trigger and grip, single action, steel frame, target model, 40 oz. Imported 1991-1993.

$375	$295	$260	$220	$185	$165	$150

Last MSR was $450.

EUROPEAN 32 (320) - .32 ACP cal., 3.88 in. barrel, 7 shot mag., single action, steel frame, 26 oz., blue, chrome or blue/chrome, wood grips. Importation 1991-95.

$130	$110	$95	$85	$80	$75	$70

Last MSR was $161.

Add $14 for chrome finish.

EUROPEAN 380 - .380 ACP cal., single (new 1994) or double (disc. 1994) action, 3 7/8 in. barrel, blue, brushed chrome (disc. 1996), Wonder finish (new 1997), matte blue/ chrome (disc. 1993), or blue/gold plated Duo-Tone (European Lady, disc. 1995) finish, 7 shot bottom release mag., steel construction, firing pin safety, external hammer, smooth wood or ivory rose polymer (European Lady) grips, 26 oz. Imported 1992-2001.

$145	$115	$95	$85	$75	$70	$65

Last MSR was $179.

Add $9 for Wonder finish (new 1997).
Add $67 for European Lady model (disc. 1995).
Add $32 for double action design (disc. 1994).
Add $14 for brushed chrome or matte blue/chrome (disc. 1993) finish.

This model employed a unique patented magazine gun lock system.

PISTOLS: SEMI-AUTO, WITNESS SERIES

The following Witness pistols also have a .22 LR conversion kit available for $229.

EA 38 SUPER SERIES - .38 Super cal., action patterned after the CZ-75, selective double action, 4½ in. barrel, steel or polymer frame/steel slide (new 1997), 10 (C/B 1994) or 19* shot mag., choice of Wonder (heat treated grey satin finish, new 1997), stainless steel (disc. 1996) or blue, blue/ chrome (disc. 1994), or brushed chrome (disc. 1996) finish, combat sights, black neoprene grips, 33 oz. Importation began 1994.

MSR	$449		$370	$310	$255	$225	$200	$185	$180

Subtract $20 for polymer frame.
Add $10-$20 for Wonder finish.

✳ *Model EA 38 Stainless* - similar to EA 38, except is stainless steel. Imported 1994- 96.

$525	$435	$350

Last MSR was $595.

Grading	100%	98%	95%	90%	80%	70%	60%

✳ *Model EA 38 Compact* - similar to EA 38 Super Series, except has 3 5/8 in. unported or ported barrel, choice of matte blue or Wonder finish, 30 oz. New 1999.

MSR	$449	$370	$310	$255	$225	$200	$185	$180

Subtract $20 for polymer frame.
Add $10-$20 for Wonder finish or ported barrel (polymer frame only).

EA 9 SERIES

- 9mm Para. cal., action patterned after the CZ-75, selective double action, 4½ in. unported or ported (polymer, New Frame only, new 2002) barrel, steel or polymer frame/steel slide (new 1997), 10 (C/B 1994) or 16* shot mag., choice of Wonder (new 1997), stainless steel (disc. 1996) or blue, blue/chrome (disc. 1993), or brushed chrome (disc. 1996) finish, combat sights, black neoprene grips, 33 oz. Importation began late 1990.

MSR	$449	$370	$310	$255	$225	$200	$185	$180

Subtract $20 for polymer frame, $30 for polymer New Frame.
Add $10-$20 for Wonder finish.

✳ *Model EA 9 Stainless* - similar to EA 9, except is stainless steel. Imported 1992-96.

		$420	$350	$295				

Last MSR was $480.

Model EA 9 (L) Compact - similar to EA 9, except has 3 5/8 in. unported or ported (polymer frame only, new 2002) barrel and 10 (C/ B 1994) or 13* shot mag.

MSR	$449	$370	$310	$255	$225	$200	$185	$180

Subtract $10 for polymer frame.
Add $10-$20 for Wonder finish or ported barrel (polymer frame only).

EA 40 SERIES

- .40 S&W cal., action patterned after the CZ-75, selective double action, 4½ in. barrel, steel or polymer frame/steel slide (new 1997), 10 (C/B 1994) or 12* shot mag., choice of Wonder (new 1997), stainless steel (disc. 1996) or blue, blue/chrome (disc.), or brushed chrome (disc. 1996) finish, combat sights, black neoprene grips, 33 oz. Importation began late 1990.

MSR	$449	$370	$310	$255	$225	$200	$185	$180

Subtract $20 for polymer frame.
Subtract $30 for polymer New Frame.
Add $10-$20 for Wonder finish.

✳ *Model EA 40 Stainless* - similar to EA 40, except is stainless steel. Imported 1992- 96.

		$455	$365	$295				

Last MSR was $509.

✳ *Model EA 40 (L) Compact* - similar to EA 40, except has 3 5/8 in. unported or ported barrel and 9 shot mag.

MSR	$449	$370	$310	$255	$225	$200	$185	$180

Subtract $20 for polymer frame.
Add $10-$20 for Wonder finish or ported barrel (polymer frame only).

EA 10 SUPER SERIES

- 10mm cal., action patterned after the CZ-75, selective double action, 4½ in. barrel, steel frame, 10 or 12* shot mag., choice of stainless steel (disc.), blue, chrome (disc.), or Wonder (new 1999) finish, combat sights, black neoprene grips, 33 oz. Imported 1994 only, resumed 1999.

MSR	$449	$370	$310	$255	$225	$200	$185	$180

Add $10 for Wonder finish.
Add $30 for chrome finish (disc.).
Add $65 for stainless steel (disc.).

✳ *Model EA 10 Stainless* - similar to EA 10, except is stainless steel.

		$495	$425	$350				

Last MSR was $566.

Grading	100%	98%	95%	90%	80%	70%	60%

✳ Model EA 10 Carry Comp - similar to EA 10, except has 4½ in. compensated barrel, blue finish only. New 1999.

MSR	$489		$415	$350	$285	$240	$215	$190	$180

✳ Model EA 10 Compact - similar to EA 10, except has 3 5/8 in. barrel and 8 shot mag.

MSR	$449		$370	$310	$255	$225	$200	$185	$180

Add $10 for Wonder finish.

EA 41 SERIES - .41 Action Express cal., action patterned after the CZ-75, selective double action, 4½ in. barrel, steel frame, 11 shot mag., blue, blue/chrome, or brushed chrome finish, combat sights, black neoprene grips, 33 oz. Importation disc. 1993.

		$450	$375	$325	$275	$250	$225	$200

Last MSR was $595.

Add $40 for blue/chrome or brushed chrome finish.

✳ Model EA 41 Compact - similar to EA 41, except has 3½ in. barrel and 8 shot mag.

		$495	$425	$375	$325	$295	$260	$230

Last MSR was $625.

Add $40 for blue/chrome or brushed chrome finish.

EA 45 SERIES - .45 ACP cal., action patterned after the CZ-75, selective double action, 4½ in. standard or compensated (new 1998) barrel, steel frame or polymer frame/steel slide (new 1997), 10 (C/ B 1994) or 11* shot mag., choice of Wonder (new 1997), stainless steel (disc. 1996) or blue, blue/chrome (disc. 1993), or brushed chrome (disc. 1996) finish, combat sights, walnut grips, 35 oz. Importation began late 1990.

MSR	$449		$370	$310	$255	$225	$200	$185	$180

Subtract $20 for polymer frame.
Add $10 for Wonder finish.
Add $30 for carry configuration with compensator.
Add $40 for ported barrel (steel only, with Wonder finish).

✳ Model EA 45 Stainless - similar to EA 45, except is stainless steel. Imported 1992- 96.

		$510	$430	$350				

Last MSR was $595.

✳ Model EA 45 (L) Compact - similar to EA 45, except has 3 5/8 in. unported or ported barrel and 8 shot mag.

MSR	$449		$370	$310	$255	$225	$200	$185	$180

Subtract $20 for polymer frame.
Add $10 for Wonder finish.
Add $30 for ported barrel (polymer frame only).
Add $50 for single port barrel compensator or carry configuration with compensator (disc.).

WITNESS CARRY COMP GUN - .38 Super (disc. 1997), 9mm Para. (disc. 1997), .40 S&W cal. (disc. 1997), 10mm (disc. 1994, reintroduced 1999), or .45 ACP cal., full size frame with compact slide and 1 in. compensator, 10 (C/B 1994), 12* (.40 S&W), or 16* (9mm Para.) shot mag., Wonder (new 1997), blue or Duo-Tone (disc. 1994) finish. Importation began 1992.

MSR	$479		$425	$360	$310	$270	$235	$210	$195

Add $10 for Wonder finish.

WITNESS SPORT - .38 Super, 9mm Para., .40 S&W, 10mm (disc. 1994), or .45 ACP cal., 4½ in. barrel, full size frame, standard slide length, Duo-Tone finish, extended safety and high capacity mag., target sights. Imported 1994-95.

		$535	$470	$400	$375	$350	$325	$295

Last MSR was $616.

Add $86 for .38 Super, 10mm, or .45 ACP cal.

Grading	100%	98%	95%	90%	80%	70%	60%

WITNESS SPORT LONG SLIDE - .38 Super, 9mm Para., .40 S&W, 10mm (disc. 1994), or .45 ACP cal., long slide variation of the EA Series, except has 4¾ in. ported or unported barrel and slide, Duo-Tone finish, extended safety and high capacity mag., competition sights, 34½ oz. Importation disc. 1995.

	$595	$500	$450	$395	$350	$325	$295

Last MSR was $681.

Add $79 for .38 Super, 10mm, or .45 ACP cal.

WITNESS LIMITED CLASS - .38 Super, 9mm Para., .40 S&W, or .45 ACP cal., match frame, competition grips, high capacity mag., single action trigger, long slide with match barrel and super sight, extended safety, blue finish only. Imported 1994-98.

	$855	$715	$610	$500	$450	$400	$375

Last MSR was $967.

WITNESS COMBO PACKAGE - includes one built up frame and 9mm Para./.40 S&W complete conversion kits, blue, chrome, or Duo-Tone (disc. 1994) finish, full size variation with 4½ in. barrel. Imported 1992-97.

	$515	$460	$400	$375	$350	$325	$295

Last MSR was $588.

Add $29 for chrome or Duo-Tone finish.

* **Witness Combo Package (L) Compact** - similar to Witness Combo Package, except has 3 5/8 in. barrels, blue only. Imported 1994-97.

	$515	$460	$400	$375	$350	$325	$295

Last MSR was $588.

WITNESS MULTI-CLASS PISTOL PACKAGE - .38 Super, 9mm Para., 9x21mm, .40 S&W, or .45 ACP cal., consists of one Witness Limited Class Pistol and complete Unlimited Class top half (slide and barrel), dual chamber steel compensator, blue finish only. Imported 1994 only.

	$1,450	$1,200	$1,025	$895	$775	$650	$525

Last MSR was $1,638.

WITNESS TRI-CALIBER PACKAGE - includes one built up frame and caliber conversions (9mm Para., .40 S&W, and .41 AE) that include slide, barrel, recoil guide, and spring, matte blue or chrome finish, compact or full size variations, includes carry case. Imported 1992-1993 only.

	$975	$825	$700	$575	$495	$425	$375

Last MSR was $1,195.

Add $40 for chrome finish.

WITNESS SILVER TEAM - .38 Super, 9mm Para., 9x21mm, 10mm (disc. 1994), .40 S&W, or .45 ACP cal., dual comp. chambers, S/A trigger, super sight and drilled and tapped for scope mount, competition features include hammer, extended safety, paddle mag. release, black rubber grips, double-dip blue finish, high capacity mag. Imported 1992-98.

	$855	$710	$600	$500	$425	$375	$325

Last MSR was $967.

WITNESS GOLD TEAM - .38 Super, 9mm Para., 9x21mm, 10mm (disc. 1994), .40 S&W, or .45 ACP cal., triple comp. chambers, S/A trigger, super sight and drilled and tapped for scope mount, top-of-the-line competition model featuring hand-fitted major components and 25 LPI checkering, hard chrome finish. Imported 1992-98.

	$1,875	$1,525	$1,250	$995	$825	$700	$575

Last MSR was $2,150.

This model was also available as a frame only - retail was $389.

Grading	100%	98%	95%	90%	80%	70%	60%

F.A.B. 92 - 9mm Para. or .40 S&W cal., double action featuring hammer drop safety and decocker (Witness style), 4½ in. barrel, 16* (9mm Para.) or 12* (.40 S&W), or 10 (C/B 1994) shot mag., all steel construction, blue, chrome (disc. 1993), or Duo-Tone (disc. 1993) finish, smooth wood grips, 33 oz. Imported 1992-95.

	$335	$280	$235	$210	$190	$170	$155

Last MSR was $386.

Add $40 for chrome or Duo-Tone finish.
Add $29 for .40 S&W cal.

F.A.B. designates Foreign American Brands.

✳ **F.A.B. 92 Compact** - similar to F.A.B. 92, except has 3 5/8 in. barrel, 13* (9mm Para.), 10 (9mm only, C/B 1994), or 9 (.40 S&W) shot mag., 30 oz. Imported 1992- 95.

	$335	$280	$235	$210	$190	$170	$155

Last MSR was $386.

Add $40 for chrome or Duo-Tone finish.
Add $29 for .40 S&W cal.

REVOLVERS: DOUBLE ACTION, WINDICATOR SERIES

STANDARD GRADE - .22 LR (disc.), .22LR/.22 Mag. combo. (disc.), .22 Mag. (disc.), .32 H&R (disc. 1993), .357 Mag. (new 1994), or .38 Spl. (alloy frame only) cal., 2 (.32 H&R, .357 Mag., or .38 Spl. only), 4 (new 1997), or 6 (disc.) in. squared off barrel, blue or chrome (.38 Spl. only, new 1994) finish, steel or alloy frame, 6 (.38 Spl.), 7 (.32 H&R), or 8 (.22 LR/.22 Mag.) shot, finger grooved rubber grips. Importation from Germany began 1992.

MSR	$249		$205	$170	$145	$125	$110	$85	$75

Add $10 for .357 Mag.
Add $10-$20 for 4 in. barrel.
Add $78 for .22 LR/.22 Mag. combo. (disc.).

TACTICAL GRADE - .38 Spl. cal. only, fixed sights, 6 shot, 2 in. (bobbed hammer) or 4 in. compensated barrel, blue finish only. Imported 1992-1993.

	$220	$190	$165	$145	$130	$115	$105

Last MSR was $295.

Add $80 for 4 in. compensated barrel.

TARGET GRADE - .22 LR, .357 Mag., or .38 Spl. cal., 6 or 8 (.22 LR) shot, 6 in. squared off barrel, finger grooved hardwood stocks, adj. trigger pull and rear sight, blue finish only, 3.1 lbs. Imported 1992-1993.

	$425	$325	$260	$220	$200	$185	$170

Last MSR was $550.

REVOLVERS: SAA, BOUNTY HUNTER SERIES

MODEL EASAB - .22 LR cal., single action revolver, 6 shot, 4¾ in. barrel, blued or chrome (disc. 1991) finish, wood grips. Importation disc. 1995.

	$70	$55	$50	$45	$40	$35	$30

Last MSR was $85.

Add $20 for chrome finish.

MODEL EASAMB COMBO - includes .22 LR and .22 Mag. cal. cylinders, 4¾ (standard), 6, or 9 in. barrel, blue finish, wood grips. Importation disc. 1995.

	$85	$75	$65	$55	$50	$45	$40

Last MSR was $100.

Add $14 for 9 in. barrel.
Add $40 for gold backstrap and trigger guard (disc.).

Grading	100%	98%	95%	90%	80%	70%	60%

BIG BORE BOUNTY HUNTER - .357 Mag., .44 Mag., or .45 LC cal., 4½ (new 1994), 5½ (disc. 1993), or 7½ in. barrel, 6 shot, choice of blue, chrome (mfg. 1994-95), nickel (new 1998), or case colored finish, gold trigger guard/backstrap (disc. 1994), or gold (disc.) finish, 32-41 oz. New 1992.

	MSR	$369		$315	$255	$205	$175	$165	$155	$150

Add $10 for .44 Mag. or .45 LC cal.
Add $30 for nickel finish.
Add $20 for chrome finish (disc.).
Add $15 for gold-plated grip strap and trigger guard (disc.).
Add approx. $100 for gold plated finish (disc.)

* *Small Bore Bounty Hunter Combo* - includes .22 LR/.22 Mag. cal. cylinders, 4¾ or 6¾ in. barrel, half cock mechanism and transfer bar safety, choice of 6 or 8 shot, blue or nickel (new 1998) finish. New 1997.

	MSR	$269		$210	$175	$150	$130	$110	$95	$85

Add $30 for nickel finish.

RIFLES

EAA rifles were manufactured by Sabatti in Italy (est. 1674), Lu-Mar in Italy, and H. Weihrauch in Germany (see separate listing in the H. Weihrauch section). Imported 1992-96.

SP1822 SPORTER - .22 LR cal., semi-auto, 18½ in. barrel, wood stock and forearm, adj. sights, 10 shot box mag., 5¼-6½ lbs. Imported 1994-96.

	$180	$145	$120	$100	$90	$80	$70

Last MSR was $206.

* *SP1822 Thumbhole* - similar to Sporter, except has one-piece Bell & Carlson green synthetic thumbhole stock, without sights. Importation disc. 1995.

	$310	$260	$230	$200	$175	$150	$135

Last MSR was $358.

ROVER 870 - .22-250 Rem., .243 Win., .25-06 Rem., .270 Win., .30-06, .308 Win., 7mm Rem. Mag., .300 Win. Mag., or .338 Win. Mag. cal., bolt action rifle featuring all- steel construction with 22 in. hammer-forged rifled barrel, staggered 5 shot internal mag., open sights. Imported 1993 only.

	$795	$695	$600	$550	$495	$450	$395

Last MSR was $995.

SHOTGUNS: O/U

SCIROCCO BASIC - 12 ga. only, single trigger, extractors, 26 or 28 in. fixed choke VR barrels, boxlock action, nickel engraved frame. Imported 1994-95.

	$425	$350	$315	$285	$260	$240	$220

Last MSR was $478.

This model was mfg. by Lu-Mar located in Italy.

SCIROCCO SPORTING CLAYS - 12 ga. only, 28 or 30 in. barrels with 5 choke tubes and wide VR, SST, ejectors, Raybar front sight, nickel engraved frame. Imported 1994- 95.

	$650	$550	$495	$450	$400	$350	$315

Last MSR was $734.

This model was mfg. by Lu-Mar located in Italy.

Grading	100%	98%	95%	90%	80%	70%	60%

FALCON - 12, 20 ga., or .410 bore, 3 in. chambers, 26, 28, or 30 in. fixed choke VR barrels, boxlock action, single or double trigger, extractors or ejectors, checkered pistol grip and forend. Imported 1993 only.

	$650	$525	$450	$375	$325	$295	$260

Last MSR was $795.

Add $80 for .410 bore.
Add $100 for SST and ejectors.

SPORTING CLAYS PRO GOLD - 12 ga. only, 2¾ in. chambers, 28 or 30 in. screw-in choke barrels with wide VR, boxlock action, SST, ejectors, blued frame with engraving, recoil pad with custom carry case. Imported 1993-1994.

	$850	$725	$650	$575	$525	$475	$425

Last MSR was $978.

SHOTGUNS: SxS

SABA -12, 20, 28 ga., or .410 bore, 3 in. chambers, boxlock action with scrolled nickel finish, DT or SST, 26 or 28 in. fixed choke barrels with raised matted rib, ejectors, checkered stock and forearm with sling swivels. Imported 1993 only.

	$950	$825	$700	$575	$495	$425	$375

Last MSR was $1,195.

Add $100 for SST.

SHOTGUNS: SEMI-AUTO

BUNDA SERIES - 12 ga. only, 2¾ or 3 in. chamber (depending on barrel) gas operated, 19, 26, 28 or 30 in. barrel with 4 choke tubes, choice of black synthetic or Turkish walnut stock and forearm, aluminum receiver. Limited importation 1998 only.

	$360	$300	$275	$250	$225	$200	$185

Last MSR was $406.

Add $9 for Turkish walnut stock and forearm.

SHOTGUNS: SLIDE ACTION

MODEL PM2 - 12 ga. only, slide action, unique 7 shot detachable mag., 20 in. barrel, black wood stock and composite forearm, dual action bars, cross-bolt safety on triggerguard, available in matte blue or chrome finish, 6.81 lbs. Imported 1992 only.

	$550	$450	$395	$335	$295	$260	$230

Last MSR was $695.

Add $200 for night sights.
Add $75 for matte chrome finish.

EVANS, WILLIAM, GUN & RIFLE MAKERS

Please refer to the W section in this text.

EVOLUTION USA

Current rifle manufacturer located in White Bird, ID since 1993. Distributor and dealer sales.

RIFLES: BOLT ACTION

ARGALI - most short action cals., trued Rem. Model 700 action, Krieger ultra light barrel, synthetic stock, 5½ lbs. New 2000.

MSR	$1,874		$1,625	$1,425	$1,200	$950	$775	$675	$600

Grading	100%	98%	95%	90%	80%	70%	60%

COYOTE - available in various cals., blue printed Rem. Model 700 action, Grand Master (disc. 1999) or Kreiger match barrel with cryogenic treatment, Kevlar/graphite stock. New 1996.

	MSR	$1,758		$1,525	$1,325	$1,125	$900	$750	$650	$575

PHANTOM II - various cals., heavy varmint/sniper model, Evolution M1000 stainless steel action, stainless match barrel, Kevlar/graphite stock. New 1999.

	MSR	$3,092		$3,000	$2,725	$2,350	$2,025	$1,650	$1,325	$1,050

E

YELLOW WOLF - available in various cals., designed for big game, blue printed Rem. Model 700 action, Kreiger match barrel, Kevlar/graphite stock. New 1996.

	MSR	$1,795		$1,550	$1,300	$1,075	$900	$725	$650	$575

IMPALA - most popular cals., Rem. Model 700 trued action w/o floor plate, lightweight sporter, Kevlar graphite stock. Mfg. 1998-99.

				$1,275	$1,050	$950	$750	$650	$575	$500

Last MSR was $1,456.

KUDU - most standard length cals., Winchester Pre-64 Model 70 action, stainless steel match barrel, sporter style Kevlar graphite stock. New 1998.

	MSR	$2,231		$1,950	$1,725	$1,500	$1,275	$1,050	$875	$725

Add $1,500 for presentation walnut stock.

SHI-AWELA - various cals., medium weight sporter, Evolution M1000 stainless action, stainless match barrel, Kevlar/graphite stock. New 1999.

	MSR	$3,052		$2,600	$2,000	$1,750

MBOGO - .375 H&H, .416 Rem., or .458 Win. Mag. cal., choice of Sako (disc.), Dakota (disc.), Rem. Model 700, Win. Pre-64 Model 70, or stainless steel Evolution M1000 action, stainless steel match barrel, express style Kevlar graphite stock. New 1998.

This rifle with Evolution action requires 11% federal excise tax.

* **Sako (disc.) or Remington Action**

	MSR	$1,828		$1,550	$1,325	$1,100	$925	$750	$650	$575

* **Win. Pre-64 Model 70 or Evolution Stainless Action**

	MSR	$3,000		$2,575	$1,975	$1,700	$1,325	$1,100	$900	$800

Subtract $89 for Win. Pre-64 Model 70 action.
Add $2,000 for presentation walnut stock.

* **Dakota Action**

				$2,775	$2,400	$2,000	$1,750	$1,500	$1,250	$1,000

Last MSR was $3,142.

RIFLES: SxS

NYATI - .375 H&H, .416 NE, .470 NE, or .500 NE (disc. 2000) cal., reinforced Anson & Deeley action, choice of color case hardened or coin finished engraved receiver, blue chrome moly barrels, various wood grades available, express sights. New 1999. Custom order only.

	MSR	$6,500		$5,950	$5,250	$4,500	$4,000	$3,500	$3,000	$2,650

Add $1,768 for .470 NE cal.

NYALA - various standard cals., including .300 Win. Mag., 3 grades available, 7 lbs., 9 oz. New 2001.

Please contact Evolution USA directly regarding more information and current pricing on this model.

Grading	100%	98%	95%	90%	80%	70%	60%

RIFLES: SEMI-AUTO

WOLVERINE - .22 LR cal., Grand Master barrel, Kevlar/graphite stock. Mfg. 1996-2000.

$730	$650	$565	$515	$455	$400	$360

Last MSR was $850.

GRENADA - .223 Rem. cal., paramilitary design based on the AR-15 with flat upper receiver, 17 in. stainless steel match barrel with integral muzzle brake, NM trigger. Disc. 2000.

$985	$825	$675	$600	$525	$465	$400

Last MSR was $1,195.

DESERT STORM - similar to Grenada, except has 21 in. match barrel.

MSR	$1,189						
		$975	$825	$665	$560	$500	$450	$400

IWO JIMA - features carrying handle incorporating iron sights, 20 in. stainless steel match barrel, A2 HBAR action, tubular handguard. Limited mfg.

$1,000	$875	$775	$700	$600	$475	$425

RIFLES : SINGLE SHOT

IMPALA - various standard cals., including .300 Win. Mag., 5 grades available, similar appearance and handling as Nyala. New 2001.

> Please contact Evolution USA directly regarding more information and current pricing on this model.

PHANTOM III SINGLE SHOT - .50 BMG cal., Evolution M-2000 stainless single shot action, Lilja match barrel with flutes and muzzle brake. New 2000.

MSR	$3,550						
		$3,250	$2,750	$2,375	$2,000	$1,850	$1,675	$1,500

EXCAM

Previous importer and distributor located in Hialeah, FL that went out of business late 1990. Excam distributed Dart, Erma, Tanarmi, Targa, & Warrior exclusively for the U.S. These trademarks will appear under Excam only in this book. All importation of Excam firearms ceased in 1990.

All Targa and Tanarmi pistols were manufactured in Gardone V.T., Italy. All Erma and Warrior pistols and rifles were manufactured in W. Germany. Senator O/U shotguns were manufactured by A. Zoli located in Brescia, Italy.

HANDGUNS: TANARMI MFG.

TA 38SB O/U DERRINGER - .38 Spl. cal. only, O/U derringer-copy of Rem. Model 41, 3 in. barrels, 14 oz., with safety, blue finish only, checkered nylon grips. Importation disc. 1985.

$90	$75	$65	$55	$50	$45	$40

Last MSR was $80.

MODEL TA 22 SAA - .22 LR cal., 6 shot, 4¾ in. barrel, brass trigger guard and grip straps, blued finish, wood grips, 34 oz.

$85	$70	$60	$55	$50	$45	$40

Last MSR was $99.

MODEL TA 76 SAA - .22 LR cal., single action revolver, 4¾ in. barrel, 6 shot, blue finish only, wood grips, 32 oz.

$85	$65	$55	$50	$45	$40	$35

Last MSR was $95.

Add $4 for chrome finish or brass backstrap and trigger guard.

Grading	100%	98%	95%	90%	80%	70%	60%

✴ *Model TA 76M Combo* - includes .22 LR and .22 Mag. cal. cylinders, 4¾ (standard), 6, or 9 in. barrel, blue finish, wood grips.

	$95	$75	$65	$60	$55	$50	$45

Last MSR was $105.

Add $6 for chrome plated finish (4¾ in. barrel only).
Add $10 for 6 (Model TA 766) or 9 (Model TA 769) in. barrel.
Add $16 for brass backstrap and trigger guard (N/A in 9 in. barrel).

TA 41 SERIES SEMI-AUTO - .41 Action Express cal., action similar to TA 90 Series, 11 shot mag., matte blue (Model TA 41B) or matte chrome (Model TA 41C) finish, combat sights, black neoprene grips, 38 oz. Imported 1989-90.

	$450	$390	$360	$330	$295	$265	$240

Last MSR was $490.

Add $70 for adj. target sights (Model TA 41BT).

✴ *Model TA 41C* - matte chrome finish.

	$485	$430	$395	$360	$330	$295	$270

Last MSR was $550.

Add $50 (retail) for adj. target sights (Model TA 41CT).

✴ *Model TA 41 SS* - .41 AE cal., compensated variation of the Model TA 41 except has 5 in. ported barrel and slide, blue/chrome finish, competition sights, 40 oz. Import 1989-90.

	$575	$450	$420	$385	$350	$325	$300

Last MSR was $650.

TA 90 SERIES SEMI-AUTO - 9mm Para. cal., double action, copy of the CZ-75, 4¾ in. barrel, steel frame, 15 shot mag., matte blue (Model TA 90B) or matte chrome finish (Model TA 90C), combat sights, wood (disc. 1985) or neoprene grips, 38 oz. New 1985.

	$365	$300	$260	$225	$205	$190	$180

Last MSR was $415.

Add $85 for adj. target sights (TA 90BT).
Earlier models featured a polished blue finish and nickel steel alloy frame (35 oz.).

✴ *Model TA 90C* - matte chrome finish.

	$380	$315	$270	$235	$210	$190	$180

Last MSR was $430.

Add $95 for adj. target sights (TA 90CT).

✴ *Model BTA 90B and C* - 9mm Para. cal., smaller version of TA 90, 3½ in. barrel, 12 shot mag., neoprene grips. Imported 1986-90.

	$380	$315	$270	$235	$210	$190	$180

Last MSR was $430.

Add $20 for chrome finish (BTA 90C).

✴ *Model TA 90 SS* - 9mm Para. cal., compensated variation of the Model TA 90 except has 5 in. ported barrel and slide, blue/chrome finish, competition sights, 40 oz. Imported 1989-90.

	$575	$450	$420	$385	$350	$325	$300

Last MSR was $650.

✴ *TA 90BK* - convertible kit including 2 barrels (9mm and .41 AE) and 2 mags. While advertised, this combination never saw production.

PISTOLS: SEMI-AUTO, ERMA MFG.

RX 22 - .22 LR cal. only, double action-Walther copy, 3¼ in. barrel, 8 shot mag., blue only, plastic grips, 17 oz. Assembled in the U.S. Disc. 1986.

	$140	$125	$105	$95	$90	$85	$80

Last MSR was $139.

Grading	100%	98%	95%	90%	80%	70%	60%

KGP 22 - .22 LR cal. only, Luger type toggle action, 3.78 in. barrel, 8 shot mag., blue only, plastic grips, 29 oz. Importation disc. 1986.

| | $220 | $195 | $175 | $155 | $135 | $120 | $105 |

Last MSR was $220.

KGP 380 - .380 ACP cal. only, Luger type toggle action, 3½ in. barrel, 5 shot mag., blue only, plastic grips, 23 oz. Disc. 1986.

| | $250 | $215 | $185 | $160 | $145 | $135 | $125 |

Last MSR was $230.

PISTOLS: SEMI-AUTO, TARGA MFG.

GT 22 SERIES - .22 LR cal., 3.88 in. barrel, 10 shot mag., single action 26 oz., steel frame, either satin chrome (GT 22C) or standard blue (GT 22B) finish, wood grips became standard in 1986. GT 22T is 6 in. barrel target version (12 shot mag.).

| | $170 | $140 | $125 | $110 | $95 | $80 | $70 |

Last MSR was $200.

Add $15 for chrome finish (Model GT 22C).

GT 26 and GT 27B OR C - .25 ACP cal., 2½ in. barrel, 6 shot mag., single action, 13 oz., available in standard blue alloy, satin chrome alloy (GT 27B or C), or steel frame (GT 26S), wood grips became standard in 1986.

| | $50 | $45 | $35 | $30 | $30 | $25 | $25 |

Last MSR was $56.

Add $59 for steel frame (Model GT 26S).
Add $13 for chrome alloy (Model GT 27C).

GT 28 SERIES - .25 ACP cal., 2½ in. barrel, 5 shot mag., single action, blue alloy, wood grips. Imported 1990 only.

| | $45 | $35 | $30 | $30 | $25 | $25 | $20 |

Last MSR was $51.

Add $18 for chrome finish (Model GT 28C).

GT 32 SERIES - .32 ACP cal., 3.88 in. barrel, 7 shot mag., single action, steel frame, 26 oz., either satin chrome (GT 32C) or standard blue (GT 32B), wood grips became standard in 1986.

| | $170 | $140 | $125 | $110 | $95 | $80 | $70 |

Last MSR was $200.

Add $15 for chrome finish (Model GT 32C).

GT 380 ACP SERIES - .380 ACP cal., 3.88 in. barrel, 6 shot mag., single action, steel frame, 26 oz., either satin chrome (GT 380C) or standard blue (GT 380B), wood grips became standard in 1986.

| | $175 | $145 | $135 | $125 | $115 | $105 | $95 |

Last MSR was $212.

Add $8 for chrome finish (Model GT 380C).

* **GT 380 LW** - similar to GT 380 Series except has light alloy receiver and 3¼ in. barrel.

| | $100 | $85 | $70 | $60 | $55 | $50 | $45 |

Last MSR was $119.

* **GT 380 BE or CE** - engraved models, either blue (BE) or chrome (CE) finish, wood grips. Importation disc. 1989.

| | $180 | $155 | $145 | $135 | $125 | $115 | $105 |

Last MSR was $220.

Add $25 for chrome finish (Model GT 380 CE).

Grading	100%	98%	95%	90%	80%	70%	60%

GT 380 XE - .380 ACP cal., 3.88 in. barrel, 11 shot mag., blue only, wood grips, 28 oz.

	$190	$165	$155	$145	$135	$125	$115

Last MSR was $235.

✳ *GT 32 XEB* - .32 ACP cal., similar to GT 380 XE, 12 shot mag. Disc. 1985.

	$165	$145	$135	$125	$115	$100	$95

Last MSR was $189.

REVOLVERS

E

RX 38 B - .38 Spl. cal., double action, 6 shot, 2 in. barrel, blue finish only. Imported 1990-disc.

	$85	$65	$55	$50	$45	$40	$35

Last MSR was $95.

ALDO UBERTI CATTLEMAN SA REVOLVER - .357 Mag., .44 Mag., or .45 LC cal., 6 shot, single action, 5½, 6, or 7½ in. barrels, target sights, wood grips, blued finish. New 1985. Disc. 1986.

	$295	$250	$195	$165	$150	$140	$130

Last MSR was $222.

Add $10 for .44 Mag. cal.

ALDO UBERTI DA INSPECTOR - .38 Spl., double action, 3 or 4 in. barrel, blue finish, wood grips, 6 shot. Disc. 1986.

	$325	$250	$200	$180	$165	$150	$140

Last MSR was $240.

Add $17 for adj. sights.

WARRIOR DOUBLE ACTION MODEL W 722 (B) - .22 LR or .22 Mag. cal. only, double action, 6 in. barrel, 8 shot, blue only, plastic grips, 35 oz. Disc. 1986.

	$100	$80	$70	$65	$60	$55	$50

Last MSR was $98.

Add $50 for .22 Mag. extra cyl.

WARRIOR DOUBLE ACTION MODEL W 384 (B) - .38 Spl. cal. only, double action, 4 or 6 in. barrels, 6 shot, blue only, plastic grips, 30 oz. Vent. rib standard. Disc. 1986.

	$135	$110	$100	$90	$80	$70	$65

Last MSR was $125.

Add $5 for 6 in. barrel (W 386 B).

WARRIOR DOUBLE ACTION MODEL W 357 - .357 Mag. cal. only, double action, 4 or 6 in. barrels, 6 shot, blue only, plastic grips, 36 oz. Vent. rib standard. 6 in. barrel (W 3576). Disc. 1986.

	$190	$165	$145	$135	$130	$125	$120

Last MSR was $185.

RIFLES: ERMA MFG.

EG 712 - .22 LR cal. only, lever action copied after the Win. Model 92, 18½ in. barrel, 15 shot, iron sights. Disc. 1985.

	$180	$160	$140	$125	$115	$100	$90

Last MSR was $204.

EG 712L - .22 LR cal. only, lever action copied after the Win. Model 92, 18½ in. octagonal barrel, deluxe walnut silver plated receiver and barrel bands, 15 shot, iron sights. Disc.

	$300	$241	$220	$180	$150	$130	$115

Grading	100%	98%	95%	90%	80%	70%	60%

EG 73 - .22 Mag. cal. only, lever action copied after the Win. Model 92, 19¼ in. barrel, 12 shot, iron sights, blue only. Disc. 1985.

	$205	$185	$160	$140	$130	$120	$105

Last MSR was $229.

EG 722 - .22 LR cal. only, slide action, 18½ in. barrel, 15 shot, iron sights, blue only. Disc. 1985.

	$180	$160	$140	$125	$115	$100	$90

Last MSR was $204.

EM 1 CARBINE - .22 LR or .22 Mag. cal., gas semi-auto, copy of the original M1 carbine, 19½ in. barrel, 15 shot, iron sights, blue only. ESG 22 is .22 Mag. (12 shot). Disc. 1985.

	$175	$155	$140	$125	$115	$100	$90

Last MSR was $195.

Add $100 for ESG 22, .22 Mag.

SHOTGUNS: O/U

SENATOR MODEL - 12, 20 ga., or .410 bore, 3 in. chambers, 26 or 28 in. F/M barrels, folding action, double triggers, extractors, vent. barrels and rib, checkered walnut stock and fore-arm, engraved silver finished receiver. Imported 1986-1987.

	$235	$200	$180	$165	$150	$140	$130

Last MSR was $275.

EXEL ARMS OF AMERICA, INC.

Previous importer located in Gardener, MA. Exel Arms previously imported Lanber (Series 100), Ugartechea (Series 200), and Laurona (Series 300) shotguns. Please refer to the appropriate sections for more information on this series.

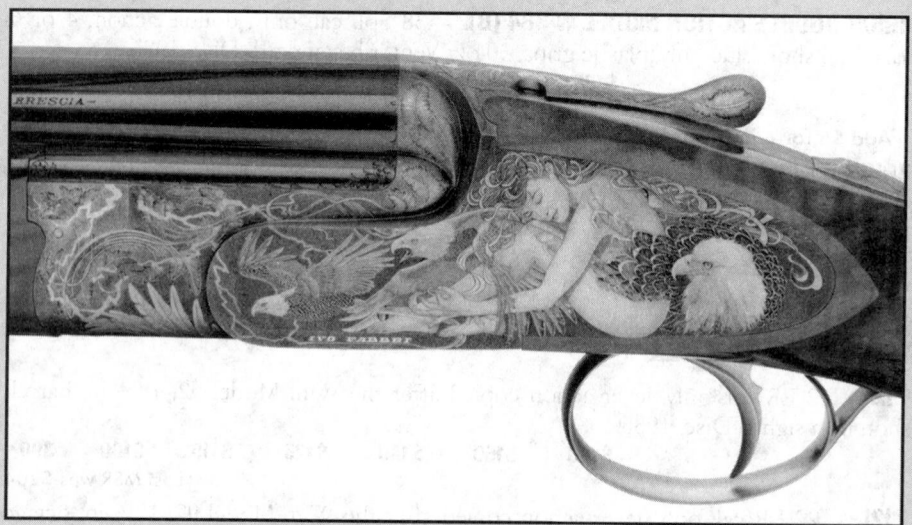

E is for engraving. The unique fantasy engraving on this Fabbri O/U was expertly done by Creative Art, located in Gardone, Italy.

F SECTION

F. DARNE FILS AINÉ

Previous manufacturer located in St. Etienne, France.

Francisque Darne was the eldest son of Regis Darne, who developed the sliding breech gun. In 1910, Francisque left his father's company to form his own, "F.Darne Fils AinÉ", producing high quality versions of the original 1894 patent "R" model Darne. Regis Darne updated most of his designs in 1909 and allowed the older patents to become public domain.

Francisque Darne died in 1917, but his company remained in production until 1955 under at least four different owners. As is usually the case, the earlier production guns are by far the highest quality. Wide variations in quality exist in this marque, depending on the financial health of the owners at the time of production.

F

Grading	100%	98%	95%	90%	80%	70%	60%

SHOTGUNS: SxS, PRE-WAR MODELS

CLASSIC MODEL - 12 or 16 ga., an exact copy of the first Darne patent of 1894. Available in four grades.

* ***Type A*** - standard French proof barrels, very light engraving, color case hardened, no quality stamps on barrel flats.

	$1,200	$1,000	$800	$700	$600	$500	$450

* ***Type B*** - French gray hardened or color case hardened, somewhat more engraving, 1 quality stamp on barrel flats.

	$1,700	$1,400	$1,200	$900	$700	$600	$500

* ***Type C*** - French gray hardening over modern or old English engraving, double proofed barrels with two quality stamps on barrel flats.

	$2,000	$1,650	$1,350	$1,000	$800	$650	$550

* ***Type E*** - French gray hardening over elaborate engraving. Better quality wood in either English or semi-pistol grip. Double proof barrels with four quality stamps on barrel flats.

	$2,400	$2,000	$1,600	$1,300	$1,000	$900	$800

MODEL T - 12 or 16 ga., stylistic improvements to the 1894 patent R model. Two-piece stock, barrels removed by holding a button on forend, 4 grades, all were originally color case hardened, never blued.

Both the T 32 and T 34 were available in 10 ga. with 70mm or 75mm chambers and 72cm or 76cm barrels on special order. The barrels would carry triple proof in 10 ga.

* ***Type T 32*** - lightly engraved, 3 quality stamps on barrel flats.

	$1,950	$1,700	$1,250	$950	$700	$600	$500

Add 30% for 10 ga.

* ***Model T 34*** - better engraving and wood, 5 quality stamps on barrel flats.

	$2,100	$1,800	$1,500	$1,100	$850	$675	$575

Add 30% for 10 ga.

* ***Model T 35*** - mono bloc barrels of superior French proof steel, better engraving and wood, 6 quality stamps on barrel flats.

	$2,500	$2,200	$1,800	$1,400	$1,200	$1,000	$800

* ***Model T 36*** - mono bloc barrels of superior French proof steel, top-of-the-line T model, 7 quality stamps on barrel flats.

	$2,800	$2,500	$2,100	$1,700	$1,400	$1,200	$850

Grading	100%	98%	95%	90%	80%	70%	60%

MODEL FIXED - 12 or 16 ga., further tinkering with the 1894 R model, these located the barrels in a rectangular block cut near the flats. Two grades.

✳ *Type No. 3* - color case hardened or French gray hardened. Good quality engraving and wood. For pricing, see Type T 34.

✳ *Type No. 4* - better wood and engraving. For pricing, see Type T 35.

MODEL PLATINUM - 12 or 16 ga., based on the model Fixed, these were top-of-the-line sliding breech guns. Four grades.

✳ *Type No. 5* - mono bloc barrels, English or art nouveau style engraving, chisled fences.

	$3,100	$2,800	$2,500	$2,200	$1,700	$1,400	$1,100

✳ *Type No. 6* - mono bloc barrels, English rose and scroll engraving or game scene or art nouveau style, high grade wood.

	$3,400	$2,900	$2,600	$2,350	$1,900	$1,600	$1,200

✳ *Type No. 7* - mono bloc barrels of top quality French proof steel, engraved in English rose and scroll or deep chisled art nouveau style, superior wood. Pigeon model.

	$3,800	$3,500	$3,000	$2,800	$2,200	$1,900	$1,500

✳ *Type No. 8* - mono bloc barrels of top quality French proof steel. Top-of-the-line model with all details to customer's wishes. Very rare in any condition. Rarity precludes accurate pricing.

SHOTGUNS: SxS, POST-WAR MODELS

Note: the model name of the following post-war guns is usually engraved on the side of the gun in front of the safety lever.

CLASSIC MODEL - 12 or 16 ga. with modified and full choke on 70 cm barrels, simple case colored gun with no engraving and plain wood in semi-pistol grip or straight stock, 2 quality stamps.

	$1,250	$1,000	$850	$700	$600	$525	$400

BARONNET-BROUSSARD - 12,16, or 20 ga. with 70 cm barrels (two-piece stock on 12 and 16 ga.), lightly engraved with satin chrome receiver finish, Broussard model featured 80 cm barrels but was essentially the same, 3 quality stamps.

	$1,400	$1,200	$1,000	$800	$675	$550	$475

Add 20% for Broussard model.

GOUVERNEUR MODEL - 12, 16, or 20 ga., better engraving and one-piece stock of select walnut, French gray receiver, choice of barrel lengths in 12 ga. (70 cm, 72 cm, or 74 cm.) classic or modern style engraving, 5 quality stamps.

	$1,800	$1,650	$1,200	$1,000	$750	$600	$550

GOUVERNEUR PLUME AND PLUME MAGNUM - same as above, but with plume (swamped rib) on Plume Model, plume rib and 76mm chambers included on Plume Magnum Model. Prices about 10% higher than previous models due to these having six quality stamps on flats of barrels in spite of being the same basic gun.

RAMBOUILLET MODEL - 12 or 16 ga., double sears in a large key action somewhat similar to the Darne V models stylistically, one-piece stock of select walnut, in semi-pistol grip or straight style, light engraving on color case hardening, choice of rib, 8 quality stamps.

	$1,500	$1,300	$1,100	$900	$700	$650	$575

AMBASSADEUR MODEL - 12 or 16 ga., large key model with double sears. French gray finish on breech with excellent engraving, one-piece stock of good quality walnut, top- of-the-line production model, 10 quality stamps.

	$2,700	$2,400	$2,200	$1,800	$1,500	$1,100	$850

F

Grading	100%	98%	95%	90%	80%	70%	60%

PRESTIGE MODEL - top-of-the-line custom gun, mono bloc barrels of Jacob Holtzer steel with plume swamped rib. Large key action with silent operation and double sears, one-piece stock of best quality walnut, in straight style only, 72 cm barrels, excellent full coverage engraving, eight month minimum wait, 12 quality stamps.

		100%	98%	95%	90%	80%	70%	60%
		$3,500	$3,100	$2,900	$2,600	$2,200	$1,700	$1,200

F.A.I.R. TECNI-MEC (I. RIZZINI)

Current manufacturer established in 1971 (F.A.I.R. stands for Fabbrica Armi Isidoro Rizzini) and located in Marcheno, Italy (owned by Isidoro Rizzini). Currently imported and distributed exclusively by New England Arms Corp. located in Kittery Point, ME.

SHOTGUNS: O/U

Techni-Mec manufactures a wide variety of shotguns, rifles, and combinations guns, including O/Us and single shots in assorted models. Some models, however, are not being imported into the U.S. at this time. For more information on the complete Techni-Mec model line-up, please contact New England Arms Corp.

Beginning 1999, Models 500, 600, 702, and 900 in 16 ga. have their own size frame (approx. 6¼ lbs). A smaller 28 ga. frame was introduced in 2000 (also used for .410 bore), and weighs approx. 5¾ lbs. Prices on these models include custom dimensions – numerous options are available.

MODEL PREMIERE EM - 12, 20, 28 ga., or .410 bore, standard model with ST, ejectors, vent. rib barrels, blued frame. Importation began 1998.

		100%	98%	95%	90%	80%	70%	60%
MSR	$850	$775	$650	$550	$500	$450	$400	$360

MODEL 500 - 12, 16, 20, 28 ga., or .410 bore, boxlock action with case colored frame and game scene engraving, choke tubes (5) except for .410 bore. Importation began 1998.

		100%	98%	95%	90%	80%	70%	60%
MSR	$2,250	$2,000	$1,750	$1,525	$1,275	$1,075	$950	$825

Add $275 for Model 500 Gold (includes gold inlays on receiver).

MODEL 600 GOLD - same gauges as Model 500, features case colored or coin finished receiver with engraved and gold inlaid sideplates. Importation began 1998.

		100%	98%	95%	90%	80%	70%	60%
MSR	$2,995	$2,650	$2,225	$1,900	$1,675	$1,400	$1,150	$925

MODEL S 610 - 10 ga., 3½ in. Mag., O/U boxlock action, double underlug locking, 32 in. VR barrels, SST, ejectors, checkered walnut stock and forearm. Imported 1991-97.

		100%	98%	95%	90%	80%	70%	60%
		$925	$825	$750	$675	$595	$525	$450

Last MSR was $1,000.

MODEL SPL 640 - 12, 16, 20, 28 ga., or .410 bore, folding O/U design, DT, 26 in. VR barrels. Importation disc. 1997.

		100%	98%	95%	90%	80%	70%	60%
		$465	$390	$325	$260	$215	$180	$160

Last MSR was $500.

MODEL 702 - 12, 16, 20, 28 ga., or .410 bore, O/U boxlock with sideplates, standard interchangeable chokes available, case colored receiver with hand inlaid 24Kt. gold wire outlines on sideplates, SST, ejectors. Importation began 1995.

		100%	98%	95%	90%	80%	70%	60%
MSR	$3,995	$3,500	$2,450	$2,000	$1,750	$1,500	$1,350	$1,225

MODEL 900 - similar to Model 702, except has upgraded wood and hand executed Bulino/scroll engraving on coin finished receiver, game scenes vary with each ga. Importation began 1995.

		100%	98%	95%	90%	80%	70%	60%
MSR	$3,995	$3,500	$2,450	$2,000	$1,750	$1,500	$1,350	$1,225

Grading	100%	98%	95%	90%	80%	70%	60%

✴ *Model 900 EL* - same general specifications as the Model 900, except has full engraving coverage with individually signed Bullio game scene engraving. Importation began 2001.

	MSR	$5,995		$5,500	$4,500	$4,000	$3,500	$2,450	$2,000	$1,750

✴ *Model 900 EELL* - same general specifications as Model 900 EL, top-of-the-line model with Turkish walnut, extensive engraving, cased. Importation began 2001.

	MSR	$7,500		$6,875	$6,000	$5,500	$4,500	$4,000	$3,500	$2,450

MODEL 902 - similar to Model 900, except has sideplates. Importation began 2001.

	MSR	$4,750		$4,275	$3,250	$2,650	$2,100	$1,825	$1,500	$1,350

✴ *Model 902 EL* - same general specifications as the Model 902, except has full engraving coverage on sideplates. Importation began 2001.

	MSR	$6,995		$6,275	$5,300	$4,500	$3,900	$2,700	$2,300	$2,100

✴ *Model 902 EELL* - same general specifications as Model 902 EL, top-of-the-line model with Turkish walnut, extensive Bullino game scene engraving with signature, cased. Importation began 2001.

	MSR	$8,995		$8,350	$7,500	$6,500	$5,600	$4,600	$3,600	$2,750

F.A.V.S. di FRANCESCO GUGLIELMINOTTI

Current manufacturer established in 1957, and located in Villar Focchiardo, Italy. No current U.S. importation. F.A.V.S. is an abbreviation for Fabbrica Armi Valle Susa.

RIFLES: SINGLE SHOT

STRADIVARI – various cals., unique "shorty" bullpup configuration utilizing a break open single-shot action and pivoting wood buttstock that opens/closes breech, finger grooved pistol grip wood stock with short forend, scope is mounted on front portion of barrel, 19¾ in., 24 in., or 29 in. barrel with muzzleweight.

Please contact the manufacturer directly regarding U.S. importation and current pricing.

FAS

Current pistol manufacturer located in Milan, Italy. No current U.S. importation. Previously imported and distributed by Nygord Precision Products located in Prescott, AZ, and Mandall Shooting Supplies, located in Scottsdale, AZ. Previously imported by Beeman Precision Arms, Inc. located in Santa Rosa, CA and Osborne's located in Cheboygan, MI.

PISTOLS: SEMI-AUTO

MODEL 601 - .22 Short cal. only, competition pistol, 5½ in. barrel, 5 shot mag., wraparound match wood grips, 41½ oz.

	$1,025	$875	$695	$640	$565	$500	$450

Last MSR was $1,250.

MODEL 602 - .22 LR cal. only, competition pistol, 5.6 in. barrel, 5 shot mag., ergonomically designed match wood grips, 40 oz. Importation disc. 1994.

	$895	$800	$625	$600	$525	$475	$425

Last MSR was $1,100.

MODEL 603 - .32 S&W Wadcutter cal. only, competition pistol, 5.6 in. barrel, 5 shot mag., ergonomically designed adj. or non-adj. match wood grips, 40 oz.

	$975	$875	$695	$640	$565	$500	$450

Last MSR was $1,175.

Grading	100%	98%	95%	90%	80%	70%	60%

MODEL 607 - .22 LR cal. only, semi-auto competition pistol, similar to Model 602, except has removable barrel weights.

	$975	$875	$695	$640	$565	$500	$450

Last MSR was $1,175.

FEG

Current manufacturer located in Hungary (FEG stands for Fegyver es Gepgyar) since circa 1900. Currently imported and distributed K.B.I., Inc. located in Harrisburg, PA, and Century International Arms located in St. Albans, VT (see additional information under the Century International Arms in this text). Previously imported and distributed until 1998 by Interarms located in Alexandria, VA.

PISTOLS: SEMI-AUTO, INTERARMS IMPORTED

All FEG pistols were supplied with two mags.

MARK II AP22 - .22 LR cal., double action, 3.4 in. barrel, 8 shot mag., blue finish, black plastic grips, 23 oz. Imported 1997-98.

	$235	$200	$175	$160	$145	$130	$115

Last MSR was $269.

MARK II AP - .380 ACP cal., double action, patterned after the Walther PP, 3.9 in. barrel, 7 shot mag., blue finish, black plastic grips, 27 oz. Imported 1997-98.

	$235	$200	$175	$160	$145	$130	$115

Last MSR was $269.

MARK II APK - .380 ACP cal., similar to Mark II AP, except is patterned after the Walther PPK/S, 3.4 in. barrel, 7 shot mag., blue finish, black plastic grips, 25 oz. Imported 1997-98.

	$235	$200	$175	$160	$145	$130	$115

Last MSR was $269.

PISTOLS: SEMI-AUTO, RECENT IMPORTATION

In addition to the following imported models, FEG also makes additional models available mostly in Europe. Currently, these pistols include the RL61 (.22 LR cal.), the P9R/P9RK (9mm Para. cal.), AP9/APK9 (.380 ACP cal.), P9RZ Compact (9mm Para cal.), and the AC/ACK (.45 ACP cal.).

MODEL PMK-380 - .380 ACP cal., patterned after Walther PP, alloy frame, double action, 4 in. barrel, plastic grips with thumbrest, blued finish, 21 oz. Importation by K.B.I. began 1992.

MSR	$239	$205	$180	$160	$135	$120	$110	$100

MODEL SMC-380 - .380 ACP cal., double action semi-auto, patterned after Walther PPK, alloy frame, 3½ in. barrel, 6 shot mag., plastic grips with thumbrest, blue finish, 18½ oz. Importation by K.B.I. began 1993.

MSR	$239	$205	$180	$160	$135	$120	$110	$100

* **Model SMC-22** - .22 LR cal., 8 shot mag., otherwise similar to Model SMC-380. Importation disc. 1997.

	$210	$195	$180	$165	$150	$135	$115

Last MSR was $235.

Grading	100%	98%	95%	90%	80%	70%	60%

MODEL SMC-918 - 9x18 Makarov cal., double action, semi-auto, 7 shot mag. Importation disc. 1997.

	$210	$195	$180	$165	$150	$135	$115

Last MSR was $235.

MODEL R-9 - 9mm Para. cal., patterned after Browning Hi-Power, double action, 13 shot mag., blued finish, steel construction, checkered wood grips. Imported 1986-87 only.

	$275	$230	$200	$180	$165	$155	$145

Last MSR was $375.

MODEL PPH - .380 ACP cal., patterned after Walther PP, alloy frame, double action, plastic grips with thumbrest, blued finish. Imported 1986-87 only.

	$200	$170	$140	$125	$115	$105	$95

Last MSR was $225.

MODEL MBK-9HP - 9mm Para. cal., patterned after Browning Hi-Power, double action, 4 2/3 in. barrel, 14 shot mag., blued finish, steel construction, checkered wood grips, 36 oz. Imported 1992 only.

	$315	$270	$250	$225	$200	$185	$170

Last MSR was $349.

✳ Model MBK-9HPC - compact variation of the Model MBK-9HP with 4 in. barrel, 34 oz. Imported 1992 only.

	$325	$275	$250	$225	$200	$185	$170

Last MSR was $359.

MODEL PJK-9HP - 9mm Para. cal., patterned after Browning Hi-Power, single action, all steel construction, 4¾ in. barrel, thumb safety, 10 (C/B 1994) or 13* shot mag. and cleaning rod, 32 oz. Importation by K.B.I. began 1992.

MSR	$295		$250	$225	$195	$175	$150	$130	$120

Add approx. $60 for industrial hard chrome finish (Model PJK-9HPC - includes Uncle Mike's rubber grips, disc. 1999).

MODEL GKK-92C - 9mm Para. cal., double action semi-auto, 4 in. barrel, 14 shot mag., improved variation of MBK models, includes same accessories as PJK-9H, 34 oz. Importation disc. 1993.

	$315	$280	$255	$230	$200	$185	$170

Last MSR was $369.

MODEL GKK-40C - .40 S&W cal., 9 shot mag., otherwise similar to GKK-45. Imported 1995-96.

	$300	$265	$230	$200	$180	$160	$145

Last MSR was $349.

MODEL GKK-45 - .45 ACP cal., double action semi-auto, all steel, 4¼ in. barrel, blue (disc. 1994) or chrome (Model GKK-45C) finish checkered walnut grips, 8 shot mag., approx. 37 oz. Imported 1993-96.

	$300	$265	$230	$200	$180	$160	$145

Last MSR was $349.

RIFLES: SEMI-AUTO

MODEL SA-85M - 7.62x39mm cal., sporter rifle utilizing AKM action, 16.3 in. barrel, 6 shot detachable mag., thumbhole stock, 7 lbs. 10 oz. Imported 1991, banned 1998.

	$350	$315	$280	$250	$225	$200	$185

Last MSR was $429.

Grading	100%	98%	95%	90%	80%	70%	60%

SA-2000M - .223 Rem. or 7.62x39mm cal., sporter rifle with skeletonized Choate synthetic stock, 17¾ in. barrel with muzzle brake, 10 shot detachable mag. Imported 1999- 2000.

	$330	$285	$250	$225	$200	$185	$170

Last MSR was $365.

    Add approx. $100 for .223 Rem. cal.

FIAS

Current long gun and related components manufacturer located in Brescia, Italy. FIAS is an abbreviation for Fabbrica Italiana Armi Sabatti. No current U.S. importation. Please contact FIAS directly (see listing in Trademark Index) to obtain current information on their models and prices.

FIAS belongs to the Sabatti family, and is based in Gardone VT, Brescia. Both companies produce SxS and O/U shotguns and rifles, in addition to providing local gunmakers with many components.

F.I.E.

Previous importer (F.I.E. is the acronym for Firearms Import & Export) located in Hialeah, FL until 1990.

F.I.E. filed bankruptcy in November of 1990 and all models are discontinued. Some parts or service for these older firearms may be obtained through Heritage Manufacturing, Inc. located in Opa Locka, FL or Gun Parts Corp. located in (see Trademark Index), even though all warranties on F.I.E. guns are void.

DERRINGERS

MODEL D38 - .38 Spl. cal., O/U, chrome finish only, no transfer bar. Disc. 1985.

	$70	$60	$55	$45	$40	$35	$30

Last MSR was $82.

    Add $17 for walnut grips.

MODEL D86 - .38 Spl. cal., single shot, 3 in. barrel, internal transfer bar safety, ammo storage compartment, blue or Dyna-chrome finish, 11 oz. Mfg. 1986 - disc.

	$80	$65	$55	$50	$45	$40	$35

Last MSR was $95.

    Add $9 for Dyna-chrome finish.
    Add $25 for deluxe model (walnut stocks).
    Add $60 for Misty Gold finish (disc.).

PISTOLS: SEMI-AUTO, TITAN SERIES

TITAN II (E32 SERIES) - .32 ACP (disc. 1988), or .380 ACP, single action, blue (standard) or chrome finish. Mfg. in USA - disc.

	$195	$160	$135	$120	$105	$95	$85

Last MSR was $220.

    Add $25 for walnut grips.
    Add $10 for chrome finish.

This series was redesigned in 1988 to be shorter and more compact. Older series Titans are worth approx. $50 less than values shown above.

SUPER TITAN II - .32 ACP (disc. 1988), or .380 ACP cal., single action, 12 shot mag. in .32 ACP, 11 for .380 cal., walnut grips, standard blue only. Mfg. U.S. - disc.

	$215	$185	$155	$135	$120	$105	$95

Last MSR was $260.

Grading	100%	98%	95%	90%	80%	70%	60%

.22 TITAN II (E22) - .22 LR cal., single action, 10 shot mag., blue finish only. Walnut grips standard. Mfg. 1990 only.

	$130	$105	$90	$80	$70	$65	$60

Last MSR was $161.

✳ *Lady .22* - similar to .22 TITAN II except has combination blue/gold finish with scrimshawed red rose on ivory polymer grips. New 1990.

	$185	$155	$130	$120	$105	$95	$85

Last MSR was $208.

THE BEST (A27) - .25 ACP cal., single action, blue only, deluxe finish, walnut grips, steel frame, 6 shot mag. Mfg. in Spain by Astra. Importation disc. 1988.

	$125	$105	$90	$80	$70	$65	$60

Last MSR was $155.

.25 TITAN (E27 SERIES) - .25 ACP cal., single action, blue (disc. 1989) or Dyna- chrome finish (standard 1990).

	$60	$50	$45	$40	$35	$30	$30

Last MSR was $77.

Subtract $5 for blued finish.
Add $26 for gold trim (new 1986).
Add $62 for Misty Gold finish (1988 only).

✳ *Titan Tigress* - similar to .25 Titan except is entirely gold plated and cased, ladies pistol. Imported 1989-90 only.

	$130	$110	$95				

Last MSR was $153.

.25 TITAN (E38 SERIES) - .25 ACP cal., similar to E27 series except has standard blue finish. Mfg. 1990 only.

	$50	$45	$40	$35	$30	$30	$25

Last MSR was $59.

Add $9 for Dyna-chrome finish.

SSP SERIES - .32 ACP or .380 ACP cal., single action semi-auto, 3 1/8 in. barrel, 5 shot mag., blue or chrome finish, composition grips, 25 oz. Mfg. in U.S. - 1990 only.

	$120	$95	$85	$75	$65	$60	$55

Last MSR was $146.

Add $19 for chrome finish.

✳ *Lady SSP* - similar to SSP except has gold trimmed parts, scrimshawed red rose on ivory polymer grips, and gold case. Mfg. 1990 only.

	$210	$180	$155	$135	$120	$105	$95

Last MSR was $250.

TZ-75 - 9mm Para. cal., double action, 4.72 in. barrel, steel frame and slide, 15 shot mag., patterned after the CZ-75 action, 35 oz. Imported 1982-1989. This model was updated in 1988 (Series 88).

	$375	$325	$290	$270	$250	$235	$220

Last MSR was $440.

Add $20 for satin chrome finish (new 1986).
Add $20 for black rubber grips.

TZ-75 SERIES 88 - 9mm Para. or .41 Action Express cal., improved TZ-75 action, 4.72 in. barrel, steel frame and slide, 11 (.41 AE) or 17 (9mm Para.) shot mag., fixed removable rear sight, choice of matte blue, satin chrome, or blue slide/chrome frame finish, updated CZ-75 action, 35 oz. Mfg. 1988-90.

	$435	$360	$330	$295	$280	$260	$240

Last MSR was $519.

Grading	100%	98%	95%	90%	80%	70%	60%

Add $97 for .41 Action Express cal.

Add $20 for satin chrome on 9mm Para., $29 on .41 AE.

Add $14 for black rubber grips.

This model was also available with a blue slide/chrome frame (I.P.S.C. configuration) at no extra charge.

The TZ-75 Series 88 was re-engineered in 1988 to include: frame mounted sear locking safety (cocked and locked), Colt style firing pin safety block, improved recessed slide serrations, muzzle barrel swell, bobbed hammer design, elongated combat style slide stop, new mag. release, and removable rear sight.

* **TZ-75 Combo** - includes both .41 Action Express and 9mm Para. barrels. Mfg. 1990 only.

	$615	$535	$475	$430	$395	$370	$350

Last MSR was $709.

Add $29 for satin chrome or blue slide/chrome frame finish.

* **TZ-75 Series 88 Govt. Model** - 9mm Para. cal. only, compact variation of the TZ-75 Series 88, 3 3/5 in. barrel, 12 shot mag., checkered walnut grips, 33½ oz. Mfg. 1990 only.

	$435	$360	$330	$295	$280	$260	$240

Last MSR was $519.

Add $20 for satin chrome or blue slide/chrome frame finish.

* **TZ-75 Series 88 with ported barrel** - similar to the TZ-75 Series 88 except has 5 in. ported barrel and slide. Mfg. 1990 only.

	$615	$535	$475	$430	$395	$370	$350

Last MSR was $709.

* **Compensated TZ-75 Series 88** - similar to the TZ-75 Series 88 except has 5¾ in. compensated barrel, 42 oz. Mfg. 1990 only.

	$700	$615	$535	$475	$430	$395	$370

Last MSR was $804.

MODEL 722 TP SILHOUETTE PISTOL - .22 LR cal., bolt action target pistol, 10 in. free-floating barrel, 4-way adj. trigger, micro adj. rear sight, 6 or 10 shot mag., stippled pistol grip and forearm, supplied with 2-piece scope mount, 3.4 lbs. Mfg. 1990 only.

	$220	$190	$160	$140	$125	$115	$100

Last MSR was $263.

SPECTRE PISTOL - 9mm Para. or .45 ACP cal., double action, unique triple action blowback system with two piece bolt, 6 in. barrel, military style configuration, adj. sights, 30 or 50 (optional with unique 4 column configuation) shot mag., 4.8 lbs. Mfg. 1989-90 only.

	$675	$600	$525	$480	$440	$400	$360

Last MSR was $718.

Add $14 for mag. loading tool.

KG-99 - 9mm Para. cal., paramilitary design pistol, 36 shot mag. Mini-99 also available with 20 shot mag. and 3 in. barrel. Disc. 1984.

	$550	$475	$440	$400	$365	$330	$300

This model was not manufactured but sold by F.I.E.

REVOLVERS: DOUBLE ACTION, ARMINIUS SERIES

All pistols under this heading were manufactured in W. Germany under the trademark Arminius. .22 cal. is 8 shot, .32 S&W is 7 shot, all others 6 shot.

MODEL 522TB - .22 LR cal., blue finish, 4 in. barrel, 8 shot.

	$130	$100	$85	$75	$70	$65	$60

Last MSR was $174.

Add $23 for walnut grips.

Grading	100%	98%	95%	90%	80%	70%	60%

722 SERIES - .22 LR cal., blue (standard) or chrome finish (disc. 1985), 6 in. barrel, 8 shot.

	$125	$100	$90	$80	$70	$65	$60

Last MSR was $161.

> **Add $23 for walnut grips.**
> **Add $49 for .22 LR/.22 Mag. combo.**
> **Add $15 for chrome finish.**

STANDARD REVOLVER - .22 LR, .22 Mag., .32 Mag. or .38 Spl. cal., 2 or 4 in. barrel, blued finish, fixed sights, without ejector assembly. U.S. mfg. 1989-90.

	$80	$70	$65	$60	$55	$50	$45

Last MSR was $101.

> **Add $19 for chrome finish (2 in. barrel only).**
> **Add $38 for gold plated finish (2 in. barrel only).**
> **Add $23 for .22 Combo package (2 cylinders - 4 in. barrel only).**
> Models with 4 in. barrels were available in blued finish only.

MODEL 532TB - .32 S&W cal., blue (standard) or chrome finish (disc. 1985), adj. sights, 4 in. barrel, 7 shot.

	$145	$120	$100	$80	$75	$70	$65

Last MSR was $183.

> **Add $23 for walnut grips.**
> **Add $15 for chrome finish.**

MODEL 732B - similar to Model 532TB, except has 6 in. barrel and fixed sights. Imported 1988 only.

	$120	$100	$90	$80	$70	$65	$60

Last MSR was $140.

MODEL N-38 (TITAN TIGER) - .38 Spl. cal., blue (standard) or chrome finish (disc. 1985), 2 or 4 in. barrel, fixed sights. Disc. 1990.

	$130	$110	$95	$80	$75	$65	$60

Last MSR was $176.

> **Add $23 for walnut grips.**
> **Add $15 for chrome finish.**

ZEPHYR - .38 Spl. cal., 5 shot, aluminum construction, 2 in. barrel, blue finish, checkered grips, 14 oz. Mfg. 1990 only.

	$145	$120	$100	$80	$75	$70	$65

Last MSR was $189.

✴ *Lady Zephyr* - similar to Zephyr, except has gold trimmed parts, scrimshawed red rose on ivory polymer grips, and gold case. Mfg. 1990 only.

	$250	$210	$180	$155	$135	$115	$95

Last MSR was $295.

MODEL 384TB - .38 Spl. cal., blue (standard) or chrome finish (disc. 1985), 6 shot, 4 in. barrel.

	$150	$125	$105	$85	$80	$70	$65

Last MSR was $195.

> **Add $23 for walnut grips.**
> **Add $13 for chrome finish.**

MODEL 386TB - .38 Spl. cal., blue (standard) or chrome finish (disc. 1985), 6 shot, 6 in. barrel.

	$150	$125	$105	$85	$80	$70	$65

Last MSR was $195.

> **Add $23 for walnut grips.**
> **Add $13 for chrome finish.**

Grading	100%	98%	95%	90%	80%	70%	60%

.357 MAG. SERIES - .357 Mag. cal., blue (standard) or chrome finish (disc. 1985), 6 shot, 3 (Model 3573TB), 4 (Model 3574TB), or 6 (Model 3576TB) in. barrels.

	$200	$170	$135	$120	$110	$100	$90

Last MSR was $255.

Add $23 for walnut grips.
Add $15 for chrome finish.

Revolvers: Double Action, Snub-Nose

Previously manufactured 2 in. snub-nosed revolvers are listed in the previous category under Standard Revolver, Titan Tiger, and Zephyr.

222 SERIES - .22 LR & .22 Mag. cal., blue (standard) or chrome finish, 2 in. snub-nose barrel. Disc. 1985.

	$135	$115	$90	$85	$75	$65	$60

Last MSR was $120.

Add $15 for walnut grips.
Add $45 for .22 LR/.22 Mag. combo.

* **222B SERIES** - .22 LR cal. only 1989, similar to 222 Series. Reintroduced 1987- 1989.

	$150	$120	$105	$85	$80	$70	$65

Last MSR was $185.

Add $45 for .22 LR/.22 Mag. combo (disc. 1988).

232 SERIES - .32 S&W cal., blue (standard) or chrome finish, 2 in. barrel. Disc.

	$120	$90	$85	$75	$65	$60	$55

Add $15 for walnut grips.
Add $14 for adj. sights.
Add $28 for chrome finish.

* **232B SERIES** - similar to 232 Series, 2 in. barrel. Reintroduced 1987-1989.

	$150	$125	$110	$95	$85	$75	$70

Last MSR was $185.

Add $5 for adj. sights.

MODEL 382TB - .38 Spl. cal., blue (standard) or chrome finish, 2 in. barrel. Disc. 1985.

	$125	$110	$100	$90	$80	$75	$65

Last MSR was $145.

Add $15 for walnut grips.
Add $16 for chrome finish.

MODEL 3572 - .357 Mag. cal., blue (standard) or chrome finish, 2 in. barrel. Disc. 1984.

	$223	$170	$160	$135	$125	$115	$100

Add $15 for walnut grips.
Add $17 for chrome finish.

REVOLVERS: SINGLE ACTION

Combo designations on the following models indicate 2 cylinders (.22 LR/.22 Mag.).

COWBOY - .22 LR or .22 LR/Mag. cal. combo, 3¼ or 6 in. barrel, blued finish, square butt grip, without ejector tube, fixed sights. U.S. mfg. 1989-90.

	$75	$65	$50	$45	$40	$35	$30

Last MSR was $95.

Add $23 for combo.

Grading	100%	98%	95%	90%	80%	70%	60%

GOLD RUSH - .22 LR or .22 LR/Mag. cal. combo, 3¼, 4¾, or 6½ in. barrel, round (3¼ in. barrel only) or square butt grip, gold band on barrel and cylinder, ivory-tex grips. U.S. mfg. 1989-90.

	$155	$125	$110	$95	$85	$75	$70

Last MSR was $189.

Add $47 for combo.

TEXAS RANGER (TEX 22 SERIES) - .22 LR or .22 Mag. cal.(combo only), 3¼ (new 1986), 4¾, 6½ (new 1989), 7, or 9 in. barrel, 6 shot, blue only. U.S. mfg. - disc.

	$80	$70	$60	$50	$45	$40	$35

Last MSR was $108.

Add $23 for combo.
Add $6 for 9 in. barrel.
This model with a 3¼ in. barrel is called the Little Ranger.

BUFFALO SCOUT (E15 SERIES) - .22 LR or .22 Mag. cal., blue (standard) or chrome finish, 4¾ in. barrel. Mfg. in Brescia, Italy - disc.

	$75	$55	$45	$35	$35	$30	$30

Last MSR was $98.

Add $23 for walnut grips.
Add $23 for combo.
Add $9 for chrome or blue/gold finish.

✻ *The Yellow Rose Combo* - all metal parts 24 Kt. gold plated, smooth walnut grips. Mfg. 1986-90.

	$130	$110	$95				

Last MSR was $161.

Add $151 for scrimshawed ivory polymer grips - walnut cased (new 1989).

LEGEND SAA (PL-22 SERIES) - .22 LR or .22 Mag. cal., blue only. Mfg. in Brescia, Italy. Disc. 1984.

	$120	$90	$85	$75	$65	$60	$55

Add $3 for walnut grips.
Add $17 for combo.

HOMBRE MODEL - .357 Mag., .44 Mag., or .45 LC cal., color case hardened receiver, 5½ (disc. 1985), 6, or 7½ in. barrel, 45 oz., smooth walnut grips. Previously mfg. W. Germany.

	$220	$180	$145	$130	$120	$110	$100

Last MSR was $265.

Add $25 for brass back strap and trigger guard (disc.).

✻ *Golden Hombre* - same general specifications as Hombre, except all metal surfaces are plated in 24 Kt. gold.

	$300	$210	$145				

Last MSR was $350.

Add $65 for ivory polymer grips (new 1989).

RIFLES: BOLT-ACTION

MODEL 122 - .22 LR cal., 6 or 10 shot box mag., 21 in. tapered barrel, Monte Carlo walnut stock, adj. sights. Mfg. by Hamilton & Hunter. Mfg. 1986-disc.

	$100	$80	$70	$60	$55	$50	$45

Last MSR was $115.

MODEL 322 - .22 LR cal., competition model, 26.2 in. floating barrel, adj. trigger, 6 or 10 shot mag., stippled pistol grip, 7 lbs. Mfg. 1990-disc.

	$580	$425	$380	$340	$295	$260	$230

Last MSR was $665.

Grading	100%	98%	95%	90%	80%	70%	60%

MODEL 422 - similar to Model 322 except has heavy barrel, 9 lbs. Mfg. 1990-disc.

| | $580 | $425 | $380 | $340 | $295 | $260 | $230 |

Last MSR was $665.

RIFLES: SEMI-AUTO

GR-8 BLACK BEAUTY - .22 LR cal., 14 shot, 19½ in. barrel, 64 oz., tubular feed, black nylon stock, patterned after Rem. Nylon 66. Mfg. by C.B.C. of Brazil. F.I.E. Importation disc. 1988.

| | $90 | $75 | $70 | $65 | $60 | $55 | $50 |

Last MSR was $100.

PARA RIFLE - .22 LR cal., paramilitary designed rifle with tube stock (is also magazine), includes green cloth case with white stenciled letters, takedown, 11 shot mag., matte black receiver finish, approx. 4 lbs. Mfg. by L. Franchi between 1979-1984. Imported into the U.S. from 1985-88.

| | $250 | $225 | $195 | $155 | $130 | $110 | $95 |

Last MSR was $225.

8,000 of this model were manufactured by L. Franchi. 5,000 went to the Italian Government and were used as training rifles (with German scopes). The remainder were imported by F.I.E. (without scopes).

SPECTRE CARBINE - 9mm Para. cal., same action as Spectre pistol, paramilitary design carbine, collapsible metal butt stock, 30 or 50 (opt.) shot mag., adj. rear sight, with pistol and forearm grip. Mfg. 1989 - disc.

| | $525 | $425 | $365 | $300 | $275 | $250 | $225 |

Last MSR was $700.

SHOTGUNS

All currently manufactured Franchi shotguns can be located in the Franchi section of this text.

S.O.B. - 12, 20 ga., or .410 bore, 18½ in. single barrel, pistol grip only. Disc. 1984.

| | $100 | $90 | $80 | $70 | $60 | $55 | $50 |

THE STURDY O/U - 12 or 20 ga., 3 in. chambers, 28 in. barrels, vent. rib and barrels, engraved silver finish receiver, double triggers, extractors, manufactured by Maroccini of Italy. Imported 1985-1988.

| | $300 | $275 | $250 | $235 | $220 | $205 | $190 |

Last MSR was $350.

✴ **Sturdy Deluxe Priti** - similar to The Sturdy model except has deluxe walnut. Importation disc. 1988.

| | $325 | $290 | $260 | $240 | $225 | $205 | $195 |

Last MSR was $380.

Add $70 for ejectors, SST, and choke tubes.

✴ **Model 12 Deluxe** - 12 ga. only, SST, auto ejectors, multi-choked barrels, select walnut. Imported 1988 only.

| | $320 | $290 | $260 | $240 | $225 | $205 | $195 |

Last MSR was $380.

THE BRUTE - 12, 20 ga, or .410 bore, 19 in. barrels, 30 in. overall length. Side-by-side action, disc. 1984.

| | $195 | $150 | $140 | $120 | $110 | $100 | $90 |

SPAS-12 - this model appears under the Franchi heading in the F section.

SAS-12 - this model appears under the Franchi heading in the F section.

Grading	100%	98%	95%	90%	80%	70%	60%

LAW-12 - this model appears under the Franchi heading in the F section.

FMJ

Previous manufacturer located in Copperhill, TN, until circa 1998.

Little information is available regarding FMJ firearms (including short barrel derringers and pistols), except they were inexpensive shooters and are not collectible. Their production records were turned in to the BATF during 1998.

FTL

Previously manufactured by Wilkinson Arms located in Covina, CA for the FTL Marketing Corp. located in N. Hollywood, CA.

PISTOLS: SEMI-AUTO

FTL AUTO NINE - .22 LR cal., single action, hammerless, blowback action, 8 shot mag., checkered plastic grips, fixed sights. Disc.

$200	$160	$125	$105	$95	$85	$75

FABARM, S.p.A.

Current manufacturer established in 1900 and located in Brescia, Italy. Currently imported and distributed by Heckler & Koch, Inc. beginning 1998. Certain models had limited importation by Ithaca Acquisition Corp. located in King Ferry, NY during 1993-95. Previously imported and distributed (1988-90) by St. Lawrence Sales, Inc. located in Lake Orion, MI. Previously imported until 1986 by Beeman Precision Arms, Inc. located in Santa Rosa, CA.

Fabarm currently manufactures approx. 35,000 shotguns annually.

SHOTGUNS: O/U

FIELD MODEL- 12 ga. only, 29 1/8 in. VR barrels, single trigger, ejectors, silver finished receiver, also available in Skeet and Trap models. Disc. 1985.

$695	$595	$550	$500	$460	$420	$390

Last MSR was $795.

SKEET/TRAP COMBINATION SET - 12 ga. only, is supplied with both skeet and trap barrel assemblies, cased. Disc. 1986.

$1,050	$900	$840	$780	$720	$670	$600

Last MSR was $1,195.

Add $39 for high gloss wood finish.
Add $30 for auto safety.

The following models have boxlock actions with coin finished receivers and light engraving.

GAMMA FIELD - 12 or 20 (disc.) ga., SST, ejectors, 26, 28, 29, 30, or 32 in. VR barrels, fixed or innerchokes, checkered walnut stock and forearm, 6½ lbs. Imported 1989-95.

$840	$715	$660	$600	$550	$450	$375

Last MSR was $1,044.

Add $28 for 5 innerchokes with wrench (3 in. chambers in 12 ga.).
Add $50 for 20 ga. (3 in. chambers).

* **Gamma AL Superlight** - 12 ga. only, similar to Gamma Field except receiver is made from Ergal light alloy, 6 lbs. Imported 1989-1990.

$875	$760	$695	$625	$550	$450	$375

Last MSR was $970.

Add $41 for 5 innerchokes with wrench.
Add $66 for 20 ga. with 3 in. chambers. New 1990.

This model is chambered for 2¾ in. shells only.

Grading	100%	98%	95%	90%	80%	70%	60%

GAMMA SPORTING CLAYS COMPETITION - 12 ga. only, designed for sporting clays competition, SST, 28, 29, or 30 in. VR, (10mm) and barrels supplied with 5 innerchokes, special recoil pad, ejectors, checkered walnut stock and forearm. Imported 1989- 95.

	$950	$825	$725	$650	$575	$495	$400

Last MSR was $1,175.

Add $17 for trap stock and forearm (disc. - includes 28 in. barrels with 5 choke tubes).

GAMMA SKEET - 12 ga. only, 27½ or 28 in. VR barrels, SST, ejectors, supplied with 5 innerchokes, special recoil pad, checkered walnut stock and forearm, reversed Skeet chokes new 1994. Imported 1989-95.

	$875	$735	$695	$635	$550	$450	$375

Last MSR was $1,107.

GAMMA TRAP - 12 ga. only, 29 or 30 in. VR barrels with special trap chokes and 10mm rib, SST, ejectors, checkered Monte Carlo stock and forearm, 7½ lbs. Imported 1989- 95.

	$875	$735	$695	$635	$550	$450	$375

Last MSR was $1,107.

GAMMA PARADOX - 12 ga. only, 25 in. VR barrels with top barrel rifled and lower barrel supplied with 3 innerchokes, SST, ejectors, checkered walnut stock and forearm, 6 lbs. 6 oz. Imported 1989-1990.

	$850	$750	$695	$625	$550	$450	$375

Last MSR was $945.

* *Gamma Paradox AL Superlight* - similar to Gamma Paradox except receiver is made from Ergal light alloy, 5 lbs. 7 oz. Imported 1989-1990.

	$875	$760	$695	$625	$550	$450	$375

Last MSR was $960.

EURALFA - 12 ga., 2¾ in. chambers, 26 or 28 in. VR barrels with fixed chokes, DT or SNT, extractors, blued receiver with photo engraving, 6½ lbs. Imported 1989-1990.

	$495	$460	$420	$390	$350	$310	$275

Last MSR was $571.

* *Euralfa AL Superlight* - 12 ga., similar to Euralfa except receiver is made from Ergal light alloy, 6 lbs. Imported 1989-1990.

	$515	$475	$430	$400	$360	$320	$285

Last MSR was $603.

* *Euralfa Trap* - 12 ga. only, 3 in. chambers, 30 in. barrels bored IM/F. Imported 1990.

	$550	$495	$460	$430	$400	$360	$320

Last MSR was $636.

* *Euralfa Magnum* - 12 ga., 3 in. chambers, 26, 28, or 29 in. VR (10mm wide) barrels with fixed chokes, rubber recoil pad. Imported 1989-1990.

	$515	$475	$430	$400	$360	$320	$285

Last MSR was $587.

* *Euralfa Innerchoke* - 12 ga. only, 3 in. chambers, 28 in. barrels. Imported 1990 only.

	$560	$500	$460	$430	$400	$360	$320

Last MSR was $652.

* *Euralfa Slug* - 12 ga. only, 24 in. barrels bored cyl./cyl. Imported 1990.

	$500	$475	$430	$400	$360	$320	$285

Last MSR was $571.

EURALFA PARADOX - 12 ga. only, similar to Euralfa except 25 in. VR barrels with top barrel rifled and lower barrel supplied with 3 innerchokes, 6 lbs. 6 oz. Imported 1989- 1990.

	$550	$495	$460	$430	$400	$360	$320

Last MSR was $636.

F

Grading	100%	98%	95%	90%	80%	70%	60%

✻ **Euralfa Paradox AL Superlight** - similar to Euralfa Paradox except receiver is made from Ergal light alloy, 5 lbs. 7 oz. Imported 1989-1990.

	$550	**$495**	**$460**	**$430**	**$400**	**$360**	**$320**

Last MSR was $636.

SILVER LION - 12 or 20 ga., similar to Max Lion, except has standard wood and lockable hard plastic case, ported 26 in. TriBore barrels became optional during 1999, standard in 2000, 6.8-7.7 lbs. Importation began 1998.

MSR	**$1,299**	**$1,125**	**$975**	**$850**	**$725**	**$600**	**$500**	**$400**

Subtract 10% if w/o TriBore system barrels.

✻ **Silver Lion Cub Model** - similar to Silver Lion, except has youth dimensions, steel receiver, ported 24 in. TriBore vent. barrels standard, mid rib bead, approx. 6 lbs. New 1999.

MSR	**$1,299**	**$1,125**	**$975**	**$850**	**$725**	**$600**	**$500**	**$400**

ULTRA MAG LION - 12 ga. only, 3½ in. chambers, 28 in. standard or ported TriBore (new 1999) barrels, choice of non-glare matte metal finish (disc. 2000) or 100% Advantage Wetlands camo coverage, black colored walnut stock and forearm, non-automatic ejectors, 7.9 lbs., includes lockable plastic case. Importation began 1998.

MSR	**$1,299**	**$1,125**	**$975**	**$850**	**$725**	**$600**	**$525**	**$450**

CAMO TURKEY MODEL - 12 ga. only, 3½ in. chambers, 20 in. separated barrels, unique Picatinny rail on top of receiver allows convenient scope mounting, 100% Advantage extra brown camo coverage, includes two ultra-full ported choke tubes, locking fitted luggage case, approx. 7½ lbs. Imported 1999-2000, reintroduced 2002.

MSR	**$1,199**	**$995**	**$875**	**$775**	**$700**	**$600**	**$550**	**$500**

SUPER LIGHT LION - 12 ga. only, 3 in. chambers, lightweight alloy receiver, blue finish, 24 in. vent. standard (disc. 1999) or ported TriBore (new 1999, standard 2000) barrels with VR, standard checkered walnut stock and forearm, includes lockable hard plastic case, 6½ lbs. Imported 1998-2000.

	$975	**$850**	**$775**	**$700**	**$600**	**$550**	**$500**

Last MSR was $1,159.

Subtract $100 if w/o ported TriBore barrels (disc. 1999).

✻ **Super Light Lion Cub (Youth) Model** - similar to Silver Lion Youth Model, except has Ergal 55 aluminum receiver, approx. 5¾ lbs. Imported 1999-2000.

	$925	**$825**	**$765**	**$685**	**$600**	**$550**	**$500**

Last MSR was $1,099.

SPORTING CLAYS COMPETITION LION - 12 or 20 ga., 3 in. chambers, 28 or 30 (12 ga. only, new 2000) in. vent. ported TriBore barrels with 10mm VR, recoil reducer in buttstock, checkered walnut stock and forearm, adj. SST, includes locking fitted luggage case. Importation began 1999.

	$1,185	**$1,025**	**$875**	**$745**	**$630**	**$525**	**$425**

Last MSR was $1,419.

✻ **Sporting Clays Competition Lion Extra** - 12 ga. only, 28 or 30 in. ported TriBore VR barrels, regular walnut or black competition checkered stock and forearm, adj. cheekpiece, 100% carbon fiber metal finish, includes 8 choke tubes, locking fitted luggage case, approx. 7.8 lbs. New 2000.

MSR	**$1,749**	**$1,575**	**$1,325**	**$1,100**	**$900**	**$825**	**$750**	**$675**

Grading	100%	98%	95%	90%	80%	70%	60%

BLACK LION COMPETITION - 12 or 20 ga., competition model featuring blued receiver, 26, 28, or 30 (12 ga. only) in. vent. standard or ported TriBore (new 1999) barrels with VR, deluxe checkered wood, 6.8-7.8 lbs. Imported 1998-99.

		$1,300	$1,025	$875	$775	$675	$600	$550

Last MSR was $1,529.

Add $66 for ported TriBore barrels.

MAX LION - 12 or 20 ga., 3 in. chambers, engraved boxlock action with nickel finish, 26, 28, or 30 (12 ga. only) in. vent. standard (disc. 1999) or ported TriBore (new 1999, standard 2000) barrels with VR, rebounding hammers, deluxe checkered stock and forearm, with vent. recoil pad, choke tubes, gold SST, non-automatic safety, includes locking fitted luggage case, 6.8-7.8 lbs. Importation began 1998.

MSR	$1,899		$1,695	$1,425	$1,200	$975	$850	$750	$675

Subtract $100 if w/o ported TriBore barrels (disc. 1999).

✷ ***Max Lion Light*** - 12 or 20 (new 2001) ga., similar to Max Lion, except has 24 (disc. 2000, reintroduced 2002) or 26 (mfg. 2001 only) in. barrels with TriBore system and gold game birds on satin finished receiver sides, 7-7.2 lbs. New 2000.

MSR	$1,899		$1,695	$1,425	$1,200	$975	$850	$750	$675

✷ ***Max Lion Paradox*** - 12 or 20 ga., features 24 in. upper smoothbore barrel with TriBore and lower barrel with paradox rifling, case colored receiver, select walnut, sling studs, 7.6 lbs. New 2002.

MSR	$1,199		$1,050	$900	$800	$700	$625	$550	$500

SHOTGUNS: SxS

The following models have boxlock actions with added sideplates.

BETA MODEL - 12 ga. only, 2¾ in. chambers, standard model with checkered walnut stock and forearm, ST, ejectors. Imported 1989 only.

		$695	$625	$550	$450	$375	$300	$250

Last MSR was $920.

This model was replaced by the Beta Lux in 1990.

BETA LUX - 12 ga. only, 3 in. chambers, SST, ejectors, boxlock action, 24, 26, 28, or 30 in. barrels bored F/M, 6.6 lbs. Imported 1990-95.

		$1,100	$875	$725	$625	$550	$475	$400

Last MSR was $1,270.

Add $30 for 5 Innerchokes.
Add $114 for competition trap/pigeon model (disc.).

BETA EUROPE - 12 ga. only, deluxe model with coin finished game scene engraved sideplates, 26½ or 27½ in. barrels with fixed chokes, ejectors, DT or SST, checkered English stock and splinter forearm, 6 lbs. 6 oz. Imported 1989-1990.

		$1,400	$1,100	$850	$700	$575	$495	$450

Last MSR was $1,711.

Add $33 for semi-beavertail forend.
Add $130 for competition trap/pigeon model.

CLASSIC LION - 12 ga. only, 3 in. chambers, boxlock action, SST or DT, ejectors, TriBore barrels with 5 choke tubes, approx. 7 lbs. Importation began 1998.

✷ ***Grade I*** - features standard grade wood, 26, 28, or 30 in. VR barrels, English (DT) or pistol grip (disc.) stock, engraved nickel finished receiver, gold SST.

MSR	$1,499		$1,250	$1,025	$800	$700	$625	$550	$500

Grading	100%	98%	95%	90%	80%	70%	60%

* *Grade II* - features deluxe wood and removable sideplates with engraving, SST, fitted lugage case.

	MSR	$2,249		$1,900	$1,525	$1,225	$950	$850	$750	$675

◇*Grade II Bill Hanus Birdgun Model* - similar to Grade II, except has best quality wood. New 2000.

	MSR	$2,599		$2,275	$1,925	$1,550	$1,225	$995	$875	$800

This model is available through Bill Hanus Birdguns, LLC only.

* *Classic Lion Elite* - features case colored receiver, DT, select checkered straight grip stock and splinter forearm, 26 or 28 in. fixed choke barrels, 7¾ lbs.

	MSR	$1,599		$1,325	$1,100	$850	$750	$650	$550	$500

SHOTGUNS: SEMI-AUTO

The following models are gas operated, self compensating, have 4 shot mags., aluminum receivers, twin action bars, blued receiver with photo etched game scene engraving, and checkered walnut stock and forearm.

Add $25 for De Luxe engraving or camouflage wood finish.

DEER GUN - 12 ga. only, 3 in. chamber, 24 in. rifled barrel with front and rear rifle sights, 5 shot mag., 7 lbs. Limited importation 1994-95.

	$695	$475	$425	$375	$325	$300	$285

Last MSR was $775.

ELLEGI STANDARD - 12 ga. only, 28 in. VR barrel with fixed choke, blued receiver, gold trigger, 6 lbs. 9 oz. Imported 1989-1990.

	$525	$450	$375	$325	$300	$275	$250

Last MSR was $619.

* *Ellegi Multichoke* - similar to Ellegi Standard except 5 different choke tubes extend length of barrel up to 6 in., average weight is 6 lbs. 9 oz. Imported 1989-1990.

	$540	$475	$395	$350	$325	$300	$265

Last MSR was $644.

The standard barrel length on this model is 24½ in. (30½ in. with full extra-long choke tube).

* *Ellegi Innerchoke* - 12 ga. only, 3 in. chamber, 28 in. VR barrel with 5 innerchokes supplied, 7 lbs. Imported 1989-1990.

	$540	$475	$395	$350	$325	$300	$265

Last MSR was $644.

* *Ellegi Magnum* - 12 ga. only, 3 in. chamber, 30 in. VR barrel with fixed choke, recoil pad, 7¼ lbs. Imported 1989-1990.

	$525	$450	$375	$325	$300	$275	$250

Last MSR was $619.

* *Ellegi Super Goose* - 12 ga. only, 3 in. chamber, 35½ in. VR (12mm wide) barrel with fixed choke, adj. rifle rear sight, supplied with rail for mounting scope rings, rubber recoil pad, designed especially for long range shooting, 7½ lbs. Imported 1989-1990.

	$625	$495	$425	$375	$340	$315	$280

Last MSR was $734.

* *Ellegi Slug* - 12 ga. only, 24½ in. barrel, adj. rear sight and bead front, 6 lbs. 9 oz. Imported 1989- 1990.

	$545	$475	$395	$350	$325	$300	$265

Last MSR was $652.

Add $200 for combo set (includes innerchoked 28 in. barrel).

Grading	100%	98%	95%	90%	80%	70%	60%

✳ Ellegi Police - 12 ga. only, 20 in. cylinder bored barrel, matte black receiver, non-glare stock and forearm. Imported 1989-1990.

	$495	$425	$360	$300	$275	$250	$225

Last MSR was $587.

TACTICAL SEMI-AUTO - 12 ga. only, 3 in. chamber, 20 in. barrel with TriBore choke system, tactical configuration with large cocking handle, oversized safety, black polymer stock and forearm, Picatinny rail with integral rear sight, 5 shot mag., 6.6 lbs. Importation began 2001.

MSR	$999		$865	$750	$650	$575	$515	$450	$400

RED LION MARK II - 12 ga. only, 3 in. chamber, gas operated, alloy receiver, 24, 26, or 28 in. VR standard (disc. 1999) or ported TriBore (standard 2000) barrel, matte finish, reversible safety (oversize beginning 2000), checkered walnut stock and forearm, red receiver logo, lockable plastic case, approx. 7 lbs. Imported 1998-2000.

	$710	$635	$550	$500	$450	$400	$360

Last MSR was $820.

During 2000, the model nomenclature changed to Red Lion Mark II.

GOLD LION MARK II - similar to Red Lion, except has select walnut stock with olive wood pistol grip cap, ported barrel, gold trigger and receiver logo. Importation began 1998.

MSR	$849		$750	$675	$595	$550	$500	$450	$400

During 2000, the model nomenclature changed to Gold Lion Mark II.

REX LION - 12 ga. only, limited edition of the Gold Lion Mark II, features black and silver finished receiver with gold medallions, checkered Turkish walnut stock, 26 or 28 in. barrel, 7¾ lbs. New 2002.

MSR	$1,049		$900	$775	$700	$625	$550	$500	$450

CAMO LION - 12 ga. only, 3 in. chamber, 20, 24, 26, or 28 in. ported TriBore VR barrel, features 100% Advantage Wetlands camo coverage, approx. 7 lbs. New 1999.

MSR	$979		$850	$725	$650	$575	$510	$450	$400

SPORTING CLAYS LION - 12 ga. only, 28 in. ported TriBore VR barrel, deluxe checkered walnut stock and forearm with olive wood pistol grip cap, matte finish with gold accents on receiver sides, approx. 7.2 lbs. Imported 1999-2000.

	$865	$745	$645	$565	$510	$450	$400

Last MSR was $999.

✳ Sporting Clays Lion Extra - similar to Sporting Clays Lion, 28 or 30 in. barrel, except has carbon fiber metal finish, stock recoil reducer, adj. cheekpiece on checkered walnut or black (new 2002) stock and forearm, includes 6 choke tubes and locking fitted luggage case. New 2000.

MSR	$1,249		$1,025	$895	$775	$695	$600	$550	$500

SHOTGUNS: SINGLE BARREL

The following models have receivers made out of aluminum alloy, rear trigger guard safety, and matte black finish metal surfaces.

OMEGA STANDARD - 12, 20 ga., or .410 bore, 3 in. chamber, 26 or 28 (12 ga. only) in. barrel, checkered beech stock and forearm, approx. 5 lbs. 5 oz. Imported 1989-1990.

	$120	$95	$80	$70	$60	$55	$50

Last MSR was $139.

✳ Goose Gun - 12 ga. only, similar to Omega Standard, except has a 35½ in. barrel, 6 lbs. Imported 1989-1990.

	$135	$115	$90	$80	$70	$60	$55

Last MSR was $156.

Grading	100%	98%	95%	90%	80%	70%	60%

MONOTRAP SHOTGUN - 12 ga. only, 2¾ in. chamber, lightweight 20 ga. frame with nickel finish, 30 (disc. 2001) or 34 (ported, new 2001) in. over single VR barrel with TriBore system and 3 competition choke tubes, adj. trigger, checkered walnut stock and forearm with adj. cheekpiece, recoil system, 6 lbs. New 2000.

MSR $1,799		$1,625	$1,375	$1,150	$950	$825	$725	$625

SHOTGUNS: SLIDE ACTION

The following models are variations of the same action based on a twin bar slide system, alloy receiver with anti-glare finish (including barrel), rear trigger guard safety, and 2¾ or 3 in. shell interchangeability.

Add $25 for camouflage wood finish on the following models.

MODEL S.D.A.S.S. - 12 ga. only, 3 in. chamber, originally designed for police and self defense use, 8 shot tube mag., 20 or 24½ in. barrel threaded for external choke tubes, approx. 6 lbs. 6 oz. Imported 1989-1990.

$325	$285	$260	$230	$195	$160	$140

Last MSR was $415.

This model with 24½ in. barrel is threaded for external multi-chokes which can add up to 6 in. to the barrel length - available for a $17 extra charge.

✳ *Special Police* - similar to Model S.D.A.S.S. except has special heavy 20 in. cylinder bored barrel, VR, cooling jacket, 6 shot mag., rubber recoil pad. Imported 1989- 1990.

$340	$295	$265	$230	$195	$160	$140

Last MSR was $440.

✳ *Martial* - 12 ga. only, 18, 20, 28, 30, or 35½ (disc. 1989) in. barrel, fixed sights and choke, approx. 6¼ lbs. Imported 1989-1990.

$330	$290	$260	$225	$190	$160	$140

Last MSR was $424.

Add $41 for VR.
Add $20 for 35½ (disc. 1989) in. barrel.
Add $33 for multi-choke (plain rib with 1 choke and wrench).
Add $65 for innerchoke (includes 1 choke and wrench - VR barrel only).

FP6 - 12 ga. only, 3 in. chamber, 20 or 28 (new 2001) in. barrel (non-ported TriBore system became standard 2000) with vent. heat shield, camo (new 2001), matte, or carbon fiber (new 2000) finished metal, 100% Mossy Oak camo (new 2001) or black synthetic stock and forearm, various security configurations, includes locking plastic case, 6½ - 7 lbs. Importation began 1998.

MSR $499		$430	$385	$350	$315	$285	$260	$240

Subtract $30 for 100% Mossy Oak Break-up camo coverage.
Subtract $100 for Field FPS with matte black finish and 28 in. barrel (new 2001).FABARM, S.p.A., cont.

FABBRI s.n.c.

Current manufacturer established during 1965, and currently located in Concesio, Italy (previously located in Brescia). The factory should be contacted directly (see Trademark Index) for more information regarding current information and prices on the following models.

Fabbri s.n.c. relocated from Brescia to Concesio during 1969 and underwent a name change from Armi Fabbri to Fabbri s.n.c. during 1989. Currently, Fabbri s.n.c. engravers include Creative Art, Pedersoli, Torcoli, and Francassi. Fabbri manufactures perhaps the highest quality shotguns available in today's marketplace - approx. 20-30 guns are mfg. annually. Delivery times range from 2- 4 years.

Grading	100%	98%	95%	90%	80%	70%	60%

SHOTGUNS: CUSTOM

SxS SHOTGUN - 12 or 20 ga., one of the world's best sidelock SxS shotguns, ejectors, full engraving, E prefix ser. no., two types of back action. Disc.

> Currently, Fabbri SxS shotguns manufactured within the last decade and in mint condition are priced in the $30,000-$38,500 range (type II). Subtract $15,000 for scroll engraving, and/or approx. 25% for type I action.

O/U SHOTGUN - 12 or 20 ga., top-of-the-line quality with advanced CNC metal fabrication, any combination of engraving, wood, and other options. Current retail starts at approx. $72,000 FOB Italy, w/o engraving.

> Mint guns mfg. 1967-1983 are currently priced in the $35,000-$38,500 range, guns mfg. between 1983-1989 are priced in the $50,000-$55,000 range, and mfg. within the last 10 years are currently priced in the $67,500 - $75,000 range. As a final note on Fabbri pricing - hook up the right gauge and engraver, and it's possible to pay $350,000 for one shotgun!

FABRIQUE NATIONALE

Current manufacturer located in Herstal, near Liege, Belgium. The current company name is "Group Herstal", however, the company is better known by "Fabrique Nationale" or Fabrique Nationale d'Armes de Guerre". FN established their first contract with John M. Browning in 1897 for the manufacture of their first pistol, the FN 1899 Model. Additional contracts were signed and the relationship further blossomed with the manufacture of the A-5 shotgun. FN was acquired by GIAT of France in 1992. In late 1997, the company was purchased by the Walloon government of Belgium. Additional production facilities are located in Portugal (assembly) and Japan.

Also See: Browning Arms under Rifles, Shotguns, and Pistols.

The author would like to express his sincere thanks to Anthony Vanderlinden from the Browning Collector's Association for making FN contributions to this edition.

PISTOLS: SEMI-AUTO

For FN Models 1900, 1903, 1905, 1910, 1922 (10/22), Baby Model, and the Model 10/ 71, please refer to the Browning Pistol section in this text.

PISTOLS: SEMI-AUTO, HI-POWER VARIATIONS

The F.N. Hi-Power (also known as P-35) was Browning's last pistol design. A 9mm Para., single action, semi-auto pistol, it was the first to incorporate a staggered high capacity magazine. It has a 4 21/32 in. barrel, 13 shot mag., hammer and mag. safeties, a wide variety of finishes and sight options. It's probably the most widely used military pistol in the world.

PRE-WAR COMMERCIAL HP - 9mm Para. cal., single action, blue, wood grips, tangent rear sight, slotted (original) for stock with tangent rear sight, 13 shot mag.

Tangent sight & slotted	$1,875	$1,200	$995	$850	$600	$450	$375

> Add $400 for original flat board stock in 98%+ condition.
> Add $600 for original flat board stock with matching numbers of pistols – beware of reproductions.

PRE-WAR FOREIGN MILITARY CONTRACTS - mfg. under military contract for various countries.

Grading	100%	98%	95%	90%	80%	70%	60%
Lithuanian Crest	N/A	$1,950	$1,500	$995	$700	$600	$500
Estonian Contract ("E.V." or "K.L.")	N/A	$1,950	$1,500	$995	$700	$600	$500
Finnish Contract ("SA" marked)	N/A	$1,750	$1,250	$985	$600	$550	$475
Chinese refinished imports	$700	$650	$575	$500	$450	$400	$350

Add $800 for matching flat board stock (ser. no. range 11,000-15,000) with attached holster as shipped to Finland.

Add $550 for matching flat board stock (ser. no. range 11,000-15,000) with holster removed.

Pre-war Belgian military HPs are priced similarly to the pre-war Commercial Model. Most Finnish contract guns can be identified by the "SA" stamp on frame and/or slide, and/or magazine. 2,400 pistols were shipped to Finland in 1940. All pistols fall in the 11,000 – 15,000 serial number range.

Chinese contract pistols can sometimes be identified by Chinese added inventory markings. Chinese contract pistols are in the 5,000 – 10,000 and 20,000 – 21,000 ser. no. range. Many Chinese contract pistols have been refinished, and all are recent imports.

WWII PRODUCTION: WAFFENAMT PROOFED

There is a range of finishes during Nazi production that varies from the excellent pre-war commercial finish on early guns assembled from captured parts to the roughly milled, poorly finished specimens mfg. late in the war. Values listed assume all major parts (slide, barrel, and frame) are matching with original magazine.

In recent years, some Nazi production Hi-Powers have had the rear grip strap milled out and slotted to accept a shoulder stock. Careful observation is advised before purchasing a "rare" (and expensive) slotted and tangent sight specimen. Many HPs have been restored, since the restoration is easily accomplished by professionals.

✳ Type I: Tangent sights - slotted - taken from existing pre-war Belgian army pistols, quality is excellent, correct ser. range is quite limited, approx. 40,000-47,000. Ser. range for production under German occupation is 50,001-53,000. All are proofed WaA 613.

	N/A	$2,750	$2,400	$2,000	$1,500	$1,250	$995

Beware of restorations.

✳ Type II - tangent rear sight only, approx. 90,000 mfg. with generally good quality finish, pistols are proofed WaA613, WaA103, some are WaA140.

	N/A	$1,100	$850	$600	$550	$450	$400

Add 25% if pistol is marked WaA613.
Add 15% if pistol is marked WaA103.

✳ Type III Standard Fixed Sights - most common HP pistol produced during the war.

$700	$550	$450	$395	$325	$300	$200

Add 15% for late war Bakelite/synthetic grips.
Add 20% for eagle N proof instead of WaA140 proof.

POST-OCCUPATION PRODUCTION - commercial mfg. began 1944, first imported with BAC markings in 1954 (see Browning HP section). Military mfg. from 1944-present. Early (1944) models are identifiable by an "A" serial number prefix and are not fitted with a magazine safety. In 1947, the rear slide bushing became hardened by a new heat treatment process. Other design modifications were added in 1950. Many thousands manufactured under various government contracts, many will have a T prefix.

Add $50 if round hammer.
Add $200-$2,000 for military pistols with crests, depending on condition and variation.

✳ Tangent sight only

$775	$600	$500	$400	$350	$325	$300

Add $100 for "T" prefix.

Grading	100%	98%	95%	90%	80%	70%	60%

❋ ***Tangent sight*** - slotted for stock, military mfg.

	$1,200	$1,050	$950	$700	$600	$500	$400

Add $150 for "T" prefix.
Add $150 for internal extractor.

❋ ***Fixed sight*** - most common variation.

	$600	$500	$450	$400	$350	$325	$300

Add $50 for round hammer.
Add $50 for internal extractor.

MUSCAT AND OMAN CONTRACT

❋ ***First Model*** - 9 pistols.

	$6,000	$5,000	$4,000

❋ ***Second Model*** - 27 pistols.

	$4,500	$3,500	$2,000

INGLIS MANUFACTURED HI-POWERS - SEE INGLIS SECTION.

RIFLES: BOLT ACTION

F.N. MAUSER SPORTER DELUXE - available in popular American and European calibers, 24 in. barrel, adj. sight, checkered pistol grip stock. Mfg. 1947-1963.

	$650	$550	$495	$460	$300	$275	$250

F.N. PRESENTATION GRADE - similar to Deluxe, except engraved and select wood.

	$1,150	$935	$855	$770	$500	$475	$450

F.N. SUPREME - .243 Win., .270 Win., 7mm Rem. Mag., .308 Win. cal., or .30-06, 24 in. barrel, peep sight, checkered pistol grip stock. Mfg. 1957-1975.

	$650	$550	$495	$460	$300	$275	$250

F.N. SUPREME MAGNUM - .264 Mag., 7mm Rem. Mag., or .300 Win. Mag. cal., similar to Bolt Action.

	$675	$575	$540	$495	$325	$275	$250

FN SNIPER RIFLE (MODEL 30) - .308 Win. cal., this model was a Mauser actioned Sniper Rifle equipped with 20 in. extra heavy barrel, flash hider, diopter sights, Hensoldt 4X scope, hard case, bipod, and sling. 51 were imported into the U.S. with the last retail price (1988) being $2,950. When encountered today, values will range from $3,500 and higher (depending on condition).

RIFLES: SEMI-AUTO

MODEL 1949 - 7x57mm Mauser (8,003 mfg. for Venezuela), 7.65mm (approx. 5,500 mfg. for Argentina), 7.92mm, or .30-06 cal., gas operated, 10 shot mag., 23 in. barrel, military rifle, tangent rear sight, military stock. Mfg. 160,000.

	$700	$575	$450	$300	$250	$225	$175

Add 10% for .30-06 cal.
Add 100% for sniper variation.
Add 10% for slotted receivers (to accept scope mount).
Add $650 for correct scope, rings, and mount.
Subtract 20% for recently assembled Egyptian parts models.

RIFLES: SEMI-AUTO, FAL/LAR/FNC SERIES

After tremendous price increases between 1985-1988, Fabrique Nationale decided in 1988 to discontinue this series completely. Not only are these rifles not exported to the U.S. any longer, but all

Grading	100%	98%	95%	90%	80%	70%	60%

production has ceased in Belgium as well. The only way FN will produce these models again is if they are given a large military contract - in which case a "side-order" of commercial guns may be built. 1989 Federal legislation regarding this type of paramilitary design also helped push up prices to their current level. FAL rifles were also mfg. in Israel by I.M.I.

F.N. FAL - semi-auto, French designation for the FN L.A.R. (light automatic rifle), otherwise similar to LAR.

	$2,375	$2,050	$1,750	$1,550	$1,375	$1,200	$1,025

✱ **F.N. FAL G** - most desirable FAL model.

	$3,750	$3,000	$2,600	$2,375	$2,050	$1,750	$1,550

F.N. L.A.R. COMPETITION (50.00, LIGHT AUTOMATIC RIFLE) - .308 Win. (7.62x51mm) cal., semi-auto, competition rifle with match flash hider, 21 in. barrel, adj. 4 position fire selector on automatic models, wood stock, aperture rear sight adj. from 100-600 meters, 9.4 lbs. Mfg. 1981-83.

	$2,000	$1,750	$1,600	$1,450	$1,300	$1,175	$1,000

This model was designated by the factory as the 50.00 Model.

Mid-1987 retail on this model was $1,258. The last MSR was $3,179 (this price reflected the last exchange rate and special order status of this model).

✱ **Heavy barrel rifle (50.41 & 50.42)** - barrel is twice as heavy as standard L.A.R., includes wood or synthetic stock, short wood forearm, and bi-pod, 12.2 lbs. Importation disc. 1988.

	$2,500	$2,150	$1,850	$1,600	$1,425	$1,250	$1,075

Add $400 for walnut stock.

There were 2 variations of this model. The Model 50.41 had a synthetic butt stock while the Model 50.42 had a wood butt stock with steel butt plate incorporating a top extension used for either shoulder resting or inverted grenade launching.

Mid-1987 retail on this model was $1,497 (Model 50.41) or $1,654 (Model 50.42). The last MSR was $3,776 (this price reflected the last exchange rate and special order status of this model).

✱ **Paratrooper rifle (50.63 & 50.64)** - similar to L.A.R. model, except has folding stock, 8.3 lbs. Mfg. 1950-1988.

	$3,300	$2,650	$2,300	$2,150	$1,900	$1,700	$1,500

There were 2 variations of the Paratrooper L.A.R. Model. The Model 50.63 had a stationary aperture rear sight and 18 in. barrel. The Model 50.64 was supplied with a 21 in. barrel and had a rear sight calibrated for either 150 or 200 meters. Both models retailed for the same price.

Mid-1987 retail on this model was $1,310 (both the Model 50.63 and 50.64). The last MSR was $3,239 (this price reflected the last exchange rate and special order status of this model).

FNC MODEL - .223 Rem. (5.56mm) cal., lightweight combat carbine, 18½ in. barrel, NATO approved, 30 shot mag., 8.4 lbs. Disc. 1987.

	$2,150	$1,775	$1,425	$1,250	$1,050	$950	$825

Add $50 for Paratrooper model (16 or 18½ in. barrel).

While rarer, the 16 in. barrel model incorporated a flash hider that did not perform as well as the flash hider used on the standard 18½ in. barrel.

Mid-1987 retail on this model was $749 (Standard Model) and $782 (Paratrooper Model). The last MSR was $2,204 (Standard Model) and $2,322 (Paratrooper Model) - these prices reflected the last exchange rate and special order status of these models.

FALCO, S.R.L.

Current shotgun manufacturer established circa 1960, and located in Marcheno, Italy. Currently, K.B.I. imports some of the models manufactured by Falco.

Falco manufactures a variety of good quality, small gauge shotguns (20 ga., 28 ga., or .410 bore only) in various configurations, including O/U, SxS, and single shot. Falco is well

Grading	100%	98%	95%	90%	80%	70%	60%

known for their folding action design. Currently, K.B.I. is importing certain models and configurations – please contact K.B.I. directly for more information and pricing. Please contact the factory directly for those models not currently being imported by K.B.I.

FALCON FIREARMS

Previous manufacturer located in Northridge, CA from 1986-1990.

PISTOLS: SEMI-AUTO

PORTSIDER - .45 ACP cal., patterned after Colt M 1911 A-1, stainless steel, fixed sights, 5 in. barrel, 7 shot mag., available in left-hand only. Mfg. 1986-90.

$500 $425 $375

Last MSR was $580.

* ***Portsider Set*** - features right and left-hand models with matching serial numbers. Only 100 sets mfg. 1986-1987.

$1,300 $1,100 $895

Last MSR was $1,400.

GOLD FALCON - .45 ACP cal., machined receiver made from solid 17 Kt. gold alloy, stainless steel slide, diamond sighting system, choice of grips, standard or personalized engraving options. Only 50 mfg.

$25,000 $17,500 $11,500

Last MSR was $30,500.

FAMARS di ABBIATICO & SALVINELLI SRL

Current manufacturer located in Gardone, Italy. Exclusively distributed by Robin Hollow Outfitters, located in Addieville, RI. Previously distributed by The First National Gun Banque, located in Colorado Springs, CO. Previously imported by A&S of America, located in Jefferson Boro, PA.

A&S Famars manufactures some of the world's finest rifles and shotguns – approx. 100 are fabricated annually. Most Famars guns include a lifetime warranty. Values listed are for base models with no extra embellishments or special orders. Because every A&S Famars longarm is an individual custom order, each Famars firearm must have its value ascertained on an individual appraisal basis.

All A&S Famars shotguns incorporate a patented A&S Famars mechanism, and are available in Hunting, Trap, Skeet, Sporting Clays, and Pigeon configurations. All models except the Excalibur O/U have chopper lump barrels.

RIFLES: SxS, CUSTOM MFG.

Boxlock and sidelock rifles are all best quality and range in calibers between .22 LR and .600 Nitro Express. Each gun is manufactured per individual customer special order, and the following values reflect base model pricing with no additional special order features (most models can be ordered with 6 levels of engraving/ornamentation). Further information and price quotations are available by contacting the distributor directly.

AFRICAN EXPRESS

MSR	$31,325	$27,850	$20,250	$16,750	$13,000	$11,750	$10,250	$9,250

VENUS EXPRESS PROFESSIONAL

MSR	$41,050	$35,950	$29,750	$25,250	$21,500	$18,500	$16,500	$13,000

VENUS EXPRESS EXTRALUSSO - top-of-the-line model.

Prices start at $65,000 on this model.

Grading	100%	98%	95%	90%	80%	70%	60%

SHOTGUNS: O/U, CUSTOM MFG.

O/U SIDELOCK MODELS

* **Jorema** - 12 or 20 ga. Disc. 1999.

	100%	98%	95%	90%	80%	70%	60%
	$25,000	$19,750	$13,500	$10,250		$8,750	$7,500
$6,250							

Last MSR was $25,650.

Add 10% for 20 ga.

* **Sovereign (Jorema Royal, Aries)**

MSR	$38,875	$34,000	$23,750	$17,750	$13,000	$10,000	$8,500	$7,250

Add 20% for 28 ga. or .410 bore.

This model was originally called the Jorema Royal, then renamed the Aries in 2000, and renamed the Sovereign in 2002.

* **Royale SH** - 12, 20, 28 ga., or .410 bore, bar action.

MSR	$38,875	$34,000	$23,750	$17,750	$13,000	$10,000	$8,500	$7,250

Add 20% for 28 ga. or .410 bore.

O/U COMPETITION MODELS - various gauges, current models include the BL, BLE (Extra), BLP (Prestige), BLX (sideplate), BLXE, BLXP, SL (sidelock), SLE, and SLP.

* **Excalibur BL** - detachable locks, monobloc barrels.

MSR	$10,800	$9,750	$8,000	$7,000	$6,000	$4,950	$4,250	$3,600

* **Excalibur BLX** - detachable locks, with sideplates and monobloc barrels.

MSR	$15,236	$13,950	$9,950	$8,950	$7,500	$6,250	$5,500	$4,650

* **Excalibur SL** - sidelock action, monobloc barrels.

MSR	$23,750	$21,000	$17,500	$13,250	$9,750	$8,200	$7,500	$6,750

Add 25% for 28 ga. or .410 bore.

4-BARREL MODEL

* **Rombo Quattrocanne** - 28 ga. or .410 bore, barrels are arranged in a quad pattern.

MSR	$54,000	$48,500	$39,500	$32,750	$26,250	$21,750	$17,750	$14,750

SHOTGUNS: SxS

Add 25% for small gauges.

CASTORE HAMMER GUN - various gauges, double barrel, exposed hammers, double triggers,.

MSR	$28,075	$24,750	$21,250	$17,250	$14,650	$11,850	$10,000	$8,000

BOXLOCK MODELS - various gauges, available with Anson-Deeley boxlock action, scalloped or rounded frame, various engraving patterns available.

* **Zeus** - 12 or 20 ga., features round action.

MSR	$23,750	$20,150	$14,250	$10,750	$8,950	$7,600	$6,500	$5,250

* **Tribute** - 12, 20, 28 ga., or .410 bore, scalloped back drop lock action.

MSR	$22,755	$20,750	$14,750	$10,500	$8,500	$7,000	$5,750	$5,000

SIDELOCK MODELS

* **Highline (Veneri)** - various gauges, round body, back action. Disc. 1999.

	$27,000	$20,000	$16,000	$12,250	$10,000	$8,500	$7,250

Last MSR was $30,000.

* **Venus** - back action.

MSR	$35,650	$31,250	$22,000	$17,000	$13,000	$10,250	$8,500	$7,250

Grading	100%	98%	95%	90%	80%	70%	60%

FANZOJ, JOHANN

Current long gun manufacturer located in Ferlach, Austria.

Johann Fanzoj is the 9th generation in his family to manufacture top quality long arms. Today's configurations include double rifles (mostly over .300 cal.), double shotguns, stalking rifles, drillings, and the new Tri-Bore three barrel shotgun. Fanzoj is also a member of the Ferlach Guild. Prices range from $15,000 - $150,000, and almost anything is possible through custom order. Please contact the factory directly for current model availability, pricing, and to order a catalog.

FAUSTI STEFANO SRL

Current manufacturer located in Marcheno, Italy. Currently imported beginning in 2000 by Traditions, located in Old Saybrook, CT.

S. Fausti manufactures a variety of good quality shotguns in O/U, SxS, and single shot configurations. Please refer to the Traditions section for current information on recent Fausti importation. New importation by Traditions can be determined by the Fausti Stefano SRL markings. Previously imported until 1999 by American Arms located in N. Kansas City, MO (Fausti, Cav., Stefano & Figlie snc.).

FAUSTI® STEFANO s.r.l.

FEATHER INDUSTRIES, INC.

Previous manufacturer located in Boulder, CO until 1995.

DERRINGERS

GUARDIAN ANGEL CENTERFIRE - 9mm Para. or .38 Spl. cal., O/U design, stainless steel, double action backup derringer. Mfg. 1988-1989 only.

$130	$95	$75

Last MSR was $140.

This model has interchangeable loading blocks that allow shooting 9mm Para. or .38 Spl. There is no exposed hammer and trigger is totally enclosed.

GUARDIAN ANGEL RIMFIRE - .22 LR or .22 Mag. cal., design is similar to 9mm Para./.38 Spl. model, loading block breech, 2 in. barrel, fixed sights, 12 oz. Mfg. 1990-95.

$100	$75	$60

Last MSR was $120.

Add $30 for individual extra loading blocks.

This model has interchangeable loading blocks that allow shooting .22LR or .22 Mag. There is no exposed hammer and the trigger is totally enclosed.

PISTOLS: SEMI-AUTO

MINI-AT - .22 LR cal., pistol variation of the AT-22, 5½ in. shrouded barrel, 20 shot mag., approx. 2 lbs. Mfg. 1986-1989.

$195	$165	$145	$135	$130	$125	$115

Last MSR was $220.

RIFLES: SEMI-AUTO

AT-22 - .22 LR cal., semi-auto blowback action, 17 in. detachable shrouded barrel, collapsible metal stock, adj. rear sight, with sling and swivels, 20 shot mag., 3¼ lbs. Mfg. 1986-95.

$225	$175	$155	$145	$135	$125	$115

Last MSR was $250.

Grading	100%	98%	95%	90%	80%	70%	60%

F2 - similar to AT-22, except is equipped with a fixed polymer buttstock. Mfg. 1992-95.

| | $245 | $190 | $165 | $150 | $135 | $125 | $115 |

Last MSR was $280.

AT-9 - 9mm Para. cal., semi-auto blowback action, 16 in. barrel, paramilitary design, available with 10 (C/B 1994), 25*, 32 (disc.), or 100 (disc. 1989) shot mag., 5 lbs. Mfg. 1988-95.

| | $700 | $625 | $550 | $495 | $450 | $400 | $350 |

Last MSR was $500.

Add $250 for 100 shot drum mag.

F9 - similar to AT-9, except is equipped with a fixed polymer buttstock. Mfg. 1992-95.

| | $575 | $525 | $450 | $395 | $335 | $295 | $260 |

Last MSR was $535.

SATURN 30 - 7.62x39mm Kalashnikov cal., semi-auto, gas operated, 19½ in. barrel, composite stock with large thumbhole pistol grip, 5 shot detachable mag., drilled and tapped for scope mounts, adj. rear sight, 8½ lbs. Mfg. in 1990 only.

| | $650 | $550 | $475 | $425 | $375 | $325 | $280 |

Last MSR was $695.

KG-9 - 9mm Para. cal., semi-auto blowback action, 25 or 50 shot mag., paramilitary configuration. Mfg. 1989 only.

| | $750 | $675 | $600 | $550 | $500 | $450 | $400 |

Last MSR was $560.

Add $100 for 50 shot mag.

SAR-180 - .22 LR cal., semi-auto blowback action, 17½ in. barrel, 165 shot drum mag., fully adj. rear sight, walnut stock with combat style pistol grip and forend, 6¼ lbs. Mfg. 1989 only.

| | $495 | $425 | $375 | $325 | $275 | $240 | $200 |

Last MSR was $500.

Add $250 for 165 shot drum mag.
Add $200 for retractable stock.
Add $395 for laser sight.

This variation was also manufactured for a limited time by ILARCO (Illinois Arms Company), previously located in Itasca, IL.

KG-22 - .22 LR cal., similar to KG-9, 20 shot mag. Mfg. 1989 only.

| | $295 | $250 | $200 | $175 | $155 | $145 | $135 |

Last MSR was $300.

FEDERAL ENGINEERING CORPORATION

Previous manufacturer located in Chicago, IL.

RIFLES: SEMI-AUTO

XC-220 - .22 LR cal., semi-auto paramilitary design rifle, 16 5/16 in. barrel, 28 shot mag., machined steel action, 7½ lbs. Mfg. 1984-89.

| | $495 | $450 | $400 | $350 | $320 | $295 | $275 |

XC-450 - .45 ACP cal. only, semi-auto paramilitary design carbine, 16½ in. barrel length, 30 shot mag., fires from closed bolt, machined steel action, 8½ lbs. Mfg. 1984-89.

| | $950 | $825 | $750 | $675 | $600 | $550 | $500 |

XC-900 - 9mm Para. cal., semi-auto paramilitary design carbine, 16½ in. barrel length, 32 shot mag., fires from closed bolt, machine steel action, 8 lbs. Mfg. 1984-89.

| | $950 | $825 | $750 | $675 | $600 | $550 | $500 |

Grading	100%	98%	95%	90%	80%	70%	60%

FEDERAL ORDNANCE, INC.

Previous manufacturer, importer, and distributor located in South El Monte, CA from 1966- 1992. Brickley Trading Co. bought the remaining assets of Federal Ordnance, Inc. in late 1992, and continued to import various firearms until circa 1998.

Federal Ordnance imported and distributed both foreign and domestic military handguns and rifles until 1992. In addition, they also fabricated firearms using mostly newer parts.

PISTOLS: SEMI-AUTO

In addition to the following Broomhandle models, Federal Ordnance also manufactured other special editions. These models include the British Model, Cut-Away, Cartridge Counter, Para La Guerra, and others. Prices are in the $800-$950 range (retail).

F

MODEL 714 BROOMHANDLE - 7.63 Mauser or 9mm Para. cal., 5½ in. barrel, new frame, exterior completely refinished, 10 shot detachable mag., "fair" bore, adj. rear sight. Mfg. 1986-1991.

$550	$500	$450	$400	$350	$325	$300

Last MSR was $820.

Add $100 for new barrel.

✳ *Model 714 Para La Guerra* - 7.63 Mauser or 9mm Para. cal., remanufactured to duplicate Spanish Civil War configuration Broomhandle, includes 10 in. barrel with "Para La Guerra" engraved on side. Mfg. 1990-91 only.

$575	$525	$450	$400	$350	$325	$300

Last MSR was $890.

✳ *Model 714 Bolo* - similar to Model 714 Broomhandle, except has smaller grips, 3.9 in. barrel, 10 shot mag. standard. Mfg. 1988 only.

$550	$500	$450	$400	$350	$325	$300

Last MSR was $890.

STANDARD BROOMHANDLE - 7.63 Mauser or 9mm Para. cal., refurbished (new barrels, completely refinished, etc.) C-96 pistols, replaced springs, includes original Chinese shoulder/holster stock. Disc. 1991.

$525	$485	$450	$420	$390	$380	$360

Last MSR was $735.

Subtract $150 without shoulder/holster stock.

✳ *Standard Bolo* - similar to Standard Broomhandle, except Bolo configuration (3.9 in. barrel and smaller grips). Includes original Chinese shoulder/holster stock. Mfg. 1990-91 only.

$480	$450	$420	$390	$380	$370	$360

Last MSR was $530.

RANGER 1911A1 GI - .45 ACP cal., 5 in. barrel, 7 shot mag., steel construction throughout, checkered walnut grips, 40 oz. Mfg. 1988-92.

$385	$350	$310	$280	$260	$240	$200

Last MSR was $440.

Add $20 for Ranger Extended Model (40 oz. - new 1990).
Add $40 for Ranger Ambo (ambidextrous safety, 40 oz. - new 1990).
Add $15 for lightweight Ranger Lite Model (32 oz. - new 1990).
These pistols are patterned after the Colt 1911A1 Govt. Model.

✳ *Ranger Ten* - 10mm cal., otherwise similar to regular Ranger 1911A1. Mfg. 1990- 91 only.

$675	$525	$475	$450	$420	$395	$370

Last MSR was $780.

Grading	100%	98%	95%	90%	80%	70%	60%

RANGER SUPERCOMP - .45 ACP or 10mm cal., compensated variation of the Ranger 1911A1 with 6 in. compensated barrel, slide, tuned trigger, and other competition features, 42 oz. Mfg. 1990-91 only.

	$1,250	$875	$775	$675	$600	$550	$495

Last MSR was $1,390.

Add $10 for 10mm cal.

THE RANGER ALPHA - .38 Super, 10mm, or .45 ACP cal., 5 or 6 in. barrel, patterned after the Colt Govt. Model. Mfg. 1990-91 only.

	$895	$775	$675	$575	$475	$425	$380

Last MSR was $1,000.

Add $16 for 10mm cal.
Add $16 for 6 in. barrel.
Add $9-$25 for ported 5 or 6 in. barrel depending on cal.

RIFLES/CARBINES

ALL AMERICAN SPORTER BOLT ACTION - .30-06 cal., Springfield M1903 receiver, new sporter stock, drilled and tapped for scope base (included), blued finish. Mfg. late 1991-92.

	$165	$145	$120	$100	$90	$80	$75

MODEL 713 DELUXE MAUSER SEMI-AUTO CARBINE - 7.63 Mauser or 9mm Para. cal., 16 in. barrel, detachable stock, one 10 shot and one 20 shot detachable mag., deluxe walnut, leather case with accessories, adj. sights to 1,000 meters, 5 lbs. 1,500 mfg. 1986-92.

	$1,495	$1,250	$1,050				

Last MSR was $1,986.

* ***Field Grade Mauser Carbine*** - 7.63 Mauser or 9mm Para. (new 1989) cal., 16 in. barrel, 10 shot fixed mag., nondetachable walnut stock. Mfg. 1987-92.

	$750	$675	$600	$525	$475	$425	$400

Last MSR was $1,200.

M-14 SEMI-AUTO - .308 Win. cal., legal for private ownership (no selector), 20 shot mag., refinished original M-14 parts, available in either filled fiberglass, G.I. fiberglass, refinished wood, or new walnut stock. Mfg. 1986-91.

	$625	$550	$495	$450	$395	$335	$285

Last MSR was $700.

Add $50 for filled fiberglass stock.
Add $110 for refinished wood stock.
Add $190 for new walnut stock with handguard.

During the end of production, Chinese parts were used on this model. Values are the same.

TANKER GARAND SEMI-AUTO - .30-06 or .308 Win. cal., original U.S. GI parts, 18 in. barrel, new hardwood stock, parkerized finish. Mfg. began late 1991.

	$675	$525	$475	$450	$420	$395	$370

CHINESE RPK 86S-7 SEMI-AUTO - 7.62x39mm cal., semi-auto version of the P.R.C.- RPK light machine gun, 75 shot drum mag., 23¾ in. barrel, with bipod. Imported 1989 only.

	$1,000	$875	$725	$650	$575	$525	$475

Last MSR was $500.

Add $100 for 75 shot drum mag.

FEINWERKBAU

Current airguns and firearms manufacturer established circa 1951, and located in Oberndorf, Germany. Feinwerkbau firearms have had limited importation by Beeman Precision Airguns, located in Huntington Beach, CA.

Grading	100%	98%	95%	90%	80%	70%	60%

Feinwerkbau manufactures some of the world's finest quality target rifles and pistols (.22 LR rimfire and airgun). Target rifles and pistols have had limited importation into the U.S., and as this edition went to press, a decision had yet to be finalized on future Feinwerkbau firearms importation.

For more information and current pricing on both new and used Feinwerkbau airguns, please refer to the 2nd Ed. Blue Book of Airguns by Dr. Robert Beeman & John Allen (now online also).

PISTOLS: SEMI-AUTO, RIMFIRE

MODEL AW-93 - .22 LR cal., 6 in. barrel, 5 shot mag., ergonomically designed stippled walnut grips with adj. heel, unique damper prevents muzzle jump and recoil, satin nickel finish, top-of- the-line Target pistol, approx. 2½ lbs. New 1993.

MSR	$1,695	$1,525	$1,350	$1,150	$950	$850	$750	$625

RIFLES: BOLT ACTION, RIMFIRE

MODEL 2000 - .22 LR cal. only, single shot, match target bolt action rifle, fully adj. trigger, walnut stocks, four variations featuring different specifications. Importation disc. 1988.

* ***Universal Model*** - 26 3/8 in. barrel, aperture sights, stippled pistol grip and forearm, 9¾ lbs.

	$1,150	$925	$850	$735	$650	$595	$550

Last MSR was $1,395.

Add $350 for electronic trigger.
Add $160 for left-hand variation.

* ***Mini 2000 (Junior)*** - 22 in. barrel, aperture sights, stippled pistol grip, 9 1/8 lbs.

	$1,025	$875	$825	$700	$625	$575	$525

Last MSR was $1,225.

Add $350 for electronic trigger.
Add $150 for left-hand variation.

* ***Match Model*** - 26¼ in. barrel, adj. cheekpiece on stock, stippled pistol grip and forearm, aperture sights.

	$1,075	$895	$825	$700	$625	$575	$525

Last MSR was $1,285.

Add $390 for electronic trigger.
Add $113 for left-hand variation.

* ***Running Target*** - adj. cheekpiece on stock, thumbhole stippled pistol grip, no sights, for running boar competition.

	$1,150	$925	$850	$735	$650	$595	$550

Last MSR was $1,398.

Add $142 for left-hand variation.

MODEL 2600 UNIVERSAL - .22 LR cal. only, similar design to Model 600 air rifle, single shot, 26.3 in. barrel, aperture sights, 10.6 lbs. Imported 1986-94.

	$1,425	$1,125	$925	$850	$735	$650	$595

Last MSR was $1,695.

Add $160 for left-hand variation.

MODEL 2600 ULTRA MATCH FREE RIFLE - .22 LR cal., single shot match gun based on Model 2600 action, 26.1 in. barrel, laminated stock with thumbhole, fully adj. aperture sights, 14 lbs. 1 oz. Mfg. 1986-94.

	$2,175	$1,750	$1,400	$1,150	$925	$850	$735

Last MSR was $2,498.

Add $250 for electronic trigger (disc. 1988).
Add $152 for left-hand variation.

Grading	100%	98%	95%	90%	80%	70%	60%

MODEL 2602 UNIVERSAL (UIT) RIFLE - .22 LR cal., designed for Match competition, state-of-the-art Target rifle with different color wood laminations possible. New 1997.

MSR	$1,615	$1,450	$1,275	$1,125	$975	$850	$725	$600

Add $125 for left-hand action.

MODEL 2602 FREE RIFLE - .22 LR cal., standard Match rifle with state-of-the-art laminated wood stock with thumbhole, adj. cheekpiece, adj. buttplate, and adj. hand rest, features 16¾ in. barrel with unique 13¾ in. squared-off barrel sleeve with sight, diopter sights, top-of-the-line competition rifle, approx. 13.86 lbs. New 1997.

MSR	$2,365	$2,035	$1,800	$1,575	$1,350	$1,175	$1,000	$850

Add $155 for left-hand action.

MODEL 2602 SUPER MATCH - .22 LR cal., Super Match variation featuring state- of- the-art design, adj. stock, comb, LOP, and trigger pull.

MSR	$2,370	$2,050	$1,800	$1,575	$1,350	$1,175	$1,000	$850

Add $130 for left-hand action.
Subtract $130 for Model 2602 Sport RT.

MODEL 2602 SPORT - .22 LR cal., sporter variation of the Model 2602, repeater action. New 2000.

MSR	$2,240		$1,950	$1,750	$1,525	$1,325	$1,175	$1,000	$850

FEMARU

Previously manufactured by Femaru-Fegyver-es Gepgyar R.T. located in Budapest, Hungary.

PISTOLS: SEMI-AUTO

MODEL 1910 - 7.65mm Roth/Steyr cal., rare and only infrequently encountered. Estimated serial range 1-10,000.

		$2,350	$1,900	$1,500	$1,150	$975	$850	$725

MODEL 1929 (29M) - .380 ACP cal., 3.93 in. barrel, 8 shot mag., identifiable by squared- off rear slide with vertical serrations, 2 piece walnut grips, approx. 50,000 mfg.

		$400	$340	$275	$215	$185	$165	$145

MODEL 1937 (37M) - .32 ACP or .380 ACP cal., 3.93 in. barrel, 8 shot mag., commercial blue finish, left slide marking "FEMARU FEGYVER ES GEPYAR RT. 37M", vertically grooved 2-piece walnut grips, approx. 200,000 mfg. (.380 ACP cal.) for Hungarian service before Nazi variations began (dubbed "Pistole Modell 37 (ung)", c. 1941), Nazi marked jhv 41 or jhv 44, 27 oz.

		$350	$295	$225	$190	$175	$160	$145

Add 50% for Waffenamt proofing (.32 ACP only).
Add another 60% if with holster and 2 matching mags.

FROMMER STOP POCKET AUTO - .32 ACP or .380 ACP cal., 6 or 7 shot, 3 7/8 in. barrel, fixed sights, blue, rubber grips, locked breech, outside hammer. Mfg. 1912-1920.

		$300	$250	$180	$150	$120	$100	$80

Add 50% for .380 ACP cal.

FROMMER BABY POCKET AUTO - similar to Stop Pocket Auto, except 2 in. barrel, 5 or 6 shot.

		$250	$215	$180	$150	$115	$90	$70

Grading	100%	98%	95%	90%	80%	70%	60%

FROMMER LILIPUT AUTO - .25 ACP cal., blowback action, 6 shot, 2.14 in. barrel, blue, hard rubber grips. Mfg. in early 1920s.

	100%	98%	95%	90%	80%	70%	60%
	$400	$300	$200	$145	$115	$90	$75

FERLACH GUNS

Includes those firearms manufactured in Ferlach, Austria from 1558 to present. Currently, the Ferlach Guild (Genossenschaft) represents most of Ferlach's gunmakers, and has no exclusive U.S. importation.

Many people are confused that Ferlach is a trademark - it is not. Rather, it is a small village in Austria where a gun guild was started as early as 1558. At that time, it was absolutely necessary that all the people involved in fabricating a firearm were located together in close proximity. This enabled the barrel maker, the stock maker, and the lock mechanism maker to work together closely to ensure that everyone was performing their task(s) correctly, effectively and efficiently. As the individual skills became better and more refined, more and more firearms were manufactured. Eventually, individual gunsmiths began to put their name on the barrel or frame of those guns which they had either manufactured solely or with the help of their fellow Ferlach craftsmen. Since all Ferlach firearms are essentially hand made per individual special order, very few are exactly alike. In the past, the gunsmiths of Ferlach have produced almost every type of shoulder arm imaginable, including such modern weapons as superposed and juxtaposed rifles and shotguns, hammerless drillings, repeating rifles, 3 barrel rifles, combination guns, 4 barrel rifles/ shotguns/combination guns (called Vierlings), hammer guns of every type, etc. Some of these specimens represent the highest refinement in the gunmakers trade. Because of the almost unlimited variety of Ferlach variations, it is recommended that a COMPETENT appraisal is procured before buying or selling a specimen.

As is the case with many other European weapons, those models with desirable American features will generally outperform those with European specifications (i.e. a Ferlach sidelock combination gun that is 20 ga. x .243 Win. will be more valuable than a similar specimen chambered for 16 ga. x 5.6 by 50Rmm with sling swivels). Original condition and overall beauty are the primary factors to consider when contemplating buying or selling a Ferlach longarm. Other considerations include: type of action, difficulty of fabrication (Vierlings are very complicated to construct), caliber/gauge desirability, notoriety of gunsmith on barrel legend, elaborateness of embellishments, condition, rarity, accessories, and any provenance a specimen might have.

Today's master gunsmiths of Ferlach carry on the Old World tradition of quality in every respect. Most guns manufactured today are by individual special order with a wide range of calibers/gauges and other special features and options. As of this writing, these gunsmiths in alphabetical order are: LUDWIG BOROVNIK, JOHANN FANZOJ, WILFRIED GLANZNIG, JOSEF HAMBRUSCH, KARL HAUPTMANN, GOTTFRIED JUCH, JOSEF JUST, JAKOB KOSCHAT, PETER MICHELITSCH, JOHANN & WALTER OUTSCHAR, HERBERT SCHEIRING, BENEDIKT WINKLER, AND JOSEF WINKLER. Anyone wishing to contact these master gunmakers should either write to the Guild or address them individually at: Ferlach Genossenschaft der Büchsenmachermeister reg.Gen.m.b.H., Waagplatz 6, A-9170 Ferlach, AUSTRIA. Please allow at least 4-6 weeks for a response.

FERLIB

Current manufacturer etablished circa late 1940s, and located in Gardone V.T., Italy. Currently imported and distributed by Dakota Arms, Inc. since late 1999, and located in Sturgis, SD. Previously distributed until 1999 by Hi-Grade Imports located in Gilroy, CA.

Ferlib currently manufactures approx. 20 best quality guns annually. All are special order, and all engraving is quoted individually.

Grading	100%	98%	95%	90%	80%	70%	60%

SHOTGUNS: O/U

BOSS MODEL - features Boss style action, custom order gun, many engraving options.
Prices for this model start at $29,500, w/o engraving (quoted separately).

SHOTGUNS: SxS

The following models are available in 10, 12, 16, 20, 24, 28, 32 ga., or .410 bore. Also available for an additional charge are extra quality wood and upgraded engraving.
    Add 10% for 24, 28, 32 ga., or .410 bore.
    Add $250 for single trigger.
    Add $650 for leather case.

MIGNON HAMMER MODEL - back action, exposed hammers, extensive scroll engraving, deluxe checkered walnut stock and forearm.
Prices for this model start at $19,000.

MODEL F.VI - 12, 16, 20, 28 ga., or .410 bore, Anson & Deeley scalloped boxlock action, ejectors, double triggers, case hardened frame, select checkered stock and forearm. Disc. 1992.

	$3,500	$2,950	$2,275	$1,975	$1,600	$1,250	$1,000

Last MSR was $3,250.

MODEL 7 (F.VII) - 12, 16, 20, 28 ga., or .410 bore, Anson & Deeley scalloped boxlock action, ejectors, double triggers, coin finish, full coverage English scroll or game scene engraving, select checkered stock and forearm.

MSR	$10,950		$9,950	$8,750	$7,600	$6,500	$5,400	$4,500	$3,400

✱ *Model 7 Rex* - similar to Model 7, except has sideplates with extensive engraving. Importation began 2000.

MSR	$14,950		$13,300	$10,650	$9,150	$8,100	$7,000	$6,000	$5,000

✱ *Model 7 Premier* - top-of-the-line boxlock model, similar to Model 7 Rex, except more extensive engraving with gold inlays, best quality walnut. Importation began 2000.

MSR	$16,950		$15,000	$12,750	$10,950	$9,250	$8,100	$7,100	$6,100

MODEL F.VII/SC - 12, 16, 20, 28 ga., or .410 bore, Anson & Deeley scalloped boxlock action, ejectors, double triggers, coin finish, game scene with scroll accent engraving with gold inlays, select checkered stock and forearm. Importation disc. 1999.

	$6,200	$5,500	$5,000	$4,500	$3,800	$3,300	$2,750

Last MSR was $7,800.

SIDE PLATE MODEL (F.VII SIDEPLATE) - 12, 16, 20, 28 ga., or .410 bore, Anson & Deeley boxlock action with sideplates, ejectors, single trigger, coin finish, extensive English scroll or game scene and scroll accent engraving, select checkered stock and forearm.

MSR	$14,400		$12,950	$10,500	$9,000	$8,000	$7,000	$6,000	$5,000

Subtract $400 if English scroll engraved.

✱ *F.VII/SC Gold* - similar to F.VII Sideplate, except with gold inlays.

MSR	$15,100		$13,450	$10,950	$9,250	$8,100	$7,100	$6,100	$5,100

PRINCE MODEL - various ga.'s, contoured Anson & Deeley action with rounded frame, choice of top or side lever opening, DT, deluxe checkered walnut stock and forearm. Importation began 2000.

MSR	$11,950		$10,600	$9,250	$8,100	$6,800	$5,550	$4,600	$3,500

Add $2,550 for side lever opening.

Grading	100%	98%	95%	90%	80%	70%	60%

SIDELOCK MODEL - various models and ga.'s, full H&H sidelock action, special order to customer specifications. Importation began in 2000.

Prices for this model start at $20,000 w/o engraving. The Esposizione & L'Inglesina models retail for $25,500, and the Model E Fantasy currently lists at $39,500 (including engraving).

FIALA OUTFITTERS INCORPORATED
Previous manufacturer located in New York City, NY.

PISTOLS: SLIDE ACTION

FIALA REPEATING PISTOL - .22 LR cal., 10 shot, 3, 7½, or 20 in. barrel, blue, plain wood grips, resembles an auto loader, but is actually hand operated by moving the slide to eject, load and cock. Mfg. 1920-1923.

	100%	98%	95%	90%	80%	70%	60%
	$475	$400	$340	$280	$230	$200	$175

Add 50% for 3-barrel set.
Add $150 for original case.
Add $250 for stock.
Add $300 for canvas holster stock.

FINNISH LION
Previous trademark manufactured by Valmet (now Tikka) located in Sweden. Limited importation into the U.S. by Mandall's Shooting Supplies, Inc. in Scottsdale, AZ.

RIFLES: BOLT ACTION

MATCH MODEL - .22 LR cal., bolt action, single shot, 29 in. barrel, extended aperture sight, globe front sight, thumbhole stock, adj. hook butt. Mfg. 1937-1972.

	$495	$415	$360	$305	$250	$210	$195

CHAMPION FREE MODEL - .22 LR cal., bolt action, single shot, 29 in. barrel, double set trigger, full target stock and accessories. Mfg. 1965-1972.

	$580	$495	$440	$385	$330	$290	$265

STANDARD ISU TARGET MODEL - .22 LR cal., bolt action, single shot, 27 in. barrel, full target stock and accessories. Mfg. 1966-1977.

	$330	$275	$250	$205	$180	$165	$150

TARGET MODEL - .22 LR cal., target rifle with adj. stock and trigger, bolt action, single shot, aperture sights.

	$725	$595	$495	$440	$385	$340	$295

Last MSR was $795.

FIOCCHI OF AMERICA, INC.
Previous firearms importer and distributor located in Ozark, MO.

Fiocchi of America imported Pardini target pistols until 1990, and continues to manufacture a wide variety of ammunition domestically. Fiocchi also imported Antonio Zoli shotguns until 1988. These trademarks can be found in their respective sections of this text.

FIREARMS INTERNATIONAL (F.I.)
Previous importer and assembler located in Washington, D.C.

F.I. manufactured and imported various shotguns and pistols including the Star D and Iver Johnson Pony handguns. F.I. sold less than 100 .380 ACPs that were marked Colt before the Mustang was introduced - these are rare. While some models are relatively rare, collectability to date has been minimal and most models sell in the $125-$250 range.

Grading	100%	98%	95%	90%	80%	70%	60%

FIREARMS INTERNATIONAL, INC.

Current manufacturer established in 1997, and located in Houston, TX. Dealer sales.

While IAI (Israel Arms International) was originally established to market firearms manufactured by Israel Arms, Ltd. through Firearms International, Inc., IAI defaulted on this agreement without any sales being made.

PISTOLS: SEMI-AUTO

During 1999, Firearms International, Inc. obtained permission to use older High Standard model nomenclature (Crusader & Supermatic Trophy) for use with their M-1911 pistols. Currently manufactured pistols are marked Firearms International Inc. on the frame, and High Standard on the slide.

Sharpshooter .45 ACP to .22 LR cal. conversion units are also available – fixed sight model retails for $280, adj. rear sight model retails for $340.

MODEL 1911 CRUSADER (CUSTOM SERIES) - 38 Super (new 2002, Two-tone finish only) or .45 ACP cal., 5 in. barrel, 7 shot mag., many shooting enhancements are standard, stainless steel, blue, or Two-tone (new 2001) finish, adj. sights, 40 oz. New 2000.

MSR	$655	$585	$525	$475	$425	$400	$375	$350

Add $10 for stainless steel.
Add $40 for .38 Super cal.
Subtract $10 for blue finish.

❋ **Crusader Combat** - similar to M-1911 Crusader, except has 4¼ in. barrel and choice of fixed or adj. (disc. 2000) sights, 38 oz. New 2000.

MSR	$655	$575	$500	$460	$425	$400	$375	$350

Add $20 for stainless steel.
Subtract $10 for blue finish.

❋ **Crusader Compact** - 4 in. barrel, similar to Crusader Combat, except has shorter grip frame, 6 shot mag., 36 oz. Limited mfg. 2000 only.

			$715	$600	$500	$475	$425	$375	$325

Last MSR was $775.

SUPERMATIC TROPHY MATCH (MATCH MODEL) - similar to M-1911 Crusader, except has National Match 5 or 6 in. barrel and bushing, polished feed ramp and throated barrel, lowered/flared ejection port, 40 oz. New 2000.

MSR	$995	$850	$700	$600	$525	$475	$425	$375

Subtract $100 for blue finish (disc. 2001).
Subtract $80 if w/o sights and no finish (disc.).

CAMP PERRY MODEL - .45 ACP cal., 5 in. barrel, mil-spec slide, barrel and barrel bushing, blue or TuTone (mfg. 2001 only) finish only, competition tuned, beveled mag. well, 40 oz. New 2000.

MSR	$995	$895	$675	$600	$550	$495	$450	$400

G-MAN - .45 ACP cal., 5 in. barrel, special tolerances, including frame to slide fit, match grade stainless barrel and National Match bushing, polished feed ramp, throated barrel, slotted hammer, lightweight trigger, lowered and flared ejection port, beveled mag. well, checkered American walnut grips, black Teflon finish, includes two 8 shot mag., 39 oz. New 2001.

MSR	$1,225	$1,075	$900	$825	$750	$675	$600	$550

Grading	100%	98%	95%	90%	80%	70%	60%

GI MODEL - .45 ACP cal., 5 in. barrel, parkerized finish, fixed sights, classic WWII style (1911A1 frame), 7 shot mag. Introduced 2002.

	MSR	$498		$450	$395	$365	$335	$300	$285	$270

ARMY SPECIAL - .45 ACP cal., 5 in. barrel, blue or parkerized finish, 7 shot mag., fixed sights, 39 oz. Limited mfg. 2000.

		$485	$435	$395	$365	$330	$300	$285

Last MSR was $549.

NAVY MODEL - similar to Army Special, except is stainless steel, 39 oz. Limited mfg. 2000.

		$535	$465	$425	$395	$350	$325	$300

Last MSR was $599.

AIR CREW MODEL - similar to Army Special, except is titanium, 26 oz. New 2000.

While advertised, this model was never manufactured.

RIFLES: SEMI-AUTO

M1 CARBINE - .30 Carbine cal., 18 in. barrel, parkerized finish, wood stock, adj. rear sight, 10 shot mag., mfg. in the U.S., and patterned after the WWII design, 5½ lbs. Limited mfg. beginning 2001.

	MSR	$575		$500	$425	$375	$335	$300	$275	$250

P50 RIFLE/CARBINE - .50 BMG cal., designed by Robert Pauza, gas operation, 24 or 29 in. barrel, MOA accuracy at 1,000 yards, includes two 5 shot mags. and hard case, 25 (carbine) or 30 lbs. Limited mfg. beginning 2001.

	MSR	$7,950		$7,500	$6,750	$5,750	$5,000	$4,500	$4,000	$3,500

FIRESTORM

Current trademark of pistols manufactured by Industria Argentina. Imported and distributed beginning late 2000 by SGS Imports, International Inc., located in Wanamassa, NJ.

PISTOLS: SEMI-AUTO

FIRESTORM SERIES (.22 LR & .380 ACP) - .22 LR or .380 ACP cal., double action, 3½ in. barrel, matte or duo-tone finish, 7 (.380 ACP) or 10 (.22 LR) shot mag., 3 dot combat sights, anatomic rubber grips, 23 oz. Importation began 2001.

	MSR	$249		$220	$190	$170	$155	$145	$135	$125

Add $25 for duo-tone finish.

MINI-FIRESTORM - 9mm Para., .40 S&W, or .45 ACP (new 2002) cal., double action, 3½ in. barrel, nickel, matte or duo-tone finish, 7 (.45 ACP cal.) or 10 shot mag., 3 dot sights, polymer grips, safeties include manual, firing pin, and decocking, 24½ oz. Importation began 2001.

	MSR	$367		$315	$270	$240	$210	$195	$180	$165

Add $8 for duo-tone finish.
Add $25 for nickel finish.
Add $8 for .45 ACP cal.

FIRESTORM 45 GOVERNMENT - .45 ACP cal., single action, 5 1/8 in. barrel, matte or duo-tone finish, 7 shot mag., anatomic rubber grips, 36 oz. Importation began 2001.

	MSR	$315		$270	$240	$210	$190	$175	$165	$155

Add $10 for duo-tone finish.

F

Grading	100%	98%	95%	90%	80%	70%	60%

❋ *Firestorm 45 Compact* - .45 ACP cal., 4¼ in. barrel, otherwise similar to Firestorm 45 Government, 34 oz. Importation began 2001.

MSR **$315**		**$270**	**$240**	**$210**	**$190**	**$175**	**$165**	**$155**

Add $10 for duo-tone finish.

❋ *Firestorm Mini Compact* - .45 ACP cal., 3 1/8 in. barrel, chrome or matte or duo- tone finish, 10 shot staggered mag., polymer grips, 31 oz. Imported 2001 only.

$280	**$245**	**$215**	**$195**	**$180**	**$170**	**$155**

Last MSR was $324.

Add $17 for chrome finish.

FLODMAN GUNS

Current manufacturer established in 1978 and located in Järsta, Sweden. In 1992, Skullman Enterprise AB took over Flodman Guns. No current U.S. importation.

O/U: LONG GUNS

Flodman manufactures a variety of high quality shotguns, combination guns, and double rifles. They offer three designs – hunting, sporting, and luxury. All Flodman O/Us utilize a low profile, boxlock, stainless steel self-opening action, patented ejector (allows dry firing w/o ejector movement), and have no hammer, rather a primed firing pin which moves perpendicular, allowing 2/1000 of a second detonation time. Barrels are available in either titanium or Sandvik steel, and are equipped with choke tubes. Prices for the Standard Model start at $9,800, while Titanium barrels start at $15,500. Please contact the factory directly for more information regarding an individual price quotation and delivery time.

FORT WORTH FIREARMS

Previous manufacturer located in Fort Worth, TX 1995-2000.

PISTOLS: SEMI-AUTO, RIMFIRE

MATCH MASTER STANDARD - .22 LR cal., 3 7/8, 4½, 5½, 7½, or 10 in. bull barrel, double extractors, includes upper push button and standard mag. release, beveled mag. well, angled grip, flared slide, low profile frame. Mfg. 1995-2000.

$310	**$265**	**$230**	**$200**	**$185**	**$170**	**$160**

Last MSR was $389.

Add $84 for 10 in. bull barrel.

❋ *Match Master Dovetail* - similar to Match Master Standard, except has 3 7/8, 4½, or 5½ barrel with dovetail rib. Mfg. 1995-2000.

$385	**$325**	**$285**	**$240**	**$215**	**$190**	**$170**

Last MSR was $473.

❋ *Match Master Deluxe* - similar to Match Master Standard, except has Weaver rib on barrel. Mfg. 1995-2000.

$450	**$365**	**$315**	**$280**	**$240**	**$215**	**$190**

Last MSR was $538.

Add $92 for 10 in. barrel.

SPORT KING - .22 LR cal., 4½ or 5½ in. barrel, blued finish, military grips, drift sight, 10 shot mag. Mfg. 1995-2000.

$275	**$245**	**$225**	**$200**	**$185**	**$170**	**$160**

Last MSR was $313.

Grading	100%	98%	95%	90%	80%	70%	60%

CITATION - .22 LR cal., 5½ in. bull or 7¼ in. fluted barrel, military grips, 10 shot mag. Mfg. 1995-2000.

| | $310 | $265 | $230 | $200 | $185 | $170 | $160 |

Last MSR was $389.

TROPHY - .22 LR cal., 5½ or 7¼ in. bull barrel, blued finish, military grips, 10 shot mag. Mfg. 1995-2000.

| | $330 | $285 | $240 | $200 | $185 | $170 | $160 |

Last MSR was $411.

Add $41 for left-hand action (5½ in. barrel only).

VICTOR - .22 LR cal., 3 7/8, 4½ (VR or Weaver rib), or 5½ (VR or Weaver rib), 8 (Weaver rib), or 10 (Weaver rib) in. barrel, blued finish, military grips, 10 shot mag. Mfg. 1995-2000.

| | $385 | $325 | $285 | $240 | $215 | $190 | $170 |

Last MSR was $473.

Add $65 for 4½ or 5½ in. Weaver rib barrel.
Add approx. $148 for 8 or 10 in. Weaver rib barrel.

OLYMPIC - .22 LR or Short cal., 6¾ in. fluted barrel, blued finish, military grips, 10 shot mag. Mfg. 1995-2000.

| | $525 | $465 | $415 | $360 | $330 | $295 | $265 |

Last MSR was $600.

SHARP SHOOTER - .22 LR cal., 5½ in. bull barrel, blued finish, military grips, 10 shot mag. Mfg. 1995-2000.

| | $300 | $260 | $230 | $200 | $185 | $170 | $160 |

Last MSR was $380.

RIFLES: BOLT ACTION

YOUTH RIFLE - .22 LR cal., bolt action, single shot, shortened stock dimensions. Mfg. 1995-96.

| | $120 | $105 | $90 | $80 | $70 | $60 | $50 |

Last MSR was $138.

SHOTGUNS: SLIDE ACTION

GL 18 - 12 ga. only, security configuration with 18 in. barrel with perforated shroud, thumb operated laser/xenon light built into end of 7 shot mag. tube, ammo storage. Mfg. 1995-96.

| | $295 | $265 | $240 | $210 | $190 | $170 | $160 |

Last MSR was $347.

FOX, A.H.

Current manufacturer located in New Britain, CT. The A.H. Fox trademark was brought to life once again during 1993 when the Connecticut Shotgun Manufacturing Company, began producing an A.H. Fox 20 gauge in 5 different grades. Previously manufactured in Philadelphia, PA 1903-1930, and in Utica, NY from 1930-approx. 1946. Manufactured by Savage 1930-1988.

Depending on the remaining A.H. Fox factory data, a factory letter authenticating the configuration of a particular Fox shotgun (not to be confused with the more recent Savage/Stevens designed Fox doubles) may be obtained by contacting John T. Callahan (see Trademark Index for listings and address). If a model number is not known, please include a photo, the ser. no., gauge, barrel length and style, stock and forearm style, markings, patent dates, inspector stamps, etc. The charge for this service is $25.00 for the Sterlingworth Model, and $30.00 for graded models - please allow 2-4 weeks for an adequate response.

Mr. Ansley H. Fox first started manufacturing shotguns in circa 1896. This first company was called the Fox Gun Co. located in Baltimore, MD. Relatively few guns were made and surviving specimens today are very rare. After this venture, he was employed by the Baltimore Gun Co. for several years (circa 1900-1903). Following this period, he formed the Philadelphia Gun Co. where the predecessors to the A.H. Fox Gun Co. models were manufactured. These Philadelphia Gun Co. models (circa 1904) were the same as the newer Fox shotguns except that the hinge pin was removed. Sources indicate that the lowest grade was an "A" with the highest being an "E" (fully engraved and ultra rare). Following this tenure, Mr. Fox went on to form the A.H. Fox Gun Co. that was started approx. 1905. In addition to being an entrepreneur and trend setter, Mr. Fox also had the reputation of being an expert shot in his own right, winning more than a few events on the East Coast around the turn of the century.

The A.H. Fox Gun Company of Philadelphia, Pennsylvania, began production in 1905 and produced high quality double barrel shotguns until 1930. The Savage Arms Company, then of Utica, New York, acquired the Fox Company and produced these guns until 1942, when all but the utilitarian model B series guns were discontinued.

A.H. Fox guns are considered an American classic comparable to L.C. Smith, Parker, and others. Collector interest is high and will undoubtedly grow. The guns do not command quite as high a price as the Smith and Parker guns, but represent a fine investment collectible value.

Savage made guns from 1930-1942 are usually valued similarly as the early A.H. Fox guns. The recent production B series are just not in the same class and are obviously not intended to be. They are lower priced by today's standards and are designed as a utility grade hunting gun.

FOX COMPANY CHRONOLOGY

1906 - Company formed January 1906, A, B & C Grades introduced in 12 ga. only. D and F Grades introduced in 12 ga. in 1907. Ejector guns introduced in 1908. 1910 saw the introduction of the 12 ga. Sterlingworth - William H. Gough takes over as Chief of Engraving. Ansley Fox resigns in 1911 - first catalog showing Sterlingworth Model (called Model 1911). A-F Grades released in 16 and 20 ga. during 1912, as well as the addition of a 20 ga. Sterlingworth. 16 ga. Sterlingworth introduced in 1913. Fox/Kautsky single trigger introduced in 1914 - engineering transition complete. During 1915, the XE Grade was introduced. The B Grade was dropped in 1918. Single barrel trap guns (J, K, and L Grades) were introduced in 1919. 1920 saw the introduction of the M Grade single barrel trap. In 1922, both the G and HE Grades were released. Beavertail forend and vent. rib were introduced in 1927. 1929 was the Savage buy-out (November), GE Grade dropped. Company moved from Philadelphia, PA to Utica, NY in 1930. Skeeter Grade introduced in 1931 while the 20 ga. HE Grade was disc. 1932 saw the introduction of both the Trap Grade Double and SP Grade. Wildfowl Grade was introduced in 1934. 1935 was the last year of the K and L single barrel trap guns. 1937 was the last year for the J Grade single barrel trap gun. The last 16 and 12 ga. Sterlingworths were built in 1939. The outbreak of the war in 1941 saw the last FE Grade shipped, the Wildfowler Grade dropped, and the introduction of the Model B. 1942 was the last retail catalog. Factory records indicate that the last 12 ga. was shipped in 1945 and the last 20 ga. was shipped during 1946 (SP Grade shipped in December, 1946). However, guns continued to be assembled from left-over parts as late as the 1960s.

FOX SERIAL NUMBER ASSIGNMENTS

The publisher wishes to express his thanks to Mr. Gurney Brown for providing the model serialization and years of mfg. in this section.

Ser. # range 50,000-200,000 - 12 ga. Sterlingworth - 111,556 mfg.
Ser. # range 350,000-400,000 - 16 ga. Sterlingworth - 28,481 mfg.
Ser. # range 250,000-300,000 - 20 ga. Sterlingworth - 21,304 mfg.

Grading	100%	98%	95%	90%	80%	70%	60%

Ser. # range 1-50,000 - 12 ga. A-F Grades - 35,280 mfg.
Ser. # range 300,000-350,000 - 16 ga. A-F Grades - 3,875 mfg.
Ser. # range 200,000-250,000 - 20 ga. A-F Grades - 3,974 mfg.
Ser. # range 400,000-400,568 - 12 ga. Single Barrel Traps - 568 mfg.

FOX MODELS BY YEARS IN MFG.

Sterlingworth - 1910-1942 mfg. - 32 years.
Wildfowler - 1934-1940 mfg. - 6 years.
Trap Double - 1932-1942 mfg. - 10 years.
Skeeter - 1931-1942 mfg. - 11 years.
SP - 1932-1946 mfg. - 14 years.
A - 1906-1942 mfg. - 36 years.
B - 1906-1919 mfg. - 13 years.
C - 1906-1942 mfg. - 36 years.
D - 1907-1942 mfg. - 35 years.
F - 1907-1940 mfg. - 33 years.
G - 1922-1929 mfg. - 7 years.
H - 1922-1939 mfg. - 17 years.
J - 1919-1937 mfg. - 18 years.
K - 1919-1935 mfg. - 16 years.
L - 1919-1935 mfg. - 16 years.
M - 1920-1937 mfg. - 17 years.
X - 1915-1942 mfg. - 27 years.

SHOTGUNS: SxS, CURRENT MFG.

Delivery time for custom orders is currently 10-14 months, depending on gauge and grade.

The following models are manufactured by the Connecticut Manufacturing Co. located in New Britain, CT. These finely made shotguns have the following standard features: automatic safety, auto ejectors, DTs, Chromox 26, 28, or 30 in. barrels, individual barrel chokings, 2¾ in. chambers, scalloped receiver, Turkish Circassian walnut with hand-rubbed oil finish, choice of straight, semi-pistol or full-pistol grip stock with custom dimensions, splinter forearm, ivory bead sights. Special order options are as follows: Krupp steel barrels ($200), Fox SST ($1,200), walnut upgrades ($300-$2,200), custom initials ($200-$350), personalized gold inlays on barrel ($500), skeleton steel buttplate ($650), beavertail forearm ($650), and traditional leather trunk case with accessories ($850). Multi-barrel sets (same or multi-gauge) are also available with prices ranging from $4,500-$8,200, depending on the grade.

Add $1,500 for 28 ga. and .410 bore guns on the following models (except Exhibition Grade).

CE GRADE - 16 (new 1995), 20, 28 ga. (new 1995), or .410 bore (new 1995), engraved with fine scroll and game scenes, Grade I Turkish Circassian walnut. New 1993.

	MSR	$11,000		$11,000	$8,500	$6,250	$5,250	$4,500	$3,350	$2,700

XE GRADE - ga.'s similar to CE Grade, scroll work and engraved game scenes, Grade II Turkish Circassian walnut. New 1993.

	MSR	$12,500		$12,500	$9,250	$6,500	$5,500	$4,750	$3,500	$3,000

DE GRADE - ga.'s similar to CE Grade, intricate and extensive engraving, Grade III highly figured Turkish Circassian walnut. New 1993.

	MSR	$15,000		$15,000	$11,500	$9,500	$7,750	$6,250	$5,000	$4,000

FE GRADE - ga.'s similar to CE Grade, gold inlays surrounded by different types of scroll work, Grade IV highly figured Turkish Circassian walnut with finest checkering. New 1993.

	MSR	$20,000		$20,000	$16,500	$12,750	$9,750	$8,000	$6,250	$4,750

100%	98%	95%	90%	80%	70%	60%	50%	40%	30%	20%	10%

EXHIBITION GRADE - ga.'s similar to CE Grade, individually built per customer specifications on a "cost-no-object" basis, includes best-quality leather trunk case with full accessories, Exhibition Grade Turkish Circassian walnut. New 1993.

> This model is a special order only, and the base price is $30,000. Please contact the company directly for an individual price quotation and available options.

SHOTGUNS: SxS, DISC.

STERLINGWORTH - 12, 16, or 20 ga., 26, 28, or 30 in. barrels, various chokes, boxlock, extractors, double trigger, checkered pistol grip stock. Mfg. 1905-1930.

N/A	$1,250	$1,050	$875	$750	$650	$500	$450	$400	$365	$325	$275

Add 33% for auto ejectors.

Add 50% for 20 ga.

> A single trigger is a very desirable option on this model.

> Ser. no. range on 12 ga. Sterlingworths is 50,000-200,000, 16 ga. is 350,000-400,000, and 20 ga. is 250,000-300,000.

STERLINGWORTH DELUXE - similar to Sterlingworth, with recoil pad and ivory bead, 32 in. barrel available.

N/A	$1,500	$1,200	$995	$900	$825	$725	$650	$550	$475	$425	$395

Add 33% for auto ejectors.

Add 50% for 20 ga.

> A single trigger was not an option on this model.

STERLINGWORTH SKEET - similar to Sterlingworth, with 26 or 28 in. skeet boring, straight grip stock.

> This model is very scarce (only several are known) and the extreme rarity factor precludes accurate price evaluation.

SUPER HE GRADE - 12 ga., 2¾ (very rare) or 3 in. chambered long range gun, 30 and 32 in. full choke, auto ejectors, otherwise similar to Sterlingworth.

N/A	$5,200	$4,800	$4,400	$3,950	$3,400	$2,850	$2,300	$1,900	$1,625	$1,475	$1,300

Add $300 for SST.

> Original 3 in. chambered HE grades are marked "not warranteed, see instruction tag" on barrel flats. The HE grade was also manufactured in 20 ga. but is extremely rare. 2¾ in. chambers are rarer than 3 in. guns in this model.

HIGHER GRADE MODELS (A-F) - the following higher grade Fox shotguns are similar to the Sterlingworth in configuration. The grades differ in engraving and inlays, grade of wood and general workmanship. The E designation means auto ejectors.

> Early A and B grades have very little engraving and are much less desirable than later models. The following values are for later guns.

> **VALUES ARE FOR 12 GA.**

> **Add 50% for 16 ga. (made on same frame as 20 ga.).**

> **Add 75% for 20 ga.**

> **Add $200-$1,000 for SST, depending on grade.**

> **Add $200-$1,000 for beavertail forearm, depending on grade.**

> Note: These guns were disc. in 1942 by Savage Arms after they mfg. them for 12 years. Pre- 1930 guns were made by A.H. Fox Company.

✱ A Grade

N/A	$2,175	$1,875	$1,625	$1,375	$1,075	$900	$825	$725	$650	$600	$525

✱ AE Grade (ejectors)

N/A	$2,700	$2,400	$2,075	$1,675	$1,400	$1,150	$1,000	$900	$850	$825	$725

100%	98%	95%	90%	80%	70%	60%	50%	40%	30%	20%	10%

* **BE Grade (ejectors)**

| N/A | N/A | $4,450 | $3,950 | $3,475 | $2,950 | $2,500 | $2,250 | $1,975 | $1,800 | $1,675 | $1,550 |

This model is rarely encountered.

* **CE Grade (ejectors)**

| N/A | N/A | $5,200 | $4,650 | $4,150 | $3,750 | $3,300 | $3,000 | $2,700 | $2,425 | $2,150 | $1,875 |

* **XE Grade (ejectors)**

| N/A | N/A | $7,350 | $6,750 | $5,950 | $5,225 | $4,625 | $4,100 | $3,650 | $3,200 | $2,750 | $2,400 |

* **DE Grade (ejectors)**

| N/A | N/A | $11,650 | $9,675 | $8,750 | $7,500 | $6,750 | $6,000 | $5,300 | $4,750 | $4,300 | $3,750 |

* **FE Grade (ejectors)** - top-of-the-line model, only infrequently encountered.

| N/A | N/A | $19,500 | $16,450 | $14,150 | $12,000 | $10,500 | $9,750 | $9,150 | $9,000 | $8,750 | $8,250 |

SINGLE BARREL TRAP - 12 ga., 30 or 32 in. vent. rib barrel, full choke, boxlock, auto ejector, checkered trap style stock and recoil pad. The grades differ in wood, engraving, and overall quality. ME grade is custom built and extremely high quality with gold inlays. These models were disc. 1942. 568 single barrel trap guns were mfg. between 1932-1942 and have a ser. range of 400,000-400,568, with Monte Carlo stock.

Even though trap guns may be rarer than their SxS counterparts, to date their desirability is less since there are simply fewer collectors.

* **JE Grade**

| N/A | $3,860 | $3,550 | $3,200 | $2,800 | $2,500 | $2,100 | $1,800 | $1,600 | $1,500 | $1,425 | $1,325 |

* **KE Grade**

| N/A | $5,200 | $4,650 | $4,000 | $3,500 | $3,200 | $2,800 | $2,600 | $2,400 | $2,250 | $2,100 | $1,975 |

* **LE Grade**

| N/A | N/A | $6,500 | $5,750 | $5,000 | $4,500 | $4,100 | $3,750 | $3,300 | $3,000 | $2,650 | $2,300 |

* **ME Grade**

Extreme rarity factor precludes accurate percentage pricing on this model.

Grading	100%	98%	95%	90%	80%	70%	60%

MODEL B DOUBLE BARREL - 12, 16, 20 ga., or .410 bore, 24-30 in. barrels, various chokes, vent rib on newer models, boxlock, extractors, double triggers, handcut or pressed checkered pistol grip stock and forearm. Mfg. 1940-1986.

			$395	$350	$295	$265	$235	$200	$180

Last MSR was $250.

Add 20% for 20 ga., 35% for .410 bore.

MODEL B-ST - similar to model B, with single trigger. Mfg. 1955-1966.

			$500	$425	$350	$315	$290	$260	$230

Add 20% for 20 ga., 35% for .410 bore.

MODEL B-DL - similar to model B-ST, with satin chrome frame, select wood. Mfg. 1962-1965.

			$600	$475	$425	$350	$315	$275	$250

Add 20% for 20 ga., 35% for .410 bore.

MODEL B-DE - similar to B-DL, with less checkering. Mfg. 1965-1966.

			$550	$450	$400	$325	$300	$275	$250

Add 20% for 20 ga., 35% for .410 bore.

Grading	100%	98%	95%	90%	80%	70%	60%

MODEL B-SE - 12, 20 ga., or .410 bore, single trigger, selective ejectors, vent. rib, beavertail forearm, select walnut with press checkering. Mfg. 1966-88.

| | $750 | $675 | $600 | $550 | $475 | $400 | $325 |

Last MSR was $525.

Add 20% for 20 ga., 35% for .410 bore.

Even though there were multiple series designations assigned to this model, there seems to be little difference in desirability. For that reason, other designations will be priced similarly to values shown above.

FRANCHI, LUIGI

Current manufacturer established during the mid-1860s, and located in Brescia, Italy. This trademark has been imported for approx. the past 50 years. Currently imported exclusively by Benelli USA, located in Accokeek, MD, since 1998. Previously imported and distributed by American Arms, Inc. located in North Kansas City, MO. Some models were previously imported by FIE firearms located in Hialeah, FL.

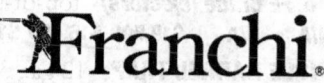

Also see Sauer/Franchi heading in the S section.

RIFLES: SEMI-AUTO

CENTENNIAL MODEL - .22 LR cal., 21 in. barrel, open sight to commemorate Franchi's 100th anniversary. Mfg. 1968 only.

| | $330 | $250 | $220 | $195 | $165 | $150 | $140 |

* **Engraved deluxe model**

| | $415 | $330 | $305 | $275 | $240 | $200 | $165 |

* **Gallery model**

| | $220 | $195 | $160 | $120 | $100 | $80 | $60 |

SHOTGUNS: O/U

Currently manufactured Franchi O/U shotguns are supplied with a custom-fitted hard case, and use choke tubes that are compatible with both Beretta and Benelli.

DE LUXE MODEL PRITI - 12 or 20 ga., boxlock action, ST, ejectors, 26 or 28 in. VR barrels with fixed chokes. Imported 1988-1989 only.

| | $395 | $350 | $315 | $285 | $240 | $215 | $185 |

Last MSR was $460.

This model was imported exclusively by FIE Firearms located in Hialeah, FL.

ALCIONE MODEL - 12 ga., 28 in. barrels, less engraving than Alcione SL, separated barrels. Importation disc. 1989.

| | $675 | $550 | $495 | $460 | $430 | $380 | $335 |

Last MSR was $800.

Previously designated Diamond Model.

This model was imported exclusively by FIE Firearms located in Hialeah, FL.

ALCIONE SL - 12 ga., 27 or 28 in. barrels, 6 lbs. 13 oz., separated barrels, ejectors, single trigger, silver finished frame engraved with luggage case. Importation disc. 1986.

| | $1,150 | $995 | $875 | $800 | $725 | $640 | $550 |

Last MSR was $1,595.

Grading	100%	98%	95%	90%	80%	70%	60%

ALCIONE 2000 SX (FIELD MODEL) - 12 ga., 3 in. chambers, 28 in. barrels, SST, separated barrels, ejectors, single trigger, engraved silver finished frame with gold accents, with case, 7 lbs. 4 oz. Imported 1997 only.

	$1,675	$1,495	$1,275	$1,025	$875	$750	$650

Last MSR was $1,895.

ALCIONE FIELD - 12 ga. only, 3 in. chambers, nickel finished steel alloy frame with game bird etching, SST, ejectors, 26, or 28 in. interchangeable barrels with choke tubes, checkered satin finished walnut stock and forearm, includes hard case, 7.4 lbs. New 1998.

MSR $1,275		$1,100	$950	$800	$700	$600	$500	$425

This model was previously designated 97-12 IBS.

* *Alcione LF* - 12 or 20 ga., 3 in. chambers (20 ga. only), lightweight alloy receiver with etching and gold fill, approx. 6.8 lbs. Mfg. 2000-2002.

	$1,150	$975	$875	$775	$650	$550	$425

Last MSR was $1,305.

ALCIONE SL SPORT - 12 ga. only, 2¾ in. chambers (can also be fitted for barrels with 3 in. chambers), polished stainless steel receiver, blued barrels, SST, manual safety, ejectors, 30 in. target rib ported barrels with choke tubes, detachable sideplates, includes hard case, 7.7 lbs.

MSR $1,650		$1,400	$1,200	$950	$850	$725	$625	$475

This model was previously designated SL IBS.

ALCIONE SX - 12 ga. only, 3 in. chambers, 26 or 28 in. interchangeable vent. barrels with VR and 3 choke tubes, deluxe walnut, removeable sideplates with etched game scenes, gold trigger, approx. 7.2 lbs. Importation began 2001.

MSR $1,800		$1,500	$1,350	$1,050	$925	$800	$700	$575

Add $450-$500 for extra set of barrels.

ALCIONE TITANIUM (T) - 12 or 20 ga., 3 in. chambers, features receiver manufactured from aluminum alloy coupled with titanium inserts, 26 or 28 in. interchangeable vent. barrels with VR and 3 choke tubes, deluxe walnut, removeable sideplates with etched game scenes, gold trigger with selector switch, approx. 6.8 lbs. Importation began 2002.

MSR $1,425		$1,225	$1,050	$950	$875	$800	$750	$695

VELOCE - 20 or 28 ga., 3 in. chambers on 20 ga., 26 or 28 (20 ga. only) in. barrels with 3 choke tubes, aluminum alloy steel reinforced frame, etched game scene receiver with gold filled inlays, deluxe oil finished checkered pistol grip or English (new 2002) stock and forearm, mechanical gold SST, 5½ (28 ga.) or 5.8 (20 ga.) lbs. Importation began 2001.

MSR $1,425		$1,250	$1,050	$925	$825	$725	$600	$550

Add $75 for 28 ga.

BLACK MAGIC SPORTING HUNTER - 12 ga. only, 3 in. chambers, 28 in. separated barrels with VR and Franchokes, black frame with gold accents and trigger, SST, ejectors, checkered walnut stock and forearm, 7 lbs. Imported 1989-91.

	$995	$875	$800	$725	$650	$575	$495

Last MSR was $1,249.

The Black Magic Model Series was imported exclusively by American Arms, Inc. located in North Kansas City, MO.

* *Black Magic Lightweight Hunter* - similar to Black Magic Sporting Hunter except 2¾ in. chambers only, 26 in. separated barrels with VR and Franchokes, alloy frame, 6 lbs. Imported 1989- 91.

	$975	$850	$775	$700	$625	$550	$475

Last MSR was $1,209.

Grading	100%	98%	95%	90%	80%	70%	60%

SPORTING 2000 - 12 ga. only, design for sporting clays or hunting, 28 in. vent. ported (disc. 1993) or unported (new 1997) barrels with target VR and choke tubes, SST, ejectors, select walnut with checkering, solid pad, hard case, 7¾ lbs. Imported 1992-1993, resumed 1997, disc. 1998.

	$1,275	$1,025	$875	$750	$650	$575	$500

Last MSR was $1,495.

ARISTOCRAT FIELD - 12 ga., 26, 28, or 30 in. barrels, various chokes, vent. rib, auto ejectors, boxlock, selective single trigger, checkered pistol grip stock. Mfg. 1960-1969.

	$660	$470	$440	$395	$375	$340	$310

ARISTOCRAT MAGNUM - similar to Field, except 32 in. barrel, 3 in. chamber, full choke, pad. Mfg. 1962-1965.

	$660	$470	$440	$395	$375	$340	$310

ARISTOCRAT SKEET - similar to Field, but 26 in. vent. rib, bored skeet no. 1 and no. 2. Mfg. 1960-1969.

	$715	$525	$495	$450	$430	$395	$365

ARISTOCRAT TRAP - 30 in. vent. rib barrel, bored mod. and full, trap stock Mfg. 1960- 1969.

	$745	$550	$525	$480	$455	$415	$380

ARISTOCRAT SILVER KING - select wood, engraved coin finished frame. Mfg. 1962- 1969.

	$750	$560	$535	$485	$470	$430	$400

ARISTOCRAT DELUXE - finer wood, more engraving. Mfg. 1960-1966.

	$990	$870	$835	$810	$770	$715	$660

ARISTOCRAT SUPREME - gold inlaid game birds. Mfg. 1960-1966.

	$1,430	$1,265	$1,155	$1,075	$990	$935	$880

ARISTOCRAT IMPERIAL - high grade wood, more engraving. Mfg. 1967-1969.

	$2,640	$2,200	$2,090	$1,925	$1,815	$1,650	$1,430

ARISTOCRAT MONTE CARLO - highest grade wood, elaborate engraving and inlay, mfg. 1967-1969.

	$3,520	$3,080	$2,915	$2,640	$2,420	$2,090	$1,870

FALCONET S - 12 ga., lightweight model of the Alcione SL, 27 or 28 in. barrels, 6 lbs. 1 oz., separated barrels, moderate engraving on silver finish frame. Disc. 1985.

	$895	$765	$660	$560	$510	$460	$410

Last MSR was $1,015.

FALCONET FIELD - 12, 16, 20, 28 ga., or .410 bore, 24-30 in. barrels, various chokes, auto ejectors, select single trigger, engraved alloy frame, checkered walnut stock. Mfg. 1968-1975.

	100%	98%	95%	90%	80%	70%	60%
Buckskin (light)	$550	$495	$470	$440	$415	$385	$360
Ebony (black)	$550	$495	$470	$440	$415	$385	$360
Silver	$605	$550	$525	$495	$470	$415	$385

Add 25% for 28 ga. or .410 bore.

FALCONET SKEET - 26 in. barrels, bored skeet no. 1 and no. 2, wide vent. rib, case hardened steel frame. Mfg. 1970-1974.

	$935	$855	$825	$770	$715	$690	$650

FALCONET INTERNATIONAL SKEET - higher grade wood, more engraving. Mfg. 1970-1974.

	$1,045	$935	$865	$825	$770	$745	$700

FALCONET STANDARD TRAP - 12 ga., 30 in. mod. and full, wide vent. rib, trap stock, pad. Mfg. 1970-1974.

	$935	$855	$825	$770	$715	$690	$650

Grading	100%	98%	95%	90%	80%	70%	60%

FALCONET INTERNATIONAL TRAP - higher grade wood, more engraving. Mfg. 1970-1974.

	$1,045	$935	$865	$825	$770	$745	$700

FALCONET 2000 - 12 ga. only, boxlock with alloy frame featuring silver finish with gold plated game scenes, 26 in. separated barrels with VR and choke tubes, SST, ejectors, select checkered walnut stock and forearm, hard case, 6 lbs. Imported 1992-97.

	$1,245	$975	$850	$725	$650	$575	$500

Last MSR was $1,375.

FALCONET 97-12 IBS - 12 ga. only, 2¾ in. chambers, ultra light alloy frame with gold inlays, scroll engraving, and nickel finish, SST, ejectors, 26 in. barrels with Franchokes, checkered walnut stock and forearm, includes hard case. Imported 1998-2000.

	$875	$750	$625	$550	$500	$450	$400

Last MSR was $965.

PEREGRINE MODEL 451 - 12 ga., 26-28 in. barrels, various chokes, vent. rib, auto ejectors, alloy frame, selective single trigger, checkered pistol grip stock. Mfg. 1975.

	$605	$550	$525	$495	$440	$415	$360

PEREGRINE MODEL 400 - similar to 451, except steel frame. Mfg. 1975.

	$660	$605	$570	$540	$495	$460	$385

MODEL 2003 TRAP - 12 ga., 30 or 32 in. barrels, imp. mod. and full, or full and full, boxlock, auto ejectors, single selective trigger, high vent. rib, trap style stock, pad, cased. Mfg. 1976. Disc.

	$1,205	$1,090	$1,045	$910	$855	$770	$660

MODEL 2004 TRAP - similar to 2003, except single barrel, cased. Mfg. 1976. Disc.

	$1,205	$1,090	$1,045	$910	$855	$770	$660

MODEL 2005 COMBINATION TRAP - two sets of barrels, one single, one O/U, cased. Mfg. 1976. Disc.

	$1,815	$1,595	$1,515	$1,320	$1,210	$1,075	$935

MODEL 2005/3 COMBINATION TRAP - three sets of barrels, cased. Mfg. 1976. Disc.

	$2,420	$2,090	$1,980	$1,705	$1,515	$1,485	$1,320

UNDERGUN MODEL 3000 - radical competition trap, very high rib separated barrels, under single and O/U, drop in set screw chokes (hex drive), set aluminum cased. Disc.

	$2,750	$2,530	$2,310	$2,090	$1,980	$1,870	$1,760

SHOTGUNS: SxS

AIRONE - 12 ga., choice of barrel length and chokes, box lock, Anson & Deeley, auto ejectors, double triggers, checkered English style stock, engraved. Mfg. 1940-1950.

	$1,320	$1,100	$935	$825	$745	$715	$660

ASTORE - similar to Airone, except less engraving, extractors. Mfg. 1937-1960.

	$990	$910	$770	$715	$635	$580	$550

ASTORE 5 - similar to Astore, except higher grade wood, more engraving, auto ejectors. Disc.

	$2,200	$1,925	$1,650	$1,540	$1,460	$1,375	$1,320

ASTORE II - similar to Astore 5, except less elaborate, currently mfg. in Spain for Franchi.

	$1,210	$1,045	$935	$880	$800	$715	$660

Grading	100%	98%	95%	90%	80%	70%	60%

SIDELOCK DOUBLE BARREL - 12, 16, or 20 ga., barrels and choke custom order, stock to order, hand detachable side lock, self-opening action, auto ejectors, six grades offered, they differ only in overall quality and ornamentation, and grade of wood used.

	100%	98%	95%	90%	80%	70%	60%
Condor	$7,700	$6,600	$6,050	$5,720	$5,500	$4,620	$3,960
Imperial	$10,450	$9,350	$8,800	$8,250	$7,480	$6,600	$5,720
Imperiales	$10,670	$9,570	$9,020	$8,470	$7,700	$6,820	$5,940

SIDE-LOCK DOUBLE BARREL - the following models are available through the Beretta Galleries and selected premium dealers only (see Trademark Index).

٭ No. 5 Imperial Monte Carlo

MSR	$27,500	N/A	$13,750	$11,000	$9,900	$8,900	$7,750	$6,500

٭ No. 17 Imperial Monte Carlo

MSR	$35,000	N/A	$15,250	$12,500	$10,500	$9,350	$8,000	$7,000

٭ Imperial Monte Carlo Extra

Note: Imperial Monte Carlo Extra is currently being mfg. on special order only. Prices range from $53,000 - $90,000.

SHOTGUNS: SEMI-AUTO

BLACK MAGIC GAME - 12 ga. only, 3 in. chamber with gas metering system, interchangeable shell handling without adjustments, two-tone black alloy receiver with gold accents and trigger, 24, 26, or 28 in. VR barrel with Franchokes, checkered walnut stock and forearm, 7 lbs. Imported 1989- 91.

$550	$450	$395	$330	$300	$270	$240

Last MSR was $659.

٭ Black Magic Skeet - skeet variation of the Black Magic Game, 2¾ in. chamber, 26 in. ported VR barrel with fixed Tula skeet choke, skeet dimensioned stock, 7¼ lbs. Imported 1989-91.

$580	$475	$425	$350	$325	$295	$265

Last MSR was $699.

٭ Black Magic Trap - trap variation of the Black Magic Game, 2¾ in. chamber, 30 in. VR barrel with Franchoke system, trap dimensioned stock, 7½ lbs. Imported 1989- 91.

$615	$495	$430	$350	$325	$295	$265

Last MSR was $739.

48 AL FIELD MODEL - 12 (disc. 2001), 20, or 28 (new 1996) ga., 2¾ in. chamber, 24, 26, 28, or 30 (disc. in 1990) in. VR barrel with (beginning 1989) or w/o choke tubes, long recoil operation, alloy receiver, checkered pistol grip walnut stock and forearm, VR standard, standard choke tubes became available in 1989, 12 ga., 6 lbs. 9 oz. and 20 ga., 5 lbs. 6 oz. Mfg. 1950-present.

MSR	$715	$585	$530	$430	$325	$295	$265	$235

Add $100 for 28 ga.
Add $30 for 12 ga. 24 in. slug barrel (disc. 1994).
Subtract 10% if without choke tubes.

This model is also available as a Youth Model (12½ LOP, 20 ga. only). Starting in 1990, black receiver, gold accents, and choke tubes became standard.

٭ AL 48 Deluxe - 20 or 28 ga., 26 in. barrel, similar to AL 48 Standard, except has a high polish blue finish and upgraded walnut pistol grip or English (new 2002) stock and forearm, gold trigger and receiver accents. New 2000.

MSR	$940	$775	$625	$525	$400	$350	$300	$265

Add $150 for 28 ga.

Grading	100%	98%	95%	90%	80%	70%	60%

STANDARD MAGNUM (48/AL) - similar to Standard, except has 3 in. chamber with 28 in. (disc. 1988) or 32 in. VR barrel, recoil pad. Mfg. 1954-1990.

	$415	$360	$300	$270	$250	$230	$210

Last MSR was $482.

This model was slated to be replaced with the Combo S/T - however, while advertised, the Combo S/T was never mfg.

HUNTER MODEL (48/AL) - similar to Standard, except etched receiver, better wood, VR standard, Franchokes became available in 1989. Mfg. 1950-1990.

	$415	$360	$300	$270	$250	$230	$210

Last MSR was $482.

Add $35 for internal Franchokes (3).

This model was imported exclusively by FIE Firearms located in Hialeah, FL.

HUNTER MAGNUM - mfg. 1954-1973.

	$430	$380	$370	$340	$315	$290	$275

PRESTIGE MODEL - 12 ga. only, gas operated, vent. rib, various barrel lengths, alloy receiver, Franchokes became available in 1989. Imported 1985-1989.

	$575	$475	$395	$325	$310	$295	$275

Last MSR was $720.

Add $40 for internal Franchokes (3).

This model was imported exclusively by FIE Firearms located in Hialeah, FL.

* ***Turkey Model*** - similar to Prestige Model except has dull matte black finish, Franchokes standard. Imported 1989 only.

	$615	$515	$425	$350	$320	$300	$280

Last MSR was $760.

This model was imported exclusively by FIE Firearms located in Hialeah, FL.

ELITE MODEL - same general specifications as the Prestige Model, only etched receiver, Franchokes became available in 1989. Imported 1985-1989.

	$595	$500	$425	$350	$320	$300	$280

Last MSR was $740.

Add $45 for internal Franchokes (3).

This model was imported exclusively by FIE Firearms located in Hialeah, FL.

610 VS - 12 ga., incorporates gas-operated Variopress System, adjusts for both 2¾ and 3 in. shells, 4 lug rotating breech bolt, alloy receiver, non-glare finish, 26 or 28 in. VR barrels with Franchokes, checkered walnut stock and forearm. Imported 1997 only.

	$650	$550	$425	$325	$275	$250	$225

Last MSR was $750.

Add $45 for engraved receiver and bolt (Model 610 VSL).

MODEL 612/620 (VS) - 12 (Model 612) or 20 (Model 620) ga., 3 in. chamber, features Vario-System/Variomax gas operation utilizing reversable gas adjustment collar on mag. tube, advanced safety system, black receiver with (disc. 2001) or w/o gold borders (new 2002), 24, 26, or 28 in. barrel with choke tubes, last shot hold open, choice of checkered satin walnut, black synthetic stock and forearm, 100% Realtree X-tra brown (disc. 1999), Realtree HD Timber (new 2002), or Advantage (mfg. 2000-2002) camo coverage, 5.9-7 lbs. New 1998.

MSR	$710	$595	$495	$425	$350	$325	$300	$275

Add $40 for satin finished walnut stock and forearm.
Add $115 for 100% camo coverage (Models 612/620 VS Camo).
Add $20 for Youth Model (20 ga. only, 12½ LOP stock).

This model was previously designated the Variopress 612/620.

Grading	100%	98%	95%	90%	80%	70%	60%

✳ *Model 612 Sporting* - 12 ga. only, features blue receiver with gold logo (new 2002), or silver receiver with black border and gold small parts (disc. 1998) or matte black receiver with green logo (mfg. 2000-2002), 28 (disc. 1998) or 30 (new 2000) in. ported target rib barrel with Franchokes, select checkered walnut stock and forearm, 7.1 lbs. Limited mfg. 1998, reintroduced 2000.

MSR	$1,275	$1,075	$875	$750	$625	$525	$450	$375

This model was previously designated the Variopress 612 Sporting.

MODEL 612 DEFENSE - 12 ga. only, 18½ in. barrel with cyl. bore, matte finish metal with black synthetic stock and forearm, 6½ lbs. New 2000.

MSR	$635	$525	$450	$375	$325	$285	$265	$245

This model was previously designated the Variopress 612 Defense.

MODEL 912 - 12 ga. only, 3½ chamber, VarioSystem/Variomax gas operation utilizing reversable gas adjustment collar on mag. tube, lightweight alloy receiver, 24, 26, 28, or 30 in. VR barrel with 3 choke tubes, choice of satin walnut stock (new 2002), black synthetic or 100% Advantage Timber HD camo coverage, magazine cutoff, includes hard case, 7.5-7.8 lbs. Importation began 2001.

MSR	$940	$825	$725	$625	$525	$450	$375	$325

Add $50 for camo coverage.
Add $60 for satin finished walnut stock and forearm.
This model was previously designated the Variopress 912.

SPAS-12 - 12 ga., 2¾ in. chamber, combat shotgun that offers pump or semi-auto operation, 5 (new 1991) or 8 (disc.) shot tube mag., alloy receiver, synthetic stock with built- in pistol grip (limited quantities were also mfg. with a folding stock or metal fixed stock), one-button switch to change from semi-auto to slide action operation, 21½ in. barrel, 8¾ lbs. Importation disc. 1994.

		$675	$575	$475	$400	$350	$300	$280

Last MSR was $769.

This model was imported exclusively by FIE Firearms located in Hialeah, FL until 1990.

SPAS-15 - 12 ga. only, 2¾ in. chamber, operates as either semi-auto or slide action that is convertible with a one-button switch, 6 shot detachable box mag., 21½ in. barrel, lateral folding skeleton stock, carrying handle, 10 lbs. Limited importation 1989 only.

This model had very limited importation (less than 200) as the BATF disallowed further importation almost immediately. Even though the retail was in the $700 range, demand and rarity have pushed prices past the $2,000 level.

SAS-12 - 12 ga. only, 3 in. chamber, slide action only, synthetic stock with built-in pistol grip, 8 shot tube mag., 21½ in. barrel, 6.8 lbs. Imported 1988-90 only.

		$415	$360	$300	$270	$250	$230	$210

Last MSR was $473.

This model was imported exclusively by FIE Firearms located in Hialeah, FL.

LAW-12 - 12 ga. only, 2¾ in. chamber, gas operated semi-auto, synthetic stock with built- in pistol grip, 5 (new 1991) or 8 (disc.) shot tube mag., 21½ in. barrel, 6¾ lbs. Imported 1988-94.

		$570	$485	$400	$360	$320	$300	$280

Last MSR was $719.

TURKEY GUN - 12 ga., similar to Standard Mag., 3 in. chamber only, turkey scene engraved. Mfg. 1963-1965.

		$415	$385	$370	$340	$315	$290	$275

Grading	100%	98%	95%	90%	80%	70%	60%

SLUG GUN - 22 in. plain barrel, and rifle sights.

| | $360 | $330 | $315 | $295 | $275 | $255 | $240 |

SKEET GUN - 26 in. skeet choke, vent. rib, select wood. Mfg. 1972-1974.

| | $385 | $370 | $350 | $330 | $310 | $285 | $265 |

ELDORADO - fancy wood and gold filled engraved receiver. Mfg. 1954-1975.

| | $450 | $420 | $395 | $380 | $360 | $340 | $320 |

CROWN GRADE - engraved hunting scene. Mfg. 1954-1975.

| | $1,540 | $1,320 | $1,210 | $1,045 | $965 | $910 | $855 |

DIAMOND GRADE SILVER INLAID SCROLL - mfg. 1954-1975.

| | $1,980 | $1,735 | $1,540 | $1,430 | $1,210 | $1,045 | $965 |

IMPERIAL GRADE - gold inlaid hunting scene.

| | $2,420 | $2,090 | $1,925 | $1,760 | $1,595 | $1,485 | $1,320 |

Note: Standard, Skeet and Slug with steel frame mfg. 1965-1972, designated "Dynamic" 12 ga., values are the same.

MODEL 500 STANDARD - 12 ga., 26 or 28 in. barrel, various chokes, vent. rib, gas operated, checkered pistol grip stock. Mfg. 1976-disc.

| | $330 | $310 | $305 | $265 | $230 | $195 | $165 |

MODEL 520 DELUXE - engraved receiver.

| | $385 | $365 | $330 | $290 | $260 | $220 | $195 |

MODEL 520 ELDORADO GOLD - fine wood, engraved gold, inlaid receiver. Mfg. 1977- disc.

| | $990 | $770 | $715 | $660 | $580 | $525 | $470 |

MODEL 530 AUTO TRAP - similar to 500, except 30 or 32 in. full choke barrels, very high rib, special trap stock, pad.

| | $660 | $550 | $525 | $440 | $415 | $385 | $330 |

FRANCOTTE, AUGUSTE & CIE. S.A.

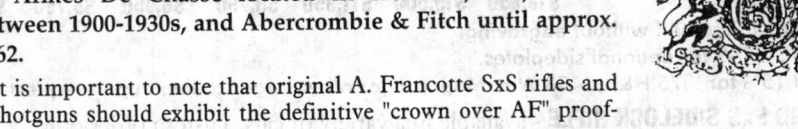

Current manufacturer located in Leige, Belgium since 1805. No current U.S. importation. Previously imported until 1999 by Armes De Chasse located in Hertford, NC, VL&O between 1900-1930s, and Abercrombie & Fitch until approx. 1962.

It is important to note that original A. Francotte SxS rifles and shotguns should exhibit the definitive "crown over AF" proof-mark on water table.

As this edition went to press, Francotte production has decreased due to a labor shortage, reducing their annual output to approx. 15-20 guns.

REVOLVERS

Francotte manufactured Pryse-type revolvers at the end of the 19th century, and these revolvers bore the name of the well-known British retailer. Encountered only infrequently domestically, these specimens found overseas are usually priced in the $150-$650 range.

RIFLES

All newly mfg. rifles in this section are custom made to the purchaser's individual specifications. Francotte takes advantage of 5 different frame sizes for its double rifles. The following values reflect the most recent U.S. pricing.

Grading	100%	98%	95%	90%	80%	70%	60%

BOLT ACTION MODEL - many calibers available between .18 Bee and .505 Gibbs Mag., selec checkered walnut stock, engraved mag. floor plate, gold inlays optional, the following val ues assume engraving.

* *Short Bolt Action* - cals. with shorter cartridges.

MSR	N/A	$9,400	$7,350	$6,000	$4,950	$4,100	$3,300	$2,700

  Subtract $3,250 if without engraving.

* *Standard Model* - cals. with medium cartridge lengths.

MSR	N/A	$7,825	$6,100	$4,975	$4,100	$3,300	$2,700	$2,000

  Subtract $2,675 if without engraving.

* *Magnum Action* - cals. with longer cartridge lengths.

MSR	N/A	$13,750	$10,850	$9,350	$7,750	$6,400	$4,950	$3,950

  Subtract $7,850 if without engraving.

SINGLE SHOT MOUNTAIN RIFLE - available in a variety of cals., boxlock or sidelock action custom order only.

* *Boxlock Mountain Rifle* - 6.5x50R, 7x57R, or 7x65R cal.

MSR	N/A	$13,900	$11,000	$9,450	$7,850	$6,500	$5,000	$4,000

  Subtract $4,800 if without engraving.
  Add 10% for optional sideplates.

* *Sidelock Mountain Rifle* - 7x65R or 7mm Rem. Mag. cal.

MSR	N/A	$24,800	$20,350	$16,650	$13,000	$10,500	$9,000	$8,000

  Subtract $5,725 if without engraving.

BOXLOCK SxS RIFLE - .30-06, .375 H&H, .470 NE, .500-3 in. or 9.3x62mm cal., ejectors, case colored frame with border engraving (including screws), quarter rib on barrel, deluxe checkered pistol grip walnut stock and forearm. New 1997.

MSR	N/A	$11,850	$9,700	$8,500	$7,250	$6,000	$4,950	$4,100

SIDELOCK SxS RIFLE - .30-06, .375 H&H, .470 NE, .500-3 in. or 9.3x62mm cal., ejectors, case colored frame with border engraving (including screws), quarter rib on barrel, deluxe checkered pistol grip walnut stock and forearm. New 1997.

MSR	N/A	$16,250	$14,250	$12,500	$10,250	$8,750	$7,250	$6,500

STANDARD SxS BOXLOCK RIFLE - available in a variety of cals., custom order only.

MSR	N/A	$18,650	$15,500	$11,350	$8,750	$6,950	$5,750	$5,000

  Subtract $7,600 if without engraving.
  Add $1,449 for optional sideplates.
  Add 15% for .375 H&H, .458 Win. Mag. cal., or other larger calibers upon request.

STANDARD SxS SIDELOCK RIFLE - available in a variety of cals., custom order only.

MSR	N/A	$29,450	$25,000	$20,250	$16,500	$13,000	$10,500	$9,000

  Subtract $7,000 if without engraving.

SHOTGUNS: SxS

All newly manufactured shotguns in this section are custom made to purchaser's individual specifi-cations. Basic types listed are also available in 24 or 32 ga. upon special order. Francotte takes advantage of 5 different action sizes, one for each gauge. Auguste Francotte does not manufacture guns by model - all guns are custom order.

Original A. Francotte SxS shotguns must have the "Francotte Choke Bore" marking on the water table. Be wary of fake barrel and frame markings, as some guns have recenty surfaced that are not Francotte, but have the Francotte name.

The following values reflect the most recent U.S. pricing.

Grading	100%	98%	95%	90%	80%	70%	60%

BOXLOCK MODEL - 12, 16, 20, 28 ga., or .410 bore, premium grade Belgium side-by-side, double triggers standard, auto ejectors, English scroll engraving, Anson & Deeley boxlock action.

MSR N/A	$15,450	$11,250	$8,000	$6,250	$5,000	$4,000	$3,250

Subtract $5,925 if without engraving.
Add 10% for 28 ga. or .410 bore.
Add $1,159 for sideplates with engraving.

* ❋ **Deluxe Anson & Deeley** - gold inlaid game scenes, and engraving is by customer's personal preference.

  Prices and options are quoted per individual request.

SIDELOCK MODEL - 12, 16, 20, 28 ga., or .410 bore, true sidelock action, Arabesque scroll engraving, various chokes and barrel lengths, custom order only.

MSR N/A	$27,300	$22,000	$18,750	$15,150	$12,000	$9,000	$7,750

Subtract $4,850 if without engraving.
Add 10% for 28ga. or .410 bore.

* ❋ **Deluxe Sidelock** - gold inlaid game scenes and engraving are by customer's personal preference.

  Prices and options are quoted per individual request.

JUBILEE MODEL - case colored frame with hand engraving.

	100%	98%	95%	90%	80%	70%	60%
	$2,250	$1,875	$1,525	$1,325	$1,100	$975	$850
No. 14	$2,750	$2,250	$1,975	$1,775	$1,600	$1,450	$1,150
No. 18	$2,950	$2,550	$2,250	$1,925	$1,700	$1,550	$1,225
No. 20	$3,450	$2,900	$2,575	$2,275	$1,900	$1,725	$1,375
No. 25	$4,000	$3,500	$3,000	$2,500	$2,150	$1,925	$1,575
No. 30	$5,450	$4,975	$4,500	$4,000	$3,500	$2,500	$2,200

KNOCKABOUT MODEL - disc. circa 1975.

	$2,350	$1,850	$1,575	$1,265	$1,100	$935	$825

Add 75% for 20 ga.
Add approx. 200%-250% for 28 ga. or .410 bore.

NO. 45 EAGLE GRADE MODEL - this model can be identified by the gold eagle on frame bottom, disc. circa 1977.

	$7,650	$6,700	$5,850	$4,950	$4,250	$3,800	$3,000

FRASER, DANL. & CO.

Current trademark owned by Dickson & MacNaughton located in Edinburgh, Scotland. Previously imported and distributed by Flying G Ranch, located in Carrizo Springs, TX.

Danl. Fraser & Co. has manufactured rifles since 1873 (originally located in Edinburgh, Scotland).

RIFLES: SINGLE SHOT

HIGHLANDER SINGLE SHOT - .22 LR or .22 Hornet cal., underlever falling block action (color case hardened), 24 in. (½ round, ½ octagon) barrel, folding express-style sights, pistol grip walnut stock with fine checkering. Disc.

$415	$335	$300	$280	$260	$240	$220

Last MSR was $475.

* ❋ **Royal Highlander** - .22 LR or .22 Hornet cal., mfg. in Scotland, rose and scroll engraving with 18 Kt. inlays. Special order only.

Grading	100%	98%	95%	90%	80%	70%	60%

FRASER FIREARMS CORP.

Previously manufactured by R.B. Industries, Ltd. until 1990. Previously distributed by Fraser Firearms Corp. located in Fraser, MI.

PISTOLS: SEMI-AUTO

FRASER 25 CAL. - .25 ACP cal. only, copy of the Bauer semi-auto pocket model, 6 shot mag., 2¼ in. barrel, stainless steel construction.

$120 $100 $90

Last MSR was $133.

Add $17 for Model 2 (black nylon grips).
Add $115 for Model 3 (24 Kt. gold plated).

FREEDOM ARMS

Current manufacturer established during 1983, and located in Freedom, WY. Consumer direct and dealer sales.

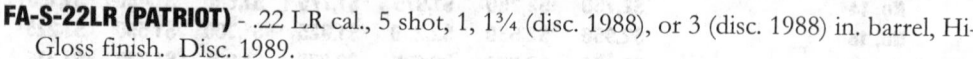

REVOLVERS: MINI, STAINLESS STEEL

Because Freedom Arms' manufacturing capacity has been maximized due to the success of the .454 Casull revolver, the mini-revolver series was discontinued beginning 1989.

FA-S-22LR (PATRIOT) - .22 LR cal., 5 shot, 1, 1¾ (disc. 1988), or 3 (disc. 1988) in. barrel, Hi-Gloss finish. Disc. 1989.

$175 $135 $100

Last MSR was $153.

Add $15 for 3 in. barrel model (FA-BG-22LR, Minute-Man, disc. 1988).

FA-S-22M (IRONSIDES) - .22 Mag. cal., 4 shot, 1, 1¾ (disc. 1988), or 3 in. barrel, Hi Gloss finish. Disc. 1989.

$200 $150 $110

Last MSR was $177.

Add $43 for 3 in. barrel model (Bostonian).

FA-S-22-LR BUCKLE/REVOLVER COMBINATION - .22 LR cal., 1 in. barrel, pistol is housed in belt buckle. Disc. 1989.

$295 $225 $185

Last MSR was $193.

✳ **.22 Mag. cal.**

$350 $250 $200

Last MSR was $216.

REVOLVERS: SA, STAINLESS STEEL

Freedom Arms also offers a complete line of accessories and factory installed options. The factory should be contacted directly for an up-to-date listing and prices. Beginning in 1999, all revolvers are equipped with a locking safety device which slides into the muzzle and locks into the chamber under the firing pin, making it impossible to either load the top chamber or turn the cylinder. The Model 83 uses a sliding bar safety, while the Model 97 has a transfer bar safety.

Add $264 per interchangeable cylinder in different cals on most of the following centerfire models.
Add $140 for 4 port Mag-na-ported barrel.
Add $106 for 2 port Mag-na-ported barrel.
Add $455 for octagon barrel.

Grading	100%	98%	95%	90%	80%	70%	60%

Add $78 for non-standard barrel length.
Subtract $91 (Field Grade) or $124 (Premier Grade) for no sight, centerfire models.
Subtract $124 (Varmint Class) or $158 (Silhouette Class) for no sight, centerfire models.

MODEL 83 (252 VARMINT, .22 LR) - .22 LR cal., 5 shot, unique two point firing pin, choice of 5 1/8 or 7½ in. barrel, includes express sights, black/green laminated hardwood grips, approx. 3¾ lbs. New 1991.

MSR	$1,828	$1,525	$1,125	$825

Add $264 for extra .22 Mag. cylinder.

* *Model 83 (252 Silhouette)* - silhouette variation featuring 10 in. barrel with competition sights (adj. front sight blade and ISGW silhouette competition rear sight) and black micarta grips.

MSR	$1,879	$1,575	$1,175	$875

Add $23 for front sight hood.

MODEL 83 (353 FIELD GRADE, .357 MAG.) - .357 Mag. cal., 5 shot, 4¾, 6, 7½, 9 in. barrel on non-glare field grade finish, Pachmayr grips, adj. sights, 3¾ lbs. New 1992.

MSR	$1,527	$1,325	$995	$750

* *Model 83 (353 Premier Grade)* - similar to Field Grade, except has premier grade brushed finish and impregnated hardwood grips. New 1992.

MSR	$1,976	$1,650	$1,225	$825

* *Model 83 (353 Silhouette)* - includes silhouette competition sights, 9 in. barrel, field grade finish, Pachmayr grips and trigger overtravel screw. New 1992.

MSR	$1,635	$1,375	$1,025	$775

MODEL 83 (654 FIELD GRADE, .41 REM. MAG.) - .41 Rem. Mag. cal., 5 shot, 4¾, 6, 7½, or 10 in. barrel. New 1998.

MSR	$1,527	$1,325	$995	$750

* *Model 83 (654 Premier Grade)* - adj. sight, 4¾, 6, 7½, or 10 in. barrel. New 1998.

MSR	$1,976	$1,650	$1,225	$825

* *Model 83 (654 Silhouette)* - field grade finish with silhouette competition sights, 10 in. barrel only, includes Pachmayr grips.

MSR	$1,635	$1,375	$1,025	$775

MODEL 83 (FIELD GRADE, .44 REM. MAG.) - .44 Rem. Mag. cal., 5 shot, 4¾, 6, 7½, or 10 in. barrel.

MSR	$1,527	$1,325	$995	$750

* *Model 83 (44 Premier Grade)* - adj. sight, 4¾, 6, 7½, or 10 in. barrel.

MSR	$1,976	$1,650	$1,225	$825

Subtract $66 for fixed sight.

* *Model 83 (44 Silhouette)* - field grade finish with silhouette competition sights, 10 in. barrel only, includes Pachmayr grips.

MSR	$1,635	$1,375	$1,025	$775

MODEL 83 (.45 LC) - .45 LC only. Disc. 1990.

	$1,200	$900	$700

MODEL 83 (CASULL FIELD GRADE, .454 CASULL) - .454 Casull cal., 5 shot, 4¾ (fixed sight only), 6, 7½, or 10 in. barrel, stainless steel matte finish with Pachmayr presentation grips. New 1988.

MSR	$1,591	$1,375	$995	$750

Subtract $35 for fixed sight.

Grading	100%	98%	95%	90%	80%	70%	60%

✳ *Model 83 (.454 Casull Silhouette Model)* - .454 Casull cal., includes 10 in. barrel, Pachmayr grips, field grade finish, silhouette competition sights, and trigger over travel screw.

$1,600 $1,150 $850

Last MSR was $1,958.

✳ *Model 83 Silhouette Pak* - .44 Mag. cal., includes 10 in. barrel, silhouette competition sight, honed action with 3 lb. trigger pull, plastic grips, locking aluminum carrying case with cleaning kit and tool. Mfg. 1990 only.

$1,000 $850 $750

Last MSR was $1,242.

MODEL 83 (CASULL PREMIER GRADE, .454 CASULL) - .454 Casull cal., 5 shot, stainless steel with brushed finish, single action revolver, 4¾, 6, 7½, or 10 in. standard barrel, laminated hardwood grips, adj. sights. Mfg. 1983-present.

MSR $2,058 $1,725 $1,250 $900

Subtract $64 for fixed sight.

✳ *Model 83 Silhouette Pak* - .454 Casull cal., includes 10 in. barrel, silhouette competition sight, honed action with 3 lb. trigger pull, hardwood grips, locking aluminum carrying case with cleaning kit and tool. Mfg. 1990 only.

$1,275 $995 $850

Last MSR was $1,522.

MODEL 83 (757 FIELD GRADE, .475 LINEBAUGH) - .475 Linebaugh cal., 5 shot, stainless steel, matte finish, Pachmayr grips, 4¾, 6, or 7½ barrel. New 1999.

MSR $1,591 $1,375 $995 $750

✳ *Model 83 (757 Premier Grade)* - adj. sights, brushed finish, impregnated hardwood grips. New 1999.

MSR $2,058 $1,725 $1,250 $900

MODEL 83 (555 FIELD GRADE, .50 AE) - .50 AE cal., 5 shot, stainless steel, matte finish, Pachmayr grips, 4¾, 6, 7½, or 10 in. barrel. New 1994.

MSR $1,591 $1,375 $995 $750

✳ *Model 83 (555 Premier Grade)* - adj. sights, brushed finish, impregnated hardwood grips. New 1994.

MSR $2,058 $1,725 $1,250 $900

MODEL 83 HUNTER PAK FIELD GRADE - .357 Mag., .44 Rem. Mag., or .454 Casull cal., 7½ in. barrel, plastic grips, field grade low profile adj. sight or no front sight base, sling and studs, locking aluminum carrying case with cleaning kit and tool. Mfg. 1990-1993.

$1,075 $925 $775

Last MSR was $1,333.

Add $76 for low profile adj. sight and Pachmayr grips.

✳ *Model 83 Hunter Pak Premier Grade* - .357 Mag., .44 Rem. Mag., or .454 Casull cal., 7½ in. barrel, ebony micarta grips, no sights or premier grade adj. sight, sling and studs, locking aluminum carrying case with cleaning kit and tool. Mfg. 1990-1993.

$1,395 $1,025 $850

Last MSR was $1,611.

Add $100 for adj. sights.

Grading	100%	98%	95%	90%	80%	70%	60%

MODEL 97 - .22 LR (new 2002), .357 Mag., .41 Rem. Mag. (new 2000), .45 LC (new 1999) cal., 5 (.45 LC) or 6 (.22 LR or .357 Mag.) shot, mid-size frame, 4¼ (new 2000), 5½, 7½, or 10 (.22 LR cal. only) in. barrel, satin stainless finish, smooth wood grips, choice of fixed or adj. rear sight. New 1997.

   MSR $1,668   **$1,425 $1,050 $775**

   Subtract $76 for fixed sights.
   Add $64 for .22 LR cal. with sporting chambers.

U.S. DEPUTY MARSHAL - 3 in. barrel only with no ejector, fixed or adj. sights, U.S. Marshal medallion in left hardwood grip. Mfg. 1990-1993.

                          $1,325 $900 $750

                                    Last MSR was $1475 (fixed sights).
                                    Last MSR was $1,558 (adj. sights).

   Add approx. $80 for adj. sights.

SIGNATURE EDITION - .454 Casull cal., high polish stainless steel, 7½ in. barrel only, rosewood grips, cased with accessories, only 93 of 100 were actually mfg.

                     $2,300 $1,750 $1,300

                                    Last MSR was $2,684.

PRIMUS INTER PARES - 1 of every 100 guns is made in this variation, includes octagonal barrel, ivory grips, 7½ in. barrel, and cased. Disc. 1993.

   Rarity factor precludes accurate pricing.

FRENCH MILITARY

   Various configurations manufactured in several locations in France.

PISTOLS: SEMI-AUTO

MODEL 1935A AUTO PISTOL - 7.65mm French Long cal., 8 shot, 4.3 in. barrel, fixed sights, blue, checkered wood grips, French service sidearm. Mfg. 1935-1945.

                     $275 $225 $180 $135 $110 $100 $90

   Add 50% if Nazi proofed.

* **MODEL 1935S** - 7.65mm French Long cal., 4 1/3 in. barrel, enamel finish, Colt Govt. Model locking system, 26 oz.

                     $325 $295 $260 $225 $195 $170 $150

M.A.B. MODEL C - 7.65mm French Long cal., design based on FN Browning Model 1910, 6.1 in. barrel. Introduced 1933.

                     $250 $220 $190 $170 $150 $125 $110

M.A.B. MODEL D - 7.65mm French Long cal., 3.96 in. barrel, single action, similar to Model C, mfg. commercially 1933-1940, many thousands mfg. for the German military during WWII (marked "Pistole MAB Kaliber 7.65mm").

                     $275 $225 $200 $175 $150 $125 $110

MODEL M.A.B. PA - 15 - 9mm Para. cal., single action, 16 shot, currently used by French military.

                     $550 $500 $450 $400 $365 $335 $300

   Subtract 10% for phosphate.

MODEL M.A.B. PA - 15 TARGET - rare target variation of PA-15, adj. sight, 6 in. barrel, cased.

                     $1,250 $1,000 $750 $675 $600 $550 $500

Grading	100%	98%	95%	90%	80%	70%	60%

RIFLES: BOLT ACTION

MODEL 1886 LEBEL - 8mm Lebel cal., 32 in. barrel, adj. sight, military stock. Mfg. 1886-WWII.

	$125	$100	$75	$65	$50	$40	$25

1936 MAS MILITARY RIFLE - 7.5mm MAS cal., 22 in. barrel, adj. sight, military stock, bayonet in forearm. Mfg. 1936-1940.

	$300	$225	$175	$145	$125	$100	$80

MODEL 45 - .22 LR cal., may have Mauser parts, aperture rear sight, post war mfg.

	$400	$360	$330	$275	$235	$200	$175

FRIGON GUNS, INC.

Previously manufactured by Marocchi in Italy. Previously imported by Frigon Guns, Inc. located in Clay Center, KS.

SHOTGUNS

FT-I - 12 ga. only, single barrel trap gun, blued finish, 32 or 34 in. VR barrel, quick-change stock. Mfg. 1986-94.

	$925	$675	$525	$435	$375	$350	$295

Last MSR was $1,100.

FT-C - 12 ga. only, quick-change stock, trap combination gun includes 1 single barrel and 1 set of O/U barrels, cased. Mfg. 1986-94.

	$1,700	$1,325	$1,050	$875	$775	$685	$620

Last MSR was $1,975.

FS-4 - 4-barrel skeet set including 12, 20, 28 ga., or .410 bore, individual forearms, quick-change stock, vent. barrels (except for .410 bore), cased. Mfg. 1986-94.

	$2,575	$1,975	$1,675	$1,475	$1,350	$1,250	$1,150

Last MSR was $2,890.

FROMMER PISTOLS

Previously manufactured by Femaru-Fegyver-es Gepgyar R.T., Budapest, Hungary.

Please refer to the Femaru listing in this section.

FURR ARMS

Current manufacturer located in Orem, UT.

Please refer to the Gatling Gun listing in this text.

G SECTION

GALAZAN

Current trademark established in 1995, and manufactured by Connecticut Shotgun Manufacturing Co., located in New Britain, CT. Consumer direct sales.

The Galazan trademark has established itself as one of the premier names in best quality O/U shotguns and double rifles. All guns are custom order. For more information regarding current firearms manufacturing, please refer to the Connecticut Shotgun Manufacturing Co. listing in this text.

GALEF SHOTGUNS

Previous importer of Zabala Hermanos (Spanish) and Antonio Zoli (Italian) shotguns.

Grading	100%	98%	95%	90%	80%	70%	60%

SHOTGUNS

COMPANION FOLDING SINGLE BARREL - 12, 16, 20, 28 ga., or .410 bore, 28 in. barrel, full choke, 30 in. full, 12 ga. only, hammerless, underlever, checkered pistol grip stock.

	100%	98%	95%	90%	80%	70%	60%
	$155	$125	$100	$85	$75	$65	$55

MONTE CARLO TRAP SINGLE BARREL - 12 ga., 32 in. full vent. rib, hammerless, underlever, recoil pad, checkered pistol grip Monte Carlo stock. Disc.

	100%	98%	95%	90%	80%	70%	60%
	$225	$185	$175	$150	$135	$125	$100

SILVER SNIPE O/U - 12 or 20 ga., 3 in. chambers, 26, 28, or 30 in. barrels, imp. cyl. and mod. or full and mod. vent. rib, checkered pistol grip stock, boxlock, extractors, single trigger, mfg. by Angelo Zoli, disc.

	100%	98%	95%	90%	80%	70%	60%
	$525	$500	$475	$400	$375	$325	$275

GOLDEN SNIPE O/U - similar to Silver Snipe, except has auto ejectors.

	100%	98%	95%	90%	80%	70%	60%
	$595	$525	$500	$475	$375	$350	$300

SILVER HAWK SxS - 12 or 20 ga., 3 in. chambers, 26, 28, or 30 in. barrels, imp. cyl. and mod. or mod. and full, boxlock, extractors, checkered pistol grip and beavertail forearm. Mfg. by Angelo Zoli, 1968-1972.

	100%	98%	95%	90%	80%	70%	60%
	$450	$400	$375	$350	$300	$275	$250

GALEF ZABALA SxS - 10, 12, 16, or 20 ga., 22, 26, 28, or 30 in. barrels, boxlock, extractors.

	100%	98%	95%	90%	80%	70%	60%
10 gauge	$250	$230	$200	$175	$150	$140	$125
Other gauges	$200	$175	$150	$130	$120	$110	$100

GALENA INDUSTRIES INC.

Please refer to the AMT and Automag listings.

GALIL

Current trademark manufactured by Israel Military Industries (IMI). No current consumer importation. Recent Galil semi-auto sporterized rifles and variations with thumbhole stocks were banned in April, 1998. Beginning late 1996, Galil rifles and pistols were available in selective fire mode only (law enforcement, military only) and are currently imported by UZI America, Inc., a subsidiary of O.F. Mossberg & Sons, Inc. Previously imported by Action Arms, Ltd. located in Philadelphia, PA until 1994. Previously imported by Springfield Armory located in Geneseo, IL and Magnum Research, Inc., located in Minneapolis, MN.

Magnum Research importation can be denoted by a serial number prefix "MR", while Action Arms imported rifles have either "AA" or "AAL" prefixes.

RIFLES: SEMI-AUTO

Models 329, 330 (Hadar II), 331, 332, 339 (sniper system with 6x40 mounted Nimrod scope), 361, 372, 386, and 392 all refer to various configurations of the Galil rifle.

Grading	100%	98%	95%	90%	80%	70%	60%

MODEL AR - .223 Rem. cal. or .308 Win. cal., semi-auto paramilitary design rifle, gas operated - rotating bolt, 16.1 in. (.223 Rem. cal. only) or 19 in. (.308 Win. cal. only) barrel, parkerized, folding stock. Flip-up Tritium night sights. 8.6 lbs.

	$2,250	$1,750	$1,500	$1,250	$1,100	$900	$775

Last MSR was $950.

MODEL ARM - similar to Model AR, except includes folding bi-pod, vented hardwood hand-guard, and carrying handle.

	$2,625	$2,200	$1,900	$1,600	$1,350	$1,100	$975

Last MSR was $1,050.

GALIL SPORTER - similar to above, except has one-piece thumbhole stock, 4 (.308 Win.) or 5 (.223 Rem.) shot mag., choice of wood (disc.) or polymer hand guard, 8½ lbs. Imported 1991-1993.

	$995	$900	$800	$725	$600	$525	$475

Last MSR was $950.

HADAR II - .308 cal., gas operated, paramilitary type configuration, 1 piece walnut thumbhole stock with pistol grip and forearm, 18½ in. barrel, adj. rear sight, recoil pad, 4 shot (standard) or 25 shot mag., 10.3 lbs. Imported 1989 only.

	$1,195	$975	$825	$700	$600	$500	$450

Last MSR was $998.

SNIPER OUTFIT - .308 Win. cal., semi-auto, limited production, sniper model built to exact I.D.F. specifications for improved accuracy, 20 in. heavy barrel, hardwood folding stock (adj. recoil pad and adj. cheekpiece) and forearm, includes Tritium night sights, bi-pod, detachable 6x40mm Nimrod scope, two 25 shot mags., carrying/storage case, 14.1 lbs. Imported 1989 only.

	$4,500	$4,000	$3,650	$3,150	$2,650	$2,150	$1,750

Last MSR was $3,995.

GAMBA, RENATO

Current manufacturer established in 1748, and located in Gardone V.T., Italy. Currently imported by Renato Gamba U.S.A. Corp., located in New York, NY. Gamba of America, a subsidiary of Firing Line, located in Aurora, CO, was the exclusive importer and distributor for Renato Gamba long guns from 1996-2000. Pistols were previously imported and distributed (until 1990) by Armscorp of America, Inc. located in Baltimore, MD. Shotguns were previously (until 1992) imported by Heckler & Koch, Inc. located in Sterling, VA.

RENATO GAMBA

Filli Gamba (Gamba Brothers) was founded in 1946. G. Gamba sold his tooling to his brother, Renato, in 1967 when Renato Gamba left his brothers and S.A.B. was formed. Filli Gamba closed in 1989 and the Zanotti firm was also purchsed the same year.

Renato Gamba firearms have had limited importation since 1986. In 1989, several smaller European firearms companies were purchased by R. Gamba and are now part of the Renato Gamba Group. The importation of R. Gamba guns changed in 1990 to reflect their long term interest in exporting firearms to America. Earlier imported models may be rare but have not enjoyed much collectability to date.

PISTOLS: SEMI-AUTO

All the following models were discontinued for importation approx. 1990.

SAB G90 STANDARD - .30 Luger/7.65 Para. (disc.), 9x18mm Ultra (disc.), or 9mm Para. cal., double action, 4.72 in. barrel, 10 (C/B 1994) or 15* shot side release mag., blue or chrome (disc.) finish, hammer drop safety on frame, smooth walnut grips, 2.2 lbs.

	$625	$375	$325	$295	$275	$250	$225

Last MSR was $736.

Add $65 for chrome finish (disc.).

Grading	100%	98%	95%	90%	80%	70%	60%

❋ *SAB G90 Competition* - 9mm Para. cal., similar to SAB G90 Standard, except has adj. rear sight, "cocked and locked" operation, and checkered walnut grips. Imported 1990 only.

	$1,175	$425	$375	$325	$300	$275	$250

Last MSR was $1,364.

Add $205 for stainless steel (SAB G90 Service Competition).

SAB G91 COMPACT - similar to SAB G90, except has 3.54 in. barrel, 12 shot mag., 1.87 lbs.

	$625	$375	$325	$295	$275	$250	$225

Last MSR was $736.

Add $65 for chrome finish (disc.).

❋ *SAB G91 Competition* - 9mm Para. cal., similar to SAB G91 Compact, except has adj. rear sight, "cocked and locked" operation, and checkered walnut grips. Imported 1990 only.

	$450	$395	$330	$300	$275	$250	$225

Last MSR was $575.

SAB G2001 - .380 ACP cal., double action, mfg. from forged and milled steel, high polish blue, neoprene grips, slide mounted manual safety with firing pin block, 10 shot mag.

	$615	$395	$325	$295	$275	$250	$225

Last MSR was $699.

REVOLVERS

The following models were discontinued for importation approx. 1990.

TRIDENT FAST ACTION - .32 S&W or .38 Spl. cal., 2½ or 3 in. barrel, double action, blued frame with checkered walnut grips, 6 shot, 23 oz.

	$550	$425	$360	$330	$295	$270	$245

Last MSR was $630.

TRIDENT SUPER - .32 S&W or .38 Spl. cal., 4 in. vent. rib barrel, 6 shot, double action, checkered walnut grips, 25 oz.

	$585	$450	$375	$340	$310	$280	$250

Last MSR was $683.

TRIDENT MATCH 900 - .32 S&W Long W.C. or .38 Spl. cal., match gun featuring 6 in. heavy barrel and anatomically compatible checkered walnut grips, target sights, 2.2 lbs.

	$750	$660	$595	$525	$475	$430	$390

Last MSR was $895.

❋ *Trident Match 901* - similar to Trident Match 900.

	$750	$660	$595	$525	$475	$430	$390

Last MSR was $895.

RIFLES

SAFARI EXPRESS SxS - 7x65R, 9.3x74R, or .375 H&H cal., 25 in. barrels with open sights, underlug locking with Greener crossbolt, ejectors except on .375 H&H, coin finished frame with scroll work and game scene engraving, DTs, deluxe checkered walnut stock with cheekpiece and recoil pad, 9.9 lbs.

	$5,685	$4,575	$3,950	$3,575	$3,175	$2,850	$2,500

Last MSR was $6,630.

CONCORDE EXPRESS O/U - .30-06, 8x57JRS, or 9.3x74R cal., monoblock frame, Boss type action, ejectors, cased.

MSR	$8,500	$7,500	$5,350	$4,700	$4,200	$3,825	$3,350	$2,950

Add $300 for automatic double safety system.

DAYTONA SL EXPRESS O/U - .30-06, .375 H&H, or 9.3x74R cal., monoblock frame with Boss type improved action, detachable Gamba trigger assembly, hand engraved sideplates with game scenes and English scroll.

MSR	$9,900	$8,850	$6,350	$5,400	$4,600	$4,200	$3,750	$3,350

Grading	100%	98%	95%	90%	80%	70%	60%

EXPRESS MAXIM SxS - .375 H&H, .458 Win. Mag., .470 N.E., or .458 Lott (new 1995) cal., sidelock action, fine engraving with big game scenes signed by the master engraver, includes leather case.

	MSR	$56,200	$50,750	$43,000	$35,500	$27,000	$21,000	$17,500	$13,000

MUSTANG EXTRA SINGLE SHOT - 5.6x50mm (disc.), 5.6x57R (disc.), 6.5x57R, 7x65R, .222 Rem. (disc.), .243 Win., .270 Win., or .30-06 cal., single 25½ in. barrel configuration with highly engraved sidelock action featuring triple-bite double Purdey locking system with Greener crossbolt, extra fine vine leaf Renaissance engraving (game scene upon request), double-set triggers, best quality checkered walnut stock and forearm, 6.17 lbs.

	MSR	$32,400	$28,500	$15,250	$11,500	$7,950	$6,900	$6,100	$5,500

RGZ 1000 BOLT ACTION - 7x64mm, .270 Win., 7mm Rem. Mag., or .300 Win. Mag. cal., modified Mauser K-98 action, 20½ in. barrel, pistol grip stock with cheekpiece, 7 lbs.

$1,100	$885	$825	$760	$700	$640	$575

Last MSR was $1,310.

* **RGX 1000 Express** - similar to RGZ 1000, except has 23¾ in. barrel and double set triggers, 7.7 lbs.

$1,255	$960	$875	$795	$725	$650	$575

Last MSR was $1,475.

SHOTGUNS: O/U

Most of the following O/U models (except for the Daytona Trap and Concorde Model) were discontinued in 1990 when H&K became the exclusive importer for R. Gamba shotguns.

Add on values for the following models represent the manufacturer's suggested retail on those items, not necessarily the value in the secondary marketplace.

EUROPA 2000 - 12 ga. only, engraved, silver finished boxlock action with sideplates, vent. rib, single trigger, ejectors, deluxe checkered stock and forearm, 6.84 lbs.

$1,250	$995	$895	$835	$775	$715	$650

Last MSR was $1,475.

EDINBURGH SUPER SLUG - 12 ga. only, trap model, SST, ejectors, engraved action, deluxe checkered stock and forearm.

$1,225	$980	$895	$835	$775	$715	$650

Last MSR was $1,425.

GRIFONE SPORTING TRAP - 12 ga. only, trap model, SST, ejectors, moderately engraved action, deluxe checkered stock and forearm.

$975	$900	$850	$800	$750	$700	$650

Last MSR was $1,425.

GRINTA TRAP/SKEET - 12 ga. only, trap/skeet model, SST, ejectors, medium engraving coverage.

$900	$825	$725	$650	$575	$500	$450

Last MSR was $1,710.

VICTORY TRAP/SKEET - similar to Grinta Model, except has better walnut and more engraving.

$1,200	$1,075	$950	$850	$750	$650	$550

Last MSR was $1,905.

EDINBURG MATCH - similar to Victory Model, except has different style of engraving.

$1,200	$1,075	$950	$850	$750	$650	$550

Last MSR was $1,930.

MONTREAL MODEL 90/91 - 12 ga. only, boxlock, interchangeable trigger assembly, select walnut, vent. rib. Available in International Trap, American Skeet, Sporting, and Field models.

$2,650	$2,275	$1,700	$1,400	$1,100	$1,000	$900

Add $200 for single selective trigger.

The Model 90 has a flat-sided receiver, while the Model 91 has a Daytona sculpted receiver.

Grading	100%	98%	95%	90%	80%	70%	60%

MONTREAL 90/91 AMERICAN TRAP COMBO - 12 ga. only, 32 in. barrels and adj. impact, single 34 in. barrel, interchangeable trigger assembly.

	$2,800	$2,100	$1,820	$1,540	$1,400	$1,260	$1,120

SINGLE BARREL TRAP-MODEL 496 - 12 ga. only, boxlock, vent. rib.

	$1,150	$865	$750	$635	$575	$520	$460

HUNTER II - 12 ga. only, boxlock action with alloy frame, reinforced barrels including 5 choke tubes, SST, ejectors, checkered walnut stock and forearm, approx. 6 lbs. New 2002.

MSR	$1,390		$1,275	$995	$850	$725	$600	$500	$425

LE MANS SPORTING - 12 ga. only, boxlock action with steel frame, reinforced barrels including 5 choke tubes, SST, ejectors, checkered walnut stock and forearm, approx. 6 lbs. New 2002.

MSR	$1,580		$1,425	$1,100	$950	$850	$725	$600	$500

CONCORDE GAME MODEL - 12 or 20 ga., Boss type improved locking system, ejectors, 26¾ or 28 in. VR barrels, 2nd generation Concorde with fixed trigger group started 2002. Importation began 1995.

MSR	$6,100		N/A	$3,250	$2,750	$2,350	$2,000	$1,750	$1,500

Add $2,000 for Trap combo (disc.).

✳ Grade 7 - includes engraving featuring game scenes and English scroll.

MSR	$10,410		N/A	$5,950	$5,000	$4,400	$3,850	$3,250	$2,575

Add $821 for Sporting Clays Model.

✳ Grade 8 - features top-of-the-line English scroll engraving.

MSR	$8,180		N/A	$5,000	$4,250	$3,600	$2,925	$2,400	$2,100

Add $821 for Sporting Clays Model.

DAYTONA (2K NEW SERIES) & VARIATIONS - 12 ga. only, monolithic boxlock action, SST, ejectors, detachable trigger group, blue or chrome finish standard, available in either Hunting, Skeet, Pigeon, Sporting Clays, Olympic Trap, or American Trap configuration, deluxe walnut with fine English scroll engraving with game scenes. New Daytona series started in 2000. Importation began 1990.

MSR	$7,600		N/A	$4,300	$3,700	$2,950	$2,400	$1,900	$1,500

Add $900 for Sporting Clays Model.
Add $1,250 for New American Trap configuration.
Add $200 for Pigeon Electrocible Model.
Add $2,000 for Daytona combo package.
Add $3,550 for extra set of O/U barrels.

✳ Grade 4 Daytona Model - most elaborately engraved numbered Daytona model, choice of eagle panel scene or fine scroll engraving.

MSR	$18,450		N/A

Add $300 for Luxe game scene and fine English scroll engraving.
Limited after market availability in used condition precludes accurate pricing in 60%-98% condition factors on this model.

✳ Grade 5/5E Daytona Model - one grade below Grade 4.

MSR	$17,900		N/A	$7,850	$6,500	$4,500	$3,850	$3,250	$2,750

✳ Grade 6/6 SCE Daytona Model - one grade below Grade 5, choice of duck game scene or tight scroll engraving.

MSR	$15,900		N/A	$6,250	$5,600	$4,250	$3,850	$3,250	$2,750

Add $2,560 for game scene engraving (Grade 6 SCE).

✳ Grade 7 Daytona Model - one grade below Grade 6, oval game scene engraving with English scroll on perimeter.

MSR	$15,660		N/A	$5,250	$4,675	$3,950	$3,750	$3,250	$2,750

✳ Grade 8 Daytona Model - features English scroll engraving.

MSR	$13,700		N/A	$6,200	$4,800	$3,700	$3,300	$2,950	$2,350

G

Grading	100%	98%	95%	90%	80%	70%	60%

DAYTONA SL - deluxe variation of the Daytona Model, except has sideplates with extensive engraving, new mfg. has detachable trigger group, available in the same configurations as the Daytona Model, includes case. Limited importation 1990-94, reintroduced 2000.

MSR	$24,400	N/A	$10,500	$9,450	$8,150	$6,600	$5,000	$4,250

✳ *Grade Royale* - top-of-the-line Daytona Model.

MSR	$27,000	N/A	$12,500	$10,750	$9,150	$7,400	$5,800	$4,650

Limited after market availability in used condition precludes accurate pricing in 60%-98% condition factors on this model.

✳ *Grade Purdey* - features Purdey locking system.

MSR	$26,400	N/A	$12,000	$10,250	$8,950	$7,300	$5,700	$4,550

Limited after market availability in used condition precludes accurate pricing in 60%-98% condition factors on this model.

✳ *SLE Tiger* - features sideplates with African game scenes.

MSR	$36,800	N/A	$17,950	$14,950	$12,950	$10,250	$8,750	$7,500

Limited after market availability in used condition precludes accurate pricing in 60%-98% condition factors on this model.

DAYTONA SLE BEST - features elaborate scroll and 24 Kt. gold game scene inlays.

MSR	$42,100	N/A	$19,750	$17,150	$14,000	$10,500	$8,750	$7,300

DAYTONA SLE VENUS - features elaborate scroll and game scene engraving.

MSR	$38,500	N/A	$17,250	$15,000	$12,750	$11,000	$9,000	$7,000

✳ *Grade 1 SL* - elaborate engraving with 24 Kt. gold game scene engraving.

MSR	$36,800	N/A	$16,650	$14,000	$12,750	$11,000	$9,000	$7,000

✳ *Grade 2 SL* - elaborate scroll and game scene engraving, w/o gold inlays.

MSR	$28,000	N/A	$12,000	$9,950	$8,400	$6,700	$5,100	$4,250

✳ *Grade 3 SL* - features hand engraved sideplates with English scroll and game scenes. Importation began 1995.

MSR	$24,400	N/A	$10,500	$9,450	$8,150	$6,600	$5,000	$4,250

DAYTONA SLHH - 12 or 20 ga., H&H style sidelock action with Boss improved lock-up, top-of-the-line model, game or competition configuration, includes leather case. Importation began in 1990.

MSR	$41,000	N/A	$18,550	$15,500	$13,500	$12,000	$9,500	$7,500

✳ *Grade 1* - similar to Grade 2, except has better engraving.

MSR	$48,300	N/A	$20,000	$16,000	$14,250	$12,500	$9,500	$7,500

✳ *Grade 2* - available in either Hunting (12 ga. only), Skeet, Trap, Pigeon, or Sporting Clays configuration.

MSR	$43,650	N/A	$19,250	$16,000	$13,850	$12,250	$9,500	$7,500

✳ *Grade 3* - features elaborate scroll and game scene engraving.

MSR	$41,000	N/A	$18,550	$15,550	$13,500	$12,000	$9,500	$7,500

Add $800 for floral English scroll engraving.

DAYTONA VENUS SLEHH - boxlock action with engraved sideplates featuring relief scroll and Goddess of the Hunt engraving.

MSR	$53,500	N/A	$25,000	$21,000	$16,500	$13,750	$10,750	$8,750

DAYTONA SLHH "THE BEST" - sidelock action with elaborate engraving and multiple 24 Kt. gold game scene inlays.

MSR	$58,600	N/A	$29,950	$25,000	$20,000	$15,000	$12,000	$9,950

ONE OF THOUSAND - top-of-the-line model with every possible refinement, Boss action, individually special ordered only.

This model starts out at $85,000.

Grading	100%	98%	95%	90%	80%	70%	60%

BAYERN 88 COMBINATION GUN - 12 ga. over same cals. listed for Mustang Model, coin finished boxlock action with game scene engraving, double DTs, extractors, deluxe checkered walnut stock with recoil pad, 7 ½ lbs.

	$1,000	$875	$775	$700	$650	$600	$550

Last MSR was $1,595.

SHOTGUNS: SxS

Previous to 1989, most of the following models were available in 28 ga. on a 28 ga. frame by option.
Add 20%+ for 28 ga. on the following models.

HUNTER SUPER - 12 ga. only, Anson & Deeley engraved boxlock action with silver finish, DTs, extractors, 6.84 lbs.

	$1,750	$1,275	$895	$760	$630	$575	$525

Last MSR was $1,506.

PRINCIPESSA - 12 or 20 ga., similar to Hunter Super except has English straight grip stock and better engraving, 6.62 lbs. Importation disc. 1994.

	$2,750	$1,900	$1,525	$1,250	$995	$800	$625

Last MSR was $2,495.

Add $200 for single trigger.

S. VINCENT 580 EXTRA DELUXE - 12 ga. only, custom made to individual preferences, very high quality, sidelock action, engraving coverage 100%.

	$4,950	$4,250	$3,500	$2,750	$2,125	$1,775	$1,625

OXFORD 90 - 12 or 20 ga., boxlock action with Purdey locking system, DTs, ejectors, scroll engraving on sideplates, deluxe checkered straight grip walnut stock with recoil pad or checkered butt, 6.84 lbs. Disc. 1998.

	$3,250	$2,925	$2,500	$2,100	$1,700	$1,250	$1,025

Last MSR was $4,300.

Add $245 for single trigger.

OXFORD EXTRA - 12 or 20 ga., double Purdey locking system, includes elegantly engraved sideplates, ejectors, and better quality hand checkered stock and forearm. Importation began 1992.

MSR	$5,500	N/A	$2,875	$2,475	$2,100	$1,750	$1,400	$1,175

Add $500 for single trigger.

MODEL 624 PRINCE - 12 or 20 ga. (disc.), boxlock action, ejectors, choice of English scroll or with woodcock (Model 624 Prince Beccaccia) on bottom of frame, hand checkered walnut stock and forearm. Importation began 1992.

MSR	$5,500	N/A	$2,875	$2,475	$2,100	$1,750	$1,400	$1,175

Add $450 for single trigger.

MODEL 624 PRINCE EXTRA - similar to Model 624 Prince, except has deep floral hand engraving.

MSR	$9,450	N/A	$3,500	$2,850	$2,400	$1,950	$1,500	$1,200

NEW LONDON GOLD - 12 or 20 ga., H&H side-lock system, ejectors, DT or SST, chopper lump barrels, English scroll engraving, deluxe checkered straight grip stock and forearm, 6.84 lbs.

MSR	$13,800	N/A	$6,250	$5,500	$4,750	$3,300	$2,500	$1,750

Add $950 for single trigger.

LONDON ROYAL - similar to London Model except has less extensive game scene engraving.

	$9,000	$8,000	$7,000	$5,750	$4,750	$3,950	$3,475

Last MSR was $6,730.

ZANOTTI 1625 MAXIM - 12 or 20 ga., H&H sidelock system, ejectors, demibloc barrels, coin finished action with royal English scroll engraving, cased. New 2002.

MSR	$27,000	N/A	$12,000	$10,000	$8,500	$7,350	$6,250	$5,200

Grading	100%	98%	95%	90%	80%	70%	60%

AMBASSADOR MODEL - 12 or 20 ga., H&H sidelock system, available with either gold- line engraving on barrels and frame with blued receiver (Gold and Black Model) or English scroll engraving (English Engraved Model), single trigger, ejectors, deluxe checkered walnut stock and forearm, cased, 6.4 lbs.

MSR	$33,700	N/A	$14,000	$11,750	$9,000	$7,850	$6,700	$5,600

Add $800 for English scroll engraving.

Subtract 25% for 12 ga. in used condition only.

This model is also available in either Field or Sporting versions upon special request.

AMBASSADOR EXECUTIVE - 12 or 20 ga. only, top-of-the-line model, made to individual order only, every possible refinement.

MSR	$43,400	N/A	$19,950	$16,000	$12,000	$10,000	$8,850	$7,000

Subtract 25% for 12 ga. in used condition only.

SHOTGUNS: SLIDE ACTION

MODEL 2100 - 12 ga., 3 in. chamber, 19½ in. barrel, 7 shot mag., law enforcement configuration with matte black metal and wood, 6.62 lbs. Limited importation.

$450	$375	$325	$295	$275	$250	$225

Last MSR was $715.

GARBI, ARMAS

Current manufacturer located in Eibar, Spain. Imported and distributed exclusively by W.L. Moore & Co. located in Scottsdale, AZ. Distributor sales.

Currently, Garbi is mfg. 100-125 shotguns per year.

RIFLES: SxS

Garbi also manufactures a deluxe SxS double rifle in 7x65R, 8x57JRS, 9.3x74R, .300 H&H, or .375 H&H cal. Currently, the base retail price for this Express Rifle is $16,900. Please contact the importer or factory directly for more information (including special orders and prices) on this model.

SHOTGUNS: SxS, DISC.

MODEL 51 A - 12 ga. only, extractors, case hardened finish, straight grip.

$450	$350	$325	$300	$280	$260	$240

MODEL 51 B - 12, 16, or 20 ga., ejectors, case hardened or coin finish frame, straight grip.

$850	$650	$590	$540	$500	$460	$420

MODEL 60 A - 12 ga. only, extractors, case hardened finish, true sidelock, large scroll engraving, cocking indicators, hand checkered butt, choice of grip.

$725	$575	$530	$475	$440	$400	$360

MODEL 60 B - 12, 16, or 20 ga., ejectors, case hardened or coin finish frame, extensive engraving, straight grip.

$1,200	$850	$790	$735	$680	$630	$575

MODEL 62 A - 12 ga. only, extractors, case hardened finish, true sidelock, light engraving, cocking indicators, hand checkered butt, choice of grip.

$725	$575	$530	$475	$440	$400	$360

MODEL 62 B - 12, 16, or 20 ga. only, ejectors, case hardened or coin finish frame, extensive engraving, straight grip.

$1,200	$850	$790	$735	$680	$630	$575

Grading	100%	98%	95%	90%	80%	70%	60%

MODEL 71 - 12, 16, or 20 ga., Holland-pattern detachable sidelock ejector double, fine English scroll engraving, oil finish, select walnut, articulated trigger. Importation disc. 1988.

	$2,250	$1,825	$1,500	$1,300	$1,075	$980	$900

Last MSR was $2,600.

MODEL 102 - 12, 16, 20, or 28 ga., Holland-pattern sidelock ejector double with chopper lump barrels, Holland-type large scroll engraving, selected walnut stock. Importation disc. 1993.

	$5,700	$4,500	$3,450	$2,700	$2,350	$2,000	$1,750

Last MSR was $7,100.

MODEL 120 - 12, 16, 20, or 28 ga., Holland-pattern sidelock ejector double with chopper lump barrels of nickel-chrome steel, H&H type easy opening mechanism, game scene engraving-3 patterns available. Well figured walnut stock. Importation disc. 1994.

	$7,500	$6,000	$4,875	$4,125	$3,375	$2,600	$2,200

Last MSR was $9,400.

SPECIAL WLM - 12, 16, 20, or 28 ga., top-of-the-line Holland-pattern sidelock ejector double with chopper lump barrels, full coverage large scroll engraving, fancy-figured walnut stock. Importation disc. 1994.

	$7,500	$6,000	$4,875	$4,125	$3,375	$2,600	$2,200

Last MSR was $9,400.

SPECIAL AG - 12, 16, 20, or 28 ga., top-of-the-line Holland-pattern sidelock ejector double with chopper lump barrels, large scroll engraving patterned after Lebeau-Courally, fancy figured walnut stock. Disc.

	$8,000	$6,350	$5,200	$4,300	$3,550	$2,750	$2,300

Last MSR was $9,200.

SHOTGUNS: SxS, RECENT MFG.

On the following models, add 5% for 28 ga., $675 for single trigger, $500-$1,500 for English or Turkish walnut wood upgrade, $150-$300 for beavertail forearm, $1,000-$2,100 per extra set of barrels (depending on grade), and $200 for Churchill style level file-cut rib.

MODEL 100 - 12, 16, or 20 ga., Holland-pattern detachable sidelock ejector double, Purdey style scroll engraving, chopper lump barrels, oil finish, select walnut, articulated trigger.

MSR	$3,700	$3,700	$3,250	$2,350	$1,700	$1,450	$1,200	$1,025

MODEL 101 - 12, 16, or 20 ga., round body action and smooth wood now standard, Holland-pattern sidelock ejector double with chopper lump barrels, scroll engraving, selected walnut stock.

MSR	$4,750	$4,750	$4,100	$3,025	$2,375	$1,900	$1,650	$1,400

MODEL 103A SPECIAL - 12, 16, 20, or 28 ga., Holland-pattern sidelock ejector double with chopper lump barrels, H&H royal style fine scroll and rosette engraving, selected walnut stock.

MSR	$5,900	$5,900	$4,925	$3,575	$2,800	$2,350	$2,000	$1,750

✴ *Model 103A Royal* - deluxe variation of the Model 103A, features engraving patterned after the H&H "Royal" rose and scroll styles, extra fancy walnut, gold stock oval plate and matted concave rib.

MSR	$8,800	$8,800	$7,400	$6,825	$5,350	$4,350	$3,500	$2,750

MODEL 103B SPECIAL - 12, 16, 20, or 28 ga., Holland-pattern sidelock ejector double with chopper lump barrels of nickel-chrome steel, H&H type easy opening mechanism, H&H royal type fine scroll and rosette engraving, well figured walnut stock.

MSR	$8,200	$8,200	$7,000	$6,400	$4,950	$3,950	$3,350	$2,600

G

Grading	100%	98%	95%	90%	80%	70%	60%

✳ *Model 103B Royal* - deluxe variation of the Model 103B, features engraving patterned after the H&H "Royal" rose and scroll styles, extra fancy walnut, gold stock oval plate and matted concave rib.

MSR	$11,800		$11,800	$10,000	$8,850	$6,750	$5,350	$4,350	$3,750

MODEL 200 - 12, 16, 20, or 28 ga., Holland-pattern sidelock ejector double with chopper lump barrels of nickel-chrome steel, heavy-duty locks, magnum proofed, very fine Continental style floral and scroll engraving, well figured walnut stock.

MSR	$8,000		$8,000	$6,350	$5,000	$4,225	$3,400	$2,600	$2,200

GASTINNE RENETTE

Current manufacturer and retailer established 1812, and located in Paris, France.

Currently being manufactured with limited importation and distribution. Gastinne Renette should be contacted directly (see Trademark Index) for an up-to-date quotation or information on their current model line-up.

RIFLES: BOLT ACTION

Values listed are base prices for each model - since all guns are made to individual order, the customer can choose the wood, level of engraving, and other special features, all at additional cost. Gastinne Renette should be contacted directly (see Trademark Index) for an individual price quotation.

STANDARD MODEL MAUSER ACTION

MSR	$6,000		$6,000	$5,150	$4,450	$3,850	$3,150	$2,550	$1,900

DELUXE MAUSER ACTION

MSR	$12,000		$12,000	$10,750	$7,850	$6,850	$5,750	$4,750	$3,900

RIFLES: SxS, DOUBLE

BOXLOCK MODEL - variety of cals., features Anson & Deeley boxlock mechanism, color case hardened frame. New 1993.

MSR	$10,000		$10,000	$7,750	$6,950	$5,850	$4,950	$4,100	$3,200

EUROPEAN SIDELOCK

MSR	$36,000		$36,000	$31,000	$27,000	$22,500	$18,750	$15,000	$12,500

AFRICAN SIDELOCK - various Mag. cals. New 1993.

MSR	$40,000		$40,000	$33,000	$28,750	$23,500	$19,250	$15,500	$12,750

STANDARD TYPE G - 9.3x74R, 7.65R, .30-06, or .375 H&H cal., double bolt action, ejectors, reinforced stock, 23¾ in. barrels, bouquet style engraving with deluxe walnut stock and forearm, 7 lbs. 6 oz.

			$2,995	$2,500	$2,150	$1,700	$1,560	$1,480	$1,340

DELUXE TYPE R - 9.3x74R, 7.65R, .30-06, or .375 H&H cal., double bolt action, true sideplates, ejectors, reinforced stock, 23¾ in. barrels, animal engraving with deluxe walnut stock and forearm, 7 lbs. 6 oz.

			$3,875	$3,325	$2,700	$2,175	$1,850	$1,700	$1,525

PRESIDENT TYPE PT - 9.3x74R, 7.65R, .30-06, or .375 H&H cal., double bolt action, true sideplates, ejectors, reinforced stock, 23¾ in. barrels, light engraving with gold line inlays, best quality walnut, 7 lbs. 6 oz.

			$4,250	$3,725	$3,200	$2,650	$2,250	$1,825	$1,600

RIFLES: SINGLE SHOT

FALLING BLOCK MODEL

MSR	$14,000		$14,000	$12,000	$9,750	$8,250	$6,750	$5,900	$5,000

Grading	100%	98%	95%	90%	80%	70%	60%

SIDELOCK MODEL - features breakdown action. New 1993.

	MSR	$34,000						
		$34,000	$29,500	$25,750	$21,250	$18,000	$14,750	$11,350

SHOTGUNS: SxS

MODEL 105 - 12 or 20 ga., Anson and Deeley type triple bolt action, ejectors, double triggers, case hardened frame, 6 lbs. 8 oz.

$2,250	$1,800	$1,400	$1,250	$1,125	$1,000	$900

MODEL 98 - 12 and 20 ga., Purdey type triple bolt action, ejectors, double triggers, case hardened frame, 6 lbs. 8 oz.

$2,995	$2,500	$2,000	$1,850	$1,580	$1,430	$1,260

MODEL 202 - 12 or 20 ga., Purdey type triple bolt action, sidelocks, fine English engraving, first grade French walnut, ejectors, double triggers, coin finished frame, 6 lbs. 10 oz.

MSR	$5,250						
		$4,500	$3,950	$3,250	$2,500	$2,175	$1,875	$1,650

MODEL 353 - 12 or 20 ga., Purdey type triple bolt action, hand detachable sidelocks, Chopper lump barrels, fine English engraving, first grade French walnut, ejectors, double triggers, case hardened frame, best quality, 6 lbs. 10 oz.

MSR	$19,950						
		$17,500	$13,650	$11,000	$8,900	$6,700	$6,250	$5,750

GATLING GUN COMPANY

Currently manufactured and distributed by Furr Arms, established 1961, and located in Orem, UT.

The Furr Arms-Gatling Gun Company manufactures high quality 1/6, 1/3, ½, ¾, and full scale brass reproductions of famous, antique Gatling guns and cannons. Model Gatling guns include various models and scales from 1874 to 1893. Model cannons include the British Naval Cannon and the James Six Pounder. Prices vary according to the complexity of each model and are available by contacting Furr Arms.

Except for Models 1876 Carriage Gatling (½ scale) and 1876 Camel Tripod (½ scale), all the models listed may be purchased on a special order basis from the factory. 100% values represent the current manufacturer's suggested retail.

Due to the limited manufacture and delivery times on the following models, after market asking prices can be 10%-25% over the 100% values. Gatling Gun Company has not made any reproductions since 1999, but will make them on special order with short delivery time.

REPRODUCTIONS: CANNONS

	100%	98%	95%
James Six Lb. Cannon 1/6	$900	$750	$575
James Six Lb. Cannon 1/5	$2,200	$1,850	$1,400
James Six Lb. Cannon 1/3	$3,200	$2,550	$2,000
* H.M.S. Victory Naval Cannon 1/10			
	$500	$375	$325

* **H.M.S. Victory Naval Cannon 1/10** - this cannon is mounted on an oak ship deck section complete with planking, port lid, and working block and tackle.

	$900	$750	$575

* **H.M.S. Victory Naval Cannon 1/3**

	$3,200	$2,550	$2,000

REPRODUCTIONS: GATLING GUNS

	100%	98%	95%
1874 Carriage 1/6	$5,000	$4,000	$3,500
1874 Carriage Gatling 1/3	$11,000	$8,750	$6,500
1876 Carriage Gatling ½	$15,000	$11,500	$8,575
1876 Carriage Gatling ¾	$19,000	$15,000	$12,000
1874 Camel Tripod 1/6	$4,000	$3,000	$2,500

Grading	100%	98%	95%	90%	80%	70%	60%
1874 Camel Tripod 1/3	$4,500	$3,500	$2,800				
1876 Camel Tripod ½	$8,000	$6,500	$5,250				
1876 Camel Tripod ¾	$12,000	$9,000	$7,500				
1876 Camel Tripod (Full)	$18,000	$14,500	$11,500				
1893 Police Gatling 1/6	$2,500	$2,100	$1,650				
1893 Police Gatling 1/3	$3,200	$2,550	$2,000				
1883 Carriage Gatling 1/6	$5,000	$4,000	$3,500				
1883 Carriage Gatling 1/3	$6,500	$5,250	$4,250				

GAUCHER

Current manufacturer located in St. Etienne, France. No current U.S. importation. Previously imported and distributed by Mandall Shooting Supplies located in Scottsdale, AZ.

During 1997, Gaucher released four shooting rifles with unique sound suppression (approx. 71 dB) in 9mm Para., 12mm cal., or .410 bore - prices are in the $311-$372 range. Additionally, Gaucher manufactures rifles (O/U and SxS double, bolt action rimfire, and semi-auto rimfire), shotguns (SxSs, single shot), and 22 LR cal. target pistols. To date, there has been little importation of Gaucher firearms. Please contact the Gaucher factory directly (see Trademark Index) for more information and up-to-date pricing regarding their current lineup of firearms.

PISTOLS: SINGLE SHOT, TARGET

MODEL GN1 - .22 LR cal., single shot silhouette pistol featuring 10 in. barrel, adj. sights, anatomically shaped grips, monobloc lever cocking, 2.42 lbs. Limited importation.

	100%	98%	95%	90%	80%	70%	60%
	$360	$325	$290	$260	$230	$200	$185

Last MSR was $380.

MODEL GP - similar to Model GN1, except has forearm integrated into grip. Limited importation.

	100%	98%	95%	90%	80%	70%	60%
	$300	$275	$250	$225	$200	$185	$160

Last MSR was $323.

GAZELLE ARMS

Current trademark established circa 1970, and manufactured by Hisar Avcilik & Doga Sporlasi San Ve Tic. Ltd. Sti., located in Konak-Izmir, Turkey. No current U.S. importation.

Gazelle Arms currently includes an extensive lineup of good quality shotguns, including semi-autos, SxSs, single shots, and O/Us. Please contact the company directly for more information.

GAVAGE

Previous manufacturer located in Liege, Belgium circa 1936-1943.

PISTOLS: SEMI-AUTO

GAVAGE PISTOL - .32 ACP/7.65mm cal., patterned after the "Clement", fixed barrel, limited mfg.

	100%	98%	95%	90%	80%	70%	60%
	$375	$325	$250	$200	$175	$150	$125

This pistol is very rare if encountered with Waffenamt proofmarks - healthy premiums are being asked.

Grading	100%	98%	95%	90%	80%	70%	60%

GENTRY, DAVID - CUSTOM GUNMAKER

Current custom rifle maker located in Belgrade, MT.

David Gentry is a current custom rifle builder who usually fabricates rifles to individual custom order requests. Current models include Gentry's Black Beauty, Mountain "70", Gray Ghost, and the Outfitter's Rifle. The Rough Rider Model was disc. 1994. David Gentry also manufactures top quality muzzle brakes, stainless steel Featherlight scope rings (1 in. and 30mm), and performs custom metal-work. Mr. Gentry should be contacted directly (see Trademark Index) for more information on options/prices.

GERMAN P.38 MILITARY & COMMERCIAL PISTOLS

Previously manufactured P.38s from various German companies, circa 1938-1946.

Also See: Fabrique Nationale, Luger, Mauser, and Walther for other military pistols.

PISTOLS: SEMI-AUTO

P.38 - 9mm Para. cal., double action, 5 in. barrel, 8 shot mag., fixed sights, brown or black composite grips, blued finish. Many variations exhibiting a variety of metal finishes and codings, 34 oz. Over 1,000,000 manufactured during WW II.

Note: This model was adopted as the standard service pistol of the German Military in 1938. The P.38 was manufactured by Walther - code "ac" (mfg. 1939-1945), Mauser - code "byf" (mfg. Nov. of 1942-1945), and Spreewerke - code "cyq" (mfg. 1943-1945). The finish on most WWII 1942 and later P.38s is not of the same quality as the pre and early war Walther guns with the Spreewerke (cyq) models being the poorest. Pre-war Walther commercial manufactured P.38s (Models AP and Walther Banner HPs) are comparable to Zero Series - 3rd Issue values listed.

HP "HEERES PISTOLE" - 9mm Para. cal., early Walther commercial production, high polish until approx. 13,000 ser. no. range, approx. 24,000 mfg. from 1938-1944.

It is recommended that early variations are evaluated and priced by an expert. Watch for fakes.

* **"Concealed Extractor" HP** - 7.65mm or 9mm Para., first experimental production ser. range 1026-approx. 1080, hand made glossy finish, approx. 20 mfg.

N/A	$12,000	$10,000	$8,000	$7,000	$6,000	$5,000

Add 20% for 7.65mm Para. cal.
Add 30% for dural aluminum frame.

* **"Swedish" HP** - experimental first production HP for Swedish trials, ser. range H1,001-H2,065, H prefix, rectangular firing pin and crown/N proofs, thin sight, thick safety lever, superb polish, hand made craftsmanship.

$3,000	$2,500	$2,000	$1,700	$1,400	$1,100	$900

Add 30% for rare matched magazines.

* **Standard HP Production** - ser. range 2,080-approx. 24,000, high gloss finish until approx. ser. no. 13,000 - then changed to military blue (1944).

$2,000	$1,750	$1,275	$1,000	$800	$700	$600

Add 20% for Nazi "359" military proof (scarce).
Add 10% for matching mag.
Add 20% for high polish finish.

* **7.65mm Para HP Production** - 7.65mm Para cal., single or double action, very limited mfg., rarest collector category for standard production P.38s.

N/A	$9,500	$8,500	$7,500	$6,500	$5,500	$4,500

Add 100% for single action.

* **Late War HP Production** - marked "MOD P38" on left slide, rough military blue finish, some frames show heavy tool marks, ser. range 24,000-25,990, w/o matching mags.

$1,800	$1,500	$1,300	$1,000	$800	$600	$500

ZERO-SERIES - 9mm Para. cal., features Walther banner, high polish finish, 5-digit number w/o suffix. Mfg. 1940.

Add 10% for matching mag.

Grading	100%	98%	95%	90%	80%	70%	60%

✳ **Zero Series** - 1st Issue - internal extractor, square firing pin, ser. range 01-01,000.

	$7,500	$5,750	$4,400	$3,500	$2,900	$1,800	$1,500

✳ **Zero Series** - 2nd Issue - external extractor, square firing pin, ser. range 02,001- 03,445, more difficult to find than 1st Issue.

	$6,000	$4,650	$3,400	$2,500	$1,900	$1,300	$1,000

✳ **Zero Series** - 3rd Issue - external extractor, round firing pin, 03,446-013,725, after ser. no. 10,000, some models had brown military style grips.

	$2,750	$2,000	$1,500	$850	$750	$600	$500

✳ **480 code** - "480" appears on slide, first military contract P.38, approx. 7,200 mfg. with ser. range 1-7,665, rare in any condition above 90%.

	$5,250	$3,500	$2,900	$2,200	$1,750	$1,200	$1,000

ac-NO DATE (UNDATED) - 9mm Para. cal., ac (Walther code) appears on slide without date, "ac" on triggerguard, 2,800 mfg. with ser. range 7,356-9,691, rarest military coded P.38, rarely encountered in 90% or better original condition.

	$5,500	$4,200	$3,900	$2,800	$2,300	$1,800	$1,300

Add 20% for matching mag.

✳ **ac-40 Surcharge** - hand-stamped "40" before regular ac-40 production, ser. range 9,691-9,978 A, 10,000 mfg., high polish, rare in any condition above 90%.

	$4,000	$3,500	$3,000	$2,500	$2,000	$1,500	$1,000

Add 20% for matching mag.

ac-40 CODE - 9mm Para. cal., indicates 1940 mfg., the 480 code was dropped in October of 1940, and the "ac" code was started, approx. 10,000 mfg. with ser. range 1B-9,900B.

	$2,000	$1,600	$1,400	$1,100	$700	$600	$500

Add 20% for matching mag.

✳ **ac-41 1st and 2nd Variation** - last military high polish guns, only 1st var. (ser. range 1-4,833 B) has "ac" on left triggerguard, 2nd var. continues to ser. no. 4,527 I.

	$1,500	$1,350	$1,100	$800	$700	$550	$500

Add 20% for matching mag.

ac-41 3RD VAR. or ac-42 CODE - 9mm Para. cal., dull military finish, ser. range (approx.) ac-41, 4,500 I to ac-42, 9,200 K. Matching magazines stop at approx. ac-42, 2,000 B.

	$1,250	$1,100	$900	$700	$600	$500	$450

Add 20% for matching mag.

"byf" CODED 42 - 9mm Para. cal., dull military finish, approx. 15,000 mfg.

	$1,100	$1,000	$900	$700	$600	$500	$400

Add 30% for early "135" proofed parts.

"byf" POLICE CODED 43 or 44 - 9mm Para. cal., eagle F or L.

	$1,600	$1,200	$900	$750	$650	$550	$450

Add 20% for "dual tone" phosphate finish.

"ac" or "byf" CODED 43-45 - 9mm Para. cal., letters are followed by two digit code corresponding to year of mfg. 1943-1945. Two line codes are more desirable than single line models. Highest P.38 production occurred in 1943 and 1944.

	$700	$600	$550	$500	$450	$425	$400

Add up to 50% for "dual tone" (blue and phosphate finish - byf-44 date) – if in 95+ or better condition.

"cyq" CODE AND "ac-45" MISMATCH - 9mm Para. cal., cyq variation typically exhibits rough machining with visible circular milling marks, mismatched slide and frame on ac- 45 model.

	$475	$400	$375	$350	$325	$300	$275

Add 30% for A or B prefix on serialization.

Grading	100%	98%	95%	90%	80%	70%	60%

LATE WAR (1945) - 9mm Para. cal., Zero Series with rough milled finish, ser. range 025,960-027,659.

	$1,100	$925	$795	$650	$500	$425	$350

1945 "svw" CODE - 9mm Para. cal., Nazi proofed only, most dual tone finish, some all blue or all gray.

	$1,100	$925	$700	$600	$500	$450	$400

Add 20% for all blue or all gray.
Subtract 50% for French production (Star proof).

1946 "svw" CODE - 9mm Para. cal., Mauser mfg. 1946 with French controlling production.

	$450	$365	$315	$285	$260	$245	$225

Lower condition prices for this model are usually based on shooting value.

GEVARM

Previous manufacturer located in Saint Etienne, France.

RIFLES: SEMI-AUTO

E-1 AUTOLOADING RIFLE - .22 LR cal., 19 in. barrel, open sights, walnut pistol grip stock.

	$300	$250	$225	$195	$180	$165	$150

GIB

Previous trademark manufactured in Spain.

SHOTGUNS: SxS

10 GAUGE MAGNUM - 10 ga., 3½ in. chambers, 32 in. full choke barrel, case hardened frame, matted rib, rubber pad, checkered pistol grip walnut stock. Disc.

	$275	$250	$235	$220	$200	$175	$150

GIBBS GUNS, INC.

Previously manufactured by Volunteer Enterprises in Knoxville, TN and previously distributed by Gibbs Guns, Inc. located in Greenback, TN.

CARBINES

MARK 45 CARBINE - .45 ACP cal. only, based on M6 Thompson machine gun, 16½ in. barrel, 5, 15, 30, or 90 shot mag., U.S. mfg. Disc. 1988.

	$575	$495	$450	$375	$330	$300	$285

Last MSR was $279.

Add $150 for 90 shot mag.
Add $60+ for nickel plating.

GIBBS RIFLE COMPANY, INC.

Current manufacturer, importer, and distributor located in Martinsburg, WV. Gibbs manufactured rifles with the Gibbs trademark in Martinsburg, WV 1991-94, in addition to importing Mauser-Werke firearms until 1995. Dealer and distributor sales.

In the past, Gibbs Rifle Company, Inc. imported a variety of older firearms, including British military rifles and handguns (both original and refurbished condition), a good selection of used military contract pistols and rifles, in addition to other shooting products and accessories, including a bi-pod patterned after the Parker-Hale M- 85.

Gibbs Rifle Company, Inc. currently imports and manufactures military collectibles, historical remakes, and sport speciality rifles. All rifles are carefully inspected, commercially cleaned and boxed to ensure their quality, and all have a limited lifetime warranty. Gibbs Rifle Company, Inc. also offers membership in the Gibbs Military Collectors Club, an organization dedicated to military firearms collectors. Please contact them directly for more information, including membership (refer to Firearms Associations listing).

Grading	100%	98%	95%	90%	80%	70%	60%

RIFLES: BOLT ACTION

M-71/84 MAUSER - 11mm Mauser cal., 31½ in. barrel, available in good original or refurbished condition, 10 lbs. Importation began 1999.

	MSR	$190		$165	$135	$120	$110	$100	$90	$85

Add $110 for refurbished condition (all parts are historically correct and have been cleaned and hand inspected).

This rifle cannot be safely shot with modern ammunition.

M-1888 MAUSER - 8mm Mauser (7.92x57mm) cal., good original condition, 30 in. barrel, 10 lbs. Importation began 1999.

	MSR	$100		$85	$75	$65	$55	$45	$40	$35

This rifle cannot be safely shot with modern ammunition.

M-98K ISRAELI MAUSER - .308 Win. cal., rebarreled by the Israeli Arsenal Ha'as, various makers, 23.6 in. barrel, original condition (offered in 3 grades), 9 lbs. Importation began 1999.

	MSR	$170		$150	$125	$115	$105	$95	$90	$85

Add $10 for Grade 2, or $20 for Grade 1.

M-98 MAUSER SPORTER - .270 Win. or .30-06 cal., Mauser M-98 type action, blue finish, sporterized checkered hardwood stock and forend, 24 in. Wilson barrel. Mfg. in Martinsburg, WV 1998-99.

	$295	$265	$245	$225	$210	$195	$180

Last MSR was $330.

2A HUNTER RIFLE/CARBINE - .308 Win. cal., sporterized action features black enamel refinish, synthetic stock, 12 shot mag, and choice of 18 (carbine) or 22½ (rifle) in. barrel with Parker-Hale muzzle brake, approx. 10 lbs. Mfg. 1999 only.

	$235	$200	$180	$165	$155	$145	$140

Last MSR was $275.

ENFIELD NO. 5 JUNGLE CARBINE - .303 British cal., older No. 4 Enfield barrel action with newly manufactured stock, bayonette lug and flash hider have been added, 20 in. barrel, 7¾ lbs. Importation began 1999.

	MSR	$205		$175	$155	$125	$115	$105	$95	$90

ENFIELD NO. 7 JUNGLE CARBINE - .308 Win. cal., older 2A action with reconfigured original wood, flash hider and bayonet lug have been added, 20 in. barrel, 8 lbs. Importation began 1999.

	MSR	$200		$170	$150	$125	$115	$105	$95	$90

QUEST EXTREME CARBINE - .303 British cal., updated No. 5 Enfield action with 20 in. barrel with compensator and flash hider, electroless nickel metal finish, new buttstock with survival kit packaged in butt trap, 7¾ lbs. New 2000.

	MSR	$250		$215	$185	$170	$160	$150	$140	$130

QUEST II - .308 Win. cal., modern 2A Enfield barreled action, mfg. from chrome vanadium steel, 20 in. barrel with compensator/flash-hider and adj. rear sight, front sight protector, pre-fitted, see-through scope mount accepts all Weaver based optics and accessories, electroless nickel finish, hardwood stock with survival kit included, 12 shot mag., 8 lbs. Importation began 2001.

	MSR	$280		$235	$200	$185	$170	$160	$155	$150

QUEST III - .308 Win. cal., similar to Quest II, except has black syntetic stokc, w/o survival kit. Importation began 2002.

	MSR	$300		$250	$220	$200	$185	$170	$160	$155

Grading	100%	98%	95%	90%	80%	70%	60%

SUMMIT .45-70 CARBINE - .45-70 Govt. cal., remanufactured No. 4 Enfield action, new 21 in. button rifled barrel with front sight, blued action and barrel, checkered hardwood sporting stock, 3 shot mag., 8½ lbs. Importation began 2000.

MSR	$385	$330	$280	$255	$230	$210	$195	$180

GIBBS ECONOMY SPORTER - 8mm Mauser cal., sporterized military action with good barrel and sporting sights, walnut finished checkered hardwood stock. Mfg. 1993- 94.

	$185	$150	$135	$120	$100	$85	$70

Last MSR was $205.

GIBBS MAUSER SPORTER - .243 Win., .270 Win., .30-06, or .308 Win. cal., features M-98 action, walnut finished checkered hardwood stock, action is drilled and tapped, flip-up rear sight and ramp front. Mfg. 1993-94.

	$250	$220	$195	$175	$150	$135	$120

Last MSR was $295.

MODEL 81 CLASSIC - available in 11 cals. between .22-250 Rem. and 7mm Rem. Mag., 24 in. barrel, open sights, 4 shot mag., select checkered walnut with sling swivels, 7¾ lbs.

	$795	$595	$475	$395	$340	$300	$280

Last MSR was $900.

❋ *Model 81 African* - .375 H&H or 9.3x62mm cal., similar specifications as Model 81 Classic with quarter rib and express sights, engraved action, Pachmayr recoil pad, 9 lbs.

	$925	$725	$600	$500	$425	$360	$330

Last MSR was $1,050.

MODEL 85 SNIPER RIFLE - .308 Win. cal., bolt action, 24 in. heavy barrel, 10 shot mag., camo green synthetic McMillan stock with stippling, built in adj. bi-pod and recoil pad, enlarged contoured bolt, adj. sights, 12 lbs. 6 oz.

	$1,825	$1,450	$1,275	$1,050	$875	$750	$625

Last MSR was $2,050.

MODEL 87 TARGET - .243 Win., 6.5x55mm, .308 Win., .30-06, or .300 Win. Mag. cal., target stock, aperture sights. Mfg. disc. 1992.

	$1,375	$1,100	$900	$775	$650	$550	$495

Last MSR was $1,500.

MODEL 1000 STANDARD - .22-250 Rem., .243 Win., 6mm Rem., 6.5x55mm, 7x57mm, 7x64mm, .270 Win., .30-06, or .308 Win. cal., 22 in. barrel, 4 shot built in mag., checkered walnut stock with cheekpiece, open sights, 7¼ lbs.

	$425	$375	$325	$290	$260	$240	$220

Last MSR was $495.

❋ *Model 1000 Clip* - similar to Model 1000 Standard, except has detachable 4 shot mag.

	$460	$395	$350	$300	$270	$240	$220

Last MSR was $535.

MODEL 1100 LIGHTWEIGHT - available in 9 cals. between .22-250 Rem. and .308 Win., 22 in. barrel, open sights, 4 shot mag., 6½ lbs.

	$435	$380	$325	$290	$260	$240	$220

Last MSR was $510.

❋ *Model 1100M African* - .375 H&H, or .458 Win. Mag. cal., 24 in. barrel, 4 shot mag., 9½ lbs.

	$825	$650	$575	$500	$450	$425	$400

Last MSR was $930.

MODEL 1200 SUPER - .22-250 Rem., .243 Win., 6mm, 6.5x55mm, 7x64mm, .270 Win., .30-06, or .308 Win. cal., bolt action, Mauser type action, 24 in. barrel, folding sight, skip checkered walnut stock, pad swivels, rosewood pistol grip cap and forend tip.

	$495	$400	$350	$325	$285	$270	$255

Last MSR was $595.

Grading	100%	98%	95%	90%	80%	70%	60%

✷ Model 1200 Super Clip - similar to Model 1200 Super, except has detachable 4 shot box mag.

	$525	$425	$375	$350	$300	$280	$265

Last MSR was $640.

MODEL 1300S SCOUT - .243 Win. or .308 Win. cal., 20 in. barrel with muzzle brake, internal 5 shot or detachable 5/10 shot mag., laminated checkered birchwood stock, sling swivels, 8½ lbs.

	$425	$375	$325	$290	$260	$240	$220

Last MSR was $495.

Add $30 for detachable mag. (Model 1300C).

MODEL 1500S SURVIVOR - .308 Win. cal., bolt action, matte stainless construction, black composite (Kevlar/fiberglass) stock, 22 in. barrel, 4 shot mag., 7 lbs. Mfg. began 1993. Disc.

	$395	$350	$300	$270	$240	$210	$185

Last MSR was $450.

Add $30 for detachable mag. (Model 1500C).

This model was made for the Gibbs Rifle Co. by Bell & Carlson, Inc.

RIFLES: BOLT ACTION, MIDLAND SERIES

MODEL 2100 MIDLAND DELUXE - similar to Model 2600 Midland, except has checkered walnut stock and pistol grip cap.

	$335	$280	$235	$210	$190	$180	$170

Last MSR was $390.

MODEL 2600 MIDLAND - .22-250 Rem., .243 Win., 6mm Rem. (disc. 1994), 6.5x55mm (disc. 1994), 7x57mm (disc. 1994), 7x64mm (disc. 1994), .270 Win., .30- 06, or .308 Win. cal., 22 in. barrel, 4 shot mag., checkered hardwood stock with Monte Carlo cheekpiece, open sights, drilled and tapped action, 7 lbs. Disc. 1997.

	$350	$275	$225	$200	$180	$165	$150

Last MSR was $400.

This model was re-introduced during late 1996, utilizing a 1903 Springfield action with choice of 5 shot fixed mag. with hinged floorplate or 3 shot detachable mag.

MIDLAND 2700 LIGHTWEIGHT - lightweight variation of the Model 2100 Midland Deluxe featuring tapered barrel, anodized aluminum trigger housing and lightened stock with full pistol grip and recoil pad, Schnabel forend, 6½ lbs.

	$350	$285	$245	$225	$200	$190	$180

Last MSR was $415.

MIDLAND 2800 - similar to Model 2600 Midland, except has laminated birchwood stock, re-introduced during late 1996, utilizing a 1903 Springfield action, 7 lbs. Disc. 1997.

	$360	$295	$250	$215	$195	$185	$175

Last MSR was $430.

SHOTGUNS: SINGLE SHOT

MIDLAND STALKER - 12 ga., trigger bar safety, unique squeeze break open action and cocking system, 28½ in. barrel bored F, hardwood stock and forearm, 6 lbs.

	$90	$65	$55	$45	$35	$30	$25

Last MSR was $110.

GIL, ANTONIO & CO.

Current manufacturer located in Eibar, Spain. Imported and distributed exclusively beginning late 2000 by New England Arms Corp., located in Kittery Point, ME.

All Antonio Gil shotguns are hand made, and built to each customer's exact measurements at no extra cost.

Grading	100%	98%	95%	90%	80%	70%	60%

SHOTGUNS: SxS

Add 10% for 20, 28 ga. or .410 bore.
Add $500-$1,500 for wood upgrade.
Add $1,000-$1,250 per extra set of barrels.
Add $500 for non-selective trigger.

LAGA - 12, 16, 20, 28 ga. or .410 bore, sidelock action with color case hardened receiver and scroll engraving, demi-bloc barrels, DT, deluxe checkered walnut stock and forearm. Importation began 2001.

MSR	$2,495		$2,250	$1,750	$1,500	$1,350	$1,200	$1,100	$995

OLIMPIA - 12, 16, 20, 28 ga. or .410 bore, sidelock action, features traditional rose and scroll engraving on coin finished receiver. Importation began 2001.

MSR	$2,995		$2,575	$2,250	$1,750	$1,500	$1,350	$1,200	$1,050

ALHAMBRA - 12, 16, 20, 28 ga. or .410 bore, sidelock action, features elaborate full coverage floral scroll engraving on coin finished receiver and wood upgrade. Importation began 2001.

MSR	$3,995		$3,625	$3,150	$2,575	$2,250	$1,750	$1,500	$1,350

DIAMOND - 12, 16, 20, 28 ga. or .410 bore, sidelock action, top-of-the-line model with best engraving and best quality wood. Importation began 2001.

MSR	$5,995		$5,475	$4,650	$4,125	$3,625	$3,050	$2,500	$2,000

GLISENTI

Please refer to the Italian Military Arms section in this text.

GLOCK

Currently manufactured by Glock GmbH in Austria beginning 1983. Exclusively imported and distributed by Glock, Inc., located in Smyrna, GA. Distributor and dealer sales.

All Glock pistols have a "safe action" safety system (double action only) which includes trigger safety, firing pin safety, and drop safety. Glock pistols have only 35 parts for reliability and simplicity of operation.

PISTOLS: SEMI-AUTO

MODEL 17/17C SPORT/SERVICE - 9mm Para. cal., double action, polymer frame, mag., trigger and other pistol parts, 4.49 in. steel hexagonal rifled barrel with (Model 17C, new 1999) or w/o ports, steel slide and springs, 10 (C/B 1994), 17*, or 19* shot mag., adj. (Sport Model) or fixed (Service Model) rear sight, includes lockable pistol box, cable lock, cleaning rod, and other accessories, extra mag. and spare rear sight, 24 ¾ oz. Importation began late 1985.

MSR	$641	$495	$425	$345

Add $30 (Model 17C) or $30 (Model 17) for adj. rear sight.
Add $80 for fixed Meprolight sight.
Add $105 for fixed Trijicon sight.
Add $119 for competition model w/ adj. sights (Model 17CC, new 2000).

* ***Model 17L Competition Model*** - 9mm Para. cal., competition version of the Model 17, includes internally compensated 6.02 in. barrel, recalibrated trigger pull (3½ lb. pull), adj. rear sight, 26.3 oz. Mfg. 1988-1999.

	$650	$545	$425

Last MSR was $795.

Add $28 for adj. sight.

Early models with barrel ports matched to relieved slide will command a small premium.

Grading	100%	98%	95%	90%	80%	70%	60%

✹ Glock 17 Desert Storm Commemorative - 9mm Para. cal., features coalition forces listing on top of barrel, inscription on side of slide "NEW WORLD ORDER", 1,000 mfg. in 1991 only.

				$995	$825	$600	

Last MSR was $795.

MODEL 19/19C COMPACT SPORT/SERVICE - 9mm Para. cal., similar to Model 17, except has scaled down dimensions with 4.02 in. ported (Model 19C, new 1999) or unported barrel and serrated grip straps, 10 (C/B 1994), 15*, or 17* shot mag., fixed (Service Model) or adj. (Sport Model) rear sight, 23 ½ oz. New 1988.

MSR	$641		$495	$425	$345	

Add $30 (Model 19C) or $30 (Model 19) for adj. rear sight.
Add $80 for fixed Meprolight sight.
Add $105 for fixed Trijicon sight.
Add $119 for competition model w/ adj. sights (Model 19CC, new 2000).
During 1996, AcuSport Corp. commissioned Glock to make a special production run of matching 9mm Para. cal. sets. Each set consists of a Model 19 and 26 with serialization as follows: Model 19 (ser. range AAA0000-AAA0499) and Model 26 (ser. range AAB0000- AAB0499).

MODEL 20/20C SPORT/SERVICE - 10mm Norma cal., similar action to Model 17, features 4.6 in. ported (Model 20C, new 1999) or unported barrel, 10 (C/B 1994) or 15* shot mag., larger slide and receiver, fixed (Service Model) or adj. (Sport Model) rear sight, 30 oz. New 1990.

MSR	$700		$600	$485	$425	

Add $30 for adj. rear sight.
Add $80 for fixed Meprolight sight.
Add $105 for fixed Trijicon sight.
Add $35 for compensated barrel (Model 20C).
Add $145 for competition model w/ adj. sights (Model 20CC, new 2000).

MODEL 21/21C SPORT/SERVICE - .45 ACP cal., similar to Model 20, except has octagonal profile, right hard twist, 10 (C/B 1994) or 13* shot mag., 29 oz. Introduced May 1991.

MSR	$700		$600	$485	$425	

Add $30 for adj. rear sight.
Add $80 for fixed Meprolight sight.
Add $105 for fixed Trijicon sight.
Add $35 for compensated barrel (Model 21C).
Add $145 for competition model w/ adj. sights (Model 21CC, new 2000).

MODEL 22/22C SPORT/SERVICE - .40 S&W cal., similar to Model 17, except has locking block pin above trigger guard, 4.49 in. barrel, 10 (C/B 1994) or 15* shot mag., 25½ oz. Introduced 1990.

MSR	$641		$495	$425	$345	

Add $25 (Model 22C) or $30 (Model 22) for adj. rear sight.
Add $80 for fixed Meprolight sight.
Add $105 for fixed Trijicon sight.
Add $34 for compensated barrel (Model 22C).
Add $119 for competition model w/ adj. sights (Model 22CC, new 2000).
200 Model 22s were originally shipped with serial numbers beginning with "NY-1". Somehow, they probably were erroneously numbered at the factory (probably thinking that they somehow were part of the New York State Troopers shipment of Model 17s) during 1990. Premiums will occur on this variation.

MODEL 23/23C COMPACT SPORT/SERVICE - .40 S&W cal., compact variation of the Model 22 with 4.02 in. ported (Model 23C, new 1999) or unported barrel and 10 (C/B 1994) or 13* shot mag., 23½ oz. New 1990.

MSR	$641		$495	$425	$345	

Add $30 for adj. rear sight.
Add $80 for fixed Meprolight sight.

Grading	100%	98%	95%	90%	80%	70%	60%

Add $105 for fixed Trijicon sight.
Add $34 for compensated barrel (Model 23C).
Add $119 for competition model w/ adj. sights (Model 23CC, new 2000).
During 1996, AcuSport Corp. commissioned Glock to make a special production run of matching .40 S&W cal. sets. Each set consists of a Model 23 and 27 with serialization as follows: Model 23 (ser. range AAC0000-AAC1499) and Model 27 (ser. range AAD0000- AAD1499).

MODEL 24/24C - .40 S&W cal., similar to Model 17L Competition, choice of standard or ported (Model 24C) barrel and fixed or adj. rear sight. Mfg. 1994-99.

| | **$665** | **$525** | **$415** |

Last MSR was $795.

Add $40 for compensated barrel.
Add $28 for adj. rear sight.

MODEL 25 - .380 ACP cal., similar to Model 19 with 4.02 in. barrel, 10 shot mag., 22½ oz. New 1999.
This model is available for law enforcement only.

MODEL 26 - 9mm Para. cal., sub-compact variation of the Model 19, except has shortened grip, 3½ in. barrel, 10 shot mag., 21¾ oz. New 1995.

| **MSR** | **$641** | | **$495** | **$425** | **$345** |

Add $30 for adj. rear sight.
Add $80 for fixed Meprolight sight.
Add $105 for fixed Trijicon sight.

MODEL 27 - .40 S&W cal., sub-compact variation of the Model 23, except has shortened grip, 3½ in. barrel, 9 shot mag., 21¾ oz. New 1995.

| **MSR** | **$641** | | **$495** | **$425** | **$345** |

Add $30 for adj. rear sight.
Add $80 for fixed Meprolight sight.
Add $105 for fixed Trijicon sight.

MODEL 28 - .380 ACP cal., similar to Model 26/27/33, except has scaled down dimensions with 3.46 in. barrel, approx. 20 oz. New 1999.
This model is available for law enforcement only.

MODEL 29 - 10mm Norma cal., sub-compact model featuring 3.78 in. barrel, 10 shot mag., 27 oz. New 1997.

| **MSR** | **$700** | | **$585** | **$490** | **$425** |

Add $30 for adj. rear sight.
Add $80 for fixed Meprolight sight.
Add $105 for fixed Trijicon sight.

MODEL 30 - .45 ACP cal., compact Model 21, 10 shot mag., features octagon rifling and extension on mag., 26.5 oz. New 1997.

| **MSR** | **$700** | | **$585** | **$490** | **$425** |

Add $30 for adj. rear sight.
Add $80 for fixed Meprolight sight.
Add $105 for fixed Trijicon sight.

MODEL 31/31C - .357 Sig cal., similar to Model 17, 4.49 in. ported (Model 31C, new 1999) or unported barrel, fixed sights, 10 shot mag., 26 oz. New 1998.

| **MSR** | **$641** | | **$495** | **$425** | **$345** |

Add $30 for adj. rear sight.
Add $80 for fixed Meprolight sight.
Add $105 for fixed Trijicon sight.
Add $34 for compensated barrel (Model 31C).
Add $119 for competition model w/ adj. sights (Model 31CC, new 2000).

Grading	100%	98%	95%	90%	80%	70%	60%

MODEL 32/32C - .357 Sig cal., similar to Model 19, 4.02 in. ported (Model 32C) or unported barrel, 24 oz. New 1998.

MSR	$641	$495	$425	$345

Add $30 for adj. rear sight.
Add $80 for fixed Meprolight sight.
Add $105 for fixed Trijicon sight.
Add $34 for compensated barrel (Model 32C).
Add $119 for competition model w/ adj. sights (Model 32CC, new 2000).

MODEL 33 - .357 Sig cal., compact variation of Models 31 & 32, features 3½ in. barrel with shortened frame and magazine housing, 10 shot mag., 22 oz. New 1998.

MSR	$641	$495	$425	$345

Add $30 for adj. rear sight (new 2000).
Add $80 for fixed Meprolight sight (new 2000).
Add $105 for fixed Trijicon sight (new 2000).

MODEL 34 - 9mm Para. cal., similar construction to Model 17, except has 5.32 in. barrel, extended slide stop lever and magazine catch, fixed sights, target grips with finger grooves, thumbrest, receiver has rails for mounting accessories, 10 shot mag., 25¾ oz. New 1998.

MSR	$770	$655	$555	$475

MODEL 35 - .40 S&W cal., 27¼ oz., otherwise similar to Model 34. New 1998.

MSR	$770	$655	$555	$475

MODEL 36 - .45 ACP cal., similar to Model 30, except has single column 6 shot mag., 22 ½ oz. New 1999.

MSR	$700	$585	$490	$425

Add $30 for adj. rear sight.
Add $80 for fixed Meprolight sight.
Add $105 for fixed Trijicon sight.

GOLAN

See KSN Industries Ltd. listing.

GOLDEN EAGLE

Previous trademark of rifles/shotguns produced by Nikko Limited located in Tochigi, Japan, circa 1975-1981.

Please refer to the Nikko Firearms Limited listing in this text for a complete chronological history of Nikko - Japan's previous long gun manufacturer.

RIFLES: BOLT ACTION

MODEL 7000 GRADE I - bolt action, all popular American calibers, including .270 Win., and .300 Wby. Mag., 24 or 26 in. barrels, select skipline checkered walnut stock, rosewood forend tip, golden eagle head engraved in pistol grip cap, recoil pad. Mfg. 1976-1981.

	$600	$550	$525	$450	$375	$340	$290

MODEL 7000 GRADE I AFRICAN - .375 H&H and .458 Win. Mag. cal., similar to 7000, open sights.

	$650	$590	$555	$480	$400	$365	$315

MODEL 7000 GRADE II - scroll engraving, better grade wood.

	$690	$625	$590	$510	$430	$395	$340

SHOTGUNS: O/U

MODEL 5000 GRADE I (FIELD) - 12 or 20 ga., 26, 28, or 30 in. barrels, various chokes, vent. rib, engraved frame, gold eagle head inlay, auto ejectors, SST, checkered pistol grip beavertail stock. Mfg. 1975-1981.

	$850	$775	$700	$625	$560	$510	$440

Grading	100%	98%	95%	90%	80%	70%	60%

MODEL 5000 GRADE I SKEET - similar to 5000 Field, except 26 or 28 in. skeet bored, wide rib.

	$875	$800	$725	$650	$580	$510	$440

MODEL 5000 GRADE I TRAP - similar to 5000 Field, except 30 or 32 in. barrel, mod. and full, imp. mod. and full, or full and full choke, wide rib, trap stock with pad.

	$875	$800	$725	$650	$580	$510	$440

MODEL 5000 GRADE II - available in Field, Trap, and Skeet, more engraving, better grade wood, with screaming eagle on frame in gold.

	$950	$875	$790	$710	$630	$540	$460
Skeet	$975	$895	$810	$725	$640	$540	$460
Trap	$975	$895	$810	$725	$640	$540	$460

GRANDEE GRADE III - similar to 5000 Grade II, except elaborate engraving, inlays, and better grade wood.

	$2,500	$2,200	$1,900	$1,575	$1,250	$1,000	$850

GOLDEN STATE ARMS

Previous importer located in Pasadena, CA. Golden State Arms imported and subcontracted various firearms constructed by European and Japanese manufacturers - achieving private label status on some guns. Most firearms previously imported by Golden State Arms (including private labels) are not that collectible. In many cases, the shooting value will determine the price of a specimen. In some models or configurations which are currently desirable, however, premiums may exist.

GONCZ ARMAMENT, INC.

Previous manufacturer located in North Hollywood, CA circa 1984-1990.

While advertised, BATF records indicate very few Goncz pistols or carbines were actually produced. All of these guns were prototypes or individually hand-built and none were ever mass produced through normal fabrication techniques.

In 1990, Claridge Hi-Tec, Inc. purchased Goncz Armament, Inc.

GRANGER, G.

Current manufacturer established during 1902, and located in Saint Etienne, France. Current U.S. agent is Jean-Jacques Perodeau, located in Enid, OK.

All guns are made on a custom order basis. Please contact the U.S. agent directly for more information (please refer to Trademark Index).

SHOTGUNS: SxS, SIDELOCK

GRANGER SxS - 12, 16, 20, or 28 ga., case hardened receiver, Granger sidelock mechanism and plates, DT or SNT, choice of pistol or straight grip, deluxe French walnut stock and forearm, prices will vary per older customer specifications and appointments, delivery time is 12-36 months. Limited mfg.

MSR	$30,198	$29,250	$25,000	$21,000	$18,000	$15,000	$12,000	$9,000

Add $4,767 for fine English engraving.
Add $1,783 for Aiglon fastening action.

GRANT, STEPHEN

Current trademark manufactured by Atkin, Grant & Lang, established in 1821, and located in Hertfordshire, England.

The Stephen Grant trademark is responsible for mostly custom order SxS rifles and shotguns. Shotguns can be top or side lever and are equipped with sidelocks and a self-opening mechanism. Please contact the company directly for current information, availability, delivery time, and custom order pricing.

Atkin, Grant & Lang provide a useful historical research service on older Stephen Grant shotguns and rifles. The charge for this service is £25 per gun, and the company will give you all pertinent factory information regarding the history.

Grading	100%	98%	95%	90%	80%	70%	60%

RIFLES: SxS

Prices indicated are for manufacturer's suggested retail and 100% condition factors are listed in English pounds. All new prices do not include VAT or importation costs. Values for used guns in 98%-60% condition factors are priced in U.S. dollars.

SIDELOCK MODEL - various cals. between .300 H&H - .577 NE, best quality sidelock, individually made per customer specifications.

	MSR	£34,000		£34,000	$39,250	$35,000	$31,000	$27,000	$24,000	$20,500

SHOTGUNS: O/U

SIDELOCK MODEL - 12, 16, 20, 28 ga., or 410 bore, best quality sidelock ejector, individually made per customer specifications.

	MSR	N/A		N/A	$18,500	$15,000	$12,000	$10,000	$8,850	$7,500

Add 20% for 20 ga., 30% for 28 ga. and .410 bore.

SHOTGUNS: SxS

SIDELOCK MODEL - 12, 16, 20, 28 ga., or .410 bore, best quality sidelock ejector, top or side lever opening, individually made per customer specifications.

	MSR	N/A		N/A	$12,000	$9,900	$8,700	$7,500	$6,250	$5,000

Add 20% for 20 ga., 30% for 28 ga. and .410 bore.

GREAT WESTERN ARMS COMPANY

Previous importer located in Los Angeles, CA. Founded by Mr. William R. Wilson.

Originated probably in early 1953. When Colt Firearms Company ceased production of what is known today as "First Generation Single Action Army Revolvers". After several trips to the Colt factory to ascertain Colt's intent of reviving their production of the S.A. Army, and being assured it would never be revived, he founded the G.W. Arms Co. The main change between the Colt S.A. and the G.W. Frontier was removing the firing pin from the hammer and the design of a rebounding firing pin inserted in the revolver frame. This firm also redesigned the Remington Double Derringer and produced a derringer in 2 cals., .38 S&W and .38 S&W Special. Approx. 2,000 of these were mfg. Production of the Frontier probably did not exceed 23,000. When the Colt Company resumed production of their 2nd Generation S.A. 1873 Revolver, it rang the death knell of Great Western Arms Co. products, and the G.W. Arms Co. soon disappeared with its last sales of their "Frontier" being sold as unassembled "Kit Guns" to be assembled by the purchaser.

DERRINGERS

GREAT WESTERN DERRINGER - .38 S&W or .38 S&W Spl. cal. (not interchangeable). Basically an improved version of the Remington Double Derringer frame.

			$300	$275	$250	$225	$200	$180	$160

REVOLVERS: SINGLE ACTION

FRONTIER MODEL SAA - .45 LC, .44-40 WCF, .44 Mag., .44 Spl., .357 Atomic, .357 Mag., .38 S&W Spl., .32-20 WCF, .22 Hornet, or .22 Rimfire cal., 3½, 5½, or 7½ in. barrel, blue with case hardened colors on frame, gate and hammer, all blue, satin blue, nickel, black nickel, copper plated black oxide, gold, silver, gold and silver and parkerizing, grips were imitation stag (plastic), wood, pearl, ivory and sterling silver on special order. Unfinished "Kit Guns" were also sold, allowing buyer to assemble and finish.

			$500	$450	$400	$350	$300	$265	$235

Add 50% for flattop model.

Great Western Arms Company had a wide variety of factory special order features and options. They will act both independently and interdependently to determine the premiums on values listed.

Grading	100%	98%	95%	90%	80%	70%	60%

GREENER, W.W., LIMITED

Current manufacturer located in Birmingham, England since 1829. No current U.S. importation. Until 1994, Gibbs Rifle Co. located in Martinsburg, WV was the U.S. agent.

RIFLES: SxS, CURRENT MFG.

Boxlock and sidelock rifle quotations may be obtained by writing the company directly (see Trademark Index). A complete choice of calibers, engraving options, and walnut selection are available on a special order basis only.

SHOTGUNS: SINGLE SHOT

GENERAL PURPOSE - 12 ga., improved Martini action, single shot, 26, 30, or 32 in. barrel, full or mod., auto ejectors, straight checkered stock.

	100%	98%	95%	90%	80%	70%	60%
	$330	$305	$275	$220	$195	$165	$160

GP MK II - 12 ga. only, famed general purpose (GP) English shotgun configuration featuring Greener Martini action, 28 or 30 in. barrel, walnut stock and forearm. Mfg. resumed in 1991.

MSR	$522	98%	95%	90%	80%	70%	60%
	$522	$450	$400	$350	$300	$250	$195

Older, used military contract variations of this model have been imported recently - typically seen in the $165-$200 range.

SHOTGUNS: SxS, DISC.

FARKILLER GRADE F35 - 12 ga., 28, 30, or 32 in. barrels, hammerless boxlock, checkered straight or semi-pistol grip stock.

	100%	98%	95%	90%	80%	70%	60%
	$2,420	$2,200	$2,090	$1,870	$1,760	$1,650	$1,540
Auto ejectors	$3,300	$3,025	$2,750	$2,475	$2,035	$1,925	$1,650

FARKILLER GRADE F35 LARGE BORE - 8 or 10 ga., similar to F35.

	100%	98%	95%	90%	80%	70%	60%
	$2,750	$2,585	$2,310	$2,090	$1,980	$1,815	$1,650
Auto ejectors	$3,575	$3,300	$3,080	$2,860	$2,640	$2,090	$1,925

HAMMERLESS EJECTOR MODELS - 12, 16, 20, 28 ga., or .410 bore, 26, 28, or 30 in. barrels supplied with any choke combination, auto ejectors, single or double triggers, straight or semi-pistol grip stock, grades differ as follows:

* *Jubilee Grade DH35*

	100%	98%	95%	90%	80%	70%	60%
	$2,420	$2,255	$2,090	$1,925	$1,650	$1,540	$1,375

* *Sovereign Grade DH40*

	100%	98%	95%	90%	80%	70%	60%
	$2,860	$2,695	$2,420	$2,200	$1,980	$1,815	$1,595

* *Crown Grade DH55*

	100%	98%	95%	90%	80%	70%	60%
	$3,300	$3,080	$2,915	$2,750	$2,420	$2,035	$1,760

* *Royal Grade DH75*

	100%	98%	95%	90%	80%	70%	60%
	$4,400	$4,180	$3,850	$3,300	$3,080	$2,915	$2,640

Add $400 for SST.

Note: Degree of engraving and grade of wood are the basic differences between models.

EMPIRE - 12 ga. only, 2¾ or 3 in., any choke, 28, 30, or 32 in. barrel, hammerless, boxlock, straight stock or semi pistol grip.

	100%	98%	95%	90%	80%	70%	60%
	$1,760	$1,540	$1,320	$1,100	$935	$825	$770
Auto ejectors	$1,980	$1,760	$1,540	$1,320	$1,155	$1,045	$990

EMPIRE DELUXE - similar to Empire, only better grade wood.

	100%	98%	95%	90%	80%	70%	60%
	$1,980	$1,760	$1,540	$1,320	$1,155	$1,045	$990
Auto ejectors	$2,200	$1,980	$1,760	$1,540	$1,375	$1,265	$1,100

G

Grading	100%	98%	95%	90%	80%	70%	60%

SHOTGUNS: SxS, CURRENT MFG.

Various hard and soft cases are available for the following models with prices ranging from $500 up to $3,200.

NO. 5 NEEDHAM EJECTOR - 12, 16, 20 ga., or .410 bore, scalloped boxlock action, DT, any barrel length.

MSR	$4,470	$4,470	$3,750	$3,175	$2,750	$2,250	$1,825	$1,475

This model has been re-introduced to commemorate the takeover of J. V. Needham by W.W. Greener in 1874.

DH 40 - similar to No. 5 Needham Ejector, except has better engraving and deluxe walnut stock and forearm.

MSR	$6,705	$6,705	$5,900	$5,000	$4,250	$3,500	$2,850	$2,100

DH 75 - 12 ga. only, 2¾ in. chambers, Greener "Facile Princeps" scalloped boxlock action 27, 28, or 30 in. barrels, case hardened receiver, choice of engraving (game scene or fine scroll work).

MSR	$11,175	$11,175	$9,950	$8,450	$7,250	$6,000	$4,950	$3,875

DOH 90 - 12, 16, 20 ga., or .410 bore, 2½, 2¾ or 3 in. Mag. chambers, best boxlock featuring Anson & Deeley scalloped boxlock action with Greener easy-opening device, French walnut stock, DT.

MSR	$14,900	$14,900	$12,500	$9,750	$8,250	$7,000	$5,850	$4,675

L 120 - 12, 16, 20 ga., or .410 bore, best sidelock ejector model with dovetail lump barrels, fine scroll engraving with choice of bright or color case hardened frame finish.

MSR	$22,350	$22,350	$19,500	$16,000	$13,000	$10,000	$7,850	$6,000

L 150 - 12, 16, 20 ga., or .410 bore, 2½ or 3 in. chambers, very best sidelock ejector model with chopper lump barrels and easy-opening device, bright or color case hardened frame finish.

MSR	$29,800	$29,800	$24,000	$21,000	$17,000	$14,000	$11,000	$8,500

L 500 - 12, 16, 20 ga., or .410 bore, new St. George sidelock ejector model incorporating top-of-the- line carved engraving, walnut, and workmanship.

Because this model is entirely custom ordered per individual choice, a price quotation is necessary on every order.

GREIFELT AND COMPANY

Previous manufacturer located in Suhl, E. Germany.

COMBINATION GUNS

COMBINATION MODEL - 12, 16, 20, 28 ga., or .410 bore, shotgun barrel, rifle in any rimmed caliber, 24 or 26 in. solid rib barrel, pre-WWII.

			$5,200	$4,800	$4,400	$4,000	$3,600	$3,150	$2,800

Add $700 for auto ejectors.
Subtract 10% for 16 ga.
Add 20% for 28 ga. or .410 bore.
Subtract 40-50% for obsolete rifle caliber.
Above values for 12 or 20 ga. over obtainable rifle cartridge.

DRILLINGS

DRILLING MODEL - 12, 16, or 20 ga., SxS shotgun over rimmed rifle caliber, 26 in. barrels, boxlock, extractors, double triggers, rifle sight activated by barrel selector, pre- WWII.

			$3,500	$3,000	$2,750	$2,550	$2,300	$2,000	$1,750

Subtract 10% for 16 ga.
Subtract 40-50% for obsolete cals.
Above values for 12 or 20 ga. over obtainable rifle cartridge.

Grading	100%	98%	95%	90%	80%	70%	60%

SHOTGUNS: O/U

GRADE NO. 1 - 12, 16, 20, 28 ga., or .410 bore, O/U, any barrel 26-32 in., choke, vent. or solid rib, Anson & Deeley boxlock, auto ejectors, checkered pistol grip or English stock, pre-war.

12 or 20 ga.	$3,600	$3,200	$2,850	$2,500	$2,100	$1,750	$1,500

Subtract 10% for 16 ga.
Add 30% for 28 ga. or .410 bore.
Add $300 for vent. rib.
Add $400 for SST.

GRADE NO. 3 - similar to No. 1, except less elaborate engraving, pre-WWII.

12 or 20 ga.	$2,850	$2,500	$2,200	$2,000	$1,650	$1,350	$1,200

Subtract 10% for 16 ga.
Add 20% for 28 ga. or .410 bore.
Add $300 for vent. rib.
Add $400 for SST.

MODEL 143E - similar to No. 1, except not as high quality as pre-war model, not available in 28 ga. or .410 bore. Mfg. post-WWII.

	$2,400	$2,150	$1,850	$1,550	$1,350	$1,175	$1,000

Add 10% for vent. rib and SST.

SHOTGUNS: SxS

MODEL 22 - 12 or 20 ga., 28 or 30 in. mod. and full, hammerless, boxlock, false sideplates, extractors, checkered pistol grip or English style stock, post-WWII.

	$2,200	$1,760	$1,595	$1,320	$1,100	$990	$825

MODEL 22E - similar to Model 22, except has auto ejectors.

	$2,750	$2,200	$1,980	$1,760	$1,540	$1,430	$1,265

MODEL 103 - 12 or 16 ga., 28 or 30 in. mod. and full, extractors, double triggers, checkered pistol grip or English stock, post-war.

	$1,980	$1,650	$1,485	$1,210	$990	$880	$715

MODEL 103E - similar to Model 103, except has auto ejectors.

	$2,200	$1,760	$1,595	$1,320	$1,100	$990	$825

GRENDEL, INC.

Previous manufacturer located in Rockledge, FL circa 1990-95.

PISTOLS: SEMI-AUTO

MODEL P-10 SERIES - .380 ACP cal., blowback double action, 10 shot mag., small dimensions, hammerless, matte blue finish, 15 oz. Mfg. disc. 1991.

	$140	$125	$115	$105	$95	$90	$85

Last MSR was $155.

Add $15 for electroless nickel finish.
Add $15 for nickel green finish.
Green finish was available at no extra charge.

MODEL P-12 - .380 ACP cal., double action only, 3 in. barrel, steel construction with polymer grip area, no external safety, 11 shot Zytel mag., blue or electroless nickel finish, 11 lb. trigger pull, 13 oz. Mfg. 1992-95.

	$155	$135	$120	$110	$100	$90	$80

Last MSR was $175.

Add $20 for nickel finish.
Add $50 for threaded barrel with muzzle brake parts option.

G

Grading	100%	98%	95%	90%	80%	70%	60%

MODEL P-30 - .22 Mag. cal., blowback similar action to P-12, 5 in. barrel, hammerless, matte black finish, 10 (C/B 1994) or 30* shot mag., 21 oz. Mfg. 1990-95.

	$240	$200	$175	$155	$140	$125	$115

Last MSR was $225.

Add $25 for electroless nickel finish (disc. 1991).
Add $35 for scope mount (Weaver base).

✳ *Model P-30M* - similar to Model P-30, except has 5.6 in. barrel with removable muzzle brake. Mfg. 1990-95.

	$250	$210	$180	$160	$140	$125	$115

Last MSR was $235.

Add $25 for electroless nickel finish (disc. 1991).

MODEL P-30L - similar to Model P-30, except has 8 in. barrel with removable muzzle brake, 22 oz. Mfg. 1991-92.

	$275	$235	$200	$180	$160	$140	$125

Last MSR was $280.

Add $15 for Model P-30LM that allows for fitting various accessories.

MODEL P-31 - .22 Mag. cal., same action as P-30, except has 11 in. barrel, enclosed synthetic barrel shroud and flash hider, 48 oz. Mfg. 1990-95.

	$350	$315	$275	$240	$215	$185	$160

Last MSR was $345.

RIFLES & CARBINES

MODEL R-31 - similar design to Model P-31, except has 16 in. barrel and telescoping stock, 64 oz. Mfg. 1991-95.

	$365	$325	$275	$235	$210	$185	$165

Last MSR was $385.

SRT-20F COMPACT - .243 Win. or .308 Win. cal., bolt action based on the Sako A-2 action, 20 in. match grade finned barrel with muzzle brake, folding synthetic stock, integrated bi-pod rest, no sights, 9 shot mag., 6.7 lbs. Disc. 1989.

	$575	$525	$475	$395	$365	$340	$320

Last MSR was $525.

Grendel previously manufactured the SRT-16F, SRT-20L, and SRT-24 - all were disc. 1988. Values are approx. the same as the SRT-20F.

GRIFFIN & HOWE

Current custom gunsmith, rifle manufacturer, and importer established 1923, and located in New York, NY and Bernardsville, NJ.

Griffin & Howe

Founded in 1923 by Seymour Griffin and James Howe, Griffin & Howe continues to build its custom rifles as well as providing the full spectrum of gunsmithing services and importation of fine English guns.

Griffin & Howe has been building custom rifles since 1923. They also perform a variety of custom gunsmithing services. Prices may vary greatly depending on configuration, desirability, condition and special features. Most used Griffin & Howe Custom Rifles in average condition and without special engraving start at $3,150+ and rise according to condition and nature of the individual gun. Since 1923, fewer than 2,800 have been made. In 1930, Griffin & Howe became a subsidiary of Abercrombie & Fitch and remained with them until 1976, when it became a privately held company. Because all Griffin & Howe rifles are essentially special ordered, accurate pricing can be ascertained only by examining each individual gun. Elaborate specimens by this maker trademark will command over $10,000. Engraving by Joseph Fugger, Winston Churchill, Bob Swartley or Kornbrath will add considerably to the value.

Pricing on new custom rifles, with a wide selection of options, is available directly from Griffin & Howe.

Grading	100%	98%	95%	90%	80%	70%	60%

RIFLES: BOLT ACTION

Values represent a base gun with customer supplied action, normal wood and no options.

G&H CLASSIC FRENCH WALNUT STOCK - most popular cals., custom honed action with lapped lugs, Douglas premium barrel, hand engraving, French walnut sporter stock with ebony forend tip, G&H pistol grip cap, "Griffin & Howe, New York" barrel address, custom order.

	100%	98%	95%	90%	80%	70%	60%
MSR $7,000	$7,000	$5,750	$5,150	$4,650	$4,250	$3,850	$3,500

G&H PRE-'64 MODEL 70 CLASSIC SYNTHETIC STOCK - most popular cals., features glass bedded synthetic classic sporter stock in black or woodgrain finish, Douglas premium barrel, "Griffin & Howe, New York" barrel address, custom order. Disc. 2002.

	95%	90%	80%	70%	60%
	$2,250	$1,900	$1,650	$1,400	$1,175	$995	$850

Last MSR was $2,250.

WIN M70 STANDARD ACTION - for .243 Win., .270 Win., .30-06, or .308 Win. cal.

	$7,000	$5,000	$4,500	$3,500	$3,200	$2,800	$2,500

WIN M70 MEDIUM -.300 Win. Mag., 7mm Rem. Mag., or .338 Win. Mag. cal.

	$5,950	$5,350	$4,600	$3,750	$3,400	$3,100	$2,750

WIN M70 MAGNUM -.375 H&H or .416 Rem. cal.

	$6,250	$5,650	$4,850	$3,950	$3,500	$3,000	$2,850

WIN M52 -.22 LR cal.

	$3,500	$3,000	$2,500	$2,300	$2,000	$1,650	$1,450

WIN HIGHWALL

	$2,500	$2,250	$1,750	$1,650	$1,450	$1,300	$1,100

SPRINGFIELD 1903

	$2,450	$2,150	$1,750	$1,550	$1,350	$1,250	$1,100

SPRINGFIELD 1922

	$2,450	$2,150	$1,750	$1,550	$1,350	$1,250	$1,100

MAUSER STANDARD

	$3,600	$3,200	$2,850	$2,250	$2,000	$1,750	$1,600

MAUSER MAGNUM

	$7,750	$6,800	$5,700	$5,250	$4,750	$4,300	$3,875

SAVAGE 99

	$1,850	$1,650	$1,250	$1,150	$1,025	$950	$850

SHOTGUNS: O/U

MADISON - 12, 20, 28 ga., or .410 bore, case hardened frame, 26½, 28, or 30 in. VR barrels, scroll engraved with gold accents. Mfg. by the Belgian Browning custom shop using a B25 action beginning 1999.

	100%	98%	95%	90%	80%	70%	60%
MSR $9,750	$9,000	$8,250	$7,750	$7,150	$6,450	$5,500	$4,500

CLAREMONT - 12 ga. only, case hardened frame, shallow frame BOSS style lock-up, 30 in. VR barrels standard length, scroll engraving with gold accents. Mfg. by Gamba beginning 1999.

MSR $8,750	$8,250	$7,750	$7,150	$6,500	$5,900	$5,400	$4,700

EXTRA FINISH CLAREMONT - similiar to Claremont, except has coin finished frame with full coverage acanthus scroll engraving and drop out trigger group. Importation began 1999.

MSR $11,500	$10,800	$9,500	$8,250	$7,000	$6,000	$5,500	$4,800

CLAREMONT LUSSO - similar to Extra Finish Claremont, except has fully engraved sideplates. Importation began 2000.

MSR $18,000	$16,750	$14,250	$12,500	$9,950	$8,500	$7,200	$6,000

G

Grading	100%	98%	95%	90%	80%	70%	60%

BROADWAY - 12 or 20 ga., case hardened frame, 26, 28, or 30 in. VR barrels, scroll engraving with gold accents. Mfg. by the Belgian Browning custom shop using a B125 action beginning 1999.

	MSR	$5,750		$5,400	$4,600	$4,150	$3,550	$2,950	$2,400	$1,900

SHOTGUNS: SxS

ROUND BODY GAME GUN - 12, 16, 20, 28 ga., or .410 bore, features case colored round frame with sidelock action and 3rd fastener, H&H style selective ejectors, 25-30 in. barrels, double triggers, checkered straight grip stock and splinter forearm, G&H name gold inlaid, cased, mfg. by Arrieta.

	MSR	$5,750		$5,300	$4,600	$4,100	$3,500	$2,900	$2,400	$1,850

Add $200 for 28 ga. or .410 bore.

G **EXTRA FINISH ROUND BODY GAME GUN** - similar to Round Body Game Gun, except has coin finished frame and game scene engraving with gold accents. Importation began 1999.

	MSR	$8,500		$8,150	$7,400	$6,750	$5,950	$5,200	$4,500	$3,900

Add $350 for 28 ga. or .410 bore.

GRIFFON

Currently manufactured by Continental Weapons (Pty) Ltd. established in 1996, and located in Midrand, Johannesburg, South Africa. Currently imported and distributed by Griffon USA, Inc., a subsidiary of 21st Century Technologies, Inc., located in Ft. Worth, TX. Previously imported and distributed by First Defense International located in San Clemente, CA.

PISTOLS: SEMI-AUTO

GRIFFON 1911 A1 COMBAT - .45 ACP cal., patterned after the Colt M1911, single action, 4.13 in. barrel, 7 shot mag., ported barrel/slide, black Teflon finish, Commander hammer, Tritium sights, 36.5 oz. Importation began 1997.

	MSR	$495		$445	$375	$335	$300	$275	$250	$225

GRIFFON CW 11 - 9mm Para. cal., 8 shot mag., 4 in. barrel without porting, combo blue/chrome finish, perforated trigger, 3 dot sighting system. Importation began 1997.

	MSR	$495		$445	$375	$335	$300	$275	$250	$225

GRULLA ARMAS

Current manufacturer located in Eibar, Spain since 1932. Currently imported and distributed since 1994 by Hi-Grade Imports, located in Gilroy, CA, by Lion Country Supply, located in Port Matilda, PA, by Kevin's (double rifles only) located in Tallahassee, FL, and by Dale Decoy Service, located in Nelsonville, OH.

Grulla Armas manufactures a complete line of quality SxS shotguns in addition to both SxS and double rifles.

RIFLES

C-95 BOLT ACTION - .338 Win. Mag. or .375 H&H cal., deluxe bolt action featuring extensively scroll engraved square bridge receiver with elongated upper tang, octagon barrel with quarter rib and express sights, deluxe checkered wood with ebony forend tip, custom made per individual order. New 1996.

			$6,950	$6,400	$5,750	$4,950	$4,300	$3,600	$2,750

Last MSR was $7,500.

Grading	100%	98%	95%	90%	80%	70%	60%

E-95 SxS DOUBLE RIFLE - 9.3x74R or .375 H&H cal., top-of-the-line double rifle utilizing H&H type sidelocks with scroll engraving, skeleton steel buttplate, regulated barrels, beavertail forend, custom made per individual order. New 1996.

MSR $20,000	$18,000	$15,750	$13,250	$11,750	$9,650	$8,500	$7,250

SHOTGUNS: SxS, SIDELOCK

The following models are currently available in 12, 16, 20, 28 ga., or .410 bore. All guns have double triggers with hinged front, selective auto-ejectors, and straight grip stock with splinter forearm. Values represent standard models with no options.

MODEL 209 - HOLLAND - coin finished frame with scroll engraving.

MSR $3,450	$2,950	$2,525	$2,125	$1,800	$1,500	$1,325	$1,100

MODEL 215 - similar to Model 209, except has rose and scroll engraving with 3rd lever fastener and better wood.

MSR $4,050	$3,600	$3,000	$2,500	$2,100	$1,800	$1,500	$1,325

MODEL 216 - features delicate scroll engraving with border designs.

MSR $4,550	$4,000	$3,550	$2,975	$2,475	$2,100	$1,800	$1,500

MODEL 219 - similar to Model 216, except has more elaborate engraving and better wood.

	$5,325	$4,650	$4,000	$3,550	$2,950	$2,475	$1,995

Last MSR was $6,050.

CONSORT - features easy-opening H&H style action, scroll engraving with border fences.

MSR $6,475	$5,875	$5,150	$4,575	$3,850	$3,275	$2,650	$2,200

WINDSOR - similar to Consort Model, except has more engraving.

MSR $6,995	$6,225	$5,600	$4,975	$4,350	$3,750	$3,000	$2,400

MODEL 219-P

	$7,050	$6,225	$5,600	$4,850	$4,100	$3,200	$2,600

Last MSR was $7,750.

SUPER MH - features Boss style fine engraving with rosettes.

MSR $12,395	$11,400	$9,500	$8,475	$7,425	$6,200	$5,000	$4,150

NUMBER 1 - next to the top-of-the-line gun with best quality features.

MSR $15,550	$13,175	$10,625	$8,800	$7,575	$6,350	$5,150	$4,200

ROYAL - top-of-the-line model with H&H style scroll engraving.

MSR $16,950	$15,100	$12,850	$10,500	$8,750	$7,575	$6,350	$5,150

GRÜNIG & ELMIGER AG

Current rifle manufacturer located in Malters, Switzerland. No current U.S. importation.

Grünig & Elmiger AG manufacture high quality competition and sporting rifles. Please contact the factory directly for current U.S. availability and pricing.

GUN WORKS, LTD.

Previous manufacturer and distributor located in Buffalo, NY. Early guns were made in Tonawanda, NY.

HANDGUNS

X-CALIBER - .44 Mag. cal., single shot, tip up pistol, 8 in. barrel, matte type blue finish, ergonomic hardwood grips, probably used older Sterling Arms parts and restamped the barrel address. Limited mfg.

$350	$300	$260	$230	$200	$175	$150

Grading	100%	98%	95%	90%	80%	70%	60%

MODEL 9 - .357 Mag., 9mm Para., .38 Super, or .38 Spl. cal., O/U derringer, electroless nickel finish, 2½ in. barrel, wood grips, Millett sights, 15 oz. Disc. 1986.

	$135	$120	$105	$95	$65	$55	$50

Last MSR was $149.

GUSTAF, CARL
See listing under Carl Gustaf.

GYROJET
See MBA Gyrojet listing in the M Section of this text.

Griffin & Howe's Joe Prather may have shotgun shells on his tie, but the double rifle in his hands is getting all his attention.

H SECTION

HHF

Current manufacturer established in 1922 and located in Huglu, Turkey. HHF designates Huglu Hunting Firearms. Currently imported by Armsco, located in Des Plaines, IL. Previously imported 1993-96 by Turkish Firearms Corp., located in Allentown, PA and Alex Imports (1997 only), located in Chula Vista, CA.

Armsco currently imports a wide variety of HHF shotguns in all configurations. Retail prices/ranges are as follows: O/U - $430 - $1,290 MSR, SxS - $520 - $1,250 MSR, Semi-Auto - $469 - $499 MSR, Slide Action - $469 MSR, and Single Shot - $210 MSR. All O/U, SxS, semi-auto, and slide action models include interchangeable choke tubes. Additionally, many engraving options are available on O/U and SxS models, as well as Turkish walnut upgrades ($250 - $750). Please contact the importer directly for more information, a price quotation, and current availability.

SHOTGUNS: DISC.

All 12 and 20 ga. O/U shotguns listed were supplied with five choke tubes. All 12, 16, and 20 ga. shotguns were equipped with automatic ejectors - extractors were available for $200 less. SxS models were also available in 12, 16, 20, 28 ga. or .410 bore. Values for these older guns will be slightly less than their current equivilants.

H.J.S. INDUSTRIES, INC.

Previous manufacturer located in Brownsville, TX.

Grading	100%	98%	95%	90%	80%	70%	60%

DERRINGERS

FRONTIER FOUR - .22 LR cal., 4 shot derringer, stainless steel construction, 5½ oz.

	100%	98%	95%
	$115	$90	$80

LONE STAR - .38 S&W cal., single shot derringer, stainless steel construction, 6 oz.

	100%	98%	95%
	$137	$105	$95

H & R 1871, LLC. (Harrington & Richardson)

Current manufacturer and holding company located in Gardner, MA since 1991. During 2000, Marlin Firearms Co. purchased the assets of H&R 1871, Inc., and the name was changed to H&R 1871, LLC. Production of H&R products will continue at the factory located in Gardner, MA.

H & R 1871 LLC utilizes the original H & R trademark and does not accept warranty work for older (pre-1986 mfg.) Harrington & Richardson, Inc. firearms. Distributor sales only.

The use of the original Harrington & Richardson trademark was permitted during 1991. All new manufacture will use this trademark, but older H & Rs manufactured by Harrington & Richardson, Inc. are not the responsibility of H & R 1871, LLC.

REVOLVERS

Additional revolvers using the New England Firearms trademark may be located in the N section of this text. During 1997-99, all H & R 1871, Inc. revolvers were supplied with a lockable plastic case.

929 SIDEKICK - .22 LR cal., 9 shot, blue metal, swing-out cylinder, 4 in. heavy barrel, square butt with brown laminate grips, fixed sights, 30 oz. Mfg. 1996-99.

	100%	98%	95%	90%	80%	70%	60%
	$150	$120	$100	$85	$75	$65	$55

Last MSR was $173.

Grading	100%	98%	95%	90%	80%	70%	60%

✳ 929 Sidekick Trapper Edition - similar to 929 Sidekick, except has grey laminate grips and special barrel markings, limited mfg. 1996 only, distributed through 1996.

	$150	$115	$95	$85	$75	$65	$55

Last MSR was $175.

939 PREMIER WESTERN TARGET - .22 LR cal., 9 shot, blue metal, swing-out cylinder, target model with ribbed 6 in. heavy barrel and adj. rear sight, hardwood grips, 36 oz. Mfg. 1995-99.

	$150	$125	$105	$90	$75	$65	$55

Last MSR was $190.

FOURTY-NINER (WESTERN 949) - .22 LR cal., 9 shot fixed cylinder, case colored frame, 5½ or 7½ in. barrel, hardwood grips, fixed sights, approx. 37 oz. Mfg. 1995-99.

	$150	$125	$105	$90	$75	$65	$55

Last MSR was $190.

SPORTSMAN 999 - .22 LR cal., single or double action, top break action with auto shell ejection, 9 shot, 4 or 6 in. barrel with fluted solid rib, smooth hardwood stocks, transfer bar safety, blue finish, adj. sights, 30-34 oz. Mfg. 1991-99.

	$230	$180	$145	$125	$115	$100	$90

Last MSR was $285.

RIFLES: SINGLE SHOT

H&R 1871 began providing the Trigger Guardian trigger locking system beginning Dec. 1, 1999 at no extra charge.

ULTRA MODEL - .22 Mag. (new 2002), .22-250 Rem. (disc. 1994), .223 Rem. (disc. 1997, reintroduced 2002), .25-06 Rem. (new 1995), .243 Win., .308 Win. (new 1995), .357 Rem. Max. (mfg. 1996-98), .450 Marlin (new 2001), 7x57mm (mfg. 1997 only), or 7x64mm (mfg. 1997 only) cal., single shot break- open action, side-lever release, 22 in. heavy (.22-250 Rem. or .223 Rem.), 22 in. normal (.22 Mag., .308 Win. or .450 Marlin), or 26 in. (.25-06 Rem.) barrel with scope mount rail, checkered curly maple (disc. 1994) or laminated cinammon hardwood Monte Carlo stock with black line recoil pad, sling swivel studs, 7-8 lbs. New 1993.

MSR	$324	$260	$200	$155	$120	$110	$95	$85

Subtract $30 for metric cals. (disc.).

This model features a scope rail on .25-06 Rem. and .308 Win. cals.

✳ Ultra .22 Mag. - .22 Mag. cal. only, 22 standard or 24 in. heavy (disc.) in. barrel.

MSR	$189	$150	$125	$100	$90	$85	$80	$75

✳ Ultra Varmint Model - .223 Rem. or .243 Win. cal., features heavy 24 in. barrel, blue finish, natural finish cinammon laminate Monte Carlo stock, includes scope mount rail. New 1998.

MSR	$324	$260	$200	$155	$120	$110	$95	$85

✳ Ultra Comp. Model - .270 Win. or .30-06 cal., features 23 in. barrel with integral compensator, blue finish, multi-color checkered laminate wood stock and forearm. Approx. 7-8 lbs. New 1997.

MSR	$362	$300	$235	$190	$150	$125	$105	$95

✳ Rocky Mountain Elk Foundation Commemorative 1st Ed. - .280 Rem. cal., 26 in. blue barrel, features RMEF medallion in stock, high gloss bluing, 7-8 lbs. Mfg. 1995-96.

	$220	$175	$135

Last MSR was $270.

✳ Rocky Mountain Elk Foundation Commemorative 2nd Ed. - .35 Whelen cal., 26 in. blue barrel, features RMEF medallion in multi-color laminate stock and forearm, high gloss bluing, 7- 8 lbs. Mfg. 1996-97.

	$260	$215	$160

Last MSR was $300.

Grading	100%	98%	95%	90%	80%	70%	60%

WHITETAILS UNLIMITED COMMEMORATIVE RIFLE - .30-30 (new 1998) or .45-70 Govt. cal., Topper style break-open action, 22 in. barrel, blue frame with special etching, checkered American walnut stock (with medallion) and forearm. 7 lbs. Mfg. 1997-98.

	$250	$210	$170

Last MSR was $290.

HARRINGTON & RICHARDSON BUFFALO CLASSIC - .45-70 Govt. cal., top lever break open action, 32 in. barrel, case hardened frame, checkered walnut stock and forearm, 8 lbs. New 1995.

MSR	$409		$345	$265	$225

This model was also produced under the Wesson & Harrington trademark.

HARRINGTON & RICHARDSON TARGET RIFLE - .38-55 WCF cal., 28 in. barrel, target sights, blue finish. New 1998.

MSR	$409		$345	$265	$225

This model was also produced under the Wesson & Harrington trademark.

SHOTGUNS: SINGLE SHOT

H&R 1871 began providing the Trigger Guardian trigger locking system beginning Dec. 1, 1999 at no extra charge.

TOPPER 098 - 12, 16 (new 1992), 20, 28 (mfg. 1992-95, reintroduced 1998) ga., or .410 bore, 2¾ or 3 in. chamber, 26 or 28 in. barrel, break open side lever release action, transfer bar safety, ejector, satin nickel frame with blue barrel, black finish hardwood stock with full pistol grip and forearm, 5-6 lbs. Mfg. began 1991.

MSR	$140	$110	$90	$80	$70	$60	$50	$40

* **Topper Deluxe** - 12 ga. only, 3½ in. chamber, satin nickel frame with blue barrel, 28 in. barrel with 1 choke tube, black finish hardwood stock (with recoil pad) and forearm, 5-6 lbs. New 1991.

MSR	$164	$130	$110	$90	$80	$70	$60	$50

* **Topper Deluxe Rifled Slug Gun** - 12 ga. only, 3 in. chamber, 24 in. compensated barrel, rifle sights, dark American hardwood stock and forearm, satin nickel frame, approx. 5½ lbs. Mfg. 1996-99.

	$150	$115	$95	$85	$75	$65	$55

Last MSR was $170.

* **Topper Jr.** - 20 ga. or .410 bore, smaller variation of the Topper 098 with youth dimensions including 22 in. barrel and shortened stock with recoil pad, satin nickel frame with blue barrel, 12½ in. LOP, 5-6 lbs. Mfg. began 1991.

MSR	$147	$110	$95	$80	$70	$60	$50	$40

* **Topper Jr. Classic** - 20, 28 ga., or .410 bore, 22 in. barrel, checkered American black walnut stock and forearm, recoil pad, 12½ in. LOP. Mfg. began 1991.

MSR	$180	$150	$115	$95	$80	$70	$65	$60

* **NWTF Turkey Mag.** - 10 (mfg. 1996 only) or 12 (mfg. 1991-95) ga., 3½ in. chamber, 24 in. drilled and tapped barrel with 1 choke tube, entire gun is covered in mossy oak camo, includes sling and swivels, 6 lbs. Mfg. 1991-96.

	$145	$120	$100	$85	$75	$65	$55

Last MSR was $180.

This model was part of the National Wild Turkey Federation (NWTF) sponsorship program.

* **1994 NWTF Youth Turkey Gun** - 20 ga., 3 in. chamber, 22 in. full choke barrel, features Realtree camo finish and sling, limited mfg. 1994-95.

	$140	$110	$95	$85	$75	$65	$55

Last MSR was $160.

Grading	100%	98%	95%	90%	80%	70%	60%

✱ *2000 NWTF/Youth Edition* - 12 or 20 ga., 3 in. chamber, 20 ga. is NWTF Youth Edition with 22 in. barrel, camo finished laminate stock and forend with NWTF laser engraved frame, includes sling and swivels. New 2000.

	MSR	$203		$175	$130	$115	$95	$80	$70	$60

Add $9 for 12 ga. with 24 in. barrel.

THE TAMER - .410 bore, 3 in. chamber, synthetic thumbhole stock is designed to hold 4 shells, transfer bar system, 20 in. full choke barrel, electroless nickel finish. New 1994.

	MSR	$157		$130	$110	$90	$80	$70	$60	$50

SB1-920 ULTRA SLUG HUNTER - .20 ga. only, utilizes 12 ga. action and barrel that has been under-bored to 20 ga. and fully rifled, hardwood Monte Carlo stock and forearm, matte black frame. Mfg. 1996-Disc.

				$190	$155	$125	$100	$85	$75	$65

Last MSR was $225.

ULTRA SLUG HUNTER - 12 or 20 ga., 3 in. chamber, 22 (20 ga., Youth Model) or 24 in. fully rifled heavy barrel, side-release lever, black Monte Carlo hardwood stock with recoil pad, matte finished frame, 8-9 lbs. New 1995.

	MSR	$249		$210	$165	$130	$105	$90	$75	$65

✱ *Ultra Slug Hunter Deluxe* - similar to Ultra Slug Hunter, except has checkered camo laminate wood and scope mount rail, adj. rear sight. New 1997.

	MSR	$306		$255	$200	$165	$130	$105	$90	$80

WHITETAILS UNLIMITED RIFLE SLUG GUN - 12 ga., 3 in. chamber, 24 in. fully rifled heavy barrel, hand checkered Monte Carlo black laminate stock and forend, Whitetails medallion, hammer extension, swivels and sling. Mfg. 1998-99.

				$220	$185	$145	$120	$100	$85	$75

Last MSR was $255.

H-S PRECISION, INC.

Current custom pistol and rifle manufacturer established 1990 and located in Rapid City, SD. H-S Precision, Inc. also manufactures synthetic stocks and custom machine barrels as well. Dealer and consumer direct sales.

In addition to the following models, H-S Precision, Inc. will also build rifles using a customer's action (Remington 700 ADL or 700 BDL, Sako, Weatherby, or Winchester). These models will be approx. 33% less expensive than values listed (not available in Sniper Model).

PISTOLS: SINGLE SHOT

PRO-SERIES 2000 P - .17 Rem., .22-250 Rem., .223 Rem., .243 Win., .257 Roberts, .260 Rem., .308 Win., .35 Rem., 6mm PPC, 7mm-08 Rem., or 7mm BR cal., stainless steel receiver, 15 in. fluted stainless steel barrel, 3 position safety, laminated composite Pro-Series stock, Teflon coated receiver and barrel, choice of varmint (no sights) or silhouette (drilled and tapped for sights) configuration, choice of stock colors. New late 1997.

	MSR	$1,350		$1,250	$1,075	$995	$875	$750	$650	$575

RIFLES: BOLT ACTION, PRO-SERIES 2000

All H-S Precision rifles feature Kevlar/graphite laminate stocks, cut rifle barrels, and other high tech innovations including a molded in aluminum bedding block system. Beginning in 1999, H-S Precision began utilizing their H-S 2000 action, and model nomenclature was changed to begin with Pro-Series 2000.

Grading	100%	98%	95%	90%	80%	70%	60%

PRO-SERIES 2000 VARMINT TAKEDOWN (VTD) - .22-250 Rem., .270 Win., .308 Win., or .300 Win. Mag. cal., accurized Remington Model 700 receiver (disc. 1999) or H-S 2000 action (new 2000), H-S stainless steel cut rifled and fluted barrel, 5 or 10 shot detachable mag., Teflon coated metal finish. New 1997.

MSR	$2,500		$2,250	$1,675	$1,400	$1,000	$800	$650	$575

Add $1,250-$1,450 for extra barrel, depending on head size.
Add $250 for left hand action.

PRO-SERIES 2000 SPORTER/VARMINT (VAR/SPR) - .223 Rem., .22 PPC, .22-250 Rem., .243 Win., 6mm PPC, 7mm-08 Rem., or .308 Win. cal. are available in short action, .270 Win., .30-06, 7mm Rem. Mag., .300 Win. Mag., or .338 Win. Mag. cal. are available in long action, Remington ADL action only, each rifle is built per individual specifications. New 1990.

MSR	$1,950		$1,750	$1,500	$1,225	$900	$750	$650	$575

Add $150 for left-hand action.
Add $880 for extra stainless barrel (disc.).

PRO-SERIES 2000 PRO-HUNTER RIFLE (PHR) - available in 10 Safari cals., 24 or 26 in. fluted stainless steel barrel with cut rifling, Teflon finish, Pro-Series sporter stock, long action only.

MSR	$2,200		$1,975	$1,625	$1,325	$1,000	$800	$675	$575

Add $400 for Pro-Hunter takedown rifle (PTD).

PRO-SERIES 2000 LONG RANGE (TACTICAL MARKSMAN, HTR) - .223 Rem., .243 Win., .30-06, .308 Win., 7mm Rem. Mag., or .300 Win. Mag. cal., stainless fluted barrel standard, Remington BDL (disc. 1999) or Pro-Series 2000 (new 2000) action. New 1990.

MSR	$2,100		$1,875	$1,550	$1,275	$950	$775	$650	$575

Add $150 for left-hand action.

PRO-SERIES 2000 TAKEDOWN TACTICAL LONG RANGE (TTD) - .22-250 Rem., .243 Win., 7mm-08 Rem., or .308 Win. cal. in short action, .25-06 Rem., .270 Win., .30-06, 7mm Rem. Mag., .300 Win. Mag., or .338 Win. Mag. cal. in long action, stainless steel barrel, Remington BDL takedown action, matte blue finish. New 1990.

MSR	$2,800		$2,550	$2,050	$1,575	$1,250	$950	$825	$700

Add $1,250-$1,450 for extra barrel, depending on head size.

PRO SERIES 2000 RAPID DEPLOYMENT RIFLE (RDR) - .308 Win. cal., Pro-Series 2000 stainless steel short action only, 20 in. fluted barrel, black synthetic stock with or w/o thumbhole, black teflon metal finish, approx. 7½ lbs. New 2000.

MSR	$1,975		$1,800	$1,525	$1,250	$900	$750	$650	$575

Add $125 for PST60A Long Range stock.
Add $150 for left hand action.

TAKEDOWN LONG RANGE (TACTICAL MARKSMAN) - .223 Rem., .243 Win., .30-06, .308 Win., 7mm Rem. Mag., .300 Win. Mag., or .338 Win. Mag. cal., includes "kwik klip" and stainless fluted barrel. Mfg. 1990-97.

			$2,895	$2,225	$1,675	$1,350	$995	$850	$750

Last MSR was $2,895.

A complete rifle package consisting of 2 calibers (.308 Win. and .300 Win. Mag.), scope and fitted case was available for $5,200 retail.

HWP INDUSTRIES

Previous manufacturer located in Milwaukee, WI circa 1989.

REVOLVERS

THE SLEDGEHAMMER - .500 HWP Mag. cal., 5 shot revolver, double action, stainless steel, full shrouded 4 in. barrel (quick change), Pachmayr grips. Limited mfg. 1989 only.

			$1,150	$895	$750				

Last MSR was $1,295.

Grading	100%	98%	95%	90%	80%	70%	60%

HAENEL, C.G.

Previous manufacturer located in Suhl, Germany. Haenel mfg. many varieties of firearms between 1925-circa 1940. Currently, Haenel continues to manufacture airguns, mostly for Europe. Presently not imported into the U.S.

During 1925-WWII, C.G. Haenel manufactured a variety of sporting longarms, mostly concentrating on bolt action rifles, drillings, and SxS shotguns. Some of these guns are extremely well executed, and must be appraised individually. If quality, condition, and overall desirability are at a level similar to pre-war Sauers, Krieghoffs, etc., Haenel values could be similar to the trademarks just mentioned. However, a standard grade Haenel rifle/shotgun/drilling, in an obscure metric caliber with no engraving in 70% or less original condition, gets priced for its utilitarian shooting value as opposed to adding a collector premium.

For more information and current pricing on both new and used Haenel, C.G., airguns, please refer to the 2nd Ed. Blue Book of Airguns by Robert Beeman & John Allen (now online also).

PISTOLS: SEMI-AUTO

SCHMEISSER MODEL 1 & 2 - .25 ACP cal., similar to Baby Browning.

	$385	$340	$300	$275	$230	$200	$180

MODELS 200-205 - see Hämmerli-Walther.

RIFLES: BOLT ACTION

MAUSER-MANNLICHER SPORTING RIFLE - 7x57mm, 8x57R, or 9x57R cal., M/88 Mauser type action, 22 or 24 in. octagon barrel, Mannlicher box mag., double set triggers, raised rib on barrel, leaf sight, sporter stock.

	$440	$360	$330	$275	$250	$220	$165

88 MAUSER SPORTER - similar to Mauser-Mannlicher, with Mauser 5 shot mag.

	$525	$450	$375	$325	$275	$240	$200

HAMBRUSCH JAGDWAFFEN GmbH

Current manufacturer established in 1752, and located in Ferlach, Austria. Currently imported and distributed exclusively by CONCO Arms, located in Emmaus, PA.

Hambrusch Jagdwaffen is a member of the Ferlach Gun Guild, and manufactures many types of high-grade long arms including SxS shotguns, combination guns, drillings, double rifles, and single shot rifles. The combinations of these configurations are almost endless. During 2002, Hambrusch introduced a new proprietary big game cartridge, the .600/538 MM (Mega Magnum with 722 grain bullet). Please contact the CONCO Arms (see Trademark Index) for current model information and price quotations. Please allow 2 weeks for a reply.

HÄMMERLI AG

Current manufacturer located in Lenzburg, Switzerland. Currently imported and distributed by SIG Arms Inc. located in Exeter, NH, and Larry's Guns, located in Portland, ME. Previously imported until 1995 by Hämmerli Pistols USA, located in Groveland, CA, and by Beeman Precision Arms located in Santa Rosa, CA.

For more information and current pricing on both new and used Hämmerli airguns, please refer to the 2nd Edition Blue Book of Airguns by Dr. Robert Beeman & John Allen (now online also).

PISTOLS: SINGLE SHOT, RIMFIRE

FP-10 FREE PISTOL - .22 LR cal., current top-of-the-line Hämmerli pistol. Importation began 2000.

MSR	$1,750		$1,525	$1,200	$950	$850	$750	$650	$575

Grading	100%	98%	95%	90%	80%	70%	60%

MODEL 33MP - .22 LR cal., similar to the Model 100, except not available in a deluxe model. Mfg. 1933-1949.

	$925	$725	$650	$550	$470	$440	$385

MODEL 100 FREE PISTOL - .22 LR cal., 11½ in. octagon barrel, blue, martini action single shot, set trigger, micro rear sight, walnut stock and forearm. Mfg. 1950-1956.

	$880	$660	$605	$550	$470	$440	$385

Add 15%-20% for Olympic rings, "London", and "1948" markings (indicative of Swiss shooting team).

* **Deluxe model** - carved stock.

	$990	$770	$715	$660	$580	$550	$495

MODEL 101 - similar to Model 100, but heavy round barrel, improved action and sights, matte finish. Mfg. 1956-1960.

	$880	$660	$605	$550	$470	$440	$385

MODEL 102 - similar to Model 101, except high polished finish. Mfg. 1956-1960.

	$880	$660	$605	$550	$470	$440	$385
Deluxe model	$990	$770	$715	$660	$580	$550	$495

MODEL 103 FREE PISTOL - similar to Model 101, except lighter octagon polished barrel. Mfg. 1956-1960.

	$935	$715	$660	$605	$580	$550	$495

MODEL 104 MATCH PISTOL - similar to Model 103, except lighter round barrel, redesigned stock, mfg. 1961-1965.

	$760	$660	$550	$495	$470	$440	$385

MODEL 105 MATCH PISTOL - similar to Model 103, except redesigned action and stock, octagon barrel. Mfg. 1962-1965.

	$935	$715	$660	$605	$580	$550	$495

MODEL 106 MATCH PISTOL - similar to Model 105, except improved trigger.

	$910	$690	$580	$525	$495	$470	$415

MODEL 107 MATCH PISTOL - similar to Model 105, except improved trigger.

	$990	$770	$660	$550	$525	$495	$440

* **Deluxe model** - engraved and carved wood.

	$1,320	$990	$880	$660	$635	$605	$550

MODEL 120-1 SINGLE SHOT FREE PISTOL - .22 LR cal., bolt action, 9.9 in. barrel, blue barrel and receiver, side lever operated, anodized aluminum lever and frame, walnut checkered grips.

	$600	$540	$475	$425	$375	$325	$295

MODEL 120-2 - similar to 120-1, except stocks hand contoured.

	$600	$540	$475	$425	$375	$325	$295

MODEL 120 HEAVY BARREL - similar to 120-1, with 5.7 in. bull barrel.

	$600	$540	$475	$425	$375	$325	$295

MODEL 150 FREE PISTOL - .22 LR cal., 11.3 in. barrel, improved Martini-type action, set trigger, innovative design incorporating many unusual features. Disc. 1989.

	$1,850	$1,495	$1,275	$1,120	$980	$900	$850

Last MSR was $1,980.

Add $113 for left-hand variation.

The Model 150 was replaced by the Model 160.

MODEL 151 FREE PISTOL - replacement for the Model 150 Free Pistol. Imported 1990-1993.

	$1,850	$1,495	$1,275	$1,120	$995	$900	$800

Last MSR was $1,980.

Grading	100%	98%	95%	90%	80%	70%	60%

MODEL 152 FREE PISTOL - .22 LR cal., 11.3 in. barrel. improved Martini-type action, electronic trigger release, innovative design incorporating many unusual features. State of the art target pistol. Disc. 1992.

	$1,995	$1,600	$1,350	$1,195	$1,090	$990	$895

Last MSR was $2,105.

Add $57 for left-hand variation.

MODEL 160 FREE PISTOL - .22 LR cal., similar to Model 150, except has poly-carbon fiber forend, includes carrying case. Mfg. 1993-2002.

	$1,725	$1,475	$1,175	$900	$800	$700	$595

Last MSR was $1,850.

Add $290 for smaller adj. grips.

MODEL 162 FREE PISTOL - .22 LR cal., replacement for the Model 152 Free Pistol, includes poly-carbon fiber forend, includes carrying case. Imported 1993-2000.

	$2,150	$1,700	$1,375	$1,125	$900	$800	$700

Last MSR was $2,410.

Add $290 for smaller adj. grips.

PISTOLS: SEMI-AUTO

MODELS 200-205 - see Hämmerli-Walther.

INTERNATIONAL MODEL 206 - .22 Short or .22 LR cal., semi-auto, 7 1/16 in. barrel with muzzle brake, adj. sights, walnut grips, blue. Mfg. 1962-1969.

	$675	$625	$525	$450	$395	$365	$330

INTERNATIONAL MODEL 207 - similar to 206, except adj. grip heel.

	$725	$650	$550	$475	$425	$375	$350

INTERNATIONAL MODEL 208 - .22 LR cal., 9 shot, 6 in. barrel, blue, adj. sights, checkered walnut grips with adj. heel. Mfg. 1966-1988.

	$1,600	$1,300	$1,050	$950	$880	$835	$770

Last MSR was $1,755.

This model was replaced by the Model 208S.

* ***Model 208S*** - similar to Model 208, except has redesigned triggerguard and safety with interchangeable rear sight element. Imported 1988-2000.

	$1,750	$1,300	$995	$900	$775	$675	$575

Last MSR was $2,021.

Add $125 for factory scope mount.
Add $180 for smaller adj. grips.

* ***Model 208 Deluxe*** - similar to Model 208, except has carved grips and elaborate engraving. Importation disc. 1988.

	$2,995	$2,500	$1,995

Last MSR was $3,250.

* ***Model 208C (Commemorative)*** - limited edition commemorative. Disc. 1987.

	$2,100	$1,750	$1,400

Last MSR was $2,225.

INTERNATIONAL MODEL 209 - .22 Short cal., semi-auto, 5 shot, 4¾ in. barrel, muzzle brake, adj. sights, blue, walnut stock. Mfg. 1966-1970.

	$800	$690	$635	$550	$525	$485	$440

INTERNATIONAL MODEL 210 - similar to 209, but grips have adj. heel. Mfg. 1966- 1970.

	$800	$715	$660	$590	$540	$525	$495

MODEL 211 - .22 LR cal., semi-auto, 9 shot, 6 in. barrel, adj. sights, blue, similar to Model 208 except non-adj. walnut stocks. Importation disc. 1990.

	$1,550	$1,275	$1,050	$950	$880	$835	$770

Last MSR was $1,669.

Grading	100%	98%	95%	90%	80%	70%	60%

MODEL 212 HUNTER - .22 LR cal., semi-auto, hunter's pistol, 9 shot, 5 in. barrel, adj. sights, blue, walnut stocks. Importation disc. 1993.

		$1,250	$1,000	$875	$775	$675	$575	$475

Last MSR was $1,395.

MODEL 215 - .22 LR cal., semi-auto, Model 208 specs on commercial target model, 9 shot, 5 in. barrel, adj. sights, blue, walnut stocks. Importation disc. 1990.

		$1,395	$1,050	$895	$775	$695	$650	$600

Last MSR was $1,505.

MODEL 230 RAPID FIRE PISTOL - .22 S cal., semi-auto, 5 shot, 6.3 in. barrel, blue, adj. sights, smooth walnut grips. Mfg. 1970-1983.

	$705	$635	$580	$530	$485	$450	$415

MODEL 230-2 - similar to 230, except checkered grips with adj. heel. Mfg. 1970-1983.

	$735	$655	$605	$570	$515	$485	$470

MODEL 232-1 RAPID FIRE PISTOL - .22 S cal., semi-auto, 6 shot, 5.1 in. barrel, blue, adj. sights, contoured walnut grips. Importation disc. 1993.

		$1,395	$1,125	$950	$850	$750	$700	$650

Last MSR was $1,505.

Add $25 for wraparound grips sizes S-M-LG (Model 232-2).

MODEL 280 - .22 LR or .32 S&W Wadcutter cal., new modular pistol design utilizing carbon fiber synthetic material to replace frame and other critical parts, adj. grips, trigger, and rear sight, 4.6 in. barrel, 5 or 6 shot mag., approx. 2.2 lbs. Imported 1988-2000.

		$1,450	$1,125	$900	$800	$675	$575	$475

Last MSR was $1,643.

Add $200 for .32 S&W Wadcutter cal.
Add $765 (.22 LR) or $965 (.32 S&W Wadcutter) for conversion kit.
Add $200 for smaller adj. grips.
A package is also available with both calibers, magazines, and hard case for $2,595.

MODEL SP 20 - .22 LR or .32 S&W Wadcutter cal., replacement for Model 280, features low-level sight line, colored alloy receiver (blue, red, gold, violet, or black), adj. "JPS" buffer system that varies recoil characteristics per individual preference, black Hi-Grip anatomical grips. New 1998.

MSR	$1,450		$1,325	$1,075	$875	$775	$675	$575	$475

Add $110 for .32 S&W Wadcutter cal.
Add $620 for .22 LR conversion, $720 for .32 S&W Wadcutter conversion.

MODEL SP 20 RRS - .22 LR cal., state-of-the-art target pistol featuring composite frame with redesigned ergonomic grips, RRS designates recoil reducing system, fully hand adj. rear sight, various slide colors available. New 2002.

As this edition went to press, prices had yet to be established on this model.

MODEL P-240 - see SIG-Hämmerli for this model.

TRAILSIDE - .22 LR cal., single action, 4½ or 6 in. barrel, two-tone finish, choice of ultralight polymer composite grips or target variation which includes wood grips and adj. rear sight, 10 shot mag., cased with trigger lock, 28 or 30 oz. New 1999.

MSR	$449		$395	$350	$300	$275	$250	$225	$200

Add $80 for 4½ in. barrel with target sights, or $100 for 6 in. barrel in target sights.
This model is available from SIGARMS.

* **Trailside Competition** - includes 6 in. barrel with anatomical stipled grips and adj. bottom rest, cased with trigger lock, 37.2 oz. New 2000.

MSR	$699		$575	$500	$400	$350	$300	$265	$225

HÄMMERLI

Grading	100%	98%	95%	90%	80%	70%	60%

RIFLES: BOLT ACTION, TARGET

OLYMPIC 300 METER - .30-06 cal., bolt action, single shot free rifle, U.S.A. import, 7x57mm overseas, 20½ in. heavy barrel, double set trigger, aperture rear sight, globe front, free rifle stock with thumbhole pistol grip, beavertail forearm, Swiss style target butt. Mfg. 1945-1959.

	$880	$745	$605	$550	$470	$440	$415

HÄMMERLI-TANNER 300 METER FREE RIFLE - similar to Olympic 300 , except 7.5mm standard, also was available in other calibers. Mfg. 1962-disc.

	$895	$825	$770	$715	$660	$580	$520

Last MSR was $935.

MODEL 45 SMALLBORE MATCH RIFLE - .22 LR cal., bolt action, single shot, 27½ in. heavy barrel, same sights and stock type as Hämmerli-Tanner. Mfg. 1945-1957.

	$660	$550	$470	$440	$385	$360	$330

MODEL 54 SMALLBORE MATCH RIFLE - similar to 45 Smallbore, except adj. butt. Mfg. 1954-1957.

	$670	$560	$480	$450	$395	$370	$340

MODEL 503 SMALLBORE FREE RIFLE - similar to 54 Smallbore, except free style stock.

	$660	$550	$470	$440	$385	$360	$330

MODEL 505 MATCH RIFLE - match stock with aperture sights.

	$690	$580	$495	$470	$415	$385	$360

MODEL 506 SMALLBORE MATCH RIFLE - similar to 503 Smallbore. Mfg. 1963- 1966.

	$690	$580	$495	$470	$415	$385	$360

SPORTING RIFLE - various calibers, set triggers, Mauser repeating action.

	$725	$650	$490	$425	$360	$325	$300

HÄMMERLI-WALTHER

Previously manufactured semi-auto target pistols made under joint effort from Hämmerli and Walther.

PISTOLS: SEMI-AUTO, RIMFIRE

MODEL 200 OLYMPIA - .22 Short or LR cal., 7½ in. barrel, 1952 type, adj. sights, barrel weight, blue, checkered walnut grips. Mfg. 1952-1958.

	$660	$605	$550	$440	$415	$385	$360

MODEL 200 OLYMPIA - 1958 type, similar to 1952 type, except has muzzle brake. Mfg. 1958-1963.

	$715	$605	$550	$495	$470	$415	$385

MODEL 201 - similar to 200, 1952 type, except 9½ in. barrel. Mfg. 1955-1957.

	$660	$605	$550	$440	$415	$385	$360

MODEL 202 - similar to 201, except adj. heel grips. Mfg. 1955-1957.

	$715	$605	$550	$495	$470	$415	$385

MODEL 203 - similar to 200, except has adj. heel grip.

✳ *1955 Type* - no muzzle brake.

	$715	$605	$550	$495	$470	$415	$385

✳ *1958 Type* - muzzle brake.

	$770	$660	$605	$550	$525	$470	$440

MODEL 204 - similar to 200, except .22 LR cal. only.

✳ *1956 Type* - no muzzle brake.

	$745	$635	$580	$525	$495	$470	$440

Grading	100%	98%	95%	90%	80%	70%	60%
✳ **1958 Type** - muzzle brake.	$800	$690	$635	$550	$525	$495	$470

MODEL 205 - .22 LR cal., similar to 204, except adj. heel grips.

	100%	98%	95%	90%	80%	70%	60%
✳ **1956 Type** - no muzzle brake.	$800	$690	$635	$550	$525	$495	$470
✳ **1958 Type** - muzzle brake.	$855	$745	$715	$635	$580	$525	$495

HARRINGTON & RICHARDSON, INC.

Previous manufacturer located in Gardner, MA - formerly from Worchester, MA. Successors to Wesson & Harrington, manufactured from 1871 until January 24, 1986. H & R 1871, LLC. was formed during 1991 (see their listing in the front of this section). H & R 1871, LLC. is not responsible for the warranties or safety of older pre-1986 H & R firearms.

A manufacturer of utilitarian firearms for over 115 years, H & R ceased operation on January 24, 1986. Even though new manufacture (under H & R 1871, LLC.) is utilizing the H & R trademark, the discontinuance of older models in either NIB or mint condition may command slight asking premiums, but probably will not affect values on those handguns only recently discontinued. Most H & R firearms are still purchased for their shooting value rather than collecting potential.

Please refer to H & R listing in the Serialization section for alphabetical suffix information on how to determine year of manufacture for most H & R firearms between 1940-82.

COMBINATION GUNS: SINGLE SHOT

MODEL 058 - 20 ga./.30-30, .22 Rem. Jet, .22 Hornet, .357 Mag., or .44 Mag. cal. combination, 2 separate barrels supplied, blue only. Disc. 1985.

$155	$130	$110	$95	$85	$75	$65

Last MSR was $145.

MODEL 258 COMBINATION HANDY GUN II - supplied with 20 ga., 22 in. barrel and 22 in. rifle barrel in .22 Hornet, .30-30 Win., or .357 Mag. cal., electroless, matte nickel finish, side lever action release, cased, 6½ lbs. Disc. 1985.

$175	$155	$140	$130	$120	$100	$95

Last MSR was $195.

COMMEMORATIVES, SPECIAL EDITIONS, & LIMITED MFG.

ABILENE ANNIVERSARY .22 REVOLVER - 300 mfg. 1967.

$150	$115	$75

Last MSR was $83.50 (1967).

H&R 100TH ANNIVERSARY OFFICER'S MODEL - 1871-1971, Commemorative Officer's Model, Springfield 1873 Replica, Trapdoor, .45-70 Govt. cal., engraved metal work, 26 in. barrel, anniversary plaque on stock, 10,000 mfg. in 1971.

$595	$550	$500

Last MSR was $250.

MODEL 171 AND 171 DELUXE - please refer to listings under Rifles section.

MODEL 172 CARBINE - .45-70 Govt. cal., 22 in. barrel, Trapdoor action, walnut stock, silver plated grip cap, tang sight. Mfg. 1978-1982.

$1,250	$1,000	$750

MODEL 173 RIFLE - .45-70 Govt. cal., similar to Officer's Model, no plaque on stock. Mfg. 1972-1983.

$495	$425	$325

H

Grading	100%	98%	95%	90%	80%	70%	60%

MODEL 174 CARBINE (LITTLE BIG HORN) - .45-70 Govt. cal., Little Big Horn Commercial Carbine. Quantity unknown.

	$395	$325	$250

Last MSR was $220 (1972).

MODEL 178 - .45-70 Govt. cal., Infantry Musket Replica, 32 in. barrel. Mfg. 1973-1984.

	$375	$325	$250

1873 SPRINGFIELD TRAPDOOR - .45-70 Govt. cal., unknown quantities mfg. 1973.

	$450	$350	$275

Last MSR was $250.

CUSTER MEMORIAL ISSUE - .45-70 Govt. cal., limited production, deluxe walnut stock, highly engraved, gold inlaid, mahogany display case and two volumes on Custer history. Each weapon bears the name of one who fell at Little Big Horn.

✴ **Officer's Model** - 25 mfg., must be new with original box/accessories.

	$3,995	$3,150	$2,400

Last MSR was $3,000 (1973).

✴ **Enlisted Men's Model** - 243 mfg., must be new with original box/accessories.

	$1,995	$1,400	$900

Last MSR was $2,000 (1973).

HANDGUNS: PRE-1942

MODEL 4 - .32 S&W Long 6 shot, or .38 S&W Long 5 shot cal., (1904), double action, 2½, 4½, and 6 in. barrels, blue or nickel, hard rubber grips, solid frame, fixed sights. Mfg. 1904-1941.

	$95	$85	$70	$55	$45	$35	$30

MODEL 5 - .32 S&W Long cal., 5 shot only, (1905), double action, same as Model 4. Mfg. 1905-1939.

	$95	$85	$70	$55	$45	$35	$30

MODEL 6 - .22 LR cal., 7 shot only, (1906), double action, similar to Model 4. mfg. 1906-1941.

	$95	$85	$70	$55	$45	$35	$30

AMERICAN - .32 S&W, .38 S&W, or .44 S&W cal., 5 or 6 (.32 S&W cal.) shot, double action, 2½, 4, or 6 in. barrel, fixed sights, blue or nickel.

	$95	$85	$70	$55	$45	$35	$30

YOUNG AMERICAN - .22 Long, 7 shot, or .32 S&W, 5 shot cal., double action, 2, 4½, or 6 in. barrel, fixed sights, blue or nickel. Mfg. 1887-1941.

	$95	$85	$70	$55	$45	$35	$30

VEST POCKET - double action, 1 1/8 in. barrel, blue or nickel, solid frame, spurless hammer.

	$95	$85	$70	$55	$45	$35	$30

HUNTER - .22 LR cal., double action, 10 in. octagon barrel, 9 shot, checkered walnut grips.

	$140	$110	$100	$85	$65	$55	$45

TRAPPER - .22 LR cal., double action, 7 shot, 6 in. octagon barrel, checkered walnut stocks.

	$175	$135	$100	$85	$65	$55	$45

MODEL 922 - .22 LR cal., first issue, 9 shot, 10 in. octagon barrel on early models, 6 in. round barrel on later models, checkered walnut grips.

	$140	$120	$100	$85	$65	$55	$45

Some early guns were marked "22 SPECIAL" on left barrel.

AUTOMATIC EJECTING - .32 S&W cal., 6 shot, .38 S&W, 5 shot, double action, 3¼, 4, 5, or 6 in. barrels, hinged top break, blue or nickel finish, fixed sights, black rubber grips. Mfg. 1896-disc.

	$160	$150	$105	$90	$75	$65	$55

Grading	100%	98%	95%	90%	80%	70%	60%

PREMIER - .22 LR, 7 shot, or .32 S&W, 5 shot cal., double action, break open, small frame.

	$95	$85	$70	$55	$45	$35	$30

HAMMERLESS - .22 LR, 7 shot, or .32 S&W, 5 shot cal., double action, 2, 3, 4, 5, or 6 in. barrels, small frame, top break, blue or nickel, black rubber grips.

	$125	$110	$100	$85	$65	$55	$45

HAMMERLESS - .32 S&W, 6 shot, or .38 S&W, 5 shot cal., double action, 3¼, 4, 5, or 6 in. barrels, large frame, break open.

	$125	$110	$100	$85	$65	$55	$45

TARGET MODEL - .22 LR, or .22 WRF cal., 7 shot, double action, 6 in. barrel, fixed sights, break open, small frame, blue only, walnut grips.

	$140	$120	$100	$85	$70	$60	$50

.22 SPECIAL - .22 LR, or .22 WRF cal., 9 shot, double action, 6 in. barrel, break open, large frame, blue only, gold plated front sight, walnut grips.

	$165	$140	$120	$100	$85	$70	$60

EXPERT - double action, similar to .22 Special, except 10 in. barrel.

	$150	$140	$120	$100	$85	$70	$60

SPORTSMAN NO. 199 - .22 LR cal., 9 shot, single action, 6 in. barrel, adj. target sights, break open, blue only, checkered walnut grips.

	$275	$235	$195	$165	$140	$110	$90

DEFENDER - .38 S&W cal., double action, 4 or 6 in. barrel, fixed sights, blue, break open, black plastic grips, made during WWII for police reserves and major corporation guards.

	$140	$120	$110	$100	$85	$65	$55

ULTRA SPORTSMAN - .22 LR cal., 9 shot, single action, 6 in. barrel, blue, break open, adj. sights, walnut grips, short cylinder action, wide hammer spur.

	$220	$200	$180	$150	$120	$100	$85

NEW DEFENDER - .22 LR cal., 9 shot, double action, 2 in. barrel, break open, adj. sights, blue, round butt, checkered walnut grip.

	$220	$200	$180	$150	$120	$100	$85

USRA SINGLE SHOT TARGET - .22 LR cal., 7, 8, or 10 in. barrel, blue, hinged break open, adj. sights, walnut grips. Approx. 3,300 mfg. 1928-1941.

	$440	$415	$385	$330	$290	$250	$195

> **Subtract 25% for 1928-1930 mfg.**
> This model had many production changes and manufacturing variances. Pistols made from 1928-1930 do not have the USRA markings, and are not worth as much as later guns with more features.

.25 CAL. SELF LOADING PISTOL - .25 ACP cal., 6 shot, 2 in. barrel, blue, black rubber grips. 16,630 mfg. 1912-1916.

	$375	$330	$305	$250	$195	$165	$140

.32 CAL. SELF LOADING PISTOL - .32 ACP cal., 8 shot, 3½ in. barrel, fixed sights, black rubber grips. Mfg. 1916-1924.

	$330	$305	$250	$195	$165	$140	$110

> **Add 20% for type I models if in 90%+ original condition.**
> Type I models with 12 slide pull grooves are serialized 1-3,025. Type II (more common) are serialized 3,026 - 34,500.

HANDY-GUN - smooth bore (mfg. 1921-1934) or rifled-barrel(mfg. 1931-1934) pistol, single shot, top lever break open, available in either 8 or 12¼ in. choked or unchoked barrel in either .410 bore or 28 ga., case colored (Tiger stripe colors resulting from hot cyanide method) or blue frame. Rifled barrel (.22 LR in blue frame or .32- 20 WCF cal. in case colored frame, 12¼ in. barrel only) is rare. Early smooth bore guns bear only manufacturer's

Grading	100%	98%	95%	90%	80%	70%	60%

name, later blue and case-colored guns are stamped H. & R. "Handy-Gun" on left side and manufacturer's name on right side, as are all rifled barrel models. Ser. nos. on barrel lug and frame should match. Smooth bore Handy-Guns (more than 50 variations have been documented) not currently registered with ATF cannot be legally owned and are subject to seizure. Rifled barrels are exempt if not w/shoulder stock.

* **Smooth bore** - ser. no. range is 1 - 53,933.

	100%	98%	95%	90%	80%	70%	60%
	$595	$495	$400	$350	$295	$250	$200

* **.22 Rimfire** - ser. no. range is 1 - approx. 223.

	$900	$750	$650	$550	$500	$450	$350

* **.32-20 WCF** - ser. no. range is approx. 43,851-43,937.

	$1,200	$1,000	$800	$650	$550	$500	$450

Add $50-$250 for original box, and $75-$200 for original H&R holster.

Values for smooth bore are for the most common variation (.410 with 12¼ in. choked barrel), premiums of 25%-200% or more for rare variations (8 in. barrel, 28 ga., hooked trigger guard, optional detachable shoulder stock), rarest (just a few were made) is a .410 bore with 18 in. choked barrel mfg. in 1934. "Private branded" or "trade-branded" variations command 25%- 100% premiums. An optional detachable wire stock was available, but not commonly ordered. Most smooth bore variations were not drilled for a shoulder stock.

REVOLVERS: RECENT MFG.

MODEL 504 SQUARE BUTT - .32 H&R Mag. cal., 5 shot, 4 or 6 in. bull barrels, adj. rear sight, swing out cylinder, blue, black plastic and walnut grips. Mfg. 1984 and 1985.

	$165	$145	$135	$120	$110	$100	$90

Last MSR was $185.

* **Model 504 Round Butt** - compact design available with 3 or 4 in. barrel only. Disc. 1985.

	$165	$145	$135	$120	$110	$100	$90

Last MSR was $185.

MODEL 532 - .32 H&R Mag. cal., 5 shot, 2½ and 4 in. barrels, solid frame revolver, blue, pull pin cylinder, black plastic and walnut grips. Mfg. 1984 and 1985.

	$100	$90	$80	$70	$60	$50	$45

Last MSR was $115.

MODEL 586 - .32 H&R Mag. cal., 5 shot, Western-style revolver, double action, 4½, 5½, 7½, or 10 in. barrels, adj. rear sight, fixed cylinder, antique finish, black plastic or walnut grips. Made 1984 and 1985.

	$175	$155	$135	$120	$110	$100	$90

Last MSR was $195.

MODEL 603 - .22 Mag. cal., 6 in. barrel, double action. Disc.

	$159	$120	$110	$95	$90	$80	$70

MODEL 604 - same specifications as the Model 603, only has 6 in. bull barrel.

	$170	$130	$115	$95	$90	$80	$70

MODEL 622 - .22 Short, Long, or LR cal., solid frame, 6 shot, 2½, 4, or 6 in. barrels, blue, plastic grips. Mfg. 1957-1985.

	$95	$82	$70	$60	$55	$50	$45

Last MSR was $104.

MODEL 623 - same basic specifications as the Model 622, nickel finish only. Disc.

	$115	$95	$75	$60	$55	$50	$45

MODEL 632 GUARDSMAN - .32 S&W cal., 6 shot, 2½ or 4 in. barrel, solid frame, checkered tenite grips, blue. Mfg. 1953-1984.

	$104	$82	$70	$60	$55	$50	$45

Grading	100%	98%	95%	90%	80%	70%	60%

MODEL 633 - same basic specifications as the Model 632, only nickel finish. Disc.

| | $115 | $95 | $75 | $60 | $55 | $50 | $45 |

MODEL 642 - .22 Mag cal., 2½ or 4 in. barrel. Disc.

| | $95 | $70 | $65 | $60 | $50 | $45 | $40 |

MODEL 649 CONVERTIBLE - .22 LR or .22 Mag. cal., furnished with extra cylinder, Western style, double action, side loading, 5½ or 7½ in. barrel, 6 shot, walnut grips, blue finish. Mfg. 1976-1985.

| | $140 | $120 | $110 | $95 | $90 | $80 | $70 |

Last MSR was $160.

MODEL 650 CONVERTIBLE - similar to Model 649, except with nickel finish and only available with 5½ in. barrel. Disc. 1985.

| | $150 | $130 | $115 | $100 | $90 | $80 | $70 |

Last MSR was $175.

MODEL 666 - .22 LR or .22 Win. Mag. cal., 6 shot, 6 in. barrel, blue, plastic grips, convertible. Mfg. 1976-1982.

| | $100 | $90 | $70 | $50 | $45 | $35 | $30 |

MODEL 676 - .22 LR or .22 Win. Mag. cal., 6 shot, 4½, 5½, 7½, or 12 in. barrel, side load and eject, convertible (includes .22 LR/.22 Mag. cylinders), blue, case hardened frame, one piece walnut stock. Mfg. 1976-1982.

| | $140 | $120 | $100 | $85 | $60 | $45 | $35 |

MODEL 686 CONVERTIBLE - .22 LR or .22 Mag. cal., furnished with extra cylinder, Western style, double action, side loading, 5½, 7½, 10 or 12 in. barrel, 6 shot, walnut grips, color case hardened frame, adj. rear sight, 12 in. barrel. Disc. 1984.

| | $185 | $160 | $140 | $125 | $110 | $90 | $80 |

MODEL 732 - .32 S&W or .32 H&R Mag. cal., 6 shot, 2½ and 4 in. barrels, fixed sights, swing out cylinder, blue, black plastic grips. Add $15 for .32 H&R Mag. cal. Mfg. 1958- disc.

| | $127 | $100 | $85 | $75 | $65 | $55 | $45 |

MODEL 733 - same specifications as the Model 732, only nickel finish and available only with 2½ in. barrel. Add $15 for .32 H&R Mag. cal.

| | $140 | $125 | $110 | $85 | $75 | $60 | $50 |

MODEL 900 - .22 S, L, or LR cal., 9 shot, 2½, 4, or 6 in. barrels, snap out cylinder, blue, black plastic grips. Mfg. 1962-1973.

| | $90 | $85 | $70 | $55 | $50 | $40 | $30 |

MODEL 901 - similar to 900, but chrome with white tenite grips. Mfg. 1962-1963.

| | $110 | $100 | $90 | $70 | $50 | $40 | $30 |

MODEL 904 - .22 S, L, LR cal., double action, 4 or 6 in. bull barrel, target grade, 9 shot. Disc. 1985.

| | $150 | $135 | $120 | $105 | $95 | $80 | $70 |

Last MSR was $168.

MODEL 905 - similar to Model 904, except with nickel finish and 4 in. barrel only. Disc. 1985.

| | $160 | $140 | $125 | $105 | $95 | $80 | $70 |

Last MSR was $185.

MODEL 922 - .22 LR cal., Second Issue, 9 shot, 2½, 4, or 6 in. barrels, solid frame, blue, plastic grips. Mfg. 1950-1982.

| | $85 | $70 | $60 | $45 | $40 | $30 | $25 |

MODEL 923 - similar to 922, only nickel.

| | $90 | $75 | $65 | $50 | $45 | $35 | $30 |

Grading	100%	98%	95%	90%	80%	70%	60%

MODEL 925 DEFENDER - .38 S&W cal., 5 shot, 2½ in. barrel, blue, break open, adj. sight, wrap-around one piece grip. Mfg. 1964-1984.

	$130	$120	$100	$85	$70	$60	$50

Model 935 - similar to Model 925, except with nickel finish.

	$145	$135	$115	$100	$70	$60	$50

MODEL 926 - .22 LR or .38 S&W cal., 5,(.38 S&W) or 9 (.22LR)shot, 4 in. barrel, blue, adj. rear sight, break open, walnut grips. Mfg. 1968-1982.

	$130	$120	$100	$85	$70	$60	$50

✱ **Model 926 Abilene Kansas Centennial** - .22 LR cal., barrel is marked "Abilene Kansas" and "1869 Centennial 1969," mfg. 1969 only.

	$175	$155	$125	$105	$90	$80	$70

MODEL 929 SIDEKICK - .22 LR cal., 9 shot, 2½, 4, or 6 in. barrels, swing out cylinder, plastic grips, blue. Mfg. 1956-1985.

	$115	$100	$70	$55	$45	$35	$30

Last MSR was $127.

MODEL 930 SIDEKICK - similar to 929 Sidekick, only nickel finish and not available with 6 in. barrel. Disc. 1985.

	$125	$110	$80	$65	$55	$45	$40

Last MSR was $140.

MODEL 939 ULTRA SIDEKICK - .22 S, L, or LR cal., 9 shot, 6 in. barrel, swing out cylinder, vent rib, adj. sights, blue. Mfg. 1958-1982.

	$110	$100	$85	$70	$55	$45	$30

MODEL 940 ULTRA SIDEKICK - similar to 939, only round barrel. Disc.

	$105	$95	$75	$65	$50	$40	$30

MODEL 949 "FORTY NINER" - .22 S, L, or LR cal., 5½ in. barrel, double action, solid frame, 9 shot, side load and Western style ejection, adj. rear sight, walnut grips. Mfg. 1960-1985.

	$115	$100	$85	$70	$55	$50	$45

Last MSR was $127.

MODEL 950 - similar to Model 949, except with nickel finish. Disc. 1985.

	$125	$105	$90	$70	$55	$50	$45

Last MSR was $145.

MODEL 976 - similar to 949, only color case hardened frame. Disc.

	$100	$90	$85	$70	$60	$50	$35

MODEL 999 SPORTSMAN - 22 LR cal., Second Issue, 9 shot, 4 or 6 in. vent. rib barrel, top-break action, adj. sights, walnut grips. Mfg. 1950-1985.

	$195	$170	$155	$140	$125	$110	$95

This model was also made in a Sportsman Centennial Commemorative. Add 15%-25% if NIB.

MODEL 999 ENGRAVED - similar to 999, only engraved throughout, 6 in. barrel only. Disc. 1985.

	$425	$375	$300	$260	$225	$190	$175

Last MSR was $525.

RIFLES

REISING MODEL 60 - .45 ACP cal., semi-auto, 12 or 20 shot, 18¼ in. barrel, detachable mag. Mfg. 1944-1946.

	$550	$500	$450	$400	$360	$330	$295

MODEL 65 MILITARY - .22 LR cal., 10 shot mag., 23 in. barrel, Redfield aperture rear sight. Mfg. 1944-1946 for USMC.

	$250	$230	$200	$165	$145	$130	$110

Grading	100%	98%	95%	90%	80%	70%	60%

MODEL 150 - .22 LR cal., semi-auto, 5 shot. Mfg. 1949-1953.

| | $95 | $85 | $70 | $55 | $40 | $35 | $30 |

MODEL 155 - .44 Mag. or .45-70 Govt. cal., single shot, break open. Mfg. 1972-disc.

| | $150 | $130 | $115 | $95 | $75 | $55 | $45 |

MODEL 157 - .22 Mag., .22 Hornet, or .30-30 cal., single shot, break open, Mannlicher stock. Mfg. 1976-84.

| | $165 | $150 | $135 | $100 | $80 | $65 | $45 |

MODEL 158 - .22 Jet, .22 Hornet, .30-30, .357 Mag or .44 Mag. cal., single shot break open, 22 in. barrel, side or top lever action release, ejector, case hardened frame. Disc. 1985.

| | $150 | $135 | $125 | $90 | $80 | $60 | $50 |

Last MSR was $115.

✳ *Model 158 Combination* - supplied with rifle barrel and 20 ga., 26 in. barrel. Disc. 1985.

| | $195 | $175 | $150 | $135 | $115 | $100 | $90 |

Last MSR was $145.

MODEL 165 - .22 LR cal., 10 shot. Mfg. 1945-1961.

| | $120 | $110 | $95 | $85 | $70 | $55 | $50 |

MODEL 171 - .45-70 Govt. cal., Model 1873 Trapdoor copy, 22 in. barrel, Model 174 is the deluxe model. Disc.

| | $350 | $300 | $270 | $250 | $230 | $210 | $195 |

MODEL 171-DL - .45-70 Govt. cal., single shot, Springfield copy, 22 in. barrel. Mfg. 1984-1985.

| | $400 | $350 | $295 | $250 | $225 | $200 | $185 |

Last MSR was $385.

MODEL 174

| | $400 | $375 | $325 | $300 | $250 | $210 | $195 |

MODEL 300 ULTRA - .22-250 Rem., .243 Win., .270 Win., .30-06, .308 Win., 7mm Mag., or .300 Win. Mag. cal., bolt action, 22 or 24 in. barrel. Mfg. 1965-1978.

| | $495 | $450 | $425 | $400 | $350 | $325 | $295 |

MODEL 301 CARBINE - similar to 300, but 18 in. barrel, full length Mannlicher stock, N/A .22-250 Rem. cal.

| | $440 | $415 | $360 | $305 | $250 | $220 | $195 |

MODEL 317 ULTRA WILDCAT - .17 Rem., .17-223, .222 Rem., or .223 Rem. cal., short action Sako, 20 in. barrel, no sights. Mfg. 1968-1976.

| | $550 | $525 | $500 | $450 | $400 | $350 | $325 |

MODEL 317P PRESENTATION - similar to 317, but deluxe wood basketweave checkering. Mfg. 1968-1976.

| | $625 | $550 | $495 | $440 | $400 | $360 | $305 |

MODEL 322 - .222 Rem. cal., short throw bolt action, 6 shot mag., 24 in. barrel, checkered hardwood Monte Carlo stock with cheekpiece, drilled and tapped, approx. 6¾ lbs. Mfg. circa 1973-1980.

| | $325 | $275 | $245 | $220 | $200 | $180 | $165 |

MODEL 333 - 7mm Mag. cal., similar to 300, plainer version. Mfg. 1974 only.

| | $250 | $230 | $215 | $180 | $160 | $140 | $120 |

MODEL 340 - .243 Win., .270 Win., .30-06, .308 Win., 7mm Mauser cal., bolt action, 5 shot, 22 in. barrel, checkered walnut. Mfg. 1982-1984.

| | $395 | $300 | $275 | $240 | $220 | $200 | $180 |

MODEL 360 ULTRA AUTOMATIC - .243 Win. or .308 Win. cal., 3 shot, 22 in. barrel. Mfg. 1965-1978.

| | $395 | $350 | $325 | $300 | $275 | $250 | $225 |

H

Grading	100%	98%	95%	90%	80%	70%	60%

MODEL 370 ULTRA MEDALIST TARGET - .22-250 Rem., .243 Win., or 6mm Rem. cal., Varmint Rifle, 5 shot mag., 24 in. varmint weight barrel, unchecked target stock with rollover cheekpiece and semi-beavertail forearm, 9½ lbs. Mfg. 1968-1973.

| | $475 | $425 | $385 | $360 | $340 | $325 | $295 |

MODEL 422 - .22 S, L, or LR cal., slide action. Mfg. 1956-1958.

| | $110 | $100 | $85 | $65 | $45 | $40 | $30 |

✻ *Model 450* - similar to Model 451 Medalist only no sights.

| | $150 | $140 | $120 | $110 | $95 | $70 | $55 |

MODEL 451 MEDALIST - .22 LR cal., bolt action, 5 shot, 26 in. barrel. Mfg. 1948- 1961.

| | $165 | $150 | $140 | $110 | $100 | $85 | $55 |

MODEL 700 - .22 Win. Mag. cal., semi-auto, 5 shot, clip mag., 22 in. barrel. Mfg. 1977- 1985.

| | $275 | $250 | $225 | $200 | $175 | $150 | $125 |

Last MSR was $210.

MODEL 700DL - similar to Model 700 except deluxe checkered walnut. 4-power scope is standard, recoil pad. Disc. 1985.

| | $395 | $350 | $325 | $300 | $275 | $250 | $200 |

Last MSR was $360.

MODEL 750 - .22 LR cal. single shot bolt action, 22 in. barrel, open sights, youth stock dimensions. Disc. 1985.

| | $85 | $75 | $60 | $50 | $45 | $40 | $35 |

Last MSR was $95.

MODEL 865 - .22 LR cal. bolt action, 5 shot mag., 22 in. barrel. Disc. 1985.

| | $90 | $80 | $65 | $55 | $50 | $45 | $40 |

Last MSR was $105.

MODEL 5200 TARGET - .22 LR cal. target rifle, heavy 28 in. barrel, adj. trigger, no sights, single shot. 11 lbs. Disc. 1985.

| | $475 | $450 | $400 | $350 | $300 | $275 | $250 |

Last MSR was $450.

MODEL 5200 SPORTER - .22 LR cal., bolt action, 5 shot, 24 in. barrel, adj. sights, checkered walnut. Disc. 1983.

| | $595 | $550 | $500 | $475 | $450 | $400 | $350 |

SHOTGUNS

HARRICH NO. 1 - 12 ga., single barrel Trap Gun, 32 or 34 in. full choke, high quality, engraved, vent. rib. Mfg. by Ferlach of Austria from 1971-1975.

| | $1,650 | $1,595 | $1,485 | $1,320 | $1,100 | $880 | $770 |

MODEL 3 HAMMERLESS - similar to Model 8, but no visible external hammer. Mfg. 1908-1942.

| | $85 | $75 | $70 | $55 | $45 | $40 | $30 |

MODEL 5 LIGHTWEIGHT - 24, 28 ga., or .410 bore only. Mfg. 1908-1942.

| | $95 | $90 | $75 | $65 | $55 | $40 | $35 |

MODEL 6 HEAVY BREECH - similar to Model 8, only 10 ga. - 20 ga., heavier barrels. Mfg. 1908-1942.

| | $95 | $85 | $75 | $60 | $50 | $45 | $35 |

MODEL 7 OR 9 BAY STATE - similar to Model 8, only 12, 16, 20 ga., or .410 bore, rounded pistol grip. Mfg. 1908-1942.

| | $85 | $75 | $70 | $55 | $45 | $40 | $30 |

Grading	100%	98%	95%	90%	80%	70%	60%

MODEL 8 STANDARD - 12, 16, 20, 24, 28 ga., or .410 bore, single shot, 26-32 in. barrels, plain pistol grip stock, auto ejector, break open. Mfg. 1908-1942.

| | $150 | $125 | $95 | $75 | $65 | $60 | $55 |

Add 100% for 28 ga. or .410 bore.

FOLDING GUN - 12, 16, 20, 28 ga., or .410 bore, hinged frame, barrel folds against stock. Mfg. 1908-1942.

| | $195 | $175 | $150 | $125 | $100 | $85 | $60 |

Add 75% for 28 ga. or .410 bore.

TOPPER - 12, 16, 20 ga., or .410 bore, single shot, top or side lever break open action, 10 different variations of this shotgun, all are very similar and values run too close to differentiate, with ejector. Mfg. 1946-disc.

| | $145 | $125 | $100 | $85 | $70 | $55 | $45 |

Add 15% for Topper Deluxe (Model 488, chrome finish).

This model was also designated the Model 48, Model 158 (not in 28 ga.), Model 162 Buck gun with open sights, and Model 198 (28 ga. or .410 bore only).

MODEL 088 - 12, 16, 20, 28 ga., or .410 bore, single shot, hammer model, ejector, top or side lever break open action, blue barrel finish with case hardened frame. Disc. 1985.

| | $85 | $75 | $55 | $50 | $45 | $40 | $35 |

Last MSR was $95.

MODEL 099 - 12, 16, 20 ga., or .410 bore, similar to Model 088, only electroless nickel finish, ejector, top or side lever break open action. Disc. 1984.

| | $95 | $80 | $60 | $55 | $50 | $45 | $40 |

MODEL 162 - 12 or 20 ga., single shot, 24 in. slug barrel with rifle sights, case hardened frame, top or side lever break open action. Disc. 1984.

| | $115 | $105 | $90 | $80 | $65 | $55 | $45 |

MODEL 176 - 10 (3½ in.), 12, or 20 ga., Mag., single shot, 32-36 in. heavy barrel, top or side lever break open action. Mfg. 1977-1985.

| | $110 | $95 | $80 | $70 | $60 | $50 | $45 |

Last MSR was $125.

MODELS 348/349 BOLT ACTION - 12 or 16 ga., 3 shot tube mag., 28 in. barrel (Model 349 has adj. vari-choke), walnut stock, 7½ lbs. Disc.

| | $115 | $90 | $75 | $60 | $50 | $45 | $40 |

MODEL 400 PUMP ACTION - 12, 16, or 20 ga., 28 in. full choke. Mfg. 1955-1967.

| | $155 | $145 | $125 | $110 | $90 | $75 | $55 |

MODEL 401 PUMP - similar to 400, but H&R variable choke. Mfg. 1956-1963.

| | $165 | $155 | $140 | $120 | $100 | $90 | $65 |

MODEL 402 PUMP - .410 bore, similar to 400, lightweight. Mfg. 1959-1967.

| | $175 | $165 | $150 | $140 | $110 | $100 | $85 |

MODEL 403 AUTOLOADER - .410 bore, 26 in. full choke, takedown. Mfg. 1964 only.

| | $195 | $180 | $165 | $155 | $120 | $100 | $85 |

MODEL 404 - 12, 20 ga., or .410 bore, double barrel, SxS, 26 or 28 in. barrel, boxlock, extractors, double triggers. Mfg. by Rossi of Brazil 1969-1972.

| | $185 | $175 | $165 | $145 | $110 | $90 | $70 |

MODEL 404C - similar to 404, only checkered stock.

| | $200 | $185 | $175 | $155 | $120 | $100 | $85 |

MODEL 440 - 12, 16, or 20 ga., pump action, 26, 28, or 30 in. barrels, available in various chokes, plain pistol grip and slide. Mfg. 1968-1973.

| | $145 | $130 | $110 | $100 | $85 | $70 | $55 |

Grading	100%	98%	95%	90%	80%	70%	60%

MODEL 442 - pump action, similar to 440, only vent. rib, checkered stock. Mfg. 1969- 1973.

	$175	$165	$155	$140	$100	$85	$65

MODEL 490 - 20 ga. or .410 bore, made for junior shooters, Greenwing finish - add $10. Disc. 1984.

	$85	$65	$60	$50	$45	$40	$40

MODEL 1212 - 12 ga., O/U, Field, 2¾ in., 28 in. vent. rib barrels, various chokes, checkered walnut stocks. Mfg. by Lanber Arms, Spain, from 1976-disc.

	$310	$295	$275	$250	$200	$175	$155

MODEL 1212 WATERFOWL - 12 ga., 3 in. chamber, similar to Model 1212, 30 in. barrel.

	$320	$310	$285	$260	$210	$185	$165

HARRIS GUNWORKS

Previous firearms manufacturer located in Phoenix, AZ 1995-March 31, 2000. Previously named Harris-McMillan Gunworks and G. McMillan and Co., Inc. (please refer to the M section for more information on these two trademarks).

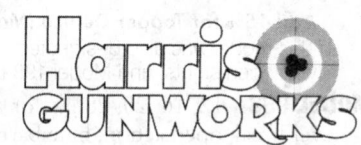

RIFLES: BOLT ACTION

BENCHREST COMPETITOR - .222 Rem. (disc.), .243 Win., 6mm Rem., 6mm PPC, 6mm BR, or .308 Win. cal., benchrest configuration. Mfg. 1993-2000.

	$2,675	$2,425	$1,950	$1,675	$1,425	$1,200	$1,025

Last MSR was $3,050.

NATIONAL MATCH COMPETITOR - .308 Win., or 7mm-08 Rem. cal. Mfg. 1993- 2000.

	$3,125	$2,675	$2,300	$1,875	$1,650	$1,325	$1,100

Last MSR was $3,500.

LONG RANGE TARGET MODEL - .300 Win. Mag., .300 Phoenix, .30-378 Wby. Mag., .30-416 Rigby, .338 Lapua, or 7mm Rem. Mag. cal., black synthetic fully adj. stock, w/ o sights, grey barrel finish. Mfg. 1996-2000.

	$3,225	$2,700	$2,325	$1,900	$1,650	$1,325	$1,100

Last MSR was $3,620.

TALON SPORTER - available in various cals. between .22-250 Rem. and .416 Rem., receiver available in either 4340 chrome molybdenum or 17-4 stainless steel, drilled and tapped, match grade barrel. Mfg. 1992-2000.

	$2,600	$2,075	$1,725	$1,375	$1,050	$895	$800

Last MSR was $2,900.

The Talon action is patterned after the Winchester pre-64 Model 70. It features a cone breech, controlled feed, claw extractor, and 3 position safety.

SIGNATURE CLASSIC SPORTER - various cals. available between .22-250 Rem. and .416 Rem., premium wood stock, matte metal finish, buttoning used on rifling for 22 or 24 in. stainless steel barrel, McMillan action made from 4340 chrome moly steel (either left or right-handed), 3 or 4 shot mag. supplied with 5 shot test target. Mfg. 1988-2000.

	$2,450	$2,000	$1,675	$1,325	$1,000	$895	$800

Last MSR was $2,700.

SIGNATURE VARMINTER - similar to Signature Model, except is available in 12 cals. between .22-250 Rem. and .350 Rem. Mag., hand bedded fiberglass stock, adj. trigger, 26 in. heavily contoured barrel. Mfg. 1988-2000.

	$2,450	$2,000	$1,675	$1,325	$1,000	$895	$800

Last MSR was $2,700.

Grading	100%	98%	95%	90%	80%	70%	60%

SIGNATURE TITANIUM MOUNTAIN RIFLE - .270 Win., .280 Rem., .30-06, .300 Win. Mag., .338 Win. Mag., or 7mm Rem. Mag. cal., lighter weight variation with shorter stainless steel or graphite/steel composite barrel, 5¾ (w/graphite barrel), or 6½ lbs. Mfg. 1990-2000.

		$2,950	$2,575	$2,300	$1,925	$1,650	$1,325	$1,100

Last MSR was $3,300.

   Add $400 with graphite barrel.

SIGNATURE ALASKAN - available in many cals. between .270 Win. and .458 Win. Mag. Mfg. 1990-2000.

		$3,425	$2,725	$2,275	$1,650	$1,250	$1,125	$900

Last MSR was $3,800.

TALON SAFARI - available in many cals. between .300 Win. Mag. and .460 Wby. Mag., hand bedded fiberglass stock, 4 shot mag., 24 in. stainless steel barrel, matte black finish, 9½ lbs. Mfg. 1988-2000.

		$3,650	$2,850	$2,500	$2,150	$2,000	$1,850	$1,700

Last MSR was $3,900.

   Add $300 for .300 Phoenix, .30-416 Rigby, .30-378 Wby. Mag., .338 Lapua, .335-378, .338- 378, .378 Wby. Mag., .416 Wby. Mag. or Rigby, or .460 Wby. Mag. cal.

   The Talon action is patterned after the Winchester pre-64 Model 70. It features a cone breech, controlled feed, claw extractor, and 3 position safety. Older Signature action rifles do not have this new Talon action.

M-40 SNIPER RIFLE - .308 Win. cal., Remington action with McMillan match grade heavy contour barrel, fiberglass stock with recoil pad, 4 shot mag., 9 lbs. Mfg. 1990- 2000.

		$1,825	$1,450	$1,125	$925	$800	$700	$600

Last MSR was $2,000.

M-86 SNIPER RIFLE - .300 Phoenix (disc. 1996), .30-06 (new 1989), .300 Win. Mag. or .308 Win. cal., fiberglass stock, variety of optical sights. Mfg. 1988-2000.

		$2,450	$2,000	$1,675	$1,325	$1,000	$895	$800

Last MSR was $2,700.

   Add $300 for .300 Phoenix cal. with Harris action (disc. 1996).
   Add $200 for takedown feature (mfg. 1993-96).

.300 PHOENIX - available in most popular .30 cals., special fiberglass stock with adj. cheekpiece and buttplate, right- or left-hand action, 12½ lbs. Mfg. 1997-2000.

		$3,025	$2,650	$2,325	$1,925	$1,675	$1,325	$1,100

Last MSR was $3,380.

M-87 LONG RANGE SNIPER RIFLE - .50 BMG cal., stainless steel bolt action, 29 in. barrel with muzzle brake, single shot, camo synthetic stock, accurate to 1500 meters, 21 lbs. Mfg. 1988-2000.

		$3,450	$2,800	$2,375	$2,000	$1,850	$1,700	$1,575

Last MSR was $3,885.

   ✳ M-87R - same specs. as Model 87, except has 5 shot fixed box mag. Mfg. 1990-2000.

		$3,725	$2,950	$2,550	$2,200	$2,000	$1,850	$1,700

Last MSR was $4,000.

M-88 U.S. NAVY - .50 BMG cal., reintroduced U.S. Navy Seal Team shell holder single shot action with thumb hole stock (one-piece or breakdown two-piece), 24 lbs. Mfg. 1997-2000.

		$3,250	$2,600	$2,200	$1,625	$1,250	$1,125	$900

Last MSR was $3,600.

   Add $300 for two-piece breakdown stock.

M-89 SNIPER RIFLE - .308 Win. cal., 28 in. barrel with suppressor (also available without), fiberglass stock adj. for length and recoil pad, 15¼ lbs. Mfg. 1990-2000.

		$2,875	$2,525	$2,250	$1,875	$1,650	$1,325	$1,100

Last MSR was $3,200.

   Add $425 for muzzle suppressor (disc. 1996).

Grading	100%	98%	95%	90%	80%	70%	60%

M-92 BULL PUP - .50 BMG cal., bullpup configuration with shorter barrel. Mfg. 1993- 2000.

| | $4,300 | $3,250 | $2,750 | $2,300 | $2,050 | $1,850 | $1,700 |

Last MSR was $4,770.

M-93 - .50 BMG cal., similar to M-87, except has folding stock and detachable 5 or 10 shot box mag. Mfg. 1993-2000.

| | $3,800 | $3,250 | $2,750 | $2,300 | $2,000 | $1,850 | $1,700 |

Last MSR was $4,150.

Add $300 for two-piece folding stock or dovetail combo. quick disassembly fixture.

M-95 TITANIUM/GRAPHITE - .50 BMG cal., features titanium alloy M-87 receiver with graphite barrel and steel liner, single shot or repeater, approx. 18 lbs. Mfg. 1997-2000.

| | $4,650 | $4,175 | $3,475 | $2,875 | $2,300 | $2,050 | $1,850 |

Last MSR was $5,085.

Add $165 for fixed mag.
Add $315 for detachable mag.

M-96 SEMI-AUTO - .50 BMG cal., gas-operated with 5 shot detachable mag., carry handle scope mount, steel receiver, 30 lbs. Mfg. 1997-2000.

| | $6,200 | $5,625 | $5,075 | $4,650 | $4,175 | $3,475 | $2,875 |

Last MSR was $6,800.

RIFLES SxS

BOXLOCK MODEL - various cals. from .270 Win. - .500 NE, engraved boxlock action, 3 leaf express rear sights, AAA wood, high polish barrel blue, equipped with aluminum case and chain, custom order. Mfg. 1998-2000.

| | $12,000 | $10,000 | $8,500 | $7,000 | $6,000 | $5,000 | $4,000 |

Last MSR was $12,000.

Add $1,000 for quick detachable claw scope mounts.
Add $6,000 for additional set of rifle barrels.
Add $5,000 for additional set of shotgun barrels.

SIDELOCK MODEL - various cals. from .375 H&H - .577 NE, engraved sidelock action, 3 leaf express rear sights, AAA wood, high polish barrel blue, equipped with aluminum case and chain, custom order. Mfg. 1998-2000.

| | $18,200 | $15,750 | $12,000 | $10,000 | $8,500 | $7,000 | $6,000 |

Last MSR was $18,200.

Add $1,000 for quick detachable claw scope mounts.
Add $6,000 for additional set of rifle barrels.
Add $5,000 for additional set of shotgun barrels.

HARTFORD ARMS & EQUIPMENT COMPANY

Previous manufacturer located in Harford, CT circa 1929-1932. Hartford Arms was the forerunner of High Standard Arms Co., who acquired them in 1932.

PISTOLS: SEMI-AUTO, RIMFIRE

HARTFORD AUTOMATIC TARGET - .22 LR cal., 10 shot, 6¾ in. barrel, blue, black rubber grips. Mfg. 1929-1930.

| | $650 | $575 | $500 | $450 | $375 | $300 | $275 |

HARTFORD REPEATING PISTOL - .22 LR cal., similar in appearance to Automatic, except a hand operated repeater. Mfg. 1929-1930.

| | $495 | $425 | $360 | $310 | $260 | $250 | $225 |

HARTFORD SINGLE SHOT TARGET - .22 LR cal., similar in appearance to Automatic, 6¾ in. barrel, target sights, case colored frame and slide, blue barrel, rubber or wood grips. Mfg. 1929-1930.

| | $475 | $390 | $350 | $310 | $260 | $250 | $225 |

Grading	100%	98%	95%	90%	80%	70%	60%

HARTMANN & WEISS GmbH

Current manufacturer established during 1965 and located in Hamburg, Germany.

Hartmann and Weiss manufactures only top quality longarms, including sidelock SxS shotguns and rifles, falling block single shot rifles (including the Heeren action), and bolt action rifles. Please contact the manufacturer directly for more information and/or a price quotation.

HASKELL MANUFACTURING

Previous manufacturer of .45 ACP cal. semi-auto pistols located in Lima, OH. Previously distributed by MKS Supply located in Mansfield, OH.

Refer to listing under Hi-Point Firearms.

HATFIELD GUN CO., INC.

Previous manufacturer located in St. Joseph, MO. The following shotguns were previously manufactured until 1996 by the Hatfield Gun Co., Inc. (designated Hatfield Rifle Works until 1986).

SHOTGUNS: O/U

BOXLOCK - 20 ga. only, boxlock action with satin grey finished receiver, maple stock. Mfg. 1995-96.

$3,350	$2,950	$2,550	$2,175	$1,725	$1,450	$1,100

Last MSR was $3,749.

Add $1,425 for extra 28 ga. barrels.

SHOTGUNS: SxS

In addition to Grades I and II, Hatfield also offered custom order shotguns built per individual special order - prices started at $3,000.

GRADE I UPLANDER - 20 or 28 ga., 3 in. chambers, 26 in. IC/M, matted rib barrels, case hardened boxlock action, single trigger, ejectors, deluxe checkered straight grip maple stock and forearm, 5¾ lbs, cased. Mfg. 1987-96.

$1,975	$1,700	$1,500	$1,325	$1,150	$900	$725

Last MSR was $2,249.

Add $800 for extra 28 ga. barrels.

✳ Collector's Grade I - mfg. 1990-92.

$1,475	$1,200	$1,000	$875	$700	$550	$475

Last MSR was $1,625.

Add $400 for extra 28 ga. barrels.

GRADE II PIGEON - similar to Grade I, except has scroll engraving on top lever, sides, floor plate, and triggerguard, cased. Mfg. 1987-96.

$2,650	$2,250	$1,825	$1,475	$1,100	$900	$775

Last MSR was $2,995.

Add $995 for extra 28 ga. barrels.

✳ Collector's Grade II - mfg. 1990-92.

$2,675	$2,000	$1,600	$1,250	$1,050	$875	$775

Last MSR was $3,025.

Add $400 for extra 28 ga. barrels.

GRADE III SUPER PIGEON - includes heavy relief scroll engraving (total coverage) on frame, top lever, floor plate, and triggerguard, leather cased. Mfg. 1987-disc.

$2,350	$1,900	$1,495	$1,200	$1,025	$900	$775

Last MSR was $3,500.

Add $900 for extra 28 ga. barrels.

Grading	100%	98%	95%	90%	80%	70%	60%

✳ *Collector's Grade III* - mfg. 1990-disc.

	100%	98%	95%	90%	80%	70%	60%
	$3,000	$2,500	$2,000	$1,750	$1,400	$1,175	$995

Last MSR was $4,375.

Add $900 for extra 28 ga. barrels.

GRADE IV GOLDEN QUAIL - more extensive engraving including six 24 Kt. gold inlays on frame and floor plate, 2 gold barrel bands, leather cased. Mfg. 1987-disc.

	100%	98%	95%	90%	80%	70%	60%
	$3,995	$3,575	$2,900	$2,350	$1,900	$1,600	$1,300

Last MSR was $5,500.

Add $900 for extra 28 ga. barrels.

✳ *Collector's Grade IV* - mfg. 1990-disc.

	100%	98%	95%	90%	80%	70%	60%
	$4,475	$3,900	$3,300	$2,650	$2,175	$1,800	$1,500

Last MSR was $6,625.

Add $1,350 for extra 28 ga. barrels.

GRADE V WOODCOCK - previous top-of-the-line model with best quality engraving and multiple gold inlays, leather cased. Mfg. 1987-disc.

	100%	98%	95%	90%	80%	70%	60%
	$4,600	$4,400	$3,350	$2,700	$2,175	$1,800	$1,500

Last MSR was $6,900.

Add $1,500 for extra 28 ga. barrels.

✳ *Collector's Grade V* - mfg. 1990-disc.

	100%	98%	95%	90%	80%	70%	60%
	$6,200	$5,700	$4,475	$3,900	$3,300	$2,650	$2,200

Last MSR was $8,500.

Add $2,000 for extra 28 ga. barrels.

GRADE VI BLACK WIDOW - mfg. 1990-disc.

	100%	98%	95%	90%	80%	70%	60%
	$5,200	$4,875	$3,700	$3,000	$2,500	$2,100	$1,800

Last MSR was $7,900.

GRADE VII ROYALE - mfg. 1990-disc.

	100%	98%	95%	90%	80%	70%	60%
	$5,200	$4,875	$3,700	$3,000	$2,500	$2,100	$1,800

Last MSR was $7,900.

GRADE VIII TOP HAT - top-of-the-line model with best quality wood and extensive engraving with gold inlays. Built to individual customer specifications. Mfg. 1990-disc.

	100%	98%	95%	90%	80%	70%	60%
	$12,000	$9,750	$8,750	$7,500	$6,500	$5,500	$4,500

Last MSR was $17,500.

SIDELOCK MODEL - 20 ga. only, satin grey finished receiver, full engraving. Mfg. 1995- 96.

	100%	98%	95%	90%	80%	70%	60%
	$10,750	$8,750	$7,500	$6,250	$5,000	$4,850	$3,600

Last MSR was $12,000.

✳ *Grade II Sidelock* - features high relief full coverage engraving, color case hardened receiver, multiple gold and silver inlays.

	100%	98%	95%	90%	80%	70%	60%
	$15,000	$12,000	$10,750	$8,750	$7,000	$5,750	$4,650

Last MSR was $17,500.

KARL HAUPTMANN JAGDWAFFEN

Current manufacturer located in Ferlach, Austria. Consumer direct sales.

Karl Hauptmann is a member of the Ferlach Guild, and manufactures high quality shotguns, combination guns, and double rifles, and a very unique, three barrel SxSxS rifle. Since every gun is custom made according to each customer specifications, please contact the factory directly for an individual price quotation and delivery time.

HAWES FIREARMS

Previously manufactured by J.P. Sauer & Sohn in Eckernforde, Germany. Previously imported by Hawes Firearms in Van Nuys, CA.

Rather than give an individual listing of the various single action and double action (including Medallion models) revolvers that have been imported, a generalized price range is as follows: centerfire single actions usually are in the $150-$275 range, centerfire double actions are $175-$295, while .22 rimfire models are typically valued between $60- $140.

Grading	100%	98%	95%	90%	80%	70%	60%

HECKLER & KOCH

Current manufacturer located in Oberndorf/Neckar, Germany. Currently imported and distributed by Heckler & Koch, Inc. (U.S. headquarters) located in Sterling, VA (previously located in Chantilly, VA). In early 1991, H & K was absorbed by Royal Ordnance, a division of British Aerospace located in England.

PISTOLS: SEMI-AUTO, RECENT MFG.

Add $19-$35 for ambidextrous control lever (safety/decocking lever on right side) on the following currently manufactured USP models.

HK4 - .380 ACP, .32 ACP, .25 ACP, and .22 LR cals., double action auto, available with all caliber conversion units, 3 1/3 in. barrel, blue, plastic grips. Disc. 1984.

	100%	98%	95%	90%	80%	70%	60%
.25 ACP or .32 ACP cal.	$295	$260	$230	$215	$180	$150	$130
.22 LR or .380 ACP cal.	$430	$345	$300	$250	$195	$160	$140

This model was also available as a H & R commemorative model with gold tone plaque on slide and came in a plastic presentation box. Add approx. 25% to .22 LR or .380 ACP cal. prices if mint or NIB only.

✳ *.380 ACP with .22 LR conversion*

	$480	$385	$350	$325	$310	$290	$280

✳ *.380 ACP with all conversions*

	$650	$550	$450	$420	$390	$375	$360

This model was also mfg. in a French model in .22 LR and/or .32 ACP (about 500 imported).

P9S - .45 ACP or 9mm Para. cal., double action combat model, 4 in. barrel, phosphate finish, sculptured plastic grips, fixed sights. Although production ceased in 1984, limited quantities were available until 1989.

	$650	$525	$400	$360	$320	$290	$265

Last MSR was $1,299.

Add 25% for .45 ACP.

P9S TARGET - .45 ACP or 9mm Para. cal., 4 in. barrel, phosphate finish, adj. sights and trigger. Although production ceased in 1984, limited quantities were available until 1989.

	$1,000	$800	$600	$540	$500	$465	$430

Last MSR was $1,382.

P9S COMPETITION KIT - 9mm Para. or .45 ACP (rare) cal., similar to P9S Target, except extra 5½ in. barrel and weight, competition walnut grip, 2 slides. Disc. 1984.

	$1,150	$950	$875	$800	$720	$640	$550

Last MSR was $2,250.

P7 PSP - 9mm Para. cal., older variation of the P7 M8, without extended trigger guard, ambidextrous mag. release (European style), or heat shield. Standard production ceased 1986. A re-issue of this model was mfg. in 1990, with approx. 150 produced. Limited quantities remained through 1999.

	$750	$650	$550	$460	$410	$390	$370

Last MSR was $1,111.

P7 M8 - 9mm Para. cal., unique squeeze cocking single action, extended square combat type trigger guard with heat shield, 4.13 in. fixed barrel with polygonal rifling, 8 shot mag., ambidextrous mag. release, fixed 3-dot sighting system, stippled black plastic grips, black phosphate or nickel (mfg. 1992-2000) finish, includes 2 mags., 28 oz.

MSR	$1,472	$1,100	$925	$775	$650	$550	$500	$450

Add $94 for Tritium sights (various colors, new 1993).
Add $566 for .22 LR conversion kit (barrel, slide, and two mags., disc. 1999).

HK

Grading	100%	98%	95%	90%	80%	70%	60%

P7 M13 - similar to P7 M8, only with staggered 13 shot mag., 30 oz. Disc. 1994.

	$1,200	$995	$800	$675	$575	$525	$475

Last MSR was $1,330.

Add $85 for Tritium sights (various colors, new 1993).

P7 M10 - .40 S&W cal., similar specifications as P7 M13, except has 10 shot mag., 39 oz. Mfg. 1991-94.

	$975	$800	$725	$650	$600	$550	$495

Last MSR was $1,315.

Add $85 for Tritium sights (various colors, new 1993).

P7 K3 - .22 LR or .380 ACP cal., uses unique oil-filled buffer to decrease recoil, 3.8 in. barrel, matte black or nickel (less common) finish, 8 shot mag. (includes 2), 26½ oz. Mfg. 1988-94.

	$840	$715	$600	$525	$450	$410	$390

Last MSR was $1,100.

Add $525 for .22 LR conversion kit.
Add $228 for .32 ACP conversion kit.
Add $85 for Tritium sights (various colors, new 1993).

P 2000 - 9mm Para. cal., SA or DA, various configurations (V1-V4), 10 shot mag., combat defense action, interchangeable rear grip panels, black finish. European introduction 2002.
As this edition went to press, U.S. availability and pricing had yet to be determined on this model.

USP 357 COMPACT - .357 SIG cal., similar to USP 40 Compact, 10 shot mag., black finish, approx. 28 oz. Importation began 2001.

MSR	$786	$680	$535	$475	$430	$375	$335	$300

USP 9 - 9mm Para. cal., available in regular DA/SA mode or DA only (10 variants), 4.13 in. barrel with polygonal rifling, Browning-type action with H&K recoil reduction system, polymer frame, all metal surfaces specially treated, can be carried cocked and locked, stippled synthetic grips, bobbed hammer, 3-dot sighting system, multiple safeties, 10 (C/B 1994) or 16* shot polymer mag., 26½ oz. New 1993.

MSR	$766	$670	$540	$485	$430	$365	$330	$295

Add $94 for Tritium sights (various colors, new 1993).

* **USP 9 Stainless** - similar to USP 9, except has satin finished stainless steel slide. Mfg. 1996-2001. Limited quantities remain.

MSR	$817	$700	$565	$475

USP 9 COMPACT - 9mm Para. cal., compact variation of the USP 9 featuring 3.58 in. barrel, 25½ oz. New 1997.

MSR	$786	$680	$540	$475	$430	$375	$335	$300

* **USP 9 Compact Stainless** - similar to USP 9 Compact, except has satin finished stainless steel slide. New 1997.

MSR	$878	$750	$590	$500

USP 40 - .40 S&W cal., similar to USP 9, 9 variants of DA/SA/DAO, 10 (C/B1994) or 13* shot mag., 27¾ oz. New 1993.

MSR	$766	$670	$540	$485	$430	$365	$330	$295

Add $94 for Tritium sights (various colors, new 1993).

* **USP 40 Stainless** - similar to USP 40, except has satin finished stainless steel slide. Mfg. 1996-2001. Limited quantities remain.

MSR	$817	$700	$565	$470

USP 40 COMPACT - .40 S&W cal., compact variation of the USP 40 featuring 3.58 in. barrel, 27 oz. New 1997.

MSR	$786	$680	$540	$475	$430	$375	$335	$300

* **USP 40 Compact Stainless** - similar to USP 40 Compact, except has satin finished stainless steel slide. New 1997.

MSR	$878	$750	$590	$500

Grading	100%	98%	95%	90%	80%	70%	60%

✳ *USP 40 Compact LEM* - LEM designates law enforcement modification, DAO, unique trigger mechanism decreases trigger pull to 7½ - 8½ lbs, blue only. Importation began 2002.

MSR	$821		$720	$575	$495	$450	$400	$350	$315

USP 45 - .45 ACP cal., similar to USP 9, 9 variants of DA/SA/DAO, 10 (C/B 1994) or 13* shot mag., 27¾ oz. New 1995.

MSR	$827		$725	$590	$500	$450	$395	$350	$315

Add $94 for Tritium sights (various colors, new 1993).

✳ *USP 45 Stainless* - similar to USP 45, except has satin finished stainless steel slide. Mfg. 1996-2001. Limited quantities remain.

MSR	$888		$760	$600	$500

✳ *USP 45 Match Pistol* - .45 ACP cal., features 6.02 in. barrel with polygonal rifling, micrometer adj. high relief and raised rear sight, raised target front sight, 10 shot mag., barrel weight, fluted, and ambidextrous safety, choice of matte black or stainless steel slide, supplied with additional o-rings and setup tools, 38 oz. Mfg. 1997-98.

		$1,275	$1,025	$825	$750	$675	$550	$500

Last MSR was $1,369.

Add $72 for stainless steel slide model.

USP 45 COMPACT - .45 ACP cal., compact variation of the USP 45, featuring 3.8 in. barrel, 28 oz. New 1998.

MSR	$857		$750	$590	$500	$450	$400	$350	$315

Add $18-$32 for control lever (safety/decocking lever on right side).

✳ *USP 45 Compact Stainless* - similar to USP 45 Compact, except has satin finished stainless steel slide. New 1998.

MSR	$909		$790	$615	$510

✳ *USP 45 Compact 50th Anniversary* - commemorates the 50th year of H&K (1950-2000), 1 of 1,000 special edition featuring high polish blue slide with 50th Anniversary logo engraved in gold and silver, supplied with presentation wood case and commemorative coin. Limited mfg. 2000 only.

		$1,150	$895	$795

Last MSR was $999.

USP 45 TACTICAL PISTOL - .45 ACP cal., enhanced variation of the USP 45, similar to Mark 23, except has 4.92 in. threaded barrel with rubber o-ring, adj. target type sights and trigger, limited availability, 36 oz. New 1998.

MSR	$1,124		$995	$875	$775	$675	$600	$525	$495

USP EXPERT - .40 S&W (new 2002) or .45 ACP cal., features new slide design with 5.2 in. barrel, match grade SA or DA trigger pull, recoil reduction system, reinforced polymer frame, adj. rear sight, approx. 30 oz. New 1999.

MSR	$1,499		$1,375	$1,125	$900	$800	$700	$600	$525

Add $34 for .45 ACP cal.

MARK 23 SPECIAL OPERATIONS PISTOL - .45 ACP cal., 5.87 in. barrel, polymer frame and integral grips, 3-dot sighting, 10 shot mag., squared off trigger guard, 2.6 lbs., limited availability. New 1996.

MSR	$2,444		$2,175	$1,875	$1,550	$1,225	$975	$800	$675

"MK23" is the official military design. Not available to civilians.

SP 89 - 9mm Para. cal., recoil operated delayed roller-locked bolt system, 4.5 in. barrel, 15 shot mag., adj. aperture rear sight (accepts HK claw-lock scope mounts), 4.4 lbs. Mfg. 1990-1993.

		$3,250	$3,000	$2,850	$2,600	$2,300	$2,000	$1,650

Last MSR was $1,325.

Grading	100%	98%	95%	90%	80%	70%	60%

VP 70Z - 9mm Para. cal., 18 shot, double action only, 4½ in. barrel, parkerized finish, plastic receiver/grip assembly. Disc. 1984.

	100%	98%	95%	90%	80%	70%	60%
	$550	$475	$400	$350	$325	$275	$250

Add 100% if frame cut for shoulder stock (Model VP 70M, NFA Class III).

RIFLES: BOLT ACTION

BASR - .22 LR, .22-250 Rem., 6mm PPC, .300 Win. Mag., .30-06, or .308 Win. cal., Kevlar stock, stainless steel barrel, limited production. Special order only. Mfg. 1986 only.

	100%	98%	95%	90%	80%	70%	60%
	$5,750	$5,000	$4,500	$4,000	$3,650	$3,300	$2,600

Last MSR was $2,199.

Less than 135 of this variation were manufactured and they are extremely rare. Contractual disputes with the U.S. supplier stopped H&K from receiving any BASR models.

RIFLES: SEMI-AUTO

Most of the models listed, being of a paramilitary design, were disc. in 1989 due to Federal legislation. Sporterized variations mfg. after 1994 with thumbhole stocks were banned in April, 1998.

In 1991, the HK-91, HK-93, and HK-94 were discontinued. Last published retail prices (1991) were $999 for fixed stock models and $1,199 for retractable stock models.

In the early '70s, S.A.C.O. importers located in Virginia sold the Models 41 and 43 which were the predecessors to the Model 91 and 93, respectively. Values for these earlier variations will be higher than values listed.

SR-9 - .308 Win. cal., semi-auto sporting rifle, 19.7 in. barrel, Kevlar reinforced fiberglass thumbhole stock and forearm, 5 shot mag., diopter adj. rear sight, accepts H&K claw-lock scope mounts. Mfg. 1990-1993.

	100%	98%	95%	90%	80%	70%	60%
	$1,775	$1,450	$1,150	$995	$850	$725	$650

Last MSR was $1,199.

While advertised again during 1998, this model was finally banned in April, 1998.

SR-9T - .308 Win. cal., precision target rifle with adj. MSG 90 buttstock and PSG-1 trigger group, 5 shot mag. Mfg. 1992-1993.

	100%	98%	95%	90%	80%	70%	60%
	$2,495	$2,100	$1,800	$1,550	$1,150	$995	$850

Last MSR was $1,725.

While advertised again during 1998, this model was finally banned in April, 1998.

SR-9TC - .308 Win. cal., similar to SR-9T except has PSG-1 adj. buttstock. Mfg. 1993 only.

	100%	98%	95%	90%	80%	70%	60%
	$2,995	$2,600	$2,300	$2,000	$1,675	$1,250	$1,050

Last MSR was $1,995.

While advertised again during 1998, this model was finally banned in April, 1998.

PSG-1 - .308 Win. cal. only, high precision marksman's rifle, 5 shot mag., adj. buttstock, includes accessories and case (Hensholdt illuminated 6X x 42mm scope), 17.8 lbs. Importation disc. 1998.

	100%	98%	95%	90%	80%	70%	60%
	$9,950	$8,675	$7,500	$6,500	$5,500	$4,500	$3,850

Last MSR was $10,811.

MODEL 41 A-2 - .308 Win. cal., predecessor to the Model 91 A-2, originally imported by Golden State Arms.

	100%	98%	95%	90%	80%	70%	60%
	$2,500	$2,250	$1,850	$1,600	$1,350	$1,100	$995

MODEL 43 A-2 - successor to the Model 41 A-2. Disc.

	100%	98%	95%	90%	80%	70%	60%
	$2,500	$2,250	$1,850	$1,600	$1,350	$1,100	$995

MODEL 91 A-2 - .308 Win. cal., semi-auto paramilitary design rifle, delayed roller lock bolt system, antennuated recoil, black cycolac stock, 17.7 in. barrel, 20 shot mag., 9.7 lbs. Importation disc. 1989.

Grading	100%	98%	95%	90%	80%	70%	60%

* **Fixed stock model**

	$2,100	$1,850	$1,600	$1,350	$1,100	$995	$875

Last MSR was $999.

Add $200 for desert camo finish.
Add $275 for NATO black finish.

* **Model 91 SBF (Semi-Beltfed)** - supplied with bi-pod and M60 link (200 shot with starter tab) and MG42 modified belt (49 shot with fixed starter tab), limited mfg. Disc.

	$8,500	$7,500	$6,500

* **Model 91 A-3** - with retractable metal stock.

	$2,375	$2,100	$1,850	$1,600	$1,350	$1,100	$995

Last MSR was $1,114.

Add $775 for .22 LR conversion kit.

* **Model 91 A-2 Package** - includes A.R.M.S. mount, B-Square rings, Leupold 3x9 compact scope with matte finish. Importation disc. 1988.

	$3,000	$2,600	$2,250	$2,000	$1,750	$1,550	$1,325

Last MSR was $1,285.

Add 30% for retractable stock.

MODEL 93 A-2 - .223 Rem. cal., smaller version of the H&K 91, 25 shot mag., 16.14 in. barrel, 8 lbs.

* **Fixed stock model**

	$2,100	$1,850	$1,600	$1,350	$1,100	$995	$875

Last MSR was $946.

Add 10% for desert camo finish.
Add 15% for NATO black finish.

* **Model 93 A-3** - with retractable metal stock.

	$2,375	$2,100	$1,850	$1,600	$1,350	$1,100	$995

Last MSR was $1,114.

* **Model 93 A-2 Package** - includes A.R.M.S. mount, B-Square rings, Leupold 3x9 compact scope with matte finish. Importation disc. 1988.

	$3,000	$2,600	$2,250	$2,000	$1,750	$1,550	$1,325

Last MSR was $1,285.

Add 10% for retractable stock.

MODEL 94 CARBINE A-2 - 9mm Para. cal., semi-auto carbine, 16.54 in. barrel, aperture rear sight, 15 shot mag. New 1983.

* **Fixed stock model**

	$3,150	$2,775	$2,450	$2,150	$1,750	$1,450	$1,250

Last MSR was $946.

* **Model 94 Carbine A-3** - retractable metal stock.

	$3,400	$2,950	$2,600	$2,300	$2,000	$1,750	$1,500

Last MSR was $1,114.

* **Model 94 A-2 Package** - includes A.R.M.S. mount, B-Square rings, Leupold 3x9 compact scope with matte finish. Importation disc. 1988.

	$4,150	$3,650	$3,250	$2,825	$2,400	$2,100	$1,850

Last MSR was $1,285.

Add 10% for retractable stock.

* **Model 94 SGI** - 9mm Para. cal., target rifle, aluminum alloy bi-pod, Leupold 6X scope, 15 or 30 shot mag. Imported 1986 only.

	$2,850	$2,500	$2,200	$1,900	$1,675	$1,475	$1,275

Last MSR was $1,340.

H

Grading	100%	98%	95%	90%	80%	70%	60%

MODEL 270 - .22 LR cal., sporting rifle, 19.7 in. barrel with standard or polygonal rifling, 5 or 20 shot mag., high luster blue, plain walnut stock, approx. 5.7 lbs. Disc. 1985.

	$475	$400	$350	$300	$275	$250	$225

Last MSR was $200.

MODEL 300 - .22 Mag. cal., 5 or 15 shot, polygonal rifling standard, otherwise similar to H&K 270 with checkered walnut stock. Importation disc. 1989.

	$900	$775	$625	$550	$450	$400	$375

Last MSR was $608.

Add $250-$300 for factory H&K scope mount system.

✷ *Model 300 Package* - includes A.R.M.S. mount, B-Square rings, Leupold 3x9X compact scope with matte finish. Importation disc. 1988.

	$1,150	$975	$850	$725	$575	$500	$450

Last MSR was $689.

MODEL 630 - .223 Rem. cal., delayed roller lock bolt system, 17.7 in. barrel with or w/o muzzle brake (early mfg.), reduced recoil, checkered walnut, 4 or 10 shot mag., 7.04 lbs. Importation disc. 1986.

	$1,175	$995	$875	$750	$650	$550	$500

Last MSR was $784.

Add $250-$300 for factory H&K scope mount system.
The .222 Rem. cal. was also available in this model. Most were French contracts.

MODEL 770 - .308 Win. cal., 3 or 10 shot mag., 19.7 in. barrel with or w/o muzzle brake (early mfg.), otherwise similar to Model 630, 7.92 lbs. Importation disc. 1986.

	$1,825	$1,500	$1,275	$1,050	$950	$850	$750

Last MSR was $797.

Add $250-$300 for factory H&K scope mount system.
Significant price increases stopped the importation of this model.
Approx. 6 Model 770s were imported in .243 Win. cal. during 1984. Values for the .243 Win. cal. will be considerably higher than listed for the .308 Win. cal.

MODEL 911 - .308 Win. cal., earlier importation. Disc.

	$1,750	$1,550	$1,350	$1,175	$950	$850	$725

MODEL 940 - .30-06 cal., 21.6 in. barrel with or w/o muzzle brake (early mfg.), otherwise same as Model 770, 8.62 lbs. Importation disc. 1986.

	$1,950	$1,750	$1,500	$1,250	$995	$875	$750

Last MSR was $917.

Add $250-$300 for factory H&K scope mount system.
Cals. 7x64mm and 9.3x62mm were also available in this model.
Significant price increases stopped the importation of this model.

✷ *Model 940K* - similar to Model 940, except has 16 in. barrel and higher cheekpiece. Two imported 1984 only.
Rarity precludes accurate price evaluation.

SLB 2000 - .30-06 cal. (same bolt system allows cartridge changeability), short stroke piston actuated gas operating system, alloy receiver with black weather resistant coating, gold accents on receiver, 19.69 in. barrel (interchangeable), checkered walnut stock and specially angled pistol grip, tang mounted safety blocks hammer and trigger, 2, 5, or 10 shot mag., iron sights, 7.28 lbs. Importation began 2001.

MSR	$1,399	$1,225	$1,025	$925	$850	$775	$700	$650

MODELS SL6 & SL7 CARBINE - .223 Rem. or .308 Win. cal., 17.71 in. barrel, delayed roller lock bolt system, reduced recoil, vent. wood hand guard, 3 or 4 shot mag., 8.36 lbs., matte black metal finish, HK-SL6 is .223 Rem. cal., HK-SL7 is .308 Win. cal. Importation disc. in 1986.

	$775	$675	$575	$495	$460	$430	$400

Add $250-$300 for factory H&K scope mount system.
These models are the only sporter variations H&K manufactures - no U.S. importation since 1986.

Grading	100%	98%	95%	90%	80%	70%	60%

MODEL SL8-1 - .223 Rem. cal., short stroke piston actuated gas operating system, advanced grey carbon fiber polymer construction based on the German Army G36 rifle, thumbhole stock with adj. cheekpiece and buttstock, 10 shot mag., modular and removable Picatinny rail sight, removable sights from rail, 20.8 cold hammer forged heavy barrel, adj. sights, 8.6 lbs. Importation began 2000.

MSR	$1,249	$1,085	$950	$875	$800	$750	$700	$650

    Add $338 for carrying handle with 1.5X – 3X optical sights.

    Add $624 for carrying handle with 1.5X – 3X optical sights and red dot reflex sight.

MODEL USC .45 ACP CARBINE - .45 ACP cal., similar design/construction as the Model SL8-1, except is blowback action, and has 16 in. barrel and grey skeletonized buttstock, 10 shot mag., 6 lbs. Importation began 2000.

MSR	$1,249	$1,085	$950	$875	$800	$750	$700	$650

SHOTGUNS: SEMI-AUTO

Previously imported H&K Benelli shotguns can be found under their own heading.

MODEL 512 - 12 ga. only, mfg. by Franchi for German military contract, rifle sights, matte finished metal, walnut stock, fixed choke pattern diverter giving rectangular shot pattern. Importation disc. 1991.

	$1,500	$1,300	$1,100	$925	$800	$700	$600

                        Last Mfg.'s Wholesale was $1,895.

SLS 2002 - 12 ga. only, 3 in. chamber, IQ-port gas operation (excess gas is vented forward through forearm cap), various barrel lengths, including slug barrel, double slide rails, deluxe checkered walnut stock and forearm, phosphate black finish, approx. 6 3/4 lbs. European introduction 2002.

As this edition went to press, U.S. availability and pricing had yet to be determined on this model.

HEINIE SPECIALTY PRODUCTS

Current pistol and related components manufacturer located in Quincy, IL

Heinie manufactures both scratch built personal defense and tactical/carry 1911 packages in a wide variety of chamberings. Almost any combination of special orders and features are available, and the Tactical/Carry model lists at $2,315. Please contact the factory directly for information regarding current pricing and availability.

HELWAN

Previous trademark imported by Navy Arms Co. and Interarms until 1995.

PISTOLS: SEMI-AUTO

BRIGADIER - 9mm Para. cal., single action, 4.5 in. barrel, all steel construction, 8 shot mag. with finger extension, black plastic grips, 32.6 oz. Imported 1988-94.

	$195	$150	$125	$115	$105	$95	$85

                      Last MSR was $260.

This model is patterned after the Beretta Model 1952. They were manufactured at the Helwan arsenal in Egypt.

HENDRY, RAMSAY & WILCOX

Current manufacturer located in Perth, Scotland.

Hendry, Ramsay & Wilcox manufactures top quality shotguns and rifles and are priced per individual quotation. Please contact the factory directly (see Trademark Index) for more information on this trademark.

HENRY, ALEX

Current trademark owned and manufactured by Dickson & MacNaughton, located in Edinburgh, Scotland.

Please contact Dickson & MacNaughton directly for more information regarding this trademark, including current availability and pricing.

Grading	100%	98%	95%	90%	80%	70%	60%

HENRY REPEATING ARMS COMPANY

Current rifle manufacturer established during 1997, and located in Brooklyn, NY. Distributor and dealer sales.

RIFLES

HENRY MINI-BOLT - .22 LR cal., single shot, stainless steel receiver and barrel, Williams fire sights, manual safety, 11½ in. LOP, black synthetic stock, 3¼ lbs. New 2002.

MSR	$170	$145	$125	$115	$105	$95	$90	$85

HENRY LEVER ACTION - .22 LR or .22 Mag. (new 2000) cal., side ejection, blue steel receiver, 18¼ (.22 LR only) or 19¼ (.22 Mag. only) in. barrel, 11 (.22 Mag.) or 15 (.22 LR) shot mag., deluxe American walnut stock and forearm, adj. rear sight and hooded front, 5½ lbs. New 1997.

MSR	$250	$210	$185	$165	$150	$140	$130	$120

Add $50 for .22 Mag. cal.

This model is also available as a Youth Model, with 13 in. LOP and shorter barrel.

* ***Henry Carbine*** - similar to Henry Lever Action, except has shorter barrel and large loop lever. New 1998.

MSR	$260	$215	$190	$170	$150	$140	$130	$120

* ***Henry Golden Boy Lever Action***- features brasslite receiver, buttplate, and rear sight, 20 in. octagon barrel, 16 shot mag. New mid-1999.

MSR	$380	$335	$275	$220	$195	$175	$160	$140

Add $70 for .22 Mag. cal. (new 2002).

HENRY PUMP ACTION - .22 LR cal., blue grooved receiver, 18¼ in. barrel, walnut straight grip stock and forearm, 15 shot mag., adj. rear sight, approx. 5½ lbs. New 1999.

MSR	$250	$210	$185	$165	$155	$140	$130	$120

HENRY U.S. SURVIVAL .22 SEMI-AUTO - .22 LR cal., patterned after the Armalite AR-7 with improvements, takedown design enables receiver, 2 mags., and barrel to stow in ABS plastic stock, 100% Mossy Oak Break-Up camo (new 2000) or weather resistant silver or black (new 1999) stock/metal finish, two 8 shot mags., adj. sights, 16½ in. long when disassembled and stowed in stock, approx. 2½ lbs. New 1997.

MSR	$165	$150	$135	$125	$115	$105	$95	$90

Add $65 for 100% camo finish (new 2000).

HENRY RIFLE

Please refer to the Winchester section in this text for this model.

HERITAGE MANUFACTURING, INC.

Current manufacturer located in Opa Locka, FL since 1992. Dealer and distributor sales.

PISTOLS: SEMI-AUTO

H-25/25S - .25 ACP cal., 6 shot mag. with finger extension, single action, exposed hammer, choice of blue or blue/gold finish, 13½ oz. Mfg. 1995-99.

		$125	$95	$80	$65	$55	$50	$45

Last MSR was $150.

Add $10 for nickel steel.
Add $10 for Model H-25G (blue/gold finish with checkered grips).

Grading	100%	98%	95%	90%	80%	70%	60%

STEALTH SHADOW COMPACT - 9mm Para. or .40 S&W cal., striker firing mechanism, stainless steel slide and 3.9 in. barrel, black all polymer frame, manual safety, 10 shot mag. with finger extension, fixed sights, choice of stainless slide, two-tone stainless slide, or all black (Shadow) finish, 20.5 oz. Mfg. 1996-2000.

	$255	$220	$190	$165	$150	$135	$110

Last MSR was $300.

Add $30 for .40 S&W cal.

REVOLVERS

ROUGH RIDER SAA SERIES - .22 LR or .22 LR/.22 Mag. cal. combo, SAA design with choice of alloy (33.4 oz.) or steel (35 oz., new 2000) frame, hammer block safety, blue, nickel (disc. 2001), black satin (new 2002), or satin (new 2001) finish, 4¾, 6½, or 9 (combo only) in. barrel, fixed or adj. (new 2001) rear sight, smooth wood grips, approx. 33½ oz. New 1993.

MSR	$200		$165	$125	$95	$80	$70	$60	$50

Add $51 for nickel finish (combo package only, disc. 2001).
Add $10 for 9 in. barrel (available with combo package only).
Subtract $50 for alloy frame with combo package.

✱ *Rough Rider SAA Fixed Sight Series* - .22 LR/.22 Mag. cal. combo only, 4¾, 6½ or 9 in. barrel.

MSR	$159		$130	$110	$95	$80	$70	$60	$50

Add $40 for stain or black satin finish.
Add $25 for faux pearl grips.
Add $40 for steel frame.

✱ *Rough Rider SAA Adjustable Sight Series* - .22 LR/.22 Mag. cal. combo only, 4¾, 6½ or 9 in. barrel.

MSR	$189		$155	$135	$110	$95	$80	$70	$60

Add $50 for stain or black satin finish.
Add $30 for steel frame.

✱ *Rough Rider SAA Illuminator Series* - .22 LR/.22 Mag. cal. combo only, features AdcoHot Shot Red Dot frame mounted sight, 6 ½ in. barrel only.

MSR	$189		$155	$135	$110	$95	$80	$70	$60

✱ *Rough Rider SAA with Birds Head Grip* - .22 LR/.22 Mag. cal. combo only, choice of 2¾ (disc. 1997), 3 (disc. 1994), 3½, or 4¾ in. barrel. New 1993.

MSR	$159		$130	$110	$95	$80	$70	$60	$50

Add $30 for nickel finish (disc. 2001).
Add $25 for faux pearl grips.
Add $40 for steel frame.

SENTRY DA SERIES - .22 Mag. (disc. 1996), .32 Mag. (disc. 1996), .38 Spl., or 9mm Para. (disc. 1996) cal., snubnose design, with 2 or 4 (.22 LR or .38 Spl.) in. barrel, 6 (centerfire) or 8 (rimfire) shot, transfer bar safety, blue or nickel finish, black polymer grips, ramp front sight. Mfg. 1993-97.

	$110	$85	$70	$55	$50	$45	$40

Last MSR was $130.

Add $10 for nickel finish.

HEROLD RIFLE

Previously manufactured by Franz Jaeger, located in Suhl, Germany.

RIFLES: BOLT ACTION

SPORTING RIFLE - .22 Hornet cal., miniature Mauser action, 24 in. barrel, leaf sight, double set trigger, select checkered stock, imported by Daly & Stoeger, pre-WWII.

	$990	$880	$825	$770	$660	$550	$495

Grading	100%	98%	95%	90%	80%	70%	60%

HERTERS

Previous importer, distributor, and retailer headquartered in Waseca, MN from early 1960s - 1979. Herters also had additional retail stores scattered throughout the upper Midwest.

Herters subcontracted various manufacturers (mostly European) to fabricate Powermag revolvers, U- 9/J-9 rifles, and shotguns which were mostly patterned after more famous original models. Most of these copies were designed to undersell the competition at the time and while quality in most cases was quite good, consumer sales were not strong enough to continue production. While many Herters models are relatively rare, collectibility to date has been minimal. Herters model values are usually under the original trademarks from which they were derived and to date have been based more on the shooting utility than the collector potential.

HESSE ARMS

Current manufacturer located in Inver Grove Heights, MN. Dealer and consumer sales.

PISTOLS: SEMI-AUTO

HAR-15 - .223 Rem. cal., features carbon/Aramid fiber flattop upper receiver, 7½ in. barrel, 100% parts interchangeability with AR-15 type firearms. New 2002.

MSR	$850	$775	$700	$650	$600	$550	$500	$475

RIFLES: BOLT ACTION

M98 V5 - .220 Swift, .22-250 Rem., or .308 Win. cal., Mauser M98 action, 26 in. barrel with recessed crown and fully stressed relieved, competition stock with vent forearm, fully adj. trigger. New 1999.

MSR	$640	$575	$515	$460	$395	$360	$330	$295

HBR 50 - .50 BMG cal., single shot action, 34 in. match barrel with muzzle brake, adj. buttstock and trigger. New 2001.

MSR	$1,650	$1,595	$1,450	$1,350	$1,275	$1,200	$1,150	$1,100

RIFLES: SEMI-AUTO, RIMFIRE

H22 SERIES - .22 LR cal., stainless steel Ruger 10/22 action, various configurations and features. Models included the Standard (last MSR $460), Wildcat (last MSR $559), Competition (last MSR $560), and Tiger Shark (last MSR $830). Very limited mfg. 1997-2000.

RIFLES: SEMI-AUTO, CENTERFIRE

HAR-15A2 SERIES - .223 Rem. cal., AR-15 type action, various configurations, barrel lengths and options. New 1997.

* ***Standard Rifle/Carbine*** - features mil-spec parts, 16 (carbine) or 20 (rifle) in. heavy match grade barrel. New 1997.

MSR	$779	$695	$585	$510	$450	$395	$360	$330

* ***Bull Gun*** - features 1 in. stainless steel barrel with special front sight base. New 1997.

MSR	$825	$735	$645	$560	$500	$450	$395	$360

* ***Dispatcher*** - features 16 in. barrel with full length hand guards, 7.9 lbs. New 1999.

MSR	$799	$710	$595	$515	$450	$395	$360	$330

* ***.50 Action Express*** - .50 AE cal., 16 or 20 in. barrel, fixed tube stock, 10 shot mag., 6.9-7.3 lbs. New 1999.

MSR	$1,100	$995	$850	$750	$665	$575	$500	$450

* ***X-Match*** - features 20 in. heavy barrel with A3 flattop receiver, free floating aluminum forearm tube, 16 or 20 in. barrel, 8.7-9.6 lbs. New 1999.

MSR	$799	$710	$595	$515	$450	$395	$360	$330

Grading	100%	98%	95%	90%	80%	70%	60%

* *National Match* - features ½ minute match sights, CMP legal free float hand guards, match bolt carrier, adj. trigger, individually tested. New 1997.

MSR	$1,100	$995	$850	$750	$665	$575	$500	$450

* *Omega Match* - top-of-the-line features including 1 in. stainless steel barrel, hooked style stock with pistol grip, flat-top receiver, capable of ¼ in. groups. New 1997.

MSR	$1,100	$995	$850	$750	$665	$575	$500	$450

* *High Grade* - custom built per individual order. New 1997.

MSR	$1,399	$1,275	$1,050	$925	$800	$725	$650	$575

ULTRA RACE - 24 in. stainless barrel, vented free floating hand guard, flattop upper receiver, Palma style rear sight, globe front sight, fully adj. skeleton stock. New 2001.

MSR	$1,999	$1,825	$1,675	$1,400	$1,200	$995	$875	$725

FAL/FALO SERIES - .308 Win. cal., action patterned after the F.N. FAL, various barrel lengths and configurations. New 1997.

* *FAL-H/FALO Standard Rifle* - features 24 in. barrel, synthetic stock. New 1997.

MSR	$1,100	$995	$850	$750	$665	$575	$500	$450

* *FAL-H/FALO Congo Carbine* - features 16 in. barrel. New 1997.

MSR	$1,150	$1,025	$875	$765	$665	$575	$500	$450

* *FALO Tactical* - features free floating handguard assembly, flat-top receiver. New 1997.

MSR	$1,400	$1,225	$1,025	$875	$750	$675	$600	$500

* *FAL-H/FALO High Grade* - custom built per individual order. New 1997.

MSR	$1,400	$1,225	$1,025	$875	$750	$675	$600	$500

H91 RIFLE SERIES - .308 Win. cal., 18¼ in. barrel, action patterned after the H&K 91, approx. 9 lbs. New 2000.

MSR	$1,250	$1,100	$925	$795	$675	$575	$500	$450

Add $600 for Marksman Rifle variation (special receiver with strengthening rails).

* *H91 Precision* - 26 in. barrel, tuned "set" trigger, free floating polymer forearm, receiver has specially designed inserts for strength and stability, 12.4 lbs. New 2000.

MSR	$3,250	$2,950	$2,600	$2,300	$2,000	$1,850	$1,700	$1,650

H94 CARBINE - .9mm Para. cal., copy of H&K MP5, stamped steel receiver, integral scope mount, 9 in. (A2 or pinned telescoping stock), or 5.5 in. barrel (fixed folding stock). New 2002.

MSR	$1,850	$1,675	$1,450	$1,350	$1,275	$1,200	$1,150	$1,100

M14H STANDARD RIFLE - .308 Win. cal., semi-auto version of the M14 rifle, choice of walnut or wrinkle coat synthetic stock, supplied with extra 10 shot mag. and original M14 stock. Mfg. 1997-99.

		$925	$800	$725	$650	$575	$500	$450

Last MSR was $999.

Add $110 for M14HE2 variation.

* *M14H Brush Rifle* - features black synthetic stock with 18 in. barrel. Mfg. 1997-99.

		$975	$825	$735	$650	$575	$500	$450

Last MSR was $1,059.

MODEL 47 RIFLE - 7.62x39mm or .308 Win. (new 2000) cal., Kalashnikov type action in various configurations, including RPK and STG 940, black synthetic stock, 16¼, 20 (disc. 1999), or 22 (.308 Win.) in. barrel. New 1997.

MSR	$570	$500	$440	$395	$355	$330	$300	$275

Add $270 for RPK or STG 940 configuration.
Add $329 for .308 Win. cal.

Grading	100%	98%	95%	90%	80%	70%	60%

HEYM WAFFENFABRIK GmbH

Current manufacturer established in 1865 and located in Gleichamberg, Germany since 1995. Currently imported beginning 1999 by New England Custom Gun Service, Ltd., located in Plainfield, NH. During 1998, Heym underwent a management change. Previously manufactured in Muennerstadt, Germany circa 1952-1995 and Suhl, Germany between 1865-1945. Originally founded in 1865 by F.W. Heym. Previously imported by JagerSport, Ltd. located in Cranston, RI 1993-94 only, Heckler & Koch, Inc. (until 1993) located in Sterling, VA, Heym America, Inc. (subsidiary of F.W. Heym of W. Germany) located in Fort Wayne, IN, and originally by Paul Jaeger, Inc. 1970-1986.

Please contact New England Custom Gun Service Ltd. for more information and availability regarding currently imported Heym models (see Trademark Index listing).

Pre-war guns in 95%+ original condition will bring a premium over values listed.

H | COMBINATION GUNS

MODEL 22 S2 O/U - rifle/shotgun combination, 12, 16, or 20 ga. (3 in.), under rifle (17 cals. available), single set trigger, takedown feature (standard 1990), coin finish with engraving, 5½ lbs.

$3,675	$3,000	$2,450	$1,875	$1,575	$1,325	$1,100

Last MSR was $4,125.

Subtract $380 without engraving.

This model featured a dampened rifle barrel which prevents the "climbing" of groups, thereby enhancing accuracy.

MODEL 25 O/U - rifle/shotgun combination, 12, 16, or 20 ga. over various rifle cals., 23¾ in. barrels with iron sights, checkered walnut stock and forearm, 5.9 lbs.

MSR	$2,650						
		$2,425	$1,725	$1,350	$1,125	$950	$800	$700

Add $800 for deluxe game scene engraving.

MODEL 55 BF O/U - rifle/shotgun combination, popular U.S. and European cals., shotgun barrels interchangeable in 12 (disc.), 16, or 20 ga., 25 or 28 in. barrels, boxlock, auto ejectors, silver finish, fine German engraving, folding leaf sight, checkered pistol grip stock.

$6,500	$5,400	$4,950	$4,525	$3,950	$3,615	$3,210

Last MSR was $7,485.

Add $3,250 for O/U rifle and $2,250 for O/U shotgun or shotgun/rifle combination extra barrels.

MODEL 88 BF SxS - 2 barrel set with 20 ga. barrels and an extra set of rifle barrels available in cals. .375 H&H Mag., .458 Win. Mag., .470 N.E., or .500 N.E.

$13,100	$10,750	$9,600	$8,150	$6,900	$5,850	$4,850

Last MSR was $15,060.

This model is a larger frame variation of the Model 88 B.

✻ *Model 88B/F Safari* - includes set of rifle and shotgun barrels, choice of .375 H&H, .458 Win. Mag., .470 NE, or .500 NE cal. and extra set of 20 ga. 3 in. chamber barrels.

$16,150	$14,100	$11,950	$10,250	$8,950	$6,750	$5,250

Last MSR was $18,530.

MODEL 88 F SxS - available in various cals. and 20 ga. with 2¾ or 3 in. chambers.

$13,300	$11,250	$10,100	$9,400	$8,000	$6,950	$5,800

Last MSR was $14,650.

Grading	100%	98%	95%	90%	80%	70%	60%

DRILLINGS

MODEL 33 BOXLOCK STANDARD - 16 or 20 ga., boxlock, Arabesque engraving, shotgun barrels over popular European cals., and .222 Rem., .243 Win., .270 Win., .308 Win., and .30- 06 cal. rifle barrel, 25 in. full and mod. barrels, set trigger on rifle, checkered pistol grip stock.

	MSR	$6,650	$6,075	$5,300	$4,525	$3,950	$3,350	$2,750	$2,150

❋ ***Model 33 Deluxe*** - same specifications as Standard Model, only hunting scene engraved.

	MSR	$7,075	$6,450	$5,425	$4,650	$4,025	$3,400	$2,750	$2,150

MODEL 35 STANDARD - 3 barrels, (two rifle and one shotgun), choice of cals. with top barrel either 16 or 20 ga., light border engraving, 8¼ lbs.

$13,650	$11,000	$9,250	$8,000	$6,850	$5,700	$4,600

Last MSR was $15,100.

Add $2,430 for hunting scene engraving.

MODEL 37 SIDELOCK STANDARD - shotgun barrels (12, 16, or 20 ga.) over rifle, detachable sidelocks, select French walnut, border engraving, 8 lbs.

MSR	$9,200	$8,650	$7,850	$6,950	$6,000	$5,000	$4,000	$2,950

❋ ***Model 37 Deluxe*** - similar to Model 37 Standard, except has large engraved hunting scenes.

MSR	$10,500	$9,650	$8,700	$7,600	$6,500	$5,400	$4,300	$3,200

MODEL 37 B STANDARD - rifle barrels over shotgun (20 ga.), sidelock, border engraved, about 8.6 lbs.

$13,250	$10,875	$9,500	$8,400	$7,550	$6,500	$5,650

Last MSR was $15,065.

❋ ***Model 37 B Deluxe*** - similar to Model 37 B Standard, except has large hunting scene engraving.

$15,600	$12,750	$10,700	$9,450	$8,200	$7,050	$5,750

Last MSR was $17,620.

RIFLES: BOLT ACTION

On most of the models listed, the "N" suffix in the model denotes standard calibers, whereas "G" refers to Mag. cals. Heym currently manufactures approx. 100 bolt actions per month, with 54 company personnel.

MODEL SR 10 SPORTER - various cals., originally mfg. by H&K. Limited mfg.

$1,325	$1,100	$950	$850	$750	$650	$550

MODEL SR 20N & CLASSIC - available in 18 cals., Mauser type bolt action, single trigger, French walnut, 24 in. Krupp steel barrel except Mag. (25 in.). Importation disc. 2001.

$1,825	$1,425	$1,100	$900	$800	$700	$600

Last MSR was $2,100.

Subtract $70 without iron sights.
Add $430 for left-hand variation.
Add $300 for Mag. cals. (G suffix).
Add $1,140 for .375 H&H cal. (Model SR20 G Etoscha).
Add $260 for Classic Model.
Add $300 for carbine Classic Model.

❋ ***Model SR 20 Hunter*** - similar to Model SR 20N, except has classic style fiberglass stock with either matte blue or parkerized metal finish. Imported 1988-90.

$1,500	$1,225	$1,050	$900	$800	$700	$600

Last MSR was $1,750.

❋ ***Model SR 20L*** - Mannlicher style stock, European configuration, 18 in. barrel, 7 lbs.

$1,475	$1,225	$985	$895	$785	$720	$650

Last MSR was $1,700.

Grading	100%	98%	95%	90%	80%	70%	60%

SR 20 TROPHY - available in all SR 20 cals., bolt action, 22 or 24 (Mag. cals. only) in. octagonal barrel, classic stock configuration with cheekpiece and recoil pad. Importation began 1989.

	$2,550	$2,100	$1,800	$1,500	$1,250	$985	$895

Last MSR was $2,815.

Add $120 for Mag. cals.
This model was also available in either right hand or left-hand action.

SR 20G CLASSIC SPORTER - available in various cals., bolt action, 22 or 24 in. round barrel, steel grip cap. Importation began 1989.

	$1,875	$1,600	$1,300	$1,050	$900	$785	$720

Last MSR was $2,235.

Subtract $70 without iron sights.
This model was also available in either right hand or left-hand action.

SR 20 ALPINE - available in standard cals. between .243 Win. and 9.3x62mm, mountain style rifle with Mannlicher forend and classic buttstock, supplied with mounted open sights. Importation began 1989.

	$1,900	$1,650	$1,325	$1,075	$925	$800	$750

Last MSR was $2,165.

This model was also available in either right hand or left-hand action.

SR 20 MATCH - .308 Win. cal., 24 in. heavy barrel, target stock with accessory rail, large bolt handle, supplied without sights, 9 lbs. Imported 1991-94.

	$1,860	$1,600	$1,300	$1,050	$900	$785	$720

Last MSR was $2,200.

SR 20 CLASSIC SAFARI - .375 H&H, .404 Jeffery (disc.), .425 Express, or .458 Win. Mag. cal., 24 in. barrel only, express rear sight and large front post sights, tight grained walnut. Imported 1989-94.

	$2,150	$1,650	$1,250	$1,050	$875	$800	$700

Last MSR was $2,530.

This model was also available in either right hand or left-hand action.

SR 21 N - 26 standard and metric cals., traditional bolt action that is bascially a Mauser M90 design with modern extractor recessed in the bolt face, single set trigger, unique interchangeable barrel/receiver, detachable mag., 3 position side safety, right or left hand action, iron sights, approx. 7 lbs. New 2001.

MSR	$2,275	$1,950	$1,500	$1,175	$950	$825	$725	$625

Add $325 for carbine (Model SR 21 N Classic).
Add $1,325 for Model SR 21 N Concorde.
Add $110 for Model SR 21 N Keiler.

SR 30 N - various cals., straight pull bolt with lock in the receiver head, iron sights, deluxe checkered walnut stock with rosewood pistol grip cap and forend tip, sling swivels, available in various configurations, 7-7½ lbs.

MSR	$2,495	$2,100	$1,750	$1,325	$1,100	$900	$825	$725

Add $264 for SR 30 N Classic Model (carbine).
Add $1,505 for SR 30 N Concorde Model.
Add $155 for SR 30 N Wild Boar Model.

EXPRESS SERIES RIFLE - .338 Lapua Mag., .375 H&H, .378 Wby. Mag., .404 rimless Jeffery (disc. 1992), .416 Rigby, .450 Ackley, .460 Wby. Mag., .500 NE (new 1994), .500 A-Square, or .505 Gibbs cal., express sights, Timney single trigger. New 1989.

MSR	$6,125	$5,500	$4,800	$4,050	$3,150	$2,500	$2,150	$1,875

Add $525 for .460 Wby. Mag. - .505 Gibbs cal.
Add $375 for muzzle brake (includes installation).
Add $555 for left-hand action (disc. 1992).

Grading	100%	98%	95%	90%	80%	70%	60%

✳ **.577 NE & .600 NE Cals.** - .577 NE or .600 NE cal., 24 in. barrel, reinforced action, 2 shot mag. New 1991.

MSR $10,375	$9,550	$8,350	$7,250	$6,100	$5,000	$3,750	$2,950

Add $1,125 for .600 NE cal.

RIFLES: O/U

MODEL 55 BOXLOCK - various cals., engraving similar to Model 55 BF.

MSR $7,400	$6,350	$5,400	$4,500	$3,750	$3,250	$2,750	$2,450

Add $500 for deluxe game scene engraving.

MODEL 55 SIDELOCK - O/U rifle only with different caliber for each barrel, double set triggers, "Bergstutzen" design.

MSR $10,500	$9,350	$8,000	$6,850	$5,950	$5,125	$4,500	$3,975

Add $1,000 for Deluxe Model.

RIFLES: SxS

MODEL 80 B - various cals., modified boxlock action with top sear bars, regular or manual cocking, 23¾ in. barrels with quarter rib and iron sights, DT or ST, deluxe checkered walnut stock and forearm, 6.6 lbs.

MSR $6,600	$6,025	$5,300	$4,550	$3,950	$3,350	$2,750	$2,150

Add $600 for ST with hand cocking, $700 for DT with hand cocking.

MODEL 88 B SAFARI CLASSIC - available in most safari cals. between .300 Win. Mag. - .458 Win. Mag. boxlock action, Krupp steel barrels, double underlocking lugs with Greener crossbolt, ejectors, checkered circassian walnut, built to customer specifications, 7½ lbs.

MSR $13,300	$11,650	$9,750	$8,600	$7,100	$6,125	$5,420	$4,575

Add $550 for .416 Rigby - .500 NE cal.

✳ *Model 88 B Safari Classic Sidelock (BSS)* - sidelock model with interceptor sears.

MSR $17,400	$15,500	$13,000	$10,250	$8,750	$7,425	$6,300	$5,175

This model is also available in both .577 NE and .600 NE cal. Prices start at $28,575 for the .577 NE, and $32,500 for .600 NE.

✳ *Model 88 B Safari Classic Boxlock* - available in various safari cals., double safety bar, 24 in. barrels, 9.9 lbs.

MSR $10,600	$9,850	$8,600	$7,400	$6,300	$5,175	$4,500	$3,750

Add $1,150 for .300 Win. Mag. - .500 NE cal.

✳ *Model 88 B Safari Sidelock* - sidelock model with interceptor sears.

MSR $15,200	$13,750	$10,500	$8,850	$7,500	$6,300	$5,175	$4,250

RIFLES: SINGLE SHOT

MODEL HR 30N - available in many cals., Ruger No. 1 falling block action, 24 in. barrel, French walnut with Bavarian cheekpiece, round barrel, Sporter or full length carbine style French walnut stock, engraved coin finished receiver, 6.6 lbs.

	$3,500	$2,975	$2,350	$1,950	$1,675	$1,350	$1,175

Last MSR was $4,040.

Add $440 for Mag. cals.
Add $1,710 for Mannlicher stocked Carbine Model.
Add $850 for hunting scene engraving (minimum extra charge).

Grading	100%	98%	95%	90%	80%	70%	60%

MODEL HR 38 N - available in many cals., Ruger No. 1 falling block action 24 in. barrel, octagon barrel, French walnut with Bavarian cheekpiece, Sporter or full length carbine style French walnut stock, engraved coin finished receiver, 6.6 lbs.

			$4,150	$3,450	$2,875	$2,300	$1,950	$1,675	$1,350

Last MSR was $4,835.

> Add $235 for Mag. cals.
> Add $2,400 for sideplates with engraved large game hunting scenes.

MODEL 44 B - various standard and metric cals., single lock action with thumbpiece and sideplates, open sights with barrel quarter rib, deluxe checkered stock and forearm, 6.6 lbs.

MSR	$5,400		$4,900	$4,350	$3,550	$3,025	$2,350	$2,000	$1,750

> Add $1,100 for Deluxe Model.

SHOTGUNS: O/U

MODEL 55 F - 16 or 20 ga., ejectors, engraved, 6.6 lbs. Importation disc. 1992.

		$5,100	$4,525	$3,950	$3,615	$3,200	$2,775	$2,300

Last MSR was $5,500.

MODEL 55 SS - sidelock version of Model 55 F, large engraved hunting scenes.

		$4,500	$3,825	$3,300	$2,850	$2,400	$2,000	$1,700

Last MSR was $4,890.

MODEL 200 - 20 ga., 3 in. chambers, boxlock action, DTs, 28 in. VR barrels, light engraving, previous importation.

		$895	$795	$700	$650	$600	$550	$500

VIERLINGS

MODEL 37 V - 4 barrel configuration, various cals. and gauges, special order only. Limited mfg.

MSR	$16,300		$14,500	$11,000	$9,000	$7,750	$6,500	$5,500	$4,500

> Add $1,700 for Deluxe Model.

HI-POINT FIREARMS

Current trademark marketed by MKS Supply, Inc. located in Dayton, Ohio. Hi-Point firearms have been manufactured since 1988. Dealer and distributor sales.

HI-POINT FIREARMS

Prior to 1993, trademarks sold by MKS Supply, Inc. (including Beemiller, Inc., Haskell Manufacturing, Inc., Iberia Firearms, Inc., and Stallard Arms, Inc.) had their own separate manufacturers' markings. Beginning in 1993, Hi-Point Firearms eliminated these individualized markings and chose instead to have currently manufactured guns labeled Hi-Point Firearms.

CARBINES

MODEL 995 - 9mm Para. or .40 S&W (mfg. late 2000-2001) cal., 16½ in. barrel, one-piece camo or black polymer stock features pistol grip, 10 shot mag., aperture rear sight, parkerized or chrome finish. New 1996.

MSR	$199		$170	$135	$115	$95	$85	$75	$70

> Add approx. $40 for .40 S&W cal.
> Add $10 for chrome finish.
> Add $11 for camo stock (new 2002).
> Add $71 for detachable compensator, laser, and mount (new 1999).

PISTOLS: SEMI-AUTO

Beginning 2000, all compact models feature magazine disconnect safety and last shot hold open, and all pistols are shipped with a rear adj. aperture sight (which can replace the standard rear adj. sight).

Grading	100%	98%	95%	90%	80%	70%	60%

MODEL CF-380 POLYMER - .380 ACP cal., single action, 3½ or 4 (new 2002) in. barrel, polymer frame, 3-dot adj. sights, 8 shot mag. with thumb activated release, chrome slide or two-tone black satin finish, 29 oz. New 1995.

MSR $100	$85	$75	$65	$55	$50	$45	$40

Add $25 for 4 in. barrel with compensator and two mags.

JS-9 - 9mm Para. cal., single action, 4½ in. barrel, thumb safety, fixed (disc. 1999) or adj. (new 2000) sights, 8 shot mag., non-glare military blue finish (early mfg.) or black satin finish (new 1991), copolymer synthetic grips, 39 oz. New 1990.

	$140	$110	$95	$80	$70	$65	$60

Last MSR was $159.

Add 10% for nickel finish (disc.).

This model is manufactured by Beemiller, Inc. located in Mansfield, OH.

✳ ***JS-9 Compact (Model C-9)*** - compact variation of the Model JS-9 with 3½ in. barrel and 8 shot mag., choice of alloy or polymer (new 1994, various slide/frame finishes) frame, 3-dot adj. sights became standard in 2000, 32 (polymer) or 29 oz. New 1993.

MSR $137	$110	$90	$80	$70	$65	$60	$55

This model is manufactured by Beemiller, Inc. located in Mansfield, OH.

✳ ***JS-9 Comp*** - features 4 in. barrel with compensator, with (new 1999) or w/o laser sight package, adj. sights, 10 shot mag. New 1998.

MSR $169	$140	$115	$100	$90	$80	$75	$70

Add $50 for laser sights.

JS-40/JC-40 - .40 S&W cal., single action, black finish, 4½ in. barrel, 3-dot adj. sights, 8 shot mag., 39 oz. New 1992.

MSR $169	$140	$115	$100	$90	$80	$75	$70

This model is manufactured by Iberia Firearms, Inc. located in Iberia, OH.

Add $7 for nickel finish (disc. 1994).

JS-45/JH-45 - .45 ACP cal., single action, similar to JS-9, except has 7 shot mag. and 4½ in. barrel, adj. sights, 39 oz. New 1991.

MSR $169	$140	$115	$100	$90	$80	$75	$70

Add $10 for nickel finish (disc. 1994).

This model is manufactured by Haskell Mfg., Inc. located in Lima, OH.

HIGGINS, J.C.

Previous trademark used on Sears & Roebuck rifles and shotguns manufactured between 1946-1962.

The J.C. Higgins trademark has appeared literally on hundreds of various models (shotguns and rifles) sold through the Sears & Roebuck retail network. Most of these models were manufactured through subcontracts with both domestic and international firearms manufacturers. Typically, they were "spec." guns made to sell at a specific price to undersell the competition. Most of these models were derivatives of existing factory models (i.e., Browning, High Standard, Marlin, Mossberg, Savage, Stevens, Winchester, etc.) with less expensive wood and perhaps missing the features found on those models from which they were derived.

To date, there has been minimal interest in collecting J.C. Higgins guns, regardless of rarity. Rather than list J.C. Higgins models, a general guideline is that values generally are under the models of their "1st generation relatives" (listed above). The Ranger trademark was also used by Sears & Roebuck - it is not any more desirable than those guns marked J.C. Higgins. As a result, prices are ascertained by the shooting value of the gun, rather than its collector value.

For converting J.C. Higgins models to the sub-contracted manufacturers, please refer to the Store Brand Crossover List after the Serialization section.

Grading	100%	98%	95%	90%	80%	70%	60%

HIGH STANDARD

Previous manufacturer located in Hamden, Hartford, and East Hartford, CT. High Standard Mfg. Co. was founded in 1926. They purchased Hartford Arms and Equipment Co. in 1932. The original plant was located in New Haven, CT from 1932-1952 until they moved to a larger facility at Hamden, CT from 1951-1976. High Standard also operated another Hamden, CT plant between 1940-1949. In 1968 the company was sold to the Leisure Group, Inc. A final move was made to East Hartford, CT in 1977 where they remained until the doors were closed in January, 1984.

High Standard values have risen dramatically over the past several years. Many collectors have realized the rarity and quality factors this trademark has earned (Models C, A, D, E, H-D, H-E, H-A, H-B First Model, G-380, GB, GD, GE, GO - 13 different variations had a total production of less than 43,000 pistols). For these reasons, top condition High Standard pistols are getting more difficult to find each year.

Note: catalog numbers were not always consistent with design series, and in 1966-1967 changed with accessories offered, but not design series.

The approx. ser. number cut-off for New Haven, CT marked guns is 43X,XXX.

The approx. ser. number cut-off for Hamden, CT manufacture is 44X,XXX - 2,495,000 and G or ML 010000 - G or ML 25,000.

The approx. ser. number range for E. Hartford, CT manufacture is ML 25,000 - ML 87,000 and SH 10,000 and SH 35,000.

COMMEMORATIVES, SPECIAL EDITIONS, & LIMITED MFG.

PRESIDENTIAL DERRINGER - limited mfg. in 1974-77. Cased.

$550 $450 $350

Last MSR was $150.

CRUSADER REVOLVER 50TH ANNIVERSARY - .44 Mag. or .45 LC cal., approx. 50 mfg. for each cal. in 8 3/8 in. barrel with 1/3 coverage engraving (ser. no. 0-50), blue or gold finish. Also, advertising materials at the time listed 450 revolvers of each cal. in a 6 in. barrel (ser. no. 51-500). Cased. Mfg. in 1977 only.

Standard Model

w/o engraving	$850	$650	$500
8 3/8 in. barrel	$1,700	$1,200	$1,000

Add 25% for single digit serial number.

Limited availability might affect asking prices considerably. Two gun sets with matching serial numbers were also available - current asking prices are over $3,250.

DERRINGERS

DERRINGER MODELS - .22 or .22 WMR cal., double action only O/U, 2 shot, 3½ in. barrels, The first derringer was mfg. about 1962 in Hamden, CT.

* ***First Issue*** - "D-100" or "DM-101" appears on left side of frame, "Hi-Standard Derringer" with eagle logo on left side of barrel, blue with white grips introduced 1962.

$250 $215 $190 $155 $135 $110 $100

.22 cal. listed as "D-100" in catalog #9193. .22 WMR cal. listed as "DM-101" in catalog #9194.

* ***Gold plated*** - with black grips, includes presentation case, introduced 1964.

$600 $500 $400

.22 cal. listed as "D-100" in catalog #9195. .22 WMR cal. listed as "DM-101" in catalog #9196.

* ***Matched Set*** - gold plated, consecutive serial numbers, includes presentation case.

$1,100 $990 $770

.22 cal. listed as "D-100" in catalog #9197. .22 WMR cal. listed as "DM-101" in catalog #9198.

Grading	100%	98%	95%	90%	80%	70%	60%

✴ ***Second Issue*** - "D-100" or "DM-101" on left side of frame, "Hi-Standard Derringer" with trigger logo on left side of barrel, blue finish with white grips introduced 1967.

	$225	$195	$175	$145	$125	$100	$90

.22 cal. listed as "D-100" in catalog #9193. .22 WMR cal. listed as "DM-101" in catalog #9194.

✴ ***Third Issue*** - "D-101" or "DM-101" appears on left side of frame, "Derringer" on left side of barrel, blue with white grips mfg. 1970-77.

	$225	$195	$175	$145	$125	$100	$90

.22 cal. listed as "D-101" in catalog #9193. .22 WMR cal. listed as "DM-101" in catalog #9194.

✴ ***Blue Finish*** - with black grips.

	$200	$175	$155	$130	$110	$90	$75

.22 cal. listed in catalog #9193, introduced 1982, E. Hartford. .22 WMR cal. listed in catalog #9194, introduced 1979, E. Hartford.

✴ ***Nickel Finish*** - with black grips, introduced 1970.

	$275	$240	$215	$180	$155	$125	$110

.22 cal. listed as "D-101" in catalog #9305. .22 WMR cal. listed as "DM-101" in catalog #9306.

✴ ***Electroless Nickel Finish*** - with black grips, frame and sideplates are electroless nickel, introduced 1974 in E. Hartford.

	$275	$240	$215	$180	$155	$125	$110

.22 cal. listed in catalog #9305. .22 WMR cal. listed in catalog #9306.

✴ ***Cased Set*** - blue finish with white grips, and nickel finish with black grips, with black grips, includes presentation case. Introduced 1974.

	$700	$550	$400

.22 WMR cal. listed as "DM-101" in catalog #9194 & 9306.

✴ ***Gold Plated*** - with walnut grips, includes presentation case, ser. no. has "GP" prefix, introduced 1980 in E. Hartford.

	$500	$450	$350

.22 WMR cal. listed in catalog #9196.

✴ ***Silver Plated*** - with grey grips, includes presentation case, ser. no. has "SP" prefix, introduced 1981 in E. Hartford, 501 were mfg.

	$550	$495	$350

.22 WMR cal. listed in catalog #9341.

✴ ***Electroless Nickel Finish*** - with walnut grips, introduced 1982 in E. Hartford.

	$300	$250	$200

.22 cal. listed in catalog #9420. .22 WMR cal. listed in catalog #9421.

PISTOLS: SEMI-AUTO, RIMFIRE

Pre-war High Standard Semi-Automatic pistols had 3 different takedown types.

TYPE I-A MFG. 1932-38. Takedown lever on left side of frame next to safety. Round retracting rod on rear of slide. This takedown was used on Models B & C.

TYPE I-B MFG. 1938. Similar to I-A Type except has strengthened rectangular rod on rear of slide.

TYPE II MFG. 1939. Takedown lever located on right side of frame. Round pick-up rod on top of slide.

> As a final note on High Standard pistols, original factory boxes have become very desirable. Prices can range from $75-$100 for a good condition Model 106 or 107 factory box to over $150 for an older box of a desirable model.

Pistols: Hammerless Fixed Barrel Series

This series consists of the 5 original pistols mfg. in 1932-1942. All serial numbers are located on forestrap of frame. This series is also sometimes referred to as the "Letter Models".

Grading	100%	98%	95%	90%	80%	70%	60%

MODEL B - .22 LR cal., original High Standard pistol, basically the same gun as Hartford Arms 1925 Automatic, small frame, 4½ or 6¾ in. light weight barrel, fixed Patridge type front and rear sights, checkered hard rubber grips with or without H.S. monogram, 10 shot mag. Beginning ser. no. 5,000. Approx. 65,000 mfg. 1932-42.

	$525	$375	$250	$200	$175	$150	$100

Add $75 for I-B Type takedown.

Less than 14,000 pistols with this takedown were mfg.

MODEL S - .22 LR cal., chambered for .22 LR shot shell cartridge, essentially a Model B with a 6¾ in. smooth bore barrel only without choke, left side of slide is stamped "HI- STAN-DARD MODEL S .22 LR SHOT ONLY", this variation was never a production model with approx. 5-10 guns mfg. total, 10 shot mag., a second variation using Model C slides was called the Model C/S - also not a production model with approx. 5 mfg. Mfg. 1939 only.

Because of the extreme rarity factor of this model, a specimen in almost any condition will bring $3,000 - $5,000. This model was used primarily for pest control.

MODEL C - .22 Short cal.only, identical to Model B in appearance, small frame, 4½ or 6¾ in. light weight barrel, fixed rear sight, checkered hard rubber grips with or without H.S. monogram, this action was adapted for the decreased power of the .22 Short cartridge. Beginning ser. no. 500 to 31XX, later beginning ser. no. 42XXX. Approx. 4,700 mfg. 1936-42.

	$950	$690	$510	$375	$275	$230	$200

Add $100 for I-A takedown.
Add $250 for I-B takedown.

This model was used primarily for plinking and gallery shooting. The Model C was made in all 3 variations of takedowns - I-A, I-B, and Type 2 (but less than 100 were mfg. in I-B).

MODEL A - .22 LR cal., similar to Model B, except enlarged frame, squared-off butt, 4½ or 6¾ in. light weight barrel, adj. rear sight, checkered walnut grips, automatic slide lock, trigger stop, 10 shot mag. Beginning ser. no. 33XXX. Approx. 7,300 mfg. 1938- 42.

	$750	$550	$450	$325	$260	$220	$200

Add $250 for I-B takedown.

MODEL D - .22 LR cal., identical to Model A except 4½ or 6¾ in. medium weight barrel, adj. sights, walnut grips, slide lock trigger stop, 10 shot mag. Beginning ser. no. 33XXX. Approx. 2,500 mfg. 1938-42.

	$950	$625	$510	$400	$300	$250	$215

Add $250 for I-B takedown.

MODEL E - .22 LR cal., high quality, deluxe model of the hammerless series, adj. sight, 4½ or 6¾ in. heavy bull barrel, checkered walnut target grips with thumbrest, automatic slide lock, 10 shot mag. Beginning ser. no. 34XXX. Approx. 2,600 mfg. 1938-42.

	$1,150	$900	$650	$500	$440	$360	$300

Add $250 for I-B takedown.

Pistols: Exposed Hammer – Fixed Barrel Series

This series consists of 4 pistols that were introduced in 1940. Frame and slide modified to accommodate external hammer. All ser. numbers located on forestrap of frame. Prefix "H" added to standard model designation with the exception of Model C. Mfg. 1940-42. This series has very low production numbers. May also be referred to as the "Hammer Letter Models".

MODEL H-D - .22 LR cal., first exposed hammer model, similar to Model D, 4½ or 6¾ in. medium weight barrel, adj. sight, target or standard walnut grips, no external safety, 10 shot mag. High quality pistol. Beginning ser. no. 45,463. Approx. 2,000 mfg. 1940- 42.

	$950	$700	$600	$500	$400	$300	$250

This variation is infrequently encountered.

Grading	100%	98%	95%	90%	80%	70%	60%

MODEL H-E - .22 LR cal., high quality, deluxe model of exposed hammer series, 4½ or 6¾ in. heavy barrel, adj. sight, deluxe hand checkered walnut grips with thumbrests, no external safety, 10 shot mag. Rarest of the H.S. pistols. Beginning ser. no. 51,802. Approx 1,000 mfg. 1941-42.

	$2,275	$1,600	$1,200	$950	$725	$600	$500

MODEL H-A - .22 LR cal., similar to Model A, 4½ or 6¾ in. light weight barrel, adj. sight, plain checkered walnut grips, no external safety, 10 shot mag. Very rare gun. Beginning ser. no. 53,176. Approx. 1,000 mfg. 1940-42.

	$1,050	$895	$750	$475	$365	$295	$250

MODEL H-B - .22 LR cal., duplicate of Model B with external hammer, 4½ or 6¾ in. light weight barrel, fixed sight, checkered hard rubber grips with or without H.S. monogram, no external safety, 10 shot mag. This first Model H-B had beginning ser. no. 52,405. Approx. 2,200 mfg. 1940-42.

	$600	$500	$400	$355	$275	$235	$200

* *Model H-B Second Model* - H.S. reintroduced a H-B second model similar to first model, except with external safety. Ser. no. range 274,197 – 311,535. Mfg. 1949-1954.

	$550	$450	$375	$310	$235	$200	$170

Pistols: U.S. Military Series

These models are earlier H.S. pistols adapted as training guns during WWII. They were the sole suppliers of the .22 cal. pistol for military training. Ser. numbers located on forestrap of frame.

MODEL B-US - .22 LR cal., adapted Model B with minor changes, available in 4½ in. barrel only, checkered hard rubber grips, fixed sight, marked "Property of U.S." on right side of frame and on top of barrel. Ordnance acceptance crossed cannon stamped on right side of frame above trigger guard, 10 shot mag. Approx. ser. no. range 95XXX – 111,631. Approx. 14,000 mfg. 1942-43.

	$875	$725	$575	$350	$275	$235	$195

USA-MODEL-HD - .22 LR cal., this model was developed because the government needed a training pistol similar to the Colt Model 1911 .45 ACP, the result was a Model HD with external safety and fixed sight, 4½ in. medium weight barrel, barrel is marked "Property of USA", black checkered hard rubber grips. First models mfg. had high gloss blue finish, changed to a Parkerized finish near ser. no. 130XXX. Ser. no. range 108,586-145,700. Approx. 44,000 mfg. 1943-46.

	$725	$625	$525	$320	$250	$200	$170

Add 20% for early blue finish.

MODEL USA-HD-MS - .22 LR cal., variation of the USA-Model-HD with attached silencer, mfg. for U.S. Government covert operations, original ownership required NFA transfer, approx. 2,000 mfg.

	$3,850	$3,350	$2,900	$2,500	$2,250	$1,995	$1,750

MODEL H-D MILITARY - .22 LR cal., though called H-D Military, this model was not mfg. for the government, essentially a USA-HD with the addition of adj. sights, 4½ or 6¾ in. barrel, plastic (early mfg.) or checkered walnut grips (later mfg.), external safety, 10 shot mag. Ser. no. range 145,196 – 334,751 . Approx. 150,000 mfg. 1946-55.

	$600	$425	$300	$250	$200	$190	$160

Add 20% for all-blue finish.

MODEL G-380 CENTERFIRE - .380 ACP cal., this is H.S.'s only in-house production of a centerfire pistol, transition model to the G-series using a lever takedown, has exposed hammer, fixed sights, checkered black plastic grips, external safety, 5 in. barrel only, 6 shot mag. Beginning ser. no. 100. Approx. 7,400 mfg. 1947-50.

	$550	$450	$400	$325	$245	$210	$180

Grading	100%	98%	95%	90%	80%	70%	60%

Pistols: G-Series

This series is hammerless with interchangeable target barrel, 6¾ in. and plinking barrel, 4½ in., consists of 4 pistols, all using lever takedown. An adaptation of the G-380 design. Ser. numbers on right side of slide and rear right side of frame. Mfg. 1949-50.

MODEL GB - .22 LR cal., similar to Model B with light barrel, small frame, external safety, fixed sight, checkered brown plastic grips, interchangeable 4½ or 6¾ in. barrel with lever takedown, 10 shot mag. Beginning ser. no. 311XXX. Approx. 4,900 mfg. 1949-50.

	$550	$400	$350	$250	$200	$185	$155

Add 15-20% for both barrels.

MODEL GD - .22 LR cal., large frame with medium weight with interchangeable 4½ or 6¾ in. barrel with lever takedown, featured new adj. "Davis" sight, named for designer G.F. Davis. Grips avail. in plain checkered walnut or deluxe with thumbrest grips, 10 shot mag. Beginning ser. no. 311XXX. Approx. 3,300 mfg. 1949-50.

	$925	$795	$625	$385	$295	$245	$205

Add 15-20% for both barrels.

This sight is adjustable for both windage and elevation.

MODEL GE - .22 LR cal., deluxe top-of-the-line quality .22 LR pistol, large frame with interchangeable 4½ or 6¾ in. heavy "bull" barrel with lever takedown, "Davis" adj. sight, deluxe walnut hand checkered grips with thumbrest, 10 shot mag. Beginning ser. no. 312XXX. Approx. 2,900 mfg. 1949-50.

	$1,345	$1,150	$875	$555	$425	$360	$300

Add 15-20% for both barrels.

MODEL G-O - .22 Short cal. cal., adaptation of Model GE in .22 Short cal., also known as First Model Olympic. First fired in Olympic competition in 1948. Deluxe top-of-the- line quality, interchangeable 4½ or 6¾ in. heavy "bull" barrel with lever takedown, "Davis" adj. sight, deluxe hand checkered walnut grips with thumbrests. First High Standard large production gun with aluminum slide. Has unique curved magazine, flat milled surface on top of barrel. Rare. Beginning ser. no. 307XXX. Approx. 1,200 mfg. 1949-50.

	$1,695	$1,350	$1,050	$625	$475	$395	$345

Add 15-20% for both barrels.

This model has a grooved fore and rear strap.

Pistols: Supermatic Series

All of this series were mfg. at the New Haven, CT plant from 1951-53. Consisted of 4 guns, featuring the lever takedown introduced in the G-Series. Hammerless, new positive lock safety, use of one screw to attach grips, no production figures available. Approximate serial range of this series is 340,000- 440,000.

SPORT-KING (FIRST MODEL) - .22 LR cal., 10 shot mag., similar to Field-King but has fixed sight and lightweight interchangeable 4½ or 6¾ in. barrel featuring lever takedown.

	$450	$325	$250	$200	$175	$145	$125

Add 10-15% for extra barrel.

Add $50 w/o slide lock.

This model was available with or without slide lock.

The High Standard catalog number for this model was 9080-81, while both barrels were numbered 9082.

FIELD-KING (FIRST MODEL) - .22 LR cal., plain version of Supermatic, 10 shot mag., interchangeable 4½ or 6¾ in. barrels with lever takedown, "Davis" adj. sight, 10 shot mag.

	$600	$500	$425	$300	$260	$210	$175

Add 10-15% for both barrels.

The High Standard catalog number for this model was 9090-91, while both barrels were numbered 9092.

H

Grading	100%	98%	95%	90%	80%	70%	60%

SUPERMATIC (FIRST MODEL) - .22 LR cal., 10 shot mag., 4½ or 6¾ in. interchangeable barrel with lever takedown, "Davis" adj. sight, slide lock, front and back straps grooved, serrated rib between front and rear sight, adj. 2 oz. and 3 oz. weights which dovetail into and beneath barrel.

	$650	$525	$400	$325	$280	$225	$195

Add 15-20% for both barrels.

The High Standard catalog numbers for this model were 9070-71, while both barrels were numbered 9072.

OLYMPIC (SECOND MODEL) - .22 Short cal., identical in all respects to the Supermatic, except has aluminum slide for rapid recoil, interchangeable 4½ or 6¾ in. barrel with lever takedown, "Davis" adj. sight, adj. 2 oz. and 3 oz. weights, 10 shot mag.

	$1,175	$950	$775	$485	$375	$315	$265

Add 15-20% for both barrels.

The High Standard catalog numbers for this model were 9043-44, while both barrels were numbered 9045.

QUICK CHANGE CONVERSION KIT - avail. in 1951 to let you shoot both .22 LR or .22 Short in the Supermatic, Olympic, or Field-King models. Featured factory fitted barrel, slide, barrel weights and magazine.

	$550	$450	$350

This kit featured all components fitted neatly into a small maroon and yellow box.
Cat.# 9150 Supermatic/Field King to 22 short, 4½ Bbl.
Cat.# 9151 Supermatic/Field King to 22 short, 6¾ Bbl.
Cat.# 9152 Olympic to Supermatic 22 L.R., 4½ Bbl.
Cat.# 9153 Olympic to Supermatic 22 L.R., 6¾ Bbl.
Cat.# 9154 Olympic to Field King 22 L.R., 4½ Bbl.
Cat.# 9155 Olympic to Field King 22 L.R., 6¾ Bbl.

Pistols: M-100 & M-101 Series

All of this series were mfg. at the Hamden, CT plant from 1954-57. Hammerless design consisting of 5 pistols featuring a new push-button type takedown. The beginning ser. no. for .22 LR pistols only in this series was 443,611. This series featured slanted plastic grips as standard issue. The serial range for this series was 443,XXX-770,XXX. Conversion unit factory nomenclature for this series is as follows:

Cat.# 9150 Supermatic/Field King to 22 short, 4½ Bbl.
Cat.# 9151 Supermatic/Field King to 22 short, 6¾ Bbl.
Cat.# 9152 Olympic to Supermatic 22 L.R., 4½ Bbl.
Cat.# 9153 Olympic to Supermatic 22 L.R., 6¾ Bbl.
Cat.# 9154 Olympic to Field King 22 L.R., 4½ Bbl.
Cat.# 9155 Olympic to Field King 22 L.R., 6¾ Bbl.

M-100/M-101 Conversion unit pricing is similar to the M-102, M-103, and M-104 Conversion units (please refer to that section).

DURA-MATIC - .22 LR cal., 4½ or 6¾ in. barrels, fixed sight, oversized plastic grips. M-100 or M-101 stamped on right side of slide. Mfg. 1954-70. The Duramatic was sold by Sears Roebuck & Co. as the J. C. Higgins Model 80. This Sears variation had some minor exterior differences, but mechanically it was the same. Unique thumb screw takedown, push-button mag. release and oversized trigger guard.

	$300	$225	$200	$160	$125	$105	$90

Add 20% for extra barrel.
Add 10% for M-100 (has push button to release thumb screw).

The High Standard catalog number for this model was 9124-25, while both barrels were numbered 9126.

Grading	100%	98%	95%	90%	80%	70%	60%

SPORT-KING (SECOND MODEL) - .22 LR cal., SK 100 stamped on right side of slide, similar to Flite-King but with steel slide and frame, front and rear grip straps on this model are smooth, fixed rear sight.

	$400	$325	$260	$185	$140	$120	$100

Add 15-20% for both barrels.
Add 20% for nickel finish.
The High Standard catalog number for this model was 9100-01, while both barrels were numbered 9102.

SPORT-KING LIGHTWEIGHT - .22 LR cal., similar to standard Sport-King, except has forged aluminum alloy frame. The word "Lightweight" is inscribed in script on the left side of frame on the Model 100. Also avail. in nickel. Mfg. 1956-64.

	$530	$450	$315	$225	$175	$150	$125

Add 20% for nickel finish (H.S. number 9166-67, both barrels - 9168).
Add 15 - 20% for both barrels.
The High Standard catalog number for this model was 9156-57, while both barrels were numbered 9158.

FLITE-KING (FIRST MODEL) - .22 Short cal., LW 100 stamped on right side of slide, 10 shot mag., 4½ or 6¾ in. interchangeable light weight barrel with push-button takedown, alloy slide, front and rear grip straps on this model are smooth. First commercial use of aluminum alloy for frame. Fixed rear sight. Mfg. until 1960.

	$500	$425	$380	$275	$210	$175	$150

Add 15-20% for both barrels.
The High Standard catalog number for this model was 9103-04, while both barrels were numbered 9105.

FIELD-KING (SECOND MODEL) - .22 LR cal., FK 100 or FK 101 stamped on right side of slide, 10 shot mag. 4½ or 6¾ in. interchangeable barrel with push-button takedown, front and rear grip straps on this model are smooth. Slotted stabilizer 6¾ in. target barrel was an option. Adj. rear sight.

	$625	$500	$400	$300	$265	$215	$180

Add $250 for Models marked FK100.
The High Standard catalog number for this model was 9115-16, while both barrels were numbered 9117.

SUPERMATIC (SECOND MODEL) - .22 LR cal., S 100 or S 101 stamped on right side of slide, 10 shot mag., 4½ or 6¾ in. interchangeable barrel with push-button takedown, adj. 2 oz. or 3 oz. weights. Integral slotted stabilizer with 6¾ in. target barrel was an option. Adj. rear sight.

	$700	$575	$400	$325	$275	$230	$195

Add $75 for models marked S100.
The High Standard catalog number for this model was 9118-19, while both barrels were numbered 9120.

OLYMPIC (THIRD MODEL) - .22 Short cal., 0-100 or 0-101 stamped on right side of alloy slide, 10 shot mag., 4½ or 6¾ in. interchangeable barrel with push-button takedown, adj. 2 oz. or 3 oz. weights. Integral slotted stabilizer 6¾ in. target barrel was an option. Adj. rear sight.

	$1,025	$825	$650	$425	$325	$275	$235

Add $75 for models marked O-100.
The High Standard catalog number for this model was 9121-22, while both barrels were numbered 9123.

Pistols: Model 102 & 103 Series

This series included the following and were mfg. in Hamden, CT. The words "Model 102" or "Model 103" and the serial number were inscribed on the right side of slide, and the serial number was duplicated on the right side of the new and longer frame. A new and larger push-button takedown enabling easier use was another improvement. A grooved and wider trigger in addition to a new rear sight were also added on the target models. The 102 Series was mfg. from 1957-1960 and

Grading	100%	98%	95%	90%	80%	70%	60%

the serial range was approx. 770,XXX-1,100,XXX. The 103 Series was mfg. between 1960-1963 and the approximate serial range was 1,100,XXX-1,330,XXX. Plastic grips were standard and checkered walnut grips with thumbrest were optional.

Original cased 102/103 Series Trophy, Olympic Trophy, Olympic Citation models, and Special Presentation combinations in 98%+ condition are currently in great demand and are bringing premiums with asking prices in the $1,500-$2,600 range.

SPORT-KING - .22 LR cal., similar to the Series 100/101, but stamped Model 102 or Model 103, nickel finish on the Lighweight Sport King only was available (disc. 1960), the Lightweight Sport King was still available but was disc. in 1964, this basic Sport- King was mfg. from 1958-77.

	100%	98%	95%	90%	80%	70%	60%
	$350	$300	$230	$165	$125	$100	$85

Add 50% for nickel finish on Sport King Lightweight only (catalog nos. 9166-9167, both barrels 9168).
Add 25% for Sport King Lightweight (catalog nos. 9156-9156, both barrels 9158).
Add 20% for 102 Models.
The High Standard catalog number for this model was 9200-9201, while both barrels - (102 only) were numbered 9202.

FLITE-KING - .22 LR cal., similar to Series 100/101, this variation of the Flite-King featured an all steel frame with an alloy slide. Mfg. 1958-1965.

	100%	98%	95%	90%	80%	70%	60%
	$475	$400	$345	$265	$215	$175	$150

Add 10% for 102 Models.
The High Standard catalog number for this model was 9220-21, while both barrels (102 only) were numbered 9222.

SUPERMATIC TOURNAMENT - .22 LR cal., 10 shot, 4½, 5½ bull (avail. 1963), or 6¾ in. straight barrel, brown diamond checkered plastic slant grips, adj. sight, push-button takedown, this model featured smooth front and back grip straps. The govt. ordered approx. 1,000-2,000 Mod. 102 Tournaments for training. These were marked "US" on right side of frame. Mfg. 1958-1965.

	100%	98%	95%	90%	80%	70%	60%
	$625	$500	$425	$300	$265	$220	$185

The High Standard catalog number for this model was 9270-71, while both barrels were numbered 9272.
103 series pistols were numbered 9271-9275, (5½).

SHARPSHOOTER - .22 LR cal., 10 shot, 5½ in. bull barrel. Introduced 1969.

	100%	98%	95%	90%	80%	70%	60%
	$575	$450	$375	$275	$230	$190	$160

Add $50 for Sport King frame.
The High Standard catalog no. was 9205. First Models used a Sport King frame - Model 103 only.

SUPERMATIC CITATION - .22 LR cal., 10 shot, 6¾, 8, and 10 in. tapered barrels, diamond checkered plastic slant grips, adj. sight, push-button takedown, one grade above Tournament, grooved front and back grip straps, adj. sight located on 8 and 10 in. barrel (a 5½ in. target bull barrel became avail. in 1962), detachable stabilizer and 2 or 3 oz. barrel weights available. Mfg. 1958-65.

	100%	98%	95%	90%	80%	70%	60%
	$675	$500	$400	$300	$250	$225	$210

Add $125 for 8 in. barrel.
Add $225 for 10 in. barrel.
The High Standard catalog number for this model was 9260-61-62. 8 in. and 10 in. barrel set, 9262-8, 5½ bull barrel, 103 only - 9263. The govt. ordered a quantity of Mod. 102 Citations for training and are marked "U.S." on left side of frame.

Grading	100%	98%	95%	90%	80%	70%	60%

SUPERMATIC TROPHY - .22 LR cal., 10 shot, 6¾ in., 8 in. and 10 in. tapered barrels, 5½ bull and 7¼ in. fluted barrels became avail. in 1962, detachable barrel weights and stabilizer were also available, walnut checkered grips. Features gold trigger, gold safety button and gold inlaid lettering, adj. sight and push-button takedown. Mfg. 1958-63.

	$1,150	**$950**	**$725**	**$525**	**$400**	**$325**	**$275**

Add $150 for 8 in. barrel.
Add $250 for 10 in. barrel.
This variation was High Standard's Top-of-the-Line Target pistol.
The High Standard catalog number for this model was 9250-51-52. 8 in. and 10 in. barrel set, 9252-8, 5½ bull barrel (103 only) - 9254, 7¼ fluted barrel (103 only) - 9255.

ISU OLYMPIC - .22 Short cal., this is the model used to win the 33rd Gold Medal in the Rome Olympics in 1960. 10 shot, 6¾ in. barrel with integral stabilizer, checkered walnut grips, high luster finish, alloy slide. Top-of-the-line Olympic model. Complies with all rapid-fire International Shooting Union regulations. Mfg. 1961-66.

	$1,150	**$925**	**$675**	**$430**	**$330**	**$280**	**$240**

Add $1,000 for Model 9289 marked "Olympic Trophy" if in 98% or better condition.
The High Standard catalog number for this model was 9289-9299, 9289 (103 only).

OLYMPIC - .22 Short cal., same basic gun as Citation but is of lesser quality finish. Adj. sight located on 8 in. barrel. Mfg. 1958-65.

	$1,075	**$895**	**$625**	**$395**	**$315**	**$265**	**$225**

Add $350 for Model 9280-81-82 marked "OLYMPIC CITATION".
Add $150 for 8 in. barrel.
Add $250 for 10 in. barrel.
This model has also been observed with markings "OLYMPIC CITATION". Numbering was 9280-81-82, 8 in. and 10 in. barrel set 9282-8, 5½ bull barrel (Model 103, 1963 only) - 9294.

Pistols: Model 104 Series

This series was mfg. from 1964-1972. This is the last series to feature the slant grip trophy pistol. Serial No. range is approx. 1,330,000-2,330,000.

SUPERMATIC TOURNAMENT - .22 LR cal., similar to Model 102/103 series. Mfg. 1964-65.

	$600	**$525**	**$450**	**$325**	**$290**	**$245**	**$210**

The High Standard catalog number for this model was 9271-9275.
The 104 Tournament is quite rare.

SHARPSHOOTER - .22 LR cal., 10 shot, 5½ in. bull barrel. Mfg. 1969-72 (numbered 104) and 1973 (unnumbered).

	$550	**$450**	**$375**	**$275**	**$250**	**$225**	**$210**

The High Standard catalog number for this model was 9205. The 104 Sharpshooter is very rare.

SUPERMATIC CITATION - .22 LR cal., similar to Model 102/103 series, brown plastic grips or walnut checkered grips, grooved front and back straps.

	$650	**$500**	**$400**	**$300**	**$250**	**$225**	**$210**

Add $150 for 8 in. barrel.
Add $250 for 10 in. barrel.
The 5½ in. bull barrel, 9263 - disc. 1966 (supplied with extra mag). The 5½ in. bull barrel, 9244 - available 1966. The 6¾ in. tapered barrel, 9260 - disc. 1965. The 8 in. tapered barrel, 9261 - disc. 1965. The 10 in. tapered barrel, 9262 - disc. 1965.

SUPERMATIC TROPHY - .22 LR cal., similar to Model 102/103 series, Top-of-the-line target, 5½ in. bull, 7¼ in. fluted barrel available, extra mag., muzzle brake and weights were supplied with gun, grooved front and back straps, checkered walnut grips. Mfg. 1964-65.

	$1,095	**$895**	**$595**	**$425**	**$325**	**$275**	**$235**

Add $50 for high blue finish.
The High Standard catalog number for this model was 9254-55.

Grading	100%	98%	95%	90%	80%	70%	60%

OLYMPIC - .22 LR cal., similar to Model 102/103, grooved front and back straps, checkered walnut grips were optional.

	$1,095	$895	$650	$425	$330	$280	$240

Add $100 for catalog number 9295.
Add $150 for 8 in. barrel.

The 5½ in. bull barrel, 9294 - disc. 1964. The 5½ in. bull barrel, 9295 - avail. 1964-65, was supplied with muzzle brake and weights. The 8 in. tapered barrel, 9281 - disc. 1964.

ISU OLYMPIC - .22 Short cal., similar to Model 102/103 Olympic series, grooved front and back straps, 6¾ in. barrel with det. muzzle brake & wts. avail., brown plastic grips standard or walnut checkered grips optional.

	$1,150	$950	$695	$430	$330	$280	$240

The High Standard catalog number for this model was 9237-9299.

CONVERSION KITS MODEL 102/103/104 - Cat. # 9263 Olympic to Supermatic Citation, 6¾ Bbl., Cat. # 9264 Olympic to Supermatic Citation, 8 Bbl., Cat. # 9265 Olympic to Supermatic Citation, 10 Bbl., Cat. # 9283 Supermatic Citation to Olympic, 6¾ Bbl., Cat. # 9284 Supermatic Citation to Olympic, 8 Bbl., Cat. # 9285 Supermatic Citation to Olympic, 10 Bbl., Cat. # 9286 Supermatic Trophy to Olympic, 6¾ Bbl., Cat. # 9287 Supermatic Trophy to Olympic, 8 Bbl., Cat. # 9288 Supermatic Trophy to Olympic, 10 Bbl.

	$500	$450	$400	$325	$275	$225	$195

Add $250 for Trophy Conversions.
Add $125 for 8 in. barrel.
Add $225 for 10 in. barrel.

These conversion kits have the Trophy High Luster finish.

Pistols: High Standard did not have a Model 105 Series

Pistols: 106 Series, Military Models

This series was mfg. 1965-1968. This new military model featured a walnut checkered grip and a frame that has the exact heft and feel of the famous Military 45. This military model features a new slide and a new adj. rear bridge or saddle type sight, permanently fixed to the frame. Front and rear grip straps were stippled and a new design magazine had an extension foot. Removable stabilizer and wts. were available on all models. Beginning serial no. for 106 series was approx. 1,436,000 to 2,030,000.

SUPERMATIC TOURNAMENT MILITARY - .22 LR cal., bottom of the line target pistol, smooth front & back straps, slide mounted rear sight instead of bridge sight, 5½ in. bull or 6¾ in. straight barrel with military grips.

	$550	$425	$325	$250	$215	$180	$155

Add $50 for 9230-31.

The High Standard catalog no. 9230-31 was disc. early 1966 (supplied with extra mag). 9232-33 became available 1966.

SUPERMATIC CITATION MILITARY - .22 LR cal., middle of the line target pistol, stippled front & back straps, 5½ in. bull barrel or 7¼ in. fluted barrel, new rear bridge or saddle type sight.

	$595	$550	$450	$350	$270	$230	$195

Add $100 for 9240-41.

The High Standard catalog no. 9240-41 was disc. early 1966, (supplied with extra mag., muzzle brake, and weights). 9242-43 became available 1966.

SUPERMATIC TROPHY MILITARY - .22 LR cal., top-of-the-line target pistol, stippled front and back straps, 5½ bull or 7¼ in. fluted barrel avail., gold plated trigger, safety and magazine release, gold filled lettering.

	$925	$825	$575	$425	$325	$275	$235

Add $125 for 9245-46.

The High Standard catalog number for this model 9245-46 was disc. early 1966, (supplied with extra mag., muzzle brake, weights, wrench and cleaning tool). 9247-48 became available 1966.

Grading	100%	98%	95%	90%	80%	70%	60%

OLYMPIC MILITARY - .22 Short cal., target pistol, 5½ in. bull barrel, back & front straps, stippled alloy slide, bridge rear sight, military grips, supplied with extra mag. and weights. Disc. early 1966.

	$1,095	$895	$675	$425	$325	$275	$235

The High Standard catalog number for this model was 9235.

OLYMPIC ISU MILITARY - .22 Short cal., target pistol, 6¾ in. tapered barrel with integral stabilizer and wts., front and back straps stippled, rear bridge or saddle type sight, military grips, supplied with extra mag. and weights. Disc. 1966.

	$1,150	$950	$675	$425	$325	$275	$235

Add $75 for 9236.

The High Standard catalog number for this model was 9236. The Model 9238 became available 1966.

Pistols: Model 107 Series

The Military 107 Series was mfg. 1968-1972. However, 107 unmarked variations were mfg. 1973-75. ML prefix variations were mfg. 1975 - mid-1981 are also covered within this grouping. The 107 series is basically identical to the Military Model 106 Series. Serial no. range is approx. 2,030,000-2,300,000.

SUPERMATIC TOURNAMENT MILITARY - .22 LR cal., similar to Model 106 series, this was the last of the Tournament pistols, adj. sight replaced the bridge sight, 5½ bull or 6¾ in. tapered barrel. Disc. 1971.

	$525	$425	$325	$250	$195	$165	$135

The High Standard catalog number for this model was 9232-33.

SUPERMATIC CITATION MILITARY - .22 LR cal., similar to Model 106 series, middle of the line target pistol, 7¼ fluted and 5½ in. bull barrel available.

	$575	$500	$400	$325	$275	$220	$185

The High Standard catalog number for this model was 9242-43.

SUPERMATIC TROPHY MILITARY - .22 LR cal., similar to Model 106 series, top-of- the-line target pistol.

	$895	$750	$550	$400	$315	$250	$210

The High Standard catalog number for this model was 9247-48.

OLYMPIC ISU MILITARY - .22 Short cal., target pistol for Olympic Style Rapid Fire Events. 6¾ in. fluted barrel with integral stabilizer and two detachable weights.

	$1,100	$950	$775	$475	$375	$305	$255

The High Standard catalog number for this model was 9238.

THE VICTOR - .22 LR cal., introduced 1972, newest and most expensive production target pistol, all steel vented rib running length of barrel until 1974 when it changed to an alloy VR/SR, early adj. sight located on rear of barrel on rib., .22 long rifle built on a military frame, walnut grips, available in 4½ or 5½ in. barrel, push-button takedown, stippled front and rear straps, 10 shot mag., barrel slab sided, wts. are rectangular. Mfg. in Hamden, CT. Stamped "THE VICTOR" on left side of barrel.

	$825	$700	$575	$350	$275	$225	$195

Add $100 for 4½ in. barrel.

The High Standard catalog number for the vent. rib model was catalog number 9216-17.

Pistols: Numbered Series

In 1973, High Standard stopped marking the series numbers (either 104 or 107) on the guns. These guns just carry the normal seven digit serial number and are sometimes referred to as "NUMBERED SERIES", "UNNUMBERED SERIES", or "SEVEN-NUMBER SERIES". These pistols include the following - the Sport King, Sharpshooter, Supermatic Citation, Supermatic Trophy, The Victor, and the ISU Olympic (in both military and slant grip models). The serial number range for these guns is 2,330,000 to 2,500,000.

Grading	100%	98%	95%	90%	80%	70%	60%

PLINKER - .22 LR cal., introduced in 1970-73. Successor to Duramatic and identical in almost all aspects. Thumb screw takedown.

	$295	$225	$200	$160	$115	$100	$85

Early guns were marked M-101, R.H. slide 1970-71.
The High Standard catalog number for this model was 9214-15.

SPORT KING - .22 LR cal., similar to Series 102/103, 4½ or 6¾ in. barrel.

	$295	$250	$200	$165	$125	$100	$85

The High Standard catalog number for this Model was 9200-01.

SPORT KING (NICKEL PLATED) - .22 LR cal., this was a nickel plated Sport King with black slanted plastic grips with silver medallion insert on grip. Mfg. 1974-77.

	$475	$390	$280	$200	$155	$130	$110

The High Standard catalog number for this Model was 9208-09.

SHARPSHOOTER - .22 LR cal., successor to the Tournament, introduced in 1969 as part of the Model 103 Series, new model using the slant model grip frame, 5½ in. bull barrel only.

	$495	$425	$300	$250	$195	$165	$140

The High Standard catalog number for this Model was 9205.

SUPERMATIC CITATION - .22 LR cal., identical to 104 Series, 5½ in. bull barrel only.

	$625	$495	$425	$375	$290	$245	$210

The High Standard catalog number for this Model was 9244.

SUPERMATIC CITATION MILITARY - .22 LR cal., similar to 107 Series.

	$575	$495	$400	$325	$275	$220	$185

The High Standard catalog number for this Model was 9242-43.

SUPERMATIC TROPHY MILITARY - .22 LR cal., similar to 107 Series.

	$875	$725	$525	$375	$290	$245	$210

The High Standard catalog number for this Model was 9247-48.

ISU OLYMPIC - .22 LR cal., identical to 104 Series, 6¾ in. barrel.

	$1,150	$950	$650	$395	$325	$265	$225

The High Standard catalog number for this Model was 9237.

ISU OLYMPIC MILITARY - .22 Short cal., otherwise identical to 107 series.

	$1,150	$950	$650	$395	$325	$265	$225

The High Standard catalog number for this Model was 9238.

THE VICTOR (SLANT GRIP) - .22 LR cal., slant grip, mfg. 1973-74.

	$3,150	$2,575	$1,875	$1,350	$1,025	$850	$715

Add $75 for early steel rib.
Add $200 for solid rib.
Add $150 for 4½ in. barrel.
The High Standard catalog numbers for this model were: 4½ vent. rib, 9218 mfg. 1973-74. 5½ vent. rib, 9219 mfg. 1973-74. 4½ solid rib, 9226 mfg. 1974 only. 5½ solid rib, 9229 mfg. 1974 only.

THE VICTOR - .22 LR cal., similar to 107 series, Hamden mfg., military grips, in 1974, an aluminum vent. rib was used to lighten this variation, a solid rib was also available.

	$795	$625	$550	$315	$245	$200	$335

Add $150 for solid rib.
Add $75 for steel rib.
Add $100 for 4½ in. barrel.
The High Standard catalog number for the solid rib with military grips was 9206-11. The vent. rib model was catalog number 9216-17.

Pistols: G Prefix Series

Identical to 103/104 series (most models retained the same HS catalog no.) Due to the GCA of 1968, High Standard decided to serialize their rifles and shotguns beginning with ser. no. 3,000,000. In 1975, handgun serialization (pistols, revolvers, and derringers) was up to ser. no. 2,500,000 and

Grading	100%	98%	95%	90%	80%	70%	60%

High Standard felt they needed an alternate serial number system before handgun serialization reached 3,000,000. They decided to use the following prefixes - G for slant grip pistols, ML for military grip pistols, R for revolvers, and D for derringers. These prefixes were followed by the 5 digit ser. no. This is the last of the slant grip pistols.

SPORT KING - .22 LR cal., identical to 102/103 series, 4½ or 6¾ in. barrel. Disc. 1977.

	$295	$250	$200	$165	$125	$100	$85

The High Standard catalog numbers for this model were 9200-01.

SPORT KING (NICKEL PLATED) - .22 LR cal., identical to 102/103 series, nickel plated, 4½ or 6¾ in. barrel. Disc. 1977.

	$475	$395	$275	$200	$155	$130	$110

The High Standard catalog numbers for this model were 9208-09.

SHARPSHOOTER - .22 LR cal., identical to 103 series, 5½ in. bull barrel only. Disc. 1977.

	$495	$425	$300	$250	$195	$165	$140

The High Standard catalog number for this Model was 9205.

SUPERMATIC CITATION - .22 LR cal., identical to numbered series, 5½ in. bull barrel only. Disc. 1976.

	$625	$495	$425	$375	$295	$245	$210

The High Standard catalog number for this model was 9244.

OLYMPIC ISU - .22 LR cal., identical to numbered series, 6¾ in. tapered barrel. Disc. 1977.

	$1,150	$950	$650	$425	$315	$270	$230

The High Standard catalog no. for this Model was 9237.

Pistols: ML Prefix Series

As mentioned in the G Prefix section, High Standard revised their serial numbering system in 1975 from a 7 digit serial number to a five digit serial number with an ML prefix. These guns are basically identical to the guns listed in the 107 series category, but are listed here for chronological and value reasons. Mfg. mid-1975 through 1981. Guns with serial numbers between ML1,000 and ML24,999 were manufactured in Hamden, CT. Guns with serial numbers between ML25,000 and ML87,000 were manufactured in East Hartford, CT.

SPORT KING - .22 LR cal., similar to previous Sport Kings, but they now use military grips. Some of these Sport Kings were labeled "SPORT KING-M". Mfg. 1977-1981 in East Hartford only.

	$295	$250	$195	$135	$105	$85	$70

The High Standard catalog number for this model was 9258-59.

SHARPSHOOTER - .22 LR cal., some of the Sharpshooters with military grips were labeled "SHARPSHOOTER-M". Mfg. 1979-1981 in East Hartford only.

	$450	$365	$275	$200	$155	$125	$105

The High Standard catalog number for this model was 9210.

✻ **Sharpshooter Survival Pack** - introduced 1981, includes Sharpshooter-M pistol, electroless nickel, push-button take down, packaged in canvas carrying case with extra nickel magazine, 5½ in. bull barrel.

	$595	$495	$415	$300	$230	$195	$165

The High Standard catalog number for this model was 9424.

SUPERMATIC CITATION MILITARY - .22 LR cal., similar to previous model.

	$525	$425	$350	$275	$215	$165	$140

Subtract 10% for East Hartford model.

The High Standard catalog number for this model was 9242-43.

SUPERMATIC TROPHY MILITARY - .22 LR cal., similar to previous series.

	$750	$625	$475	$340	$265	$215	$180

Subtract 10% for East Hartford model.

The High Standard catalog number for this model was 9247-48.

Grading	100%	98%	95%	90%	80%	70%	60%

SUPERMATIC ISU OLYMPIC MILITARY - .22 Short cal., target pistol, similar to previous model. Disc. 1981.

	$925	$750	$575	$425	$325	$260	$220

Subtract 10% for East Hartford model.
The High Standard catalog number for this model was 9238 (disc. 1977).

THE VICTOR - .22 LR cal., similar to previous model, military grip, vent. or solid rib. Last solid rib mfg. in 1977. Later Victors in this series were stamped simply "VICTOR" above trigger guard.

	$635	$525	$450	$275	$220	$180	$150

Add $150 for solid rib models.
Add $100 for 4½ in. barrel length.
Subtract 10% for East Hartford models.
The High Standard catalog number for this model was 9216-17, catalog number for the solid rib model was 9206-9211 (disc. 1977).

10X - .22 LR cal., specifically designed for top flight shooting, 5½ in. bull barrel, push-button takedown. This model used hand-picked parts and was precisely assembled by a High Standard Master Gunsmith (with his initials under the left grip of each gun). Black matte finish, black painted walnut grips, stippled front and back straps. Mfg. 1980 in East Hartford.

❋ *Push Button Barrel Release*

	$2,350	$2,000	$1,625	$1,195	$925	$715	$595

The High Standard catalog number for this model was 9372.

Pistols: SH Series

This was the last series of High Standard pistols and can be differentiated from the 107/Unnumbered/ML series by the mechanical differences within the frame assembly. Mfg. from mid 1981-1984. Serial No. range was approx. 10,000-35,000 and is prefixed "SH". Features a new barrel release in place of the push button takedown. An allenhead screw attached the frame to the barrel. A few guns were mfg. with push-button takedown from parts left over from the previous series. Also, some guns in this series have a "V" suffix.

SPORT KING - .22 LR cal., similar to ML series, except has allen screw take down, 4½ or 6¾ in. barrel.

	$250	$195	$175	$125	$95	$75	$65

The High Standard catalog number for this model was 9258-59 (disc. 1983).

SPORT KING (SH PREFIX) - .22 LR cal., SH prefix serial no. with allen screw takedown, military grips with new electroless nickel model available. Mfg. 1982-84.

	$325	$275	$225	$145	$115	$95	$80

This model was also called the "SPORT KING-M".
The High Standard catalog number for this model was 9450-51.

SHARPSHOOTER - .22 LR cal., SH prefix serial no. with allen screw takedown, military grips. Mfg. 1982.

	$375	$300	$235	$170	$135	$110	$95

This model was also sometimes called "SHARPSHOOTER-M".
The High Standard catalog number for this model was 9210 (disc. 1982).

SUPERMATIC CITATION MILITARY - .22 LR cal., SH prefix, similar to previous Citation model with allen screw takedown, military grips. Disc. May 1982.

	$495	$395	$325	$225	$175	$140	$120

The High Standard catalog number for this model was 9242-43.

Grading	100%	98%	95%	90%	80%	70%	60%

CITATION II - .22 LR cal., 10 shot, new variation of the Supermatic Citation, 5½ and 7¼ in. barrels, checkered military-type wood grips, allen screw takedown, SH prefix serial no., slab sided barrel, electroless nickel model also available, this model replaced the Sharpshooter. Mfg. 1983-84.

	$475	$400	$325	$265	$205	$165	$140

The High Standard catalog number for this model was 9348-49.

SUPERMATIC TROPHY MILITARY - .22 LR cal., similar to previous Trophy Model with SH prefix, allen screw takedown, military grips.

	$650	$535	$395	$295	$225	$175	$150

The High Standard catalog number for this model was 9247-48.

VICTOR - .22 LR cal., similar to previous Victor, new allen screw takedown, SH prefix, military grips, 5½ in. vent. barrel only mfg. in this Victor Series, some Victor ser. numbers had a "V" suffix.

	$550	$450	$350	$250	$195	$155	$130

The High Standard catalog number for this model was 9217.

10X - .22 LR cal., high quality gun similar to previous 10X, but with allen screw takedown, a High Standard 10X Victor was also offered. These had a 5½ in. vented Victor rib; only a few were mfg., limited mfg. also in 7¼ in. fluted barrel.

* **Allen Screw Barrel Release**

	$2,000	$1,750	$1,425	$995	$795	$675	$575

Add $1,250 for Victor VR model.
Add $1,000 for fluted barrel.
The High Standard catalog number for this model was 9234-9249-9372.

SURVIVAL PACK - .22 LR cal., Sharpshooter "M" or Citation II electroless nickel, allen screw takedown, packaged in canvas carrying case with extra nickel magazine. Disc. 1984.

	$575	$475	$395	$275	$215	$185	$160

The High Standard catalog number for this model was 9424.

Pistols: Commemorative Models

1972 OLYMPIC COMMEMORATIVE - .22 LR cal., a highly engraved version of a Supermatic Trophy Military, Model 107, has 5 Olympic gold rings on right side of receiver, Ser. no. has a "T" prefix, high polish blue finish, 5½ in. bull barrel, lined presentation case avail. Limited edition of 1,000 guns, but it is believed only about 175-200 of these pistols were manufactured due to their high price, issue price was $550. Mfg. 1972-1974 only.

	$6,000	$4,000	$2,000

1974 retail on this model was $605. Early models were marked "MODEL 107", and were not hi-polished.
The High Standard catalog number for this model was 9207.

1980 OLYMPIC COMMEMORATIVE - .22 Short, an ISU Olympic Military with 6¾ in. tapered barrel with integral stabilizer and weights. Has 5 Olympic gold rings on right side of receiver. Produced in a limited edition of 1,000 guns. Ser. no. has a "USA" prefix, blue finish, lined presentation case avail. Mfg. 1980 only.

	$1,395	$900	$700

The High Standard catalog number for this model was 9239.

Pistols: Conversion Kits

These kits for conversion of .22 LR to .22 Short contained an alloy slide with vent. rib, barrel weight, and two Short mags., kit comes in "gun size box" set in styrofoam. These kits were designated either #9370 or #9371 when mfg., depending on the pistol to be converted.

VICTOR KIT - this model was designated #9370 when in mfg.

	$550	$450	$350

Grading	100%	98%	95%	90%	80%	70%	60%

TROPHY/CITATION KIT - this kit also includes a stabilizer. This model was designated #9371 when in mfg.

	$550	$450	$350				

REVOLVERS

Add 20% for extra convertible cylinder (.22 LR/.22 Mag.) on those models listed that apply.

Revolvers: Police Style

SENTINEL - .22 LR cal., 9 shot, swing out cylinder, 3, 4, or 6 in. barrel, aluminum frame, various Dura-tone colors, made 1955-1956.

	100%	98%	95%	90%	80%	70%	60%
Blue finish	$120	$110	$100	$95	$85	$70	$55
Blue/Green finish	$135	$120	$100	$95	$85	$70	$55
Nickel finish	$150	$135	$115	$105	$95	$85	$65
Pink finish	$325	$290	$250	$200	$180	$160	$140
Gold finish	$310	$280	$250	$200	$180	$160	$140

SENTINEL IMPERIAL - similar to Sentinel, with adj. sights, walnut grips, made 1962- 1965.

Blue finish	$140	$125	$115	$110	$100	$90	$75
Nickel finish	$150	$140	$125	$120	$110	$100	$90

SENTINEL DELUXE - similar to Sentinel, except adj. sights, wide trigger, 4 and 6 in. barrel, square butt, 24 or 26 oz. Mfg. 1965-1974.

Blue finish	$140	$125	$115	$110	$100	$90	$75
Nickel finish	$165	$150	$130	$120	$110	$100	$90

SENTINEL SNUB - similar to Deluxe, except checkered bird's-head grip, choice of blue, nickel, gold, turquoise, or pink Dura-tone color, 2 3/8 in. barrel, mahogany finished case with colors, 20 oz.

Blue finish	$145	$140	$130	$120	$110	$90	$85
Nickel finish	$155	$150	$145	$130	$120	$100	$95
Pink or Turquoise finish	$325	$290	$250	$200	$180	$160	$140
Gold finish	$310	$280	$250	$200	$180	$160	$140

KIT GUN - .22 LR cal., swing out cylinder, 9 shot, 4 in. barrel, adj. sights, blue, walnut grips, made 1970-1973.

	$195	$170	$150	$125	$115	$105	$85

CAMP GUN DOUBLE ACTION - .22 LR or .22 Win. Mag. cal., 6 in. barrel, blue, adj. rear sight, checkered walnut grips, made 1976-1984.

	$250	$185	$165	$145	$125	$110	$100

SENTINEL MARK I DOUBLE ACTION - .22 LR cal., 2, 3, and 4 in. barrel, 9 shot, smooth walnut grips, made 1974-1984.

Blue finish	$235	$180	$160	$140	$120	$105	$90
Nickel finish	$275	$250	$195	$150	$130	$110	$95

Add $15 for blue finish w/adj. sights.

SENTINEL MARK IV DOUBLE ACTION - similar to Sentinel 1, except .22 WRM cal.

Blue finish	$275	$240	$200	$175	$150	$125	$100
Nickel finish	$300	$260	$220	$195	$170	$145	$110

Add $25 for adj. sights.

SENTINEL POWER PLUS - .38 Spl. cal., 5 shot, swing out cylinder, 3 in. barrel, based on Sentinel Mark IV, approx. 300 mfg. 1981.

	$350	$300	$250	$200	$175	$150	$125

SENTINEL MARK II DOUBLE ACTION - .357 Mag. cal., 6 shot, double action, 2½, 4, and 6 in. barrel, blue, fixed sights, wood grips, made 1974-1976 by Dan Wesson.

	$275	$250	$200	$175	$150	$140	$130

H

Grading	100%	98%	95%	90%	80%	70%	60%

SENTINEL MARK III DOUBLE ACTION - similar to Mark II, except adj. sights, mfg. by Dan Wesson.

	$300	$270	$225	$200	$170	$160	$150

CRUSADER - .357 Mag., .44 Mag. or .45 LC cal., double action employing gear assembly, swing out cylinder, unique action, adj. sights, limited mfg. starting 1976 because of expensive fabrication.

> Only a few prototypes of this model exist. No regular Crusaders were ever made - only serial numbers 0-500 of the 50th Anniversary Model.

Revolvers: Western Style

DURANGO - .22 LR cal., double action, alloy frame, 4½ and 5½ in. barrel, wood grips, mfg 1971-1973.

	100%	98%	95%	90%	80%	70%	60%
Blue finish	$175	$150	$125	$100	$85	$70	$55
Nickel finish	$190	$160	$140	$110	$95	$85	$65

HOMBRE DOUBLE ACTION - similar to Double Nine alloy frame, but no ejector rod housing, 4½ in. barrel, mfg. 1971-1973.

	100%	98%	95%	90%	80%	70%	60%
Blue finish	$170	$140	$120	$105	$95	$85	$65
Nickel finish	$180	$150	$130	$115	$105	$95	$75

LONGHORN - .22 LR or .22 WRM cal., Western style double action, 4½, 5½, or 9½ in. barrel, 9 shot swing out cylinder, fixed sights except for one model.

* *1958-1970 Mfg.* - .22 LR cal. only, aluminum frame, simulated stag, ebony, or ivory grips.

	$250	$225	$180	$150	$110	$90	$80

* *1971-1984 Mfg.* - steel frame, 9½ in. barrel only, walnut grips.

	$375	$295	$235	$190	$150	$125	$100

> Add $50 for adj. front sight.

DOUBLE NINE - .22 LR or .22 WRM cal., Western style double action, 5½ in. barrel, 9 shot swing out cylinder.

* *1958-1970 Mfg.* - .22 LR cal. only, aluminum frame, simulated stag, ebony, or ivory grips.

	100%	98%	95%	90%	80%	70%	60%
Blue finish	$190	$170	$150	$125	$100	$80	$70
Nickel finish	$200	$180	$160	$125	$100	$80	$70

* *1971-1984 Mfg.* - steel frame, walnut grips.

	100%	98%	95%	90%	80%	70%	60%
Blue finish	$250	$200	$175	$150	$125	$100	$90
Nickel finish	$275	$225	$200	$150	$125	$100	$90

HIGH SIERRA - similar to Double Nine steel frame, except 7 in. octagon barrel, gold plated grip frame. Mfg. 1973-1984.

Fixed sights	$350	$300	$275	$225	$200	$175	$125

> Add $10 for adj. sights.

POSSE - similar to Double Nine aluminum, except 3½ in. barrel, blue, brass grip frame, walnut grips, made 1961-1966.

	$170	$150	$120	$100	$90	$80	$70

NATCHEZ - similar to Double Nine aluminum, except has bird's-head grip, made 1961-1966.

	$250	$200	$175	$150	$125	$100	$80

MARSHAL - .22 LR cal., similar to Double-Nine, alloy frame w/o ejector housing, 5½ in. barrel, stag grips, included leather holster. Mfg. 1971-1973.

	$220	$180	$160	$135	$110	$90	$80

> Subtract $35 if w/o holster.

Grading	100%	98%	95%	90%	80%	70%	60%

RIFLES

SPORT KING FIELD MODEL - .22 S (Hi-Speed), .22 L, .22 LR cal., semi-auto, tube mag., 22 in. barrel, open sight, plain pistol grip stock, made 1960-1966.

	$100	$90	$85	$75	$65	$55	$45

SPORT KING SPECIAL - similar to Field, except beavertail forearm and Monte Carlo stock.

	$180	$140	$95	$90	$75	$65	$55

SPORT KING CARBINE - similar to Field, except 18 in. barrel, straight grip, barrel band and sling, made 1964-1973.

	$200	$160	$120	$110	$100	$90	$85

SPORT KING DELUXE - similar to Special, but stock checkered, made 1966-1975.

	$225	$175	$140	$115	$90	$75	$65

HI-POWER FIELD BOLT ACTION - .270 Win. or .30-06 cal., Mauser type action, 4 shot mag., 22 in. barrel, folding rear sight, plain stock, made 1962-1966.

	$400	$300	$210	$195	$180	$165	$150

HI-POWER DELUXE - similar to Field, except checkered Monte Carlo stock, swivels, made 1962-1966.

	$475	$350	$300	$220	$205	$195	$165

FLITE KING SLIDE ACTION - .22 S, L, or LR cal., 24 in. barrel, tube mag., hammerless, Patridge sight, Monte Carlo stock with pistol grip, semi beavertail forearm, made 1974- 1975.

	$210	$160	$110	$85	$65	$60	$50

SHOTGUNS: O/U

SUPERMATIC INDY - 12 ga., this model was mfg. in Japan by Nikko and imported in 1974 and 1975, boxlock, fully engraved receiver, selective auto ejectors and single trigger, 27½ sk & sk, 29½ imp. mod. and full, or full and full, trap variation allows air flow with aluminum vent. rib, checkered (skipline) pistol grip stock with pad and vent. forearm.

	$925	$830	$760	$700	$645	$590	$530

SUPERMATIC SHADOW SEVEN - similar to Indy O/U, except less elaborate engraving, unvented forearm, standard vent. rib, regular checkering, no recoil pad, imported 1974-1975.

	$760	$685	$615	$540	$490	$440	$400

SHOTGUNS: SEMI-AUTO

SUPERMATIC FIELD GRADE - 12 ga., 28 and 30 in. barrel, mod. or full, gas operated semi-auto, plain pistol grip stock, made 1960-1966.

	$205	$185	$175	$160	$145	$140	$120

SUPERMATIC SPECIAL - 12 ga., similar to Field, 27 in. barrel, adj. choke, made 1960- 1966.

	$210	$195	$180	$165	$150	$145	$125

SUPERMATIC DELUXE - similar to Field, except vent. rib, checkered stock and forearm, made 1961-1966.

	$265	$225	$200	$175	$160	$155	$140

SUPERMATIC TROPHY - similar to Deluxe, except 27 in. barrel, adj. choke.

	$235	$215	$205	$180	$165	$160	$145

SUPERMATIC DUCK - similar to Field, except 3 in. Mag., 30 in. full barrel, recoil pad, made 1961-1966.

	$275	$235	$190	$160	$145	$125	$110

Grading	100%	98%	95%	90%	80%	70%	60%

SUPERMATIC DUCK VENT RIB - similar to Duck, vent. rib, checkered stock and forearm, made 1961-1966.

	$295	$250	$210	$175	$150	$130	$115

SUPERMATIC DEER GUN - similar to Field, except 22 in. cylinder bore barrel, rifle sights, checkered stock and forearm, recoil pad, made 1965.

	$230	$210	$200	$185	$165	$155	$140

SUPERMATIC SKEET - similar to Deluxe Rib, except 26 in. barrel, skeet bore, made 1962- 1966.

	$300	$260	$225	$195	$175	$160	$150

SUPERMATIC TRAP - similar to Skeet, except 30 in. full barrel, trap stock with pad, made 1962-1966.

	$245	$230	$220	$205	$185	$170	$160

Note: All preceding models, except Deer and Trap, were also chambered for 20 ga., 3 in. Mag. Values are approx. $20 higher.

High Standard restyled the Supermatic Autoloader in 1966. The new model Supermatics are recognized by the new checkering pattern and jeweled bolt. All models previously listed were offered, 12 and 20 ga. values are $25 higher per model. All are considered deluxe models. They were discontinued in 1975.

MODEL 10A/10B - 12 ga. combat shotgun, 18 in. barrel, semi-auto, unique design incorporates raked pistol grip in front of receiver and metal shoulder pad attached directly to rear of receiver, black cycolac plastic shroud and pistol grip, folding carrying handle, provisions made for attaching a Kel-lite flashlight to receiver top, extended blade front sight, very compact size (28 in. overall). Disc.

	$925	$825	$700	$550	$450	$375	$325

Subtract 15% for Model 10B w/o flashlight.
The Model 10A had the Kel-lite flashlight built in.

RIOT SHOTGUN - 18 or 20 in. barrel, police riot gun, available with or without rifle sights, 12 ga. only on the Flite/Sport King Action. Disc. 1975.

	$195	$165	$155	$140	$130	$120	$115

SUPERMATIC SHADOW - 12 and 20 ga., 2¾ or 3 in. chambers in 12 ga., air flow rib, 26 in. imp. cyl. or skeet, 28 in. mod., imp. mod. or full and 30 in. full or trap, checkered walnut stock, gas operated, imported 1974-1975.

	$390	$340	$290	$260	$225	$195	$165

SHOTGUNS: SLIDE ACTION

MODEL 322P - similar to Flite King/Sport King Field, except was mfg. 1956-1960.

	$165	$150	$140	$130	$120	$110	$100

FLITE KING/SPORT KING PUMP FIELD GRADE - 12, 20, 28 ga., or .410 bore, slide action, 26, 28, or 30 in. barrel, imp. cyl., mod., or full choke, plain pistol grip stock and slide, mfg. 1960-1973.

	$165	$150	$140	$130	$120	$110	$100

This model was designated the Flite King Pump 1960-63, then changed to Sport King Pump 1964-1973.

FLITE/SPORT KING PUMP SPECIAL - 12, 20, 28 ga., or .410 bore, similar to Pump Field, except 27 in. barrel, adj. choke, made 1960-1966.

	$155	$130	$120	$110	$100	$90	$80

FLITE/SPORT KING PUMP DELUXE - 12, 20, 28 ga., or .410 bore, similar to Pump Special, except vent. rib, checkered stock, made 1961-1966.

	$195	$175	$170	$165	$155	$140	$125

FLITE/SPORT KING PUMP TROPHY - 12, 20, 28 ga., or .410 bore, similar to Deluxe Rib, except 27 in. vent. rib barrel, adj. choke, made 1960-1966.

	$200	$180	$175	$170	$160	$145	$130

Grading	100%	98%	95%	90%	80%	70%	60%

FLITE/SPORT KING PUMP BRUSH - 12 ga. only, similar to Field, except 18 or 20 in. cylinder bore barrel, rifle sights, made 1962-1964.

	$185	$170	$165	$160	$150	$140	$120

FLITE/SPORT KING PUMP BRUSH DELUXE - 12 ga. only, similar to Brush, except adj. aperture rear sight, checkered stock, recoil pad, swivels and sling, 20 in. barrel only, made 1964-1966.

	$265	$230	$195	$170	$155	$145	$130

FLITE/SPORT KING PUMP SKEET - 12, 20, 28 ga., or .410 bore only, similar to Deluxe Rib, except 26 in. vent. rib, skeet bore, made 1962-1966.

	$265	$230	$195	$170	$155	$145	$130

Add 35% for 28 ga. or .410 bore.

FLITE/SPORT KING PUMP TRAP - 12 ga. only, similar to Deluxe, except 30 in. vent. rib, full choke and pad, made 1962-1966.

	$250	$220	$195	$165	$150	$140	$125

Note: Flite King was available in 16 ga. also, except for the Brush, Skeet, and Trap models. Values are about $20 less per model. A .410 bore was offered in all models that were offered in 20 ga., except the Special and Trophy models. Values are generally the same per model.
High Standard restyled the Flite King in 1966. The new models have a jeweled bolt and new checkering pattern. These new guns were available as Deluxe, Deluxe Rib, Brush, Brush Deluxe, Skeet Deluxe, and Trap Deluxe. Their values are about $20 higher per model.
The new redesigned Flite King was also offered in Deluxe, Deluxe Rib, and Deluxe Skeet, in 20, 28 ga., and .410 bore.

HIGH STANDARD MANUFACTURING CO.

High Standard is a current trademark of firearms manufactured by High Standard Manufacturing Co., F.I. Inc. - Dept. HS, established in 1993 and located in Houston, TX.

This company was formed during 1993, utilizing many of the same employees and original material vendors that the original High Standard company used during their period of manufacture (1926-1984). Currently, some variations within the expanded High Standard commercial model lineup might be hard to get, since the company is in the process of fulfilling military contracts.

PISTOLS: SEMI-AUTO, RIMFIRE

SPORT KING - .22 LR cal., 4½ or 6¾ in. barrel, blue finish, military grips, 10 shot mag.
While advertised during 1996, this model was produced in very limited quantites.

SUPERMATIC CITATION - .22 LR cal., 5½ or 7¼ (disc. 1995) in. barrel, matte blue (disc. 1996) or parkerized finish, military grips, open sights (disc. 2001) or univeral scope base, 9 shot mag., 44 oz. New 1994.

MSR	$490		$415	$325	$260	$225	$200	$185	$170

Add $317 for .22 Short conversion kit (includes barrel, slide, and 2 mags.).

SUPERMATIC CITATION MS - .22 LR cal., features 10 in. barrel, mounting bracket with scope base, designed for the Metallic Silhouette shooter, 54 oz. New 1997.

MSR	$696		$625	$550	$475	$400	$350	$300	$265

Add approx. $119 for RPM sights (scope base only).

SUPERMATIC CITATION 10X - .22 LR cal., 5½ in. barrel, blue finish, military grips, High Standard's most accurate pistol, choice of either factory or Shea custom tuning, 10 shot mag., approx. 45 oz., custom shop only. New 1994.

* *Factory Tuned 10X*

MSR	$925		$795	$650	$575	$475	$425	$350	$300

* *Custom Shea 10X* - limited mfg. (approx. 150 pistols annually), hand-built by Bob Shea. New 1995.

MSR	$1,160		$995	$850	$750	$650	$550	$450	$375

H

Grading	100%	98%	95%	90%	80%	70%	60%

SUPERMATIC TOURNAMENT - .22 LR cal., choice of 4½ (disc. 1995), 5½, or 6¾ (disc. 1995) in. barrel, matte blue, non-adj. trigger, approx. 44 oz. Mfg. 1995-97.

	$400	$315	$255	$225	$200	$185	$170

Last MSR was $468.

SUPERMATIC TROPHY - .22 LR cal., 5½ or 7¼ in. barrel, blue finish, scope base became standard on 5½ in. barrel in 2000, 2002 for 7¼ in. barrel, with or w/o iron sights, military grips, 10 shot mag., 44 or 46 oz. New 1994.

MSR	$540	$475	$395	$315	$260	$220	$200	$185

Add $63 for iron sights.
Add $85 for 7¼ in. barrel.
Add $317 for .22 Short conversion kit (includes barrel, slide, and 2 mags.).

VICTOR - .22 LR cal., 4½ or 5½ in. barrel, blue or parkerized (new 1995, 5½ in. barrel only) finish, military grips, with open sight rib or universal mount (HSUM, blue only, new 1996), 10 shot mag., approx. 45 oz., custom shop only. New 1994.

MSR	$564	$495	$400	$325	$265	$225	$200	$185

Add $61 for open sights (5½ in. barrel only).
Add $317 for .22 Short conversion kit (includes VR barrel, slide, and 2 mags.).

✳ ***Victor 10X*** - factory tuned and individually tested, includes test target signed by the gunsmith, 46 oz. New 1997.

MSR	$1,027	$925	$725	$625	$525	$425	$375	$325

✳ ***Victor 10X Shea*** - parkerized finish, 5½ in. barrel only, 150 built by Bob Shea annually, 46 oz. New 1996.

MSR	$1,265	$1,150	$950	$825	$750	$625	$550	$475

HSCA LIMITED EDITIONS - during 1996, High Standard offered several HSCA limited editions. They included the Victor (fully engraved, 6 mfg., $1,862 MSR), the Tournament (non-engraved, 26 mfg., $608 MSR), and the engraved Tournament (50% engraved, 6 mfg. $1,062 MSR). Additionally, only 5 sets were mfg. with 4 guns included – the Olympic 8 in. Space Gun, Tournament, Flite King, and Victor. Retail was $3,200 (non-engraved) or $7,200 (engraved). A 3 gun set was also available (w/o Olympic) for $2,150 (non-engraved) or $5,150 (engraved).

Extreme rarity of these guns precludes accurate pricing.

OLYMPIC I.S.U. - .22 Short cal., 6¾ in. fluted barrel with integral muzzle brake, blue finish, military grips, 10 shot mag. Mfg. 1994-95 only.

	$550	$450	$385	$315	$250	$200	$185

Last MSR was $625.

OLYMPIC MILITARY - .22 Short cal., 5½ in. fluted bull barrel with removable stabilizer, aluminum alloy slide with steel frame, scope base or open sights. New 1995.

MSR	$564	$495	$400	$325	$265	$225	$200	$185

Add $61 for open sights.

OLYMPIC RAPID FIRE - .22 Short cal., 4 in. VR barrel with integral muzzle brake and forward mounted compensator, gold-plated small parts, matte finish, special grips with rear support, adj. trigger, 46 oz., custom shop only. New 1996.

MSR	$1,027	$925	$725	$625	$525	$425	$375	$325

HIGH TECH CUSTOM RIFLES

Current manufacturer of bolt action rifles located in Colorado Springs, CO. Consumer direct sales.

High Tech Custom Rifles currently manufactures a complete line of custom built, high quality bolt action rifles, including the Shadow, Shadow II, Falcon Series, Varmint Hunter, and Mountain Hunter. They also manufacture and install their own proprietary muzzle brake (60%-80% noise reduction). For current model availability, features, special orders, and pricing information (including a custom quotation and delivery time), please contact the factory directly (see Trademark Index).

Grading	100%	98%	95%	90%	80%	70%	60%

HILL COUNTRY RIFLE COMPANY

Current manufacturer of bolt action rifles located in New Braunfels, TX. Consumer direct sales.

Hill Country Rifles currently manufactures a complete line of custom built, high quality bolt action rifles, including the Custom Hunter, Custom Sheep, Custom Varmint, and American Classic. Hill Country Rifles also accurizes rifles and performs complete gunsmithing services. For current model availability, features, special orders, and pricing information (including a custom quotation and delivery time), please contact the factory directly (see Trademark Index).

HISPANO ARGENTINO FABRICA DE AUTOMOVILES SA (HAFDASA)

Previous car manufacturer located in Buenos Aires, Argentina.

This company accepted and sold both commercial and military pistols manufactured by Ballester-Rigaud initially, followed by Ballester-Molina.

PISTOLS: SEMI-AUTO

BALLESTER-MOLINA/RIGAUD - .45 ACP or .22 LR cal., 5 in. barrel, patterned after the Colt M-1911A1 except has pinned trigger, is without grip safety, has different sear mechanism, and distinctive pattern retracting grooves in slide. Circa 1930-mid 1940s. Probably an unauthorized copy at the time.

$500	$400	$360	$330	$300	$275	$225

Add 100% for .22 LR.

GEORGE HOENIG, INC.

Current custom rifle builder located in Boise, ID.

George Hoenig builds a unique rotary round action O/U rifle, shotgun, or combination gun. Opening is achieved by rotating barrels right quarter turn to the right, then sliding barrel assembly forward. Because of this, there is no top opening lever. Prices for a 28 ga. game gun start at $20,000 (approx. 6 lbs., 12 month delivery time), while the double rifle and combination guns have a base price of $25,000. For more information, delivery time, and current pricing, please contact George Hoenig directly (see Trademark Index).

HOFER-JAGDWAFFEN, PETER

Current master gunsmith located in Ferlach, Austria. Custom order only, best quality rifles (most configurations) and shotguns (O/U and SxS) made per individual order - prices usually start in the $20,000 range, and can go up to over $600,000! Information (including an individualized quotation) can be obtained by contacting Mr. Hofer directly (see Trademark Index).

P.L. HOLEHAN, INC.

Current custom rifle manufacturer located in Tucson, AZ. Consumer direct sales.

P.L. Holehan, Inc. is a custom rifle maker fabricating best quality bolt action rifles only. The company is also known for its integral return to zero scope mounting system. All guns are essentially built per individual custom order and the company should be contacted directly for more information, including special order options/features.

RIFLES: BOLT ACTION

SAFARI HUNTER - various Safari cals., features Win. M-70 controlled feed claw extractor, double square bridge action, premium grade barrel, satin blue metal finish, choice of fiberglass or oil finished English walnut stock with ebony forend tip, Pachmayr decelerator pad, hinged floor plate, 9½ lbs.

MSR	$6,025		$6,025	$5,225	$4,275	$3,600	$3,150	$2,650	$2,100

Subtract $750 for fiberglass stock.

Grading	100%	98%	95%	90%	80%	70%	60%

AFRICAN HUNTER - various Safari cals., similar to Safari Hunter, except features Dakota Magnum action. New 2002.

	MSR	$7,950	$7,950	$6,950	$5,500	$4,500	$3,750	$3,350	$2,750

CLASSIC HUNTER - similar to Safari Hunter, except available in most popular non- Safari cals., hinged floor plate, standard or blind box mag., 7½ - 8 lbs.

	MSR	$4,950	$4,950	$4,200	$3,650	$3,075	$2,500	$2,000	$1,600

Add $300 for standard box mag.
Subtract $700 for fiberglass stock.

LONG RANGE HUNTER - various cals., action similar to Classic Hunter, except has 26 in. fluted barrel, satin blue or matte Teflon metal finish, 8¾ lbs.

	MSR	$5,025	$5,025	$4,350	$3,700	$3,150	$2,550	$2,000	$1,650

Subtract $500 for fiberglass stock.

LIGHTWEIGHT CLASSIC HUNTER - various cals., features short action, Win. M-70 controlled feed claw extractor, lightweight 22 in. barrel, standard or blind box mag., 6½ - 7 lbs.

	MSR	$4,850	$4,850	$4,125	$3,600	$3,050	$2,500	$2,000	$1,600

Subtract $700 for fiberglass stock.
Add $300 for standard box mag.

ALPINE HUNTER - various cals., Win. M-70 short or standard length action with controlled feeding, blind box mag., fiberglass or Kevlar stock, approx. 6 – 6¾ lbs. New 2000.

	MSR	$3,300	$3,300	$2,900	$2,600	$2,200	$1,800	$1,500	$1,250

HOLLAND & HOLLAND LTD.

Current manufacturer established in 1835 and located in London, England since 1835. All H&H long guns are built per individual special order. Orders may be placed directly with their office located in New York, NY or directly with the factory in England. Please refer to these listings in the Trademark Index for address, telephone, or fax information.

HOLLAND & HOLLAND
Established 1835

> Holland & Holland over the years has justly earned the reputation of producing some of the finest firearms ever manufactured. Their double rifles chambered for the black powder express cartridges are still among the most powerful rifles ever made, while exhibiting outstanding quality and superior craftsmanship. Most of these fine arms were made to order for the famous, wealthy, or royalty of their day. Because of the individual nature of each firearm, these early guns, as with any high grade item, must be individually appraised.
>
> The early double rifles were proofed and regulated with the black powder ammunition of their day. These exposed hammer rifles were almost exclusively sold cased with accessories by Holland & Holland. They are seldom found on the market, and then not in the best of condition. Purchase of these as well as any high grade firearm should include trusted appraisal.

RIFLES: MODERN

As this edition went to press, 2002 retail prices had yet to be formally established, and the following MSRs have been approximated per the company's request.

ROOK RIFLE - .250, .295/.300, .360, .380 black powder cals., single shot, break-open action, various levels of embellishment - Royal Models were made but most Rook rifles were base models with few extra features. Values today range from $600 (average condition, small cal.) to $2,500 (larger cal., engraving, better wood, perhaps cased). Disc.

BEST QUALITY MAGAZINE RIFLE - Mauser 98 (current mfg.) or Enfield (disc.) action, various cals., incl. .300 H&H, .375 H&H, built per individual customer specifications, checkered French walnut stock available in traditional configuration or with Monte Carlo pattern.

	MSR	$27,000	$27,000	$18,550	$15,750	$11,750	$9,000	$7,750	$6,500

Subtract 25% for Enfield action.
Add $2,200 for full length carbine stock.

Grading	100%	98%	95%	90%	80%	70%	60%

Add $2,500+ for deluxe grade walnut.

The values listed represent the standard model without additional options or engraving (of which there are a wide array).

DE LUXE MAGAZINE RIFLE - similar to Best Quality, except with deluxe grade walnut and various engraving options, very limited mfg.

There is no standard base price on this model - rather, individual options are custom ordered and are individually priced.

DOMINION GRADE NO. 2 MODEL DOUBLE RIFLE SxS - various British and American cals., 24-28 in. barrels, sidelock, folding leaf sight, checkered French walnut stock, auto ejectors.

	100%	98%	95%	90%	80%	70%	60%
	$15,000	$13,000	$11,000	$10,000	$9,000	$7,000	$6,500

ROYAL DOUBLE SxS RIFLE - OLDER MFG. - similar to No. 2, except has deluxe finish and more engraving.

	100%	98%	95%	90%	80%	70%	60%
.300 H&H cal. or less	$40,000	$35,000	$30,000	$25,000	$22,000	$19,500	$17,500
Up to .375 H&H cal.	$45,000	$40,000	$35,000	$30,000	$25,000	$22,000	$19,500
Up to .470 NE cal.	$55,000	$50,000	$45,000	$40,000	$35,000	$30,000	$26,000
Up to .600 NE cal.	$60,000	$55,000	$50,000	$45,000	$40,000	$35,000	$30,000

Subtract 15% if w/o ejectors.

Subtract 20% if w/o reinforced action.

ROYAL DE LUXE SxS RIFLE - LATEST PRODUCTION - same cals. as the Royal Double SxS, top-of-the-line model, every refinement, built to individual order only with almost any option possible.

* **.240 H&H, 7mm H&H, or 8mm cal.**

	MSR	100%	98%	95%	90%	80%	70%	60%
	$113,000	$113,000	$93,200	$62,750	$43,500	$36,250	$31,000	$27,000

* **.275 H&H, .300 H&H, or 9.3mm cal.**

	MSR	100%	98%	95%	90%	80%	70%	60%
	$118,800	$118,800	$97,850	$66,000	$45,500	$39,000	$33,000	$28,750

* **.375 H&H or .465 H&H cal.**

	MSR	100%	98%	95%	90%	80%	70%	60%
	$124,500	$124,500	$102,000	$69,500	$49,500	$42,000	$35,500	$30,000

* **.577 NE or .600 NE cal.**

	MSR	100%	98%	95%	90%	80%	70%	60%
	$143,000	$143,000	$118,450	$86,750	$56,500	$46,000	$40,000	$32,500

H&H .700 BORE DOUBLE RIFLE - .700 H&H cal., 1,000 grain jacketed bullet, approx. 19 lbs. with 26 in. barrels chambered 3½ in. This is the largest caliber rifle available in the world today.

* **Royal Model** - this model is not currently mfg. 1997 retail was $115,920.

* **Royal De Luxe Model**

	MSR	100%	98%	95%
	$192,500	$192,500	$125,000	$100,000

SHOTGUNS: O/U

ROYAL OLD MODEL - 12 ga., customer specifications as to barrel length and choke, hand detachable sidelocks, auto ejectors, checkered straight grip stock. Mfg. until 1951. Very rare, very few mfg.

	100%	98%	95%	90%	80%	70%	60%
	$37,500	$32,000	$28,000	$23,500	$20,000	$18,000	$16,500

Add 5% for single trigger.

ROYAL NEW MODEL - similar to Old Model, with improved narrow action. Mfg. until 1960, fewer than 30 mfg.

	100%	98%	95%	90%	80%	70%	60%
	$36,000	$31,000	$27,000	$22,500	$19,000	$17,000	$15,500

ROYAL SIDELOCK GAME GUN - 12, 20, 28 (new 1997) ga., or .410 bore (new 1997), somewhat similar to New Model, with improved cocking, striking and ejection, slimmer action body, DT, 25 to 30 in. game or VR barrels, 2¾ in. chambers, finest checkered walnut straight hand or pistol grip stock, scroll engraved receiver with color case hardened or bright finish, proto-

Grading	100%	98%	95%	90%	80%	70%	60%

type testing has finished and guns are available for demonstration, 5 lbs. 1 oz - 7 lbs. 8 oz. Written quotations on this re-released model are available by contacting H&H directly (see Trademark Index). Values listed are for base models only and reflect the most recent factory information. Limited availability.

   Add $2,020 for single trigger.
   Add $17,000 per extra set of barrels.

✳ ***12 or 20 ga.***

	MSR	$94,500		$94,500	$53,000	$39,500	$30,000	$23,500	$20,000	$18,000

✳ ***28 ga. or .410 bore***

	MSR	$100,000		$100,000	$58,750	$44,000	$33,750	$26,000	$22,500	$19,500

ROYAL DE LUXE MODEL - similar to Royal Sidelock Game Gun, except choice of more elaborate engraving and exhibition wood.

   This model is quoted per individual special order only.

SPORTING MODEL - 12, 16, 20, or 28 ga., 2³⁄₄ or 3 in. chambers, designed with a trigger plate action, Game or Sporting Clays configuration featuring detachable SST mechanism, 25 to 32 in. game or VR barrels. Options on specifications to include screw-in chokes, 12 ga. - 7¹⁄₄-8 lbs., 28 ga. - 6 lbs. New 1993. Values listed reflect most recent factory information. Limited availability.

	MSR	$51,150		$51,150	$35,000	$29,000	$23,000	$18,000	$14,000	$11,000

   Add $1,820 for color case hardened action with gold name inlay.
   Add $12,300 per extra set of barrels.

SPORTING DE LUXE MODEL - similar to Sporting O/U Model, except with choice of more elaborate engraving and exhibition wood. New 1993.

   This model is quoted per individual special order only.

SHOTGUNS: SxS

Holland & Holland currently manufactures the Royal De Luxe Game Gun and Royal Game Gun (limited mfg.) models in sidelock configuration. In addition to the sidelock models, H&H also manufactured the boxlock models Cavalier, Cavalier De Luxe, Northwood, and Northwood De Luxe until recently. The following values assume standard model with double triggers, game rib, standard walnut, or casing. Additional special order features will add considerable value to the price of a new custom order.

In 1988, Holland & Holland absorbed W & C Scott and manufactured the Chatsworth, Bowood, and Kinmount boxlock models until they were discontinued in late 1990. H&H has phased this trademark out, and more information can be found in the W & C Scott section of this text.

NORTHWOOD SxS BOXLOCK - 12, 16 (disc. 1992), 20, or 28 (disc. 1992) ga., 28 or 30 in. barrels, scalloped-case colored receiver, boxlock, auto ejectors, double triggers, border engraving, checkered pistol grip or straight stock. The values shown are for standard model. Disc. 1993.

	$5,950	$5,200	$4,450	$3,850	$3,300	$2,800	$2,300

   Last MSR was $6,705.

   Add approx. 10% for 20 ga.
   Add approx. 20% for 28 ga.

✳ ***Northwood De Luxe*** - 12, 16, 20, or 28 ga., scalloped-case colored receiver with moderate engraving and select walnut, double triggers. Disc. 1993.

	$6,375	$5,450	$4,600	$3,950	$3,350	$2,850	$2,400

   Last MSR was $7,450.

   Add approx. 10% for 20 ga.
   Add approx. 20% for 28 ga.

Grading	100%	98%	95%	90%	80%	70%	60%

CAVALIER SxS BOXLOCK - 12, 20, or 28 (disc. 1992) ga., best quality model boxlock with scalloped frame, double triggers, ejectors, and case colored receiver. Disc.

| | $9,500 | $7,750 | $6,350 | $5,500 | $4,850 | $4,100 | $3,500 |

Last MSR was $11,175.

Add approx. 10% for 20 ga.
Add approx. 20% for 28 ga.

* *Cavalier De Luxe* - similar to Cavalier Model, except has deluxe walnut and better engraving. Disc. 1993.

| | $9,950 | $8,000 | $6,500 | $5,600 | $4,950 | $4,200 | $3,600 |

Last MSR was $11,920.

Add approx. 10% for 20 ga.
Add approx. 20% for 28 ga.

DOMINION GAME GUN - 12, 16, or 20 ga., 25-30 in. barrels, any choke, sidelock, auto ejectors, double triggers, checkered straight grip stock. Disc. 1990.

| | $6,150 | $5,650 | $4,750 | $4,150 | $3,650 | $3,250 | $2,850 |

Add 20% for 20 gauge.

ROYAL HAMMERLESS EJECTOR SIDELOCK (NON-SELF OPENING) - 12, 16, 20, 28 ga., or .410 bore, non-self opening, customer specifications as to barrel length and chokes, hand detachable sidelocks, stocked in pistol grip or straight style to specifications. Mfg. 1885-disc.

| | $20,000 | $17,500 | $14,750 | $12,500 | $10,000 | $9,000 | $8,000 |

Add 20% for 20 ga.
Add 40% for 28 ga.
Add 60% for .410 bore.
Values listed are for older, previously manufactured specimens.

ROYAL GAME GUN - 12, 16, 20, 28 ga., or .410 bore, best quality sidelock self opening game gun. Mfg. per individual customer specifications. The following values reflect most recent factory information. Mfg. 1922 to date. Limited availability.

* *12, 16, or 20 ga.*

| MSR $74,250 | $74,250 | $40,000 | $35,000 | $30,000 | $23,000 | $18,000 | $13,000 |

* *28 ga. or .410 bore*

| MSR $79,200 | $79,200 | $45,000 | $40,000 | $35,000 | $29,000 | $25,000 | $20,000 |

Add $5,750 for ST.
Add $14,700 per extra set of barrels.
Add $3,100 for VR (disc.).

ROYAL DE LUXE GAME GUN - 12, 16, 20, 28 ga., or .410 bore, top-of-the-line sidelock self opening shotgun. Mfg. per individual customer specifications. Current production.
This model is quoted per individual special order only.
Older mfg. is sometimes referred to as the De Luxe Model.

BADMINTON SIDELOCK - similar to Royal model, without self opening action. Disc.

| | $10,500 | $9,000 | $8,000 | $7,000 | $6,000 | $5,000 | $4,000 |

Add 20% for 20 ga.
Add 40% for 28 ga.
Add 60% for .410 bore.
Add $1,000 for SST.
Values listed are for older, previously manufactured specimens.

* *Badminton Game Gun* - 12 or 20 ga., double or single trigger. Disc. 1988.

| | $20,000 | $17,000 | $14,500 | $12,250 | $10,000 | $8,500 | $6,750 |

Last MSR was $28,000.

RIVIERA SIDELOCK - similar to Badminton model, with two sets of barrels. Mfg. until 1967.

| | $15,000 | $11,500 | $9,500 | $7,950 | $7,100 | $6,350 | $5,600 |

Add 20% for 20 ga.
Add 40% for 28 ga.
Add 60% for .410 bore.

Grading	100%	98%	95%	90%	80%	70%	60%

CENTENARY SIDELOCK - 12 ga., 2 in. chambers, lightened version of Royal, Badminton, and Dominion grades. The values would be the same as for the standard models, mfg. until 1962.

SHOTGUNS: SINGLE SHOT

SINGLE BARREL TRAP GUN - 12 ga., 30 or 32 in. full choke barrel, vent. rib, boxlock, auto ejector, Monte Carlo pistol grip stock, pad. Disc.

	100%	98%	95%	90%	80%	70%	60%
	$15,000	$12,000	$10,000	$8,500	$7,500	$6,750	$4,850

Last MSR was $28,420.

❋ *Trap Guns - Older Mfg.*

	100%	98%	95%	90%	80%	70%	60%
Standard Grade	$5,000	$4,500	$4,000	$3,250	$2,500	$2,250	$2,000
De Luxe Grade	$8,250	$7,000	$6,250	$5,000	$4,500	$3,750	$3,000
Exhibition Grade	$10,500	$8,950	$7,500	$6,000	$5,500	$5,000	$4,250

HOLLOWAY & NAUGHTON

Current trade name of shotguns manufactured since the late 1800s in England. No current U.S. importation.

Please contact the factory directly (see Trademark Index) for more information including individual quotations. Holloway & Naughton makes 7-10 best quality, custom order only guns annually. They also perform all services, including engraving, in-house.

SHOTGUNS: CUSTOM

BOXLOCK O/U MODEL - 12 or 20 ga., Anson & Deeley boxlock action, moderate engraving, special order only, approx. 12 month delivery time.
   Prices start for this model at $14,000.

SIDELOCK O/U MODEL - 12, 16, 20, 28 ga. or .410 bore, various configurations including field and sporting clays, features lightweight true Boss coin finished action with reinforced forearm, SST, exhibition grade wood, engraving per customer specifications, special order only, approx. 12 month delivery time.
   Prices for this model start at $48,000 (Sporting Clays, 12 or 20 ga.), add $5,000 for lightweight game, $10,000 for .410 bore in lightweight game.

BOXLOCK SxS MODEL - 12 or 20 ga., Anson & Deeley boxlock action, moderate engraving, special order only, approx. 12 month delivery time.
   Prices start for this model at $18,000.

HOLLOWAY ARMS CO.

Previous manufacturer located in Fort Worth, TX.

Holloway firearms did not make many rifles or carbines before operations ceased.

RIFLES: SEMI-AUTO

HAC MODEL 7 RIFLE - .308 Win. cal., gas operated semi-auto paramilitary design rifle, 20 in. barrel, adj. front and rear sights, 20 shot mag., side folding stock, right or left hand action. Mfg. 1984-1985 only.

	100%	98%	95%	90%	80%	70%	60%
	$1,200	$1,050	$895	$795	$695	$595	$525

Last MSR was $675.

❋ *Model 7C Carbine* - 16 in. carbine, same general specifications as Model 7. Disc. 1985.

	100%	98%	95%	90%	80%	70%	60%
	$1,200	$1,050	$895	$795	$695	$595	$525

Last MSR was $675.

Also available from the manufacturer were the models 7S and 7M (Sniper and Match models).

HOLMES FIREARMS

Previous manufacturer located in Wheeler, AR. Previously distributed by D.B. Distributing, Fayetteville, AR.

Grading	100%	98%	95%	90%	80%	70%	60%

PISTOLS: SEMI-AUTO

These pistols were mfg. in very limited numbers, most were in prototype configuration and exhibit changes from gun to gun. These models were open bolt and subject to 1988 federal legislation regulations.

MP-83 - 9mm Para. or .45 ACP cal., paramilitary design pistol, 6 in. barrel, walnut stock and forearm, blue finish, 3½ lbs.

	100%	98%	95%	90%	80%	70%	60%
	$700	$600	$500	$450	$400	$375	$350

Last MSR was $450.

> **Add 10% for deluxe package.**
> **Add 40% for conversion kit (mfg. 1985 only).**

MP-22 - .22 LR cal., 2½ lbs., steel and aluminum construction, 6 in. barrel, similar appearance to MP-83. Mfg. 1985 only.

	100%	98%	95%	90%	80%	70%	60%
	$395	$360	$320	$285	$250	$230	$210

Last MSR was $400.

SHOTGUNS

COMBAT 12 - 12 ga., riot configuration, cylinder bore barrel. Disc. 1983.

	100%	98%	95%	90%	80%	70%	60%
	$795	$720	$650	$595	$550	$500	$450

Last MSR was $750.

HOPKINS & ALLEN ARMS COMPANY, 1902-1914

Previous manufacturer located in Norwich, CT. H&A started their firearms business in 1867, manufacturing percussion revolvers. Before 1870, they were producing rimfire cartridge guns and eventually centerfire handguns and long guns. Prior to 1896, H&A guns were marked "HOPKINS & ALLEN MANUFG. CO. NORWICH CONN." or other private tradenames, including Merwin, Hulbert & Company. Hopkins & Allen guns are about equally priced with Stevens, N.R. Davis, Crescent Firearms Co., etc. There are many exceptions due to the numerous limited production guns, examples are the AA GRADE double shotgun and the "PARROT BEAK" Derringer. Hopkins & Allen also manufactured firearms which were not described in their catalogs.

Compiled from Hopkins & Allen catalogs by Charles E. Carder.

HANDGUNS

Most H&A handguns were nickel plated, with blue finish originally costing $.50 extra, grips were hard rubber, wood or pearl. Some had engraving from low to very good quality. Revolver barrel lengths varied from 1¾-6 in. Calibers were .22 rimfire (.22 S, L, or LR) up to .38-40 WCF. Specific calibers have not been listed in this section.

FOREHAND MODEL - .32 cal., breaktop, double action, five shot.

$190	$160	$140	$120	$100	$85	$75

FOREHAND MODEL - similar to above except hammerless. (This model was offered in large and small frame).

$190	$160	$140	$120	$100	$85	$75

FOREHAND MODEL - large frame as above in .32 and .38 centerfire cal. with full hammer or "bobbed" hammer.

$190	$160	$140	$120	$100	$85	$75

FOREHAND MODEL - solid frame and hard rubber grips, otherwise as above in small frame.

$170	$140	$120	$100	$85	$75	$65

Grading	100%	98%	95%	90%	80%	70%	60%

FOREHAND MODEL - similar to above models, with "folding hammer". .22 rimfires were seven shot, while .32 and .38 centerfires were five shot. By 1909, the Forehand logo was dropped from these revolvers.

| | $170 | $140 | $120 | $100 | $85 | $75 | $65 |

H&A NEW MODEL AUTOMATIC HAMMER REVOLVER - similar to breaktop with hammer, produced in small and large frame, in .22 rimfire, .32 and .38 centerfire cal.

| | $170 | $140 | $120 | $100 | $85 | $75 | $65 |

H&A SOLID FRAME - .32 and .38 centerfire cal., five shot, double action, hammer or "bobbed" hammer.

| | $175 | $140 | $120 | $100 | $85 | $70 | $55 |

H&A XL MODEL - similar to above in .22, .32 and .38 cal.

| | $140 | $120 | $100 | $85 | $75 | $60 | $45 |

H&A RANGE MODEL - .22, .32 and .38 cal., solid frame, loading gate on right side, wood target style grips, single or double action. (Two models, large and small frames.)

| | $200 | $175 | $140 | $120 | $100 | $85 | $70 |

H&A TRIPLE ACTION SAFETY POLICE REVOLVER - .22, .32 and .38 cal.,breaktop with newly design locking mechanism, hard rubber or pearl grips (considered to be one of the best designed breaktops in its time). Other options for this model, include hammerless, engraved, wood target or pearl grips.

| | $240 | $210 | $175 | $140 | $120 | $100 | $85 |

H&A NEW VEST POCKET DERRINGER - .22 Short rimfire cal., single shot, tip up, single action, 3½ in. overall length, folding trigger, blue or nickel finish, wood or pearl grips with golden monograms. This model was first listed about 1910 and known as the "Parrot Beak". An estimate of less than one thousand were produced and they are very rare.

| | $2,375 | $2,100 | $1,800 | $1,550 | $1,250 | $950 | $650 |

H&A NEW MODEL TARGET PISTOL - .22 rimfire cal., single shot breaktop with the same new locking mechanism as the Safety Police Revolver, wood target grips with golden monograms, blue finish and 6, 8 or 10 in. barrels.

| | $565 | $495 | $440 | $375 | $325 | $285 | $250 |

H&A NEW MODEL SKELETON STOCK TARGET PISTOL - similar to above, with rounded hard rubber grips with logo, detachable "skeleton metal stock", 18 in. barrel and blue finish.

| | $850 | $775 | $675 | $600 | $550 | $500 | $465 |

RIFLES

Hopkins & Allen started building "falling block" rifles circa 1887-1914 with the buy- out of the Baystate Arms Company. Most commonly seen is the "Junior" model, known after 1902 as 922, 925, and 932. These numbers were in reference to the catalog numbers, not model numbers. In the very late 1890s or early 1900s, the Number 722, 822, and 832 rifles were added. In 1906, a "bolt action" repeater was added to their line, followed in 1909 by a "bolt action" single shot "military". Specific calibers have not been listed in this section.

Add $60-$75 for Lyman tang sights on the following models.

NUMBER 922 - falling block, lever operated, .22 cal. rimfire, with round bbl.

| | $310 | $245 | $195 | $195 | $165 | $125 | $110 |

NUMBER 925 - similar to above in .25 cal. rimfire.

| | $390 | $310 | $245 | $195 | $150 | $110 | $95 |

NUMBER 932 - similar to above in .32 cal. rimfire.

| | $310 | $245 | $195 | $150 | $110 | $95 | $80 |

NUMBER 938 - similar to above in .38 S&W centerfire.

| | $440 | $350 | $285 | $225 | $200 | $175 | $150 |

Grading	100%	98%	95%	90%	80%	70%	60%

NUMBER 1922 - similar to above in .22 cal. rimfire with octagon bbl.

	$310	$250	$200	$180	$165	$150	$125

NUMBER 1932 - similar to above in .32 cal. rimfire.

	$310	$250	$200	$165	$125	$110	$90

NUMBER 2922 - similar to above in .22 cal. rimfire, with checkering.

	$420	$335	$265	$225	$195	$175	$150

NUMBER 2932 - similar to above in .32 cal. rimfire.

	$420	$335	$265	$225	$195	$175	$150

NUMBER 3922 - similar to above in .22 cal. rimfire, "SCHUETZEN RIFLE", nickeled Swiss butt plate, octagon barrel. (Schuetzen rifles in good cond., are somewhat rare.)

	$775	$620	$495	$450	$400	$365	$325

NUMBER 3925 - similar to above in .25-20 WCF. (This caliber rifle is more rare than the .22 cal. rimfire).

	$1,010	$810	$650	$600	$550	$500	$450

NUMBER 44XL - chambered for the 44XL shotshell, similar to Number 922, except has smooth bore. (Referred to as, "TAXIDERMIST'S" or "LADIES GUN").

	$530	$430	$350	$325	$275	$235	$200

NUMBER 722 - .22 cal. rimfire, rolling block, thumb operated.

	$300	$240	$195	$165	$125	$110	$90

SCOUT MILITARY RIFLE - similar to above with military style stock and with a "Bonneted Indian" stamped on the left side of frame. (These are somewhat rare).

	$505	$405	$325	$285	$250	$200	$175

NUMBER 822 - .22 cal. rimfire, rolling block, lever operated,

	$300	$240	$195	$175	$150	$125	$100

NUMBER 832 - .32 cal. rimfire, otherwise similar to Model 822 (This model was offered first with "pig tail" type levers and later with "loop" type levers. The "loop levers" are somewhat rare.)

	$350	$280	$225	$200	$175	$150	$125

NUMBER 4922 - .22 rimfire cal., bolt action, repeater.

	$260	$205	$165	$135	$120	$100	$80

NUMBER 5022 - similar to above with deluxe checkering.

	$340	$270	$215	$175	$150	$135	$100

MILITARY RIFLE - similar to above, except single shot with military style stock and sling. (In good condition, these are somewhat rare.)

	$490	$395	$315	$250	$225	$200	$185

NOISELESS - .22 rimfire, similar to the Number 922, except for checkered wood and the addition of a noise suppressor attached to the muzzle, by means of mating threads inside of suppressor and outside of barrel. The job is so well fitted, that it is difficult to recognize the suppressor. The front sight is attached to a dovetail slot in the suppressor. (These rifles are listed under the National Firearms Act of 1934 and must have proper licensing. Very rare.)

	$690	$625	$575	$500	$450	$395	$325

SHOTGUNS: SxS

Hopkins & Allen purchased Forehand Arms Co. and W.H. Davenport, and continued to produce their line of firearms, and after a few years dropped the Forehand name. In 1902, they offered the Forehand double boxlocks with or without outside hammers. Most models were offered in 12, 16 & 20 gauge. Sidelocks were added 1906-09. In 1902, the AA GRADE, a very high quality boxlock, was offered for $100 to $125. It had fine Damascus barrels, straight grip, plain or automatic ejectors,

Grading	100%	98%	95%	90%	80%	70%	60%

fine wood and engraving and was competitive with some Remingtons, L.C. Smiths, Bakers and other fine guns of that era. This gun was very short lived and today is rare. One feature found on all H&A double barrel guns is the "rib extension" or "doll's head."

BOXLOCK - Anson & Deeley type frame, damascus, twist, and steel barrels.

| | $315 | $275 | $235 | $195 | $160 | $130 | $95 |

BOXLOCK - similar to above, except with outside hammers.

| | $315 | $275 | $235 | $195 | $160 | $130 | $95 |

SIDELOCK - hammerless, damascus, twist, and steel barrels.

| | $315 | $275 | $235 | $195 | $160 | $130 | $115 |

SIDELOCK - similar to above, except with outside hammers.

| | $315 | $275 | $235 | $195 | $160 | $130 | $95 |

SHOTGUNS: SINGLE SHOT

H&A produced a "falling block" shotgun in most gauges circa 1887 - early 1900s. Falling Blocks (FBs) in 12 ga. were built on heavy frames with the 20 and 16 gauges sharing a medium frame. Prior to 1902, some FBs were chambered for .45-70 shotshells and, today, these are rare if in good condition. From the 1890s through 1914, 38XL, 44XL shotshell guns were periodically offered in the Junior frame. After 1902, "tip-over" single shotguns were offered in Forehand designs and, later, the Davenport designs.

FALLING BLOCK - lever operated, outside hammer.

| | $275 | $235 | $210 | $180 | $160 | $145 | $125 |

BOXLOCK - with outside hammer, damascus, twist, and steel barrels.

| | $190 | $170 | $150 | $130 | $110 | $95 | $80 |

BOXLOCK - hammerless, top safety.

| | $190 | $170 | $150 | $130 | $110 | $95 | $80 |

GOOSE GUNS - outside hammer, 8, 10, or 12 ga., were offered with barrels up to 40 inches long.

| | $250 | $225 | $190 | $170 | $150 | $135 | $115 |

"SAFETY SINGLE GUN" - engraved with outside hammer and top safety. (Was offered in 1911 and recommended for trap shooting for $15.00).

| | $250 | $225 | $195 | $175 | $155 | $140 | $125 |

HORTON, LEW, DIST. CO.

See Lew Horton Dist. Co. listing.

HOWA

Current manufacturer established in 1967, and located in Tokyo, Japan. Howa sporting rifles currently imported beginning Oct., 1999 by Legacy Sports International (LSI), LLC, located in Alexandria, VA. Previously imported until 1999 by Interarms/Howa, located in Alexandria, VA, Weatherby (Vanguard Series only), Smith & Wesson (pre-1985), and Mossberg (1986-87).

RIFLES: BOLT ACTION

MODEL 1500 HUNTER - various cals., 3 (Mag. cals. only) or 5 shot, 22 or 24 in. barrel, adj. rear sight and trigger, checkered walnut stock, blue metal finish or stainless steel (new 1999) construction, approx. 7.6 lbs. Imported by Interarms 1988 only, reintroduced during 1999.

| MSR | $500 | $410 | $320 | $280 | $240 | $210 | $175 | $160 |

Add $22 for Mag. cals.
Add $88 for stainless steel.

Grading	100%	98%	95%	90%	80%	70%	60%

❋ *Model 1500 Lightning* - .270 Win., .30-06, .300 Win. Mag., or 7mm Rem. Mag. cal., light-weight variation of the Model 1500 Hunter featuring lightweight Carbolite (synthetic) stock, 7 lbs. Imported 1988-91.

	$415	$335	$290	$260	$240	$225	$205

Last MSR was $539.

Add $20 for Mag. cals.

MODEL 1500 LIGHTNING RIFLE - various cals., 22 or 24 in. barrel, black synthetic Carbolite stock with cheekpiece and pressed checkering, no sights, 3 or 5 shot mag., high luster bluing or stainless steel, approx. 7.6 lbs. Importation began 1993.

MSR	$478	$370	$310	$260	$230	$200	$175	$160

Add $22 for Mag. cals.
Add $87 for stainless steel.

MODEL 1500 ULTRALIGHT - .243 Win. cal., 20 in. barrel, short bolt throw, non-glare blue or blue/black metal finish, black finished hardwood stock, 5 shot mag., w/o sights, 6.4 lbs. Importation began 2002.

MSR	$511	$425	$325	$285	$250	$225	$185	$165

MODEL 1500 VARMINT - .22-250 Rem., .223 Rem., or .308 Win. (mfg. 1990-92, reintroduced 2001) cal., 24 in. heavy barrel without sights, 5 shot mag., blue steel or stainless steel (new 1999) construction, black polymer (new 1999) or walnut stock, approx. 9.3 lbs. Imported 1988-92, reintroduced 1999-2001.

	$415	$335	$275	$230	$200	$175	$160

Last MSR was $496.

Add $22 for wood stock.
Add $64 for stainless steel.

MODEL 1500 CUSTOM - .300 Win. Mag. or .300 WSM cal., 22 or 24 (.300 Win. Mag. cal. only) in. barrel, black polymer or laminate wood in either the Classic JSR or thumbhole configuration, 3 shot mag., blue (.300 Win. Mag. cal. only) or stainless steel barrel and action, 7.6 – 8.1 lbs. Importation began 2002.

MSR	$855	$775	$695	$625	$550	$500	$465	$435

Add $35 for .300 WSM cal. in stainless steel with polymer stock.
Add $105 for regular laminate stock, $135 for thumbole laminate stock.

MODEL 1500 TEXAS SAFARI - .270 Win. or .300 Win. Mag. cal., features Howa M-1500 barreled action that Bill Wiseman recontours the bolt sleeve and receiver, machines a new bolt release, and adds his own 3-position safety, 3 or 5 shot mag., non-glare blue Teflon metal finish, brown laminate glass bedded stock, individually test fired, approx. 7.8 lbs. Importation began 2002.

MSR	$1,522	$1,295	$1,100	$925	$800	$675	$575	$500

Add $231 for .300 Win. Mag. cal.

This model is also available as a complete custom rifle with many options and special orders – please contact the importer directly for a price quotation and delivery time.

MODEL 1500 PCS - .308 Win. cal., police counter sniper rifle featuring 24 in. barrel, choice of blue metal or stainless steel, black synthetic or checkered walnut stock, no sights, approx. 9.3 lbs. Imported 1999-2000.

	$385	$315	$265	$225	$195	$175	$160

Last MSR was $465.

Add $20 for wood stock.
Add $60 for stainless steel.

Grading	100%	98%	95%	90%	80%	70%	60%

MODEL 1500 TROPHY - .22-250 Rem., .223 Rem., .243 Win., .270 Win., .308 Win., .30-06, .300 Win. Mag., .338 Win. Mag. or 7mm Rem. Mag. cal., 3 (Mag. cals. only) or 5 shot, 22 or 24 in. barrel, adj. rear sight and trigger, select Monte Carlo stock with skipline checkering. Imported 1988-92.

	$528	$410	$335	$290	$260	$240	$225

Last MSR was $528.

Add $20 for Mag. cals.

LIGHTNING WOODGRAIN - .243 Win., .270 Win., .30-06, .308 Win., or 7mm Rem. Mag. cal., features lightweight Carbolite synthetic stock with simulated wood grain and checkering, 22 in. barrel, 5 shot mag., no sights, 7.5 lbs. Imported 1994 only.

	$450	$395	$365	$320	$275	$250	$225

Last MSR was $537.

Add $19 for 7mm Rem. Mag. cal.

REALTREE CAMO RIFLE - .270 Win. or .30-06 (disc. 1993) cal., 22 in. barrel, 5 shot mag., monobloc receiver, drilled and tapped, thumb safety, entire rifle is coated with a Realtree brown leaf camo pattern, no sights, 8 lbs. Imported 1993-94.

	$495	$400	$350	$325	$300	$280	$260

Last MSR was $620.

HUG-SAN

Current shotgun manufacturer located in Huglu, Turkey. No current U.S. importer.

Hug-San manufactures slide action, semi-auto, and O/U shotguns, in various configurations and gauges. Please contact the factory (see Trademark Index) for more information.

HUGLU

Current shotgun manufacturer established in 1962, and located in Huglu, Turkey. Currently imported beginning 1999 by Huglu USA, located in Rigby, ID.

Huglu makes a wide variety of quality O/U, semi-auto, and SxS shotguns available in all gauges. The shotguns imported by Huglu USA are a specially designed Premium Grade line, not available overseas. For more information, including current models, prices, and U.S. availability, please contact the importer directly (see Trademark Index).

HUNTER ARMS COMPANY

Previous manufacturer located in Fulton, NY circa 1891-1945.

The Hunter Arms Company was formed to manufacture L.C. Smith shotguns. Please refer to the L.C. Smith section in this text for further information regarding this manufacturer (including Fulton, Fulton Special, and Hunter Special models.)

HUSQVARNA

Previous manufacturer located in Husqvarna, Sweden.

Also see: Lahti Pistols.

RIFLES: BOLT ACTION

HI-POWER - .220 Swift, .270 Win., or .30-06 cal., Mauser type action, open sight, checkered beech wood. Mfg. 1946-1951, early models found in 6.5x55mm, 8x57R, 9.3x57mm cals.

	$395	$365	$330	$295	$265	$235	$200

MODEL 1951 - similar to Hi-Power, except high profile stock.

	$425	$385	$340	$300	$270	$240	$210

SERIES 1100 DELUXE - similar to Model 1951, except has European walnut and jeweled bolt. Mfg. 1952-1956.

	$440	$360	$330	$310	$290	$275	$250

SERIES 1000 SUPER GRADE - similar to Model 1951, has walnut Monte Carlo stock. Mfg. 1952-1956.

	$440	$360	$330	$310	$290	$275	$250

Grading	100%	98%	95%	90%	80%	70%	60%

SERIES 3100 CROWN GRADE - .243 Win., .270 Win., .30-06, 7x57mm, or .308 Win. cal., improved HVA Mauser action, 24 in. barrel, walnut stock, black forend tip and pistol grip cap. Mfg. 1954-1972.

	$470	$385	$360	$330	$315	$305	$275

SERIES 3000 CROWN GRADE - similar to 3100, except has Monte Carlo stock.

	$470	$385	$360	$330	$315	$305	$275

SERIES 4100 LIGHTWEIGHT - HVA Mauser action, calibers same as 3100, 20½ in. barrel, open sights, lightweight walnut stock, pistol grip, Schnabel forend. Mfg. 1954- 1972.

	$470	$385	$360	$330	$315	$305	$275

SERIES 4000 LIGHTWEIGHT - similar to 4100, except has Monte Carlo stock, no sights.

	$470	$385	$360	$330	$315	$305	$275

MODEL 456 LIGHTWEIGHT - similar to 4000/4100, except full length stock. Mfg. 1959-1970.

	$495	$415	$385	$360	$330	$310	$290

SERIES 6000 IMPERIAL GRADE - similar to 3100, except has select wood, 3 leaf folding sight. Mfg. 1968-1970.

	$580	$495	$470	$440	$395	$365	$330

SERIES 6000 IMPERIAL LIGHTWEIGHT - similar to 6000 Imperial, except 20½ in. barrel, lightweight stock.

	$580	$495	$470	$440	$395	$365	$330

SERIES P-3000 PRESENTATION - similar to Crown, except engraved action, special wood. Mfg. 1968-1970.

	$770	$660	$635	$605	$550	$510	$485

MODEL 9000 CROWN GRADE - cals. similar to Model 3100 Crown Grade, except also available in .300 Win. Mag. cal., Husqvarna action, 23½ in. barrel, adj. trigger, adj. sight, walnut stock. Mfg. 1971-1972.

	$470	$385	$360	$330	$315	$305	$275

MODEL 8000 IMPERIAL - similar to 9000, but jeweled bolt, engraved floor plate, no sights and deluxe stock. Mfg. 1971-1972.

	$605	$525	$495	$470	$415	$385	$350

HY-HUNTER INC. FIREARMS MANUFACTURING CO.

Previous manufacturer located in W. Germany, imported by Hy-Hunter Inc.

Previous importer of single action revolvers in various calibers. Typically, prices are determined by their shooting value rather than their collector value. Prices generally range from $100-$175 depending on caliber and finish.

HYPER

Previous manufacturer located in Jenks, OK.

RIFLES: SINGLE SHOT

SINGLE SHOT RIFLE - all calibers, all standard lengths and contours, falling block trigger guard lever activated, adj. trigger, no sights, stocked to customer specifications, in AA grade walnut. Disc. 1984.

	$2,200	$1,980	$1,925	$1,870	$1,650	$1,540	$1,375

Add $75 for stainless barrel.
Add $85 for octagon barrel.

NOTES

No Safari Club International (SCI) Show would be complete without stopping by Holland & Holland's elegant and well appointed booth to see Daryl Greatrex, the H&H director for the New York sales office.

I SECTION

I A B

Currently manufactured by Industria Armi Bresciane, located in Sarezzo, Brescia, Italy. No current U.S. importation. Previously imported by American Arms, located in Kansas City, MO. Previously distributed by Sporting Arms International, Inc. located in Indianola, MS.

I A B manufactures shotguns (O/U and single barrel trap or skeet) in various styles and configurations including combo sets. These guns employ a boxlock action, have ejectors, and various amounts of engraving. Prices for 100% condition usually start in the $650- $1,000 price range. I A B shotguns are not being imported currently - values for older models will be determined by the prices shooters, not collectors, are willing to pay for them. I A B has also manufactured Sharps and rolling block rifles for various importers and distributors over the years.

IAI

Please refer to Intrac Arms International LLC listing.

IAI INC. – AMERICAN LEGEND

Current manufacturer, importer, and distributor located in Houston, TX. Firearms are manufactured by Israel Arms International, Inc., located in Houston, TX. IAI designates Israel Arms International, and should not be confused with Irwindale Arms, Inc. (also I A I).

The models listed are part of an American Legend Series that are patterned after famous American and Belgian military carbines/ rifles and semi-auto pistols.

Grading	100%	98%	95%	90%	80%	70%	60%

CARBINES

MODEL 888 M1 CARBINE - .22 LR or .30 Carbine cal., 18 in. barrel, mfg. from new original M1 parts and stock by IAI (barrel bolt and receiver) and unused GI parts, 10 shot mag., choice of birch or walnut stock, parkerized finish, metal or wood handguard, 5½ lbs. Mfg. by IAI in Houston, TX beginning 1998.

	MSR	$557	$485	$425	$395	$365	$335	$295	$260

Add $11 for .22 LR cal.
Add $31 for walnut stock.
Add $46 for walnut stock and forearm.

PISTOLS: SEMI-AUTO

MODEL 2000 -.45 ACP cal., patterned after the Colt Govt. 1911, 5 or 4¼ (Commander configuration, Model 2000-C) in. barrel, parkerized finish, plastic or rubber grips, 36-38 oz. Mfg. in South Africa. New 2002.

	MSR	$465	$415	$365	$325	$295	$275	$250	$225

I A I

Please refer to the Irwindale Arms, Inc. heading in this section.

IAR, Inc.

Current importer and distributor since 1995 located in San Juan Capistrano, CA.

IAR, Inc. imports and distributes a wide variety of firearms, including revolvers, derringers, rolling block pistols, rifle reproductions, and exposed hammer shotguns. Please contact them directly regarding their current product lineup and consumer pricing.

Grading	100%	98%	95%	90%	80%	70%	60%

I G A SHOTGUNS

Current trademark with manufacturing facilities located in Veranopolis, Brazil (O/U and SxS shotguns only), and by Vursan Manufacturing (semi- auto shotguns only) beginning in 2000, located in Istanbul, Turkey. Currently imported by Stoeger Industries, Inc. located in Accokeek, MD. Previously located in Wayne, NJ.

During 2000, Stoeger Industries was purchased by Beretta USA Corp., located in Accokeek, MD.

SHOTGUNS: O/U

CONDOR MODEL - 12 ga. only, single trigger, ejectors, presentation walnut, chrome lined bores. Disc. 1985.

	100%	98%	95%	90%	80%	70%	60%
	$580	$500	$450	$410	$375	$350	$325

Last MSR was $667.

CONDOR I SINGLE TRIGGER - 12 or 20 ga., 3 in. chambers, boxlock action, deluxe checkered walnut, 26 or 28 in. VR separated barrels, 7.7 lbs.

MSR	$390		$350	$315	$265	$230	$210	$195	$180

Choke tubes became standard 1992.

CONDOR II DOUBLE TRIGGER - 12 or 20 (disc.) ga., boxlock action, VR, checkered walnut, separated barrels. Disc. 1997.

	$350	$295	$260	$230	$195	$170	$150

Last MSR was $459.

CONDOR I SPECIAL - similar to Condor I, except features matte nickel finish, oil finished hardwood stock and forearm. Importation began 2002.

MSR	$430		$380	$335	$275	$235	$215	$195	$180

CONDOR SUPREME - 12 or 20 ga., boxlock action, single trigger, ejectors, 26 or 28 in. VR barrels with choke tubes, deluxe checkered walnut stock and forearm. Imported 1995-2000.

	$500	$450	$395	$360	$320	$280	$240

Last MSR was $629.

CONDOR SUPREME DELUXE - 12 or 20 ga., 3 in. chambers, 24 (20 ga. only), 26, or 30 (disc. 2001) in. VR barrels with choke tubes, high polish blue, gold SST, AE, checkered American walnut stock and forearm, approx. 7.7 lbs. Importation began 2000.

MSR	$490		$450	$395	$360	$330	$300	$285	$265

HUNTER CLAYS MODEL - 12 ga. only, ST, ejectors, 28 in. barrels with choke tubes, deluxe checkered stock and forearm, gold trigger. Mfg. 1997-99.

	$595	$515	$435	$375	$335	$300	$270

Last MSR was $699.

TURKEY SERIES - 12 ga. only, 3 in. chambers, 26 in. VR barrels with choke tubes, ST, ejectors, Advantage camo on wood and metal (except receiver). Mfg. 1997-2000.

	$615	$525	$450	$380	$335	$300	$270

Last MSR was $729.

WATERFOWL SERIES - 12 ga. only, 3 in. chambers, similar to Turkey Series, except has 30 in. barrels. Mfg. 1998-2000.

	$615	$525	$450	$380	$335	$300	$270

Last MSR was $729.

TRAP SERIES - 12 ga., features SST, ejectors, 30 in. VR barrels with choke tubes, deluxe checkered Monte Carlo stock and forearm. Mfg. 1998-99.

	$595	$515	$435	$375	$335	$300	$270

Last MSR was $699.

Grading	100%	98%	95%	90%	80%	70%	60%

ERA 2000 MODELS - 12 ga. only, 26 or 28 in. VR barrels with choke tubes, single trigger. Imported 1992-94.

		100%	98%	95%	90%	80%	70%	60%
		$585	$375	$315	$250	$215	$195	$180

Last MSR was $710.

SHOTGUNS: SxS

UPLANDER MODEL - 12, 16 (new 1996), 20, 28 ga., or .410 bore, 3 in. chambers, DT, underlug lockup, checkered pistol grip or straight English (20 ga. or .410 bore only) stock, Youth Model also available in 20 ga. and .410 bore, double triggers, extractors.

MSR	$325	$295	$230	$185	$150	$130	$115	$100

Add $20 for choke tubes (12 or 20 ga.).

UPLANDER SPECIAL - 12, 20, or 28 ga., 3 in. chambers (not available in 28 ga.), features straight grip Brazilian hardwood checkered English stock and forearm, DT, approx. 7.3 lbs. New 2002.

MSR	$365	$335	$295	$260	$230	$200	$165	$125

UPLANDER SUPREME - 12 or 20 ga., 3 in. chambers, 24 (20 ga. only), 26, or 28 in. barrels with choke tubes, AE, gold SST, high gloss checkered walnut stock and forearm. Importation began 2000.

MSR	$435	$390	$350	$300	$265	$230	$200	$175

DELUXE MODEL - 12, 20, 28 ga., or .410 bore, features better quality checkered walnut stock and forearm, gold triggers, 12 and 20 ga. have choke tubes, 28 ga. and .410 bore have fixed chokes. Mfg. 1997-99.

		$425	$365	$310	$270	$230	$195	$170

Last MSR was $559.

Subtract $40 for 28 ga. or .410 bore (fixed chokes only).

COACH GUN MODEL - 12, 20 ga., or .410 (new 1991) bore, hammerless, choice of blue or nickel (new 1996) finish, 20 in. fixed choke barrels only (IC/M), choice of dark (nickel finish only) or light hardwood stock, 6½ lbs.

MSR	$310	$275	$235	$195	$165	$135	$110	$100

Add $55 for nickel finish.
Add $64 for engraved stagecoach scene on stock (mfg. 1996-99).

* ***Coach Deluxe*** - similar to Coach Gun Model, includes deluxe checkered walnut stock and forearm, fixed (IC/M) or choke tubes (new 1998), gold triggers. Mfg. 1997-99.

		$385	$325	$290	$260	$230	$195	$170

Last MSR was $499.

SILVERADO COACH GUN - similar to Coach Gun, except features a matte nickel metal finish and oil finished hardwood pistol grip or straight English stock and forearm. Importation began 2002.

MSR	$365	$315	$265	$215	$180	$150	$130	$110

TURKEY SERIES MODEL - 12 ga. only, 3 in. chambers, 24 in. barrels, DT, choke tubes. Mfg. 1997-2000.

		$425	$365	$310	$270	$230	$195	$170

Last MSR was $559.

Grading	100%	98%	95%	90%	80%	70%	60%

SHOTGUNS : SEMI-AUTO

MODEL 2000 - 12 ga. only, 3 in. chambers, inertia recoil operating system, 26, 28, or 30 in. VR barrel with 5 choke tubes, checkered walnut or black synthetic (new 2002) stock and forearm, matte metal or 100% Advantage Timber HD camo (new 2002) finish, approx. 7.1 lbs. Mfg. by Vursan Manufacturing located in Istanbul, Tukey, with importation beginning 2001.

MSR	$499	$430	$355	$325	$295	$275	$250	$225

Add $51 for 100% camo coverage.

Add $121 for Model 2000 Deluxe with upgraded wood and floral etched receiver trim.

This model is also available as a combo package which includes a smoothbore slug barrel with screw in IC choke and rifle sights.

SHOTGUNS : SINGLE BARREL

REUNA SINGLE BARREL - 12, 20 ga., or .410 bore, exposed hammer with half-cock, extractor. Disc. 1998.

	$95	$70	$60	$50	$45	$40	$35

Last MSR was $120.

Add $22 for choke tubes (12 ga. new 1992, 20 ga. new 1993).

* ***Reuna Single Barrel Youth*** - 20 ga. or .410 bore, 22 in. barrel, features rubber recoil pad. Imported 1993-98.

	$100	$75	$60	$50	$45	$40	$35

Last MSR was $132.

SINGLE BARREL - 12, 20 ga., or .410 bore, 3 in. chamber, break open action activated by moving triggerguard rearward, exposed hammer, 26 or 28 in. barrel, hardwood stock and forend, matte metal finish, Youth Model also available in 20 ga. or .410 bore (13 LOP), approx. 5.5 lbs. New 2002.

MSR	$109	$90	$75	$65	$55	$45	$40	$35

IBERIA FIREARMS

Current manufacturer of .40 S&W cal. pistols located in Iberia, OH. Distributed by MKS Supply located in Dayton, OH. Distributor sales only.

Please refer to the Hi-Point section in this text.

IMPERIAL GUN CO. LTD

Previous manufacturer located in Surrey, Great Britain circa 1992-95. The Imperial Gun Co. Ltd. had limited importation into the U.S.

Imperial Gun secondary marketplace values must be based realistically on their competitive shooting value, not collectibility.

INDIAN ARMS

Previous trademark manufactured by Indian Arms Corporation located in Detroit, MI.

PISTOLS: SEMI-AUTO

INDIAN ARMS .380 - .380 ACP cal., patterned after Walther PPK, stainless steel, 3¼ in. barrel, 6 shot mag., natural or blue finish, with (early specimens) or without key lock safety, with or without VR barrel, walnut grips, 20 oz. Mfg. 1975-1977.

	$395	$285	$230

This model had limited manufacture with approx. 1,000 guns being made.

Grading	100%	98%	95%	90%	80%	70%	60%

INDUSTRIA ARMI GALESI
Previous manufacturer located in Brescia, Italy.

PISTOLS: SEMI-AUTO

GALESI MODEL 6 POCKET AUTO - .22 LR or .25 ACP cal., 6 shot, 2¼ in. barrel blue, fixed sights, plastic grips. Mfg. 1930-disc.

	$130	$120	$105	$90	$75	$65	$55

Add 100% if chrome engraved.

GALESI MODEL 9 POCKET AUTO - .22 LR, .32 ACP, or .380 ACP cal., 8 shot, 3¼ in. barrel, blue, fixed sights, plastic grips. Mfg. 1930-disc.

	$165	$130	$110	$100	$85	$65	$55

Add 100% if chrome engraved.

INFALLIBLE
Previous trademark manufactured by Warner Arms Corp. located in Norwich, CT and Davis- Warner Arms Corp. located in Assonet, MA.

PISTOLS: SEMI-AUTO

INFALLIBLE PISTOL - .32 ACP cal., 3.2 in. barrel, 7 shot mag., 24.7 oz.

* ✱ *Type I* - mfg. and marked "Warner Arms Corp., Norwich, Conn.", serial range is 501-2,299.

	$325	$295	$270	$250	$225	$200	$180

* ✱ *Type II* - marked "Davis-Warner Arms Corporation, Assonet, Massachusetts", serial range is 2,300- 5,299.

	$295	$270	$250	$225	$195	$170	$150

* ✱ *Type III* - marked "Warner Arms Corporation, Norwich, Connecticut", serial range is 5,300-7,400.

	$295	$270	$250	$225	$195	$170	$150

INFINITY FIREARMS
Current trademark manufactured by Strayer-Voight Inc. since 1994 and located in Grand Prairie, TX. Distributor and dealer sales.

PISTOLS: SEMI-AUTO

Strayer-Voight manufactures a complete line of custom high quality M1911 based semi-auto pistols in a wide variety of finishes, materials (including titanium), options, and special orders. Their curent lineup includes the Tiki Pistol, Titanium Model, Bushing Pistol, Comp. Gun, Hybricomp, IED 1911, Duotone 1911, PPC Masterpiece, and Competition Gun. Please contact Strayer-Voight directly for more information on pricing and availability regarding Infinity firearms (see Trademark Index).

INGLIS HI-POWERS
Previously manufactured by John Inglis Co. Limited of Toronto, Canada. Over 151,000 Inglis Hi-Powers were manufactured between February 1944 and September 1945 under military contractual agreements.

PISTOLS: SEMI-AUTO

CHINESE CONTRACT PATTERN 35

Grading	100%	98%	95%	90%	80%	70%	60%

✴ ***Chinese No. 1*** - 9mm Para. cal., large Chinese characters (6) on left slide, slotted for stock and tangent sights, can be denoted by no numerical prefix before the "CH" in serial number.

	$3,350	$2,950	$2,350	$1,500	$1,000	$750	$600

Add approx. $350 for original wood holster stock (beware of reproductions).
Add $350-$450 for early front sight (approx. first 100 pistols only).

CH SERIES MILITARY

✴ ***MK 1-No. 1 Inglis*** - 9mm Para. cal., tangent sight, slotted, contracts included Canadian, Chinese, and other countries.

	$1,325	$1,050	$875	$725	$650	$550	$450

Add 10%-20% for decal on front strap.
Add approx. $350 for original wood holster stock. Beware of reproductions.
This model has been recently imported again. Most recent imports have been painted black or refinished, and are priced in the $350-$575 range.

T SERIES CANADIAN MILITARY

✴ ***MK 1-No. 2 Inglis*** - 9mm Para. cal., fixed sight, without slot, numerical prefix references (0-10) the number of guns in increments of 10,000. Scarcer variations include: 0, 9, and 10.

	$900	$675	$500	$400	$350	$295	$275

Add 10%-20% for decal on front strap.
Add 15% for O variation.
Add 10% for 9 variation prefix.
Add 30% for 10 variation (ser. no. prefix).
Since the original decals are very fragile, most are observed with approx. 10%-90% of the decal remaining.
This model has been recently imported again. Most recent imports are priced $350-$650.

✴ ***Inglis "DIAMOND" logo*** - refers to Inglis trademark in diamond shaped logo on left side of slide, only a few prototypes were mfg. 1946-47.

	$3,000	$2,750	$2,000	$1,500	$1,200	$800	$600

Add 50% for polished steel (parkerized finish is more common).
Add 50% for 5 CH Series.
All Inglis diamond variations are in the 5CH or 9T ser. no. range.
Be careful of fakes!

✴ ***MK 1-No. 2 Inglis*** - fixed sight, slotted. Inspect slot very carefully, and provenance verification is advised.

	$1,950	$1,250	$1,100	$900	$800	$650	$500

INGRAM

Previously manufactured until late 1982 by Military Armament Corp. (MAC) located in Atlanta, GA.

PISTOLS: SEMI-AUTO

MAC 10 - .45 ACP or 9mm Para. cal., open bolt, semi-auto version of the sub machine gun, 10 (.45 ACP cal.), 16 (9mm Para cal.), 30 (.45 ACP cal.), or 32 (9mm Para cal.) shot mag., compact all metal welded construction, rear aperture and front blade sight. Disc. 1982.

	$850	$775	$700	$650	$600	$550	$495

Add approx. $160 for accessories (barrel extension, case, and extra mag).

MAC 10A1 - similar to MAC 10 except fires from a closed bolt.

	$295	$275	$250	$230	$215	$200	$190

MAC 11 - similar to MAC 10 except in .380 ACP cal.

	$650	$595	$550	$525	$500	$480	$460

Grading	100%	98%	95%	90%	80%	70%	60%

INTERARMS

Previous importer and distributor located in Alexandria, VA from circa 1962-1999.

Interarms imported a multitude of trademarks and models since the early 1960s. Most of the models listed were recent imports. The FEG, Howa, Rossi, and Walther trademarks will be found in their own sections listed alphabetically in this text.

PISTOLS: SEMI-AUTO, FEG & HELWAN MFG.

Please refer to the FEG & HELWAN sections in this text.

REVOLVERS: SA, VIRGINIAN SERIES

Virginian Revolvers were previously imported from Europe by various manufacturers (including Hämmerli of Switzerland). They were also manufactured in Midland, VA from 1976-1984. Older models with exceptional quality (including Hämmerli guns) are worth a premium over values listed.

VIRGINIAN DRAGOON STANDARD - .44 Mag. or .45 LC (mfg. 1982-84) cal., improved action patterned after Colt SAA design, 6 shot, 6, 7½, 8 3/8, or 12 (Buntline) in. barrel, blue finish, smooth walnut grips, adj. rear sight, 51 oz. with 7½ in. barrel.

| $255 | $225 | $205 | $190 | $180 | $170 | $160 |

Last MSR was $315.

Add 15% for Buntline Model.

* ***Dragoon Standard Stainless*** - .44 Mag. or .45 LC cal., 6 (disc.), 7½ (disc.), or 8 3/8 in. barrel, same general specifications as Standard Dragoon.

| $265 | $230 | $210 |

Last MSR was $315.

DRAGOON SILHOUETTE - .357 Mag. or .44 Mag. cal., stainless steel, 7½, 8 3/8, or 10½ in. (standard on .357 Mag.) barrel, special sights and grips.

| $365 | $320 | $275 |

Last MSR was $425.

DRAGOON ENGRAVED - .44 Mag. cal. only, choice of stainless steel or blue finish, 6 or 7½ in. barrel.

| $545 | $470 | $430 | $395 | $360 | $320 | $285 |

Last MSR was $625.

Add $75 for presentation case.

DRAGOON "DEPUTY" - .357 Mag. or .44 Mag. cal., blued barrel, case hardened frame, 5 in. barrel only.

| $250 | $215 | $195 | $180 | $165 | $155 | $145 |

Last MSR was $295.

* ***Stainless Deputy*** - similar to above, except .44 Mag. available in 6 in. barrel only, stainless steel.

| $255 | $225 | $205 |

Last MSR was $295.

VIRGINIAN .22 CONVERTIBLE - .22 LR/.22 Mag. cal. cylinders, 5½ in. barrel only, adj. rear sight, 38 oz.

| $185 | $155 | $145 | $135 | $125 | $115 | $105 |

Last MSR was $219.

* ***Virginian .22 Convertible Stainless*** - stainless steel fabrication, otherwise similar to above.

| $200 | $170 | $155 |

Last MSR was $239.

Grading	100%	98%	95%	90%	80%	70%	60%

RIFLES: BOLT ACTION, DISC.

MODEL JW-15 - .22 LR cal., 5 shot detachable mag., 23.8 in. barrel, open sights, blued finish, Model 70 style safety, patterned after the Brno Model ZKM, 5.5 lbs. Mfg. by Norinco. Imported 1990- 96.

	100%	98%	95%	90%	80%	70%	60%
	$85	$70	$60	$50	$40	$35	$30

Last MSR was $109.

ENFIELD NO. 4 - .303 British cal., genuine British Commonwealth issue, 25¼ in. barrel, 10 shot box mag., 9 lbs. Importation disc. 1996.

	100%	98%	95%	90%	80%	70%	60%
	$75	$60	$50	$40	$35	$35	$35

Last MSR was $86.

RIFLES: BOLT ACTION, HOWA MFG.

Please refer to the Howa section in this text.

RIFLES: BOLT ACTION, MAUSER ACTIONS

Whitworth rifles were mfg. in England. Mark X rifles were mfg. in Yugoslavia by Zastava Arms until late 1997.

MARK X VISCOUNT - .22-250 Rem. (disc. 1993), .243 Win. (disc. 1993), .25-06 Rem. (disc. 1993), .270 Win. (disc. 1993), 7x57mm (disc. 1993), 7mm Rem. Mag. (disc. 1994), .308 Win. (disc. 1994), .30-06, or .300 Win. Mag. (disc. 1994) cal., 5 shot, 3 shot mag., 24 in. barrel, adj. rear sight and trigger, classic style Monte Carlo stock. Disc. 1983, re-introduced 1985 - disc. 1996.

	100%	98%	95%	90%	80%	70%	60%
	$375	$300	$265	$240	$225	$205	$190

Last MSR was $471.

Add $15 for 7mm Rem. Mag. or .300 Win. Mag. cal.

This model is often referred to as the Viscount. Early manufacture was done in Manchester, England. Recent manufacture is in Yugoslavia. Earlier Manchester guns (before approx. 1980) will bring a slight premium over the values listed.

Mini Mark X - .223 Rem. or 7.62x39mm (new in 1990) cal., miniature M98 Mauser System action, 20 in. barrel with iron sights, checkered hardwood stock, 5 shot mag., adj. trigger, 6.35 lbs. Imported 1987-94.

	100%	98%	95%	90%	80%	70%	60%
	$360	$295	$265	$240	$225	$205	$190

Last MSR was $455.

✳ Lightweight Mark X - .22-250 Rem. (new 1994), .270 Win. (disc.), .30-06 (disc. 1994), or 7mm Rem. Mag. (disc.) cal., similar to Mark X Viscount, except has Carbolite (synthetic) stock and 20 in. barrel, 7 lbs. Imported 1988-90, reintroduced 1994-97.

	100%	98%	95%	90%	80%	70%	60%
	$350	$290	$265	$240	$225	$205	$190

Last MSR was $438.

CAVALIER - similar to Viscount, except modern style stock, roll-over cheekpiece, rosewood pistol grip cap and forend tip, recoil pad. Disc.

	100%	98%	95%	90%	80%	70%	60%
	$365	$330	$305	$290	$265	$230	$195

MANNLICHER STYLE CARBINE - similar to Cavalier, except 20 in. barrel, full length stock, no Magnum or varmint calibers. Disc.

	100%	98%	95%	90%	80%	70%	60%
	$365	$330	$305	$290	$265	$230	$195

CONTINENTAL CARBINE - similar to Mannlicher Style, except with double set trigger. Disc.

	100%	98%	95%	90%	80%	70%	60%
	$395	$365	$330	$310	$285	$255	$220

THE MARQUIS - .243 Win., .270 Win., .308 Win., 7x57mm, or .30-06 cal., 20 in. barrel, adj. trigger. Mannlicher style carbine. Disc. 1984.

	100%	98%	95%	90%	80%	70%	60%
	$430	$325	$300	$275	$250	$230	$215

Grading	100%	98%	95%	90%	80%	70%	60%

ALASKAN - similar to Mark X, except .375 H&H or .458 Win. Mag. cal., recoil pad and extra stock crossbolt. Disc. 1984.

| | $460 | $350 | $330 | $310 | $290 | $250 | $210 |

MARK X REALTREE - .270 Win. or .30-06 cal., features Realtree Camo finish. Imported 1994-96.

| | $460 | $390 | $365 | $320 | $275 | $250 | $225 |

Last MSR was $549.

MARK X WHITWORTH -.270 Win., .30-06, and .300 Win. Mag. cals, Mauser action, 24 in. barrel, open sights, 5 shot mag. (.300 Win. Mag. is only 3), checkered deluxe walnut with ebony forearm tip, thumb safety with sling swivels, adj. trigger, rubber recoil butt plate, 7 lbs. Imported 1984-96.

| | $475 | $400 | $365 | $320 | $275 | $250 | $225 |

Last MSR was $565.

Add $19 for 7mm Rem. Mag. (disc.) or .300 Win. Mag. cal.

This model was the Whitworth American Field Series until 1987. Early manufacture was done in Manchester, England. Recent manufacture is by Zastava located in Yugoslavia. Earlier Manchester guns (before approx. 1980) will bring a slight premium over the values listed.

WHITWORTH MANNLICHER STYLE CARBINE - .243 Win., .270 Win., .308 Win., 7x57mm, or .30-06 cal., bolt action with full length walnut Mannlicher style stock, open sights, sling swivels, thumb safety, 20 in. barrel, 5 shot mag., 7 lbs. Imported 1984- 87.

| | $570 | $495 | $455 | $410 | $375 | $340 | $310 |

Last MSR was $675.

WHITWORTH EXPRESS RIFLE - .375 H&H (disc. 1993) or .458 Win. Mag. cal., 3 shot, 24 in. barrel, 3 leaf express sight, English style walnut stock, checkered pistol grip and forend, 8½ lbs. Imported 1974-96.

| | $600 | $540 | $465 | $425 | $395 | $375 | $350 |

Last MSR was $703.

RIFLES: SEMI-AUTO

22-ATD - .22 LR cal. only, patterned after the Browning Semi-Auto, 19.4 in. barrel, 11 shot mag. in stock, blued finish, checkered hardwood stock, take-down design, adj. rear sight, 4.6 lbs. Mfg. by Norinco 1987-96.

| | $110 | $95 | $90 | $80 | $75 | $70 | $65 |

Last MSR was $121.

Add $16 for camo case (disc.).

INTERDYNAMIC OF AMERICA, INC.

Previous distributor located in Miami, FL 1981-84.

PISTOLS: SEMI-AUTO

KG-9 - 9mm Para. cal., 3 in. barrel, open bolt, paramilitary design pistol. Disc. approx. 1982.

| | $750 | $700 | $650 | $600 | $575 | $550 | $525 |

KG-99 - 9mm Para. cal., 3 in. barrel, semi-auto paramilitary design pistol, closed bolt, 36 shot mag., 5 in. vent. shroud barrel, blue only, a stainless steel version of the KG-9. Mfg. by Interdynamic 1984 only.

| | $375 | $325 | $275 | $230 | $200 | $180 | $160 |
| KG-99M, mini pistol | $450 | $400 | $350 | $285 | $235 | $200 | $180 |

INTRAC ARMS INTERNATIONAL LLC

Current importer located in Knoxville, TN. Intrac imports trademarks manufactured by Arsenal Bulgaria, and by IM Metal Production facility in Croatia beginning late 2000. Currently imported by HS America, located in Knoxville, TN. Distributor and dealer sales.

Grading	100%	98%	95%	90%	80%	70%	60%

PISTOLS: SEMI-AUTO

HS 2000 - 9mm Para, .357 SIG, or .40 S&W cal., short recoil locked breech mechanism, polymer frame, trigger and grip safety, 3 dot low profile sights, loaded chamber indicator, black finish, 23 oz. Importation from Croatia began 2000.

	MSR	$419		$350	$295	$250	$225	$200	$185	$175

MAKAROV - .380 ACP or 9x18mm cal., double action, black phosphate finish, black grips, supplied with two 8 shot mags. and holster. Importation began 2002.

	MSR	$159		$145	$125	$110	$95	$85	$80	$75

RIFLES: SEMI-AUTO

ROMAK 1 & 2 - 7.62x39mm (Romak 1) or 5.45x39mm (Romak 2) cal., AK-47 copy with 16½ in. barrel and scope mount on left side of receiver, wood thumbhole stock, includes 5 and 10 shot mags., and accessories. Importation began 2002.

	MSR	$329		$285	$250	$215	$190	$175	$160	$145

SLR-101 - similar to Romak, except has 17¼ in. cold hammer forged barrel and black polymer stock and forearm, includes 2 mags. and accessories. Importation began 2002.

	MSR	$359		$310	$265	$220	$195	$180	$165	$145

ROMAK 3 - 7.62x54R cal., based on current issue PSL/FPK sniper configuration, 5 or 10 shot mag., last shot bolt hold open, 26½ in. barrel with muzzle brake, mil-spec scope with range finder, bullet drop compensator and illuminated recticle. Importation began 2002.

	MSR	$899		$800	$725	$650	$600	$550	$500	$450

INTRATEC

Previous manufacturer circa 1985-2000 located in Miami, FL.

PISTOLS: SEMI-AUTO

PROTEC-25 - .25 ACP. cal., double action only, 2½ in. barrel, 8 shot mag., 13 oz. Disc. 2000.

	$110	$80	$65	$45	$35	$30	$25

Last MSR was $137.

Add $5 for Tec-Kote finish or black slide/frame finish (disc.).

TEC-DC9 - 9mm Para. cal., paramilitary design pistol, 5 in. shrouded barrel, matte black finish, 10 (C/B 1994) or 32* shot mag. Mfg. 1985-94.

	$245	$175	$155	$140	$130	$120	$110

Last MSR was $269.

* **TEC-9DCK** - similar to TEC-9, except has new durable Tec-Kote finish with better protection than hard chrome. Mfg. 1991-94.

	$250	$185	$160	$140	$130	$120	$110

Last MSR was $297.

* **TEC-DC9S** - matte stainless version of the TEC-9. Disc. 1994.

	$300	$240	$185

Last MSR was $362.

Add $203 for TEC-9 with accessory package (deluxe case, 3-32 shot mags., paramilitary design grip, and recoil compensator).

TEC-DC9M - mini version of the Model TEC-9, including 3 in. barrel and 20 shot mag. Disc. 1994.

	$245	$175	$155	$140	$130	$120	$110

Last MSR was $245.

Grading	100%	98%	95%	90%	80%	70%	60%

✳ **TEC-DC9MK** - similar to TEC-9M, except has Tec-Kote rust resistant finish. Mfg. 1991-1994.

	$255	$185	$155	$140	$130	$120	$110

Last MSR was $277.

✳ **TEC-DC9MS** - matte stainless version of the TEC-9M. Disc. 1994.

	$275	$225	$180				

Last MSR was $339.

TEC-22 "SCORPION" - .22 LR cal., paramilitary design, 4 in. barrel, ambidextrous safety, military matte finish, or electroless nickel, 30 shot mag., adj. sights, 30 oz. Mfg. 1988- 94.

	$190	$165	$150	$135	$120	$100	$90

Last MSR was $202.

Add $20 for TEC-Kote finish.

✳ **TEC-22N** - similar to TEC-22, except has nickel finish. Mfg. 1990 only.

	$200	$175	$160	$140	$125	$105	$95

Last MSR was $226.

Add $16 for threaded barrel (Model TEC-22TN).

TEC-22T - threaded barrel variation of the TEC-22 "Scorpion". Mfg. 1991-94.

	$145	$125	$110	$100	$90	$80	$70

Last MSR was $161.

Add $23 for Tec-Kote finish.

SPORT-22 - .22 LR cal., 4 in. non-threaded barrel, 10 shot Ruger styled rotary mag., matte finish, adj. rear sight, 29½ oz. New 1995.

	$140	$110	$95	$80	$65	$55	$45

Last MSR was $170.

Add $15 for stainless steel barrel.

CAT-9, CAT-45, CAT-380 - .380 ACP (new 1995), 9mm Para., or .45 ACP (new 1995) cal., double action only, black finish, polymer frame with top sight channel, only 27 parts, blowback action on 9mm Para., locked breech on .45 ACP, 6 (.45 ACP cal.) or 7 (.380 ACP or 9mm Para.) shot mag., 3 or 3¼ (.45 ACP only) in. barrel, 18-21 oz. Mfg. 1993-2000.

	$215	$180	$155	$135	$120	$100	$90

Last MSR was $260.

Subtract $25 for .380 ACP cal.
Add $20 for .45 ACP cal.
Add $15 for Fire Sights.
This series was designed by N. Sirkis of Israel.

AB-10 - 9mm Para. cal., paramilitary design, 2¾ in. non-threaded barrel, choice of 32 (limited supply) or 10 shot mag., black synthetic frame, firing pin safety block, black or stainless steel finish, 45 oz. Mfg. 1997-2000.

	$200	$180	$160	$150	$135	$120	$105

Last MSR was $225.

Add $20 for stainless steel (new 2000).
Add $55 for 32 shot mag.

INTRATEC U.S.A.

Previous manufacturer located in Miami, FL.

DERRINGERS

TEC-38 DERRINGER - .22 Mag., .32 H&R Mag., or .38 Spl. cal., O/U, 3 in. barrel, blue frame, double action, 13 oz. Mfg. 1986-1988.

	$110	$95	$85	$75	$65	$60	$55

Last MSR was $125.

Grading	100%	98%	95%	90%	80%	70%	60%

PISTOLS: SEMI-AUTO

PROTEC-22 - while advertised for $112 MSR during 1993, this model was never mfg.

TEC-9 - 9mm Para. cal., paramilitary design, 5 in. shrouded barrel, 32 shot mag., disc.

	$450	$400	$350	$315	$275	$235	$195

TEC-9C - 9mm Para. cal., carbine variation with 16½ in. barrel, 36 shot mag. Only 1 gun mfg. 1987 - extreme rarity precludes pricing.

INVESTARM, s.p.a.

Current manufacturer located in Marcheno, Italy. No current U.S. importation. Please contact the factory directly (please refer to Trademark Index listing).

Investarm manufactures a wide variety of shotguns in various configurations, including folding single shots, folding O/Us, a range of high quality competition and hunting models (including the new Sydney Models), in addition to muzzle loading black powder rifles and pistols.

INVESTMENT ARMS INC.

Current company specializing in limited/special editions located in Fort Collins, CO.

Investment Arms Inc. subcontracts various gun manufactures to produce their own limited editions/special editions. These guns are typically limited by county or state, and feature various engraving motifs, configurations, and other embellishments. Please contact the company directly for more information on quantities, original issue prices, and dates of manufacture (refer to Trademark Index). Secondary marketplace liquidity is difficult to determine, based on their relative rarity and overall collectibility.

IRWINDALE ARMS, INC. (IAI)

Previous manufacturer located in Irwindale, CA 1988-1991.

PISTOLS: SEMI-AUTO

In June, 1991, AMT reacquired the manufacturing rights to all IAI models. Please refer to the AMT section for current models.

AUTOMAG III - .30 Carbine or 9mm Win. Mag. (mfg. 1990-92) cal., stainless steel only, 6 3/8 in. barrel, patterned after Colt Govt. Model, Millett adj. sights with white outline, grooved Lexan grips, 8 shot mag., 43 oz. Mfg. 1989-91.

	$550	$475	$395

Last MSR was $606.

AUTOMAG IV - .45 Win. Mag., or 10mm cal., semi-auto, 6½ or 8 5/8 (mfg. 1991) in. barrel, 7 shot mag., Millett adj. sights, stainless steel only, 46 oz. Mfg. 1990-91.

	$565	$485	$500

Last MSR was $630.

JAVELINA - 10mm cal., semi-auto, 5 (disc. 1991) or 7 in. barrel, 8 shot mag., Millett adj. sights, wraparound Neoprene grips, stainless steel, wide adj. trigger, long grip safety, 48 oz. Mfg. 1990-91.

	$525	$450	$375

Last MSR was $570.

BACKUP PISTOL - .380 ACP cal., semi-auto action, 2½ in. barrel, stainless steel, Lexan grips, 5 shot mag., 18 oz. Older disc. walnut grip models are worth a slight premium. Disc. 1989.

	$200	$165	$135

Last MSR was $243.

ISRAEL ARMS INTERNATIONAL

Current importer (please refer to IAI listing) and manufacturer located in Houston, TX, beginning 1997.

Grading	100%	98%	95%	90%	80%	70%	60%

ISRAEL ARMS LTD.

Previous manufacturer located in Kfar Saba, Israel. Imported and distributed exclusively by Israel Arms International, Inc. located in Houston, TX 1997-2001.

PISTOLS: SEMI-AUTO

MODEL 1500 HI POWER - 9mm Para. cal., single action, 3.85 (Compact) or 4.64 (Standard, disc. 1998) in. barrel, two-tone finish, rubberized grips, regular or Meprolite sights, 10 shot mag., 33.6 oz. Imported 1997-98 only.

$360	$305	$255	$225	$200	$185	$170

Last MSR was $413.

Add approx. $160 for two-tone finish with Meprolite sights.

✱ *Model 1500/1501 Hi-Power Compact* - 9mm Para. or .40 S&W cal., compact variation with 3.85 in. barrel, choice of two-tone (Model 1500) or blue (Model 1501) finish, 32.2 oz. Imported late 1999-2000.

$360	$305	$255	$225	$200	$185	$170

Last MSR was $412.

MODEL 2500 - 9mm Para. or .40 S&W cal., single or double action, ambidextrous safety with decocking feature, steel slide with alloy frame, 3 7/8 in. barrel, 10 shot mag., matte black finish, 34 oz.

While advertised during 1999, this model had very limited importation.

MODEL 3000 - 9mm Para cal., double action. Limited importation 2000-2001.

$335	$295	$260	$230	$200	$175	$150

Last MSR was $374.

MODEL 4000 - .40 S&W cal., double action. Limited importation 2000-2001.

$335	$295	$260	$230	$200	$175	$150

Last MSR was $374.

MODEL 5000/5001 COMBAT - .45 ACP cal., single action, 4¼ in barrel, combat configuration with ambidextrous safety, competition trigger, hammer, and slide stop, front and rear slide serrations, blue (Model 5001) or two-tone (Model 5000) finish, wraparound rubber grips, 42 oz., mfg. in Phillipines. Imported 1999-2001.

$395	$365	$330	$295	$265	$235	$210

Last MSR was $448.

MODEL 6000/6001 STANDARD - .45 ACP cal., single action, 5 in. stainless steel barrel, features beveled feed ramp, extended slide stop, safety and magazine release, ambidextrous safety, beavertail grip safety and combat style hammer, blue (Model 6001) or two- tone (Model 6000, disc. 2000) finish, 38 oz., mfg. in Phillipines. Imported 1999-2001.

$395	$365	$330	$295	$265	$235	$210

Last MSR was $448.

MODEL 7000/7001 WIDE FRAME - .45 ACP cal., single action, similar to Model 6000/ 6001, except has double stack mag., blue (Model 7001) or two-tone (Model 7000) finish, 40 oz. Imported 1999-2000.

$445	$395	$350	$300	$255	$225	$200

Last MSR was $490.

RIFLES

MODEL 333 M1 GARAND - .30-06 cal., 24 in. barrel, parts remanufactured to meet GI and mil specs, parkerized finish, 8 shot en-bloc mag., 9½ lbs. Mfg. 2000-2001.

$640	$550	$495	$450	$400	$365	$335

Last MSR was $852.

Grading	100%	98%	95%	90%	80%	70%	60%

MODEL 444 FAL - .308 Win. cal., patterned after the FN FAL model, mfg. by Imbel, located in Brazil, 2000-2001.

	$675	$595	$535	$475	$425	$375	$350

Last MSR was $897.

ISRAELI MILITARY INDUSTRIES (IMI)

Current manufacturer located in Israel. Limited importation currently.

IMI manufactured guns (both new and disc. models) include Galil, Jericho, Magnum Research, Timberwolf, Uzi, and others, and can be located in their respective sections.

ITALIAN MILITARY ARMS

Previous Italian popular military models mfg. since 1891.

PISTOLS: SEMI-AUTO

GLISENTI MODEL 1910 - 9mm Glisenti cal., 4 in. barrel, 7 shot mag., checkered wood grips, official Italian service pistol of both WWI and WWII, 32 oz.

	$800	$675	$550	$400	$325	$265	$235

Warning: 9mm Para. ammunition (9x18mm) cannot be used in this pistol - only 9mm Glisenti, as it is approx. 25% less powerful than the 9mm Para.

BRIXIA - similar to Glisenti Model 1910, except utilizes simplified mfg. techniques, mostly sold to civilians.

	$925	$750	$575	$425	$350	$325	$300

SOSSO - 9mm Para. cal., large experimental semi-auto, early pistols were double action and marked "Sosso", late guns were single action and built by FNA. All Sosso pistols feature a unique continuous "chain link" 19 or 21 shot mag. Approx. 5 guns mfg.

Extreme rarity factor precludes accurate price evaluation.

RIFLES: BOLT ACTION

MODEL 1891 MANNLICHER-CARCANO - 6.5x52mm Carcano cal., 6 shot, 31 in. barrel, straight handle, adj. sight, military stock.

	$120	$100	$85	$70	$55	$40	$30

MODEL 38 TERNI MILITARY RIFLE - 7.35x52mm Carcano cal., similar to 1891, except turned down bolt handle, 21 in. barrel and folding bayonet.

	$120	$100	$85	$70	$55	$40	$30

ITHACA CLASSIC DOUBLES

Current SxS shotgun manufacturer established during late 1998, and currently located in Victor, NY. Previously located in Mendon, NY until 1999. Consumer direct and dealer sales.

Ithaca
CLASSIC DOUBLES
The Legend Returns

SHOTGUNS: SxS

All Ithaca Classic Doubles shotguns feature state-of-the-art manufacturing techniques, Italian or U.S. hand engraving (using the original William McGraw patterns), Doug Turnbull bone/charcoal case colors and metal finish, and top quality American feather crotch walnut with precise hand checkering. Each gauge has its own frame size, and serial numbers are continued from the last gun Ithaca manufactured in 1948 (ser. no. 469,999). Please contact the company directly regarding special orders and options.

The Ithaca custom shop is also available to produce custom orders, including special options and features. For more information on these custom services, please contact the manufacturer directly (see Trademark Index).

Add $3,000 (4E, 5E, 6E) and $3,750 (Grades 7E & Sousa) for extra set of 16 (20 ga. frame) or 28 (.410 bore frame) ga. barrels.

Add $600-$2,150 for canvas, canvas and leather, leather, or oak and leather cases.

Grading	100%	98%	95%	90%	80%	70%	60%

SPECIAL FIELD/SKEET GRADE - 16 (new 2001), 20, 28 ga., or .410 bore, designed for field and clay shooting, DT, ejectors, 26, 28, or 30 in. barrels with fixed chokes, light perimeter hand engraving with metal stippling on shoulders and in front of top opening lever, Turnbull bone and charcoal case colors, checkered pistol grip or English feather crotch walnut stock and forearm, 5lbs. 5 oz. – 6 lbs. 6 oz. New late 1998.

MSR	$3,465	$3,250	$2,700	$2,200	$1,800	$1,500	$1,250	$1,100

Add 10% for 28 ga. or .410 bore.

CLASSIC COMPETITION GRADE - all gauges, competition features. New 2002.

MSR	$5,995	$5,500	$4,750	$3,750	$3,250	$2,650	$2,175	$1,775

GRADE 4E CLASSIC - 16 (new 2001), 20, 28 ga., or .410 bore, features gold plated triggers, jewelled barrel flats, hand tuned locks, hand engraved three game scenes with floral scroll, deluxe walnut stock and forearm with fleur de lis pattern and 22 LPI checkering, other specifications similar to Special Field/Skeet Grade. New late 1998.

MSR	$5,995	$5,500	$4,750	$3,750	$3,250	$2,650	$2,175	$1,775

GRADE 5E CLASSIC - step up from Grade 4E, with more elaborate frame engraving and gold inlays on frame sides, upgraded walnut. New 2002.

MSR	$7,500	$6,995	$5,750	$4,750	$3,750	$3,250	$2,650	$2,175

GRADE 6E CLASSIC - step up from Grade 5E, with fine scroll engraving and gold dog inlays on frame sides, upgraded walnut. New 2002.

MSR	$8,999	$8,450	$7,150	$5,950	$4,850	$3,950	$3,250	$2,650

GRADE 7E CLASSIC - 16 (new 2001), 20, 28 ga., or .410 bore, features hand engraved oak leaf scroll on frame and barrels, and 24 Kt. flat gold game scene inlays, including a bald eagle on floor plate, exhibition grade American walnut with 12 checkered panels in fleur-de-lis pattern, other specifications similar to Special Field/Skeet Grade. New late 1998.

MSR	$9,900	$9,150	$7,400	$6,375	$5,400	$4,675	$3,975	$3,400

SOUSA GRADE - 16 (new 2001), 20, 28 ga., or .410 bore, top-of-the-line model with every possible refinement, each gun individually hand fitted, jewelled, and polished, includes famous 24 Kt. Sousa mermaid on trigger guard, other specifications similar to Special Field/Skeet Grade. Special order only, new late 1998.

MSR	$15,125	$13,550	$11,250	$9,250	$8,150	$6,875	$5,950	$5,100

SUPERLATIVE CLASS - custom order, best quality model with a wide choice of engraving options and inlays, exhibition grade walnut, approx. 10-15 guns mfg. annually. New 2002.

Prices for this model start at $20,000. Please contact the company directly for an individual price quotation and delivery time.

ITHACA GUN COMPANY LLC

Current manufacturer established during 1996 and located in King Ferry, NY. Ithaca Gun Company, LLC has resumed production on the Model 37 slide action shotgun and variations. Previously manufactured in Ithaca, NY, 1883 to Nov. of 1986. In the past, Ithaca also absorbed companies including Syracuse Arms Co., Lefever Arms Co., Union Fire Arms Co., Wilkes-Barre Gun Co., as well as others.

COMBINATION GUNS

LSA-55 TURKEY GUN - O/U shotgun-rifle combo, 12 ga., .222 Rem., 24½ in. ribbed barrel, exposed hammer, folding rear sight, checkered Monte Carlo stock. Mfg. by Tikka, Finland 1970- 1981.

	$650	$575	$475	$450	$425	$385	$330

Grading	100%	98%	95%	90%	80%	70%	60%

HANDGUNS

ITHACA WWII MILITARY MFG. - .45 ACP cal., mfg. for WWII military M1911A1 contracts, 7 shot mag. 5 in. barrel, ser. no. ranges 856,405 - 916,404, 1,208,674 - 1,279,673, 1,441,431 - 1,471,430, 1,743,847 - 1,890,503, 2,075,104 - 2,134,403, and 2,619,014 - 2,693,613. Parkerized finish.

$800	$600	$500	$450	$375	$350	$325

Add 20% with original shipping carton.

For more information on other WWI and WWII M1911/A1 military contracts, please refer to the Colt's Manufacturing section Pistols: Semi-Auto, Govt. Model 1911/1911A1 Military Variations in this text.

ITHACA 50TH SEMI-AUTO ANNIVERSARY MODEL - .45 ACP cal., 5 in. match barrel with bushing, blue polished or tactical matte finish, checkered diamond pattern walnut grips, extended beavertail grip safety, includes plastic case and certificate, only 125 mfg. with special serialization 1995- 97. Disc.

$695	$625	$550	$500	$450	$400	$360

Last MSR was $795.

This model was offered exclusively by All American Sales, Inc. located in Memphis, TN.

X-CALIBER SINGLE SHOT - .22 LR or .44 Mag. cal., break open action with contoured wood grip and forearm, 8, 10 or 15 in. barrel, unique dual firing pin detonates both rimfire and centerfire cartridges. While advertised in 1988, Models 20 and 30 were never sold, even though approx. 300 units were mfg. in 22 cal. only. Production was ceased due to unsolvable manufacturing problems.

RIFLES: BOLT ACTION

LSA-55 STANDARD - .222 Rem., .22-250 Rem., 6mm Rem., .243 Win., or .308 Win. cal., Mauser type action, 22 in. barrel, leaf sight, 3 shot mag., checkered Monte Carlo stock. Mfg. in Finland by Tikka from 1969 to 1977.

$400	$375	$350	$310	$275	$250	$230

The LSA Model designation stands for Light, Strong, Accurate.

LSA-55 DELUXE - similar to Standard, except rollover cheekpiece, rosewood pistol grip cap and forend tip, skipline checkering, no sights, scope mounts furnished.

$495	$450	$425	$400	$365	$345	$325

LSA-55 HEAVY BARREL - similar to LSA-55, except .222 Rem. or .22-250 Rem. cal. only, target heavy barrel, special beavertail stock 8½ lbs.

$450	$425	$400	$375	$350	$325	$300

LSA-65 - similar to LSA-55, except long action for calibers .25-06 Rem., .270 Win., or .30-06. Mfg. 1969 to 1977.

$400	$375	$350	$310	$275	$250	$230

LSA-65 DELUXE - similar to LSA-55, except has deluxe checkered walnut stock, .25-06 Rem., .270 Win., or .30-06.

$495	$450	$425	$400	$365	$345	$325

RIFLES: LEVER ACTION

MODEL 49 SADDLEGUN - .22 LR or .22 Mag. cal., lever action, single shot. Mfg. 1961- 1978. Martini-style action.

$145	$130	$110	$80	$65	$50	$40

Add 15% for .22 Mag. cal.
Add 20% for Deluxe Model.

Grading	100%	98%	95%	90%	80%	70%	60%

MODEL 49R - similar to Model 49 Saddlegun, except is slide action repeater. Mfg. 1965-1971.

	$265	$250	$235	$200	$175	$150	$125

Add 15% for .22 Mag. cal.

MODEL 49 PRESENTATION - similar to Model 49 Saddlegun, except gold-plated trigger, hammer, engraved receiver, fancy walnut. Mfg. 1962-1974.

	$295	$275	$250	$235	$200	$165	$135

MODEL 49 ST. LOUIS BICENTENNIAL - like Deluxe Model 49, except inscription on receiver, 200 mfg. 1964.

	$325	$255	$215				

Last MSR was $35.

MODEL 72 SADDLEGUN - .22 or .22 Mag. cal., lever action, 18½ in. barrel, hooded front sight. Mfg. 1973-1978 by Erma Werke, W. Germany.

	$325	$275	$225	$175	$145	$130	$120

MODEL 72 DELUXE - similar to Model 72, except has silver finished engraved receiver, deluxe walnut, octagon barrel. Mfg. 1974-1976.

	$395	$325	$250	$225	$175	$145	$130

RIFLES: SEMI-AUTO

MODEL X5-C - .22 LR cal., 7 shot mag., grooved forearm, Model X5-T has tube mag. Mfg. 1958-1964.

	$195	$165	$125	$100	$80	$70	$60

MODEL X-15 - .22 LR cal., similar to X5-C, except forearm is not grooved. Mfg. 1964-1967.

	$195	$165	$125	$100	$80	$70	$60

RIFLES: SINGLE SHOT

MODEL 89 - .243 Win., .30-06, .375 H&H, .416 Rigby, or 7x57mm cal., falling block action, 26 or 28 in. Shilen barrel, full-length uncheckered walnut stock.

While advertised at $658 MSR during 1994, this model was never mfg.

SHOTGUNS: O/U, PREVIOUS IMPORTATION

Note: Ithaca was the sole importer for Perazzi in the '70s. All new and used models will be in the P section under Perazzi. Perazzi currently distributes their own firearms.

Note: Please refer to the Fabarm section in this text for those models previously imported by Ithaca (imported 1994-95).

Note: SKB shotguns previously imported by Ithaca can be found under the SKB heading.

SHOTGUNS: SxS, 1880-1948 MFG.

AUTO & BURGLAR SxS - 20 ga. smooth bore with 10 in. double barrels, case hardened finish, pistol grip, Model A (approx. 2,500 mfg.) has grip spur, Model B (approx. 2,000 mfg.) has squared grip; both were mfg. in lots of about 100 according to demand, and serial numbers are mixed with those of regular Ithaca shotguns. Guns not currently registered with BATF cannot be legally owned and are subject to seizure. Mfg. 1922-1934.

✳ *Model A* - serial no. range is 343,336-398,365.

	$1,850	$1,450	$1,200	$975	$775	$675	$575

✳ *Model B* - serial no. range is 425,000-464,699.

	$1,450	$1,200	$975	$775	$675	$575	$465

Add $300-$500 for original holster (very rare). Prototype or special order guns (in 16, 28 ga., or .410 bore) are extremely rare and command premiums of 100%+.

100%	98%	95%	90%	80%	70%	60%	50%	40%	30%	20%	10%

ITHACA HAMMERLESS - 12, 16, 20, 28 ga., or .410 bore, 26-32 in. fluid steel or damascus barrels, boxlock, extractors, double triggers, any standard choke, checkered pistol grip stock and forearm, grades shown differ in overall quality, ornamentation, grade of wood, and style of checkering. In 1925, the rotary bolt and stronger frame were adapted (ser. numbers after 400,000 - commonly referred to as NID or New Ithaca Double). Values are the same as for pre-400,000 serial range shotguns. Ithaca doubles incorporated a number of design changes made on the action - they are referred to as the Lewis, Crass, Flues, and Minier frame variations.

Values below are for guns mfg. between 1925-1948.

Add $200 for SST.

Add $150 for SNT.

Add $350 for VR on Grades 4, 5, 7, and $2,000 Grade.

Add $200 for VR - lower grades.

Add $175 for beavertail forearm.

Add 33% for auto ejectors on Grades No. 1, 2, and 3.

Subtract 33% if without ejectors on Grades 4E-7E.

Early hammer doubles in average condition are approx. valued between $175-$450. However, if 60% condition remains (including original case colors), values can approximate those listed.

FIELD GRADE

✳ 10 ga. Mag.

100%	98%	95%	90%	80%	70%	60%	50%	40%	30%	20%	10%
N/A	N/A	$1,500	$1,400	$1,300	$1,200	$1,100	$950	$825	$775	$675	$630

3½ in. chambered 10 ga. Mags. are serial numbered over 500,000. Total mfg. was approx. 850 guns for all grades. 2 7/8 in. chambered 10 ga.'s are priced the same as a 12 ga. A 12 ga., 3 in. model was also made on the 10 ga. frame - only 87 were mfg. and specimens are noted in the 500,000 serial range.

✳ 12 ga.

100%	98%	95%	90%	80%	70%	60%	50%	40%	30%	20%	10%
$1,000	$800	$600	$550	$500	$450	$415	$380	$350	$325	$300	$280

✳ 16 ga.

100%	98%	95%	90%	80%	70%	60%	50%	40%	30%	20%	10%
$1,100	$900	$800	$750	$700	$650	$600	$550	$500	$425	$375	$340

✳ 20 ga.

100%	98%	95%	90%	80%	70%	60%	50%	40%	30%	20%	10%
$1,400	$1,200	$1,000	$900	$850	$800	$750	$700	$600	$550	$500	$440

✳ 28 ga.

100%	98%	95%	90%	80%	70%	60%	50%	40%	30%	20%	10%
N/A	N/A	$2,850	$2,500	$2,200	$2,000	$1,800	$1,700	$1,600	$1,500	$1,400	$1,200

✳ .410 bore

100%	98%	95%	90%	80%	70%	60%	50%	40%	30%	20%	10%
$3,800	$3,400	$2,850	$2,500	$2,200	$2,000	$1,800	$1,700	$1,600	$1,500	$1,400	$1,200

GRADE NO. 1 - manufactured in both Flues and NID models, similar to Field Grade.

✳ 12 ga.

100%	98%	95%	90%	80%	70%	60%	50%	40%	30%	20%	10%
$1,225	$1,000	$800	$600	$550	$500	$450	$415	$380	$350	$325	$315

✳ 16 ga.

100%	98%	95%	90%	80%	70%	60%	50%	40%	30%	20%	10%
$1,375	$1,150	$925	$825	$750	$700	$650	$600	$550	$500	$425	$395

✳ 20 ga.

100%	98%	95%	90%	80%	70%	60%	50%	40%	30%	20%	10%
$1,700	$1,400	$1,200	$1,000	$900	$850	$800	$750	$700	$600	$550	$525

✳ 28 ga.

100%	98%	95%	90%	80%	70%	60%	50%	40%	30%	20%	10%
N/A	N/A	$2,750	$2,200	$2,000	$1,800	$1,700	$1,600	$1,500	$1,400	$1,200	$1,125

✳ .410 bore

100%	98%	95%	90%	80%	70%	60%	50%	40%	30%	20%	10%
N/A	N/A	$2,850	$2,250	$2,000	$1,800	$1,700	$1,600	$1,500	$1,400	$1,200	$1,125

GRADE NO. 2

✳ 10 ga. Mag.

100%	98%	95%	90%	80%	70%	60%	50%	40%	30%	20%	10%
$2,400	$2,000	$1,800	$1,600	$1,400	$1,300	$1,200	$1,100	$950	$900	$800	$735

3½ in. chambered 10 ga. Mags. are serial numbered over 500,000. Total mfg. was approx. 850 guns for all grades. 2 7/8 in. chambered 10 ga.'s are priced the same as a 12 ga.

100%	98%	95%	90%	80%	70%	60%	50%	40%	30%	20%	10%
✳ 12 ga.											
$1,500	$1,200	$1,000	$800	$600	$550	$500	$450	$415	$380	$350	$335
✳ 16 ga.											
$1,500	$1,200	$1,000	$900	$800	$750	$700	$650	$600	$550	$500	$475
✳ 20 ga.											
$1,800	$1,500	$1,200	$1,100	$1,000	$900	$850	$800	$750	$700	$650	$580
✳ 28 ga.											
N/A	N/A	$3,250	$2,500	$2,000	$1,950	$1,850	$1,750	$1,650	$1,550	$1,450	$1,350
✳ .410 bore											
N/A	N/A	$3,250	$2,500	$2,000	$1,950	$1,850	$1,750	$1,650	$1,550	$1,450	$1,350

GRADE NO. 3

100%	98%	95%	90%	80%	70%	60%	50%	40%	30%	20%	10%
✳ 10 ga. Mag.											
$3,500	$2,900	$2,300	$1,850	$1,600	$1,400	$1,300	$1,200	$1,100	$950	$825	$735

3½ in. chambered 10 ga. Mags. are serial numbered over 500,000. Total mfg. was approx. 850 guns for all grades. 2 7/8 in. chambered 10 ga.'s are priced the same as a 12 ga.

100%	98%	95%	90%	80%	70%	60%	50%	40%	30%	20%	10%
✳ 12 ga.											
$1,850	$1,500	$1,200	$1,000	$800	$750	$700	$650	$600	$550	$500	$475
✳ 16 ga.											
N/A	$1,500	$1,200	$1,000	$900	$850	$800	$750	$700	$650	$600	$575
✳ 20 ga.											
N/A	N/A	$1,500	$1,300	$1,200	$1,100	$1,000	$900	$850	$800	$750	$735

✳ 28 ga. - only 5 mfg.
Extreme rarity factor precludes accurate pricing evaluation.

✳ .410 bore - only 7 mfg.
Extreme rarity factor precludes accurate pricing evaluation.

GRADE NO. 4E - auto ejectors.

100%	98%	95%	90%	80%	70%	60%	50%	40%	30%	20%	10%
✳ 10 ga. Mag.											
$4,650	$3,950	$3,250	$2,600	$2,100	$1,975	$1,875	$1,750	$1,650	$1,550	$1,450	$1,350

3½ in. chambered 10 ga. Mags. are serial numbered over 500,000. Total mfg. was approx. 850 guns for all grades. 2 7/8 in. chambered 10 ga.'s are priced the same as a 12 ga.

100%	98%	95%	90%	80%	70%	60%	50%	40%	30%	20%	10%
✳ 12 ga.											
N/A	$3,000	$2,500	$2,100	$1,700	$1,550	$1,325	$1,200	$1,100	$995	$875	$800
✳ 16 ga.											
N/A	N/A	$3,000	$2,400	$2,000	$1,875	$1,650	$1,550	$1,450	$1,325	$1,200	$1,050
✳ 20 ga.											
N/A	$4,000	$3,700	$3,500	$3,300	$3,100	$2,950	$2,700	$2,300	$1,975	$1,650	$1,400

✳ 28 ga.
Extreme rarity factor precludes accurate pricing evaluation.

✳ .410 bore
Extreme rarity factor precludes accurate pricing evaluation.

GRADE NO. 5E - auto ejectors.

✳ 10 ga. - only 9 mfg.
Extreme rarity factor precludes accurate pricing evaluation.

100%	98%	95%	90%	80%	70%	60%	50%	40%	30%	20%	10%
✳ 12 ga.											
N/A	N/A	$3,200	$3,000	$2,700	$2,200	$1,875	$1,650	$1,325	$1,200	$1,100	$1,050
✳ 16 ga.											
N/A	N/A	$2,800	$2,500	$2,200	$1,875	$1,750	$1,550	$1,425	$1,325	$1,200	$1,150
✳ 20 ga.											
N/A	$4,500	$4,000	$3,700	$3,300	$3,000	$2,875	$2,650	$2,325	$2,100	$1,875	$1,700

100%	98%	95%	90%	80%	70%	60%	50%	40%	30%	20%	10%

✳ 28 ga.
Extreme rarity factor precludes accurate pricing evaluation.

✳ .410 bore
Extreme rarity factor precludes accurate pricing evaluation.

GRADE NO. 7E - auto ejectors, only 22 mfg. in all gauges.
Extreme rarity factor precludes accurate pricing evaluation on this model.

$2,000 GRADE - 12 ga., top-of-the-line model, auto ejectors, single selective trigger.

100%	98%	95%	90%	80%	70%	60%	50%	40%	30%	20%	10%
N/A	N/A	$8,450	$7,400	$6,500	$5,650	$4,750	$4,000	$3,250	$2,600	$2,100	$1,700

Rarity on 16 or 20 ga. precludes accurate pricing.

PRE-WAR $1,000 GRADE - 12 ga., top-of-the-line models, auto ejectors, single selective trigger.

100%	98%	95%	90%	80%	70%	60%	50%	40%	30%	20%	10%
N/A	N/A	$9,500	$8,450	$7,400	$6,500	$5,650	$4,750	$4,000	$3,250	$2,600	$2,250

Rarity on 16 or 20 ga. precludes accurate pricing.

SOUSA GRADE - has mermaids on trigger guard in gold, only 11 manufactured (including one .410 bore). This model is very rare and prices are hard to establish. Recently, the price range has been approx. $15,000-$40,000, depending on gauge and original condition.
The famous band director and composer, John Phillip Sousa, assisted in the development of this model.

Grading	100%	98%	95%	90%	80%	70%	60%

SHOTGUNS: SEMI-AUTO

MODEL 51A FEATHERLIGHT STANDARD - 12 or 20 ga., 30 in. full, 28 in. full or mod., 26 in. imp. cyl., gas operated, autoloading, checkered pistol grip stock. Mfg. 1970-1985. Vent. rib became standard during late production.

	100%	98%	95%	90%	80%	70%	60%
Older models (no VR)	$250	$230	$200	$180	$165	$150	$130
Recent production (w/VR)	$295	$265	$235	$210	$190	$175	$165

Last MSR with VR was $477.

MODEL 51A MAGNUM - similar to 51 Standard, except 3 in. shells only, blue finish, recoil pad, VR became standard in 1984. Disc. 1985.

	100%	98%	95%	90%	80%	70%	60%
Older models w/o VR	$265	$235	$220	$205	$180	$165	$150
Vent. rib	$325	$275	$250	$225	$200	$185	$170

MODEL 51A MAGNUM WATERFOWLER - similar to 51 Standard, except 3 in. shells only, matte finished metal & flat finished walnut, recoil pad. Vent. rib standard. Mfg. 1984-1986.

100%	98%	95%	90%	80%	70%	60%
$325	$295	$275	$250	$230	$200	$180

Last MSR was $625.

Add $40 for camouflaged exterior finish (mfg. 1986 only).

MODEL 51A SUPREME TRAP - similar to 51 Standard, except 12 ga. only, 30 in. barrel, 7 post rib, full choke, select wood, pad, trap style stock. Add $36 for Monte Carlo. Mfg. 1970-1986.

100%	98%	95%	90%	80%	70%	60%
$450	$375	$325	$295	$270	$250	$230

Last MSR was $869.

MODEL 51A SUPREME SKEET - similar to 51 Standard, except 26 in. VR barrel, skeet choke, select wood. Mfg. 1970-present. 20 ga. was available 1983. Disc. 1986.

100%	98%	95%	90%	80%	70%	60%
$465	$395	$340	$300	$280	$260	$240

Last MSR was $858.

MODEL 51A DEERSLAYER - similar to 51 Standard, with 24 in. slug barrel, rifle sights, recoil pad, no rib. Mfg. 1972-1983.

100%	98%	95%	90%	80%	70%	60%
$350	$300	$260	$230	$195	$180	$165

Last MSR was $477.

Grading	100%	98%	95%	90%	80%	70%	60%

MODEL 51A TURKEY GUN - 12 ga. Mag. only, 26 in. barrel, matte finish, sling and swivels included. Mfg. 1984-1986.

	100%	98%	95%	90%	80%	70%	60%
	$360	$305	$275	$265	$250	$230	$210

Last MSR was $625.

MODEL 51 DUCKS UNLIMITED - similar to 51 Deluxe, with D/U emblem on receiver.

	$425	$375	$335	$300	$280	$260	$230

MODEL 51 PRESENTATION - 12 ga., blued, engraved, gold engraved receiver with deluxe walnut. Mfg. 1984-1986.

	$1,325	$1,050	$875	$700	$575	$450	$325

Last MSR was $1,658.

MODEL XL 300 - 12 or 20 ga., gas operated, various barrel lengths with or w/o VR, mfg. 1973-76.

	$250	$230	$200	$180	$165	$150	$130

Add 15% for VR barrel.

MODEL XL 900 - 12 or 20 ga., gas operated, various barrel lengths with VR, mfg. 1973-78.

	$295	$275	$245	$210	$185	$170	$150

Add 10% for skeet, trap, or slug variations.

Shotguns: Semi-Auto, Mag-10 Series

All Ithaca Mag-10s were disc. 1986.

MAG-10 - 10 ga., 3½ in. Mag., various barrel lengths, stainless steel breech block assembly, gas operated, various chokes, plain barrel, 11 lb. Mfg. 1975-1986.

100% values assume NIB condition - if without, subtract 10%.

✳ *Standard Grade* - no checkering, ribless barrel, dull finished wood.

	$600	$550	$500	$460	$430	$395	$375

Last MSR was $726.

✳ *Standard Grade with VR* - available in 22, 26, 28, or 32 in. barrel lengths - otherwise similar to Standard Grade.

	$625	$550	$495	$450	$400	$360	$330

Last MSR was $781.

Add $60 for camouflaged exterior finish.
Add $60 for interchangeable choke tubes (3) - became available in 1986.

✳ *Deluxe Vent* - select checkered walnut stock and forearm, 22, 26, 28, or 32 in. barrels, high lustre wood finish.

	$675	$600	$550	$495	$450	$400	$350

Last MSR was $924.

✳ *Supreme Grade* - extra-select checkered walnut stock and forearm, otherwise similar to Deluxe Vent.

	$795	$725	$675	$595	$550	$495	$450

Last MSR was $1,124.

✳ *Mag. 10 Roadblocker* - 22 in. cylinder bored ribless barrel, parkerized finish.

	$750	$625	$575	$500	$460	$430	$400

Last MSR was $741.

✳ *National Wild Turkey Fed. Special Edition* - mfg. in 1985 only.

	$950	$795	$625				

MAG-10 PRESENTATION OR CENTENNIAL - 10 ga. Mag., blued, engraved, gold inlaid receiver, extra fancy walnut. Limited production. Approx. 200 mfg. in Presentation Grade 1983-1986.

	$1,875	$1,550	$1,300	$1,050	$915	$830	$745

Last MSR was $1,727.

This configuration was also offered as a 3 gun set - a NIB set is currently selling in the $4,750 range.

Grading	100%	98%	95%	90%	80%	70%	60%

SHOTGUNS: SINGLE SHOT, LEVER ACTION

MODEL 66 - 12, 20 ga., or .410 bore single shot lever action, field gun only. Mfg. 1963- 1978.

| | $125 | $95 | $90 | $75 | $70 | $65 | $55 |

Add 33% to .410 bore.
Add 25% for VRs that were also available on special order.

* *Model 66 RS* - 20 ga. slug gun with 22 in. barrel and rifle type sights, recoil pad.

| | $195 | $165 | $135 | $115 | $90 | $80 | $70 |

Add 25% for special order VR.

SHOTGUNS: SINGLE BARREL TRAP

CENTURY TRAP - 12 ga., 32 or 34 in. VR barrel, engraved, auto ejector, full choke, checkered walnut stock. Mfg. 1973 and 1976 by SKB.

| | $550 | $525 | $470 | $440 | $385 | $360 | $320 |

CENTURY II TRAP - improved trap stock version of Century, Monte Carlo stock.

| | $600 | $550 | $495 | $470 | $415 | $385 | $350 |

SINGLE BARREL TRAP - 12 ga., 30, 32, or 34 in. barrels, VR, boxlock, auto ejector, checkered pistol grip and forearm, grades differ in engraving, overall workmanship, and grade or wood and checkering. Values on these models sometimes vary greatly depending on originality of finish, customer alterations, and other variations trap shooters might use to alter dimensions for their particular shooting requirements. Values represent trap guns in original, unaltered condition.

Note: Flues model mfg. prior to 1921 with serial numbers under 400,000 generally have better engraving than NID (New Ithaca Double) models over serial number 400,000 (also referred to as Knick models).

Trap guns under 60% original condition will be within 25% of the value shown in the 60% column.

* *Victory Grade* - disc. 1938.

| | $995 | $850 | $775 | $675 | $575 | $495 | $440 |

* *No. 4E* - disc. 1976.

| | $2,450 | $2,200 | $2,000 | $1,825 | $1,625 | $1,475 | $1,350 |

* *No. 5E* - 12 ga., 32 or 34 in. barrel, custom order only, elaborate engraving, quality workmanship throughout. Originally mfg. 1925-1986, mfg. resumed 1988-91.

| | $2,950 | $2,550 | $2,175 | $1,900 | $1,725 | $1,495 | $1,300 |

Last MSR was $7,500.

* *No. 6E* - this model was available by special order only. Rarity factor precludes accurate pricing.

* *No. 7E* - disc. 1964.

| | $5,500 | $4,700 | $4,000 | $3,500 | $3,000 | $2,500 | $2,200 |

* *Dollar Grade* - 12 ga., 32 or 34 in. barrel. Top-of-the-line model custom built to customer specifications. Original mfg. was stopped 1986 and resumed 1988-91.

| | $5,950 | $5,200 | $4,600 | $3,850 | $3,250 | $2,775 | $2,250 |

Last MSR was $10,000.

* *$5,000 Grade* - similar to Pre-War $1,000 grade.

| | $9,500 | $8,900 | $8,175 | $7,650 | $6,725 | $5,825 | $4,950 |

* *Sousa Grade* - extremely rare.

Extreme rarity factor precludes accurate pricing evaluation. Prices will be higher than the $5,000 Grade.

Grading	100%	98%	95%	90%	80%	70%	60%

SHOTGUNS: SLIDE ACTION

During late 1996, Ithaca Gun Co., LLC resumed manufacture of the Model 37, while discontinuing the Model 87. In 1987, Ithaca Acquisition Corp. reintroduced the Model 37 as the Model 87. Recently manufactured Model 87s are listed in addition to both new and older Model 37s (produced pre-1986).

Over 2 million Model 37s have been produced to date.

Model 37s will ser. nos. above 855,000 will accept both 2¾ and 3 in. chambered barrels interchangeably. Earlier guns have incompatible threading for the magnum barrels.

MODEL 37 TRENCH AND RIOT GUNS - see separate listing under Trench Guns in the T Section.

MODEL 37 DS POLICE SPECIAL - 12 ga. only, 18½ in. barrel with rifle sights, Parkerized finish on metal, oil finished stock, typically subcontracted by police departments or law enforcement agencies, with or without unit code markings.

	$325	$275	$235	$200	$185	$170	$160

MODEL 37 FEATHERLIGHT STANDARD - 12, 16, or 20 ga., bottom ejection, 4 shot mag., 26, 28, or 30 in. barrel, hammerless, take down, any standard choke. Mfg. 1937-disc.

	$250	$225	$195	$175	$160	$140	$125

Add 25% for 16 or 20 ga.

MODEL 37 $1000 GRADE - all gauges, deluxe engraving and checkering, gold inlaid, select figured walnut, hand-finished parts. Mfg. 1937-1940.

	$5,750	$5,200	$4,750	$4,250	$3,750	$3,250	$2,650

MODEL 37 $5000 GRADE - similar to $1000 Grade, post-war designation. Mfg. 1947- 1967.

	$5,250	$4,850	$4,250	$3,850	$3,250	$2,850	$2,250

MODEL 37V - similar to 37, except VR. Mfg. 1962-disc.

	$315	$260	$240	$195	$180	$170	$165

All currently manufactured Model 37s have the Featherlight designation. Prices are for older manufactured Model 37s.

MODEL 37D - similar to 37, except recoil pad, beavertail forearm, checkered. Mfg. 1954-1981.

	$295	$275	$235	$200	$185	$175	$160

MODEL 37DV - similar to 37D, except VR. Mfg. 1962-1981.

	$375	$325	$265	$225	$200	$185	$170

MODEL 37 ULTRA FEATHERLIGHT - 20 ga. only, bottom ejection, 4 shot mag., 26 or 28 in. VR barrel, standard choke, approx. 4¾ lbs. Disc.

	$395	$340	$275	$235	$210	$190	$175

MODEL 37 FIELD GRADE MAGNUM - 12 or 20 ga., 3 in. chambers, VR, walnut stock and corncob forearm, supplied with three choke tubes. Mfg. 1984-1986.

	$300	$240	$195	$180	$170	$165	$150

Last MSR was $428.

MODEL 37 FIELD GRADE STANDARD - 12 or 20 ga., economy model, corncob forearm, 26, 28, or 30 in. barrel. Mfg. 1983-1985 only.

	$245	$225	$195	$175	$160	$140	$120

Last MSR was $298.

MODEL 37 ULTRALITE - 12 (disc.) or 20 ga., new manufacture features checkered pistol grip (with Sid Bell red grip cap) and forearm, most recent mfg. is in deer configuration, 20 ga. only with 20 or 25 in. smooth bore barrel. New 1996.

MSR	$600	$475	$380	$340	$300	$275	$250	$225

MODEL 37 ENGLISH ULTRALITE - 12 or 20 ga., 25 or 26 in. barrels, world's lightest pump, 20 ga. weighs 4¾ lb., 12 ga. weighs 5½ lbs., checkered straight stock. Mfg. 1983-1986, production resumed 1999.

MSR	$600	$475	$380	$340	$300	$275	$250	$225

Grading	100%	98%	95%	90%	80%	70%	60%

MODEL 37R - 12, 16, or 20 ga., solid rib. Mfg. 1937-1967.

	100%	98%	95%	90%	80%	70%	60%
Plain stock	$295	$200	$175	$145	$130	$110	$90
Checkered stock	$335	$245	$200	$175	$165	$145	$120

Add 20% for 16 or 20 ga.

TURKEYSLAYER - 12 or 20 (new 2000) ga., choice of matte blue or 100% camo coverage in Realtree Hardwoods, Realtree Timber, or Advantage (disc. 2001) pattern, 22 in. barrel with extended choke tube, 7 lbs. New late 1996.

MSR	$615	$500	$375	$295	$225	$175	$160	$145

Add $20 for ported choke tube.

✳ *Youth Turkeyslayer* - 20 ga. only, features 22 in. barrel and shortened youth dimension stock. New 1998.

MSR	$615	$500	$375	$295	$225	$175	$160	$145

WATERFOWLER - 12 ga. only, features Wetlands camo treatment and 28 in. barrel designed for shooting steel shot. New 1998.

MSR	$680	$540	$400	$315	$250	$185	$175	$155

MODEL 37R DELUXE - similar to 37R, except fancy wood. Mfg. 1937-1955.

	$425	$350	$275	$250	$225	$195	$165

▌MODEL 37 DELUXE - 12, 16 (Featherlight, new 1999), or 20 ga., similar to Model 87 Field Grade except has cut checkering, 26, 28, or 30 in. VR barrel, high gloss lacquer finish, and gold trigger, newer mfg. includes 3 choke tubes. New 1996.

MSR	$600	$485	$365	$275	$225	$175	$160	$145

Add $30 for 20 ga. Youth Model.

✳ *Model 37 Deluxe English* - 12 (new 2000) or 20 ga., features 24, 26, or 28 in. English style vent. rib barrel, approx. 7 lbs. New 1998.

MSR	$600	$485	$365	$275	$225	$175	$160	$145

Add $30 for 20 ga.

MODEL 37 NEW CLASSIC - 12, 16 (Featherlight, new 1999), or 20 ga., features knuckle cut receiver, corn cob forearm, hand checkering, and sunburst recoil pad, 26 or 28 in. VR barrel with choke tubes. Limited production beginning 1998.

MSR	$780	$665	$525	$400	$350	$275	$240	$200

Add $20 for 20 ga.

MODEL 37 SUPREME - 12, 16, or 20 ga., deluxe checkered walnut stock and forearm, 28 or 30 in. VR barrel, engraved receiver, approx. 7¾ lbs. Originally mfg. 1967-1986, reintroduced late 1996-disc. 1997.

	$675	$575	$495	$425	$375	$325	$295

Last MSR was $750.

MODEL 37S SKEET GRADE - similar to 37, except Knicker VR, large forearm, fancy wood. Mfg. 1937-1955.

	$495	$445	$375	$335	$300	$275	$250

Add 20% for 16 or 20 ga.

MODEL 37 SPORTING CLAYS - 12 ga. only, 24, 26, 28, or 30 (disc.) in. VR ported (standard 2001) or unported (disc. 2000) barrel with 3 Briley choke tubes, similar in appearances and features to Model 37 Trap. New 2000.

MSR	$1,360	$1,175	$1,025	$900	$775	$625	$500	$425

MODEL 37T TRAP GRADE - similar to 37S, except trap stock, select walnut, recoil pad. Mfg. 1937-1955.

	$475	$425	$375	$325	$295	$275	$250

Add 20% for early models with Fleur-de-lis checkering.

Grading	100%	98%	95%	90%	80%	70%	60%

MODEL 37 TRAP - 12 ga. only, 30 in. VR ported (standard 2001) or unported (disc. 2000) barrel with 3 Briley choke tubes, antique silver finished receiver with scroll style engraving and gold inlays on receiver sides, optional adj. cheekpiece stock. New 2000.

MSR	$1,360	$1,175	$1,025	$900	$775	$625	$500	$425

MODEL 37T TARGET GRADE - replaced 37S and 37T. Mfg. from 1955-1961.

		$475	$425	$375	$325	$295	$275	$250

MODEL 37 DEERSLAYER - 12, 16, or 20 ga., original Deerslayer, smooth bore with fixed choke only, rifle sights, mfg. c. 1962-1986.

		$300	$240	$195	$180	$170	$165	$150

MODEL 37 SUPER DELUXE DEERSLAYER - similar to Model 37 (87) Deerslayer, except fancy wood. Mfg.1962-1985.

		$375	$335	$300	$270	$235	$210	$185

Last MSR was $447.

MODEL 37 DEERSLAYER DELUXE - 12, 16 (new 1999 - smooth bore only, rifled beginning 2000) or 20 ga., 20 or 25 in. smooth bore or rifled barrel, current manufacture has choice of 100% Realtree Hardwoods 20/200 camo (new 2000, 12 ga. only) or walnut stock and forearm with cut checkering, light receiver engraving. Production resumed late 1996.

MSR	$565	$475	$395	$325	$285	$240	$210	$185

Add $50 for Hardwoods camo.
Add $35 for 20 ga.

DEERSLAYER II - 12, 16 (new 2001), or 20 ga., 20 or 25 in. barrel with 1:34 rifling (also available with fast twist 1:25 rifling, 12 ga. only), Monte Carlo stock and forearm with cut checkering, receiver is drilled and tapped for scope mounting, 7 lbs. New late 1996.

MSR	$615	$500	$375	$295	$225	$175	$160	$145

MODEL 37 BICENTENNIAL - 12 ga., engraved, fancy wood, cased with pewter buckle, 1,776 mfg. 1976, 100% value assumes NIB condition with case and belt buckle.

		$595	$450	$325				

MODEL 37 2500 SERIES CENTENNIAL - 12 ga., customized version of the Model 37 commemorating Ithaca's 100th year anniversary, silver plated, etched antique finish receiver, deluxe walnut. Mfg. 1980-1984.

		$775	$625	$450				

Last MSR was $919.

LIMITED EDITION MODEL 37 60TH ANNIVERSARY - 20 ga., scroll engraving by A&A Engraving on both sides of nickel receiver with dog game scene/eagle motif, supreme grade wood, includes case. 200 mfg. 1997 only.

		$1,450	$850	$475				

Last MSR was $2,000.

MODEL 37 PRESENTATION - 12 ga., blued, engraved, gold mounted receiver with extra-fancy walnut, cased, limited production. Mfg. 1981-86.

		$1,500	$1,245	$1,080	$915	$830	$745	$665

Last MSR was $1,658.

A 3 gun set was also available - an NIB set is currently priced in the $1,750 range.

MODEL 37 DUCKS UNLIMITED - 12 ga., VR.

		$385	$305	$275				

MODEL 37 60TH ANNIVERSARY - 20 ga., 3 in. chamber, 26 in. VR barrel, checkered Supreme wood, engraved, cased. 200 mfg. 1997 only.

		$1,750	$1,250	$850				

Grading	100%	98%	95%	90%	80%	70%	60%

MODEL 87 FIELD (BASIC) - 12 or 20 ga., 3 in. chamber, economy model, walnut stock and forearm with pressed checkering, 26, 28, or 30 (disc.) in. barrel with 3 choke tubes standard. Reintroduced 1987-1996.

	$360	$290	$240	$195	$170	$160	$145

Last MSR was $477.

* *Model 87 Basic Field Combo* - 12 or 20 ga., includes 20/25 in. deer barrel with special bore and 28 in. VR multi-choke field barrel, uncheckered walnut stock and corncob forearm, 7 lbs. Mfg. 1989-92.

	$400	$315	$275	$235	$210	$190	$170

Last MSR was $459.

Add $32 for rifled bore barrel.
Add $104 for laminated wood (includes rifle bored barrel).

* *Model 87 Camo Field* - 12 ga. only, 3 in. chamber, 24, 26, or 28 in. VR barrel, camo-seal rust resistant finish on exterior parts. Available in either green or brown camo finish. Mfg. began 1986, resumed 1988-disc. 1996.

	$425	$315	$260	$200	$175	$160	$145

Last MSR was $542.

* *Model 87 Turkey Field* - 12 ga. only, 24 in. VR barrel with choice of fixed full choke or full choke tube, camo or matte blue finish. Mfg. 1989-1996.

	$365	$285	$235	$190	$170	$160	$145

Last MSR was $466.

Add $85 for camo finish.
Add $43 for full choke tube.

MODEL 87 ULTRALITE FIELD - 12 or 20 ga., 3 in. chamber, aluminum receiver, 20 (disc. 1988), 24, 25 (disc. 1988), or 26 in. barrel. 20 ga. weighs 5 lbs., 12 ga. weighs 5¾ lbs, multi-chokes (3) became standard in 1989. Originally mfg. 1985-86, reintroduced 1988-90.

	$445	$375	$295	$240	$210	$190	$170

Last MSR was $481.

Add $50 for slim grip model (12½ in. stock - disc. 1985).
Subtract $42 if without multiple choke feature.
The 20 and 25 in. barrels were disc. when mfg. was resumed 1988.

* *Model 87 Ultra Deluxe* - similar to Ultralite Field except has cut checkering, high gloss lacquer finish, and gold trigger. Mfg 1989-91.

	$425	$360	$300	$250	$220	$190	$170

Last MSR was $514.

MODEL ENGLISH 87 - 20 ga. only, 3 in. chamber, 24 or 26 in. VR barrel with 3 choke tubes, steel receiver, checkered walnut stock and forearm, recoil pad, 6¾ lbs. Mfg. 1991-96.

	$425	$315	$260	$200	$175	$160	$145

Last MSR was $545.

MODEL 87 DELUXE - similar to Model 87 Field Grade except has cut checkering, 26, 28, or 30 in. VR barrel, high gloss lacquer finish, and gold trigger, newer mfg. includes 3 choke tubes. Mfg. 1989-1996.

	$415	$310	$255	$200	$175	$160	$145

Last MSR was $533.

Add $54 for combo package (includes 20 in. special bore deer barrel, disc. 1992).
Add $87 for combo package with 20 or 25 in. rifled bore deer barrel, disc. 1992.

* *Model 87 Deluxe Magnum* - 12 or 20 ga., 3 in. chambers, VR, deluxe wood with checkered forearm. Mfg. 1981-1986, production resumed 1988 only.

	$320	$270	$230	$210	$200	$185	$165

Last MSR was $395.

Add $77 for Combo package (extra 28 in. barrel).
New mfg. 20 ga. shotguns were available with a 25 in. barrel only (with choke tubes).

Grading	100%	98%	95%	90%	80%	70%	60%

MODEL 87 SUPREME GRADE - 12 or 20 ga., presentation walnut, high luster blue, limited production, previously available in either trap, skeet, or field models, fixed chokes. Mfg. 1988-1996.

	$640	$475	$395	$325	$295	$270	$250

Last MSR was $809.

BASIC DEERSLAYER - 12 ga. only, 20 or 25 in. special bore or rifled barrel, oil finished stock and corncob forearm with no checkering, iron sights, matte metal finish, 7 lbs. Mfg. 1989-1996.

	$345	$280	$240	$195	$175	$160	$145

Last MSR was $425.

    Add $40 for rifled barrel.

MODEL 87 FIELD DEERSLAYER - 12 or 20 ga., rifle slug barrel, 20 or 25 in. special smooth bore barrel with open sights. Mfg. 1959-86, reintroduced 1988-1993.

	$300	$250	$210	$180	$160	$150	$140

Last MSR was $364.

MODEL 87 DELUXE DEERSLAYER - similar to Field Deerslayer except has cut checkering, high gloss lacquer finish, and gold trigger. Mfg. 1989-1996.

	$365	$285	$235	$190	$170	$160	$145

Last MSR was $465.

    Add $34 for rifled bore.
    Add $120 for combo package (28 in. multi-choke barrel).

✳ ***Model 87 Ultra Deerslayer*** - similar to Deluxe Deerslayer except has aluminum frame. Mfg. 1989-90 only.

	$350	$285	$245	$200	$175	$160	$145

Last MSR was $444.

MONTE CARLO DEERSLAYER II - 12 ga. only, 20 or 25 in. barrel with rifling, Monte Carlo stock and forearm with cut checkering, receiver is drilled and tapped for scope mounting, 7 lbs. Mfg. 1989-1996.

	$445	$335	$270	$210	$175	$160	$145

Last MSR was $567.

DEERSLAYER II FAST TWIST - 12 ga. only, 25 in. rifled permanently fixed barrel, Monte Carlo stock with checkering, receiver is drilled and tapped. Mfg. 1992-1993.

	$440	$385	$325	$275	$235	$200	$180

Last MSR was $550.

MODEL 87 MILITARY & POLICE - 12 (3 in.) or 20 (new 1989) ga., short barrel Model 37 w/normal stock or pistol grip only, 18½, 20, or 24¾ (scarce) in. barrel, choice of front bead or rifle sights, front blade was usually a flourescent orange plastic, 5, 8, or 10 shot. Originally disc. 1983, reintroduced 1989-1995.

	$265	$230	$200	$180	$170	$160	$150

Last MSR was $323.

    Add $104 for nickel finish (mfg. 1991-92 only).
    Subtract $35 without parkerizing (disc.).

IVER JOHNSON ARMS, INC.

Previously manufactured in Fitchburg, MA, 1883-1984 and Jacksonville, AR 1984-1993. Formerly Johnson Bye & Co. 1871-1883. Renamed Iver Johnson & Co. in 1871 until 1891. Renamed Iver Johnson's Arms & Cycle Works in 1891 with manufacturing moving to Fitchburg, MA. In 1975 the name changed to Iver Johnson's Arms, Inc., and two years later, company facilities were moved to Middlesex, NJ. In 1982, production was moved to Jacksonville, AR under the trade name Iver Johnson Arms, Inc. In 1983, Universal Firearms, Inc. was acquired by Iver Johnson Arms, Inc.

    Iver Johnson Arms was sold in March of 1987 and was acquired by American Military Arms Corporation (AMAC). AMAC ceased operations in early 1993.

Grading	100%	98%	95%	90%	80%	70%	60%

PISTOLS: SEMI-AUTO

AMAC also manufactured a Super Enforcer .30 Carbine, Delta 786 9mm Para. (disc. 1989), and the M-2 machine gun in .30 Carbine which are not listed in this text.

TRAILSMEN PISTOL - .22 LR cal. only, all steel construction, 4½ or 6 in. barrel, blue finish, black checkered composition grips, 10 shot mag., approx. 30 oz. Mfg. 1985-86 and reintroduced 1990 only.

	$200	$165	$145	$130	$120	$110	$100

Last MSR was $230.

Add $20 for hardwood stocks and high polish blue (disc. 1990).

PONY PISTOL (PO380 SERIES) - .380 ACP cal. only, semi-auto single action, 3 in. barrel, 6 shot mag., all steel construction, blue or matte blue finish, 20 oz. Mfg. 1985-1986 (by Firearms International) and reintroduced 1990 only.

	$290	$245	$210	$185	$170	$155	$140

Last MSR was $330.

* **Pony .380 Stainless** - similar to Pony Pistol, except is stainless steel construction. New 1990 only.

	$315	$280	$240

Last MSR was $365.

* **Nickel Pony** - with nickel finish. Mfg. 1985 only.

	$260	$230	$215	$200	$185	$170	$160

Last MSR was $290 for nickel finish.

POCKET PISTOL (TP SERIES) - .22 LR or .25 ACP cal., semi-auto, double action, 3 in. barrel, 7 shot finger tip extension mag., black plastic grips, fixed sights, blue or matte finish, 15 oz. Previously mfg. 1985-86, reintroduced 1988-90.

	$145	$125	$110	$100	$90	$80	$70

Last MSR was $165.

Add $15 for nickel finish (disc. 1989).

AMAC-22/25 COMPACT - .22 Short (disc.) or .25 ACP cal., semi-auto, single action, 5 shot mag., 2 in. barrel, all steel construction, plastic grips, 9.3 oz. Disc. 1993.

	$165	$135	$115	$100	$90	$80	$70

Last MSR was $200.

Add $10 for nickel finish (disc. 1990).

* **Compact Elite Engraved** - similar to .25 ACP Compact, except has extensive engraving. Mfg. 1991-93.

	$850	$600	$475

Last MSR was $1,000.

SILVER HAWK - .22 LR or .25 ACP cal., double action semi-auto, similar to TP-22 Series, except is stainless steel. Mfg. 1990-93.

	$215	$185	$160

Last MSR was $250.

SUPER ENFORCER (MODEL 3000) - .30 Carbine cal. only, pistol version of the Carbine with 11 in. shrouded barrel. Mfg. 1985-1986 only.

	$400	$350	$325	$300	$200	$175	$160

Last MSR was $255.

Add $40 for stainless steel (disc. for 1986).

* **Enforcer** - similar to Super Enforcer model, except has 10½ in. barrel. Reintroduced 1988-disc. 1993.

	$450	$400	$300	$275	$225	$200	$175

Last MSR was $417.

Grading	100%	98%	95%	90%	80%	70%	60%

REVOLVERS

CATTLEMAN MAGNUM - .357 Mag., .44 Mag., or .45 LC cal., single action, 6 shot, Colt replica, 4¾, 5½, or 7½ in. barrel, case color frame, blue barrel, and brass grip frame, smooth walnut grips, fixed sights. Disc. 1984.

	100%	98%	95%	90%	80%	70%	60%
	$190	$175	$150	$140	$130	$125	$110
.44 Mag.	$220	$190	$175	$165	$145	$135	$125

BUCKHORN MAGNUM - similar to Cattleman, except flat top, adj. sights.

	$210	$190	$175	$165	$145	$140	$125

BUNTLINE BUCKHORN MAGNUM - similar to Buckhorn, only 18 in. barrel, detachable stock.

	$345	$310	$295	$275	$260	$250	$225
.44 Mag.	$375	$325	$310	$295	$280	$275	$250

TRAIL BLAZER - .22 LR, or .22 Mag. cal., interchangeable cylinder, 5½ or 6½ in. barrel, blue.

	$175	$145	$130	$120	$110	$100	$80

MODEL 1900 - .22 L, S, LR, .32 S&W, or .38 S&W cal., double action, 2½, 4½, or 6 in. barrel, fixed sights, blue or nickel, rubber grips. Mfg. 1900-1947.

	$125	$80	$70	$60	$55	$45	$40

MODEL 1900 TARGET - .22 LR cal., 6 shot, 6 or 9½ in. barrel, blue, fixed sights. Mfg. 1925-1942.

	$140	$90	$80	$70	$65	$55	$50

TARGET SEALED 8 - .22 LR cal., 8 shot, 6 or 10 in. barrel, blue, fixed sights, rubber grips. Mfg. 1931-1957.

	$150	$100	$95	$80	$75	$65	$60

TARGET 9 SHOT - similar to Target Sealed 8, except 9 shot. Mfg. 1929-1946.

	$145	$90	$80	$70	$65	$55	$50

SAFETY HAMMER MODEL - .22 LR, .32 S&W, or .38 S&W cal., 2 or 3 in. barrel standard, 4, 5, or 6 in. available at extra cost, fixed sights, blue (standard) or nickel, break open. Mfg. 1892-1950.

	$125	$80	$70	$60	$55	$45	$40

SAFETY HAMMERLESS - .32 S&W or .38 S&W cal., 2, 3 (.32 only), 3¼, 4, 5, or 6 in. barrel, double action only, break open, fixed sights, rubber grips, blue or nickel. Mfg. 1895-1950.

	$125	$100	$95	$80	$75	$65	$60

.22 SUPERSHOT - .22 LR cal., 6 in. barrel, blue, fixed sights, checkered wood grips, break open, no counterbore. Mfg. 1929-1949.

	$150	$80	$70	$60	$55	$45	$40

TRIGGER COCKING SINGLE ACTION - .22 LR cal., 8 shot, 6 in. barrel, break open, counterbored, blue, checkered wood grips, first pull on trigger cocks, second fires. Mfg. 1940- 1947. Rare in 100% condition.

	$250	$200	$175	$125	$100	$85	$75

.22 TARGET SINGLE ACTION - .22 LR cal., 8 shot, 6 in. barrel, break open, counterbored, checkered wood, adj. grips and sights. Mfg. 1938-1948.

	$250	$225	$200	$175	$150	$125	$100

SUPERSHOT SEALED 8 - .22 LR cal., 8 shot, break open, blue, adj. sights, checkered wood grips. Mfg. 1931-1957.

	$175	$130	$120	$110	$90	$85	$75

SUPERSHOT 9 - similar to Sealed 8, only 9 shot, not counterbored. Mfg. 1929-1949.

	$135	$90	$80	$75	$60	$50	$40

Grading	100%	98%	95%	90%	80%	70%	60%

PROTECTOR SEALED 8 - .22 LR cal., 8 shot, 2½ in. barrel, break open, fixed sights, blue, wood grips. Mfg. 1933-1949.

	$175	$135	$125	$110	$90	$80	$75

SUPERSHOT MODEL 844 - .22 LR cal., 8 shot, 4½ or 6 in. barrel, adj. sights, break open, blue, wood grips. Mfg. 1955-1956.

	$100	$90	$85	$80	$75	$60	$50

ARMSWORTH MODEL 855 - .22 LR cal., single action, 8 shot, 6 in. barrel, break open, blue, adj. sights, wood grips, adj. finger rest. Mfg. 1955-1957.

	$250	$225	$200	$175	$150	$125	$100

MODEL 55A TARGET - .22 LR cal., 8 shot, 4½ or 6 in. barrel, solid frame, blue, fixed sights, wood grips, loading gate. Mfg. 1955-1984.

	$100	$75	$65	$50	$40	$35	$25

CADET - .22 LR, .22 WRM, .32 S&W, .38 S&W, or .38 Spl. cal., 2½ in. barrel, blue, fixed sights, plastic grips. Mfg. 1955-1984.

	$110	$90	$80	$75	$65	$55	$50

MODEL 57A TARGET - .22 LR cal., 8 shot, 4½ or 6 in. barrel, solid frame, blue, adj. sights, wood grips. Mfg. 1955-1975.

	$100	$80	$75	$65	$55	$45	$40

MODEL 66 TRAILSMAN - .22 LR cal., 6 in. barrel, break open, blue, adj. sights, rebounding hammer, wood grips. Mfg. 1958-1975.

	$110	$90	$85	$75	$65	$55	$50

SIDEWINDER - .22 LR cal., 6 or 8 shot, 4¾ or 6 in. barrel, solid frame, blue, nickel, or case hardened finish, plastic grips, wood on case color model. Mfg. 1961-disc. 8 shot pre-1975.

	$110	$90	$85	$75	$65	$55	$50

SIDEWINDER S - similar to Sidewinder, except .22 WMR, interchangeable cylinder.

	$125	$100	$95	$85	$75	$65	$60

MODEL 67 VIKING - .22 LR cal., 8 shot, 4½ or 6 in. barrel, break open, blue, adj. sights, wood grips with thumbrest. Mfg. 1964-1975.

	$135	$110	$100	$95	$85	$75	$65

MODEL 67S VIKING - .22 LR, .32 S&W, or .38 S&W cal., 8 shot in .22, 5 shot in .32 or .38, 2¾ in. barrel, break open, adj. sights, plastic grips. Mfg. 1964-1975.

	$130	$100	$95	$85	$75	$60	$50

AMERICAN BULLDOG - .22 LR, .22 WRM, or .38 Spl. cal., 6 shot in .22, 5 shot in .38, 2½ or 4 in. barrel, blue or nickel, adj. sights, plastic grips. Mfg. 1974-1976.

	$135	$110	$100	$90	$80	$65	$60

ROOKIE - .38 Spl. cal., 5 shot, 4 in. barrel, solid frame, blue or nickel, plastic grips. Mfg. 1975-1984.

	$100	$80	$75	$65	$55	$45	$35

SPORTSMAN - .22 LR cal., 6 shot, 4¾ or 6 in. barrel, solid frame, blue, fixed sights, plastic grips. Mfg. 1974-1976.

	$100	$80	$75	$65	$55	$45	$35

DELUXE TARGET - similar to Sportsman, adj. sights. Mfg. 1975-1976.

	$110	$90	$85	$75	$65	$55	$40

SWING OUT - .22 LR, .22 WRM, .32 S&W, or .38 S&W cal., 6 shot in .22, 5 shot in .32 or .38, 2, 3, or 4 in. barrel, VR, 4 or 6 in., blue or nickel, fixed or adj. sights. Mfg. 1977-1984.

	$130	$110	$100	$90	$80	$75	$65

* *VR Barrel* - 4 or 6 in. VR barrel, adj. sights.

	$170	$150	$140	$130	$125	$120	$100

Grading	100%	98%	95%	90%	80%	70%	60%

RIFLES

MODEL X - .22 Short, Long, or LR cal., bolt action, single shot, 22 in. barrel, open sight, pistol grip with knob forend. Mfg. 1928-1932.

	$150	$140	$125	$100	$75	$50	$40

This model was mfg. both in the U.S. and Canada (by Cooey). Canadian models generally have birch stocks.

* ***Model XA*** - same as Model X, except equipped with Lyman No. 55J receiver peep sight, ivory bead, swivels and leather sling strap, scarce. Mfg. 1928-1932.

	$200	$175	$150	$125	$100	$75	$60

MODEL 2X - improved Model X, 24 in. heavy barrel, larger stock, adj. sights. Mfg. 1932-1955.

	$175	$150	$135	$125	$75	$50	$40

* ***Model 2XA*** - sames as the Model 2X, except equipped with Lyman No. 55J receiver peep sight, ivory bead, swivels and leather sling, scarce. Mfg. 1932-1945.

	$280	$225	$200	$150	$120	$125	$100

Add 25% for factory checkered stock.

LI'L CHAMP - .22 LR cal. only, single shot bolt action, 16¼ in. barrel, black molded stock, nickel plated bolt, youth dimensions, (32½ in. overall length), 3 lbs. Introduced 1986, reintroduced 1988 only.

	$75	$60	$50	$45	$40	$35	$35

Last MSR was $92.

LONG RANGE RIFLE - .308 Win. (new 1991) or .50 BMG cal., bolt action design, single shot, 29 in. stainless steel fluted barrel with muzzle brake, adj. trigger pull, built in bipod, adj. rail stock, includes Leupold M-1 Ultra 20X scope, 36 lbs. Limited mfg. between 1988-1993.

	$4,350	$3,500	$3,150	$2,750	$2,400	$2,100	$1,800

Last MSR was $5,000.

9MM PARA. CARBINE (JJ9MM SERIES) - 9mm Para. cal. only, copy of U.S. military M1, 16 in. barrel, blue finish only, 20 shot mag. Mfg. 1985-86 only.

* ***Hardwood Stock Model*** - disc. 1986.

	$230	$200	$180	$170	$160	$150	$140

Last MSR was $255.

* ***Standard Model*** - with plastic stock. Disc. 1985.

	$225	$200	$180	$170	$160	$150	$140

Last MSR was $250.

* ***Folding Plastic Stock Model*** - disc. 1985.

	$255	$225	$200	$180	$170	$160	$150

Last MSR was $281.

DELTA-786 CARBINE - 9mm Para. cal., semi-auto, patterned after the U.S. military M1 Carbine, 16 in. barrel, matte black finish. Mfg. 1989 only.

	$575	$425	$360	$325	$295	$260	$230

Last MSR was $665.

.30 CARBINE CAL. - .30 Carbine or 9mm Para. (new 1991) cal., semi-auto, 18 or 20 (new 1991) in. barrel, available in various stock configurations, hardwood stock. Mfg. 1985-1986, reintroduced 1988-disc. 1993.

	$285	$215	$190	$165	$150	$140	$130

Last MSR was $350.

Add $16 for 9mm Para. cal.
Add $35 for walnut stock, Parkerized finish (disc. 1990), or 20 in. barrel (new 1991).

Grading	100%	98%	95%	90%	80%	70%	60%

❋ *Paratrooper Model* - similar to standard model, except has folding synthetic stock. Disc. 1993.

| | $345 | $270 | $225 | $195 | $165 | $150 | $140 |

Last MSR was $433.

❋ *Stainless Steel Variation* - disc. 1985.

| | $230 | $200 | $180 |

Last MSR was $250.

❋ *5.7mm Johnson (Spitfire) Cal.* - remilled, add $30 for stainless steel.

| | $195 | $175 | $165 | $155 | $145 | $135 | $125 |

Last MSR was $219.

.22 CAL. U.S. CARBINE - .22 LR or .22 Mag. cal., 18½ in. barrel, except for Mag. (19.3 in.), 5.8 lbs., 15 shot mag., sling swivels. Mfg. in Germany by Erma 1985-1986, reintroduced 1988 only.

| | $150 | $120 | $110 | $100 | $90 | $85 | $80 |

Last MSR was $166 for .22 LR cal.
Last MSR was $183 for .22 Mag. cal.

Add $120 for .22 Mag. model (gas operated - disc. 1986).

TARGETMASTER SLIDE ACTION - .22 LR or .22 Mag. (disc. 1986) cal., 18½ in. barrel, 12 shot (LR) tube mag., 5¾ lbs. Mfg. in Germany by Erma 1985 only, reintroduced 1988-90.

| | $175 | $140 | $125 | $115 | $100 | $90 | $80 |

Last MSR was $209.

This model was designated EW.22 HBP previously.

MODEL EW.22 HBL LEVER ACTION (WAGONMASTER) - .22 S, L, and LR or .22 Mag. cal., 18½ in. barrel, walnut finish, hardwood stock, blue finish, 5¾ lbs., grooved for scope mounts. Mfg. in Germany by Erma 1985-1986, reintroduced 1988-90.

| | $175 | $140 | $125 | $115 | $100 | $90 | $80 |

Last MSR was $209.

Add $23 for .22 Mag. cal. (19 in. barrel).

This model was also available in a Junior variation with smaller dimensions; values same as listed.

TRAIL BLAZER SEMI-AUTO (MODEL IJ.22 HB) - .22 LR cal. only, 10 shot mag., 18½ in. barrel, 5.8 lbs. Mfg. 1985 only.

| | $115 | $100 | $90 | $85 | $80 | $75 | $70 |

Last MSR was $125.

SHOTGUNS

CHAMPION - 10, 12, 16, 20, 24, 28, 32 ga., or .410 bore, also available in .44, .45, 12mm, or 14mm rifle cal., single barrel shotgun or rifle, 26-32 in. full barrel, exposed hammer, auto ejector, plain pistol grip stock. Mfg. 1909-1956.

| | $175 | $150 | $125 | $100 | $75 | $50 | $40 |

Subtract 25% for birch stock (12 ga. only, 1970s mfg.).

Values on both smaller gauge shotguns and rifles would be considerably higher than those listed. A mint .32 ga. might command 400% more than the listed values. Rifles will also bring premiums over values listed.

MATTED RIB GRADE - similar to Champion, except not available in 10, 24, 28, or 32 ga., solid rib, checkered stock. Mfg. 1909-1948.

| | $200 | $175 | $150 | $125 | $100 | $75 | $60 |

This model has either a semi-octagon (with top matted) or jacketed breech.

TRAP GRADE - similar to Matted Rib, except 32 in. full barrel, super select wood, 12 ga., vent rib. Mfg. 1926-1942.

| | $350 | $300 | $250 | $200 | $150 | $125 | $100 |

Grading	100%	98%	95%	90%	80%	70%	60%

HERCULES GRADE - 12, 16, 20, 28 ga., or .410 bore, 26-32 in. barrels, hammerless, boxlock, various chokes, extractors and double triggers standard, checkered pistol grip or straight stock. Mfg. 1918-1943.

	$795	$525	$450	$425	$375	$335	$310

Add $100 for auto ejectors.
Add $200 for Miller SST.
Add 10% for 16 ga.
Add 20% for 20 ga.
Add 200% for 28 ga.
Add 100% for .410 bore.
Add 200%+ for rare factory engraved specimens.

The Hercules Model was mfg. in both USA and Canada by Cooey. The Hercules name was dropped in 1936 and became known as the "Iver Johnson Hammerless" until the end of production. Case colored frames were standard until 1936, blued frames were standard 1937-1943. A special run of Hercules Doubles was built in the 1930s for Montgomery Ward under the "Western Field" Model 53 nomenclature. All Western Field guns had a beavertail forearm, twin ivory sights, and recoil pad. Hercules 28 ga. SxS's are extremely rare.

SKEET-ER MODEL - 12, 16, 20, 28 ga., or .410 bore, similar to Hercules Model, except has blued receiver, super select wood and beavertail forearm, many Skeeters were special order guns with options including selective or non-selective Miller trigger, custom stock, barrel chokes, chamber lengths, checkering and wood finishes, sling swivels, recoil pad, checkered butt, VR, and various engraving patterns. Approx. 1,200 mfg. 1933-1942.

	$1,595	$1,295	$900	$800	$700	$600	$500

Add 20% for auto ejectors.
Add 40% for SST.
Add 50% for factory VR.
Add 20% for 20 ga.
Add 100% for 16 ga., 28 ga. or .410 bore.
Add 200% for rare factory engraving.
Add 50% for scarce factory case colors (be wary of new colors).

.410 bore is the most commonly encountered gun and was made on a special small frame. This model was probably responsible for more Skeet records than any other American .410 bore SxS shotgun.

SUPER TRAP - 12 ga. only, 32 in. full VR, boxlock, extractors, checkered pistol grip stock, beavertail forend and recoil pad. Mfg. 1928-1942. Scarce.

	$1,095	$750	$550	$475	$415	$395	$370

Add $100 for auto ejectors.
Add $100 for SST.

SILVER SHADOW - O/U, 12 ga., 26 or 28 in. barrels, various chokes, extractors, vent rib, checkered pistol grip stock, Italian mfg. Disc.

	$375	$325	$300	$275	$225	$185	$175

IZHMASH

Current manufacturer and trademark imported from Russia and distributed by European American Armory (certain models only), located in Sharpes, FL. Other models are also imported by Kalashnikov USA, located in Port St. Lucie, FL. Currently distributed by Interstate Arms Corp., located in Billerica, MA, and by L.A. Austin International, Inc., located in Surprise, AZ.

Other Izhmash trademarks include Saiga, Hesse-Saiga, Krebs-Saiga, Romak, Sobol (not imported) , Korshun (not imported), LOS (not imported), Maral (not imported), and Dragunov. Please contact the distributors directly for more information on the most current releases and availability.

Grading	100%	98%	95%	90%	80%	70%	60%

RIFLES: BOLT ACTION

URAL 5-1 MATCH RIFLE - .22 LR cal., single shot, competition model with eccentric bolt, adj. cheekpiece, trigger, and buttplate, 26½ in. barrel with aperture sights, 11.3 lbs. Importation began 2000.

MSR	$1,225	$1,100	$950	$825	$700	$600	$500	$425

URAL 6-1 MATCH RIFLE - .22 LR cal., U.I.T. configuration with adj. buttplate and 26¾ in. barrel, aperture sights, various accessories included, 10 2/3 lbs. Importation began 2000.

MSR	$625	$550	$500	$450	$400	$360	$330	$300

URAL 6-2 MATCH RIFLE - .22 LR cal., features laminated stock. Importation began 2000.

MSR	$1,125	$1,000	$875	$750	$650	$550	$450	$350

BIATHLON BASIC - .22 LR cal., entry level biathlon model, beech stock, heavy barrel with Weaver rail, 6.1 lbs. Importation began 2002.

MSR	$339	$295	$265	$235	$195	$175	$160	$145

BIATHLON 7-4 - .22 LR cal., features pivoting crank action, extra mags. that can be stored on the stock, 19.7 in. barrel with aperture sights, includes biathlon harness, spare mags., and counter weights, 9.1 lbs. Importation began 2000.

MSR	$979	$875	$725	$650	$550	$450	$350	$300

CM-2 - .22 LR cal., light match rifle, similar overall to Ural 6-1. Importation began 2000.

MSR	$495	$450	$400	$360	$330	$300	$260	$220

LOS 7-1 SPORTER - .223 Rem., .308 Win., or 7.62x39mm cal., 21.8 in. hammer forged barrel with two lug bolt lockup, detachable 5 shot mag., adj. trigger, checkered hardwood stock with vent. recoil pad, 7.3 lbs. Importation began 2000.

MSR	$395	$360	$330	$300	$270	$240	$210	$190

Add $99 if w/o scope.

SHOTGUNS

Kalashnikov USA also imports some Saiga 12 ga. shotguns. Please contact the distributors directly for more information on the most current releases and availability.

Ithaca Classic Double's Steve Lamboy (seated) with elaborate wood case containing cleaning accessories. The talented engravers of Creative Art, Ugo Tacenti (l), Giacomo Fausti (center), and Ferlib's master gunsmith, Ivano Tanfoglio are also having fun at IWA, Europe's answer to the SHOT Show.

J SECTION

J.O. ARMS
Previous importer of KSN Industries, Ltd. pistols until 1997.

JMC FABRICATION & MACHINE, INC.
Previous manufacturer located in Rockledge, FL 1997-99.

Grading	100%	98%	95%	90%	80%	70%	60%

RIFLES: BOLT ACTION

MODEL 2000 M/P - .50 BMG cal., rapid takedown, 30 in. barrel, matte black finish, cast aluminum stock with Pachmayr pad, fully adj. bipod, 10 shot staggered mag., two-stage trigger, includes 24X U.S. Optics scope, prices assume all options included, 29½ lbs. Limited mfg. 1998-99.

	$7,950	$7,400	$6,800	$6,150	$5,500	$4,900	$4,200

Last MSR was $8,500.

Subtract $2,800 if w/o options.

JP ENTERPRISES, INC.
Current manufacturer and customizer located in White Bear Lake, MN beginning 2000. Previously located in Vadnais Heights, MN 1998-2000, and in Shoreview, MN 1995-98. Distributor, dealer, and consumer sales.

JP Enterprises also customizes Remington shotgun models 11-87, 1100, and 870, the Remington bolt action Model 700 series, Glock pistols, and the Armalite AR-10 series. Please contact the company directly or refer to their web site (www.jpart5.com) for more information regarding these customizing services.

PISTOLS: SEMI-AUTO

Level I & Level II custom pistols were manufactured 1995-97 using Springfield Armory slides and frames. Only a few were made, and retail prices were $599 (Level I) and $950 (Level II).

RIFLES: SEMI-AUTO

BARRACUDA 10/22 - .22 LR cal., features customized Ruger 10/22 action with reworked fire control system, choice of stainless bull or carbon fiber superlight barrel, 3 lb. trigger, color laminated "Barracuda" skeletonized stock. New 1997.

MSR	$1,195	$1,075	$950	$775	$650	$575	$475	$400

A-2 MATCH - .223 Rem. cal., JP-15 lower receiver with JP fire control system, 20 in. JP Supermatch cryo-treated stainless barrel, standard A-2 stock and pistol grip, DCM type free float tube, Mil-Spec A-2 upper assembly with Smith National Match rear sight. New 1995.

MSR	$1,095	$995	$875	$750	$625	$550	$500	$450

GRADE I (A-3 FLAT TOP) - .223 Rem. cal., features Eagle Arms (disc. 1999), DPMS (disc. 1999) or JP15 lower assembly with JP fire control system, Mil-spec A-3 type upper receiver with 18 or 24 in. JP Supermatch cryo-treated stainless barrel, JP vent. two-piece free float tube, JP adj. gas system and recoil eliminator. New 1995.

MSR	$1,495	$1,350	$1,175	$1,025	$900	$800	$700	$600

Add $400 for NRA Hi-Power version with 24 in. bull barrel and sight package.
Add $200 for laminated wood thumbhole stock.

✳ *Grade I IPSC Limited Class* - similar to Grade I, except has quick detachable match grade iron sights, Versa-pod bipod. New 1999.

MSR	$1,795	$1,675	$1,400	$1,150	$995	$775	$625	$550

Grading	100%	98%	95%	90%	80%	70%	60%

✳ *Grade I Tactical/SOF* - similar to Grade I, all matte black non-glare finish, 18, 20, or 24 in. Supermatch barrel. New 1999.

	MSR	$1,595		$1,425	$1,225	$1,050	$925	$800	$700	$600

Add $798 for Trijicon A-COG sight with A-3 adapter.

GRADE II - .223 Rem. cal., features Mil-spec JP lower receiver with upper assembly finished in a special two-tone color anodizing process, JP fire control and gas system, 18- 24 in. cryo treated stainless barrel, composite skeletonized stock, Harris bipod, choice of multi-color or black receiver and handguard, includes hard case. New 1998.

	MSR	$1,895		$1,750	$1,450	$1,200	$1,025	$825	$700	$600

Add $200 for laminated wood thumbhole stock.

GRADE III (THE EDGE) - .223 Rem. cal., RND machined match upper/lower receiver system, 2-piece free floating forend, standard or laminated thumbhole wood stock, 18 to 24 in. barrel (cryo treated beginning 1998) with recoil eliminator, includes Harris bipod, top of the line model, includes hard case. New 1996.

	MSR	$2,795		$2,550	$2,125	$1,750	$1,450	$1,150	$875	$750

Add $250 for laminated thumbhole stock (when ordered with gun).

MODEL AR-10T - .243 Win. or .308 Win. cal., features Armalite receiver system with JP fire control, flat-top receiver, vent. free floating tube, 24 in. cryo treated stainless barrel, black finish. New 1998.

	MSR	$2,695		$2,475	$2,075	$1,725	$1,450	$1,150	$875	$750

Add $150 for anodized upper assembly in custom color.

Add $350 for laminated wood thumbhole stock.

✳ *Model AR-10LW* - lightweight variation of the Model AR-10T, includes 16-20 in. cryo treated stainless barrel, composite fiber tube, black finish only, 7-8 lbs. New 1998.

	MSR	$2,195		$2,000	$1,600	$1,250	$1,025	$825	$750	$650

Add $200 for detachable sights.

J R DISTRIBUTING

Current manufacturer located in Moorpark, CA. J R Distributing is a division of J R Sports Distribution Corporation. Dealer and consumer sales.

RIFLES: SEMI-AUTO

.22 MAG. CUSTOM RIFLE - .22 Mag. cal., choice of Ruger 10/22 or AMT action, 20 in. bull barrel with laminate or synthetic stock, 9 shot rotary mag., supplied with hard case. New 1998.

	MSR	$795		$725	$650	$550	$500	$450	$400	$360

JSL (HEREFORD)

Previous manufacturer located in Hereford, England. Imported until 1994 by Specialty Shooters Supply, Inc. located in Fort Lauderdale, FL.

PISTOLS: SEMI-AUTO

SPITFIRE (G1) - 9mm Para. or 9x21mm cal., patterned after the Czech CZ-75/85, 3.7 in. barrel, ambidextrous safety, commander style hammer, black non-slip rubberized grip panels, investment cast stainless steel fabrication, 10 (C/B 1994) or 15* shot mag., 2.2 lbs. Imported 1992-94.

✳ *Spitfire Standard* - includes fixed rear sight, 2 mags., presentation case, and allen key.

				$1,332	$1,100	$925

Last MSR was $1,332.

Add $81 for adj. rear sight (Sterling Model).

Grading	100%	98%	95%	90%	80%	70%	60%

JACKSON HOLE FIREARMS
Previous manufacturer located in Jackson Hole, WY circa mid-70s.

RIFLES: BOLT ACTION

STANDARD RIFLE - various cals., Mauser 98 action utilizing patented system for interchangeable barrels, checkered walnut stock.

	$1,050	$875	$800	$725	$650	$575	$495

Jackson Hole Firearms manufactured a limited quantity of their unique interchangeable barrel bolt action rifles. Collectibility to date has been minimal, and values are affected by the J.P. Sauer Models 90 and 200 which also feature the interchangeable barrel design.

JAGD-UND SPORTWAFFEN SUHL GmbH
Current manufacturer located in Suhl, Germany since 1535.

Currently, the famous Merkel trademark (mfg. by Jagd-Und Sportwaffen Suhl GmbH) is imported by Gun South Inc. located in Trussville, AL. Please refer to the Merkel listing in this text for current information regarding this older European trademark. See the Trademark Index in this text for current factory information.

JANZ GmbH
Current revolver manufacturer established in 2000, and located in Malente, Germany. No current U.S. importation.

REVOLVERS

JTL-S - .357 Mag./.38 Spl., .44 Mag., .454 Casull/.45 LC cal., DA, 6 or 7 (.357 Mag.) shot, unique interchangeable barrels and cylinders allows cals. to be changed rapidly, 4 in – 10 in. barrel with full lug, ergonomic wood grips, target sights. New 2000.
Please contact the factory directly for U.S. pricing and availability.

JAPANESE MILITARY
Previously manufactured prior and during WWII in Japan by various manufacturers.

PISTOLS: SEMI-AUTO

Please refer to the Nambu section for further information on Nambus and variations.

HAMADA VARIATIONS
* **Type I** - .32 ACP cal., similar to FN Model 1910, except has 9 shot mag., early production pistols have chrysanthemum and Japanese characters on left slide, salt blue. Mfg. estimated at 5,000, but examples are scarce and usually in the 2,000-3,000 ser. range.

	$3,500	$3,000	$2,600	$2,200	$1,850	$1,500	$1,250

Add 10% for early variation.
* **Type II** - 8mm cal., designed to replace the Type 94 Nambu, larger than Type I and with a more squared profile, essentially a pre-production gun, all known examples are roughly finished in the white and are serial numbered 1-50.

	$4,500	$4,000	$3,250	$2,800	$2,500	$2,200	$1,900

REVOLVERS

1893 REVOLVER (MODEL 26) - 9mm Japanese cal., double action only, 4.7 in. barrel, blue, wood grips. Approx. 59,000 mfg. 1893-1925.

	$650	$475	$325	$200	$150	$135	$120

Subtract 25% for arsenal rework.
Add 150% for early mfg. with internal numbers (approx. first 300 revolvers).

Grading	100%	98%	95%	90%	80%	70%	60%

RIFLES: MILITARY

Subtract 20% if National Crest (chrysanthemum flower) has been ground off front receiver ring.

Subtract 20% if serial numbers are not matching (does not apply to sniper rifles, as they are only rarely found with matching scopes and mounts).

Subtract 10%-40% for training rifles of each type.

MODEL 38 ARISAKA RIFLE - 6.5X51R Arisaka cal., Jap. Mauser type action, 31 in. barrel, adj. sight, adopted 1905.

	100%	98%	95%	90%	80%	70%	60%
	$625	$525	$400	$300	$225	$125	$75

MODEL 38 CAVALRY CARBINE - 6.5x51R Arisaka cal., similar to Model 38 Rifle, except shorter barrel. Mfg. 1911.

	100%	98%	95%	90%	80%	70%	60%
	$625	$525	$400	$300	$225	$125	$75

Add 300% for paratrooper variation with hinged stock (often referenced as Type I, has crude construction and cast iron hinge).

MODEL 44 CAVALRY ARISAKA CARBINE - 6.5x51R Arisaka cal., similar to T38 Carbine, features 19 in. barrel and folding bayonet.

	100%	98%	95%	90%	80%	70%	60%
	$750	$600	$500	$400	$325	$240	$135

MODEL 97 SNIPER RIFLE - based on Model 38.

	100%	98%	95%	90%	80%	70%	60%
	$2,500	$2,200	$1,950	$1,650	$1,375	$1,100	$950

MODEL 99 SERVICE RIFLE - 7.7x58mm Arisaka cal., WWII version of Model 38, mostly encountered with shorter barrels than the Model 38 Arisaka Rifle.

	100%	98%	95%	90%	80%	70%	60%
	$375	$275	$225	$195	$150	$90	$65

Add 20% for monopod.

Add 400% for sniper variation with 4X scope.

Add $1,000 for externally adjustable scope.

Add 75% for long barrel.

PARATROOPER TAKEDOWN VERSION - 7.7x58mm Arisaka cal., adopted 1940, crossbolt barrel lock.

Type 2	100%	98%	95%	90%	80%	70%	60%
	$1,350	$1,200	$1,000	$800	$700	$600	$500

JARRETT RIFLES, INC.

Current manufacturer established in 1979, and located in Jackson, SC. Direct custom order sales only.

HANDGUNS

CUSTOM XP-100 HUNTER - various cals., re-machined Remington XP-100 action, Jarrett match grade stainless steel barrel, McMillan fiberglass stock, various options.

MSR	$3,450						
		$3,250	$2,650	$2,150	$1,750	$1,350	$1,050	$995

ULTIMATE REDHAWK - .44 Mag. cal., features Hogue grips and muzzle brake. Mfg. 1995-2000.

	100%	98%	95%	90%	80%	70%	60%
	$1,150	$1,025	$850	$675	$575	$500	$450

Last MSR was $1,150.

RIFLES: BOLT ACTION

Jarrett rifles are justifiably famous for their well-known Beanfield rifles (refers to shooting over a beanfield at long targets). A Jarrett inovation is the Tri-Lock reciver, which has 3 locking lugs, and a semi-integral recoil lug. Jarrett blueprints every action for proper dimensioning and rigid tolerances, and explains why their rifles have set rigid accuracy standards.

A wide variety of options are available for Jarrett custom rifles (holders of 16 world records in rifle accuracy). The factory should be contacted directly (see Trademark Index) for pricing and availability regarding these special order options. Custom gunsmithing services for Jarrett rifles are also available and again, the manufacturer should be contacted directly for gunsmith quotations.

Grading	100%	98%	95%	90%	80%	70%	60%

STANDARD HUNTING RIFLE - various cals., Remington Model 700 right-hand or left- hand action, McMillan fiberglass stock, blue receiver, Jarrett satin finish match grade barrel, sling studs and leather sling, rings and base, weights vary.

MSR	$3,550	$3,350	$2,750	$2,150	$1,750	$1,375	$1,200	$1,050

WALK ABOUT - various cals. in short action only, features Remington Model 7 action (left- hand utilizes Rem. Model 700 short action), weights vary. New 1995.

MSR	$3,550	$3,350	$2,750	$2,150	$1,750	$1,375	$1,200	$1,050

TRUCK GUN - various small bore cals., 19-20 in. barrel, black synthetic stock. New 1999.

MSR	$3,550	$3,350	$2,750	$2,150	$1,750	$1,375	$1,200	$1,050

BENCHREST/YOUTH/TACTICAL - various cals., various configurations depending on application. New 1999.

MSR	$3,550	$3,350	$2,750	$2,150	$1,750	$1,375	$1,200	$1,050

SERIES RIFLE - various cals., various configurations, only 100 made of each series. New 1993.

✳ *Standard Series Rifle* - various cals.

MSR	$4,195	$3,850	$3,350	$2,850	$2,350	$1,950	$1,750	$1,450

✳ *Coup de Grace* - various cals. Mfg. 1996-99.

		$3,295	$2,750	$2,300	$1,800	$1,500	$1,250	$995

Last MSR was $3,495.

✳ *Nombre Unique Series* - various cals., 100 mfg. 1999 only.

		$3,495	$2,900	$2,400	$1,850	$1,550	$1,250	$995

Last MSR was $3,695.

WINDWALKER SERIES - various cals. up to .30 cal., Rem. M-700 ADL action only, lightweight design, Brown Precision stock, muzzle brake step, 7¼ lbs. New 1999.

MSR	$4,395	$4,100	$3,350	$2,700	$2,100	$1,700	$1,500	$1,350

Add $790 for Swarovski 3X-10X (42mm) scope.

PROFESSIONAL HUNTER - Mag. cals. to customer's specifications, features Winchester controlled round feed Model 70 action with claw extractor and 3 position bolt shroud safety, Jarrett match grade stainless steel barrel, McMillan stock, quarter rib with iron sights, includes 2 sets of detachable rings and two 1.5X-5X Leupold scopes, takedown action.

MSR	$6,700	$6,450	$5,450	$4,550	$3,700	$3,000	$2,500	$2,150

.50 CAL. - .50 BMG cal., McMillan custom receiver, choice of repeater or single shot, 30 or 34 in. barrel with muzzle brake, 28-45 lbs. New 1999.

MSR	$6,700	$6,450	$5,450	$4,550	$3,700	$3,000	$2,500	$2,150

Add $250 for repeater action.

CLASSIC SERIES - various cals., 100 mfg. 1989 only.

		$3,195	$2,650	$2,100	$1,650	$1,375	$1,150	$875

INVESTOR SERIES - various cals., 100 mfg. 1989 only.

		$3,195	$2,650	$2,100	$1,650	$1,375	$1,150	$875

ACCURACY LEGEND SERIES - various cals., similar to Jarrett Custom Rifle, except has many accuracy tune-ups incorporated as well as muzzle brake. 100 mfg. 1993 only.

		$3,495	$2,850	$2,300	$1,850	$1,500	$1,250	$995

Last MSR was $3,495.

COUP de MAIM - various cals., similar to the Jarrett Custom Rifle, includes muzzle brake, matte black or olive drab finish, Model 70 style bolt release. 100 mfg. 1995 only.

		$2,750	$2,300	$1,800	$1,500	$1,250	$995	$775

Last MSR was $3,495.

PRIVATE COLLECTION - various cals., similar quality as the Jarrett Custom Rifle, except many extra cost special order options are included, ser. numbered 1-100. Mfg. 1994 only.

		$3,495	$2,850	$2,300	$1,850	$1,500	$1,250	$995

Last MSR was $3,495.

Grading	100%	98%	95%	90%	80%	70%	60%

SILENT PARTNER SERIES - various cals., only 10 mfg. 1994 only.

	100%	98%	95%	90%	80%	70%	60%
	$3,495	$2,850	$2,300	$1,850	$1,500	$1,250	$995

ULTIMATE HUNTER SERIES - various cals., 100 mfg. 1989 only.

	100%	98%	95%	90%	80%	70%	60%
	$3,495	$2,850	$2,300	$1,850	$1,500	$1,250	$995

RIFLES: RIMFIRE, SEMI-AUTO

SQUIRREL KING - .22 LR cal., reworked Ruger 10/22 action, 18 in. barrel, McMillan or Brown Precision synthetic stock. New 1999.

	MSR	$1,800						
			$1,650	$1,300	$1,050	$900	$700	$575	$475

Add $195 for Target King variation.

SHOTGUNS: SLIDE ACTION

JARRETT ULTIMATE SHOTGUN - 12 ga., Remington Model 870 action with 21 in. hand lapped barrel with interchangeable chokes, 8 shot mag. extension, matte black or olive drab green finish. Disc. 1999.

	100%	98%	95%	90%	80%	70%	60%
	$900	$825	$675	$550	$450	$350	$295

Last MSR was $1,000.

JEFFERY, W.J. & CO. LTD

Previous manufacturer located in London, England.

In addition to making a complete line of their own shotguns and rifles, W.J. Jeffery also was subcontracted by many other exporters, distributors, and retailers (including London's famous Army & Navy department store). Many models were produced and rather than list them individually, a generalized format has been adopted for determining values on both rifles and shotguns.

RIFLES

SINGLE SHOT - various cals., falling block action, checkered walnut stock and forearm, usually multiple folding leaves rear sight (also tangent), excellent quality. Prices start in the $600 range for poor condition specimens in obsolete or undesirable cals. and can go up to $5,000 for 100% condition in .600 Nitro Express.

Subtract substantially for the Martini action variation.

BOXLOCK DOUBLE RIFLE - many cals., various engraving patterns, top or under (usually large cals.) lever opening, multiple folding leaves rear sight, checkered walnut stock and forearm. Prices usually start in the $1,500 range for poor condition in undesirable cals. and can exceed $8,000 if encountered with elaborate engraving in .475 Express or larger cals.

Subtract approx. 40% if with hammers, over 50% if with damascus barrels.

SIDELOCK DOUBLE RIFLE - various cals., available in No. 1 or No. 2 grade, top-lever opening, best quality engraving, deluxe checkered walnut stock and forearm, almost any custom order could be filled. Prices start in the $3,250 range for 60% condition in smaller cals. and can easily go to $12,000+ when found in excellent condition in the larger cals.

Subtract approx. 40% if with hammers, over 50% if with damascus barrels.

SHOTGUNS: SxS

BOXLOCK SHOTGUN - most ga.'s, many combinations of options available, top-lever opening, many ranges of engraving, high quality and worksmanship. Values usually start in the $650 range if in poor condition and can go to $4,500+ if in a small ga. in near new condition ($1,750 for 12 ga.).

Subtract approx. 40% if with hammers, over 50% if with damascus barrels.

Grading	100%	98%	95%	90%	80%	70%	60%

SIDELOCK SHOTGUN - most ga.'s, many combinations of options available, top-lever opening, many ranges of engraving, high quality and worksmanship. Values usually start in the $1,250 range if in poor condition and can go to $8,500+ if in a small ga. in near new condition ($3,950 for 12 ga.).

JENNINGS, B.L., INC.

Previous manufacturer until 1985 located in City of Industry, CA. Currently, Jennings is the exclusive distributor for Bryco, Sundance, and Accu-Tek. The Jennings trademark is now owned by Bryco Arms.

PISTOLS: SEMI-AUTO

MODEL J-22 - .22 LR cal., 6 shot, single action, 2½ in. barrel, positive safety locks sear, satin nickel, bright chrome or black teflon finish, 13 oz. Disc. 1985.

$65	$50	$40	$35	$30	$30	$30

Last MSR was $79.

JERICHO

Previous trademark of Israeli Military Industries (I.M.I.). Previously imported by K.B.I., Inc. located in Harrisburg, PA.

PISTOLS: SEMI-AUTO

J

JERICHO 941 - 9mm Para. or .40 S&W cal.(new 1991), .41 Action Express (by conversion only), semi-auto double action or single action, 4.72 in. barrel with polygonal rifling, all steel fabrication, 3 dot Tritium sights, 11 or 16 (9mm Para.) shot mag., ambidextrous safety, polymer grips, decocking lever, 38½ oz. Imported 1990-92.

$550	$475	$425	$375	$325	$295	$260

Last MSR was $649.

Add $299 for .41 AE conversion kit.

Industrial hard chrome or nickel finishes were also available for all Jericho pistols.

✳ ***Jericho 941 Pistol Package*** - includes 9mm Para. and .40 S&W barrels, also includes .41 AE conversion kit, cased with accessories. Mfg. 1990-91 only.

$695	$625	$550	$495	$450	$400	$360

Last MSR was $775.

JOHANNSEN RIFLES

Currently manufactured by Reimer Johannsen GmbH, located in Germany, and currently imported by Johannsen, Inc., located in Plainfield, NH.

RIFLES: BOLT ACTION

Johannsen rifles feature high quality reproduction Mauser Magnum actions in 5 caliber groupings and are manufactured by Orth, using sophisticated CAD and CNC technology, in addition to Old World gunsmithing techniques. Actions are also available and start at $3,250.

Johannsen take down express rifles are unique in that the bolt locks into the barrel with the same precision every time. This design ensures that point of impact remains identical after each assembly/disassembly.

Add $4,490 for take down action on the models listed.

BASIC SQUARE BRIDGE RIFLE - various cals. between .375 H&H - .416 Rigby, double square bridge, various options available, deluxe checkered walnut stock.

MSR	$8,210						
		$8,210	$7,500	$6,500	$5,500	$4,750	$4,000	$3,300

Subtract $500 if not finished (in-the-white).

Grading	100%	98%	95%	90%	80%	70%	60%

CLASSIC SAFARI - various cals., single square bridge action with thumbcut, 8 lbs. 3 oz.

	MSR	$9,500		$9,500	$7,850	$6,750	$5,600	$4,800	$4,000	$3,300

SAFARI RIFLE - various cals., features double square bridge action w/o thumbcut, 8 lbs. 6 oz.

	MSR	$10,250		$10,250	$8,350	$7,000	$5,750	$4,900	$4,100	$3,400

TRADITION RIFLE - various cals., top-of-the-line model, 8 lbs.

	MSR	$10,550		$10,550	$8,550	$7,150	$5,800	$4,950	$4,100	$3,400

JOHNSON AUTOMATICS, INC.

Previous manufacturer located in Providence, RI. Johnson Automatics, Inc. moved many times during its history, often with slight name changes. M.M. Johnson, Jr. died in 1965, and the company continued production at 104 Audubon Street in New Haven, CT as Johnson Arms, Inc. mostly specializing in sporter semi-auto rifles in .270 Win. or 30-06.

RIFLES: SEMI-AUTO

MODEL 1941 - .30-06 or 7x57mm cal., 22 in. removable air cooled barrel, recoil operated, perforated metal handguard, aperture sight, military stock. Most were made for Dutch military, some used by U.S. Marine Paratroopers, during WWII all .30-06 and 7x57mm were ordered by South American governments.

$2,495	$2,250	$1,850	$1,575	$1,250	$995	$850

Subtract $50 for 7x57mm cal.

JUNG, WAFFEN, GMBH

Please refer to Waffen Jung GmbH.

JURRAS

Previous custom pistolsmith located in Prescott, AZ. Previously distributed by J & G Sales located in Prescott, AZ.

Ammunition for Jurras pistols was manufactured by Robert Davis, Jr. located in Athens, TN.

PISTOLS

Lee E. Jurras manufactured custom pistols in larger calibers. Almost any caliber was available by special order and the listings represent a few of his more standard items.

HOWDAH - available in .375, .416, .460, .475, .500, or .577 Jurras cals., action based on Thompson/ Center Contender receiver, 12 in. bull barrel, nitex finish, adj. rear sights, limited mfg. (100).

* **Custom Grade**

$1,150	$925	$800	$725	$650	$575	$500

* ***Presentation Grade*** - .375 Jurras or .460 Jurras cals. standard, deluxe Claro walnut stock and forearm.

$2,000	$1,750	$1,500	$1,250	$1,050	$950	$825

Special order .416, .475, .500, or .577 Jurras calibers command a premium on this model.

JUST, JOSEF

Current custom long gun manufacturer and gunsmith established in 1790, and located in Ferlach, Austria.

Josef Just is a member of the Ferlach Guild, and manufactures a variety of high quality long gun configurations (including SxSs, O/Us, drillings, vierlings, combination guns, and single shot), all to custom order. Please contact the Guild or Mr. Just directly for more information and an individual price quotation (see Trademark Index).

K SECTION

K.B.I., INC.

Current importer and distributor located in Harrisburg, PA. Distributor and dealer sales.

K.B.I., Inc. currently imports Armscor (Arms Corp. of the Philippines), Charles Daly shotguns, FEG pistols, and Liberty revolvers. These may be found within the correct alphabetical sections. K.B.I. previously imported the Jericho pistol manufactured by I.M.I. from Israel. The Jericho pistol may be found under its own heading in this text.
Please refer to the FEG section in this text.

Grading	100%	98%	95%	90%	80%	70%	60%

RIFLES: BOLT ACTION

KASSNAR GRADE I - available in 9 cals., thumb safety that locks trigger, with or w/o deluxe sights, 22 in. barrel, 3 or 4 shot mag., includes swivel posts and oil finished standard grade European walnut with recoil pad, 7½ lbs. Imported 1989-1993.

	100%	98%	95%	90%	80%	70%	60%
	$445	$385	$325	$275	$225	$195	$175

Last MSR was $499.

NYLON 66 - .22 LR cal., patterned after the Remington Nylon 66. Imported until 1990 from C.B.C. in Brazil, South America.

	100%	98%	95%	90%	80%	70%	60%
	$125	$110	$95	$85	$75	$70	$65

Last MSR was $134.

MODEL 122 - .22 LR cal., bolt action design with mag. Imported from South America until 1990.

	100%	98%	95%	90%	80%	70%	60%
	$125	$110	$95	$85	$75	$70	$65

Last MSR was $136.

MODEL 522 - .22 LR cal., bolt action design with tube mag. Imported from South America until 1990.

	100%	98%	95%	90%	80%	70%	60%
	$130	$115	$100	$85	$75	$70	$65

Last MSR was $142.

BANTAM SINGLE SHOT - .22 LR cal., youth dimensions. Imported 1989-90 only.

	100%	98%	95%	90%	80%	70%	60%
	$110	$90	$85	$75	$70	$65	$60

Last MSR was $120.

SHOTGUNS

GRADE I O/U - 12, 20, 28 ga., or .410 bore, gold plated SST, extractors, vent. rib, checkered walnut stock and forearm. Imported 1989-1993.

	100%	98%	95%	90%	80%	70%	60%
	$525	$425	$350	$295	$265	$240	$220

Last MSR was $599.

Add $70 for 28 ga. or .410 bore.
Add $50 for choke tubes (12 and 20 ga. only).
Add $150 for automatic ejectors (with choke tubes only).

GRADE II SxS - 10, 12, 16, 20, 28 ga., or .410 bore, boxlock action, case hardened receiver, English style checkered European walnut stock with splinter forearm, chrome barrels with concave rib, extractors, double hinged triggers. Imported 1989-90 only.

	100%	98%	95%	90%	80%	70%	60%
	$515	$435	$375	$325	$275	$250	$225

Last MSR was $575.

Add $95 for 28 ga. or .410 bore.
Add $85 for 10 ga.

K

Grading	100%	98%	95%	90%	80%	70%	60%

KDF, INC.

Current manufacturer (beginning 1998 again) and custom riflesmith specializing in restocking and installing muzzle brakes, in addition to supplying specialized rifle parts located in Seguin, TX. KDF utilizes Mauser K-15 actions imported from Oberndorf, Germany. Previously, KDF rifles were manufactured by Voere (until 1987) in Vöhrenbach, W. Germany.

Older KDF rifles were private labeled by Voere and marked KDF. Since Voere was absorbed by Mauser-Werke in 1987, model designations changed. Mauser-Werke does not private label (i.e. newer guns are marked Mauser-Werke), and these rifles can be found under the Mauser-Werke heading in this text.

RIFLES: BOLT ACTION, U.S. MFG.

KDF also builds custom rifles on Remington & Winchester actions, in addition to converting Rem. M700 and Winchester M70 rifles into custom rifles. Please contact the company directly for more information and pricing.

In 1989, KDF announced the release of a new American built redesigned Model K15 with many improvements. While advertised, approximately only 25 were manufactured in various cals.

K15 - .22-250 Rem. (disc. 1992), .243 Win., 6mm Rem., .25-06 Rem., .270 Win., .280 Rem., .30-06 cal. or .308 Win. cal., 60 degree short lift bolt action with 3 lugs, Kevlar composite or laminate walnut stock, adj. single stage competition trigger, box magazine, thumb activated slide safety, satin blue finish, 24 in. match grade barrel, deluxe checkered walnut stock with ebony accents and Pachmayr Decelerator recoil pad, approx. 8 lbs. Limited mfg. in U.S. starting 1989.

$1,750	$1,375	$1,150	$950	$750	$650	$575

Last MSR was $1,950.

✳ K15 Magnum - .270 Wby. Mag., .300 Win. Mag. (disc.), .300 Wby. Mag., 7mm Rem. Mag., .338 Win. Mag., .340 Wby. Mag. (disc.), .375 H&H, .411 KDF, .416 Rem. Mag. (disc.), or .458 Win. Mag. cal., similar to K15, except has 26 in. barrel. Mfg. in U.S. starting in 1989. Disc.

$1,795	$1,400	$1,175	$975	$775	$675	$600

Last MSR was $2,000.

KDF CLASSIC - cals. similar to K15, custom tuned Remington 700 action, bench rest barrel, Brown Precision stock, KDF accurizing, Arnold jewell custom trigger, matte blue finish, Pachmayr Decelerator pad, includes rings and bases.

$1,750	$1,375	$1,150	$950	$750	$650	$575

Last MSR was $1,950.

Add $50 for Mag. cals.

KDF FRONTIER - cals. similar to KDF Classic, custom tuned Winchester Model 70 action, bench rest barrel, Brown Precision stock, KDF accurizing, Arnold jewell custom trigger, matte blue finish, Pachmayr Decelerator pad, includes rings and bases.

$1,750	$1,375	$1,150	$950	$750	$650	$575

Last MSR was $1,950.

Add $50 for Mag. cals.
Add $150 for action with positive feeding claw extractor.

KDF VARMINT - varmint cals., custom tuned Remington 700 or XP action, bench rest heavy contour barrel, Brown Precision stock, KDF accurizing, Arnold jewell custom trigger, matte blue finish, Pachmayr Decelerator pad, includes rings and bases.

$2,000	$1,725	$1,425	$1,200	$950	$750	$650

Last MSR was $2,250.

Add $250 for Rem. XP action.

Grading	100%	98%	95%	90%	80%	70%	60%

KDF MAUSER 98 - .22-250 Rem. (new 2000), .243 Win. (new 2000), .25-06 Rem. (new 2000), .270 Win., .30-06, .308 Win. (new 2000), or 6.5x55mm (new 2000) cal., sporterized action, Wilson, Adams, or Bennett barrel, Butler Creek black synthetic stock, 7.5 lbs. New 1998.

	MSR	$379		$325	$275	$250	$225	$200	$185	$170

Subtract $40 for 6.5x55mm cal.

KDF CUSTOM MAUSER PACKAGE - various cals., features custom bolt shroud, adj. trigger, glass bedding, 1 in. rings, and KDF slimline muzzle brake. Mfg. 1998-99.

	$675	$550	$500	$450	$400	$360	$330

Last MSR was $750.

RIFLES: OLDER VOERE MFG. (PRE-1988)

TITAN SPORTER SERIES - various cals., 24 or 26 in. barrel, select walnut, pistol grip stock. This series was available with either European Monte Carlo high-luster stock or in classic featherweight configuration with Schnabel forend - add $50-$200.

❋ **Titan Menor** - .222 Rem. or .223 Rem. cal. Importation disc. 1987.

	$675	$615	$560	$495	$450	$395	$350

Last MSR was $765.

Add $100 for Match or Competition model (.223 Rem. cal.).

❋ **Titan II Standard** - many cals., between .243 Win. and .30-06. Disc. 1988.

	$950	$825	$725	$625	$550	$500	$450

Last MSR was $1,075.

Add $100 for Match or Competition model (.308 Win. cal.).

❋ **Titan II Magnum** - available in cals. between 7mm Rem. Mag. and .375 H&H. Disc. 1988.

	$995	$875	$750	$650	$575	$520	$475

Last MSR was $1,125.

❋ **Titan .411 KDF Mag.** - .411 KDF cal., 26 in. barrel with recoil arrestor, 3 shot mag., blue or electroless nickel finish, 9¼ lbs. Imported 1986-1988.

	$1,175	$965	$810	$725	$650	$575	$520

Last MSR was $1,300.

MODEL 2005 - .22 LR cal. only, semi-auto, 19½ in. barrel, Monte Carlo stock, 5 shot mag., iron sights, 6 lbs. Imported 1986 only.

	$235	$215	$195	$175	$160	$145	$135

Last MSR was $165.

This model was ruled no longer importable by the BATF.

❋ **Model 2005 Deluxe** - similar to Model 2005, except has deluxe checkered walnut. Mfg. 1986-87 only.

	$260	$230	$210	$185	$165	$145	$135

Last MSR was $185.

MODEL 2107 - .22 LR or .22 Mag. cal., bolt action, 19½ in. barrel, 5 shot mag., adj. iron sights, 6 lbs. Imported 1986-87 only.

	$175	$150	$125	$105	$95	$85	$80

Last MSR was $197.

Add $42 for .22 Mag. cal.

❋ **Model 2107 Deluxe (Mauser 107)** - similar to Model 2107, except has deluxe checkered walnut. Imported 1986-1988.

	$185	$165	$140	$125	$110	$105	$100

Last MSR was $219.

Add $50 for .22 Mag. cal.

This model was redesignated KDF-Mauser Model 107 when Voere distributor/dealer inventories were depleted.

K

Grading	100%	98%	95%	90%	80%	70%	60%

MODEL 2112 - .22 LR or .22 Mag. cal., similar to Model 2107, except has extra select walnut. Imported 1988 only.

	$235	$200	$180	$160	$145	$135	$125

Last MSR was $279.

Add $50 for .22 Mag. cal.

K-14 INSTA FIRE RIFLE - .22-250 Rem., .270 Win., .300 Wby. Mag., or .458 Win. Mag. cal., 24 or 26 in. barrel, no sights, ultra fast lock time, hidden detachable mag., checkered Monte Carlo stock, recoil pad. Imported 1971-78.

	$725	$650	$575	$525	$475	$425	$375
K15 (.22 cal.)	$235	$205	$175	$150	$135	$120	$105

K-15 (MODEL 225) - available in 13 cals. between .243 Win. and .300 Wby. Mag., bolt action, 60 degree bolt lift with 3 locking lugs, ultra fast lock time, adj. trigger, 24 or 26 (Mag. only) in. barrel, 3 or 5 shot mag., no sights, guaranteed ½ in. accuracy at 100 yards, many stock options available at extra cost. Left-handed action available in certain cals. at a $50 charge.

* **Deluxe Standard Sporter** - standard model available in 6 regular cals. and 9 Mag. cals. Disc. 1988.

	$1,075	$950	$810	$700	$625	$550	$495

Last MSR was $1,275.

Add $50 for Magnum action.
Add $525 for .411 KDF cal.
In addition to the 15 regular cals., it was also possible to order various other factory cals. as a $200 option.
This model was redesignated KDF-Mauser Model 225 when Voere distributor/dealer inventories were depleted.

* **K-15 Fiberstock Pro-Hunter** - similar to the K-15, except is supplied with fiberglass stock (various colors), choice of parkerized, matte blue, or electroless nickel metal finish, and recoil arrestor installed. Imported 1986-1988.

	$1,420	$1,200	$950

Last MSR was $1,680.

Add $50 for Magnum action.
This model was redesignated KDF-Mauser Model 225 when Voere distributor/dealer inventories were depleted.

* **K-15 Dangerous Game** - .411 KDF Mag. (new cartridge 1985) cal., choice of finishes, oil finished deluxe American walnut stock. Imported 1986-1988.

	$1,895	$1,500	$1,150

Last MSR was $2,100.

This model was redesignated KDF-Mauser Model 225 when Voere distributor/dealer inventories were depleted.

* **K-15 Swat Rifle** - .308 Win. cal. standard, 24 or 26 in. barrel, parkerized metal, oil finished target walnut stock, 3 or 4 shot detachable mag., 10 lbs. Importation disc. 1988.

	$1,475	$1,250	$1,000	$850	$725	$650	$575

Last MSR was $1,725.

K-16 - available in 6 standard cals. between .243 Win. and .300 Win. Mag. in addition to optional cals., modified Remington Model 700 action, standard features include KDF accurizing and Insta Fire ignition, single stage adj. trigger, Dupont Rynite stock (camel or grey), choice of finishes (high-gloss blue standard), recoil pad and quick detachable sling swivels, many options available. Imported 1988 only.

	$765	$675	$615	$560	$495	$450	$395

Last MSR was $876.

Add $120 for KDF muzzle brake.
Add $250 for optional cals.
Add $350 for .411 KDF Mag. cal.

Grading	100%	98%	95%	90%	80%	70%	60%

K-22 (MAUSER 201) - .22 LR or .22 Mag. cal., bolt action, free floating 21 in. barrel, 5 shot mag., adj. trigger, scaled down version of the K-15, unusual action incorporates two front-located locking lugs on bolt face that engage Stellite inserts on the front receiver portion, guaranteed 1 in. groupings at 100 yards, blue only, no sights, select walnut stock with cheek-piece, standard model disc. 1987.

	$310	$285	$260	$240	$225	$210	$195

Last MSR was $345.

Add $50 for .22 Mag. cal.

* **K-22 Deluxe (Mauser 201)** - better walnut and stock options. Model notation changed in 1988.

	$410	$360	$295	$275	$250	$235	$210

Last MSR was $495.

Add $50 for .22 Mag. cal.

This model was redesignated KDF-Mauser Model 201 when Voere distributor/dealer inventories were depleted.

* **K-22 Deluxe Custom** - richly layered walnut and stock options. Importation disc. 1987.

	$655	$595	$550	$495	$450	$395	$350

Last MSR was $725.

Add $50 for .22 Mag. cal.

* **K-22 Deluxe Special Select** - top-of-the-line bolt action, double set triggers. Importation disc. 1987.

	$1,060	$950	$850	$750	$695	$650	$595

Last MSR was $1,225.

Add $50 for .22 Mag. cal.

SHOTGUNS

CONDOR O/U - 12 ga., 28 in. barrel, various chokes, selective single trigger, auto ejectors, wide VR, boxlock, checkered pistol grip stock, Italian made.

	$660	$635	$605	$580	$525	$470	$415

BRESCIA SxS - 12 ga., 28 in. barrel, full and mod., double triggers, engraved, checkered pistol grip stock.

	$330	$305	$275	$250	$195	$165	$140

K.F.C.

Previously manufactured by Kawaguchiya Firearms Co., Ltd. Previously imported and distributed by La Paloma Marketing, Inc. located in Tucson, AZ.

SHOTGUNS

MODEL 250 SEMI-AUTO - 12 ga. only, semi-auto incorporating a patented, cushioned piston assembly, 26, 28, or 30 in. barrel, matte blue finish, vent. rib standard, checkered premium walnut, 7 lbs. Manufactured 1980-86.

	$360	$290	$270	$250	$235	$220	$205

Last MSR was $485.

Add $60 for multi-chokes.

* **Model 250 Deluxe Semi-Auto** - same specifications as Model 250, except has scrolled acid etching panels on both sides of normally black receiver. Disc. 1986.

	$395	$310	$290	$270	$250	$225	$210

Last MSR was $520.

FIELD GUN O/U - 12 ga. only, VR, premium grade walnut, semi pistol grip stock, F&IC chokes. Disc. 1986.

	$645	$565	$530	$495	$470	$445	$410

Last MSR was $748.

Grading	100%	98%	95%	90%	80%	70%	60%

E-1 TRAP OR SKEET O/U - 12 ga. only, VR, oil finished premium grade walnut, semi pistol grip stock, engraved. Disc. 1986.

	$935	$800	$750	$700	$625	$550	$495

Last MSR was $1,070.

E-2 TRAP OR SKEET O/U - 12 ga. only, VR, oil finished premium grade walnut, semi pistol grip stock, detailed engraving. Disc. 1986.

	$1,450	$1,250	$1,075	$950	$850	$750	$650

Last Mfg. Sug. Retail was $1,660.

KSN INDUSTRIES LTD.

Previous distributor (1952-1996) located in Houston, TX. Previously imported until 1996 exclusively by J.O. Arms, Inc. located in Houston, TX. Currently mfg. Israel Arms, Ltd. pistols may be found under their individual listing.

PISTOLS: SEMI-AUTO

The pistols listed below were mfg. by Israel Arms, Ltd.

KAREEN MK II - 9mm Para. or .40 S&W (new late 1994) cal., single action, 3.85 (Compact) or 4.64 (Standard) in. barrel, two-tone finish, rubberized grips, regular or Meprolite sights, 10 (C/B 1994), 13*, or 15* shot mag., 33 oz. Imported 1993-96.

	$360	$305	$255	$225	$200	$185	$170

Last MSR was $411.

Add approx. $160 for two-tone finish with Meprolite sights.

✱ *Kareen Mk II Compact* - compact variation with 3.85 in. barrel. Imported 1993-96.

	$415	$360	$315	$255	$225	$200	$185

Last MSR was $497.

GOLAN MODEL - 9mm Para. or .40 S&W cal., single or double action, ambidextrous safety with decocking feature, steel slide with alloy frame, 3 7/8 in. barrel, matte black finish, 29 oz. Imported 1994-96.

	$565	$515	$460	$410	$360	$330	$295

Last MSR was $650.

Add $35 for .40 S&W cal.

KAHR ARMS

Current manufacturer established 1993, with headquarters located in Blauvelt, NY, and manufacturing in Worchester, MA. Distributor and dealer sales.

PISTOLS: SEMI-AUTO

All Kahr pistols are supplied with two 7 shot mags., hard polymer case, trigger lock, and lifetime warranty.

K9 COMPACT - 9mm Para. cal., trigger cocking, double action only with passive striker block, locked breech with Browning type recoil lug, steel construction, 3½ in. barrel with polygonal rifling, 7 shot mag., wraparound black polymer grips, matte black, black titanium (Black-T, mfg. 1997-98), or electroless nickel (mfg. 1996-99) finish, 25 oz. New 1993.

MSR	$580	$510	$450	$410	$370	$320	$285	$250

Add $74 for electroless nickel finish (disc.).
Add $126 for black titanium finish (Black-T, disc.).
Add $88 for tritium night sights (new 1996).

K

Grading	100%	98%	95%	90%	80%	70%	60%

✳ ***Economy K9*** - features black matte finish, shipped with one mag. only. Limited mfg. 1999 only.

	$350	$300	$275	$250	$230	$210	$190

Last MSR was $399.

✳ ***K9 Stainless*** - similar to Kahr K9, except is matte finished stainless steel. New 1998.

MSR	$638	$530	$460	$400

Add $97 for tritium night sights.

✳ ***K9 Elite 98 Stainless*** - similar to K9, except has high polish slide and specially designed combat trigger utilizing shorter trigger stroke. New 1998.

MSR	$694	$580	$475	$425

Add $97 for tritium night sights.

✳ ***K9 Wilson Custom Package*** - includes Wilson customizing with Metalloy hard chrome frame, black slide, checkered front strap and beveled mag. well. Limited quantities mfg. 1998.

	$1,175	$995	$875	$775	$700	$625	$550

Last MSR was $1,310.

✳ ***Kahr Lady K9*** - similar to Kahr K9, except has lightened recoil spring, not available in black titanium finish, 25 oz. Mfg. 1997-99.

	$480	$435	$395	$365	$315	$285	$250

Last MSR was $545.

Add $74 for electroless nickel finish.
Add $85 for tritium night sights (new 1996).

P9 POLYMER COMPACT - 9mm Para cal., similar to Kahr K9, except has lightweight polymer frame, matte stainless slide, 17.9 oz. New 1999.

MSR	$599	$520	$450	$400	$365	$325	$285	$250

Add $88 for tritium night sights (new 2000).

✳ ***P9 Polymer Covert*** - similar to Kahr K9 Polymer Compact, except has ½ in. shorter frame, supplied with one 6 and one 7 (with grip extension) shot mag., 16.9 oz. Limited mfg. 1999, reintroduced 2002.

MSR	$599	$520	$450	$400	$365	$325	$285	$250

Add $88 for tritium night sights (new 2000).

MK9 MICRO SERIES - 9mm Para. cal., micro compact variation of the K9 featuring 3 in. barrel, double action only with passive striker block, overall size is 4 in. H x 5½ in. L, duo-tone finish with stainless frame and black titanium slide, includes two 6 shot flush floor plate mags. Mfg. 1998-99.

	$650	$575	$515	$465	$425	$395	$375

Last MSR was $749.

Add $85 for tritium night sights.

✳ ***MK9 Stainless*** - similar to MK9, except is stainless steel. New 1998.

MSR	$638	$530	$465	$415

Add $97 for tritium night sights.

✳ ***MK9 Elite 98 Stainless*** - similar to Kahr MK9, except has high polish slide and specially designed combat trigger utilizing shorter trigger stroke. New 1998.

MSR	$694	$575	$485	$425

Add $97 for tritium night sights.

✳ ***MK9 Elite 2000 Stainless*** - similar to MK9 Elite 98 Stainless, except features black stainless frame and slide, black Roguard finish. New 2001.

MSR	$694	$575	$485	$425

K

Grading	100%	98%	95%	90%	80%	70%	60%

MP9 COMPACT POLYMER - 9mm Para cal., features lightweight polymer frame and matte stainless steel slide, 3 in. barrel, DAO with passive striker block, supplied with 6 and 7 shot mag with grip extension, includes hard case and trigger lock, 15.9 oz. New 2002.

	MSR	$599	$520	$450	$400	$365	$325	$285	$250

Add $88 for tritium night sights.

E9 - 9mm Para. cal., economized version of the K9, matte black finish, supplied with one mag. Mfg. 1997 only.

	$395	$365	$335	$300	$280	$265	$250

Last MSR was $433.

K40 COMPACT - .40 S&W cal., similar to Kahr K9, except has 6 shot mag., matte black or electroless nickel finish (disc. 1999), 26 oz. New 1997.

	MSR	$580	$510	$460	$400	$370	$320	$285	$250

Add $88 for tritium night sights (new 1997).
Add $74 for electroless nickel finish (disc. 1999).
Add $126 for black titanium finish (Black-T, disc. 1998).

* **K40 Stainless** - similar to Kahr K40, except is stainless steel. New 1997.

	MSR	$638	$530	$465	$415

Add $97 for tritium night sights.

* **K40 Elite 98 Stainless** - similar to Kahr K40, except has high polish slide and specially designed combat trigger utilizing shorter trigger stroke. New 1998.

	MSR	$694	$575	$485	$425

Add $97 for tritium night sights.

* **K40 Wilson Custom Package** - includes Wilson customizing with Metalloy hard chrome frame, black slide, checkered front strap and beveled mag. well. Limited quantities mfg. 1998.

	$1,175	$995	$875	$775	$700	$625	$550

Last MSR was $1,310.

* **K40 Covert Stainless (KS40 Small Frame)** - .40 S&W cal., similar to Kahr K40, except grip is ½ in. shorter, supplied with 5 and 6 shot mags., 25 oz. Mfg. 1998- 2000.

	$500	$440	$400

Last MSR was $580.

Add $88 for tritium night sights.

P40 COMPACT POLYMER - .40 S&W cal., similar to P9 Compact, 6 shot mag., 18.9 oz. New 2001.

	MSR	$599	$520	$450	$400	$365	$325	$285	$250

Add $88 for tritium night sights.

* **P40 Polymer Covert** - similar to Kahr P40 Compact Polymer, except has ½ in. shorter frame, matte stainless slide, supplied with one 6 and one 7 (with grip extension) shot mag., 16.9 oz. New 2002.

	MSR	$599	$520	$450	$400	$365	$325	$285	$250

Add $88 for tritium night sights.

MK40 MICRO - .40 S&W cal., micro compact variation of the Kahr K40, featuring 3 in. barrel, matte stainless frame and slide, supplied with one 5 shot and one 6 shot (with grip extension) mag. New 1999.

	MSR	$638	$530	$465	$415

Add $88 for tritium night sights.

* **Kahr MK40 Elite Stainless** - similar to Kahr MK40, except has high polish slide and specially designed combat trigger utilizing shorter trigger stroke. New 2000.

	MSR	$694	$575	$485	$425

Add $88 for tritium night sights.

Grading	100%	98%	95%	90%	80%	70%	60%

KASSNAR IMPORTS, INC.

Previous importer and distributor located in Harrisburg, PA. Kassnar Imports operations ceased April, 1989.

Kassnar also imported Churchill and Omega shotguns which can be found in their individual section.

PISTOLS: SEMI-AUTO

PJK-9HP - 9mm Para. cal., single action, patterned after the Browning Hi-Power, 4¾ in. barrel, 13 shot mag., cone hammer, checkered walnut grips, 32 oz.

	$225	$200	$185	$175	$165	$155	$145

Add $15 for VR barrel.

This pistol was imported from Hungary. Approx. 18,000 (including the MBK-9HP) were imported until importation was disc. because of Federal ramifications.

MBK-9HP - 9mm Para. cal., double action, patterned after the Browning Hi-Power, 4 2/3 in. barrel, spur hammer, blue metal, checkered walnut grips, 14 shot mag., 36 oz. Limited importation was stopped in late 1985.

	$295	$260	$230	$190	$175	$165	$155

PMK-380 - .380 ACP cal., double action, patterned after the Walther PP, plastic grips with thumbrest, 4 in. barrel, 7 shot mag., 21 oz. Limited importation.

	$275	$235	$200	$185	$175	$165	$155

This model was imported in very limited quantities before Interarms began exclusive importation.

KEBERST INTERNATIONAL

Previously manufactured and distributed by Kendall International located in Paris, KY.

RIFLES: BOLT ACTION

KEBERST MODEL 1A - .338 Lapua Mag., .338-416 Rigby, or .338-06 cal., muzzle brake and unique recoil pad, camouflaged synthetic stock, package includes 3-9 power Leupold scope, stainless steel cleaning rod, custom designed case, built to special order only. Mfg. 1987-1988 only.

	$3,475	$2,850	$2,475	$2,100	$1,750	$1,400	$1,150

Last MSR was $3,750.

Add $275 for 10X Ultra scope.

KEL-TEC CNC INDUSTRIES, INC.

Current manufacturer established in 1991, and located in Cocoa, FL. Dealer and distributor sales.

CARBINES: SEMI-AUTO

SUB-9/SUB-40 CARBINE - 9mm Para. or .40 S&W cal., unique pivoting 16.1 in. barrel rotates upwards and back, allowing overall size reduction and portability (16 in. x 7 in.), interchangable grip assembly will accept most popular, double column, high capacity handgun mags., tube stock with polymer buttplate, matte black finish, 4.6 lbs. Mfg. 1997-2000.

	$325	$295	$265	$240	$215	$195	$180

Last MSR was $700.

Add $25 for .40 S&W cal.

SUB-2000 CARBINE - 9mm Para cal., similar to Sub-9. New 2001.

MSR	$383		$325	$295	$265	$240	$215	$195	$180

Grading	100%	98%	95%	90%	80%	70%	60%

PISTOLS: SEMI-AUTO

P-11 - 9mm Para. cal., double action only, locked breech design, 3.1 in. barrel, composite frame with steel slide, transfer bar safety, matte blue, parkerized (new 1997), hard chrome (new 1999), or electroless nickel (disc. 1995) finish, black, grey, or green (disc. 1998) synthetic grips, 10 shot double column mag., 14.4 oz. New 1995.

	MSR	$314	$265	$210	$180	$165	$150	$135	$125

Add $80 for night sights (new 1997).
Add $41 for parkerized finish (choice of grips).
Add $54 for hard chrome finish (new 1999).
Add $30 for electroless nickel finish (disc. 1995).
Add $175 for 9mm Para. to .40 S&W cal. conversion kit.

✴ **P-11 Stainless** - similar to P-11, except is stainless steel, available with black (P- 11SB), grey (P- 11SGY), or green (P-11SGN) grips. Mfg. 1996-98.

	$350	$275	$230

Last MSR was $408.

P-32 - .32 ACP cal., double action only with internal hammer block safety, composite frame with steel slide, 2.68 in. barrel, choice of parkerized, blue, or hard chrome finish, 6.6 oz. New 1999.

	MSR	$300	$255	$200	$175	$160	$150	$135	$125

Add $40 for parkerized finish.
Add $55 for hard chrome finish.

P-40 - .40 S&W cal., double action only with internal hammer block safety, composite frame with steel slide, 3.3 in. barrel, choice of parkerized, blue, or hard chrome finish, 9 or 10 shot mag., 15.8 oz. Mfg. 1999-2001.

	$275	$225	$190	$175	$160	$140	$130

Last MSR was $331.

Add $41 for parkerized finish.
Add $58 for hard chrome finish.

KEMEN

Current competition shotgun manufacturer established in 1990, and located in Elgoibar, Spain. Currently imported by New England Custom Gun Service (Model KM-4 only), located in Plainfield, NH, by Fieldsport, located in Traverse City, MI, Target Shotguns, located in Arden, NC, American Shooting Centers, located in Houston, TX, and by Fly and Field, located in Bend, OR. Gun service is available through Briley.

SHOTGUNS: O/U

Kemen shotguns are built to individual customer specifications. 250-300 special order guns are made annually – delivery time is 4-6 months. Their unique metal finish makes them almost impervious to any type of oxidation or rust.

Add 7% for 20 ga. on models listed below.

KM-4 STANDARD - 12 or 20 ga., boxlock action, competition shotgun various length vent. or separated barrels with VR and Briley choke tubes, detachable trigger group, blue receiver with gold accents, checkered walnut stock and forearm, wood upgrades available, cased, 8-8½ lbs.

	MSR	$5,900		$5,000	$4,425	$3,800	$3,400	$2,850	$2,375	$1,875

Grading	100%	98%	95%	90%	80%	70%	60%

KM-4 LUXE A/B - similar to KM-4 Standard, except has nickel finished receiver with choice of fine scroll or game scene engraving.
    MSR $9,995 $9,000 $8,000 $7,100 $6,200 $5,300 $4,475 $3,600
    Subtract $500 for KM-4 Luxe B.

KM-4 SUPER LUXE A/B/C - similar to KM-4 Luxe A/B, except has nickel finished receiver with more elaborate game scene engraving, A suffix features game scene engraving, B suffix includes gold line engraving, C suffix has high relief scroll work and gold trigger.
    MSR $11,999 $10,250 $8,900 $7,850 $6,750 $5,950 $4,950 $4,000
    Add $1,000 for Super Luxe B variation.

KM-4 EXTRA LUXE A/B/C - similar to KM-4 Super Luxe, except has nickel finished receiver with sideplates and choice of Purdey style fine scroll (Extra Luxe A), extra fine game scene (Extra Luxe B), or gargoyle motif (Extra Luxe C) engraving.
    MSR $12,495 $11,000 $9,250 $8,000 $7,000 $6,000 $5,000 $4,400
    Add $1,400 for Extra Luxe B variation.
    Add $5,005 for Extra Luxe C variation.

KM-4 EXTRA GOLD A/B - 12 or 20 ga., features engraved sideplate action with multiple gold inlays, select wood.
    MSR $17,500 $15,000 $12,000 $9,950 $8,750 $7,500 $6,500 $5,750
    Add $1,000 for Extra Gold B variation.

SUPREMA AX/BX/CX - 12 or 20 ga., top-of-the-line model, sidelock action, Suprema AX features English fine scroll engraving, custom ordered to individual specifications.
    MSR $29,950 $26,000 $22,000 $18,000 $14,500 $11,000 $9,250 $8,000
    Add $2,000 for Suprema AX Model.

K

SHOTGUNS: SxS

IMPERIAL PARALELAS - best quality sidelock model, many options available.
    MSR $17,500 $15,000 $12,000 $9,950 $8,750 $7,500 $6,500 $5,750

KENDALL INTERNATIONAL

Previous importer and distributor located in Paris, KY. Kendall International also imported Australian Automatic Arms, and the Keberst Rifle, Air rifles can be found in the 2nd Edition Blue Book of Airguns by Dr. Robert Beeman & John Allen.

KENTUCKY RIFLES

U.S. flintlock/percussion long rifle configuration originating in Pennsylvania. Kentucky rifles are a field unto themselves, and should be evaluated by an experienced and known source for accurate identification and/or price evaluation.

KENTUCKY RIFLES INDENTIFICATION & PRICING

The author wishes to express his thanks once again to Mr. James Buelow for updating the following information.

The Kentucky rifle was the creation of early settlers from Europe. This new American configuration combined the architectural elements of the English Fowler with the ornamental features of the German Jaeger.

The earliest recorded use of the term "Kentucky rifle" was in a ballad written after the battle of New Orleans. The battle was won by the American Long Rifle, in the hands of 2,000 frontiersmen. During that period, the area west of the 13 colonies was known as Kentucky; hence the name Kentucky rifle.

Kentucky rifles began appearing around the middle of the 18th century and disappeared by the middle of the 19th century. Their origin is credited to eastern Pennsylvania, but soon spread to many other states, including Maryland, Virginia, Tennessee, North Carolina, and areas where the

Grading	100%	98%	95%	90%	80%	70%	60%

rifle maker found a market for his skills.

The styles vary, but they have two things in common: they are long, and most had curly maple stocks. The bores are found both rifled and smooth. The rifles most prized by the collector are the ones that have relief or incised carving. Carved Kentucky rifles are considered one of America's earliest art forms and are now considered Americana personified. Present values may range from as low as $1,000 all the way up to $50,000+! Non-carved or plain Kentuckys are most often encountered.

The present value of an uncarved, original flintlock Kentucky rifle in average condition is approx. $3,000. An uncarved percussion specimen in average original condition is approx. $2,000. These prices diminish when the Kentucky rifle lacks a maker's name, usually found on the top of the barrel, or if it does not have a patch box. Kentucky rifle values vary greatly, due to maker popularity, quality of carving, condition, rifle style, and a mulititude of other factors.

During the past several decades, many fine contemporary Kentucky rifles have been built by craftsmen who understand the trade. Many of these guns are now available in the secondary marketplace. A large percentage have outstanding craftsmanship, and are highly sought after. These specimens sell in the $2,000- $10,000 range, depending on the notoriety of the builder and the sophistication of the work. Because of this, these guns have to be evaluated one at a time.

The best way to find out the value of a Kentucky rifle is to seek out a knowledgeable Kentucky rifle collector. To find such a person in your area, contact the Kentucky Rifle Association's Administrative Assistant: Ruth Collis, 2319 Sue Ann Dr., Lancaster, PA, 17602.

For information regarding contemporary Kentucky rifles makers (with some contact information), visit the Contemporary Longrifle Association at www.longrifle.ws, or see their listing under Firearms Associations.

K KEPPELER TECHNISCHE ENTWICKLUNG GmbH

Current rifle manufacturer located in Fichtenberg, Germany. No current U.S. importation.

Keppeler manufactures a wide variety of top quality rifles, in many target configurations (including UIT-CISM, Prone, Free, and Sniper Bullpup). Both metric and domestic calibers are available as well as a variety of special order options. Keppeler also manufactures precision caliber conversion tubes for the shotgun barrel(s) on combination guns and drillings. Please contact the factory directly for more information and current pricing (see Trademark Index).

KEPPLINGER, ING. HANNES

Please refer to the Kufsteiner Waffenstube section.

KESSLER ARMS CORPORATION

Previous manufacturer located in Silver Creek, NY.

SHOTGUNS

LEVERMATIC MODEL - 12, 16, or 20 ga., lever action, 26 or 28 in. full choke, takedown, plain pistol grip stock. Disc. 1953.

	100%	98%	95%	90%	80%	70%	60%
	$175	$150	$125	$100	$85	$65	$55

BOLT ACTION MODEL - 12, 16, or 20 ga., 26 or 28 in. full, takedown, plain stock. Mfg. 1951-1953.

	100%	98%	95%	90%	80%	70%	60%
	$90	$65	$50	$45	$35	$35	$35

Grading	100%	98%	95%	90%	80%	70%	60%

KEYSTONE SPORTING ARMS, INC.

Current rifle manufacturer established 1996, and located in Milton, PA.
Distributor and dealer sales.

RIFLES: BOLT ACTION

CRICKETT SPORTER - .22 LR or .22 Mag. (new 2001) cal., manually cocked single shot, 16 1/8 in. barrel with adj. rear aperture sight, steel or stainless steel (new 1999) construction, 11½ in. LOP (youth dimension), choice of walnut, colored laminate, or molded black synthetic stock, stainless or blue barrel and receiver, 30 in. overall length, 2½ lbs. New 1997.

MSR	$165		$150	$135	$120	$105	$95	$85	$75

Add $20 for solid walnut stock.
Add $45-$60 for color laminated stock (various colors).
Add $35 for stainless steel, and $20 for bull barrel.
Add $25 for .22 Mag. cal.

✳ *Crickett Custom/Deluxe Sporter* - features deluxe hand checkered stock. Mfg. 1998-2000.

$225	$195	$175	$150	$135	$120	$105

Last MSR was $250.

Add $10 for deluxe configuration.KEYSTONE SPORTING ARMS, INC., cont.

J. KIMBALL ARMS CO.

Previous manufacturer located in Detroit, MI circa 1958.

PISTOLS: SEMI-AUTO

AUTOMATIC PISTOL - .30 Carbine or .22 Hornet (very rare) cal., 7 shot, 3 in. (Combat Model) or 5 in. (Target Model) barrel, approx. 32 oz. Less than 300 mfg. in 1958 only.

$950	$850	$725	$600	$500	$395	$300

Functional weaknesses of this pistol caused discontinuance. Surviving specimens should be checked carefully for slide failures and other potential problems. Values assume no operational damage to the pistol. .22 Hornet cal. rarity factor precludes accurate price evaluation.

KIMBER

Current trademark manufactured by Kimber Mfg., Inc., established during 1997, with company headquarters and manufacturing located in Yonkers, NY. Previous manufacture was by Kimber of America, Inc., located in Clackamas, OR circa 1993-97. Dealer sales.

PISTOLS: SEMI-AUTO, CLASSIC & CDP SERIES

All Kimber pistols are shipped with lockable high impact synthetic case with cable lock and one mag., beginning 1999. During 2001, all Kimber Classic pistols were converted to "Series II". These models include the Kimber Firing Pin Safety System. Inclusion of this new system can be determined by the Roman numeral "II" after the model name. This conversion was completed by February, 2002, and all Kimber pistols were Series II.

Add $300 for .22 LR cal. conversion kit for all mil-spec 1911 pistols (includes complete upper assembly, lightweight aluminum slide, premium bull barrel, and 10 shot mag.). Available in satin black and satin silver.

Grading	100%	98%	95%	90%	80%	70%	60%

CUSTOM II - .45 ACP cal., patterned after the Colt Government Model 1911, 5 in. barrel, various finishes, 7 shot mag., forged steel or polymer (new 1997) frame, match grade barrel, chamber, bushing, and trigger group, dovetail mounted sights, frame, slide, and barrel machined from steel forgings, high ride beavertail grip safety, choice of rubber, walnut or rosewood (new 1999) grips, 38 oz. New 1995.

	MSR	$730	$610	$525	$440	$375	$335	$300	$275

Add $22 for walnut or rosewood (disc.) grips.
Add $137 for night sights.
Add $156 for Royal II finish (polished blue and rosewood grips).

* **Custom Target II** - similar to Custom II, except features Kimber adj. rear sight. New 1998.

	MSR	$837	$720	$595	$515	$450	$395	$340	$300

* **Stainless II** - .38 Super (advertised in 1999, never mfg.), 9mm Para (advertised in 1999, never mfg.), .40 S&W (new 1999), or .45 ACP cal., similar to Custom II, except is stainless steel slide and frame.

	MSR	$832	$700	$585	$475

Add $38 for .40 S&W cal.
Add $137 for night sights.
Subtract $27 for Stainless Limited Edition marked "Stainless LE" (disc. 1998).

* **Stainless Target II** - similar to Stainless II, except is available in .38 Super (new 2002) cal., features Kimber adj. rear sight. New 1998.

	MSR	$945	$785	$645	$535

Add $30 for .40 S&W cal.

* **Heritage Edition** - special edition for the NSSF Heritage Foundation, approximately 1,000 units produced beginning 2001.

	MSR	$1,076	$950	$825	$675

GOLD MATCH II - .45 ACP cal., features Kimber adj. sight, stainless steel match barrel and bushing, premium aluminum match grade trigger, ambidextrous thumb safety became standard in 1998, 8 or 10 (disc. 1998) shot mag., fancy checkered rosewood grips in double diamond pattern, hand fitted, high polish blue, hand fitted in the Kimber Custom Shop, 38 oz.

	MSR	$1,168	$1,035	$875	$740	$630	$525	$450	$400

* **Stainless Gold Match II** - .38 Super (advertised in 1999, never mfg.), 9mm Para (advertised in 1999, never mfg.), .40 S&W (new 1999), or .45 ACP cal., similar to Gold Match, except is stainless steel, 38 oz.

	MSR	$1,315	$1,130	$975	$785

Add $30 for .40 S&W cal.

* **Polymer Gold Match II** - .45 ACP cal. only, similar to Gold Match, except has polymer frame, supplied with 10 shot mag., 34 oz. Mfg. 1999-2001.

	$925	$850	$725	$650	$550	$450	$400

Last MSR was $1,041.

◇**Polymer Gold Match Stainless II** - similar to Gold Match Stainless, except has polymer frame, 34 oz. Mfg. 1999-2001.

	$1,025	$900	$750

Last MSR was $1,177.

GOLD COMBAT II - .45 ACP cal. only, 5 in. barrel, full size carry pistol based on the Gold Match, steel frame and slide, stainless steel match grade barrel and bushing, KimPro finish, tritium night sights, checkered walnut grips, 38 oz. New 1999.

	MSR	$1,681	$1,450	$1,100	$950	$800	$675	$575	$400

* **Gold Combat Stainless II** - similar to Gold Combat, except is all stainless steel. New 1999.

	MSR	$1,623	$1,400	$1,050	$925

Grading	100%	98%	95%	90%	80%	70%	60%

SUPER MATCH II - .45 ACP cal. only, 5 in. barrel, top-of-the-line model, two-tone stainless steel construction, KimPro finish on slide, match grade trigger, custom shop markings, 38 oz. New 1999.

    MSR   **$1,927**   **$1,500**   **$1,125**   **$975**

LPT II - .45 ACP cal., designed for Limited Ten competition, external extractor, steel frame and slide, KimPro finish, 30 LPI front strap checkering, 20 LPI checkering under triggerguard, titanium guide rod, flat top serrated slide, beveled mag. well, ambidextrous thumb safety, adj. sight. Mfg. by Custom Shop beginning 2002.

    MSR   **$2,036**   **$1,800**   **$1,575**   **$1,275**   **$995**   **$875**   **$750**   **$625**

POLYMER MODEL II - .45 ACP cal., features widened black polymer frame offering larger mag. capacity, choice of fixed McCormick (Polymer Model) or adj. Kimber target (Polymer Target Model, disc. 1999) rear sight, matte black slide, 10 shot mag., 34 oz. Mfg. 1997-2001.

                $675   **$575**   **$525**   **$475**   **$425**   **$375**   **$330**

Last MSR was $795.

    Add $88 for Polymer Target Model.

✳ *Polymer Stainless II* - .38 Super (advertised in 1999, never mfg.), 9mm Para (advertised in 1999, never mfg.), .40 S&W (mfg. 1999 only), or .45 ACP cal., similar to Polymer Model, except has satin finish stainless steel slide. Mfg. 1998-2001.

                $745   **$625**   **$550**

Last MSR was $856.

    Add $88 for Polymer Stainless Target Model (disc. 1999).

✳ *Polymer Gold Match II* - .45 ACP cal. only, similar to Gold Match, except has polymer frame, supplied with 10 shot mag., 34 oz. Mfg. 1999-2001.

                $925   **$850**   **$725**   **$650**   **$550**   **$450**   **$400**

Last MSR was $1,041.

✳ *Polymer Pro Carry II* - .45 ACP cal. only, 4 in. bushingless bull barrel, steel slide, 32 oz. Mfg. 1999-2001.

                $725   **$650**   **$575**   **$485**   **$435**   **$375**   **$330**

Last MSR was $814.

    ◇**Polymer Pro Carry Stainless II** - similar to Polymer Pro Carry, except has stainless steel slide. Mfg. 1999-2001.

                $755   **$625**   **$550**

Last MSR was $874.

✳ *Ultra Ten II* - .45 ACP cal., black polymer frame with aluminum frame insert, stainless slide, shorter, 3 in. barrel, 10 shot staggered mag., McCormick low profile sights, lighter version of the Polymer Series frame, Kimber Firing Pin Safety, 24 oz.

While advertised during 2001 with an MSR of $896, this model was never manufactured.

COMPACT II - .45 ACP cal., features 4 in. barrel, .4 in. shorter aluminum or steel frame, 7 shot mag., Commander style hammer, single recoil spring, McCormick low profile combat sights, choice of walnut or checkered black synthetic grips, 28 (aluminum) or 34 (steel) oz. Mfg. 1998-2001.

                $635   **$535**   **$455**   **$395**   **$365**   **$325**   **$295**

Last MSR was $764.

✳ *Compact Stainless II* - .40 S&W (mfg. 1999-2001) or .45 ACP cal., features stainless steel slide, 4 in. barrel, 4 in. shorter aluminum frame, 7 shot mag., Commander style hammer, single recoil spring, McCormick low profile combat sights, black synthetic grips, 28 oz. New 1998.

    MSR   **$870**   **$725**   **$585**   **$480**

    Add $32 for .40 S&W cal.

K

Grading	100%	98%	95%	90%	80%	70%	60%

❋ **Compact Aluminum Stainless II** - .40 S&W or .45 ACP cal., features aluminum frame and stainless steel slide, 28 oz. Mfg. 1999-2001.

	$700	$575	$475				

Last MSR was $837.

Add $36 for .40 S&W cal.

COMBAT CARRY - .40 S&W or .45 ACP cal., 4 in. barrel, carry model featuring aluminum frame and trigger, stainless steel slide, tritium night sights, and ambidextrous thumb safety, 28 oz. Limited mfg. 1999 only.

	$940	$815	$675	$600	$500	$450	$400

Last MSR was $1,044.

Add $30 for .40 S&W cal.

PRO CARRY II - .40 S&W (disc. 2001) or .45 ACP cal., 4 in. barrel, features full length grip similar to Custom Model, aluminum frame (except Pro Carry HD), steel slide, 7 or 8 shot mag., 28 oz. New 1999.

MSR	$773		$645	$550	$450	$395	$355	$325	$295

Add $35 for .40 S&W cal.

❋ **Stainless Pro Carry II** - similar to Pro Carry, except has stainless steel slide. New 1999.

MSR	$845		$715	$600	$475				

Add $36 for .40 S&W cal.

❋ **Pro Carry HD II** - .38 Super (new 2002) or .45 ACP cal., similar to Pro Carry Stainless, except has heavier, stainless steel frame, 35 oz. New 2001.

MSR	$879		$745	$625	$485				

Add $40 for .38 Super cal.

ULTRA CARRY II - .40 S&W (disc. 2001) or .45 ACP cal., 3 in. barrel, aluminum frame, 7 shot mag., 25 oz. New 1999.

MSR	$767		$645	$550	$495	$440	$395	$350	$325

Add $39 for .40 S&W cal.

❋ **Stainless Ultra Carry II** - similar to Ultra Carry, except has stainless steel slide. New 1999.

MSR	$841		$725	$615	$475				

Add $43 for .40 S&W cal.

ELITE II SERIES - .45 ACP cal., Custom Shop pistol, stainless steel slide and frame, matte finish with brush polished flat surfaces for elegant two-tone finish, Tritium night sights, target models have adj. Bar/Dot sights, silver/grey laminated double diamond grips, black small parts, 30 LPI front strap checkering, include Eclipse Ultra II (3 in. barrel, short grip), Eclipse Pro II and Eclipse Pro-Target II (4 in. barrel, standard grip), Eclipse Custom II, and Eclipse Target II (full size). New 2002.

MSR	$1,052		$975	$835	$725	$635	$525	$450	$400

Add $19 for Eclipse Custom II.
Add $101 for Eclipse Target II or Eclipse Pro-Target II.

A similar Custom Shop version of these pistols was mfg. during late 2001, featuring an ambidextrous thumb safety, and "Custom Shop" markings on left side of slide, several thousand were mfg.

TEN II SERIES - .45 ACP cal., high capacity polymer frame, Custom Shop pistol, stainless steel slide with satin finish, impressed front grip strap checkering and serrations under trigger guard, textured finish, polymer grip safety and mainspring housing, 10 round double stack mag., includes Ultra Ten II (3 in. barrel, short grip), Pro Carry Ten II (4 in. barrel, standard grip), Stainless Ten II (full size), and Gold Match Ten II (stainless steel barrel, polished stainless steel slide flats, hand fitted barrel/bushing to slide, adj. sight), 14 (pre-ban) round mags. also available, accepts magazines from older Kimber mfg. polymer pistols. New 2002.

MSR	$812		$700	$600	$475	$425	$395	$365	$345

Add $16 for Pro-Carry Ten II, $38 for Ultra Ten II, or $306 for Gold Match Ten II.

Grading	100%	98%	95%	90%	80%	70%	60%

CDP II (CUSTOM DEFENSE PACKAGE) - .40 S&W or .45 ACP cal., Custom Shop pistol featuring Tritium night sights, stainless steel slide with black anodized aluminum frame, 3 (Ultra CDP II only), 4 (Pro CDP II or Compact CDP II), or 5 (Custom CDP II, 31 oz.) in. barrel, melt-down treatment, ambidextrous thumb safety, double diamond pattern checkered rosewood grips, checkered front strap and two-tone finish, 25 (Ultra CDP II) or 28 (Pro II or Compact II) oz. New 2000.

MSR $1,084	$995	$850	$725	$635	$525	$450	$400

Add $36 for .40 S&W cal., available in Ultra CDP II configuration only.

The Pro CDP has a full length grip frame.

RIFLES: BOLT ACTION

Kimber .22 Cal. - Repeating and Single Shot

HUNTER - . 22 LR cal., similar to Classic, except has lower grade walnut and different barrel contour, 6.7 lbs. New 2002.

MSR $678	$595	$550	$495	$450	$395	$365	$335

YOUTH - . 22 LR cal., similar to Hunter, except has 12¼ in. LOP. New 2002.

MSR $746	$650	$575	$495	$450	$395	$365	$335

Kimber will contribute $50 to the NRA's Youth Education Endowment for each Youth rifle sold.

CLASSIC - .22 LR cal., Mauser claw extractor with 2 position Model 70 type safety, unique eccentric bolt that allows a "centerfire-type" firing pin for faster lock time and greater strength, AA Claro walnut sporter stock with 20 LPI 4-point panel checkering and hand rubbed oil finish, 22 in. match grade sporter barrel with match chamber and Custom Sporter contour, 5 shot mag., steel grip cap, pillar bedding, bead blasted blue finish, adj. trigger, approx. 6½ lbs. New 1999.

MSR $949		$820	$695	$595	$500	$425	$375	$330

Through 2002, all Kimber .22 cal. Classic rifles had a claro walnut stock, 2-point checkering pattern, urethane finish, and straight taper contour.

NEW CLASSIC - .22 LR cal., similar to Classic, except has deluxe AA walnut and new barrel. New 2002.

MSR $1,085	$975	$850	$725	$635	$525	$450	$400

SUPERAMERICA MODEL - .22 LR cal., top-of-the-line model with AAA Claro walnut with 24 LPI full wrap checkering, hand rubbed oil finish, Custom Sporter barrel contour, ebony forend tip, and black recoil pad, 5 shot mag., 6½ lbs. New 2001.

MSR $1,764	$1,500	$1,250	$950	$800	$700	$600	$525

Through 2001, all Superamerica rifles had urethane finish and straight taper barrel contour.

SVT (SHORT VARMINT/TARGET) MODEL - .22 LR cal., 18 in. fluted stainless steel bull barrel, uncheckered grey laminate wood stock with high comb target design, matte blue action and satin stainless steel barrel, 5 shot mag., no sights, 7½ lbs. New 1999.

MSR $949	$825	$575	$465	

HS (HUNTER SILHOUETTE) MODEL - .22 LR cal., features 24 in. half-fluted medium sporter match grade barrel w/o sights, checkered walnut high comb Monte Carlo stock with hand rubbed oil finish, adj. trigger, matte blue finish, 7 lbs. New 1999.

MSR $813	$700	$625	$525	$450	$395	$350	$300

Through 2001, all HS Models had urethane finish.

MODEL 82C CLASSIC - .22 LR cal., 22 in. drilled and tapped receiver, repeater with 4 shot mag., A Claro checkered walnut stock, polished and blue metal, 6½ lbs. Mfg. 1995-99.

$775	$625	$550	$475	$400	$360	$330

Last MSR was $917.

The C suffix on this model designates manufacture by Kimber of America.

Grading	100%	98%	95%	90%	80%	70%	60%

✳ *Stainless Classic* - .22 LR cal., features stainless steel barrel with matte blue action. Approx. 600 mfg. 1997-98.

	$800	**$650**	**$565**				

Last MSR was $968.

✳ *Varmint Stainless* - .22 LR cal., features 20 in. fluted stainless steel barrel, A Claro walnut with 18 LPI side panel checkering. Approx. 1,000 mfg. 1995-98.

	$825	**$675**	**$575**				

Last MSR was $1,002.

MODEL 82C SVT - .22 LR cal., single shot, features 18 in. fluted heavy stainless barrel with uncheckered high comb target style walnut stock, matte blue action, 7½ lbs. Mfg. 1997 only.

	$675	**$550**	**$495**				

Last MSR was $825.

SVT designates Short Varmint/Target.

MODEL 82C HS - while advertised during 1997, this model was never manufactured.

MODEL 82C SUPERAMERICA - .22 LR cal., 22 in. drilled and tapped barrel, 4 shot mag., AAA Claro checkered walnut stock with steel pistol grip cap, polished and blue metal, 6½ lbs. Mfg. 1993-99.

	$1,275	**$995**	**$875**	**$750**	**$650**	**$575**	**$400**

Last MSR was $1,488.

MODEL 82C CUSTOM MATCH - .22 LR cal., features AA French walnut with 22 LPI wraparound checkering, steel Neidner-style buttplate, matte rust blue finish. Mfg. 1995- 99.

	$1,900	**$1,525**	**$1,225**	**$975**	**$775**	**$650**	**$525**

Last MSR was $2,158.

MODEL 82C SUPER CLASSIC - .22 LR cal., features AAA Claro walnut with 18 LPI side panel checkering, polished and blue metal. Mfg. 1995-96.

	$975	**$875**	**$775**	**$675**	**$600**	**$550**	**$450**

Last MSR was $1,090.

Centerfire Models

The models below feature a Mauser style action with controlled round feeding and extraction.

MODEL 84C SINGLE SHOT CLASSIC - while advertised during 1996-97, this model was never manufactured.

MODEL 84C SINGLE SHOT SUPERAMERICA - while advertised during 1996-97, this model was never manufactured.

MODEL 84C SINGLE SHOT VARMINT STAINLESS - while advertised during 1997, this model was never manufactured.

MODEL 84C SINGLE SHOT VARMINT - .17 Rem. or .223 Rem. cal., features 24 (first 200 rifles only), or 25 in. stainless match grade fluted barrel with recess crown, matte blue receiver finish, checkered A Claro walnut stock with beavertail forend, 7½ lbs. Mfg. 1997-99.

	$895	**$765**	**$625**				

Last MSR was $1,032.

Add $150 for .17 Rem. cal. (less than 100 mfg.).

MODEL 84M REPEATER - .22-250 Rem., .243 Win., .260 Rem., .308 Win., or 7mm- 08 Rem. cal., true Mauser action, much improved version of the Model 84C, longer and stronger receiver, 2 position Model 70 type safety, 22 in. light sporter (Classic), 24 in. heavy stainless steel fluted sporter (.308 Win. cal., LongMaster Classic, new 2002), 26 in. heavy stainless steel fluted sporter (Varmint), or 26 in. stainless bull (.22-250 Rem. cal., LongMaster VT) match grade barrel, match grade trigger, 5 shot mag. with sculpted steel floorplate0, grey/black

Grading	100%	98%	95%	90%	80%	70%	60%

laminate target stock with high comb and extended pistol grip (LongMaster VT) or checkered walnut stock and forend, 5 lbs., 10 oz. (Sporter), 7 lbs., 5 oz. (Varmint and LongMaster
Classic), or 10 lbs (LongMaster VT). New 2001.

MSR **$917**	**$810**	**$665**	**$555**	**$450**	**$395**	**$350**	**$300**

Add $84 for Model 84M Varmint or LongMaster Classic (.308 Win. cal.).
Add $205 for LongMaster VT (.22-250 Rem. cal.).

MODEL K770 CLASSIC - while advertised during 1997, this model was never manufactured.
Prototypes only.

MODEL K770 SUPER AMERICA - while advertised during 1997, this model was never manufactured. Prototypes only.

Mauser 96 Sporters

MODEL 96 SPORTER - .308 Win. cal., features M-96 action with stainless steel fluted heavy barrel. Mfg. 1995-97.

$450	**$415**	**$365**

Last MSR was $520.

During 1995-96, Kimber began sporterizing the Swedish Mauser Model 96 military surplus rifles.
They featured stainless steel fluted barrels and a black synthetic Ramline stock, receivers were
drilled and tapped to accept Weaver scope mounts, bead blasted bluing, and original reprofiled
military bolt. The Sporter configuration included .243 Win., 6.5x55mm, or .308 Win. cal., while the
heavy fluted barrel models were available in .22-250 Rem. or .308 Win. (Varmint or Heavy Barrel).
Retail prices ranged from $340-$415 for the Standard Sporter, while the Varmint/Heavy barrel variation was priced at approx. $510. Sporter variations were also available as a combo package with
scope and hardshell case - add approx. $30.

Mauser 98 Sporters

MODEL 98 SPORTER - .220 Swift (100 mfg.), .257 Roberts (100 mfg.), .270 Win., .280 Rem. (100
mfg.), .30-06, .300 Win. Mag., .338 Win. Mag., or 7mm Rem. Mag. cal., features Mauser M-
98 action with stainless match grade fluted barrel, choice of synthetic or Claro walnut stock,
and Warne bases, matte black finish receiver. Mfg. 1996-98.

$465	**$425**	**$375**

Last MSR was $535.

Add $25 for Mag. cals.
Add $100 for Claro walnut stock.

* *Mauser Model 98 Sporter Matte* - .300 Win. Mag., .338 Win. Mag., or 7mm Rem. Mag. cal.,
features 25 in. non-fluted sporter barrel, synthetic stock, and Weaver style bases. Disc.
1998.

$275	**$250**	**$225**	**$200**	**$185**	**$170**	**$155**

Last MSR was $339.

SHOTGUNS: O/U

AUGUSTA SERIES - 12 ga., 2¾ (Trap & Skeet) or 3 (Sporting & Field) in. chambers, BOSS type
boxlock action with shallow frame, blue (Trap & Skeet) or polished metal (Field & Sporting)
frame, ejectors, SST, tang safety with ejector, 26-34 in. vent. barrel lengths with VR back-
bored to .736 in., available in Field, Sporting, Skeet, and Trap variations, beavertail or Schnabel forend, Pachmayr decelerator recoil pad, 7 lbs., 2 oz – 7 lbs., 13 oz. Mfg. in Italy
beginning 2002.

As this edition went to press, prices had yet to be established on this series.

K

Grading	100%	98%	95%	90%	80%	70%	60%

KIMBER OF OREGON, INC.

Previous manufacturer located in Clackamas, OR circa 1980-1991.

> Kimber of Oregon went out of business with its final sale in 1991. Rare models are starting to attract premiums already. In some models, magazines for these fine quality rifles are getting extremely hard to find with healthy premiums being asked. Once "B" suffix models were introduced, older manufacture started being referred to as "A" models.

PISTOLS: BOLT ACTION

PREDATOR MODEL - .221 Fireball, .223 Rem., 6mm TCU (disc. 1987), 7mm TCU, or 6x45mm (disc. 1987) cal., single shot Model 84 action with shortened 14 7/8 in. barrel, scope use only, one piece deluxe walnut stock with contoured pistol grip, 5¼ lbs., rare cals. will command a premium. Approx. 200 mfg. 1987-1988 only.

* ***Hunter Grade*** - AA Claro walnut without checkering. Disc. 1988.

	$1,775	$1,500	$1,275	$1,025	$875	$750	$675

Last MSR was $995.

* ***Super Grade*** - similar to Hunter Grade, except has select French walnut with ebony forend tip and 22 lines/in. checkering. Disc. 1988.

	$2,500	$2,275	$1,950	$1,750	$1,500	$1,300	$1,050

Last MSR was $1,195.

RIFLES: BOLT ACTION

Note: No suffix in Kimber models denotes pre-1986 action design, "B" suffix models incorporate the new action with improved cocking system, faster lock time, swept-back bolt design, improved recoil lug, and are right-handed.

> Add $175 for skeleton grip cap on models listed below.
> Add $275 for skeleton buttplate on models listed below.
> Add $100 for checkered bolt handle on models listed below.
> Add $300 for raised quarter rib.
> Add $100 for forend tip.
> Extra fancy walnut on any Kimber will always command a premium.

Model 82, .22 Cal. Series

STANDARD MODEL 82 - .22 LR, .22 Mag., or .22 Hornet cal., Mauser type rear locking bolt action, 3 (.22 Hornet), 4 (.22 Mag.), or 5 (.22 LR) shot mag., 22 in. (Sporter) or 24 in. (Varmint) barrel, deluxe claro walnut, steel butt plate, rocker style safety, right or left hand action, 6½ lbs.

* ***Classic Model*** - disc. 1988.

	$885	$745	$650	$525	$450	$375	$335

Last MSR was $750.

> Add $100-$200 for .22 Hornet or .22 Mag. cal., depending on the variation.
> Add $100 for Cascade Model (Monte Carlo cheekpiece, 34 mfg.).

* ***Custom Classic Model*** - higher grade claro walnut, ebony forearm tip, Niedner style steel butt plate. Disc. 1988.

	$965	$795	$665	$550	$475	$400	$350

Last MSR was $995.

> Add 25% for .218 Bee cal. (approx. 130 standard mfg.).
> Add 100% for 36 Mashburn mfg.

Also available in .25-20 (approx. 200 mfg. single shot only) cals. Mfg. 1985 only (retail price was $695).

Grading	100%	98%	95%	90%	80%	70%	60%

* ***Deluxe Grade*** - .22 LR cal. only, similar to Custom Classic Model, AA walnut, 5 or 10 (optional) shot mag., 6½ lbs. Mfg. 1989-90 only.

	$1,050	$925	$725	$625	$525	$450	$395

Last MSR was $1,195.

A left-hand variation was also available at no extra charge, but had limited mfg. in 1990.

SPORTER MODEL - .17 Ackley Hornet (approx. 9 mfg.), .17 K. Hornet (approx. 88 mfg.), or .22 LR cal., includes Model 82A action, 22 in. sporter weight barrel, 4 shot mag., round top receiver with bases, checkered stock and forend, 6½ lbs. Mfg. 1991 only.

	$940	$785	$675	$575	$500	$450	$395

Last MSR was $995.

Add approx. 50% for .17 K Hornet or .17 Ackley Hornet cals.

RIMFIRE VARMINTER - .22 LR cal. only, Model 82A action, free floating 25 in. medium heavy barrel, laminated stock, 5 or optional 10 shot mag., rubber butt pad, 8¼ lbs. Mfg. 1990-91 only.

	$835	$700	$575	$500	$440	$385	$350

Last MSR was $795.

HUNTER GRADE - .22 LR cal. only, similar to Rimfire Varminter with Super America configured barrel and action with low glare metal finish. Mfg. 1990 only.

	$785	$625	$535	$455	$395	$340	$295

Last MSR was $895.

MINI CLASSIC - .22 LR cal. only, Model 82 action, 18 in. barrel, steel butt plate, sling swivels. Mfg. 1988 only.

	$600	$495	$430	$385	$350	$300	$275

Last MSR was $795.

K

GOVERNMENT MODEL 82A TARGET - .22 LR cal. only, specifically designed for U.S. Army training, 25 in. heavy target barrel including scope blocks, oversized stock, some rifles are "star" marked indicating an accuracy guarantee, 10¾ lbs. Mfg. 1987-91.

	$735	$600	$515	$460	$410	$350	$325

Last MSR was $595.

20,000 rifles were mfg. 1987-1989 to fill the initial U.S. government contract. U.S. property marked guns do exist in private hands - all within a low serial number range (watch markings carefully). Commercial guns were manufactured for the private sector with values listed.

ALL AMERICAN MATCH - .22 LR cal. only, precision rifled 25 in. free floating target grade barrel, stock is adj. both vertically and for length of pull, fully adj. single stage trigger, approx. 9 lbs. Mfg. 1990-91 only.

	$790	$625	$540	$465	$400	$340	$295

Last MSR was $895.

CONTINENTAL - .22 LR, .22 Mag., or .22 Hornet cal., Sporter action only, full length Mannlicher stock, open sights, deluxe walnut. Add $200 for .22 Mag. or .22 Hornet cal. New 1987.

This model was only available as a special order with prices on request from the factory.

* ***Super Continental*** - similar to Continental, except has AAA claro walnut with 22 lines/in. checkering. Mfg. 1987-1988.

	$1,525	$1,325	$1,050	$900	$800	$700	$625

Last MSR was $1,465.

Three laminated stock variations with cheekpieces were mfg.

SUPER AMERICA - top-of-the-line model, includes detachable scope mounts, Niedner checkered steel butt plate and best quality walnut, available in Sporter configuration only. This model was disc. 1988, and reintroduced 1990-91.

	$1,125	$975	$800	$650	$575	$475	$425

Last MSR was $1,295.

Grading	100%	98%	95%	90%	80%	70%	60%

✴ ***Super Grade*** - similar to Super America, AAA walnut, beaded cheekpiece, 5 or 10 (optional) shot mag., 6½ lbs. Mfg. 1989 only.

| | $1,125 | $975 | $800 | $650 | $575 | $475 | $425 |

Last MSR was $1,295.

CUSTOM MATCH - .22 LR or .22 Mag. cal., limited edition of 217 rifles, match dimension chamber, French walnut stock with 22 L.P.I. checkering, rust blued finish, other custom rifle features. Introduced 1984.

| | $1,825 | $1,425 | $1,075 | $925 | $825 | $725 | $650 |

Add $200 for .22 Mag. cal.

BROWNELL - .22 LR cal., only 500 mfg. to commemorate the late Leonard Brownell, Mannlicher style extra deluxe claro walnut stock. Mfg. 1986 only.

| | $1,625 | $1,275 | $875 |

Last MSR was $1,500.

CENTENNIAL - .22 LR cal. only, limited edition (100 rifles) to commemorate centennial of .22 LR cal., includes hand-picked checkered walnut, moderate engraving, special Wilson Arms match barrel, skeleton butt plate and other refinements, serial numbered C1- C100. Mfg. 1987 only.

| | $2,875 | $2,500 | $1,875 |

Last MSR was $2,950.

TENTH ANNIVERSARY ISSUE - .22 LR cal., limited edition, French walnut stock featuring slim forend design with shadowed cheekpiece, Neidner steel buttplate and other refinements. Mfg. 1989 only.

| | $1,650 | $1,325 | $995 |

Add $100 for matte finish.

Model 84 Centerfire Series

Model 84 caliber rarity is as follows: .222 Rem. and .223 Rem. are common. 6x45mm or 47mm, .221 Fireball, .17 Rem., and .17 Mach IV are less common and more desirable. .223 Rem. Mag. is rare, while 5.6x50mm is extremely rare.

Add $75 for forend tip - option A. Add $300 for iron sights - option B. Add $100 for checkered bolt handle - option C. Add $200 for skeleton grip cap - option D. Add $300 for skeleton buttplate - option G. Add $250-$300 for 3-position safety in this series.

STANDARD MODEL 84 - .17 Rem., .17 Mach IV (disc. 1987), 6x45 or 47mm (disc. 1987), 5.6x50mm (disc. 1987), .221 Fireball, .222 Rem., .222 Rem. Mag. (disc. 1987), or .223 Rem. cal., "Mini-Mauser" type head locking bolt action, 5 shot mag., 22 (Sporter) or 24 (Varmint) in. barrel, deluxe Claro walnut, steel buttplate, rocker style safety, 6½ lbs.

✴ ***Classic Model*** - disc. 1988.

| | $995 | $800 | $650 | $575 | $485 | $425 | $375 |

Last MSR was $885.

Add $55 for disc. Cascade Model (Monte Carlo cheekpiece).
Add 20% for left-hand action.

Also available in left-hand action in .22 Hornet, .222 Rem., .223 Rem., 6x45mm, 6x47mm, .17 Rem., and .17 Mach IV (very limited mfg.).

CUSTOM CLASSIC MODEL - higher grade Claro walnut, ebony forearm tip, Niedner style steel butt plate. Disc. 1988.

| | $1,200 | $1,000 | $825 | $665 | $560 | $475 | $425 |

Last MSR was $1,130.

✴ ***Deluxe Grade Sporter*** - .17 Rem., .221 Rem., or .223 Rem. cal., Mauser action, AA walnut, similar to Custom Classic Model, 6¼ lbs. Mfg. 1989-90.

| | $1,125 | $995 | $800 | $640 | $550 | $475 | $425 |

Last MSR was $1,295.

Also available in left-hand action (.223 Rem. cal. only), limited mfg.

Grading	100%	98%	95%	90%	80%	70%	60%

CONTINENTAL - .221 Fireball (extremely rare, mfg. 1988 only) .222 Rem. or .223 Rem. cal., Sporter action only, full length Mannlicher stock, open sights, deluxe walnut. New 1987.
> This model was only available as a special order with prices on request from the factory.

✳ ***Super Continental*** - similar to Continental (same cals.), except has AAA Claro walnut with 22 lines/in. checkering. Mfg. 1987-1988.

	100%	98%	95%	90%	80%	70%	60%
	$1,650	$1,325	$975	$875	$775	$695	$625

Last MSR was $1,600.

> Three laminated stocks were mfg. in .223 Rem. cal.

HUNTER GRADE - .17 Rem., .222 Rem., or .223 Rem. cal., laminated stock, Super America configured action and barrel with low glare metal finish. Mfg. 1990 only.

	$875	$675	$575	$500	$440	$395	$360

Last MSR was $995.

SPORTER - .17 Rem., .22 Hornet, .222 Rem., .22-250 Rem., or .223 Rem. cal., 22 in. sporter weight barrel, A grade Claro walnut, round top receiver with bases, 4 shot mag., hand checkering. Mfg. 1991 only.

	$1,020	$850	$725	$625	$550	$500	$495

Last MSR was $1,095.

> This model was available in either right or left-hand action.

✳ ***Big Bore Sporter*** - .250 Savage or .35 Rem. cal., similar action to Sporter Model, except has ¾ in. red Pachmayr Decelerator recoil pad. Mfg. 1991 only.
> Extreme rarity precludes accurate price evaluation - consult an expert when buying/selling this model. This model was available in either right or left-hand action.

Last MSR was $1,095.

SUPER AMERICA/SUPER GRADE - .17 Rem., .17 MK IV, .221 Fireball, .22 Hornet, .222 Rem., .222 Rem. Mag., .22-250 Rem., .223 Rem., 5.6x56mm, or 6x47mm cal., 22 in. sporter weight barrel, top-of-the-line, with detachable scope mounts, available in Sporter configuration only, 4 shot mag., right or left-hand action. Disc. 1988, reintroduced 1990-91.

	$1,575	$1,250	$940	$865	$775	$695	$625

Last MSR was $1,495.

> Be careful when buying rare cals. and/or options on this model.

✳ ***Big Bore Super America*** - .250 Savage or .35 Rem. cal., similar action to Super America Model, except has ¾ in. red Pachmayr Decelerator recoil pad. Mfg. 1991 only.

	$2,100	$1,775	$1,425	$1,125	$925	$800	$700

Last MSR was $1,495.

CUSTOM MATCH - .222 Rem. or .223 Rem. cal., limited edition of 200 rifles, match dimension chamber, French walnut stock with 22 L.P.I. checkering, rust blue finish, other custom rifle features. Introduced 1986.

	$2,250	$1,725	$1,425	$1,050	$875	$750	$650

TENTH ANNIVERSARY ISSUE - .223 Rem. cal., limited edition, French walnut stock featuring slim forend design with shadowed cheekpiece, 22 in. barrel, roundtop receiver with mounts, Neidner steel buttplate and other refinements. Mfg. 1989 only.

	$1,995	$1,650	$1,250				

Add $100 for matte finish.

ULTRA VARMINTER - .17 Rem., .22 Hornet (rare, new 1991), .221 Rem. (disc. 1990), .222 Rem., .22-250 Rem. (rare), or .223 Rem. cal., 24 in. medium weight stainless steel barrel, laminated birch stock, plain buttstock, right or left-hand action, 7¾ lbs. Mfg. 1989-91 only.

	$1,425	$1,150	$975	$800	$650	$550	$475

Last MSR was $1,295.

✳ ***Super Varminter*** - similar to Ultra Varminter except has steel barrel, AAA walnut stock with beaded cheekpiece, 7¼ lbs. Mfg. 1989-91 only.

	$1,595	$1,350	$1,050	$925	$775	$650	$525

Last MSR was $1,495.

K

Grading	100%	98%	95%	90%	80%	70%	60%

Model 89 Centerfire, Big Game Series

Fewer than 5,000 Model 89 BGRs were mfg.

MODEL 89 BGR - .270 Win., .280 Rem., 7mm Rem. Mag., .30-06, .300 Win. Mag., .338 Win. Mag., or .375 H&H cal., new action incorporates features from both Mauser 98 and Win. pre-64 Model 70, three position safety, 22 or 24 in. barrel, matte blue finish will command a premium. Introduced late 1988.

* *Classic Model* - deluxe Claro walnut checkered 18 lines/in. with steel butt plate. Disc. 1988.

	$875	$725	$600	$500	$415	$350	$300

Last MSR was $985.

Add $200 for .375 H&H cal.
Add $100 for matte finish.

* *Custom Classic Model* - higher grade Claro walnut, ebony forearm tip, Niedner style steel butt plate. Disc. 1988.

	$1,125	$950	$775	$650	$525	$450	$375

Last MSR was $1,230.

Add $200 for .375 H&H cal.

DELUXE GRADE - similar to Custom Classic Model, round top receiver with Model 70 scope mount hole configuration, AA walnut stock with ebony forend tip and rubber recoil pad (no cheekpiece), 22 or 24 in. barrel, 7½-8½ lbs. New 1989.

* *Featherweight Barrel Model* - .257 Roberts (rare), .25-06 Rem., 7x57mm (rare, disc. 1990), .270 Win., .280 Rem., or .30-06 cal., 5 shot mag., 22 in. Featherweight barrel, right-hand action only, 7½ lbs. Disc. 1990.

	$1,600	$1,225	$1,000	$850	$700	$600	$525

Last MSR was $1,795.

Add $470 for Super America Grade with square bridge, dovetail receiver.
Add $100 for matte finish.

The Super America Grade will accept Kimber double lever scope mounts and has one grade better wood than the Deluxe Grade with beaded cheekpiece.

* *Medium-weight Barrel Model* - .300 Win. Mag., .300 H&H (rare, disc. 1990), .300 Wby. Mag. (very rare, new 1991), .338 Win. Mag., .35 Whelen (rare, disc. 1990), or 7mm Rem. Mag. cal., 3 shot mag., 24 in. medium-weight barrel, right- hand action only, 7¾-8½ lbs. Disc. 1990.

	$1,675	$1,250	$1,025	$875	$725	$625	$550

Last MSR was $1,895.

Add $495 for Super America Grade with square bridge, dovetail receiver.
Add $100 for matte finish.

The Super America Grade will accept Kimber double lever scope mounts and has one grade better wood than the Deluxe Grade with beaded cheekpiece.

* *Heavy-weight Barrel Model* - .375 H&H Mag. cal., 3 shot mag., 24 in. heavy weight barrel, right-hand action only, 9 lbs. Disc. 1990.

	$1,775	$1,325	$1,075	$925	$775	$700	$650

Last MSR was $1,995.

Add $495 for Super America Grade with square bridge, dovetail receiver.
Add $100 for matte finish.

The Super America Grade will accept Kimber double lever scope mounts and has one grade better wood than the Deluxe Grade with beaded cheekpiece.

Grading	100%	98%	95%	90%	80%	70%	60%

SPORTER MODEL - same cals. as Deluxe/Super America Models, 22 in. featherweight or 24 in. medium or heavy barrel, double square bridge dovetail receiver, A grade Claro walnut stock with ¾ in. red Pachmayr Decelerator recoil pad (Mag. cals. only with 24 in. barrel). Mfg. 1991 only.

	$1,395	$1,050	$900	$775	$650	$500	$450

Last MSR was $1,595.

Add $100 for medium Magnum action.
Add $200 for heavy Magnum action (.375 H&H and .458 Win. Mag. cals.).

HUNTER GRADE - .270 Win., .30-06, .300 Win. Mag., .338 Win. Mag., or 7mm Rem. Mag. cal., laminated stock, Super America configured action and barrel with low glare metal finish. Mfg. 1990-91 only.

	$1,325	$1,025	$895	$750	$625	$525	$450

Last MSR was $1,495.

Add $100 for Mag. cals.

SUPER GRADE - similar to Super America Model, square top frame, AAA walnut, 22 or 24 in. barrel, plain buttstock, 7½-8½ lbs. Mfg. 1989 only.

	$1,575	$1,325	$995	$825	$695	$550	$500

Last MSR was $1,495.

Add $100 for .375 H&H cal.
Add $100 for matte blue metal finish.
The 24 in. barrel was available in Mag. cals. only.

LIMITED WILDLIFE EDITION SERIES - series of 5 guns, includes .257 Roberts (Whitetail Deer Edition), .270 Win. (Mule Deer Edition), .338 Win. Mag. (Rocky Mt. Elk Edition), 7mm Rem. Mag. (Big Horn Sheep Edition), and .375 H&H (Grizzly Bear Edition) cals. included, hand select walnut, special Shilen Rifle barrel, gold plated trigger, receivers are stamped "Wildlife Edition", special prefix serialization, only 25 sets were to be manufactured in 1991 only, includes rings, swivels, and hard case.

While advertised, only one .270 Win. Mule Deer model was mfg. Retail price was scheduled to be $3,595.

MODEL 89 AFRICAN - .375 H&H (rare), .416 Rigby (most common) cal., or .505 Gibbs (rare) cal., Magnum action, 24 in. heavy barrel, AA English walnut stock with beaded cheekpiece and rubber recoil pad, includes twin recoil cross bolts, express sights on quarter rib, drop box magazine, 10-10½ lbs. Mfg. 1990-91 only.

	$4,500	$3,875	$3,350	$2,625	$2,100	$1,750	$1,550

Last MSR was $3,595.

.375 H&H or .505 Gibbs cal. will command a premium.

KIMEL INDUSTRIES, INC.

Previously manufactured until late 1994 by AAArms located in Monroe, NC. Previously distributed by Kimel Industries, Inc. located in Matthews, NC.

CARBINES

AR-9 CARBINE - 9mm Para. cal., carbine variation of the AP-9 with 16½ in. barrel, 20 shot mag., and steel rod folding stock. Mfg. 1991-94.

	$550	$475	$425	$365	$315	$275	$220

Last MSR was $384.

PISTOLS: SEMI-AUTO

AP-9 PISTOL - 9mm Para. cal., paramilitary design, blowback action with bolt knob on left side of receiver, 5 in. barrel with vent. shroud, front mounted 10 (C/B 1994) or 20* shot detachable mag., black matte finish, adj. front sight, 3 lbs. 7 oz. Mfg. 1989-94.

	$425	$365	$325	$275	$250	$225	$200

Last MSR was $279.

Grading	100%	98%	95%	90%	80%	70%	60%

✴ **Mini AP-9** - compact variation of the AP-9 Model with 3 in. barrel, blue or nickel finish. Mfg. 1991-94.

	$475	$425	$350	$295	$275	$250	$225

Last MSR was $273.

✴ **Target AP-9** - target variation of the AP-9 with 12 in. match barrel with shroud, blue finish only. Mfg. 1991-94.

	$495	$462	$375	$325	$295	$275	$250

Last MSR was $294.

✴ **P-95** - similar to AP-9, except without barrel shroud and is supplied with 5 shot mag., parts are interchangeable with AP-9. Mfg. 1990-91 only.

	$350	$295	$265	$235	$195	$165	$135

Last MSR was $250.

KING'S GUN WORKS, INC.

Current custom handgun and accessories manufacturer established during 1949 and currently located in Glendale, CA. Dealer and consumer direct sales.

King's Gun Works manufactures a complete line of custom pistols patterned after Colt M-1911, in addition to many related accessories and/or after-market parts. Please contact the company directly for current information and prices (see Trademark Index listing).

KLEINGUENTHER FIREARMS CO.

Previous custom rifle manufacturer located in Seguin, TX until circa 2001. The original KDF Co. was started by Mr. Robert Kleinguenther and sold in the early 1980s. Mr. Kleinguenther then started a new company called Kleinguenther Firearms Co.

RIFLES: BOLT ACTION

Values listed below are for base model only with no additional customer special order options. Mr. Keinguenther also custom built rifles utilizing customer actions.

BOLT ACTION RIFLE - various cals., individual customer special order rifle with a variety of options, guns are guaranteed to shoot ½ M.O.A., choice of actions, various weights. Currently, the manufacturer does not have availability on either the Winchester Model 70 Custom or the Mauser K-15 action.

✴ **Winchester Model 70 Custom**

	$975	$800	$675	$575	$500	$450	$400

Last MSR was $975.

✴ **Sako Action** - various cals., newer guns feature the ballistic recoil muzzle brake system (60-70% recoil reduction), most newer stocks are mfg. out of high tech laminated wood with 28-32 resin coated panels.

	$1,550	$1,325	$1,100	$950	$825	$725	$625

Last MSR was $1,750.

Add $155 for ballistic recoil muzzle brake system.

✴ **K-15**

	$1,375	$1,100	$950	$800	$675	$575	$500

Last MSR was $1,375.

Grading	100%	98%	95%	90%	80%	70%	60%

KNIGHT'S MANUFACTURING COMPANY

Current manufacturer established in 1993, and located in Vero Beach, FL. Dealer and consumer direct sales.

RIFLES: SEMI-AUTO

Some of the models listed below were also available in pre-ban configurations.

STONER SR-15 M-5 RIFLE - .223 Rem. cal., 20 in. standard weight barrel, flip-up low profile rear sight, two-stage target trigger, 7.6 lbs. New 1997.

MSR	$1,595	$1,425	$1,150	$975	$875	$800	$725	$650

✳ ***Stoner SR-15 M-4 Carbine*** - similar to SR-15 rifle, except has 16 in. barrel, choice of fixed synthetic or non-collapsible buttstock. New 1997.

MSR	$1,495	$1,325	$1,100	$950	$850	$775	$700	$650

Add $100 for non-collapsible buttstock (SR-15 M-4 K-Carbine).

STONER SR-15 MATCH RIFLE - .223 Rem. cal., features flat-top upper receiver with 20 in. free floating barrel, two-stage match trigger, 7.9 lbs. New 1997.

MSR	$1,795	$1,600	$1,375	$1,125	$950	$850	$750	$700

STONER SR-25 SPORTER - .308 Win. cal., 20 in. lightweight barrel, AR-15 configuration with carrying handle, 5, 10, or 20 (disc. per C/B 1994) shot detachable mag., less than 2 MOA guaranteed, non-glare finish, 8.8 lbs. Mfg. 1993-97.

		$2,650	$2,250	$1,900	$1,600	$1,300	$1,000	$850

Last MSR was $2,995.

✳ ***Stoner SR-25 Carbine*** - 16 in. free floating barrel, grooved non-slip handguard, removable carrying handle, 7¾ lbs. New 1995.

MSR	$2,995	$2,650	$2,250	$1,900	$1,600	$1,300	$1,000	$850

Add $250 for Rail Adapter System (RAS) forearm - new 1999.

SR-25 MATCH - similar to SR-25 Standard, except has 24 in. free floating match barrel and flat-top receiver, less than 1 MOA guaranteed, 10¾ lbs. New 1993.

MSR	$2,995	$2,650	$2,250	$1,900	$1,600	$1,300	$1,000	$850

Add $250 for Rail Adapter System (RAS) forearm - new 1999.

Over 3,000 SR-25s have been made to date.

✳ ***SR-25 Lightweight Match*** - features 20 in. medium contour free floating barrel, 9½ lbs. New 1995.

MSR	$2,995	$2,650	$2,250	$1,900	$1,600	$1,300	$1,000	$850

Add $250 for Rail Adapter System (RAS) forearm - new 1999.

"DAVID TUBB" COMPETITION MATCH RIFLE - .260 Rem. or .308 Win. cal., incorporates refinements by David Tubb, top-of-the-line competition match rifle, including adj. and rotating buttstock pad. Mfg. 1998 only.

		$5,200	$4,000	$3,600	$3,150	$2,700	$2,300	$1,995

Last MSR was $5,995.

STONER SR-50 - .50 BMG cal., features high strength materials and lightweight design, fully locked breech and two lug rotary breech bolt, horizontal 5 shot box mag., tubular receiver supports a removable barrel, approx. 31 lbs. Limited mfg. 2000 only.

		$6,300	$5,400	$4,200	$3,600	$3,150	$2,700	$2,300

Last MSR was $6,995.

KODIAK CO.

Previous manufacturer located in North Haven, CT circa 1963-66.

Kodiak Co. was in business for only a short time. They produced the first .22 Mag. semi- auto rifle (Model 260), as well as a centerfire bolt action (Model 158 Deluxe), and a slide action shotgun (Model 458). While Kodiak long guns are rare and extremely well made, collectability to date has been minimal with most specimens selling at a slight premium over similar quality

K

Grading	100%	98%	95%	90%	80%	70%	60%

trade name counterparts of that era. Prior to 1963, Kodiak firearms were marketed under the trade name of Jefferson.

KOLIBRI

Previous trademark manufactured 1914-1925 by Georg Grabner located in Rehberg, Austria.

PISTOLS: SEMI-AUTO

KOLIBRI PISTOL - 2.7 or 3mm centerfire cal., unrifled barrel, 5 shot box mag., world's smallest semi-auto centerfire pistol.

	$2,250	$1,950	$1,750	$1,500	$1,350	$1,175	$1,000

Add approx. $300 for original case.
Add approx. 40% for nickel finish (rare).

Individual rounds of 2.7 or 3mm (more rare) ammunition are currently trading in the $75 range as it has the distinction of being the world's smallest centerfire shell (shooting a 3 grain bullet at approx. 475 fps and generating 1.75 ft./lbs. of muzzle energy!).

KONGSBERG

Previous manufacturer circa 1814-1998 located in Kongsberg, Norway. Previously imported and distributed 1996-98, by Kongsberg America L.L.C. located in Fairfield, CT, and by Lew Horton Distributing Co., Inc. until 1996, located in Westboro, MA.

RIFLES: BOLT ACTION

Add $50 for iron sights on models listed below.

393 SERIES - .22-250 Rem., .243 Win., .270 Win., .30-06, .308 Win., 6.5x55 Swedish, 7mm Rem. Mag., .300 Win. Mag., or .338 Win. Mag. cal., available in either Classic, De Luxe, Thumbhole (.22-250 Rem. or 308 Win. only), or Select (Standard) configuration, checkered pistol grip, forend mounted recoil lug which connects to stock, 3-position rear safety, fixed rotary mag., fully adj. trigger. Imported 1994-98.

* *Classic Model*

	$875	$750	$675	$575	$495	$440	$385

Last MSR was $995.

Add $114 for Mag. cals.
Add $138 for left-hand action.

* *Select Model (Standard Model in Europe)*

	$860	$735	$660	$560	$495	$440	$385

Last MSR was $980.

Add $113 for Mag. cals.
Add $138 for left-hand action.

* *De Luxe Model*

	$940	$795	$700	$595	$515	$450	$395

Last MSR was $1,124.

Add $112 for Mag. cals.
Add $137 for left-hand action.

* *Thumbhole Model* - .22-250 Rem. or .308 Win. cal., features thumbhole stock. Mfg. 1996-98.

	$1,350	$1,175	$1,000	$875	$750	$625	$500

Last MSR was $1,580.

Add $138 for left-hand action.

Grading	100%	98%	95%	90%	80%	70%	60%

KORA BRNO

Current revolver trademark manufactured by Kroko a.s., located in Brno, Czech Republic. No current U.S. importer.

To date, the Kora Brno revolver line has had little or no importation into the U.S. Models include many configurations of both .22 LR and .38 Spl. cals. Please contact the factory directly for more information (see Trademark Index).

KORRIPHILA

Current trademark manufacturered by Intertex, located in Eislingen, Germany. Currently imported beginning 1999 by Korriphila, Inc., located in Pineville, NC. Previously imported and distributed by Osborne's located in Cheboygan, MI until 1988.

PISTOLS: SEMI-AUTO

Less than 30 Korriphila pistols are made annually.

HSP 701 - 7.65 Luger (disc.), .38 Spl. (disc.), 9mm Para., 9mm Police (disc.), 9mm Steyr (disc.), .45 ACP, or 10mm Norma (disc.) cal., double action, Budischowsky delayed roller block locking system assists in recoil reduction, 40% stainless steel parts, 4 or 5 in. barrel, blue or satin finish, walnut grips, 7 or 9 shot mag., approx. 2.6 lbs, very limited production.

MSR	$7,590	$6,500	$5,500	$3,750	$2,950	$2,150	$1,850	$1,675

❋ **HSP 701 Odin's Eye (Damascus)** - similar to HSP 701, except is completely made from one block of Damascus stainless steel, rosewood grips with Manta skin inlays, custom order only, the world's most expensive currently manufactured semi-auto pistol.

MSR	$13,900	$12,250	$10,250	$8,500

KORTH

Current manufacturer established 1954, and located in Ratzeburg, Germany. Currently imported beginning 2000 by Korth USA, a division of Earl's Repair Service, Inc., located in Tewksbury, MA. Previously imported 1997-99 by Keng's Firearms Specialty, Inc. located in Atlanta, GA. Previously imported by Mandall Shooting Supplies, Inc. located in Scottsdale, AZ, Beeman Precision Arms, located in Santa Rosa, CA and by Osborne's in Cheboygan, MI.

Korth handguns are very high quality and are literally manufactured one-at-a-time, resulting in limited mfg. (less than 100 annually) and importation.

Retail values listed below reflect the most recent U.S. pricing from Korth USA.

PISTOLS: SEMI-AUTO

KORTH SEMI-AUTO - 9mm Para., .357 SIG, .40 S&W, or 9x21mm IMI cal., double action, 4, 4½ threaded, or 5 in. barrel, all steel construction, 9 (.40 S&W and .357 SIG) or 10 (9mm Para. or 9x21mm IMI) shot mag., adj. sights, checkered walnut grips, top quality manufacture throughout. Introduced 1986 with first guns shipped 1988.

MSR	$4,921	$4,500	$3,950	$3,500	$2,950	$2,500	$2,000	$1,750

Add $215 for plasma coated silver matte finish.
Add $562 for plasma coated silver polished finish.
Add $1,200 per interchangeable barrels.
Add $300 for combat trigger guard.
Add $150 for extra mag.
Blue, charcoal, and gold plasma finish are also available at an additional cost – please contact the importer directly for a price quotation.
Base values are for high polish blue finish.

K

Grading	100%	98%	95%	90%	80%	70%	60%

REVOLVERS

The crane of the main cylinder and of the extra cylinder (.22 LR/.22 Mag. or .357 Mag./9mm Para.) are cut from the same billet of steel, and for reasons of smallest tolerance that Korth guarantees, once a gun is made with a single cylinder, the extra convertible cylinder cannot be ordered at a later date. Korth currently produces the world's most expensive revolver.

Add $541 for interchangeable cylinder in bright blue finish.
Add $192 for plasma coated silver matte finish.
Add $393 for plasma coated silver polished finish.
Add $1,900 for arabesk engraving.
Add $2,000 for platinum engraving.

COMBAT MODEL - .22 LR, .22 Mag., .38 Spl., or .357 Mag. cal., 3 (solid only), 4 VR, 5¼ VR, 6 VR, or 8 in. barrel, 6 shot, combat sights fully adj., full length shrouded ejector rod, adj. trigger, checkered and oil finished walnut grips, 2.6 lbs. Introduced 1967.

	MSR	$4,677		$4,150	$3,750	$2,850	$2,150	$1,850	$1,600	$1,400

Add 20% for stainless steel (disc., limited mfg.).

SPORT MODEL - .22 LR, .32 S&W Long, .38 Spl., or .357 Mag. cal., 2½ (disc., scarce), 4, 5¼, 6 VR, or 8 in. barrel, 5 (early mfg.) or 6 shot, micro adj. sights, full length shrouded ejector rod, adj. trigger, checkered and oil finished walnut grips, 2.6 lbs. Introduced 1967.

	MSR	$4,766		$4,225	$3,775	$2,850	$2,150	$1,850	$1,600	$1,400

Subtract approx. 10%-15% for 5 shot, depending on condition.

❋ ***Model Everest, 40 Years Korth, Ltd. Ed.*** - .357 Mag., 5¼ in. barrel only, deeply engraved frame and barrel with gold inlays, smooth select walnut grips, cased, only 25 mfg. 1994 only.

		$8,950	$6,350	$4,500

Last MSR was $8,500.

TARGET MODEL - .22 LR, .32 S&W Long, .38 Spl., or .357 Mag. cal., 5¼ or 6 VR in. barrel, 6 shot, micro adj. sights, adj. trigger, stippled oversized target walnut grips, 2.6 lbs.

	MSR	$4,947		$4,450	$3,900	$3,000	$2,350	$2,050	$1,850	$1,650

Add $538 for interchangeable cylinder in bright blue finish.
Add $193 for plasma coated silver matte finish.
Add $390 for plasma coated silver polished finish.

ANNO DOMINI 2000 - 357 Mag., 4 in. combat model, PVD gold plasma coating, deep relief engraving featuring thorns, only 10 mfg. during 2000.

Extreme rarity precludes accurate pricing on this model – manufacturer's suggested retail was $10,000.

CUSTOM PRESENTATION MODEL - deluxe variation of Sport/Combat model.

This variation is available with engraving and other special options that are priced per individual quotation from the importer.

KRAG-JORGENSEN

Previous U.S. magazine fed military rifle. First U.S. (.30-40 Krag) military repeating rifle to shoot smokeless powder ammunition. Manufactured 1894-1904.

There have been many conversions of Krag-Jorgensen rifles - many of which are hard to identify. As a rule, these conversions are not as desirable as the specific models listed below.

RIFLES: BOLT ACTION

M1892-DATED 1894 - .30-40 Krag cal., mfg. by Springfield Armory, with cleaning rod. Note: This model is designated Type I, and has a wide, solid upper barrel band.

	$8,950	$7,500	$6,250	$5,250	$4,250	$3,500	$2,750

Grading	100%	98%	95%	90%	80%	70%	60%

✷ Receivers dated 1894 or 1895 with 1894, 1895 or 1896 stock cartouche - .30-40 Krag, designated Type II. Upper band has double strap instead of being solid as in Type I. Model 1892 rifles were dated in two places - receiver dates of 1894 or 1895 and stock cartouche dates of 1894, 1895 or 1896. The final 1892s were completed in 1896. These rifles retained a number of Model 1892 features such as a barrel with a flat muzzle, a stock with a thin wrist, and a one piece cleaning rod. They also have a number of Model 1896 features, including a stock with a rounded toe, and an early Model 1896 rear sight with a lug leaf. These last Model 1892 rifles are in the 20,000 ser. no. range. They will have 1894 dated receivers with 1896 stock cartouche date.

	$7,500	$6,500	$5,500	$4,500	$3,750	$3,000	$2,250

ARSENAL-ALTERED TO M1896 STYLE

	$750	$550	$450	$400	$375	$325	$295

M1896 - .30-40 Krag cal., receivers marked 1896 and Model 1896 with 1896, 1897, 1898 stock cartouche dates. 1,300 rifles were mfg. in this configuration before July 1, 1896 and can be denoted by observing the receiver having the "1896" date w/o the word Model.

	$700	$550	$425	$350	$300	$275	$250

M1896 CARBINE

	$1,000	$900	$800	$600	$550	$500	$475

M1895 CARBINE - .30-40 Krag cal., this is a variant that has receiver dates of 1894, 1895, and 1896 and omits the word "Model". 7,111 carbines were mfg. in a crash program to rearm the regular cavalry. Mfg. mid 1895 to May of 1896. Stock cartouche is dated 1896. Early variation have stocks drilled for two cleaning rods in the butt trap (rare).

	$1,500	$1,250	$1,000	$850	$750	$700	$650

M1896 CADET RIFLE - .30-40 Krag cal., two variations are encountered, the first variation included 400 guns that were issued to the Service Academy, most of which were converted to a standard service rifle configuration. Observed specimens of these converted Cadet rifles are in the 18,000-19,000 ser. no. range. Converted Cadet rifles are easily identified by the filled band spring inletting in the band stock (with 1896 cartouche) - no known unmodified examples. The second variation appears to consist of only 4 guns, only 3 are known to exist.

✷ Type I - ser. no. range 18,000-20,000, arsenal altered to Model 1896 configuration.

	$3,025	$2,750	$2,530	$2,200	$1,815	$1,500	$1,200

✷ Type II - ser. no. range 35,XXX, unaltered Cadet configuration, only 3 known to exist. Extreme rarity factor precludes accurate price evaluation. A recent specimen sold for over $40,000.

M1898 RIFLE

	$1,875	$1,625	$1,350	$1,000	$850	$650	$450

M1898 CARBINE - .30-40 Krag cal., most legitimate guns fall within the ser. no. range 125,XXX-135,XXX, original guns should have matching cartouche, sights, and ser. no. Most of these guns were converted to the M1899 configuration by replacing the stocks, handguards, and sights.

	$1,875	$1,625	$1,350	$1,000	$850	$650	$450

M1898 NRA CARBINE - features carbine stock and hardware, shortened rifle (22 in.) barreled action, identifiable by full band front sight.

	$850	$725	$600	$525	$450	$375	$325

M1899 CARBINE

	$750	$635	$525	$495	$465	$430	$395

K

Grading	100%	98%	95%	90%	80%	70%	60%

M1899 CARBINE, PHILIPPINE CONSTABULARY - .30-40 Krag cal., 4,980 Model 1899 Krag Carbines were purchased by the Insular government of the Phillipines for use by the constabulary and modified by the U.S. Army at the Manila Ordnance Depot. "JFC" or "CV" were modified by the U.S. Army at Springfield and were school guns, not constabulary carbines. The stateside school variation was named "United States Magazine Carbine, Model of 1899, modified for use with knife bayonet and gun sling."

	$1,500	$1,200	$1,000	$950	$900	$850	$700

Watch yourself - many counterfeits have surfaced in recent years.

KRICO

Current trademark manufactured by Kriegeskorte Handels GmbH, located in Pyrbaum, Germany. Currently distributed by Precision Sales, Int'l, located in Westfield, MA, beginning in late 1999. Previously manufactured in Vohburg-Irsching, Germany 1996-1999, and in Fürth-Stadeln, Germany by Sportwafeenfabrik Kriegeskorte GmbH pre-1996.

During 2000, Krico was purchased by Marocchi. Krico has been imported/distributed by over ten U.S. companies/individuals. Krico manufactures high quality rifles, and to date, has mostly sold their guns in Europe. Many of the discontinued models listed below may still be current within the European marketplace.

RIFLES: BOLT ACTION

Values and information below reflect the most current information available to the publisher. Please contact either Precison Sales Int'l or the factory directly for current pricing and model availability.

SPORTING RIFLE - .22 Hornet or .222 Rem. cal., miniature Mauser action, 4 shot, 22, 24, or 26 in. barrel, single or double set triggers, open sights, checkered walnut stock, pistol grip. Mfg. 1956- 1962.

	$605	$550	$495	$440	$400	$360	$305

CARBINE - similar to Sporting Rifle, except 20 or 22 in. barrel, full length stock.

	$635	$580	$415	$470	$420	$375	$320

SPECIAL VARMINT RIFLE - similar to Sporting Rifle, except heavy barrel, no sights.

	$605	$550	$495	$440	$400	$360	$300

MODEL 300 SPORTER - .22 LR, .22 Mag., or .22 Hornet cal., select walnut with straight, checkered stock and fuller forearm, 23½ in. barrel, 5 shot mag., grooved receiver, 6½ lbs. Importation disc. 1999.

	$550	$495	$450	$410	$380	$350	$320

Last MSR was $595.

Add $30 for .22 Mag. cal.
Add $155 for .22 Hornet cal.
This model was designated Model 302 Sporter until 1986.

❋ *Model 300 Deluxe* - similar to Model 300 Standard, except has deluxe wood and checkering. Imported 1991-99.

	$625	$550	$480	$430	$385	$350	$320

Last MSR was $695.

Add $25 for .22 Mag. cal.
Add $200 for .22 Hornet cal.

MODEL 311 SMALL BORE RIFLE - .22 LR cal. only, bolt action, 5 or 10 shot, 22 in. barrel, single or double set trigger, open sights, checkered stock. Disc.

	$330	$275	$250	$220	$195	$165	$155

Add 30% for Kahles 2½ power scope.

Grading	100%	98%	95%	90%	80%	70%	60%

MODEL 320 MANNLICHER SPORTER - .22 LR, .22 Mag., or .22 Hornet cal., full stock sporter, 19½ in. barrel, 5 shot mag., double set triggers, 6 lbs. Importation disc. 1999.

	$650	$575	$500	$460	$430	$395	$370

Last MSR was $750.

Add $25 for .22 Mag. cal.
Add $150 for .22 Hornet cal.

This model was designated Model 304 Mannlicher Sporter until 1986. In 1991 it was redesignated the Model 320 Stutzen.

MODEL 340 S ST - .22 LR cal. only, silhouette model, 21 in. bull barrel, match trigger, no sights, 5 shot mag., stippled pistol grip and forearm, 7½ lbs. Importation disc. 1999.

	$750	$625	$550	$500	$450	$375	$325

Last MSR was $795.

✴ *Model 340 Kricotronic* - similar to above, except with Krico electronic trigger. Importation disc. 1988.

	$1,295	$995	$900	$800	$690	$600	$550

Last MSR was $1,450.

✴ *Model 340 Mini-Sniper* - non-glare wood and metal finish, military style barrel with muzzle brake, vent. forearm, no sights, match trigger (interchangeable), 5 shot, raised cheekpiece. Importation disc. 1988.

	$1,050	$825	$725	$600	$550	$500	$450

Last MSR was $1,200.

BIATHLON MODEL 360 S - .22 LR cal., standard biathlon configuration with conventional straight pull bolt. Importation disc. 1999.

	$1,375	$1,075	$925	$750	$625	$550	$500

Last MSR was $1,695.

BIATHLON MODEL 360 S2 - .22 LR cal., biathlon competition rifle featuring unique pistol grip operated rapid fire action, includes 5 mags., aperture sights, snow guards, and black stock. Importation disc. 1999.

	$1,300	$1,050	$900	$750	$625	$550	$500

Last MSR was $1,595.

MODEL 400 SPORTER - .22 LR or .22 Hornet cal., 23½ in. barrel, select checkered walnut with European style curved cheekpiece, 5 shot mag., open sights, 6.8 lbs. Importation disc. 1999.

	$840	$750	$625	$550	$500	$450	$375

Last MSR was $895.

Add $55 for .22 Hornet cal.

✴ *Model 400 Match Single Shot* - .22 LR only, match rifle configuration. Importation disc. 1999.

	$875	$750	$625	$550	$500	$450	$375

Last MSR was $950.

✴ *Model 400 Silhouette* - .22 LR only, designed for silhouette shooting, no sights. Importation disc. 1999.

	$725	$615	$550	$500	$450	$375	$325

Last MSR was $775.

MODEL 420 L ST MANNLICHER SPORTER - .22 Hornet only, full stock sporter, 19½ in. barrel, double set triggers, 5 shot, 6½ lbs.

	$875	$750	$625	$550	$500	$450	$375

MODEL 440 - .22 Hornet, otherwise similar to Model 340. Importation disc. 1988.

	$900	$725	$575	$525	$450	$400	$360

Last MSR was $1,025.KRICO, cont.

Grading	100%	98%	95%	90%	80%	70%	60%

MODEL 600 HUNTING - .222 Rem., .223 Rem., .22-250 Rem., .243 Win., .308 Win., or 5.6x50 Mag. cal., 23½ in. barrel, select checkered walnut with curved European style cheekpiece and vent. forend, 3 or 4 shot mag., open sights, single set trigger, 7 lbs. Importation disc. 1999.

	$1,100	$975	$850	$750	$625	$550	$500

Last MSR was $1,295.

Add $55 for Model 600 SC.
Add $300 for Model 600 Benchrest.
Add $355 for Model 600 in sniper configuration.

This model was also available in single shot configuration at no extra charge as well as in a Match Model Group I & II - add $100 for Group II.

MODEL 620 MANNLICHER SPORTER - same cals. as Model 600, full stock sporter, 20¾ in. barrel, double set triggers, 3 shot mag., 6.8 lbs. Importation disc. 1988.

	$1,165	$965	$875	$760	$695	$650	$590

Last MSR was $1,300.

MODEL 640 S ST VARMINT - .22-250 Rem., .222 Rem., or .223 Rem. cal., 23¾ in. heavy barrel, high Monte Carlo comb and full cheekpiece, rosewood forearm tip and grip cap, Wundhammer hand swell, double set triggers, 4 shot mag., 9.6 lbs. Importation disc. 1990.

	$875	$750	$625	$550	$500	$450	$375

Last MSR was $950.

❋ *Model 640 Sniper* - similar to Model 640, except has non-adj. cheekpiece. Importation disc. 1988.

	$1,325	$1,075	$965	$875	$760	$695	$650

Last MSR was $1,500.

K

MODEL 640 DELUXE/SUPER SNIPER - .223 Rem. or .308 Win. cal., 23 in. barrel, select walnut stock has stippled hand grip, adj. cheekpiece and vent. forearm, engine turned bolt assembly, 3 shot mag., match trigger, 10 lbs. Importation disc. 1988.

	$1,495	$1,175	$1,025	$875	$760	$695	$650

Last MSR was $1,725.

This model was known as the 650 Sniper/Match until 1986.

MODEL 700A ECONOMY - .222 Rem., .243 Win., or .308 Win. cal. (Group I) or 6.5x55mm, 7x64mm, .270 Win., or .30-06 cal. (Group II), without sights, single trigger. Imported 1991-99.

	$900	$775	$650	$550	$500	$450	$375

Last MSR was $995.

Add $70 for Group II cals.

MODEL 700 SERIES - .17 Rem., .22-250 Rem., .222 Rem., .222 Rem. Mag., .223 Rem., 5.6x50mm Mag., .243 Win., .308 Win., or 5.6x57 RWS cal. (Group I), 6.5x55mm, 7x57mm, .270 Win., 7x64mm, .30-06, or 9.3x72 cal. (Group II), or 6.5x68mm, 7mm Rem. Mag., .300 Win. Mag., 8x68S, 7.5mm Swiss, or 6x62mm Freres (Group III) cal., matte black metal finish, open sights, approx. 7 lbs. Imported 1991-99.

❋ *Model 700 Hunting* - available in Group I or II cals. only, walnut hunting stock with Bavarian cheekpiece, recoil pad, and palm swell grip. Importation disc. 1999.

	$1,075	$950	$850	$750	$625	$550	$500

Last MSR was $1,249.

Add $50 for Group II cals.

❋ *Model 700 DeLuxe* - similar to Model 700 Hunting, except has better grade walnut and is available in Group III cals. also. Importation disc. 1999.

	$1,150	$1,000	$875	$750	$625	$550	$500

Last MSR was $1,379.

Add $20 for Group II cals.
Add $71 for Group III cals.
Add $150 for left-hand action.
Add $346-$516 for repeating variation in Groups I-III.

Grading	100%	98%	95%	90%	80%	70%	60%

* **Model 700 Stutzen** - full stock variation (Mannlicher) of the Model 700 DeLuxe. Importation disc. 1999.

	100%	98%	95%	90%	80%	70%	60%
	$1,200	$1,025	$895	$750	$625	$550	$500

Last MSR was $1,450.

Add $39 for Group II cals.
Add $160 for Group III cals.
Add $275 for DeLuxe variation (includes better wood and finish).

MODEL 700 DL R SPORTER - .270 Win. or .30-06 cal., 23½ in. barrel, curved European cheek-piece, select walnut, 3 shot Mag., single set trigger, open sights, 7 lbs. Importation disc. 1990.

	$925	$800	$650	$575	$500	$450	$375

Last MSR was $1,025.

Subtract $30 for Model 700 DM ST.
Add $470 for Model 700 DLM.

MODEL 720 MANNLICHER SPORTER - similar to Model 700, only has 20¾ in. barrel, double set triggers, 6.8 lbs. Importation disc. 1990.

	$1,100	$975	$850	$750	$625	$550	$500

Last MSR was $1,295.

* **Model 720 Limited Editio00n** - .270 Win. cal. only, 24Kt. gold scroll work on bolt handle, receiver, barrel and mounts. Trigger and front sight are gold plated. Serial numbered in gold. Disc. 1986.

	$2,310	$1,990	$1,700	$1,450	$1,200	$1,050	$950

Last MSR was $2,659.

MODEL 902 DELUX GRADE I - .222 Rem., .243 Win., .270 Win., .30-06, 6.5x55mm, 7x64mm, 8x68mm, 9.3x64mm, or 7mm Rem. Mag. cal., 22¼ or 24¼ in. barrel, Oxidal deep black or satin finish, various grades, checkered walnut stock and forend. Importation began late 1999.

	MSR	$1,740		$1,650	$1,400	$1,200	$995	$875	$750	$625

* **Grade II**

	MSR	$3,440		$3,100	$2,750	$2,375	$2,050	$1,750	$1,450	$1,150

* **Grade III**

	MSR	$4,400		$3,950	$3,500	$3,100	$2,750	$2,375	$2,050	$1,750

* **Grade IV**

	MSR	$5,480		$4,950	$4,450	$3,800	$3,200	$2,600	$2,250	$1,875

* **Grade V** - custom model, individually built per customer specifications, POR.

RIFLES: SEMI-AUTO

MODEL 260 SPORTER - .22 LR cal. only, standard features. Importation began 1991.

	MSR	$595		$550	$495	$450	$410	$380	$350	$320

H. KRIEGHOFF GUN CO.
(SHOTGUNS OF ULM)

Current manufacturer located in Ulm, Germany since circa 1954. Previous manufacture was in Suhl, Germany 1886-1947. Currently imported and distributed by Krieghoff International Inc. located in Ottsville, PA. Dealer direct sales only.

Currently, Krieghoff manufacturers 2,000 guns annually, in all configurations.

WWII Krieghoff Lugers will appear in the Luger section of this text.

KRIEGHOFF

DRILLINGS

H. Krieghoff drillings can be ordered with a variety of cals. (.222 Rem., .243 Win., .270 Win., or .30-06) and special order features. Prices shown below are for standard guns with no options. Better

Grading	100%	98%	95%	90%	80%	70%	60%

models will have a finer grade walnut and exhibit more elaborate deep relief engraving.

Add $450 for free floating rifle barrels on Trumpf and Neptun Models listed below (both regular steel frame and Dural variations).

Add $1,290 for 3-claw scope mount system.

PLUS MODEL - 12 or 20 ga. over rifle barrel (.222 Rem., .243 Win., .270 Win., or .30-06 cal.) boxlock action, light engraving, current mfg. utilizes free floating rifle barrel with adj. poin of impact (Thermo TS Stabil). New 1988.

	MSR $5,975	$4,900	$3,550	$2,750	$2,175	$1,825	$1,525	$1,200

TRUMPF MODEL - 12, 16, or 20 ga. O/U, or rifle shotgun combo., various cals., boxlock, 25 in. barrels, 7½ lbs.

	MSR $9,950	$8,300	$6,300	$5,350	$4,250	$3,300	$2,750	$2,200

Add $1,850 for single trigger.

* **Trumpf Dural** - Dural aluminum frame variation of the Trumpf, 6.8 lbs., cased.

	MSR $9,950	$8,300	$6,300	$5,350	$4,250	$3,300	$2,750	$2,200

NEPTUN MODEL - 12 or 20 ga., variety of cals., elaborate engraving, sidelocks.

	MSR $16,500	$13,250	$10,400	$9,000	$7,550	$6,200	$5,100	$4,150

* **Neptun Dural** - Dural aluminum frame variation of the Neptun, cased.

	MSR $16,500	$13,250	$10,400	$9,000	$7,550	$6,200	$5,100	$4,150

NEPTUN PRIMUS MODEL - similar to Neptun Model, only hand detachable sidelocks and elabo- rate deep relief engraving.

	MSR $24,500	$18,500	$13,650	$10,450	$8,400	$7,100	$5,850	$4,950

* **Neptun Primus Dural** - Dural aluminum frame variation available at no extra charge.

	MSR $24,500	$18,500	$13,650	$10,450	$8,400	$7,100	$5,850	$4,950

RIFLES: DOUBLE, O/U & SxS

Various grades differ in style and amount of engraving, choice of walnut and various options that can be special ordered.

Add $1,950 for 4-claw scope mount (standard or European).

TECK O/U - .30-06, .300 Win. Mag. (disc. 1994), .308 Win., 7x56R (disc. 1994), 7x65R (new 1995), 8x57JRS, 8x75RS (new 1995), 9.3x74R, .375 H&H (disc. 1988), or .458 Win. Mag. cal., 25 in. barrels, boxlock action, cocking indicators, hard case included.

	MSR $10,500	$8,725	$6,475	$5,200	$4,300	$3,650	$3,300	$3,000

Add $1,400 for .375 H&H or .458 Win. Mag. cal.

Add $990 for DTs with front set trigger.

* **Teck-Handspanner** - 7x65R, .30-06, or .308 Win. cal. on 16 ga. receiver frame, manual cock- ing.

	MSR $12,495	$10,200	$7,950	$6,675	$5,175	$4,375	$3,950	$3,200

ULTRA O/U - various cals. up to 9.3x74R, features unique manual cocking/self cocking device and interchangeable muzzle wedge for adjustable point of impact. New 1993.

	MSR $6,970	$6,300	$5,625	$4,950	$4,250	$3,500	$2,950	$2,250

CLASSIC O/U - same standard cals. as Teck O/U, boxlock action, light engraving. New 1995.

	MSR $7,850	$6,975	$5,900	$5,150	$4,300	$3,500	$2,950	$2,250

* **Classic Big Five O/U (Big Bore)** - .375 H&H, .375 Flanged Mag. NE, .500/.416 NE, .458 Win. Mag., .470 NE, or .500 NE/3 in. cal. New 1995.

	MSR $9,450	$8,250	$6,925	$5,950	$5,000	$4,150	$3,350	$3,150

Grading	100%	98%	95%	90%	80%	70%	60%

ULM O/U - similar to Teck Double Rifle, except has any combination of cals., with sidelocks and more elaborate engraving.

MSR $17,900	$14,300	$10,350	$8,550	$6,900	$6,100	$5,500	$4,950

Add $695 for hand detachable sidelocks.
Add $1,775 with single/double trigger.

✳ *Ulm Dekor* - sidelock with light scroll engraving. Importation disc. 1991.

$10,450	$9,150	$8,000	$6,750	$5,600	$5,000	$4,400

Last MSR was $12,500.

✳ *Ulm Primus* - deluxe sidelock.

MSR $26,000	$19,750	$13,000	$10,250	$8,100	$6,550	$5,700	$5,300

TRUMPF SxS - boxlock action, similar to Teck model, except in .30-06, 8x57JRS, or 9.3x74R cal. Disc. 1994.

$13,200	$9,700	$8,350	$6,900	$6,100	$5,500	$4,950

Last MSR was $16,150.

CLASSIC SxS STANDARD - same standard cals. as Teck O/U, boxlock action, 21½ (optional) or 23½ in. regulated barrels, DTs, Combi cocking device, removable wedge and integrated front sight in cals. up to .375 H&H, extractors, choice of standard or bavarian style stock, light engraving, with or w/o sideplates, various engraving options, 7½-11 lbs. New 1995.

MSR $7,850	$6,950	$5,950	$5,150	$4,350	$3,500	$2,950	$2,250

Add $3,200 for a set of 20 ga./3 in. barrels.
Add $4,500 per set of interchangeable rifle barrels.
Add $1,950 for sideplates with standard scroll engraving.

✳ *Classic SxS Big Five (Big Bore)* - .375 H&H (disc. 1999), .375 Flanged Mag. NE (new 1996), .416 Rigby (disc. 1999), .458 Win. Mag. (disc. 1999), .470 NE, .500/ .416 NE (new 1996) or .500 NE cal., hinged front trigger, non-removable muzzle wedge, 23 ½ in. barrel with express style quarter rib, 9½ -10½ lbs. New 1995.

MSR $9,450	$8,300	$6,975	$5,975	$5,000	$4,150	$3,350	$3,150

Add $3,200 for a set of 20 ga./3 in. barrels.
Add $5,500 per set of interchangeable rifle barrels.
Add $1,950 for sideplates with standard scroll engraving.

NEPTUN SxS - sidelock double rifle, same features as the Ulm model. Importation disc. 1991.

$12,750	$10,400	$8,700	$7,350	$6,000	$5,450	$4,995

Last MSR was $15,500.

RIFLES: SINGLE SHOT

HUBERTUS RIFLE - available in .22-250 Rem., 222 Rem., 243 Win., .270 Win., .30-06, .308 Win., .270 Wby. Mag. (disc.), .300 Win. Mag., 7mm Rem. Mag., and in 12 metric cals. between 5.6x50R Mag.-8x57RS, single shot stalking rifle with Kickspanner (unique manual cocking device), engraved boxlock action, 23½ in. barrel with quarter rib, fast lock time, double underlugs, approx. 6½ lbs. Importation began 1997-99.

MSR $5,850	$5,375	$4,650	$3,975	$3,400	$2,950	$2,575	$1,850

Add $1,000 for Mag. cals.
Add $1,950 for sideplates with standard scroll engraving.

SHOTGUNS: O/U

Subtract 20%-50% for shotguns mfg. before 1960.

MODEL 32 STANDARD - 12, 20, 28 ga., or .410 bore, O/U, 28-32 in. high rib barrels, ejectors, boxlock, single trigger, select wood. Disc. 1983.

Standard	$3,500	$3,000	$2,700	$2,400	$2,100	$1,800	$1,500
San Remo	$7,000	$6,000	$5,000	$4,000	$3,000	$2,600	$2,200

Grading	100%	98%	95%	90%	80%	70%	60%
Monte Carlo	$9,000	$7,500	$6,500	$5,500	$4,000	$3,000	$2,500
Crown	$10,000	$8,000	$7,000	$6,000	$4,500	$3,500	$3,000
Super Crown	$12,000	$10,000	$8,000	$7,000	$5,000	$4,000	$3,500

✳ *Low Rib* - 28 ga. or .410 bore.

	$3,950	$3,575	$2,875	$2,650	$2,200	$1,900	$1,600

Add 50% for two-barrel set.

MODEL 32 4-BARREL SKEET SET - 12, 20, 28 ga., or .410 bore, O/U, matched barrels in case, grades differ in engraving and wood quality. Disc. 1983.

	100%	98%	95%	90%	80%	70%	60%
Standard	$11,250	$9,950	$8,650	$7,450	$6,200	$4,950	$3,700
München Grade	$13,250	$11,250	$9,500	$8,300	$6,600	$5,775	$5,225
San Remo Grade (unmarked)	$16,995	$13,750	$11,000	$9,000	$7,800	$6,600	$6,325
Monte Carlo (Silver Crown, 50 mfg.)	$18,750	$16,000	$13,750	$11,000	$9,000	$7,800	$6,600
Crown Grade (400 mfg.)	$24,995	$21,000	$17,750	$14,750	$12,100	$10,350	$9,650
Super Crown Grade (48 mfg.)	$29,995	$25,750	$20,750	$16,750	$14,775	$12,650	$10,350

K-20 SPORTING AND FIELD - 20, 28 ga., or .410 bore, compact 20 ga. frame, incorporates all of the technical refinements of the K-80, nickel plated receiver with satin grey finish and classic scroll engraving, 28 or 30 in. separated barrels (28 ga. and .410 bore barrels can be purchased separately w/o fitting) with tapered flat rib, SST, AE, checkered walnut stock and Schnabel forearm, includes 5 choke tubes, approx. 7¼ lbs., includes fitted aluminum case. Importation began 2000.

MSR	$8,150						
		$7,500	$6,500	$5,500	$4,750	$4,000	$3,250	$2,650

Add $275 for 28 ga. or .410 bore.
Add $3,300 for extra set of 20 ga. barrels, $3,575 for 28 ga. or .410 bore.
Add $475-$2,700+ for wood upgrades, depending on quality.

A 20/28 ga. set with 10 choke tubes and hard case is also available for $11,725. A 3 gauge set (20, 28 ga. and .410 bore) with 15 choke tubes and hard case is also available for $15,325.

Additional options for the K-20 include case colors ($1,275), and engraving options are Super Scroll ($2,250), Suhl Scroll ($3,500), Parcours Special ($3,950), Gold Super Scroll (coin or blue finish, $4,700), Bavaria ($5,150), Gold Uplander (coin or blued finish, $7,950), Gold Plantation Scroll (coin or blue finish, $6,950), Plantation Scroll/Uplander (nickel or blue finish, $4,650), and Bavaria Suhl ($8,500).

K-80 TRAP - 12 ga. only, available in O/U, Unsingle, Top Single (single top barrel), and Combo (O/U with extra trap barrel) configurations, standard model has silver finished receiver, adj. rib allowing variable points of impact (new 1993). In O/U configuration the barrels are separated, about 8½ lbs. A wide variety of custom order options can be ordered on this model.

For the Model K-80 Trap, extra barrels (fixed chokes) cost $2,900 for O/Us, $2,950 for top single (disc. 1999), and $3,575 for unsingle barrel.

Beginning 2000, options for the K-80 Trap include case colors ($1,275), and engraving options are Super Scroll ($2,250), Suhl Scroll ($3,500), Parcours Special ($3,950), Gold Super Scroll (coin or blue finish, $4,700), Gold Uplander (coin or blued finish, $7,950), Gold Plantation Scroll (coin or blue finish, $6,950), Plantation Scroll/Uplander (nickel or blued finish, $4,650), and Bavaria Suhl ($8,500).

$650 for O/U screw-in chokes (5 tubes).
Add $425 for 3 screw-in chokes (single barrel guns only).
Add $425 for single release trigger or $750 for double release trigger.

✳ *Standard Unsingle* - 32 or 34 in. lower barrel with either fixed choke or choke tubes.

MSR	$7,950						
		$6,600	$5,300	$4,350	$3,550	$3,000	$2,600	$2,295

Add approx. 30% for Combo (includes unsingle and O/U barrels).

Grading	100%	98%	95%	90%	80%	70%	60%

* ***Standard O/U*** - 30 or 32 in. barrels with either fixed chokes or choke tubes.
  MSR $7,375   **$6,200**   **$5,025**   **$4,250**   **$3,550**   **$3,000**   **$2,600**   **$2,295**
  Add 40% for Combo Standard K-80 variations.
  Subtract 20% for top single variation (very limited mfg.).

* ***Bavaria Suhl*** - game scene engraved silver receiver with light scroll perimeter scroll work, select walnut. Special order only for Top Single.
  MSR $15,875   **$13,250** **$10,000**   **$8,000**   **$6,750**   **$5,500**   **$4,750**   **$4,250**
  Add 5% for Unsingle, or 24% for Combo Bavaria variations.

* ***Danube Model*** - fine English scrollwork on receiver sides and floor plate. Special order only for Top Single.
  MSR $23,625   **$19,325** **$13,950** **$10,750**   **$9,000**   **$7,150**   **$6,570**   **$5,850**
  Add 4.5% for Unsingle, or 20% for Combo Danube variations.

* ***Gold Target Model*** - deep chiseled scroll engraving with gold line accents, 100% coverage finest quality walnut. Special order only for Top Single.
  MSR $27,170   **$22,000** **$15,500** **$12,750**   **$9,500**   **$7,750**   **$7,000**   **$6,650**
  Add 3% for Unsingle, and 14% for Combo Gold Target variations.

* ***Centennial Model*** - 12 ga. only, available in combo configuration only, 100 only mfg. 1986 to commemorate Krieghoff's centennial year, ser. no. 14501-14600. H. Krieghoff's signature inlaid in gold on frame sides.
      $6,000   **$5,000**   **$4,400**

  Last MSR was $5,995.

K-80 SKEET/SKEET SPECIAL - 12 ga. only, available in Standardweight (8mm rib) or International (12mm rib) configuration, 28 or 30 in. barrels, approx. 8¾ lbs.

For the Model K-80 Skeet, add $675 for Skeet Special (choke tubes & tapered flat rib).
Beginning 2000, options for the K-80 Skeet include case colors ($1,275), and engraving options are Super Scroll ($2,250), Suhl Scroll ($3,500), Parcours Special ($3,950), Gold Super Scroll (coin or blue finish, $4,700), Gold Uplander (coin or blued finish, $7,950), Gold Plantation Scroll (coin or blue finish, $6,950), Plantation Scroll/Uplander (nickel or blue finish, $4,650), and Bavaria Suhl ($8,500). Additonally, custom engraving options (added to the Standard Grade price) are also available. Add $5,150 for Bavaria, $12,150+ for Gold Bavaria, $16,250 for Danube, $19,975 for Gold Target, $9,500 for Waterfowl Medallion, and $7,000 for Millenium. Crown, Majestic, and San Remo Bulino engraving are POR.

* ***Standard Model*** - available in Standardweight frame, hard case optional.
  MSR $6,900   **$5,850**   **$4,475**   **$3,375**   **$2,850**   **$2,450**   **$2,125**   **$1,900**
  Add $675 for Skeet Special (choke tubes & tapered flat rib).
  Add $2,650 per extra set of barrels with fixed chokes, $3,300 with choke tubes (Skeet Special).

* ***Centennial Skeet*** - available in skeet configuration - special features as noted above on Centennial Model description listed under K-80 Trap. Mfg. 1986 only.
      $3,675   **$3,150**   **$2,700**

  Last MSR was $3,980.

K-80 2-BARREL LIGHTWEIGHT SKEET SET - 12 ga., includes one set of 28 in. barrels with Tula chokes and one set of carrier barrels allowing use of sub-gauge tubes (carrier barrels cannot be used for 12 ga.), 8mm rib, hard case standard. Mfg. 1988-1999.

* ***Standard Grade***
        $9,400   **$7,000**   **$5,150**   **$4,300**   **$3,875**   **$3,300**   **$3,000**
  Last MSR was $11,840.

  Subtract $1,845 for heavy barrel variation, which does not include sub-gauge tubes.
  Retail price for 2 barrel heavy set with choke tubes was $9,995.

Grading	100%	98%	95%	90%	80%	70%	60%

✳ *Bavaria Model* - game scene engraved silver receiver with light perimeter scroll work, select walnut. Imported 1988-1999.

	$14,975	$11,250	$8,575	$7,200	$6,200	$5,250	$4,800

Last MSR was $16,990.

Subtract $1,845 for heavy barrel variation, which does not include sub-gauge tubes.
Retail price for 2 barrel heavy set with choke tubes was $15,145.

✳ *Danube Model* - fine English scroll work on receiver sides and floor plate. Imported 1988-1999.

	$22,945	$15,250	$17,750	$9,400	$7,750	$7,000	$6,650

Last MSR was $28,090.

Subtract $1,845 for heavy barrel variation, which does not include sub-gauge tubes.
Retail price for 2 barrel heavy set with choke tubes was $26,245.

✳ *Gold Target Model* - deep chiseled scroll engraving with gold line accents, 100% coverage finest quality walnut. Importation disc. 1999.

	$25,975	$20,500	$15,950	$12,375	$9,950	$8,700	$7,500

Last MSR was $31,635.

Subtract $1,845 for heavy barrel variation.
Retail price for 2 barrel heavy set with choke tubes was $29,790.

K-80 4-BARREL SKEET SET - 1 barrel each of 12, 20, 28 ga., and .410 bore, 12 ga. is Tula choked (even patterning), 8mm tapered flat or standard VR, includes hard case. Since most shooters prefer different gauge insert tubes (Briley, etc.) rather than barrel sets, values have gone down considerably recently for these 4 gauge sets.

✳ *Standard Grade* - satin finished receiver with skeet scroll engraving. Importation disc. 1999.

	$13,150	$7,625	$6,275	$5,350	$4,500	$4,000	$3,650

Last MSR was $16,950.

✳ *Bavaria Model* - game scene engraved silver receiver with light perimeter scrollwork, select walnut. Importation disc. 1999.

	$18,200	$12,500	$9,750	$8,250	$6,900	$5,400	$4,350

Last MSR was $22,100.

✳ *Danube Model* - fine English scroll work on receiver sides and floor plate. Importation disc. 1999.

	$26,100	$17,000	$13,000	$10,500	$8,700	$7,500	$6,250

Last MSR was $33,200.

✳ *Gold Target Model* - deep chiseled scroll engraving with gold line accents, 100% coverage finest quality walnut. Importation disc. 1999.

	$29,650	$17,350	$13,000	$10,500	$8,700	$7,500	$6,250

Last MSR was $36,745.

K-80 PIGEON - 12 ga. only, available with 28 or 30 in. barrels, standard tapered step rib, IM/F choking, available in Standardweight configuration.

Beginning 1992, the K-80 Pigeon Model is available by special order only. Rather than list the various Pigeon models separately, their current values will be approximately the same as the corresponding K-80 Trap/Skeet Models listed.

K-80 SPORTING CLAYS - 12 ga. only, 28, 30 (new 1991), or 32 (new 1993) in. barrels with 5 choke tubes, choice of 8mm VR skeet, tapered flat (broadway) or step rib (special order), sporting clay stock dimensions. New 1988.

For options on the Model K-80 Sporting, please refer to the options on the K-80 Skeet, as they are the same.

✳ *Standard Grade* - satin finished receiver with sporting scroll engraving.

MSR	$8,150		$6,750	$5,425	$4,500	$3,650	$3,000	$2,600	$2,100

Add $3,300 for extra set of O/U barrels with 5 choke tubes.

ULM-P LIVE PIGEON - 12 ga. only, live pigeon gun with hand detachable sidelocks, 28 or 30 in.

Grading	100%	98%	95%	90%	80%	70%	60%

VR barrels, standard grade has light scrollwork engraving.

MSR $22,500 $17,500 $12,000 $9,175 $7,700 $6,000 $5,450 $4,995

✻ ***Bavaria Grade*** - similar to Ulm-P, only with elaborate game scene engraving.

MSR $29,500 $22,000 $14,750 $11,450 $8,750 $6,750 $5,700 $5,300

KS-2 SERIES - any ga., full H&H type sidelocks, priced by individual special order. Prices start at $24,000. Custom order only with substantial wait.

SHOTGUNS: O/U OR COMBINATION GUNS

Add $695 for hand detachable sidelocks (Ulm only).
Add $1,290 for 4-claw scope mount system.

TECK MODEL - 12 and 16 ga., O/U shotgun or rifle/shotgun combo., various cals. (7x57R, 7x64mm, 7x65R, .30-06, or .308 Win.), boxlock action, Kersten double crossbolt, auto ejectors, 7½ lbs.

MSR $7,750 $6,650 $5,100 $4,400 $3,550 $3,000 $2,600 $2,295

✻ ***Teck Dural*** - Dural aluminum frame variation of the Teck, 6.8 lbs.

MSR $7,750 $6,625 $5,100 $4,400 $3,550 $3,000 $2,600 $2,295

ULM - similar to Teck, except sidelock and fully engraved with leaf arabesques.

MSR $14,500 $11,700 $8,975 $7,600 $6,350 $5,250 $4,400 $3,500

✻ ***Ulm Dural*** - Dural aluminum frame variation of the Ulm.

MSR $14,500 $11,700 $8,975 $7,600 $6,350 $5,250 $4,400 $3,500

ULM PRIMUS - similar to Ulm, except game scene engraved with English arabesques.

MSR $22,850 $18,100 $12,850 $9,000 $7,000 $5,975 $5,450 $4,995

✻ ***Ulm Primus Dural*** - Dural aluminum frame variation of the Ulm Primus.

MSR $22,850 $18,100 $12,850 $9,000 $7,000 $5,975 $5,450 4,995

ULTRA COMBINATION GUN - 12 ga. only, combination O/U, various calibers (lower barrel), 25 in. barrels, "Kickspanner" mechanism allows manual cocking from thumb safety, satin finish receiver, VR, 6 lbs. New 1985.

MSR $4,950 $3,975 $2,575 $1,850 $1,400 $1,200 $1,050 $900

✻ ***Ultra-B*** - similar to Ultra, except features a selector to switch the front set trigger to the top shotgun barrel. Disc. 1995.

$4,050 $2,675 $1,925 $1,550 $1,350 $1,150 $1,000

Last MSR was $4,990.

SHOTGUNS: SINGLE BARREL TRAP

MODEL 32 - 12 ga., same action as Model 32 O/U, 32-34 in. barrel, VR, mod., imp. mod., or full choke.

$3,150 $2,700 $2,500 $2,200 $1,900 $1,625 $1,350

KS-5 - 12 ga. only, 32 or 34 in. barrel, adj. point of impact, innovative trigger configuration, optional choke tubes, redesigned streamlined receiver (new 1993). Mfg. 1985-1999.

$3,175 $2,775 $2,475 $2,125 $1,875 $1,625 $1,400

Last MSR was $3,675.

Add $2,100 per additional barrel.
Add $425 for screw-in choke option.
Add $395 for factory adj. comb stock.
Add $425 for aluminum case.

Adj. point of impact on this model is achieved by means of different, optional front hangers.

K

Grading	100%	98%	95%	90%	80%	70%	60%

✻ *KS-5 Special* - 12 ga. only, 32 or 34 in. barrel, features adj. rib and comb stock, cased. Mfg. 1990- 99.

	$4,100	$3,550	$2,975	$2,475	$2,050	$1,750	$1,500

Last MSR was $4,695.

Add $2,750 per additional barrel.
Add $425 for screw-in choke option.

KX-5 - 12 ga. only, 34 in. barrel only, adj. point of impact, innovative adj. trigger, adj. stock comb, includes choke tubes and aluminum case. New 2002.

MSR	$4,200	$3,700	$3,200	$2,650	$2,350	$2,150	$1,850	$1,550

KUFSTEINER WAFFENSTUBE

Current rifle manufacturer located in Kufstein, Austria. No current U.S. importation.

RIFLES

Kepplinger rifles are essentially built per individual order. In addition to his unique bolt action, he also makes other bolt action designs and O/U rifles as well. It is recommended that Mr. Kepplinger of Kufsteiner Waffenstube be contacted for more information, including price quotations on his quality, custom order rifles (please refer to the Trademark Index).

Additionally, Kepplinger also manufactures an entire range of set triggers for many popular domestic rifles - these are distributed through Brownell's, located in Montezuma, IA. The company also makes double stage triggers for Mauser M-98 rifles.

3-S SYSTEM BOLT ACTION RIFLE - various cals., unique short action allows for straight on cartridge loading, high strength alloy main parts, grip safety on lower pistol grip, unique uncocking device allowing manual cocking/decocking of the firing pin spring, 23.6 in. standard barrel, 3 shot detachable mag., iron sights, receiver drilled for scope mounts, best quality wood, available in either Schnabel forearm or Mannlicher configuration, many styles of engraving are optional, 7.14 lbs.

Please contact the factory directly regarding a price quotation for this model.

K

L SECTION

L.A.R. MANUFACTURING, INC.

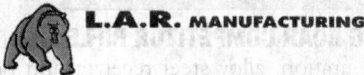

Current rifle manufacturer located in West Jordan, UT. Dealer sales.

Grading	100%	98%	95%	90%	80%	70%	60%

PISTOLS: SEMI-AUTO

GRIZZLY WIN. MAG. MARK I - .357 Mag., .357/.45 Grizzly Win. Mag. (new 1990), .45 ACP, 10mm, or .45 Win. Mag. cal., single action, based on the Colt 1911 design, 5.4 in. (new 1986), 6½ in., 8 in. (new 1987), or 10 in. (new 1987) barrel, parkerized finish, 7 shot mag., ambidextrous safeties, checkered rubber grips, adj. sights, 48 oz. empty. Also can be converted to .45 ACP, 10mm (new 1988), .357 Mag., or .30 Mauser (disc.). Mfg. 1984-1999.

* ***Short Barrel Lengths*** - 5.4 or 6.5 in. barrel.

	$875	$675	$625	$525	$495	$475	$450

Last MSR was $1,000.

Add $14 for .357 Mag. cal.
Add $150 for hard chrome or nickel frame.
Add $260 for full hard chrome or nickel frame.
Add $233-$248 for cal. conversion units.
Conversion units include .357 Mag., 10mm, .40 S&W (1991-1993 only), and .45 ACP cals.

* ***Long Barrel Lengths*** - .357 Mag., .45 Win. Mag., or .357/.45 Grizzly Win. Mag. (new 1990) cal., 8 or 10 in. barrel, extended slides. Disc. 1995.

	$1,195	$975	$895	$800	$725	$650	$575

Last MSR was $1,313.

Add $62 for 10 in. barrel.
Add $24 for .357 Mag.
Add $143 for scope mounts (disc.).
Add $110 for muzzle compensator.

* ***Grizzly State Special Edition*** - .45 Grizzly Win. Mag., 50 mfg. beginning 1998 to commemorate each state (ser. numbers match the order each state was admitted to the union), features gold etchings on frame, gold small parts, faux mother-of-pearl grips, cased. Limited mfg. 1998-99.

Regional demand/interest preclude accurate pricing on this model.

GRIZZLY .44 MAG. MARK 4 - .44 Mag. cal., choice of lusterless blue, parkerized, chrome, or nickel finish, 5.4 or 6½ in. barrel, adj. sights. Mfg. 1991-99.

	$875	$715	$635	$550	$495	$475	$450

Last MSR was $1,014.

GRIZZLY .50 MARK 5 - .50 Action Express cal., single action semi-auto, 5.4 or 6½ in. barrel, 6 shot mag., checkered walnut grips, 56 oz. Mfg. 1993-99.

	$1,025	$865	$720	$615	$525	$495	$475

Last MSR was $1,152.

Add $178-$189 per coversion unit (new 1996).

GRIZZLY WIN. MAG. MARK II - similar to Mark I, except has fixed sights, standard safeties, and different metal finish. Mfg. 1986 only.

	$625	$550	$525	$495	$475	$450	$425

Last MSR was $550.

Add $25 for .357 Mag.

Grading	100%	98%	95%	90%	80%	70%	60%

RIFLES: BOLT ACTION

BIG BOAR COMPETITOR RIFLE - .50 BMG cal., single shot, bolt action design in bullpup configuration, alloy steel receiver and bolt, 36 in. heavy barrel with compensator, thumb safety,
match or field grade, includes bipod, scope mount, leather cheek pad and hard carry case,
30.4 lbs. New 1994.

MSR	$2,570		$2,295	$1,750	$1,400	$1,275	$1,100	$995	$895

Add $100 for parkerizing.
Add $250 for nickel frame.
Add $350 for full nickel.
Add approx. $500 for redesigned (2002) tripod and pintle mount.

L E S INCORPORATED

Previous manufacturer located in Morton Grove, IL.

PISTOLS: SEMI-AUTO

P-18 ROGAK - 9mm Para. cal., double action, 18 shot, 5½ in. barrel, stainless steel, black plastic
grips with partial thumb rest. Disc.

	$350	$295	$265

High polish finish

	$395	$330	$295

This pistol was patterned after the Steyr Model GB. Approx. 2,300 P-18s were mfg. before being
disc.

LABANU INCORPORATED

Labanu, Inc. SKSs were manufactured by Norinco in China, and imported exclusively
until 1998 by Labanu Inc., located in Ronkonkoma, NY.

RIFLES: SEMI-AUTO

MAK 90 SKS SPORTER RIFLE - 7.62x39mm cal., sporterized variation of the SKS with thumbhole stock, 16½ in. barrel, includes accessories, 5 lbs. Importation began 1995, banned 1998.

	$150	$135	$120	$100	$90	$85	$80

Last MSR was $189.

LAHTI PISTOL

Previous manufacturer located in Husqvarna, Sweden. Also mfg. by Vkt (state rifle
factory) in Jyvaskyla, Finland.

PISTOLS: SEMI-AUTO

SWEDISH MODEL 40 - 9mm Para. cal., 4¾ in. barrel, blue finish, fixed sights, plastic grips, mfg.
1940-1944.

	$450	$375	$300	$275	$260	$250	$240

Add 10% for Holster-Rig.
Note: It is important to note that there are diversely marked variations of this pistol, such as RPLT
(Danish State Police); such police markings reduce value by about 10%.

FINNISH L-35 - 9mm Para., 4 basic variations - only the first 2 types have the more desireable
shoulder stock lug. Military pistols are usually "SA" marked, approx. 9,100 mfg. 1938-1954.

* ✱ *1st Variation* - can be identified by "hump" for yoke locking piece and loaded indicator, ser.
  no. range 1001 - 3700.

	$2,500	$2,250	$2,000	$1,650	$1,400	$1,100	$800

Grading	100%	98%	95%	90%	80%	70%	60%

* ✱ *2nd Variation* - does not have the "hump" for yoke locking piece, scarcer than 1st Variation, ser. no. 3701 - 4700.

	$2,200	$2,000	$1,800	$1,600	$1,400	$1,100	$800

* ✱ *3rd Variation* - can be identified by small changes in loaded indicator, most are marked "Valmet", ser. no. range 4701 - 6800.

	$1,200	$1,000	$850	$750	$700	$650	$600

* ✱ *4th Variation* - w/o loaded indicator, marked "Valmet", and sold commercially, ser. no. range 6801 - 9100.

	$1,100	$900	$850	$750	$700	$650	$600

* ✱ *Shoulder Stocks* - the shoulder stock for this model (w/o serial numbers) features a sheet metal compartment which contains a cleaning rod and extra magazine. Original stocks (only 50 mfg.) are currently selling in the $3,000-$3,500 range, while more recently manufactured stocks utilizing original hardware are currently priced in the $1,800-$2,250 range.

LAKE FIELD ARMS LTD.

Previous manufacturer located in Ontario, Canada. Lake Field Arms Ltd. was acquired by Savage Arms, Inc. during late 1994. Distributor sales only through most major U.S. distributors.

Lake Field rifles manufactured after the Savage acquisition are marked Savage - please refer to the Savage section for current mfg.

RIFLES: .22 RIMFIRE

MARK I - .22 LR cal., single shot bolt action, 20¾ in. rifled or smooth bore barrel, adj. rear sight, thumb rotary safety, walnut finish hardwood stock, 5½ lbs. Disc.

	$110	$75	$65	$55	$50	$40	$30
							Last MSR was $135.

Add $14 for left-hand variation.

This model was also available in youth dimensions (19 in. barrel) at no extra charge (Model Mark I-Y).

MARK II - .22 LR cal., bolt action, 10 shot mag., 20¾ in. barrel, adj. rear sight, thumb rotary safety, walnut finish hardwood stock, 5½ lbs. Disc.

	$120	$80	$70	$60	$50	$40	$30
							Last MSR was $140.

Add $15 for left-hand variation (mfg. 1993-95).

This model was also available in youth dimensions (19 in. barrel) at no extra charge (Model Mark II-Y).

MODEL 64B - .22 LR cal., semi-auto, side ejection, 10 shot mag., 20¼ in. barrel, adj. rear sight, thumb rotary safety, walnut finish hardwood stock, 5½ lbs. Disc.

	$120	$85	$75	$65	$55	$45	$40
							Last MSR was $143.

MODEL 90B (BIATHLON) - .22 LR cal., biathlon rifle, includes five 5-shot mags., 21 in. barrel, aperture sights, one-piece natural finish hardwood stock, 8¼ lbs. Mfg. 1991-95.

	$430	$300	$225	$195	$170	$150	$130
							Last MSR was $570.

Add $55 for left-hand variation (new 1993).

MODEL 91T - .22 LR cal., target rifle, single shot, 25 in. barrel with aperture sights, dark hardwood finished stock, 8 lbs. Mfg. 1991-95.

	$340	$255	$215	$175	$150	$135	$115
							Last MSR was $455.

Add $45 for left-hand variation (mfg. 1993-95).

Grading	100%	98%	95%	90%	80%	70%	60%

✵ **Model 91TR** - repeater version of the Model 91T, 5 shot mag. Mfg. 1993-95.

	$360	$265	$215	$175	$150	$135	$115

Last MSR was $485.

Add $45 for left-hand variation (mfg. 1993-95).

MODEL 92S - .22 LR cal., 5 shot detachable mag., 21 in. barrel, hardwood stock with Monte Carlo cheekpiece, 8 lbs. Mfg. 1993-95.

	$300	$240	$200	$175	$160	$150	$135

Last MSR was $388.

Add $37 for left-hand variation.

MODEL 93M - .22 Mag. cal., 5 shot mag., thumb operated rotary safety, 20¾ in. barrel, hardwood stock, 5¾ lbs. Mfg. 1995 only.

	$140	$120	$100	$85	$75	$65	$55

Last MSR was $168.

LAKELANDER

Previous trademark circa 1976-1999. Manufacture was by MIPRO AB (c. 1946-1999) in Sweden. Previously imported and distributed 1996-98 by Lakelander U.S.A., Inc. located in Gulfport, MS.

RIFLES: BOLT ACTION

LAKELANDER 389 - .270 Win., .30-06, or .308 Win. cal., unique design with many shooter enhancements, 4 shot integrated mag. with rotary swing plate, 3 configurations including Premium (22 in. barrel with skip-line checkering and Monte Carlo stock), Classic (22 in. barrel, standard stock with checkering), Match-Maker (target model with 21.7 in. barrel and competition stock and adj. cheekpiece, .308 Win. only), 7.3-8.4 lbs. Mfg. 1996-98.

	$1,425	$1,225	$995	$850	$700	$600	$500

Last MSR was $1,599.

Add $500 for Match-Maker Model.

LAMBOY, S.R. & CO. INC.

Current importer located in Victor, NY. S.R. Lamboy imports Renato Caem, and other high quality, low production longguns from Italy. Please refer to the individual listing in this text, as well as contacting the company directly regarding current importation.

LAMES

Previous manufacturer located in Italy.

SHOTGUNS: O/U

FIELD MODEL - 12 ga., 26, 28, or 30 in. barrels, various chokes, VR, engraving, SST, auto ejectors, checkered pistol grip stock with pad.

	$400	$380	$365	$350	$325	$300	$275

Add 25% for separated barrels.

STANDARD TRAP - similar to Field, 30 or 32 in. various trap bore barrels, with wide VR, trap style Monte Carlo stock.

	$600	$575	$550	$525	$425	$400	$450

CALIFORNIA TRAP - similar to Standard Trap, with separated barrels.

	$700	$675	$650	$625	$525	$500	$450

SKEET MODEL - similar to Field, with 26 in. skeet bore barrels, skeet stock and separated barrels.

	$600	$575	$550	$525	$425	$400	$350

L

Grading	100%	98%	95%	90%	80%	70%	60%

LANBER

Current shotgun (O/U and semi-auto only) trademark manufactured by ComLanber, S.A., located in Zaldibar, Spain. Beginning 1999, O/U shotguns are imported by Wingshooting Adventures, located in Grand Rapids, MI. Previously imported 1996-99 by ITC International, Inc. located in Marietta, GA. Previously imported and distributed until 1994, by Eagle Imports, Inc. located in Wanamassa, NJ. Previously imported by Exel Arms of America, Inc., located in Gardener, MA, and by Lanber Arms of America located in Adrian, MI.

Lanber makes a wide range of quality O/U and semi-auto shotguns.

SHOTGUNS: O/U, DISC.

Please refer to 19th-21st Editions of the *Blue Book of Gun Values* for more information on those Lanber models imported until 1987.

SHOTGUNS: O/U, CURRENT IMPORTATION

MODEL 2077 - 12 ga. only, 2¾ in. chambers, boxlock action, SST, black receiver finish, 26 in. VR barrels with 5 choke tubes, ejectors, checkered walnut stock and forearm, 6.2 lbs. Importation began 2000.

MSR	$825		$750	$650	$575	$525	$475	$400	$350

MODEL 2087 - similar to Model 2077, except has 3 in. chambers, engraved receiver and 28 in. barrels, 7 lbs. Importation began 2000.

MSR	$800		$725	$625	$550	$495	$450	$375	$325

MODEL 2088 - 12 ga. only, 2¾ in. chambers, sporting clays configuration, 28 in. VR barrels with 5 choke tubes, oil finished top quality European walnut, 7½ lbs. Importation began 2000.

MSR	$1,499		$1,350	$1,175	$950	$825	$750	$625	$500

MODEL 2097 - 12 ga. only, 3 in. chambers, sporting clays configuration, engraved receiver, 28 or 30 in. VR barrels with 5 choke tubes, 7¾ lbs. Importation began 2000.

MSR	$900		$800	$700	$600	$525	$465	$415	$365

MODEL 2098 - 12 ga. only, 2¾ in. chambers, top-of-the-line sporting clays model with engraved coin finished sideplates, 7 lbs., 10 oz. Importation began 2000.

MSR	$1,899		$1,650	$1,325	$1,075	$950	$825	$750	$625

LANG, JOSEPH

Current trademark manufactured by Atkin, Grant & Lang, located in Hertfordshire, England. No current U.S. importation.

Prices indicated are for manufacturer's suggested retail and 100% condition factors are listed in English pounds. All new prices do not include VAT. Values for used guns in 98%-60% condition factors are priced in U.S. dollars.

Please contact the factory directly for more information and model availability. Atkin, Grant & Lang provide a useful historical research service on older Joseph Lang shotguns and rifles. The charge for this service is £25 per gun, and the company will give you all pertinent factory information regarding the history.

RIFLES: SxS

JOSEPH LANG DOUBLE RIFLE - available in cals. between .300 H&H - .577 NE, best quality double rifle, individually made per customer specifications.

MSR	£19,000		£19,000	$21,950	$19,000	$16,250	$13,750	$11,750	$10,250

Grading	100%	98%	95%	90%	80%	70%	60%

SHOTGUNS: SxS

IMPERIAL SIDELOCK EJECTOR - 12, 16, 20, 28 ga., or .410 bore, best quality sidelock ejector model, individually made per customer specifications.

	MSR	£25,000		£25,000	$28,875	$24,750	$20,750	$17,250	$15,000	$13,250

LASALLE

Previous manufacturer located in France.

SHOTGUNS

SLIDE ACTION SHOTGUN - 12 or 20 ga., 26, 28, or 30 in. barrels, various chokes, alloy frame, checkered pistol grip stock.

	$250	$225	$200	$175	$150	$125	$100

SEMI-AUTO SHOTGUN - 12 ga., 26, 28, or 30 in. barrels, various chokes, gas operated, checkered pistol grip stock.

	$300	$275	$250	$225	$200	$175	$150

LASERAIM ARMS, INC.

Previous distributor located in Little Rock, AR. Previously manufactured until 1999 in Thermopolis, WY. Laseraim Arms, Inc. was a division of Emerging Technologies, Inc.

PISTOLS: SEMI-AUTO

SERIES I - .40 S&W, .400 Cor-Bon (new 1998), .45 ACP, or 10mm cal., single action, 3 3/8 (Compact Model), 5, or 6 in. barrel with compensator, ambidextrous safety, all stainless steel metal parts are Teflon coated, beveled mag. well, integral accessory mounts, 7 (.45 ACP) or 8 (10mm or .40 S&W) shot mag., 46 or 52 oz. Mfg. 1993-99.

	$325	$295	$265

Last MSR was $349.

Add $120 for wireless laser combo (new 1997).

* **Compact Series I** - .40 S&W or .45 ACP cal., features 3 3/8 in. non-ported slide and fixed sights. Mfg. 1993-99.

	$325	$295	$265

Last MSR was $349.

Series I Illusion and Dream Team variations were made during 1993-94. Retail prices respectively were $650 and $695.

SERIES II - .40 S&W (disc. 1994), .45 ACP, or 10mm cal., similar technical specs. as the Series I, except has non-reflective stainless steel finish, fixed or adj. sights, and 3 3/8 (Compact Model, .45 ACP only), 5, or 7 (.45 ACP only) in. non-compensated barrel, 37 or 43 oz. Mfg. 1993-96.

	$485	$385	$300

Last MSR was $550.

Series II Illusion and Dream Team variations were made during 1993-94. Retail prices respectively were $500 and $545.

SERIES III - .45 ACP cal., 5 in. ported barrel, serrated slide, Hogue grips. Mfg. 1994- Disc.

	$595	$465	$415	$375	$345	$310	$275

Last MSR was $675.

SERIES IV - .45 ACP cal., 3 3/8 (Compact Model) or 5 in. ported barrel, serrated slide, diamond checkered wood grips. Mfg. 1994-Disc.

	$550	$450	$400	$360	$330	$300	$265

Last MSR was $625.

Grading	100%	98%	95%	90%	80%	70%	60%

LAURONA

Current trademark established in 1941, and manufactured by Armas Eibar, S.A.L., located in Eibar, Spain. No current U.S. importation. Previously imported until 1993 by Galaxy Imports located in Victoria, TX. Galaxy Imports still services Laurona shotguns (no warranty, see Trademark Index).

Laurona was founded in Eibar during 1941 by four craftsmen (hence the name Laurona, which in Basque means "of the four"), each a specialist in a discipline of shotgun mfg. Laurona made SxS guns until 1978, at which time they discontinued mfg. to concentrate on the O/U marketplace.

Laurona manufactures high quality O/U shotguns and O/U express rifles/combination guns. Beginning 1992, Laurona switched from a one-piece, demi-block type of fabrication to a monobloc system which has improved strength characteristics while reducing weight in their X-Series line of shotguns and express rifles.

Laurona long guns come standard with a Black Chrome metal finish that is extremely resistant to oxidation. Left hand stocks are available for the 83 MG Super Game, 85 MS Super Game, Trap, and Super Skeet, Silhouette Trap models, and Silhouette Sporting Clays.

Suffix designations on Laurona shotguns refer to the following: G - twin non-selective triggers, S - selective single trigger, M - multi-chokes, T - Tulip, BV - beavertail, U - single non-selected triggers.

All Super Game Models were available with a deluxe package which includes a recoil pad, mid-bead sight, and select wood for an additional $250. Special order dull matte finished barrels (with multi- chokes) were available for an additional $200 - extra barrels were priced between $635 (20 ga.) or $800 (12 ga.) per set.

If more information is required on an older Laurona model not listed in this publication (including ser. no. dating), please contact Galaxy Imports (see Trademark Index). For an accurate appraisal, please send a complete description of your specimen (including Laurona model name, serial number, and other pertinent data - include photos if possible). The charge for this service is $25 per serial number.

RIFLES: O/U CURRENT MFG.

MODEL 2000X EXPRESS RIFLE - .30-06, 8x57JRS, 8x57RS, 9.3x74R, or .375 H&H cal., monobloc construction, 24 in. separated barrels featuring quarter rib sight and convergency adjustment at muzzle, matte black chrome finish, open sights, ejectors or extractors, SST or DT, approx. 8.1 lbs. New 1992.

This model must be custom ordered - please contact Galaxy Imports for more information.

This model accepts Leupold or European styled ring mounts.

* ***Model 2000X Combo*** - includes choice of cals. listed, except for .375 H&H cal. with 12 ga. under-barrel. New 1992.

This model must be custom ordered.

SHOTGUNS: O/U, RECENT MFG.

The author wishes to express his thanks to Thomas E. Barker for making the following information available.

1967 Series (Earliest O/U Model)

MODEL 67 (VERSIONS G & U) - 12 ga., first O/U model mfg. with manual extractors, G designation stands for Gemini for twin select trigger system (triggers will function as single or double), front trigger is non-selective firing in bottom to top sequence, and back trigger in top to bottom sequence, U designation stands for non-selective single triggers, boxlock action and barrel bluing, light walnut stock, skip diamond checkering.

$500	$400	$350	$300	$250	$200	$150

Grading	100%	98%	95%	90%	80%	70%	60%

1971 Series

MODEL 71 (VERSIONS G & U) - similar to Model 67 with minor improvements, bright chrome receiver with rolled engraved game scene, earlier models had traditional solid center ribbed blue barrels, later models had solid ribbed barrels with Black Chrome finish. G & U designations are the same as Model 67.

This model was imported and sold by Sears & Roebuck in 1973-74.

	$500	$400	$350	$300	$250	$200	$150

1982 Series

12 ga. only, similar to Model 71 with auto-ejectors. (Manual extractors were disc.) Firing pins changed to traditional round type, many internal parts were improved for better reliability. Skip diamond and standard checkering. All SUPER Series barrels separated (w/o center rib) with Black Chrome finish and hard chrome bores with long forcing cones in chambers. In most respects, the 82 Models are representative to present day Laurona O/U shotguns and will share most internal parts. G & U designations are the same as Model 67.

MODEL 82 GAME (VERSIONS G & U) - 12 ga, 28 in. black chromed barrels, 2¾ or 3 in. chambers, long forcing cones, solid side ribs, hard chrome bores, 5mm vent. rib, chokes ****/** or ***/ * (IC/IM/M/F), Imperial nickel receiver with Louis XVI style engraving, tulip forend, field stock drop 35/65mm with plastic butt plate, 7 lbs.

	$550	$475	$400	$350	$300	$250	$200

MODEL 82 TRAP COMBO (VERSIONS G & U) - 12 ga., similar to 82 Game, except has 28 (chokes ***/*) or 29 (chokes **/*) in. barrels, steel rib, 8mm trap buttstock drop 35/ 55mm with rubber special trap recoil pad, 8 lbs.

	$550	$475	$400	$350	$300	$250	$200

82 TRAP COMPETITION (VERSION U) - 12 ga., similar to 82 Trap Combo, except has 13mm aluminum rib with long white sight, engraved motif on receiver, beavertail fluted forend, Monte Carlo trap stock drop 35/35/55mm with black rubber special trap recoil pad, 8 lbs.

	$600	$550	$475	$400	$350	$300	$250

82 PIGEON COMPETION (VERSION U) - 12 ga., similar to 82 Trap Competition, excpet has 28 in. barrels choked ****/** or ***/*. Recoil pad special competiton Pachmayr with imitation leather face, 7 lbs, 13 oz.

	$650	$600	$550	$475	$400	$350	$300

Model 82 Super Series

The Super Models listed have nickel finished receivers with full coverage, delicate scroll engraving with Black Chrome relief and forend iron. All barrels are split (w/o side ribs), and have very durable rust resistance Black Chrome finish.

82 SUPER GAME (VERSIONS G & U) - 12 ga., similar to 82 Game, except has more elaborate fine scroll engraving.

	$575	$475	$400	$350	$300	$250	$200

82 SUPER TRAP (VERSION U) - 12 ga., similar to 82 Trap Competition, except has special trap Pachmayr recoil pad with imitation leather face and fine scroll engraving.

	$675	$600	$550	$475	$400	$350	$300

82 SUPER SKEET - 12 ga., similar to 82 Super Trap, except has 28 in. barrels choked Skeet/ Skeet, buttstock drop 35/65mm with plastic buttplate, 7 lbs.

	$600	$550	$475	$400	$350	$300	$250

82 SUPER PIGEON - 12 ga., similar to 82 Super Trap, except has 28 in. barrels choked ****/** or ***/*, 7 lbs, 9 oz.

	$675	$600	$550	$475	$400	$350	$300

Grading	100%	98%	95%	90%	80%	70%	60%

Model 83 Super Series

83MG SUPER GAME - 12 or 20 ga., 3 in. chambers, 26 (20 ga. only) or 28 in. barrels, 8mm rib, similar to 82 Super Game, except had Laurona's new multi-choke, not compatible with any other brand of screw in chokes because of the Black Chrome plating of the metric threads, 7 lbs.

	$995	$675	$600	$550	$475	$400	$350

Model 84 Super Series

The Super Game Models listed were available with an extra set of 26 or 28 in. 20 ga. multi-choke barrels and cast-on stocks for left-handed shooters.

Add $400 for multi-choke barrels.
Add $50 for left hand stock.

84S SUPER GAME - 3 in. chambers, similar to 82 Super Game, except for new single selective trigger, ejectors, 28 in. barrels choked IC/IM or M/F, 8mm rib, 7 lbs.

	$750	$675	$600	$550	$475	$400	$350

Add $400 for extra set of 20 ga. multi-choke barrels.

84S SUPER SKEET - 12 ga. only, 2¾ in. chambers, with elongated forcing cones, 28 in. separated barrels choked Skeet/Skeet, 13mm aluminum rib, extensive fine scroll engraving, rust resistant Black Chrome finish, 7 lbs. Imported 1988-1990.

	$995	$675	$600	$550	$475	$400	$350

84S SUPER TRAP - 12 ga., 29 in. barrels with 2¾ in. chambers and long forcing cones, chokes IM and full, 13mm aluminum rib, auto ejectors, nickel plated receiver with fine scroll engraving, Black Chrome relief, beavertail forearm, MC or standard trap stock, 7 lbs., 12 oz.

	$1,250	$975	$875	$750	$625	$550	$475

Model 85 Super Series

85MS SUPER GAME - 12 or 20 ga., 3 in. chambers, similar to 83MG Super Game, except for single selective trigger, 7 lbs.

	$995	$675	$600	$550	$475	$400	$350

85MS SUPER TRAP - similar to 84S Super Trap, except for multi-choke in bottom barrel with fixed full on top, 7 lbs., 12 oz.

	$1,250	$975	$875	$750	$625	$550	$475

85MS SUPER PIGEON - similar to 85MS Super Trap, except for 28 in. barrels with fixed IM choke on top with multi-choke on bottom, intended for live bird competition, 7 lbs., 4 oz.

	$1,250	$975	$875	$750	$625	$550	$475

85MS SPECIAL SPORTING - similar to 85MS Super Pigeon, except field butt stock with plastic buttplate, intended for upland game, 7 lbs., 4 oz.

	$1,250	$975	$875	$750	$625	$550	$475

Excel 300 Series

EXEL 300 SERIES - 12 or 20 ga. The Model 301 is basic field gun, and the Model 310 was the highest grade.

❂ *Models 301 and 302* - 12 ga., double selective trigger system, ejectors, pistol grip, vent. rib, lightly engraved chrome finish receiver, various chokes and barrel lengths. Importation disc. 1986.

	$485	$415	$380	$340	$300	$275	$250

Last MSR was $553.

Grading	100%	98%	95%	90%	80%	70%	60%

❋ *Models 303 and 304* - 12 ga., similar to 301/302, except has better engraving on coin finish receiver, vent. barrels. Importation disc. 1987.

| | $545 | $470 | $430 | $385 | $340 | $315 | $270 |

Last MSR was $623.

Previously designated Model 82G Super.

❋ *Models 305(A) and 306(A)* - 12 or 20 ga., similar to 303/304, except has better engraving on coin finish receiver, screw-in choke tubes. Importation disc. 1987.

| | $625 | $535 | $470 | $430 | $390 | $350 | $315 |

Last MSR was $711.

Previously designated Models 83MG and 85MS.

❋ *Models 307 and 308* - 12 ga., trap model, 29 in. barrels, extensive engraving, Monte Carlo stock. Importation disc. 1987.

| | $580 | $500 | $460 | $420 | $380 | $340 | $300 |

Last MSR was $668.

Previously designated Model 82U Trap.

❋ *Models 309 and 310* - super trap model, 29 in. vent. barrels, more extensive engraving than Models 307/308. Importation disc. 1987.

| | $630 | $545 | $495 | $460 | $415 | $385 | $340 |

Last MSR was $726.

Previously designated Model 82 S. Trap.

Silhouette 300 Series

These shotguns are basically the same as the Super Series, with the following exceptions; this series was readily indentifiable by their white and black chrome striped receiver, with the model engraved on the receiver side. Barrels were multi-choked on both bores and had an 11mm steel rib. Two types of chokes were used. Some guns came with knurl head type as in the Super Models, and others were made with flush Invector style. A later option for ease of changing chokes was the knurl long choke, which is a flush type with the knurl head added. Both later type chokes (flush and knurl long), can be used in the early multi-choke models with some extension showing.

SILHOUETTE 300 TRAP - 12 ga., 2¾ in. chambers, 29 in. 11mm VR barrels with long forcing cones and hard chrome bores, beavertail forearm and straight comb trap stock with vent. black rubber recoil pad, 8 lbs.

| | $1,250 | $975 | $875 | $775 | $700 | $650 | $595 |

SILHOUETTE 300 SPORTING CLAYS - 12 ga., 3 in. chambers, similar to 300 Trap, except has 28 in. barrels and butt stock is field type with plastic buttplate or hard rubber sporting clays pad, 7½ lbs.

| | $1,250 | $975 | $875 | $775 | $700 | $650 | $595 |

SILHOUETTE 300 ULTRA MAGNUM - 12 ga. 3½ in. chambers, similar to 300 Sporting Clays, Black Chrome finish, 7½ lbs.

| | $1,300 | $1,025 | $875 | $775 | $700 | $650 | $595 |

SHOTGUNS: SxS, BOXLOCK

Shotguns mfg. after 1975 with "X" after the model number featured Black Chrome barrels and action with hard chrome bores. 28 ga. and .410 bore could be special ordered. SxS shotguns were disc. by Laurona during 1978 in an effort to concentrate on the O/U marketplace.

MODEL 11 - 12, 16, or 20 ga., triple Greener type round crossbolt with independent firing pins bushed into the face of the action, Bellota steel barrels.

| | $400 | $350 | $315 | $260 | $210 | $175 | $140 |

MODEL 13 - 12, 16, or 20 ga., similar to Model 11, except utilizes Purdey type bolt system, extractors are of double radius, sold through Sears & Roebuck.

| | $400 | $350 | $315 | $260 | $210 | $175 | $140 |

Grading	100%	98%	95%	90%	80%	70%	60%

* **Model 13 E** - similar to Model 13, except has ejectors.

| | $500 | $450 | $395 | $350 | $315 | $260 | $210 |

* **Model 13 X** - similar to Model 13, except has Black Chrome finished barrels and action with hard chrome bores.

| | $500 | $450 | $395 | $350 | $315 | $260 | $210 |

* **Model 13 XE** - similar to Model 13 E, except has Black Chrome finish and hard chrome bores .

| | $600 | $525 | $450 | $395 | $350 | $315 | $260 |

MODEL 15 ECONOMIC PLUMA - 12, 16, or 20 ga., similar to Model 13, except was first model to have hard chrome bores.

| | $450 | $395 | $350 | $315 | $260 | $210 | $175 |

* **Model 15 E Economic Pluma** - similar to Model 15 Economic Pluma, except has ejectors.

| | $550 | $475 | $400 | $350 | $315 | $260 | $210 |

* **Model 15 X** - similar to Model 15 Economic Pluma, except has Black Chrome finish and hard chrome bores.

| | $500 | $450 | $395 | $350 | $315 | $260 | $210 |

* **Model 15 XE** - similar to Model 15 E, except has ejectors.

| | $600 | $525 | $450 | $395 | $350 | $315 | $260 |

MODEL 52 PLUMA - 12, 16, or 20 ga., back of actions scalloped and engraved in fine English scroll, Churchill rib and double radius extractors, hard chrome bores, 6 lbs.

| | $750 | $675 | $600 | $525 | $450 | $395 | $350 |

* **Model 52 E Pluma** - similar to Model 52 Pluma, except has ejectors, 6 lbs., 2 oz.

| | $850 | $750 | $675 | $600 | $525 | $450 | $395 |

SHOTGUNS: SxS, SIDELOCK

Models listed were available in 12, 16, or 20 ga. 28 ga. and .410 bore were available by special order.

MODEL 103 - 12, 16, or 20 ga., blue sidelocks with light border engraving, triple Purdey type bolt system, double radius extractors, Bellota steel barrels with hard chrome bores.

| | $895 | $800 | $675 | $575 | $525 | $475 | $425 |

* **Model 103-E** - similar to Model 103 except with ejectors.

| | $995 | $895 | $800 | $675 | $575 | $525 | $475 |

MODEL 104 X - 12, 16, or 20 ga., case colored sidelock with Purdey type bolting system, double radius extractors, fine double safety sidelocks, gas relief vents, articulated trigger, hard chromed bore, demi-block barrels of special Bellota steel, Black Chrome barrels.

| | $1,200 | $1,075 | $925 | $825 | $700 | $600 | $525 |

* **Model 104 XE** - same as Model 104 X, but with H&H style automatic selective ejectors.

| | $1,350 | $1,200 | $1,075 | $925 | $825 | $700 | $575 |

MODEL 105 X FEATHER - 12, 16, or 20 ga., similar to Model 104 X, except has concave rib, approx. 6 lbs. 2 oz. (12 ga.).

| | $1,250 | $1,100 | $950 | $875 | $800 | $725 | $650 |

* **Model 105 XE Feather** - similar to Model 105 X, except has H&H automatic selective ejectors.

| | $1,400 | $1,225 | $1,075 | $925 | $850 | $775 | $700 |

Grading	100%	98%	95%	90%	80%	70%	60%

MODEL 502 FEATHER - 12, 16, or 20 ga., Purdey type bolting system, hand detachable side-locks, gas relief vents, H&H style automatic selective ejectors, articulated trigger, inside hard chromed demi-block barrels of special Bellota steel, Black Chrome finish, fine English scroll engraving, marble grey or Laurona Imperial finish, Churchill or concave type rib, 6.4 lbs. (12 ga.).

	$2,200	$2,050	$1,875	$1,650	$1,525	$1,400	$1,275

MODEL 801 DELUXE - 12, 16, or 20 ga., similar to Model 502 Feather, except engraving is true deluxe Renaissance style, fully hand made with Laurona Imperial finish, best qulaity checkered walnut stock and forearm.

	$4,400	$4,150	$3,650	$3,250	$2,900	$2,600	$2,250

MODEL 802 EAGLE - 12, 16, or 20 ga., similar to Model 801 Deluxe, except features highly artistic bas-relief engraving of hunting scenes, hand engraved with burin and chisel.

	$5,000	$4,400	$3,900	$3,375	$2,825	$2,375	$1,875

LAW ENFORCEMENT ORDNANCE CORPORATION

Previous manufacturer located in Ridgway, PA until 1990.

SHOTGUNS: SEMI-AUTO

STRIKER-12 - 12 ga. Mag., paramilitary design shotgun featuring 12 shot rotary mag., 18¼ in. barrel, semi-auto, alloy shrouded barrel with PG extension, folding or fixed paramilitary design stock, 9.2 lbs., limited mfg. 1986-1990.

	$850	$750	$625	$550	$495	$450	$375

Last MSR was $725.

Add $150 for folding stock.
Add $100 for Marine variation ("Metal Life" finish).

Earlier variations were imported and available to law enforcement agencies only. In 1987, manufacture was started in PA and these firearms could be sold to individuals (18 in. barrel only). This design was originally developed in South Rhodesia.

HARRY LAWSON CO.

Current custom gun manufacturer and customizer established during 1965 and currently located in Tucson, AZ. Consumer direct sales.

Harry Lawson Co. is well known for custom stock work. This company also manufactures their own line of sporting rifles, most feature an innovative thumbole stock design. Please contact the factory directly for more information regarding custom model availability/configuration and current pricing.

RIFLES: BOLT ACTION

LAWSON 650 SERIES - various Wby. Mag. cals., features Wby. Mark V barreled action with choice of Burris scope, mounts, custom stabilizer sling, and Doskocil hardshell case, prices include new Mark V .340 Wby. Mag. action with black fiberglass "Cochise" stock. Many wood stock options available.

MSR	$2,995		$2,700	$2,225	$1,775	$1,525	$1,350	$1,225	$1,100

LAWSON 650 MOUNTAINEER & ULTRALITE SERIES - various cals., features Rem. Model 700 barreled action, otherwise similar to Lawson 650 Series, prices include new Rem. Model 700 action with black fiberglass "Cochise" stock. Many wood stock options available.

MSR	$2,555		$2,275	$1,950	$1,625	$1,425	$1,250	$1,100	$995H

L

Grading	100%	98%	95%	90%	80%	70%	60%

LAZZERONI ARMS COMPANY

Current manufacturer located in Tucson, AZ since 1995.
Direct/ dealer sales.

LAZZERONI

RIFLES: BOLT ACTION

Lazzeroni ammunition is precision loaded in Lazzeroni's Tucson facility under rigid tolerances. All ammunition is sealed for absolute weatherproofing. Lazzeroni proprietary calibers are already established as being extremely effective at long distances.

SAKO MODEL TRG-S - 7.21 Firebird (.284, new 2002) or 7.82 Warbird (.308) cal., features Sako TRG action with free floating 26 in. barrel, 3 shot detachable mag., fully adj. trigger, and scope rings, 7.9 lbs. New 1999.

> MSR $950 $875 $775 $675
>
> Add $350 for metal finish upgrade or $1,150 for metal finish upgrade with Burris 4-16X mil-dot scope.

SAVAGE 16LZ - 7.21 Tomahawk (.284, disc. 2001) or 7.82 Patriot (.308) cal., stainless steel action with 2 locking lugs, 24 in. stainless barrel, detachable box mag., injection molded composite stock, 6.8 lbs. New 2001.

> MSR $750 $685 $600 $550
>
> Add $100 for left hand action.

MODEL 700ST - various Lazzeroni cals., Rem. M-700 action, features remachined bolt face, squared recoil lug and receiver, mag. and follower are replaced with Lazzeroni style units, steel (disc.) or stainless steel (new 1999) action, blue steel or stainless steel 24 in. barrel. Mfg. 1998-99.

> $2,150 $1,750 $1,425
>
> Last MSR was $2,395.

L

MODEL 2000 SERIES - available in either Lazzeroni short magnum (6.17 Spitfire - .243 cal., 6.71 Phantom - .264 cal., 7.21 Tomahawk - .284 cal., 7.82 Patriot - .308 cal., 8.59 Galaxy - .338 cal., or 10.57 Maverick - .416 cal.) or Lazzeroni long magnums (6.53 Scramjet - .257 cal., 7.21 Firebird - .284 cal., 7.82 Warbird - .308 cal., 8.59 Titan - .338 cal., or 10.57 Meteor - .416 cal.), features precision machined steel (disc.) or stainless steel (new 1999) receiver, helically fluted bolt with heavy duty extractor, stainless steel match barrel with integral muzzle brake, adj. benchrest trigger, matte finish metal, 3 position firing pin safety on most models (new 1999), 2 or 3 (new 1999) shot internal mag., various stock configurations. New 1996.

✻ Model L2000ST - features 27 in. barrel with conventional fiberglass stock, 8.1 lbs.

> MSR $5,000 $4,450 $3,725 $3,000

✻ Model L2000ST-28 - .308 Warbird cal., shoots 130 grain BarnesX boattail at 4,000 fps, 28 in. stainless steel fluted barrel, includes Schmidt & Bender 4X-16X x 50mm scope, stainless action, black synthetic stock, approx. 8.3 lbs. Mfg. 1999-2001.

> $5,875 $5,250 $4,750
>
> Last MSR was $6,310.

This model was advertised as the flattest shooting hunting rifle currently manufactured, and is zeroed in at 100, 200, and 300 yards.

✻ Model L2000ST-W - features 27 in. barrel with conventional black wood laminate stock. Mfg. 1996 only.

> $4,400 $4,050 $3,600
>
> Last MSR was $4,795.

✻ Model L2000ST-WF Package - features 27 in. barrel with one conventional fiberglass and one black wood laminate stock. Disc. 1997.

> $4,875 $4,450 $4,050
>
> Last MSR was $5,295.

Grading	100%	98%	95%	90%	80%	70%	60%

✳ *Model L2000DG* - .375 Saturn or .416 Meteor cal. only, features Fibergrain stock finish, removable muzzle brake, 3 shot mag., 24 in. barrel, includes sling swivels, 10.1 lbs. New 1998.

MSR	$5,000	$4,450	$3,725	$3,000

✳ *Model L2000SA* - .243 Spitfire, .264 Phantom, .284 Tomahawk, .308 Patriot, .338 Galaxy, .358 Eagle, .375 Hellcat, or .416 Maverick cal., short action cals. only, lightweight mountain configuration with 24 in. fluted barrel, 6.8 lbs. New 1998.

MSR	$5,000	$4,450	$3,725	$3,000

✳ *Model L2000SLR* - features 28 in. extra heavy fluted barrel and conventional fiberglass stock, not chambered in .338 Titan. Disc. 1999.

$3,775	$3,400	$2,975

Last MSR was $4,195.

✳ *L2000SP* - 25 in. fluted barrel, thumbhole fiberglass stock, 7.8 lbs.

MSR	$5,000	$4,450	$3,725	$3,000

✳ *L2000SP-W* - 23 in. barrel, thumbhole black wood laminate stock.

$4,400	$4,050	$3,600

Last MSR was $4,795.

✳ *L2000SP-FW Package* - features 23 in. barrel with one thumbhole fiberglass and one black wood laminate thumbhole stock. Disc. 1997.

$4,875	$4,450	$4,050

Last MSR was $5,295.

LEBEAU-COURALLY

Current manufacturer established during 1865 and located in Liege, Belgium. Currently imported by William Larkin Moore, located in Scottsdale, AZ. Previously imported until 1998 by New England Arms Co. located in Kittery Point, ME.

Lebeau-Courally manufactures only best quality rifles and shotguns. Approximately 50 are manufactured annually. Prices do not include engraving. Please contact the importer directly for a firm quotation on a Lebeau-Courally rifle or shotgun.

RIFLES: SxS

BOXLOCK EJECTOR - 8x57JRS or 9.3x74R cal., Anson & Deeley boxlock, ejectors, select French walnut stock, quarter rib with ramp front sight, about 8 lbs. Importation disc. 1988, resumed 1993.

The importer or manufacturer should be contacted directly (see Trademark Index) for current information and prices regarding this model.

SIDELOCK EJECTOR EXPRESS RIFLE - 7x65R, 8x57JRS, 9.3x74R, .30-06, .375 H&H, .458 Win. Mag., .470 NE (new 1991), or .577 NE (new 1992) cal., chopper lump barrels, reinforced action, select French walnut stock, quarter rib with ramp front sight, engraving not included, approx. 8 lbs.

MSR	$41,000	$36,500	$31,000	$25,750	$20,000	$16,500	$13,750	$11,000

RIFLES: SINGLE SHOT

SINGLE SHOT - 6.5x57R, 7x65R, or other metric cals., best quality, boxlock or sidelock action.

The importer should be contacted directly (see Trademark Index) for current information and prices regarding this model.

SHOTGUNS: O/U

SIDELOCK - 12, 20, or 28 ga., Greener locking system.

MSR	$37,600	$33,800	$29,000	$24,500	$20,750	$17,500	$14,500	$11,850

Grading	100%	98%	95%	90%	80%	70%	60%

BOSS-VEREES - 12 or 20 ga., Boss pattern sidelock with low profile action, prices do not include engraving, top-of-the-line O/U individually made to customer specifications.

MSR $65,000	$59,000	$47,000	$41,000	$34,000	$28,000	$23,500	$18,950

SHOTGUNS: SxS

For currently manufactured shotguns - add $2,500 for single trigger. Older mfg. Lebeau-Courally shotguns have a completely different action and locking system than the newer models.

SOLOGNE - 12, 16, or 20 ga., Anson & Deeley boxlock action, various chokes and barrel lengths, select walnut, no engraving.

MSR $14,650	$13,250	$11,250	$9,350	$7,500	$6,250	$5,150	$4,350

GRAND RUSSE MODEL - grade up from Sologne Model.

MSR $18,820	$16,480	$13,000	$10,750	$8,475	$7,375	$5,250	$4,450

BOXLOCK EJECTOR - 12, 16, or 20 ga., choice of classic or rounded action, with or without sideplates, select French walnut stock, choice of numerous engraving patterns (optional), 26, 28, or 30 in. barrels, double trigger.

MSR $18,500	$16,750	$14,000	$11,500	$9,950	$8,500	$7,250	$6,000

✳ *Boxlock with sideplates*

MSR $15,500	$13,850	$11,650	$9,650	$7,700	$6,250	$5,150	$4,350

SIDELOCK EJECTOR - 12, 16, 20, 28 ga., or .410 bore, choice of classic or rounded action, chopper lump barrels, select French walnut stock, choice of numerous engraving patterns (optional), 26, 28, or 30 in. barrels, double triggers.

MSR $37,500	$33,000	$26,250	$22,500	$18,000	$15,000	$12,500	$11,000

LEFEVER ARMS COMPANY

Previous shotgun manufacturer located in Syracuse, NY circa 1885-1948.

100%	98%	95%	90%	80%	70%	60%	50%	40%	30%	20%	10%

SHOTGUNS: SxS

The Lefever was the first commercially successful hammerless double barrel shotgun made in America. They were made in Syracuse, NY from 1885-1916, at which time the company was acquired by Ithaca Gun Company. Ithaca made the Lefever after 1916. In 1921, the Box Lock Nitro Special was introduced and in 1934, the Lefever Grade A was introduced. Production of Lefever guns ceased in 1948.

The following is a percentage breakdown of gauges made between 1885-1916 (totaling 100%): 8 ga.-½%, 10 ga.-25%, 12 ga.-60%, 14 ga.-½%, 16 ga.-8%, 20 ga.-6%. Total manufacture was approx. 72,000 during this period. Damascus specimens of this trademark are worth approximately the same if in 60% or better original condition as their fluid steel barrel counterparts because of the rarity and desirability factors. Subtract 10%-30% on values with respective condition factors 50%- 10%. Prices shown for 90% and up condition are very difficult to evaluate and are meant as a guide only - any Lefever shotgun is rare and hard to evaluate if in over 95%.

SIDELOCK MODELS - 10, 12, 16, or 20 ga., 26-32 in. barrels, any choke, boxlock action (even though model nomenclature referred to sidelock model), cocking indicators on all but DS and DSE grades, double triggers standard, checkered straight or pistol grip stock, auto ejectors designated by letter E after grade. Mfg. 1885-1919.

Add 50% for 16 ga.
Add 100% for 20 ga.
Add 10% for SST.

✳ *I Grade*

$1,375	$1,250	$1,025	$925	$850	$775	$700	$630	$565	$500	$425	$350

100%	98%	95%	90%	80%	70%	60%	50%	40%	30%	20%	10%
✳ **DS Grade**											
$1,375	$1,250	$1,025	$925	$850	$775	$700	$630	$565	$500	$425	$350
✳ **DSE Grade**											
$1,800	$1,525	$1,250	$1,100	$950	$850	$775	$715	$650	$600	$540	$475
✳ **H Grade**											
$1,975	$1,650	$1,300	$1,200	$1,100	$1,000	$950	$900	$800	$750	$650	$550
✳ **HE Grade**											
$2,750	$2,350	$1,800	$1,600	$1,400	$1,250	$1,100	$1,000	$900	$850	$800	$700
✳ **G Grade**											
N/A	$1,975	$1,600	$1,500	$1,400	$1,300	$1,200	$1,100	$1,000	$900	$800	$600
✳ **GE Grade**											
N/A	$2,850	$2,200	$1,800	$1,700	$1,500	$1,400	$1,300	$1,200	$1,100	$1,000	$900
✳ **F Grade**											
N/A	$2,150	$1,700	$1,600	$1,500	$1,400	$1,100	$1,000	$900	$800	$700	$650
✳ **FE Grade**											
N/A	$2,950	$2,400	$2,000	$1,800	$1,600	$1,400	$1,300	$1,100	$1,000	$900	$800
✳ **E Grade**											
N/A	$2,700	$2,300	$2,100	$1,900	$1,800	$1,600	$1,400	$1,200	$1,100	$900	$800
✳ **EE Grade**											
N/A	$3,800	$3,200	$3,000	$2,700	$2,500	$2,300	$2,100	$1,900	$1,800	$1,600	$1,500
✳ **D Grade**											
N/A	$3,300	$2,500	$2,200	$2,000	$1,800	$1,600	$1,500	$1,400	$1,200	$1,100	$1,000
✳ **DE Grade**											
N/A	$4,850	$4,000	$3,700	$3,200	$2,700	$2,200	$2,000	$1,800	$1,600	$1,400	$1,200
✳ **C Grade**											
N/A	$4,850	$4,000	$3,200	$2,700	$2,400	$2,200	$2,000	$1,900	$1,800	$1,600	$1,300
✳ **CE Grade**											
N/A	N/A	$7,000	$5,500	$4,700	$4,200	$4,000	$3,400	$3,000	$2,500	$2,100	$1,750
✳ **B Grade**											
N/A	N/A	$4,850	$4,425	$4,050	$3,675	$3,175	$$2,750	$2,600	$2,400	$2,200	$2,000
✳ **BE Grade**											
N/A	N/A	$8,250	$7,500	$6,750	$5,950	$5,100	$4,400	$3,700	$3,500	$3,200	$3,000
✳ **A grade** - auto ejectors standard.											
N/A	N/A	$15,500	$13,750	$11,250	$9,250	$8,150	$7,200	$6,300	$5,400	$4,700	$4,200
✳ **AA grade** - auto ejectors standard.											
N/A	N/A	$21,750	$18,750	$15,500	$12,750	$10,250	$8,250	$7,150	$6,500	$6,000	$5,500

✳ ***Optimus Grade*** - auto ejectors standard. Extreme rarity precludes accurate percentage pricing.

✳ ***Thousand Dollar Grade*** - auto ejectors standard. Extreme rarity precludes accurate percentage pricing.

Grading	100%	98%	95%	90%	80%	70%	60%

NITRO SPECIAL - 12, 16, 20 ga., or .410 bore, 26-32 in. barrels, various chokes, boxlock, extractors, checkered pistol grip stock. Mfg. 1921-1948.

	100%	98%	95%	90%	80%	70%	60%
	$450	$395	$350	$300	$250	$225	$200

Add $75 for ST.
Add 20% for 16 ga.
Add 50% for 20 ga.
Add 200% for .410 bore.
Add 50%+ for beavertail.

Grading	100%	98%	95%	90%	80%	70%	60%

GRADE A FIELD MODEL - 12, 16, 20 ga., or .410 bore, 26-32 in. barrels, various chokes, boxlock, checkered pistol grip stock. Mfg. 1934-1942.

	100%	98%	95%	90%	80%	70%	60%
	$880	$770	$715	$660	$550	$495	$440

> Add 33% for auto ejectors.
> Add $75 for ST.
> Add $75 for beavertail forearm.
> Add 20% for 16 ga.
> Add 50% for 20 ga.
> Add 200% for .410 bore.

GRADE A SKEET MODEL - similar to Grade A, with 26 in. skeet bore barrels, auto ejector, single trigger and beavertail forearm standard.

	100%	98%	95%	90%	80%	70%	60%
	$1,155	$1,045	$990	$935	$825	$770	$715

> Add 50% for 16 ga.
> Add 100% for 20 ga.
> Add 200% for .410 bore.

SHOTGUNS: SINGLE BARREL

TRAP GUN - 12 ga. only, 30 or 32 in. VR barrel, full choke, boxlock, auto ejector, checkered pistol grip stock. Disc. 1942.

	100%	98%	95%	90%	80%	70%	60%
	$550	$440	$385	$330	$275	$250	$195

LONG RANGE FIELD - 12, 16, 20 ga., or .410 bore, 26-32 in. barrel, boxlock, extractor, checkered pistol grip stock. Disc. 1942.

	100%	98%	95%	90%	80%	70%	60%
	$330	$275	$250	$220	$165	$140	$120

LEFEVER, D.M. & SON

Previous manufacturer located in Bowling Green, OH circa 1901-1906.

SHOTGUNS

"Uncle Dan" Lefever, founder of Lefever Arms, designed and manufactured the first breech loading double hammerless shotgun made in the U.S. Production started in 1872 and continued in the Syracuse, NY plant until he sold his interest in the Lefever Arms Company during the early 1900s. He then moved to Ohio and started another factory under the name D.M. Lefever & Son. After his death a few years later the Ohio factory was closed, while his old company (Lefever Arms Co.) continued manufacturing Lefevers until being sold to Ithaca Gun Company in the early 1920s. From that point, Lefever Arms Co. was a branch of Ithaca and continued to make shotguns until shortly after WWII.

Total production on D.M. Lefever shotguns between 1901-1904 totaled less than 1,200. Because of their inherent rarity, values listed show only 10%-80% condition specimens. D.M. Lefever specimens are so rare in 80%+ condition that prices cannot be accurately ascertained.

100%	98%	95%	90%	80%	70%	60%	50%	40%	30%	20%	10%

SHOTGUNS: SxS

NEW LEFEVER MODEL - 12, 16, or 20 ga., boxlock action, any length barrel and choke on order, auto ejectors standard on all grades except O Excelsior, double triggers standard on all except Uncle Dan grade, optional single triggers available, checkered walnut pistol grip or straight stock, grades differ as to engraving, wood, checkering and overall quality. Mfg. 1904-1906.

> Add 50% for 16 ga.
> Add 10% for SST.

✳ O Excelsior Grade

100%	98%	95%	90%	80%	70%	60%	50%	40%	30%	20%	10%
N/A	N/A	N/A	N/A	$2,365	$1,925	$1,650	$1,475	$1,350	$1,175	$950	$750

100%	98%	95%	90%	80%	70%	60%	50%	40%	30%	20%	10%

✳ Excelsior Grade w/ejectors

| N/A | N/A | N/A | N/A | $2,640 | $2,310 | $1,925 | $1,595 | $1,450 | $1,300 | $1,045 | $825 |

✳ F Grade, No. 9

| N/A | N/A | N/A | N/A | N/A | $2,640 | $2,310 | $1,925 | $1,725 | $1,575 | $1,300 | $1,000 |

✳ E Grade, No. 8

| N/A | N/A | N/A | N/A | N/A | $3,350 | $2,875 | $2,300 | $2,075 | $1,800 | $1,575 | $1,250 |

✳ D Grade, No. 7

| N/A | N/A | N/A | N/A | N/A | $4,125 | $3,850 | $3,375 | $2,975 | $2,750 | $2,500 | $1,925 |

✳ C Grade, No. 6

| N/A | N/A | N/A | N/A | N/A | $4,400 | $4,125 | $3,850 | $3,575 | $3,175 | $2,750 | $2,420 |

✳ B Grade, No. 5

| N/A | N/A | N/A | N/A | N/A | $5,500 | $4,600 | $4,275 | $3,975 | $3,750 | $3,450 | $3,100 |

✳ AA Grade, No. 4

| N/A | N/A | N/A | N/A | N/A | $7,700 | $6,600 | $5,500 | $4,850 | $4,400 | $3,700 | $3,350 |

UNCLE DAN GRADE - extreme rarity factor precludes accurate pricing.

SHOTGUNS: SINGLE BARREL TRAP

TRAP GUN - 12 ga., 26-32 in. full choke, auto ejector, boxlock, checkered pistol grip stock. Mfg. 1904-1906.

Extreme rarity factor precludes accurate pricing.

LE FORGERON

Previous manufacturer located in Belgium. Previously imported and distributed by Midwest Gun Sport in Zebulon, NC.

Grading	100%	98%	95%	90%	80%	70%	60%

RIFLES: SxS

MODEL 6020 - 9.3x74R cal., boxlock action, beavertail forearm, pistol grip stock.

	$4,450	$4,025	$3,750	$3,475	$3,100	$2,800	$2,550

Last MSR was $4,900.

Add $700 for sideplates (Model 6040).

MODEL 6030 - sidelock action, engraved action with deluxe French walnut stock and forearm.

	$8,475	$7,900	$7,100	$6,300	$5,500	$4,700	$4,000

Last MSR was $8,950.

SHOTGUNS: SxS

Prices represent the last import information available (1989).

BOXLOCK EJECTOR - 20 or 28 ga. only, with or without sideplates, select French walnut stock, choice of engraving patterns (optional), single trigger.

	$3,975	$3,650	$3,325	$2,995	$2,600	$2,250	$1,900

Last MSR was $4,400.

Add $1,000 for sideplates.

SIDELOCK EJECTOR - 20 or 28 ga. only, select French walnut stock, choice of engraving patterns (optional), rounded action, single trigger.

	$10,200	$9,250	$8,500	$7,900	$7,100	$6,300	$5,500

Last MSR was $11,600.

Grading	100%	98%	95%	90%	80%	70%	60%

LE FRANCAIS PISTOLS

Previously manufactured by Francais d'Armes Et Cycles located in Saint Etienne, France.

PISTOLS: SEMI-AUTO

STAFF OFFICER MODEL AUTOMATIC - .25 ACP cal., 2½ in. barrel, blue, fixed sights, rubber grips, no visible cocking piece. Mfg. 1914-disc.

	$275	$230	$200	$165	$140	$115	$80

POLICEMAN MODEL AUTOMATIC - .32 ACP cal., double action, 7 shot, 3½ in. barrel, hinged finned barrel, blue, fixed sights, rubber grips. Mfg. 1950s.

	$850	$800	$700	$575	$435	$350	$275

ARMY MODEL AUTOMATIC - 9mm Browning Long cal., 8 shot, 5 in. barrel, blue, fixed sights, checkered walnut grips. Mfg. 1928-1938. Early model with tapered barrel, later model with finned barrel.

	$1,500	$1,100	$850	$700	$550	$425	$350

LEITNER-WISE RIFLE CO. INC.

Current manufacturer located in Alexandra, VA beginning 1999. Dealer sales.

RIFLES: SEMI-AUTO

LW 15.22 - .22 LR or .22 Mag. cal., paramilitary configuration patterned after the AR-15, forged upper and lower receivers, choice of carry handle or flat-top upper receiver, forward bolt assist, last shot hold open, 16½ or 20 in. barrel, 10 or 25 shot mag. New 2000.

MSR	$775		$725	$650	$575	$525	$475	$435	$400

Add $20 for A2 carrying handle.

LW 15.499 - .499 (12.5x40mm) cal., receiver action patterned after the AR-15, mil spec standards, 16½ in. barrel, flat-top receiver, 5 or 10 shot mag. New 2000.

MSR	$865		$800	$750	$675	$600	$550	$500	$475

LES BAER CUSTOM, INC.

Current manufacturer and customizer established in 1992, and located in Hillsdale, IL. Dealer sales only.

PISTOLS: SEMI-AUTO

Les Baer has been customizing and manufacturing M1911 type pistols for decades. The company should be contacted directly (see Trademark Index) for an up-to-date price sheet and catalog on their extensive line-up of high quality competition/combat pistols that range in price from $1,390 - $2,690, except for Presentation Grades. A wide range of competition parts and related gunsmithing services are also available.

RIFLES: SEMI-AUTO

CUSTOM ULTIMATE AR .223 - .223 Rem. cal., individual rifles are custom built with no expense spared, everything made in-house ensuring top quality and tolerances, all models are guaranteed to shoot ½ - ¾ in. MOA groups, various configurations include Varmint Model, Super Varmint Model, NRA Match Rifle, Super Match Model (new 2002), M4 Flattop Model, and IPSC Action Model. New 2001.

MSR	$2,195		$2,000	$1,700	$1,500	$1,250	$1,050	$925	$800

Add $800 - $1,100 for scope package (includes Leupold Vari-X III 4.5-14x40mm scope). Subtract approx. $200 for Super Varmint Model.

Make/Model	Qty. Made	Year Issue	Retail Price

LEW HORTON DIST. CO.

Current firearms distributor located in Westboro, MA. While Lew Horton is not a manufacturer or an importer, this company has been responsible for many special and limited editions that are listed with quanities, but without prices, since they may vary greatly from region to region. Special/Limited Editions began in 1983.

SPECIAL/LIMITED EDITIONS

BERETTA

Make/Model	Qty. Made	Year Issue	Retail Price
Lady Beretta	100	1985	$285

COLT MODELS

Make/Model	Qty. Made	Year Issue	Retail Price
SAA Horse Pistol	100	1983	$1,100
Presidential - Gold SAA & Det. Spec. w/Gold Eye	600	1985	$525
Colt Boa (includes complete production run of 4 & 6 in. barrel)	600	1985	$525
Ultimate Officer's .45 ACP	500	1989	$777
Lt. Commander .45 ACP	800	1985	$590
Combat Cobra 2½ in.	1,000	1987	$500
Lady Colt (MK IV .380 ACP)	1,000	1989	$547
Night Commander .45 ACP	250	1989	$725
El Presidente .38 Super Govt.	350	1990	$800
El Comandante .38 Super Govt.	500	1991	$800
El General .38 Super Govt.	500	1991	$850
El Capitan .38 Super	500	1991	$875
Detective Special	100	1992	$430
Elite Ten/Forty	100	1992	$900
El Patron	500	1992	$850
El Jefe	500	1992	$849
El Dorado	750	1992	$1,099
El Teniente	400	1992	$1,037
El Teniente	300	2001	N/A
El Coronel	750	1993	$900
Classic Gold Cup	300	1993	$1,285
Classic Single Action	180	1993	$680
Night Officer	350	1993	$680
El Presidente Premier Edition	10	1993	$3,000
Classic Government	300	1993	$965
Night Government	300	1993	$705
El Caballero	500	1994	$986
El Potro	500	1994	$1,025
Frontier Six Shooter	100	1994	$1,849
McCormick Factory Racer	500	1994	$1,149
Springfield Armory Bicentennial Edition	400	1994	$1,000
Springfield Armory Premier Bicentennial	200	1994	$1,213
Classic 45 Special Edition	500	1995	$960
Comp Commander .45 ACP Ported	350	1998	$889
Defender Custom .45 ACP 3in. w/4 Ports	100	1998	$900
Delta 98 10mm 5in. Matte SS	100	1998	$800
El Aquila Supreme .38 Sup. Engraved	20	1999	$3,000
El Aquila 39 Sup. 5 in. RB	350	1999	$1,000
El Cabo .38 Sup. 5 in. Bright SS	350	1999	$1,200
El Campcon .38 Super Blue	550	1997	$870
El Centauro .38 Sup. BTS	350	1997	$798
El Embajador .38 Sup. BTS/Gold	350	1998	$1,000
El General 5 Star Deluxe 38 Sup. Engr.	10	1997	$2,000
El Jefe Supremo Supreme 38 Sup. Engr.	20	1999	$3,000

Make/Model	Qty. Made	Year Issue	Retail Price
El Jefe Supremo 38 Sup BSTS/Fire Bl.	350	1999	$1,410
El Oficial .38 Sup R/Blue w/gold	450	1998	$1,003
El Sargento .38 Sup 5 RB/SS	350	1999	$1,000
El Soldado 38 Super 5 Ryl Blue/Pearlite grips	350	2000	$1,020
El Soldado Supreme 38 Super A Engraved	20	2000	$2,996
El Soldado Supreme	20	2001	N/A
El Soldado Supreme Proposed	20	2001	N/A
El Senador	350	2001	N/A
El Senador Supreme	20	2001	N/A
El Toro 38 Super Bl w/jeweled parts	350	2000	$1,020
El Toro	350	2001	N/A
El Toro Supreme	20	2001	N/A
El Obra Maestra .38 Super Royal Blue/Gold	350	2001	$1,130
El Matadore .38 Super 5 in. Bright Stainless w/Gold	350	2001	$1,425
El Rey Hi Polish Stainless Steel Blue .38 Super	350	2001	$1,050
McCormick Combat Cmdr 45 Engr.	50	1995	$1,213
McCormick Combat Cmdr 45 Chrome	500	1995	$1,073
McCormick Officer Cmdr 45 Chrome	300	1995	$1,073
Night Officer II Chrm 45 Night Sight	100	1994	$829
Night Officer III SS/Matte 45	200	1996	$810
Officers Ultimate .45 ACP Bl/SS	500	1995	$900
Officers Ultimate .45 ACP Engr.	10	1995	$1,995
SAA CC/B Mop. Std. Eng.	15	1999	$5,345
SAA .45 LC Nickel Bird's Head Mother-of-Pearl, Std. C	30	2001	$5,715
U.S. Shooting Team .45 ACP	750	1995	$1,150

EUROPEAN AMERICAN ARMORY

Make/Model	Qty. Made	Year Issue	Retail Price
Witness Competitor 45 Ported	100	1998	$460
Witness Competitor Polymer 45 Ported	100	1998	$460
Witness Defender II 45 Ported	100	1998	$460
Witness Defender Polymer 45 Ported	100	1998	$496
Witness Tactical .40 S&W 12rd	300	1997	$400
Witness Tactical .45 ACP 10rd	300	1997	$400

H&R 1871, INC.

Make/Model	Qty. Made	Year Issue	Retail Price
999 Premier Edition	100 pr.	1993	$345

MOSSBERG

Make/Model	Qty. Made	Year Issue	Retail Price
Night Persuader Special Edition	300	1990	N/A

REMINGTON

Make/Model	Qty. Made	Year Issue	Retail Price
Model 541J Curly Maple	500	1994	$500

SIGARMS

Make/Model	Qty. Made	Year Issue	Retail Price
P220 Premium Edition .45 ACP	200	1994	$850

SMITH & WESSON - Lew Horton is a major distributor of S&W's Heritage Series and Performance Center models. Please contact Lew Horton directly to find out more information on this wide variety of handguns, including current availability and pricing.

Make/Model	Qty. Made	Year Issue	Retail Price
Model 25-3 Lew Horton Special	100	1977	$500
Model 29-3 Lew Horton Special	5,000	1984	$425
Model 629-3 Lew Horton Special	5,000	-	$400
Model 24-3 Lew Horton Special	5,000	1983-84	$380
Model 686 Lew Horton Special	-	1984	$450
Model 657-3 Lew Horton Special	5,000	1986	$410
Model 624-2 Lew Horton Special	7,000	1986-87	$395
Model 640 Carry Comp	250	1991	$750
.40 Compensated	150	1992	$1,699
.40 Tactical	200	1992	$1,499
Shorty Forty	-	1992	$950
Model 629 Hunter	200	1992	$1,234
Model 629 Carry Comp	300	1992	$1,000
Model 686 Carry Comp 4 in.	300	1992	$1,000
Model 657 Classic Hunter	350	1993	$545
Model 356 Shorty	-	1993	$999

Make/Model	Qty. Made	Year Issue	Retail Price
Model 356 Tactical	-	1993	$1,350
Model 629 Hunter II	200	1993	$1,234
Model 629 Carry Comp II	100	1993	$1,000
Model 686 Carry Comp 3 in.	300	1993	$1,000
Model 686 Competitor	400	1993	$1,100
Model 686 Hunter	200	1993	$1,153
Model 5906 Shorty Nine	200	1993	$999
Model 60 Carry Comp	300	1993	$800
Model 629 Unfluted	300	1993	$1,234
Model 629 Hunter III	300	1994	$1,234
Springfield Armory Bicentennial Edition	500	1994	$775
Model 640 Paxton Quigley	250	1994	$800
Model 625 Classic Snub	300	1994	$603
Model 629 Classic Hunter	500	1994	$1,234
Model 629 Quad-magnaported .44 Mag.	150	1994	$900
Shorty Forty Mark II	150	1995	$999
Shorty .40 Mark III	500	1997	$1,025
Shorty .45	225	1997	$1,096
Shorty .45 Mark II	N/A	1997	N/A
Model 625 Hunter .45 LC Fluted	150	1997	$1,234
Model 629 Hunter .44 Mag. Unfluted	500	1997	$1,234
Model 686 Hunter 7 Shot Unfluted	300	1997	$1,234
Model 640 Quadport .357 Mag. 2 in. Brl	500	1997	$836
Model 681 Quadport .357 Mag. 7 Shot	300	1997	$700
PC M627 357 2 5/8 in. 8 shot RRWO Unfluted	450	2000	$1,025
Model 686 7 Shot Night Sight	300	1997	$1,000
F Comp. 3 in. Comp. Barrel	500	1997	$800
Model 629 Classic Carry 3 in. Unfluted	300	1997	$590
M625 .45 LC 3 in. Rosewood Red ramp WO	400	1998	$755
M625 45 Colt 3 FL Rosewood RRWO	150	2000	$755
M627 Classic Hunter 41 Mg 6.5 in. wood flt.	150	1997	$614
M627 Classic Hunter 41 Mg 6.5 in. wood unfl	400	1997	$614
PC M629 44 6 in. Hunter w/barrel cut out, unfluted	350	2000	$1,300
PC M629 44 12 in. barrel FL w/sling, Bomar sights	400	2000	$1,059
PC M1006 Classic SER 10mm 5 9 shot	28	1998	$550
PC M27 .357 Mag. 5 in. fluted cyl. SB	16	1999	$670
PC M29 Classic SER .44 Mag. 7.5 wood c/s	19	1998	$1,060
PC M41 Classic Ser .22 LR 7 S&W sights	14	1998	$801
PC M4516 Classic Ser .45 ACP 3 3/4	7	1998	$866
PC M4563 CQB .45 ACP 4 Alloy Frame	100	1998	$1,235
PC M4563 CQB .45 ACP 4 two-tone	200	1998	$1,235
PC M4566 CQB .45 ACP 4 SS frame	100	1998	$1,235
PC M4567 Classic Ser .45 4.5 two-tone	14	1998	$1,010
PC M627 Htr .357 6 in. 8 shot unf. wood	200	1997	$1,060
PC M627 .357 Mg. 5 in 8 shot ported	100	1997	$1,050
PC M627 .357 2 5/8 8 shot RRWO unflt.	300	1999	$1,025
PC M627 .357 5 in. 8 shot unf. wood cmbt	1,200	1997	$1,000
PC M627 .357 5 in. 8 shot unf. rosewood	200	1998	$1,000
PC M627 .357 6.5 in. 8 shot fluted rosewood	200	1998	$1,025
PC M629 .44 Mg. 6½ in. flt. 6 shot RMB	200	1998	$1,020
PC M629 .44 Mg. 2 5/8 in. 6 sht rosewood	300	1999	$1,026
PC M629 6 Htr w/bbl CO Unf port	100	1999	$1,060
PC M657 Classic Ser .41 Mg. 3	7	1994	$550
PC M657 Classic Ser .41 Mg. 4	25	1998	$550
PC M657 41 Mg. 6½ in. FL 6 sht	200	1998	$1,020
PC M686 .357 3 in. 7 sht ss night sights	500	1996	$1,000
PC M686 .357 6 in. 7 sht Hntr w/port	175	1996	$1,024
PC M686 .357 Mg. 7 sht profile bbl	125	1998	$1,025
PC M9 Shorty 9 MKII 9mm Compact	150	1995	$1,050
M15 .38 Spl. 4 in. color case blue	200	2001	$770
M15 .38 Spl. 4 in. nickel	200	2001	$750
M15 .38 Spl. 5 in. nickel McGivern	150	2001	$1,070

Make/Model	Qty. Made	Year Issue	Retail Price
M15 .38 Spl. 6 in. blue McGivern	150	2001	$1,040
M15 .38 Spl. 6 in. color case blue	100	2001	$1,070
M17 .22 LR 6 in. AS blue	200	2001	$1,040
M17 .22 LR 6 1/2 in. color case blue	150	2001	$1,070
M24 .44 Spl.6 1/2 in. color case frame	300	2001	$1,110
M24 .44 Spl.6 1/2 in. fluted blue	150	2001	$1,050
M25 (1917) .45 ACP 5 1/2 in. 6 shot	200	2001	$1,047
M25 .45 Colt 6 1/2 in. color case blue frame	150	2001	$1,111
M25 .45 Colt 6 1/2 in. fluted blue	150	2001	$1,050
M25 (1917) .45 ACP 5 1/2 in. color case blue	100	2001	$1,110
M25 (1917) .45 ACP 5 1/2 in. Military	150	2001	$1,050
M29 .44 Mag. 6 1/2 in. blue	250	2001	$1,045
M29 .44 Mag. 6 1/2 in. nickel	200	2001	$1,070
Schofield M3 .45 S&W	100	2001	$1,520
Schofield 7 in. bright nickel	100	2001	$1,520

SPRINGFIELD

Night Light Compact 1911 A1 Lightweight	500	1997	$749
Night Light Standard 1911 A1 Lightweight	300	1997	$749
M1911 Ltw Compact .45 ACP bi-tone 7rd	125	1998	$675
M1911 Ltw Std. .45 ACP bi-tone 8rd	300	1998	$675

SAVAGE

10FP Tactical .223 Rem. Short Action	200	1999	$492
10FP Tactical .308 Win. HB 20	550	1999	$500
30 ^ Joshua Stevens .22 LR	250	2001	$400

TAURUS

Model PT-92AF	250	1990	N/A
Model 85 3 in. Ported Blue	500	1995	$229
Model 85 3 in. Ported Stainless	500	1995	$349

In addition to the special/limited editions listed, Lew Horton also subcontracted special editions that were sold from company flyers and other promotional materials. They include the following Smith & Wesson Models - Classic Hunter M29 (500 mfg. 1989), Model 63 2 in. (500 mfg. 1989), Model 36 2nd Amendment (200 mfg. 1989), Model 60 25th Anniversary (100 mfg. 1989), Model 629 Classic Hunter (mfg. 1986), Model 5967 (500 mfg. 1990), and the Model 3914 (200 mfg. 1990). There are two Remington models - the M1100 Special Field (200 mfg. 1987-88) and the M700 BDL .257 Roberts cal. (500 mfg. 1990). There are three Colt models - the Combat Python (750 mfg. 1987-88), the Pocketlite (350 mfg. 1989), and the Custom Cobra Stainless Sets (2 sizes, mfg. 1989).

LIBERATOR

Previously manufactured by the Guide Lamp Corporation (division of General Motors) circa 1942.

Grading	100%	98%	95%	90%	80%	70%	60%

PISTOLS: SINGLE SHOT

LIBERATOR PISTOL - .45 ACP cal., simplistic design and action utilizing nonstrategic WWII materials, mfg. for European resistance movement during WWII (most were issued or air-dropped in Europe), each gun was individually packaged in a paraffin- coated cardboard box which included the gun, a graphics only (no English) instruction sheet, wood ram rod, and 10 rounds of .45 ACP ammo stored in the gun's butt, 4 in. smooth bore barrel, sheet steel stamping mfg. with welds, 1 million mfg. 1942 only.

$1,175	$995	$850	$725	$650	$525	$450

Add $500 if in original box with instructions.

Even though 1 million of these pistols were mfg., remaining specimens brought into the U.S. with the listed accessories are rare since all were delivered overseas. While the Liberator's appearance is crude, remember that the entire production run (1 million) was mfg. and ready for overseas shipment in 13 weeks.

Grading	100%	98%	95%	90%	80%	70%	60%

LIBERTY

Current trademark imported beginning 1997 by K.B.I., Inc. located in Harrisburg, PA. Distributor and dealer sales.

REVOLVERS: SAA

FRONTIER MODEL - .38-40 Win. (disc. 1998), .357 Mag. (disc. 1998, reintroduced 2000 only), .44- 40 WCF (disc. 2000), or .45 LC cal., 4¾, 5½, or 7½ in. barrel, case hardened, bright nickel, or antique silver (new 1999) frame, choice of brass or steel backstrap and trigger guard, mfg. by Uberti. Imported 1997-2001.

	100%	98%	95%	90%	80%	70%	60%
	$295	$250	$235	$210	$195	$175	$160

Last MSR was $339.

Add $45 for steel backstrap and trigger guard.
Add $80 for antique silver finish (new 1999).
Add $25 for bright nickel finish (.44-40 WCF or .45 LC only).

TARGET MODEL - similar to Frontier Model, except is not available in .357 Mag. cal., and has adj. rear sight. Imported 1997-98.

	100%	98%	95%	90%	80%	70%	60%
	$300	$265	$240	$220	$200	$180	$165

Last MSR was $319.

BISLEY MODEL - .44-40 WCF or .45 LC cal., features Bisley grip configuration, 4¾, 5½, or 7½ in. barrel, case hardened or bright nickel finish, steel backstrap and trigger guard. Limited importation 1999 only.

	100%	98%	95%	90%	80%	70%	60%
	$415	$365	$325	$295	$260	$230	$200

Last MSR was $459.

Add $60 for bright nickel finish.

RIFLES: LEVER ACTION

MODEL 1892 CARBINE - .357 Mag. or .45 LC cal., choice of case hardened or brass plated receiver, 20 in. round barrel. Limited importation 2000 only.

	100%	98%	95%	90%	80%	70%	60%
	$595	$525	$475	$425	$395	$360	$330

Last MSR was $665.

Add $15 for brass plated receiver.

MODEL 1892 RIFLE - .357 Mag., .44-40 WCF, or .45 LC cal., choice of case hardened, brass plated, or antique silver finished receiver, 24 in. octagon barrel. Limited importation 2000 only.

	100%	98%	95%	90%	80%	70%	60%
	$610	$535	$485	$430	$400	$360	$330

Last MSR was $680.

RIFLES: REPRODUCTIONS

SHARPS TRAPDOOR CARBINE/RIFLE/BUSINESS - .45-70 Govt. cal., case hardened receiver finish, choice of 22 (Carbine), 28 (Rifle), or 32 (Business, limited importation 2000 only) in. round barrel, single or double set triggers. Imported from Pedersoli 2000-2001.

	100%	98%	95%	90%	80%	70%	60%
	$675	$575	$500	$450	$400	$350	$300

Last MSR was $769.

Add $20 for Hunter rifle.
Add $60 for Business Model (limited importation 2000 only).

ROLLING BLOCK CARBINE/RIFLE - .357 Mag., .45 LC, or .45-70 Govt. cal., case hardened receiver finish, 22 in. round (Carbine) or 28 in. octagon (Rifle) barrel. Imported from Pedersoli 2000-2001.

	100%	98%	95%	90%	80%	70%	60%
	$615	$550	$475	$425	$375	$325	$275

Last MSR was $689.

Add $10 for Rifle.

Grading	100%	98%	95%	90%	80%	70%	60%

SPRINGFIELD TRAPDOOR CARBINE/RIFLE - .45-70 Govt. cal., case hardened receiver finish, 22 (Carbine) or 26 (Rifle) in. round barrel. Imported from Pedersoli 2000-2001.

	$725	$650	$600	$550	$475	$425	$375

Last MSR was $815.

> **Add $34 for rifle with 26 in. barrel.**

RIFLES: SxS

LIGHTNING EXPRESS DOUBLE RIFLE - .44-40 WCF, .45 LC, or .45-70 Govt. cal., exposed hammers, 22 in. barrels, choice of case hardened, bright nickel (disc.) or antique silver (new 2000) finish. Limited importation 1999-2000.

	$750	$650	$550	$475	$425	$375	$325

Last MSR was $840.

> **Add $40 for antique silver finish.**

SHOTGUNS: SxS

LIBERTY COACH GUN - 12 ga. only, exposed hammers, 20 or 24 (disc. 2000, reintroduced 2002) in. barrels, choice of case hardened or antique silver finish, fixed chokes (cyl./cyl., 20 in. barrels only, or IC/M, 24 in. barrels only). Importation began 1999.

MSR	$659	$575	$485	$435	$375	$345	$315	$285

* *Liberty Coach Gun/Express Rifle Combination Set* - includes 20 in. 12 ga. barrels, and choice of 22 in. rifle barrels in any Lightning Express cal., blue finish only. Limited importation 1999 only.

	$1,025	$875	$750	$625	$550	$475	$425

Last MSR was $1,159.

LIBERTY ARMS WORKS, INC.

Previous manufacturer located in West Chester, PA circa 1991-1996.

PISTOLS: SEMI-AUTO

L.A.W. ENFORCER - .22 LR, 9mm Para., 10mm, .40 S&W (new 1994), or .45 ACP cal., patterned after the Ingram MAC 10, single action, 6¼ in. threaded barrel, closed bolt operation, manual safety, 10 (C/B 1994) or 30* shot mag., 5 lbs. 1 oz. Mfg. 1991-96.

	$575	$500	$450	$415	$385	$335	$295

Last MSR was $545.

LIEGEOISE D'ARMES

Previous manufacturer located in Belgium.

Small manufacturer that specialized in boxlock shotguns, normally engraved and with ejectors. Prices usually range from $600-$1,200, depending on condition and engraving.

LIGNOSE (BERGMAN)

Previous manufacturer located in Suhl, Germany.

PISTOLS: SEMI-AUTO

EINHAND MODEL 2A POCKET AUTOMATIC - 6.35mm/.25 ACP cal., 6 shot, 2 in. barrel, blue, rubber grips, can be cocked by rearward pressure on triggerguard.

	$350	$295	$225	$165	$140	$110	$85

MODEL 3 POCKET AUTOMATIC - similar to 3A, except without one hand cocking trigger guard.

	$250	$220	$195	$165	$140	$110	$85

MODEL 3A POCKET AUTOMATIC - similar to 2A, except longer grip, 9 shot capacity.

	$395	$325	$250	$200	$140	$110	$85

Grading	100%	98%	95%	90%	80%	70%	60%

MODEL 2 POCKET AUTOMATIC - similar to 2A, without one hand cocking triggerguard.

	$325	$265	$215	$165	$90	$75	$55

LILIPUT

Previous trademark manufactured by August Menz, located in Suhl, Germany.

PISTOLS: SEMI-AUTO

4.25mm cal. - 4.25mm centerfire Liliput cal. (shoots 12 grain bullet), blue or nickel finish, limited 1920s mfg.

	$700	$550	$425	$385	$340	$300	$280

6.35mm cal. - .25 ACP cal., mfg. in large quantities pre-WWII.

	$250	$200	$140	$110	$90	$75	$55

LITTLE SHARPS RIFLE MFG.

Current rifle manufacturer established in 1996, and located in Big Sandy, MT. Consumer direct sales.

RIFLES: SINGLE SHOT

LITTLE SHARPS RIFLE - various cals. between .22 LR and .38-55 WCF, features scaled down frame for smaller cals. (20% smaller than original Sharps), octagon barrel. New 1998.

MSR	$2,950	$2,950	$2,600	$2,250	$1,850	$1,550	$1,275	$1,050

Add $100+ for English walnut wood upgrade.
Add $250 for set trigger.

LJUNGMAN

Previously manufactured by Carl Gustaf, located in Eskilstuna, Sweden.

RIFLES: SEMI-AUTO

AG 42 - 6.5x55mm Swedish cal., 10 shot mag., wood stock, tangent rear sight, hooded front, bayonet lug, designed in 1941. This was the first mass produced, direct gas operated rifle. This weapon was also used by the Egyptian armed forces and was known as the Hakim, and chambered in 8x57mm Mauser.

	$850	$700	$600	$495	$450	$400	$365

LJUTIC INDUSTRIES, INC.

Current shotgun manufacturer established circa 1955 and located in Yakima, WA. Dealer direct sales only.

Prior to 1960, Ljutic Industries, Inc. was doing business as Ljutic Gun Co.

SHOTGUNS: O/U

LM 6 - 12 ga. only, supplied with one set of O/U barrels, deluxe wood and checkering, separated barrels on O/U.

MSR	$19,995		$19,995	$15,750	$11,000	$9,250	$8,400	$7,500	$6,600

Add $6,000 for extra set of O/U barrels.
Add $6,000 for top single barrel (includes 2 pull trigger groups, and 2 forearms).

DYNA BI GUN - 12 ga. only, includes one set of O/U barrels, deluxe checkered walnut stock and forearm. New 2000.

MSR	$15,995		$15,995	$12,000	$9,250	$8,400	$7,500	$6,600	$5,700

Add $2,000 for stainless steel construction.

Grading	100%	98%	95%	90%	80%	70%	60%

SHOTGUNS: SEMI-AUTO

BI MATIC AUTO LOADER - 12 ga., 2 shot, 26-32 in. barrels, low recoil, trap or skeet models available, stock and choking to customer specifications. Limited mfg. until 1999.

	$5,995	$4,450	$2,500	$2,100	$1,750	$1,250	$900

Last MSR was $5,995.

Add $2,000 for extra barrel.
Add $750 for extra release trigger.

SHOTGUNS: SINGLE BARREL TRAP

To date approx. 12,750 target shotguns have been manufactured total (all models).

DYNATRAP MODEL - 12 ga., 33 in. barrel, full choke, push button opening, extractor, trap stock.

	$2,500	$2,150	$1,600	$1,475	$1,300	$1,200	$1,100

Add $300 for release trigger.
Add $400 for extra release trigger.
Add $250 for extra pull trigger.

MODEL X-73 MODEL - 12 ga., 33 in. barrel. full choke, push button opening, high rib fancy Monte Carlo stock.

	$2,500	$2,250	$2,000	$1,850	$1,700	$1,600	$1,500

Add $300 for extra pull trigger.
Add $500 for extra release trigger.

DYNOKIC MODEL - 12 ga., 32 (disc.) or 33 in. barrel with 2 choke tubes, patented recoil reduction system reduces felt recoil by 50%, checkered walnut stock, many options available. New 1997.

MSR	$4,795	$4,795	$4,000	$3,450	$2,900	$2,500	$2,000	$1,650

Add $1,000 for stainless steel construction.

❋ **Dynokic Supreme** - similar to Dynokic Model, except has deluxe walnut stock with checkering. New 2000.

MSR	$5,595	$5,595	$4,250	$3,400	$3,000	$2,650	$2,300	$1,900

Add $1,000 for stainless steel construction.

MONO GUN - 12 ga., 34 in. barrel, custom choked, custom stocked, pull or release trigger, a "built to customers specifications" trap gun. Also known as Standard Rib or Medium Rib.

❋ **Standard, Medium, or Olympic Rib Model**

MSR	$5,995	$5,995	$4,550	$3,450	$3,225	$2,650	$2,300	$1,900

Add $400 for stainless choke tubes.
Add $1,000 for stainless steel construction.
Add $2,700 for stainless steel SLE Pro Model.
Add $1,700 for SLE Pro Package (includes Laib adj. comb, adj. alum. base plate with 2 pads, and Pro barrel with special bore).
Approximately 3,100 Mono Guns have been manufactured to date.

❋ **LTX (Deluxe Mono Trap)** - similar to Mono Gun except has 33 (disc.) or 34 in. medium rib barrel and exhibition wood and checkering.

MSR	$7,495	$7,495	$6,500	$5,600	$4,700	$3,800	$2,900	$2,350

Add $500 for extra pull trigger.
Add $650 if with release trigger.
Add $300 for choke tube barrel with 2 chokes.
Add $850 for extra release trigger.
Add $2,499 for extra barrel.
Add $1,200 for stainless steel package.

L

Grading	100%	98%	95%	90%	80%	70%	60%

✷ **Pro 3 (Deluxe Mono Trap)** - similar to Mono Gun except is lighter weight, 34 in. medium rib barrel, exhibition wood and checkering, Briley Series 12 choke tubes. New 2000.

| | MSR | $8,995 | $8,995 | $7,750 | $6,500 | $5,600 | $4,700 | $3,800 | $2,900 |

Add $500 for extra pull trigger.
Add $650 if with release trigger.
Add $850 for extra release trigger.
Add $2,599 for extra barrel with fixed chokes.
Add $1,000 for stainless steel Pro 3 Package.

SPACE GUN - 12 ga. only, single barrel, unusual design permits in-line round stock with recoil pad, circular forearm wraps around barrel, high post rib on muzzle half of barrel, patented recoil reduction system reduces recoil by 50%. Disc. 1999.

| | | $5,995 | $4,150 | $3,375 | $2,825 | $2,300 | $2,000 | $1,750 |

Last MSR was $5,995.

LLAMA - Gabilondo y Cia, S.A.

Current manufacturer located in Vitoria, Spain. Currently distributed by Import Sports, Inc. located in Wanamassa, NJ. Previously imported and distributed by Stoeger Industries, Inc. located in South Hackensack, NJ until 1993.

PISTOLS: SEMI-AUTO

MODEL IIIA - .380 ACP cal., 7 shot, 3 in. barrel, adj. sights, blue, plastic grips. Mfg. 1951-disc.

| | $235 | $200 | $180 | $160 | $140 | $120 | $110 |

MODEL XA - similar to Model IIIA, except .32 ACP.

| | $235 | $200 | $180 | $160 | $140 | $120 | $110 |

MODEL XV - similar to Model XA, except .22 LR.

| | $235 | $200 | $180 | $160 | $140 | $120 | $110 |

Add 50% for airweight.

MODELS C-IIIA, C-XA, C-XV - similar to Model C, except engraved chrome.

| | $350 | $300 | $250 | $205 | $180 | $155 | $140 |

MODELS BE-IIIA, BE-XA, BE-XV - similar to Model CE, except engraved, blue.

| | $365 | $315 | $250 | $205 | $180 | $155 | $140 |

Deluxe Models, all blue or chrome engraved with simulated pearl grips, add $20.

MODEL G-IIIA - similar to IIIA, except gold damascened, simulated pearl grips.

| | $1,515 | $880 | $825 | $660 | $550 | $440 | $330 |

MODEL VIII - .38 Super cal., 9 shot, 5 in. barrel, fixed sights, wood grips. Mfg. 1952-disc.

| | $305 | $255 | $220 | $195 | $180 | $165 | $140 |

MODEL IXA - similar to Model VIII, except .45 ACP.

| | $305 | $255 | $220 | $195 | $180 | $165 | $140 |

MODEL XI - similar to Model IXA, except 9mm Para..

| | $305 | $255 | $220 | $195 | $180 | $165 | $140 |

MODELS C-VIII, C-IXA, C-XI - similar to Model VIII, except satin chrome.

| | $360 | $315 | $285 | $260 | $220 | $195 | $165 |

MODELS CE-VIII, CE-IXA, CE-XI

| | $425 | $350 | $310 | $285 | $265 | $220 | $195 |

MODELS BE-VIII, BE-IXA, BE-XI - similar to Model CE, except blue, engraving.

| | $495 | $395 | $295 | $275 | $250 | $210 | $180 |

Deluxe Models are similar, except simulated pearl grips - add $20.

Grading	100%	98%	95%	90%	80%	70%	60%

OMNI - .45 ACP or 9mm Para. cal., double action, all steel construction, 2 sear bars, 3 safeties, 4¼ in. barrel, 7 shot mag. in .45 cal., 13 shot mag. in 9mm Para., blue finish. Importation disc. 1986.

9mm Para.	$440	$380	$330	$295	$260	$225	$200

Last MSR was $546.

.45 ACP Caliber	$395	$360	$320	$285	$250	$220	$195

Last MSR was $500.

SMALL FRAME MODEL - .22 LR (disc. 1994), .32 ACP (disc. 1993), or .380 ACP cal., Colt 1911A1 design, single action, 3 11/16 in. barrel, 7 shot mag., 23 oz. Also available in satin chrome, optional engraving patterns. Disc. 1997.

	$220	$180	$155	$135	$120	$110	$100

Last MSR was $259.

Add $60 for duo-tone finish (.380 ACP only, mfg. 1991-1993).
Add $33 for satin chrome finish (not avail. in .32 ACP cal.).

COMPACT FRAME MODEL (IX-D) - 9mm Para. (disc.) or .45 ACP cal., scaled down variation of the Large Frame Model, 4¼ in. barrel, 7 or 9 shot mag., 34 or 37 oz. Mfg. 1986-1997.

	$325	$255	$200	$180	$160	$155	$150

Last MSR was $409.

Add $16 for satin chrome finish.
Add $90 for duo-tone finish (mfg. 1990-1993).

GOVERNMENT MODEL (IX-C) - 9mm Para. (disc.), .38 Super (mfg. 1988-1996), or .45 ACP cal., similar to Small Frame Model, 5 1/8 in. barrel, 36 oz., 9 shot mag. in 9mm Para., 7 shot mag. in .45 ACP. Engraved and deluxe models available also. Disc. 1997.

	$325	$255	$200	$180	$160	$150	$140

Last MSR was $409.

Add $16 for satin chrome finish (.45 ACP only).
Add $90 for duo-tone finish (.45 ACP only, mfg. 1991-1993).

MAX I MODEL - 9mm Para. or .45 ACP cal., patterned after the Colt Govt. Model, single action only, 4¼ (Compact Model) or 5½ in. barrel, 3-dot combat sights, 7 (.45 ACP) or 9 (9mm Para.) shot mag., matte blue, satin chrome, or duo-tone finish, rubber grips, 34 or 36 oz. Mfg. 1995-99.

	$265	$225	$200	$180	$160	$150	$140

Last MSR was $299.

Add $10 for duo-tone finish (.45 ACP cal. only).
Add $16 for satin chrome finish (new 1996).

 ✳ *Max-I Compensated* - .45 ACP only, 7 or 10 shot mag., features compensated barrel. Disc. 1997.

	$445	$385	$330	$250	$200	$180	$160

Last MSR was $492.

Add $25 for 10 shot model.

MINI-MAX - 9mm Para. (disc. 1999), .40 S&W, or .45 ACP cal., mini-compact variation featuring 6-8 shot mag., choice of matte, satin chrome, duo-tone (.45 ACP only), or stainless steel finish/construction. New 1996.

MSR $325		$290	$245	$210	$185	$165	$150	$140

Add $17 for satin chrome finish.
Add $9 for duo-tone finish (.45 ACP only).
Add $66 for stainless steel construction (disc.).

Grading	100%	98%	95%	90%	80%	70%	60%

✳ *Mini-Max Sub Compact* - 9mm Para. (disc. 2000), .40 S&W (disc. 2000), or .45 ACP cal., 3.14 in. barrel, all steel construction, 3-dot combat sights, 10 shot mag., polymer grips, choice of matte, satin chrome, or duo-tone finish, 31 oz. New 1999.

	MSR	$350	$310	$255	$215	$185	$160	$150	$140

Add $9 for satin chrome finish.
Add $10 for duo-tone finish (.45 ACP cal. only).

MICRO-MAX - .32 ACP (new 1999, matte finish only) or .380 ACP cal., features standard or lightweight steel design, polymer grips, 3 dot combat sights, slimline slide and frame, non-glare matte or satin chrome finish. New 1998.

	MSR	$282	$255	$220	$200	$170	$160	$150	$140

Subtract $15 for Ultra Lite Model (disc.).
Add $17 for satin chrome finish (.380 ACP cal. only, beginning 1999).

MODEL 82 - 9mm Para. cal., double action, 4¼ in. barrel, blue finish, 3-dot sighting system, 15 shot mag., ambidextrous safety, loaded chamber indicator, black polymer grips, 39 oz. Imported 1988- 1993.

	$650	$600	$550	$495	$450	$395	$365

Last MSR was $975.

MODEL 87 COMPETITION - 9mm Para. cal., competition variation of the Model 82, includes built in ported compensator, oversize magazine and safety release, fixed barrel bushing, beveled rapid load magazine well, 14 shot mag., extended and serrated triggerguard, and adj. trigger. Imported 1989-1993.

	$1,275	$995	$850	$750	$650	$575	$500

Last MSR was $1,450.

REVOLVERS: DOUBLE ACTION

MARTIAL MODEL - .22 LR or .38 Spl. cal., 6 shot, 4 and 6 in. barrels, target sights, blue, checkered wood grips. Mfg. 1969-1976.

	$220	$200	$180	$165	$140	$120	$100

DELUXE MARTIAL - similar to Martial, except finish as follows:

	100%	98%	95%	90%	80%	70%	60%
Satin chrome	$275	$250	$220	$195	$165	$140	$120
Chrome, engraved	$305	$275	$250	$220	$195	$165	$140
Blue, engraved	$290	$265	$235	$210	$180	$155	$120
Gold, damascened	$1,430	$880	$770	$660	$550	$495	$415

COMANCHE I - .22 LR cal., similar to Martial DA, mfg. 1977-1982.

	$255	$220	$195	$165	$155	$140	$110

COMANCHE II - .38 Spl. cal., similar to Martial DA, mfg. 1977-1982 and 1986 in .22 LR and .22 Mag. only.

	$240	$220	$195	$165	$155	$140	$110

Last MSR was $272.

COMANCHE III - .22 LR (disc.) or .357 Mag. cal., 6 shot, 4, 6, or 8½ (disc. 1986) in. barrel, blue, adj. sights, checkered walnut grips. Mfg. 1975-95. Before 1977, it was called "Comanche".

	$280	$245	$200	$165	$155	$140	$130

Last MSR was $339.

✳ *Satin Chrome Finish (disc.)*

	$330	$270	$230	$205	$185	$170	$160

Last MSR was $395.

✳ *Gold Finish (disc.)*

	$1,100	$880	$825	$660	$550	$440	$330

Grading	100%	98%	95%	90%	80%	70%	60%

SUPER COMANCHE IV - .44 Mag. cal., 6 or 8½ in. VR barrel, adj. sights, blue only. Disc. 1998.

| | $350 | $285 | $235 | $220 | $205 | $185 | $175 |

Last MSR was $440.

SUPER COMANCHE V - .357 Mag. cal., 6 shot, 4, 6, or 8½ in. VR barrel, adj. sights, blue only. Importation disc. 1988.

| | $335 | $275 | $230 | $210 | $200 | $190 | $180 |

Last MSR was $414.

LONE STAR RIFLE CO., INC.

Current rifle manufacturer established 1992 and located in Conroe, TX, specializing in Remington Rolling Block rifle reproductions. Dealer and consumer direct sales.

RIFLES: REPRODUCTIONS

REMINGTON ROLLING BLOCK SERIES - various black powder cartridge cals., configurations, and options, case colored or nickel plated receiver, rust or nitre blue barrel, extra select checkered walnut, single, single set, and double set triggers.

* *Creedmoor* - features competition long range 34 in. full octagon or half octagon/ half round barrel with pistol grip and shotgun butt, single trigger set at 3 lbs., per Creedmoor rules, 10 lbs.

| MSR $1,995 | | $1,850 | $1,550 | $1,250 | $995 | $875 | $725 | $600 |

* *Silhouette (Target)* - designed for silhouette competition, with 30, 32, or 34 in. full octagon or half octagon/half round barrel with pistol grip and shotgun butt.

| MSR $1,995 | | $1,850 | $1,550 | $1,250 | $995 | $875 | $725 | $600 |

* *Silhouette Standard Rifle* - .40-65 or .45-70 Govt. cal., similar to #5 Sporting Standard Rifle, except has 32 or 34 in. barrel, steel shotgun butt plate, pistol grip stock, and shortened forearm, 11 lbs. New 1999.

| MSR $1,495 | | $1,325 | $1,100 | $875 | $725 | $600 | $550 | $475 |

* *Cowboy Action Rifle* - .32-40 WCF, .38-55 WCF, .40-65 WCF, .44-77, .45 LC, .45-70 Govt., or .50-70 cal., similar to #5 Sporting Standard Rifle, except has heavy 28 in. barrel, 8½ lbs. New 1999.

| MSR $1,495 | | $1,325 | $1,100 | $875 | $725 | $600 | $550 | $475 |

* *#5 Sporting Standard Rifle* - .25-35 WCF (new 2002), .30-30 Win. (new 2000) or .30-40 Krag cal., 26 in. round barrel, single trigger, case colored frame, standard American walnut stock and forearm, 6 lbs. New 1999.

| MSR $1,495 | | $1,325 | $1,100 | $875 | $725 | $600 | $550 | $475 |

* *#7 Sporting Rifle* - as this edition went to press, more information was not available on this model. New 2002.

| MSR $2,500 | | $2,225 | $1,850 | $1,550 | $1,250 | $975 | $850 | $725 |

* *Sporting Rifle* - various cals., standard sporting rifle designed for accuracy, 28, 30, or 32 in. barrel, straight grip stock.

| MSR $1,995 | | $1,850 | $1,550 | $1,250 | $975 | $850 | $725 | $600 |

* *Deluxe Sporting Rifle* - deluxe variation of the Sporting Rifle with 28, 30, or 32 in. full octagon or half octagon/half round barrel with pistol grip and shotgun butt, buckhorn rear sight and choice of front sight.

| MSR $1,995 | | $1,850 | $1,550 | $1,250 | $975 | $850 | $725 | $600 |

* *Custer Rifle* - .50-70 cal., an exact reproduction of Gen. G.A. Custer's original Remington Rolling Block, 28 in. octagon barrel with SST, straight grip, crescent buttplate, and rounded forearm tip.

| MSR $2,900 | | $2,575 | $2,225 | $1,875 | $1,625 | $1,400 | $1,200 | $1,000 |

L

Grading	100%	98%	95%	90%	80%	70%	60%

✳ **Buffalo Rifle** - .50-90 cal., features relic finish enabling a new gun to appear somewhat worn, double set triggers, exact copy of the original, 16 lbs. 100% refers to NIB condition, not finish.

	MSR	$2,900		$2,575	$2,225	$1,875	$1,625	$1,400	$1,200	$1,000

✳ **Take Down Model** - features take down action. New 2001.

	MSR	$4,000		$3,600	$3,150	$2,750	$2,300	$1,995	$1,700	$1,375

GOVE ROLLING BLOCK - various cals., new rolling block with underlever design by Carlos Gove. New 1998.

	MSR	$2,995		$2,650	$2,250	$1,875	$1,625	$1,400	$1,200	$1,000

LORCIN ENGINEERING CO., INC.

Previous handgun manufacturer located in Mira Loma, CA, 1989-1999.

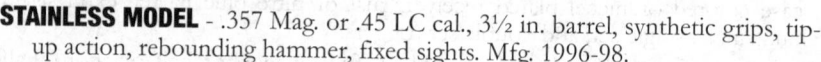

DERRINGERS: O/U

STAINLESS MODEL - .357 Mag. or .45 LC cal., 3½ in. barrel, synthetic grips, tip-up action, rebounding hammer, fixed sights. Mfg. 1996-98.

	$95	$80	$65

Last MSR was $110.

PISTOLS: SEMI-AUTO

During the height of production in the mid-90s, Lorcin was making 40,000 semi-auto pistols a month. One year, their production totalled 400,000 units.

L-22 MODEL - .22 LR cal., similar to L-25 Model, except 2.55 in. barrel and 9 shot mag., black or chrome finish, 16 oz. Mfg. 1992-99.

	$75	$60	$50	$45	$40	$35	$35

Last MSR was $89.

L-25 MODEL - .25 ACP cal., single action, 6 shot mag., 2.4 in. barrel, anatomically designed grips to fit hand better, choice of black and gold, chrome and pearl, satin chrome and pearl, Teflon camo finish (new 1992), or black and pearl finish, 13.5 oz. Mfg. 1989-1999.

	$65	$50	$45	$40	$35	$35	$35

Last MSR was $79.

Add $20 for lightweight frame (Model LT 25, new in 1990).

✳ **Lady Lorcin** - same specifications as the L-25 Model, except is available in chrome, satin chrome, or black exterior finish with pink grips. Mfg. 1990-99.

	$70	$60	$50	$45	$40	$35	$35

Last MSR was $79.

L-32 - .32 ACP cal., single action, 7 shot mag., 3.5 in. barrel, available in black or chrome finish, 23 oz. Mfg. 1992-99.

	$80	$70	$60	$50	$45	$40	$35

Last MSR was $89.

L-380 - .380 ACP cal., single action, 7 shot mag., 3.5 in. barrel, available in black or chrome finish, 23 oz. Mfg. 1992-99.

	$85	$75	$65	$55	$50	$45	$40

Last MSR was $100.

LH-380 - .380 ACP cal., similar to L9MM, 36 oz. Mfg. 1995-99.

	$125	$115	$100	$90	$85	$80	$75

Last MSR was $149.

Grading	100%	98%	95%	90%	80%	70%	60%

L9MM - 9mm Para. cal., single action, 10 (C/B 1994) or 13* shot mag., 4½ in. barrel, grip safety, black finish, 3-dot sights, 36 oz. Mfg. 1994-99.

	$125	$115	$100	$90	$85	$80	$75

Last MSR was $149.

Add $20 for disc. 13 shot mag. variation.

LUCCHINI, SANDRO

Current manufacturer located in Sarezzo (Brescia), Italy.

Lucchini manufactures high quality, made to order, double rifles and shotguns (approx. 10-12 guns annually). Shotguns starting prices are as follows (does not include engraving – simple English scroll is approx. $1,000, elaborate ornate or game scene engraving by a master engraver can be up to $12,000): $6,000 for Anson action without sideplates (add $1,000 for sideplates), $14,000 for standard sidelock, hammer guns base prices are $7,000 (manual cocking extractor) up to $14,000 (self cocking ejector). Add 10% for 28 ga. or .410 bore, and $500 for single trigger. All shotgun barrels are demi-bloc construction. Double rifles start at $24,000 for calibers less than .375 H&H, and are available up to .600 NE. All are constructed with Ferlach barrels. Add approx. $4,500 per extra set of shotgun barrels. Please contact the manufacturer directly for more current information.

LUGERS WITH VARIATIONS

Currently manufactured trademark of both pistol and shotgun configurations. Pistol design originated by Georg Luger, circa 1899. This trademarked name is currently manufactured/marketed by Stoeger Industries, located in  Wayne, NJ. Previous post-WWII manufacture (through 1997) was by Mauser- Werke Oberndorf Waffensysteme, located in Oberndorf, Germany. Many previous manufacturers - see main text for more information.

Note: The Luger section in this book is arranged chronologically by year of manufacture (1900 models to Post-War production), under individual manufacturer headings.

Often times, year of production can be hard to nail down, especially on commercial models. An easier way to initially identify your Luger is to categorize by toggle marking first - then by chamber marking within groups (chronologically for dated chambers). Once you know period of manufacture, simply refer to the appropriate subheading in this section. While some rare variations will be excluded in this generalized overview, it will be very helpful to establish correct, basic knowledge about your particular Luger.

While many recently imported Lugers would make workable shooters, they have in no way lowered prices on 90%+ condition specimens due to normal collector activity in top quality only pistols. Recently imported Lugers should have the importer's name visibly stamped on an exterior surface. Most of these imports are in the 9mm Para. - 4 in. barrel configuration.

Every year more and more reblue, restrawed, regripped, reframed, rebarreled Lugers are sold to unknowing military handgun collectors as rare variations. On any expensive contract variation, careful inspection on all parts must be made before potentially purchasing. If in doubt, secure 2 or 3 additional appraisals/observations from qualified individuals. Lugers are a field in themselves and an experienced Winchester dealer would not be qualified to guesstimate the originality of these German handguns.

A final note on Lugers: Original pistols in 95%-100% condition have not been affected by the influx of recent imports as these newly imported guns are usually in 80% and lower condition or have been reblue.

It seems that every year the prices of top quality (98%+ condition) original Lugers get more expensive and less predictable. For this reason, the 100% values on some vintage Lugers have been omitted intentionally, since rarity precludes accurate price evaluation in this condition factor. In many cases, a mint original Luger can double the 98% price listed.

Values for all variations of Lugers listed assume a proper magazine and matching parts.

DWM TOGGLE IDENTIFICATION

* **DWM MODELS** - mfg. from 1900 to 1930 in Berlin, Germany.
* **1900 Models** - grip safety and "Dished" Toggles, ser. nos. 1-24,999.
* **1906 Models** - grip safety, many chamber markings, ser. nos. 25,000-74,000.
* **1908 Commercial Models** - no grip safety, 9mm Para., ser. nos. 39,000-74,000.
* **1908 Military Models** - no stock lug.
* **1914 Military Models** - stock lug, dated 1913-1918.
* **1920 Commercial Models** - no grip safety, usually 3 7/8 in. barrel. Most common Luger, undated chamber, 7.65mm Para. or 9mm Para.
  Note: Lugers with 4 inch barrels are most frequently encountered in military and commercial models. 6 in. barrels usually denote "Navy" models. 8 in. barrels usually denote "Artillery" models. Guns with barrels over 8 inches are rare and should be checked carefully for originality.

DWM COMMERCIAL LUGERS

DWM MEANS DEUTSCHE WAFFEN & MUNITIONS FABRIKEN

These are models manufactured from 1900-1923 found in the five digit serial range.

MODEL 1900 - ser. range 1-20,000. Configuration: 4¾ in. x .30 Commercial, American Eagle, Swiss.

MODEL 1900 - ser. range 20,001-21,000. Configuration: 4¾ in. x .30 Bulgarian.

MODEL 1902 - ser. range 21,001-25,000. Configuration: 9mm Para. x 4 in. "Fat Barrels" and 11¾ in. x 7.65mm Para. Carbine models, intermixed with 4¾ x 7.65mm Para. American Eagles and Commercials.

MODEL 1906 - ser. range 25,001-39,000. Configuration: Commercial American Eagle, Navy Commercial and Swiss, both 4¾ in. x 7.65mm Para. and 9mm Para. x 4 in. grip safety models.

MODEL 1908 - ser. range 39,001-71,000. Configuration: First 9mm Para. x 4 in. without grip safety, M1908 Commercials were interspersed with 7.65mm Para. and 9mm Para. Eagles, Commercials, Navy Commercials, and a few Carbines and Swiss.

MODEL 1914 - ser. range 71,001-74,000. Configuration: Last pre-WWI Commercial Lugers, made with stock lug, with a few 9mm Para. Commercials mixed in.

MODEL 1920 - ser. range 2,000i-9,999u. Configuration: Post-WWI Commercials, mostly 3 7/ 8 in. x 7.65mm Para. cal.

MODEL 1923 - ser. range 89,001-91,000. Configuration: The last thousand or so made have "safe" on lever and "loaded" on the extractor, 3 7/8 in. x 7.65mm Para. barrels

ERFURT TOGGLE IDENTIFICATION

ERFURT MODELS

Produced from 1911-1914 and 1916-1918 in Erfurt, Germany. Military Model - Chamber dated 1911- 1914 and 1916-1918. Erfurt models exhibit the most proof marks and individual parts numbering. Walnut grips.

SIMSON & CO. TOGGLE IDENTIFICATION

SIMSON & CO.

Manufactured 1922 to 1934 in Suhl, Germany. Most Simson Lugers are military models (9mm - 4 in. barrels). During this 12 year period, Simson supplied the German Army Lugers exclusively. Can be dated 1925-1928. Many reworks of WWI DWM Military Lugers were refurbished by Simson, and can be detected by the Simson "Eagle-over-6" proof on repaired parts. A very few Simsons made in 1934 have just an "S" on the toggle (very rare).

SWISS TOGGLE IDENTIFICATION

SWISS BERN MODELS

Manufactured 1924 to 1929 by WAFFENFABRIK Bern, Switzerland. Relatively rare - these Swiss models have "improved" changes (flat and curved front grip strap), 4¾ in. barrels, walnut or plastic grips, grip safety. 1929 model (flat front grip strap) has Swiss Cross in shield on front link.

MAUSER TOGGLE IDENTIFICATION

MAUSER VARIATIONS

Manufactured 1934-1942 in Oberndorf, Germany. Between 1930 and 1934 Mauser Werke was primarily engaged in reworking older Lugers, since transfer of machinery and personnel to the DWM plant in Berlin was completed in 1931. Mauser "Banner" models were made from 1934 to 1942, many are dated from 1939-1942 on the chamber. S/42 models are MOSTLY MILITARY contract guns manufactured between 1934 and 1940, usually chamber marked. "42" toggle marked guns (Mauser code) were mfg. 1939 and 1940 and are dated. "byf" marked toggles indicate guns made for German military use after 1940 and are more common than other military models. The Mauser Werke trademark also appears on those Lugers made in the 1970s.

KRIEGHOFF TOGGLE IDENTIFICATION

KRIEGHOFF MODELS

Manufactured between 1934-1946 in Suhl, Germany. Early Krieghoffs are side frame inscribed. The German Luftwaffe contracted with Krieghoff for military guns in 1935. Early military Krieghoffs have "S" marked chambers, most are chamber dated between 1936 and 1945. Krieghoff Lugers are prized for their quality fit and finish and command higher prices because of their rarity factor.

Grading	100%	98%	95%	90%	80%	70%	60%

VICKERS TOGGLE IDENTIFICATION

VICKERS
LTD.

VICKERS

Manufactured by Vickers, Ltd., circa 1921, in England from DWM parts for military contract sale to the Netherlands. Added barrel date is a date of arsenal refinish or refurbishing. Distinguishable by Vickers toggle and "rust" marked safety. Serial range is 1-10,100. Grips can be finely checkered with shallow contour or very coarsely checkered. Configuration is 9mm Para., 4 in. barrel, and grip safety.

PISTOLS: SEMI-AUTO, LUGERS & VARIATIONS

Lugers: Pre-1900 & 1900 DWM Mfg.

Values on most 100% Lugers have been omitted intentionally since rarity precludes accurate price evaluation in this condition factor.

1898/99 BORCHARDT LUGER TRANSITIONAL - 7.65mm Para. cal., 5 in. barrel, this is perhaps one of the most desirable Lugers, only few mfg. Examples scarce, no reported sales, an original example would command a price in the 5-figure range.

1899/1900 SWISS TEST MODEL - 7.65mm Para. cal., 4¾ in. barrel, 100 or less mfg., the very first true Luger. Engraved "Swiss Cross" chamber marking.

	N/A	$35,000	$30,000	$22,000	$16,000	$12,000	$8,500

Approx. 50 pistols serial numbered in the 1-50 range.
Buyers should be very cautious when considering a purchase of this rare model, as good fakes do exist.

1900 COMMERCIAL DWM - 7.65mm Para. cal., 4¾ in. barrel, 5,500 mfg.

	N/A	$3,000	$2,500	$2,000	$1,650	$1,325	$950

1900 SWISS COMMERCIAL DWM - 7.65mm Para. cal., 4¾ in. barrel, 2,000 commercially mfg. and 3000 military mfg.

	N/A	$3,750	$3,000	$2,450	$1,750	$1,350	$975

Add 15% for wide trigger (found only in ser. no. range 4,000).

1900 AMERICAN EAGLE DWM - 7.65mm Para. cal., 4¾ in. barrel, approx. 12,000 mfg.

	N/A	$2,950	$1,650	$1,250	$1,000	$850	$650

Add 40% for U.S. Test Model (approx. ser. no. range 6,100-7,100).

1900 BULGARIAN DWM - 7.65mm Para. cal., 4¾ in. barrel, 1,000 mfg., very rare in U.S., most often seen in the 60% and lower condition.

	N/A	$8,750	$5,250	$3,750	$3,150	$2,650	$2,150

Deduct 30% if rebarreled.

Lugers: 1902-DWM Mfg.

1902 COMMERCIAL - 9mm Para. cal., 4 in. barrel, serial number range 22,300-22,400 and 22,900-23,500 (500-600 mfg.). Commonly called "Fat Barrel" model.

	N/A	$8,000	$6,500	$4,650	$3,950	$3,350	$2,750

1902 AMERICAN EAGLE - 9mm Para. cal., 4 in. barrel, 600-700 mfg., commonly called the "Fat Barrel". Same ser. range as 1902 Commercial Model.

	N/A	$8,500	$6,500	$4,850	$4,000	$3,500	$3,000

Grading	100%	98%	95%	90%	80%	70%	60%

1902 CARTRIDGE COUNTER AMERICAN EAGLE - 9mm Para. cal., only 50 mfg. with the Powell Indication Device; be extremely wary of fakes. Ser. no. range 22,401- 22,450.

	N/A	$26,000	$16,500	$12,250	$9,750	$8,650	$7,500

1902 DANZIG TEST - 7.65mm Para. or 9mm Para. cal., blank toggle, 4 in. barrel, Crown D proofs.

	N/A	$6,500	$5,000	$4,250	$3,400	$2,950	$2,200

1902 CARBINE - 7.65mm Para. cal., 11¾ in. barrel, approx. 2500 mfg.

Gun w/matching stock	N/A	$13,750	$10,000	$8,250	$6,500	$5,250	$4,500
Gun only	N/A	$7,500	$5,950	$3,500	$2,700	$2,200	$1,800

Add approx. 40% for American Eagle variation.
Subtract 20% for non-matching stock.

1902/06 TRANSITIONAL CARBINE - 11¾ in. barrel, 50-100 mfg., may have new model frame. Ser. nos. start at 50,000.

	N/A	$9,000	$6,250	$4,500	$4,200	$4,000	$3,800

Subtract 30% if without matching stock.

1903 COMMERCIAL - 7.65mm Para. cal., 4 in. barrel, 50 mfg., extractor marked "charge". Ser. range 25,000-25,050, with 90 degree toggle checkering.

	N/A	$6,500	$6,000	$5,500	$5,000	$3,000	$2,500

Lugers: 1904-DWM Mfg.

1904 NAVY DWM - 9mm Para. cal., 6 in. barrel, limited mfg., a Transitional Navy, "Fat Barrel" with 90 degree toggle checkering and toggle lock, should have 2-digit ser. no.
Extreme rarity precludes pricing for individual condition factors. Good condition (70%-95%), no problem, original specimens are currently selling in the $28,000-$35,000 range. Most of these pistols available for sale are fakes - buyer beware!

Lugers: 1906-DWM Mfg.

1906 COMMERCIAL 7.65mm Para. W/"GESICHERT" MARKED SAFETY - 7.65mm Para. cal., 4¾ in. barrel, "GESICHERT" marked safety, long frame. Approx. 750 mfg.

	N/A	$2,750	$1,950	$1,500	$1,125	$900	$750

1906 COMMERCIAL 9mm Para. - 9mm Para. cal., 4 in. barrel, 3,500-4,000 mfg. Scarcer than 7.65mm Para.

	N/A	$2,800	$1,850	$1,200	$900	$775	$650

1906 COMMERCIAL 7.65mm Para. - 7.65mm Para. cal., 4¾ in. barrel, area under safety polished bright, 5000 mfg.

	N/A	$2,400	$1,500	$950	$775	$625	$550

1906 AMERICAN EAGLE - 9mm Para. - 9mm Para. cal., 4 in. barrel, American Eagle stamped in front of breech, 3,000 mfg.

	N/A	$2,800	$2,000	$1,275	$975	$800	$650

1906 AMERICAN EAGLE - 7.65mm Para. - 7.65mm Para. cal. , 4¾ in. barrel, 7,500- 8,000 mfg. Add 40% for long frame.

	N/A	$2,600	$2,000	$1,200	$850	$725	$600

1906 NAVY COMMERCIAL - 9mm Para. cal., 6 in. barrel, approx. 2,500 mfg.

	N/A	$3,800	$3,000	$1,800	$1,600	$1,200	$950

Add 50% for 7.65mm Para. cal. with 6 in. barrel.

1906 NAVY MILITARY FIRST ISSUE - 9mm Para. cal., 6 in. barrel, first issue, 19,000 mfg., mostly altered safety marking - "GESICHERT" in upper position. Ser. no. range 1-9,000a.

	N/A	$3,800	$3,000	$2,400	$1,200	$875	$600

Add 10% for Navy unit markings.
Add 25% for unaltered safety variation.

Grading	100%	98%	95%	90%	80%	70%	60%

1906 NAVY MILITARY SECOND ISSUE - 9mm Para. cal., 6 in. barrel, second issue, 2,000 mfg. Ser. range 9,000a-1,000b.

	N/A	$4,000	$3,400	$2,000	$1,600	$1,200	$1,000

Add 10% for Navy unit markings.

Lugers: 1906-1918 DWM & Erfurt Mfg.

Most common variations in good supply within this section in 50% or less condition will approximate the 60% value. This reflects its value as a representative shooter rather than a higher priced collector's gun.

1906 SWISS COMMERCIAL - 7.65mm Para. or 9mm Para. cal., 4¾ in. barrel, less than 1,000 mfg., Swiss "Cross in Sunburst," short frame.

	N/A	$2,400	$1,750	$1,500	$1,350	$1,200	$1,100

Add 20% for "Cross in Shield".

1906 SWISS MILITARY - 7.65mm Para. cal., 4¾ in. barrel, long frame, Swiss Police has Cross in Shield. Either "Cross in Shield" or "Cross in Sunburst".

	N/A	$2,400	$1,600	$1,200	$900	$800	$700

1906/23 DUTCH - 9mm Para. cal., 4 in. barrel, approx. 4,000 mfg., often seen as arsenal rework.

	N/A	$1,600	$1,400	$900	$750	$600	$525

Add 200% for original finish and barrel.

1906 BRAZILIAN - 7.65mm Para. cal., 4¾ in. barrel, 5,000 mfg., extremely rare in fine condition.

	N/A	$2,500	$1,800	$1,000	$800	$700	$650

1906 BULGARIAN - 7.65mm Para. cal., 4¾ in. barrel, 1,500 mfg., most rebarrelled to 9mm Para. (deduct 60%).

	N/A	$4,750	$3,500	$3,500	$2,000	$1,850	$1,450

This is the rarest Bulgarian - most are fakes or have been restored.

1908 BULGARIAN - 9mm Para. cal., 4 in. barrel, DWM on chamber, 10,000 mfg., extremely rare in mint condition.

	N/A	$2,500	$1,800	$1,000	$825	$750	$675

1906 PORTUGUESE ARMY - 7.65mm Para. cal., 4¾ in. barrel, Manuel II crest on chamber. Approx. 5,000 mfg.

	N/A	$1,800	$1,400	$900	$600	$500	$400

1906 ROYAL PORTUGUESE NAVY - 9mm Para. cal., 4 in. barrel, Anchor & Crown on chamber, very rare. Most are fakes.

	N/A	$9,500	$6,000	$4,000	$2,500	$2,000	$1,500

1906 REPUBLIC OF PORTUGAL NAVY - 7.65mm Para. cal., Anchor R.P. on chamber, very rare. Most are fakes.

	N/A	$9,500	$6,000	$4,000	$2,500	$2,000	$1,500

1906 RUSSIAN - 9mm Para. cal., 4 in. barrel, approx. 1,000 mfg., only 6 reported.

	N/A	$15,000	$9,950	$8,100	$6,400	$5,500	$4,600

1906 VICKERS DUTCH - 9mm Para., 4 in. barrel, approx. 10,000 assembled by Vickers Ltd. from DWM supplied parts.

	N/A	$2,800	$2,000	$1,500	$1,200	$800	$700

1906 FRENCH COMMERCIAL - 7.65mm Para. cal., 4¾ in. barrel.

	N/A	$2,350	$1,800	$1,575	$1,400	$1,200	$995

Add 100% if cased with accessories.

1908 DWM COMMERCIAL AND MILITARY - 9mm Para. cal., 4 in. barrel, Test/Acceptance Model, approx. 500 mfg. Ser. no. range 69,000-71,200.

	N/A	$1,200	$800	$700	$575	$475	$400

Grading	100%	98%	95%	90%	80%	70%	60%

1908 NAVY COMMERCIAL - 9mm Para. cal., 6 in. barrel.

	N/A	$4,500	$3,000	$2,400	$1,800	$1,500	$1,300

Add 50% for 7.65mm Para. with 6 in. barrel.

1908 DWM MILITARY - 9mm Para. cal., 4 in. barrel, approx. 95,000 mfg each year, undated 1st issue or dated 1910-1913, no stock lug, except for a few late 1913 mfg. guns.

	N/A	$1,200	$750	$525	$450	$400	$350

Add 20%+ for Imperial unit markings (depends on history of unit).
Add 20% for undated or for 1913 date w/stock lug.
Approx. 25,000 1st issue pistols were mfg., 20,000 dated 1910, 15,000 dated 1911, 10,000 dated 1912, 25,000 dated 1913.

1908 DWM COMMERCIAL - 9mm Para. cal., 4 in. barrel, no stock lug or hold open, blank chamber.

	N/A	$1,200	$800	$650	$600	$500	$400

1910-1914 DATED 1908 ERFURT MILITARY - 9mm Para. cal., 4 in. barrel (dated 1910-1914), 1911, 1912, and most 1913 chamber dates do not have stock lugs.

	N/A	$1,200	$800	$650	$600	$500	$400

Add 20%+ for Imperial unit markings (depends on history of unit).
Add 20% for 1913 chamber date with stock lug.

WWI ERFURT MILITARY SERIAL RANGES

CHAMBER DATE	OBSERVED LOW SERIAL	OBSERVED HIGH SERIAL	APPROXIMATE QTY. MADE
1911	575	9548	10,000
1912	255	866b	22,000
1913	575	2563b	25,000
1914	2137	539A	25,000
1915	none observed		
1916	13	5764b	80,000
1917	844	2854n	150,000
1918	304	5816s	180,000

Production data appears courtesy of Jan C. Still.

1908 NAVY - 9mm Para. cal., 6 in. barrel, scarce. Ser. No. range 1,000B-10,000B, 9,000 mfg.

	N/A	$5,500	$3,500	$2,400	$1,750	$1,500	$1,350

1908 BOLIVIAN CONTRACT - 9mm Para. cal., 4 in. barrel.

	N/A	$3,000	$2,500	$1,700	$1,300	$1,100	$900

1913 COMMERCIAL DWM - 9mm Para. cal., 4 in. barrel, grip safety and stock lug, horizontal "N" proof mark, 71,000 ser. no. range, rare.

	N/A	$2,250	$1,500	$1,050	$900	$780	$700

1914 COMMERCIAL DWM - 9mm Para. cal., 4 in. barrel, undated, stock lug, horizontal crown-N proofed.

	N/A	$1,600	$1,200	$975	$875	$750	$600

1914 NAVY - 9mm Para. cal., 6 in. barrel, scarce. Dated 1916 and 1917.

	N/A	$3,250	$2,250	$1,600	$1,200	$1,000	$900

Add 20% for 16 date.
Watch for fakes made from 1920 Commercials with new barrels and rear toggles added. Crown M proofs and date will look "fresh" (16 date usually encountered).

Grading	100%	98%	95%	90%	80%	70%	60%

1916-1918 DATED ERFURT MILITARY - 9mm Para. cal., 4 in. barrel, dated 1916- 1918 - there are no known 1915 chamber dated Erfurts.

| | N/A | $1,100 | $800 | $600 | $500 | $475 | $450 |

Add 20% for 1914 date.
Add $75 for original holster in average+ condition.
Add 10% for matching mag.
Add 100% for 2 matching mags.
Add 20%+ for Imperial unit markings (depends on history of unit).
Note: Date stamped on top frame is date of production; thus dates could be 1914, 1916, 1917, or 1918. All are Military P.08s, however, 99%-100% Erfurts are rare.

1914 ERFURT ARTILLERY - 9mm Para. cal., 1914 date is only one seen, 8 in. barrel.

| | N/A | $2,500 | $1,750 | $1,100 | $995 | $875 | $750 |

Add 20%+ for Imperial unit markings (depends on history of unit).

1912-1918 DATED WWI DWM MILITARY - 9mm Para. cal., 4 in. barrel. 1912-1918 dated. Most frequently encountered WWI military Luger, stock lug.

| | N/A | $1,100 | $700 | $600 | $500 | $475 | $450 |

Add $75 for original holster in average+ condition.
Add 20% for matching mag.
Add 100% for 2 matching mags.
Add 20%+ for Imperial unit markings (depends on history of unit).
Note: Date stamped on top frame is date of production; thus, dates could be 1914, 1915, 1916, 1917, or 1918. All are Military P.08s, however.

WWI DWM MILITARY SERIAL RANGES

CHAMBER DATE	OBSERVED LOW SERIAL	OBSERVED HIGH SERIAL	APPROXIMATE QTY. MADE
1908	(undated) 34	2636b	25,000
1910	5095b	5358d	20,000
1911	1524c	4825e	13,000
1912	599	9974	10,000
1913	2617	3850d	25,000
1914	282	6212c	40,000
1915	1398	2557d	100,000
1916	287	5438q	180,000
1917	587	3521m	60,000
1918	3690	9018n	190,000

Production data appears courtesy of Jan C. Still.

1914-1918 DATED DWM ARTILLERY - 9mm Para. cal., 8 in. barrel. Dated 1914- 1918.

| | N/A | $2,200 | $1,800 | $1,200 | $1,000 | $900 | $800 |

Add $350 for matching stock.
Add $200 for proper non-matching stock.
Add $200 for original leather holster with shoulder strap.
Add 200% for rare 1914 chamber date.
Add 20% for 1915 chamber date.
Add 20%+ for Imperial unit markings (depends on history of unit).

Lugers: 1920-1930 DWM

Most common variations in good supply within this section in 50% or less condition will approximate the 60% value. This reflects its value as a representative shooter rather than a higher priced collector's gun.

Grading	100%	98%	95%	90%	80%	70%	60%

1920 DWM OR ERFURT - 9mm Para. cal., 4 in. barrel, military and police, reworked and issued to police units, many thousand reworked, double date also, 1920 and 1921 dated.

	N/A	$900	$700	$600	$500	$475	$450

1920 COMMERCIAL - 7.65mm Para. or 9mm Para. cal., 3 7/8-4 in. barrel, available in many configurations, since these guns were assembled using the parts of previously manufactured Lugers, including 1900-1906 mfg. with the grip safety on the frame.

	N/A	$825	$625	$450	$395	$350	$295

Add 25% for 9mm Para. cal.
These prices reflect original condition, and are not to be confused with recent imports (with import markings).

1920 NAVY COMMERCIAL - 9mm Para. cal., 6 in. barrel, very rare rework, Navy rear sight.

	N/A	$2,500	$1,800	$1,200	$1,000	$800	$700

Add 20% for 7.65mm Para. with 6 in. barrel.

1920 COMMERCIAL ARTILLERY - 9mm Para. cal., 8 in. barrel, very rare rework.

	N/A	$1,800	$1,500	$1,000	$900	$800	$700

While this variation is undoubtedly rarer than the 1914-1918 military Artillery models, it is less desirable.

1920 "LONG BARREL" COMMERCIAL - 7.65mm Para. or 9mm Para. cal., 10-20 in. barrel, extremely rare.

	N/A	$3,000	$2,500	$1,400	$750	$655	$600

Watch for fakes - these guns have to be evaluated one at a time. Barrel should have matching nos. and Crown N proof.

1920 NAVY CARBINE - 7.65mm Para. cal., 11¾ in. barrel, long frame (if short frame, be wary of fakes, very few produced). Navy rear sight, no forearm under barrel.

	N/A	$3,500	$2,500	$1,500	$1,025	$950	$850

1920 CARBINE - 7.65mm Para. cal., 11¾ in. barrel, very rare.

Gun only	N/A	$5,450	$4,750	$4,000	$3,000	$2,500	$2,000
Gun with stock	N/A	$9,250	$7,250	$6,400	$5,500	$4,650	$3,650

1920 SWISS REWORK - 7.65mm Para. cal., 3 5/8-6 in. barrel, several hundred produced.

	N/A	$1,650	$1,250	$1,000	$750	$655	$600

ABERCROMBIE & FITCH COMMERCIAL - 7.65mm Para. or 9mm Para. cal., long frame, 4¾ in. barrel, 100 mfg., total for both cals.

	N/A	$5,750	$4,350	$3,500	$3,000	$2,575	$2,200

Add 30% for 6 in. barrels (rare).
Inspect barrel legend very carefully (as in beware of fakes) - must have reinforced frame (look for rib in rear frame well).

1920/21-DWM - 9mm Para. cal., 4 in. barrel.

	N/A	$700	$600	$450	$400	$350	$300

Deduct 20% if arsenal reworked.

1920/23 STOEGER AMERICAN EAGLE - 7.65mm Para. or 9mm Para. cal., 3 5/ 8-24 in. barrels, less than 1,000 mfg., made by DWM for Stoeger, sold in USA, longer barrel models have higher value.

3 7/8 - 6 in. barrels	N/A	$2,500	$1,450	$1,200	$1,050	$950	$825
8 in. barrel	N/A	$4,500	$2,300	$2,000	$1,650	$1,200	$995

Add 50% for Mauser mfg., safe and loaded extractor, or V ser. no. suffix.
Be extremely careful when examining the frame markings on this variation as there are many fakes in the marketplace.

1923 DWM COMMERCIAL - 7.65mm Para. cal., 3 5/8 in. barrel, 14,000 mfg. ser. range 74,000-89,000.

	N/A	$825	$525	$385	$335	$285	$250

Grading	100%	98%	95%	90%	80%	70%	60%

1923 DWM "SAFE AND LOADED" COMMERCIAL - 7.65mm Para. cal., "safe and loaded" marked on frame and ejector, 7.65mm Para. cal., 3 7/8 in. barrel, safety and extractor marked in English, 2,000 mfg. ser. range 89,000-91,000.

	N/A	$1,450	$1,000	$850	$600	$500	$420

1923 FINNISH LUGER - 7.65mm Para. cal., approx. 5,000-7,000 units made for Finnish military contract (Army and Navy), marked "SA" surrounded by a rectangle, most have been recently imported into the U.S.

	N/A	$600	$450	$375	$325	$300	$275

Lugers: Krieghoff Mfg.

Add 20% for matching mag. on Krieghoff Models listed .

1923 DWM/KRIEGHOFF COMMERCIAL - 7.65mm Para. (3 7/8 in. barrel only) or 9mm Para. (4 in. barrel only), few mfg., reworked by Krieghoff, chamber dated 1921 or unmarked, most in "i" range, Krieghoff stamped on back-frame. Be wary of fakes.

	N/A	$1,650	$1,300	$1,100	$880	$770	$660

DWM/KRIEGHOFF COMMERCIAL - 7.65mm Para. or 9mm Para. cal., 4 in. barrel, a few hundred made, side frame marked Krieghoff. Most are fake.

	N/A	$2,700	$2,000	$1,650	$1,300	$1,000	$800

KRIEGHOFF COMMERCIAL SIDE FRAME - 7.65mm Para. or 9mm Para. cal., 4 or 6 in. barrel, 1500 mfg., 1,000 with side frame marked, and 500 without. "P" prefix ser. nos.

	N/A	$2,750	$2,100	$1,600	$995	$800	$700

Add 30% for side frame marked 7.65mm Para.

KRIEGHOFF S CODE EARLY - 9mm Para. cal., 4 in. barrel, 1,800 mfg., German Luftwaffe. Has fat walnut grips, "H-K Suhl" toggle.

	N/A	$3,250	$2,400	$1,600	$1,200	$995	$895

KRIEGHOFF S CODE MID SERIES - 9mm Para. cal., 4 in. barrel, 500-700 mfg., Luftwaffe, ser. no. range 1600-2500, fine-checkered plastic grips.

	N/A	$3,250	$2,400	$1,600	$1,200	$995	$895

KRIEGHOFF S CODE LATE - 9mm Para. cal., 4 in. barrel, 1,800 mfg., Luftwaffe, ser. no. range 2300-4200.

	N/A	$2,500	$1,800	$1,200	$750	$600	$500

KRIEGHOFF 36 DATE - 9mm Para. cal., 4 in. barrel, 500-700 made, Luftwaffe military, 2 digit date, coarse checkered plastic grips.

	N/A	$3,000	$2,500	$1,800	$1,300	$1,000	$800

KRIEGHOFF 1936-1945 DATED - 9mm Para. cal., 4 in. barrel, approx. 9,000 mfg., 4 digit chamber date, 1936, 1937 and 1940 most common; 1938 and 1941 through 1944 dates command 70-200% premiums. 1945 is extremely rare - add 500%.

	N/A	$3,000	$2,500	$1,800	$1,320	$1,225	$1,100

The 1941 "large date" is very rare - watch for fakes (re-dated frames) on this model in general.

POST-WAR KRIEGHOFF TYPE I - 9mm Para. cal., 4 in. barrel, 150 mfg. for occupation forces, H-K marked toggle link.

	N/A	$2,500	$1,700	$1,350	$1,050	$950	$850

POST-WAR KRIEGHOFF TYPE II - 9mm Para. cal., 4 in. barrel, 150 mfg., unmarked toggle link, many parts proofed "Eagle-over-2".

	N/A	$2,400	$1,600	$1,200	$995	$875	$775

POST-WAR KRIEGHOFF COMMERCIAL - 7.65mm Para. cal., 4 in. barrel, 100- 200 mfg., unmarked toggle, many parts proofed "Eagle-over-2".

	N/A	$1,800	$1,400	$1,000	$900	$800	$775

Grading	100%	98%	95%	90%	80%	70%	60%

Lugers: Mauser Mfg.

Most common variations in good supply within this section in 50% or less condition will approximate the 60% value. This reflects its value as a representative shooter rather than a higher priced collector's gun.

1935-06 PORTUGUESE GNR - 7.65mm Para. cal., 4¾ in. barrel, 564 mfg., GNR on chamber, Portuguese marked safety and extractor.

	N/A	$2,600	$1,600	$1,300	$1,050	$800	$525

1934/06 MAUSER SWISS COMMERCIAL - 7.65mm Para. cal., 4¾ in. barrel, a few hundred produced, "Cross in Sunburst" or blank chamber, grip safety.

	N/A	$3,150	$2,450	$2,000	$1,500	$1,250	$850

1934 MAUSER BANNER COMMERCIAL - 7.65mm Para. or 9mm Para. cal., 4 in. barrel, hundreds produced, unmarked chamber, "v" suffix to ser. no.

	N/A	$2,600	$1,800	$1,425	$1,150	$950	$725

Add 15% for "Kal. 7.65" barrel marking.

S/42 K DATE - 9mm Para. cal., 4 in. barrel, approx. 10,000 mfg. during 1934 only for military.

	N/A	$4,500	$3,800	$2,500	$1,800	$1,500	$1,200

Add 100% for "large eagle over M Navy" proofmark.

S/42 G DATE - 9mm Para. cal., 4 in. barrel, many thousand produced 1935 only.

	N/A	$1,325	$900	$675	$525	$450	$400

Add 20% for Navy markings.

S/42 DATED CHAMBER - 9mm Para. cal., 4 in. barrel, many thousands produced, "S/ 42" stamped rear toggle, chamber dated 1936-1940. One of the most frequently encountered WWII military Lugers.

	N/A	$1,000	$775	$600	$475	$400	$350

Add $100 for original holster in average+ condition.
Add 50% for matching mag.
Add 100% for 2 matching mags.
Add 100% for Navy markings.
Add 20% for 1936 date.
Add 30% for "strawed" 1937 date.
The last regular production S/42 Models were mfg. approx. April of 1939.

MAUSER PERSIAN (IRANIAN) CONTRACT - 9mm Para. cal., 4 and 8 in. barrels, 1,000 - 8 in. mfg., and 1,000 - 4 in. mfg., Farsi numerals.

4 in. barrel	N/A	$3,750	$3,200	$2,750	$2,250	$2,000	$1,750
Artillery (8 in.)	N/A	$2,400	$2,000	$1,800	$1,650	$1,475	$1,200

Add 50% for Artillery with matching rig.
This variation became less desirable after the U.S. hostage situation occurred in Iran.

1936-1942 DATED MAUSER BANNER - 9mm Para. cal., 4 in. barrel, over 1,000 mfg., commercial and contract sales. No sear safety, often have strawed small parts.

	N/A	$1,500	$1,050	$800	$700	$600	$500

MAUSER BANNER DUTCH CONTRACT - 9mm Para. cal., 4 in. barrel, 1,000 mfg., safety marked "Rust". Dated 1936-1940.

	N/A	$2,800	$1,700	$1,000	$600	$500	$400

Add 25% for 1936, 1937, 1938, or 1939 chamber date.

MAUSER BANNER SWEDISH CONTRACT - 275 mfg. in 9mm Para. cal., 4¾ in. barrels, dated 1938, 25 mfg. in 9mm Para. cal., dated 1939, 30 mfg. in 7.65mm Para. cal., dated 1939, very rare in 7.65mm Para. dated 1940.

	N/A	$2,700	$1,800	$1,200	$695	$600	$500

Add 15% for 7.65mm Para. cal. (4¾ in. barrel).

L

Grading	100%	98%	95%	90%	80%	70%	60%

CODE "S/42" COMMERCIAL CONTRACT - 9mm Para. cal., 4 in. barrel, a few hundred produced, dated 1938. Commercial proof marks only.

	N/A	$1,350	$975	$750	$650	$550	$500

CODE "42" - 9mm Para. cal., 4 in. barrels, dated 1939-1940, rear toggle marked "42". One of the most frequently encountered WWII military Lugers.

	N/A	$1,100	$800	$700	$600	$500	$475

Add 100% for Navy markings.
Add $125+ for original holster in average condition.

MAUSER BANNER POLICE - 9mm Para. cal., approx. 30,000 mfg., dated 1939-1942, police contract, have sear safeties, blue small parts. A few observed dated 1938.

	N/A	$1,650	$1,000	$600	$500	$400	$350

Add 30% with 1938 chamber date (rare).

CODE "41-42" - 9mm Para. cal., 4 in. barrel, 2-digit date, approx. 7,000 mfg. in January of 1941, "41" dated chamber, "42" code, most 42 dates are reworks.

	N/A	$1,500	$950	$650	$425	$375	$350

Add $150+ for original holster in average condition.

CODE "byf" - 9mm Para. cal., 4 in. barrel, thousands made, chamber dated 41 and 42. Rear toggle is stamped "byf", standard magazine was "fxo" marked and had an un-numbered plastic bottom. One of the most frequently encountered WWII military Lugers.

	N/A	$1,200	$900	$700	$600	$500	$475

Add 30% for original black bakelite grips.
Add $150 for original holster in average condition.

Code "byf" Lugers with black bakelite grips are referred to as the "Black Widow" variation.

AUSTRIAN BUNDES HEER - 9mm Para. cal., 4 in. barrel, several hundred produced, Austrian Federal Army, no serial letter suffix-same ser. placement as KU. Rarely encountered in mint condition.

	N/A	$1,800	$1,200	$950	$825	$750	$650

MAUSER 1934 CODE BYF, S/42 AND 42 KU - 9mm Para. cal., 3,500 mfg. Post-1942 Luftwaffe subcontract.

	N/A	$1,875	$1,300	$950	$825	$750	$650

Lugers: Reworks

DEATH'S HEAD REWORK - 9mm Para. cal., 4 in. barrel, very rare, possible early SS unit issue. Most are fakes.

	N/A	$2,500	$1,800	$1,500	$1,400	$1,200	$1,000

SIMSON REWORK - 9mm Para. cal., 4 in. barrel, DWM toggles, Simpson Eagle proofs on reworked parts.

	N/A	$850	$700	$500	$475	$450	$400

DOUBLE DATED DWM/ERFURT - 9mm Para. cal., 4 or 8 in. barrel, very scarce. 1920 over 1910-1918 chamber dates. Often with sear safety and mag. safety remnant.

	N/A	$900	$750	$550	$500	$425	$400

Add 100% for intact mag. safety.
Add 40% for 8 in. barrel.

KONZENTRATION LUGER REWORK - 9mm Para. cal., 4 in. barrel, 200-300 marked "KI 1933" and issued to guards working in the first concentration camps - most went to Dachau. Most are fakes.

	N/A	$1,800	$1,500	$1,200	$1,000	$700	$600

Grading	100%	98%	95%	90%	80%	70%	60%

Lugers: Simson Mfg.

SIMSON & COMPANY - 7.65mm Para. or 9mm Para. cal., 3 7/8 or 4 in. barrel, military and limited commercial sales, many thousands produced, but rarely found.

	N/A	$1,450	$800	$650	$500	$450	$375

SIMSON MILITARY DATED - 9mm Para. cal., 4 in. barrel, 2,000 mfg., dated 1925.

	N/A	$2,500	$2,000	$1,000	$800	$675	$550

This model is most commonly encountered with a 1925 chamber date.

SIMSON S CODE - 9mm Para. cal., 4 in. barrel, less than 1,000 mfg. Rare.

	N/A	$1,850	$1,300	$975	$675	$550	$475

Lugers: Swiss Bern

1906 BERN - 7.65mm Para. cal., 4¾ in. barrel, "Waffenfabrik Bern" on toggle, Swiss military, bordered checkered walnut grips, exactly 17,874 mfg.

	N/A	$2,375	$1,700	$1,200	$900	$700	$600

1929 SWISS BERN - 7.65mm Para. cal., 4¾ in. barrel, 29,857 mfg., many machining changes to simplify production, straight front grip strap, P prefix designates commercial model, brown or black plastic grips.

	N/A	$1,750	$1,100	$900	$800	$600	$500

Add 20% for red plastic grips and mag. bottom.

Lugers: KDF, Interarms, Stoeger, & Recent Import

Note: Post-WWII Lugers have been manufactured by Mauser Werke in Oberndorf, W. Germany during the 1970s, and by both Stoeger Industries and Mitchell Arms (see separate listing under Mitchell Arms) in recent years. Currently, the Stoeger Luger is the only Luger available for sale domestically. Earlier Mauser importation was by Precision Imports, Inc. located in San Antonio, TX and Interarms of Alexandria, VA (and so marked on these guns).

Prices for 100% condition Lugers assume NIB status. If without box and accessories, deduct 25%.

INTERARMS MAUSER P.08 - 7.65mm Para. or 9mm Para. cal., 4 or 6 in. barrel, fully- contoured front grip strap.

$850	$675	$550	$425	$375	$350	$300

INTERARMS "SWISS-STYLE" MAUSER EAGLE - 7.65mm Para. or 9mm Para. cal., "straight" front grip strap, American eagle logo on top of frame.

$775	$600	$425	$375	$350	$325	$275

Add 10% for 6 in. barrel in 9mm Para.

STOEGER .22 CAL. LUGER - .22 LR cal., toggle action, all steel construction, 4½ in. barrel, 10 shot mag. capacity, previously mfg. in the U.S. until 1985.

$150	$125	$100	$85	$70	$60	$50

Last MSR was $200.

✳ **"1 of 1,000"** - .22 LR cal., 1,000 mfg. in 1984-85, includes wooden box and extra mag.

$295	$225	$175

STOEGER LUGER - 9mm Para. cal., choice of 4 or 6 (Navy) in. barrel, stainless steel construction, choice of polished stainless or matte black (new 1996) upper frame finish, American eagle engraved on top of frame, curved front grip strap, 7 shot mag., plastic mag. bottom, approx. 30 oz. Mfg. 1994-disc..

$640	$350	$275

Last MSR was $720.

Add $79 for matte black finish.

Grading	100%	98%	95%	90%	80%	70%	60%

NEW MODEL CARBINE WITH STOCK - 9mm Para. cal., authentic reproduction of the original Luger Carbine complete with matching stock, accessories, and case. Inventory was depleted during 1998.

$4,995 $3,850 $2,000

Last MSR was $7,431.

CARTRIDGE COUNTER - 9mm Para. cal., left grip is slotted and contains a numbered metal strip. Manufacture began 1983, and inventory was depleted during 1998.

$2,650 $1,550 $950

Last MSR was $3,865.

COMMEMORATIVE BULGARIAN - 9mm Para. cal., 100 available on U.S. market.

$1,800 $1,200 $800

COMMEMORATIVE RUSSIAN - 9mm Para. cal., 100 available on U.S. market.

$1,800 $1,200 $800

✳ *Matched pair of each*

$4,000 $2,550 $1,850

MAUSER SPORT PARABELLUM - 7.65mm Para. or 9mm Para. cal., imported target barrel and adj. sights. 10 mfg. of each cal.

$2,500 $2,000 $1,250

✳ *Mauser Sport Consecutive Pair* - 7.65mm Para. or 9mm Para. cal.

$4,250 $3,175 $1,950

Lugers: Special Interest

SPANDAU LUGER - Beware of fakes, since they are all fake!

M04/05 G.L. BABY LUGER - 7.65mm Para. or 9mm Para. cal., 3¼ in. barrel, G.L. proofed, hand-made under Georg Luger's supervision, two known to exist. Made with shortened barrel, mag., and grip frame.

BABY LUGER 1925/26 - .380 ACP/.32 ACP cal., prototype, 4 mfg., only one known is .380. Only Luger documented by the manufacturer.

VONO REWORK - 7.65mm Para. or 9mm Para. cal., 4 in. barrel, commercial, rework by W.P. Von Nordheim, extremely rare variation.

$1,500 $1,275 $1,050 $900 $800 $700 $600

1900 DWM CARBINE - 7.65mm Para. cal., 11¾ in. barrel, 100 mfg., only one known to exist. Characterized by "Ski slope" sight on rear toggle.

1907 U.S. ARMY TEST TRIAL - .45 ACP cal., at least four mfg., three known to exist. BIG buck$ (read that $10x10 to the fifth power!)

CONVERSIONS: JOHN MARTZ - John Martz of Lincoln, CA has converted WWII P.38s and WWI or WWII Lugers into various configurations since 1968. These conversions are known for their quality workmanship and functional accuracy. Below is a generalized listing of variations he has fabricated and their values to date with production totals.

✳ *.380 ACP Baby Luger* - 6 fabricated. (disc.).

$6,000 $3,200 $2,400

✳ *7.65mm Para. Baby Luger (Grip Safety)* - 21 fabricated 3 in. barrel.

$3,000 $2,500 $1,900

✳ *9mm Para. Baby Luger* - 159 fabricated, 2, 2¼, 2½, 2 5/8, or 3 in. barrel.

$2,500 $2,000 $1,500

✳ *Big-Bore .45 ACP Luger* - 74 fabricated (5 are babies), .45 ACP cal., fixed sights, 2¾, 4, 6, or 8 in. barrel.

$5,500 $3,350 $2,400

Grading	100%	98%	95%	90%	80%	70%	60%

* ***Navy Model*** - .45 ACP cal., 6 or 8 in. barrel, adj. rear Navy sight, estimated mfg. is 25 pistols (Disc.).

	$6,000	$4,450	$3,300				

Add 10% for Navy Model with 100-200 meter rear sight.

* ***Navy Model Ltd. Edition*** - .38 Super cal., 6 in. barrel, adj. rear Navy sight, 10 fabricated (disc.).

	$5,000	$3,950	$3,100				

Subtract 10% for fixed rear sight (standard model with 4 in. barrel).

* ***Standard Model*** - .38 Super cal., 4 to 8 in. barrel, fixed sight, 3 fabricated.

	$4,500	$3,150	$2,400				

* ***Target Luger*** - .22 Mag. cal., 6 or 9 in. barrel, fixed sight, 11 fabricated. (disc.).

	$7,500	$5,400	$3,400				

* ***Luger Carbines (with shoulder stock)*** - .22 Mag. (disc.), 7.65mm Para., 9mm Para., or .38 Super cal., 11-18 in. barrel with adj. rear sights. Disc.

	$7,900	$5,650	$3,600				

Add 20% for .22 Mag. cal. (2 fabricated).

83 Luger carbines with 16 in. barrels were fabricated with shoulder stocks.
42 Luger carbines with 12 in. barrels were fabricated w/o shoulder stocks.

* ***Experimental Lugers*** - experimental pistols have been made in .40 S&W (disc.), .41 AE (disc.), and .357 Mag. Most have 8 in. barrels (except for .40 S&W cal., disc.). Extreme rarity (and not for sale status) precludes accurate price evaluation.

LUGERS: ACCESSORIES

CONVERSION UNITS - .22 cal.

ERMA - postwar-green cardboard box.

	$350	$320	$295	$275	$250	$225	$200

ERMA-PREWAR IN WOODEN BOX - Pre-war in wooden box - deduct 20% for mismatched. Add 50% for Nazi Navy property numbered.

	$950	$825	$700	$550	$550	$430	$400

Detachable Stocks

ARTILLERY TYPE FLAT BOARD

	$350	$250	$200	$165	$135	$120	$110

ARTILLERY HOLSTER RIG, COMPLETE

	$1,000	$775	$575				

Subtract 20% if shoulder strap is missing.

NAVAL-TYPE FLAT BOARD

	$1,500	$995	$750	$600	$450	$410	$350

NAVAL HOLSTER RIG, COMPLETE

	$4,500	$4,000	$3,000	$2,500	$1,800	$1,500	$1,200

Subtract 20% if shoulder strap is missing.

CARBINE CONTOURED (ORIGINAL)

	$3,500	$3,000	$2,500	$1,800	$1,200	$900	$700

IDEAL TELESCOPING WITH GRIPS - mfg. U.S. by Ideal Corp.

	$1,800	$1,500	$1,000	$700	$600	$550	$500

"Snail" Drum Magazines

1ST ISSUE

	$1,200	$850	$700				

L

Grading	100%	98%	95%	90%	80%	70%	60%

2ND ISSUE

	$950	$700	$600				

LOADING TOOL

	$775	$675	$500				

SHOTGUNS: O/U

CLASSIC MODEL - 12 ga., 3½ in. chambers, engraved boxlock action, 26, 28, or 30 in. vent. barrels with VR and 3 choke tubes, gold SST, AE, checkered walnut stock and forearm, approx. 7½ lbs.

While advertised by Stoeger Industies during 2000, this model was never imported.

SHOTGUNS: SEMI-AUTO

ULTRA-LIGHT MODEL - 12 ga. only, 3 in. chamber, gas operated, 26 or 28 in. VR barrel with 3 choke tubes, checkered walnut stock and forearm, approx. 6½ lbs.

	$295	$260	$230	$210	$195	$180	$165

While advertised by Stoeger Industies during 2000, this model was never imported by Stoeger Industries. However, it has had limited importation to date from domestic distributors.

LU-MAR s.r.l.

Current shotgun manufacturer located in Gardone, Italy. No current U.S. importation.

Lu-Mar makes a wide variety of O/U shotguns. In addition to their fine O/U lineup, Lu-Mar also manufactures SxS shotguns. Please contact the factory directly (see Trademark Index) for more information on Lu-Mar's complete line of quality O/U shotguns.

LUNA

Previous manufacturer located in Germany.

PISTOLS: SINGLE SHOT

MODEL 200 FREE PISTOL - .22 LR cal., 11 in. barrel, blue, target sights, checkered target grips, pre-WWII.

	$1,100	$990	$855	$770	$660	$605	$525

RIFLES: SINGLE SHOT

TARGET RIFLE - falling block action, .22 LR or .22 Hornet cal., 20 in. barrel, adj. sights, target type stocks, pre-WWII.

	$990	$880	$800	$690	$605	$550	$495

M Section

MAB

Please refer to listings under the French Military heading.

MAC (MILITARY ARMAMENT CORP.)

Please refer to FMJ and Ingram sections in this text. MAC is located in Ducktown, TN (please refer to the FMJ listing in the Trademark Index for current information).

MAS

Previously manufactured by D'Armes St. Etienne (MAS) located in France.

Please refer to the French Military heading in this text.

MBA GYROJET

Previous manufacturer circa 1966-1969 located in San Ramon, CA.

Grading	100%	98%	95%	90%	80%	70%	60%

PISTOLS: SEMI-AUTO

MARK I GYROJET PISTOL - 12mm or 13mm (no cartridge case) cal., uses spin-stabilized rocket projectiles that accelerate to 1,250 FPS in .12 seconds, 2 in. (rare) or 5 in. barrel, 6 shot semi-auto action drives rocket projectile (primer activated) into fixed firing pin, smooth walnut grips, black, antique nickel, or gold-plated finish, 13 or 16 oz., "A" prefix until ser. no. 49, "B" prefixes followed, there are also other variations and experimental models in addition to the production models listed. Not particularly accurate.

The rocket ammunition for this model is rare and typically sells in the $20-$25/round range per shell.

* ***Mark I Model A Cased*** - 13mm, black finish, smooth walnut grips, walnut cased with 10 rounds and medal.

	100%	98%	95%	90%	80%	70%	60%
	$1,450	$1,300	$1,100	$950	$875	$795	$700

* ***Mark I Model B Cased*** - 13mm, black, nickel, satin, or green finish, many variations with different grips, casings, and barrel lengths, wood cased.

	$1,195	$1,000	$900	$800	$700	$600	$500

Add approx. 25% for satin finish.

* ***Mark I Model B Uncased or Cardboard*** - either with cardboard case or no case, black finish.

	$650	$525	$450	$400	$360	$330	$300

* ***Mark II Model C Uncased or Cardboard*** - 12mm, black finish, walnut grips.

	$650	$525	$450	$400	$360	$330	$300

This variation was manufactured in 12mm to conform with the 1968 GCA, since any caliber over .50 was classified as a destructive device (i.e., 12mm = .49 cal. and 13mm = .51 cal.). In 1982, the 13mm guns were reclassified as curios and relics.

* ***Mark I Presentation Model*** - cased with 10 dummy/live rounds and bronze medal honoring rocket pioneers Robert H. Goddard and Joseph J. Stubbs.

	$2,250	$1,600	$995

RIFLES: SEMI-AUTO, CARBINES

MARK I MODEL A or B CARBINE - 13mm cal., same action as Mark I pistol, black (Model A) or satin (Model B) finish, full stock with pistol grip extension, 18 in. barrel, nickel finish, 4½ lbs. Limited mfg.

	100%	98%	95%	90%	80%	70%	60%
Model A	$1,695	$1,600	$1,475	$1,350	$1,225	$1,100	$1,000
Model B	$1,195	$925	$800	$700	$600	$550	$500

M

Grading	100%	98%	95%	90%	80%	70%	60%

M-K SPECIALTIES INC.

Current rifle manufacturer established in 2000 located in Grafton, WV. Dealer sales only.

RIFLES: SEMI-AUTO

M-14 A1 - .308 Win. cal., new production forged M-14 steel receiver using CNC machinery to original government specifications, available as Rack Grade, Premier Match, or Tanker Model, variety of National Match upgrades are available at extra cost, base price is for Rack Grade. New 2000.

MSR	$1,595		$1,400	$1,200	$995	$875	$750	$625	$500

National Match upgrades range from $345-$955.

MK ARMS INC.

Previous manufacturer located in Irvine, CA circa 1992.

CARBINES

MK 760 - 9mm Para. cal., paramilitary design carbine configuration, steel frame, 16 in. shrouded barrel, fires from closed bolt, 14, 24, or 36 shot mag., parkerized finish, folding metal stock, fixed sights. Mfg. 1983-approx. 1992.

		$675	$625	$575	$525	$475	$415	$375

Last MSR was $575.

MKE

Previous manufacturer located in Ankara, Turkey. Previously distributed by Mandall Shooting Supplies, Inc., located in Scottsdale, AZ.

PISTOLS: SEMI-AUTO

KIRIKKALE AUTOMATIC - 7.65mm Para. (disc.) or .380 ACP cal., double action, 7 shot, blue, fixed sights, checkered plastic grips, this is a close copy of Walther's PP and the Turkish Army's standard service pistol. Disc. 1987.

		$365	$295	$240	$215	$185	$170	$155

Last MSR was $395.

M.O.A. CORPORATION

Current manufacturer located in Eaton, OH. Dealer direct sales only.

PISTOLS: SINGLE SHOT

Approx. 500-600 Maximum pistols are produced annually.

MAXIMUM - available in 30 standard chamberings between .22 Rimfire and .454 Casull cal., additional custom calibers are also available upon special order, single shot lever action pistol, falling block action, Chromoly receiver (disc. 1991), Armoloy coated Chromoly (disc. late 1992), or stainless steel (new 1991, standard 1992) receiver, 8¾ (new 1989), 10½, or 14 in. interchangeable barrel, transfer bar safety, adj. open sights, walnut grips and forearm. New 1986.

MSR	$799		$695	$575	$495	$450	$400	$375	$350

Subtract 10% for older steel receiver.
Add $60 for scope mounts.
Add $84 for stainless steel barrel on either receiver.
Add $125 for muzzle brake.
Add $254 per extra steel barrel.
Add $317 per extra stainless steel barrel.

Grading	100%	98%	95%	90%	80%	70%	60%

Barrels must be fitted to individual receivers at the factory initially. Afterwards, they can be changed by the customer with the spanner wrench (included with extra barrels).

✳ ***Carbine Model*** - cals. up to .250 Sav., stainless receiver, otherwise similar to Maximum, except has 18 in. barrel. Mfg. began 1986, and production has been disc. several times.

	MSR	$909		$825	$725	$650	$575	$525	$475	$425

MTs ARMS

Current trademark manufactured by the State Unitary Enterprise, Instrument Design Bureau, a subsidiary of Sporting and Hunting Gun Central Design and Research Bureau (GUP "KBP" - "TsKIB SOO"), located in Tula, Russia. No current U.S. importation.

MTs Arms manufactures a variety of firearms, including SxS and O/U shotguns, combination guns, slide action shotguns, bolt action rifles, drillings, competition guns, and semi-auto rifles TsKIB SOO is the only manufacturer of quality hunting guns in Russia and the countries of the CIS (Commonwealth of Independent States). Please contact the company directly for more information regarding this trademark (see Trademark Index).

JAMES MacNAUGHTON & SONS

Current trademark owned and manufactured by Dickson & MacNaughton, located in Edinburgh, Scotland.

The firm of James MacNaughton was founded in Edinburgh, Scotland in 1864. During 1947, the company was acquired by John Dickson and during 1996, the ownership of the company changed again, having purchased the manufacturing rights from Dickson. In 1999, the directors of James MacNaughton & Sons acquired the whole share capital of John Dickson & Son, and the two companies now trade as one under the name of Dickson & MacNaughton. Please contact Dickson & MacNaughton directly for more information regarding this trademark, including current availability and pricing.

RIFLES: SxS

SIDELOCK RIFLE - .375 H&H or .470 NE cal., specifications per individual customer order.
Prices currently start at approx. $27,125 for this model.

SHOTGUNS

SxS SIDELOCK MODEL - 20 or 28 ga., lightweight construction.
Prices currently start at approx. $36,000 for this model.

MAADI-GRIFFIN CO.

Current rifle manufacturer located in Mesa, AZ. Consumer direct sales.

RIFLES: SEMI-AUTO

MODEL MG-6 - .50 BMG cal., gas operated, bullpup configuration, one piece cast lower receiver, 5, 10, or 15 shot side mounted mag., 26-30 in. barrel, includes bipod, hard carrying case, and 3 mags. 23 lbs. New 2000.

	MSR	$5,950		$5,500	$4,750	$3,850	$3,250	$2,600	$2,200	$1,800

Add $450 for MK-IV tripod.

RIFLES: SINGLE SHOT

MODEL 89 - .50 BMG cal., one piece cast lower receiver, 36 in. barrel, felt recoil is less than 12 ga., tig-welded interlocking assembly, no screws, tripod optional, 22 lbs. New 1990.

	MSR	$3,150		$2,900	$2,600	$2,300	$2,000	$1,750	$1,500	$1,250

Add $600 for stainless steel.

Grading	100%	98%	95%	90%	80%	70%	60%

MODEL 92 CARBINE - .50 BMG cal., 20 in. barrel, 5 lbs. trigger pull, 18½ lbs. New 1990.

MSR	$2,990	$2,800	$2,500	$2,200	$1,850	$1,650	$1,400	$1,200

Add $650 for stainless steel.

MODEL 99 - .50 BMG cal., similar to Model 89, except has 44 in. barrel, 28 lbs. New 1999.

MSR	$3,350	$3,150	$2,725	$2,450	$2,050	$1,775	$1,500	$1,250

Add $650 for stainless steel.

MAGNUM RESEARCH, INC.

Current trademark of pistols and rifles with company headquarters located in Minneapolis, MN. Centerfire pistols (Desert Eagle Series) are again mfg. by IMI, located in Israel. Previously mfg. by Saco Defense located in Saco, ME during 1995-98, and by TAAS/IMI (Israeli Military Industries) 1986-1995. .22 Rimfire semi-auto pistols (Mountain Eagle) were previously manufactured by Ram-Line. Single shot pistols (Lone Eagle) were manufactured by Magnum Research sub-contractors. Distributed by Magnum Research, Inc., in Minneapolis, MN. Dealer and distributor sales.

MRI CUSTOM SHOP

In addition to the models listed, Magnum Research can also provide a variety of special order options through their custom shop including a choice of nine different finishes listed, in addition to various sight systems and grips.

MRI's current custom shop finish options with MSRs are as follows: Add $225 for polished hard chrome (PC), matte hard chrome (MC), brushed hard chrome (BC), bright nickel (BN), satin nickel (SN), polished blue (PB), or gold accents. 24 Kt. gold (GO) finish, titanium gold finish (TG, new 2000), or titanium carbon nitride (TCN, new 2002) is also available for an additional $500.

PISTOLS: SEMI-AUTO, RIMFIRE

THE MOUNTAIN EAGLE - .22 LR cal., single action, 6 (new 1995) or 6½ (disc. 1994) in. polymer and steel barrel, features alloy receiver and polymer technology, matte black finish, adj. rear sight, 15 or 20 shot mag. 21 oz. Mfg. 1992-96.

		$185	$155	$135	$115	$100	$85	$75

Last MSR was $239.

✳ *Mountain Eagle Compact Edition* - similar to Mountain Eagle, except has 4½ in. barrel with shortened grips, adj. rear sight, 10 or 15 shot mag., plastic case, 19.3 oz. Mfg. 1996 only.

		$165	$135	$120	$105	$95	$80	$70

Last MSR was $199.

✳ *Mountain Eagle Target Edition* - .22 LR cal., Target variation of the Mountain Eagle, featuring 8 in. accurized barrel, 2- stage target trigger, jeweled bolt, adj. sights with interchangeable blades, 23 oz. Mfg. 1994-96.

		$235	$185	$150	$135	$120	$105	$95

Last MSR was $279.

PISTOLS: SEMI-AUTO, CENTERFIRE

BARAK SP-21 - 9mm Para., .40 S&W, or .45 ACP cal., DAO, delayed blow back action, polymer frame with ergonomic design, 3.9 in. barrel with polygonal rifling, 10 shot mag., reversible mag. release, multiple safeties, matte black finish, decocking feature, approx. 29 oz. Importation from IMI began 2002.

MSR	$499	$425	$375	$335	$300	$280	$260	$240

Grading	100%	98%	95%	90%	80%	70%	60%

PISTOLS: SEMI-AUTO, CENTERFIRE - EAGLE SERIES

Magnum Research also offers a Collector's Edition Presentation Series. Special models include a Gold Edition (serial numbered 1-100), a Silver Edition (serial numbered 101-500), and a Bronze Edition (serial numbered 501-1,000). Each pistol from this series is supplied with a walnut presentation case, 2 sided medallion, and certificate of authenticity. Prices are available upon request by contacting Magnum Research directly.

Alloy frames on the Desert Eagle Series of pistols were discontinued in 1992. However, if sufficient demand warrants, these models will once again be available to consumers at the same price as the steel frames.

Beginning late 1995, the Desert Eagle frame assembly for the .357 Mag., .44 Mag., and .50 AE cals. is based on the .50 caliber frame. Externally, all three pistols are now identical in size. This new platform called the Desert Eagle Pistol Mark XIX Component System enables .44 Mag. and .50 AE conversions to consist of simply a barrel and a magazine - conversions to or from the .357 Mag. also include a bolt.

Individual Desert Eagle Mark XIX barrels are either $339 (6 in.) or $419 (10 in.).

THE BABY EAGLE - 9mm Para., .40 S&W, .41 AE (disc.), or .45 ACP (3.7 in. barrel only, new 2000) cal., double action, all steel or polymer (3.5 in. barrel, 9mm Para. or .40 S&W only) frame construction, 3.5 (new 2000), 3.62 (mfg. 1993-99), 3.7 (new 2000), or 4.72 in. barrel, short recoil operation, polygonal rifling, combat styled trigger guard, decocking slide safety or frame mounted safety (Model 9mmF), blued (disc. 1995), standard black (new 1996), or chrome (disc. 1999) finish, 10 (C/B 1994), 16* (9mm Para.), 11* (.41 AE), or 10 (.40 S&W) shot mag., 38½ oz. Imported 1991-96. Reintroduced mid 1999.

MSR	$499	$415	$350	$300	$265	$230	$210	$190

Add $239 for conversion kit (9mm Para. to .41 AE or .41 AE to 9mm Para., includes barrel, spring, and mag.) – disc. 1996.

* ***Baby Eagle Compact*** - 9mm Para. or .40 S&W cal., same general specifications as Baby Eagle, except has 3.5 in. barrel and polymer frame only.

MSR	$499	$415	$350	$300	$265	$230	$210	$190

MARK XIX .357 MAG. DESERT EAGLE - features .50 cal. frame and slide, standard black finish, 6 or 10 in. barrel, mfg. by Saco 1995-98, and IMI again beginning 1998.

MSR	$1,199	$1,025	$875	$725	$575	$475	$400	$350

Add $100 for 10 in. barrel.

MARK VII .357 MAG. DESERT EAGLE - .357 Mag. cal., gas operated, 6 (standard barrel length), 10, or 14 in. barrel length with 3/ 8 in. rib, steel (58.3 oz.) or alloy (47.8 oz.) frame, adaptable to .44 Mag. with optional kit, 9 shot mag. (8 for .44 Mag.). Mfg. 1983-95, limited quantities were made available again during 1998 and 2001.

	$850	$650	$525	$475	$425	$395	$375

Last MSR was $929.

Add approx. $150 for 10 or 14 in. barrel (disc. 1995).
Add $495 for .357 Mag. to .41 Mag./.44 Mag. conversion kit (6 in. barrel). Disc. 1995.
Add approx. $685 for .357 Mag. to .44 Mag. conversion kit (10 or 14 in. barrel). Disc. 1995.

* ***Whitetail Special .357 Mag.*** - 14 in. barrel, includes scope mount, target walnut grips, and Desert Eagle premiums. Mfg. 1990-1992.

	$925	$750	$650	$550	$450	$400	$375

Last MSR was $1,088.

Add $50 for stainless steel frame.

* ***Stainless Steel .357 Mag.*** - similar to .357 Mag. Desert Eagle, except has stainless steel frame, 58.3 oz. Mfg. 1987-95.

	$750	$650	$550

Last MSR was $839.

Add approx. $150 for 10 or 14 in. barrel.

M

Grading	100%	98%	95%	90%	80%	70%	60%

MARK VII .41 MAG. DESERT EAGLE - .41 Mag. cal., similar to .357 Desert Eagle, 6 in. barrel only, 8 shot mag., steel (62.8 oz.) or alloy (52.3 oz.) frame. Mfg. 1988-95, limited quanitites available during 2001.

		$785	**$675**	**$565**	**$500**	**$465**	**$420**	**$390**

Last MSR was $899.

Add $395 for .41 Mag. to .44 Mag. conversion kit (6 in. barrel only).

* ✳ *Stainless Steel .41 Mag.* - similar to .41 Mag. Desert Eagle, except has stainless steel frame, 58.3 oz. Mfg. 1988- 95.

		$825	**$700**	**$550**

Last MSR was $949.

MARK XIX .44 MAG. DESERT EAGLE - features .50 cal. frame and slide, standard black finish, 6 or 10 in. barrel, mfg. by Saco 1995-98, and by IMI again beginning 1998.

MSR	**$1,199**	**$1,025**	**$875**	**$725**	**$575**	**$475**	**$400**	**$350**

Add $100 for 10 in. barrel.

MARK VII .44 MAG. DESERT EAGLE - .44 Mag. cal., similar to .357 Desert Eagle, 8 shot mag., steel (62.8 oz.) or alloy (52.3 oz.) frame. Originally mfg. 1986-95, re-released 1998-2000.

		$925	**$700**	**$565**	**$585**	**$430**	**$395**	**$375**

Last MSR was $1,049.

Add $100 for 10 (current) or 14 (disc. 1995) in. barrel.
Add $475 for .44 Mag. to .357 Mag. conversion kit (6 in. barrel). Disc. 1995.
Add $675 for .44 Mag. to .357 Mag. conversion kit (10 or 14 in. barrel). Disc. 1995.
Add $395 for .44 Mag. to .41 Mag. conversion kit (6 in. barrel). Disc. 1995.

* ✳ *Stainless Steel .44 Mag.* - similar to .44 Mag. Desert Eagle, except has stainless steel frame, 58.3 oz. Mfg. 1987- 95.

		$825	**$700**	**$550**

Last MSR was $949.

Add approx. $210 for 10 or 14 in. barrel.

M

HUNTER EDITION MARK VII - .357 or .44 Mag. cal., 6 in. barrel with extra 14 in. hunting barrel, includes Leupold 2X EER scope, scope mount. Mfg. late 1987-1993.

		$1,200	**$975**	**$825**	**$675**	**$550**	**$475**	**$425**

Last MSR was $1,350.

Add $110 for .44 Mag. cal.

MARK VII .50 MAG. DESERT EAGLE - .50 AE cal., 6 in. barrel with 7/8 in. rib with cross slots for Weaver style rings, steel only, black standard finish, frame slightly taller than the Mark VII .357 Mag./.44 Mag., 7 shot mag., 72.4 oz. Mfg. 1991-95 by IMI, limited quantities were made available again during 1998 only.

		$950	**$825**	**$700**	**$575**	**$500**	**$450**	**$400**

Last MSR was $1,099.

This cartridge utilized the same rim dimensions as the .44 Mag. and was available with a 300 grain bullet. The .50 Action Express cal. has 60% more stopping power than the .44 Mag., with a minimal increase in felt recoil.

MARK XIX CUSTOM 440 - .440 Cor-Bon cal., similar to Mark XIX .44 Mag. Desert Eagle, 6 or 10 in. barrel, standard black finish, rechambered by MRI Custom Shop, limited mfg. 1999-2001.

		$1,175	**$995**	**$850**	**$725**	**$575**	**$500**	**$450**

Last MSR was $1,389.

Add $40 for 10 in. barrel.

MARK XIX .50 MAG. DESERT EAGLE - features .50 AE cal., larger frame, standard black finish, 6 or 10 in. barrel, mfg. by Saco 1995-98, and by IMI again beginning 1998.

MSR	**$1,199**	**$1,025**	**$875**	**$725**	**$575**	**$475**	**$400**	**$350**

Add $100 for 10 in. barrel.

Grading	100%	98%	95%	90%	80%	70%	60%

MARK XIX 3 CAL. COMPONENT SYSTEM - includes Mark XIX .44 Mag. Desert Eagle and 5 barrels including .357 Mag. (6 and 10 in.), .44 Mag., and .50 AE (6 and 10 in.) cals., .357 bolt assembly and ICC aluminum carrying case. New 1998.

MSR	$3,691	$3,290	$2,800	$2,350	$1,950	$1,650	$1,300	$1,050

* **Mark XIX Component System** - includes component Mark XIX system in 6 or 10 in. barrel only. New 1998.

MSR	$2,395	$2,115	$1,800	$1,650	$1,475	$1,250	$1,000	$850

Add $260 for 10 in. barrels.

PISTOLS: SINGLE SHOT

LONE EAGLE (SSP-91) - .22 LR (disc. 1992), .22 Mag. (disc. 1992), .22 Hornet, .22- 250 Rem., .223 Rem., .243 Win., .260 Rem. (new 1997), .30-30 Win., .30-06, .300 Win. Mag. (Ltd. ed., mfg. 1997- 99), .308 Win., 6mmBR (disc. 1992), 7mm-08 Rem., 7mmBR, .35 Rem., .357 Max. (disc. 1997, reintroduced 2001), .358 Win., .44 Mag., .440 Cor-Bon (new 1999), .444 Marlin, or 7.62x39mm (new 1996) cal., circular rear breech action, quick change 14 in. barrels (drilled and tapped), black or chrome (new 1997) finish, black synthetic Valox ambidextrous pistol grip, 4 lbs. 3 oz. - 4 lbs. 7 oz. Mfg. 1991-2001.

		$380	$315	$275	$230	$200	$185	$170

Last MSR was $438.

Add $40 for chrome finish.
Add $35 for adj. hunting sights.
Add $129 for adj. silouhette sights by RPM.
Add $319 for standard black finish barrel, $418 for standard barrel with muzzle brake, $359 for chrome barrel, and $469 for chrome barrel with muzzle brake.

The grip assembly ($119) and barreled actions were available individually on this model.

REVOLVERS

BFR LONG CYLINDER (MAXINE) - .444 Marlin, .45 LC/.410 bore, .450 Marlin (new 2002, 10 in. barrel only), or .45-70 Govt. cal., single action, 5 shot, stainless steel, 7½ (.45 LC/.410 bore and .45-70 Govt.) or 10 (.444 Marlin, .450 Marlin, or .45-70 Govt.) in. barrel, checkered rubber grips, 4 lbs. – 4.36 lbs. New 1999.

MSR	$999	$875	$750	$650

This model was originally advertised as the BFR Maxine, then was changed to BFR (Biggest Finest Revolver).

BFR SHORT CYLINDER (LITTLE MAX) - .22 Hornet, .45 LC+P (disc. 2001), .454 Casull, .480 Ruger (new 2002), or .50 AE (disc. 2001) cal., similar to BFR Model, 6½ (.45 LC+P, .454 Casull, or .480 Ruger cal.), 7½, or 10 (not available in .50 AE or .45 LC+P cal.) barrel, 3.2 – 4.36 lbs. New 1999.

MSR	$999	$875	$750	$650

This model was originally advertised as the BFR Little Max, then was changed to BFR (Biggest Finest Revolver).

M

Grading	100%	98%	95%	90%	80%	70%	60%

RIFLES: BOLT-ACTION

MOUNTAIN EAGLE RIFLE - ...223 Rem. (new 2000), 270 Win., .280 Rem., .30-06, 7mmSTW (mfg. 1998-99), .300 Win. Mag., .300 Wby. Mag., .338 Win. Mag., .340 Wby. Mag. (disc. 1997), 7mm Rem. Mag., .375 H&H, or .416 Rem. Mag. cal., Sako action, adj. trigger, 4 or 5 shot mag., match grade Krieger barrel with cut rifling, H-S Precision composite stock with aluminum bedding block, includes carrying case. Mfg. 1994-2000.

	$1,325	$1,075	$900	$775	$625	$550	$495

Last MSR was $1,499.

Add $200 for muzzle brake.
Add $50 for left-hand action.
Add $300 for .375 H&H or .416 Rem. Mag. cal.

* *Varmint Mountain Eagle* - .222 Rem. or .223 Rem. cal., 26 in. stainless steel heavy fluted barrel, w/o sights, approx. 9¾ lbs. Mfg. 1996-2000.

	$1,425	$1,100	$925				

Last MSR was $1,629.

MOUNTAIN EAGLE MAGNUM LITE - .223 Rem. (varmint only), .22-250 Rem. (varmint only), .280 Rem., .30-06, .300 Win. Mag., or 7mm Rem. Mag. cal., custom built Sako action with one-piece forged bolt, adj. trigger, 24 in. sport tapered or 26 in. varmint bull graphite barrel with stainless steel liner, no sights, black swirl H-S Precision Kevlar graphite stock, 4 or 5 shot mag, approx. 7.9 lbs. New 2001.

MSR	$2,295	$1,995	$1,700	$1,400	$1,100	$825	$700	$575

Magnum Lite graphite barrels are available in 3 configurations for $799.

MOUNTAIN EAGLE TACTICAL RIFLE - .223 Rem. (new 2002), .22-250 (new 2002), .308 Win., .300 Win. Mag., or .300 WSM (new 2002) cal., accurized Rem. M-700 action, 26 in. Magnum Lite barrel, H-S Precision tactical stock, adj. stock and trigger, 9 lbs., 4 oz. New 2001.

MSR	$2,400	$2,075	$1,750	$1,425	$1,125	$850	$700	$575

RIFLES: SEMI-AUTO

Magnum Lite .22 graphite barrels are also available individually for $269.
Add $140 for Clark custom upgrade (includes Clark deluxe trigger kit, tuned extractor, and bolt release) on the models listed (.22 LR cal. only).

MAGNUM LITE RIFLE - .22 LR or .22 Mag. (new 2000) cal., features Ruger 10/22 receiver with Acculite (disc.) or graphite (new 1999) barrel utilizing uni-directional graphite carbon fiber with stainless steel liner, barrel weighs 13 oz. New 1997.

* *Magnum Lite Rifle w/Hogue or Fajen Stock* - choice of black Hogue Overmolded or Fajen high stock (disc. 1999) in either midnight or coffee color, 4.3 (.22 LR cal.) or 5.4 (.22 Mag. cal.) lbs. with Hogue stock. New 1997.

MSR	$599		$525	$450	$395	$360	$330	$275	$250

Add $200 for .22 Mag. cal.

* *Magnum Lite Rifle w/Fajen Thumbhole Stock* - features choice of Fajen thumbhole sporter or thumbhole silhouette in midnight or coffee color. Mfg. 1997-99.

	$625	$525	$450	$395	$360	$330	$275

Last MSR was $699.

Add $100 for thumbhole silhouette stock configuration.

* *Magnum Lite Rifle w/Turner Barracuda Stock* - features skeletonized sporter stock in choice of green or coffee laminate, 4.4 (.22 LR cal.) or 5.4 (.22 Mag.) lbs. New 1997.

MSR	$799		$695	$575	$475	$425	$375	$350	$325

Add $200 for .22 Mag. cal.

Grading	100%	98%	95%	90%	80%	70%	60%

MAGTECH

Current importer and distributor of CBC (Companhia Brasileria de Cartuchos) ammunition and firearms located in Centerville, MN. Previously located in Madison, CT 1999-2001 and in Las Vegas, NV until 1999. Manufactured by CBC located in Brazil. Distributor sales only.

CARBINES: SEMI-AUTO

MODEL 7022 - .22 LR cal., Ruger 10/22 style action, 10 shot, 18 in. barrel, choice of hardwood or synthetic stock. New 2001.

No MSR	$120	$100	$85	$75	$70	$65	$60	$55

RIFLES: BOLT ACTION

MODEL 122 - .22 LR cal., 6 shot detachable mag., safety lever disconnects trigger from firing mechanism, uncheckered hardwood stock, 5.7 lbs. Imported 1992 only.

		$115	$95	$80	$70	$60	$50	$40

Last MSR was $131.

SHOTGUNS

MODEL 151 SINGLE SHOT - 12, 16, 20 ga., or .410 bore, 26, 28, or 30 in. barrel, exposed hammer, ejector, front triggerguard opening mechanism, some plastic used for buttons, levers, and bushings, 5 - 6½ lbs. Imported 1992 only.

	$95	$80	$70	$60	$50	$40	$35

Last MSR was $109.

MODEL 199 – 12, 16, 20, 28 ga., or .410 bore, all steel construction, exposed hammer with underlever opening, unique hammer/firing pin safety, 24 or 28 in. barrel, uncheckered Brazilian stock and forearm, recoil pad supplied on Youth Models (20 ga. or .410 bore only), New 2001.

No MSR		$100	$85	$75	$70	$65	$60	$55

MODEL MT-586-2 SLIDE ACTION - 12 ga. only, 3 in. chamber, standard Field model shotgun, 28 in. barrel with fixed chokes, hardwood stock and forearm, double slide bars. Imported 1993-95.

	$190	$175	$160	$140	$130	$120	$110

Last MSR was $229.

The Model MT-586 preceded the MT-586-2, the MT-586 was disc. 1994.

❋ *Model MT-586-2-VR Slide Action* - similar to Model MT-586, except has choice of 26 or 28 in. VR barrel with interchangeable chokes. Imported 1993-95.

	$220	$185	$170	$155	$140	$130	$120

Last MSR was $259.

MODEL MT-586 SLIDE ACTION SLUG - 12 ga. only, slug gun featuring 24 in. cylinder bore barrel with rifle sights, matte finished metal parts, and special Monte Carlo stock. Imported 1993-95.

	$195	$180	$165	$145	$130	$120	$110

Last MSR was $239.

MODEL MT-586-2P - 12 ga. only, 3 in. chamber, slide action, 19 in. cylinder bore barrel, 7 shot mag., double slide bars, steel construction, hardwood stock, 7.3 lbs. Imported 1992-96.

	$185	$170	$155	$140	$130	$120	$110

Last MSR was $219.

M

Grading	100%	98%	95%	90%	80%	70%	60%

MAJESTIC ARMS, LTD.

Current manufacturer established during 2000, and located on Staten Island, NY. Dealer sales only.

CARBINES: SEMI-AUTO

MA 2000 - .22 LR cal., Henry Repeating Arms Co. AR-7 take down action, fiber optic sights, American walnut forearm, pistol grip, and buttplate, fixed tubular stock with butt bag, 16¼ in. barrel with crown, black teflon or silver bead blast finish, 4 lbs. New 2000.

MSR	$459		$395	$350	$295	$250	$225	$195	$175

MAKAROV

Pistol design originating from Russia. Russian mfg. Makarovs may be found under the "Russian Service Pistol and Rifle" heading in this text. Pistols listed have recently been imported by various companies, including Century International Arms, Inc. located in St. Albans, VT.

PISTOLS: SEMI-AUTO

MAKAROV COPIES - 9mm Makarov cal., patterned after the Soviet PM pistol, mfg. in eastern Germany, Bulgaria, and China, double action, blowback design, all steel, slide mounted safety that doubles as a decocking lever, 3.6 in. barrel, 8 shot mag., 25 oz.

No MSR		$185	$145	$125	$105	$95	$85	$75

Add approx. $35-$40 for polished blue or silver matte finish (Bulgarian mfg. only).

The importation of this type of pistol increased beginning 1992.

MALIN, F.E.

Previous manufacturer located in England. Previously imported by Saxon Arms, Inc. located in Clearwater, FL. Charles Boswell purchased Malin shortly before manufacture stopped.

SHOTGUNS: SxS, CUSTOM

BOXLOCK - made to individual order, choice of game scene engraving, Anson & Deeley boxlock actions, select European hybrid walnut, double triggers, leather cased. Prices started at $3,750 and each shotgun was priced per individual special order.

SIDELOCK - made to individual order, choice of game scene engraving, H&H sidelock action, select European hybrid walnut, double triggers, leather cased. Prices started at $5,000 and each shotgun were priced per individual special order.

MAMBA

Previously manufactured by Viper Mfg. Co. (a division of Sandock Austral Boksburg) located in South Africa.

PISTOLS: SEMI-AUTO

AUTO PISTOL - 9mm Para. cal., double action, 5 in. barrel, 14 shot mag., designed in Rhodesia, manufacture was not successful due to the non-hardened steel used in the investment cast construction process, poor exterior finish, less than 80 imported into the U.S., and 25 prototypes were built for Navy Arms.

Rarity factor precludes accurate pricing, values vary greatly in different regions.

Grading	100%	98%	95%	90%	80%	70%	60%

MANCHESTER ARMS INC.

Previous manufacturer located in Lenoir, TN.

PISTOLS: SEMI-AUTO

COMMANDO MARK 45 - .45 ACP cal., paramilitary type design with detachable mag., wood pistol grip, 5 in. barrel with muzzle brake. Disc.

	$525	$450	$395	$350	$300	$265	$235

MANDALL SHOOTING SUPPLIES, INC.

Current importer, distributor, and retailer located in Scottsdale, AZ.

Mandall Shooting Supplies distributes/imports various firearms including pistols, revolvers, rifles, shotguns, as well as other models. Mandall Shooting Supplies, Inc. should be contacted directly for current pricing and special order questions.

MANNLICHER PISTOLS

Previously manufactured in Austria and Switzerland starting circa 1894.

PISTOLS: SEMI-AUTO

MODEL 1894 - 6.5mm or 7.6mm cal., unique blow forward design, fewer than 100 mfg. by Fabrique d' Armes in Neuhausen and OWG, Steyr.

	$13,500	$11,000	$9,500	$8,500	$7,500	$6,000	$5,000

MODEL 1897 - 7.63mm Mannlicher cal., first Mannlicher pistol with detachable mag. (matching), unique cocking lever on right frame, approx. 1,000 mfg.

	$6,500	$5,500	$4,800	$4,250	$3,750	$3,250	$2,750

Subtract 15% for carbine version.
Add 150% for Model 1896 prototype in similar configuration, but with fixed mag.

MODEL 1899 - rear sight mounted on barrel, large safety lever on left frame, approx. 300 mfg.

	$6,500	$5,500	$4,800	$4,000	$3,500	$2,850	$2,500

MODEL 1901 - rear sight mounted on barrel, safety on rear of right slide, approx. 1,000 mfg.

	$2,500	$1,800	$1,200	$900	$600	$500	$400

MODEL 1905 - final and most common variation.

	$1,650	$1,200	$800	$500	$400	$350	$300

ARGENTINE MODEL 1905 - 7.65mm cal., Argentine crest on left panel is usually machined off. Values assume matching numbers but removed crest.

	$400	$350	$300	$255	$220	$185	$150

❋ *Argentine Model 1905* - with Original Military Crest

	$2,000	$1,600	$1,200	$850	$650	$500	$400

MANNLICHER SCHOENAUER SPORTING RIFLES

Currently manufactured by Steyr, Mannlicker, A.G., in Austria from 1850s-present. Please refer to Steyr-Mannlicher in this text for currently manufactured rifles.

RIFLES: BOLT ACTIONS, PRE-WWII

Add approx. 50%-75% for all takedown pre-war models.

MODEL 1903 CARBINE - 6.5x54mm Mannlicher Schoenauer cal., 5 shot, 17.7 in. barrel, rotary mag., two leaf rear sight, double set trigger, full length stock.

	$3,900	$3,500	$3,000	$1,200	$600	$500	$400

This caliber may also be referred to as 6.5x53mm.
This model is normally encountered in poor condition.

M

Grading	100%	98%	95%	90%	80%	70%	60%

MODEL 1905 CARBINE - similar to Model 1903, except 9x56mm Mannlicher Schoenauer cal. only, 19.7 in. barrel.

	100%	98%	95%	90%	80%	70%	60%
	$1,200	$775	$695	$650	$550	$495	$450

This model is normally encountered in poor condition. It is perhaps the least desirable of pre-war models because of the wide variation in bore diameters.

MODEL 1908 CARBINE - similar to Model 1905, except in 8x56mm Mannlicher Schoenauer cal. only.

	100%	98%	95%	90%	80%	70%	60%
	$1,500	$1,200	$1,000	$800	$550	$495	$450

This model is frequently noticed in better condition factors. Some exceptional takedown variations also exist within this model.

MODEL 1910 CARBINE - similar design to the Model 1905, except originally chambered for 9.5x56mm Mannlicher, .375 Express, or 9.5x57mm Mauser cal., this model was the predecessor of the post-war Model 1924.

	100%	98%	95%	90%	80%	70%	60%
	$1,500	$1,200	$900	$700	$600	$525	$475

MODEL 1924 CARBINE - similar to 1905, except .30-06.

	100%	98%	95%	90%	80%	70%	60%
	$1,650	$1,450	$1,300	$1,150	$800	$600	$475

HIGH VELOCITY SPORTING RIFLE - 7x64 Brenneke, .30-06, 8x60mm Mag., 9.3x62mm, or 10.75x68mm cal., 23.6 in. barrel, 3 leaf sight, half stock.

	100%	98%	95%	90%	80%	70%	60%
	$2,500	$2,100	$1,700	$1,100	$700	$500	$400

Add $200 for 10.75x68mm, 7x64 Brenneke, or 8x60mm Mag. cal.

RIFLES: BOLT ACTION, POST-WWII

Values below represent standard models with no engraving. Original engraving will add at least $500-$1,500 to prices listed with some heavily engraved Premier & Alpine models selling for large premiums. A variation of the 1950-1952 Series is called the "GK" because of its traditionally styled European stock - which is a variant of the pre-war style and approaches the design of the Model 1951 MCA. Of the calibers listed for post-WWII models, the 6.5x54mm is considered one of the most desirable, as well as the 9.3x62mm.

In 1951, Steyr (at Stoeger's request) made the following changes to the Model 1950 (named Improved Model 1950). These include: an ebony tip and fuller forend, left-side dummy plate cuts for side mount, left-side of receiver was flattened to facilitate side scope mount, and flatter bolt handle requiring slot inside of stock.

In 1952, changes included a carved cheekpiece, change from ¾ in. sling swivels to 1 in., swept back bolt handle, wood on left-side of stock over the dummy sideplate cutout thickened to strengthen the stock with a side mount in place, and removal of loading ears and clip guides, thereby streamlining the receiver and enabling lower scope mounting.

At one time Stoeger listed 18 versions of the M1950-52 family defined as #S-1 through #S-18 with three major differences existing within each block of Model 1950, Improved Model 1950, and Model 1952. The differences were: single and double set triggers (DST), rifle or carbine style, 6.5mm Carbine, single trigger or DST.

MODEL 1950 - various cals. including .244 Rem., .257 Roberts, .270 Win., .280 Rem., .30-06, .358 Win., 6.5x54mm (very desirable), 7x57mm, 8x57mm Mauser, or 9.3x62mm Mauser, bolt action, 5 shot rotary mag., 23.6 in. barrel, low bolt handle, half length stock, ebony forearm tip. Mfg. 1950-1952.

	100%	98%	95%	90%	80%	70%	60%
	$1,450	$1,325	$1,000	$850	$650	$495	$450

MODEL 1950 CARBINE - similar to Model 1950, except has 20 in. barrel, full length stock. Mfg. 1950-1952.

	100%	98%	95%	90%	80%	70%	60%
	$1,950	$1,700	$1,400	$950	$800	$550	$450

M

Grading	100%	98%	95%	90%	80%	70%	60%

MODEL 1950 CARBINE 6.5 - similar to Model 1950 Carbine, except 6.5x54mm cal., 18½ in. barrel. Mfg. 1950-1952.

	$1,800	$1,600	$1,200	$950	$800	$500	$400

Deduct 50% if encountered with oversized bore (over .265 in.).

IMPROVED MODEL 1952 - same specifications as Model 1950, except swept back bolt handle. Mfg. 1952-1956.

	$1,450	$1,200	$1,000	$700	$500	$400	$300

IMPROVED MODEL 1952 CARBINE - .257 Roberts, .270 Win., 7x57mm, or .30- 06 cal., swept bolt handle, otherwise similar to Model 1950 Carbine.

	$1,950	$1,295	$1,000	$700	$600	$400	$300

IMPROVED MODEL 1952 6.5 CARBINE - similar to Model 1952 Carbine, except 6.5mm cal., 18½ in. barrel. Mfg. 1952-1956.

	$1,050	$950	$750	$675	$600	$550	$495

MODEL 1956 RIFLE - similar to Improved Model 1952, except .243 Win. and .30-06 cals., new high comb stock design, 22 in. barrel, half length stock. Mfg. 1956-1960.

	$1,150	$1,000	$850	$500	$400	$300	$200

✻ *Model 1956 Magnum* - includes .257 Wby. Mag., .264 Win. Mag., .458 Win. Mag., 6.5x68mm, or 8x68mm cal.

	$2,100	$1,800	$1,600	$1,200	$900	$700	$500

MODEL 1956 CARBINE - similar to Model 1956 Rifle, except .243 Win., 6.5x53mm, .257 Roberts, .270 Win., 7mm Rem. Mag., .30-06, or .308 Win. cal., 20 in. barrel, full length stock. Mfg. 1956- 1960.

	$850	$775	$675	$600	$550	$495	$450

MODEL 1961 MCA RIFLE - similar to Model 1956 Rifle, except Monte Carlo stock. Mfg. 1961-1971.

	$1,650	$1,200	$1,100	$800	$600	$500	$400

MODEL 1961 MCA CARBINE - similar to Model 1956 Carbine, except Monte Carlo stock. Mfg. 1961-1971.

	$2,000	$1,800	$1,500	$1,300	$1,000	$800	$500

M

RIFLES: BOLT ACTION, CURRENT PRODUCTION

Current production guns are now called Steyr-Mannlicher models and can be located under this trademark in the S section.

MANU-ARM

Current rifle and airgun manufacturer located in Veauche, France. No current U.S. importation.

Manu-Arm manufactures good quality utilitarian .22 cal. bolt action and semi-auto rifles, in addition to an O/U in 9mm Para., .410 bore, and .32 ga. Please contact the factory directly for more information, including U.S. availability and pricing.

MANUFRANCE

Current manufacturer established circa 1887 and located in St. Etienne, France. No current U.S. importation.

Manufrance currently manufactures both SxS rifle and shotgun variations (the Robust Models being the most popular) that are not being currently imported in the U.S. Please contact the factory directly for more information, including model availability, parts, and domestic prices.

Grading	100%	98%	95%	90%	80%	70%	60%

SEMI-AUTO MODEL - 12 ga., 26, 28, or 30 in. imp. cyl., mod. and full, 2¾ or 3 in. chamber, gas operated, walnut stock, black matte receiver, VR.

	$330	$305	$290	$275	$255	$240	$220

FALCOR O/U - 12 ga., VR, 26 in. imp. cyl. and mod., 28 in. mod. and full, SST, auto ejector, chrome lined barrel, walnut checkered stock.

	$715	$665	$635	$605	$550	$495	$470

MANURHIN

Current trademark manufactured by Manufacture d. Armes de tir Chapuis beginning in 1998, and located in Saint Bonnet Le Chateau, France. No current U.S. importation. During 1998, Chapuis Armes purchased Manurhin, and new revolvers are currently being manufactured in the new Manufacture d. Armes de tir Chapuis facility located in Saint Bonnet Le Chateau, France, utilizing the original production machinery. Previously manufactured by Manurhin Equipment 1972-1998, located in Mulhouse, France. Currently available by contacting the factory directly. Previously owned by Matra Manurhin Defense. Previously imported and distributed by Sphinx U.S.A. located in Meriden, CT. Previously imported (1984-86) directly by Matra-Manurhin International, Inc., located in Fort Lauderdale, FL.

Manurhin in France has been manufacturing models PP, PPK, and PPK/S since 1952. Previously, they were imported by Interarms out of Alexandria, VA. In 1984, Manurhin imported their new models directly and they were marked Manurhin on the left front slide assembly. This differs from the previous Walther stamped guns. Also, no Interarms logo appears on the right side.

P-1 - 9mm Para. cal., similar to W. German P-38, double action, 5 in. barrel.

	$350	$325	$300	$275	$230	$215	$200

MODEL P4 - 9mm Para. cal., P.38 variation issued to the French Police when in Berlin during post- WWII.

	$375	$340	$300	$245	$230	$215	$200

MODEL PP - .22 LR, .32 ACP, or .380 ACP cal., 3 7/8 in. barrel, 10 shot mag.-.22 LR, 8 shot mag.-.32 ACP, 7 shot mag.-.380 ACP, blue only, all steel construction, double action with positive steel hammer block safety, 24 oz. Add $10 for .22 LR cal., $46 for Durgarde finish. Imported 1984-86.

	$360	$320	$275	$230	$205	$185	$170

Last MSR was $419.

✴ *Collector Model* - blue finish, special engraving. Imported 1986 only.

	$465	$415	$350				

Last MSR was $529.

✴ *Presentation Model* - blue finish, special ornamentation. Imported 1986 only.

	$720	$650	$500				

Last MSR was $819.

Also available with various engraving options in either blue, nickel, or gold finish - prices range from $222 - $540.

MODEL PPK/S - .22 LR, .32 ACP, or .380 ACP cal., 3¼ in. barrel, 10 shot mag.-.22 LR, 8 shot mag.-.32 ACP, 7 shot mag.-.380 ACP, blue only, all steel construction, double action with positive steel hammer block safety, 23 oz. Add $10 for .22 LR cal. Imported 1984-86.

	$360	$320	$275	$230	$205	$185	$170

Last MSR was $419.

Grading	100%	98%	95%	90%	80%	70%	60%

✻ *PPK/S Durgarde* - similar to PPK/S, only with bonded brushed chrome finish. Add $14 for .22 LR cal.

	$410	$365	$325	$290	$265	$250	$240

Last MSR was $465.

✻ *Collector Model* - blue finish, special engraving. Imported 1986 only.

	$465	$415	$350

Last MSR was $529.

✻ *Presentation Model* - blue finish, special ornamentation. Imported 1986 only.

	$720	$650	$500

Last MSR was $819.

Also available with various engraving options in either blue, nickel, or gold finish - prices range from $222-$540.

PP SPORT - .22 LR cal. only, double action, 6.1 or 8.1 in. barrel, blue finish only, precision adj. sights, contoured plastic grips with thumb rest, 25 oz. New Manurhin design for 1985. Imported 1984- 86.

	$675	$525	$430	$385	$325	$290	$270

Last MSR was $635.

Add 10% for 8.1 in. barrel.

✻ *PP Sport-C* - similar to PP Sport, except has single action with lightened trigger pull.

	$650	$500	$415	$370	$310	$280	$260

Last MSR was $635.

REVOLVERS

MODEL 73 DEFENSE - .357 Mag./.38 Spl. cal., 6 shot, 2½, 3, or 4 in. barrel, checkered wood stocks, mfg. to precise tolerances, 31-33½ oz. Importation began 1988.

MSR	N/A	$1,200	$1,000	$850	$725	$600	$500	$425

MODEL 73 GENDARMERIE - .357 Mag./.38 Spl. cal., 6 shot, similar to Model 73 Defense except has adj. sighting components and also is offered in 5¼, 6, or 8 in. barrel lengths. Manufactured for police requirements. Importation began 1988.

MSR	N/A	$1,675	$1,125	$900	$750	$625	$525	$450

MODEL 73 SPORT - .357 Mag./.38 Spl. cal., 6 shot, sport shooting features include minimized hammer stroke, micrometer rear sight, and free release trigger with fitted adj. sights. Importation began 1988.

MSR	N/A	$1,675	$1,125	$900	$750	$625	$525	$450

MODEL 73 CONVERTIBLE - includes choice of .22 LR/.38 Spl. or .22 LR/.32 Long cal. cylinders and barrels (5¾ in. for .38 Spl. and 6 in. for .22 LR/.32 Long). Imported 1988-95.

	$1,925	$1,675	$1,325	$1,125	$950	$800	$700

Last MSR was $2,200.

✻ *3 Cylinder Model 73 Convertible* - similar to Model 73 Convertible except includes 3 calibers (.22 LR, .32 Long, and .38 Spl.). Imported 1988-95.

	$2,375	$1,950	$1,700	$1,375	$1,150	$975	$850

Last MSR was $2,690.

MODEL 73 SILHOUETTE - .22 LR or .357 Mag. cal., Silhouette variation with fully adj. rear sight and either 10 (.22 LR) or 10¾ (.357 Mag.) in. heavy barrel with full shroud, contoured wooden target grips, approx. 4 lbs. Importation began 1988.

MSR	N/A	$1,750	$1,175	$925	$750	$625	$525	$450

Add $13 for .357 Mag. cal.

MODEL MR 88 - .357 Mag. cal., stainless steel, 4, 5, or 6 in. barrel, fixed sights, rubber grips. Importation began 1996.

MSR	N/A	$775	$625	$450

Grading	100%	98%	95%	90%	80%	70%	60%

MODEL MR 96 - .357 Mag. cal., black finish, 3, 4, 5, or 6 in. VR barrel, adj. rear sight, ergonomic rubber grips. Importation began 1996.

MSR	N/A	$750	$615	$425	$375	$350	$325	$295

This model allows the user to unlock, swing the cylinder out, and eject the cases with one movement of the hand.

MARATHON PRODUCTS, INC.

Previously manufactured by Santa Barbara Armaments exclusively for Marathon Products, Inc. Most of the models listed were also available in kit form, but are not shown in this book.

PISTOLS: SINGLE SHOT

HOT SHOT MODEL - .22 LR cal., single shot, fixed sights, 14¾ in. barrel, hardwood stock with target grip configuration. Mfg. 1986-87.

		$55	$45	$40	$35	$35	$30	$30

Last MSR was $60.

RIFLES: BOLT ACTION

.22 FIRST SHOT - .22 LR cal., single shot, 16½ in. barrel, hardwood stock, open sights, 31 in. total length, 3.8 lbs. Mfg. 1985-87.

		$55	$45	$40	$35	$35	$30	$30

Last MSR was $60.

✳ **.22 Super Shot** - similar to First Shot, except with 24 in. barrel and regular dimension stock. Mfg. 1985- 87.

		$55	$45	$40	$35	$35	$30	$30

Last MSR was $60.

CENTERFIRE MODEL - .243 Win., .270 Win., 7x57mm, 7mm Rem. Mag., .30-06, .300 Win. Mag., or .308 Win. cal., Mauser type action, 5 shot fixed box mag., 24 in. barrel, select walnut with recoil pad, adj. trigger, open sights, 7.9 lbs. Available 1985-86 only.

		$295	$240	$215	$195	$180	$170	$160

Last MSR was $320.

MARBLE ARMS & MFG. CO.

Previous firearms manufacturer circa 1907-late 1950s, located in Gladstone, MI. Marble Arms is still in business, manufacturing sights, knives, and compasses.

In addition to axes and compasses, Marble Arms & Mfg. Co. also manufactured their Game Getter O/ U combination gun from approx. 1907 to the early 1950s. During this period of production, the gun underwent quite a few changes including sights (an aperture sight mounted on the rear backstrap was optional in 1908), different configuration folding metal stock, and other changes.

GAME GETTER MODELS - starting manufacture in 1908, 2 variations of the model 1908 Game Getter were offered, the 1908A featured a flexible rear sight mounted behind the hammer, the 1908B had a filler blank in that space. The 1908s featured a .22 cal. rifled top barrel, and in standard configuration, a smooth bored bottom barrel chambered for the .44 round ball or .44 shot. Very late in production, chambering for the 2 in. .410 could be ordered. Standard barrel lengths were 12 in., 15 in., and 18 in., but Marbles was ready to please their customers, and on special order, 8 in., 10 in., 17 in., and 22 in. barrels were made, some were even shipped from the factory fitted with silencers, a very few guns ordered were not milled for the round tubular folding stock. A pivoting striker on the hammer was used to select the barrel to be fired, and the tip-up barrels were opened by pressing the trigger guard to the rear. The top frame featured a folding leaf sight, and the front barrel band incorporated the front sight, the grips were checkered black hard rubber with fleur-de-lis design. On very early 1908

Grading	100%	98%	95%	90%	80%	70%	60%

guns, the buttplate was a separate piece secured to the tubing with 2 screws, later stocks were all one piece, with bottom barrels chambered for .25-20 & .32-20, but these are very rare. The gun was shipped in a dovetailed wooden box with sliding lid, and included a shoulder holster, cleaning rod, and directions for use. The first 1908 was shipped from the factory June 21, 1909, and serial letters A-M were used. Then starting with serial number 1, they continued through 9981, the last gun was shipped from the factory May 22, 1918.

	$1,850	$1,650	$1,450	$1,200	$1,050	$950	$875

Add $250 for Model 1908A with original flexible tang sight.

Add $100-$150 for original holster, depending on condition of leather.

✱ *1921 Model* - the 1921 was an entirely new gun, with similar barrel lengths (12, 15, or 18 in.), not nearly as pleasing in appearance as the 1908. The same barrel lengths were standard, but the bottom was chambered for the 2 in. .410. In 1924, the standard chamber was changed to 2½ in. .410. It featured a bag style, oiled walnut grip, and a unique "Triple Combination Rear Sight", which was developed and made only for this model. A number of guns in the 14,000 to 16,000 serial number range can be found with brown plastic grips, conventional rear sight, and v notch with screw adjustment for elevation. The 1921 featured a folded and hinged 3 piece stock with an improved lock that eliminated wobble, but had no adjustment for drop. It also had a shorter action than the 1908, which was a faster action, and the hammer rebounded to a safety notch after firing. As with the 1908 Model, Marbles would accomodate the wishes of the customer, and barrels as short as 8 in. can be found. Some guns were ordered choke bored, some were chambered just for .44 Game Getter on the bottom barrel. A few had no provision for stock, at least 2 were shipped in .32-20, and as records are not complete, other calibers such as .25-20 and .38-40 may also exist. Supplied with a heavy cardboard box, shoulder holster, cleaning rod and instructions. First shipment was serial number 10,001 - shipped to William L. Marble, the west coast representative, on Oct. 4, 1921. Serial range 10,000-20,076.

	$1,500	$1,350	$1,200	$1,000	$900	$800	$750

Values assume legal 18 in. barrels or correct registration. If not legal configuration, the gun is basically a black market item subject to BATF confiscation. The U.S. government and foreign countries continued to purchase 15 in. guns after the 1934 law was passed, and the last gun was shipped during the mid 1950s.

M

MARCEL THYS & SONS

Current SxS rifle and shotgun manufacturer established in 1960 and located in Crisnée, Belgium. The U.S. agent is currently Jean-Jacques Perodeau, located in Enid, OK.

Marcel Thys & Sons manufactures fine quality double rifles and shotguns, with many engraving options and special orders. Prices range from $12,000-$85,000, w/o engraving. Since these guns are custom made per individual order, please contact the U.S. agent or the factory directly (see Trademark Index) for current information, availability, and a firm price quotation.

MARGOLIN

Original pistol design by M.V. Margolin developed after WWII as a training firearm for members of the Russian shooting team. The Margolin is currently manufactured at the Izhevsk mechanical plant located in Izhevsk, Russia as the "MTsN" sporting pistol. Limited importation.

PISTOLS: SEMI-AUTO

TARGET MODEL - .22 LR cal., originally developed from the TT (Tula Tokarev), manufactured to precise tolerances, many specimens are made to individual shooters specifications, seldom encountered in the U.S.A., while rare, desirability to date has been limited, current mfg. - limited importation.

Margolin pistols are typically priced in the $475-$850 range, depending on features and assuming 95%+ original condition. While currently imported Chinese copies are considerably less expensive, they do not have the quality (or accuracy) of the Russian Margolins.

MARLIN FIREARMS COMPANY

Current manufacturer located in North Haven, CT. Marlin has been manufacturing firearms since 1870. Recent manufacture (1969-present) is in North Haven, CT. Previously, Marlin was manufactured (1870-1969) in New Haven, CT. Distributor sales only.

On Nov. 10th, 2000, Marlin Firearms Company purchased H&R 1871, Inc. This includes the brand names Harrington & Richardson, New England Firearms, and Wesson & Harrington (please refer to individual sections in this text).

PISTOLS: DERRINGERS AND REVOLVERS

Many of these variations in average condition sell in the $150-$250 range, while rarer specimens with 90%+ original condition will be priced considerably higher.

100%	98%	95%	90%	80%	70%	60%	50%	40%	30%	20%	10%

RIFLES: LEVER ACTION, ANTIQUE

Factory information by individual serial number may be available from the Cody Firearms Museum in Cody, WY on the following models: Model 1888, Models 1889 and 1892 (ser. no. range 4,001- 355,504 only), Models 1893, 1894, 1895, and 1897 may be researched, since Marlin only had one series of serial numbers for all lever action rifles mfg. 1883-1906.

Values below are for standard models only without special order features. 98% and 100% prices have been intentionally replaced with N/As (not applicable), since these condition factors are seldom encountered and hard to accurately price, as their values have dramatically increased during the past 3-5 years.

Add a premium for all mint condition guns with strong, case colored frames.

MODEL 1881 - .32-40 WCF, .38-55 WCF, .40-60 WCF, .45-70 Govt., or .45-85 Marlin cal., tube mag., 28 in. octagonal barrel standard, top ejection, blued finish with case hardened hammer, lever, and butt plate. Approx. 20,000 mfg. between 1881- 1892.

N/A	N/A	$1,800	$1,425	$1,000	$900	$800	$650	$550	$500	$450	$400

This model came in 3 frame styles for various calibers.

Add approx. 15% for .45-70 cal.

Add 200-300% premium for rare First models (pre ser. no. 600).

Add a premium for very early First models with hand engraved script barrel markings - approx. first 60 rifles mfg.

MODEL 1888 - .32-20 WCF, .38-40 WCF, or .44-40 WCF cal., 24 in. octagonal barrel most frequently encountered, top ejection, blued finish with case hardened hammer, lever, and butt plate, short throw lever action principle. Approx. 4,800 mfg. between 1888-1889. Ser. range approx. 19,560 - 27,850.

N/A	N/A	$2,400	$2,000	$1,700	$1,475	$1,250	$1,000	$875	$750	$625	$500

Add 40% for half-round, half-octagon barrel (23 mfg.).

Add 20% for round barrel (266 mfg.).

Add 25% for half magazine (78 mfg.).

100%	98%	95%	90%	80%	70%	60%	50%	40%	30%	20%	10%

MODEL 1889 - .25-20 WCF (very rare), .32-20 WCF, .38-40 WCF, .38-55 WCF, or .44-40 WCF cal., 24 (approx. 39,300 mfg.) or 28 (approx. 2,260 mfg.) in. octagonal barrel most frequently encountered, side ejection with solid top frame, blued finish with case hardened hammer, lever, and butt plate, short throw lever action principle. Approx. 55,000 mfg. between 1889-1899. Ser. range approx. 25,000-100,000.

N/A	N/A	$1,100	$800	$600	$500	$400	$340	$295	$260	$230	$200

Add 300-500% for Musket.
Add 25% for carbine.
Add 15% for .44-40 WCF cal.
Factory special orders/features will add premiums, depending on the desirability of each option(s), and the gun's original condition factor.
Also available as Carbine with either a 15 in. (only 367 mfg.) or 20 in. (approx. 10,000 mfg.) barrel or Musket (30 in. barrel - very rare).

MODEL 1891 - .22 Rimfire and .32 Rimfire/Centerfire cal., 24 in. octagonal barrel most often encountered, choice of side loading (1st variation) or tube loading (2nd variation), blued finish with case hardened hammer, lever, and butt plate, sear safety system on lever action. Approx. 18,650 mfg. between 1891-1897. Ser. No. range is approx. 37,500- 118,000.

N/A	N/A	$1,700	$1,300	$1,100	$950	$875	$775	$695	$625	$550	$475

Add 50% for deluxe, pistol grip checkered model.
Subtract 40% for tube loading model (.32 Centerfire).
Add $100 each for special sights (including correct Lyman, Marbles, Beeches combo, etc.).
Factory special orders/features will add premiums, depending on the desirability of each option(s), and the gun's original condition factor.

MODEL 1892 - .22 S, L, or LR, .32 S or L cal., 16, 24, 26, or 28 in. barrel, tubular mag., open sight, plain straight stock. Mfg. 1892-1916.

N/A	N/A	$1,350	$975	$775	$700	$600	$525	$475	$425	$385	$340

Add 10% for .22 cal.
Subtract 10% for .32 cal.
Add $100 each for special sights (including correct Lyman, Marbles, Beeches combo, etc.).
Factory special orders/features will add premiums, depending on the desirability of each option(s), and the gun's original condition factor.
.22 cals. will bring a premium in this model.

M

MODEL 1893 RIFLE - .25-36 Marlin, .30-30 Win., .32 Spl., .32-40 WCF, or .38-55 WCF cal., 20-32 in. round or octagonal barrels, case colored receiver, 10 shot tube mag., straight grip stock. Mfg. 1893-1936. Musket model also mfg. - 30 in. barrel and military style forearm.

N/A	N/A	$2,500	$1,800	$1,400	$1,050	$825	$625	$450	$400	$375	$350

Add 100% for Musket.
Add %15-20% for calibers other than .30-30 Win. or .32 Spl.
Add 15%-20% for takedown model, depending on condition.
Add approx. 20% for special Lightweight Model.
Subtract 50%-60% for the Model B with blue receiver.
Factory special orders/features will add premiums, depending on the desirability of each option(s), and the gun's original condition factor.
Strong, original case colors over 95% condition can result in $2,500 asking prices.
Although incorrect, more than a few people refer to all 20 in. barrels as "Lightweight" models. Technically, the Lightweight variation has a 7½ in. forearm rather than the standard 9 in.
Later production guns were marked "Model '93" and have less value. This model had two barrel variations - one was marked "special smokeless steel" while the other was marked "for Black Powder". The latter (also known as Model B) are 1st Models only and have blue receivers rather than case colored.

100%	98%	95%	90%	80%	70%	60%	50%	40%	30%	20%	10%

MODEL 1893 CARBINE - .30-30 Win., .32 Spl., .32-40 WCF cal., or .38-55 WCF cal., 15 (only 61 mfg.) or 20 in. round barrel, case colored receiver, 7 shot tube mag., straight or pistol grip stock. Mfg. 1893-1935.

> **Add %15-20% for calibers other than .30-30 Win. or .32 Spl.**
> **Factory special orders/features will add premiums, depending on the desirability of each option(s), and the gun's original condition factor.**

> ✳ **1st Model** - with saddle ring. Mfg. 1893-1915.

N/A	N/A	$1,600	$1,300	$1,100	$900	$750	$600	$500	$400	$375	$350

> Strong, original case colors over 95% condition can result in $2,500 asking prices.

> ✳ **2nd Model** - .30-30 Win. or .32 HPS cal., has "Bulls-eye" in stock, no saddle rings. Mfg. 1922- 1935.

N/A	N/A	$850	$725	$600	$475	$425	$385	$350	$325	$300	$285

> ✳ **Model 1893 Sporting Carbine** - .30-30 Win. or .32 Spl. cal., 20 in. round barrel, 2/3 mag., 5 shot, carbine style front sight, Rocky Mountain rear, straight stock, hard rubber buttplate, bullseye in stock. Mfg. 1923-1935.

N/A	N/A	$1,375	$1,100	$900	$750	$700	$550	$475	$400	$375	$350

> **Subtract 40% for 2nd Model made in 1935 with "S" steel buttplate and ivory bead front sight.**

MODEL 1894 - .25-20 WCF, .32-20 WCF, .38-40 WCF, or .44-40 WCF cal., case colored receiver, 10 shot tube mag., 24 in. round or octagon barrel, straight or pistol grip stock. Mfg. 1894- 1934.

N/A	N/A	$2,500	$1,995	$1,650	$1,250	$875	$625	$450	$400	$375	$350

> **Add 25% for saddle ring carbine.**
> **Add 10% for .44-40 WCF cal.**
> **Add 40% for Baby Carbine.**
> **Add 15%-20% for takedown model, depending on condition.**
> **Add 100% for Musket.**
> **Factory special orders/features will add premiums, depending on the desirability of each option(s), and the gun's original condition factor.**
> Strong, original case colors over 95% condition can result in $2,500 asking prices.
> Later production guns were marked "Model '94" and have less value. This model was also available in both a Carbine and Musket variation.

MODEL 1895 - .33 WCF, .38-56 WCF, .40-65 WCF, .40-70 WCF, .40-82 WCF, or .45- 70 Govt. cal., case colored receiver, 9 shot tube mag., 24 or 26 in. round or octagon barrel standard, other lengths were available, open sights, plain straight or pistol grip stock. Mfg. 1895-1915.

N/A	N/A	$3,000	$2,000	$1,575	$1,150	$900	$800	$700	$650	$600	$550

> **Add 15%-20% for takedown model, depending on condition.**
> **Premiums exist for .40-70 WCF (approx. 60 mfg.), .45-70 Govt., and .45-90 WCF cal.**
> **Factory special orders/features will add premiums, depending on the desirability of each option(s), and the gun's original condition factor.**
> Strong, original case colors over 95% condition can result in $3,500 asking prices.
> In 1912, a lightweight variation was introduced with hard rubber butt plate and half-magazine, cals. were .33 WCF and .45-70 Govt.(commands a premium), and round barrels were either 22 or 24 in. A Carbine variation was also offered with approx. 200 mfg. - premiums may run as high as 150% over rifle values listed.

MODEL 1897 - .22 S, L, or LR cal., tube mag., 16, 24, 26, or 28 in. barrel, case colored receiver, takedown, open sights, plain straight or pistol grip stock. Mfg. 1897-1922.

N/A	N/A	$2,500	$1,750	$1,475	$1,000	$850	$625	$450	$400	$375	$350

> **Add 100% for 16 in. barrel "Bicycle Rifle."**
> **Add 15%-20% for takedown model, depending on condition.**
> **Add $100 each for special sights (including correct Lyman, Marbles, Beeches combo, etc.).**
> **Factory special orders/features will add premiums, depending on the desirability of each option(s), and the gun's original condition factor.**
> Strong, original case colors over 95% condition can result in $2,500 asking prices.

Grading	100%	98%	95%	90%	80%	70%	60%

RIFLES: MODERN PRODUCTION

Year of manufacture can be determined from 1946-1968 by the following letter/ numeral prefix: 1946-C, 1947-D, 1948-E, 1949-F, 1950-G, 1951-H, 1952-J, 1953-K, 1954-L, 1955-M, 1956-N, 1957-P, 1958-R, 1959-S, 1960-T, 1961-U, 1962-V, 1963-W, 1964-Y,Z, 1965-AA, 1966-AB, 1967- AC, 1968-AD, 1969-69, 1970-70, 1971-71, 1972-72. Starting in 1973, the year can be determined by subtracting the first 2 numbers of the serial number from 100.

The models below are listed in numerical sequence to assist quick access.

Machine cut checkering became standard on many Marlins beginning 1995. Safety locks have been shipped with every new rifle/shotgun beginning 1999.

MODEL MR-7 BOLT ACTION - .22-250 Rem. (advertised in 1998, but never mfg.), .243 Win. (advertised in 1998, but never mfg.), .25-06 Rem. (new 1997), .270 Win., .280 Rem. (new 1998) .30- 06, or .308 Win. (advertised in 1998, but never mfg.) cal., 4 shot box mag. with removable hinged floorplate, 3 position safety, adj. 3-6 lb. trigger, 22 in. barrel, checkered American walnut stock, cocking indicator, forged receiver, damascened bolt, includes sling swivels, with or without sights, approx. 7½ lbs. Mfg. 1996- 99.

	$495	$440	$375	$315	$275	$240	$215

Last MSR was $603.

Add $40 for open sights (.270 Win., .280 Rem., or .30-06).

* ***Model MR-7B*** - .270 Win. or .30-06 only, similar to Model MR-7, except has birch stock and forearm with cut checkering. Mfg. 1998-99.

	$380	$250	$185	$165	$150	$130	$125

Last MSR was $483.

Add $40 for open sights (mfg. 1998 only).

MODEL 9 CAMP CARBINE SEMI-AUTO - 9mm Para. cal. only, 16½ in. barrel, 12 or 20 shot mag. (disc. 1989), 4 shot mag. became standard in 1990, sand blasted steel receiver, open sights, last shot automatic hold-open, 6¾ lbs. Mfg. 1985-1999.

	$340	$230	$170	$150	$140	$130	$125

Last MSR was $443.

Add 10% for nickel plating (mfg. 1991-94, Model 9N).

A new high visibility orange front sight post with cutaway hood was added in 1989.

MODEL 15YN "LITTLE BUCKAROO" SINGLE SHOT - .22 S, L, or LR cal., single shot, 16¼ in. barrel, youth dimensions with 12 LOP, adj. rear sight, grooved receiver, pressed checkering, 4¼ lbs.

MSR	$204	$150	$130	$105	$80	$75	$70	$65

* ***Model 15YS Stainless Steel*** - similar to Model 15YN, except is stainless steel and has Fire Sights. New 2002.

MSR	$228	$170	$145	$115

MODEL 17V BOLT ACTION - .17 HMR (Hornady Mag. Rimfire) cal., 7 shot detachable mag., 22 in. heavy barrel, walnut finished checkered hardwood Monte Carlo stock and forend, red cocking indicator, grooved receiver, includes scope mounts, 6 lbs. New 2002.

MSR	$263	$215	$195	$180	$170	$160	$145	$130

* ***Model 17VS*** - similar to Model 17V, except has bead blasted stainless steel barrel and receiver, laminated black/grey hardwood Monte Carlo stock, New 2002.

MSR	$392	$325	$265	$225

MODEL 18 SLIDE ACTION - .22 S, L, or LR cal., tube mag., 20 in. round or octagon barrel, open sight, exposed hammer, plain straight grip stock. Mfg. 1906-1909.

	$450	$325	$225	$175	$135	$100	$85

MODEL 20 SLIDE ACTION - .22 S, L, or LR cal., 24 in. octagon barrel, open sight, exposed hammer, takedown, plain straight grip stock. Mfg. 1907-1922.

	$395	$295	$200	$165	$125	$100	$85

M

Grading	100%	98%	95%	90%	80%	70%	60%

MODEL 25 SLIDE ACTION - .22 S or L cal., tube mag., 23 in. barrel, open sight, exposed hammer, takedown, plain straight grip stock. Mfg. 1909-1910.

	$425	$315	$215	$170	$150	$120	$95

MODEL 25MB BOLT ACTION - .22 Mag. cal., bolt action, 16¼ in. micro-groove barrel, 7 shot mag., hardwood stock, takedown action, 6 lbs. Mfg. 1987-88 only.

	$145	$115	$95	$85	$75	$70	$65

Last MSR was $173.

This model included both a scope and gun case.

MODEL 25MG GARDEN GUN - please refer to the Marlin bolt action shotgun section for information on this model.

MODEL 25MN BOLT ACTION - .22 Mag. cal., bolt action, 7 shot mag., 22 in. barrel, choice of walnut finished hardwood or Mossy Oak Breakup camo (new 2001) stock (pressed checkering became standard 1994), grooved receiver, adj. rear sight (new 1995), 6 lbs. New 1989.

MSR	$235	$180	$135	$105	$85	$75	$70	$65

Add $6 for 4X scope (disc. 2000).

Add $37 for Mossy Oak Breakup camo stock.

MODEL 25N BOLT ACTION - .22 LR cal., 7 shot mag., 22 in. barrel, press checkered Monte Carlo stock, 5½ lbs.

MSR	$205	$150	$130	$110	$80	$75	$70	$65

Add $8 for 4X scope.

✳ *Model 25NC Bolt Action* - similar to Model 25N, except has Mossy Oak Breakup camo stock.

MSR	$241	$185	$140	$105	$85	$75	$70	$65

MODEL 27 SLIDE ACTION - .25-20 WCF, or .32-20 WCF cal., 2/3 tube mag., 7 shot, 24 in. octagon barrel, open sight, plain straight grip stock. Mfg. 1910-1911.

	$400	$325	$250	$200	$165	$140	$125

Subtract 15% for .25RF cal.

M

MODEL 27S - .25RF, .25-20 WCF, or .32-20 WCF cal., similar to Model 27, except has safety button on right side of receiver, round or octagonal barrel added in 1913.

	$350	$275	$200	$150	$110	$100	$85

MODEL 29 SLIDE ACTION - similar to Model 20, with 23 in. round barrel, ½ tube mag. Mfg. 1913-1916.

	$400	$325	$250	$200	$165	$140	$125

MODEL 30/30A LEVER ACTION - .30-30 Win. cal., 20 in. barrel, promotional Glenfield model with birch stock and pressed checkering. Mfg. 1964-1983.

	$220	$185	$160	$135	$120	$110	$100

This model was replaced by the Model 30AS in 1983.

MODEL 30AS/336A/336AS LEVER ACTION - .30-30 Win. cal. only, 20 in. barrel, walnut finished birch stock (pressed checkering became standard 1995, cut checkering became standard 1998), open sights (adj. rear sight became standard 1995), no frills version of the 336CS, 7 lbs. New 1983.

MSR	$441	$335	$255	$160	$140	$125	$120	$115

Add $46 for 4X scope.

Prior to 2000, this was designated the Model 30AS. The Model 30AS was formerly part of the Glenfield line. During 2001, this model's nomenclature was changed from 336AS to 336A.

✳ *Model 30AW/336W* - similar to Model 30AS, except has carbine style barrel band and gold trigger.

MSR	$447	$340	$260	$165	$145	$130	$120	$115

Add $8 for 4X scope.

This model was previously sold to Wal-Mart only. Model nomenclature was changed during 1998.

Grading	100%	98%	95%	90%	80%	70%	60%

✳ *Model 336CC* - similar to Model 336W, except has Mossy Oak Breakup camo stock and forearm, 7 lbs. New 2001.

MSR	$491		$355	$280	$185	$150	$135	$125	$115

MODEL 32 SLIDE ACTION - .22 S, L, or LR cal., 2/3 tube mag., 24 in. octagon barrel, open sight, plain pistol grip stock, hammerless. Mfg. 1914-1915.

		$600	$525	$425	$350	$300	$225	$150

MODEL 1936 - .30-30 Win. or .32 HPS (High Power Special) cal., 6 shot, 20 or 24 in. barrel, tubular mag., open sights, pistol grip stock, barrel band, leaf mainspring, thinner "perch belly" forearm, case colored or blued receiver, upper tang, buttstock has a fluted comb and flat hard rubber buttplate. Mfg. 1936-1937.

	$750	$650	$500	$350	$275	$200	$150

Add 10% for vivid case colors with strong greens, reds, and yellows.
Add 10% for rifles and sporting carbines.
Rifles have "A" suffix, sporting carbine has "SC" suffix, and regular and carbine has "RC" suffix.
The Model 1936 has an upper tang inscription "Model 1936" and a case colored receiver. Also, the Model 1936 did not have a letter prefix in the ser. no.

MODEL 36 - 1ST VARIATION - same as Model 1936, except has a coil mainspring. Mfg. 1937-1940.

	$600	$550	$450	$300	$225	$175	$150

Add 10% for rifles and sporting carbines.
The Model 36 - 1st Variation has an upper tang inscription "Model 1936" and a case colored receiver. Also, the Model 36 - 1st variation did not have a letter prefix in the ser. no.

MODEL 36 - 2ND VARIATION - similar to Model 1936, still has case colored receiver with "Model 1936" on upper tang, buttstock is heavier style and no longer has fluted comb, buttplate is a thicker, slightly curved style - hard rubber, forearm is a heavier beaver-tailed style, "B" prefix in ser. no. Mfg. 1941 only.

	$550	$450	$375	$275	$250	$200	$165

Add 10% for rifles and sporting carbines.

MODEL 36ADL DELUXE RIFLE - similar to Model 1936, case colored receiver, checkered pistol grip buttstock and forearm, pistol grip cap, Winchester quick detachable swivels with 1 in. sling, "B" prefix in ser. no., has "Model 1936" on upper tang. Less than 50 mfg. in 1941 only.

	$1,150	$1,000	$800	$600	$400	$275	$250

Both the rear and front swivel bases are attached with two wood screws and are not inletted into the wood.

MODEL 36 - 3RD VARIATION - .30-30 Win. or .32 SPEC cal., blued receiver, no upper tang markings, model no. and cal. marked on barrel, rifles have "A" suffix, Deluxe rifle has "ADL" suffix, Sporting Carbine has "SC" suffix, and regular carbine has "RC" suffix. Mfg. 1946-1947.

	$500	$425	$350	$225	$165	$150	$125

Add 10% for rifles and sporting carbines.
Deluxe rifles (ADL) had a checkered pistol grip stock and forearm with no pistol grip cap. Deluxe rifles also have swivel round studs in buttstock and forearm cap with quick detachable swivels and a 1 in. sling. Also, some standard rifles may have the "ADL" barrel markings in 1946- 47. 1946 mfg. has a lower case "c" prefix and 1947 mfg. has a capital "D" prefix in ser. no.

✳ *Model 36 ADL Deluxe* - similar to Model 36 3rd Variation, has checkered pistol grip stock and forearm, forearm has checkering on sides and underneath, round swivel stud in buttstock and on forearm cap, deluxe quick detachable swivels and 1 in. leather sling, does not have model designation on upper tang or pistol grip cap, hooded front ramp screw on front sight, Rocky Mountain rear, letter prefix in ser. no. is "C" or "D".

	$850	$700	$550	$450	$400	$375	$350

M

Grading	100%	98%	95%	90%	80%	70%	60%

MODEL 37 SLIDE ACTION - similar to Model 29, with 24 in. barrel, full length tube mag. Mfg. 1913-1916.

	$395	$325	$250	$200	$150	$125	$100

MODEL 38 SLIDE ACTION - .22 S, L, or LR cal., 2/3 tube mag., 24 in. octagon barrel, open sights, hammerless, takedown, plain pistol grip stock. Mfg. 1920-1930.

$350	$300	$225	$175	$125	$100	$85

MODEL 39 LEVER ACTION - .22 S, L, or LR cal., 24 in. octagon barrel with tube mag., open sights, takedown, case hardened receiver and lever, S-shaped pistol grip stock, bluing on barrel, forend tip, mag. tube, bolt, hammer, and screws, various qualities of walnut (X, 2X, or 3X), hard rubber buttplate. Approx. 40-50,000 mfg. 1922-1938.

N/A	N/A	$2,500	$1,575	$1,325	$1,050	$825

Early models with fancy 2X-3X wood will bring a considerable premium.

Excellent original condition in this model is extremely hard to find since most specimens were well used due to the 16/25 shell mag. capacity, reliability, and the fact that the balance point of the gun (the receiver) normally wore first due to carrying wear. Earlier guns without a prefix or with an S prefix are noted for their superior workmanship and fine finish. Later HS prefix (High Speed) are not quite as valuable as these earlier guns.

MODEL 39A - similar to Model 39, with case hardened receiver (mfg. 1939-1945), includes 1st and 2nd Models with round barrel. 3rd Model 1st Variation was introduced in 1946 and has blue receiver, 3rd Model 2nd Variation has flutes in buttstock comb and was introduced in 1951, and 3rd Model 3rd Variation has Micro-Groove rifling, no pistol grip cap, and was introduced in 1954.

✳ *1st Model* - case colored frame, no prefix. Mfg. 1939 only.

$1,500	$1,000	$900	$775	$650	$500	$400

The first variation of the Model 39A mfg. in 1939 is distinguishable by a buttstock and lever similar to those on earlier Model 39s.

✳ *2nd Model* - case colored frame, "B" prefix. Mfg. 1940-45.

$800	$725	$650	$575	$450	$395	$350

The second variation had a rounded lever like current production and no "S" shape to bottom of pistol grip.

✳ *3rd Model 1st Variation* - features blued receiver, new ramp front sight, hard rubber buttplate, and continued Ballard rifling. Mfg. 1946-1950.

$350	$325	$295	$275	$250	$225	$200

✳ *3rd Model 2nd Variation* - similar to 3rd Model 1st Variation, except has flutes in buttstock comb, white plastic spacer next to buttplate, and pistol grip cap with white spacer and brass insert. Mfg. 1951-1953.

$350	$325	$295	$275	$250	$225	$200

✳ *3rd Model 3rd Variation* - similar to 3rd Model 2nd Variation, except has Micro-Groove rifling, and no pistol grip cap. Mfg. 1954-57.

$300	$275	$250	$225	$150	$125	$100

GOLDEN 39A - similar to Model 39A, with gold-plated trigger, sling swivels. Mfg. 1957- 1987.

$300	$275	$250	$225	$150	$125	$100

Add 30% to pre-1970 (oil finished stock) models.

GOLDEN 39M - similar to Golden 39A, except is carbine variation.

$300	$275	$250	$225	$150	$125	$100

MODEL 39A "MOUNTIE" - straight grip stock, slim forearm, otherwise similar to 39A. Mfg. 1953-1972.

$350	$325	$275	$250	$150	$125	$100

✳ *Model 39A "MOUNTIE" with K prefix* - 24 in. barrel and slender forearm. 4,335 mfg. 1953 only.

$750	$650	$550	$475	$425	$350	$300

M

Grading	100%	98%	95%	90%	80%	70%	60%

90TH ANNIVERSARY 39A - 24 in. chrome barrel and action, select checkered walnut stock, carved squirrel on side of butt stock. 500 mfg. in 1960.

	$1,200	$1,000	$750	$500	$425	$350	$250

Last MSR was $100.

90TH ANNIVERSARY MODEL 39M MOUNTIE CARBINE - similar to 90th Anniversary Model 39A, except 20 in. barrel, straight stock. 500 mfg. in 1960.

	$1,200	$1,000	$750	$600	$400	$350	$250

Last MSR was $100.

MODEL 39A-DL - similar to 90th Anniversary, with blue barrel and action, regular production. Mfg. 1960-1963.

	$900	$800	$750	$500	$400	$300	$200

This model is also known as the "Marlin 39A Squirrel Gun."

MODEL 39A OCTAGON - similar to Golden 39A, with octagon barrel, no pistol grip cap, 2,551 rifles and 2,140 carbines were produced. Mfg. 1973.

	$595	$550	$475	$425	$360	$295	$250

MODEL 39 CARBINE - similar to 39M, with light barrel, ¾ tube mag. 9,695 mfg. 1963-1967.

	$450	$325	$275	$225	$175	$150	$110

MODEL 39D - similar to 39M, with pistol grip stock. Mfg. 1971-1973.

	$225	$195	$175	$150	$135	$115	$90

MODEL 39A/AS - .22 LR cal., current production model, lever action, tube mag., 19-26 shot, 24 in. barrel, walnut stock (cut checkering became standard 1994), open sights, gold trigger, takedown, 6½ lbs.

MSR	$540	$405	$280	$190	$160	$130	$110	$100

This model was previously designated the Model 39A. In 1988, the Model 39AS became the standard production model and included a rebounding hammer and hammer block safety. In 2001, the model nomenclature was changed back to the Model 39A.

MODEL 39TDS - .22 LR cal., carbine variation of the Model 39AS, 16½ in. barrel with open sights, 5¼ lbs. Mfg. 1988-95.

	$450	$350	$200	$175	$150	$125	$110

Last MSR was $443.

MODEL 39M - carbine version of Model 39A, 20 in. lightweight barrel, 16 shot tube mag., squared finger lever, 6 lbs. Disc. 1987.

	$350	$325	$295	$250	$200	$175	$150

Last MSR was $304.

MODEL 39M OCTAGON - similar to Model 39M, with octagon barrel. Mfg. 1973.

	$550	$495	$475	$425	$360	$295	$250

MODEL 39 CENTURY LTD - Marlin Centennial 1870-1970 Commemorative, 20 in. octagon barrel, select walnut straight stock, brass forearm cap and butt plate, name plate in butt. 35,388 mfg. 1970.

	$400	$350	$275	$200	$175	$150	$125

MODEL 39A ARTICLE II - NRA Centennial Commemorative 1871-1971, "Right to Bear Arms" medallion in receiver, 24 in. octagon barrel, fancy pistol grip stock, brass butt plate and forearm cap. 6,244 mfg. 1971.

	$450	$395	$375	$350	$295	$250	$195

MODEL 39M ARTICLE II CARBINE - similar to 39A Article II, with 20 in. barrel, straight grip stock. Mfg. 3,824.

	$450	$395	$375	$350	$295	$250	$195

Grading	100%	98%	95%	90%	80%	70%	60%

MODEL 45 CARBINE - .45 ACP cal. only, 7 shot mag., sandblasted steel receiver, 16½ in. barrel, last shot hold open device, press checkering, adj. rear sight, 6¾ lbs. Mfg. 1986-1999.

	$340	$230	$175	$150	$140	$130	$125

Last MSR was $443.

A new high visibility orange front sight post with cutaway hood was added in 1989.

MODEL 56 - similar to Model 57 Levermatic, 22 or 24 in. barrel, with mag. Mfg. 1955- 1964.

	$295	$245	$200	$150	$125	$100	$85

MODEL 57 LEVERMATIC - .22 S, L, or LR cal., tube mag., 22 in. barrel, open sight, Monte Carlo pistol grip stock. Mfg. 1959-1965.

	$295	$245	$200	$150	$125	$100	$85

MODEL 57M - .22 Mag. cal., similar to Model 57 Levermatic, except has 24 in. barrel.

	$350	$300	$225	$175	$135	$125	$110

MODEL 60 SEMI-AUTO - .22 LR cal., 14 shot (LR) tube mag., entry level rifle with 22 in. Micro-Groove barrel, hardwood stock with pressed checkering, approx. 5½ lbs. New 1960.

MSR	$181	$145	$120	$95	$80	$75	$65	$60

Add $7 for 4X scope.

✳ *Model 60C* - similar to Model 60SS, except has full coverage Mossy Oak Breakup camo stock, 5½ lbs. New 2000.

MSR	$216	$165	$130	$100	$80	$75	$65	$60

MODEL 60SS SEMI-AUTO STAINLESS - .22 LR cal., 14 shot tube mag., stainless steel construction with laminated black/gray birch stock with Monte Carlo cheekpiece, Mar- Shield finish, 22 in. barrel, most recent mfg. has adj. semi-buckhorn folding rear with high visibility post and removable cutaway Wide-scan hood front sight, 5½ lbs. New 1993.

MSR	$290	$220	$185	$145

✳ *Model 60SB* - similar to Model 60SS, except has uncheckered (mfg. 1998 only) or press-checkered (new 1999) birch Monte Carlo stock. New 1998.

MSR	$231	$170	$155	$130

Add $13 for 4X scope.

This model was previously sold to Wal-Mart only.

✳ *Model 60SSK* - similar to Model 60SS, except has black fiberglass stock with Monte Carlo cheekpiece. New 1998.

MSR	$252	$200	$170	$140

Add $15 for 4X scope (disc. 2001).

MODEL 62 LEVERMATIC - .256 Mag. or .30 Carbine cal., 4 shot mag., 23 in. barrel, open sight, pistol grip Monte Carlo stock. Mfg. 1963-1969.

.256 Mag.	$475	$375	$325	$275	$225	$195	$175
.30 Carbine	$375	$335	$300	$250	$200	$175	$150

MODEL 70P (PAPOOSE) SEMI-AUTO - .22 LR cal. only, semi-auto, takedown carbine with 16¼ in. barrel, 7 shot mag., rustproof receiver, bolt hold open, is supplied with floating nylon carrying case. Mfg. 1986-94.

	$170	$125	$90	$75	$65	$60	$55

Last MSR was $225.

Subtract $25 if without 4X scope (became standard 1993).

✳ *Model 70PSS* - similar to Model 70P, except has stainless steel construction with black checkered synthetic stock with swing swivels, last shot hold-open became standard in 1996, 3¼ lbs. New 1995.

MSR	$297	$225	$180	$135

✳ *Model 70HC* - .22 LR cal., semi-auto, carbine with 18 in. barrel. Mfg. 1988-1995.

	$185	$155	$130	$120	$110	$100	$90

M

Grading	100%	98%	95%	90%	80%	70%	60%

MODEL 81TS BOLT ACTION - .22 S, L, or LR cal., 22 in. barrel with 17-25 shot tube mag., black synthetic stock with molded checkering, adj. rear sight, 6 lbs.

	MSR	$207		$160	$125	$95	$80	$75	$65	$60

MODEL 83TS BOLT ACTION - .22 Mag. cal., 22 in. barrel, 12 shot mag., otherwise similar to Model 81TS, 6 lbs.

	MSR	$252		$190	$145	$120	$95	$85	$75	$70

MODEL 322 BOLT ACTION VARMINT - .222 Rem. cal., Sako Mauser type action, 3 shot mag., 24 in. medium weight barrel, 2 position aperture sight, checkered stock. Mfg. 1954-1957.

$550	$500	$475	$400	$325	$300	$250

MODEL 336A RIFLE - improved 36A, .30-30 Win., .35 Rem., or .32 Spl. cal., round breech bolt, 24 in. barrel with 2/3 mag. Mfg. 1948-1962, re-introduced 1973-1980.

$350	$300	$250	$225	$195	$175	$150

Add 20% for 1st Model mfg. 1948-1952.
Add 10% for 1953-1962 mfg.
The .35 Rem. cal. was added in 1950, .32 Spl. was disc. in 1962.

✷ *Model 336ADL Rifle* - similar to Model 336A Rifle, except has deluxe checkered walnut stock and forearm, quick detachable swivels and 1 in. sling. Mfg. 1948-1962.

$500	$450	$375	$325	$275	$230	$200

Add 20% for 2nd Model.
The 336ADL 1st Model (mfg. 1948-1956) did not have a raised comb or cheekpiece. The 2nd Model (mfg. 1957-1962) is identifiable by a Monte Carlo butt stock with raised comb and cheekpiece. Wood was supplied by Bishop.

MODELS 336A/336AS/336CC/336W - these models are listed previously under the Model 30AS.

MODEL 336RC CARBINE - .30-30 Win., .32 Spl., or .35 Rem. cal., standard model carbine. Mfg. 1948-68.

$300	$275	$200	$175	$155	$140	$120

Add 10% for 1st Model mfg. 1948-1952.

MODEL 336C CARBINE - .30-30 Win., .32 Spl., or .35 Rem. cal., standard model carbine with 20 in. barrel. Mfg. 1969-1983.

$250	$210	$185	$160	$150	$135	$115

MODEL 336SC SPORTING CARBINE - similar to Model 336C, with 20 in. barrel and 2/3 length mag. tube, raised comb butt stock (1957-1963). Mfg. 1948-1963.

$350	$295	$250	$225	$195	$185	$165

Add 10% for 1st Model mfg. 1948-1952.

MODEL 336SC .219 ZIPPER - similar to Model 336SC, in .219 Zipper cal., 5 shot mag. 3,230 mfg. 1955-1960.

$500	$475	$400	$350	$300	$250	$220

MODEL 336SD CARBINE (SPORTING DELUXE) - .30-30 Win., .32 Spl., or .35 Rem. cal., deluxe sporting carbine with 20 in. barrel, checkered stock and forearm, raised comb, no cheekpiece, quick detachable swivels and 1 in. sling. Mfg. 1954-1962.

$595	$525	$400	$275	$200	$185	$165

MODEL 336C (336CS) CARBINE LEVER ACTION - .30-30 Win., or .35 Rem. cal., 6 shot tube mag., 20 in. barrel, hammer block safety, American black walnut pistol grip stock (cut checkering became standard 1994), 7 lbs. Introduced 1984.

	MSR	$518		$395	$270	$210	$195	$175	$165	$150

During 2001, this model's nomenclature was changed from 336CS to 336C.

M

Grading	100%	98%	95%	90%	80%	70%	60%

MODEL 336SS (336M) - .30-30 Win. cal. only, similar to Model 336W/30AW, except is stainless steel, 6 shot tube mag., 7 lbs. New 2000.

	MSR	$627	$510	$435	$380

During 2001, this model's nomenclature was changed from 336M to 336SS.

MODEL 336 LTD - .35 Rem. cal., blue metal finish, 18½ in. ported barrel with 5 shot tube mag., checkered straight grip walnut stock and forearm, includes letter of authenticity. 1,001 mfg. in 2000 only.

			$425	$275	$220	$200	$180	$170	$160

Last MSR was $515.

This model was distributed exclusively by Davidson's.

MODEL 336LTS CARBINE - .30-30 Win. cal. only, 16¼ in. barrel, 5 shot tube mag., 6½ lbs. 2,671 mfg. 1988-89 only.

			$450	$400	$350	$200	$175	$165	$150

Last MSR was $346.

MODEL 336 COWBOY - .30-30 Win. or .38-55 WCF cal., 8 shot tube mag., squared off finger lever, 24 in. tapered octagon barrel with deep cut Ballard-type rifling (6 grooves), cut checkered (disc. 2001) straight grip walnut stock and forearm, adj. Marbles semi-buckhorn rear and carbine front sight, ser. no. is on left side of receiver, instead of on tang, 7½ lbs. New 1999.

	MSR	$719	$585	$470	$380	$310	$275	$250	$225

MODEL 336ER (EXTRA RANGE) - .356 Win. cal., 5 shot tube mag., 20 in. barrel, walnut pistol grip stock, open sights, 7 lbs. 2,441 mfg. 1983-86.

		$525	$450	$325	$225	$200	$175	$150

Last MSR was $350.

Although advertised, the .307 cal. was never manufactured in this model.

MODEL 336T CARBINE "TEXAN" - .30-30 Win., .35 Rem., or .44 Mag. (1965-1967 only) cal., similar to 336C, with straight stock, 18½ (1983 only) or 20 in. barrel, saddle ring (1965-1971 only). Mfg. 1954-1983.

		$300	$275	$200	$165	$155	$140	$120

MODEL 336DT CARBINE (DELUXE TEXAN) - .30-30 Win. or .35 Rem. cal., select stock version of 336T, longhorn and map of Texas carved on butt stock. Mfg. 1962-1963.

		$700	$625	$450	$300	$200	$150	$135

Add 10% for .35 Rem. cal.

MODEL 336TS TEXAN - similar to 336 CS, except is .30-30 Win. cal., 18½ in. barrel, straight grip stock and squared finger lever, crossbolt safety. Mfg. 1984-87.

		$250	$200	$175	$150	$140	$130	$120

Last MSR was $314.

MODEL 336 OCTAGON RIFLE - .30-30 Win. cal. only, with 22 in. octagon barrel, standard model. 2,414 mfg. 1973 only.

		$500	$425	$300	$250	$200	$175	$150

MODEL 336 MARAUDER CARBINE - .30-30 Win. or .35 Rem. cal., 16¼ in. barrel. 5,856 mfg. 1963-1964.

		$450	$400	$350	$275	$235	$210	$185

Add 10% for .35 cal.

Approx. 65% were mfg. in .30-30 Win. cal., and 35% were mfg. in .35 Rem. cal.
Be careful of re-barreled examples of this model.

MODEL 336 MAGNUM CARBINE - .44 Mag. cal., 20 in. standard carbine configuration, w/o saddle ring. 2,823 mfg. 1963- 1964 only.

		$375	$325	$250	$225	$195	$170	$160

Grading	100%	98%	95%	90%	80%	70%	60%

MODEL 336T - .44 Mag. cal., with saddle ring, 13,895 mfg. 1965-1967.

| | $325 | $275 | $225 | $200 | $175 | $160 | $150 |

MODEL 336 ZANE GREY CENTURY CARBINE - .30-30 Win. cal., similar to 336 Octagon, 22 in. octagon barrel, Zane Grey medallion inlaid in receiver, select walnut stock, pistol grip, brass butt plate and forearm cap. 7,871 mfg. in 1971.

| | $425 | $350 | $300 |

This model was mfg. to commemorate the 100th anniversary of the birth of Zane Grey.

MODEL 336 PRESENTATION RIFLE - .30-30 Win. cal., 22 in. octagon barrel, engraved action, sold with Model 39 Presentation. Mfg. 1970 only.

| | $995 | $700 | $475 |

Add a premium for serial numbers under 100.

MARLIN CENTENNIAL MATCHED PAIR - Model 336 and Model 39 serial numbered the same, .30-30 Win. or .22 LR cal., engraved by Robert Kain and Winston Churchill, deluxe wood, inlaid medallions, cased. 1,000 mfg. sets in 1970.

| | $1,500 | $1,350 | $900 |

Last MSR was $750.

MODEL 375 - similar to Model 336 CS, except is .375 Win. cal. 16,315 mfg. 1980-83.

| | $350 | $295 | $225 | $200 | $175 | $160 | $150 |

MODEL 444 LEVER ACTION - .444 Marlin cal., 4 shot tube mag., 24 in. barrel, open sights, straight grip, Monte Carlo stock, recoil pad, swivels, sling. Mfg. 1965-1971.

| | $375 | $325 | $250 | $225 | $200 | $185 | $160 |

✴ *Model 444S* - similar to Model 444, except has pistol grip stock. Mfg. 1972-1983.

| | $325 | $265 | $225 | $200 | $185 | $165 | $150 |

MODEL 444P OUTFITTER - .444 Marlin cal., 5 shot tube mag., 18½ in. ported barrel with deep cut Ballard-type rifling (6 grooves), adj. semi-buckhorn folding rear sight with ramp front, checkered straight grip walnut stock and forearm, tapped for scope mount, approx. 7 lbs. New 1999.

| MSR | $631 | $495 | $395 | $315 | $245 | $195 | $180 | $170 |

M

MODEL 444 (444SS) SPORTER - .444 Marlin cal., similar to Model 444, with 22 in. barrel and hammer block safety, pistol grip stock without Monte Carlo configuration (cut checkering became standard 1994), 7½ lbs. Mfg. 1984-present.

| MSR | $618 | $450 | $300 | $275 | $225 | $195 | $180 | $170 |

During 2001, this model's nomenclature was changed from 444SS to 444.

MODEL 455 BOLT ACTION SPORTER - .30-06, or .308 Win. cal., FN Mauser action with Sako trigger, 24 in. barrel, stainless steel barrel, Lyman aperture sight, checkered Monte Carlo pistol grip stock. 1,079 were mfg. in 30.06 cal., 59 in .308 Win. cal. Mfg. 1957-1959.

| | $550 | $400 | $350 | $250 | $220 | $195 | $165 |

Add 20% for .308 Win. cal.

MODELS 780, 781, 782, and 783 BOLT ACTION - .22 LR or .22 Mag. (Models 782 and 783) cal., tube or mag., 22 in. barrel. Disc. 1988.

| | $110 | $85 | $75 | $70 | $65 | $55 | $50 |

Last MSR was $162.

Add $17-$25 for Models 782 and 783.

MODEL 795 SEMI-AUTO - .22 LR cal., 10 shot mag., 18 in. barrel, black synthetic Monte Carlo stock, grooved receiver, last shot bolt hold open, approx. 5 lbs.

| MSR | $173 | $125 | $100 | $80 | $75 | $65 | $60 | $55 |

✴ *Model 795SS* - similar to Model 795, except has stainless steel barrel and nickel plated parts. New 2002.

| MSR | $231 | $170 | $145 | $120 |

MODELS 880/881 BOLT ACTION - .22 LR or .22 Mag. cal., replacements for Models 780, 781, Model 880 is .22 LR with 7 shot detachable mag. and 22 in. barrel, (cut checkering became standard 1994), Model 881 is .22 LR with 17 shot tube mag. and 22 in. barrel, 6 lbs. Mfg. 1989-1997.

| | $185 | $145 | $100 | $85 | $75 | $70 | $65 |

Last MSR was $251.

Add $10 for Model 881.

* **Model 880SS** - similar to Model 880, except is stainless steel, black fiberglass synthetic stock, approx. 6 lbs. New 1994.

| MSR | $308 | | $235 | $170 | $115 |

* **Model 880SQ (Squirrel Rifle)** - similar to Model 880, except has black fiberglass filled synthetic stock with checkering and heavy 22 in. barrel, without sights and grooved receiver, matte finish, 7 lbs. New 1996.

| MSR | $322 | | $240 | $185 | $130 | $100 | $80 | $70 | $65 |

MODELS 882/883 BOLT ACTION - .22 Win. Mag. cal., 7 shot detachable (Model 882) or 12 shot tube mag. (Model 883), 22 in. barrel, checkered (cut checkering became standard 1994), black walnut Monte Carlo stock with Mar-Shield finish, adj. semi-buckhorn rear sight and hooded front, thumb safety, 6 lbs. New 1989.

| MSR | $314 | | $235 | $180 | $125 | $95 | $85 | $75 | $70 |

Add $14 for Model 883.

Add $35 for nickel finish on Model 883N (disc. 1993).

The Models 882 and 883 are the replacements for Models 782 and 783.

* **Model 882SS** - .22 Win. Mag. cal., similar to Model 882, except is stainless steel and stock is black synthetic with molded-in checkering, fire sights (red fiber optic inserts with cutaway hood) became standard 1998, approx. 6 lbs. New 1995.

| MSR | $336 | | $245 | $185 | $130 |

* **Model 882SSV** - .22 Win. Mag. cal., features 22 in. bead blasted stainless barrel and receiver with black fiberglass reinforced synthetic stock, 7 shot mag., grooved receiver, w/o sights, ring mounts included, 7 lbs. New 1997.

| MSR | $330 | | $240 | $180 | $125 |

* **Model 882L** - similar to Model 882, except has two-tone brown laminated hardwood stock, 6¼ lbs. New 1992.

| MSR | $333 | | $245 | $195 | $135 | $95 | $85 | $75 | $70 |

* **Model 883SS** - .22 Win. Mag. cal., 12 shot tube mag., similar to Model 883, except barrel is stainless steel and stock is laminated two-tone brown birch with Monte Carlo cheekpiece. New 1993.

| MSR | $348 | | $260 | $200 | $140 |

MODEL 922M SEMI-AUTO - .22 Win. Mag. cal., 7 shot detachable mag., 20½ in. barrel, Garand style safety, alloy receiver, hold-open device, uncheckered or checkered (became standard 1994) walnut stock with solid pad, blue steel (hard coated on receiver), 6½ lbs. Mfg. 1993-2001.

| | $360 | $295 | $240 | $200 | $185 | $175 | $165 |

Last MSR was $454.

MODEL 990 SEMI-AUTO - .22 LR cal. only, 18 shot tube mag., 22 in. barrel, last shot automatic bolt hold-open, Monte Carlo American black walnut stock with pistol grip, 5½ lbs. Disc. 1987.

| | $115 | $90 | $75 | $65 | $60 | $55 | $50 |

Last MSR was $159.

M

Grading	100%	98%	95%	90%	80%	70%	60%

MODEL 990L SEMI-AUTO - .22 LR cal., 14 shot tube mag., 22 in. barrel, laminated two-tone brown Monte Carlo stock, gold trigger, adj. rear sight, grooved receiver, 5¾ lbs. Mfg. 1993-94.

	$180	$160	$145	$130	$120	$110	$100

Last MSR was $223.

MODEL 995 SEMI-AUTO - .22 LR cal., 7 shot mag., 18 in. barrel, Monte Carlo walnut stock, 5 lbs. Disc. 1994.

	$160	$125	$85	$70	$65	$60	$55

Last MSR was $206.

✳ ***Model 995SS*** - .22 LR cal., stainless steel barrel and nickel-plated small parts, black fiberglass stock with molded-in checkering, adj. rear sight, last shot hold-open new 1996, 5 lbs. Mfg. 1995-99.

	$195	$145	$110				

Last MSR was $255.

MODEL 1894 - .44 Spl. or .44 Mag. cal., 20 in. bbl., 10 shot tube mag., adj. sights, straight grip walnut stock and forearm, 6 lbs. Mfg. 1969-1984.

	$375	$300	$250	$195	$165	$145	$130

MODEL 1894C CARBINE - .357 Mag. (introduced in 1979), .44 Spl., or .44 Mag. cal., 18½ in. barrel, w/o hammer block safety, 6 lbs. Mfg. 1979-1984.

	$350	$275	$225	$180	$160	$145	$130

MODEL 1894 SPORTER - .44 Mag. cal. only, 6 shot half mag. tube, crescent shaped hard rubber buttplate, 1,398 mfg. 1973 only.

	$475	$425	$360	$300	$250	$200	$175

MODEL 1894C CARBINE (1894CS) - copy of original Model 1894, .357 Mag./.38 Spl. cal., 9 shot mag., 18½ in. round barrel, open sights (hooded front became standard 1999), straight grip stock (cut checkering became standard 1994), squared finger lever, 6 lbs. Mfg. 1984-present.

MSR $544	$425	$310	$220	$180	$150	$140	$130

During 2001, this model's nomenclature was changed from 1894CS to 1894C.

✳ ***Model 1894CC41-LTD*** - .41 Mag. cal., 20 in. tapered octagon barrel, blue finish, Marble sights, 10 shot full length tube mag., includes letter of authenticity. 1,001 mfg. in 1999.

	$575	$475	$400	$350	$300	$275	$250

Last MSR was $715.

This models was distributed exclusively by Davidson's.

✳ ***Model 1894CP Carbine*** - similar to Model 1894C, except has 16¼ in. ported round barrel, 8 shot mag., approx. 5¾ lbs. New 2001.

MSR $566	$440	$320	$235	$185	$150	$140	$130

MODEL 1894P CARBINE - .44 Mag./.44 Spl. cal., 16¼ in. ported barrel with deep-cut Ballard type 6 groove rifling, 8 shot tube mag., checkered straight grip walnut stock with vent. recoil pad, 5¾ lbs. New 2000.

MSR $566	$440	$320	$235	$185	$150	$140	$130

✳ ***Model 1894S Limited*** - .44 Mag./.44 Spl. cal., features 16¼ in. barrel with "The Marlin Limited" roll stamped on barrel, approx. 1,500 mfg. 1996 only.

	$450	$400	$350				

✳ ***Model 1894SC 44/45 LTD*** - .44 Mag./.44 Spl. or .45 LC cal., features 16 in. barrel, 8 shot tube mag., includes letter of authenticity, approx. 1,550 mfg. in .44 Mag. cal. 1996 only, 1,050 mfg. in .45 LC cal. 1997 only.

	$425	$325	$240	$190	$160	$150	$140

Last MSR was $460.

These models were distributed exclusively by Davidson's.

Grading	100%	98%	95%	90%	80%	70%	60%

MODEL 1894 (1894S) - .41 Mag. (disc. 1991), .44 Mag./.44 Spl., or .45 LC (mfg. 1988- 91) cal.,
Model 1894 with addition of cross bolt (S suffix) and hammer block safety, 20 in. barrel, 10 shot tube mag., adj. sights, straight grip walnut stock and forearm (cut checkering became standard 1994), 6 lbs.

MSR	$544	$425	$310	$220	$180	$150	$140	$130

During 2001, this model's nomenclature was changed from 1894S to 1894.

MODEL 1894SS - .44 Mag./.44 Spl. cal., stainless steel, 20 in. barrel, 10 shot tube mag., straight
grip, checkered black walnut stock and forearm, off set hammer spur, approx. 6 lbs. New 2002.

MSR	$665	$525	$395	$300

MODEL 1894 COWBOY/COWBOY II - .357 Mag. (new 1997), .44-40 WCF (mfg. 1997-99), .44
Mag. (new 1997), or .45 LC cal., 10 shot tube mag., incorporates "cowboy shooter" features, straight grip stock w/o or with checkering (disc. 2001), adj. Marbles-type rear sight, blued finish, 24 in. tapered octagon barrel, 7½ lbs. New 1996.

MSR	$802	$630	$495	$390	$325	$265	$225	$195

The Model 1894 Cowboy II refers to the three new cals. introduced 1997.

✱ *Model 1894 Cowboy Competition* - .38 Spl. cal., 10 shot tube mag., 20 in. tapered barrel with
deep cut Ballard type rifling, hammer block safety, Marbles sights, case colored receiver, lever, and bolt. New 2002.

MSR	$965	$750	$650	$500	$425	$375	$325	$295

✱ *Model 1894 Cowboy Carbine* - .44-40 WCF cal., 20 in. tapered octagon barrel with 10 shot
full length tube mag., uncheckered straight grip walnut stock and forearm, adj. Marble rear sight, includes letter of authenticity. Only 325 mfg. in 2000.

		$580	$480	$400	$365	$310	$280	$260

Last MSR was $715.

This model was distributed exclusively by Davidson's.

MODEL 1894M (.22 MAG.) - .22 Mag. cal., with 20 in. barrel, 11 shot tube mag., straight grip
walnut stock and forearm, 6¼ lbs. Disc. 1989.

		$450	$395	$350	$250	$200	$175	$150

Last MSR was $358.

MODEL 1894CL - .218 Bee (new 1990), .25-20 WCF or .32-20 WCF cal., 6 shot (two- thirds
length) tube mag., 22 in. barrel, 6¼ lbs. Mfg. 1988-94.

		$450	$395	$350	$250	$200	$175	$150

Last MSR was $502.

Add 10% for .218 Bee cal.

MODEL 1894 CENTURY LIMITED (EMPLOYEE SPECIAL EDITION) - employee special edition
featuring gold inlaid Marlin horse and rider logo. 100 mfg. 1994-95 in ser. no. range 1-100.

		$1,750	$1,450	$995

MODEL 1894 CENTURY LIMITED - .44-40 WCF cal., limited edition commemorative mfg. to cel-
ebrate the Model 1894's 100th Anniversary, 24 in. tapered octagon barrel with full 12 shot tube mag., features Giovanelli engraved receiver, bolt, and lever, receiver is case colored using traditional methods, checkered straight grip stock and forearm, crescent butt plate, 6½ lbs. 2,500 mfg. 1994 only.

		$1,100	$900	$600

Last MSR was $1,088.

MODEL 1894 OCTAGON - similar to 1894 Carbine, with octagon barrel. Mfg. 1973.

		$450	$400	$350	$275	$225	$200	$185

MODEL 1895M - .450 Marlin Mag. cal. (belted), 4 shot tube mag., 18½ in. ported barrel, check-
ered straight grip walnut stock and forearm, vent. recoil pad, 7 lbs. New 2000.

MSR	$680	$555	$450	$375	$315	$275	$250	$225

Grading	100%	98%	95%	90%	80%	70%	60%

MODEL 1895 LEVER ACTION - .45-70 Govt. cal., 4 shot tube mag., 22 in. barrel, open sights, straight grip stock with curved buttplate, forearm cap, sling and swivels. Mfg. 1972-1984.

	100%	98%	95%	90%	80%	70%	60%
	$350	$300	$275	$200	$185	$165	$140

Early new Model 1895 Marlins had cut rifling suitable for cast bullets, while later mfg. was switched to Marlin's "Micro Groove" shallow rifling. Changes were also made from a straight stock to a pistol grip stock and from a traditional receiver to one with the newer hammer- block, push-button safety. Early guns with a straight grip stock, traditional receiver, and cut rifling command premiums over later mfg. Cut rifling occured during the first year of production only - these guns have a ser. no. prefix of B.O. More recently mfg. models have pistol grip, Micro Groove rifling, and hammer-block safety - these newer guns are the least desirable from a collector's standpoint.

✳ Model 1895S - similar to Model 1895, except has pistol grip stock and straight buttpad.

	100%	98%	95%	90%	80%	70%	60%
	$300	$275	$250	$200	$175	$150	$140

MODEL 1895 (1895SS) - similar to Model 1895S only with hammer block safety, cut checkering became standard 1994, 7½ lbs. New 1983.

	MSR	$618	98%	95%	90%	80%	70%	60%
			$475	$345	$250	$180	$155	$140	$130

During 2001, this model's nomenclature was changed from 1895SS to 1895.

✳ Model 1895SS Cody Stampede 75th Anniversary - .45-70 cal., includes semi- fancy checkered walnut stock with medallion, serial numbered CS-001 - CS-200, 200 mfg. 1994 only.

	100%	98%	95%
	$750	$500	$400

Last MSR was $695.

✳ Model 1895 LTD I/II - .45-70 Govt. cal., 24 in. half round/half octagon (LTD I) or 24 in. full octagon (LTD II) barrel, uncheckered (LTD I) or checkered (LTD II) walnut pistol grip (LTD II) or straight (LTD I) stock and forearm. 1,001 of each model mfg. 1997-98.

	100%	98%	95%	90%	80%	70%	60%
	$525	$450	$375	$325	$290	$260	$230

Last MSR was $671.

These models were distributed exclusively by Davidson's.

✳ Model 1895 LTD III - .45-70 Govt. cal., 18 ½ tapered octagon barrel, uncheckered straight grip walnut stock and forearm, Marble sights, 5 shot full length tube mag., includes letter of authenticty. 1,001 mfg. in 1991 only.

	100%	98%	95%	90%	80%	70%	60%
	$575	$475	$400	$350	$300	$275	$250

Last MSR was $715.

M

This model was distributed exclusively by Davidson's.

✳ Model 1895 LTD IV - .45-70 Govt. cal., 24 in. full octagon barrel with full length 8 shot tube mag., uncheckered straight grip walnut stock and forearm, Marble sights, includesletter of authenticity. Only 1,001 mfg. in 2000.

	100%	98%	95%	90%	80%	70%	60%
	$595	$495	$415	$365	$310	$280	$260

Last MSR was $729.

This model was distributed exclusively by Davidson's.

MODEL 1895 COWBOY - .45-70 Govt., features 26 in. tapered octagon barrel and 9 shot tube mag., uncheckered straight grip walnut stock and forearm, marble front and rear (adj.) sights, 8 lbs. New 2001.

	MSR	$802	98%	95%	90%	80%	70%	60%
			$630	$510	$430	$355	$315	$280	$255

MODEL 1895G GUIDE GUN - .45-70 Govt. cal., features 18½ in. ported barrel with Ballard style cut rifling, cut checkered American stock and forearm, 4 shot tube mag., vent. recoil pad, approx. 7 lbs. 2,500 to be mfg. beginning 1998.

	MSR	$631	98%	95%	90%	80%	70%	60%
			$495	$365	$250	$185	$155	$140	$130

Model 1895GS - similar to Model 1895G, except is stainless steel. New 2001.

	MSR	$744	98%	95%	90%
			$565	$410	$280

Grading	100%	98%	95%	90%	80%	70%	60%

MODEL 1895 CENTURY LIMITED (CLTD) - .45-70 cal., commemorates Marlin's 125th Anniversary, engraving includes grizzly bear on left side, Marlin horse and rider logo on right, 24 in. half-round half- octagonal barrel, crescent buttplate, satin finished receiver, checkered walnut stock and forearm. Approx. 2,500 mfg. 1995 only.

	$1,100	$850	$550

Last MSR was $1,104.

A Marlin Collector's Association Edition was also mfg. and was the same as the Model 1895 Century Limited.

✷ *Model 1895 Century Limited (CLTD) Employee Edition* - features 3 elk on left side and gold inlaid Marlin horse and rider logo on right. 100 mfg. 1995-96 in ser. no. range 1-100.

	$1,600	$1,100	$850

MODEL 1897 COWBOY - .22 S, L, or LR cal., takedown action, 19 shot (.22 LR cal.), tube mag., rebounding hammer with block safety, 24 in. tapered octagon barrel with Micro-Groove (16 grooves) rifling, cut checkered walnut stock and forearm, adj. Marble semi-buckhorn rear and carbine front sight with brass bead, high polish blue, 6½ lbs. Mfg. 1999-2001.

	$625	$495	$400	$350	$295	$265	$235

Last MSR was $708.

MODEL 1897T - .22 S, L, or LR cal., 14-21 shot mag., 20 in. tapered octagon barrel, hammer block safety, Marble front and rear sights, 6 lbs. New 2002.

MSR	$732		$575	$425	$360	$325	$285	$240	$195

MODEL 1897 CENTURY LIMITED LEVER ACTION - .22 LR cal., 100th anniversary of the Model 1897, features extensive receiver engraving and gold accenting, 24 in. half round/half octagon barrel with open sights, checkered fancy walnut stock and forearm. Limited mfg. 1997 only, limited quantities remained through 1999.

	$950	$800	$650

Last MSR was $1,055.

✷ *Model 1897 Century Limited Employee Edition* - .22 LR, features gold scroll work on lever, less than 100 mfg. 1997 only in ser. no. range 1-100.

	$1,500	$1,000	$850

MODEL 1897 ANNIE OAKLEY - .22 LR cal., features 18½ in. tapered octagon barrel with marble sights, blue receiver with rolled scroll engraving featuring gold Annie Oakley etched name on bolt, deluxe checkered walnut stock and forearm. Mfg. 1998 only.

	$675	$600	$500

Last MSR was $1,054.

Add $100 for employee variation.

An employee variation of this model was made with gold inlays on finger lever, 100 mfg. total.

MODEL 2000 TARGET BOLT ACTION - .22 LR cal., single shot (can be converted), 22 in. heavy barrel with match chambered and Lyman adj. sights, 2 stage target trigger, molded synthetic stock made from fiberglass and Kevlar with twice baked blue enamel, adj. buttplate, aluminum forearm rail, 8 lbs. Mfg. 1991-95.

	$495	$410	$350	$300	$275	$250	$225

Last MSR was $602.

Add $34 for 5-shot conversion unit (for summer biathlon competition).

✷ *Model 2000A Target* - similar to Model 2000 Target, except has adj. comb, ambidextrous pistol grip, and molded-in logo. Mfg. 1994 only.

	$525	$425	$365	$315	$290	$260	$230

Last MSR was $625.

✷ *Model 2000L* - .22 LR cal., updated version of the Model 2000, featuring grey/black laminated stock, adj. aperture rear and aperture insert front sight, double bedding screws, factory test target supplied with each gun, 8 lbs. New 1996.

MSR	$745		$600	$475	$380	$320	$280	$250	$225

M

MODEL 7000 SEMI-AUTO - .22 LR cal., 10 shot detachable mag., 18 in. heavy barrel without sights and recessed muzzle, black fiberglass, synthetic stock with molded-in checkering, grooved receiver, no sights, last shot hold open, scope mounts provided, 5½ lbs. New 1997.

MSR	$245		$200	$180	$160	$140	$130	$120	$110

* **Model 7000T** - .22 LR cal., target model with 18 in. heavy barrel, red, white and blue laminated hardwood stock with adj. pad, two stage target trigger with stop, aluminum forend rail with adj. stop, grooved receiver w/o sights, 7½ lbs. Mfg. 1999-2001.

$365	$300	$240	$200	$185	$175	$165

Last MSR was $465.

MARLIN PROMOTIONAL MODELS - Models 15 (disc.), 15Y (disc.), 15N (mfg. 1998-99, last MSR $188), 15YN (refer to individual listing), 25 (disc.), 25M (disc.), 25N (refer to individual listing), 25NC (refer to individual listing),, 70 (disc.), 70HC (mfg. 1989-95, last 1995 MSR was $167), 75C (disc.), 81TS (refer to individual listing), and 795 Semi-Auto (refer to individual listing), are inexpensive, utilitarian .22 LR or .22 Mag. cal. (Model 25M only), rifles designed for inexpensive shooting.

Series 15 and 25 Models designate bolt action, Series 60 and 70 designate semi-auto design.

RIFLES: .22 CAL.

Between 1930 to date, Marlin has made a number of .22 cal. rimfire rifles, bolt action single shots, bolt action repeaters and auto loaders. These have normally been good quality, inexpensive weapons. In 1960, the name Glenfield was also used in connection with these guns. We will list these models for reference purposes with price ranges appearing at the end of each listing.

BOLT ACTION, SINGLE SHOT

Model 65 - 1932-1938. Price Range $35 - $65.
Model 65E - 1932-1938. Price Range $45 - $75.
Model 100 - 1936-1941. Price Range $45 - $75.
Model 100S Tom Mix Special - disc. Price Range $125 - $250.
Model 100SB - 1936-1941. Price Range $50 - $85.
Model 101 - 1951-disc. Price Range $45 - $75.
Model 101 DL - disc. Price Range $60 - $90.
Model 101 Crown Prince - 1959. Price Range $75 - $150.
Model 101G - 1960-1965, Marlin Glenfield. Price Range $40 - $70.
Model 10 - 1966-disc., Marlin Glenfield. Price Range $40 - $65.
Model 122 - 1966-disc. Price Range $40 - $65.

BOLT ACTION: REPEATING RIFLES

Model 80 - 1934-1939. Price Range $45 - $85.
Model 80E - 1934-1940. Price Range $50 - $90.
Model 80C - 1940-1970. Price Range $50 - $90.
Model 80DL - 1940-1965. Price Range $60 - $95.
Model 80G - 1960-1965, Marlin Glenfield. Price Range $40 - $70.
Model 20 - 1966-disc., Marlin Glenfield. Price Range $40 - $70.
Model 780 - 1971-1988. Price Range $45 - $75.
Model 781 - 1971-1988. Price Range $45 - $75.
Model 782 - 1971-1988, .22 WRM. Price Range $65 - $100.
Model 783 - 1971-1988, .22 WRM. Price Range $65 - $100.
Model 980 - 1962-1970, .22 WRM. Price Range $65 - $100.
Model 81 - 1937-1940. Price Range $25 - $50.
Model 81E - 1937-1940. Price Range $60 - $85.
Model 81C - 1940-1970. Price Range $60 - $85.
Model 81DL - 1940-1965. Price Range $65 - $90.
Model 81G - 1960-1965 Marlin Glenfield. Price Range $50 - $75.

AUTOLOADING RIFLES

Model 50 - 1931-1935. Price Range $75 - $125.
Model 50E - 1931-1934. Price Range $75 - $135.
Model A-1 - 1936-1940. Price Range $75 - $125.

M

Grading	100%	98%	95%	90%	80%	70%	60%

Model A-1E - 1935-1946. Price Range $75 - $135.
Model A-1C - 1941-1946. Price Range $65 - $125.
Model A-1DL - 1941-1946. Price Range $65 - $135.
Model 88-C - 1948-1956. Price Range $65 - $135.
Model 88-DL - 1953-1956. Price Range $65 - $135.
Model 89-C - 1948-1961. Price Range $65 - $135.
Model 89-DL - 1950-1961. Price Range $65 - $135.
Model 98 - 1957-1959. Price Range $65 - $135.
Model 99 - 1959-1960. Price Range $65 - $135.
Model 99C - 1961-1978. Price Range $65 - $135.
Model 99G - 1960-1965, Marlin Glenfield. Price Range $65 - $135.
Model 60 - 1960-present, Marlin Glenfield (2000 MSR $172).
Model 99DL - 1960-1964. Price Range $65 - $135.
Model 49 - 1968-1970. Price Range $65 - $135.
Model 49DL - 1971-1978. Price Range $65 - $135.
Model 99M1 - 1964-1978. Price Range $65 - $135.
Model 989M2 - 1966-disc. Price Range $65 - $135.
Model 989 - 1962-1965. Price Range $65 - $135.
Model 70 (HC) - 1966-1995, Marlin Glenfield. Price Range $75 - $145.
Model 989G - 1962-1964, Marlin Glenfield. Price Range $65 - $135.
Model 990 - disc. Price Range $65 - $135.

SHOTGUNS: BOLT ACTION

MODEL 25MG GARDEN GUN - .22 Mag. shot shell, features 22 in. smooth bore barrel with high visibility bead front sight only, 7 shot detachable mag., black synthetic stock, thumb safety, 6 lbs. New 1999.

	100%	98%	95%	90%	80%	70%	60%
MSR $245	$190	$155	$130	$110	$100	$90	$80

MODEL 50 DL - 12 ga. only, upland game model, 28 in. barrel bored M, black Rynite stock with molded- in checkering, 2 shot mag., 7½ lbs. Mfg. 1997-99.

100%	98%	95%	90%	80%	70%	60%
$255	$195	$150	$125	$115	$100	$90

Last MSR was $330.

MODEL 55 - 12, 16, or 20 ga., 2 shot detachable mag., 26 and 28 in. full choke barrel, plain pistol grip stock. Mfg. 1950-1965.

	100%	98%	95%	90%	80%	70%	60%
	$90	$70	$55	$40	$35	$30	$25
With adj. choke	$100	$85	$65	$50	$45	$40	$30

MODEL 55 GOOSE GUN - similar to Model 55, except 12 ga. only, 36 in. full choke barrel, 3 in. chamber, 2 shot mag., leather carrying strap and detachable swivels, walnut stock with rubber recoil pad, 8 lbs. Mfg. 1962-96.

100%	98%	95%	90%	80%	70%	60%
$235	$185	$145	$125	$115	$100	$90

Last MSR was $308.

✱ *Model 55 GDL* - similar to Model 55 Goose Gun, except has black Rynite synthetic stock. Mfg. 1997- 2000.

100%	98%	95%	90%	80%	70%	60%
$330	$240	$200	$180	$160	$145	$130

Last MSR was $396.

MODEL 55 SWAMP GUN - similar to Model 55, 12 ga., 20 in. adj. choke barrel, 3 in. mag. Mfg. 1963-1965.

100%	98%	95%	90%	80%	70%	60%
$105	$90	$70	$55	$50	$45	$35

MODEL 55S SLUG GUN - 24 in. barrel, cylinder bore, rifle sights. Mfg. 1974-1983.

100%	98%	95%	90%	80%	70%	60%
$140	$120	$110	$95	$85	$55	$40

Grading	100%	98%	95%	90%	80%	70%	60%

MODEL 512 SLUGMASTER - 12 ga., 3 in. chamber, bolt action, 2 shot box mag., 21 in. rifled barrel, adj. rear sight, receiver is drilled and tapped for scope mount (included), walnut finished birch stock with pressed checkering and vent. recoil pad, 8 lbs. Mfg. 1994-99.

	$295	$220	$195	$175	$160	$145	$130

Last MSR was $361.

* ***Model 512DL Slugmaster*** - similar to Model 512 Slugmaster, except has black Rynite stock, Fire Sights (with red fiber optic inserts) became standard 1998. Disc. 1998.

	$310	$230	$200	$180	$160	$145	$130

Last MSR was $372.

* ***Model 512P Slugmaster*** - 12 ga., 3 in. chamber, features 21 in. ported fully rifled barrel with front and rear Fire Sights (high visibility red and green fiber optic inserts), 2 shot detachable box mag., black fiberglass synthetic stock with molded-in checkering, receiver is drilled and tapped, 8 lbs. Mfg. 1999-2001.

	$315	$235	$200	$180	$165	$155	$145

Last MSR was $388.

MODEL 5510 - 10 ga., 3½ in. mag., 2 shot mag., 34 in. barrel, leather carrying strap and detachable swivels, rubber recoil pad, 10½ lbs. Mfg. 1976-1985.

	$220	$170	$160	$150	$140	$130	$120

Last MSR was $282.

SHOTGUNS: LEVER ACTION

MODEL .410 LEVER ACTION - .410 bore, 22 or 26 in. barrel, full choke, lever action, similar to 1893, exposed hammer, plain pistol grip stock. Mfg. 1929-1932 as a stockholders promotional firearm.

	$1,400	$1,200	$950	$675	$550	$500	$425

Add 20% for 22 in. barrel.

* ***Model .410 Deluxe*** - includes deluxe checkered walnut stock and forearm.

	$1,800	$1,600	$1,250	$1,000	$850	$700	$600

Deluxe forearm does not have flute in it.

M

SHOTGUNS: O/U

MODEL 90 - 12, 16, 20 ga., or .410 bore shotgun or combination gun configuration (12 ga. over .30/ 30 barrels), 26, 28, or 30 in. barrels, boxlock, extractors, checkered pistol grip stock. Mfg. 1937-1958. Guns made from 1937-1949 had vent. separated barrels, after 1949, solid barrels.

	$450	$385	$360	$330	$290	$265	$230

Add 50% for combination gun configuration.

* ***With single trigger***

	$550	$495	$470	$440	$400	$375	$340

Add 25% for .410 bore.

SHOTGUNS: SINGLE SHOT

MODEL 60 - 12 ga., 30 or 32 in. barrel, full choke, top lever, break open, exposed hammer, pistol grip stock. Approx. 3,000 mfg.

	$195	$165	$140	$120	$110	$100	$90

SHOTGUNS: SLIDE ACTION, 1898-1963 PRODUCTION

During 1998, Marlin issued a service bulletin recommending that slide action exposed hammer Models 1898, 16, 17, 19, 19S, 19G, 19N, 21, 24, 24G, 26, 30, 42, 49, and 49N, in addition to hammerless Models 28, 31, 43, 44, 53, and 63 should not be fired, as many of these guns are 70-100 years old, and system failures can and do happen.

Grading	100%	98%	95%	90%	80%	70%	60%

MODEL 1898 - 12 ga., 5 shot tube mag., 26-32 in. barrels, various chokes, exposed hammer, pistol grip stock, grades differ in quality of wood and engraving on C and D. Mfg. 1898-1905.

	100%	98%	95%	90%	80%	70%	60%
Grade A	$325	$275	$225	$200	$165	$150	$140
Grade B	$580	$495	$440	$415	$360	$305	$275
Grade C	$880	$715	$635	$580	$525	$495	$440
Grade D	$1,760	$1,540	$1,320	$1,210	$1,045	$965	$880

Factory information by individual ser. no. from the Cody Firearms Museum may be available for this model in the ser. range 19,601-67,000.

MODEL 16 - 16 ga. only, 26 or 28 in. barrel, various chokes, takedown, pistol grip stock. Mfg. 1904- 1910.

	100%	98%	95%	90%	80%	70%	60%
Grade A	$325	$275	$225	$200	$165	$150	$140
Grade B	$495	$415	$360	$330	$305	$275	$250
Grade C	$635	$525	$495	$440	$415	$385	$330
Grade D	$1,320	$1,100	$990	$825	$715	$635	$550

MODEL 17 - 12 ga., 30 or 32 in. full choke barrel, solid frame, straight stock. Mfg. 1906- 1908.

100%	98%	95%	90%	80%	70%	60%
$335	$275	$235	$200	$165	$150	$140

MODEL 17 BRUSH GUN - similar to Model 17, with 26 in. cylinder bore barrel. Mfg. 1906-1908.

100%	98%	95%	90%	80%	70%	60%
$325	$275	$235	$200	$165	$150	$140

MODEL 17 RIOT GUN - similar to Model 17, with 20 in. barrel. Mfg. 1906-1908.

100%	98%	95%	90%	80%	70%	60%
$325	$275	$235	$200	$165	$150	$140

MODEL 19 - improved lightened version of Model 1898, matte top surface on barrel. Mfg. 1906- 1907.

	100%	98%	95%	90%	80%	70%	60%
Grade A	$325	$275	$235	$200	$165	$150	$140
Grade B	$495	$415	$360	$330	$305	$275	$250
Grade C	$635	$525	$495	$440	$415	$385	$330
Grade D	$1,320	$1,100	$990	$825	$715	$635	$550

MODEL 21 - straight grip version of Model 19.

	100%	98%	95%	90%	80%	70%	60%
Grade A	$325	$275	$235	$200	$165	$150	$140
Grade B	$495	$415	$360	$330	$305	$275	$250
Grade C	$635	$525	$495	$440	$415	$385	$330
Grade D	$1,320	$1,100	$990	$825	$715	$635	$550

MODEL 24 - improved 21, takedown, automatic recoil lock on slide, solid matte rib. Mfg. 1908- 1915.

	100%	98%	95%	90%	80%	70%	60%
Grade G	$295	$265	$225	$195	$165	$150	$140
Grade A	$325	$275	$235	$200	$165	$150	$140
Grade B	$525	$440	$385	$360	$330	$305	$275
Grade C	$660	$550	$525	$470	$440	$415	$360
Grade D	$1,375	$1,155	$1,045	$880	$770	$660	$580

MODEL 26 - similar to Model 24 Grade A, with solid frame, 30 or 32 in. full choke barrel. Mfg. 1909- 1915.

100%	98%	95%	90%	80%	70%	60%
$275	$230	$210	$195	$165	$150	$140

MODEL 26 BRUSH GUN - 26 in. cylinder bore barrel. Mfg. 1909-1915.

100%	98%	95%	90%	80%	70%	60%
$275	$230	$210	$195	$165	$150	$140

MODEL 26 RIOT GUN - 20 in. cylinder bore barrel. Mfg. 1909-1915.

100%	98%	95%	90%	80%	70%	60%
$250	$195	$180	$165	$150	$140	$120

M

Grading	100%	98%	95%	90%	80%	70%	60%

MODEL 28 HAMMERLESS - 12 ga., 26-32 in. barrels, various chokes, takedown, matte top barrel, pistol grip stock. Mfg. 1913-1922.

	100%	98%	95%	90%	80%	70%	60%
Grade A	$295	$265	$235	$200	$165	$150	$140
Grade B	$495	$415	$360	$330	$305	$275	$250
Grade C	$635	$525	$495	$440	$415	$385	$330
Grade D	$1,320	$1,100	$990	$825	$715	$635	$550

MODEL 28TS TRAP GUN - similar to Model 28, with 30 in. matte rib barrel, full choke, high comb straight grip stock. Mfg. 1915.

	$415	$330	$275	$250	$220	$195	$165

MODEL 28T - similar to Model 28TS, with fancy wood, checkering, better finish. Mfg. 1915.

	$605	$525	$495	$470	$415	$360	$305

MODEL 30 - similar to Model 16, with automatic recoil lock on slide, also mfg. in 20 ga. 1915-1917 (Model 30-20). Mfg. 1910-1914.

	100%	98%	95%	90%	80%	70%	60%
Grade A	$325	$275	$235	$200	$165	$150	$140
Grade B	$495	$415	$360	$330	$305	$275	$250
Grade C	$635	$525	$495	$440	$415	$385	$330
Grade D	$1,320	$1,100	$990	$825	$715	$635	$550

MODEL 30 FIELD GRADE - similar to Model 30 Grade B, with 25 in. mod. barrel, straight stock. Mfg. 1913-1917.

	$335	$275	$220	$180	$160	$130	$115

MODEL 31 - scaled down small ga. (16 and 20 ga.) version of the Model 28, has 26 and 28 in. barrels, various chokes, Model 31-16 was mfg. 1914-1917, Model 31-20 was mfg. 1911-1923.

	100%	98%	95%	90%	80%	70%	60%
Grade A	$385	$305	$250	$220	$195	$165	$140
Grade B	$495	$415	$360	$330	$305	$275	$250
Grade C	$636	$525	$495	$440	$415	$385	$330
Grade D	$1,320	$1,100	$990	$825	$715	$635	$550

MODEL 31F FIELD GUN - 25 in. mod. barrel. Mfg. 1915-1917.

	$395	$350	$325	$295	$265	$225	$200

MODEL 42A - similar to Model 24, but lesser quality finishing. Mfg. 1922-1934.

	$250	$220	$195	$165	$140	$120	$100

MODEL 43 HAMMERLESS - similar to Model 28, with lesser quality finish. Mfg. 1923- 1930.

	$275	$225	$200	$175	$150	$125	$100

MODEL 43TS - similar to Model 28T, lower quality.

	$525	$440	$415	$385	$360	$305	$275

MODEL 44A - similar to Model 31 Grade A, 20 ga. only. Mfg. 1923-1935.

	$360	$275	$250	$220	$195	$165	$140

MODEL 44S - select checkered stock.

	$470	$385	$360	$330	$195	$165	$140

MODEL 49 - lower priced version of Model 42A. They were given to purchasers of 4 shares of Marlin stock. 3,000 mfg. in 1925-1928.

	$440	$360	$305	$275	$220	$195	$165

MODEL 53 - similar to Model 43 Hammerless. Mfg. 1929-1930.

	$330	$275	$250	$220	$195	$165	$140

MODEL 63 - similar to Model 43 Hammerless, later model. Mfg. 1931-1935.

	$330	$250	$220	$195	$165	$140	$110

MODEL 63TS - similar to Model 43TS, with trap style stock.

	$385	$305	$250	$220	$195	$165	$140

M

Grading	100%	98%	95%	90%	80%	70%	60%

MODEL 120 MAGNUM - slide action, 12 ga., 3 in. chamber, 26-38 in. barrel, takedown, various chokes, checkered pistol grip stock. Mfg. 1971-1985.

	100%	98%	95%	90%	80%	70%	60%
	$290	$225	$215	$205	$195	$180	$165

Last MSR was $370.

  Subtract $35 if without VR.

MODEL 778 - 12 ga. Mag. slide action, 20-38 in. barrels, 7¾ lbs. Disc. 1984.

	$225	$190	$175	$155	$140	$125	$110

PREMIER MARK I - 12 ga. only, aluminum receiver, takedown, manufactured in France for Marlin.

	$200	$180	$160	$150	$140	$120	$95

PREMIER MARK II - similar to Mark I, except with engraved receiver and checkering. Mfg. 1960-1963 in France.

	$275	$235	$200	$175	$150	$125	$100

PREMIER MARK IV - similar to Mark II, only deluxe grade with better wood, more engraving. Mfg. 1960-1963 in France.

	$305	$250	$220	$195	$165	$140	$110
With VR	$330	$275	$250	$220	$195	$165	$140

MAROCCHI

Current trademark established in 1922, and currently manufactured by CD Europe SRL, located in Sarezzo, Italy. Currently distributed by Precision Sales International, Inc. located in Westfield, MA.

ARMI ⚒ MAROCCHI

Marocchi O/U shotguns are high quality, and currently have limited U.S. importation. Discontinued Frigon guns (manufactured by Marocchi) appear under the F section in this text.

COMBINATION GUNS

VALLEY COMBO - 12 ga. over .222 Rem. cal., 23½ in. separated barrels with VR, 3 in. chamber, fold down rear sight and will accept claw scope mounts, fixed cylinder choke, DTs, engraved silver receiver, satin finish walnut Monte Carlo stock with checkering and recoil pad, 8¼ lbs. Disc. 1994.

	$585	$480	$415	$375	$325	$295	$275

Last MSR was $700.

SHOTGUNS: O/U, 1995 & EARLIER

FIELD MASTER I - 12 ga. only, 26 or 28 in. VR barrels and rib with choke tubes, engraved coin finished receiver, extractors, SNT, checkered walnut stock and forearm. Disc. 1994.

	$455	$395	$325	$275	$240	$215	$200

Last MSR was $530.

  This model was imported exclusively by Sile Distributors.

 ✱ *Field Master II* - similar to Field Master I except has SST and choke tubes. Disc. 1994.

	$475	$350	$295	$260	$225	$210	$190

Last MSR was $550.

SKEET MODEL - 12 ga. only, 26 in. barrels bored SK/SK. Disc. 1994.

	$445	$395	$325	$275	$240	$215	$200

Last MSR was $520.

  This model was imported exclusively by Sile Distributors.

TRAP MODEL - 12 ga. only, 30 in. barrels bored M/F, ejectors. Disc. 1994.

	$560	$485	$415	$360	$300	$260	$230

Last MSR was $630.

  This model was imported exclusively by Sile Distributors.

Grading	100%	98%	95%	90%	80%	70%	60%

AVANZA - 12 or 20 (disc. 1993) ga., 3 in. chambers, monobloc boxlock action, 26 or 28 in. vent. barrels with VR (with or without choke tubes), SST, ejectors, deluxe checkered walnut stock and forearm with vent. recoil pad, high polish bluing with gold accents, all steel lightweight mfg., 6 lbs. 5 oz. - 6 lbs. 13 oz. Imported 1990-95.

		$775	**$675**	**$575**	**$525**	**$475**	**$425**	**$375**

Last MSR was $829.

> **Add $45 for 20 ga. (disc. 1993).**
> **Subtract 10% if without choke tubes (3).**
> This model was imported exclusively by Precision Sales International, Inc.

* ✱ *Avanza Sporting Clays* - 12 ga. only, 3 in. chambers, built on 20 ga. frame, 28 in. vent. barrels with VR and choke tubes, select checkered walnut stock with deluxe recoil pad and forearm, gold- plated trigger, 7 lbs. Mfg. 1991-95.

		$825	**$725**	**$600**	**$550**	**$495**	**$450**	**$400**

Last MSR was $889.

> **Add $99 for Premier Grade (disc., included select walnut and gold etched triggerguard).**
> This model features a trigger that is adjustable for length and pull without special tools.

SHOTGUNS: O/U, RECENT PRODUCTION

In the U.S., Conquista shotguns are identical in specifications and features to the Marocchi Classic Doubles sold in Europe, with the exception of Classic Doubles U.S.A.

GOLDEN SNIPE III FIELD - 12 ga. only, 3 in. chambers, field configuration with 28 in. VR barrels and choke tubes. New 1998.

MSR	$800	$725	$675	$625	$575	$525	$475	$425

GOLDEN SNIPE III SPORTING - 12 ga. only, entry level sporting clays model with 28 or 30 in. VR barrels with choke tubes, checkered walnut stock and forearm. Importation began 1999.

MSR	$950	$850	$750	$675	$625	$575	$525	$450

CONQUISTA FIELD MAGNUM GRADE I - 12 ga. only, 3 in. chambers, features 28 in. 8mm VR barrels with choke tubes, nickel finished receiver, SST, checkered walnut stock and forearm with smooth rosewood buttplate, approx. 7¼ lbs. Imported 1999-2001.

		$1,275	**$1,025**	**$900**	**$800**	**$700**	**$625**	**$550**

Last MSR was $1,490.

CONQUISTA USA SPORTING - 12 ga. only, 3 in. chambers, features 30 in. vent. barrels with 10mm VR, muzzle porting, back boring, and lengthened forcing cones, blued barrels and receiver with gold accents, checkered standard or adj. walnut stock and forearm, approx. 8 lbs. New 1999.

MSR	$1,490	$1,275	$1,025	$900	$800	$700	$625	$550

> **Add $100 for adj. stock.**

CONQUISTA SPORTING CLAYS - 12 ga. only, boxlock action with brushed coin finish, SST, ejectors, adj. trigger, choice of 28, 30, or 32 in. 10mm VR barrels with choke tubes, right or left-hand (Grade I only) action, checkered walnut stock and forearm with recoil pad, 7 7/8 lbs. Imported 1994- 2000.

* ✱ *Grade I* - features coin finished receiver with perimeter line engraving.

		$1,725	**$1,450**	**$1,200**	**$1,000**	**$850**	**$700**	**$550**

Last MSR was $1,995.

> **Add $125 for left-hand variation.**
> **Add $151 for adj. stock (new 1999).**

* ✱ *Lady Sport* - 12 ga. only, features lighter weight specialized stock designed to fit women, cased, 7½ lbs. Mfg. 1995-99.

		$1,800	**$1,525**	**$1,250**	**$1,000**	**$850**	**$700**	**$550**

Last MSR was $2,120.

> **Add $180 for left-hand variation (Sport Spectrum only).**
> **Add $79 for Lady Sport Spectrum (partially colored receiver).**

Grading	100%	98%	95%	90%	80%	70%	60%

* **Grade II** - features better walnut and game scene engraving on receiver.

	$1,995	$1,675	$1,425	$1,200	$1,000	$850	$700

Last MSR was $2,330.

Add $355 for left-hand variation.

* **Grade III** - features more elaborate game scene engraving on receiver sides and fine scroll-work throughout rest of action, includes hard gun case and stock wrench.

	$3,225	$2,650	$2,250	$1,875	$1,650	$1,400	$1,175

Last MSR was $3,599.

Add $396 for left-hand variation.

* **Grade IV** - top-of-the-line Sporting Clays model. Importation began 1997. Price available by request only.

CONQUISTA TRAP MODEL - 12 ga. only, Trap configuration, 30 or 32 (disc. 1997, reintroduced 2000) in. 10mm VR barrels with fixed chokes, 8¼ lbs. Imported 1994- 2000.

* **Grade I** - features coin finished receiver with perimeter line engraving.

	$1,725	$1,475	$1,225	$1,000	$850	$700	$550

Last MSR was $1,995.

Add $151 for adj. stock (new 1999).

* **Grade II** - features better walnut and game scene engraving on receiver.

	$1,995	$1,675	$1,450	$1,200	$1,000	$850	$700

Last MSR was $2,330.

* **Grade III** - features more elaborate game scene engraving on receiver sides and fine scroll-work throughout rest of action, includes hard gun case and stock wrench.

	$3,225	$2,650	$2,250	$1,875	$1,650	$1,400	$1,175

Last MSR was $3,599.

* **Grade IV** - top-of-the-line Trap model. Importation began 1997. Price available by request only.

CONQUISTA SKEET MODEL - 12 ga. only, Skeet configuration, 28 in. 10mm VR barrels with fixed Skeet chokes, 7¾ lbs. Imported 1994-2000.

* **Grade I** - features coin finished receiver with perimeter line engraving.

	$1,725	$1,475	$1,225	$1,000	$850	$700	$550

Last MSR was $1,995.

* **Grade II** - features better walnut and game scene engraving on receiver.

	$1,995	$1,675	$1,450	$1,200	$1,000	$850	$700

Last MSR was $2,330.

* **Grade III** - features more elaborate game scene engraving on receiver sides and fine scroll-work throughout rest of action, includes hard gun case and stock wrench.

	$3,225	$2,650	$2,250	$1,875	$1,650	$1,400	$1,175

Last MSR was $3,599.

* **Grade IV** - top-of-the-line Skeet model. Importation began 1997. Price available by request only.

CLASSIC DOUBLES MODEL 92 - 12 ga. only, 3 in. chambers, sporting clays configuration featuring 30 in. vented barrels with VR, back-boring, elongated forcing cones, and three screw-in chokes, low profile blued receiver, checkered walnut stock, and Schnabel forearm, adj. trigger, gold receiver accents and trigger. Imported 1996-98.

	$1,450	$1,175	$950	$850	$775	$700	$650

Last MSR was $1,598.

MODEL 99 SPORTING - 12 ga. only, 2¾ in. chambers, boxlock action with brushed coin finish, SST, ejectors, adj. trigger, choice of 28, 30, or 32 in. 10mm VR barrels with choke tubes, right hand action only, deluxe checkered walnut stock and forearm with recoil pad, approx. 7 7/8 lbs. New 2000.

Grading	100%	98%	95%	90%	80%	70%	60%

✴ Grade I
  MSR $2,350 $1,995 $1,750 $1,500 $1,250 $1,000 $875 $750

✴ Grade II - features better walnut and engraving on receiver.
  MSR $2,870 $2,475 $2,125 $1,725 $1,400 $1,100 $925 $800
  Add $155 for gold inlays.

✴ Grade III - features more elaborate engraving and wood upgrade.
  MSR $3,275 $2,925 $2,400 $2,000 $1,600 $1,350 $1,075 $900
  Add $185 for gold inlays.

MODEL 99 SKEET - 12 ga. only, 2¾ in. chambers, boxlock action with brushed coin finish, SST, ejectors, adj. trigger, 28 in. 10mm VR barrels with choke tubes, right hand action only, deluxe checkered walnut stock and forearm with recoil pad, approx. 7 7/8 lbs. New 2000.

✴ Grade I
  MSR $2,350 $1,995 $1,750 $1,500 $1,250 $1,000 $875 $750

✴ Grade II - features better walnut and engraving on receiver.
  MSR $2,870 $2,475 $2,125 $1,725 $1,400 $1,100 $925 $800
  Add $155 for gold inlays.

✴ Grade III - features more elaborate engraving and wood upgrade.
  MSR $3,275 $2,925 $2,400 $2,000 $1,600 $1,350 $1,075 $900
  Add $175 for gold inlays.

MODEL 99 TRAP - 12 ga. only, 2¾ in. chambers, boxlock action with brushed coin finish, SST, ejectors, adj. trigger, 30 or 32 in. VR barrels with choke tubes, right hand action only, deluxe checkered walnut stock and forearm with recoil pad, approx. 7 7/8 lbs. New 2000.

✴ Grade I
  MSR $2,350 $1,995 $1,750 $1,500 $1,250 $1,000 $875 $750

✴ Grade II - features better walnut and engraving on receiver.
  MSR $2,870 $2,475 $2,125 $1,725 $1,400 $1,100 $925 $800
  Add $155 for gold inlays.

✴ Grade III - features more elaborate engraving and wood upgrade.
  MSR $3,275 $2,925 $2,400 $2,000 $1,600 $1,350 $1,075 $900
  Add $175 for gold inlays.

MODEL 99 CUSTOM GRADES - 12 ga. only, 2¾ in. chambers, available in either Sporting, Trap, or Skeet configuration, deluxe Model 99 with best quality walnut and elaborate engraving options per model - base model is the Blackgold (non-engraved with gold line frame accents), 28, 30, or 32 in. barrels. Importation began 2000.
  MSR $4,150 $3,650 $3,200 $2,600 $2,100 $1,650 $1,350 $1,100
  Add $975 for engraved Loadstar or Britannia Model.
  Add $2,200 for top-of-the-line Diana Model with game scene engraving.

SHOTGUNS: SINGLE SHOT

MODEL 2000 - 12 ga. only, 3 in. chamber, hammer, 28 in. barrel, ejector, lightly engraved receiver. Importation disc. 1991.
                     $80 $70 $60 $50 $45 $40 $35
                                              Last MSR was $94.

MARTIN, ALEX

Current trademark owned and manufactured by Dickson & MacNaughton, located in Edinburgh, Scotland.

Please contact Dickson & MacNaughton directly for more information regarding this trademark, including current availability and pricing.

Grading	100%	98%	95%	90%	80%	70%	60%

MASTERPIECE ARMS, INC.

Current manufacturer of derringers established in 2000, and located in Carrollton, GA.

Masterpiece Arms manufactures derringers in both steel and stainless steel configuration. Please contact the company directly for more information, availability, and pricing (see Trademark Index).

MASQUELIER S.A.

Previous manufacturer located in Belgium. Previously distributed (until 1986) by Ambel Ltd., Inc. located in Sugarland, TX.

RIFLES: SxS

CARPATHE - .243 Win., .270 Win., .30-06, 7x57R, or 7x65R cal., single shot, hair trigger, push-down cocking system. Importation disc. 1986.

	100%	98%	95%	90%	80%	70%	60%
	$3,500	$3,200	$2,900	$2,600	$2,300	$2,100	$1,850

Last MSR was $3,850.

EXPRESS - .270 Win., .30-06, 8x57JRS, or 9.3x74R cal., O/U configuration, SST, ejectors. Add $800 for extra set of 20 ga. barrels. Importation disc. 1986.

	100%	98%	95%	90%	80%	70%	60%
	$3,300	$3,000	$2,800	$2,600	$2,300	$2,100	$1,850

Last MSR was $3,600.

ARDENNES MODEL - top-of-the-line model, custom order only. Importation disc. 1986.

	100%	98%	95%	90%	80%	70%	60%
	$6,600	$6,000	$5,400	$4,800	$4,300	$3,900	$3,450

Last MSR was $7,250.

SHOTGUNS:SxS

BOXLOCK - 12 ga. only, 2¾ in. chambers, Anson & Deeley boxlock action, ejectors, fine scroll engraving with French walnut. Importation disc. 1986.

	100%	98%	95%	90%	80%	70%	60%
	$4,400	$4,000	$3,650	$3,300	$2,995	$2,600	$2,200

Last MSR was $4,780.

SIDELOCK - 12 ga. only, 2¾ in. chambers, H&H style sidelocks, auto ejectors, English style fine scroll engraving with French walnut. Importation disc. 1986.

	100%	98%	95%	90%	80%	70%	60%
	$12,500	$10,000	$8,750	$7,600	$6,700	$5,800	$5,000

Last MSR was $15,850.

MATCHGUNS srl

Current manufacturer established during 2001, and located in Parma, Italy. No current U.S. importation.

During 2001, Cesare Morini left Morini Competition Arm S.A. of Switzerland and started a new company, Matchguns srl, with headquarters in Parma, Italy.

PISTOLS: SEMI-AUTO

Matchguns srl will also be releasing a new .32 S&W Wadcutter cal. semi-auto target pistol during 2002.

MG2 - .22 LR cal., innovative new action with patented compact mechanism allowing recoil reduction of up to 50% w/o the use of counterweights or muzzle brakes, 6 in. barrel, fully adj. rear sight, fully adj. anatomical walnut grips, 5 shot mag., blue only, adj. trigger from 60 grams - 950 grams, approx. 2 lbs. New mid-2002.

As this edition went to press, U.S. pricing had yet to be established on this model.

Grading	100%	98%	95%	90%	80%	70%	60%

MATCH GRADE ARMS & AMMUNITION

Current custom rifle manufacturer located in Spring, TX. Consumer direct sales.

REVOLVERS

MGA CUSTOM - .45 LC+P, .475 Linebaugh, or .500 Linebaugh cal., Ruger frame, stainless 5 shot cylinder, custom barrels. New 2000.

Prices for this model range from $1,195-$1,495, depending on custom features.

RIFLES: BOLT ACTION

ULTRA-LIGHT MODEL - various cals., lightened and skeletonized Wby. Vanguard action, MGA button rifled barrel, Teflon metal finish, camo epoxy stock with Pachmayr decelerator pad, Super Eliminator muzzle brake, 5½ lbs.

	MSR	$1,895		$1,850	$1,600	$1,350	$1,050	$875	$700	$550

MGA VARMINTER - various cals., squared and lapped Rem. M700 action, stainless steel National Match barrel with Super Eliminator muzzle brake, black Teflon metal finish, camo epoxy stock.

	MSR	$1,995		$1,995	$1,750	$1,500	$1,250	$995	$850	$700

SIGNATURE CLASSIC - various cals., Nesika Hunter action, Hart barrel, Jewell trigger, fiberglass or claro walnut stock. Limited mfg. (approx. 10 guns per year) beginning 2000.

	MSR	$4,500		$4,300	$4,000	$3,600	$3,200	$2,800	$2,400	$2,000

MATEBA

Current trademark manufactured by Mateba srl, located in Pavia, Italy. Currently imported by American Western Arms, located in Delray Beach, FL. Previously imported 2000-2001 by Keisler's Wholesale, located in Jeffersonville, IN, and by American Arms, Inc. until late 1999. Previously manufactured by Macchine Termo Balistiche located in Italy. Older mfg. has had little domestic importation.

M

REVOLVERS

MATEBA REVOLVER - various cals. (older mfg.), most recent mfg was .357 Mag./.38 Spl. cal., combination semi-auto pistol and revolver, action allows cylinder and slide assembly to move back when fired, causing the cylinder to rotate, unique design permits barrel to fire lowest shell in cylinder (6 o'clock position), mechanism to rear of cylinder, single or double action, 6, 7 (older mfg.), or 8 (older mfg.) shot, 4, 6 (mfg. 1998-2000), or 8 (mfg. 1998-2000) in. barrel, steel/alloy frame, blue finish, flared ergonomic walnut grips, interchangeable barrels, 2¾ lbs.

	MSR	$1,295		$1,150	$895	$800	$675	$525	$450	$400

Add 15% for older mfg.

MATHELON ARMES

Current SxS double rifle and drilling manufacturer located in Rumilly, France. No current U.S. importation.

Currently, Mathelon Armes manufactures a boxlock drilling, and SxS double rifle in 8x57JRS and 9.3x64R cal. Please contact the factory directly (see Trademark Index) for more information and current pricing.

MATRA MANURHIN DEFENSE

Please refer to the Manurhin heading in this section.

MAUSER JAGDWAFFEN GmbH

Current trademark established during 1871, and currently owned by San Swiss Arms AG beginning late 2000. Mauser Model 98 Magnum bolt action rifles are currently manufactured by Mauser Jagdwaffen GmbH, located in Isny, Germany. Currently imported by SIG Arms, located in Exeter, NH. Current handgun production is manufactured by SIG, located in Switzerland. The former transition name was Mauser Jagd-und Sportwaffen GmbH. On January 1, 1999, Mauser transferred all production and distribution rights of both hunting and sporting weapons to SIG-Blaser. SIG was purchased by San Swiss Arms AG. Mauser-Werke Oberndorf Waffensysteme GmbH continues to manufacture military defense contracts (including making small bore barrel liners for tanks), in addition to other industrial machinery.

Previously imported exclusively by Brolin Arms, located in Pomona, CA during 1997-98 only. During 1998, the company name was changed from Mauser-Werke Oberndorf Waffensysteme GmbH. During 1994, the name was changed from Mauser-Werke to Mauser-Werke Oberndorf Waffensysteme GmbH. Previously imported by GSI located in Trussville, AL, until 1997, Gibb's Rifle Co., Inc. until 1995, Precision Imports, Inc. located in San Antonio, TX until 1993, and KDF located in Seguin, TX (1987-89).

HANDGUNS: EARLY PRODUCTION

MODEL 1877 SINGLE SHOT - 9mm cal., single shot, barrel release in usual hammer position and safety on left side, examples are rare.

$10,000	$8,500	$7,000	$6,000	$5,000	$4,000	$3,000

MODEL 1878 "ZIG-ZAG" REVOLVER - 7.6mm, 9mm(most common) or 10.6mm cal., Zig-Zag refers to Z-pattern grooves cut into cylinder, earliest revolvers were solid frame, gate loaded, and chambered in 9mm, most were designed with a hinged frame, third and last version had an "improved" sliding release on the forward frame, most revolvers had a rust blue frame and barrel complementing a fire blue cylinder, grips were checkered or hard rubber with a floral pattern.

7.6mm	$4,500	$3,750	$2,500	$2,000	$1,850	$1,700	$1,400
9mm	$5,250	$4,250	$3,500	$3,000	$2,250	$1,900	$1,500
10.6mm	$6,500	$5,000	$4,000	$3,200	$2,400	$2,000	$1,600

Add 10% for earliest pistols with "midnight blue" finish. Premiums exist for solid frame, late improved model, and factory cased guns.

PISTOLS: SEMI-AUTO, DISC.

The Models 1906-08, 1912-14, and HSv are very rare and only infrequently encountered. A competent appraisal is advisable before buying or selling these models.

MODEL 1906-08 - 9mm Export (9x25mm) cal., detachable mag., incorporates features of both the pocket pistols and Model 1896 Broomhandle. Ser. range 1-100 (est.).

N/A	$35,000	$29,500	$25,000	$19,500	$15,000	$9,950

MODEL 1912-14 - generally chambered for 9mm Para. cal., similar to pocket pistol configuration, but considerably larger, earliest specimens have inscribed slide legend. Those under serial number 100 (approx.) are not slotted for shoulder stock while those over 100 are generally slotted. Ser. range 1-175 (est.).

N/A	$20,000	$16,000	$12,000	$10,000	$8,000	$6,000

Add 50% if slotted with matching shoulder stock.
This variation is very rare in .45 ACP cal. or with a tangent rear sight.

Grading	100%	98%	95%	90%	80%	70%	60%

WTP MODEL I VEST POCKET AUTOMATIC - 6.35mm cal., 6 shot, 2½ in. barrel, blue, rubber grips. Mfg. 1922-1937.

	$495	$325	$250	$200	$160	$140	$100

WTP MODEL II - similar to Model I, but 2 in. barrel. Mfg. 1938-1940.

	$650	$525	$450	$350	$250	$200	$150

POCKET MODEL 1910 - 6.35mm or 7.65mm cal., 9 shot, 3 in. barrel, blue fixed sights, checkered walnut or hard rubber grips. Mfg. 1910-1934.

	$425	$300	$180	$165	$150	$140	$130

Add 30% for sidelatch variation.

POCKET MODEL 1914 - similar to Model 1910, but 7.65mm cal., 3.4 in. barrel. Mfg. 1914-1934.

	$425	$300	$175	$165	$150	$145	$135

Add 10% for military acceptance proof by rear sight (Prussian eagle WWI proofs and/or crown D).
Add 500% for the "humpback" model.

POCKET MODEL 1934 - similar to Model 1914, but reshaped grip. Mfg. 1934-1939.

	$450	$325	$210	$175	$160	$150	$140

Add 50% for Waffenamt or Nazi Police.
Add 100% for Nazi Navy marked.

MODEL HSv - 9mm Para. cal., limited mfg., similar features to Model HSc, except has larger dimensions.

	N/A	$15,000	$10,000	$8,500	$7,000	$6,500	$5,500

Mauser Pistols: HSc Models

MODEL HSc DOUBLE ACTION - 7.65mm (8 shot) or .380 ACP (7 shot) cal., 3.4 in. barrel, blue or nickel, fixed sights, checkered walnut grips. Mfg. 1938-disc. (most recent mfg. was by R. Gamba in Italy circa 1996).

Mauser Pistols: HSc WWII Military Mfg.

* **Low Grip Screw** - very rare, first variation with ser. numbers starting at 700,000, less than 2,000 mfg.

	$4,000	$3,000	$1,850	$1,200	$1,000	$800	$650

Add 20% if Navy marked.

* **Early Nazi Army** - proofed 655 and 135.

	$750	$550	$425	$265	$225	$200	$185

Add 50% for small 655 additonally test-proofed on left tang.

* **Early Nazi Navy** - marked on front grip strap.

	$1,000	$800	$540	$500	$440	$395	$350

* **Early Nazi Police** - Eagle L proof only.

	$650	$450	$360	$320	$285	$245	$200

* **Wartime Nazi Army** - proof 135 and WaA 135. Eagle N proofed also.

	$450	$350	$290	$250	$200	$180	$150

* **Wartime Nazi Navy** - proofed on left side of triggerguard.

	$700	$550	$400	$340	$295	$260	$230

* **Wartime Nazi Police** - proofed Eagle L.

	$500	$395	$360	$320	$285	$245	$200

Add 10% if Eagle F.

* **Wartime Commercial** - standard WWII Commercial Model.

	$400	$325	$290	$265	$200	$180	$150

* **Swiss Commercial** - ser. range 800,000-900,000. Very rare.

	$1,400	$1,250	$1,125	$995	$900	$850	$600

Grading	100%	98%	95%	90%	80%	70%	60%

* **Cutaways** - mfg. to visibly show mechanism. Should not be proofed.

	100%	98%	95%	90%	80%	70%	60%
	$1,495	$1,000	$900	$850	$800	$750	$700

Mauser Pistols: HSc Post-WWII Mfg.

* **French Manufacture** - frequently encountered in poor condition - post-WWII production.

		$375	$300	$245	$220	$180	$155	$130

* **Mauser Production** - .32 or .380 cal., 15 shot, mfg. 1968-1981.

	$350	$295	$260	$225	$180	$150	$130

Deduct 20% if not boxed or in .32 cal.

* **Interarms Import** - imported by Interarms from 1983-1985 (Italian mfg. by Gamba).

	$325	$275	$250	$220	$180	$150	$125

Last MSR was $415.

* **One of Five Thousand Edition** - American Eagle edition (marked on gun), 5,000 total mfg. (serial numbered 1-5000).

	$400	$325	$275

* **Armes De Chasse Import** - previously imported by Armes De Chasse located in Chadds Ford, PA on a limited basis.

	$475	$425	$330	$300	$260	$240	$220

Last MSR was $695.

Add $195 for Limited Series.
Add $58 For G15 variation (9 shot).

* **E.A.A. Import** - imported by European American Armory, distributed by RSR Wholesale.

	$265	$225	$195	$175	$150	$125	$110

* **Recent Gamba Mfg.** - .32 ACP or .380 ACP cal., steel construction, double action, double safety, stippled walnut grips, recently imported by Gamba, USA until approx. 1996.

	$395	$330	$300	$260	$240	$220	$200

Last MSR was $699.

M Mauser Pistols: Luger Mfg.

The original Mauser Luger P.08 is still being currently mfg. at the factory, with very limited domestic importation. Both pre-war and post-war Mauser manufactured Lugers will be found in the Luger section of this book.

PISTOLS: SEMI-AUTO, RECENT IMPORTATION

MODEL 80 SA - .380 ACP or 9mm Para. cal., semi-auto single action patterned after the Browning Hi-power, 4 2/3 in. barrel, blue finish with checkered walnut grips, round hammer, steel construction, 10 (C/B 1994) or 13* shot mag., 1.95 lbs. Mfg. by FEG in Hungary, imported 1992-96.

	$450	$325	$275	$240	$215	$185	$165

Last MSR was $520.

MODEL 90 DA - similar to Model 80 SA, except is double action, spur hammer, and has 10 (C/B 1994) or 14* shot mag., 2.15 lbs. Mfg. by FEG, imported 1992-96.

	$445	$325	$275	$240	$215	$185	$165

Last MSR was $516.

* **Model 90 DAC** - similar to Model 90 DA, except is compact model with 4 1/8 in. barrel, 2.05 lbs. Imported 1992-96.

	$450	$325	$275	$240	$215	$185	$165

Last MSR was $520.

Grading	100%	98%	95%	90%	80%	70%	60%

M-2 - .357 SIG (disc. 2001), .40 S&W, or .45 ACP cal., short recoil operation, striker fired operating system, rotating 3.54 in. barrel lockup, 8 (.45 ACP) or 10 shot, DAO, hammerless, aluminum alloy frame with nickel chromium steel slide, black finish, includes case and trigger lock, approx. 29 oz. Mfg. by SIG in Europe, importation began 2000.

	MSR	$491						
			$435	$385	$340	$300	$275	$250	$225

PISTOLS: SEMI-AUTO, MODEL 1896 BROOMHANDLES

Note: Manufactured in Oberndorf, Germany between 1897 & 1938.

While many variations of the famous 1896 Broomhandle exist, most common Broomhandles are pre-war Commercials, Model 1930 Commercials, Red 9s, and Bolos. They can be found in chronological order in this section. Holster stocks are a very popular accessory in this model. Commercial stocks may be matching or may not be serial numbered to gun (proper stock). Add $300+ for stock depending on overall original condition and if matching/non-matching.

In 1984, Federal legislation once again allowed importation of non-domestic WWI and WWII military handguns. While many of these newer imports would make workable shooters, they have in no way lowered prices on 90%+ condition specimens due to normal collector activity in top quality only pistols. Recently imported Broomhandles should have the importer's name visibly stamped on an exterior surface.

Mauser Broomhandles: Conehammer Variations

STANDARD CONEHAMMER - 7.63 Mauser cal., distinguishable by circular machined upper hammer with concentric rings. 5.5 in. barrel, 23 groove wooden grips, rear adjustable sight available in 1-10, 50-500, 100-300, 50-300, 50-700 meter configurations, 10 shot mag.

	$3,250	$2,500	$1,850	$1,200	$1,050	$925	$700

Add 40% for matching stock.

FIXED SIGHT CONEHAMMER - 7.63 Mauser cal., similar to Standard Conehammer, except has fixed rear sight.

	$4,200	$3,000	$1,800	$1,300	$1,100	$925	$700

6 SHOT CONEHAMMER - FIXED SIGHT - 7.63 Mauser cal., 4¾ in. barrel, 6 shot mag., rare.

	$7,500	$6,000	$4,500	$3,500	$3,000	$2,500	$2,000

* *6 Shot Conehammer w/adjustable sight* - 7.63 Mauser cal., 5.5 in. barrel, very rare.

	$11,000	$8,500	$6,000	$5,000	$4,000	$3,000	$2,500

Sales of this variation are extremely limited.

TURKISH CONEHAMMER - 7.63 Mauser cal., 5.5 in. barrel, 10 shot mag. Approx. 1,000 mfg. for Turkey in 1898, Farsi serial numbers.

	$6,500	$4,500	$3,000	$2,400	$2,100	$1,800	$1,500

"SYSTEM MAUSER" CONEHAMMER - 7.63 Mauser cal., "SYSTEM MAUSER" marked on top of chamber, improved 5.5 in. tapered barrel, 10 shot mag.

	$15,000	$11,000	$6,000	$5,000	$4,000	$3,500	$3,000

* *Stepped barrel variation* - similar to System Mauser variation, except has older 5.5 in. stepped barrel with no taper.

	$22,500	$16,000	$10,000	$8,000	$7,000	$6,000	$5,000

Add 40% for "SYSTEM MAUSER" stock.

20 SHOT CONEHAMMER - 7.63 Mauser cal., 20 shot non-detachable mag., frame can either be flatside or have milled panels, 5.5 in. tapered barrel, extremely rare.

	$30,000	$25,000	$15,000	$12,000	$9,000	$8,000	$7,000

Add 20% for milled panel variation.
Add 40% for matching stock cut for 20 shot mag.
Several restored guns have recently sold in the $10,000 range.
Many fake 20 shot pistols (especially flat side) have surfaced over the last few years. Use extreme caution when considering purchase.

M

Grading	100%	98%	95%	90%	80%	70%	60%

EARLY TRANSITIONAL LARGE RING HAMMER - 7.63 Mauser cal., distinguishable by large, open centered ring, 10 shot mag., 5.5 in. barrel.

	$3,000	$2,250	$1,550	$1,200	$1,050	$925	$700

This variation is normally found in the 12,000-15,000 serial range only.

Mauser Broomhandles: Flatside Variations

Add approximately $500 for a matching shoulder stock on the following models, $350 for non-matching.

ITALIAN CONTRACT FLATSIDE - 7.63 Mauser cal., distinguishable by flatside frame and DV/AV proofmarks, 10 shot mag., 5.5 in. barrel.

	$3,500	$2,500	$1,600	$1,300	$1,100	$900	$700

This variation is found in the 1-5,000 serial range only.

FLATSIDE COMMERCIAL - 7.63 Mauser cal., 5.5 in. barrel, 23 groove walnut grips, adj. rear sight typically marked 1- 10 or 50-1,000.

	$2,700	$2,000	$1,500	$1,000	$800	$600	$400

Early specimens may have pinned rear sights. Found in serial range 20,000-30,000.

Mauser Broomhandles: Post-1900 Variations

Add approximately $400 for a matching shoulder stock on the following models, $325 for non-matching. This assumes excellent condition - exceptions are noted.

PRE-WAR LARGE RING BOLO - 7.63 Mauser cal., 3.9 in. barrel, floral grips, usually found in 29,000 and 40,000 serial range.

	$4,000	$3,000	$2,000	$1,450	$1,000	$700	$450

Add $850 for short pre-war bolo stock, $1,500 if stock matches pistol.

LARGE RING SHALLOW MILLING - 7.63 Mauser cal., 5.5 in. barrel, 23 groove walnut or hard rubber grips, normally found in the 30,000-33,000 ser. range.

	$2,500	$1,600	$1,000	$750	$625	$500	$400

M

LARGE RING DEEP MILLING - 7.63 Mauser cal., 5.5 in. barrel, 35 groove walnut or hard rubber grips, normally found in the 34,000 ser. range.

	$2,650	$1,650	$1,000	$750	$625	$500	$400

PRE-WAR SMALL RING BOLO - 7.63 Mauser cal., 3.9 in. barrel, floral/checkered rubber or 31-36 groove walnut grips, usually found in 40,000-44,000 serial range.

	$3,250	$2,300	$1,600	$1,200	$800	$575	$400

Add $850 for short pre-war bolo stock, $1,500 if stock matches pistol.

6-SHOT BOLO - 7.63 Mauser cal., distinctive 6 shot mag., 3.9 in. barrel, either fixed rear sight (more common) or adjustable, could have either large ring or small ring hammer.

	$6,500	$5,000	$3,500	$3,000	$2,600	$2,200	$1,500

Add $850 for short pre-war bolo stock, $1,500 if stock matches pistol.

STANDARD PRE-WAR COMMERCIAL - 7.63 Mauser cal., 5.5 in. barrel, 10 shot mag., 34 groove walnut or checkered black rubber grips, typically 50-1,000 meter adj. rear sight.

	$1,800	$1,350	$850	$725	$600	$500	$400

This variation is the most commonly encountered of all M1896 broomhandles. It can be encountered in the 39,000-274,000 serial range. Early guns below serial no. 100,000 are often Von Lengerke and Detmold marked and can be encountered with hard rubber grips. Rifling changed from 4 groove to 6 groove at approx. serial no. 100,000.

Note: This model is once again being imported by domestic distributors/dealers. Condition is somewhat poor, and prices usually start in the $250 range. These specimens usually have been reblued in addition to other reworking because the original condition has generally been very poor.

Grading	100%	98%	95%	90%	80%	70%	60%

MAUSER BANNER CHAMBER MARKED - 7.63 Mauser or 9mm Export/9mm Mauser (rare) cal., 5.5 in. barrel, distinguishable by Mauser banner trademark on top of chamber, 32 groove walnut grips. Approx. 10,000 mfg. in serial range 84,000-94,000.

	$2,700	$1,900	$1,250	$850	$725	$600	$500

This model is very similar in appearance to the Pre-War Commercial.

PERSIAN CONTRACT - 7.63 Mauser cal., 5.5 in. barrel, distinguished by Persian lion crest in left rear frame panel, must be in the 154,000 serial range, 50-1,000 meter adj. rear sight.

	$3,750	$2,800	$2,200	$1,600	$1,100	$850	$700

This variation is frequently faked - pay close attention to serial no. and Persian crest.

STANDARD WARTIME COMMERCIAL - 7.63 Mauser cal., 5.5 in. barrel, 10 shot mag., 30 groove walnut grips, adj. 50-1,000 meter rear sight.

	$1,500	$1,000	$750	$650	$550	$450	$350

This variation is encountered almost as frequently as the Standard Pre-War Commercial. It is usually found in the 290,000-440,000 serial range. It was the first model to utilize the "new safety" design, and can be noticed by the "NS" marking on the back of hammer. Similar features as the Pre-War Commercial, except finish and polishing exhibit more machine and tooling marks.
Note: This model is once again being imported by domestic distributors/dealers. Condition is somewhat poor, and prices usually start in the $250 range. These specimens usually have been reblued in addition to other reworking because the original condition has generally been very poor.

RED-9 ADJ. SIGHT - 9mm Para. cal., 5.5 in. barrel, 10 shot mag., 24 groove walnut grips usually marked with large red no. 9, adj. 50-500 meter rear sight, standard WWI military contract model with separate serial range 1-150,000, generally poorly finished. Mfg. 1916-1918.

	$1,950	$1,400	$1,000	$850	$750	$650	$550

Add $600 for matching stock.
Add $350 for non-matching stock.
Add $200 for original leather.
Add 10% if Prussian Eagle proofed on front of magazine well.
Note: Be cautious for originality since metal refinishing is prevalent in this model. The last 10,000 guns of this German military contract are not military proofed, are better polished, and will command a slight premium.

RED-9 FIXED SIGHT - 9mm Para. cal., 3.9 in. barrel, this is a 1920 commercial rework of the Red-9 military, may be dated 1920 and/or have police markings on front grip strap.

	$1,100	$850	$650	$550	$475	$400	$350

Because of the Treaty of Versailles following WWI, barrels had to be shortened to less than 4 inches and the adj. rear sight removed.

FRENCH GENDARME - 7.63 Mauser cal., 3.9 in. barrel, distinguished by Bolo barrel length on large frame, hard rubber or walnut (rare) grips, found in the serial range 431,000-434,000, adj. 50-500 meter rear sight.

	$2,850	$2,000	$1,250	$850	$700	$550	$400

EARLY POST-WAR BOLO - 7.63 Mauser cal., 3.9 in. barrel, shot extractor, small ring hammer, usually found in the 440,000-500,000 serial range. Fit with full-size stock.

	$2,350	$1,650	$925	$725	$600	$500	$375

Add 50% for long barrel Bolos in approx. the 475,000 serial range.

LATE POST-WAR BOLO - 7.63 Mauser cal., 3.9 in. barrel, similar features of Early Post- War Bolo except has Mauser banner trademark on left rear frame panel, usually encountered in the 500,000- 700,000+ serial range. Fit with full-size stock.

	$2,600	$1,750	$1,250	$800	$625	$500	$375

Add 10% for late pistols with high polish salt blue finish.

Mauser Broomhandles: Post-1930 Variations

Add approximately $500 for a Mauser banner marked stock. These late stocks were not marked with a serial number.

M

Grading	100%	98%	95%	90%	80%	70%	60%

EARLY MODEL 1930 COMMERCIAL

EARLY MODEL 1930 COMMERCIAL - 7.63 Mauser cal., 5.2 (common) or 5.5 in. stepped barrel, 12 groove walnut grips, adj. 50-1,000 meter rear sight, usually found in the 800,000- 890,000 serial range.

	$2,450	$1,650	$950	$750	$625	$500	$375

This broomhandle variation had a high polish, salt blue finish. Small parts are still fire blue and milling grooves were machined in receiver rails.

LATE MODEL 1930 COMMERCIAL - 7.63 Mauser cal., 5.5 in. stepped barrel, similar appearance to early 1930 Commercial except has solid receiver rails and various small parts are salt blued. Ser. range 890,000- 921,000 with production ending in late 1930s.

	$2,350	$1,550	$950	$750	$625	$500	$375

This model is serial numbered on rear top of barrel extension assembly.

MODEL 1930 REMOVABLE MAG. - 7.63 Mauser cal., 5.5 in. stepped barrel, 12 groove walnut grips, adj. 50-1,000 meter rear sight, very rare.

	$18,000	$15,000	$9,000	$5,000	$4,000	$3,200	$2,500

Original specimens of this variation have frames without the extra cuts required for the selector switch. Fakes are usually welded up Schnellfeuers made to look original. Only a very few are known in the 84,000-88,000 serial range. They are not slotted for the shoulder stock. Also known as the Model 711.

SCHNELLFEUER (MODEL 712) - 7.63 Mauser cal., 5.5 in. stepped barrel, 12 groove walnut grips, adj. 50-1,000 meter rear sight, switchable full auto variation generally with selector switch, separate serial range 1- 100,000, 10 or 20 shot detachable mag. 712 stock is internally grooved for selector switch.

	$4,000	$3,250	$2,600	$2,200	$1,800	$1,500	$1,200

Add $750 for correct stock.
Deduct 60% if Class III transferable only (dealer sample).
The Model 712 is classified as a machine gun and is subject to registration and payment of a $200 transfer tax.

Broomhandle Carbines

FLUTED BARREL MODEL - marked "July 1897".

	$28,000	$16,000	$12,000	$8,000	$6,000	$5,000	$4,000

FLATSIDE CONE HAMMER - 7.63mm cal., 11¾ in. barrel, experimental variation.

	$20,000	$17,500	$12,250	$7,000	$6,000	$5,000	$4,000

FLATSIDE TRANSITIONAL - 7.63mm cal., 11¾ in. barrel.

	$18,500	$14,000	$9,000	$7,000	$6,000	$5,000	$4,000

LARGE RING HAMMER TRANSITIONAL - 7.63mm cal., 11¾ in. barrel.

	$16,000	$12,500	$9,000	$7,000	$6,000	$5,000	$4,000

LARGE RING HAMMER - 7.63mm cal., 14½ in. barrel.

	$16,000	$12,500	$9,000	$8,000	$7,000	$6,000	$5,000

SMALL RING HAMMER - 7.63mm cal., 14½ in. barrel.

	$15,000	$11,500	$8,500	$8,000	$7,000	$6,000	$5,000

M

Grading	100%	98%	95%	90%	80%	70%	60%

Broomhandles: Copies from Other Countries

These pistols are Chinese manufactured copies of the original German design.

HAND-MADE MAUSER CHINESE MARKED AND OTHERS - 9mm Para. or .45 ACP cal., copies of the Mauser Broomhandle, many thousands made, fixed (.45 ACP cal.) or detachable (9mm Para.) mag., quality can vary significantly, recent imports will have import markings. IAR, Inc. imported these recently.

9mm Para.	$625	$550	$475	$400	$325	$275	$250
.45 ACP	$1,200	$950	$740	$680	$600	$500	$400

Add $100 for reproduction shoulder stock holster (with or w/o leather).
Subtract 25% for poor quality (QC with slave labor only goes so far).

HAND-MADE UNMARKED - poor quality.

$400	$360	$330	$300	$275	$250	$225

ASIATIC FLATSIDE UNMARKED - better quality, not exceedingly rare.

$1,200	$950	$740	$680	$600	$500	$400

TAKU-NAVAL DOCKYARD FLATSIDE - machine-made, better quality, not exceedingly rare, approx. 6,000 mfg.

$1,500	$1,100	$740	$680	$600	$500	$400

Add 30% with correct stock.
Add 5% if with holster.

SHANSEI ARSENAL .45 CAL. - .45 ACP cal., approx. 8,500 mfg., scarce and desirable in excellent condition, as most remaining original pistols are in rough condition, original stripper clips for this model are rare.

N/A	$5,500	$4,250	$3,000	$1,700	$1,600	$1,475

Recently, a small number of currently manufactured pistols have been marketed as "restorations". Buyer beware! These newly made guns are currently priced in the $1,000-$1,500 range. Also, fake stocks have recently surfaced.

Broomhandles: Spanish Copies

VERY EARLY ASTRA-900 - Bolo grips, frame has single-line address, approx. 1,200 mfg.

$3,000	$2,500	$2,200	$2,000	$1,750	$1,600	$1,475

EARLY ASTRA-900 - single-line address, approx. ser. range 1,200-12,000.

$2,750	$2,000	$1,350	$850	$700	$525	$425

LATE ASTRA-900 - two and three-line address, two-line address ser. range is approx. 12,000-20,000, three- line address ser. range is approx. 20,000-34,400.

$2,650	$1,850	$1,350	$850	$700	$525	$425

Add 20% for Japanese character variation in the 27,000 serial range or if in Nazi procurement range.

ROYAL SEMI-AUTO - early Royals are mostly seen in semi-auto with round bolts.

$3,000	$2,450	$1,900	$1,300	$850	$700	$600

There were many variations of the Royals and values assume standard variation.

ROYAL SELECTIVE FIRE - 7.63mm cal., most of approx. 25,000 Royals manufactured were selective fire, several variations, Class III transferable only.

Class III	$2,500	$2,200	$2,000	$1,800	$1,700	$1,600
$1,475						

Add 20% if detachable mag., 100% if equipped with pneumatic rate retarder.
This model had either a fixed mag. or detachable mag. May have been fit with pneumatic rate retarder.

M

Grading	100%	98%	95%	90%	80%	70%	60%

RIFLES: BOLT ACTION, MILITARY PRODUCTION

Subtract 30% if bolt is not matching or contract crests have been removed.
Add 20%-25% if with matching bayonet.

ARGENTINA

	100%	98%	95%	90%	80%	70%	60%
Model 1891 Rifle Argentine pattern	$400	$350	$300	$250	$150	$110	$90
Model 1891 Carbine	$400	$350	$300	$210	$145	$115	$90
Model 1909 Rifle	$500	$450	$425	$350	$250	$140	$90
Model 1909 Cavalry Carbine	$450	$375	$300	$195	$140	$125	$80
Model 1909 Mountain Carbine	$450	$375	$300	$210	$150	$100	$80
FN Mle 24 Short Rifle	$400	$350	$290	$250	$190	$150	$100
FN Mle 30 Short Rifle	$400	$350	$290	$250	$190	$150	$100

AUSTRIA

	100%	98%	95%	90%	80%	70%	60%
Model 1914 Rifle	N/A	N/A	$1,300	$1,100	$900	$500	$350

BELGIUM

	100%	98%	95%	90%	80%	70%	60%
Model 1889 Rifle	$600	$550	$475	$350	$140	$125	$75
Model 1889 Carbine	$550	$500	$425	$350	$125	$125	$75
Model 1889 Carbine Hopkins & Allen	$600	$550	$500	$375	$175	$150	$100
Model 1889 Carbine with "yataghan"	$550	$500	$425	$350	$200	$150	$100
Model 1889 Carbine Lightened	$550	$500	$425	$350	$200	$150	$100
Model 1916 Carbine	$500	$475	$425	$325	$200	$125	$95
Model 1935 Short Rifle	$600	$550	$450	$325	$295	$150	$90
Model 1889/36 Short Rifle	$550	$475	$395	$325	$295	$150	$90
Model 35/46 & 50 SH. Rifles .30-06 cal.	$450	$400	$360	$250	$150	$100	$80

BOLIVIA

	100%	98%	95%	90%	80%	70%	60%
Model 1895 Rifle, (Argentine M1891 Rifle)	$375	$335	$250	$200	$160	$110	$75
Model 1907 Rifle	$450	$375	$300	$240	$200	$140	$100
Model 1907 Short Rifle	$450	$375	$300	$240	$200	$140	$100
Czech marked Model VZ 24 Short Rifle	$500	$425	$350	$275	$180	$125	$70
Standard Model Mauser Banner Short Rifle	$400	$350	$280	$200	$175	$140	$100
Model 1950 Rifle Series B-50	$500	$425	$350	$295	$200	$150	$100

BRAZIL

	100%	98%	95%	90%	80%	70%	60%
Model 1894 Rifle	$450	$325	$250	$200	$170	$140	$110
Model 1894 Carbine	$450	$325	$250	$200	$170	$140	$110
Model 1904 Mauser Vergueiro Rifle	$475	$325	$300	$250	$175	$120	$90

M

Grading	100%	98%	95%	90%	80%	70%	60%
Model 1907 Rifle	$425	$315	$300	$250	$175	$120	$100
Model 1907 Carbine	$425	$315	$250	$200	$160	$125	$90
Model 1908 Rifle	$425	$300	$250	$175	$125	$100	$60
Model 1908 Short Rifle	$350	$275	$220	$195	$125	$90	$60
Model 1922 Carbine	$375	$335	$250	$175	$90	$80	$70
Model 1924 VZ 24 Carbine	$350	$275	$240	$190	$120	$80	$70
Model 1924/34 Czech Carbine	$450	$325	$275	$200	$150	$100	$80
Model 1908/34 Rifle .30-06 cal.	$450	$325	$275	$200	$150	$100	$80
Model 1935 Mauser Banner Rifle	$650	$425	$475	$400	$170	$130	$100
Model 1935 Mauser Banner Carbine	$650	$425	$475	$400	$170	$130	$100
Model M954 Rifle .30-06 cal.	$450	$300	$250	$200	$120	$100	$80

CHILE

Grading	100%	98%	95%	90%	80%	70%	60%
Model 1893 Rifle - Bent bolt handle	$425	$350	$240	$200	$140	$115	$90
Model 1895 Rifle - Army	$450	$375	$240	$200	$140	$115	$90
Model 1895 Rifle - Anchor crest	$425	$350	$240	$200	$140	$120	$100
Model 1895 Short Rifle	$450	$375	$240	$200	$140	$120	$95
Model 1895 Carbine	$400	$325	$265	$220	$180	$150	$100
Model 1912 Rifle	$375	$325	$295	$225	$160	$120	$100
Model 1912 Rifle (7.62 NATO)	$375	$325	$295	$225	$160	$120	$100
Model 1912 Short Rifle	$375	$325	$295	$225	$160	$120	$100
Model 1912 Rifle (7.62 NATO)	$425	$350	$285	$225	$160	$120	$100
Model 1935 Carbine (7.62 NATO)	$425	$350	$285	$225	$160	$120	$100
Mauser Banner	$500	$520	$480	$350	$275	$225	$150

CHINA

Grading	100%	98%	95%	90%	80%	70%	60%
Gew 1871 Rifle - Chinese marked	$550	$520	$380	$325	$290	$275	$250
Kar 1871 Carbine - Chinese marked	$550	$520	$400	$350	$300	$275	$250
Kar 98a Carbine	$550	$520	$475	$390	$300	$275	$250
Model 1907 Rifle - China contract	$600	$550	$450	$375	$300	$275	$250
Model 1907 Carbine	$600	$550	$450	$375	$300	$275	$250
Model 98/22 Rifle	$400	$350	$325	$300	$260	$225	$195
Model 24/30 FN Short Rifles	$275	$240	$210	$190	$160	$125	$90
Model 21 Chinese-made VZ 24	$400	$350	$325	$300	$250	$195	$160
Std. Modell 1933 Mauser Banner Rifle	$550	$500	$475	$400	$300	$225	$120
Std. Model 1933 Mauser Banner Carbine	$550	$500	$475	$400	$300	$225	$120
Chiang Kai-Shek Rifle - Chinese copy	$500	$450	$390	$250	$160	$100	$80
Chinese VZ 24 P prefix - "1937" SH. Rifle	$400	$350	$300	$225	$175	$140	$110
Chinese copy VZ 24 w/Jap. folding byt.	$600	$550	$495	$400	$350	$300	$275

M

Grading	100%	98%	95%	90%	80%	70%	60%
COLOMBIA							
Model 1891 Rifle -							
Argentine pattern	$325	$290	$225	$180	$160	$120	$95
Model 1912 Rifle - Steyr	$400	$375	$300	$225	$185	$150	$120
Model 1912 Short Rifle - Steyr	$450	$375	$320	$275	$220	$180	$150
Model 24 FN Short Rifle	$300	$280	$230	$160	$125	$90	$65
Model 30 FN Short Rifle	$300	$280	$230	$160	$125	$90	$865
Model VZ 24 Short Rifle	$325	$300	$240	$200	$160	$110	$90
Model 29 Short Rifle - Steyr	$500	$450	$375	$295	$225	$175	$120
Model 1950 Rifle - FN .30-06 cal.	$400	$375	$280	$200	$160	$120	$100
COSTA RICA							
Model 1895 Rifle	$350	$325	$250	$180	$140	$110	$90
Model 1910 Rifle	$450	$400	$325	$280	$225	$180	$90
Model 24 FN Short Rifle	$400	$375	$300	$220	$175	$110	$95
CZECHOSLOVAKIA							
Model 1919 Mauser - Jelen Rifle	N/A	N/A	$2,500	$2,300	$2,000	$1,800	$1,600
Model 1921 Mauser - Jelen Rifle	N/A	N/A	$2,400	$2,100	$2,000	$1,800	$1,600
Model 98/22 Rifle	$400	$375	$320	$295	$220	$150	$90
Model VZ 23 Short Rifle	$400	$375	$320	$280	$210	$160	$120
Model VZ 23A Short Rifle	$400	$375	$320	$280	$210	$160	$120
Model VZ 24 Short Rifle	$400	$350	$275	$180	$135	$90	$70
Model 98/29 Rifle	$500	$450	$325	$270	$200	$140	$100
Model VZ 08/33 Carbine	$350	$290	$220	$175	$110	$90	$80
Model VZ 12/33 Carbine -							
light VZ 24	$400	$375	$290	$220	$160	$120	$90
Model VZ 16/33	$500	$450	$390	$340	$275	$195	$145
Model "JC" Short Rifle	$600	$525	$450	$400	$350	$300	$250
Model "L" SH. Rifle cal.,							
.303, Lithuania	N/A	$1,200	$900	$775	$675	$600	$550
DOMINICAN REPUBLIC							
M1953 Rifle - Ex-Brazil M1908	$500	$460	$275	$190	$125	$90	$70
M1953 SH. Rifle -							
Ex-Brazil M1908 SHR.	$500	$460	$275	$190	$125	$90	$70
ECUADOR							
Model 71/84 Rifle	$500	$400	$275	$180	$125	$80	$50
Model 1891 Rifle -							
Argentine pattern	$350	$310	$270	$220	$180	$130	$80
Model 1907 Rifle	$400	$375	$325	$275	$250	$195	$150
Model VZ 23 Short Rifle	$400	$375	$340	$290	$250	$190	$150
Model VZ 24 Short Rifle	$400	$375	$300	$250	$180	$135	$90
Model VZ 12/33 Carbine	$400	$375	$290	$200	$175	$100	$80

M

Grading	100%	98%	95%	90%	80%	70%	60%
Model 24/30 FN Short Rifle	$300	$280	$230	$160	$125	$90	$65

EL SALVADOR

Model 1895 Rifle - Chilean pattern	$300	$275	$225	$180	$140	$110	$90
Model VZ 12/33 Carbine	$400	$380	$330	$260	$200	$100	$80
Standard Model 1935 Export	$400	$350	$325	$290	$250	$195	$150
FN M50 Israeli Short Rifle	$395	$360	$320	$260	$200	$125	$90

ESTONIA
Czech Model "L"

Short Rifle - .303 cal.	N/A	$1,200	$900	$775	$675	$600	$550

ETHIOPIA

Model 24 FN Short Rifle	$700	$675	$600	$500	$425	$350	$250
Model 24 FN Carbine	$700	$675	$600	$500	$425	$350	$250
Model 1933 Standard Model Rifle	$800	$775	$700	$600	$500	$450	$350

svw MB | ✢ **FRANCE**

Modified 98K

Carbine - Hex. stacking rod	$500	$475	$400	$325	$250	$200	$100

GERMANY

Model 1871 Rifle - Gew 71	$900	$860	$800	$675	$600	$400	$295
Model 1871 Carbine - Kar 71	$1,000	$975	$900	$825	$750	$600	$295
Model 1871 Short Rifle - Jaeger 71	$1,000	$950	$900	$800	$750	$600	$295
Model 1871/84 Rifle	$950	$875	$700	$550	$425	$275	$150
Model 1888 Commission Rifle	$500	$450	$380	$300	$250	$150	$70
Model 1888/05 Commission Rifle	$500	$450	$375	$300	$225	$125	$70
Model 1888/14 Commission Rifle	$500	$450	$375	$300	$225	$125	$70
Model 1888 Commission Carbine	$500	$475	$400	$300	$225	$175	$140
Model 1891 Comm. Carbine w/stacking hook	$500	$475	$400	$300	$225	$175	$140
Model 1888/97 Rifle	N/A	N/A	N/A	$5,000	$4,500	$3,200	$2,800
Model 1898 Rifle - Gew 98	$750	$700	$650	$500	$350	$225	$100
Model 1898 Carbine - Kar. 98, 16.9 in. bbl.	N/A	$6,000	$4,500	$4,000	$3,500	$3,200	$2,800
Model 1898/17 Rifle	N/A	N/A	N/A	$4,500	$4,000	$3,200	$2,800
Model 1898/18 Rifle	N/A	N/A	N/A	$4,500	$4,000	$3,200	$2,800
Model 1909 Self Loading Carbine	N/A	$7,000	$5,000	$4,500	$4,200	$3,800	$3,500
Model 1898A Carbine	$700	$650	$500	$400	$290	$150	$100
Model 1898AZ Carbine (also Model 98a)	$700	$650	$500	$400	$290	$150	$100
Model 1898b Carbine	$900	$850	$675	$500	$350	$290	$175
Model Gew. 98 (Transitional)	$600	$525	$450	$300	$250	$180	$130
Model K98k Carbine (1936-45, coded mfg.)	$800	$750	$650	$400	$350	$290	$175
Model K98k, Para-troop model	$3,000	$2,800	$2,400	$1,800	$1,200	$800	$700
Model K98k "Kriegsmodell"	$500	$460	$400	$295	$195	$140	$110
Model 33/40 Carbine ("945" 1940)	$1,000	$950	$850	$650	$500	$450	$400
Model 33/40 Carbine							

M

Grading	100%	98%	95%	90%	80%	70%	60%
("DOT" 1941-43)	$1,000	$950	$825	$650	$500	$400	$300
Model 24 (T) Rifle	$600	$550	$450	$350	$275	$200	$175
Model 98/40	$650	$600	$500	$400	$300	$200	$175
Model 29 (0) Rifle L/W issue	$875	$825	$750	$675	$550	$500	$460
Model VG-1	N/A	NA/	N/A	$1,000	$950	$850	$500
G 43 Semi-Automatic Rifle	$1,500	$1,300	$1,000	$900	$800	$650	$500
G 41M Semi-Automatic Rifle	$4,000	$3,800	$3,400	$3,000	$2,600	$2,300	$2,000
G 41W Semi-Automatic Rifle	$3,400	$3,300	$3,000	$2,500	$2,100	$1,800	$1,500

GREECE

	100%	98%	95%	90%	80%	70%	60%
Model 1930 FN Short Rifle	$500	$475	$375	$290	$200	$150	$90

GUATEMALA

	100%	98%	95%	90%	80%	70%	60%
Czech VZ 24 Short Rifle	$600	$580	$500	$325	$190	$135	$90
M1895 Rifle	$325	$300	$275	$200	$150	$110	$80

ARMEE D'HAITI

HAITI

	100%	98%	95%	90%	80%	70%	60%
Model 1930 FN Short Rifle	$400	$350	$275	$225	$175	$125	$90

IRAN (PERSIA)

	100%	98%	95%	90%	80%	70%	60%
Model 1895 Rifle	$500	$460	$410	$300	$220	$150	$90
Model 98/29 Rifle	$650	$620	$550	$475	$380	$300	$200
Model 98/29 Short Rifle	$650	$620	$550	$475	$380	$300	$200
Model 49 Carbine	$600	$575	$480	$420	$310	$250	$175

IRAQ

	100%	98%	95%	90%	80%	70%	60%
Model 1948 98k Carbine	$400	$380	$330	$280	$225	$185	$90

ISRAEL

	100%	98%	95%	90%	80%	70%	60%
German 98k with Israeli marks	$400	$375	$325	$275	$210	$120	$90
Czech 98k w/large triggerguard	$400	$375	$325	$275	$210	$120	$90
Model 1954 Short Rifle	$450	$420	$380	$325	$250	$180	$130

LATVIA

	100%	98%	95%	90%	80%	70%	60%
Czech VZ 24 Short Rifle	$700	$675	$630	$550	$275	$225	$160

LIBERIA

	100%	98%	95%	90%	80%	70%	60%
Model 24 FN Short Rifle	N/A	N/A	$395	$325	$275	$225	$160

GUKLU FONDAS
1937
24L

LITHUANIA

	100%	98%	95%	90%	80%	70%	60%
Czech "L" Model Short Rifle (.303)	N/A	N/A	$775	$675	$600	$550	$500
Model VZ 24 Short Rifle	N/A	N/A	$700	$650	$575	$495	$425
Model 30 FN Short Rifle	N/A	N/A	$700	$650	$575	$495	$425
Model 1900 Rifle	$595	$550	$495	$450	$395	$325	$275

M

Grading	100%	98%	95%	90%	80%	70%	60%
MANCHURIA							
Mukden Arsenal Rifle	$1,500	$1,400	$1,200	$1,000	$850	$700	$400
MEXICO							
Model 1895 Rifle	$350	$300	$225	$190	$145	$110	$60
Model 1895 Carbine	$350	$300	$225	$190	$145	$110	$60
Model 1902 Rifle	$1,200	$1,100	$950	$700	$500	$250	$85
Model 1907 Rifle	$395	$320	$250	$210	$145	$115	$90
Model 1910 Rifle	$350	$295	$250	$200	$140	$110	$85
Model 1910 Carbine	$350	$295	$250	$200	$140	$110	$85
Model 1912 Rifle	$350	$295	$250	$200	$140	$110	$85
Model 1912 Short Rifle	$350	$295	$250	$200	$140	$110	$85
Model 1924 FN Short Rifle	$350	$300	$250	$185	$125	$100	$80
Model 1924 Carbine	$350	$300	$250	$190	$145	$110	$85
Model 1936 Short Rifle	$400	$375	$325	$275	$200	$150	$80
Model 1954 Short Rifle	$400	$375	$325	$275	$200	$150	$80
MOROCCO							
Model 1950 FN Carbine							
(.308 Win. or .30-06)	$500	$475	$425	$350	$295	$150	$120
NETHERLANDS							
Model 1950 Carbine							
"W"or"J" crest	$500	$470	$420	$375	$325	$290	$250
NICARAGUA							
Model VZ 12/33 Short Rifle	$600	$575	$375	$295	$220	$120	$100
Model VZ 24 Short Rifle	$450	$400	$350	$295	$225	$190	$150
ORANGE FREE STATE							
Model 1896 Rifle							
(OVS marked), DWM	$900	$860	$780	$600	$300	$175	$125
Model 1896 Rifle (OVS marked),							
Loewe & Sons	$850	$800	$750	$600	$300	$175	$125
Model 1896 Rifle, Chile overmark	$450	$400	$350	$280	$210	$175	$125
Model 1895 Short Rifle	$450	$400	$350	$280	$210	$175	$125
Model 1895 Carbine	$450	$400	$350	$280	$210	$175	$125
PARAGUAY							
Model 1895 Rifle	$375	$325	$295	$210	$160	$110	$90
Model 1907 Rifle (DWM)	$500	$450	$400	$350	$250	$125	$90
Model 1907 Carbine (Full-stocked)	$500	$475	$425	$375	$275	$150	$120
Model 1927 Rifle (Oviedo)	$300	$260	$230	$195	$150	$90	$75

Grading	100%	98%	95%	90%	80%	70%	60%
Model 1927 Short Rifle	$300	$260	$230	$195	$150	$90	$75
Model 1927 Carbine (Full-stocked)	$400	$375	$325	$220	$185	$140	$100
Model 1933 Standard Model Rifle	$450	$425	$380	$320	$230	$120	$95
M24 "Model 1935" FN Short Rifle	$450	$425	$380	$320	$230	$125	$100

PERU

	100%	98%	95%	90%	80%	70%	60%
Model 1891 Rifle (Lange sight)	$400	$360	$300	$250	$175	$100	$60
Model 1891 Carbine (Lange sight)	$400	$360	$300	$250	$175	$100	$60
Model 1909 Rifle	$900	$875	$825	$750	$290	$195	$120
Model VZ 24 Short Rifle (Model 32)	$450	$420	$380	$290	$195	$150	$125
Model VZ 32 Short Rifle (Model 32)	$475	$450	$400	$320	$250	$150	$125
Model 1935 FN Short Rifle (7.65mm/.30-06)	$500	$475	$425	$350	$250	$150	$120

POLAND

	100%	98%	95%	90%	80%	70%	60%
Model 1898 Rifle	$500	$475	$420	$340	$280	$200	$150
Model 1898 Carbine (Kar 98a)	$425	$375	$320	$250	$190	$120	$80
Model 1929 Short Rifle (Wz 29)	$600	$575	$550	$450	$300	$200	$125

PORTUGAL

	100%	98%	95%	90%	80%	70%	60%
Model 1904 Mauser-Verguiero Rifle	$600	$575	$520	$420	$300	$200	$100
Model 1937 Short Rifle	$500	$460	$350	$295	$220	$160	$110
Model 937a Short Rifle	$550	$500	$450	$395	$360	$280	$150
Model 1941 Short Rifle	$600	$575	$550	$480	$390	$300	$200

ROMANIA

	100%	98%	95%	90%	80%	70%	60%
Model VZ 24 Short Rifle, "M" or "C" Crest	$600	$575	$540	$420	$300	$180	$120

SAUDI ARABIA

	100%	98%	95%	90%	80%	70%	60%
Model 1930 FN Short Rifle	N/A	N/A	$300	$250	$195	$110	$65

SERBIA

	100%	98%	95%	90%	80%	70%	60%
Model 1878/80 Rifle	$1,400	$1,200	$1,000	$850	$600	$400	$250
Model 1885 Cavalry Carbine	$1,150	$1,100	$1,000	$850	$600	$400	$250
Models 1886/6C and 1880/7C	$1,200	$1,100	$1,000	$850	$350	$280	$225
Model 1899 Rifle	$550	$500	$475	$390	$275	$200	$110
Model 1889/07 Rifle	$500	$475	$430	$325	$250	$125	$90
Model 1899/08 Rifle	$500	$475	$430	$325	$250	$125	$90
Model 1899C Short Rifle	$500	$475	$430	$325	$250	$125	$80

Grading	100%	98%	95%	90%	80%	70%	60%
Model 1899/08 Carbine	$600	$560	$540	$450	$350	$280	$150
Model 1910 Rifle	$450	$420	$390	$300	$225	$160	$125

SIAM (THAILAND)

Model 1902 Rifle (Type 45)	$460	$440	$400	$360	$270	$175	$100
Model 1923 Short Rifle (Type 66)	$460	$440	$400	$360	$270	$175	$100

SLOVAK REPUBLIC

Model VZ 24 Short Rifle	$700	$650	$600	$500	$375	$300	$180

SOUTH AFRICAN REPUBLIC

Model 1896 Rifle "ZAR" marked	N/A	$500	$450	$400	$300	$195	$150

SPAIN

Model 1891 Rifle	$600	$550	$500	$400	$290	$195	$100
Model 1892 Rifle	$600	$575	$525	$450	$290	$185	$110
Model 1892 Carbine	$500	$475	$425	$360	$290	$185	$120
Model 1893 Rifle	$400	$380	$350	$300	$240	$175	$110
Model 1895 Carbine (Full-stocked)	$450	$420	$380	$300	$195	$110	$80
Model 1916 Short Rifle	$350	$295	$220	$180	$140	$115	$95
Model 1943 Short Rifle	$400	$375	$350	$285	$190	$130	$95

SWEDEN

Model 1894 Carbine	$600	$575	$550	$420	$360	$190	$120
Model 1896 Rifle	$400	$375	$340	$300	$220	$185	$120
Model 1938 Short Rifle	$325	$275	$220	$190	$130	$100	$80
Model 1940 Short Rifle (8mm)	$600	$550	$500	$450	$375	$325	$275

SYRIA

Model 1948 Carbine	$400	$375	$340	$290	$190	$120	$80

TURKEY

Model 1887 Rifle	$1,100	$1,000	$950	$750	$600	$375	$250
Model 1887 Carbine	$1,100	$1,000	$950	$750	$600	$375	$250
Model 1890 Rifle	$750	$700	$675	$600	$450	$380	$290
Model 1893 Rifle	$500	$475	$425	$380	$290	$200	$120
Model 1903 Rifle 7.65mm	$700	$675	$650	$600	$450	$380	$200
Model 1905 Carbine	$700	$675	$650	$600	$450	$380	$225
Model VZ 98/22 Rifle	$450	$420	$380	$300	$200	$140	$90
Model 1888 Rifle (Turkish marked)	$300	$280	$250	$200	$150	$110	$70
Model 1888/38 Rifle (improved)	$300	$280	$250	$200	$150	$110	$70
Model 1938 Rifle 8mm	$300	$280	$250	$200	$150	$90	$60
Model 1938 Short Rifle	$300	$280	$250	$200	$150	$90	$60

M

Grading	100%	98%	95%	90%	80%	70%	60%

URUGUAY

	100%	98%	95%	90%	80%	70%	60%
Model 1895 Rifle	$495	$460	$425	$375	$295	$125	$95
Model 1904 Rifle	$525	$495	$450	$395	$325	$260	$210
Model 1908 Rifle	$550	$520	$500	$450	$400	$300	$250
Model 1980 Short Rifle	$550	$520	$500	$450	$400	$300	$250
Czech VZ 32 Short Rifle (Model 1934)	$500	$475	$425	$350	$290	$200	$120
Czech VZ 24 Short Rifle (Model 1934)	$600	$575	$550	$500	$390	$300	$260
Mle 24 FN Short Rifle	$400	$375	$350	$280	$225	$175	$120

VENEZUELA

	100%	98%	95%	90%	80%	70%	60%
Model 1910 Rifle	$400	$380	$350	$290	$240	$130	$90
Czech VZ 24/26 Short Rifle	$500	$475	$440	$385	$300	$250	$180
Mle 24/30 FN Short Rifle	$675	$650	$620	$575	$475	$385	$275
Mle 24/30 FN Carbine	$650	$650	$620	$575	$475	$385	$275

YEMEN

	100%	98%	95%	90%	80%	70%	60%
Mle 30 Short Rifle (Markings unknown)	N/A	N/A	$400	$375	$300	$250	$190

YUGOSLAVIA

	100%	98%	95%	90%	80%	70%	60%
M90T Short Rifle (ex-Turkish M1890)	N/A	$450	$430	$400	$325	$275	$190
Model M24B Rifle (ex-Mexican M1912)	N/A	$450	$420	$390	$300	$250	$200
Mle 22 FN Short Rifle	$450	$420	$390	$300	$200	$150	$120
Mle 24 FN Short Rifle	$450	$420	$390	$300	$200	$150	$120
Czech VZ 24 Short Rifle	$475	$450	$420	$360	$250	$160	$135
Model 1924 Short Rifle (Kragujevac)	$500	$475	$450	$380	$300	$220	$150
Model 30 FN Short Rifle	$450	$420	$390	$310	$240	$190	$130
Model 30 FN Carbine	$450	$420	$390	$310	$240	$190	$130
M24B Carbine	$500	$475	$400	$325	$250	$200	$150

Approx. 125,000 commercial sporting Mausers were built between 1898 and 1946. Three action lengths; overall measurements: Short (Kurz) 8¼ in., Standard 8¾ in., and Magnum 9¼ in. Optional squarebridge receiver rings for custom sight mounting. Innumerable variations of triggers, barrels, sights and checkering.

Add $350-$550 for conversion unit.
Add 50% for single squarebridge action.
Add 100% for double squarebridge action.
Add 100% for Short (Kurz) action, except on Type K below.
Add 100% for Magnum action, except on African Type below.

Grading	100%	98%	95%	90%	80%	70%	60%

SPECIAL RIFLE, TYPE A - expressly made for English market, superior finish, with round tapered barrel, silver-bead front sight on sleeved-on block with matted surface, hinged floorplate, pear shaped bolt knob, horn forend tip and PG cap, sling eyes.

	$4,000	$3,500	$3,000	$2,000	$1,100	$750	$575

NORMAL RIFLE, TYPE B - 24 in. barrel, steel-capped PG, Schnabel forend, sling swivels, pear shaped bolt knob, hinged floorplate.

	$2,750	$2,400	$1,650	$1,300	$900	$700	$500

LIGHT SHORT RIFLE, TYPE K - 6.5x54 Mauser, 8x51mm, or .250-3000 Savage cal., short action, 22 in. barrel, steel PG cap, sling swivels, pear shaped bolt knob, hinged floorplate, hard rubber buttplate.

	$4,250	$3,675	$3,100	$2,550	$1,500	$1,250	$1,250

CARBINE, TYPE S - 20 or 24 in. barrel stocked to muzzle, steel PG cap, horn buttplate, sling swivels, pear shaped bolt knob, hinged floorplate.

	$3,750	$2,875	$2,200	$1,650	$1,100	$750	$575

CARBINE, TYPE M - 20 in. barrel stocked to muzzle with steel forend cap, steel PG cap, trapdoor steel buttplate holding sectional cleaning rod, butterknife bolt handle, hinged floorplate.

	$3,750	$2,875	$2,200	$1,650	$1,100	$750	$575

MILITARY SPORTING RIFLE, TYPE C - stepped round barrel, round bolt knob, half grip, banner Mauser imprint in side of buttstock.

	$750	$600	$500	$450	$400	$350	$295

AFRICAN TYPE - 28 in. round barrel, stocked to 4 in. from muzzle, Magnum action, pear shaped bolt knob.

	$5,000	$4,000	$3,000	$2,500	$2,250	$2,000	$2,000

RIFLES: BOLT ACTION, RECENT PRODUCTION

During April, 2001, SIG-Blaser completed the purchase production and distribution rights of Mauser sporting and hunting weapons.

Add $150 for double set triggers on all current models.

MODEL 66A - similar to Model 66S except has American configured laminate stock (wood grain), cals., action, and features are the same as the Model 66S. Imported 1988- 89 only.

❋ *Standard Calibers*

	$1,900	$1,425	$1,150	$925	$800	$700	$650

Last MSR was $2,100.

Add $630 per interchangeable barrel.
The A suffix on this model denotes American.

❋ *Magnum Calibers* - includes Weatherby Mag. cals. also.

	$2,050	$1,500	$1,200	$975	$825	$700	$650

Last MSR was $2,270.

Add $670 per interchangeable barrel.

❋ *Big Game Calibers* - includes most popular Mag. cals. up to .458 Win. Mag.

	$2,350	$1,900	$1,425	$1,150	$950	$825	$750

Last MSR was $2,700.

M

Grading	100%	98%	95%	90%	80%	70%	60%

MODEL 66S STANDARD - telescoping short action, 5.6x57mm, 6.5x57mm, 7x57mm Mauser (disc. 1992), 7x64mm, 9.3x62mm, .243 Win., .270 Win., .30-06, or .308 Win. cal., 24 in. barrel, standard interchangeable barrels, single or double set triggers, adj. and detachable sights, Monte Carlo walnut stock with checkering, swivels, new safety, rosewood tipped forearm and pistol grip, rubber recoil pad, 7½ lbs. Mfg. 1974-1995.

	$2,350	$1,275	$995	$875	$775	$695	$625

Last MSR was $2,722.

✳ *Model 66 Magnum* - 28 in. barrel, 6.5x68mm, 8x68S, 9.3x64mm, 7mm Rem. Mag., .300 Win. Mag., or .300 Wby. Mag. cal., 7.9 lbs. Disc. 1995.

	$2,500	$1,325	$1,050	$900	$795	$695	$625

Last MSR was $2,925.

✳ *Model 66 Carbine (Stutzen-Mannlicher)* - .243 Win., .270 Win., .30-06, 7x64mm, or 9.3x62mm cal., 21 in. barrel, full-stock (Mannlicher only) and half- stock (disc. in 1989), double or single triggers, 7.5 lbs. Disc. 1995.

	$2,500	$1,325	$1,050	$900	$795	$695	$625

Last MSR was $2,925.

This model was available in a half-stock "Ultra" variation until 1989. Values are similar to those listed.

✳ *Model 66S Diplomat* - similar cals. as the Model 66S Standard, except not available in 5.6x57mm, similar features, except includes selected walnut and special engraving including deer and wild boar game scenes. Disc. 1995.

	$4,650	$3,850	$3,350	$2,750	$2,250	$1,850	$1,400

Last MSR was $5,317.

Add $390 for Mag. cals. (similar to Model 66S Magnum).

✳ *Safari/Big Game Model 66* - .375 H&H or .458 Win. Mag. cal., single trigger, 9.3 lbs. Disc. 1995.

	$2,950	$1,850	$1,350	$1,025	$875	$775	$650

Last MSR was $3,487.

M

MODEL 66SM - telescoping short action, .243 Win. (disc.), .270 Win., 7x57mm Mauser (disc.), 7x64mm, .308 Win., .30-06, or 6.5x57mm cal. (disc.), 24 in. barrel, standard interchangeable barrels, set trigger, adj. and detachable sights, Monte Carlo walnut stock with checkering, swivels, new safety, anatomical gripped select walnut stock with Mauser-nose, cocking lever on tang, rubber recoil pad, 7¼ lbs. Importation 1981-95.

	$2,875	$1,800	$1,325	$1,025	$875	$775	$650

Last MSR was $3,398.

✳ *Model 66SM Ultra* - all standard cals., 21 in. barrel, 7¼ lbs.

	$1,625	$1,325	$1,140	$920	$760	$650	$550

Last MSR was $1,903.

✳ *Model 66SM Magnum* - cals. similar to Model 66S Magnum, except not available in 9.3x64mm cal., 26 in. barrel, 8.4 lbs. Disc. 1995.

	$3,025	$1,925	$1,375	$1,025	$875	$775	$650

Last MSR was $3,578.

✳ *Model 66SM Diplomat* - similar cals. as the Model 66SM Standard, similar features, except includes selected walnut and special engraving including deer and wild boar game scenes. Disc. 1995.

	$5,075	$3,975	$3,450	$2,775	$2,250	$1,850	$1,400

Last MSR was $5,943.

Add $382 for Mag. cals. (similar to Model 66SM Magnum).

Grading	100%	98%	95%	90%	80%	70%	60%

✳ *Model 66SM Carbine (Mannlicher type full stock)* - .30-06 cal., 21 in. barrel, 7 lbs. Disc. 1995.

	$3,025	$1,925	$1,375	$1,025	$875	$775	$650

Last MSR was $3,578.

These models were previously available on a custom order only basis through KDF, Inc. located in Seguin, TX.

MODEL 66SL - similar to Model 66SM, except features extra select walnut with special graining, 7¼ lbs. Disc. 1985.

	$1,370	$1,275	$890	$720	$580	$475	$420

Last MSR was $1,470.

✳ *Model 66SL Ultra* - 7x64mm or .30-06 cal., 21 in. barrel, 7¼ lbs. Disc. 1985.

	$1,475	$1,325	$940	$750	$600	$450	$400

Last MSR was $1,520.

✳ *Magnum Calibers* - similar to Model 66 S, 8.4 lbs. Disc. 1985.

	$1,475	$1,325	$940	$750	$600	$450	$400

Last MSR was $1,520.

✳ *Mannlicher Type Full Stock* - 21 in. barrel, 7 lbs. Disc. 1985.

	$1,475	$1,325	$940	$750	$600	$450	$400

Last MSR was $1,520.

MODEL 66SL DIPLOMAT - same specifications as Model 66SM, except includes selected walnut and special engraving including deer and wild boar game scenes.

Add $93 for Mannlicher full-stock (21 in. barrel).
Add $387 for Mag. cals.

This model was available on an individual custom order basis only. The last published retail price (1988) for a standard model without options was $3,167.

MODEL 660 - U.S. designation of 66S. Imported 1971-1973.

	$925	$820	$720	$600	$500	$450	$400

MODEL 66S DELUXE - special order engraved and inlaid, select wood. Priced per individual customer order. All guns are custom made only.

MODEL 66P - imported 1995 only.

	$4,250	$3,575	$3,075	$2,600	$2,075	$1,700	$1,375

Last MSR was $4,888.

MODEL 66SP SUPER MATCH - .300 Win. Mag. or .308 Win. cal., telescoping short action, 27½ in. heavy barrel with muzzle brake, no sights, match trigger, 3 shot mag., select European walnut stock with stippling and thumbhole, adj. cheekpiece and butt plate, includes premium scope, 12 lbs. Never imported domestically.

	$4,150	$3,500	$3,050	$2,600	$2,075	$1,700	$1,375

Last MSR was $4,737.

MODEL 77 - .243 Win., .270 Win., 6.5x57mm, 7x64mm, .308 Win., or .30-06 cal., 24 in. barrel, set trigger on tang, adj. and detachable sights, walnut stock with European cheekpiece and hand checkering, swivels, new safety, steel detachable box mag., rubber recoil pad, 7¼ lbs. Disc.

	$1,130	$950	$875	$810	$750	$675	$595

Last MSR was $1,331.

✳ *Model 77 Ultra* - 6.5x57mm, 7x64mm or .30-06 cal., 20 in. barrel, 7.7 lbs. Disc.

	$1,175	$975	$895	$835	$760	$675	$595

Last MSR was $1,394.

✳ *Magnum Calibers* - similar to Model 66S, 8 1/8 lbs. Disc.

	$1,175	$975	$895	$835	$760	$675	$595

Last MSR was $1,394.

M

Grading	100%	98%	95%	90%	80%	70%	60%

❋ ***Mannlicher type full stock*** - 20 in. barrel, Mauser-set trigger, 7.7 lbs. Disc.

	$1,175	$975	$895	$835	$760	$675	$595

Last MSR was $1,394.

❋ ***Big Game Model*** - .375 H&H cal., 26 in. barrel, 8 1/8 lbs. Disc.

	$1,075	$1,000	$900	$795	$675	$575	$475

Last MSR was $1,150.

MODEL 77 SPORTSMAN - .243 Win. or .308 Win. cal., sports version of the Model 77, set trigger on tang, no sights, 24 in. barrel, 9 lbs. Disc.

	$1,495	$1,230	$1,075	$985	$895	$820	$740

Last MSR was $1,754.

Add $430 for Zeiss 2½-10X scope and mounts.

MODEL 83 MATCH SINGLE SHOT - .308 Win. cal. only, cylinder locking action with 3 locking lugs in rear, match trigger, anatomical match stock with select walnut, adj. comb and butt plate. Disc.

	$2,170	$1,815	$1,660	$1,545	$1,400	$1,195	$925

Last MSR was $2,594.

This model is a UIT standard rifle for 300-meter competition.

MODEL 83 MATCH UIT FREE RIFLE - .308 Win. cal. only, cylinder locking action with 3 locking lugs in rear, match trigger, anatomical match stock with select walnut, adj. comb and butt plate. Disc.

	$2,320	$1,940	$1,760	$1,600	$1,430	$1,195	$925

Last MSR was $2,771.

MODEL 83 STANDARD RIFLE - similar to Model 83 Match, except has removable 10 shot steel mag., 26 in. barrel. Disc.

	$2,320	$1,950	$1,800	$1,625	$1,460	$1,250	$1,000

Last MSR was $2,766.

MODEL 86 LAMINATED/FIBERGLASS (SR) - .308 Win. cal., updated version of the Model 83 action, 25.6 (disc.) or 28¾ (new 1997) in. fluted barrel with muzzle brake, black laminate wood (with thumbhole) or fiberglass (disc.) stock with rail in forearm, adj. trigger, 9 shot detachable mag., cased, 10.8 lbs. Imported 1989-1996, recent mfg. included a 2½x10 power Zeiss tactical scope with detachable mount.

	$10,750	$8,900	$7,700	$6,500	$5,500	$4,500	$3,500

Last MSR was $11,795.

MODEL SR 93 - .300 Win. Mag. cal., precision rifle employing skeletonized cast magnesium/aluminum stock, combination right-hand/left-hand bolt, adj. ergonomics, 27 in. fluted barrel with muzzle brake, integrated bi-pod, 4 or 5 shot mag., approx. 13 lbs. without accessories. Disc. 1996.

	$20,000	$17,250	$14,750	$11,950	$8,700	$6,500	$5,000

Last MSR was $21,995.

MODEL 94 - .243 Win., .270 Win., .30-06, .308 Win., .300 Win. Mag., 7x64mm, 7mm Rem. Mag., 8x68S (disc. 1996), 9.3x62 Mag. cal., 22 or 24 in. interchangeable barrel, aluminum block in stock bedding system, 60 degree bolt, 6 lug locking system, checkered walnut stock and forearm, 3 or 4 shot mag., lateral slide safety, approx. 7¼ lbs. Mfg. began 1994, U.S. importation was disc. 1995, resumed 1997 only.

	$1,925	$1,550	$1,325	$1,100	$925	$850	$775

Last MSR was $2,295.

Add $799 per interchangeable barrel assembly.

Grading	100%	98%	95%	90%	80%	70%	60%

MODEL 96 - .25-06 Rem. (new 1997), .270 Win., .30-06, .308 Win. (new 1997), 7x64mm (new 1997), .300 Win. Mag. (new 1997), or 7mm Rem. Mag. (new 1997) cal., 16 lug bolt slides straight back allowing for low scope mounts, 22 or 24 (Mag. cals., new 1997) in. barrel, safety mechanism in bolt in addition to rear 3-position tang safety, checkered walnut stock, 4 (Mag. cals., new 1997) or 5 shot top loading mag., w/o sights, 6¼ lbs. Imported 1996-97.

| | $625 | $550 | $500 | $450 | $400 | $360 | $330 |

Last MSR was $699.

MODEL 98 COMMERCIAL - various cals., features original breech mechanisms refurbished to new condition, barrel, trigger system, and stock are new from factory.

This model was mostly distributed in Europe with no domestic MSR.

MODEL 1898 COMMEMORATIVE - 8x57mm Mauser cal., special limited edition model mfg. to commemorate the 100th anniversary of the original M-98, bright royal blue on most major metal parts, bolt and receiver have silver satin finish, checkered select European walnut. 1,998 mfg. 1998 only.

| | $2,175 | $1,775 | $1,500 |

Last MSR was $2,300.

MODEL 98 MAGNUM SAFARI - .375 H&H, .416 Rigby, .450 Dakota (new 2001), .458 Lott (new 2001), or .500 Jeffrey (new 2001) cal., original M-98 Magnum square bridge action with 3 lugs, Model 70 style wing safety, folding express sights, 24 in. barrel, features custom workmanship, extra select checkered walnut stock, 8.8 lbs. Limited mfg. beginning 1998.

| MSR | $9,500 | | $8,750 | $5,500 | $4,250 | $3,250 | $2,850 | $2,450 | $2,150 |

Add $1,000 for .500 Jeffrey cal.

This is the only Mauser model rifle currently manufactured (in Isny, Germany).

MODEL 99 - 5.6x57mm, 6.5x57mm, 7x57mm, 7x64mm, .243 Win., .25-06 Rem., .270 Win., .30-06 or .308 Win. cal., bolt action with 60 degree throw, 24 in. free-floating barrel, jeweled bolt, available in either hand-rubbed oil or high-luster lacquer finish for stock, mini-claw extractor, adj. single stage trigger, 4 shot detachable mag., no sights, 8 lbs. Imported 1989- disc.

* **Classic Lacquer Finish** - high-luster lacquer finish for stock.

| | $1,110 | $925 | $850 | $775 | $700 | $625 | $550 |

Last MSR was $1,272.

This model was available with either a Schnabel forearm with regular stock or rosewood capped forearm with American Monte Carlo stock.

* **Classic Oil Finish** - hand-rubbed oil finish for stock. Disc.

| | $1,130 | $995 | $875 | $775 | $700 | $625 | $550 |

Last MSR was $1,130.

This model was available with either a Schnabel forearm with regular stock or rosewood capped forearm with American Monte Carlo stock.

MODEL 99 MAGNUM - 8x68S, 9.3x64mm, 7mm Rem. Mag., .257 Wby. Mag., .270 Wby. Mag., .300 Wby. Mag., .300 Win. Mag., .338 Win. Mag., or .375 H&H cal., similar specifications as Model 99, except has 26 in. barrel and 3 shot mag. Imported 1989- disc.

* **Classic Lacquer Finish** - high-luster lacquer finish for stock.

| | $1,135 | $950 | $875 | $775 | $700 | $625 | $550 |

Last MSR was $1,322.

This model was available with either a Schnabel forearm with regular stock or rosewood capped forearm with American Monte Carlo stock.

* **Classic Oil Finish** - hand-rubbed oil finish for stock.

| | $1,025 | $895 | $795 | $725 | $625 | $550 | $495 |

Last MSR was $1,180.

This model is available with either a Schnabel forearm with regular stock or rosewood capped forearm with American Monte Carlo stock.

M

Grading	100%	98%	95%	90%	80%	70%	60%

MODEL 225 - available in 13 cals. between .243 Win. and .300 Wby. Mag., bolt action, 60 degree bolt lift with 3 locking lugs, ultra fast lock time, adj. trigger, 24 or 26 (Mag. only) in. barrel, 3 or 5 shot mag., no sights, guaranteed ½ in. accuracy at 100 yards, many stock options available at extra cost.

* ***Deluxe Standard Sporter*** - standard model available in 6 regular cals. and 9 Mag. cals. Importation disc. 1989.

	100%	98%	95%	90%	80%	70%	60%
	$1,275	$1,000	$875	$750	$625	$550	$495

Last MSR was $1,400.

Add $90 for Mag. cals.

This model was formerly the KDF Model K-15.

MODEL 226 - left-handed variation of the Model 225 with slight changes. Disc. 1989.

	100%	98%	95%	90%	80%	70%	60%
	$1,275	$1,000	$875	$750	$625	$550	$495

Last MSR was $1,400.

MODEL 2000 (DISC.) - .270 Win., .308 Win., or .30-06 cal., 5 shot mag., 24 in. barrel, leaf rear sight, checkered walnut stock. Mfg. by F.W. Heym for Mauser, 1969-1971.

	100%	98%	95%	90%	80%	70%	60%
	$495	$475	$450	$400	$375	$350	$325

MODEL 2000 CLASSIC - .270 Win., .30-06, .308 Win., .300 Win. Mag., or 7mm Rem. Mag. cal., features new design allowing interchangeable calibers from standard to standard and Magnum to Magnum models, bolt locks directly into barrel, detachable mag., deluxe walnut stock with checkering and rosewood forend, double function set trigger, high polish blue, includes studs. Limited importation 1998 only.

	100%	98%	95%	90%	80%	70%	60%
	$1,595	$1,375	$1,125	$950	$825	$700	$575

Last MSR was $1,800.

* ***Model 2000 Varmint*** - .22-250 Rem. or .243 Win. cal., choice of black synthetic or special varmint wood stock with accessory rail, heavy fluted barrel. Limited importation 1998 only.

	100%	98%	95%	90%	80%	70%	60%
	$1,900	$1,550	$1,350	$1,100	$900	$775	$650

Last MSR was $2,200.

* ***Model 2000 Sniper*** - .300 Win. Mag. or .308 Win. cal., features heavy fluted barrel, special set trigger system, bi-pod rail, and other special shooting performance features, satin blue metal finish, custom built with individual certificate. Limited importation 1998 only.

	100%	98%	95%	90%	80%	70%	60%
	$1,900	$1,550	$1,350	$1,100	$900	$775	$650

Last MSR was $2,200.

* ***Model 2000 Professional*** - .300 Win. Mag. or .308 Win. cal., features recoil reduction compensator, camo all- weather special pistol grip stock, satin blue metal finish, custom built with individual certificate. Limited importation 1998 only.

	100%	98%	95%	90%	80%	70%	60%
	$3,175	$2,725	$2,400	$2,100	$1,800	$1,500	$1,250

Last MSR was $3,500.

MODEL 3000 - .243 Win., .270 Win., .308 Win., or .30-06 cal., 5 shot mag., 22 in. barrel, no sights, walnut Monte Carlo style stock, rosewood forearm and pistol grip, skipline checkering, recoil pad and swivels. Mfg. 1971-1974.

	100%	98%	95%	90%	80%	70%	60%
	$525	$475	$450	$425	$395	$335	$285

MODEL 3000 MAGNUM - similar to 3000, except 7mm Rem. Mag., .300 Win. Mag., or .375 H&H cal., 3 shot mag., 26 in. barrel.

	100%	98%	95%	90%	80%	70%	60%
	$575	$525	$475	$450	$415	$350	$295

This model was mfg. by Heym for Mauser.

MODEL 4000 VARMINT RIFLE - similar to 3000, except smaller action, .222 Rem. or .223 Rem. cal., folding leaf rear sight, rubber butt plate.

	100%	98%	95%	90%	80%	70%	60%
	$425	$400	$375	$350	$300	$260	$225

This model was mfg. by Heym for Mauser.

Grading	100%	98%	95%	90%	80%	70%	60%

LIGHTNING MODEL - .308 Win. or 7.62x39mm cal., slide-bolt action, locking bolt similar to M-16 enabling locking directly onto free floating short barrel, fixed internal mag., specially bedded receiver, satin blue finish or stainless steel, open sights, synthetic stock available in black, light grey, blue, or NATO green. Limited importation 1998 only.

	$495	$425	$375	$325	$295	$275	$250

Last MSR was $550.

LIGHTNING HUNTER MODEL - .243 Win., .270 Win., .30-06, .308 Win., .300 Win. Mag., or 7mm Rem. Mag. cal., slide-bolt mechanism, detachable mag., choice of satin blue or bright blue metal finish, checkered satin or high gloss walnut stock, with or w/o sights, free floating barrel, bedded receiver. Limited importation 1998 only.

	$650	$575	$500	$450	$400	$360	$330

Last MSR was $730.

Add $50 for open sights.
Add $20 for bright blue metal finish with high gloss stock.

✳ *Lightning Hunter Stainless Steel Model* - similar to Lightning Hunter Model, except has satin finish stainless steel receiver and barrel, checkered satin finished walnut stock. Limited importation 1998 only.

	$665	$585	$500				

Last MSR was $750.

Add $50 for open sights.

LIGHTNING HUNTER ALL-WEATHER MODEL - similar to Lightning Hunter, except has black synthetic stock, satin blue metal finish, scope mounts included, with or w/o sights. Limited importation 1998 only.

	$625	$550	$475	$400	$350	$325	$295

Last MSR was $700.

Add $50 for open sights.

✳ *Lightning All-Weather Stainless Steel* - similar to Lightning Hunter All-Weather Model, except is satin stainless steel. Limited importation 1998 only.

	$650	$575	$500				

Last MSR was $730.

Add $50 for open sights.

LIGHTNING VARMINT MODEL - .22-250 Rem., .243 Win., features slide-bolt action, free floating heavy fluted barrel, satin blue metal finish, choice of special varmint wood or synthetic stock. Limited importation 1998 only.

	$895	$775	$675	$600	$525	$475	$425

Last MSR was $1,000.

✳ *Lightning Varmint Model Stainless* - similar to Lightning Varmint Model, except is satin stainless steel. Limited importation 1998 only.

	$895	$775	$675				

Last MSR was $1,000.

LIGHTNING SNIPER MODEL - .300 Win. Mag. or .308 Win. cal., slide-bolt action, features free floating heavy fluted barrel w/o sights, special wood or synthetic stock with built in bi-pod rail, detachable mag., satin blue metal finish. Limited importation 1998 only.

	$895	$775	$675	$600	$525	$475	$425

Last MSR was $1,000.

✳ *Lightning Sniper Model Stainless* - similar to Lightning Sniper Model, except is satin stainless steel. Limited importation 1998 only.

	$895	$775	$675				

Last MSR was $1,000.

M

Grading	100%	98%	95%	90%	80%	70%	60%

LIGHTNING PROFESSIONAL MODEL - .300 Win. Mag. or .308 Win. cal., slide- bolt action, features special black or camo synthetic adj. stock with pistol grip, special tuned trigger system, free floating heavy fluted barrel, recoil reduction compensator. Limited importation 1998 only.

		$1,595	$1,375	$1,125	$950	$825	$700	$575

Last MSR was $1,800.

RIFLES: BOLT ACTION, .22 CAL.

MODEL 20/22 - .22 LR or .22 Mag. cal., bolt action, features free floating barrel, precision trigger, standard or deluxe checkered walnut stock with stock. Limited importation 1998 only.

	$625	$550	$475	$400	$350	$325	$295

Last MSR was $700.

Add $100 for Deluxe Model.

MODEL 107 STANDARD - .22 LR cal. only, bolt action, 19½ in. barrel, 5 shot mag., adj. iron sights, 6 lbs. Imported 1988-89, reintroduced 1993 only.

	$300	$260	$215	$185	$170	$155	$140

Last MSR was $356.

This model is the same as KDF's previous Model 2107 mfg. by Voere.

✱ *Model 107 Deluxe* - .22 LR or .22 Mag. cal., similar to Model 107, except has deluxe checkered walnut. Imported 1988-89 only.

	$290	$240	$210	$175	$150	$135	$120

Last MSR was $320.

Add $90 for .22 Mag. cal.

This model is the same as KDF's previous Model 2107 Deluxe mfg. by Voere.

MODEL 201 - .22 LR or .22 Mag. cal., bolt action, free-floating 21 in. barrel, 5 shot mag., adj. trigger, scaled-down version of the K-15, unusual action incorporates two front- located locking lugs on bolt face that engage Stellite inserts on the front receiver portion, blue only, no sights, beechwood stock with cheekpiece, 6½ lbs. Disc. 1997.

	$635	$515	$465	$415	$365	$315	$260

Last MSR was $716.

Add $19 for sights (disc.).
Add $77 for .22 Mag. cal. (Model 201-SM).

This model is the same as KDF's disc. Model K-22 mfg. by Voere. Before 1989, this model came standard with a walnut stock.

✱ *Model 201 Luxus* - similar to the Model 201 except has walnut stock with rosewood forend. Disc. 1997.

	$710	$650	$550	$475	$425	$375	$295

Last MSR was $809.

Add $27 for sights (disc.).
Add $67 for .22 Mag. cal.

This model is the same as KDF's previous Model K-22 Deluxe mfg. by Voere.

MODEL DSM34 - .22 LR cal., bolt action, 25.98 in. barrel. "Deutsches Sportmodell" lightweight trainer, side sling, no bayonet lug.

	$625	$375	$325	$300	$260	$225	$200

MODEL MS 420B - .22 LR Sporter cal., bolt action, pre-war, 5 shot mag.

	$1,425	$875	$725	$625	$525	$450	$395

Add 15%-25% for double set triggers (rare).

MODEL ES340 - .22 LR cal., single shot, bolt action, 25½ in. barrel, adj. sights, checkered pistol grip, grooved forearm, pre-1935.

	$725	$425	$350	$325	$295	$260	$230

M

Grading	100%	98%	95%	90%	80%	70%	60%

MODEL ES350 - .22 LR cal., single shot, bolt action, 27½ in. barrel, championship rifle, micrometer rear sight, ramp front sight, checkered full target stock, swivels, pre-1935.

| | $925 | $550 | $500 | $460 | $430 | $400 | $375 |

    Add 15%-25% for double set triggers (rare).

MODEL M410 - .22 LR cal., bolt action, repeating, 5 shot detachable mag., 23½ in. barrel, adj. sights, sporter stock, checkered pistol grip, swivels, pre-1935.

| | $1,425 | $875 | $725 | $625 | $525 | $450 | $395 |

    Add 15%-25% for double set triggers (rare).

MODEL M420 - .22 LR cal., bolt action, repeating, 5 shot detachable mag., 25½ in. barrel, adj. sights, sporter stock, checkered pistol grip, swivels, pre-1935.

| | $1,425 | $875 | $725 | $625 | $525 | $450 | $395 |

    Add 15%-25% for double set triggers (rare).

MODEL EN310 - .22 LR cal., single shot, bolt action, 19¾ in. barrel, fixed sights, plain pistol grip stock, pre-1935.

| | $625 | $365 | $315 | $280 | $260 | $225 | $200 |

MODEL EL320 - .22 LR cal., single shot, bolt action, 23½ in. barrel, fixed sights, checkered pistol grip stock.

| | $695 | $395 | $330 | $295 | $275 | $250 | $225 |

MODEL KKW - .22 LR cal., single shot, bolt action, target, 26 in. barrel, tangent rear sight, military style stock with bayonet lug. This weapon was also produced by Walther, Gustloff, and Anschütz. It was used as a training rifle in addition to commercial sales. Deduct 15% for 4mm KKW Models.

| | $625 | $375 | $325 | $300 | $260 | $225 | $200 |

MODEL MS350B - .22 LR cal., bolt action, repeating, 5 shot mag., 26¾ in. barrel, grooved receiver for scope or sight, micrometer rear sight, ramp front sight, target stock, checkered pistol grip and forearm, swivels.

| | $1,200 | $725 | $650 | $550 | $495 | $450 | $395 |

MODEL ES350B - .22 LR cal., bolt action, single shot, 5 shot mag., 26¾ in. barrel, grooved receiver for scope or sight, micrometer rear sight, ramp front sight, target stock, checkered pistol grip and forearm, swivels.

| | $750 | $425 | $350 | $325 | $295 | $260 | $230 |

MODEL ES340B - .22 LR cal., bolt action, single shot, 26¾ in. barrel, adj. sight, plain pistol grip stock.

| | $650 | $375 | $325 | $300 | $260 | $225 | $200 |

MODEL MM410BN - .22 LR cal., bolt action sporter, 5 shot mag., 23½ in. barrel, adj. sights, lightweight stock, checkered pistol grip, swivels.

| | $1,295 | $775 | $675 | $575 | $475 | $400 | $375 |

MODEL MS420B - .22 LR cal., bolt action target, 5 shot mag., 26¾ in. barrel, adj. sights, target style stock, checkered pistol grip, swivels.

| | $1,100 | $650 | $575 | $500 | $450 | $400 | $365 |

RIFLES: SEMI-AUTO, .22 LR

MODEL 105 STANDARD - .22 LR cal. only, 10 shot mag., approx. 5 lbs. Imported 1995-97.

| | $285 | $250 | $205 | $180 | $170 | $155 | $140 |

    Last MSR was $330.

M

Grading	100%	98%	95%	90%	80%	70%	60%

SHOTGUNS

Mauser shotguns were sub-contracted to various European firms and were made in various O/U (including field and target), SxS (both boxlock and sidelock), and single shot configurations. While they are relatively rare (these shotguns had limited importation into the U.S. by Bauer located in Michigan - models included the 496 single shot, 496 SxS, 580 SxS, 610 O/U, 620 O/U, 71E O/U, and others), collectability to date has been minimal. Values will depend on the grade, configuration, features, engraving, and overall desirability. Most of these shotguns have been priced in the $395-$1,350 range, depending on the configuration's desirability.

MAVERICK ARMS, INC.

Currently manufactured by Maverick Arms, Inc. located in Eagle Pass, TX. Administrative offices are at O.F. Mossberg & Sons, located in North Haven, CT. Distributor sales only.

SHOTGUNS

Beginning 1992, all Maverick slide action shotguns incorporate twin slide rails in the operating mechanism.

MODEL 60 SEMI-AUTO - while advertised, this model was never manufactured.

MODEL 88 FIELD SLIDE ACTION - 12 ga. only, 3 in. chamber, slide-action, 24 (Deer Model with iron sights), 28, or 30 in. plain or VR barrel, wood (disc.) or black synthetic stock and forearm with recoil pad, fixed or Accu-chokes (disc. 1997, reintroduced 2002), 6 shot (w/2¾ in. shot shells), aluminum alloy receiver, crossbolt safety, approx. 7¼ lbs. New 1989.

MSR	$229	$195	$160	$140	$125	$115	$105	$100

Add $14 for Deer Model (24 in. cyl. bore barrel, disc. 1996).
Add $20 for Accu-choke barrel with single tube.

* ***Model 88 Deer Combos*** - includes various combinations of extra Deer barrels with rifle sights, 28 in. plain or VR barrel, or extra 18½ in. cyl. bore barrel. Mfg. 1990-95.

		$245	$190	$160	$130	$120	$110	$105

Last MSR was $294.

Add $10 for VR barrel.
Add $17 for Accu-choke barrel.
Add $29 for wood stock and forearm (mfg. 1992 only).

* ***Model 88 Security*** - 12 ga., 18½ in. barrel with cyl. bore choke, regular or pistol grip (disc. 1997) synthetic stock, 6 or 8 shot, plain synthetic forearm. New 1993.

MSR	$221	$185	$150	$130	$115	$110	$105	$100

Add $98 for Bullpup configuration (6 or 9 shot) (disc. 1994).
Add $47-$65 for combo package (disc.).

* ***Model 88 Combat*** - 12 ga. only, combat design featuring pistol grip stock and forearm, black synthetic stock is extension of receiver, 18½ in. cyl. bore barrel with vented shroud with built- in carrying handle, open sights. Mfg. 1990-92.

		$375	$335	$285	$250	$225	$200	$185

Last MSR was $282.

MODEL 91 SLIDE ACTION - 12 ga. only, 3½ in. chamber, 18½ cyl. bore or 28 in. VR barrel with 1 choke tube, otherwise similar to Model 88. Mfg. 1991-95.

		$230	$190	$170	$160	$150	$140	$130

Last MSR was $269.

Add $2 for VR barrel.

Grading	100%	98%	95%	90%	80%	70%	60%

MODEL 95 BOLT ACTION - 12 ga. only, 3 in. chamber, synthetic stock with recoil pad, 25 in. barrel bored mod., cross-bolt triggerguard safety. Mfg. 1995-97.

	$155	$135	$115	$100	$90	$80	$70

Last MSR was $184.

McMILLAN BROS. RIFLE CO.

Current manufacturer located in Phoenix, AZ since 1993. Dealer and consumer direct sales. During 1998, the company name changed from McBros Rifles to McMillan Bros. Rifle Co.

RIFLES: BOLT ACTION

AMERICAN HUNTER - available in 16 cals. between .22-250 Rem. and .416 Rem. Mag. (disc. 1997), camouflaged fiberglass stock, match grade stainless steel barrel, choice of MCRT (Rem. Model 700 custom type action mfg. to aerospace standards) or MCR (disc., Rem. Model 700 BDL action that has been trued). New 1993.

MSR	$3,400	$2,925	$2,450	$2,100	$1,825	$1,550	$1,375	$1,100

✳ *Yukon Hunter* - available in 6 Mag. cals. between .300 Wby. Mag. and .458 Win. Mag., built to aerospace tolerances for any hunting situation, barrel band sling swivel, folding leaf sight, black synthetic stock. New 1993.

MSR	$3,700	$3,350	$2,800	$2,400	$2,050	$1,775	$1,500	$1,350

✳ *Outdoorsman* - .30-378 Wby. Mag. or .338-378 Wby. Mag. (disc. 1997) cal., RT action only. New 1996.

MSR	$3,700	$3,350	$2,800	$2,400	$2,050	$1,775	$1,500	$1,350

MCR TACTICAL - .308 Win. or .300 Win. Mag. cal. New 1993.

MSR	$3,100	$2,700	$2,250	$1,825	$1,500	$1,250	$1,050	$925

This model was formerly designated the MCR Sniper Model.

✳ *MCRT Tactical* - similar to MCR Tactical, except is also available in .338 Lapua (new 1998). New 1993.

MSR	$3,400	$2,925	$2,450	$2,100	$1,825	$1,550	$1,375	$1,100

Add $600 for .338 Lapua Mag (muzzle brake is standard).
This model was formerly designated the MCRT Sniper Model.

BENCHREST COMPETITOR - .222 Rem., 6mm PPC, 6mm BR, 7mm BR, or .308 Win. cal., benchrest configuration. Mfg. 1993-99.

	$2,400	$1,925	$1,575	$1,275	$1,050	$900	$775

Last MSR was $2,800.

1000 YARD BENCHREST (NATIONAL MATCH COMPETITOR) - .300 Win. Mag. (new 1996), .30-378 Wby. Mag. (new 1996), 7.82 Warbird (new 1996), .308 Win. (disc. 1995) or .338-378 Wby. Mag. (mfg. 1996-97) cal. Mfg. 1993-99.

	$2,450	$1,950	$1,575	$1,275	$1,050	$900	$775

Last MSR was $2,875.

TUBB 2000 - .243 Win., .260 Rem., 7mm-08 Rem., 6mmX, or .308 Win. cal., target rifle featuring metal 4 way adj. stock, Picatinny rail, hand lapped Schneider match barrel, Anschütz 2 stage trigger, state-of-the-art action, vent. handguard, 12 lbs. New 2000.

MSR	$2,650	$2,375	$1,925	$1,525	$1,250	$1,025	$875	$750

Add $300 for Tubb 2000 C (includes four 10 shot mags., cleaning rod guide, etc.).

Grading	100%	98%	95%	90%	80%	70%	60%

BOOMER - .50 BMG cal., available as either single shot sporter, repeater sporter, light benchrest, or heavy benchrest variation. New 1993.

	MSR	$4,800	$4,250	$3,650	$3,050	$2,550	$2,125	$1,825	$1,525

    Add $200 for repeating action.
    Add $400 for Tactical 50 variation.
    Add $100 for single shot.
    Add $100 for heavy benchrest variation.
    Subtract $100 for light benchrest variation.

McMILLAN, G. & CO., INC.

    Previous trademark established circa 1988, located in Phoenix, AZ.

    G. McMillan & Co., Inc. had various barrel markings from 1988-1995 including G. McMillan, Harris - McMillan, and Harris Gunworks.

HANDGUNS

WOLVERINE - available in 9mm Para., 10mm, .38 Super, .38 Wad Cutter, .40 S&W, .45 ACP, or .45 Italian cal., interchangeable barrels, competition ready handgun patterned after the Colt 1911. Imported 1992-95.

✳ *Combat Wolverine* - combat features including 5½ in. compensated barrel.

	$1,600	$1,350	$1,025	$875	$750	$625	$550

                                                 Last MSR was $1,700.

✳ *Competition Match Wolverine* - competition features including 6 in. non-compensated barrel.

	$1,600	$1,350	$1,025	$875	$750	$625	$550

                                                 Last MSR was $1,700.

SIGNATURE JR. BOLT ACTION - available in a variety of cals., utilizes Signature benchrest short action, choice of stainless steel barrel lengths, right or left-hand action, single shot or repeater, McMillan design fiberglass stock, choice of electroless nickel or Teflon finish, 5 lbs. Mfg. 1992-95.

	$2,175	$1,775	$1,350	$995	$895	$800	$700

                                                 Last MSR was $2,400.

    This model was also available in all titanium.

RIFLES: BOLT ACTION

The models listed were also available with custom wood stocks at varying prices. McMillan also manufactured a custom rifle from a supplied action - features included new barreling, a fiberglass stock, matte black finish, and range testing to guarantee ¾ M.O.A. Prices started at $1,400.

    Add $150 for stainless steel receiver on most models.

TALON SPORTER - available in various cals. between .22-250 Rem. and .416 Rem., receiver available in either 4340 chrome molybdenum or 17-4 stainless steel, drilled and tapped, match grade barrel. Mfg. 1992-95.

	$2,375	$1,950	$1,650	$1,325	$1,000	$895	$800

                                                 Last MSR was $2,600.

    The Talon action was patterned after the Winchester pre-64 Model 70. It features a cone breech, controlled feed, claw extractor, and 3 position safety.

SIGNATURE CLASSIC SPORTER - various cals. available between .22-250 Rem. and .416 Rem., premium wood stock, matte metal finish, 22 or 24 in. stainless steel barrel with button rifling, McMillan action made from 4340 chrome moly steel (either left or right-handed), 3 or 4 shot mag. supplied with 5 shot test target. Mfg. 1988-95.

	$2,250	$1,850	$1,350	$950	$850	$750	$675

                                                 Last MSR was $2,400.

Grading	100%	98%	95%	90%	80%	70%	60%

SIGNATURE VARMINTER - similar to Signature Model, except is available in 10 cals. between .22-250 Rem. and .350 Rem. Mag., hand bedded fiberglass stock, adj. trigger, 26 in. heavy contour barrel. Mfg. 1988-95.

	$2,250	$1,850	$1,350	$995	$895	$800	$700

Last MSR was $2,400.

SIGNATURE TITANIUM MOUNTAIN RIFLE - .270 Win., .280 Rem., .30-06, .300 Win. Mag., .338 Win. Mag., or 7mm Rem. Mag. cal., lighter weight variation with shorter barrel. Mfg. 1990-95.

	$2,750	$2,195	$1,850	$1,450	$1,100	$925	$825

Last MSR was $3,000.

Add $605 for titanium alloy light contour match grade barrel.

SIGNATURE ALASKAN - available in 11 cals. between .270 Win. and .416 Rem. Mfg. 1990- 95.

	$3,050	$2,475	$2,100	$1,575	$1,200	$1,000	$900

Last MSR was $3,300.

TALON SAFARI - available in 15 cals. between .300 Win. Mag. and .460 Weatherby, hand-bedded fiberglass stock, 4 shot mag., 24 in. stainless steel barrel, matte black finish, 9½ lbs. Mfg. 1988- 95.

	$3,275	$2,675	$2,300	$1,675	$1,300	$1,100	$950

Last MSR was $3,600.

Add $600 for .300 Phoenix, .338 Lapua, .378 Wby. Mag., .416 Wby. Mag. or Rigby, or .460 Wby. Mag. cal.

The Talon action was patterned after the Winchester pre-64 Model 70. It featured a cone breech, controlled feed, claw extractor, and 3-position safety. Older Signature action rifles did not have this new Talon action.

M-40 SNIPER RIFLE - .308 Win. cal., Remington action with McMillan match grade heavy contour barrel, fiberglass stock with recoil pad, 4 shot mag., 9 lbs. Mfg. 1990-95.

	$1,675	$1,375	$1,050	$895	$800	$700	$600

Last MSR was $1,800.

M-86 SNIPER RIFLE - .300 Phoenix, .30-06 (new 1989), .300 Win. Mag. or .308 Win. cal., fiberglass stock, variety of optical sights. Mfg. 1988-95.

	$1,725	$1,400	$1,075	$925	$825	$725	$625

Last MSR was $1,900.

Add $550 for .300 Phoenix cal.
Add $200 for takedown feature (new 1993).

❋ *M-86 Sniper System* - includes Model 86 Sniper Rifle, bipod, Ultra scope, rings, and bases. Cased. Mfg. 1988-92.

	$2,460	$2,050	$1,825	$1,600	$1,350	$1,100	$950

Last MSR was $2,665.

M-87 LONG RANGE SNIPER RIFLE - .50 BMG cal., stainless steel bolt action, 29 in. barrel with muzzle brake, single shot, camo synthetic stock, accurate to 1500 meters, 21 lbs. Mfg. 1988-95.

	$3,350	$2,750	$2,350	$2,000	$1,850	$1,700	$1,575

Last MSR was $3,735.

❋ *M-87 Sniper System* - includes Model 87 Sniper Rifle, bipod, 20X Ultra scope, rings, and bases. Cased. Mfg. 1988-92.

	$3,950	$3,400	$3,000	$2,750	$2,450	$2,200	$2,000

Last MSR was $4,200.

❋ *M-87R* - same specs. as Model 87, except has 5 shot fixed box mag. Mfg. 1990-95.

	$3,750	$2,950	$2,550	$2,200	$2,000	$1,850	$1,700

Last MSR was $4,000.

Add $300 for Combo option.

Grading	100%	98%	95%	90%	80%	70%	60%

M-89 SNIPER RIFLE - .308 Win. cal., 28 in. barrel with suppressor (also available without), fiberglass stock adj. for length and recoil pad, 15¼ lbs. Mfg. 1990-95.

	$2,075	$1,675	$1,375	$1,050	$895	$800	$700

Last MSR was $2,300.

Add $425 for muzzle suppressor.

M-92 BULLPUP - .50 BMG cal., bullpup configuration with shorter barrel. Mfg. 1993- 95.

	$3,750	$2,950	$2,550	$2,200	$2,000	$1,850	$1,700

Last MSR was $4,000.

M-93SN - .50 BMG cal., similar to M-87, except has folding stock and detachable 5 or 10 shot box mag. Mfg. 1993-95.

	$3,950	$3,250	$2,750	$2,300	$2,000	$1,850	$1,700

Last MSR was $4,300.

.300 PHOENIX LONG RANGE RIFLE - .300 Phoenix cal., special fiberglass stock featuring adj. cheekpieces to accommodate night vision optics, adj. buttplate, 29 in. barrel, conventional box mag., 12½ lbs. Mfg. 1992 only.

	$2,700	$2,195	$1,850	$1,450	$1,100	$925	$825

Last MSR was $3,000.

.300 Phoenix was a cartridge developed to function at ranges in excess of 800 yards. It produces muzzle velocities of 3100 ft. per second with a 250 grain bullet.

COMPETITION MODELS - available in Metallic Silhouette (.308 Win. or 7mm-08 Rem. cal. - disc. 1989), National Match (.308 Win. cal. only), Long Range (.300 Win. Mag. only), or Bench Rest (shooter's choice). Each model made specifically for individual competition events. Mfg. 1988-95.

MSR	$2,600	$2,325	$1,775	$1,450	$1,100	$895	$800	$700

Last MSR was $2,600.

Add $200 for Benchrest Model.
Subtract $300 for Metallic Silhouette model (disc. 1989).

M MEDWELL & PERRETT LIMITED

Current long gun manufacturer located in Suffolk, England. Consumer direct sales.

Medwell & Perrett manufactures best quality bolt action and double rifles, in addition to O/U shotguns. Delivery time is approx. 6-18 months, depending on caliber and configuration.

RIFLES

MEDWELL & PERRETT BOLT ACTION - various cals. up to .505 Gibbs, Medwell & Perrett action, Timney adj. trigger, select checkered walnut stock and forend, custom order only.

MSR	$9,480	$9,480	$8,600	$7,500	$6,500	$5,500	$4,500	$3,500

Add $820 for Mag. length action.
Add $2,340 for .500 Jeffrey or .505 Gibbs cal.
Add $1,770 for take down action.

MEDWELL & PERRETT SQUARE BRIDGE BOLT ACTION - various cals. up to .505 Gibbs, square bridge action, integral telescopic mount system, barrel quarter rib, adj. trigger, deluxe checkered walnut stock and forend.

MSR	$15,320	$15,320	$12,950	$9,950	$8,500	$7,250	$6,000	$5,500

Add $815 for Mag. length action.
Add $1,530 for .500 Jeffrey or .505 Gibbs cal.

Grading	100%	98%	95%	90%	80%	70%	60%

DOUBLE RIFLE SxS - most cals. up to .600 NE, back action, sidelock, ejectors, reinforced bolsters, DT, 22-26 in. chopper lumb barrels with folding express sights, oil finished checkered walnut stock and forearm, 8 lbs. , 14 oz. – 14 lbs., 4 oz.

MSR $42,000	$42,000	$38,000	$32,000	$26,500	$21,000	$16,000	$12,000

Add $525 for detachable sidelocks.
Add $3,750 for cals over .375 H&H - .470 NE.
Add $9,180 for cals. over .470 NE - .577 NE.
Add $12,500 for .600 NE cal.

SHOTGUNS

O/U SIDELOCK - 12, 16, 20, 28 ga. or .410 bore, back action, sidelock, ejectors, ST, 25- 30 in. barrels, oil finished deluxe walnut stock and forearm, house engraving pattern is standard, 5 lbs., 6 oz. – 7 lbs., 4 oz.

MSR $39,420	$39,420	$35,000	$30,000	$25,000	$20,000	$16,000	$13,500

Add $4,560 for 28 ga. or .410 bore.
Add $7,200 for an extra set of interchangeable barrels (if ordered with new gun).
Add $630 for Teague choke tubes.

SxS SIDELOCK - 12, 16, 20, 28 ga. or .410 bore, ejectors, best quality SxS. New 2001.

MSR $34,750	$34,750	$31,000	$26,000	$22,000	$18,000	$14,000	$11,000

Add $4,440 for 28 ga. or .410 bore.

MENZ, AUGUST

Previous manufacturer located in Suhl, Germany.

Please refer to listings in the Liliput section of this text.

MERCURY

Previous importer of Spanish manufactured shotguns.

SHOTGUNS: SxS

MAGNUM MODEL - 10, 12, or 20 ga. Mag., 28 and 32 in. barrels, full and mod., boxlock, extractors, double triggers, engraved frame, checkered pistol grip stock.

	100%	98%	95%	90%	80%	70%	60%
12 or 20 ga.	$300	$275	$250	$225	$200	$180	$150
10 ga.	$400	$375	$325	$300	$275	$225	$200

MERCURY

Previous manufacturer located in Belgium. Previously imported 1962-68 by Tradewinds, Inc. located in Tacoma, WA.

PISTOLS: SEMI-AUTO

MERCURY MODEL - .22 LR cal., 7 shot mag., steel frame, fixed sights.

	100%	98%	95%	90%	80%	70%	60%
	$400	$375	$325	$300	$275	$225	$200

MERKEL

Current trademark manufactured by Suhler Jagd-und Sportwaffen GmbH located in Suhl, Germany since circa 1898. Currently imported exclusively by GSI located in Trussville, AL. Previously imported (until 1992) by Armes De Chasse located in Chadds Ford, PA.

Merkel

For many years Merkel shotguns had a unfair disadvantage in this country because of the politics of importing firearms from communist bloc countries (goods were subject to a 65% non-favored nation tax). With the reunification of Germany in 1991, this trademark has become more competitive domestically. Merkel continues to manufacture high quality guns. Merkel is

M

Grading	100%	98%	95%	90%	80%	70%	60%

currently owned by the Steyr Group, located in Austria.

Beginning 1995, Merkel serialization employs an alpha numeric date code for year of manufacture, making it difficult to determine year of manufacture by serial number. Higher grade models (including the 300 Series) continue to be manufactured one at a time by hand, with less than 30 being mfg. annually.

Many Merkel collectors are now categorizing older production guns into 3 different categories. The first is guns made before 1962, when the Berlin Wall was created. The second is the GDR guns (German Democratic Republic). The last is after the Berlin wall came down (post-1991). Premiums are paid on pre-WWII manufacture and some GDR guns. These older production models should be appraised by a knowledgeable person, since there are a lot of things to consider when evaluating these earlier Merkels. Some guns made up for the Nürnberg and Leipzig trade shows have top quality workmanship, especially the engraving.

On all factory engraved Merkels manufactured since 1992, the engraver's signature will appear.

COMBINATION GUNS

O/U MODEL - 12, 16, or 20 ga. (2¾ in. chamber) over 5.6x50R, 5.6x52R, 6.5x55mm, 6.5x57R, 7x57R, 7x65R, 8x57JRS, 9.3x74R, .22 Hornet (disc. 1997), .222 Rem., .243 Win., .30-06, .308 Win., or .375 H&H (disc. 1994) cal., 25.6 in. barrels, various chokes. Disc. 1999.

* ***Model 210E***

$5,700	$4,600	$3,700	$3,150	$2,600	$2,100	$1,800

Last MSR was $6,195.

* ***Model 211E***

$6,650	$4,750	$3,900	$3,300	$2,775	$2,275	$1,925

Last MSR was $7,495.

* ***Model 213E*** - disc. 1997.

$13,000	$10,750	$8,250	$6,975	$5,825	$4,600	$3,550

Last MSR was $14,795.

* ***Model 313E*** - disc. 1997.

$19,350	$14,950	$12,500	$9,950	$8,350	$7,100	$5,900

Last MSR was $22,795.

MODEL 314 - 12 ga. over 8x60mm Mag. cal., detachable H&H sidelock system, elaborate scroll engraving. Disc. pre-WWII.

$21,250	$15,750	$13,000	$10,000	$8,500	$7,200	$6,200

SxS MODEL - similar gauges and cals. to O/U Combination Gun, boxlock models included 8EI and 9EI, 10EI is a sidelock, boxlock models ranged in MSRs from $5,500- $7,000 and the Model 10EI MSR was $9,500. Importation disc. 1990.

DRILLINGS

Previously, the Drilling Models 90 (disc. 1994), 90S (disc. 1997), 90K (disc. 1997), 95 (disc. 1994), 95K (disc. 1998), and 95S (disc. 1997) were also imported. Models differ in the amount of engraving, cocking systems, and quality of wood.

MODEL 96K - choice of 12, 16, or 20 ga., with the rifle barrel being bored in most popular U.S. and metric cals. between .22 Hornet and 9.3x74R (disc.), 23.6 in. barrels, current models are boxlocks with Greener crossbolt and double under barrel locking lugs, extractors, tang mounted cocking for rifle, case hardened receiver with Arabesque scroll engraving, DT, fitted leather case.

MSR	$7,495		$6,875	$5,700	$4,600	$3,550	$3,000	$2,500	$1,995

Add $1,100 for hunting scene engraving (Model 96K Engraved).

MERKEL ANSON DRILLING - usually 2 shotguns over rifle, although 2 rifles over shotgun have been noted, 12, 16, or 20 ga., calibers 7x57R, 8x57JR, and 9.3x74R cals. most common, others noted, 25.6 in. or 21.6 in. barrels, boxlock, Anson & Deeley system, double triggers, extractors, checkered pistol grip stock, pre-WWII.

Grading	100%	98%	95%	90%	80%	70%	60%

MODEL 142 - engraved.

	$5,000	$4,000	$3,000	$2,750	$2,500	$2,200	$2,000

MODEL 142 - less ornamentation.

	$4,000	$3,500	$3,000	$2,500	$2,250	$2,100	$2,000

MODEL 145 - least ornamentation.

	$3,000	$2,800	$2,700	$2,600	$2,500	$2,100	$1,900

RIFLES: BOLT ACTION

MODEL 190 - various cals., Mauser M-98 system, checkered walnut stock and extended forend, values depend on caliber and action size. Disc. pre-WWII.

	$7,500	$6,500	$5,275	$4,200	$3,200	$2,350	$1,500

Premiums exist for Magnum or Kurz (short) action.

RIFLES: SINGLE SHOT

MODEL K1 LIGHTWEIGHT STALKING RIFLE - available in 9 cals. between .243 Win. - 9.3x74R, Franz Jaeger break open action, cocking/uncocking slide type safety, matte silver receiver, adj. trigger pull, 23.6 in. barrel, pistol grip, includes 1 in. or 30mm quick detachable mounts, silver border engraving is standard, 5 lbs., 5 oz. Importation began 2002.

MSR $3,795		$3,400	$2,950	$2,600	$2,250	$1,900	$1,600	$1,300

Add $300 for Premium Model with light arabesque scroll engraving.
Add $600 for Jagd Model with fine hunting scene engraving.

MODEL 180 - various cals., with (Model 180E) or w/o ejector, double triggers, checkered walnut stock and extended forend, values depend on caliber and action size. Disc. pre- WWII.

	$8,500	$7,250	$5,775	$4,600	$3,750	$3,000	$2,500

MODEL 183E - various cals., top of the line rifle with elaborate engraving. Disc. pre- WWII.

	$12,500	$10,750	$8,250	$6,975	$5,825	$4,600	$3,550

RIFLES: DOUBLE

O/U MODEL - same cals. as the O/U Combination Gun, various actions, engraving options, and other special orders.

* ***Model 220E Boxlock*** - boxlock Blitz action, scroll engraved case hardened receiver, DTs, pistol grip with cheekpiece. Importation disc. 1994.

	$9,575	$8,250	$7,150	$6,100	$5,100	$4,250	$3,500

Last MSR was $10,795.

* ***Model 221E Boxlock*** - similar to 220E, except has silver-grey receiver with hunting scene engraving. Disc. 1998.

	$9,975	$8,450	$7,450	$6,300	$5,100	$4,250	$3,350

Last MSR was $10,895.

* ***Model 223E Sidelock*** - sidelock action with arabesque engraving featuring large scrolls, sideplates removed without tools. Disc. 1997.

	$16,250	$13,650	$11,000	$9,750	$8,500	$7,400	$6,250

Last MSR was $17,895.

* ***Model 323E Sidelock*** - similar to 223E Sidelock, except has medium scrollwork engraving, top-of-the-line O/U double rifle. Disc. 1997.

	$23,300	$20,000	$17,500	$13,500	$11,250	$9,750	$8,350

Last MSR was $27,195.

M

Merkel

Grading	100%	98%	95%	90%	80%	70%	60%

MODEL 324 O/U - 8x60mm Mag. cal., premium quality pre-WWII double rifle, elaborate scroll engraving and best quality walnut. Disc. pre-WWII.

	$26,500	$23,000	$20,000	$17,500	$13,500	$11,250	$9,750

SxS MODEL - same cals. as listed for the O/U Combination Gun.

✱ ***Model 140-1*** - Anson & Deeley boxlock action with cocking indicators, double triggers, engraved case hardened receiver. Importation began 1994.

MSR	$6,695		$5,725	$4,250	$3,175	$2,525	$2,000	$1,825	$1,675

Subtract approx. $400 if w/o H&H ejectors (pre-2002).
Add approx. $200 for set front trigger.
Add $1,100 for engraved hunting scenes on silver/grey receiver (Model 140-1.1).

✱ ***Model 140-2*** - .375 H&H, .416 Rigby, or .470 NE cal., similar to Model 140-1, except has scroll engraved silver grey receiver and positive extractors, includes fitted leather luggage case. Importation began 2000.

MSR	$9,495		$8,100	$6,850	$5,575	$4,400	$3,600	$3,100	$2,600

◇**Model 140-2.1** - similar to Model 140-2, except has Africa game scene engraving. Importation began 2000.

MSR	$10,595		$9,025	$7,275	$5,450	$4,600	$3,800	$3,350	$2,850

✱ ***Model 150-1*** - Anson & Deeley boxlock action with cocking indicators and sideplates, double triggers, silver grayed receiver with Arabesque engraving. Imported 1994-98.

	$6,500	$5,275	$4,375	$3,750	$3,250	$2,675	$2,100

Last MSR was $7,495.

Add $385 for H&H ejectors.
Add approx. $200 for set front trigger.

◇**Model 150-1.1** - similiar to Model 150-1, except has elaborate hunting scene engraving. Importation disc. 2000.

	$7,750	$5,350	$4,250	$3,550	$2,900	$2,400	$2,000

Last MSR was $8,995.

✱ ***Model 160S-1*** - sidelock action with Greener crossbolt featuring fine Arabesque engraving, H&H ejectors, DTs, pistol grip stock with cheekpiece. Disc. 1998.

	$11,400	$9,350	$7,675	$6,500	$5,300	$4,400	$3,550

Last MSR was $13,295.

Add $415 for H&H ejectors.
Add approx. $500 for set front trigger.
Add approx. $1,000 for single non-selective trigger.

◇**Model 160-1.1** - similiar to Model 150-1, except has elaborate hunting scene engraving on silver-grey receiver. Importation disc. 2000.

	$13,250	$11,000	$9,000	$7,775	$6,600	$5,400	$4,750

Last MSR was $14,995.

◇**Model 160-2.1** - .375 H&H, .416 Rigby, or .470 NE cal., features octagon barrels, African game scene engraving with gold wire inlays on silver receiver, includes fitted leather luggage case, special order only. Importation began 2002.

MSR	$24,995		$22,750	$18,750	$15,500	$12,500	$10,000	$8,950	$7,750

MODEL 132 SxS - various cals., boxlock action with triple Greener cross bolt system, barrels, mfg. from Bohler steel, extractors (Model 132) or H&H system ejectors (Model 132E), DT, elaborate engraving and premium checkered walnut stock and forearm, pre-WWII mfg.

	$12,000	$10,500	$8,500	$6,500	$5,750	$4,900	$4,150

Add 20% for ejectors (Model 132E).

Grading	100%	98%	95%	90%	80%	70%	60%

SHOTGUNS: O/U, DISC.

MODEL 100 - 12, 16, or 20 ga., various barrel lengths and chokes, boxlock, Greener cross bolt, double triggers, extractors, checkered pistol grip or English style stock, pre-WWII.

	100%	98%	95%	90%	80%	70%	60%
Plain	$1,850	$1,675	$1,450	$1,250	$1,000	$925	$850
Ribbed	$1,950	$1,775	$1,550	$1,300	$1,050	$950	$875

MODEL 101 - similar to 100, except selective extractors, rib barrel, some English style scroll engraving, pre-WWII.

	100%	98%	95%	90%	80%	70%	60%
	$2,050	$1,850	$1,600	$1,325	$1,100	$1,000	$900

MODEL 101E - similar to 100, except auto ejectors, pre-WWII.

	100%	98%	95%	90%	80%	70%	60%
	$2,200	$2,000	$1,750	$1,425	$1,250	$1,150	$1,000

MODEL 400 - similar to 101, except arabesque engraving and Kersten double cross bolt, pre-WWII.

	100%	98%	95%	90%	80%	70%	60%
	$2,075	$1,875	$1,650	$1,350	$1,200	$1,100	$975

MODEL 400E - similar to 400, except auto ejector, pre-WWII.

	100%	98%	95%	90%	80%	70%	60%
	$2,250	$2,050	$1,800	$1,450	$1,325	$1,175	$1,025

MODEL 410 - similar to 400, except more engraving and fancier wood, pre-WWII.

	100%	98%	95%	90%	80%	70%	60%
	$2,200	$2,000	$1,750	$1,425	$1,250	$1,150	$1,000

MODEL 410E - similar to 410, except auto ejectors, pre-WWII.

	100%	98%	95%	90%	80%	70%	60%
	$2,325	$2,175	$1,900	$1,600	$1,450	$1,225	$1,100

MODEL 200 - 12, 16, 20, 24, 28, or 32 ga., ribbed barrels in various lengths, Kersten double cross bolt, scalloped frame, boxlock, double triggers, extractors, cocking indicators, either pistol grip or English style checkered stock.

	100%	98%	95%	90%	80%	70%	60%
	$2,175	$1,975	$1,700	$1,350	$1,100	$990	$770

MODEL 210 - similar to 200, except engraved and better grade wood, pre-WWII.

	100%	98%	95%	90%	80%	70%	60%
	$2,375	$2,175	$1,900	$1,500	$1,300	$1,075	$895

MODEL 201 - 12, 16, or 20 ga., Greener crossbolt, hunting engraving or fine arabesque, dark walnut.

	100%	98%	95%	90%	80%	70%	60%
	$2,600	$2,300	$2,000	$1,600	$1,425	$1,200	$995

MODEL 201E - similar to 201, except with auto ejectors, pre-WWII.

	100%	98%	95%	90%	80%	70%	60%
	$3,050	$2,775	$2,400	$1,825	$1,600	$1,400	$1,200

MODEL 202 - similar to 201, except with false sideplates, higher quality wood, more profuse engraving, pre-WWII.

	100%	98%	95%	90%	80%	70%	60%
	$3,575	$3,225	$2,800	$2,400	$2,035	$1,700	$1,450

MODEL 202E - similar to 202, with auto ejectors, pre-WWII.

	100%	98%	95%	90%	80%	70%	60%
	$4,100	$3,675	$3,200	$2,800	$2,485	$2,050	$1,700

MODEL 203E - similar to 202E, except better engraving and wood.

	100%	98%	95%	90%	80%	70%	60%
	$5,150	$4,600	$4,000	$3,400	$2,900	$2,500	$2,100

MODEL 204E - similar to 203E, but fine English scroll engraving and Merkel sidelocks, ejectors, pre- WWII.

	100%	98%	95%	90%	80%	70%	60%
	$7,150	$6,500	$5,650	$4,900	$4,300	$3,850	$3,300

MODEL 300 - 12, 16, 20, 24, 28, or 32 ga., various lengths and choke ribbed barrels, Merkel-Anson boxlock, Kersten double cross bolt, two underlugs, scalloped frame, either English or pistol grip style stock, cocking indicators, pre-WWII.

	100%	98%	95%	90%	80%	70%	60%
	$2,650	$2,400	$2,100	$1,900	$1,700	$1,550	$1,375

This model is usually encountered without engraving and has standard wood.

M

Grading	100%	98%	95%	90%	80%	70%	60%

MODEL 300E - similar to Model 300, with auto ejectors, pre-WWII.

	$3,175	$2,875	$2,500	$2,250	$1,900	$1,750	$1,500

This model is usually encountered without engraving and has standard wood.

MODEL 301 - similar to Model 300, but more profusely engraved and better grade wood, pre-WWII.

	$6,600	$6,000	$5,250	$4,250	$3,995	$3,500	$3,000

MODEL 310E - similar to Model 300, with auto ejectors, pre-WWII.

	$7,950	$7,200	$6,250	$5,300	$4,450	$3,900	$3,400

MODEL 302 - similar to Model 301, but has auto ejectors and more elaborate ornamentation, false sideplates and better grade wood.

	$14,000	$12,000	$10,500	$8,500	$6,500	$5,750	$4,900

MODEL 304E - special order version of Model 303E, higher quality and more ornamentation, top of Merkel O/U line.

	$22,500	$18,750	$15,750	$12,000	$10,500	$8,750	$7,500

SHOTGUNS: O/U, RECENT PRODUCTION

MODEL 200E BOXLOCK - 12, 16, or 20 ga., case hardened scalloped boxlock action with minor scroll engraving, 26 (disc.), 26¾, or 28 in. barrels, checkered European walnut stock and forearm, ejectors, SST or DT, pistol grip or English style stock, solid rib, 6-7 lbs. Importation disc. 1994, quantities remained until 1998.

	$3,600	$2,750	$2,150	$1,900	$1,600	$1,300	$1,100

Last MSR was $3,995.

❋ **Model 200ES Skeet** - 12 ga. only, 26¾ in. VR barrels bored skeet/skeet. Imported 1993-94.

	$4,550	$3,950	$3,500	$3,000	$2,500	$2,100	$1,625

Last MSR was $4,995.

❋ **Model 200ET Trap** - 12 ga. only, 30 in. VR barrels bored full/full (other choke configurations available upon request). Importation disc. 1994.

	$4,400	$3,750	$3,300	$2,800	$2,300	$2,000	$1,550

Last MSR was $5,195.

MODEL 2000EL - 12, 20, or 28 (new 1999) ga., Kersten double cross-bolt lock, scroll engraved, silver receiver, modified Anson & Deeley boxlock action, 26 or 28 in. fixed choke barrels, ejectors, ST or DT, select checkered walnut with pistol grip or English style stock, 3 piece forearm, 6.4-7 lbs. Importation began 1998.

MSR	$5,795	$5,200	$4,100	$3,550	$2,850	$2,300	$1,775	$1,600

❋ **Model 2000EL Sporter** - similar to Model 2000EL, except chokes are SK/IC only. Importation began 1999.

MSR	$5,795	$5,200	$4,100	$3,550	$2,850	$2,300	$1,775	$1,600

MODEL 2001EL (201E) - 12, 16 (disc. 1997), 20, or 28 (new 1995) ga., similar to Model 200E, except has coin finished action with light game scene engraving.

MSR	$7,295	$6,275	$5,150	$3,875	$3,375	$2,900	$2,375	$2,125

This model's nomenclature was changed from 201E to 2001EL during 1998.

❋ **Model 2001EL Sporter** - similar to Model 2001EL, except chokes are SK/IC only. Importation began 1999.

MSR	$7,295	$6,275	$5,150	$3,875	$3,375	$2,900	$2,375	$2,125

❋ **Model 201ES Skeet** - 12 ga. only, 26¾ in. VR barrels bored skeet/skeet. Imported 1993-97.

	$7,850	$6,675	$5,400	$4,300	$3,450	$2,900	$2,250

Last MSR was $8,495.

Grading	100%	98%	95%	90%	80%	70%	60%

✳ **Model 201ET Trap** - 12 ga. only, 30 in. VR barrels bored full/full (other choke configurations available upon request). Importation disc. 1997.

		$7,850	$6,675	$5,400	$4,300	$3,450	$2,900	$2,250

Last MSR was $8,495.

MODEL 2002EL (202E) - similar to Model 201E/2001EL, except has fine hunting scenes with arabesque engraving on silver false sideplates, 3 piece forearm, choice of pistol grip of English straight grip stock, includes fitted luggage case. Importation began 1993.

MSR	$10,995	$9,625	$7,500	$5,750	$4,850	$3,850	$3,350	$2,850

This model's nomenclature was changed from 202E to 2002EL during 1998.

MODEL 203E SIDELOCK - 12, 16 (disc. 1997), or 20 ga. (24, 28, and 32 ga.'s were once available but are now disc.), 26 (disc.), 26¾, or 28 in. barrels, VR, H&H ejectors, SST (current) or DT, elaborate scroll engraving on coin finished receiver, sidelock screws are H&H style but the removable sidelocks are not, choice of English or pistol grip stock, 6- 7 lbs. Disc. 1998.

	$9,750	$6,450	$4,950	$3,900	$3,400	$2,550	$2,150

Last MSR was $11,995.

✳ **Model 203ES Skeet** - 12 ga. only, 26¾ in. VR barrels bored skeet/skeet. Imported 1993-97.

	$12,050	$9,100	$7,300	$5,975	$4,950	$3,950	$3,500

Last MSR was $14,595.

✳ **Model 203ET Trap** - 12 ga. only, 30 in. VR barrels bored full/full (other choke configurations available upon request). Importation disc. 1997.

	$12,050	$9,100	$7,300	$5,975	$4,950	$3,950	$3,500

Last MSR was $14,595.

MODEL 303EL (LUXUS) - 12, 20, or 28 (new 1998) ga., similar to Model 203EL, except has H&H type sidelock action with hidden thumbnail detachable sidelocks, double underlugs, more ornamentation and better wood, DT with articulated front.

MSR	$19,995	$17,250	$14,500	$11,750	$9,500	$8,100	$7,000	$5,800

Luxus variations are also encountered in the 201 and 203 series in addition to older pre-war models.

SHOTGUNS: SxS, PRE-WWII PRODUCTION

Merkel began manufacturing SxS shotguns during 1914.

MODEL 126E - 12, 16, or 20 ga., similar action as the Model 127, except features game scene and other engraving patterns, H&H style system ejectors, pre-WWII mfg.

	$28,250	$24,725	$21,500	$16,500	$12,500	$10,000	$8,800

MODEL 127E - 12, 16, or 20 ga., various barrel lengths and chokes, H&H style hand detachable sidelocks, auto ejectors, double triggers, pistol or English style stock, elaborate scroll engraving only, this is a best grade gun, pre-WWII mfg.

	$28,250	$24,725	$21,500	$16,500	$12,500	$10,000	$8,800

MODEL 128E - 12, 16, or 20 ga., scalloped Anson & Deeley action featuring engine turned removeable locks and hinged floorplate, DT, H&H system ejectors, elaborate scroll and game scene engraving (including scroll work on barrels), deluxe checkered walnut stock and forearm, pre-WWII mfg.

	$14,500	$12,000	$9,500	$7,500	$6,350	$5,400	$4,600

MODEL 130 - 12, 16, or 20 ga., various barrel lengths and chokes, Anson & Deeley action with false side plates, boxlock, auto ejectors, English style or pistol grip stock, elaborate game scenes and arabesque engraving, pre-WWII mfg.

	$16,250	$13,800	$12,000	$9,500	$7,500	$6,350	$5,400

M

Merkel

Grading	100%	98%	95%	90%	80%	70%	60%

SHOTGUNS: SxS, RECENT PRODUCTION

Add $895 for left hand stocking on models.

MODEL 8 - 12, 16 (disc.), or 20 ga., case hardened scalloped boxlock action with light engraving, Greener crossbolt with chopper lump extension, extractors, SST (current) or DT, standard walnut with checkering, pistol grip or English style stock, sling swivels (disc. 1992). Disc. 1994.

| | $1,150 | $950 | $795 | $700 | $625 | $550 | $475 |

Last MSR was $1,695.

MODEL 47E - 12, 16 (disc. 2001), or 20 ga., case hardened scalloped boxlock action with chopper lump extension and Greener crossbolt, 26 (disc.), 26¾, or 28 in. barrels with fixed chokes, SST (current) or DT, ejectors, deluxe checkered walnut, pistol grip or English style stock, sling swivels (disc. 1992), 5.9-6.8 lbs.

| MSR | $3,295 | $2,675 | $1,950 | $1,425 | $1,100 | $875 | $750 | $650 |

MODEL 47SL - 12, 16 (disc. 2001), 20, 28 (disc.) ga., or .410 (disc.) bore, coin finished sidelock action with scroll engraving, Greener crossbolt, ST (current) or DT, deluxe walnut stock (with cheekpiece) and forearm, sling swivels (disc. 1992).

| MSR | $5,995 | $5,200 | $4,425 | $3,675 | $2,875 | $2,325 | $1,975 | $1,625 |

Add approx. $600 for 28 ga. or .410 bore (mfg. 1992 only).

MODEL 76E - top-of-the-line boxlock shotgun. Importation disc. 1992.

| | $2,600 | $2,100 | $1,850 | $1,600 | $1,325 | $995 | $775 |

Last MSR was $3,500.

MODEL 147 - 12, 16, 20, or 28 (new 1995, 147E only) ga., 26¾ or 28 in. barrels, Anson & Deeley boxlock, any choke, SST (current) or DT, extractors, straight or pistol grip stock, hunting scene engraved. Disc. 1998, some inventory remained until 1999.

| | $2,400 | $1,875 | $1,425 | $1,100 | $875 | $750 | $650 |

Last MSR was $2,995.

Add $200 for H&H style auto ejectors (Model 147E).

✳ *Model 147E* - 12 or 20 ga., similar to Model 147, except has ejectors, 5.8-6.8 lbs.

| MSR | $3,995 | $3,350 | $2,725 | $2,250 | $1,900 | $1,550 | $1,325 | $1,150 |

✳ *Model 147EL* - similar to Model 147E, except has luxury grade wood upgrade. Importation began 1999.

| MSR | $4,995 | $4,300 | $3,500 | $2,950 | $2,525 | $2,100 | $1,700 | $1,400 |

MODEL 122 - 12, 16, or 20 ga., Anson & Deeley boxlock action with silver greyed false sideplates, H&H ejectors, SST or DT, fine hunting scenes with arabesque engraving, pistol grip or English style stock. Imported 1993-99.

| | $3,750 | $3,375 | $3,000 | $2,600 | $2,300 | $2,000 | $1,600 |

Last MSR was $4,495.

MODEL 122E - 12, 16, or 20 ga., coin finished sidelock action with Greener crossbolt and chopper lump extension, cocking indicators, ejectors, DTs, deluxe game scene engraving. Importation disc. 1991.

| | $4,100 | $3,650 | $3,200 | $2,800 | $2,250 | $1,950 | $1,650 |

Last MSR was $3,500.

MODEL 147SL - 12, 16 (disc. 2001), 20, 28 ga., or .410 (mfg. 1992 only) bore, coin finished sidelock action with Greener crossbolt and chopper lump extension, 25 ½ (disc.), 26 (disc.), 26 ¾, or 28 in. barrels, ejectors, ST (current) or DT, deluxe game scene engraving, 6-7 lbs.

| MSR | $7,995 | $6,995 | $4,900 | $3,925 | $3,300 | $2,750 | $2,250 | $1,850 |

Add $750 for .410 bore (mfg. 1992 only).

| MSR | $8,495 | $7,400 | $6,350 | $5,650 | $4,800 | $4,100 | $3,400 | $2,600 |

Grading	100%	98%	95%	90%	80%	70%	60%

MODEL 247SL - 12, 16 (disc. 2001), 20, or 28 ga., similar to Model 147SL, except has deluxe scroll engraving. Importation disc. 1991, resumed 1993.

MSR	$7,995		$6,995	$4,900	$3,925	$3,300	$2,750	$2,250	$1,850

MODEL 280 PETITE FRAME - 28 ga. only, Anson & Deeley boxlock action with Greener cross-bolt and double under barrel locking lugs, scroll engraving, case hardened receiver, H&H ejectors, DT, English style stock, 28 in. barrels bored IC/M, includes fitted luggage case. Importation began 2002.

MSR	$3,695		$3,175	$2,150	$1,550	$1,125	$875	$750	$650

* ✳ *Model 280/360 2 Barrel Set* - includes 28 in. 16 and 20 ga. barrels bored IC/M. Importation began 2002.

MSR	$5,795		$4,995	$4,450	$4,000	$3,500	$3,000	$2,500	$2,000

MODEL 280E PETITE FRAME - similar to Model 280 Petite Frame, except has fine hunting scenes engraved on silver receiver. Importation began 2002.

MSR	$4,395		$3,675	$2,450	$1,775	$1,300	$1,000	$850	$750

MODEL 280EL PETITE FRAME - 28 ga. only, Anson & Deeley boxlock action with Greener crossbolt and double under barrel locking lugs, fine hunting scene engraving, ejectors, DT, pistol grip or English style stock, 28 in. barrels bored IC/M, includes fitted luggage case, 5.2 lbs. Importation began 2000.

MSR	$5,795		$5,125	$4,100	$3,475	$2,850	$2,250	$1,750	$1,600

MODEL 280EL/360EL COMBO - consists of both 28 ga. and .410 bore barrels with fitted luggage case. Importation began 2000.

MSR	$8,295		$7,250	$6,300	$5,600	$4,800	$4,050	$3,400	$2,600

MODEL 280SL PETITE FRAME - 28 ga. only, H&H style sidelock action with Greener crossbolt and double under barrel locking lugs, English style arabesque engraving featuring small scrolls, ejectors, DT, pistol grip or English style stock, 28 in. barrels bored IC/M, includes fitted luggage case, 5.2 lbs. Importation began 2000.

MSR	$8,495		$7,400	$6,350	$5,650	$4,800	$4,100	$3,400	$2,600

* ✳ *Model 280SSL Petite Frame* - similar to Model 280SL Petite Frame, except has quick detachable sideplates. Importation began 2002.

MSR	$9,495		$8,150	$6,850	$5,875	$5,000	$4,300	$3,600	$3,200

MODEL 347SL - 12, 16, or 20 ga., similar to Model 247S, except has more elaborate engraving and better walnut. Importation disc. 1991, resumed 1993-97.

			$7,000	$4,850	$3,950	$3,350	$2,775	$2,275	$1,925

Last MSR was $7,895.

MODEL 360 PETITE FRAME - .410 bore, 28 in. barrels bored IC/F, otherwise similar to Model 280 Petite Frame. Importation began 2002.

MSR	$3,695		$3,175	$2,150	$1,550	$1,125	$875	$750	$650

MODEL 360E PETITE FRAME - similar to Model 360 Petite Frame, except has fine hunting scenes engraved on silver receiver. Importation began 2002.

MSR	$4,395		$3,675	$2,450	$1,775	$1,300	$1,000	$850	$750

MODEL 360EL PETITE FRAME - .410 bore, otherwise similar to Model 280EL, 5.5 lbs. Importation began 2000.

MSR	$5,795		$5,125	$4,100	$3,475	$2,850	$2,250	$1,750	$1,600

MODEL 360SL PETITE FRAME - .410 bore, otherwise similar to Model 280SL, 5.5 lbs. Importation began 2000.

MSR	$8,495		$7,400	$6,350	$5,650	$4,800	$4,100	$3,400	$2,600

* ✳ *Model 360SSL Petite Frame* - similar to Model 360SL Petite Frame, except has quick detachable sideplates. Importation began 2002.

MSR	$9,495		$8,150	$6,850	$5,875	$5,000	$4,300	$3,600	$3,200

M

Merkel

Grading	100%	98%	95%	90%	80%	70%	60%

MODEL 280SL/360SL 2 BARREL SET - consists of both 28 ga. and .410 bore barrels with fitted luggage case. Importation began 2000.

MSR	$11,995		$10,700	$9,375	$8,200	$6,900	$5,600	$4,400	$3,400

MODEL 280SSL/360SSL 2 BARREL SET - similar to 280SL/360SL 2 barrel set, except has quick detachable sideplates. Importation began 2002.

MSR	$12,995		$11,450	$9,875	$8,500	$7,200	$5,900	$4,900	$3,700

MODEL 447SL - similar to Model 347S, except is also available in 28 ga. and has more delicate scroll engraving. Importation disc. 1991, resumed 1993.

MSR	$9,995		$8,500	$5,750	$4,500	$3,700	$2,950	$2,400	$2,000

MODEL 1620 - 16 ga. only, Anson & Deely boxlock action, Greener crossbolt with double underbarrel locking lugs, 28 in. barrels with IC/Mod. fixed chokes, case hardened receiver with scroll engraving, H&H style ejectors, DT, English straight grip stock, includes fitted luggage case. Importation began 2002.

MSR	$3,695		$3,175	$2,150	$1,550	$1,125	$875	$750	$650

✱ *Model 1620 2 Barrel Set* - includes 28 in. 16 and 20 ga. barrels bored IC/M. Importation began 2002.

MSR	$5,795		$4,995	$4,450	$4,000	$3,500	$3,000	$2,500	$2,000

MODEL 1620EL - similar to Model 1620, except has finely engraved hunting scenes on silver receiver and luxury wood upgrade. Importation began 2002.

MSR	$5,795		$4,995	$4,450	$3,900	$3,400	$2,850	$2,350	$1,850

✱ *Model 1620EL 2 Barrel Set* - includes 28 in. 16 and 20 ga. barrels bored IC/M. Importation began 2002.

MSR	$8,295		$7,400	$6,500	$5,750	$5,000	$4,250	$3,500	$2,950

MODEL 1620SL - similar to Model 1620EL, except has sidelock action. Importation began 2002.

MSR	$8,495		$7,550	$6,600	$5,750	$4,950	$4,250	$3,400	$2,850

✱ *Model 1620SL 2 Barrel Set* - includes 28 in. 16 and 20 ga. barrels bored IC/M. Importation began 2002.

MSR	$11,995		$10,700	$9,375	$8,350	$7,200	$6,300	$5,100	$4,300

SHOTGUNS: SPORTING CLAYS

MODEL 47LSC SxS SPORTING CLAYS - 12 ga. only, features Anson & Deely boxlock action with scroll engraved case hardened receiver, 28 in. barrels with Briley screw- in chokes, H&H style ejectors, SST adj. for length of pull, select grade checkered walnut stock with pistol grip and beavertail forearm, competition recoil pad. Disc. 1994.

			$2,725	$2,400	$2,050	$1,725	$1,450	$1,125	$925

Last MSR was $2,995.

MODEL 200SC O/U SPORTING CLAYS - 12 ga. only, 3 in. chambers, 30 in. VR fixed choke barrels with lengthened forcing cones, Kersten double cross-bolt lock, color case hardened receiver, Blitz action, SST, fitted luggage case. Imported 1995-96.

			$6,750	$4,600	$3,750	$3,200	$2,625	$2,175	$1,850

Last MSR was $7,495.

Add $500 for Briley choke tubes (5 total).

MERRILL

Previous manufacturer located in Tucson, AZ. This original pistol design was by Jim Rock, who then joined R.P.M.

A newer variation of the Sportsman, now designated the XL and Hunter Model XL was offered by R.P.M. Please refer to the R.P.M. listing for more information.

Grading	100%	98%	95%	90%	80%	70%	60%

PISTOLS: SINGLE SHOT

SPORTSMAN MODEL - .22 S, L, or LR, .22 Mag., .22 Rem. Jet., .22 Hornet, 30 Herrett, .38 Spl., .357 Mag., .256 Win. Mag., .45 LC, .44 Mag., or .30-30 Win. cal., 9 in. barrel, hinged break open available, smooth walnut grips.

	$650	$575	$525	$450	$395	$350	$300

> **Add $70 for interchangeable barrels.**
> **Add $25 for wrist support.**

MERWIN HULBERT & CO.

Previous company with headquarters located in New York, NY circa 1874-1891.

Merwin Hulbert offered very high quality revolvers which were serious competitors with the Colt, Smith & Wesson, and Remington large frame single actions during this era. Their guns are believed to have been manufactured in a separate section of the Hopkins & Allen plant. Most will have both Merwin Hulbert and Hopkins & Allen markings on the barrel.

Merwin revolvers have a unique twist-open mechanism. The latch on the bottom of the frame is pushed towards the rear, while barrel & cylinder are twisted clockwise and pulled forward. This design was intended to allow selective ejection of empty cases while leaving unfired cartridges in the cylinder.

Merwins will often found with a distinctive and colorful unusual "punch dot" style engraving, often with some sort of simple panel scene (an animal, bird, flowers, etc.) on one or (rare) both sides of the frame. These will usually bring perhaps a 50% premium in lower grades, while in higher condition may bring double or triple what an undecorated gun will bring.

100%	98%	95%	90%	80%	70%	60%	50%	40%	30%	20%	10%

REVOLVERS: LARGE FRAME

All chambered for either .44 Merwin Hulbert (usually no caliber markings), .44 Russian (usually marked "Russian Model"), or .44-40 (marked "Calibre Winchester 1873"). Blue finish is rare and will being a premium.

The Merwin Hulbert system was copied by various Spanish & possibly other makers. These foreign copies will bring significantly less than original Merwins.

FIRST MODEL FRONTIER ARMY SA - .44 cal., square butt, open-top, scoop flutes on cylinder, 7½ in. barrel, 2 screws above triggerguard.

N/A	N/A	$3,500	$2,750	$1,800	$1,600	$1,400	$1,200	$1,050	$950	$875	$750

SECOND MODEL FRONTIER ARMY SA - similar to First Model, except has only one screw above triggerguard.

$5,500	$4,650	$3,250	$2,500	$1,700	$1,500	$1,250	$1,100	$995	$900	$800	$700

SECOND MODEL POCKET ARMY SA - similar to Second Model Frontier Army, except has birdshead butt instead of square butt, 3½ in. or 7 (scarce) in. barrel, may be marked "POCKET ARMY".

$5,000	$4,250	$3,000	$2,500	$1,250	$1,100	$1,000	$900	$800	$700	$600	$500

> **Add 10% for 7 in. barrel.**
> There are no First Model Pocket Army models.

THIRD MODEL FRONTIER ARMY SA - .44 cal., square butt, top strap, usually has conventional fluting on cylinder, but some have scoop flutes, 7 in. round barrel with no rib.

$5,000	$4,250	$3,000	$2,500	$1,250	$1,100	$1,000	$900	$800	$700	$600	$500

THIRD MODEL FRONTIER ARMY DA - similar to Third Model Frontier Army SA, except is double action.

$4,750	$3,950	$2,750	$2,250	$1,150	$1,000	$900	$800	$700	$625	$550	$450

> There are no First or Second Model Army double action models.

100%	98%	95%	90%	80%	70%	60%	50%	40%	30%	20%	10%

THIRD MODEL POCKET ARMY SA - .44 cal., single action,. birdshead butt, top strap, 3½ in. or 7 in. round barrel with no rib.

| $4,750 | $3,950 | $2,750 | $2,250 | $1,150 | $1,000 | $900 | $800 | $700 | $625 | $550 | $450 |

THIRD MODEL POCKET ARMY DA - similar to Third Model Pocket Army SA, except is double action.

| $4,750 | $3,950 | $2,750 | $2,250 | $1,150 | $1,000 | $900 | $800 | $700 | $625 | $550 | $450 |

FOURTH MODEL FRONTIER ARMY SA - .44 cal., 3½, 5 (most common), or 7 in. unique ribbed barrel, square butt, top strap, conventional flutes.

| $6,500 | $5,750 | $5,000 | $4,250 | $3,500 | $2,500 | $1,750 | $1,250 | $1,050 | $925 | $850 | $750 |

FOURTH MODEL FRONTIER ARMY DA - similar to Fourth Model Frontier Army SA, except is double action.

| $6,000 | $5,250 | $4,750 | $3,500 | $2,750 | $2,150 | $1,650 | $1,150 | $975 | $875 | $725 | $625 |

FOREIGN COPIES OF LARGE FRAME REVOLVERS - .44 cal.

These models may be based on any configuration, but 2nd & 3rd Frontier Army styles are probably the most commonly found. The words "Merwin Hulbert" (such as "Sistema Merwin Hulbert") may appear somewhere on the revolver, but rarely, if ever, found with the Hopkins & Allen marking. These will usually bring half or less what a comparable genuine Merwin will bring.

REVOLVERS: MEDIUM & SMALL FRAME

Medium frame revolvers were usually 5 shot in .38 cal., or 7 shot in .32 cal. The small frame was a 5 shot in .32 cal. Models chambered for .38 MH or .32 MH cal. are very similar to the black powder loadings of the .38 S&W and .32 S&W cal.

FIRST POCKET MODEL SA - .38 cal., 5-shot, spur-trigger, w/ cyl. pin exposed at the front of the frame, distinguishing feature is round loading hole in recoil shield, with no loading gate.

| $1,500 | $1,200 | $825 | $750 | $625 | $550 | $495 | $450 | $375 | $325 | $275 | $225 |

SECOND POCKET MODEL SA - .38 cal., 5-shot, similar to First Model, except has sliding loading gate.

| $1,350 | $1,100 | $750 | $675 | $600 | $500 | $460 | $425 | $360 | $315 | $260 | $215 |

THIRD POCKET MODEL SA - .38 cal., 5-shot, similar to First Model, except has enclosed cylinder pin.

| $1,250 | $1,000 | $700 | $650 | $575 | $475 | $440 | $415 | $350 | $300 | $255 | $210 |

THIRD POCKET MODEL SA WITH TRIGGERGUARD - .38 cal., 5-shot, similar to Third Pocket Model, except has conventional triggerguard.

| $1,250 | $1,000 | $700 | $650 | $575 | $475 | $440 | $415 | $350 | $300 | $255 | $210 |

MEDIUM FRAME DA POCKET MODEL - .38 cal., 5 shot, double action, may have folding hammer spur.

| $950 | $775 | $500 | $450 | $415 | $365 | $335 | $300 | $275 | $250 | $225 | $200 |

Add 10% for folding hammer spur.

MEDIUM FRAME DA POCKET MODEL - .32 cal., 7 shot, double action.

| $1,100 | $875 | $675 | $625 | $550 | $450 | $425 | $395 | $340 | $295 | $250 | $210 |

SMALL FRAME DA POCKET MODEL - .32 cal., 5 shot, double action.

| $950 | $775 | $500 | $450 | $415 | $365 | $335 | $300 | $275 | $250 | $225 | $200 |

TIP-UP .22 MODEL - .22 rimfire cal., 7 shot, spur trigger, closely patterned after the S&W Model One. Very scarce.

| $1,100 | $875 | $675 | $625 | $550 | $450 | $425 | $395 | $340 | $295 | $250 | $210 |

RIFLES: SINGLE SHOT

These rifles were generally patterned after the Hopkins & Allen single shots.
The Merwin Hulbert name marking may bring a 25%-50% over models that do not have this marking.

Grading	100%	98%	95%	90%	80%	70%	60%

MICHIGAN ARMS

Previous manufacturer located in Michigan until circa 1981.

PISTOLS: SEMI-AUTO

GUARDIAN - SS - .380 ACP cal., patterned after the Walther PPK, bears close resemblance to the Indian Arms .380 semi-auto, 3¼ in. barrel, checkered walnut grips with medallion, 6 shot finger extension mag., fixed sights. Limited mfg.

$375	$295	$225	$210	$190	$170	$150

This model was mfg. by using Indian Arms tooling.

M1911 A1 - .45 ACP cal., patterned after the Colt M1911 A1, fixed sights, 7 shot mag. Disc.

$450	$395	$350	$275	$225	$210	$190

MIDLAND RIFLES

Previous trademark of rifles manufactured by Gibbs Rifle Co. (please refer to the G section for previous models and pricing) and older models mfg. by Parker-Hale, Ltd. (please refer to the P section).

MIIDA

Previous manufactured by Nikko Firearms, Ltd. in Tochigi, Japan. Previously imported by Marubeni America Corp. located in New York, NY circa 1972-1974.

SHOTGUNS: O/U

MODEL 612 FIELD - 12 ga., 26 or 28 in. barrels, VR, various chokes, boxlock, auto ejectors, single selective trigger, checkered pistol grip stock. Mfg. 1972-1974.

$800	$725	$650	$575	$510	$440	$400

MODEL 2100 SKEET GUN - similar to Model 612, with 27 in. VR, skeet bore barrels, more elaborate engraving. Mfg. 1972-1974.

$875	$775	$700	$615	$550	$465	$425

MODEL 2200T TRAP GUN - similar to Model 2100, except with 29¾ in. imp. mod. and full choke barrels, wide VR, 60% engraved coverage and select wood. Mfg. 1972-1974.

$925	$825	$750	$665	$595	$500	$450

MODEL 2200S SKEET GUN - similar to Model 2200T, except with 27 in. skeet bore barrels.

$925	$825	$750	$665	$595	$500	$450

MODEL 2300 SERIES TRAP OR SKEET - similar to Model 2200 Trap/Skeet but with more engraving. Mfg. 1972-1974.

$975	$875	$800	$715	$630	$550	$500

MODEL GRT GRANDEE TRAP GUN - 12 ga., 29¾ in. full choke barrels, single selective trigger, auto ejector, boxlock with side plates, receiver fully engraved as well as breech ends of barrel, triggerguard and locking lever, gold inlaid, extensive silver line inlays, high grade select walnut stock. Mfg. 1972-1974.

$2,500	$2,200	$1,900	$1,575	$1,250	$1,000	$850

MODEL GRS GRANDEE SKEET GUN - similar to Model GRT, with 27 in. skeet bored barrels.

$2,500	$2,200	$1,900	$1,575	$1,250	$1,000	$850

MILLER, DAVID CO.

See David Miller Co. listing.

M

Grading	100%	98%	95%	90%	80%	70%	60%

MIL-SPEC INDUSTRIES CORP.

Current pistol manufacturer and related components supplier located in Roslyn Heights, NY since 1996. Dealer sales.

PISTOLS: SEMI-AUTO

MIL-SPEC 1911 A1 - 9mm Para., 9x21mm, 9x22mm, .40 S&W, .45 HP, or .45 ACP cal., high tech polymer and stainless steel frame, beavertail grip safety, aluminum trigger, 10 shot mag., 3 15/16 (Compact), 5 5/16 (Combat with compensator), or 5 (Government) in. barrel, choice of wood, plastic, or rubber grips, 39½-46 oz. New late 1996.

MSR	$690		$625	$550	$500	$450	$400	$360	$330

Add $5 for parkerized finish.
Add $45 for electroless nickel finish.
Add $50 for hard chrome finish.

MILTEX, INC.

Previous handgun importer located in La Plata, MD. Miltex imported commercial Makarovs until approx. 2000.

MIROKU FIREARMS MFG. CO.

Current manufacturer established during 1893 and located in Kochi, Japan. Miroku currently manufactures long arms for Browning and Winchester (please refer to individual sections), in addition to their own line of firearms mostly distributed in Europe.

Shotguns marked Miroku only without another trademark listing represent that period of manufacture before Miroku began manufacturing shotguns for other companies (i.e. Charles Daly, SKB, Browning, and others). Most guns marked Miroku only were made on a limited basis and although somewhat rare, collector desirability to date has been minimal. Since model notations were not specified in most instances (many shotguns were made to test market demand), a model rundown is virtually impossible. Values can be approx. ascertained by comparing a Miroku shotgun of similar gauge, features, engraving/ wood, and condition to an equivalent Japanese Charles Daly model. Miroku also manufactured revolvers up until approx. 1964 which may be designated Liberty Chief - limited importation into the U.S.

MITCHELL ARMS, INC.

Current manufacturer, importer, and distributor located in Fountain Valley, CA. Distributor sales only.

DERRINGERS: O/U

GUARDIAN ANGEL - .22 LR or .22 Mag. cal., double action, hammerless, choice of blue, satin, nickel, or gold finish. Mfg. 1996-97.

		$125	$105	$95	$85	$80	$75	$70

Last MSR was $150.

Add $10 for .22 Mag. cal.
Add $20 for blue or nickel finish.
Add $40 for gold finish.
Add $10 for Deluxe Model with case and angel charm.

PISTOLS: SEMI-AUTO

AMERICAN EAGLE LUGER - 9mm Para. cal., 4 in. barrel, stainless steel with toggle action, checkered American walnut grips, American Eagle version, contoured front grip strap. Disc. 1994.

	$590	$475	$400

Last MSR was $695.

Grading	100%	98%	95%	90%	80%	70%	60%

ROLLING BLOCK PISTOL - .22 LR, .22 Mag., .223 Rem., .357 Mag., or .45 LC cal., reproduction of the Remington Rolling Block design, 10 in. barrel. Mfg. 1991-92 only.

	$340	$285	$240	$210	$185	$170	$150

Last MSR was $395.

Mitchell .22 Cal. Target Pistols

Mitchell Arms manufactured High Standard marked pistols during 1993-94. Due to litigation, the High Standard logo was dropped in 1994, and High Standard model nomenclature was dropped in 1996. These guns feature push button barrel takedown and usually, a choice between stainless steel or royal blue steel construction. Mitchell Arms is not responsible for the older High Standard pistols manufactured in New Haven and East Hartford, CT, even though Mitchell parts are interchangeable with original High Standard pistols.

MONARCH (CITATION II) - .22 LR cal., 5½ bull or 7¼ in. fluted barrel, frame mounted bridge rear sight, checkered walnut grips with thumb rest, push button take down, stippled front and rear grip straps, adj. trigger, travel, and weight, stainless steel or royal blue finish. Mfg. 1993-2000.

	$395	$295	$245	$215	$190	$170	$150

Last MSR was $490.

MEDALIST (OLYMPIC I.S.U.) - .22 S or LR (new 1994) cal., military grip style, 6¾ in. special barrel with internal stabilizer, adj. barrel weights, other features similar to Citation II, stainless steel or blue finish. Mfg. 1993-2000.

	$625	$550	$425	$375	$325	$275	$22

Last MSR was $700.

BARON (SHARPSHOOTER II) - .22 LR cal., 5½ in. bull barrel, standard trigger, adj. rear sight, smooth grip frame, stainless steel or blue (disc.) finish. Mfg. 1993-2000.

	$320	$280	$240	$210	$185	$160	$135

Last MSR was $400.

SPORTSTER (SPORT KING II) - .22 LR cal., 4½ or 6¾ in. tapered barrel, military black checkered plastic grips, stainless steel only, adj. rear sight. Mfg. 1993-2000.

	$270	$220	$185	$160	$135	$120	$110

Last MSR was $330.

MEDALLION (TROPHY II) - .22 LR cal., 5½ in. bull or 7¼ in. fluted barrel, military grips with full checkering and thumb rest, bridge rear sight, gold-plated trigger safety and mag. release, stippled front and rear grip straps, stainless steel or royal blue (disc. 1997) finish. Mfg. 1993-2000.

	$425	$350	$275	$225	$190	$170	$150

Last MSR was $500.

SOVEREIGN (VICTOR II) - .22 LR cal., 4½ or 5½ in. full length VR or black rib barrel, checkered walnut grips with thumb rest, stainless steel became standard 1998, gold- plated trigger, safety, mag. release, and side lock, rib mounted sights. Mfg. 1993-2000.

	$500	$425	$375	$325	$275	$225	$195

Last MSR was $600.

Add $80 for Weaver style base built into VR.

HIGH STANDARD COLLECTORS ASSOCIATION SPECIAL EDITIONS

* **HSCA-SE Trophy II** - .22 LR cal., 100 mfg. 1993 only, cased.

	$450	$375	$300

* **HSCA-SE Victor II**

	$495	$400	$325

* **HSCA-SE Citation II**

	$435	$365	$285

M

Grading	100%	98%	95%	90%	80%	70%	60%

* **HSCA-SE Three Gun Set** - includes Trophy II, Olympic II, and Victor II.

| | $1,495 | $1,295 | $1,050 | | | | |

* **HSCA-SE Six Gun Set** - includes 6¾ in. I.S.U. Olympic (.22 Short), 4½ in. Victor, 7¼ in. Citation, 5½ in. Sharpshooter, 4½ in. Sport King, and Trophy Model. Special engraving, cased, HSCA prefix with 2-digit serial number, 19 sets total mfg. 1994 only.

| | $2,650 | $2,100 | $1,675 | | | | |

Last MSR was $2,995.

Mitchell Centerfire Pistols

MODEL 57A (TOKAREV DESIGN) - .30 Mauser cal., single action semi-auto, 9 shot mag., hammer block and mag. safety, all steel construction. Imported from Yugoslavia 1990 only.

| | $240 | $215 | $180 | $160 | $145 | $135 | $120 |

Last MSR was $280.

MODEL 70A (TOKAREV DESIGN) - 9mm Para. cal., otherwise similar to Model 57A. Imported from Yugoslavia 1990 only.

| | $240 | $215 | $180 | $160 | $145 | $135 | $120 |

Last MSR was $280.

88A OFFICERS MODEL (TOKAREV DESIGN) - 9mm Para. cal., newer slenderized variation issued to the Officers Corps., short slide and frame, finger extension mag. Imported from Yugoslavia 1990 only.

| | $255 | $225 | $190 | $165 | $145 | $135 | $120 |

Last MSR was $300.

SKORPION - while advertised during 1987, this model was never mfg.

SPECTRE - while advertised during 1987, this model was never mfg.

1911 GOLD/SIGNATURE SERIES (STANDARD) - .45 ACP cal., features new tapered barrel slide lock-up, wide body accepts staggered mag., full length guide rod recoil buffer assembly, beveled mag. well, blue (disc. 1995) or stainless steel, 8 shot mag., walnut checkered grips, fixed or adj. sights. New 1994-disc.

| Blue Finish | $465 | $395 | $350 | $325 | $295 | $270 | $250 |

Last MSR was $535.

* **Stainless Steel** - disc. 1997.

| | $675 | $585 | $525 | | | | |

Last MSR was $675

* **Tactical Model** - stainless steel, features elongated grip safety and serrated front slide, fixed or adj. rear sight. Mfg. 1996-97.

| | $640 | $550 | $500 | | | | |

Last MSR was $735.

Add $40 for adj. rear sight.

* **Bullseye Model** - similar to Tactical Model, except has fully adj. rear sight. Mfg. 1996-97.

| | $850 | $700 | $575 | | | | |

Last MSR was $950.

* **IPSC Limited Model** - choice of ghost ring or adj. rear sight. Mfg. 1996-97.

| | $1,075 | $875 | $675 | | | | |

Last MSR was $1,195.

Add $45 for ghost ring sight.

1911 GOLD/SIGNATURE SERIES (WIDE BODY) - .45 ACP cal., features new tapered barrel slide lock-up, full length guide rod recoil buffer assembly, beveled mag. well, blue (disc. 1995) or stainless steel, 10 (C/B 1994) or 13* shot mag., walnut checkered grips, fixed or adj. sights. Mfg. 1994-97.

| Blue Finish | $595 | $525 | $475 | $425 | $375 | $335 | $295 |

Last MSR was $685.

Grading	100%	98%	95%	90%	80%	70%	60%

* **Standard Model** - stainless steel, fixed sights, smooth grips. Mfg. 1996-97.

  $765 $650 $550

  Last MSR was $840.

* **Tactical Model** - stainless steel, features elongated grip safety and serrated front slide, adj. rear sight. Mfg. 1996-97.

  $795 $675 $575

  Last MSR was $895.

MITCHELL .44 - .44 Mag. cal., 5½ in. barrel, blue finish, 7 shot mag., checkered walnut grips, adj. rear sight. Mfg. 1996-97.

$1,050 $900 $800 $725 $650 $575 $495

Last MSR was $1,190.

JEFF COOPER SIGNATURE/COMMEMORATIVE MODEL - .45 ACP cal., blue finish. Mfg. 1996-97.

* **Signature Model**

  $725 $625 $560 $500 $450 $415 $375

  Last MSR was $795.

* **Commemorative Model** - 1,000 mfg. 1996-97.

  $1,650 $1,400 $1,200 $1,000 $800 $675 $550

  Last MSR was $1,895.

ALPHA SERIES - while advertised in 1995, this model was never mfg.

REVOLVERS: SINGLE ACTION

SINGLE ACTION ARMY - .22 LR (disc.), .357 Mag., .44-40 WCF (new 1998), .44 Mag. (disc.), .45 ACP (disc.), or .45 LC cal., 4¾, 5½, 6 (disc. 1993), or 7½ in. barrel lengths, hammer block safety mechanism, steel construction, case hardened frame, one-piece walnut stock. Imported 1986-94, re-introduced 1997.

* **Cowboy Model** - .357 Mag., .44-40 WCF, .45 ACP (disc.), or .45 LC cal., 4¾ in. barrel.

  MSR $450 $395 $350 $315 $275 $260 $245 $230

  Add $50 for nickel finish.
  Add $50 for adj. rear sight (disc.).
  Add $150 for dual cylinder (.357 Mag./9mm Para., .45 LC/.45 ACP, or .44-40 WCF/.44 Spl.).
  Add $95 for steel back strap and triggerguard (disc.).
  This model is also available in a Bat Masterson variation.

* **U.S. Army Model** - similar to Cowboy Model, except has 5½ in. barrel.

  MSR $450 $395 $350 $315 $275 $260 $245 $230

  Add $50 for nickel finish.
  Add $150 for dual cylinder (.357 Mag./9mm Para., .45 LC/.45 ACP, or .44-40 WCF/.44 Spl.).

* **U.S. Cavalry Model** - similar to Cowboy Model, except has 7½ in. barrel.

  MSR $450 $395 $350 $315 $275 $260 $245 $230

  Add $150 for dual cylinder (.357 Mag./9mm Para., .45 LC/.45 ACP, or .44-40 WCF/.44 Spl.).
  Add $50 for nickel finish.

* **.44 Mag.** - .44 Mag. cal., fully adj. target sights. Disc. 1992.

  $425 $350 $295 $250 $200 $180 $165

  Last MSR was $495.

* **Rimfire Model** - .22 LR cal. Importation disc. 1989.

  $230 $200 $180 $160 $145 $130 $120

  Last MSR was $280.

  Add $30 for adj. rear sight.

M

Grading	100%	98%	95%	90%	80%	70%	60%

* *Silhouette Model* - available with 10, 12, or 18 in. barrel in .44 Mag. or .45 LC cal. Importation disc. 1991.

	$395	$325	$260	$220	$195	$170	$155

Last MSR was $450.

Add $175 for shoulder stock (available with 18 in. barrel only).
The shoulder stock is available with .44 Mag./.44-40 WCF cals. only.

* *Dual Cylinder* - available in either .22 LR/.22 Mag. (disc.), .22 LR/.22 Mag. stainless (disc. 1988), .357 Mag./9mm Para. (disc. 1993), .44 Mag./.44-40 WCF (disc. 1991), or .45 LC/.45 ACP (new 1990) cal. Imported 1986-94.

	$475	$415	$365	$335	$300	$275	$250

Last MSR was $549.

Add $50 for adj. rear sight (disc.).
Add $39 for nickel finish.
Add $93 for for steel backstrap.

* *Stainless Model* - available in .22 LR or .357 Mag. (disc. 1987) cal. only, adj. sights. Imported 1986- 1988 only.

	$260	$225	$195

Last MSR was $301.

Add $25 for .357 Mag.

BAT MASTERSON MODEL - .45 LC cal., 4¾ , 5½ or 7½ in. barrel with full ejector rod housing, nickel-plated, one- piece walnut stocks, hammer-block safety, rear sight is square notch in frame, two-piece backstrap. Imported 1989-94.

	$375	$285	$240	$210	$185	$170	$150

Last MSR was $450.

Add $156 for extra .45 ACP cylinder.

MODEL 1875 REMINGTON - .357 Mag. or .45 LC cal., royal blue finish with color case hardened frame, walnut grips. Imported 1990-91.

	$345	$285	$245	$210	$185	$170	$150

Last MSR was $399.

Add $76 for nickel finish.
Add $51 for extra convertible .45 ACP cylinder.

REVOLVERS: DOUBLE ACTION

TITAN II - .357 Mag. cal., 6 shot, 2, 4, or 6 in. barrel, blue or stainless, fixed sights, shrouded ejector rod, target hammer. Mfg. 1995 only.

	$285	$250	$220	$190	$170	$150	$135

Last MSR was $339.

TITAN III - similar to Titan II, except has adj. rear sight. Mfg. 1995 only.

	$340	$285	$245	$200	$175	$150	$135

Last MSR was $429.

GUARDIAN II - .38 Spl. cal., 6 shot, 3 or 4 in. barrel, fixed sights, blue only, target or combat grips. Mfg. 1995 only.

	$240	$215	$185	$165	$145	$130	$120

Last MSR was $275.

GUARDIAN III - similar to Guardian II, except has adj. rear sight, and 6 in. barrel. Mfg. 1995 only.

	$260	$230	$195	$175	$155	$140	$130

Last MSR was $305.

RIFLES: BOLT ACTION, RECENT MAUSER IMPORT

Beginning 1999, Mitchell Arms imports a sizeable quantity of WWII Mauser 98Ks manufactured in Yugoslavia during/after WWII. These guns are basically in new condition, having been only test

Grading	100%	98%	95%	90%	80%	70%	60%

fired over the past 50 years. They are supplied with bayonet and scabbard, military leather sling, original field cleaning kit, and leather ammo pouch. Caliber is 8mm Mauser (7.9x57mm), and all parts numbers match on these rifles. Basic retail on the Standard Grade is $225, w/o accessories. Additionally, a Collector Grade is $395, and apremium grade rifle is available for $495. (both include accessories).

RIFLES: DISC.

MODEL 15/22 OR 20/22 SEMI-AUTO CARBINE - .22 LR cal., American walnut stock, high polish blue, detachable 10 shot mag. Mfg. 1994-95.

	100%	98%	95%	90%	80%	70%	60%
	$155	$125	$105	$95	$85	$75	$65

Last MSR was $179.

> Subtract $40 for 20/22 Special.
> Add $20 for Deluxe model (includes deluxe walnut, rosewood accents, and fine line checkering).

LW22 SEMI-AUTO - .22 LR cal., 10 shot mag., composite or skeleton stock, patterned after Feather Industries semi-auto. Limited mfg. 1996-97.

	100%	98%	95%	90%	80%	70%	60%
	$240	$220	$195	$175	$160	$145	$130

Last MSR was $275.

> Add $30 for composite stock.

LW9 SEMI-AUTO - 9mm Para. cal., semi-auto, blowback action, composite or skeleton stock, patterned after Feather Industries 9mm Para. semi-auto. Limited mfg. 1996-97.

	100%	98%	95%	90%	80%	70%	60%
	$450	$395	$360	$330	$300	$270	$240

Last MSR was $500.

> Add $35 for composite stock.

MODEL 9303/9304/9305 STANDARD BOLT ACTION - .22 LR (9303) or .22 Mag. (9304, new 1995) cal., standard or deluxe variation, 10 shot mag. Mfg. 1994-95.

	100%	98%	95%	90%	80%	70%	60%
	$240	$195	$180	$160	$145	$130	$120

Last MSR was $275.

> Add $14 for .22 Mag. cal.
> Subtract $76 for special bolt action (9305).

MODEL 9301/9302 DELUXE BOLT ACTION - similar to 9304/9305, except includes deluxe walnut, rosewood accents, and fine line checkering. Mfg. 1994-95.

	100%	98%	95%	90%	80%	70%	60%
	$265	$220	$190	$170	$150	$135	$125

Last MSR was $313.

> Add $12 for .22 Mag. cal.

M-16A3 - .22 LR, .22 Mag. (disc. 1987), or .32 ACP cal., patterned after Colt's AR-15. Mfg. 1987-94.

	100%	98%	95%	90%	80%	70%	60%
	$235	$195	$175	$160	$145	$130	$120

Last MSR was $266.

> Add $100 for .22 Mag. cal. or .32 ACP (disc. 1988).

CAR-15/22 - .22 LR cal., carbine variation of M-16 with shorter barrel and collapsible stock. Mfg. 1990-94.

	100%	98%	95%	90%	80%	70%	60%
	$235	$195	$175	$160	$145	$130	$120

Last MSR was $266.

GALIL - .22 LR or .22 Mag. cal., patterned after Galil semi-auto paramilitary design rifle, choice of wood stock or folding stock (new 1992). Mfg. 1987-1993.

	100%	98%	95%	90%	80%	70%	60%
	$285	$240	$195	$160	$150	$140	$130

Last MSR was $359.

M

Grading	100%	98%	95%	90%	80%	70%	60%

MAS - .22 LR or .22 Mag. cal., patterned after French MAS rifle. Mfg. 1987-1993.

	$285	$240	$195	$160	$150	$140	$130

Last MSR was $359.

Add $75 for .22 Mag. cal. (disc. 1988).

PPS-30/50 - .22 LR cal., patterned after the Russian WWII PPS military rifle, full length barrel shroud, 20 shot banana mag., adj. rear sight, walnut stock. Mfg. 1989-94.

	$235	$195	$175	$160	$145	$130	$120

Last MSR was $266.

Add $100 for 50 shot drum magazine.

SPECTRE CARBINE - while advertised during 1987, this model was never mfg.

AK-22 - .22 LR or .22 Mag. (new 1988) cal., copy of the famous Russian AK-47, fully adj. sights, built in cleaning rod, high quality European walnut or folding stock, 20 shot mag. Mfg. 1985-94.

	$235	$195	$175	$160	$145	$130	$120

Last MSR was $266.

Add $40 for folding stock.

AK-47 - 7.62x39 cal., copy of the original Kalashnikov AK-47, semi-auto, teak stock and forend, 30 shot steel mag., last shot hold open. Mfg. Yugoslavia. Imported 1986-1989.

	$595	$550	$495	$450	$400	$360	$310

Last MSR was $675.

Add $23 for steel folding butt stock.
Add $150 for 75 shot steel drum mag.

.308 WIN. NATO AK-47 (M77B1) - .308 Win. cal., milled receiver, adj. gas port, otherwise similar to AK-47 except has scope rail, day/night Tritium sights, and 20 shot mag. Imported 1989 only.

	$900	$800	$700	$595	$525	$475	$425

Last MSR was $775.

Add $600 for military issue sniper scope and rings.

M76 - similar to AK-47, except is 7.92mm cal. and has longer barrel and frame set up for scope mount, counter sniper design, 10 shot mag., mfg. to mil. specs. Imported 1986-1989.

	$1,725	$1,535	$1,350	$1,100	$900	$820	$760

Last MSR was $1,995.

SKS-M59 - 7.62x39 cal., copy of the SKS-M59 standard rifle, full walnut stock, fully adj. sights, gas operated. Mfg. in Yugoslavia. Imported 1986-1989.

	$610	$525	$465	$410	$360	$315	$260

Last MSR was $699.

R.P.K. - 7.62x39mm or .308 Win. cal., forged heavy barrel with cooling fins, teak stock, detachable bipod, mil. specs. Importation disc. 1992.

	$1,050	$875	$725	$650	$575	$525	$475

Last MSR was $1,150.

Add $845 for .308 Win. cal.

MODEL M-90 - 7.62x39mm or .308 Win. cal., AK-47 type action, in various configurations (heavy barrel, folding or fixed stock, finned barrel, etc.), plastic thumbhole stock, 5 shot mag., limited importation from Yugoslavia 1991-92.

	$750	$650	$550	$495	$450	$395	$350

Last MSR was $829.

Add 20% for folding stock.
Add 10% for .308 Win. cal. (wood stock only).

This model was subjected to modification due to ATF regulations after arrival in the U.S.

Grading	100%	98%	95%	90%	80%	70%	60%

RIFLES: REPRODUCTIONS

HENRY RIFLE - .44-40 WCF cal., polished brass frame, octagonal barrel, original loading system. Imported 1990.

	$840	$650	$585	$520	$465	$415	$375

Last MSR was $999.

Iron frame also available at extra charge.

MODEL 1866 - .22 LR (disc.), .38 Spl. (disc.), or .44-40 WCF cal., patterned after the Winchester Model 1866 rifle, solid brass frame, octagon barrel. Imported 1990-1993.

	$715	$535	$465	$415	$375	$335	$295

Last MSR was $829.

This model was also available in a carbine variation.

MODEL 1873 - .22 LR (disc.), .38 Spl.(disc), .357 Mag. (disc.), .44-40 WCF (disc.), or .45 LC cal., patterned after the Winchester 1873 rifle, octagon barrel, solid steel frame. Imported 1990-1993.

	$810	$640	$550	$515	$465	$415	$375

Last MSR was $950.

This model was also available in a carbine variation until 1992.

SHOTGUNS: SLIDE ACTION

MODEL 9104/9105 - 12 ga. only, features 20 in. barrel with bead sights, 5 shot mag. tube, uncheckered walnut stock and forearm. Mfg. 1994-96.

	$240	$195	$175	$160	$145	$130	$120

Last MSR was $279.

Add $20 for adj. rear rifle sight (Model 9105).
Add $20 for interchangeable choke tube (Model 9104 only).

MODEL 9108/9109 - 12 ga. only, all-purpose self-defense model featuring 20 in. barrel with 7 shot mag., choice of military green (special order), brown walnut, or black regular or pistol grip stock and forearm. Mfg. 1994-96.

	$240	$195	$175	$160	$145	$130	$120

Last MSR was $279.

Add $20 for adj. rear rifle sight (Model 9109).
Add $20 for interchangeable choke tube (Model 9108 only).

MODEL 9111/9113 - 12 ga. only, 18½ in. barrel with bead sights, 6 shot mag., choice of brown or green synthetic (special order), brown walnut or black regular or pistol grip stock and forearm. Mfg. 1994-96.

	$240	$195	$175	$160	$145	$130	$120

Last MSR was $279.

Add $20 for adj. rear rifle sight (Model 9113).
Add $20 for interchangeable choke tube (Model 9111 only).

MODEL 9114 - 12 ga. only, designed for police and riot control, choice of synthetic pistol grip or top folding (disc. 1994) buttstock, 20 in. barrel with iron sights, 6 shot mag. Mfg. 1994-96.

	$295	$255	$210	$180	$160	$145	$130

Last MSR was $349.

MODEL 9115 - 12 ga. only, design based on Special Air Services riot gun, 18½ in. barrel with vent. heat shield, parkerized finish, 6 shot mag., stealth grey stock featuring 4 shell storage. Mfg. 1994- 96.

	$295	$255	$210	$180	$160	$145	$130

Last MSR was $349.

Add $20 for interchangeable choke tube.

Grading	100%	98%	95%	90%	80%	70%	60%

MOLL, M.F.

Current custom rifle manufacturer and gunsmith located in Moenchengladbach, Germany. Consumer direct sales.

M.F. Moll manufactures high quality reproductions of the Sharps Model 1874 rifle. He also provides many gunsmithing services, including his own proprietary color case hardening process. Please contact him directly for more information, including an individual price quotation and U.S. availability.

MONTANA ARMORY, INC.

Current distributor of C. Sharps Arms Co. Inc. rifles located in Big Timber, MT. Please refer to the C. Sharps Arms Co. listing in the S section for more information.

MONTGOMERY WARD

Catalog sales/retailer that has subcontracted various domestic and international manufacturers to private label various brand names under the Montgomery Ward conglomerate.

Montgomery Ward shotguns and rifles have appeared under various labels and endorsers, including Western Field and others. There have literally been hundreds of various models (shotguns and rifles) sold through the Montgomery Ward retail network. Most of these models were manufactured through subcontracts with both domestic and international firearms manufacturers. Typically, they were "spec." guns made to sell at a specific price to undersell the competition. Most of these models were derivatives of existing factory models with less expensive wood and perhaps missing the features found on those models from which they were derived. Please refer to the Store Brand Crossover Section in the back of this book under Western Field for converting Montgomery Ward models to the respective manufacturer.

To date, there has been very little interest in collecting Montgomery Ward guns, regardless of rarity. Rather than list Montgomery Ward models, a general guideline is that values generally are under those of their "1st generation relatives". As a result, prices are ascertained by the shooting value of the gun, rather than its collector value.

MORINI COMPETITION ARM SA

Current target pistol manufacturer located in Bedano, Switzerland. Currently imported and distributed by Nygord Precision Products located in Prescott, AZ, and Pilkington Competition Equipment, LLC, located in Monteagle, TN. Previously imported and distributed by Osborne's, located in Cheboygan, MI.

For more information and current pricing on both new and used Morini airguns, please refer to the 2nd Ed. *Blue Book of Modern Airguns* by Dr. Robert Beeman & John Allen (now online also).

PISTOLS: .22 CAL. TARGET

Morini was one of the first companies to develop a sophisticated anatomical grip for handgun target shooting, and continues to be a leader in grip design.

CM-22 - .22 LR cal., design for NRA or ISSF "standard pistol" competition, split trigger guard, direct bullet feed, fully adj. rear sight and trigger, 6 shot mag., 5.1 in. barrel, alloy and steel construction, adj. anatomical wood grips. New 2000.

	100%	98%	95%	90%	80%	70%	60%
No MSR	$1,295	$1,150	$925	$825	$725	$625	$525

CM-32 - .32 S&W Wadcutter cal., otherwise similar to CM-22. New 2000.

	100%	98%	95%	90%	80%	70%	60%
No MSR	$1,395	$1,225	$995	$875	$775	$675	$575

CM-80 STANDARD SINGLE SHOT - .22 LR cal. only, adj. grips, frame, and sights. Importation disc. 1989.

100%	98%	95%	90%	80%	70%	60%
$925	$825	$725	$650	$585	$520	$465

Last MSR was $1,015.

Add $50 for left-hand model.

* **CM-80 Super Competition** - similar to CM-80 Standard, except has deluxe finish, and unique plexiglass front sighting system. Importation disc. 1989.

100%	98%	95%	90%	80%	70%	60%
$1,085	$920	$800	$690	$590	$520	$450

Last MSR was $1,196.

Add $50 for left-hand model.

Grading	100%	98%	95%	90%	80%	70%	60%

CM-84E FREE PISTOL - .22 LR cal., single shot, anatomical grips, unique electronic trigger features optic beam safety.

MSR	$1,450		$1,325	$1,100	$925	$800	$675	$575	$495

MODEL CM-102E SEMI-AUTO - .22 LR cal., advanced rapid fire competition pistol featuring updated ergonomic grips and flared trigger guard, first target pistol to utilize an electronic trigger. Mfg. 1992-97.

$1,525	$1,250	$995	$895	$795	$695	$595

Last MSR was $1,695.

MORTIMER, THOMAS

Current trademark owned and manufactured by Dickson & MacNaughton, located in Edinburgh, Scotland.

Please contact Dickson & MacNaughton directly for more information regarding this trademark, including current availability and pricing.

MOSSBERG, O.F. & SONS, INC.

Current manufacturer located in North Haven, CT, 1962-present and New Haven, CT, 1919-1962.

Oscar Mossberg developed an early reputation as a designer and inventor for the Iver Johnson, Marlin- Rockwell, Stevens and Shattuck Arms companies. In 1915, he began producing a 4-shot, .22 palm pistol known as the "Novelty", with revolving firing pin. After producing approx. 600 of these pistols, he sold the patent to C.S. Shattuck, which continued to manufacture under the name "Unique". The first 600 had no markings except serial numbers, and were destined for export to South America. Very few of these original "Novelty" pistols survived in this country, and are extremely rare specimens.

Since 1985, O.F. Mossberg & Sons, Inc. has produced only shotguns and accessories. Mossberg acquired Advanced Ordnance Corp. during 1996, a high quality manufacturer utilizing state-of-the-art CNC machinery.

DERRINGERS

M

BROWNIE - .22 LR cal., top break open action, rotating firing pin, 4-bbl. derringer, double action, 4- shot, approx. 32,000 mfg. 1919-1932.

$350	$300	$275	$250	$205	$175	$150

RIFLES: DISC.

The models listed appear alphabetically first, followed by numerical models in sequence.

MODEL K - .22 S, L and LR cal., tube mag., hammerless, 22 in. bbl., takedown, open sights, plain straight stock. Mfg. 1922-1931.

$250	$225	$200	$175	$150	$100	$85

MODEL M - similar to Model K, except has 24 in. octagonal bbl. Mfg. 1928-1931.

$285	$250	$200	$175	$150	$100	$85

MODEL S - similar to Model K, except has shorter mag. tube and 19¾ in. bbl., very rare. Mfg. 1927- 1931.

$350	$275	$225	$200	$175	$150	$135

MODEL L - .22 S, L and LR cal., falling block action, single shot, 24 in. takedown bbl., open sights, pistol grip stock. Mfg. 1929-1932.

$450	$350	$300	$275	$200	$185	$165

MODEL L-1 - rare target version of Model L with Lyman 2A tang sight and factory sling.
Add $50 to Model L values.

Grading	100%	98%	95%	90%	80%	70%	60%

MODEL R - .22 S, L and LR cal., bolt action, 24 in. round bbl., first tube feed, ivory bead front sight, open sporting bbl. sight. Mfg. 1930-1932.

| | $250 | $225 | $200 | $175 | $150 | $100 | $85 |

MODEL RM-7 - .30-06 or 7mm Rem. Mag. cal., bolt action, 22 inch (.30-06) or 24 inch (7mm Rem. Mag.) round barrel, three-position safety, folding leaf rear sight, gold bead front sight, hand- checkered American walnut with grip cap, built on imported Swedish rotary magazine action, cartridge release lever for unloading magazine from top. 3(7mm Rem. Mag.) or 4 (.30-06) shot mag. Mfg. approx. 1979-1980.

| | $325 | $290 | $265 | $245 | $230 | $215 | $200 |

MODEL B - .22 S, L and LR cal., single shot, bolt action, 22 in. round tapered bbl. Mfg. 1930-1932.

| | $175 | $130 | $100 | $75 | $60 | $50 | $35 |

MODEL C - .22 S, L and LR cal., single shot, 24 in. bbl., ivory bead front sight, open sporting rear sight. Mfg. 1931-1932.

| | $175 | $130 | $100 | $75 | $60 | $50 | $35 |

MODEL C-1 - target version of Model C, Lyman front and rear sights, leather sling and swivels, special walnut stock, rare.

Add $100 to Model C values.

MODELS 10, 14, 20, 21, 25, 25A, 125 - .22 S, L and LR cal., single shot models. Mfg. 1933-1938.

| | $175 | $130 | $100 | $75 | $60 | $50 | $35 |

Add 25% to prices for models equipped with aperture sights.

MODEL 26B - .22 S, L and LR cal., entirely new design in single shot rifles, easily identified by bolt handle at extreme rear of bolt, 26 in. tapered bbl., hooded ramp front sight, No. 4 rear peep, open bbl. sight, swivels. Mfg. 1938-1941.

| | $175 | $130 | $100 | $75 | $60 | $50 | $35 |

MODEL 26-C - similar to Model 26B with less expensive sights. Mfg. 1938-1941.

| | $150 | $125 | $85 | $70 | $55 | $45 | $35 |

MODEL 26M (OR B26M) - rare version of 26 series model with two-piece Mannlicher- style stock. Mfg. 1938.

| | $350 | $300 | $265 | $200 | $175 | $150 | $100 |

MODEL 30 - .22 S, L and LR cal., single shot, 24 in. bbl., rear peep and ramp front sights, swivels. Mfg. 1933-1935.

| | $150 | $125 | $100 | $75 | $65 | $55 | $45 |

MODEL 34 - similar to Model 30, except with heavy stock, target style. Mfg. 1934-1935.

| | $165 | $125 | $100 | $85 | $70 | $55 | $45 |

MODEL 35 - .22 S, L, LR cal., single shot, first full target model, 26 in. heavy target bbl., walnut stock, hooded front ramp, No. 4 rear peep with adj. aperture, approx. 9½ lbs. Mfg. 1935-1937.

| | $325 | $275 | $250 | $225 | $200 | $150 | $110 |

MODEL 35A - revised version of Model 35, with all-new "master action", approx. 8¼ lbs. Mfg. 1937.

| | $325 | $275 | $250 | $225 | $200 | $150 | $110 |

Add 40% for Model 35A-LS with Lyman sights.

MODEL 40 - .22 S, L, and LR cal., repeater with tube mag., 16 shot, 24 in. bbl., No. 3 Mossberg aperture sight, hooded ramp front sight, swivels, approx. 5 lbs. Mfg. 1933- 1935.

| | $175 | $150 | $125 | $90 | $70 | $65 | $60 |

MODEL 44 - similar to Model 40, but with heavier target stock, approx. 6 lbs. Mfg. 1934- 1935.

| | $250 | $200 | $150 | $110 | $90 | $80 | $75 |

Grading	100%	98%	95%	90%	80%	70%	60%

MODEL 42 - .22 S, L, and LR cal., first model with 7 rd. magazine, 24 in. bbl., front ramp, sporting bbl., rear aperture sights, 42 in. overall length, approx. 5 lbs. Mfg. 1935- 1937.

	$150	$125	$100	$80	$70	$65	$60

MODEL 42A - redesign of Model 42, new master action with shorter bolt and receiver. Mfg. 1937-1938.

	$150	$125	$100	$90	$80	$70	$65

MODEL 42B - same basic specs. as Model 42A, approx. 6 lbs. Mfg. 1938-1941.

	$150	$125	$100	$90	$80	$70	$65

MODEL 42C - similar to Model 42B, with open bbl. and bead front sights. Mfg. 1938- 1941.

	$125	$100	$90	$80	$65	$55	$45

MODEL 42M - .22 S, L and LR cal., 7-shot magazine, bolt action, two-piece Mannlicher- style stock, 23 in. bbl., 40 in. overall length, 6¾ lb., front ramp, open bbl., receiver aperture sights, trapdoor buttplate for extra mag. in butt stock. Mfg. 1940-1944.

	$175	$150	$135	$110	$100	$75	$50

Add $40 for extra magazine in butt stock.

MODELS 42M(a), 42M(b), 42M(c) - similar to Model 42M with minor changes in extractors and sights. Mfg. 1944-1950.

	$175	$150	$135	$110	$100	$75	$50

MODEL 42MB - military version of the Model 42M, approx. 50,000 mfg. for US and British troops as a training rifle. US Property marked with serial number, usually found w/o bbl. sight. Mfg. 1942-1943.

	$200	$175	$150	$135	$110	$100	$75

Add $50 for Lend-Lease models with British proofs.

MODEL L42A - left-handed version of Model 42A with true left-handed aperture sight, walnut stock, 1¼ in. swivels. Mfg. 1937-1938.

	$300	$250	$200	$150	$135	$125	$100

MODEL 43 - .22 S, L and LR cal., target rifle, 7-round magazine, external trigger adjustment, 13/ 16 in. diameter barrel, 26 in. long walnut stock with four-position 1¼ in. swivels in front, Lyman 17A front sight, Lyman 57 MS receiver peep sight, rare. Mfg. 1937-1938.

	$300	$250	$200	$185	$175	$150	$135

Add $25 for 43S Model and $50 for 43SS Model.

MODEL L43 - left-handed version of Model 43 target rifle with left-handed Lyman 57 MS rear aperture sight, rare. Mfg. 1937-1938.

	$400	$350	$300	$275	$250	$225	$200

Add $75 for models with true left-handed Mossberg scope.

MODEL 44B - .22 S, L, LR cal. target model, mag. fed, 26 in. heavy bbl., 43 in. overall length, approx. 8 lbs., front ramp and No. 4 receiver aperture sights, four-position front swivels, walnut stock. Mfg. 1938-1941.

	$250	$225	$200	$185	$175	$150	$135

MODEL 44US - .22 S, L, LR cal. target model, 7 round magazine, bolt action, 26 in. heavy bbl., overall length 43 in., approx. 8½ lbs., ramp front sight with hood, rear aperture sight, detachable swivels. Mfg. 1943-45.

	$325	$275	$175	$165	$150	$135	$125

MODEL 44US (US PROPERTY MARKED) - used by all branches of military for target training, approx. 53,000 mfg. 1943-1944.

	$250	$225	$200	$175	$150	$125	$100

MODELS 44US(a), 44US(b), 44US(c), 44US(d) - same rifle as 44US with minor changes in sights and extractors. Mfg. 1944-1949.

	$200	$185	$175	$165	$150	$135	$125

M

Grading	100%	98%	95%	90%	80%	70%	60%

MODEL 45 - .22 S, L and LR cal., tube fed, bolt action, 24 in. heavy target bbl., overall length 42½ in., approx. 6¾ lbs., hooded front sight, sporting bbl. sight, receiver aperture sight. Mfg. 1935- 1937.

	$175	$150	$135	$125	$100	$85	$65

MODEL 45-A - similar to Model 45 with newer, master action. Mfg. 1937-38.

	$175	$150	$135	$125	$100	$85	$65

MODEL L45-A - similar to Model 45-A, true left-handed version. Mfg. 1937-1938.

	$300	$275	$250	$200	$150	$125	$100

MODEL 46 - .22 S, L and LR cal., tube fed, bolt action, 26 in. heavy bbl., overall 44½ in., beavertail walnut stock, hooded ramp front, rear aperture sight, 7½ lbs. Mfg. 1935- 1937.

	$175	$150	$135	$125	$100	$85	$65

MODEL 46T - similar to Model 46 with heavier bbl. and stock. Mfg. 1936-1937.

	$200	$175	$150	$135	$125	$100	$75

MODEL 46A - similar to Model 46 with master action. Mfg. 1937-1938.

	$175	$150	$135	$125	$100	$85	$65

MODEL 46-ALS - similar to Model 46-A with Lyman 17A front sight and 57 MS rear aperture, rare. Mfg. 1937-1938.

	$250	$225	$200	$175	$150	$125	$100

MODEL L46-ALS - similar to Model 46-ALS with true left-handed action and left- handed Lyman rear sight, very rare. Mfg. 1937-1938.

	$325	$300	$275	$250	$225	$200	$175

MODEL 46B - .22 S, L and LR cal., tube fed, new streamlined design, 43 1/3 in. overall, walnut stock, 7 lbs. Mfg. 1938-1945.

	$150	$135	$110	$100	$85	$75	$65

MODEL 46B-T - heavy barrel and stock, target version of Model 46-B, rare. Mfg. 1938.

	$200	$175	$150	$135	$110	$95	$85

MODEL 46M - .22 S, L and LR cal., bolt action, tube fed, with two-piece Mannlicher- style walnut stock, 23 in. bbl., overall 40 in., hooded front, sporting bbl., rear aperture sight, 7 lbs. Mfg. 1940- 1945.

	$200	$175	$150	$125	$110	$95	$80

MODELS 46M(a), 46M(b) - similar to Model 46M with minor changes in sights. Mfg. 1945-1952.

	$200	$175	$150	$125	$110	$95	$80

MODEL 50 - .22 S, L, LR cal., semi-auto, tube fed through butt stock, 24 in. bbl., overall 43¾ in., hooded front sight, open bbl. sight, no swivels, 6¾ lbs. Mfg. 1939-1942.

	$165	$150	$135	$125	$110	$85	$65

MODEL 51 - similar to Model 50 with receiver aperture sight, heavier, beavertail stock, q.d. swivels, 7¼ lbs. Mfg. 1939.

	$165	$150	$135	$125	$110	$85	$65

MODEL 51M - similar to Model 51 with two-piece Mannlicher style walnut stock, 20 in. bbl, 40 in. overall, front ramp, rear aperture, sporting bbl. sights, 7 lbs. Mfg. 1939-1946.

	$185	$150	$135	$125	$110	$95	$80

MODEL 140B - .22 S, L and LR cal., bolt action, mag. fed, 24½ in. bbl., 42 in. overall, walnut stock, front ramp, sporting bbl., rear aperture sight, 5¾ lbs. Mfg. 1957-1958.

	$165	$150	$135	$125	$110	$85	$65

MODEL 140K - similar to Model 140B with post front and no aperture sight. Mfg. 1955- 1958.

	$150	$125	$100	$80	$70	$60	$50

Grading	100%	98%	95%	90%	80%	70%	60%

MODEL 142A - .22 S, L and LR cal., bolt action, 7 round mag., carbine model with fold down forearm, walnut stock with sling, 18 in. bbl., 27 in. overall length, rear aperture sight and military front sight, no bbl. sight, early models had "T" shaped bolt handles and wood forearms, later models had round knob bolt handle and black plastic forearm, 5 lbs. Mfg. 1949-1957.

	$190	$160	$140	$125	$110	$85	$65

MODEL 142K - similar to Model 142A with less expensive sights, sporting barrel and post front type. No aperture sight. Mfg. 1953-1957.

	$175	$150	$125	$100	$80	$75	$55

MODEL 144 - .22 S, L, LR cal., full target rifle, heavy 26 in. bbl., 43 in. overall length, 8 lbs., q.d. swivels, four-position front swivels, rear aperture, front ramp sights, "T" shaped bolt handle. Mfg. 1949-1954.

	$200	$185	$165	$150	$135	$125	$110

MODEL 144LS - similar to Model 144, with round knob handle, Lyman 57 MS rear aperture and 17A front sight. Mfg. 1954-1960.

	$250	$235	$220	$200	$185	$165	$150

MODEL 144LS-A - similar to Model 144LS, with Mossberg S 130 rear aperture in place of Lyman 57 MS. Mfg. 1960-1979.

	$250	$235	$220	$200	$185	$165	$150

MODEL 144LS-B - last generation of 144 series, 27 in. bbl., 15/16 in. diameter, 44 in. overall length, new Mossberg S 331 aperture, Lyman 17A front sight, 8½ lbs. Mfg. 1979-1985.

	$275	$250	$235	$210	$190	$175	$165

MODEL 146-B - .22 S, L and LR cal., bolt action, tube fed, capacity of 30S, 23L, 20LR, 26 in. bbl., overall length 43¼ in., ramp front sight, leaf bbl. and rear aperture sight, walnut Monte Carlo stock with cheekpiece, QD swivels, adj. trigger, Schnabel forend, 7 lbs. Mfg. 1949-1954.

	$180	$150	$135	$125	$100	$85	$65

MODEL 146B-A - similar to Model 146-B, with different bbl. sight. Mfg. 1954-1958.

	$180	$150	$135	$125	$100	$85	$65

MODEL 151-K - .22 S, L, LR cal., semi-auto, butt fed, 24 in. bbl., overall 44 in., open sights, walnut Monte Carlo stock with cheekpiece and Schnabel forend, 6 lbs. Mfg. 1950-1951.

	$175	$150	$135	$100	$80	$70	$60

MODEL 151(M) - .22 S, L, LR cal., semi-auto butt fed, capacity 15LR, 20 in. bbl., overall 40 in., two-piece Mannlicher-style walnut stock, QD swivels, steel butt plate, hooded ramp front, sporting rear, micro-click aperture sights, 7 lbs. Mfg. 1946-1947.

	$175	$150	$135	$125	$100	$85	$65

MODELS 151M(a), 151M(b), 151M(c) - similar to Model 151M with minor changes in butt plate and sights. Mfg. 1947-1958.

	$175	$150	$135	$125	$100	$85	$65

MODEL 152 - .22 S, L, LR cal., semi-auto, mag. fed with 7 round capacity, carbine model with hinged, fold-down forend, Monte Carlo stock with adj. sling, 18 in. bbl., 27 in. overall, receiver aperture and military post front sights, 5 lbs. Mfg. 1948-1952.

	$175	$150	$135	$125	$100	$85	$65

MODEL 152K - similar to Model 152 with open sights. Mfg. 1950-1957.

	$150	$125	$110	$100	$90	$75	$50

MODEL 320B - .22 S, L, LR cal., single shot, junior target model, bolt action, new closed breech design, 24 in. bbl., overall 43½ in., 5¾ lbs., walnut finish Monte Carlo stock with swivels and pistol grip, front ramp, rear aperture and sporting bbl. sights. Mfg. 1960-1971.

	$165	$140	$125	$110	$85	$75	$55

M

Grading	100%	98%	95%	90%	80%	70%	60%

MODELS 320K, 320K-A - similar to Model 320B with open sights, no swivels, later models marked 321, 321K. Mfg. 1960-1980.

| | $125 | $100 | $80 | $70 | $60 | $55 | $50 |

MODELS 340B, 340B-A - .22 S, L, LR cal., bolt action, 7 round magazine, 24 in. bbl., 43½ in. overall length, walnut, Monte Carlo stock with cheekpiece and pistol grip, front ramp, sporting bbl., rear aperture sights, 6½ lbs. Mfg. 1958-1980.

| | $165 | $140 | $125 | $110 | $85 | $75 | $55 |

> At least one example of a Model 340B smoothbore gun is known. This particular specimen was factory fitted with a stock that lacked a magazine cut-out, so the gun could only be fired as a single shot. The muzzle was not threaded to accept any sort of barrel adaptor.

MODELS 340K, 340K-A - similar to Model 340B with open sights, later models marked 341. Mfg. 1958-1980.

| | $125 | $100 | $80 | $70 | $60 | $55 | $50 |

MODEL 340M - .22 S, L, LR cal. bolt action, mag. fed, same operating design as other 340 series, with one-piece, walnut Mannlicher-style Monte Carlo stock with pistol grip and swivels, 18½ in. bbl., 38½ in. overall, open rear and bead front sights, rare, 5¼ lbs. Mfg. 1970-1972.

| | $300 | $275 | $250 | $200 | $185 | $175 | $165 |

MODEL 342 - .22 S, L and LR cal., bolt action, mag. fed, carbine model with hinged, black plastic, fold- down forend, walnut Monte Carlo stock with swivels and sling, 18 in. bbl., 38 in. overall, military post front and rear aperture sight, 5 lbs. Mfg. 1957-1959.

| | $175 | $150 | $125 | $110 | $85 | $75 | $55 |

MODELS 342K, 342K-A - similar to Model 342 with open sights. Mfg. 1958-1971.

| | $150 | $125 | $100 | $75 | $60 | $55 | $50 |

MODELS 344, 344K - .22 S, L, LR cal., bolt action, mag. fed, walnut finish, checkered stock, 344K is carbine length. Mfg. 1985.

| | $165 | $140 | $125 | $110 | $85 | $75 | $55 |

MODEL 346B - .22 S, L, and LR cal., bolt action tube feed, closed-breech design, walnut Monte Carlo stock with cheekpiece, QD swivels, capacity 25S, 20L, 18LR, 24 in. bbl., 42½ in. overall, rear aperture, sporting bbl., hooded front ramp sights, 6½ lbs. Mfg. 1958-1960.

| | $165 | $140 | $125 | $110 | $85 | $75 | $55 |

MODELS 346K, 346K-A - similar to Model 346B w/open sights. Mfg. 1958-1968.

| | $135 | $120 | $110 | $100 | $80 | $70 | $55 |

MODEL 350K - .22 LR cal., semi-auto, LR only, mag. fed, walnut Monte Carlo stock with pistol grip and cheekpiece, 23½ in. bbl., overall 43½ in., open sights, 6 lbs. Mfg. 1958- 1960.

| | $150 | $125 | $100 | $65 | $60 | $50 | $40 |

MODEL 350 K-A - similar to Model 350K with dovetail bbl. sight. Mfg. 1960-1968.

| | $150 | $125 | $100 | $65 | $60 | $50 | $40 |

MODEL 351K - .22 LR cal., semi-auto, tube fed through stock, walnut Monte Carlo stock with pistol grip, 24 in. bbl., 43 in. overall, 6 lbs. Mfg. 1958-1960.

| | $150 | $125 | $100 | $65 | $60 | $50 | $40 |

MODEL 351K-A - similar to Model 351K with dovetail bbl. sight. Mfg. 1960-68.

| | $150 | $125 | $100 | $65 | $60 | $50 | $40 |

MODEL 352 - .22 LR cal., mag. fed, carbine model with fold-down black plastic forend, walnut Monte Carlo stock, pistol grip, swivels, web strap, 18 in. bbl., overall 38 in., rear peep, post front sights, 5 lbs. Mfg. 1957-1959.

| | $150 | $125 | $100 | $85 | $75 | $65 | $55 |

MODELS 352K, 352 K-A, 352K-B - similar to Model 352 with open sights. Mfg. 1960- 1971.

| | $140 | $120 | $90 | $75 | $70 | $65 | $55 |

Grading	100%	98%	95%	90%	80%	70%	60%

MODEL 377, "PLINKSTER" - .22 LR cal., semi-auto, tube fed, synthetic stock with "thumb hole", capacity 15 rds., 20 in. bbl., overall 40 in., 6.25 lbs., equipped with 4X scope. Mfg. 1977- 1979.

| | $175 | $150 | $135 | $100 | $85 | $75 | $65 |

MODELS 380, 380S - same basic design as Model 377, only with solid, wood stock, open sights. Model 480 same in 1985. Mfg. 1980-1985.

| | $135 | $115 | $100 | $85 | $75 | $65 | $55 |

MODEL 400 "PALAMINO" - .22 S, L and LR cal., lever action, tube fed, walnut, beavertail stock and forearm, cross bolt safety, 24 in. bbl., overall length, 41 in., bead front, open rear sights, 5½ lbs. Mfg. 1959-1964.

| | $250 | $200 | $175 | $150 | $135 | $100 | $85 |

Model 400-A similar to in specs and value, dovetail.

MODEL 402 - carbine version of Model 400, bbl. 20 in. Mfg. 1961-1971.

| | $250 | $200 | $175 | $150 | $135 | $100 | $85 |

MODEL 430 - .22 LR cal., semi-auto, tubular mag. under bbl. with capacity of 18 LR, walnut checkered Monte Carlo stock and checkered forend, 24 in. bbl., overall length 43½ in., open sights, 6.25 lbs. Mfg. 1970-1971.

| | $135 | $115 | $100 | $85 | $75 | $65 | $55 |

MODEL 432 - similar to Model 430 with 20 in. bbl., straight grip, smooth stock and forend, walnut finish. Mfg. 1970-1971.

| | $135 | $115 | $100 | $75 | $65 | $60 | $50 |

MODEL 472 - .30-30 Win. or .35 Rem. cal., lever action carbine, 20 in. barrel, open sights, pistol grip or straight stock, saddle ring on straight model. Mfg. 1972-disc.

| | $180 | $155 | $145 | $130 | $120 | $110 | $90 |

MODEL 472 RIFLE - similar to Carbine, except 24 in. barrel, pistol grip stock. Mfg. 1974- 1976.

| | $195 | $165 | $155 | $145 | $130 | $120 | $100 |

MODEL 472 BRUSH GUN - similar to Carbine, except 18 in. barrel, straight stock only. Mfg. 1974-1976.

| | $195 | $165 | $155 | $145 | $130 | $120 | $100 |

MODEL 472 ONE IN FIVE THOUSAND - similar to Brush Gun, except Indian scene etched on receiver, brass butt plate, saddle ring and barrel bands, select stock, only 5,000 mfg., 1974.

| | $415 | $210 | $195 | $175 | $165 | $145 | $120 |

MODEL 479 PCA - .30-30 Win. cal., lever action, 20 in. barrel, 6 shot capacity.

| | $195 | $135 | $120 | $110 | $95 | $85 | $75 |

MODEL 479 RR - limited edition "Roy Rogers" signature model, gold trigger, barrel bands, 5,000 total mfg. New 1983.

| | $350 | $275 | $215 | | | | |

MODEL 479 - .30-30 Win. cal. only, lever action, 6 shot tube mag., 20 in. barrel with adj. sights, 7 lbs. Mfg. 1985 only.

| | $190 | $175 | $160 | $150 | $145 | $140 | $135 |

Last MSR was $232.

Mossberg also has made several .22 bolt action and semi-auto sporters that are in the $115 - $130 price range. While they are good shooting models, they are not covered in this section as they are not collectible.

MODEL 480 - similar to Models 380 and 380S.

| | $135 | $115 | $100 | $85 | $75 | $65 | $55 |

Grading	100%	98%	95%	90%	80%	70%	60%

MODEL 620K - .22 Mag. cal., single shot, bolt action, walnut Monte Carlo stock, pistol grip, cheekpiece, sling swivels, 24 in. bbl., overall 44¾ in., open rear, post front sights, 6 lbs. Mfg. 1959- 1960.

	$150	$135	$115	$100	$85	$75	$65

MODEL 620K-A - similar to Model 620K with change in bbl. sight. Mfg. 1960-1968.

	$150	$135	$115	$100	$85	$75	$65

MODELS 640K, 640K-S - similar to 620 series, but 5 shot mag. repeater. Mfg. 1959- 1984.

	$195	$150	$135	$125	$105	$90	$75

MODEL 640KS - similar to Model 640K with deluxe checkered stock and gold trigger. Mfg. 1960-1968.

	$225	$200	$185	$150	$135	$120	$110

MODEL 640M - full length, Mannlicher-styled stock, version of 640, checkered stock, Monte Carlo, cheekpiece, pistol grip, swivels and leather strap, heavy receiver, jeweled bolt, 20 in. bbl., overall 40¾ in., open rear sights, bead front, 6 lbs. Mfg. 1971.

	$300	$275	$225	$200	$175	$165	$150

MODEL 642K - .22 Mag. cal., carbine style, bolt action, 5 rd. mag., fold-down forend, walnut stock with web sling, 18 in. bbl., overall 38¼ in., open bbl. and bead front sights, 5 lbs. Mfg. 1960- 1968.

	$225	$200	$185	$150	$135	$120	$110

MODEL 800 - .222 Rem., .22-250 Rem., .243 Win., or .308 Win. cal., bolt action, 22 in. barrel, folding sight, checkered pistol grip stock. Mfg. 1967-disc.

	$220	$195	$165	$110	$85	$55	$45

MODEL 800VT - similar to 800, except .222 Rem., .22-250 Rem., or .243 Win. cal., 24 in. heavy barrel, no sights. Mfg. 1968-disc.

	$220	$195	$165	$110	$85	$55	$45

MODEL 800M - similar to 800, except 20 in. barrel, full length stock, spoon bolt handle. Mfg. 1969-1972.

	$275	$240	$220	$205	$175	$160	$145

MODEL 800D - similar to 800, with roll-over combination and cheekpiece, checkered stock with rosewood forearm tip and pistol cap, no .222 Rem. available. Mfg. 1970- 1973.

	$325	$300	$275	$250	$225	$200	$165

MODEL 810 - .270 Win., .30-06, 6.5mm Rem. Mag., or .338 Win. Mag. cal., bolt action, 22 or 24 in. barrel, rear leaf sight, checkered Monte Carlo stock. Mfg. 1970-disc.

	$300	$275	$250	$225	$200	$175	$150

RIFLES: BOLT ACTION, RECENT PRODUCTION

In 1985, Mossberg purchased the parts inventory and importing rights for those rifles that Smith & Wesson imported from Howa of Japan. These new models were identical to those models which S&W disc.

MODEL 1500 MOUNTAINEER GRADE I - .223 Rem., .243 Win., .270 Win., .30- 06, or 7mm Rem. Mag. cal., bolt action, 22 or 24 (7mm Rem. Mag. only) in. barrel, 5 or 6 shot mag., available with or without sights, hardwood stock is satin finished, blued finish, about 7 lbs. 10 oz. Imported 1986-87 only.

	$285	$250	$225	$195	$180	$165	$150

Last MSR was $335.

Add $15 for 7mm Rem. Mag. cal., $25 for iron sights.

M

Grading	100%	98%	95%	90%	80%	70%	60%

✳ **Model 1500 Varmint** - .22-250 Rem., .223 Rem., or .308 Win. cal., similar to Model 1500 Grade I, except has 24 in. heavy barrel only, Monte Carlo stock. Imported 1986-87 only.

	$360	$300	$270	$235	$205	$190	$175

Last MSR was $457.

Add $10 for parkerized finish (oil finished stock with swivels - not available in .22-250 Rem. cal.).

Blue finish and high gloss wood finish available with .22-250 Rem. or .223 Rem. cal. only. Parkerized variation is available in .223 Rem. or .308 Win. cal. only (matte wood finish, includes swivels).

MODEL 1500 MOUNTAINEER GRADE II -- similar to Grade I Mountaineer, except has select checkered American walnut stock. Also available in .300 Win. Mag. or .338 Win. Mag. cal. Imported 1986-87 only.

	$315	$270	$235	$205	$190	$175	$160

Last MSR was $368.

Add $15 for Mag. cals.
Add $25 for iron sights.

MODEL 1550 - similar to Model 1500, except has detachable mag. and available in standard cals. (.243 Win., .270 Win., or .30-06), with or without sights. Imported 1986-87 only.

	$330	$280	$245	$210	$190	$175	$160

Last MSR was $391.

Add $24 for iron sights.

MODEL 1700 LS - .243 Win., .270 Win., or .30-06 cal., no sights, jeweled bolt body and knurled bolt handle, detachable mag., Schnabel forend, deluxe checkering, 7 lbs. Imported 1986-87 only.

	$405	$365	$310	$275	$240	$205	$190

Last MSR was $492.

Mossberg "Targo" Smoothbore Models

These dual-purpose smoothbore rifles were designed to fire both .22 RF bullets and shotshell ammunition. Targo barrels are threaded either externally (Models 26T, 42TR, 42T, B42T) or internally (Models 320TR, 340TR) at the muzzle for attachment of rifled and smoothbore adapters which enable the shooter to use the gun as a standard rifle, or (with the smoothbore adapter installed) as a miniature shotgun. Mossberg produced a line of Targo accessories including a barrel-mounted miniature clay target launcher, a pistol grip hand trap frame, a hand thrower, a target carrier, clay targets, hard rubber "practice" targets, and a target catching net. The presence of one or more of these accessories augments the value of any model Targo gun. Prices quoted below are for guns with all listed features exclusive of Targo accessories.

MODEL 26-T SINGLE SHOT - .22 RF/shotshell cal., bolt action, thumb lever safety located at rear of bolt, black plastic buttplate and contoured black plastic triggerguard (#R413), rifle-style open rear sight with screw adjustments for windage and elevation, shotgun style elevated front bead sight with removable sight hood, smoothbore and rifled screw-on barrel adapters and spanner wrench for adapter removal and installation, stock generally provided with sling swivels, forend necks down toward muzzle, takedown screw has retaining bail to facilitate removal by hand. Mfg. 1940-42 (only 873 mfg.).

	$600	$450	$375	$335	$280	$245	$220

100% price is estimated since an example would be extremely rare.

MODEL 42T BOLT ACTION REPEATER - .22 RF/shotshell cal., box magazine (7- round) fitted with adapter screw to enable firing of .22 Short cartridges, same safety, buttplate, optional stock swivels, and shotgun style front sight as Model 26T, #R145 contoured black plastic triggerguard, supplied with the smoothbore barrel adapter only (rifled adapter, open rear sight, and front sight hood were not provided), produced 1940-42 (906 guns made), examples in 95% or better condition are uncommon.

	$440	$325	$310	$295	$260	$235	$200

Grading	100%	98%	95%	90%	80%	70%	60%

MODEL 42TR BOLT ACTION REPEATER - .22 RF/shotshell cal., produced before and after WWII until roughly 1949. Pre-War (1940-42) guns identical to Model 42T except rifled adapter, open rear sight, and front sight hood were provided, and no stock swivels. The earliest pre-War 42TRs were marked using a 42T barrel stamp and a separate "R" (stamped to the right of the "T"). Post-War (1946-49) guns have slotted takedown screw, magazine plate, shorter unnecked forend, and (frequently) a blue bolt knob. The most common of all Targo guns. A total of 6,577 guns were produced during the period 1940-42 (post-War production figures are not available). Both early and late versions of this model are comparably priced.

	$415	$345	$295	$280	$245	$190	$175

Add $250 for cased gun with clay targets and Targo accessories.

Note: A very small number of 42TRs were supplied with fitted cases and Targo accessories and were used as dealer displays. Several variations in the internal compartmentalization of these cases have been noted. The pre-War 42TR display guns came in a hard (plywood) luggage case. The post-War guns were supplied in a semi-hard (fiberboard) luggage case.

MODEL B42T BOLT ACTION REPEATER - .22 RF/shotshell cal., identical to the Model 42TR, except stock has sling swivels and metal buttplate with trapdoor for magazine storage. Gun was supplied with extended 15- round box magazine in addition to the standard 7-round mag. A comparatively scarce model marketed exclusively through mail order stores (e.g., Spiegel) in the early 1940s. According to factory records, only 250 guns were made, all in 1940.

	$465	$385	$350	$325	$285	$250	$210

The 15 round magazine originally supplied with this model is scarce – good specimens are currently selling for approx. $85-$120 (may exceed legal limits, depending on state).

MODEL 320TR SINGLE SHOT BOLT ACTION - .22 RF/shotshell, automatic safety with thumb lever located on right side of receiver, black plastic buttplate and contoured black plastic triggerguard. Rifle-style ("U" notch) rear sight adjustable for elevation (via sliding wedge) and windage (by deflecting sight arm laterally by hand). Sporting type vertical blade front sight. Gun supplied with rifled and smoothbore screw-in barrel adapters. A wire target carrier and a hand thrower for launching miniature clay targets were included with each gun. Limited mfg. 1961-62.

	$320	$240	$225	$190	$150	$135	$115

Factory records indicate that only 962 guns were sold during the production period.

MODEL 340TR BOLT ACTION REPEATER - .22 RF/shotshell cal., 7-round box magazine featuring adjustable top bar to accommodate feeding of .22 S, L, and LR cartridges. Two known variations of thumb lever safety markings (words "OFF"/"ON" and red dot). Other features identical to Model 320TR. Limited mfg. 1961-62.

	$345	$265	$240	$215	$165	$145	$125

Factory records indicate that only 2,026 guns were sold during the production period.

RIFLES: LEVER ACTION

MODEL SSi-ONE (RIFLE/SHOTGUN) - .22-250 Rem., .223 Rem., .243 Win., .270 Win., .30-06, or .308 Win. cal., also available in 12 ga., design allows interchangeable rifle/shotgun barrels, single shot, satin finished checkered walnut stock and forearm, matte blue metal, 24 in. regular or heavy (.22-250 Rem. or .223 Rem. cal.) rifle barrel with ejector or 12 ga. (3 in. chamber with rifled bore for Slug, 3½ in. chamber for Turkey) ported barrel, break open action, cocking indicator, drilled and tapped intergral scope base, automatic safety, approx. 8 (regular) or 10 (heavy) lbs. New 2001.

MSR	$469	$390	$310	$250	$225	$200	$180	$160

Add $233 per interchangeable rifle barrel and $290 for SSi-One Slug Model barrel.
Add $21 for heavy barrel or 12 ga. Slug (fully rifled bore) variation.

Grading	100%	98%	95%	90%	80%	70%	60%

SHOTGUNS: BOLT ACTION - DISC.

MODELS G-4, 70, 73, 73B - .410 bore, single shot, mfg. 1932-1940.

	$110	$100	$85	$70	$60	$50	$40

MODELS 80, 83, 83B, 83D - .410 bore, 3 or 4 shot, internal top-loading mag., mfg. 1933-1946.

	$135	$110	$95	$75	$60	$50	$40

MODELS 75, 75A, 75B - 20 ga., bolt action, single shot, mfg. 1933-1940.

	$110	$100	$85	$70	$60	$50	$40

MODELS 85, 85A, 85B, 85D - 20 ga., 2 or 3 shot mag., mfg. 1934-1940.

	$110	$100	$85	$70	$60	$50	$40

MODELS 173, 173A, 173Y - .410 bore, single shot, "Y" designates youth model, mfg. 1957-1973.

	$110	$100	$85	$70	$60	$50	$40

MODELS 183, 183D, 283D(a), 183D-B, 183D-C, 183D-D, 183D-E, 183D-F, 183K, 183K-B, 183K-C, 183T, 184T, 184TY, 283T, 284T, 284TY - .410 bore, bolt action shotgun, 2 or 3 shot mag., various screw-on or C-Lect choke on some models, mfg. 1948-1985.

	$125	$110	$95	$75	$60	$55	$50

MODELS 185, 185D, 185D-A, 185D-B, 185D-C, 185K, 185K-A, 185K-B - 20 ga., 2 shot 2¾ in. mag., various screw-on or C-Lect chokes, mfg. 1947-1959.

	$125	$110	$95	$75	$60	$55	$50

MODELS 190, 190D, 190D-A, 190K-A, 190K-B - 16 ga., bolt action, 2 shot 2¾ in. mag., various screw-on or C-Lect choke, mfg. 1955- 1958.

	$125	$110	$95	$75	$60	$55	$50

MODELS 195, 195A, 195K-A, 195D - same as model 185 Series, only 12 ga. version, mfg. 1954-1968.

	$125	$110	$95	$75	$60	$55	$50

MODELS 385, 385K, 385KA, 385T, 485A, 485B - 20 ga., bolt action, 3 in. chamber, detachable box mag., mfg. 1960-1986.

	$125	$110	$95	$75	$60	$55	$50

M

MODELS 390, 390K-A, 390K-B, 490A - 16 ga., 3 in. chamber, detachable box mag., mfg. 1971-1976.

	$125	$110	$95	$75	$60	$55	$50

MODELS 395, 395K, 395KA, 395S, 395 SPL., 495A, 495B - 12 ga., 3 in. chamber, detachable box mag., mfg. 1963-1983.

	$125	$110	$95	$75	$60	$55	$50

Add $40 for slug barrel ("S" designation) or 38 in. barrel (spl.).

MODELS 595, 595K - 12 ga., bolt action, special police stock, 4 shot mag., mfg. 1983- 1985.

	$175	$150	$135	$110	$95	$85	$75

Add $40 for 38 in. barrel (Spl.).

SHOTGUNS: RECENT PRODUCTION

In 1985, Mossberg purchased the parts inventory and manufacturing rights for the shotguns that Smith & Wesson discontinued in 1984. These new models (manufactured in Japan) are identical to those models which S&W discontinued. Parts and warranties are not interchangeable. Beginning 1989, all Mossbergs sold in the U.S. and Canada have been provided with a Cablelock which goes through the ejection port, making the gun's action inoperable.

To celebrate its 75th anniversary, Mossberg released a new Crown Grade variation within most models during 1994, including the slide action 500 and 835 Series. These can be differentiated from previous manufacture by cut checkering, redesigned walnut or American hardwood stocks and forearms, screw-in choke tubes, and 4 different camo patterns. The Crown Grade was discontinued in 2000.

MODEL 200K SLIDE ACTION - slide action shotgun, 12 ga., 28 in., select choke, plain pistol grip stock, black nylon slide handle. Mfg. 1955-1959.

	$175	$150	$125	$90	$65	$55	$40

MODEL 200D - similar to 200K, except interchangeable choke tubes (2). Mfg. 1955- 1959.

	$175	$150	$125	$90	$65	$55	$40

MODEL 500 SLIDE ACTION FIELD (1962-1998 MFG.) - 12, 20 ga., or .410 bore, slide action, 24 in. (with rifle sights) or 20-28 in. barrel (with various chokes), upper receiver slide safety, C-Lect (disc.) & Accu-Choke (became standard 1994) choke system, checkered hardwood pistol grip stock after 1973. Mfg. 1962-1998.

	$250	$200	$165	$135	$120	$110	$100

Last MSR was $309.

Subtract 10% if without VR (disc.).
Subtract 10% for fixed choke barrel in 12 or 20 ga.
For recent Model 500 information and values, please refer to Model 500 Field – Current Mfg. later in this section.

✳ **Model 500 Slugster** - 12 or 20 (disc. 1997) ga., 24 in. cyl. (disc. 1997) or rifled bore (became standard 1998) barrel, barrel porting became standard in 1998, choice of sights, walnut finished hardwood stock and forearm. Disc. 1998.

	$270	$220	$175	$145	$125	$110	$100

Last MSR was $336.

Subtract $75 if w/o barrel porting or rifled bore.

✳ **Model 500 Bantam** - 20 ga. or .410 bore (new 1991) only, 22 in. (20 ga.), 24 in. fixed choke barrel (.410 bore), or 26 in. VR barrel with Accu-choke(s), blue or blue matte (disc.), Bantam Jake with Realtree Camo finish in 20 ga./22 in. VR barrel only (disc.), 20 ga. has walnut finish stock and .410 bore has synthetic stock (both stocks are tailored for youth dimensions), 6.9 lbs. Mfg. 1990-96, reintroduced 1998 only.

	$240	$195	$165	$135	$120	$110	$100

Last MSR was $312.

Subtract $12 for .410 bore.
Add $45 for Bantam Jake configuration (disc. 1993).

✳ **Model 500 Turkey** - 12 or 20 (new 1995) ga., 22 (20 ga. only), or 24 in. barrel, Woodlands metal/wood camo finish. Disc. 1997.

	$265	$195	$150				

Last MSR was $324.

Subtract $15 for 20 ga.
Add $60 for 24 in. VR barrel with Ghost Ring Sight (12 ga. only).

✳ **Model 500 Muzzleloader Combo** - 12 ga. only, includes 24 in. (rifled bore only, new 1993) or 28 in. VR Accu-choke barrel and additional 24 in. .50 cal. muzzleloader conversion barrel with rifled bore and iron sights, walnut finished hardwood stock and forearm, 7.2 lbs. Mfg. 1991-96.

	$335	$280	$240	$200	$180	$160	$145

Last MSR was $385.

✳ **Model 500 Quail Unlimited** - 20 ga. only, 26 in. VR barrel with Accu-II chokes (3), engraved receiver and hand selected stock and forearm, 3,500 mfg. in 1991 to commemorate the 10th anniversary of Quail Unlimited.

	$295	$240	$195				

Last MSR was $359.

M

Grading	100%	98%	95%	90%	80%	70%	60%

❋ ***Model 500 Sporting Steel Shot*** - 12 ga. only, 3 in. chamber, 28 in. VR Accu- choke barrel with special Accu-steel tube for shooting steel shot. Mfg. 1987-90.

| | $250 | $200 | $175 | $165 | $155 | $145 | $135 |

Add $29 for camo stock (disc. 1989).

This model was phased out of production in 1990 since all Mossberg shotguns currently manufactured are capable of shooting steel shot safely. The last MSR was $295.

MODEL 500 REGAL SERIES - 12 or 20 ga., slide action, 26 or 28 in. barrel, select checkered walnut, VR. Disc. 1987.

| | $240 | $195 | $175 | $165 | $155 | $145 | $135 |

Last MSR was $286.

Add $39 for Combo pack (includes 1 extra 24 in. slugster barrel).
Add $19 for Accu-choke.

MODEL 500 CAMPER - 12, 20 ga., or .410 bore only, 18½ in. barrel, synthetic pistol grip (no stock), camo carrying case optional, blued finish. Mfg. 1986-90 only.

| | $235 | $190 | $175 | $165 | $155 | $145 | $135 |

Last MSR was $276.

Add $25 for .410 bore.
Add $30 for camo case.

MODEL 500 HI-RIB TRAP - 12 ga. only, high post trap rib, 28 or 30 in. barrel. Disc. 1986.

| | $285 | $250 | $230 | $200 | $175 | $155 | $140 |

Last MSR was $334.

Add $20 for Accu-choke.

MODEL 500 SUPER GRADE - similar to Model 500 Field, except VR and checkered, no 16 ga. Mfg. 1965-1976.

| | $250 | $215 | $180 | $170 | $160 | $140 | $130 |

MODEL 500 ATR SUPER GRADE - similar to Model 500 Field, except 12 ga., VR, 30 in. full, checkered Monte Carlo. Mfg. 1968-1971.

| | $295 | $260 | $230 | $200 | $175 | $155 | $140 |

MODEL 500 PIGEON GRADE - similar to 500 Super Grade, except etched and scroll engraving, select wood, floating VR. Mfg. 1971-1975.

| | $385 | $330 | $305 | $250 | $210 | $185 | $165 |

MODEL 500 APTR PIGEON GRADE TRAP - similar to 500 ATR, except trap style stock. Mfg. 1971-1975.

| | $440 | $415 | $330 | $250 | $220 | $200 | $175 |

MODEL 500 DSPR DUCK STAMP COMMERCIAL - similar to Pigeon Grade, except wood duck etching. 1,000 mfg. 1975.

| | $525 | $330 | $310 | $285 | $260 | $220 | $195 |

MODEL 500L SERIES - similar to 500 Field Grade, except no 16 ga., etched receiver, new style stock and slide. Mfg. 1977-1983.

| | $250 | $220 | $210 | $200 | $175 | $165 | $140 |

MODEL 500 BULLPUP - 12 ga., 18½ (6 shot) or 20 (9 shot) in. barrel, bullpup configuration, 6 or 9 shot mag., includes shrouded barrel, carrying handle, ejection port in stock, employs high impact materials. Mfg. 1986-1990.

| | $475 | $425 | $385 | $350 | $320 | $290 | $260 |

Last MSR was $425.

Add $15 for 8 shot mag. (disc.).

MODEL 500 SPECIAL HUNTER - 12 or 20 ga., 3 in. chamber, 26 or 28 in. VR barrel with or w/o porting and Accu-Chokes set, parkerized metal finish, black synthetic stock and forearm. New 1999.

| MSR | $327 | $260 | $210 | $170 | $140 | $120 | $110 | $100 |

M

Grading	100%	98%	95%	90%	80%	70%	60%

MODEL 500 VIKING - 12 or 20 ga., 24 (12 ga. only, with rifled barrel and sights, porting became standard in 1997), 26 (20 ga. only) or 28 (12 ga. only, porting became standard in 1997) in. ported (new 1997, 12 ga. only) or unported VR barrel with one Accu- Choke and twin bead sights, matte finish with green synthetic stock and forearm, approx. 7 lbs. Mfg. 1996-98.

	$230	$190	$155	$135	$120	$110	$100

Last MSR was $287.

Add $40 for 12 ga. rifled barrel.
Add $108 for Slug Shooting System with ported barrel.

* **Model 500 Viking Turkey** - 12 ga. only, 24 in. ported VR barrel, green synthetic stock, matte finish, Accu-Choke. Mfg. 1997-98.

	$230	$190	$155	$135	$120	$110	$100

Last MSR was $286.

MODEL 500 FIELD – CURRENT MFG. - 12, 20 ga., or .410 bore, 3 in. chamber, choice of regular or Bantam (shorter stock, 13 in. LOP, 12 ga. Bantam was introduced 2001) configuration, 22 (Bantam, 20 ga. only), 24, 26, or 28 in. ported (new 1997, 12 ga. only, 26 or 28 in. barrel) or unported VR (unless with rifle sights) barrel, Slug model (12 ga. with 24 in. ported barrel with rifle sights was introduced in 2001), blue finish, walnut finished or synthetic (.410 bore only) stock, safety on back of receiver top, Accu- chokes except for .410 bore, supplied with 1 Accu-Choke, 6-7½ lbs.

MSR	$307	$250	$200	$170	$150	$145	$140	$135

Add approx. $59-$103 for 10 various combo packages, depending on configuration.
This model also includes the Crown Grade, manufactured 1994-2000.

* **Model 500 Slugster** - 12 or 20 ga., 24 in. ported (standard 1997) or unported (disc. 1996) barrel with choice of cyl. (disc. 2000) or rifled bore, blue or Marinecote (mfg. 1995-97) finish, choice of rifle (Bantam Model in 20 ga.), Truglo fiber optic sights (12 ga. only), or Trophy Slugster intregral scope base, press checkered hardwood stock and forearm, 6½ - 7¼ lbs.

MSR	$375	$295	$225	$175	$145	$120	$110	$100

Add $31 for Truglo fiber optic sights (new 1998).
Add $31 for integral scope base.
Add $125 for Marinecote finish (with synthetic stock, disc.).
This model also includes the Crown Grade Slugster, manufactured 1994-2000.

* **Model 500 Synthetic** - 12 or 20 ga., 3 in. chamber, 24 (slug barrel with ported barrel with cylinder bore choke and adj. rifle sights, new 2001), 26 (20 ga. only), or 28 (12 ga. ported only) in. VR barrel, black parkerized metal finish, black synthetic stock and forearm, 7-7½ lbs.

MSR	$307	$250	$200	$170	$150	$145	$140	$135

* **Model 500 Camo** - 12 ga. only, 100% camo finishes include parkerized camo (disc.), OFM Camo (standard, mfg. 1991-96), or Woodlands (new 1995) metal and synthetic stock coverage, 24 (disc.), 26 (disc.), 28, or 30 (disc.) in. ported (standard 1997) or unported (disc. 2000) VR barrel (choice of cylinder bore with rifle sights or Accu-II chokes), includes swivels, camo sling, and drilled and tapped receiver, older Speedfeed stock (disc. 1990) holds 4 extra shells, 7½ lbs. New 1986.

MSR	$382	$295	$220	$155				

Subtract 10% if without Accu-II choke system.
Add $30 for Speedfeed in synthetic stock (disc. 1990).
Accu-chokes became standard in 1991. Current models are supplied with 2 choke tubes.

* **Model 500 Camo Turkey** - 12 ga. only, 24 in. ported barrel with fiber optic sights and XX-full choke tube only, synthetic stock and forearm with Woodlands camo treatment, 7¼ - 7½ lbs. New 1999.

MSR	$395	$310	$220	$165				

M

Grading	100%	98%	95%	90%	80%	70%	60%

◇**Model 500 Camo Turkey Bantam** - 20 ga. only, 22 in. VR barrel with fiber optic sights and Accu-II X-full choke only, 6½ lbs. New 1997.

MSR	$395		$310	$220	$165		

✳ *Model 500 Camo Combo* - 12 or 20 ga., includes a wide variety of extra barrel combinations including slug barrel options, prices vary slightly depending on the configuration (gauge/ barrel/ choke set- up). Rifled bores, VR barrels, and Accu- chokes became standard in the combo package late 1994. Disc. 1998.

		$375	$295	$250	$200	$180	$160	$145

Last MSR was $434.

MODEL 500 HOME SECURITY - 20 (1996 only) ga. or .410 bore, 3 in. chamber, 18½ in. barrel with spreader choke, Model 500 slide-action, 5 shot mag., blue metal finish, synthetic field stock with pistol grip forearm, 6¼ lbs. New 1990.

MSR	$345		$280	$230	$200	$175	$150	$125	$110

✳ *Laser Home Security .410* - includes laser sighting device in right front of forearm. Mfg. 1990-1993.

		$400	$350	$315	$280	$250	$225	$195

Last MSR was $451.

MODEL 500 PERSUADER - 12 or 20 (new 1995) ga., 6 or 8 shot, 18½ in. plain barrel, cyl. bore or Accu-Chokes (new 1995), optional rifle (12 ga./20 in. cyl. bore barrel only) or ghost ring (new 1999) sights, blue or parkerized (12 ga. with ghost ring sights only) finish, Speedfeed stock was disc. 1990, optional bayonet lug, plain pistol grip wood or synthetic stock, approx. 6¾ lbs.

MSR	$330		$265	$205	$175	$155	$145	$135	$120

Add $12 for pistol grip stock kit.
Add $112 for parkerized finish and ghost ring sights.
Add $40 for combo with pistol grip (disc.).
Add $23 for rifle sights (disc., 12 ga. only).

✳ *Night Persuader Special Edition* - 12 ga. only, includes synthetic stock and factory installed Mepro-Light night sight bead sight, only 300 mfg. for Lew Horton Distributing in 1990 only.

		$295	$250	$200	$175	$150	$130	$115

Last MSR was $296.

MODEL 500 SPECIAL PURPOSE - 12 ga. only, 18 in. cylinder bored barrel, choice of blue or parkerized finish, synthetic stock with or without Speedfeed. Disc. 1996.

		$330	$270	$240	$220	$200	$175	$160

Last MSR was $378.

Add $21 for Speedfeed stock.
Add $76 for ghost ring sight (parkerized finish only).

MODEL 500 CRUISER - 12, 20, or .410 (new 1993) ga., 14 (12 ga. only, Law Enforcement Model, disc. 1995), 18½, 20, or 21 (20 ga. only - new 1995) in. cylinder bore barrel, shroud is available in 12 ga. only, 6 or 8 shot mag., pistol grip forearm only. New 1989.

MSR	$335		$270	$205	$180	$150	$145	$135	$120

Add $12 for 20 in. barrel with heat shield (12 ga. only).
Add $12 for heat shield/barrel shroud (12 ga. only).
Add $96 for 14 in. barrel (disc.).
Add approx. $34 for camper case (1993-96).

✳ *Mil-Spec Cruiser* - 12 ga. only, 20 in. cylinder bored barrel with bead sights, built to Mil-Specs., parkerized finish. Mfg. 1997 only.

		$395	$350	$325	$295	$275	$250	$225

Last MSR was $478.

M

Grading	100%	98%	95%	90%	80%	70%	60%

MODEL 500 GHOST RING SIGHT - 12 ga. only, 3 in. chamber, 18½ or 20 in. cyl. bore or Accu-Choke (20 in. only - new 1995) barrel, 6 or 9 shot tube mag., blue or parkerized finish, synthetic field stock, includes ghost ring sighting device. Mfg. 1990-97.

	$270	$225	$180	$160	$150	$140	$130

Last MSR was $332.

Add $53 for parkerized finish.
Add $49 for 9 shot mag. (20 in. barrel only).
Add $123 for Accu-choke barrel (parkerized finish only).
Add $134 for Speedfeed stock (new 1994 - 9 shot, 20 in. barrel only).

MODEL 500 MARINER - 12 ga. only, 3 in. chamber, 18½ or 20 in. cyl. bore barrel, 6 or 9 shot, Marinecote finish on all metal parts (more rust-resistant than stainless steel), black synthetic stock and forearm, fixed or ghost ring (mfg. 1995-99) sights, approx. 6¾ lbs.

MSR	$482		$400	$300	$225		

Add $17 for 9 shot model.
Add $68 for ghost ring sights (disc. 1999).
Add $23 for Speedfeed stock (mini-combo only - disc.).

MODEL 500/590 INTIMIDATOR LASER - 12 ga. only, 3 in. chamber, 18½ (Model 500) or 20 (Model 590) in. cyl. bore barrel, 6 (Model 500) or 9 (Model 590) shot tube mag., blue or parkerized finish, synthetic field stock, includes laser sighting device. Mfg. 1990-1993.

❋ *Model 500 Intimidator*

	$440	$375	$340	$295	$260	$230	$195

Last MSR was $505.

Add $22 for parkerized finish.

❋ *Model 590 Intimidator*

	$495	$440	$375	$340	$295	$260	$230

Last MSR was $556.

Add $45 for parkerized finish.

MODEL 590 SPECIAL PURPOSE SLIDE ACTION - similar to Model 500, except has 9 shot mag., 20 in. cyl. bore barrel with or w/o ¾ shroud, and bayonet lug, blue or parkerized finish, regular black synthetic stock, with or w/o Speedfeed, 7¼ lbs. New 1987.

MSR	$406		$335	$275	$225	$190	$165	$145	$125

Add $57 for parkerized finish.
Add $85 for heavy barrel with metal triggerguard and safety.
Add $33 for Speedfeed (blue, disc. 1999) or $98 for Speedfeed (parkerized) stock.
Add $121 or $162 (includes Speedfeed stock) for ghost ring sights (new 1998) and parkerized finish.

❋ *Model 590 Mariner* - similar to Model 500 Mariner except is 9 shot and has 20 in. barrel. Mfg. 1989-1993.

	$310	$250	$200	$185	$165	$145	$125

Last MSR was $353.

Add $17 for Speedfeed stock (disc. 1990).
Add $15 for pistol grip adapter (mini combo - disc.).

❋ *Model 590 Bullpup* - similar to Model 500 Bullpup except is 9 shot and has 20 in. barrel. Mfg. 1989-90 only.

	$425	$360	$300	$250	$225	$195	$175

Last MSR was $497.

❋ *Model 590A1* - 12 ga., marked 590A1 on receiver, parkerized, ghost ring rear sight, synthetic stock and forend, ramp front sight. Disc. 1997.

	$450	$395	$360	$330	$295	$260	$230

Grading	100%	98%	95%	90%	80%	70%	60%

* ❋ *Model 590 Double Action* - 12 ga. only, 3 in. chamber, world's first double action shotgun (long trigger pull), 18½ or 20 in. barrel, 6 or 9 shot, bead or ghost ring sights, black synthetic stock and forearm, top tang safety, parkerized metal finish, 7- 7¼ lbs. New 2000.

MSR	$510		$450	$415	$360	$330	$295	$260	$230

Add $31 for 9 shot capacity.
Add $48 for ghost ring sights.
Add $124 for Speedfeed stock (20 in. barrel with ghost ring sights only).

MODEL 695 BOLT ACTION
12 ga. only, with detachable 2 shot mag., 3 in. chamber, 22 in. barrel with fully rifled and ported (new 1999) or Accu-Choke (disc. 1998) barrel, black synthetic or Woodlands camo (with bead sights, disc. 2001) on stock and forearm, rifle or Truglo fiber optic sights, 7½ lbs. New 1996.

MSR	$345		$275	$220	$185	$150	$135	$120	$115

Subtract approx. $50 for Accu-choke barrel.
Add $22 for Truglo fiber optic sights (new 1998).
Add $52 for Truglo fiber optic sights and Woodlands camo finish (disc. 2001).

MODEL 712 SEMI-AUTO
12 ga. only, gas operated, shoots 2¾ and 3 in. shells interchangeably, plain barrel or VR, top of receiver safety, checkered hardwood stock, rubber recoil pad, fixed or Accu-Choke II choking. Mfg. 1986-1988 only.

			$285	$250	$220	$200	$190	$175	$160

Last MSR was $345.

Subtract $25 without Accu II choking.
Add $90 for combo pack (includes 1 extra 24 in. slugster barrel).

* ❋ *Model 712 Steel Shot* - similar to Model 712, except has Accu-Steel choking system for steel shot, 28 in. VR barrel. Mfg. 1988 only.

			$290	$250	$220	$200	$190	$175	$160

Last MSR was $349.

* ❋ *Model 712 Camo/Speedfeed* - 12 ga. only, similar to Model 712, except has camo finished metal parts, stock, and forearm, 24 or 28 in. barrel. Mfg. 1986-87 only.

			$340	$295	$240				

Last MSR was $390.

Add $20 for Accu II choke.

MODEL 712 REGAL SEMI-AUTO
12 or 20 ga., action same as Model 712, special bright bluing, VR only, deluxe checkered walnut stock and forearm, gold trigger, inlaid medallion on receiver, top of receiver safety. Mfg. 1986-87 only.

			$310	$280	$250	$225	$200	$185	$170

Last MSR was $366.

Add $20 for Accu II choke.

NEW HAVEN BRAND
similar to previous models, except plainer finish. Disc.

Values are 20% less per model.

MODEL 835 ULTI-MAG SLIDE ACTION
12 ga. with 3½ in. chamber (new 1988), slide action, 24 (Turkey Model - new 1990) or 28 in. VR barrel with Accu-Mag choke tubes, 6 shot mag., safety on top rear of receiver, choice of camo synthetic or checkered hardwood stock. Introduced late 1988, disc. 1991.

			$375	$310	$265	$220	$190	$165	$150

Last MSR was $430.

Add $30 for synthetic camo field stock.

Various Combo packages were available in this model with prices ranging from $469-$534 depending on barrel chokings and scope base options.

This model was followed by the 835 Regal Series introduced in late 1991.

M

Grading	100%	98%	95%	90%	80%	70%	60%

ULTI-MAG 835 FIELD GRADE SLIDE ACTION - 12 ga. only, 3½ in. chamber, 24 in. cyl. bore (disc.), 24 in. VR (Turkey Special, disc. 1993), or 28 in. ported (new 1997) or unported VR barrel with 1 Accu-Mag choke, walnut finish stock and forearm (pressed checkering became standard 1994), blue finish, approx. 7½ lbs. Disc. 1998.

	$270	$230	$200	$185	$165	$145	$125

Last MSR was $331.

Add $40 for combo package (disc. 1993).

ULTI-MAG 835 SYNTHETIC (SPECIAL HUNTER) - 12 ga. only, 3½ in. chamber, 26 (disc. 1999) or 28 in. VR ported barrel with mod. Accu- Mag choke, parkerized finish, black synthetic stock, 7¾ lbs. New 1998.

MSR	$382						
		$310	$255	$215	$185	$165	$145	$125

MODEL 835 FIELD SLIDE ACTION (CROWN GRADE) - similar to Field Grade, except has gold trigger and cut checkering on walnut finished hardwood stock, blue or OFM Woodland camo (24 in. Turkey only) finish, ported (standard 1997) or unported (disc.) VR barrel, 7¾ lbs. New 1994.

MSR	$382						
		$310	$255	$215	$185	$165	$145	$125

❋ *Model 835 Turkey* - 12 ga. only, 24 in. ported VR barrel, parkerized finish, walnut finished stock and forearm. Mfg. 1997-2000.

	$320	$255	$215	$190	$165	$145	$125

Last MSR was $378.

❋ *Model 835 New Turkey* - 12 ga. only, 24 in. ported barrel with Ulti-full choke only, choice of Realtree Advantage Timber (new 2001), Realtree Hardwoods (mfg. 2000 only), Realtree Xtra brown (disc. 1999) or Woodlands (disc. 1999) 100% camo finish, fiber optic sights, 7½ lbs. Mfg. 1999-2001.

	$450	$380	$345	$300	$270	$235	$210

Last MSR was $525.

❋ *Ulti-Mag 835 Crown Grade* - 12 ga. only, 3½ in. chamber, 28 in. VR ported (standard 1997) or unported barrel, walnut stock and forearm, Accu-Mag choke. Disc. 1998.

	$365	$300	$260	$230	$200	$180	$160

Last MSR was $421.

Add $7 for duo-comb stock.

MODEL 835 VIKING - 12 ga. only, 28 in. VR ported (standard 1997) or unported (1996 only) barrel with one Accu-Choke and twin bead sights, matte blue finish with green synthetic stock and forearm, 7.7 lbs. Mfg. 1996-98.

	$260	$225	$200	$185	$165	$145	$125

Last MSR was $316.

MODEL 835 CAMO TURKEY & WATERFOWL - 12 ga. only, 3½ in. chamber, OFM Woodland Camo (all-purpose camo, combo. only mfg. 1997-99), Realtree (mfg. 1993- 99), Realtree AP (all purpose grey, mfg. 1996-99), Realtree X-tra Brown (mfg. 2000-2002), Brown Leaf (disc. 1999), Woodlands (new 2000), Mossy Oak Shadow Grass (new 2000, Waterfowl only), Realtree Hardwwods (new 2002, Turkey only), Advantage Timber (mfg. 2001-2002), or Mossy Oak (mfg. 1994-99) finish, 24 (Turkey Special) or 28 (Waterfowl only) in. VR ported (new 1997) or unported (disc. 2000) barrel with 6 choke tubes, dual comb wood (Turkey/Deer combo only) or synthetic stock, approx. 7½ lbs. New 1991.

MSR	$541						
		$460	$385	$350	$300	$270	$235	$210

Subtract $104 for Woodlands camo finish.
Add $49 for Turkey/Deer combo with TruGlo fiber optic sights and synthetic stock.
Subtract $41 for 28 in. barrel with Mossy Oak Shadow Grass and hunter set of chokes (Waterfowl Model).
Subtract $122 for 28 in. barrel with Woodlands camo finish (Waterfowl Model).
OFM Woodland camo finish on this model included a dual comb stock.

Grading	100%	98%	95%	90%	80%	70%	60%

MODEL 835 WALNUT ULTI-MAG (REGAL) SLIDE ACTION

- 12 ga., 3½ in. chamber, 28 in. VR barrel with Accu-Mag chokes (disc. 1996) or 24 in. rifled slug barrel, single (new 1993) or dual comb (2 comb inserts are provided for the stock affording different shooting positions), aluminum receiver, back-bored barrel, double slide bars, high gloss walnut stock with recoil pad, approx. 7½ lbs. Mfg. 1991-96.

	$350	$290	$260	$230	$200	$175	$160

Last MSR was $404.

Add $8 for dual comb stock.
Add $30 for 24 in. slug barrel with trophy scope base and dual comb stock.
Add $72-$83 for combo package (includes extra slug barrel with choice of sights).

MODEL 835 WILD TURKEY FED. LIMITED EDITION

- 12 ga. with 3½ in. chamber, 24 in. VR barrel with Accu-Mag. chokes, camo finish, includes camo sling, medallion in stock, and 10-pack of Federal Turkey loads. Mfg. 1989 only.

	$425	$360	$295

Last MSR was $477.

MODEL 835 NWTF SPECIAL EDITION

- 12 ga. only, 24 in. VR barrel with Accu- Mag chokes, features Realtree camo finish, drilled and tapped receiver, 7½ lbs. Mfg. 1991 only to commemorate the National Wild Turkey Federation.

	$380	$300	$225

Last MSR was $436.

MODEL 835 WATERFOWL LIMITED EDITION

- 12 ga. with 3½ in. chamber, 28 in. VR barrel with Accu-Mag. chokes, camo finish, synthetic stock, camo sling. Mfg. 1990 only.

	$425	$360	$295

Last MSR was $480.

MODEL 1000 SEMI-AUTO

- 12 or 20 ga., gas semi-auto, 2¾ in. chamber, scroll engraved aluminum alloy receiver, plain or VR barrel, also available in trap and skeet configuration, checkered walnut stock and forearm. Imported 1986-87 only. VR became standard in 1987.

	$410	$345	$300	$270	$245	$220	$200

Last MSR was $472.

Add $28 for Multi-Choke II.
Deduct $50 if without VR.
Model 1000 barrels are not interchangeable with Model 1000 Super barrels.

- ✳ *Model 1000 Junior* - similar to Model 1000, except 20 ga. only, shortened stock, and 22 in. VR Multi- Choke barrel. Imported 1986-87 only.

	$425	$355	$310	$275	$250	$220	$200

Last MSR was $499.

- ✳ *Model 1000 Slug* - 12 or 20 ga., 22 in. barrel with rifle sights, recoil pad. Imported 1986-87 only.

	$405	$340	$295	$270	$245	$220	$200

Last MSR was $464.

- ✳ *Model 1000 Skeet* - 12 or 20 ga., steel receiver, 26 in. VR barrel bored skeet. Mfg. 1986 only.

	$395	$335	$295	$270	$245	$220	$200

Last MSR was $439.

MODEL 1000 SUPER SEMI-AUTO

- 12 or 20(Super 20) ga., gas semi-auto, 3 in. chambers, shoots 2¾ and 3 in. shells interchangeably, steel receiver, vent. recoil pad, select checkered walnut stock and forearm, Multi-Choke II is standard (except on slug barrel). Slug models are approx. the same price as values listed directly below. Imported 1986-87 only.

	$495	$405	$365	$330	$295	$270	$245

Last MSR was $577.

Model 1000 Super barrels are not interchangeable with Model 1000 barrels.

Grading	100%	98%	95%	90%	80%	70%	60%

✴ *Model 1000 Super Waterfowler* - 12 ga. only, matte finished wood and metal, includes swivels and camouflaged sling, 28 in. Multi-Choke barrel. Imported 1986- 87 only.

	$510	**$430**	**$370**				

Last MSR was $605.

✴ *Model 1000 Super Skeet* - 12 or 20 ga., 25 in. barrel, jug choking. Imported 1986-87 only.

	$575	**$495**	**$450**	**$410**	**$375**	**$330**	**$295**

Last MSR was $658.

✴ *Model 1000 Super Trap* - 12 ga. only, 30 in. Multi-Choke II barrel with high VR, Monte Carlo stock, recoil pad. Mfg. 1986 only.

	$470	**$380**	**$345**	**$320**	**$285**	**$270**	**$250**

Last MSR was $560.

MODEL 3000 SLIDE ACTION - 12 or 20 ga. only, 3 in. chamber, slide action, steel receiver, double action bars, various chokes and VR barrel lengths, checkered walnut stock and forearm, vent. recoil pad. This model was introduced in 1986 and the field version was disc. in 1987.

	$325	**$275**	**$250**	**$220**	**$200**	**$185**	**$170**

Last MSR was $360.

Add $25 for Multi-Choke II.

✴ *Model 3000 Waterfowler* - 12 ga. only, similar to Model 3000, except has dull matte finish on wood and metal, includes swivels and camouflaged sling, VR only. Mfg. 1986 only.

	$340	**$295**	**$265**				

Last MSR was $386.

Add $30 for Multi-choke II option, $70 for camo/speedfeed stock.

✴ *Model 3000 Law Enforcement* - 12 or 20 ga. only, 18½ or 20 in. cylinder bore only, rifle or bead sights. Mfg. 1986-87 only.

	$325	**$275**	**$250**	**$220**	**$200**	**$185**	**$170**

Last MSR was $362.

Add $25 for rifle sights.
Add $33 for black speedfeed stock.

MODEL 5500 SEMI-AUTO - 12 ga., 2¾ or 3 in. mag., gas operated, 18½ - 30 in. barrels. Disc. 1985.

	$250	**$235**	**$205**	**$185**	**$170**	**$155**	**$140**

Last MSR was $307.

Add $20 for VR.

✴ *Model 5500 Mag.* - 12 ga. only, 3 in. chamber, 30 in. VR barrel. Disc. 1985.

	$275	**$250**	**$225**	**$205**	**$190**	**$175**	**$160**

Last MSR was $325.

MODEL 5500 MKII SEMI-AUTO - 12 ga. only, supplied with 2 VR barrels - 26 in./2¾ in. chamber or 28 in./3 in. chamber VR barrel, includes choice of Accu-II choke tubes (lead shot only) or Accu-Steel choke tubes, blue or camo finish (new 1990), checkered hardwood stock and forearm, top receiver safety, recoil pad, 7½ lbs. Mfg. 1989-92.

	$260	**$225**	**$200**	**$180**	**$160**	**$140**	**$125**

Last MSR was $294.

Add $10 for 24 in. rifled bore barrel.
Add $43 for camo metal finish and synthetic stock.
Add $30 for Turkey Model (24 in. barrel, camo finish, and synthetic stock).

This model was also available with different Combo options. Prices varied between $463- $484, depending on configuration of barrel choking.

✴ *Model 5500 U.S. Shooting Team* - 2¾ in. chamber, 26 in. non-Mag. barrel with VR and Accu-II chokes, blue finish, checkered walnut stock and forearm, 7½ lbs. Mfg. 1991-92.

	$325	**$250**	**$225**	**$200**	**$185**	**$170**	**$160**

Last MSR was $376.

Grading	100%	98%	95%	90%	80%	70%	60%

✳ ***NWTF Special Edition*** - 12 ga. only, 3 in. chamber, 24 in. VR barrel with 1 choke tube, Mossy Oak Camo finish with synthetic stock and forearm, 7.3 lbs. Mfg. 1991- 92.

	$365	$300	$265	$235	$200	$175	$160

Last MSR was $428.

MODEL 6000 SEMI-AUTO - 12 ga. only, 2¾ or 3 in. chamber 28 in. VR barrel with Accu-choke, economical model with walnut finish stock, blue finish, 7.7 lbs. Mfg. 1993 only.

	$280	$240	$215	$200	$185	$165	$145

Last MSR was $321.

MODEL 9200 CROWN SEMI-AUTO - 12 ga. only, 3 in. chamber, gas operated, shoots any shell interchangeably, 18½ (SP only), 22 (Bantam only), 24 in. rifled, 24 (Turkey), 26 (U.S. Shooting Team variation, new 1993), or 28 in. VR barrel with 3 Accu-chokes, engraved aluminum receiver, synthetic (18½ in. barrel only) or walnut stained hard wood stock (1 in. shorter on Bantam Model) and forearm, top tang safety, approx. 7½ lbs. Mfg. 1992-2001.

	$460	$335	$275	$225	$190	$170	$160

Last MSR was $574.

Add approx. $73-$95 for combo package.
Add $33 for Truglo fiber optic sights (mfg. 1998 only).
Add $23 for 24 in. rifled bore barrel with trophy scope base.
Subtract $90 for synthetic stock (Special Purpose with matte blue finish, 18½ in. barrel).

✳ ***Model 9200 Viking*** - 12 ga. only, 28 in. VR barrel with one Accu-Choke and twin bead sights, matte finish with green synthetic stock and forearm, 7.7 lbs. Mfg. 1996- 98.

	$365	$310	$270	$230	$200	$175	$160

Last MSR was $429.

✳ ***Model 9200 Special Hunter*** - 12 ga. only, 28 in. VR barrel with Accu-II choke set, parkerized finish, black synthetic stock. Mfg. 1998-2001.

	$425	$345	$285	$245	$200	$175	$160

Last MSR was $491.

✳ ***Model 9200 Camo*** - 12 ga. only, similar to Model 9200, except is supplied with OFM (disc. 1996), Mossy Oak (disc. 1999), Realtree (mfg. 1994-95), Realtree AP (mfg. 1996-99) or Woodlands (new 1995) camo finish, 24 (Turkey) or 28 in. VR barrel. Mfg. 1992-99.

	$445	$320	$265	$230	$195	$170	$160

Last MSR was $556.

Subtract approx. $40 for Turkey Model with Woodlands camo and one choke tube.

✧**Model 9200 New Turkey Camo** - 12 ga. only, 24 in. VR barrel with XX-full choke tube only and fiber optic sights, choice of 100% Woodlands or Mossy Oak Shadow Branch camo treatment. Mfg. 1999-2001.

	$415	$300	$250	$225	$195	$170	$160

Last MSR was $517.

Add approx. $95 for Mossy Oak Shadow Branch camo coverage.

✳ ***Model 9200 Jungle Gun*** - 12 ga. only, 18½ in. plain barrel with cyl. bore, parkerized metal, synthetic stock. Mfg. 1998-2001.

	$610	$500	$360	$300	$250	$225	$200

Last MSR was $704.

MOUNTAIN RIFLERY

Current custom rifle builder located in Pocatello, ID. Consumer direct sales.

John Bolliger has been producing top quality, custom made bolt action rifles for over 30 years. Currently, Mountain Riflery is concentrating on 3 series of rifles: the Signature Series, the Excalibur Series, and the Crown Series. Since almost all rifles are special ordered per customer specifications (with many options also available), please contact Mountain Riflery directly for more information, including prices.

M

Grading	100%	98%	95%	90%	80%	70%	60%

MOUNTAIN RIFLES INC.

Previous rifle manufacturer located in Palmer, AK 1995-98.

RIFLES: BOLT ACTION

MOUNTAINEER - various cals., choice of M-700 Rem. or M-70 Win. action, Chrome Moly barrel with ultra muzzle brake, Timney trigger, parkerized finish, fiberglass stock with decelerator pad, 5½ lbs. Limited mfg. 1995-98.

$1,825	$1,475	$1,100	$900	$750	$675	$550

Last MSR was $1,995.

SUPER MOUNTAINEER - similar to the Mountaineer, except has Kevlar epoxy bedded stock with steel cross-bolts on Mag. cals., 4¼ lbs. Limited 1995-98.

$2,575	$2,025	$1,475	$1,100	$900	$750	$675

Last MSR was $2,895.

PRO MOUNTAINEER K.S. - various cals., Winchester M-70 controlled feed action, choice of fiberglass pillar epoxy bedded, Kevlar, or KSDB (Kevlar Stock Drop Box mag.) stock with decelerator pad, parkerized finish. 6 lbs. Limited mfg. 1995-98.

$2,395	$1,950	$1,425	$1,050	$875	$725	$650

Last MSR was $2,695.

Add $500 for KSDB stock with drop mag.

PRO SAFARI - various cals., Winchester M-70 controlled feed action, high gloss bluing, exhibition grade English walnut with decelerator pad, 4 shot detachable mag. 7-9 lbs. Limited mfg. 1995- 98.

$3,795	$3,350	$2,875	$2,350	$1,775	$1,450	$1,200

Last MSR was $3,995.

ULTRA MOUNTAINEER - various cals., features stainless steel match grade barrel with black Kevlar/Graphite thumbhole stock, approx. 5 lbs. New 1997.

$2,650	$2,075	$1,500	$1,100	$900	$750	$675

Last MSR was $2,995.

Add $500 for Rigby length.

MUSGRAVE

Current manufacturer located in the Republic of South Africa since 1951. No current U.S. importation.

Newer models manufactured by Musgrave (imported into Austria and Switzerland) include the Model 90 (features Musgrave action) Standard Rifle, Model 90 Light Rifle, Mini-90, Model 90 Varmint, Model 90 De Luxe Rifle, and Magnum Rifle, in addition to the same series in the Mauser 98 action. More information can be obtained (including prices and availability) by contacting the company directly (see Trademark Index).

RIFLES: BOLT ACTION

VALIANT BOLT ACTION RIFLE - .243 Win., .270 Win., .30-06, .308 Win., or 7mm Rem. Mag. cal., 24 in. barrel, leaf sight, skip checkered straight stock, pistol grip. Mfg. 1971-1976.

$375	$325	$275	$250	$220	$195	$175

PREMIER - similar to Valiant, with 26 in. barrel, select Monte Carlo stock, rosewood pistol grip cap and forearm tip.

$425	$365	$315	$275	$250	$225	$200

RSA SINGLE SHOT TARGET RIFLE - .308 Win. cal. only, 26 in. heavy barrel, target sights and stock. Mfg. 1971-1976.

$425	$365	$315	$275	$250	$225	$200

M

Grading	100%	98%	95%	90%	80%	70%	60%

MUSKETEER RIFLES

Previous trademark of rifles previously imported by Firearms International Company (FIC), located in Washington, D.C.

RIFLES: BOLT ACTION

SPORTER - .243 Win., .25-06 Rem., .270 Win., .264 Win. Mag., .308 Win., .30-06, 7mm Rem. Mag., or .300 Win. Mag. cal., bolt action, FN Mauser action, 24 in. barrel, no sights, checkered Monte Carlo stock. Mfg. 1963-1972.

	100%	98%	95%	90%	80%	70%	60%
	$375	$325	$275	$250	$220	$195	$175

SPORTER DELUXE - adj. trigger, select wood, tear drop pistol grip, skipline checkering.

	100%	98%	95%	90%	80%	70%	60%
	$425	$365	$315	$275	$250	$225	$200

CARBINE - similar to Sporter, except 20 in. barrel and full length stock.

	100%	98%	95%	90%	80%	70%	60%
	$375	$325	$275	$250	$220	$195	$175

M

NOTES

_____
_____
_____
_____
_____
_____
_____
_____
_____
_____

Not many people know more about currently manufactured Marlin firearms than Marlin's Tony Aeschliman (r). Richard Jacobson (l), group publisher for Primedia (i.e., Guns & Ammo, Hunting, etc.), looks on during a recent NASGW (National Association of Sporting Goods Wholesalers) show.

N Section

NS FIREARMS CORP.

Previous importer located in Atlanta, GA until 1994. NS Firearms was a division of KFS, Inc. located in Atlanta, GA. Previously manufactured in China.

Grading	100%	98%	95%	90%	80%	70%	60%

RIFLES: SEMI-AUTO

MODEL 522 SPORTER - .22 LR cal., 21 in. cold hammer forged barrel, 5 shot detachable mag., grooved receiver, checkered walnut stock, 7¾ lbs. Imported 1994 only.

	100%	98%	95%	90%	80%	70%	60%
	$250	$215	$185	$165	$145	$125	$110

Last MSR was $299.

NAMBU PISTOLS

Previously manufactured in Japan for the Japanese military between 1902-1945.

PISTOLS: SEMI-AUTO

Please refer to Japanese Military Pistols for the Hamada variations.

TYPE 14 - 8mm Nambu cal., recoil operated, 4.7 in. barrel, blue, wood grips, 8 shot mag., a simply designed pistol used by Japanese armed forces from 1925-1945.

Type 14 Nambus have a 3 or 4 digit number just forward of the lanyard ring on the right side of frame (on back of grip). Earliest Taisho era pistols are dated 15.11 or 15.12 from the Nagoya arsenal - can be identified by small trigger guard and other early features. Fewer than 100 mfg. To determine year and month of manufacture for most type 14 pistols, add "1925" to the first two digits and the last number will indicate the month (i.e. code 13.3 indicates a gun built in March of 1938).

Add 25% for 3.X date Tokyo.
Add 50% for 2.X date Nagoya.
Add 400% for early Taisho era pistols dated 15.11 or 15.12 from Nagoya arsenal.
Add 10% for matching mag. on models listed.

✳ *1925-1930 Mfg.*

	100%	98%	95%	90%	80%	70%	60%
	$700	$500	$360	$320	$265	$230	$200

✳ *1930-1939 Mfg.* - small trigger guard.

	100%	98%	95%	90%	80%	70%	60%
	$500	$400	$260	$220	$200	$180	$165

✳ *1939-1945 Mfg.* - large trigger guard.

	100%	98%	95%	90%	80%	70%	60%
	$295	$260	$215	$195	$180	$165	$150

Add 10% for strawed trigger and safety.

TYPE 94 - 8mm Nambu cal., recoil operated, 3.8 in. barrel, blue, and bakelite wood grips, 6 shot mag. Mfg. 1935-1945.

	100%	98%	95%	90%	80%	70%	60%
	$275	$225	$185	$160	$150	$135	$120

Add 300% for 10.X date, 200% for 11.X date, 100% for 12.X date, 30% if pre-WWII, and 20% if late square back.

HAMADA NAMBU - .32 ACP or 8mm Nambu (scarce) cal., available with rough (early production, mostly prototypes) or polished (production) finish, very rare.

	100%	98%	95%	90%	80%	70%	60%
	$3,250	$2,800	$2,400	$2,000	$1,800	$1,600	$1,475

Add 10% for "in the white" 8mm Nambu.

BABY NAMBU - 7mm Nambu cal., 3¼ in. barrel, blue, wood grips, grip safety, one of the most desirable Japanese handguns.

	100%	98%	95%	90%	80%	70%	60%
	$2,700	$2,250	$1,800	$1,600	$1,475	$1,300	$1,050

Add 10% for matching mag.
Add 50% for chamber marked "TGE" (Tokyo Gas & Electric).

N

Grading	100%	98%	95%	90%	80%	70%	60%

PAPA NAMBU (MODEL 1904) - 8mm Nambu cal., 4.7 in. barrel, wood grips, grip safety, 8 shot
mag., essentially the same action as the Baby, but a larger version. Mfg. 1904-1925.

	$1,600	$1,400	$1,200	$1,000	$800	$675	$550

Add 10% for matching mag.
Add 50% for chamber marked "TGE" (Tokyo Gas & Electric).

GRANDPA NAMBU - 8mm Nambu cal., similar to Papa Nambu, except has smaller trigger guard
and fixed lanyard ring, cherry wood based mag., issued with 2 matching mags. Early Tokyo
arsenal or later Thai issue, all Grandpa frames are slotted.

	$5,500	$4,350	$3,200	$2,600	$2,150	$1,850	$1,500

Add 100% for matching shoulder stock.
Add $3,500 for spare stock alone.
Add 10% for second matching mag.
Original stocks are rare and expensive.

1893 REVOLVER (MODEL 26) - 9mm Japanese cal., double action only, 4.7 in. barrel, blue, wood
grips. Approx. 59,000 mfg. 1893-1925.

	$450	$350	$250	$200	$150	$135	$120

Subtract 25% for arsenal rework.
Add 150% for early mfg. with internal numbers (approx. first 300 revolvers), or final
Kokura assembled pistols in 58,971-59,183 serial range.

NATIONAL WILD TURKEY FEDERATION

Current national organization located in Edgefield, SC.

Although the National Wild Turkey Federation is not a manufacturer or importer, this organization has been responsible for many special and limited editions that are listed with quanities
but without prices since they may vary greatly from region to region. Also, many are sold at
auction, making predictible pricing difficult to determine. During 2001, the NWTF purchased
23,000 guns total (includes the gun of the year). NWTF suffix after model name indicates
National Wild Turkey Federation gun of the year. Some of the models (and current values) may
be listed under manufacturer listings in this text.

Manufacturer	Model	Quantity	Year	Issue Price

SHOTGUNS: AUCTION/TRADE EDITIONS

Manufacturer	Model	Quantity	Year	Issue Price
Navy Arms	Black Powder 12 ga. NWTF	500	1983	$350
Winchester	Model 101	300	1985	$1,895
Browning	BPS 12 ga. NWTF	500	1986	$495
American Arms	SxS 10 ga. 3½ in.	150	1985/86	$695
Winchester	Model 1300 Win-Cam 12 ga.	500	1987/88	$449
Winchester	Model 1300 12 ga. Trade Gun	-	-	$458
Beretta	Model A-303 12 ga. NWTF	500	1988/89	$695
Winchester	Model 1300 12 ga. Win-Cam NWTF	500	1989	$479
Winchester	Model 1300 12 ga. Trade Gun	-	-	$458
Browning	Model A5 12 ga. NWTF	500	1990	$925
Mossberg	Model 835 12 ga. Auction	500	1991	$567
Mossberg	Model 835 12 ga. Trade Gun	-	-	$436
Remington	Model 11-87 12 ga. Auction	00	1992	-
Remington	Model 11-87 12 ga. Trade Gun	-	-	$698
Winchester	Model 1300 12 ga. Auction	500	1993	$671
New England Firearms	SxS 20 ga. Auction	-	-	$167
New England Firearms	SxS 12 ga. Trade Gun	-	-	$200
New England Firearms	SxS 10 ga. Trade Gun	-	-	$240
American Arms	Model Turkey 12 ga. Auction	300	1993	-

Manufacturer	Model	Quantity	Year	Issue Price
Mossberg	Model 9200 12 ga. Auction	600	1994	$690
Mossberg	Model 9200 12 ga. Trade	-	1994	-
Luigi Franchi	Model 610 12 ga. Auction	600	1995	-
Fausti	O/U 12 ga. Auction	720	1996	-
New England Firearms	Topper Jr. 20 ga. Auction	-	1996	-
Fausti	O/U 12 ga. Auction	900	1997	-
New England Firearms	Jakes Topper Jr. 20 ga. Auction	-	1997	-
Remington	Model 870 12 ga. Auction	1200	1998	-
Beretta	Model AL390 12ga.	1400	1999	-
Ithaca	Model 37 12ga.	1700	2000	-
Browning	BPS 12 ga.	1900	2001	-
Winchester	Super X2	2100	2002	-

NAVY ARMS COMPANY

Current importer established during 1958, and located in Union City, NJ, beginning 2001. Previously located in Ridgefield, NJ. Navy Arms imports are fabricated by various manufacturers including the Italian companies Davide Pedersoli & Co., Pietta & Co., and Uberti & Co. Distributor and dealer sales.

Until recently, Navy Arms has also sold a wide variety of original military firearms in used condition. Handguns included the Mauser Broomhandle, Japanese Nambu, Colt 1911 Government Model, Tokarev, Browning Hi-Power, S&W Model 1917, and others. Rifles included Mauser contract models, Japanese Type 38s, Enfields, FNs, Nagants, M1 Carbines, M1 Garands, Chinese SKSs, Egyptian Rashids, French MAS Model 1936s, among others. Most of these firearms are priced in the $75-$500 price range depending on desirability of model and condition.

For more information and up-to-date pricing regarding current Navy Arms black powder models, please refer to Colt Blackpowder Reproductions and Replicas, and the 2nd Ed. Blue Book of Modern Black Powder Values, by Dennis Adler. These books feature hundreds of color photographs and support text of the most recent black powder models available, as well as a complete pricing and reference guide. A tear out order form (located up front in this printed product) has also been provided.

Grading	100%	98%	95%	90%	80%	70%	60%

N

PISTOLS

TU-711 MAUSER - 9mm Para. cal., patterned after Mauser 711 (semi-auto version of the Model 712 Schnellfeuer), 5¼ in. barrel, 712 upper receiver that has been converted to 9mm Para. and mounted on new lower receiver, supplied with 10 and 20 shot detachable mag., mfg. in China, 2 lbs. 11 oz. Imported 1992 only.

$575	$475	$425	$375	$325	$295	$275

Last MSR was $650.

TT-OLYMPIA - .22 LR cal., patterned after the Walther Olympia that won 1936 Olympics, 4 5/8 in. barrel, checkered walnut grips, mfg. in China, 27 oz. Imported 1992-98.

$255	$225	$195	$175	$160	$150	$140

Last MSR was $290.

TU-90 PISTOL - .30 Tokarev or 9mm Para. cal., patterned after the rare Tokagypt variation (improved TT-33 Tokarev), 4½ in. barrel, single action, wraparound synthetic grips, unique forward motion safety, mfg. in China, 30 oz. Imported 1992-98.

$115	$100	$90	$80	$70	$60	$50

Last MSR was $130.

Add $15 for 9mm Para. cal.
Add $40 for pistol combo (includes both cals.).

Grading	100%	98%	95%	90%	80%	70%	60%

LUGER MODEL - .22 LR cal. only, 10 shot mag., Luger toggle type action, available in blue or matte finish, 4, 6, or 8 in. barrel, checkered walnut stocks. Mfg. in U.S. 1986- 87 only.

	$140	$120	$95	$85	$75	$70	$65

Last MSR was $165.

GRAND PRIX SILHOUETTE - .30-30 Win., 7mm Spl., .44 Mag., or .45-70 Govt. cal., 13¾ in. barrel, non-glare matte blue finish, walnut forearm and grips, adj. heat dispersing aluminum rib, adj. target sights, 4 lbs. Mfg. 1985 only.

	$320	$280	$240	$220	$195	$175	$150

Last MSR was $375.

REVOLVERS: REPRODUCTIONS

1872 OPEN TOP - .38 Spl. cal., 5½ or 7½ in. barrel, case colored frame with blue cylinder and barrel, silver plated brass trigger guard and backstrap, 2½ - 2¾ lbs. Limited importation 2000 only.

	$335	$275	$220	$185	$165	$150	$135

Last MSR was $390.

1873 SINGLE ACTION ARMY - .32-20 WCF (new 2002), .357 Mag. (new 1998), .44-40 WCF or .45 LC cal., reproduction of the Colt SAA, case hardened frame with blue or nickel (disc. 1998) finish, 3 (Sheriff's Model - mfg. 1992-98), 4¾, 5½, or 7½ in. barrel, approx. 36 oz.

MSR	$405		$345	$280	$220	$180	$160	$145	$130

Add $65 for nickel finish.
Add $30 for Pinched Frame Model (7½ in. barrel, .45 LC, disc. 2002).
Subtract $20 for brass trigger guard and backstrap (disc.).

* **1873 SAA Economy** - .44-40 WCF or .45 LC cal., 3, 4¾, 5½, or 7½ in. barrel, brass trigger guard and backstrap, 2-piece walnut grips. Imported 1993-96.

	$295	$230	$185	$160	$145	$130	$120

Last MSR was $345.

* **Deputy SAA** - .44-40 WCF or .45 LC cal., patterned after the Colt 1877 Thunderer double action, birds head grips, 3, 3½, 4, or 4¾ in. barrel, case colored frame. Imported 1997-98 only.

	$340	$270	$215	$180	$160	$145	$130

Last MSR was $405.

* **1873 Flat Top Target Model** - .45 LC cal. only, features flat top frame, 7½ in. barrel only, adj. spring loaded front sight and dovetailed rear sight, 30 oz. Importation began 1999.

MSR	$450		$380	$310	$270	$235	$205	$175	$150

* **1873 Shootist Model** - .357 Mag., .44-40 WCF, or .45 LC cal., interchangeable parts with original Colt 1st and 2nd Generation SAAs, designed for Cowboy Action Shooting, 4¾, 5½, or 7½ in. barrel, case colored frame and hammer, blue cylinder barrel, trigger guard and backstrap. Limited importation 2000 only.

	$330	$265	$210	$180	$160	$145	$130

Last MSR was $385.

* **Bisley Model** - .44-40 WCF or .45 LC cal., patterned after the Colt Bisley, 4¾, 5½, or 7½ in. barrel, case colored frame, spur hammer, walnut grips. Importation began 1997.

MSR	$425		$345	$295	$235	$190	$160	$145	$130

◇ **Bisley Flat Top Target Model** - .44-40 WCF or .45 LC cal., features flat top frame, adj. front sight, and dovetailed rear sight, 40 oz. Imported 1999-2000.

	$380	$330	$300	$265	$235	$200	$175

Last MSR was $435.

* **1873 SAA Cavalry Model** - .45 LC cal. only, exact replica of the original U.S. Government issue SAA, 7½ in. barrel, arsenal stampings, inspector's cartouche on walnut stocks.

MSR	$485		$425	$340	$305	$270	$230	$200	$175

Grading	100%	98%	95%	90%	80%	70%	60%

✳ *1895 SAA Artillery Model* - similar specifications to the Cavalry Model, except has 5½ in. barrel.

	MSR	$485		$425	$340	$305	$270	$230	$200	$175

1875 REMINGTON REVOLVER - .44-40 WCF or .45 LC cal., reproduction of the 1875 Remington revolver, 7½ in. barrel, case colored frame, 41 oz. Importation disc. 1991, resumed 1994-2000.

	$360	$295	$260	$230	$200	$175	$150

Last MSR was $435.

1890 REMINGTON REVOLVER - .44-40 WCF or .45 LC cal., reproduction of the 1890 Remington revolver, 5½ in. barrel, brass trigger guard and lanyard loop, 39 oz. Importation disc. 1991, resumed 1994-2000.

	$370	$295	$260	$230	$200	$175	$150

Last MSR was $445.

1875 SCHOFIELD CAVALRY MODEL - .44-40 WCF or .45 LC cal., patterned after the original Schofield Cavalry Model, 7½ in. barrel, 37 oz. New 1994.

	MSR	$695		$600	$525	$450	$375	$325	$250	$195

1875 SCHOFIELD WELLS FARGO MODEL - .44-40 WCF or .45 LC cal., 5½ in. barrel, 35 oz.. New 1994.

	MSR	$695		$600	$525	$450	$375	$325	$250	$195

1875 SCHOFIELD HIDEOUT MODEL - .44-40 WCF or .45 LC cal., similar to Wells Fargo Model, except has 3½ in. barrel, 34 oz. New 1999.

	MSR	$695		$600	$525	$450	$375	$325	$250	$195

1875 ENGRAVED SCHOFIELD - .44-40 WCF or .45 LC cal., similar to Deluxe Schofield, except does not have gold inlays, extensive B or C coverage scroll engraving on both frame, cylinder, and barrel. Special order only beginning 1999.

	MSR	$1,565		$1,425	$1,225	$1,000	$875	$750	$625	$525

Add $215 for C engraving.

1875 DELUXE SCHOFIELD - .44-40 WCF or .45 LC cal., available in Cavalry, Wells Fargo, or Hideout configurations, with light scroll engraving on frame and cylinder with extensive frame, barrel, and cylinder gold line inlays and scroll motifs. Special order only beginning 1999.

	MSR	$1,875		$1,675	$1,450	$1,250	$995	$875	$750	$625

NEW MODEL RUSSIAN - .44 Russian cal., patterned after the S&W Model 3 Russian Third Model Single Action, 6½ in. barrel, blue metal with case colored trigger, trigger guard, and hammer, smooth walnut grips, 40 oz. Importation began 1999.

	MSR	$769		$655	$565	$475	$385	$335	$250	$195

REVOLVERS: REPRODUCTIONS, COLT CARTRIDGE CONVERSIONS

1851 NAVY CONVERSION - .38 Spl. or .38 Colt cal., patterned after the Colt 1851 Navy Conversion, 5½ or 7½ in. barrel, case colored frame and hammer, blue cylinder and barrel, brass back strap and trigger guard, 40 or 44 oz. Imported 1999-2000.

	$320	$255	$200	$175	$160	$145	$130

Last MSR was $365.

1860 ARMY CONVERSION - .38 Spl. or .38 Colt cal., patterned after the Colt 1860 Army Conversion, other specifications similar to 1851 Navy Conversion. Imported 1999-2000.

	$320	$255	$200	$175	$160	$145	$130

Last MSR was $365.

N

Grading	100%	98%	95%	90%	80%	70%	60%

1861 NAVY CONVERSION - .38 Spl. or .38 Colt cal., patterned after the Colt 1861 Navy Conversion, other specifications similar to 1851 Navy Conversion. Imported 1999-2000.

| | $320 | $255 | $200 | $175 | $160 | $145 | $130 |

Last MSR was $365.

RIFLES: REPRODUCTIONS

REVOLVING CARBINE - .357 Mag., .44-40 WCF, or .45 LC cal., 6 shot cylinder, 20 in. barrel, case hardened frame, straight stock. Mfg. 1968-1984.

| | $575 | $475 | $425 | $375 | $325 | $275 | $225 |

REMINGTON ROLLING BLOCK BUFFALO RIFLE - .444 Marlin (disc.), .45-70 Govt., or .50-70 (disc.) cal., replica of Remington Rolling Block, 26 or 30 in. heavy octagon or ½ round/½ octagon barrel (disc. 2000), open sight, straight grip stock. Mfg. 1971-present.

| MSR | $825 | $635 | $450 | $345 | $260 | $195 | $160 | $140 |

Brass fittings were disc. during 1998, and replaced with steel fittings.

* **Buffalo Carbine** - similar to Rifle, with 18 in. barrel. Disc. 1985.

| | $385 | $325 | $280 | $230 | $180 | $160 | $140 |

Last MSR was $375.

* **Rolling Block Baby Carbine** - .22 LR, .22 Hornet, .357 Mag., or .44-40 WCF cal., replica of small frame Remington, 20 in. octagon or 22 in. round barrel, open sight, straight stock. Mfg. 1968-1984.

| | $215 | $175 | $140 | $110 | $90 | $65 | $55 |

REMINGTON ROLLING BLOCK BODINE RIFLE

| MSR | $1,385 | $1,175 | $995 | $875 | $750 | $625 | $500 | $400 |

ROLLING BLOCK PLAINS RIFLE - .45-70 Govt. cal., features 30 in. tapered octagon barrel with straight grip stock, bright polished receiver with steel furniture, 9 lbs. Imported 1997-98 only.

| | $650 | $500 | $400 | $285 | $195 | $175 | $150 |

Last MSR was $800.

* **Deluxe Rolling Block Plains Rifle** - similar to Plains Rifle, except has hand engraved coin finished receiver and trigger guard, rust blue barrel with German silver forearm tip. Imported 1997-98.

| | $1,475 | $1,250 | $1,050 | $850 | $725 | $600 | $525 |

Last MSR was $1,625.

ROLLING BLOCK NO. 2 CREEDMOOR TARGET - similar to Buffalo Rifle, in .45-70 Govt. or .50-70 (disc.) cal., with Creedmoor tang sight, color case hardened receiver, checkered walnut.

| MSR | $995 | $785 | $585 | $425 | $300 | $200 | $175 | $150 |

* **Deluxe Rolling Block No. 2 Creedmoor Target** - featured hand engraved coin finished receiver and trigger guard, rust blue barrel and German silver forearm tip. Imported 1997-98.

| | $1,625 | $1,400 | $1,200 | $1,000 | $850 | $725 | $600 |

Last MSR was $1,875.

1874 SHARPS PLAINS RIFLE - .45-70 Govt. cal., 32 in. octagon barrel, case hardened receiver, checkered stock and forearm, double set triggers, 9½ lbs. New 1996.

| MSR | $1,175 | $1,020 | $900 | $800 | $725 | $625 | $575 | $525 |

Add $75 for vernier rear tang or $55 for globe sight.

* **Engraved Sharps Plains Rifle** - .45-70 Govt. cal., features hand engraved coin finished receiver. Imported 1997-98.

| | $2,325 | $2,000 | $1,800 | $1,600 | $1,400 | $1,200 | $995 |

Last MSR was $2,500.

Add $700 for gold inlays (Deluxe Model).

Grading	100%	98%	95%	90%	80%	70%	60%

1874 SHARPS BUFFALO RIFLE - .45-70 Govt. or .45-90 (disc. 2000) cal., 28 in. octagon heavy barrel, case colored receiver, checkered stock, 10 lbs. 10 oz. New 1996.

MSR	$1,200		$1,035	$925	$825	$725	$625	$575	$525

Add $75 for vernier rear tang or $55 for globe sight.

* ✳ *Engraved Sharps Buffalo Rifle* - .45-70 Govt. or .45-90 cal., features hand engraved coin finished receiver. Imported 1997-98.

	$2,325	$2,000	$1,800	$1,600	$1,400	$1,200	$995

Last MSR was $2,515.

Add $700 for gold inlays (Deluxe Model).

SHARPS SPORTING RIFLE - .45-70 Govt. cal., similar to Plains Rifle, except has pistol grip stock. Importation began 1997.

MSR	$1,200		$1,035	$925	$825	$725	$625	$575	$525

1874 SHARPS QUIGLEY - Importation began 2002.

MSR	$1,385		$1,175	$995	$875	$750	$625	$500	$400

1874 SHARPS NO. 2 CREEDMOOR - Importation began 2002.

MSR	$1,300		$1,100	$975	$850	$750	$650	$575	$525

1874 SHARPS NO. 3 LONG RANGE - .45-70 Govt. cal., 34 in. medium weight octagon barrel with globe front target sight, shotgun buttplate, double set triggers, German silver forearm cap, 10 lbs. 14 oz. Importation began 2000.

MSR	$1,885		$1,600	$1,325	$1,175	$1,000	$875	$725	$600

1874 SHARPS SNIPER/INFANTRY RIFLE - .45-70 Govt. cal., patterned after the 3- band military sniper rifle, 30 in. barrel, color case hardened frame, hammer, and furniture, ST or DST (Sniper rifle, disc. 1995). Mfg. 1994-2000.

	$895	$780	$650	$475	$395	$350	$325

Last MSR was $1,060.

Add $55 for DST (Sniper).

* ✳ *1874 Sharps Cavalry Carbine* - .45-70 Govt. cal., patterned after Sharps Cavalry carbine, 22 in. barrel, color case hardened frame, hammer, patchbox, and furniture. New 1994.

MSR	$1,000		$785	$560	$415	$300	$200	$175	$150

1873 SPRINGFIELD INFANTRY RIFLE - .45-70 Govt. cal., 32½ in. barrel, 8 lbs, 4 oz. Imported 1997-2000.

	$840	$750	$650	$475	$395	$350	$325

Last MSR was $995.

* ✳ *1873 Springfield Cavalry Carbine* - similar to the 1873 Springfield Rifle, except has 22 in. barrel, 1 barrel band, 7 lbs. Importation began 1997.

MSR	$930		$775	$550	$400	$285	$195	$175	$150

KODIAK MARK IV DOUBLE RIFLE - .45-70 Govt. cal., patterned after the Colt Double rifle, semi-regulated barrels, hammers, folding leaf rear sight, 24 in. barrels, color cased hardened receiver, 10 lbs. 3 oz. Mfg. 1996-2000.

	$2,450	$2,250	$2,000	$1,800	$1,600	$1,400	$1,200

Last MSR was $2,815.

* ✳ *Deluxe Kodiak Mark IV* - similar to Kodiak Mark IV Double rifle, except has brown barrels and hand engraved satin finished receiver. Mfg. 1996-2000.

	$3,300	$2,900	$2,600	$2,375	$2,000	$1,750	$1,500

Last MSR was $3,690.

HENRY RIFLE - .44-40 WCF, .44 Rimfire (disc. 1989), or .45 LC (new 1998) cal., reproduction of Winchester's famous Henry Rifle, brass or iron frame. New 1985.

* ✳ *Military Rifle* - 24 in. barrel, brass frame, blue barrel, walnut stock, original style sling swivels, 9¼ lbs. New 1985.

MSR	$989		$775	$600	$475	$375	$285	$225	$195

N

Grading	100%	98%	95%	90%	80%	70%	60%

* **Union Pacific Railroad Commemorative** - .44-40 WCF cal., only 100 mfg.

	$795	$575	$475				

Last MSR was $695.

* **Engraved Rifle** - limited mfg., extensive engraving on brass frame. Disc. 1988.

	$1,510	$1,275	$1,100	$900	$750	$650	$550

Last MSR was $1,850.

Add $100 for steel frame.

* **Carbine** - 24 in. barrel, limited edition of 1,000 units including 50 engraved specimens, no swivels, 8¼ lbs. Importation disc. 2002.

	$685	$540	$450	$350	$275	$225	$195

Last MSR was $875.

* **Engraved Carbine** - limited production, only 50 mfg. Disc. 1988.

	$1,450	$1,225	$1,075	$900	$750	$650	$550

Last MSR was $1,750.

* **Trapper Model** - 16½ in. barrel, 7¼ lbs., 34¼ in. overall length. Disc. 2000.

	$685	$540	$450	$350	$275	$225	$195

Last MSR was $875.

* **Iron Frame Model** - with steel frame and butt plate, 24 in. blue barrel, select walnut, 9¼ lbs.

MSR	$1,035	$825	$715	$585	$495	$430	$360	$295

This model is available with either blue or color case hardened receiver.

MODEL 1866 YELLOWBOY CARBINE/RIFLE

.22 LR (disc.), .357 Mag. (disc.), .38 Spl. (new 1998), .44-40 WCF, or .45 LC (new 1998) cal., choice of rifle (24¼ in. octagon barrel), short rifle (20 in. octagon barrel), or carbine (19 in. round barrel), case hardened receiver, replica of the Winchester Model 1866. Mfg. 1972-1984, re-introduced.

MSR	$761	$625	$500	$375	$275	$215	$485	$150

Subtract $15 for carbine variation.

YELLOWBOY TRAPPER

.44-40 WCF cal., 16½ in. barrel. Disc.

	$575	$475	$425	$375	$325	$275	$225

MODEL 1873 STANDARD CARBINE/RIFLE

.357 Mag. (new 1998), .44-40 WCF or .45 LC cal., choice of rifle (24 in. octagon barrel) or carbine (19 in. round barrel), replica of the Winchester Model 1873.

MSR	$869	$750	$635	$530	$435	$350	$295	$250

Add $21 for rifle variation.

* **Model 1873 Trapper** - .44-40 WCF cal., similar to Carbine, with 16½ in. barrel. Disc.

	$575	$475	$425	$375	$325	$275	$225

* **Model 1873 Border Model Rifle** - .357 Mag., .44-40 WCF, or .45 LC cal., features 20 in. short octagon rifle barrel, case hardened receiver with blue barrel, 7 lbs. 6 oz. Importation began 1999.

MSR	$890	$770	$650	$550	$450	$350	$295	$250

* **Model 1873 Deluxe Border Model Rifle** - similar to Model 1873 Deluxe Sporting Rifle, except has 20 in. barrel. Importation began 2001.

MSR	$1,005	$875	$725	$565	$435	$325	$275	$225

* **Model 1873 Deluxe Sporting Rifle** - deluxe variation of the Model 1873 featuring case hardened receiver, lever, and hammer, checkered pistol grip stock, and choice of 24¼ or 30 (not available in .357 Mag. cal., disc. 2002) in. barrel, 8 lbs. 4 oz. or 8 lbs., 14 oz. New 1992.

MSR	$1,005	$875	$725	$565	$435	$325	$275	$225

Add $30 for 30 in. barrel (disc. 2002).

* **Model 1873 1 of 1,000** - only 1,000 mfg., deluxe wood, special engraving.

	$1,000	$775	$550				

Grading	100%	98%	95%	90%	80%	70%	60%

MODEL 1892 STANDARD CARBINE/RIFLE - .357 Mag., .44-40 WCF, or .45 LC cal., features 20 (carbine, w/o forearm cap, disc. 2001) or 24 (rifle) in. octagon barrel, choice of brass (disc.), blue, or case hardened receiver and crescent butt plate, uncheckered straight grip walnut stock and forearm, 5 lbs. 14 oz. or 7 lbs. Importation began 1999.

MSR	$545		$450	$375	$325	$275	$240	$210	$185

Subtract approx. $65 for carbine configuration (disc. 2001).

* ✷ *Model 1892 Stainless Carbine/Rifle* - similar to Standard Model 1892, except is stainless steel, not available in .44-40 WCF cal. Importation began 2000.

MSR	$515		$425	$350	$295

Add $70 for rifle configuration.

* ✷ *Model 1892 Short Rifle* - .32-20 WCF cal. (new 2002), similar to Model 1892 Standard Rifle, except has 20 in. short barrel, not available with brass frame, approx. 6¼ lbs. Importation began 1999.

MSR	$545		$445	$350	$295	$260	$215	$185	$155

* ✷ *Model 1892 Stainless Short Rifle* - similar to Model 1892 Short Rifle, except is stainless steel. Importation began 2000.

MSR	$585		$475	$355	$295

MODEL 1885 HIGH WALL RIFLE - .45-70 Govt. cal., available with 30 in. medium heavy octagon barrel with crescent butt plate or 28 in. round barrel with shotgun style butt plate, standard or open target sights, case hardened frame and lever, uncheckered European walnut stock and forearm, 9¼ or 10 lbs. Importation began 1999.

MSR	$920		$800	$635	$530	$430	$350	$295	$275

Add $75 for 30 in. octagon barrel.
Add $100 for rear tang sight.

RIFLES: MODERN PRODUCTION

In addition to the models listed, Navy Arms in late 1990 purchased the manufacturing rights of the English firm, Parker-Hale. In 1991, Navy Arms built a manufacturing facility located in Martinsburg, WV and produced these rifles domestically 1991-1994. The name of this company is Gibbs Rifle Co., and the current models listed are made in this location (see Gibbs Rifle Co. listing for more info).

N

TU-KKW TRAINING RIFLE - .22 LR cal., replica of the German "KKW" Gewehr training rifle, full sized Mauser 98K action with military sights, 26 in. barrel, detachable 5 shot mag., mfg. in China, 8 lbs. Imported 1992-94.

			$210	$180	$150	$135	$120	$105	$90

Last MSR was $310.

Add $125 for 2¾ power Type 89 quick mount scope (Sniper Trainer).

TU-33/40 CARBINE - .22 LR or 7.62x39mm cal., based on WWII Mauser G33/40 mountain carbine, 20¾ in. barrel, includes sling, adj. rear sight, mfg. in China, 7 lbs. 7 oz. Imported 1992- 94.

			$180	$150	$135	$120	$105	$90	$75

Last MSR was $210.

JW-15 RIFLE - .22 LR cal., sporter bolt action based on Brno Model 5 action, 24 in. barrel, detachable 5 shot mag., receiver top is dove-tailed, mfg. in China, 5 lbs. 12 oz. Imported 1992-94.

			$85	$70	$60	$50	$40	$35	$30

Last MSR was $100.

MARTINI TARGET RIFLE - .444 Marlin or .45-70 Govt. cal., single shot, 26 or 30 in. octagon barrel, tang sight, pistol grip stock. Mfg. 1972-1984.

			$480	$420	$350	$250	$195	$175	$150

Grading	100%	98%	95%	90%	80%	70%	60%

RPKS-74 - .223 Rem. or 7.62x39mm (new 1989) cal., semi-automatic version of the Chinese RPK Squad Automatic Weapon, Kalashnikov action, 19 in. barrel, integral folding bipod, 9½ lbs. Imported 1988-1989 only.

	$525	$445	$350	$250	$195	$175	$150

Last MSR was $649.

MODEL 1 CARBINE/RIFLE - .45-70 Govt. cal., action is sporterized No. 1 MKIII Enfield, choice of 18 (carbine) or 22 (rifle) in. barrel with iron sights, black Zytel Monte Carlo (rifle) or straight grip walnut (carbine) stock, 7 (carbine) or 8½ (rifle) lbs. Limited importation 1999 only.

	$325	$255	$200	$175	$160	$145	$130

Last MSR was $375.

MODEL 4 CARBINE/RIFLE - .45-70 Govt. cal., action is sporterized No. 4 MKI Enfield, choice of 18 (carbine) or 22 (rifle) in. barrel, blue metal, choice of checkered walnut Monte Carlo (rifle) or uncheckered straight grip (carbine, disc. 1999) stock, 7 or 8 lbs. Mfg. 1999-2001.

	$325	$255	$200	$175	$160	$145	$130

Last MSR was $375.

✳ *Deluxe No. 4 Enfield Sporter* - .303 British cal., synthetic Zytel Monte Carlo stock, 25 in. barrel with original military sights, approx. 8½ lbs. Mfg. 1999-2001.

	$115	$95	$85	$75	$65	$55	$50

Last MSR was $125.

2A HUNTER CARBINE/RIFLE - .308 Win. cal., action is sporterized 2A Enfield, 18 (carbine) or 22 (rifle) in. barrel with Parker-Hale style muzzle brake, includes scope mount, 12 shot mag., black enamel synthetic Zytel stock, 6¾ or 10¼ lbs. Mfg. 1999-2001.

	$240	$210	$190	$175	$160	$145	$130

Last MSR was $275.

Add $50 for rifle variation.

✳ *Deluxe 2A Enfield Sporter* - .308 Win. cal., 25 in. barrel, black Zytel Monte Carlo stock, original 2A Enfield military sights, approx. 8½ lbs. Mfg. 1999-2001.

	$130	$110	$95	$85	$75	$65	$55

Last MSR was $150.

N

SHOTGUNS: O/U, RECENT IMPORTATION

Importation of the models listed was disc. in 1990.

MODEL 83 - 12 or 20 ga., manufactured in Italy by R. Luciano, 3 in. chambers, extractors, double triggers, engraved chrome receiver, vent. barrels (bored M/F or IC/M) and rib. Introduced 1985.

	$280	$240	$215	$195	$170	$160	$150

Last MSR was $320.

MODEL 93 - 12 or 20 ga., manufactured in Italy by R. Luciano, 3 in. chambers, ejectors, double triggers, engraved chrome receiver, vent. barrels (bored M/F or IC/M) and rib. Introduced 1985.

	$325	$285	$250	$220	$200	$185	$160

Last MSR was $380.

MODEL 95 - similar to Model 93, except with single trigger and multi-chokes (includes 5 tubes), extractors.

	$375	$330	$295	$265	$235	$210	$190

Last MSR was $420.

MODEL 96 SPORTSMAN - 12 ga. only, 3 in. chambers, vent. barrels and rib, engraved chrome receiver, gold-plated receiver, multi-choked with 5 choke tubes, ejectors. Introduced 1985.

	$470	$425	$375	$330	$295	$260	$230

Last MSR was $530.

Grading	100%	98%	95%	90%	80%	70%	60%

MODEL 100 - 12, 20, 28 ga., or .410 bore, 3 in. chambers, 26 in. VR barrels, photo engraved hard chrome receiver, single trigger, extractors, checkered walnut stock and forearm, approx. 6¼ lbs. Introduced 1985.

$225	$205	$190	$170	$160	$150	$140	

Last MSR was $250.

SHOTGUNS: SxS, RECENT IMPORTATION

MODEL 100 - 12 or 20 ga., 3 in. chambers, 27½ in. barrels, checkered European walnut, double triggers, extractors, 6½ or 7 lbs. Imported 1985-1987 only.

$380	$330	$290	$260	$230	$200	$170

Last MSR was $475.

MODEL 150 - similar to Model 100, except with ejectors. Imported 1985-1987 only.

$455	$395	$350	$310	$280	$250	$220

Last MSR was $574.

SHOTGUNS: SINGLE SHOT

MODEL 105 SINGLE BARREL - 12, 20 ga,, or .410 bore, 26 or 28 in. full choke barrel only, folding action, engraved chrome receiver, checkered hardwood stock and forearm. New 1985.

$80	$70	$65	$60	$55	$50	$45

Last MSR was $90.

This model was designated the Model 600 before 1988.

❋ *Model 105 Deluxe* - similar to Model 105, except has European walnut stock and VR.

$95	$85	$75	$65	$60	$55	$50

Last MSR was $105.

This model was designated the Model 600 Deluxe before 1988.

P.V. NELSON, (GUNMAKERS)

Current manufacturer located in Bucks, England.

P.V. Nelson manufactures best quality shotguns and double rifles per individual customer order. Double rifles feature back action locks, and bolsters for extra strength. Side-by-side and over/under shotguns are available in most gauges, with a choice of rounded or regular action. Please contact the company directly (see Trademark Index) to find out more information about this quality English manufacturer.

NESIKA

Current trademark of rifle actions manufactured by Nesika Bay Precision, Inc., located in Poulsbo, WA. Dealer and consumer sales.

Nesika makes some of the most advanced rifle actions available today. As this edition went to press, the company had plans to start manufacturing complete rifles in the near future. Please contact the factory directly for a price list on their actions (7 different types), in addition to more information on their upcoming rifle production.

NEW DETONICS MANUFACTURING CORPORATION

Previous manufacturer located in Phoenix, AZ 1989-1992. Formerly named Detonics Firearms Industries (previous manufacturer located in Bellevue, WA 1976-1988). Detonics was sold in early 1988 to the New Detonics Manufacturing Corporation, a wholly owned subsidiary of "1045 Investors Group Limited."

PISTOLS: SEMI-AUTO, STAINLESS

MARK I - .45 ACP cal., matte blue. Disc. 1981.

$550	$450	$395

Grading	100%	98%	95%	90%	80%	70%	60%

MARK II - .45 ACP cal., satin nickel finish. Disc. 1979.

	$495	$375	$300				

MARK III - .45 ACP cal., hard chrome finish. Disc. 1979.

	$520	$390	$325				

MARK IV - .45 ACP cal., polished blue. Disc. 1981.

	$539	$410	$360				

COMBATMASTER MC1 (FORMERLY MARK I) - .45 ACP, 9mm Para., or .38 Super cal., 3½ in. barrel, two-tone (slide is non-glare blue and frame is matte stainless) finish, 6 shot mag., fixed sights, 28 oz. Disc. 1992.

	$775	$575	$450				

Last MSR was $920.

Add $15 for OM-3 model (polished slide - disc. 1983).
Add $100 for 9mm Para. or .38 Super cal. (disc. 1990).
This model was originally the MC1, then changed to the Mark I, then changed back to the MC1.

COMBATMASTER MARK V - .45 ACP, 9mm Para., or .38 Super cal., matte stainless finish, fixed sights, 6 shot mag. in .45 ACP, 7 shot in 9mm Para. and .38 Super, 3½ in. barrel, 29 oz. empty. This model was disc. 1985.

	$620	$550	$495				

Last MSR was $689.

Add $100 for 9mm Para. or .38 Super cal.

COMBATMASTER MARK VI - .45 ACP, 9mm Para., or .38 Super cal., 3½ in. barrel, 6 shot mag., adj. sights and polished stainless slide sides. Disc. 1989.

	$685	$575	$450				

Last MSR was $795.

Add $100 for 9mm Para. or .38 Super cal.

✳ **.451 Detonics Mag. Cal.** - limited mfg. 1,000. Disc. 1985.

	$1,000	$900	$775				

Last MSR was $1,165.

N

COMBATMASTER MARK VII - similar to Mark VI, only no sights, special order only, 25 oz.

	$895	$775	$600				

Add $100 for 9mm Para. or .38 Super cal.
Add $350 for .451 Detonics Mag., (disc. 1982).

MILITARY COMBAT MC2 - .45 ACP, 9mm Para., or .38 Super cal., dull, non-glare combat finish, fixed sights. Comes with camouflaged pile-lined wallet, and Pachmayr grips. Disc. 1984.

	$621	$560	$500				

Add $55 for 9mm Para. or .38 Super.

O.S. MODEL - .45 ACP cal. only, emergency backup pistol, similar to Combatmaster, 6 shot mag., choice of satin stainless or all black finish. 2 mfg. 1991 only.
Extreme rarity precludes accurate price evaluation.

SCOREMASTER - .45 ACP or .451 Mag. cal., match gun with closer tolerances, 5 or 6 in. barrel. Millett adj. sights, grip safety, 7 or 8 shot mag., 42 oz. Disc. 1992.

	$995	$850	$695				

Last MSR was $1,178.

Add $40 for 6 in. barrel.

COMPMASTER - .45 ACP cal. only, similar to Scoremaster, except is fully compensated. Mfg. 1988-92.

	$1,995	$1,575	$1,250				

Last MSR was $1,550.

This model was called the Janus Competition Scoremaster in 1988-1989.

Grading	100%	98%	95%	90%	80%	70%	60%

COMPETITION MASTER T.F. - .45 ACP cal., competition model with dual port compensator, rotational torque compensating vents, patented coned barrel system, hand tuned trigger, includes all competition modifications. Disc. 1992.

	$1,995	$1,575	$1,250

Last MSR was $1,550.

SERVICEMASTER - .45 ACP cal. only, shortened version of the Scoremaster, non-glare combat finish, 4¼ in. barrel, coned barrel system, 8 shot mag., interchangeable front and adj. rear sights, 39 oz. Disc. 1986.

	$825	$675	$575

Last MSR was $686.

* *Servicemaster II* - similar to Servicemaster, except has polished stainless steel finish. Mfg. 1986- 92.

	$925	$750	$625

Last MSR was $998.

POCKET 9 - 9mm Para. cal., double action, 3 in. barrel, 6 shot mag., soft matte sheen finish, 26 oz. Limited mfg. 1985-86 only.

	$495	$400	$335

Last MSR was $458.

The entire Pocket 9 series was disc. 1986.

* *Pocket 9 LS* - similar to Pocket 9, except has 4 in. barrel. Limited mfg. 1986 only.

	$575	$450	$375

Last MSR was $458.

* *Pocket .380* - similar to Pocket 9, except is .380 ACP cal., 23 oz. Limited mfg. 1986 only.

	$575	$450	$375

Last MSR was $458.

POWER 9 - 9mm Para. cal., similar to Pocket 9, except has polished slide sides and is supplied with 2 mags. Disc. 1986.

	$575	$450	$375

Last MSR was $509.

New Detonics Ladies Escort Series

This series was designed specifically to suit a woman's shooting requirements. Note that all prices have been listed as N/A - this is because there has been some speculation on these rare models recently, with reports of $2,500 and up paid for NIB specimens. Because this is a niche market, prices can be very volatile, and unpredictability is the rule.

ROYAL ESCORT - .45 ACP cal., action similar to Combatmaster, 3½ in. barrel, 6 shot mag., black frame, slide and grips are iridescent purple, hammer and trigger are 24 Kt. gold-plated. Less than 25 were mfg. 1990-92.

	N/A	N/A	$650

Last MSR was $990.

MIDNIGHT ESCORT - similar to Royal Escort, except is stainless with a black slide and smooth black grips. Less than 30 were mfg. 1990-92.

	N/A	N/A	$750

Last MSR was $1,090.

JADE ESCORT - similar to Midnight Escort, except has stainless frame, jade colored slide and grips. Less than 10 were mfg. 1990 only.

	N/A	N/A	$600

Last MSR was $918.

N

Grading	100%	98%	95%	90%	80%	70%	60%

NEW ENGLAND ARMS CORP.

Current importer, distributor, and retailer established during 1975, and located in Kittery Point, ME.

New England Arms Corp. imports, distributes, or retails the following trademarks: Arrieta, P. Arrizabalaga, Bertuzzi, Luciano Bosis, Cosmi, Henri Dumoulin, Fair Techni-Mec (I. Rizzini), Antonio Gil, Lebeau-Courally, F.lli Rizzini, B. Rizzini, Luciano Rota, S.I.A.C.E., and Fabio Zanotti. These trademarks may be found under their own headings in this text. For further information regarding any one of these manufacturers, please contact the company directly. New England Arms Corp. also offers quality restoration services on best quality shotguns and rifles executed by trained European craftsmen, in addition to performing firearms appraisals and evaluation work.

New England Arms Corp. should not be confused with New England Firearms.

NEW ENGLAND CUSTOM GUN SERVICE, LTD.

Current company importing and/or selling Johannsen rifles and Heym long arms from Germany, AYA and Kemen shotguns from Spain, Krieghoff double rifles, and custom made guns from small makers in Suhl, Germany, including Adamy-Jagdwaffen.

NECG, Ltd. specializes in custom gun services including checkering, stock fitting/alterations, claw mount scope installation and repair, detachable rifle scope mounts, and other gunsmithing services. Please contact the company directly regarding more information on their extensive line of products and services.

NEW ENGLAND FIREARMS

Current trademark established during 1987, and located and manufactured in Gardner, MA. Distributor sales only.

During 2000, Marlin Firearms Co. purchased the assets of H&R 1871, Inc., and the name was changed to H&R 1871, LLC. Brand names include Harrington & Richardson, New England Firearms, and Wesson & Harrington. Production will remain at the Gardner, MA plant.

All NEF firearms utilize a transfer bar safety system and have a $10 service plan which guarantees lifetime warranty.

New England Firearms should not be confused with New England Arms Corp.

REVOLVERS: DOUBLE ACTION

Ultra Models listed were available in blue finish only. All Ultras were supplied with a lockable storage case beginning 1993.

STANDARD REVOLVER .22 (MODEL R92) - .22 S, L, and LR cal., 9 shot, swing out cylinder, 2½ (disc. 1997), 3 (new 1998) or 4 in. barrel, blue or nickel finish, hardwood stocks, fixed rear sight, 25-28 oz. Mfg. 1988-1999.

$125	$95	$85	$70	$60	$55	$40

Last MSR was $144.

Add $10 for nickel finish.

✴ **Standard Revolver .32 H&R Mag. (Model R73)** - .32 H&R Mag. cal. similar to Standard Revolver .22, except has 5 shot cylinder, 2½ (disc.), 3, or 4 in. barrel, choice of blue or nickel finish (not available with 4 in. barrel), 23-26 oz. Mfg. 1988-1999.

$125	$95	$85	$70	$60	$55	$40

Last MSR was $144.

Add $10 for nickel finish (2½ or 3 in. barrel only).

ULTRA MODEL - .22 S, L, or LR cal., 9 shot, swing-out cylinder, 4 or 6 in. solid rib target-grade barrel with rebated muzzle and fully adj. rear sight, blue finish, smooth hardwood grips, 36 oz. Disc. 1999.

$150	$115	$95	$80	$70	$60	$55

Last MSR was $180.

Grading	100%	98%	95%	90%	80%	70%	60%

ULTRA MAG (MODEL R22) - .22 Mag. cal., 6 shot, 4 (disc. 1997) or 6 in. solid rib barrel, adj. rear sight, swing-out cylinder, blue finish, 36 oz. Mfg. 1988-1999.

	$150	$115	$95	$80	$70	$60	$55

Last MSR was $180.

LADY ULTRA - .32 H&R Mag. cal., swing-out cylinder, 5 shot, blue finish, 3 (disc. 1997, reintroduced 1999) or 4 (mfg. 1998 only) in. barrel with rib, adj. sights, thinner contoured grips, 31 oz. Mfg. 1991-99.

	$150	$115	$95	$80	$70	$60	$55

Last MSR was $180.

RIFLES: SINGLE SHOT

HANDI-RIFLE - .22 Hornet, .22-250 Rem. (mfg. 1992-94), .223 Rem., .243 Win. (new 1992), .270 Win. (new 1993), .280 Rem. (new 1996), .30-30 Win., .30-06 (new 1992), .308 Win. (new 1998), .357 Mag. (new 1999), .44 Rem. Mag. (new 1996), .45-70 Govt., 7x57mm Mauser (new 1998), or 7x64mm Brenneke (new 1998) cal., break open single shot action, 22 or 26 (.280 Rem. only) in. regular or bull (.223 Rem., .243 Win., or .22-250 Rem.) barrel, blue receiver, walnut stained hardwood stock, scope mount rail or ramp front and adj. rear sights, sling swivels, 7 lbs. New 1989.

MSR	$264	$215	$165	$125	$105	$80	$70	$60

Add $20 for Handi-Rifle .243 Win./Huntsman .50 cal. black powder muzzleloader rifle combo.

This model in .22-250 Rem., .223 Rem., or .243 Win. cal. is supplied with heavy barrel, scope mount, and no sights.

* ***Handi-Rifle Synthetic*** - .22 Hornet, .223 Rem., .243 Win., .270 Win., .280 Rem., .30-30 Win., .30-06, .357 Mag. (new 2002), .44 Rem. Mag., or .45-70 Govt. cal., 22 or 26 (.280 Rem. only) in. barrel, blue finish, features black synthetic stock and forearm, adj. sights on some cals., scope base mount only on others. New 1998.

MSR	$274	$220	$170	$130	$110	$85	$80	$75

* ***Handi-Rifle Youth*** - .223 Rem. or .243 Win. cal, features 22 in. barrel and shortened stock dimensions (13½ in. LOP), blue finish. New 1998.

MSR	$264	$215	$165	$125	$105	$80	$70	$60

* ***10th Anniversary Handi-Rifle*** - same cals. as Handi-Rifle, limited edition features scroll engraving by Ken Hurst, deep bluing on receiver, steel trigger guard and forearm spacer, select hand checkered walnut, less than 100 mfg. 1997 only.

	$695	$475	$350				

Last MSR was $750.

* ***Handi-Rifle NTA Anniversary Edition*** - .223 Rem. only, 24 in. heavy barrel w/o sights, features checkered black/grey laminate stock and forearm with NTA (National Trapper's Association) medallion in stock. Limited production 1999 only.

	$225	$200	$175	$160	$145	$135	$125

Last MSR was $272.

SUPER LIGHT HANDI-RIFLE - .22 Hornet, .223 Rem., or .243 Win. cal., break open single shot, black synthetic stock and forearm, recoil pad, 20 in. special contour barrel with rebated muzzle, .22 Hornet has sights (Model SB2-SL4), .223 Rem. has scope base and hammer extension (Model SB2-SL3), approx. 5½ lbs. New 1997.

MSR	$274	$220	$170	$130	$110	$85	$80	$75

This model is also available as a Youth Model with shorter stock dimensions (11¾ in. LOP).

SPORTSTER - .17 HMR (new 2002), .22 LR or .22 Mag. (new 2001) cal., 20 (mid-weight) or 22 (.17 HMR cal. only, heavy) in. barrel with Weaver style scope rail, available in either adult or youth dimensions, black polymer stock and forearm. New 1999.

MSR	$147	$120	$100	$85	$75	$60	$50	$45

Add $13 for .17 HMR cal.

Grading	100%	98%	95%	90%	80%	70%	60%

SURVIVOR - .223 Rem., .308 Win. (new 1999), .357 Mag. (disc. 1998) cal., similar in design to the Survivor Series shotgun, 22 in. barrel, blue or nickel (disc. 1998) finish, .357 Mag. cal. has open sights, .223 Rem. and .308 Win. cal. have heavy barrels and scope mount rail, 6 lbs. New 1996.

MSR	$277	$225	$180	$140	$110	$90	$80	$70

Add approx. $15 for nickel finish (disc.).

SHOTGUNS: SINGLE SHOT

PARDNER - 12, 16 (new 1989), 20, 28 ga.(new 1991), or .410 bore, 2¾ or 3 in. chamber (12, 20 ga., and .410 bore), single shot, break open action, safety transfer bar mechanism on hammer, side lever release, color case hardened receiver, 14 in. LOP, 24 (disc.), 26, 28, or 32 in. fixed choke barrel, extractor, walnut stained hardwood stock and forearm, 5-6 lbs. New 1987.

MSR	$128	$110	$90	$75	$65	$55	$45	$40

Add $15 for 32 in. barrel (12 ga. only).
Add $65 for Pardner 12 ga. Shotgun/Huntsman .50 cal. black powder muzzleloader combo.

* **Pardner Youth** - 12 (new 1998), 20, 28 ga., or .410 bore, similar to Pardner, except has 22 in. barrel and straight grip stock with recoil pad, 12½ in. LOP.

MSR	$136	$115	$95	$80	$70	$55	$45	$40

Add $29 for Pardner Youth .22 cal./.410 bore Versa-Pack combo.

* **Pardner Youth Turkey** - 20 ga. only, features 22 in. full choke barrel and camo painted wood. New 1999.

MSR	$183	$150	$115	$95	$80	$65	$55	$50

* **Pardner Special Purpose** - 10 or 12 (new 2002) ga., 3½ in. chamber, 28 or 32 (10 ga. only, new 1996) in. barrel, blue barrel and receiver, walnut or Mossy Oak Break Up camo (new 2002) finish on stock and forearm, recoil pad, 9½ lbs. New 1988.

MSR	$161	$135	$115	$95	$75	$65	$55	$45

Add $47 for 10 ga. with walnut finish.
Add $102 for 10 ga. with Mossy Oak Break Up camo finish (new 2002).

* **Pardner Turkey Gun** - 10 or 12 ga. only, 3 (disc.) or 3½ in. chamber, 24 in. barrel with fixed or full choke tube, camo or matte black wood finish, 6 or 9 (10 ga.) lbs. New 1999.

MSR	$175	$145	$120	$100	$80	$70	$60	$50

Add $8 for camo 12 ga. with full choke bore.
Add $60 for 10 ga. in black matte wood finish.
Add $85 for 10 ga. with camo wood finish.

* **Pardner NRA Foundation Youth** - 20, 28 (disc. 2001) ga. or .410 bore, 22 in. barrel, high luster bluing, features "NRA Foundation Youth Endowment Edition" laser etched in black on stock, approx. 5½ lbs. New 1999.

MSR	$161	$130	$105	$90	$75	$65	$55	$45

* **National Wild Turkey Federation (NWTF)** - 10 or 20 (new 1993) ga., 22 (20 ga. only) or 24 in. barrel with full screw-in choke, full Mossy Oak camo treatment, includes swivels and sling. Mfg. 1992-96.

		$190	$160	$135	$110	$95	$80	$70

Last MSR was $230.

Subtract $80 for 20 ga.
This model was drilled and tapped for scope mounts.

Grading	100%	98%	95%	90%	80%	70%	60%

SURVIVOR SERIES - 12, 20 ga., or .410/.45 LC (new 1995) bore, 3 in. chamber, 20 (.410/.45 LC) or 22 in. barrel with Mod. choke, blue or electroless nickel finish, synthetic thumbhole designed hollow stock with pistol grip, removable forend holds additional ammo, sling swivels, and black nylon sling, 13¼ in. LOP, 6 lbs. Mfg. 1992-93, reintroduced 1995.

	MSR	$157		$125	$100	$80	$65	$55	$45	$40

   Add $26 for electroless nickel finish.
   Add $42 for .410/.45 LC bore.

TRACKER SLUG MODEL - 10 ga. (mfg. 1994 only), 12, or 20 ga., 3 (12 or 20 ga.) or 3 ½ (10 ga. only) in. chamber, 24 in. cylinder bore barrel, case colored receiver, includes recoil pad and adj. sights, 6 lbs. Mfg. 1992-2001.

			$120	$90	$75	$60	$50	$45	$40

   Last MSR was $143.

✷ *Tracker II* - 12 or 20 ga., 3 in. chamber, similar to Tracker Slug Model except has 24 in. rifled bore barrel, 14 in. LOP, 5¼ lbs. New 1995.

	MSR	$180		$145	$115	$85	$70	$60	$50	$45

   Add $44 for Tracker II 12 ga. Slug Gun/Huntsman .50 cal. black powder muzzleloader.

NEW ULTRA LIGHT ARMS LLC

Current rifle manufacturer located in Morgantown, WV. Dealer sales.

RIFLES: BOLT ACTION

   Add $100 for left-hand action on the models listed.

ULTRA LIGHT RIFLE - caliber to customer specs., various actions, 2-position 3-function safety in top of stock, Timney trigger, Douglas barrel, no sights, Kevlar stock reinforced with graphite, recoil pad, Dupont Imron epoxy finish, designed to customer specifications, includes hard case, 5¼-5¾ lbs.

MODEL 20 - various short action centerfire cals. available between .17 Rem. and .358 Win, 5¼ lbs.

	MSR	$2,500		$2,225	$1,675	$1,225	$950	$800	$700	$640

✷ *Model 20 RF* - .22 LR cal., single shot or repeater, 5¼ lbs.

	MSR	$800		$750	$650	$550	$475	$400	$350	$300

   • Add $50 for repeater action.

MODEL 24 - various cals. between .25-06 Rem. - .35 Whelen, 5¼ lbs.

	MSR	$2,600		$2,325	$1,775	$1,300	$995	$825	$700	$640

MODEL 28 MAGNUM - various Mag. cals. between .264 Win. Mag. - .338 Win. Mag., 5¾ lbs.

	MSR	$2,900		$2,625	$1,975	$1,550	$1,225	$950	$700	$600

MODEL 40 MAGNUM - .300 Wby. Mag. or .416 Rigby cal., otherwise similar to Model 28 Magnum.

	MSR	$2,900		$2,625	$1,975	$1,550	$1,225	$950	$700	$600

NEWTON ARMS CO.

Previous manufacturer located in Buffalo, NY circa 1913-1932.

RIFLES: BOLT ACTION

NEWTON-MAUSER - .256 Newton - .30 Adolph Express cals., Oberndorf 98 bolt action, 24 in. barrel, sporting style stock, various grades and variations, some with double set triggers. A small shipment of these commerical rifles were built in Germany during 1914.

			$1,200	$1,050	$950	$850	$750	$650	$550

Grading	100%	98%	95%	90%	80%	70%	60%

1922 NEWTON MAUSER - .256 Newton cal., commercial Mauser 98 action, double set triggers opposed in guard, stock and/or barrels marked "Made in Germany", some barrels marked "Chas. Newton Rifle Corp., Buffalo, NY", leaf type rear sight. Approx. 100 rifles imported.

	N/A	$1,250	$1,050	$875	$775	$675	$575

This model can can vary quite a bit from specimen to specimen.

FIRST TYPE STANDARD - .22 Newton, .256 Newton, .30 Newton, .33 Newton, .35 Newton, or .30-06 cal., 24 in. standard barrel, open barrel sight, bolt peep sight was optional, checkered pistol grip stock, segmentally rifled barrels are marked "Newton Arms Co., Buffalo, NY", double set triggers. Approx. 4,000 mfg. 1917-1919.

$1,200	$950	$850	$750	$600	$550	$500

SECOND TYPE STANDARD - prototype only, this model was never produced.

BUFFALO NEWTON - .256 Newton, .30-06, .30 Newton, or .35 Newton cal., checkered sporting stock, reversed double set triggers, Enfield style bolt handle, open sights, 24 in. parabolically rifle barrel marked "Buffalo Newton Rifle Corp., New Haven Conn.". Approx. 1,000 mfg. 1923-1929 in New Haven, CT.

$750	$675	$625	$575	$525	$450	$385

There is little collector interest in this model.

NEWTON SPRINGFIELD - kit consisting of a Marlin-made sporting stock and .256 Newton barrel, customer supplied Springfield 1903 action and sights, original kit guns will have conventional square cut rifled barrels marked "Newton Arms Co. Buffalo, NY". Mfg. 1914-1917.

$595	$540	$495	$450	$410	$375	$330

Due to the low numbered Springfield receivers and the fact that many of these barrels were customer fitted, it is not advisable to fire these rifles until a competent gunsmith has performed an inspection.

NIKKO FIREARMS CO., LTD.

Previous manufacturer located in Tochigi, Japan circa 1958-1989.

NIKKO HISTORY AND GENERAL INFORMATION

The publisher wishes to thank the Golden Eagle Collectors Association located at 11144 Slate Creek Road, Grass Valley, CA 95945 for providing this publication with the information listed. Please refer to the Golden Eagle heading in this text for information on Nikko manufactured Golden Eagle firearms.

Both Nikko Firearms Co., Ltd. and Nikko Arms Co., Ltd. were trade names used by the Kodensha Co., Ltd. of Tochigi, Japan on products they manufactured and distributed worldwide. Nikko is the name of the Prefecture, or district, in which Tochigi City is located, about 50 miles north of Tokyo. The word Nikko translates to English as "sunshine". Kodensha first manufactured or distributed under the Nikko name in April 1955, and exported out of Japan beginning in August 1958. Nothing is known of the origin of the Kodensha Co.

Kodensha first approached the American shotgun market in about 1958 or '59 using the Japanese export marketing firm of Kyowa-Boeki-Bussan. They contacted various US distributors, and in about 1959 or '60, Continental Arms Co. of New York City began importing the Nikko "Grade 5". Continental imported these Nikko over/unders, in various models and configurations, until about 1972.

In 1962, the Kodensha Co. Ltd. formed a joint venture with Olin/Winchester of New Haven, CT to produce the Winchester Model 101 over/under shotgun. This venture was known as the Olin-Kodensha Co. Ltd. Added a little later was the side-by-side Model 23, and the Model 96 Xpert (a budget priced 101). The "pre-Olin" Kodensha factory was considerably outdated, and the joint venture began a complete modernization process, with the financial and technical assistance of Olin. Millions of dollars of machinery and technology were brought in, and the entire manufacturing process was upgraded to the then current standards.

One of the conditions of the joint venture was that Kodensha restrict their own products (made in the same factory, but recorded separately from the joint venture) to sale in Japan only. At the outset of the 25 years that the joint venture existed, Kodensha was probably amenable to this, as they were reaping huge financial and technical benefits from Olin. But, by the mid '60s, when the factory was in place and running smoothly, Kodensha essentially ignored that condition of the agreement, leaving Olin at somewhat of a disadvantage, not wanting to jeopardize their investment or production source. Additionally, Olin/Winchester was allowed only 2 permanent personnel, hardly enough to monitor the activities of a factory which employed up to 400 people. As an example, when walnut stock blanks arrived from France, Kodensha took first pick, and Olin got what was left over.

Kodensha converted an existing building near the manufacturing plant into an assembly area for Nikko, and other brands of guns. This building was probably the "true" Nikko Firearms Co., Ltd. Manufactured components from the Olin-Kodensha factory were carted to the Nikko plant for final assembly and fitting. This "dual-factory" arrangement continued until the mid-1980s. In 1981, for an unknown reason, the Olin-Kodensha name was changed to OK Firearms Co. Ltd. In October 1987, Olin/Winchester sold their interest in OK Firearms to Classic Doubles International, which continued making the 101 style shotgun under their own name. For reasons unknown, Classic Doubles went out of business in December 1988. Shortly thereafter, the entire factory was torn down, and all that remains today is a vacant lot.

During the "dual-factory" days, Nikko produced firearms for the following distributors or retailers: 1) Kanematsu Gosho of Arlington Heights, IL approx. 1974-1982 - distributed Nikko brand shotguns, Golden Eagle brand shotguns and rifles (1975 through March 1977 only); 2) Golden Eagle Firearms, Houston, TX March 1977 through early 1981 - Golden Eagle shotguns and rifles; 3) Tradewinds, Inc. of Tacoma, WA exported from Japan by Caspoll International, Tokyo January 1971 through December 1972 - Shadow Seven; Shadow Indy (Model 707); Gold, Silver, and Black Shadow over/ under shotguns; 4) Marubeni America, Inc. of New York City 1972-1974 - Miida brand over/under shotguns; 5) Winchester GMBH of West Germany, manufactured by Olin-Kodensha (dates unknown - early '80s) - Winchester Model 777 rifle (Golden Eagle look-alike); 6) Parker Reproduction shotguns, distributed in the US by Reagent Chemical & Research, Inc. 1984-1988; 7) International Star Commerce Corp. (ISCC) of Salt Lake City, Utah approx. 1982 - distributor of Nikko brand shotguns; 8) Moore Supply Co. of Salt Lake City, UT beginning mid- 1981 - distributor of Nikko brand shotguns; 9) USA Nikko, Inc. of Los Angeles, CA (factory reps and distributors of Nikko shotguns), initial date unknown, through December 1981; 10) Weatherby, Inc. of Los Angeles, CA May 1972 to 1981. Centurion semi-auto and Patrician pump shotguns, some Mark 22 rifles. Olympian O/U shotgun and possibly other O/Us from 1978-81. Model 82 semi-auto and Model 92 pump shotguns; 11) Savage Industries of Hamden, CT 1981-1982 - Savage/Fox FA-1 and FP-1 shotguns; 12) Charles Daly. "Automatic" distributed by Sloan's (Japanese made only) mid-1980s; 13) Sears, Roebuck Co. Ted Williams Model 400 and possibly others; 14) Churchill semi-auto, imported by Kassnar mid- 1980s; 15) High Standard of Hamden, CT 1974-75 - Supermatic Shadow Indy (Model 707, an O/U), Supermatic Shadow Seven (also O/U), and Supermatic Shadow semi-auto.

NOTE: ALL of the semi-auto shotguns used essentially the same design. Each distributor may have made a few cosmetic or dimensional embellishments to differentiate their gun. Differences exist in barrel/breech fit, magazine caps, pistol grip caps, checkering pattern, piston size, ejector location, fluted bolt. Use caution if interchanging parts. Generally, the same statement can be made about the pump versions also.

NOBLE MFG. CO.

Previous manufacturer located in Haydenville, MA circa 1950-1970.

Noble manufactured both semi-auto, lever, and slide action rifles in addition to both slide action and SxS shotguns. While most models were relatively inexpensive, good working, utilitarian guns, there has been little collectability to date and most rifles are seen priced in the $35-$85 price range while the shotguns are priced in the $65-$175 range.

NORINCO

Current manufacturer located in China. Currently imported and distributed by Interstate Arms Corp., located in Billerica, MA. Previous importers have included: Norinco Sports U.S.A., located in Diamond Bar, CA, Century International Arms, Inc. located in St. Albans, VT; China Sports, Inc. located in Ontario, CA; Interarms located

Grading	100%	98%	95%	90%	80%	70%	60%

in Alexandria, VA; KBI, Inc. located in Harrisburg, PA; and others. Dealer and distributor sales only.

Norinco pistols, rifles, and shotguns are manufactured in the People's Republic of China by Northern China Industries Corp. (Norinco has over 100 factories).

PISTOLS: SEMI-AUTO

MODEL 213 - 9mm Para. cal., single action, satin blue finish. Imported 1988 only.

	$185	$150	$135	$125	$115	$105	$100

Last MSR was $200.

TYPE 54-1 TOKAREV STANDARD - 7.62x25mm Tokarev or .38 Super cal., single action semi-auto, 4.5 in. barrel, 8 shot mag., fixed sights, blue finish, 29 oz. Imported 1989-95.

	$125	$100	$80	$70	$65	$60	$55

Last MSR was $145.

* **Type 54-1 Double Column** - similar to Standard Model, except is also available in 9mm Para. cal. and has 10 (C/B 1994) or 13* shot mag., 35 oz. Imported 1991-95.

	$155	$135	$120	$110	$100	$90	$80

Last MSR was $185.

* **Type 54-1 Compact** - .38 Super, 9mm Para., or 7.62x25mm Tokarev cal., 3.8 in. barrel, 8 shot mag., 27 oz. Imported 1991-95.

	$155	$135	$120	$110	$100	$90	$80

Last MSR was $185.

TYPE 59 MAKAROV - 9x18mm Makarov or .380 ACP cal., double action semi-auto, 3.5 in. barrel, 8 shot bottom release mag., checkered plastic grips, PPK design with additional features, adj. rear sight, 24 oz. Imported 1989-95.

	$150	$135	$125	$115	$95	$85	$75

Last MSR was $185.

TYPE 77B - 9mm Para. cal., semi-auto single action, action patterned after the older German Lignose (unique design permits one handed operation utilizing "trigger guard cocking" enabling the slide to be moved backward cocking the hammer), 5 in. barrel, 8 shot mag., adj. rear sight, 34 oz. Limited importation 1991-95.

	$350	$295	$250	$225	$195	$165	$135

Last MSR was $285.

MODEL 1911 A1 - .45 ACP cal. only, patterned after the Colt 1911 A1, 5 in. barrel, 7 shot mag., fixed sights, blue or parkerized finish, wood grips, 39 oz. Imported 1991-95.

	$275	$245	$220	$195	$180	$165	$150

Last MSR was $320.

RIFLES: SEMI-AUTO

TYPE 84S AKS RIFLE - .223 Rem. cal., semi-auto Kalashnikov action, 16.34 in. barrel, hardwood stock and pistol grip, 30 shot mag., 1,000 meter adj. rear sight, includes bayonet and sheath, 8.87 lbs. Imported 1988-1989 only.

	$575	$450	$400	$360	$330	$300	$285

Last MSR was $350.

* **Type 84S-1** - similar to Type 84S AK except has under-folding metal stock. Imported 1989 only.

	$700	$625	$550	$475	$425	$385	$350

Last MSR was $350.

* **Type 84S-3** - similar to Type 84S AK except has composite fiber stock (1½ in. longer than wood stock). Imported 1989 only.

	$650	$575	$500	$425	$400	$360	$330

Last MSR was $365.

N

Grading	100%	98%	95%	90%	80%	70%	60%

✳ *Type 84S-5* - similar to Type 84S AK except has side-folding metal stock. Imported 1989 only.

	$1,125	$995	$850	$725	$650	$575	$500

Last MSR was $350.

NHM-90/91 (AK-47 THUMBHOLE) - .223 Rem. or 7.62x39mm cal., features new thumbhole stock for legalized import, 5 shot mag. Imported 1991-1993, configuration was restyled and renamed NHM-90/91 in 1994.

	$495	$450	$400	$360	$330	$285	$250

Last MSR was $375.

NHM-90/91 SPORT - 7.62x39mm cal., choice of 16.34 (NHM-90) or 23.27 (NHM-91) in. barrel, hardwood thumbhole stock, NHM-91 has bipod, 5 shot mag., 9-11 lbs. Imported 1994-95.

	$450	$400	$360	$330	$285	$250	$225

The .223 Rem. cal. was also available for the Model NHM-90. Each Model NHM-90/91 was supplied with three 5 shot mags., sling, and cleaning kit.

MODEL B THUMBHOLE - 9mm Para. cal., patterned after the Uzi, features sporterized thumbhole wood stock, 10 shot mag. Importation 1995 only.

	$550	$485	$440	$400	$360	$330	$295

Last MSR was $625.

R.P.K. RIFLE - 7.62x39mm cal., includes bipod. Importation disc. 1993.

	$850	$775	$700	$640	$595	$550	$500

Last MSR was $600.

TYPE SKS - .223 Rem. or 7.62x39mm cal., SKS action, 20.47 in. barrel, 10 (C/B 1994) or 30* shot mag., 1,000 meter adj. rear sight, hardwood stock, new design accepts standard AK mag., with or w/o folding bayonet, 8.8 lbs. Imported 1988-1989, re-introduced 1992-95 with Sporter configuration stock.

	$150	$135	$120	$100	$90	$85	$80

Last MSR was $150.

Add $100 for synthetic stock and bayonet.
Subtract 15% if refinished.

TYPE 81S AKS RIFLE - 7.62x39mm cal., semi-auto Kalashnikov action, 17.5 in. barrel, 5, 30, or 40 shot mag., 500 meter adj. rear sight, fixed wood stock, hold open device after last shot, 8 lbs. Imported 1988-1989.

	$995	$850	$725	$650	$575	$500	$450

Last MSR was $385.

✳ *Type 81S-1* - similar to Type 81S AK except has under-folding metal stock. Imported 1988-1989.

	$1,100	$995	$850	$725	$650	$575	$500

Last MSR was $385.

TYPE 56S-2 - 7.62x39mm cal., older Kalashnikov design with side-folding metal stock. Importation disc. 1989.

	$1,150	$1,050	$875	$750	$650	$575	$500

Last MSR was $350.

TYPE 86S-7 RPK RIFLE - 7.62x39mm cal., AK action, 23.27 in. heavy barrel with built- in bipod, in-line buttstock, 11.02 lbs. Imported 1988-1989.

	$1,195	$1,050	$900	$825	$750	$650	$550

Last MSR was $425.

Grading	100%	98%	95%	90%	80%	70%	60%

TYPE 86S BULLPUP RIFLE - 7.62x39mm cal., bullpup configuration with AK action, under-folding metal stock, 17¼ in. barrel, ambidextrous cocking design, folding front handle, 7 lbs. Imported 1989 only.

	$1,100	$995	$850	$725	$650	$575	$500

Last MSR was $400.

DRAGUNOV (MODEL 350 NDM-86) - 7.62x54mm Russian, sniper variation of the AK-47, features 24 in. barrel with muzzle brake, special laminated skeletonized wood stock with vent. forearm, detachable 10 shot mag., 8 lbs. 9 oz. Importation disc. 1995.

	$2,775	$2,350	$1,925	$1,575	$1,275	$1,050	$900

Last MSR was $3,080.

This model was also imported by Gibbs Rifle Co. located in Martinsburg, WV.

✳ ***Dragunov Carbine*** - similar to Dragunov rifle, except shorter barrel, various accessories including a lighted scope were also offered, plastic furniture.

	$1,700	$1,500	$1,300	$1,100	$995	$875	$750

OFFICERS NINE - 9mm Para. cal., 16.1 in. barrel, action patterned after the IMI Uzi, 32 shot mag., black military finish, 8.4 lbs. Limited 1988-1989.

	$1,100	$995	$850	$725	$650	$575	$500

Last MSR was $450.

RIFLES: .22 CAL.

MODEL EM-321 - .22 LR cal., slide action, 19.5 in. barrel, 10 shot tube mag., hardwood stock and forearm, fixed sights, 6 lbs. Importation began 1989-90, resumed 1994 - disc.

	$135	$115	$95	$85	$75	$65	$55

TYPE EM-332 - .22 LR cal., bolt action, 18½ in. barrel with adj. rear sight, mag. holder on stock holds two extra 5 shot mags., Monte Carlo stock with cheekpiece and recoil pad, 4½ lbs. Imported 1991-1993.

	$225	$195	$165	$140	$120	$95	$80

SHOTGUNS: O/U

TYPE HL12-203 - 12 ga. only, 2¾ in. chambers, boxlock action, ejectors, 30 in. vent. barrels and rib, single trigger, multi-chokes, checkered stock and forearm, 7½ lbs. Imported 1989-1993.

	$400	$350	$300	$265	$225	$200	$185

SHOTGUNS: SxS

MODEL 99 COACH GUN - 12 ga. only, 2¾ in. chambers, exposed hammers, 20 in. barrels with F/M fixed chokes, blue finish with checkered stock and forearm, 7.2 lbs. Limited importation beginning 1999.

MSR	$270		$225	$200	$185	$170	$155	$145	$130

Add $20 for American walnut stock and forearm.

SHOTGUNS: SEMI-AUTO

MODEL 2000 FIELD - 12 ga. only, 2¾ in. chamber, steel receiver and aluminum alloy trigger guard, 26 or 28 in. VR barrel with M choke tube, choice of black synthetic or checkered hardwood stock and forearm, approx. 7½ lbs. Limited importation 1999 only.

	$260	$230	$200	$185	$170	$160	$150

Last MSR was $299.

Add $8 for wood stock and forearm.

Choke tubes are interchangable with the WinChoke system.

Grading	100%	98%	95%	90%	80%	70%	60%

✳ *Model 2000 Defense* - 12 ga. only, 2¾ in. chamber, 18½ in. barrel with cyl. choke tube and choice of bead, rifle, or ghost ring sights, matte black metal finish, black synthetic stock and forearm with recoil pad. Limited importation 1999 only.

	$245	$225	$190	$175	$160	$155	$145

Last MSR was $282.

Add $5 for rifle sights.
Add $17 for ghost ring sights.

SHOTGUNS: SLIDE ACTION

TYPE HL12-102 - 12 ga. only, 2¾ in. chamber, 28.4 in. barrel, 3 shot mag., crossbolt safety on rear trigger guard, fixed chokes, 9.3 lbs. Imported 1989-1993.

	$230	$200	$175	$165	$150	$135	$120

MODEL 97 HAMMER - 12 ga. only, patterned after the Win. Model 97, hammer, 20 in. plain barrel with cylinder bore fixed choke, solid frame, hardwood stock with grooved "corn cob" forearm. Importation began 2001.

MSR	$360		$310	$275	$240	$215	$190	$175	$160

Add $30 for American walnut stock and forearm.

MODEL 97 WWI TRENCH GUN - 12 ga. only, authentic reproductin of the original Winchester WWI Trench Gun, complete with shrouded barrel, proper markings, finish and wood. Importation began mid-2002.

As this edition went to press, prices had yet to be determined on this model.

MODEL 98 FIELD - 12 ga. only, 3 in. chamber, 26 or 28 in. VR barrel with M choke tube, choice of black synthetic or uncheckered hardwood stock and forearm with recoil pad, approx. 7 lbs. Limited importation 1999 only.

	$185	$160	$140	$125	$110	$100	$90

Last MSR was $205.

Add $8 for wood stock and forearm.
Add $55 for Field Combo (includes extra 18½ in. barrel) or $82 for Field Combo with 22 in. slug or turkey barrel.

✳ *Model 98 Turkey* - similar to Model 98 Field, except has 22 in. VR barrel with extra full choke tube, black synthetic stock and forearm only. Limited importation 1999 only.

	$190	$165	$140	$125	$110	$100	$90

Last MSR was $216.

✳ *Model 98 Defense* - 12 ga. only, 3 in. chamber, 18½ in. barrel with cyl. choke tube and choice of bead, rifle, or ghost ring sights, matte black metal finish, black synthetic stock and forearm with recoil pad. Limited importation 1999 only.

	$170	$150	$130	$115	$100	$90	$80

Last MSR was $190.

Add $15 for ghost ring sights.

MODEL 981/982 - 12 ga. only, 3 in. chamber, defense configuration with 18½ in. cylinder bore barrel with fixed choke, black synthetic stock and forearm, matte black metal finish. Importation began 2001.

MSR	$220		$190	$165	$145	$125	$115	$95	$85

Add $10 for ghost ring sights (Model 982).

MODEL 983 - 12 ga. only, 22 in. barrel with external rifled choke tube and adj. rifle sights, synthetic black stock. Importation began 2002.

MSR	$230		$215	$170	$155	$135	$125	$105	$95

N

Grading	100%	98%	95%	90%	80%	70%	60%

MODEL 984/985/987 - 12 ga. only, 3 in. chamber, field series with 26 or 28 in. VR barrel and M choke tube, black synthetic or uncheckered hardwood stock and forearm, matte black metal finish. Importation began 2001.

MSR $235	$200	$170	$155	$135	$125	$105	$95

Add $10 for hardwood stock (Models 985 & 987).

NORSMAN SPORTING ARMS

Current rifle manufacturer/customizer located in Havre, MT since 1999. Previously located in Bismarck, ND until 1999. Consumer direct sales.

Norsman specializes in both wood and synthetic take-down rifles and multiple barrel/caliber configurations, along with a complete line of built to order custom double rifles. Please contact the factory directly (see Trademark Index) for additional information and prices.

RIFLES: BOLT ACTION

VIKING GRADE - most standard cals., unique NSA takedown action, many options, including left hand models, custom orders also available.

MSR $6,000	$5,750	$5,250	$4,500	$3,750	$3,000	$2,500	$2,000

Add $1,500 per interchangable barrel.

VIKING GRADE MAGNUM - most standard Mag. cals., unique NSA takedown action, many options and custom orders available, including left hand.

MSR $9,000	$8,600	$8,000	$7,000	$6,000	$5,000	$4,000	$3,000

Add $2,000 per interchangable barrel.

FIELD GRADE SYNTHETIC - most standard cals., unique NSA takedown action, many options and custom orders available.

MSR $3,500	$3,250	$2,850	$2,500	$2,100	$1,850	$1,500	$1,250

Add $1,200 per interchangeable barrel.

RIFLES: SxS

VIKING GRADE - most standard cals. including .30-30 WCF, .30-40 Krag, .375 Win., .444 Marlin, .45-70 Govt., as well as traditional European NE cals. up to .600 NE, built per individual custom order. New 2000.

MSR $20,000	$19,600	$16,400	$14,000	$12,000	$10,000	$8,500	$7,250

NORTH AMERICAN ARMS, INC.

Current manufacturer established circa 1976, and currently located in Provo, UT. Distributor and dealer sales.

North American Arms was originally founded under the name Rocky Mountain Arms circa 1974-75 by noted handgun entrepreneur Dick Casull. During 1976-77, the company's name was changed to North American Arms, and it became part of the Tally Corp. of Newbury Park, CA. North American Arms was relocated from Salt Lake City to Provo, UT in 1978, and moved again in 1984 to Spanish Fork, UT. During 1986-87, Teleflex Corp., an aerospace company, bought North American Arms parent company, the Tally Corp. In 1992, Teleflex decided to sell off the gunmaking company, and North American Arms was purchased by Sandy Chisholm, a Teleflex employee. The company relocated again in 1994 to Provo, UT.

PISTOLS: SEMI-AUTO

In addition to many accessories being available for the Guardian Pistol Series, there is also a Guardian Custom Shop that offers consumers a customized Guardian model, with a wide variety of finish, slide, sight, grips, and serialization options. Please contact the company directly for more information on these custom shop special orders and options.

Grading	100%	98%	95%	90%	80%	70%	60%

NAA .32 GUARDIAN - .32 ACP cal., double action only, hammerless, stainless steel construction, 6 shot mag., 2.185 in. barrel, fixed low profile sights, dimpled black synthetic grips, 13½ oz. New 1999.

	MSR	$408		$355	$285	$245

NAA .380 GUARDIAN - .380 ACP cal., double action only, larger version of the NAA .32 Guardian, 2.49 in. barrel, 6 shot mag., dimpled black grips, mfg. in partnership with Kahr Arms, 18.7 oz. New 2001.

	MSR	$449		$385	$300	$250

REVOLVERS: MINI SERIES

All NAA mini revolvers are manufactured to highest quality control standards and have half-way notches cut on the front cylinder face allowing the hammer to lock up the cylinder between cartridges. This allows the gun to be carried fully loaded without the danger of accidental discharge.

NAA .22 S/LR - .22 Short (new 1994) or .22 LR cal., 5 shot, single action, spur trigger, 1 1/8, 1 5/8, or 2½ (disc.) in. barrel, stainless steel, plastic (disc.) or laminated rosewood grips, approx. 4½ oz. Mfg. 1975-present.

	MSR	$186		$150	$115	$95

Add $15 for 2½ in. barrel (disc.).
Add $35 for holster grip accessory.
Add $39 for quick-release belt buckle option.
The optional holster grip allows the pistol to fold forward allowing concealability, safety, and has a clip which allows it to be attached to a belt.

NAA .22 MAGNUM - similar to .22 LR, except in .22 Mag. cal.

	MSR	$205		$170	$130	$110

Add $18 for 2½ in. barrel (disc.).
Add $34 for quick-release belt buckle option.

NAA .22 MAGNUM CONVERTIBLE - similar to NAA .22 Mag., except has extra LR cylinder in pouch.

	MSR	$245		$205	$170	$120

Add $18 for 2½ in. barrel (disc.).
Add $33 for holster grip accessory.

MINI-MASTER TARGET REVOLVER - .22 LR or .22 Mag. cal., 5 shot, 4 in. heavy vent. barrel, unfluted bull cylinder, spur trigger, fixed or adj. white outline rear sight, oversize black rubber Mini-master grip, 10.7 oz. New 1990.

	MSR	$286		$245	$200	$170

Add $38 for extra combo cylinder.
Add $18 for adj. rear sight (elevation only).
This model was also available in hot fuschia colored oversized grips.

MINI-MASTER BLACK WIDOW - .22 LR or .22 Mag. cal., 2 in. heavy VR barrel, full size black rubber grip, fixed or adj. rear sight, unfluted cylinder, 8.8 oz. New 1991.

	MSR	$256		$215	$170	$130

Add $38 for extra combo cylinder.
Add $18 for adj. rear sight (elevation only).
This model was also available in hot fuschia colored oversized grips.

NAA STANDARD SET - 3 gun set (.22 Short, .22 LR, and .22 Mag. cals.) in walnut display case with matching serial numbers, high polish finish with matte contours.

	MSR	$748		$545	$455	$365

NAA DELUXE SET - 3 gun set (.22 Short, .22 LR, and .22 Mag. cals.) in walnut display case with matching serial numbers, high polish finish on entire gun.

	MSR	$825		$690	$555	$410

N

Grading	100%	98%	95%	90%	80%	70%	60%

CASED .22 MAG. - includes .22 Mag. cal. model in walnut display case with high polish finish with matte contours.

MSR	$376	$310	$225	$180

NAA SINGLE ACTION REVOLVER - .45 Win. Mag. or .450 Mag. Express cal., polished stainless steel, transfer bar safety inside the hammer, 5 shot, 7½ in. barrel, walnut grips, includes presentation case. Disc. 1984.

Matte finish	$1,200	$950	$700
High polish finish	$1,400	$1,100	$850
Both cylinders	$1,650	$1,275	$975

Last MSR was $650.

This model was also available by special order with 10½ in. barrel and optional scope. Extra cylinders were also available at $75-$100 and were fitted to the gun. A set including 2 cylinders could also be ordered. North American Arms cannot perform any repair work on .450 Mag. Express revolvers.

NORTH AMERICAN SAFARI EXPRESS

Previous trademark for those rifles (SxS) assembled by A. Francotte of Belgium for exclusive importation by Armes De Chasse located in Chadds Ford, PA.

NORTHWEST ARMS

Please refer to Wilkinson Arms listing.

NOWLIN MFG., INC.

Current custom handgun and components manufacturer established in 1982, and located in Claremore, OK. Dealer or consumer direct sales.

Nowlin Mfg., Inc. manufactures a complete line of high quality M1911 A1 styled competition and defense pistols, available in 9mm Para., 9x23mm, .38 Super, .40 S&W, or .45 ACP cal. Various frame types are available, including a variety of Nowlin choices. Recent models (available in blue or nickle finish) include the NRA Bianchi Cup (approx. 1997 retail was $2,750 - disc.), 007 Compact ($1,395 - disc.), Compact X2 ($1,436 - disc.), Match Classic ($1,295), Crusader ($1,589), Avenger w/STI frame ($1,849), Challenger ($1,669), World Cup PPC ($1,819), STI High Cap. Frame ($1,595 - disc. 1999), Mickey Fowler Signature Series ($1,987), Compact Carry ($1,695 - disc. 1999), Compact 4¼ in. ($1,750, .45 ACP), Gladiator ($1,447 in .45 ACP cal.), Match Master ($2,395), and the Custom Shop Excaliber Series ($2,529), Please contact the factory directly for more information, including specific pricing (see Trademark Index).

N

O Section

O.D.I. (OMEGA DEFENSIVE INDUSTRIES)

Previous manufacturer located in Midland Park, NJ circa 1981-82.

Essex Arms located in Island Pond, VT has acquired the remaining O.D.I. Viking inventory of parts for the Viking pistol (see Trademark Index), in addition to being a components supplier (slides and receivers) for M-1911 styled pistols. Previously, Randco Manufacturing located in Monrovia, CA was providing service (and had parts) for these older O.D.I. Pistols.

Grading	100%	98%	95%	90%	80%	70%	60%

PISTOLS: SEMI-AUTO

VIKING & VIKING COMBAT - .45 ACP or 9mm Para. (advertised, but never mfg.) cal., Viking Model is Government size and the Combat Model is Commander size. All stainless steel construction, the design utilizes the Seecamp double action, teakwood grips. 5 in. barrel on the Viking Model and 4 1/4 in. barrel on the Viking Combat Model, 7 shot mag., 39 oz. Approx. 200-300 Viking Combat Models were made from kits.

	$495	$385	$295				

Last Mfg.'s Retail was $579.

Add $100 for slide with cross bolt safety.

OBREGON

Previously manufactured by Fabrica de Armas Mexico located in Mexico City, Mexico.

PISTOLS: SEMI-AUTO

OBREGON - 11.35mm cal., patterned somewhat after the Colt Model 1911A1, features tubular slide and Savage/Steyr type action, 1,000 pistols mfg. in Mexico for commercial sale during and after WWII, slide marked "Sistema Obregon Cal 11.35mm".

$4,750	$4,250	$3,750	$3,250	$2,750	$2,250	$1,750

OHIO ORDNANCE WORKS, INC.

Current rifle manufacturer established in 1997, and located in Chardon, OH.

RIFLES: SEMI-AUTO

MODEL BAR 1918A3 - .30-06 cal., patterned after the original Browning BAR (M1918A2) used during WWI, all steel construction utilizing original parts except for lower receiver, 24 in. barrel, original folding type rear sight, 20 shot mag., matte metal and wood finish, 20 lbs. Limited mfg.

MSR	$2,650		$2,450	$2,250	$1,900	$1,600	$1,400	$1,100	$875

MODEL 1928 BROWNING - .30-06, 7.65mm, .308 Win., or 8mm cal., semi-auto action patterned after the 1928 Browning watercooled machine gun, blue or parkerized finish, includes tripod, water hose, ammo can, 3 belts, and belt loader. Production began late 2001.

MSR	$5,950		$5,450	$4,850	$4,450	$4,000	$3,650	$3,450	$3,150

Add $200 for .308 Win. or 8mm cal.
Subtract $2,100 for parkerized finish.

OLD-WEST GUN CO.

Previous importer and distributor that took over the inventory of Allen Firearms after they went out of business in early 1987. Old-West Gun Co. changed their name to Cimarron Arms in late 1987. Please refer to Cimarron Arms in this text for approximate prices on similar models from Old-West Gun Co.

Grading	100%	98%	95%	90%	80%	70%	60%

OLYMPIC ARMS, INC.

Current manufacturer established during 1976, and located in Olympia, WA. Dealer direct sales.

In late 1987, Olympic Arms, Inc. acquired Safari Arms of Phoenix, AZ.

PISTOLS: SEMI-AUTO

There is no post-ban OA-93 pistol.

OA-93 PISTOL - .223 Rem. (most common) or 7.62x39mm (very limited mfg.) cal., semi-auto, gas operated without buffer tube stock, or charging handle, 6 (most common), 9, or 14 in. free-floated match barrel, upper receiver utilizes integral scope mount base, 30 shot mag., 4 lbs. 3 oz., approx. 500 mfg. before Crime Bill discontinued mfg. Mfg. 1993-94 only.

	$2,450	$2,200	$1,925	$1,700	$1,500	$1,300	$1,100

Last MSR was $2,700.

Add $800 for 7.62x39mm cal.

OA-96 AR PISTOL - .223 Rem. cal., 6 in. barrel only, similar to OA-93 Pistol, except has pinned (fixed) 30 shot mag. and rear takedown button for rapid reloading, 5 lbs. Mfg. 1996-2000.

	$860	$775	$650	$575	$495	$450	$395

Last MSR was $860.

OA-98 PISTOL - .223 Rem. cal., skeletonized, lightweight version of the OA-96, 10 shot fixed mag., denoted by perforated appearance, 3 lbs. New 1998.

MSR	$1,020		$1,020	$850	$775	$650	$575	$495	$450

RIFLES: BOLT ACTION

In 1993, Olympic Arms purchased the rights, jigs, fixtures, and machining templates for the Bauska Big Bore Magnum Mauser action. Please contact Olympic Arms (see Trademark Index) for more information regarding Bauska actions both with or without fluted barrels.

ULTRA MAG BBK-01 - various cals. between .300 Win. Mag.-.505 Gibbs, custom order rifle available with many barrel options and other special order features, price on request from the factory.

This model was formerly the Bauska BBK-02.

BOLT ACTION SAKO - various cals. between .17 Rem.-.416 Rem. Mag., 26 in. fluted barrel, various stock configurations, values represent base price with no options. Disc. 2000.

	$660	$575	$500	$450	$400	$360	$330

Last MSR was $660.

ULTRA CSR TACTICAL RIFLE - .308 Win. cal., Sako action, 26 in. broach cut heavy barrel, Bell & Carlson black or synthetic stock with aluminum bedding, Harris bipod, carrying case. Mfg. 1996-2000.

	$1,140	$900	$740	$625	$550	$500	$450

Last MSR was $1,140.

RIFLES: SEMI-AUTO

On the models listed, the PCR (Politically Correct Rifle) variations refer to those guns manufactured after the Crime Bill was implemented in September, 1994. PCR rifles have smooth barrels (no flash suppressor), a 10 shot mag., and fixed stocks. Older, discontinued named models refer to the original, pre-ban model nomenclature. All pre-ban commercial inventory is now depleted, and values reflect current secondary marketplace prices.

Grading	100%	98%	95%	90%	80%	70%	60%

COMPETITOR RIFLE - .22 LR cal., Ruger 10/22 action with 20 in. barrel featuring button cut rifling, Bell & Carlson thumbhole fiberglass stock, black finish and matte stainless fluted barrel, includes bipod, 6.9 lbs. Mfg. 1996-99.

	$575	$500	$450	$400	$360	$330	$300

Last MSR was $575.

ULTRAMATCH/PCR-1 - .223 Rem. cal., AR-15 action with modifications, 20 or 24 in. match stainless steel barrel, picatinny flattop, Williams set trigger optional, scope mounts, 10 lbs. 3 oz. New 1985.

✳ PCR-1

MSR	$1,040	$960	$825	$725	$600	$550	$500	$460

✳ PCR-1P - .223 Rem. cal., premium grade ultramatch rifle with many shooting enhancements, including Maxhard treated upper and lower receiver, 20 or 24 in. broach cut Ultramatch bull barrel, 1x10 in. or 1x8 in. rate of twist. New 2001.

MSR	$1,299	$1,075	$925	$800	$700	$600	$550	$500

✳ Ultramatch

	$1,400	$1,200	$1,000	$875	$775	$675	$550

Last MSR was $1,515.

While still available to law enforcement, military, and qualified export agencies, this model is now discontinued for commerical sales, and no inventory remains.

INTERCONTINENTAL - .223 Rem. cal., features synthetic wood-grained thumbhole butt stock and aluminum handguard, 20 in. ultra match barrel (free floating). Mfg. 1992-93.

	$1,650	$1,350	$1,050	$875	$750	$600	$550

Last MSR was $1,371.

INTERNATIONAL MATCH - .223 Rem. cal., similar to Ultramatch, except has custom aperture sights. Mfg. 1991-93.

	$1,475	$1,150	$950	$800	$675	$575	$525

Last MSR was $1,240.

SERVICE MATCH/PCR SERVICE MATCH - .223 Rem. cal., AR-15 action with modifications, 20 in. SS Ultramatch barrel, carrying handle, standard trigger, choice of A1 or A2 flash suppressor (Service Match only), 8¾ lbs.

✳ PCR Service Match

MSR	$1,060	$975	$845	$700	$600	$530	$495	$450

✳ Service Match

	$1,075	$875	$725	$625	$550	$500	$450

Last MSR was $1,200.

While still available to law enforcement, military, and qualified export agencies, this model is now discontinued for commerical sales, and no inventory remains.

MULTIMATCH ML-1/PCR-2 - .223 Rem. cal., tactical short range rifle, 16 in. Ultramatch barrel, aluminum collapsible (Multimatch ML-1) or fixed (PCR-2) stock, carrying handle, stealth vortex flash suppressor (Multimatch ML-1 only), 5 lbs. 14 oz. New 1991.

✳ PCR-2

MSR	$960	$895	$775	$650	$575	$495	$450	$400

✳ Multimatch ML-1

	$1,075	$875	$725	$625	$550	$500	$450

Last MSR was $1,200.

While still available to law enforcement, military, and qualified export agencies, this model is now discontinued for commerical sales, and no inventory remains.

MULTIMATCH ML-2/PCR-3 - .223 Rem. cal., featurespicatinny flattop upper receiver with SS 16 in. Ultramatch barrel, carrying handle, 5 lbs. 14 oz. New 1991.

✳ PCR-3

MSR	$960	$895	$775	$650	$575	$495	$450	$400

Grading	100%	98%	95%	90%	80%	70%	60%
✳ Multimatch ML-2	$1,075	$875	$725	$625	$550	$500	$450

Last MSR was $1,200.

While still available to law enforcement, military, and qualified export agencies, this model is now discontinued for commerical sales, and no inventory remains.

AR-15 MATCH/PCR-4 - .223 Rem. cal., patterned after the AR-15 with 20 in. barrel and solid synthetic stock, 8 lbs. 5 oz. New 1975.

✳ PCR-4							
MSR $800	$725	$650	$575	$525	$475	$425	$395
✳ AR-15 Match	$995	$875	$775	$650	$575	$495	$450

Last MSR was $1,075.

CAR-15/PCR-5 - modified AR-15 with choice of 11½ (disc. 1993) or 16 in. barrel, stow-away pistol grip and collapsible stock (CAR-15 only), 7 lbs. Mfg. 1975-1998, PCR-5 reintroduced 2000.

✳ PCR-5 - .223 Rem., 9mm Para. (new 1996), .40 S&W (new 1996), or .45 ACP (new 1996) cal. Disc. 1998, reintroduced 2000.

MSR $750	$695	$650	$550	$475	$450	$400	$375

Add $45 for 9mm Para., .40 S&W, or .45 ACP cal.

✳ CAR-15 - .223 Rem., 9mm Para., .40 S&W, .45 ACP, or 7.62x39mm cal.

	$960	$860	$775	$650	$575	$495	$450

Last MSR was $1,030.

Add $170 for pistol cals.

While still available to law enforcement, military, and qualified export agencies, this model is now discontinued for commerical sales, and no inventory remains.

PCR-6 - 7.62x39mm cal., 16 in. barrel, post-ban only, A-2 stowaway stock, carrying handle, 7 lbs. Mfg. 1995-2002.

	$795	$725	$650	$500	$475	$425	$375

Last MSR was $870.

PCR-7 ELIMINATOR - .223 Rem. cal., similar to PCR-4, except has 16 in. barrel, 7 lbs. 10 oz. New 1999.

MSR $800	$740	$650	$575	$500	$475	$425	$375

PCR-8 - .223 Rem. cal., same configuration as the PCR-1, except has standard 20 in. stainless steel heavy bull barrel with button rifling. New 2001.

MSR $904	$825	$725	$625	$550	$495	$450	$425

PCR-9/10/40/45 - 9mm Para., 10mm, .40 S&W, or .45 ACP cal., similar to PCR-5 Carbine except for pistol cals, A2 upper standard, 16 in. barrel, A2 buttstock, Mil-Spec lower. New 2001.

MSR $834	$765	$665	$585	$510	$480	$425	$375

PLINKER - .223 Rem. cal., similar to PCR-5, except has 16 in. button rifled barrel standard, A1 sights, cast upper/lower receiver, 100% standard Mil-Spec parts, 7 lbs. New 2001.

MSR $599	$550	$495	$460	$430	$410	$390	$375

CAR-97 - .223 Rem. cal., 9mm Para., 10mm, .40 S&W, or .45 ACP cal., similar to PCR-5, except has 16 in. button rifled barrel, A2 sights, fixed CAR stock, standard with post-ban muzzle brake, approx. 7 lbs. New 1997.

MSR $780	$725	$650	$575	$495	$450	$415	$360

Add approx. $65 for 9mm Para., .40 S&W, or .45 ACP cal.

FAR-15 - .223 Rem. cal., featherweight model with lightweight 16 in. barrel, fixed collapsible stock, A1 contour lightweight button rifled barrel, 9.92 lbs. New 2001.

MSR $822	$755	$660	$580	$510	$480	$425	$375

Grading	100%	98%	95%	90%	80%	70%	60%

OA-93 CARBINE - .223 Rem. cal., 16 in. barrel, design based on OA-93 pistol, aluminum folding stock, flat-top receiver, Vortex flash suppressor, 7½ lbs. Mfg. 1995 - civilian sales disc. 1998.

	$1,400	$1,200	$1,000	$875	$775	$675	$550

Last MSR was $1,550.

While still available to law enforcement, military, and qualified export agencies, this model is now discontinued for commerical sales, and no inventory remains.

COUNTER SNIPER RIFLE - .308 Win. cal., bolt action utilizing M-14 mags., 26 in. heavy barrel, camo-fiberglass stock, 10½ lbs. Disc. 1987.

	$1,100	$900	$775	$695	$550	$440	$410

Last MSR was $1,225.

SURVIVOR I CONVERSION UNIT - .223 Rem. or .45 ACP cal., converts M1911 variations into carbine, bolt action, collapsible stock, 16¼ in. barrel, 5 lbs.

	$275	$225	$195

This kit is also available for S&W and Browning Hi-Power models.

OMEGA

Previous trademark manufactured by Armero Specialistas Reunidas, located in Eibar, Spain, circa 1920s.

PISTOLS: SEMI-AUTO

SEMI AUTOMATIC PISTOL - 6.35mm or 7.65mm cal., "Eibar" type action, marked Omega on slide, 6 shot mag.

	100%	98%	95%	90%	80%	70%	60%
6.35 cal.	$225	$180	$130	$110	$70	$55	$40
7.65 cal.	$250	$195	$135	$115	$80	$70	$55

OMEGA FIREARMS

Previous manufacturer located in Flower Mound, TX circa 1965-1969.

RIFLES: BOLT ACTION

SINGLE SHOT RIFLE - various cals., premium walnut. Disc. late 1960s.

	$775	$650	$575	$495	$425	$360	$295

OMEGA PISTOL

Previously manufactured and distributed by Springfield Armory located in Geneseo, IL. Omega conversion kits only were available until 1996 from Safari Arms located in Olympia, WA under license from Peters-Stahl in Germany.

PISTOLS: SEMI-AUTO

OMEGA - .38 Super, 10mm Norma, or .45 ACP cal., single action, ported slide, 5 or 6 in. interchangeable ported or unported barrel with Polygon rifling, special lock-up system eliminates normal barrel link and bushing, Pachmayr grips, dual extractors, adj. rear sight. Mfg. 1987-90.

	$625	$560	$495	$425	$360	$295	$265

Last MSR was $849.

Add $663 for interchangeable conversion units.
Add $336 for interchangeable 5 or 6 in. barrel (including factory installation).
Each conversion unit includes an entire slide assembly, one mag., 5 or 6 in barrel, recoil spring guide mechanism assembly, and factory fitting.

Grading	100%	98%	95%	90%	80%	70%	60%

OMEGA RIFLES/SHOTGUNS

Previous trademark of select rifles/shotguns imported by K.B.I., Inc. located in Harrisburg, PA, until 1994.

RIFLES

To date, there has been little collector interest for Omega rifles. Values are mostly determined by the shooting value rather than collector value.

SHOTGUNS

STANDARD O/U - 12, 20 (disc.), 28 (disc.) ga., or .410 (disc) bore, boxlock action, folding design, SNT, 26 or 28 in. VR barrels, extractors, checkered walnut stock and forearm, 5½-7 lbs. Disc. 1994.

	100%	98%	95%	90%	80%	70%	60%
	$425	$330	$295	$260	$230	$200	$180

✻ **Deluxe O/U** - 12 ga. only, similar to Standard Model except has better walnut. Importation disc. 1990.

	100%	98%	95%	90%	80%	70%	60%
	$335	$290	$255	$220	$185	$160	$140

Last MSR was $379.

STANDARD SxS - 20, 28 ga., or .410 bore, boxlock action, folding design, double triggers, hardwood stock and forearm, 26 in. barrels, extractors, 5½ lbs. Disc. 1989.

	100%	98%	95%	90%	80%	70%	60%
	$190	$165	$140	$120	$110	$100	$90

Last MSR was $229.

Add $40 for 28 ga. or .410 bore.

✻ **Deluxe SxS** - .410 bore only, similar to Standard Model except has better walnut. Disc. 1989.

	100%	98%	95%	90%	80%	70%	60%
	$200	$185	$170	$155	$140	$130	$120

Last MSR was $249.

SINGLE BARREL - 12, 20 ga., or .410 bore, various barrel lengths, matte blue finish, extractor. Importation disc. 1987.

	100%	98%	95%	90%	80%	70%	60%
	$85	$75	$65	$55	$45	$40	$35

Last MSR was $95.

STANDARD FOLDING SINGLE BARREL - 12, 16, 20, 28 ga., or .410 bore, 28 or 30 in. barrel, checkered hardwood stock, matte chrome receiver, approx. 5½ lbs. Importation disc. 1987.

	100%	98%	95%	90%	80%	70%	60%
	$160	$135	$115	$100	$85	$70	$65

Last MSR was $180.

DELUXE FOLDING SINGLE BARREL - 12, 16, 20, 28 ga., or .410 bore, similar to Standard Model, except has checkered walnut stock and forearm, blue receiver. Importation disc. 1987.

	100%	98%	95%	90%	80%	70%	60%
	$195	$160	$135	$115	$100	$85	$70

Last MSR was $220.

OMEGA WEAPONS SYSTEMS INC.

Current shotgun manufacturer established circa 1998, and located in Tucson, AZ. Distributed by Defense Technology, Inc., located in Lake Forest, CA.

SHOTGUNS: SEMI-AUTO

OMEGA SPS-12 - 12 ga. only, 2¾ in. chamber, features gas operation and 5 shot detachable mag., 20 in. barrel, protected ghost ring sights, synthetic stock (with or w/o pistol grip) and forearm, 9 lbs. New 1998.

	MSR	$495	100%	98%	95%	90%	80%	70%	60%
	MSR	$495	$450	$400	$360	$330	$300	$275	$250

Grading	100%	98%	95%	90%	80%	70%	60%

OMNI

Previous manufacturer located in Riverside, CA 1992-1998. During 1998, Omni changed its name to E.D.M. Arms. Previously distributed by First Defense International located in CA.

RIFLES: BOLT ACTION

LONG ACTION SINGLE SHOT - .50 BMG cal., competition single shot, chrome-moly black finished receiver, 32-34 in. steel or stainless steel barrel with round muzzle brake, benchrest fiberglass stock, designed for FCSA competition shooting, 32 lbs. Mfg. 1996-98.

$3,200	$2,800	$2,500	$2,150	$1,800	$1,500	$1,250

Last MSR was $3,500.

Add $400 for painted stock (disc. 1996).

SHELL HOLDER SINGLE SHOT - similar to Long Action Single Shot, except has fiberglass field stock with bipod, 28 lbs. Mfg. 1997-98.

$2,525	$2,150	$1,800	$1,500	$1,250	$1,100	$925

Last MSR was $2,750.

MODEL WINDRUNNER - .50 BMG cal., long action, single shot or 3 shot mag., 1-piece I-beam receiver, chrome-moly black finish, 36 in. barrel with round muzzle brake, fiberglass tactical stock, 35 lbs. Mfg. 1997-98.

$6,950	$6,425	$5,875	$5,325	$4,750	$4,175	$3,500

Last MSR was $7,500.

Add $750 for 3 shot repeater.

MODEL WARLOCK - .50 BMG or 20mm cal., single, 3 (20mm), or 5 (.50 BMG) shot fixed mag., massive receiver design, fiberglass field stock, chrome-moly black finished receiver, muzzle brake, 50 lbs. Mfg. 1997-98.

$10,750	$8,950	$7,750	$6,750	$5,500	$4,750	$3,950

Last MSR was $12,000.

E.D.M. ARMS MODEL 97 - available in most cals. up to .308 Win., single shot or repeater (cals. .17 Rem. through .223 Rem. only), wire-cut one-piece design, black tactical stock with pillar-bedded chrome-moly barrel, black finished receiver, unique trigger with safety, 9 lbs. Mfg. 1997-98.

$2,525	$2,150	$1,800	$1,500	$1,250	$1,100	$925

Last MSR was $2,750.

E.D.M. ARMS WINDRUNNER WR50 - .50 BMG cal., sniper rifle, 5 shot mag., removable tactical adj. stock, take-down removable barrel, wire-cut one-piece receiver, titanium muzzle brake, blackened chrome moly barrel, approx. 29 lbs. Mfg. 1998 only.

$11,750	$10,250	$9,500	$8,250	$7,000	$5,750	$4,500

Last MSR was $12,900.

OPUS SPORTING ARMS, INC.

Previous manufacturer located in Long Beach, CA.

RIFLES: BOLT ACTION

OPUS ONE - .243 Win., .270 Win., or .30-06 cal., U.S.R.A. Co. Model 70 action, 24 in. barrel, deluxe checkered walnut stock with ebony forend cap, 6¾ lbs., Halliburton cased. Mfg. 1987-1988 only.

$2,350	$1,995	$1,675	$1,250	$1,000	$875	$795

Last MSR was $2,700.

Grading	100%	98%	95%	90%	80%	70%	60%

OPUS TWO - similar to Opus One, except in 7mm Rem. Mag. or .300 Win. Mag. cal., 7¼ lbs., cased. Mfg. 1987-1988 only.

		$2,350	$2,050	$1,705	$1,300	$1,000	$875	$795

Last MSR was $2,700.

OPUS THREE - similar to Opus Two, except in .375 H&H or .458 Win. Mag. cal., 10¼ lbs., cased. Mfg. 1987-1988 only.

		$2,600	$2,275	$1,800	$1,375	$1,050	$900	$825

Last MSR was $2,850.

OREGON ARMS

Please refer to the Chipmunk Rifles, Inc. section.

ORTGIES PISTOLS

Previous trademark of pistols manufactured by Deutsche Werke A.G. located in Erfurt, Germany.

PISTOLS: SEMI-AUTO

VEST POCKET AUTOMATIC - .25 ACP cal., 6 shot, 2¾ in. barrel, blue or nickel finish, fixed sights, wood grips. Mfg. 1921-1928.

	$275	$200	$165	$145	$125	$110	$100

POCKET AUTOMATIC - .32 ACP cal. (8 shot) mfg. 1920-1928 or .380 ACP cal. (7 shot) mfg. 1922-1926, 3¼ in. barrel, blue or nickel finish, fixed sights, wood grips.

	$300	$225	$175	$150	$130	$115	$105

Add 20% for .380 ACP cal. or double safety variation.

ORVIS

Current catalog retailer and importer of private label subcontracted shotguns located in Manchester, VT and many other locations.

ORVIS

Orvis imports various shotguns under subcontract with various international manufacturers. Typical custom order delivery time is 2-8 months. Most of these private label models will approximate the values of the equivalent model manufactured by the subcontractor unless there are additional features and/or options which will add to the value.

SHOTGUNS: O/U

SKB GREEN MOUNTAIN UPLANDER (MODEL 555) - 12, 20, 28 ga., or .410 bore, 25-27 in. barrels, blue frame, straight stock with leather covered recoil pad. Disc.

	$750	$675	$600	$550	$500	$450	$400

Last MSR was $995.

Add 15% for 28 ga. or .410 bore.

UPLANDER SERIES - 12 (disc. 1998), 20, or 28 ga., boxlock action, 26 in. barrels with choke tubes (except 28 ga.), SST, straight grip, select American black walnut with 24 LPI checkering, leather covered recoil pad since 1992, 6-7 lbs. Mfg. by P. Beretta of Italy.

MSR	$3,200		$3,200	$2,450	$2,000	$1,550	$1,200	$995	$875

Add $1,250 for 28/20 ga. combo with case.

WATERFOWLER - 12 ga. only, 3 in. chambers, matte metal finish, 28 in. barrels with choke tubes, steel shot compatible, 7½ lbs. Mfg. by P. Beretta of Italy.

MSR	$3,450		$3,450	$2,650	$2,150	$1,650	$1,250	$1,025	$900

SPORTING CLAYS - 12 ga. only, 30 in. vented barrels with VR and choke tubes, adj. trigger, oil finished checkered walnut stock and forearm. New 1994.

MSR	$3,300		$3,300	$2,550	$2,000	$1,550	$1,175	$995	$875

This model is also available in a women's configuration in 20 ga. with lightweight frame - includes carrying case.

Grading	100%	98%	95%	90%	80%	70%	60%

SUPER FIELD - 12 or 20 ga., 26 (Uplander 20 ga. only), 28 (All Rounder), or 30 (Sporting Clays) in. VR barrels, configurations include Uplander 20 ga. with straight grip stock, All Rounder 12 ga. with 28 in. barrels and pistol grip stock, and Sporting Clays 12 ga. with 30 in. barrels, wide rib, and pistol grip stock, blue receiver, choke tubes, mfg. in Italy. Limited importation 1995 only.

	$1,495	$1,250	$1,000	$875	$750	$625	$500

Last MSR was $2,150.

PREMIER GRADE - 12 or 20 ga., 3 in. chambers, 20 ga. features 28 in. barrels with straight grip stock, 12 ga. features pistol grip stock, select oil-finished European stock and forearm, choke tubes, blue frame with scrolled engraving, adj. trigger, cased, mfg. in Belgium 1995-98.

	$6,450	$5,875	$5,250	$4,675	$4,000	$3,450	$2,675

Last MSR was $6,450.

Add $100 for Premier Grade Sporting.

This model is also available as a 20 ga. Superlight with straight grip stock and 26 in. barrels.

ORVIS DELUXE GRADE - similar to Uplander and Waterfowler, except has engraved bird scenes and scroll work on antique coin-finished receiver, deluxe checkered walnut stock and forearm, case. Imported 1993-94 only.

	$4,250	$3,575	$2,950	$2,300	$1,900	$1,500	$1,275

Last MSR was $4,950.

RUGER/ORVIS MODEL - 12 or 20 ga., 3 in. chambers, Red Label Ruger action with customized Orvis features including blue receiver and straight grip English checkered stock. Importation disc. 1993.

	$1,295	$975	$850	$725	$600	$495	$450

Last MSR was $1,295.

SHOTGUNS: SxS

WATERFOWLER - 12 ga. only, 3 in. chambers, matte metal finish, 28 in. barrels with choke tubes, 7¾ lbs. Mfg. by P. Beretta of Italy until 1993.

	$1,950	$1,725	$1,475	$1,125	$950	$825	$700

Last MSR was $1,950.

CUSTOM UPLANDER - 12, 16, 20, 28 ga., or .410 bore, traditional frame, 25 or 27 in. barrels only, case colored or blue sidelock action with light engraving, DT, custom ordered gun, mfg. by Arrieta located in Spain.

MSR	$3,100	$3,100	$2,525	$2,250	$1,950	$1,650	$1,450	$1,025

Add $950 for SNT.

Add $1,200 for extra set of barrels (same ga.).

FINE GRADE - 12, 16, 20, 28 ga., or .410 bore, custom ordered gun, custom order barrel lengths, sidelock action, DT, mfg. by Arrieta located in Spain. Disc. 1999.

	$4,650	$3,775	$3,150	$2,500	$1,995	$1,500	$1,150

Last MSR was $4,650.

Add $950 for SNT.

Add $1,950 for extra set of barrels (same ga.).

ROUNDED ACTION - similar to Fine Grade, except sidelock action has rounded corners and finer engraving (100% coverage) and wood upgrade, leather cased, mfg. by Arrieta located in Spain.

MSR	$6,700	$6,700	$5,550	$4,250	$3,775	$3,300	$2,550	$1,995

✷ **Rounded Action Uplander** - similar to Rounded Action, except has less engraving, blue or case hardened frame. New 2000.

MSR	$4,900	$4,900	$4,450	$3,950	$3,500	$3,000	$2,500	$2,000

NOTES

O

O is for Ordnance - in this case, heavy ordnance. .50 BMG is still the hot cal. in big bore bolt actions. With its formidable firepower, is this a fad, futuristic fantasy, potential BATF victim, or here to stay?

P Section

P.A.F.

Previous manufacturer located in S. Africa. P.A.F. stands for Pretoria Arms Factory.

Grading	100%	98%	95%	90%	80%	70%	60%

PISTOLS: SEMI-AUTO

.25 ACP PISTOL - .25 ACP cal., patterned after the Baby Browning, blue finish. Approx. 10,000 mfg.

$300	$275	$250	$235	$225	$200	$180

P.A.W.S., INC.

Current manufacturer located in Salem, OR. Distributor and dealer sales. Previously distributed by Sile Distributors, Inc. located in New York, NY.

CARBINES

ZX6/ZX8 CARBINE - 9mm Para. or .45 ACP cal., semi-auto paramilitary design carbine, 16 in. barrel, 10 or 32* shot mag., folding metal stock, matte black finish, aperture rear sight, partial barrel shroud, 7½ lbs. New 1989.

MSR	$800		$715	$635	$550	$475	$375	$300	$250

The ZX6 is chambered for 9mm Para., while the ZX8 is chambered for .45 ACP.

PKP, INC.

Previous manufacturer and distributor located in Tempe, AZ. Dealer or consumer direct sales.

PISTOLS

POWELL KNIFE PISTOL MR-38 - .38 Spl., unique knife-pistol design allows barrel to be incorporated into the upper rear portion of the break-action blade assembly, 1¾ in. barrel, stainless steel with wood handles, 17 oz. Limited mfg. 1997-98.

$415	$350	$275

Last MSR was $450.

P.S.M.G. GUN COMPANY

Previous manufacturer located in Arlington, MA.

PISTOLS: SEMI-AUTO

SIX IN ONE SUPREME - .22 LR, 7.65mm Luger, .38 Super, .38 Spl., 9mm Para., or .45 ACP cal., single action, 3¼, 5, or 7½ in. barrel with solid cooling rib, adj. rear sight, limited mfg. Mfg. 1988-89.

$700	$600	$500	$450	$400	$365	$330

Last MSR was $895

Add $20-$55 for caliber options.
Add $25 for 7½ in. barrel.
Add $35 for satin nickel plating.
Add $225 per extra barrel.
Add $450 per individual conversion unit.

P.V. NELSON, (GUNMAKERS)

Please refer to the N section for this manufacturer.

P

Grading	100%	98%	95%	90%	80%	70%	60%

PTK INTERNATIONAL, INC.

Previous distributor located in Atlanta, GA.

Please refer to listing under Poly-Technologies in this section.

P.38s

Standard German military 9mm Para. handgun beginning 1938. On older WWII German models, please refer to the German WWII Military Pistols section of this text.

PISTOLS: SEMI-AUTO

P.38 - JOHN MARTZ CONVERSIONS

* ✻ **Baby P.38** - 9mm Para. cal., shortened barrel (3 in.) grip, and two 7 shot mags., 56 fabricated.

$2,500	$2,000	$1,500

* ✻ **P.38** - .38 Super (4 or 6 in. barrel, 8 fabricated) or .45 ACP (4 or 7½ in. barrel, 22 fabricated) cal.

$4,500	$2,750	$1,950

* ✻ **P.38 Carbine** - 9mm Para. cal., 16 in. barrel, adj. rear sight, 30 fabricated w/shoulder stocks. Disc.

$7,900	$5,950	$3,925

PARAMOUNT

Previous trademark manufactured by Imperial Gun Co., Ltd. located in Surrey, England. Actions were previously imported by O.K. Weber, Inc. located in Eugene, OR and Olympic Arms, Inc. located in Olympia, WA.

RIFLES: SINGLE SHOT

THE IMPERIAL - .308 Win. cal., single shot target rifle featuring thumbhole stock and CPE aperture rear sight, fully adj. trigger, vent. forearm. Disc. 1994.

$3,250	$2,700	$2,250	$1,850	$1,400	$1,000	$795

Last MSR was $3,400.

RANGEMASTER - various cals., single shot design, steel frame, contoured walnut grips, satin chrome finish, 8½ lbs. Limited importation 1992-94.

$1,600	$1,400	$1,200	$995	$895	$795	$695

Last MSR was $1,800.

PARA-ORDNANCE MFG. INC.

Current manufacturer located in Scarborough, Ontario, Canada. Various U.S. distributors. Distributor sales only.

Para-Ørdnance.

PISTOLS: SEMI-AUTO

LDA/6.45 LDA - 9mm Para., .40 S&W, or .45 ACP cal., double action, 5 in. barrel, 10 shot single (new 2001, .45 ACP cal. only, Model 6.45 LDA) or double stack mag., stainless (new 2001) or black carbon steel with matte metal finish. New 1999.

MSR	$775		$650	$525	$450	$400	$350	$325	$295

Add $49 for stainless steel (new 2001).

Grading	100%	98%	95%	90%	80%	70%	60%

✳ *LDA/6.45 LLDA Limited Series* - 9mm Para., .40 S&W, or .45 ACP cal., available in black carbon or stainless steel, features patented lightning double action trigger, 6 (6.45 LLDA Model) or 10 shot mag., 3 (6.45 LLDA Model) or 5 in. barrel, front slide serrations, full length recoil guide, adj. rear sight, ambidextrous safety, 40 oz. New 2001.

	MSR	$899	$795	$675	$535	$460	$400	$350	$325

Add $30 for stainless steel.

P10 - 9mm Para. (new 1998), .40 S&W, .45 ACP, 10mm (mfg. 1998 only, stainless steel) cal., single action, super compact variation featuring 3 in. barrel and shortened grip, 10 shot double column mag., 3-dot sights, choice of alloy (matte black), steel (matte black), or stainless (Duo-Tone – disc. 2000, or bright finish) frame, 31 oz. with steel frame or 24 oz. with alloy frame. New 1997.

	MSR	$740		$625	$500	$435	$390	$350	$325	$295

Add $10 for steel frame.
Add $49 for stainless steel.
Add $45 for stainless steel with Duo-Tone finish (disc. 2000).

S10 LIMITED - similar to P10, except has competition shooting features, including beavertail grip safety, competition hammer, tuned trigger, match grade barrel, front slide serrations, choice of steel or alloy frame with matte black finish or stainless steel, 40 oz. New 1999.

	MSR	$865		$765	$650	$525	$450	$395	$350	$325

Add $10 for steel receiver.
Add $24 for stainless steel.

P12 - .40 S&W or .45 ACP cal., compact variation of the P14 featuring 10 (C/B 1994) or 11* shot mag. and 3½ in. barrel, 33 oz. with steel frame or 24 oz. with alloy frame. New 1990.

	MSR	$740		$625	$500	$435	$390	$350	$325	$295

Add $10 for steel frame.
Add $49 for stainless steel.
Add $45 for stainless steel with Duo-Tone finish (disc. 2000).

S12 LIMITED - similar to P12, except has competition shooting features, including beavertail grip safety, competition hammer, tuned trigger, match grade barrel, front slide serrations, choice of steel or alloy frame, matte black or stainless steel finish, 40 oz. New 1999.

	MSR	$865		$765	$650	$525	$450	$395	$350	$325

Add $10 for steel receiver.
Add $24 for stainless steel.

P13 - .40 S&W (disc. 2000) or .45 ACP cal., similar to P14, except has 10 (C/B 1994) or 12* shot mag., 4¼ in. barrel, 35 oz. with steel frame or 25 oz. with alloy frame. New 1993.

	MSR	$740		$625	$500	$435	$390	$350	$325	$295

Add $10 for steel frame.
Add $49 for stainless steel.
Add $45 for stainless steel with Duo-Tone finish (disc. 2000).

S13 LIMITED - similar to P13, except has competition shooting features, including beavertail grip safety, competition hammer, tuned trigger, match grade barrel, front slide serrations, choice of steel or alloy frame, matte black or stainless steel finish, 40 oz. New 1999.

	MSR	$865		$765	$650	$525	$450	$395	$350	$325

Add $10 for steel receiver.
Add $24 for stainless steel.

P

Grading	100%	98%	95%	90%	80%	70%	60%

P14 - .40 S&W (mfg. 1996-2000) or .45 ACP cal., patterned after the Colt Model 1911A1 except has choice of alloy (matte black), steel (matte black), or stainless steel (stainless or Duo-Tone finish) frame that has been widened slightly for extra shot capacity (13* shot), 10 shot (C/B 1994) mag., single action, 3- dot sight system, rounded combat hammer, 5 in. ramped barrel, 38 oz. with steel frame or 28 oz. with alloy frame. Introduced 1990.

	MSR	$740	$625	$500	$435	$390	$350	$325	$295

Add $10 for steel frame.
Add $49 for stainless steel.
Add $45 for stainless steel with Duo-Tone finish (disc. 2000).

S14 LIMITED - similar to P14, except has competition shooting features, including beavertail grip safety, competition hammer, tuned trigger, match grade barrel, front slide serrations, matte black or stainless steel, 40 oz. New 1998.

	MSR	$875	$775	$660	$525	$450	$395	$350	$325

Add $24 for stainless steel.

P15 - .40 S&W cal., otherwise similar to P13, 36 oz. with steel frame or 28 oz. with alloy frame. Mfg. 1996-99.

		$625	$500	$435	$390	$350	$325	$295

Last MSR was $740.

Add $10 for steel frame.
Add $59 for stainless steel.
Add $45 for stainless steel with Duo-Tone finish.

P16 - .40 S&W cal., otherwise similar to P14, steel or stainless steel (new 1997) frame only. New 1995.

	MSR	$750	$640	$515	$435	$385	$350	$325	$295

Add $49 for stainless steel.
Add $35 for Duo-Tone stainless steel (disc. 2000).

S16 LIMITED - similar to P16, except has competition shooting features, including beavertail grip safety, competition hammer, tuned trigger, match grade barrel, front slide serrations, matte black steel or stainless steel, 40 oz. New 1998.

	MSR	$875	$775	$660	$525	$450	$395	$350	$325

Add $24 for stainless steel.

P18 - 9mm Para. cal., 5 in. ramped barrel, stainless steel, solid barrel bushing, flared ejection port, quadruple safety, adj. rear sight, 40 oz. New 1998.

	MSR	$850	$725	$575	$450

PARDINI, ARMI S.r.l.

Current manufacturer located in Lido di Camaiore, Italy. Currently imported by Nygord Precision Products located in Prescott, AZ. Previously imported and distributed until 1996 by Mo's Competitor Supplies & Range, Inc. located in Brookfield, CT and until 1990 by Fiocchi of America, Inc., located in Ozark, MO.

For more information and current pricing on both new and used Pardini airguns, please refer to the *Blue Book of Modern Airguns* by Dr. Robert Beeman & John Allen (now online also).

PISTOLS: SEMI-AUTO

PC45 - .40 S&W, .45 ACP, or 9x21mm cal., single action mechanism designed for stock competition category, adj. trigger pull. Limited importation starting 2000.

	MSR	N/A	$1,050	$840	$715	$575	$500	$440	$415

* **PC45S** - similar to PC, except has compensator and optic sight with scope mount. Importation began 2000.

	MSR	N/A	$1,250	$1,100	$950	$850	$725	$600	$475

Grading	100%	98%	95%	90%	80%	70%	60%

✳ **PCS-Open** - similar to PCS, except w/o scope and frame mount, top-of-the-line semi-auto. Importation began 2000.

	MSR	N/A	$1,400	$1,250	$1,100	$950	$850	$725	$600

PISTOLS: TARGET

Pardini pistols have always been known for their technological improvements developed from ongoing design research. During 1991, the entire Pardini pistol line was modified both internally and externally to improve function and reliability - these changes included the addition of grooves on the barrel shroud to accept scope mounts directly.

MODEL SP (STANDARD PISTOL) - .22 LR cal. only, target grips, adj. sights, 4.92 in. barrel, interchangable grips, detachable mag. New 1991.

	MSR	N/A	$950	$715	$575	$475	$425	$395	$375

Add $145 for SP Master Model.

LADIES PISTOL - similar to Standard Pistol, except grips are suitable for smaller hands. Importation disc. 1999.

			$850	$700	$600	$520	$460	$410	$380

Last MSR was $995.

MODEL GP (RAPID FIRE PISTOL) - .22 Short cal., features enclosed style grip assembly, adj. sights, 5.12 in. barrel. New 1991.

	MSR	N/A	$1,095	$975	$850	$725	$600	$475	$425

Add $500 for "Schumann" Model (Model GP-S, special muzzle ports, sights, weights, etc.).

MODEL HP (CENTERFIRE PISTOL) - .32 S&W Wadcutter cal., otherwise similar to Standard Pistol, 4.92 in. barrel. New 1991.

	MSR	N/A	$1,050	$840	$715	$575	$500	$440	$415

MODEL K22 - .22 LR cal., top-of-the-line target pistol, toggle bolt pushes cartridge into chamber, unique ventilated front sight assembly that also supports counterweights, cocking lever action. Importation began 2000.

	MSR	N/A	$1,295	$1,125	$975	$850	$725	$600	$475

MODEL K50 (FREE PISTOL) - .22 LR cal., single shot, sliding rotating bolt, 9.06 in. barrel, tilted anatomical grip, top-of-the-line match pistol. Mfg. 1991-99.

			$925	$750	$600	$500	$450	$420	$395

Last MSR was $1,050.

PARDINI/NYGORD MASTER - .22 LR cal., designed for NRA bullseye shooting, micrometer rear sight and red-dot sight, includes small Adco sight, anatomical target grips. Importation began late 2000.

	MSR	N/A	$1,095	$840	$715	$575	$500	$440	$415

PARKER BROTHERS

Previously manufactured in Meriden, CT from 1866-1934. Remington took over production in 1934, and in 1938, the plant was moved to Ilion, NY. Over 4,500 "Transition Guns" (exhibiting Meriden and Ilion characteristics) were produced in Meriden between 1934-1937 and about 4,500 Parkers were manufactured at the Ilion location before production stopped. Total production reached approx. 242,487.

95% of the original Parkers bought and sold each year are in 30% or less condition (referring to original case colors). Percentages on following pages refer to the amount of original case colors remaining on frame.

SHOTGUNS, SxS, DAMASCUS BARRELS

Parker damascus barreled shotguns (hammer or hammerless) are very collectible if original condition is over 40%. Specimens in 90% or better condition with strong case colors can approximate values of the steel barrel models if the bores are in excellent condition also (no pitting). Values for under 40% specimens fall off rapidly and are no longer comparable to steel barrel guns. As an example, a steel "D" Grade (without ejectors) might range from $1,500 to $7,000 (10%-100%) with a rather even downward progression of values in between the high and low values. A 100% damascus "D" Grade could have a $3,500+ price tag hanging from the trigger guard while 5%-15% condition specimen is typically seen priced in the $375-$550 range. Remember, the guns are not rare but their condition is.

SHOTGUNS, SxS, FLUID STEEL BARRELS

Values listed in the 95%-100% condition columns can vary a lot as there is very little supply and strong demand for these high condition "cream puffs".

Note: Values are for non-ejector guns through the CH grade, ejectors assumed on BHE and better models. Add 15% - 30% for vent. ribs. Skeet model has beavertail forearm and single selective trigger valued at approx. 50%-75% higher than values shown. Higher grade guns typically had ejectors, and will not make as much difference percentage-wise in the overall value as those lower grades with ejectors. Ejectors typically will add 50% or more value to a Parker in common grades. Also, lower condition high grade models sometimes have their values established by the potential gain in refurbishing these specimens.

Due to the extremely high value of Parker Guns, extreme care should be taken in their purchase. There are many upgraded and refinished guns represented as original; expert advice should always be sought. Many collectors would rather own a specimen with 30% original case colors than a refinished gun that is 100% (regardless who did the work). Many advanced collectors will discount a refinished Parker's value 40%-60% of the price for an original gun. Misrepresentation of refinished or upgraded Parkers is rampant today - especially case colors. Believe it or not, also beware of fake boxes and hanging tags - if the box and Parker shotgun are an original "pair", the value is enhanced tremendously. If the box/hanging tag is fake, you could pay as much as $1,500 to learn this lesson! In other words, do your homework, be careful, shop carefully, and above all, get a receipt for exactly what you are purchasing.

Frame size on Parker shotguns is determined by the number on the bottom of the rear barrel lug on breech. Frame sizes (from largest to smallest) include 7, 6, 5, 4, 3, 2, 1½, 1, ½, 0, 00, and 000. 8 ga. guns typically are framed 6 or 7. 10 ga. guns typically are 3 or 4. 12 ga. guns typically range from 2 through 1 (more desirable). "½" frame 12 ga. guns are very rare and desirable. 20 and 16 ga.'s range from 2 through 0 (more desirable). 28 ga. guns are either 0 or 00 (more desirable and twice as expensive). .410 bore shotguns are 00 or 000 (most common and most desirable). 8 and 10 ga. steel barreled shotguns are very rare, and prices can equate .410 bore values if the original condition is there.

The grade on Parker shotguns is a number or initials located on the water table of the frame. An alphabetical designation would indicate the grade immediately. For numerals, a "2" would indicate a GH, while an "8" would specify an A-1 Special - interpolate for the others (numbers 3 through 7). Parker shotguns manufactured by Remington will have date codes stamped on left barrel flat that correspond to the month and the year (see Remington serialization in the Serialization Section). Also, if a Parker gun was returned to Remington for repair, alteration, or refinishing, it will usually have the date code stamped with a suffix of 3 (i.e., OK3 represents some type of rework completed in either July of 1941 or 1963). There is some ambiguity with the year as the year codes repeat.

A note about Parker condition: Percentages of condition indicate the amount of original case colors remaining on the frame, but sometimes these colors are faded and the rest of the gun is excellent - hence, all the separate condition factors must be considered when determining overall condition.

A Parker IS NOT 60% if the barrel bluing and stock/forearm varnish are 60% but case colors are only 10%. Typically, a 60% case color Parker shotgun will have 90%+ blue and varnish, yet this does not mean the gun is 90% overall. Similarly, a 20% case color Parker will probably have 90% barrel bluing remaining. Strong, original case colors are the key in determining Parker condition and subsequent values.

"The Parker Story, Vol. I", was published in late 1998. This book has production statistics derived from factory records, and the quantities manufactured listed in this text for steel-barreled hammerless Parker guns are taken from this book. This new publication also has more detailed production statistics on Parker guns produced from 1869-1942, including a break down by action type (lifter, top lever, and hammerless), grade, barrel steel, gauge, and barrel length. Some grades, gauges, etc., are fewer in number than previously estimated (i.e., there are only two 28 ga. Trojans). All the grades are pictured in color, including the Invincible. Parker Reproductions are also covered in detail, including production statistics. Vol. II was published in late 2000. If interested in Parkers, these publications will be invaluable. The author wishes to thank Mr. Charles Price, William Mullins, Roy Gunther, Louis C. Parker III, and Daniel Cote for sharing the following Parker production statistics with this publication.

The Parker Gun Collectors Association can also provide research letters on certain Parkers. Please refer to their listing under Firearms Organizations in the back of this text for contact information.

    Add 20% for SST.
    Add 20% for beavertail forearm.
    Add 20%-50% for VR (rare on smaller gauges).
    Add 20% for straight English stock.
    Add 20% for skeleton steel butt plate.
    Add 20% for short barrels (26 in. with open chokes).

100%	98%	95%	90%	80%	70%	60%	50%	40%	30%	20%	10%

TROJAN - Parker's lowest-priced gun, single or double triggers, but no auto ejectors available, very rarely found in mint condition because they were used a lot, a genuine utility gun, introduced 1912-13 with approx. 33,000 total mfg.

✱ **12 ga.**

N/A	$2,000	$1,500	$1,175	$950	$850	$750	$650	$600	$575	$525	$500

✱ **16 ga.**

N/A	$2,750	$2,000	$1,750	$1,500	$1,200	$1,050	$950	$750	$700	$650	$600

✱ **20 ga.**

N/A	$3,375	$2,500	$1,800	$1,700	$1,600	$1,500	$1,400	$1,300	$1,200	$1,100	$900

VH - Parker's biggest selling model, offered with all options, the most commonly found Parker. Approx. 79,000 mfg. 10 ga. is very rare in this model.
    Add 60% for ejectors (VHE Model).

✱ **12 ga.**

N/A	$2,975	$2,200	$1,750	$1,450	$1,200	$1,100	$1,000	$900	$800	$750	$700

✱ **16 ga.**

N/A	$2,975	$2,200	$1,750	$1,450	$1,200	$1,100	$1,000	$925	$850	$775	$700

✱ **20 ga.**

N/A	$3,950	$3,500	$3,200	$3,000	$2,800	$2,400	$2,200	$2,000	$1,800	$1,600	$1,400

✱ **28 ga.**

N/A	$6,550	$5,750	$5,150	$4,600	$3,900	$3,600	$3,100	$2,850	$2,650	$2,475	$2,425

✱ **.410 bore.**

N/A	$17,250	$14,000	$12,250	$10,000	$8,750	$7,900	$7,200	$6,800	$6,300	$5,800	$5,100

PH - offered for a very short time, most had twist barrels, prices here are for fluid steel barrels only. Approx. 1,400 mfg. A very few .410 bores were mfg. 10 ga. with fluid steel barrels is very rare in this model.
    Add 60% for ejectors (PHE Model).

✱ **12 ga.**

N/A	$2,975	$2,600	$2,350	$2,100	$1,850	$1,625	$1,400	$1,150	$995	$900	$825

✱ **16 ga.**

N/A	$2,975	$2,600	$2,350	$2,100	$1,850	$1,625	$1,400	$1,150	$995	$900	$825

✱ **20 ga.**

N/A	$4,600	$4,000	$3,750	$3,350	$2,950	$2,600	$2,350	$2,175	$1,900	$1,650	$1,400

✱ **28 ga.**

N/A	$8,250	$7,400	$7,000	$6,500	$6,000	$5,750	$5,500	$5,000	$4,500	$3,750	$3,000

GH - very popular model, barrels marked Parker Special Steel, engraved moderately with all options available. 10 ga. with fluid steel barrels is very rare in this model, approx. 4,300 mfg.
    Add 60% for ejectors (GHE Model).

✱ **12 ga.**

N/A	$3,775	$3,150	$2,475	$1,850	$1,625	$1,500	$1,300	$1,100	$950	$900	$800

100%	98%	95%	90%	80%	70%	60%	50%	40%	30%	20%	10%

✲ 16 ga.

| N/A | $4,000 | $3,400 | $2,600 | $2,175 | $1,850 | $1,650 | $1,350 | $1,150 | $1,050 | $950 | $900 |

✲ 20 ga.

| N/A | $4,250 | $3,700 | $3,400 | $3,100 | $2,800 | $2,500 | $2,300 | $2,200 | $1,800 | $1,600 | $1,500 |

✲ 28 ga.

| N/A | $6,650 | $5,750 | $5,125 | $4,550 | $4,200 | $3,800 | $3,600 | $3,300 | $3,000 | $2,750 | $2,600 |

✲ .410 bore.

| N/A | N/A | $15,350 | $12,850 | $10,500 | $8,525 | $8,000 | $7,500 | $7,000 | $6,500 | $6,000 | $5,500 |

DH - the most popular higher grade gun, very tastefully engraved and flawlessly finished, approx. 9,400 mfg.

Add 50% for ejectors (DHE Model).

✲ 12 ga.

| N/A | $5,250 | $4,300 | $3,450 | $2,675 | $2,175 | $1,850 | $1,625 | $1,450 | $1,325 | $1,150 | $995 |

✲ 16 ga.

| N/A | $5,375 | $4,450 | $3,500 | $2,675 | $2,175 | $1,850 | $1,625 | $1,450 | $1,325 | $1,150 | $995 |

✲ 20 ga.

| N/A | $6,150 | $5,500 | $5,300 | $5,000 | $4,800 | $4,000 | $3,500 | $3,150 | $2,750 | $2,200 | $1,650 |

✲ 28 ga.

| N/A | $9,550 | $8,175 | $7,800 | $7,500 | $7,000 | $6,700 | $6,500 | $6,200 | $6,000 | $5,500 | $5,000 |

✲ .410 bore.

| N/A | N/A | $28,250 | $22,000 | $18,950 | $16,350 | $14,000 | $12,750 | $10,650 | $9,100 | $8,000 | $7,250 |

CH - scarce because they were only slightly more decorative than the DH, Acme steel barrels. Approx. 1,100 mfg. 10 ga. is very rare in this model.

Add 50% for ejectors (CHE Model).

✲ 12 ga.

| N/A | N/A | $4,775 | $4,000 | $3,350 | $2,600 | $2,400 | $2,200 | $2,000 | $1,800 | $1,650 | $1,425 |

✲ 16 ga.

| N/A | N/A | $4,850 | $4,050 | $3,350 | $3,000 | $2,700 | $2,600 | $2,400 | $2,200 | $1,975 | $1,650 |

✲ 20 ga.

| N/A | N/A | $6,375 | $5,550 | $4,950 | $4,500 | $4,300 | $4,000 | $3,800 | $3,650 | $3,300 | $2,750 |

✲ 28 ga.

| N/A | N/A | $13,850 | $10,500 | $9,250 | $8,175 | $7,000 | $6,375 | $5,750 | $5,125 | $4,550 | $3,895 |

✲ .410 bore. - very rare, approx. 6 are known to exist.

| N/A | N/A | $35,250 | $28,250 | $23,250 | $19,950 | $17,250 | $14,450 | $12,950 | $11,000 | $9,950 | $8,950 |

BH - quite popular and decorative, 4 styles of engraving available, Acme steel barrels. Approx. 700 mfg. 10 ga. is very rare in this model.

Add 50% for ejectors (BHE Model).

✲ 12 ga.

| N/A | N/A | $7,425 | $6,375 | $5,550 | $4,950 | $4,300 | $3,750 | $3,100 | $2,800 | $2,500 | $2,000 |

✲ 16 ga.

| N/A | N/A | $7,600 | $6,400 | $5,550 | $4,950 | $4,300 | $3,750 | $3,100 | $2,800 | $2,500 | $2,000 |

✲ 20 ga.

| N/ | N/A | $12,000 | $10,250 | $9,300 | $8,275 | $7,100 | $6,375 | $5,650 | $5,200 | $4,700 | $4,000 |

✲ 28 ga.

| N/A | N/A | N/A | $17,500 | $13,850 | $10,500 | $9,250 | $8,175 | $7,000 | $6,275 | $5,350 | $4,550 |

✲ .410 bore. - only 2 guns are known in this gauge. Extreme rarity precludes accurate price evaluation, but will be VERY expensive.

AHE - a scarce gun, extremely decorative and flawlessly executed, Acme steel barrels. Approx. 300 mfg. 10 ga. is very rare in this model.

Subtract 25% if w/o ejectors (AH Model).

✲ 12 ga.

| N/A | N/A | $16,100 | $12,250 | $9,250 | $8,000 | $7,150 | $6,500 | $6,000 | $5,500 | $5,000 | $4,500 |

✲ 16 ga.

| N/A | N/A | $17,000 | $13,000 | $9,375 | $8,100 | $7,500 | $7,000 | $6,500 | $6,000 | $5,500 | $5,000 |

100%	98%	95%	90%	80%	70%	60%	50%	40%	30%	20%	10%

✳ 20 ga.

| N/A | N/A | $21,000 | $17,500 | $13,850 | $10,500 | $9,250 | $8,500 | $8,000 | $7,500 | $7,000 | $6,500 |

✳ 28 ga.

| N/A | N/A | N/A | $31,500 | $23,750 | $18,975 | $16,000 | $14,000 | $12,250 | $10,750 | $9,000 | $8,250 |

✳ .410 bore - 1 gun known in this gauge. Any questions?

AAHE - very elaborate model, early AAs have Whitworth barrels, late ones have Peerless. Approx. 240 mfg.

> **Subtract 20% if without ejectors (AAH Model).**

✳ 12 ga.

| N/A | N/A | $28,500 | $26,000 | $23,000 | $21,000 | $19,000 | $17,000 | $15,500 | $13,750 | $12,000 | $10,500 |

✳ 16 ga.

| N/A | N/A | $32,000 | $28,500 | $26,000 | $23,000 | $21,000 | $19,000 | $17,000 | $15,500 | $13,750 | $12,000 |

✳ 20 ga.

| N/A | N/A | $50,000 | $45,000 | $40,250 | $35,000 | $31,050 | $28,000 | $24,750 | $21,000 | $19,550 | $17,250 |

✳ 28 ga.

| N/A | N/A | N/A | $68,500 | $63,250 | $58,750 | $53,475 | $46,000 | $39,500 | $33,925 | $28,175 | $25,875 |

A-1 SPECIAL GRADE - 100% engraved, all were special ordered, each one inspected by the company president before being shipped. Approx. 80 mfg.

✳ 12 ga.

| N/A | N/A | $61,000 | $57,000 | $51,750 | $46,250 | $40,250 | $36,175 | $31,050 | $28,500 | $26,450 | $22,000 |

✳ 16 ga.

| N/A | N/A | $61,000 | $57,000 | $51,750 | $46,250 | $40,250 | $36,175 | $31,050 | $28,500 | $26,450 | $22,000 |

✳ 20 ga.

| N/A | N/A | N/A | $90,000 | $82,000 | $76,000 | $70,000 | $64,000 | $57,500 | $53,000 | $46,500 | $40,000 |

✳ 28 ga. - extreme rarity and desirability factors preclude accurate price evaluation by condition factors. 70% original condition A-1 Specials HAVE sold for over $125,000.

INVINCIBLE GRADE - only 3 documented mfg,.$1,250 MSR circa 1930, extreme rarity and desirability factors preclude accurate price evaluation on this model.

SHOTGUNS: SINGLE BARREL TRAP

12 or 20 (rare) ga., 26 (20 ga. only, rare), 28 (very rare), 30 (rare), 32, or 34 (rare) in. barrels, any boring was available, as was stock configuration, boxlock, auto ejector. The grades differ only in engraving, checkering and wood finish.

It should be noted that single barrel trap guns cannot be compared to the SxS models as they are not as desirable, even though they are more rare. Approximately 1,900 Parker single barrel trap guns were manufactured, mostly in SC Grade. Most SxS collectors are not that interested in single barrel trap models and very few collectors specialize in single barrels.

> **Add 15% for 30 or 34 in. barrel.**

S.C. GRADE

| $4,000 | $3,600 | $3,100 | $2,700 | $2,350 | $1,875 | $1,625 | $1,400 | $1,150 | $995 | $900 | $825 |

S.B. GRADE

| $4,825 | $4,300 | $3,750 | $3,475 | $3,100 | $2,700 | $2,350 | $1,875 | $1,625 | $1,400 | $1,150 | $995 |

S.A. GRADE

| N/A | $5,000 | $4,375 | $3,875 | $3,425 | $3,050 | $2,675 | $2,275 | $1,875 | $1,550 | $1,200 | $1,050 |

S.A.A. GRADE

| N/A | N/A | $5,500 | $4,750 | $4,000 | $3,575 | $3,050 | $2,675 | $2,375 | $1,850 | $1,575 | $1,350 |

S.A.-1 SPECIAL GRADE

| N/A | N/A | N/A | $13,000 | $10,000 | $9,150 | $8,350 | $7,425 | $6,375 | $5,550 | $4,950 | $4,300 |

PARKER PISTOLS

Refer to the Wyoming Arms section in this text.

Grading	100%	98%	95%	90%	80%	70%	60%

PARKER REPRODUCTIONS

Previously imported by the Parker Reproduction Division of Reagent Chemical & Research, Inc., located in Middlesex, NJ. Previously distributed by Parker Reproductions located in Webb City, MO.

These shotguns were manufactured in Japan to original Parker specifications by Winchester until the factory closed in January, 1989.

In 1984, Winchester was contracted by Reagent Chemical & Research, Inc. to manufacture a new Parker shotgun. The new SxS was a DHE model, available in 20 and 28 ga. initially. These models were fabricated in Japan to original Parker specifications, and the reproduction was so authentic that most parts are interchangeable with original Parker guns. Mfg. 1984-89. In 1993, a 16/20 ga. combo was introduced in some models. On Sept. 17, 1999, a flood destroyed all remaining inventory including parts.

SHOTGUNS: SxS

Because of the high quality and limited mfg. of these reproductions, they have become very collectible, as they offer the shooter the only realistic alternative to using an original Parker Bros. shotgun.

Currently, higher grade Parker Reproductions in smaller gauges are very desirable, and 95%-100% values are getting harder to accurately determine.

DHE GRADE - 12 (new 1986), 20, or 28 (new 1984) ga., 26 or 28 in. barrels, boxlock action, ejectors, single selective or double triggers, beavertail or splinter forend, straight or pistol grip stock, skeleton steel butt plate, engraving in original DH style, case hardened frame, rust blue barrels. Supplied with leather trunk case, canvas and leather cover, and snap caps. Disc.

$3,250	$2,850	$2,500	$2,250	$2,000	$1,800	$1,675

Last MSR was $3,370.

Add 10% for 20 ga.
Add $150 for beavertail forend.
Add $650 for Sporting Clays Model w/choke tubes.
Add $850-$1,150 per extra set of barrels, depending on gauge, configuration, and condition.

Quantities mfg. for this model are as follows: 12 ga. - 2,137 mfg., 20 ga. - 6,050 mfg., 28 ga. - 4,203 mfg.

* **DHE Steel Shot Special** - similar to 12 ga. D Grade, except has strengthened No. 1½ barrels, 3 in. chambers, and 28 in. chrome lined barrels, 7¼-7½ lbs. Approx. 350 mfg. 1987-89.

$3,500	$3,150	$2,700	$2,475	$2,100	$1,850	$1,700

Last MSR was $3,370.

Add $100 for beavertail forend.

* **DHE Small Gauge Combo** - available in either 28 ga./.410 bore (disc.) or 16/20 ga. (mfg. 1993-97) combo with 2 barrels and 2 forends. Less than 160 mfg. of the 28 ga./.410 bore combo. Disc.

* **28 ga./.410 bore Combo**

$6,500	$5,750	$4,500	$4,000	$3,625	$3,150	$2,900

Last MSR was $4,970.

* **16/20 ga. Combo** - new 1994 - disc.

$5,000	$4,650	$4,000	$3,600	$3,300	$2,950	$2,600

Last MSR was $4,870.

* **DHE 3-Barrel Set** - includes two 28 ga. and one .410 bore barrels, cased. Disc.

$7,500	$6,750	$5,500	$5,000	$4,500	$3,750	$3,500

Last MSR was $5,630.

Grading	100%	98%	95%	90%	80%	70%	60%

BHE GRADE LIMITED EDITION - 12, 20, 28 ga. or 410 bore, original Parker BH specifications, single selective or double trigger(s), 26 or 28 in. barrels, straight or pistol grip stock, engraved skeleton butt plate, bank note scroll engraving around game scenes, cased. Only 100 manufactured in each gauge during late 1987-89. Disc.

		100%	98%	95%	90%	80%	70%	60%
		$5,000	$4,650	$4,150	$3,750	$2,750	$2,150	$1,800

Add $1,000 for 20 ga.
Add $4,000 for 28 ga. or .410 bore.
Add $1,000 for extra set of barrels.
Add $150 for beavertail forend.

Last MSR was $3,970.

A 28 ga./.410 bore combo was also available with 2 forends. Only seven 28 ga.'s were mfg. in this model.

A-1 SPECIAL - 12, 16/20 ga. combo (introduced 1993), 20, or 28 ga., original Parker A-1 specifications, 26 or 28 in. barrels, single selective or double trigger(s), fine scroll engraving with game scenes, 32 lines/in. checkering, cased with accessories. Limited mfg. 1988-89.

		$10,500	$8,500	$7,250	$6,000	$5,475	$4,800	$4,350

Last MSR was $11,200.

Add $3,000+ for 28 ga.
Add $1,000 for extra set of barrels.
Add $200 for beavertail forend.
Add $1,700 for 16 ga. barrel (splinter model only).

Fourteen 3 barrel sets were mfg. in this grade. Rarity factor precludes accurate pricing.

* **A-1 Special Custom Engraved** - custom (per individual special order) engraving, available with two sets of barrels only, cased with accessories. Limited mfg. 1988-89. Prices started at $11,000 and go up according to individualized special features.

* **Federal Duck Stamp Collector's Series** - available in 12 or 20 ga., A-1 Special specifications, authorized by U.S. Department of Interior. Mfg. was limited to 10 per year in 1988-89 only.

	$13,500	$10,000	$8,000

This model included special case and 2 barrels per buyer's specifications.

Last MSR was $14,000.

PARKER-HALE LIMITED

Previous gun manufacturer located in Birmingham, England. Rifles were manufactured in England until 1991 when Navy Arms purchased the manufacturing rights and built a plant in West Virginia for fabrication. This new company is called Gibbs Rifle Company and they manufactured models very similar to older Parker-Hale rifles during 1992-94. Shotguns were manufactured in Spain and imported by Precision Sports, a division of Cortland Line Company, Inc. located in Cortland, NY until 1993.

Parker-Hale Ltd. continues to make a wide variety of high quality firearms cleaning accessories for both rifles and shotguns, including their famous bi-pod.

RIFLES: BOLT ACTION

All Parker-Hale rifle importation was discontinued in 1991. Parker-Hale bolt action rifles utilize the Mauser K-98 action and were offered in a variety of configurations. A single set trigger option was introduced in 1984 on most models, which allows either "hair trigger" or conventional single stage operation - add $85.

Grading	100%	98%	95%	90%	80%	70%	60%

MODEL 81 CLASSIC - available in 11 cals. between .22-250 Rem., and 7mm Rem. Mag., 24 in. barrel, open sights, 4 shot mag., select checkered walnut with sling swivels, 7¾ lbs. New 1985.

	$715	$565	$475	$395	$340	$300	$280

Last MSR was $860.

✱ *Model 81 African* - .375 H&H or 9.3x62mm Mauser cal., similar specifications as Model 81 Classic and has engraved action. New 1986.

	$875	$700	$600	$500	$425	$360	$330

Last MSR was $1,110.

MODEL 84 TARGET - .308 Win. cal., match rifle with special sights, adj. cheekpiece on stock. Importation disc. 1990.

	$1,080	$875	$760	$680	$610	$530	$465

Last MSR was $1,300.

MODEL 85 SNIPER RIFLE - .308 Win. cal., bolt action, extended heavy barrel, 10 shot mag., camo green synthetic stock with stippling, built in adj. bipod, enlarged contoured bolt, adj. recoil pad. Importation began 1989.

	$1,750	$1,425	$1,275	$1,050	$875	$750	$625

Last MSR was $1,975.

MODEL 86 TARGET - .308 Win. cal., 27½ in. barrel, 5 shot mag., stippled stock and forend, aperture front and rear sights, 11¼ lbs. Distributed 1986 only by North American Precision.

	$980	$830	$760	$690	$610	$530	$465

Last MSR was $1,149.

MODEL 87 TARGET - .243 Win., 6.5x55mm Swedish, .308 Win., .30-06, or .300 Win. Mag. cal., target stock, aperture sights. Importation began 1987.

	$1,375	$1,100	$900	$775	$650	$550	$495

Last MSR was $1,525.

MODEL 1000 STANDARD - available in 9 cals. between .22-250 Rem. and .308 Win., 22 in. barrel, 4 shot mag., walnut stock with cheekpiece, 7¼ lbs. Disc. 1988.

	$400	$330	$285	$255	$230	$215	$195

Last MSR was $500.

MODEL 1100 LIGHTWEIGHT - available in 9 cals. between .22-250 Rem. and .30-06, 22 in. barrel, open sights, 4 shot mag., 6½ lbs. New 1985.

	$495	$400	$350	$325	$285	$270	$255

Last MSR was $595.

✱ *Model 1100M African* - .375 H&H, .404 Jeffery, or .458 Win. Mag. cal., 24 in. barrel, 4 shot mag., 9½ lbs.

	$800	$650	$575	$500	$450	$425	$400

Last MSR was $960.

MODEL 1200 SUPER - bolt action, Mauser type action, .22-250 Rem., .243 Win., 6mm Rem., .25-06 Rem., .270 Win., .30-06, .300 Win. Mag., 7mm Rem. Mag., or .308 Win. cal., 24 in. barrel, folding sight, skip checkered walnut stock, sling swivels, rosewood pistol grip cap and forend tip. New 1968 - disc..

	$540	$450	$375	$330	$295	$275	$260

This model in Magnum cals. was called the 1200 M Super Magnum.

Last MSR was $680.

✱ *Model 1200 C (Super Clip)* - similar to Model 1200 Super, except has detachable 4 shot box mag.

	$590	$500	$400	$350	$300	$280	$265

Last MSR was $740.

MODEL 1200P PRESENTATION - similar to 1200, except .243 Win. or .30-06 cal., scroll engraved, no sights. Mfg. 1969-1975.

	$495	$425	$395	$340	$315	$305	$275

Grading	100%	98%	95%	90%	80%	70%	60%

MODEL 1200 SUPER VARMINT - similar to 1200, except .22-250 Rem., 6mm Rem., .25-06 Rem., or .243 Win. cal., 24 in. heavy barrel, no sights. Disc. 1988.

	$525	$425	$365	$325	$285	$270	$255

Last MSR was $660.

MODEL 1300 C SCOUT - shorter barrel variation.

	$695	$550	$450	$385	$330	$300	$275

Last MSR was $785.

MODEL 2100 MIDLAND (HYBRID ACTION) - available in 11 cals. between .22-250 Rem. - .300 Win. Mag. cal., 22 in. barrel, 4 shot mag., open sights, 7 lbs.

	$325	$270	$230	$200	$190	$180	$170

Last MSR was $365.

✳ *Model 2100 Midland Magnum* - .300 Win. Mag., or 7mm Rem. Mag. cal., 24 in. barrel, 4 shot mag., 9½ lbs. Imported 1989-90 only.

	$380	$325	$295	$270	$260	$250	$240

Last MSR was $430.

MODEL 2600 MIDLAND SPECIAL - .243 Win., .270 Win., .308 Win., or .30-06 cal., Midland Gun Co. action, iron sights. New 1989.

	$295	$250	$225	$200	$190	$180	$170

Last MSR was $330.

MIDLAND 2700 LIGHTWEIGHT - lightweight variation of the Model 2600.

	$340	$285	$240	$200	$190	$180	$170

Last MSR was $390.

SHOTGUNS: SxS

Parker-Hale shotguns were manufactured by Ugartechea in Eibar, Spain and imported as Parker-Hale models by Precision Sports located in Cortland, NY until 1994. Please refer to the Ugartechea section of this text.

PASTUSEK INDUSTRIES

Previous manufacturer located in Fort Worth, TX 1993-2000.

PISTOLS: SEMI-AUTO

HSK (SPORT KING) - .22 LR cal., 4½ or 5½ in. barrel. Mfg. 1995-2000.

	$275	$250	$225	$195	$175	$150	$135

Last MSR was $312.

HSS (SHARPSHOOTER) - .22 LR cal., 5½ in. bull barrel. Mfg. 1995-2000.

	$315	$275	$240	$210	$190	$165	$150

Last MSR was $379.

HSC (SUPERMATIC CITATION) - .22 LR cal., 5½ bull or 7¼ in. fluted barrel. Mfg. 1995-2000.

	$340	$295	$265	$230	$210	$180	$165

Last MSR was $388.

Add $22 for 7¼ in. fluted barrel.
This model was also available with an 8, 10, or 12 in. bull barrel.

HST (SUPERMATIC TROPHY) - .22 LR cal., 5½ bull or 7¼ in. fluted barrel. Mfg. 1995-2000.

	$400	$340	$275	$240	$220	$180	$165

Last MSR was $494.

This model was also available with an 8, 10, or 12 in. bull barrel. Left-hand ejection is also an option on this model.

P

Grading	100%	98%	95%	90%	80%	70%	60%

HSV (VICTOR) - .22 LR cal., 3 7/8, 4½, 5½, 8 (optional), or 10 (optional) in. VR barrel. Mfg. 1995-2000.

	$475	$375	$300	$250	$230	$185	$165

Last MSR was $569.

Add $30 for dove tail rib on 5½ in. barrel only.
Add $79 for Weaver rib on 5½ in. barrel only.

HSO (OLYMPIC) - .22 S or .22 LR cal., 6¾ in. barrel only. Mfg. 1995-2000.

	$495	$395	$325	$265	$245	$195	$170

Last MSR was $599.

PAUZA SPECIALTIES

Previously manufactured by Pauza Specialties circa 1991-96, and located in Baytown, TX. Previously distributed by U.S. General Technologies, Inc. located in South San Francisco, CA.

Pauza currently manufactures the P50 semi-auto rifle for Firearms International, Inc. – please refer to that section for current information.

RIFLES

P50 SEMI-AUTO - .50 BMG cal., semi-auto, 24 (carbine) or 29 (rifle) in. match grade barrel, 5 shot detachable mag., one-piece receiver, 3-stage gas system, takedown action, all exterior parts Teflon coated, with aluminum bipod, 25 or 30 lbs. Mfg. 1992-96.

	$5,950	$5,250	$4,600	$4,100	$3,650	$3,200	$2,800

Last MSR was $6,495.

PEACE RIVER CLASSICS

Previous manufacturer located in Bartow, FL until 2001. Peace River Classics was a division of Tim's Guns.

RIFLES: SEMI-AUTO

PEACE RIVER CLASSICS SEMI-AUTO - .223 Rem. or .308 Win. (new 1998) cal., available in 3 configurations including the Shadowood, the Glenwood, and the Royale, hand-built utilizing Armalite action, patterned after the AR-15, matched parts throughout, special serialization, laminate thumbhole stock. Mfg. 1997-2001.

	$2,575	$2,275	$2,000	$1,775	$1,525	$1,250	$995

Last MSR was $2,695.

Add $300 for .308 Win. cal.

P PEDERSEN CUSTOM GUNS

Previously manufactured circa 1973-1975 by O.F. Mossberg located in North Haven, CT. Pedersen Custom Guns was a division of O.F. Mossberg.

RIFLES: BOLT ACTION

MODEL 3000 - .270 Win., .30-06, 7mm Rem. Mag., or .338 Win. Mag. cal., Mossberg Model 810 action, 22 or 24 in. barrel, open sights, checkered Monte Carlo stock.

* *Grade III* - no engraving.

	$550	$495	$470	$440	$420	$385	$330

* *Grade II* - moderately engraved.

	$660	$580	$525	$495	$440	$420	$385

* *Grade I* - heavily engraved and inlaid, with select wood.

	$990	$770	$745	$690	$635	$560	$495

* *Presentation Model* - top-of-the-line model.

	$1,250	$1,000	$895	$800	$745	$690	$635

Grading	100%	98%	95%	90%	80%	70%	60%

MODEL 4700 - custom deluxe lever action, (Model 472 Mossberg), .30-30 Win. or .35 Rem. cal., 5 shot, tube mag., 24 in. barrel, open sight, black walnut stock.

	$250	$195	$165	$155	$145	$130	$120

SHOTGUNS: O/U

MODEL 1500 HUNTING GUN - 12 ga., 2¾ or 3 in. chambers, 26 in. imp. cyl. and mod., 28 in. mod. and full, 30 in. mod. and full barrels, boxlock, auto ejectors, selective or non-selective single trigger, checkered pistol grip stock. Mfg. 1973-1975.

	$700	$575	$500	$440	$415	$385	$365

MODEL 1500 SKEET - similar to Hunting Gun, except 27 in. skeet barrel, skeet stock. Mfg. 1973-1975.

	$725	$600	$525	$450	$425	$400	$385

MODEL 1500 TRAP - similar to Hunting Gun, except 30 and 32 in. full barrels, trap Monte Carlo stock. Mfg. 1973-1975.

	$650	$550	$475	$435	$410	$375	$350

MODEL 1000 HUNTING GUN - 12 or 20 ga., 26, 28, or 30 in. barrels, various chokes, boxlock, auto ejectors, SST, checkered select walnut stock, silver inlays, more engraving. Mfg. 1973-1975.

	100%	98%	95%	90%	80%	70%	60%
Grade I	$2,200	$1,980	$1,870	$1,700	$1,540	$1,460	$1,375
Grade II	$1,815	$1,540	$1,430	$1,265	$1,185	$1,100	$1,045

MODEL 1000 TRAP GUN - similar to Hunting Gun, but 12 ga., 30 or 32 in. mod. and full barrels, Monte Carlo trap stock. Mfg. 1973-1975.

	100%	98%	95%	90%	80%	70%	60%
Grade I	$2,100	$1,800	$1,650	$1,500	$1,350	$1,200	$995
Grade II	$1,650	$1,500	$1,375	$1,200	$1,050	$900	$725

MODEL 1000 SKEET - similar to Hunting Gun, except 26 or 28 in. barrels, bored skeet. Mfg. 1973-1975.

	100%	98%	95%	90%	80%	70%	60%
Grade I	$2,255	$2,145	$2,035	$1,870	$1,705	$1,625	$1,540
Grade II	$1,980	$1,705	$1,595	$1,430	$1,350	$1,265	$1,210

SHOTGUNS: SxS

MODEL 200 - 12 or 20 ga., 26 in. imp. cyl. and mod., 28 in. mod. and full, 30 in. mod. and full barrels, boxlock, auto ejectors, SST. Mfg. 1973-1974.

	100%	98%	95%	90%	80%	70%	60%
Grade I	$2,420	$2,175	$2,090	$1,955	$1,790	$1,705	$1,625
Grade II	$2,200	$1,955	$1,815	$1,735	$1,625	$1,540	$1,485

MODEL 2500 - 12 or 20 ga., 26 in. imp. cyl. and mod., 28 in. mod. and full barrels, auto ejectors, boxlock, checkered pistol grip stock and forearm.

	$470	$385	$360	$305	$275	$260	$240

SHOTGUNS: SLIDE ACTION

MODEL 4000 - custom Mossberg Model 500, 12, 20 ga., or .410 bore, 3 in. chamber, 26 in. imp. cyl. or skeet, 28 in. full or mod. barrel, 30 in. full, vent. rib, floral engraved, checkered select walnut stock. Mfg. 1975.

	$460	$375	$330	$305	$265	$230	$220

MODEL 4000 TRAP - similar to 4000, except 12 ga., 30 in. full barrel, Monte Carlo trap stock and pad. Mfg. 1975.

	$485	$395	$350	$325	$285	$255	$240

MODEL 4500 - similar to 4000, less engraving.

	$420	$330	$305	$275	$240	$200	$175

P

Grading	100%	98%	95%	90%	80%	70%	60%

MODEL 4500 TRAP - similar to 4000 Trap, less engraving.

	$440	$350	$310	$280	$240	$210	$200

PEDERSOLI, DAVIDE & C. Snc.

Current manufacturer of modern, black powder, and older historically significant firearms located in Brescia, Italy. Currently full-line distributors include Flintlocks, Etc., located in Richmond, MA, Cherry's Fine Guns, located in Greensboro, NC, and Dixie Gun Works, Inc., located in Union City, TN. Current importers include Cabela's, located in Sidney, NE, Cape Outfitters, located in Cape Girardeau, MO, Cimarron, FA Co., located in Fredricksburg, TX, E.M.F., located in Santa Ana, CA, and Navy Arms, located in Ridgefield, NJ.

D. Pedersoli manufactures top quality black powder replicas and other high quality firearms reproductions. Most of their production domestically is subcontracted by other U.S. firms. Please refer to the individual importer/distributor listings in this text for both model information and pricing.

For more information and up-to-date regarding current Pedersoli black powder models, please refer to *Colt Blackpowder Reproductions and Replicas*, and the *Blue Book of Modern Black Powder Values*, by Dennis Adler. These books feature hundreds of color photographs and support text of the most recent black powder models available, as well as a complete pricing and reference guide.

PENTHENY de PENTHENY

Current manufacturer and gunsmith located in Santa Rosa, CA. Established in 1987.

RIFLES: BOLT ACTION

The rifles listed include ebony forend tips, old English style black recoil pads, steel skeleton grip caps, four panels of 22 LPI checkering, and other custom features. These models are built on a U.S.R.A. Model 70 action.

THE INVADER - small and medium bore cals., classic styled Claro walnut stock, blue finish.

MSR	$3,850		$3,850	$2,975	$2,400	$1,975	$1,500	$1,150	$875

THE NORMAN - Mag. cals., classic styled English walnut stock, blue finish.

MSR	$3,850		$3,850	$2,975	$2,400	$1,975	$1,500	$1,150	$875

THE CONQUEROR - large bore cals., classic styled English walnut stock, blue finish, rifle has secondary recoil lug, dual steel reinforcing bolts, and express sights including fixed and folding leaves.

MSR	$4,700		$4,700	$3,650	$3,000	$2,400	$1,975	$1,500	$1,150

P PERAZZI

Current manufacturer established in 1952, and located in Brescia, Italy. Imported and distributed by Perazzi USA, Inc. located in Monrovia, CA (previously located in Rome, NY).

Note: Previously, Perazzi shotguns were imported by both Winchester and Ithaca during the 1960s and 1970s. The company now has its own distribution network and its current model line-up is extensive. Perazzi shotguns are well known for their quality control standards and reliability in clay target championships and in-field conditions.

SHOTGUNS: DISC.

Perazzi shotguns have incorporated many improvements during their manufacture. One of the most important changes has been the modification of the forearm design. Basically, there have been 4 different types: Type 1 has a serial range of 30,000 - 33,250, Type 2 is serial numbered 33,251 - 35,450, Type 3 has a range of 35,451 - 51,242, Type 4 started at 51,243 and is still current as of this writing. Differences include changes in the forearm iron and barrel lug attachment. Because of these forearm changes (and other parts modifications), the desirability factor on a Type 4 forearm

Grading	100%	98%	95%	90%	80%	70%	60%

shotgun as opposed to a Type 1 is much greater. Competition shooters prefer Types 3 or 4 as they are the current design. If a Type 1 or 2 competition gun develops problems, they are automatically retrofitted to the Type 4 design - and these modifications are expensive. For these reasons, the serial number of a Perazzi competition gun will determine its type. Since Types 1 through 3 are discontinued, Types 1 and 2 will be less desirable (and less expensive) than the values listed for Type 3.

As a final note on older Perazzi shotguns, the most collectable models will be those specimens which exhibit the highest quality and are equally rare. Older SCO grades on small frames with older style "V" springs are at the top for desirability. Also, any older SPECIAL GUNS were all custom made - usually engraved by master engravers with Angelo Galeazzi being considered the best. These models are exceedingly rare, with prices going over the $40,000 level in today's marketplace.

COMPETITION ONE TRAP GRADE - single shot, 12 ga., auto ejector, VR, cased.

$2,250	$1,975	$1,725	$1,600	$1,450	$1,300	$1,175

COMPETITION ONE O/U TRAP - similar to Competition, except O/U double.

$3,750	$3,400	$3,200	$2,800	$2,500	$2,150	$1,850

COMPETITION ONE SKEET

$3,500	$3,100	$2,900	$2,500	$2,000	$1,800	$1,450

SINGLE BARREL TRAP - 12 ga., 34 in. VR, full choke barrel, boxlock, auto ejector, checkered pistol grip stock, recoil pad. Mfg. 1971-1972.

$2,050	$1,895	$1,725	$1,575	$1,450	$1,300	$1,175

LIGHT GAME MODEL O/U FIELD - 12 ga., 27½ in. VR barrels, mod. and full or imp. cyl. and mod., boxlock, auto ejectors, field stock. Mfg. 1972-1974.

$3,350	$3,000	$2,850	$2,500	$2,150	$1,850	$1,600

MT-6 GRADE - 12 ga., VR, auto ejector, cased, five interchangeable choke tubes. Disc. 1983.

$3,000	$2,400	$2,250	$1,950	$1,675	$1,500	$1,400

This model was also manufactured in DHO and SHO models as well. Please refer to those models listed in the current manufacture section for approximate values.

Perazzi Shotguns Information

Not until 1988 did most single barrel trap guns have a "Special" option package which includes an adjustable trigger group (designated P4). This P4 trigger is now standard. Non-adj. trigger is a special order. Values assume shotguns with the "Special" designation (became standard in 1988).

Models listed in the following sections assume a Type 4 forearm attachment design and are serial numbered 51,243 and above. Models that are serial numbered below 51,243 are an older design and will be priced less than the newer Type 4 models (see explanation under SHOTGUNS: DISC.).

Rather than describe all the following models individually, descriptions will appear only once and are listed. The various grades have similar features and engraving (i.e., an SCO Grade Sideplate in American Skeet would appear similar to an American Trap SCO Grade Sideplate, except for stock dimensions of course).

Older SHO (Type 3s) and DHO models with rebounding hammers (disc.) are perhaps the most collectable Perazzi shotguns currently.

> **SC3 and other higher grade models have not been listed due to space consideration. The 14th edition does include all pertinent information (including 1993 pricing) pertaining to Perazzi higher grade models.**

Recently, some Model MX8s have been modified by adding sideplates and other markings of the Extra Gold and SCO Models. These forgeries usually have the original markings polished off and have not been reproofed. Perazzi will verify any gun suspected of upgrading.

Perazzi discontinued "Mirage" model nomenclature during 1998.

Perazzi Grades and Descriptions

Due to space considerations and relative low manufacture, the higher grade Perazzis have been described but not individually priced. Please contact Perazzi, USA for more information and prices on these higher grades (see Trademark Index).

Perazzi

Grading	100%	98%	95%	90%	80%	70%	60%

GRADES AND DESCRIPTIONS

* ***Special Model*** - introductory level model with high polished blue on barrels and receiver, normally listing model name on lower frame sides in gold letters and numerals. Checkered walnut stock (interchangeable) and forearm, all have adjustable trigger assembly.

* ***Gold Outline Model*** - similar to Standard Model, except has gold line engraving around perimeter of frame, also features better grade of walnut. This configuration is very rare.

* ***SC3 Model*** - features coin finished receiver with two different styles of scroll engraving and four different patterns of game scene engraving (snipe, grouse, pointing bird dog, or woodcock). Better grade of walnut than the Gold Outline Model.

* ***SCO Model*** - more elaborate than SC3 Model in that it features two different styles of scroll engraving (deep relief "gargoyles" or fine English scroll) and four different game scene engraving patterns (two different styles of ducks, grouse, or woodcock). Again, a better grade of walnut (in addition to finer checkering) is utilized.

* ***SCO Gold Grade Model*** - differentiated from SCO Model in that it has six engraving patterns featuring multiple gold inlays on receiver sides (including two different duck scenes, two separate grouse scenes, one woodcock, and one deep relief "gargoyle").

* ***SCO Grade Sideplate Model*** - includes coin finished receiver with game scene engraved sideplates (with boxlock action). Game scene engraving choices include three different duck scenes, one grouse, one "Chisel" relief scroll, and a Diana Goddess of the Hunt pattern.

* ***SCO Gold Grade Sideplate Model*** - similar to SCO Grade Sideplate Model, except has game figures on sideplates in relief gold. Patterns include three different grouse scenes, two separate ducks patterns, and dogs flushing upland game. This model can also be ordered with detachment lever for sideplates.

* ***Extra Grade Model*** - denoted by top-of-the-line fine bank note style game scene engraving with elaborate scroll and relief work on metal perimeters. Game scene choices include two different dog scenes, one grouse, and one duck. Top quality Circassian walnut finely checkered.

* ***Extra Gold Grade Model*** - top-of-the-line boxlock model that differs from Extra Grade Model in that birds/dogs are in gold relief. This model can also be ordered with detachment lever for sideplates.

* ***SHO Over & Under Model*** - features sidelock action with coin finished receiver and intricate bank note game scene engraving with choices including three different duck patterns and one pheasant. Top quality walnut and checkering. Type One SHOs have non-rebounding firing pins, while Type Two guns have rebounding firing pins (since 1985).
  This model is individually hand made per customer's specifications. Currently, no orders are being taken for this series.

* ***SHO Gold Over & Under Model*** - similar to SHO Over & Under Model, except features game scene of wildlife in relief gold. This model is the best sidelock special order grade that Perazzi currently offers for sale.
  This model is individually hand made per customer's specifications. Currently, no orders are being taken for this series.

* ***DHO SxS Models*** - top-of-the-line sidelock model in 12 ga. only for DHO and DHO Gold grades. DHO Extra and DHO Gold Extra grades have similar engraving to Extra Grade and Extra Gold Grade models and are available in all gauges. The DHO Gold Extra is the most elaborate, highly finished SxS shotgun that an individual can currently special order from any company. The DHO model is exceedingly rare, and specimens should be appraised individually.
  This model is entirely hand made per customer's specifications. Currently, no orders are being taken for this series.

Some descriptions on the Standard Models listed have not been duplicated into the other Perazzi sections because of space consideration.

Grading	100%	98%	95%	90%	80%	70%	60%

SHOTGUNS: SINGLE BARREL, AMERICAN TRAP

12 ga. only, 32 or 34 in. barrel, high post rib, select walnut, more expensive models vary in the amount of engraving, grade of walnut, and other special order features.

NOTE: Combination guns (Combo Models) listed include either a 32 or 34 in. single barrel and a set of either 29½ or 31½ in. O/U barrels. Current combination guns (Combo Models) include MX6, MX7, MX11, MX14, MX8 Special, DB81 Special, and MX10.

Subtract $600 for shotguns without the "Special" model designation (pre-1988).

STANDARD GRADE MODELS

Add 35%-43% for Combo Models depending on model variation.

* *TM1 Special* - features normal trap rib. Disc. 1995.

	100%	98%	95%	90%	80%	70%	60%
	$3,600	$3,350	$3,050	$2,100	$1,875	$1,750	$1,600

Last MSR was $6,150.

* *TMX Special* - features high post trap rib. Disc. 1998.

	100%	98%	95%	90%	80%	70%	60%
	$3,600	$3,350	$3,050	$2,100	$1,875	$1,750	$1,600

Last MSR was $6,790.

* *MX3 Special* - features rib similar to TM1 Special. Disc. 1992.

	100%	98%	95%	90%	80%	70%	60%
	$3,500	$3,150	$2,850	$2,200	$2,000	$1,775	$1,575

Last MSR was $6,150.

* *MX6* - removable trigger group, 32 or 34 in. barrel. Imported 1995-96.

	100%	98%	95%	90%	80%	70%	60%
	$2,950	$2,725	$2,525	$1,950	$1,825	$1,700	$1,475

Last MSR was $6,270.

* *MX7* - non-removable trigger group, barrel selector, 32 or 34 in. barrel. Mfg. 1995 only.

	100%	98%	95%	90%	80%	70%	60%
	$3,100	$2,875	$2,550	$1,875	$1,675	$1,500	$1,250

Last MSR was $5,650.

* *MX8 Special* - has tapered stepped rib and adj. trigger. Disc. 1994.

	100%	98%	95%	90%	80%	70%	60%
	$3,800	$3,650	$3,300	$2,850	$2,500	$2,000	$1,700

Last MSR was $7,300.

* *MX9* - 12 ga., 32 or 34 in. barrel with choke tubes, unique VR on vent. barrel features removable center inserts significantly changing the point of shot pattern impact, fully adj. cheekpiece. Mfg. 1993-94.

	100%	98%	95%	90%	80%	70%	60%
	$4,250	$4,075	$3,875	$3,400	$2,900	$2,350	$2,000

Last MSR was $9,200.

* *MX9 Combo* - includes a set O/U barrels and top single trap barrel, features new rib design with interchangeable middle bead inserts to change point of impact. Mfg. 1992-94.

	100%	98%	95%	90%	80%	70%	60%
	$5,500	$5,150	$5,000	$4,875	$4,550	$3,850	$3,300

This model was available with or without choke tubes. Choke tubes include 5 chokes and 5 rib inserts (3 in. pattern per insert).

Last MSR was $12,800.

* *MX10* - 12 ga., 32 or 34 in. barrel featuring center-pivoting VR allowing for adj. point of impact, fixed chokes, fully adj. cheekpiece, removable trigger. Mfg. 1993-94.

	100%	98%	95%	90%	80%	70%	60%
	$4,600	$4,550	$4,400	$4,250	$3,800	$3,600	$3,200

Last MSR was $9,450.

This model is still available by special order only.

MX11 - removable trigger group, adj. comb, 32 or 34 in. barrel. Imported 1995-96.

	100%	98%	95%	90%	80%	70%	60%
	$3,900	$3,600	$2,650	$2,350	$2,150	$1,850	$1,675

Last MSR was $7,620.

This model is still available by special order only.

P

Perazzi

Grading	100%	98%	95%	90%	80%	70%	60%

* **MX14** - removable trigger group, adj. comb, unsingle configuration, 32 or 34 in. barrel. Imported 1995-96.

| | **$3,850** | **$3,600** | **$3,200** | **$2,450** | **$2,250** | **$1,975** | **$1,700** |

Last MSR was $7,030.

This model is still available by special order only.

* **Grand American 88 Special** - features MX3 high ramped rib and grooved forearm. Mfg. 1988- 92.

| | **$3,900** | **$3,550** | **$3,600** | **$2,850** | **$2,450** | **$2,100** | **$1,825** |

Last MSR was $7,000.

* **DB81 Special** - features ultra high ramped rib. Disc. 1994.

| | **$5,100** | **$4,650** | **$4,250** | **$3,500** | **$3,000** | **$2,500** | **$2,100** |

Last MSR was $7,600.

This model is still available by special order only.

SHOTGUNS: O/U, INTERNATIONAL/OLYMPIC TRAP

12 ga. only, unless indicated otherwise. Current barrel lengths include 29½, 30¾, or 31½ in.

STANDARD GRADE MODELS

The MX2/MX2L configuration is available mainly for the European marketplace. Values for this model represent recent pricing - Perazzi U.S.A. should be contacted directly for an up-to- date price quotation.

Models with "Special" nomenclature feature Perazzi's new, adjustable (4 positions) trigger group introduced on certain models beginning 1988.

* **MX3 Special** - includes 6.4mm high ramped rib and separated barrels. Disc. 1992.

| | **$3,700** | **$3,400** | **$3,200** | **$2,950** | **$2,675** | **$2,350** | **$1,975** |

Add $380 for MX3C Model (includes choke tubes).

Last MSR was $6,500.

* **MX6** - removable trigger group. Mfg. 1995-98.

| | **$3,050** | **$2,650** | **$2,300** | **$1,975** | **$1,700** | **$1,500** | **$1,350** |

Last MSR was $5,700.

* **MX7C** - 29½ or 31½ in. barrels, features fixed coil spring trigger mechanism, safety incorporates selector switch, non-removable trigger group. Mfg. 1993-98.

| | **$3,750** | **$3,300** | **$2,950** | **$2,600** | **$2,300** | **$1,950** | **$1,650** |

Last MSR was $6,100.

* **MX8** - denoted by low profile rib, vent. barrels and grooved forearm.

| **MSR** | **$8,670** | **$4,250** | **$3,700** | **$3,250** | **$2,875** | **$2,600** | **$2,375** | **$2,050** |

This model is also available with standard triggers.

* **MX8 Special** - similar to MX8, except four position adj. trigger (P4S).

| **MSR** | **$9,180** | **$3,850** | **$3,500** | **$3,250** | **$2,875** | **$2,600** | **$2,375** | **$2,050** |

* **MX8/20** - 20 ga., 29½ in. barrels with fixed chokes, flat VR with removable trigger group. New 1993.

| **MSR** | **$8,670** | **$4,350** | **$4,000** | **$3,650** | **$3,250** | **$2,875** | **$2,600** | **$2,375** |

* **MX9** - 29½ or 31½ in. barrels with choke tubes, unique VR on vent. barrels features removable center inserts significantly changing the point of shot pattern impact, fully adj. cheekpiece, removable trigger. Mfg. 1993-94.

| | **$5,050** | **$4,725** | **$4,400** | **$3,900** | **$3,500** | **$3,000** | **$2,650** |

Last MSR was $9,600.

* **MX10** - 12 or 20 ga., 29½ in. barrels featuring center-pivoting VR allowing for adj. point of impact, fixed chokes, fully adj. cheekpiece, removable trigger. New 1993.

| **MSR** | **$11,050** | **$5,850** | **$5,500** | **$4,950** | **$4,500** | **$4,000** | **$3,500** | **$3,000** |

* **MX11** - removable trigger group and adj. comb. New 1995.

| **MSR** | **$8,180** | **$3,650** | **$3,350** | **$3,100** | **$2,700** | **$2,250** | **$1,950** | **$1,750** |

P

Grading	100%	98%	95%	90%	80%	70%	60%

✳ Grand American 88 Special - features high ramped rib, separated barrels, and grooved forearm. Disc. 1992.

		$4,100	$3,850	$3,700	$3,250	$2,750	$2,350	$2,000

Last MSR was $7,400.

✳ DB81 Special - features ultra high ramped rib and vent. barrels.

MSR	$9,450		$4,650	$4,500	$4,250	$4,000	$3,500	$3,150	$2,650

✳ MX2/MX2L - denoted by 8.2mm high rib, Monte Carlo stock, and vented side ribs. Model
MX2L designates light weight model and has no side ribs. Disc. 1992.

		$3,900	$3,500	$3,050	$2,750	$2,400	$2,075	$1,750

Last MSR was $5,510.

✳ MX16 - 12 ga., nonremovable trigger group, barrel selector on top of frame, with hard case.
New 1998.

MSR	$7,210		$3,250	$2,800	$2,400	$2,150	$1,850	$1,600	$1,400

Add $2,280 for combo package.

O/U SIDELOCK MODELS - older models without rebounding hammers are not as desirable. The
most desirable configurations in this model are the Skeet, Pigeon, and Sporting variations
(pricing follows new SHO Gold values). All SHO sidelock models were disc. 1992.

✳ SHO Older Mfg.

		$19,000	$16,750	$12,250	$9,500	$8,500	$7,600	$6,800

Add $6,000 for game scene engraving.

✳ SHO Newer Mfg.

		$35,000	$27,750	$25,750	$23,750	$21,750	$19,750	$17,750

Last MSR was $43,000.

✳ SHO Gold Older Mfg.

		$25,000	$21,000	$18,000	$15,000	$13,000	$11,000	$9,250

✳ SHO Gold Newer Mfg.

		$55,000	$49,500	$45,500	$40,000	$35,500	$30,000	$25,000

Last MSR was $48,000.

✳ SHO Extra - while advertised, none were sold.

Last MSR was $80,000.

✳ SHO Gold Extra - while advertised, none were sold.

Last MSR was $86,000.

SHOTGUNS: O/U, AMERICAN SKEET

12 ga. only, 26, 27 5/8 (standard and most common), or 28 3/8 in. separated barrels, select walnut,
more expensive models vary in the amount of engraving, grade of walnut, and other special order
features.

STANDARD GRADE MODELS

✳ MX3 Special - introductory skeet model, detachable and adj. four position P4S trigger, flat
rib. Barrel lockup is same as MX8. Disc. 1992.

		$3,800	$3,550	$3,100	$2,800	$2,675	$2,350	$1,975

Last MSR was $6,500.

Previous to 1988, this model was designated the MX3. It did not have the P4 adj. selective trigger
group.

✳ MX6 - removable trigger group. Mfg. 1995-96.

		$2,775	$2,500	$2,250	$1,925	$1,700	$1,500	$1,350

Last MSR was $6,270.

P

Grading	100%	98%	95%	90%	80%	70%	60%

* **MX7C** - 27 5/8 or 28 3/8 in. barrels with choke tubes, features fixed coil spring trigger mechanism, safety incorporates selector switch, non-removable trigger group. Mfg. 1993-95.

		$2,850	$2,550	$2,300	$1,950	$1,725	$1,525	$1,375

Last MSR was $6,100.

* **MX8** - 12 or 20 ga., 27 5/8 in. barrels bored SK/SK, flat VR with removable trigger group. New 1993.

MSR	$8,670	$3,800	$3,750	$3,100	$2,700	$2,500	$2,300	$2,100

* **MX8 Special** - evolved from Olympic Skeet Model, features detachable and adj. four position trigger.

MSR	$9,180	$3,900	$3,525	$3,100	$2,700	$2,500	$2,300	$2,100

* **MX10** - removable trigger group, adj. rib and comb. New 1995.

MSR	$11,050	$4,850	$4,700	$4,500	$4,000	$3,650	$3,350	$2,950

* **MX11** - removable trigger group, adj. comb. New 1995.

MSR	$8,180	$2,550	$2,500	$2,450	$1,975	$1,800	$1,700	$1,475

* **MX16** - 12 ga., nonremovable trigger group, barrel selector on top of frame, with hard case. New 1998.

MSR	$7,210	$3,200	$2,975	$2,800	$2,600	$2,350	$2,100	$1,875

SHOTGUNS: O/U, 4-GAUGE SKEET SETS

STANDARD GRADE MODELS

* **MX3 Special**

		$5,200	$4,875	$4,650	$4,500	$4,150	$3,650	$3,150

Last MSR was $15,400.

* **Mirage Special** - disc. 1994.

		$5,850	$5,500	$4,850	$4,600	$4,200	$3,700	$3,200

Last MSR was $17,500.

SHOTGUNS: O/U, INTERNATIONAL/OLYMPIC SKEET

Available in 12 ga. only. Usually supplied with 29½ in. barrels.

Since the international skeet variations are similar to the American skeet models, rather than duplicating these models (with the exception of the Mirage MX8), please refer to pricing in the American Skeet Shotguns section for corresponding values and information. Only the Model MX8 remains, since there is no similar American model.

STANDARD GRADE MODELS

Older Mirage Models (without the "Special" designation) do not have the adjustable 4 position trigger.

Subtract $250-$500 on values listed for these older variations.

* **MX8** - developed especially for Olympic Skeet Competition featuring vent. barrels with optional muzzle brakes on sides, grooved forearm, interchangeable trigger groupings with non-adj. trigger.

MSR	$8,090	$5,900	$4,400	$3,600	$3,100	$2,700	$2,500	$2,300

O/U SIDELOCK MODELS - older models without rebounding hammers are not as desirable.

* **SHO Older Mfg.**

		$18,000	$15,750	$12,000	$9,500	$8,500	$7,600	$6,800

* **SHO Newer Mfg.**

		$35,850	$30,000	$25,000	$20,000	$17,000	$14,500	$12,750

Last MSR was $43,000.

* **SHO Gold Older Mfg.**

		$18,000	$15,750	$12,000	$9,500	$8,500	$7,600	$6,800

Grading	100%	98%	95%	90%	80%	70%	60%

✱ SHO Gold Newer Mfg.

	$45,000	$34,500	$27,250	$22,000	$18,500	$15,950	$13,750

Last MSR was $48,000.

✱ SHO Extra - imported 1985-1992.

	$68,750	$54,700	$38,100	$32,000	$26,500	$21,250	$18,000

Last MSR was $80,000.

✱ SHO Gold Extra - similar to SHO Extra, except has gold inlays. Imported 1992 only.

	$72,750	$56,500	$39,500	$33,000	$27,000	$22,000	$18,500

Last MSR was $86,000.

SHOTGUNS: O/U, COMPETITION SPORTING

12 ga. only, unless indicated otherwise, designed for sporting clays competition.

The Mirage Sporting Classic Models listed replace the Mirage Special Sporting and incorporate several new improvements. Perazzi discontinued the Mirage nomenclature during 1998.

STANDARD GRADE MODELS

The MX1/MX1B configuration is available mainly for the European marketplace. Values for this model represent recent pricing - Perazzi USA should be contacted directly for an up-to- date price quotation.

Choke tubes became standard on Perazzi's Sporting shotguns beginning in 1992. Subtract $400 - $500 for older variations without choke tubes (Models without the "C" suffix nomenclature). Older specimens without the "Special" designation do not have adjustable 4 position trigger group - subtract $400 from values without this feature.

✱ MX3C Special Sporting - features VR and barrels, includes adj. four position trigger, and 5 interchangeable choke tubes. Disc. 1992.

	$4,000	$3,650	$3,350	$2,900	$2,500	$2,250	$1,900

Last MSR was $6,880.

✱ MX6 - removable trigger group, external selector, 7 chokes. Mfg. 1995-98.

	$3,350	$2,950	$2,700	$2,400	$2,100	$1,875	$1,675

Last MSR was $6,740.

✱ MX7C Sporting - sporting configuration, includes 5 choke tubes. Imported 1992-95.

	$3,575	$3,100	$2,800	$2,550	$2,150	$1,900	$1,700

Last MSR was $6,670.

✱ MX8 - 12 or 20 ga., 27 5/8, 28 3/8, or 29½ in. barrels with fixed or screw-in chokes. New 1993.

MSR	$9,600	$3,200	$3,500	$3,250	$2,875	$2,500	$2,150	$1,800

✱ MX10 - 12 or 20 ga., 27 5/8 in. barrels with fixed chokes. New 1993.

MSR	$12,180	$5,375	$5,100	$4,900	$4,400	$3,950	$3,450	$2,950

✱ MX11 - removable trigger group, adj. comb, external selector, 7 chokes. New 1995.

MSR	$9,110	$3,000	$2,700	$2,500	$2,150	$1,875	$1,600	$1,400

✱ MX16 - 12 ga., nonremovable trigger group, barrel selector on top of frame, with hard case. New 1998.

MSR	$7,830	$3,600	$3,300	$2,800	$2,550	$2,150	$1,900	$1,700

✱ Mirage Special Sporting - 28 3/8 in. barrels with choke tubes, external SST (non- adj.), special sporting dimension stock and forend, Schnabel forearm. Disc. 1998.

	$4,250	$4,100	$3,650	$3,200	$2,800	$2,400	$2,000

Last MSR was $9,160.

✱ Mirage Special Sporting Classic - similar to Mirage Sporting, except has engraving package, SC3 quality wood, and SST. Disc. 1998.

	$5,250	$4,700	$4,175	$3,650	$3,150	$2,800	$2,500

Last MSR was $10,200.

P

Grading	100%	98%	95%	90%	80%	70%	60%

* ***MX1/MX1B Sporting*** - 12 ga. only, MX1 has high tapered ramped rib and separated barrels. MX1B has lower profile flat rib.

	MSR	$8,090		$3,750	$3,500	$3,100	$2,675	$2,300	$2,000	$1,850

SHOTGUNS: O/U, PIGEON-ELECTROCIBLES

STANDARD GRADE MODELS - 12 ga. only.

This configuration specifically made for pigeon/electrocibles competition shooting and is currently available in the MX1B, Mirage (MX8), Mirage Special (MX8 Special), MX10, and MX11 Models. **Subtract $1,000 for 27½ in. barrels, or $500 for 28 3/8 in. barrels.**

* ***MX1B*** - removable trigger group, 27½ in. barrels. New 1995.

MSR	$8,090	$3,500	$3,150	$2,700	$2,475	$2,175	$1,850	$1,625

* ***Standard Grade*** - removable trigger group, 27½, 28 3/8, 29½, or 31½ in. barrels. New 1995.

MSR	$7,850	$3,900	$3,450	$2,900	$2,600	$2,225	$1,875	$1,625

* ***Standard Grade Special*** - removable trigger group, adj. trigger, 28 3/8, 29½, or 31½ in. barrels. New 1995.

MSR	$8,570	$3,900	$3,450	$2,900	$2,600	$2,225	$1,875	$1,625

* ***MX10*** - removable trigger group, adj. rib and comb, 27½ or 29½ in. barrels. New 1995.

MSR	$11,050	$5,500	$4,950	$4,500	$3,950	$3,450	$3,000	$2,650

* ***MX11*** - removable trigger group, adj. comb., 27½ in. barrels. New 1995.

MSR	$8,620	$3,500	$3,150	$2,700	$2,475	$2,175	$1,850	$1,625

* ***MX16*** - 12 ga., nonremovable trigger group, barrel selector on top of frame, with hard case. New 1998.

MSR	$7,210	$3,200	$2,950	$2,500	$2,275	$1,975	$1,700	$1,500

SHOTGUNS: O/U, HUNTING - BOXLOCK ACTION

12, 20, 28 ga., or .410 bore, 26 (disc. on MX8/12 ga. and MX12 1994), 26¾, or 27½ in. barrels only, choice of chokes. These small frame shotguns are available in 20, 28 ga., or .410 bore but choke tubes (MX20C designation) are optional only in 20 ga.

STANDARD GRADE MODELS

* ***MX8*** - 12 or 20 ga., removable trigger group, separated barrels with fixed or screw-in chokes. New 1993.

MSR	$8,670	$3,950	$3,475	$3,100	$2,750	$2,425	$2,100	$1,850

* ***MX12*** - 12 ga. only, 2¾ in. chambers only, separated barrels with VR, coil springs, SST (fixed trigger group), Schnabel forearm, light receiver border engraving.

MSR	$8,650	$4,650	$4,350	$3,950	$3,600	$3,100	$2,700	$2,450

Vented side rib guns with flushed chokes are available beginning 1993.

* ***MX16*** - 12 or 16 ga., nonremovable trigger group, barrel selector on top of frame, with hard case. New 1998.

MSR	$7,210	$3,850	$3,375	$3,150	$2,775	$2,500	$2,225	$1,975

* ***MX20*** - similar to MX12, except 20, 28 ga., or .410 bore on smaller frame, 2¾ or 3 in. chambers.

MSR	$8,670	$4,500	$4,300	$3,650	$3,100	$2,700	$2,450	$2,150

* ***MX28/MX410*** - 28 ga. or .410 bore, small frame, 3 in. chambers on .410 bore, flat VR barrels with fixed chokes, fixed trigger (non-removable), straight grip, satin nickel receiver. New 1993.

MSR	$17,330	$8,100	$7,750	$7,250	$6,250	$5,400	$4,600	$3,800

Grading	100%	98%	95%	90%	80%	70%	60%

SHOTGUNS: O/U, HUNTING - SIDELOCK MODELS

All SHO models were disc. in 1992 (they were available through special order only).

SHO MODELS

* **SHO Older Mfg.** - older models without rebounding hammers are not as desirable.

	$18,000	$15,750	$12,000	$9,500	$8,500	$7,600	$6,800

* **SHO Newer Mfg.** - 12 ga. only, introductory sidelock O/U model with bank note game scene engraving on coin finished receiver.

	$35,500	$29,950	$25,000	$20,000	$17,000	$14,500	$12,750

  Last MSR was $43,000.

* **SHO Gold Older Mfg.** - older models without rebounding hammers are not as desirable.

	$18,000	$15,750	$12,000	$9,500	$8,500	$7,600	$6,800

* **SHO Gold Newer Mfg.** - similar to SHO, except has game scenes in gold relief.

	$38,650	$31,500	$26,500	$21,250	$18,000	$15,500	$13,750

  Last MSR was $48,000.

* **SHO Extra** - importation began 1992.

	$68,750	$54,700	$38,100	$32,000	$26,500	$21,250	$18,000

  Last MSR was $80,000.

* **SHO Gold Extra** - similar to SHO Extra, except has gold inlays. Importation began 1992.

	$72,750	$56,500	$39,500	$33,000	$27,000	$22,000	$18,500

  Last MSR was $86,000.

SHOTGUNS: SxS, HUNTING - SIDELOCK MODELS

DHO Models have not been included within the scope of this text due to the extreme rarity factor. Please contact Perazzi, USA for more information on these models and current pricing.

Subtract 40% without rebounding hammers on older DHO models.

PEREGRINE INDUSTRIES, INC.

Previous company located in Huntington Beach, CA circa 1991.

While advertised, Peregrine never manufactured the Falcon Model.

PERUGINI-VISINI

Current manufacturer established during 1968 and located in Brescia, Italy. No current U.S. importation. Rifles were previously imported and distributed until 1992 by William Larkin Moore & Co., previously located in Westlake Village, CA. All other models listed were previously imported and distributed by Armes De Chasse located in Chadds Ford, PA until 1988. Please contact the factory directly for more information, including current domestic pricing (see listing in Trademark Index).

P

RIFLES

Many of the models listed are currently manufactured. Information and pricing reflects the last year of domestic importation (1992). Please contact the factory directly for current availability and pricing.

STANDARD MODEL: BOLT ACTION - available in most U.S. and metric cals., Mauser 98K action, 24 or 26 in. barrel, 3 shot mag.(non-detachable), matte finished European walnut, high polish bluing, no sights. Importation disc. 1987.

	$4,250	$3,800	$3,400	$2,950	$2,500	$2,000	$1,800

Last MSR was $4,250.

DELUXE MODEL: BOLT ACTION - similar to Standard Model, except has finely checkered oil finished walnut stock, sights, knurled bolt handle, and is cased. Importation disc. 1987.

	$4,250	$3,800	$3,400	$2,950	$2,500	$2,000	$1,800

Last MSR was $4,250.

Grading	100%	98%	95%	90%	80%	70%	60%

MODEL EAGLE: SINGLE SHOT - available in most U.S. and metric cals., Anson & Deeley type action, ejector, sights, adj. trigger, oil finished finely checkered European walnut stock, 24 or 26 in. Hämmerli barrel. Importation disc. 1987.

	$5,255	$4,500	$3,800	$3,400	$2,950	$2,500	$2,000

Last MSR was $5,255.

MODEL VICTORIA M SxS - .30-06 (disc.), 7x57R, 7x65R, or 9.3x74R cal., Anson & Deeley type boxlock action, border engraving, ejectors, folding leaf rear sight, DTs, 24 or 26 in. monobloc barrels with chopper lumps, leather cased. Importation disc. 1992.

	$7,000	$5,700	$4,600	$3,500	$2,950	$2,500	$2,000

Last MSR was $7,900.

✳ **Model Victoria D Mag. SxS** - similar to Model Victoria, except in .375 H&H, .458 Win., .470 NE, or .500-3 in. NE cal., demi-bloc barrels, and has elaborate engraving. Importation disc. 1992.

	$10,950	$9,150	$8,200	$7,400	$6,600	$5,800	$5,100

Last MSR was $13,750.

MODEL SELOUS SxS - 9.3x74R, .375 H&H, .458 Win. Mag., .470 NE, or .500 3 in. NE cal., H&H style detachable sidelock action, ejectors, folding leaf rear sight, border engraving with best quality checkered walnut, top-of-the-line model, leather cased. Importation disc. 1992.

	$23,000	$18,500	$15,000	$12,000	$10,000	$9,000	$8,150

Last MSR was $26,000.

BOXLOCK EXPRESS SxS - .444 Marlin or 9.3x74R cal., Anson & Deeley boxlock action, ejectors, color case hardened frame, iron sights. Importation disc. 1989.

	$3,150	$2,800	$2,500	$2,200	$1,950	$1,700	$1,475

Last MSR was $3,500.

BOXLOCK MAGNUM O/U - .270 Win., .375 H&H, or .458 Win. Mag. cal., Anson & Deeley boxlock action, ejectors, monobloc barrels, select walnut. Importation disc. 1989.

	$5,500	$4,900	$4,300	$3,750	$3,100	$2,600	$2,200

Last MSR was $6,100.

SIDELOCK SUPER EXPRESS SxS - choice of 9 different cals. including .470 Nitro Express, H&H patterned sidelocks, chopper lump barrels, third lever fastener, multi-leaf express sights, coin finished or case hardened receiver, engraving patterns optional. Importation disc. 1989.

	$9,500	$8,400	$7,400	$6,850	$6,100	$5,600	$5,000

Last MSR was $10,500.

P | SHOTGUNS

AUSONIA SxS - 12 or 20 ga., exposed hammers with double Purdey type sidelock action, various engraving options, demibloc barrels. Disc.

	$7,140	$6,500	$5,750	$4,950	$4,200	$3,500	$2,550

Last MSR was $7,140.

LIBERTY MODEL SxS - 12, 20, 28 ga., or .410 bore, scalloped Anson & Deeley type engraved action, 28 in. chopper lump barrels, double Purdey-type lock, ejectors, leather cased. Disc.

	$7,140	$6,500	$5,750	$4,950	$4,200	$3,500	$2,550

Last MSR was $7,140.

CLASSIC MODEL SxS - 12 or 20 ga., H&H style scroll engraved sidelock action, 28 in. chopper lump barrels, double Purdey-type lock, best quality checkered walnut stock and forearm, top-of-the-line model, leather cased. Disc.

	$16,600	$13,000	$10,250	$8,650	$7,500	$6,500	$5,500

Last MSR was $16,600.

Grading	100%	98%	95%	90%	80%	70%	60%

MAESTRO O/U - various gauges, boxlock action, removeable adj. trigger group, monobloc barrels, ejectors, deluxe checkered walnut stock and forearm, various engraving options. Disc.

	$6,545	$5,750	$4,950	$4,300	$3,700	$3,100	$2,400

Last MSR was $6,545.

NOVA O/U - various gauges, H&H style scroll engraved sidelock action, demibloc barrels, top-of-the-line model, leather cased.

Prices were quoted per individual order.

PETERS STAHL GmbH

Current pistol manufacturer located in Paderborn, Germany. No current U.S. importation. Previously distributed by Swiss Trading GmbH, located in Bozeman, MT. Previously imported 1998-99 by Peters Stahl, U.S.A. located in Delta, UT, and by Franzen International Inc. located in Oakland, NJ until 1998. Dealer direct sales only.

PISTOLS: SEMI-AUTO

Peters Stahl manufactures high quality semi-auto pistols based on the Model 1911 design, but to date, has had limited U.S. importation. Current models include the Multicaliber, 92-Sport, O7-Sport, HC-Champion and variations, 1911-Tactical/Classic, PLS, and a .22 LR. Peters-Stahl also manufactures multicaliber conversion kits of the highest quality. Recent models previously imported (until 2000) included the Model Millennium (MSR was $2,195), Match 22 LR (MSR was $1,995), Trophy Master (MSR was $1,995), Omega Match (MSR was $1,995), High Capacity Trophy Master (MSR was $1,695), O7 Multicaliber (MSR was $1,995), and the 92 Multicaliber (MSR was $2,610-$2,720). In the past, Peters Stahl has manufactured guns for Federal Ordnance, Omega, Schuetzen Pistol Works, and Springfield Armory. The factory should be contacted directly (see Trademark Index) for current model information, U.S. availability, and pricing.

PHELPS MFG. CO.

Previous manufacturer located in Evansville, IN circa 1978-1996.

Phelps Manufacturing Company began shipping guns in early 1978. Phelps guns were investment cast in 4140 steel, with basic single-action simplicity, using a transfer bar in the action.

REVOLVERS

HERITAGE I - .45-70 cal., single action revolver, incorporates transfer bar hammer safety, blue finish (standard), nickel (optional), adj. rear sight, 8 in. barrel standard, other barrel lengths up to 20 in. available, 6 lbs. Disc. 1996.

	$2,050	$1,675	$1,425

Last MSR was $2,250.

Add $20 for each additional in. of barrel.

EAGLE I - .444 Marlin cal., single action revolver, blue finish, adj. rear sight, barrel options same as Heritage I, 6 lbs. Disc. 1996.

	$2,050	$1,675	$1,425

Last MSR was $2,250.

PATRIOT - .375 Win. cal., single action revolver, blue finish, adj. rear sight, barrel options are the same as Heritage I. Limited mfg. 1993-94.

	$1,925	$1,550	$1,350

Last MSR was $2,225.

GRIZZLY .50-70 - .50-70 cal., otherwise similar to Heritage I. Mfg. 1992-96.

	$2,300	$1,875	$1,500

Last MSR was $2,580.

Add $20 for each additional in. of barrel.

P

Grading	100%	98%	95%	90%	80%	70%	60%

PHILLIPS & ROGERS, INC.

Current manufacturer established 1992, and located in Huntsville, TX since 1997. Previously located in Conroe, TX circa 1992-97. Dealer direct sales.

In addition to manufacturing the firearms listed, Phillips & Rogers also made a multi-caliber conversion cylinder for all Ruger, .357 Mag., new model Blackhawk revolvers (disc. 1996) - the retail price was $145. Multi-caliber conversion cylinders are also available for the Ruger new Model Blackhawk (allows shooting .45 LC, .45 Win. Mag., or .45 ACP - retail price is $185) and the Ruger Super Blackhawk (converts .44 Mag. to .50 AE - $550). A new version of the Ruger .50 AE conversion is also available for $995.

REVOLVERS

MEDUSA MODEL 47 REVOLVER - multi-caliber, over 25 cals. in the .355 - .380 diameter range (including .357 Mag., .38 Super, .38 Spl., 9mm Para., etc.), unique design does not utilize half-moon clips or cylinder/barrel changes, 2½, 4, 5, 6, or 8 in. barrel, 6 shot, double action, matte blue finish, rubber or wood grips. New 1993.

MSR	$599		$525	$475	$435	$400	$375	$350	$325

Add $95 for 8 in. barrel.

RIFLES: BOLT ACTION

WILDERNESS EXPLORER - .218 Bee, .22 Hornet, .44 Mag., or .50 AE cal., bolt action, features 18 in. match grade barrel, quick change bolt face and barrel allowing interchangeable calibers, white speckled black synthetic stock, side safety, 5½ lbs. Mfg. 1997 only.

			$925	$825	$725	$650	$575	$500	$425

Last MSR was $995.

PHOENIX ARMS

Current manufacturer located in Ontario, CA since 1992. Distributor sales only.

PISTOLS: SEMI-AUTO

RAVEN - .25 ACP cal., single action, 2 7/16 in. barrel, 6 shot mag., alloy frame, choice of finishes and grips. Disc. 1998.

			$69	$50	$45	$40	$35	$30	$25

Last MSR was $79.

This model was supplied with a magazine disconnect lock.

HP MODEL - .22 LR or .25 ACP cal., single action, 3 in. VR barrel, 10 (.25 ACP), 10 (C/B 1994), or 11* (.22 LR) shot staggered mag., alloy frame, firing pin block safety, adj. rear sight, choice of polished blue or satin nickel finish, keyed mag. lock and safety cable lanyard, 20 oz. New 1994.

MSR	$128		$100	$80	$70	$60	$50	$45	$40

Add $99 for laser sight and mount (new 1998).
Add $45 for 2-in-1 target barrel and magazine conversion kit.

❊ HP Rangemaster Target Kit - includes HP Model in .22 LR with 5 in. extended barrel, extended mag., locking plastic storage case (compartmentalized during 2000), and cleaning kit. New 1998.

MSR	$169		$140	$115	$100	$90	$75	$65	$55

❊ HP Rangemaster Deluxe Target Kit - similar to HP Rangemaster Target Kit, except has 3 and 5 in. barrels and extended mag. New 1999.

MSR	$200		$180	$165	$135	$110	$100	$90	$80

PHOENIX ARMS CO.

Previous importer located in Lowell, MA.

PISTOLS: SEMI-AUTO

PHOENIX - .25 ACP cal., Belgian semi-auto, previously manufactured by Robar et DeKerkhove located in Liege, Belgium.

This trademark is rarely encountered - values would start at $350 and go up according to original condition.

PIETTA, F.LLI

Current black powder and firearms manufacturer located in Gussago, Italy. Various U.S. importation and distribution.

Pietta manufactures good quality black powder and modern firearms reproductions in many configurations for various American companies including Navy Arms, Dixie Gun Works, Cabela's, and others. During 2000-2001, Pietta developed their own proprietary centerfire bottleneck cartridge – the .30-357 AeT, manufactured by Lapua. They have also completed a modern SAA revolver capable of shooting this new cartridge, and will be announcing U.S. importation shortly. Please visit their web site for current information or to request a comprehensive catalog listing of the wide assortment of firearms this company manufactures (see Trademark Index).

For more information and up-to-date regarding current Pietta black powder models, please refer to *Colt Blackpowder Reproductions and Replicas*, and the *Blue Book of Modern Black Powder Values*, by Dennis Adler. These books feature hundreds of color photographs and support text of the most recent black powder models available, as well as a complete pricing and reference guide.

PIOTTI

Current manufacturer located in Brescia, Italy. Currently imported and distributed exclusively by William Larkin Moore & Co. located in Scottsdale, AZ.

Fratelli Piotti is one of Italy's premier gunmakers. These shotguns meet the highest British standards of craftsmanship and are made to customer specifications. Variety of gauges, engraving, styles, chokes, etc.

SHOTGUNS: O/U

PIOTTI BOSS - 12, 16, 20, or 28 ga., 26-32 in. barrels, single or double triggers, standard with King 2 engraving, Turkish Circassian walnut, various engraving patterns available, 6 lbs - 20 ga., approx. 7½ 12 ga. New 1995.

MSR	$34,000						
	$34,000	$28,750	$23,650	$18,950	$15,450	$12,950	$10,200

Add $2,400 for 16 or 20 ga.
Add $6,600 for 28 ga.

SHOTGUNS: SxS

For the following models - add $1,950 (SxS) or $2,300 (O/U) for single trigger, $7,300 for H&H type self-opening mechanism, $800-$1,300 for hand-detachable locks, add $650 for pinless action, approx. $1,000-$1,400 for leather case, $700 for 16 or 20 ga., $1,000 for 28 ga. or .410 bore boxlock, $1,900 for 28 ga. or .410 bore sidelock.

HAMMER GUN - 12 ga. only, self cocking ejector model, DT, exposed hammers, back action with fine scroll engraving. Importation began 2001.

MSR	$23,200						
	$23,200	$18,750	$12,250	$10,000	$8,700	$6,800	$5,600

PIUMA (BSEE) - 12, 16, 20, 28 ga., or .410 bore, Anson & Deeley boxlock ejector double with chopper lump barrels, level file-cut rib, light scroll and rosette engraving, scalloped frame.

MSR	$10,900						
	$10,900	$9,500	$8,400	$7,000	$5,750	$4,500	$3,400

P

Grading	100%	98%	95%	90%	80%	70%	60%

WESTLAKE - 12, 16, 20, 28 ga., or .410 bore, H&H sidelock action, moderate scroll engraving. Mfg. disc. 1989.

	$8,500	$7,500	$6,050	$5,300	$4,700	$4,200	$3,750

Last MSR was $8,400.

MONTE CARLO - 12, 16, 20, 28 ga., or .410 bore, best-quality H&H pattern sidelock ejector double with chopper lump barrels, Purdey style scroll and rosette engraving. Importation disc. 1990.

	$10,500	$9,250	$8,200	$7,100	$6,000	$5,000	$4,500

Last MSR was $11,400.

KING NUMBER 1 - 12, 16, 20, 28 ga., or .410 bore, best-quality H&H pattern sidelock ejector double with chopper lump barrels, level file-cut rib, very fine, full coverage scroll engraving with small floral bouquets, gold crest in forearm, gold crown in top lever, name in gold and finely figured wood.

MSR $20,900	$20,900	$17,750	$13,500	$10,050	$7,750	$6,600	$5,500

LUNIK - 12, 16, 20, 28 ga., or .410 bore, best-quality H&H pattern sidelock ejector double with lump (demi-bloc) barrels, level file-cut rib, Renaissance style large scroll engraving in relief, gold crown in top lever, gold name, and gold crest in forearm, finely figured wood.

MSR $21,900	$21,900	$18,750	$14,250	$11,250	$8,700	$6,950	$5,850

KING EXTRA - 12, 16, 20, 28 ga., or .410 bore, best-quality H&H pattern sidelock ejector double with chopper lump barrels, level file-cut rib, choice of either bulino game scene engraving or standard cameo game scene engraving with gold inlays, engraved and signed by a master engraver, exhibition grade wood.

MSR $25,900	$25,900	$22,000	$16,250	$12,000	$9,250	$7,250	$5,850

MONACO NUMBER 1 OR 2 - 12, 16, 20, 28 ga., or .410 bore, best-quality H&H pattern sidelock ejector double with lump (demi-bloc) barrels, level file-cut rib, Renaissance style large scroll engraving in relief, gold crown in top lever, gold name, and gold crest in forearm, finely figured wood.

MSR $27,000	$27,000	$22,350	$17,000	$12,500	$9,500	$7,500	$6,000

MONACO NUMBER 3 - next to top-of-the-line model.

MSR $29,000	$29,000	$24,000	$18,500	$13,250	$9,750	$7,750	$6,250

MONACO NUMBER 4 - top-of-the-line model with every refinement incorporated. Custom order only and extremely rare.

MSR $35,000	$35,000	$31,500	$25,250	$20,750	$16,000	$13,750	$11,000

PIRANHA

Previous trademark that was advertised circa 1996, but never manufactured by Recoilless Tech, Inc. located in Phoenix, AZ.

POLY TECHNOLOGIES, INC.

Previously distributed by PTK International, Inc. located in Atlanta, GA. Previously imported by Keng's Firearms Specialty, Inc., located in Riverdale, GA. Manufactured in China by Poly Technologies, Inc.

Poly Technologies commercial firearms are made to Chinese military specifications and have excellent quality control.

These models were banned from domestic importation due to 1989 Federal legislation.

RIFLES: SEMI-AUTO

POLY TECH AKS-762 - 7.62x39mm or .223 Rem. cal., 16¼ in. barrel, semi-auto version of the Chinese AKM (Type 56) paramilitary design rifle, 8.4 lbs., wood stock. Imported 1988-89.

	$995	$840	$750	$675	$600	$550	$500

Last MSR was $400.

Add $100 for side-fold plastic stock.

This model was also available with a downward folding stock at no extra charge.

Grading	100%	98%	95%	90%	80%	70%	60%

CHINESE SKS - 7.62x39mm cal., 20 9/20 in. barrel, full wood stock, machine steel parts to Chinese military specifications, 7.9 lbs. Imported 1988-89.

	$295	$270	$230	$200	$175	$140	$130

Last MSR was $200.

RUSSIAN AK-47/S (LEGEND) - 7.62x39mm cal., 16 3/8 in. barrel, semi-auto configuration of the original AK-47, fixed, side-folding, or under-folding stock, with or w/o spike bayonet, 8.2 lbs. Imported 1988-89.

	$1,150	$1,025	$925	$850	$775	$700	$650

Last MSR was $550.

Add $50 for folding stock.
The "S" suffix in this variation designates third model specifications.

✻ *National Match Legend* - utilizes match parts in fabrication.

	$1,300	$1,150	$1,025	$925	$850	$775	$700

RPK - 7.62x39mm cal. Disc.

	$1,300	$1,150	$1,025	$925	$850	$775	$700

U.S. M-14/S - .308 Win. cal., 22 in. barrel, forged receiver, patterned after the famous M-14, 9.2 lbs. Imported 1988-89.

	$675	$625	$550	$495	$420	$385	$360

Last MSR was $700.

POWELL, WILLIAM & SON (GUNMAKERS) LTD.

Please refer to the W Section for this trademark.

PRAIRIE GUN WORKS

Current manufacturer established in 1992, and located in Winnipeg, Manitoba, Canada. Dealer and consumer direct sales.

RIFLES: BOLT ACTION

Prairie Gun Works manufactures approx. 50-60 guns annually. They also sell their actions separately for $900-$1,800.

M-15 Ti ULTRA LITE - various cals., titanium (denoted by Ti model suffix) or re- machined Rem. 700 (disc.) short action, 20 in. barrel, Kevlar stock with glass bedding, matte metal finish, approx. 4½ - 6¼ lbs. New 1996.

MSR	$2,800	$2,650	$2,300	$2,000	$1,750	$1,750	$1,525	$1,375

Subtract $400 for benchrest or varmint single shot.
Add $100 for tactical stainless.
Add $200 for stainless steel (disc.).
Add $120 for Ultra Lite muzzle brake (disc.).
Add $200 for teflon black finish.
Add $100 for electroless nickel plating (disc.).
This model is also available in a hunter tactical configuration (Model M-15 Ti/HT) at no extra charge.

M-18 Ti ULTRA LIGHT - most long action cals. to .340 Wby. Mag., titanium or re-machined Rem. Model 700 long (disc.) action, 22 in. barrel, matte metal finish, approx. 4¾ lbs. New 1996.

MSR	$2,900	$2,725	$2,350	$2,025	$1,750	$1,750	$1,525	$1,375

Add $100 for stainless steel.
Add $200 for teflon black finish.
Add $120 for Ultra Lite muzzle brake (disc.).
Add $100 for electroless nickel plating (disc.).

P

Grading	100%	98%	95%	90%	80%	70%	60%

TAKEDOWN MODEL – various cals., New 2001.

	MSR	$4,000	$3,675	$3,200	$2,800	$2,400	$2,000	$1,650	$1,350

Add $1,500 per additional barrel assembly.

LRT-2 PGW/GIBBS - various large cals. starting with .378, designed for dangerous game, 4½ in. mag. box, one piece bolt, Sako type extraction, choice of Safari style or A-2 stock, 10-18 lbs. New 1999.

	MSR	$3,800	$3,500	$3,100	$2,800	$2,500	$2,250	$1,950	$1,750

Add $100 for A-2 stock.

LRT-3 PGW/GIBBS - .50 BMG cal., single shot action, Big Mac stock. New 1999.

	MSR	$4,200	$3,800	$3,500	$3,100	$2,800	$2,500	$2,250	$1,950

PRANDELLI-GASPERINI

Previous manufacturer located in Brescia, Italy. Previously imported by Richland Arms located in Blissfield, MI.

Prandelli-Gasperini made both O/U and SxS shotguns in either sidelock or boxlock. Currently, older boxlock models start at approx. $550 (assuming 80% or better original condition). Sidelock models in similar condition usually start at $1,450, depending on gauge, embellishments, and condition.

Approx. 250 specimens of this trademark were imported during Richland Arms importation.

PRECISION SMALL ARMS, INC. ("PSA")

Current manufacturer esstablished in 1979, and made under F.N. license in Irvine, CA. Previously manufactured in Charlottesville, VA until 1999. Dealer and distributor sales.

PISTOLS: SEMI-AUTO

PSP-25 PISTOL - .25 ACP, single action, Baby Browning design mfg. in the U.S., 2 1/8 in. barrel, 6 shot mag., checkered black polymer grips, all steel construction with choice of polished blue (new 1999), black oxide (disc. 1999), brushed satin white nickel (Nouveau satin), or highly polished white nickel finish (Nouveau mirror), dual safety system, 7¼-9½ oz. New 1989.

	MSR	$269	$230	$210	$185	$170	$155	$140	$130

Add $40 for highly polished white nickel finish.

This pistol is mfg. in the U.S. under license from Fabrique Nationale.

✷ PSP-25 Stainless Steel - features stainless steel construction. Mfg. 1996 only.

			$285	$230	$195				

Last MSR was $327.

✷ PSP-25 Featherweight - features aircraft aluminum frame with high polish nickel slide and mag., gold-plated trigger, smooth pearlescent polymer grips. New 1996.

	MSR	$405	$375	$325	$275	$225	$195	$175	$160

✷ PSP-25 Diplomat - features blue, high polish frame and slide, 24 Kt. gold plated external components, ivory grips. New 1999.

	MSR	$625	$575	$525	$450	$400	$350	$295	$250

✷ PSP-25 Montreux - high polish 24 Kt. gold plated frame, slide, and external components, ivory grips. New 1999.

	MSR	$692	$625	$575	$525	$450	$400	$350	$275

✷ PSP-25 Presidential - features highly polished 24 Kt. gold plated slide, frame, magazine, and trigger, Dendrite ivory grips. Disc. 1999.

			$600	$475	$375				

Last MSR was $725.

✷ PSP-25 Renaissance - features chrome receiver with full coverage scroll engraving. New 1996.

	MSR	$1,115	$995	$775	$525				

Grading	100%	98%	95%	90%	80%	70%	60%

✱ **PSP-25 Imperiale** - features hand inlaid 24 Kt. gold scroll pattern on frame and slide by Angelo Bee, black oxide finish, ivory grips. Limited mfg.

MSR	**$3,600**		**$3,300**	**$2,600**	**$2,100**		

✱ **PSP Signature Editions** - similar to Imperiale, except has "Michael B. Kassnar" signature on left slide top in gold. Mfg. 1989-91.

		$325	$295	$260	$230	$200	$175	$160

Last MSR was $385.

There were also two Limited Signature Editions (less than 10 mfg.) which retailed for $1,458 and approx. $2,150.

PREMIER

Previous trademark manufactured in Italy and Spain by various companies.

SHOTGUNS: SxS

Note: Premier is a trade name for guns that have been produced in both Spain and Italy for various importers.

REGENT MODEL - 12, 16, 20, 28 ga., or .410 bore, 26, 28, or 30 in. barrels, various chokes, checkered pistol grip stock and beavertail forearm. Mfg. 1955-disc.

	$275	$250	$220	$195	$140	$110	$100

REGENT MAGNUM EXPRESS - 12 ga., 3 in. chambers only, 30 in. full barrel, recoil pad. Mfg. 1957-disc.

	$305	$275	$250	$220	$165	$140	$110

REGENT 10 GAUGE MAGNUM - similar to 12 ga. Mag., but 10 ga., 3½ in. chamber, 32 in. full and full barrel. Mfg. 1975-disc.

	$330	$305	$275	$250	$195	$165	$140

BRUSH KING - 12 or 20 ga., 22 in. imp. cyl. and mod. barrels, straight grip stock. Mfg. 1959- disc.

	$275	$250	$220	$195	$140	$110	$100

MONARCH SUPREME GRADE - 12 or 20 ga., 26 or 28 in. barrels, various chokes, boxlock, auto ejectors, select stock. Mfg. 1959-disc.

	$440	$385	$360	$330	$275	$250	$200

PRESENTATION CUSTOM GRADE - custom made, gold and silver game scene. Mfg. 1959-disc.

	$1,100	$990	$880	$825	$715	$605	$495

AMBASSADOR MODEL - 12, 16, 20 ga., or .410 bore, 26 or 28 in. barrels, mod. and full choke, checkered pistol grip stock. Mfg. 1957-disc.

	$385	$360	$330	$305	$250	$220	$195

PRINZ

Previous manufacturer of bolt action rifles, single shot rifles, and combination guns. Previously imported and distributed by Helmut Hofmann Inc. located in Placitas, NM.

RIFLES

GRADE 1 BOLT ACTION - .243 Win., .30-06, .308 Win., .300 Win. Mag., or 7mm Rem. Mag. cal., single or double set trigger(s), oil finished walnut stock.

	$495	$440	$385	$360	$330	$275	$250

✱ **Grade 1 Carbine** - similar to Grade 1 except has carbine barrel.

	$570	$495	$435	$390	$360	$330	$275

GRADE 2 BOLT ACTION - similar to Grade 1 except has rosewood forend cap.

	$545	$485	$425	$385	$360	$330	$275

Grading	100%	98%	95%	90%	80%	70%	60%

TIP-UP RIFLE - available in 8 cals. between .222 Rem. and .30-06, high quality and limited mfg. Importation began 1989.

	$2,175	$1,900	$1,675	$1,375	$1,100	$950	$775

PRINCESS MODEL 85 - combination gun available in 12 ga. (2¾ in. chamber) and choice of 8 cals. between .222 Rem. and .30-06.

	$1,450	$1,275	$1,100	$925	$800	$775	$650

This model came standard with a leather case.

PROFESSIONAL ORDNANCE INC.

Current manufacturer located in Lake Havasu City, AZ since 1998. Previously manufactured in Ontario, CA circa 1996-1997. Distributor sales only.

PISTOLS: SEMI-AUTO

CARBON-15 TYPE 20 - .223 Rem. cal., Stoner type operating system with recoil reducing buffer assembly, carbon fiber upper and lower receiver, hard chromed bolt carrier, 7¼ in. unfluted stainless steel barrel with ghost ring sights, 30 shot mag. (supplies limited), also accepts AR-15 type mags., 40 oz. Mfg. 1999-2000.

	$800	$725	$650	$575	$525	$475	$425

Last MSR was $1,500.

CARBON-15 TYPE 21 - .223 Rem cal., ultra lightweight carbon fiber upper and lower receivers, 7¼ in. "Profile" stainless steel barrel, quick detachable muzzle compensator, ghost ring sights, 10 shot mag., also accepts AR-15 type mags., Stoner type operating sytem, tool steel bolt, extractor and carrier, 40 oz. New 2001.

MSR	$899	$825	$750	$675	$600	$550	$500	$450

CARBON-15 TYPE 97 - similar to Carbon 15 Type 20, except has fluted barrel and quick detachable compensator, 46 oz. New 1996.

MSR	$964	$875	$825	$750	$650	$575	$500	$450

RIFLES: SEMI-AUTO

CARBON-15 TYPE 20 - .223 Rem. cal., same operating system as the Carbon-15 pistol, 16 in. unfluted stainless steel barrel, carbon fiber buttstock and forearm, includes mil spec optics mounting base, 3.9 lbs. Mfg. 1998-2000.

	$850	$795	$725	$650	$550	$475	$425

Last MSR was $1,550.

CARBON-15 TYPE 21 - .223 Rem. cal., ultra light weight carbon fiber upper and lower receivers, 16 in. "Profile" stainless steel barrel, quick detachable muzzle compensator, Stoner type operating system, tool steel bolt, extractor and carrier, optics mounting base, quick detachable stock, 10 shot mag., also accepts AR-15 type mags., 3.9 lbs. New 2001.

MSR	$988	$895	$840	$765	$665	$585	$500	$450

CARBON-15 TYPE 97/97S - .223 Rem. cal., ultra lighweight carbon fiber upper and lower receivers, Stoner type operating system, hard chromed tool steel bolt, extractor and carrier, 16 in. fluted stainless steel barrel, quick detachable muzzle compensator, optics mounting base, quick detachable stock, 30 shot mag. (limited quantities), also accepts AR-15 type mags., 3.9 lbs. 2001.

MSR	$1,120	$995	$900	$825	$750	$675	$600	$550

Add $165 for Model 97S (includes Picatinny rail and "Scout" extension, double walled heat shield foregrip, ambidextrous safety, and multi-carry silent sling).

Grading	100%	98%	95%	90%	80%	70%	60%

PUMA RIFLES

Current trademark of rifles imported by Legacy Sports International, located in Alexandria, VA.

RIFLES: LEVER ACTION

MODEL 92 - 357 Mag./.38 Spl., .44 Mag., .45 LC, or .454 Casull (new 2002, carbine only) cal., 20 in. round or 24 in. octagon barrel, choice of blue, black/brass, case colored, or stainless steel receiver, unchecked walnut stock and forearm. Importation began 2001.

* *Round Barrel Carbine* - blue, black brass, or stainless steel finish, 20 in. barrel.

MSR	$407		$350	$295	$260	$225	$200	$175	$155

Add $55 for stainless steel construction.
Add $7 for black brass (.357 Mag./.38 Spl. or .45 LC cal. only).

* *Octagon Barrel Rifle* - choice of blue/case colored, stainless steel, or stainless steel/brass (not available in .44 Mag. cal.) finish.

MSR	$500		$395	$350	$300	$265	$235	$200	$180

Add $27 for .357 Mag. or .45 LC cal.
Add $7 for blue/case colored finish.
Add $29 for BHS/SR (new 2002).
Add $54 for stainless steel construction.
Add $61 for stainless steel/brass construction.

PURDEY, JAMES & SONS, LTD.

Current manufacturer established in 1814, and located in **London, England**. Annual production is approximately 75 guns.

Purdey guns have long been regarded as among the finest in the world. They have typically been made to customer specifications, and as such, should be appraised individually for purposes of evaluation. Values vary with gauge, barrel length, chamber length and age. Listed are the modern models and approximate values for reference purposes.

Prices indicated are for manufacturer's suggested retail and 100% condition factors are listed in English pounds. All new prices do not include VAT. Values for used guns in 98%-60% condition factors are priced in U.S. dollars.

RIFLES: CUSTOM ORDER & OLDER PRODUCTION

New rifle prices represent the base price with standard fine scroll and bouquet engraving.

PURDEY DOUBLE RIFLE - various English Nitro Express cals., 25½ in. barrels, folding leaf sight, checkered pistol grip stock, recoil pad, sidelock, auto ejectors. Mfg. pre-WWII and post-war.

* *Smaller calibers* - .300 H&H or .375 H&H cal.

MSR	£69,500		£69,500	$69,000	$58,000	$45,000	$33,750	$26,500	$21,500

* *Large calibers*

  ◇.416 Rigby - .500 NE.

MSR	£76,500		£76,500	$82,500	$70,000	$50,000	$38,750	$30,250	$26,500

  ◇577 NE & .600 NE.

MSR	£84,700		£84,700	$96,500	$83,750	$67,000	$49,000	$37,500	$30,250

The values represent base price only. Since each Purdey is basically a special order, new gun pricing is calculated per individual customer work order.

MAGAZINE RIFLE - cals. up to .375 H&H are built on Mauser action, 24 in. barrel, folding leaf sight, checkered best quality walnut pistol grip stock, indivdually built per customer specifications.

MSR	£15,750		£15,750	$18,250	$14,750	$12,000	$9,750	$8,500	$7,000

P

Grading	100%	98%	95%	90%	80%	70%	60%

MAGNUM MAGAZINE RIFLE - .375 H&H, .416/450, and .500 cal., built on Purdey's dedicated Magnum action, individually built per customer's specifications.

	MSR £16,950	£16,950	$20,000	$16,750	$13,750	$11,250	$9,650	$8,500

SHOTGUNS: CUSTOM ORDER & OLDER PRODUCTION

New shotgun prices represent the base price with standard fine scroll and bouquet engraving.

BEST QUALITY GAME GUN SxS - 10, 12, 16, 20, 28 ga., or .410 bore, best quality sidelock action. 26-30 in. barrels, any choke and style of rib, checkered straight or pistol grip stock. Mfg. 1880-present, auto ejector gun, best quality only.

	MSR £40,100	£40,100	$43,000	$35,000	$30,500	$22,000	$17,500	$14,250

Add £2,300 for 28 ga. or .410 bore on new mfg.
Add £9,400-£9,600 for extra set of barrels depending on gauge.
10 ga. is POR.

* *Older mfg.*

		100%	98%	95%	90%	80%	70%	60%
Game gun		$23,450	$19,750	$16,750	$13,000	$10,750	$9,250	$7,950
Heavy Duck gun		$20,500	$17,000	$14,000	$11,000	$9,500	$8,750	$7,500

Add 50% for 20 ga.
Add 35%-50% for 28 ga. or .410 bore, depending on condition.
Subtract 10%-15% if not cased with accessories.
Add $1,000 for SST.

O/U GUN - 12, 16, 20, 28 ga., or .410 bore best quality sidelock action. 26-30 in. barrels, any choke, auto ejectors, ST, checkered straight or pistol grip stock. Since WWII, Purdey has taken over the Woodward Company, and later guns have the Woodward O/U action. Very few early actions.

	MSR £51,100	£51,100	$53,250	$42,000	$30,000	$25,000	$21,000	$18,500

Add £2,850 for 28 ga. or £6,300 for .410 bore.
Add £13,925 for extra set of barrels.

* *Older mfg.*

		$37,500	$33,000	$30,000	$26,000	$21,500	$17,750	$15,000

Add $3,000 for Woodward action.
Add 25% for 20 ga.
Add 60%+ for 28 ga.
Add 10% for SST.

SINGLE BARREL TRAP GUN - 12 ga. Purdey action only, similar to O/U specifications. Mfg. prior to WWII.

		$11,250	$10,000	$8,750	$7,900	$7,200	$6,750	$5,950

P

Q Section

QFI (QUALITY FIREARMS INC.)
Previous manufacturer located in Opa Locka, FL circa December 1990-1992.

Grading	100%	98%	95%	90%	80%	70%	60%

PISTOLS: SEMI-AUTO

MODEL LA380 - .380 ACP cal., single action, 6-shot, magazine disconnect, hammer, trigger, and firing pin block safety, 3¼ in. barrel, blue or chrome finish. Mfg. 1991-1992.

	100%	98%	95%	90%	80%	70%	60%
	$125	$100	$90	$80	$70	$60	$55

Last MSR was $147.

Add $23 for chrome finish.

❋ *Model LA380SS* - stainless steel variation of the Model LA380. Mfg. 1992 only.

	100%	98%	95%
	$195	$165	$135

Last MSR was $220.

MODEL SA 25 - .25 ACP cal., single action, 2½ in. barrel, 6-shot, includes inertial firing pin, external exposed hammer with half cock, and trigger blocking thumb safety, blue, Dynachrome, or blue/gold finish, smooth walnut grips. Mfg. 1991 only.

	100%	98%	95%	90%	80%	70%	60%
	$55	$45	$40	$35	$30	$25	$25

Last MSR was $55.

Add $50 for blue/gold finish.
Add $10 for chrome finish with pearlite plastic grips.

TIGRESS MODEL - .25 ACP or .380 ACP cal., single action, 2½ (.25 ACP) or 3¼ (.380 ACP) in. barrel, blue frame with gold-plated slide, 6-shot with finger extension on mag., white polymer grips with a red rose scrimshawed on both sides, designed for women, supplied with zippered gold pouch, 14 or 25 oz. Mfg. 1991 only.

	100%	98%	95%	90%	80%	70%	60%
	$130	$100	$90	$80	$70	$60	$55

Last MSR was $155.

Add $85 for .380 ACP cal.

REVOLVERS: DOUBLE ACTION

All revolvers under this heading are 6-shot.

RP SERIES STANDARD REVOLVER - .22 LR, .22 Mag., .32 S&W Long, .32 H&R Mag or .38 Spl. cal., 2 or 4 in. barrel, blue or chrome finish, fixed sights, hammer block safety, without ejector assembly, composition grips. Mfg. in U.S. 1990-disc.

	100%	98%	95%	90%	80%	70%	60%
	$85	$70	$65	$60	$55	$50	$45

Last MSR was $105.

Add $15-20 for chrome finish.
Add approx. $5 for 4 in. barrel.

MODEL SO 38 - .38 Spl. cal., swing out cylinder, 6-shot, 2 in. SR or 4 in. VR barrel, hammer block safety, composition grips. Mfg. 1991 only.

	100%	98%	95%	90%	80%	70%	60%
	$175	$135	$115	$95	$80	$75	$65

Last MSR was $175.

Q

Grading	100%	98%	95%	90%	80%	70%	60%

REVOLVERS: SINGLE ACTION

SAA WESTERN RANGER - .22 LR cal., 6-shot, 3, 4 (disc. 1991), 4¾ (new 1992), 6 (disc. 1991), 6½ (new 1992), 7 (disc. 1991), or 9 in. barrel, blue finish with gold accenting, walnut grips. Mfg. 1991-1992.

	$85	$70	$65	$60	$55	$50	$45

Last MSR was $105.

Add approx. $5 for 7 (disc.) or $7 for 9 in. barrel.
Add approx. $15-$35 for .22 Mag. extra cylinder (combo).

SAA PLAINS RIDER - similar to Western Ranger, except has black composition grips and no gold accenting. Mfg. 1991-1992.

	$80	$65	$55	$50	$45	$40	$35

Last MSR was $100.

Add $11 for 9 in. barrel.
Add approx. $26 for .22 Mag. extra cylinder (combo).

SAA HORSEMAN SERIES - .357 Mag., .44 Mag., or .45 LC cal., 6-shot, 6½ or 7½ in. barrel, color case hardened or blue (Dark Horseman only) finish, walnut or black composition grips, hammer block safety. Mfg. 1991 only.

	$250	$220	$190	$170	$150	$130	$115

Last MSR was $250.

The Dark Horseman had an extended grip frame with black composition grips and an adj. rear sight.

QUACKENBUSH, H.M.

Previous rifle manufacturer circa 1886-1922, and located in Herkimer, NY. Quackenbush also manufactured airguns 1871-1943.

For more information on Quackenbush airguns, including the combination rimfire/airgun, please refer to the 2nd Ed. *Blue Book of Airguns*, by Dr. Robert Beeman & John Allen (now online also).

RIFLES: .22 CAL., RIMFIRE

Only one breech mechanism was used on all H.M. Quackenbush .22 cal. rimfire rifles, the company's only rifle configuration. These models were supplied in several different boxes, and often came with a cleaning rod. These and other accessories will significantly add to the value of the firearms prices listed. No serial numbers were applied to Quackenbush guns. Many variations of these models are encountered, which can also add premiums to the values listed. Quackenbush also manufactured heavy metal targets for these rifles 1884-1931.

SAFETY MODEL - single shot, swinging breech, walnut stock. Mfg. 1886-1922.

	$600	$500	$425	$375	$350	$325	$300

Add 10% for heavy cast iron buttplate, original factory blue finish, optional Town & Country combination rear and front sights, or for barrel and optional sights where rear sight is approx. 1 in. forward of the breech end of the barrel.

JUNIOR SAFETY MODEL - similar to Safety Model, except smaller and has tubular receiver, wire stocked, swinging breech. Mfg. 1890-1920.

	$800	$700	$600	$500	$400	$375	$350

Add 10% for original factory blue finish.

BYCYCLE MODEL - similar to Safety Model, except smaller and has a wire pistol grip. Mfg. 1896-1919.

	$1,800	$1,700	$1,400	$1,200	$1,000	$800	$600

Add 10% for original factory blue finish.

BYCYCLE MODEL W/STOCK - single shot, wire grip with retractable shoulder stock, fixed rear

Grading	100%	98%	95%	90%	80%	70%	60%

sight, swinging breech. Mfg. 1896-1919.

| | $1,000 | $900 | $800 | $700 | $600 | $500 | $400 |

Add 10% for original factory blue finish.

QUAIL UNLIMITED, INC.

Current national conservation organization with national headquarters located in Edgefield, SC.

Although Quail Unlimited, Inc. is not a manufacturer or importer, this organization has been responsible for many special and limited editions that are listed below with quantities, but without secondary market prices, since they may vary greatly from region to region. Some of the models (and current values) may be listed under manufacturer listings in this text. Because of the relatively low quantities involved with these special editions, most of the models listed below have premiums currently being asked over issue prices - the amount will vary with the region and acceptance by Quail Unlimited members. Quail Unlimited designated their special editions as follows: 1986 - Grand Slam I - Bobwhite Edition, 1987 - Grand Slam II - California Edition, 1988 - Grand Slam III - Gambel Edition, 1989 - Grand Slam IV - Mountain Quail Edition, 1990 - Grand Slam V - Scaled Quail Edition, 1992 - Gun Dog I - Pointer Edition, 1993 - Gun Dog II - Setter Edition, 1994 - Gun Dog III - Brittany Edition, 1995 - Gun Dog IV - German Shorthair Edition, 1996 - Gun Dog V - Belgian Edition. 1994 - Golden Covey I - Full Covey Edition, 1995 - Golden Covey II - Bobwhite Edition, 1997 - Upland I - Ruffed Grouse Edition.

Manufacturer	Model	Quantity	Year	Issue Price
Browning	Superposed 20 ga.	100	1986	$2,850
Winchester	Model 101 28 ga.	100	1987	$2,195
Browning	Sweet 16 16 ga.	100	1988	$1,895
Winchester	Model 23 12 ga.	100	1989	$2,885
Browning	Citori Lightning .410 bore	100	1990	$2,295
Add $500 to issue price for silver finish (standard finish was nickel).				
Add $700 to issue price for gold finish (standard finish was nickel).				
Browning	Model A-5 20 ga.	100	1992	$1,795
Browning	Citori Lightning 28 ga.	100	1993	$2,395
Browning	Model A-5 20 ga.	100	1993	$1,795
Browning	Model A-5 20 ga.	100	1994	$1,895
Browning	Citori Lightning .410 bore	100	1994	$2,395
Browning	Model A-5 20 ga.	100	1995	$1,895
Belgian Browning	Model A-5 20 ga. 3 in. GRIII	75	1996 (15th Anniv.)	$2,195
Belgian Browning	Model A-5 20 ga. 3 in. GRV	25	1996 (15th Anniv.)	$3,995
Rizzini	SxS 20 ga.	100	1996 (15th Anniv.)	$2,850
Rizzini	SxS 20 ga. (Gold)	15	1996 (15th Anniv.)	$4,250
Browning	Citori Superlight 20 ga.	100	1997	$2,495
Winchester	Model 12 20 ga.	100	1997	$995
Winchester	Model 12 20 ga.Chevy/QU Exclusive	400	1997	$995
Browning	Citori Superlight 28 ga.	100	1998	$2,495
Browning	Model A-5 Chevrolet	400	1998	$1,495
Franchi	620 VS 20 ga.	100	1999	$1,195
Browning	Citori Upland 12 ga.	100	1999	$2,495
Browning	Citori Superlight 20 ga.	100	2000	$2,495
Sturm Ruger	Red Label 28 ga. Chevrolet	400	2000	$1,995
Franchi	Feniche 28 ga. 20th Anniversary	125	2000	$1,195
Ithaca Gun	Model 37 16 ga. 20th Anniversary	200	2000	$995
Franchi	620 VS 20 ga. Chevrolet	400	2001	$1,395
Browning	Citori Superlight .410 bore	100	2001	$2,495

Q

Manufacturer	Model	Quantity	Year	Issue Price
Franchi	Feniche 28 ga. Encore	100	2001	$1,295
Browning	Triton Upland Special 20 ga.	50	2002	$1,695
Browning	Citori Feather 20 ga.	100	2002	$2,595

QUALITY ARMS, INC.

Current importer and sales agent located in Houston, TX.

Quality Arms currently imports and distributes Arrieta shotguns. They also carry Beretta, Merkel, and Perazzi shotguns, and many fine high quality pre-owned guns. Quality Arms also imports European gun cases and shooting accessories. Please contact them directly for pricing and availability on these items.

QUALITY PARTS CO./BUSHMASTER

Quality Parts Co. is a division of Bushmaster Firearms, Inc. located in Windham, ME that manufactures AR-15 type paramilitary rifles and various components and accessories for them. Distributor and dealer sales. Please refer to the Bushmaster section in this text for model listings and values.

Q is for quality. And certainly, nobody understands quality better than Feinwerkbau's Reiner Altenburger, pictured with the company's new underhammer black powder pistol. Feinwerkbau in Deutsche literally means the "House of Fine Work". Feinwerkbau also makes some of the world's finest air rifles and pistols (see the 2nd Ed. Blue Book of Airguns by Dr. Robert Beeman & John Allen and the 2nd Ed. Blue Book of Modern Black Powder Values by Dennis Adler).

R Section

RAF

Previous manufacturer of shotguns and rifles located in St. Etienne, France circa 1994-96.

RAF manufactured superposed rifles, shotguns, combination guns, and semi-auto rimfire rifles.

RND MANUFACTURING

Current manufacturer located in Longmont, CO. Previously distributed by Mesa Sportsmen's Association, L.L.C. located in Delta, CO. Dealer or consumer direct sales.

Grading	100%	98%	95%	90%	80%	70%	60%

RIFLES: SEMI-AUTO

THE EDGE SERIES - .223 Rem. (RND 400), .308 Win. (RND 800) or .338 Lapua Mag. (RND 2000, new 1999) cal., patterned after the AR-15, CNC machined, 18, 20, or 24 in. barrel, choice of synthetic (Grade I), built to individual custom order, hand-made laminated thumbhole (Grade II, disc. 1998), or custom laminated thumbhole with fluted barrel (Grade III, disc. 1998) stock, vented aluminum shroud, approx. 11 1/2-16 lbs., custom order only, values represent base model. New 1996.

	MSR	$2,395		$2,275	$2,075	$1,775	$1,575	$1,375	$1,200	$1,075

Add $355 for Grade II.
Add $605 for Grade III or .308 Win. cal.
Add $1,855 for .338 Lapua Mag. cal.

R.F.M.

Current shotgun manufacturer established in 1956, and located in Brescia, Italy. No current U.S. importation.

R.F.M. manufactures a complete line of both O/U and SxS shotguns, in many configurations. Please contact the factory directly for current information and domestic pricing (see Trademark Index).

R.G. INDUSTRIES

Previous importer located in Miami, FL. Operations ceased in January of 1986.

HANDGUNS

R.G. Industries manufactured and imported plain utilitarian revolvers and semi- auto pistols. Unfortunately, because of a product liability situation, R.G. Industries was litigated out of business during 1986. Whereas their models represent good values, they are not collectible, and a generalized listing is provided.

RG 14 S, RG 23, RG 31

	$95	$80	$70	$60	$55	$50	$45

RG 40, RG 74, & HIGHNOON S.A.

	$125	$115	$95	$80	$70	$60	$55

RG 26 SEMI-AUTO - .25 ACP cal., 6 shot mag., 2¼ in. barrel, plastic grips, single action, 12 oz.

	$65	$55	$50	$40	$35	$30	$25

Last MSR was $66.

RPB INDUSTRIES

Current company located in Avondale, GA. RPB Industries guns are made by Masterpiece Arms. Consumer and dealer sales.

R

Grading	100%	98%	95%	90%	80%	70%	60%

CARBINES: SEMI-AUTO

RPB CARBINE - .45 ACP cal., closed bolt blowback action, 16¼ in. barrel, fixed skeletonized stock and forearm pistol grip, accepts M-3 mags., black finish, 9½ lbs. New 2000.

No MSR	$450	$375	$325	$285	$260	$235	$210

Add $75 for Deluxe Model with EZ cocker and installed scope mount.

RPM

Current manufacturer located in Tuscon, AZ. Direct sales only.

PISTOLS: SINGLE SHOT

XL PISTOL - many cals. available, tip-up action, 8, 10¾, 12, or 14 in. barrel, positive thumb safety, steel frame, cocking indicator, right or left-hand action. Disc.

$785	$675	$600	$550	$500	$450	$395

Last MSR was $858.

XL HUNTER - over 40 cals., stainless steel frame, 5 1/16 in. under-lug, 12 or 14 in. Douglas barrel, ISGW rear and Patridge or hooded front sight, with (became standard 2000) or w/o external positive extractor. New 1995.

MSR	$1,592	$1,425	$1,050	$775

Add $160 for muzzle brake.
Add $50 for left-hand action.
Add $407-$547 per extra barrel, depending on length.

RWS

Current trademark of Dynamit Nobel GmbH which has been manufacturing firearms in Nurenberg Stadeln and Troisdorf, Germany since 1865. RWS firearms were imported until 1995 by Dynamit Nobel of America, Inc. located in Closter, NJ. Other trademarks (including Rottweil) by Dynamit Nobel can be located under individual heading names in this text.

For more information and current pricing on both new and used RWS airguns produced by Dianawerk, Mayer, and Grammelspacher, please refer to the Blue Book of Modern Airguns by Dr. Robert Beeman & John Allen (now online also).

RIFLES: BOLT ACTION, TARGET

MODEL 820 L - .22 LR cal. only, 24 (disc.) or 26 in. barrel, no. 100 aperture sight, oil polished stock for 3 position match, stippled pistol grip and forearm, recoil pad, adj. trigger, 10.6 lbs. Disc. 1994.

$1,275	$1,000	$850	$700	$575	$475	$400

Last MSR was $1,500.

Previous to 1986 this model was designated the 820 S and was supplied with a no. 75 aperture rear sight.

❋ Model 820 S - with Model 82 aperture sight.

$1,100	$895	$795	$650	$560	$480	$420

Last MSR was $995.

MODEL 820 F MATCH - similar to Model 820 L, except has heavy match barrel, 15.4 lbs. Disc. 1994.

$1,750	$1,400	$1,275	$1,000	$850	$700	$575

Last MSR was $2,000.

❋ Model 820 SF - with Model 820 L aperture sight. Disc.

$1,125	$900	$795	$650	$560	$480	$420

Last MSR was $1,010.

Grading	100%	98%	95%	90%	80%	70%	60%

MODEL 820 K - .22 LR cal. only, made for running boar competition, 24 in. barrel, stock similar to Model 820 SF, no sights, 9½ lbs. without barrel weight or scope. Importation disc. 1986.

	100%	98%	95%	90%	80%	70%	60%
	$900	$775	$695	$615	$540	$470	$420

Last MSR was $870.

RADOM

Currently manufactured by Z.M. Lucznik (Radom Factory) in Radom, Poland. Currently imported by Dalvar of USA, located in Henderson, NV. Previously located in Richardson, TX. 1931-1939 production also by the Polish Arsenal, located in Radom, Poland.

REVOLVERS

RADOM REVOLVER - Nagant design, dated 1931-1936.

	100%	98%	95%	90%	80%	70%	60%
	$1,100	$850	$700	$550	$400	$300	$200

PISTOLS: SEMI-AUTO, 1935-1939 PRODUCTION

P-35 AUTOMATIC - 9mm Para. cal., 8 shot, 4¾ in. barrel, blue, fixed sights, plastic grips. Mfg. 1935-WWII.

* *Polish Eagle* - dated 1936, 1937 (scarcest date), 1938, or 1939.

	100%	98%	95%	90%	80%	70%	60%
	$2,350	$1,600	$1,000	$700	$500	$400	$300

Add 15% for 1937 mfg.
Add 10% for 1936 mfg.

* *Polish Eagle Nazi Capture*

	100%	98%	95%	90%	80%	70%	60%
	N/A	$1,825	$1,200	$900	$700	$600	$500

Beware of fakes!

* *Nazi Type I Slotted*

	100%	98%	95%	90%	80%	70%	60%
	$900	$700	$450	$295	$230	$180	$150

* *Nazi Type II No Slot w/Takedown Lever*

	100%	98%	95%	90%	80%	70%	60%
	$550	$375	$275	$225	$200	$185	$150

* *Nazi Type III No Slot, No Takedown Lever*

	100%	98%	95%	90%	80%	70%	60%
	$375	$300	$240	$200	$180	$160	$140

* *Nazi Type III* - parkerized with wood grips, small parts blue.

	100%	98%	95%	90%	80%	70%	60%
	$1,000	$800	$600	$400	$300	$200	$175

Note: Certain Radoms with German acceptance marks will bring a premium.

PISTOLS: SEMI-AUTO, CURRENT PRODUCTION

VIS P-35 - 9mm Para. cal., patterned after the 1937 P-35, large Polish eagle stamped on left side of slide, with or w/o slotted rear grip strap for shoulder stock, 4½ in. barrel, 36 oz. Limited mfg. 1997 only.

	100%	98%	95%	90%	80%	70%	60%
	$2,600	$1,425	$850	$625	$450	$375	$300

Last MSR was $2,999.

R

VANAD P-83 - 9x18mm Makarov cal., 8 shot mag., available in Standard Military Issue or Special Eagle Limited Edition, loaded chamber indicator, firing pin block safety, steel receiver with external hammer, 3½ in. barrel, drift adj. target sights, checkered composition grips, 26 oz. Importation began 1994 (Standard Military Issue) or 1997.

MSR	$390						
		$350	$290	$265	$235	$210	$190	$170

Add $46 for Standard Military Issue.

Grading	100%	98%	95%	90%	80%	70%	60%

MAG 95 - 9mm Para. cal., single or double action with firing pin block, external hammer, ambidextrous hammer drop safety, 4½ in. barrel, 37 oz. Limited importation 1997 only.

| | | $650 | $550 | $450 | $400 | $350 | $300 | $275 |

Last MSR was $749.

RAM-LINE, INC.

Previous manufacturer located in Grand Junction, CO until 1995.

In addition to the Ram-Tech pistol, Ram-Line, Inc. also manufactured a complete line of synthetic and wood stocks for a variety of firearms. Ram-Line continues to manufacture a complete line of magazines for most popular pistols and rifles.

PISTOLS: SEMI-AUTO

EXACTOR PISTOL - .22 LR cal., single action, aircraft alloy receiver with 5½ in. polymer VR barrel and steel liner, unique two-motion safety featuring blocks on hammer, trigger, and sear, 15 shot mag., matte finish, easy disassembly, injected molded grip, fixed sight, 20.3 oz., supplied with case. Mfg. 1990-93.

| $195 | $165 | $135 |

Last MSR was $225.

✱ *Target Exactor* - similar to above, except has 7½ in. barrel, 23 oz. Disc. 1993.

| $265 | $230 | $195 |

Last MSR was $300.

RAM-TECH PISTOL - similar to Exactor pistol, except 4½ in. barrel w/o VR. Mfg. 1994-95.

| $175 | $145 | $125 |

Last MSR was $200.

RAMO DEFENSE SYSTEMS

Current rifle manufacturer established in 1999 and located in Nashville, TN. Dealer direct sales.

RIFLES: BOLT ACTION

TACTICAL .308 - .308 Win. cal., Rem. M-700 long action, match grade stainless steel barrel, skeletonized black synthetic stock with cheekpad, matte black metal finish, 4 shot mag., 16 lbs. New 1999.

| MSR | $2,495 | | $2,495 | $2,100 | $1,850 | $1,600 | $1,400 | $1,200 | $995 |

M91/M91A2 - .308 Win. or .300 Win. Mag. cal., Rem. M-700 long action, black Kevlar and fiberglass stock, matte black metal finish, 4 shot mag., 14 lbs. New 1999.

| MSR | $2,695 | | $2,695 | $2,250 | $1,950 | $1,675 | $1,475 | $1,250 | $995 |

Add $200 for .300 Win. Mag. cal.

M600 SINGLE SHOT - .50 BMG cal., single shot, twin tube skeletonized stock with pistol grip and cheekpiece, 32 in. barrel with fins at breech and muzzle brake, 23 lbs. New 1999.

| MSR | $4,195 | | $4,195 | $3,700 | $3,200 | $2,750 | $2,250 | $1,950 | $1,675 |

M650 REPEATER - .50 BMG cal., repeater action with 6 shot detachable rotary mag., stock and barrel (30 in.) similar to M600, approx. 30 lbs. New 1999.

| MSR | $6,395 | | $6,395 | $5,750 | $5,150 | $4,500 | $3,750 | $3,000 | $2,250 |

RANDALL FIREARMS COMPANY

Previously manufactured in Sun Valley, CA. Manufactured between June 7, 1983 and December 15, 1984 - final plant closing was June 15, 1985.

Before manufacturing ceased in May of 1985, 24 models with 12 variations in 3 different calibers had been produced. In some instances, production on certain models was very limited and premiums for these low volume niches are starting to develop.

Between June of 1983 and May of 1984, 9,968 handguns were manufactured with 75% of all 9mm Para. pistols being exported to Europe, and 35% of 9mm Para. production employing a 10 groove barrel. Models manufactured after 1984 came equipped with an extended slide stop, long trigger and beavertail grip safety. Production ser. numbers started at 02000 for right hand models and 02100 for left hand models. All but the first 200 (approx.) serial numbers started with "RF" and ended with "C" or "W". A few rare mis-marks are in circulation. Total mfg. for all models and variations was 9,968. Randall prototype serialization starts with a "T" - less than 45 were manufactured and these specimens command up to a 50% premium. In addition, 78 serial numbers under 2,000 were manufactured by special order.

For a Randall letter of authenticity, please refer to the Randall Firearms listing in the Trademark Index.

Models listed are generally described with values per specific variations listed afterward.

PISTOLS: SEMI-AUTO

The following is a complete listing for Randall Firearms variations including production statistics. Values shown represent recent aftermarket prices, but it should be noted regional interest can change these prices significantly.

All original Randall pistols had no blue parts. Only the front and rear sights were finished in black oxide.

100% Randall prices assume NIB condition with paperwork.

Add 50% for prototypes with "T" serial numbers.

COMBAT MODEL - same size as Service Model, ribbed top fixed sight slide, Pachmayr grips on right hand model only, left hand models had Herrett walnut grips. While this model was advertised as having a flat mainspring housing, it was never produced.

Last MSR was $549.

RAIDER/SERVICE MODEL-C - 9mm Para. or .45 ACP cal., Colt Commander Model design, 4¼ in. barrel, 36 oz., total stainless steel construction. Add $130 for adj. sights/ ribbed slide, available in either right-hand or left-hand (only 2 mfg.) model. Roll- marked Service Model-C in 1983 and Raider in 1984.

Last MSR was $460.

❋ *Raider/Service Model-C Featherweight* - .45 ACP cal. only, alloy receiver, stainless steel slide, roll-marked Service Model-C, T-type serial numbers, 29 oz. Disc. 1984, only 4 mfg.

FULL SIZE SERVICE MODEL - .38 Super, 9mm Para., or .45 ACP cal., Colt Model 1911 A1 design, 5 in. barrel, total stainless steel construction, 38 oz. Available in either right-hand or left-hand model.

Last MSR was $460.

CURTIS E. LEMAY 4-STAR MODEL - 9mm Para. or .45 ACP cal., Gen. Curtis E. LeMay design, 4¼ in. barrel, 6 (.45 ACP) or 7 (9mm Para.) shot mag., total stainless steel construction, 35 oz. Available in either right-hand or left-hand model, left-hand models are a true mirror image with over 17 major parts changes.

Last MSR was $533.

This model was ½ in. shorter in magazine well and had a cast, squared off triggerguard compared to the Colt 1911A1 design.

❋ *Curtis E. LeMay Featherweight Model* - .45 ACP cal. only, alloy receiver, stainless steel slide, T-type serial numbers, 28 oz. Disc. 1984 (only one mfg.).

RANDALL MATCHED SETS - .45 ACP cal. only, each set consisted of a right-hand and a left-hand Service Model with matching serial numbers. Only 4 sets were mfg. on a special order basis. A111/B111 model configuration.

Last MSR was $1,250.

Randall Variations & Identification

Randall pistols are denoted by a four-character model notation, starting with an alphabetical prefix followed by three digits. The alphabetical prefix will be either A, B, or C - A designates right-hand configuration only, B designates left-hand configuration only, and C designates right-hand lightweight model. The first digit will be 1, 2, or 3 - 1 denotes Service Model, 2 denotes Service Model-C or Raider, 3 represents the C.E. LeMay Model. The second digit again will be either 1, 2, or 3 - 1 designates round top and fixed sight slide, 2 denotes flat top fixed sight slide, and 3 represents adj.

Grading	100%	98%	95%	90%	80%	70%	60%

sights, flat top frame. The third digit again, is either 1, 2, or 3 - 1 denotes .45 ACP cal., 2 designates 9mm Para., and 3 represents .38 Super. Hence, if you had a left-hand Randall in the service model size with a flat top adj. sight slide, and in .45 ACP cal., your model would be a B131. These model codes are not marked on the pistols.

A111 - 3,421 mfg.

$680	$595	$510	$465

Five A111s were mfg. with Austrian proofmarks with premiums existing.

A112 - 301 mfg.

$895	$795	$650	$525

A121 - 1,067 mfg.

$700	$625	$510	$465

A122 - 19 mfg.

$1,325	$1,125	$940	$795

A131 - 2,083 mfg.

$725	$640	$535	$495

A211 - 992 mfg.

$750	$660	$535	$480

A212 - 76 mfg.

$925	$815	$600	$500

A231 - 574 mfg.

$850	$750	$535	$505

A232 - 5 mfg.

$1,500	$1,075	$990	$775

A311 - 361 mfg.

$1,100	$950	$725	$575

Most LeMay models (4¼ in. barrel) were shipped in gun rugs without a factory box. Original factory LeMay boxes are rare - add 10% premium. Beware of Randall LeMay and service model pistols made from parts kits. There were 226 LeMay receivers and 322 service model receivers (all right hand) sold that could be parts guns.

A312 - 1 mfg.
Too rare to evaluate.

A331 - 293 mfg.

$1,200	$1,075	$700	$595

The note that appears for the Model A311 also applies to this variation.

A332 - 9 mfg.

$1,450	$1,275	$975	$825

B111 - 297 mfg.

$1,250	$1,100	$850	$750

B121 - 110 mfg.

$1,500	$1,325	$1,075	$895

B122 - 2 mfg.
Extreme rarity precludes accurate price evaluation.

B123 - 2 mfg.
Extreme rarity precludes accurate price evaluation.

B131 - 225 mfg.

$1,450	$1,250	$925	$775

B311 - 52 mfg.

$1,575	$1,325	$895	$750

R

Grading	100%	98%	95%	90%	80%	70%	60%

B312 w/.45 ACP FACTORY CONVERSION - 1 mfg.
Rarity precludes accurate price evaluation.

B312 - 9 mfg.

	$2,750	$2,300	$1,800	$1,550

B321 - 1 mfg.
Rarity precludes accurate price evaluation. The B321 was the only factory 3-slide set. It was fitted with the 3 different LH LeMay slides available (B311, B321, & B331). This model was mirror polished, engraved, and had ivory grips with the Randall logo.

B331 - 45 mfg.

	$1,775	$1,495	$1,050	$875

B2/321 - 1 mfg.
Rarity precludes accurate price evaluation. This was the only factory model variation to leave Randall Firearms. This was a Left-hand Raider with the C.E. LeMay slide.

C211 - 5 mfg.
Rarity precludes accurate price evaluation.

C331 - 1 mfg.
Rarity precludes accurate price evaluation.

C332 - 4 mfg.
Rarity precludes accurate price evaluation.

* ***Matched Sets*** - large premiums exist for different models with the same serial number if NIB condition. Only 4 were mfg.

RANGER ARMS INC.
Previous manufacturer located in Gainesville, TX until the early 1970s.

Ranger Arms Inc. manufactured good quality, bolt action rifles in various calibers and configurations. Although somewhat rare in that there were not a large number manufactured, collectibility to date has been limited with specimens in 90%+ condition, typically priced in the $375-$500 range.

RAPTOR ARMS CO., INC.
Previous rifle manufacturer located in Shelton, CT, approx. 1997-mid 1999. Previously distributed by Davidson's and Jerry's Sport Centers.

RIFLES: BOLT ACTION

RAPTOR SPORTING RIFLE - .243 Win., .25-06 Rem., .270 Rem., .30-06, or .308 Win. cal., features "Taloncote" or blue (mfg. 1998 only) finished barreled action, black checkered fiberglass reinforced synthetic stock, adj. trigger, with or w/o sights. Mfg. 1997-99.

$230	$195	$175	$160	$150	$140	$130

Last MSR was $259.

Add $30 for sights (disc.).
Add $15 for blue finish (disc.).
Add $36 for heavy barrel.
Add $50 for stainless steel barreled action with sights (new 1999).

* ***Peregrine Deluxe Sporting Rifle*** - similar to Raptor Sporting Rifle, except has deluxe checkered or plain hardwood stock. Mfg. 1998 only.

$265	$225	$195	$175	$160	$150	$140

Last MSR was $309.

Subtract $10 for plain hardwood stock and no sights (blue finish only).

R

Grading	100%	98%	95%	90%	80%	70%	60%

RAVELL

Previous manufacturer located in Barcelona, Spain.

RAVELL *LTD.*

RIFLES: SxS

MAXIM DOUBLE RIFLE - .375 H&H or 9.3x74R cal., H&H type sidelock action with automatic ejectors, Purdey scroll engraving, 23 in. barrels, deluxe walnut with full pistol grip and rubber butt plate, double articulated triggers. Importation disc. circa 1998.

$6,600	$6,100	$5,000	$4,000	$3,500	$2,950	$2,600

Last MSR was $7,000.

Add 10% for .375 H&H cal.

RAVEN ARMS

Previous manufacturer located in Industry, CA circa 1970-1991. **Approximately 2 million were mfg.**

PISTOLS: SEMI-AUTO

RAVEN ARMS

P-25 - .25 ACP cal., single action, 2 7/16 in. barrel, 6 shot mag., walnut grips, available in nickel, blue, or chrome finish, 15 oz. Disc. 1984.

$70	$60	$50	$40	$30	$25	$25

MP-25 - similar to Model P-25, except die-cast slide serrations are slightly different. Disc. 1992.

$60	$50	$45	$40	$35	$30	$25

Last MSR was $70.

Walnut, slotted plastic, or ivory colored grips were available for this model. In 1987, a new sear-block safety was incorporated into manufacture.

RECORD-MATCH

Previously manufactured by Anschütz, located in Zella-Mehlis, Germany circa pre-WWII.

PISTOLS: SINGLE SHOT, TARGET

MODEL 210 FREE PISTOL - .22 LR cal., Martini action, 11 in. barrel, single shot, blue, carved and checkered walnut grips and forearm, set trigger (button release), micrometer rear sight, deluxe target pistol, pre-WWII.

$1,320	$1,265	$1,210	$1,100	$880	$745	$550

MODEL 210A - similar to 210, but alloy frame.

$1,265	$1,210	$1,155	$1,045	$825	$690	$495

MODEL 200 FREE PISTOL - similar to Model 210, but less deluxe features and spur trigger guard, pre-WWII.

$990	$935	$770	$660	$525	$440	$360

R GARY REEDER CUSTOM GUNS

Current custom pistol manufacturer located in Flagstaff, AZ. Consumer direct sales.

Gary Reeder specializes in customizing revolvers from various companies, and is building over 40 different series of custom hunting handguns, cowboy guns, and hunting rifles. He has also produced Custom Contenders for almost 20 years, including the development of many custom calibers for the Thompson Contender. Current MSR for the full Custom Contender is $995. For more information on on his extensive range of custom guns, including the Master Hunter ($995), Night Rider ($995), Alaskan Survivalist ($995), Gambler's Classic ($995), and the African Hunter ($1,495), please contact the factory directly (see Trademark Index).

Grading	100%	98%	95%	90%	80%	70%	60%

REISING ARMS COMPANY

Previous manufacturer originally located in Hartford, CT and later in New York, NY.

PISTOLS: SEMI-AUTO

TARGET AUTOMATIC PISTOL - .22 LR cal., 12 shot, 6¾ in. barrel, blue, brown hard rubber grips, hinged frame, outside hammer. Mfg. 1921-1924.

$475	$395	$340	$315	$265	$220	$195

This model was mfg. in Hartford, CT from serial number 1,001-4,000. The New York, NY address occurs in the serial range 10,000-12,000.
Warning: This pistol's slide may crack if modern high speed .22 ammo is used.

REMINGTON ARMS COMPANY, INC.

Current manufacturer established in 1816, with factories currently located in Ilion, NY, and Mayfield, KY. Originally founded by E. Remington II, and originally located in Litchfield, Herkimer County, NY circa 1816-1828.  Remington moved to the area which would later be known as Ilion, NY in 1828, where they continue to manufacture a variety of sporting shotguns and rifles. Corporate offices were moved to Madison, NC in 1996. The Hickory, KY plant opened in 1997.

REMINGTON TRADEMARKS - 1816-PRESENT

1816-1847 - Remington (mostly barrel and lock markings)
1847-1856 - E. Remington & Son
1856-1888 - E. Remington & Sons
1888-1911 - Remington Arms Company
1911-1916 - Remington Arms & Ammunition Company, Inc.
1916-1920 - Remington Arms - Union Metallic Cartridge Co., Inc.
1920 to date - Remington Arms Company, Inc.

100%	98%	95%	90%	80%	70%	60%	50%	40%	30%	20%	10%

HANDGUNS: 1857-1945 PRODUCTION

BEALS' FIRST MODEL POCKET REVOLVER - percussion .31 cal., 5 shot, smooth cylinder, 3 in. octagon barrel, blue finish, 1-piece Gutta Percha grip, brass or iron trigger guard. Approx. 3,000 produced, 1857-1858.

N/A	N/A	$1,600	$1,200	$1,000	$800	$700	$600	$500	$450	$350	$300

BEALS' SECOND MODEL POCKET REVOLVER - percussion .31 cal., 5 shot, smooth cylinder, 3 in. octagon barrel, blue finish, 2-piece Gutta Percha grips, spur trigger. Less than 1,000 produced 1858-1861. Quite rare.

N/A	N/A	$6,000	$5,000	$4,500	$4,000	$3,500	$3,000	$2,500	$2,250	$2,000	$1,850

BEALS' THIRD MODEL POCKET REVOLVER - percussion .31 cal., 5 shot, smooth cylinder, 4 in. octagon barrel, blue finish, 2-piece Gutta Percha grips, spur trigger, first Remington revolver with loading lever. Approx. 1,000 mfg. between 1859-1861.

N/A	N/A	$1,500	$1,400	$1,200	$1,050	$900	$800	$700	$600	$500	$500

BEALS' NAVY REVOLVER - percussion .36 cal., 6 shot, smooth cylinder, 7½ in. octagon barrel, blue finish, 2-piece walnut grips, some martially marked with inspector's initials and cartouche on grips. Approx. 15,000 produced, 1861-1862. Barrel address is "Beals' Patent, Sept. 14, 1858 - Manufactured by Remingtons', Ilion, N.Y."

R

100%	98%	95%	90%	80%	70%	60%	50%	40%	30%	20%	10%

❋ *Commercial Model* - single wing base pin (very rare), less than 400 mfg. Serial range under 200, very desirable.

N/A	N/A	$4,750	$4,500	$4,000	$3,000	$2,500	$2,000	$1,750	$1,500	$1,250	$1,200

❋ *Commercial Model* - several variations with serialization 1-15,500, most were purchased by military but were not inspected.

N/A	N/A	$4,000	$3,750	$3,000	$2,500	$2,000	$1,750	$1,500	$1,250	$1,000	$850

Subtract 20% for cartridge conversion.

❋ *Martially marked* - serial range 13,500-15,500.

N/A	N/A	$4,500	$4,000	$3,500	$3,250	$3,000	$2,750	$2,500	$2,000	$1,500	$1,250

BEALS' ARMY REVOLVER - percussion .44 cal., 6 shot, smooth cylinder, 8 in. octagon barrel, blue finish, 2-piece walnut grips. Barrel address is "Beals' Patent, Sept. 14, 1858 - Manufactured by Remingtons', Ilion, N.Y."

N/A	$5,000	$4,500	$4,000	$3,500	$3,000	$2,500	$2,000	$1,500	$1,250	$1,000	$850

Subtract 20% for cartridge conversions.

❋ *Martially marked* - serial range is 850-1,900 inspected by "WAT" or "CGC", very desirable.

N/A	N/A	$6,000	$5,500	$4,750	$4,500	$4,000	$3,500	$3,000	$2,250	$1,750	$1,500

RIDER'S DOUBLE-ACTION POCKET REVOLVER - percussion .31 cal., 5 shot, unusual "mushroom-shaped" cylinder, 3 in. octagon barrel, blue finish, 2-piece Gutta Percha grips, brass triggerguard, no loading lever. One of the earliest double-action handguns produced. Approx. 20,000 produced, 1860-1870.

N/A	N/A	$1,500	$1,250	$1,000	$750	$600	$500	$425	$375	$350	$300

Subtract 30% for cartridge conversion.

RIDER'S SINGLE-SHOT DERRINGER - percussion .17 cal., all brass construction, grips included. Less than 1,000 produced, 1859-1863. MANY FAKES, caveat emptor.

N/A	N/A	$6,000	$5,500	$5,000	$4,250	$3,750	$3,250	$2,750	$2,500	$2,300	$2,100

MODEL OF 1861 NAVY REVOLVER - percussion .36 cal., 6 shot, unfluted cylinder, 7½ in. octagon barrel, blue finish, 2-piece walnut grips. Loading lever has slot allowing cylinder pin to be pulled forward without lowering lever. Approx. 6,000 produced 1862- 1863 in serial range 15,000-21,000. Barrel address "Patented Dec. 17, 1861, 1858 - Manufactured by Remingtons', Ilion, N.Y.".

❋ *Commercial Model*

N/A	N/A	$4,000	$3,750	$3,250	$2,750	$2,000	$1,750	$1,500	$1,100	$900	$800

Subtract 30% for cartridge conversion.

❋ *Martially Marked* - over 4,000 martially inspected "CGC".

N/A	N/A	$4,500	$4,000	$3,500	$3,000	$2,500	$2,000	$1,750	$1,500	$1,250	$1,000

MODEL OF 1861 ARMY REVOLVER - percussion .44 cal., 6 shot, unfluted cylinder, 8 in. octagon barrel, blue finish, 2-piece walnut grips. Majority are martially inspected "CGC". Loading lever has slot allowing cylinder pin to be pulled forward without lowering lever. Approx. 10,000 produced 1862-1863 in serial range 1,900-12,000. Barrel address "Patented Dec. 17, 1861, 1858 - Manufactured by Remingtons', Ilion, N.Y.".

N/A	N/A	$4,000	$3,750	$3,250	$2,750	$2,000	$1,750	$1,500	$1,100	$900	$800

Subtract 30% for cartridge conversion.

NEW MODEL ARMY REVOLVER - percussion .44 cal., 6 shot, unfluted cylinder, 8 in. octagon barrel, blue finish, 2-piece walnut grips. Approx. 135,000 produced 1863-1888 in serial range 12,000-148,000. Barrel address "Patented Sept. 14, 1858 - Manufactured by Remingtons', Ilion, N.Y. - New Model". Early models lack "New Model" markings on barrel and have transition features from "1861" model.

N/A	N/A	$4,000	$3,750	$3,250	$2,750	$2,000	$1,750	$1,500	$1,100	$900	$800

Add 25% for cartridge conversion (most are in .44 rimfire).
Add 25% for martially inspected.

100%	98%	95%	90%	80%	70%	60%	50%	40%	30%	20%	10%

NEW MODEL NAVY REVOLVER - percussion .36 cal., 6 shot, unfluted cylinder, 7½ in. octagon barrel, blue finish, 2-piece walnut grips. Approx. 18,000 produced in percussion from 1863-1878 with serial range 21,000-48,000. None were martially marked at time of mfg. Approx. 4,000 were purchased by U.S. Navy during 1863-1865 in serial range 21,000-32,000. Barrel address "Patented Sept. 14, 1858 - Manufactured by Remingtons', Ilion, N.Y. - New Model". Early specimens lack "New Model" markings on barrel and have transition features from "1861" model.

N/A	N/A	$3,750	$3,500	$3,000	$2,250	$2,000	$1,750	$1,500	$1,250	$1,000	$800

Subtract 20% for cartridge conversion if in less than 50%+ original condition.
No premium for martial markings.

NEW MODEL BELT REVOLVER, SINGLE ACTION - percussion .36 cal., 6 shot, unfluted or fluted cylinder, 6½ in. octagon barrel, blue or nickel finish, 2-piece walnut grips. Approx. 5,000 produced 1863-1872.

N/A	N/A	$2,000	$1,750	$1,500	$1,300	$1,100	$900	$800	$700	$600	$500

Add 50% for fluted cylinder (cylinder numbered to the gun).
Subtract 30% for cartridge conversion (mfg. 1870-1886).

NEW MODEL BELT REVOLVER, DOUBLE ACTION - percussion .36 cal., 6 shot, smooth or fluted cylinder, 6½ in. octagon barrel, blue or nickel finish, 2-piece walnut grips. Approx. 2,500 produced 1863-1872.

N/A	N/A	$1,900	$1,700	$1,400	$1,200	$1,000	$800	$700	$600	$500	$400

Add 100% for fluted cylinder (most not numbered to the gun).
Subtract 30% for cartridge conversion.

NEW MODEL POLICE REVOLVER - percussion .36 cal., 5 shot, smooth cylinder, 3 to 6½ in. octagon barrels, blue or nickel finish, 2-piece walnut grips. Approx. 18,000 produced 1863-1872.

N/A	N/A	$1,900	$1,700	$1,400	$1,200	$1,000	$800	$700	$600	$500	$400

Add 10% for 6½ in. barrel.
Subtract 40% for cartridge conversion.

NEW MODEL POCKET REVOLVER - percussion .31 cal., 5 shot, smooth cylinder, spur trigger, 3 to 4½ in. octagon barrel, blue or nickel finish, 2-piece walnut grips. Approx. 25,000 produced, 1863-1888.

N/A	N/A	$1,900	$1,700	$1,400	$1,200	$1,000	$800	$700	$600	$500	$400

Add 25%-50% for brass frame and/or trigger sheath.
Subtract 40% for cartridge conversion.

ZIG-ZAG DERRINGER - cartridge .22 S-L-LR cal., 6 shot, 6 barrel cluster (rotating), ring trigger, 3 in. barrel cluster, blue finish, 2-piece hard rubber grips. Less than 1,000 produced, 1861-1863. Reputed to be Remington's first cartridge handgun.

N/A	N/A	$2,750	$2,500	$2,100	$1,800	$1,500	$1,300	$1,100	$975	$900	$800

ELLIOT'S FIVE SHOT DERRINGER - cartridge .22 S-L-LR cal., 5 shot, 5 barrel cluster (fixed), 3 in. barrel cluster, blue and/or nickel finish, 2-piece hard rubber, walnut, ivory or pearl grips, ring trigger. Approx. 25,000 produced (combined production total with .32 cal.).

N/A	N/A	$1,750	$1,500	$1,250	$1,000	$900	$800	$700	$600	$500	$425

ELLIOT'S FOUR SHOT DERRINGER - cartridge .32 cal., 4 shot, 4 barrel cluster (fixed), ring trigger, 3 3/8 in. barrel cluster, blue and/or nickel finish, 2-piece hard rubber, walnut, ivory or pearl grips. Approx. 25,000 produced (combined production with .22 cal.).

N/A	N/A	$1,500	$1,400	$1,250	$1,100	$975	$850	$750	$625	$525	$450

VEST POCKET DERRINGER - cartridge .22, .30, .32, or .41 cal., single shot, various barrel lengths, blue or nickel finish, 2-piece walnut grips, spur trigger.

* **.22 Rimfire** - approx. 25,000 produced, 1865-1888.

N/A	N/A	$1,300	$1,200	$1,050	$900	$800	$700	$600	$500	$400	$300

Subtract 25% for guns lacking company name.

* **.30 or .32 Rimfire** - number produced unknown, 1865-1888.

N/A	N/A	$1,500	$1,400	$1,300	$1,150	$900	$800	$700	$600	$500	$400

R

100%	98%	95%	90%	80%	70%	60%	50%	40%	30%	20%	10%

✳ .41 Rimfire - approx. 25,000 produced, 1865-1888.

| N/A | N/A | $1,400 | $1,300 | $1,200 | $1,050 | $850 | $750 | $650 | $550 | $450 | $350 |

OVER AND UNDER DERRINGER - cartridge .41 Rimfire cal., 2 shot, 3 in. superimposed barrels, oscillating firing pin, spur trigger, blue and/or nickel finish, hard rubber, walnut, ivory or pearl 2-piece grips. Approx. 150,000 produced, 1866-1934. A.k.a. Double Derringer or Model 95.

  ✳ Type One, Early Variation - maker's name and patent data stamped between the barrels, made without extractor. 1866-1888.

| N/A | N/A | $2,250 | $2,000 | $1,750 | $1,500 | $1,200 | $1,000 | $900 | $750 | $600 | $500 |

  ✳ Type One, Late Variation - maker's name and patent data stamped between the barrels, made with extractor. 1866-1888.

| N/A | N/A | $2,400 | $2,200 | $2,150 | $1,750 | $1,400 | $1,100 | $975 | $775 | $650 | $550 |

  ✳ Type Two - two line markings atop barrels, maker's name and patent data. 1866- 1888.

| N/A | N/A | $1,500 | $1,400 | $1,250 | $1,100 | $1,000 | $900 | $800 | $700 | $600 | $500 |

  ✳ Type Three - marked on top of barrel, single line, "REMINGTON ARMS CO., ILION, N.Y." 1888-1911.

| N/A | N/A | $1,500 | $1,400 | $1,250 | $1,100 | $1,000 | $900 | $800 | $700 | $600 | $500 |

  ✳ Type Four - marked on top of barrel, single line, "REMINGTON ARMS-U.M.C. CO. ILION, N.Y."

| N/A | N/A | $1,500 | $1,400 | $1,250 | $1,100 | $1,000 | $900 | $800 | $700 | $600 | $500 |

MODEL 1866 NAVY ROLLING BLOCK PISTOL - cartridge .50 Rimfire cal., single shot, 8½ in. round barrel, spur trigger, walnut grip and forearm, blue finish. Approx. 6,500 produced, 1866-1867. Erroneously designated as, "Model of 1865 Navy".

  ✳ Martially Marked

| N/A | N/A | $5,000 | $4,500 | $4,000 | $3,500 | $3,000 | $2,500 | $2,000 | $1,750 | $1,500 | $1,400 |

  Subtract 30% if not martially marked (Commercial Model mfg. 1866-1875).
  Subtract 15% for centerfire breech block.
  Less than 150 remain in original condition.

COMBINATION PISTOL-SHOTGUN - 20 ga., 11¾ in. single barrel with smooth bore, rolling block action, designed as a pistol or shotgun (with detachable shoulder stock). Mfg. circa mid 1920s by an unknown manufacturer (possibly Bannerman's). Rolling block receivers appear to have been from foreign made military rifles.

  Extreme rarity factor precludes accurate pricing information.
  In either configuration, this model is an NFA firearm that cannot be legally owned unless registered with the BATF.

MODEL 1870 NAVY ROLLING BLOCK PISTOL - cartridge .50 Centerfire cal., single shot, 7 in. round barrel, standard trigger with triggerguard, walnut grip and forearm, blue finish. Approx. 6,400 produced 1870-1875. Modified by Remington for the Navy from the Model 1866.

| N/A | N/A | $3,000 | $2,500 | $2,000 | $1,750 | $1,500 | $1,300 | $1,200 | $1,100 | $1,000 | $900 |

  Add approx. 20% for 8 in. commercial version (approx. 200-400 mfg.) without inspector's marks.

MODEL 1871 ARMY ROLLING BLOCK PISTOL - cartridge .50 Centerfire cal., single shot, 8 in. round barrel, standard trigger with triggerguard, walnut grip and forearm, blue finish. Approx. 5,000 produced, 1871-1872.

| N/A | $3,500 | $3,000 | $2,500 | $2,000 | $1,750 | $1,500 | $1,300 | $1,200 | $1,100 | $1,000 | $900 |

  Subtract 10% for Commercial Model.
  Pistols produced between 1871-1872 are martially marked.

100%	98%	95%	90%	80%	70%	60%	50%	40%	30%	20%	10%

MODEL 1887 TARGET ROLLING BLOCK PISTOL
- cartridge .22, .25 Rimfire and .32, .50 Centerfire cals., single shot, 8 in. round barrel, standard trigger with triggerguard, walnut grip and forearm, blue finish. Approx. 900 produced 1887-1891. A.K.A. "Plinker Model of 1887".

N/A	$2,500	$2,250	$2,000	$1,750	$1,500	$1,250	$1,000	$900	$800	$700	$600

Add 10% for Navy framed.

Navy framed 1887s are discernible by military proofs on right side of frame, Remington altered from original Navy Model 1870. Estimated mfg. of 100.

MODEL 1891 TARGET MODEL ROLLING BLOCK PISTOL
- cartridge .22, .25 Rimfire and .32 Centerfire cals., single shot, 10 in. part octagon, part round barrel, standard trigger with triggerguard, smooth walnut grip and forearm, blue finish. Approx. 100 produced 1891-1900.

N/A	$2,500	$2,250	$2,000	$1,750	$1,500	$1,250	$1,000	$900	$800	$700	$600

MODEL 1901 TARGET ROLLING BLOCK PISTOL
- cartridge .22 S and L, .25 Rimfire and, .32 Centerfire, or .44 S&W Russian cal., single shot, 10 in. part octagon, part round barrel, standard trigger with triggerguard, checkered walnut grip and forearm, blue finish. Approx. 800 produced 1900-1909.

N/A	$2,500	$2,250	$2,000	$1,750	$1,500	$1,250	$1,000	$900	$800	$700	$600

Add $200 for S&W Russian.

RIDER'S MAGAZINE PISTOL
- cartridge .32 cal., 5 shot, 3 in. octagon barrel, spur trigger, walnut, rosewood, ivory or pearl grips. Approx. 10,000 produced, 1871-1888.

N/A	$2,000	$1,800	$1,600	$1,300	$1,200	$1,000	$900	$800	$700	$600	$500

Add 50% with case hardened magazine.

ELLIOT'S SINGLE SHOT DERRINGER
- cartridge .41 Rimfire cal., single shot, 2½ in. round barrel, spur trigger, walnut 2-piece grips, blue and/or nickel finish. Approx. 10,000 produced, 1867-1888. A.K.A. "Mississippi Derringer".

N/A	$1,500	$1,400	$1,300	$1,000	$900	$750	$675	$600	$500	$400	$300

NUMBER ONE (SMOOT PATENT) REVOLVER
- cartridge .30 Rimfire cal., 5 shot, 2¾ in. octagon barrel, spur trigger, walnut, hard rubber, pearl or ivory 2-piece grips. Number produced debatable, 1873-1888.

N/A	$1,000	$900	$800	$700	$550	$500	$400	$300	$250	$200	$150

Add 100% on early #1s with revolving recoil shield.

On Number One through Number Four Revolvers, ivory grips refer to Remington Celluloid, not genuine ivory. Only in rare instances does ivory appear.

NUMBER TWO (SMOOT PATENT) REVOLVER
- cartridge .30 or .32 Rimfire cal., 5 shot, 2¾ in. octagon barrel, spur trigger, hard rubber, pearl or ivory 2-piece grips. Number produced debatable, 1873-1888.

N/A	$1,000	$900	$800	$700	$550	$500	$400	$300	$250	$200	$150

NUMBER THREE (SMOOT PATENT) REVOLVER
- cartridge .38 Rimfire or .38 Centerfire cal., 3¾ in. octagon barrel with or without barrel rib, spur trigger, hard rubber, ivory or pearl 2-piece grips, "Bird-Head and SawHandle" grip frame with Remington logo "R" on the "saw-handle" hard rubber grips, Bird-Head referred to models with or without a barrel rib. Number produced debatable, 1875-1888.

N/A	$1,000	$900	$800	$700	$550	$500	$400	$300	$250	$200	$150

Add small premiums on Centerfire Number 3s.

NUMBER FOUR REVOLVER
- cartridge .38 and .41 Rimfire or .38 and .41 Centerfire cals., 5 shot, 2½ in. round barrel, hard rubber, pearl or ivory 2-piece grips. Number produced debatable, 1877-1888.

N/A	$1,000	$900	$800	$700	$550	$500	$400	$300	$250	$200	$150

Add small premiums on Centerfire Number 4's.

R

100%	98%	95%	90%	80%	70%	60%	50%	40%	30%	20%	10%

IROQUOIS REVOLVER - cartridge .22 Rimfire cal., 7 shot, 2¼ in. round barrel, spur trigger hard rubber, pearl or ivory 2-piece grips, fluted or non-fluted cylinder. Approx. 10,000 produced between, 1878-1888.

N/A	$1,200	$1,100	$1,000	$800	$700	$550	$350	$300	$250	$200	$175

Subtract 33% if unmarked.
Add 20% for fluted cylinder.
Add 50% for U.S. government markings.

MODEL 1875 SINGLE ACTION REVOLVER - cartridge .44 or .45 Centerfire cal., 6 shot, 7½ or 5¾ in. round barrel, standard trigger with triggerguard, blue or nickel finish, walnut, ivory, or pearl 2-piece grips. Approx. 25,000 produced, 1875-1888.

N/A	N/A	$6,000	$5,000	$3,500	$3,000	$2,500	$2,000	$1,750	$1,500	$1,250	$1,000

Add 25% for blue finish.
Add 10% for government markings.
Add 10% for .45 cal.
There is some debate over originality of the 5¾ in. barrel.

MODEL 1888 SINGLE ACTION REVOLVER - cartridge .44 Centerfire cal., resembles 1890 SA, has "E. Remington & Sons" barrel address, 5¾ in. barrel, nickel finish with walnut grips, perhaps mfg. during Remington's period of bankruptcy and receivership (circa late 1880s).

N/A	N/A	$6,000	$5,000	$3,500	$3,000	$2,500	$2,000	$1,750	$1,500	$1,250	$1,000

This model was never listed in a Remington catalog or price list. Rather, it first appeared in a Hartly Graham ad during late 1888. It is assumed this revolver was made from parts of Models 1875 & 1890 pistols. Model nomenclature has been created by collectors, not the factory.

MODEL 1890 SINGLE ACTION REVOLVER - cartridge .44 Centerfire cal., 6 shot, 7½ or 5¾ in. round barrel, standard trigger with trigger guard, hard rubber 2-piece grips with Remington monogram, ivory or pearl grips on special order, blue or nickel finish. Approx. 2,000 produced, 1891-1894.

❖**Blue Finish**

N/A	$9,000	$8,500	$8,000	$7,000	$6,000	$5,000	$4,000	$3,000	$2,000	$1,500	$1,000

❖**Nickle Finish**

N/A	$8,000	$7,500	$7,000	$6,000	$5,000	$4,000	$3,500	$3,000	$2,000	$1,500	$1,000

MODEL 51 SEMI-AUTO - .32 ACP or .380 ACP cal., 8 shot (7 in mag., 1 in chamber), hard rubber 2-piece grips with company's name, dull black finish. Approx. 65,000 mfg. 1918-1927, parts clean-up 1927-1934 (11 mfg.).

$650	$525	$450	$335	$300	$275	$225	$200	$175	$165	$150	$125

Add 25% for .32 ACP cal.
Add 20% for original box, brochure, oiler, and cleaning rod.
Note: .380 ACP cal. much more common than .32 ACP cal.

MODEL 1911 REMINGTON - UMC - .45 ACP cal., WWI M1911 military contract, over 21,500 mfg. (ser. numbered 1-21,676) in 1918-1919 only, blue finish.

N/A	$4,000	$3,750	$3,000	$2,500	$2,000	$1,500	$1,000	$750	$500	$400	$300

The cut-off serial number for 1918 mfg. is 13,152.

MODEL 1911A1 REMINGTON RAND - approx. 1,086,624 mfg. 1943-1945 in Syracuse, NY, ser. no. ranges 916,405 - 1,041,404, 1,279,649 - 1,441,430, 1,471,431 - 1,609,528, 1,743,847 - 1,816,641, 1,890,504 - 2,075,103, 2,134,404 - 2,244,803, and 2,380,014 - 2,619,013. Parkerized finish. Mfg. by Remington Rand Corp.

$795	$625	$525	$425	$375	$350	$325	$300	$285	$260	$250	$250

Add 20% with original shipping carton.
Note: This model was not manufactured by Remington Arms Co., Inc.

MARK III SIGNAL PISTOL - 10 ga., single shot, brass frame, 9 in. round steel barrel, spur trigger, walnut 2-piece grips. Approx. 25,000 produced, 1915-1918.

N/A	N/A	$300	$265	$230	$210	$190	$175	$160	$145	$130	$110

R

Grading	100%	98%	95%	90%	80%	70%	60%

HANDGUNS: POST-WWII PRODUCTION

Model XP-100 & Variations

Manufacture stopped on the XP-100 at the end of 1994, and resumed briefly during 1998-99 (Model XP-100R).

MODEL XP-100 - .221 Rem. Fireball cal., single shot bolt action pistol, one-piece Dupont Zytel (nylon) pistol grip stock, adj. sights, drilled and tapped for receiver sight and scope, 3¾ lbs. Mfg. 1963-1985.

	100%	98%	95%	90%	80%	70%	60%
	$425	$385	$325	$215	$185	$165	$150

MODEL XP-100 VARMINT SPECIAL - single shot bolt action pistol, .223 Rem. (new 1986) cal., 14½ in. barrel, drilled and tapped for receiver sights and scope, one-piece pistol grip nylon stock, 4 1/8 lbs. Mfg. 1986-1992.

	$495	$395	$330	$295	$240	$210	$185

Last MSR was $419.

Add $100 for original hard zipper case.

XP-SILHOUETTE - .35 Rem. (mfg. 1987-1992) or 7mm BR Rem. (mfg. 1980-1992) cal., bench rest model, 14½ in. barrel, drilled and tapped, nylon (disc. 1992) or walnut (new 1992) stock, 3 7/8 lbs. Disc. 1992.

	$535	$455	$400	$360	$330	$270	$220

Last MSR was $427.

Add $15 for .35 Rem. cal.

MODEL XP-100 HUNTER - .223 Rem., 7mm BR Rem., 7mm-.08 Rem., or .35 Rem. cal., 14½ in. barrel, drilled and tapped for sights, laminated wood stock, 4 3/8 lbs. New 1993-94.

	$550	$475	$410	$350	$300	$230	$195

Last MSR was $548.

MODEL XP-100 WALNUT - 7mm BR Rem. cal., 10½ in. barrel, solid American walnut stock and target sights, 3 7/8 lbs. Mfg. 1993-94.

	$625	$545	$475	$410	$360	$330	$275

Last MSR was $625.

XP-100R KS - .22-250 Rem. (new 1992), .223 Rem., .250 Savage (new 1991), 7mm-08 Rem., .308 Win. (new 1992), .35 Rem., or .350 Rem. Mag. (new 1991) cal., repeater variation, Kevlar synthetic stock, right hand action only, open sights (except for .223 Rem. and .250 Savage) 4 1/8 lbs. Mfg. 1990- 94.

	$850	$750	$675	$595	$495	$400	$365

Last MSR was $840.

This model was available through Remington's Custom Shop only.

MODEL XP-100R - .22-250 Rem., .223 Rem., .260 Rem., or .35 Rem. cal., right hand repeater with 4 or 5 shot blind mag., fiberglass composite stock, 14½ in. barrel, drilled and tapped receiver, approx. 4½ lbs. Mfg. 1998-99.

	$595	$550	$500	$450	$400	$360	$330

Last MSR was $665.

XP-100 CUSTOM - .22-250 Rem. (new 1992), .223 Rem., .250 Savage, 6mm BR Rem., 7mm BR Rem., .308 Win. (new 1992), .35 Rem., or 7mm-08 Rem. cal., choice of standard or heavy barrel, available through custom gun shop only, choice of right or left- hand action, wood stock with contoured pistol grip, without sights. Mfg. 1986-94.

	$950	$800	$700	$600	$550	$500	$450

Last MSR was $945.

R

100%	98%	95%	90%	80%	70%	60%	50%	40%	30%	20%	10%

RIFLES: DISC.

REVOLVING PERCUSSION RIFLE - .36 or .44 cal., 6 shot unfluted cylinder, 24 or 28 in. octagon barrel, walnut stock with crescent butt, scroll triggerguard, blue with case hardened frame. Less than 1,000 mfg., 1866-1872.

> **Subtract 20% for conversion to .38 long rimfire cartridge.**
>
> Due to poor percussion sales, most of the remaining factory stock was converted to .38 R.F., factory conversions will be serial numbered similarly on the recoil plate and cylinder.

❋ *.36 Caliber*

| N/A | N/A | $5,000 | $4,750 | $4,000 | $3,500 | $3,000 | $2,500 | $2,250 | $2,000 | $1,750 | $1,500 |

❋ *.44 Caliber* - very rare.

| N/A | N/A | $10,000 | $9,500 | $8,500 | $7,000 | $5,500 | $4,500 | $4,000 | $3,500 | $3,000 | $2,500 |

MODEL 1862 "ZOUAVE RIFLE" - .58 cal., muzzle loading percussion, 33 in. round barrel, two barrel bands, blue barrel, case hardened lock, brass furniture. Mfg. 12,501, 1862-1865.

| N/A | $4,500 | $4,250 | $4,000 | $3,500 | $2,750 | $2,250 | $2,000 | $1,750 | $1,500 | $1,250 | $1,000 |

U.S. NAVY ROLLING BLOCK CARBINE - .50-70 cal., 23¼ in. barrel, open sight, blue with case hardened frame, bar and ring on frame, walnut straight grip stock. Mfg. 5,000, 1868-1869. Mfg. by Springfield Armory from receivers made by E. Remington & Sons in Ilion, NY.

| N/A | N/A | $3,000 | $2,750 | $2,500 | $2,000 | $1,750 | $1,500 | $1,250 | $1,000 | $750 | $500 |

LONG RANGE "CREEDMOOR" - rolling block, .44-90, .44-100, or .45-70, cal., barrel 1/3 octagon, long range tang sight, globe front sight, checkered pistol grip stock, blue. Approx. 500 mfg., 1873-1886.

| N/A | N/A | $9,800 | $8,825 | $6,250 | $4,475 | $3,875 | $3,175 | $2,700 | $2,475 | $2,150 | $1,800 |

> Add premiums for higher grade guns with select wood, additional checkering, and other deluxe features.

NO. 1 SPORTING RIFLE - rolling block, .40-50, .40-70, .44-70, .44-77, .45-70, .50-45, or .50-70 centerfire, .38 or .46 rimfire cal., 28 or 30 in. octagon barrels, folding leaf sight, straight grip stock. Approx. 10,000 mfg., 1868-1886.

| N/A | $5,000 | $4,500 | $3,500 | $3,000 | $2,500 | $2,000 | $1,500 | $1,000 | $750 | $500 | $300 |

> Subtract 15% for rimfire cals.
> Add 20% for .44-77, .45-70, or .50-70 cal. (primary buffalo hunting cals.).

NO. 1½ SPORTING RIFLE - .22, .25 Stevens, .25 Long, .32, and .38 Long & Extra Long rimfire cal., also in .32-20 WCF, .38-40 WCF, and .44-40 WCF, 24-28 in. octagon medium weight barrel, straight grip walnut stock, somewhat lighter than the No. 1 Sporting. Several thousand mfg., 1888-1897.

| N/A | $3,500 | $3,000 | $2,500 | $1,750 | $1,250 | $900 | $800 | $650 | $550 | $450 | $300 |

> Subtract 15% for rimfire cals.

NO. 2 SPORTING RIFLE - available in many rimfire cals. between .22 and .38 as well as centerfire cals. between .22 to .38-40 WCF, blue finish with case hardened frame, perch belly style walnut stock, many special orders available, smaller size action than the No.1 and rear of frame is curved, mfg. 1873-1909.

| N/A | $1,750 | $1,500 | $1,200 | $900 | $750 | $500 | $400 | $300 | $250 | $200 | $150 |

> Subtract 15% for rimfire cals.

LIGHT BABY CARBINE - rolling block, .44-40 WCF cal., 20 in. lightweight round blue barrel with band, straight stock, nickel receiver. Few thousand mfg., 1892-1902, a few are known to exist in .44 long rimfire cal.

| N/A | $5,000 | $4,750 | $4,000 | $3,500 | $2,750 | $2,250 | $1,750 | $1,500 | $1,000 | $750 | $600 |

> Add 20% for blue barrel with color case hardened receiver.

REMINGTON - HEPBURN NO. 3 - falling block, single shot, side lever actuated, blue barrel, case hardened actions, patented 1879, first introduced 1880, many custom features were offered, variations as follows:

R

100%	98%	95%	90%	80%	70%	60%	50%	40%	30%	20%	10%

NO. 3 SPORTING & TARGET - various cals. from .22 Win. to .50-90 Sharps, 26, 28, or 30 in. round or octagon barrel, open sight, semi-pistol grip stock. Mfg. 1883-1907.

N/A	$3,500	$3,000	$2,750	$2,250	$1,750	$1,500	$1,000	$900	$800	$700	$600

NO. 3 MATCH RIFLE A QUALITY - similar to Sporting and Target, with target match sights (tang), and Schuetzen stock. Less than 1,000 mfg., 1883-1907.

N/A	$4,500	$4,000	$3,500	$3,000	$2,250	$1,800	$1,500	$1,250	$1,000	$850	$700

* ***B Quality*** - select grade wood and vernier rear tang sight.

N/A	$5,400	$4,800	$4,200	$3,600	$2,700	$2,150	$1,800	$1,500	$1,200	$1,000	$850

NO. 3 LONG RANGE CREEDMOOR - .44-40 WCF cal., 32 or 34 in. octagon barrel, tang sight, otherwise similar to Target Model. A few hundred mfg., 1880-1907.

N/A	N/A	$9,800	$8,825	$6,250	$4,475	$3,875	$3,175	$2,700	$2,475	$2,150	$1,800

NO. 3 MID RANGE CREEDMOOR - similar to Long Range, in .40-65 WCF cal., 28 in. barrel.

N/A	$6,000	$5,750	$5,000	$4,000	$3,000	$2,500	$2,000	$1,750	$1,500	$1,250	$1,000

NO. 3 LONG RANGE MILITARY - similar to Creedmoor, with 34 in. full musket stock, in .44-75-520 Rem. cal., military sights, rarely encountered. Mfg. c. 1880s.

N/A	N/A	$9,800	$8,825	$6,250	$4,475	$3,875	$3,175	$2,700	$2,475	$2,150	$1,800

NO. 3 WALKER-HEPBURN SCHUETZEN MATCH - under-lever action, 30 or 32 in. barrel, tang sight, palm rest, target stock, approx. 23 mfg. in 1903, perhaps the rarest single shot American rifle.

Extreme rarity factor precludes accurate price evaluation but a few have been observed with price tags in the $5,000-$20,000+ range, depending on condition.

* ***With False Muzzle***
Add a premium according to condition - very rare.

NO. 4 ROLLING BLOCK RIFLE - .22 S-L-LR, .25 Stevens (barrels marked "25-10"), or .32 Short or Long cal. rimfire, 22½ octagon barrel standard with round barrels available late in the series, smooth bore barrel was introduced approx. 1911, blue finish with case hardened frame, solid frame initially followed by takedown in 2 different types (lever release introduced approx. 1901, screw in approx. 1926), this model was Remington's smallest rolling block. Approx. 350,000 mfg. 1890-1933.

N/A	$900	$800	$700	$500	$400	$275	$200	$175	$150	$100	$75

Solid frame variations will command a premium, especially if over 90% original condition.

* ***Model 4-S "Boy Scout"***

N/A	N/A	$1,750	$1,500	$1,100	$900	$800	$750	$600	$500	$400	$300

* ***Model 4-S Military*** - .22 S,L, LR cal., either marked "MILITARY MODEL" (most common) or "AMERICAN BOY SCOUT" (rare), 28 in. round barrel with musket type forend (1 barrel band), thought to have been used by military academies to train their young cadets.

N/A	N/A	$1,500	$1,400	$1,000	$750	$700	$600	$450	$300	$275	$250

Bayonets are an extremely rare accessory for this model.

NO. 6 ROLLING BLOCK RIFLE - .22 S-L-LR or .32 Short or Long rimfire cal., 20 in. round barrel, boy's gun with small dimensions, takedown action, case hardened (early mfg.) or blue finish, also available in smooth bore, 497,000 mfg. 1901-1933.

N/A	$600	$500	$450	$300	$275	$250	$175	$150	$125	$100	$75

Add 25% for smooth bore barrel.
Original case colors will bring a premium on this model.

R

100%	98%	95%	90%	80%	70%	60%	50%	40%	30%	20%	10%

NO. 7 ROLLING BLOCK RIFLE - .22 S, .22 LR, or .25-10 Stev. rimfire cal., constructed on Rem. Model 1871 SS pistol action frame, 24, 26, or 28 in. ½ round, ½ octagon tapered barrels, marked 'REMINGTON ARMS CO. ILION, NY USA" on barrel top flat, distinctive long tang pistol grip stock, checkered pistol grip and forearm, hard rubber buttplate, available in Target or Sporting configurations, with or w/o special Lyman tang mounted sight, ser. no. range 300,000. Last of the Rolling Block Rifles. Approx. 350 mfg. 1903-1910.

| N/A | N/A | $6,950 | $6,250 | $5,500 | $4,900 | $4,400 | $3,900 | $3,600 | $3,300 | $3,000 | $2,700 |

Add $300 for Lyman folding tang sight.

REMINGTON KEENE MAGAZINE BOLT RIFLE - .45-70 Govt., .40, or .43 cal. Approx. 5,000 mfg. 1880-1888.

 * **Frontier Model** - those made for U.S. Dept. of Interior (Indian Police), marked U.S.I.D. will command a 50% premium.

| N/A | N/A | $3,500 | $3,000 | $2,500 | $2,000 | $1,500 | $1,000 | $750 | $500 | $300 | $250 |

 * **Carbine Model** - 22 in. full stock.

| N/A | N/A | $3,500 | $3,000 | $2,500 | $2,000 | $1,500 | $1,000 | $750 | $500 | $300 | $250 |

 * **Army Rifle** - 32½ in. barrel, full stock.

| N/A | N/A | $3,250 | $2,750 | $2,500 | $1,750 | $1,250 | $900 | $700 | $500 | $300 | $250 |

 * **Sporter Rifle** - ½ oct. barrel, full or "BUTTON" mag. Add for pistol grip and select wood variations.

| N/A | N/A | $3,250 | $2,750 | $2,500 | $1,750 | $1,250 | $900 | $700 | $500 | $300 | $250 |

 * **Navy Rifle** - 29½ in. barrel, full stock.

| N/A | N/A | $3,250 | $2,750 | $2,500 | $1,750 | $1,250 | $900 | $700 | $500 | $300 | $250 |

Grading			100%	98%	95%	90%	80%	70%	60%

RIFLES: ROLLING BLOCK, RECENT MFG.

The following models are manufactured in limited quantities by the Remington Custom Shop.

NO. 1 ROLLING BLOCK CREEDMOOR - .45-70 Govt. cal., rolling block action, patterned after the original Remington No. 1 mid-range Creedmore-style configuration, 30 in. half-round half-octagon tapered 30 in. barrel, includes rear tang aperture and front globe sight with four interchangeable inserts, checkered walnut stock and forearm, SST, case colored receiver, cased, 9 7/8 lbs. Mfg. 1997-98.

			$2,400	$1,900	$1,600				

Last MSR was $2,799.

NO. 1 ROLLING BLOCK MID-RANGE SPORTER - .30-30 Win. (disc. 1998), .444 Marlin (disc. 1998), or .45-70 Govt. cal., 30 in. round barrel, checkered pistol grip sporter stock and forearm, blue barrel end and receiver, adj. buckhorn rear sight, 8¾ lbs. New 1998.

MSR	$1,429		$1,185	$1,025	$925	$775	$675	$600	$550

NO. 1 ROLLING BLOCK SILHOUETTE - .45-70 Govt. cal., meets BPCR silhouette requirements, similar to No. 1 Rolling Block Mid-Range Sporter, except has 30 in. round heavy barrel w/o sights and single set trigger. New 2000.

MSR	$1,537		$1,260	$1,075	$950	$825	$675	$600	$550

RIFLES: SEMI-AUTO - CENTERFIRE

The models have been listed in numerical sequence for quick reference.

MODEL FOUR - 6mm Rem., .243 Win., .270 Win., .280 Rem., .30-06, .308 Win. (disc. 1984), or 7mm Express (mfg. 1981-83) cal., gas operation with metering system, 22 in. barrel, 4 shot detachable mag., deluxe Monte Carlo stock and forend, detachable sights. Mfg. 1981-1987.

	$395	$360	$325	$275	$250	$225	$195

Last MSR was $475.

Grading	100%	98%	95%	90%	80%	70%	60%

✻ *Special Model Four Diamond Anniversary* - .30-06 cal. only, less than 1,500 mfg. in 1981 only to commemorate 75th anniversary of the Model 8, laser engraved with gold and premium checkered walnut stock and forearm. One grade only.

	$1,000	$795	$600				

MODEL 8 - .25 Rem., .30 Rem., .32 Rem., or .35 Rem. cal., 22 in. barrel, open sights, 5 shot non-detachable box mag., plain stock. Approx. 60,000 mfg. 1906-1936.

	$425	$365	$295	$220	$195	$165	$140

Add 15% for .25 cal.
Add premiums for higher grades C through F.

MODEL 74 SPORTSMAN - .30-06 cal. only, 22 in. barrel, 4 shot mag., uncheckered hardwood stock and forearm, open sights, 7½ lbs. Mfg. 1984-1987.

	$295	$260	$235	$210	$190	$175	$160

Last MSR was $353.

MODEL 81 "WOODSMASTER" - .30 Rem., .32 Rem., .35 Rem., or .300 Savage cal., semi-auto, takedown action, 5 shot, non-detachable box mag., 22 in. round barrel, notched elevator rear sight. An improvement of the Model 8; was available in 5 grades. Better grades bring higher prices. 56,091 mfg. 1936-1950.

	$400	$350	$300	$250	$200	$175	$150

Add 20% for .25 cal.
The .32 Rem. cal. was dropped after WWII and the .300 Savage was added in 1940. While a few specimens have been observed in .25 Rem. cal., it is probably the result of part swapping as the Remington Co. cannot verify this cal.

MODEL 740 WOODMASTER & 740A - .244 Rem. (mfg. 1957-59), .280 Rem. (mfg. 1957-59), .30-06 (first caliber, introduced 1955) or .308 Win. (introduced 1956) cal., 22 in. barrel, open sight, box mag., gas operated, plain pistol grip stock. Mfg. 1955-59.

	100%	98%	95%	90%	80%	70%	60%
.244 Rem. or .30-06 cal.	$295	$250	$225	$210	$200	$190	$180
.280 Rem. or .308 Win. cal.	$295	$250	$225	$210	$200	$190	$180

Add 15% for carbine version.

MODEL 740ADL - similar to 740A, with checkered stock, grip cap and swivels. Mfg. 1955-59.

	100%	98%	95%	90%	80%	70%	60%
.244 Rem. or .30-06 cal.	$375	$325	$280	$250	$225	$200	$180
.280 Rem. or .308 Win. cal.	$415	$350	$300	$275	$250	$225	$200

Add 15% for carbine version.

MODEL 740BDL - similar to 740ADL, with select wood.

	100%	98%	95%	90%	80%	70%	60%
.244 Rem. or .30-06 cal.	$395	$340	$295	$250	$225	$200	$180
.308 Win. cal.	$425	$375	$350	$325	$275	$225	$200

Add 15% for carbine version.
BDLs were not listed in the 1958 or 1959 Remington price list.

MODEL 742 (A) "WOODSMASTER" - 6mm Rem. (mfg. 1963), .243 Win. (mfg. 1968), .280 Rem. (marked 7mm Express 1979-1980), .30-06, or .308 Win. cal., 22 in. barrel, open sights, 4 shot box mag., gas operated, checkered pistol grip stock. Mfg. 1960-1980.

	$325	$290	$275	$250	$235	$210	$185

Add 10% for .280 Rem. cal.

MODEL 742ADL DELUXE - similar to the Model 742A, except has fine checkering, sling swivels and engraved game scenes on receiver.

	$350	$300	$275	$260	$235	$215	$195

MODEL 742 CARBINE - similar to 742, except .280 Rem., .30-06, or .308 Win. cal. only, 18½ in. barrel. Mfg. 1961-1980.

	$350	$300	$275	$260	$235	$215	$195

R

Grading	100%	98%	95%	90%	80%	70%	60%

MODEL 742BDL - similar to Model 742, except .30-06 or .308 Win. cal., step receiver, right hand action with choice of right hand or left hand cheekpiece, Monte Carlo basket weave stock and forend, black pistol grip cap and forend tip. Mfg. 1966-1980.

	$350	$300	$275	$260	$235	$215	$195

MODEL 742D PEERLESS GRADE - similar to Model 742, with scroll engraving and fancy wood. Mfg. 1961-1980.

	$2,000	$1,870	$1,200

MODEL 742F PREMIER GRADE - similar to Model 742, with extensive hand engraved game scenes and scroll work, best grade wood.

	$4,200	$3,860	$2,650

MODEL 742F PREMIER GRADE (WITH INLAYS) - gold inlaid model.

	$6,500	$5,785	$4,180

MODEL 742 150TH YEAR ANNIVERSARY - .30-06 cal. only. 11,409 Mfg. 1966 only.

	$395	$325	$300

MODEL 742 CANADIAN CENTENNIAL - 1,000 mfg. in 1967. Issue price was $200.

	$395	$325	$300

REMINGTON/RUGER CANADIAN CENTENNIAL SET - please refer to the Sturm Ruger section of this text.

MODEL 742 BICENTENNIAL - similar to 742, with inscription on receiver. 10,108 Mfg. 1976 only.

	$400	$325	$300	$275	$225	$200	$185

MODEL 7400 - 6mm Rem. (disc. 1987), .243 Win., .270 Win., 7mm Express (mfg. 1981-83), .280 Rem. (introduced 1984, disc. 2000), .30-06, .308 Win., or .35 Whelen (mfg. 1993-95) cal., modified Model 742 action, gas operation, 22 in. barrel, 4 shot detachable mag., pressed checkered Monte Carlo walnut stock, 7½ lbs. Mfg. 1981 to date.

MSR	$624	$495	$400	$315	$255	$230	$210	$185

Add 15% for .35 Whelen cal.

Beginning in 1991, a high gloss wood finish became available in cals. .270 Win. and .30-06 (Model 7400 High Gloss). Beginning 1997, receiver panels have photo etched game scene engraving.

❋ *Model 7400 Carbine* - .30-06 cal. only, similar to Model 7400 Rifle, except has 18½ in. barrel, 7¼ lbs. New 1988.

MSR	$624	$495	$400	$315	$255	$230	$210	$185

❋ *Model 7400 SP (Special Purpose)* - .270 Win. or .30-06 cal., similar to Model 7400, except has non-reflective matte finish on both wood and metalwork. Mfg. 1993-94.

	$435	$370	$300	$255	$230	$210	$185

Last MSR was $524.

❋ *Model 7400 Synthetic* - same cals. as Model 7400, features black fiberglass reinforced synthetic stock and forend, matte black metal finish, 22 in. barrel only. New 1998.

MSR	$520	$415	$355	$315	$280	$260	$240	$220

◇*Model 7400 Synthetic Carbine* - similar to Model 7400 Synthetic, except has 18½ in. barrel. 7¼ lbs. New 1998.

MSR	$520	$415	$355	$315	$280	$260	$240	$220

❋ *Model 7400 175th Anniversary* - .30-06 cal. only, Anniversary Model with light engraving and high gloss finish. 4890 Mfg. in 1991 only.

	$435	$365	$300

Last MSR was $515.

A limited quantity of .270 Win. cal. were specially made in this 175th Anniversary Model for distributor Bill Hicks in MN. Pricing varies, since these rifles are a special edition.

Grading	100%	98%	95%	90%	80%	70%	60%

✴ **Model 7400 ADF Limited Edition** - .30-06 cal. only, special edition 1997 only featuring Buckmaster's American Deer Foundation, special ADF engraving. Mfg. 1997 only.

| | **$495** | **$400** | **$315** | | | | |

Last MSR was $600.

✴ **Model 7400 Engraved** - the engraved Model 7400s were introduced 1988.

✴ **D Grade (Peerless)**

| MSR | **$3,323** | **$2,600** | **$1,875** | **$1,300** | | | |

✴ **F Grade (Premier)**

| MSR | **$6,845** | **$5,700** | **$4,200** | **$2,750** | | | |

✴ **F Grade w/gold inlays (Premier Gold)** - top-of-the-line Custom Shop model.

| MSR | **$10,263** | **$8,750** | **$4,950** | **$3,325** | | | |

RIFLES: SLIDE ACTION, CENTERFIRE

MODEL SIX - 6mm Rem. (disc. 1985), .243 Win., .270 Win., .30-06, or .308 Win. (disc. 1984) cal., pump action, laser engraved, detachable sights, 4 shot mag. Mfg. 1981- 1987.

| | **$400** | **$360** | **$290** | **$265** | **$235** | **$215** | **$195** |

Last MSR was $439.

✴ **D Peerless Grade** - custom shop hand-engraved.

| | **$1,975** | **$1,870** | **$1,200** | | | | |

Last MSR was $2,291.

✴ **F Premier Grade**

| | **$4,150** | **$3,835** | **$2,650** | | | | |

Last MSR was $4,720.

✴ **F Premier Gold Grade** - with gold inlays.

| | **$6,420** | **$5,735** | **$4,000** | | | | |

Last MSR was $7,079.

MODEL 14/14A - .25 Rem., .30 Rem., .32 Rem., or .35 Rem. cal., 22 in. barrel, open sight, plain pistol grip stock. Mfg. 1912-1935.

| | **$400** | **$340** | **$295** | **$195** | **$165** | **$130** | **$110** |

Add 100% for "fingernail" safety.
Add 15% for .25 Rem.

MODEL 14R CARBINE - similar to 14A, with 18½ in. barrel, straight grip stock.

| | **$650** | **$600** | **$550** | **$500** | **$450** | **$400** | **$350** |

Add 10% for .25 Rem. or .35 Rem. cals.

MODEL 14½ RIFLE - similar to 14A, with 22½ in. barrel, .38-40 WCF or .44-40 WCF cal. Mfg. began Dec. 5, 1913-1934.

| | **$800** | **$725** | **$650** | **$600** | **$550** | **$500** | **$450** |

Add 10% for .44-40 WCF cal.

Quantities mfg. of this model are unknown, as serial numbers were intermixed with the Model 14.

MODEL 14½ R CARBINE - similar to 14½ Rifle, with 18½ in. barrel.

| | **$1,600** | **$1,450** | **$1,300** | **$1,200** | **$995** | **$850** | **$725** |

Add 100% for "fingernail safety".

MODEL 25/25A SLIDE ACTION - .25-20 WCF or .32-20 WCF cal., 24 in. barrel, open sight, tube mag., plain pistol grip stock. Mfg. 1923-1935.

| | **$440** | **$385** | **$350** | **$300** | **$250** | **$225** | **$200** |

MODEL 25R CARBINE - similar to 25A, with 18 in. barrel and straight stock.

| | **$495** | **$425** | **$350** | **$275** | **$225** | **$200** | **$175** |

R

Grading	100%	98%	95%	90%	80%	70%	60%

MODEL 76 SPORTSMAN SLIDE ACTION - .30-06 cal. only, 22 in. barrel, 4 shot mag., unchecked ered hardwood stock and forearm, open sights, 7½ lbs. Mfg. 1984-87.

	100%	98%	95%	90%	80%	70%	60%
	$255	$225	$195	$180	$170	$160	$150

Last MSR was $319.

MODEL 141/141A SLIDE ACTION RIFLE - .25 Rem. (very few mfg. during 1936 only), .30 Rem., .32 Rem., or .35 Rem. cal., 24 in. barrel, takedown, open sight, plain pistol grip stock. Mfg. 1936-1950.

	$425	$350	$295	$240	$195	$165	$140

Add 20% for .25 Rem. cal.
Add 10% for .35 Rem. cal.

MODEL 141 CARBINE - mfg. 1936-1942.

	$750	$700	$650	$600	$550	$500	$450

MODEL 760 "GAMEMASTER" RIFLE - .222 Rem. (mfg. 1958-1961), .223 Rem. (200 mfg. 1964-68), 6mm Rem. (introduced 1969), .243 Win. (introduced 1968), .244 (mfg. 1957-1961), .257 Roberts (mfg. 1955-1961), .270 Win., .280 Rem. (marked 7mm Express 1979-80), .30-06, .300 Sav., .308 Win., or .35 Rem. (mfg. 1952-1967, and 1980) cal., 22 in. barrel, detachable mag., uncheckered pistol grip stock. Mfg. 1952- 1980.

	100%	98%	95%	90%	80%	70%	60%
	$375	$325	$275	$250	$225	$200	$175
.222 Rem. cal.	$1,150	$900	$800	$725	$650	$575	$500
.223 Rem. cal.	$1,350	$995	$850	$775	$700	$625	$575
.257 Roberts cal.	$850	$695	$575	$450	$400	$350	$300

Add 10% for .300 Savage or .35 Rem. cal.

The Model 760 seems to have regional pricing differences in the rare calibers. Values in the Eastern U.S. seem to be quite a bit higher than prices encountered in the Midwest and West. Hence, values on the .222 Rem., .223 Rem., and .257 Roberts cals. reflect a nationalized average rather than one region's high or another's low. A few Model 760s were also mfg. in .244 cal. (before going to 6mm Rem.) - very rare with pricing unpredictable.

MODEL 760 CARBINE - .270 Win. (introduced 1969), .280 Win., .30-06, .308 Win., or .35 Rem. cal., 18½ in. barrel.

	$450	$400	$375	$325	$300	$275	$250

Subtract 10% for .30-06 cal.

MODEL 760D PEERLESS GRADE - similar to 760, with hand engraving and fancy wood. Mfg. 1953-1980.

	$1,100	$935	$825	$770	$690	$605	$525

MODEL 760F - similar to 760, with extensive hand engraved game scenes, best grade wood.

	$2,420	$1,980	$1,760	$1,650	$1,485	$1,375	$1,100

✳ *Gold Inlaid Model*

	$5,500	$4,675	$4,180	$3,960	$3,300	$2,750	$2,200

MODEL 760 150 YEAR ANNIVERSARY - .30-06 cal. only. 4610 Mfg. 1966 only.

	$395	$325	$300	$275	$225	$200	$185

MODEL 760 BICENTENNIAL - similar to 760, with commemorative inscription engraved on receiver. 3,800 Mfg. 1976 only.

	$395	$325	$300	$275	$225	$200	$185

MODEL 760ADL - .30-06 cal., similar to 760A, except with checkered pistol grip, deluxe wood and sling swivels. Mfg. 1953-1963.

	$395	$350	$325	$300	$275	$250	$225

MODEL 760BDL - similar to 760, except .270 Win., .30-06, or .308 Win. cal. only, step receiver, available with right or left hand cheekpiece on Monte Carlo stock (basket weave checkering pattern became standard mid-'70s), black pistol grip and forend tip. Mfg. 1953-1982.

	$425	$375	$350	$300	$275	$250	$225

Add 20% for .308 Win. cal.

Grading	100%	98%	95%	90%	80%	70%	60%

MODEL 7600 - 6mm Rem. (disc. 1984), .243 Win., .270 Win., .280 Rem. (mfg. 1988- 2000), .30-06, .308 Win., or .35 Whelen (mfg. 1988-96) cal., modified 760 action, 22 in. barrel, detachable mag., pressed checkered pistol grip stock and forearm, 7½ lbs. Mfg. 1981 to date.

MSR $588		$470	$390	$295	$235	$205	$185	$165

Add 10% for .35 Whelen cal.

Beginning in 1990, a high gloss wood finish became available in cals. .270 Win. and .30-06 (Model 7600 High Gloss). Beginning 1997, receiver panels have photo etched game scene engraving.

* *Model 7600 Carbine* - .30-06 cal. only, similar to Model 7600 Rifle, except has 18½ in. barrel, 7¼ lbs.

MSR $588		$470	$390	$295	$235	$205	$185	$165

* *Model 7600 SP (Special Purpose)* - .270 Win. or .30-06 cal., similar to Model 7600, except has non-reflective matte finish on wood and metalwork. Mfg. 1993-94.

		$420	$360	$280	$230	$205	$185	$165

Last MSR was $496.

* *Model 7600 Synthetic* - same cals. as Model 7600, features black fiberglass reinforced synthetic stock and forend, matte black metal finish, 22 in. barrel only, 7½ lbs. New 1998.

MSR $484		$385	$335	$290	$270	$255	$240	$225

* ✧*Model 7600 Synthetic Carbine* - similar to Model 7600 Synthetic, except has 18½ in. barrel. 7¼ lbs. New 1998

MSR $484		$385	$335	$290	$270	$255	$240	$225

* *Model 7600 175th Anniversary* - 1,000 mfg. 1991 only.

	$625	$525	$375

* *Model 7600 ADF Limited Edition* - .30-06 cal. only, special edition 1997 only featuring Buckmaster's American Deer Foundation, special ADF engraving. Mfg. 1997 only.

	$460	$385	$295

Last MSR was $567.

* *Model 7600 Engraved* - hand engraved Model 7600s were introduced 1988.
* *D Grade (Peerless)*

MSR $3,323		$2,600	$1,875	$1,300

* *F Grade (Premier)*

MSR $6,845		$5,700	$4,200	$2,750

* *F Grade w/gold inlays (Premier Gold)* - top-of-the-line Custom Shop model.

MSR $10,263		$8,750	$4,950	$3,325

RIFLES: RIMFIRE, DISC. & CURRENT PRODUCTION

From 1930-1960 Remington produced a number of bolt action .22 cal. Rimfire rifles, both single shot and repeaters. They were good quality, serviceable weapons with many slight variations upon a basic design. Whenever possible, models have been listed in numerical sequence.

	100%	98%	95%	90%	80%	70%	60%
Model 33	$200	$150	$125	$100	$85	$75	$60
Model 33 NRA	$300	$225	$200	$175	$150	$125	$100
Model 33-P	$250	$200	$175	$150	$125	$100	$75

263,557 of the Model 33 were mfg. 1932-1935.

	100%	98%	95%	90%	80%	70%	60%
Model 34	$200	$150	$125	$100	$85	$75	$60
Model 34-P	$300	$225	$200	$175	$150	$125	$100
Model 34 NRA	$450	$400	$350	$300	$275	$250	$200

162,941 of the Model 34 were mfg. 1932-1936.

	100%	98%	95%	90%	80%	70%	60%
Model 341 A	$150	$125	$100	$90	$85	$80	$75
Model 341 P	$175	$150	$125	$100	$85	$75	$70
Model 341 SB	$275	$235	$200	$175	$140	$125	$110

131,604 of the Model 341 "Sportsmaster" were mfg. 1936-1940.

R

Grading	100%	98%	95%	90%	80%	70%	60%
Model 41 A	$150	$125	$100	$75	$65	$60	$55
Model 41 AS							
(.22 Rem. Spec. cal.)	$225	$200	$175	$150	$140	$125	$110
Model 41 P	$150	$125	$100	$85	$65	$60	$55
Model 41 SB	$250	$200	$175	$160	$140	$125	$110

306,880 of the Model 41 "Targetmaster" were produced 1936-1939.

Model 411	$400	$375	$350	$300	$250	$225	$200

The Model 411 is similar to the Model 41 single shot, but in CB Cap or .22 Short and without safety on rear of bolt. Eye screw for gallery use. 1,316 mfg. 1937- 1939 (although never cataloged). Add 50% premium for .22 Short.

Model 510 A	$125	$110	$90	$75	$65	$60	$55
Model 510 C (Carbine)	$175	$150	$95	$85	$75	$65	$60
Model 510 P	$175	$150	$95	$85	$75	$65	$60
Model 510 Routledge/Smoothbore	$200	$165	$150	$120	$110	$100	$90

Add 15% for Mo-Skeet-O Bore

These models were mfg. 1939-1962. There were no ser. nos. until 1954 – approx. 545,000 were mfg.

Model 511 A	$150	$135	$120	$100	$85	$80	$75
Model 511 P	$200	$165	$125	$110	$100	$90	$85

These models were mfg. 1939-1962. There were no ser. nos. until 1954 – approx. 375,000 mfg.

Model 512 A	$150	$135	$120	$100	$85	$80	$75
Model 512 P	$200	$165	$125	$110	$100	$90	$85

These models were mfg. 1940-1962. There were no ser. nos. until 1954 – approx. 395,000 mfg.

Model 510-X	$140	$125	$110	$90	$80	$70	$60
Model 510-X SB	$200	$175	$150	$135	$125	$120	$110
Model 511-X (29,120 mfg.)	$175	$150	$125	$100	$90	$80	$70
Model 512-X (30,670 mfg.)	$175	$150	$125	$100	$90	$80	$70

These models were mfg. 1964-1966. 19,901 Model 510-Xs were mfg. and mixed with the Model 512-X.

Model 514 (1948-1970)	$135	$110	$90	$75	$65	$55	$40
Model 514 P (1952-1971)	$175	$165	$145	$120	$85	$75	$65
Model 514 Boy's Rifle (1961-1970)	$155	$135	$120	$100	$85	$75	$65
Model 514 Routledge/Smoothbore	$185	$150	$125	$120	$115	$110	$100

These models were mfg. 1951-1969 – 5,557 were mfg. Serialization began in 1968 – approx. 780,000 mfg.

MODEL 12A SLIDE ACTION RIFLE - .22 S, L, and LR cal., hammerless, 22 in. round or octagon barrel, open sights, tube mag., plain grip stock, approx. 840,000 (all variations) were mfg. 1909-1936.

$450	$400	$300	$270	$220	$210	$200

Originally this model was designated "The New .22 Repeater", and did not have a model number. It was also available in Grades 1-6.

MODEL 12B (GALLERY SPECIAL) - similar to 12C, except in .22 Short cal., all had octagon barrels.

$700	$650	$550	$500	$425	$375	$350

Add 15% for extended mag. tube.

MODEL 12C - similar to 12A, except 24 in. octagon barrel.

$600	$550	$450	$325	$300	$275	$250

Add premiums for grades D, E, and F.

R

Grading	100%	98%	95%	90%	80%	70%	60%

MODEL 12C NRA TARGET - limited manufacture.

	$1,000	$900	$750	$650	$500	$450	$400

MODEL 12CS - similar to 12C, chambered for .22 Rem. Spl. (.22 WRF) cal.

	$600	$550	$450	$325	$300	$275	$250

MODEL 16/16A AUTOLOADING RIFLE - .22 Rem. Autoloading cal., 22 in. barrel, open sight, tube mag. in butt stock, straight stock. 17,738 mfg. 1914-1928.

	$600	$550	$450	$325	$300	$275	$250

Add premiums for higher grades C, D, and F.

MODEL 24/24A AUTOLOADING RIFLE - .22 S or LR cal., 19 in. barrel, open sights, Browning semi-auto design, bottom ejection, tube mag. through butt stock, takedown, plain pistol grip stock. Approx. 131,000 mfg. 1922-1935.

	$400	$300	$250	$175	$150	$125	$115

Add premiums for higher grades C Special, D Peerless, E Expert, and F Premier.

MODEL 37 "RANGEMASTER" BOLT ACTION TARGET RIFLE - .22 LR cal., 5 shot with single shot adapter, 28 in. barrel, target sight and scope bases, target stock, 12½ lbs. Mfg. 1937-1940.

	$800	$750	$600	$550	$475	$425	$400

MODEL 37 - 1940 - improved trigger and stock design. Mfg. 1940-1954.

	$800	$750	$600	$550	$475	$425	$400

Total manufacture of the Model 37 was 12,198.

MODEL 121A SLIDE ACTION RIFLE - hammerless, .22 S, L, or LR cal., 24 in. round barrel, tube mag., plain pistol grip stock. 201 were mfg. 1936-1954.

	$425	$325	$275	$250	$225	$215	$200

Originally designated Model 121.

MODEL 121S - similar to 121A, except chambered for .22 Rem. Spl. (rare) cal..

	$550	$450	$400	$325	$275	$225	$200

MODEL 121SB/ROUTLEDGE - similar to 121A, except smooth bore for .22 shot, at least 5 different chamberings and barrel markings. 557 were mfg.

	$650	$550	$500	$400	$375	$350	$325

MODEL 241/241A SPEEDMASTER SEMI-AUTO - .22 S or LR cal., 24 in. barrel, replaced the Model 24, open sights, takedown, tube mag. through stock, non-checkered walnut stock and forearm. Approx. 132,000 mfg. 1935-1949.

	$400	$300	$250	$175	$150	$125	$115

Add premiums for Special, Peerless, Expert, and Premier Grade models.

MODEL 513T (TARGET) "MATCHMASTER" BOLT ACTION - .22 LR cal., 27 in. barrel, Redfield aperture sight, target stock, 6 shot, sling swivels, approx. 166,000 were mfg. 1940-1968.

	$395	$300	$250	$200	$150	$115	$95

A TR suffix on this gun indicated with sights, a TX indicated w/o sights, a TS indicated sporter. Most 513s are marked either 513T (Target) or 513S (Sporter).

MODEL 513S (SPORTER) - similar to 513T, with Marbles open sight and checkered sporter stock. 13,677 were mfg. 1941-1956.

	$650	$600	$550	$500	$450	$400	$350

MODEL 521TL JR. BOLT ACTION - .22 LR cal., 25 in. barrel, Lyman target sights, takedown, 6 shot mag., target stock, approx. 67,000 were mfg. 1947-1968.

	$300	$275	$225	$175	$125	$100	$90

These models had no ser. no. until 1954.

R

Grading	100%	98%	95%	90%	80%	70%	60%

MODEL 522 VIPER SEMI-AUTO - .22 LR cal., semi-auto blowback action, 20 in. barrel, full-length black synthetic resin stock with beavertail forend, 10 shot mag., cocking indicator, adj. rear sight, grooved synthetic receiver, 4 5/8 lbs. Mfg. 1993-97.

	$125	$110	$100	$90	$80	$70	$60

Last MSR was $152.

MODEL 540X RIMFIRE - .22 LR cal., single shot bolt action, 26 in. heavy barrel, no sights, target stock, adj. butt, approx. 5,115. Mfg. 1969-1974.

	$350	$325	$300	$250	$200	$185	$175

MODEL 540XR - similar to 540X, with large position style stock with adj. butt plate. Mfg. 1974-1983.

	$350	$325	$300	$250	$200	$185	$175

✸ *Model 540XR JR* - jr. size with 1½ in. shorter stock. Mfg. 1974-1983.

	$350	$325	$300	$250	$200	$185	$175

MODEL 541S CUSTOM BOLT ACTION - .22 S, L, or LR cal., bolt action, 24 in. barrel, no sights, 5 shot mag., scroll engraved receiver and triggerguard, checkered walnut stock with rosewood pistol grip cap and forend tip. Mfg. 1972-1984.

	$650	$575	$500	$425	$375	$325	$275

MODEL 541T BOLT ACTION - .22 LR cal. only, 5 shot mag., 24 in. standard or heavy (new 1993) barrel, checkered American walnut stock with satin finish, barrel is drilled and tapped, 5 7/8 lbs. Mfg. 1986-99.

	$380	$300	$235	$200	$180	$165	$150

Add $27 for heavy barrel.

Last MSR was $465.

MODEL 541X - .22 LR cal. only, bolt action, U.S. military training rifle, 27 in. barrel, 5 shot mag., ser. no. scribed by hand on bolt, 9,077 mfg. 1984-86.

	$500	$450	$400	$375	$350	$325	$300

Lower values on this model reflect recent sales through DCM program.

MODEL 550A SEMI-AUTO - .22 S, L, or LR cal., 24 in. barrel, open sight, shell deflector, 2 extractors, tube mag., plain one piece pistol stock. 764,573 Mfg. 1941-1946.

	$195	$150	$110	$90	$80	$70	$60

This model replaced the Model 241.

MODEL 550-1 - similar to 550A, except has single extractor. Approx. 220,000 mfg. 1946-1970.

	$150	$125	$100	$85	$75	$65	$55

These models had no ser. no. until 1954.

MODEL 550P - similar to 550-1, with aperture (peep) sight.

	$200	$175	$150	$130	$110	$100	$85

MODEL 550-2G - .22 Short cal., similar to 550-1, except 22 in. barrel and eye screw for counter chain in shooting gallery.

	$200	$175	$150	$130	$110	$100	$85

MODEL 552A SPEEDMASTER SEMI-AUTO - .22 S, L, or LR cal., 23 in. barrel, semi-auto open sight, tube mag., pistol grip stock. Mfg. 1957-disc.

	$160	$135	$120	$100	$85	$75	$65

This model was also mfg. in a 150th Anniversary Model (1966 only) and a 175th Anniversary (1991 only). Slight premiums are being asked if condition is 98% or better.

MODEL 552C - similar to 552A, with 21 in. barrel. Mfg. 1961-1977.

	$170	$145	$130	$110	$95	$85	$75

✸ *Model 552 BDL Deluxe Speedmaster* - similar to Model 552A, except checkered walnut Monte Carlo stock and forearm. Mfg. 1966 to date.

MSR	$385		$295	$215	$165	$125	$105	$90	$75

Grading	100%	98%	95%	90%	80%	70%	60%

MODEL 552 175th ANNIVERSARY - 1,000 mfg. 1991 only.

	100%	98%	95%
	$395	$275	$200

MODEL 572 LIGHTWEIGHT SLIDE ACTION - .22 S, L, LR cal., slide action, anodized alloy receiver and barrel, steel sleeved, checkered "Sun-Grain" stock and forend, 4 lbs. Offered in 3 colors. Approx. 34,785 mfg., 1958-1962.

	100%	98%	95%	90%	80%	70%	60%
Buckskin Tan	$275	$250	$200	$150	$120	$110	$100
Crow-Wing Black	$375	$345	$295	$195	$150	$125	$100
Teal-Wing Blue	$700	$600	$425	$300	$250	$225	$200

MODEL 572SB/ROUTLEDGE - similar to 572A, except smooth bore.

	100%	98%	95%	90%	80%	70%	60%
	$350	$300	$275	$225	$200	$175	$150

MODEL 572 FIELDMASTER - .22 S, L, or LR cal., slide action, 21 in. barrel, walnut stock and forearm, tube mag., 5½ lbs. Mfg. 1955-1988.

	100%	98%	95%	90%	80%	70%	60%
	$160	$145	$125	$105	$90	$75	$65

Last MSR was $176.

This model was also mfg. in a 150th Anniversary Model (1966 only). 20% premiums if condition is 98% or better.

* ***Model 572 BDL Deluxe Fieldmaster*** - similar to Model 572, except with checkered walnut Monte Carlo stock and forearm. Mfg. 1966 to date.

MSR	$399	98%	95%	90%	80%	70%	60%
	$305	$220	$170	$125	$105	$90	$75

MODEL 572 175th ANNIVERSARY - 300 mfg. 1991 only.

	100%	98%	95%
	$425	$295	$225

MODEL 580 SINGLE SHOT - .22 S, L or LR cal., bolt action, 24 in. barrel, open sights, Monte Carlo stock. Mfg. 1967-1978.

	100%	98%	95%	90%	80%	70%	60%
	$150	$125	$105	$100	$90	$80	$75

Add 50% for smooth bore (Model 580SB).

MODEL 580BR - Boy's Model, 1 in. shorter stock. Mfg. 1971-1978.

	100%	98%	95%	90%	80%	70%	60%
	$175	$150	$125	$100	$75	$65	$50

MODEL 581 BOLT ACTION - .22 LR cal., bolt action, 6 shot mag., converts to single shot. Mfg. 1967-1983.

	100%	98%	95%	90%	80%	70%	60%
	$165	$135	$135	$100	$90	$70	$60

MODEL 581 SPORTSMAN - .22 LR cal., bolt action, 5 shot mag., 24 in. barrel, hardwood uncheckered stock, 4¾ lbs. Mfg. 1986-1999.

	100%	98%	95%	90%	80%	70%	60%
	$200	$170	$145	$125	$105	$90	$75

Last MSR was $239.

MODEL 582 BOLT ACTION - similar to 581, with tube mag. Mfg. 1967-1983.

	100%	98%	95%	90%	80%	70%	60%
	$175	$150	$125	$115	$100	$85	$75

MODEL 591 BOLT ACTION - 5mm Rimfire Mag. cal., 24 in. barrel, open sight, 5 shot mag., Monte Carlo stock. Approx. 27,000 mfg. 1970-1974.

	100%	98%	95%	90%	80%	70%	60%
	$175	$125	$100	$85	$75	$65	$50

5mm rimfire ammo has been disc. for some time, and as a result, collectibility on this model is mostly for 95% or better condition, since there is little shooter utility in lower conditions, because the discontinued ammo has become too expensive. Original 5mm ammo is selling for $35-$50 per box.

MODEL 592 BOLT ACTION - similar to 591, with tube mag. Approx. 25,000 mfg. 1970- 1974.

	100%	98%	95%	90%	80%	70%	60%
	$175	$125	$100	$85	$75	$65	$50

MODEL 597 SEMI-AUTO - .22 LR cal., alloy receiver with nickel plated bolt, matte black metal finish, one-piece dark grey smooth synthetic stock, 20 in. free-floating barrel, 10 shot staggered detachable mag., adj. iron sights, new trigger design, 5½ lbs. New 1997.

MSR	$163	98%	95%	90%	80%	70%	60%
	$135	$115	$100	$90	$80	$70	$60

R

Grading	100%	98%	95%	90%	80%	70%	60%

❋ *Model 597 Sporter* - similar to Model 597, except has hardwood stock, includes sling swivel studs. Mfg. 1998-2000.

	$160	$135	$115	$100	$90	$80	$70

Last MSR was $199.

❋ *Model 597 Stainless Sporter* - similar to Model 597 Sporter, except has stainless steel barrel and hardwood stock. Mfg. 2000 only.

	$190	$155	$130

Last MSR was $239.

❋ *Model 597 SS* - similar to Model 597, except is stainless synthetic with satin finished receiver and barrel, beavertail style forend. New 1998.

MSR	$217		$175	$145	$125

❋ *Model 597 LSS* - similar to Model 597, except has stainless steel barrel with matching alloy receiver, and satin finished brown wood laminate stock, 5½ lbs. New 1997.

MSR	$272		$230	$185	$160

❋ *Model 597 HB* - similar to Model 597 LSS, except has 20 in. heavy steel barrel. New 2001.

MSR	$265		$225	$180	$155

MODEL 597 CUSTOM TARGET - .22 LR cal., 20 in. custom contoured satin finish heavy stainless free floating barrel w/o sights, match chamber, special green laminated stock with Monte Carlo profile and beavertail forend. Mfg. 1998-2000.

	$495	$400	$300

Last MSR was $599.

❋ *Model 597 Custom Target* - .22 Mag. cal. Disc. 2000.

	$600	$450	$350

Last MSR was $745.

MODEL 597 MAGNUM - .22 Mag. cal., similar in appearance to Model 597, 9 shot mag., 20 in. barrel, black synthetic stock with sling swivel studs, 6 lbs. New 1997.

MSR	$321		$265	$230	$190	$160	$140	$125	$110

❋ *Model 597 Magnum LS* - .22 Mag. cal., features brown laminate stock with sling swivel studs and steel barrel. New 1998.

MSR	$377		$315	$265	$230	$190	$160	$140	$125

❋ *Model 597 Magnum Target* - .22 Mag. cal., similar to Model 597 Magnum LS, except has 20 in. heavy barrel. New 2001.

MSR	$399		$330	$280	$240	$195	$160	$140	$125

RIFLES: RIMFIRE - "NYLON SERIES"

NYLON 10 SINGLE SHOT - .22 S, L, or LR cal., bolt action. 8,606 were mfg. 1962-1964.

	$250	$200	$150	$110	$60	$50	$40

❋ *Nylon 10-SB* - similar to Nylon 10, except smooth bore barrel used for .22 shot cartridges. 2,064 mfg.

	$550	$450	$300	$200	$175	$155	$135

This model is infrequently encountered.

MOHAWK 10-C - similar to Model 77, renamed after changing to a 10 shot mag, approx. 129,000 were mfg. 1971-1978.

	$125	$100	$70	$65	$60	$55	$50

MODEL 11 NYLON - .22 S, L, or LR cal., bolt action repeater, 6 or 10 shot mag., 4½ lbs. 22,423 were mfg. 1962-1964.

	$250	$200	$150	$110	$75	$50	$40

MODEL 12 NYLON - similar to 11, with tube mag. 27,551 were mfg. 1962-1964.

	$250	$200	$150	$110	$75	$50	$40

Grading	100%	98%	95%	90%	80%	70%	60%

NYLON 66 AUTOLOADER - .22 LR cal., 19 5/8 in. barrel, open sights, butt stock tube mag. holds 14 shells, 4 lbs. Stock made from Zytel plastic in black, brown, or green. 1,050,336 were mfg. 1959-1990.

	$140	$115	$95	$80	$70	$60	$50

Add 25% for Black Diamond (56,000 mfg.).
Add 30% for Apache black or chrome finish (221,000 mfg.).
Add 50% for Seneca green (45,000 mfg.).

Last MSR was $124.

NYLON 66 150TH ANNIVERSARY - 3,792 mfg. in 1966 only with 150th Anniversary Remington logo on receiver.

	$250	$200	$150	$100	$85	$70	$60

NYLON 66 BICENTENNIAL - inscription on receiver, 10,268 mfg. 1976 only, brown nylon stock only.

	$225	$185	$150	$100	$85	$70	$60

NYLON 76 LEVER ACTION - similar appearance to Nylon 66 with brown or black stock, short throw lever action, 25,312 mfg. in standard finish, 1,615 mfg. in black chrome finish 1962-1964 only.

	100%	98%	95%	90%	80%	70%	60%
Standard finish (25,312 mfg.)	$250	$200	$150	$115	$80	$65	$60
Apache Black/chrome finish (1,615 mfg.)	$400	$350	$275	$200	$150	$135	$125

The Nylon 76 "Trail Rider" is the only lever action repeating rifle ever mfg. by Remington.

NYLON 77 - similar to Nylon 66, except with 5 shot mag. 15,327 were mfg. 1970-1971 only.

	$165	$130	$100	$75	$65	$55	$45

NYLON APACHE 77 - similar to Model 10-C, but bright green stock. Mfg. for K-Mart in 1987-89.

	$135	$100	$65	$55	$50	$45	$40

RIFLES: BOLT ACTION, CENTERFIRE

The models in this section have been listed in numerical sequence for quick reference.

MODEL SEVEN LIGHTWEIGHT - compact bolt action available in .17 Rem. (mfg. 1993-95), .222 Rem. (disc. 1984), .223 Rem. (disc. 1984), .243 Win., .260 Rem. (new 1997), 6mm Rem. (disc. 1995), 7mm-08 Rem., or .308 Win. cal., 18½ in. barrel, 6¼ lbs., 4 or 5 shot mag., individually test fired, oil finished American walnut, adj. rear and ramp front sight (w/o sights on .17 Rem.). Mfg. 1982-1999.

	$475	$370	$275	$225	$205	$180	$165

Last MSR was $585.

Add 5%-10% for .17 Rem. cal.
Add 10% for .222 Rem. cal.

All steel Model Sevens (including floor plate and triggerguard) are currently commanding a small premium.

* **Model Seven LS Lightweight** - .223 Rem., .243 Win., .260 Rem. (disc. 2001), .308 Win., or 7mm-08 Rem. cal., features brown laminated stock, 20 in. steel barrel, matte barrel and satin wood finish, 6½ lbs. New 2000.

MSR	$677	$550	$435	$315	$255	$225	$200	$180

* **Model Seven LS Magnum** - .300 Rem. Ultra Mag. or 7mm Rem. Ultra Mag. cal., short action, 22 in. barrel, blue action and barrel, 3 shot mag. with detachable floor plate, brown laminated stock, sling swivel studs, 7 1/8 lbs. New 2002.

MSR	$717	$575	$435	$340

R

Grading	100%	98%	95%	90%	80%	70%	60%

* **Model Seven LSS** - .22-250 Rem., .243 Win. (disc. 2001), or 7mm-08 Rem. cal., similar to Model Seven LS, except has stainless steel barrel w/o sights. New 2000.

MSR	$770		$610	$445	$325			

* **Model Seven SS** - .223 Rem. (new 1997), .243 Win., .260 Rem. (new 1997), .308 Win., or 7mm-08 Rem. cal., features stainless steel construction, 20 in. barrel w/o sights, and synthetic stock. New 1994.

MSR	$703		$555	$420	$310			

* **Model Seven SS Magnum** - .300 Rem. Ultra Mag. or 7mm Rem. Ultra Mag. cal., short action, satin finished stainless steel action and 22 in. barrel, 3 shot mag. with detachable floor plate, black synthetic stock, sling swivel studs, 7 1/8 lbs. New 2002.

MSR	$743		$595	$450	$350			

* **Model Seven Youth** - .223 Rem. (new 2000), .243 Win., 6mm Rem. (disc. 1995), .260 Rem. (new 1998), .308 Win. (disc.), or 7mm-08 Rem. (new 1994) cal., uncheckered hardwood stock shortened 1 in., 6 lbs. New 1993.

MSR	$531		$425	$360	$295	$230	$205	$180	$165

* **Model Seven FS** - .243 Win., 7mm-08 Rem., or .308 Win. cal., 18½ in. parkerized blue barrel, grey or grey camo Kevlar fiberglass stock, adj. rear sight, 5¼ lbs. Mfg. 1987-89 only.

		$525	$455	$415	$375	$335	$310	$285

Last MSR was $600.

* **Model Seven Custom MS (Mannlicher Stock)** - .222 Rem., .22-250 Rem., .223 Rem., .243 Win., .250 Savage, .257 Roberts, .260 Rem. (new 1997), .308 Win., .35 Rem., .350 Rem. Mag., 6mm Rem., or 7mm-08 Rem. cal., features 20 in. custom shop barrel with Model 7 action bedded to a Mannlicher style laminate full stock. New 1994.

MSR	$1,312	$1,115	$825	$600	$495	$425	$385	$340

This model is available from the Custom Shop only (special order).

* **Model Seven Custom KS** - .223 Rem. (new 1989), .260 Rem. (new 1998), 7mm BR Rem. (mfg. 1989-1993), 7mm-08 Rem. (new 1989), .308 Win. (new 1991), .35 Rem., or .350 Rem. Mag. cal., 20 in. barrel with (.35 Rem. or .350 Rem. Mag.) or w/o sights, synthetic Kevlar stock with solid recoil pad. New 1987.

MSR	$1,294	$1,080	$815	$575	$485	$425	$385	$340

This model is available from the Custom Shop only (special order).

* **Model AWR (Alaskan Wilderness Rifle)** - .300 Rem. Ultra Mag. or 7mm Rem. Ultra Mag. cal., short action, stainless steel action and 22 in. barrel with matte black Teflon satin finish, 3 shot mag. with detachable floor plate, fiberglass matte black stock, sling swivel studs, 6 1/8 lbs. New 2002.

MSR	$1,524	$1,350	$1,150	$800	$650	$550	$450	$375

This model is available from the Custom Shop only (special order).

MODEL 30A BOLT ACTION RIFLE - .25 Rem., .30 Rem., .30-06 (original cal.), .32 Rem., .35 Rem., or 7x57mm Mauser (introduced 1931), Enfield M/1917 type action, 22 in. barrel, checkered pistol grip stock. Mfg. 1921-1940.

	$550	$475	$400	$350	$300	$260	$200

MODEL 30R CARBINE - .25 Rem., .30 Rem., .32 Rem., .35 Rem., or .30-06 cal., similar to Model 30A, with 20 in. barrel. Introduced 1927.

	$575	$500	$450	$375	$325	$275	$225

MODEL 30 EXPRESS - .25 Rem., .30 Rem., .32 Rem., .35 Rem., or .30-06 cal. Introduced 1926.

	$550	$475	$400	$350	$300	$260	$200

MODEL 30S (SPECIAL GRADE) - .25 Rem. rimless (introduced 1931), .257 Roberts (new 1934), 7x57mm Mauser (introduced 1931), or .30-06 (original cal.) cal., deluxe version of Model 30A, 22 or 24 in. barrel, Lyman receiver sight, special stock, 7½ lbs. Mfg. 1930-1940.

	$675	$550	$500	$450	$375	$300	$250

The Model 30S Express Rifle was introduced in 1934 in .257 Roberts cal.

Grading	100%	98%	95%	90%	80%	70%	60%

MODEL 78 SPORTSMAN BOLT ACTION - .223 Rem., .243 Win., .270 Win., .30- 06, or .308 Win. cal., 22 in. barrel, 4 shot mag., unchecked hardwood stock, open sights, 7 lbs. Mfg. 1984- 89.

	100%	98%	95%	90%	80%	70%	60%
	$300	$250	$210	$190	$170	$160	$150

Last MSR was $333.

MODEL 600 BOLT ACTION - .222 Rem., .223 Rem. (very rare), 6mm Rem., .243 Win., .308 Win., or .35 Rem. cal., 18½ in. VR barrel, dog leg bolt handle, checkered pistol grip stock. 94,086 were mfg. 1964-1968.

	100%	98%	95%	90%	80%	70%	60%
Reg. cals.	$450	$350	$275	$210	$195	$175	$155
.35 Rem.	$575	$495	$350	$320	$295	$270	$250
.222 Rem.	$495	$465	$425	$385	$350	$325	$295
.223 Rem.	$995	$825	$700	$500	$400	$350	$325

315 Model 600s in .223 Rem. cal. were mfg.

❋ *Model 600 Montana Centennial* - 6mm Rem., 1,020 mfg. in 1964 only.

	100%	98%	95%
	$900	$700	$600

Last MSR was $125.

MODEL 600 MAGNUM - 6.5mm Rem. Mag. or .350 Rem. Mag. cal., laminated walnut/ beech stock with or without recoil pad (early mfg. walnut stocks did not have recoil pad). Mfg. 1965- 1968.

	100%	98%	95%	90%	80%	70%	60%
	$975	$875	$775	$675	$575	$475	$425

MODEL 600 MOHAWK - .222 Rem., 6mm Rem., .243 Win., or .308 Win. cal., this variation was a promotional model, 18½ in. barrel with no rib. 94,920 were mfg. 1971- 1979.

	100%	98%	95%	90%	80%	70%	60%
	$395	$325	$285	$265	$240	$225	$200

MODEL 660 BOLT ACTION - .222 Rem., 6mm Rem., .243 Win., or .308 Win. cal., 20 in. barrel, open sight, dog leg bolt handle, checkered pistol grip stock, black pistol grip cap and forend tip. 50,536 were mfg. 1968-1971.

	100%	98%	95%	90%	80%	70%	60%
	$495	$465	$425	$385	$350	$325	$295

Add 10% for .222 Rem. cal.

❋ *.223 Rem. cal.* - 227 total mfg. This cal. was never listed in a Remington catalog.

	100%	98%	95%	90%	80%	70%	60%
	$1,100	$875	$725	$600	$500	$400	$350

MODEL 660 MAGNUM - 6.5mm Rem. Mag. or .350 Rem. Mag. cal., laminated stock and recoil pad.

	100%	98%	95%	90%	80%	70%	60%
	$875	$700	$600	$450	$400	$350	$300

MODEL 710 SPORTSMAN - .270 Win. or .30-06 cal., unique bolt to barrel lockup design utilizing 3 locking lugs on bolt face that lock directly in an integrated rear barrel design (as opposed to locking into the receiver), polymer receiver sleeve, adj. trigger, detachable 4 shot box mag, 60 degree bolt throw, 22 in. ordnance grade steel barrel with matte finish, grey synthetic stock with solid pad, supplied with bore sighted 3-9 power x 40mm Bushnell Sharpshooter scope and mounts, ISS (Integrated Security System) locking bolt safety, 7 1/8 lbs. New 2001.

		100%	98%	95%	90%	80%	70%	60%
MSR	$425	$350	$315	$290	$260	$250	$240	$230

MODEL 720A BOLT ACTION - Enfield type action, .257 Roberts, .270 Win., or .30- 06 cal., 22 in. barrel, open sights, 5 shot, checkered pistol grip stock, 2,500 mfg. 1941- 1944.

	100%	98%	95%	90%	80%	70%	60%
	$1,200	$995	$850	$700	$600	$500	$400

Add 50%+ for .270 Win. cal.
Add 100%+ for .257 Roberts cal.

920-1,000 Model 720As were purchased by the Dept. of Navy during 1942 and used as trophies - these are discernible by crossed cannon proofs on wood.

Most of this model was chambered for .30-06 cal. Approx. 100 were chambered for .270 Win. and 20 or less were chambered for the .257 Roberts.

R

Grading	100%	98%	95%	90%	80%	70%	60%

MODEL 720R - similar to 720A, except with 20 in. barrel.

	$1,400	$1,100	$900	$750	$650	$550	$450

This is the rarest variation in the Model 720 Series.

MODEL 720S - similar to 720A, except with 24 in. barrel.

	$1,475	$1,125	$900	$750	$600	$500	$400

MODEL 721 BOLT ACTION - .270 Win., .280 Rem. (new 1960), or .30-06 cal., 24 in. barrel, open sights, 4 shot, plain pistol grip stock. Mfg. 1948-1962.

	$395	$300	$225	$200	$165	$155	$145

.280 Rem. (688 mfg.) and .264 Win. Mag. (1,115 mfg.) are rare in this model. 100% condition on these calibers could bring $700+.

MODEL 721ADL - similar to Model 721A, except has deluxe checkered stock.

	$395	$360	$330	$300	$250	$200	$175

This model's suffix does not appear on the gun. ADL features will determine the model.

MODEL 721BDL - similar to 721ADL, except has extra select wood.

	$475	$425	$375	$325	$300	$275	$250

This model's suffix does not appear on the gun. BDL features will determine the model.

MODEL 721A MAGNUM - .264 Win. Mag. or .300 H&H cal., 26 in. heavy barrel, recoil pad, 3 shot mag., 8¼ lbs.

	$495	$450	$360	$320	$295	$275	$260

Add 15% for .264 Win. Mag. cal.

MODEL 721ADL MAGNUM - 264 Win. Mag., similar to 721A Mag., checkered. 1,115 mfg. 1961-62, not cataloged.

	$550	$495	$400	$350	$315	$290	$275

MODEL 721BDL MAGNUM - similar to 721ADL Mag., select wood.

	$600	$550	$475	$425	$385	$360	$330

MODEL 722(A) - short action version of 721A, .222 Rem. (mfg. 1950-1962), .222 Rem. Mag. (mfg. 1958-1962), ..243 Win. (mfg. 1960-1962), .244 Rem. (mfg. 1957-1962), .257 Roberts (disc. 1960), .300 Savage (disc. 1959), or .308 Win. (mfg. 1956- 1962) cal., 7 lbs. Mfg. 1948-1962.

	$350	$300	$275	$250	$225	$200	$180

Subtract 10% for .300 Savage cal.
Add 20% for .257 Roberts or .308 Win. cal.

.222 Rem. Mag. (3,803 mfg.) and .243 Win. (2,186 mfg.) are rare in this model. Add approx. 25% to values for these cals.

MODEL 722ADL - similar to Model 722(A), except with deluxe checkered wood.

	$400	$350	$300	$275	$225	$200	$180

This model's suffix does not appear on the gun. ADL features will determine the model.

MODEL 722BDL - similar to Model 722ADL, except features extra select wood.

	$550	$500	$400	$340	$300	$265	$245

This model's suffix does not appear on the gun. BDL features will determine the model.

MODEL 725ADL BOLT ACTION - .222 Rem., .243 Win., .244 Rem., .270 Win., .280 Rem., or .30-06 cal., 22 in. barrel, open sights, 4 shot, checkered Monte Carlo stock. 16,635 mfg. 1958-1961.

	100%	98%	95%	90%	80%	70%	60%
.30-06 cal.	$575	$450	$375	$350	$325	$300	$280
.270 Win.	$700	$575	$450	$400	$375	$350	$325
.280 Rem.	$800	$650	$525	$450	$400	$350	$325
.222 Rem.	$750	$625	$500	$450	$400	$350	$325

R

Grading	100%	98%	95%	90%	80%	70%	60%
.244 Rem.	$750	$650	$500	$450	$400	$350	$325
.243 Win.	$750	$650	$500	$450	$400	$350	$325

Caliber mfg. breakdown is as follows: 7,657 in .30-06; 2,784 in .280 Rem.; 2,818 in .270 Win.; 840 in .244 Rem.; 1,478 in .222 Rem.; 998 in .243 Win.

MODEL 725 KODIAK - .375 H&H Mag. or .458 Win. Mag. cal., 26 in. barrel, 3 shot, recoil reducer in muzzle, deluxe checkered Monte Carlo stock, black pistol grip cap and forend tip. 52 mfg. 1961 only.

$4,000	$3,200	$2,700	$2,250	$2,000	$1,800	$1,650

Only 24 rifles in .458 Win. Mag. were mfg. and 28 rifles in .375 H&H Mag.

MODEL 788 BOLT ACTION - .222 Rem., .22-250 Rem., .223 Rem., 6mm Rem., .243 Win., .308 Win., .30-30 Win., 7mm-08 Rem., or .44 Mag. cal., 18½ (Carbine), 22, or 24 in. barrel, open sight, plain pistol grip Monte Carlo stock. Mfg. 1967-1983.

	100%	98%	95%	90%	80%	70%	60%
Rifle	$375	$275	$250	$225	$210	$200	$185
Carbine (18½ in. barrel)	$375	$275	$250	$225	$210	$200	$185

Add 10% for .30-30 Win. cal.
Add 15% for 7mm-08 Rem. cal.
Add 30% for .44 Mag. cal.
Add 10% for left-hand action (6mm Rem. and .308 Win. cal. only).

RIFLES: BOLT ACTION, MODEL 700 & VARIATIONS

MODEL 700 TITANIUM ULTIMATE LIGHTWEIGHT - .260 Rem., .270 Win., .30-06, .308 Win. (new 2002) or 7mm-08 Rem cal., titanium receiver (drilled and tapped), spiral cut breech bolt with flutes and skeleton handle, 22 in. stainless steel barrel, satin stainless finish on receiver and barrel, ultra lightweight carbon-fiber matte finished Kevlar reinforced stock, 3-4 shot fixed mag., sling swivel studs, 5¼ - 5½ lbs. New 2001.

MSR	$1,239	$1,115	$865	$710

MODEL 700 AS - .22-250 Rem., .243 Win., .270 Win., .280 Rem., .30-06, .308 Win., 7mm Rem. Mag., or .300 Wby. Mag. cal., synthetic stock is made from Arylon resin, matte black finished stock and metal, 22 or 24 in. barrel, 6½ lbs. Mfg. 1989-91 only.

			$445	$370	$310	$275	$250	$220	$195

Last MSR was $528.

Add $21 for 7mm Rem. Mag. or .300 Wby. Mag. cal.

MODEL 700 FS - .243 Win., .270 Win., .30-06, .308 Win., or 7mm Rem. Mag. cal., 22 in. polished blue barrel, grey or grey camo Kevlar fiberglass stock with solid recoil pad, iron sights, 6¼ lbs. Mfg. 1987-1988 only.

		$530	$460	$415	$375	$335	$310	$285

Last MSR was $613.

Add $20 for 7mm Rem. Mag. cal. (24 in. barrel).

MODEL 700 RS - .270 Win., .280 Rem., or .30-06 cal., 22 in. polished blue barrel, grey or grey camo DuPont Rynite synthetic stock with smooth cheekpiece and solid recoil pad, iron sights, 7¼ lbs. Mfg. 1987-1988 only.

		$500	$450	$410	$370	$335	$310	$285

Last MSR was $547.

Add 30% for .280 Rem. cal.
In 1987 less than 500 rifles were dual barrel marked - 7mm EXP REM .280 REM. These specimens will command a 40% premium.

R

Grading	100%	98%	95%	90%	80%	70%	60%

MODEL 700 CAMO SYNTHETIC - .22-250 Rem. (disc. 1993), .243 Win., .270 Win. (disc. 1993), .280 Rem. (disc. 1993), 7mm-08 Rem. (disc. 1993), 7mm Rem. Mag., .30-06, .308 Win. (disc. 1993), or .300 Wby. Mag. (disc. 1993) cal., 22 or 24 (Mag. only) in. barrel, features synthetic stock and is fully camouflaged in Mossy Oak Bottomland pattern, iron sights, approx. 7¼ lbs. Mfg. 1992-94.

	$490	$425	$350	$315	$285	$265	$250

Last MSR was $581.

Add $27 for Mag. cals.

MODEL 700ADL DELUXE RIFLE - .22-250 Rem. (disc. 1991), .222 Rem. (disc.), .222 Rem. Mag. (disc.), .25-06 Rem. (disc. 1991), 6mm Rem. (disc.), .243 Win. (disc. 1997), .270 Win., .280 Rem. (disc. 1997 - marked 7mm Express 1979-82), .30-06, .308 Win. (disc. 2001), or 7mm Rem. Mag. cal., 20 (disc.), 22, or 24 in. barrel, open sights, 4 shot mag., checkered Monte Carlo stock or brown laminated stock (new 1988). Mfg. 1962-present.

MSR	$559		$445	$350	$275	$225	$175	$165	$155

Add $26 for 7mm Rem. Mag. cal.
Add 20% for 20 in. barrel (mfg. 1962-63).
Add 50% for .222 Rem. Mag. or .280 Rem. cal. 20 in barrel.
Add 15% for 7mm Rem. Mag., .264 Win. Mag., or .300 Win. Mag. cal. with stainless steel barrel (mfg. 1962-1970).

During 1962-63, the 20 in. barrel was standard on .222 Rem., .222 Rem. Mag., .243 Win., .270 Win., .280 Rem., .30-06, or .308 Win. cal. In 1964, these cals. had a standard barrel length of 22 in.; 24 in. barrels were standard on 7mm Rem. Mag. and .264 Win. Mag. cals.

Remington, in 1987-89, introduced a Model 700 Gun Kit that enabled the owner to assemble the stock to the barreled action. All metal work is completely finished and wood finishing is all that is required. This kit was available in most popular cals. - last MSR price was $333 (1989).

✱ *Model 700ADL Synthetic* -.22-250 Rem. (new 1999), .223 Rem., .243 Win., .270 Win., .30-06, .308 Win., .300 Win. Mag. (new 1999), or 7mm Rem. Mag., features fiberglass reinforced synthetic stock with positive checkering, black matte finish on metal/wood, open sights, approx. 7 3/8 lbs. New 1996.

MSR	$484		$380	$295	$240	$210	$185	$170	$155

Add $27 for .300 Win. Mag. or 7mm Rem. Mag. cal.

✱ *Model 700ADL Synthetic Youth* -.243 Win. or .308 Win. cal., similar to Model 700ADL Synthetic, except has 20 in. barrel and 1 in. shorter LOP.

MSR	$484		$380	$295	$240	$210	$185	$170	$155

✱ *Model 700ADL/LS* - .243 Win. (new 1989), .270 Win. (new 1989), .30-06, or 7mm Rem. Mag. cal., brown laminate stock with checkering. Mfg. 1988-1993.

	$400	$345	$275	$230	$210	$195	$165

Last MSR was $485.

Add $27 for 7mm Rem. Mag. cal.

MODEL 700BDL CUSTOM DELUXE - .17 Rem., .22-250 Rem., .222 Rem., .223 Rem., .243 Win., .25-06 Rem., .264 Win. Mag. (disc.), .270 Win., .280 Rem. (mfg. 1992-95, resumed 2000), .300 Savage (mfg. 1992 only), .30-06, .308 Win. (disc. 1995), .35 Whelen (mfg. 1989-94), 6mm Rem. (disc. 1994), 7mm-08 Rem. (disc. 1994, reintroduced 2000), 7mm Rem. Mag., .300 Win. Mag., .300 Rem. Ultra Mag (new 1999), .338 Win. Mag. (mfg. 1988-94, resumed 1997), .338 Rem. Ultra Mag. (new 2000), .375 Rem. Ultra Mag. (new 2001), 7mm Rem. Ultra Mag. (new 2001), or 8mm Mag. (disc.) cal., similar to 700ADL Deluxe, except with hinged floorplate, cut skipline checkering, black pistol grip cap and forend tip, receiver and floorplate fine line engraving was standard 1997-2001, supplied with iron sights first year.

MSR	$661		$530	$420	$345	$285	$250	$220	$195

Add $27-$67 for left-hand model (available in certain cals. only, short action .22-250 Rem. and .243 Win. cals. are scarce in left-hand).
Add $27 for .17 Rem., 7mm Rem. Mag., .300 Win. Mag. or .338 Win. Mag. cal.
Add $40 for .300 Rem. Ultra Mag., .338 Ultra Mag., .375 Rem. Ultra Mag., or 7mm Rem. Ultra Mag. cal.

Grading	100%	98%	95%	90%	80%	70%	60%

Add 15% for 7mm Rem. Mag., .264 Win. Mag., or .300 Win. Mag. cal. with stainless steel barrel (mfg. 1962-1970).

In 1962, the 20 in. barrel was standard on .222 Rem., .222 Rem. Mag., .243 Win., .270 Win., .280 Rem., .30-06, or .308 Win. cal. In 1964, these cals. had a standard barrel length of 22 in. 24 in. barrels were standard on 7mm Rem. Mag. and .264 Win. Mag. cals.

Remington mfg. the Model 700BDL in .350 Rem. Mag. and 6.5mm Rem. Mag. (1,584 mfg. between 1969-1975). 1,558 were assembled in 1969, and sold through 1975. The .350 Rem. Mag. mfg. in 1969 is 3 times rarer than the 1985 Model 700 Classic chambered for .350 Rem. Mag.

.222 Rem. Mag.	$550	$475	$400	$340	$300	$280	$260
.350 Rem. Mag.	$695	$525	$425	$350	$325	$300	$275
6.5mm Rem. Mag.	$695	$525	$425	$350	$325	$300	$275

MODEL 700BDL CLASSIC (LTD EDITION) - similar to 700BDL, except has classic straight stock, high polish bluing, has been offered in .17 Rem., .220 Swift, .221 Fireball (new 2002), .222 Rem., .22-250 Rem. (Classic only), .223 Rem., .250 Savage (250/3000), 6.5x55mm Swedish, 6mm Rem. (Classic only), 7x57mm Mauser, 8mm Rem. Mag., .243 Win. (Classic only), .25-06 Rem., .257 Roberts, .264 Win. Mag., .270 Win. (Classic only), .280 Rem., .300 Win. Mag., .300 Wby. Mag., .30-06 (Classic only), 7mm-08 Rem., 7mm Wby. Mag., .338 Win. Mag., .350 Rem. Mag., .35 Whelen, .300 H&H, or .375 H&H cal. The original Model 700 Classic was mfg. 1978-1985. Limited edition calibers were introduced during 1981 (see listings), and continue to be produced annually, receiver and floorplate fine line engraving was standard 1997-2001.

MSR	**$661**	$540	$440	$360	$280	$250	$220	$195

The Model 700 Classic was originally introduced in 1978 in .22-250 Rem., 6mm Rem., .243 Win., .270 Win., .30-06, and 7mm Rem. Mag., and was part of the standard Remington product lineup until 1985. Limited editions were introduced during 1981, and are still being produced today.

This model is produced in limited quantities of a different caliber each year. Add premiums for several calibers in NIB condition only (including 7x57mm Mauser, .257 Roberts, .300 H&H, and .375 H&H).

The following is a list of annual Limited Classic calibers offered previously with year of manufacture: 7x57mm Mauser (1981), .257 Roberts (1982), .300 H&H (1983), .250 Savage (1984), .350 Rem. Mag. (1985), .264 Win. Mag. (1986), .338 Win. Mag. (1987), .35 Whelen (1988), .300 Wby. Mag. (1989), .25-06 Rem. (1990), 7mm Wby. Mag. (1991), .220 Swift (1992), .222 Rem. (1993), 6.5x55mm Swedish (new 1994), .300 Win. Mag. (1995), .375 H&H Mag. (1996), .280 Rem. (1997), 8mm Rem. Mag. (1998), .17 Rem. (1999), .223 Rem. (2000), 7mm-08 Rem. (2001), and .221 Fireball (2002).

MODEL 700BDL DM (DETACHABLE MAG.) - .243 Win. (disc. 1999), .25-06 Rem. (disc. 1997), .270 Win., .280 Rem. (disc. 1999), 6mm Rem. (disc. 1996), 7mm Rem. Mag., 7mm-08 Rem. (disc. 1999), .30-06, .308 Win. (disc. 1996), .300 Win. Mag., or .338 Win. Mag. (disc. 1996) cal., Monte Carlo walnut stock with 20 LPI skip-line checkering, high polish bluing, black forend cap, receiver and floorplate fine line engraving was standard 1997-2001, open sights, 3-4 shot detachable mag. New 1995.

MSR	**$728**	$585	$470	$385	$330	$285	$265	$250

Add $27 for .300 Win. Mag. and 7mm Rem. Mag. cals.

Left-hand actions on this model were disc. in 1999. Their last retail prices ranged from $665- $692, depending on caliber.

R

* ***Model 700BDL Lew Horton Special Edition*** - .257 Roberts cal., 500 mfg. in 1990 only, first time the 700BDL has been offered in .257 Roberts cal.

	$575	$525	$450	$395	$360	$325	$280

Last MSR was $580.

Grading	100%	98%	95%	90%	80%	70%	60%

MODEL 700BDL SS (STAINLESS SYNTHETIC) - .223 Rem. (mfg. 1993-94), .243 Win. (mfg

1993-94), .25-06 Rem. (disc. 1994), .270 Win., .280 Rem. (disc. 1995), .30-06, . 308 (disc 1994), 7mm Rem. (mfg. 1993-94), 7mm-08 Rem. (mfg. 1993-94), .300 Win. Mag. (new 1993) .300 Rem. Ultra Mag. (new 1999), .300 Wby. Mag. (mfg. 1993-94), .338 Win. Mag. (mfg 1993-94, resumed 1997), .338 Rem. Ultra Mag. (new 2000), 7mm Rem. Mag., 7mm Rem Ultra Mag. (new 2001), 7mm Wby. Mag. (scarce, disc. 1994), .375 Rem. Ultra Mag. (new 2001), or .375 H&H (new 1997) cal., features matte finished 416 stainless steel barrel, receiver, and bolt, black synthetic stock with checkering, drilled and tapped, hinged floorplate mag., 24 in. barrel, no sights, 6¼ - 7 lbs. New 1992.

	MSR $735		$585	$470	$355

Add $13 for Mag. cals., except 7mm Rem. Mag.
Add approx. $100 for .223 Rem. cal., $150 for 7mm Wby. Mag. cal.
Subtract $27 for .270 Win. or .30-06 cal.

✱ Model 700LSS - .270 Win. (left-hand only, disc. 2000), .300 Win. Mag., .300 Rem. Ultra Mag. (new 1999), .338 Rem. Ultra Mag. (new 2000), .30-06 (left-hand only, disc. 2000), 7mm Rem. Ultra Mag., 7mm Rem. Mag., or .375 Rem. Ultra Mag. cal., stainless steel barreled action, grey tinted laminate Monte Carlo wood stock, 24 in. barrel, w/o sights, 7½ lbs. New 1996.

	MSR $803		$645	$500	$385

Add $13 for Rem. Ultra Mag. cals.
Add $40 for Mag. cals. in left-hand action.

✱ Model 700BDL SS DM (Detachable Mag.) - .243 Win. (disc. 1997), .25-06 Rem., .260 Rem. (mfg. 1997-2000), .270 Win., .280 Rem., 6mm Rem. (disc. 1995), 7mm Rem. Mag., 7mm-08 Rem. (disc. 1998, resumed 2000-2001), .30-06, .308 Win. (disc. 1999), .300 Win. Mag., .300 Wby. Mag. (disc. 2000), or .338 Win. Mag.(disc. 1996) cal., features 3-4 shot detachable mag., stainless steel, 24 in. barrel, satin finish metalwork, black non-reflective stock with checkering, receiver and floorplate fine line engraving was standard in 1997-2001, w/o sights, 7 3/8 lbs. New 1995.

	MSR $775		$650	$550	$455

Add $26 for Mag. cals.
Add $89 for muzzle brake (Model 700BDL SS DM-B, mfg. 1996-2001, available in 7mm STW, 7mm Rem. Mag. (disc. 1999) or .300 Win. Mag. cals. only).

MODEL 700BDL VARMINT SPECIAL - .22-250 Rem., .222 Rem., .223 Rem., .25- 06 Rem.(disc.),

6mm Rem., .243 Win., .308 Win., or 7mm-08 Rem. cal., 24 in. heavy barrel, checkered walnut stock, no sights. Mfg. 1967-1994.

	$480	$420	$350	$315	$285	$265	$250

Last MSR was $565.

✱ Model 700VS (Varmint Synthetic) - .220 Swift (disc. 1996), .22-250 Rem., .223 Rem., .243 Win. (mfg. 1997-98), or .308 Win. cal., composite, textured black and grey synthetic stock features Kevlar, fiberglass, and graphite, matte metal finish, 26 in. heavy barrel w/o sights, 9 lbs. New 1992.

	MSR $788		$635	$460	$405	$325	$295	$265	$250

Add $27 for left-hand action.
The right hand model was disc. 1998, but resumed in 2000.

✱ Model 700VS SF/SF-P (Varmint Synthetic Stainless Fluted/Ported) - .220 Swift (ported barrel only until 2000), .22-250 Rem., .223 Rem. (w/o porting), .308 Win. (ported barrel only, disc. 1999) or .338 Rem. Ultra Mag. (mfg. 2000 only) cal., stainless steel action with 26 in. barrel with flutes, 2 barrel ports became an option in some cals. during 1998-99 only (Model SF-P). New 1994.

	MSR $949		$800	$590	$465

Add 5% for ported barrel (Model 700VS SF-P, disc. 1999).

Grading		100%	98%	95%	90%	80%	70%	60%

✳ Model 700 VLS (Varmint Laminated Stock) - .222 Rem. (mfg. 1995 only), .22- 250 Rem., .223 Rem., .243 Win., 6mm Rem. (new 1998), .260 Rem. (disc. 1999), .308 Win., or 7mm-08 Rem. (mfg. 1997-99) cal., 26 in. heavy barrel, blue metalwork, w/o sights, brown laminated stock with skip line checkering, beavertail shaped forend became standard 1998, 9 3/8 lbs. New 1995.

MSR	$705	$575	$465	$370	$320	$285	$265	$250

MODEL 700BDL SS CAMO - .300 Rem. Ultra Mag. cal., Realtree Hardwoods camo stock treatment, satin finished receiver and round barrel, special edition for the Rocky Mountain Elk Foundation. New 2001.

MSR	$808	$660	$515	$400				

MODEL 700BDL MOUNTAIN RIFLE DM (DETACHABLE MAG.) - .243 Win. (disc. 1997), .260 Rem. (new 1998), .25-06 Rem., .270 Win., .280 Rem., 7mm-08 Rem., or .30-06 cal., detachable mag., satin finished American walnut stock, satin bluing, without sights, 6¾ lbs. New 1995.

MSR	$728	$585	$470	$380	$330	$285	$265	$250

✳ Model 700BDL Mountain LSS - .260 Rem., .270 Win., .30-06, or 7mm-08 Rem. cal., features stainless action and 22 in. barrel w/o sights, brown laminate stock, approx. 6½ lbs. New 1999.

MSR	$776	$635	$500	$395				

MODEL 700BDL MOUNTAIN RIFLE (FIXED MAG.) - .243 Win. (new 1988), .25- 06 Rem. (new 1992), .257 Roberts (new 1991), .270 Win., 7mm-08 Rem. (new 1988), .280 Rem., .30-06, .308 Win. (new 1988), or 7x57mm Mauser (new 1990) cal., 22 in. tapered barrel, checkered satin finished American walnut stock with cheekpiece and ebony forend, 4 shot mag., without sights, 6¾ lbs. Mfg. 1986-94.

		$445	$380	$315	$275	$250	$220	$195

Last MSR was $532.

✳ Model 700BDL Mountain Stainless - .25-06 Rem., .270 Win., .280 Rem., or .30-06 cal., 22 in. barrel, black synthetic stock with pressed checkering, blind mag., 7¼ lbs. Mfg. 1993 only.

		$450	$385	$315				

Last MSR was $532.

MODEL 700BDL EUROPEAN - .243 Win., .270 Win., .280 Rem., 7mm-08 Rem., 7mm Rem. Mag., .30-06, or .308 Win. cal., Monte Carlo stock with hand-rubbed oil finish, 22 or 24 (Mag. cals. only) in. barrel, hinged floorplate, iron sights, approx. 7¼ lbs. Disc. 1994.

		$445	$375	$325	$280	$250	$220	$195

Last MSR was $532.

Add $27 for 7mm Rem. Mag. cal.

MODEL 700 SENDERO SPECIAL - .25-06 Rem., .270 Win. (disc. 2001), .300 Win. Mag., or 7mm Rem. Mag. cal., similar to Model 700 VS, except has long action for Mag. cals., 24 (non-cataloged) or 26 in. barrel, 9 lbs. New 1994.

MSR	$788	$635	$510	$420	$335	$295	$265	$250

Add $27 for Mag. cals.
Add approx. $100 for fluted barrel (not cataloged).

✳ Model 700 Sendero SF (Stainless Fluted) - .25-06 Rem., .300 Win. Mag., .300 Wby. Mag. (mfg. 1997-2001), .300 Rem. Ultra Mag. (new 1999), .338 Rem. Ultra Mag. (new 2000), 7mm STW (new 1997), 7mm Rem. Mag., or 7mm Rem. Ultra Mag. (new 2001) cal., 26 in. varmint type fluted barrel, approx. 8½ lbs. New 1996.

MSR	$976	$815	$630	$470				

Add $13 for Mag. cals., except for 7mm Rem. Mag.
Subtract $27 for .25-06 Rem. cal.

R

Grading	100%	98%	95%	90%	80%	70%	60%

MODEL 700 SENDERO COMPOSITE - .25-06 Rem., .300 Win. Mag., or 7mm STW cal., features 26 in. composite barrel, matte black finished steel action, Kevlar reinforced black synthetic stock, 7 7/8 lbs. Mfg. 1999 only.

	$1,395	$1,125	$750	$650	$575	$525	$475

Last MSR was $1,665.

MODEL 700VS COMPOSITE - .22-250 Rem., .223 Rem., or .308 Win. cal., similar to Model 700 Sendero Composite, except is available in short action only. Mfg. by Custom Shop 1999-2000.

	$1,550	$1,225	$825	$700	$600	$550	$500

Last MSR was $1,912.

MODEL 700 ETRONX VS SF - .220 Swift, .22-250 Rem., or .243 Win. cal., features patented Etronx technology utilizing an electronic discharge for virtually instant cartridge ignition, CPU located in stock incorporates standard 9V battery, and allows electric signal to be passed through a ceramic coated firing pin, which in turn activates the specially designed electronic primer. There are no moving parts in this system, and therefore, nothing to delay ignition. Electronic trigger mechanism enables almost zero lock time. LED on top of grip indicates system status (fire or safe mode), chamber status (loaded or not loaded), low battery indicator, and any possible system malfunction. 26 in. heavy stainless steel barrel with black flutes, alumiunum bedding, Kevlar reinforced composite stock with matte black finish, 8 7/8 lbs. Introduced late 1999.

MSR	$1,999		$1,875	$1,650	$1,500		

Because the Etronx ignition system uses an electronic primer the same size as a standard rifle primer, reloading is no different than using standard cases, powder, and bullets. The only thing that has changed is the electronic primer.

MODEL 700 CUSTOM KS MOUNTAIN RIFLE - .270 Win., .280 Rem., .300 Win. Mag., .300 Wby. Mag. (new 1989), .300 Rem. Ultra Mag. (new 1999), .30-06, .338 Win. Mag. (new 1986), .338 Rem. Ultra Mag. (new 2000), .35 Whelen (new 1989), 7mm STW (new 1999), 7mm Rem. Mag., 7mm Rem. Ultra Mag. (new 2001), 8mm Rem. Mag. (new 1986), .375 Rem. Ultra Mag. (new 2001), or .375 H&H cal., 22 in. barrel, features extra lightweight Kevlar fiber-reinforced stock, available in either right or left-hand action. New 1986.

MSR	$1,294		$1,030	$850	$625	$525	$450	$385	$350

Add $79 for left-hand action.

This model is available from the Custom Shop only (special order).

❋ *Model 700 Custom KS Mountain Stainless Rifle* - similar to Model 700 Custom KS Mountain Rifle, except has stainless steel action and barrel, not available in .35 Whelen or 8mm Rem. Mag. cal., not available in left-hand action. New 1995.

MSR	$1,477		$1,235	$940	$725				

❋ *Model 700 Mountain Rifle Custom KS Wood Grained Kevlar* - similar to Model 700 Custom KS Safari Grade, except has wood grained Kevlar stock. Mfg. 1992-1993.

	$1,000	$875	$750	$650	$550	$485	$430

Last MSR was $1,109.

Add $63 for left-hand action.

MODEL 700 SAFARI GRADE - .375 H&H, 8mm Rem. Mag. (new 1986), .416 Rem. Mag. (new 1989), or .458 Win. Mag. cal., heavier 700BDL barrel, 3 shot mag., 24 in. barrel, available with either Classic or Monte Carlo stock configuration, custom shop special order only, 9 lbs. Mfg. 1962-2000.

	$1,015	$800	$595	$440	$415	$385	$330

Last MSR was $1,225.

Add $73 for left-hand model (Classic stock only).

❋ *Model 700 Custom KS Safari Grade* - 8mm Rem. Mag., .375 H&H, .416 Rem. Mag., or .458 Win. Mag. cal., stock made from Kevlar and fiberglass, 24 in. barrel. New 1989.

MSR	$1,497		$1,260	$975	$760	$660	$575	$500	$450

Add $80 for left-hand model.

R

Grading	100%	98%	95%	90%	80%	70%	60%

❋ *Model 700 Custom KS Safari Stainless* - .375 H&H, .416 Rem. Mag., or .458 Win. Mag. cal., features fiberglass and Kevlar stock and stainless steel action. Introduced 1993.

	MSR	$1,672		$1,365	$1,050	$725			

MODEL 700 ABG (AFRICAN BIG GAME) - .375 H&H, .375 Rem. Ultra Mag., .416 Rem. Mag., or .458 Win. Mag. cal., straight line 3 shot detachable box mag., checkered brown lamniate stock with right hand cheekpiece, matte finished steel receiver, 26 in. barrel, custom shop special order only, 9½ lbs. New 2001.

	MSR	$1,726		$1,475	$950	$750	$525	$475	$425	$395

MODEL 700 APR (AFRICAN PLAINS RIFLE) - .300 Win. Mag., .300 Wby. Mag., .300 Rem. Ultra Mag. (new 1999), .338 Win. Mag., .338 Rem. Ultra Mag. (new 2000), .375 H&H, 7mm Rem. Mag, 7mm Rem. Ultra Mag. (new 2001), or .375 Rem. Ultra Mag. (new 2001) cal., custom shop variation with 26 in. custom shop barrel, satin finish metal and brown, pressure laminated, checkered wood stock with satin finish and butt pad, machined steel triggerguard and floor plate. New 1994.

	MSR	$1,690		$1,425	$1,125	$965	$785	$650	$550	$485

MODEL 700 AWR (ALASKAN WILDERNESS RIFLE) - .300 Win. Mag., .300 Wby. Mag., .300 Rem. Ultra Mag. (new 1999), .338 Win. Mag., .338 Rem. Ultra Mag. (new 2000), .375 H&H, 7mm STW (new 1998), 7mm Rem. Mag., 7mm Rem. Ultra Mag. (new 2001), or .375 Rem. Ultra Mag. (new 2001) cal., black synthetic fiberglass with Kevlar stock, black stainless steel action. New 1994.

	MSR	$1,569		$1,395	$1,100	$950			

MODEL 700C GRADE (CUSTOM SHOP) - from custom shop, no engraving, deluxe checkered wood with rosewood forearm cap. Mfg 1964-1983.

		$850	$775	$695	$635	$510	$440	$400

MODEL 700D PEERLESS GRADE (CUSTOM SHOP) - scroll engraving, best wood. Mfg. 1962-1983.

		$1,700	$1,425	$1,200	$1,000	$880	$825	$690

MODEL 700F PREMIER GRADE (CUSTOM SHOP) - elaborate engraving, best wood. Mfg. 1962-1983.

		$3,250	$2,750	$2,420	$2,200	$2,035	$1,870	$1,760

MODEL 700 CUSTOM GRADE - special order only, grades differ in amount of engraving and type of walnut. Available as a custom order only through Remington. Values reflect 1991 information. The Remington Custom Shop should be contacted for a current price quotation and the availability of options.

Special order Model 700s mfg. between early '60s - 1982 were designated C Grade, D Grade, or F Grade. Values will approximate Custom Grade Models I-III listed. In 1991, Remington discontinued Custom Grade Model designations.

❋ *Model 700 Custom Grade Model I* - mfg. 1983-1991.

	$1,200	$1,000	$795

Last MSR was $1,314.

❋ *Model 700 Custom Grade Model II* - mfg. 1983-1991.

	$1,995	$1,675	$1,295

Last MSR was $2,335.

❋ *Model 700 Custom Grade Model III* - mfg. 1983-1991.

	$2,900	$2,150	$1,750

Last MSR was $3,650.

❋ *Model 700 Custom Grade Model IV* - mfg. 1983-1991.

	$4,875	$4,100	$2,950

Last MSR was $5,695.

R

Grading	100%	98%	95%	90%	80%	70%	60%

MODEL 700 CUSTOM RIFLE - the Remington Custom Shop should be contacted directly (see Trademark Index) for current information regarding this model. New 1992.

MSR	$2,897	$2,350	$1,950	$1,375	$1,075	$875	$750	$625

Beginning 1992, Remington stopped Custom Grade Model designations in favor of individualized quotations per work order. The suggested retail price for this model is the starting price with the minimum number of options. The Custom Shop should be contacted directly regarding special order pricing (see Trademark Index).

RIFLES: BOLT ACTION, MODEL 40X & VARIATIONS

MODEL 40X SPORTER - .22 LR cal. only, sporterized version of the 40X Target Rifle, 5 shot mag., custom 700 stock, a special order only gun from the factory. Rare, less than 700 mfg. 1969-1977, parts clean-up to 1980.

	$1,850	$1,325	$925	$800	$720	$650	$595

Add 10% if NIB.

This model was last listed in the 1977 Remington catalog - retail was $525.

MODEL 40X TARGET RIFLE (RANGEMASTER) - .22 LR cal., 28 in. heavy barrel, Redfield Olympic sights, scope bases, target stock, rubber butt, first production rifle with built in bedding device and adjustment screws, 12¾ lbs. Mfg. 1956-1964.

	$800	$700	$600	$525	$450	$375	$325
No sights	$750	$650	$550	$475	$400	$350	$300

MODEL 40X STANDARD BARREL (RANGEMASTER) - similar to 40X Target Rifle, with lighter barrel, 10¾ lbs.

	$550	$475	$380	$310	$250	$220	$190
No sights	$495	$450	$360	$295	$240	$200	$180

MODEL 40X CENTERFIRE (RANGEMASTER) - similar to Model 40X Rim Fire, except in .222 Rem., .222 Rem. Mag., .30-06, or .308 Win. cal. Mfg. 1961-1964.

	$550	$475	$380	$310	$250	$220	$190
No sights	$495	$450	$360	$295	$240	$200	$180

MODEL 40-XB RANGEMASTER RIMFIRE - .22 LR cal., bolt action single shot, 28 in. light or heavy barrel, no sights, target stock with guide rail, rubber butt. Mfg. 1964-1974.

	$575	$525	$420	$335	$275	$220	$195

Add a premium for this model equipped with a mag.

MODEL 40-XB RANGEMASTER CENTERFIRE - available in 18 cals. between .22 BR Rem. and .300 Rem. Ultra Mag., custom made, 27¼ in. barrel (current production is stainless steel action and barrel), single shot or repeater (5 shot mag.), walnut stock, test fired, 10½ - 11 lbs. Mfg. 1964-present.

MSR	$1,612	$1,310	$1,025	$735	$550	$450	$375	$325

Add $122 for repeater model.

Add $62 for left-hand action (disc. 1994).

An International Free Rifle was also offered - only 107 were mfg. with premiums being paid.

MODEL 40-XB KS (KEVLAR STOCK) - 15 short action cals. between .220 Swift and .300 Win. Mag., 27¼ in. bright finished stainless steel barrel, single shot or repeater, black finish Kevlar stock, no sights, 9¾ lbs. New 1987.

MSR	$1,821	$1,560	$1,095	$760

Add $27 for bench rest model (Model 40-XBBR KS).

Add $120 for repeater model.

Add $197 for 2 oz. trigger.

MODEL 40-XC KS - .223 Rem. (mfg. 1995-99) or .308 Win. cal., National Match Course repeater rifle, adj. trigger pull, wood (disc. 1989) or fiberglass with Kevlar (standard 1990) stock.

MSR	$1,794	$1,525	$1,050	$750

Subtract approx. $120 for wood stock.

Grading	100%	98%	95%	90%	80%	70%	60%

MODEL 40-XRBR/KS RIMFIRE SINGLE SHOT - .22 LR cal., 24 in. heavy barrel, no sights, adj. butt plate and palm stop, target wood (disc. 1989) or fiberglass with Kevlar (became standard 1990, now available only in benchrest configuration) stock. Mfg. 1974-present.

	MSR	**$1,866**		**$1,585**	**$1,100**	**$775**		

Subtract 20% for wood stock.

MODEL 40-XR KS SPORTER - .22 LR or .22 Mag. cal., Model 40-XR action, match chambered, custom sporter contoured 24 in. barrel, fiberglass with Kevlar stock, drilled and tapped receiver, w/o sights, special order. Mfg. 1994-99.

			$1,375	**$1,100**	**$750**	**$625**	**$550**	**$500**	**$450**

Last MSR was $1,638.

MODEL 40-XB THUMBHOLE - available in 18 centerfire cals. between .22 BR Rem. - .300 Rem. Ultra Mag, 27¼ in. heavy stainless barrel, laminated thumbhole stock. New 1999.

	MSR	**$1,821**		**$1,535**	**$1,095**	**$785**		

Add $120 for repeater action (new 2000).

MODEL 40-XR CUSTOM SPORTER - .22 LR or .22 Win. Mag. (new 2000) cal., top-of-the-line sporter from the custom shop, individually made per customer's specifications.

	MSR	**$3,333**		**$2,925**	**$2,400**	**$1,900**	**$1,600**	**$1,325**	**$1,100**	**$925**

MODEL 40-XR CUSTOM SPORTER HIGH GRADES - .22 LR cal. only, single shot, available on special order from Remington's Custom Shop only, Grades I-IV (disc. 1991) increase by amount of engraving, quality of wood, and other special order options/features. Mfg. 1986-1991.

Values for Custom Grades listed reflect 1991 (the year of discontinuance) price information. The Remington Custom Shop should be contacted directly regarding current values and options.

✳ *Model 40-XR Custom Grade Model I* - mfg. 1986-1991.

	$1,100	**$925**	**$795**	

Last MSR was $1,314.

✳ *Model 40-XR Custom Grade Model II* - mfg. 1986-1991.

	$1,995	**$1,675**	**$1,295**	

Last MSR was $2,335.

✳ *Model 40-XR Custom Grade Model III* - mfg. 1986-1991.

	$2,900	**$2,150**	**$1,750**	

Last MSR was $3,650.

✳ *Model 40-XR Custom Grade Model IV* - mfg. 1986-1991.

	$4,875	**$4,100**	**$2,950**	

Last MSR was $5,695.

SHOTGUNS: O/U

Values listed for Model 3200s assume NIB condition - subtract 10%-15% if without box, warranty card, and original shipping container (with packing materials).

MODEL 32 - 12 ga., double lock action, SST, separated barrels, 26, 28, or 30 in. barrels without rib, SR, or VR. Approx. 6,050 mfg. (ser. range approx. 0001-6,053) 1931-1947. There is a discrepancy as to when serialization started on this model.

			$1,950	**$1,675**	**$1,425**	**$1,275**	**$925**	**$825**	**$795**

Add 10% for SST.
Add 10% for vent. or solid rib.
Add 20% for VR on 28 in. barrels.

MODEL 32 SERIALIZATION IS AS FOLLOWS: 1931 - 0001-1,009; 1932 - 1,010-1,903; 1933 - 1,904-1,948; 1934 - 1,949-2,727; 1935 - 2,728-3,610; 1936 - 3,611-4,259; 1937 - 4,260-4,755; 1938 - 4,756-4,958; 1939 - 4,959-5,202; 1940 - 5,203-5,425; 1941 - 5,426-5,741; 1942 - 5,742-6,020; 1943 - 6,021-6,031; 1944 - 6,032-6,049; 1945 to 1947 - 6,050-6,053.

MODEL 32D TOURNAMENT

			$3,750	**$3,000**	**$2,500**	**$2,000**	**$1,750**	**$1,400**	**$1,175**

R

Grading	100%	98%	95%	90%	80%	70%	60%

MODEL 32E EXPERT - less than 35 mfg.

	$4,500	$3,950	$3,500	$2,975	$2,650	$2,200	$1,875

MODEL 32F PREMIER

	$6,500	$5,500	$5,000	$4,500	$3,520	$2,750	$2,300

Note: Grades differ in quality, grade of wood, and amount of engraving.

MODEL 32 SKEET - similar to 32A, with 26 or 28 (more desirable) in. skeet bored barrels, SST. Mfg. 1932-1942.

	$1,600	$1,400	$1,200	$1,000	$950	$875	$800

Add 10% for VR.
Add 10%-15% for 28 in. barrels.

MODEL 32TC TARGET - similar to 32A, with 30 or 32 in. VR full choke barrels, trap style stock. Mfg. 1932-1942.

	$3,000	$2,300	$1,800	$1,700	$1,600	$1,475	$1,300

Add 10% for 30 in. VR barrels.

MODEL 300 IDEAL - 12 ga. only, 3 in. chambers, boxlock action, features unique forearm latching system that incorporates barrel selector switch, 26, 28, or 30 in. 8mm VR barrels with twin beads and Rem. chokes (3), engraved receiver sides, gold SST, high polish blue, checkered satin finished American walnut stock and forearm with English style solid recoil pad, 7 3/8 - 7 7/8 lbs. Mfg. 2000-2001.

	$1,150	$995	$875	$800	$750	$700	$650

Last MSR was $1,332.

MODEL 332 - 12 ga. only, 3 in. chambers, new modified boxlock action with underlock custom shop design, low profile receiver with Model 32 type styling, 26, 28, or 30 in. VR light contour barrels with Remchokes, glass-bead blasted black oxide metal finish with resembles Model 32 rust bluing, satin finished checkered walnut stock and forearm with solid rubber recoil pad, mechanical SST, ejectors, 7½ - 8 lbs. Mfg. in Ilion beginning late 2001.

MSR	$1,532		$1,250	$995	$875	$750	$625	$550	$475

MODEL 396 SKEET/SPORTING CLAYS - 12 ga. only, satin finished boxlock action with engraved sideplates, 28 or 30 in. barrels with 10mm VR and Rem. chokes, select checkered walnut stock and target style forend, Sporting Clays Model has ported barrels, SST, ejectors, approx. 7½ lbs. Mfg. 1996-98.

✳ *Model 396 Skeet*

	$1,750	$1,475	$1,250	$1,075	$925	$800	$700

Last MSR was $1,993.

✳ *Model 396 Sporting Clays*

	$1,875	$1,575	$1,300	$1,100	$950	$825	$725

Last MSR was $2,126.

MODEL 3200 FIELD - 12 ga., 26, 28, or 30 in. barrels, VR, various chokes, boxlock, auto ejectors, single selective trigger, checkered pistol grip stock, separated barrels. Mfg. 1973-1977.

	$1,100	$1,000	$950	$900	$850	$800	$750

During 1998, the custom shop once again started manufacturing the Model 3200 from existing parts. Supplies are limited - please contact the Remington Custom Shop for availability and pricing.

Model 3200s with shorter barrels (26 or 28 in.) and open choking are more desirable than 30 in. tubes bored F/M.

MODEL 3200 SERIALIZATION IS AS FOLLOWS: 1973 - 4,200-16,667; 1974 - 16,668-27,393; 1975 - 27,394-35,303; 1976 - 35,304-39,216; 1977 - 39,217-41,432; 1978 - 41,433-42,813; 1979 - 42,814-44,278; 1980 - 44,279-45,504; 1981 - 45,505-45,974; 1982 - 45,975-47,200; 1983 - 47,201-47,308.

MODEL 3200 MAGNUM - 12 ga., 3 in. chambers, 30 in. heavy wall barrels (steel shot compatible), less than 1,000 mfg. 1975-1977.

	$1,695	$1,575	$1,475	$1,200	$1,050	$950	$850

Grading	100%	98%	95%	90%	80%	70%	60%

MODEL 3200 SKEET - similar to 3200 Field, with 26 or 28 in. skeet bored barrels, skeet style stock. Mfg. 1973-1980.

	$1,295	$1,050	$950	$850	$750	$650	$575

28 in. barrels will command a premium on this model.

This model was also mfg. in a 28 in. IM/F configuration with gold pigeon on bottom for live pigeon shooting. Since less than 300 were mfg., prices in the $2,700 range are being asked if NIB condition. This model generally had a trap style rib, but there have been some field ribs as well. Originally, it was called the "Competition Live Pigeon" and was mfg. with a competition receiver and trap grade style wood.

❋ *Model 3200 Competition Skeet Four Ga. Set* - includes 12, 20, 28 ga., or .410 bore, cased. Mfg. 1980-83.

	$5,500	$5,000	$4,600	$4,200	$4,000	$3,800	$3,500

Add 10%-15% for 28 in. barrels.

28 in. barrels will command a premium on this model.

MODEL 3200 COMPETITION SKEET - similar to 3200 Skeet, with scroll engraved frame and trigger guard, select wood. Mfg. 1976-1983.

	$1,700	$1,450	$1,250	$995	$950	$850	$750

Add 10%-15% for 28 in. VR barrels.

MODEL 3200 TRAP - similar as 3200 Field, with 30 or 32 in. barrels choked IM/F or F/ F, stock and rib. Mfg. 1973-1977.

	$1,375	$1,100	$950	$875	$800	$750	$700

30 in. barrels are more desirable than 32 in.

MODEL 3200 SPECIAL TRAP - similar to 3200 Trap, except fancy wood. Mfg. 1973- 1980.

	$1,450	$1,300	$1,200	$1,000	$875	$800	$750

MODEL 3200 COMPETITION TRAP - similar to 3200 Trap, with scroll engraving. Mfg. 1976-1983.

	$1,950	$1,800	$1,675	$1,450	$1,200	$950	$875
Pigeon Grade	$2,450	$2,150	$1,850	$1,500	$1,250	$995	$900

The Pigeon Grade featured a gold pigeon on receiver bottom - approx. 250 mfg. 1979-1983. There was a special production of this model during 1991-92 which was limited to approx. 100 guns.

MODEL 3200 PREMIER - 12 ga., sold through Remington's International Division, 500 mfg. 1975 only, patterned after "One of 1000" series, regular or Monte Carlo stock.

	$2,900	$2,500	$2,150	$1,800	$1,500	$1,200	$1,025

Add 125% for engraving (only 116 mfg., engraving was done in Belgium).

MODEL 3200 "ONE OF 1000" - limited edition, elaborate engraving, fancy wood, supplied with hard case, made in both skeet and trap models. Mfg. 1,000 each model: 1973 (Trap) and 1974 (Skeet).

Trap (30 IM/F or F/F)	$2,150	$1,750	$1,475	$1,325	$1,200	$1,075	$875
Skeet (26 or 28 in. SK/SK)	$1,925	$1,675	$1,475	$1,325	$1,200	$1,075	$875

Add 10% for 28 in. barrels on the Skeet Model.

PEERLESS FIELD GRADE - 12 ga. only, 3 in. chambers, 26, 28, or 30 in. VR barrels with Rem. chokes, boxlock with engraved sideplates, SST, ejectors, high-gloss checkered walnut stock and forearm with vent. recoil pad, 3.28 milliseconds lock time, blue metal, approx. 7½ lbs. Mfg. 1993- 98.

	$1,000	$900	$850	$800	$750	$700	$650

Last MSR was $1,172.

This model is an entirely new design not sharing any parts with either the Models 32 or 3200.

R

100%	98%	95%	90%	80%	70%	60%	50%	40%	30%	20%	10%

SHOTGUNS: SxS

The author wishes to express thanks to Charles Semmer for once again updating the following section on older Remington SxS Shotguns.

Because E. Remington & Sons shotguns are classified as antique, it may be helpful to consult the "NRA Antique Condition Standards" section in the front of this text to convert to the Percentage Grading System listed.

MODEL 1873 "HAMMER LIFTER" - 10 or 12 ga., also known as Whitmore Hammer Lifter, 28 or 30 in. decarbonized, twist, or damascus barrels, top "thumb lever" action activated by pushing upward to open, rib top marked "E. REMINGTON & SONS, ILION, N.Y.", patented "AUG. 8, 1871, APRIL 16, 1872", steel buttplate, pistol grip was optional, grades above 3 were made to order. Approx. 5,000 mfg. from 1873 to 1878, starting with ser. no. 1.

✳ *Grade 1* - decarbonized steel barrels, no checkering or engraving.

$1,800	$1,500	$1,200	$1,000	$950	$800	$600	$500	$375	$300	$250	$225

✳ *Grade 2* - twist steel barrels, checkering, no engraving.

$2,200	$2,000	$1,700	$1,500	$1,200	$1,000	$900	$750	$650	$500	$350	$275

✳ *Grade 3* - twist or damascus steel barrels, checkering and engraving.

$3,500	$3,200	$2,200	$1,750	$1,500	$1,200	$1,100	$1,000	$750	$650	$450	$350

Add 10%-20% to Grade 3 prices for higher grades (extra fine engraving).

MODEL 1875 AND 1876 "LIFTER" (WHITMORE LIFTER) - 10 or 12 ga., 28 or 30 in. decarbonized, twist, or damascus barrels, top "thumb lever" action activated by pushing upward to open, rib top marked "E. REMINGTON & SONS, ILION, N.Y.", patented "AUG. 8, 1871, APRIL 16, 1872", steel buttplate, pistol grip was optional, the Model 1875 started with ser. no. 1, and went to approx. 3,350, the Model 1876 started with ser. no. 3,350 and went to approx. 5,900. Approx. 5,900 Model 1875s & 1876s were mfg. from 1875-1882.

✳ *Grade 1* - decarbonized steel barrels, no checkering or engraving.

$1,800	$1,500	$1,200	$1,000	$950	$800	$600	$500	$375	$300	$250	$225

✳ *Grade 2* - twist steel barrels, checkering, no engraving.

$2,000	$1,800	$1,500	$1,200	$1,000	$900	$750	$650	$550	$500	$350	$275

✳ *Grade 3* - twist or damascus steel barrels, checkered and engraving.

$3,200	$2,900	$1,900	$1,500	$1,200	$1,000	$900	$750	$650	$550	$450	$350

✳ *Grade 4* - twist or damascus steel barrels, checkered and extra fine engraving.

$3,500	$3,200	$2,500	$2,100	$1,500	$1,200	$1,000	$900	$750	$650	$475	$350

✳ *Grade 5* - damascus steel barrels, checkered and superior engraving.

$4,000	$3,700	$3,200	$2,600	$2,300	$1,800	$1,200	$1,000	$900	$800	$550	$400

Add 100% to the few Model 1873s and 1875s that are rib marked "NEW YORK & LONDON".

Add 100% for double rifles and combination guns in Models 1873, 1875, and 1876.

There were very few double rifles and combination guns made in Models 1873, 1875, and 1876 - they are very rare, and be aware of fake double rifles.

R **MODEL 1878 HAMMER (HEAVY DUCK GUN)** - 10 ga., called the Heavy Duck Gun, 30-32 in., 9¾ and 10 lbs., "thumb-lever" action, thick bolsters, top extension rib, no flash fences, steel buttplate. Approx. 2,500 mfg. from 1878 to 1882, starting with ser. no. 1.

✳ *Grade 1* - decarbonized steel barrels, no checkering, no engraving.

$1,800	$1,500	$1,200	$1,000	$950	$800	$600	$500	$375	$300	$250	$250

✳ *Grade 2* - twist steel barrels, checkered, no engraving.

$2,100	$1,800	$1,500	$1,200	$1,000	$900	$750	$650	$550	$500	$375	$375

✳ *Grade 3* - laminated steel barrels, checkered, engraved.

$3,500	$3,200	$2,500	$2,100	$1,500	$1,200	$1,000	$900	$750	$650	$475	$475

✳ *Grade 4* - damascus steel barrels, checkered, engraved.

$4,000	$3,700	$3,300	$3,000	$2,500	$2,000	$1,500	$1,200	$1,000	$900	$650	$600

100%	98%	95%	90%	80%	70%	60%	50%	40%	30%	20%	10%

MODEL 1879 SxS HAMMER - usually 12 ga., top extension rib, no flash fences, steel buttplate, only Whitmore model with Deeley & Edge forend catch. Ser. nos. within the Model 1878.

Add 40% for this scarce variation to Model 1878 listed prices.

MODEL 1882 SxS HAMMER - (includes the unique Model 1883), 10 or 12 ga., 30 or 32 in. decarbonized, twist or damascus steel barrels, rib marked "E. REMINGTON & SONS, ILION, N.Y.", typical top lever, all grades have checkered pistol grip and forend with various designs according to grade. All contain Deeley & Edge forend catch. Approx. 16,000 Model 1882s, possibly 1,000 Model 1883s were mfg. from 1882-1888. Started with ser. no. 1,000.

❋ Grade 1 - decarbonized steel barrels, no enraving, steel buttplate.

$1,500	$1,300	$1,200	$1,000	$750	$650	$550	$450	$350	$275	$250	$200

❋ Grade 2 - twist steel barrels, no engraving, steel buttplate.

$1,400	$1,200	$1,100	$900	$750	$650	$550	$450	$350	$275	$250	$200

❋ Grade 3 - laminated steel barrels, engraved, steel buttplate.

$1,800	$1,600	$1,400	$1,200	$1,000	$875	$750	$650	$550	$400	$350	$250

❋ Grade 4 - damascus steel barrels, engraved, steel buttplate.

$2,000	$1,800	$1,600	$1,400	$1,200	$1,000	$800	$700	$600	$500	$400	$300

❋ Grade 5 - fine damascus steel, finely engraved, superior rubber buttplate.

$3,000	$2,800	$2,400	$2,200	$2,000	$1,700	$1,400	$1,000	$800	$700	$600	$500

❋ Grade 6 - extra fine damascus, fine scroll engraved, superior rubber buttplate.

$5,000	$4,800	$4,200	$3,700	$3,200	$2,700	$2,500	$2,000	$1,500	$1,200	$1,000	$800

Add 25% for optional auxiliary rifle barrel insert.

MODEL 1883 - identified by its hammer shape which is different that the Model 1882.

Add 40% to the values for this model.

MODEL 1885/1887 SxS HAMMER - 10, 12, or 16 ga., different hammer style variation of the Model 1882, 28, 30, or 32 in. decarbonized, twist or damascus steel barrels, rib marked "E. REMINGTON & SONS, ILION, N.Y.", top lever, all grades are checkered pistol grip and forend with various designs according to grade, Deeley & Edge forend catch, rubber buttplate with ERS logo. Approx. 7,000 mfg. from 1885-1888. Ser. nos. started at 16,700. Guns before ser. no. 20,200 are considered Model 1885s, ser. nos. after are Model 1887s.

❋ Grade 1 - decarbonized steel barrels, no engraving.

$1,800	$1,600	$1,400	$1,200	$1,000	$700	$600	$500	$400	$300	$275	$225

❋ Grade 2 - twist steel barrels, no engraving.

$1,700	$1,500	$1,300	$1,000	$850	$750	$650	$550	$450	$375	$300	$225

❋ Grade 3 - damascus steel barrels, no engraving.

$1,800	$1,600	$1,400	$1,200	$1,000	$875	$750	$650	$550	$400	$350	$250

❋ Grade 4 - damascus steel barrels, engraved.

$2,000	$1,800	$1,600	$1,400	$1,200	$1,000	$800	$700	$600	$500	$400	$300

❋ Grade 5 - fine damascus steel barrels, finely engraved.

$3,000	$2,800	$2,400	$2,200	$1,700	$1,500	$1,200	$900	$750	$650	$500	$400

❋ Grade 6 - extra fine damascus barrels, fine scroll engraved.

$5,000	$4,800	$4,200	$3,700	$3,200	$2,700	$2,500	$2,000	$1,500	$1,200	$900	$700

❋ Grade 7 - superior damascus barrels, extra fine scroll engraved, game scene.

$7,500	$7,300	$7,100	$6,500	$6,000	$5,500	$5,000	$4,000	$3,500	$3,000	$2,000	$1,000

Add 25% for optional auxiliary rifle barrel insert.

Add 30% for 16 ga.

R

100%	98%	95%	90%	80%	70%	60%	50%	40%	30%	20%	10%

MODEL 1889 SxS HAMMER - 10, 12, or 16 ga., 28, 30, or 32 in., a few 26 in. are known. Decarbonized, twist, or damascus barrels, exposed "circular" hammers, rib marked "REMINGTON ARMS CO. ILION, N.Y. U.S.A.", top lever, all grades have checkered pistol grip and forend with various designs according to grade, Deeley & Edge forend catch. Grade number is stamped on water table left of the ser. no. Rubber buttplate with RACo logo. 134,200 mfg. 1889-1908. Ser. range from 30,000 to 100,000. After the year 1900, ser. nos. are in the 200,000 range.

✱ *Grade 1* - decarbonized steel barrels, no engraving.

$1,500	$1,300	$1,200	$1,000	$750	$650	$550	$450	$350	$300	$275	$225

✱ *Grade 2* - twist steel barrels, no engraving.

$1,600	$1,400	$1,300	$1,000	$750	$750	$650	$550	$450	$350	$300	$225

✱ *Grade 3* - damascus steel barrels, no engraving.

$1,700	$1,500	$1,400	$1,100	$950	$850	$750	$650	$500	$400	$350	$250

✱ *Grade 4* - damascus steel barrels, engraved.

$3,000	$2,800	$2,400	$2,200	$2,000	$1,700	$1,400	$1,000	$800	$700	$600	$500

✱ *Grade 5* - damascus steel barrels, finely engraved.

$5,000	$4,800	$4,200	$3,700	$3,200	$2,700	$2,500	$2,000	$1,500	$1,200	$1,000	$800

✱ *Grade 6* - extra fine damascus barrels, fine scroll engraved.

$7,500	$7,300	$7,100	$6,500	$6,000	$5,500	$5,000	$4,000	$3,500	$3,000	$2,000	$1,000

✱ *Grade 7* - superior damascus barrels, extra fine scroll engraved, game scene.

$15,000	$13,000	$10,000	$9,000	$8,000	$7,000	$6,000	$5,000	$4,000	$3,500	$2,500	$1,500

Add 20% for 16 ga.

Hardly any exist of the special ordered Grades 4 through 7.

MODEL 1894 SxS HAMMERLESS - 10, 12, or 16 ga., 26 to 32 in. "Remington", "Ordnance", or Damascus steel barrels, auto ejectors, boxlock, double triggers, checkered pistol grip or straight stock, Purdey forend snap. Grades A, B, F, and C have RACo hard rubber butt, Grade D, horn butt, Grade E, horn or heel and toe plates. Grade is usually stamped on the water table. 16 and especially 10 ga., are considered scarce and will command a higher value. 41,194 mfg. between 1894 and 1910 in the 100,000 block serial range.

✱ *Grade AE* - no engraving.

$1,500	$1,300	$1,200	$1,100	$1,000	$850	$700	$600	$500	$400	$300	$200

✱ *Grade BE* - scroll and line engraving.

$3,000	$2,800	$2,500	$2,200	$2,000	$1,700	$1,400	$1,000	$700	$500	$400	$300

✱ *Grade FE Trap* - scroll and line engraving.

$3,000	$2,800	$2,500	$2,200	$2,000	$1,700	$1,400	$1,000	$700	$500	$400	$300

✱ *Grade CE* - extra scroll engraving, silver name plate.

$4,500	$4,300	$4,000	$3,600	$3,300	$3,000	$2,500	$2,000	$1,500	$1,000	$600	$500

✱ *Grade DE* - fine scroll and game engraving, silver name plate.

$9,000	$8,000	$7,500	$7,000	$6,500	$6,000	$5,000	$4,000	$3,000	$2,000	$1,500	$1,000

✱ *Grade EE* - finest quality scroll, bird and game engraving, gold name plate.

$18,000	$17,000	$15,000	$12,000	$10,000	$8,000	$7,000	$6,500	$5,000	$3,500	$2,500	$2,000

Subtract 20% for non-ejector guns.

Add 25% for "Ordnance" barrels.

A few Remington SPECIAL grade guns were produced; they are so rare, it is not practical to attempt a value.

MODEL 1900 SxS HAMMERLESS - 12 or 16 ga., 28 or 30 in. "Remington" or damascus steel barrels, lower priced gun to meet market competition, quality a cut below the Model 1894, but mechanically the same, snap forend. No engraving was offered on this model. 98,475 mfg. between 1900 and 1910 in the 300,000 block serial range.

✱ *Grade K and KD* - Remington or Damascus steel barrels, non-ejector.

$1,000	$900	$825	$750	$675	$625	$575	$525	$475	$295	$250	$200

100%	98%	95%	90%	80%	70%	60%	50%	40%	30%	20%	10%

✳ Grade KE and KED - Remington or Damascus steel barrels, ejectors.

$1,300	$1,200	$1,100	$1,000	$900	$800	$700	$600	$500	$300	$250	$200

PARKER AHE - while advertised, the Remington re-issue of the original Parker AHE Model was never mfg. due to product liability considerations. Older Remington manufactured Parkers may be found in the Parker section of this text.

Grading	100%	98%	95%	90%	80%	70%	60%

SHOTGUNS: SEMI-AUTO, DISC.

REMINGTON AUTOLOADING SHOTGUN (PRE-MODEL 11) - 12 ga. only, original Remington mfg. of the Browning A-5, 5 shot, various grades, 20 (riot), 26, or 28 in. plain or matted rib barrel. Mfg. 1905-1910.

	$350	$275	$225	$175	$160	$135	$110

Add 20% for matted rib.

MODEL 11A AUTOLOADER 5-SHOT - 12, 16 (introduced 1931), or 20 (introduced 1930) ga., 26-32 in. barrels, takedown, various chokes, Browning type, checkered pistol stock. Approx. 300,000 mfg., 1911-1948.

	100%	98%	95%	90%	80%	70%	60%
Plain barrel	$295	$240	$215	$185	$165	$150	$120
Solid rib	$395	$315	$235	$200	$185	$165	$140
Vent. rib	$440	$360	$335	$305	$275	$220	$165

Add 35% for barrels marked "Long Range" - beware of fakes.
This model was mfg. under patent agreement with John Browning.

MODEL 11B SPECIAL - higher grade wood with hand checkered stock and forearm.

	$525	$440	$385	$360	$305	$250	$195

MODEL 11D TOURNAMENT

	$950	$850	$725	$550	$495	$470	$440

MODEL 11E EXPERT

	$1,175	$975	$875	$775	$675	$595	$525

MODEL 11F PREMIER

	$1,850	$1,550	$1,375	$1,100	$975	$850	$750

Note: Grades differ in quality, grade of wood, and amount of engraving.

SPORTSMAN MODEL SEMI-AUTO - 12, 16, or 20 ga., 26 (3 shot only) in. barrel, skeet choke, beavertail forend. Mfg. 1931-1949.

	100%	98%	95%	90%	80%	70%	60%
Plain barrel	$325	$275	$250	$195	$165	$140	$120
Solid rib	$400	$350	$300	$250	$200	$180	$150
Vent. rib	$470	$415	$360	$330	$275	$250	$220

This model was manufactured in Field, Riot, and Skeet configurations.

MODEL 48 SPORTSMAN - 12, 16, or 20 ga., 26, 28, or 32 in. barrels, 3 shot, mechanical (solid breech) ejection system, various chokes, rounded receiver, checkered pistol grip stock with cap. Approx. 275,000 mfg., 1949-1960.

	$300	$225	$200	$185	$175	$165	$140
VR barrel	$325	$275	$250	$200	$175	$165	$140

R

MODEL 48B SELECT

	$420	$360	$310	$290	$245	$220	$195

MODEL 48D TOURNAMENT

	$1,100	$825	$715	$660	$605	$440	$415

MODEL 48F PREMIER

	$2,420	$2,035	$1,540	$1,210	$990	$770	$715

Grading	100%	98%	95%	90%	80%	70%	60%

MODEL 48A RIOT GUN - 12 ga. only, 20 in. plain barrel.

	100%	98%	95%	90%	80%	70%	60%
	$275	$220	$195	$165	$150	$140	$110

MODEL 48SA SKEET - 26 in. barrel, skeet bore, ivory bead. Mfg. 1949-1960.

	100%	98%	95%	90%	80%	70%	60%
	$305	$275	$255	$230	$210	$195	$165
With VR barrel	$395	$350	$300	$260	$230	$210	$195

MODEL 48SC SKEET - "C" suffix designates C-grade wood.

	100%	98%	95%	90%	80%	70%	60%
	$385	$360	$330	$305	$275	$250	$220

MODEL 48SD TOURNAMENT - custom shop engraved.

	100%	98%	95%	90%	80%	70%	60%
	$1,100	$825	$715	$660	$605	$440	$415

MODEL 48SF PREMIER - custom shop engraved.

	100%	98%	95%	90%	80%	70%	60%
	$2,200	$1,925	$1,650	$1,210	$990	$770	$715

MODEL 11-48 SEMI-AUTO - 12, 16, 20, 28 (introduced 1952) ga., or .410 (introduced 1954) bore, recoil operated action, walnut stock. Approx. 429,000 mfg., 1949- 1968.

	100%	98%	95%	90%	80%	70%	60%
Plain barrel	$300	$225	$200	$185	$175	$165	$140
VR barrel	$325	$275	$250	$200	$175	$165	$140

Add 15% - 40% for 28 ga. or .410 bore, depending on condition.

MODEL 58ADL "SPORTSMAN - 58" SEMI-AUTO - 12, 16, or 20 ga., 26, 28, or 30 in. barrel, gas operation, various chokes, 3 shot, checkered pistol grip stock, scroll game scene engraved. Approx. 271,000 mfg., 1956-1963.

	100%	98%	95%	90%	80%	70%	60%
Plain barrel	$275	$250	$220	$195	$140	$120	$110
VR barrel	$360	$305	$275	$250	$220	$165	$140

Add 5% for Magnum in 12 ga.

MODEL 58 X-SERIES (SUNGRAIN) - similar to Model 58ADL semi-auto, except has blonde stock, available in Field (special order only), Skeet, or Trap configuration.

	100%	98%	95%	90%	80%	70%	60%
	$275	$250	$220	$195	$160	$140	$120

MODEL 58BDL - similar to 58ADL, with select wood.

	100%	98%	95%	90%	80%	70%	60%
Plain barrel	$295	$275	$250	$225	$210	$195	$165
VR barrel	$375	$335	$300	$275	$250	$200	$175

MODEL 58SA SKEET GUN - similar to 58ADL, with 26 in. skeet bore VR barrel, skeet stock.

	100%	98%	95%	90%	80%	70%	60%
	$360	$330	$305	$275	$250	$200	$175

MODEL 58SC SKEET - "C" suffix designates C-grade wood.

	100%	98%	95%	90%	80%	70%	60%
	$495	$440	$415	$385	$330	$305	$275

MODEL 58D TOURNAMENT - custom shop engraved.

	100%	98%	95%	90%	80%	70%	60%
	$825	$715	$635	$580	$525	$470	$440

MODEL 58F PREMIER - custom shop engraved.

	100%	98%	95%	90%	80%	70%	60%
	$1,650	$1,375	$1,210	$1,045	$965	$880	$800

Note: Models differ in grade of wood, amount of engraving, and gold inlays.

R MODEL 878A "AUTOMASTER" - 12 ga. gas operated semi-auto, 26, 28, or 30 in. barrels, action similar to Model 58. Approx. 62,000 mfg., 1959-1962. Add 15% for VR.

	100%	98%	95%	90%	80%	70%	60%
	$235	$200	$185	$170	$160	$150	$135

Barrels on this model are interchangeable with those on the Model 58.

Grading	100%	98%	95%	90%	80%	70%	60%

SHOTGUNS: SEMI-AUTO, CURRENT/RECENT PRODUCTION

MODEL SP-10 - 10 ga., 3½ in. chamber, semi-auto stainless steel gas system operation, lighter recoil than most 12 ga. Mags., 26 or 30 in. barrel with 3/8 in. VR and Rem. chokes (2), checkered stock and forearm with low gloss satin finish, matte metal finish, crossbolt safety, recoil pad, supplied with camo sling, approx. 11 lbs. Introduced 1989.

MSR	$1,292	$970	$860	$780	$650	$575	$550	$475

Add $317 (factory MSR) per extra Model SP-10 barrel.

The first 5,000 SP-10s were assigned special serialization (LE89 prefix) - no premiums exist at this time, however.

This model is NOT a re-designed Ithaca Mag-10 and the parts are NOT interchangeable. The SP-10 is a new design.

✴ *Model SP-10 Camo* - 23 (Turkey Model, mfg. 1999-2000), or 26 in. VR barrel, choice of Mossy Oak (disc. 1996), full coverage Mossy Oak Break-Up (new 1997), or Bottomland (mfg. 1994-96) Camo finish. New 1993.

MSR	$1,412	$1,045	$860	$780	$665	$585	$550	$475

✴ *Model SP-10 Magnum Synthetic* - features lightweight black synthetic stock and forearm, matte non-reflective metal finish, 26 in. barrel only, 10 lbs. New 2000.

MSR	$1,292	$970	$860	$780	$650	$575	$550	$475

✴ *Model SP-10 Turkey Camo NWTF 25th Anniversary* - 12 ga., limited mfg. to commemorate the 25th Anniversary of the NWTF during 1998, Truglo fiber optic sights. Mfg. 1998 only.

	$1,050	$925	$775				

Last MSR was $1,225.

✴ *Model SP-10 Turkey Combo* - includes choice of either 26 or 30 VR regular barrel and extra 22 in. deer barrel with rifle sights. Mfg. 1991-94.

	$1,295	$1,125	$925	$775	$700	$650	$625

Last MSR was $1,132.

Remington Shotguns: Semi-Auto, Model 1100 & Variations

3 in. shells (12 or 20 ga.) may be shot in Magnum receivers only, regardless of what the barrel markings may indicate (the ejection port is larger in these Magnum models with M suffix serialization).

Add $667 for custom shop Etchen stock and forearm installed on new Model 1100s (new 2000).

SPORTSMAN 12 AUTO - 12 ga. only, 2¾ in. chamber, 28 or 30 in. VR barrel, similar to Model 1100 action, hardwood stock and forearm, 7¾ lbs. Mfg. 1985-86 only.

	$300	$260	$220	$195	$170	$160	$150

Last MSR was $405.

Add 10% for Rem. chokes (mfg. 1986 only).

MODEL 1100 FIELD - 12 (disc. 1987), 16 (disc. 1980), or 20 ga., 26, 28, or 30 in. barrels, various chokes, gas operated, checkered pistol grip stock, Rem. chokes became standard 1987 (introduced 1986 as $40 option), VRs became standard in 1985 on this model, 20 ga. lightweight frame became standard 1972, prices assume VR and Rem. chokes. Mfg. 1963-1988.

	$350	$295	$265	$225	$200	$185	$170

Last MSR was $545.

Subtract $40 if without VR.
Subtract $45 if without Rem. chokes.

The Model 1100 20 ga. Standard (12 ga. frame) was disc. in 1969 (mahogany wood stock and forearm – advertised as a Lightweight), except for Skeet A & B grades. This model was produced only in a Lightweight or Mag. 20 (3 in. chamber), 28 ga., or .410 bore, before the release of the Model 11-87.

R

Grading	100%	98%	95%	90%	80%	70%	60%

MODEL 1100 SPECIAL FIELD - 12, 20 ga., or .410 (limited mfg., disc.) bore, 21 (disc. 1993) or 23 (new 1994) in. VR barrel, various chokes, gas operated, checkered straight grip stock, VR standard, high gloss wood finish (1991 only) or satin wood finish. Rem. chokes became standard in 1987. Mfg. 1983-1999.

	$510	$415	$325	$265	$230	$210	$180

Last MSR was $665.

Subtract 10% if without Rem. chokes.
Add 15%-20% for .410 bore.
Two hundred .410 bores were mfg. for National Shooting Supplies in Houston, TX.

MODEL 1100 SMALL GAUGE - 28 ga. or .410 bore, 25 in. barrel, scaled down receiver, skeet and field fixed choke, VR standard. Mfg. 1969-1994.

	$550	$475	$425	$365	$300	$275	$250

Last MSR was $647.

MODEL 1100 LW-20 (LIGHTWEIGHT) - 20 ga. only, 2¾ in. chamber, lightweight scaled down receiver, mag. tube, and barrel, similar to 28 ga./.410 bore frame, standard length ejection port, with mahogany stock, 26 or 28 in. barrel, 6½ lbs. Mfg. 1970-76.

	$510	$415	$325	$265	$230	$210	$180

Subtract 10% if w/o VR.
Remington introduced a lightweight 20 ga. Model 1100 in 1961, with standard frame, mahogany stock and forearm. This model was disc. in Dec., 1969.

MODEL 1100 LT-20 - 20 ga. only, variation of Model 1100 LW-20, 2¾ in. chamber, has opened ejection port and barrel extension similar to 12 ga. (long), lightened receiver, 23, 26 (disc., gloss wood only) or 28 (disc., satin wood only) in. barrel, VR became standard 1985, hi-gloss (disc.) or satin finish walnut stock and forearm, 6½ lbs. Mfg. 1977-1995.

	$510	$415	$325	$265	$230	$210	$180

Last MSR was $665.

Subtract 10% if without VR.
Subtract $34 for gloss walnut.
Please refer to the Model 1100 Synthetic for currently manufactured LT-20 values/information. Rolled scroll receiver engraving became standard on 20 ga. in 1998.

MODEL 1100 LT-20 YOUTH - 20 ga. only, similar to Model 1100 Lightweight, except stock is 1 in. shorter and 21 in. barrel only. Disc. 1998.

	$500	$415	$325	$265	$230	$210	$180

Last MSR was $659.

	$495	$415	$325	$265	$230	$210	$180

Last MSR was $652.

MODEL 1100 LT-20 MAG. (LIGHTWEIGHT MAGNUM) - chambered for 3 in. 20 ga. Mag., 20 (disc.), 26 (disc.), or 28 in. barrel, Rem. chokes became standard 1987. Introduced 1977, disc. 1998.

	$500	$415	$325	$265	$230	$210	$180

Last MSR was $659.

Subtract 10% if without VR.

MODEL 1100 MAGNUM DUCK GUN - similar to 1100, in 12 (disc. 1987) or 20 ga., 3 in. chamber, recoil pad, VR became standard 1984, Rem. chokes became standard 1987. Mfg. 1963-1988.

	$400	$325	$280	$260	$220	$200	$180

Last MSR was $533.

Add $80 for left-hand model (disc. 1986).
Subtract $40 if without VR.
Subtract $45 if without Rem. chokes.

Grading	100%	98%	95%	90%	80%	70%	60%

✳ *Model 1100 Magnum Special Purpose (SP)* - 12 ga. only, low luster finish on stock and fore-arm, sand blasted metal parts. Mfg. 1985-86 only.

	$395	$350	$295	$265	$235	$200	$180

Last MSR was $550.

Add $40 for Rem. chokes

MODEL 1100 SYNTHETIC (INCLUDING LT-20)

- 12 or 20 (LT-20) ga., 2¾ in. chamber, 26 (20 ga. only) or 28 (12 ga. only) in. VR barrel with Rem. choke, checkered black synthetic stock and forearm, matte metal finish, 7-7½ lbs. New 1996.

MSR	$549		$430	$340	$275		

Add $157-$296 (factory MSR) per extra barrel (2¾ in. chamber only), depending on configuration.

✳ *Model 1100 LT-20 Synthetic Youth* - features 21 in. VR barrel, matte black synthetic stock and forearm. New 1999.

MSR	$549		$430	$340	$275		

Add $63 for Youth Turkey Camo (includes 3 in. chamber and 100% Realtree Advantage Camo on stock and forearm).

✳ *Model 1100 Synthetic Deer* - 12 or 20 ga., 21 in. fully rifled barrel with choice of cantilever scope mount (12 ga. only) or rifle sight (20 ga. only), 7 or 7½ lbs. New 1997.

MSR	$583		$460	$355	$290		

Add $46 for cantilever scope mount (12 ga. only).

MODEL 1100 "1 OF 3,000" FIELD

- 12 ga. only, limited edition, serial numbered 1- 3,000, deluxe walnut, gold washed etched hunting scenes on receiver, 28 in. modified VR barrel. Mfg. 1980.

	$1,100	$900	$600	$500	$425	$350	$300

MODEL 1100 DEER GUN

- 12 (disc. 1987) or 20 ga., 20 (disc.), 21 in. (20 ga. only) or 22 (disc.) in. imp. cyl. barrel with rifle sights. Disc. 1996.

	$435	$345	$270	$225	$200	$185	$165

Last MSR was $584.

Add $80 for left-hand model (disc. 1986).
Add $117 for 21 in. fully rifled Cantilever deer barrel.

✳ *Model 1100 Special Purpose Deer (SP)* - similar to Model 1100 Deer Gun, except has low luster finish on stock and forearm, sandblasted metal parts. Mfg. 1986 only.

	$335	$295	$275	$255	$220	$200	$180

Last MSR was $495.

MODEL 1100 LT-20 (TOURNAMENT SKEET)

- 12 or 20 (LT-20) ga., 26 in. skeet bored or Rem. choke barrel, optional Cutts Compensator available from Jan. 1964 to Dec. 1976. Mfg. 1963-1994, reintroduced 1996, disc. 1997.

	$625	$525	$450	$375	$325	$275	$225

Last MSR was $732.

Add $40 for left-hand model (disc. 1986).

MODEL 1100 SMALL GAUGE SKEET

- 28 ga. or .410 bore, 25 or 26 (disc.) in. VR barrel, 6½-7¼ lbs. Mfg. 1969-1994.

	$550	$450	$415	$375	$300	$265	$230

Last MSR was $692.

2½ in. chamber is standard on the .410 bore (Skeet only).

MODEL 1100 SKEET MATCHED PAIR

- 28 ga. and .410 bore, walnut stock and forearm. 5,067 cased Skeet sets were mfg. 1969 and 1970 only.

	$1,250	$995	$875				

MODEL 1100 SPORTING

- 12 (new 2000), 20 (new 1998) or 28 ga., 25 (28 ga. only) or 28 (20 ga. only) in. VR barrel with Rem. chokes, 12 ga. has lightweight 28 in. VR target barrel, high gloss checkered deluxe walnut stock and forearm, 6½ lbs. New 1996.

MSR	$868		$720	$550	$475	$375	$325	$275	$225

R

Grading	100%	98%	95%	90%	80%	70%	60%

MODEL 1100 TA TRAP - 12 ga., 30 in. barrel, recoil pad on regular stock, available in left or right-hand. Mfg. 1979-86.

	$410	$330	$295	$270	$230	$210	$190

Last MSR was $570.

Add 5% for Monte Carlo stock.
Add $50 for left-hand model.

MODEL 1100 TB TRAP - 12 ga., 30 in. VR full choke barrel, special trap stock, select wood. Mfg. 1963-1981.

	$475	$400	$325	$300	$245	$210	$190
Monte Carlo stock		$495	$415	$340	$310	$280	$235
$220							

MODEL 1100 TOURNAMENT TRAP - 12 ga., 30 in. VR full choke barrel, special trap stock, extra select wood. Mfg. 1979-86.

	$550	$495	$425	$365	$325	$285	$250

Last MSR was $675.

Add 5% for Monte Carlo stock.

MODEL 1100 CLASSIC TRAP - 12 ga. only, features 30 in. VR light contour target barrel, high gloss checkered walnut Monte Carlo stock and forearm, high polish blue, receiver features fine line engraving and gold inlays, 8¼ lbs. New 2000.

MSR	**$895**		$730	$570	$485	$385	$325	$275	$225

MODEL 1100 150TH ANNIVERSARY - limited mfg. in 1966 only.

	$400	$340	$290

MODEL 1100 BICENTENNIAL - 12 ga. only, configurations include Trap, Skeet, and Trade, mfg. to commemorate U.S. Bicentennial (1776-1976).

Trap or Skeet	$450	$375	$325
Trade	$375	$295	$225

In 1976, the 1100 Bicentennial Trap retailed for $320 ($330 w/Monte Carlo stock), the Skeet retailed for $285, and the Trade retailed for $270.

MODEL 1100 DUCKS UNLIMITED - "DU" in serial number.

Remington has offered many variations of the Model 1100 specifically manufactured according to individual DU chapter specifications. The price of a DU 1100 varies substantially from the "DU point of purchase" to real market conditions. When contemplating a DU gun it is always important to know how many of that particular variation were manufactured. The Remington factory normally has this information unless the special DU work was subcontracted elsewhere.

While most DU guns are good vehicles for fund raising, their collectability to date has been minimal. Actual market conditions indicate that unless production is truly limited, most DU firearms sell very close to the models they were derived from. Also, any collectability that does exist is for 100% guns new in the box with warranty papers. Used DU guns have values comparable to the standard model from which they were derived.

In addition to regular DU guns, Remington has also produced special editions including the 1982 Atlantic Flyway (dinner gun) and a 1981 DU Lt. 20 ga. and 12 ga. (dinner gun - 2,400 mfg. each), and a 1973 dinner gun (600 mfg.). These were rarer DU shotguns, and current values could vary significantly.

MODEL 1100 D-GRADE (TOURNAMENT) - custom order only, any gauge. Mfg. 1963-present.

MSR	**$3,323**		$2,600	$1,875	$1,300

MODEL 1100 F-GRADE (PREMIER) - custom order only, any gauge. Mfg. 1963- present.

MSR	**$6,845**		$5,700	$4,200	$2,750

MODEL 1100 F-GRADE W/GOLD (GOLD PREMIER) - with gold inlay, custom order only. Mfg. 1963-present.

MSR	**$10,263**		$8,750	$4,950	$3,325

Note: Grades differ in quality, grade of wood, amount of engraving, and gold inlays.

R

Grading	100%	98%	95%	90%	80%	70%	60%

Remington Shotguns: Semi-Auto, Model 11-87 & Variations

Add $667 for custom shop Etchen stock and forearm installed on new Model 11-87s (new 2000).

Remington MSRs on extra barrels (3 in. chamber standard) for the following currently manufactured models range from $192-$324 per barrel, depending on configuration.

MODEL 11-87 PREMIER - 12 or 20 (new 1999) ga. (3 in. chamber), 26, 28, 30 (12 ga. only, new 2000) or 32 (disc. 1996) in. VR Rem. choked barrel, successor to Model 1100, gas compensating action adaptable to all loads, stainless steel magazine tube, polished blue finish, high gloss or satin (current mfg. is in 12 ga./28 in. barrel only) finished and checkered walnut stock and forearm, a high gloss wood finish option became available in 1991 at N/C, and is now standard, fine line receiver engraving (referred to as embellished receiver) became standard during 1999, solid recoil pad, 8 1/8-8 3/8 lbs. Introduced 1987.

	MSR	$765		$590	$465	$395	$350	$315	$275	$250

Add $80 for 21 in. fully rifled Cantilever deer barrel.

Add $54 for left-hand action (12 ga. only).

Note: Model 11-87 Premier barrels are not interchangeable with Model 1100 barrels.

* ***Model 11-87 Premier Upland Special*** - 12 or 20 ga., 3 in. chamber, 23 in. (light contour barrel on 12 ga.) VR barrel, straight grip satin finished checkered walnut stock and forearm, high polish metal with engraving, 6½ or 7¼ lbs. New 2000.

MSR	$765		$590	$465	$395	$350	$315	$275	$250

MODEL 11-87 PREMIER 3½ IN. SUPER MAGNUM - 12 ga. only, 3½ in. chamber, 28 in. VR barrel with Rem. chokes, blue high polish non-embellished receiver and barrel, checkered high gloss walnut stock and forearm, 8¼ lbs. New 2001.

MSR	$852		$685	$485	$425	$365	$325	$300	$280

MODEL 11-87 SP (SPECIAL PURPOSE) - 12 ga. only, 3 in. chamber, 26, 28, or 30 (disc.) in. VR Rem. choked barrel, parkerized metal with satin finish wood stock and forearm, vent. recoil pad, included camouflaged nylon sling, 8¼ lbs. New 1987.

MSR	$765		$590	$465	$395	$350	$315	$275	$250

MODEL 11-87 SP (SPECIAL PURPOSE) 3½ IN. SUPER MAGNUM - 12 ga. only, 3½ in. chamber, non- reflective black matte finish on barrel and receiver, 26 or 28 in. VR barrel with Rem. choke, satin finished stock and forearm, approx. 8 1/8 lbs. New 2000.

MSR	$852		$685	$485	$425	$365	$325	$300	$280

MODEL 11-87 SPS (SPECIAL PURPOSE SYNTHETIC) - see individual sub-models listed below.

* ***Model 11-87 SPS 3 in. Magnum*** - similar to Model 11-87 SP 3 in. Mag., except is supplied with black synthetic stock and forearm.

MSR	$765		$590	$465	$395	$350	$315	$275	$250

* ***Model 11-87 SPS Camo (Special Purpose Synthetic Camo)*** - 12 ga. only, 3 in. chamber, 21 (new 1999), 26 or 28 (disc. 1998) in. VR barrel with Rem. choke, available in Mossy Oak Bottomland (disc. 1996) or Mossy Oak Break-Up (new 1997) finish. New 1994.

MSR	$879		$700	$500	$435	$365	$325	$300	$280

* ***Model 11-87 SPS-BG Camo (Special Purpose Synthetic Big Game)*** - 12 ga. only, 21 in. plain barrel with rifle sights and Rem. choke. Mfg. 1994 only.

			$555	$425	$350	$290	$250	$225	$200

Last MSR was $692.

R

Grading	100%	98%	95%	90%	80%	70%	60%

✱ **Model 11-87 SP/SPS (Special Purpose Deer Gun)** - 12 ga. only, 3 in. chamber, 21 in. IC or Rem. choked (Model SP, new 1989) or fully rifled (new 1993) barrel with iron sights, parkerized metal with matte finished wood or black synthetic (Model SPS, new 1993) stock and forearm, vent. recoil pad, includes camouflaged nylon sling, 7¼ lbs. New 1987.

	MSR	$745		$575	$455	$385	$340	$300	$270	$250

Add $100 for Cantilevered rifled deer barrel with Rem. choke (Model SPS).
Add $54 for fully rifled deer barrel.
Subtract 10% for fixed choke barrel.
Rem. chokes became standard on this model in 1989.

✱ **Model 11-87 SPS-T (Special Purpose Turkey)** - 12 ga. only, 3 or 3½ (new 2002) in. chamber, 21 or 23 (3 ½ in. chamber only) in. VR barrel with Rem. choke (turkey superfull choke included with 3½ in.), available in flat black (disc. 2000) or 100% camo treatment in Mossy Oak (disc. 1996), Mossy Oak Break Up (new 1999), Realtree X-tra Brown (mfg. 1997 only), or Greenleaf (disc. 1996) finish, TruGlo rifle sights became standard in 2002 (Model SPS-T Turkey Gun RS/TG).

	MSR	$897		$715	$515	$440	$375	$325	$300	$280

Add $38 for 3½ chamber (new 2002).
Add $10 for cantilevered scope mount with superfull choke tube (Model SPS-T Turkey Gun Cantilever, new 2001).
Add $324 for Leupold Gilmore red dot sights, Monte Carlo stock and superfull choke tube (mfg. 2000 only).
Subtract approx. $20 if w/o TruGlo rifle sights.

◇**Model 11-87 SPS Turkey Camo NWTF** - 20 ga. only, features 100% Mossy Oak Break-Up camo finish, TruGlo fiber optic sights, 6½ lbs. Mfg. 1998 only.

				$675	$575	$450	$395	$325	$290	$265

Last MSR was $832.

MODEL 11-87 SPS 3½ IN. SUPER MAGNUM - choice of 26 or 28 in. VR barrel with Rem. choke, black synthetic stock and forearm, approx. 8 1/8 lbs. New 2000.

	MSR	$852		$685	$485	$425	$365	$325	$300	$280

✱ **Model 11-87 SPS-T 3½ in. Super Magnum Turkey** - 12 ga. only, 3½ in. chamber, full coverage Mossy Oak Break-Up camo treatment, 23 in. barrel with TruGlo rifle sights and Rem. choke tube, 8 1/8 lbs. New 2001.

	MSR	$935		$750	$550	$475	$425	$375	$335	$300

MODEL 11-87 SPORTING CLAYS - 12 ga. only, 26 (disc. 1996) or 28 in. VR barrel with extended Rem. chokes (knurled extension chokes allow for no-wrench field changes), specially balanced, satin finished walnut, top metal surfaces have fine matte finish, radiused recoil pad, twin bead sights on 5/16 wide VR, 7½ lbs. Mfg. 1992-99.

				$675	$575	$450	$395	$325	$290	$265

Last MSR was $833.

✱ **Model 11-87 Sporting Clays NP** - 12 ga. only, features matte nickel plated receiver with engraving, satin finished checkered stock and forearm, 28 (new 1998) or 30 in. VR ported barrel with extended choke tubes, 7¾ lbs. Mfg. 1997-2001.

				$775	$650	$525	$450	$375	$325	$295

Last MSR was $948.

MODEL 11-87 PREMIER SKEET - 12 ga. only, 26 in. VR Rem. choked barrel, deluxe walnut with quality cut checkering, 7¾ lbs. Mfg. 1987-1999.

				$650	$550	$475	$425	$375	$325	$275

Last MSR was $799.

Add approx. $70 for left-hand action.
Subtract 10% if without Rem. chokes.

Grading	100%	98%	95%	90%	80%	70%	60%

MODEL 11-87 PREMIER TRAP - 12 ga. only, 30 in. raised VR Rem. choked barrel, deluxe walnut stock (Monte Carlo became standard in 1996) with quality cut checkering, 8¼ lbs. Mfg. 1987-1999.

		$660	$565	$440	$385	$300	$275	$260

Last MSR was $833.

Subtract $30 if without Monte Carlo stock.
Add approx. $40 for left-hand action (disc. 1994).
Subtract 10% if without Rem. chokes.

MODEL 11-87 175TH ANNIVERSARY - 12 ga. only, 28 in. barrel with Rem- chokes, 175th Anniversary Model (1816-1991) with light engraving and high gloss wood finish. 4,606 1991 mfg. only.

$515	$425	$335

Last MSR was $618.

MODEL 11-87 D-GRADE (TOURNAMENT) - custom order only, any gauge. Mfg. 1963-present.

MSR	$3,323		$2,600	$1,875	$1,300

MODEL 11-87 F-GRADE (PREMIER) - custom order only, any gauge. Mfg. 1963- present.

MSR	$6,845		$5,700	$4,200	$2,750

MODEL 11-87 F-GRADE W/GOLD (GOLD PREMIER) - with gold inlay, custom order only. Mfg. 1963-present.

MSR	$10,263		$8,750	$4,950	$3,325

Note: Grades differ in quality, grade of wood, and amount of engraving.

Remington Shotguns: Semi-Auto, Model 11-96

MODEL 11-96 EURO LIGHTWEIGHT - 12 ga. only, steel receiver with distinctive slight hump over chamber, 26 or 28 in. 6mm VR Rem. choked barrel, checkered walnut stock and forearm, receiver panel engraving, approx. 7 lbs. Mfg. 1996 only.

		$715	$615	$550	$475	$395	$335	$295

Last MSR was $852.

100%	98%	95%	90%	80%	70%	60%	50%	40%	30%	20%	10%

SHOTGUNS: SINGLE BARREL

MODEL NO. 3 RIDER SINGLE BARREL - 10, 12, 16, 20, 24, or 28 ga., single barrel, 30 or 32 in. barrels, top lever break open, plain pistol grip stock. Approx. 25,000 mfg. 1893-1905.

$325	$290	$260	$230	$200	$170	$140	$110	$85	$65	$50	$35

MODEL NO. 9 RIDER SINGLE BARREL - similar to No. 3, with auto ejector. Mfg. 1902-1910.

$375	$325	$290	$260	$230	$200	$170	$140	$110	$85	$65	$50

Grading	100%	98%	95%	90%	80%	70%	60%

R

MODEL 90-T (TRAP) - 12 ga., 32 (disc. 1993) or 34 in. full choke VR barrel with fixed full choke, matte black receiver and wood around tang area, deluxe checkered stock and forearm, short throw top-lever release, elongated forcing cone, approx. 8¾ lbs. Mfg. 1992-97.

		$1,850	$1,550	$1,375	$1,175	$1,025	$925	$850

Last MSR was $3,199.

Add $50 for factory porting.

✻ *Model 90-T HPAR (High Post w/adj. Rib)* - features high post, adj. rib. Mfg. 1994-97.

		$2,300	$1,875	$1,700	$1,550	$1,450	$1,325	$1,075

Last MSR was $3,992.

Grading	100%	98%	95%	90%	80%	70%	60%

MODEL 310 SKEET - .32 Rimfire case loaded with No. 12 leadshot, break open single shot, .310 bore shotgun, used in conjunction with a self-operated trap set which threw half-size clay targets, entire set-up included gun, shooting booth, ammunition, and trap thrower, 5½ lbs., mfg. circa late '60s.

Gun only	$425	$350	$300	$250	$195	$175	$150

Add 25%-75% depending on the amount of original accessories included.

This model was mfg. by CBC in Brazil, and imported into the U.S. as the .310 Skeet. This model was never mass produced, but test marketed for approx. 5 years in CT, NJ, PA, and TX primarily at amusement parks. It failed commercially due to lack of sales. Aprrox. 500 units imported.

SHOTGUNS: SLIDE ACTION, DISC.

REMINGTON REPEATING SHOTGUN - 12 ga., hammerless, bottom ejection, takedown, plain barrel only, blue finish, sight notch on receiver top, marked "REMINGTON ARMS CO." with February 3rd, 1903 and May 18th, 1905 patent dates, walnut pistol grip stock and short forearm, hard rubber buttplate, 7½ lbs., approx. 10,000 mfg. 1908-1910.

	$295	$225	$200	$175	$150	$125	$110

Add 10% for 32 in. barrel.

There were 7 grades of this model (Numbers 0-6) that were originally priced from $27 to approx. $140. This model was renamed the Model 10 in 1911.

MODEL 10A SLIDE ACTION - 12 ga., 26-32 in. barrels, various chokes, takedown, plain pistol grip stock. Mfg. 1907-1929.

	$300	$275	$200	$175	$150	$125	$110

Add 10% for 32 in. full choke barrel.
Add 35% for guns marked "Long Range"- beware of fakes.

MODEL 17A SLIDE ACTION - 20 ga., 26-32 in. barrel, various chokes, takedown, bottom ejection, 4 shot mag., plain grip stock. Approx. 48,000 mfg., 1917-1933.

Plain barrel	$350	$275	$220	$195	$165	$140	$110
Solid. rib	$450	$375	$325	$290	$270	$250	$210

Grades range from A - F in suffix form, F being the highest. Large premiums are paid for mint condition, higher grade models.

MODEL 29A SLIDE ACTION - 12 ga., 26-32 in. barrel, bottom ejection, various chokes, takedown, 5 shot mag., checkered pistol grip stock. Approx. 24,000 mfg., 1929- 1933.

	$325	$265	$235	$200	$150	$120	$100

Add 15% for solid rib, 25% for VR.

✱ *32 in. Long Range barrel* - should be marked "Long Range" - beware of fakes.

	$525	$475	$425	$350	$250	$200	$180

Grades range from A - C and TA - TF, lowest to highest. Premiums exist for finer condition upper grades. The Model 29 was similar in appearance to the Model 10.

MODEL 29S - "Trap Special" with trap style straight grip stock, matted or VR rib.

	$500	$450	$425	$375	$350	$325	$300

Add 20% for VR rib.

MODEL 31A SLIDE ACTION - 12, 16, or 20 ga., side ejection, 2 or 4 shot mag., 26-32 in. barrels, various chokes, takedown, pistol grip stock. Approx. 160,000 mfg., 1931- 1949.

Plain barrel	$395	$345	$300	$265	$225	$185	$150
Solid rib	$455	$385	$345	$300	$270	$230	$190
Vent. rib	$475	$415	$375	$320	$290	$250	$210

Add 15% for 20 ga.

Grades range from A - F suffixes. Higher grades will bring considerable premiums in excellent condition. TC suffix is Target Model. A Model 31L (lightweight) was mfg. 1948-1950 and while rare, demand dictates to subtract 20% for this variation. Early models will command a small premium in this model.

R

Grading	100%	98%	95%	90%	80%	70%	60%

MODEL 31B "SPECIAL" - higher grade wood and hand checkered pistol grip stock and forearm.

	$650	$550	$440	$385	$360	$305	$275

MODEL 31R "RIOT" GRADE - features shortened barrel.

	$425	$365	$325	$295	$270	$230	$190

MODEL 31D TOURNAMENT - features scroll engraving.

	$1,100	$880	$715	$580	$525	$495	$470

MODEL 31E EXPERT - features scroll engraving with game scene on left side of receiver.

	$1,320	$1,100	$935	$880	$770	$660	$605

MODEL 31F PREMIER - features scroll engraving and game scenes on both sides of receiver. Introduced 1942.

	$2,100	$1,800	$1,600	$1,500	$1,300	$1,050	$875

Add 20% for 20 ga.

Note: Grades differ in quality, grade of wood, and amount of engraving.
This model was also available with a Cutts compensator 1940-49, or a Poly Choke on special order from 1941-49.

MODEL 31TC TRAP - similar to 31A, with 12 ga. only, 30 or 32 in. barrel, vent. rib, full choke, trap stock and beavertail forend, pad.

	$875	$795	$675	$575	$450	$375	$300

Subtract 10% for lightweight receiver.
TC stands for Trap with C Grade wood.

MODEL 31S TRAP SPECIAL - solid rib barrel, plainer wood.

	$550	$500	$450	$400	$365	$345	$325

MODEL 31H HUNTER - similar to 31S, with sporter stock. Mfg. 1941-disc.

	$395	$350	$300	$275	$250	$220	$195

MODEL 31L LIGHTWEIGHT - features an alloy receiver, available in both field and skeet, introduced 1941.

	$350	$325	$300	$275	$250	$225	$200

MODEL 31 SKEET - similar to 31A, with 26 in. skeet bored barrel, standard solid rib, beavertail forend.

	100%	98%	95%	90%	80%	70%	60%
Plain barrel	$495	$450	$395	$365	$335	$265	$220
Vent. rib	$650	$550	$495	$425	$375	$340	$295

Subtract 10% for lightweight receiver.
Add 20% for 20 ga. with VR barrel.

SHOTGUNS: SLIDE ACTION, MODEL 870 & VARIATIONS

3 in. shells (12 or 20 ga.) may be shot in Magnum receivers only regardless of what the barrel markings may indicate (the ejection port is larger in these Magnum models with M suffix serialization).

Add $667 for custom shop Etchen stock and forearm installed on new Model 870s (new 2000).

Add 25%-35% for 16 ga. on older mfg., depending on original condition.

Remington MSRs on extra barrels (3 in. chamber is standard, except for Skeet barrel) for the following currently manufactured models range from $148-$321 per barrel, depending on configuration.

MODEL 870AP SLIDE ACTION - "Wingmaster", 12, 16, or 20 ga., 26, 28, or 30 in. barrel, 5 shot, various chokes, plain pistol grip stock. Mfg. 1950-1963.

	100%	98%	95%	90%	80%	70%	60%
Plain barrel	$220	$195	$175	$165	$140	$120	$110
Vent. rib	$250	$220	$200	$195	$165	$150	$140

Add 15% for "Sungrain" blonde maple wood (mfg. 1959-1961).

R

Grading	100%	98%	95%	90%	80%	70%	60%

MODEL 870ADL - deluxe checkered version of 870AP. Mfg. 1950-1963.

Plain barrel	$250	$220	$200	$180	$165	$140	$120
Matted top barrel	$275	$250	$220	$210	$195	$165	$140
Vent. rib	$300	$275	$250	$225	$200	$175	$150

MODEL 870BDL - select walnut stock.

Plain barrel	$275	$250	$220	$200	$180	$165	$140
Vent. rib	$315	$290	$260	$240	$210	$195	$165

SPORTSMAN 12 PUMP - 12 ga. only (3 in. chamber), 28 or 30 in. barrel, recoil pad, VR standard, hardwood stock and forearm, Model 870 type action, 7½ lbs. Mfg. 1984- 86.

	$275	$235	$195	$175	$160	$150	$140

Last MSR was $270.

Add $35 for Rem. chokes.

MODEL 870 EXPRESS - 12, 16 (new 2002), 20 (new 1991), 28 ga. (disc., reintroduced 2002), or .410 bore (disc., reintroduced 2002), 3 in. chamber, 20, 25 (28 ga. or .410 bore only), 26, or 28 in. VR Rem. choked (12 or 20 ga., supplied with Mod. Rem. choke) barrel, parkerized metal, matte finished hardwood stock and forearm, solid recoil pad, 7¼ lbs. New 1987.

MSR $332	$265	$215	$180	$160	$145	$135	$130

Add $27 for 28 ga. or .410 bore.

Add $27 for left-hand action (12 ga., 28 in. barrel only, new 1998).

Various combination Express packages are available in both 12 and 20 ga. Retail prices range from $443-$476.

✳ *Model 870 Synthetic Express* - 12 ga. only, 26 or 28 in. VR barrel with 1 Rem. choke, features black synthetic stock and forearm. New 1994.

MSR $332	$265	$215	$180	$160	$145	$135	$130

◇*Model 870 Synthetic Express Deer* - 12 ga. only, features 20 in. fully rifled barrel with rifle sights. New 2002.

MSR $372	$295	$225	$185	$165	$145	$135	$130

✳ *Model 870 Turkey Express* - 12 ga. only, choice of wood with flat finish or Realtree Advantage camo (new 1998) stock and forearm, 21 in. VR barrel with Rem. turkey choke, 7¼ lbs.

MSR $345	$270	$215	$185	$160	$145	$135	$130

Add $54 for camo stock and forearm.

✳ *Model 870 Express Deer Gun* - 12 ga. only, 20 in. IC choked barrel or fully rifled barrel with rifle sights, Monte Carlo stock. Introduced in 1991.

MSR $332	$265	$215	$180	$160	$145	$135	$130

Add $33 for fully rifled deer barrel.

Add $78 for cantilever scope system and IC Rem. choke (disc. 1991).

✳ *Model 870 Youth* - 20 ga. only, 21 in. VR barrel with Rem. choke, 13 in. LOP with recoil pad, choice of RealTree Advantage camo (new 1998) or regular wood finish on stock and forearm, 6 lbs.

MSR $332	$265	$215	$180	$160	$140	$130	$125

Add $33 for Youth Deer Gun (fully rifled 20 in. barrel). New 1994.

Add $67 for Youth Turkey with RealTree Advantage Camo.

✳ *Model 870 Express Synthetic HD (Home Defense)* - 12 ga. only, 18 in. cyl. choked barrel with bead sights, black synthetic stock and forend. Introduced 1991.

MSR $319	$250	$205	$170	$155	$140	$130	$125

R

Grading	100%	98%	95%	90%	80%	70%	60%

MODEL 870 EXPRESS SUPER MAGNUM - 12 ga., 3½ in. chamber, choice of checkered natural hardwood, black synthetic, or 100% RealTree Advantage camo stock and forearm, 23 (camo only), 26 (synthetic only), or 28 (wood only) in. VR barrel, matte or 100% camo finish metal, recoil pad, approx. 7¼ lbs. New 1998.

MSR $376	$295	$230	$190	$165	$145	$135	$130

Add $13 for synthetic Turkey Model with 23 in. barrel (new 1999).
Add $147 for combo package (includes 26 in. regular and 20 in. fully rifled deer barrel).

* *Model 870 Express Super Magnum Turkey Camo* - features 100% RealTree Advantage camo on metal and stock/forearm, 23 in. VR barrel only with Turkey extra full Rem. choke. New 1998.

MSR $500	$395	$315	$250	$210	$175	$160	$145

* *Model 870 Express Super Magnum Synthetic Camo* - 12 ga., 3½ in. chamber, 23 or 26 in. VR barrel with Rem. choke, 100% Mossy Oak Break Up camo coverage, wood or synthetic stock and forearm. Mfg. 1999 only.

$385	$320	$265	$240	$220	$200	$180

Last MSR was $532.

MODEL 870 FIELD WINGMASTER - 12, 16 (disc. 1980, reintroduced late 2001), 20 (LW-20), 28 (disc. late 1994, reintroduced 1999) ga., or .410 (disc. late 1994, reintroduced 1999) bore, various barrel lengths (26, 28, and 30 are current mfg.), incorporates twin slide rails, 3 in. chamber in 12 ga. became standard in 1985, Rem. chokes became standard in 1987, lightweight frame on 20 ga. was introduced 1972, checkered walnut stock and forearm, a choice of high gloss or satin (28 in. barrel only) wood finish became available in 1991. Mfg. 1964- present.

Plain barrel	$250	$225	$205	$190	$175	$160	$150

* *Vent. rib* - became standard in 1985.

MSR $579	$410	$340	$285	$250	$215	$190	$175

Subtract 10% without Rem. chokes.
Add $48 for left-hand model (12 ga. only, disc. 1994).
Add $80 for 20 in. fully rifled Cantilever deer barrel (12 ga. - mfg. 1992-99 or 20 ga. - mfg. 1992-95).
Beginning 1998, rolled scroll engraving started to appear on 20 ga. guns only.

* *Small Gauge Model 870 Wingmaster* - 28 ga. or .410 bore, scaled down 870 on lightweight smaller frame, 25 in. fixed (F or M, .410 bore only) or Rem. choke (28 ga. only, new 1999) barrel, VR became standard 1984, 6-6½ lbs. Mfg. 1969-1994, reintroduced 1999.

MSR $605	$530	$440	$385	$325	$295	$260	$240

Add $54 for 28 ga.
Subtract 10% if w/o VR.

* *Wingmaster 3½ in. Super Magnum* - 12 ga. only, 28 in. VR barrel with choke tubes, high polish blue with receiver engraving, high gloss walnut stock and forearm with cut checkering, 7½ lbs. New 2000.

MSR $659	$555	$470	$395	$340	$300	$265	$250

* *Wingmaster Fiftieth Anniversary Classic Trap* - 12 ga. only, 2¾ in. chamber, features high polish blue fine line receiver engraving with gold inlays, 30 in. low profile light contour barrel, checkered high gloss semi-fancy walnut stock and forearm with cut checkering, 8 lbs. New 2000.

MSR $784	$680	$555	$465	$395	$340	$300	$265

MODEL 870 MAGNUM DUCK GUN - 3 in. chamber, 12 or 20 ga., 26, 28, or 30 in. full or mod. barrel, recoil pad. Mfg. 1964-present. 3 in. chambers became standard on all Model 870s starting in 1985. Rem. chokes became standard 1987 (introduced 1986 as $40 option).

Please refer to Model 870 Field Wingmaster prices.

R

Grading	100%	98%	95%	90%	80%	70%	60%

MODEL 870 SPECIAL PURPOSE - 12 ga. only, differs only in that metal parts are sand blasted, choice of Mossy Oak Camo (new 1992), black synthetic, or checkered wood stock with low luster finish, 21 (Turkey barrel), 26, or 28 in. VR barrel. Rem. chokes were introduced 1986.

Add $75 for wood stock and forearm (disc. 1992).
Subtract 10% without Rem. chokes.

✱ *Model 870 Special Purpose Synthetic Camo* - 12 ga. only, 26 or 28 (disc. 1995) in. VR barrel with Rem. choke, available in either Mossy Oak (disc. 1995) Bottomland (disc. 1996), or full coverage Mossy Oak Break Up finish (1997). New 1994.

MSR $572	$430	$340	$275	$240	$210	$180	$170

✱ *Model 870 SPS-BG Camo (Special Purpose Synthetic Big Game)* - 12 ga. only, 20 in. plain barrel with rifle sights and Rem. choke. Mfg. 1994 only.

	$350	$285	$235	$200	$170	$150	$130

Last MSR was $442.

✱ *Model 870 Special Purpose Turkey (SPS-T)* - 12 ga. only, 20 (new 2002) or 21 in. VR barrel with Rem. choke, available in flat black, Mossy Oak (disc. 1996, reintroduced 2002), Greenleaf (disc. 1996), or Realtree X-tra Brown (full SPS-T-camo, mfg. 1997 only) finish. Disc. 1999, reintroduced 2002.

MSR $576	$435	$345	$280	$240	$210	$180	$170

This model is also available beginning 2002 in a Youth Model with 1 in. shorter LOP.

✱ *Model 870 SPS-T (Turkey) Super Magnum* - 12 ga. only, features 3½ in. chamber, choice of 23, 26, or 28 (new 2001) in. VR barrel with Rem. chokes, fully camouflaged in Mossy Oak Break-Up pattern, choice of wood or synthetic (26 in. barrel only) stock. New 2000.

MSR $572	$430	$340	$280	$240	$210	$180	$170

Add $19 for Cantilever scope mount (new 2001) with Turkey super full choke tube.
Add approx. $330 if with Leupold Gilmore red dot sights and Turkey super full choke tube - 23 in. barrel only (mfg. 2000 only).

✱ *Model 870 Special Purpose Deer Gun (SPS-Deer)* - 12 ga. only, 3 in. chamber, 20 in. Rem. choke barrel (disc. 1992) or fully rifled barrel with iron sights (new 1993), satin finished (disc. 1992) or black synthetic (new 1993) stock and forearm, matte black metal, 7¼ lbs. Mfg. 1989-1999.

	$345	$275	$225	$195	$175	$160	$145

Last MSR was $436.

Add $28 for Cantilever deer barrel with Rem. choke (disc. 1996).
Add $60 for fully rifled Cantilever deer barrel.
Add $65 for Cantilever scope mount system (disc. 1992).

✱ *Model 870 Special Purpose Super Slug Deer* - 12 ga. only, 3 in. chamber, 23 in. fully rifled Cantilever barrel, matte black metal finish, black synthetic Monte Carlo stock and forearm, approx. 8 lbs. New 1999.

MSR $561	$455	$365	$300	$250	$225	$195	$175

MODEL 870 LIGHTWEIGHT - 20 ga. only, lighter and shorter mahogany stock than magnum model, 23 in. barrel. Mfg. 1972-1983.

	$270	$230	$210	$190	$175	$165	$155

Add $30 for VR.

MODEL 870 LIGHTWEIGHT (MAGNUM) - 20 ga., 3 in. chamber, 26 or 28 in. barrel, 6 lbs. Mfg. 1972-1994. Rem. chokes became standard 1987.

	$365	$320	$260	$225	$200	$175	$160

Last MSR was $460.

Subtract 10% without Rem. chokes.
Subtract $40 without VR.

R

Grading	100%	98%	95%	90%	80%	70%	60%

MODEL 870 SPECIAL FIELD - 12 or 20 (LW-20) ga., lighter straight grip stock with solid recoil pad, 21 (disc. 1993) or 23 (new 1994) in. VR barrel, 6¼ or 7 lbs. New 1984. Rem. chokes became standard 1987 (introduced 1986 as $40 option). Disc. 1995.

		$380	$320	$265	$230	$210	$190	$175

Last MSR was $473.

Subtract 10% without Rem. chokes.

MODEL 870 BRUSHMASTER - 12 or 20 (disc.) ga., 20 in. barrel with imp. cyl. (disc.) or Rem. choke and rifle sights, 3 in. chamber standard for 1985, normal bluing with satin finished wood. Disc. 1994.

	$355	$310	$255	$225	$200	$175	$160

Last MSR was $452.

Add $43 for left-hand model.

MODEL 870 MARINE MAGNUM - 12 ga. only, 3 in. chamber, 18 in. plain barrel bored cyl., features electroless nickel plating on all metal parts, supplied with 7 shot mag., sling swivels and Cordura sling, 7½ lbs.

MSR	$555	$415	$345	$270	$235	$210	$185	$175

MODEL 870 POLICE - 12 ga. only, 18 or 20 in. plain barrel, choice of blue (18 in. barrel only) or parkerized finish, bead or rifle (disc. 1995, 20 in. barrel only) sights, Police cylinder (disc.) or IC choke. New 1994.

MSR	$452	$350	$295	$230	$195	$175	$160	$145

Add $13 for parkerized finish.
Add $44 for rifle sights.

MODEL 870 RIOT - 12 ga. only, 18 or 20 in. barrel, choice of blue or parkerized metal finish. Disc. 1991.

	$295	$265	$225	$200	$170	$150	$130

Last MSR was $355.

Add $40 for police rifle sights (20 in. barrel only).

MODEL 870 D-GRADE (TOURNAMENT) - custom order only, any gauge. Mfg. 1950-present.

MSR	$3,323	$2,600	$1,875	$1,300

MODEL 870 F-GRADE (PREMIER) - custom order only, any gauge. Mfg. 1950- present.

MSR	$6,845	$5,700	$4,200	$2,750

MODEL 870 F-GRADE W/GOLD (GOLD PREMIER) - with gold inlays, custom order only. Mfg. 1950-present.

MSR	$10,263	$8,750	$4,950	$3,325

Note: Grades differ in quality, grade of wood, and amount of engraving. Prices also vary accordingly.

MODEL 870 DUCKS UNLIMITED - "DU" in serial number, disc.

	$335	$270	$195

Remington has offered many variations of the Model 870 specifically manufactured according to individual DU chapter specifications. The price of a DU 870 varies substantially from the "DU point of purchase" to real market conditions. When contemplating a DU gun it is always important to know how many of that particular variation were manufactured. The Remington factory normally has this information unless the special DU work was subcontracted elsewhere.

While most DU guns are good vehicles for fund raising, their collectability to date has been minimal. Actual market conditions indicate that unless production is truly limited, most DU firearms sell very close to the model which they were derived from. Also, any collectability that does exist is for 100% guns new in the box with warranty papers. Used DU guns have values comparable to the standard model from which they were derived.

In addition to regular DU guns, Remington has also produced special editions including the 1982 Mississippi Edition (dinner gun) and a 1974 DU (dinner gun - first 500 mfg.).

MODEL 870 150TH ANNIVERSARY - 12 ga. only, 2,534 mfg. 1966 only.

	$400	$325	$275

R

Grading	100%	98%	95%	90%	80%	70%	60%

MODEL 870 BICENTENNIAL - 12 ga. only, configurations include Trap, Skeet, and Trade, mfg. to commemorate U.S. Bicentennial (1776-1976).

Trap or Skeet	$425	$350	$295				
Trade	$375	$295	$225				

In 1976, the 870 Bicentennial Trap retailed for $255 ($265 w/Monte Carlo stock), and the Skeet retailed for $220.

MODEL 870 SC SKEET - 12, 16 (disc. 1960), or 20 ga., 26 in. VR skeet bore barrel. Mfg. 1950-1979.

	100%	98%	95%	90%	80%	70%	60%
	$395	$325	$275	$225	$200	$185	$170

MODEL 870 SKEET MATCHED PAIR - includes .410 bore and 28 ga., 1,503 cased sets mfg. 1969 only.

	100%	98%	95%
	$1,150	$995	$895

MODEL 870 TA TRAP - 12 ga. trap model, deluxe walnut, VR. Add $15 for Monte Carlo stock. Mfg. 1978-1986.

	100%	98%	95%	90%	80%	70%	60%
	$425	$375	$325	$275	$250	$225	$200

Last MSR was $430.

MODEL 870 TB TRAP - similar to 870, with 28 or 30 in. VR full choke barrel, trap stock, recoil pad. Mfg. 1950-1981.

	100%	98%	95%	90%	80%	70%	60%
	$425	$375	$325	$275	$250	$225	$200

MODEL 870 TC TRAP - higher grade walnut and special VR, Rem. chokes became standard 1987. Mfg. 1950-1979, reintroduced 1996-99.

	100%	98%	95%	90%	80%	70%	60%
	$600	$475	$400	$350	$275	$240	$220

Last MSR was $680.

Subtract 5% if w/o Monte Carlo stock.
Add 20% for early Model 870 TC Trap guns with hand cut checkering.

MODEL 870 COMPETITION TRAP - 12 ga. single shot competition model, reduced recoil, competition walnut stock with cut checkering, VR. Mfg. 1980-1986.

	100%	98%	95%	90%	80%	70%	60%
	$550	$475	$395	$350	$315	$275	$250

Last MSR was $680.

MODEL 870 ALL AMERICAN TRAP - 30 in. full choke barrel, engraved receiver, triggerguard and barrel, deluxe trap stock. Approx. 1,000 mfg., 1972-1976.

	100%	98%	95%	90%	80%	70%	60%
	$795	$700	$650	$605	$495	$440	$385

RENATO GAMBA
Please refer to the Gamba section in this text.

RENETTE, GASTINNE
Please refer to the Gastinne Renette section of this text.

REPUBLIC ARMS, INC.
Previous manufacturer 1997-2001, and located in Chino, CA.

PISTOLS: SEMI-AUTO

THE PATRIOT - .45 ACP cal., double action only, ultra compact with 3 in. barrel, 6 shot mag., black polymer frame with stainless steel slide (either brushed or with black Melonite coating, new 2000), locked breech action, checkered grips, 20 oz. New 1997.

	100%	98%	95%	90%	80%	70%	60%
	$265	$230	$210	$185	$175	$165	$155

Last MSR $299.

Grading	100%	98%	95%	90%	80%	70%	60%

REPUBLIC ARMS OF SOUTH AFRICA

Current manufacturer located in Jeppestown, Union of South Africa. Exclusively imported by TSF Ltd., located in Fairfax, VA.

PISTOLS: SEMI-AUTO

RAP 401 - 9mm Para. cal., 8 shot mag., otherwise similar to Rap-440. New 1999.

MSR	$495	$425	$375	$350	$325	$300	$275	$250

RAP-440 - .40 S&W cal., compact double action, 3½ in. barrel with high contrast 3 dot sights, last shot hold open, hammer drop safety/decocking lever, firing pin block safety, 7 shot mag., all steel construction, 31½ oz., includes case, spare magazine, and lock. New 1998.

MSR	$545	$475	$425	$395	$375	$330	$300	$275

Add $50 for Trilux tritium night sights.

SHOTGUNS: SLIDE ACTION

MUSLER MODEL - 12 ga., lightweight shotgun, polymer reinforced stock and forearm, action opening release lever, action locks open after the last round. New 1998.

MSR	$549	$475	$425	$395	$375	$330	$300	$275

REXIO

Current trademark of guns manufactured in Argentina beginning late 1999. Exclusively imported and distributed by VAM Distribution Company, LLC, located in Wooster, OH. Distributor and dealer direct sales.

PISTOLS: SINGLE SHOT

OUTFITTER RC-SERIES - various cals., including .45 LC/.410 bore, tip-up action, 6 or 10 in. barrel, synthetic SAA style grip and full forearm, opening release lever in front of trigger-guard, transfer bar safety, with or w/o (.45 LC/.410 bore only) sights, manual locking safety, 2.2 - 3 lbs. Importation began 2000.

MSR	$205	$185	$165	$145	$130	$120	$110	$100

REVOLVERS

RJ-22 SERIES - .22 LR cal., 9 shot, 4 or 6 in. VR barrel with full shroud, choice of wood or synthetic grips with finger grooves, adj. sights, 2.1 - 2.6 lbs. Importation began 2000.

MSR	$170	$150	$135	$125	$115	$105	$100	$95

RJ-38 SERIES - .38 Spl. cal., 6 shot, 3 or 4 in. VR barrel with full shroud, choice of wood or synthetic grips with finger grooves, 1.8-2 lbs. Importation began 2000.

MSR	$170	$150	$140	$125	$115	$110	$105	$100

RS-22 SERIES - .22 LR or .22 Mag. cal., 8 (.22 Mag.) or 9 (.22 LR) shot, alloy or steel frame, blue finish, rubber grips with finger grooves, 4 or 6 in. VR barrel with full shroud, fixed or adj. sights, supplied with plastic case. Importation began 2000.

MSR	$175	$155	$140	$125	$115	$110	$105	$100

Add $12 for adj. sights.

✳ *RS-22 Series Stainless* - similar to RS-22 Series, except is stainless steel. Importation began 2000.

MSR	$200	$175	$150	$130				

Add $12 for adj. sights.

RS-357 SERIES - .357 Mag. cal., 6 shot, alloy or steel frame, 3, 4, or 6 in. VR barrel with full shroud, fixed or adj. sights, supplied with plastic case. Importation began 2000.

MSR	$175	$155	$140	$125	$115	$110	$105	$100

Add $12 for adj. sights.

R

Grading	100%	98%	95%	90%	80%	70%	60%

★ **RS-357 Series Stainless** - similar to RS-357 Series, except is stainless steel. Importation began 2000.

MSR	$200	$175	$150	$130

Add $12 for adj. sights.

RHODE ISLAND ARMS COMPANY

Previous manufacturer located in Hope Valley, RI.

SHOTGUNS: O/U

MORRONE MODEL - 12 or 20 ga., 26 or 28 in. plain barrels, boxlock, extractors, single trigger, checkered straight or pistol grip stock. Mfg. 1949-1953, only 500 of these guns were mfg., 450 in 12 ga., and 50 in 20 ga., very few with VR, they are quite rare although collector interest is not overwhelming.

	$1,100	$880	$770	$660	$550	$495	$440

Add 20% for 20 gauge.
Add 20% for VR.

RIB MOUNTAIN ARMS, INC.

Previous rifle manufacturer circa 1992-2000, and located in Beresford and Sturgis, SD.

RIFLES: BOLT ACTION

MODEL 92 - .50 BMG cal., match grade barrel with muzzle brake, long action, walnut thumbhole stock, Timney trigger, approx. 28 lbs. Mfg. 1997-2000.

	$3,175	$2,725	$2,275	$2,000	$1,750	$1,575	$1,300

Last MSR was $3,475.

MODEL 93 - similar to Model 92, except has short action with removable shell holder bolt, approx. 25 lbs. Mfg. 1997-2000.

	$3,175	$2,725	$2,275	$2,000	$1,750	$1,575	$1,300

Last MSR was $3,475.

RICHLAND ARMS COMPANY

Previous importer (until 1986) located in Blissfield, MI. The models listed were made by various manufacturers located in either Italy or Spain.

SHOTGUNS

MODEL 80 LS SINGLE SHOT - 12, 20 ga., or .410 bore, 26 or 28 in. full choke barrel. Mfg. 1986 only.

	$140	$120	$110	$100	$90	$80	$70

Last MSR was $162.

MODEL 711 MAGNUM SxS - 10 ga., 3½ in. chamber, 12 ga., 3 in. chamber, 32 in. full and full, 30 in. full and full, 20, 28 ga., and .410 bore also available on special order, hammerless, boxlock, extractors, checkered, walnut stock, recoil pad. Mfg. 1963-1985 in Spain.

	100%	98%	95%	90%	80%	70%	60%
10 gauge	$400	$325	$275	$250	$230	$210	$190
12 gauge	$340	$295	$265	$250	$230	$210	$190
20 gauge	$450	$340	$295	$260	$230	$210	$195

MODEL 707 DELUXE SxS - 12 or 20 ga., 3 in. chambers, 26, 28, or 30 in. barrels, various chokes, boxlock, extractors, double triggers, checkered stock and forend. Mfg. 1963-1972 in Spain.

	$330	$305	$290	$275	$250	$230	$210

R

Grading	100%	98%	95%	90%	80%	70%	60%

MODEL 200 FIELD GRADE SxS - 12, 16, 20, 28 ga., or .410 bore, 22, 26, and 28 in. barrels, various chokes, Anson & Deeley boxlock, extractors, double triggers, checkered stock, 6 lbs. 2 oz. - 7 lbs. 4 oz. Mfg. 1963-1985 in Spain.

	$320	$285	$255	$225	$195	$175	$150

Last MSR was $379.

MODEL 202 ALL PURPOSE SxS - similar to Field, except 2 sets of barrels, 12 and 20 ga. only. Mfg. 1963-disc. in Spain.

	$305	$260	$230	$220	$195	$165	$150

MODEL 41 ULTRA O/U - 20, 28 ga., or .410 bore, 3 in. chambers (.410 bore only), single non-selective trigger, 26 or 28 in. barrels, extractors, VR, engraved silver finished receiver, select checkered walnut stock and forearm, 6 lbs. 2 oz. Importation disc. 1986.

	$265	$220	$210	$200	$190	$180	$170

Last MSR was $298.

MODEL 747 O/U - 12 or 20 ga. only, 3 in. chambers, Greener crossbolt, boxlock action, VR and barrels, SST, extractors. Importation disc. 1986.

	$420	$350	$325	$310	$295	$280	$265

Last MSR was $464.

MODEL 757 O/U - 12 ga., 3 in. chambers, boxlock action with Greener crossbolt, vent. barrels and rib, double triggers, extractors, walnut stock and forearm, 7 lbs. 4 oz. New 1986. Importation disc. 1986.

	$290	$260	$230	$215	$200	$185	$170

Last MSR was $325.

Add $70 for multi-chokes (Model 7570).

MODEL 787 O/U - 12 ga. only, 3 in. chambers, boxlock action with silver finish, single trigger, vent. barrels and rib, extractors, walnut stock with recoil pad, is supplied with 5 interchangeable choke tubes, 7¼ lbs. Made 1986 only.

	$435	$375	$340	$310	$295	$280	$265

Last MSR was $471.

MODEL 808 O/U - 12 ga., 26, 28, or 30 in. barrels, various chokes, boxlock, extractors, checkered stock. Mfg. 1963-1968 in Italy.

	$420	$360	$330	$315	$290	$270	$230

MODEL 810 O/U - 10 ga., 3½ in. chambers, ST, extractors.

	$600	$550	$500	$460	$430	$395	$360

MODEL 828 O/U - 28 ga., single non-selective trigger, extractors, engraved, only 250 imported.

	$550	$500	$450	$400	$350	$325	$300

RIEDL RIFLE COMPANY

Previous single shot rifle manufacturer.

RIFLES: SINGLE SHOT

SINGLE SHOT RIFLE - many cals., 22-30 in. barrel, rack and pinion action, lever trigger guard activated, fully adj. trigger, select walnut stock, basically custom made.

	$495	$470	$440	$415	$385	$330	$305

✱ Stainless barrel

	$560	$535	$505	$480	$450	$395	$370

RIFLES, INC.

Current manufacturer located in Pleasanton, TX. Previously located in Cedar City, UT. Dealer or direct consumer sales.

Grading	100%	98%	95%	90%	80%	70%	60%

RIFLES: BOLT ACTION

CLASSIC - various cals., features Remington or Winchester stainless steel controlled round action, stainless lapped barrel, matte stainless finish, laminated fiberglass stock with pillar glass bedding, approx. 6½ lbs. New 1996.

    MSR $2,500   **$2,275** **$1,650** **$1,225**

    Add $100 for left-hand action.

LIGHTWEIGHT STRATA STAINLESS - various cals., lightened stainless Remington action, match grade barrel with slimbrake, matte stainless finish, 5 lbs. New 1996.

    MSR $2,850   **$2,625** **$2,025** **$1,650**

    Add $150 for left-hand action.

TITANIUM STRATA - various cals., based on lightened and blue printed Rem. 700 action, titanium receiver, 4 1/2 lbs. New 2002.

    MSR $3,850   **$3,450** **$2,750** **$2,000**

LIGHTWEIGHT 70 - most cals. up to .375 H&H, features Winchester Model 70 stainless controlled round feeding blue printed action, match grade stainless steel barrel with muzzle brake, matte stainless finish, laminated Kevlar/boron/graphite stock with glass bedding, approx. 5½ lbs. New 1997.

    MSR $2,750   **$2,525** **$1,950** **$1,600**

    Add $150 for left-hand action.

VARMINT/TARGET - similar to Classic, except has different stock design and dimensions, different barrel contour. Mfg. 1998-99.

                $1,800 **$1,375** **$1,075**

Last MSR was $1,900.

    Add $250 for Varmint brake.

MASTER SERIES - various cals. up to .300 Wby. Mag., designed for long range accuracy, blue printed Rem. Model 700 action, fiberglass stock, guaranteed to shoot ½ MOA. New 1998.

    MSR $2,950   **$2,725** **$2,075** **$1,650**

SIGNATURE SERIES - .300 Rem. Ultra Mag. cal., blue printed, Rem. M-700 stainless receiver, honed trigger assembly, 27 in. fluted match grade stainless steel barrel with matte finish, w/o sights, synthetic McMillan sporter stock, each gun is signed by Lex Webernick on the floorplate, guaranteed ½ in. MOA. Limited mfg. beginning 2000.

    MSR $2,800   **$2,600** **$2,050** **$1,700**

    Add $175 for slimbrake.

    Add $150 for left hand action.

SAFARI - .375 H&H, .416 Rem., or .458 Lott cal., features Winchester Model 70 controlled round feeding action, match grade barrel with slimbrake, matte stainless or black Teflon finish, various options are available. New 1996.

    MSR $2,700   **$2,525** **$1,975** **$1,650**

R RIGANIAN, RAY (RIFLEMAKER)

Current custom riflemaker and gunsmith established in 1988 and located in Glendale, CA. Consumer direct sales.

RIFLES: BOLT ACTION

Ray Riganian manufactures a Peerless Series (I & II) of custom rifles, using the customer's Win. Model 70, Rem. 700, or Sako action. The Peerless I retails for $2,250 (subtract $150 for Sako action). The Peerless II retails for $3,750 (subtract $450 for Sako action). Peerless II dangerous game cals. (.375 H&H, .416 Rem. Mag., .458 Win. Mag., or .458 Lott) range from $5,200-$5,600 w/o action. He also makes a best quality sporter rifle based on a Win. Model 70 or large ring Mauser 98

Grading	100%	98%	95%	90%	80%	70%	60%

action ($7,000 starting price), in addition to a best quality drop box magazine express rifle that starts at $9,000. Please contact the company directly for more information, current pricing, and delivery time.

RIGBY, JOHN & CO. (GUNMAKERS), INC.

Current manufacturer established during 1735 in Dublin, Ireland. Currently manufactured in Paso Robles, CA since 1997. Previously manufactured in London, England. Currently and distributed domestically by John Rigby & Co. (Gunmakers), Inc., located in Paso Robles, CA. Previously imported by Griffin & Howe until 1998.

Original trade name was W. & J. Rigby circa 1820-1865, during the percussion era. Rigby has always been well known for its dueling pistols. The first London Branch of J. Rigby was opened in 1865, and the Dublin Premises were closed during 1895. The firm became a company in 1900, and has been responsible for many of the large caliber developments in both rifles and ammunition. During 1997, Rigby was acquired by an American investment group located in Paso Robles, CA.

Rigby is one of the world's finest weapons makers. A good portion of the guns they manufacture were custom built to customer specifications. They were chambered for the large black powder express cartridges used for dangerous game in Africa and Asia. The modern Rigby guns follow this same tradition.

We will list the modern Rigby Guns with approximate values but strongly urge that if purchase or sale is contemplated, a professional appraisal be utilized.

RIFLES

Please contact the company directly for more information on the currently manufactured models listed, including delivery time. Values listed for currently manufactured rifles do not include F.E.T.

SINGLE SHOT STALKING RIFLE - .22 Hornet - .500 NE cals., Farquharson lever actuated falling block action, 24 in. barrel, extractor, checkered pistol grip stock, deluxe finish and engraving. Reintroduced 2000.

MSR	$9,750	$9,250	$8,500	$7,500	$6,500	$5,500	$4,500	$3,500

.350 MAGNUM MAGAZINE RIFLE - .350 Magnum cal. originally, most were rechambered to .375 H&H Mag. cal.

		$3,995	$3,400	$2,950	$2,600	$2,300	$2,000	$1,700

Values assume out of production models.

RIGBY EXPRESS MAGAZINE RIFLE - various cals. include .300 H&H, .416 Rigby, .458 Win. Mag., or .505 Gibbs, other calibers are available upon request, new double square bridge Mauser action (pre-1939), claw extraction bolt action, 3-5 shot mag., 20- 28 in. barrel, exhibition grade checkered walnut, full pistol grip stock.

MSR	$17,000	$15,750	$12,000	$9,750	$7,750	$6,750	$5,950	$4,800

Many options include wood upgrades, engraving, express sights, telescopic sight, case, or other details.

STANDARD MAGAZINE RIFLE - similar to Rigby Express Magazine rifle, except in small cals.

MSR	$12,500	$11,250	$9,750	$8,500	$7,000	$6,000	$5,000	$4,000

Many options include wood upgrades, engraving, express sights, telescopic sight, case, or other details.

R

BEST QUALITY SIDELOCK EJECTOR DOUBLE RIFLE - currently mfg. cals. include .375 H&H Flanged, .416/500 Flanged, .470 NE, .500 NE, or .577 NE, older cals. have included .22 LR, .275 Mag., .350 Mag., .416 Rigby, .458 Win. Mag., .465, or .470 NE cal., 24-28 in. barrels, case colored contoured and reinforced Greener sidelock action with cross bolt, deluxe finish and engraving.

MSR	$34,750	$31,500	$26,750	$22,000	$18,000	$14,000	$12,000	$10,500

Many options include wood upgrades, engraving, express sights, telescopic sight, case, or other details.

Grading	100%	98%	95%	90%	80%	70%	60%

BEST QUALITY BOXLOCK EJECTOR DOUBLE RIFLE - current production cals. include .375 H&H Flanged, .416/500 Flanged, .470 NE, .500 NE, or .577 NE cal., 22- 26 in. barrels, Greener cross bolt Anson & Deeley action.

	MSR	$19,450		$18,100	$15,250	$13,000	$10,750	$8,750	$7,500	$6,500

Add $1,500 for .500 NE cal.
Add $3,000 for .577 NE cal.

SECOND QUALITY BOXLOCK EJECTOR DOUBLE RIFLE - similar to Best Quality, with less select wood and engraving. Disc.

			$12,750	$10,750	$9,750	$8,750	$7,350	$6,350	$5,000

Subtract 35% without ejectors.
Values are for larger calibers, smaller cals. could have less value than listed.

SHOTGUNS: O/U

BEST QUALITY SIDELOCK - 12 ga. only, true sidelock action with double safety sears, configured for clay pigeon sports, live bird, or field use, all working parts are titanium nitrate coated, various length vent. barrels with VR, exhibition grade English walnut and various stock configurations, case colored, rust blue, or coin finished is standard, 100% small English scroll engraved. New 2000.

	MSR	$28,000		$25,000	$22,000	$18,500	$15,500	$12,750	$10,500	$9,250

SHOTGUNS: SxS

Please contact the company directly for more information on the currently manufactured models listed, including delivery time. Values listed for currently manufactured shotguns do not include F.E.T.

BEST QUALITY SIDELOCK - CURRENT PRODUCTION - 12, 16, 20, 28 ga. or 410 bore, case colored or coin finished contoured sidelock action, current engraving includes fine frame and border English scroll, also available with optional game scene engraving on both sidelocks.

	MSR	$34,750		$31,500	$26,750	$22,000	$18,000	$14,000	$12,000	$10,500

BOXLOCK SHOTGUN - all ga.'s, barrel lengths and chokes to order, checkered stock to order, auto ejectors, double triggers.

* *Chatsworth Grade*

		$4,500	$3,500	$3,000	$2,500	$2,000	$1,600	$1,200

* *Sackville Grade* - deluxe engraved.

		$5,900	$5,000	$4,500	$3,750	$3,100	$2,650	$2,200

Add 20% for 20 ga.
Add 40% for 28 ga.
Add 60% for .410 bore.

SIDELOCK SHOTGUN - PRE-1997 PRODUCTION - all ga.'s, barrel lengths and chokes to specifications, double triggers, auto ejectors stocked to order.

* *Sandringham Grade*

		$9,500	$7,500	$6,000	$5,000	$4,450	$3,775	$2,950

* *Regal Grade* - deluxe engraved.

		$12,500	$10,000	$8,750	$7,500	$6,400	$5,250	$4,250

Add 20% for 20 ga.
Add 40% for 28 ga.
Add 60% for .410 bore.

Grading	100%	98%	95%	90%	80%	70%	60%

RIZZINI, BATTISTA

Current manufacturer established during 1965, and located in Marcheno, Italy. Imported in the U.S. by William Larkin Moore & Co. located in Scottsdale, AZ, and New England Arms Corp. located in Kittery Point, ME.

RIFLES: O/U

EXPRESS 90L - various cals., ST, ejectors, deluxe wood and features, includes case.

	MSR	$3,650		$3,650	$3,300	$2,975	$2,600	$2,300	$1,950	$1,625

EXPRESS 92EL - similar to Express 90, except has sideplates with more elaborate engraving, includes Nizzoli case, custom dimensions available.

	MSR	$7,500		$7,500	$6,750	$6,000	$5,200	$4,500	$3,900	$3,300

SHOTGUNS: O/U

AURUM - 12, 16, or 20 ga., boxlock action, light engraving, cased. New 1996.

	MSR	$1,500		$1,500	$1,325	$1,125	$900	$775	$650	$525

✳ ***Aurum Light*** - 16 ga. only, standard dimensions only, cased. Importation began 2000.

	MSR	$1,600		$1,600	$1,400	$1,175	$950	$825	$675	$550

ARTEMIS - similar to Aurum, except has better engraving and wood, cased. New 1996.

	MSR	$1,700		$1,700	$1,475	$1,225	$975	$850	$700	$575

ARTEMIS DELUXE - all gauges, game scene engraving with gold inlays.

	MSR	$3,700		$3,700	$3,300	$2,825	$2,450	$1,975	$1,600	$1,275

ARTEMIS EL - top-of-the-line gun with hand engraving. Importation disc. 2000.

				$12,000	$10,000	$9,200	$8,300	$6,900	$5,900	$4,850

Last MSR was $15,625.

780 FIELD SERIES - 10, 12, or 16 ga., boxlock action, DTs, extractors, checkered walnut stock and forearm. Importation disc. 1998.

				$1,075	$875	$750	$675	$595	$525	$450

Last MSR was $1,225.

Add $550 for 10 ga.
Add $150 for ejectors (Model S780 E).
Add $200 for SST with ejectors (Model S780 EM).
Add $350 for SST, ejectors, and upgraded wood (Model S780 EML).
A Model S780 EMEL is also available that is entirely hand-finished and engraved for $5,995.

✳ ***780 Competition Series*** - includes Skeet, Trap, and Sporting Clays configuration. Importation disc. 1998.

				$1,375	$1,050	$925	$825	$725	$625	$525

Last MSR was $1,600.

✳ ***780 Small Gauge Series*** - includes 20, 28, or 36 ga., DTs, ejectors. Importation disc. 1998.

				$1,275	$975	$875	$800	$725	$625	$525

Last MSR was $1,500.

Add $50 for SST (Model 780 EM).

S 780 EMEL - includes Nizzoli case.

	MSR	$7,800		$7,800	$6,800	$5,900	$5,000	$4,200	$3,400	$2,600

R

Grading	100%	98%	95%	90%	80%	70%	60%

782 EM FIELD SERIES - 12 or 16 ga., boxlock action with sideplates, SST ejectors, extractors, checkered walnut stock and forearm. Importation disc. 1998.

| | $1,450 | $1,150 | $995 | $875 | $750 | $675 | $550 |

Last MSR was $1,700.

Add $450 for Slug variation (Model 782 EM Slug).
Add $350 for better engraving and wood (Model 782 EML).
A Model S7820 EMEL is also available that is entirely hand-finished and engraved for $12,000.

✳ **S 782 EMEL Deluxe** - all gauges, individually made per customer specifications, 27½ in. VR barrels with choke tubes (except .410 bore), coin finished receiver with side plates featuring elaborate Bulino game scene engraving with gold inlays and fine scroll borders, deluxe English walnut, Nizzoli best leather case. Importation began 1994.

| MSR | $9,500 | | $9,500 | $8,525 | $7,200 | $6,300 | $5,350 | $4,400 | $3,500 |

790 SERIES COMPETITION - 12 or 20 ga., choice of Trap, Skeet, or Sporting Clays configuration, features black frame outlined with gold line engraving. Importation disc. 1999.

| | $1,975 | $1,575 | $1,300 | $1,050 | $925 | $825 | $695 |

Last MSR was $2,275.

Subtract $150 for 20 ga. Trap.
Subtract $50 for 20 ga. Skeet.
Add $1,050 for 20 ga. Sporting (includes sideplates and quick detachable stock).
A Model 790 Trap EL is also available that is entirely hand-finished with 18 Kt. gold and hand engraving - prices begin at $5,650 in 12 ga., $5,200 in 20 ga.

✳ **790 Small Gauge Series** - similar to 790 Competition Series, except in 20, 28, or 36 ga., SST and ejectors standard. Importation disc. 2000.

| | $1,475 | $1,150 | $995 | $875 | $750 | $675 | $550 |

Last MSR was $1,750.

A Model 790 EMEL was also available that was entirely hand-finished with 18 Kt. gold and hand engraving - prices began at $9,600.

✳ **S 790 EL** - includes multichokes and case. Importation disc. 2000.

| | $5,650 | $5,225 | $4,750 | $4,150 | $3,500 | $3,000 | $2,500 |

Last MSR was $6,250.

✳ **S 790 EMEL Deluxe** - all gauges, individually made per customer specifications, 27½ in. VR barrels with choke tubes (except .410 bore), color case hardened or coin finished receiver with ornate ornamental engraving and Rizzini crest, deluxe English walnut, Nizzoli best leather case. Importation began 1994.

| MSR | $7,800 | | $7,800 | $6,800 | $5,900 | $5,000 | $4,200 | $3,400 | $2,600 |

792 SMALL GAUGE MAG. SERIES - 20, 28, or 36 ga., Mag. chambers, SST, ejectors, includes engraved sideplates. Importation disc. 1998.

| | $1,700 | $1,275 | $1,050 | $895 | $750 | $675 | $595 |

Last MSR was $2,000.

A Model 792 EMEL is also available that is entirely hand-finished with 18 Kt. gold and hand engraving - prices begin at $8,250.

✳ **S 792 EMEL Deluxe** - all gauges, individually made per customer specifications, 27½ in. VR barrels with choke tubes (except .410 bore), coin finished receiver with side plates featuring upgraded Bulino game scene engraving and fine scroll borders, deluxe English walnut, Nizzoli leather case. Importation began 1994.

| MSR | $7,500 | | $7,500 | $6,600 | $5,650 | $4,700 | $4,000 | $3,200 | $2,400 |

MODEL 2000 TRAP - 12 ga. only, includes nickel finished receiver with sideplates, gold trigger, VR barrels and rib. Importation disc. 1998.

| | $1,900 | $1,500 | $1,275 | $1,025 | $925 | $825 | $695 |

Last MSR was $2,200.

A Model 2000 Trap EL was also available that was entirely hand finished with 18 Kt. gold and hand-engraving - prices began at $5,290.

Grading	100%	98%	95%	90%	80%	70%	60%

MODEL 2000-SP - 12 ga. only, 26, 28, 30, or 32 in. overbored barrels with choke tubes, includes engraved sideplates, semi-fancy select walnut with quick detachable stock, cased. Imported 1994-98.

	$3,250	$2,800	$2,400	$1,975	$1,600	$1,300	$1,000

Last MSR was $3,650.

PREMIER SPORTING - 12 or 20 ga., 28, 29½, or 32 in. multi-choke (5 chokes) barrels, hard cased, custom dimensions upon application. Importation began 1994.

MSR	$2,200		$2,200	$1,950	$1,675	$1,500	$1,375	$1,175	$875

SPORTING EL - includes multichokes and case. Importation disc. 2000.

	$3,425	$2,850	$2,500	$2,225	$1,950	$1,675	$1,500

Last MSR was $3,750.

UPLAND EL - all gauges, 27½ in. VR barrels with choke tubes (except .410 bore), case hardened receiver, deluxe walnut, hard case. Importation began 1994.

MSR	$2,800		$2,800	$2,400	$2,100	$1,800	$1,500	$1,200	$995

RIZZINI, EMILIO

Current shotgun manufacturer established during the mid-1950s and located in Brescia, Italy. Currently imported by Tristar Sporting Arms, Ltd., located in N. Kansas City, MO.

All Emilio Rizzini shotguns are equipped with a patented Four Locks locking system. Models listed were introduced during 1999. Most Emilio Rizzini field shotguns are available with internal choke tubes.

SHOTGUNS: O/U

CLASS MODEL - 12, 16, 20, 28 ga., or 410 bore, boxlock action with reinforced frame, hand engraving, select wood, ejectors, SST. Importation disc. 2000.

	$1,625	$1,400	$1,125	$975	$875	$750	$675

Last MSR was $1,870.

Add $70 for sideplates and case (Class SL Model).

CLASS DE LUXE MODEL - 12, 16, 20, 28 ga., or 410 bore, boxlock action with reinforced frame, hand finished game scene engraving with gold inlays, ejectors, SST, cased. Importation disc. 2000.

	$3,675	$3,325	$2,975	$2,625	$2,300	$1,950	$1,675

Last MSR was $4,185.

Add $170 for sideplates (Class SL De Luxe Model.)

BRIXIAN DE LUXE - all gauges, top-of-the-line model, boxlock action with reinforced frame, master fine scroll engraving, ejectors, SST, deluxe English wood, individually made per customer's specifications, leather cased. Importation disc. 2000.

	$8,350	$7,600	$6,950	$5,700	$4,500	$3,650	$2,950

Last MSR was $8,975.

Add $1,986 for sideplates and best leather case (Brixian SL DE Luxe).

TR-I FIELD (NOVA I) - 12 or 20 ga., blue boxlock action, SST, extractors, 26 or 28 vent. barrels with 7mm VR and fixed chokes, checkered standard grade walnut stock and forearm, gold trigger, approx. 7¼ lbs. Imported 1998-2001.

	$585	$485	$430	$375	$330	$300	$275

Last MSR was $687.

✳ **TR-I Plus** - 12 or 20 ga., 3 in. chambers, includes choke tubes, 7mm vent. rib, Importation began 2000.

MSR	$748		$625	$550	$465	$425	$375	$330	$300

R

Grading	100%	98%	95%	90%	80%	70%	60%

TR-II FIELD (NOVA II) - 12, 16 (fixed chokes), 20, 28 ga. or .410 bore (fixed chokes), similar to Nova I, except has choke tubes and ejectors. New 1998.

MSR $879	$760	$660	$555	$465	$410	$355	$300

Add $45 for 20, 28 ga., or .410 bore.

TR-MAG. (NOVA MAG.) - 10 (new 2000) or 12 ga. only, 3½ in. chambers, SST, ejectors or extractors (10 ga. only), 24 or 28 in. vent. barrels with 7mm VR and choke tubes, matte finished wood and metal or Mossy Oak/Shadowgrass camo wood finish (new 2000), 7¼ - 9¼ lbs. New 1998.

MSR $764	$625	$550	$465	$425	$375	$330	$300

Add $178 for camo (new 2000).
Add $368 for 10 ga. with camo (new 2000).

SHOTGUNS: O/U, COMPETITION SERIES

The following models are available in either Trap, Skeet, or Sporting Clays configuration. Sporting Clays models have 5 internal multichokes.

COMPACT MODEL - 12, 16, or 20 ga., boxlock action with reinforced frame, ejectors, SST, model and company name inlaid on black finished action, select checkered walnut stock and forearm, cased. Importation disc. 2000.

	$1,900	$1,750	$1,450	$1,100	$900	$775	$700

Last MSR was $2,135.

GARA MODEL - similar to Compact, except has hand engraving and wood upgrade. Importation disc. 2000.

	$3,325	$2,975	$2,600	$2,200	$1,800	$1,400	$1,250

Last MSR was $3,765.

Add $351 for Gara Cup Model (company logo inlaid in gold).
Add $1,022 for Gara SL Model (includes engraved sideplates).

GARA DE LUXE - top-of-the-line competition model, ornamental pattern engraved by master engraver, deluxe wood, best leather case. Importation disc. 2000.

	$6,600	$5,750	$5,250	$4,400	$3,500	$2,750	$2,450

Last MSR was $7,375.

SHOTGUNS: O/U, SPORTING CLAYS

TR-SC (NOVA SC) - 12 or 20 (new 1999) ga. only, 3 in. chambers, sporting clays model, silver finished boxlock action, gold SST, 28 or 30 in. vent. barrels with 10mm VR and mid-rib sight beads, fancy checkered walnut stock and forearm, approx. 7½ lbs. Importation began 1998.

MSR $996	$845	$745	$645	$555	$450	$395	$350

Add $77 for 20 ga. (new 1999).

TR-L - similar to Nova SC, except has stock dimensions for female shooter (13 1/2 LOP), also available in 20 ga., approx. 7¾ lbs. Importation began 1999.

MSR $1,014	$850	$750	$650	$575	$450	$395	$350

TR-ROYAL - 12, 20, or 28 ga., 3 in. chambers, similar to the TR-SC, except has special dimension stock designed to reduce recoil, 28 or 30 in. VR barrels with 7mm-10mm tapered rib and rhino ported extended choke tubes, ejectors, silver finished boxlock action, deluxe checkered walnut stock and forearm, silver frame with gold accents, approx. 7½ lbs. Importation began 1999.

MSR $1,340	$1,075	$935	$825	$700	$600	$500	$400

Subtract $82 for 20 or 28 ga.

TR-CLASS SL - 12 ga. only, 2¾ in. chambers, features select materials, silver finished boxlock action with engraved sideplates, ejectors, SST, 28 or 30 VR barrels with choke tubes, 7¾ lbs. Importation began 1999.

MSR $1,775	$1,525	$1,275	$1,025	$900	$800	$700	$575

Grading	100%	98%	95%	90%	80%	70%	60%

RIZZINI, F.LLI

Current manufacturer located in Magno di Gardone V.T., Italy. Currently imported and distributed by William Larkin Moore & Co. located in Scottsdale, AZ, L. Michael Weatherby, located in Laguna Niguel, CA, and by New England Arms Corp. located in Kittery Point, ME.

In the past, this manufacturer collaborated with Antonio Zoli to make "spec" guns that were usually imported by Abercrombie & Fitch or Von Lengerke & Detmold. These guns are normally marked on the water table "Zoli-Rizzini" or "F.lli Rizzini" (in the latter case, most of the time these guns have the Abercrombie & Fitch, etc. logo as well). These guns are not to be confused with the quality of current Rizzini F.lli mfg. Normally, these older Field Grade models (non-ejector, boxlock actions in 12, 16, 20, 28 ga., or .410 bore) sell in the $500- $1,200 range, with a 25% premium for 28 ga. or .410 bore. Deluxe Field Models with a scalloped boxlock action and ejectors are currently valued in the $1,500-$2,500 range, with a 30% premium for 28 ga. or .410 bore. The Extra Lusso Model (top-of-the-line) currently sell in the $3,500 range in 12 ga., $4,250 in 20 ga., $4,750 in 28 ga., and $4,250 in .410 bore.

Rizzini shotguns are made to individual custom order only (about 25 are made a year). Prices do not include engraving (prices range from $8,700-$21,700, substantially more for famous name engravers such as Fracassi, Torcoli, etc.) and may be subject to fluctuation in exchange rates.

SHOTGUNS: SxS, CUSTOM

Add approx. $8,000-$10,000 for fine English scroll or ornamental engraving with swans.
Add approx. $19,500-$24,375 for extra quality ornamental engraving.
Add approx. $25,000-$40,000 for Torcoli or Fracassi engraving.

R2-E BOXLOCK EJECTOR - 12, 16, or 20 ga., select walnut, detachable bottom inspection plate, various barrel lengths, without engraving. Disc. 1995.

	100%	98%	95%	90%	80%	70%	60%
	$11,500	$9,000	$8,000	$7,000	$6,200	$5,500	$4,750

Last MSR was $25,000.

✳ 28 ga. or .410 bore. - otherwise similar to above. Disc. 1995.

	100%	98%	95%	90%	80%	70%	60%
	$15,000	$12,250	$10,000	$8,750	$7,500	$6,250	$5,000

Last MSR was $27,500.

RI-E SIDELOCK EJECTOR - 12, 16, or 20 ga., H&H patterned sidelocks, select Circassian walnut, various barrel lengths, without engraving.

MSR	$49,000	$49,000	$39,000	$33,000	$28,000	$24,500	$21,250	$18,500

Add $7,000 for 28 ga. or .410 bore.

R3-E - sidelock ejector model w/o engraving. Importation began 2000.

MSR	$35,000	$35,000	$30,000	$24,500	$19,750	$16,000	$14,750	$11,750

RIZZINI, I.

Please refer to the Fair Tecni-Mec listing.

THE ROBAR COMPANIES, INC.

Current manufacturer established during 1986, and located in Phoenix, AZ.

Robar is a leader in custom metal finishing, including combination finishes. These include the Roguard black finish, NP3 surface treatment, and additional finishes including bluing, electroless nickel, blackening stainless steel, phosphating/parkerizing, Polymax camoflauge, and Polymax dry film. Please contact Robar directly (see Trademark Index) for more information, including current prices on their lineup of firearms, custom metal and wood finishes, and customizing services, including shotguns.

PISTOLS: SEMI-AUTO

Robar manufactures a complete line of semi-auto, .45 ACP pistols in various configurations including the Super Deluxe Pistol Package ($2,300), Robar Combat Master ($1,250), Thunder Ranch Pis-

Grading	100%	98%	95%	90%	80%	70%	60%

tol ($1,100), .45 Super, or Basic Carry ($850). These guns are built up from other makers including Springfield and Colt to provide the configuration/modifications necessary.

RIFLES

Robar also manufactures a complete line of rifles including the SR60 ($2,900), SR90 ($3,500), QR2 ($3,200), Robar RC 50 BMG ($5,500), RC50F (disc., last MSR was $4,800), Hunter, Precision Hunter, Varminter (disc., last MSR $2,400), and Thunder Ranch Package ($3,900).

SHOTGUNS

Defensive shotguns are also manufactured, and include the Robar Elite ($1,200), Robar Defender ($575), Robar S.O.F. ($870), Thunder Ranch model ($700).

ROBERTS, J. & SON (GUNMAKERS) LTD.

Current manufacturer, import agent, and dealer established during 1950, and located in London, England.

Please contact J. Roberts & Son (Gunmakers) Ltd. directly for more information on their current inventory and other services (see Trademark Index).

RIFLES

J. Roberts & Son new boxlock SxS ejector rifles are currently priced in the £14,000 - £16,000 range, depending on caliber. New Roberts magazine rifles are currently priced from £6,500 - £10,400, depending on caliber.

SHOTGUNS

Please contact the company directly for a quotation on a new shotgun (boxlock or sidelock).

ROBINSON ARMAMENT CO.

Current rifle manufacturer located in Salt Lake City, UT. Currently distributed by ZDF Import/Export, Inc., located in Salt Lake City, UT. Dealer and consumer direct sales.

RIFLES: SEMI-AUTO

Please refer to the Vepr. Rifle section for more information on Vepr. Rifles.

M96 EXPEDITIONARY RIFLE/CARBINE - .223 Rem. cal., paramilitary design, unique action allows accessory kit to convert loading from bottom to top of receiver (available later in 2000), 16 (Recon Model, new 2001), 17¼ (carbine, new 2000) or 20 in. barrel with muzzle brake, stainless steel receiver and barrel, matte black finish metal, black synthetic stock and forearm, adj. sights, gas operated with adjustment knob, last shot hold open, rotating bolt assembly, 8.5 lbs. New 1999.

MSR	$1,600	$1,495	$1,300	$1,100	$925	$850	$775	$700

Add $100 for carbine with 16 in. barrel.
Add $200 for rifle/carbine with top feed.

ROCHE, CHRISTIAN

Current manufacturer located in Veauche, France.

Christian Roche manufactures quality side-by-side shotguns and double rifles. Since all orders are per individual specifications, the factory must be contacted directly to obtain a current price quotation and information (see Trademark Index).

ROCK RIVER ARMS, INC.

Current handgun and rifle manufacturer located in Cleveland, IL. Dealer and consumer direct sales.

Grading	100%	98%	95%	90%	80%	70%	60%

PISTOLS: SEMI-AUTO

Rock River Arms makes a variety of high quality M-1911 based semi-autos. They specialize in manufacturing their own National Match frames and slides. Current models (standard cal. is .45 ACP) include the Standard Match (MSR $1,150), National Match Hardball (MSR $1,275), Bullseye Wadcutter (MSR $1,380), Basic Limited Match (MSR $1,395), Limited Match (MSR $1,795), Ultimate Match Achiever (MSR $2,255), Matchmaster Steel (disc. 2001, last MSR was $2,355), Elite Commando (MSR $1,395), Hi-Cap Basic Limited (MSR $1,895), and the Doug Koenig Signature Series (MSR $5,000, .38 Super cal.). Rock River Arms also offers additional options and parts. Please contact the factory for additional information and availability.

RIFLES: SEMI-AUTO

Rock River Arms makes a variety of paramilitary style rifles/carbines patterned after the AR-15 in .223 Rem. cal. Current models include the CAR A2 (MSR $825), Standard A2 (MSR $825), CAR A4 Flattop (MSR $800), Standard A4 Flattop (MSR $800), LE Tactical Carbine A2/A4 (MSR $850/$875), Elite LE Tactical Carbine A2/A4 (MSR $850/$875), LE TASC rifle (MSR $725), M4 Entry (MSR $875), Varmint (MSR $950), and the NM A2-DCM Legal (MSR $1,200).

ROCKY MOUNTAIN ARMS CORP.

Previous manufacturer of mini revolvers circa mid-1960s, and located in Salt Lake City, UT.

REVOLVERS

MINI REVOLVER - .22 Short cal., 6 shot, stainless steel, locking bolt is in top strap, bolt cam on left side of hammer, supplied with black velveteen case.

$275	$225	$150					

When RMAC went out of business, production was resumed by North American Arms Corp., then after another company change, Freedom Arms started production.

ROCKY MOUNTAIN ARMS, INC.

Current manufacturer located in Longmont, CO since 1990.

Rocky Mountain Arms is a quality specialty manufacturer of rifles (currently mfg.), and pistols (disc.). All firearms are finished in Dupont Teflon-S industrial coatings (Bear Coat). Direct sales only (see listing in Trademark Index for more information).

PISTOLS: SEMI-AUTO

BAP (BOLT ACTION PISTOL) - .308 Win., 7.62x39mm, or 10mm Rocky Mountain Thunderer (10x51mm) cal., features 14 in. heavy fluted Douglas Match barrel, Kevlar/ graphite pistol grip stock, supplied with Harris bipod and black nylon case. Mfg. 1993 only.

$1,425	$1,275	$1,100	$950	$825	$700	$575	

Last MSR was $1,595.

1911A1-LH - .40 S&W or .45 ACP cal., specifically designed for left-handed shooters, featuring left side ejection port and right side controls, gold cup size, stainless steel construction, hand fitted parts, integral ramp barrel, Millett adj. sights, test target. Mfg. 1991-93.

$1,295	$995	$750					

Last MSR was $1,395.

Add $100 for Bo-Mar sights.

BACKUP PLUS - .45 ACP cal., hand tuned AMT Back-up pistol, black DuPont Teflon- S finish, Tritium front night sight. Mfg. 1995-97.

$575	$515	$450	$400	$360	$330	$300	

Last MSR was $650.

Grading	100%	98%	95%	90%	80%	70%	60%

22K PISTOLS - .22 LR cal., AR style pistols featuring 7 in. barrel, choice of matte black or NATO Green Teflon-S finish, will use Colt conversion kit, choice of carrying handle or flat-top upper receiver, 10 or 30 shot mag., includes black nylon case. Mfg. 1993 only.

	$475	$425	$375	$350	$325	$295	$275

Last MSR was $525.

Add $50 for flat-top receiver with Weaver style bases.

PATRIOT PISTOL - .223 Rem. cal., AR style pistol featuring 7 in. match barrel with integral Max Dynamic muzzle brake, 21 in. overall, available with either carrying handle upper receiver and fixed sights or flat-top receiver with Weaver style bases, fluted upper receiver became an option in 1994, accepts standard AR-15 mags, 5 lbs. Mfg. 1993-94 (per C/B).

	$2,295	$1,975	$1,625	$1,425	$1,250	$1,075	$950

Last MSR was $1,795.

Add $200 for black milled upper and lower receiver w/o carrying handle.

KOMRADE - 7.62x39mm cal., includes carrying handle upper receiver with fixed sights, floating 7 in. barrel, Teflon red or black finish, 5 lbs., 5 shot mag. Mfg. 1994-95.

	$1,825	$1,650	$1,425	$1,200	$975	$850	$775

Last MSR was $1,995.

RIFLES: BOLT ACTION

PROFESSIONAL SERIES - .223 Rem., .30-06, .308 Win., or .300 Win. Mag. cal., bolt action rifle utilizing modified Mauser action, fluted 26 in. Douglas premium heavy match barrel with integral muzzle brake, custom Kevlar-Graphite stock with off-set thumbhole, test target. Mfg. 1991-95.

	$2,050	$1,650	$1,275	$995	$850	$725	$600

Last MSR was $2,200.

Add $100 for .300 Win. Mag. cal.
Add $300 for left-hand action.

PRAIRIE STALKER - .223 Rem., .22-250 Rem., .30-06, .308 Win., or .300 Win. Mag. cal., choice of Remington, Savage, or Winchester barreled action, includes Choate ultimate sniper stock, lapped bolt and match crown, "Bear Coat" all-weather finish, includes factory test target. Limited mfg. 1998 only.

	$1,595	$1,350	$1,150	$950	$875	$775	$675

Last MSR was $1,795.

❋ **Ultimate Prairie Stalker** - similar to Prairie Stalker, except custom barrel and caliber specifications are customer's choice. Limited mfg. 1998 only.

	$2,200	$1,875	$1,625	$1,400	$1,200	$1,000	$895

Last MSR was $2,495.

PRO-VARMINT - .22-250 Rem., or .223 Rem. cal., RMA action, 22 in. heavy match barrel with recessed crown, Bear Coat metal finish, Choate stock with aluminum bedding. New 1999.

MSR	$1,095	$995	$875	$800	$725	$650	$575	$450

POLICE MARKSMAN - .308 Win. or .300 Win. Mag. cal., similar to Professional Series, except has 40X-C stock featuring adj. cheekpiece and buttplate, target rail, Buehler micro-dial scope mounting system. Mfg. 1991-95.

	$2,325	$1,995	$1,650	$1,325	$1,100	$900	$700

Last MSR was $2,500.

Add $100 for .300 Win. Mag. cal.
Add $400 for left-hand action.
Add $400 for illuminated dot scope (4X-12X x 56mm).

❋ **Police Marksman II** - .308 Win. cal., RMA action, 22 in. heavy match barrel with recessed crown, Bear Coat metal finish, Choate stock with aluminum bedding. New 1999.

MSR	$1,095	$995	$875	$800	$725	$650	$575	$450

Grading	100%	98%	95%	90%	80%	70%	60%

PRO-GUIDE - .280 Rem., .35 Whelen, .308 Win., 7x57mm Mauser, or 7mm-08 Rem. cal., Scout Rifle design with 17 in. Shilen barrel, "Bear Coat" finish, approx. 7 lbs. New 1999.

	MSR	$2,295		$2,025	$1,800	$1,600	$1,425	$1,200	$1,000	$825

NINJA SCOUT RIFLE - .22 Mag. cal., takedown rifle based on Marlin action, black stock, 16½ in. match grade crowned barrel, forward mounted Weaver style scope base, adj. rear sight, 7 shot mag. Mfg. 1991-95.

	$640	$575	$525	$460	$430	$390	$360

Last MSR was $695.

Add $200 for illuminated dot scope (1.5X-4X) w/ extended eye relief.

SCOUT SEMI-AUTO - .22 Mag. cal., patterned after Marlin action. Mfg. 1993-95.

	$650	$575	$495	$395	$350	$295	$260

Last MSR was $725.

Add $200 for illuminated dot scope (1.5X-4X) w/ extended eye relief.

RIFLES: SEMI-AUTO

M-SHORTEEN - .308 Win. cal., compact highly modified M1-A featuring 17" match crowned barrel, custom front sight, mod. gas system, hand honed action & trigger, custom muzzle brake. Mfg. 1991-94.

	$1,650	$1,425	$1,175	$995	$850	$725	$600

Last MSR was $1,895.

Add $200 for Woodland/Desert camo.

VARMINTER - .223 Rem. cal. only, AR-15 styled rifle with 20 in. fluted heavy match barrel, flat-top receiver with Weaver style bases, round metal National Match hand guard with floating barrel, choice of NATO green or matte black Teflon-S finish, supplied with case and factory test target (sub-MOA). Mfg. 1993-94.

	$2,195	$1,800	$1,600	$1,400	$1,200	$1,000	$875

Last MSR was $2,495.

PATRIOT MATCH RIFLE - .223 Rem. cal., 20 in. Bull Match barrel, regular or milled upper and lower receivers, two-piece machined aluminum hand guard, choice of DuPont Teflon finish in black or NATO green, ½ MOA, hard case. Mfg. 1995-97.

	$2,375	$1,975	$1,650	$1,400	$1,200	$1,000	$895

Last MSR was $2,500.

Add approx. $325 for milled upper receiver.
Add approx. $650 for milled upper and lower receivers.

SHOTGUNS: SLIDE ACTION

870 COMPETITOR - 12 ga., 3 in. chamber, security configuration with synthetic stock, hand-honed action, ghost ring adj. sights, "Bear Coat" finish, high visibility follower. Mfg. 1996-97.

	$695	$625	$550	$500	$450	$400	$360

Last MSR was $795.

ROCKY MOUNTAIN ELK FOUNDATION

Current national conservation organization with national headquarters located in Missoula, MT.

RIFLES: BOLT ACTION

RUGER NO. 1-A LIGHT SPORTER - .35 Whelen cal., features gold inlaid elk on right side of receiver and mountain scene with gold accents on left side, engraved by Adams & Son, blue finish, deluxe wood, 50 mfg. 1995 only.

	$2,395	$1,850	$1,475

Last MSR was $2,395.

Grading	100%	98%	95%	90%	80%	70%	60%

SAUER MODEL 90 - .270 Win. or .30-06 cal., banquet offering only, total mfg. unknown.

| | | | $1,375 | $1,100 | $925 | | |

ROGAK

Please refer to the L E S Incorporated listing in this text for more information on the Rogak Pistol.

ROGUE RIVER RIFLEWORKS

Current manufacturer located in Paso Robles, CA. Dealer and consumer direct sales.

RIFLES

BOLT ACTION MODEL - 7mm STW, .300 Win. Mag., .30-378 Wby. Mag., 8mm Rem. Mag., .375 H&H, .416 Rem. Mag., or .458 Win. Mag. cal., choice of Remington M-700 or Winchester M-70 action, Pac-Nor match grade barrel (with cryogenic treatment), engraved receiver, floorplate, and grip cap, jewelled bolt, exhibition grade checkered walnut stock with ebony forend cap. New 1998.

MSR	$10,500		$9,500	$8,500	$7,500	$6,500	$5,500	$4,500	$3,250

LEVER ACTION MODEL - .243 Win., .260 Rem., 7mm-08 Rem., .308 Win., or .358 Win. cal., features rebuilt Winchester Model 88 action, match grade chrome moly barrel, exhibition grade walnut, choice of American classic or Mannlicher stock design. New 1998.

MSR	$5,100		$4,650	$4,125	$3,675	$3,100	$2,600	$2,000	$1,700

SxS MODEL - .470 NE, .500 NE, or .577 NE cal., Anson & Deely action, Purdey double locking lugs, Greener crossbolt, Southgate selective ejectors, quarter rib with rear sights, exhibition grade wood, case colored or coin finished receiver. Limited mfg. 1998- 2000.

Prices started at $12,500 for .470 NE cal. A 12, 16, or 20 ga. shotgun barrel conversion kit was also available for $3,800.

RÖHM

Previous firearms manufacturer located in Sontheim an der Brenz, Germany. Limited importation into the U.S. Röhm still manufactures gas alarm pistols, mostly for European sales.

Röhm produced inexpensive revolvers for the U.S. marketplace during the late 1960s- 1970s. Most of these guns were built as sub-contracts for U.S. companies and/or distributors (i.e., Hy-Score, a previous distributor located in Brooklyn, NY). Some of the models included are RG-7 through RG-88 (21 variations), Romo, Thalco, Valor, Vestpocket, Western Style, Zephyr, and others. Röhm also manufactured a few semi-auto pistols (RG-25 and RG-26) at approx. the same time. Currently, these guns are seen priced in the $35- $125 range, as the shooting value determines the price tag, not collector interest.

DERRINGERS

DERRINGER - .22 LR cal., blue, copy of Remington O/U derringer. Excellently made, but half-cock safety is old design and could fail if dropped.

			$150	$115	$95	$85	$75	$65	$55

ROHRBAUGH FIREARMS

Current manufacturer located in Bayport, NY. Rohrbaugh Firearms is a division of API.

PISTOLS: SEMI-AUTO

MS-9 - 9mm Para cal., DAO, features patented magnetic safety system that uses a magnetic ring worn by the shooter to unlock the gun safety, aluminum frame, 2.7 in. barrel, 6 shot mag., wood grips, 14 oz. New 2002.

MSR	$695		$625	$475	$375	

Add $100 for gold accents and wood grips.

Grading	100%	98%	95%	90%	80%	70%	60%

ROSS RIFLE COMPANY

Previous manufacturer located Quebec, Canada.

RIFLES: BOLT ACTION

CANADIAN 1907 MARK II - .303 Brit. cal., straight pull, 28 in. barrel, pre-WWII.

	$295	$250	$200	$180	$160	$140	$120

MODEL 1910 SPORTING RIFLE - .280 Ross or .303 Brit. cal., similar action as 1907, checkered Sporter stock, leaf sights. Mfg. 1910-1920.

	$375	$325	$300	$275	$225	$175	$150

Add $100 for Porter "pop-up" receiver apeture sight.

Note: Many experts state this rifle is unsafe to fire.

ROSSI

Current trademark manufactured by Amadeo Rossi S.A., located in Sao Leopoldo, Brazil. Currently imported exclusively by BrazTech, International beginning late 1998, located in Miami, FL. Previously imported by Interarms, located in Alexandria, VA.

PISTOLS: SINGLE SHOT

ROCKET SINGLE SHOT - .22 LR, .22 Hornet, .22-250 Rem., .220 Swift, .223 Rem., .30-30 Win., .357 Mag., .44 Mag., or .45 LC cal., break open single shot action. Limited importation 2000 only.

	$135	$120	$110	$100	$90	$80	$75

Last MSR was $149.

Add $36 for stainless steel.

REVOLVERS: DOUBLE ACTION

All discontinued models in this section were only imported by Interarms, not Braztech. Braztech is the exclusive North American importer for Rossi firearms.

MODEL 31 - .38 Spl., 5 shot, 4 in. medium barrel, target trigger and hammer, 22 oz. Disc. 1985. Add $5 for nickel.

	$120	$105	$95	$85	$75	$70	$65

Last MSR was $139.

MODEL 51 - .22 LR cal., 6 shot, 6 in. barrel, blue only, adj. sights. Disc. 1985.

	$125	$110	$100	$90	$85	$80	$75

Last MSR was $149.

✳ **Sportsman 511 Stainless** - .22 LR cal. only, stainless steel, 4 in. barrel, with matted rib, adj. rear sight, 6 shot, hardwood stocks, 30 oz. Imported 1986-90 only.

	$190	$160	$125				

Last MSR was $235.

MODEL 68 - .38 Spl. cal., 5 shot, 2 or 3 in. barrel, blue or nickel (3 in. barrel only), choice of wood or rubber grips with 2 in. barrel. Disc. 1998.

	$165	$135	$100	$90	$80	$70	$65

Last MSR was $225.

MODEL 69 - .32 S&W cal., 6 shot, 3 in. barrel, walnut grips. Disc. 1985.

	$120	$105	$95	$85	$75	$70	$65

Last MSR was $139.

Add $5 for nickel finish.

R

Grading	100%	98%	95%	90%	80%	70%	60%

MODEL 70 - .22 LR cal, 6 shot, 3 in. barrel. Disc. 1985.

	$120	$105	$95	$85	$75	$70	$65

Last MSR was $139.

   Add $5 for nickel finish.

MODEL 84 STAINLESS - .38 Spl. cal., 6 shot, 3 or 4 in. solid raised rib barrel, standard service sights, checkered hardwood grips, 27½ oz. Imported 1985-86 only.

	$190	$155	$125

Last MSR was $205.

MODEL 88 STAINLESS - .38 Spl. cal., 5 shot, stainless steel construction, 2 or 3 in. barrel, hardwood or rubber (2 in. barrel only) grips, 21 oz. Disc. 1998.

	$195	$145	$110

Last MSR was $255.

✷ *Model 88 Lady Rossi* - .38 Spl., 2 in. barrel, stainless steel, slim round grips. Imported 1995-98.

	$215	$175	$150

Last MSR was $285.

MODEL 89 STAINLESS - .32 S&W cal. only, 6 shot, 3 in. barrel. Imported 1985-86. Reintroduced 1989-90.

	$175	$135	$115

Last MSR was $215.

MODEL 94 - .38 Spl. cal., 6 shot, 3 or 4 in. barrel, blue finish only, 27½ oz. Imported 1985-1988.

	$160	$140	$120	$110	$95	$85	$75

Last MSR was $185.

MODEL R351 - .38 Spl.+P cal., 5 shot, 2 in. barrel, blue action, combat rubber grips, supplied with key lock, 24 oz. Importation began 1999.

MSR	$298	$240	$185	$165	$145	$130	$115	$105

MODEL R352 - similar to Model R351, except is stainless steel. Importation began 1999.

MSR	$345	$275	$220	$165

MODEL R461 - .357 Mag.+P cal., 6 shot, 2 in. barrel, blue action, combat rubber grips, supplied with key lock, 26 oz. Importation began 1999.

MSR	$298	$240	$185	$165	$145	$130	$115	$105

MODEL R462 - similar to Model R461, except is stainless steel. Importation began 1999.

MSR	$345	$275	$220	$165

MODEL 515(M) STAINLESS - .22 LR or .22 Mag. (Model 515M) cal., double action, 6 shot, classic kit gun design, stainless steel with shrouded ejector rod, adj. rear sights, checkered custom wood grips, 4 in. barrel, 30 oz. Imported 1992 only.

	$195	$145	$110

Last MSR was $248.

MODEL 515 STAINLESS - .22 Mag. cal., similar to 515(M), supplied with 2 pairs of grips (checkered wood and rubber wraparound). Imported 1994-98.

	$210	$165	$140

Last MSR was $270.

MODEL 518 STAINLESS - .22 LR cal., otherwise similar to Model 515 Stainless. Disc. 1998.

	$195	$155	$135

Last MSR was $255.

MODEL 677 FS - .357 Mag. cal., 6 shot, 2 in. heavy barrel, enclosed ejector rod, rubber combat grips, matte blue finish, 26 oz. Imported 1997-98.

	$215	$160	$135	$110	$95	$80	$70

Last MSR was $260.

Grading	100%	98%	95%	90%	80%	70%	60%

MODEL 720 STAINLESS - .44 Spl. cal., choice of hammer or hammerless (new 1994) design, 3 in. ribbed barrel, double action, 5 shot with fluted or unfluted cylinder, full ejector rod shroud, adj. rear sight, rubber combat grips, stainless, 27½ oz. Imported 1992-98.

	$220	$180	$155

Last MSR was $290.

✳ *Model 720C* - similar to Model 720 Stainless, except hammerless.

	$220	$180	$155

Last MSR was $290.

MODEL 851 - .38 Spl.+P cal., 4 in. barrel, 6 shot, integral key lock, rubber grips. Importation began 2001.

MSR	$298	$240	$185	$165	$145	$130	$115	$105

MODEL 851 STAINLESS - .38 Spl. cal., 3 (disc. 1994) or 4 in. VR barrel, 6 shot, walnut grips, adj. rear sight, 27½ oz. Mfg. 1985-98.

	$195	$155	$135

Last MSR was $255.

This model was previously designated the Model 85 Stainless.

MODEL 877 FS STAINLESS - .357 Mag. cal., 6 shot, small frame, 2 in. barrel with full ejector rod housing, rubber combat grips, 26 oz. Mfg. 1996-98.

	$220	$175	$150

Last MSR was $290.

MODEL 951 - .38 Spl. cal., 6 shot, 3 or 4 in. VR barrel, blue finish only, 27½ oz. Imported 1985-90.

	$190	$155	$135	$120	$110	$100	$90

Last MSR was $233.

This model was previously designated the Model 95.

MODEL 971 - .357 Mag. cal., 4 in. solid rib barrel with internal ejector shroud, 6 shot, adj. rear sight, blue only, hardwood grips, 36 oz. Imported 1988-1998.

	$200	$160	$145	$135	$125	$115	$105

Last MSR was $255.

✳ *Model 971 Stainless* - .357 Mag. cal., 2½ (new 1992), 4, or 6 in. solid rib barrel with full shroud, 6 shot, combat style rubber grips, adj. rear sight, 35.4 - 40.5 oz. Imported 1989-1998.

	$220	$175	$145

Last MSR was $290.

✳ *Model 971 Compensated* - .357 Mag. cal., stainless steel, 3¼ in. compensated barrel, 32 oz. Imported 1993-98.

	$220	$175	$145

Last MSR was $290.

MODEL 971 VRC STAINLESS - .357 Mag. cal., stainless steel, 6 shot, choice of 2½, 4, or 6 in. barrel with 8-port vented rib compensator and full-length ejector shroud, combat rubber grips, adj. rear sight, 30-39 oz. Mfg. 1996-98.

	$295	$220	$175

Last MSR was $340.

MODEL 971 (NEW MFG.) - .357 Mag. cal., 4 in. barrel, 6 shot, rubber grips, adj. sights, integral key lock. Importation began 2001.

MSR	$345	$275	$220	$165	$150	$135	$125	$115

MODEL 972 - similar to Model 971, except is stainless steel, 6 in. barrel only. Importation began 2001.

MSR	$391	$325	$265	$195

R

Grading	100%	98%	95%	90%	80%	70%	60%

CYCLOPS (MODEL 988 STAINLESS) - .357 Mag. cal., 6 or 8 shot, 8 or 10¾ (ported or unported, new 1998) in. full shroud barrel with 8 compensation ports, black rubber grips, 51 oz. Imported 1997-98.

	$385	$300	$230				

Last MSR was $429.

Add $50 for unported 10¾ in. barrel.
Add $60 for ported 10¾ in. barrel.

RIFLES

MODEL 65/92 SRC LEVER ACTION - .38 Spl./.357 Mag., .44 Spl./.44 Mag., .44- 40 WCF (new 1995), or .45 LC (new 1995) cal., patterned after Win. Model 92, 16 (.38 Spl./.357 Mag. only), 20 (blue or stainless) or 24 (new 1997, half round/half octagon) in. barrel, 5-5¾ lbs. Also available in matte blue finish at no extra charge. Importation disc. 1998.

	$285	$220	$165	$125	$110	$100	$90

Last MSR was $360.

Add $69 for half round/half octagonal barrel (24 in. barrel).
This model in .44 Spl./.44 Mag., .44-40 WCF, or .45 LC cal. sometimes is also known as the Model 65.

❋ *Model 92 SRC Stainless* - .38 Spl./.357 Mag. or .45 LC cal., 20 in. barrel. Mfg. 1998 only.

	$340	$265	$210	$165	$125	$110	$100

Last MSR was $415.

❋ *Model 92 SRC Large Loop* - .38 Spl./.357 Mag. or .45 LC cal., 16 in. barrel, 8 shot mag., large loop lever, 5½ lbs. Imported 1997-98.

	$285	$220	$165	$125	$110	$100	$90

Last MSR was $360.

Add $55 for stainless steel (.45 LC cal. only, new 1998).

❋ *Blue Engraved* - with etched engraving and special wood. Disc. 1989.

	$275	$225	$175				

Last MSR was $327.

❋ *Gold or Chrome Engraved* - either gold (disc. 1987) or chrome (disc.) finish with special wood.

	$280	$230	$185	$150	$130	$120	$110

Last MSR was $330.

MODEL 62 SA SLIDE ACTION - .22 LR cal., copy of Win. 1890 "gallery" model, rifle (23 in. barrel) or carbine (16½ in. barrel) available, takedown action, blue or nickel finish, round or octagon barrel, 12 or 13 shot tube mag. Importation disc. 1998.

	$185	$145	$115	$95	$85	$80	$75

Last MSR was $240.

Add $10 for nickel finish.
Add $10 for octagon barrel.

❋ *Model 62 SA Stainless* - similar to regular model, except is stainless steel. Imported 1986 only.

	$165	$145	$120				

Last MSR was $192.

MODEL 62 SAC CARBINE - similar to Model 62 SA, except has 16½ in. carbine barrel with full length mag. tube (12 shot), 4¼ lbs. Imported 1988-1998.

	$185	$145	$115	$95	$85	$80	$75

Last MSR was $240.

Add $10 for nickel finish.

R

Grading	100%	98%	95%	90%	80%	70%	60%

✳ *Model 62 SAC Carbine Stainless* - similar to Model 62 SAC Carbine, except is stainless steel. Imported 1998 only.

	$215	**$165**	**$125**				

Last MSR was $280.

MODEL 59 - .22 Mag. version of Model 62 SA, 10 shot mag., 5.5 lbs. Importation disc. 1998.

	$220	**$170**	**$130**	**$120**	**$110**	**$100**	**$90**

Last MSR was $280.

ROCKET SINGLE SHOT - .22 LR, .22 Hornet, .22-250 Rem., .220 Swift, .223 Rem., .30-30 Win., .357 Mag., .44 Mag., or .45 LC cal., action and other specifications similar to Model S12 shotgun. Limited importation 2000 only.

	$160	**$145**	**$130**	**$115**	**$100**	**$90**	**$80**

Last MSR was $179.

Add $30 for stainless steel.

FIELD GRADE SINGLE SHOT - .22 LR, .22 Mag., .223 Rem. (new 2002), .243 Win. (new 2002), .357 Mag./.38 Spl., .44 Mag., or .410/.45 LC cal., 23 in. lightweight tapered barrel with fully adj. sights, choice of matte blue with natural wood or matte stainless steel with black wood finish, manual safety, extractor (centerfire) or ejector (rimfire), Monte Carlo stock became an option in 2002, 4 3/4-6 1/4 lbs. Importation began 2001.

MSR	**$150**	**$125**	**$105**	**$95**	**$80**	**$70**	**$60**	**$60**

Add $30 for matte stainless steel.
Add $10 for .357 Mag. or .44 Mag. cal., $20 for .410/.45 LC cal.
Add $25 for .223 Rem. cal. (new 2002).
Add $30 for Monte Carlo stock (.223 Rem. or .243 Win. cal.), or for Youth Model.

SHOTGUNS: SxS

OVERLUND - 12, 20 ga., or .410 bore, exposed hammers, 20 (Coach Model), 26, or 28 in. barrels, double triggers. Importation disc. 1988.

	$275	**$230**	**$185**	**$155**	**$140**	**$125**	**$115**

Last MSR was $332.

SQUIRE - 12, 20 ga., or .410 bore, hammerless, 20, 26 or 28 in. barrels, double triggers, raised matted rib, beavertail forearm, pistol grip, hardwood stock, 3 in. chambers. Imported 1985-90.

	$300	**$245**	**$195**	**$160**	**$150**	**$140**	**$130**

Last MSR was $350.

SHOTGUNS: SINGLE SHOT

MODEL S12/S20/S41 - 12, 20 ga., or .410 bore, lightweight break open action with exposed hammer, ejector, uncheckered hardwood stock and forearm with sling swivels, blue action and 22 (Youth) or 28 (Standard) in. barrel, supplied with trigger lock, 4 lbs. 13 oz Importation began 1999.

MSR	**$101**	**$90**	**$80**	**$70**	**$60**	**$60**	**$50**	**$45**

This model is also available as a Youth Model in all gauges (.410 bore weighs approx. 4 lbs.) - prices are the same as listed.

MATCHED PAIR - includes choice of 12, 20 ga., or .410 bore single shotgun barrel and interchangable .22 LR, .223 Rem. (new 2002), or .243 Win. (new 2002) cal. rifle barrel with fully adj. front sight, manual safety. Importation began 2000.

MSR	**$140**	**$120**	**$100**	**$90**	**$80**	**$70**	**$60**	**$60**

Add $30 for polished stainless steel (.410 bore only, black wood stock and forearm).
Add $30 for matched pair carrying case.
Add $60 for centerfire rifle pair.

R

Grading	100%	98%	95%	90%	80%	70%	60%

ROTA, LUCIANO

Current manufacturer located in Brescia, Italy. Currently imported and distributed by New England Arms Corp., located in Kittery Point, ME.

SHOTGUNS: SxS

MODEL 105 - most gauges, 26-32 in. barrels, boxlock action with sideplates, floral scroll engraving, choice of case colored or coin finished receiver, fixed chokes (any combination), extractors, Circassian checkered walnut stock and forearm.

MSR	$1,595		$1,325	$1,075	$875	$750	$650	$550	$500

Add $100 for 28 ga. or .410 bore.
Add $50 for ST, or $175 for multichokes.
Add $500 for hand engraving.

MODEL 106 - all gauges, Anson & Deely type engraved boxlock action, DT or ST, ejectors, extractors, Circassian checkered walnut stock and forearm, case colored action.

MSR	$1,395		$1,225	$950	$775	$675	$550	$500	$450

Add $100 for 28 ga. or .410 bore.
Add $155 for 10 ga.
Add $50 for ST, or $175 for multichokes.
Add $300 for hand engraving.

✳ *Model 106 Slug Gun* - 12 or 20 ga., similar to Model 106, except has 25 in. barrels with express rib and folding leaf sights, with or w/o sideplates, tapered front ramp sight, choke tubes.

MSR	$1,595		$1,325	$1,075	$875	$750	$650	$550	$500

Add $200 for hand engraving.
Add $400 for sideplates.

ROTTWEIL

Current manufacturer located in Rottweil, Germany. No current U.S. importation. Previously imported by Rottweil Competition, located in Orange, CA.

SHOTGUNS

PARAGON - 12 ga. only, new design featuring boxlock action, 11 different stock configurations, detachable and interchangeable trigger action, trigger and sear safety, ejectors (switchable to extractors), various barrel lengths (30 in. standard) and rib combinations, cased. Limited importation 1993-99.

$6,950	$6,500	$5,750	$4,850	$3,950	$3,000	$2,500

Last MSR was $7,500.

Add $850 for Trap Model.
Add $3,150 per extra set of barrels.

✳ *Paragon Sporting Clays Deluxe* - 30 in. barrels only, features better quality wood and engraving. Limited importation.

$6,950	$6,500	$5,750	$4,850	$3,950	$3,000	$2,500

Last MSR was $7,500.

MODEL 650 FIELD O/U - 12 ga. only, 28 in. barrels with VR, ejectors, single trigger, select checkered walnut, multi-choked with 6 choke tubes, lightly engraved, coin finished receiver. Importation disc. 1986.

$750	$650	$595	$550	$500	$460	$435

Last MSR was $850.

MODEL 72 FIELD O/U - 12 ga. only, 28 in. vent. barrels and rib, sand blasted receiver, select walnut with checkered stock and forearm, single trigger, ejectors. Importation disc. 1987.

$1,850	$1,650	$1,450	$1,200	$1,000	$850	$700

Last MSR was $2,295.

R

Grading	100%	98%	95%	90%	80%	70%	60%

MODEL 72 AMERICAN SKEET O/U - 12 ga. only, 26¾ in. barrels, VR, ejectors, select French walnut, marginal engraving on sand blasted receiver, single trigger, 7½ lbs. Importation disc. 1987.

	$1,850	$1,650	$1,450	$1,200	$1,000	$850	$700

Last MSR was $2,295.

This model was distributed exclusively by Paxton Arms, located in Dallas, TX.

MODEL 72 AAT SINGLE BARREL TRAP - 12 ga. only, adj. American trap (AAT), barrel features adj. point of impact, 34 in. barrel bored full, high VR. Importation disc. 1986.

	$1,400	$1,200	$1,000	$850	$700	$650	$600

Last MSR was $2,295.

MODEL 72 AT O/U - 12 ga. only, 32 in. IM & F barrels, VR and barrels, sand blasted receiver, checkered select walnut stock and forearm, non-adj. point of impact, single trigger, ejectors. Importation disc. 1987.

	$1,850	$1,650	$1,450	$1,200	$1,000	$850	$700

Last MSR was $2,295.

MODEL 72 AAT COMBINATION - 12 ga. only, comes with 2 single barrels (32 and 34 in.) that have adj. impact points. Importation disc. 1986.

	$2,450	$2,100	$1,850	$1,600	$1,450	$1,250	$995

Last MSR was $2,850.

* **72 AAT Combination** - supplied with 1 single adj. barrel and 32 in. O/U barrels.

	$2,450	$2,100	$1,850	$1,600	$1,450	$1,250	$995

Last MSR was $2,850.

MODEL 72 AAT 3-BARREL SET - 12 ga. only, supplied with 2 single barrels (32 and 34 in.) with adj. impact points and 1 set of 32 in. O/U barrels bored IM & F. Importation disc. 1986.

	$2,850	$2,600	$2,300	$2,000	$1,800	$1,600	$1,400

Last MSR was $3,250.

MODEL 72 INTERNATIONAL TRAP - 12 ga. only, O/U 30 in. barrels bored IM & F with extra high rib. Importation disc. 1987.

	$1,850	$1,650	$1,450	$1,200	$1,000	$850	$700

Last MSR was $2,295.

MODEL 72 INTERNATIONAL SKEET - 12 ga. only, 26¾ in. barrels, VR, select walnut stock and forearm. Importation disc. 1987.

	$1,850	$1,650	$1,450	$1,200	$1,000	$850	$700

Last MSR was $2,295.

ROYAL AMERICAN SHOTGUNS

Previously imported by Royal Arms International, located in Woodland Hills, CA circa 1985- 87.

SHOTGUNS

MODEL 100 O/U - 12 or 20 ga., 2¾ in. chambers, double triggers, extractors, vent. rib and barrels. Imported 1985-87 only.

	$325	$265	$240	$220	$200	$180	$170

Last MSR was $390.

Add $40 for 3 in. chambers, single trigger, and auto ejectors.

MODEL 600 BOXLOCK SxS - 12, 20, 28 ga., or .410 bore, sideplates, silver finished receiver, 3 in. chambers, single trigger, auto ejectors. Imported 1985-87 only.

	$365	$295	$265	$235	$210	$195	$180

Last MSR was $420.

Subtract 25% for double triggers and 2¾ in. chambers.

Grading	100%	98%	95%	90%	80%	70%	60%

MODEL 800 SIDELOCK SxS - 12, 20, 28 ga., or .410 bore, sidelocks with sideplates, silver finished receiver, 3 in. chambers, single trigger, checkered straight grip stock with select walnut, auto ejectors. Imported 1985-87 only.

	$775	$650	$595	$550	$500	$460	$435

Last MSR was $899.

RUGER

See Sturm, Ruger, & Co. section in this text.

RUKO SPORTING GOODS, INC.

Previous importer (non-exclusive) located in Buffalo, NY that imported Arms Corp. of the Philippines firearms circa 1990-95. Ruko Sporting Goods, Inc. (previously Ruko Products) firearms were manufactured by the Arms Corporation of the Philippines. In 1991, Ruko Products, Inc. became the exclusive domestic importer for arms manufactured by Arms Corp. of the Philippines. These firearms were marked "Ruko-Armscor" on the barrels.

Please refer to the Armscor section for current importation, as well as previous importation by Armscorp Precision, Inc. and Ruko Products, Inc.

RUSSIAN SERVICE PISTOLS AND RIFLES

Previously manufactured at various Russian military arsenals (including Tula).

HANDGUNS

MODEL TT30 & TT33 TOKAREV AUTOMATIC - 7.62mm Russian cal., design borrowed from Colt 1911, Petter-type unitized trigger/hammer assembly, 8 shot, 4½ in. barrel, blue. Mfg. 1930-1954.

	$325	$290	$250	$225	$165	$145	$110

Add 20% for matching mag.
Add 50% for TT30 Model.
Values listed assume original condition - no recent imports with importer markings.

✱ **TT Recent Import** - 7.62x25mm Tokarev cal., must be stamped by importer, Russian Arsenal mfg., currently imported by Century Arms International, Inc. and others.

No MSR	$140	$110	$90	$80	$70	$60	$50

NAGANT REVOLVER - 7 shot, cylinder comes forward to seal barrel.

	$260	$225	$185	$165	$135	$115	$100

Add 10% for pre-communist Imperial marked.
"GRU" marked gun (Armed Forces Intelligence) has shorter barrel and grip frame. While rarer, there is a slight premium being asked.

MAKAROV MD - 9mm Makarov cal., mag. fed double action, post-war manufacture.

	$450	$400	$350	$300	$250	$200	$150

Recent imports or commercial models with adj. rear sight are currently selling in the $175 range.

RIFLES

During 1999, various older mfg. Russian Mosins are scheduled for importation. These include all models from the 91/30 through the M44 Carbine.

TOKAREV M38 & M40 RIFLE - semi-auto Russian issue bolt action.

	$365	$310	$270	$250	$230	$210	$195

Add 20% for M38, 100% for scoped sniper.

MOSIN-NAGANT - various cals., bolt action, many produced under various military contracts, prices assume recent importation.

	$250	$225	$185	$165	$145	$130	$120

Grading	100%	98%	95%	90%	80%	70%	60%

RUTTEN HERSTAL

Previous firearms manufacturer of O/U shotguns located in Herstal, Belgium. Previously imported by Labanu, Inc. located in Ronkonkoma, NY.

For more information and current pricing on both new and used Rutten airguns, please refer to the Blue Book of Modern Airguns by Dr. Robert Beeman & John Allen (now online also).

SHOTGUNS: O/U

MODEL RM 100 - 12 ga., 3 in. chambers, VR multi-choke barrels, ejectors, checkered walnut stock and forearm, hard case. Imported 1995-98.

$875	$775	$675	$575	$500	$450	$400

Last MSR was $1,095.

MODEL RM 285 - similar to Model RM 100, except has engraved side plates and silver engraved receiver, select walnut with Schnabel forearm, hard case. Imported 1995-98.

$1,025	$850	$725	$600	$500	$450	$400

Last MSR was $1,295.

R

NOTES

The NRA Foundation's Wayne Sheets (l), benefactor Archie Walker, and the late F.R. Rudy Etchen (r) of Remington Arms Co., one of the greatest trap shooters of all time.

S Section

S.A.C.M.

Previous company located in Cholet, France. S.A.C.M. stands for Societe Alsacienne de Construction Mechanique.

Grading	100%	98%	95%	90%	80%	70%	60%

PISTOLS: SEMI-AUTO

FRENCH MODEL 1935A - 7.65mm Long cal., 8 shot, 4.3 in. barrel, blue, fixed sights, checkered stocks, used by French troops in WWII and Indochina 1945-1954. Mfg. 1935-1945.

	$250	$220	$205	$180	$165	$150	$140

Add 50% for Nazi WWII mfg. (Waffenamt proofed).

SAE

Previous importer located in Miami, FL. SAE stands for Spain America Enterprises Inc. SAE imported Felix Sarasqueta shotguns from Spain until circa 1988.

SHOTGUNS: O/U

MODEL 70 - 12 or 20 ga., 3 in. chambers, boxlock action, single trigger, ejectors, 26 in. VR barrel, European checkered walnut stock and forearm, standard finish is blue, Model 70 multi-choke has silver finished action with Florentine engraving and low gloss stock finish. Imported 1988 only.

	$400	$275	$260	$245	$230	$215	$195

Last MSR was $598.

Add $120 for multi-chokes (27 in. barrel).

MODEL 66C - 12 ga. only, 26 in. Skeet or 30 in. F&M VR barrels, boxlock with engraved side-plates including 24 Kt. gold inlays, Monte Carlo deluxe stock and beavertail forearm. Imported 1988 only.

	$950	$725	$650	$575	$495	$450	$395

Last MSR was $1,544.

SHOTGUNS: SxS

MODEL 210S - 12, 20 ga., or .410 bore, 3 in. chambers, boxlock action, double triggers, extractors, silver finished receiver with light engraving, approx. 7 lbs. Imported 1988 only.

	$420	$280	$260	$245	$230	$215	$195

Last MSR was $638.

MODEL 340X - 12 or 20 ga., sidelock action, 26 in. barrels with 2¾ in. chambers, H&H boxlock action, case hardened finish with moderate scroll engraving, straight grip select walnut stock and forearm with high gloss finish. Imported 1988 only.

	$700	$550	$495	$460	$430	$395	$375

Last MSR was $1,170.

MODEL 209E - 12, 20 ga., or .410 bore, H&H type sidelock action, 26 or 28 in. barrels with 2¾ in. chambers, hand engraved coin finished receiver, select checkered walnut stock and forearm, double triggers. Imported 1988 only.

	$925	$700	$650	$575	$495	$450	$395

Last MSR was $1,490.

S

S.I.A.C.E.

Current shotgun manufacturer located in Brescia, Italy. Currently imported exclusively by New England Arms Corp., located in Kittery Point, ME.

Grading	100%	98%	95%	90%	80%	70%	60%

SHOTGUNS: SxS, HAMMERGUN

MODEL GARDONE - 12, 16, 20, 28 ga., or .410 bore, scalloped boxlock round frame, ejectors, DT, full coverage best hand engraving, checkered deluxe Turkish walnut and custom dimensions. Importation began 2000.

	MSR	$3,995		$3,650	$3,125	$2,700	$2,250	$1,850	$1,450	$1,250

MODEL VINTAGE - 12, 16, or 20 ga., sidelock, case hardened receiver with border edged engraving, top tang safety, DT, extractors, monobloc barrels.

	MSR	$2,950		$2,625	$1,850	$1,475	$1,100	$850	$700	$550

MODEL ETON - 12, 16, 20, 28 ga., or .410 bore, 2 ¾ in. chambers standard, DT, extractors, monobloc barrels, case colored receiver with scroll engraving, Turkish walnut, straight or pistol grip stock with splinter or semi-beavertail forearm. Importation began 2000.

	MSR	$3,995		$3,650	$3,125	$2,700	$2,250	$1,850	$1,450	$1,250

Add $1,245 for ejectors and self cocking system (Model Eton Deluxe).

MODEL 350G AURORA SUPER LUSSO - 24, 28 ga., or .410 bore, back action sidelock, case hardened receiver with finely engraved rose and scroll patterns, DT, extractors, top tang safety. Disc. 2000.

			$5,500	$4,750	$3,950	$3,150	$2,450	$1,875	$1,450

Last MSR was $5,950.

This model became part of the Juno Series.

MODEL 370B CONCORDIA - 12, 16, 20, 24, 28 or 32 ga., or .410 bore, scalloped frame back action sidelock, silver or case hardened receiver with fine scroll engraving, top tang safety, select checkered Turkish walnut, prices include custom dimensions.

	MSR	$5,995		$5,525	$4,750	$3,950	$3,150	$2,450	$1,875	$1,450

MODEL 371Q JUNO - 12, 16, 20, 24, 28, 32 ga., or .410 bore, sidelock, available with self cocking and ejectors, silver or case colored receiver, best quality rose and scroll engraving, DT or ST, top tang safety, select checkered Turkish walnut, prices include custom dimensions.

	MSR	$5,995		$5,525	$4,750	$3,950	$3,150	$2,450	$1,875	$1,450

SKB SHOTGUNS

Currently manufactured by the new SKB Arms Company located in Tokyo, Japan. Currently imported and distributed by G.U. Inc. located in Omaha, NE. SKB has been manufacturing firearms since 1855. Distributor and dealer sales.

Previously imported by Ithaca. In 1987, importation resumed on most SKB models. While the model numbers have changed, quality is similar to those models imported previously by Ithaca. In most cases, the newer models are derived closely from their previous counterparts. Listings below will differentiate older disc. models from currently imported models.

SHOTGUNS: O/U

MODEL 85 TARGET SUPER SPORT (TSS) - available in Sporting Clays (including sets), Skeet, or Trap configuration, Magna-ported barrels, Hi-Viz competiton sights, matte wood finish. New 2002.

	MSR	$1,949		$1,650	$1,400	$1,150	$950	$875	$800	$725

Add $180 for adj. comb on stock.

❋ **Model 85 Un-Single** - top un-single, fixed or adj. rib, standard or Monte Carlo stock. New 2002.

	MSR	$3,019		$2,575	$2,150	$1,750	$1,500	$1,250	$1,050	$875

Add $180 for adj. rib.
Add $180 for adj. comb on stock.

A Sporting Clays set is also available (2 barrels, MSR $3,149), in addition to a 3 gauge Skeet set (20, 28 ga. or .410 bore, MSR $4,679).

S

Grading	100%	98%	95%	90%	80%	70%	60%

MODEL 500 - 12, 20, 28 ga., or .410 bore, field grade, VR, selective ejector, 26 in. imp. cyl. and mod., 28 in. full and mod., and 30 in. full and mod. barrels, checkered stock. Mfg. in Japan by SKB 1966-1979.

	$525	$440	$395	$365	$330	$300	$275

Add 15% for 20 ga.
Add 25% for 28 ga. or .410 bore.

* **Model 500 Magnum** - 12 ga., 3 in. Mag., field grade, similar to Model 500, except 3 in. Mag. chambers.

	$625	$455	$410	$385	$355	$320	$290

MODEL 505 DELUXE FIELD - 12, 20, or 28 (disc.) ga., blue (new 1998) or silver nitride engraved receiver (disc. 1997), 3 in. chambers, 26 or 28 in. barrels (supplied with choke tubes), single selective trigger, ejectors, checkered walnut stock with recoil pad and forearm.

MSR	$1,189	$1,055	$865	$725	$600	$500	$460	$420

Add $500 for combo package (disc.).
The combo package includes either 12/20 ga. barrels with inter-chokes or 28 ga./.410 bore barrels.

* **Model 505 Sporting Clays** - 28 or 30 in. multi-choke barrels, blue receiver with light engraving, dimensioned for Sporting Clays competition, 1997 importation features Schnabel forearm, semi-wide channeled rib, and lengthened forcing cones, approx. 8¼ lbs. Older importation in addition to new model during 1997.

MSR	$1,299	$1,100	$885	$765	$650	$525	$460	$420

* **Model 505 Trap** - 12 ga., 30 or 32 in. choke tube barrels with or without Monte Carlo stock, high rib.

	$875	$725	$650	$525	$475	$430	$395

Last MSR was $995.

Add $400 for O/U Trap Combo.
The above Combo includes one set of O/U Trap barrels and a top single Trap barrel.

* **Model 505 Skeet** - 12, 20, 28 ga., or .410 bore, 28 in. barrels with multi-chokes.

	$875	$725	$650	$525	$475	$430	$395

Last MSR was $995.

* **Model 505 3-Ga. Skeet Set** - includes 20, 28 ga., and .410 bore extra Skeet barrels, aluminum case.

	$1,925	$1,575	$1,350	$1,200	$1,125	$950	$875

Last MSR was $2,195.

MODEL 585 DELUXE FIELD - 12, 20, 28 ga., or .410 (new 1995) bore, silver nitride engraved receiver, 3 in. chambers, 26 or 28 in. barrels (supplied with choke tubes), similar to 505 Series, except has .735 diameter bore on 12 ga. models and includes lengthened forcing cones with extended length "Competition Series" Inter-Choke System designed to improve shot patterns and reduce recoil, SST, ejectors, checkered walnut stock with recoil pad and forearm (Youth model is also available with shortened dimensions), 6 lbs. 10 oz. - 7 lbs. 11 oz. Importation began 1992.

MSR	$1,499	$1,255	$945	$760	$615	$525	$475	$425

Add $70 for 28 ga. or .410 bore.
Add $120 for Gold Package featuring choice of silver or blue receiver, gold plated trigger, and 2 gold game scenes with Schnabel forearm - new 1998.

S

Grading	100%	98%	95%	90%	80%	70%	60%

* **Model 585 Field Set** - includes 12/20 ga., 20/28 ga., 28 ga./.410 bore, 26 or 28 (new 1994) in. VR barrels with SKB inter-choke system (on 12, 20, and 28 ga.), silver nitride receiver with finely engraved scroll game scenes, low profile receiver, cross bolt locking system, SST, ejectors, manual safety, checkered high gloss American walnut stock and forearm.

MSR	$2,399		$2,115	$1,775	$1,475	$1,200	$995	$895	$800

Add $70 for 20/28 ga. set or 28 ga./.410 bore set.

Add $300 (12/20 ga.) or $360 (20 ga. and smaller) for Gold Package featuring choice of silver or blue receiver, gold plated trigger, and 2 gold game scenes with Schnabel forearm - new 1998.

* **Model 585 Upland** - 12, 20, or 28 ga., 3 in. chambers for 12 and 20 ga., features straight grip stock with recoil pad and 26 in. VR barrels, Schnabel forearm, 6 lbs. 10 oz. - 7 lbs. 10 oz. New 1997.

MSR	$1,499		$1,255	$945	$765	$610	$525	$475	$425

Add $70 for 28 ga.

Add $190 for Gold Package featuring choice of silver or blue receiver, gold plated trigger, and 2 gold game scenes with Schnabel forearm - new 1998.

* **Model 585 Trap** - 12 ga., 30 or 32 in. choke tube barrels with or w/o Monte Carlo stock, high rib.

MSR	$1,619		$1,310	$975	$800	$600	$500	$450	$395

Add $200 for Gold Package featuring choice of silver or blue receiver, gold plated trigger, and 2 gold game scenes with Schnabel forearm - new 1998.

Add $800 for O/U Trap Combo or $1,100 for O/U Trap Combo with Gold Package.
The above Combo includes one set of O/U Trap barrels and a top single Trap barrel.

* **Model 585 Skeet** - 12, 20, 28 ga., or .410 bore, 28 or 30 (12 ga. only - new 1994) in. barrels with multi-chokes.

MSR	$1,619		$1,310	$975	$800	$600	$500	$450	$395

Add $60 for 28 ga. or .410 bore.

Add $200 for Gold Package featuring choice of silver or blue receiver, gold plated trigger, and 2 gold game scenes with Schnabel forearm - new 1998.

* **Model 585 3-Ga. Skeet Set** - includes 20, 28 ga., and .410 bore extra Skeet barrels, aluminum case.

MSR	$3,779		$3,175	$2,550	$2,000	$1,700	$1,525	$1,400	$1,300

Add $450 for Gold Package featuring choice of silver or blue receiver, gold plated trigger, and 2 gold game scenes with Schnabel forearm - new 1998.

* **Model 585 Sporting Clays** - 12, 20, or 28 ga., 3 in. chambers (12 and 20 ga.), 28 in. (all gauges), 30 in. (12 or 20 ga.), or 32 in. (12 ga. only) multi-choke barrels, dimensioned for Sporting Clays competition, narrow rib 3/8 in. became available 1994.

MSR	$1,679		$1,410	$1,050	$850	$635	$530	$475	$425

Add $50 for 28 ga.

Add $170 for Gold Package featuring choice of silver or blue receiver, gold plated trigger, and 2 gold game scenes with Schnabel forearm - new 1998.

◇**Model 585 Sporting Clays Set** - includes 2 sets of barrels (12 ga. - 30 in., 20 ga. - 28 in.), cased. New 1996.

MSR	$2,419		$2,135	$1,775	$1,495	$1,200	$1,050	$925	$825

Add $300 for Gold Package featuring choice of silver or blue receiver, gold plated trigger, and 2 gold game scenes with Schnabel forearm - new 1998.

* **Model 585 Waterfowler** - 12 ga. only, 3½ in. chambers, oil finished stock and forearm, matte blue finish. Imported 1995-2000.

				$1,125	$850	$700	$525	$475	$430	$395

Last MSR was $1,329.

Grading	100%	98%	95%	90%	80%	70%	60%

❋ ***Model 585 Youth/Ladies*** - 12 or 20 ga., 26 or 28 (12 ga. only) in. VR barrels, features 13½ in. LOP, barrels have .735 in. bores with lengthened forcing cones. New 1994.

MSR	$1,499	$1,355	$950	$765	$585	$500	$450	$395

Add $190 for Gold Package featuring choice of silver or blue receiver, gold plated trigger, and 2 gold game scenes with Schnabel forearm - new 1998.

MODEL 600 FIELD GRADE - similar to Model 500, except silver-plated frame and select wood.

	$700	$495	$465	$440	$375	$345	$325

Add 20% for 20 ga.

An unknown quantity of Model 600s were mfg. with blue receivers - a small premium may be asked.

MODEL 600 MAGNUM - similar to Model 600 Field, except chambered for 3 in. Mag., 12 ga. Mfg. 1969-1972 by SKB.

	$720	$510	$480	$455	$415	$390	$355

MODEL 600 TRAP GRADE - similar to Model 600 Field Grade, except 12 ga. only, trap stock, recoil pad, select wood.

	$675	$555	$520	$485	$445	$410	$385

MODEL 600 DOUBLES GUN - similar to Model 600 Trap, except choked for 21 yd. and 30 yd. targets. Mfg. 1973-1975.

	$675	$555	$520	$485	$445	$410	$385

MODEL 600 SKEET GRADE - 12, 20, 28 ga., or .410 bore, 26 or 28 in. barrels, bored S&S, otherwise similar to Model 600 Trap.

	$700	$540	$510	$475	$430	$400	$370
28 ga. or .410 bore.	$850	$740	$620	$560	$485	$440	$420

MODEL 600 SKEET GRADE COMBO SET - similar to Model 600 Skeet, except fitted with matched set of 20, 28 ga., and .410 bore barrels, in fitted case.

	$2,000	$1,430	$1,265	$1,155	$935	$770	$660

MODEL 605 FIELD - similar to Model 505 Deluxe Field except has silver finished engraved receiver with better walnut. Importation disc. 1992.

	$1,075	$850	$750	$675	$575	$500	$450

Last MSR was $1,195.

Add $500 for extra set of barrels (Combo).

❋ ***Model 605 Trap*** - 12 ga., 30 or 32 in. choke tube barrel with or without Monte Carlo stock, high rib.

	$1,075	$850	$750	$675	$575	$500	$450

Last MSR was $1,195.

Add $400 for O/U Trap Combo.

The above Combo includes one set of O/U Trap barrels and a top single Trap barrel.

❋ ***Model 605 Skeet*** - 12, 20, 28 ga., or .410 bore, 28 in. barrels with multi-chokes.

	$1,100	$850	$750	$675	$575	$500	$450

Last MSR was $1,195.

❋ ***Model 605 3-Ga. Skeet Set*** - includes 20, 28 ga., and .410 bore extra Skeet barrels, aluminum case.

	$2,175	$1,650	$1,400	$1,250	$1,125	$950	$875

Last MSR was $2,395.

❋ ***Model 605 Sporting Clay*** - 28 or 30 in. multi-choke barrels, dimensioned for Sporting Clay competition.

	$1,110	$850	$750	$675	$575	$500	$450

Last MSR was $1,245.

S

Grading	100%	98%	95%	90%	80%	70%	60%

❋ *Model 605 DU Sponsor Gun* - mfg. for DU chapters - dinner auction gun, 850 mfg. in 12 ga. (1990) and 850 mfg. in 20 ga. (1991). Features gold inlays and presentation case.
DU sponsor gun values are usually hard to ascertain in the secondary marketplace. Currently, prices seem to range between $1,000-$1,450.

MODEL 680 ENGLISH - similar to Model 600 Field, except English style stock, select walnut and fine scroll engraving. Mfg. 1973-1976.

	$725	$640	$600	$555	$520	$495	$445

Add 20% for 20 ga.

MODEL 685 FIELD - similar to Model 585 Deluxe Field, except has silver finished engraved receiver with gold inlays and better walnut, engine turned monobloc.

	$1,325	$950	$795	$675	$575	$500	$450

Last MSR was $1,549.

❋ *Model 685 Field Set* - includes 12/20, 20/28 ga., 28 ga./.410 bore 26 or 28 (new 1994) in. VR barrels with SKB inter-choke system (on 12, 20, and 28 ga.), silver nitride receiver with finely engraved scroll game scenes, low profile receiver, cross bolt locking system, SST, ejectors, manual safety, checkered high gloss American walnut stock and forearm.

	$1,850	$1,650	$1,500	$1,350	$1,275	$1,100	$1,000

Last MSR was $2,149.

❋ *Model 685 Trap* - 12 ga., 30 or 32 in. choke tube barrels with or w/o Monte Carlo stock, high rib.

	$1,365	$975	$825	$700	$600	$525	$450

Last MSR was $1,595.

Add $600 for O/U Trap Combo.
The above Combo includes one set of O/U Trap barrels and a top single Trap barrel.

❋ *Model 685 Skeet* - 12, 20, 28 ga., or .410 bore, 28 or 30 (12 ga. only - new 1994) in. barrels with multi-chokes.

	$1,365	$975	$825	$700	$600	$525	$450

Last MSR was $1,595.

❋ *Model 685 3-Ga. Skeet Set* - includes 20, 28 ga., and .410 bore extra Skeet barrels, aluminum case.

	$2,550	$2,175	$1,875	$1,675	$1,450	$1,275	$1,125

Last MSR was $2,949.

❋ *Model 685 Sporting Clays* - 28 (all gauges), 30 (12 ga. only), or 32 (12 ga. only) in. multi-choke barrels, dimensioned for Sporting Clays competition, 3/8 in. narrow rib became available 1994. Importation disc. 1995.

	$1,365	$975	$825	$700	$600	$525	$450

Last MSR was $1,595.

❋ *Model 685 Sporting Clays Set* - includes one set of 12 ga. (28, 30, or 32 in. VR barrels) and 20 ga. (28 in. only) or one set of 32 and 28 in. barrels in 12 ga only. Imported 1994-95.

	$2,000	$1,675	$1,500	$1,350	$1,200	$1,025	$895

Last MSR was $2,295.

❋ *Model 685 DU Sponsor Gun* - mfg. for DU chapters - dinner auction gun, 850 mfg. in 12 ga. (1990) and 850 mfg. in 20 ga. (1991). Features gold inlays and presentation case.
DU sponsor gun values are usually hard to ascertain in the secondary marketplace. Currently, prices seem to range between $1,200-$1,700.

MODEL 700 TRAP GRADE - 12 ga., similar to Model 600 Trap, except more engraving, better grade wood, wide rib. Mfg. 1969-1975.

	$820	$770	$740	$685	$630	$595	$565

MODEL 700 DOUBLES GUN - 12 ga., similar to Model 700 Trap, except choked for 21 yd. and 30 yd. targets. Mfg. 1973-1975.

	$795	$770	$740	$685	$630	$595	$565

S

Grading	100%	98%	95%	90%	80%	70%	60%

MODEL 700 SKEET GRADE - 12 ga., similar to Model 700 Doubles, only bored S&S, available in 12 or 20 ga.

	$840	$770	$740	$685	$620	$585	$555

MODEL 785 DELUXE FIELD - 12, 20, 28 ga., or .410 bore, silver nitride engraved receiver, 3 in. chambers, 26 or 28 in. barrels (supplied with choke tubes), similar to 585 Series, except has chrome lined bores on all models and also includes lengthened forcing cones with extended length "Competition Series" Inter-Choke System designed to improve shot patterns and reduce recoil, SST, ejectors, checkered walnut stock with recoil pad and forearm, 6 lbs. 10 oz. - 7 lbs. 11 oz. Importation began 1995.

	MSR	$2,119	$1,900	$1,650	$1,400	$1,150	$1,000	$900	$800

Add $80 for 28 ga. or .410 bore.

* *Model 785 Field Set* - includes 12/20, 20/28 ga., 28 ga./.410 bore, 26 or 28 in. VR barrels with SKB inter-choke system (on 12 and 20 ga.), silver nitride receiver with finely engraved scroll game scenes, low profile receiver, cross bolt locking system, SST, ejectors, manual safety, checkered high gloss American walnut stock and forearm.

	MSR	$3,019	$2,680	$2,300	$1,925	$1,600	$1,500	$1,375	$1,275

Add $100 for 20/28 ga. set or 28 ga./.410 bore set.

* *Model 785 Trap* - 12 ga., 30 or 32 in. choke tube barrels with or w/o Monte Carlo stock, high rib.

	MSR	$2,199	$1,940	$1,625	$1,365	$1,125	$995	$895	$800

Add $880 for O/U Trap Combo.

The above Combo includes one set of O/U Trap barrels and a top single Trap barrel.

* *Model 785 Skeet* - 12, 20, 28 ga., or .410 bore, 28 or 30 (12 ga. only) in. barrels with multi-chokes.

	MSR	$2,199	$1,940	$1,625	$1,365	$1,125	$995	$895	$800

Add $40 for 28 ga. or .410 bore.

* *Model 785 3-Ga. Skeet Set* - includes 20, 28 ga., and .410 bore extra Skeet barrels, aluminum case.

	MSR	$4,439	$3,835	$2,975	$2,350	$2,000	$1,600	$1,400	$1,295

* *Model 785 Sporting Clays* - 12, 20, or 28 ga., 28 in. (all gauges), 30 in. (12 ga. only), or 32 in. (12 ga. only) multi-choke barrels, dimensioned for Sporting Clays competition with 3/8 in. narrow rib.

	MSR	$2,269	$2,000	$1,675	$1,375	$1,150	$995	$895	$800

Add $80 for 28 ga.

◇ *Model 785 Sporting Clays Set* - includes 2 sets of barrels (12 ga. - 30 in., 20 ga. - 28 in.), cased. New 1996.

	MSR	$3,149	$2,775	$2,450	$2,125	$1,825	$1,625	$1,400	$1,200

MODEL 800 TRAP GRADE - 12 ga., similar to Model 700 Trap, except more engraving, better grade wood, wide rib. Mfg. 1969-1975.

		$1,150	$875	$775	$675	$575	$500	$425

MODEL 800 SKEET GRADE - 12 or 20 ga., skeet chokes. Mfg. 1969-1975.

		$1,200	$1,000	$895	$795	$680	$595	$565

MODEL 880 CROWN GRADE - 12, 20, 28 ga., or .410 bore, coin finished receiver, extensively engraved with sideplates, SST, ejectors, select walnut with fleur-de-lis scroll style checkering, double cross bolt action. Disc. 1980.

		$1,650	$1,300	$1,150	$975	$890	$835	$750

Add 25% for 28 ga. or .410 bore.

MODEL 885 - available in either Field, Skeet, or Trap configuration, coin finished receiver featuring fine scroll engraving with game scenes, boxlock action with sideplates, beginning 1992, the 885 Series in 12 ga. features lengthened forcing cones, .735 bore, and a competition series of extended length multi-chokes. Imported 1988-94.

S

Grading	100%	98%	95%	90%	80%	70%	60%

✳ *Model 885 Field* - 12, 20, 28 ga., or .410 bore, field dimensions, barrels include choke tubes. Imported 1989-94.

	$1,600	$1,200	$975	$825	$725	$650	$595

Last MSR was $1,895.

✳ *Model 885 Trap* - 12 ga., 30 or 32 in. barrels with multi-chokes, standard or Monte Carlo stock.

	$1,650	$1,200	$975	$850	$750	$650	$595

Last MSR was $1,949.

Add $700 for O/U Trap Combo.
The above Combo includes one set of O/U Trap barrels and a top single Trap barrel.

✳ *Model 885 Skeet* - 12, 20, 28 ga., or .410 bore, 28 or 30 (12 ga. only - new 1994) in. barrels with multi-chokes.

	$1,650	$1,200	$975	$850	$750	$650	$595

Last MSR was $1,949.

✳ *Model 885 Field Set* - includes 12/20, 20/28 ga., 28 ga./.410 bore 26 or 28 (new 1994) in. VR barrels with SKB inter-choke system (on 12 and 20 ga.), silver nitride receiver with finely engraved scroll game scenes, low profile receiver, cross bolt locking system, SST, ejectors, manual safety, checkered high gloss American walnut stock and forearm.

	$2,450	$2,150	$1,750	$1,500	$1,250	$1,075	$925

✳ *Model 885 3-Ga. Skeet Set* - includes 20, 28 ga., and .410 bore extra Skeet barrels, aluminum case.

	$3,200	$2,700	$2,300	$1,975	$1,725	$1,500	$1,400

Last MSR was $3,595.

✳ *Model 885 Sporting Clays* - 28 (all gauges), 30 (12 ga. only), or 32 (12 ga. only) in. multi-choke barrels, dimensioned for Sporting Clays competition, 3/8 in. narrow rib became available 1994.

	$1,650	$1,200	$975	$850	$750	$650	$595

Last MSR was $1,949.

MODEL 5600 - 12 ga. only, available as Trap or Skeet model only, VR (Trap only) and vent. barrels (Skeet only), no engraving, select walnut. Disc. 1980.

	$575	$495	$450	$420	$390	$360	$330

✳ *Model 5700* - available as Trap or Skeet model only, light engraving, select walnut, VR. Disc. 1980.

	$750	$625	$540	$495	$460	$430	$400

✳ *Model 5800* - available as Trap or Skeet model only, more deluxe engraving, select walnut. Disc. 1980.

	$950	$800	$695	$595	$500	$450	$425

SHOTGUNS: SxS

Models 100, 150, 200, 280, 300, 400, and 480 were available in 12 and 20 ga. only, featured 25-30 in. barrels, and all had boxlock actions. More expensive models differ in the amount of engraving, grade of walnut, and style of checkering, beavertail forearm, 6¼ - 7 lbs. Disc. 1980.

MODEL 100 - 12 or 20 ga., Mag. model also, SST, extractors, blue only.

	$485	$425	$380	$340	$310	$275	$250

Add 20% for 20 ga.

MODEL 150 - similar to Model 100, except scroll engraving, beavertail forearm. Mfg. 1972-1974 by SKB.

	$520	$435	$385	$345	$310	$275	$250

Add 20% for 20 ga.

Grading	100%	98%	95%	90%	80%	70%	60%

MODEL 200 - 12 or 20 ga., Mag. model also, SST, ejectors, boxlock, scalloped frame, lightly engraved coin finished receiver.

	$795	$575	$525	$475	$395	$350	$280

Add 20% for 20 ga.

MODEL 200 (NEW PRODUCTION) - similar to original Model 200, SST, ejectors, recoil pad. Imported 1987-1988 only.

	$795	$575	$525	$475	$395	$350	$325

Last MSR was $895.

Add 25% for choke-tubes.
Add 20% for 20 ga.

This model was supplied with 3 factory choke-tubes during 1988 - only 400 were mfg. (retail was $995).

* *Model 200E (English)* - similar to New Model 200, except has straight grip stock. Importation disc. 1988.

	$895	$795	$525	$475	$395	$350	$325

Last MSR was $895.

Add 20% for 20 ga.

MODEL 280 ENGLISH - 12 or 20 ga., Mag. model also, SST, AE, lightly engraved blue receiver, straight grip.

	$1,050	$895	$795	$695	$550	$450	$395

Add 20% for 20 ga.

MODEL 300 - 12 or 20 ga., Mag. model also, SST, AE, lightly engraved coin finished receiver.

	$950	$850	$695	$550	$495	$450	$395

MODEL 385 FIELD - 12 (new 1998), 20 or 28 ga., scalloped boxlock action with silver nitride receiver, engraved scroll and game scene designs, SST, ejectors, automatic safety, semi-fancy American walnut, English or pistol grip stock, satin finish and splinter forearm became available 2002, limited quantities. Importation began 1992.

MSR	$2,049	$1,750	$1,425	$1,050	$850	$725	$600	$525

* *Model 385 Sporting Clays* - 12, 20 (new 2000), or 28 (new 2000) ga., 3 in. chambers (12 ga.), 28 in. barrels with raised VR and double bead sights, pistol grip stock, approx. 7½ lbs. New 1998.

MSR	$2,159	$1,850	$1,425	$1,050	$875	$750	$650	$550

  ⬦*Model 385 Sporting Clays Set* - includes a pair of 20 and 28 ga. 26 in. barrels. New 1999.

MSR	$2,969	$2,500	$2,075	$1,725	$1,475	$1,200	$1,050	$975

* *Model 385 Field Set* - includes a pair of 20 and 28 ga. 26 in. barrels, choice of pistol grip or English straight stock. New 1997.

MSR	$2,929	$2,475	$2,100	$1,750	$1,475	$1,200	$1,050	$975

* *Model 385 DU Commemorative* - features gold inlaid mallards on both receiver sides and gold inlaid DU duck head on receiver bottom, includes hard shell case, and signed letter from SKB president, DU proofmarks, limited mfg. - 200 sets in 1992.

	$3,950	$2,750	$1,950

Last MSR was $5,000.

This model is a DU "Collectors Series" gun.

MODEL 400 - 12 or 20 ga., Mag. model also, boxlock, SST, AE, moderately engraved coin finished receiver with sideplates.

	$895	$750	$600	$500	$430	$410	$385

Add 20% for 20 ga.

S

Grading	100%	98%	95%	90%	80%	70%	60%

MODEL 400 (RECENT PRODUCTION) - similar to original Model 400, SST, ejectors, recoil pad. Imported 1987-1988 only.

	100%	98%	95%	90%	80%	70%	60%
	$1,200	$1,050	$900	$750	$595	$525	$475

Last MSR was $1,195.

Add 20% for 20 ga.

✳ *Model 400E (English)* - similar to New Model 400, except has engraved sideplates and straight grip stock. Importation disc. 1989.

	$1,350	$1,200	$950	$775	$600	$525	$475

Last MSR was $1,195.

Add 20% for 20 ga.

MODEL 480 ENGLISH - 12 or 20 ga., Mag. model also, SST, AE, moderately engraved coin finished receiver, straight grip.

	$1,450	$1,250	$975	$795	$695	$525	$475

Add 20% for 20 ga.

MODEL 485 FIELD - 12 (new 1998), 20, or 28 ga., coin finished boxlock action with engraved upland game scene side plates, 26 in. barrels with raised VR, checkered American walnut stock and beavertail forearm, ejectors, SST, satin finish and splinter forearm became available 2002, approx. 7 lbs. New 1997.

MSR	$2,769	$2,400	$2,050	$1,725	$1,425	$1,250	$995	$850

✳ *Model 485 Field Set* - includes a pair of 20 and 28 ga. 26 in. barrels, choice of pistol grip or English straight stock. New 1998.

MSR	$3,949	$3,400	$2,825	$2,300	$2,000	$1,675	$1,375	$1,150

SHOTGUNS: SEMI-AUTO

MODEL 300 STANDARD - 12 or 20 ga., 3 in. chamber, 26 in. imp. cyl., 28 in. mod. or full barrels, 30 in. full, recoil operated, checkered pistol grip stock. Mfg. 1968-1972.

	$295	$255	$205	$165	$155	$145	$140
Vent. rib model	$320	$275	$220	$195	$165	$155	$150

MODEL 1300 UPLAND - 12 or 20 ga., 3 in. chamber, 22, 26, or 28 in. VR barrel with multichokes, matte black receiver, checkered walnut stock and forearm. Importation resumed 1988- 1996.

	$450	$385	$340	$300	$270	$240	$210

Last MSR was $495.

This model was previously designated the Model 300. The new Model 1300 was available in Slug configuration with 22 in. barrel/iron sights at no extra charge. Recent Model 1300s have a magazine cutoff system on front left side of frame.

XL 900 MR - 12 ga. only, gas operated, 26-30 in. barrels, 5 shot, alloy receiver, etched game bird scroll work on receiver, shoots both 2¾ and 3 in. shells by interchanging barrels. Disc. 1980.

	$325	$280	$260	$240	$225	$190	$175

✳ *XL 900* - similar to XL 900 MR, only in 20 ga. and no recoil pad, 6¼ lbs.

	$360	$315	$275	$250	$230	$190	$175

XL 900 TRAP GRADE - similar to XL 900 MR, 12 ga. only, scroll engraved black chrome receiver, 30 in. imp. mod. or full barrel, trap style stock, straight or Monte Carlo, recoil pad. Mfg. 1980-disc.

	$395	$350	$320	$305	$275	$265	$260

XL 900 SKEET GRADE - similar to XL 900 MR, except scroll engraved black chrome receiver, 26 in. barrel, skeet stock. Mfg. 1972-disc.

	$400	$350	$320	$305	$275	$265	$260

Grading	100%	98%	95%	90%	80%	70%	60%

XL 900 SLUG GUN - similar to XL 900 MR, except 24 in. slug barrel, rifle sights, no rib. Mfg. 1972-disc.

	$350	$310	$280	$265	$250	$220	$200

MODEL 1900 - 12 or 20 ga., 3 in. chamber, 22, 26, or 28 in. VR barrel with multi- chokes, deluxe outdoor field scene etched on receiver, gold trigger, approx. 1,000-2,000 mfg. per year. Importation disc. 1996.

	$485	$430	$395	$360	$330	$295	$260

Last MSR was $545.

This model was previously designated the Model 900. The new Model 1900 was available in Slug configuration with 22 in. barrel and iron sights or Trap Model at no extra charge. Recent Model 1900s have a magazine cutoff system on front left side of frame.

MODEL 3000 - 12 or 20 ga., 3 in. chamber, gas operated, (shoots both 2¾ and 3 in. shells interchangeably) with semi-squareback styling, elaborate game scenes etched on both sides of receiver, deluxe checkered walnut stock and forearm. Imported 1988- 90.

	$545	$475	$415	$380	$350	$315	$285

Last MSR was $597.

Add $125 for Trap model (2¾ in. chamber).
This model has not previously been imported in this configuration.

SHOTGUNS: SINGLE BARREL, TRAP

MODEL 505 TRAP - 12 ga., 32 or 34 in. barrel with multi-chokes, regular or Monte Carlo stock.

	$875	$725	$650	$525	$475	$430	$395

Last MSR was $995.

MODEL 605 TRAP - 12 ga., 32 or 34 in. barrel with multi-chokes.

	$1,075	$850	$750	$675	$575	$500	$450

Last MSR was $1,195.

SHOTGUNS: SLIDE ACTION

MODEL 7300 - 12 or 20 ga., 2¾ or 3 in. chambers, blue only, French walnut stock-hand checkered, twin action slide bars. Disc. 1980.

	$295	$250	$225	$200	$180	$165	$150

MODEL 7900 - trap or skeet variation of the Model 7300.

	$350	$310	$265	$235	$200	$180	$160

SKS

SKS designates a semi-auto rifle design originally developed by the Russian military. No current domestic importation. Currently manufactured in Russia, China, Yugoslavia, and many other countries.

SKS Development & History

SKS (Samozaryadnaya Karabina Simonova) - developed by S.G. Simonov in the late 1940s to use the 7.62 cartridge of 1943 (7.62x39mm). The SKS is actually based on an earlier design developed by Simonov in 1936 as a prototype self-loading military rifle. The SKS was adopted by the Soviet military in 1949, two years after the AK-47, and was originally intended as a complement to the AK- 47's select-fire capability. It served in this role until the mid-to-late 1950s, when it was withdrawn from active issue and sent to reserve units and Soviet Youth "Pioneer" programs. It was also released for use in military assistance programs to Soviet Bloc countries and other "friendly" governments. Much of the original SKS manufacturing equipment was shipped to Communist China prior to 1960. Since then, most of the SKS carbines produced, including those used by the Viet Cong in Vietnam, have come from China.

Like the AK-47, the Simonov carbine is a robust military rifle. It too was designed to be used by troops with very little formal education or training. It will operate reliably in the harshest climatic conditions, from the Russian arctic to the steamy jungles of Southeast Asia. Its chrome-lined bore is impervious to the corrosive effects of fulminate of mercury primers and the action

S

Grading	100%	98%	95%	90%	80%	70%	60%

is easily disassembled for cleaning and maintenance.

The SKS and a modified sporter called the OP-SKS (OP stands for Okhotnichnyj Patron) are the standard hunting rifles for a majority of Russian hunters. It is routinely used to take everything from the Russian saiga antelope up to and including moose, boar, and brown bear. The main difference between the regular SKS and the OP variant is in the chamber dimensions and the rate of rifling. The OP starts as a regular SKS, then has the barrel removed and replaced with one designed to specifically handle a slightly longer and heavier bullet.

Prior to the ban, hundreds of thousands of SKS carbines were imported into the U.S. The SKS was rapidly becoming one of the favorites of American hunters and shooters. Its low cost and durability made it a popular "truck gun" for those shooters who spend a lot of time in the woods, whether they are ranchers, farmers, or plinkers. While the Russian- made SKS is a bonafide curio and relic firearm and legal for importation, the Clinton administration suspended all import permits for firearms having a rifled bore and ammunition from the former Soviet Union in early 1994. In order to get the ban lifted, the Russian government signed a trade agreement, wherein they agreed to deny export licenses to any American company seeking SKS rifles and a variety of other firearms and ammunition deemed politically incorrect by Clinton & Gore. The BATF then used this agreement as a reason to deny import licenses for any SKS from any country.

Most of the SKS carbines imported into the U.S. came from the People's Republic of China. They were a mix of refurbished military issue, straight military surplus, and even some new manufacture. Quality was rather poor. Compared to the SKS Chinese carbines, only a few Russian made SKSs ever made it into the U.S. All are from military stockpiles and were refurbished at the Tula Arms Works, probably the oldest continuously operating armory in the world. Recently, more SKS carbines have been imported from Yugoslavia by Century International Arms. These carbines carry the former Soviet Bloc designation of "Type 58" and feature milled receivers. Quality is generally good, and values are comparable to other Russian/European SKS imports. Values for unmodified Russian and Eastern European made SKS carbines (those with the original magazines and stock) are higher than the Chinese copies.

Over 600 million SKS carbines have been manufactured in China alone, in addition to the millions manufactured in other former Soviet Bloc countries. The Simonov carbine was the best selling semi-auto rifle in America (and other countries) during 1993-94, and remains a popular choice for plinking, hunting, and protection in the new millennium.

RIFLES: SEMI-AUTO

SKS - 7.62x39mm Russian cal., semi-auto rifle, Soviet designed, original Soviet mfg. as well as copies mfg. in China, Russia, Yugoslavia, and other countries, gas operated weapon, 10 shot fixed mag., wood stock (thumbhole design on newer mfg.), with or w/o (newer mfg.) permanently attached folding bayonet, tangent rear and hooded front sight, no current importation from China, Russia, or the former Yugoslavia.

Chinese Mfg.

/thumbhole stock	$145	$130	$115	$100	$90	$85	$80
Original Russian Mfg.	$225	$190	$170	$155	$140	$130	$120

During late 1993 until the Crime Bill was enacted during September of 1994, runaway demand escalated SKS prices on recent Chinese exports to the $195-$250 range. Earlier Russian manufacture at the time was selling for $250-$325, but prices fell once the glut of Chinese imports arrived. However, as supply began equaling demand, prices fell off to their current levels. With interest waning and a current stable marketplace, SKS pricing has become more predictable, and knowledgeable shooters and collectors are now seeking out earlier Russian made SKSs, as these guns have the most quality and best fit/finish (not Chinese overall poor quality). Lately there have been a rash of lawsuits over recently imported SKS semi-auto models going full auto, and as a result, prices have gone down slightly.

This model may also be listed under those importers/distributors who import this model and are listed in this text.

SSK INDUSTRIES

Current Class II manufacturer located in Wintersville, OH. Consumer direct sales.

SSK Industries manufactures complete rifles and suppressors for police, military, and civilian use (where legal in accord with ATF regulations). Their custom shop works on virtually anything 20mm or smaller.

SSK Industries uses Thompson Center flatside frames and applies an industrial hard chrome

Grading	100%	98%	95%	90%	80%	70%	60%

finish. Most SSK handguns and rifles are extensively customized in exotic calibers, finishes, and various engraving options. Receivers and barrels may be purchased separately - values below are for complete assembled pistols.

SSK has also manufactured various limited editions including the Handgun Hunters International (HHI) Models 1, 2, and 3. Issue prices on these guns were $1,100 (Model 3), $1,200 (Model 2), and $1,300 (Model 1). Only 50 were mfg. total in 1987. SSK also customized a Ruger Super Redhawk (.44 Mag. or .45 LC cal.). This variation came with either a scoped 7½ in. octagon barrel (Beauty Model) or a 6 in. bull barrel with muzzle brake (Beast Model). Prices started at $1,430 - add $245 extra for .45 LC cal.

PISTOLS: SINGLE SHOT

Values listed are for basic models with no options or special features.

SSK-CONTENDER - over 150 cals. available from .17 Bee to .50-70, various custom barrels available, basically, this is a custom order only gun.

MSR	N/A	$1,500	$1,375	$1,250	$1,125	$1,000	$900	$825

Individual barrels are available starting at $268.
An arrestor muzzle brake is available on special order.
This model includes barrel, frame, stocks, and sights as standard equipment.

SSK-XP100 - various cals. between .17 and .50, includes TSOB mount and rings.

MSR	N/A	$1,700	$1,500	$1,300	$1,150	$1,025	$925	$850

The .50 cal. XP100 (12.9 X 50.8 JDJ) comes with SSK muzzle brake, scope, dies, and new reinforced fiberglass stock - retail price is $1,700.

RIFLES

Values listed are for basic models with no options or special features. In addition, SSK also custom manufactures a bolt action rifle available in almost any caliber and configuration - prices start at approx. $2,000 and can go as high as $6,000, depending on the customer's individual special orders. SSK also has developed a 6.5mm, 7mm, or .30 cal. upper unit conversion for AR-15s and M-16s utilizing heavy sub-sonic bullets designated "whispers".

SSK TCR 87 - .14 through .600 cals., Nitro Express cals. are also available, features Thompson Center TRC 87 receiver, and SSK custom barrels, muzzle brakes and exotic finishes are available at extra cost.

MSR	N/A	$1,700	$1,500	$1,300	$1,150	$1,025	$925	$850

SSK RUGER NO. 1 - many cals. including .577 NE (optional), custom order rifle based on a Ruger No. 1 frame.

MSR	N/A	$2,000	$1,800	$1,600	$1,400	$1,250	$1,100	$1,000

SSK BOLT ACTION - various cals., ground up custom order rifle.

MSR	N/A	$2,500	$2,250	$1,800	$1,600	$1,400	$1,250	$1,100

STI INTERNATIONAL

Current manufacturer established during 1993, and located in Georgetown, TX. Distributor and dealer sales.

In addition to manufacturing the pistols listed, STI International also makes frame kits in steel, stainless steel, aluminum, or titanium - prices range between $441-$989.

PISTOLS: SEMI-AUTO

The beginning numerals on all STI pistols designate the barrel length, and the following models are listed in numerical sequence.

3.4 BLS9/BLS40 - 9mm Para. or .40 S&W cal., blue finish, Govt. length grips, Heine low mounted sights, single stack mag. New 1999.

MSR	$844	$725	$625	$550	$450	$400	$360	$330

S

Grading	100%	98%	95%	90%	80%	70%	60%

3.4 LS9/LS40 - 9mm Para. or .40 S&W cal., blue finish, Commander length grips, single stack mag., Heine low mounted sights. New 1999.

	MSR $747	$625	$550	$500	$425	$375	$350	$325

3.9 FALCON - .38 Super, .40 S&W, or .45 ACP cal., STI standard frame, 3.9 in. barrel, size is comparable to Officers Model, adj. rear sight. Limited mfg. 1993-98.

	$1,875	$1,375	$1,175	$925	$850	$775	$675

Last MSR was $2,136.

3.9 RANGER - .45 ACP cal. only, Officer's Model with 3.9 in. barrel and ½ in. shortened grip frame, 6 shot mag., blue steel frame with stainless steel slide, low mount STI/ Heine sights, 29 oz. New 2001.

	MSR $976	$850	$725	$625	$550	$450	$400	$350

3.9 V.I.P. - .45 ACP cal. only, aluminum frame, STI modular polymer grip, stainless steel slide, 3.9 in. barrel with STI Recoilmaster muzzlebrake, 10 shot mag., STI fixed sights, 25 oz. New 2001.

	MSR $1,699	$1,500	$1,300	$1,050	$850	$825	$725	$600

4.3 HAWK - various cals., 4.3 in. barrel, STI standard frame (choice of steel or aluminum), 27 or 31 oz. Mfg. 1993-1999.

	$1,725	$1,275	$1,075	$875	$800	$700	$600

Last MSR was $1,975.

4.3 NIGHT HAWK - .45 ACP cal., 4.3 in. barrel, STI wide extended frame, blue finish, 33 oz. Limited mfg. 1997-1999.

	$1,875	$1,375	$1,175	$925	$850	$775	$675

Last MSR was $2,136.

5.0 SPARROW - .22 LR cal. only, breech blow back mechanism, STI standard extended frame, 5.1 in. ramped bull barrel, fixed sights, blue finish, 30 oz. Limited mfg. 1998-1999 only.

	$1,025	$900	$800	$700	$600	$500	$400

Last MSR was $1,090.

5.0 EAGLE - various cals., 5.1 in. barrel, STI standard frame (choice of steel or aluminum) govt. model full-size, wide body with stagger stack mag., adj. rear sight, 31 or 35 oz.

	MSR $1,699	$1,500	$1,300	$1,050	$850	$825	$725	$600

Add $266 for .40 Super with .45 ACP conversion kit.

5.0 EDGE - 9mm Para., 10mm Norma, .40 S&W or .45 ACP cal., designed for limited/ standard IPSC competition, STI wide extended frame, wide body with stagger stack mag., blue finish, 39 oz. New 1998.

	MSR $1,776	$1,575	$1,350	$1,175	$925	$850	$750	$625

5.0 EXECUTIVE - .40 S&W cal. only, STI long/wide frame, 10 shot mag., stainless construction, grey nylon polymer grips and triggerguard, hard chrome finish with black inlays, fiber optic front and STI adj. rear sights, approved for IPSC standard and USPSA limited edition. New 2001.

	MSR $2,263	$2,000	$1,725	$1,475	$1,300	$1,050	$900	$800

5.0 TROJAN - 9mm Para., .40 S&W, .40 Super, or .45 ACP, standard Govt. length grips, single stack mag. New 1999.

	MSR $970	$850	$725	$625	$550	$450	$400	$350

Add $288 for .40 Super with .45 ACP conversion kit.

5.1 LIMITED - while advertised during 1998, this model was never manufactured.

Last MSR was $1,699.

5.5 EAGLE - various cals., features STI standard frame, 5½ in. compensated barrel, 44 oz. Limited mfg. 1994-98.

	$2,100	$1,750	$1,475	$1,200	$995	$895	$775

Last MSR was $2,399.

S

Grading	100%	98%	95%	90%	80%	70%	60%

5.5 COMPETITOR - .38 Super cal. only, standard frame, classic slide with front and rear serrations, square hammer, compensator, match sear, STI "Alchin" style blast deflector mount, C-more rail scope, wide ambidextrous and grip safeties. New 1999.

	MSR	$2,499		$2,175	$1,875	$1,650	$1,425	$1,200	$995	$875

This model is also available with an STI TruBore compensator (5.5 TruBore Competitor) at no extra charge.

5.5 GRANDMASTER - .38 Super cal. standard, custom order gun with any variety of options available, 42 oz. New 2001.

	MSR	$3,297		$2,995	$2,600	$2,250	$1,900	$1,650	$1,425	$1,200

6.0 HUNTER - 10mm cal. only, 6 in. barrel, STI super extended heavy frame with single stack mag., blue finish, 51 oz. Only 2 mfg. 1998, disc. 2000.

			$2,250	$1,875	$1,650	$1,425	$1,200	$995	$895

Last MSR was $2,485.

Add $350 for Leupold 2X scope with terminator mount.

6.0 EAGLE - various competition cals., features STI super extended heavy frame, 6 in. barrel, blue finish, wide body with stagger stack mag., 42 oz. New 1998.

	MSR	$1,795		$1,625	$1,400	$1,250	$995	$875	$800	$725

Add $267 for .40 Super with .45 ACP conversion kit.

6.0 TROJAN - similar to Trojan 5.0, except has 6 in. barrel and single stack mag. New 2000.

	MSR	$1,074		$950	$825	$725	$625	$525	$450	$395

Add $143 for .40 Super with .45 ACP conversion kit.

6.0 .450 XCALIBER - .450 cal., single stack mag., V-10 barrel and slide porting, stainless grip and thumb safeties, adj. rear sight. New 2000.

	MSR	$1,122		$1,000	$850	$750	$650	$525	$450	$395

6.0 .450+ XCALIBER - .450+ cal., otherwise similar to Xcaliber 6.0 .450, except has 6 in. frame with patented polymer grip and stagger stack mag. New 2000.

	MSR	$1,998		$1,775	$1,575	$1,350	$1,175	$995	$875	$775

S.W.D., INC.

Previous manufacturer located in Atlanta, GA.

Similar models have previously been manufactured by R.P.B. Industries, Inc. (1979-82), and met with BATF disapproval because of convertibility into fully automatic operation. "Cobray" is a trademark for the M11/9 semi-automatic pistol.

CARBINES

SEMI-AUTO CARBINE - 9mm Para. cal., same mechanism as M11, 16¼ in. shrouded barrel, telescoping stock.

		$550	$495	$450	$400	$325	$275	$235

PISTOLS: SEMI-AUTO

COBRAY M-11/NINE mm - 9mm Para. cal., fires from closed bolt, 3rd generation design, stamped steel frame, 32 shot mag., parkerized finish, similar in appearance to Ingram Mac 10.

		$350	$315	$235	$200	$175	$160	$150

This model was also available in a fully-auto variation, Class III transferable only.

S

Grading	100%	98%	95%	90%	80%	70%	60%

REVOLVERS

LADIES HOME COMPANION - .45-70 Govt. cal., double action design utilizing spring wound 12 shot rotary mag., 12 in. barrel, steel barrel and frame, 9 lbs. 6 oz. Mfg. 1990-94.

	$650	$525	$400	$360	$335	$310	$290

SHOTGUNS: SINGLE SHOT

TERMINATOR - 12 or 20 ga., paramilitary design shotgun with 18 in. cylinder bore barrel, parkerized finish, ejector. Mfg. 1986-1988 only.

	$95	$80	$70	$60	$55	$50	$45

Last MSR was $110.

SABATTI s.p.a.

Current manufacturer located in Gardone, Italy with history tracing back to 1674. Some models are currently imported by European American Armory located in Sharpes, FL.

In 1960, the sons of Antonio Sabatti formed the current company, and manufacture currently includes good quality O/U and SxS shotguns, O/U combination and double rifles, bolt action and semi-auto rifles, and slide action and single shot shotguns. Sabatti should be contacted directly (see Trademark Index) regarding more information and domestic availability on their extensive firearms line-up.

SACO DEFENSE INC.

Previous firearms manufacturer located in Saco, ME. Saco Defense was purchased by General Dynamics in July of 2000, and continues to produce guns for military defense contracts currently. This company was previously owned by Colt's Manufacturing Company, Inc. during late 1998-2000.

In the past, Saco Defense utilized their high-tech manufacturing facility to produce guns for Magnum Research, Weatherby (contract ended Sept., 2001), and others.

SAFARI ARMS

Current trademark manufactured in Olympia, WA. Schuetzen Pistol Works is the custom shop division of Safari Arms. M-S Safari Arms was started in 1978 as a division of M-S Safari Outfitters. In 1987, Safari Arms was absorbed by Olympic Arms.

Safari Arms previously made the Phoenix, Special Forces, Camp Perry, and Royal Order of Jesters commemoratives in various configurations and quantities. Prices average in the $1,500 range except for the Royal Order of Jesters ($2,000).

Schuetzen Pistol Works

Some of the pistols made by Safari Arms had the "Schuetzen Pistol Works" name on them (c. 1994-96). All pistols currently manufactured are marked with the Safari Arms slide marking. All pistols, however, have been marked "Safari Arms" on the frame. The pistols formerly in this section have been moved under the PISTOLS: SEMI-AUTO category.

PISTOLS: SEMI-AUTO

S

Safari Arms currently manufactures mostly single action, semi-auto pistols derived from the Browning M1911 design with modifications.

Grading	100%	98%	95%	90%	80%	70%	60%

ENFORCER - .45 ACP cal., 3.8 in. barrel, 6 shot mag., shortened grip, available with max hard finish aluminum frame, parkerized, electroless nickel or lightweight anodized finishes, flat or arched mainspring housing, adj. sights, ambidextrous safety, neoprene or checkered walnut grips, 27 oz. (lightweight model).

MSR	$750		$725	$575	$500	$450	$425	$400	$375

This model was originally called the Black Widow. After Safari Arms became Schuetzen Pistol Works, this model was changed extensively to include stainless construction, beavertail grip safety, and combat style hammer.

MATCHMASTER - similar to the Enforcer, except has 5 or 6 in. barrel and 7 shot mag., approx. 40 oz.

MSR	$715		$675	$550	$485	$450	$425	$400	$375

Add $60 for 6 in. barrel.

BIG DEUCE - .45 ACP cal., 6 in. longslide version of the MatchMaster, matte black slide with satin stainless steel frame, smooth walnut grips, 40.3 oz. New 1995.

MSR	$835		$775	$625	$575	$500	$450	$400	$350

GI SAFARI - .45 ACP cal., patterned after the Colt Model 1911, Safari frame, beavertail grip safety and commander hammer, parkerized matte black finish, 39.9 oz. Mfg. 1991- 2000.

	$500	$455	$395	$350	$295	$275	$250

Last MSR was $550.

COHORT PISTOL - .45 ACP cal., features Enforcer slide and MatchMaster frame, 3.8 in. stainless steel barrel, beavertail grip safety, extended thumb safety and slide release, commander style hammer, smooth walnut grips with laser etched Black Widow logo, 37 oz. New 1995.

MSR	$775		$725	$600	$525	$475	$425	$400	$375

CARRYCOMP - similar to MatchMaster, except utilizes W. Schuemann designed hybrid compensator system, 5 in. barrel, available in stainless steel or steel, 38 oz. Mfg. 1993- 99.

	$1,030	$875	$750	$600	$500	$425	$375

Last MSR was $1,160.

✱ ***Enforcer CarryComp*** - similar to Enforcer, except utilizes W. Schuemann designed hybrid compensator system, available in stainless steel or steel, 36 oz. Mfg. 1993-96.

	$1,175	$1,025	$875	$750	$600	$500	$425

Last MSR was $1,300.

CARRIER - .45 ACP cal. only, reproduction of the original Detonics ScoreMaster, except has upgraded sights, custom made by Richard Niemer from the Custom Shop. New 1999-2001.

	$750	$625	$575	$500	$450	$400	$350

Last MSR was $750.

RENEGADE - .45 ACP cal., left-hand action (port on left side), 4½ (4-star, disc. 1996) or 5 (new 1994) in. barrel, 6 shot mag., adj. sights, stainless steel construction, 36-39 oz. Mfg. 1993-98.

	$955	$800	$700	$600	$525	$450	$395

Last MSR was $1,085.

Add $50 for 4-star (4½ in. barrel, disc.).

RELIABLE - similar to Renegade, except has right-hand action. Mfg. 1993-98.

	$730	$620	$525	$450	$425	$400	$375

Last MSR was $825.

Add $60 for 4-star (4½ in. barrel, disc.).

GRIFFON PISTOL - .45 ACP cal., 5 in. stainless steel barrel, 10 shot mag., standard govt. size with beavertail grip safety, full-length recoil spring guide, commander style hammer, smooth walnut grips, 40½ oz. Disc. 1998.

	$855	$725	$650	$575	$500	$450	$395

Last MSR was $920.

S

Grading	100%	98%	95%	90%	80%	70%	60%

STREET DUECE - .45 ACP cal., M1911A1 styled frame, 5 in. stainless steel National Match bushingless barrel, stainless frame, steel slide, lowered and widened ejectionport, 7 shot mag., diamond pattern checkered rosewood grips. New 2001.

	MSR	$1,195	$1,075	$950	$825	$700	$600	$500	$400

JOURNEYMAN - similar to Street Duece, except has 4 in. barrel. New 2001.

	MSR	$1,195	$1,075	$950	$825	$700	$600	$500	$400

BLACK WIDOW - .45 ACP cal., 3.9 in. barrel, hand-contoured front grip strap, schrimshawed ivory Micarta grips with Black Widow emblem, 6 shot mag., 27 oz. Inventory was depleted 1988.

$565	$510	$460	$430	$400	$375	$350

Last MSR was $595.

BILL OF RIGHTS BICENTENNIAL MATCHED SET - includes the MatchMaster Pistol and Service-Match Rifle, features beryllium receivers and special engraving. Disc.

$8,950	$6,500	$4,750

Last MSR was $7,400.

PARTNER - .22 LR cal., formerly the Whitney Wolverine, 8 shot mag., black plastic grips, non-adj. sights. New late 1997.

	MSR	$315	$275	$250	$225	$200	$185	$170	$155

MODEL 81 TARGET PISTOL - .38 Spl. or .45 ACP cal., 5 in. barrel, hand-contoured front grip strap, 2 lbs. 10 oz. Disc. 1987.

$775	$695	$550	$440	$410	$375	$350

Last MSR was $875.

Add $50 for Deluxe Model (with Herrett adj. grips).

* ***Model 81L*** - .38 Spl. or .45 ACP, 6 in. barrel, 2 lbs. 13 oz. Disc. 1987.

$850	$775	$695	$550	$440	$410	$375

Last MSR was $975.

Add $50 for Deluxe Model (with Herrett adj. grips).

* ***Model 81 NM*** - .38 Spl. or .45 ACP cal., similar frame as Model 81, except has flat front grip strap, 5 in. barrel, 2 lbs. 5 oz. Disc. 1987.

$775	$695	$550	$440	$410	$375	$350

Last MSR was $875.

* ***Model 81BP*** - .38 Spl. or .45 ACP cal., 6 in barrel, contoured front grip strap, faster cycle time, 2 lbs. 9 oz. Disc. 1987.

$875	$775	$695	$550	$440	$410	$375

Last MSR was $995.

* ***Silueta*** - .45 ACP or .38/.45 Wildcat cal., 10 in. extended barrel, designed for silhouette shooting, 2 lbs. 14 oz. Disc. 1987.

$875	$775	$695	$550	$440	$410	$375

Last MSR was $1,050.

PISTOLS: SINGLE SHOT

ULTIMATE/UNLIMITED - various cals., bolt action target pistol, 14 15/16 in. barrel, black finished metal, laminated stock. Disc. 1987.

$850	$775	$695	$550	$440	$410	$375

Last MSR was $975.

Manufacturer	Model	Quantity	Year	Issue Price

SAFARI CLUB INTERNATIONAL

SCI is an international hunting and conservation organization with headquarters located in Tucson, AZ.

Although Safari Club International (SCI) is not a manufacturer or importer, this organization is responsible for special and limited editions similar to the one listed. Additionally, SCI also has one custom-built rifle manufactured for each annual SCI convention with an auction determining the price of the rifle.

SPECIAL/LIMITED EDITIONS

Winchester	Super Grade 25th Anniversary	200	1997	$1,395

SAIGA

Current manufacturer located in Russia. Currently imported by European American Armory Corp., located in Sharpes, FL.

Grading	100%	98%	95%	90%	80%	70%	60%

RIFLES: SEMI-AUTO

SAIGA RIFLE - .223 Rem., .308 Win., or 7.62x39mm, Kalashnikov type action, black synthetic stock and forearm, 16.3-22 in. barrel length, matte black metal. Importation began 2002.

	MSR	$389		$340	$300	$275	$260	$245	$230	$215

Add $40 for .308 Win. cal.

SHOTGUNS: SEMI-AUTO

SAIGA SHOTGUN - 12, 20 ga. or .410 bore, Kalashnikov type action, black synthetic stock and forearm, 19-22 in. barrel length, matte black metal. Importation began 2002.

As this edition went to press, prices had yet to be established on this model.

SAKO, LTD.

Current rifle manufacturer established circa 1921 and located in Riihimäki, Finland. Current models are presently being imported by Beretta USA, located in Accockeek MD. Previously imported by Stoeger Industries, Inc. located in Wayne, NJ, Garcia, and Rymac.

During 2000, Sako, Ltd. was purchased by Beretta Holding of Italy. All currently produced Sakos are imported by Beretta U.S.A. Corp. located in Accokeek, MD.

Beginning 2000, all Sako rifles are shipped with a Key Concept locking device. This patented system uses a separate key to activate an almost invisible lock which totally blocks the firing pin, and prevents bolt movement.

PISTOLS: SEMI-AUTO

Less than 200 Triace pistols were imported into the United States.

TRIACE - .22 Short, .22 LR or .32 S&W Wadcutter cal., target pistol incorporating unique action, competition walnut grips with thumb rest and adj. heel, blue finish with chrome accents. Imported 1985-86 only.

		$1,300	$1,150	$950	$825	$700	$600	$500

Last MSR was $1,395.

* ***Triace Pistol Kit*** - consists of Triace frame, .22 Short, .22 LR, and .32 S&W barrels. Cased with accessories. Imported 1985-86 only.

		$2,500	$2,200	$2,000	$1,500	$1,300	$1,175	$1,025

Last MSR was $2,385.

S

Grading	100%	98%	95%	90%	80%	70%	60%

RIFLES: BOLT ACTION, DISC.

Add 10%-15% for popular Mag. cals. on rifles listed.
Note: Prices are for pre-1972 Sako rifles, unless stated otherwise. Pre-1972 Sakos utilize the L-46, L-461, L-469, L-57, and L-61 R actions.
Subtract approx. 25% for post-1972 models.

DELUXE - various cals., Monte Carlo stock, skipline checkering, long, medium, or short actions, contrasting pistol grip cap and forend tip, engraved floorplate.

	$1,045	$925	$775	$625	$450	$425	$385

STANDARD SPORTER - long, medium, and short actions.

	$850	$725	$625	$500	$450	$410	$375

HEAVY BARREL MODEL - long, medium, and short actions.

	$850	$725	$625	$500	$450	$410	$375

FULL STOCK MODELS - 20 in. carbine barrel (all actions), 23½ in. barrel on rifle (short & medium actions).

* ***Finnbear*** - long action.

	$1,100	$975	$800	$725	$550	$475	$425

* ***Forester*** - medium action.

	$1,050	$925	$775	$700	$525	$450	$400

* ***Vixen*** - short action.

	$1,050	$925	$775	$700	$525	$450	$400

L-46 action pre-Vixen Sakos had detachable mags.

MAUSER ACTION (FN) - .270 Win. or .30-06 cal., long action. Mfg. 1950-1957.

	$695	$500	$400	$345	$310	$280	$260

MAGNUM MAUSER (FN) - 8x60S, 8.2x57mm, .300 H&H, or .375 H&H cal.

	$745	$635	$580	$495	$450	$410	$375

MODEL 74 - various cals.

	$650	$575	$450	$375	$340	$320	$290

MODEL 78 - .22 LR, .22 Mag., or .22 Hornet cal., detachable mag., same size as short action Standard Model. Importation disc. 1986.

	$480	$395	$340	$310	$280	$265	$250

Last MSR was $647.

Add $30 for .22 Hornet cal.

FINNSPORT MODEL 2700 - available in long (AIII) action only, .270 Win., .300 Win. Mag. cals., select checkered walnut. Disc. 1985.

	$750	$675	$600	$560	$510	$475	$430

Last MSR was $910.

FINNWOLF - .243 Win. or .308 Win. cal., lever action, 4 shot mag. early model, 3 shot mag. later model. Mfg. 1962-1974.

	$895	$775	$550	$500	$440	$410	$375

Add 15% for early model with 4 shot mag.

ANNIVERSARY MODEL - 7mm Rem. Mag. cal. only, 1,000 mfg.

	$2,750	$1,625	$975

The 100% value on this model refers to NIB unfired condition with factory papers.

RIFLES: BOLT ACTION, RECENT PRODUCTION

All Sako left-handed models are available in medium or long action only.

S

FINNFIRE - .22 LR cal., 22 in. regular or heavy (new 1996) or 23 (Sporter and Varmint only) in. cold-hammer forged free floating barrel, single stage adj. trigger, 50 degree bolt lift, 2 position safety, European walnut stock, cocking indicator, available in Hunter, Sporter (new 1999), or Varmint configuration, 5 or 10 shot mag., integral 11mm dovetail (for scope mounting), with (new 1996) or w/o open sights, 5¾ lbs. Importation began 1994.

	MSR	$854	$715	$640	$560	$500	$450	$400	$350

Add $42 for Varmint Model with heavy barrel.
Add $97 for Sporter Model (new 1999).

HUNTER LIGHTWEIGHT RIFLE - available in short action (AI) in .17 Rem., .222 Rem., or .223 Rem. cal., medium action (AII) in .22-250 Rem., .243 Win., .308 Win., or 7mm-08 Rem. cal., or long action (AIII) in .25-06 Rem., .270 Win., .280 Rem., .30-06, .270 Wby. Mag. (disc. 1996), 7mm Wby. Mag. (disc. 1996), 7mm Rem. Mag., .300 Win. Mag., .300 Wby. Mag., .338 Win. Mag., .340 Wby. Mag. (disc. 1996), .375 H&H, or .416 Rem. Mag. (new 1991) cal., 21¼, 21¾, or 22 in. barrel, classic styled stock with choice of oil (disc. 1996) or matte lacquer finish, finely checkered French walnut. Disc. 1997.

	$850	$685	$550	$490	$460	$430	$410

Last MSR was $1,050.

Add $35 for long action.
Add $50-$70 for Mag. cals.
Add approx. $80 for left-hand action (available in all Mag. cals. - mfg. 1994-96).

* **Hunter Carbine (Handy)** - available in medium action in .22-250 Rem. (disc. 1990), .243 Win. (new 1991), .308 Win. (new 1991) cal. or long action in .25-06 Rem. (disc. 1990), 7mm Rem. Mag. (disc. 1990), .338 Win. Mag. cal., or .375 H&H (new 1990) cal., 18½ in. barrel with iron sights, oil or lacquer finished deluxe walnut stock with checkering, approx. 7 lbs. Mfg. 1986-91.

	$725	$650	$600	$490	$460	$430	$410

Last MSR was $945.

Add $50-$65 for long action (Mag. cals.).

FINNLIGHT - .243 Win., .25-06 Rem., .270 Win., .280 Rem., .30-06, .308 Win., .300 Win. Mag., 6.5x55mm, 7mm-08 Rem., or 7mm Rem. Mag. cal., stainless steel free floating fluted barrel, alloy triggerguard/mag. bottom, black synthetic stock, 4 or 5 shot detachable mag., no sights, 6½ lbs. Importation began 2001.

	MSR	$1,239	$1,050	$835	$675	$575	$500	$450	$435

Add $35 for Mag. cals.

LONG RANGE HUNTING MODEL - available in long action in .25-06 Rem., .270 Win., .300 Win. Mag., or 7mm Rem. Mag. cal., 26 in. heavy barrel only w/o sights. Mfg. 1996-97.

	$1,030	$785	$625	$545	$495	$465	$440

Last MSR was $1,275.

Add $15 for Mag. cals.

FIBERCLASS MODEL - available in medium action (disc. 1992) in .22-250 Rem., .243 Win., .308 Win., or 7mm-08 cal., or long action in .25-06 Rem., .270 Win., .280 Rem., .30-06, 7mm Rem. Mag., .300 Win. Mag., .338 Win. Mag., .375 H&H, or .416 Rem. Mag. (new 1991) cal., has black fiberglass stock. Disc. 1996.

	$1,170	$930	$785	$725	$630	$560	$510

Last MSR was $1,388.

Add $17-$37 for Mag. cals.
Subtract $40 for medium action cals. (disc. 1992).
Add $80 for left-hand action (disc. 1989).

S

Grading	100%	98%	95%	90%	80%	70%	60%

✳ **FiberClass Carbine (Handy)** - available in medium action in .243 Win. or .308 Win. cal. and long action in .25-06 Rem. (disc.), .270 Win. (disc.), .30-06, 7mm Rem. Mag. (disc.), .300 Win. Mag. (disc.), .338 Win. Mag., or .375 H&H(new 1991) cal., 18½ in. barrel with fiberglass stock. Mfg. 1986-91.

	$995	$895	$775	$725	$630	$560	$510

Last MSR was $1,239.

Add $50-$65 for Mag. cals.

LAMINATED RIFLE - available in short action (disc. 1989), medium action in .22-250 Rem., .243 Win., .308 Win., or 7mm-08 Rem. cal., or long action in .25-06 Rem., .270 Win., .280 Rem., .30-06, 7mm Rem. Mag., .300 Win. Mag., .338 Win. Mag., .375 H&H, or .416 Rem. Mag. (new 1991) cal., features laminated wood stock. Mfg. 1988- 95.

	$985	$790	$635	$550	$495	$460	$430

Last MSR was $1,200.

Add $35 for short action.
Add $55 for long action.
Add $75-$95 for Mag. cals.
Add approx. $100 for left-hand action (disc.).
The left-handed action was available in .270 Win., .280 Rem., .30-06, 7mm Rem. Mag., .300 Win. Mag., .338 Win. Mag., .375 H&H, or .416 Rem. Mag. cal.

MODEL TRG-21 - .308 Win. cal., bolt action, 25¾ in. barrel, new design features modular synthetic stock construction with adj. cheekpiece and buttplate, stainless steel barrel, cold hammer forged receiver, and resistance free bolt, 10 shot detachable mag., 10½ lbs. Imported 1993-99.

	$2,300	$2,000	$1,800	$1,600	$1,400	$1,200	$975

Last MSR was $2,699.

MODEL TRG-22 - .308 Win. cal., bolt action, 26 in. barrel, updated TRG-21 design featuring adj. modular synthetic stock (green or all black) construction with adj. cheekpiece and buttplate, choice of blue or phosphate (new 2002) metal finish, stainless steel barrel, cold hammer forged receiver, and resistance free bolt, 10 shot detachable mag., approx. 10¼ lbs. Importation began 2000.

MSR	$2,484		$2,200	$1,900	$1,725	$1,600	$1,325	$1,125	$825

Add $414 for green stock or all black configuration with phosphate finish (new 2002).

MODEL TRG-41 - .338 Lapua Mag. cal., similar to Model TRG-21, except has long action and 27 1/8 in. barrel, 7¾ lbs. Imported 1994-99.

	$2,700	$2,425	$2,150	$1,850	$1,625	$1,400	$1,200

Last MSR was $3,099.

MODEL TRG-42 - .300 Win. Mag. or .338 Lapua Mag. cal., updated TRG-41 design featuring long action and 27 1/8 in. barrel, choice of black composite/blue finish or green composite/phosphate (new 2002) finish, 5 shot mag., 11¼ lbs. Importation began 2000.

MSR	$2,829		$2,375	$2,175	$1,850	$1,625	$1,400	$1,200	$950

Add $414 for green stock with phosphate metal finish.

MODEL TRG-S - available in medium action (disc. 1993) in .243 Win. or 7mm-08 cal., or long action in .25-06 Rem. (Mfg. 1994-98), .270 Win. (disc. 2000), 6.5x55mm Swedish (disc. 1998), .30-06 (disc.), .308 Win. (disc. 1995), .270 Wby. Mag. (disc. 1998), 7mm Wby. Mag. (Mfg. 1998), 7mm Rem. Mag. (disc.), .300 Win. Mag. (disc.), .300 Wby. Mag. (mfg. 1994-99), .30-378 Wby. Mag. (new 1998, 26 in. barrel only), .338 Win. Mag. (disc. 1999), .338 Lapua Mag. (new 1994), .340 Wby. Mag. (disc. 1998), 7mm STW (26 in. barrel only, disc. 1999), .375 H&H (disc. 1998), or .416 Rem. Mag. (disc. 1998) cal., Sporter variation derived from the Model TRG- 21, 22 or 24 (Mag. cals. only) in. barrel, 3 or 5 shot detachable mag., fully adj. trigger, 60 degree bolt-lift, matte finish, 8 1/8 lbs. Importation began 1993.

MSR	$882		$755	$610	$525	$475	$440	$415	$380

S

Grading	100%	98%	95%	90%	80%	70%	60%

MANNLICHER CARBINE - available in short action (disc. 1989), medium action in .243 Win. or .308 Win. cal., or long action in .25-06 Rem. (disc. 1991), .270 Win., .30- 06, 7mm Rem. Mag. (disc. 1991), .300 Win. Mag. (disc. 1991), .338 Win. Mag., or .375 H&H cal., 18½ in. barrel, two-piece full Mannlicher style stock, open sights. Disc. 1996.

	$1,030	$785	$625	$545	$495	$465	$440

Last MSR was $1,275.

Add $35 for long action.
Add $60-$75 for Mag. cals.

PPC MODEL - 22 PPC or 6 mm PPC cal., 21¾ or 23¾ (Benchrest Model) in. barrel, single shot in Benchrest Model, 4 shot mag. in Hunter or Deluxe Model, checkered walnut stock, Deluxe Model has rosewood pistol grip and forearm caps plus skip line checkering, matte lacquer finish on Hunter and Deluxe, oiled finish on Benchrest, 6¼ or 8¾ (Benchrest Model with heavy barrel) lbs. Imported 1989-1998.

	$1,250	$950	$750	$650	$600	$540	$500

Last MSR was $1,535.

Add $320 for Deluxe Hunter Model (disc. 1993).
Add $85 for Benchrest Model (disc. 1993).

VARMINT RIFLE - available in short action (AI) in .17 Rem., .222 Rem., or .223 Rem., and medium action (AII) .22-250 Rem., .243 Win., .308 Win., or 7mm-08 cal., 22¾ in. heavy barrel, no sights. Disc. 1997.

	$1,025	$795	$615	$545	$475	$430	$400

Last MSR was $1,240.

Subtract $110 for single shot configuration (6mm PPC or .22 PPC only, disc. 1989).

CLASSIC GRADE - .243 Win., .270 Win., .30-06, or 7mm Rem. Mag. cal., short (AI, disc. 1992), medium (AII), or long (AIII) action, classic styled stock, finely checkered French walnut with matte lacquer finish. Disc. 1985, reintroduced 1992-97.

	$895	$745	$600	$545	$475	$430	$400

Last MSR was $1,050.

Add $50 for Mag. cal.
Add $35 for long action.
Add $120-$135 for left hand action (disc. 1994) (.270 Win. or 7mm Rem. Mag cal. only).
In 1992, the Classic Grade was once again imported into the U.S. in .243 Win., .270 Win., .30-06, or 7mm Rem. Mag. cal.

DELUXE LIGHTWEIGHT RIFLE - available in short action (AI) in .17 Rem., .222 Rem., or .223 Rem. cal., medium action (AII) in .22-250 Rem., .243 Win., .308 Win., or 7mm-08 Rem. cal., or long action (AIII) in .25-06 Rem., .270 Win., .280 Rem., .30- 06, 7mm Rem. Mag., .300 Win. Mag., .300 Wby. Mag., .338 Win. Mag., .375 H&H, or .416 Rem. Mag. (new 1991) cal., 21¼, 21¾, or 22 in. barrel, deluxe quality skipline checkered walnut stock with rosewood forend tip. Disc. 1997.

	$1,185	$965	$750	$650	$595	$540	$500

Last MSR was $1,475.

Add $35 for long action.
Add $50-$70 for Mag. cals.
Add $150-$175 for left-hand action (disc. 1994, available in long action only).

SAFARI GRADE - available in long (AIII) action only, .300 Win. Mag. (disc. 1989), .338 Win. Mag., .375 H&H, or .416 Rem. Mag. (new 1991) cal., deluxe walnut with sculptured cheekpiece, 22 in. barrel, 4 shot mag., open sights, sling swivels. Disc. 1996.

	$2,235	$1,785	$1,475	$1,250	$1,050	$900	$795

Last MSR was $2,765.

S

Grading	100%	98%	95%	90%	80%	70%	60%

SUPER DELUXE - a limited edition rifle available on special order only, various cals. are available in the short (AI), medium (AII), and long (AIII) actions, presentation grade walnut with both checkering and carving, rosewood forend tip. Disc. 1997.

			$2,400	$1,825	$1,475	$1,250	$1,050	$900	$795

Last MSR was $3,100.

SAKO 75 HUNTER - available in 5 action sizes, .17 Rem. (new 1998), .222 Rem. (new 1998), .223 Rem. (new 1998), .22-250 Rem., .243 Win., .308 Win., 7mm-08 Rem., .25-06 Rem., .270 Win., .280 Rem., .30-06, .270 Wby. Mag. (disc. 2001), 7mm Rem. Ultra Mag. (new 2002), 7mm Wby. Mag., 7mm STW, 7mm Rem. Mag., .300 Win. Mag., .300 Wby. Mag., .300 Rem. Ultra Mag. (new 2000), .338 Win. Mag., .340 Wby. Mag., .375 H&H, or .416 Rem. Mag. (disc. 2001) cal., hammer forged barrel, utilizes 3 locking lugs, mechanical ejector, 5 bolt sliding guides with 70 degree bolt lift, 3-position rear tang safety, available with top loading fixed mag. (hinged floorplate, .300 Rem. Ultra Mag., .416 Rem. Mag., and 7mm Rem. Ultra mag. cals. only), or detachable staggered 4-6 shot mag., checkered walnut stock, approx. 7¾ lbs. New 1997.

MSR	$1,129		$960	$780	$655	$560	$485	$430	$400

Add $34 for Mag. cals.

✳ *Sako 75 Deluxe* - same cals. as Sako 75 Hunter, features hinged floorplate and deluxe walnut stock with checkering, approx. 7¾ lbs. New 1997.

MSR	$1,653		$1,425	$1,175	$915	$735	$625	$550	$500

Add $35 for Mag. cals.

✳ *Sako 75 Stainless Synthetic* - available in .22-250 Rem., .243 Win., .25-06 Rem., .270 Win., .30-06, .308 Win., .300 Win. Mag., .300 Wby. Mag. (new 1999), .300 Rem. Ultra Mag. (new 2000), 7mm-08 Rem. (new 1998), 7mm STW (new 1998), 7mm Rem. Mag., 7mm Rem. Ultra Mag. (new 2002), .338 Win. Mag., or .375 H&H cal., 3-4 shot detachable mag. (except for floorplate with Rem. Ultra Mag. cals.), features black composite stock with soft rubber grip inserts in pistol grip and forearm area, matte stainless steel metal, 7¾ lbs. New 1997.

MSR	$1,239		$1,050	$840	$685				

Add $35 for Mag. cals.

✳ *Sako 75 Stainless Walnut* - .270 Win., .30-06, .300 Win. Mag., .300 Wby. Mag., .338 Win. Mag., 7mm STW, or 7mm Rem. Mag. cal., features checkered walnut stock and forearm. Importation began 1999.

MSR	$1,239		$1,050	$840	$685				

Add $35 for Mag. cals.

✳ *Sako 75 Varmint* - .17 Rem., .22-250 Rem., .222 Rem., .223 Rem., 22PPC (new 1999), or 6mmPPC (new 1999) cal., 23 5/8 in. heavy barrel w/o sights and beavertail forend, 5 or 6 shot detachable mag., 8 5/8 lbs. New 1998.

MSR	$1,337		$1,215	$915	$760	$655	$550	$475	$425

✳ *Sako 75 Stainless Varmint Laminated* - .22-250 Rem., .222 Rem., .223 Rem., 22PPC, 6mmPPC, or 7mm-08 Rem. (new 2002), similar to Sako 75 Varmint, features stainless steel action and barrel, lbrown aminated wood stock, 9 lbs. New 1999.

MSR	$1,448		$1,250	$1,025	$815				

✳ *Sako 75 80th Anniversary Model* - .375 H&H cal., limited edition rifle featuring Mauser style claw extractor, premium grade checkered walnut with ebony forend tip, cold hammer forged match grade barrel has ¼ rib with open sights, 5 shot internal mag. with hinged floorplate, includes Swarovski PV-1 scope and case, only 80 rifles (serial numbered 200101 – 200180) mfg. 2001 only.

MSR	$15,960		$13,750	$10,500	$8,750	$7,500			

✳ *Sako 75 Super Deluxe* - a limited edition rifle available on special order only, presentation grade walnut with both checkering and carving, rosewood forend tip.

Please contact Beretta USA Corp. directly for a price quotation on this special order model.

Grading	100%	98%	95%	90%	80%	70%	60%

SALERI, W.R. di SALERI WILLIAM & C. snc

Current longun manufacturer located in Gardone, Italy.

W.R. Saleri manufactures high quality O/U shotguns (Continental model) and single barrel rifles (Viper model). Please contact the company directly for more information, including pricing and availability (see Trademark Index).

SAMCO GLOBAL ARMS, INC.

Current importer and distributor located in Miami, FL. Dealer sales.

Samco Global Arms currently imports a variety of foreign and domestic surplus military rifles (including various contract Mausers, Loewe, Steyr, Czech, Lee Enfield, etc.). Most of these guns are in the $95-$1,500 range and they offer excellent values to both shooters and collectors. Samco also sold newly remanufactured sporting rifles (German or Spanish) in .308 Win. or 7x57mm cal. These sporters ranged in value from approx. $225-$325. During 2000, Samco also received some older Schmidt-Rubin carbines and rifles chambered in 7.5mm Swiss (Model 11 cartridge) - these are priced in the $200-$575 range, depending on configuration and condition.

SAN SWISS ARMS AG

Current company established during late 2000, with headquarters located in Neuhausen, Switzblueerland. Dealer and distributor sales.

During the end of 2000, SIG Arms AG was purchased by SAN Swiss Arms AG, a newly formed company. Unchanged are the 140 years of expertise in the development and manufacture of firearms for the military, law enforcement, and civilian market. Also firmly in place is the group of companies that represent numerous renowned brands and products. This new group includes 5 independently operational companies – Blaser Jadgwaffen GmbH located in Isny, Germany, Hämmerli AG located in Lenzburg, Switzerland, J.P. Sauer & Sohn GmbH located in Eckernförde, Germany, SIG Arms, Inc. (U.S.A.) located in Exeter, NH, and SAN Swiss Arms AG, located in Neuhausen, Switzerland. Current trademarks include: Blaser, Hämmerli, Mauser Magnum rifles, Sauer rifles, and Sig-Sauer pistols. Please refer to these individual listings for current information and pricing.

swiss
arms
SAN Swiss Arms AG

SARASQUETA, FELIX

Previous manufacturer located in Eibar, Spain. Previously imported and distributed by SAE (Spain America Enterprises), Inc. located in Miami, FL.

SHOTGUNS: O/U

MODEL MERKE - 12 ga. only, boxlock action, 22 or 27 in. separated barrels, single non- selective trigger, blue only, extractors, recoil pad. Imported 1986 only.

$255	$215	$200	$190	$180	$170	$160

Last MSR was $291.

SARASQUETA, J.J.

Previous manufacturer located in Eibar, Spain. Imported until 1984 by American Arms, Inc. located in Overland Park, KS.

SHOTGUNS: SxS

MODEL 107 E - 12, 16, or 20 ga., ejectors, various barrel lengths, checkered walnut stock and forearm, double triggers.

$360	$290	$270	$255	$240	$215	$200

Last MSR was $435.

MODELS 119E-132E-1882E - more deluxe versions of Model 107E.

$470	$375	$340	$315	$285	$255	$230

Last MSR was $570.

S

Grading	100%	98%	95%	90%	80%	70%	60%

MODEL 130 E - more deluxe version of Model 119 E.

	$800	$635	$590	$555	$515	$480	$450

Last MSR was $960.

MODEL 131 E - action similar to Model 107 E, except has deluxe engraving.

	$1,050	$845	$770	$710	$665	$620	$585

Last MSR was $1,250.

MODEL 1882 E LUXE - double triggers, moderate engraving, otherwise similar to Model 107 E.

	$825	$660	$615	$565	$520	$480	$450

Last MSR was $990.

* *Model 1882 E Luxe w/gold inlays* - SST, extensive engraving.

	$1,120	$920	$850	$790	$740	$695	$650

Last MSR was $1,320.

* *Model 1882 E Luxe w/silver inlays* - SST, extensive engraving.

	$1,055	$855	$795	$740	$700	$660	$630

Last MSR was $1,260.

MODEL 150 E - 12 or 16 ga., single trigger, ejectors, select walnut and extensive engraving.

	$1,285	$1,035	$960	$895	$835	$770	$695

Last MSR was $1,500.

* *Model 150 E Trap* - similar to Model 150 E, except trap dimensions on stock.

	$1,360	$1,125	$1,010	$940	$875	$790	$720

Last MSR was $1,600.

SARASQUETA, VICTOR

Previous manufacturer located in Eibar, Spain. Trademark was sold to Diarm S.A. circa 1986.

SHOTGUNS:SxS

MODEL 3 BOXLOCK - 12, 16, or 20 ga., all standard barrel lengths and chokes, boxlock, double triggers, checkered English style stock and forearm.

	100%	98%	95%	90%	80%	70%	60%
Extractors	$445	$395	$350	$295	$250	$215	$185
Auto ejectors	$575	$515	$450	$375	$300	$250	$225

HAMMERLESS SIDELOCK - 12, 16, 20, 28 ga., or .410 bore, SxS, barrel length and choke to order, straight English style stock, models differ as to amount of engraving, grade of wood, and overall quality as follows:

Add 25% for 28 ga.
Add 30% for .410 bore.

MODEL 4 - extractors.

	$620	$550	$525	$495	$450	$415	$360

MODEL 4E - auto ejectors.

	$680	$605	$580	$550	$505	$470	$415

MODEL 203 - extractors.

	$650	$570	$545	$515	$475	$435	$380

MODEL 203E - auto ejectors.

	$710	$625	$600	$570	$530	$490	$435

MODEL 6E

	$800	$715	$690	$660	$615	$580	$525

MODEL 7E

	$855	$770	$745	$715	$670	$635	$580

Grading	100%	98%	95%	90%	80%	70%	60%
MODEL 10E	$1,735	$1,595	$1,485	$1,405	$1,320	$1,240	$1,100
MODEL 11E	$1,870	$1,680	$1,595	$1,515	$1,430	$1,350	$1,265
MODEL 12E	$2,145	$1,900	$1,790	$1,705	$1,570	$1,430	$1,375

SARDIUS

Please refer to the Sirkis Industries section in this text.

SARRIUGARTE, FRANCISO S.A.

Previous manufacturer located in Elgoibar, Spain. Previously part of the Diarm S.A. Group which was imported and distributed by American Arms, Inc. located in North Kansas City, MO.

SARSILMAZ

Current manufacturer established during 1880, and located in Istanbul, Turkey. Currently distributed beginning 2000 by PMC, located in Boulder City, NV. Previously imported and distributed until 2000 by Armsport, Inc. located in Miami, FL.

Sarsilmaz offers a wide range of shotguns in O/U, semi-auto, and slide action configurations. Some of these models are not available in the U.S. Please contact the importer directly for more information regarding availability and U.S. pricing.

SAUER, J.P., & SOHN

Current manufacturer located in Eckernförde, Germany since 1751 (originally Prussia). Currently imported by SIG Arms located in Exeter, NH since 1995. Previously manufactured in Suhl pre-WWII. Rifles were previously imported until 1995 by the Paul Company Inc. located in Wellsville, KS and until 1994 by G.U., Inc. located in Omaha, NE.

In 1972, J.P. Sauer & Sohn entered into a cooperative agreement with SIG. During 2000, SAN Swiss Arms AG purchased SIG Arms AG, including the J.P. Sauer & Sohn trademark. Production remains in Eckernförde, Germany.

DRILLINGS & COMBINATION GUNS

SAUER MODEL 3000 DRILLING - available in either 16 ga./.30-06, 6.5x57R, 7x57R, 7x65R or 12 ga./.222 Rem. (disc.), .243 Win., .30-06, 6.5x57R, 7x57R, 7x65R, or 9.3x74R cal., Greener cross-bolt and double barrel lug locking, cocking indicators, front set trigger, automatic sight, walnut pistol grip stock with hog-back and cheekpiece, Grade III scroll engraving, 7¼ lbs. Importation disc. 1999.

	$4,300	$3,600	$3,100	$2,675	$2,200	$1,800	$1,400

Last MSR was $4,600.

This model was also previously imported by Weatherby and Colt - please refer to separate listings for more information.

* ***Luxury Grade*** - similar to Model 3000 standard, except select root timber and extensive engraving featuring two animals. Importation disc. 1999.

	$5,550	$4,875	$4,400	$3,875	$3,475	$3,000	$2,575

Last MSR was $6,100.

COMBO BBF 54 O/U - standard grade combination gun, 16 ga./.222 Rem., .243 Win., 6.5x57R, 7x57R, 7x65R, and .30-06 cals., ejectors, double triggers with front set trigger, moderate engraving on coin finished receiver, Greener cross-bolt with double barrel lugs, 6 lbs. Importation disc. 1986.

	$2,200	$2,060	$1,760	$1,565	$1,380	$1,250	$1,125

Last MSR was $2,495.

S

Grading	100%	98%	95%	90%	80%	70%	60%

✳ *Luxury Grade* - similar to Combo BBF 54, except game scene engraved and deluxe crotch walnut.

	$2,450	$2,200	$2,000	$1,785	$1,600	$1,475	$1,300

Last MSR was $2,745.

LUFTWAFFE SURVIVAL DRILLING - 12 or 16 ga. (65mm) SxS over 9.3x74R, 28 in. barrels, large eagle swastika on stock and breech end of right barrel. Originally mfg. for Luftwaffe pilots during WWII.

	$4,500	$4,000	$3,600	$3,200	$2,600	$2,400	$2,200

Add 20% for original aluminum case and accessories.

SAUER MODEL 3000E DRILLING - see listing under Colt Sauer Drilling.

PISTOLS: SEMI-AUTO

MODEL 1913 POCKET AUTOMATIC - .32 ACP cal., 7 shot, 3 in. barrel, fixed sights, blue, black rubber grips. Mfg. 1913-1930.

	$295	$225	$185	$165	$155	$145	$135

MODEL 1913 25 AUTOMATIC - .25 ACP cal., 7 shot, 2½ in. barrel, fixed sights, blue, black rubber grips. Mfg. 1913-1930.

	$325	$250	$200	$175	$150	$140	$135

MODEL 28 - .25 ACP cal., 7 shot, 3 in. barrel, fixed sights, blue, black rubber grips. Mfg. 1930-1938.

	$300	$240	$185	$170	$155	$145	$135

BEHÖRDEN "AUTHORITY" M1930 MODEL - .32 ACP cal., 3 in. barrel, blue only, black plastic grips.

	$325	$240	$200	$175	$150	$145	$135

Add $1,000 for very rare alloy frame example.

MODEL 38 H DOUBLE ACTION AUTOMATIC - .22 LR (extremely rare), .32 ACP, or .380 ACP (rare) cal., 3¼ in. barrel, fixed sights, blue, plastic grips. Mfg. 1938-1945.

.32 ACP	$395	$325	$240	$205	$185	$165	$150
.380 ACP	$3,500	$2,750	$2,000	$1,500	$1,250	$995	$775
.22 LR	$4,000	$3,000	$2,200	$1,600	$1,250	$995	$775

Add 10% for Waffenamt proofing.
Add 15%-25% for police markings.
Add 60% for alloy frame.

RIFLES: BOLT ACTION

SAUER PRE-WWII BOLT ACTION RIFLE - most popular European cals. and .30-06, 22 or 24 in. barrel, raised solid rib, Krupp steel, double set triggers, folding 3 leaf express sight, checkered sporter stock. Mfg. pre-WWII.

	$715	$550	$495	$440	$360	$330	$305

MODEL 90 STANDARD - .22-250 Rem., .222 Rem. (only 3 mfg.), .243 Win., .25-06 Rem., 6.5x55mm, .270 Win., .30-06, .308 Win. (late mfg.), .300 Win. Mag., .300 Wby. Mag., 7mm Rem. Mag., .375 H&H, or .458 Win. Mag. cal., 24 in. barrel, 3 or 4 shot detachable mag., satin, oil finished checkered walnut stock with Monte Carlo cheekpiece and rosewood forend cap, 2 stage set trigger, free floated barrel, approx. 7½ lbs. Importation disc.

	$1,000	$875	$750	$625	$550	$500	$450

Last MSR was $1,175.

Early importation rifles came standard with a half stock and barrel band, and also had European sling swivels with milled stopsin 1989, this model's designed changed to look more like the Colt Sauer rifle (w/o sights, gloss finished stock and set trigger was removed). During 1985-1989, Sauer exported to Sigarms 2,300 Model 90 rifles, 1,100 of these were in Mag. cals.

Grading	100%	98%	95%	90%	80%	70%	60%

❋ Model 90 Stutzen - .22-250 Rem., .222 Rem. (3 mfg.), or .243 Win., Mannlicher style full stock, not available in European or Mag. cals. Importation disc. 1989.

	100%	98%	95%	90%	80%	70%	60%
	$1,200	$995	$850	$750	$650	$475	$500

Last MSR was $1,225.

❋ Safari Model - .458 Win. Mag cal., 23.62 in. barrel, 10½ lbs. Imported 1986-1988 only.

	$1,250	$950	$850	$750	$650	$575	$500

Last MSR was $1,675.

MODEL 90 SUPREME (LUX) - .243 Win., .25-06 Rem., 6.5x55 Swedish, .270 Win., .30-06, .300 Win. Mag., .300 Wby. Mag., 7mm Rem. Mag., .338 Win. Mag., or .375 H&H cal., similar to Model 90, satin finished deluxe stock with Monte Carlo cheekpiece and rosewood forearm and pistol grip caps, gold trigger, no sights, 7.1 - 7.7 lbs. Importation 1987-1998.

	$1,300	$1,050	$875	$775	$650	$475	$500

Last MSR was $1,350.

Add $32 for Mag. cals.
On Models 90 Lux and Supreme add 69% for Grade I engraving, 105% for Grade II, 128% for Grade III, and 164% for Grade IV.

❋ Safari Model (Lux)
While advertised, this model was never imported. MSR was set at $1,795.

❋ Model 90 Stutzen (Lux)
While advertised, this model was never imported. MSR was set at $1,200.

MODEL 200 BOLT ACTION - available in 15 cals. between .243 Win. and .375 H&H, short and medium actions only, 23.62 in. unique interchangeable barrels, 6 lug bolt, easily detachable stock and forearm, optional set trigger, detachable mag. with hidden release button, 7.7 lbs. Production disc. 1993.

	$1,225	$925	$800	$700	$600	$525	$450

Last MSR was $1,395.

Add $100 for 7mm Rem. Mag. or .300 Win. Mag. cal.
Add $300 for extra interchangeable barrel.
During 1986-1989, Sauer exported to Sigarms 4,170 Model 200 rifles, 1,370 of these were in Mag. cals.

❋ Model 200 Lightweight - similar to Model 200, only with alloy receiver, 6.6 lbs.

	$1,225	$925	$800	$700	$600	$525	$450

Last MSR was $1,395.

Add $150 for left-hand version.

❋ Model 200 Lux - similar to Model 200, except has deluxe walnut, rosewood forend tip and pistol grip cap, marmorized bolt and gold trigger.

	$1,395	$1,175	$925	$800	$700	$600	$525

Last MSR was $1,595.

❋ American 200 Lux - similar to Model 200 Lux, except has high gloss Monte Carlo stock, 24 in. barrel, jeweled bolt, and gold trigger.

	$1,395	$1,175	$925	$800	$700	$600	$525

Last MSR was $1,595.

Add $150 for left-hand version.

❋ European 200 Lux - similar to Model 200 Lux, except has European configured stock with Schnabel forearm, 26 in. barrel.

	$1,395	$1,175	$925	$800	$700	$600	$525

Last MSR was $1,595.

Add $95 for left-hand version.

❋ Model 200 Carbon Fiber - similar to Model 200, except has carbon fiber stock. Imported 1987-88 only.

	$800	$700	$625	$565	$500	$465	$430

Last MSR was $1,200.

S

Grading	100%	98%	95%	90%	80%	70%	60%

MODEL 202 SUPREME (LUX) - .22-250 Rem. (new 2001), .243 Win. (disc. 1998, resumed 2000), .25-06 Rem., .270 Win., .30-06, .308 Win., 6.5x55mm Swedish (disc. 2000), or 7x64mm (disc. 1997) cal., steel receiver, modular design allowing barrel change within 2 minutes, dual safety, 2 piece figured walnut stock, cocking indicator, detachable 3-5 shot mag., takedown with interchangeable barrels, right or left hand action, 7.7 lbs. Importation began 1994.

MSR	$1,385		$1,175	$950	$800	$700	$600	$550	$475

Also available in left-hand action in .270 Win. (disc. 2000) or .30-06 cal.

* **Model 202 Supreme Magnum (Lux)** - .300 Win. Mag., .300 Wby. Mag., .338 Win. Mag. (disc. 1997), .375 H&H, 7mm Rem. Mag., 6.5x68mm (importation disc. 1997), or 8x68mm (inportation disc. 1997) cal., converts to 7 cals. Importation began 1994.

MSR	$1,385		$1,175	$950	$800	$700	$600	$550	$475

Was also available until 2000 in left-hand action in .300 Win. Mag. or 7mm Rem. Mag. cal.

* **Model 202 Standard** - similar to Model 202 Synthetic, except has checkered walnut stock and forearm, 7½ lbs. Importation began 2001.

MSR	$1,249		$1,120	$900	$775	$675	$575	$525	$450

* **Model 202 Synthetic** - .22-250 Rem. (new 2001), .243 Win. (new 2001), .25-06 Rem., .270 Win., .30-06, .308 Win., .300 Win. Mag., 7mm Rem. Mag. (new 2000), .300 Wby. Mag., .375 H&H, or 6.5x55mm Swedish (disc. 2000) cal., features black synthetic stock, 24 or 26 in. barrel w/o sights, 7.7 lbs. Importation began 1999.

MSR	$1,259		$1,125	$900	$775	$675	$575	$525	$450

* **Model 202 Lightweight** - .22-250 Rem., .243 Win., .25-06 Rem., .270 Win., .30-06, or .308 Win. cal., 24 in. fluted barrel w/o sights, aluminum alloy receiver with integral Weaver rail, Ilaflon coated metal, black synthetic stock. Importation began 2001.

MSR	$1,395		$1,185	$950	$800	$700	$600	$550	$475

* **Model 202 Varminter** - .22-250 Rem., .243 Win., or .25-06 Rem. cal., 24 in. match grade fluted bull barrel with no sights, 3 shot mag., matte black finish, adj. cheekpiece on checkered Turkish walnut stock, 8½ lbs. Importation began 2001.

MSR	$1,495		$1,275	$1,025	$850	$750	$625	$550	$475

* **Model 202 Super Grade**

While advertised in 1994, this model was never imported. MSR was set at $1,020.

MODEL 202 HUNTER MATCH

While advertised in 1994, this model was never imported. MSR was set at $1,495.

MODEL 202 ALASKA

While advertised in 1994, this model was never imported. MSR was set at $1,335.

MODEL 205 TR TARGET - 6.5x55mm or .308 Win. cal., true left hand variation, 200 meter diopter sights, modular design allows changing single components including caliber, free floating barrel with vent. forearm, 5 shot mag., interchangeable barrel systems, 12.1 lbs. Imported 1994-97.

	$1,775	$1,575	$1,400	$1,250	$1,100	$950	$825

Last MSR was $1,900.

SSE 3000 PRECISION RIFLE - .308 Win. cal., very accurate, law enforcement counter Sniper Rifle, built to customer specifications.

	$4,845	$3,655	$3,200	$2,850	$2,500	$2,275	$2,000

SSG 2000 - available in .223 Rem., 7.5mm Swiss, .300 Wby. Mag., or .308 Win. (standard) cal., bolt action, 4 shot mag., no sights, deluxe sniper rifle featuring thumbhole style walnut stock with stippling and thumbwheel adj. cheekpiece, 13 lbs. Importation disc. 1986.

	$2,480	$2,260	$1,950	$1,700	$1,500	$1,300	$1,100

Last MSR was $2,850.

This model was available in .223 Rem., .300 Wby. Mag., or 7.5mm cal. by special order only.

Grading	100%	98%	95%	90%	80%	70%	60%

SSG 3000 - .223 Rem., 22½ in. barrel, Parker-Hale bipod, 2-stage match trigger, includes 2½-10X x52mm Zeiss scope, 200 mfg. for Swiss police.

		100%	98%	95%	90%	80%	70%	60%
		$12,000	$10,000	$8,500	$7,000	$6,750	$5,500	$4,250

SSG 3000 PRECISION TACTICAL RIFLE (CURRENT MFG.) - .308 Win. cal., modular design, ambidextrous McMillan tactical stock with adj. comb, 23.4 in. barrel with muzzle brake, 5 shot detachable mag., supplied in 3 different levels, Level I does not have bipod or scope, cased, 12 lbs. New 2000.

	MSR	$2,560		$2,100	$1,875	$1,600	$1,375	$1,100	$975	$850

Add $930 for Level II (includes Leupold Vari-X III 3.5-10x40mm duplex scope and Harris bipod).
Add $1,940 for Level III (includes Leupold Mark 4 M1-10x40mm Mil-Dot scope and Harris bipod).
Add $750 for .22 conversion kit.

SHOTGUNS

MODEL 60 SXS - various ga.'s, boxlock action, DT, extractors, checkered walnut stock and forearm, this model was the standard model of its period.

	$975	$875	$750	$650	$550	$450	$395

Add 20% for 20 ga.

ROYAL MODEL SXS - 12, 16 or 20 ga., 26, 28, or 30 in. barrels, various chokes, boxlock, scalloped engraved frame, cocking indicators, SST, auto ejectors, Krupp steel barrel, checkered pistol grip stock. Mfg. 1955-1977.

	$1,650	$1,375	$1,210	$1,100	$880	$770	$660

Add 20% for 20 ga.

ARTEMIS SXS - 12 ga., 28 in. barrels, mod. and full choke, H&H type sidelock, SST, auto ejector, Krupp steel, checkered pistol grip stock. Mfg. 1966-1977.

✳ *Grade I* - fine line engraved.

	$5,500	$4,620	$3,850	$3,520	$3,080	$2,640	$2,200

✳ *Grade II* - extensive engraving.

	$6,600	$5,500	$4,840	$4,235	$3,850	$3,300	$3,080

GRADE 380 SXS

	$4,500	$4,000	$3,500	$3,000	$2,500	$2,200	$1,500

GRADE F-40 SXS

Rarity factor precludes accurate price evaluation.

MODEL F-45 SXS

	$12,000	$10,500	$9,000	$8,000	$6,500	$5,000	$3,200

MODEL F-60 SXS

	$23,000	$20,000	$17,000	$14,000	$12,000	$9,000	$5,000

MODEL 66 O/U FIELD GUN - 12 ga., 28 in. mod. and full, Krupp steel barrels, H&H type sidelocks, SST, auto ejectors, checkered pistol grip stock, available in three grades of engraving. Mfg. 1966-1975.

	100%	98%	95%	90%	80%	70%	60%
Grade I	$2,200	$1,760	$1,540	$1,320	$1,100	$880	$770
Grade II	$3,080	$2,420	$1,980	$1,650	$1,430	$1,210	$990
Grade III	$3,850	$3,300	$2,860	$2,420	$1,980	$1,650	$1,320

MODEL 66 O/U SKEET GUN - similar to Field Gun, with 26 in. VR skeet bored barrel and vent. forearm. Mfg. 1966-1975.

S

Grading	100%	98%	95%	90%	80%	70%	60%

MODEL 66 O/U TRAP GUN - similar to 66 Skeet, with 30 in. barrels, full and full, or mod. and full choke, trap style stock.

Grade I	$2,090	$1,760	$1,540	$1,320	$1,100	$880	$770
Grade II	$3,080	$2,420	$1,980	$1,650	$1,430	$1,210	$880
Grade III	$3,850	$3,300	$2,860	$2,420	$1,980	$1,650	$1,320

SAUER/FRANCHI STANDARD GRADE O/U - 12 ga. only, double triggers, checkered walnut stock and forearm, SST, blueblue finish only, sling swivels, VR. Importation disc. 1986.

$375	$340	$315	$290	$275	$260	$245

Last MSR was $785.

* ✱ *Regent Grade* - similar to Standard grade, except has single trigger and lightly engraved silver finished receiver. Importation disc. 1986.

$475	$395	$350	$310	$290	$275	$265

Last MSR was $825.

* ✱ *Favorit Grade* - similar to Regent Grade, except has elaborate scroll engraving on coin finished receiver, gold-plated trigger. Importation disc. 1986.

$550	$495	$450	$420	$385	$350	$300

Last MSR was $875.

* ✱ *Diplomat Grade* - similar to Favorit Grade, except has more elaborate scroll engraving and with model name gold filled on receiver sides and barrel, extra grain French walnut, cased.

$875	$750	$625	$550	$495	$460	$435

Last MSR was $1,520.

SAUER/FRANCHI SPORTING S O/U - 12 ga. only, 28 in. barrels, ejectors, SST, select European walnut with checkered stock and forearm, 10mm VR, plain silver finished receiver with model name gold filled on both sides. Importation disc. 1986.

$800	$700	$600	$500	$450	$420	$395

Last MSR was $1,375.

SAUER/FRANCHI MODEL TRAP O/U - similar to Sporting S, except has 29 in. barrels, trap chokes and stock dimensions. Importation disc. 1986.

$875	$750	$625	$550	$495	$460	$435

Last MSR was $1,375.

SAUER/FRANCHI MODEL SKEET O/U - similar to Sporting S, except has skeet chokes. Importation disc. 1986.

$875	$750	$625	$550	$495	$460	$435

Last MSR was $1,375.

SAVAGE ARMS, INC.

Current manufacturer located in Westfield, MA since 1959. Previously manufactured in Utica, NY - later manufacture was in Chicopee Falls, MA. Distributor sales only.

This company originally started in Utica, NY in 1895. The Model 1895 was initially manufactured by Marlin between 1895-1899. The company was renamed Savage Arms Co. in 1899. After WWI, the name was again changed to the Savage Arms Corporation. Savage moved to Chicopee Falls, MA circa 1946 (to its J. Stevens Arms Co. plants). In the mid- 1960s the company became The Savage Arms Division of American Hardware Corp., which later became The Emhart Corporation. This division was sold in September 1981, and became Savage Industries, Inc. located in Westfield, MA (since the move in 1960). On November 1, 1989, Savage Arms Inc. acquired the majority of assets of Savage Industries, Inc.

Savage Arms, Inc. will offer service and parts on their current line of firearms only (those manufactured after Nov. 1, 1989). These models include the 24, 99, and 110 plus the imported Model 312. Warranty and repair claims for products not acquired by Savage Arms, Inc. will remain the responsibility of Savage Industries, Inc. For information regarding the repair and/or parts of Savage Industries, Inc. firearms, please refer to the Trademark Index in the back of this

text. Parts for pre- 1989 Savage Industries, Inc. firearms may be obtained by contacting the Gun Parts Corporation located in West Hurley, NY (listed in Trademark Index). Savage Arms, Inc. has older records/info. on pistols, the Model 24, older mfg. Model 99s, and Model 110 only. A factory letter authenticating the configuration of a particular specimen may be obtained by contacting Mr. John Callahan (see Trademark Index for listings and address). The charge for this service is $15.00 per gun, and $20.00 per gun for Models 1895, 1899, and 99 rifles - please allow 2-4 weeks for an adequate response.

For more Savage model information, please refer to the Serialization section in the back of this text.

Please refer to the Blue Book of Modern Black Powder Values by Dennis Adler (now online also) for more information and prices on Savage's lineup of modern black powder models. For more information and current pricing on both new and used Savage airguns, please refer to the Blue Book of Modern Airguns by by Dr. Robert Beeman & John Allen (now online also).

COMBINATION GUNS

All Model 24s are under the domain of Savage Arms, Inc.

MODEL 24 O/U - .22 LR over .410 bore, open rifle sight, visible hammer, break open, plain pistol grip stock. Mfg. 1950-1965.

$160	$130	$110	$100	$85	$70	$55

This model featured top lever opening, except on the Models 24S and 24MS.

MODEL 24B-DL

$185	$155	$135	$120	$100	$90	$80

MODEL 24S - similar to Model 24, with 20 ga. or .410 bore barrel, sidelever, dovetail for scope. Mfg. 1964-1971.

$185	$155	$135	$120	$100	$90	$80

MODEL 24MS - similar to Model 24S, with .22 WRM barrel. Mfg. 1964-1971.

$170	$140	$120	$110	$90	$85	$70

MODEL 24DL - similar to Model 24S, with top lever, satin chrome frame and checkered stock. Mfg. 1962-1969.

$170	$140	$120	$110	$90	$85	$70

MODEL 24MDL - similar to Model 24DL, with .22 WRM barrel and chrome frame. Mfg. 1962-1969.

$175	$145	$125	$115	$95	$85	$70

MODEL 24FG - similar to Model 24D, w/o Monte Carlo stock, with top lever. Mfg. 1972-disc.

$165	$130	$110	$90	$85	$65	$55

MODEL 24 FIELD - .22 LR or .22 Mag. over 20 ga. or .410 bore, lightweight field version, 24 in. separated barrels, 3 in. chambers, 6¾ lbs. Disc. 1989.

$185	$150	$120	$100	$85	$80	$70

Last MSR was $209.

MODEL 24F (PREDATOR) - choice of .22 LR, .22 Hornet, .222 Rem. (disc. 1989), .223 Rem., or .30-30 Win. cal., over 12, 20 ga., or .410 bore (mfg. 1998-2000), 3 in. chamber, 24 in. barrels, 12 ga. barrel is available either with fixed choke or choke tube, wood (disc.) or matte black Dupont Rynite synthetic stock, hammer block safety, DTs, approx. 8 lbs. New 1989.

MSR	$504	$450	$360	$285	$240	$210	$180	$165

Add $27 for 12 ga.

Add $55 for .410 bore adaptor (12 ga. only, disc. 2000).

Add $14 for Camo Rynite stock (disc., Model 24F-T, Turkey Model-12 ga./.22 Hornet or .223 Rem. cal. only).

The .22 LR cal. is available with 20 ga. barrel only.

MODEL 24V - similar to Model 24, with .22 Hornet (disc. 1984), .222 Rem. (1967 only), .223 Rem., .30-30 Win., .357 Max., or .357 Mag.(disc.), 20ga., 3in. chamber, 24in. barrels, single trigger, 7 lbs. Mfg. 1971-89.

$300	$265	$230	$200	$175	$150	$130

S

Grading	100%	98%	95%	90%	80%	70%	60%

MODEL 24D - .22 LR or .22 Mag. over .410 bore or 20 ga., black or case hardened frame, game scene decoration was eliminated in 1974, forearm not checkered after 1976. Introduced 1971.

	$250	$220	$185	$150	$130	$115	$105

MODEL 24C CAMPER'S COMPANION - nickel finish, .22 LR over 20 ga., 20 in. barrel cylinder bore, buttplate opens to store ten .22 LR cartridges and one 20 ga. shell in buttstock, carrying case, 5¾ lbs. Mfg. 1972-1988.

	$200	$165	$130	$115	$105	$95	$80

Last MSR was $239.

Add 10% for nickel finish (Model 24CS - shipped with pistol grip stock also).

MODEL 24 VS - similar to Model 24CS, only .357 Mag. over 20 ga., nickel finish, accessory pistol grip stock is included.

	$250	$210	$185	$160	$145	$135	$120

MODEL 2400 O/U - 12 ga. full choke barrel over .222 Rem. or .308 Win. rifle barrel, 23½ in. barrels, folding leaf sight, solid rib, dovetailed for scope mount, checkered Monte Carlo stock. Mfg. by Valmet between 1975-1980.

	$605	$550	$525	$495	$440	$415	$385

MODEL 389 - 12 ga. with 3 in. chamber over choice of .308 Win. or .222 Rem., choke tubes standard, hammerless, double triggers, checkered walnut stock and forearm with recoil pad. Mfg. 1988- 90 only.

	$800	$640	$550	$495	$435	$365	$300

Last MSR was $919.

PISTOLS: BOLT ACTION

MODEL 501F SPORT STRIKER - .22 LR cal., left-hand bolt, right side ejection, 10 in. button rifled barrel with scope blocks, 10 shot mag., grey fiberglass/graphite composite stock, 4 lbs. New 2000.

MSR	$216	$185	$165	$150	$140	$130	$125	$120

Add $42 for XP package (Model 501FXP) – includes scope and mounts.

MODEL 502F SPORT STRIKER - similar to Model 501F Sport Striker, except is .22 Mag. cal., and 5 shot mag. New 2000.

MSR	$238	$205	$180	$165	$150	$140	$130	$125

MODEL 510F STRIKER - .22-250 Rem., .223 Rem. (new 1999), .243 Win., .260 Rem. (mfg. 1999-2000), .308 Win., or 7mm-08 Rem. cal., left-hand short bolt action with right hand ejection, 14 in. free floating barrel, 2 shot internal box mag., blueblue barrel action, black composite stock with grooved forend and wide bottom swell, drilled and tapped, 5 lbs. New 1998.

MSR	$440	$385	$335	$285	$240	$210	$180	$165

MODEL 516FSS STRIKER - similar to 510F Striker, except has stainless steel barreled action. Mfg. 1998-2000.

	$410	$365	$320

Last MSR was $462.

✱ *Model 516FSAK Striker* - similar to 516FSS Striker, except has adj. muzzle brake (AMB). New 1998.

MSR	$531	$475	$390	$335

✱ *Model 516FSAK Striker Camo* - .300 WSM cal., similar to 516FSAK Striker, except has camo treatment stock. New 2002.

MSR	$538	$480	$395	$335

S

Grading	100%	98%	95%	90%	80%	70%	60%

MODEL 516BSAK/BSS SUPER STRIKER - similar cals. to Model 510F Striker, features dual pillar bedded short action and custom designed thumb-hole laminate grey stock, stainless steel frame and fluted 14 in. barrel with adj. muzzle brake (AMB), new ESP (Engineered Step Performance) adj. two-stage trigger, approx. 5 lbs. Mfg. 1999-2001.

$535 $430 $350

Last MSR was $618.

Subtract aprrox. $50 if w/o muzzle brake (Model 516BSS – disc. 2000).

PISTOLS: SEMI-AUTO

MODEL 1907 AUTO PISTOL - .32 ACP or .380 ACP cal., 9 (.380 ACP) or 10 (.32 ACP) shot mag., 3 13/16 (.32 ACP) or 4 5/16 (.380 ACP) in. barrel, blue, fixed sights, metal (early mfg. on .32 ACP only until serial no. 10,980) or hard rubber grips, exposed cocking piece. Mfg. 1910-1917.

.32 ACP	$425	$300	$175	$150	$125	$115	$100
.380 ACP	$550	$450	$350	$300	$250	$200	$150

Add large premiums for factory nickel, silver, or gold finish (rare).

There were three different types of pearl grips: the early variation was a snap-on with an S/A logo, screw-on with an indianhead logo, and the flared 1917 with no logo. Asking prices for the grips alone are in the $250-$1,000 range (this also applied to the Model 1915 Hammerless and Model 1917 Automatic).

MODEL 1915 HAMMERLESS - similar to Model 1907, with grip safety and no visible cocking piece. Mfg. 1915-1917.

.32 ACP	$525	$450	$375	$300	$250	$225	$200
.380 ACP	$650	$575	$500	$400	$300	$250	$200

Add 10% with original box and instruction manual.

MODEL 1917 AUTOMATIC - similar to Model 1907, with spur cocking piece and trapezoidal grips. Mfg. 1920-1928.

.32 ACP	$300	$250	$175	$145	$130	$110	$100
.380 ACP	$445	$400	$350	$300	$250	$200	$150

Add 10% with original box and instruction manual.

M1907 U.S. ARMY TEST TRIAL .45 ACP - .45 ACP cal., large version of Model 1910, exposed hammer. Approx. 400 mfg. 1907-1911 for military trials.

$7,500 $5,500 $4,500 $3,500 $3,000 $2,500 $2,000

Add 250% for experimental M1910 and M1911.
Add 100% if in original condition.

Most pistols were repurchased from the government, reconditioned (many reblue), and resold to the public as commercial models.

PISTOLS: SINGLE SHOT

MODEL 101 - .22 LR cal., 5½ in. barrel, single action, adj. sight, swing out barrel, blue, wood grips. Mfg. 1960-1968.

$150 $120 $95 $80 $70 $60 $50

RIFLES: DISC, CENTERFIRE & RIMFIRE

S

Savage made a wide variety of inexpensive, utilitarian rifles that to date have attracted mostly shooting interest, but little collector interest. A listing of these models may be found in the back of this text under "Serialization".

Grading	100%	98%	95%	90%	80%	70%	60%

MODEL 1895 - .303 Savage cal. only, lever action, mfg. in either carbine (22 in.), rifle (26 in.), or musket (30 in.) variations, round (scarce) or octagon barrel that has Marlin proofmark under the forend, open top, solid breech, side ejecting, 6 shot rotary mag., unfired shots indicator. Originally mfg. by Marlin, marked "Savage Repeating Arms Co. Utica, N.Y. U.S.A. Pat. Feb. 7, 1893.", approx. 6,000 mfg. 1895-1899, early models had hole in top of bolt - later ones were smooth.

	$1,500	$1,250	$995	$880	$770	$660	$495

Values assume rifle configuration - add a 100%+ premium for the carbine (rare) and musket (rare).

MODEL 1899 - improvement of Model 1895 with squared off front end of breech bolt and cocking indicator as opposed to viewing hole indicator. Early model 1899s have oblong cocking indicator located on the top of the breech bolt. In approx. 1908, this was changed to a pin on the upper tang. Older models have perch belly stocks and high gloss bluing (commanding premiums of 10%- 15%). A wide variety of special order features were available including special length barrels (up to 30 in.), pistol grip stocks, checkering, woods, plating, grades of engraving, sights, etc., all of which can command a moderate to sizeable premium.

Add 15% for takedown (added 1909).
Add 20% for .25-35 WCF, .32-40 WCF, or .38-55 WCF cal.

In 1905 Savage broadened the variety of this model and added the 1899A2, CD, BC, AB, Excelsior, Leader, Crescent, Victor, Rival, Premier, and Monarch (top-of-the-line model). Prices at the time ranged from $21 to $250 - quite a range of prices. Any factory engraved Savage 99 is rare (less than 1,000 mfg. to date) with values having to be computed one gun at a time. Engraved Model 1899s range from $2,000-$40,000, depending on the level of engraving and original condition. Because of this, the above values assume standard rifle with no engraving options (Grades A through G).

All Model 1899s & 99s fall within the domain of Savage Arms, Inc.

Rifles under ser. no. 90,000 should not be fired due to possible receiver cracking at rear left corner.

✳ *Model 1899A Rifle* - .303 Savage, .30-30 Win., .25-35 WCF, .32-40 WCF, .38-55 WCF, or .300 Sav., 26 in. round barrel, straight grip stock, cresent or steel shotgun butt, takedown added 1909. Mfg. 1899-1927, Short rifle (22 in.) mfg. 1899-1922.

	$795	$675	$600	$535	$475	$400	$325

✳ *Model 1899B Rifle* - .303 Savage, .30-30 Win., .25-35 WCF, .32-40 WCF, or .38- 55 WCF, 26 in. octagon barrel, straight grip stock, cresent or steel shotgun butt. Mfg. 1899-1915.

	$895	$800	$725	$650	$575	$500	$425

✳ *Model 1899C Rifle* - .303 Savage, .30-30 Win., .25-35 WCF, .32-40 WCF, or .38- 55 WCF, 26 in. half octagon barrel, straight grip, cresent or steel shotgun butt. Mfg. 1899-1915.

	$995	$900	$825	$750	$675	$600	$525

✳ *Model 1899-D Military Rifle (Musket)* - .30-30 Win. or .303 Savage cal., 28 or 30 in. round barrel with two barrel bands, straight grip stock with bayonet lug.

	$3,500	$3,200	$2,800	$2,400	$2,000	$1,600	$1,200

✳ *Model 1899-F Carbine* - various cals., 3 different variations, the first variation was made approx. 1899-1905 with small barrel band and receiver ring (scarce), the second and third variations are more frequently encountered.

	$1,500	$1,275	$1,100	$925	$800	$700	$600

Add approx. 40% for .25-35 WCF, .32-40 WCF, or .38-55 WCF cal.
Add 50% for small barrel band variation.

✳ *Model 1899H Rifle* - .22 Hi-Power, .25-35 WCF, .30-30 Win., or .303 Savage cal., 20 in. featherweight barrel, straight grip, steel or hard rubber shotgun butt, takedown added in 1909. Mfg. 1905- 1915.

	$800	$725	$625	$550	$425	$350	$275

Add 10% for .22 Hi-Power.
Add 20% for .25-35 WCF.

Grading	100%	98%	95%	90%	80%	70%	60%

✳ Model 1899 .250-3000 Rifle - takedown frame only, pistol grip checkered stocks with corrugated steel butt, fine cross-checkered trigger (unique to this model). Mfg. 1914-1921.

	$850	$775	$675	$600	$525	$450	$375

MODEL 99A - .30-30 Win., .300 Sav., or .303 Sav. cal., lever action, 24 in. barrel, open sight, hammerless, straight grip stock, crescent butt. Mfg. 1920-1936.

	$550	$440	$330	$275	$180	$165	$150

MODEL 99A RECENT PRODUCTION - similar to original, with .243 Win., .250 Sav., .300 Sav., .308 Win., or .375 Win. (1981 only, approx. 1,500 mfg.) cal., 20 or 22 in. barrel, tang safety, conventional butt. Mfg. 1971-1981.

	$375	$340	$310	$275	$250	$225	$200

Add 10% for .375 Win. cal.

MODEL 99B - takedown version of original Model 99A, 24 (introduced 1926-27) or 26 (initial standard barrel length) in. barrel. Mfg. 1920-1934.

	$650	$600	$550	$495	$330	$250	$195

MODEL 99H CARBINE - .250-3000 Sav., .30-30 Win., .300 Sav. (scarce) or .303 Sav. cal., solid frame, carbine type stock. Mfg. 1923-1940.

	$475	$400	$350	$300	$275	$250	$225

Add 30% for .250 Sav. and .300 Sav. cal.
There were four variations of this model - the latter three had barrel bands. This variation did not have a saddle ring.

MODEL 99E - .22 Hi Power, .250-3000 Sav., .30-30 Win., .300 Sav., or .303 Sav. cal., 20, 22 or 24 in. barrel, solid frame, straight stock. Mfg. 1922-1934.

	$475	$425	$375	$300	$250	$200	$175

Add 15% for .22 Hi Power or .250 Sav. cal.

MODEL 99E CARBINE - .243 Win., .250 Sav., .300 Sav., or .308 Win. cal., 22 in. barrel, checkered pistol grip stock, 5 shot rotary mag. Mfg. 1960-1982.

	$320	$260	$230	$200	$180	$165	$150

Last MSR was $343.

MODEL 99F FEATHERWEIGHT - similar to pre-war Model 99E, except takedown and ½ pound lighter, also mfg. with .410 bore shotgun barrel. Mfg. 1920-1940.

	$550	$440	$330	$275	$220	$195	$175

Add 50% for .410 bore shotgun barrel.

MODEL 99F - .243 Win., .250-3000 Sav., .284 Win., .300 Sav., .308 Win., or .358 Win. cal., solid frame, checkered pistol grip stock. Mfg. 1955-1973.

	$350	$310	$285	$260	$230	$210	$190

Add 10% for .250-3000 Sav.
Add 10% for .358 Win. cal.
Add 15% for .284 Win. cal.
This model, in many cases, had the receiver marked "99M".

MODEL 99G - similar to Model 99E pre-war, with checkered pistol grip stock and takedown. Mfg. 1922-1941.

	$660	$565	$475	$350	$275	$235	$200

MODEL 99EG - similar to Model 99G, with solid frame and no checkering. Mfg. 1935-1941.

	$550	$440	$330	$260	$230	$210	$190

MODEL 99EG POST-WAR - .243 Win., .250 Sav., .300 Sav., .308 Win., or .358 Win. cal., checkered stock. Mfg. 1946-1960.

	$450	$400	$350	$300	$250	$225	$200

Add 20% for .358 Win. cal.
Add 10% for .250 Sav. cal.

S

Grading	100%	98%	95%	90%	80%	70%	60%

MODEL 99R PRE-WAR - .250-3000 Sav., .303 Sav., or .300 Sav. cal., 22 or 24 in. barrel, large pistol grip stock and forearm. Mfg. 1932-1942.

	$550	$500	$450	$350	$250	$220	$195

Add 10% for .250-3000 Sav. cal.

MODEL 99R POST-WAR - .250-3000 Sav., .300 Sav., .308 Win., .358 Win., or .243 Win. cal., similar to Pre-War, 24 in. barrel only, swivel studs. Mfg. 1946-1960.

	$450	$400	$350	$300	$275	$250	$225

Add 20% for .250-3000 Sav. or .358 Win. cal.

MODEL 99RS PRE-WAR - similar to Model 99R Pre-War, with Lyman aperture sight, swivels and sling. Mfg. 1932-1942.

	$650	$600	$525	$350	$275	$250	$220

MODEL 99RS POST-WAR - similar to Model 99R Post-War, with Redfield receiver sight. Mfg. 1946-1958.

	$500	$450	$400	$325	$275	$250	$225

MODEL 99T - 20 or 22 in. barrel, solid frame, lightweight, checkered pistol grip stock. Mfg. 1935-1940.

	$695	$525	$450	$400	$350	$300	$275

MODEL 99K - engraved receiver and fancy wood stock, Lyman aperture sight and folding middle sight. Mfg. 1926-1940.

	$2,200	$1,870	$1,210	$880	$770	$550	$440

MODEL 99DL - .243 Win., .250-3000 Sav., .284 Win., .300 Sav., .308 Win., or .358 Win. cal., Monte Carlo stock and sling swivels. Post-war mfg. 1960-1973.

	$350	$310	$285	$260	$230	$210	$185

Add 10% for cut checkering.
Add 10% for .250-3000 Sav. cal.
Add 20% for .284 Win. or .358 Win. cal.

MODEL 99C - similar to Model 99F Post-War, available in .22-250 Rem. (rare), .243 Win., .284 Win. (disc.), 7mm-08 (disc.), or .308 Win. cal., 22 in. barrel, Monte Carlo stock with cut checkering and recoil pad, top tang safety, cocking indicator, open sights, detachable 4 shot mag., 7¾ lbs. Mfg. 1965, 1995-97.

	$525	$430	$365	$300	$260	$230	$200

Last MSR was $629.

Add 10% for .22-250 cal.

MODEL 99CD - similar to Model 99C, with Monte Carlo cheekpiece stock. Mfg. 1975- 1981.

	$525	$450	$375	$325	$295	$260	$230

MODEL 99-358 (BRUSH GUN) - .358 Win. cal., recoil pad. Mfg. 1977-1980.

	$495	$450	$400	$325	$295	$260	$230

MODEL 99-375 (BRUSH GUN) - .375 Win. cal., recoil pad, fluted forearm. Mfg. 1980 only.

	$725	$625	$550	$500	$450	$400	$350

MODEL 99PE - elaborately engraved and plated receiver, tang, and lever, fancy wood with hand cut checkering. Mfg. 1966-1970.

	$1,320	$990	$740	$500	$375	$300	$260

This model had the receiver marked "99M".

MODEL 99DE CITATION - similar to Model 99PE, except with less engraving and pressed checkering. Mfg. 1968-1970.

	$885	$660	$495	$330	$250	$220	$195

This model had the receiver marked "99M".

MODEL 99M - while the receivers on Models 99F, 99PE, and 99DE were marked "99M" this is not a model designation. Rather, the "M" barrel designation indicated Monte Carlo stock.

S

Grading	100%	98%	95%	90%	80%	70%	60%

SAVAGE 1895 ANNIVERSARY - a replica of the original M1895, .308 Win. cal., 24 in. octagon barrel, engraved receiver, brass-plated lever, straight stock, Schnabel forend, medallion in stock, brass crescent butt plate. Mfg. 9,999 in 1970 only, to commemorate Savage's 75th year.

	$495	$350	$275				

Last MSR was $195 and mfg. by Savage Arms, Division of Emhart.

MODEL 1903 STANDARD SLIDE ACTION - .22 S, L, or LR cal., 24 in. barrel, open sights, box mag., pistol grip stock. Mfg. 1903-1922.

	$375	$315	$200	$150	$120	$100	$85

✳ **Model 1903 Grade EF** - features "B" grade checkering on fancy English walnut stock, Savage #22B front sight, and #21B micrometer open rear sight.

	$1,150	$1,000	$850	$750	$650	$550	$450

✳ **Model 1903 Expert Grade** - features "A" grade engraving on receiver, "B" grade checkering on fancy American walnut stock, standard sights.

	$850	$750	$650	$550	$475	$400	$350

✳ **Model 1903 Grade GH** - features "A" grade checkering on plain American walnut stock, no engraving, #22B front sight, and #21B micrometer open rear sight.

	$395	$325	$250	$200	$160	$120	$90

✳ **Model 1903 Gold Medal** - features animal ornamentation on receiver, less elaborate checkering on plain American walnut stock, standard sights.

	$650	$550	$475	$400	$350	$275	$200

MODEL 1909 SLIDE ACTION - similar to Model 1903, with 20 in. round barrel. Mfg. 1909-1915.

	$220	$140	$110	$90	$75	$65	$45

MODEL 1904 SINGLE SHOT - .22 S, L, or LR cal., bolt action, 18 in. barrel, straight stock. Mfg. 1904-1917.

	$140	$85	$55	$45	$35	$30	$30

MODEL 1905 SINGLE SHOT - similar to Model 1904, except 24 in. barrel, takedown. Mfg. 1905-1919.

	$140	$85	$55	$45	$35	$30	$30

MODEL 1911 - .22 S only, bolt action, 20 shot tubular mag. in buttstock, 20 in. barrel. Limited mfg. 1911-1912.

	$400	$325	$295	$240	$195	$150	$115

MODEL 1912 AUTOLOADER - .22 LR cal., semi-auto, 20 in. barrel, takedown, straight stock. Mfg. 1912-1916.

	$350	$295	$235	$190	$150	$115	$80

MODEL 1914 SLIDE ACTION - .22 S, L, and LR cal., 24 in. octagon barrel, plain pistol grip stock. Mfg. 1914-1926.

	$250	$225	$195	$135	$110	$75	$65

MODEL 19 NRA BOLT ACTION - .22 LR cal., 25 in. barrel, adj. aperture sight, 5 shot military stock. Approx. 50,000 mfg. 1919-1932.

	$220	$140	$110	$100	$90	$75	$65

Between 1943-1945 approx. 6,000 Model 19s were made under military contract - add 15%.

MODEL 19 BOLT ACTION TARGET - .22 LR cal., 25 in. barrel, speed lock, adj. aperture sight, target stock. Mfg. 1933-1946.

	$250	$165	$140	$110	$100	$90	$70

MODEL 19L - similar to Model 19, with Lyman receiver sight. Mfg. 1933-1942.

	$330	$275	$195	$140	$120	$110	$100

MODEL 19M - similar to Model 19, with 28 in. heavy barrel and scope bases. Mfg. 1933-1942.

	$330	$275	$195	$165	$140	$120	$110

S

Grading	100%	98%	95%	90%	80%	70%	60%

MODEL 19H - similar to Model 19, except .22 Hornet. Mfg. 1933-1942.

	100%	98%	95%	90%	80%	70%	60%
	$550	$495	$330	$220	$175	$165	$155

MODEL 1920 BOLT ACTION - Mauser type action, .250-3000 Sav. or .300 Sav. cal., 22 or 24 in. barrel, open sights, 5 shot, checkered pistol grip, Schnabel forend. Mfg. 1920-1931.

	100%	98%	95%	90%	80%	70%	60%
	$350	$325	$275	$225	$175	$165	$155

Add 10% for .250-3000 Sav. cal.

MODEL 1920-1926 - similar to Model 1920, with 24 in. barrel, Lyman aperture sight, Mfg. 1926-1931.

	100%	98%	95%	90%	80%	70%	60%
	$330	$250	$220	$200	$175	$165	$155

MODEL 1922 - .22 LR cal., predecessor of the Model 23A, mfg. 1922.

	100%	98%	95%	90%	80%	70%	60%
	$250	$220	$165	$140	$110	$95	$85

MODEL 23A BOLT ACTION RIFLE - .22 LR cal., 23 in. barrel, open sights, plain pistol grip stock, Schnabel forend. Mfg. 1923-1933.

	100%	98%	95%	90%	80%	70%	60%
	$220	$165	$140	$110	$95	$85	$70

MODEL 23AA - improved version of Model 23A, with speedlock and checkered stock. Mfg. 1933-1942.

	100%	98%	95%	90%	80%	70%	60%
	$275	$195	$165	$130	$110	$100	$85

MODEL 23B - .25-20 WCF cal., same configuration as Model 23A, 25 in. barrel, full forearm. Mfg. 1923-1942.

	100%	98%	95%	90%	80%	70%	60%
	$220	$140	$110	$100	$90	$75	$65

MODEL 23C - .32-20 WCF, similar to Model 23B. Mfg. 1923-1942.

	100%	98%	95%	90%	80%	70%	60%
	$220	$140	$110	$100	$90	$75	$65

MODEL 23D - with .22 Hornet, similar to Model 23B. Mfg. 1933-1947.

	100%	98%	95%	90%	80%	70%	60%
	$305	$250	$220	$195	$165	$140	$110

MODEL 25 SLIDE ACTION - .22 S, L, or LR cal., 24 in. octagon barrel, open sight, takedown, hammerless, tube mag., plain pistol grip stock. Mfg. 1925-1929.

	100%	98%	95%	90%	80%	70%	60%
	$275	$235	$200	$150	$125	$75	$65

MODEL 40 BOLT ACTION RIFLE - .250-3000 Sav., .300 Sav., .30-30 Win., or .30-06 cal., 22 or 24 in. barrel, open sight, 4 shot mag., plain pistol grip stock, Schnabel forend. Mfg. 1928-1940.

	100%	98%	95%	90%	80%	70%	60%
	$330	$220	$195	$165	$155	$140	$120

Add 10% for .250-3000 Sav. cal.

MODEL 45 SUPER - similar to Model 40, with Lyman receiver sight and checkered stock. Mfg. 1928-1940.

	100%	98%	95%	90%	80%	70%	60%
	$385	$275	$250	$200	$175	$165	$140

MODEL 29 SLIDE ACTION - .22 S, L, or LR cal., 22 in. barrel, octagon until 1940, round on post-WWII, open sights, checkered pistol grip stock on pre-war, plain on late model. Mfg. 1929-1967.

	100%	98%	95%	90%	80%	70%	60%
	$235	$200	$165	$100	$90	$75	$65
Pre-war	$295	$250	$195	$120	$110	$100	$90

MODEL 3 SINGLE SHOT - .22 S, L, or LR cal., bolt action, 26 in. barrel, 24 in. barrel on post-war, open sights, plain grip stock. Mfg. 1930-1947.

	100%	98%	95%	90%	80%	70%	60%
	$85	$65	$55	$40	$30	$30	$30

MODEL 3S - similar to Model 3, with aperture sight. Mfg. 1930-1947.

	100%	98%	95%	90%	80%	70%	60%
	$100	$85	$70	$55	$40	$30	$30

MODEL 3ST - similar to Model 3S, with swivels and sling. Mfg. 1930-1947.

	100%	98%	95%	90%	80%	70%	60%
	$110	$90	$85	$70	$45	$35	$30

S

Grading	100%	98%	95%	90%	80%	70%	60%

MODEL 4 BOLT ACTION REPEATER - .22 S, L, or LR cal., 24 in. barrel, open sight, takedown, 5 shot, checkered pistol grip stock on pre-war, plain stock on post-war. Mfg. 1933-1965.

	100%	98%	95%	90%	80%	70%	60%
	$110	$85	$70	$55	$40	$30	$30
Pre-war	$120	$95	$85	$65	$50	$40	$30

MODEL 4S - similar to Model 4, with aperture sight. Mfg. 1933-1942.

	$120	$90	$75	$65	$55	$40	$30

MODEL 4M - similar to Model 4, except .22 WRM. Mfg. 1961-1965.

	$110	$85	$70	$55	$45	$30	$30

MODEL 5 - similar to Model 4, with tubular mag. Mfg. 1938-1964.

	$110	$85	$70	$55	$45	$30	$30

MODEL 5S - similar to Model 5, with aperture sight. Mfg. 1936-1942.

	$120	$95	$85	$65	$55	$40	$30

MODEL 6 AUTOLOADER - .22 S, L, or LR cal., 24 in. barrel, tubular mag., takedown, checkered pistol grip stock on pre-war, plain stock on post-war. Mfg. 1938-1968.

	100%	98%	95%	90%	80%	70%	60%
	$140	$110	$95	$85	$65	$55	$40
Pre-war	$150	$120	$105	$95	$75	$65	$50

MODEL 6S - similar to Model 6, with aperture sight. Mfg. 1938-1942.

	$150	$120	$105	$95	$75	$65	$45

MODEL 7 AUTOLOADER - similar to Model 6, with box mag. Mfg. 1939-1951.

	100%	98%	95%	90%	80%	70%	60%
	$140	$110	$95	$65	$55	$55	$40
Pre-war	$150	$120	$105	$95	$75	$65	$50

MODEL 7S - similar to Model 7, with aperture sight. Mfg. 1938-1942.

	$150	$120	$105	$95	$75	$65	$45

MODEL 60 AUTOLOADER - .22 LR cal., 20 in. barrel, leaf sight, tubular mag., checkered Monte Carlo walnut stock. Mfg. 1969-1972.

	$95	$85	$70	$55	$45	$35	$30

MODEL 90 AUTOLOADING CARBINE - similar to Model 60, with 16½ in. barrel, plain carbine stock, with barrel band.

	$95	$85	$70	$55	$45	$35	$30

MODEL 88 AUTOLOADER - similar to Model 60, except has walnut finished hardwood stock. Mfg. 1969-1972.

	$85	$65	$55	$45	$40	$35	$30

MODEL 63/63K SINGLE SHOT - .22 S, L, or LR cal., bolt action, 18 in. barrel, open sights, trigger locks with key (only on Model 63K), full length pistol grip walnut finished hardwood stock, Model 63s were mfg. 1964-69, Model 63Ks were mfg. 1970-1972.

	$80	$65	$55	$45	$40	$35	$30

MODEL 63KM - .22 Mag. cal., similar to Model 63K.

	$90	$70	$65	$55	$45	$40	$35

MODEL 219 SINGLE SHOT - .22 Hornet, .25-20 WCF, .32-20 WCF, or .30-30 Win. cal., 26 in. barrel, open sight, hammerless, break open, top lever, plain pistol grip stock. Mfg. 1938-1965.

.30-30 Win. cal.	$140	$125	$110	$100	$90	$80	$70

Add 15% for all other cals.

MODEL 219L - similar to Model 219, with side lever. Mfg. 1965-1967.

	$100	$85	$70	$55	$45	$35	$30

S

Grading	100%	98%	95%	90%	80%	70%	60%

MODELS 221, 222, 223, 227, 228, AND 229 - single shot, similar to Model 219, only supplied with additional shotgun barrel, interchangeable, different model numbers are for different cals., ga.'s, and barrel lengths, all have been disc.

	$130	$100	$85	$65	$55	$45	$30

SAVAGE/STEVENS MODEL 65 - please refer to listing under Stevens section.

MODEL 34M - similar to Model 34, chambered for .22 WRM. Mfg. 1969-1973.

	$90	$70	$55	$45	$35	$30	$30

MODEL 35 - .22 LR cal., bolt action, 22 in. barrel, 5 shot detachable mag., open sights, hardwood Monte Carlo stock. Disc. 1985.

	$90	$80	$65	$50	$35	$30	$30

Last MSR was $100.

MODEL 36 - .22 LR cal., single shot, otherwise similar to Model 35. Mfg. 1983-84.

	$90	$80	$65	$50	$35	$30	$30

MODEL 46 - similar to Model 34, with tubular mag. Mfg. 1969-1973.

	$90	$70	$55	$45	$35	$30	$30

MODEL 65M - .22 Mag. cal., similar to Model 65.

	$95	$75	$65	$55	$45	$35	$30

SAVAGE/STEVENS MODEL 72 "CRACKSHOT" - please refer to listing under Stevens section.

SAVAGE/STEVENS MODEL 73 - similar to Model 63, w/o Monte Carlo stock. Mfg. 1964-69.

	$80	$65	$55	$45	$40	$35	$30

SAVAGE/STEVENS MODEL 89 SINGLE SHOT - please refer to listing under Stevens section.

MODEL 340 BOLT ACTION - .22 Hornet, .222 Rem., .223 Rem., or .30-30 Win. cal., 22 and 24 in. barrel, open sights, 4 or 5 shot mag., 7½ lbs., plain pistol grip stock. Mfg. 1950-1985.

	$225	$195	$170	$160	$150	$140	$130

Last MSR was $257.

EL 340C - similar to Model 340, with aperture sight, checkered stock and sling swivels. Mfg. 1952-1960.

	$235	$205	$180	$165	$155	$145	$135

MODEL 340V - .225 Win. cal., varmint configuration, 24 in. barrel. Limited mfg. in late 1960s.

	$295	$265	$235	$205	$180	$165	$150

MODEL 340S DELUXE - similar to Model 340, with aperture sight, checkered stock, sling swivels. Mfg. 1952-1960.

	$260	$225	$205	$190	$175	$160	$150

MODEL 342 AND 342S - .22 Hornet cal., similar to Model 340. Mfg. 1950-1955.

	$250	$215	$200	$185	$170	$160	$150

RIFLES: RIMFIRE, CURRENT PRODUCTION

MARK I-G SERIES BOLT ACTION RIMFIRE - .22 S-L-LR, or LR shot (Mark I- GSB) cal., single shot, self-cocking, 19 (Mark I-GY, Youth Model) or 20¾ in. barrel, checkered hardwood stock, approx. 5 lbs. New 1996.

MSR	$135		$115	$95	$80	$75	$70	$65	$60

Add $31 for Youth Color (new 2002) or Camo Youth (new 2002).
Add $19 for scope (Model Mark I-GYXP only, new 2002).

This Model is also available with left-hand action (Mark I-GL), Youth Model (Mark I-GY), Youth Color (Mark I-GLY, features blue/green/grey laminate stock, new 2002), Camo Youth (Mark I-Y Camo , new 2002), or with smooth bore barrel (Mark I-GSB).

MARK II CAMO - similar to Mark II-F, except has Realtree Hardwoods HD full camo stock treatment. New 2002.

MSR	$167		$135	$115	$95	$85	$80	$75	$65

Grading	100%	98%	95%	90%	80%	70%	60%

MARK II-F SERIES BOLT ACTION RIMFIRE - .22 LR cal., features checkered black synthetic stock, 20¾ in. barrel, blueblue barrel, 10 shot mag., 5 lbs. New 1998.

MSR	$135	$115	$95	$80	$75	$70	$65	$60

Add $6 for Mark II-FXP package (includes 4x15mm scope).

MARK II-FV - .22 LR cal., features 21 in. heavy barrel w/o sights, black synthetic stock, 5 shot detachable mag., Weaver style bases included, 6 lbs. New 1998.

MSR	$205	$170	$135	$110	$100	$90	$80	$70

Add $35 for Mark II-FVXP package (includes 4x32mm scope).

MARK II-G - .22 LR cal., similar to Mark I-G Series, except has detachable 10 shot mag., approx. 5 lbs. New 1996.

MSR	$148	$125	$105	$85	$75	$70	$65	$60

Add $7 for Mark II-GXP package (includes 4x15mm scope).
Add $7 for Mark II-GLXP package (left hand, includes 4x15mm scope).
This Model is also available with left-hand action (Mark II-GL), Youth Model (Mark II-GY), Youth Model Left Hand (Mark II-GLY) at no additional charge.

MARK II-LV - .22 LR cal., features 21 in. blueblue heavy barrel, no sights, grey laminated hardwood stock with cut checkering, 6½ lbs. New 1997.

MSR	$235	$195	$165	$140	$125	$115	$105	$100

MARK II-FSS - .22 LR cal., 20¾ stainless steel barrel with sights, black graphite/polymer stock with checkering, dove-tailed receiver, 5 lbs. New 1997.

MSR	$179	$140	$115	$95

MODEL 64G SEMI-AUTO RIMFIRE - .22 LR cal., 20¼ in. barrel with adj. rear sight, 10 shot detachable mag., checkered hardwood stock, thumb operated rotary safety, 5½ lbs. New 1996.

MSR	$142	$120	$100	$85	$75	$70	$65	$60

Add $6 for Model 64-GXP package (includes 4x15mm scope).

* **Model 64F/64FV** - .22 LR cal., similar to Model 64G, except has black graphite/polymer checkered stock, 20¼ regular or 21 (Model 64FV, new 1998) heavy barrel, 5 or 6 lbs. New 1997.

MSR	$132	$115	$100	$85	$75	$70	$65	$60

Add $41 for Model 64FV with heavy barrel.
Add $4 for Model 64-FXP package (includes 4x15mm scope).

* **Model 64FSS** - similar to Model 64F, except has stainless steel barrel and action with checkered black synthetic graphite/polymer stock, 5 lbs. New 2002.

MSR	$171	$140	$120	$95

* **Model 64FVSS** - similar to Model 64FSS, except has 21 in. heavy barrel, 6 lbs. New 2002.

MSR	$225	$180	$140	$115

MODEL 93G/GL MAGNUM BOLT ACTION - .22 Win. Mag. cal., 20¾ in. barrel with adj. rear sight, 5 shot detachable mag., checkered right or left hand (Model 93 GL) hardwood Monte Carlo stock, 5¾ lbs. New 1996.

MSR	$173	$140	$120	$95	$85	$75	$70	$65

* **Model 93F** - features 20¾ blueblue barrel with checkered black synthetic graphite polymer stock, 5 lbs. New 1998.

MSR	$166	$130	$110	$95	$85	$75	$70	$65

* **Model 93FSS** - similar to Model 93G, except has stainless steel barrel and action with checkered black synthetic graphite/polymer stock, 5 lbs. New 1997.

MSR	$209	$170	$135	$110

* **Model 93FVSS** - similar to Model 93FSS, except has 21 in. heavy barrel with recessed crown and button rifling, drilled and tapped, Weaver bases included, 6 lbs. New 1998.

MSR	$240	$200	$155	$125

Add $34 for Model 93FVSSXP package (includes 4x32mm scope and mounts).

S

Grading	100%	98%	95%	90%	80%	70%	60%

MODEL 900 SERIES - .22 LR cal., single (Target/Silhouette Model) or 5 shot (Biathlon Model 21 or 25 (Target Model) in. free floated barrel, uncheckered hardwood stock, right or left hand action, approx. 8 lbs. Mfg. 1996-2001.

* **900B Biathlon** - blonde stock, supplied with five 5-shot mags., includes shooting rail and barrel snow cover, aperture rear sight. Mfg. 1996-97.

	$445	$395	$350	$300	$265	$230	$200

Last MSR was $498.

This model was also available with left hand action (Model 900B-LH, new 1997).

* **900S Silhouette** - brown hardwood stock, heavy 21 in. barrel with muzzle crown, scope bases installed, w/o sights. Mfg. 1996-97.

	$300	$265	$230	$200	$180	$160	$140

Last MSR was $346.

This model was also available with left hand action (Model 900S-LH, mfg. 1997).

* **900TR Target** - features aperture sights, shooting rail with hand stop, 25 in. barrel. Disc. 2001.

	$395	$325	$280	$235	$200	$180	$160

Last MSR was $448.

This model was also available with left hand action (Model 900TR-LH, new 1997).

RIFLES: CENTERFIRE, CURRENT/RECENT PRODUCTION

The 110 Series was first produced in 1958. Beginning in 1992, Savage Arms, Inc. began supplying this model with a master trigger lock, earmuffs, shooting glasses (disc. 1992), and test target.

Beginning 1994, all Savage rifles employ a laser etched bolt featuring the Savage logo. During 1996 Savage began using pillar bedded stocks for many of their rifles. Savage introduced a new line of Rimfire rifles during 1996.

Recent Savage nomenclature usually involves alphabetical suffixes which mean the following: B - Brown laminated wood stock, C - detachable box mag., F - composite/ synthetic stock, G - hardwood stock, K - standard muzzle brake, AK - adj. muzzle brake with fluted barrel, L - left-hand, LE – Law Enforcement, NS - no sights, P - police (tactical) rifle, SE - safari express, SS - stainless steel, SS-S - stainless steel single shot, T - Target, U - high luster blue, blueblue metal finish and/or stock finish, V - Long Range (Varmint), XP - package gun (scope, sling, and rings/base), Y - Youth/ Ladies Model. Hence, the Model 116-FCSAK designates a 116 series firearm with composite stock, detachable stainless steel mag., and adj. muzzle brake on barrel. A 2 digit model number (10) designates new short action. A 3 digit model number (110) indicates long action.

Whenever possible, the models within this category have been listed in numerical sequence.

MODEL 10FCM SCOUT - .308 Win. or 7mm-08 Rem. cal., 20 in. barrel with removable ghost ring rear sight, one-piece barrel mount (allows long scope eye relief), 4 shot detachable mag., satin blueblue action with large ball bolt handle, black synthetic dual pillar bedded stock, includes swivel set and sling, 6 1/8 lbs. New 1999.

MSR	$559	$485	$420	$370	$330	$300	$280	$265

MODEL 10FM (SIERRA) - .243 Win., .308 Win., .300 WSM (new 2002), or 7mm-08 Rem. (new 1999) cal., short action, lightweight, features black synthetic stock with dual pillar bedding, button rifling and recessed crown, 20 (Sierra, standard weight, new 1999) or 24 (heavy only, disc. 1998) in. barrel, w/o sights, 6 lbs. New 1998.

MSR	$476	$405	$335	$280	$240	$210	$175	$160

This model is also available in left-hand action (disc.).

MODEL 10FP - .223 Rem., .260 Rem. (mfg. 1999-2001), .308 Win., or 7mm-08 (mfg. 1999-2001) cal., short action, tactical/law enforcement model, checkered black synthetic stock, features 24 in. heavy barrel w/o sights, 8 lbs. New 1998.

MSR	$502	$420	$345	$285	$250	$215	$180	$165

This model is also available in left-hand action (Model 10FLP).

S

Grading	100%	98%	95%	90%	80%	70%	60%

* **Model 10FP Duty** - similar to Model 10FP, except has open iron sights. New 2002.

MSR	$525	$435	$355	$290	$250	$215	$180	$165

* **Model 10FP LE1/LE2** - similar to Model 10FP, except has 20 or 26 in. heavy barrel with no sights. New 2002.

MSR	$511	$425	$350	$290	$250	$215	$180	$165

* **Model 10FPXP-LE** - .308 Win. cal. only, similar to Model 10FP LE, 26 in. barrel w/o sights, includes Burris 3½-10Xx50mm scope with flip covers and sling, 4 shot mag., Harris bi-pod, aluminum case, 10 ½ lbs. New 2002.

MSR	$1,100	$965	$840	$750	$650	$575	$500	$450

MODEL 10GY - .223 Rem., .243 Win., or .308 Win. cal., ladies/youth model with shorter wood stock and 22 in. barrel with open sights.

MSR	$418	$365	$305	$260	$220	$195	$175	$160

MODEL 11F HUNTER - .22-250 Rem., .223 Rem., .243 Win., .260 Rem. (mfg. 1999- 2000), .308 Win., .300 WSM (new 2002), or 7mm-08 Rem. (new 1999) cal., short action, dual pillar bedding, checkered black synthetic stock, 22 or 24 (.300 WSM cal. only) in. blueblue barrel with open sights, 6¾ lbs. New 1998.

MSR	$442	$380	$315	$265	$225	$195	$175	$160

Subtract $8 if w/o sights (Model 11FNS, not available in .300 WSM cal.).

This model is also available in left-hand action (Model 11FL).

MODEL 11FC - .22-250 Rem. .243 Win., .260 Rem. (disc. 2000), .308 Win. or 7mm-08 Rem. cal., 22 in. blue barrel and action, dual pillar bedded black synthetic stock, 6 3/8 lbs. Mfg. 1999-2001.

		$395	$325	$275	$230	$200	$175	$160

Last MSR was $468.

This model is also available in left-hand action (Model 11FLC).

MODEL 11FYXP3 - .243 Win. cal. only, similar to 11F Hunter, except is Youth Model with 12½ LOP, includes 3-9Xx40mm scope, 6 ½ lbs. New 2002.

MSR	$453	$385	$315	$270	$220	$195	$175	$160

MODEL 11G HUNTER - similar to 11F Hunter, except is also available in .300 WSM, .300 RSUM, or 7mm RSUM cal. (24 in. barrel only), wood stock with pressed fleur-de-lis checkering. New 1998.

MSR	$418	$365	$305	$260	$220	$195	$175	$160

Subtract $7 if w/o sights (Model 11GNS, not available in .260 Rem., .300 WSM, .300 RSUM, or 7mm RSUM cal.).

This model is also available in left-hand action (Model 11GL, not available in .300 RSUM or 7mm RSUM cal.)

MODEL 11GC - .22-250 Rem., .243 Win., .260 Rem. (disc. 2000), .308 Win. or 7mm- 08 Rem. cal., detachable mag., hardwood stock, open sights, 22 in. barrel, blue finish, 6 3/8 lbs. Mfg. 1999-2001.

		$375	$310	$270	$230	$200	$175	$160

Last MSR was $441.

This model is also available in left-hand action (Model 11GLC).

MODEL 12BVSS - .22-250 Rem., .223 Rem., .243 Win. (new 2002), or .308 Win. (disc. 1999, reintroduced 2001) cal., short action, 26 in. heavy fluted stainless barrel w/o sights, dual pillar bedding, brown laminated wood stock with flat beavertail forend, 9 lbs. New 1998.

MSR	$616	$530	$450	$380				

* **Model 12BVSS-S** - similar to Model 12BVSS, except is single shot and not available in .308 Win. cal. Mfg. 1998-2001.

		$515	$440	$375				

Last MSR was $595.

S

Grading	100%	98%	95%	90%	80%	70%	60%

❋ *Model 12BVSS-XP* - similar to Model 12BVSS, except not available in .243 Win. cal., target style heavy prone laminate stock with Wundhammer plam swell and black forend cap, 26 in. fluted stainless barrel w/o sights, includes Burris 16x18x37mm scope and black aluminum hard case, 12 lbs. New 2002.

	MSR	$1,100		$965	$840	$750			

MODEL 12FV - .22-250 Rem., .223 Rem., .243 Win. (new 2002), .308 Win. (new 1999) cal., short action, features 26 in. regular barrel with low luster bluing, black synthetic stock with dual pillar bedding, 5 shot top loading mag., drilled and tapped, 9 lbs. New 1998.

MSR	$481		$405	$340	$280	$240	$210	$175	$160

This model was also available in left-hand action (Model 12FLV, disc. 2001).

MODEL 12FVSS - .22-250 Rem., .223 Rem., or .308 Win. cal., short action, features 26 in. fluted heavy stainless free floating barrel w/o sights, black checkered synthetic stock with dual pillar bedding, drilled and tapped, 9 lbs. New 1998.

MSR	$569		$495	$415	$340				

This model is also available in left-hand action (Model 12FLVSS).

❋ *Model 12FVSS-S* - similar to Model 12FVSS, except is single shot and not available in .308 Win. cal. Mfg. 1998-2001.

			$480	$405	$335				

Last MSR was $549.

❋ *Model 12VSS* - .22-250 Rem., .223 Rem., or .308 Win. cal., semi-skeletonized Choate adj. black synthetic stock with cheekpiece, 24 in. fluted stainless barrel, blueblue stainless steel receiver, 4 shot mag., drilled and tapped receiver, 15 lbs. New 2000.

MSR	$900		$780	$665	$555				

MODEL 16BSS WEATHER WARRIOR - .300 WSM, .300 RSUM, or 7mm RSUM cal., 24 in. barrel w/o sights, 2 or 3 shot mag., brown laminated stock with cut checkering, stainless action and barrel, 7 ¾ lbs. New 2002.

MSR	$644		$545	$450	$350				

MODEL 16FCSS WEATHER WARRIOR - .243 Win., .260 Rem. (disc. 2000), .308 Win., or 7mm-08 Rem. cal., stainless steel barreled action with 22 in. barrel, detachable mag., dual pillar bedded black synthetic stock, 6¾ lbs. Mfg. 1999-2001.

			$460	$395	$325				

Last MSR was $532.

Also available in left-hand action at no additional charge (Model 16FLCSS).

MODEL 16FSS - .223 Rem., .243 Win., .260 Rem. (mfg. 1999-2000), .308 Win., .300 WSM (new 2002), .300 RSUM (new 2002), 7mm RSUM (new 2002), or 7mm-08 Rem. (new 1999) cal., short action, stainless steel 22 or 24 (WSM and RSUM cals only) in. barreled action w/o sights, checkered black synthetic stock with dual pillar bedding, 6¾ lbs. New 1998.

MSR	$500		$425	$380	$300				

Also available in left-hand action at no additional charge (Model 16FLSS – not available in .300 RSUM or 7mm RSUM cal.).

MODEL 16FXP3 PACKAGE - .223 Rem., .243 Win., .308 Win., or .300 WSM cal., short action, stainless action and 22 or 24 in. stainless barrel w/o sights, checkered black synthetic stock, includes nickel finished 3x9x40X scope and mounts, supplied with sling, approx. 6½ lbs. New 2002.

MSR	$534		$455	$380	$320				

MODEL 99C LEVER ACTION - .243 Win. or .308 Win. cal., detachable box mag., checkered Monte Carlo stock and forearm, high gloss bluing, 22 in. barrel with adj. rear sight, drilled and tapped, 7¾ lbs. Reintroduced 1996-97 only.

	$585	$500	$450	$400	$360	$330	$300	

Last MSR was $665.

Grading	100%	98%	95%	90%	80%	70%	60%

MODEL 99-CE (CENTENNIAL EDITION) - .300 Sav. cal. only, limited edition featuring fully engraved nickel receiver and lever, 24 Kt. gold-plated receiver figures, trigger, and safety, deluxe hand checkered walnut stock and forearm, 1,000 mfg. 1996-97 only, serial numbered AS0001- AS1000.

     $1,500   **$1,100**   **$750**

Last MSR was $1,660.

MODEL 110 SPORTER BOLT ACTION - .243 Win., .270 Win., .308 Win., or .30- 06 cal., 22 in. barrel, open sight, 4 shot, checkered pistol grip stock. Mfg. 1958-1963.

     $200   **$175**   **$145**   **$120**   **$110**   **$95**   **$85**

MODEL 110-MC - similar to Model 110, with Monte Carlo stock. Mfg. 1959-1969.

     $225   **$195**   **$160**   **$140**   **$120**   **$110**   **$95**

MODEL 110-M - similar to Model 110MC, except 7mm Rem. Mag., .264 Win. Mag., .300 Win. Mag., or .338 Win. Mag. cal., recoil pad. Mfg. 1963-1969.

     $275   **$220**   **$195**   **$150**   **$140**   **$125**   **$110**

MODEL 110-C/CL - various cals., push-button detachable mag., walnut stock. Mfg. 1966-1985.

     $300   **$265**   **$230**   **$200**   **$185**   **$170**   **$160**

MODEL 110-D - .22-250 Rem. (disc.), .223 Rem., .243 Win., .25-06 Rem. (disc.), .270 Win., .308 Win. (disc.), .30-06, 7mm Rem. Mag., .300 Win. Mag. (disc.), or .338 Win. Mag. cal., similar to Model 110B, hinged floorplate (1972-75 only), checkered walnut stock, removable and adj. rear sight, 7½ lbs. Mfg. 1966-1988.

     $340   **$290**   **$260**   **$240**   **$215**   **$190**   **$170**

Last MSR was $409.

     Add $80 for left-hand version.

MODEL 110-E - .22-250 Rem., .223 Rem., .243 Win., .270 Win., 7mm Rem. Mag., .308 Win., or .30-06 cal., 22 or 24 (Mag. only) in. barrel, open sights, uncheckered hardwood Monte Carlo stock, blind internal floorplate, 7 lbs. Mfg. 1963-1988.

     $260   **$230**   **$190**   **$175**   **$165**   **$155**   **$145**

Last MSR was $325.

     Subtract $16 without sights.

MODEL 110-F - .22-250 Rem., .223 Rem., .243 Win., .250 Sav. (new 1993), .25-06 Rem. (new 1993), .308 Win., .30-06, .270 Win., 7mm-08 Rem. (new 1993), 7mm Rem. Mag., .300 Sav. (new 1993), .300 Win. Mag., .338 Win. Mag. (new 1991) cal., 22 or 24 (Magnum) in. barrel, black DuPont Rynite stock with swivel studs and recoil pad, adj. rear sight, drilled and tapped for scope mounts, 4 or 5 shot mag., 6¾ lbs. Mfg. 1989-1993.

     $335   **$300**   **$265**   **$235**   **$210**   **$195**   **$180**

All Model 110 mfg. is in the domain of Savage Arms, Inc.

✳ *Model 110-FNS* - similar to Model 110-F, except has no sights. Mfg. 1991-1993.

     $325   **$285**   **$250**   **$225**   **$200**   **$190**   **$175**

✳ *Model 110-FXP3* - .22-250 Rem. (new 1992), .223 Rem. (new 1992), .243 Win., .270 Win., .30-06, .308 Win. (new 1992), 7mm Rem. Mag., or .300 Win. Mag. cal., similar to Model 110-F except is without sights and has integral Weaver type scope bases. Mfg. 1989-1993.

     $415   **$370**   **$325**   **$285**   **$250**   **$225**   **$195**

MODEL 110-GY - .223 Rem. (Mfg. 1993-99), .243 Win. (disc. 1999), .270 Win. (new 1994), .300 Sav. (disc. 1995), or .308 Win. (mfg. 1994-99) cal., 22 in. barrel, youth/ ladies variation with shortened classic stock, open sights, 6½ lbs. Mfg. 1991-2000.

     $350   **$300**   **$260**   **$220**   **$195**   **$175**   **$160**

Last MSR was $395.

MODEL 110-WLE - .250-3000 Sav., .300 Sav., or 7x57mm Mauser cal. Mfg. 1991- 1993.

     $425   **$390**   **$360**   **$320**   **$280**   **$250**   **$225**

Approx. 1,000 of each cal. were mfg. in this model.

Grading	100%	98%	95%	90%	80%	70%	60%

❊ *Model 110-WLE 1 of 1,000* - 7x57mm Mauser, features select walnut stock with Monte Carlo cheekpiece, high luster blue finish with laser etched Savage logo on bolt body, drilled and tapped, 1,000 mfg. beginning 1992, 7¾ lbs. Mfg. 1992-1993 only.

	$415	$370	$325	$285	$250	$225	$195

MODEL 110-FM SIERRA ULTRA LIGHT - .243 Win. (disc. 1998), .270 Win., .30-06, or .308 Win. (disc. 1998) cal., features 20 in. high gloss barrel w/o sights, black graphite/fiberglass-filled stock with non-glare finish, drilled and tapped, 6¼ lbs. Mfg. 1996-2000.

	$380	$325	$270	$230	$205	$175	$160

Last MSR was $449.

MODEL 110-FP TACTICAL POLICE RIFLE - .223 Rem. (disc. 1998), .25-06 Rem. (new 1995), .300 Win. Mag. (new 1995), .30-06 (new 1996), .308 Win. (disc. 1998), or 7mm Rem. Mag. (new 1995) cal., 24 in. heavy pillar bedded barrel tactical rifle, all metal parts are non-reflective, 4 shot internal mag., black Dupont Rynite stock, right or left-hand (new 1996) action, tapped for scope mounts, 8½ lbs. Mfg. 1990-2001.

	$410	$345	$280	$240	$210	$175	$160

Last MSR was $486.

Also available in left-hand action at no additional charge (new 1996, Model 110-FLP).

MODEL 110-G - .22-250 Rem., .223 Rem., .243 Win., .250 Sav. (new 1992), .25-06 Rem. (new 1992), .300 Sav. (new 1993), .308 Win., .30-06, .270 Win., 7mm-08 Rem. (new 1992), 7mm Rem. Mag., or .300 Win. Mag. cal., top loading internal box mag., 22 or 24 in. barrel, adj. iron sights, checkered hardwood stock, approx. 7 lbs. Mfg. 1989-1993.

	$325	$285	$250	$225	$200	$190	$175

Subtract $10-$20 if without sights (Model 110-GNS).

❊ *Model 110-GC* - .270 Win., .30-06, 7mm Rem. Mag., or .300 Win. Mag. cal., features detachable 3 or 4 shot mag., 22 or 24 in. barrel, checkered hardwood stock, adj. sights, 6¾ lbs. Mfg. 1992-1993.

	$410	$325	$275	$240	$210	$180	$165

Add $20 for Mag. cals.

❊ *Model 10GXP3/110-GXP3 Package* - .22-250 Rem., .223 Rem., .243 Win., .250 Savage (disc. 1995), .25-06 Rem., .270 Win., .300 Sav. (disc. 1995), .30-06, .308 Win., 7mm-08 Rem. (disc. 1995, reintroduced 1999), 7mm Rem. Mag., .300 Rem. Ultra Mag. (new 2002), or .300 Win. Mag. cal., similar to Model 110-G, except has no sights, includes 3x9x32 scope, rings, bases, QD swivels, and deluxe rifle sling, includes integral Weaver type scope bases. New 1989.

MSR	$476	$405	$340	$285	$240	$210	$175	$160

Also available in left-hand action at no additional charge (Model 10GLXP3/110-GLXP3, not available in .300 WSM cal.).

❊ *Model 110-GCXP3 Package* - .270 Win., .30-06, .300 Win. Mag., or 7mm Rem. Mag. cal., 22 or 24 in. barrel, checkered hardwood stock, detachable box mag., package includes 3x9x32 scope, rings, bases, QD swivels, and deluxe rifle sling, 7¼ lbs. Disc. 2001.

	$445	$375	$315	$275	$235	$190	$175

Last MSR was $524.

Was also available in left-hand action at no additional charge (Model 110-GLCXP3 – disc. 2000).

❊ *Model 110-GL* - .30-06, .270 Win., or 7mm Rem. Mag. cal., left hand variation of the Model 110-G. Mfg. 1989-1993.

	$325	$265	$225	$200	$180	$165	$150

❊ *Model 110-GLNS* - similar to Model 110-GL, except has no sights. Mfg. 1991-1993.

	$320	$260	$220	$200	$180	$165	$150

S

Grading	100%	98%	95%	90%	80%	70%	60%

MODEL 110-K - .243 Win., .270 Win., or .30-06 cal., incorporates laminated camouflage stock. Mfg. 1986-1988.

	$335	$280	$240				

Last MSR was $399.

MODEL 110-S - .308 Win. or 7mm-08 Rem. (disc.) cals., silhouette model, 22 in. heavy barrel, Wundhammer swell pistol grip with stippling, no sights, 4 shot mag., 8 lbs. 10 oz. Disc. 1985.

	$340	$290	$255	$225	$205	$190	$175

Last MSR was $385.

MODEL 110-V - .22-250 Rem. or .223 Rem. cal. only, varmint model, 26 in. heavy barrel, no sights, 5 shot mag., stippled walnut Wundhammer pistol grip stock, 9¼ lbs. Disc. 1989.

	$370	$315	$265	$230	$205	$190	$175

Last MSR was $439.

MODEL 110-GV - .22-250 Rem. or .223 Rem. cal., varmint variation, 24 in. medium barrel, no sights, checkered hardwood stock with rubber rifle pad, drilled and tapped for scope, 8¼ lbs. Mfg. 1989-1993.

	$380	$285	$250	$225	$200	$190	$175

MODEL 110-B - similar to Model 110E, except available in .243 Win., .270 Win. or .30-06 cal., select stock and pistol grip cap, features blind mag, walnut Monte Carlo stock. Reintroduced 1989 with laminate stock (Model 110-B Laminate). Mfg. 1978-1979.

	$360	$300	$265	$235	$205	$190	$175

This model was also available in left hand action (Model 110-BL).

MODEL 110-B LAMINATE - similar to Model 110-B, except is available in .300 Win. Mag. or .338 Win. Mag. cal. also, has brown laminate hardwood stock with iron sights, approx. 7½ lbs. Mfg. 1989-91.

	$385	$310	$250	$225	$200	$190	$180

Last MSR was $477.

MODEL 110-P PREMIER GRADE - similar to Model 110B, with select French walnut stock, skip checkered, rosewood forend and pistol grip cap, sling swivels, 7mm Mag. has recoil pad. Mfg. 1964-1970.

	100%	98%	95%	90%	80%	70%	60%
	$440	$330	$310	$275	$250	$220	$195
7mm Mag.	$460	$350	$330	$305	$275	$240	$220

MODEL 110-PE PRESENTATION GRADE - similar to Model 110P, with engraved receiver, floorplate and triggerguard. Mfg. 1968-1970.

	$660	$550	$525	$470	$440	$415	$385
7mm Mag.	$690	$580	$550	$495	$470	$440	$415

MODEL 111 CHIEFTAIN ACTION - .243 Win., .270 Win., 7x57mm, 7mm Mag., or .30-06 cal., 22 in. barrel, 24 in. barrel (Mag. cals.), leaf sight, 4 shot detachable mag., checkered walnut Monte Carlo stock, pistol grip cap, sling swivels. Mfg. 1974-1978.

	$375	$350	$300	$250	$225	$200	$175
Magnum	$395	$375	$325	$295	$275	$225	$195

MODEL 111-F - similar to Model 111-G, except has black graphite/fiberglass stock (with non-glare finish) and also available in .338 Win. Mag. cal., 22, 24, or 26 in. barrel, solid recoil pad, 6½ lbs. New 1994.

MSR	$442	$385	$325	$275	$230	$195	$175	$160

Subtract $48 for .270 Win., .30-06, 7mm Rem. Mag., and .300 Win. Mag. cals. (right hand).

Subtract $8 if w/o sights (Model 111-FNS, not available in .300 Rem. Ultra Mag. or 7mm Rem. Ultra Mag. cals.).

This model is also available in left-hand (Model 111-FL).

S

Grading	100%	98%	95%	90%	80%	70%	60%

Model 111-FC - .270 Win., .30-06, .300 Win. Mag., or 7mm Rem. Mag. cal., 22 or 24 in. barrel, detachable box mag., black graphite/fiberglass stock, 6½ lbs. New 1994.

MSR	$468	$400	$340	$285	$230	$195	$175	$160

This model is also available with left-hand action (Model 111-FLC).

MODEL 111-FAK EXPRESS - .270 Win., .30-06, .300 Win. Mag., .338 Win. Mag., or 7mm Rem. Mag. cal., 22 in. barrel with adj. muzzle brake, black or black matte graphite/fiberglass-filled stock, w/o sights, 6¾ lbs. Mfg. 1996-98.

		$390	$340	$285	$240	$200	$180	$165

Last MSR was $450.

MODEL 111-FCXP3 PACKAGE - .270 Win., .30-06, .300 Win. Mag. (disc. 2001), or 7mm Rem. Mag. (disc. 2001) cal., 4 shot detachable box mag., checkered black syntetic stock, 22 or 24 in. barrel, package includes bore sighted 3-9Xx32mm scope, rings, bases, QD swivels, and deluxe rifle sling, 6½ lbs. New 1994.

MSR	$436	$375	$305	$270	$230	$200	$175	$160

Add approx. $60 for Mag. cals. (disc. 2001).

This model was also available with left-hand action (Model 111-FLCXP3 – disc. 2000).

MODEL 11FXP3/111-FXP3 PACKAGE - .22-250 Rem., .223 Rem., .243 Win., .250 Savage (disc. 1996), .25-06 Rem., .270 Win., .300 Sav. (disc. 1996), .30-06, .308 Win., .300 Win. Mag., .300 WSM (new 2002) .338 Win. Mag., 7mm Rem. Mag., 7mm Rem. Ultra Mag. (new 2002), or 7mm-08 Rem. (disc. 1996, reintroduced 1999-2001) cal., 22 or 24 in. barrel, black graphite/fiberglass composite stock, non- glare finish, package consists of bore sighted 3x9x32 scope, rings, bases, QD swivels, and deluxe rifle sling, approx. 7¼ lbs. New 1994.

MSR	$502	$425	$360	$295	$240	$200	$180	$165

This model is also available with left hand action (Model 11FLXP3/111-FLXP3).

MODEL 111-G - .22-250 Rem. (disc. 1998), .223 Rem. (disc. 1998), .243 Win. (disc. 1998), .250 Savage (disc. 1996), .25-06 Rem., .270 Win., .300 Sav. (disc. 1996), .30-06, .308 Win. (disc. 1998), .300 Win. Mag., .300 Rem. Ultra Mag. (new 2002), .338 Win. Mag. (disc. 1993 - not available with wood stock), 7mm-08 Rem. (disc. 1996), 7mm Rem. Ultra Mag. (new 2002), or 7mm Rem. Mag. cal., walnut finished hardwood stock with cut checkering and vent. recoil pad, open sights, top tang safety with red dot indicator, 22, 24, or 26 in. barrel, drilled and tapped, 6 3/8 or 7 lbs. New 1994.

MSR	$418	$370	$315	$265	$225	$195	$175	$160

Subtract $7 w/o sights (Model 111-GNS, not available in .300 Rem. Ultra Mag. or 7mm Rem. Ultra Mag. cals.).

This model is also available in left-hand (Model 111-GL, not available in 7mm Rem. Ultra Mag.).

Model 111-GC - .270 Win., .30-06, .300 Win. Mag., or 7mm Rem. Mag. cal., 22 or 24 in. barrel, detachable box mag., walnut finished hardwood stock with cut checkering and vent. recoil pad. Mfg. 1994-2001.

		$385	$325	$275	$240	$210	$175	$160

Last MSR was $441.

This model was also available with left hand action (Model 111-GLC – disc. 2000).

MODEL 112V VARMINT RIFLE - .220 Swift, .222 Rem., .223 Rem. (new 1976), .22- 250 Rem., .243 Win., or .25-06 Rem. cal., single shot, bolt action, 26 in. heavy barrel, no sights, heavy select walnut stock, checkered, swivels. Mfg. 1975-1978.

		$350	$325	$300	$275	$250	$235	$225

MODEL 112 R - .22-250 Rem., .25-06 Rem., or .243 Win. cal., similar to Model 112V, except has 4 shot mag. Disc. 1980.

		$340	$305	$275	$250	$230	$210	$175

MODEL 112-BV - .22-250 Rem. or .223 Rem. cal., alloy steel construction, 26 in. barrel with recessed muzzle, 4 shot mag., brown laminate stock with ambidextrous Wundhammer style pistol grip, 9½ lbs. Mfg. 1993 only.

		$475	$430	$365	$315	$285	$250	$215

S

Grading	100%	98%	95%	90%	80%	70%	60%

MODEL 112-BVSS LONG RANGE

- .22-250 Rem. (disc. 1998), .223 Rem. (disc. 1998), .25-06 Rem. (new 1996), .30-06 (new 1996), .308 Win. (mfg. 1996-98), .300 Win. Mag. (new 1996), or 7mm Rem. Mag. (new 1996) cal., 4 shot, pillar bedded laminate wood stock with Wundhammer palm swell, 26 in. stainless steel fluted barrel, bolt handle and trigger guard, recessed muzzle, 10½ lbs. New 1994.

MSR $616	$525	$430	$365	$310	$275	$230	$200

✳ *Model 112-BVSS-S* - .220 Swift, .223 Rem. (disc. 1998), .22-250 Rem. (disc. 1998), or .300 Win. Mag. (new 1996) cal., single shot, 26 in. stainless steel fluted barrel, with target features, 10½ lbs. Mfg. 1994-2001.

	$510	$420	$360

Last MSR was $595.

MODEL 112-BT COMPETITION GRADE

- .223 Rem. or .308 Win. cal., laminated pillar bedded wood stock with adj. cheek rest and Wundhammer palm swell, vent. forend, 5 shot internal mag., alloy steel receiver with 26 in. matte black finished heavy stainless steel barrel w/o sights, drilled and tapped receiver, approx. 10 7/8 lbs. Mfg. 1994-2001.

	$930	$810	$705	$625	$550	$495	$400

Last MSR was $1,049.

✳ *Model 112-BT-S* - .300 Win. Mag. cal., single shot, otherwise similar to Model 112- BT Competition Grade. Mfg. 1995-2001.

	$930	$810	$705	$625	$550	$495	$400

Last MSR was $1,049.

MODEL 112-FV

- .22-250 Rem. or .223 Rem. cal., varmint variation with 26 in. heavy barrel, with or w/o iron sights, 4-shot mag., black Rynite synthetic stock with recoil pad, 8 7/8 lbs. Mfg. 1991- 98.

	$360	$300	$260	$235	$200	$175	$160

Last MSR was $410.

✳ *Model 112-FVS* - similar to Model 112-FV, except is single shot with solid bottom receiver and is available in .220 Swift (new 1993) cal. Mfg. 1992-93 only.

	$375	$340	$295	$265	$235	$210	$195

✳ *Model 112-FVSS (Long Range)* - .22-250 Rem. (disc. 1998), .223 Rem. (disc. 1998), .25-06 Rem. (new 1995), .30-06 (new 1996), .308 Win. (mfg. 1996-98), .300 Win. Mag. (new 1995), or 7mm Rem. Mag. (new 1995) cal., alloy receiver with 26 in. fluted stainless steel barrel, 4 shot mag., black synthetic pillar bedded sporter stock w/o sights, 8 7/8 lbs. New 1993.

MSR $569	$495	$425	$360				

This model is also available with left hand action (Model 112-FLVSS, new 1996, not available in .30-06 cal.).

✳ *Model 112-FVSS-S* - .220 Swift, .22-250 Rem. (disc. 1998), .223 Rem. (disc. 1998), or .300 Win. Mag. (new 1996) cal., single shot variation, pillar bedded stock, 8 7/8 lbs. Mfg. 1994-2001.

	$480	$415	$355	$300	$270	$230	$200

Last MSR was $549.

MODEL 114-C (CLASSIC) 114-CU (CLASSIC ULTRA)

- .270 Win., .30-06, .300 Win. Mag., or 7mm Rem. Mag. cal., 22 or 24 in. barrel, features high gloss classic American black walnut stock with cut checkering, fitted grip cap, and recoil pad, removable 3 or 4 shot staggered box mag., available with deluxe adj. sights (Model 114-CU, disc. 1995) or w/o sights (Model 114-C, new 1996), approx. 7 1/8 lbs. Mfg. 1991-2000.

	$485	$410	$355	$300	$270	$230	$200

Last MSR was $556.

MODEL 114-U

- similar to Model 114-C, except is also available in 7mm STW cal., 3 shot internal mag, no sights, approx. 7 lbs. New 1999.

MSR $532	$465	$395	$335	$275	$250	$230	$200

Grading	100%	98%	95%	90%	80%	70%	60%

MODEL 114-CE (CLASSIC EUROPEAN) - same cals. as the Model 114-C, except also available in 7mm x 64 Brenneke cal., features oil finished stock with Schnabel forend and skip-line checkering, high luster bluing, 22 or 24 in. barrel with adj. rear sight, 7 1/8 lbs. Mfg. 1996-2001.

	$480	$400	$350	$285	$260	$235	$200

Last MSR was $554.

MODEL 116-BSS WEATHER WARRIOR - .270 Win., .30-06, .300 Win. Mag., .300 Rem. Ultra Mag., or 7mm Rem. Mag. cal., long action, brown wood laminate stock with cut checkering, stainless steel action and tapered barrel, 2-4 shot internal mag., 24 or 26 in. barrel, 7-7¾ lbs. New 2001.

MSR	$644		$560	$480	$410		

MODEL 116-FSS - .22-250 Rem. (mfg. 1992 only), .223 Rem. (mfg. 1992-98), .243 Win. (mfg. 1993-98), .270 Win., .30-06, .308 Win. (disc. 1998), 7mm Rem. Mag., 7mm STW (new 2001), 7mm Rem. Ultra Mag. (new 2002), .300 Win. Mag., .300 Rem. Ultra Mag. (new 2001), .338 Win. Mag., or .375 H&H (new 2002) cal., short or long (new 2001) action, features black Dupont Rynite synthetic stock, stainless steel metal parts, drilled and tapped for scope mounting, 22 or 24 in. barrel, 3 or 4 shot mag., 6¾ lbs. New 1991.

MSR	$500		$435	$390	$330	$275	$245	$225	$200

This model is also available with left-hand action (Model 116-FLSS).

★ Model 116-FCSS - .270 Win., .30-06, 7mm Rem. Mag., or .300 Win. Mag. cal., otherwise similar to Model 116-FSS, except has removable 3 or 4 shot mag. with recessed push button release, 22 or 24 in. barrel, 6½ lbs. Mfg. 1992-2001.

	$470	$410	$360	$320	$290	$260	$230

Last MSR was $532.

This model is also available with left-hand action (Model 116-FLCSS).

★ Model 116-FSK (Kodiak) - similar cals. as Model 116-FCSS, except also available in .338 Win Mag. cal., stainless steel construction, 22 in. barrel with recoil arrester, cocking indicator, 3 shot mag., black synthetic sporter stock, no sights, 6½ lbs. Mfg. 1993-2000.

	$495	$430	$370	$325	$290	$260	$230

Last MSR was $569.

This model was also available with left-hand action (Model 116-FLSK).

MODEL 116-US (ULTRA STAINLESS) - .270 Win., .30-06, 7mm Rem. Mag., or .300 Win. Mag. cal., 24 in. barrel, checkered walnut stock and forearm with ebony tip, no sights, 7 1/8 lbs. Mfg. 1995-98.

	$625	$550	$500	$450	$400	$360	$330

Last MSR was $700.

MODEL 116-SE (SAFARI EXPRESS) - .300 Win. Mag., .300 Rem. Ultra Mag. (new 2002), .338 Win. Mag. (disc. 2001), .375 H&H (new 2000), .425 Express (mfg. 1995 only), or .458 Win. Mag. cal., stainless steel receiver and 24 in. barrel with adj. muzzle brake, controlled round feeding, select grade checkered walnut stock with solid recoil pad and ebony forend, 3-leaf express sights, 8½ lbs. New 1994.

MSR	$975		$850	$750	$675	$615	$575	$535	$475

MODEL 116-FSAK - .270 Win., .30-06, .300 Win. Mag., .300 Rem. Ultra Mag. (new 2001), .338 Win. Mag., .375 H&H (new 2002), 7mm STW (new 2001), 7mm Rem. Ultra Mag. (new 2002), or 7mm Rem. Mag. cal., short or long (new 2001) action, features 22 in. fluted stainless steel barrel with adj. muzzle brake, 6½ lbs. New 1994.

MSR	$578		$500	$445	$380	$335	$295	$265	$235

This model is also available with left-hand action (Model 116-FLSAK, not availble in 7mm STW, 7mm Rem. Ultra Mag., or .375 H&H cals.).

Grading	100%	98%	95%	90%	80%	70%	60%

MODEL 116-FCSAK - .270 Win., .30-06, .300 Win. Mag., or 7mm Rem. Mag. cal., features push button activated detachable box mag., 22 in. fluted barrel with adj. muzzle brake, 6½ lbs. Mfg. 1994-2000.

	$590	**$505**	**$430**	**$365**	**$315**	**$275**	**$245**

Last MSR was $668.

This model was also available with left-hand action (Model 116-FLCSAK).

MODEL 116FXP3 PACKAGE - 270 Win., .30-06, .300 Rem. Ultra Mag., .300 Win. Mag., .338 Win. Mag., 7mm STW, 7mm Rem. Mag., or 7mm Rem. Ultra Mag. cal., long action, stainless action 22, 24, or 26 in. stainless barrel w/o sights, checkered black synthetic stock, includes nickel finished 3x9x40X scope and mounts, supplied with sling, approx. 6½-7 lbs. New 2002.

MSR	**$534**		**$455**	**$380**	**$320**		

MODEL 170 PUMP RIFLE - .30-30 Win. or .35 Rem. (rare) cal., 22 in. barrel, folding leaf sight, 3 shot tube mag., checkered pistol grip stock. Mfg. 1970-1981.

	$180	**$155**	**$140**	**$110**	**$90**	**$65**	**$55**

This model was mfg. by Emhart.

MODEL 170C - .30-30 Win. cal. only, similar to 170, 18½ in. barrel. Mfg. 1974-1981.

	$195	**$170**	**$150**	**$115**	**$90**	**$65**	**$55**

SHOTGUNS

Most Savage shotguns (except the Model 312 Series) fall under the domain of Savage Industries, Inc.

Savage made a wide variety of inexpensive, utilitarian shotguns that to date have attracted mostly shooting interest, but little collector interest. A listing of these models may be found in the back of this text under "Serialization".

The models listed are grouped by configuration, and are not in numerical sequence.

MODEL 420 O/U - 12, 16, or 20 ga., 26-30 in. barrel, various chokes, boxlock, double trigger, extractors, plain pistol grip stock. Mfg. 1937-1943.

	$385	**$305**	**$275**	**$250**	**$210**	**$195**	**$155**
Single trigger	**$440**	**$360**	**$330**	**$305**	**$265**	**$220**	**$195**

MODEL 430 O/U - similar to Model 420, with checkered stock and solid rib, recoil pad.

	$440	**$360**	**$305**	**$275**	**$240**	**$220**	**$195**
Single trigger	**$495**	**$415**	**$360**	**$320**	**$285**	**$265**	

$220

MODEL 220 SINGLE BARREL - 12, 16, 20, 28 ga., or .410 bore, 26-32 in. barrel, various chokes, hammerless, plain pistol grip stock. Mfg. 1938-1965.

	$125	**$100**	**$85**	**$75**	**$65**	**$50**	**$40**

MODEL 220P - similar to Model 220, with poly choke, not made in .410 bore.

	$90	**$65**	**$55**	**$45**	**$35**	**$30**	**$30**

MODEL 220 AC - similar to Model 220, with Savage adj. choke.

	$100	**$85**	**$65**	**$55**	**$45**	**$35**	**$30**

MODEL 220L - similar to Model 220, with sidelever. Mfg. 1965-1972.

	$90	**$65**	**$55**	**$45**	**$35**	**$30**	**$30**

MODEL 720 AUTOLOADER STANDARD - 12 or 16 ga., Browning A-5 style semi- auto action, 26-32 in. barrels, various chokes, checkered pistol grip stock. Mfg. 1930- 1949.

	$225	**$180**	**$165**	**$155**	**$140**	**$120**	**$110**

MODEL 720 RIOT - see the "Trench/Riot Shotgun" category in the T section for more information and prices.

S

Grading	100%	98%	95%	90%	80%	70%	60%

MODEL 726 SEMI-AUTO UPLAND SPORTER - similar to Model 720, except 2 shell mag. Mfg. 1931-1949.

	$275	$195	$165	$155	$140	$120	$110

MODEL 740C SKEET GUN - similar to Model 726, with Cutts Compensator and skeet stock, 24½ in. barrel. Mfg. 1936-1949.

	$305	$230	$200	$175	$155	$140	$120

MODEL 745 LIGHTWEIGHT - similar to Model 720, with alloy receiver, 12 ga. only, 28 in. barrel. Mfg. 1940-1949.

	$275	$195	$165	$155	$140	$120	$110

MODEL 755 STANDARD SEMI-AUTO - 12 or 16 ga., 26, 28, or 30 in. barrel, various chokes, rounded off receiver, checkered pistol grip stock. Mfg. 1949-1958.

	$265	$180	$160	$150	$140	$120	$110

MODEL 755SC - similar to Model 755, with Savage Super Choke.

	$275	$195	$165	$155	$140	$120	$110

MODEL 775 LIGHTWEIGHT SEMI-AUTO - similar to Model 755, with alloy receiver. Mfg. 1950-1965.

	$275	$195	$180	$165	$150	$140	$120

MODEL 775SC - similar to Model 775, with Savage Super Choke.

	$285	$205	$195	$175	$160	$150	$130

MODEL 750 SEMI-AUTO - 12 ga., Browning patterned semi-auto, 26 or 28 in. barrels, various chokes, checkered pistol grip stock. Mfg. 1960-1969.

	$275	$195	$165	$155	$140	$120	$110

MODEL 750SC - similar to Model 750, with Savage Super Choke.

	$285	$205	$175	$165	$150	$130	$120

MODEL 750AC - similar to Model 750, with poly choke.

	$285	$205	$175	$165	$150	$130	$120

MODEL 21 SLIDE ACTION - similar to Model 28, except stock has no checkering. Mfg. 1920-28.

	$300	$265	$235	$190	$165	$150	$130

MODEL 28 SLIDE ACTION - 12, 16, or 20 ga., patterned after the Winchester Model 12. Mfg. 1927-1934.

	$300	$265	$235	$190	$165	$150	$130

This model was available in either standard configuration (Models 28A and 28B), Riot (28C), Trap (28D), or Special (28S).

MODEL 30 SLIDE ACTION - 12, 16, 20 ga., or .410 bore, 26, 28, or 30 in. barrels, various chokes, VR, plain pistol grip stock. Mfg. 1958-1970.

	$220	$175	$155	$140	$120	$100	$85
Checkered Late Model	$230	$185	$165	$150	$130	$110	$95

MODEL 30AC - similar to Model 30, with adj. choke, checkered wood, 12 ga. only. Mfg. 1959-1970.

	$240	$200	$175	$160	$145	$120	$100

MODEL 30T TRAP AND DUCK GUN - similar to Model 30, with 30 in. full barrel, 12 ga. only, Monte Carlo stock and pad. Mfg. 1963-1970.

	$230	$185	$165	$150	$130	$110	$90

MODEL 30FG TAKEDOWN ACTION - 12, 20 ga., or .410 bore, 26, 28, or 30 in. barrel, various chokes, checkered pistol grip stock. Mfg. 1970-1975.

	$175	$155	$130	$110	$95	$85	$70

Grading	100%	98%	95%	90%	80%	70%	60%

MODEL 30T TAKEDOWN TRAP - 12 ga. only, 30 in. full barrel, Monte Carlo stock with pad. Mfg. 1970-1973.

| | $195 | $175 | $155 | $140 | $110 | $100 | $85 |

MODEL 30AC TAKEDOWN - similar to Model 30FG, with adj. choke, 12 or 20 ga., 26 in. barrel. Mfg. 1971-1972.

| | $200 | $180 | $165 | $150 | $120 | $110 | $90 |

MODEL 30 TAKEDOWN SLUG GUN - similar to Model 30FG, with 32 in. cylinder bore barrel, rifle sights. Mfg. 1971-disc.

| | $195 | $175 | $160 | $140 | $110 | $100 | $85 |

MODEL 30D TAKEDOWN - similar to Model 30FG, with VR, engraved receiver and pad. Mfg. 1971-disc.

| | $200 | $180 | $165 | $150 | $120 | $110 | $90 |

MODEL 67 SLIDE ACTION - see listing under Stevens Section.

FOX MODELS B, B-SE, AND STEVENS 311 - see listing under Stevens Section.

MODEL 210F SLUG WARRIOR BOLT ACTION (MASTER SHOT) - 12 ga. only, 3 in. chamber, built on Model 100 action with controlled round feeding, 24 in. rifled barrel (1:35 twist), 2 shot detachable mag., 60 degree bolt lift, black synthetic stock with checkering and recoil pad, top tang safety, no sights, 7½ lbs. New 1997.

| MSR $416 | $365 | $315 | $275 | $235 | $215 | $195 | $180 |

❊ *Model 210FT* - similar to Model 210F, except has Advantage camo stock and mag., 24 in. smooth bore barrel accepts Win. style choke tubes. Mfg. 1997-2000.

| | $410 | $350 | $305 | $265 | $235 | $215 | $195 |

Last MSR was $466.

MODEL 242 O/U - .410 bore, single exposed hammer, single trigger, barrel selector lever, full chokes. Mfg. 1977-1981.

| | $350 | $300 | $260 | $230 | $200 | $175 | $150 |

MODEL 440/440B O/U - 12 or 20 ga., 26, 28, or 30 in. barrels, various chokes, boxlock, ST (Model 440) or SST (Model 440B), extractors, checkered pistol grip stock, VR. Imported from Italy 1968-1972.

| | $495 | $440 | $415 | $385 | $330 | $305 | $250 |

MODEL 440T - similar to Model 440, 12 ga., 30 in. barrel only, imp mod. or full choke, wide VR, trap style stock, pad. Mfg. 1969-1972.

| | $550 | $470 | $440 | $415 | $385 | $360 | $330 |

MODEL 444 DELUXE - similar to Model 440, with auto ejectors, select walnut. Mfg. 1969- 1972.

| | $550 | $470 | $440 | $415 | $385 | $360 | $330 |

MODEL 550 SxS - 12 or 20 ga., 26, 28, or 30 in. barrels (made by Valmet - rare), various chokes, boxlock, auto ejectors, single trigger, checkered pistol grip stock. Mfg. 1971- 1973.

| | $275 | $220 | $195 | $165 | $150 | $130 | $110 |

KIMEL KAMPER SINGLE SHOT - 20 ga. or .410 bore, 3 in. chamber, 18 1/2 in. barrel, pistol grip hardwood stock and forearm, buttrap holds 3 shells, bottom opening, exposed hammer. Mfg. 1979-c.1981

| | $175 | $150 | $135 | $120 | $105 | $90 | $75 |

MODEL 312 SERIES O/U - 12 ga. only, boxlock action, 3 in. chambers, vent. barrels, satin chrome finished receiver, checkered walnut stock and forearm, SST, choke tubes, approx. 7 lbs. Mfg. 1990-93.

The Model 312 Series falls under the domain of Savage Arms, Inc.

❊ *312 Field* - 26 or 28 in. VR barrels with choke tubes.

| | $585 | $520 | $485 | $435 | $395 | $360 | $330 |

S

Grading	100%	98%	95%	90%	80%	70%	60%

✳ *312 Trap* - 30 in. barrels only, Monte Carlo stock with recoil pad.

	$615	$550	$500	$460	$415	$375	$330

✳ *312 Sporting Clays* - 28 in. barrels only with 7 choke tubes provided, recoil pad.

	$595	$530	$485	$435	$395	$360	$320

MODEL 330 O/U - 12 or 20 ga., 26, 28, or 30 in. barrels, various chokes, boxlock, SST, extractors, checkered pistol grip stock. Mfg. by Valmet between 1969-1980.

	$495	$440	$385	$335	$275	$250	$220

   Add 25% for extra set of barrels.

MODEL 333T - similar to Model 330, with 30 in. VR barrels bored imp. mod. and full choke, trap stock with pad. Mfg. by Valmet between 1972-1980.

	$550	$470	$415	$385	$360	$305	$275

MODEL 333 O/U - 12 or 20 (rare) ga., 26, 28, or 30 in. VR barrels, various chokes, boxlock, SST, auto ejectors, checkered pistol grip stock. Mfg. by Valmet between 1973- 1980.

	$650	$575	$500	$450	$400	$375	$330

   Add 25% for extra set of barrels.
   Add 30% for 20 ga.

SAVIN, J.C.

Current manufacturer located in St. Etienne, France. J.C. Savin manufactures only best quality shotguns and rifles per individual order. Annual production is approx. 25 long guns. Please contact the factory directly for an individual quotation.

RIFLES: DOUBLE, CUSTOM

Available in either O/U or SxS sidelock or Anson & Deely boxlock. Available in various cals. (.30-.577NE), 24 or 26 in. barrels. Prices start at $14,000 for boxlock and $25,000 for sidelock action.

SHOTGUNS: DOUBLE, CUSTOM

Available in either O/U or SxS sidelock configuration, 12 or 20 ga., DT or ST, premier quality. Prices start at $23,000. A SxS round action Dixon model with trigger plate is also available in 12 or 20 ga., with prices starting at $2,200.

SAXONIA

Current manufacturer located in Schwarzenberg, Germany. No current U.S. importation.

Saxonia makes semi-auto pistols, security/combat shotguns, and bolt action sniper rifles in various configurations. Please contact the company directly (see Trademark Index) to obtain model information and domestic availability.

SCATTERGUN TECHNOLOGIES INC. (S.G.T.)

Current manufacturer located in Berryville, AR since 1999. Previously located in Nashville, TN 1991-99. Distributor, dealer, and consumer sales.

During 1999, Wilson Combat purchased Scattergun Technologies. S.G.T. manufactures practical defense, tactical, and hunting shotguns in 12 ga. only, utilizing Remington Models 870 and 11-87 actions in various configurations as listed. All shotguns feature 3 in. chamber capacity and parkerized finish.

SHOTGUNS: SEMI-AUTO

   Add $15 for short stock on models listed.
   Subtract $100 if w/o Armor-Tuff finish on models listed.

K-9 MODEL - 12 ga., 18 in. barrel, adj. ghost ring sight, 7 shot mag., side saddle, synthetic buttstock and forearm.

	MSR	$1,270		$1,075	$875	$775

Grading	100%	98%	95%	90%	80%	70%	60%

SWAT MODEL - 12 ga., similar to K-9 Model, except has 14 in. barrel and forearm with 11,000 CP flashlight.

    MSR $1,525 $1,275 $1,075 $895

    This model is available for military and law enforcement only.

URBAN SNIPER MODEL - 12 ga., 18 in. rifled barrel, scout optics, 7 shot mag., side saddle, synthetic butt stock, forearm and bipod. Disc. 1999.

                    $1,225 $1,075 $950

                                     Last MSR was $1,390.

SHOTGUNS: SLIDE ACTION

    Add $15 for short stock on models listed.
    Subtract $100 if w/o Armor-Tuff finish on models listed.

STANDARD MODEL - 12 ga., 18 in. barrel, adj. ghost ring sight, 7 shot mag., side saddle, synthetic buttstock and forearm with 11,000 CP flashlight.

    MSR $1,070 $950 $775 $575

PROFESSIONAL MODEL - 12 ga., similar to Standard Model, except has 14 in. barrel and 6 shot mag.

    MSR $1,095 $970 $785 $580

    This model is available for military and law enforcement only.

EXPERT MODEL - 12 ga., 18 in. barrel with Mod. choke, nickel/Teflon finished receiver, adj. ghost ring sight, forearm incorporates 11,000 CP flashlight. Mfg. 1997- 2000.

                    $1,200 $995 $775

                                       Last MSR was $1,350.

ENTRY MODEL - 12 ga., 12½ in. barrel with mod. choke, adj. ghost ring sights, 5 shot mag., side saddle, synthetic buttstock and nylon strap assisted forearm with 5,000 CP flashlight.

    MSR $1,125 $995 $800 $600

    This model is available for military and law enforcement only.

COMPACT MODEL - 12½ in. barrel with mod. choke, adj. ghost ring sight, 5 shot mag., synthetic butt stock and forearm. Mfg. 1994-99.

                    $575 $510 $420

                                       Last MSR was $635.

    This model was available for military and law enforcement only.

PRACTICAL TURKEY MODEL - 20 in. barrel with extra full choke, adj. ghost ring sight, 5 shot mag. for 3 in. shells, synthetic buttstock and forearm. Mfg. 1995-99.

                    $545 $500 $465

                                       Last MSR was $595.

LOUIS AWERBUCK SIGNATURE MODEL - 18 in. barrel with fixed choke, adj. ghost ring sight, 5 shot mag., side saddle, wood butt stock with recoil reducer and forearm. Mfg. 1994- 99.

                    $625 $490 $385

                                       Last MSR was $705.

F.B.I. MODEL - similar to Standard Model, except has 5 shot mag. Disc. 1999.

                    $715 $625 $490

                                       Last MSR was $770.

MILITARY MODEL - 18 in. barrel with vent. handguard and M-9 bayonet lug, adj. ghost ring rear sight, 7 shot mag., synthetic stock and grooved corn cob forearm. Mfg. 1997-98.

                    $625 $490 $385

                                       Last MSR was $690.

PATROL MODEL - 18 in. barrel, adj. ghost ring sight, 5 shot mag., synthetic butt stock and forearm. Disc. 1999.

                    $545 $500 $465

                                       Last MSR was $595.

S

Grading	100%	98%	95%	90%	80%	70%	60%

BORDER PATROL MODEL 20 - 12 ga., similar to Patrol Model, except has 7 shot mag.

    MSR   **$850**   **$725**   **$600**   **$525**

BORDER PATROL MODEL 21 - similar to Border Patrol Model 20, except has 14 in. barrel and 6 shot mag.

    MSR   **$870**   **$740**   **$610**   **$530**

    This model is available for military and law enforcement only.

CONCEALMENT MODEL 00 - 12½ in. barrel with fixed choke, 5 shot mag., bead sight, grooved wood forearm and pistol grip. Disc. 1998.

                $490   **$395**   **$280**

                                        Last MSR was $550.

CONCEALMENT MODEL 01 - similar to Concealment Model 00, except has synthetic finger-grooved combat forearm and pistol grip. Disc. 1993.

                $475   **$395**   **$295**

                                        Last MSR was $525.

CONCEALMENT MODEL 02 - similar to Concealment Model 00, except has Pachmayr forearm and pistol grip. Disc. 1993.

                $495   **$415**   **$315**

                                        Last MSR was $555.

CONCEALMENT MODEL 03 - similar to Concealment Model 01, except has synthetic nylon strap assisted forearm with 5,000 CP flashlight. Disc. 1993.

                $550   **$455**   **$350**

                                        Last MSR was $625.

BREACHING MODEL - similar to Concealment Model 00, except has standoff device. Disc. 1998.

                $450   **$390**   **$340**

                                        Last MSR was $500.

SCHALL

Previous manufacturer located in Hartford, CT, circa late 1920s. This company was later purchased by High Standard.

PISTOLS

REPEATING HANDGUN - .22 LR cal. only, 6½ or 7 ½ in. barrel, walnut grips, target pistol, mag. fed manual repeating action.

                $425   **$360**   **$320**   **$270**   **$220**   **$180**   **$150**

    Subtract 50% if not in working order.

SCHEIRING, GES. m.b.H.

Current custom rifle manufacturer located in Ferlach, Austria.

H. Scheiring manufactures best quality rifles (including O/U, SxS, and Stalking variations) per individual customer special order. The factory should be contacted directly for more information regarding current models and domestic availability (see Trademark Index).

SCHELLER SPEZIALWAFFEN

Previous manufacturer located in Suhl, Germany that specialized in bolt action rifles.

SCHILLING, FA. ALFRED

Current rifle manufacturer and gunsmith established in 1898, and located in Zella-Melis, Germany.

Schilling manufactures high quality target rifles, in addition to providing gunsmithing services, including color case hardening. All guns are custom order, and the standard Schilling breechblock rifle retails at $4,258, while the Aydt target model has na MSR of $2,823. Please contact the company for more information, including an individual price quotation, delivery time, and availability (see Trademark Index).

Grading	100%	98%	95%	90%	80%	70%	60%

SCHMIDT-RUBIN RIFLES

Please refer to the Swiss Military listing in this section.

SCHMITT FRERES

Previous manufacturer located in Saint Etienne, France.

This manufacturer produced copies of 1894 patent Darne R model guns until 1956. While higher grades do exist, they do not command the prices given for the later patent (1909) Darne produced guns. Lower grade guns will be priced in the same range as Soleihac and lower grade Darne R models.

SCHULTZ & LARSEN

Previous manufacturer located in Otterup, Denmark beginning 1911.

RIFLES: BOLT ACTION

NO. 47 MATCH RIFLE - .22 LR cal., single shot, 28 in. heavy barrel, target sights, set trigger, free rifle stock.

	$660	$550	$495	$440	$385	$360	$330

M61 MATCH RIFLE - .22 LR cal., single shot, 28 in. heavy barrel, target sights, set trigger, free rifle stock, palm rest.

	$895	$825	$740	$680	$600	$550	$500

M62 MATCH RIFLE - various cals., single shot, 28 in. heavy barrel, target sights, set trigger, free rifle stock, palm rest.

	$995	$875	$780	$700	$620	$550	$500

MODEL 54 FREE RIFLE - any American centerfire standard caliber, plus 6.5x55mm, 27 in. heavy barrel, target sights, free rifle stock.

	$825	$745	$690	$605	$550	$495	$440

MODEL 54J SPORTING RIFLE - .270 Win., .30-06, or 7x61 Sharpe and Hart cal., 3 shot, 24 in. barrel, checkered Monte Carlo stock, no sights.

	$650	$550	$470	$415	$360	$330	$300

MODEL 68 DL - .22-250 Rem., .243 Win., 6mm Rem., .264 Win. Mag., .270 Win., .30-06, .308 Win., 7x61 S&H, 7mm Rem. Mag., 8x57JS, .300 Win. Mag., .308 Norma Mag., .338 Win. Mag., .358 Norma Mag., or .458 Win. Mag. cal., 24 in. barrel, Bofors Steel receiver, bolt has 4 rear locking lugs, select French walnut, adj. trigger, no sights except for .458 Mag.

	$725	$650	$575	$525	$495	$460	$430

SCHUERMAN ARMS., LTD.

Current bolt action rifle manufacturer located in Scottsdale, AZ.

Schuerman manufactures the M40 bolt action rifle, a new design that incorporates controlled round feeding with a fully enclosed case. The M40 is scheduled for release in mid-2001, and the MSR is $1,500. Please contact the factory directly for more information (see Trademark Index).

SCHUETZEN PISTOL WORKS
(FORMERLY SAFARI ARMS)

Schuetzen Pistol Works is the custom shop for Safari Arms - please refer to the Safari Arms Listing for more information.

S

SCHUETZEN RIFLES

A Schuetzen Rifle is a special single shot target rifle. During the time span 1875-1945 this target configuration rifle was very popular with competition shooters. Many of these guns had elaborate locking systems, top quality sights, double set triggers, heavy barrels, palm and thumb rests, sculptured cheekpiece, Swiss style butt plate, etc. Rather than list all the various domestic and European makers (there are hundreds), it should be noted that since there are so many combinations of options for this configuration that most guns have to be examined and appraised individually. Most non-major trademarks sell in the $550- $1,500 range, depending

Grading	100%	98%	95%	90%	80%	70%	60%

on features and condition. A famous trademark specimen (Ballard, Stevens, Winchester, etc.) in a rare model with superior original condition can bring over $10,000. Schuetzen Rifles are a field in themselves and a knowledgeable dealer/collector should be consulted before buying or selling one of these guns.

SCOTT, W.C., LTD.

Previous manufacturer established during 1834 and located in Birmingham, England. All operations ceased during 1991.

Established in 1834 by William Scott, located in Birmingham, England, and remained in the family until 1897. At this time, Scott merged with P. Webley & Son to form Webley & Scott Revolver and Arms Co., Ltd. (later changed to Webley & Scott Ltd.). Even though Scott family members were no longer associated with this new company, the Scott gun-line was continued with the trademark intact until 1935. Thereafter, only a few guns were marked Scott. In 1979, Webley & Scott ceased manufacture of all firearms. A new company, W. & C. Scott, was formed in 1980 utilizing mostly employees of Webley & Scott. W. & C. Scott remained part of its parent company, Harris & Sheldon (also had controlling interest in Hardy and Churchill trademarks), until 1985 when Scott was purchased by Holland & Holland. Manufacture of Scott guns decreased substantially after the merger, and in September 1991, W. & C. Scott ceased operation all together. During its 157 years of production, Scott and Webley & Scott produced approximately, 150,000 double guns, 10,000 rifles (either double or bolt-action) and thousands of single guns and single rifles.

SHOTGUNS: SxS

All W.C. Scott Shotguns were discontinued in 1990. W.C. Scott also manufactured many hammer guns that vary in price from $250-$2,500, depending on grade and original condition.

KINMOUNT - 12, 16, 20, or 28 ga., boxlock action, ejectors, deluxe checkered walnut, scroll engraving.

$6,500	$5,750	$5,000	$4,500	$4,000	$3,000	$2,500

Last MSR was $11,000.

Add 20% for 28 ga. or .410 bore.
Add 10% for SNT.

BOWOOD - 12, 16, 20, or 28 ga., boxlock action, ejectors, deluxe checkered walnut, extensive scroll engraving.

$7,500	$6,500	$5,750	$5,000	$4,500	$4,000	$3,500

Last MSR was $12,500.

Add 20% for 28 ga. or .410 bore.
Add 10% for SNT.

CHATSWORTH - 12, 16, 20, or 28 ga., top-of-the-line boxlock action, ejectors, deluxe checkered walnut, extensive scroll engraving.

$8,750	$7,500	$6,500	$5,750	$5,000	$4,500	$4,000

Last MSR was $14,000.

Add 20% for 28 ga. or .410 bore.
Add 10% for SNT.

BLENHEIM - 12 bore only, upgraded models, custom made to individual specifications, originally priced per individual order.

Specimen rarity precludes percentage grading pricing. Individual appraisals have to be secured on this model.

SEARCY, B. & CO.

Current rifle manufacturer established in 1975 and located in Boron, CA.

RIFLES: SxS

B. Searcy & Co. manufactures a unique stainless steel double rifle in a variety of calibers. Currently, prices range from $8,500 (Field Grade boxlock) up to $50,000 (sidelock in .700 NE). Please contact the factory directly (see Trademark Index) for current model information and a price quotation.

Grading	100%	98%	95%	90%	80%	70%	60%

SEARS ROEBUCK

Catalog merchandiser that, in addition to selling major trademark firearms, also private labeled many configurations of firearms (mostly longarms) under a variety of trademarks and logos (i.e., J.C. Higgins, Ted Williams, Ranger, etc.).

A general guideline for Sears Roebuck and related labels is that values are generally lower than those of the major factory models from which they were derived. Remember, 99% of Sears Roebuck and related label guns get priced by their shootability factor in today's competitive marketplace, not collectability. An extensive crossover listing (see Storebrand Cross-Over List) has been provided in the back of this text for linking up the various Sears Roebuck models to the original manufacturer with respective "crossover" model numbers.

SECURITY INDUSTRIES

Previous manufacturer located in Little Ferry, NJ.

REVOLVERS

MODEL PSS 38 DOUBLE ACTION - .38 Spl. cal., 5 shot cylinder, 2 in. barrel, stainless steel, fixed sights, wood grips. Mfg. 1973-1978.

	$175	$150	$140	$130	$125	$110	$100

MODEL PM357 - .357 Mag. cal., similar to Model PSS 38, 2½ in. barrel. Mfg. 1975- disc.

	$225	$175	$165	$150	$140	$125	$110

MODEL PPM 357 - .357 Mag. cal., 5 shot, 2 in. barrel, spurless hammer until 1977, new models have spur. Mfg. 1965-disc.

	$225	$175	$165	$150	$140	$125	$110

SEDCO INDUSTRIES, INC.

Previous manufacturer located in Lake Elsinore, CA until 1991.

PISTOLS: SEMI-AUTO

MODEL SP-22 - .22 LR cal., single action, 2½ in. barrel, rotary safety, serrated slide, nickel, satin nickel (new 1990), or black metal finish, simulated pearl grips in white, blue, grey, or pink, 11 oz. Mfg. 1989-90 only.

	$60	$55	$50	$45	$40	$35	$35

Last MSR was $69.

SEDGLEY, R.F., INC.

Previous manufacturer located in Philadelphia, PA.

RIFLES: BOLT ACTION

SPRINGFIELD SPORTING RIFLE - .218 Bee, .220 Swift, .22-3000, .22-4000, .22 Hornet, .25-35 WCF, .250-3000 Sav., .257 Roberts, .270 Win., 7x57mm Mauser, or .30-06 cal., '03 Springfield bolt action, 24 in. barrel, Lyman receiver sight, checkered pistol grip stock, pre-WWII.

	$1,250	$1,125	$995	$875	$750	$625	$495

SPRINGFIELD CARBINE SPORTER - similar to Rifle, with 20 in. barrel, and full length stock.

	$1,450	$1,250	$1,125	$995	$875	$750	$625

SEECAMP, L.W. CO., INC.

Current handgun manufacturer located in Milford, CT. Dealer direct sales only.

All Seecamp pistols are hand machined and hand fitted from stainless steel. Manufacture has always emphasized quality over quantity - this explains why values often exceed the company's retail prices. There is simply more demand than supply.

S

Grading	100%	98%	95%	90%	80%	70%	60%

PISTOLS: SEMI-AUTO

LWS .25 ACP MODEL - .25 ACP cal., double action, 2 in. barrel, 7 shot mag., stainless steel, matte finish, no sights, 12 oz. Approx. 4,000 mfg. 1981-1985.

$400	$325	$275	$235	$220	$210	$200

Last MSR was $275.

LWS 32 MODEL - .32 ACP cal., (mfg. recommends .32 ACP Win. Silvertip ammo only), double action, 2.06 in. barrel, stainless steel, 6 shot mag., no sights, extreme backorder situation coupled with high demand has resulted in elevated 100% values, 11½ oz. Mfg. Jan. 1985-present.

MSR	$425	$575	$525	$475	$425	$395	$375	$350

This model is available in either a matte or polished finish. The polished finish carries a slight premium.

MATCHED PAIR - includes both .25 ACP and .32 ACP pistols with the same serial number, approx. 200 sets were mfg. before the BATF stopped this practice.

$1,200	$1,000	$850

This set contained a matte finished .25 ACP and a polished .32 ACP.

LWS-380 MODEL - .380 ACP cal. (mfg. recommends .380 ACP Win. Silvertip ammo only), identical in appearance to the LWS 32 Model, 2.06 in. barrel, double action only, delayed blowback mechanism, polished stainless steel, checkered black glass filled nylon grips, no sights, 11.5 oz. Very limited production beginning 2000.

MSR	$850	$850	$775	$650

SEITZ

Previous manufacturer located in Portland, OR circa mid-1980s -1993.

SHOTGUNS: SINGLE BARREL TRAP

SINGLE BARREL TRAP GUN - 12 ga. only, single barrel, various barrel lengths, pull or release trigger, only 45 guns mfg.

$18,500	$16,000	$13,000	$10,000	$8,500	$7,700	$6,950

SEMMERLING

Current trademark owned by American Derringer Corp., located in Waco, TX. Previously manufactured by Semmerling Corporation, located in Boston, MA from 1978-1982.

Less than 600 LM-4 pistols were originally mfg. by the Semmerling Corporation.

PISTOLS: SLIDE ACTION

LM-4 PISTOL - .45 ACP cal., 2 in. barrel, blue, smallest .45 ACP repeater available, slide is worked manually with thumb on serrated slide-top, extremely high quality, hand fitted and choice of finishes include chrome, electroless nickel, or high polish blue.

Chrome	$2,950	$2,600	$2,300	$2,100	$1,950	$1,725	$1,600
Electroless nickel	$3,200	$2,950	$2,600	$2,300	$2,100	$1,950	$1,725
High polish blue	$4,950	$4,500	$4,000	$3,600	$3,200	$2,800	$2,500

The original U.S. Army contract pistol mfg. by Semmerling in Boston sold for $5,000. Earlier mfg. by Lichtman will also command a premium over values listed.

✳ LM-4 Stainless Steel (Current Mfg.) - matte finish stainless steel variation of the LM-4, combat grey, satin, high polish finish, rosewood grips, limited mfg. by special order only.

MSR	$2,635	$2,350	$1,975	$1,775

SENTINEL ARMS

Previous importer of Arsenal Bulgaria pistols and rifles.

S

Grading	100%	98%	95%	90%	80%	70%	60%

C. SHARPS ARMS CO. INC.

Current manufacturer located in Big Timber, MT. Distributed by Montana Armory located in Big Timber, MT.

Montana Armory, Inc. currently distributes smokeless powder replicas of C. Sharps rifles/ carbines and the Winchester Model 1885 single shot. They are able to shoot both smokeless and black powder loads. Most models are available in the following cals.: .40-50, .40- 70, .40-90, .45-70, .45-90, .45-100, .45-110, .45-120, .50-70, .50-90, .50-100, and .50-140. All models are authentically reproduced and high quality.

RIFLES: REPRODUCTIONS, SHARPS BLACK POWDER

Currently, C. Sharps Arms Co. Inc. is experiencing a back order situation on some of their models. New Models 1875 and 1885 are experiencing a 2-4 month wait, while the New Model 1874 is currently running over 2-3 years for delivery. However, Montana Armory currently has some models in stock - call for availability and pricing (see Trademark Index).

NEW MODEL 1874 SPORTING

	MSR	$1,495	N/A	N/A	$1,175	$850	$750	$650	$550

In addition to the 1874 Sporting Model, a custom long range target rifle or Schuetzen short range target rifle is available in this model. Because of the extended back order situation on this model, premiums will probably exist for those people who would rather pay a premium than wait.

CUSTOM NEW MODEL 1874 BOSS GUN - features 34 in. No. 1 heavy tapered octagon barrel, vernier tang sight, straight grip stock with cheekrest and steel shotgun butt.

Base price is $3,950 and custom order only. Please contact the factory to obtain a custom quotation on this model.

NEW MODEL 1875 SPORTING RIFLE - similar to New Model 1875 Classic, except has receiver with round crown.

	MSR	$1,095	N/A	N/A	$925	$850	$795	$725	$650

NEW MODEL 1875 CLASSIC RIFLE - receiver with octagon top, 26, 28, or 30 in. tapered full octagon barrel, straight grip stock with steel toe plate, 9½ lbs. New 1992.

	MSR	$1,385	N/A	N/A	$1,050	$950	$875	$800	$750

NEW MODEL 1875 CARBINE - features 24 in. tapered round barrel. Mfg. 1996-98.

		$750	$675	$600	$500	$450	$375	$325

Last MSR was $810.

NEW MODEL 1875 SADDLE RIFLE - receiver with octagon top, 26 in. barrel only. Disc. 1998.

		$835	$760	$685	$625	$550	$460	$365

Last MSR was $910.

NEW MODEL 1875 BUSINESS RIFLE - receiver with round top, 28 in. heavy tapered round barrel. Disc. 1998.

		$750	$675	$600	$500	$450	$375	$325

Last MSR was $810.

Add $50 for barrel sights.

NEW MODEL 1885 HIGHWALL - .22 LR, .22 Hornet, .219 Zipper, .30-40 Krag, .32-40, .38-55 WCF, .40-65, or .45-70 cal., patterned after the Winchester Model 1885 single shot, falling block action, case colored receiver and small parts, 26-30 in. octagon barrel. New 1992.

	MSR	$1,350	$1,050	$900	$775	$650	$550	$475	$410

Add $200 for New Model 1885 Highwall Classic rifle (crescent buttplate and satin grey receiver finish).

SHARPS, CHRISTIAN

Previously manufactured by Sharps Rifle Manufacturing Company circa 1851-1855 and located in Windsor, VT. Also manufactured in Hartford, CT under same name between 1855- 1874. Reorganized as Sharps Rifle Company in 1876 with production resuming in Hartford (1876 only) and Bridgeport, CT from 1877-1881.

S

100%	98%	95%	90%	80%	70%	60%	50%	40%	30%	20%	10%

HANDGUNS

REVOLVER, PERCUSSION - made 1850s in Philadelphia, production about 2000, 3 in. octagonal tip-up barrel with rib, .25 caliber, 6 shot.

| $1,950 | $1,750 | $1,500 | $1,275 | $1,100 | $1,000 | $900 | $800 | $700 | $600 | $500 | $400 |

PEPPERBOX PISTOL - also marked Sharps and Hankins, 4-shot breech-loading, .32, .30, or .22 rimfire cal., firing pin rotates, brass frame with silver plating, or case-hardening on iron frame.

* **First Model** - 5 variations, 2½ in. barrel. Scarcer variations can be worth up to 150% more.

| $595 | $550 | $500 | $465 | $430 | $400 | $360 | $330 | $300 | $275 | $250 | $225 |

* **Second Model** - 5 variations, 3 in. barrel. Scarcer variations can be worth up to 150% more.

| $595 | $550 | $500 | $465 | $430 | $400 | $360 | $330 | $300 | $275 | $250 | $225 |

* **Third Model** - Sharps and Hankins markings, .32 rimfire short, 4 variations, 3½ in. barrel. Premium for scarcer variations.

| $750 | $700 | $650 | $600 | $560 | $520 | $480 | $440 | $400 | $360 | $320 | $280 |

* **Fourth Model** - 4 variations, 2½, 3, or 3½ in. barrel, birds head grip, .32 rimfire long. Premium for scarcer variations.

| $650 | $575 | $525 | $475 | $430 | $400 | $360 | $330 | $300 | $275 | $250 | $225 |

RIFLES: BREECH LOADING

The earliest Sharps rifles and carbines were made for Christian Sharps by A.S. Nippes, in Mill Creek, PA circa 1850, and a year later by Robbins and Lawrence Co. of Windsor, VT. Not until 1856 did the Sharps Rifle Co. of Hartford, CT begin to manufacture its own guns.

MODEL 1849 RIFLE - .36 or .44 cal., percussion breechloader, 30 in. barrels and brass patchboxes were standard, ser. numbered 1 and up, very few examples exist, less than 100 mfg. These are the first of all Sharps long guns, there is no fixed value range. Depending on condition, they could range from $5,000 to $50,000+.

MODEL 1850 RIFLE - .36 or .44 cal., incorporated the Maynard tape primer on the right side of the breech, features similar to Model 1849, approx. 150 mfg. by A.S. Nippes, very rare. Values only slightly less than Model 1849.

MODEL 1851 CARBINE - .52 cal. percussion, 21 5/8 barrel, hammer mounted inside frame, Maynard tape primer. Approx. 1,800 mfg. by Robbins and Lawrence, 200 went to U.S. Government- these will bring a premium.

| $13,200 | $12,100 | $11,000 | $9,900 | $8,800 | $7,920 | $7,100 | $6,600 | $6,050 | $5,350 | $4,840 | $4,400 |

MODEL 1852 CARBINE - this design became standard for all the Sharps for the next two decades, first to be called "slant breech", established Christian Sharps as a major gun manufacturer. Approx. 5,000 mfg. by Robbins and Lawrence, U.S. military markings will command a premium.

| $8,800 | $8,250 | $7,700 | $6,930 | $5,940 | $5,170 | $4,620 | $4,180 | $3,630 | $3,300 | $2,860 | $2,420 |

MODEL 1853 CARBINE - .52 cal., very similar to Model 1852, with walnut stock and brass patchbox, Sharps patented pellet primer feed, ser. no. range 9,000-19,000.

| $7,700 | $7,150 | $6,600 | $5,720 | $4,950 | $4,180 | $3,520 | $2,750 | $2,200 | $1,980 | $1,650 | $1,320 |

> Approx. 10,000 mfg. by Robbins and Lawrence 1854-1858, an additional 3,000 rifles mfg - subtract 25%.

MODEL 1855 CARBINE - .52 cal., U.S. military model, all with Maynard tape primer, this was the period that Robbins and Lawrence failed, and Sharps Rifle Co. took over production. 800 Mfg.

| $11,000 | $9,900 | $9,200 | $8,580 | $7,480 | $6,270 | $5,500 | $4,400 | $3,630 | $3,080 | $2,750 | $2,420 |

100%	98%	95%	90%	80%	70%	60%	50%	40%	30%	20%	10%

Sharps "New Model"

Manufactured in Hartford, CT by Sharps Rifle Manufacturing Co. circa 1859-1866. Visibly different from earlier models because of straight breech and pellet priming feature built into lock plate. Approx. 115,000 were built, all in .52 cal. breechloading paper cartridge. Carbines had 22 in. barrels, rifles came standard with 30 in. round barrels. After ser. numbers reached 100,000, a C prefix was used in the number - i.e. C500 represents ser. no. 100,500.

MODEL 1859 CARBINE - standard with all iron furniture and patchbox, first 3,000 had brass instead of iron, ser. no. range 30,000-75,000. Approx. 33,000 mfg.

100%	98%	95%	90%	80%	70%	60%	50%	40%	30%	20%	10%
$13,200	$10,800	$10,200	$9,000	$7,200	$6,000	$4,800	$4,200	$3,600	$3,000	$2,400	$1,800

MODEL 1863 CARBINE - made with and w/o iron patchbox, ser. no. range 75,000- 140,000. Approx. 65,000 mfg.- those with patchbox will bring a premium.

$11,000	$9,350	$8,800	$7,700	$6,050	$4,950	$3,850	$3,300	$2,750	$2,200	$1,650	$1,325

MODEL 1865 CARBINE - made w/o patchbox, ser. no. range 140,000-145,000. Only 5,000 mfg.

$12,000	$10,000	$9,000	$8,000	$6,500	$5,500	$4,500	$4,000	$3,500	$3,000	$2,500	$2,000

MODEL 1859 RIFLE - iron patchbox only, long forearm fastened with three barrel bands, approx. 4,300 mfg. in carbine ser. range with lug on barrel for attachment of saber bayonet. Approx. 600 were mfg. with 36 in. long barrel - these will command a premium.

$14,000	$12,000	$10,500	$9,500	$7,800	$6,500	$5,000	$4,000	$3,000	$2,500	$2,000	$1,500

COFFEE MILL MODEL - experimental variation buttstock with a grinding device and detachable handle that was fitted to several Model 1859 & 1863 Carbines. Designed to provide a quick and easy method for cavalry troops in the field to process coffee beans or corn for meals. Field trials are believed to have been in Trenton, NJ circa 1863. Very few originals known - no official records indicating government acceptance. Originals are extremely rare and values could range from $10,000- $50,000.

Buyer beware! Many fakes exist.

Model 1863 RIFLE - adapted for socket bayonet, shared ser. range with carbine. Approx. 6,000 mfg.

$13,000	$11,000	$9,500	$8,700	$6,800	$5,500	$4,500	$3,500	$2,700	$2,200	$1,800	$1,200

Model 1865 RIFLE - only 1,000 mfg. in carbine ser. range.

$15,000	$13,000	$11,500	$10,500	$8,600	$7,500	$6,000	$4,700	$3,700	$3,200	$2,800	$2,200

Sharps Cartridge Conversions

In 1867, the U.S. government decided to convert their percussion Sharps carbines and rifles to the new .50/70 metallic cartridge. Approx. 31,000 carbines and 1,000 rifles were converted by the Sharps Co. Any original, six groove barrels that were worn beyond specification had a groove liner installed. Those barrels meeting specs. remained unaltered. All buttstocks were stamped on the left side with "D.F.C." in a ribbon cartouche, the initials for the principal sub-inspector, David F. Clark. Damaged buttstocks were all replaced with the plain (no patchbox) Model 1865 buttstock, regardless of the model of the carbine; however, many of the old style buttplates with notches for patchboxes were retained.

.50/70 CARBINES - most had relined three groove barrels, approx. 31,000 remodeled. Those found with original six groove barrels will command a slight premium, as will those Model 1859s & Model 1863s with original patchbox buttstocks.

$6,000	$5,300	$4,900	$4,200	$3,300	$2,800	$2,300	$2,000	$1,800	$1,600	$1,400	$1,200

.50/70 RIFLES - all had three groove relined barrels, approx. 1,000 converted in 1867. More rare, but do not command any higher prices than their carbine counterparts.

SPRINGFIELD/SHARPS MODEL 1870-1871 - approx. 1,000 rifles and 300 carbines altered by Springfield Armory to fire .50/70 metallic cartridge, in addition to those done by Sharps Co., rifle barrels 35½ in., carbine barrels 22 in., receivers color case hardened, all other metal parts bright finish, own ser. range, and numbered on receiver tang and left side of barrel.

100%	98%	95%	90%	80%	70%	60%	50%	40%	30%	20%	10%

* **Rifles**

$6,600	$6,380	$5,720	$4,950	$4,180	$3,630	$3,190	$2,860	$2,530	$2,200	$1,870	$1,650

* **Carbines**

$6,600	$6,050	$5,390	$4,730	$3,740	$3,300	$2,750	$2,530	$2,310	$1,980	$1,760	$1,540

Sharps Metallic Cartridge Models

MODEL 1874 - mfg. in several configurations and a variety of calibers, designed to fire metallic cartridges and was not a conversion from percussion parts, made famous for its deadly accuracy at long distances and became known as the "Buffalo Rifle" of its day. Mfg. in Hartford, CT circa 1874-1876, in Bridgeport, CT circa 1881.

* **Sporting Model** - .40, .44, .45 or .50 cal., variety of barrel lengths and weights, many special order features. Approx. 6,500 mfg.

$16,000	$15,000	$13,500	$11,000	$9,000	$7,500	$6,000	$5,000	$4,200	$3,500	$3,000	$2,500

* **Business Rifle** - no frills version of the 1874 Sporting, with shorter, round barrel and open sights.

$10,000	$9,500	$9,000	$8,200	$7,300	$6,600	$5,000	$4,200	$3,500	$2,700	$2,200	$2,000

* **Military Rifle** - .45/70 or .50/70 cal., long forearm and three barrel bands. Approx. 1,700 mfg.

$8,000	$7,500	$7,000	$6,500	$5,500	$4,500	$3,700	$3,200	$2,700	$2,300	$2,000	$1,700

* **Military Carbine** - most in .50/70 cal., very similar to previous Sharps carbines. Less than 500 mfg.

$9,000	$8,500	$8,000	$7,500	$6,000	$5,000	$4,000	$3,200	$2,800	$2,400	$2,000	$1,600

* **Meachan Type Conversion** - most in .45/70 cal., very similar to Business Rifle, with both round and octagon barrels, mfg. from Civil War Sharps carbine actions and surplus, as well as new parts by several commercial firms in the 1880s after Sharps Rifle Co. closed. Sharps Co. assembled several hundred of these from 1879-1881 from existing parts on hand.

$8,500	$8,000	$7,500	$6,800	$5,700	$4,500	$3,700	$3,200	$2,800	$2,200	$1,800	$1,500

While of lesser quality than the Model 1874, these rifles were widely used on the Western frontier and have become very desirable to today's firearms collectors.

MODEL 1878 SHARPS-BORCHARDT - many cals. and barrel lengths, single trigger, hammerless action designed by Hugo Borchardt, carbines, military, sporting, and target rifles were all mfg., but sales suffered from a bolt and lever action market glut. Less than 9,000 mfg. by Sharps Rifle Co. in Bridgeport, CT circa 1878-1881.

$6,500	$6,000	$5,500	$5,000	$4,000	$3,200	$2,800	$2,500	$2,200	$1,900	$1,600	$1,300

Special order or deluxe models with other than standard features will command a premium.

Grading	100%	98%	95%	90%	80%	70%	60%

SHERIDAN PRODUCTS INCORPORATED

Previous manufacturer located in Racine, WI.

PISTOLS: SINGLE SHOT

KNOCKABOUT - .22 S-L-LR cal., 5 in. barrel, checkered plastic grips, fixed sights. Mfg. 1953-1960.

		$110	$100	$85	$75	$60	$50	$40

SHILEN RIFLES, INCORPORATED

Previous manufacturer located in Enis, TX circa 1975-mid 1980s.

Grading	100%	98%	95%	90%	80%	70%	60%

RIFLES: BOLT ACTION

Older Shilen rifles have become very desirable for target shooters and other accuracy enthusiasts. Because of their small quantities of manufacture (approx. 3,350 mfg.) and new found demand, prices have gone up considerably on this trademark. Originally, the Sporters retailed in the $600-$700 range, but at the end, prices were in the $3,500 range.

DGA SPORTER - .17 Rem., .223 Rem., .22-250 Rem., .220 Swift, 6mm Rem., .243 Win., .250 Savage, .257 Roberts, .284 Win., .308 Win., or .358 Win. cal., 3 shot mag., 24 in. barrel, no sights, claro walnut stock.

	$1,475	$1,175	$950	$800	$675	$575	$495

DGA VARMINTER - similar to Sporter, except 25 in. medium heavy barrel.

	$1,395	$1,100	$900	$775	$650	$575	$495

DGA SILHOUETTE RIFLE - similar to Varminter, .308 Win. cal. only.

	$1,395	$1,100	$900	$775	$650	$575	$495

DGA BENCHREST RIFLE - single shot, choice of cals., 26 in. heavy or medium barrel, no sights, choice of fiberglass or walnut stock, thumbhole available.

	$1,450	$1,200	$950	$800	$650	$575	$495

SHILOH RIFLE MFG. CO.

Current manufacturer located in Big Timber, MT since 1983. Previously manufactured by Shiloh Products, a division of Drovel Tool Company of Farmingdale, NY, 1976-1983. Dealer or consumer direct sales.

The Shiloh Rifle Mfg. Co. is currently manufacturing quality replicas of Sharps rifles and carbines. They are available as black powder or modern cartridge rifles - current MSRs range from $1,504 - $2,860. Please contact Shiloh Rifle Mfg. Co. directly regarding availability, pricing, and the current waiting period.

SHOOTERS ARMS MANUFACTURING INCORPORATED

Current manufacturer established in 1992, and located in Cebu, the Phillipines. No current U.S. importation.

Shooters Arms Manufacturing Incorporated makes semi-auto pistols ($350-$450 MSR), revolvers ($160-$195 MSR), and slide action shotguns ($245-$285). Please contact the factory directly for current U.S. availability and pricing.

SIDEWINDER

Previously manufactured by D-Max, Inc. located in Bagley, MN circa 1993-96. Dealer or consumer sales.

REVOLVERS

SIDEWINDER - .45 LC or 2½/3 in. .410 bore shotshells/slugs, 6 shot, stainless steel construction, 6½ or 7½ in. bull barrel (muzzle end bored for choke), Pachmayr grips, hammer bar safety, adj. rear sight, unique design permits one cylinder to shoot above listed loads, cased with choke tube, 3.8 lbs. Mfg. 1993-96.

	$695	$575	$475

Last MSR was $775.

S

Grading	100%	98%	95%	90%	80%	70%	60%

SIG ARMS AG

Current Swiss company (SIG) established during 1860 in Neuhausen, Switzerland. P 210 pistols and the SHR 970 rifle are currently imported and distributed by SIG Arms, located in Exeter, NH.

During late 2000, SIG Arms AG was purchased by SAN Swiss Arms AG, a newly formed company. This new group includes 5 independently operational companies – Blaser Jadgwaffen GmbH, Hämmerli AG, J.P. Sauer & Sohn GmbH, SIG Arms, Inc. (U.S.A.), and SAN Swiss Arms AG. Current trademarks include: Blaser, Hämmerli, Mauser Magnum rifles, Sauer rifles, and Sig-Sauer pistols. Please refer to these individual listings for current information and pricing.

PISTOLS: SEMI-AUTO

Add $700 for .22 LR conversion kit on the following models (not available on the P 210-8).

TRAILSIDE - .22 LR cal., single action, 4½ or 6 in. barrel, two-tone finish, choice of ultralight polymer composite grips or target variation which includes wood grips and adj. rear sight, 10 shot mag., cased with trigger lock, 28 or 30 oz. New 1999.

MSR	$449	$395	$350	$300	$275	$250	$225	$200

Add $80 for 4½ in. barrel with target sights, or $100 for 6 in. barrel in target sights.

This model is mfg. by Hämmerli for SIG Arms.

* ***Trailside Competition*** - includes 6 in. barrel with anatomical stipled grips and adj. bottom rest, cased with trigger lock, 37.2 oz. New 2000.

MSR	$699	$575	$500	$400	$350	$300	$265	$225

P 210 - 9mm Para. or 7.65mm Para. (disc.) cal., single action, 4¾ in. barrel, 8 shot mag., standard weapon of the Swiss Army, 2 lbs.

Originally mfg. in 1947, this pistol was first designated the SP 47/8 and became the standard military pistol of the Swiss Army in 1949. Later designated the P 210, this handgun has been mfg. continuously for over 50 years.

* ***P 210-1*** - polished finish, walnut grips, special hammer, fixed sights. Importation disc. 1986.

	$2,000	$1,675	$1,400	$1,195	$975	$850	$750

Last MSR was $1,861.

* ***P 210-2*** - matte finish, field or contrast (current mfg.) sights, plastic (disc.) or wood grips. Limited importation since 1987.

MSR	$1,680	$1,500	$1,275	$1,000	$875	$750	$625	$550

Prices are the same for West German Police Contract models with unique loaded indicator on slide. Approx. 5,000 mfg. in D prefix serial range.

* ***P 210-5*** - matte finish, heavy frame, micrometer target sights, 150mm or 180mm (rare) extended barrel, hard rubber (disc.) or wood (current mfg.) grips, very limited mfg. Limited importation since 1997.

MSR	$2,325	$1,995	$1,750	$1,400	$1,195	$975	$850	$750

* ***P 210-6*** - matte blue finish, fixed (current importation) or micrometer sights, 120mm barrel, checkered walnut grips.

MSR	$2,089	$1,875	$1,500	$1,200	$995	$875	$775	$675

* ***P 210-7*** - .22 LR or 9mm Para. cal., regular or target long barrel, limited importation. No longer in production.

	$3,375	$2,950	$2,600	$2,300	$1,950	$1,600	$1,275

* ***P 210-8*** - features heavy frame, target sights, and wood grips. Importation began 2001.

MSR	$4,289	$3,750	$3,250	$2,650	$2,300	$1,950	$1,600	$1,275

S

Grading	100%	98%	95%	90%	80%	70%	60%

✳ *P 210 Deluxe Models* - various models differ in the amount of engraving, gold inlays, carved wood grips, presentation cases, and other special order features available from the factory. P 210 Deluxe Model pricing starts at $3,500, and goes up according to special order and embellishments.

RIFLES: BOLT ACTION

SHR 970 - .25-06 Rem., .270 Win., .280 Rem., .30-06, .308 Win., .300 Win. Mag. or 7mm Rem. Mag. cal., steel receiver, standard model featuring easy take-down (requires single tool) and quick change 22 or 24 (Mag. cals. only) in. barrel, detachable 3 or 4 shot mag., 65 degree short throw bolt, 3 position safety, standard medium gloss walnut stock with checkering, ultra-fast lock time, nitrided bore, no sights, includes hard carry case, approx. 7.3 lbs. New 1998.

MSR $550	$475	$395	$350	$325	$295	$275	$250

✳ *SHR 970 Synthetic* - similar to SHR 970, except has checkered black synthetic stock with stippled grip. New 1999.

MSR $499	$445	$375	$325	$295	$275	$250	$230

STR 970 LONG RANGE - .308 Win. or .300 Win. Mag. cal., inlcudes stippled black McMillan composite stock with precision bedding blocks, 24 in. fluted heavy barrel with integral muzzle brake and non-reflective Ilaflon metal coating, cased, 11.6 lbs. New 2000.

MSR $899	$795	$700	$625	$575	$525	$475	$425

RIFLES: SEMI-AUTO

PE-57 - 7.5 Swiss cal. only, semi-auto version of the Swiss military rifle, 24 in. barrel, includes 24 shot mag., leather sling, bipod and maintenance kit. Importation disc. 1988.

$5,125	$4,500	$3,950	$3,500	$2,950	$2,500	$2,000

Last MSR was $1,745.

The PE-57 was previously distributed in limited quantities by Osborne's located in Cheboygan, MI.

SIG-AMT RIFLE - .308 Win. cal., semi-auto version of SG510-4 auto paramilitary design rifle, roller delayed blowback action, 5, 10, or 20 shot mag., 18¾ in. barrel, wood stock, folding bipod. Mfg. 1960-present. Importation disc. 1988.

$3,875	$3,250	$2,675	$2,300	$2,000	$1,750	$1,500

Last MSR was $1,795.

SG 550/551 - .223 Rem. cal. with heavier bullet, Swiss Army's semi-auto version of newest paramilitary design rifle (SIG 90), 20.8 (SG 550) or 16 in. (SG 551 Carbine) barrel, some synthetics used to save weight, 20 shot mag., diopter night sights, built-in folding bipod, 7.7 or 9 lbs.

Sig 550 (Rifle)	$7,750	$7,000	$6,250	$5,500	$4,950	$4,500	$4,000
Sig 551 (Carbine)	$9,500	$8,875	$8,000	$7,250	$6,500	$5,600	$4,500

Last MSR was $1,950.

This model has been banned from domestic importation due to 1989 Federal legislation.

SIG-HÄMMERLI

Previously manufactured by Hämmerli Ltd. in Lenzburg, Switzerland.

S

Grading	100%	98%	95%	90%	80%	70%	60%

PISTOLS: SEMI-AUTO

P240 TARGET PISTOL - .32 S&W Long Wadcutter or .38 Mid-range (disc.) cal., single action, 5 shot mag., 5.9 in. barrel, blueblue finish, thumb rest walnut grips, adj. sights and trigger, 3 lbs. Importation mostly disc. 1986.

	$1,475	$1,225	$1,000	$875	$775	$700	$660

Last MSR was $1,350.

Add $100 for Morini adj. grips.

.38 Mid-range cal. is very desirable in this model - healthy premiums (and inconsistent) are being asked.

✹ *.22 Conversion Unit*

	$550	$495	$400

Last MSR was $595.

SIG SAUER

Current firearms trademark manufactured by SIG Arms AG (Schweizerische Industrie-Gesellschaft) located in Neuhausen, Switzerland. Currently imported, manufactured (some models), and distributed by SIG Arms, Inc. located in Exeter, NH.

SIGSAUER

During late 2000, SIG Arms AG was purchased by SAN Swiss Arms AG, a newly formed company. This new group includes 5 independently operational companies – Blaser Jadgwaffen GmbH, Hämmerli AG, J.P. Sauer & Sohn GmbH, SIG Arms, Inc. (U.S.A.), and SAN Swiss Arms AG. Current trademarks include: Blaser, Hämmerli, Mauser, Sauer rifles, and Sig-Sauer pistols. Please refer to these individual listings for current information and pricing.

PISTOLS: SEMI-AUTO

Beginning 2001, add $15 for all handguns that are MA compliant. Handguns for MD are priced the same as the models listed.

P 210 - please refer to listing under SIG heading.

MODEL P220 - .22 LR (disc.), .38 Super (disc.), 7.65mm (disc.), 9mm Para. (disc 1991), or .45 ACP cal., 7 (.45 ACP) or 8 shot mag., regular double action or double action only (.45 ACP cal. only), 4.4 in. barrel, choice of matte blue, stainless steel (new 2001), K-Kote (disc. 1999), electroless nickel (disc. 1991), two- tone with nickel finished slide, or Ilaflon (mfg. 2000 only) finish, lightweight alloy frame, black plastic grips, values are for .45 ACP cal. and assume American side mag. release (standard 1986), approx. 30.4 or 41.8 (stainless steel) oz. Mfg. 1976-present.

MSR	$810		$670	$580	$490	$435	$395	$350	$310

Add $92 for Siglite night sights.
Add $41 for two-tone (nickel slide) finish. (new 1992).
Add $69 for stainless steel frame & slide (new 2001).
Add $40 for Ilaflon finish (disc. 2000).
Add $45 for factory K-Kote finish (disc. 1999).
Add $70 for electroless nickel finish (disc. 1991).
Add $680 for .22 LR conversion kit (disc.).
Subtract 10% for "European" Model (bottom mag. release - includes 9mm Para. and .38 Super cals.).

✹ *P220 Sport* - .45 ACP cal., features 4.8 in. heavy compensated barrel, stainless steel frame and slide, 10 shot mag., target sights, improved trigger pull, single or double action, 46.1 oz. Imported 1999-2000.

	$1,175	$925	$750

Last MSR was $1,320.

Grading	100%	98%	95%	90%	80%	70%	60%

MODEL P225 - 9mm Para. cal., regular double action or double action only, similar to P220, shorter dimensions, 3.85 in. barrel, 8 shot, thumb actuated button release mag., fully adj. sights, 28.8 oz. Disc. 1998.

	100%	98%	95%	90%	80%	70%	60%
	$595	$525	$450	$425	$395	$350	$310

Last MSR was $725.

Add $45 for factory K-Kote finish.
Add $105 for Siglite night sights.
Add $45 for nickel finished slide (new 1992).
Add $70 for electroless nickel finish (disc. 1991).

MODEL P226 - .357 SIG (new 1995), 9mm Para. (disc. 1997, reintroduced 1999), or .40 S&W (new 1998) cal., compact variation, choice of double action or double action only (new 1992) operation, 10 (C/B 1994) or 15* shot mag., 4.4 in. barrel, alloy frame, currently available in blackened stainless steel (Nitron finish became standard 2000) or nickel finish (stainless slide only), high contrast sights, automatic firing pin lock safety, 31.7 or 34 oz. New 1983.

	MSR	$851						
			$740	$610	$540	$450	$400	$350	$310

Add $102 for Siglite night sights.
Add $46 for two-tone finish (nickel finished stainless steel slide - new 1992).
Add $45 for K-Kote (Polymer) finish (mfg. 1992-97, 9mm Para. only).
Add $70 for electroless nickel finish (disc. 1991).
This model is also available in double action only (all finishes) at no extra charge.

✹ ***Model P226 Jubilee*** - limited edition commemorating SIG's 125th anniversary, features gold-plated small parts, carved select walnut grips, special slide markings, cased. Mfg. 1985 only.

	$1,495	$1,175	$950

Last MSR was $2,000.

MODEL P228 - 9mm Para., choice of double action or double action only (new 1992) operation, compact design, 3.86 in. (compact) barrel, 10 (C/B 1994) or 13* shot mag., automatic firing pin lock safety, high contrast sights, alloy frame, choice of blue, nickel slide (new 1991), or K-Kote finish, 29.3 oz. Mfg. 1990-97.

	$675	$575	$500	$425	$395	$350	$310

Last MSR was $750.

Add $95 for Siglite night sights.
Add $45 for K-Kote (Polymer) finish.
Add $45 for nickel finished slide (new 1992).
Add $70 for electroless nickel finish (disc. 1991).
This model is also available in double action only (all finishes) at no extra charge.

MODEL P229 - .357 SIG (new 1995), 9mm Para. (mfg. 1994-96, reintroduced 1999), or .40 S&W cal., similar to Model P228, except has blackened Nitron or satin nickel finished stainless steel slide with aluminum alloy frame, 10 (C/B 1994) or 12* shot mag., includes lockable carrying case, 31.1 or 32.4 oz. New 1991.

	MSR	$851						
			$725	$620	$540	$465	$410	$350	$310

Add $100 for Siglite night sights.
Add $46 for two-tone satin nickel finished stainless steel slide.
This model is also available in double action only at no extra charge.

✹ ***Model P229 Sport*** - .357 SIG cal., features 4.8 in. heavy compensated barrel, stainless steel frame and slide, target sights, improved trigger pull, single or double action, 43.6 oz. Mfg. 1998-2000.

	$1,175	$925	$750

Last MSR was $1,320.

S

Grading	100%	98%	95%	90%	80%	70%	60%

MODEL P230 - .22 LR (disc.)-10 shot, .32 ACP-8 shot, .380 ACP-7 shot, or 9mm Ultra (disc.) cal., 7 shot, 3.6 in. barrel, regular double action or double action only, blue, composite grips, 17.6 oz. Mfg. 1976-96.

			$425	$375	$300	$270	$240	$215	$190

Add $35 for stainless slide (.380 ACP only).

Last MSR was $510.

✳ *Model P230 SL Stainless* - similar to Model P230, except stainless steel construction, 22.4 oz. Disc. 1996.

			$480	$400	$375

Last MSR was $595.

MODEL P232 - .380 ACP cal., choice of double action or double action only, 3.6 in. barrel, 7 shot mag., aluminum alloy frame, blue or two-tone stainless slide, automatic firing pin lock safety, composite grips. New 1997.

MSR	$518		$450	$390	$315	$275	$240	$215	$190

Add $41 for Siglite night sights (new 2001).
Add $20 for stainless two-tone slide.

✳ *Model P232 Stainless* - similar to Model P232, except stainless steel construction, natural finish, 17.6 or 22.4 (stainless) oz. New 1997.

MSR	$559		$485	$430	$360

Add $41 for Siglite night sights and Hogue grips.

MODEL P239 - .357 SIG, 9mm Para., or .40 S&W (new 1998) cal., double action or double action only, blackened or two-tone stainless steel slide and aluminum alloy frame, firing pin lock safety, 3.6 in. barrel, 7 or 8 (9mm Para. only) shot mag., fixed sights, approx. 29 oz. New 1996.

MSR	$636		$500	$440	$365	$295	$255	$220	$195

Add $102 for Siglite night sights.
Add $46 for two-tone stainless slide.

MODEL P245 - .45 ACP cal., compact model featuring 3.9 in. barrel, traditional double action, 6 shot mag., blue, two-tone, Ilaflon (mfg. 2000 only), or K-Kote (disc. 1999) finish, approx. 30 oz. New 1999.

MSR	$800		$660	$575	$490	$435	$395	$350	$310

Add $71 (blue only) or $102 for Siglite night sights.
Add $51 for two-tone or K-Kote (disc.) finish.
Add $50 for Ilaflon finish (mfg. 2000 only).

MODEL SIG PRO SP2009 - 9mm Para. cal., otherwise identical to SP2340, 28 oz. New 1999.

MSR	$602		$480	$430	$350	$285	$255	$220	$195

Add $59 for Siglite night sights.
Add $25 for two-tone finish.

MODEL SIG PRO SP2340 - .357 SIG, or .40 S&W cal., features polymer frame and one-piece Nitron finished stainless steel or two-tone (new 2001) finished slide, 3.86 in. barrel, includes two interchangeable grips, 10 shot mag., approx. 30.2 oz. New 1999.

MSR	$602		$480	$430	$350	$285	$255	$220	$195

Add $59 for Siglite night sights.
Add $25 for two-tone finish.

RIFLES: BOLT ACTION

Please refer to listing in J.P. Sauer & Sohn section.

SHOTGUNS: O/U

The following Aurora shotguns are mfg. by Battista Rizzini, located in Marcheno, Italy.

Grading	100%	98%	95%	90%	80%	70%	60%

L.L. BEAN NEW ENGLANDER SERIES - 12, 20, 28 ga., or .410 bore. Importation began 2001.

MSR	$1,995	$1,775	$1,525	$1,300	$1,075	$950	$800	$675

APOLLO/AURORA TR20 FIELD - 12, 20, 28 ga., or .410 bore, 3 in. chambers except for 28 ga., 26 or 28 in. VR barrels with choke tubes, satin finished low profile boxlock receiver, monobloc construction, removable hinge pins, gold SST, ejectors, deluxe checkered round pistol grip walnut stock and forearm, 6-7 lbs. New 2000.

MSR	$1,865	$1,695	$1,450	$1,250	$1,050	$925	$800	$675

✴ *Apollo/Aurora TR20U Field* - similar to Apollo/Aurora TR20 Field, except has straight English stock (Upland Model) and color case hardened receiver. New 2000.

MSR	$1,865	$1,695	$1,450	$1,250	$1,050	$925	$800	$675

APOLLO/AURORA TR30 FIELD - similar to Apollo/Aurora TR20 Field, except has color case hardened receiver with sideplates. New 2000.

MSR	$2,240	$1,950	$1,725	$1,500	$1,300	$1,075	$950	$800

APOLLO/AURORA TR40 GOLD/SILVER - similar to Apollo/Aurora TR30 Field, except receiver and sideplates are engraved and have multiple gold bird inlays, choice of color case hardened (Gold Series) or silver receiver (Silver Series) finish, deluxe checkered walnut stock and forearm. New 2000.

MSR	$2,595	$2,250	$1,950	$1,725	$1,500	$1,300	$1,000	$825

Add $80 for color case hardened receiver (Gold Series).

✴ *Apollo/Aurora TR40U* - similar to Apollo/Aurora TR40 Gold/Silver, except has straight English grip stock and silver finished receiver only. Imported 2000 only.

	$2,250	$1,950	$1,725	$1,500	$1,300	$1,000	$825

Last MSR was $2,595.

APOLLO/AURORA TT25 COMPETITION - 12 or 20 ga., 3 in. chambers, features include polished 5 in. forcing cones and American stock dimensions with palm swell and Schnabel forearm, oil finished checkered walnut stock and forearm, matte finished 28, 30, or 32 (12 ga. only) in. VR barrels, 6¾ or 7¼ lbs. New 2000.

MSR	$1,995	$1,795	$1,525	$1,300	$1,075	$950	$825	$675

AURORA TT45 COMPETITION - 12 or 20 ga., 28, 30, or 32 (12 ga. only) in. VR barrels. Importation began 2001.

MSR	$2,795	$2,400	$2,100	$1,750	$1,525	$1,300	$1,075	$950

SA 3 - 12 or 20 (new 1998) ga., 3 in. chambers, scalloped coin finished monobloc boxlock action with game scene engraving, field or Sporting Clays (new 1998) configuration, 26, 28, or 30 (Sporting Clays only) in. separated barrels with VR and choke tubes, ejectors, SST, checkered walnut stock and forearm, approx. 7 lbs. Mfg. 1997-98 only.

	$1,175	$925	$775	$650	$550	$475	$400

Last MSR was $1,335.

SA 5 - 12 or 20 ga., 3 in. chambers, features coin finished boxlock action with hand engraved detachable side plates, ejectors, SST, select checkered walnut stock and forearm, field or Sporting Clays (new 1998) configuration, 26½, 28, or 30 (Sporting Clays only) in. barrels with VR and choke tubes, supplied with lockable case, 6 or 7 lbs. Mfg. 1997-99.

	$2,175	$1,775	$1,450	$1,225	$1,075	$900	$775

Last MSR was $2,670.

Add $130 for Sporting Clays Model (12 ga. only, 28 or 30 in. barrels).

SILE DISTRIBUTORS

Previous distributor, importer, and previous manufacturer located in New York, NY.

In addition to distributing a wide variety of firearms and related accessories (including the mfg. of stocks and grips), Sile Distributors also had some firearms "private labeled" to their specifications.

S

Grading	100%	98%	95%	90%	80%	70%	60%

SILMA SPORTING GUNS

Current manufacturer established during 1949 and located in Brescia, Italy. Currently distributed and imported beginning 2000 on a limited basis by Legacy Sports, International, LLC, located in Alexandria, VA. All Silma shotguns, double rifles, and combination models are high quality and utilize premium materials in their manufacture.

Please contact the importer directly (see Trademark Index) for current domestic model availability and pricing.

RIFLES

Currently, Silma offers one O/U double rifle (Model EX 70 N). This is also available in a combination gun (12 ga. x various cals.). Not currently imported.

SHOTGUNS

In addition to the Model 70 EJ and Superlight models listed, Silma also manufactures other Model 70 configurations. Models 70 and 80 are O/U hunting models available in either 12, 20 ga., or .410 bore. They are available with double triggers standard, extractors or ejectors (extra cost), with or without sideplates, or in superlight configuration - retail values range between $730-$980. Competition models (including T.J. 70, T.S. 81, Cobra T1, T2, or T3) are also available for trap, skeet, or sporting clays events. Values range between $1,000-$6,200 (with T.J. 70 being the least expensive, and Cobra T2 the most expensive). Two side by side models (AS/70 N and AS/70 EJ) are also available.

MODEL 70 EJ STANDARD O/U - 12 or 20 ga., 3 or 3 1/2 (12 ga. only) in. chambers, similar to Model 70 EJ Deluxe, except has standard grade walnut. Importation began 2001.

MSR	$735	$650	$575	$500	$465	$430	$395	$360

Add $122 for fixed chokes.

MODEL 70 EJ DELUXE O/U - 12, 20, 28 ga., or .410 bore, 3 (12 and 20 ga.) or 3 1/2 in. chambers, 28 in. VR barrels with either multichokes (12 ga. only) or fixed chokes, engraved coin finished boxlock receiver, gold ST, deluxe checkered walnut stock and forearm. Importation began 2001.

MSR	$817	$735	$675	$595	$550	$495	$450	$395

Add $133 for 28 ga. or .410 bore.

MODEL 70 EJ SUPERLIGHT O/U - 12 or 20 ga., 3 in. chambers, similar to Model 70 EJ Deluxe, except has separated barrels and lightweight aluminum frame. Importation began 2001.

MSR	$995	$885	$785	$695	$625	$550	$495	$450

SIMILLION, GENE

Current custom rifle maker located in Gunnison, CO. Consumer direct sales.

RIFLES: BOLT ACTION, CUSTOM

CLASSIC HUNTER RIFLE - various cals., new Winchester Model 70 Classic action, options include LOP, caliber, and barrel length, deluxe walnut, custom made to individual customer specifications.

MSR	$5,400	$5,150	$4,500	$3,750	$3,000	$2,500	$2,000	$1,650

Add $600 for Mag. cals. up to .375 H&H.
Add $1,100 for heavy Mag. cals. .375 H&H. and larger.

Grading	100%	98%	95%	90%	80%	70%	60%

PREMIER RIFLE - various cals., mostly Winchester new Model 70 action (others available), custom made to individual customer specifications, finest materials and workmanship, individually tested.

	MSR	$7,800		$7,500	$6,650	$5,600	$4,550	$3,525	$2,750	$2,000

    Add $500 for Mag. cals. up to .375 H&H.
    Add $1,250 for heavy Mag. cals. .375 H&H and larger.

SIMSEK

Current shotgun manufacturer located in Turkey. No current U.S. importation.

Simsek manufactures shotguns in O/U, SxS, and semi-auto configurations. Please contact the factory directly for U.S. model availablity and U.S. pricing.

SIRKIS INDUSTRIES, LTD.

Previous manufacturer located in Ramat-Gan, Israel. Previously imported and distributed by Armscorp of America, Inc. located in Baltimore, MD.

PISTOLS: SEMI-AUTO

S.D. 9 - 9mm Para. cal., double action mechanism, frame is constructed mostly of heavy gauge sheet metal stampings, 3.07 in. barrel, parkerized finish, loaded chamber indicator, 7 shot mag., plastic grips, 24½ oz. Imported under the Sirkis & Sardius trademarks between 1986-1990.

		$375	$295	$250	$200	$190	$180	$170

                                    Last MSR was $350.

RIFLES

MODEL 35 MATCH RIFLE - .22 LR cal. only, single shot bolt action, 26 in. full floating barrel, select walnut, match trigger, micrometer sights. Disc. 1985.

		$650	$625	$595	$550	$510	$460	$420

                                    Last MSR was $690.

MODEL 36 SNIPER RIFLE - .308 Win. cal. only, gas operated action, carbon fiber stock, 22 in. barrel, flash suppressor, free range sights. Disc. 1985.

		$670	$580	$520	$475	$430	$390	$350

                                    Last MSR was $760.

SKORPION

Please refer to Armitage International, Ltd. in the "A" section of this text.

SMITH, L.C.

Previous trademark manufactured circa 1880-1888 in Syracuse, NY., and in Fulton, NY 1890-1945 by Hunter Arms Company.

The L.C. Smith shotgun was made from 1890-1945 by the Hunter Arms Company in Fulton, New York. In 1946, the company was acquired by Marlin Firearms Company. Production continued until 1951 when it ceased for a period of 17 years. In 1968, Marlin brought the L.C. Smith back to life for a period of 5 years. Production stopped in 1973. The L.C. Smith is one of the finest American made shotguns and collector interest is very high. All values shown are for hammerless shotguns.

SHOTGUNS: SxS, HAMMERLESS - 1890-1913 PRODUCTION

All prices listed are for guns with fluid steel barrels (except A-1 grade).

It is important to note that damascus barreled guns with hammers in 90% original condition or better are very collectible and values can approximate those of steel barrel models if the bore is excellent with no pitting. Damascus specimens below 90% condition are not as collectible, however, and values fall off rapidly if under 90%. Prices shown below for 90% and up condition are very difficult to evaluate and are meant as a guide only. L.C. Smith shotguns are rare and hard to evaluate if over 95% condition in the higher grades.

S

100%	98%	95%	90%	80%	70%	60%	50%	40%	30%	20%	10%

00 GRADE - 12, 16, or 20 ga. Approx. 60,000 mfg.

| $1,500 | $1,200 | $800 | $600 | $500 | $465 | $430 | $395 | $375 | $350 | $325 | $295 |

    Add 33% for auto ejectors.
    Add 50% for 20 ga.

0 GRADE - 10, 12, 16, or 20 ga. Approx. 30,000 mfg.

| $1,600 | $1,400 | $1,000 | $775 | $675 | $600 | $550 | $515 | $460 | $400 | $350 | $300 |

    Add 50% for 20 ga.

NO. 1 GRADE - 10, 12, 16, or 20 ga. Approx. 10,000 mfg.

| N/A | $1,950 | $1,425 | $995 | $850 | $750 | $700 | $625 | $550 | $495 | $450 | $400 |

    Add 33% for auto ejectors.
    Add 50% for 20 ga.
    Add $200 for SST.

NO. 2 GRADE - 10, 12, 16, or 20 ga. Approx. 13,000 mfg.

| N/A | $2,275 | $1,700 | $1,400 | $1,200 | $1,000 | $825 | $750 | $675 | $600 | $550 | $500 |

    Add 33% for auto ejectors.
    Add 75% for 20 ga.
    Add $200 for SST.

NO. 3 GRADE - 10, 12, 16, or 20 ga. Approx. 4,000 mfg.

| N/A | N/A | $2,400 | $1,850 | $1,500 | $1,300 | $1,100 | $995 | $875 | $775 | $625 | $500 |

    Add 25% for auto ejectors.
    Add 75% for 20 ga.
    Add $200 for SST.

PIGEON GRADE - 10, 12, 16, or 20 ga. Approx. 1,200 mfg.

| N/A | N/A | $2,400 | $1,850 | $1,500 | $1,300 | $1,100 | $995 | $875 | $775 | $625 | $500 |

    Add 25% for auto ejectors.
    Add 75% for 20 ga.
    Add $200 for SST.

NO. 4 GRADE - 10, 12, 16, or 20 ga. Approx. 500 mfg., seldomly encountered.

| N/A | N/A | $5,750 | $4,500 | $3,500 | $2,650 | $2,000 | $1,775 | $1,500 | $1,375 | $1,200 | $1,095 |

    Add 25% for auto ejectors.
    Add 75% for 20 ga.
    Add $200 for SST.

A-1 GRADE - 10, 12, or 16 ga. Approx. 700 mfg. Damascus barrels only.

| N/A | N/A | $3,000 | $2,200 | $1,850 | $1,725 | $1,425 | $1,175 | $995 | $800 | $700 | $600 |

    Auto ejectors standard.
    Add $200 for SST.

NO. 5 GRADE - 10, 12, 16, or 20 ga. Approx. 500 mfg.

| N/A | N/A | $4,950 | $4,500 | $4,000 | $3,500 | $3,150 | $2,700 | $2,450 | $2,200 | $1,995 | $1,800 |

    Auto ejectors standard.
    Add $200 for SST.
    Add 75% for 20 ga., extremely rare.

MONOGRAM GRADE - 10, 12, 16, or 20 ga. Approx. 100 mfg.

| N/A | N/A | $7,400 | $6,000 | $5,500 | $5,000 | $4,600 | $4,100 | $3,800 | $3,500 | $3,250 | $3,000 |

    Auto ejectors standard.
    Add 50% for 20 ga., extremely rare.

A-2 GRADE - 10, 12, or 20 ga. Approx. 200 mfg.

| N/A | N/A | N/A | $7,000 | $6,000 | $5,200 | $4,700 | $4,200 | $3,850 | $3,500 | $3,250 | $3,000 |

    Auto ejectors standard.
    20 ga. - only 6 mfg.

S

100%	98%	95%	90%	80%	70%	60%	50%	40%	30%	20%	10%

A-3 GRADE - 10, 12, 16, or 20 ga. Approx. 20 mfg. Rarity precludes accurate pricing on this model.

> Auto ejectors standard.
> 20 ga. - only 2 mfg.

SHOTGUNS: SxS, 1914-1951 PRODUCTION

Fulton trademarked shotguns mfg. by Hunter Arms Co. were inexpensive, utilitarian shotguns designed for a price point rather than quality. Models Fulton and Fulton Special were supplied in 12, 16, 20 ga., or .410 bore (rare). When encountered today, values usually are in the $150-$350 range. The Hunter Special, although not an L.C. Smith shotgun, did employ the rotary locking bolt system. This was also a low priced gun in its day and prices today are usually in the $150-$375 range. These models had nothing in common with the L.C. Smith shotguns of that time.

L.C. SMITH DOUBLE BARREL SHOTGUN - 12, 16, 20 ga., or .410 bore, any choke, sidelock, auto ejectors standard from Crown Grade up, extractors on lower grades, double or single triggers, straight, ½ pistol grip, or pistol grip stock, grade specifications differ in grade of wood, degree of engraving, and overall quality. Featherweight models were also manufactured on a regular basis and are so marked - values will approximate those listed for standard models.

STANDARD FIELD GRADE

100%	98%	95%	90%	80%	70%	60%	50%	40%	30%	20%	10%
$1,250	$1,000	$775	$675	$600	$500	$465	$435	$395	$375	$340	$295

> Add 33% for auto ejectors.
> Add $200 for SST.
> Add 45% for 20 ga.
> Add 300% for .410 bore.

IDEAL GRADE STANDARD

100%	98%	95%	90%	80%	70%	60%	50%	40%	30%	20%	10%
$1,600	$1,400	$1,100	$900	$825	$750	$700	$650	$595	$550	$530	$495

> Add 33% for auto ejectors.
> Add $200 for SST.
> Add 45% for 20 ga.
> Add 400% for .410 bore.

TRAP GRADE

100%	98%	95%	90%	80%	70%	60%	50%	40%	30%	20%	10%
$2,000	$1,500	$1,200	$1,100	$1,000	$925	$850	$775	$675	$600	$550	$500

> Auto ejectors - add 33%.
> Add $200 for SST.
> Add 50% for 20 ga.
> Add 400% for .410 bore.

SPECIALTY GRADE

100%	98%	95%	90%	80%	70%	60%	50%	40%	30%	20%	10%
$2,950	$2,450	$1,800	$1,375	$1,100	$1,000	$925	$875	$825	$775	$695	$625

> Add $200 for SST.
> Add 50% for 20 ga.
> Add 400% for .410 bore.
> Add 33% for auto ejectors.

SKEET SPECIAL GRADE

100%	98%	95%	90%	80%	70%	60%	50%	40%	30%	20%	10%
N/A	$2,600	$1,650	$1,200	$1,100	$925	$875	$825	$775	$725	$675	$600

> Add $200 for SST.
> Add 50% for 20 ga.
> Add 400% for .410 bore.
> Add 33% for auto ejectors.

PREMIER SKEET GRADE

100%	98%	95%	90%	80%	70%	60%	50%	40%	30%	20%	10%
N/A	$2,600	$1,650	$1,200	$1,100	$925	$875	$825	$775	$725	$675	$600

> Add $200 for SST.
> Add 50% for 20 ga.
> Add 400% for .410 bore.
> Add 33% for auto ejectors.

S

100%	98%	95%	90%	80%	70%	60%	50%	40%	30%	20%	10%

EAGLE GRADE

| N/A | $4,250 | $3,500 | $2,900 | $2,350 | $1,850 | $1,500 | $1,400 | $1,300 | $1,200 | $1,100 | $1,000 |

Add $200 for SST.
Add 50% for 20 ga.

CROWN GRADE

| N/A | $4,950 | $4,250 | $4,000 | $3,500 | $3,100 | $2,700 | $2,450 | $2,225 | $2,000 | $1,900 | $1,800 |

Add $200 for SST.
20 gauge - very rare.
.410 - rare and very expensive, only 6 mfg.

MONOGRAM GRADE

| N/A | N/A | $7,750 | $6,400 | $5,650 | $5,100 | $4,650 | $4,150 | $3,775 | $3,500 | $3,250 | $3,000 |

Add 50% for 20 ga.

PREMIER GRADE - very limited mfg., rarity precludes accurate pricing on this model.

DELUXE GRADE - very limited mfg., rarity precludes accurate pricing on this model.

SINGLE BARREL TRAP GUN - 12 ga. only, 32 or 34 in. VR barrel, boxlock, auto ejector, checkered pistol grip stock, recoil pad. Approx. 2,650 mfg. 1917-1951.

✳ *Olympic Grade*

| N/A | $1,400 | $1,200 | $1,100 | $1,000 | $900 | $800 | $725 | $675 | $625 | $575 | $550 |

✳ *Specialty Grade*

| N/A | $1,700 | $1,500 | $1,400 | $1,300 | $1,200 | $1,125 | $1,075 | $1,000 | $925 | $875 | $800 |

✳ *Crown Grade*

| N/A | $3,125 | $2,750 | $2,350 | $2,100 | $2,000 | $1,900 | $1,800 | $1,700 | $1,600 | $1,500 | $1,400 |

✳ *Monogram Grade*

| N/A | N/A | $4,250 | $3,700 | $3,150 | $2,750 | $2,400 | $2,150 | $2,000 | $1,850 | $1,700 | $1,525 |

✳ *Premier Grade*

| N/A | N/A | $6,400 | $5,275 | $3,850 | $3,300 | $2,900 | $2,600 | $2,350 | $2,100 | $1,900 | $1,750 |

✳ *Deluxe Grade*

| N/A | N/A | $9,995 | $7,850 | $6,000 | $5,000 | $4,500 | $3,995 | $3,375 | $2,900 | $2,500 | $2,150 |

Grading	100%	98%	95%	90%	80%	70%	60%

SHOTGUNS: SxS, 1968-1973 PRODUCTION

1968 MODEL - 12 ga., 28 in. VR barrel, full and mod. choke, sidelock, extractors, double triggers, checkered pistol grip stock. Mfg. 1968-1973 by Marlin.

| | $725 | $600 | $550 | $495 | $425 | $350 | $275 |

1968 DELUXE MODEL - similar to Standard, with Simmons floating rib, beavertail forearm. Mfg. 1971-1973 by Marlin.

| | $995 | $825 | $725 | $600 | $495 | $400 | $350 |

SMITH & WESSON

Current manufacturer located in Springfield, MA 1857 to date. Partnership with H. Smith & D.B. Wesson 1856-1874. Family owned by Wesson 1874-1965. S & W became a subsidiary of Bangor-Punta from 1965-1983. Between 1983-1987, Smith & Wesson was owned by the Lear Siegler Co. On May 22, 1987, Smith & Wesson was sold to Tompkins, an English holding company.

Smith & Wessons have been classified under the following category names - TIP-UPS, TOP-BREAKS, SINGLE SHOTS, EARLY HAND EJECTORS (Named Models), NUMBERED

MODEL REVOLVERS (Modern Hand Ejectors), SEMI-AUTOS, RIFLES, and SHOTGUNS. Each category is fairly self-explanatory. Among the early revolvers, Tip-ups have barrels that tip up so the cylinder can be removed for loading or unloading, whereas Top-breaks have barrels & cylinders that tip down with automatic ejection.

Hand Ejectors are the modern type revolvers with swing out cylinders. In 1958, S&W began a system of numbering all models they made. Accordingly, the Hand Ejectors have been divided into two sections - the Early Hand Ejectors include the named models introduced prior to 1958. The Numbered Model Revolvers are the models introduced or continued after that date, and are easily identified by the model number stamped on the side of the frame, visible when the cylinder is open. The author wishes to express his thanks to Mr. Roy Jinks, the S&W Historian, for his updates and valuable contributions. Mr. Jim Supica and W. R. Powell are also to be thanked for the S&W revised format.

For more information and current pricing on both new and used Smith & Wesson airguns, please refer to the Blue Book of Modern Airguns by Dr. Robert Beeman & John Allen (now online also).

Factory special orders, such as ivory or pearl grips, special finishes, engraving, and other production rarities will add premiums to the values listed. After 1893, all ivory and pearl grips had the metal S&W logo medallions inserted on top.

100%	98%	95%	90%	80%	70%	60%	50%	40%	30%	20%	10%

TIP-UPS

Spur-trigger rimfires, these include the earliest S&W revolvers, made 1857-1881. A latch at the bottom front of the frame allows the hinged barrel to be tipped up and the cylinder removed for loading and unloading. These pistols are listed in order of model number (1, 1½, 2).

MODEL NO. 1 FIRST ISSUE TIP-UP - .22 Short cal., single action, 7 shot non- fluted cylinder, 3 3/16 in. octagon barrel, bottom break, spur trigger, silver-plated brass frame, blue barrel and cylinder, square rosewood grips, circular sideplate, cross-section of frame is oval with rounded frame sides. Approx. 11,500 mfg. 1857-1860.

* **First Type** - serial range approx. 1-200.
  Extreme rarity factor of this model precludes accurate pricing - a nice condition model can easily exceed $10,000.

* **Second Type** - serial range approx. 200-1130.
  Extreme rarity factor of this model precludes accurate pricing - a nice condition model can easily exceed $10,000.

* **Third Type** - serial range approx. 1130-3000.

N/A	N/A	$8,000	$7,000	$5,500	$5,000	$4,500	$3,000	$2,500	$2,000	$1,500	$1,000

* **Fourth Type** - serial range approx. 3000-4200.

N/A	$3,500	$3,000	$2,000	$1,800	$1,650	$1,600	$1,500	$1,350	$1,200	$1,000	$900

* **Fifth Type** - serial range approx. 4200-5500.

N/A	$3,500	$3,000	$2,000	$1,800	$1,650	$1,600	$1,500	$1,350	$1,200	$1,000	$900

* **Sixth Type** - serial range approx. 5,500-11,500.

N/A	$2,000	$1,900	$1,800	$1,600	$1,500	$1,400	$1,300	$1,100	$900	$800	$750

MODEL NO. 1 SECOND ISSUE TIP-UP - similar to First Issue, except flat sided frame and irregular shaped sideplate. 114,900 mfg. 1860-1868. Serial range approx. 11,500- approx. 126,000.

$1,500	$1,000	$700	$650	$600	$575	$550	$500	$450	$400	$350	$300

An early sideplate variation with 2 patent dates on cylinder occured in the serial range 11,500-12,100. The second sideplate variation with 2 patent dates occurred in the serial range 12,100-20,000.

* **Second Quality**
  Extreme rarity precludes accurate pricing on this model. May bring double or triple values over the Model No. 1 Second Issue Tip-Up. Beware of fakes!

MODEL NO. 1 THIRD ISSUE TIP-UP - similar to Second Issue, except fluted cylinder, round barrel, and birdshead grip. 131,163 mfg. 1868-1882. This model has its own serial range no. 1-131,163.

S

100%	98%	95%	90%	80%	70%	60%	50%	40%	30%	20%	10%

✳ 3 3/16 in. barrel Model. - will have markings on top of barrel.

100%	98%	95%	90%	80%	70%	60%	50%	40%	30%	20%	10%
$1,500	$1,000	$600	$500	$425	$375	$350	$300	$250	$225	$200	$175

✳ Short barrels 2 11/16 - 2¾ in. - will have markings on side of barrel.

100%	98%	95%	90%	80%	70%	60%	50%	40%	30%	20%	10%
$900	$850	$775	$720	$680	$640	$600	$560	$520	$480	$440	$400

MODEL NO. 1½ OLD MODEL - .32 rimfire, single action, 3½ or 4 (rare) in. octagon barrel, 5 shot non-fluted cylinder, bottom break, spur trigger, blue or nickel, rosewood grips, square butt. 26,300 mfg. 1865-1868. Serial range 1- approx. 26,300.

100%	98%	95%	90%	80%	70%	60%	50%	40%	30%	20%	10%
$1,200	$800	$600	$500	$425	$350	$275	$250	$225	$210	$195	$185

Early production had 2 patent dates with the barrel markings (approx. serial range 1-15,500). Later production had 3 patent dates (approx. serial range 15,501-26,300).

✳ 4 in. barrel

Extreme rarity precludes accurate pricing on this model. May bring double or triple values over the Model No. 1 1/2 Old Model. Watch for fakes (i.e. stretched barrels).

✳ Model 1½ Transitional Model - octagon barrel with birdshead grips, serial range 27,200-28,800, rare.

100%	98%	95%	90%	80%	70%	60%	50%	40%	30%	20%	10%
$3,000	$2,500	$1,800	$1,500	$1,350	$1,275	$1,200	$1,125	$1,075	$1,000	$950	$900

MODEL NO. 1½ NEW MODEL - similar to First Issue, with birdshead grips and round barrel. 100,800 mfg. 1868-1875. Serial range 26,301-127,100.

✳ Short barrel model - barrel markings on side, length varies from 2½-2¾ in. (scarce). Extreme rarity precludes accurate pricing on this model. May bring double or triple values over the Model No. 1 1/2 New Model. Beware of fakes!

✳ 3½ in. barrel model

100%	98%	95%	90%	80%	70%	60%	50%	40%	30%	20%	10%
$900	$750	$500	$400	$350	$300	$225	$200	$180	$165	$150	$135

MODEL NO. 2 ARMY TIP-UP - .32 rimfire long, similar in appearance to No. 1½ First Issue, except 6 shot cylinder, different barrel lengths, used as a sidearm during Civil War. 77,155 mfg. 1861-1874. Serial number range 1-77,155.

✳ 5 or 6 in. Standard Model

100%	98%	95%	90%	80%	70%	60%	50%	40%	30%	20%	10%
$3,000	$2,500	$1,500	$1,000	$900	$800	$700	$625	$525	$450	$400	$375

Premiums exist for early 2 pin models under ser. no. 3,000. Large premiums will be asked for 4 in. barrel - beware of fakes!

TOP-BREAKS

These revolvers have a latch just in front of the hammer, which locks the barrel to the frame. When the action is opened, the barrel & cylinder tip down, with an automatic extractor ejecting the shells. Mfg 1870-1940, they include single action (spur-trigger or trigger guard), double action, and safety hammerless designs. They are listed in order of frame size. Model 1½ is the smallest or .32 cal. pocket sized frame; Model 2 is the medium or .38 cal. belt sized frame; Model 3 is the large holster or .44 cal. frame. Within each frame size, they are listed by action type - SA, DA, or "Hammerless", as may be applicable.

Changes from one Top-Break model type to another are not necessarily definitive at a specific serial number - therefore, an overlap of serial numbers from one model to another may be observed.

.32 SINGLE ACTION - .32 S&W cal., spur trigger, top break, rebounding hammer, auto extraction. 97,599 mfg. 1878-1892. Serial range 1-97,599.

✳ Later Model - with strain screw, remainder of serial range.

100%	98%	95%	90%	80%	70%	60%	50%	40%	30%	20%	10%
$750	$500	$400	$350	$300	$275	$250	$225	$210	$200	$190	$150

Early models under ser. no. 6,000 w/o strain screw will bring a slight premium. Original 2, 8, or 10 in. barrel models with bring a large premium - watch for fakes!

.32 DOUBLE ACTION FIRST MODEL TOP BREAK - .32 S&W cal., 5 shot fluted cylinder, 3 in. round barrel, square edged side plate, blue or nickel finish, black rubber grips, one of the rarest of all S&Ws. Only 30 mfg. 1880. Serial range 1-30.

Extreme rarity precludes accurate pricing on this model.

100%	98%	95%	90%	80%	70%	60%	50%	40%	30%	20%	10%

.32 DOUBLE ACTION SECOND MODEL - similar to First Model, except irregular shaped side-plate, 3, 3¼, 4, 5, or 6 in. barrel, 22,142 mfg. 1880-1882. Serial range 31- 22,172.

100%	98%	95%	90%	80%	70%	60%	50%	40%	30%	20%	10%
$475	$425	$380	$340	$300	$260	$220	$180	$150	$120	$100	$90

.32 DOUBLE ACTION THIRD MODEL - similar to Second Model, except without groove around cylinder. 22,232 mfg. 1882- 1883. Serial range 22,173-43,405.

100%	98%	95%	90%	80%	70%	60%	50%	40%	30%	20%	10%
$475	$425	$380	$340	$300	$260	$220	$180	$150	$120	$100	$90

.32 DOUBLE ACTION FOURTH MODEL - similar to Third Model, except rounded triggerguard. 239,600 mfg. 1883-1909. Serial range 43,406-approx. 282,999.

100%	98%	95%	90%	80%	70%	60%	50%	40%	30%	20%	10%
$345	$305	$270	$240	$210	$185	$160	$135	$115	$100	$90	$85

An 8 or 10 in. barrel on this model will command a premium.

.32 DOUBLE ACTION FIFTH MODEL - similar to Fourth Model, except integral front sight. 44,641 mfg. 1909-1919. Serial range approx. 282,300-327,641.

100%	98%	95%	90%	80%	70%	60%	50%	40%	30%	20%	10%
$375	$335	$300	$270	$240	$215	$190	$165	$135	$120	$105	$90

.32 SAFETY HAMMERLESS FIRST MODEL TOP BREAK - .32 S&W cal., 5 shot fluted cylinder, 2, 3 (most common), 3¼, 3½, or 6 (rare) in. round barrel, blue or nickel, black rubber grips. This model was officially called the New Departure. 91,417 mfg. 1888-1902. Serial range 1-91,417.

Short 2 in. barrel versions known as "Bicycle model" will bring 25% to 50% premium on all Safety Hammerless models. Six inch barrels will bring a premium as well.

✳ Standard Model - 2, 3, 3¼, or 3½ in. barrel.

100%	98%	95%	90%	80%	70%	60%	50%	40%	30%	20%	10%
$500	$475	$450	$425	$400	$375	$350	$325	$275	$235	$185	$150

.32 SAFETY HAMMERLESS SECOND MODEL - 2, 3, 3¼, 3½, or 6 in. barrel. 78,500 mfg. 1902-1909. Serial range 91,418-170,000.

100%	98%	95%	90%	80%	70%	60%	50%	40%	30%	20%	10%
$450	$425	$400	$375	$350	$325	$300	$275	$235	$200	$165	$130

.32 SAFETY HAMMERLESS THIRD MODEL - 2, 3, 3¼, 3½, or 6 in. barrel. 73,000 mfg. 1909-1937. Serial range 163,082-242,981 (with some overlap from the Second Model).

100%	98%	95%	90%	80%	70%	60%	50%	40%	30%	20%	10%
$450	$425	$400	$375	$350	$325	$300	$275	$235	$200	$165	$130

.38 SINGLE ACTION FIRST MODEL (BABY RUSSIAN) TOP BREAK SPUR TRIGGER - .38 S&W cal., 5 shot fluted cylinder, 3¼, 4, 5, or 6 in. barrel, blue with wood grips, nickel with "S&W" monogram hard black or red rubber grips. 25,548 mfg. 1876-1877. Serial range 1-25,548.

✳ Standard Model

100%	98%	95%	90%	80%	70%	60%	50%	40%	30%	20%	10%
$1,750	$700	$600	$500	$400	$350	$325	$300	$275	$250	$225	$200

Substantial premiums will be asked for "Aldrich" safety models (first 50-100 guns). Add a slight premium for ser. nos. under 1,500 with filler screws on right side of frame.

.38 SINGLE ACTION SECOND MODEL - similar to above, except very short ejector housing under barrel, cal. and cylinder same as above, 3¼, 4, 5, 6, 8, or 10 in. barrel, grips same as above. 108,225 mfg. 1877-1891. Serial range 1-108,255.

✳ Standard Model

100%	98%	95%	90%	80%	70%	60%	50%	40%	30%	20%	10%
$700	$500	$375	$285	$250	$225	$210	$200	$190	$185	$180	$150

✳ 8 or 10 in. Barrel

Extreme rarity precludes accurate pricing on this model.

.38 SINGLE ACTION THIRD MODEL (MODEL OF 1891) - similar to above, except has trigger guard, cal. and cylinder same as above, 3¼, 4, 5, or 6 in. barrel (also accepts the single shot barrel), blue or nickel finish with "S&W" monogram, hard black rubber grips. 26,850 mfg. 1891-1911. Serial range 1-28,107 which also includes the serial number range of the Single Shot First Model in .22 LR, .32 S&W, .38 S&W cal. and the .38 S.A. Mexican Model described below. Barrel marked "Model of 1891".

100%	98%	95%	90%	80%	70%	60%	50%	40%	30%	20%	10%
$2,300	$1,650	$1,425	$1,250	$1,075	$950	$850	$775	$700	$625	$550	$475

Add 50%-75% for single shot barrel with matching serial number.

S

100%	98%	95%	90%	80%	70%	60%	50%	40%	30%	20%	10%

.38 SINGLE ACTION MEXICAN MODEL

.38 SINGLE ACTION MEXICAN MODEL - essentially same as above, except has inserted spur trigger, .38 S&W cal., 5 shot fluted cylinder, 3¼, 4, 5, or 6 in. barrel, blue or nickel finish, "S&W" monogram checkered hard rubber or walnut grips. Features unique to this model are flat sided hammer, half cock notch, and "inserted" spur trigger assembly (not integral with frame). This model would also accept the single shot barrel, limited mfg. 1891-1911. Serial range described above. Watch out for fakes (and conversions)!

| N/A | $4,000 | $3,500 | $2,750 | $2,000 | $1,650 | $1,400 | $1,250 | $1,150 | $1,050 | $975 | $950 |

Add 50%-75% for single shot barrel with matching serial number.

.38 DOUBLE ACTION FIRST MODEL

.38 DOUBLE ACTION FIRST MODEL - .38 S&W cal., 5 shot fluted cylinder, 3¼ or 4 in. barrel, blue or nickel finish, "S&W" monogram checkered hard rubber grips. 4,000 mfg. 1880. Serial range 1-4,000.

| $900 | $850 | $750 | $650 | $550 | $475 | $400 | $325 | $250 | $200 | $175 | $150 |

.38 DOUBLE ACTION SECOND MODEL

.38 DOUBLE ACTION SECOND MODEL - .38 S&W cal., cylinder same as above, 3¼, 4, 5, or 6 in. barrel, blue or nickel finish, "S&W" monogram checkered hard rubber grips in black or red. 115,000 mfg. 1880-1884. Serial range approx. 4,001-approx. 119,000.

| $500 | $350 | $250 | $225 | $200 | $185 | $170 | $165 | $160 | $145 | $135 | $125 |

.38 DOUBLE ACTION THIRD MODEL

.38 DOUBLE ACTION THIRD MODEL - .38 S&W cal., cylinder same as above, 3¼, 4, 5, 6, 8, or 10 in. barrel, blue or nickel finish, "S&W" monogram hard rubber grips. 203,700 mfg. 1884-1895. Serial range approx. 119,001-322,700.

| $500 | $350 | $225 | $200 | $190 | $175 | $160 | $155 | $150 | $140 | $125 | $115 |

❋ 8 or 10 in. Barrel
Extreme rarity precludes accurate pricing on this model.
A 2 in. variation, while extremely rare, was manufactured in the Third Model, Fourth Model, Fifth Model, and Perfected Models listed. Large premiums do exist ($850-$1,500) - watch for fakes!

.38 DOUBLE ACTION FOURTH MODEL

.38 DOUBLE ACTION FOURTH MODEL - .38 S&W cal., cylinder same as above, 3¼, 4, 5, or 6 in. barrel, blue or nickel finish, "S&W" monogram checkered hard rubber grips, also offered in an extended square butt target style. 216,300 mfg. 1895-1901. Serial range 322,701-539,000.

| $450 | $300 | $230 | $200 | $185 | $170 | $155 | $150 | $145 | $135 | $120 | $110 |

.38 DOUBLE ACTION FIFTH MODEL

.38 DOUBLE ACTION FIFTH MODEL - .38 S&W cal., cylinder, barrel, and grip specifications same as above with the additional availability of an extended square butt target style walnut grip as an accessory. 15,000 mfg. 1909-1911. Serial range approx. 539,001- 554,077.

| $500 | $465 | $425 | $375 | $325 | $285 | $250 | $225 | $200 | $180 | $150 | $125 |

.38 DOUBLE ACTION PERFECTED MODEL TOP BREAK

.38 DOUBLE ACTION PERFECTED MODEL TOP BREAK - .38 S&W cal., 2 (extremely rare – watch for fakes), 3¼, 4, 5, or 6 in. barrel, cylinder change in frame incorporates rolled I frame revolver and lockwork, trigger guard is integral part of frame, and side plate is on right side - not left side. The last of the S&W break open revolvers. 59,400 mfg. 1909-1920. Serial range 1-59,400. Identified by having both top latch and side latch.

| $800 | $500 | $425 | $375 | $325 | $285 | $250 | $225 | $200 | $180 | $150 | $125 |

❋ .38 Double Action Perfected Model Top Latch Only - as above, except no side latch - rare.
Extreme rarity precludes accurate pricing on this model.
Add a substantial premium for triggerguard with integral frame.

.38 SAFETY HAMMERLESS FIRST MODEL (.38 NEW DEPARTURE) TOP BREAK

.38 SAFETY HAMMERLESS FIRST MODEL (.38 NEW DEPARTURE) TOP BREAK - .38 S&W cal., 5 shot fluted cylinder, 3¼, 4, 5, or 6 in. barrel, blue or nickel finish, "S&W" monogram checkered hard rubber grips, features "Z-Bar" latch. Approx. 5,000 mfg. in 1887. Serial range 1-5,001.

| $1,200 | $800 | $700 | $550 | $485 | $435 | $375 | $325 | $275 | $250 | $225 | $150 |

Add 25% for blue finish.

❋ 6 in. Barrel
Extreme rarity precludes accurate pricing on this model.

100%	98%	95%	90%	80%	70%	60%	50%	40%	30%	20%	10%

.38 SAFETY HAMMERLESS SECOND MODEL - .38 S&W cal., cylinder same as above, 3¼, 4, 5, or 6 in. barrel, finish and grips same as above. 37,350 mfg. 1887-1890. Serial range approx. 5,001-42,483.

$600	$465	$425	$375	$325	$285	$250	$225	$200	$180	$150	$125

U.S. MARTIALLY MARKED - 100 purchased by Govt. in 1890, serial range 41,333- 41,470, serial numbers in Second Model range, but are true Third Models.
> Extreme rarity precludes accurate pricing on this model. Beware of fakes!

.38 SAFETY HAMMERLESS THIRD MODEL - .38 S&W cal., cylinder same as above, 3¼, 4, 5, or 6 in. barrel, finish and grips same as above. 73,500 mfg. 1890-1898. Serial range 24,284- 116,002.

$500	$375	$330	$300	$275	$250	$225	$200	$175	$150	$135	$110

.38 SAFETY HAMMERLESS FOURTH MODEL - .38 S&W cal., cylinder, barrel lengths, finishes and grips same as above. 104,000 mfg. 1898-1907. Serial range 116,003 to approx. 220,000.

$375	$280	$240	$205	$190	$165	$155	$145	$135	$125	$115	$100

> A 2 in. barrel in this variation is rare (Bicycle Model).

.38 SAFETY HAMMERLESS FIFTH MODEL - .38 S&W cal., cylinder same as above, 2, 3¼, 4, 5, or 6 in. barrel, blue or nickel finish, "S&W" monogram checkered hard rubber or checkered walnut grips. 41,500 mfg. 1907-1940. Serial range 220,000- 261,493.

$450	$350	$240	$205	$190	$165	$155	$145	$135	$125	$115	$100

> ❋ *2 in. Barrel*
> Extreme rarity precludes accurate pricing on this model - will bring a premium.

MODEL 3 AMERICAN FIRST MODEL - .44 S&W American or .44 rimfire Henry cal., single action, 6 shot fluted cylinder, 6, 7, or 8 in. round barrel, blue or nickel finish, walnut grips. 8,000 mfg. 1870-1872. Serial range 1-approx. 8,000. Serial number overlaps on the variations below are known to exist.
> Slight premiums will be asked for models with vent. hole in bottom rear barrel (approx. first 1,500). Original barrel lengths other than 8 in. are worth a premium - beware of cut barrels.

> ❋ *Standard Model* - without hole in extractor.

N/A	$8,000	$4,500	$3,500	$3,000	$2,500	$2,150	$1,850	$1,650	$1,450	$1,250	$1,100

> ❋ *Transitional Model* - includes locking notch on hammer, with small trigger pin, serial range 6,700-8,000.

N/A	$8,000	$4,600	$3,600	$3,100	$2,650	$2,250	$2,150	$1,850	$1,650	$1,450	$1,200

> ❋ *.44 Rimfire Henry* - limited mfg. Watch for fakes!

N/A	$8,250	$7,000	$6,000	$5,000	$4,000	$3,750	$3,500	$3,250	$3,000	$2,750	$2,500

> ❋ *U.S. Marked* - approx. 1,000 mfg., 800 in blue, and 200 in nickel finish. All nickel plated revolvers are serial numbered above 1,950 — watch for fakes.

N/A	$15,000	$10,750	$9,100	$8,100	$7,250	$6,500	$5,900	$5,375	$4,850	$4,450	$4,000

> ❋ *Nashville Police* - very rare, only 32 manufactured. Scarcity precludes accurate pricing – beware of fakes.

MODEL 3 AMERICAN SECOND MODEL - .44 S&W American or .44 rimfire Henry cal., single action, 6 shot fluted cylinder, mechanism allows the hammer to lock the barrel latch in place, larger trigger pin, 5½, 6, 6½, 7, or 8 in. barrel, blue or nickel, walnut grips. 19,635 mfg. 1872-1874, serial range approx. 8,000-32,800 which includes commercial version of Model 3 Russian First Model.

> ❋ *Standard Model* - .44 S&W American cal., 8 in. barrel.

N/A	$7,000	$3,750	$3,250	$2,750	$2,250	$2,150	$1,850	$1,650	$1,450	$1,250	$1,100

> Add 35% for 5½, 6, 6½, or 7 in. barrel.

> ❋ *Standard Model .44 Rimfire Henry* - 6, 7, or 8 in. barrel, non-locking hammer below approx. serial number 25,000. 3,014 mfg.

N/A	$8,000	$4,750	$3,750	$3,525	$3,050	$2,650	$2,250	$2,150	$1,850	$1,650	$1,450

S

100%	98%	95%	90%	80%	70%	60%	50%	40%	30%	20%	10%

MODEL 3 FIRST MODEL RUSSIAN (OLD OLD MODEL RUSSIAN) - .44 S&W Russian, 5½, 6, 7, or 8 in. barrel, Russian contract revolvers had 8 in. barrels, blue finish, and Cyrillic barrel markings, commerical mfg. had blue or nickel finish, walnut grips, looks similar to First and Second Model American. 5,165 mfg. 1871-1874 for commercial sale and 20,014 for Russian Contract (separate ser. no. range). Serial range 6,000- 32,800, see Model 3 Second Model American.

* Commercial Version - 4,665 mfg.

100%	98%	95%	90%	80%	70%	60%	50%	40%	30%	20%	10%
N/A	$5,000	$4,000	$3,250	$2,750	$2,250	$2,150	$1,850	$1,650	$1,450	$1,250	$1,100

* Reject Russian Contract - approx. 500 mfg., can be determined by the barrel, latch, and cylinder having a full serial number, rather than assembly numbers.

100%	98%	95%	90%	80%	70%	60%	50%	40%	30%	20%	10%
N/A	$5,000	$4,000	$3,250	$2,750	$2,250	$2,150	$1,850	$1,650	$1,450	$1,250	$1,100

* Russian Contract - 20,014 mfg., rare, most sent to Russia, Cyrillic marked. Serial range 1- approx. 20,014.

100%	98%	95%	90%	80%	70%	60%	50%	40%	30%	20%	10%
N/A	N/A	$6,750	$5,975	$5,125	$4,450	$3,800	$3,350	$2,950	$2,600	$2,250	$2,000

MODEL 3 SECOND MODEL RUSSIAN (OLD RUSSIAN) - 2nd and 3rd Model Russians have an extreme knuckle at the top of backstrap and trigger guard spur, 85,200 mfg. in all variations between 1873-78, 7 in. barrel, small screw in top-strap of frame, features longer ejector housing and "Russian Model" marking on top of barrel. Ser. nos. started at 32,800.

* Commercial Version - 6,200 mfg.

100%	98%	95%	90%	80%	70%	60%	50%	40%	30%	20%	10%
N/A	$3,750	$3,000	$2,375	$2,000	$1,750	$1,500	$1,300	$1,100	$995	$895	$795

* .44 Rimfire Henry - approx. 500 mfg.

100%	98%	95%	90%	80%	70%	60%	50%	40%	30%	20%	10%
N/A	$5,000	$4,500	$4,000	$3,525	$3,050	$2,650	$2,250	$2,150	$1,850	$1,650	$1,500

* Russian Contract - approx. 70,000 mfg. for Russian Military contract, cryllic marked, rare in U.S.

100%	98%	95%	90%	80%	70%	60%	50%	40%	30%	20%	10%
N/A	N/A	$3,150	$2,850	$2,525	$2,275	$2,100	$1,950	$1,800	$1,650	$1,500	$1,350

* Turkish Model - 1,000 mfg. in their own serial number range in .44 Rimfire, features rimfire hammer, but the cylinder is chambered for .44 Russian. This is probably the rarest and most valuable variation.

100%	98%	95%	90%	80%	70%	60%	50%	40%	30%	20%	10%
N/A	N/A	$5,000	$4,500	$4,000	$3,600	$3,250	$2,900	$2,675	$2,475	$2,250	$2,000

This model was converted to rimfire from .44 S&W Russian cal.

* Japanese Contract - may be marked with an anchor.

100%	98%	95%	90%	80%	70%	60%	50%	40%	30%	20%	10%
N/A	N/A	$3,200	$2,600	$2,300	$2,050	$1,825	$1,650	$1,500	$1,375	$1,250	$1,175

MODEL 3 THIRD MODEL RUSSIAN - commonly called the "New Model Russian" and is similar to old model, except has shorter extractor housing, 6½ in. barrel, large knurled screw in top-strap of frame, shorter ejector housing, butt is usually marked with an 1874 in a square, approx. 60,600 mfg. between 1874 and 1878. Values are similar to old model for comparable variations. In addition, the Tula Arsenal in Russia also mfg. 300,000- 400,000 pistols for domestic use and Ludwig & Loewe in Germany mfg. 100,000.

* Commercial Version - approx. 13,500 mfg.

100%	98%	95%	90%	80%	70%	60%	50%	40%	30%	20%	10%
N/A	$3,750	$3,000	$2,375	$2,000	$1,750	$1,500	$1,300	$1,100	$995	$895	$795

* .44 Rimfire Henry

100%	98%	95%	90%	80%	70%	60%	50%	40%	30%	20%	10%
N/A	$5,000	$4,500	$4,000	$3,525	$3,050	$2,650	$2,250	$2,150	$1,850	$1,650	$1,500

* Russian Contract - 41,138 mfg. Cyrillic lettering.

100%	98%	95%	90%	80%	70%	60%	50%	40%	30%	20%	10%
N/A	$3,500	$3,200	$2,900	$2,650	$2,400	$2,200	$2,000	$1,775	$1,575	$1,325	$1,100

* Ludwig & Loewe, & Tula Copies - copies mfg. for the Russian government.

100%	98%	95%	90%	80%	70%	60%	50%	40%	30%	20%	10%
N/A	$2,800	$2,500	$2,250	$2,000	$1,800	$1,625	$1,475	$1,350	$1,225	$1,100	$950

Add 30% for Tula copies.

* Turkish Contract - 5,000 mfg., utilizes .44 Russian cylinder - chambered for .44 Rimfire.

100%	98%	95%	90%	80%	70%	60%	50%	40%	30%	20%	10%
N/A	$4,000	$3,700	$3,425	$3,100	$2,850	$2,575	$2,325	$2,025	$1,700	$1,425	$1,200

* Japanese Contract - 1,000 made.

100%	98%	95%	90%	80%	70%	60%	50%	40%	30%	20%	10%
N/A	$3,800	$3,150	$2,300	$2,000	$1,750	$1,500	$1,300	$1,225	$1,100	$950	$800

NEW MODEL NO. 3 - features very short extractor housing under the barrel, knuckle on backstrap is less pronounced than Russian Models, 35,796 mfg. between 1878-1912.

Slight premiums will be asked for cut shoulder stock ($750-$1,250), target sights (standard non-target models only).

Add a premium for barrel lengths other than 6 1/2 in. (beware of .44 DA barrels!), and for calibers other than .44 Russian.

Early production had rack and gear extractor (serial number range 1-13,500), and will bring a slight premium over the later mfg. Also, premiums do exist for all but 6 and 6½ in. barrel lengths; premiums for unusual chamberings.

* ✳ *Commercial Version*

100%	98%	95%	90%	80%	70%	60%	50%	40%	30%	20%	10%
$8,500	$5,000	$2,850	$2,000	$1,800	$1,625	$1,475	$1,325	$1,175	$995	$795	$695

* ✳ *Japanese Navy Model* - Japan purchased approx. 1/3 of total production.
  Add 50% for Japanese characters on ejector housing, Japanese anchor brings only a small premium, if any.
* ✳ *Australian Model* - 7 in. barrel, detachable stock, for Australian Colonial Police, broad arrow marking on both pistol and stock, stocks were originally numbered to the matching pistol, but are seldom seen with matching numbers today, approx. 250 mfg., usually found in the low 12,000 - low 13,000 ser. no. range.
  Add a substantial premium if with shoulder stock.
* ✳ *Argentine Model* - unknown total production, marked "Ejercito Argentina" (very rare).
  Add a premium over the Commercial Version.
* ✳ *State of Maryland Model* - U.S. marked, serial number range 7,126-7,405.
  Add a premium over the Commercial Version.
  Add a premium for Revenue Cutter Service (Coast Guard) model, identifiable only by ser. no.

NEW MODEL NO. 3 FRONTIER - .44-40 WCF cal., single action, 4, 5, or 6½ in. barrel, blue or nickel finish, walnut or hard rubber grips. 2,072 mfg. 1885-1908.

* ✳ *Japanese Purchase* - 786 converted to .44 Russian cal., cylinder should measure 1 9/16 in., in the Frontier serial range of 1-2,072.

100%	98%	95%	90%	80%	70%	60%	50%	40%	30%	20%	10%
N/A	$5,000	$3,000	$2,250	$1,800	$1,625	$1,475	$1,325	$1,175	$995	$795	$695

* ✳ *Standard Model* - .44-40 WCF cal.

100%	98%	95%	90%	80%	70%	60%	50%	40%	30%	20%	10%
$9,000	$6,000	$3,500	$3,000	$2,500	$2,250	$2,000	$1,850	$1,600	$1,400	$1,250	$1,100

NEW MODEL NO. 3 - .38-40 WCF. - separate ser. range, only 74 mfg., ser. no. 1- 74.

Extreme rarity factor of this model precludes accurate pricing.

NEW MODEL NO. 3 TARGET MODEL - .32-44 S&W or .38-44 S&W cal., 4,333 mfg. between 1887-1910.

100%	98%	95%	90%	80%	70%	60%	50%	40%	30%	20%	10%
$6,500	$3,250	$2,500	$2,250	$1,925	$1,700	$1,500	$1,350	$1,100	$950	$800	$700

NEW MODEL NO. 3 TURKISH - .44 rimfire cal., 5,461 mfg. between 1879-1888, in separate serial number series.

100%	98%	95%	90%	80%	70%	60%	50%	40%	30%	20%	10%
N/A	$7,000	$4,675	$4,350	$4,050	$3,750	$3,450	$3,150	$2,850	$2,550	$2,275	$1,950

MODEL 3 SCHOFIELD FIRST MODEL - .45 S&W cal., single action, 7 in. barrel, 6 shot fluted cylinder, blue finish only, walnut grips, 3,035 mfg. 1875.

* ✳ *U.S. Issue* - 3,000 mfg.

100%	98%	95%	90%	80%	70%	60%	50%	40%	30%	20%	10%
N/A	$15,000	$9,000	$6,000	$4,500	$4,000	$3,600	$3,400	$3,200	$3,000	$2,600	$2,250

* ✳ *Commercial Model (not U.S. marked)* - 35 were produced without U.S. markings, very rare - beware of fakes - there could be more phony ones than real ones.
  Extreme rarity factor of this model precludes accurate pricing.

S

100%	98%	95%	90%	80%	70%	60%	50%	40%	30%	20%	10%

❊ *Wells Fargo and Company* - barrel cut to approx. 5 in. with Wells Fargo markings.

100%	98%	95%	90%	80%	70%	60%	50%	40%	30%	20%	10%
N/A	N/A	N/A	N/A	$7,000	$5,100	$4,550	$4,175	$3,750	$3,350	$3,050	$2,750

Warning - Beware of fakes! There may be more fake Wells Fargo Schofields than authentic ones. While most fakes are usually poor quality, others may be quite impressive.

Many Schofields are found with cut 5 in. barrels and no Wells Fargo marking - these will bring approx. 66% of uncut values or if they have fake WF markings their value is ½ of the uncut values.

MODEL 3 SCHOFIELD SECOND MODEL

❊ *Standard Model* - U.S. on butt.

100%	98%	95%	90%	80%	70%	60%	50%	40%	30%	20%	10%
N/A	$14,000	$8,000	$5,500	$4,500	$4,000	$3,600	$3,400	$3,200	$3,000	$2,600	$2,250

❊ *Commercial Model* - blue or nickel finish, 650 mfg.

100%	98%	95%	90%	80%	70%	60%	50%	40%	30%	20%	10%
N/A	$9,500	$7,000	$5,000	$4,500	$4,000	$3,600	$3,400	$3,200	$3,000	$2,600	$2,250

❊ *Wells Fargo and Company* - barrel cut to 5 in. with Wells Fargo markings.

100%	98%	95%	90%	80%	70%	60%	50%	40%	30%	20%	10%
N/A	N/A	N/A	N/A	$7,000	$5,100	$4,550	$4,175	$3,750	$3,350	$3,050	$2,750

Warning - Beware of fakes! There may be more fake Wells Fargo Schofields than authentic ones. While most fakes are usually poor quality, others may be quite impressive.

Many Schofields are found with cut 5 in. barrels and no Wells Fargo marking - these will bring approx. 66% of uncut values or if they have fake WF markings their value is ½ of the uncut values.

.44 DOUBLE ACTION FIRST MODEL
- .32-44 (rare), .38-44 (rare), .38 Military (rare), .44 S&W Russian (most common), and .455 (rare) cal., caliber markings on later production for .44 S&W Russian is ".44 Smith & Wesson", 6 shot fluted cylinder, 4, 5, 6, or 6½ in. barrel, blue or nickel finish, "S&W" monogram checkered hard rubber or walnut grips. Walnut grips with "S&W" inlays will be found after 1900. 53,668 mfg. 1881-1913. Serial range 1-54,668.

Add 100% for cals. other than .44 S&W Russian with target sights on sub-models listed.

❊ *Standard Model*

100%	98%	95%	90%	80%	70%	60%	50%	40%	30%	20%	10%
$4,500	$1,900	$1,500	$1,275	$1,000	$925	$825	$695	$650	$575	$475	$375

❊ *.44 Double Action Wesson Favorite* - similar to Standard Model, but in 5 in. barrel only with special front sight, blue nickel finish, patent markings are on the cylinder rather than on the barrel, grooved barrel rib, external and internal lightening cuts to reduce weight. Approx. 1,000 mfg. 1882-1883. Ser. range included with .44 Double Action First Model, between approx. 8,900- 10,100.

100%	98%	95%	90%	80%	70%	60%	50%	40%	30%	20%	10%
N/A	$10,000	$8,000	$7,000	$5,500	$4,500	$3,600	$3,200	$2,825	$2,500	$2,275	$2,000

Add 30-40% for blue finish.

.38 WIN. DOUBLE ACTION
- .38-40 WCF cal., 4, 5, 6, or 6½ in. barrel, only 276 mfg. in separate ser. range 1-276.

100%	98%	95%	90%	80%	70%	60%	50%	40%	30%	20%	10%
N/A	$6,000	$5,000	$4,000	$3,000	$2,500	$2,000	$1,750	$1,500	$1,300	$1,225	$1,125

.44 DOUBLE ACTION FRONTIER
- .44-40 WCF cal., 4, 5, 6, or 6½ in. barrel, only 15,340 mfg. in separate ser. range 1-15,340.

100%	98%	95%	90%	80%	70%	60%	50%	40%	30%	20%	10%
$4,500	$1,900	$1,500	$1,275	$1,000	$925	$825	$695	$650	$575	$475	$375

Add 100% for factory target sights.

SINGLE SHOTS

FIRST MODEL - .22 LR, .32 S&W, or .38 S&W cal., 6, 8, or 10 in. barrel marked "Model of 1891", blue or nickel, hard rubber extension grips. 1,251 mfg. 1893-1905, ser. range (same as Third Model 38 Single Action) 1-28,107. Serial number is located on the front strap.

Add a premium for early flat frame without recoil shields (ser. no. range 16,000-28,107).

❊ *.22 LR* - approx. 862 mfg.

100%	98%	95%	90%	80%	70%	60%	50%	40%	30%	20%	10%
$1,200	$800	$650	$575	$525	$475	$425	$375	$350	$325	$300	$285

Add a premium for .32 S&W or .38 S&W cals.

SECOND MODEL .22 LR - similar to First Model, but will not accommodate a revolver cylinder, flatsided frame (does not have recoil shield) 10 in. barrel only, black hard rubber extension grips, 4,617 mfg. 1905-1909. Ser. range 1-4,617 (ser. no. located on front grip strap).

100%	98%	95%	90%	80%	70%	60%	50%	40%	30%	20%	10%
$1,100	$750	$625	$575	$525	$475	$425	$375	$325	$280	$250	$225

100%	98%	95%	90%	80%	70%	60%	50%	40%	30%	20%	10%

THIRD MODEL .22 S (PERFECTED MODEL) - similar to Second Model, except is built on "I" solid frame with integral trigger guard, side plate on right side, made both single or double action, checkered walnut extension grips. 6,949 mfg. 1909-1923. Serial range 4,618-11,641 (ser. no. located on front grip strap).

$1,100	$750	$600	$550	$500	$450	$400	$350	$300	$265	$235	$210

Add 30% for Olympic Model in extra short .22 LR rifle chamber.

STRAIGHT LINE TARGET SINGLE SHOT - .22 LR cal., single shot, 10 in. barrel, sideswing barrel, blue, target sights, smooth walnut grips, shaped like an autoloader. 1,870 mfg. 1925- 1936. Ser. range 1-1,870. Values below assume case and accessories.

$1,750	$1,200	$950	$850	$750	$650	$550	$450	$415	$350	$335	$315

Subtract 30% w/o case and accessories.

EARLY HAND EJECTORS (NAMED MODELS)

Named Models. 1896-1958. Listed in order of caliber, except where newer mfg. might also include model number. These will NOT have any model number stamped on the frame. Several were continued after 1958 as Numbered Models, so be sure to check that section as well.

.22/.32 HAND EJECTOR (ALSO KNOWN AS .22/32 BEKEART MODEL) - .22 LR cal., 6 shot fluted cylinder, 6 in. barrel, blueblue, checkered walnut grips with "S&W" medallions, extension style square butt, there were several hundred thousand of the standard .22/.32 Hand Ejector mfg. The first 3,000 mfg. will be found with a separate ser. no. (1-3,000) stamped into the bottom of the wood grips. This model was cataloged as the .22/.32 heavy frame target unit in 1931.

* ***Bekeart Model*** - will be found with separate identification number on bottom of wooden grip. Serial numbers for early Bekeart models start at 138,226.

$1,075	$875	$750	$650	$550	$450	$350	$275	$200	$150	$135	$110

Slight premiums are charged over the values listed for early production with grip models in lower ser. no. range 1,001-3,000.

This model was specifically mfg. for a San Francisco retailer, Philip Bekeart. Originally, Mr. Bekeart ordered 1,000 guns to his specifications, S&W mfg. 5,000. While the first 1,000 revolvers in ser. no. range 138,226 with grip numbered 1-1,000 are accepted as "True Bekearts", only 292 were actually delivered to Philip Bekeart.

* ***Standard .22/.32 Hand Ejector Model*** - mfg. approx. 1913-1953.

$850	$675	$550	$450	$375	$325	$275	$225	$175	$135	$115	$100

.22/32 KIT GUN - similar to Standard .22/32 Hand Ejector Model, except has 2 or 4 in. barrels, round or square butt. Mfg. 1935-1953, serial number overlaps occur within this model.

$800	$700	$575	$500	$450	$400	$350	$300	$260	$230	$200	$175

MODEL .22 HAND EJECTOR (LADYSMITH) - originally chambered for .22 S&W (same as .22 Long) cal., 7 shot fluted cylinder, small frame, available in blue or nickel finish, nicknamed "Ladysmith" due to its small size. Over 26,000 mfg. between 1902- 1921.

* ***First Model*** - .22 L cal., 3, or 3½ in. barrel length, serial numbered 1-4,575, checkered hard rubber grips, round butt. 4,575 mfg. 1902-1906. Serial range 1-4,575. Identifiable by frame mounted cylinder release lever.

$2,500	$1,800	$1,500	$1,250	$975	$800	$650	$550	$475	$435	$390	$350

* ***Second Model*** - .22 L cal., 3, or 3½ in. barrel, distinguishable from first model in that cylinder locking device was placed on barrel bottom, locking both ends. 9,400 mfg. 1906-1910. Serial range 4,576- 13,950.

$2,000	$1,500	$1,275	$950	$800	$700	$600	$525	$475	$425	$375	$325

* ***Third Model*** - .22 L cal., 2½, 3, 3½, or 6 in. barrel, smooth walnut grips with "S&W" medallion inlays, square butt. 12,200 mfg. 1910-1921. Serial range 13,951- 26,154.

$2,000	$1,475	$1,250	$900	$750	$650	$550	$475	$425	$375	$325	$325

Add 85% for 6 in. barrel with target sights.
Add 95% for 6 in. barrel with plain sights.

S

100%	98%	95%	90%	80%	70%	60%	50%	40%	30%	20%	10%

.32 HAND EJECTOR FIRST MODEL (MODEL OF 1896)

.32 S&W Long cal.; 6 shot fluted cylinder, 3¼, 4¼ or 6 in. barrel, blue or nickel, black rubber grips, round butt, cylinder stop is mounted in frame top-strap, patent markings are on cylinder, rather than on barrel. 19,712 mfg. 1896-1903. Serial range 1-19,712.

| $700 | $600 | $500 | $475 | $440 | $400 | $375 | $325 | $285 | $250 | $225 | $200 |

Add 25% for short hammer variation.

.32 HAND EJECTOR (MODEL OF 1903)

.32 S&W Long cal., 6 shot fluted cylinder, 3¼, 4¼ or 6 in. barrel, blue or nickel, black rubber grips. 19,425 mfg. 1903-1904. Serial range 1-19,425.

| $400 | $340 | $300 | $275 | $250 | $225 | $200 | $175 | $150 | $130 | $115 | $100 |

✱ *.32 Hand Ejector (Model of 1903 - 1st Change)* - rubber grips. 31,700 mfg. 1904-1906. Serial range 19,426-51,126.

| $395 | $340 | $300 | $275 | $250 | $225 | $200 | $175 | $150 | $130 | $115 | $100 |

✱ *.32 Hand Ejector (Model of 1903 - 2nd Change)* - rubber grips. 44,373 mfg. 1906-1909. Serial range 51,127-95,500.

| $395 | $340 | $300 | $275 | $250 | $225 | $200 | $175 | $150 | $130 | $115 | $100 |

✱ *.32 Hand Ejector (Model of 1903 - 3rd Change)* - rubber grips. 624 mfg. 1909-1910. Serial range 95,501-96,125.

| $525 | $475 | $420 | $385 | $350 | $320 | $290 | $265 | $240 | $220 | $205 | $190 |

✱ *.32 Hand Ejector (Model of 1903 - 4th Change)* - rubber grips. 6,374 mfg. 1910. Serial range 96,126-102,500.

| $400 | $340 | $300 | $275 | $250 | $225 | $200 | $175 | $150 | $130 | $115 | $100 |

✱ *.32 Hand Ejector (Model of 1903 - 5th Change)* - rubber grips.

| $355 | $315 | $280 | $250 | $225 | $200 | $175 | $150 | $125 | $110 | $100 | $90 |

.32 HAND EJECTOR THIRD MODEL

.32 S&W Long cal., 6 shot fluted cylinder, 3¼, 4¼ or 6 in. barrel, blue or nickel finish, grips of checkered hard rubber with "S&W" monogram, round butt. 271,531 mfg. 1911-1942. Serial range approx. 263,001- 534,532.

| $350 | $310 | $275 | $250 | $225 | $200 | $175 | $150 | $125 | $110 | $100 | $90 |

Add 50% for pre-war mfg.

.32-20 WCF HAND EJECTOR FIRST MODEL

.32-20 WCF cal., 6 shot fluted cylinder, 4, 5, 6, or 6½ in. barrel, blue or nickel, case hardened trigger and hammer, hard rubber with "S&W" monogram or non-monogrammed walnut grips, round butt style.

| $520 | $475 | $450 | $425 | $400 | $375 | $350 | $325 | $305 | $290 | $260 | $230 |

.32-20 WCF HAND EJECTOR SECOND MODEL (MODEL OF 1902)

.32-20 WCF cal., 6 shot fluted cylinder, 4, 5, or 6½ in. barrel, blue or nickel, grips of hard rubber with "S&W" monogram or walnut, round butt style. 4,499 mfg. 1902-1905. Serial range 5,312- 9,811.

| $475 | $400 | $350 | $300 | $250 | $200 | $150 | $125 | $110 | $95 | $85 | $75 |

✱ *.32-20 WCF Hand Ejector Second Model (Model of 1902 - 1st Change)* - grip also available in checkered walnut. 8,313 mfg. 1903-1905. Serial range 9,812- 18,125.

| $465 | $390 | $340 | $290 | $240 | $190 | $140 | $120 | $105 | $90 | $80 | $75 |

.32-20 WCF HAND EJECTOR (MODEL OF 1905)

.32-20 WCF cal., (revolvers manufactured until approx. 1916 were marked .32 Winchester, .32 WCF between 1916-1928, and late production was marked .32/20.), cylinder and barrel specifications same as above, with round or square grip. 4,300 mfg. 1905-1906. Serial range 18,126- 22,426.

| $475 | $400 | $350 | $300 | $250 | $200 | $150 | $125 | $110 | $95 | $85 | $75 |

Add 75% for Target Models.

✱ *.32-20 WCF Hand Ejector (Model of 1905 - 1st Change)* - 4, 5, 6, or 6½ barrel, blue or nickel, grips same as above, round or square butt. 11,073 mfg. 1906-1907. Serial range 22,427 to approx. 33,500.

| $465 | $390 | $340 | $290 | $240 | $190 | $140 | $120 | $105 | $90 | $80 | $75 |

✱ *.32-20 WCF Hand Ejector (Model of 1905 - 2nd Change)* - caliber, cylinder, barrel and grip specifications same as above. 11,699 mfg. 1906-1907. Serial range 33,501-45,200.

S

100%	98%	95%	90%	80%	70%	60%	50%	40%	30%	20%	10%
$465	$390	$340	$290	$240	$190	$140	$120	$105	$90	$80	$75

※ **.32-20 WCF Hand Ejector (Model of 1905 - 3rd Change)** - caliber and cylinder same as above, 4 or 6 in. barrel, finish and grips same as above. 20,499 mfg. 1909- 1915. Serial range approx. 45,201-65,700.

$455	$380	$330	$280	$230	$180	$140	$120	$105	$90	$80	$75

※ **.32-20 WCF Hand Ejector (Model of 1905 - 4th Change)** - caliber and cylinder same as above, 4, 5, or 6 in. barrel, finish and grips same as above. 78,983 mfg. 1915- 1940. Serial range 65,701-144,684.

$375	$325	$280	$235	$200	$175	$135	$115	$100	$85	$80	$75

.38 MILITARY & POLICE FIRST MODEL (MODEL OF 1899)

.38 S&W Special cal., early Army & Navy models were marked "S&W .38 MIL.", civilian guns and standard models are 2-line barrel marked ".38 S&W SPECIAL & U.S. SERVICE CTG'S" with the "Maltese Cross" emblem stamped both before and after the caliber, these models are also referred to as .38 Hand Ejectors, 6 shot fluted cylinder, 4, 5, or 6½ in. barrel, blue or nickel finish, "S&W" monogram checkered hard rubber or checkered walnut grips with walnut grips exhibiting an impressed circle at top, left plain for civilian issue, marked with inspector's initials for military issue. 20,975 mfg. 1899- 1902. Serial range 1-20,975.

On these models, barrel markings are somewhat confusing, generally marked .38 S&W Spl. & U.S. Service cartridge, Military Issue is typically marked .38 Military. Fixed sights are referred to as Military & Police Models while target sights are referred to as .38 Hand Ejectors.

※ **Standard Model** - Civilian Issue

$650	$550	$475	$425	$375	$325	$275	$240	$205	$190	$180	$170

Add 75% for target sights.

※ **U.S. Navy Model** - 1,000 revolvers in .38 S&W Spl. cal. with 6 in. barrel, blue, checkered walnut grips, delivered in 1900. Stamped on butt "U.S.N." with an anchor and inspector's initials. All in S&W serial range 5,001-6,000. U.S. Navy serial range 1-1,000.

$1,900	$1,600	$1,375	$1,200	$1,050	$925	$825	$725	$625	$525	$435	$375

※ **U.S. Army Model** - 1,000 revolvers in .38 Military cal. with 6 in. barrel, blueblue, checkered walnut grips, inspector's initials "K.S.M. " on right grip panel with "J.T.T.1901" on left grip panel. Stamped on butt "U.S. ARMY/MODEL 1899". S&W serial range 13,001-14,000.

$1,900	$1,600	$1,375	$1,200	$1,050	$925	$825	$725	$625	$525	$435	$375

.38 MILITARY & POLICE SECOND MODEL (MODEL OF 1902)

.38 S&W Special and .38 Military cal., civilian guns and standard models are barrel 2-line marked ".38 S&W SPECIAL & U.S. SERVICE CTG'S" with the "Maltese Cross" emblem stamped both before and after the caliber, 6 shot, fluted cylinder, 4, 5, 6, and 6½ in. barrels, blue or nickel, "S&W" monogram checkered hard rubber or checkered walnut grips. 12,827 mfg. 1902-1903. Serial range 20,976-33,803.

※ **Standard Model** - civilian issue, all in .38 S&W Special cal.

$600	$470	$425	$390	$335	$320	$290	$260	$235	$210	$200	$185

Add 75% for target sights.

※ **U.S. Navy Model** - 1,000 revolvers in .38 United States Service caliber with 6 in. barrel, delivered in 1902. Stamped on butt "U.S.N." with "J.A.B.", anchor, and arrow through horizontal "S" and "No." (Naval Ser. No. designation).

$1,800	$1,575	$1,400	$1,250	$1,125	$1,000	$900	$800	$750	$700	$650	$610

.38 MILITARY & POLICE SECOND MODEL - 1ST CHANGE

.38 S&W Special cal., 6 shot fluted cylinder, 4, 5, or 6½ in. barrel, blue or nickel, "S&W" monogram checkered hard rubber or checkered walnut grips, rounded butt style. 28,645 mfg. 1903- 1905. Serial range 33,804-62,449.

Add 75% for target sights.

※ **Standard Model** - hard rubber grips, round butt.

$450	$345	$310	$275	$250	$210	$175	$150	$135	$125	$115	$100

S

100%	98%	95%	90%	80%	70%	60%	50%	40%	30%	20%	10%

❋ Standard Model - checkered walnut grips or square butt to frame style. All will have serial numbers over the 58,000 range.

| $475 | $355 | $335 | $300 | $275 | $235 | $200 | $175 | $160 | $145 | $130 | $115 |

.38 MILITARY & POLICE (MODEL OF 1905) - .38 S&W Special cal., 6 shot fluted cylinder, 4, 5, or 6½ in. barrel, blue or nickel finish, "S&W" monogram checkered hard rubber (round butt) or checkered walnut (square butt) grips. 10,800 mfg. 1905-1906. Serial range 62,450-73,250.

| $500 | $385 | $345 | $310 | $275 | $240 | $205 | $175 | $150 | $125 | $110 | $100 |

Add 50% for Target Model.

.38 MILITARY & POLICE (MODEL OF 1905 - 1ST CHANGE) - .38 S&W Special cal., 6 shot fluted cylinder, 4, 5, 6, or 6½ in. barrel, blue or nickel finish, grips same as above. 73,648 mfg. (including Model 1905 2nd change), exact quantity of both models has not been determined. The first change mfg. in 1906-1908. Serial range 73,251- unknown.

| $375 | $275 | $250 | $225 | $200 | $175 | $155 | $135 | $115 | $100 | $90 | $80 |

Add 50% for Target Model.

.38 MILITARY & POLICE (MODEL OF 1905 - 2ND CHANGE) - .38 S&W Special cal., cylinder barrel lengths, finishes and grip styles same as above. 73,648 (including Model 1905 1st change) mfg. Exact quantity unknown. The second change mfg. in 1908-1909. Serial range unknown-146,899.

| $375 | $275 | $250 | $225 | $200 | $175 | $155 | $135 | $115 | $100 | $90 | $80 |

Add 50% for Target Model.

.38 MILITARY & POLICE (MODEL OF 1905 - 3RD CHANGE) - .38 S&W Special cal., 6 shot fluted cylinder, 4, 5, or 6 in. barrel, finishes and grip styles same as above. 94,803 mfg. 1909-1915. Serial range 146,900-241,703.

| $375 | $275 | $250 | $225 | $200 | $175 | $155 | $135 | $115 | $100 | $90 | $80 |

Add 50% for Target Model.

.38 MILITARY & POLICE (MODEL OF 1905 - 4TH CHANGE) - .38 S&W Special cal., 6 shot fluted cylinder, 2, 4, 5, or 6 in. barrel, finishes and grip styles same as above. 458,296 mfg. 1915-1942. Serial range 241,704 - approx. 1,000,000.

| $350 | $255 | $230 | $205 | $180 | $165 | $140 | $125 | $110 | $100 | $90 | $80 |

Add 50% for Target Model.

.44 HAND EJECTOR FIRST MODEL (.44 HAND EJECTOR NEW CENTURY OR .44 TRIPLE LOCK) - .38-40 WCF, .44 S&W Special cal. (standard), .44-40 WCF, .44 S&W Russian, .45 LC, or .455 Mark II cal., 4, 5, 6½, or 7½ in. barrel, non-monogrammed checkered walnut grips and square butt on early production, gold monogram inlay on later production. 15,375 mfg. 1908-1917. Serial range 1-15,375 (overlapping occurs between the 1st and 2nd models, and there is some ser. no. duplication with the .455 Mark II).

❋ Special Caliber Model - .38-40 WCF, .44 Russian, .44-40 WCF, .45 LC (marking, only 21 mfg.), or .455 Mark II (commercial) cal.

| N/A | $2,275 | $1,875 | $1,650 | $1,450 | $1,275 | $1,130 | $985 | $840 | $695 | $550 | $365 |

❋ Conversion Model - .455 Mark II cal.

| $1,200 | $1,075 | $975 | $885 | $765 | $675 | $600 | $540 | $480 | $420 | $365 | $325 |

Only 808 factory conversions of .44 Special to .455 cal. were mfg. and sold to the British government.

❋ Standard Model - .44 S&W Special cal.

| $1,700 | $1,525 | $1,325 | $1,100 | $1,000 | $900 | $800 | $715 | $630 | $545 | $460 | $400 |

Add 100% for factory target sights.

❋ British Target Model Triple Lock - .455 cal., 6½ or 7½ in. barrel, with drift adj. sights (not screw operated) for shooting at Bisley, England, typically unmarked for cal.

| $3,200 | $2,950 | $2,675 | $2,350 | $1,875 | $1,650 | $1,450 | $1,275 | $1,130 | $985 | $840 | $695 |

100%	98%	95%	90%	80%	70%	60%	50%	40%	30%	20%	10%

44 HAND EJECTOR 2ND MODEL - .44 S&W Special cal. as standard, .38-40 WCF, .44-40 WCF, or .45 LC cal., 4, 5, 6, or 6½ in. barrel, blue or nickel finish, checkered walnut grips of square butt style, with or w/o "S&W" monogram inlays. 34,624 mfg. 1914-1937. Ser. range 15,376-approx. 60,000.

✱ *Standard Caliber* - .44 S&W Special cal.

$675	$595	$530	$475	$430	$385	$340	$295	$250	$210	$175	$145

Add 50% for factory target sights.

✱ *Special Calibers* - .38-40 WCF, .44-40 WCF, or .45 LC cal.

$2,450	$2,150	$1,800	$1,600	$1,400	$1,200	$1,000	$895	$795	$700	$575	$475

44 HAND EJECTOR THIRD MODEL (MODEL 1926 HAND EJECTOR THIRD MODEL) - .44 S&W Special cal., very rare in .44-40 WCF or .45 LC cal., 6 shot fluted cylinder, 4, 5, or 6½ in. barrel, finishes and grips same as above, same ser. range as the Second Model .44 Hand Ejectors, approx. 4,976 mfg. pre-war. Ser. range 28,358- S62,489.

✱ *Standard Model* - .44 S&W Special Cal.

$825	$715	$625	$550	$490	$430	$370	$310	$225	$175	$150	$125

There is also a Post-War variation of this model mfg. 1946-49 in the ser. range S62,490- S74,000 (approx. 1,432 mfg. 1946-49). These transitional guns have safety hammer blocks but long actions. The values are similar to those listed.

✱ *.44 Hand Ejector 1926 Target Model* - pre-war, target sights, blue only, otherwise same as above. Mfg. 1926-1941.

$3,950	$3,250	$2,800	$1,950	$1,725	$1,600	$1,500	$1,400	$1,250	$1,100	$975	$925

There is also a Post-War variation of this model mfg. 1946-49 in the ser. range S62,490- S74,000. These transitional guns have safety hammer blocks but long actions. The Post-War Target Model has a barrel rib and 1950s style micrometer rear sight. The values are similar to those listed.

.455 HAND EJECTOR FIRST MODEL - .455 Mark II cal., ser. range 1-5,000 in its own range, English or Canadian proofed.

$1,250	$1,100	$975	$885	$765	$675	$600	$540	$480	$420	$365	$325

Add 25% for commerically sold revolvers.
Subtract 20%-40% for conversion to American caliber.

.455 HAND EJECTOR SECOND MODEL - ser. range 5,001-74,755, generally British or Canadian proofed.

$550	$480	$420	$360	$300	$250	$235	$225	$215	$200	$185	$150

Add 25% for commerically sold revolvers.
Subtract 20%-40% for conversion to American caliber.

Grading	100%	98%	95%	90%	80%	70%	60%

K-22 OUTDOORSMAN - .22 LR cal., 6 shot, 6 in. round barrel, K frame, blue, adj. target sights, walnut grips, serial numbers are in the 600,000 range of the .38 M&P. Mfg. 1931-1940.

	$575	$500	$450	$375	$330	$285	$250

K-22 MASTERPIECE - similar to K-22 Outdoorsman, but has micro click rear sight, short action, round barrel w/o rib. 1,067 mfg. in 1940 with serial range 682,420- 696,952 in .38 Hand Ejector range.

	$1,200	$1,050	$875	$750	$675	$600	$550

.32 HAND EJECTOR POST WWII (MODEL 30) - .32 S&W Long cal., 6 shot, 2, 3, 4, or 6 in. barrel, blue or nickel, fixed sights, walnut or rubber grips. Mfg. 1946-1976.

	$275	$220	$165	$140	$110	$105	$100

This model was designated Model 30 after 1958.

REGULATION POLICE - .32 S&W cal., 6 shot, 2, 3, 4, or 6 in. barrel, square butt, walnut grips, fixed sights, blue or nickel. Mfg. 1917-1957.

	$325	$275	$225	$170	$145	$135	$125

Add 100% for Regulation Police Target (6 in. barrel only, blue).

S

Grading	100%	98%	95%	90%	80%	70%	60%

VICTORY MODEL - .38 Spl. (post-WWII commercial sales only), .38 S&W Spl. (U.S. government sales only), or .38 S&W (Lend-Lease arms to Allied Forces only) cal., mfg. in accordance with British/American Lend-Lease agreement of WWII, parkerized finish, mfg. 1942-1944.

U.S. Govt. Models	$500	$450	$400	$350	$325	$300	$275
Lend-lease mfg.	$250	$225	$200	$175	$160	$150	$140
Post-WWIICommercial sales	$425	$400	$375	$350	$330	$300	$275

Post WWII Victorys sold commercially went through the Defense Supply Commission, and had no U.S. markings. Be careful of fake markings.

U.S. AIR FORCE LIGHTWEIGHT (U.S. MODEL M 13) - .38 Spl. cal., aluminum cylinder and frame, "USAF" marked back strap. Most were destroyed by the Government. Perhaps S&W's most faked revolver!

$800	$725	$675	$525	$475	$425	$350

This model was purchased in large quantities during 1953 and early 1954 only. While S&W never assigned a model number to this variation, M 13 is marked on the top strap and thus mis-nomered as the Model 13. In 1954, a conventional steel cylinder replaced the aluminum cylinder because of cracking.
This model was based on the S&W .38 Military & Police Airweight (later became the Model 12).

.357 MAGNUM FACTORY REGISTERED - .357 Mag. cal., this model could be custom ordered with any barrel length from 3½ - 8¾ in., adj. sights, checkered walnut grips, hand fitted and registered to the buyer by a number found on the inside of the yoke, ser. no. with REG prefix. This practice was disc. 1939 (approx. 5,500 were mfg.) due to the tremendous demand for the .357 Mag. revolver. Mfg. 1935-1939.

$1,950	$1,700	$1,500	$950	$850	$700	$650

Add 40% for rare registration certificate.
Add 20% for non-standard barrel lengths.
Common barrel lengths were 3½, 4, 5, 6½, and 8¾ in.

.357 MAGNUM PRE-WAR NON-REGISTERED - similar to above, but not registered. 1,142 mfg. 1938-1941.

$1,000	$850	$725	$650	$525	$470	$385

.44 MAGNUM PRE-MODEL 29 (5 SCREW) - .44 Mag. cal., 5 screw, can be discerned by 4 screws on right sideplate, 1 located under grip, and 1 in front of the trigger guard. Approx. 6,500 mfg. during 1956-1958.

$850	$750	$650	$575	$560	$450	$400

This model was cataloged in 4 and 6½ in. barrel. The 4 in. is rare, and commands a premium. Also, a rare variation in this model is a 5 in. barrel. Only 500 were mfg. in 5 screw Pre- Model 29 variation with bright blue finish, diamond target stocks, and wood case. In NIB condition the value is $2,800 - add 25% for nickel finish.

.45 HAND EJECTOR (MODEL OF 1917) -.45 Auto Rim, or .45 ACP (in half moon clip) cal., 6 shot, 5½ in. barrel, fixed sights, satin blue on military - high gloss blue on commercial, smooth walnut on military, checkered walnut on commercial models. Early military revolvers have concentric groove cut inside of hammer (approx. serial range 1- 15,000).

✱ *Military* - 175,000 mfg., 1917-1919.

$800	$600	$475	$350	$220	$195	$165

Add 25% for early military mfg. with concentric groove cut inside of hammer.

✱ *Commercial* - mfg. 1920-1941.

$650	$500	$395	$370	$320	$285	$185

Add 200% for factory target sights.

✱ *Brazilian Contract of 1937* - Brazilian shield on right side, 25,000 originally sold to Brazil, 14,000 have been recently imported.

$175	$150	$125	$110	$100	$90	$80

Add 100% for older "non-import".
There was also a "1917 Army" commercial mfg. May 14, 1946-July 25, 1947 (approx. 991 mfg.). Denoted by safety hammer block and ser. no. "S" prefix.

Grading	100%	98%	95%	90%	80%	70%	60%

NUMBERED MODEL REVOLVERS (MODERN HAND EJECTORS)

Smith & Wesson handguns manufactured after 1958 are stamped with a model number on the frame under the cylinder yoke. The number is visible when the cylinder is open. All revolvers manufactured by S&W from 1946-1958 were produced without model numbers.

To determine which variation a particular revolver is in the following section, simply swing the cylinder out to the loading position and notice the model number inside the yoke. The designation Mod. and a two or three digit number followed by a dash and another number designates which engineering change was underway when the gun was manufactured. Hence, a Mod. 48-3 is a Model 48 in its 3rd engineering change (and should be designated when ordering parts). Usually, earlier variations are the most desirable to collectors unless a particular improvement is rare. The same rule applies to semi-auto pistols and the model designation is usually marked on the outside of the gun.

Beginning 1994, S&W started providing synthetic grips and drilled/tapped receiver for scope mounting on certain models.

S&W revolvers are generally categorized by frame size. Frame sizes are as follows: J-frame (small), K-frame (medium), L-frame (medium), and N-frame (large).

All currently manufactured S&W revolvers chambered for .38 S&W Spl. cal. will also accept +P rated ammunition.

Add 10%-15% for those models listed that are pinned and recessed (pre-1981 mfg.).

MODEL 10 M & P - .38 Spl. +P cal., 6 shot, K-frame, round or square butt (4 in. barrel only starting 1992), fixed sights, 2 (disc. 1996), 3 (disc.), 4 (standard – disc. or heavy), 5 (disc.), or 6 (disc.) in. barrels, current mfg. utilizes Uncle Mike's combat grips, 36 oz.

MSR	$496	$365	$260	$195	$155	$130	$115	$100

Add $12 for nickel finish (disc. 1991, 4 in. barrel only).

The Model 10 is currently available in 4 in. heavy barrel only (a 4 in. heavy barrel nickel square butt variation was disc. in 1992).

MODEL 12 M & P AIRWEIGHT - similar to Model 10, only alloy frame, 2 or 4 in. barrel. Disc. 1986.

		$280	$245	$210	$200	$185	$175	$150

Last MSR was $320.

Add $40 for nickel finish (disc.).

MODEL 13 M & P - .357 Mag. cal., 6 shot, fixed sights, 3 (round butt, disc. 1996) or 4 (square butt) in. heavy barrel. Disc. 1998.

		$310	$230	$165	$145	$135	$125	$120

Last MSR was $411.

Add $20 for nickel finish (disc. 1986).

✳ **Model 13 - N.Y. State Police** - .357 Mag. cal., 4 in. barrel, blueblue, fixed sights, 1,200 were mfg. for the N.Y. State Police and are marked 10-6. All 1,200 were recalled by S&W and exchanged for Model 28s.

		$375	$300	$250	$200	$175	$150	$140

MODEL 14 K-38 - .38 Spl. cal., target model, blue only. Disc. 1981.

		$300	$250	$215	$200	$185	$175	$160

Add $20 for 6 in. barrel single action.

MODEL 14 K-38 MASTERPIECE - .38 Spl. cal., 6 in. full lug barrel, adj. rear sight, combat style Morado wood square butt grips, blue finish, 47 oz. Disc. 1999.

		$385	$310	$260	$225	$200	$185	$165

Last MSR was $498.

S

Grading	100%	98%	95%	90%	80%	70%	60%

MODEL 15 COMBAT MASTERPIECE - .38 Spl. cal., adj. sights, 6 shot, square butt, 2 (disc.), 4, 6 (mfg. 1986-91), or 8 3/8 (new 1986, disc.) in. barrel. Disc. 1999.

	$340	$260	$215	$190	$180	$160	$150

Last MSR was $450.

Add $31 for TT or TH (disc. 1991).
Add $11 for 8 3/8 in. barrel (disc.).
Add $20 for nickel finish (disc. 1987).

MODEL 16 (K-32 MASTERPIECE) - .32 S&W Long cal., 6 in. barrel, adj. sights, checkered walnut, blue. Only 3630 mfg., 1947-1974.

	$1,350	$1,150	$995	$875	$750	$625	$525

✳ Pre-War K-32 (Model 16 Outdoorsman) - only 104 mfg. pre-war, scarce.

	$2,250	$1,950	$1,700	$1,475	$1,250	$1,050	$875

MODEL 16 - .32 cal./.32 Mag. cal., 6 shot, 4 (mfg. 1990-91 only), 6, or 8 3/8 (disc. 1991) in. barrel, square butt, blue finish only, TH and TT. Mfg. 1990-92.

	$335	$280	$225	$210	$200	$190	$180

Last MSR was $419.

Add 5%-10% for 8 3/8 in. barrel.

MODEL 17 K-22 MASTERPIECE - .22 LR cal., blue only, 6 shot, 4 (mfg. 1986-93), 6 (current mfg.), or 8 3/8 (disc. 1992) in. barrel. Disc. 1993, reintroduced 1996, disc. 1998.

	$390	$280	$240	$215	$200	$185	$175

Last MSR was $508.

Add $39 for full lug 6 in. long barrel (w/TT & TH, disc.).
Add $50 for full lug 8 3/8 in. long barrel (w/TT & TH, disc. 1992).

MODEL 17-2 PROTOTYPE MERCOX DART PROJECTILE GUN - .530 Dart Projectile, .22 Ramset blank gas generator, 12 in. barrel, blue finish only, 25 prototype units mfg. 1966 only.

	$3,950	$3,250	$2,750

Add $500 for handmade Safariland holster.
Add $100-$500 depending on variation of projectile (six known).

MODEL 18 .22 COMBAT MASTERPIECE - .22 LR cal., combat style adj. sights, 4 in. barrel, blue only. Disc. 1985.

	$305	$270	$225	$200	$180	$175	$165

Last MSR was $352.

Add $30 for TT and TH.

MODEL 19 .357 COMBAT MAGNUM - .357 Mag. cal., K frame, adj. sights, 2½ (round butt, disc. 1998), 4 (square butt), or 6 (square butt, disc. 1996) in. barrel, bright blue or nickel (disc. 1992) finish, drilled/tapped receiver and synthetic grips became standard 1994. Disc. 1999.

	$345	$265	$210	$190	$180	$170	$160

Last MSR was $457.

Add $9 for 4 in. or $14 for 6 in. (disc. 1996) barrel.
Add $35 for white outline rear sight (disc. 1994).
Add $20 for nickel finish - disc. 1991.
Add $60 for TS, TT, TH, RR, and WO - disc. 1991 (6 in. barrel only).

This model was supplied with a round butt on 2½ in. barrel. The 2½ and 6 in. barrels (blue finish) were disc. in 1991 along with the 4 and 6 in. nickel variations.

PRE-MODEL 20 (PRE-WAR .38/44) - .38 Spl. cal., 6 shot, 4, 5, or 6½ in. barrel lengths, fixed sights, walnut grips, blue or nickel, walnut grips. Mfg. 1930-1941 and re-introduced 1946 (with S prefix starting at serial 62,940). The 38/44 Heavy Duty became the Model 20 in 1957.

	$595	$490	$450	$415	$385	$340	$300

Add 40% for 6½ in. barrel.

Early post-war models had pre-war long action (ser. range S62,489-approx. S74,000).

Grading	100%	98%	95%	90%	80%	70%	60%

MODEL 20 - .38 Spl. cal., 6 shot, 4, 5, or 6½ in. barrel, fixed sights, blue or nickel finish, checkered walnut grips. Mfg. 1957-1964.

	$350	$285	$260	$220	$195	$145	$125

MODEL 21 (.44 HAND EJECTOR FOURTH MODEL - MODEL OF 1950 MILITARY) - .44 S&W cal., 6 shot, 4, 5, or 6½ in. barrel, large frame, blue, walnut grips, fixed sights, 1,200 mfg. scattered throughout serial range S75,000-S263,000. Mfg. 1950- 1964.

	$1,750	$1,575	$1,350	$1,100	$875	$650	$550

Add 50% for 6½ in. (rare).

MODEL 22 (.45 HAND EJECTOR MODEL OF 1950 MILITARY) - .45 Auto Rim or .45 ACP cal., same specifications as 1917 Army, except redesigned hammer block, short action, fixed sights. Approx. 1,200 mfg. 1950-1964.

	$1,500	$1,275	$1,050	$875	$725	$650	$525

MODEL 23 (.38-44 OUTDOORSMAN) - .38 Spl. cal., similar to Model 20 in .38 Spl., except with adj. sights, blue only, pre-war guns had plain barrels, post-war mfg. featured ribbed 6½ in. barrel standard. Mfg. 1930-1967.

	$650	$550	$450	$375	$300	$280	$270

Add 20% for post-war transitional variation.

Early post-war models had long action with barrel rib and micrometer sights (ser. range S62,489-approx. S74,000). There were 4,761 pre-war revolvers, 2,036 post-war transitional, and 6,039 styled after the 1950 model.

The 44 in this model's nomenclature refers to the size frame, not the caliber. This variation became designated the Model 23 after 1958.

MODEL 24 (.44 HAND EJECTOR FOURTH MODEL - 1950 TARGET) - .44 Spl., redesigned hammer, short action, 6½ in. ribbed barrel standard, satin blue or bright blue, micrometer sights, serialization begins at approx. S75,000. 5,050 mfg. 1950-1967.

	$695	$575	$500	$400	$375	$350	$320

Add 20% for bright blue.
Add 40% for 4 in. barrel.
Add 50% for 5 in. barrel.

MODEL 24-3 - .44 Spl., 4 or 6½ in. barrel, bright blue only, checkered Goncalo Alves target grips (without speedloader cutout), barrel and frame not pinned, 7,500 mfg. 1983 only.

✳ 4 in. barrel. - 2,625 mfg.

	$450	$425	$400	$375	$325	$275	$225

✳ 6½ in. barrel. - 4,875 mfg.

	$400	$375	$350	$325	$275	$225	$175

Last MSR was $359.

This model's serialization is triple alpha - 4 numeric (i.e. ABC0123).

✳ Model 24 Lew Horton Special - .44 Spl., 3 in. barrel, round butt, adj. sights, blue finish, includes special fitted holster.

	$380	$325	$250				

Subtract 10% without holster.

MODEL 25/25-2 (1955 TARGET MODEL) - .45 ACP, .45 Auto Rim or .45 LC (earlier mfg.) cal., N frame, blue finish only, target grips, 6 (later mfg.) or 6½ (earlier mfg.) in. barrel. Disc. approx. 1985.

	$450	$400	$350	$300	$235	$200	$190

Last MSR was $347.

Add $150 for 6½ in. barrel (early mfg. with pinned barrel).
Add 300% for .45 LC cal.

After 1957, the Model 25 in .45 ACP cal was designated Model 25-2.

S

Grading	100%	98%	95%	90%	80%	70%	60%

✱ *Model 25 Lew Horton Special* - .45 ACP cal., 3 in. barrel, adj. sights, blue finish, only 100 mfg.

| | | $500 | $450 | $375 | | | |

MODEL 25-5 - .45 LC cal., 4, 6, or 8 3/8 in. barrel, blue or nickel finish (no extra charge - disc. 1987). Disc. 1991.

| | $375 | $315 | $250 | $215 | $200 | $190 | $180 |

Last MSR was $429.

Add 5%-10% for 8 3/8 in. barrel.

MODEL 26 (.45 HAND EJECTOR MODEL OF 1950 TARGET) - .45 ACP, or .45 Auto Rim cal., adj. sights, thin ribbed barrel, 2,768 mfg.

| | $770 | $660 | $550 | $440 | $275 | $200 | $150 |

Add 300% for .45 Colt cal. (200 mfg.).

MODEL 27 - .357 Mag. cal., N-frame, 3½ (disc. 1977), 4 (disc. 1991), 5 (disc. 1977), 6, 6½, or 8 3/ 8 (disc. 1991) in. barrel, blue or nickel (disc. 1987) finish. Disc. 1994.

| | $380 | $300 | $235 | $220 | $205 | $190 | $180 |

Last MSR was $486.

Add 10% for pinned barrel and recessed cylinder.
Add $28 for white outline rear sight -(disc. 1991).
Add $8 for 8 3/8 in. barrel - (disc. 1991).

✱ *3½ and 5 in. barrel* - disc.

| | $425 | $365 | $275 | $265 | $240 | $230 | $180 |

MODEL 28 HIGHWAY PATROLMAN - .357 Mag. cal., "Highway Patrol" utility model, dull or brushed nickel (very rare) finish, adj. sights, standard grips, blue only, 4 or 6 in. barrel, mfg. 1954-1986.

| | $270 | $235 | $210 | $200 | $190 | $180 | $150 |

Last MSR was $306.

Add $20 for TS.
Add 30% for 5 screw variation.
Add 300% for brushed nickel finish (beware of fakes).

MODEL 29 .44 MAGNUM (4 SCREW) - .44 Mag. cal., 4 screw, can be discerned by 2 exposed screws on lower right sideplate (one is concealed by the right grip, and one in front of the trigger guard). Mfg. began 1957 after approx. ser. no. S175,000 and was disc. 1961.

| | $695 | $650 | $600 | $550 | $475 | $425 | $375 |

MODEL 29/29-2 (3 SCREW) - .44 Mag. cal., 4, 6½, or 8 3/8 in. barrel, eliminated top screw on sideplate and 1 screw in front of trigger guard. Disc.

| | $650 | $550 | $500 | $400 | $300 | $275 | $250 |

Subtract $40 if without case.

The S serial number prefix was used on this model until 1968, at which time the law required a new numbering system, and the serial number prefix was changed to N. The S prefix originally designated the additional hammer block safety.

MODEL 29 - .44 Mag. cal., 6 shot, 4 (disc. 1992), 6, or 8 3/8 in. barrel, blue or nickel (disc. 1991) finish. Disc. 1998 (long live Dirty Harry!).

| | $400 | $335 | $285 | $265 | $255 | $245 | $210 |

Last MSR was $574.

Add $12 for 8 3/8 in. barrel.
Add $11 for nickel finish (disc. 1991).
Add 10%-15% for pinned barrel and recessed cylinder, depending on condition.
Add $45 for combat grips with scope mount - disc. 1991 (8 3/8 in. barrel only).

Older Model 29 mfg. (5 screw variations) will appear under the previous subheading: "EARLY HAND EJECTORS (NAMED MODELS)".

S

Grading	100%	98%	95%	90%	80%	70%	60%

✴ *Model 29 Lew Horton Special* - similar to Model 29, except has 3 in. barrel, round butt, adj. sights.

	$425	$350	$295				

MODEL 29 CLASSIC - .44 Mag. cal., 5, 6½, or 8 3/8 in. full lug barrel, blue only, round butt with Hogue conversion square butt grips, interchangeable front sights with white outline rear sight, frame is drilled and tapped to accept scope mounts, blue finish only. Mfg. 1990-94.

$475	$375	$295	$280	$260	$240	$225

Last MSR was $591.

Add $8 for 8 3/8 in. barrel.

✴ *Model 29 Classic DX* - similar to Model 29 Classic, except supplied with 2 sets of grips, 6½ or 8 3/8 in. barrel, 5 interchangeable front sights, numbered test target, 51- 54 oz. Mfg. 1991-92.

$625	$525	$495	$425	$350	$300	$250

Add $8 for 8 3/8 in. barrel.

MODEL 29 SILHOUETTE - .44 Mag. cal., 10 5/8 in. barrel, adj. front and rear sights, bright blue only, Goncalo Alves target stocks. Mfg. 1983-91.

$550	$475	$395	$335	$290	$260	$240

Last MSR was $536.

MODEL 29 MAGNACLASSIC - .44 Mag. cal., 7½ in. full lug, ported barrel, high polish bright bluing, round butt, interchangeable front sight, supplied with cherry wood display case mfg. in England, 3,000 mfg. in 1990 only.

$850	$725	$600	$500	$450	$395	$360

Last MSR was $999.

MODEL 30 - .32 S&W cal., 6 shot, 2, 3, 4, or 6 in. barrel, square butt, walnut grips, fixed sights, blue or nickel finish. Limited mfg.

$300	$260	$220	$190	$175	$165	$150

MODEL 31 - .32 S&W Long cal., fixed sights, 2, 3 or 4 (disc.) in. barrel, blue only. Disc. 1991.

$290	$235	$195	$185	$175	$165	$150

Last MSR was $365.

Add 25% for early flatlatch models.

MODEL 32 (.38 TERRIER) - .38 S&W cal., 5 shot, 2 in. barrel, walnut or rubber grips, blue or nickel, fixed sights, built on .32 frame. Mfg. 1936-1974.

$330	$220	$175	$150	$135	$125	$115

This variation was designated the Model 32 after 1958.

MODEL 33 (.38 REGULATION POLICE) - .38 S&W cal., 5 shot, 2, 3, 4 in. barrel, square butt, walnut grips, fixed sights, blue or nickel finish. Mfg. 1917-74.

$325	$275	$225	$170	$145	$135	$125

MODEL 34 - .22 LR or .22/32 Kit Gun cal. (disc.), adj. sights in J frame, 6 shot, 2 or 4 in. barrel, round or square butt, blue or nickel (disc. 1986) finish. Disc. 1991. This model was re-issued for 2-3 years.

$300	$235	$195	$185	$175	$165	$150

Last MSR was $366.

Add $25 for nickel finish.
Add 25% for early flatlatch models.

MODEL 35 (.22/32 TARGET MODEL OF 1953) - similar to Standard .22/.32 Hand Ejector Model, except micrometer rear sight, magna target grips. Mfg. 1953-1974.

$425	$300	$265	$230	$200	$180	$160

MODEL 35 .22/.32 TARGET

$300	$250	$195	$165	$130	$110	$90

S

Grading	100%	98%	95%	90%	80%	70%	60%

MODEL 36 (CHIEFS SPECIAL) - .38 Spl. cal., 5 shot, J frame, round or square (disc. 1991) butt, 1 7/8 in. regular or 3 in. (heavy only, disc. 1994) barrel, blue or nickel (disc. 1992) finish. Disc. 1999.

	$295	$230	$180	$165	$155	$150	$145

Last MSR was $406.

Add $12 for nickel finish (disc., round butt - 2 in. barrel only).
Add 25% for early small trigger guard and grips (below ser. no. 2,500).
Note: 1st models with high polish blue and diamond grips will bring premiums when mint in original box.

MODEL 36 TARGET - similar to Model 50, 2 in. barrel, square butt, mfg. started 1955.

	$850	$725	$650	$575	$500	$400	$350

MODEL 36 LADYSMITH - .38 Spl. +P cal., 5 shot, J-frame, 1 7/8 in. regular or 3 (disc. 1991) in. heavy barrel, blue finish only, Combat Dyamondwood grips are anatomically designed for women (round butt on 1 7/8 in., wood combat grips on 3 in.), fixed sights, redesigned double action, 20-23 oz., Morocco grained (disc. 1991) or soft side jewelry case. New 1990.

MSR	$518		$395	$280	$220	$195	$175	$165	$150

MODEL 37 CHIEFS SPECIAL AIRWEIGHT - similar to Model 36 Chiefs Special, except alloy frame and 1 7/8 in. barrel only, J-frame, blue or nickel (disc. 1995) finish, barrels are marked Airweight.

MSR	$523		$410	$285	$220	$195	$175	$165	$150

Add $16 for nickel finish (disc.).

MODEL 38 BODYGUARD AIRWEIGHT - .38 S&W Spl. cal., 5 shot, alloy frame, round butt, shrouded hammer, 2 in. barrel, blue or nickel (disc. 1996) finish. Disc. 1998.

	$350	$260	$205	$190	$180	$170	$150

Last MSR was $462.

Add $15 for nickel finish (disc. 1996).

MODEL 40 CENTENNIAL - .38 S&W Spl. cal., 2 in. barrel, double action only, fully concealed hammer, grip safety, smooth walnut grips, blue or nickel. Mfg. 1953-1974.

	$475	$425	$345	$290	$260	$240	$220

This model commands a premium for the first series with no letter prefix. After 1968, L prefix series began.

MODEL 42 CENTENNIAL AIRWEIGHT - .38 S&W Spl. cal., aluminum variation of Model 40 Centennial, mfg. began 1953. Disc.

Blue	$475	$425	$395	$325	$300	$265	$240
Nickel	$1,100	$950	$875	$775	$675	$550	$475

MODEL 42 - .38 Spl. cal., blue finish only. Disc.

	$450	$400	$360	$320	$295	$270	$250

MODEL 43 (.22/32 KIT GUN AIRWEIGHT) - .22 LR cal., 3½ in. barrel, round or square butt, adj. sights, aluminum frame and cylinder, mfg. 1955-1974.

	$425	$350	$275	$240	$185	$165	$150

MODEL 45 (.22 MILITARY & POLICE) - .22 LR cal. only, originally mfg. as training gun between 1931-1957, also mfg. 500 in 1963 (Model 45).

Pre-War	N/A	N/A	$1,900	$1,600	$1,350	$1,250	$950
Post-War	$650	$550	$450	$375	$300	$280	$270

MODEL 48 K-22 MASTERPIECE - .22 Mag cal., 4, 6 or 8 3/8 in. barrel, blue only. Disc. 1986.

	$275	$245	$200	$185	$175	$165	$150

Last MSR was $320.

Add $15 for 8 3/8 in. barrel.
Add $15 for TT, TH, and TS (disc.).

Grading	100%	98%	95%	90%	80%	70%	60%

MODEL 49 BODYGUARD - similar to Model 38, only steel frame, 2 in. barrel, blue or nickel (disc.) finish. Disc. 1996.

	100%	98%	95%	90%	80%	70%	60%
	$300	$260	$180	$170	$160	$150	$145

Last MSR was $409.

Add $25 for nickel finish (disc.).

MODEL 50 (.38 CHIEFS SPECIAL TARGET) - .38 S&W Spl. cal., Chiefs Special Target, mfg. from 1955 in 2 in. (see Model 36 Target listing) or 3 (211 mfg. beginning 1973) in. barrels, target sights, most were unmarked for model number, approx. 1,100 mfg. The other variation was designated Model 36 Target.

	$795	$700	$625	$550	$475	$400	$350

The Model 50 designation was not used until 1970.

MODEL 51 - .22 Mag. cal. only, .22/32 kit gun, 3½ in. barrel, 6 shot, adj. rear sight, blue or nickel, walnut stocks. Disc.

	$400	$350	$300	$275	$250	$225	$200

MODEL 53 .22 REM. JET - .22 S, L, or LR inserts, 6 shot, 4, 6, or 8 3/8 in. barrel, blue, walnut grips, adj. sights. Mfg. 1960-1974.

	$735	$650	$550	$470	$385	$360	$330

Add 10% for 8 3/8 in. barrel.
Add $200 for extra matching .22 LR cylinder.

MODEL 57 - .41 Mag. cal., similar to Model 29, except for cal., 4 (disc. 1991), 6 or 8 3/ 8 (disc. 1991) in. barrel, blue or nickel (disc.) finish. Disc. 1993.

	$350	$255	$225	$205	$190	$175	$165

Last MSR was $466.

Add 10%-20% for S prefix serialization.
Add 10% for nickel finish if NIB.
Add $20 for 8 3/8 in. barrel.
Add 10% for pinned barrel and recessed cylinder.

MODEL 58 - .41 Mag cal., M&P, fixed sights, 4 in. barrel, blue or nickel finish. Disc.

	$495	$450	$385	$340	$315	$290	$260

Add $25 for nickel finish or "S" serial number prefix.

MODEL 60 .38 SPL. CHIEFS SPECIAL - .38 S&W Spl., stainless version of Chiefs Special, 2 or 3 in. full lug barrel. Disc. 1996.

	$335	$250	$195

Last MSR was $458.

Subtract $25 for 2 in. barrel.
Add 30% for early Model 60s without letter prefix and bright satin finish.
The full lug barrel option began in 1990 with limited mfg. It had been tested for +P+ ammo and features an adj. rear sight - 24½ oz.

MODEL 60 .357 MAG. CHIEFS SPECIAL - .357 Mag. cal., 2 1/8 or 3 (new 1997) in. barrel, round butt, stainless steel, J-frame, current production uses Uncle Mike's Combat grips, 22½ - 24 oz. New 1996.

MSR	$541	$400	$295	$210

Add $33 for 3 in. full lug barrel with adj. sight (new 1997).

MODEL 60 LADYSMITH - .38 S&W Spl. +P cal., 5 shot, 2 in. regular (disc. 1996), 2 1/ 8 (new 1997), or 3 in. heavy (disc. 1991) barrel, J-frame, frosted stainless steel finish, Combat Dymondwood grips are anatomically designed for women (round butt on 2 in., wood combat grips on 3 in.), fixed sights, redesigned double action, 20- 23 oz, Morocco grained (disc. 1991) or soft side jewelry case. New 1990.

MSR	$566	$430	$285	$215

S

Grading	100%	98%	95%	90%	80%	70%	60%

MODEL 63 .22/32 KIT GUN - .22 LR/.32 cal., stainless kit gun, 2 or 4 in. barrel, 19 oz. Disc. 1998.

	$365	$245	$195

Add $5 for 4 in. barrel.

Last MSR was $476.

MODEL 64 M & P - .38 Spl. +P cal., stainless Model 10, 6 shot, 2, 3, or 4 in. barrel, K-frame, 3 (square butt disc. 1992) and 4 in. (square butt only) barrels are heavy, current production uses Uncle Mike's combat grips, 30½ - 36 oz.

MSR	$522	$390	$265	$200

Add $10 for 3 or 4 in. heavy barrel.

MODEL 65 - .357 Mag. cal., stainless version of Model 13, K-frame, has 3 (round butt, disc. 2000) or 4 (square butt) in. heavy barrels, satin stainless steel, current production uses Uncle Mike's grips, fixed sights, 35 oz.

MSR	$531	$395	$270	$205

MODEL 65 LADYSMITH - .357 Mag. cal., K-frame, 3 in. barrel with round butt, glass beaded stainless finish, soft side jewelry case, smooth Dymondwood combat grips, 32 oz. New 1992.

MSR	$584	$450	$300	$225

MODEL 66 - .357 Mag. cal., K-frame, satin stainless version of Model 19, has 2½, 3 (disc., only 2,500 mfg.), 4, or 6 in. barrel, current production uses Uncle Mike's Combat grips, 32-39 oz.

MSR	$579	$450	$310	$225

Add $11 for 2½ in. barrel.
Add $29 for 6 in. barrel.
Add $48 for TH and TT with 4 (disc. 1991) or 6 in. barrel only (disc. 1999).

Note: Several models of the Model 66 were made - such features as an all-stainless steel rear sight and a recessed cylinder will bring a slight premium if NIB.

MODEL 67 COMBAT MASTERPIECE - .38 S&W Spl.+P cal., K-frame, stainless version of Model 15, has 4 in. barrel, current production uses Uncle Mike's Combat grips, 36 oz. Disc. 1988, reintroduced 1991.

MSR	$585	$455	$310	$225

1991 mfg. included square butt and red ramp front sight insert.

MODEL 68 - .38 S&W Spl. cal., similar in appearance to the Model 66, except is in .38 Spl. cal., 4 or 6 in. barrel, approx. 7,500 mfg.

	$750	$625	$495

This model was originally ordered by CA Highway Patrol. Add 10% for CHP markings.

MODEL 296 AIRLITE TI CENTENNIAL - .44 S&W Spl. cal., L-frame, 5 shot, 2½ barrel, similar to Model 331 in construction materials, Uncle Mike's Boot grips, 18.9 oz. New 2000.

MSR	$754	$620	$490	$355

MODEL 317 AIRLITE/KIT GUN - .22 LR cal., J-frame, 8 shot, 1 7/8 or 3 (new 1998, Hi-Viz sights became standard in 2001, Model 317 Kit Gun) in. barrel, combination of aluminum alloy and stainless steel construction, brushed aluminum finish, round butt, choice of synthetic or Dymondwood Boot (disc. 1998) grips, fixed sights, 10.5 oz. New 1997.

MSR	$550	$425	$305	$220

Add $50 for 3 in. barrel.
Add $33 for Dymondwood Boot grips.

✴ *Model 317 Airlite LadySmith* - .22 LR cal., 1 7/8 in. barrel only, includes Dymondwood Boot grips, 9.9 oz. New 1998.

MSR	$596	$445	$320	$220

S

Grading	100%	98%	95%	90%	80%	70%	60%

MODEL 331 AIRLITE TI CHIEFS SPECIAL - .32 H&R Mag. cal., J-frame, 6 shot, 1 7/8 in. barrel with stainless steel liner, features titanium cylinder and aluminum alloy frame, barrel shroud, and yoke, fixed sights, Uncle Mike's or Dymondwood Boot (disc.) wood grips, two-tone matte stainless/grey finish approx. 12 oz. New 1999.

MSR $716	$565	$435	$370	$335	$300	$275	$250

Add $24 for Dymondwood Boot grips (mfg. 1999 only).

MODEL 332 AIRLITE TI CENTENNIAL - J-frame, similar Model 331 Airlite Ti, except is hammerless and double action only, current production uses Uncle Mike's Boot grips, 12 oz. New 1999.

MSR $734	$575	$455	$390	$345	$310	$280	$250

Add $24 for Dymondwood Boot grips (mfg. 1999 only).

MODEL 337 AIRLITE TI CHIEFS SPECIAL - .38 S&W Spl.+P cal., J-frame, 5 shot, 1 7/8 in. barrel, similar design as the Model 331, 11.9 oz. New 1999.

MSR $716	$565	$435	$370	$335	$310	$280	$250

Add $24 for Dymondwood Boot grips (mfg. 1999 only).

MODEL 337 AIRLITE TI KIT GUN - .38 S&W Spl.+P cal., J-frame, 5 shot, 3 1/8 in. barrel with Hi-Viz front sight (new 2001), choice of Dymondwood or Uncle Mike's combat grips, approx. 13 oz. New 2000.

MSR $779	$600	$460	$385	$345	$315	$285	$250

MODEL 337 PD AIRLITE TI CHIEFS SPECIAL - .38 S&W Spl.+P cal., J-frame, 5 shot, 1 7/8 in. barrel, black/grey finish, black Hogue Bantam grips, 10.7 oz. New 2000.

MSR $740	$580	$450	$385	$340	$310	$280	$250

MODEL 340 AIRLITE Sc CENTENNIAL - .357 Mag. cal., J-frame, 5 shot, 1 7/8 in. barrel, Scandium alloy frame, barrel shroud, and yoke, titanium cylinder, two-tone matte stainless/grey finish, hammerless, Hogue Bantam grips, 12 oz. New 2001.

MSR $763	$595	$460	$390	$350	$315	$280	$250

MODEL 340 PD AIRLITE Sc CENTENNIAL - similar to Model 340 Airlite Sc, except has 3½ in. barrel with Hi-Viz front sight, black/grey finish, 12 oz. New 2001.

MSR $785	$605	$465	$390	$345	$315	$285	$250

MODEL 342 AIRLITE TI CENTENNIAL - similar to Model 337, except is hammerless and double action only, matte stainless/grey finish, Uncle Mike's Boot grips, 12 oz. New 1999.

MSR $734	$575	$445	$390	$345	$310	$280	$250

Add $24 for Dymondwood Boot grips (mfg. 1999 only).

MODEL 342 PD AIRLITE TI CENTENNIAL - .38 S&W Spl.+P cal., J-frame, 5 shot, double action only, aluminum alloy frame with titanium cylinder and stainless steel 1 7/8 in. barrel, hammerless, black/grey finish, Hogue Bantam grips, 10.8 oz. New 2000.

MSR $758	$595	$460	$390	$340	$310	$280	$250

MODEL 360 AIRLITE Sc CHIEFS SPECIAL - .357 Mag. cal., J-frame, 5 shot, 1 7/8 in. barrel, Scandium alloy frame with titanium cylinder, matte stainless/grey finish, Hogue Bantam grips, fixed sights, 12 oz. New 2001.

MSR $745	$585	$450	$395	$350	$310	$280	$250

MODEL 360 AIRLITE Sc KIT GUN - .357 Mag. cal., J-frame, 5 shot, 3 1/8 in. barrel with Hi-Viz front sight, Scandium alloy frame with titanium cylinder, matte stainless/grey finish, Uncle Mike's Combat grips, 14½ oz. New 2001.

MSR $876	$675	$500	$410	$360	$325	$295	$260

MODEL 386 AIRLITE Sc MOUNTAIN LITE - .357 Mag. cal., L-frame, 7 shot, 3 1/8 in. stainless barrel with Hi-Viz front sight, Scandium alloy frame with titanium cylinder, two-tone matte stainless/grey finish, Hogue Bantam grips, 18½ oz. New 2001.

MSR $799	$620	$465	$395	$355	$325	$295	$265

S

Grading	100%	98%	95%	90%	80%	70%	60%

MODEL 386 PD AIRLITE Sc - .357 Mag. cal., L-frame, 7 shot, 2½ in. stainless barrel with adj. black rear sight, scandium alloy frame with titanium cylinder, black/grey finish, Hogue Bantam grips, 17½ oz. New 2001.

	MSR	$795		$615	$470	$395	$350	$315	$285	$250

MODEL 396 AIRLITE TI MOUNTAIN LITE - .44 S&W Spl. cal., L-frame, 5 shot, 3 1/ 8 in. barrel with stainless liner and Hi-Viz front sight, aluminum alloy frame with titanium cylinder, matte stainless/grey finish, Hogue Bantam grips, 18 oz. New 2001.

	MSR	$788		$610	$465	$395	$350	$315	$285	$250

MODEL 442 CENTENNIAL AIRWEIGHT - .38 S&W Spl.+P cal., J-frame, 5 shot, double action only, 1 7/8 in. barrel only with fixed sights, hammerless, aluminum alloy/steel frame, blue or nickel (disc. 1995) finish, round butt, current production uses Uncle Mike's Boot grips, 15 oz. New 1993.

	MSR	$547		$415	$300	$225	$195	$180	$170	$150

Add $15 for nickel finish (disc.).

MODEL 520 - .357 Mag. cal., 4 in. barrel, fixed sights, N frame, originally ordered for N.Y. State Police but never purchased. Approx. 3,000 mfg. with box.

			$325	$275	$240	$210	$185	$175	$165

MODEL 547 M & P - 9mm Para. cal., 3 or 4 in. heavy barrel, 6 shot, round (3 in. barrel) or square (4 in. barrel) butt, blue only, 32 oz. Disc. 1985.

			$295	$265	$240	$210	$195	$185	$175

Last MSR was $317.

MODEL 581 - .357 Mag. cal., L-Frame, fixed sights, 4 in. barrel, 6 shot, blue or nickel finish, 38 oz. Disc. 1992.

			$275	$225	$180	$170	$160	$150	$145

Last MSR was $335.

Add $20 for nickel (disc. 1987).
This model was disc. 1985-86, and reintroduced 1987-92.

MODEL 586 (DISTINGUISHED COMBAT MAGNUM) - .357 Mag. cal., L- Frame, 4, 6, or 8 3/8 (disc. 1991) in. barrel, adj. sights, blue or nickel (disc. 1991) finish. Disc. 1999.

			$370	$285	$215	$195	$185	$175	$165

Last MSR was $494.

Add 5%-10% for nickel finish (disc.).
Add $4 for white outlined rear sight (disc. 1994).
Add $5 for 6 in. barrel.
Add $22 for 8 3/8 in. barrel (disc. 1991).
Add $35 for adj. front sight - disc. 1991 (6 in. barrel only, new 1986).

* **1985 Model 586 Iowa Highway State Patrol** - mfg. to commemorate 50th anniversary, gold etching, 4 in. barrel. Mfg. 1985 only.

			$375	$250	$225				

MODEL 610 CLASSIC - 10mm/.40 S&W cal., N-frame, 6 shot, adj. sights, 4 (new 2001) 5 (disc. 2000) or 6½ (disc. 2000) in. full lug barrel, stainless steel construction, fluted or unfluted (4 or 6½ in. barrel only) cylinder, round butt, adj. rear sight, current production uses Hogue rubber grips, target hammer optional, 50 oz., approx. 5,000 mfg. 1990 only, reintroduced 1998.

	MSR	$785		$640	$500	$395				

MODEL 617 (K-22 MASTERPIECE) - .22 LR cal., K-frame, stainless steel variation of the Model 17 (K-22 Masterpiece), 6 (6 in. barrel only beginning 1999) or 10 (new 1997) shot, 4, 6, or 8 3/8 in. barrel, satin stainless finish, combat trigger and Hogue rubber grips are standard on current production, semi-target, 41-52.5 oz. New 1990.

	MSR	$625		$470	$325	$225				

Add $19 for 4 in. barrel, add $44 for 6 in. barrel with 10 shot, or $54 for 8 3/8 in. barrel.
In 2000, this model includes target hammer with 8 3/8 in. barrel.

S

Grading	100%	98%	95%	90%	80%	70%	60%

MODEL 624 .44 TARGET - .44 S&W Spl. cal., 6 shot, 4 or 6½ in. barrel, 42 oz. Mfg. 1986-87 only.

| | $340 | $250 | $225 | | | | |

Last MSR was $449.

Add $14 for 6½ in. barrel.

* ❋ *Model 624-2 Lew Horton Special* - .44 Spl. cal., 3 in. barrel with round butt, adj. sights, includes special fitted holster.

| | $395 | $350 | $295 | | | | |

Subtract 10% if without holster.

MODEL 625 - .45 ACP cal., N-frame, stainless variation of the Model 25-2, 6 shot, 3 (disc. 1991), 4 (disc. 1991), or 5 in. barrel, round butt, frosted stainless finish, full lug barrel, Pachmayr (disc.) or Hogue rubber combat grips, 45 oz. New 1988.

| MSR | $745 | | $585 | $450 | $325 | | |

This variation has the frame stamped "625-2", roll engraved barrel with ".45 CAL MODEL OF 1988" barrel inscription.

MODEL 627 - .357 Mag. cal., also known as "Model of 1989" (stamped on barrel), N- frame, round butt, unfluted cylinder, full underlug 5½ in. barrel. Disc.

| | $545 | $425 | $325 | | | | |

MODEL 629 - .44 Mag./.44 S&W Spl. cal., N-frame, 6 shot, similar to Model 29, available with 4, 6, or 8 3/8 in. barrel, satin stainless finish, current production uses Hogue rubber combat grips, 41½ - 49½ oz.

| MSR | $717 | | $575 | $445 | $325 | | |

Add $22 for 6 in. barrel or $39 for 8 3/8 in. barrel.

Add $52 for combat grips with barrel scope mount (cut across barrel rib) - disc. 1991 (8 3/8 in. barrel only).

Add 10% for pinned barrel with recessed cylinder.

During 1978, approx. 100 pre-production revolvers were made with pinned barrels and recessed cylinders, serial range is N629,062-N629,200, includes wood box. Prices range from $650-$750, depending on condition.

* ❋ *Model 629 Classic* - satin stainless steel variation of the Model 29 Classic, 5, 6½ (with or w/o PowerPort), or 8 3/8 in. barrel, current production uses Hogue rubber combat grips, 49½ - 53½ oz. New 1990.

| MSR | $768 | | $600 | $455 | $345 | | |

Add $25 for 6½ in. barrel with white outline on rear sight or 8 3/8 in. barrel.

* ❋ *Model 629 Classic DX* - similar to Classic, except is supplied with 2 sets of grips (Hogue combat square and Morado wood round butt stocks), 6½ or 8 3/8 in. barrel, satin stainless finish, 5 interchangeable front sights, numbered test target, 51-54 oz. New 1992.

| MSR | $986 | | $795 | $635 | $510 | | |

Add $32 for 8 3/8 in. barrel.

* ❋ *Model 629 Magna Classic* - .44 Mag. cal., similar to Model 29, 3,000 mfg. during 1990 only.

| | $900 | $825 | $750 | | | | |

Last MSR was $999.

* ❋ *Model 629 Lew Horton Special* - .44 Mag. cal., 3 in. barrel with round butt, adj. sights.

| | $400 | $350 | $295 | | | | |

MODEL 631 - .32 Mag. cal., 6 shot, 2 or 4 in. barrel, combat stocks, round butt only, approx. 5,500 mfg. 1990-92.

| | $340 | $275 | $200 | | | | |

Last MSR was $386.

* ❋ *631 Ladysmith* - 2 in. barrel only, rosewood stocks.

| | $365 | $295 | $225 | | | | |

Last MSR was $400.

S

Grading	100%	98%	95%	90%	80%	70%	60%

MODEL 632 CENTENNIAL - .32 Mag. cal., 2 or 3 (mfg. 1991 only) in. barrel, stainless/ alloy construction, fully concealed hammer, small frame, Santoprene combat grips, fixed sights, 15.5 oz. Mfg. 1991-1992.

			$315	$240	$195		

Last MSR was $410.

Add 20% for 3 in. barrel.

MODEL 637 CHIEFS SPECIAL AIRWEIGHT - .38 S&W Spl.+P cal., J-frame, 5 shot, alloy frame with 1 7/8 in. satin stainless steel barrel and cylinder, current production uses Uncle Mike's Boot grips, 15 oz., 560 mfg. during 1991, reintroduced 1996.

MSR	$548		$405	$275	$210		

MODEL 638 BODYGUARD AIRWEIGHT - .38 S&W Spl.+P cal., J-frame, 5 shot, alloy frame, 1 7/8 in. stainless steel barrel and cylinder, shrouded hammer, round butt, Uncle Mike's Boot grips, 15 oz. 1,200 mfg. during 1990 only, reintroduced 1998.

MSR	$564		$420	$300	$230		

MODEL 640 CENTENNIAL - .357 Mag./.38 S&W Spl.+P cal., J-frame, 5 shot, double action only, 1 7/8 (mfg. 1998-2001), 2 1/8 (new 1991), or 3 (disc. 1992) in. barrel, hammerless, current production uses Uncle Mike's Combat grips, satin stainless finish, round butt, 23 oz. New 1991.

MSR	$599		$450	$320	$240		

MODEL 642 CENTENNIAL AIRWEIGHT - .38 S&W Spl.+P cal., J-frame, 5 shot, 1 7/8, 2 (disc. 1997), or 3 (disc. 1991) in. barrel, alloy frame with stainless steel cylinder and barrel, combat grips, hammerless, satin stainless finish, fixed rear sight, 15 oz. Mfg. 1990-1992, reintroduced 1996.

MSR	$571		$420	$300	$220		

MODEL 642 LADYSMITH AIRWEIGHT - .38 S&W Spl.+P cal., J-frame, 5 shot, 1 7/8 in. barrel, stainless steel/alloy construction, smooth wood grips, satin stainless finish, includes soft side carry or jewelry case, 14.5 oz. New 1996.

MSR	$597		$460	$315	$225		

MODEL 648 - .22 Mag. cal., 6 in. full lug barrel, combat grips, square butt, combat trigger, semi-target hammer. Mfg. 1990-94.

			$350	$250	$195		

Last MSR was $464.

MODEL 649 BODYGUARD - .357 Mag./.38 S&W Spl.+P cal., J-frame, otherwise similar to Model 49 Bodyguard, except is satin stainless steel, 1 7/8 (mfg. 1998 only), 2 (disc. 1997), or 2 1/8 (new 1998) in. barrel, shrouded hammer, current production uses Uncle Mike's Combat grips, 23 oz. New 1986.

MSR	$594		$445	$300	$220		

MODEL 650 - .22 Mag. cal., service kit gun, stainless steel, 3 or 3½ in. heavy barrel, J- Frame, fixed sights. Mfg. 1983-87.

			$250	$200	$185		

Last MSR was $305.

MODEL 651 KIT GUN - .22 Mag. cal., target kit gun, stainless steel, 4 in. barrel, J- Frame, adj. sights (same as old Model 51). Mfg. 1983-87, re-released in late 1990, disc. 1998.

			$355	$250	$195		

Last MSR was $478.

This model could be ordered with a factory fitted optional .22 LR cylinder until 1987 (last mfg. sug. retail was $295 for the cylinder alone). This variation with the extra cylinder is very desirable.

Grading	100%	98%	95%	90%	80%	70%	60%

MODEL 657 - .41 Mag. cal., N-frame, 4 (disc.), 6 (disc. 2000), 7½ (new 2001), or 8 3/ 8 (disc. 1992) in. barrel, satin stainless steel, current production uses Hogue rubber combat grips, approx. 53 oz. New 1986.

	MSR	$706	$535	$375	$290

Add $17 for 8 3/8 in. barrel (disc. 1992).

✳ *Model 657-3 Lew Horton Special* - .41 Mag. cal., 3 in. barrel with round butt, adj. sights.

$410 $360 $300

MODEL 681 DISTINGUISHED SERVICE - .357 Mag. cal., 4 in. barrel, L-Frame. Disc. 1988, reintroduced 1991-1992.

$320 $235 $195

Last MSR was $412.

1991 mfg. includes square butt.

MODEL 686 DISTINGUISHED COMBAT - .357 Mag./.38 S&W Spl.+P cal., L-Frame, similar to Model 586, except 2½ (new 1990), 4, 6 (with or w/o PowerPort), or 8 3/8 in. barrel, fixed (disc.) or adj. sights, current production uses Hogue rubber grips, 35-51 oz. New 1984.

MSR $608 $475 $320 $350

Add $24 for 4 in., $30 for 6 in. barrel, $73 for PowerPort 6 in. barrel, or $55 for 8 3/8 in. barrel.

Add $14 for white outline rear sight (disc. 1994).

✳ *Model 686 Plus* - .357 Mag./.38 S&W Spl.+P cal., L-frame, 7 shot, 2½, 4, or 6 in. barrel, synthetic or Hogue rubber grips, round (2½ in. barrel only) or square butt, white outline rear sight on 4 or 6 in. barrel, 34½ - 43 oz. New 1996.

MSR $631 $490 $330 $250

Add $22 for 4 in. or $32 for 6 in. barrel.

✳ *1984 Model 686 Lew Horton Edition* - 2½ in. barrel only, limited mfg.

$450 $275 $225

MODEL 696 - .44 S&W Spl. cal., L-frame, 5 shot, 3 in. barrel with full shroud, Hogue rubber (disc. 2000) or Uncle Mike's Combat grips, satin stainless steel, adj. rear sight, 36 oz. New 1997.

MSR $620 $485 $315 $250

MODEL 940 CENTENNIAL - 9mm Para. cal., fully concealed hammer, 2 or 3 (disc. 1992) in. barrel, fixed rear sight, Santoprene combat grips, 23-25 oz. Mfg. 1991-98.

$390 $265 $220

Last MSR was $493.

PISTOLS: SEMI-AUTO

Listed in order of model number (except .32 and .35 Automatic Pistols). Alphabetical models will appear at the end of this section.

To understand S&W 3rd generation model nomenclature, the following rules apply. The first two digits (of the four digit model number) specify caliber. Numbers 39, 59, and 69 refer to 9mm Para. cal. The third digit refers to the model type. 0 means standard model, 1 is for compact, 2 is for standard model with decocking lever, 3 is for compact variation with decocking lever, 4 is for standard with double action only, 5 designates a compact model in double action only, 6 indicates a non-standard barrel length, 7 is a non-standard barrel length with decocking lever, 8 refers to non-standard barrel length in double action only. The fourth digit refers to the material(s) used in the fabrication of the pistol. 3 refers to an aluminum alloy frame with stainless steel slide, 4 designates an aluminum alloy frame with carbon steel slide, 5 is for carbon steel frame and slide, 6 is a stainless steel frame and slide, and 7 refers to a stainless steel frame and carbon steel slide. Hence, a Model 4053 refers to a pistol in .40 S&W cal. configured in compact version with double action only and fabricated with an aluminum alloy frame and stainless steel slide. This model nomenclature does not apply to 2 or 3 digit model numbers (i.e., Rimfire Models and the Model 52).

S

100%	98%	95%	90%	80%	70%	60%	50%	40%	30%	20%	10%

.32 AUTOMATIC PISTOL - .32 ACP cal., 7 shot mag., 3½ in. barrel, blueblue with "S&W" monogram inlaid plain walnut grip. 957 mfg. 1924-1936. Serial range starting with S.N. 1.

$3,000	$2,500	$2,000	$1,750	$1,500	$1,250	$1,000	$800	$700	$600	$500	$400

.35 AUTOMATIC PISTOL (MODEL 1913) - .35 S&W Auto cal., 7 shot mag., 3½ in. barrel, blue or nickel w/"S&W" monogram inlaid in plain walnut grips. 8,350 mfg. 1913-1921. Serial range starting with No. 1.

$775	$625	$525	$450	$375	$325	$275	$235	$200	$185	$175	$165

A slight premium might exist for the first model (up to ser. no. 3,125).

Grading	100%	98%	95%	90%	80%	70%	60%

MODEL 22A SPORT SERIES - .22 LR cal., single action, 10 shot mag., aluminum alloy frame, stainless steel slide, choice of 4 standard, 5½ standard or bull, or 7 in. standard barrel with raised solid rib, adj. rear and Hi-Viz (5½ in. bull barrel only, new 2001) sights, 2-piece black polymer (hard or soft) or Dymondwood (5½ bull barrel only) grips, blueblue finish, 28-39 oz. New 1997.

MSR	$264			$210	$185	$155	$135	$110	$95	$80

Add $28 for 5½ in. standard barrel with soft-touch grips.
Add $67 for 7 in. standard barrel with thumb rest soft-touch grips.
Add $103 for 5½ in. bull barrel with Dymondwood target grips.
Add $123 for 5½ bull barrel with Hi-Viz sights (new 2001).
Add $71 for 5½ in. bull barrel with 2 piece target grips and thumbrest (disc. 2000).

MODEL 22S SPORT SERIES - .22 LR cal., single action, 10 shot mag., aluminum alloy frame, stainless steel slide, choice of 5½ standard/bull or 7 in. standard barrel with raised solid rib, adj. rear and Hi-Viz (5 ½ in. bull barrel only, new 2001) sights, 2-piece black polymer (hard or soft) or Dymondwood (5½ in. bull barrel only) grips, satin stainless finish, 41-48 oz. New 1997.

MSR	$358			$285	$235	$190	$165	$140	$125	$110

Add $37 for 7 in. standard barrel with thumb rest soft-touch grips.
Add $76 for 5½ in. bull barrel with Dymondwood target grips.
Add $95 for 5½ bull barrel with Hi-Viz sights (new 2001).
Add $44 for 5½ in. bull barrel with 2 piece target grips and thumbrest (disc. 2000).

MODEL 39 ALLOY FRAME - 9mm Para. cal., alloy frame, this model was unmarked up to ser. no. approx. 2,600, early guns had a short safety lever, checkered walnut grips, blue or nickel finish. Mfg. started 1954.

			$400	$350	$315	$260	$210	$175	$140

Add $35 for nickel finish.
Collectors report an approx. ser. no. range 1,001-105,000 with long ejector.
This model was the first commercially mfg. 9mm Para. double action semi-auto in the U.S.

✱ **Early Mfg. (Pre 39)** - short safety, first group of 298 were produced for military inspection, various markings include "Quantico, VA", approx. ser. no. range 1,001- 2,600. Mfg. 1954-55.

		$1,495	$1,250	$995	$875	$750	$625	$500

Add 50% for early manufacture original military trial guns.

MODEL 39 STEEL FRAME - 9mm Para. cal., 8 shot, 4 in. barrel, long ejector, walnut stocks, blue, adj. rear windage only sight, double action, walnut grips, 927 mfg. during 1966 only in 3 ser. no. ranges.

		$1,200	$975	$850	$735	$650	$550	$475

Grading	100%	98%	95%	90%	80%	70%	60%

MODEL 39-2 ALLOY FRAME (LATER PRODUCTION) - 7.65mm (.30 Luger) or 9mm Para. cal., double action, 8 shot mag., 4 in. barrel, checkered walnut grips, adj. sight, alloy frame, approx. 1971, the 39-2 was introduced as an improved version. Mfg. 1970-1982.

9mm Para.	$360	$325	$260	$240	$220	$200	$195

Add $35 for nickel finish.

7.65mm cal.	$1,250	$1,100	$950	$825	$700	$625	$550

The .30 Luger cal. (7.65mm) was mfg. for the European marketplace only. Very hard to find in the U.S.

MODEL 41/41-1 .22 RF - .22 S (disc., Model 41-1) or LR cal., match target pistol, single action, 10 shot mag., adj. Patridge sights, checkered walnut grips with thumbrest, 5 (disc.), 5½ (heavy) 7 (standard) or 7 3/8 in. barrel, blue finish only, 41 oz. Mfg. 1957-present.

MSR $958	$675	$535	$415	$335	$280	$245	$220

Add $100 for 5½ in. barrel with extended sight (disc.).
Add $35 for 7 3/8 in. barrel with muzzle brake (disc.).
Add 125% for .22 Short cal. with counterweight and muzzle brake (disc.).

Earlier variations (A series guns with cocking indicator, Model 41-1, etc.) will command substantial premiums over values listed.

Note: there are several disc. barrels on the Model 41. They are the 5 in. standard weight with extended sight, 7 3/8 in. with muzzle brake, and 5½ in. heavy barrel with extended sight.

MODEL 44 - 9mm Para. cal., single action design, S&W's rarest semi-auto pistol, approx. 10 mfg. Extreme rarity precludes accurate price evaluation.

MODEL 46 - .22 LR cal., 5, 5½, or 7 in. barrel, blue, nylon grips, adj. sights. Mfg. 4,000, 1957-1966.

	$450	$335	$300	$260	$225	$200	$195

This model is similar to the Model 41, but does not have high polish bluing, and has brown plastic grips.

MODEL 52-A - .38 AMU cal., same action as Model 39, 4 in. barrel. Originally mfg. for U.S. Army Marksman Training Unit, 87 mfg.

	$3,000	$2,500	$2,200	$1,950	$1,600	$1,300	$1,000

MODEL 52 - .38 S&W Spl. Wadcutter only, similar action to Model 39, except incorporates a set screw locking out the double action, 5 in. barrel, 5 shot mag. Approx. 3,500 mfg. 1961-1963.

	$875	$775	$675	$575	$475	$395	$360

MODELS 52-1 & 52-2 - .38 Spl. Mid-Range Wadcutter cal. only, single action semi- auto, 5 in. barrel, adj. sights, checkered walnut grips, blue only, 5 shot mag.

	$675	$550	$450	$400	$350	$295	$265

Last MSR was $908.

The Model 52-1 was mfg. 1963-1971, and the Model 52-2 was mfg. 1971-1993.

MODEL 59 - similar to Model 39, except has 14 shot mag., black nylon grips. Disc. 1981.

	$385	$340	$270	$250	$225	$215	$200

Add $35 for nickel finish.
Add $150 for smooth (ungrooved) grip frame.

MODEL 61 ESCORT - .22 LR cal., 5 shot, semi-auto, blue or nickel, 2½ in. barrel, plastic grips, mfg. 1970-1974.

Blue finish	$250	$210	$165	$150	$140	$110	$95
Nickel finish	$275	$230	$165	$150	$140	$110	$95

MODEL 147-A - 9mm Para. cal., 14 shot, steel frame, 4 in. barrel, black plastic grips, adj. sights for windage only, similar to Model 59, except has steel frame, 112 mfg. 1979 only.

	$1,375	$1,050	$875	$800	$725	$650	$575

This model was originally marked Model 47 for export, prefix and suffix were added. Ser. nos. were stamped, and are crude by today's standard.

S

Grading	100%	98%	95%	90%	80%	70%	60%

MODEL 410 - .40 S&W cal., traditional double action, steel slide with alloy frame, blue finish, 4 in. barrel, 10 shot mag., single side safety, 3 dot sights, straight backstrap with synthetic grips, 28.5 oz. New 1996.

	MSR	$591		$460	$330	$250	$225	$195	$175	$165

MODEL 411 - .40 S&W cal., 4 in. barrel, 11 shot mag., fixed sights, blue finish, aluminum alloy frame, manual safety. Mfg. 1993-95.

	$440	$375	$335	$310	$295	$280	$265

Last MSR was $525.

MODEL 422 .22 RF (FIELD) - .22 LR cal., single action, 4½ or 6 in. barrel, aluminum frame with steel slide, 10 shot mag., fixed sights, black plastic or wood grips, matte blue finish, 22 oz. Mfg. 1987-96.

	$185	$150	$115	$110	$105	$100	$95

Last MSR was $235.

✳ *Model 422 Target* - .22 LR cal., single action, 4½ or 6 in. barrel, aluminum frame with steel slide, 10 shot mag., adj. rear sight, checkered walnut grips, matte blue finish, 22 oz. Mfg. 1987-96.

	$225	$175	$140	$115	$110	$105	$95

Last MSR was $290.

MODEL 439 - 9mm Para. cal., double action, 4 in. barrel, blue or nickel finish, alloy frame, 8 shot mag., checkered walnut grips, 30 oz. Disc. 1988.

	$385	$315	$255	$240	$225	$210	$200

Last MSR was $472.

Add $34 for nickel finish (disc. 1986).
Add $26 for adj. sights.

MODEL 457 COMPACT - .45 ACP cal., traditional double action, alloy frame and steel slide, 3¾ in. barrel, single side safety, 3 dot sights, 7 shot mag., straight backstrap, blue finish only, black synthetic grips, 29 oz. New 1996.

	MSR	$591		$460	$335	$260	$225	$195	$175	$165

MODEL 459 - 9mm Para. cal., 14 shot version of Model 439, checkered nylon stocks, limited mfg. with squared-off triggerguard with serrations. Disc. 1988.

	$410	$345	$290	$270	$255	$240	$210

Last MSR was $501.

Add $26 for adj. sights.
Add $44 for nickel finish (disc. 1986).

✳ *Model 459 Brushed Finish* - 9mm Para. cal., 14 shot, 4 in. barrel, dull finish, fixed sights, special grips made to F.B.I. or Police specs., 803 mfg.

	$650	$600	$550	$440	$385	$330	$300

MODEL 469 "MINI" - 9mm Para. cal., double action, alloy frame, 12 shot finger extension mag., short frame, bobbed hammer, 3½ in. barrel, sandblast blue or satin nickel finish, ambidextrous safety standard (1986), molded Delrin black Grips, 26 oz. Disc. 1988.

	$370	$320	$265	$250	$235	$220	$210

Last MSR was $478.

MODEL 539 - 9mm Para. cal., double action, steel frame, 8 shot, 4 in. barrel, blue or nickel. Approx. 10,000 mfg. Disc. 1983.

	$450	$395	$375	$350	$325	$300	$275

Add $35 for nickel finish.
Add $30 for adj. rear sight.

MODEL 559 - 9mm Para. cal., double action, steel frame, 12 shot mag., 4 in. barrel, blue or nickel. Approx. 10,000 mfg. Disc. 1983.

	$485	$435	$375	$275	$250	$225	$200

Add $35 for nickel finish.
Add $30 for adj. rear sight.

Grading	100%	98%	95%	90%	80%	70%	60%

MODEL 622 .22 RF (Field) - .22 LR cal., single action, 4½ or 6 in. barrel, stainless/ alloy construction, 10 shot mag., fixed sights, black plastic grips, 21½ or 23½ oz. Mfg. 1990-96.

	$220	$175	$160

Last MSR was $284.

✳ ***Model 622 Target*** - .22 LR cal., single action, 4½ or 6 in. barrel (VR was an option in 1996 only), stainless steel construction, 10 shot mag., adj. rear sight, checkered walnut grips, 21½ or 23½ oz. Mfg. 1990-96.

	$275	$225	$175

Last MSR was $337.

MODEL 639 STAINLESS - 9mm Para. cal., similar to Model 439-only stainless steel, 8 shot mag., ambidextrous safety became standard 1986, 36 oz. Disc. 1988.

	$420	$300	$275

Last MSR was $523.

Add $27 for adj. sights.

MODEL 645 STAINLESS - .45 ACP cal. only, 5 in. barrel, 8 shot mag., squared off trigger guard, black molded nylon grips, ambidextrous safety, fixed sights, 37½ oz. New 1986. Disc. 1988.

	$475	$365	$300

Last MSR was $622.

Add $27 for adj. sight.
Approx. 150 Model 645 "Interim" pistols were mfg. in 1988 only. Add $120 to values listed.

MODEL 659 STAINLESS - 9mm Para. cal., similar to Model 459-only stainless steel, 14 shot mag., ambidextrous safety became standard 1986, 39½ oz. Disc. 1988.

	$445	$335	$300

Last MSR was $553.

Add $27 for adj. sights.
Approx. 150 Model 659 "Interim" pistols were mfg. in 1988 only. Add $150 to values listed.

MODEL 669 STAINLESS - 9mm Para. cal., smaller version of Model 659 with 12 shot finger extension mag., 3½ in. barrel, fixed sights, molded Delrin grips, ambidextrous safety standard, 26 oz. Mfg. 1986-1988 only.

	$425	$305	$275

Last MSR was $522.

Approx. 150 Model 669 "Interim" pistols were mfg. in 1988 only. Add $150 to values listed.

MODEL 745 IPSC - .45 ACP cal., single action, 5 in. barrel, stainless steel frame with steel slide, hammer, and trigger, checkered walnut stocks, fixed rear sight, 38¾ oz. Mfg. 1987-90.

	$575	$440	$335

Last MSR was $699.

Early guns had optional "IPSC" markings. Later, these markings became standard.

MODEL 908 COMPACT - 9mm Para. cal., compact variation of the Model 909/910, 3½ in. barrel, 3 dot sights, 8 shot mag., straight backstrap, 24 oz. New 1996.

MSR	$535	$420	$310	$245	$215	$190	$175	$165

MODEL 909 - 9mm Para. cal., 4 in. barrel, traditional double action, large frame, 9 shot mag., fixed sights, single side safety, alloy frame and steel slide, curved backstrap with black synthetic grips, 27 oz. Mfg. 1994-96.

	$360	$275	$225	$205	$190	$175	$165

Last MSR was $443.

MODEL 910 - similar to Model 909, except has 10 shot mag., 28 oz. New 1994.

MSR	$535	$420	$310	$245	$215	$190	$175	$165

MODEL 915 - 9mm Para. cal., 4 in. barrel, fixed sights, 10 (C/B 1994) or 15* shot mag., manual safety, aluminum alloy frame, blue finish. Mfg. 1993-94.

	$350	$255	$225	$205	$190	$175	$165

Last MSR was $467.

S

Grading	100%	98%	95%	90%	80%	70%	60%

MODEL 1006 STAINLESS - 10mm cal., double action semi-auto, stainless steel construction, 5 in. barrel, exposed hammer, 9 shot mag., fixed or adj. sights, ambidextrous safety. Mfg. 1990-1993.

	$635	$530	$400

Last MSR was $769.

Add $27 for adj. rear sight.

MODEL 1026 STAINLESS - 10mm cal., 5 in. barrel, traditional double action, features frame mounted decocking lever, 9 shot mag., straight backstrap. Mfg. 1990-91 only.

	$630	$525	$400

Last MSR was $755.

MODEL 1046 STAINLESS - 10mm cal., 5 in. barrel, fixed sights, double action only, 9 shot mag., straight backstrap. Mfg. 1991 only.

	$620	$515	$400

Last MSR was $747.

MODEL 1066 STAINLESS - 10mm cal., 4¼ in. barrel, 9 shot mag., straight backstrap, ambidextrous safety, traditional double action, fixed sights. Mfg. 1990-1992.

	$610	$515	$395

Last MSR was $730.

Add $40 for Tritium night sights - disc. 1991 (Model 1066-NS).
Only 1,000 Model 1066-NSs were manufactured.

MODEL 1076 STAINLESS - similar to Model 1026 Stainless, except has 4¼ in. barrel. Mfg. 1990-1993.

	$645	$530	$400

Last MSR was $778.

MODEL 1086 STAINLESS - similar to Model 1066 Stainless, except is double action only.

	$710	$515	$395

Last MSR was $730.

MODEL 2206 STAINLESS .22 RF (FIELD) - .22 LR cal., similar to Model 622 Field, except all stainless steel components, black plastic grips, 6 in. barrel with standard (disc. 1995) or adj. rear sight, 35 or 39 oz. Mfg. 1990-96.

	$290	$225	$175

Last MSR was $385.

Subtract $58 if w/o adj. sights.

✳ *Model 2206 Stainless Target* - similar to Model 2206 Stainless, except has adj. target sight, target stocks, and is drilled and tapped. Mfg. 1994-96.

	$360	$275	$225

Last MSR was $433.

MODEL 2213 STAINLESS .22 RF "SPORTSMAN" - .22 LR cal., single action, 3 in. barrel, alloy frame with stainless steel slide, 8 shot mag., 2 dot fixed rear sight, black plastic molded grips, 18 oz., includes holster/carry case. Mfg. 1992-99.

	$255	$200	$160

Last MSR was $340.

MODEL 2214 .22 RF "SPORTSMAN" - .22 LR cal., similar to Model 2213, except has alloy frame with blue carbon steel slide with matte black finish, and no case. Mfg. 1991- 99.

	$230	$185	$160	$150	$140	$130	$120

Last MSR was $292.

MODEL 3904 - 9mm Para. cal., double action semi-auto, aluminum alloy frame, 4 in. barrel with fixed bushing, 8 shot mag., Delrin one piece wraparound grips, exposed hammer, ambidextrous safety, beveled magazine well, extended squared off triggerguard, adj. or fixed rear sight, 3 dot sighting system, 28 oz. Mfg. 1989-91.

	$450	$385	$350	$325	$300	$280	$265

Last MSR was $541.

Add $25 for adj. rear sight.

MODEL 3906 STAINLESS - stainless steel variation of the Model 3904, 35½ oz. Mfg. 1989-91.

	$510	$435	$375

Last MSR was $604.

Add $28 for adj. rear sight.

MODEL 3913 COMPACT STAINLESS - stainless steel variation of the Model 3914, 25 oz. Mfg. 1990-99.

	$535	$440	$365

Last MSR was $662.

✳ *Model 3913NL* - similar to Model 3913 Ladysmith, except does not have Ladysmith on the slide. Disc. 1994.

	$510	$425	$365

Last MSR was $622.

✳ *Model 3913 LS (LadySmith)* - similar to Model 3913 Stainless, except has white Delrin grips and mag. does not have finger extension, includes case, 25 oz. New 1990.

MSR	$782	$630	$480	$380

MODEL 3913TSW - 9mm Para. cal., traditional double action, compact frame, 3½ in. barrel, 7 shot mag., Novak low mount 2 dot sights, stainless steel slide, aluminum alloy frame, satin stainless finish, straight black backstrap synthetic grips, 24.8 oz. Mfg. 1998-2001.

MSR	$760	$615	$475	$380

MODEL 3914 COMPACT - 9mm Para. cal., double action semi-auto, aluminum alloy frame, 3½ in. barrel, hammerless, 8 shot finger extension mag., fixed sights only, ambidextrous safety, blue finish, straight backstrap grip, 25 oz. Mfg. 1990-95.

	$465	$385	$340	$320	$295	$280	$265

Last MSR was $562.

This model was also available with a single side manual safety at no extra charge - disc. 1991 (Model 3914NL).

✳ *Model 3914 LadySmith* - similar to Model 3914, except has Delrin grips, 25 oz. Mfg. 1990-91 only.

	$485	$415	$365

Last MSR was $568.

MODEL 3953 COMPACT STAINLESS - 9mm Para. cal., double action only, aluminum alloy frame with stainless steel slide, compact model with 3½ in. barrel, 8 shot mag. Mfg. 1990- 99.

	$535	$440	$365

Last MSR was $662.

MODEL 3953TSW - similar to Model 3913TSW, except is double action only, 24.8 oz. New 1998.

MSR	$760	$615	$475	$380

MODEL 3954 - similar to Model 3953, except has blue steel slide. Mfg. 1990-1992.

	$445	$380	$340	$320	$295	$280	$265

Last MSR was $528.

MODEL 4003 STAINLESS - .40 S&W cal., traditional double action, 4 in. barrel, 11 shot mag., white dot fixed sights, ambidextrous safety, aluminum alloy frame with stainless steel slide, one piece Xenoy wraparound grips, straight gripstrap, 28 oz. Mfg. 1991- 1993.

	$585	$495	$395

Last MSR was $698.

S

Grading	100%	98%	95%	90%	80%	70%	60%

✻ *Model 4003TSW* - similar to Model 4003 Stainless, but has aluminum alloy frame, 10 shot mag., stainless steel slide, S&W tactical features, including equipment rail and Novak low mount carry sights, traditional double action only, satin stainless finish, 28½ oz. New 2000.

	MSR	$886		$740	$645	$495	$440	$400	$360	$330

MODEL 4004 - .40 S&W cal., similar to Model 4003, except has aluminum alloy frame with blue carbon steel slide. Mfg. 1991-1992.

				$540	$460	$375	$325	$295	$280	$265

Last MSR was $643.

MODEL 4006 STAINLESS - .40 S&W cal., 3½ (Shorty Forty) or 4 in. barrel, 10 (C/B 1994) or 11* shot mag., satin stainless finish, exposed hammer, Delrin one piece wraparound grips, 3 dot sights, 38½ oz. Mfg. 1990-99.

				$655	$545	$400				

Last MSR was $791.

Add $31 for adj. rear sight.
Add $115 for fixed Tritium night sights (new 1992).
The bobbed hammer option on this model was disc. in 1991.

✻ *Model 4006TSW* - similar to Model 4006 Stainless, but has aluminum alloy frame and stainless steel slide, S&W tactical features, including equipment rail, traditional double action only, 37.8 oz. New 2000.

	MSR	$907		$745	$645	$500	$450	$400	$360	$330

Add $37 if w/o Novak Low Carry mount sights (NLC).
Add $133 for night sights.

MODEL 4013 COMPACT STAINLESS - .40 S&W cal., semi-auto, standard double action, 3½ in. barrel, 8 shot mag., fixed sights, ambidextrous safety, alloy frame. Mfg. 1991-96.

				$595	$485	$385	$330	$295	$280	$265

Last MSR was $722.

MODEL 4013TSW (TACTICAL) - .40 S&W cal., semi-auto, standard double action, 3½ in. barrel, 9 shot mag. with reversible mag. catch, aluminum alloy frame with stainless steel slide, satin stainless finish, black synthetic grips, fixed 3 dot Novak Low Mount carry sights, ambidextrous safety, 26.8 oz. New 1997.

	MSR	$886		$730	$580	$420				

MODEL 4014 COMPACT - similar to Model 4013, except is steel with blue finish. Mfg. 1991-1993.

				$510	$425	$375	$330	$300	$275	$250

Last MSR was $635.

MODEL 4026 STAINLESS - .40 S&W cal., traditional double action with frame mounted decocking lever, 10 (C/B 1994) or 11* shot mag., fixed sights, curved backstrap, 36 oz. Mfg. 1991-1993.

				$620	$520	$400				

Last MSR was $731.

MODEL 4043 STAINLESS - .40 S&W cal., double action only, aluminum alloy frame with stainless steel slide, 4 in. barrel, 10 (C/B 1994) or 11* shot mag., one piece Xenoy wraparound grips, straight backstrap, white dot fixed sights, 30 oz. Mfg. 1991-99.

				$635	$510	$390				

Last MSR was $772.

✻ *Model 4043TSW* - double action only, similar to Model 4043 Stainless, but has S&W tactical features, including equipment rail, 28½ oz. New 2000.

	MSR	$886		$740	$640	$495	$445	$400	$360	$330

Grading	100%	98%	95%	90%	80%	70%	60%

MODEL 4044 - .40 S&W cal., similar to Model 4043, except has carbon steel slide. Mfg. 1991-1992.

| | $540 | $460 | $375 | $325 | $295 | $280 | $265 |

Last MSR was $643.

MODEL 4046 STAINLESS - similar to Model 4006 Stainless, except is double action only, 4 in. barrel only. Mfg. 1991-99.

| | $655 | $540 | $400 | | | | |

Last MSR was $791.

Add $115 for Tritium night sights (new 1992).

✱ *Model 4046TSW* - double action only, similar to Model 4046 Stainless, but has S&W tactical features, including equipment rail, 37.8 oz. New 2000.

| MSR | $907 | $755 | $655 | $500 | $455 | $400 | $360 | $330 |

Add $133 for night sights.

MODEL 4053 COMPACT STAINLESS - double action only variation of the Model 4013. Mfg. 1991-97.

| | $600 | $490 | $380 | | | | |

Last MSR was $734.

MODEL 4053TSW (TACTICAL) - .40 S&W cal., double action only, 3½ in. barrel, 9 shot mag. with reversible mag. catch, alloy frame with stainless steel slide, satin stainless finish, black synthetic grips, fixed sights, ambidextrous safety, 26.8 oz. New 1997.

| MSR | $886 | $730 | $580 | $425 | | | |

MODEL 4054 - double action only variation of the Model 4014. Mfg. 1991-1992.

| | $510 | $425 | $375 | | | | |

Last MSR was $629.

MODEL 4056TSW (TACTICAL) - .40 S&W cal., double action only, 3½ in. barrel, 9 shot mag. with reversible mag. catch, alloy frame with stainless steel slide, satin stainless finish, black synthetic grips, fixed sights, ambidextrous safety, 37.5 oz Mfg. 1997-2000.

| | $700 | $560 | $415 | | | | |

Last MSR was $844.

MODEL 4505 - .45 ACP cal., carbon steel variation of the Model 4506, fixed or adj. rear sight. 1,200 mfg. 1991 only.

| | $575 | $500 | $450 | $400 | $350 | $300 | $265 |

Last MSR was $660.

Add $27 for adj. rear sight.

MODEL 4506 STAINLESS - .45 ACP cal., 5 in. barrel, 8 shot mag., combat triggerguard, exposed hammer, fixed or adj. rear sight, straight backstrap (curved is optional), Delrin one-piece grips, 40.5 oz. Mfg. 1990-99.

| | $680 | $550 | $410 | | | | |

Last MSR was $822.

Add $33 for adj. rear sight.

Approx. 100 Model 4506s left the factory mismarked Model 645 on the frame. In NIB condition they are worth $700.

MODEL 4513TSW - 45 ACP cal., traditional double action, compact frame, 3¾ in. barrel, 7 shot mag., 3 dot Novak Low Mount carry sights, stainless steel slide, aluminum alloy frame, satin stainless finish, 28.6 oz. New 1998.

| MSR | $924 | $755 | $595 | $450 | | | |

S

Grading	100%	98%	95%	90%	80%	70%	60%

MODEL 4516 COMPACT STAINLESS - .45 ACP cal., hammerless compact variation of the Model 4506, 3¾ in. barrel, 7 shot mag., ambidextrous safety, fixed rear sight only, 34 oz. Mfg. 1990-97.

$655 $535 $400

Last MSR was $787.

Original model is marked 4516 while later mfg. changed slide legend to read 4516-1. Original mfg. is more collectible and slight premiums are being asked.

MODEL 4526 STAINLESS - similar to Model 4506 Stainless, except has frame mounted decocking lever. Mfg. 1990-91 only.

$635 $530 $400

Last MSR was $762.

MODEL 4536 STAINLESS - similar to Model 4516 Compact, except has frame mounted decocking lever only. Mfg. 1990-91 only.

$635 $530 $400

Last MSR was $762.

MODEL 4546 STAINLESS - similar to Model 4506 Stainless, except is double action only. Mfg. 1990-91 only.

$620 $520 $400

Last MSR was $735.

MODEL 4553TSW - similar to Model 4513TSW, except is double action only. New 1998.
MSR $924 $755 $595 $450

MODEL 4556 STAINLESS - .45 ACP cal., features double action only, 3¾ in. barrel, 7 shot mag., fixed sights. Mfg. 1991 only.

$620 $520 $400

Last MSR was $735.

MODEL 4563TSW - .45 ACP cal., traditional double action only, 4¼ in. barrel, 8 shot mag., aluminum alloy frame with stainless steel slide, satin stainless finish, includes S&W tactical features, including equipment rail and Novak 3 dot sights, synthetic black straight backstrap grips, 30.6 oz. New 2000.
MSR $921 $750 $595 $445

MODEL 4566 STAINLESS - .45 ACP cal., traditional double action with ambidextrous safety, 4¼ in. barrel, 8 shot mag. Mfg. 1990-99.

$680 $550 $410

Last MSR was $822.

✳ *Model 4566TSW* - similar to Model 4566, except has ambidextrous safety, 39.1 oz.
MSR $942 $760 $600 $445

MODEL 4567-NS STAINLESS - similar to Model 4566 Stainless, except has Tritium night sights, stainless steel frame and carbon steel slide. 2,500 mfg. in 1991 only.

$620 $520 $400

Last MSR was $735.

MODEL 4576 STAINLESS - .45 ACP cal., features 4¼ in. barrel, frame mounted decocking lever, fixed sights. Mfg. 1990-1992.

$635 $535 $410

Last MSR was $762.

MODEL 4583STW - similar to Model 4563TSW, except is double action only, 30.6 oz. New 2000.
MSR $921 $750 $595 $445

MODEL 4586 STAINLESS - .45 ACP cal., 4¼ in. barrel, double action only, 8 shot mag. Mfg. 1990-99.

$680 $550 $410

Last MSR was $822.

Grading	100%	98%	95%	90%	80%	70%	60%

✴ *Model 4586TSW* - similar to Model 4566TSW, except is double action only, 39.1 oz. New 2000.

| | MSR $942 | $760 | $600 | $445 | | | | |

MODEL 5903 - 9mm Para. cal., double action semi-auto, 4 in. barrel, stainless steel slide and alloy frame, exposed hammer, 10 (C/B 1994) or 15* shot mag., adj. (disc. 1993) or fixed rear sight, ambidextrous safety. Mfg. 1990-97.

| | | $575 | $470 | $395 | $365 | $325 | $300 | $285 |

Last MSR was $701.

Add $30 for adj. rear sight (disc).

✴ *Model 5903TSW* - 9mm Para. cal., traditional double action, aluminum alloy frame with stainless slide, satin stainless finish, includes S&W tactical features, such as equipment rail and Novak low mount carry sights, black synthetic grips with curved backstrap, 28.9 oz. New 2000.

| | MSR $841 | $695 | $560 | $420 | $375 | $325 | $275 | $250 |

MODEL 5904 - similar to Model 5903, except has steel slide and blue finish, 26½ oz. Mfg. 1989-1998.

| | | $535 | $445 | $360 | $330 | $300 | $280 | $265 |

Last MSR was $663.

Add $30 for adj. rear sight (disc. 1993).

MODEL 5905 - 9mm Para. cal., similar to Model 5904, except has carbon steel frame and slide. Approx. 5,000 mfg. 1990-91 only.

| | | $650 | $575 | $500 | $440 | $375 | $335 | $300 |

MODEL 5906 STAINLESS - stainless steel variation of the Model 5904, 37½ oz. Mfg. 1989-1999.

| | | $615 | $500 | $400 | | | | |

Last MSR was $751.

Add $37 for adj. rear sight.
Add $115 for Tritium night sights.

✴ *Model 5906TSW* - traditional double action only, similar to Model 5906 Stainless, but has S&W tactical features, including equipment rail, 38.3 oz. New 2000.

| | MSR $863 | $725 | $635 | $495 | | | | |

Add $41 if w/o NLC.
Add $132 for night sights.

MODEL 5924 - 9mm Para. cal., 4 in. barrel, features frame mounted decocking lever, 15 shot mag., 37½ oz. Mfg. 1990-91 only.

| | | $515 | $440 | $365 | $330 | $300 | $280 | $265 |

Last MSR was $635.

MODEL 5926 STAINLESS - stainless variation of the Model 5924. Disc. 1992.

| | | $580 | $480 | $395 | | | | |

Last MSR was $697.

MODEL 5943 STAINLESS - 9mm Para. cal., double action only, 4 in. barrel, aluminum alloy frame with stainless steel slide, straight backstrap, 15 shot mag. Mfg. 1990-91 only.

| | | $550 | $465 | $390 | | | | |

Last MSR was $655.

✴ *Model 5943-SSV Stainless* - similar to Model 5943 Stainless, except has 3½ in. barrel, Tritium night sights. Mfg. 1990-91 only.

| | | $580 | $485 | $395 | | | | |

Last MSR was $690.

✴ *Model 5943TSW* - double action only, aluminum alloy frame with stainless steel slide, includes S&W tactical features, equipment rail, and Novak low mount carry sights, 28.9 oz. New 2000.

| | MSR $844 | $695 | $560 | $420 | $375 | $325 | $280 | $265 |

S

Grading	100%	98%	95%	90%	80%	70%	60%

MODEL 5944 - similar to Model 5943 Stainless, except has blue finish slide. Mfg. 1990- 91 only.

	$510	$435	$360	$330	$300	$280	$265

Last MSR was $610.

MODEL 5946 STAINLESS - 9mm Para. cal., double action only, one piece Xenoy wraparound grips, all stainless steel variation of the Model 5943, 39½ oz. Mfg. 1990-99.

	$615	$500	$400				

Last MSR was $751.

✳ *Model 5946TSW* - 9mm Para. cal., double action only, includes S&W tactical features, equipment rail, and Novak low mount carry sights, 38.3 oz. New 2000.

MSR	$863		$710	$570	$425		

MODEL 6904 COMPACT - 9mm Para. cal., compact variation of the Model 5904, 3½ in. barrel, 10 (C/ B 1994) or 12* shot finger extension mag., fixed rear sight, 26½ oz. Mfg. 1989-1997.

	$510	$410	$350	$325	$300	$280	$265

Last MSR was $625.

MODEL 6906 COMPACT STAINLESS - stainless steel variation of the Model 6904, 26½ oz. Mfg. 1989-1999.

	$585	$470	$380				

Last MSR was $720.

Add $116 for Tritium night sights (new 1992).

MODEL 6926 STAINLESS - 9mm Para. cal., 3½ in. barrel, standard double action, features frame mounted decocking lever, aluminum alloy frame with stainless slide, 12 shot mag. Mfg. 1990-91 only.

	$550	$455	$375				

Last MSR was $663.

MODEL 6944 - 9mm Para., double action only, 3½ in. barrel, 12 shot mag., aluminum alloy frame with blue steel slide. Mfg. 1990-91 only.

	$480	$400	$350	$325	$300	$280	$265

Last MSR was $578.

MODEL 6946 STAINLESS - similar to Model 6944, except has stainless steel slide, semi-bobbed hammer, 26½ oz. Mfg. 1990-99.

	$585	$470	$375				

Last MSR was $720.

MODEL CS9 CHIEFS SPECIAL - 9mm Para. cal., compact design with traditional double action, hammerless, 3 in. barrel, 7 shot mag., alloy frame/stainless slide or stainless steel construction (disc. 2000), Hogue wraparound rubber grips, 3 dot Novak low mount sights, 20.8 oz. New 1999.

MSR	$680		$540	$420	$360	$310	$265	$230	$195

MODEL CS40 CHIEFS SPECIAL - .40 S&W cal., similar to Model CS9, except has 3¼ in. barrel, 24.2 oz. New 1999.

MSR	$717		$575	$435	$375	$315	$275	$230	$195

MODEL CS45 CHIEFS SPECIAL - .45 ACP cal., similar to Model CS40, except has 6 shot mag., 23.9 oz. New 1999.

MSR	$717		$575	$435	$375	$315	$275	$230	$195

SIGMA MODEL SW380 - .380 ACP cal., double action only, 3 in. barrel, fixed sights, polymer frame and steel slide, striker firing system, blue finish only, 6 shot mag., shortened grip, 14 oz. Mfg. 1996-2000.

	$285	$245	$210	$190	$180	$170	$160

Last MSR was $358.

Grading	100%	98%	95%	90%	80%	70%	60%

SIGMA MODEL SW9F SERIES - 9mm Para. cal., double action only, 4½ in. barrel, fixed sights, polymer frame and steel slide, striker firing system, blue finish only, 10 (C/B 1994) or 17* shot mag., 26 oz. Mfg. 1994-96.

	$485	$390	$345	$320	$295	$280	$265

Last MSR was $593.

Add $104 for Tritium night sights.

❋ *Compact Sigma Model SW9C* - similar to Sigma Model SW9F, except has 4 in. barrel, 25 oz. Mfg. 1996-98.

	$450	$355	$325	$295	$280	$265	$240

Last MSR was $541.

❋ *Compact Sigma Model SW9M* - features 3¼ in. barrel, 7 shot mag., fixed channel rear sight, grips integral with frame, satin black finish, 18 oz. Mfg. 1996-98.

	$300	$270	$240	$220	$195	$175	$160

Last MSR was $366.

❋ *Sigma Model SW9VE/SW9P/SW9G (SW9V)* - features 4 in. standard or ported (SW9P, new 2001) barrel, 10 shot mag., 3-dot sighting system, grips integral with grey (disc. 2000) or black polymer frame, satin stainless steel slide, 24.7 oz. New 1997.

MSR	$447		$360	$300	$250		

Add $47 for SW9P or SW9G with night sights.
Add $210 for Tritium night sights (disc. 2000).
The Enhanced Sigma Series Model SW9VE was introduced during 1999, after the SW9V was discontinued.

SIGMA MODEL SW40F - .40 S&W cal., double action only, 4½ in. barrel, fixed sights, polymer frame, blue finish only, 10 (C/B 1994) or 15* shot mag., 26 oz. Mfg. 1994-98.

	$450	$355	$325	$295	$280	$265	$240

Last MSR was $541.

Add $104 for Tritium night sights (disc. 1997).

❋ *Compact Sigma Model SW40C* - similar to Sigma Model SW40F, except has 4 in. barrel, 26 oz. Mfg. 1996-98.

	$450	$355	$325	$295	$280	$265	$240

Last MSR was $541.

❋ *Sigma Model SW40VE/SW40P/SW40G (SW40V)* - features 4 in. standard or ported (SW40P, new 2001) barrel, 10 shot mag., 3-dot sighting system, grips integral with grey (disc. 2000) or black polymer frame, satin stainless steel slide, 24.4 oz. New 1997.

MSR	$447		$360	$300	$250		

Add $210 for Tritium night sights.
Add $47 for Model SW40P or SW40G (includes night sights).
The Enhanced Sigma Series Model SW40VE was introduced during 1999, after the SW40V was discontinued.

MODEL SW99 - 9mm Para. or .40 S&W cal., traditional double action, 10 shot mag., similar to the Walter P99, black polymer frame with black stainless slide and barrel, 4 or 4 1/8 (.40 S&W cal. only), black finish, ambidextrous mag. release, decocking lever, cocking indicator, adj. 3 dot or night sights, 25.4 (9mm Para cal.) or 28.5 oz. New 2000.

MSR	$810		$680	$555	$475	$440	$400	$360	$330

Add $115 for night sights.

S

ENGRAVING OPTIONS FOR CURRENT PRODUCTION HANDGUNS

The prices listed are for original factory finished guns with no extra engraving. The listings below show most recent factory engraving costs. These prices should be added to the cost of each engraved production gun to determine the correct value.

CLASS "C" ENGRAVING-1/3 METAL COVERAGE
Pistols - add $1,108.
For J Frame - add $876.
10 5/8 in. N Frame - add $1,343.
2-5 in. K, L, or N Frame - add $1,130.
6-8 3/8 in. K, L, or N Frame - add $1,285.

CLASS "B" ENGRAVING - 2/3 METAL COVERAGE
Pistols - add $1,448.
For J Frame - add $1,430.
10 5/8 in. N Frame - add $1,672.
2-5 in. K, L, or N Frame - add $1,477.
6-8 3/8 in. K, L, or N Frame - add $1,599.

CLASS "A" ENGRAVING - FULL COVERAGE
Pistols - add $1,761.
For J Frame - add $1,501.
10 5/8 in. N Frame - add $2,006.
2-5 in. K, L, or N Frame - add $1,814.
6-8 3/8 in. K, L, or N Frame - add $1,919.

SPECIAL ENGRAVING - Also available with custom artwork: inlays, seals, scenes, lettering - prices quoted on request. Please call 1-800-331-0852, ext. 2904 – a free color brochure on custom engraving services is available.

LASERSMITH ENGRAVING - laser etching was available 1989-1990 only. This process involved a digitally controlled laser producing a variety of designs, logos, commemorative messages, or autograph on the metal surface(s). Some of these designs were made exclusively for major firearms distributors. Others were custom designed for clubs or organizations. Retail prices started at just under $18 and went as high as $150+, depending on the amount and complexity of the laser etching. To date, premiums are not being paid for these "rarer" variations.

Grading	100%	Issue Price	Qty. Made

S&W COMMEMORATIVES/SPECIAL EDITIONS

During the course of a year, I receive many phone calls and letters on special editions and limited editions that do not appear in this section. It should be noted that a commemorative issue is a gun that has been manufactured, marketed, and sold through the auspices of the specific trademark (in this case S&W). During the past several decades, hundreds of limited editions have been ordered through various police agencies, state highway patrol units, and other law enforcement organizations. Many of these variations do not have the special suffix serialization (and may not have had a retail price when issued). Since most of these special editions/ commemoratives were made for a specific organization, regional demand has a lot to do with determining values (a Model 66 Montana HP Commemorative will not sell for a premium in Alabama). For this reason, most of these guns will not appear in this section and you should contact the factory to learn more about the provenance of these special editions. Remember - values on these models can vary A LOT from one region to another and an averaged "national" single price is almost impossible. While these guns do have special interest, they do not have the collectability or desirability of many of the standard models listed.

The variations listed represent the only five factory S&W Commemoratives manufactured to date. Anything else will be a special or limited edition made for a organization, company, or special event.

MODEL 19 TEXAS RANGER - .357 Mag., with or without knife, approx. 8,000 with knife, approx. 2,000 without, cased. Mfg. 1973 only.

	$595	$250	10,000

✳ *Model 19 Texas Ranger Deluxe* - approx. 50 mfg. with a serial numbers divisible by 10, cased.

	N/A	N/A	50

Grading	100%	Issue Price	Qty. Made

125TH ANNIVERSARY COMMEMORATIVE - .45 LC cal., plain variation was called Model 25-3, 10,000 mfg. total in 1977, cased with nickel silver medallion, and Roy Jinks's book, "125th Anniversary of Smith & Wesson".

	$450	$350	10,000

✳ **125th Anniversary Commemorative Deluxe** - Model 25-4, approx. 50 mfg. with S&W prefix serial numbers divisible by 10, cased, sterling silver medallion, and a leather bound "History of Smith & Wesson" book by Roy Jinks.

	N/A	N/A	50

MODEL 29 ELMER KEITH COMMEMORATIVE - .44 Mag. cal., 4 in. barrel, standard and deluxe editions, approx. 2,500 total mfg.

	$850	N/A	2,500

50TH ANNIVERSARY OF THE .357 MAGNUM - Model 27, both standard and deluxe editions, 1987 mfg.

	$450	N/A	N/A

MODEL 544 TEXAS WAGON TRAIN COMMEMORATIVE - .44-40 WCF cal. only, 6 shot, 5 in. barrel, bright blue finish, adj. sights, 7,800 mfg. 1986 to commemorate the Texas Sesquicentennial (1836-1986). Special markings on frame and barrel, smooth Goncalo commemorative grips, ser. no. TWT001 - TWT7800 (estimated). Made 1986 only.

	$450	N/A	7,800

PERFORMANCE CENTER VARIATIONS

Over the years, S&W's Performance Center has manufactured many configurations and variations that are not listed in the annual S&W product literature. These custom order revolvers and pistols cover a wide variety of different options and special orders (over 120 different P/C models have been observed). Pricing is difficult to establish due to the amount of variations, and each model's desirability factor must be taken into consideration before a price range can be determined. Most of these performance handguns, depending on how much they have been used, carry slight premiums over the models from which they are derived – but only if in 98%+ condition.

While a lot of money can be spent on "tricking out" a custom order S&W handgun to a competitive shooter's personal specifications, most of these guns on the used market have little collector value, and must be priced according to their competitive shooting value.

100%	98%	95%	90%	80%	70%	60%	50%	40%	30%	20%	10%

RIFLES

S&W in 1984 disc. importation of all Howa manufactured rifles. Mossberg continued importation utilizing both leftover S&W parts in addition to fabricating their own.

MODEL 320 REVOLVING RIFLE - .320 S&W cal., 6 shot cylinder, 16, 18, or 20 in. round barrel, hard rubber grips, detachable shoulder stock, blue or nickel (rare, add a premium) finish. 977 mfg. 1879-1887.

✳ **16 or 20 in. barrel Model** - 239 mfg. with 16 in., and 224 with 20 in. barrel.

$12,000	$10,000	$8,700	$8,100	$7,675	$7,000	$6,375	$5,600	$4,800	$3,850	$2,950	$1,950

✳ **18 in. barrel Model** - 514 mfg.

$9,750	$9,350	$8,700	$8,100	$7,675	$7,000	$6,375	$5,600	$4,800	$3,850	$2,950	$1,950

Grading	100%	98%	95%	90%	80%	70%	60%

MODEL A BOLT ACTION RIFLE - .22-250 Rem., .243 Win., .270 Win., .308 Win., .30- 06, 7mm Mag., or .300 Win. Mag. cal., 23¾ in. barrel, folding leaf sight, checkered Monte Carlo stock with rosewood forend tip and pistol grip cap. Mfg. 1969-1972.

| | $385 | $330 | $305 | $275 | $220 | $195 | $165 |

MODEL B - similar to Model A, in .243 Win., .270 Win., or .30-06 cal., 20¾ in. barrel, Schnabel forend.

| | $425 | $305 | $275 | $250 | $195 | $165 | $140 |

MODEL C - similar to Model B, with cheekpiece.

| | $425 | $305 | $275 | $250 | $195 | $165 | $140 |

MODEL D - similar to Model C, with full length stock.

| | $550 | $385 | $360 | $305 | $250 | $220 | $195 |

MODEL E - similar to Model D, with no cheekpiece.

| | $550 | $385 | $360 | $305 | $250 | $220 | $195 |

Note: These rifles were made for S&W by Husqvarna in Sweden.

MODEL 1500 MOUNTAINEER - .222 Rem., .22-250 Rem., .223 Rem., .243 Win, .25- 06 Rem., .270 Win., .30-06, or .308 Win. cal., bolt action, 22 in. barrel 5-6 shot mag., no sights, walnut stock, approx. 7 lbs. 10 oz. New 1983.

| | $300 | $250 | $245 | $210 | $195 | $175 | $160 |

Add $27 for sights.

✳ *Model 1500 Mountaineer Magnum* - 7mm Rem. Mag. or .300 Win. Mag. cal.

| | $325 | $275 | $260 | $225 | $200 | $180 | $160 |

MODEL 1500 DELUXE - same cals. as standard 1500, Monte Carlo stock, skip-line checkering, select walnut, no sights. New 1983.

| | $350 | $300 | $260 | $220 | $200 | $180 | $160 |

Add $20 for 7mm Mag. and .300 Win. Mag.

MODEL 1500 DELUXE VARMINT - .222 Rem., .22-250 Rem., or .223 Rem. cal., heavy 24 in. barrel, skip-line checkering, no sights. New 1983.

| | $350 | $275 | $315 | $275 | $215 | $195 | $170 |

Add $15 for parkerized finish.

MODEL 1700 LS "CLASSIC HUNTER" - .243 Win, 270 Win, or .30-06 cal., 22 in. barrel, removable 5 shot mag., solid recoil pad, no sights, Schnabel forend, finely checkered. New 1983.

| | $400 | $350 | $315 | $265 | $240 | $220 | $195 |

SHOTGUNS

S&W in 1984 disc. importation of all Howa manufactured shotguns. Mossberg continued importation utilizing both leftover S&W parts in addition to fabricating their own.

MODEL 916 SLIDE ACTION SHOTGUN - 12, 16, or 20 ga., 20, 26, 28, or 30 in. barrels, various chokes, plain pistol grip stock, solid frame. Mfg. by S&W in Springfield, MA. 1972- disc.

| | $175 | $150 | $140 | $130 | $120 | $110 | $100 |

✳ *Vent. rib and pad*

| | $200 | $175 | $155 | $145 | $135 | $130 | $120 |

MODEL 916T SLIDE ACTION - similar to 916, except barrels can be interchanged.

| | $195 | $170 | $155 | $145 | $135 | $130 | $125 |

✳ *Vent. rib and pad*

| | $225 | $200 | $180 | $170 | $155 | $145 | $135 |

MODEL 96 SLIDE ACTION - various gauges, disc.

| | $125 | $110 | $100 | $90 | $75 | $70 | $65 |

Grading	100%	98%	95%	90%	80%	70%	60%

MODEL 1000 P SLIDE ACTION - 12 ga., various barrel lengths, chokes, VR.

	$350	$305	$270	$230	$210	$190	$170

This model is the same as the Model 3000.

MODEL 3000 SLIDE ACTION - 12 or 20 ga., 3 in. chambers, 22-30 in. barrels, walnut stock and forend, 6¼-7½ lbs.

	$350	$305	$270	$230	$210	$190	$170

Add $30 for multi-choke tubes.
Subtract $40 for slug gun (rifle sights on 22 in. barrel).
This model was also available in a "Waterfowler" variation - values are approx. the same as listed.

MODEL 3000 POLICE - 12 ga. only, blue or parkerized finish, many combinations of finishes, stock types, and other combat accessories were available for this model, 18 or 20 in. barrel.

	$332	$255	$215	$185	$170	$155	$140

Add $70 for folding stock.

MODEL 1000 AUTOLOADER - 12 or 20 ga., 22-30 in. barrels, various chokes, gas operated, vent rib, engraved alloy receiver, checkered pistol grip stock. Mfg. 1972-1984.

	$350	$325	$295	$260	$240	$220	$200

Add $30 for multi-choke tubes.
Add approx. $125 for slug barrel.

* *12 and 20 gauge* - Magnum 28 or 30 in. barrel, multi-chokes, steel receiver, "M" suffix.

	$375	$340	$310	$275	$255	$235	$215

* *Model 1000 Super 12* - handles all loads interchangeably, top-of-the-line model during its time.

	$500	$450	$400	$360	$330	$300	$280

Add $50 for multi-choke.

* *Model 1000 Target* - 12 or 20 ga., skeet, super skeet and trap models available. Super skeet has 15 barrel muzzle vents to reduce recoil. Trap model has multi-choke tubes, Monte Carlo select walnut stock and forend. Both alloy and steel receivers available in Skeet model, Trap is steel only.

	100%	98%	95%	90%	80%	70%	60%
Skeet/Super Skeet	$400	$390	$335	$260	$235	$215	$190
Trap (Model 1000T)	$595	$525	$450	$375	$325	$285	$235

Note: Shotguns made for S&W by Howa Machinery, Ltd., Japan.

SOMMER + OCKENFUSS GmbH

Current manufacturer located in Baiersbronn, Germany. Currently imported by Lothar Walther Precision Tool, located in Cumming, GA. Previously imported by Intertex Carousels Corporation during 1998-2000, and located in Pineville, NC.

Sommer + Ockenfuss also produces a bolt adapter to convert the Remington 700 bolt action into a straight pull repeater, enabling the addition of a firing pin safety and firing chamber lock.

PISTOLS: SEMI-AUTO

P21 - .224 HV, .9mm Para., or .40 S&W cal., 3.11 (Combat) or 3.55 (Police) in. rotating barrel, SA/DA operation, release grip safety uncocks the hammer, keyed slide lock blocks firing pin and slide, 10 shot mag., approx. 24 oz. New late 2001.

MSR	$608	$550	$495	$450	$415	$375	$340	$310

Add approx. $320 for conversion slide assemblies.

RIFLES: SLIDE ACTION

SHORTY - most popular cals., unique slide action rifle in bullpup configuration featuring a straight line design with a grip safety pistol grip that also works the slide assembly, stainless or black coated barrel, compact 6-lug bolt with a locking surface of 0.263 sq. in., with or w/ o sideplates inlet into walnut or black synthetic (new 1999) stock. Importation began 1998.

Grading	100%	98%	95%	90%	80%	70%	60%

＊ Shorty Wilderness Rifle - match trigger, polymer stock and stainless steel barrel.

   MSR $1,660   **$1,495 $1,275 $1,100 $995 $925 $850 $750**

   Add $310 for .375 H&H or .416 Rem. Mag. cal. (Shorty Safari).

   Add $200 for walnut stock (Shorty American Hunter).

   Add $210 for sight mounts.

   Add $88 for recoil brake.

＊ Shorty Marksman Rifle - similar to Wilderness Rifle, except has choice of black coated or fluted heavy match barrel and recoil brake.

   MSR $2,020   **$1,875 $1,675 $1,450 $1,275 $1,100 $995 $850**

   Add $80 for .308 Win. or .300 Win. Mag. (fluted barrel), $420 for .338 Lapua Mag. with black coated barrel, or $710 for .338 Lapua Mag. with fluted stainless barrel.

   Add $80 for stainless barrel.

   Add $210 for sight mount, $168 for bipod, $210 for Spigot stock cap.

   There are also deluxe variations, limited editions, and Marksman's packages ($4,100-$4,860 MSR) available in this model - please contact the importer directly for current availability and pricing.

SNAKE CHARMER

Currently manufactured by Verney-Carron USA, Inc. located in Clay Center, KS a joint venture of Verney-Carron SA located in Saint-Etienne, FRANCE (please refer to the separate Verney-Carron listing) and Y.B.E., Inc. located in Clay Center, KS (distributor of Hastings Barrels and Choke tubes.) Distributor sales only.

SHOTGUNS: SINGLE SHOT

SNAKE CHARMER II - .410 bore only, stainless steel, break open single shot, black molded plastic stock and forend, shell holder in stock, also available as Night Charmer (disc. 1988) and Sea Charmer (disc. 1988), 3½ lbs.

   MSR $180   **$150 $115 $95**

   Add $10 for Night Charmer (disc. 1988).

   Add $18 for Sea Charmer (disc. 1988).

   Subtract $18 for black carbon steel barrel (New Generation Model).

SOCIETA SIDERURGICA GLISENTI

Previous manufacturer located in Brescia, Italy. Also see the Italian Military Arms listing.

PISTOLS: SEMI-AUTO

GLISENTI MODEL 1910 - 9mm Glisenti cal., 7 shot, 4 in. barrel, fixed sights, blue, checkered wood, rubber or plastic grips, Italian service pistol. Mfg. 1910-WWII.

           $750 $625 $450 $325 $275 $225 $200

   Warning: While some Glisentis may chamber and fire the 9mm Para. cartridge, it is extremely dangerous to do so.

SODIA, FRANZ

Previous manufacturer located in Ferlach, Austria until 1992.

Sodia arms are superb and are often excellently engraved and inlaid. Professional appraisal should be sought before purchase, since prices are high. Sodia was famous for double-barrel shotguns as well as two and three barrel combinations of rifles and shotguns.

DRILLING

BOCKDRILLING - various cals., 2 rifle barrels and 1 shotgun, top quality workmanship.

           $7,000 $6,500 $6,000 $5,000 $4,000 $3,000 $2,500

Grading	100%	98%	95%	90%	80%	70%	60%

RIFLES: DOUBLE, CUSTOM

DOPPELBÜCHSE - various cals., SxS double rifle, top quality workmanship.

	$5,000	$4,500	$4,000	$3,000	$2,000	$1,800	$1,600

O/U RIFLE - various cals., top quality workmanship.

	$4,500	$4,250	$4,000	$3,500	$3,000	$2,000	$1,800

SHOTGUNS; O/U

TRAP SHOTGUN - 12 ga. only, boxlock action, various degrees of engraving and ornamentation.

	$2,500	$1,850	$1,475	$1,100	$900	$750	$600

SOKOLOVSKY CORPORATION SPORT ARMS (SCSA)

Previous manufacturer until 1990 located in Sunnyvale, CA.

PISTOLS: SEMI-AUTO

SOKOLOVSKY .45 AUTOMASTER - .45 ACP cal. only, stainless steel, single action, 6 in. barrel, 6 shot mag., adj. Millett sights, unique action, is free of external devices, 55 oz. Mfg. 1984- 90.

	$2,700	$2,200	$1,850				

Last MSR was $3,300.

Total production on this model is 50 pistols.

SOLEIHAC ARMURIER

Previous manufacturer located in Saint Etienne, France.

This manufacturer produced copies of 1894 patent Darne R model guns until 1950. The guns produced were generally simple and less expensive than other manufacturers' sliding breech guns. Most unmarked sliding breech guns were probably manufactured by Soleihac Armurier. Quality and pricing will be similar to low grade (Halifax and RIO model) Darne guns in average condition.

SPECIAL WEAPONS LLC

Current paramilitary rifle manufacturer established in 1999, and located in Mesa, AZ. Previously located in Tempe, AZ.

CARBINES: SEMI-AUTO

OMEGA 760 - 9mm Para. cal., reproduction of the S&W Model 76, 16 1/4 in. partially shrouded barrel, fixed wire stock, 30 shot mag., 7 1/2 lbs. New 2002.

MSR	$575	$495	$450	$425	$395	$375	$350	$325

SW-5 CARBINE - 9mm Para. cal., paramilitary configuration styled after the HK-94 (parts interchangeable), stainless steel receiver, plastic lower housing, 16¼ in. stainless steel barrel, A2 style black synthetic stock with wide forearm, 10 shot mag. (accepts high capacity HK-94/MP-5 mags also), approx. 6¾ lbs. New 2000.

MSR	$1,600	$1,475	$1,225	$1,025	$875	$800	$750	$695

SW-45 CARBINE - .45 ACP cal., otherwise similar to SW-5 Carbine. New 2000.

MSR	$1,700	$1,550	$1,275	$1,050	$895	$825	$775	$725

RIFLES: SEMI-AUTO

SW-3 - .308 Win. cal., paramilitary configuration styled after the HK-91 (parts interchangeable), tooled receiver, metal steel lower trigger housing, 17.71 stainless steel barrel, A2 style stock, approx. 10 lbs. New 2000

MSR	$1,550	$1,425	$1,175	$995	$850	$800	$750	$695

S

Grading	100%	98%	95%	90%	80%	70%	60%

✱ *SW-3 SP* - similar to SW-3, except has PSG-1 style trigger assembly, 22 in. custom target barrel and Weaver rail welded to top. New 2000.

MSR	$2,500		$2,250	$1,975	$1,700	$1,500	$1,250	$1,050	$895

SPENCER REPEATING RIFLES CO.

Previously manufactured by Spencer Repeating Rifle Company located in Boston, MA between 1860-1868. Spencer manufactured approximately 144,000 rimfire rifles and carbines, of which approximately 107,000 were contracted to the United States Government during the Civil War.

The brainchild of young Christopher Miner Spencer, more than 13,500 Spencer M1860 Army rifles, 800 M1860 Navy rifles, and 48,000 M1860 Army carbines saw action during the Civil War.

In late 1864, the Chief of Ordnance directed modifications, including reducing the bore from .52 to .50 caliber, and shortening the barrel from 22 inches to 20 inches. The new carbine was designated the Spencer M1865 carbine. Nearly 19,000 were produced by the Spencer Repeating Rifle Company, and another 30,500 by the Burnside Rifle Company, although all were delivered too late to see action in the Civil war. Model 1865 carbines and re-furbished M1860 carbines became the mainstay of America's troops on the Western Frontier until replaced by "Trap-Door" Springfield carbines after 1873.

The author wishes to express his thanks to Mr. Roy Marcot for providing most of the information listed.

100%	98%	95%	90%	80%	70%	60%	50%	40%	30%	20%	10%

RIFLES: LEVER ACTION

SMALL-FRAME MILITARY CARBINES AND SPORTING RIFLES - fewer than four dozen prototype small-frame .38 cal. sporting rifles and .44 cal. military carbines were made by Christopher Spencer in Hartford between 1860 and 1861. They are exceedingly rare, and only a few are in private hands.

N/A	$15,000	$14,000	$12,000	$9,500	$8,500	$7,500	$6,500	$5,500	$4,500	$4,000	$3,500

MODEL 1860 NAVY RIFLES - the rarest of production Spencer firearms, 803 Spencer Model 1860 Navy rifles with sword-type bayonets were produced for the U.S. Navy Bureau of Ordnance between 1862 and 1863.

N/A	$12,000	$11,000	$9,000	$6,000	$4,000	$3,500	$3,250	$3,000	$2,750	$2,500	$2,000

Add $350-$750 for sword-type bayonets.

MODEL 1860 ARMY RIFLES - between 1863 and 1864, the Spencer factory in Boston produced 11,471 Spencer M1860 Army rifles for the Federal Ordnance Department, another 200 for the U.S. Navy, and approximately 2,000 for private purchase. All were issued with Pattern M1855 angular bayonets which fit only these rifles.

N/A	$10,000	$9,000	$7,000	$5,000	$3,750	$3,250	$2,800	$2,500	$2,200	$2,000	$1,800

Add $200-$450 for angular bayonets.

MODEL 1860 CARBINES - beginning in October 1863, the Spencer factory began delivering the first of 45,733 Spencer M1860 carbines to the Ordnance Department for use by Federal cavalrymen. As many as 3,000 additional M1860 carbines went to private purchasers, and also saw action in the war. Because Spencer carbines were so important to the Federal war effort, nearly all saw hard use during the last 18 months of fighting. This resulted in very few weapons available today in excellent condition, and fewer yet with case colors remaining on the receiver.

N/A	$9,000	$8,000	$6,000	$5,000	$3,750	$2,750	$2,500	$2,250	$1,750	$1,500	$1,200

Subtract 25% for Springfield Armory reconditioned Spencer Model 1860 carbines (after the war).

100%	98%	95%	90%	80%	70%	60%	50%	40%	30%	20%	10%

MODEL 1865 CARBINES - in 1865 and 1866, the Spencer factory delivered 18,959 Spencer M1865 carbines to the Federal Ordnance Department. Concurrently, the Burnside Rifle Company of Providence, Rhode Island manufactured and delivered 30,502 Spencer M1865 carbines to the Ordnance Department.

N/A	$6,000	$5,000	$4,000	$3,000	$2,750	$2,500	$2,000	$1,750	$1,500	$1,200	$1,000

MODEL 1865 ARMY RIFLES - as many as 3,000 Spencer M1865 Army rifles were made by the Spencer factory in 1865. While none were ordered by the U.S. Army Ordnance Department, 2,000 went to the Commonwealth of Massachusetts National Guard, and another 1,000 went to Canadian troops and to private purchasers.

N/A	$6,000	$5,000	$4,000	$3,000	$2,750	$2,500	$2,000	$1,750	$1,500	$1,200	$1,000

SPRINGFIELD ARMORY RIFLE MUSKET CONVERSION OF SPENCER CARBINES - in 1871, General Dyer, Chief of Ordnance, directed that 1,109 Spencer M1865 carbines be converted to two-band muskets. Each was fitted with Springfield .50 caliber barrels which held standard M1855 pattern bayonet.

N/A	$6,000	$5,000	$4,000	$3,500	$3,000	$2,800	$2,500	$2,200	$1,800	$1,200	$1,000

MODEL 1867 ARMY RIFLES AND CARBINES - in 1867, the Spencer factory produced approx. 1,000 M1867 Army rifles and 12,000 carbines. All were intended for private domestic or foreign military sales.

N/A	$4,000	$3,000	$2,500	$2,000	$1,900	$1,750	$1,500	$1,400	$1,200	$1,000	$900

NEW MODEL ARMY RIFLES AND CARBINES - in their final year of production, 1868, the Spencer Repeating Rifle Company produced approx. 1,000 Army rifles and 5,000 carbines. These too, were intended for private domestic or foreign military sales.

N/A	$4,000	$3,000	$2,500	$2,000	$1,900	$1,750	$1,500	$1,400	$1,200	$1,000	$900

SPORTING RIFLES - between 1864 and 1868, the Spencer factory produced approximately 2,000 sporting rifles for the civilian trade. The initial 200 or so were made from surplus military M1860 Army rifle receivers. Thereafter, approximatley 1,800 sporting rifles were made expressly as such. The majority chambered the Spencer 56-46 bottleneck rimfire cartridge, but a small number were produced in .50 caliber, chambering 56-50 and the 56-52 cartridges. Spencer sporting rifles missing the rear tang sight are worth approximately 25% less than those listed.

N/A	$7,000	$6,000	$5,000	$4,000	$3,000	$2,500	$2,000	$1,500	$1,300	$1,250	$1,000

Grading	100%	98%	95%	90%	80%	70%	60%

SPHINX SYSTEMS LTD.

Current manufacturer presently located in Matten b. Interlaken, Switzerland. No current U.S. importation. Previously manufactured by Sphinx Engineering S.A. located in Porrentruy, Switzerland. Previously imported by Sphinx U.S.A., located in Meriden, CT until 1996. Previously imported by Sile Distributors located in New York, NY.

SPHINX

PISTOLS

MODEL AT-380 - .380 ACP cal., semi-auto double action only, 3.27 in. barrel, stainless steel frame, two-tone finish, 10 shot mag. with finger extension, checkered walnut grips. Disc. 1996.

		$435	$375	$350	$325	$295	$275	$250

Last MSR was $494.

Add $20 for black finish.
Add $71 for N/Pall finish.

Grading	100%	98%	95%	90%	80%	70%	60%

MODEL 2000S STANDARD - 9mm Para. or .40 S&W (new 1993) cal., semi-auto in standard double action or double action only, 4.53 in. barrel, stainless steel fabrication, 10 (C/B 1994), 15* (9mm Para.), or 11* (.40 S&W) shot mag., checkered walnut grips, fixed sights, 35 oz.

MSR N/A	$965	$750	$625	$525	$450	$410	$375

Add $117 for .40 S&W cal.

✴ *Model 2000PS Police Special* - similar to Model 2000S, except has compact slide and 3.66 in. barrel.

MSR N/A	$850	$625	$525	$450	$410	$380	$350

Add $40 for .40 S&W cal.
Add $87 for N/Pall finish.

✴ *Model 2000P Compact* - similar to Model 2000 Standard, except has 3.66 in. barrel and 13 shot mag., 31 oz.

MSR N/A	$850	$625	$525	$450	$410	$380	$350

Add $40 for .40 S&W cal.
Add $87 for N/Pall finish.

✴ *Model 2000H Sub-Compact* - similar to Model 2000 Compact, except has 3.34 in. barrel and 10 shot mag., 26 oz. Disc. 1996.

	$850	$625	$525	$450	$410	$380	$350

Last MSR was $940.

Add $40 for .40 S&W cal.
Add $87 for N/Pall finish.

MODEL 2000 MASTER - 9mm Para., 9x21mm, or .40 S&W cal., single action only, two-tone finish only, designed for Master's stock class competition.

	$1,795	$1,350	$1,100	$995	$895	$775	$650

Last MSR was $2,035.

MODEL AT-2000CS COMPETITOR - 9mm Para., 9x21mm, or .40 S&W cal., single or double action, competition model featuring many shooting improvements including 5.3 in. compensated barrel, 10 (C/B 1994), 11* (.40 S&W), or 15* shot mag., Bo-Mar adj. sights, two-tone finish. Imported 1993-96.

	$1,725	$1,275	$1,050	$950	$850	$750	$675

Last MSR was $1,902.

Add $287 for Model AT-2000C (includes Sphinx scope mount).
Add $1,538 for AT-2000K conversion kit (new 1995).
Add $1,490 for Model AT-2000CKS (competition kit to convert AT-2000 to comp. pistol, disc. 1994).

MODEL 2000 COMPETITION - similar to Model 2000 Master, except is SA only and includes more advanced competitive shooting features, Bo-Mar sights, top-of-the-line competition model. Imported 1993-96.

	$2,475	$1,925	$1,725	$1,500	$1,250	$1,050	$895

Last MSR was $2,894.

Add $78 for Model AT-2000GM (includes Sphinx scope mount).

MODEL 3000 SERIES - 9mm Para., 9x21mm, .40 S&W, or .45 ACP cal., SA/DA, available in standard (4.53 in. barrel) or tactical (3 3/4 in. barrel) configuration, solid titanium frame, front/rear grip strap stippling, two-tone finish. New 2001.

Please contact the manufacturer directly for current availability and pricing.

SPHINX COMPETITION MODELS - currently available in either an Open (extended barrel with 3 port compensator and Aimpoint scope), or Modified (2 port compensator and rear sight optics). Please contact the company directly for more information on these models, including U.S. availability and pricing.

Grading	100%	98%	95%	90%	80%	70%	60%

SPITFIRE

See listing under JSL (Hereford) in this text.

SPRINGFIELD ARMORY

America's first federal armory located in Springfield, MA. Production began in 1795 and an Act of Congress made it an official federal arsenal in 1872. Not associated with the private firm of the same name located in Geneseo, IL.

In recent years, collectors have realized that military specimens in 98%-100% original condition are very rare and desirable in most cases. Since the supply of these guns is so limited, values listed for these condition factors may not be indicative of current market conditions. As always, many collectors agree that it is hard to overpay for a mint, original, military specimen.

CARBINES/RIFLES

MODEL 1870 ROLLING-BLOCK RIFLE, U.S.N. - .50 cal. centerfire, 32 5/8 in. barrel, not serial numbered, 22,013 mfg.

N/A	$2,200	$1,950	$1,500	$1,100	$900	$750

MODEL 1871 ROLLING-BLOCK RIFLE, U.S.A. - .50 cal. centerfire, 36 in. barrel, not serial numbered, 10,001 mfg.

N/A	$1,750	$1,350	$1,000	$900	$750	$650

MODEL 1873 RIFLE "TRAPDOOR" - .45-70 Govt. cal., 32 5/8 in. barrel, 2 bands. Approx. 73,000 mfg. between 1873-1877. Subtract 20% if stock cartouche faint or absent.

$2,150	$1,800	$1,500	$1,150	$775	$650	$450

MODEL 1884 RIFLE "TRAPDOOR" - .45-70 Govt. cal., 32 5/8 in. barrel, 2 bands. Approx. 232,000 mfg. between 1885-1890. Subtract 20% if stock cartouche faint or absent.

$1,850	$1,450	$975	$725	$625	$525	$425

MODEL 1873 CARBINE - 22 in. barrel, half stock, single barrel band/stacking swivel, 20,000 made, but semi-scarce. Pre-Custer serial numbers below 43,700, add up to 50%. (Pre-1876 mfg.).

N/A	$5,250	$4,250	$3,250	$2,750	$2,250	$2,000

MODEL 1873 CADET RIFLE - .45-70 Govt. cal., 29½ in. barrel, stacking swivel, no sling swivels.

$1,600	$1,300	$1,050	$900	$775	$650	$600

Subtract $100 for variation with sling-swivels.
Subtract 25-35% if restocked with butt plate and hole drilled for cleaning tools.

MODEL 1875 OFFICER'S RIFLE FIRST TYPE - .45-70 Govt. cal., mfg. 477 between 1875 and 1886, 26 in. barrel, single barrel band. Not serial numbered, some dated, non-issue.

N/A	$35,000	$27,000	$23,000	$20,000	$15,000	$10,000

Subtract 15-20% for types 2 and 3.
Approx. 25 rifles were mfg. prior to the standardization of this model.

MODEL 1877 RIFLE - .45-70 Govt. cal., mfg. 3,943.

N/A	$2,650	$2,250	$1,875	$1,625	$1,325	$1,175

MODEL 1877 CARBINE - .45-70 Govt. cal., 22 in. barrel, "C" rear sight to 1,200 yards. Mfg. 2,946.

N/A	$4,250	$3,850	$3,300	$2,850	$2,450	$2,100

MODEL 1877 CADET RIFLE - .45-70 Govt. cal., 29½ in. barrel. 1,050 mfg.

N/A	$1,200	$1,000	$950	$900	$800	$700

MODEL 1879 RIFLE - .45-70 Govt. cal., mfg. approx. 140,000.

$1,350	$1,150	$950	$850	$700	$650	$450

MODEL 1879 CARBINE - .45-70 Govt. cal., no stacking swivel. Approx. 15,000 mfg.

N/A	$2,500	$2,150	$1,900	$1,500	$1,000	$850

S

Grading	100%	98%	95%	90%	80%	70%	60%

MODEL 1879 CADET RIFLE - .45-70 Govt. cal., stacking swivel but no sling swivels. 5,000 mfg.

	$995	$850	$750	$650	$600	$550	$500

MODEL 1880 - .45-70 Govt. cal., combination triangular, sliding type, bayonet-ramrod. 1,001 mfg..

	N/A	$2,900	$2,600	$2,400	$2,000	$1,800	$1,650

MODEL 1881 FORAGER - 20 ga., 1,376 mfg. 1881-1885. Be cautious when purchasing.

	N/A	$2,250	$1,800	$1,500	$1,300	$1,150	$1,000

PISTOLS: SEMI-AUTO

M1911 MILITARY MFG. SPRINGFIELD ARMORY - approx. 30,000 mfg. between 1914-1915, blueblue finish.

	N/A	$2,575	$1,525	$975	$725	$600	$550

Serialization is 72,751-83,855, 102,597-107,596, 113,497-120,566, and 125,567-133,186.
Most mint/100% specimens encountered in this model have been refinished - be careful.

KRAG-JORGENSEN VARIATIONS MFG. BY SPRINGFIELD

Please refer to the Krag-Jorgensen section.

U.S. MODEL 1903 SPRINGFIELD - .30-06 cal., bolt action, mfg. by Springfield Armory and Rock Island Arsenal, 24 in. barrel. Mfg. 1903-1930.

* **Pre-WWI Mfg.** - values below represent original rifles.

	$5,000	$4,250	$3,650	$3,000	$2,250	$1,850	$1,650

Subtract 80% if reworked.

* **Serialized 800,000 - 1,275,767** - double heat treated receiver.

	$3,950	$3,250	$2,750	$2,500	$2,100	$1,650	$1,300

* **Serialized 1,275,768+** - nickel steel receiver.

	$1,450	$1,250	$995	$850	$800	$750	$700

U.S. MODEL 1903 MARK I - .30-06 cal., similar to U.S. Model 1903 Springfield, except altered for the Pedersen device, a slot is milled into the left side of receiver to act as an ejection port for use of the semi-auto bolt insert, value without device.

	$1,850	$1,650	$1,400	$1,200	$1,000	$850	$750

1903-A1 - .30-06 cal., similar to U.S. Model 1903 Springfield, except type C pistol grip stock. Mfg. 1930-1939. In 1941 Remington mfg. approx. 350,000.

	$1,250	$1,100	$950	$800	$700	$600	$550

* **Remington produced**

	$795	$725	$650	$575	$500	$450	$395

1903-A1 NATIONAL MATCH

	$2,250	$1,950	$1,500	$1,250	$995	$895	$825

1903-A3 - .30-06 cal., similar to 1903, with production modifications, aperture rear sight, no finger groove in forestock, lower quality finish, stamped floorplate and barrel band. Mfg. WWII by Remington and Smith Corona.

	$525	$435	$395	$360	$330	$300	$275

Add 25% for Smith Corona mfg.

1903-A3 NATIONAL MATCH - 200 mfg., known as the "unmatched" match rifle.

	$1,500	$1,300	$1,000	$850	$750	$675	$600

1903-A4 SNIPER - .30-06 cal., with M73B1 or M84 scope in Redfield mount, no front sight.

	$2,500	$2,000	$1,670	$1,200	$950	$700	$500

Subtract 25% if reworked with parkerized small parts.

S

Grading	100%	98%	95%	90%	80%	70%	60%

1903 MARINE SNIPER - .30-06 cal., includes 8X Unertl scope.

	$5,500	$3,950	$3,000	$2,500	$2,000	$1,800	$1,650

If this model is verified as an original, large premiums (double or triple) are currently being asked on values listed.

1903 NRA SPORTING RIFLE - .30-06 cal., over 4,000 mfg.

	$875	$750	$650	$550	$450	$375	$295

1903 NRA NATIONAL MATCH - .30-06 cal., similar to 1903, with hand selected and custom fit parts, produced for target shooting. "NRA" and flaming bomb proofed on trigger guard. 1915 date.

	$1,950	$1,650	$1,450	$1,150	$995	$850	$725

1903 SPORTER - .30-06 cal., similar to National Match, with sporter stock and Lyman sight.

	$1,850	$1,600	$1,400	$1,050	$925	$825	$700

1903 MATCH STYLE T - .30-06 cal., similar to Sporter, with heavy barrel, globe sight, target bases, 26, 28, or 30 in. barrel.

Because original specimens are extremely rare, pricing is very hard to determine. Excellent original condition specimens have been seen with asking prices in the $8,000-$9,000 range.

1903 FREE RIFLE TYPE A - .30-06 cal., similar to Style T, with 28 in. barrel, and Swiss hook butt.

Because original specimens are extremely rare, pricing is very hard to determine. Excellent original condition specimens have been seen with asking prices in the $8,000-$9,000 range.

1903 FREE RIFLE TYPE B - .30-06 cal., similar to Type A, with double set triggers, cheekpiece stock, modified firing pin.

Because original specimens are extremely rare, pricing is very hard to determine. Excellent original condition specimens have been seen with asking prices in the $8,000-$9,000 range.

MODEL 1922-M1 - .22 LR cal., Target Rifle, 5 shot mag., 24 in. barrel, modified 1903, Lyman receiver sight, sporter stock, issued 1927.

	$995	$900	$825	$725	$625	$550	$495

MODEL 1922 NRA VARIATION - not tapped for scope, without forend grooves.

	$2,500	$2,250	$1,925	$1,725	$1,500	$1,250	$1,000

M2 .22 TARGET RIFLE - similar to 1922 M1, except improved lock time, adj. head space, bolt design.

	$1,000	$900	$800	$700	$600	$550	$500

SPRINGFIELD ARMORY (MFG. BY SPRINGFIELD INC.)

Current trademark manufactured by Springfield Inc., located in Geneseo, IL. Springfield Inc. has also imported a variety of models. This company was named Springfield Armory, Geneseo, IL until 1992.

Springfield Inc. manufactures commercial pistols and rifles, including reproductions of older military handguns and rifles.

SPRINGFIELD, INC.

COMBINATION GUNS

S

M6 SCOUT RIFLE - .22 LR, .22 Mag. (disc.), or .22 Hornet cal. over smoothbore .410 bore w/3 in. chamber, O/U Survival Gun, 14 (legal transfer needed) or 18¼ in. barrels, parkerized or stainless steel (new 1995), approx. 4 lbs.

MSR	$185	$155	$130	$105	$85	$75	$70	$65

Add $34 for stainless steel.
Add $24 for lockable Marine flotation plastic carrying case.
Older mfg. does not incorporate a trigger guard while newer production has a trigger guard.

Grading	100%	98%	95%	90%	80%	70%	60%

M6 SCOUT PISTOL/CARBINE - .22 LR or .22 Hornet cal. over .45 LC/.410 bore, 16 in. barrels parkerized or stainless steel. New 2002.

MSR	$183	$155	$130	$105	$85	$75	$70	$65

Add $26 for stainless steel.

This model is also available with an optional detachable stock (not legal with a rifled barrel less than 16 in. or smoothbore less than 18 in.).

M6 SCOUT PISTOL - .22 LR or .22 Hornet cal. over .45 LC/.410 bore, 10 in. barrels, parkerized or stainless steel. New 2002.

MSR	$169	$145	$130	$110	$90	$80	$70	$65

Add $20 for stainless steel.

PISTOLS: SEMI-AUTO

OMEGA PISTOL - .38 Super, 10mm Norma, or .45 ACP cal., single action, ported slide, 5 or 6 in. interchangeable ported or unported barrel with Polygon rifling, special lock-up system eliminates normal barrel link and bushing, Pachmayr grips, dual extractors, adj. rear sight. Mfg. 1987-90.

		$775	$650	$575	$495	$425	$360	$295

Last MSR was $849.

Add $663 for interchangeable conversion units.

Each conversion unit includes an entire slide assembly, one mag., 5 or 6 in barrel, recoil spring guide mechanism assembly, and factory fitting.

Add $336 for interchangeable 5 or 6 in. barrel (including factory installation).

OMEGA MATCH - same cals. as Omega, except has low profile combat sights, 8 shot mag., and beveled mag. well. Mfg. 1991-1992.

	$925	$775	$660	$535	$460	$420	$385

Last MSR was $1,103.

Pistols: Semi-Auto - P9 Series

MODEL P9 - 9mm Para., 9x21mm (new 1991) .40 S&W (new 1991), or .45 ACP cal., patterned after the Czech CZ-75, selective double action design, blue (standard beginning 1993), parkerized (standard until 1992), or duotone finish, various barrel lengths, checkered walnut grips. Mfg. in U.S. starting 1990.

* **P9 Standard** - 4.72 in. barrel, 15 shot (9mm Para.), 11 shot (.40 S&W), or 10 shot (.45 ACP) mag., parkerized finish standard until 1992 - blueblue finish beginning 1993, 32.16 oz. Disc. 1993.

	$430	$375	$335	$295	$275	$240	$215

Last MSR was $518.

Add $61 for .45 ACP cal.
Add $182 for duotone finish (disc. 1992).
Subtract $40 for parkerized finish.

In 1992, Springfield added a redesigned stainless steel trigger, patented sear safety which disengages the trigger from the double action mechanism when the safety is on, lengthened the beavertail grip area offering less "pinch", and added a two piece slide stop design.

* **P9 Stainless** - similar to P9 Standard, except is constructed from stainless steel, 35.3 oz. Mfg. 1991-1993.

	$475	$425	$350

Last MSR was $589.

Add $50 for .45 ACP cal.

Grading	100%	98%	95%	90%	80%	70%	60%

✳ **P9 Compact** - 9mm Para. or .40 S&W cal., 3.66 in. barrel, 13 shot (9mm Para.) or 10 shot (.40 S&W) mag., shorter slide and frame, rounded triggerguard, 30½ oz. Disc. 1992.

	$395	$350	$300	$275	$250	$225	$200

Last MSR was $499.

Add $20 for .40 S&W cal.
Add $20-$30 for blue finish depending on cal.
Add $78 for duotone finish.

✳ **P9 Sub-Compact** - 9mm Para. or .40 S&W cal., smaller frame than the P9 Compact, 3.66 in. barrel, 12 shot (9mm Para.) or 9 shot (.40 S&W) finger extension mag., squared off triggerguard, 30.1 oz. Disc. 1992.

	$395	$350	$300	$275	$250	$225	$200

Last MSR was $499.

Add $20 for .40 S&W cal.
Add $20-$30 for blue finish depending on cal.

✳ **P9 Factory Comp** - 9mm Para., .40 S&W, or .45 ACP cal., 5½ in. barrel (with compensator attached), extended sear safety and mag. release, adj. rear sight, slim competition checkered wood grips, choice of all stainless (disc. 1992) or stainless bi-tone (matte black slide), dual port compensated, 15 shot (9mm Para.), 11 shot (.40 S&W), or 10 shot (.45 ACP) mag., 33.9 oz. Mfg. 1992-1993.

	$595	$525	$450	$420	$390	$360	$330

Last MSR was $699.

Add $36 for .45 ACP cal.
Add $75-$100 for all stainless finish.

✳ **P9 Ultra IPSC (LSP)** - competition model with 5.03 in. barrel (long slide ported), adj. rear sight, choice of parkerized (standard finish until 1992 when disc.), blueblue (disc. 1992), bi-tone (became standard 1993), or stainless steel (disc. 1992) finish, extended thumb safety, and rubberized competition (9mm Para. and .40 S&W cals. only) or checkered walnut (.45 ACP cal. only) grips, 15 shot (9mm Para.), 11 shot (.40 S&W), or 10 shot (.45 ACP) mag., 34.6 oz. Disc. 1993.

	$555	$475	$415	$350	$300	$275	$250

Last MSR was $694.

Add $30 for .45 ACP cal.

✳ **P9 Ultra LSP Stainless** - stainless steel variation of the P9 Ultra LSP. Mfg. 1991-92.

	$675	$525	$425				

Last MSR was $769.

Add $30 for .40 S&W cal.
Add $90 for .45 ACP cal.

✳ **P9 World Cup** - see listing under 1911-A1 Custom Models heading.

Pistols: Semi-Auto - R-Series

PANTHER MODEL - 9mm Para., .40 S&W, or .45 ACP cal., semi-auto single or double action, 3.8 in. barrel, hammer drop or firing pin safety, 15 shot (9mm Para.), 11 shot (.40 S&W), or 9 shot (.45 ACP) mag., Commander hammer, frame mounted slide stop, narrow profile, non-glare blue finish only, walnut grips, squared off triggerguard, 29 oz. Mfg. 1992 only.

	$535	$450	$395	$350	$300	$275	$250

Last MSR was $609.

S

Grading	100%	98%	95%	90%	80%	70%	60%

FIRECAT MODEL - 9mm Para. or .40 S&W cal., single action, 3.5 in. barrel, 3 dot low profile sights, all steel mfg., firing pin block and frame mounted ambidextrous safety, 8 shot (9mm Para.) or 7 shot (.40 S&W) mag., checkered combat style triggerguard and front/rear grip straps, non-glare blue finish, 35¾ oz. Mfg. 1992-1993.

	$495	$425	$375	$330	$295	$275	$250

Last MSR was $569.

BOBCAT MODEL - while advertised in 1992, this model was never mfg.

LINX MODEL -while advertised in 1992, this model was never mfg.

Pistols: Semi-Auto - Disc. 1911-A1 Models

MODEL 1911-A1 STANDARD MODE - .38 Super, 9mm Para., 10mm (new 1990), or .45 ACP cal., patterned after the Colt M1911-A1, 5.04 (Standard) or 4.025 (Commander or Compact Model) in. barrel, 7 shot (Compact), 8 shot (.45 ACP), 9 shot (10mm), or 10 shot (9mm Para. and .38 Super) mag., walnut grips, parkerized, blue, or duotone finish. Mfg. 1985-1990.

	$400	$360	$330	$300	$280	$260	$240

Last MSR was $454.

Add $35 for blueblue finish.
Add $80 for duotone finish.

This model was also available with a .45 ACP to 9mm Para. conversion kit for $170 in parkerized finish, or $175 in blueblue finish.

* ***Defender Model*** - .45 ACP cal. only, similar to Standard 1911-A1 Model, except has fixed combat sights, beveled mag. well, extended thumb safety, bobbed hammer, flared ejection port, walnut grips, factory serrated front strap and two stainless steel magazines, parkerized or blue finish. Mfg. 1988-90.

	$485	$435	$375	$340	$300	$280	$260

Last MSR was $567.

Add $35 for blue bluefinish.

* ***Commander Model*** - .45 ACP cal. only, similar to Standard 1911-A1 Model, except has 3.63 in. barrel, shortened slide, Commander hammer, low profile 3-dot sights, walnut grips, parkerized, blueblue, or duotone finish. Mfg. in 1990 only.

	$450	$415	$350	$325	$285	$260	$245

Last MSR was $514.

Add $30 for blue finish.
Add $80 for duotone finish.

* ***Combat Commander Model*** - .45 ACP cal. only, 4¼ in. barrel, bobbed hammer, walnut grips. Mfg. 1988-89.

	$435	$385	$325	$295	$275	$250	$230

Add $20 for blue finish.

* ***Compact Model*** - .45 ACP cal. only, compact variation featuring shortened Commander barrel and slide, reduced M1911 straight grip strap frame, checkered walnut grips, low profile 3-dot sights, extended slide stop, combat hammer, parkerized, blue, or duotone finish. Mfg. 1990 only.

	$450	$415	$350	$325	$285	$260	$245

Last MSR was $514.

Add $30 for blue finish.
Add $80 for duotone finish.

* ***Custom Carry Gun*** - .38 Super (special order only), 9mm Para., 10mm (new 1990), or .45 ACP cal., similar to Defender Model, except has tuned trigger pull, heavy recoil spring, extended thumb safety, and other features. Mfg. 1988 - Disc.

	$860	$725	$660	$535	$460	$420	$385

Last MSR was $969.

Add $130 for .38 Super Ramped, 10mm was POR.

Grading	100%	98%	95%	90%	80%	70%	60%

* **National Match Hardball Model** - .38 Super (disc.), 9mm Para. (disc.), or .45 ACP cal., National Match barrel and bushing, specially fitted frame and slide, Bo-Mar adj. rear sight, Herrett walnut grips, plastic cased. Mfg. 1988-90.

	$780	$650	$565	$515	$460	$415	$385

Last MSR was $897.

This model was made specifically for DCM competition shooting.

* **Bullseye Wadcutter Model** - .45 ACP cal. only, designed for wadcutter loads only, 5 or 6 (ported or unported) in. barrel, Bo-Mar rib mounted on slide, checkered grip straps, match trigger, beavertail grip safety, polished feed ramp and throated barrel. Mfg. 1989 - Disc.

	$1,415	$1,200	$1,025	$925	$825	$750	$675

Last MSR was $1,599.

Add $25 for 6 in. barrel.
Add $80 for 6 in. ported barrel.

* **Trophy Master Competition Pistol** - .38 Super, 9mm Para. (disc.), 10mm (new 1990), or .45 ACP cal., competition model which includes low profile combat sights, ambidextrous safety, long match trigger, bobbed hammer, Pachmayr wraparound grips. Mfg. 1988-90.

	$1,300	$1,100	$950	$875	$800	$730	$660

Last MSR was $1,443.

Add $130 for .38 Super with supported chamber, 10mm was POR.

* **Trophy Master Competition Expert Model** - .38 Super, 9mm Para. (disc.), 10mm (new 1990), or .45 ACP cal., mfg. for IPSC competition shooting, dual chamber compensator system on match barrel, blue finish, ambidextrous thumb safety, beveled and polished mag. well, lowered and flared ejection port, wraparound Pachmayr grips, shock buffer, includes 2 mags. and plastic carrying case. Mfg. 1988-90.

	$1,664	$1,450	$1,225	$1,025	$950	$890	$850

Last MSR was $1,664.

Add $130 for .38 Super with supported chamber, 10mm was POR.
This model was an improved variation of the Master Grade Competition Pistol "A".

* **Trophy Master Competition Distinguished Model** - similar to Expert Model, except has brushed hard chrome finish, checkered grip straps and trigger guard, top-of- the-line competition model. Mfg. 1988-90.

	$2,000	$1,675	$1,450	$1,225	$1,025	$950	$875

Last MSR was $2,275.

Add $130 for .38 Super with supported chamber, 10mm was POR.
Subtract $130 for "B" Model.
This model was an improved variation of the Master Grade Competition Pistol "B-1".

Pistols: Semi-Auto - 1911-A1 90s Series

The initials "PDP" refer to Springfield's Personal Defense Pistol series.
Beginning in 2000, Springfield Armory started offering a Loaded Promotion package on their 1911-A1 pistol line. Many of these features and options are found on the FBI's Hostage Rescue Teams (HRT) pistol contract with Springfield Armory. Standard features of this Loaded Promotion package are hammer forged premium air-gauged barrel, front and rear cocking serrations, Novak patented low profile sights or Bo-Mar type adj. sights, extended thumb safety, tactical beavertail, flat mainspring housing, Cocobolo grips, High Hand grip, lightweight match trigger, full length guide rod, and machine beveled mag. well. This promotion includes all pistols except the Mil-Spec Model 1911 A-1.
In 2001, Springfield's Custom Loaded 1911-A1 Series pistols came equipped standard with Springfield's integral locking system, carry bevel, hammer forged premium air-gauged barrel, front and rear cocking serrations, Novak patented low profile sights (some models come equipped with Tritium sights or Bomar type adj. sights), extended thumb safety, tactical beavertail, flat mainspring housing, cocobolo grips, high hand grip, lightweight adj. match trigger, full length guide rod, machine beveled magwell, and a "loaded" coupon ($600 consumer savings). These Custom Loaded

Grading	100%	98%	95%	90%	80%	70%	60%

features will vary by model. All models with less than a 5 in. and all alloy pistols supplied with ramped, fully supported barrels.

Beginning 2002, every Springfield pistol is equipped with a patented integral locking system (I.L.S., keyed in the rear grip strap) at no extra charge.

MODEL 1911-A1 90s EDITION - .38 Super, 9mm Para., 10mm (disc. 1991), .40 S&W, or .45 ACP cal., patterned after the Colt M1911-A1, except has linkless operating system, 5.04 (Standard) or 4 (Champion or Compact Model) in. barrel, 7 shot (Compact), 8 shot (.40 S&W or .45 ACP Standard), 9 shot (9mm Para., 10mm, or .38 Super), or 10 shot (.38 Super) mag., checkered walnut grips, parkerized (.38 Super beginning 1994 or .45 ACP beginning 1993), blue or duotone (disc. 1992) finish. New 1991.

✱ *Mil-Spec 1911-A1* - .38 Super or .45 ACP cal., blue (disc.) or parkerized finish, 3 dot Hi-Viz fixed combat sights, 35.6 oz.

	MSR	$559		$465	$375	$325	$300	$280	$250	$225

Add $17 for blue finish (disc. 2001).
Add $123 for .38 Super cal.

✱ *Mil-Spec Operator 1911-A1* - .45 ACP cal. only, similar to Mil-Spec 1911 A-1, except has Picatinny light mounting system forged into lower front of frame, parkerized finish only.

	MSR	$756		$615	$475	$425	$365	$325	$285	$255

✱ *Loaded Operator 1911-A1* - .45 ACP cal. only, similar to full size service model, except has Picatinny light mounting platform, forged into lower front of frame, checkered hardwood grips, Novak low mount tritium sights. New 2002.

	MSR	$836		$700	$575	$500	$450	$400	$350	$300

✱ *Standard or Lightweight Model* - Standard model has parkerized, blue, or OD Green (new 2002) finish, Custom Loaded features became standard in 2001, Lightweight Model was introduced 1995 with either matte or blue (mfg. 1993-disc.) finish, current mfg. is w/ either Novak low mount or night sights, 28.6 or 35.6 oz.

	MSR	$799		$650	$500	$425	$365	$325	$285	$255

Add $78 for Lightweight Model (matte finish with night sights).
Subtract approx. 10%-25% if w/o Custom Loaded features (new 2001), depending on condition.
Add $25 for blue finish on Standard model.
Add $30 for OD Green finish on Standard model (new 2002).

✱ *Stainless Standard Model* - 9mm Para. (new 1994), .38 Super (disc.), .40 S&W (new 2001), or .45 ACP cal., 7 (.45 ACP cal.), 8 (.40 S&W), or 9 (9mm Para.) shot mag., Custom Loaded features became standard in 2001, wraparound rubber (disc.) or checkered hardwood grips, Novak low mount or Bo-Mar type (mfg. 1996-2001) sights, beveled mag. well, 39.2 oz. New 1991.

	MSR	$828		$675	$525	$450				

Add $4 for 9mm Para. cal., or $32 for .40 S&W cal.
Add $50 for Bo-Mar type sights (disc. 2001).
Add $202 for long slide variation in .45 Super cal. with V16 porting and Bo-Mar sights (disc.).

✱ *Stainless Super Tuned Standard* - .45 ACP cal. only, super tuned by the Custom Shop, 7 shot mag., 5 in. barrel, Novak fixed low mount sights, 39.2 oz. Mfg. 1997-99.

			$875	$750	$600					

Last MSR was $995.

✱ *Target Model* - 9mm Para. or .45 ACP cal., includes Custom Loaded features, stainless steel, with (.45 ACP cal. only) or w/o V12 ported barrel, adj. sights, 38 oz. New 2001.

	MSR	$873		$725	$550	$450				

Add $4 for V12 ported barrel (.45 ACP cal. only).
Add $20 for 9mm Para. cal.

Grading	100%	98%	95%	90%	80%	70%	60%

✳ Trophy Match - .40 S&W (new 2001) or .45 ACP cal. only, top-of-the-line pistol featuring improved trigger pull, adj. rear sight, match grade barrel and bushing, Custom Loaded features became standard in 2001, choice of Armory Kote (.40 S&W cal. only, new 2001), stainless steel, bi-tone (disc.), or blue finish, 35.6 oz. New 1994.

	MSR	$1,148	$940	$775	$625	$550	$495	$450	$395

Add $71 for stainless steel.
Add $10 for bi-tone finish.
Add $8 for High Capacity Trophy Match (disc.).

✳ Standard High Capacity - 9mm Para. (disc.) or .45 ACP cal., 5 in. barrel, blue (disc. 2001) or matte parkerized (new 1996) finish with plastic grips, 3 dot fixed combat sights, 10 shot (except for law enforcement) mag. New 1995.

MSR	$807	$685	$550	$475	$425	$375	$335	$295

Add $50 for blue finish (disc.).

✳ Stainless High Capacity - similar to Standard High Capacity, except is stainless steel. Mfg. 1996-2000.

		$675	$540	$475				

Last MSR was $819.

✳ XM4 High Capacity Model - 9mm Para. or 45 ACP cal., features widened frame for high capacity mag., blue (mfg. 1993 only) or stainless finish only. Mfg. 1993-94.

		$595	$550	$500				

Last MSR was $689.

MODEL 1911-A1 LONG SLIDE CUSTOM LOADED STAINLESS - .45 ACP or .45 Super (mfg. 2001 only) cal., 6 in. ported or unported barrel, 7 shot mag., checkered wood grips, adj. sights, 41 oz. New 2001.

MSR	$1,049	$865	$675	$550

Add $72 for ported barrel (V16).
Add $403 for Trophy Match Model.

PDP DEFENDER MODEL - .40 S&W (disc. 1992) or .45 ACP cal., standard pistol with slide and barrel shortened to Champion length, tapered cone dual port compensator system, fully adj. sights, Videcki speed trigger, rubber grips, Commander style hammer, serrated front strap, parkerized (disc. 1992), duotone/bi-tone, or blue (disc. 1993) finish. Mfg. 1991-98.

	$850	$735	$630	$550	$495	$450	$425

Last MSR was $992.

✳ PDP Factory Comp - .38 Super (disc.) or .45 ACP cal. only, entry level IPSC gun, featuring 5 5/8 in. barrel with compensator attached, adj. rear sight, Videki speed trigger, checkered walnut grips, beveled mag. well, 10 shot (.38 Super) or 8 shot (.45 ACP) mag., blue finish only, 40 oz. Mfg. 1991-2000.

	900	$685	$585	$500	$450	$420	$390

Last MSR was $1,049.

✳ PDP High Capacity Factory Compensated - .38 Super (disc.) or .45 ACP cal. only, blue finish. Mfg. 1995-2000.

	$955	$795	$655	$575	$500	$450	$395

Last MSR was $1,109.

1911-A1 TACTICAL RESPONSE (TRP SERIES) - .45 ACP only, 5 in. standard or bull (Operator Model only) barrel, 7 shot mag., matte Armory Kote finish or stainless steel, checkered rosewood grips, Novak or HiViz (disc., Operator Model only) 3 dot Tritium (disc. 2001) sights, 36 oz. New 1999.

MSR	$1,370	$1,125	$950	$775	$675	$600	$550	$475

Add $25 for Armory Kote finish.
Add $103 for Operator Model with integral light mounting rail and adj. night sights.

S

Grading	100%	98%	95%	90%	80%	70%	60%

1911-A1 COMMANDER MODEL - .45 ACP cal. only, similar to Standard 1911-A1 Model, except has 3.63 in. barrel, shortened slide, Commander hammer, low profile 3-dot sights, walnut grips, parkerized, blue, or duotone finish. Mfg. 1991-92.

	$425	$365	$330	$300	$275	$250	$225

❋ *Combat Commander Model* - .45 ACP cal. only, 4¼ in. barrel, bobbed hammer, walnut grips. Mfg. 1991 only.

	$425	$365	$330	$300	$275	$250	$225

1911-A1 CHAMPION MODEL - .380 ACP (Model MD-1, mfg. 1995 only) or .45 ACP cal., similar to Standard Model, except has 4 in. barrel and shortened slide, blue (disc. 2000) or parkerized (Mil-Spec Champion, new 1994) finish, Commander hammer, checkered walnut grips, 3 dot sights (Novak night sights became standard 2001), 7 shot mag., 33½ oz. New 1992.

MSR	$856	$695	$500	$400	$350	$325	$295	$275

Subtract approx. 10%-25% if w/o Custom Loaded features (new 2001), depending on condition.
Subtract approx. $150 for .380 ACP cal. (Model MD-1, disc.).
Add $30 for Ultra Compact slide (mfg. 1997-98).
Add $79 for ported Champion V10 with Ultra Compact slide (disc.).

❋ *Stainless Champion Model* - .45 ACP cal. only, stainless steel variation of the Champion Model. New 1992.

MSR	$870	$700	$495	$395

Add $119 for Ultra Compact slide (mfg. 1997-98).
Add $52 for ported Champion V10 with Ultra Compact slide (disc. 2000).
Subtract approx. 10%-25% if w/o Custom Loaded features (new 2001), depending on condition.

❋ *TRP Champion* - .45 ACP cal., 4 in. barrel, otherwise similar to TRP Tactical Response. Mfg. 1999-2001.

	$1,045	$875	$700	$600	$500	$450	$395

Last MSR was $1,249.

❋ *Champion Lightweight* - .45 ACP cal., aluminum frame, matte metal finish, night sights became standard during 2001. New 1999.

	$700	$495	$395	$345	$310	$275	$240

Last MSR was $867.

Subtract approx. 10%-25% if w/o Custom Loaded features (new 2001), depending on condition.

❋ *PDP Champion Comp* - .45 ACP cal. only, compensated version of the Champion Model, blue. Mfg. 1993-98.

	$780	$690	$600	$550	$500	$450	$395

Last MSR was $869.

❋ *Super Tuned Champion* - .45 ACP cal., super tuned by the Custom Shop, 7 shot mag., 4 in. barrel, blue or parkerized finish, Novak fixed low mount sights, 36.3 oz. Mfg. 1997-99.

	$850	$725	$575	$500	$450	$400	$365

Last MSR was $959.

Add $30 for blue finish.

❋ *Champion XM4 High Capacity* - 9mm Para. or .45 ACP cal., high capacity variation. Mfg. 1994 only.

	$615	$555	$500

Last MSR was $699.

Grading	100%	98%	95%	90%	80%	70%	60%

1911-A1 COMPACT MODEL - .45 ACP cal. only, compact variation featuring shortened 4 in. barrel and slide, reduced M1911-A1 curved grip strap frame, checkered walnut grips, low profile 3-dot sights, 6 or 7 shot mag., extended slide stop, standard or lightweight alloy (new 1994) frame, combat hammer, parkerized, blue, or duotone (disc. 1992) finish, standard or lightweight (new 1995) configuration, 27 or 32 oz. Mfg. 1991- 1996.

| | $415 | $355 | $300 | $275 | $250 | $225 | $200 |

Last MSR was $476.

Add $66 for blue finish.
Add $67 for Compact Lightweight Model (matte finish only).

* **Stainless Compact Model** - stainless steel variation of the Compact Model. Mfg. 1991-1996.

| | $495 | $420 | $350 | | | | |

Last MSR was $582.

* **Compact Lightweight** - .45 ACP cal., forged alloy frame, matte metal finish, 6 shot mag., Novak night sights became standard 2001. New 1999.

| MSR | $782 | | $625 | $495 | $425 | $375 | $325 | $295 | $275 |

Subtract approx. 10%-25% if w/o Custom Loaded features (new 2001), depending on condition.

◇**Compact Lightweight Stainless** - similar to Compact Lightweight, except is stainless steel. Disc. 2001.

| | $725 | $550 | $475 | | | | |

Last MSR was $900.

Subtract approx. 10%-25% if w/o Custom Loaded features (new 2001), depending on condition.

* **Compact Comp Lightweight** - compensated version of the Compact Model, bi-tone or matte finish, regular or lightweight alloy (new 1994) frame. Mfg. 1993-98.

| | $775 | $685 | $600 | $550 | $500 | $450 | $395 |

Last MSR was $869.

* **High Capacity Compact** - blue or stainless steel, 3 dot fixed combat sights, black plastic grips, 10 shot (except for law enforcement) mag. Mfg. 1995-1996 only.

| | $540 | $465 | $425 | $395 | $360 | $330 | $295 |

Last MSR was $609.

Add $39 for stainless steel.

* **PDP High Capacity Compact Comp** - .45 ACP cal. only, features compensated 3½ in. barrel, 10 shot (except law enforcement) mag., blue finish only. Mfg. 1995-1996 only.

| | $830 | $725 | $625 | $550 | $495 | $450 | $425 |

Last MSR was $964.

ULTRA COMPACT 1911 A-1 - .380 ACP (Lightweight only, mfg. 1995 only), 9mm Para. (new 1998, lightweight stainless only), or .45 ACP cal., 3½ in. barrel, bi-tone (.45 ACP only, disc.), matte (.380 ACP, MD-1), or parkerized (Mil-Spec Ultra Compact) finish, 6, 7 (.380 ACP cal.) or 8 (9mm Para. cal.) shot mag., Custom Loaded features and night sights became standard in 2001, 24 or 30 oz. New 1995.

| MSR | $817 | | $665 | $475 | $375 | $325 | $295 | $265 | $235 |

Add $110 for bi-tone finish (disc.).
Subtract $50 for MD-1 variation (.380 ACP only).
Subtract approx. 10%-25% if w/o Custom Loaded features (new 2001), depending on condition.

* **Ultra Compact Mil-Spec** - .45 ACP cal., parkerized finish, similar to full size Mil-Spec Model, 6 shot mag., does not include Custom Loaded features, checkered grips, 3 dot fixed HiViz combat sights. New 2001.

| MSR | $589 | | $485 | $385 | $330 | | | | |

S

Grading	100%	98%	95%	90%	80%	70%	60%

✳ Ultra Compact Stainless - .45 ACP cal., stainless steel, Novak night sights became standard 2001. New 1998.

MSR	$884	$745	$525	$425			

Subtract $21 for V10 ported barrel (includes Novak low mount sights).

Subtract approx. 10%-25% if w/o Custom Loaded features (new 2001), depending on condition.

✳ Ultra Compact Lightweight - .45 ACP cal., aluminum frame, matte metal finish, night sights became standard 2001. Mfg. 1999-2001.

	$695	$495	$395	$345	$310	$275	$240

Last MSR was $867.

Subtract approx. 10%-25% if w/o Custom Loaded features (new 2001), depending on condition.

✳ V10 Ultra Compact Lightweight Ported - .45 ACP cal., bi-tone finish. Mfg. 1999- 2001.

	$750	$550	$425	$365	$335	$300	$275

Last MSR was $737.

◇V10 Ultra Compact Lightweight Stainless - 9mm Para. or .45 ACP (exclusive) cal., similar to Ultra Combat Lightweight, except is stainless steel, Novak low mount sights. New 1999.

MSR	$870	$725	$525	$425			

Add $31 for night sights (.45 ACP cal. only).

Subtract approx. 10%-25% if w/o Custom Loaded features (new 2001), depending on condition.

✳ High Capacity Ultra Compact - 9mm Para. (disc.) or .45 ACP cal., parkerized (Mil-Spec) or blue (disc.) finish, and stainless steel (disc.) construction, 10 shot mag., 3 dot fixed combat (disc.) or Novak low mount (new 2002) sights, black plastic grips. New 1996.

MSR	$909	$735	$525	$425	$365	$325	$300	$275

Add $98 for stainless steel.

Add $145 for stainless steel with V10 ported barrel (disc.).

Subtract approx. 10%-25% if w/o Custom Loaded features (new 2001), depending on condition.

✳ V10 Ultra Compact Ported - .45 ACP cal. only, 3½ in. specially compensated barrel/slide, blue (disc.), bi-tone, or parkerized (Mil-Spec Ultra Compact) finish, Novak low mount or 3 dot combat sights, 30 oz. New 1995.

MSR	$853	$690	$485	$395	$345	$310	$275	$240

Subtract approx. 10%-25% if w/o Custom Loaded features (new 2001), depending on condition.

✳ V10 Super Tuned Ultra Compact Ported - .45 ACP cal. only, super tuned by the Custom Shop, 3½ in. ported barrel, bi-tone finish or stainless steel (exclusive), Novak fixed low mount sights, 32.9 oz. Mfg. 1997-99.

	$925	$775	$600	$525	$475	$425	$385

Last MSR was $1,049.

Add $70 for stainless steel (exclusive).

MICRO COMPACT 1911-A1 - .45 ACP cal. only, 3 in. tapered barrel w/o bushing, matte finish, checkered grips, 6 shot mag., Novak low mount Tritium sights. New 2002.

MSR	$749	$625	$475	$375	$325	$295	$265	$235

✳ Micro Compact Lightweight 1911 A-1 - similar to Micro Compact 1911 A-1, except has bi-tone finish with forged steel slide (grey) and aluminum alloy frame (blue), checkered cocobolo grips, 24 oz. New 2002.

MSR	$1,060	$875	$725	$595	$535	$475	$425	$375

S

Grading	100%	98%	95%	90%	80%	70%	60%

;ULF VICTORY SPECIAL EDITION - .45 ACP cal., special edition featuring presentation grade blue finish, gold etching on slide and other gold-plated small parts, includes specially padded and embroidered storage case with jacket patch, window decal, and cloisonne medallion honoring all U.S. Armed Forces. Mfg. 1991-1992.

	$750	$600	$475				

Last MSR was $869.

Pistols: Semi-Auto - 1911-A1 Custom Models

In addition to the models listed, Springfield also custom builds other configurations of Race Guns that are available through Springfield dealers. Prices range from $2,245-$2,990.

Add $100 for all cals. other than .45 ACP.

* **Custom Carry Gun** - .45 ACP (other cals. available upon request) cal., similar to Defender Model, except has tuned trigger pull, 7 shot mag., heavy recoil spring, extended thumb safety, available in blue or phosphate (disc.), finish. New 1991.

MSR	$1,430	$1,275	$995	$875	$750	$650	$550	$475

* **Custom Operator** - .45 ACP cal. New 2001.

MSR	$2,495	$2,125	$1,725	$1,375	$1,075	$950	$825	$725

* **Basic Competition** - .45 ACP (other cals. available upon request) cal., Bo-Mar adj. rear sight, blue finish, checkered walnut grips. New 1994.

MSR	$1,535	$1,350	$1,050	$900	$775	$675	$550	$475

* **Professional Model** - .45 ACP cal. New 1999.

MSR	$2,395	$2,050	$1,675	$1,350	$1,075	$950	$825	$725

* **NRA PPC** - .45 ACP (other cals. available upon request) cal., designed to comply with NRA PPC competitive rules/regulations, factory test target, custom carrying case. New 1995.

MSR	$1,625	$1,450	$1,250	$975	$875	$750	$650	$575

* **1911-A1 Custom Compact** - .45 ACP cal. only, carry or lady's model with shortened slide and frame, compensated, fixed 3 dot sights, Commander style hammer, Herrett walnut grips, other custom features, blue only.

		$1,615	$1,325	$1,100	$950	$850	$750	$675

Last MSR was $1,815.

* **1911-A1 Custom Champion** - similar to Custom Compact, except is based on Champion model with full size frame and shortened slide.

		$1,615	$1,325	$1,100	$950	$850	$750	$675

Last MSR was $1,815.

* **National Match Hardball** - .45 ACP cal. only, National Match barrel and bushing, specially fitted frame and slide, blue only, Bo-Mar adj. rear sight, Herrett walnut grips, plastic cased.

MSR	$1,470	$1,300	$1,025	$895	$775	$650	$550	$475

This model is made specifically for DCM competition shooting.

* **Bullseye Wadcutter** - .45 ACP (other cals. available upon request) cal., specifically designed for wadcutter loads, Bo-Mar rib mounted on slide top, 5 or 6 in. barrel.

MSR	$1,650	$1,475	$1,225	$975	$875	$750	$650	$575

* **Entry Level Wadcutter** - .38 Super, .40 S&W, 10mm, or .45 ACP cal., 5 in. barrel, standard competition features.

		$925	$800	$700	$600	$550	$475	$425

Last MSR was $1,049.

Add $200 for .38 Super cal.
Add $391 for 10mm or .40 S&W cal.
This model features supported chamber in all cals. except .45 ACP.

S

Grading	100%	98%	95%	90%	80%	70%	60%

✳ Trophy Master "Competition" - .45 ACP (other cals. available upon request) cal., competition model which includes low profile combat sights, ambidextrous safety, long match trigger, bobbed hammer, Pachmayr wraparound grips. Disc. 1996.

	$1,420	$1,125	$950	$875	$800	$725	$650

Last MSR was $1,598.

✳ Expert - .45 ACP (other cals. available upon request) cal., mfg. for IPSC competition shooting, dual chamber compensator system on match barrel, duotone finish.

MSR	$1,895	$1,700	$1,450	$1,200	$995	$850	$750	$675

Subtract $120 for Limited Class variation.

This model is an improved variation of the Trophy Master Competition Model.

✳ Distinguished - similar to Expert Model, except has brushed hard chrome finish, checkered grip straps and triggerguard, top-of-the-line competition model.

MSR	$2,690	$2,375	$2,000	$1,625	$1,250	$995	$850	$750

Subtract $110 for Limited Class variation.

✳ Full House Race Gun - .45 ACP cal., high capacity frame, chrome finish only. New 1998.

MSR	$2,950	$2,600	$2,250	$1,975	$1,700	$1,500	$1,350	$1,200

Add $150 for STI/SV style frame.

✳ P9 World Cup - 9mmx21 or .40 S&W cal., state-of-the-art competition pistol, based on factory P9 Race gun, hard chrome finish only.

	$2,550	$2,100	$1,775	$1,500	$1,250	$975	$795

Last MSR was $2,935.

Pistols: Semi-Auto – XD Series

XD SERIES (X-TREME DUTY) - 9mm Para., .357 SIG, or .40 S&W cal., cold hammer forged 4 or 5 in. barrel, lightweight polymer frame, matte black OD Green finish, steel slide, single action striker fired with U.S.A. trigger system, firing pin and loaded chamber indicators, dual recoil spring system, integral accessory rails standard on frame, ambidextrous mag. release, grip safety, front and rear slide serrations, approx. 23 oz. New 2002.

MSR	$489	$425	$375	$350	$325	$295	$265	$235

Add $23 for 5 in. barrel (not available in 9mm Para. cal.).

Add $23 for ported V10 barrel (black only, not available in 9mm Para cal.).

PISTOLS: SINGLE SHOT, 1911-A2 SASS SERIES

1911-A2 SASS - various cals., single shot break open action featuring interchangeable barrels, Pachmayr grips, adj. front and rear sights, blue finish only, 61-66 oz. Mfg. 1990- 1992.

✳ 10¾ in. barrel - .22 LR, 7mm BR, .243 Win., .357 Mag., or .44 Mag. cal.

	$650	$560	$495	$450	$420	$390	$360

Last MSR was $749.

Add $399 per interchangeable conversion unit (includes barrel).

✳ 15 in. barrel - .22 LR, .223 Rem., .243 Win. (new 1991), 7mm BR, 7mm-08 Rem., .308 Win., or .358 Win. cal.

	$650	$560	$495	$450	$420	$390	$360

Last MSR was $749.

Add $399 per interchangeable conversion unit (includes barrel).

RIFLES: BOLT ACTION

MAUSER M98 - 7x57mm Mauser cal., surplus rifles with standard military dimensions and features. Importation disc. 1989.

✳ Hunting/Utility Grade

	$70	$50	$45	$45	$40	$40	$35

Last MSR was $75.

Grading	100%	98%	95%	90%	80%	70%	60%
✳ Collector Grade	$105	$90	$80	$70	$60	$50	$40

Last MSR was $116.

	100%	98%	95%	90%	80%	70%	60%
✳ Premium Grade	$170	$150	$130	$115	$100	$90	$80

Last MSR was $194.

CZ 98 HUNTER CLASSIC - .243 Win., .270 Win., .30-06, .308 Win., 6.5x55mm, 7x57 Mauser, 7x64mm, 7.29x57mm, .300 Win. Mag., or 7mm Rem. Mag. cal., features Mauser 98 Large Ring action, mfg. by CZ in the Czech Republic and Springfield Armory, controlled feeding, 24 in. hammer forged barrel, adj. trigger, choice of walnut or synthetic stock, 7.7 lbs. Limited mfg. 1995 only.

	$345	$315	$285	$260	$240	$220	$195

Last MSR was $411.

Add $38 for walnut stock.

RIFLES: SEMI-AUTO, MILITARY DESIGN

M1 GARAND AND VARIATIONS - .30-06 Springfield, .270 Win. (disc. 1987), or .308 Win. cal., semi-auto, 24 in. barrel, gas operated, 8 shot mag., adj. sights, 9½ lbs.

* **✳ Garand Rifle** - .30-06 or .308 Win. cal., mfg. with original U.S. government issue parts, with new walnut stock, 8 shot mag., 24 in. barrel. Limited mfg. beginning 2002.

MSR	$1,061	$895	$750	$625	$550	$475	$425	$375

* **✳ Standard Model** - supplied standard with camo GI fiberglass stock.

	$725	$650	$575	$525	$485	$450	$425

Last MSR was $761.

Subtract $65 if with GI stock.

* **✳ National Match** - walnut stock, match barrel and sights.

	$850	$775	$700	$650	$600	$550	$495

Last MSR was $897.

Add $240 for Kevlar stock.

* **✳ Ultra Match** - match barrel and sights, glass bedded stock, walnut stock standard.

	$950	$850	$725	$675	$610	$550	$500

Last MSR was $1,033.

Add $240 for Kevlar stock.

* **✳ M1-D Sniper Rifle** - .30-06 or .308 Win. cal., limited quantities, with original M84 scope, prong type flash suppressor, leather cheek pad and slings.

	$950	$850	$725	$675	$610	$550	$500

Last MSR was $1,033.

* **✳ Tanker Rifle** - similar to T-26 authorized by Gen. MacArthur at the end of WWII, 18¼ in. barrel, .30-06 or .308 Win. cal., GI stock standard.

	$725	$675	$600	$525	$460	$380	$335

Last MSR was $797.

Add $23 for walnut full stock.

BM 59 - .308 Win. cal., mfg. in Italy and machined and assembled in the Springfield Armory factory, 19.32 in. barrel, 20 shot box mag., 9½ lbs.

* **✳ Standard Italian Rifle** - with grenade launcher, winter trigger, tri-compensator, and bipod.

	$1,750	$1,400	$1,200	$1,000	$895	$850	$800

Last MSR was $1,950.

* **✳ Alpine Rifle** - with Beretta pistol grip type stock.

	$2,025	$1,625	$1,350	$1,150	$1,000	$925	$850

Last MSR was $2,275.

This model was also available in a Paratrooper configuration with folding stock at no extra charge.

Grading	100%	98%	95%	90%	80%	70%	60%

✳ *Nigerian Rifle* - similar to BM 59, except has Beretta pistol grip type stock.

	$2,075	$1,650	$1,375	$1,150	$1,000	$925	$850

✳ *E Model Rifle*

	$1,975	$1,595	$1,325	$1,125	$975	$900	$825

Last MSR was $2,340.

Last MSR was $2,210.

M1A RIFLES - .243 Win. (disc.), .308 Win., or 7mm-08 Rem. (1991 mfg. only) cal., patterned after the original Springfield M14 - except semi-auto, walnut or fiberglass stock, 22 in. barrel, fiberglass handguard, "New Loaded" option (see separate listing) beginning 2001 includes NM air gauge barrel, trigger group, front and rear sights, and flash supressor or Springfield proprietary muzzle brake, 9 lbs.

✳ *Standard/Basic Model* - above specifications, choice of Collector (original GI stock, disc. 2001), new walnut (M1A Standard Model beginning 1993), black fiberglass (M1A Basic Model), camo fiberglass (disc.), GI wood (disc. 1992), and brown (disc.) or black laminated (M1A Standard Model mfg. 1996-2000) stock, regular or National Match (disc.) barrel.

MSR	$1,319		$1,095	$865	$765	$635	$560	$495	$450

Add $129 for new walnut stock.
Add $56 for Collector GI stock (disc.).
Add $44 for stainless steel barrel (disc.).
Add $74 for bipod and stabilizer (disc.).
Add $125 for black or $159 for brown laminated stock (disc.).
Add $59 for National Match barrel (disc.).
Add $155 for National Match barrel and sights (disc.).
Add $200 for folding stock (disc. 1994).
Subtract $58 for camo fiberglass stock (disc.).
Standard (entry level model) stock configuration for 1996 was black or camo fiberglass.

✳ *M1A E-2* - standard stock is birch. Disc.

	$975	$825	$745	$650	$590	$550	$495

Last MSR was $842.

Add $30 for walnut stock.
Add $120 for Shaw stock with Harris bipod.

✳ *M1A Bush Rifle* - .308 Win. cal., 18 in. shrouded barrel, 8 lbs. 12 oz., collector GI, walnut, black fiberglass folding (disc. 1994 per C/B), and black fiberglass or laminated black stock. Disc. 1999.

	$1,195	$935	$800	$675	$575	$500	$450

Last MSR was $1,381.

Add $29 for walnut stock.
Add $15 for black fiberglass stock.
Add $86 for black laminated stock.
Add $235 for National Match variation.
Add $525 for Super Match variation.

✳ *National Match* - National Match sights, steel or stainless steel (new 1999) barrel, mainspring guide, flash suppressor, and gas cylinder, special glass bedded oil finished match stock, tuned trigger, walnut stock became standard in 1991, 9 lbs.

MSR	$1,995		$1,700	$1,225	$950	$800	$700	$600	$550

Add $45 for stainless steel barrel.
Add $155 for heavy composition stock (disc.).
Add $250 for either fiberglass or fancy burl wood stock (disc.).
.243 Win. and 7mm-08 Rem. cals. are also available at extra charge.

Grading	100%	98%	95%	90%	80%	70%	60%

✹ ***Super Match*** - similar to National Match, except has air-gauged Douglas or Hart heavy barrel, oversized walnut (disc.) or fiberglass super match stock, and modified operating rod guide, rear lugged receiver beginning 1991, approx. 11½ lbs.

	MSR	$2,449	$2,050	$1,350	$1,100	$900	$775	$725	$650

Add $126 for stainless steel Douglas barrel.
Add $250 for Krieger or Hart barrel.
Add $446 for McMillian black or Marine Corps camo fiberglass stock.
Add $200 for fancy burl walnut (disc.) stock.
.243 Win. and 7mm-08 Rem. cals. are also available at extra charge.

✹ ***M21 Tactical*** - .308 Win. cal., 22 in. barrel, tactical variation of the Super Match mfg. with match grade parts giving superior accuracy, adj. cheekpiece stock, 11.6 lbs. New 1990.

	MSR	$2,975	$2,550	$2,100	$1,775	$1,550	$1,275	$1,050	$875

Add $320 for Krieger barrrel.

✹ ***M25 "White Feather" Tactical Rifle*** - .308 Win. cal., includes black fiberglass M3A McMillan stock, 22 in. Kreiger heavy carbon barrel standard, Rader trigger, White Feather logo and Carlos Hathcock II signature, 10 shot box mag., includes Harris bi-pod, 12¾ lbs. New 2001.

	MSR	$3,995	$3,550	$2,975	$2,500	$2,150	$1,850	$1,550	$1,250

M1A LOADED STANDARD - .308 Win. cal., 22 in. National Match steel or stainless steel barrel, features shooting upgrades such as National Match trigger assembly, front and rear sights, and National Match flash suppressor, 10 shot mag., black fiberglass, Collector GI walnut (disc. 2000), or new walnut stock, approx. 9½ lbs. New 1999.

	MSR	$1,569	$1,335	$1,025	$875	$725	$625	$525	$475

Add $150 for new walnut stock.
Add $60 for stainless steel barrel.
Add $100 for Collector GI walnut (disc. 2000).

M1A "GOLD SERIES" - .308 Win. cal., heavy walnut competition stock, gold medal grade heavy Douglas barrel. Add $126 for Kevlar stock, add $390 for special Hart stainless steel barrel, add $516 for Hart stainless steel barrel with Kevlar stock. Mfg. 1987 only.

	$1,944	$1,750	$1,375	$1,150	$975	$850	$740

Last MSR was $1,944.

M1A SCOUT SQUAD - .308 Win. cal., 18 in. barrel, choice of GI Collector (disc. 1998), new walnut, black fiberglass, or black laminated (disc. 1998) stock, muzzle stabilizer standard, supplied with Scout mount and handguard, approx. 9 lbs. New 1997.

	MSR	$1,529	$1,300	$985	$845	$725	$625	$525	$475

Add $110 for walnut stock.

SAR-8 - .308 Win. cal., patterned after the H & K Model 91, recoil operated delayed roller lock action, fluted chamber, rotary adj. rear aperture sight, 18 in. barrel, supplied with walnut (disc. 1994) or black fiberglass thumbhole sporter stock, 10 (C/B 1994) or 20 (disc. 1994) shot detachable mag., 8.7 lbs. Mfg. in U.S. starting 1990, disc. 1998.

	$1,015	$835	$750	$675	$600	$550	$500

Last MSR was $1,204.

SAR-8 parts are interchangeable with both SAR-3 and HK-91 parts.

✹ ***SAR-8 Tactical Counter Sniper Rifle*** - .308 Win. cal., tactical sniper variation of the SAR-8. Mfg. 1996-98.

	$1,325	$1,000	$825	$725	$650	$575	$525

Last MSR was $1,610.

S

Grading	100%	98%	95%	90%	80%	70%	60%

SAR-48/SAR-4800 SPORTER MODEL - .223 Rem. (new 1997) or .308 Win. cal., authentic model of the Belgian semi-auto FAL/LAR rifle, 18 (.223 Rem. cal. only) or 21 in. barrel, adj. gas operation, 10 (C/B 1994) or 20 (disc.) shot mag., walnut (disc.) or black fiberglass thumbhole sporter stock, adj. sights, sling, and mag. loader. Mfg. 1985- 1998.

	$1,080	$915	$785	$675	$625	$575	$525

Last MSR was $1,249.

Add $70 for Paratrooper model with folding stock.
Add $17 for Compact Sporter Model.

The SAR-48 was disc. in 1989 and reintroduced as the Model SAR-4800 in 1990. All SAR- 4800 parts are interchangeable with both SAR-48 and FN/FAL parts. This model is an updated variation of the pre-WWII FN Model 49.

✻ **SAR-48/SAR-4800 Bush Rifle Sporter Model** - similar to standard model, except has 18 in. barrel.

	$1,085	$900	$795	$695	$640	$595	$550

Last MSR was $1,216.

✻ **SAR-48 .22 Cal.** - .22 LR cal., variation of the Sporter Model. Disc. 1989.

	$725	$660	$595	$540	$495	$450	$400

Last MSR was $760.

DR-200 SPORTER RIFLE - while advertised, this model was never mfg. ($687 was planned MSR).

STALLARD ARMS

Current manufacturer of 9mm Para. pistols located in Mansfield, OH since 1991. Distributed by MKS Supply, Inc. located in Dayton, OH.

Please refer to the Hi-Point listing in this text.

STANDARD ARMS & STANDARD ARMS MFG. CO.

Standard Arms started production in Wilmington, DE, in Sept., 1909, and the company folded in 1912. The company was restarted in 1913 as Standard Arms Mfg. Co., and closed in April, 1914.

Nearly 5,000 rifles were manufactured at the actual factory. At the time the plant closed, approx. 2,200 rifles were in various stages of production, and a supply of parts remained. These were primarily purchased by Numrich Arms, made into complete rifles and sold. Total production (Standard Arms, Standard Arms Mfg. Co. & those assembled by Numrich Arms) reached approx. 7,000 rifles. The highest known serial number is 9012. Within serialization, it is noted that large blocks of numbers were abandoned, and this is thought to be due to changes and improvements made during production. In addition, as the factory folded with a large number of rifles in partial stages of production, it is often not possible to determine which rifles were actually made and completed at the factory, and which were completed outside the factory at a later date.

Many special order options were available, such as checkering, pistol grip, deluxe grades of woods, special sights, etc. Several grades of engraving were available, including Rocky Mountain, Adirondack, Sierra, and Selkirk. Lower priced "etched" models were also available and less frequently encountered that engraved models. A .50 caliber "Camp Carbine" was offered in smooth bore, slide action only. Approx. 25-30 were manufactured and utilized a special cartridge similar to the .50-70 shot cartridge. These are rarely encountered, although they are known to exist in collections.

RIFLES: SEMI-AUTO

MODEL G AUTOLOADER - .25-35 WCF, .30-30 Win., .25 Rem., .30 Rem., or .35 Rem. cal., bottom loading box mag., 22 in. barrel, open sight, straight stock. This was the first gas operated rifle in the U.S.A. Gas port can be closed and gun will function as a slide action, mfg. 1910.

	$475	$400	$300	$275	$250	$225	$200

Subtract 10% for slide action only (Model M).

Grading	100%	98%	95%	90%	80%	70%	60%

STANDARD ARMS OF NEVADA, INC.
Previous manufacturer 1999-2000, and located in Reno, NV.

PISTOLS: SEMI-AUTO

SA-9 - 9mm Para. cal., double action only, sub compact design, 10 shot mag., 3.1 in. barrel, black polymer frame with matte black steel slide, 14 oz. Mfg. 1999-2000.

$220	$190	$175	$165	$150	$140	$130

Last MSR was $249.

STANDARD 380 - while advertised, this model was never produced. MSR was $176.

STAR, BONIFACIO ECHEVERRIA S.A.
Previous manufacturer located in Eibar, Spain. Star, Bonifacio Echeverria S.A. closed its doors on July 28th, 1997, due to the intense financial pressure the Spanish arms industry has been experiencing during the past several years. Previously imported by Interarms, located in Alexandria, VA.

PISTOLS: SEMI-AUTO

MODEL H - similar to Model HN, except 7.65mm, 7 shot.

$350	$250	$170	$120	$100	$90	$75

MODEL HN - .380 ACP cal., 6 shot, 2¾ in. barrel, blue, fixed sights, plastic grips. Mfg. 1934-1941.

$375	$265	$180	$120	$100	$90	$75

MODEL I - .32 ACP cal., 9 shot, 4¾ in. barrel, blue, fixed sights, plastic grips. Mfg. 1934-1936.

$350	$250	$170	$120	$100	$85	$70

MODEL IN - similar to Model I, except .380 ACP, 8 shot, 4¾ in. barrel, blue.

$395	$265	$180	$125	$105	$90	$75

MODEL 1920 - 9mm Bergmann Bayard or .38 Super cal., easily identified by unusual safety located on left rear slide. Issued to Spanish Guardia Civil.

$550	$400	$325	$280	$275	$185	$150

MODEL 1921 - 9mm Bergmann Bayard cal., this model was fitted with a grip safety that was later dropped when standardizing the Model A production. Issued to Spanish Guardia Civil.

$475	$350	$300	$250	$225	$185	$150

MODEL 1922 - designation for the early Model A. Issued to Spanish Guardia Civil.

$375	$285	$240	$215	$180	$145	$135

MODEL A - .38 Super cal., modified Government Colt, 5 in. barrel, no grip safety, blue, checkered wood grips. Mfg. 1934-disc.

$325	$275	$240	$215	$180	$145	$135

Add 50% for Spanish Air Force issue if in original box.

MODEL A CARBINE - usually 7.63mm cal., unusual variation, slotted with tangent rear sight and extended barrel.

$1,750	$1,350	$1,050	$825	$700	$575	$450

Add $500 for original stock (different from MB and MMS stock).

MODEL B - similar to Model A, but 9mm Para. cal. Mfg. 1934-1975.

$295	$250	$205	$170	$150	$140	$115

Add 50% for post-war German police if with 2 matching magazines.
Add 150% if Waffenamt proofed (WaA251).

S

Grading	100%	98%	95%	90%	80%	70%	60%

MODEL M - similar to Model A, except has large frame, available in 9mm Bergmann Bayard, 9mm Para., 8 shot, and .45 ACP, 7 shot, 5 in. barrel, blue, fixed sights, checkered wood or plastic grips.

	$325	$275	$240	$215	$185	$160	$140

Add 100% for early variation with ser. no. under 4,835.

MODEL P - .45 ACP cal. only, similar to Model A, except has large frame, 7 shot mag. Mfg. 1934-1975.

	$350	$285	$240	$215	$185	$160	$140

Add 100% for early variation with ser. no. under 5,112.

MODELS SUPER A (9mm Largo), M (9mm Largo), & P (.45 ACP) - similar to Models A, M, & P, except has loaded chamber indicator, mag. safety, and easier takedown feature. Mfg. 1946-1989.

	$395	$325	$215	$180	$160	$145	$125

Last MSR was $340.

Add 100% for Super M and Super P.

The Super A was a Spanish Service pistol. Recent imports in 80% condition were available in the $150 range.

MODEL SUPER B - 9mm Para. cal., similar to Model B, except has loaded chamber indicator, mag. safety and easier takedown feature, choice of blue or Starvel finish on Model B, late production models are poorly polished and have parkerized small parts. Importation disc. in 1990.

	$325	$250	$210	$185	$160	$140	$120

Last MSR was $330.

Add $30 for Starvel finish.

SUPER TARGET MODEL - similar to Star Super, but target sights, extended trigger guard, modified trigger. Rare.

	$1,250	$950	$800	$700	$600	$500	$400

MODEL MB - 9mm Para. cal., late production Model M cut for shoulder stock, mag. safety.

	$1,295	$975	$675	$565	$450	$365	$250

Add $300 for shoulder stock.

MODEL MMS - 7.63mm cal., late production Model M cut for shoulder stock, mag. safety.

	$1,000	$750	$460	$400	$325	$260	$200

Add $300 for shoulder stock.

MODEL SI - .32 ACP cal., 8 shot, 4 in. barrel, blue, without grip safety, small version of Government .45 in appearance, plastic grips. Mfg. 1941-1965.

	$200	$190	$160	$135	$115	$100	$80

MODEL S - similar to Model SI, except .380 ACP cal., 9 shot, mfg. 1941-1965. Importation of these Police contract models was disc. 1991.

	$235	$200	$160	$135	$115	$100	$80

Last MSR was $237.

Add $30 for Starvel finish.

Add 100% for guns issued to the Spanish Air Force with original box and 2 matching mags.

In 1989, Interarms imported factory reconditioned used Spanish Police Contract Model S pistols - these guns were available in either blue or Starvel finish and were supplied with a plastic box with accessories.

MODELS SUPER SI AND S - similar to Model S, with Super Star improvements. Mfg. 1946-1972.

	$240	$230	$210	$195	$165	$140	$120

MODEL SUPER SM - similar to Model Super S, except adjustable sight and wood grips. Mfg. 1973-1981.

	$275	$235	$220	$200	$175	$145	$125

Grading	100%	98%	95%	90%	80%	70%	60%

MODEL CO POCKET - .25 Auto cal., 2¾ in. barrel, blue, fixed sights, plastic grips. Mfg. 1929-1956.

| | $250 | $190 | $165 | $145 | $120 | $110 | $90 |

MODEL CU STARLET - .25 Auto cal., 2 3/8 in. barrel, alloy frame, fixed sights, plastic grips, blue, or chrome slide, frame anodized in black, blue, green, grey, or gold. Mfg. 1957-1972.

| | $235 | $200 | $165 | $145 | $120 | $110 | $90 |

Minor changes prompted a model redesignation as CK during 1973.

MODEL D - .380 ACP cal., small steel frame version of the Model A with several minor variations, 40,416 mfg. 1922-1947.

| | $550 | $475 | $400 | $350 | $300 | $250 | $200 |

MODEL DK (STARFIRE) - .380 ACP cal., 3 1/8 in. barrel, fixed sights, plastic stocks, finished in same color availability as Model CU. Mfg. 1957-1972, U.S. import ceased as of 1968 due to Federal GCA legislation.

| | $400 | $350 | $295 | $255 | $225 | $180 | $155 |

Add 10% for unusual alloy colors.

Minor changes prompted a redesignation as DKL (.380 ACP) 1972 and DKI (.32 ACP) 1972.

MODEL HK LANCER - similar to Model Starfire, except .22 LR cal.. Mfg. 1955-1968.

| | $245 | $215 | $180 | $160 | $140 | $120 | $110 |

MODEL F - .22 LR cal., 10 shot, 4 in. barrel, fixed sights, blue, plastic grips. Mfg. 1942-1967.

| | $325 | $225 | $140 | $110 | $95 | $85 | $55 |

MODEL FS - similar to Model F, except 6 in. barrel, adj. sights. Mfg. 1942-1967.

| | $325 | $225 | $150 | $120 | $100 | $90 | $65 |

MODEL F OLYMPIC RAPID FIRE - .22 Short cal., 9 shot, 7 in. barrel, adj. sight, aluminum slide, barrel weights and muzzle brake, blue, plastic grips. Mfg. 1942-1967.

| | $450 | $325 | $210 | $175 | $155 | $140 | $130 |

MODEL FR - restyled Model F, with "squared" barrel, adj. sight and slide stop. Mfg. 1967-1972.

| | $325 | $225 | $150 | $120 | $100 | $90 | $65 |

Add 15% for chrome finish.

MODELS FR SPORT AND MODEL FR TARGET - similar to Model FR, except FR Sport has 150mm barrel, and the Model FR Target has 180mm barrel, 65,534 mfg. 1967-1983.

| | $350 | $250 | $150 | $120 | $100 | $90 | $65 |

Add 15% for chrome finish.

MODEL FM - similar to Model FR, except heavier frame, web ahead of trigger guard, 4½ in. barrel. 8,799 mfg. 1972-1983.

| | $300 | $225 | $150 | $120 | $100 | $90 | $65 |

MODEL BKS STARLIGHT - 9mm Para. cal., 8 shot, 4¼ in. barrel, plastic grips. Mfg. 1970-1981.

| **Blue** | $265 | $230 | $210 | $180 | $160 | $145 | $130 |

Add 10% for chrome finish.

MODEL BM SEMI-AUTO - 9mm Para. cal., single action, 8 shot mag., 4 in. barrel, steel frame, Colt 1911 action, blue, chrome (disc. 1989), or Starvel (new 1990) finish, plastic grips, 35 oz. Importation disc. 1991.

| | $285 | $245 | $205 | $180 | $165 | $155 | $145 |

Last MSR was $415.

Add $30 for Starvel or chrome (disc. 1990) finish.
Add $150 for Navy issue with escutcheon grips.

MODEL BKM - identical to Model BM, except lightweight duraluminum frame, blue finish only, 26 oz. Importation disc. 1991.

| | $310 | $270 | $225 | $200 | $180 | $170 | $155 |

Last MSR was $415.

S

Grading	100%	98%	95%	90%	80%	70%	60%

MODEL PD - .45 ACP cal., 6 shot mag., single action, 4 in. barrel, adj. rear sight, blue or Starvel (new 1990) finish only, walnut grips, alloy frame, 25 oz. Mfg. 1975-importation disc. 1991.

	$345	$290	$250	$215	$195	$170	$160

Last MSR was $475.

Add $20 for Starvel finish (new 1990).
Add 20% for late variation with 30M rear sight.

MODEL 28 - 9mm Para. cal., double action, 15 shot mag., 4¼ in. barrel, blue finish only, advanced design, 40 oz. Mfg. 1983 and 1984 only.

	$400	$335	$325	$275	$250	$225	$200

Note: Model 28 is interesting since no screws are used in its manufacture. Hammer assembly (including spring, cocking lever, sear, disconnector and ejector) is housed under removable back-strap.

MODEL 30M - 9mm Para. cal. only, successor to the Model 28, double action, 4.33 in. barrel, 15 shot mag., blue finish only, adj. rear sight, checkered wraparound plastic grips, steel frame, 40 oz. New 1985. Importation disc. 1991.

	$350	$295	$275	$255	$235	$215	$195

Last MSR was $495.

MODEL 30 PK DURAL FRAME - similar to Model 30M, except slightly shorter duraluminum frame, 3.86 in. barrel, 30 oz. Disc. 1989.

	$350	$295	$270	$250	$225	$210	$195

Last MSR was $580.

MODEL 31P (STEEL FRAME)/31PK (DURAL FRAME) - 9mm Para. (disc. 1993) or .40 S&W (new 1990) cal., compact variation utilizing double action, features Acculine barrel (3.86 in.), 14 shot mag., ambidextrous safety with decocking lever, blue or Starvel finish, all steel construction, 39.4 oz. Imported 1990-94.

	$350	$295	$270	$250	$225	$210	$195

Last MSR was $398.

Add $30 for Starvel finish (disc. 1993).
Prices are the same for Model 31PK Dural Frame (imported 1990-93).

MODEL M40 FIRESTAR - .40 S&W cal., single action, 6 shot mag., 3.39 in. Acculine barrel, checkered rubber grips, compact design utilizing all steel construction, 3 dot sighting system with adjustable rear sight, blue, Starvel, or nickel (new 1997) finish, 30.35 oz. Mfg. 1990-disc.

	$295	$250	$200	$180	$165	$150	$135

Last MSR was $306.

Add $17 for nickel finish.
Add $20 for Starvel finish.

* Model M40 Firestar Plus - similar to M40 Firestar, except incorporates alloy frame, new grip design, ambidextrous easy-view safety, and fast button release 10 shot mag. Mfg. 1995 - Disc.

	$650	$550	$500	$450	$400	$350	$300

Last MSR was $527.

Add $25 for Starvel finish.
This model was never released for commercial sale.

MODEL M43 FIRESTAR - 9mm Para. cal., 7 shot mag., otherwise similar to Model M40 Firestar. Disc.

	$295	$265	$235	$200	$185	$170	$155

Last MSR was $296.

Add $17 for nickel finish.
Add $20 for Starvel finish.

Grading	100%	98%	95%	90%	80%	70%	60%

* **Model M43 Firestar Plus** - similar to M43 Firestar, except incorporates alloy frame, new grip design, ambidextrous easy-view safety, and fast button release 10 shot double stack mag. Mfg. 1995- 97.

| | $325 | $265 | $235 | $200 | $185 | $170 | $155 |

Last MSR was $351.

> Add $12 for nickel finish.
> Add $25 for Starvel finish.

MODEL M45 FIRESTAR - .45 ACP cal., single action, ultra compact design featuring 4 barrel lugs, steel frame and slide, 3.6 in. reverse taper Acculine barrel, 6 shot mag., black synthetic grips, blue or Starvel finish, 35 oz. Mfg. 1992-97.

| | $325 | $295 | $250 | $200 | $185 | $170 | $155 |

Last MSR was $351.

> Add $12 for nickel finish.
> Add $20 for Starvel finish.

* **Model M45 Firestar Plus** - similar to M45 Firestar, except incorporates alloy frame, new grip design, ambidextrous easy-view safety, and fast button release 10 shot mag. Mfg. 1995 only.

| | $650 | $550 | $500 | $450 | $400 | $350 | $300 |

Last MSR was $554.

> Add $26 for Starvel finish.
> This model was never released for commercial sale.

MEGASTAR - 10mm or .45 ACP cal., larger variation of the Firestar featuring 4.6 in. barrel and 12 (.45 ACP) or 14 (10mm) shot mag., 47.6 oz. Imported 1992-94.

| | $450 | $375 | $350 | $325 | $295 | $275 | $250 |

Last MSR was $653.

> Add $29 for Starvel finish.

ULTRASTAR - 9mm Para. or .40 S&W (new 1996) cal., compact double action design, 3.57 in. barrel, 9 shot mag., blue steel metal, triple dot sights, steel internal mechanism, polymer exterior construction, 26 oz. Mfg. 1994-97.

| | $295 | $250 | $225 | $200 | $175 | $165 | $155 |

Last MSR was $296.

STEEL CITY ARMS, INC.

Previous manufacturer located in Pittsburgh, PA until 1990. In 1991, the name was changed to Desert Industries, Inc. and manufacture was moved to Las Vegas, NV. Very few guns exist with Steel City markings.

PISTOLS: SEMI-AUTO

DOUBLE DEUCE - .22 LR cal. only, double action, matte finish stainless steel, 2½ in. barrel, 7 shot mag., unchecked rosewood grips, 18 oz. Mfg. 1984-90.

| | $265 | $230 | $200 |

Last MSR was $290.

> Various select hardwood stocks were also available at extra cost ($20-100).

STERLING

Previous manufacturer located in Gasport and Lockport (1978-1986), NY until 1986.

PISTOLS

Rather than list individual models, the following generalizations will help in ascertaining values for this trademark. Models 300, 302 and 402 will average between $75 and $150 if in 70%+ condition, Models 283, 284, 285 (Husky), and 286 (Trapper) are semi-auto .22 cal. pistols with various barrel lengths - values will range between $90-$150. Models 400 (.380 ACP), PPL (.380 ACP short barrel), and 450 (.45 ACP, prototype only - no mfg.) usually range in the $150-$275 range.

Grading	100%	98%	95%	90%	80%	70%	60%

STERLING ARMAMENT, LTD.

Previous manufacturer established c. 1900, and located in Essex, England. Previously imported and distributed by Cassi Inc. located in Colorado Springs, CO until 1990.

CARBINES: SEMI-AUTO

AR-180 - .223 Rem. cal., side-folding stock. Disc.

	$850	$775	$695	$625	$550	$495	$450

STERLING MK 6 - 9mm Para. cal., blowback semi-auto with floating firing pin, shrouded 16.1 in. barrel, side mounted mag., folding stock, 7½ lbs.

	$595	$525	$475	$425	$375	$340	$310

Last MSR was $650.

PISTOLS; SEMI-AUTO

PARAPISTOL MK 7 C4 - 9mm Para. cal., 4 in. barrel, semi-auto paramilitary design pistol, crinkle finish, same action as MK. 6 Carbine, fires from closed bolt, 10, 15, 20, 30, 34 or 68 shot mag., 5 lbs.

	$500	$435	$375	$350	$325	$295	$265

Last MSR was $600.

PARAPISTOL MK 7 C8 - 9mm Para. cal., similar to C4, except has 7.8 in. barrel, 5¼ lbs.

	$525	$450	$390	$365	$330	$300	$275

Last MSR was $620.

STEVENS, J., ARMS COMPANY

J. Stevens Arms Company was founded in 1864 at Chicopee Falls, MA as J. Stevens & Co. In 1886 the name was changed to J. Stevens Arms and Tool Co. In 1916, the plant became New England Westinghouse, and tooled up for Mosin-Nagant Rifles. In 1920, the plant was sold to the Savage Arms Corp. and manufactured guns were marked "J. Stevens Arms Co.". This designation was dropped in the late 1940s, and only the name "Stevens" has been used up to 1990. Beginning in 1999, Savage Arms, Inc. began manufacturing the Stevens Favorite again as the Model 30G.

Depending on the remaining Stevens factory data, a factory letter authenticating the configuration of a particular specimen may be obtained by contacting Mr. John Callahan (see Trademark Index for listings and address). The charge for this service is $15.00 per gun - please allow 2-4 weeks for an adequate response.

For more Stevens model information, please refer to the Serialization section in the back of this text.

COMBINATION GUNS

MODEL 22-410 - .22 LR cal. over .410 bore, selector on right side of frame, Tenite stock. Introduced mid-1939 - disc.

	$165	$140	$120	$110	$100	$90	$80

PISTOLS

NO. 10 TARGET SINGLE SHOT - .22 LR cal., 8 in. barrel, blue, adj. sights, rubber grips, squared off like an automatic pistol, tip up action. Mfg. 1919-1939.

	$220	$200	$185	$165	$140	$120	$100

NO. 35 TARGET SINGLE SHOT - .22 LR or .25 Rimfire cal., 6, 8, 10, or 12¼ in. barrel, blue, walnut grips. Mfg. 1907-1939.

	$350	$300	$265	$220	$200	$185	$165

Grading	100%	98%	95%	90%	80%	70%	60%

NO. 35 "OFF-HAND" SHOTGUN - .410 smoothbore cal., 8 or 12¼ in. barrel. Mfg. 1923-1935.

	$350	$300	$250	$225	$200	$150	$125

If this model is not currently registered with the ATF, it cannot be legally owned, and is subject to seizure.

NO. 35 "OFF-HAND" AUTOSHOT - similar to Off-hand shotgun. Mfg. 1929-1934.

	$300	$250	$225	$200	$150	$125	$100

RIFLES

Stevens made a wide variety of inexpensive, utilitarian rifles that to date have attracted mostly shooting interest, but little collector interest. A listing of these models may be found in the back of this text under "Serialization".

TIP-UP RIFLES - .22 S, .22 LR, .25 Stevens, .32, .38, or .44 Long RF or CF, variations No. 1- No. 15 feature various weights, wood styles, sights, and other differences, later series has full loop at rear triggerguard, circa 1870s-1895.

* **Basic Model No. 1 without forearm**

	$500	$475	$425	$375	$300	$250	$200

* **Model 101** - .44 shot cartridge, built on the No. 12 Marksman action, lever action opening, straight grip stock, 26 in. barrel. Mfg. 1914-1920.

	$250	$225	$195	$175	$150	$125	$100

NO. 14 ½ LITTLE SCOUT - .22 RF cal., 18 or 20 in. barrel, rolling breech block action, iron sights. Mfg. 1909-1936.

	$250	$225	$195	$175	$150	$125	$100

POCKET RIFLES - detachable serially numbered nickel-plated stock, variations found within each frame size.

* **Small Frame** - .22 cal. (various issues).

	$450	$400	$350	$300	$275	$235	$200

* **Without Stock**

	$300	$250	$200	$150	$125	$100	$80

* **Medium Frame** - .22, .32, .38, .44 cals. (various issues).

	$500	$450	$400	$350	$300	$250	$200

* **Without Stock**

	$300	$250	$200	$150	$125	$100	$75

* **Large Frame** - .22 to .44 cals.

	$600	$550	$500	$450	$400	$350	$300

* **Without Stock**

	$425	$375	$325	$275	$225	$200	$175

MODEL 44 IDEAL SINGLE SHOT - .22 LR through .44-40 WCF cals., rolling block, lever action, takedown, 24 or 26 in. barrels, straight grip stock and forearm. Mfg. 1894- 1932.

	$600	$550	$500	$425	$325	$300	$275

Subtract 20% for Rimfire cals.

MODEL 44½ IDEAL SINGLE SHOT - similar to Model 44, except .22 LR through .44-40 WCF cals., falling block, lever action, takedown, 24 or 26 in. barrels, straight grip stock and forearm, action redesigned 1903. Mfg. 1903-1916.

	$850	$775	$675	$575	$500	$425	$350

MODELS 45-54 SINGLE SHOTS - .22 LR through .44-40 WCF cals., rolling and falling block receivers, lever action, takedown, deluxe versions of the Models 44 and 44½, many special order features, including double set triggers, types of finish, engraving, length and weight of barrels, stock configuration could be special ordered. The higher grade Schuetzens and Stevens-Pope are very collectible and command premiums. These models have to be taken one at a time for determining value. Therefore, no prices are shown. Mfg. 1896-1916.

Grading	100%	98%	95%	90%	80%	70%	60%

MODEL 322 BOLT ACTION (INCLUDING A, B, C & S) - .22 Hornet cal., otherwise similar to Model 325. Mfg. 1947-1950.

| | $450 | $395 | $335 | $275 | $225 | $185 | $150 |

The Model 322S had an apeture sight.

MODEL 325 BOLT ACTION (INCLUDING A, B, C) - .30-30 Win. cal., 4 shot detachable mag., introduced 1947 - disc. 1950.

| | $375 | $335 | $275 | $225 | $185 | $150 | $135 |

NO. 414 ARMORY MODEL - .22 LR or .22 Short cal. only, lever action, 26 in. barrel, single shot, Lyman aperture sight. Mfg. 1912-1932.

| | $450 | $400 | $375 | $330 | $290 | $250 | $220 |

MODEL 416 - .22 LR cal., bolt action, 25 in. medium barrel, 5 shot mag. Disc.

| | $140 | $120 | $110 | $100 | $90 | $80 | $70 |

This model was also mfg. as a U.S. military training rifle. Can be denoted by "U.S. Property" on rear of bolt housing. Healthy premiums exist for this variation. Originally, 10,000 were mfg. at a cost of $22.42 each.

NO. 417 WALNUT HILL MODEL - .22 LR, .22 Short, and .22 Hornet cal., lever action, 28 or 29 in. extra heavy barrel, target stock with full pistol grip, beavertail forend, made in 0-3 suffix variations (different sights). Mfg. 1932-1947.

| | $875 | $675 | $525 | $475 | $440 | $395 | $360 |

NO. 417½ WALNUT HILL MODEL - similar to No. 417, except available in .25 rimfire also. Mfg. 1932-1940.

| | $875 | $675 | $525 | $475 | $440 | $395 | $360 |

NO. 418 WALNUT HILL MODEL - .22 LR or .22 Short only, 26 in. barrel, pistol grip stock, semi beavertail forearm. Mfg. 1932-1940.

| | $595 | $400 | $295 | $260 | $230 | $200 | $180 |

NO. 425 HIGH POWER LEVER ACTION RIFLE - .25, .30, .32, or .35 Rem. cals., 22 in. round barrel with 2/3 length mag. tube, side ejection, blue only, plain walnut stock and forearm, originally designed by John Redfield. Approx. 26,000 mfg. 1910-1917.

| | $650 | $595 | $535 | $465 | $400 | $350 | $295 |

Variations of the No. 425 include the No. 430 (deluxe checkered stock and forearm), No. 435 (extra fancy checkered stock and forearm with engraved designs on receiver borders and lever), or No. 440 (best quality checkered walnut with fully engraved game scenes, and engraved forearm tip and lever). Values range respectively from $450-$950, $650-$1,400, and $1,000-$2,950.

STEVENS FAVORITE NO.'S 17-29 - .22 LR, .25 RF or .32 RF cal., 24 in. barrel most common, other lengths available, Rocky Mountain front sight, straight grip stock, small tapered forearm. Mfg. 1894-1935. Octagonal barrels command a 33% premium.

| | $195 | $165 | $145 | $125 | $100 | $80 | $65 |

STEVENS FAVORITE MODEL 30G/30GM - .22 LR or .22 Mag. (Model GM, new 2002) cal., lever action falling block with inertia firing pin, new mfg. began in late 1998 by Savage Arms, Inc., 21 in. half octagon (Model 30G) or full octagon (Model GM) barrel, uncheckered wood stock and forearm, open sights, 4¼ lbs. New 1998.

| MSR $214 | $175 | $150 | $130 | $110 | $100 | $80 | $65 |

Add $37 for .22 Mag. cal. (new 2002).

STEVENS MODEL 65 - .22 LR cal., bolt action, 20 in. barrel, open sights, 5 shot mag., checkered walnut stock. Mfg. 1969-disc.

| | $90 | $70 | $55 | $45 | $35 | $30 | $30 |

NO. 70 "VISIBLE LOADING" SLIDE ACTION RIFLE - .22 S, L, or LR cal., exposed hammer, 22 in. barrel, open sights, straight grip stock, tube mag., grooved slide handle. Other variations with different barrel lengths and sights will command slight premiums.

| | $250 | $175 | $150 | $130 | $115 | $100 | $90 |

Grading	100%	98%	95%	90%	80%	70%	60%

MODEL 71 "STEVENS FAVORITE" COMMEMORATIVE - .22 LR cal., replica of original, 22 in. octagon barrel, plain straight stock, medallion inlaid, crescent butt. 1,000 mfg. in 1971.

	$250	$195	$150				

Last MSR was $75.

SIDE LEVER CRACKSHOT - .22 RF or .32 RF cal., boys type single shot rifle, breech block is operated by a small lever on the side of the frame, side lever opening, 20 in. round barrel with fixed sights. Mfg. 1898-1910.

	$250	$225	$195	$175	$150	$125	$100

NO. 26 CRACKSHOT - .22 RF or .32 RF cal., boys type single shot rifle, under lever opening, 18 in. round barrel, hardwood straight grip stock and forend, open sights. Mfg. 1913-1941.

	$250	$225	$195	$175	$150	$125	$100

MODEL 72 CRACKSHOT - .22 LR cal., single shot falling block action, 22 in. octagon barrel, open sights, color case hardened frame, straight stock. Mfg. 1972-1989.

	$145	$125	$110	$100	$90	$80	$70

Last MSR was $165.

MODEL 74 - similar to Model 72 Crackshot, except has round barrel. Mfg. 1972-1989.

	$140	$120	$110	$100	$90	$80	$70

Last MSR was $165.

MODEL 987 - .22 LR cal. only, semi-auto, 15 shot tube mag., 20 in. barrel, hardwood Monte Carlo stock, adj. rear sight, 6 lbs. Disc. 1989.

	$95	$80	$70	$60	$50	$40	$45

Last MSR was $119.

MODEL 89 LEVER ACTION - .22 LR cal., single shot, 18½ in. barrel, Martini type action, Western style lever, straight stock. Mfg. 1976-disc.

	$85	$65	$60	$50	$45	$40	$35

SHOTGUNS

Stevens made a wide variety of inexpensive, utilitarian shotguns that to date have attracted mostly shooting interest, but little collector interest. A listing of these models may be found in the back of this text under "Serialization".

NO. 20 FAVORITE - .22 RF or .32 RF smooth bore, 24 in. barrel, smooth bore variation of the No. 17 rifle.

	$225	$175	$150	$125	$95	$85	$75

NO. 26½ CRACKSHOT - .22 RF or .32 RF smooth bore, smooth bore variation of the No. 26 rifle.

	$175	$150	$125	$95	$85	$75	$65

NO. 200 SLIDE ACTION - 20 ga., 3 in. chamber, tube mag., 26, 28, 30, or 32 in. barrel, takedown, 5 shot, 6½ lbs., c. 1910.

	$225	$190	$180	$150	$125	$95	$85

MODEL 520 SLIDE ACTION - this model was designed by John M. Browning, slight humpback in receiver.

	$190	$180	$150	$125	$95	$85	$75

MODEL 520-30 TRENCH/RIOT MILITARY SHOTGUNS - see the "Trench/Riot Shotgun" category in the T section for more information and prices.

MODEL 620 SLIDE ACTION - an improved version of the Model 520 with streamlined receiver.

	$325	$290	$250	$225	$175	$150	$100

MODEL 620 TRENCH/RIOT MILITARY SHOTGUNS - see the "Trench/ Riot Shotgun" category in the T section for more information and prices.

Grading	100%	98%	95%	90%	80%	70%	60%

MODEL 77 SLIDE ACTION W/ J, K, M, OR SC SUFFIX - 12 (J suffix), 16 (K suffix), or 20 (M suffix)ga. or .410 bore, "SC" designates Super Choke.

	$175	$160	$140	$120	$100	$80	$60

MODEL 124 SLIDE ACTION - 12 ga. only, straight pull action, 28 in. barrel, 3 shot, Tenite butt stock and forearm, circa 1950.

	$215	$190	$175	$155	$145	$135	$125

MODEL 67 SLIDE ACTION - 12, 20 ga., or .410 bore, all are 3 in. chambered, steel receiver, 5 shot, upper receiver safety, 6¼ - 7½ lbs. Recent mfg. by Stevens. Disc. 1989.

	$200	$180	$170	$155	$145	$135	$125

Last MSR was $229.

Add $30 for choke tubes (with VR).
Add $10 for VR only.

* **Model 67 VTR-K Camo** - 12 or 20 ga., 28 in. VR barrel with choke tubes, laminated camo stock. Mfg. 1986-1988.

	$250	$220	$190	$170	$155	$145	$135

Last MSR was $295.

* **Slug Model** - 12 ga. only, 21 in. barrel, rifle sights. Disc. 1989.

	$200	$165	$140	$110	$100	$90	$80

Last MSR was $245.

* **Model 67 VRT-Y** - 20 ga. only, 22 in. VR barrel with choke tubes, youth model with smaller stock dimensions. Mfg. 1987-1988.

	$205	$170	$140	$110	$100	$90	$80

Last MSR was $259.

MODEL 675 SLIDE ACTION - 12 ga. only, 24 in. VR multi-choked barrel with iron sights (including removable rear ramp), hardwood stock with recoil pad, 6½ lbs. Mfg. 1987-1988.

	$250	$220	$190	$170	$155	$145	$135

Last MSR was $295.

MODEL 240 O/U - .410 bore, split hammers, double trigger.

	$350	$300	$250	$220	$190	$170	$155

MODEL 69-RXL SLIDE ACTION - 12 ga. only, law enforcement version of the Model 67, 18¼ in. cylinder bore barrel with recoil pad, 6½ lbs. Disc. 1989.

	$200	$165	$140	$110	$100	$90	$80

Last MSR was $245

MODEL 311 SxS - 12, 16, 20 ga., or .410 bore, 3 in. chambers, double triggers, extractors, VR. Disc. 1989.

	$245	$205	$185	$150	$140	$125	$115

Last MSR was $309.

Add 30% for .410 bore.
Add 20% for 16 or 20 ga.

* **Model 311-R** - 12 ga. only, similar to Model 311, except has 18¼ in. cylinder bore barrels for law enforcement use, 3 in. chambers, 6¾ lbs. Disc. 1989.

	$245	$205	$185	$150	$140	$125	$115

Last MSR was $309.

MODEL 315 SxS - 12, 16, 20 ga. or .410 bore, DT, extractors, hammerless, case colored frame, walnut stock and forearm, model identification is on top lever, this model also was mfg. under various trade names, including Riverside and Springfield.

	$225	$185	$150	$140	$125	$115	$100

FOX/STEVENS MODEL B SxS - 12, 16, 20 ga., or .410 bore, double triggers, VR, extractors, 24, 26, 28, or 30 in. barrels, 7 lbs. Disc. 1986.

	$315	$280	$240	$220	$200	$180	$160

Last MSR was $369.

Add 25% for BDE Model (with ejectors).

Grading	100%	98%	95%	90%	80%	70%	60%

FOX/STEVENS MODEL B-SE SxS - 12, 16, 20 ga., or .410 bore, single trigger, selective ejectors, VR, beavertail forearm, select walnut. Disc. 1989.

	$415	$370	$325	$280	$240	$210	$180

Last MSR was $525.

Add 20% for .410 bore.

MODEL 94 - 12, 16, 20, 28 ga., or .410 bore, single shot breakopen, hammer, 6¼ lbs. Mfg. 1929-disc.

	$95	$85	$75	$60	$50	$45	$40

Last MSR was $92.

MODEL 9478 - 10, 12, 20 ga., or .410 bore, single shot break open, inertia firing pin, external hammer. Mfg. 1978-1985.

	$95	$85	$75	$60	$50	$45	$40

STEYR AUSTRIAN MILITARY

Previously manufactured for the Austrian military in Steyr, Austria.

RIFLES: BOLT ACTION

MODEL 95 RIFLE - 8x50R Mannlicher cal., straight pull bolt action, 30 in. barrel, adj. sights, military full stock.

	$140	$110	$100	$85	$65	$55	$40

MODEL 90 CARBINE - similar to Model 95, except 19½ in. barrel.

	$155	$125	$110	$95	$85	$65	$45

STEYR DAIMLER PUCH A.G.

Previous manufacturer located in Steyr, Austria 1911 to circa 1960.

PISTOLS

POCKET AUTO - .25 ACP or .32 ACP cal., tip up barrel, mag. fed. Disc.

	$325	$265	$200	$150	$140	$130	$120

Add 10% for .32 ACP cal.

ROTH STEYR AUTO (MODEL 1907) - 8mm Steyr cal.

	$850	$650	$475	$350	$300	$250	$200

Add 30% for "Budapest" markings.

STEYR-HAHN MODEL 1911 AUTOMATIC - 9mm Steyr cal., 8 shot, 5.1 in. barrel, fixed magazine top loaded by stripper clip, blue, checkered wood grips. Mfg. 1911-1919. In 1938, the Germans confiscated and converted a quantity of these to 9mm Para., "08" was stamped on the left side of these guns.

	$450	$375	$325	$275	$225	$195	$175

Add 100% if marked "08" or with Rumanian Crest.

MODEL SP - .32 ACP cal., semi-auto, trigger cocking mechanism, very rare - mfg. in 1959 only.

	$650	$595	$540	$495	$450	$400	$350

STEYR MANNLICHER

Currently manufactured by Steyr-Mannlicher AG & Co. KG in Austria. Founded by Ferdinand Ritter Von Mannlicher and Otto Schoenauer in 1903. Previously imported and distributed by Gun South, Inc. located in Trussville, AL.

Note: also see Mannlicher Schoenauer in the M section for pre- WWII models. For more information and current pricing on both new and used Steyr airguns, please refer to the 2nd Edition Blue Book of Modern Airguns by Dr. Robert Beeman & John Allen (now online also).

S

Grading	100%	98%	95%	90%	80%	70%	60%

PISTOLS: SEMI-AUTO

As this edition went to press, GSI had limited quantites of the following Steyr models available.

MODEL GB - 9mm Para. cal., double action, 18 shot mag., gas delayed blowback action, non-glare checkered plastic grips, 5¼ in. barrel with Polygon rifling, matte finish, steel construction, 2 lbs. 6 oz. Importation disc. 1988.

	100%	98%	95%	90%	80%	70%	60%
Commercial	$600	$525	$475	$425	$375	$335	$300
Military	$550	$450	$395	$350	$300	$280	$260

Last MSR was $514.

In 1987, Steyr mfg. a military variation of the Model GB featuring a phosphate finish - only 937 were imported into the U.S.

MODEL SPP - 9mm Para. cal., single action semi-auto, delayed blow back system with rotating 5.9 in. barrel, 15 or 30 shot mag., utilizes synthetic materials and advanced ergonomics, adj. sights, grooved receiver for scope mounting, matte black finish, 44 oz. Limited importation 1992-93.

	$800	$675	$600	$550	$495	$450	$400

Last MSR was $895.

MODEL M - 9mm Para., .357 SIG, or .40 S&W cal., features first integrated limited access key lock safety in a semi-auto pistol, 3 different safety conditions, black synthetic frame, 10 shot mag., matte black finish, loaded chamber indicator, triangle/trapezoid sights, 28 oz. New 1999.

MSR	$610		$550	$500	$460	$420	$385	$350	$325

MODEL S - similar to Model M, except has 3.5 in. barrel and shorter grip frame, 10 shot mag., 22½ oz. New 2000.

MSR	$610		$550	$500	$460	$420	$385	$350	$325

RIFLES: BOLT ACTION, RECENT PRODUCTION

Current production guns are now called Steyr-Mannlicher models. For models manufactured 1903-1971, please refer to the Mannlicher Schoenauer Sporting Rifles section in this text.

The recenty discontinued models SL, L, M, S, and S/T listed have 4 different action lengths and model designations stand for the following: SL=Super Light, L=Light, M=Medium, S=Magnum, S/T=Magnum with heavy barrel. These sporting rifles were available with left-hand stock - add $109 and with either single set or double set triggers - add $125.

ZEPHYR 22 - .22 LR cal., features full length Mannlicher stock, single or double set triggers, open sights, checkered walnut stock with horn cap, sling swivels. Mfg. circa 1955- 1971.

	$1,350	$1,200	$1,000	$850	$725	$600	$525

MODEL M72 L/M RIFLE - .243 Win., .308 Win., .270 Win., .30-06, 7x57mm, and 7x64mm cals., 23 in. barrel, single or double set triggers. Mfg. 1972-1980.

	$795	$725	$650	$575	$500	$460	$420

MODEL SL - .222 Rem.,.222 Rem. Mag. (disc.), .223 Rem., .22-250 Rem. (disc. 1992), or 5.6x50mm (disc. 1991) cal., bolt action, 23.6 in. barrel, double set triggers, rotary mag. Available in full- stock (Carbine), half stock (rifle), or varmint version (vent. square forearm). Disc. 1996.

	$1,875	$1,325	$950	$775	$675	$600	$540

Last MSR was $2,250.

* ***Carbine Model (Full Stock)*** - skipline checkered full stock, 20 in. barrel. Disc. 1996.

	$1,995	$1,400	$995	$825	$700	$600	$540

Last MSR was $2,450.

S

Grading	100%	98%	95%	90%	80%	70%	60%

* **Varmint Rifle** - .222 Rem. (disc.), .223 Rem. (new 1993), or .22-250 Rem. (disc. 1992) cal., 26 in. heavy barrel, stippled pistol grip, vent. forearm, no sights. Disc. 1996.

	$1,995	$1,400	$995	$825	$700	$600	$540

Last MSR was $2,450.

MODEL L - 5.6x57mm (disc. 1991), .243 Win., or .308 Win. cals., available in .22-250 and 6mm Rem. on special order only, otherwise same general specifications as Model SL. Disc. 1996.

	$1,875	$1,325	$950	$775	$675	$600	$540

Last MSR was $2,250.

* **Carbine Model (Full Stock)** - skip-line checkered full stock, 20 in. barrel. Disc. 1996.

	$1,995	$1,400	$995	$825	$700	$600	$540

Last MSR was $2,450.

* **Varmint Rifle** - .222 Rem. (disc. 1991), .22-250 Rem., .243 Win. (disc.), or .308 Win. (disc.) cal., 26 in. heavy barrel, stippled pistol grip, vent. forearm, no sights. Disc. 1996.

	$1,995	$1,400	$995	$825	$700	$600	$540

Last MSR was $2,450.

* **Model L Luxus** - 5.6x57mm, .243 Win., or .308 Win. cal., full or half stock only, .22-250 Rem. and 6mm Rem. available on special order, 3 shot mag. Disc. 1996.

	$2,495	$1,750	$1,325	$1,000	$800	$700	$650

Last MSR was $2,950.

* **Model L Luxus Carbine (Full Stock)** - similar to L Luxus rifle, except has full stock and 20 in. barrel. Disc. 1996.

	$2,625	$1,825	$1,350	$1,025	$800	$700	$650

Last MSR was $3,150.

MODEL M - 6.5x55mm, 6.5x57mm, 7x64mm, .270 Win., .30-06, or 9.3x62mm cal., bolt action, full stock or half stock, rotary mag., double set triggers. Disc. 1996.

	$1,875	$1,325	$950	$775	$675	$600	$540

Last MSR was $2,250.

Add $400 for left-hand action.

* **Carbine Model (Full Stock)** - skipline checkered full stock, 20 in. barrel. Disc. 1996.

	$1,995	$1,400	$995	$825	$700	$600	$540

Last MSR was $2,450.

Add $400 for left-hand action.

* **Professional Rifle** - .270 Win., 7x57mm (disc. 1991), 7x64mm, .30-06, or 9.3x62mm cal., 23.6 in. barrel, Cycolac synthetic stock, 7½ lbs. Disc. 1993.

	$1,500	$1,025	$850	$700	$600	$540	$495

Last MSR was $1,710.

Add $469 for left hand action with half stock (rifle).
Add $625 for left hand action with full stock (carbine).
This variation is also available in .270 Win. or .30-06 cal. with half stock and 20 in. barrel (carbine).

* **Model M Luxus** - 6.5x55mm, 6.5x57mm (disc.), 7x64mm, .270 Win., or .30-06 cal., special order in 6.5x55mm and 7.5mm Swiss. Disc. 1996.

	$2,495	$1,750	$1,325	$1,000	$800	$700	$650

Last MSR was $2,950.

* **Model M Luxus Carbine (Full Stock)** - similar to Model M Luxus, except with full stock and 20 in. barrel. Disc. 1996.

	$2,625	$1,825	$1,350	$1,025	$800	$700	$650

Last MSR was $3,150.

* **Carbine - 1000 Year Commemorative** - 1984 only, .30-06 cal.

	$4,200	$3,620	$2,835

S

Grading	100%	98%	95%	90%	80%	70%	60%

M-III PROFESSIONAL - .25-06 Rem. (new 1996), .270 Win., .30-06, or 7x64mm cal., features black synthetic half stock, 23.6 in. barrel, no sights. Imported 1994-1996.

	$900	$800	$700	$600	$525	$450	$375

Last MSR was $995.

Add $130 for stippled checkered European wood stock.

JAGD MATCH - .222 Rem., .243 Win., or .308 Win. cal., features shortened action, 23.6 in. heavy barrel with iron sights, 5 shot rotary mag., laminated checkered half- stock, recoil pad, designed for European Match events limited to hunting rifles, double set triggers, 8½ lbs. Imported 1995-1996.

	$2,025	$1,375	$1,025	$825	$675	$600	$540

Last MSR was $2,450.

MODEL S (MAGNUM) - 6.5x68mm, 8x68S, .300 Win. Mag., .338 Win. Mag. (disc. 1992), .375 H&H, or 7mm Rem. Mag. cal., half-stock, 26 in. barrel, bolt action. Disc. 1996.

	$2,075	$1,400	$1,050	$850	$725	$625	$550

Last MSR was $2,550.

MODEL S/T - available in 9.3x64 (disc. 1992), .300 H&H, .375 H&H, or .458 Win. Mag. cal., half-stock, 26 in. heavy barrel. Disc. 1996.

	$2,325	$1,575	$1,125	$925	$775	$675	$595

Last MSR was $2,850.

* **Tropical Rifle** - .300 H&H, .375 H&H and .458 Win. Mag. cals., 26 in. heavy barrel. Disc. 1985.

	$1,150	$900	$810	$730	$660	$600	$550

Last MSR was $1,332.

* **Luxus S** - available in 6.5x68mm, 8x68S, 7mm Rem. Mag., or .300 Win. Mag. cal., 26 in. barrel, half-stock only, 3 shot mag., 8 lbs. Disc. 1996.

	$2,700	$1,900	$1,475	$1,125	$875	$750	$675

Last MSR was $3,250.

STEYR SCOUT PACKAGE - .223 Rem. (new 2000), .243 Win. (mfg. 2000 only), .308 Win., 7mm-08 Rem. (new 2000), or .376 Steyr (mfg. 1999-2000) cal., designed by Jeff Cooper, features black synthetic Zytel stock, 19¼ in. fluted barrel, Picatinny optic rail, integral bipod, includes Leupold M8 2.5x28 IER scope with factory Steyr mounts, and luggage case. New 1998.

	MSR	$2,699						
			$2,150	$1,825	$1,625	$1,325	$1,100	$995	$875

Add $100 for .376 Steyr cal. (disc. 2000).
Add $100 for Jeff Cooper grey stock.

* **Steyr Scout Jeff Cooper Package** - .308 Win. or .376 Steyr (disc. 2000) cal., grey synthetic Zytel stock with Jeff Cooper logo and integral bipod, certificate of authenticity with test target, includes Leupold M8 2.5x28 IER scope with factory Steyr mounts, and luggage case. New 1999.

	MSR	$2,699						
			$2,150	$1,825	$1,625	$1,325	$1,100	$995	$875

Add $100 for .376 Steyr cal. (disc. 2000).

* **Steyr Scout** - .243 Win. cal., similar to Jeff Cooper Package, except does not include scope, mounts, or case. New 1999.

	MSR	$1,969						
			$1,525	$1,350	$1,200	$1,050	$900	$750	$625

Add $100 for .376 Steyr cal. (black stock only, disc. 2000).
Add $100 for Jeff Cooper grey stock.

* **Steyr Scout Tactical** - .223 Rem. (new 2000) or .308 Win. cal., similar to Steyr Scout, except has black synthetic stock with removable spacers, oversized bolt handle, and emergency ghost ring sights. New 1999.

	MSR	$2,069						
			$1,600	$1,400	$1,250	$1,050	$900	$750	$625

S

Grading	100%	98%	95%	90%	80%	70%	60%

◇**Steyr Scout Tactical Stainless** - similar to Steyr Scout Tactical, except has stainless steel barrel. New 2000.

MSR $2,159	$1,650	$1,425	$1,150				

SBS PROHUNTER MODEL

SBS PROHUNTER MODEL - .243 Win., .25-06 Rem., .260 Rem. (new 2000), .270 Win., .280 Rem. (new 2000), .30-06, .308 Win., 7mm-08 Rem., 6.5x55mm, 6.5x57mm (disc. 1999), 7x64mm (disc. 1999), or 9.3x62mm (disc. 1999) cal., features safe bolt system (SBS), detachable mag., black synthetic or camo (new 2000) stock, matte blue finish, 23.6 in. barrel without sights. New 1997.

MSR $769	$700	$635	$565	$500	$450	$395	$350

Add $60 for camo stock (new 2000).

✳ *SBS ProHunter Magnum* - .300 Win. Mag., 7mm Rem. Mag., 6.5x68mm (disc. 1999), or 8x68S (disc. 1999) cal., similar to SBS Pro Hunter Model, except has 25.6 in. barrel. New 1997.

MSR $799	$720	$650	$580	$515	$455	$395	$350

Add $60 for camo stock (new 2000).
Add $150 for metric cals (disc.).

✳ *SBS ProHunter SS* - similar to SBS ProHunter, except has stainless steel barrel with matte finish. New 2000.

MSR $859	$735	$645	$575				

Add $60 for camo stock (new 2000).

◇**SBS ProHunter SS Magnum** - similar to SBS ProHunter Magnum, except has stainless steel barrel with matte finish. New 2000.

MSR $889	$760	$665	$585				

Add $60 for camo stock (new 2000).

✳ *SBS ProHunter .376 Steyr* - .376 Steyr cal. only, 20 in. barrel with iron sights, black synthetic or camo (new 2000) stock, matte blue finish. New 1999.

MSR $859	$740	$650	$575	$500	$450	$395	$350

Add $60 for camo.

✳ *SBS ProHunter Compact (Youth/Ladies) Rifle* - .243 Win., .260 Rem. (new 2000) 7mm-08 Rem., or .308 Win. cal., shortened stock with 2 butt spacers for adj. length, 20 in. barrel with iron sights, matte blue finish. New 1999.

MSR $819	$710	$640	$570	$500	$450	$395	$350

✳ *SBS ProHunter Compact (Youth/Ladies) SS* - similar to ProHunter Compact, except has stainless steel barrel with matte finish. New 2000.

MSR $909	$780	$675	$600				

✳ *SBS ProHunter Mountain Rifle* - .243 Win., .25-06 Rem., .260 Rem. (new 2000), .270 Win., .30- 06, .308 Win., 7mm-08 Rem., or 6.5x55mm (new 2000) cal., 20 in. barrel, no sights, matte blue finish, black or camo (new 2000) synthetic stock, detachable mag. New 1999.

MSR $769	$680	$615	$565	$510	$450	$395	$350

Add $60 for camo stock.

✳ *SBS ProHunter Mountain Rifle SS* - similar to ProHunter Mountain Rifle, except has stainless steel barrel with matte finish. New 2000.

MSR $859	$740	$655	$575				

Add $60 for camo stock.

SBS FORESTER MODEL

SBS FORESTER MODEL - similar to SBS Pro Hunter Model, except has wood stock and standard blue finish. New 1997.

MSR $799	$695	$630	$575	$510	$450	$395	$350

S

Grading	100%	98%	95%	90%	80%	70%	60%

✳ SBS Forester Mountain Rifle - .243 Win., .25-06 Rem., .260 Rem. (new 2000), .270 Win., .30- 06, .308 Win., 7mm-08 Rem., 6.5x55mm (new 2000) cal., 20 in. barrel, no sights, matte blue finish, checkered walnut stock, detachable mag. New 1999.

	MSR	$829	$720	$635	$565	$510	$450	$395	$350

✳ SBS Forester Magnum - .300 Win. Mag., 7mm Rem. Mag., 6.5x68mm (disc. 1999), or 8x68S (disc. 1999) cal., similar to SBS Forester Model, except has 25.6 in. barrel. New 1997.

	MSR	$829	$720	$635	$565	$510	$450	$395	$350

SBS CLASSIC AMERICAN - .243 Win., .25-06 Rem., .260 Rem., .270 Win., .280 Rem., .30-06, .308 Win., 7mm-08 Rem., or 6.5x55mm cal., features deluxe checkered walnut stock with full pistol grip and forend cap, deep blue finish, 23.6 in. barrel with exterior hammer forged swirls, no sights. New 2000.

	MSR	$1,549	$1,360	$1,140	$935	$830	$725	$600	$550

✳ SBS Classic American Magnum - .300 Win. Mag. or 7mm Rem. Mag. cal., 25.6 in. barrel. New 2000.

	MSR	$1,579	$1,380	$1,155	$945	$830	$725	$600	$550

✳ SBS Classic Mannlicher - similar to SBS Classic American, also available in 7x57mm Mauser cal., has deluxe full length stock and 20 in. barrel with sights. New 2000.

	MSR	$1,749	$1,510	$1,225	$1,000	$860	$750	$625	$575

SBS TACTICAL - .308 Win. cal. only, 20 in. barrel w/o sights, features oversized bolt handle and high capacity 10 shot mag. with adapter, matte blue finish. New 1999.

	MSR	$969	$840	$735	$625	$550	$500	$450	$395

✳ SBS Tactical Heavy Barrel - .300 Win. Mag. (new 2000) or .308 Win. cal., features 20 (carbine, new 2000, .308 Win. only) or 26 in. heavy barrel w/o sights and oversized bolt handle, matte blue finish or stainless steel (carbine only, new 2000). New 1999.

	MSR	$1,019	$865	$745	$635	$550	$500	$450	$395

Add $30 for .300 Win. Mag. cal.
Add $40 for stainless steel.

✳ SBS Tactical McMillan - similar to SBS Tactical Heavy barrel, except has custom McMillan A- 3 stock with adj. cheekpiece and oversized bolt handle, matte blue finish. New 1999.

	MSR	$1,669	$1,465	$1,245	$1,035	$850	$725	$600	$550

Add $30 for .300 Win. Mag. cal.

✳ SBS Tactical CISM - .308 Win. cal., 20 in. heavy barrel w/o sights, laminated wood stock with black lacquer finish, adj. cheekpiece and buttplate, 10 shot detachable mag., vent. forend. New 2000.

	MSR	$3,499	$3,050	$2,650	$2,300	$1,950	$1,600	$1,300	$1,150

This model was also available as a Swiss contract CISM Match in 7.5x55mm cal. with match diopter sights and 23½ in. barrel. Only 100 were imported. NIB Prices are in the $1,850 range.

SBS TACTICAL ELITE - .223 Rem. or .308 Win. cal., 20 (carbine) or 26 in. barrel with full length Picatinny spec mounting rail, oversize bolt handle, two 5 shot detachable mags. (with spare buttstock storage), adj. black synthetic stock, matte blue finish or stainless steel. New 2000.

	MSR	$2,399	$2,050	$1,750	$1,450	$1,225	$1,025	$850	$750

Add $100 for 26 in. stainless steel barrel.
Add $1,100 for heavy barrel package (includes factory installed ZF optic).

MANNLICHER SBS EUROPEAN MODEL - .243 Win., .25-06 Rem., .270 Win., .30-06 (disc. 1998), .308 Win., 7mm-08 Rem., 6.5x55mm, 6.5x57mm, 7x64mm, 7.5x55mm, or 9.3x62mm cal., features safe bolt system (SBS), 23.6 in. barrel with sights, checkered walnut stock and forearm. Mfg. 1997-99.

	$2,300	$1,850	$1,600	$1,325	$1,100	$925	$850

Last MSR was $2,795.

S

Grading	100%	98%	95%	90%	80%	70%	60%

* **Mannlicher SBS Magnum European Model** - .300 Win. Mag., 7mm Rem. Mag., 6.5x68mm, or 8x68S cal., 25.6 in. barrel with sights, checkered walnut stock and forearm. Mfg. 1997-99.

| | $2,375 | $1,900 | $1,625 | $1,350 | $1,100 | $925 | $850 |

Last MSR was $2,895.

* **Mannlicher SBS European Model** - "Goiserer" - similar to Mannlicher SBS European Model, except has 20 in. barrel. Mfg. 1997-99.

| | $2,500 | $2,000 | $1,650 | $1,350 | $1,100 | $925 | $850 |

Last MSR was $2,995.

* **Mannlicher SBS European Model** - Full Stock - similar to Mannlicher SBS European Model, except has full-length Mannlicher stock. Mfg. 1997-99.

| | $2,500 | $2,000 | $1,650 | $1,350 | $1,100 | $925 | $850 |

Last MSR was $2,995.

MODEL SSG - .243 Win. (disc., PII Sniper only) or .308 Win cal., for competition or law-enforcement use. Marksman has regular sights, rotary mag., teflon coated bolt with heavy duty locking lugs, synthetic stock has removable spacers, parkerized finish. Match version has heavier target barrel and "match" bolt carrier, can be used as single shot. Extremely accurate.

* **PI Rifle** - 26 in. barrel, 3 shot mag., black or green ABS Cycolac synthetic stock.

| MSR | $1,699 | $1,525 | $1,300 | $1,100 | $975 | $850 | $725 | $600 |

Add 15% for walnut stock (disc. 1992, retail was $448).

* **PII/PIIK Sniper Rifle** - .243 Win. (disc.) or .308 Win. cal., 20 in. heavy (Model PIIK) or 26 in. heavy barrel, no sights, green or black synthetic Cycolac or McMillian black fiberglass stock, modified bolt handle, choice of single or set triggers.

| MSR | $1,699 | $1,525 | $1,300 | $1,100 | $975 | $850 | $725 | $600 |

Add $600 for black McMillian fiberglass stock.
Add 15% for walnut stock (disc. 1992, retail was $448).

* **PIII Rifle** - .308 Win. cal., 26 in. heavy barrel with diopter match sight bases, H-S Precision Pro-Series stock in black only. Importation 1991-93.

| | $2,600 | $1,875 | $1,425 | $1,050 | $825 | $700 | $600 |

Last MSR was $3,162.

* **PIV (Urban Rifle)** - .308 Win. cal., carbine variation with 16½ in. heavy barrel and flash hider, ABS Cycolac synthetic stock in green or black. Importation began 1991.

| MSR | $2,659 | $2,285 | $1,625 | $1,275 | $975 | $775 | $700 | $650 |

* **Jagd Match** - .222 Rem., .243 Win., or .308 Win. cal., hunting rifle that features checkered wood laminate stock, 23.6 in. barrel, Mannlicher sights, double set triggers, supplied with test target. Mfg. 1991-92.

| | $1,550 | $1,050 | $950 | $800 | $675 | $600 | $540 |

Last MSR was $1,550.

* **Match Rifle** - .308 Win. only, 26 in. heavy barrel, brown ABS Cycolac stock, Walther Diopter sights, 8.6 lbs. Mfg. disc. 1992.

| | $2,000 | $1,500 | $1,225 | $925 | $800 | $700 | $600 |

Last MSR was $2,306.

Add $437 for walnut stock.

* **Model SPG-T** - .308 Win. cal., Target model. Mfg. 1993-98.

| | $3,225 | $2,850 | $2,550 | $2,200 | $1,850 | $1,500 | $1,200 |

Last MSR was $3,695.

* **Model SPG-CISM** - .308 Win. cal., 20 in. heavy barrel, laminated wood stock with adj. cheek-piece and black lacquer finish. Mfg. 1993-99.

| | $2,995 | $2,600 | $2,300 | $1,950 | $1,700 | $1,450 | $1,200 |

Last MSR was $3,295.

S

Grading	100%	98%	95%	90%	80%	70%	60%

✱ Match UIT - .308 Win. cal. only, 10 shot steel mag., special single set trigger, free floating barrel, Diopter sights, raked bolt handle, 10.8 lbs. Disc. 1998.

$3,600	$3,150	$2,750	$2,400	$2,050	$1,700	$1,400

Last MSR was $3,995.

UIT stands for Union Internationale de Tir.

RIFLES: SEMI-AUTO

AUG S.A. - .223 Rem. cal., semi-auto paramilitary design rifle, design incorporates use of advanced plastics, integral Swarovski scope, 16, 20, or 24 in. barrel, bullpup configuration, 7.9 lbs.

$1,375	$975	$875	$750	$650	$575	$525

Last MSR was $1,575.

This model was available in limited quantities only to law enforcement agencies until 2000, due to 1989 Federal legislation banning the importation for commercial sales.

✱ AUG S.A. Commercial - similar to AUG S.A., except values reflect price increases due to consumer demand after Federal legislation banned the commercial importation in 1989, grey (3,000 mfg. circa 1997), green or black finish.

	100%	98%	95%	90%	80%	70%	60%
SP receiver (Stanag metal.)	$2,250	$2,150	$1,850	$1,700	$1,600	$1,500	$1,400
Grey finish	$2,200	$2,000	$1,850	$1,700	$1,600	$1,500	$1,400
Green finish (last finish)	$3,250	$2,875	$2,575	$2,300	$2,000	$1,800	$1,675

Last MSR was $1,362 (1989).

	100%	98%	95%	90%	80%	70%	60%
Black finish	$4,125	$3,750	$3,300	$2,950	$2,750	$2,500	$2,250

STOCK, FRANZ

Previous manufacturer located in Berlin, Germany.

PISTOLS: SEMI-AUTO

.22 LR PISTOL - .22 LR cal.. Mfg. in Germany 1920-1940.

$295	$250	$225	$175	$125	$100	$75

.25 ACP PISTOL - .25 ACP or .32 ACP cal.. Mfg. in Germany 1920-1940.

$295	$225	$175	$150	$100	$90	$80

STOCKWORKS

Current custom rifle manufacturer located in Mesa, AZ. Consumer direct sales only.

RIFLES: BOLT ACTION

LIGHTWEIGHT RIFLES SLR - various cals., Rem. long or short action, Kevlar/fiberglass MPI stock, match grade Pac-Nor barrel, straight flutes in bolt body, Timney trigger, straight line muzzle brake, pillar bedded action in floating barrel, "window" cuts in action for lightening, black oxide finish on blue or stainless steel, English or Claro deluxe checkered stock, custom order only - allow 3-4 months. Approx. 4¾ - 5 lbs.

MSR	$2,600						
		$2,600	$2,300	$2,000	$1,800	$1,600	$1,400	$1,200

Add $200 for stainless steel.

SHARPSHOOTER - various cals., Win. Model 70 action with controlled feeding, precision long range hunting rifle with Schnieder stainless steel fluted barrel, laminated stock with ebony forend tip, titanium firing pin, pillar glass bedded with free floating barrel, includes Leupold 6.5Xx20mm scope, custom order only.

MSR	$5,950						
		$5,950	$5,100	$4,500	$3,900	$3,400	$2,850	$2,150

Blue Book of Airguns™

Second Edition

by Dr. Robert D. Beeman and John Allen

Blue Book of
Modern Black Powder Values™

Second Edition

by Dennis Adler

STOEGER INDUSTRIES, INC.

Current importer located in Accokeek, MD. Previously located in Wayne, NJ until 2000. Please refer to the IGA listing for currently imported Stoeger shotgun models.

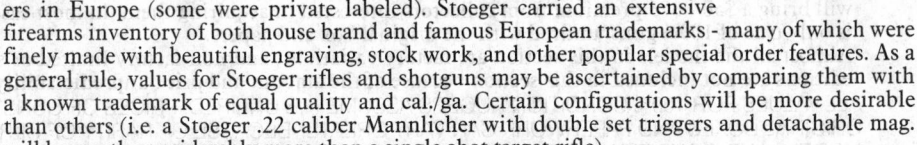

During 2000, Stoeger Industries, Inc. was purchased by Beretta Holding of Italy.

Stoeger has imported a wide variety of firearms during the past seven decades. Most of these guns were good quality and came from known makers in Europe (some were private labeled). Stoeger carried an extensive firearms inventory of both house brand and famous European trademarks - many of which were finely made with beautiful engraving, stock work, and other popular special order features. As a general rule, values for Stoeger rifles and shotguns may be ascertained by comparing them with a known trademark of equal quality and cal./ga. Certain configurations will be more desirable than others (i.e. a Stoeger .22 caliber Mannlicher with double set triggers and detachable mag. will be worth considerably more than a single shot target rifle).

Perhaps the best reference works available on these older Stoeger firearms (not to mention the other trademarks of that time) are the older Stoeger catalogs themselves - quite collectible in their own right. It is advised to purchase these older catalogs (some reprints are also available), if more information is needed on not only older Stoeger models, but the other firearms being sold at that time.

PISTOLS: SEMI-AUTO

PRO SERIES 95 - .22 LR cal., target pistol with choice of either 5½ or 7¼ VR, fluted, or bull barrel, adj. rear sight, adj. trigger, push-button takedown, Pachmayr rubber grips, gold accents, 10 shot mag., 45-47 oz. Mfg. 1995-96.

◇ **5½ in. bull barrel**

	100%	98%	95%	90%	80%	70%	60%
	$440	$375	$335	$300	$275	$250	$225

Last MSR was $495.

◇ **5½ in. VR barrel**

	100%	98%	95%	90%	80%	70%	60%
	$515	$425	$365	$325	$285	$255	$225

Last MSR was $595.

◇ **7¼ in. fluted barrel**

	100%	98%	95%	90%	80%	70%	60%
	$455	$385	$340	$300	$275	$250	$225

Last MSR was $525.

STONER RIFLE

Please refer to the Knight's Manufacturing Company listing in this text.

STRAYER TRIPP INTERNATIONAL

Please refer to the STI International listing in this section.

STRAYER-VOIGT, INC.

Current manufacturer of Infinity pistols located in Grand Prairie, TX. See the Infinity listing for more information.

STREET SWEEPER

Previously manufactured by Sales of Georgia, Inc. located in Atlanta, GA.

SHOTGUNS

STREET SWEEPER - 12 ga. only, 12 shot rotary mag., paramilitary configuration with 18 in. barrel, double action, folding stock, 9¾ lbs. Restricted sales following the ATF classification as a "destructive device". Mfg. 1989-approx. 1995.

	100%	98%	95%	90%	80%	70%	60%
	$750	$650	$550	$475	$400	$360	$330

Unless this model was registered with the ATF before May 1st, 2001, it is subject to seizure with a possible fine/imprisonment.

S

Grading	100%	98%	95%	90%	80%	70%	60%

STURM, RUGER & CO., INC.

Current manufacturer with production facilities located in Newport, NH (rifles and shotguns) beginning 1993 and Prescott, AZ (handguns) beginning 1986. Previously manufactured in Southport, CT 1949-1993 (office headquarters remain at this location).

NOTE: In 1976, Ruger stamped "Made in the 200th year of American Liberty" on the side of all of the guns they produced for this one year only. These Bicentennial or "Liberty Model" guns will bring a $50 - $75 premium from collectors interested in acquiring them. In most cases this is only true of 100% guns, unfired with the original box and papers.

Almost all the models in this section are factory variations, and non-factory limited or special editions are not included in this section because of the amount and price unpredictability.

ALL VALUES FOR 100% CONDITION RUGERS ASSUME NIB UNFIRED. PRICES OF GUNS WITH ORIGINAL BOXES AND PAPERWORK CAN VARY GREATLY BECAUSE OF RARITY OF CERTAIN MODELS AND CONDITION OF BOX OR ACCESSORIES. INDIVIDUAL APPRAISALS NEEDED.

Beginning 1998, all handguns are supplied with a case and lock.

Please refer to the Blue Book of Modern Black Powder Values (now online also) for more information and prices on Sturm Ruger black powder models.

PISTOLS: SEMI-AUTO, RIMFIRE

Many distributors and customizers have produced special/limited editions on this popular series of .22 cal. pistols. Individual companies should be contacted for current pricing and special order features/prices.

"RED EAGLE" - approx. 29,000 mfg. 1949-1952, most production occurred prior to Alexander Sturm's death (1951).

	100%	98%	95%	90%	80%	70%	60%
Standard	$525	$425	$375	$300	$265	$235	$200
Target	$500	$425	$375	$350	$300	$275	$225

Add 100%+ in 100% condition factor only for early Red Eagle with wood "salt cod" box.

Distinguishable by recessed red enamel eagle in left hand grip. Produced until early 1952. Serialized approx. 0001 - 35,000 with Mark I Auto occupying blocks from 15,000 - 17,000 and 25,000 - 25,300.

STANDARD MODEL - .22 LR cal., 9 shot, 4¾ in. or 6 in. barrel, blue, fixed sights, checkered wood or rubber grips. Mfg. 1951-1982.

			95%	90%	80%	70%	60%
			$195	$175	$150	$125	$100	$90	$80

Corrected:

	98%	95%	90%	80%	70%	60%
	$195	$175	$150	$125	$100	$90	$80

Variations marked "Hecho En Mexico" are rare. 98%+ condition specimens have sold for as much as $1,500.

✷ Stainless Steel 1 of 5,000

	95%	90%	80%
	$395	$350	$300

MARK I TARGET - similar to Standard, except has 5½ in. heavy barrel, 5¼ tapered (scarce) barrel, or 6 7/8 heavy tapered barrel, adj. rear sights, target sight. Mfg. 1951- 1982.

	98%	95%	90%	80%	70%	60%
	$250	$200	$175	$150	$140	$130	$120

Add 100% if U.S. marked.
Add 100% for 5¼ in. tapered barrel.
Add $100 for Ruger addressed muzzle brake.

MARK II STANDARD - .22 LR cal., 4¾ or 6 in. barrel, checkered black Delrin synthetic grips, blue finish, 10 shot mag., approx. 2¼ lbs. Mfg. 1982 to date.

MSR	$289		98%	95%	90%	80%	70%	60%
			$220	$170	$135	$115	$110	$100	$95

✷ Stainless Steel - variation of the Mark II Standard.

MSR	$379	98%	95%	90%
		$290	$210	$175

Serial numbers start approx. at 18-00001.

Grading	100%	98%	95%	90%	80%	70%	60%

MARK II STANDARD 50TH ANNIVERSARY - .22 LR cal., features blue receiver machined to same contour as original production, stainless steel bolt with Ruger medallion on rear, 50th Anniversary Ruger crest on top of frame in front of ejection port, black grips with Ruger medallion in red background, lockable red case. Approx. 35,000 mfg. 1999 only.

		$235	$185	$150	$125	$115	$110	$100

Last MSR was $287.

MARK II TARGET - .22 LR cal., 4 (mfg. 1996-99) bull, 5¼ (disc. 1994), 5½ bull, 6 7/8 standard, or 10 in. bull barrel, single action, 2 5/8 - 3¼ lbs. depending on barrel.

MSR	$349	$275	$240	$200	$165	$130	$120	$110

Add $16 for 4 in. bull barrel.
Add $8 for 10 in. bull barrel.

* **Stainless Steel** - stainless variation of the Mark II Target, includes choice of 5¼ (disc. 1994), 5½ bull, 6 7/8 standard, or 10 in. bull barrel.

MSR	$439	$340	$270	$205

Add $6 for 10 in. bull barrel.

GOVERNMENT TARGET MODEL (MK678G) - commercial variation of the government training model without "U.S." markings, 6 7/8 in. bull barrel, adj. rear sight, blue finish, black plastic grips, 46 oz., individually test targeted. New 1987.

MSR	$425	$335	$270	$205	$175	$155	$140	$125

* **Military "U.S." Marked** - issued to U.S. military personnel, must be factory verified. Disc. 1999.

		$550	$500	$450	$400	$360	$330	$300

Last MSR was $600.

* **Stainless Government Target Model** - 6 7/8 in. bull barrel only. New 1993.

MSR	$509	$395	$310	$230

Add $20 for 6 7/8 in. slab side bull barrel with scope rings and base.

MODEL 22/45 - .22 LR cal. only, semi-auto single action, Zytel frame is patterned after the Model 1911 .45 ACP Gov't, 4 regular, 4¾ regular, 5¼ regular (Target, disc.), or 5½ in. bull barrel, 10 shot mag. (push-button release), fixed (4¾ in. barrel only) or adj. sights, 28-35 oz. New 1993.

* **Blue Finish** - 4 in. regular barrel with adj. sights (Model P4, new 1997) or 5½ in. bull barrel with adj. sights (Model P512). New 1994.

MSR	$275	$215	$185	$160	$135	$125	$115	$100

* **Stainless Steel** - 4¾ in. regular barrel with fixed sights (Model KP4, new 1997) or 5½ in. bull barrel with adj. sights (Model KP512).

MSR	$305	$245	$210	$180

Add $54 for adj. sights (5½ in. bull barrel only).

PISTOLS: SEMI-AUTO, CENTERFIRE

P85 MARK II - 9mm Para. cal., double action, 4½ in. barrel, aluminum frame with steel slide, 3-dot fixed sights, 15 shot mag., ambidextrous safety or decocking levers, oversized trigger, polymer grips, matte black finish, 2 lbs. Mfg. 1987-92.

		$335	$295	$265	$235	$215	$200	$185

Last MSR was $410.

Subtract $30 if without case and extra mag.

* **KP85 Mark II Stainless Steel** - stainless variation of the P85. Mfg. 1990-92.

		$350	$315	$280

Last MSR was $452.

Subtract $30 if without case and extra mag.
Variants included a decocking or double action only version at no extra charge.

S

Grading	100%	98%	95%	90%	80%	70%	60%

P89 - 9mm Para. cal., improved variation of the P85 Mark II, 10 (C/B 1994) shot mag., ambidextrous safety or decocker, blue finish, 32 oz. New 1992.

MSR	$475	$380	$330	$280	$250	$215	$200	$185

Variants were available in a decocking (P89DC) or double action only (P-89DAO) version at no extra charge.

* **KP89 Stainless** - stainless variation of the P89, also available in double action only. New 1992.

MSR	$525	$425	$360	$305

Add $45 for convertible 7.65mm Luger cal. barrel (disc).

P90 - .45 ACP cal., similar to KP90 Stainless, except has blue finish.

MSR	$525	$425	$360	$305	$250	$215	$200	$185

KP90 STAINLESS - .45 ACP cal., double action, 4½ in. barrel, oversized trigger, aluminum frame with stainless steel slide, 7 shot single column mag., ambidextrous safety (KP90) or decocking (KP90D), polymer grips, 3 dot fixed sights. New 1991.

MSR	$565	$435	$370	$315

This model was previously available in a double action only variation (KP90C, disc. 1992).

KP91 STAINLESS - .40 S&W cal., similar to Model KP-90 Stainless, except is not available with external safety and has 11 shot double column mag. Mfg. 1992-94.

		$385	$335	$295

Last MSR was $489.

This model was available in a decocking variation (KP91D) or double action only (KP91DAO).

P93D BLUE - similar to KP93 Stainless, except has blue finish, ambidextrous decocker, 31 oz. New 1998.

MSR	$495	$395	$330	$285	$240	$215	$200	$185

KP93 STAINLESS - 9mm Para. cal., compact variation with 3 9/10 in. tilting barrel - link actuated, matte blue or REM (new 1996) finish, 3 dot sights, 10 (C/B 1994) or 15* shot mag., available with ambidextrous decocking or double action only, 31 oz. New 1994.

MSR	$575	$450	$370	$315

P94 BLUE - similar to KP94 Stainless, except has blue finish. New 1998.

MSR	$495	$395	$330	$285	$240	$215	$200	$185

KP94 STAINLESS - 9mm Para. cal., available with ambidextrous safety, matte blue or REM (new 1996) finish, ambidextrous decocker, or double action only, 10 (C/B 1994), or 15* (9mm Para.) shot mag., 33 oz. New 1994.

MSR	$575	$450	$370	$315

P95 BLUE - 9mm Para. cal., available in ambidextrous decocker (D suffix), ambidextrous safety (new 2001) or double action only configuration (DAO suffix), polymer frame, 3 9/10 in. barrel, fixed sights, blue finish, 10 shot mag., 27 oz. New 1997.

MSR	$425	$345	$280	$230	$190	$165	$150	$135

* **KP95 Stainless** - stainless variation of Model P95. New 1997.

MSR	$475	$380	$305	$245

P97D - .45 ACP cal., ambidextrous decocker, 8 shot mag., blue finish, 30½ oz. New 2002.

MSR	$460	$370	$315	$275	$235	$215	$200	$185

* **KP97 Stainless** - .45 ACP cal., similar to KP95 Stainless, except has 8 shot mag., 27 oz. New 1999.

MSR	$495	$395	$315	$265

P944 - .40 S&W cal., similar to P93, ambidextrous safety, blue finish, 34 oz. New 1999.

MSR	$495	$395	$330	$280	$235	$215	$200	$185

* **KP944 Stainless** - similar to P944, except is stainless steel. New 1999.

MSR	$575	$450	$375	$320

S

Grading	100%	98%	95%	90%	80%	70%	60%

REVOLVERS: SINGLE ACTION, OLD MODELS

Note: The following Rugers are known as "Old Models" (mfg. 1953 - early 1973) and are instantly recognized by the three screws through the frame and the four clicks emitted upon cocking. They are now actively sought by collectors and some shooters who desire the smoother operation they afford.

SINGLE SIX REVOLVER - .22 LR cal., 4 5/8, 5½, 6½, or 9½ in. barrel, XR-3 grip frame disc. in 1962, fixed sights, rubber or wood grips, blue. Mfg. 1953-1972.

* **5 1/2, 6 1/2 in. barrel, XR-3**

	$300	$225	$175	$130	$120	$110	$100

◇**Early 4 5/8 in. Barrel, XR-3 frame** - single cylinder, ser. no. range 127,000-198,000.

	$475	$400	$350	$300	$250	$200	$175

An extra convertible cylinder will command a premium on this model.

◇**Early 9½ in. Barrel, XR-3 frame** - single cylinder, ser. no. range 127,000-198,000.

	$450	$400	$350	$300	$250	$200	$175

An extra convertible cylinder will command a premium on this model.

* ***Flat loading gate*** - 5½ in. barrel only, approx. 61,000 mfg. from 1953-1957. Four variations.

	$350	$300	$250	$200	$175	$160	$150

Add 100% for non-serrated front sight (ser. no. 1-2,000)

* ***Factory Engraved Model***

Approx. 250 factory cased, engraved Single Six models have been mfg. Seldom seen and among the rarest of Ruger revolvers, prices have been reported in the $2,500-$3,500 range.

* ***.22 Mag.*** - 6½ in. barrel only, mfg. only three years, serial numbered between 300,000 - 342,000. Frame stamped Mag. only.

	$300	$250	$200	$175	$165	$160	$150

Add 20% for extra .22 LR cylinder in Mag. only marked guns.

SINGLE SIX CONVERTIBLE - similar to Single Six, except .22 LR and .22 Mag. interchangeable cylinders, 4 5/8, 5½, 6½, or 9½ in. barrel with 4 5/8 in. being the rarest. Mfg. 1962-1972.

	$295	$245	$195	$170	$160	$135	$120

* ***Convertible Single Six*** - XR-3 red (redesigned) grip frame. Mfg. 1963-1972.

◇**5 1/2, 6 1/2 in. barrel**

	$295	$240	$195	$130	$120	$110	$100

◇**4 5/8 or 9 1/2 in. barrel**

	$350	$300	$250	$200	$175	$160	$150

LIGHTWEIGHT SINGLE SIX - similar to Single Six, except alloy frame, 4 5/8 in. barrel, made 1956-1958. 200,000 - 212,000 serial range, can have alloy or steel cylinder.

	$500	$400	$300	$250	$200	$175	$150

Add $100 if all blue with blue alloy cyl.
Add 100% for verifiable factory second ("S") marking.

SUPER SINGLE SIX CONVERTIBLE - similar to Single Six Convertible, except adj. sights. Mfg. 1964-1972.

	$275	$250	$200	$155	$140	$120	$105

This model in 4 5/8 in. barrel is the rarest with prices ranging between $800-$1,000 in blue finish. Nickel finish 6½ in. barrel specimens are trading for $1,200-$2,250.

S

Grading	100%	98%	95%	90%	80%	70%	60%

BLACKHAWK SINGLE ACTION "FLAT-TOP"
.357 Mag. cal., 6 shot, 4 5/8, 6½, and 10 in. barrel, flat top cylinder strap, adj. sight, blue, black rubber or walnut grips. Approx. 43,000 mfg. between 1955-1963.

	100%	98%	95%	90%	80%	70%	60%
4 5/8 in. barrel	$500	$450	$375	$300	$250	$225	$200
6½ in. barrel	$700	$550	$450	$375	$350	$300	$250
10 in. barrel	$1,200	$1,050	$950	$850	$700	$600	$500

BLACKHAWK SINGLE ACTION
.30 Carbine, .357 Mag., .41 Mag., .44 Mag., or .45 LC cal., this model is the 1962 variation with hooded rear sight and 4 5/8 (.357 Mag., .41 Mag. or .45 LC), 6½ (.357 Mag. or .41 Mag.), or 7½ (.30 Carbine or .45 LC) in. barrel.

	100%	98%	95%	90%	80%	70%	60%
	$350	$300	$250	$215	$180	$160	$140

Add $50 for .41 Mag. or $75 for .45 LC cal.
Add 75% for factory verifiable installed brass grip frame (rare).

BLACKHAWK CONVERTIBLE
similar to Blackhawk, with extra cylinder, .357 Mag. and 9mm Para., and .45 LC and .45 ACP cals.

	100%	98%	95%	90%	80%	70%	60%
.357 Mag./9mm Para.	$400	$350	$295	$250	$225	$195	$175

Add $100 for NIB .357 Mag./9mm Para. with non-prefix ser. no.

	100%	98%	95%	90%	80%	70%	60%
.45 LC/.45 ACP	$500	$450	$395	$350	$325	$295	$275

BLACKHAWK FLAT-TOP .44 MAGNUM
similar to Blackhawk Flat-Top, except heavier frame and cylinder, .44 Mag., 6½, 7½, and 10 in. barrels. Approx. 28,000 mfg. between 1956-1963.

	100%	98%	95%	90%	80%	70%	60%
6½ in. barrel	$650	$575	$495	$400	$350	$300	$250
7½ in. barrel	$850	$775	$700	$625	$550	$475	$400
10 in. barrel	$1,200	$1,050	$925	$800	$700	$600	$500

Distinguishable from Super Blackhawk by fluted cylinder and rounded triggerguard.

SUPER BLACKHAWK
.44 Mag. cal., 6½ (rare) or 7½ in. barrel, larger grip frame and square back triggerguard, unfluted cylinder, adj. sights, walnut grips. Mfg. 1959-1972.

	100%	98%	95%	90%	80%	70%	60%
	$375	$300	$250	$200	$190	$185	$175

✳ ***Super Blackhawk Early Variations***

	100%	98%	95%	90%	80%	70%	60%
Brass grip frame	$750	$700	$650	$600	$500	$400	$300
Dragoon frame 6½ bbl.	$750	$700	$650	$600	$500	$400	$300
Dragoon frame white cardboard case/sleeve	$1,000	$900	$800	$700	$600	$500	$400
Dragoon frame, mahogany cased	$900	$850	$750	$650	$500	$400	$300
Long frame, mahogany cased	$1,200	$1,100	$1,000	$900	$800	$700	$650

OLD MODEL BEARCAT
.22 LR cal., 6 shot, 4 in. barrel, alloy frame, brass trigger guard, blue, wood grips with medallion, 17 oz. Mfg. 1958-1973.

	100%	98%	95%	90%	80%	70%	60%
	$350	$300	$275	$225	$200	$180	$170
w/alphabetical prefix	$400	$350	$325	$275	$250	$230	$215

Add 100%+ for blue aluminum triggerguard variation (73,000-77,000 ser. no. range).
Numerous variations exist within this model incorporating production changes.

OLD MODEL SUPER BEARCAT
similar to Bearcat, except steel frame, made with brass trigger guard (early model), or blue steel guard, 25 oz. Mfg. 1971-1973.

	100%	98%	95%	90%	80%	70%	60%
	$330	$290	$250	$225	$200	$180	$165

HAWKEYE SINGLE SHOT
.256 Mag. cal., single shot, round cylinder replaced by rectangular rotating breech block, 8½ in. barrel, blue, walnut grips, adj. sight, very rare, 45 oz., approx. 3,300 mfg. Mfg. 1963-1964.

	100%	98%	95%	90%	80%	70%	60%
	$1,300	$1,100	$900	$700	$600	$550	$500

Grading	100%	98%	95%	90%	80%	70%	60%

REVOLVERS: SINGLE ACTION, NEW MODELS

The following single actions are known as "New Models". They have 2 pins through the frame and cock without the clicks associated with the single action. The change over occurred as a result of desire for safety features. The "New Models" have a transfer bar similar to those found on modern double action revolvers and do not accidentally discharge if dropped. Manufacture started 1973. During certain years of manufacture, Ruger's changes in production on certain models (cals., barrel markings, barrel lengths, etc.) have created rare variations that are now considered premium niches. These areas of low manufacture will add premiums to the values listed on standard models. Beginning 1996, Ruger started supplying all New Model revolvers with a case and lock.

SINGLE SIX CONVERTIBLE - .22 S, L, or LR cal., includes interchangeable .22 Mag. cylinder, 5½ or 6½ in. barrel, fixed sights, blue finish, approx. 34 oz. New 1994.

	MSR	$379	$290	$220	$170	$140	$120	$110	$100

* ***Single Six Convertible Stainless Steel*** - similar to Single Six Convertible, except is stainless steel. Mfg. 1994-97, reintroduced 1999 only.

	$325	$255	$185

Last MSR was $415.

SUPER SINGLE SIX CONVERTIBLE - .22 LR cal., includes interchangeable .22 Mag. cylinder, 4 5/8, 5½, 6½, or 9½ in. barrel, 6 shot, similar to old Super Single Six, except has new interlocking safety mechanism previously described, adj. rear sight, 33 oz (w/5½ in. barrel). Mfg. 1973- present.

	MSR	$389	$295	$225	$170	$140	$120	$110	$100

* ***Super Single Six Stainless Steel*** - similar to Super Single Six, except stainless steel construction, 4 5/8 (disc. 1976), 5½, 6½, or 9½ (disc.-rare) in. barrel.

	MSR	$469	$365	$280	$200

Values for 4 5/8 or 9½ in. barrel are approx. $575 if NIB.

* ***Super Single Six "Star" Model*** - .22 LR cal., so named because of star stamped on bottom of frame, blue or stainless, single cylinder (not convertible). Mfg. 1974-75 only.

	100%	98%	95%	90%	80%	70%	60%
Blue 5½ or 6½ in. bbl.	$450	$400	$350	$295	$275	$250	$225
Blue 9½ in. bbl. (rare)	$550	$500	$450	$400	$350	$300	$250
Blue 4 5/8 in. bbl. (very rare)	$800	$750	$700	$625	$550	$475	$395
Stainless 5½ or ½ in. bbl.	$350	$300	$250				
Stainless 9½ in. bbl.	$500	$450	$400				
Stainless 4 5/8 in. bbl. (rare)	$600	$550	$500				

* ***Super Single Six High Gloss Stainless*** - 5½ (disc. 1996) or 6½ in. barrel, features high gloss stainless steel finish, simulated ivory grips became standard 1997. Mfg. 1994-97.

	$335	$265	$195

Last MSR was $425.

Subtract approx. 8% if without simulated ivory grips.

* ***Colorado Centennial Super Single Six*** - 15,000 mfg. 1975 only, includes walnut case with medallion insert, stainless steel grip frame, 6½ in. barrel, issue price was $250.

	$295	$245	$200

This model also was a U.S. Bicentennial gun as well as the Colorado Centennial Pistol. Most specimens do not have the Bicentennial statement on the barrel and are rarer with that stamping.

S

Grading	100%	98%	95%	90%	80%	70%	60%

NEW MODEL .32 H&R MAG. (SUPER SINGLE SIX SSM) - .32 H&R Mag. cal., 4 5/8, 5½ (disc. 1996), 6½ (disc. 1996)or 9½ (disc. 1996) in. barrel, blue (disc. 1996), case colored frame (new 2002), or high gloss stainless steel (new 2001), 6 shot, fixed (new 2001) or adj. (disc. 1996) sights, choice of bird's head with black Micarta grips (new 2002) or regular grips (simulated ivory became standard 2001), 32-35 oz. Disc. 1996, reintroduced 2001.

	MSR	$576	$445	$330	$270	$240	$210	$175	$145

Add 50% if cylinder frame is marked "SSM".

BLACKHAWK - .30 Carbine (disc. 1996, reintroduced 1998), .357 Mag., .41 Mag. (disc. 1996, reintroduced 1999), or .45 LC cal., similar to old Model Blackhawk, with new interlocking safety mechanism, 6 shot, 4 5/8, 6½, or 7½ in. (.30 Carbine and .45 LC only) barrel, 40-44 oz. Mfg. 1973-present.

	MSR	$435	$330	$245	$190	$160	$145	$135	$125

✳ **Blackhawk Convertible** - similar to New Model Blackhawk, except interchangeable cylinders, .357 Mag./9mm Para. (current), .44 Mag./.44-40 WCF (disc.), or .45 LC/.45 ACP (disc. 1985, reintroduced 1999) cal., 4 5/8, 5½ (.45 LC/.45 ACP only), or 6½ in. barrel.

	MSR	$489	$370	$295	$245	$200	$170	$160	$150

Add 30% for disc. convertible cals.

✳ **Buckeye Special** - .32-20 WCF/.32 H&R Mag. cal., 6½ in. barrel. Mfg. 1989.

			$450	$350	$295	$250	$220	$200	$180

Subtract 10% for limited edition Buckeye Special in .38-40 WCF/10mm auto (mfg. by Buckeye Sports in 1990).

✳ **Blackhawk Stainless Steel** - .357 Mag. or .45 LC (new 1993) cal., 4 5/8, 6½, or 7½ (.45 LC only) in. barrel.

	MSR	$530	$450	$325	$270

300 .357 Mag./9mm Para. convertible pistols were made in this model - NIB prices have ranged $500-$750.

New Model .357 Mag. Blackhawks are serial numbered 32-00001 on up. New Model .45 LC Blackhawks are ser. numbered 46-00001 on up.

✳ **Blackhawk High Gloss Stainless Steel** - .357 Mag. or .45 LC cal., 4 5/8, 6½ (.357 Mag. only), or 7½ (.45 LC only) in. barrel, features high gloss stainless steel finish. Mfg. 1994-96.

	$395	$295	$250

Last MSR was $443.

BLACKHAWK-SRM - similar to New Model Blackhawk, except is chambered for .357 Rem. Maximum, 7½ or 10½ in. barrels available, target sights, 53 oz., 11,500 mfg. 1982 only - production suspended due to unresolvable engineering problems.

	$500	$450	$400	$325	$300	$250	$225

SUPER BLACKHAWK - .44 Mag. cal., 4 5/8 (new 1994), 5½ (new 1987), 7½ or 10½ bull in. barrel, 6 shot, blue finish, walnut grips, similar to old model in appearance, but has new action, steel ejector housing was introduced in 2000. Mfg. 1973-present. The new model started with serial number 81-00001.

	MSR	$519	$385	$295	$240	$195	$170	$160	$150

Add $10 for 10½ in. bull barrel (not cased).

✳ **Super Blackhawk Stainless Steel** - stainless variation of the Super Blackhawk.

	MSR	$535	$420	$335	$240

Add $10 for 10½ in. bull barrel (not cased).

Add $16 for hunter grip frame with laminate grip panels (disc.).

✳ **Super Blackhawk High Gloss Stainless Steel** - high gloss stainless steel finish, not available in 10½ in. bull barrel. Mfg. 1994-96.

	$365	$300	$220

Last MSR was $450.

S

Grading	100%	98%	95%	90%	80%	70%	60%

✳ **Super Blackhawk Stainless Hunter** - 7½ in. ribbed barrel only, black laminated wood grips, includes scope rings and integral scope mounts (new 2002). Mfg. 1992-95, reintroduced 2002.

MSR	$639		$550	$475	$375		

VAQUERO - .357 Mag. (new 1997), .44-40 WCF (new 1994), .44 Mag. (new 1994), or .45 LC cal., 6 shot, 4 5/8, 5½, or 7½ (not available in .357 Mag.) in. barrel, color case hardened frame, blue steel grip frame, barrel, and cylinder, steel ejector housing became standard in 2000, transfer bar hammer safety, smooth rosewood, smooth bird's head (mfg. 2001 only) or black Micarta bird's head, (.45 LC cal. only, 4¾ in. barrel, new 2002), or simulated ivory (new 1996) grips, patterned after the Colt SAA, fixed sights, 39-41 oz. New 1993.

MSR	$535		$420	$320	$260	$220	$190	$170	$160

Add $41 for black Micarta bird's head grips (new 2002).
Add $41 for simulated ivory grips (new 1996).
Add approx. $150 for simulated ivory grips and engraved cylinder (mfg. 1998-99).

✳ **Vaquero High Gloss Stainless Steel** - high gloss stainless steel finish, black Micarta bird's head grips became optional 2002. New 1994.

MSR	$535		$420	$320	$260			

Add $41 for black Micarta bird's head grips.
Add $41 for simulated ivory grips (new 1996).

BISLEY VAQUERO - .357 Mag. (new 1999, 5½ in. barrel only), .44 Mag. or .45 LC cal., 4 5/8 (new 1999) or 5½ in. barrel, case colored frame with blue steel grips, barrel, and cylinder, steel ejector housing became standard in 2000, fixed sights, approx. 40 oz. New 1998.

MSR	$535		$420	$335	$270	$230	$200	$180	$160

Add $41 for simulated ivory grips.

✳ **Bisley Vaquero Stainless** - similar to Bisley Vaquero, except is stainless steel.

MSR	$555		$425	$320	$260			

Add $44 for simulated ivory grips.

BISLEY MODEL - .22 LR, .32 H&R Mag. (disc. 1996), .357 Mag., .41 Mag. (disc. 1996), .44 Mag., or .45 LC cal., 6 shot, incorporates Bisley features (flat-top frame, raked hammer, longer grip frame), 6½ (.22 LR or .32 H&R Mag. only) or 7½ in. barrel, fixed (disc. 1992, except for .32 H&R Mag.) or adj. sights, available with fluted/ unfluted or roll-marked/unmarked (disc.) cylinders, satin blue finish only, Goncalo Alves smooth grips. New 1986.

✳ **.22 LR or .32 H&R Mag. (disc.)**

MSR	$422		$335	$250	$195	$175	$160	$150	$140

Add $50 for .32 H&R Mag. (disc. 1996).

✳ **Other cals.**

MSR	$535		$420	$335	$275	$230	$200	$180	$160

NEW BEARCAT - .22 LR cal., includes interchangeable .22 Mag. cyl. (disc. 1996), frame slightly longer than old Bearcat, 4 in. barrel, transfer bar hammer safety, blue finish, smooth walnut grips, fixed sights, 24 oz. New 1994.

MSR	$379		$310	$250	$195	$140	$125	$115	$105

Add a 200% premium for early production New Bearcats with convertible cylinders (the factory recalled them).

✳ **New Bearcat Bright Stainless Steel** - similar to New Bearcat, except is stainless steel. New 2002.

MSR	$429		$345	$255	$200			

S

REVOLVERS: DOUBLE ACTION

During certain years of manufacture, Ruger's changes in production on certain models (cals., barrel markings, barrel lengths, etc.) have created rare variations that are now considered premium niches. These areas of low manufacture will add premiums to the values listed on standard models.

Grading	100%	98%	95%	90%	80%	70%	60%

SPEED SIX (MODELS 207, 208 and 209) - .38 Spl., .357 Mag., or 9mm Para. cal., 2¾ or 4 in. barrel, fixed sights, checkered walnut grips, round butt, blue finish, some guns have factory speed hammer (no hammer spur). Mfg. 1973-1988. Model 207 and 208 disc. 1988.

	$230	$205	$190	$170	$160	$150	$140

Last MSR was $292.

Add $40 for 9mm Para. (Model 209 disc. 1984).

❋ **Models 737 and 738** - stainless steel versions of Models 207 and 208, .357 Mag and .38 Spl. cals., 2¾ or 4 in. barrel. Disc. 1988.

	$280	$245	$220				

Last MSR was $320.

❋ **Model 739** - stainless steel, 9mm Para. Disc. 1984.

	$300	$250	$230				

SECURITY SIX (MODEL 117) - .357 Mag. cal., 6 shot, 2¾, 4 (heavy), or 6 in. barrel, adj. sights, checkered walnut grips, square butt. Mfg. 1970-1985.

	$250	$225	$195	$185	$160	$150	$140

Last MSR was $309.

Add $15 for target grips.

500 of this model were mfg. for the California Highway Patrol during 1983 (.38 Spl. cal.) in stainless steel only. They are distinguishable by a C.H.P. marking. Other Security Six Model 117 special editions have been made for various police organizations - premiums might exist in certain regions for these variations.

❋ **Model 717** - stainless steel version of Model 117. Disc. 1985.

	$295	$255	$230				

Last MSR was $338.

POLICE SERVICE SIX - .357 Mag, .38 Spl., or 9mm Para. cal., blue finish only, square butt, fixed sights, checkered walnut grips.

❋ **Model 107** - .357 Mag, 2¾ or 4 in. barrel, fixed sights. Disc. 1988.

	$250	$220	$200	$190	$180	$170	$165

Last MSR was $287.

❋ **Model 108** - .38 Spl., 4 in. barrel, fixed sights. Disc. 1988.

	$250	$220	$200	$190	$180	$170	$165

Last MSR was $287.

❋ **Model 109** - 9mm Para., 4 in. barrel, fixed sights. Disc. 1984.

	$275	$230	$205	$195	$185	$180	$175

POLICE SERVICE SIX STAINLESS STEEL - stainless construction, 4 in. barrel only, fixed sights, checkered walnut grips.

❋ **Model 707** - .357 Mag., square butt. Disc. 1988.

	$270	$235	$210				

Last MSR was $310.

❋ **Model 708** - .38 Spl., square butt. Disc. 1988.

	$270	$235	$210				

Last MSR was $310.

GP-100 - .357 Mag. or .38 Spl. cal., 3 (new 1990, fixed sights and .357 Mag. cal. only), 4, or 6 (.357 Mag. cal. only) in. standard or heavy barrel, 6 shot, strengthened design intended for constant use with all .357 Mag. ammunition, rubber cushioned grip panels with polished Goncalo Alves wood inserts, fixed or adj. (.357 Mag. only) sights with white outlined rear and interchangeable front, 35-46 oz. depending on barrel configuration. New 1986.

MSR	$489		$400	$315	$260	$225	$200	$185	$170

Add $10 for adj. rear sight (.357 Mag. cal., 4 or 6 in. barrel only).

❋ **GP-100 Stainless Steel** - similar to GP-100, except is stainless steel. New 1987.

MSR	$529		$425	$325	$265				

Add $10 for adj. rear sight (.357 Mag. cal. only).

Grading	100%	98%	95%	90%	80%	70%	60%

✳ **GP-100 High Gloss Stainless Steel** - .357 Mag. only, high gloss stainless steel finish, 3 or 4 in. heavy barrel. Mfg. 1996 only.

	$375	$295	$250

Last MSR was $457.

SP-101 STAINLESS STEEL - .22 LR (6 shot - new 1990), .32 H&R (6 shot - new 1991), .38 Spl. (5 shot), 9mm Para. (5 shot – mfg. 1991-2000), or .357 Mag. (5 shot - new 1991) cal., 2¼, 3 1/16, or 4 (new 1990) in. barrel, small frame variation of the GP- 100 Stainless, fixed or adj. (new 1996) sights, 25-34 oz. New 1989.

MSR	$482	$385	$295	$245

Ruger introduced adj. sights in 1996 available in .22 LR or .32 H&R cal. only.
Ruger introduced a .357 Mag./2¼ in. (new 1993) or .38 Spl./2¼ (new 1994) in. configuration featuring a spurless hammer, double action only.
SP-101 barrel lengths are as follows: .22 cal. is available in 2¼ or 4 in. standard or heavy barrel, .32 H&R is available in 3 1/16 or 4 (new 1994) in. heavy barrel, .38 Spl. is available in 2¼ or 3 1/16 in. length only, 9mm Para. is available in 2¼ (new 1992) or 3 1/16 in. only, and .357 Mag. is available in 2¼ or 3 1/16 in. only.

✳ **SP-101 High Gloss Stainless Steel** - .38 Spl. (disc. 1996), 9mm Para. (disc. 1996), or .357 Mag. cal., similar to SP-101 Stainless Steel, except has high gloss stainless steel finish. Mfg. 1996-97.

	$360	$280	$240

Last MSR was $443.

Ruger introduced adj. sights in 1996 available in .22 LR or .32 H&R cal. only.

REDHAWK - .357 Mag. (disc. 1985), .41 Mag. (disc. 1992), or .44 Mag. cal., 6 shot, this is a redesigned large frame handgun, 5½ and 7½ in. barrel, square butt, smooth hardwood grips, 49-54 oz.

MSR	$585	$480	$380	$310	$260	$215	$180	$165

Add $40 for scope rings.
.357 Mag. and .41 Mag. cals. will bring collector premiums if NIB.

✳ **Redhawk Stainless Steel** - .44 Mag or .45 LC (new 1998) cal., stainless steel construction, 49 –54 oz.

MSR	$645	$515	$405	$325

Add $40 for scope rings.
This model was also available as a KRH-35, and is marked both "Redhawk" and ".357 Magnum". Mfg. was circa 1984-1991.

SUPER REDHAWK STAINLESS - .44 Mag., .454 Casull (new 1999), or .480 Ruger (new 2001) cal., 6 shot, 7½ or 9½ in. barrel, fluted (.44 Mag. cal. only) or non-fluted cylinder, choice of regular or high gloss (new 1997) stainless steel, adj. rear sight, cushioned grip panels (GP-100 style), stainless steel scope rings, 53-58 oz. New late 1987.

MSR	$685	$550	$415	$300

Add $90 for .454 Casull or .480 Ruger (new 2001) cal.

RIFLES: BOLT ACTION, RIMFIRE

MODEL 77/17 - .17 HMR cal. only, 22 in. barrel, checkered walnut stock. New 2002.

MSR	$565	$435	$360	$285	$240	$210	$190	$175

MODEL 77/22-R/RS - .22 LR cal only, 10 shot rotary mag., 20 in. barrel, all steel construction, 3 position safety, checkered walnut stock, blue finish, non-adj. trigger, available with either optional iron sights or plain barrel (no sights) with scope rings (included), 2.7 millisecond lock time on trigger, 6 lbs. 2 oz. New 1984.

MSR	$565	$435	$360	$285	$240	$210	$190	$175

Add $20 for iron sights.
Add 125% if w/o 77/22 roll mark or with green laminated stock.

S

Grading	100%	98%	95%	90%	80%	70%	60%

✳ *Model 77/22-RP/RSP All-Weather Stainless* - similar to Model 77/22 LR, except has stainless steel metal with matte black DuPont Zytel synthetic stock, 5 lbs. 14 oz. New 1989.

> MSR $565 $435 $360 $285
> Add $20 for iron sights.

✳ *Model 77/22-VBZ Varmint Stainless Laminated* - similar to Model 77/.22 LR, stainless steel, heavy stainless barrel with dull finish, laminated brown hardwood stock. New 1995.

> MSR $599 $460 $370 $295

MODEL 77/22-RM/RSM MAG. - similar to Model 77/22-R/RS, except in .22 Win. Mag. cal., 9 shot rotary mag., blue finish, checkered walnut stock. New 1990.

> MSR $565 $435 $360 $285 $240 $210 $190 $175
> Add $20 for iron sights.

✳ *Model 77/22-RMP/RSMP Mag. All-Weather Stainless* - similar to Model 77/22- RM/RSM Mag., except has stainless steel metal with matte black Dupont Zytel synthetic stock. New 1990.

> MSR $565 $435 $360 $285
> Add $20 for iron sights.

✳ *Model 77/22-VMBZ Mag. Varmint Stainless Laminated* - similar to Model 77/ .22 Mag., stainless steel, heavy stainless barrel with dull finish, laminated brown hardwood stock. New 1993.

> MSR $599 $460 $365 $295

RIFLES: BOLT ACTION, CENTERFIRE

During certain years of manufacture, Ruger's changes in production on certain models (cals., barrel markings, barrel lengths, etc.) have created rare variations that are now considered premium niches. These areas of low manufacture will add premiums to the values listed on standard models. Earlier flat-bolt models (pre-1972) are desirable in the rarer cals. and will command a 100% premium if in 98%+ original condition.

MODEL 77/22-RH/RSH HORNET - .22 Hornet cal., features lengthened receiver, detachable 6 shot rotary mag. (not interchangeable with other 77/22 mags.), 20 in. blue barrel, checkered American walnut stock, includes scope rings, 6 lbs. New 1994.

> MSR $589 $460 $380 $300 $250 $225 $195 $180
> Add $20 for iron sights.

✳ *Model 77/22-VHZ Hornet Varmint Stainless Laminated* - similar to Model 77/ .22 Hornet, stainless steel, 24 in. heavy stainless barrel with dull finish and no sights, laminated brown hardwood stock, 6 5/8 lbs. New 1995.

> MSR $625 $480 $390 $305

MODEL 77/44 - .44 Mag. cal., 18½ in. barrel, rotary mag., plain birch or checkered walnut stock, open sights, 6 lbs. New 1998.

> MSR $599 $485 $360 $300 $265 $245 $200 $200

✳ *Model 77/44 Stainless* - .44 Mag. cal., black synthetic stock, stainless steel construction, open sights. New 1999.

> MSR $599 $485 $360 $300

Grading	100%	98%	95%	90%	80%	70%	60%

MODEL 77R - .22-250 Rem., .220 Swift, 6mm Rem. (disc.), .243 Win. (disc.), .250 Savage (disc.), .257 Roberts, .25-06 Rem., .270 Win., 7x57mm, 7mm-08 (disc.), 6.5mm Rem. Mag. (scarce), 7mm Rem. Mag., .280 Rem., .284 Win., .308 Win. (disc.), .30-06, .300 Win. Mag., .338 Win Mag., .350 Rem. Mag., or .358 Win. cal., long or short action, blue finish, 5 shot mag., 3 shot in Mag. cals., 22 or 24 in. barrel, available with integral bases or round top, some models supplied with sights, stock is checkered walnut with red rubber butt plate, approx. 7 lbs. Mfg. 1968-1992.

	$420	$395	$325	$265	$245	$200	$200

Last MSR was $558.

Add 10-15% for .284 cal.
Add 20%-30% for .350 Rem. Mag. cal.

* **Model 77 RL** - .22-250 Rem. (disc.), .243 Win., .250 Sav., .257 Roberts, .270 Win., .30-06, or .308 Win. cal., ultra light variation weighing 6 lbs., black forearm tip. Disc. 1992.

	$445	$375	$325	$270	$250	$225	$205

Last MSR was $592.

* **Model 77 RS** - .243 Win., .250 Sav., 6mm Rem., 6.5mm Rem. Mag., 7x57mm, .25-06 Rem. (disc.), 270 Win., .280 Rem., .284 Win., .30-06, .308 Win., 7mm Rem. Mag., 300 Win. Mag., .338 Win. Mag., .35 Whelen, .350 Rem. Mag., or .358 Win. cal., similar to Model 77R, except has open sights. Disc. 1992.

	$460	$425	$350	$300	$265	$230	$210

Last MSR was $616.

Add 20%-30% for .284 Win. or .350 Rem. Mag. cal.

* **Model 77PL** - .25-06 Rem., .270 Win., .30-06, .300 Win., .338 Win. Mag., 7mm Rem. Mag., or 7x57mm cal., differs from R Model in that it has a round top, drilled to take Redfield scope mounts, w/o sights.

	$420	$395	$325	$265	$245	$200	$200

* **Model 77ST** - .25-06 Rem., .257 Roberts, 7x57mm, .300 Win. Mag., .338 Win. Mag., 7mm Rem. Mag., .30-06, or .270 Win. cal., differs from RS Model in that is has round top drilled to take Redfield scope mounts with iron sights on barrel.

	$460	$425	$350	$300	$265	$230	$210

* **Model 77V Varmint** - .22-250 Rem., .220 Swift, .243 Win. (disc.), 6mm Rem. (disc.), .25-06 Rem., .280 Rem., .308 Win., or .30-06 cal., 24 in. heavy barrel (26 in. on .220 Swift), drilled and tapped for target bases, approx. 9 lbs. Mfg. 1968-92.

	$430	$395	$325	$265	$245	$210	$200

Last MSR was $574.

* **Model 77 RS African** - similar to Model 77R, except in .458 Win. Mag. cal. Disc. 1991.

	$550	$475	$400	$365	$335	$315	$300

Last MSR was $680.

This model was supplied standard with a steel triggerguard and steel floor plate.

* **Model 77 RSC** - similar to Model 77 RS African, except has Circassian walnut stock (C suffix). Mfg. 1976-78.

	$675	$575	$500	$450	$400	$365	$335

* **Model 77 RLS** - .243 Win. (disc. 1989), .270 Win., .30-06, or .308 Win. cal. (disc. 1989), ultra light, 18½ in. barrel, open sights, 6 lbs. Mfg. 1987-93.

	$445	$395	$310	$280	$260	$230	$210

Last MSR was $592.

* **Model 77 RSI** - .22-250 Rem. (disc. 1991), .243 Win. .250-3000 Sav. (reintroduced 1990), .270 Win., .30-06, .308 Win. (disc. 1991), 7x57mm (rare), or 7mm-08 Rem. cal., International Mannlicher (full length stock) with 18½ in. barrel and open sights (includes scope rings), approx. 7 lbs. Disc. 1993.

	$470	$400	$325	$295	$265	$230	$210

Last MSR was $623.

Add 20% for 7mm-08 cal.

S

Grading	100%	98%	95%	90%	80%	70%	60%

MODEL 77R MARK II SERIES - various cals. as listed in the submodels below, evolutionary design of the Ruger Model 77R featuring slenderized proportioning, 3 position swing-back safety, new trigger, trigger guard and floor plate latch, stainless steel bolt with Mauser extractor design, various barrel lengths, integral base receiver, hand checkered American walnut stock, includes scope rings, various weights. New 1989.

* ✱ *Model 77R* - .220 Swift (new 1995), .22-250 Rem. (new 1993), .223 Rem. (new 1992), .243 Win., .25-06 Rem. (new 1993), .257 Roberts (new 1993), .260 Rem. (new 1999), .270 Win. (new 1993), .280 Rem. (new 1993), 6mm Rem., 6.5x55mm Swedish (new 1993), 7x57mm (new 1993), .30-06 (new 1993), .308 Win., 7mm Rem. Mag. (new 1993), 7mm Rem. Short Ultra Mag. (new 2002), .300 Win. Mag. (new 1993), .300 Rem. Short Ultra mag. (new 2002), or .338 Win. Mag. (new 1993) cal., checkered walnut stock is standard, 22 or 24 in. barrel, standard model of the new Mark II Series, approx. 7 lbs.

MSR	$675		$460	$375	$315	$280	$245	$200	$200

* ◇*Model 77 LR* - .270 Win., .30-06, .300 Win. Mag., or 7mm Rem. Mag. cal., left hand variation of the Model 77R. New 1991.

MSR	$675		$460	$375	$315	$280	$245	$200	$200

* ✱ *Model 77 RL* - .223 Rem., .243 Win., .257 Roberts (new 1993), .270 Win. (new 1993), .30-06 (new 1993), or .308 Win. cal., 20 in. barrel, black forend tip, ultra light variation weighing approx. 6 lbs. New 1990.

MSR	$729		$500	$415	$325	$285	$250	$225	$205

* ✱ *Model 77 RLFP Stainless* - .243 Win., .270 Win. or .30-06 cal., 20 in. barrel, black synthetic stock, ultralight variation of the Model 77, w/o sights, 6½ lbs. New 1999.

MSR	$675		$460	$375	$315				

* ✱ *Model 77 RS* - 6mm Rem., .243 Win., .25-06 Rem. (new 1993), .270 Win. (new 1993), .30-06 (new 1993), .308 Win., 7mm Rem. Mag. (new 1993), .300 Win. Mag. (new 1993), .338 Win Mag. (new 1993), or .458 Win. Mag. (mfg. 1994-98) cal., 22 or 24 in. barrel, similar to Model 77R, except has open sights. New 1990.

MSR	$759		$540	$425	$350	$300	$270	$230	$210

* ✱ *Model 77 CR Compact* - .223 Rem., .243 Win., .260 Rem., .308 Win., or 7mm-08 Rem. cal., features 16½ in. barrel, checkered walnut stock, includes scope rings, no sights, approx. 5¾ lbs. New 2002.

MSR	$675		$460	$375	$315	$280	$245	$200	$200

* ◇*Model 77 CRBBZ Compact Stainless* - stainless variation of the Model 77 CR Compact, black laminate stock. New 2002.

MSR	$729		$500	$415	$325				

* ✱ *Model 77 RSI* - .243 Win., .270 Win., .30-06, or .308 Win. cal., International Mannlicher (full length stock) with 18½ in. barrel and open sights (includes scope rings), approx. 7 lbs. New 1993.

MSR	$769		$550	$435	$360	$310	$270	$230	$210

* ✱ *Model 77 RLS* - .243 Win. or .308 Win. cal., ultra light, 18½ in. barrel, open sights. Mfg. 1990 only.

			$460	$375	$310	$280	$260	$230	$210

Last MSR was $564.

* ✱ *Model K77 RFP All-Weather Stainless* - .22-250 (new 1996), .223 Rem., .243 Win., .25-06 Rem. (new 1999), .260 Rem. (new 1999), .270 Win., .280 Rem. (new 1993), 7.62x39mm (disc. 2000), .30-06, .308 Win., 7mm Rem. Mag., 7mm Rem. Short Ultra Mag. (new 2002), .300 Win. Mag., .300 Rem. Short Ultra mag. (new 2002), or .338 Win. Mag. (new 1992) cal., 22 or 24 in. barrel, similar to Model 77R Mark II except has stainless steel metal with matte black DuPont Zytel synthetic stock, no sights. New 1990.

MSR	$675		$465	$380	$305				

S

Grading	100%	98%	95%	90%	80%	70%	60%

* ***Model K77 RSFP All-Weather Stainless*** - .223 Rem. (new 2002), .243 Win., .270 Win., .30-06, 7mm Rem. Mag., .300 Win. Mag., or .338 Win. Mag. cal., otherwise similar to Model K77 RFP All-Weather Stainless, except has open sights.

    MSR **$759**   **$510**   **$415**   **$350**

* ***Model K77 RBZ Satin Stainless*** - .22-250 Rem. (new 1999), .223 Rem., .243 Win., .270 Win., .280 Rem., .30-06, .308 Win., 7mm Rem. Mag., .300 Win. Mag., or .338 Win. Mag. cal., features brown wood laminate stock with sling swivels, 22 or 24 in. barrel without sights, approx. 7 5/16 lbs. New 1997.

    MSR **$729**   **$485**   **$400**   **$345**

* ***Model K77 RSBZ*** - .243 Win., .270 Win., .30-06, .300 Win. Mag., .338 Win. Mag., or 7mm Rem. Mag. cal., 22 or 24 in. barrel, laminated stock, open sights, includes scope rings, approx. 7 3/8 lbs.

    MSR **$799**   **$500**   **$460**   **$350**

* ***Model K77 VT (VBZ)*** - .22 PPC (disc. 1996), .220 Swift, .22-250 Rem., .223 Rem., .243 Win., .25-06 Rem., .308 Win., or 6mm PPC (disc. 1996) cal., 26 in. heavy barrel, features stainless steel construction, laminated stock, approx. 9 3/4 lbs. New 1993.

    MSR **$819**   **$515**   **$470**   **$360**

    This model's nomenclature changed from VBZ to VT during 1994.

* ***Model 77 LRBBZ Stainless*** - .270 Win., .30-06, or 7mm Rem. Mag. cal., 22 in. barrel, uncheckered grey laminated stock, includes scope rings. New 1999.

    MSR **$729**   **$485**   **$400**   **$345**

MODEL 77 RSM - .375 H&H, .404 Jeffery (mfg. 1994-95), .416 Rigby, or .458 Lott (new 2002) cal., 23 in. barrel, premium grade Circassian walnut with hand cut checkering and ebony forend tip, integral barrel and sighting quarter rib, approx. 9½ lbs. New 1990.

    MSR **$1,695**   **$1,350** **$1,000** **$895**   **$800**   **$750**   **$675**   **$595**

MODEL 77 RS EXPRESS - .270 Win., .30-06, 7mm Rem. Mag., .300 Win. Mag., or .338 Win. Mag. (new 1994) cal., 22 or 24 in. barrel, 3 or 4 shot mag., similar construction to Model 77RSM with premium grade wood and other materials, 7½ lbs. New 1991.

    MSR **$1,625**   **$1,250** **$875**   **$815**   **$750**   **$700**   **$675**   **$595**

RIFLES: LEVER ACTION

MODEL 96 CARBINE - .22 LR, .22 Mag., or .44 Mag. cal., 18½ in. barrel with single barrel band, uncheckered hardwood stock with curved butt plate, 10 (.22 LR), 9 (.22 Mag.), or 4 (.44 Mag.) shot detachable rotary mag., cross-bolt safety on trigger guard, adj. rear sight, .44 Mag. has case hardened lever, rimfire receivers are drilled and tapped while the .44 Mag. has an integral base receiver with scope rings (became standard 1997), approx. 5¼-5 7/8 lbs. New 1996.

    MSR **$349**   **$280**   **$215**   **$185**   **$160**   **$145**   **$135**   **$125**

    Add $26 for .22 Mag. cal.

    Add approx. $40 for .44 Mag. cal. w/o scope rings (disc.).

    Add $176 for .44 Mag. cal. with scope rings.

RIFLES: SEMI-AUTO

During certain years of manufacture, Ruger's changes in production on certain models (cals., barrel markings, barrel lengths, etc.) have created rare variations that are now considered premium niches. These areas of low manufacture will add premiums to the values listed on standard models. The Model 10/22 has been mfg. in a variety of limited production models including a multi-colored or green laminate wood stock variation (1986), a brown laminate stock (1988), a Kittery Trading Post Commemorative (1988), a smoke or tree bark laminate stock (1989), a Chief AJ Model, Wal-Mart (stainless with black laminated hardwood stock - 1990), etc. These limited editions will com-

Grading	100%	98%	95%	90%	80%	70%	60%

mand premiums over the standard models listed, depending on the desirability of the special edition.

Note: All Ruger Rifles, except Stainless Mini-14, all Mini-30s, and Model 77-22s were made during 1976 in a "Liberty" version. Add $50 - $75 when in 100% in the original box condition.

10/22 STANDARD CARBINE - .22 LR cal., 10 shot rotary mag., 18½ in. barrel, birch, black synthetic (new 1999), or optional deluxe hand checkered walnut stock, folding rear sight. Mfg. 1964-present.

MSR	$239	$190	$150	$120	$100	$80	$60	$55

Add $20 for uncheckered walnut stock (mfg. 1964-1980 and 1987-1989).
Add $60 for deluxe checkered walnut sporter stock (Model 10/22 DSP).

※ **10/22RB Standard Carbine Stainless** - similar to Standard Carbine, except has stainless barrel and choice of birch or black synthetic (new 1997) stock. New 1992.

MSR	$279	$210	$175	$125

10/22-T TARGET MODEL - .22 LR cal., features brown laminated American hardwood stock, blue hammer-forged spiral finish barrel, w/o sights. New 1996.

MSR	$425	$350	$280	$225

※ **K10/22-T Target Model Stainless** - similar to 10/22T Target Model, except is stainless steel. New 1998.

MSR	$485	$400	$310	$250

※ **K10/22-TNZ Target Stainless** - features 20 in. barrel w/o sights, stainless steel action and barrel, laminated thumbhole stock with slanted forend, 7 lbs. New 2001.

MSR	$649	$450	$375	$300

10/22 FINGERGROOVE SPORTER - similar to Standard, except Monte Carlo stock and beavertail forearm. Mfg. 1966-1971.

	$400	$350	$300	$250	$225	$200	$175

Add 200% for checkered stock in NIB condition.

10/22 INTERNATIONAL (OLD PRODUCTION) - similar to Standard, except walnut full stock Mannlicher style. Mfg. 1966-1969.

	$550	$475	$425	$375	$350	$325	$300

Add 50% for checkered stock.

10/22RBI INTERNATIONAL (NEW PRODUCTION) - features Mannlicher style international birch full stock. New 1994.

MSR	$279	$220	$180	$135	$105	$95	$80	$65

※ **K10/22RBI Stainless** - stainless variation of the 10/22RBI International.

MSR	$299	$235	$190	$140

10/22 CANADIAN CENTENNIAL - 2,000 mfg. in 1967.

	$450	$400	$350

Last MSR was $100.

10/22 MAGNUM - .22 Mag. cal., steel receiver, longer and heavier bolt, 10 shot rotary mag., 18½ in. barrel, uncheckered birch stock, blue metal, folding rear sight, 5 9/16 lbs. New 1999.

MSR	$499	$405	$350	$300	$260	$230	$200	$185

RUGER/REMINGTON CANADIAN CENTENNIAL MATCHED NO. 3 SET - includes a Remington Model 742 in .308 Win. cal. and a Ruger 10/22 Sporter with special commemorative appointments, cased. 1,000 sets mfg. 1967 only.

$700	$525	$425

※ **Ruger Canadian Centennial Matched No. 2 Set** - 70 sets mfg. 1967 only.

$950	$775	$550

※ **Ruger Canadian Centennial Matched No. 1 Special Deluxe Set** - 30 sets mfg. 1967 only.

$1,150	$895	$675

Grading	100%	98%	95%	90%	80%	70%	60%

MODEL 44 STANDARD CARBINE - .44 Mag. cal., 4 shot mag., 18½ in. barrel, blowback action, folding sight, curved butt. Mfg. 1961-1985.

	$395	$350	$325	$295	$275	$250	$225

Last MSR was $332.

✳ ***Deerstalker Model*** - approx. 3,750 mfg. with "Deerstalker" marked on rifle until Ithaca lawsuit disc. manufacture (1962).

	$650	$600	$550	$475	$400	$325	$250

✳ ***25th Year Anniversary Model*** - mfg. 1985 only, limited production, has medallion in stock.

	$500	$425	$375

Last MSR was $495.

MODEL 44RS - similar to 44, but has aperture sight and swivels.

	$525	$450	$400	$350	$300	$275	$250

MODEL 44 FINGERGROOVE SPORTER - Monte Carlo stocked version of 44 Standard. Mfg. until 1971.

	$600	$550	$500	$450	$400	$350	$300

Add 100% for factory checkered stock.

MODEL 44 INTERNATIONAL - similar to Standard, except full length Mannlicher style stock. Mfg. until 1971.

	$750	$650	$600	$550	$475	$400	$350

Add 50% for factory checkered stock.

MODEL 99/44 DEERFIELD CARBINE - .44 Mag. cal., 4 shot rotary mag., 18½ in. barrel with folding aperture rear sight, rotating bolt with dual front locking lugs, blue finish only, uncheckered hardwood stock, includes intergral scope mounts and rings, 6¼ lbs. New 2000.

MSR	$675		$525	$440	$400	$370	$335	$300	$260

RUGER CARBINE - 9mm Para. (PC9) or .40 S&W (PC4) cal., 16¼ in. barrel, black synthetic stock, matte metal finish, with or w/o sights, with fully adj. rear sight or rear receiver sight, crossbolt safety, 6 lbs. New 1998.

MSR	$605		$500	$410	$355	$305	$265	$240	$215

Add $23 for adj. rear receiver sight.

MINI-14 - .223 Rem. or .222 Rem. (disc.) cal., 5 (standard mag. starting in 1989), 10, or 20* shot detachable mag., 18½ in. barrel, gas operated, blue finish, aperture rear sight, military style stock, approx. 6¾ lbs. Mfg. 1976-present.

MSR	$636		$515	$425	$355	$315	$270	$240	$215

Add $125 for folding stock (disc. 1989).
Add 25% for Southport Model with gold bead front sight.

Due to 1989 Federal legislation and public sentiment, the Mini-14 is now being shipped with a 5 shot detachable mag. only. This model was also available as a Mini-14 GB (primarily used for law enforcement), and was equipped with a flash hider and bayonet lug.

✳ ***Mini 14 Stainless*** - mini stainless steel version, choice of wood or black synthetic (new 1999) stock.

MSR	$696		$550	$435	$375

Add $125 for folding stock (disc. 1990).

MINI-14 RANCH RIFLE - .223 Rem. cal., 18½ in. barrel, folding rear sight, receiver cut for factory rings, similar to Mini-14, supplied with scope rings, approx. 6½ lbs.

MSR	$675		$525	$440	$400	$375	$335	$300	$260

Due to 1989 Federal legislation and public sentiment, the Mini-14 Ranch Rifle is now being shipped with a 5 shot detachable mag. only.

S

Grading	100%	98%	95%	90%	80%	70%	60%

✳ ***Stainless Ranch Rifle*** - stainless steel construction, choice of wood or black synthetic (new 1999) stock. New 1986.

MSR	$745	$580	$470	$385

Add $125 for folding stock (disc. 1990).

MINI-THIRTY - 7.62x39mm Russian cal., 18½ in. barrel, 5 shot detachable mag., hardwood stock, includes scope rings, 7 lbs. 3 oz. New 1987.

MSR	$675	$525	$440	$400	$375	$335	$300	$260

✳ ***Mini-Thirty Stainless*** - steel variation of the Mini-Thirty, new 1990.

MSR	$745	$580	$470	$385

XGI - while advertised, this model was never shipped commercially because it could not maintain Ruger accuracy standards.
MSR was originally targeted at $425.

RIFLES: SINGLE SHOT

During certain years of manufacture, Ruger's changes in production on certain models (cals., barrel markings, barrel lengths, etc.) have created rare variations that are now considered premium niches. These areas of low manufacture will add premiums to the values listed on standard models.
Pre-1969, non prefix rifles with long action cals. will command a 30%-50% premium (ser. no. 1-8xxx).

NO. 1-A LIGHT SPORTER - similar to No. 1-B Standard, .22 Hornet (disc., 355 mfg.), .243 Win., .270 Win., 7x57mm, or .30-06 cal., 22 in. barrel, folding sight on quarter rib, ramp front sight, no rings, Alexander Henry forearm, front swivel in barrel band, 7¼ lbs. Mfg. 1966-present.

MSR	$850	$660	$520	$440	$350	$280	$245	$215

The "A" suffix designates an Alexander Henry classic forearm with light barrel.

NO. 1-B STANDARD - falling block action with curved Farquharson lever, popular cals. include .218 Bee, .22 Hornet (new 1988), .22-250 Rem., .220 Swift, .223 Rem., .257 Roberts, .243 Win., 6mm Rem, .25-06 Rem., .270 Win., .280 Rem., .30-06, .308 Win. (new 2002), 6.5mm Rem. Mag. (disc.), 7mm Rem. Mag., .270 Wby. Mag. (new 1990), .300 Wby. Mag. (new in 1990), .300 Win. Mag., or .338 Win. Mag., 22 or 26 in. barrel, quarter rib with integral scope bases, supplied with rings and no sights, checkered stock and semi beavertail forearm. Mfg. 1966-present.

MSR	$850	$660	$520	$440	$350	$280	$245	$215

The "B" suffix designates semi-beavertail forearm with medium barrel and is available in all cals. under .375 H&H except 7x57mm.

NO. 1-H TROPICAL RIFLE - similar to Medium Sporter, except .375 H&H, .404 Jeffery (mfg. 1993-95), .416 Rem. (new 1993), .416 Rigby (new 1991), or .458 Win. Mag. cal., 24 in. heavy barrel, open sights, approx. 9 lbs.

MSR	$850	$660	$520	$475	$410	$375	$340	$300

NO. 1 K1-B-BBZ STAINLESS - various cals. and configurations, satin stainless steel action and barrel, grey laminate hardwood stock with black recoil pad, drilled and tapped rear quarter rib w/o sights. New 2001.

✳ ***No. 1 K1-B-BBZ Standard*** - .243 Win., .25-06 Rem., .30-06, .308 Win. (new 2002), .300 Win. Mag., 7mm STW, or 7mm Rem. Mag. cal., 26 in. barrel, 8 lbs. New 2001.

MSR	$885	$685	$545	$485

✳ ***No. 1 K1-H-BBZ Tropical*** - .375 H&H, .416 Rigby (new 2002), or .458 Lott (new 2002) cal., 24 in. barrel, 9 lbs. New 2001.

MSR	$885	$685	$545	$485

✳ ***No. 1 K1-S-BBZ Sporter*** - .45-70 Govt. cal. only, 22 in. barrel with iron sights, 7¼ lbs. New 2001.

MSR	$885	$685	$545	$485

S

Grading	100%	98%	95%	90%	80%	70%	60%

✳ ***No. 1 K1-V-BBZ Varmint*** - .22-250 Rem. cal. only, 24 in. barrel, 9 lbs. New 2001.

    MSR $885 $685 $545 $485

NO. 1-RSI INTERNATIONAL - .243 Win., .270 Win., 7x57mm, or .30-06 cal., features 20 in. light-weight barrel with full length Mannlicher stock, includes swivels and open sights, 7¼ lbs.

    MSR $865 $675 $540 $440 $350 $280 $245 $215

NO. 1-S MEDIUM SPORTER - similar to Light Sporter, only .218 Bee, 7mm Rem. Mag., .45-70 Govt., .300 Win. Mag., or .338 Win. Mag. cal., 22 (.45-70 Govt. cal. only) or 26 in. medium barrel, open sights, 7¼ - 8 lbs.

    MSR $850 $660 $520 $445 $350 $280 $245 $215

✳ ***No. 1-S 50th Anniversary*** - .45-70 Govt. cal. only, engraved action with gold inlays, including the Ruger logo and 50 years, William B. Ruger signature on receiver bottom, checkered Circassian wlanut stock and forearm. 1,500 mfg. 1999 only.

            $1,950 $1,700 $1,500 $1,250 $995 $850 $700

                                         Last MSR was $1,950.

NO. 1-V VARMINT - similar to No. 1-B Standard, except .22 PPC (mfg. 1993-96), .22-250 Rem., .220 Swift, .223 Rem., .243 Win. (disc.), .25-06 Rem., 6mm Rem., 6mm PPC (mfg. 1993-96), or .280 Rem. (disc.) cal., 24 or 26 (.220 Swift only) in. heavy barrel, without rib, checkered walnut stock and forearm, target scope blocks, 9 lbs. Mfg. 1966-present.

    MSR $850 $660 $520 $445 $350 $280 $245 $215

NO. 3 CARBINE - same basic action as No. 1, except simpler lever design, uncheckered stock, available in .22 Hornet, .30-40 Krag, .45-70 Govt. (only cal. available 1986), .223 Rem., .44 Mag., or .375 Win. cal., 22 in. barrel, folding sight. Mfg. 1972-1987.

            $450 $400 $350 $300 $250 $200 $150

                                         Last MSR was $284.

SHOTGUNS: O/U

RED LABEL - 12, 20, or 28 (new 1994) ga., 3 in. chambers (except 28 ga.), various barrel lengths and choke (including skeet) combinations, boxlock, SST, 26 or 28 in. VR barrels, auto ejectors, choice of checkered pistol grip or English straight grip (new 1992, Red Label English Field) stock, stainless steel frame became standard on 12 ga. 1985 (not available in 20 ga.), choke tubes became optional in 1988, standard 1990. Mfg. 1977-present.

✳ ***Standard Grade***

    MSR $1,489 $1,125 $860 $725 $640 $565 $500 $450

    Add $550 for .410 bore Briley conversion tube set for 28 ga. only.

    Subtract 15%-20% without choke tubes.

    During late 1994, some 12 and 20 ga. Red Label boxes were marked "EZ", indicating the new easy-opening feature (this is not mechanically spring-assisted, but rather works on tight machining tolerances). All Red Label shotguns have the "EZ"-opening feature beginning 1995.

    Earlier all-steel 12 ga. models (approx. 500 mfg.) with short field tubes could command 10%- 15% premiums over values listed from collectors interested in acquiring this variation. 20 ga. models w/o choke tubes are blue only.

✳ ***Red Label All Weather Stainless*** - 12 ga. only, stainless steel receiver and barrels, checkered black synthetic stock and forearm, 26, 28, or 30 in. VR barrels with choke tubes, 7½ lbs. New 1999.

    MSR $1,489 $1,125 $860 $715

    Add $56 for 30 in. barrels.

✳ ***Red Label Sporting Clays*** - 12 or 20 (new 1994) ga., features 30 in. separated barrels, Briley chokes with forcing cones back bored to .744 in., 3/8 in. VR with middle bead, sporting clays recoil pad. New 1992.

    MSR $1,545 $1,145 $995 $775 $650 $560 $500 $450

S

Grading	100%	98%	95%	90%	80%	70%	60%

◇**Red Label Sporting Clays Engraved** - available in 12 ga. only with 1/3 engraving pattern. Mfg. 1997.

	$2,500	$2,200	$1,900	$1,650	$1,300	$1,000	$850

Last MSR was $3,068.

✳ *Red Label English Field* - 12, 20, or 28 (new 1995) ga., similar to Red Label, except has English style straight grip stock. Mfg. 1992-2000.

	$965	$775	$685	$600	$550	$500	$450

Last MSR was $1,276.

✳ *Red Label Engraved (Current Mfg.)* - available in 12, 20, or 28 ga., 26, 28, or 30 in. barrels, 4 different gold inlay options (depending on ga.) with receiver scroll engraving, available in Standard Model, All Weather Stainless, and Sporting Clays configurations. New 2001.

MSR	$1,650	$1,225	$1,050	$815	$660	$555	$500	$450

Add $75 for 30 in. barrels (available in Sporting Clays and All Weather Stainless only.

✳ *Red Label Engraved (1997-2000 Mfg.)* - available in 12, 20, or 28 ga., available in 3 different engraving patterns (pattern engraving standard). Mfg. 1997-2000.

	$2,200	$1,900	$1,650	$1,300	$1,000	$850	$725

Last MSR was $2,552.

Add $190 for 1/3 engraving coverage.

Add $532 for 2/3 engraving coverage (12 ga. only, disc.).

RED LABEL "WOODSIDE"
- 12 ga. only, 3 in. chambers, 26, 28, or 30 (Sporting Clays Model only with special chokes, new 1996) in. barrels, straight or pistol grip stock, features premium checkered walnut, satin nickel finish, unique stock design permitting wood to fill-in where frame boxlock action would normally be, hand-engraving available at extra cost, 7½ - 8 lbs. New 1995.

MSR	$1,889	$1,525	$1,250	$1,000	$800	$625	$550	$500

✳ *Red Label "Woodside" Engraved* - available with patterned engraving only with pistol grip and 26 or 28 in. barrels. New 1997-disc.

	$2,200	$2,050	$1,725	$1,350	$1,050	$875	$750

Last MSR was $2,805.

WILDLIFE FOREVER SPECIAL EDITION
- 12 ga. only, limited edition to celebrate the 50th anniversary of Wildlife Forever, features Baron & Son engraving with gold pheasant and mallard inlays on receiver sides, 300 mfg. 1993 only.

	$1,595	$900	$775

Last MSR was $1,595.

Add $125 for hard case.

SHOTGUNS: SxS

GOLD LABEL - 12 ga. only, 3 in. chambers, 28 in. barrels with solid rib and choke tubes, rounded stainless boxlock action, SST, blue barrel finish, ejectors, choice of deluxe 22 LPI checkered English straight grip or pistol grip stock and splinter forearm, 6 1/3 lbs. New 2002.

MSR	$1,950	$1,575	$1,275	$1,000	$800	$625	$550	$500

SHOTGUNS: SINGLE BARREL

TRAP MODEL - 12 ga., 34 in. stainless barrel with straight grooves and 2 choke tubes, fully adj. high post rib, engraved stainless receiver with gold Ruger name, adj. deluxe checkered walnut stock, beavertail forearm, adj. trigger, 9 lbs. New 2000.

MSR	$2,850	$2,225	$2,075	$1,725	$1,350	$1,050	$875	$750

SUHLER JAGDGEWEHR MANUFAKTUR GmbH

Previous manufacturer and firearms restorer located in Suhl, Germany.

Suhler Jagdgewehr manufactured a variety of SxS shotguns, in addition to restoring both antique and historical guns.

Grading	100%	98%	95%	90%	80%	70%	60%

SUNDANCE INDUSTRIES, INC.

Current manufacturer located in Valencia, CA. Distributor sales only.

DERRINGERS

POINT BLANK DERRINGER - .22 LR cal., O/U design, double action, 3 in. barrels, black matte finish, 8 oz. Mfg. began mid-1994.

MSR	$99	$80	$60	$50	$45	$40	$35	$30

PISTOLS: SEMI-AUTO

MODEL A-25 - .25 ACP cal., single action design, 2 7/16 in. barrel, 7 shot mag., rotary safety, lower grip push button mag. release, satin nickel (disc.), bright chrome, or black teflon finish, choice of simulated pearl with different colors or grooved black grips, serrated slide. New 1989.

MSR	$79	$65	$55	$45	$40	$35	$30	$25

LADY LASER/LASER 25 - .25 ACP cal., similar to Model A-25, except has factory installed and sighted 5mW Laser sight with no exposed wiring or switch, polished chrome or black finish (Laser 25 only), dual safety switch. New 1995.

MSR	$220	$195	$160	$135	$115	$95	$80	$70

The Laser Lady was disc. during 1998.

MODEL BOA - similar to Model A-25, except has patented squeeze grip safety. New in 1990.

MSR	$95	$75	$60	$50	$45	$40	$35	$30

SUPERIOR AMMUNITION

Current custom rifle manufacturer located in Sturgis, SD. Consumer direct sales only.

RIFLES: BOLT ACTION

SUPERIOR CLASSIC LIGHTWEIGHT - various cals. up to .375 H&H, Rem. 700, Win. Mod. 70 Classic, or Dakota Mod. 76 action, blind box mag. or hinged floorplate, approx. 5¾ lbs.

MSR	$2,000	$2,000	$1,650	$1,350	$1,100	$900	$750	$625

SUPERIOR VARMINT MODEL - various smaller cals., Rem. 700, Dakota Varmint,or Searcy action, stainless match grade barrel, heavy or light variations.

MSR	$2,100	$2,100	$1,725	$1,400	$1,125	$900	$750	$625

SUPERIOR PROFESSIONAL MODEL - various large cals. up to .470 Capstick, only available in Win. Mod. 70 Classic or Dakota Mod. 76 action, blind box mag. (optional) or hinged floorplate.

MSR	$2,500	$2,500	$2,150	$1,850	$1,600	$1,350	$1,150	$900

SUPER SIX LIMITED

Previous manufacturer located in Brookfield, WI until 1992.

REVOLVERS

GOLDEN BISON SERIES - .45-70 Govt. cal., 6 shot revolver, 8 or 10½ in. octagon barrel, large size (overall length 15-17½ in.), manganese bronze frame, cross bolt manual safety, smooth hardwood grips, approx. 6 lbs. 177 total mfg. (including special/limited editions). Disc. approx. 1992.

		$1,675	$1,475	$1,275	$1,000	$875	$775	$675

Last MSR was $1,895.

Low serialization specimens (ser. numbers 1-15) have asking prices of $2,250-$2,950.

✱ *Centennial Limited Edition* - features special engraving and case. 20 total mfg.

		$2,950	$2,275	$1,675

Last MSR was $3,995.

SUPER SIX LLC

Current manufacturer established during 1999, and located in Milwaukee, WI. Consumer direct sales.

During late 1998, Super Six LLC purchased the previous trademark of Super Six Limited. As this edition went to press, no manufacture of the Golden Bison series has occurred. Please contact the company directly (see Trademark Index) for current information, including model availability and pricing.

SURVIVAL ARMS, INC.

Previous manufacturer established in 1990 located in Orange, CT. Previously located in Cocoa, FL until 1995.

In 1990, Survival Arms, Inc. took over the manufacture of AR-7 Explorer rifles from Charter Arms located in Stratford, CT.

RIFLES: SEMI-AUTO

AR-7 EXPLORER RIFLE - .22 LR cal., takedown or normal wood stock, takedown barreled action stores in Cycolac synthetic stock, 8 shot mag., adj. sights, 16 in. barrel, black matte finish on AR-7, silvertone on AR-7S, camouflage finish on AR-7C, 2½ lbs. Disc.

| $120 | $100 | $85 | $75 | $65 | $55 | $50 |

Last MSR was $150.

AR-20 SPORTER - similar to AR-22, except has shrouded barrel, tubular stock with pistol grip, 10 or 20 shot mag. Mfg. 1996-98.

| $165 | $140 | $120 | $105 | $95 | $80 | $70 |

Last MSR was $200.

AR-22/AR-25 - .22 LR cal., 16 in. barrel, black rifle features pistol grip with choice of wood or metal folding* stock, includes 20 (1995 only) or 25 (disc. 1994) shot mag. Disc. 1995.

| $155 | $120 | $95 | $80 | $70 | $60 | $55 |

Last MSR was $200.

Subtract $50 for wood stock model.

SVENDSEN, ERL, F.A. MFG. CO.

Previous manufacturer located in Itasca, IL.

DERRINGERS

LITTLE ACE - .22 S cal., patterned after the Ethan Allen "HIDE-A-WAY", bronze frame, blue steel barrel with case hardened hammer and spur trigger.

| $85 | $75 | $70 | $65 | $60 | $55 | $50 |

4-ACES - .22 S cal., 4 barrel derringer with rotating firing pin and spur trigger, bronze frame with blue rifled steel barrels and case hardened parts.

| $175 | $150 | $135 | $120 | $105 | $90 | $75 |

SWING

Previously manufactured by Schutzen Bohme GmbH located in Rintein, Germany.

RIFLES: BOLT ACTION

SWING BOLT ACTION - .308 Win. cal., target bolt action rifle with thumbhole stock and vented forearm, target sights, 30 in. barrel, 12.1 lbs. Mfg. 1994.

| $850 | $750 | $650 | $575 | $500 | $450 | $395 |

Grading	100%	98%	95%	90%	80%	70%	60%

SWISS MILITARY

Previously manufactured Swiss military rifles.

RIFLES: BOLT ACTION

The models below were manufactured by Schmidt-Rubin, unless otherwise indicated.

MODEL 1889 - usually encountered between 85%-95% condition.

	100%	98%	95%	90%	80%	70%	60%
	$350	$325	$285	$260	$230	$210	$185

MODEL 1911 - available in either carbine or rifle configuration.

	100%	98%	95%	90%	80%	70%	60%
	$450	$325	$200	$185	$170	$160	$150

Add 125% for carbine configuration.

MODEL 1931

	100%	98%	95%	90%	80%	70%	60%
	$650	$600	$525	$450	$285	$250	$225

Add 500% for sniper variations.
Subtract 30% if import marked.

VETTERLI - .41 Swiss or 10.4mm Swiss cal., not mfg. by Schmidt-Rubin.

	100%	98%	95%	90%	80%	70%	60%
	$450	$400	$360	$320	$285	$250	$225

SYMES & WRIGHT LTD.

Previous manufacturer located in London, England.

Symes & Wright Ltd. manufactured approx. 25 best quality shotguns and double rifles annually. Values must be determined after evaluating each firearm individually.

SZECSEI & FUCHS FINE GUNS GmbH

Current long gun manufacturer established in 1986, and located in Innsbruck, Austria. North American headquarters are located in Windsor, Canada.

Szecsei & Fuchs manufactures extremely high quality and unique long guns, including combination guns, drillings, bolt action and double rifles, and SxS shotguns. The company is well known for its unique magazine fed SxS double rifle, which utilizes a single bolt to load/unload both chambers. Many options are available, including a titanium bolt trigger system. At a recent European trade show, Szecsei & Fuchs exhibited a show stopper – a solid titanium O/U .700 NE double bolt rifle with side mount magazine! Please contact the North American office directly for more information on their current models (virtually anything is possible), including pricing, availability, delivery time, and U.S. pricing.

RIFLES: BOLT ACTION

DOUBLE BARREL REPEATER - various cals., unique action allows single bolt to chamber both barrels from one twin column detachable titanium mag., titanium bolt face, right or left-hand, various engraving and wood options available. Base price is $33,900 w/o options or special orders. Base weight is approx. 13 lbs.
Add $2,100 for titanium.

S

NOTES

S if for SHOT Show and shooting. The legendary Jim Carmichel, longtime Shooting Editor for Outdoor Life, and Midway USA's Sara Potterfield take a digital break at the recent Las Vegas SHOT (Shooting, Hunting, Outdoor, Trade) Show.

T Section

TNW, INC.
Current rifle manufacturer located in Vernonia, OR. Consumer direct sales.

RIFLES: SEMI-AUTO

TNW makes a belt fed semi-auto variation of the original Browning M2 HB machine gun in .50 BMG cal. Current price is $6,990. They also make a semi-auto Model 1919 A4 in .30-06 or .308 Win. cal. Retail pricing is in the $2,485 range. Please contact the company directly for more information regarding these semi-auto working replicas of famous American machine guns (see Trademark Index).

TACONIC FIREARMS, LTD.
Current rifle manufacturer located in Cambridge, NY. Consumer direct sales.

Grading	100%	98%	95%	90%	80%	70%	60%

RIFLES: BOLT ACTION, CUSTOM

TACONIC 98 ULTIMATE MOUNTAIN HUNTER - various cals., features double square bridge, titanium alloy M-98 action, XXX Grade English or Circassian walnut, stainless or chrome moly barrel, matte finished metal, available with a variety of options, base prices are listed below.

MSR	$5,995		$5,750	$5,100	$4,500	$4,000	$3,500	$3,000	$2,500

TALON INDUSTRIES, INC.
Previous pistol manufacturer located in Ennis, MT until 2001.

PISTOLS: SEMI-AUTO

T100 - .380 ACP cal., double action only, 3.3 in. barrel, black polymer frame with choice of black (T100B) or satin (T100S) slide finish, alloy frame and slide, 10 shot mag., fail safe loaded chamber indicator positioned on top of slide in back of breech bolt, 3 dot sights, 20½ oz. Mfg. 2000-2001.

	$115	$95	$85	$75	$65	$55	$50

Last MSR was $135.

T200 - 9mm Para. cal., otherwise similar to Model T100. Mfg. 2000-2001.

	$145	$125	$100	$90	$75	$65	$55

Last MSR was $170.

TANFOGLIO, FRATELLI, S.r.l.
Current pistol manufacturer located in Gardone, Italy.

Tanfoglio manufactures a wide variety of high quality semi-auto pistols. In addition to currently being imported by European American Armory Corp. and K.B.I. (see individual listings), Tanfoglio also manufactures their own complete line which, to date, has been mostly distributed in Europe.

TANNER, ANDRÉ
Current manufacturer located in Switzerland. No current U.S. importation. Previously imported and distributed by Mandall Shooting Supplies, Inc. located in Scottsdale, AZ, and by Osborne's located in Cheboygan, MI.

Tanner rifles are noted for their superior accuracy and limited production - less than 150 are mfg. each year.

T

Grading	100%	98%	95%	90%	80%	70%	60%

RIFLES: BOLT ACTION

300 METER MATCH RIFLE - 7.5 Swiss (special order) or 7.62mm cal. only, single shot, top-of-the-line 300 meter match rifle incorporating all match shooting features including deluxe palm rest, aperture sights. Importation disc.

$4,650	$3,995	$3,400	$2,775	$2,250	$1,900	$1,600

Last MSR was $4,900.

Add $100 for adj. cheekpiece.
Subtract $190 for repeating model with similar features.

* ***300 Meter UIT Standard*** - similar to Model 300, except is without palm rest and adj. Swiss butt plate, 10 shot mag., aperture sights. Importation disc.

$4,450	$3,850	$3,350	$2,750	$2,225	$1,925	$1,600

Last MSR was $4,700.

Add $100 for adj. cheekpiece.

SUPERMATCH MODEL 50 M - .22 LR cal. only, 50 meter free rifle, deluxe palm rest, adj. butt plate, thumbhole stock. Importation disc.

$3,600	$3,200	$2,850	$2,450	$2,050	$1,800	$1,600

Last MSR was $3,900.

Add $100 for adj. cheekpiece.

TAR-HUNT CUSTOM RIFLES, INC.

Current custom rifled shotgun manufacturer established in 1990, and located in Bloomsburg, PA. Dealer and consumer direct sales.

SHOTGUNS: BOLT ACTION

PROFESSIONAL MODEL RSG-12 - 12 (RSG-12) ga., 2¾ in. chamber, bolt action slug gun featuring 21½ in. Shaw barrel and 2 lug bolt, 1 round down in mag. (new 1998), matte black finish, McMillan fiberglass stock with Pachmayr Decelerator rifle pad, receiver drilled and tapped for standard Leupold windage bases (included, new 1997), muzzle brake became standard 1994, various finish options, 7¾ lbs. New 1991.

MSR	$1,885	$1,675	$1,400	$1,125	$950	$800	$700	$600

* ***RSG-12 Combo Slug Gun*** - includes standard Professional RSG-12 Slug Gun and a second benchrest McMillan heavy weight stock. New 1994.

MSR	$2,075	$1,825	$1,500	$1,250	$1,050	$900	$800	$700

* ***RSG-12/RSG-20 10th Anniversary*** - 12 or 20 ga., hand selected actions and barrels, Jewell custom adj. trigger, NP-3 nickel/Teflon metal finish, black McMillan stock with Pachmayr Decelerator pad. Only 25 mfg. during 2000 only.

MSR	$2,300	$2,075	$1,825	$1,500	$1,250	$1,050	$900	$800

MATCHLESS MODEL RSG-12 - upgraded variation featuring 400 grit polished gloss metal finish and the McMillan regular or "Fiber" grain stock (wood grain finish, disc. 2000). New 1995.

MSR	$1,899	$1,725	$1,465	$1,150	$900	$800	$750	$700

PEERLESS MODEL RSG-12 - upgraded variation featuring NP-3 (nickel/Teflon) metal finish by Robar of Phoenix, AZ, McMillan regular or "Fiber"-grain stock (wood grain finish, disc. 2000). New 1995.

MSR	$2,145	$1,900	$1,550	$1,275	$1,050	$900	$800	$700

MOUNTAINEER MODEL RSG-20 - 20 (RSG-20) ga., 2¾ in. chamber, features 21 in. Shaw rifled barrel and 2 lug bolt, one shot mag., matte black finish only, McMillan fiberglass stock with Pachmayr Decelerator pad, receiver drilled and tapped for Rem. 700 long action style bases, muzzle brake standard, 6½ lbs. New 1997.

MSR	$1,885	$1,675	$1,425	$1,125	$950	$800	$700	$600

Grading	100%	98%	95%	90%	80%	70%	60%

RSG-TACTICAL (SNIPER) MODEL - 12 ga. only, similar to RSG-12, except has M-86 McMillan fiberglass black tactical stock with Pachmayr Decelerator pad and heavy barrel. Mfg. 1992-98.

	$1,495	$1,250	$995	$875	$750	$700	$650

Last MSR was $1,595.

> **Add $150 for Bi-pod.**

BLOCK CARD MODEL - 12 ga., 2¾ in. chamber, various barrel lengths, cartage type chokes, special McMillan fiberglass stock, Pachmayr Decelerator pad, fluted barrels optional, special chambers, weighted stocks optional, single shot actions. Disc.

	$1,625	$1,425	$1,125	$900	$800	$750	$700

Last MSR was $1,775.

TAURUS INTERNATIONAL

Currently manufactured by Taurus Forjas S.A., located in Porto Alegre, Brazil. Currently imported by Taurus International, located in Miami, FL since 1982. Distributor sales only.

All Taurus products are known for their innovative design, quality construction, proven value, and are backed by a lifetime repair policy. Taurus order number nomenclature is as follows: the first digit followed by a dash refers to type (1 = pistol, 2 = revolver, 3 = rifle/carbine, 5 = magazines, accessories, or grips, and 10 = scope mount bases), the next 2 or 3 digits refer to model number, the next digit refers to type of hammer (O = exposed, 1 = concealed), the next digit refers to barrel length, the last digit refers to finish (1 = blue, 9 = stainless), and the suffix at the end refers to special feature (T = total titanium, H = case hardened, M = matte finish, UL = Ultra-Lite, C = compensator (ported), G = gold accent, R = rosewood grips, PRL = mother-of-pearl grips, and NS = night sights). Hence, 2-454089M refers to a revolver in .454 Casull cal. with exposed hammer, and an 8 3/8 in. barrel in stainless steel with matte finish.

PISTOLS: SEMI-AUTO

From 1990-1992, certain models became available with a Laser Aim LA1 sighting system that included mounts, rings (in matching finish), a 110 volt AC recharging unit, a 9 volt DC field charger, and a high impact custom case.

Taurus incorporated their keyed Taurus security system on most models during 2000, except the PT-22 and PT-25. When the security system is engaged (via a keyed button on the bottom of rear grip strap), the pistol cannot be fired, cocked, or disassembled, and the gun's manual safety cannot be disengaged. This security key also works for the revolver.

> **Add approx. $30 for the Deluxe Shooter's Pack option (included extra mag. and custom case) on the 92, 99, 100, and 101 Series (disc. 2000).**

PT-22 - .22 LR cal., double action only, tip-up 2¾ in. barrel, 8 shot mag., fixed sights, blue, nickel (new 1995), blue/nickel (mfg. 1997-2000), Duo-tone (new 2000), or deluxe blue/gold (new 1997) finish, wood (new 1999), mother-of-pearl (new 2000, deluxe blue/gold finish only), or rosewood grips, 12.3 oz. New 1992.

MSR	$215		$175	$135	$115	$95	$80	$70	$60

> **Add $15 for blue/gold finish with rosewood or mother-of-pearl grips.**
> **Subtract $25 for wood grips.**

PT-25 - .25 ACP cal., similar to PT-22, except has 9 shot mag. New 1992.

MSR	$215		$175	$135	$115	$95	$80	$70	$60

> **Add $15 for blue/gold finish with rosewood or mother-of-pearl grips.**
> **Subtract $25 for wood grips.**

T

Grading	100%	98%	95%	90%	80%	70%	60%

PT-58 - .380 ACP cal., similar to PT-99AF, except in .380 ACP cal., 4 in. barrel, 10 (C/B 1994) or 12* shot mag. Mfg. 1988-96.

	$325	$275	$235	$215	$200	$190	$180

Last MSR was $429.

Add $32 for satin nickel finish (disc. 1994).

Beginning 1993, the PT-58 utilized the Taurus Tri-Position safety system which features a hammer-drop, "cocked-and-locked" option system.

✳ **PT-58SS (Stainless Steel)** - similar to PT-58, except is stainless steel. Mfg. 1992- 96.

	$385	$310	$260

Last MSR was $470.

PT-91AF - .41 Action Express cal., action similar to PT-92AF, except is in .41 AE cal., 10 shot mag., 34 oz. Imported 1990 only.

	$365	$300	$250	$225	$200	$190	$180

Last MSR was $446.

Add $36 for satin nickel finish.
Add $25 for shooter's pack (includes custom case and extra mag.).

PT-92AF - 9mm Para. cal., semi-auto double action, design similar to Beretta Model 92 SB-F, exposed hammer, ambidextrous safety, 5 in. barrel, 10 (C/B 1994) or 15* shot mag., smooth Brazilian walnut (disc.) or checkered rubber (new 1999) grips, blue, nickel (disc.), or stainless steel finish, fixed or night (new 2000) sights, 34 oz.

MSR	$575	$430	$340	$275	$235	$210	$195	$180

Add $40 for satin nickel finish (disc. 1994).
Add $415 for Laser Aim Sight (disc. 1991).
Add $80 for night sights.
Add $266 for blue or stainless conversion kit to convert 9mm Para. to .22 LR (new 1999).

✳ **PT-92SS (Stainless Steel)** - similar to PT-92AF, except is fabricated from stainless steel. New 1992.

MSR	$595	$440	$350	$280

Add $75 for night sights.

✳ **PT-92 Deluxe** - choice of blue/gold finish or stainless steel with gold, rosewood, or mother-of-pearl (new 2000) grips. New 1999.

MSR	$625	$485	$370	$285	$245	$215	$200	$190

Add $20 for stainless steel.
Add $20 for mother-of-pearl grips.

✳ **PT-92AFC** - compact variation of the Model PT-92AF, 4 in. barrel, 10 (C/B 1994) or 13* shot mag., fixed sights. Disc. 1996.

	$335	$285	$235	$225	$200	$190	$180

Add $38 for satin nickel finish (disc. 1993).

Last MSR was $449.

✳ **PT-92AFC (Stainless Steel)** - similar to PT-92AFC, except stainless steel. Mfg. 1993-96.

	$400	$310	$260

Last MSR was $493.

✳ **PT-92AF Lew Horton Special Edition** - 9mm Para. cal., matte satin finished frame with high polish stainless steel slide, blue barrel, hammer, trigger, mag. release, safety, and slide release. 250 mfg. in 1990 only.

	$395	$350	$295	$250	$225	$210	$190

Last MSR was $454.

PT-99AF - similar to Model PT-92AF, except has adj. rear sight.

MSR	$595	$465	$355	$290	$250	$215	$200	$190

Add $45 for satin nickel finish (disc. 1994).
Add $266 for blue or stainless conversion kit to convert 9mm Para. to .22 LR (new 1999) or .40 S&W (new 2000).

This action is similar to the Beretta Model 92SB-F.

Grading	100%	98%	95%	90%	80%	70%	60%

* ***PT-99SS (Stainless Steel)*** - similar to PT-99AF, except is fabricated from stainless steel. New 1992.

MSR	$610		$475	$385	$295		

PT-100 - .40 S&W cal., semi-auto, standard double action, 5 in. barrel, 10 (C/B 1994) or 11* shot mag., safeties include ambidextrous manual, hammer drop, inertia firing pin, and chamber loaded indicator, choice of blue, satin nickel (disc. 1994), or stainless steel finish, smooth Brazilian hard wood (disc.) or rubber grips, 34 oz. Mfg. 1992-97, reintroduced 2000.

MSR	$575		$450	$345	$275	$240	$215	$200	$190

Add $40 for satin nickel finish (disc. 1994).
Add $80 for night sights (new 2000).
Add $266 for blue or stainless conversion kit to convert .40 S&W to .22 LR cal.

* ***PT-100SS (Stainless Steel)*** - similar to PT-100, except is fabricated from stainless steel. Mfg. 1992-96, reintroduced 2000.

MSR	$595		$465	$355	$285			

Add $75 for night sights.

* ***PT-100 Deluxe*** - choice of blue/gold finish or stainless steel with gold, rosewood, or mother-of-pearl grips. New 2000.

MSR	$625		$485	$370	$290	$255	$225	$210	$200

Add $20 for stainless steel or $20 for mother-of-pearl grips.

PT-101 - similar to PT-100, except has adj. sights. Mfg. 1992-96, reintroduced 2000.

MSR	$595		$465	$355	$285	$245	$215	$200	$190

Add $266 for blue or stainless conversion kit to convert .40 S&W to .22 LR cal.
Add $45 for satin nickel finish (disc. 1994).

* ***PT-101SS (Stainless Steel)*** - similar to PT-101, except is stainless steel. Mfg. 1992-96, reintroduced 2000.

MSR	$610		$470	$375	$295			

MODEL PT-111 MILLENNIUM - 9mm Para. cal., double action only, 3¼ in. barrel with fixed 3 dot sights, black polymer frame with steel slide, striker fired, 10 shot mag. with push button release, 18.7 oz. New 1998.

MSR	$425		$355	$290	$235	$190	$155	$135	$120

Add $75 for night sights (new 2000).

* ***Model PT-111 Millennium Stainless*** - similar to Model PT-111, except has stainless steel slide. New 1998.

MSR	$435		$355	$290	$235			

Add $65 for night sights (new 2000).

* ***Model PT-111 Millennium Titanium*** - similar to Model PT-111, except has titanium slide and night sights. New 2000.

MSR	$585		$475	$350	$275			

PT-132 MILLENNIUM - .32 ACP cal., double action only, 3¼ in. barrel, black polymer frame, manual safety, 10 shot mag., fixed 3 dot sights, blue steel slide, 18.7 oz. New 2001.

MSR	$425		$355	$290	$235	$190	$155	$135	$120

* ***Model PT-132 Millennium Stainless*** - similar to Model PT-132, except has stainless steel slide. New 2001.

MSR	$435		$355	$290	$235			

PT-138 MILLENNIUM - .380 ACP cal., double action only, 3¼ in. barrel, black polymer frame, manual safety, 10 shot mag., fixed 3 dot sights, blue steel slide, 18.7 oz. New 1999.

MSR	$425		$355	$290	$235	$190	$155	$135	$120

Add $75 for night sights (new 2000).

T

Grading	100%	98%	95%	90%	80%	70%	60%

❋ *Model PT-138 Millennium Stainless* - similar to Model PT-138, except has stainless steel slide. New 1999.

MSR $435 $355 $290 $235

Add $85 for night sights (new 2000).

PT-140 MILLENNIUM - .40 S&W cal., double action only, 3¼ in. barrel, black polymer frame, manual safety, 10 shot mag., fixed 3 dot sights, blue steel slide, 18.7 oz. New 1999.

MSR $455 $370 $295 $235 $190 $155 $135 $120

Add $80 for night sights (new 2000).

❋ *Model PT-140 Millennium Stainless* - similar to Model PT-140, except has stainless steel slide. New 1999.

MSR $475 $380 $305 $245

Add $80 for night sights (new 2000).

PT-145 MILLENNIUM - .45 ACP cal., otherwise similar to PT-140 Millenium, 23 oz. New 2000.

MSR $490 $395 $320 $250 $200 $165 $145 $135

Add $70 for night sights (new 2000).

❋ *Model PT-145 Millennium Stainless* - similar to Model PT-140, except has stainless steel slide. New 1999.

MSR $500 $400 $325 $260

Add $75 for night sights (new 2000).

PT-400 - .400 Cor-Bon cal., similar to PT-940, except has 4¼ in. ported barrel and 8 shot mag., 29½ oz. Mfg. 1999 only.

              $415 $325 $270 $235 $210 $200 $190

Last MSR was $523.

❋ *Model PT-400 Stainless* - similar to Model PT-400, except has stainless steel slide. Mfg. 1999 only.

              $415 $330 $275

Last MSR was $539.

PT-908 - 9mm Para. cal., compact version of the PT-92 with 3.8 in. barrel and 8 shot mag., fixed sights, blue or nickel finish. Mfg. 1993-97.

              $330 $285 $235 $215 $200 $190 $180

Last MSR was $435.

❋ *PT-908D SS (Stainless Steel)* - similar to Model PT-908, except is stainless steel. Mfg. 1993-97.

              $385 $310 $260

Last MSR was $473.

PT-911 COMPACT - 9mm Para. cal., single or double action, 4 in. barrel, 10 shot mag., checkered rubber grips, fixed sights, 28.2 oz. New 1997.

MSR $525 $415 $335 $275 $225 $200 $185 $170

Add $75 for night sights.

❋ *PT-911 SS (Stainless Steel)* - stainless variation of the PT-911 Compact.

MSR $535 $420 $325 $275

Add $85 for night sights.

❋ *PT-911 Deluxe* - choice of blue/gold finish or stainless steel with gold, rosewood, or mother-of-pearl grips. New 2000.

MSR $570 $450 $365 $290 $255 $225 $210 $200

Add $15 for stainless steel with gold.

Add $15 for mother-of-pearl grips.

PT-938 COMPACT - .380 ACP cal., 3¾ in. barrel, ambidextrous safety, 10 shot mag., blue finish, rubber grips, fixed sights, 26.7 oz. New 1997.

MSR $500 $400 $335 $275 $235 $200 $180 $170

Grading	100%	98%	95%	90%	80%	70%	60%

✳ **PT-938 SS (Stainless Steel)** - stainless variation of the PT-938 Compact.
    MSR $530 $420 $345 $285

PT-940 - .40 S&W cal., compact version of the PT-100 with 3 5/8 in. barrel and 10 shot mag., fixed sights, 28.2 oz. New 1996.
    MSR $525 $425 $355 $290 $240 $210 $190 $180
    Add $75 for night sights.

✳ **PT-940 SS (Stainless Steel)** - similar to PT-940, except is stainless steel. New 1996.
    MSR $535 $435 $360 $295
    Add $85 for night sights.

✳ **PT-940 Deluxe** - choice of blue/gold finish or stainless steel with gold, rosewood, or mother-of-pearl grips. New 2000.
    MSR $570 $465 $385 $310 $260 $230 $210 $200
    Add $15 for stainless steel with gold.
    Add $15 for mother-of-pearl grips.

PT-945 - .45 ACP cal., compact double action, 4¼ in. ported (new 1997) or unported barrel, 8 shot single stack mag., ambidextrous 3 position safety, chamber loaded indicator, 3 dot sights, 29.5 oz. New 1995.
    MSR $560 $450 $365 $305 $260 $230 $210 $200
    Add $75 for night sights.
    Add $40 for ported barrel.

✳ **PT-945 SS (Stainless Steel)** - stainless steel variation of the PT-945. New 1995.
    MSR $580 $475 $385 $310
    Add $75 for night sights.
    Add $40 for ported barrel.

✳ **PT-945 Deluxe** - choice of blue/gold finish or stainless steel, mother-of-pearl (new 2000), or rosewood grips. New 1999.
    MSR $610 $485 $390 $320
    Add $15 for stainless steel with gold.
    Add $15 for mother-of-pearl grips.

PT-957 - .357 SIG cal., compact model with 3 5/8 in. ported (available only with night sights or in 957 Deluxe beginning 2002) or non-ported (new 2002) barrel and slide, 10 shot mag., ambidextrous 3 position safety, blue finish, checkered rubber grips, fixed sights, 28 oz. New 1999.
    MSR $525 $425 $355 $290 $240 $210 $190 $180
    Add $90 for night sights.
    Add $40 for ported barrel (disc. 2002).

✳ **PT-957 SS (Stainless Steel)** - stainless steel variation of the PT-957. New 1999.
    MSR $535 $430 $360 $295
    Add $40 for ported (disc. 2001) barrel, or $130 for ported barrel and night sights.

✳ **PT-957 Deluxe** - choice of blue/gold finish or stainless steel with gold, rosewood, or mother-of- pearl grips. New 2000.
    MSR $610 $475 $385 $310 $260 $230 $210 $200
    Add $15 for stainless steel.
    Add $15 for mother-of-pearl grips.

REVOLVERS: RECENT PRODUCTION

From 1990-1992, certain models became available with a Laser Aim LA1 sighting system that included mounts, rings (in matching finish), a 110 volt AC recharging unit, a 9 volt DC field charger, and a high impact custom case.

The following Taurus revolvers have been listed in numerical order. All currently manufactured

Grading	100%	98%	95%	90%	80%	70%	60%

revolvers listed are rated for +P ammunition.

All currently manufactured Taurus revolvers are equipped with their patented Taurus Security System, introduced in 1998, which utilizes an integral key lock on the back of the hammer, locking the action.

> **Add $50 for scope base mount on currently produced models that offer this option.**
> **Add $30 for carrying case on Raging Bull & Raging Hornet Models listed.**

MODEL 22H RAGING HORNET - .22 Hornet cal., 8 shot, stainless steel construction, 10 in. VR barrel with full shroud, fully adj. sights, scope mount bases included, contoured rubber grips, 50 oz. New 1999.

	MSR	$898		$795	$700	$600

MODEL 44 - .44 Mag. cal., 6 shot, integral porting compensator, exposed or concealed (3 in. barrel only, mfg. 1997-98) hammer, bright blue finish, adj. sights, 3 (mfg. 1997-98), 4, 6½ (VR), or 8 3/8 (VR) in. barrel, 45-57 oz. New 1994.

MSR	$500		$400	$325	$265	$225	$190	$160	$130

> **Add $25 for 6½ or 8 3/8 in. ported barrel.**

❋ *Model 44SS (Stainless Steel)* - similar to Model 44, except matte finished stainless steel. New 1994.

MSR	$565		$455	$365	$295

> **Add $10 for 6½ or 8 3/8 in. ported barrel.**
> **Add $46 for 3 in. ported barrel with fixed sights and round butt grips (mfg. 1996-97).**

MODEL 45 RAGING BULL - .45 LC cal., 6 shot, 6½ or 8 3/8 in. VR ported barrel, adj. sights, soft rubber grips, 53 or 63 oz. Mfg. 1999-2001.

$475	$415	$375	$335	$300	$280	$260

Last MSR was $575.

❋ *Model 45 .45 LC Raging Bull Stainless* - similar to Model 45 Raging Bull, except is stainless steel. Disc. 2001.

$530	$435	$360

Last MSR was $630.

MODEL 65 - .357 Mag./.38 Spl. cal., double action, 6 shot, fixed sights, 2½ (mfg. 1993- 97), 3 (disc. 1992) or 4 in. barrel, blue finish, checkered walnut (disc.) or rubber (new 1999) grips, 38 oz. Disc. 1997, reintroduced 1999.

MSR		$345	$260	$195	$140	$125	$100	$90 $85

> **Add $15 for satin nickel finish (disc.).**

❋ *Model 65SS (Stainless Steel)* - similar to Model 65, except is matte finished stainless steel. Mfg. 1993-97, reintroduced 1999.

MSR	$395		$305	$235	$195

MODEL 66 - .357 Mag./.38 Spl. cal., double action, 6 (disc. 2001) or 7 (new 1999) shot, 2½ (mfg. 1993-97), 3 (disc. 1992), 4, or 6 in. barrel, checkered walnut (disc. 1999) or rubber (new 2000) grips, blue finish, adj. sights, 38-40 oz. Disc. 1997, reintroduced 1999.

MSR	$395		$305	$235	$200	$165	$140	$120	$100

> **Add $15 for satin nickel finish (disc.).**
> **Add $10 for 4 or 6 in. compensated (66CP) barrel (mfg. 1993-94).**

❋ *Model 66SS (Stainless Steel)* - similar to Model 66, but in stainless steel. Mfg. 1987-97, reintroduced 1999.

MSR	$435		$345	$245	$195

> **Add $10 for 4 or 6 in. compensated (66CP) barrel (mfg. 1993-94).**

❋ *Model 66 Silhouette* - .357 Mag./.38 Spl. cal., 7 shot, 12 in. barrel with adj. sights, rubber grips, includes scope mount. New 2001.

MSR	$414		$320	$235	$200	$165	$140	$120	$100

T

Grading	100%	98%	95%	90%	80%	70%	60%

* ***Model 66 Silhouette SS (Stainless Steel)*** - similar to Model 66 Silhouette, except is matte finished stainless steel. New 2001.

| | MSR | $461 | | $370 | $300 | $245 | | |

MODEL 73 - .32 Long cal. only, double action, 6 shot, 3 in. heavy barrel only, checkered walnut grips, 20 oz. Disc. 1992.

| | | | $175 | $150 | $125 | $115 | $105 | $95 | $85 |

Last MSR was $223.

Add $20 for satin nickel finish.

MODEL 76 - .32 H&R Mag. cal., double action, 6 shot, 6 in. heavy barrel with solid rib, fully adj. rear sight, transfer bar safety, checkered hard wood grips, blue only, 34 oz. Mfg. 1991-94.

| | | | $240 | $190 | $155 | $130 | $115 | $100 | $90 |

Last MSR was $308.

MODEL 80 - .38 Spl. cal. only, double action, 6 shot, 3 or 4 in. barrel, checkered walnut grips, fixed sights, 30 oz. Disc. 1996.

| | | | $190 | $145 | $115 | $105 | $95 | $85 | $80 |

Last MSR was $252.

Add $15 for satin nickel finish (disc. 1992).

* ***Model 80SS (Stainless Steel)*** - similar to Model 80, except stainless steel. Mfg. 1993-97.

| | | | $245 | $180 | $135 | | | | |

Last MSR was $313.

MODEL 82 - .38 Spl. cal. only, double action, 6 shot, 3 (disc. 1998) or 4 in. heavy barrel, checkered walnut (disc.) or rubber (new 1999) grips, full underlug, fixed sights, 34 oz.

| | MSR | $325 | | $235 | $170 | $130 | $105 | $95 | $85 | $80 |

Add $15 for satin nickel finish (disc.).

* ***Model 82SS (Stainless Steel)*** - similar to Model 82, except is polished stainless steel. New 1993.

| | MSR | $375 | | $285 | $200 | $140 | | | |

MODEL 83 - .38 Spl. cal. only, double action, 6 shot, 4 in. heavy barrel, checkered walnut grips, adj. sights, 34½ oz. Disc. 1998.

| | | | $215 | $155 | $125 | $115 | $105 | $95 | $80 |

Last MSR was $278.

Add $13 for satin nickel finish.

* ***Model 83SS (Stainless Steel)*** - similar to Model 83, except stainless steel. Mfg. 1993-98.

| | | | $250 | $185 | $135 | | | | |

Last MSR was $324.

MODEL 85 - .38 Spl. cal. only, double action, 5 shot, 2 or 3 (disc. 2001) in. heavy ported (new 1997) or unported barrel, hammer forged frame, exposed hammer, checkered walnut (disc. 2000) or soft rubber grips, fixed sights, 21-24½ oz.

| | MSR | $345 | | $265 | $200 | $150 | $125 | $105 | $95 | $85 |

Add $15 for ported barrel.
Add $20 for satin nickel finish (3 in. barrel only, disc. 1992).

* ***Model 85 Ultra-Lite*** - ultra-lightweight version of Model 85 using an alloy frame, 17 oz.

| | MSR | $375 | | $290 | $215 | $165 | $135 | $110 | $100 | $90 |

◇**Model 85SSUL Ultra-Lite Stainless** - matte stainless variation of the Model 85 Ultra-Lite, 17 oz.

| | MSR | $425 | | $325 | $235 | $175 | | | |

◇**Model 85 Ultra-Lite Deluxe** - ported barrel, choice of blue/gold or stainless/gold, mother-of-pearl (new 2000) or rosewood grips, 17 oz. New 1999.

| | MSR | | $410 | $315 | $230 | $170 | | | |

Add $15 for stainless/gold.
Add $25-$35 for mother-of-pearl grips.

T

Grading	100%	98%	95%	90%	80%	70%	60%

✴ *Model 85SS (Stainless Steel)* - stainless version of Model 85.

    MSR   **$395**   **$305**   **$225**   **$170**

    Add $10 for ported barrel (new 1997).

✴ *Model 85CH (Blue or Stainless)* - similar to Model 85, except has Brazilian hardwood combat (disc. 2000) or soft rubber grips and spurless concealed hammer that fits flush with the frame, 2 in. barrel, double action only, 21 oz. New 1992.

    MSR   **$345**   **$265**   **$200**   **$150**   **$125**   **$105**   **$95**   **$85**

    Add $15 for ported barrel.

    Add $50 for polished stainless steel.

✴ *Model 85 Ultra-Lightweight* - features titanium cylinder and choice of matte aluminum or stainless steel (disc. 2001) small frame, fixed sight, rubber grips, choice of hammer or concealed hammer (Police Model 85). New 1999.

    MSR   **$515**   **$435**   **$365**   **$315**

✴ *Model 85B2 Special Edition/Deluxe* - features blue finish with gold trim or stainless/gold trim, ported 2 in. barrel, rosewood or mother-of-pearl grips, includes integral key lock. New 1998.

    MSR   **$380**   **$280**   **$245**   **$175**   **$130**   **$110**   **$95**   **$85**

    Add $25 for mother-of-pearl grips.

    Add $55 for stainless/gold trim.

MODEL 85T - similar to Model 85, except 100% titanium construction, 2 in. ported barrel only, choice of bright spectrum blue, matte spectrum blue, matte spectrum gold, stealth grey (mfg. 2000 only), or shadow grey (new 2000) finish, 15.4 oz. New 1999.

    MSR   **$530**   **$460**   **$420**   **$350**

MODEL 86 CUSTOM TARGET - .38 Spl. cal. only, double action target model, 6 shot, 6 in. barrel, specially contoured smooth walnut grips, adj. rear sight, blue only, 34 oz. Disc. 1994.

               $270   **$200**   **$160**   **$150**   **$140**   **$130**   **$120**

                                                            Last MSR was $352.

    This model was available in either single or double action with adj. counterweight and interchangeable front sight inserts.

MODEL 94 - .22 LR cal., double action, 9 shot, 2 (new 1997), 3 (mfg. 1991-98), 4, or 5 (new 1996) in. barrel, full underlug on 4 or 5 in. barrel, blue finish, adj. rear sight, target features, 25 oz. New 1989.

    MSR   **$325**   **$245**   **$180**   **$140**   **$120**   **$105**   **$95**   **$85**

✴ *Model 94 Ultra-Lite* - ultra light hammer forged frame, 2 in. barrel, available in matte blue or bright stainless steel, 18 oz. New 1999.

    MSR   **$375**   **$280**   **$205**   **$155**   **$125**   **$105**   **$95**   **$85**

    Add $45 for matte stainless steel construction.

✴ *Model 94SS (Stainless Steel)* - stainless version of Model 94. New 1990.

    MSR   **$375**   **$290**   **$210**   **$155**

MODEL 96 TARGET SCOUT - .22 LR cal. only, double action, 6 shot, 6 in. barrel, checkered walnut grips, same features as Model 86, 34 oz. Disc. 1998.

               $275   **$200**   **$160**   **$150**   **$140**   **$130**   **$120**

                                                            Last MSR was $376.

MODEL 415 - .41 Mag. cal., 5 shot, similar to Model 415T, except has matte stainless steel construction, Ribber grips, 30 oz. New 1999.

    MSR   **$475**   **$410**   **$340**   **$280**

MODEL 415T - .41 Mag. cal., 5 shot, all titanium construction, 2½ in. ported barrel with fixed sights, choice of bright spectrum blue (disc. 2001), matte spectrum blue (disc. 2001), matte gold (mfg. 1999 only), stealth grey (mfg. 2000 only), or shadow grey (new 2000) finish, Ribber grips. New 1999.

    MSR   **$600**   **$500**   **$440**   **$360**

Grading	100%	98%	95%	90%	80%	70%	60%

MODEL 425 TRACKER - .41 Mag. cal., similar to Model 415T, 4 in. ported barrel with full shroud, adj. sights with red inserts, Ribber grips, stainless steel with matte finish. New 2000.

MSR **$500** **$430** **$355** **$285**

MODEL 425T TRACKER - similar to Model 425 Tracker, except is all titanium construction, choice of stealth grey (mfg. 2000 only) or shadow grey finish, adj. sights. New 2000.

MSR **$690** **$560** **$465** **$350**

MODEL 431 - .44 Spl. cal., 5 shot, 2 (new 1995), 3, or 4 in. barrel, blue only, fixed sights. Mfg. 1993-97.

$220 **$170** **$145** **$130** **$115** **$100** **$90**

Last MSR was $286.

✳ *Model 431SS (Stainless Steel)* - similar to Model 431, except stainless steel. Mfg. 1993-97.

$285 **$215** **$180**

Last MSR was $368.

MODEL 441 - similar to Model 431, except has 3, 4, or 6 in. barrel, adj. sights. Mfg. 1993-97.

$240 **$180** **$145** **$130** **$115** **$100** **$90**

Last MSR was $313.

✳ *Model 441SS (Stainless Steel)* - similar to Model 441, except is stainless steel. Mfg. 1993-97.

$350 **$250** **$195**

Last MSR was $468.

MODEL 444 RAGING BULL - .44 Mag. cal. only, 6 shot, 6½ or 8 3/8 in. VR ported barrel with full shroud, soft rubber grips, 53 or 63 oz. New 1999.

MSR **$575** **$485** **$415** **$370** **$335** **$300** **$280** **$260**

✳ *Model 444 Raging Bull Stainless* - similar to Model 444, except is matte stainless steel. New 1999.

MSR **$630** **$530** **$460** **$365**

MODEL 445 - .44 Spl. cal., 5 shot, 2 in. ported (new 1999) or standard barrel, fixed sights, blue or stainless, Ribber or rubber grips, 28 oz. New 1997.

MSR **$345** **$270** **$205** **$165** **$145** **$115** **$100** **$90**

Add $15 for ported barrel (new 1999).

✳ *Model 445 Concealed Hammer* - similar to Model 445, except w/o hammer, ported or unported barrel. New 1999.

MSR **$345** **$270** **$205** **$165** **$145** **$115** **$100** **$90**

Add $15 for ported barrel.

✳ *Model 445 Concealed Hammer Stainless* - similar to Model 445 Concealed Hammer, except is stainless steel. New 1999.

MSR **$395** **$300** **$225** **$155**

Add $5 for ported barrel.

✳ *Model 445 SS (Stainless Steel)* - stainless variation of the Model 445. New 1997.

MSR **$395** **$300** **$225** **$155**

Add $5 for ported barrel.

✳ *Model 445 Ultra-lite Stainless* - features ported 2 in. barrel and matte stainless steel. New 1999.

MSR **$500** **$370** **$285** **$230**

✳ *Model 445 Ultra-lite Concealed Carry* - features stainless steel or titanium frame, ported 2 in. barrel, walnut combat grips. New 2002.

MSR **$500** **$370** **$285** **$230**

Add $100 for titanium construction.

T

Grading	100%	98%	95%	90%	80%	70%	60%

MODEL 445T - .44 Spl. cal., 5 shot, all titanium construction, 2 in. ported barrel with fixed sights, choice of bright spectrum blue, matte spectrum blue, matte gold (mfg. 1999 only), stealth grey (new 2000), or shadow grey (new 2000) finish, Ribber grips. New 1999.

| | MSR | $600 | | $500 | $440 | $360 | | |

MODEL 450 - .45 LC cal., similar to Model 450T, except is matte stainless steel, also available in Ultra-Lite variation, 28 oz. New 1999.

| | MSR | $470 | | $410 | $340 | $280 | | |

Add $55 for Ultra-Lite Model.

MODEL 450T - .45 LC cal., 5 shot, all titanium construction, 2 in. ported barrel with fixed sights, choice of bright spectrum blue, matte spectrum blue, matte gold (mfg. 1999 only), stealth grey (new 2000), or shadow grey (new 2000) finish, Ribber grips. New 1999.

| | MSR | $600 | | $500 | $440 | $360 | | |

MODEL 454 CASULL RAGING BULL - .454 Casull cal., single or double action, 5 shot, front and rear cylinder locks, bright blue or case colored (new 1999) finish, 5 (case colored, disc. 2000, or stainless), 6½ or 8 3/8 in. full lug ported barrel with integral VR, soft black rubber grips with recoil absorbing insert, micrometer adj. rear sight, transfer bar ignition, integral key lock, 53-63 oz. New 1998.

| | MSR | $785 | | $725 | $645 | $585 | $530 | $475 | $450 | $425 |

Add $96 for case colored frame.

* **✱ *Model 454 Casull Raging Bull Stainless*** - similar to Model 454 Casull Raging Bull, except is stainless steel, with either satin (6½ in. barrel only, disc. 2000) or matte (new 1999) stainless finish. New 1998.

| | MSR | $855 | | $780 | $710 | $635 | | |

MODEL 455 TRACKER - .45 ACP cal., 5 shot, 4 or 6 in. ported barrel, adj. rear sight, matte stainless steel, Ribber grips. New 2002.

| | MSR | $525 | | $450 | $360 | $295 | | |

MODEL 480 RUGER RAGING BULL - .480 Ruger cal., 5 shot, 5, 6½, or 8 3/8 in. barrel, matte stainless finish only, otherwise similar to Model 454 Casull. New 2001.

| | MSR | $855 | | $750 | $650 | $600 | | |

MODEL 605 - .357 Mag. cal., 5 shot, 2 in. unported (new 2002), 2¼ or 3 (mfg. 1996-98) in. barrel, blue or stainless, 4 port compensated barrel (2¼ in. only) with fixed sights, exposed or concealed (Model 605CH, new 1997, 2¼ in. barrel) hammer, full barrel shroud, oversized finger grooved rubber grips, 24½ oz. New 1995.

| | MSR | $345 | | $270 | $205 | $150 | $125 | $105 | $95 | $85 |

Add $15 for ported barrel.

* **✱ *Model 605 SS (Stainless Steel)*** - stainless variation of the Model 605.

| | MSR | $395 | | $295 | $225 | $165 | | |

Add $10 for ported barrel.

MODEL 606 - .357 Mag. cal., 6 shot, 2 or 2¼ in. uncompensated or compensated barrel, exposed or concealed hammer, fixed sights. Mfg. 1997-98.

| | | | | $235 | $180 | $140 | $120 | $105 | $95 | $85 |

Last MSR was $296.

Add $19 for ported barrel (2 in. only).

* **✱ *Model 606 SS (Stainless Steel)*** - stainless variation of the Model 606. Disc. 1998.

| | | | | $260 | $185 | $140 | | |

Last MSR was $344.

Add $20 for ported barrel (2 in. only).

Grading	100%	98%	95%	90%	80%	70%	60%

MODEL 607 - .357 Mag. cal., 7 shot, 4 or 6½ (VR) in. compensated barrel, adj. rear sight, Santo-prene synthetic grips, 44 oz. Mfg. 1995-97.

| | $335 | $280 | $240 | $205 | $185 | $160 | $150 |

Last MSR was $447.

Add $18 for 6½ in. VR barrel.

✳ *Model 607SS (Stainless Steel)* - stainless variation of the Model 607. Mfg. 1995- 97.

| | $375 | $325 | $265 | | | | |

Last MSR was $508.

Add $20 for 6½ in. VR barrel.

MODEL 608 - .357 Mag. cal., 8 shot, 3 (mfg. 1997-98), 4, 6½ (VR), 8 3/8 (VR, new 1997) in. bar-rel with integral compensator, exposed or concealed (new 1997, 3 in. barrel) hammer, adj. sights, 44-56 oz. New 1996.

| MSR | $445 | $340 | $285 | $245 | $205 | $185 | $160 | $150 |

Add $20 for 6½ or 8 3/8 in. VR ported barrel.

✳ *MODEL 608SS (Stainless Steel)* - stainless variation of the Model 608. New 1996.

| MSR | $510 | $380 | $330 | $270 | | | | |

Add $15 for 6½ or 8 3/8 in. VR barrel.

MODEL 617 - .357 Mag. cal., 7 shot, double action, 2 in. regular or ported barrel, fixed sights, exposed (integral key lock) or concealed hammer, rubber grips, 28.3 oz. New 1998.

| MSR | $375 | $310 | $260 | $220 | $185 | $150 | $135 | $120 |

Add $20 for ported barrel.

✳ *Model 617SS (Stainless Steel)* - similar to Model 617, except is polished stainless steel. New 1998.

| MSR | $420 | $325 | $240 | $180 | | | | |

Add $20 for ported barrel.

✳ *Model 617 ULT* - similar to Model 617, except is 5 shot, aluminum alloy receiver and tita-nium cylinder, matte stainless finish, 2 in. regular or ported barrel, soft rubber grips. New 2001.

| MSR | $530 | $455 | $365 | $290 | $260 | $220 | $185 | $150 |

Add $15 for ported barrel.

MODEL 617T - .357 Mag. cal., 7 shot, all titanium construction, 2 in. ported barrel with fixed sights, choice of bright spectrum blue, matte spectrum blue (disc. 2001), matte gold (mfg. 1999 only), stealth grey (mfg. 2000 only), or shadow grey (new 2000) finish, Ribber grips, 19.9 oz. New 1999.

| MSR | $600 | $500 | $440 | $360 | | | | |

MODEL 627 TRACKER - .357 Mag. cal., 7 shot, 4 or 6 (new 2001) in. ported barrel with adj. sights, and heavy full underlug, stainless steel with matte finish, Ribber grips, 28.8 or 40 oz. New 2000.

| MSR | $500 | $395 | $280 | $210 | | | | |

MODEL 627T TRACKER - .357 Mag. cal., 7 shot, all titanium construction, 4 or 6 (new 2001) in. ported barrel with adj. sights, choice of stealth grey (disc. 2001) or shadow grey finish, Rib-ber grips, 24.3 or 28 oz. New 2000.

| MSR | $690 | $560 | $475 | $385 | | | | |

MODEL 650 CIA - .357 Mag. cal., 5 shot, double action only, hammerless, 2 in. barrel with fixed sights, rubber boot grips, blue finish. New 2001.

| MSR | $375 | $295 | $220 | $160 | $130 | $110 | $95 | $85 |

✳ *Model 650 CIA SS (Stainless Steel)* - similar to Model 650 CIA, except is matte stainless steel. New 2001.

| MSR | $422 | $325 | $240 | $180 | | | | |

T

Grading	100%	98%	95%	90%	80%	70%	60%

MODEL 669 - similar to Model 66 except has fully shrouded 4 or 6 in. barrel, blue finish, 37 oz. Disc. 1998.

	$260	$190	$145	$125	$115	$100	$90

Last MSR was $344.

Add $10 for VR barrel (mfg. 1989-1992).
Add $400 for Laser Aim Sight (offered 1990-1992).
Add $19 for compensated (669CP) barrel (new 1993).

* ***Model 669SS (Stainless Steel)*** - similar to Model 669, but in stainless steel. Disc. 1998.

	$325	$245	$190

Last MSR was $421.

Add $21 for compensated (669CP) barrel (new 1993).

MODEL 689 - similar to Model 669, except has VR. Disc. 1998.

	$265	$195	$145	$125	$115	$100	$90

Last MSR was $358.

Add $390 for Laser Aim Sight (mfg. 1990-91 only).

* ***Model 689SS (Stainless Steel)*** - similar to Model 669, but in stainless steel. Disc. 1999.

	$340	$255	$190

Last MSR was $435.

MODEL 731 ULTRA-LITE - .32 H&R Mag. cal., double action, 6 shot, matte stainless steel, 2 in. ported barrel, fixed sights, rubber boot grips, 17 oz. New 1998.

MSR	$425		$325	$230	$170

MODEL 731T - .32 H&R Mag. cal., 6 shot, all titanium construction, 2 in. ported barrel with fixed sights, bright blue, matte blue, or matte gold finish, rubber grips. Mfg. 1999 only.

	$460	$400	$350

Last MSR was $529.

MODEL 741 - .32 H&R Mag. cal., 6 shot, 3 or 4 in. barrel, blue only, adj. sights. Mfg. 1993-94.

	$205	$155	$125	$115	$100	$90	$85

Last MSR was $254.

* ***Model 741SS (Stainless Steel)*** - similar to Model 741, except is stainless steel. Mfg. 1993-94.

	$275	$215	$185

Last MSR was $342.

MODEL 761 - .32 H&R Mag. cal., 6 shot, 6 in. barrel, blue only, adj. sights. Mfg. 1993- 94.

	$250	$185	$145	$125	$115	$100	$90

Last MSR was $326.

MODEL 817 ULTRA-LITE - .38 Spl. cal., 7 shot, 2 in. ported or unported solid rib barrel, soft rubber grips, bright blue finish, 21 oz. New 1999.

MSR	$375		$295	$215	$155	$135	$110	$100	$90

Add $20 for ported barrel.

* ***Model 817 Ultra-Lite Stainless*** - similar to Model 817 Ultra-Lite, except is stainless steel. New 1999.

MSR	$420		$320	$245	$180

Add $20 for ported barrel.

MODEL 827 - .38 Spl. cal., 7 shot, 4 in. heavy SR barrel, fixed sights, rubber grips, 36½ oz. Mfg. 1999 only.

	$240	$215	$170	$130	$110	$100	$95

Last MSR was $317.

* ***Model 827 Stainless*** - similar to Model 827, except is stainless steel. Mfg. 1999 only.

	$280	$220	$170

Last MSR was $364.

T

Grading	100%	98%	95%	90%	80%	70%	60%

MODEL 850 CIA - .38 Spl. cal., 5 shot, hammerless, double action only, 2 in. barrel with fixed sights, rubber grips, blue finish. New 2001.

MSR	$375	$295	$220	$160	$130	$110	$95	$85

✴ *Model 850 CIA SS (Stainless Steel)* - similar to Model 850 CIA, except is matte stainless steel. New 2001.

MSR	$422	$325	$240	$180

MODEL 850T - .38 Spl. cal., similar to Model 850 CIA, except has shadow grey finish and all titanium construction. New 2001.

MSR	$563	$465	$415	$375

MODEL 941 - .22 Mag. cal., 8 shot, 2 (new 1997), 3 (disc. 1998), 4, or 5 in. barrel, blue only, adj. sights, full underlug on 4 and 5 in. barrels, soft rubber or wood (disc. 2000, 5 in. barrel only) grips, 24-27½ oz. New 1993.

MSR	$345	$260	$190	$145	$120	$105	$95	$85

✴ *Model 941 Ultra-Lite* - ultra light hammer forged frame, available in matte blue or bright stainless steel, 18.5 oz. New 1999.

MSR	$375	$280	$205	$155	$125	$105	$95	$85

Add $50 for matte stainless steel construction.

✴ *Model 941SS (Stainless Steel)* - similar to Model 941, except is polished stainless steel. New 1993.

MSR	$395	$295	$220	$160

MODEL 970 TRACKER SS (STAINLESS STEEL) - .22 LR cal., double action, 7 shot, 6½ in. heavy barrel with VR and adj. rear sight, Ribber grips, matte stainless steel. New 2001.

MSR	$375	$280	$210	$160

MODEL 971 TRACKER SS (STAINLESS STEEL) - .22 Mag. cal., otherwise similar to Model 970 Tracker. New 2001.

MSR	$391	$315	$235	$195

MODEL 980 SILHOUETTE SS (STAINLESS STEEL) - .22 LR cal., 7 shot, double action, 12 in. heavy barrel with adj. rear sight, Ribber grips, includes scope mount. New 2001.

MSR	$398	$325	$240	$200

MODEL 981 SILHOUETTE SS (STAINLESS STEEL) - .22 Mag. cal., otherwise similar to Model 980 Silhouette SS. New 2001.

MSR	$414	$340	$250	$205

RIFLES: SLIDE ACTION

MODEL 62 RIFLE/CARBINE - .22 LR or .22 Mag. (disc. 2000) cal., patterned after the Win. Model 62, 16½ (carbine) or 23 (rifle) in. barrel with open adj. sights, 11 or 12 shot tube mag., includes switchable manual firing pin block on top of receiver bolt and integral Taurus Security System lock on hammer, uncheckered hardwood stock and grooved forearm, blue or case colored receiver, approx. 5 lbs. Importation began 1999.

MSR	$280	$250	$220	$190	$170	$155	$140	$125

Add $70 for rear tang sight (new 2002).
Add $16 for Taurus Rimfire Recharger (2 pack w/o ammo, new 2002).
Add $40 for scope base mount.

✴ *Model 62 Rifle/Carbine Stainless* - similar to Model 62 Rifle/Carbine, except is stainless steel. New 2000.

MSR	$295	$260	$230	$200

Add $70 for rear tang sight (new 2002).
Add $16 for Taurus Rimfire Recharger (2 pack w/o ammo, new 2002).
Add $40 for scope base mount.

T

Grading	100%	98%	95%	90%	80%	70%	60%

✳ *Model 62 Rifle/Carbine Youth/Adult Combo* - similar to Model 62 Rifle/Carbine, except is available with both youth (shortened LOP), and adult stocks. New 2002.

	MSR	$310	$270	$235	$200

Add $10 for stainless steel.
Add $16 for Taurus Rimfire Recharger (2 pack w/o ammo, new 2002).
Add $40 for scope base mount.

MODEL 72 RIFLE/CARBINE - .22 Mag. cal., 10 or 11 shot tube mag., otherwise similar to Model 62 Rifle/Carbine. Importation began 2001.

	MSR	$295	$260	$225	$195	$175	$155	$140	$125

Add $70 for rear tang sight (new 2002).
Add $16 for Taurus Rimfire Recharger (2 pack w/o ammo, new 2002).
Add $40 for scope base mount.
Beginning 2001, this model's nomenclature changed from Model 62 to Model 72 (.22 Mag. cal. only).

✳ *Model 72 Rifle/Carbine Stainless* - similar to Model 72 Rifle/Carbine, except is stainless steel. Importation began 2001.

	MSR	$310	$270	$235	$200

Add $80 for rear tang sight (new 2002).
Add $16 for Taurus Rimfire Recharger (2 pack w/o ammo, new 2002).
Add $40 for scope base mount.

TAYLOR, F.C. FUR CO.

Previous company which marketed animal trap guns circa 1921-1941.

PISTOLS: SINGLE SHOT

.22 CAL. TAYLOR FUR GETTER - .22 LR cal., designed to shoot animal at close range once trigger mechanism has been activated (usually with bait attached to a lever). Mfg. by O.F. Mossberg for Taylor, ser. range 1-3,100.

	N/A	$650	$600	$560	$530	$500	$475

Add 10%-15% for low ser. no. with two-piece swiveling stake.

.38 CAL. TAYLOR FUR GETTER - .38 cal., mfg. on 1914 patent of C.D. Lovelace, believed to have been mfg. by Hopkins & Allen, markings cast in top of frame (brass) with iron barrel - all bearing the 1914 patent date.

	N/A	$550	$500	$460	$430	$400	$375

Add 10%-15% premium for alloy frame with top plate attached with two screws and uncracked frame.

TAYLOR'S & CO., INC.

Current importer and distributor established during 1988, and located in Winchester, VA.

Taylor's & Co. is an importer of both black powder and firearms reproductions, in addition to being the exclusive U.S. distributor for Armi Sport, located in Brescia, Italy. Please contact the company directly for current pricing and model availability (see Trademark Index).

For more information and up-to-date regarding current Taylor's & Co., Inc. black powder models, please refer to *Colt Blackpowder Reproductions and Replicas*, and the 2nd Edition *Blue Book of Modern Black Powder Values*, by Dennis Adler. These books feature hundreds of color photographs and support text of the most recent black powder models available, as well as a complete pricing and reference guide.

REVOLVERS: REPRODUCTIONS, SAA

The 1873 Cattleman single action is available in 7 different calibers, in 4¾, 5½, or 7½ in. barrel with different metal finishes. Retail values are currently in the $375- $435 range.

Grading	100%	98%	95%	90%	80%	70%	60%

RIFLES: REPRODUCTIONS

Taylor's Sharps reproduction models are manufactured by Armi Sport, located in Brescia, Italy. There are available in an 1874 Standard and Deluxe Sporting Rifle in 45-70 Govt. cal., in addition to other variations, including the Berdan and Cavalry Models.

Currently, Taylor's is also importing a Henry rifle, available in either brass or iron frame, a Model 1866 brass frame sporting rifle and carbine, Model 1873 rifle with case colored receiver and deluxe uncheckered walnut, and an 1885 High Wall and Low Wall single shot rifle.

For more information on Taylor's complete lineup of Sharps & Winchester reproduction rifles and accessories, including availability and pricing, please contact Taylor's directly (see Trademark Index).

MODEL 1865 SPENCER CARBINE (MODEL 160) - .44 Russian, .45 Schofield, or .56-50 cal., reproduction of the Civil War Spencer carbine, case colored receiver, lock, and hammer, 20 in. barrel, walnut stock and forearm, includes slings. Importation began 2002.

MSR	$1,600		$1,325	$1,100	$975	$825	$700	$600	$500

TECHNO ARMS (PTY) LIMITED

Previous manufacturer located in Johannesburg, S. Africa circa 1994-96. Previously imported by Vulcans Forge, Inc. located in Foxboro, MA.

SHOTGUNS: SLIDE ACTION

MAG-7 SLIDE ACTION SHOTGUN - 12 ga. (60mm chamber length), 5 shot detachable mag. (in pistol grip), 14, 16, 18, or 20 in. barrel, stock or pistol grip, matte finish, 8 lbs. Imported 1995-96.

	$795	$675	$625	$550	$500	$450	$400

Last MSR was $875.

TERRIER ONE

Previous trademark distributed by Serrifile located in Lancaster, CA.

REVOLVERS

TERRIER ONE - .32 S&W cal., double action, 2¼ in. barrel, 5 shot, nickel-plated, 17 oz. Mfg. 1984-87.

	$45	$35	$30	$25	$25	$25	$25

Last MSR was $55.

TEXAS ARMS

Previous manufacturer located in Waco, TX, until circa 1999.

DERRINGERS: O/U

DEFENDER - .357 Mag., .38 Spl., 9mm Para., .44 Mag., .45 ACP, or .45 LC/.410 bore shotshell, features 3 in. interchangeable SS octagon barrels, spur trigger, shell ejector for rimmed cartridges, rebounding hammer and retracting firing pins, crossbolt safety, bead blasted grey finish, 16-21 oz. Mfg. 1993 - circa 1999.

	$275	$235	$200	$175	$160	$145	$130

Last MSR was $310.

Add $100 per interchangeable set of barrels.

T

Grading	100%	98%	95%	90%	80%	70%	60%

TEXAS GUNFIGHTERS

Previous importer located in Irving, TX circa 1988-1990.

REVOLVERS: SINGLE ACTION

SHOOTIST EDITION - .45 LC cal., patterned after the Colt SAA, 4¾ in. barrel, nickel- plated black powder frame, one piece walnut grips, mfg. by A. Uberti of Italy. New 1988.

* **Standard Model** - 1,000 total mfg., cased.

$625	$525	$440

Last MSR was $649.

* **1 of 100 Edition** - 100 total mfg., fully engraved, genuine mother-of-pearl one piece grips, cased.

$1,275	$1,050	$775

Last MSR was $1,395.

This model was also supplied with an extra set of walnut grips.

TEXAS LONGHORN ARMS, INC.

Previous manufacturer located in Richmond, TX circa 1988-1997.

REVOLVERS

SINGLE-ACTION - various cals., patterned after Colt's SAA, except the ejection port has been moved to left side of frame enabling left-hand loading, mfg. from 4140 steel, 1- piece grip, adj. trigger, case-hardened and blue, entirely hand-made, supplied with lifetime warranty. Models included the Texas Border Patrol (last MSR was $1,595), South Texas Army (last MSR was $1,595), Texas Flattop (last MSR was $1,595), Grover's Northpaw (last MSR was $685), and Grover's Improved Number Five (last MSR was $1,195). Special editions and sets were also advertised (ranging from $1,500 MSR - $7,650 MSR), but very few were actually built. Mint examples are currently in the $1,350-$1,500 range, except for Grover's Northpaw, which is in the $650 range. While production plans called for 1,000 of each model to be manufactured, very few pistols were actually made.

THOMAS

Previous trademark manufactured by Alexander James Ordnance, Inc. located in Covina, CA.

Please refer to listing under A.J. Ordnance in this text.

THOMPSON & CAMPBELL

Current rifle manufacturer located in Rosshire, Scotland. No current U.S. importation. Consumer direct sales.

RIFLES: BOLT ACTION

Thompson & Campbell manufactures high quality bolt action rifles featuring the patented Inver action, which utilizes a rear extension plate and reinforcement rod that is inletted into the stock for additional strength. Individual models include the Inver, Cromie, the Islay, and Jura (Mannlicher configuration). Thompson & Campbell manufactures approx. 20-24 rifles annually. Please contact the factory directly for more information, current pricing, and delivery times.

THOMPSON CARBINES & PISTOLS

See Auto Ordnance Corp. section of this book.

T

Grading	100%	98%	95%	90%	80%	70%	60%

THOMPSON/CENTER ARMS CO., INC.

Current manufacturer established during 1967, and located in Rochester, NH. Distributor and dealer sales.

Please refer to the *Blue Book of Modern Black Powder Values* by Dennis Adler (now online also) for more information and prices on Thompson/Center's lineup of modern black powder models.

PISTOLS: SINGLE SHOT

Caution: older and newer TC components do not interchange safely. Although parts will fit, they may not function properly. Special ordering of barrels, frames, and calibers started in 1988.

G2 CONTENDER - various rimfire and centerfire cals., replacement for the Contender model, features finger groove grips, will accept older Contender barrels w/o frame alteration, automatic hammer block safety with built-in interlock, hammer recocking w/o breaking open the gun, opening has been made easier, approx. 3 1/4 lbs. New late 2002.

As this edition went to press, prices had yet to be established on this model.

CONTENDER - .22 LR, .22 Rem., 5mm Rem., .218 Bee, .22 Hornet, .22 Jet, .221 Fireball, .222 Rem., .25-35 WCF, .256 Mag., .30 Carbine, .30-30 Win., .38 Spl., .357 Mag., .17 Ackley Bee, .17 Bumblebee, .17 Hornet, .17K Hornet, .17 Rem., .300 Whisper (new 1994), .30 Herrett, .357 Herrett, .357-44 B&D, 7x30 Waters, .32 H&R Mag., .32-20 WCF, 6mm TCU, 6.5mm TCU, or 9mm Para. cal., barrels are interchangeable, 8¾ (disc.), 10, or 14 in. barrel, hinged break open, triggerguard, action lever, blue, .44, .357 Mag., and .45 Colt available with detachable choke for hot shot cartridges, VR, 10 in. barrel available, 10 in. bull barrel, adj. sights, checkered walnut grip and forearm. Mfg. 1967-2000.

The Contender action was made in 3 variations, and a wide variety of changes were made to grips, stocks, sights, etc. during 1967-2000. These production variances do not necessarily add premiums to values listed.

✱ *Bull Barrel* - available in 13 cals. between .17 Rem. and .45 Win. Mag., 10 in. round barrel only.

	100%	98%	95%	90%	80%	70%	60%
	$380	$295	$220	$190	$170	$160	$150

Last MSR was $510.

Add $22 for .45 Colt/.410 bore with internal chokes.
Add $11 for .22 LR match grade chamber (new 1996).
Add approx. $230-$267 per additional barrel.

✱ *Armour Alloy II Bull Barrel* - 7 cals. between .22 LR and .30-30 Win., similar to regular Bull Barrel, except has Armour Alloy II satin finish which is harder than stainless steel. Mfg. 1986-89.

	100%	98%	95%
	$320	$285	$230

Last MSR was $415.

Add $5 for .45 Colt/.410 bore internal choke.

✱ *Vent. Rib* - .357 Mag. (disc.), .44 Mag. (disc.) or .45 Colt/.410 bore, 10 in. VR barrel only, adj. front and flip up rear sight, internal choke became standard in 1985.

	100%	98%	95%	90%	80%	70%	60%
	$400	$300	$225	$185	$170	$160	$150

Last MSR was $533.

✱ *Armour Alloy Vent. Rib* - .45/.410 internal choke, has Armour Alloy II satin finish which is harder than stainless steel. Mfg. 1986-disc.

	100%	98%	95%
	$350	$295	$230

Last MSR was $435.

T

Grading	100%	98%	95%	90%	80%	70%	60%

* *Stainless Steel* - various cals., 10 in. bull barrel. Mfg. 1993-2000.

	$435	$315	$220				

Last MSR was $578.

Add approx. $240 per additional barrel.
Add $5 for .45/.410 with adj. sights.
Add $20 for .45/.410 with VR.

* *Octagon Barrel* - .22 LR, .22 Mag. (disc.), .22 Hornet (disc.), .22K Hornet (disc.), .222 Rem. (disc.), or .357 Mag. (disc.) cal., 10 in. barrel. Disc. 1998.

	$355	$260	$200	$180	$170	$160	$150

Last MSR was $474.

* *Match Grade Barrel* - .22 LR cal. only, choice of 10 or 14 in. match barrel. Mfg. 1992-98.

	$350	$265	$200	$180	$170	$160	$150

Last MSR was $460.

Add $10 for 14 in. barrel.

CONTENDER SHOOTERS PACKAGE - .22 LR Match, .223 Rem., .30-30 Win., or 7-30 Waters cal., includes blue frame and 14 in. barrel w/o sights, 2.5-7X scope, composite grips and forend, Weaver style base and rings, pistol case. Mfg. 1998-2000.

	$650	$575	$550	$450	$400	$360	$330

Last MSR was $754.

CONTENDER SUPER - 13 cals. available from .17 Rem. - .45 Win. Mag. (disc.), 14 or 16 in. bull barrel only, special grips, beavertail forearm, adj. sight, 3½ lbs. Disc. 1997.

	$360	$265	$200	$180	$170	$160	$150

Last MSR was $474.

Add $5 for 16 in. barrel.
Add $31 for .17 Rem. cal. (new 1992).
Add $10 for .45-70 Govt. cal. in 16 in. barrel only with muzzle brake (new 1992).
Add approx. $224 per additional barrel.
Add $31 for VR barrel (.45 LC/.410 bore only).
Thompson Center will also make special order guns in different cals. other than those listed above. If factory work, these pistols will be worth a premium.

* *Stainless Contender Super* - various cals., choice of 14 or 16 in. barrel. Mfg. 1993-97.

	$385	$275	$215				

Last MSR was $505.

Add $5 for 16 in. barrel.
Add $25 for .45-70 Govt. bull barrel with muzzle tamer.
Add $30-$35 for .45 LC/.410 bore with internal choke.
Add approx. $240 per additional barrel.

* *Armour Alloy II Super Contender* - 5 cals. between .22 LR and 7mm Rem. Mag., similar to regular Super Contender, except has Armour Alloy II satin finish which is harder than stainless steel. Mfg. 1986-89.

	$355	$295	$240				

Last MSR was $425.

SUPER CONTENDER - various cals. between .22 LR - .45-70 Govt., wood grips with rear stippling, barrel configurations include 14 or 16 in. bull (with or w/o VR), adj. sights, blue finish only. Mfg. 1999-2000.

	$410	$345	$285	$255	$220	$195	$170

Last MSR was $520.

Add $35 for 14 in. VR barrel.
Add $5 for 16 in. tapered barrel.

T

Grading	100%	98%	95%	90%	80%	70%	60%

✳ **Super Contender Stainless** - similar to Super Contender, except is only available in 14 in. barrel. Mfg. 1999-2000.

	$430	$320	$215				

Last MSR was $578.

Add $35 for VR barrel.
Add $22 for .45/.410 ga. barrel.

CONTENDER HUNTER PACKAGE - .223 Rem., .7-30 Waters, .30-30 Win., .35 Rem., .357 Rem. Max. (disc. 1994), .375 Win. Mag. (new 1992), .44 Mag., or .45-70 Govt. cal., special 12 (disc.) or 14 (new 1992) in. barrel with muzzle brake, 2.5X power scope with lighted reticle, walnut grip has nonslip rubber insert to cushion recoil, includes studs, swivels, sling, and deluxe carrying case, approx. 4 lbs. Mfg. 1990-97.

	$695	$575	$495	$430	$365	$315	$275

Last MSR was $798.

CONTENDER 25TH ANNIVERSARY - .22 LR cal. only, 10 in. octagon barrel, laser etched anniversary logo on receiver sides and barrel, checkered stock and forearm, limited mfg. in 1992 only.

	$610	$535	$465	$410	$360	$315	$275

Last MSR was $700.

✳ **Contender 25th Anniversary Cased Set** - cased set with 5 barrels including .22 LR, .22 Mag., .22 Jet, .22 Hornet, and .38 Spl. cal., 50 sets mfg. 1992 only.

	$1,850	$1,550	$1,225	$1,050	$900	$775	$650

Last MSR was $1,975.

ENCORE - various cals., .480 Ruger new 2002, features walnut grip with finger grooves and forend, blue finish, 10 (disc. 1999), 12 (new 1999), or 15 in. barrel with adj. sights, VR barrel on .45 LC/.410 bore, hammer block safety with bolt interlock, 4-4½ lbs. New 1998.

MSR	$555		$430	$365	$290	$255	$220	$195	$170

Add $8 for 15 in. barrel on most cals.
Add $228 for extra 10 in. (disc.) or $253 for extra 15 in. barrel.
Add $22 for .480 Ruger cal.
Add approx. $23-$40 for .45 LC/.410 bore barrel, depending on barrel length.
Encore pistol barrels ARE NOT interchangeable with Contender pistol barrels.

✳ **Encore Stainless** - .22-250 Rem., .223 Rem., .308 Win., or 7mm-08 Rem. cal., available in 15 in. barrel only, black synthetic finger groove grips and forearm. New 1999.

MSR	$611		$485	$370	$260			

✳ **Encore Hunter Package** - .22-250 Rem., .270 Win., or .308 Win. cal., features 15 in. barrel w/o sights and 2.5-7X scope, Weaver base and rings, composite grip and forend, includes case. New 1998.

MSR	$818		$700	$600	$565	$465	$400	$360	$330

RIFLES

ENCORE RIFLE - available in many cals. between .22-250 Rem. and .45-70 Govt., interchangeable standard 24 or heavy 26 in. barrel, automatic hammer block, trigger guard opening lever, choice of black synthetic (new 1999) or American walnut uncheckered forearm and Monte Carlo stock with pistol grip, adj. rear sight, approx. 7 lbs. New 1997.

MSR	$588		$470	$360	$285	$235	$195	$180	$170

Add $26 for walnut stock and forearm.
Add $10 for .45-70 Govt. cal.
Add $262 per extra blue finish barrel.
Encore rifle barrels ARE NOT interchangeable with Contender Carbine barrels.

T

Grading	100%	98%	95%	90%	80%	70%	60%

❋ **Encore Stainless** - similar to Encore Rifle, except has black synthetic stock and forearm only, and is stainless steel. New 1999.

MSR $657	$525	$375	$265				

Add $301 per extra barrel.
Add $11 for .45-70 Govt. cal.

❋ **Encore Katahdin Carbine** - .444 Marlin, .450 Marlin, or .45-70 Govt. cal., 18 in. barrel with muzzle tamer, blue steel, black composite stock and forearm, fiber optic sights, drilled and tapped, 6 lbs., 10 oz. New 2002.

MSR $606	$485	$365	$250	$235	$195	$180	$170

❋ **Encore Hunter Package** - .300 Win. Mag., or .308 Win. cal., includes 3-9x40mm scope, Weaver style base and rings, and hard case. New 2002.

MSR $870	$740	$625	$575	$475	$400	$360	$330

CONTENDER CARBINE - available in 15 cals. between .17 Rem. and .44 Rem. Mag., also .410 bore (3 in.), Contender action with pistol grip full stock and forearm, 21 in. interchangeable barrel, drilled for scope mounts, iron sights standard. Mfg. 1986-2000.

	$415	$315	$255	$215	$190	$175	$160

Last MSR was $540.

Add $31 for .17 Rem. cal. (disc. 1997).
Add $21 for .410 bore barrel. (disc. 1997).
Add approx. $244 per extra barrel.
Add $11 for match grade .22 LR barrel.
Subtract $36 for Youth Model (16¼ in. barrel w/o VR - disc. 1998).
Add $175 for Survival Carbine System (disc. - includes Rynite stock, 16¼ .223 Rem. barrel, extra .45 Colt/.410 barrel, and soft camo cordura case).

❋ **Rynite Contender Carbine** - similar to Contender Carbine, except has Rynite stock and forend. Mfg. 1990- 1993.

	$335	$270	$220	$195	$180	$165	$155

Last MSR was $425.

Add $30 for .17 Rem. cal.
Add $10 for match grade barrel.
Add $25 for 21 in. VR smooth bore .410 bore barrel.

❋ **Contender Carbine Stainless** - various cals., 21 in. barrel, choice of walnut (disc. 1993) or Rynite synthetic stock. Mfg. 1993-2000.

	$415	$310	$230				

Last MSR was $546.

Add $35 for walnut stock (disc.).
Add $11 for .22 LR match barrel (new 1995).
Add $26 for .410 smooth bore barrel with screw-in full choke (disc.).

This model was also available in a Youth Model with walnut stock at no extra charge (disc. 1993).

HUNTER RIFLE MODEL - single shot, top lever break open action w/interchangeable barrels, .22 Hornet, .223 Rem., .22-250 Rem., .243 Win., .270 Win., 7x57mm, .30-06, .308 Win., .375 H&H (new 1992), or .416 Rem. Mag. (new 1992) cal., 23 in. barrel, 6 lbs. 14 oz., checkered walnut stock, choice of medium or light sporter weight barrel. New 1983 and improved in 1987. Available in left-hand at no extra charge. Disc. 1992.

	$500	$415	$350	$295	$265	$240	$220

Last MSR was $595.

Add $20 for .375 H&H or .416 Rem. Mag. cal.
Add approx. $275 per extra rifle barrel.

❋ **Hunter Deluxe Rifle Model** - similar to Hunter Model, except features double triggers and upgraded walnut stock and forearm. Mfg. 1992 only.

	$550	$450	$375	$325	$285	$250	$225

Last MSR was $675.

Add $20 for .375 H&H or .416 Rem. Mag. cal.

T

Grading	100%	98%	95%	90%	80%	70%	60%

* ❋ **Hunter Shotgun Model** - same action as Hunter Rifle, except is supplied with 12 ga. barrel (field choke with 3½ in. chamber or slug with 3 in. chamber and iron sights) or 10 ga. barrel (3½ in. chamber). Disc. 1992.

	$500	$415	$350	$295	$265	$240	$220

Last MSR was $595.

Add $275 per additional shotgun barrel.

TCR '83 ARISTOCRAT - similar to Hunter Model, except stock has cheekpiece and forearm is checkered, stainless steel, double set triggers. Disc. 1986.

	$425	$370	$345

Last MSR was $475.

Add $175 for each additional barrel(s) (including 12 ga. slug).

RIFLES: SEMI-AUTO

CLASSIC - .22 LR cal., blowback action, all steel construction, 8 shot mag., 22 in. match grade barrel with muzzle crown, adj. rear sight, blue finish, uncheckered Monte Carlo walnut stock, 5½ lbs. New 2000.

MSR	$349	$285	$250	$215	$190	$160	$140	$120

SHOTGUNS: SINGLE SHOT

ENCORE SHOTGUN - 20 ga., 3 in. chamber, 26 in. VR barrel with three choke tubes, recoil pad. New 1998.

MSR	$656	$555	$475	$380	$310	$250	$200	$175

Add $299-$346 per additional shotgun barrel with choke tubes.

* ❋ **Encore Slug Gun** - 12 or 20 ga. only, 3 in. chamber, 24 or 26 in. rifled barrel with fiber optic sights, walnut stock and forearm. New 2000.

MSR	$625	$535	$450	$375	$310	$250	$225	$200

Add $27 for 12 ga.

* ❋ **Encore Turkey Gun** - 12 ga. only, 3 in. chamber, 24 in. smoothbore barrel with screw in turkey choke tube, 100% Advantage Timber camo coverage, and fiber optic sights. New 2002.

MSR	$726	$575	$500	$400	$325	$275	$225	$200

THUNDER-FIVE

Previous trademark manufactured by Holston Enterprises, Inc., located in Piney Flats, TN. Various current distributors. Previously manufactured by Mil, Inc. located in Piney Flats, TN. Previously distributed by C.L. Reedy & Associates, Inc. located in Jonesborough, TN.

While previously advertised as the Spectre Five (not mfg.), this firearm was re-named the Thunder Five.

REVOLVERS

THUNDER-FIVE - .45 LC cal./.410 bore with 3 in. chamber or .45-70 Govt. cal. (new 1994), single or double action, unique 5 shot revolver design permits shooting .45 LC or .410 bore shotshells interchangeably, 2 in. rifled barrel, phosphate finish, external ambidextrous hammer block safety, internal draw bar safety, combat sights, hammer, trigger, and trigger guard, Pachmayr grips, includes padded plastic carrying case, 48 oz., serialization starts at 1,101. Mfg. 1992-2000.

	$425	$400	$375	$350	$325	$300	$275

Last MSR was $450.

Sub-caliber sleeve inserts were available for 9mm Para., .357 Mag./.38 Spl., and .38 Super cals.

Grading		100%	98%	95%	90%	80%	70%	60%

TIKKA

Current trademark imported by Beretta U.S.A. Corp., located in Accokeek, MD. Previously imported until 2000 by Stoeger Industries, located in Wayne, NJ. Rifles are currently manufactured by Sako, Ltd. located in Riihimäki, Finland. Previously manufactured by Oy Tikkakoski Ab, of Tikkakoski, Finland (pre-1989).

During 2000, Tikka was purchased by Beretta Holding of Italy. All currently produced Tikkas are imported by Beretta U.S.A. Corp., located in Accokeek, MD.
Also see listings under Ithaca LSA for older models.

COMBINATIONS GUNS: O/U

Previously manufactured in Jyvaskyla, Finland. In 1989, under a joint venture agreement made in Italy, the 412 O/U shooting system was manufactured in Italy. Older models may be found in the Valmet trademark section of this text.

During 1993, the new models of the 512S series replaced the older 412S series. Separate listings have not been provided, since they are almost identical in most respects.

MODEL 512S SHOOTING SYSTEM - interchangeable barrel assemblies permit a double rifle, shotgun/rifle, and O/U shotgun configuration, user installed interchangeable barrels, monobloc locking, rifle barrel positioning by adjustment, SST, extractors or ejectors, checkered walnut stock and forend, cocking indicators, blue finish.
The 412S Model nomenclature was changed to 512S in late 1993.

* ***Model 512S Field Grade*** - 12 ga. only, 3 in. chambers, auto ejectors, screw-in choke tubes (includes 5), 26 or 28 in. barrels, matte nickel finish. New 1986-importation disc. 1997, reintroduced 2000 only.

		$1,050	$750	$595	$550	$475	$440	$400

Last MSR was $1,134.

Subtract 10% for Standard Grade.
Add $45 for Sporting Clays Model (new 2000).
Add $659 per extra set of shotgun/rifle barrels.
The Premium Grade became standard issue beginning 1995. This model was reintroduced in 2000 only, and new features included back boring and ported barrels (Sporting Clays Model only).

* ***Model 412ST Trap*** - 12 ga., Monte Carlo stock, 30 in. barrels, screw-in chokes standard.

		$1,125	$925	$725	$650	$580	$540	$475

Last MSR was $1,325.

This variation was made by Valmet in Finland.

* ***Model 412ST Premium Grade Trap*** - similar to Model 412ST Trap, except has better walnut and checkering.

		$1,425	$1,000	$875	$750	$625	$580	$515

Last MSR was $1,665.

This variation was made by Valmet in Finland.

* ***Model 512S Sporting Clays*** - 12 ga. only, sporting clays configuration with 28 or 30 (new 1994) in. VR barrels and choke tubes. Imported 1992-97.

		$1,160	$950	$735	$650	$580	$540	$475

Last MSR was $1,360.

* ***Model 512S Combination Gun*** - combination rifle/shotgun, 12 ga, 3 in. chambers, 24 in. barrels, under rifle barrel has choice of .222 Rem., .30-06, or .308 Win. cal., extractors. Importation disc. 1997.

		$1,425	$1,025	$775	$675	$600	$525	$475

Last MSR was $1,770.

T

Grading	100%	98%	95%	90%	80%	70%	60%

✳ *Model 512S Double Rifle* - .30-06 (new 1994), .308 Win. (new 1994), 9.3x74R cal., 24 in. barrels, extractors. Importation disc. 1997.

	$1,525	$1,125	$825	$750	$625	$550	$500

Last MSR was $1,890.

Add $745-$765 for extra shotgun barrels (includes screw-in chokes), $810 for extra shotgun/ rifle combo, and $1,040 for double rifle barrels.

RIFLES: BOLT ACTION

NEW GENERATION RIFLE - .22-250 Rem., .223 Rem., .243 Win., .270 Win., .30- 06, .308 Win., 7mm Rem. Mag., .300 Win. Mag., or .338 Win Mag. cal., 22½ (non- Mag.) or 24½ (Mag. cals.) in. barrel, detachable 3 (standard) or 5 (optional) shot mag., forged and milled action in two lengths, checkered walnut stock, 7-7½ lbs. Sako mfg. 1989-94.

	$725	$600	$550	$500	$450	$400	$360

Last MSR was $835.

Add $25 for Mag. cals.
Cals. .22-250 Rem., .308 Win., and .300 Win. Mag. were introduced in late 1989.

PREMIUM GRADE MODEL - same cals. as New Generation Rifle, stock is select walnut with roll-over cheek-piece and rosewood pistol grip cap and forend tip, high polished barrel blue. Imported 1989-94.

	$860	$715	$600	$550	$500	$450	$400

Last MSR was $1,030.

Add $40 for Mag. cals.

VARMINT MODEL - .22-250 Rem., .223 Rem., .243 Win., or .308 Win. cal., 24½ in. heavy barrel, no sights. Mfg. 1991-94.

	$895	$750	$625	$550	$500	$450	$400

Last MSR was $1,090.

WHITETAIL HUNTER/SYNTHETIC (BATTUE) - .22-250 Rem. (new 1995), .223 Rem. (new 1995), .243 Win. (new 1995), .25-06 Rem.(new 1995), .270 Win., .30-06, .308 Win. (not available in synthetic), 6.5x55mm Swedish (new 2002), 7mm Rem. Mag., 7mm-08 Rem. (new 1999), .300 Win. Mag., or .338 Win. Mag. cal., 20½ (disc. 1994), 22½ (new 1995), or 24½ (new 1995, Mag cals. only), in. barrel, 3 or 5 (optional) shot detachable mag., choice of wood or black synthetic (new 1996) stock, no sights (Hunter Model), or open sights on raised rib (disc., Battue Model), approx. 7¼ lbs. New in 1991.

MSR	$615	$525	$450	$390	$350	$325	$300	$275

Add $30 for Mag. cals.
Add $60 for carved elk or deer game scene stock (mfg. 1996-97).
Add $65 for left-hand action (new 2000).

✳ *Whitetail Hunter/Battue Stainless* - similar cals. as Whitetail Hunter, except not available in 6.5x55mm Swedish cal., black synthetic stock only and satin finished stainless steel, 7¼ lbs. New 1997.

MSR	$680	$590	$530	$460

Add $30 for Mag. cals.

✳ *Whitetail Hunter Stainless Laminate* - .25-06 Rem., .270 Win., .30-06, .300 Win. Mag., or 7mm Rem. mag. cal., similar to Whitetail Hunter Stainless, except has grey laminate wood stock and forend with checkering, satin finished stainless steel, 3 shot detachable mag., 7¼ lbs. New 2002.

MSR	$745	$650	$565	$500

Add $30 for Mag. cals.

✳ *Whitetail Hunter Deluxe* - similar cals. as Whitetail Hunter, gloss finished deluxe checkered walnut stock and forearm with rollover cheekpiece. Importation began 1999.

MSR	$745	$650	$565	$500	$460	$400	$360	$330

Add $30 for Mag. cals.

T

Grading	100%	98%	95%	90%	80%	70%	60%

CONTINENTAL VARMINT MODEL - .17 Rem. (new 2000), .22-250 Rem., .223 Rem., or .308 Win. cal., heavy 26 in. barrel, adj. trigger, quick release 3 shot detachable mag., integral scope mount rails, recoil pad spacer system, 8 1/8 lbs. New 1996.

MSR $720	$615	$520	$460	$400	$350	$325	$300

CONTINENTAL LONG RANGE HUNTER - .25-06 Rem., .270 Win., 7mm Rem. Mag., or .300 Win. Mag. cal., heavy 26 in. barrel w/o sights, checkered walnut stock and forend, 8 3/8 lbs. New 1996.

MSR $720	$615	$520	$460	$400	$350	$325	$300

Add $30 for Mag. cals.

SPORTER MODEL - .22-250 Rem., .223 Rem., .308 Win., 7mm-08 Rem. (new 2002), cal., 23 3/8 in. barrel w/o sights, competition style stock with adj. buttplate and cheekpiece, detachable 5 shot mag., stippled pistol grip and forend, 9 lbs. New 1998.

MSR $950	$845	$765	$660	$580	$515	$450	$395

TIMBERWOLF

Previous trademark manufactured by I.M.I. (Israel Military Industries) located in Israel. Previously imported and distributed by Action Arms located in Philadelphia, PA until 1994.

RIFLES: SLIDE ACTION

TIMBERWOLF - .357 Mag. or .44 Mag. (disc.) cal., slide action, straight grip shotgun style stock with adj. drop, blue or satin chrome finish, takedown, 18½ in. barrel, 10 shot tube mag., sear locking and firing pin safeties, integral scope base, approx. 5½ lbs. Imported 1989-1993.

.357 Mag.	$260	$230	$195	$180	$160	$145	$130
.44 Mag. (blue only)	$425	$375	$335	$300	$275	$250	$225

Last MSR was $299.

Add $80 for satin chrome finish.

This model was designed by Evan Whilden, and imported/distributed by Action Arms Ltd. Springfield Armory imported 1,000 .44 Mag. Timberwolf models during 1990-1991.

TIME PRECISION ARMS

Current custom riflemaker located in Brookfield, CT. Consumer direct sales.

RIFLES: BOLT ACTION

Time Precision rifles feature SLV/ALV actions and are available in over 30 different types, in cals. from .22 LR - .416 Rigby, prices range from $834-$1,062. All guns are made per individual custom order, but are basically available in 3 different configurations - Hunting, Benchrest, and Target rifles. Base prices begin at $2,202 (add $100 for Mag. cals.), and $1,980 for .22 Sporter. with a wide range of special order options. Actions are also available starting at $924. Please contact the company directly regarding delivery times and other information.

TIPPMAN ARMS CO.

Previous manufacturer located in Fort Wayne, IN.

Tippman Arms manufactured ½ scale semi-auto working models of famous machine guns. All models were available with an optional hardwood case, extra ammo cans, and other accessories. Mfg. 1986-1987 only.

REPRODUCTIONS: SEMI-AUTO

MODEL 1919 A-4 - .22 LR cal. only, copy of Browning 1919 A-4 Model, belt fed, closed bolt operation, 11 in. barrel, includes tripod, 10 lbs.

		$3,125	$2,950	$2,700	$2,350	$2,000	$1,725	$1,500

Last MSR was $1,325.

Grading	100%	98%	95%	90%	80%	70%	60%

MODEL 1917 - .22 LR cal. only, copy of Browning M1917, watercooled, belt fed, closed bolt operation, 11 in. barrel, includes tripod, 10 lbs.

	$6,375	$6,000	$5,500	$5,000	$4,350	$3,750	$3,250

Last MSR was $1,830.

MODEL .50 HB - .22 Mag. cal. only, copy of Browning .50 cal. machine gun, belt fed, closed bolt operation, 18¼ in. barrel, includes tripod, 13 lbs.

	$6,625	$6,400	$5,950	$5,400	$4,950	$4,500	$4,000

Last MSR was $1,929.

TOKAREV

See Russian Service Pistols and Rifles section.

TOLLEY, J & W

Current trademark manufactured by Premier English Shotguns, Ltd., located in Leicestershire, England.

RIFLES: SxS

J & W TOLLEY SIDELOCK - various cals. between .375 H&H - .600 NE, true H&H style action, approx. 12-18 months delivery time.

Prices in this model range from $55,000-$70,000, depending on caliber, options, and/or special orders.

TORNADO

Currently manufactured by AseTekno located in Helsinki, Finland.

RIFLES: BOLT ACTION

TORNADO MODEL - .338 Lapua Mag. cal., unique straight line design with free floating barrel, 5 shot mag., pistol grip assembly is part of frame, limited importation into the U.S.

The factory should be contacted directy regarding domestic availability and pricing (see Trademark Index).

TOZ

Current manufacturer established in 1712, and located in Tula, Russia. Limited U.S. importation. Previously imported by Tula Firearms, located in San Diego, CA. TOZ is an abbreviation for Tulsky Oruzheiny Zavod. Dealer sales.

TOZ manufactures a wide variety of quality O/U, SxS, single shot, and semi-auto shotguns, in addition to both rifles and combination guns. TOZ also provides a complete line of custom services, including elaborate inlays (gold, silver, and platinum) and wood carving. Please contact the importer directly for more information regarding the TOZ trademark, including current U.S. model availability and pricing.

PISTOLS: SINGLE SHOT

TOZ-35 FREE PISTOL - .22 LR cal., employs virtually every shooting refinement possible in a single shot target pistol, fully adj. target grips, limited mfg.

MSR	$995		$875	$795	$725	$650	$575	$475	$375

This model is currently available from Nygord Precision.

TRADEWINDS

Previous importer located in Tacoma, WA.

RIFLES

HUSKY MODEL 5000 - .22-250 Rem., .243 Win., .270 Win., .308 Win., or .30-06 cal., bolt action, 23¾ in. barrel, adj. sight, removable mag., hand-checkered walnut stock.

	$325	$310	$290	$250	$225	$200	$175

T

Grading	100%	98%	95%	90%	80%	70%	60%

MODEL 311-A - .22 LR cal., bolt action, 5 shot, 22½ in. barrel, folding leaf rear sight, walnut checkered stock.

	$180	$170	$150	$130	$120	$100	$85

MODEL 260-A - .22 LR cal., semi-auto, 5 shot, 22½ in. barrel, 3 leaf folding sight, checkered walnut stock.

	$200	$190	$175	$150	$130	$120	$100

SHOTGUNS: SEMI-AUTO

MODEL H-170 - 12 ga., 2¾ in. chamber, 26 in. mod. or 28 in. full, recoil operated action, alloy receiver, 5 shot, tube mag., VR, checkered walnut stock.

	$275	$265	$250	$225	$200	$180	$150

TRADITIONS PERFORMANCE FIREARMS
Current importer located in Old Saybrook, CT. Distributor and dealer sales.

Traditions Performance Firearms imports a wide variety of quality Stefano Fausti O/U & SxS shotguns from Italy, a semi-auto shotgun, and a complete line of imported lever action (Uberti mfg.) and single shot (Pedersoli mfg.) rifles and accessories. Please contact the company directly for more information (see Trademark Index) on their rifles and accessories.

Please refer to the *Blue Book of Modern Black Powder Values* by Dennis Adler (now online also) for more information and prices on Traditions' lineup of modern black powder models.

RIFLES

Traditions currently imports the Pedersoli 1874 Sharps and Remington rolling block sporting rifle reproductions. Prices range from $769 for the rolling block, to $769-$1,995 for the Sharps Standard/Deluxe Model 1874 sporting rifle. Traditions also imported Uberti black powder guns until 2002, including the Henry, Model 1866, and Model 1873. Prices ranged from $669-$969, depending on the model.

SHOTGUNS: O/U

CLASSIC FIELD SERIES - 12, 16, 20, 28 ga., or .410 bore, boxlock action, vent. barrels, vent. recoil pad, various configurations. Mfg. by Fausti, importation began 2000.

* **Field Hunter** - 12 or 20 ga., 3 in. chambers, 26 or 28 in. VR barrels with 2 choke tubes included, SST, extractors, checkered walnut stock and forearm, blue finish, 6 lbs. 7 oz. - 7 lbs. 4 oz.

MSR	$669	$610	$560	$500	$465	$430	$395	$375

* **Field I** - 12, 20, 28 ga., or .410 bore, 3 in. chambers (except for 28 ga.), 26 or 28 in. VR barrels with fixed chokes, gold SST, extractors, coin finished receiver with etched engraving, checkered walnut stock and forearm, blue finish, 6 lbs. 5 oz. - 7 lbs. 4 oz.

MSR	$619	$555	$505	$470	$435	$395	$375	$350

* **Field II** - 12, 16 (mfg. 2001 only), 20, 28 ga., or .410 bore, 3 in. chambers (12 and 20 ga. only), 26 or 28 in. VR barrels with 3 choke tubes (except 28 ga. and .410 bore) included, coin finished receiver with etched engraving, gold SST, ejectors, checkered walnut stock and forearm, blue finish, 6 lbs. 5 oz. - 7 lbs. 4 oz.

MSR	$789	$695	$625	$570	$530	$475	$425	$400

* **Field III Gold** - 12 ga. only, 3 in. chambers, 26 or 28 in. VR barrels with 3 choke tubes included, gold SST, ejectors, coin finished receiver with 3 gold engraved pheasants, deluxe checkered walnut stock and forearm, blue finish, protective gun sock and molded hard gun case became standard 2002, approx. 7 lbs. 5 oz.

MSR	$999	$890	$785	$680	$605	$550	$500	$450

T

Grading	100%	98%	95%	90%	80%	70%	60%

CLASSIC UPLAND SERIES - 12 or 20 ga., boxlock action, gold SST, vent. recoil pad, various configurations. Mfg. by Fausti, protective gun sock and molded hard gun case became standard 2002. Importation began 2000.

> ✳ *Upland II* - 3 in. chambers, 24 or 26 in. VR barrels with 3 choke tubes included, blue engraved receiver, traight English grip walnut stock with Schnabel forearm, 6 lbs. 3 oz. - 7 lbs. 3 oz.

	MSR	$839		$730	$650	$600	$550	$500	$465	$435

> ✳ *Upland III* - 3 in. chambers, 26 in. VR barrels with 3 choke tubes included, blue engraved receiver with gold pheasant inlays, checkered pistol grip walnut stock with Schnabel forearm, 7 lbs. 3 oz.

	MSR	$1,059		$945	$825	$715	$630	$580	$525	$475

CLASSIC SERIES SPORTING CLAYS II - 12 ga. only, 28 or 30 in. wide VR ported barrels with 4 extended choke tubes, SST, ejectors, coin finished receiver with perimeter engraving, checkered walnut stock with Schnabel forearm, approx. 8 lbs.

	MSR	$959		$855	$775	$685	$560	$510	$460	$420

> ✳ *Classic Series Sporting Clays III* - 12 or 20 ga., 28 or 30 in. wide VR ported barrels, SST, ejectors, hand finished silver engraved receiver with gold inlays, premium checkered walnut stock with Schnabel forearm, protective gun sock and molded hard gun case, approx. 7½ - 8 lbs. Importation began 2002.

	MSR	$1,189		$1,050	$900	$800	$725	$650	$575	$495

MAG. 350 SERIES - 12 ga. only, 3½ in. chambers, SST, ejectors, vent. recoil pad, various configurations.

> ✳ *Mag. Hunter II* - 28 in. vent. barrels with VR, matte black metal finish, matte finished checkered walnut stock and forearm, 3 choke tubes, sling swivels, 7 lbs. 2 oz.

	MSR	$799		$700	$630	$575	$530	$480	$425	$400

> ✳ *Waterfowl II* - 28 in. vent. barrels with VR, matte black receiver with Advantage Wetlands wood and barrel coverage, 3 choke tubes, sling swivels, 7¼ lbs.

	MSR	$899		$785	$680	$615	$560	$505	$465	$435

> ✳ *Turkey II* - 24 or 26 in. vent. barrels with VR, matte black receiver with Mossy Oak Breakup wood and barrel coverage, 3 choke tubes, sling swivels, approx. 7 lbs.

	MSR	$889		$780	$685	$610	$555	$505	$465	$435

SHOTGUNS: SxS

ELITE SERIES - 12, 20, 28 ga., or .410 bore, boxlock action, 3 in. chambers (except 28 ga.), fixed or multichoke tubes, SST. Mfg. by Fausti, importation began 2000.

> ✳ *Elite Field Hunter* - 12 or 20 ga. only, 26 in. barrels with 4 choke tubes, gold SST, blue finish with etched engraving, checkered walnut stock and forearm, approx. 6 or 6½ lbs.

	MSR	$999		$890	$785	$700	$575	$525	$475	$425

> ✳ *Elite Field I* - 26 in. barrels with fixed chokes, DT or ST, extractors, coin finished receiver with etched engraving, checkered walnut stock and forearm, 5 lbs. 12 oz. - 6 lbs. 8 oz.

	MSR	$789		$695	$625	$570	$530	$475	$425	$400

> Add $130 for gold SST.
> Add $80 for 28 ga. or .410 bore.

> ✳ *Elite Field III* - 28 ga. or .410 bore only, 26 in. barrels with fixed chokes, gold SST, ejectors, coin finished receiver with multiple gold inlays, deluxe checkered straight grip walnut stock and forearm, approx. 6¼ lbs.

	MSR	$2,099		$1,825	$1,550	$1,275	$1,000	$875	$750	$625

T

Grading	100%	98%	95%	90%	80%	70%	60%

SHOTGUNS: SEMI-AUTO

AL 2100 SERIES - 12 or 20 ga., 3 in. chamber, various VR barrel lengths, lightweight alloy receiver, gas operation, choke tubes in most models. Importation from Europe began 2000.

* **ALS Field Model** - checkered walnut stock and forearm, blue metal, multichokes, also available in Youth Model, 5 lbs. 10 oz. - 6 lbs. 5 oz.

MSR	$479	$430	$390	$355	$315	$285	$260	$230

* **ALS Hunter Model** - similar to ALS Field Model, except has black synthetic stock and forearm, not available in Youth Model, approx. 6¼ lbs.

MSR	$459	$410	$375	$335	$300	$270	$250	$225

* **ALS Hunter Combo** - includes 28 in. VR barrel and choice of 24 in. rifled slug barrel and walnut or synthetic stock and forearm. Importation began 2002.

MSR	$579	$540	$485	$450	$425	$395	$375	$350

Add $20 for cantilever scope mount and $30 for walnut stock and forearm.

* **ALS Slug Hunter Model** - similar to ALS Hunter Model, except is 12 ga. only, 24 in. rifled barrel with choice of rifle sights or cantilever scope mount, Turkish walnut or black synthetic stock and forearm. Importation began 2002.

MSR	$499	$435	$385	$340	$305	$275	$250	$225

Add $30 for cantilever scope mount or walnut stock and forearm.

* **ALS Turkey/Waterfowl Hunter Model** - 21 (Turkey Model with Mossy Oak Breakup, disc. 2001) or 28 (Waterfowl Model with Advantage Wetlands) in. barrel, 100% camo coverage.

MSR	$529	$465	$410	$365	$335	$300	$275	$250

* **ALS Turkey Hunter Model** - 12 ga. only, 26 in. barrel, 100% Mossy Oak Breakup camo coverage. Importation began 2002.

MSR	$519	$455	$400	$360	$330	$300	$275	$250

* **ALS 2100 Home Security Model** - 12 ga. only, 20 in. barrel bored IC, black synthetic stock and forearm, bead sights. Importation began 2002.

MSR	$399	$335	$295	$275	$250	$230	$210	$195

TRENCH/RIOT SHOTGUNS

The following is a chronological listing beginning with WWI of the various U.S. commercial Riot and military Trench and Riot shotguns mfg. to date.

The publisher wishes to express thanks to the late Pat Redmond and Rick Crosier for the information in this section.

Some 100% values have been intentionally omitted in this section as they are seldomly seen or sold.

All Trench/Riot shotguns listed are in 12 ga. only.

SHOTGUNS: MILITARY TRENCH, WWI

WINCHESTER MODEL 1897 MILITARY TRENCH GUN - high-polish commercial blue finish, solid frame with 6 row ventilated handguard for bayonet attachment, walnut high comb stock with hard rubber buttplate (no cartouches in stock). Guns used by the U.S. Army for trench warfare in WWI, originally did not have military markings. A "U.S." and ordnance bomb were hand stamped on the right side of the receiver on trench guns kept in the Army's inventory after the war. Military markings were added in the 1920s to about 10% of the total production. Serial range 650,000-695,000.

Trench Gun	N/A	$3,500	$2,400	$1,400	$1,000	$800	$700
Trench Gun w/military markings	N/A	$5,800	$4,350	$3,000	$1,800	$1,500	$1,250

Grading	100%	98%	95%	90%	80%	70%	60%

REMINGTON MODEL 10 MILITARY TRENCH GUN - high polish commercial blue finish with wood handguard on top of barrel, separate bayonet adaptor attaches to front of barrel for bayonet attachment. "U.S." and ordnance bomb marked on left side receiver, stock is unmarked. Extremely rare Trench gun and hard to find complete and in original condition. Trench gun barrel length is 22 in. as compared to 20 in. Riot gun. Prices quoted only for complete guns with wood handguard and bayonet adaptor. Serial range 160,000-165,000.

Trench Gun	N/A	$10,000	$8,500	$4,800	$3,500	$2,000	$1,800
Riot Gun	N/A	$1,900	$1,500	$1,200	$650	$500	$400

SHOTGUNS: MILITARY RIOT/TRENCH, WWII

ITHACA MODEL 37 MILITARY SHOTGUNS - rarest of all Trench shotguns, high polish commercial blue finish, RLB and ordnance bomb on left side of receiver, ordnance bomb on barrel, stocks not proofed, blue vent. handguard for bayonet attachment, only 1,420 Trench guns were ordered in 1941. Ithaca supplied mostly long barrel martially marked shotguns. Serial range 49,000-62,000.

Trench Gun	N/A	$8,500	$6,000	$5,000	$3,000	$2,500	$1,800
Riot Gun	N/A	$3,000	$2,500	$2,000	$1,000	$750	$600
Long Barrel	N/A	$1,850	$1,500	$1,000	$750	$600	$500

REMINGTON MODEL 31 MILITARY SHOTGUNS - commercial blue finish (high polish and flat blue finishes noted). Can be marked "U.S. Property" on receiver and/or barrel. Some examples noted with only ordnance mark on stock. Serial range 39,500- 60,500.

Riot Gun	N/A	$1,800	$1,500	$1,000	$750	$650	$500
Long Barrel	N/A	$1,200	$1,000	$650	$500	$400	$300
Shotguns w/compensator	N/A	$1,300	$1,100	$750	$600	$500	$400

REMINGTON MODEL 11 MILITARY SHOTGUNS - this is the most commonly found military shotgun. Examples of 5 shot and 3 shot Sportsman Model. Examples with plain or engraved receivers and plain or fancy checkered wood. Military marked with "U.S." and ordnance bomb on receiver and barrel. Later models are marked Military Finish. These shotguns all have highly polished commercial blue finish and ordnance marked stocks. Serial range 450,000-500,000 and 700,000-711,000.

Riot Guns	N/A	$1,000	$650	$450	$400	$350	$300
Long Barrel	N/A	$850	$500	$350	$300	$250	$200

* ***Riot Gun*** - this configuration was sold by the government as surplus as late as the 1970s and can occasionally be found NIB with packing materials and instruction manual. Mint in factory box - $2,000.

SAVAGE MODEL 720 MILITARY SHOTGUNS - appears identical to Remington Model 11. This was mfg. by Stevens/Savage in very limited quantities, plain and engraved receivers noted with high quality commercial blue finish. Stocks are unmarked and must have ramp sights to be original. Watch for altered guns made into Riots. Serial range 69,000-90,000.

Riot Gun	N/A	$1,850	$1,500	$1,100	$900	$750	$600
Long Barrel	N/A	$1,000	$800	$750	$500	$350	$300

STEVENS MODEL 620 MILITARY SHOTGUNS - this was the current model being sold by Stevens and has a commercial blue finish, but not of the same quality as the other companies. Trench guns are equipped with handguards that have a definite purple/reddish color to the front and dark blue vent. shaft. Model 620s are much rarer than 520s and have "U.S." and ordnance bomb on receiver, ordnance bomb on barrel and unmarked stock. Serial range 1,000-30,000.

Trench Gun	N/A	$3,200	$2,000	$1,500	$1,200	$800	$600
Riot Gun	N/A	$900	$750	$450	$400	$350	$250
Long Barrels	N/A	$500	$400	$250	$200	$175	$150

T

Grading	100%	98%	95%	90%	80%	70%	60%

STEVENS 520-30 MILITARY SHOTGUNS - this model was resurrected due to available machinery and is the most commonly found Trench gun. Riot guns in minty condition are hard to find. Same finish as Model 620, "U.S." and ordnance bomb on receiver, ordnance bomb on barrel and no proofing on stocks, except for reworks. Trench gun has same style handguard as Model 620. Serial range 30,000-70,000.

Trench Gun	N/A	$2,500	$1,800	$1,200	$800	$600	$500
Riot Gun	N/A	$1,000	$750	$350	$300	$250	$200
Long Barrels	N/A	$500	$400	$225	$175	$150	$125

STEVENS SINGLE & DOUBLE BARREL MILITARY SHOTGUNS - these guns were procured by the government from distributors and gun dealers. "U.S." and oversized flaming bomb hand stamped on left side receiver.

Single Barrel	N/A	$750	$600	$400	$350	$300	$250
Double Barrel	N/A	$950	$800	$600	$400	$350	$300

WINCHESTER MODEL 97 MILITARY SHOTGUNS - takedown model, high polish commercial blue finish, finger groove walnut stock with hard rubber buttplate. All early riot and trenchguns have WB and ordnance bomb catouches on the left side of stock, left side of receiver is machined marked "U.S." with or w/o ordnance bomb. All WB trenchguns have a 6 row ventilated handguard. All 97s will have ordnance bomb on top of barrel. Around serial range 950,000, receivers were all marked on left side with a machined "U.S." and ordnance bomb proofs, ventilated handguard was changed to a 4 row, GHD and ordnance bomb cartouches on left side of stock. During this transition, a very few examples with 6 row handguards have been found. Serial range 920,000- 960,000.

Riot Gun-WB marked	N/A	$1,800	$1,500	$800	$600	$500	$400
Trench Gun-WB marked	N/A	$4,500	$3,500	$2,800	$1,500	$1,200	$1,000
Trench Gun-GHD marked	N/A	$4,200	$3,200	$2,700	$1,800	$1,200	$1,000
Long Barrel	N/A	$1,500	$1,200	$800	$650	$500	$400

WINCHESTER MODEL 12 MILITARY SHOTGUNS - takedown model with improved hammerless receiver. These were made to supplement Model 97 production. Riot guns and Trench guns share same serial range. Finished in high polished commercial blue, Trench guns (only) were the only WWII shotguns to have factory parkerized finishes. All Model 12s have "U.S." and ordnance bomb on right side of receiver, ordnance bomb on barrel and ordnance mark and inspector initials on left side of stock. Trench guns have 4 row vent. handguards.

✳ *Blue finish* - serial range 926,000-1,030,000.

Trench Gun	N/A	$4,200	$3,400	$2,000	$1,600	$1,400	$1,000
Riot Gun	N/A	$1,850	$1,500	$750	$650	$500	$400
Long Barrel	N/A	$1,200	$1,000	$750	$600	$450	$350

✳ *Parkerized finish* - serial range 1,030,000-1,040,000.

Trench Gun	N/A	$4,500	$3,800	$3,000	$2,000	$1,500	$1,200

WINCHESTER MODEL 37 MILITARY SHOTGUNS - high polish, commercial blue, single barrel, procured from Winchester. "U.S." and ordnance bomb proofmarks were applied to left side of receiver. Winchester records show shipment of 5,410 guns to the military - very few examples of this model have ever been found.

Single Barrel	N/A	$2,000	$1,500	$1,200	$1,000	$750	$500

SHOTGUNS: MILITARY RIOT/TRENCH, VIETNAM

T

ITHACA MODEL 37 - parkerized finish with "U.S." marks on right side of receiver. Receiver and barrel are also marked "P". Serial range, applied on gun upside-down, is from S1,000-S23,500. Used in the Vietnam era. A very few original Trench guns with parkerized handguards have been noted.

Riot Gun	N/A	$1,500	$1,200	$500	$400	$350	$300
Trench Gun	N/A	$2,500	$2,200	$800	$600	$500	$450

Grading	100%	98%	95%	90%	80%	70%	60%

SAVAGE 77E - parkerized finish with sling swivels and red rubber butt pad. U.S. marked on right side of receiver and military "P" proofmark on receiver and barrel. Hard to find in excellent condition.

Riot Gun	N/A	$1,000	$750	$400	$300	$250	$225

WINCHESTER MODEL 1200 - parkerized barrel, mag. tube, and bayonet adapter with U.S. marking on barrel. Aluminum receiver with black or matte type finish, "U.S." is marked under serial number. Very rare as few examples have been released by the government due to its continued use by military forces.

Trench Gun	N/A	$2,950	$2,500	$1,200	$800	$600	$500

SHOTGUNS: RIOT/TRENCH GUN, COMMERCIAL SALES

WINCHESTER MODEL 12 RIOT - thousands mfg. between late '30s-'60s.

	N/A	$550	$450	$395	$350	$295	$240

WINCHESTER MODEL 97 - commercial high polish blue, changed from solid frame to takedown in 1935. Trench guns made through 1945 and Riot gun mfg. continued until 1960s.

❋ *Solid Frame* - Serial range 700,000+

Trench Gun	N/A	$2,500	$2,000	$1,500	$1,200	$1,000	$750
Riot Gun	N/A	$1,000	$900	$750	$600	$500	$300

❋ *Takedown* - Serial range 800,000+

Trench Gun	N/A	$2,500	$2,000	$1,300	$1,100	$900	$600
Riot Gun	N/A	$800	$700	$600	$500	$400	$300

REMINGTON MODEL 10 - commercial high polish blue, sold in the 1920s to various government and banking agencies.

Riot Gun	N/A	$400	$350	$300	$275	$250	$200

REMINGTON MODEL 11 - made in 1930s for law enforcement use.

Riot Gun	N/A	$400	$350	$300	$275	$250	$200

MODEL 31R RIOT GUN - similar to 31A, with 20 in. barrel.

	N/A	$300	$200	$175	$150	$130	$110

ITHACA MODEL 37 - parkerized models made in 1960s for police agencies and commercial sales.

Trench Gun	N/A	$1,200	$900	$700	$600	$500	$400
Riot Gun	N/A	$275	$250	$225	$175	$150	$125

U.S. MILITARY SHOTGUN ACCESSORIES

WWI BAYONETS - military acceptance proofs, leather scabbards and two variation of attachment to belt, two-toned blue handle and parkerized blade.

Winchester 1917 date
Prices range from $150-$300, depending on original condition.

Remington 1917-1918 dates
Prices range from $125-$250, depending on original condition.

LEATHER SLING - WWI dates, w/brass hardware.
Prices range from $75-$150, depending on original condition. Mint condition will bring $250.

SHOTGUN SHELL POUCHES

32 round pouch w/sling
Prices range approx. $500, depending on original condition.

12 round pouches dated 1921-1922
Prices range approx. $400, depending on original condition.

T

Grading	100%	98%	95%	90%	80%	70%	60%

WWII BAYONETS - same as from WWI, but have plastic scabbard w/large ordnance bomb, or orginal WWI leather scabbard.

> Prices range approx. $125-$300, depending on original condition.

LEATHER SLING - WWII dates, w/steel hardware.

> Prices range from $50-$125, depending on original condition. Mint condition will bring $250.

SHOTGUN SHELL POUCHES - 12 round pouches with contract dates from 1960s- 1990s.

> Prices range from $50-$125.

SHOTGUN SHELL POUCHES - 12 round pouches dated 1942-1945, various manufacturers, watch for recent 1943 JQMD fake pouches - they have extreme two-tone colors.

> Prices range approx. $350, depending on original condition.

VIETNAM BAYONETS - new contracts to supplement large quantities of shotguns being sent to Vietnam, black plastic handles, green plastic scabbards, marked M-1917.

> Gen. Cut - mfg. by General Cutlery prices range from $150-$250.
> CA – mfg. by Canadian Arsenal prices range from $150-$300.

TRISTAR SPORTING ARMS, LTD.

Current importer established in 1994, and located in N. Kansas City, MO. Distributor and dealer sales.

> Tristar also imports Uberti lever action Winchester and Colt SAA reproductions.

RIFLES: BOLT ACTION

PEE-WEE .22 - .22 LR cal., single shot, manual cocking bolt, 16½ in. barrel, steel construction, blue finish with adj. rear leaf sight, 12 in. LOP, uncheckered walnut stock with Monte Carlo, 2¾ lbs. Limited mfg. 1998 only.

$170	$140	$130	$120	$110	$100	$90

Last MSR was $189.

SHOTGUNS: LEVER ACTION

Tristar also imports the ADI Model 1887. Please refer to the Australian International Arms listing for more information and current pricing.

MODEL 1887 - 12 ga. only, patterned after the Winchester Model 1887, "WRA Co." logo on left side of receiver, 30 in. barrel, 5 shot tube mag., blue finish, 2-piece walnut forearm and rounded pistol grip stock, 8 lbs. Limited importation 1997-98.

$535	$475	$435	$400	$360	$330	$295

Last MSR was $599.

SHOTGUNS: O/U

Tristar also currently imports a wide variety of Emilio Rizzini O/U shotguns. Please refer to the Emilio Rizzini section for more information.

MODEL 300 - 12 ga. only, 3 in. chambers, under-lug action, double triggers, extractors, etched engraving, standard checkered Turkish walnut stock and forearm, 26 or 28. in. VR barrels with fixed chokes. Imported 1994-98 from Turkey.

$375	$330	$300	$275	$250	$225	$200

Last MSR was $429.

T MODEL 333 FIELD GRADE - 12 or 20 ga., 3 in. chambers, engraved boxlock receiver with satin finish, SST, ejectors, fancy grade Turkish walnut with hand-cut checkering, 26 (12 ga. only), 28, or 30 in. VR barrels, supplied with 5 choke tubes, approx. 7½ lbs. Imported from Turkey 1994-98.

$735	$625	$550	$500	$450	$400	$360

Last MSR was $800.

Grading	100%	98%	95%	90%	80%	70%	60%

✴ *Model 333 Sporting Clays* - similar to Model 333 Field Grade, except has sporting recoil pad, elongated forcing cones, 28 or 30 in. ported barrels with extended stainless steel choke tubes, 7¾ lbs. Imported from Turkey 1994-97.

		$825	$725	$625	$550	$500	$450	$400

Last MSR was $900.

✴ *Model 333SCL Ladies Sporting Clays* - similar to Model 333 Sporting Clays, except is fitted with special ladies stock, 28 in. barrels only with four choke tubes. Imported from Turkey. Disc. 1997.

		$825	$725	$625	$550	$500	$450	$400

Last MSR was $900.

MODEL 330 - 12 or 20 ga., 3 in. chambers, etched satin finished receiver, SST, extractors, fixed chokes, checkered standard Turkish walnut stock and forearm, approx. 7½ lbs. Imported from Turkey 1994-99.

		$475	$415	$375	$325	$295	$280	$265

Last MSR was $549.

✴ *Model 330D* - similar to Model 330, except has ejectors, and three choke tubes. Imported from Turkey 1994-99.

		$615	$525	$495	$450	$400	$360	$330

Last MSR was $689.

SILVER HUNTER - 12 or 20 ga., 3 in. chambers, under-lug action, SST, extractors, silver receiver with etched engraving, standard checkered Turkish walnut stock and forearm, 26 or 28. in. VR barrels with choke tubes, 7 lbs. Importation from Spain began 2002.

MSR	$507	$450	$415	$385	$365	$345	$325	$295

SILVER II - 12, 16, or 20 ga., similar to Silver Hunter, except has SST and ejectors. Importation from Spain began 2002.

MSR	$566	$485	$435	$400	$375	$350	$325	$295

SILVER CLASSIC - 12 ga., similar to Silver II, except has case colored receiver and long forcing cones. Importation from Spain began 2002.

MSR	$673	$575	$500	$450	$400	$375	$350	$325

SILVER SPORTING - 12 ga., similar to Silver II, except has 2 3/4 in. chambers and ported barrels with broadway VR, 7 lbs., 6 oz. Importation from Spain began 2002.

MSR	$765	$675	$575	$525	$465	$435	$395	$375

WS/OU MAGNUM - 12 ga., 3 ½ in. chambers, ejectors, SST, 28 in. VR barrels with choke tubes, matte black metal and checkered black finished walnut stock and forearm. 7 lbs. 2 oz. Importation began 2002.

MSR	$610	$535	$465	$425	$395	$375	$350	$325

SHOTGUNS: SxS

MODEL 311 - 12 or 20 ga., 3 in. chambers, Greener boxlock action, 26 or 28 in. barrels, standard checkered Turkish walnut stock and forearm, DTs, supplied with five choke tubes, white chrome frame finish, extractors. Imported 1994-97 from Turkey.

		$535	$475	$435	$400	$360	$330	$295

Last MSR was $599.

✴ *Model 311R* - 12 or 20 ga., 20 in. cylinder bore barrels designed for cowboy re-enactment shooting or home defense, other features similar to Model 311. Imported from Turkey. Disc. 1997.

		$375	$325	$300	$275	$250	$225	$200

Last MSR was $429.

T

Grading	100%	98%	95%	90%	80%	70%	60%

MODEL 411 - 12, 16 (new 1999), 20, 28 ga., or .410 bore, 3 in. chambers (except 28 ga.), 26 or 28 (12 ga. only) in. barrels with (12 and 20 ga.) or w/o (28 ga. or .410 bore) choke tubes, DT, extractors, steel shot compatible, case colored frame, checkered walnut stock and forearm with recoil pad, 6½ - 7¼ lbs, mfg. by Luciano Rota (R.F.M.). Importation began 1998.

	MSR	$849		$710	$650	$575	$525	$450	$400	$350

✳ *Model 411D* - similar to Model 411, except not available in 16 ga., features engraved case colored frame, single trigger, ejectors, and English style stock, 6½ - 7¼ lbs. New 1999.

	MSR	$1,110		$915	$800	$700	$600	$500	$400	$325

✳ *Model 411F* - 12, 20, 28 ga., or .410 bore, 3 in. chambers (except 28 ga.), silver engraved frame, gold SST, English straight stock with cut checkering, ejectors, choke tubes (except for 28 ga. and .410 bore), 6½ - 7¼ lbs., mfg. by Luciano Rota. Importation began 2000.

	MSR	$1,602		$1,425	$1,200	$995	$850	$725	$650	$575

✳ *Model 411R Coach Gun* - 12 or 20 ga., 3 in. chambers, hammerless, 20 in. fixed choke (C/C) barrels, case colored frame, DT, extractors, 6-6½ lbs. Importation began 1999.

	MSR	$745		$650	$575	$525	$475	$425	$375	$325

This model is designed for both cowboy competition shooting and quail hunting.

DERBY CLASSIC - 12 or 20 ga., 3 in. chambers, true sidelock case colored action, DT, ejectors, checkered straight grip stock and splinter forearm, 7 3/4 lbs. Mfg. by Zabala Hermanos in Spain beginning 2002.

	MSR	$1,059		$950	$825	$725	$650	$575	$500	$465

SHOTGUNS: SEMI-AUTO

PHANTOM SERIES - 12 ga. only, 3 or 3½ (Phantom Field/Synthetic Mag. only) in. chamber, various VR (except Phantom HP) barrel lengths with choke tubes, available in Field (blue metal finish, gold accents, and checkered walnut stock and forearm), Synthetic (black non-glare matte metal and flat black synthetic stock and forearm), or HP (home security with open sights, mate finished metal, and synthetic stock and forearm), 6 lbs. 13 oz. - 7 lbs. 6 oz. Italian mfg., importation began 2001.

	MSR	$425		$385	$350	$315	$285	$265	$245	$225

Subtract $44 for Phantom Synthetic.
Add $74 for 3½ in. Mag. (Field).
Add $44 for Mag. Synthetic.

TRUVELO ARMOURY

Current manufacturer located in Midrand, South Africa. Truvelo Armoury is a division of the Truvelo Manufacturers (Pty) Ltd. No current U.S. importation.

Truvelo Armoury manufactures a variety of firearms, including hunting and sporting rifles and pistols. Currently, they have several bolt action rifles available in the $475- $1,000 range. Please contact the factory directly (see Trademark Index) for more information.

TULA ARMS PLANT

Current manufacturer located in Tula, Russia. Limited U.S. importation. Previously distributed by Tulsky Souvenir, LLC, located in San Diego, CA.

The Tula Arms Plant is one of the world's oldest and largest gun manufacturing facilities. Many millions of military weapons have been manufactured at this facility, and currently, Tula is getting more aggressive in providing sporting arms to western countries. For more information and current pricing on the wide variety of firearms produced by this world famous manufacturing facility, please contact the factory directly (see Trademark Index).

TURKISH FIREARMS CORPORATION

Please refer to the HHF section in this text.

Grading	100%	98%	95%	90%	80%	70%	60%

DOUG TURNBULL RESTORATION, INC.

Current firearms restoration company located in Bloomfield, NY, that specializes in the accurate recreation of historic metal finishes on period firearms, from initial polishing to final finishing. These finishes include bone charcoal color case hardened, charcoal bluing, and Nitre bluing.

Turnbull Restoration has reworked current Colt SAAs to look like a pre-1920 SAA. These guns have special, factory assigned serial numbers beginning with 000DT. The retail price is $2,200, not including many options. Additonally, the company has also produced a special run of Colt SAAs in .45 LC, 5 ½ in. barrel configuration, that are serial numbered EHBM01-EHBM50. These guns have color case hardened frames with charcoal bluing, large flutes (1st Generation), beveled cylinder, and ejector housing. Retail price is $2,150.

Turnbull Restoration has performed extensive restoration work on Colt 1911s, A.H. Foxes, Parkers, L.C. Smiths, and lever action Winchesters (including upgrades and antique finishes to duplicate natural aging). These guns have been provided with documentation.

In 2000, the Miller Single Trigger Company was purchased, and Doug Turnbull Restoration is now installing this famous mechanical trigger on many SxS and O/U shotguns, both in selective and non-selective configurations, as well as forward and rear positions.

Please contact the company directly for more information on the wide variety of services available (see Trademark Index).

T

NOTES

T is for trouble in the Taurus booth! In this case, trouble being the annual chili pepper eating contest held in the Taurus booth during the SHOT Show. Anita Carson from FMG seems to be having no problems eating her umpteenth flame producing chili pepper (she finished second, the winner ate 27!).

U Section

U.S. ARMS COMPANY
Previous manufacturer located in Riverhead, NY.

Grading	100%	98%	95%	90%	80%	70%	60%

REVOLVERS: SINGLE ACTION

ABILENE .357 MAG. - 6 shot, 4 5/8, 5½, or 6½ in. barrel, adj. sights, transfer bar ignition, smooth walnut grips, blue finish only. Mfg. 1976-1983.

	$275	$240	$200	$185	$170	$155	$140

* *Abilene .357 Mag. Stainless Steel* - similar to Abilene, only in stainless steel.

	$325	$275	$225

ABILENE .44 MAG. - 7½ and 8½ in. barrel, unfluted cylinder blue finish only, otherwise similar to .357 Mag.

	$325	$265	$240	$220	$200	$165	$150

* *Abilene .44 Mag. Stainless Steel* - similar to Abilene .44 Mag., only stainless steel.

	$375	$330	$290

U.S. GENERAL TECHNOLOGIES, INC.
Previous manufacturer located in S. San Francisco, CA circa 1994-96.

RIFLES: SEMI-AUTO

P-50 SEMI-AUTO - .50 BMG cal., includes 10 shot detachable mag., folding bipod, muzzle brake, matte black finish. Mfg. 1995-96.

	$5,600	$4,950	$4,475	$3,975	$3,500	$3,050	$2,600

Last MSR was $5,995.

U.S. HISTORICAL SOCIETY
Previous organization which marketed historically significant firearms reproductions until April, 1994. Located in Richmond, VA. Most firearms were manufactured by the Williamsburg Firearms Manufactory and the Virginia Firearms Manufactory.

On April 1, 1994, the Antique Arms Division of the U.S. Historical Society was acquired by America Remembers located in Mechanicsville, VA. America Remembers' affiliates include the Armed Forces Commemorative Society, American Heroes & Legends, and the United States Society of Arms and Armor. Issues that were not fully subscribed are now available through America Remembers (please refer to listing in A section).

The information listed below represents current information up until America Remembers acquired the Antique Arms Division of the U.S. Historical Society.

Please refer to the *Blue Book of Modern Black Powder Values* by Dennis Adler (now online also) for more information and prices on U.S. Historical Society's modern black powder models.

Manufacturer	Model	Quantity	Year	Issue Price

PISTOLS: SPECIAL EDITIONS

Manufacturer	Model	Quantity	Year	Issue Price
Uberti	Secret Service Museum Edition	500	1988	$2,750
Uberti	Secret Service Investigator's Edition	1,000	1988	$1,250
N/A	George Jones SAA	950	1993	$1,675
N/A	Richard Petty Silver Edition SAA	1,000	1992	$1,675
Colt	King Richard Hand Engraved Colt .45 SAA	100	1993	$4,500
N/A	Charlton Heston SAA	500	1993	$1,850
N/A	Hopalong Cassidy Cowboy Edition SAA	950	1993	$1,675

U

Manufacturer	Model	Quantity	Year	Issue Price
Colt	Hopalong Cassidy Premier Colt Edition	100	1993	$4,500
Colt	Mel Torme Colt SAA	100	1992	$4,500
N/A	Roy Rogers Cowboy Edition SAA	2,500	1990	$1,350
N/A	Roy Rogers Premier Edition SAA	250	1990	$4,500
Armi San Marco	U.S. Marshals Wyatt Earp SAA	2,500	1991	$1,250
N/A	National Cowboy Hall of Fame SAA	1,000	1992	$1,600
Colt	Interpol Colt SAA	154	1991	$4,500
Springfield	Eisenhower .45 Auto	1,000	1992	$1,675
Colt	"Don't Give Up the Ship" Model .45 Auto	1,997	1993	$1,485
Colt	American Eagle Colt .45 Auto	2,500	1993	$1,950

REVOLVERS: MINIATURE SPECIAL EDITIONS

Uberti	SA Army Presidential Edition	1,500	1988	$1,550
Uberti	SA Army Classic Edition	1,500	1988	$575

SHOTGUNS: SPECIAL EDITIONS

Bertuzzi	Chuck Yeager Tribute	100	1989	$12,500
Reanto Telo	Arnold Palmer Tribute	100	1990	$9,750
Antonio Zoli	Christopher Columbus Tribute	200	1991	$12,500

U.S. M1 CARBINES/RIFLES

Previous manufacture for the military by various makers listed below.

Grading	100%	98%	95%	90%	80%	70%	60%

CARBINES: SEMI-AUTO

U.S. M1 CARBINE (MILITARY & COMMERCIAL) - .30 Carbine cal., 18 in. barrel, 15 or 30 shot box mag., wood stocked, two or four position aperture rear, blade front sight with protective ears, with or without bayonet lug. This weapon was designed by Winchester for the U.S. government, over 6 million were produced by 10 different companies, while Plainfield was mfg. after the war for civilian sales. It is a gas operated lightweight carbine that was also used by other countries' armed forces. Makers and values as follows. Values are for original, unmodified carbines, with proper parts makers and stock cartouches. Some variations have the type III barrel band.

Values below are for original mfg. only, not recent imports (usually denoted by visible import markings and/or alterations to original finish).

Subtract 30% for original finish guns that have been changed back to the original configuration by switching parts.

Subtract 50% for modified guns with adj. sight and bayonet lug.

	100%	98%	95%	90%	80%	70%	60%
Underwood	$850	$675	$495	$400	$350	$300	$275
S.G. Saginaw	$825	$650	$475	$400	$350	$300	$275
Quality Hardware	$850	$675	$495	$415	$370	$325	$295
Nat'l Postal Meter	$950	$775	$525	$425	$375	$325	$295
IBM	$950	$775	$525	$425	$370	$325	$295
Standard Products	$800	$650	$495	$415	$370	$325	$295
Inland	$850	$675	$495	$415	$370	$325	$295
SG Grand Rapids	$950	$775	$525	$425	$375	$325	$295
Winchester	$1,150	$850	$750	$550	$425	$350	$325
Irwin Pedersen	$1,700	$1,400	$995	$850	$775	$675	$580

U

Grading	100%	98%	95%	90%	80%	70%	60%
Rockola	$995	$925	$700	$525	$425	$350	$325
Plainfield (Commercial only)	$195	$175	$160	$150	$140	$130	$120

M1 A1 PARATROOPER CARBINE - .30 Carbine cal., mfg. by Inland - WWII production, folding stock, crossed cannon proofed on bottom, 140,000 mfg. between 1942-1945. Stock folds to 26½ in. overall.

$1,700	$1,450	$1,250	$950	$750	$650	$550

RIFLES: SEMI-AUTO

M1 GARAND - .30-06 cal., semi-auto, 8 shot en bloc clip fed, gas operated, adj. aperture sight, wooden stock. Made 1937-1957 by Springfield, Winchester, H&R, and International Harvester.

$1,250	$1,050	$900	$775	$675	$575	$475

Add 100% for pre-WWII Winchester or Springfield mfg.
Add 25% for WWII date.
Subtract 50% if rewelded or 20% if mismatched.

✳ *M1-C or M1-D Sniper* - with scope and mounts (be wary of fakes and rewelds).

	100%	98%	95%	90%	80%	70%	60%
M1-D	$2,100	$1,750	$1,550	$1,350	$1,150	$975	$900
M1-C	N/A	N/A	$3,650	$3,250	$2,850	$2,500	$2,150

If verified original, asking prices may be considerably higher than values listed above.

M1 GARAND NATIONAL MATCH - target version of the Garand, using National Match barrel and sights, glass bedding, etc. Must have serialized N.M. paperwork for prices listed below.

$2,100	$1,550	$1,250	$950	$750	$525	$460

RIFLES: BOLT ACTION

U.S. MODEL 1917 ENFIELD RIFLE - .30-06 cal., bolt action, 5 shot, 26 in. barrel, original finish was blue, adj. sights, military stock, derived from English P14 Enfield, over two million produced in 1917 and 1918.

$700	$600	$500	$400	$350	$315	$265

Add 10% for Winchester mfg.

This model was manufactured primarily by Remington at the Eddystone plant in Eddystone, PA (Eddystone marked), the Ilion Remington plant, and by Winchester in New Haven, CT.

U.S. MILITARY

See listings under Colt, Springfield Armory, and Winchester. U.S. Military Trench and Riot guns may be found under the "Trench/Riot Shotguns" category in the T section of this text.

U.S. ORDNANCE

Current rifle manufacturer located in Reno, NV.

RIFLES: SEMI-AUTO

U.S. Ordnance manufactures semi-auto reproductions (BATF approved) of the .303 Vickers ($4,495 MSR w/o tripod), M-60/M-60E3 ($5,995 MSR/$6,495 MSR)), and Browning M-19 ($1,995 MSR). These belt fed variations are machined to military specifications, and have 5 year warranties. Please contact the company directly for more information (see Trademark Index).

USAS 12

Previous trademark manufactured by International Ordnance Corporation located in Nashville, TN circa 1992-95. Previously manufactured (1990-91) by Ramo Mfg., Inc. located in Nashville, TN. Previously distributed by Kiesler's Wholesale located in Jeffersonville, IN until 1994. Originally designed and previously distributed in the U.S.

U

Grading	100%	98%	95%	90%	80%	70%	60%

by Gilbert Equipment Co., Inc. located in Mobile, AL. Previously manufactured under license by Daewoo Precision Industries, Ltd. located in South Korea.

SHOTGUNS: SEMI-AUTO

USAS 12 - 12 ga. only, gas operated action available in either semi or fully auto versions, 18¼ in. cylinder bore barrel, closed bolt, synthetic stock, pistol grip, and forearm, carrying handle, 10 round box or 20 drum (disc.) mag., 2¾ in. chamber only, parkerized finish, 12 lbs. Mfg. 1987-95.

	$925	$850	$750	$650	$575	$500	$400

Last MSR was $995.

Add $150 for extra 20 shot drum magazine (banned by the BATF).

Values above are for a semi-auto model. This model is currently classified as a destructive device and necessary paperwork must accompany a sale.

U.S.R.A.

Previous organization (United States Revolver Association) that established certain rules for target pistol shooting. Target pistols were manufactured by Harrington & Richardson.

Readers interested in obtaining more information about specific U.S.R.A. pistols, or have information to share are encouraged to contact Mr. L. Richard Littlefield (see Trademark Index).

PISTOLS: SINGLE SHOT

The author would like to express his thanks to Mr. Richard Littlefield for providing the following information.

MATCH TARGET PISTOL (MODEL 195) - .22 LR cal., many configurations, including 14 different stocks (including variations by Walter Roper), 5 trigger guards, 3 triggers, 2 hammers, 2 extractors, 3 barrel lengths (7, 8, or 10 inch), and 3 barrel rib designs, approx. 3,500 mfg. by H&R 1928-1941.

* *Variation 1 Pre-U.S.R.A.* - not marked "U.S.R.A.", known as the H&R Single Shot Pistol, no finger rest between the trigger guard and the front grip strap, advertised with a "sawhandle" shape grip copied from the Model 1 or 2 smoothbore H&R Handy Gun, mfg. with a 10 in. barrel with deeply undercut rib. First 500 pistols mfg. 1928-1930.

	$500	$450	$400	$350	$300	$250	$200

* *Variation 2 U.S.R.A. Keyhole Barrel* - standard early model marked U.S.R.A., finger rest, non-sawhandle grips, optional grip shapes, grip screw goes from rear of grip into threaded hold in back grip strap. Mfg. 1930-31.

	$500	$450	$400	$350	$300	$250	$200

* *Variation 3 Modified Keyhole Barrel* - modification of Variation 2 to improve rear sight, barrel catch changed, reduced spent cartridge force by replacing cylindrical extra ctor with less powerful hinged type, hammer cocking spur and finger rest were wider, 8 in. optional or 10 in. standard barrel, optional grip shapes, transition model between early Variation 2 and final Variation 4 designs. Mfg. 1931.

	$500	$450	$400	$350	$300	$250	$200

* *Variation 4 Tapered Slabside Barrel* - new "truncated teardrop" barrel cross section shape, 7 in. standard or 10 in. optional barrel, adj. trigger, new sear, grips screw location was changed to front of grip, front sight was adj for elevation, trigger design changed from curved to straight beveled type with relocated cocking surfaces, 13 optional grip shapes, front sight protector standard, optional luggage style case. Mfg. 1931-1941.

	$550	$495	$450	$400	$350	$200	$250

This model was introduced circa 1931, the 1932 advertisements describe a fully redesigned gun, but pictured the Variation 2, indicating that H&R probably did not rephotograph the new design.

Grading	100%	98%	95%	90%	80%	70%	60%

The final variation had a special, tight bore .217 inches in diameter, with bullet seating .03125 in (1-32 in.) into rifling, and is among the most accurate single shot .22 cal. pistols. The Model 195 U.S.R.A. was expensive, costing approx. $30 in 1932, and increased to more than $36 by the time production had ended in 1941, yet was the least expensive of all single shot quality .22 cal. target pistols during this time.

UBERTI, A. S.r.l.

Current firearms, black powder, and accessories manufacturer established in 1959 and located in Serezzo, Italy. Imported and distributed by Uberti USA, Inc., located in Lakeville, CT.

In late 1999, Beretta purchased Aldo Uberti & Co. S.r.l., and U.S. importation has not changed. Many other companies are currently importing and/or distributing Uberti firearms and black powder models. These models may be listed within the individual company listings.

For more information and up-to-date regarding current Aldo Uberti black powder models, please refer to *Colt Blackpowder Reproductions and Replicas*, and the *Blue Book of Modern Black Powder Values*, by Dennis Adler. These books feature hundreds of color photographs and support text of the most recent black powder models available, as well as a complete pricing and reference guide.

REVOLVERS: REPRODUCTIONS, SAA & VARIATIONS

These guns can be ordered with either black powder or modern configured frames. Factory engraving and other embellishments or finishes (including antique charcoal blue, white steel, nickel, etc.) can be special ordered by contacting the importer directly.

Add $85 for antique patina finish.
Add $45 for antique charcoal blue finish on all Cattleman variations.
Add $130 for silver-plating.
Add $40 for white finish.
Add $85 for nickel plating (not available on Schofield).
Add $85 for select grade walnut one-piece fitted grips (disc.), $250 or $575 (solid silver) for Army/Navy Tiffany grips.
Add $45 for checkered grips.
Add $50 for stag horn grips (disc.), $150 for black buffalo grips (disc.), or $350 for mother-of-pearl grips (disc.).
Add $650-$1,450 for Cattleman engraving, depending on amount, and if with gold inlays.

1871 RICHARDS/MASON CONVERSION - .38 Spl., .38 LC, .44 Colt (8 in. barrel only), or .45 Schofield cal., choice of brass (New Model) or steel BS/TG (Old Model), 5 ½, 7 ½, or 8 in. round or octagon barrel, one piece walnut grips, approx. 2.6 lbs. New 2002.

MSR $450	$385	$350	$315	$275	$250	$225	$200

1871-1872 OPEN TOP EARLY/LATE MODEL - .38 Spl., .38 LC, .44 Russian, .44 Colt, .44 Spl., .45 Schofield, or .45 LC cal., open top frame, 5 ½ (Early Model only) or 7 ½ in. octagon barrel, Army (Late Model) or Navy (Early Model) size grips. New 2002.

MSR $450	$385	$350	$315	$275	$250	$225	$200

Add $25 for Late Model.

CATTLEMAN VARIATIONS - available in .22 LR (disc. 1990), .22 Mag. (disc. 1990), .32-20 WCF (new 2001), .357 Mag., .38 Spl., .38-40 WCF (new 1989), .44 Spl., .44-40 WCF, or .45 LC cal., 3¾ (.45 LC only), 4 (.45 LC only), 4¾, 5½, and 7½ in. barrel lengths, brass (New Model frame) or steel (Old Model frame) backstrap and trigger guard.

✳ ***Steel backstrap and trigger guard*** - choice of new or old model frame, old model frame not available in .357 Mag. cal.

MSR $410	$345	$265	$210	$175	$160	$150	$135

Add $75 for convertible cylinder (.45 LC/.45 ACP, .22 LR/.22 Mag. in 5½ in. barrel only).
Add $64 for stainless steel construction (disc. 1989).

U

Grading	100%	98%	95%	90%	80%	70%	60%

* *Sheriff's Model* - .44-40 WCF or .45 LC cal., 3 or 4 in. barrel.

MSR $410	$345	$265	$210	$175	$160	$150	$135

* *Brass backstrap and trigger guard* - .357 Mag., .38-40 WCF (new 2001), .44 Mag. (new 2001), .44 Spl. (new 2001), .44-40 WCF, or .45 LC cal., 3¾ (.45 LC only), 4 (.45 LC only), 4¾, 5½, or 7½ in. barrel.

MSR $369	$315	$250	$195	$165	$150	$140	$130

Add $51 for convertible cylinder (.45 LC/.45 ACP).
Add $10 for .44 Spl. or .44-40 WCF cal.

* *Sheriff's Model* - .44-40 WCF or .45 LC cal., 3 or 4 in. barrel.

MSR $359	$310	$240	$190	$165	$150	$140	$135

◇**Cattleman Millenium.** - .45 LC cal., 4¾ in. barrel. New 2000.

MSR $300	$245	$200	$180	$160	$145	$130	$120

* *Target Model* - similar to standard Cattleman Model, only fully adj. rear blade sight, brass backstrap. Importation disc. 1990.

	$315	$245	$200	$185	$170	$150	$135

Last MSR was $335.

Add $25 for steel backstrap and trigger guard.
Add $60 for stainless steel construction (disc.).

CATTLEMAN "FIRST ISSUE" - .357 Mag. (new 2001, flattop only), .38-40 WCF, .44-40 WCF, or .45 LC cal., 4¾, 5½, or 7½ in. barrel, choice of regular or flattop receiver. New 1997.

MSR $435	$365	$310	$240	$195	$175	$160	$150

CATTLEMAN BIRDHEAD - .357 Mag. (new 2001), .44 Spl., .44-40 WCF, or .45 LC cal., 3 (Sheriff's Model, .44-40 WCF or .45 LC cal. only), 3½, 4 (Sheriff's Model, .44-40 WCF or .45 LC cal. only), 4 (new 2001), 4¾, or 5½ in. barrel, patterned after the Colt 1877 Thunderer, case colored frame, checkered walnut birdhead grips. New 1997.

MSR $435	$365	$310	$240	$195	$175	$160	$150

* *Cattleman Birdhead Sabre (Old Model)* - .357 Mag. (new 2001), .44 Spl. (disc. 2000), .44-40 WCF, or .45 LC cal., 3 (Sheriff's Model, .44-40 WCF or .45 LC cal. only, disc. 2000), 3½, 4 (Sheriff's Model, .44-40 WCF or .45 LC cal. only, disc. 2000), 4½ (disc. 2000) or 4¾ (new 2001), in. barrel, similar to Cattleman Sabre, except has old model frame (vertical screw holding cylinder pin). New 1997.

MSR $435	$365	$310	$240	$195	$175	$160	$150

CATTLEMAN BISLEY - .357 Mag., .38-40 WCF, .44 Spl., .44-40 WCF, or .45 LC cal., patterned after the Colt Bisley Model, 4¾, 5½, or 7½ in. barrel, case colored frame, wood grips. New 1997.

MSR $435	$365	$310	$240	$195	$175	$160	$150

* *Cattleman Bisley Flattop* - similar to Cattleman Bisley, except has flattop frame with fixed or target (.44-40 WCF or .45 LC cal., 7½ in. barrel only) sights. New 1997.

MSR $435	$365	$310	$240	$195	$175	$160	$150

Add $25 for target sights (disc.).

CATTLEMAN BUNTLINE - .22 LR/.22 Mag. combo (disc. 2000), .357 Mag., .44-40 WCF, .44 Mag. (new 2001), or .45 LC cal., 12 (new 2001, .45 LC only) or 18 in. barrel, steel backstrap cut for shoulder stock. Importation disc. 1989, re-introduced 1993.

MSR $455	$375	$310	$240	$195	$175	$160	$150

Subtract $56 for New Model frame with brass backstrap and triggerguard.

U

Grading	100%	98%	95%	90%	80%	70%	60%

✳ *Buntline Carbine* - similar to Cattleman Buntline, 18 in. barrel, includes non-detachable shoulder stock with brass hardware and lanyard ring. Importation disc. 1989, re-introduced 1993-95.

	$390	$310	$245	$200	$175	$160	$150

Last MSR was $475.

Add $34 for target sights.
Add $34 for .22 LR/.22 Mag. combo. (disc. 1989).
Add $175 for detachable shoulder stock.

SA REVOLVER CARBINE - .357 Mag., .44-40 WCF, or .45 LC cal., 19 in. barrel, fixed stock with brass rifle butt plate, finger rest extension on trigger guard, choice of quick detachable mounts or target sights, 4.4 lbs. New 1997.

MSR	$475	$395	$310	$240	$195	$175	$160	$150

Add $14 for target sights.

BUCKHORN - .44 Mag., .44 Spl. (disc.), or .44-40 WCF (disc.) cal., 4¾, 5 ½ (new 2002) 6 (disc.), or 7½ in. barrel, brass or steel backstrap.

✳ *Buckhorn New Model Frame* - steel or brass backstrap and triggerguard.

MSR	$410	$345	$265	$210	$175	$160	$150	$135

Add $69 for convertible cylinder.
Add $40 for Target Model (disc.).
Subtract $51 for New Model frame (brass BG & TG).

✳ *Buckhorn Buntline* - .44-40 WCF (disc.) or .44 Mag. cal., 18 in. barrel, includes non-detachable shoulder stock with brass hardware and lanyard ring. Importation disc. 1989, resumed 2001.

MSR	$455	$375	$310	$240	$195	$175	$160	$150

Add $40 for target sights.
Add $40 for extra .44-40 WCF cylinder combo (disc.).
Add $122 for detachable shoulder stock (disc.).
Subtract $45 for New Model frame (brass BS & TG).

STALLION 1873 COLT - .22 LR/.22 Mag. cal. combo only, 4¾, 5½, or 6½ in. barrel, case hardened frame, 1-piece walnut grip, 2.4 lbs. Importation disc. 1989.

	$300	$210	$195	$170	$155	$140	$120

Last MSR was $325.

Add $27 for steel backstrap and trigger guard.
Add $26 for Target Model.

✳ *Stainless Stallion* - similar to standard Stallion, except is stainless steel. Importation disc. 1989.

	$370	$275	$225

Last MSR was $425.

STALLION 1873 STEEL BS/TG - .22 LR (new 2000) or .38 Spl. cal., 3½, 4¾, or 5½ in. barrel, small frame. Importation 1999.

MSR	$320	$285	$255	$230	$210	$190	$165	$150

Add $39 for Target Model (38 Spl. cal. only, not available with 3 ½ in. barrel).
Add $55 for .22 LR/.22 Mag. combo.
Add $45 for .38 Spl. cal.

✳ *Stallion 1873 Brass BS/TG* - .22 LR cal. only, 5½ in. barrel.

MSR	$310	$285	$245	$225	$200	$190	$165	$150

Add $39 for dual cylinder (.22 LR/.22 Mag.).
Add $39 for Target Model, or $90 for Target Model with dual cylinder.

U

Grading	100%	98%	95%	90%	80%	70%	60%

1875 "OUTLAW" REMINGTON - .357 Mag., .44-40 WCF, .45 ACP (new 1992, extra cylinder only), or .45 LC cal., 5½ (disc. 1995, resumed 2001) or 7½ in. barrel, brass or steel (new 1993) trigger guard.

	MSR	$483		$395	$295	$225	$175	$160	$150	$135

Add $42 for convertible cylinder (.45 LC/.45 ACP).

* **Model 1875 Carbine** - same cals. as Outlaw 1875, 18 in. barrel, includes non-detachable shoulder stock with brass hardware and lanyard ring. Importation disc. 1989.

	$425	$285	$230	$200	$185	$180	$175

Last MSR was $440.

Add $110 for nickel plating.

1890 "POLICE" REMINGTON - .357 Mag., .44-40 WCF, .45 ACP (new 1993, dual cylinder only), or .45 LC cal., 5½ or 7½ (disc. 1995) in. barrel, brass or steel (new 1993) trigger guard.

	MSR	$483		$395	$295	$225	$175	$160	$150	$135

Add $42 for dual cylinder.

PHANTOM MODEL - .357 or .44 Mag. cal. only, 10½ in. barrel for silhouette use. Imported 1985-89.

	$475	$395	$325	$290	$260	$230	$215

Last MSR was $509.

REVOLVERS: DOUBLE ACTION

INSPECTOR MODEL - .32 S&W or .38 Spl. cal., 3, 4, or 6 in. barrels, double action, blue or chrome finish. Imported 1985-89.

	$390	$295	$245	$210	$170	$145	$125

Last MSR was $406.

Add $35 for target sights.
Add $25 for chrome plating.

REVOLVERS: REPRODUCTIONS

1871 ROLLING BLOCK TARGET PISTOL - available in .22 LR, .22 Mag., .22 Hornet, .357 Mag. or .45 LC (Navy Model with open sights only, mfg. 1992-95) cal., 9½ in. barrel.

	MSR	$410		$335	$275	$230	$195	$175	$155	$135

Add $80 for carbine model (22 in. barrel - not available in .45 LC cal).

1874 SCHOFIELD RUSSIAN - .44 Russian cal., 6 shot, top-break, 6 (disc.) 6 ½ (new 2002) or 7 (new 2002) in. barrel. New 2000.

	MSR	$800		$675	$585	$475	$425	$365	$300	$275

1875 SCHOFIELD - .44-40 WCF or .45 LC cal., 3, 5, or 7 in. barrel. New 2000.

	MSR	$750		$635	$550	$465	$400	$350	$300	$275

RIFLES: REPRODUCTIONS

Add $140 for antique patina finish.
Add $80 for charcoal blue finish.
Add $75 for white finish.
Add $235 for silver plating.
Add $210 for nickel plating.
Add $90 for checkered wood, $210 for select wood, or $475 for deluxe wood.
Add $850-$3,500 for hand-engraving options, depending on the amount of engraving and gold inlays.

U

Grading	100%	98%	95%	90%	80%	70%	60%

HENRY RIFLE/CARBINE - .44-40 WCF or .45 LC (rifle only) cal., brass or steel (.44-40 WCF only) frame, 24½ in. barrel on rifle, 22½ in. barrel on carbine, available in modern gun blue, charcoal blue, white, or chrome finish.

	MSR $980		$875	$650	$525	$425	$360	$320	$260

Add $70 for steel frame on rifle only.
The carbine was disc. in 1989, re-introduced 1992.

* **Henry Trapper** - similar to above, except has 16½ or 18½ in. barrel. Limited importation began in 1990.

	MSR $980		$875	$650	$525	$425	$360	$320	$260

* **Henry 1 of 1,000** - disc. several years ago.

			$1,450	$1,150	$975	$850	$700	$575	$425

1866 CARBINE - .22 LR (disc. 1989), .22 Mag. (disc. 1989), .38 Spl., .44-40 WCF, or .45 LC cal., brass receiver, 19 in. round barrel. Importation disc. 1995.

			$640	$525	$425	$360	$310	$275	$240

Last MSR was $587 for .22 Mag. or .22 LR (disc. 1989).
Last MSR was $720.

* **1866 Trapper Carbine** - .22 LR, .38 Spl., or .44-40 WCF cal., 16 in. barrel. Importation disc. 1989.

			$650	$475	$395	$340	$285	$260	$235

Last MSR was $686.

* **1866 Yellowboy Indian Carbine** - .22 LR, .22 Mag., .32-20 WCF (new 2002), .38 Spl., .44-40 WCF, or .45 LC (new 1996) cal., 19 in. barrel. Limited importation.

	MSR $760		$670	$535	$430	$360	$310	$275	$240

Subtract $50 without brass tacks (disc.).

* **Red Cloud Commemorative Carbine** - same cals., special engraving and brass tacks in forearm and stock. Importation officially disc. 1989.

			$720	$600	$475	$400	$350	$330	$300

Last MSR was $850.

1866 SPORTING RIFLE - .22 LR (new 2001), .22 Mag. (new 2001), .32-20 WCF (new 2002), .38 Spl., .38-40 WCF (new 2002), .44-40 WCF, or .45 LC (new 1996) cal., brass receiver, 20 (new 2001, .38 Spl., .44-40 WCF, or .45 LC only) or 24¼ in. round (new 1993) or octagon barrel.

	MSR $839		$740	$575	$485	$385	$300	$260	$235

* **1866 Deluxe Uberti Model** - .44-40 WCF cal., features high polished receiver with fire-blue small parts, ladder rear sight, open edition beginning 1995.

	MSR $895		$895	$675	$525				

This model is sold exclusively by Cherry's, located in Greensboro, NC.

* **1866 "L.D. Nimschke" Special Edition** - .44-40 WCF cal., receiver, buttplate, and forend cap feature recreations of Nimschke scroll-engraving by Giovanelli of Italy, silver-plated, deluxe walnut, optional 2nd Edition of Nimschke pattern book by R. L. Wilson ($100), only 300 mfg. beginning 1995. Disc.

			$1,495	$1,000	$650				

Last MSR was $1,495.

This model was sold exclusively by Cherry's, located in Greensboro, NC.

* **1866 Yellowboy Indian Rifle** - .22 LR (disc. 1989), .22 Mag. (disc. 1989), .38 Spl., or .44-40 WCF cal., 24¼ in. barrel. Importation disc. 1989, reintroduced 1993-95.

			$700	$560	$475	$385	$300	$260	$235

Last MSR was $800.

1866 MUSKET - .44-40 WCF or .45 LC cal., features 27 in. barrel with barrel bands. Importation began 1999.

	MSR $910		$810	$600	$500	$425	$360	$320	$280

U

Grading	100%	98%	95%	90%	80%	70%	60%

1873 CARBINE - .22 LR (disc. 1991), .22 Mag. (disc. 1991), .32-20 WCF (new 2001), .357 Mag., .38 Spl. (disc. 1991) .38-40 (new 2002), .44-40 WCF, or .45 LC (new 1992) cal., steel receiver, 19 in. round barrel.

| MSR $910 | | $800 | $600 | $500 | $425 | $360 | $320 | $280 |

Add $35 for case colored frame (disc.).

* **1873 Trapper Carbine** - .357 Mag., .44-40 WCF, or .45 LC cal. only, 16 1/8 in. barrel. Importation disc. 1990.

| | | $695 | $550 | $475 | $400 | $360 | $320 | $280 |

Last MSR was $750.

1873 SPORTING RIFLE - .32-20 WCF (new 2001), .357 Mag. (new 1995),.38-40 WCF (new 2002), .44-40 WCF (new 1995), or .45 LC cal., case hardened receiver, 20 in. octagon (new 1990), 24¼ in. octagon (.357 Mag. only) or half-round/half-octagon, or 30 (new 1990) in. octagon barrel, can be drilled and tapped for Uberti rear tang aperture sight (new 1993).

| MSR $973 | | $850 | $365 | $525 | $425 | $360 | $320 | $260 |

Add $17 for 30 in. barrel (.44-40 WCF or .45 LC cal. only).

Add $26 for Deluxe Model with hand-checkered pistol grip stock - $77 for Deluxe Model with 30 in. barrel.

MODEL 1873 125th ANNIVERSARY - .44-40 WCF cal., special anniversary offering featuring engraved gold plated metal with fire blue receiver and small parts, long rifle configuration with deluxe pistol grip and forearm. 125 mfg. 1998 only, marketed exclusively by Cherry's.

| | | $3,250 | $2,500 | $1,750 | | | | |

Last MSR was $3,500.

1873 MUSKET - .44-40 WCF or .45 LC cal., features 30 in. round barrel with barrel bands. Importation began 1999.

| MSR $999 | | $875 | $700 | $575 | $450 | $375 | $325 | $300 |

RIFLES: SINGLE SHOT

1885 CARBINE/RIFLE - .30-30 Win., .38-55 WCF, .40-65 WCF, .44-40 WCF, .45 LC, .45-70 Govt., .45-90 WCF or .45-120 cal., 28 (carbine) round or 30 (rifle) in. octagon barrel, case colored receiver, straight grip walnut stock and forearm, 8.8 or 9.5 lbs. Importation began 1999.

| MSR $835 | | $740 | $575 | $485 | $385 | $300 | $260 | $235 |

Add $75 for rifle.

Add $164 for Deluxe Model with pistol grip and aperture sights (30 or 32 in. barrel).

1871 ROLLING BLOCK TARGET CARBINE/RIFLE - available in .22 LR, .22 Mag., .22 Hornet, or .357 Mag. cal., 22 (carbine) or 26 in. barrel.

| MSR $410 | | $335 | $275 | $230 | $195 | $175 | $155 | $135 |

Add $100 for rifle model.

SHOTGUNS: SxS

DOUBLE BARREL - 12 ga. only, 2¾, 3, or 3½ in. chambers, 20, 21½ , 24, or 26 in. barrels, exposed hammers, checkered walnut pistol grip stock and forearm. Imported 1999-2001.

| | | $875 | $700 | $575 | $450 | $375 | $325 | $300 |

Last MSR was $999.

UGARTECHEA, ARMAS

Current manufacturer located in Eibar, Spain. Currently being imported by Lion Country Supply, located in Port Matilda, PA, and Aspen Outfitting Co., located in Aspen, CO. Formerly known as Ugartechea, Ignacio.

Currently, Aspen Outfitting Co. imports Models 116, 119, 1000, 1030, 1042, and AOC/SG.

Grading	100%	98%	95%	90%	80%	70%	60%

SHOTGUNS: SxS

MODEL AOC/SG - 12, 16, 20, 28 ga., or .410 bore, 2¾ in. chambers, Anson & Deeley boxlock action with extra polishing and fitting of parts, scalloped action shaping, 28 in. chopper lump barrels, IC/M choke, front bead sight, concave rib, DT w/articulating front trigger, southgate auto ejectors, auto safety, free floating firing pins, engraved receiver with border scroll, upgraded European straight grip walnut stock and splinter forend with plunger release, hand checkered buttstock, initial shield, case hardened action finish, long tang trigger guard with comfort roll, upgraded wood finish, Importation began in 1999.

| MSR | $1,995 | $1,900 | $1,750 | $1,575 | $1,425 | $1,275 | $1,150 | $975 |

BILL HANUS BIRDGUN - 16, 20, 28 ga., or .410 bore, boxlock action, 26 in. barrels bored SK1/SK2, Churchill raised rib, SNT, ejectors, case colored receiver, checkered straight grip walnut stock and semi-beavertail forearm, oil finish, lifetime operational warranty, 5¼-6½ lbs. Imported 1995-97.

| | | $1,425 | $1,250 | $1,050 | $880 | $750 | $635 | $540 |

Last MSR was $1,695.

Add $100 for 28 ga.
Add $150 for .410 bore.

BILL HANUS BIRDGUN CLASSIC - 20, 28 ga., or .410 bore, similar to Birdgun Model, except has double triggers with hinged front trigger, 27 in. barrels, splinter forearm and English leather handguard. Imported 1996-97.

| | | $1,355 | $1,220 | $1,035 | $880 | $750 | $635 | $540 |

Last MSR was $1,595.

Add $100 for 28 ga.
Add $200 for .410 bore.

UPLAND CLASSIC GRADE I (MODEL 30) - 12, 16, 20, 28 ga., or .410 bore, Anson & Deeley boxlock action, DT, concave rib, extractors, case colored receiver, hand checkered straight grip walnut stock and splinter forend.

| MSR | $995 | $950 | $875 | $750 | $600 | $475 | $400 | $325 |

Add $100 for 28 ga.
Add $150 for .410 bore.
This model is imported exclusively by Lion Country Supply.

UPLAND CLASSIC GRADE II (MODEL 40) - 12, 16, 20, or 28 ga., Anson & Deeley boxlock action, DT, coin finished and engraved receiver, hand checkered straight grip walnut stock and splinter forend.

| MSR | $1,195 | $1,075 | $950 | $875 | $750 | $600 | $475 | $400 |

Add $100 for 28 ga.
This model is imported exclusively by Lion Country Supply.

UPLAND CLASSIC GRADE III (MODEL 40 NEX) - 12, 16, 20, or 28 ga., Anson & Deeley boxlock action, DT or SST, case colored and engraved receiver, hand checkered straight grip walnut stock and splinter forend.

| MSR | $1,550 | $1,400 | $1,200 | $1,000 | $875 | $750 | $600 | $500 |

Add $200 for SST.
Add $100 for 28 ga.
This model is imported exclusively by Lion Country Supply.

SHOTGUNS: SxS, SIDELOCK

Ugartechea sidelocks are best quality guns. Currently, Lion Country Supply stocks the Upland Classic Series. Additionally, custom orders are available through both Lion Country Supply and Aspen Outfitting.

U

Grading	100%	98%	95%	90%	80%	70%	60%

UPLAND CLASSIC GRADE IV - 12, 16, or 20 ga., best quality true sidelock with intercepting sears, DT or SST with hinged front trigger, case colored or coin finished receiver with English style scroll engraving, auto ejectors, upgraded wood with hand rubbed oil finish.

MSR	$2,195	$2,000	$1,700	$1,475	$1,200	$1,000	$875	$750

Add $200 for SST (20 ga. only).

This model is imported exclusively by Lion Country Supply.

UPLAND CLASSIC GRADE V (MODEL 110) - 12, 16, 20, or 28 ga., best quality round body game gun, true sidelock with intercepting sears, DT or SST with hinged front trigger, case colored or coin finished receiver with English style scroll engraving, auto ejectors, upgraded wood with hand rubbed oil finish.

MSR	$2,995	$2,675	$2,300	$1,900	$1,600	$1,350	$1,100	$925

Add $200 for SST.
Add $100 for 28 ga.

This model is imported exclusively by Lion Country Supply.

MODEL 75/75EX - 12, 16, or 20 ga., case colored finish with minimal engraving, oil finished deluxe walnut stock and forearm. Importation began 1999.

MSR	$1,995	$1,900	$1,750	$1,575	$1,425	$1,275	$1,150	$975

Add $200 for SST.

MODEL 116 - 12, 16, 20, 28 ga., or .410 bore, sidelock action, antique silver finish with elaborate floral engraving, deluxe oil finished walnut stock and forearm.

MSR	$5,340	$5,000	$4,400	$3,800	$3,200	$2,600	$2,000	$1,500

Add $340 for 28 ga. or .410 bore.

MODEL 119 - 12, 16, 20, 28 ga., or .410 bore, sidelock action with coin finish or case hardend frame, Purdey style engraving, deluxe oil finished walnut stock and forearm.

MSR	$5,560	$5,150	$4,550	$3,950	$3,250	$2,600	$2,000	$1,500

Add $335 for 28 ga. or .410 bore.

MODEL 1000 - 12, 16, or 20 ga., sidelock action with coin finish or case hardened frame, Churchill style deep relief engraving, deluxe oil finished walnut stock and forearm.

MSR	$6,405	$5,950	$5,250	$4,500	$3,750	$3,000	$2,350	$1,750

MODEL 1030 - 12, 16, or 20 ga., coin finished or case hardened frame, Woodward style scalloped fences and engraving. Importation began 1994.

MSR	$7,350	$6,875	$6,000	$5,150	$4,550	$3,950	$3,250	$2,450

MODEL 1042 - 12, 16, or 20 ga., sidelock action, coin finished or case hardened frame, exquisite full coverage fine scroll engraving, deluxe oil finished walnut stock and forearm.

MSR	$8,550	$7,850	$7,000	$6,000	$5,100	$4,200	$3,350	$2,850

SPECIAL MODELS - available in all gauges with game scene engraving and/or gold inlays to customer specifications. POR only.

UGARTECHEA, IGNACIO

Previous manufacturer located in Eibar, Spain. Previously imported exclusively by Aspen Outfitting Company, located in Aspen, CO.

Ignacio Ugartechea was founded in 1922 and is the oldest maker of side-by-side sidelock and boxlock shotguns in Spain (please refer to Armas Ugartechea for current information). From 1970 until the Parker-Hale name was sold in 1990 to Navy Arms, Ugartechea manufactured the popular line of Anson Deeley boxlocks imported by Precision Sports in Cortland, NY. Precision Sports continued to import these guns under the Classic "600" name until 1994. Previously imported by Precision Sports, Inc. located in Cortland, NY until 1994. Previously imported by Exel Arms in Gardener, MA until 1987 as the Exel Model 200 series.

SHOTGUNS: SxS, BOXLOCK

Due to space considerations, the individual Ignacio Ugartechea models have not been listed in this edition. Please refer to older editions for more information on these previously imported models. The importation of Parker-Hale shotguns was disc. in 1993.

Grading	100%	98%	95%	90%	80%	70%	60%

ULTIMATE
Please refer to Camex-Blaser USA in the C section of this text.

ULTRA LIGHT ARMS, INC.
Previous manufacturer located in Granville, WV. Ultra Light Arms, Inc. was purchased by C.F. Holding Corp. in 1999. No manufacture has occurred.

PISTOLS: BOLT-ACTION

MODEL 20 HUNTERS PISTOL - various cals., 14 in. Douglas heavy barrel, 5-shot mag., Kevlar graphite reinforced stock in choice of 4 colors, Timney trigger, left-hand or right-hand bolt, approx. 4 lbs. Mfg. 1987-89.

$1,295	$1,150	$975	$850	$700	$640	$575

Last MSR was $1,600.

MODEL 20 REB - popular cals. from .22-250 Rem. through .308 Win. (other cals. on request), 14 in. Douglas #3 barrel, 5 shot mag., composite Kevlar graphite reinforced stock, green, brown, black, or camo Dupont Imron paint, Timney adj. trigger, includes hard case, 4 lbs. Mfg. 1994-95, reintroduced 1998 only.

$1,475	$1,200	$1,000	$875	$750	$625	$500

Last MSR was $1,600.

RIFLES: BOLT ACTION

ULTRA LIGHT RIFLE - caliber to customer specs., various actions, 2-position 3-function safety in top of stock, Timney trigger, Douglas 22 or 24 in. barrel, no sights, graphite reinforced stock with recoil pad, matte finish standard, other finishes at extra cost. Many special order features and services were available on these models, 4¾-5¾ lbs. Mfg. 1985-1999.

MODEL 20 - many cals. available between .17 Rem. and .358 Win., short action, Kevlar stock.

$2,225	$1,675	$1,225	$950	$800	$700	$640

Last MSR was $2,500.

Add $100 for left-hand action.

* ***Model 20 RF*** - .22 LR cal., convertible from repeater to single shot, 22 in. Douglas premium barrel, DuPont composite stock with Imron paint (some color options available), no sights, drilled and tapped, 5¼ lbs. Mfg. 1983-1999.

$750	$650	$550	$475	$400	$350	$300

Last MSR was $800.

Add $50 for repeater action.
The first 100 pre-production rifles in this model were marked "1-of-100" consecutively, with owner's initials.

MODEL 24 - .25-06 Rem., .270 Win., .280 Rem. (mfg. 1992 only), .30-06, or 7mm Exp. cal., long action, Kevlar stock, 5¼ lbs. Disc. 1999.

$2,325	$1,775	$1,300	$995	$825	$700	$640

Last MSR was $2,600.

Add $100 for left-hand action.

MODEL 28 MAGNUM - .264 Win. Mag., .300 Win. Mag., .338 Win. Mag., 7mm Rem. Mag., or .416 Rigby (mfg. 1992 only) cal., Kevlar stock, 5¾ lbs. Disc. 1999.

$2,625	$1,975	$1,550	$1,225	$950	$700	$600

Last MSR was $2,900.

Add $100 for left-hand action.

MODEL 40 MAGNUM - .300 Wby. Mag. or .416 Rigby cal., otherwise similar to Model 28 Series. Mfg. 1993-99.

$2,625	$1,975	$1,550	$1,225	$950	$700	$600

Last MSR was $2,900.

Add $100 for left-hand action.

U

Grading	100%	98%	95%	90%	80%	70%	60%

ULTRAMATIC

Previous trademark with manufacture located in Enzesfeld, Austria. Ultramatic Productions, GmbH, changed its name to Wolf Sporting Pistols in 1997.

PISTOLS: SEMI-AUTO

ULTRAMATIC PISTOL - 9mm Para. cal., double action semi-auto, various barrel lengths, competition model with muzzle brake. Disc. approx. 1996.

	$1,150	$975	$850	$700	$640	$575	$500

UMAREX SPORTWAFFEN GmbH & Co. KG.

Current firearms, airguns, and signal pistol manufacturer located in Arnsberg, Germany.

Umarex purchased Walther during 1996, and also manufactures ammunition, optics, and accessories.

Please refer to the Walther listing for currently imported Walther firearms. For more information on currently manufactured Umarex airguns, please refer to the *Blue Book of Airguns* by Dr. Robert Beeman & John Allen (now online also).

UNIQUE

Current manufacturer located in Hendaye, France. Currently imported by Nygord Precision Products located in Prescott, AZ.

In addition to the current models listed below, Unique also manufactures additional models not currently imported into the U.S., but distributed mostly in Europe (Models I.S., DES 2000U, DES 69U, T3000 rifle, T/SM, T, and X51.

PISTOLS: SEMI-AUTO

All currently manufactured Unique pistols are supplied with leatherette case, weights are additional.

KRIEGSMODELL L - 7.65mm cal., 9 shot, 3.2 in. barrel, blue, plastic grips, fixed sights. Mfg. 1940-1945, during German occupation of France, has German acceptance marks.

	$325	$250	$220	$200	$180	$160	$140

MODEL RR - post-war commercial version of Kriegsmodell, higher quality finish. Mfg. 1951-disc.

	$180	$170	$155	$130	$120	$110	$90

Add 15% for .22 LR.

MODEL B/CF - 7.65mm cal., 9 shot, or .380 auto cal., 8 shot, 4 in. barrel, blue, plastic thumbrest grips. Mfg. 1954-disc.

	$205	$195	$175	$155	$145	$130	$110

MODEL D6 - .22 LR cal., 10 shot, 6 in. barrel, adj. sights, blue, plastic grips. Mfg. 1954-disc.

	$300	$250	$200	$160	$145	$135	$120

MODEL D2 - similar to D6, except 4½ in. barrel.

	$300	$250	$200	$160	$145	$135	$120

MODEL L - .22 LR cal., 10 shot, 7.65mm cal., 7 shot, and .380 ACP cal., 6 shot, 3.3 in. barrel, fixed sights, steel and alloy frame offered, plastic grips. Mfg. 1955-disc.

	$250	$200	$150	$130	$115	$100	$90

Add $500 for .22 LR cal. pistol-rifle combination.

MODEL MIKROS POCKET - .22 Short and .25 ACP cal., 6 shot, fixed sights, blue, plastic grips, steel or alloy frame. Mfg. 1957-disc.

	$200	$155	$140	$120	$100	$90	$75

U

Grading	100%	98%	95%	90%	80%	70%	60%

MODEL DES/32U - .32 S&W Wadcutter cal., 5.9 in. barrel, dry firing device, ergonomically designed French walnut grips with adj. hand rest, 5 or 6 shot mag., 40.2 oz.

MSR N/A	$1,350	$1,225	$1,025	$900	$775	$625	$500

MODEL DES/69 MATCH - .22 LR cal. target pistol, wraparound grips, adj. features. Imported 1986-1988.

	$995	$850	$725	$625	$550	$490	$445

Last MSR was $1,198.

Add $62 for left-hand model.

MODEL DES/69U STANDARD MATCH - .22 LR cal., 5 shot mag., 5.9 in. barrel, adj. rear sight, adj. target stippled stocks, blue finish only. Imported 1969-1999.

	$1,150	$995	$875	$750	$625	$500	$450

Last MSR was $1,250.

Add $30 for left-hand model.

MODEL DES/96U - .22 LR cal., replacement for the Model DES/69U, top loading model, thinner grips, features gold plated slide. New 1996.

MSR N/A	$1,350	$1,225	$1,025	$900	$775	$625	$500

MODEL DES/823-U RAPID FIRE MATCH - .22 Short cal., 5 shot, 6 in. barrel, adj. sight, adj. trigger, adj. walnut target grips, squared barrel assembly, dry fire mechanism. Imported 1974-1988.

	$1,100	$850	$725	$625	$550	$490	$445

Last MSR was $1,300.

Add $60 for left-hand model.

MODEL 2000-U - .22 Short cal. only, specifically designed for rapid fire U.I.T. competition, 5.9 in. barrel, ergonomic styled grips with adj. hand rest, 5 shot mag. (inserted in top), 43.4 oz. Importation disc. 1995.

	$1,300	$1,050	$925	$775	$625	$500	$450

Last MSR was $1,450.

Add $30 for left-hand model.

RIFLES: BOLT ACTION

T66 MATCH RIFLE - .22 LR cal., single shot, bolt action, 25½ in. barrel, micro rear and globe front sight, full target stock. Mfg. 1966-disc.

	$425	$410	$390	$350	$300	$280	$250

MODEL F 11 - .22 LR cal., military trainer, adj. sights, target walnut stock. Limited importation.

	$560	$435	$350	$285	$260	$240	$220

Last MSR was $695.

MODEL T DIOPTRA - .22 LR or .22 Mag. cal., bolt action Sporter with 23.6 in. barrel and adj. rear sight, 5 (.22 Mag. only) or 10 shot mag., grooved receiver for scope, checkered French walnut Monte Carlo stock, approx. 6.4 lbs. Importation disc. 1995.

	$795	$700	$600	$525	$450	$375	$300

Last MSR was $890.

MODEL T/SM - .22 LR or .22 Mag cal., bolt action Target variation with 20½ in. barrel, no sights, 5 (.22 Mag. only) or 10 shot mag., stippled pistol grip stock and forearm, right or left-hand action, 6.6 lbs. Importation disc. 1995.

	$850	$735	$625	$525	$450	$375	$300

Last MSR was $960.

Add $50 for left-hand action.

U

Grading	100%	98%	95%	90%	80%	70%	60%

MODEL T/STANDARD UIT - .22 LR cal., designed for UIT competition, single shot, aperture sights, adj. cheekpiece and buttplate on stippled walnut stock, right or left-hand action, 10.8 lbs. Importation disc. 1995.

	$1,350	$1,125	$975	$850	$725	$625	$525

Last MSR was $1,450.

Add $50 for left-hand action.

MODEL 2000 FREE RIFLE - .22 LR cal., Free Rifle variation of the Model T/Standard UIT.

MSR N/A	$2,600	$2,250	$1,875	$1,500	$1,250	$1,000	$850

UNITED SPORTING ARMS, INC.

Previous manufacturer located in Tucson, AZ. Manufacture ceased in early 1986.

REVOLVERS: SINGLE ACTION

SEVILLE - .357 Mag., .41 Mag., .44 Mag., or .45 LC cal., single action revolver, 4 5/8, 5½, 6½, or 7½ in. barrels, adj. sights, smooth walnut grips.

	$395	$350	$315	$280	$260	$240	$220

Last MSR was $435.

* **Stainless steel** - all stainless version of the Seville.

	$395	$350	$315

Last MSR was $435.

* **Silver Seville** - similar to Seville, except has blue barrel, and high polish stainless steel grip frame.

	$425	$370	$330

Last MSR was $460.

* **Stainless .357 Maxi** - available in 5½ or 7½ in. barrel only.

	$575	$475	$395

Last MSR was $465.

* **Stainless .375 USA** - only in 7½ in. barrel.

	$625	$525	$425

Last MSR was $490.

* **Stainless .454 Mag.** - only in 7½ in. barrel, 5 shot.

	$700	$600	$500

Last MSR was $595.

Note: In late 1986, some .454 Mags. were made up from parts purchased from the manufacturer. Unfortunately, while the exterior appearance might seem normal, they were not involved with any type of factory quality control program. As a result, shooting these non-factory revolvers could be dangerous, and careful inspection should be made before purchasing/shooting this particular specimen.

* **Eldorado Stainless** - .44 Mag., 10½ in. barrel, adj. sights.

	$700	$600	$500

SILVER SEVILLE SILHOUETTE - .357 Mag., .41 Mag., or .44 Mag. cal., single action revolver, 10½ in. barrel, adj. sights, Pachmayr grips, blue barrel finish with stainless grip frame.

	$445	$370	$330	$295	$270	$250	$230

Last MSR was $485.

* **Stainless steel** - stainless version of the Silver Seville Silhouette.

	$425	$370	$330

Last MSR was $460.

* **Stainless .357 Maxi** - available in 10½ in. barrel only.

	$575	$475	$395

Last MSR was $480.

* **Stainless .375 USA** - available in 10½ in. barrel only.

	$625	$525	$425

Last MSR was $515.

Grading	100%	98%	95%	90%	80%	70%	60%

✳ Stainless .454 Mag. - available in 10½ in. barrel only, 5 shot.

	$700	$600	$500				

Last MSR was $620.

SHERIFF MODEL - .357 Mag., .38 Spl., .44 Spl., .44 Mag., or .45 LC cal., single action revolver, 3½ in. barrel, adj. sights, smooth walnut grips.

	$395	$350	$315	$280	$260	$240	$220

Last MSR was $435.

✳ Stainless steel - stainless version of the Sheriff Model.

	$395	$350	$315				

Last MSR was $435.

UNITED STATES FIRE ARMS MANUFACTURING COMPANY, INC.

Current manufacturer established during 1995 and located in Hartford, CT (at Colt's original old armory).

REVOLVERS: SAA

Add $110 for .38-40 WCF, .44-40 WCF, .38 S&W Spl., or .44 S&W Spl. cal. on SAAs.
Add $150 for .41 LC or .32-20 WCF cal. on SAAs.

COLT 1851 RICHARDS NAVY CONVERSION - .38 Spl. only, 7½ in. barrel with ejector, Old Armoury Bone case hardened frame, gate, hammer, and conversion ring, Dome Blue barrel, cylinder, and ejector housing, smooth walnut grips.

MSR	$1,300	$1,175	$950	$825	$700	$600	$500	$400

SINGLE ACTION ARMY - .22 LR (mfg. 1996-2001), .22 Mag. (mfg. 1996-2001), .32-20 (new 1998), .357 Mag. (disc. 1998), .38-40 WCF, .41 Colt (new 1999), .44-40 WCF, .45 ACP, or .45 LC cal., 3 (no ejector), 4 (no ejector), 4¾, 5½, 7½, or 10 (new 1997) in. barrel, original screw cylinder release, choice of Full Dome Blue, Dome Blue/Old Armory Bone Case, or nickel finish.

MSR	$1,225	$1,025	$850	$725	$600	$500	$400	$300

Add $100 for Dome Blue/Old Armory Bone Case finish (disc.).
Add $250 for nickel finish.

✳ Flattop Target SAA - similar to SAA, except has flattop receiver with target sights and two-piece rubber grips, full dome blue finish is standard. New 1997.

MSR	$1,349	$1,050	$925	$775	$675	$550	$450	$400

Add $100 for Dome Blue/Old Armory Bone Case finish.
Add $150 for Armory Blue/ Old Armory Bone Case finish.
Add $170 for nickel finish.

✳ U.S. Pre-War SAA - various cals., most historically correct and accurate pre-war SAA available. New 2000.

MSR	$1,495	$1,175	$995	$825	$725	$575	$475	$425

✳ Henry Nettleton Cavalry Revolver - .45 LC cal., faithful Cavalry Model reproduction following the original U.S. Government inspector specifications. Disc. 1998, reintroduced 2000.

MSR	$1,225	$1,075	$895	$750	$650	$525	$425	$325

✳ New Buntline Special - .45 LC cal. only, 16 in. barrel, includes correct skeleton shoulder stock, ser. numbered 28,8xx and up. New 2000.

MSR	$2,199	$1,850	$1,675	$1,500	$1,250	$1,000	$900	$800

Add $396 for nickel finish.

U

Grading	100%	98%	95%	90%	80%	70%	60%

BISLEY MODEL SAA - same cals. as SAA, 4¾, 5½, 7½, or 10 in. barrel, patterned after the Colt Bisley Model. Disc. 1998, reintroduced 2000.

MSR	$1,650		$1,375	$1,075	$850	$750	$625	$525	$450

Add $195 for Armory Blue/Old Armory Bone Case finish.
Add $85 for nickel finish.

BIRDSHEAD MODEL SAA - same cals. as SAA, patterned after the Colt Model 1877 Thunderer, 3½, 4, or 4¾ in. barrel with ejector, case colored frame. New 1997.

MSR	$1,150		$975	$825	$725	$625	$525	$425	$325

Add $149 for nickel finish.

CHINA CAMP - various cals., designed for competition shooting, silver steel competition finish with two-piece hard rubber grips. New 2000.

MSR	$1,200		$975	$850	$725	$625	$525	$425	$325

RODEO - .45 LC only, 4 3/4 or 5 ½ in. barrel, blue satin finish, fixed firing pin, square notch rear sight, hard rubber grips, entry level cowboy action shooting model. New 2002.

MSR	$505		$450	$420	$390	$375	$360	$345	$330

OMNI-POTENT SIX SHOOTER/SNUBNOSE - various cals., 2, 3, 4¾, 5½, or 7½ in. barrel, Old Armory Bone Case and Armory blue finish, checkered Bisley style walnut grips with round butt and lanyard loop. New 2000.

MSR	$1,340		$1,175	$950	$800	$675	$575	$475	$375

Add $105 for Omni-Target Six Shooter.

UNIVERSAL FIREARMS

Previous division of Iver Johnson's Arms, Inc. that was established during 1982. Formerly imported out of Hialeah, FL. Previously manufactured in Jacksonville, AR.

PISTOLS: SEMI-AUTO

MODEL 3000 ENFORCER PISTOL - .30 Carbine cal., walnut stock, 11¼ in. barrel, 17¾ in. overall, 15, and 30 shot. Mfg. 1964-1983. Also see listing under Iver Johnson.

	100%	98%	95%	90%	80%	70%	60%
blue finish	$275	$235	$200	$185	$170	$160	$150
Nickel-plated	$295	$250	$235	$220	$200	$185	$165
Gold-plated	$350	$275	$250	$225	$200	$185	$165
Stainless	$375	$300	$225				

Add $50 for Teflon-S finish.

RIFLES: SEMI-AUTO, CARBINES

MODEL 440 VULCAN - .44 Mag. cal., slide action, 18¼ in. barrel with adj. rear and front ramp sight, 5 shot detachable mag.

		$325	$275	$230	$195	$175	$150	$135

1000 MILITARY - .30 Carbine cal., "G.I." copy, satin blue, birch stock, 18 in. barrel. Disc.

		$229	$180	$170	$160	$150	$135	$125

MODEL 1003 - 16, 18, or 20 in. barrel, .30 M1 copy, blue finish, adj. sight, birch stock, 5½ lbs. Also see listing under Iver Johnson.

		$285	$250	$225	$200	$180	$160	$140

Last MSR was $203.

* **Model 1010** - nickel finish, disc.

		$300	$265	$240	$210	$180	$155	$120

* **Model 1015** - gold electroplated, disc.

		$325	$275	$250	$215	$185	$160	$130

Add $45 for 4X scope.

Grading	100%	98%	95%	90%	80%	70%	60%

1005 DELUXE - .30 Carbine cal., custom Monte Carlo walnut stock, high polish blue, oil finish on wood.

	100%	98%	95%	90%	80%	70%	60%
	$325	$275	$250	$225	$200	$180	$170

1006 STAINLESS - .30 Carbine cal., stainless steel construction, birch stock, 18 in. barrel, 6 lbs.

	$350	$300	$265

Last MSR was $234.

1020 TEFLON - .30 Carbine cal., Dupont Teflon-S finish on metal parts, black or grey color, Monte Carlo stock.

	$325	$275	$250

1256 "FERRET" - .256 Win. Mag. cal., M1 Action, satin blue, birch stock, 18 in. barrel, 5½ lbs.

	$275	$250	$175	$165	$155	$145	$135

Last MSR was $219.

2200 LEATHERNECK - .22 LR cal., recoil operated action, birch stock, satin blue, 18 in. barrel, 5½ lbs.

	$240	$190	$180	$170	$160	$145	$135

5000 PARATROOPER - .30 Carbine cal., metal folding extension, walnut stock, 16 or 18 in. barrel.

	$375	$325	$285	$250	$225	$200	$130

Last MSR was $234.

5006 PARATROOPER STAINLESS - similar to 5000, only stainless with 18 in. barrel only.

	$395	$340	$295

Last MSR was $281.

1981 COMMEMORATIVE CARBINE - .30 Carbine cal., "G.I Military" model, cased with accessories. Mfg. for 40th Anniversary 1941-1981.

	$650	$490	$400

SHOTGUNS

All Universal shotguns were disc. after 1982.

MODEL 7312 O/U - 12 ga., 30 in. full and mod., VR barrel, boxlock, vent. barrel spacer, SST, auto ejectors, barrels ported to reduce recoil, engraved, color case hardened receiver, trap or skeet style, checkered select stock.

	$1,650	$1,540	$1,485	$1,430	$1,320	$1,210	$1,045

MODEL 7412 O/U - similar to 7312, without ejectors, blue and silver receiver.

	$1,430	$1,210	$1,155	$1,100	$9,900	$880	$825

MODEL 7712 O/U - 12 ga., 26 or 28 in. barrel, VR, non-selective single trigger, extractors, light engraving, checkered pistol grip stock.

	$440	$415	$385	$360	$330	$275	$220

MODEL 7812 O/U - similar to 7712, with auto ejectors and more engraving.

	$605	$580	$550	$525	$470	$415	$385

MODEL 7912 O/U - similar to 7812, with selective single trigger and gold damascene engraving.

	$1,210	$1,155	$1,100	$1,045	$965	$880	$825

MODEL 7112 SxS - 12 ga., 26 or 28 in. barrels, various chokes, boxlock, extractors, engraved case hardened frame, checkered pistol grip stock.

	$330	$305	$275	$250	$195	$165	$140

DOUBLE WING SxS - 10, 12, 20 ga., or .410 bore, 26, 28, or 30 in. barrels, various chokes, double triggers, boxlock, extractors, checkered pistol grip stock.

	$330	$305	$275	$250	$195	$165	$140
10 gauge.	$385	$360	$330	$305	$250	$220	$165

U

Grading	100%	98%	95%	90%	80%	70%	60%

MODEL 7212 SINGLE BARREL TRAP - 12 ga., 30 in. full, Simmons type VR, engraved case colored frame, vent. barrel to reduce recoil, boxlock, auto ejector, select checkered trap style stock.

	$1,100	$990	$935	$880	$770	$715	$605

UZI

Currently manufactured by Israeli Military Industries (IMI). No commercial U.S. importation currently. During 1996-1998, Mossberg imported the Uzi Eagle pistols. These models were imported by UZI America, Inc., subsidiary of O.F. Mossberg & Sons, Inc. Previously imported by Action Arms, Ltd., located in Philadelphia, PA until 1994.

Serial number prefixes used on Uzi Firearms are as follows: "SA" on all 9mm Para. semi-auto carbines Models A and B; "45 SA" on all .45 ACP Model B carbines; "41 SA" on all .41 AE Model B carbines; "MC" on all 9mm Para. (only cal. made) semi-auto mini-carbines; "UP" on all 9mm Para. semi-auto Uzi pistols; "45 UP" on all .45 semi-auto Uzi pistols (disc. 1989). There are also prototypes or experimental Uzis with either "AA" or "AAL" prefixes - these are rare and will command premiums over values listed below.

CARBINES: SEMI-AUTO

CARBINE MODEL A - 9mm Para. cal., semi-auto, 16.1 in. barrel, parkerized finish, 25 shot mag., mfg. by IMI 1980-1983 and ser. range is SA01,001-SA037,000.

	$1,350	$1,125	$975	$875	$750	$650	$600

Approx. 100 Model As were mfg. with a nickel finish. These are rare and command considerable premiums over values listed above.

CARBINE MODEL B - 9mm Para., .41 Action Express (new 1987), or .45 ACP (new 1987) cal., semi-auto carbine, 16.1 in. barrel, baked enamel black finish over phosphated (parkerized) base finish, 16 (.45 ACP), 20 (.41 AE) or 25 (9mm Para.) shot mag., metal folding stock, includes molded case and carrying sling, 8.4 lbs. Mfg. 1983 - until Federal legislation disc. importation 1989 and ser. range is SA037,001-SA073,544.

	$1,275	$1,050	$925	$825	$725	$650	$600

Last MSR was $698.

Subtract approx. $150 for .41 AE or .45 ACP cal.
Add $150 for .22 cal. conversion kit (new 1987).
Add $215 for .45 ACP to 9mm Para./.41 AE conversion kit.
Add $150 for 9mm Para. to .41 AE (or vice-versa) conversion kit.
Add $215 for 9mm Para. to .45 ACP conversion kit.

MINI CARBINE - 9mm Para. cal., similar to Carbine except has 19¾ in. barrel, 20 shot mag., swing-away metal stock, scaled down version of the regular carbine, 7.2 lbs. New 1987. Federal legislation disc. importation 1989.

	$2,375	$2,175	$1,850	$1,600	1,350	$1,150	$995

Last MSR was $698.

PISTOLS: SEMI-AUTO

UZI PISTOL - 9mm Para. or .45 ACP cal. (disc.), semi-auto pistol, 4½ in. barrel, parkerized finish, 10 (.45 ACP) or 20 (9mm Para.) shot mag., supplied with molded carrying case, sight adj. key and mag. loading tool, 3.8 lbs. Importation disc. 1993.

	$975	$850	$795	$750	$700	$650	$600

Last MSR was $695.

Add $285 for .45 ACP to 9mm Para./.41 AE conversion kit.
Add $100 for 9mm Para. to .41 AE conversion kit.
Add approx. 30%-40% for two-line slide marking "45 ACP Model 45".

Grading	100%	98%	95%	90%	80%	70%	60%

UZI EAGLE SERIES - 9mm Para., .40 S&W, or .45 ACP cal., semi-auto double action, various configurations, matte finish with black synthetic grips, 10 shot mag. Mfg. 1997-1998.

* *Full-Size Eagle* - 9mm Para. or .40 S&W cal., 4.4 in. barrel, steel construction, decocking feature, Tritium sights, polygonal rifling. Imported 1997-98.

	100%	98%	95%	90%	80%	70%	60%
	$485	$440	$400	$365	$335	$330	$275

Last MSR was $535.

* *Short Slide Eagle* - 9mm Para., .40 S&W, or .45 ACP cal., similar to Full-Size Eagle, except has 3.7 in. barrel. Imported 1997-98.

	100%	98%	95%	90%	80%	70%	60%
	$485	$440	$400	$365	$335	$330	$275

Last MSR was $535.

Add $31 for .45 ACP cal.

* *Compact Eagle* - 9mm Para. or .40 S&W cal., available in double action with decocking or double action only, 3½ in. barrel. Imported 1997-98.

	100%	98%	95%	90%	80%	70%	60%
	$485	$440	$400	$365	$335	$330	$275

Last MSR was $535.

* *Polymer Compact* - similar to Compact Eagle, except has compact polymer frame. Imported 1997-98.

	100%	98%	95%	90%	80%	70%	60%
	$485	$440	$400	$365	$335	$330	$275

Last MSR was $535.

U

NOTES

U

U is for the United States and being United - now more than ever.

V Section

VALKYRIE ARMS LTD.

Current manufacturer located in Olympia, WA. Dealer sales.

Valkyrie Arms Ltd. manufacturers copies of the M3A1, Browning 1919 and DeLisle Commando Carbine. For more information, including availability and pricing, please contact the company directly (see Trademark Index).

VALMET, INC.

Previous manufacturer located in Jyvaskyla, Finland. Previously imported by Stoeger Industries, Inc. located in South Hackensack, NJ.

The Valmet line was discontinued in 1989 and replaced by Tikka (please refer to the Tikka section in this text) in 1990.

Grading	100%	98%	95%	90%	80%	70%	60%

RIFLES: SEMI-AUTO

HUNTER MODEL - .223 Rem., .243 Win., or .308 Win. cal., gas operated semi-auto, Kalashnikov action, 20½ in. barrel, checkered walnut stock and forearm, matte finished metal, 5, 9, or 20 shot mag., 8 lbs. New 1986, Federal legislation disc. importation 1989.

	$895	$795	$700	$625	$550	$500	$450

Last MSR was $795.

M-62S PARAMILITARY DESIGN RIFLE - 7.62x39 Russian, semi-auto version of Finn M-62, 15 or 30 shot mag., 16 5/8 in. barrel, gas operated, rotary bolt, adj. rear sight, tube steel or wood stock. Mfg. 1962-disc.

	$1,800	$1,575	$1,375	$1,175	$975	$875	$775

M-71S - similar to M-62S, except .223 Rem. cal., reinforced resin or wood stock.

	$1,450	$1,325	$1,175	$975	$875	$775	$675

MODEL 76 - .223 Rem., 7.62x39mm, or .308 Win. cal., gas operated semi-auto paramilitary design rifle, 16¾ in. or 20½ (.308 only) in. barrel, 15 or 30 (7.62x39mm only) shot mag., parkerized finish. Federal legislation disc. importation 1989.

	$1,450	$1,325	$1,175	$975	$875	$775	$675

Last MSR was $740.

Add $300 for folding, or $95-$125 for synthetic stock.

MODEL 78 - .308 Win. cal. only, similar to Model 76, except has 24½ in. barrel, wood stock and forearm, and barrel bipod, 11 lbs. New 1987. Federal legislation disc. importation 1989.

	$1,625	$1,475	$1,200	$995	$875	$775	$675

Last MSR was $1,060.

MODEL 82 BULLPUP - .223 Rem. cal., limited importation.

	$2,500	$1,950	$1,550	$1,250	$1,000	$825	$700

SHOTGUNS: O/U

LION MODEL - 12 ga., 26, 28, or 30 in. barrels, various chokes, boxlock, SST, checkered stock. Mfg. 1947-1968.

	$415	$370	$340	$320	$305	$275	$240

MODEL 412 O/U SHOOTING SYSTEM - interchangeable barrel assemblies permit a double rifle, shotgun/rifle, and O/U shotgun configuration, user installed interchangeable barrels, monobloc locking, rifle barrel positioning by adjustment, SST, extractors or ejectors, checkered walnut stock and forend, cocking indicators, blue finish. Importation on all models was disc. 1989.

Add $100 for synthetic stock on all 412 models.

V

Grading	100%	98%	95%	90%	80%	70%	60%

✳ Model 412S Field Grade - 12 ga. was standard, auto ejectors, screw-in choke tubes, matte nickel finish. Imported 1986-89.

	$855	$670	$580	$540	$475	$440	$400

Last MSR was $999.

Add 15% for 20 ga.

✳ Model 412S Field and Target - 12 ga. only, 2¾ and 3 in. chambers, ejectors. Disc. 1988.

	$775	$660	$580	$540	$475	$440	$400

Last MSR was $874.

✳ Model 412ST Trap and Skeet - 12 ga., Monte Carlo stock on Trap model, 28 in. barrels on Skeet model, screw-in chokes standard.

	$1,040	$875	$695	$650	$580	$540	$475

Last MSR was $1,215.

✳ Model 412ST Premium Grade Target - similar to Model 412ST Trap and Skeet, except has better walnut and checkering. Imported 1987-89.

	$1,355	$1,050	$865	$750	$640	$580	$515

Last MSR was $1,550.

✳ Model 412S Combination Gun - combination, 12 ga, 3 in. chamber over choice of .222 Rem., .223 Rem., .243 Win., .30-06, or .308 Win. cal., extractors.

	$1,025	$850	$675	$600	$550	$475	$440

Last MSR was $1,615.

✳ Model 412S Double Rifle - .243 Win. (disc. 1987), .30-06, .308 Win. (disc. 1987), .375 H&H Mag. (disc. 1987), or 9.3x73R cal., extractors, 24 in. barrels.

	$1,060	$895	$725	$650	$580	$540	$475

Last MSR was $1,275.

Add $100 for 9.3x74R cal. or .375 H&H Mag. cal.

This model in .30-06 cal. has extractors only while in 9.3x74R cal. ejectors are standard.

✳ Model 412K Double Rifle - .30-06 or .308 Win. cal. only, 24 in. separated barrels, extractors. Importation disc. 1986.

	$800	$660	$580	$540	$475	$440	$400

Last MSR was $899.

✳ Model 412 Engraved - satin finish, receiver extensively bank note engraved in choice of 4 patterns, select Triple-X wood hand-checkered - choice of field or target, available in any Valmet model.

This model had limited availability and prices were on request from the manufacturer.

Add $85 for shotgun rifle, $320 for double rifle.

✳ Extra Barrel Assemblies (Model 412 O/U) - $505 - $605 each for shotgun (includes screw-in chokes), $579 each for shotgun/rifle combo, $660 each for double rifle (add $100 for ejectors).

VALTRO

Current manufacturer established during 1988 and located in Brescia, Italy. Currently imported by Valtro USA, Inc., located in San Rafael, CA.

Valtro manufactures both excellent quality slide action and semi-auto shotguns, in addition to a semi-auto pistol, and a variety of signal pistols. Please contact Valtro USA Inc. (see Trademark Index listing) directly for more product information and availability.

1998 A1 .45 ACP - .45 ACP cal., forged National Match frame and slide, 5 in. barrel, deluxe wood grips, 8 shot mag., ambidextrous safety, blue finish, flat checkered mainspring housing, front and rear slide serrations, beveled mag. well, speed trigger, 40 oz. New 1998.

MSR	$1,295		$1,095	$850	$675	$600	$500	$425	$375

Grading	100%	98%	95%	90%	80%	70%	60%

SHOTGUNS: SLIDE ACTION

TACTICAL 98 SHOTGUN - 12 ga. only, 18½ or 20 in. barrel featuring MMC ghost ring sights and integral muzzle brake, 5 shot mag., internal chokes, receiver sidesaddle holds 6 exposed rounds, pistol grip or standard stock, matte black finish, lightweight. New 1998.

MSR	$865	$790	$630	$525	$475	$425	$400	$360

VARBERGER

Previous rifle manufacturer located in Varberg, Sweden. Previously imported by Hill Country Wholesale, Inc. located in Austin, TX, and distributed by Paul & Associates, located in Wellsville, KS until late 1995.

VARBERGER PRECISION PRODUCTS AB

RIFLES: BOLT ACTION

MODEL 711 GRADE 1 - available in 19 cals. between .22 PPC and .358 Norma, bolt action design featuring specially designed and manufactured receiver, rotary mag., 6 lug engine-turned bolt, and stock featuring metal retainer plate, individually test fired. Imported 1994-98.

		$950	$850	$750	$650	$550	$450	$375

Last MSR was $1,080.

MODEL 717 GRADE 1 MAGNUM - available in 11 Mag. cals. between .257 Wby. Mag. and .375 H&H. Imported 1994-98.

		$980	$875	$765	$650	$550	$450	$375

Last MSR was $1,130.

MODEL 757 GRADE 2 DELUXE - deluxe variation of the Model 711. Imported 1994-98.

	$1,775	$1,500	$1,250	$995	$895	$795	$695

Last MSR was $2,035.

Add $45 for Mag. cals.

MODEL 77 GRADE 3 PREMIER - top-of-the-line model. Imported 1994-98.

	$1,995	$1,675	$1,350	$1,050	$925	$795	$695

Last MSR was $2,375.

Add $65 for Mag. cals.

VARNER SPORTING ARMS, INC.

Previous manufacturer located in Marietta, GA circa 1988-89.

RIFLES: SINGLE SHOT

VARNER FAVORITE HUNTER - .22 LR cal., patterned after J. Stevens Favorite Model, ½ round - ½ octagon 21½ in. takedown barrel, blue frame, walnut stock and forearm, aperture rear sight, 5 lbs. Mfg. 1988-89.

		$325	$270	$220	$185	$150	$130	$110

Last MSR was $369.

✱ *Hunter Deluxe* - similar to Favorite Hunter, except has case colored frame and lever, and deluxe walnut stock and forearm. Mfg. 1988-89.

		$450	$375	$285	$225	$175	$150	$135

Last MSR was $500.

✱ *Presentation Grade* - includes target hammer and trigger, AAA quality checkered stock and forearm, includes takedown case. Mfg. 1988-89.

		$480	$400	$310	$250	$195	$170	$155

Last MSR was $569.

PRESENTATION ENGRAVED - previously available in a No. 1 Grade for $649, a No. 2 for $779, or a No. 3 for $1,099.

V

Grading	100%	98%	95%	90%	80%	70%	60%

VEKTOR

Current trademark established during 1953 as part of LIW (Lyttelton Engineering Work). Currently manufactured in South Africa. In 1995, Vektor became a separate division of Denel.

Vektor has been manufacturing high quality and reliable firearms, including semi-auto and slide action rifles, for South African law enforcement for quite some time, in addition to having secured contracts with many foreign countries.

Since Vektor does not currently have any U.S. importation, the values listed represent the last domestic MSRs.

PISTOLS: SEMI-AUTO

All Vektor pistols feature polygonal rifling, excluding the Z88.

MODEL CP1 - 9mm Para. cal., 4 in. barrel, compact model with unique aesthetics and ergonomic design allowing no buttons or levers on exterior surfaces, hammerless, striker fire system, black or nickel finished slide, 10 shot mag., approx. 25½ oz. Importation began 1999.

MSR	$480	$440	$400	$360	$330	$300	$280	$260

Add $20 for nickel slide finish.

MODEL Z88 - 9mm Para. cal., double action, patterned after the M92 Beretta, 5 in. barrel, steel construction, black synthetic grips, 10 shot mag., 35 oz. Importation began 1999.

MSR	$620	$550	$495	$450	$400	$360	$330	$295

MODEL SP1 - 9mm Para. cal., double action, 5 in. barrel with polygonal rifling, wraparound checkered synthetic grips, matte blue or normal black finish, 2.2. lbs. Importation began 1999.

MSR	$600	$535	$485	$445	$395	$360	$330	$295

Add $30 for natural anodized or nickel finish.
Add $230 for Sport Pistol with compensated barrel.

* **Model SP1 Compact (General's Model)** - similar to Model SP1, except is compact variation with 4 in. barrel, 25.4 oz. Importation began 1999.

MSR	$650	$575	$510	$460	$410	$360	$330	$295

* **Model SP1 Sport Pistol/Tuned** - similar to Model SP1, except has is available with tuned action or target pistol features. Importation began 1999.

MSR	$1,200	$1,050	$900	$775	$650	$525	$400	$350

Add $100 for Target Pistol with dual color finish.

MODEL SP2 - .40 S&W cal., otherwise similar to Model SP1. Importation began in 1999.

MSR	$650	$575	$510	$460	$410	$360	$330	$295

Add $190 for 9mm Para. conversion kit.

* **Model SP2 Compact (General's Model)** - similar to Model SP2, except is compact variation. Importation began 1999.

MSR	$650	$575	$510	$460	$410	$360	$330	$295

* **Model SP2 Competition** - competition variation of the Model SP2 featuring 5 7/8 in. barrel, additional magazine guide, enlarged safety levers and mag catch, and straight trigger, 35 oz. Importation began 2000.

MSR	$1,000	$850	$775	$675	$575	$510	$460	$395

STOCK GUN - 9mm Para. cal., normal black finish. Importation began 2000.

MSR	$1,000	$850	$775	$675	$575	$510	$460	$395

ULTRA MODEL - 9mm Para. or .40 S&W (new 2000) cal., top-of-the-line double action with most performance features, optional Lynx (disc. 1999) or Tasco (new 2000) scope. Importation began 1999.

MSR	$2,150	$1,950	$1,700	$1,500	$1,300	$1,100	$900	$700

Subtract $150 if w/o Tasco scope.

Grading	100%	98%	95%	90%	80%	70%	60%

RIFLES: BOLT-ACTION

K98 - standard cals are .243 Win., .270 Win., .30-06, .308 Win., 7x57mm Mauser, 7x64 Bren., Mag. cals. include .300 Win. Mag., .300 H&H, .416 Rigby, .470 Capstick, .458 Win. Mag., or 9.3x62mm, 5 shot staggered mag., non-rotating long extractor, positive bolt stop, checkered walnut stock, hammer forged barrel, iron sights on Mag. cals. only. Importation began 2000.

MSR $1,149	$995	$850	$775	$675	$575	$510	$460

Add $100 for Mag. cals.

RIFLES: SLIDE ACTION

H5 - .223 Rem. cal., 18 or 22 in. barrel, rotating bolt, uncheckered forearm and thumbhole stock with pad, includes 4X scope with long eye relief, 9 lbs., 7 oz. - 10¼ lbs. Importation began 2000.

MSR $850		$775	$650	$575	$510	$460	$410	$350

VEPR. RIFLES

Currently manufactured by Molot JSC (Vyatskie Polyany Machine Building Factory) located in Russia. Currently imported exclusively by ZDF Import/Export, Inc., located in Salt Lake City, UT.

RIFLES: SEMI-AUTO

VEPR II CARBINE/RIFLE - .223 Rem., .308 Win., or 7.62x39mm (new 2001) cal., features Vepr.'s semi-auto action, 20½ (carbine, .308 Win. only) or 23¼ (rifle) in. barrel with adj. rear sight, scope mount rail built into receiver top, checkered thumbhole walnut stock with recoil pad and forend, paddle mag. release, 5 or 10 shot mag., approx 9 lbs. Importation began 1999.

MSR $550		$495	$460	$430	$395	$360	$330	$300

Add $30 for .223 Rem. cal. (rifle only), $50 for .308 Win. cal.

SUPER VEPR .308 - .308 Win. cal., New 2001.

MSR $900		$800	$725	$650	$600	$550	$500	$450

VERNEY-CARRON

Current manufacturer of shotguns and rifles established during 1820, and located in St. Etienne, France. Currently imported by Verney-Carron U.S.A., Inc., located in Clay Center, KS. Currently distributed by the Graystone Group, located in Chicago, IL. Previously imported by Yellow Brick Entreprises, located in Clay Center, KS during 1998 only.

Established during 1820 by Claude Verney-Carron, whose ancestors were "Faiseur de fusils" - gunmakers - since at least 1650. Verney-Carron is proud to reflect on six generations of family ownership, and is the largest French manufacturer of hunting shotguns and rifles. Please contact the distributor directly for more information, including current model availability and domestic pricing regarding these fine firearms (see Trademark Index).

In 2000, Verney-Carron SA and Y.B.E., Inc. located in Clay Center, KS (distributor of Hastings Barrels & Choke Tubes) established a joint venture, Verney-Carron USA, Inc., located in Clay Center, KS. This joint venture purchased Sporting Arms Manufacturing, Inc., the manufacturer of the Snake Charmer II shotgun. During 2001, Sporting Arms Manufacturing was dissolved, and the Snake Charmer II is now manufactured by Verney-Carron USA, Inc. Please refer to the separate Snake Charmer listing.

V

Grading	100%	98%	95%	90%	80%	70%	60%

RIFLES

Current models include the Sagittaire O/U (with or w/o sideplates) and the Impact Plus bolt action with vent. quarter rib, front and rear sight, as well as the new semi-auto Impact Auto Rifle.

SHOTGUNS

Verney-Carron makes a wide variety of shotgun models and configurations, including the Super 9II O/U (with or w/o sideplates, (many options are available), Sagittaire O/U series, Alto 6 semi-auto, and the J.E.T. SxS.

VERONA

Current manufacturer located in Italy. Currently imported by B.C. Outdoors, located in Boulder City, NV.

Verona manufactures good quality O/U shotguns. Please contact the importer directly for more information, including pricing and model availability (see Trademark Index).

SHOTGUNS: O/U

Verona current models include the LX501 Hunting Model, the LX680 (Sporting and Competition), the LX692G (in Hunting, Sporting, and Competition configurations, including combos), and the LX702G (with Turkish Walnut).

VICKERS LIMITED

Previous manufacturer located in Crayford/Kent, England.

RIFLES: SINGLE SHOT, TARGET

JUBILEE SINGLE SHOT TARGET RIFLE - Martini type action, .22 LR cal., 28 in. heavy barrel, target sights, one piece pistol grip, target stock, pre-WWII.

$440	$330	$305	$275	$250	$220	$165

EMPIRE MODEL - similar to Jubilee, with 27 or 30 in. barrel, straight grip stock.

$415	$310	$285	$260	$220	$195	$150

VICTOR ARMS CORPORATION

Previous manufacturer located in Houston, TX.

Victor Arms Corporation manufactured limited quantities of a .22 LR upper unit for the AR-15. It works by removing the standard .223 upper, and replacing it with the V22 upper assembly and magazine. Additionally, a complete protoype gun was also manufactured.

VICTORY ARMS CO. LIMITED

Previously manufactured in prototype format only by Modern Manufacturing Company located in Phoenix, AZ.

PISTOL: SEMI-AUTO

MODEL MC5 - while a few prototypes were mfg. for trade shows (circa 1991-92), this model was never commercially manufactured. Last advertised retail was $465.

VIERLINGS

The German word Vierling denotes a four barrel long arm configuration mostly manufactured in Germany and Austria.

This configuration of long arm has four barrels, typically with a .22 caliber barrel incorporated in the center rib or stacked below two SxS shotgun barrels and a lower, larger caliber rifle barrel. Vierlings typically have two triggers, both single set. Barrel selectors are usually on the top

Grading	100%	98%	95%	90%	80%	70%	60%

tang. This unusual configuration is mostly of German mfg., although there are a few Austrian specimens also (the gunmakers of Ferlach still custom make this model). All Vierlings are mfg. one at a time, with fabrication being very complicated, lengthy, and expensive. As a result, every Vierling must be appraised individually - most specimens, however, are priced approx. $3,500 - $7,500 range, if not elaborate.

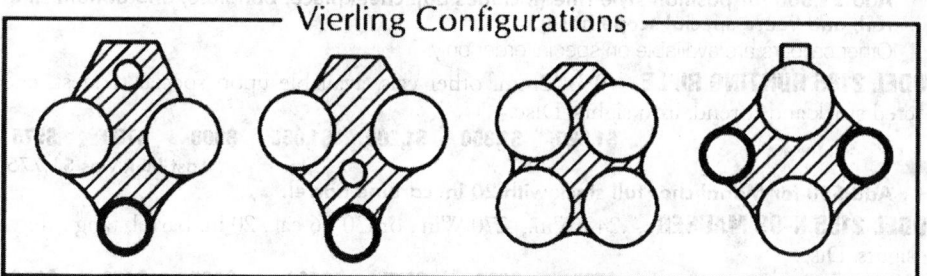

Vierling Configurations

VIRGIN VALLEY CUSTOM GUNS

Current manufacturer of custom bolt action rifles located in Hurricane, UT.

RIFLES: BOLT ACTION

SAFARI RIFLE - various big game cals., choice of Dakota Mod. 76, Mauser, or Win. Mod. 70 action, individually custom ordered.

Prices for this model range $3,100 - $4,100. Please contact the company directly for a individual price quotation and delivery time.

VIRGINIAN

This trademark can be located under the Interarms section in this text.

VIS

Currently manufactured by the F.B. Radom arsenal in Radom, Poland. Please refer to the Radom section in this text.

VOERE (AUSTRIA)

Current manufacturer established during 1965, and located in Kufstein, Austria. No current U.S. importation.

Voere of Austria is not associated with the Voere trademark of Germany that was taken over by Mauser-Werke after going bankrupt. Voere manufactures a complete line of quality rimfire semi-auto and centerfire bolt-action/semi-auto rifles. Their caseless ammunition released in 1991 was a unique step in the development of ammunition. More information on this trademark, including current models and U.S. availability and pricing, can be obtained by contacting the company directly (see Trademark Index for information).

RIFLES

MODEL VEC 91 BOLT ACTION - 5.7x26 UCC caseless ammo, unique ignition system requires electrical impulse to activate semi-conducting primer that ignites propellant (2 small batteries are housed in the pistol grip capable of igniting 5,000 shots), 5 shot detachable mag., 20 in. free floating barrel, twin forward locking lugs, 2-stage electrical trigger adj. from ½ oz. to 7 lbs, 55 grain bullet achieves 3,300 fps with no loss in accuracy over normal mechanical primer ignited cartridges, 6 lbs. New 1992.

$2,300	**$2,050**	**$1,850**	**$1,500**	**$1,225**	**$1,100**	**$995**

Last MSR was $2,540.

Unfortunately, BATF import certificates have made it very expensive to bring UCC caseless ammunition in small quantities into this country. This model is currently being distributed in Europe and other countries.

V

Grading	100%	98%	95%	90%	80%	70%	60%

MODEL 2185 MATCH SEMI-AUTO - .308 Win. cal., gas operated, free floating barrel, 3 or 5 shot detachable mag., manual safety, iron sights, laminate wood, 11 lbs. Disc.

	$2,525	$2,275	$1,975	$1,650	$1,350	$1,225	$1,050

Last MSR was $2,715.

Add $1,500 for position style rifle (includes adj. cheekpiece, buttplate, and bottom sling rail, and Voere special scope base).

Other calibers are available on special order only.

MODEL 2185 HUNTING RIFLE - 9.3x62mm, other cals. available upon special request, checkered stock and forend, iron sights. Disc.

	$1,625	$1,350	$1,200	$1,050	$900	$700	$575

Last MSR was $1,775.

Add $50 for Mannlicher full stock with 20 in. carbine barrel.

MODEL 2155 K-98 MAUSER - .243 Win., .270 Win., or .30-06 cal., 20 in. barrel, tang safety, no sights. Disc.

	$725	$650	$575	$500	$450	$400	$350

Last MSR was $780.

Add $50 for Mag. cals. (7mm Rem. Mag. or .300 Win. Mag.).

✷ *Model 2165 K-98 Mauser Deluxe* - same cals. as K-98 Mauser, European traditional style bolt action, 22 in. barrel, detachable 5 shot mag., hand-checkered deluxe walnut. Disc.

	$995	$875	$750	$675	$600	$525	$450

Last MSR was $1,110.

Add $50 for Mag. cals. (24 in. barrel).

AMERICAN CUSTOM CLASSIC K-98 MAUSER - .22-250 Rem., .243 Win., .270 Win., 7x57mm, 7x64mm, .30-06, or .308 Win. cal., 3 position safety, hinged floorplate, deluxe walnut with hand-rubbed oil finish and checkering. Mfg. 1996 only.

	$1,575	$1,450	$1,300	$1,150	$995	$850	$675

Last MSR was $1,795.

Add $50 for Mag. cals. (.300 Win. Mag., .338 Win. Mag., 7mm Rem. Mag., or 9.3x64mm).
Add $100 for .375 H&H or .458 Win. Mag. cal.

.22 SEMI-AUTO - .22 LR cal., open (disc.) or closed bolt design, 10 shot mag., checkered hardwood stock, adj. rear sight and trigger. Limited importation.

	$585	$535	$460	$400	$350	$300	$250

Last MSR was $645.

Add $50 for Deluxe Model.

VOERE (GERMAN)

Previous manufacturer located in Vohrenvach, Germany. Voere was absorbed by Mauser- Werke circa 1986, and most of the company machinery was moved to Oberndorf during that time. Voere of Germany should not be confused with the current Austrian firm of the same name.

Voere of Germany manufactured a wide variety of rifles in many configurations, including both bolt action and semi-auto (closed and open bolt) .22 cal. rifles. Bolt action centerfire rifles were also produced in many styles and calibers, including some private label contracts with such firms as Shikar, Frankonia, Akah, and others. While not considered as highly collectible today, most German Voere rifles were noted for their quality craftsmanship and above average accuracy. Secondary values today depend on the desirability of the rifle configuration (stock design, finish, caliber, etc.) and original condition.

VOLQUARTSEN CUSTOM, LTD.

Current rifle customizer and manufacturer located in Carroll, IA. Dealer sales.

PISTOLS: SEMI-AUTO, CONVERSION

Volquartsen manufactures a wide variety of custom pistols based on the Ruger Mark II action. Prices range from $640 - $1,063, depending on the configuration. Please contact the company directly for more information on these conversions.

V

Grading	100%	98%	95%	90%	80%	70%	60%

VOLQUARTSEN SEMI-AUTO PISTOL - .22 Mag. cal., prototypes only, as the ATF ruled against making this a production model.

RIFLES: SEMI-AUTO

Volquartsen manufactures a wide variety of custom rifles based on the Ruger 10/22 action. Prices range from $625 - $1,019, depending on the configuration. Please contact the company directly for more information on these conversions.

STANDARD 22 L.R. - .22 LR cal., similar to .22 Mag., stainless steel receiver, available in Standard, Lightweight, Deluxe, and Onyx models.

MSR	$920	$840	$765	$685	$600	$550	$500	$450

Add $70 for Lightweight or Deluxe model.
Add $425 for Onyx model.
Add $150 for fiberglass thumbhole or sporter stock.

STANDARD 22 MAG. - .22 Mag. cal., choice of standard (18½ in. stainless steel), deluxe (20 in. fluted), or lightweight (16½ in. aluminum) barrel, Monte Carlo laminated wood or Hogue Overmolded composite stock, available in Standard, Lightweight, Deluxe, Signature Series (top-of-the-line), VG-1, and Onyx models. approx. 7½ lbs.

MSR	$950	$870	$765	$685	$600	$550	$500	$450

Add $70 for Lightweight (carbon fiber or all metal tensioned barrel) or Deluxe model.
Add $425 for Onyx model.
Add $525 for VG-1 model.
Add $150 for fiberglass thumbhole or sporter stock.

SIGNATURE SERIES - .22 Mag. cal., top-of-the-line model, many options are available.

MSR	$1,995	$1,775	$1,525	$1,350	$1,075	$875	$700	$600

VOLUNTEER ENTERPRISES

Previous manufacturer located in Knoxville, TN.

Volunteer Enterprises became Commando Arms after 1978.

CARBINES

COMMANDO MARK III CARBINE - .45 ACP cal., semi-auto, blowback action, 16½ in. barrel, aperture sight, stock styled after the Auto-Ordnance "Tommy Gun". Mfg. 1969-1976.

	$425	$365	$315	$280	$225	$195	$160
Vertical grip	$440	$365	$320	$280	$225	$195	$160

COMMANDO MARK 9 - similar to Mark III in 9mm Para. cal.

	$440	$375	$325	$285	$230	$195	$160
Vertical grip	$440	$365	$320	$280	$225	$195	$160

VOUZELAUD

Previous manufacturer located in France. Previously imported by Waverly Arms Co. located in Suffolk, VA.

SHOTGUNS: SxS

MODEL 315 E - 12, 16 or 20 ga., boxlock, 28 in. barrels, auto ejectors, straight grip French walnut stock, double triggers, case colored receiver, light engraving. Importation disc. 1987.

Values generally range between $1,350-$2,000 for this model.

MODEL 315 EL - similar to Model 315 E, except has satin finish receiver engraved with bouquets of fine English scroll work, trigger guard and forearm also engraved. Importation disc. 1987.

Values generally range between $1,475-$2,250 for this model.
Add $600 for 28 ga. or .410 bore (Model 315 EL-S, special order only).

V

Grading	100%	98%	95%	90%	80%	70%	60%

MODEL 315 EG - 12, 16 or 20 ga., sidelock, 28 in. barrels, selective ejectors, double triggers, extensive scroll engraving on coin finish receiver, English style stock of extra fancy French walnut. Importation disc. 1987.

Values generally range between $1,750-$2,750 for this model.

MODEL 315 EGL-S - same general features as the Model 315 EGL, except monobloc barrel construction, extensive game scene engraving, and grand deluxe walnut stock and forearm with extra fine hand-checkering. Importation disc. 1987.

Values generally range between $1,950-$2,950 for this model.

Last MSR was $5,895.

W Section

WAFFENSTUBE GUGGI

Current longun manufacturer and custom order stock carver established during 1981, and located in Graz, Austria. No current U.S. importation.

Waffenstube Guggi manufactures custom order sidelock combination guns, single and SxS rifles, bolt action rifles, and shotguns. They also perform outstanding stock carving and checkering services. Please contact the company directly for more information and an individual price quotation (see Trademark Index).

WAFFEN JUNG GMBH

Current rifle manufacturer located in Lohmar, Germany. No current U.S. importation.

Waffen Jung GmbH manufactures a Stutzen style Rominten edition bolt action rifle. Please contact the company directly for more information, including U.S. availability and pricing.

WAFFEN VERATSCHNIG

Current manufacturer located in Ferlach, Austria.

Waffen Veratschnig manufactures a variety of high grade, made to individual special order, rifles, shotguns, combination guns, drillings, and vierlings. A wide variety of engraving scenes, wood carvings, and other special features are available at extra cost. Currently, they do not have U.S. importation and for more information, please contact them directly (see Trademark Index).

WALTHER

Current manufacturer located in Ulm, Germany, 1953 to date. Pistols are currently imported and distributed beginning 2002 by Smith & Wesson, located in Springfield, MA., and by Earl's Repair Service, Inc., located in Tewksbury, MA. Walther target pistols are currently  being imported by Champions Choice located in La Vergne, TN and Earl's Repair Service, Inc. beginning 1994 located in Tewksbury, MA, target rifles are imported by Champion's Choice. Previously imported and distributed 1998-2001 by Walther USA LLC, located in Springfield, MA, and by Interarms located in Alexandria, VA. Previously manufactured in Zella-Mehlis, Germany 1886 to 1945. Walther was sold to Umarex Sportwaffen GmbH circa 1996, and headquarters are located in Arnsberg, Germany.

The calibers listed in the Walther Pistol sections are listed in American caliber designations. The German metric conversion is as follows: .22 LR - 5.6mm, .25 ACP - 6.35mm, .32 ACP - 7.65mm, .380 ACP - 9mm kurz. The metric caliber designations in most cases will be indicated on the left slide legend for German mfg. pistols listed in the Walther section.

For more information and current pricing on both new and used Walther airguns, please refer to the *Blue Book of Modern Airguns* by Dr. Robert Beeman & John Allen (now online also).

Grading	100%	98%	95%	90%	80%	70%	60%

PISTOLS: SEMI-AUTO, PRE-WAR

MODEL 1 - .25 ACP cal., 2.1 in. barrel, fixed sights, blue, checkered hard rubber grips, pre-WWI. Mfg. 1908.

	100%	98%	95%	90%	80%	70%	60%
	$650	$525	$400	$300	$250	$225	$200

MODEL 2 - .25 ACP cal., 2.1 in. barrel, fixed sights, blue, hard rubber grips, pop-up rear sight on early models, fixed on late models. Mfg. 1909.

	100%	98%	95%	90%	80%	70%	60%
	$450	$425	$330	$225	$175	$135	$125

This model can usually be distinguished by its knurled barrel ring.

Grading	100%	98%	95%	90%	80%	70%	60%

✳ *Early Model* - differentiated by its pop-up rear sight.

	$1,395	$995	$950	$775	$675	$550	$400

MODEL 3 - .32 ACP cal., 2.6 in. barrel, blue, fixed sights, hard rubber grips, ejection port on left side. Mfg. 1910.

	$1,500	$1,250	$1,100	$800	$550	$500	$400

MODEL 4 - .32 ACP cal., 8 shot, 3½ in. barrel, blue, hard rubber grips, ejection port on left side. Mfg. 1910-1928.

	$400	$325	$250	$200	$125	$100	$80

Add 10% for WWI "Eagle" proofs.

MODEL 5 - better quality version of Model 2, fixed rear sight. Mfg. 1913.

	$485	$425	$375	$225	$145	$135	$125

MODEL 6 - 9mm Para. cal., 4 7/8 in. barrel, blue, hard rubber grips, ejection port on right side. Mfg. 1915-1917. Some are Imperial proofed.

	$6,000	$4,500	$3,000	$2,300	$1,500	$1,050	$800

MODEL 7 - .25 ACP cal., 3 in. barrel, blue, fixed sights, hard rubber grips, ejection port on right side. Mfg. 1917-1918.

	$650	$500	$425	$350	$250	$200	$125

MODEL 8 - .25 ACP cal., 2 7/8 in. barrel, blue or nickel finish, fixed sights, black checkered plastic grips with round medallions. Mfg. 1920-1943.

	$495	$450	$395	$265	$200	$150	$125

Add 20% for nickel.
Add 10% for "Eagle N" proofing.
Add 25% for engraved slide.

MODEL 9 VEST POCKET - .25 ACP cal., engineering revision of Model 1, 2 in. barrel, blue finish standard, upward ejection, 6 shot bottom release mag., fixed sights, black checkered plastic grips with round medallions, safety lever on left frame side behind trigger, 9 oz. Mfg. 1921-1945.

	$600	$525	$445	$325	$240	$160	$140

Add 40% for engraved slide, 20% for nickel.
Add 10% for "Eagle N" proofing.

MODEL PP DOUBLE ACTION - .22 LR, .25 ACP, .32 ACP, or .380 ACP cal., PP designates "Polizei Pistole", 3 7/8 in. barrel, blue, fixed sights, plastic grips. Mfg. 1929- 1945. Crown N proof until 1939. Eagle N Nazi commercial proof until 1945.

	100%	98%	95%	90%	80%	70%	60%
.22 LR cal.	$995	$825	$700	$600	$525	$450	$375
.25 ACP cal.	$3,450	$3,100	$2,650	$2,000	$1,500	$1,200	$1,000
.32 ACP cal.	$495	$425	$375	$350	$275	$225	$200
.380 ACP cal.	$1,250	$995	$750	$675	$600	$550	$500

Add 15% for alloy frame.
Original nickel finished Model PPs are very rare; this precludes accurate price evaluation.
Values assume original guns without import markings. Recently imported WWII/surplus Police used guns are stamped on the frame or receiver, indicating the current importer and address - subtract 20%-30% from values listed for these recent imports.

✳ *.32 ACP Bottom Release Magazine* - safety rotates 90 degrees.

	$995	$850	$625	$600	$525	$425	$395

✳ *.380 ACP Bottom Release Magazine* - safety rotates 90 degrees.

	$1,200	$1,050	$895	$825	$700	$600	$500

✳ *Pre-War Persian proofed* - 9mm kurz BMR.

	$2,000	$1,800	$1,600	$1,450	$1,250	$995	$825

Subtract 75% for recent imports which have been relisted.

W

Grading	100%	98%	95%	90%	80%	70%	60%

✱ Pre-War verchromt .32 ACP cal. - add 50% for .380 ACP cal.

	$1,600	$1,400	$1,000	$750	$675	$485	$395

✱ Pre-War Stoeger - .32 ACP cal. only.

	$1,450	$1,200	$925	$800	$600	$425	$325

✱ Nairobi - Chas. Heyer.

	$1,450	$1,200	$850	$725	$575	$400	$300

✱ Aluminum frame - safety rotates 90 degrees.

	$695	$650	$525	$400	$275	$235	$200

✱ Allemagne - French Comm.

	$1,200	$1,000	$825	$720	$600	$425	$325

MODEL PP WARTIME PRODUCTION - mfg. 1940-1945, "Eagle N" Proof (Nazi commercial nitro proof after April 1940) or "Crown N" proof (German commercial proof mark used to April, 1940) found on pre-WWII military production. Variations are listed either by proof marks or frame/slide markings.

✱ "Waffenamt" Proofed - .32 ACP or .380 ACP cal., "Eagle N", military acceptance marking.

	100%	98%	95%	90%	80%	70%	60%
.32 ACP cal. (milled finish)	$550	$465	$395	$300	$250	$220	$200
.380 ACP cal.	$1,250	$995	$800	$700	$600	$550	$500

Add 25%-50% if Waffenamt proofed, depending on condition (late war PPs are sometimes encountered with Walther marked beechwood grips).

✱ Eagle N Proofed - .22 LR or .32 ACP cal., with lanyard loop.

	100%	98%	95%	90%	80%	70%	60%
.32 ACP cal.	$495	$425	$375	$300	$250	$200	$150
.22 LR cal.	$925	$825	$675	$550	$495	$450	$395

Add 50% to .32 ACP cal., Waffenamt proofed PPs that are hi-gloss finish (all .380s are hi-gloss).
In most cases, the .380 ACP cal. has the bottom mag. release.
After WWII the French added a lanyard to the left side of the grip. Subtract 25% for this alteration.

✱ Eagle C & F Marked (Nazi Police) - .32 ACP cal., "Eagle F or C" proofed on left side of frame.

	$825	$695	$625	$500	$450	$380	$300

Add 25% if Eagle C marked. All hi-gloss are early productions.

✱ RFV Marked - .32 ACP cal., "Crown N". Mfg. for "Reichsfinanzverwaltung" Reich Finance Administration.

	$925	$725	$625	$500	$400	$325	$225

✱ RJ Marked - .32 ACP cal., "Crown N". Mfg. for "Reichsjustizministerium" Reich Justice Ministry.

	$975	$825	$625	$500	$450	$325	$225

✱ SA Marked - .22 LR or .32 ACP cal., "Crown N". Mfg. for SA (Sturm Abteilung - group leaders) of the Nazi party.

	$2,275	$1,925	$1,550	$1,200	$900	$600	$425

Add 20% for .22 LR.
Rare SA markings may bring as much as 50% more over values listed.
There are 28 SA groups.

✱ NSKK Marked - .32 ACP cal., "Crown N or Eagle N" proofed. Mfg. for "National- sozialis-tischer Kraftfahrkorps" Nazi Party Transport Corps, rare.

	$2,875	$2,050	$1,500	$1,025	$875	$700	$550

✱ RRZ proofed - .32 ACP cal., mfg. for for "Reichsrundfunkzentrale" Reich Radio Broadcasting - only 3 known.

	$3,650	$3,050	$2,500				

Grading	100%	98%	95%	90%	80%	70%	60%

✳ **PDM Marked** - .32 ACP cal., "Crown N", for "Polizeidirektion München" Munich Police Department, all have bottom mag. release.

| | $1,550 | $1,325 | $1,000 | $650 | $500 | $400 | $350 |

✳ **AC Marked** - .32 ACP cal., replaced Walther Banner during 1945, "Eagle N".

| | $500 | $400 | $300 | $250 | $200 | $150 | $125 |

Some are mismatched (assembled at factory by GIs after the factory was captured). Subtract 20% if mismatched.

✳ **Czech. Contract** - stamped Rampant Lion.

| | $1,125 | $900 | $800 | $700 | $600 | $500 | $400 |

✳ **Panagraph Slide**

| | $850 | $750 | $695 | $630 | $550 | $385 | $275 |

✳ **Danish Rplt.**

| | $995 | $925 | $825 | $775 | $700 | $625 | $400 |

MODEL PP LIGHTWEIGHT - aluminum alloy version.

Add 20% to Standard Model prices.
Add 20%-40% for original nickel finish (very rare).
Add 25% for early hi-gloss finish.

MODEL PPK PRE-WAR PRODUCTION - .22 LR, .25 ACP, .32 ACP, or .380 ACP cal., PPK designates "Polizei Pistole Kurz", 3¼ in. barrel, blue, gold, nickel, or chrome silver, fixed sights, plastic grips. Mfg. 1931- 1940.

.22 LR cal.	$1,275	$925	$750	$700	$650	$525	$400
.25 ACP cal.	$5,150	$4,550	$3,800	$3,400	$2,800	$2,100	$1,475
.32 ACP cal.	$675	$600	$500	$395	$300	$250	$225
.380 ACP cal.	$2,600	$2,000	$1,700	$1,500	$900	$700	$500

Add 60% for bottom release mag (.32 ACP cal.).

MODEL PPK WARTIME PRODUCTION - mfg. 1940-1945, "Eagle N" proofed after April 1940, "Crown N" proofs appear on pre-1940 production with frame/slide markings. Variations are listed either by proof marks, frame/slide markings, or type of finish.

✳ **Commercial "Eagle N" Proofed** - .22 LR, .32 ACP, or .380 ACP cal., Nazi Eagle over N (standard Nazi commercial acceptance proof).

.22 LR cal.	$1,250	$1,100	$800	$600	$525	$460	$420
.32 ACP cal.	$650	$475	$375	$350	$300	$250	$225
.380 ACP cal.	$2,600	$2,250	$1,800	$1,000	$600	$500	$400

This variation is normally encountered with semi-polished, exterior metal showing milling marks to various degrees.

✳ **Waffenamt Proofed With High Polish**

| | $1,450 | $1,200 | $950 | $650 | $425 | $330 | $275 |

✳ **Eagle C Marked** - .32 ACP cal., "Crown N - Eagle C", mfg. for Nazi Police.

| | $925 | $650 | $535 | $450 | $335 | $260 | $200 |

Add 25% for high polish finish.

✳ **Eagle F Marked** - .32 ACP cal., "Crown N - Eagle F", Nazi Police, all have the light weight aluminum frame.

| | $1,250 | $900 | $600 | $475 | $375 | $300 | $250 |

✳ **RZM Marked** - .32 ACP cal., "Crown N", proof marking for "Reichszeugmeisterei" Reich Party Purchasing Office.

| | $1,475 | $1,150 | $875 | $600 | $350 | $275 | $225 |

W

Grading	100%	98%	95%	90%	80%	70%	60%

* **Party Leader** - .32 ACP cal., named because grips (brown or black plastic) have the German eagle holding a Swastika, "Crown N" or "Eagle N" proofed, honor weapon awarded 3rd Reich political leaders, rare. Be very wary of fake grips (especially black color) as reproductions have been made recently. Unfortunately, the grips on a Party Leader (mfg. 1936-1941) are the only distinguishing feature on this very desirable configuration.

	$3,750	$3,000	$1,800	$1,500	$1,200	$1,100	$1,000

* **RZM With Party Leader Grips** - .32 ACP cal., RZM marked, "Crown N" proofed.

	$3,950	$3,350	$2,700	$2,200	$1,300	$1,200	$1,100

* **RFV Marked** - .32 ACP cal., "Crown N". Mfg. for "Reichsfinanzverwaltung" Reich Finance Administration.

	$1,300	$1,050	$825	$750	$800	$700	$675

* **PDM Marked** - .32 ACP cal., "Crown N". Mfg. for "Polizeidirektion München" Police Dept. Munich. All have the bottom mag. release.

	$1,600	$1,200	$995	$750	$600	$500	$395

* **DRP Marked** - .32 ACP cal., "Crown N". Mfg. for "Deutsche Reichspost" German Postal Service.

	$1,250	$1,000	$800	$600	$420	$350	$260

* **Panagraph Slide**

	$875	$750	$675	$525	$450	$375	$300

* **Verchromt** - .32 ACP or 380 ACP cal., differentiated by dull silver satin type finish.

	$2,100	$1,600	$1,300	$1,000	$800	$650	$500

Add 50% for .380 ACP cal.

* **"K" suffix** - "K" beneath ser. no.

	$650	$525	$475	$375	$300	$275	$250

* **"W" suffix** - .32 ACP cal., "Crown N" proofed, W-suffix ser. no.

	$650	$550	$475	$375	$300	$275	$250

* **Early 90 degree safety**

	$700	$625	$525	$425	$325	$260	$195

* **Early bottom release Mag.**

	$1,300	$925	$775	$650	$500	$475	$375

* **PPK Marked PP**

	$2,650	$2,150	$1,850	$1,600	$1,400	$1,180	$900

* **7-digit ser. no.**

	$750	$700	$650	$600	$550	$400	$300

* **Dural frame** - .22 LR, .32 ACP, or .380 ACP cal., chrome finish (very rare), "Eagle N".

	$725	$625	$600	$525	$400	$325	$275

Add 200% for .380 ACP.
Add 100% in .22 LR cal.

* **Czech. Contract** - Rampant Lion stamped.

	$1,075	$900	$750	$625	$550	$425	$325

* **Danish Rplt.**

	$1,075	$900	$750	$625	$550	$425	$325

* **Allemagne** - French Commercial - rare.

	$1,250	$1,100	$1,000	$800	$550	$425	$325

MODEL PPK LIGHTWEIGHT - aluminum alloy version.
Add 20% to .32 cal. commercial price listing.

SPORT MODEL 1926 - .22 S or LR cal. (known as Standard Model in Germany).

	$1,125	$900	$800	$675	$595	$550	$495

Grading	100%	98%	95%	90%	80%	70%	60%

1932 OLYMPIA MODEL - .22 S or LR cal., 10 shot, 6 or 9 in. barrel, target sights, one- piece grip, introduced in 1928 and used in 1932 Olympics. Marketed by Stoeger and Chas. Heyer-Nairobi.

| | $1,150 | $995 | $895 | $700 | $550 | $450 | $395 |

OLYMPIA SPORT MODEL - .22 LR cal., 4 or 7.4 in. barrel, adj. target sights, blue, wood grips, 4 barrel weights available. Mfg. 1936-1940.

| | $975 | $825 | $725 | $600 | $475 | $420 | $375 |

Add 20% for weight set.

1936 OLYMPIA "JÄGERSCHAFTS" HUNTING MODEL - similar to Sport, with 4 in. barrel. Mfg. 1936-1940. Also seen with Eagle N proofs.

| | $1,600 | $1,200 | $995 | $625 | $495 | $440 | $360 |

OLYMPIA RAPID FIRE MODEL - .22 Short cal. only, 7.4 in. barrel, blue, adj. sight, wood grip, has alloy slide. Mfg. 1936-1940.

| | $1,600 | $1,200 | $995 | $600 | $520 | $460 | $380 |

1936 OLYMPIA FÜNFKAMPF MODEL - .22 Short or LR cal., 9¼ in. barrel, blue, adj. sight, wood grips, barrel weights, circa 1936.

| | $1,725 | $1,400 | $1,200 | $875 | $575 | $500 | $440 |

MODEL HP COMMERCIAL DOUBLE ACTION - 9mm Para. cal., pre-war version of P-38, 5 in. barrel, fixed sight, blue, wood or plastic grips. Mfg. 1937-1944. Many variations, including several different finishes.

See German WWII Military Pistols section for values on this model.

PISTOLS: SEMI-AUTO, POST-WAR

MODEL PP DOUBLE ACTION - .22 LR, .32 ACP, or .380 ACP cal., specifications similar to pre-war PP, 3 7/8 in. barrel. Imported 1963-2000. German manufacture.

* **.380 ACP cal.** - 7 shot mag.

| | $950 | $800 | $600 | $350 | $300 | $275 | $250 |

Last MSR was $999.

* **.32 ACP cal.** - 8 shot mag.

| | $825 | $475 | $395 | $295 | $275 | $250 | $225 |

Last MSR was $999.

* **.22 LR cal.** - 10 shot mag., disc. 1984.

| | $925 | $800 | $625 | $400 | $325 | $300 | $275 |

Last MSR was $783.

* **Blue Engraved** - .22 LR (disc.) or .380 ACP cal. Disc. 1984.

| | $1,375 | $1,100 | $950 | | | | |

Last MSR was $1,650.

Add 5% for .22 LR cal.

* **Chrome Engraved** - .22 LR or .380 ACP cal. Disc. 1984.

| | $1,400 | $1,100 | $950 | | | | |

Last MSR was $1,600.

Add $50 for .22 LR cal.

* **Silver Engraved** - .22 LR (disc.) or .380 ACP cal. Disc. 1984.

| | $1,650 | $1,150 | $1,000 | | | | |

Last MSR was $1,948.

* **Gold Engraved** - .22 LR (disc.) or .380 ACP cal. Disc. 1984.

| | $1,800 | $1,450 | $1,150 | | | | |

Last MSR was $2,053.

Grading	100%	98%	95%	90%	80%	70%	60%

✳ Manurhin PP - .22 LR, .32 ACP, or .380 ACP cal. Disc. 1984.

| | $450 | $395 | $325 | $225 | $180 | $165 | $150 |

Add 10% for .380 ACP cal.

✳ Model PP 50th Anniversary Commemorative - .22 LR., .32 ACP, or .380 ACP cal., gold-plated parts, hand carved grips, presentation case. 500 imported to U.S. 1979. 800 mfg.

| | $1,575 | $1,150 | $650 | | | | |

Last MSR was $1,700.

✳ Model PP "100 Jahre" 1886-1986 - 100th anniversary PP edition, primarily made for the German marketplace, inscription marked on right side of slide.

| Plastic Grips | $995 | $750 | $625 | | | | |
| Extended Wood Grips | $1,095 | $825 | $675 | | | | |

✳ PP Last Edition - supplied with fitted hard case, certificate; and video Walther history, 400 mfg. in .32 ACP cal., 100 mfg. in .380 ACP cal., 500 total mfg. in Germany 1999 only.

| | $1,295 | $1,050 | $900 | | | | |

This model was the last of the PP, PPK, PPK/S models to be manufactured when Germany stopped production in 1999.

PP SPORT - double action, thumbrest grips, round hammer with spur, adj. rear sight, 6.1 or 8.1 in. barrel, 25.6 or 27.2 oz. Mfg. 1953-1970.

Manurhin manufacture	$700	$650	$625	$550	$495	$425	$350
Mark II (mfg. 1955-1957)	$800	$700	$650	$600	$545	$500	$450
Walther manufacture	$875	$775	$750	$625	$575	$525	$450

Subtract 10% if not marked.

Add $75 for barrel weight, $100 for factory case, 20% for factory nickel, 5% for single action.

✳ PP Sport "C" Model C - mfg. for competition shooting, single action, 7 5/8 in. barrel, spur hammer.

| | $895 | $815 | $725 | $675 | $575 | $525 | $450 |

MODEL PPK - similar to pre-war PPK, .22 LR, .32 ACP, or .380 ACP cal., 3.31 in. barrel. Mfg. post-war - 1999, U.S. import stopped by GCA 68 on W. German and French production.

.32 ACP cal.	$750	$550	$425	$350	$325	$295	$275
.22 LR cal.	$1,050	$750	$600	$525	$450	$375	$325
.380 ACP cal.	$1,050	$725	$600	$475	$425	$350	$300
Blue engraved	$1,650	$1,300	$950				
Silver engraved	$1,925	$1,400	$1,000				
Gold engraved	$2,250	$1,675	$1,250				

100% column assumes NIB condition - subtract 15% if not boxed.

MODEL PPK LAST EDITION - similar to PP Last Edition, but was never imported into the U.S.

MODEL PPK LIGHTWEIGHT - similar to Standard, with dural frame, .22 LR or .32 ACP cal.

| | $900 | $675 | $475 | $375 | $325 | $295 | $275 |

Add 20% for .22 LR cal.

MODEL PPK-1986 U.S. PRODUCTION - .380 ACP cal. only, 3.35 in. barrel, similar specifications as previous W. German and French manufacture, blue or bright nickel (new 1997) finish, 7 shot finger extension mag., black plastic grips, 21 oz. Made in the U.S. Mfg. 1986-2001, limited quantities available.

| MSR $543 | $475 | $365 | $320 | $295 | $270 | $250 | $225 |

Manufacture in the U.S. was under an exclusive licensing agreement with Walther of Germany.

✳ PPK Stainless - .32 ACP (new 1998) or .380 ACP cal., stainless steel construction. Mfg. 1986-2001.

| | $475 | $365 | $320 | | | | |

Last MSR was $543.

Grading	100%	98%	95%	90%	80%	70%	60%

MODEL PPK/E - .380 ACP cal., 3.4 in. barrel., high polish blue, 7 (.380 ACP) or 8 (.32 ACP) shot mag., 23 oz.

> While advertised in America during 2000 with a MSR of $294, this model was distributed in Europe only, and was produced with the cooperation of F.E.G., located in Hungary. Only 6 were imported into the U.S. for the SHOT Show.

MODEL PPK/S - .22 LR, .32 ACP, or .380 ACP cal., similar to PPK, except has larger PP frame to meet import requirements of 1968, 3¼ in. barrel, production in W. Germany, Manurhin of France (disc. 1986), and in the U.S. (mfg. under license from Walther by Interarms). 10 (.22 LR) or 8 (.32 ACP and .380 ACP) shot, double action, fixed sights.

* ❋ *American PPK/S* - .380 ACP cal. only, blue finish, 8 shot, one finger extension and one flat bottom mag. Disc. 2001.

	$475	$365	$320	$295	$270	$250	$225

Last MSR was $543.

* ❋ *Stainless PPK/S* - .32 ACP (new 1998) or .380 ACP cal., American manufacture, introduced July of 1983, disc. 2001, limited quantities available

MSR	$543	$475	$365	$320

* ❋ *W. German PPK/S* - .22 LR (disc.), .32 ACP (currently mfg.), or .380 ACP (currently mfg.) cal.

	100%	98%	95%	90%	80%	70%	60%
.22 LR cal. (disc. 1984)	$950	$725	$595	$450	$375	$325	$300
.32 ACP cal.	$875	$675	$550	$400	$325	$295	$275
.380 ACP cal.	$875	$675	$550	$400	$325	$295	$275

* ❋ *American PPK/S* - blue engraved. Disc. 1985.

	$875	$850	$800

Last MSR was $990.

* ❋ *American PPK/S Gold-Engraved Commemorative* - 500 total mfg. Disc. 1987.

	$1,000	$875	$700

Last MSR was $1,200.

* ❋ *American PPK/S Gold-Engraved* - disc. 1985.

	$975	$850	$700

Last MSR was $1,070.

* ❋ *W. German PPK/S Blue Engraved* - inventory depleted 1990.

	$1,475	$1,050	$850

Last MSR was $1,550.

* ❋ *W. German PPK/S Chrome Engraved* - importation disc. 1991.

	$1,525	$1,075	$950

Last MSR was $1,700.

* ❋ *W. German PPK/S Silver Engraved* - disc. 1988.

	$1,675	$1,150	$975

Last MSR was $1,700.

* ❋ *W. German PPK/S Gold Engraved* - disc. 1985.

	$1,950	$1,250	$1,000

Last MSR was $1,800.

MANURHIN PPK/S - see listings under Manurhin section.

MODEL PP SUPER - 9x18mm, (Police) or .380 ACP cal., 3.6 in. barrel, 7 shot, fixed sights, plastic grips, blue, 1,000 mfg. in .380 ACP cal., 26.8 oz. Mfg. 1973-1979.

	$895	$725	$550	$395	$285	$250	$235

Subtract 25% if in 9x18mm cal. (4,000 mfg.).

* ❋ *PP Super-Cutaway*

	$750	$625	$550

Grading	100%	98%	95%	90%	80%	70%	60%

MODEL TP - .22 LR or .25 ACP cal., updated version of Model 9, 6 shot, 2.6 in. barrel, concealed hammer, 12 oz. Mfg. 1961- 1971.

.22 LR cal.	$775	$625	$435	$350	$300	$260	$210
.25 ACP cal.	$695	$500	$350	$300	$250	$220	$185

MODEL TPH - .22 LR or .25 ACP cal., double action 2.8 in. barrel, 6 shot, alloy frame, blue, fixed sights, plastic grips, 11.5 oz. Mfg. 1968-1998 in W. Germany, U.S. import stopped by GCA of 1968.

.22 LR cal.	$795	$625	$550	$475	$350	$300	$250
.25 ACP cal.	$895	$700	$600	$500	$400	$325	$275

Subtract 10% on the 100% values if not boxed with all accessories.
TPH cutaways were also mfg. in small quantities for instructional use. Current pricing for a mint specimen is approx. $1,500.
100% price assumes NIB condition.

AMERICAN MODEL TPH - .22 LR or .25 ACP (new 1992) cal., blue finish or stainless steel, double action, black plastic grips, 6 shot mag., 2¼ in. barrel, 14 oz. Mfg. 1987-2000.

$365	$335	$280	$250	$225	$200	$185

Last MSR was $460.

✳ *American Model TPH Stainless* - stainless steel fabrication. Disc. 2000.

$365	$335	$280

Last MSR was $460.

MODEL P38 - post-war version of P38 Military, .22 LR (disc.), 7.65 (disc.), or 9mm Para. cal., 5 in. barrel, 8 shot, alloy frame, matte black finish, 28 oz. W. German manufacture. Mfg. 1956-present, not currently imported into the U.S. See German WWII Military Pistols for wartime listings.

$775	$600	$500	$375	$325	$275	$225

Last MSR was $824.

Note: Due to the release of large numbers of W. German Police and Army trade-ins of P.38 9mm Para. and PP .32 ACP cal. models, the actual value of original models in 90% or less condition has decreased somewhat. The two models most affected are the P-1 variation of the P.38, and the German PP in .32 ACP cal.

✳ *P38 Long Barrel Special Edition* - 9mm Para. cal., steel frame, 6, 7, or 8, in. barrel, wood grips, 50 mfg. 1988.

$3,500	$3,200	$2,750

✳ *Steel Frame P38* - 7.65mm Luger or 9mm Para. cal., similar to regular P.38, except has steel frame, 34 oz. Imported 1987-89 only, and in limited quantities to present.

$995	$850	$650

Last MSR was $1,400.

Add 30% for 7.65mm Luger cal.

✳ *P38 in .22 LR cal.* - disc. 1989.

$975	$650	$550	$475	$375	$325	$225

Last MSR was $1,050.

MODEL P38 II - similar to the Standard P.38, except has reinforced slide.

$600	$500	$450	$375	$325	$275	$225

MODEL P38K - 7.65mm Luger or 9mm Para. cal., shortened 2.8 in. barrel variation of P.38, front sight on slide, adj. rear sight, 27.9 oz. 3,000 mfg. 1974-1981.

$695	$600	$500	$425	$350	$275	$225

Add 30% for 7.65mm Luger cal.

Grading	100%	98%	95%	90%	80%	70%	60%

MODEL P38 SPECIAL EDITIONS/ENGRAVED

✳ ***P38 50th Year Commemorative*** - steel frame, carved grips, presentation engraved with deluxe walnut presentation case. Introduced 1987, inventory depleted 1992.

	$2,325	$1,750	$1,250

Last MSR was $950.

✳ ***P38 60th Year Commemorative*** - 9mm Para. or 7.65mm (.30 Luger) cal., special production, high polish, wood grips, includes wood presentation case. Approx. 100 mfg. in each caliber. Mfg. 1998.

	$2,325	$1,750	$1,250

Add 10% for 7.65mm cal.

✳ ***P38 100th Year Commemorative*** - 9mm Para. cal., alloy frame with slide engraving "100 Jahre Walther 1886-1986".

	$850	$725	$475

✳ ***Blue Engraved*** - .22 LR, 7.65mm Luger, or 9mm Para. cal.

9mm Para.	$1,850	$1,325	$1,125
7.65mm Luger	$2,200	$1,875	$1,450
.22 LR (disc.)	$2,000	$1,675	$1,350

Last MSR was $1,850.

✳ ***Chrome Engraved*** - .22 LR, 7.65mm Luger, or 9mm Para. cal., still imported.

	$1,475	$1,175	$925

Last MSR was $2,125.

✳ ***Silver Engraved*** - .22 LR, 7.65mm Luger, or 9mm Para. cal., still imported.

	$1,450	$1,175	$925

Last MSR was $2,100.

✳ ***Gold Engraved*** - .22 LR, 7.65mm Luger, or 9mm Para. cal., still imported.

	$1,800	$1,500	$1,000

Last MSR was $2,050.

MODEL P1 - 9mm Para. cal., post-war commercial variation of the P.38 with steel slide and alloy frame, 5 in. barrel, 8 shot mag., blue or phosphate finish, black plastic grips, Disc.

	$650	$550	$400	$300	$250	$215	$165

MODEL P4 - 9mm Para. cal., modernized variation of the original P.38, 4½ in. barrel, 8 shot mag., updates include reinforced steel slide and alloy frame, includes decocking lever and automatic safeties, rear sight, 29 oz. Mfg. 1975-1981, importation disc. 1982.

	$695	$595	$525	$425	$300	$250	$200

Add 20% for commercial variation.

MODEL P5 - 7.65mm Luger, 9mm Para., or 9x21mm cal., double action, alloy frame, frame mounted decocking lever, 3½ in. barrel, adj. rear sight, blue finish only, 8 shot mag., auto safeties, 28 oz. New 1977-disc.

	$775	$650	$525	$475	$450	$425	$375

Last MSR was $900.

P-5 cutaways were also mfg. in small quantities for instructional use. Current pricing for a mint specimen is approx. $2,000.

✳ ***P5 Compact*** - compact variation of P-5 with 3.1 in. barrel, 26½ oz. Limited importation 1987- present.

	$950	$825	$600	$525	$450	$425	$375

✳ ***P5 Long*** - special edition, 5.3 in. barrel, wood grips, 29.6 oz. 50 mfg. 1988 only.

	$3,500	$2,750	$2,000

✳ ***P5 100th Year Commemorative*** - marked "1886-1986 100 Jahre" with Walther banner, elaborate grip carving, presentation walnut case. Imported 1986-91.

	$2,650	$1,750	$1,100

Last MSR was $2,890.

Grading	100%	98%	95%	90%	80%	70%	60%

MODEL P88 - 9mm Para. or 9x21mm cal., double action, alloy frame, 4 in. barrel, 15 shot button release mag., fully ambidextrous, decocking lever, matte finish, adj. rear sight, internal safeties, plastic grips, 31½ oz. Mfg. 1987-1993.

	$1,325	$1,175	$700	$575	$490	$450	$400

Last MSR was $1,129.

P88 cutaways were also mfg. in small quantities for instructional use. Current pricing for a mint specimen is approx. $2,000.

✳ *P88 Compact* - 9mm Para. or 9x21mm cal., 3.93 in. barrel, 14* (disc.) or 10 (C/B 1994) shot mag., 29 oz. Importation began 1993.

MSR	$900	$850	$725	$625	$550	$500	$475	$450

This model had a substantial price decrease beginning 1996 (1994 retail price was $1,725).

✳ *P88 Champion* - 9mm Para. only, 6 in. barrel, SA only, 14* shot mag., 30.9 oz. Very limited mfg. 1992-disc.

	$2,250	$1,850	$1,500	$1,250	$995	$775	$625

✳ *P88 Competition* - similar to P99 Champion, except has 4 in. barrel, SA only, 14* shot mag., 28.2 oz. Very limited mfg. 1992-disc.

	$1,750	$1,500	$1,250	$995	$775	$625	$550

✳ *P88 Sport* - .22 LR cal. only, 6 in. barrel, SA only, 10 shot mag. Very limited mfg. 1995-disc.

	$2,350	$1,900	$1,550	$1,250	$995	$775	$625

P99 - 9mm Para., 9x21mm (limited importation 1996), or .40 S&W (new 1999) cal., traditional double action only, 4 in. barrel, polymer frame, standard or quick action (QA, allowing consistent SA trigger performance) trigger, decocking, and internal striker safeties, 10 shot mag., cocking and loaded chamber indicators, choice of matte black or QPQ (new 1999) finished (silver colored) slide, ambidextrous mag. release, ergonomic black or green (Military model, new 1999) synthetic grips with interchangable backstrap, adj. rear sight, 25 oz. Importation began 1995.

MSR	$733	$550	$475	$425	$385	$350	$325	$295

✳ *P99 QSA* - 9mm Para. or .40 S&W cal., first introduced before the QA, slide marked with QSA inscription, large decocking plate. Very few mfg.

	$900	$750	$525

✳ *P99 2000 Commemorative* - 9mm Para. or .40 S&W cal., features high polish blue slide with laser inscription "Commemorative for the year 2000". Limited mfg. 1,000 (only 500 for the U.S.) of each cal. in 2000 only, cased with Walther videotape.

MSR	$840	$800	$650	$495

✳ *P99 La Chasse DU Engraved* - 9mm Para. or .40 S&W cal., similar to Model P- 99 Military, except has laser engraved slide, luminescent sights. Mfg. 1998-2000.

	$900	$800	$725

Last MSR was $1,078.

✳ *P99 La Chasse Engraved* - features choice of elaborate oak leaf, arabesque, or English style hand scroll engraving on polished slide. Mfg. 1998-2000.

	$1,995	$1,600	$1,400

Last MSR was $2,126.

✳ *P99 Canada Edition* - 9mm Para. cal. only, 105mm barrel, black finish only, scarce in the U.S.

	$1,000	$750	$600

P990 - similar to P99, except is double action only, features Walther's constant pull trigger system, black, QPQ slide finish, or Military Model (green), 25 oz. New 1998.

MSR	$733	$550	$475	$425	$385	$350	$325	$295

PISTOLS: SEMI-AUTO, TARGET

Walther target pistols are currently being imported by Champions Choice located in La Vergne, TN and Earl's Repair Service since 1994 located in Tewksbury, MA. Previously imported by Interarms until 1993 and Nygord Precision Products until 1996.

Add 10% to the values listed for left-hand stocks (available on most models).

P22 - .22 LR cal., 3/4 scale of the P99, hammer fired, black polymer frame with grooved and stippled grip, SA or DA, matte black finish, internal trigger lock with loaded chamber indicator and mag. disconnect, 10 shot mag., firing pin drop safety, 3.42 (standard) or 5 in. (target) fixed barrel, 15.2 or 18.5 oz. New 2001.

MSR	$239		$210	$190	$175	$165	$155	$145	$125

Add $48 for target model with 5 in. barrel.

MODEL GSP TARGET STANDARD - .22 LR cal., 4½ in. barrel, single action, 5 shot mag. standard, 8 or 10 shot mag. optional, adj. sights, nickel, two-tone, or blue finish, walnut target grips, 2-stage trigger became optional in 1995, optional carrying case, 42.3 oz. Mfg. 1969-2001.

			$1,395	$1,200	$995	$650	$550	$475	$425

Last MSR was $1,450.

This model also comes as a complete international package, including a GSP with .22 Short and .32 S&W Wadcutter conversion units, including triggers. MSR was approx. $3,100.

* *Model GSP Junior* - similar to GSP Target, except has slimmer 4¼ in. barrel design, smaller walnut grips, 40.1 oz. Importation disc. 1992.

			$1,450	$1,350	$995	$775	$600	$500	$425

Last MSR was $1,810.

* *Model GSP-C* - similar to Model GSP Target, except in .32 S&W Wadcutter, and 4¼ in. barrel, 49.4 oz. Mfg. 1971-2001.

			$1,475	$1,025	$800	$650	$550	$475	$425

Last MSR was $1,595.

Add $1,095 for OSP-2000 .22 Short conversion unit.
Add $895 for GSP .22 LR cal. conversion unit.
Add $1,195 for GSP-C .32 S&W Wadcutter conversion unit.

* *Model GSP Expert* - .22 LR cal. only, similar to GSP Standard, except for recoil compensation system located in barrel weight, sight radius has been changed, and sights are located further to the rear of the gun, modified frame (cut on an angle) in the trigger area, stippled blonde/blue ergonomic laminated wood grips, 42.3 oz. New 2001.

MSR	N/A		$1,495	$1,025	$800	$650	$550	$475	$425

* *Model GSPC Expert* - similar to Model GSP Expert, except available in .32 S&W Wadcutter cal., 45.1 oz. New 2001.

MSR	N/A		$1,595	$1,100	$850	$675	$575	$495	$450

* *Model GSP 25th Year Commemorative Special Limited Edition* - .22 LR cal., aluminum carrying case, options included two-tone finish, laminated Canadian black birch grip, titanium plated bolt, special 70 gr barrel weight with "25 Jahre GSP" engraved, adj. front sight, two- stage trigger, 3 lbs. 1,000 mfg. 1994.

			$2,500	$2,150	$1,850				

* *Model GSP Atlanta* - .22 LR cal., special edition for the 1996 Olympic Games, Atlanta inscribed on right side of bolt housing, black laminate grips, titanium plated bolt, otherwise same as GSP Target Standard.

			$1,800	$1,450	$1,000				

* *Model GSP-C 25th Year Commemorative Special Limited Edition* - similar to GSP 25th Year Commemorative, except in .32 S&W Wadcutter, engraved 65 gr. barrel weight, 1,000 mfg. as complete pistols or conversion units. Mfg. 1996 only.

			$2,500	$2,150	$1,850				

Grading	100%	98%	95%	90%	80%	70%	60%

❈ ***Model GSP Special Anniversary Pistol/Rifle Combination*** - only 50 pieces mfg. for 2000, includes scope, pistol, and rifle conversion kit.

	MSR	$5,500		$5,500	$3,750	$2,750		

❈ ***Model GSP Rifle Conversion Kit*** - .22 LR cal., unique conversion allows taking a GSP action and inserting it into a rifle stock, includes 16¾ in. (18¼ with GSP compensator) stainless barrel, black, brown, camo, Walther blue, laminate stock, right or left hand, 5, 8, or 10 shot mag. New 1997.

	MSR	$995		$995	$850	$725		

Add $155 with Super Match stock.
Add $300 for Super Match Kit.
Add $75 for left hand stock.

This rifle conversion kit is only available from Earl's Repair Service, Inc.

MODEL KSP 200 - .22 LR cal., Walther's semi-auto pistol with adj. laminated ergonomic grips, target trigger and sights, two-tone slide finish, mfg. in cooperation with Baikal. New 2000.

	MSR	$575		$500	$450	$415	$385	$350	$325	$295

MODEL OSP - similar to GSP, in .22 Short cal.. Mfg. 1961-1994 for international competition (meets ISU and NRA regs.), 3.35 (1994-present, current model is OSP 2000) or 4¼ in. barrel, 44.4 oz.

	MSR	$1,595		$1,475	$1,025	$800	$650	$550	$475	$425

Add $200 for extended sight radius and semi-wraparound grip (Model OSP 2000).

FREE PISTOL - .22 LR cal., single shot, electronic trigger, 11.8 in. heavy barrel, advanced target design with fully adj. grips and sights, 49.4 oz. Mfg. 1977-1991.

				$1,450	$1,200	$1,000	$850	$675	$575	$500

Last MSR was $2,140.

P38 WWII MILITARY MFG. - see German Military for breakdown.

HÄMMERLI-WALTHER - see Hämmerli.

REVOLVERS

MODEL R99 - .357 Mag. cal., 6 shot, double action, 3 in. barrel, adj. rear sight, blue or stainless steel, unique Duo-grip allows for different hand sizes (2 grips included), 28½ oz. Mfg. by Smith & Wesson 1999 only for the European market with no U.S. importation.

This model was basically a variation of the S&W Models 19 (blue) or 66 (stainless).

RIFLES: DISC.

MODEL B - .30-06 cal., bolt action, post-war mfg., 22 in. barrel. Disc.

				$450	$420	$380	$340	$300	$275	$250

Add 20% for double set triggers.

MODEL 1 AUTOLOADING - .22 LR cal., Carbine model, autoloading, detachable mag., 20½ in. barrel, 5 or 9 (optional) shot mag., could be used as bolt action or semi- auto, checkered pistol grip, walnut sporter stock, 5½ lbs.

				$695	$600	$500	$400	$300	$250	$200

MODEL 2 AUTOLOADING - .22 LR cal., similar to Model 1, except has 24½ in. barrel, finger grooved forearm, tangent sight, adj. trigger, checkered sporter stock, pre-war, 7 lbs.

				$775	$625	$500	$400	$300	$250	$200

MODEL V CHAMPION - similar to Model V Single Shot, with micrometer adj. sight and checkered pistol grip stock.

				$550	$495	$425	$385	$330	$305	$250

Grading	100%	98%	95%	90%	80%	70%	60%

MODEL DSM 34 - .22 LR cal., single shot, military stock, tangent sight. Pre-war and wartime mfg.

	$650	$550	$500	$450	$375	$300	$250

Add 100% for stamp in stock.
Add 50% for AS stamp in stock.

MODEL KKM INTERNATIONAL MATCH - .22 LR cal., single shot bolt action, 28 in. heavy barrel, adj. aperture sight, adj. hook butt, thumbhole stock, accessory rail, post-war mfg.

	$880	$770	$715	$660	$550	$495	$440

MODEL KKM-S - similar to KKM, with adj. cheekpiece.

	$935	$825	$770	$715	$605	$550	$495

MODEL KKJ SPORTER - .22 LR cal., bolt action, 5 shot, 22½ in. barrel, open sight, checkered sporter stock, post-war.

	$1,250	$995	$650	$550	$450	$385	$330

Add 20% for double set triggers.

MODEL KKJ-MA - .22 Mag. cal.

	$1,250	$1,100	$775	$650	$550	$450	$385

MODEL KKJ-HO - .22 Hornet cal.

	$1,450	$1,225	$825	$700	$575	$450	$385

Add 20% for double set triggers.

MODEL KKW - .22 LR cal., single shot, military stock, tangent sight, pre-war and wartime mfg.

	$750	$600	$420	$300	$260	$220	$195

Add 50% for SA stamp on stock.

MODEL SSV VARMINT - .22 LR cal., single shot bolt action, 25½ in. barrel, no sights, Monte Carlo pistol grip stock, post-war mfg.

	$700	$600	$525	$495	$415	$360	$330
.22 Hornet	$825	$725	$600	$550	$475	$415	$385

MODEL UIT BV UNIVERSAL - .22 LR cal., single shot bolt action, 25.6 in. heavy barrel, adj. aperture sight, target stock with palm rest, adj. butt, meets ISU regs., 11 lbs. Disc. 1990.

	$1,325	$1,050	$850	$700	$635	$580	$530

Last MSR was $1,700.

This model was previously known as the Model UIT Special.

GX-1 - similar to Model UIT Match, 25 in. barrel with fully adj. free rifle stock, all accessories included, 16½ lbs. Importation disc. 1991.

	$1,895	$1,375	$1,125	$985	$860	$775	$680

Last MSR was $2,350.

MODEL KK/MS SILHOUETTE - .22 LR cal. only, designed for silhouette shooting with no sights, thumbhole stock with adj. butt, fully stippled forend and stock grip, front barrel weight, 23.6 in. barrel, 16.3 lbs. Imported 1984-91.

	$975	$795	$625	$560	$495	$435	$395

Last MSR was $1,175.

RUNNING BOAR MODEL 500 - similar to KK/MS, no sights, thumbhole stock with adj. wood buttplate and cheekpiece, 23.6 in. barrel, 8.4 lbs. Disc. 1990.

	$1,195	$900	$675	$575	$500	$435	$395

Last MSR was $1,300.

MODEL WA-2000 - .300 Win. Mag. or .308 Win. cal., ultra-deluxe semi-auto, 25.6 in. barrel, 5 or 6 shot mag., optional extras include aluminum case, spare mags., integral bipod, adj. tools and leather sling, regular or night vision scope, special order only, 16¾ lbs. Disc. 1988.

	$18,000	$12,500	$10,750	$9,000	$8,000	$7,000	$6,250

Grading	100%	98%	95%	90%	80%	70%	60%

MODEL UIT MATCH - similar to Model UIT, except with improved stock design which includes fully stippled lower forearm and pistol grip, 25.6 in. barrel, 8.6 lbs. Importation disc. 1993.

	$1,125	$925	$800	$660	$610	$555	$510

Last MSR was $1,400.

✴ *Model UIT-E* - electronic trigger, 25.6 in. barrel, 10.4 lbs. Disc. 1986.

	$1,350	$940	$860	$770	$670	$630	$560

Last MSR was $1,250.

MODEL PRONE 400 - similar to UIT Match, with Prone style competition stock and no sights. Disc.

	$750	$635	$580	$525	$415	$360	$305

RIFLES: CURRENT/RECENT MFG.

MODEL KK200 - .22 LR cal., available in standard rifle laminated stock, power match, and sport configurations, top-of-the-line competition model, 19.7 in. barrel, 11.57 lbs.

MSR N/A		$1,490	$1,275	$1,000	$850	$725	$600	$550

Add $1,200 for machined KK200 Power Match model with nickel plated stippled stock and forend, 25.5 in. barrel, 13 lbs. (limited mfg. 1995).
Add $420 for KK200 S (sport configuration).
Add $265 for electronic trigger on power match or sport models.

MODEL KK CLUB SPORT RIFLE - .22 LR cal. New 2000.

MSR N/A		$525	$450	$400	$350	$275	$260	$230

MODEL GSP RIFLE CONVERSION - .22 LR cal., utilizes GSP sport pistol action, 16¾ in. stainless fluted barrel, through engraved compensator, laminated "silhouette style" thumbhole stock, 5 shot standard, 8 or 10 shot optional, optics or scope optional, 8.55 lbs. Introduced 1997.

MSR $2,590		$2,400	$2,100	$1,800	$1,500	$1,250	$1,125	$1,000

SHOTGUNS: SxS

MODEL WSF - 12 or 16 ga., checkered walnut stock, double triggers, boxlock, sling swivels, 28.4 in. barrel. Introduced 1932-disc.

	$600	$450	$395	$325	$275	$240	$200

MODEL WSFD - 12 or 16 ga., cheekpiece, checkered walnut stock, double triggers, boxlock, sling swivels, 6.3 (16 ga.) or 6.6 (12 ga.) lbs. Introduced 1932-disc.

	$800	$575	$500	$425	$375	$340	$300

SHOTGUNS: SEMI-AUTO

WALTHER SEMI-AUTO - 12 ga. only, 2 3/4 in. chamber, 25.5 in. barrel, crossbolt safety, checkered walnut stock and forearm. Mfg. in Zella-Mehlis 1921-1931.

	$875	$775	$650	$550	$450	$375	$295

WALTHER, FRENCH-MADE BY MANURHIN

Previously manufactured in Mulhouse, France. Previously imported 1984-86 by Matra- Manurhin International, Inc. located in Alexandria, VA.

PISTOLS: SEMI-AUTO

Manufacture of these Walther pistols commenced in France in 1951. They were marked MANURHIN on the slide until 1954. Since then they were designated Walther MKII. They were imported into the USA by Interarms up to 1983. In 1984, Manurhin was imported directly with no Interarms logo or Walther trademark appearing on Models PP and PPK/S. Importation was discontinued 1986.

Grading	100%	98%	95%	90%	80%	70%	60%

MODEL PP - .22 LR, .32 ACP, or .380 ACP cal., 3 7/8 in. barrel, 10 shot mag.-.22 LR, 8 shot mag.-.32 ACP, 7 shot mag.-.380 ACP, blue only, all steel construction, double action with positive hammer block safety, 24 oz.

	$400	$350	$300	$230	$205	$185	$170

Last MSR was $419.

Add $25 for .22 LR or .380 ACP cal.
Add $46 for Durgarde finish.

* *Collector Model* - blue finish, special engraving. Imported 1986 only.

	$465	$415	$350

Last MSR was $529.

* *Presentation Model* - blue finish, special ornamentation. Imported 1986 only.

	$720	$650	$500

Last MSR was $819.

* *Interarms import*

	$350	$325	$285

Also available with various engraving options in either blue, nickel, or gold finish - prices range from $222 - $540.

PP SPORT - .22 LR cal. only, double action, 6.1 or 8.1 in. barrel, blue finish only, precision adj. sights, contoured plastic grips with thumb rest, 25 oz. New Manurhin design beginning 1985-disc.

	$545	$485	$430	$385	$325	$290	$270

Last MSR was $635.

* *PP Sport-C* - similar to PP Sport, except is single action.

	$540	$475	$415	$370	$310	$280	$260

Last MSR was $635.

MODEL PPK - .22 LR, .32 ACP, or .380 ACP cal., 3¼ in. barrel, 10 shot mag.-.22 LR, 8 shot mag.-.32 ACP, 7 shot mag.-.380 ACP, blue only, all steel construction, double action with positive hammer block safety, 23 oz.

	$550	$475	$425	$375	$350	$325	$300

Add $25 for .22 LR or .380 ACP cal.

MODEL PPK/S - .22 LR, .32 ACP, or .380 ACP cal., 3¼ in. barrel, 10 shot mag.-.22 LR, 8 shot mag.-.32 ACP, 7 shot mag.-.380 ACP, blue only, all steel construction, double action with positive hammer block safety, 23 oz.

	$400	$350	$300	$230	$205	$185	$170

Last MSR was $419.

Add 10% for .22 LR cal.

* *PPK/S Durgarde* - similar to Model PPK/S, only with bonded brushed chrome finish.

	$450	$400	$350	$300	$275	$250	$240

Last MSR was $465.

Add 10% for .22 LR cal.

* *Collector Model* - blue finish, special engraving. Imported 1986 only.

	$465	$415	$350

Last MSR was $529.

* *Presentation Model* - blue finish, special ornamentation. Imported 1986 only.

	$720	$650	$500

Last MSR was $819.

* *Interarms import*

	$395	$340	$300

Was also available with various engraving options in either blue, nickel, or gold finish - prices range from $222 - $540.

Grading	100%	98%	95%	90%	80%	70%	60%

WARNER ARMS CORPORATION
Previous manufacturer located in Norwich, CT.

PISTOLS: SEMI-AUTO

INFALLIBLE POCKET AUTO PISTOL - .32 ACP cal., 7 shot, 3 in. barrel, fixed sights, rubber grips. Mfg. 1917-1919.

$450	$350	$250	$150	$125	$100	$90

WATSON BROS.
Current long gun manufacturer established in 1885, and located in London, England.

Watson Bros. manufactures distinct round body actions with self-opening locks in both SxS and O/U shotgun configurations. Back action sidelock double rifles are also available. Please contact the factory directly (see Trademark Index) for more information including current pricing.

WEATHERBY
Current trademark manufacturerd and imported by Weatherby located in Atascadero, CA since 1995. Previously located in South Gate, CA, 1945 - 1995. Weatherby began manufacturing rifles in the U.S. during early 1995. Dealer and distributor sales.

Weatherby is an importer and manufacturer of long arms. Earlier production was from Germany and Italy, and German mfg. is usually what is collectible. Current rifle production is from the U.S., while shotguns are made in Japan. Workmanship in all instances is excellent. Weatherby is well known for their high-velocity proprietary rifle calibers.

Early Weatherby rifles used a Mathieu Arms action in the 1950s - primarily since it was available in left-hand action. Right-handed actions were normally mfg. from the FN Mauser type.

DRILLINGS

WEATHERBY DRILLING - mfg. by J. P. Sauer during the late 1960s-early 1970s for Weatherby importation (marked Weatherby on right barrel), identical to Sauer Model 3000, except was not available in all metric cals. Disc.

$2,850	$2,450	$2,100	$1,800	$1,500	$1,250	$1,000

PISTOLS: BOLT ACTION

SILHOUETTE PISTOL - .22-250 Rem. or .308 Win. cal., mfg. in Japan during late 1970s, 14½ in. barrel, Lyman or Williams sights, fitted case. Only 50 were mfg. in .22- 250 Rem. and 150 in .308 Win. cal. Disc. 1981.

$3,750	$3,300	$2,750	$2,450	$2,100	$1,850	$1,650

MARK V CFP (CENTERFIRE PISTOLS) - .22-250 Rem., .223 Rem. (new 2000), .243 Win., 7mm-08 Rem., or .308 Win. cal., features 15 in. fluted stainless barrel with recessed crown, ambidextrous designed multi-layer brown laminate stock with finger grooves and swivel studs, blue Mark V lightweight action, no sights, 3 shot internal mag., 5¼ lbs. Mfg. 1997-2000.

$935	$815	$735	$650	$600	$550	$500

Last MSR was $1,099.

✳ Mark V Accumark CFP - same cals. as Mark V CFP, features specially designed synthetic stock with Kevlar and other fibers, matte black gel coat finish with grey spider web pattern, 5 lbs. Limited mfg. 2000 only.

$935	$815	$735	$650	$600	$550	$500

Last MSR was $1,099.

Grading	100%	98%	95%	90%	80%	70%	60%

RIFLES: .22 LR CAL.

ACCUMARK CLASSIC & DELUXE BOLT ACTION - while these models were advertised in 1990 ($635 retail), they were never manufactured.

MARK XXII CLIP MAG SEMI-AUTO - .22 LR cal., mag. feed, skipline checkered walnut stock with rosewood forearm and pistol grip caps, 5 or 10 shot detachable mag., 24 in. barrel, open sights, 6 lbs. Disc. 1989.

	100%	98%	95%	90%	80%	70%	60%
Japanese mfg.	$395	$320	$265	$245	$215	$195	$180
Italian mfg.	$495	$440	$365	$325	$275	$240	$210
U.S. mfg. (approx. 200 mfg.)	$750	$675	$575	$495	$440	$365	$325

Last MSR was $454.

The Mark XXII clip mag. was originally mfg. in Italy - a slight premium might be asked. This model featured a receiver slide-switch that allowed semi-auto operation to be converted to single shot mode.

MARK XXII TUBE MAG SEMI-AUTO - .22 LR cal., same general specifications as Mark XXII Clip Mag. model, except tube-feed, 15 shot, 6 lbs. Disc. 1989.

	100%	98%	95%	90%	80%	70%	60%
	$395	$320	$265	$245	$215	$195	$180

Last MSR was $454.

RIFLES: BOLT ACTION, MARK V SERIES

In 1992, 24 in. barrels were disc. on most calibers of .300 or greater (including Models Mark V Deluxe, Fibermark, Lazermark, and Euromark). Since 1957, the Mark V Action has been manufactured in Germany, Japan, and the U.S.

All Weatherby Magnums in .30-378, .338-378, .378, .416, and .460 cal. are equipped with an Accubrake installed.

MARK V DELUXE - .22-250 Rem. (new 1999), .240 Wby. Mag. (disc. 1996, reintroduced 1999), .243 Win. (new 1999), .25-06 Rem. (new 1999), .257 Wby. Mag., .270 Win. (new 1999), .270 Wby. Mag., .280 Rem. (new 1999), 7mm Wby. Mag., 7mm-08 Rem. (new 1999), .30-06 (disc. 1996, reintroduced 1999), .308 Win. (new 1999), .300 Wby. Mag., .340 Wby. Mag., or .375 H&H (mfg. 1993 only) cal., bolt action, 3-5 shot mag., 24 or 26 in. barrel, deluxe skip line checkered pistol grip walnut stock with rosewood tipped forearm and pistol grip, no sights, 8 lbs. Left-hand actions (.270 Wby. Mag. and .300 Wby. Mag.) were available at no extra charge through 1997.

Add 15%-25% for German manufacture in calibers under .35 if condition is 95% or better.

✴ **Short Action Cals.** - .22-250 Rem., .243 Win., .240 Wby. Mag., .25-06 Rem., .270 Win., .280 Rem., .30-06, .308 Win., or 7mm-08 Rem. short action cals. New 1999.

MSR	$1,715	$1,355	$925	$700	$600	$515	$450	$410

✴ **Wby. Mag. Cals.** - includes cals. between .257 Wby. Mag. - .340 Wby. Mag.

MSR	$1,767	$1,400	$950	$725	$625	$525	$465	$415

Add approx. $200 for .375 H&H cal. (disc. 1993).

✴ **.378 Wby. Mag.** - 26 in. barrel only, 8½ lbs.

	MSR							
	$2,079	$1,625	$1,025	$800	$675	$550	$475	$425
German mfg.		$1,650	$1,425	$1,250	$1,000	$900	$825	$750

German mfg. in this model used the .375 Wby. Mag. cal.

✴ **.416 Wby. Mag.** - first new caliber (introduced 1989) since the .240 Mag. was released 1965.

MSR	$2,079	$1,625	$1,025	$800	$675	$550	$475	$425

✴ **.460 Wby. Mag.** - 24 or 26 in. barrel, includes custom stock, integral muzzle brake, 10 lbs. No extra charge for left-hand.

MSR	$2,443	$1,975	$1,450	$1,075	$850	$675	$625	$550

Grading	100%	98%	95%	90%	80%	70%	60%

ACCUMARK (MAG. CALS.) - .257 Wby. Mag., .270 Wby. Mag., .300 Win. Mag., .300 Wby. Mag., .30-378 Wby. Mag. (new 1997), .338-378 Wby Mag. (new 1998), 7mm STW (new 1998), 7mm Rem. Mag., 7mm Wby. Mag., or .340 Wby. Mag. cal., features Bell & Carlson hand laminated Kevlar/fiberglass stock with Pachmayr Decelerator pad, 26 in. stainless steel fluted barrel, aluminum bedding plate, custom trigger, approx. 8 lbs. New 1996.

	MSR	$1,507		$1,210	$995	$775		

Add $217 for .30-378 Wby. Mag. or .338-378 Wby. Mag. cals.
Add approx. $52 for left-hand action (available in most cals., new 1999).

✳ ***Accumark Lightweight*** - .22-250 Rem., .223 Rem. (new 2000), .243 Win., .240 Wby. Mag., .25-06 Rem., .270 Win., .280 Rem., 7mm-08 Rem., .30-06, or .308 Win. cal., features weight saving construction, including extra wide barrel flutes, skeletonized bolt handle, and hand laminated Kevlar/fiberglass stock with Pachmayr Decelerator pad, 24 in. stainless barrel w/o sights, 5¾ lbs. New 1998.

	MSR	$1,455		$1,215	$1,025	$860	$750	$650	$600	$550

CLASSICMARK I - available in 9 Wby. Mag. cals. in addition to .270 Win., 7mm Rem. Mag., .30-06, or .375 H&H cal., oil finished American Claro walnut stock with no cheekpiece and ebony forend cap, 1 in. solid recoil pad, panel point checkering. Mfg. 1992-1993.

	$1,075	$750	$625	$525	$475	$450	$410

Last MSR was $1,295.

Add $15 for 26 in. barrel.
Add $130 for .375 H&H cal.

✳ ***.300 or .340 Wby. Mag.*** - 26 in. barrel only, right or left-hand action, 8½ lbs.

	$1,095	$775	$625	$525	$475	$450	$410

Last MSR was $1,323.

✳ ***.378 Wby. Mag.*** - 26 in. barrel only, right or left-hand action, 8½ lbs.

	$1,125	$795	$625	$525	$475	$450	$410

Last MSR was $1,356.

✳ ***.416 Wby. Mag.*** - 26 in. barrel only, right or left-hand action, integral muzzlebrake.

	$1,150	$825	$650	$550	$495	$460	$430

Last MSR was $1,411.

✳ ***.460 Wby. Mag.*** - 26 in. barrel only, includes custom stock, integral muzzle brake, 10 lbs. No extra charge for left-hand.

	$1,250	$900	$675	$575	$525	$475	$430

Last MSR was $1,573.

CLASSICMARK II - available in 9 Wby. Mag. cals. in addition to .270 Win., 7mm Rem. Mag., or .30-06, similar to Classicmark I, except has deluxe American walnut with 22 LPI multiple point checkering, steel grip cap, satin finished wood and metal, guaranteed 1½ in. or less 3 shot grouping at 100 yards, right hand action only. Mfg. 1992 only.

	$1,525	$1,175	$975	$800	$650	$600	$550

Last MSR was $1,775.

Add $28 for 26 in. barrel.

✳ ***.300 or .340 Wby. Mag.*** - 26 in. barrel only.

	$1,550	$1,175	$975	$800	$650	$600	$550

Last MSR was $1,803.

✳ ***.378 Wby. Mag.*** - 26 in. barrel only.

	$1,700	$1,250	$1,000	$800	$650	$600	$550

Last MSR was $1,976.

✳ ***.416 Wby. Mag.*** - 26 in. barrel only, integral muzzlebrake.

	$1,875	$1,375	$1,050	$825	$650	$600	$550

Last MSR was $2,128.

* **.460 Wby. Mag.** - 26 in. barrel only, includes custom stock, integral muzzle brake, 10 lbs.

	100%	98%	95%	90%	80%	70%	60%
	$1,925	$1,400	$1,050	$825	$650	$600	$550

Last MSR was $2,207.

* **Safari Classic** - .375 H&H cal., 24 in. barrel only, right-hand action, limited edition featuring custom action, quarter rib express and front ramp sights, barrel band swivel and engraved floor plate, stock similar to Classicmark II. Mfg. 1992 only.

	$2,300	$1,850	$1,650	$1,450	$1,300	$1,175	$995

Last MSR was $2,693.

EUROMARK - available in most cals. as the Sporter Model, also includes .378 Wby. Mag. and .416 Wby. Mag., differs from Mark V Deluxe in that it has an oil finished, hand checkered, deluxe American claro walnut pistol grip cap stock with ebony forend tip, low luster bluing, and solid black recoil pad. Mfg. 1986-92, re-introduced 1995.

MSR	$1,819	$1,410	$975	$740	$585	$475	$450	$410

Add $312 for either .378 Wby. Mag. or .416 Wby. Mag. cal.

* **.460 Wby. Mag.** - 24 or 26 in. barrel, includes custom stock, internal muzzle brake, no extra charge for left-hand. Disc. 1992.

	$1,450	$1,100	$925	$775	$650	$600	$550

Last MSR was $1,708.

FIBERMARK - available in .240 Wby. Mag., .257 Wby. Mag., .270 Wby. Mag., .30-06, 7mm Wby. Mag., .300 Wby. Mag., or .340 Wby. Mag. cal., black non-glare fiberglass with wrinkle finish stock, metal has non-glare matte finish, 24 or 26 in. barrel, available in right (disc. 1991) or left-hand action, 7¼ lbs. Mfg. 1983-1992.

	$1,195	$875	$725	$600	$525	$475	$450

Last MSR was $1,376.

Add $118 for .300 or .340 Mag. cal.

This model was available in left-hand action (22 in. barrel) in .270 Win. or .30-06 cal. only.

FIBERMARK (CURRENT MFG.) - available in 21 cals. between .22-250 Rem. - .375 H&H, pillar bedded black composite Monte Carlo stock of Kevlar and unidirectional fiberglass, matte blue metal, 24, 26 (Mag. cals. only), or 28 (.30-378 Wby. Mag. cal. only) in. steel barrel, 6¾ - 8½ lbs. New 2001.

MSR	$1,070	$875	$675	$595	$450	$400	$350	$325

Add $52 for Mag. cals.
Add $277 for .30-378 Wby. Mag. cal.

* **Mark V Fibermark Stainless** - similar to Mark V Fiberglass, except has stainless steel action and barrel with matte finish. New 2001.

MSR	$1,165	$950	$725	$625

Add $52 for Mag. cals.
Add $225 for .30-378 Wby. Mag. cal.

LAZERMARK - various cals., differs from the Mark V Deluxe in that stock and forearm have been laser carved, 24 or 26 in. barrel. New 1985.

MSR	$1,923	$1,600	$1,100	$800	$650	$525	$475	$450

* **.378 Wby. Mag. or .416 Wby. Mag.** - first new caliber (introduced 1989) since the .240 Mag. was released 1965, includes muzzle brake.

MSR	$2,266	$1,850	$1,300	$1,025	$825	$650	$575	$525

* **.460 Wby. Mag.** - 24 (disc. 2000), 26 (disc. 2000), or 28 in. barrel, includes custom stock, internal muzzle brake, no extra charge for left-hand.

MSR	$2,661	$2,150	$1,500	$1,200	$925	$650	$600	$550

* **Varmintmaster** - .22-250 Rem. or .224 Varmintmaster cal., 24 or 26 in. barrel. Disc. 1991.

	$1,085	$815	$675	$575	$500	$460	$425

Last MSR was $675.

Add $25 for 26 in. barrel.
Not available in left-hand action.

Grading	100%	98%	95%	90%	80%	70%	60%

ULTRAMARK - .240 Wby. Mag., .257 Wby. Mag., .270 Wby. Mag., .30-06, 7mm Wby. Mag., .300 Wby. Mag., .378 Wby. Mag. (mfg. 1989 only), or .416 Wby. Mag. (mfg. 1989 only) cal., fancy American walnut, individually hand-bedded, high luster finish, customized action, 24 or 26 in. barrel, basket weave checkering (including pistol grip). Imported 1989-90 only.

	$1,125	$925	$800	$700	$630	$590	$550

Last MSR was $1,315.

> Add $25 for 26 in. barrel.
> Add $220 for .378 Wby. Mag. cal. (26 in. barrel only).
> Add $325 for .416 Wby. Mag. cal. (26 in. barrel only).

WEATHERMARK - available in various Wby. Mag. cals. from .240 (disc. 1996) to .340 and .257 Roberts (disc. 1994), .270 Win., 7mm Rem. Mag., .300 Win. Mag., .30-06, .338 Win. Mag., or .375 H&H (disc.) cal., design is similar to Classicmark II, except is fitted with black checkered composite stock, satin finish black metal, 22 (disc. 1995, .270 Win. or .30-06 only), 24, or 26 in. barrel, right-hand only, 7½ lbs. Mfg. 1992-94.

	$685	$540	$475	$400	$360	$330	$300

Last MSR was $799.

SYNTHETIC (MAG. CALS.) - .257 Wby. Mag., .270 Wby. Mag., .300 Wby. Mag., .30-378 Wby. Mag. (new 1998), .300 Win. Mag., .338 Win. Mag., .338-.378 Wby. Mag. (new 2001), .340 Wby. Mag., 7mm Wby. Mag., 7mm Rem. Mag., 7mm STW (new 2001), or .375 H&H cal., 24, 26, or 28 in. barrel, features lightweight black synthetic stock, bead blasted matte metal finish, approx. 8 lbs. New 1997.

MSR	$975	$825	$625	$525	$450	$375	$335	$300

Add $176 for .30-378 Wby. Mag. or .338-.378 Wby. Mag. cal. (28 in. barrel only).

* **Light Weight Synthetic** - .22-250 Rem., .243 Win., .240 Wby. Mag., .25-06 Rem., .270 Win., .280 Rem., .30-06, .308 Win., or 7mm-08 Rem. cal., features raised comb, matte black injection mold synthetic stock, no sights, 20 (carbine, .243 Win., .308 Win., or 7mm-08 Rem.) or 24 in. barrel, approx. 6½ lbs. New 1997.

MSR	$923	$775	$575	$495	$425	$350	$330	$300

* **Fluted Synthetic** - .257 Wby. Mag., .270 Wby. Mag., .300 Wby. Mag., .300 Win. Mag., 7mm Wby. Mag., or 7mm Rem. Mag. cal., features 24 or 26 in. fluted barrel, black synthetic stock with Monte Carlo cheekpiece, approx. 7½ lbs. Mfg. 1997-98.

	$785	$635	$550	$495	$450	$395	$350

Last MSR was $949.

* **Weathermark Alaskan Model** - same cals. as Weathermark, similar to Weathermark, except has non-glare electroless nickel-plated metal parts, right or left-hand (mfg. 1992 only) action. Mfg. 1992-94.

	$750	$635	$560	$495	$450	$400	$360

Last MSR was $875.

> Add $37 for Wby. Mag. cals.
> Add $164 for .375 H&H cal.
> Add $375 for left-hand action (disc.).

SYNTHETIC STAINLESS MODEL (MAG. CALS.) - same cals. as Synthetic, except not available in .338-.378 Wby. Mag. or 7mm STW, features bead blasted matte stainless construction, synthetic Monte Carlo stock. New 1995.

MSR	$1,070	$910	$700	$575

Add $167 for .30-378 Wby. Mag. (28 in. barrel only).

* **Synthetic Stainless Light Weight** - .22-250 Rem., .243 Win., .240 Wby. Mag., .25-06 Rem., .270 Win., .280 Rem., .30-06, .308 Win., or 7mm-08 Rem. cal., features raised comb, matte black injection molded synthetic stock, no sights, 20 (carbine, .243 Win., .308 Win., or 7mm-08 Rem. cal.) or 24 in. stainless barrel and action, approx. 6½ lbs. New 1997.

MSR	$1,018	$845	$675	$560

Grading	100%	98%	95%	90%	80%	70%	60%

* **Fluted Stainless** - .257 Wby. Mag., .270 Wby. Mag., .300 Wby. Mag., .300 Win. Mag., 7mm Wby. Mag., or 7mm Rem. Mag., features 24 or 26 in. fluted stainless barrel and action, black synthetic stock with Monte Carlo cheekpiece, approx. 7½ lbs. Mfg. 1997-98.

	$1,025	$925	$825

Last MSR was $1,149.

EUROSPORT - various cals., features hand-rubbed satin oil finished claro walnut stock with low luster blue metal work. New 1995.

MSR	$1,143		$915	$695	$595	$510	$450	$395	$350

MARK V SLS (STAINLESS LAMINATE SPORTER) - .257 Wby. Mag., .270 Wby. Mag., .300 Wby. Mag., .300 Win. Mag., .338 Win. Mag., .340 Wby. Mag., 7mm Wby. Mag., or 7mm Rem. Mag. cal., 24 or 26 (Wby. Mag. cals. only) in. barrel, features brown laminate stock with recoil pad, stainless steel with matte blue finish, approx. 8½ lbs. New 1997.

MSR	$1,393		$1,125	$915	$700

SPORTER (LONG ACTION) - .240 Wby. Mag. (mfg. 1996 only), .257 Wby. Mag., .270 Wby. Mag., 7mm Wby. Mag., 7mm Rem. Mag., .270 Win. (mfg. 1996 only), .30-06 (disc. 1996), .300 Wby. Mag., .300 Win. Mag., .338 Win. Mag., .340 Wby. Mag., or .375 H&H cal., 24 or 26 in. barrel, similar features as the Mark V, except has checkered walnut stock without forearm or pistol grip caps, low luster metalwork, vent. recoil pad, no sights, approx. 8 lbs. New 1993.

MSR	$1,143		$935	$725	$625	$525	$450	$400	$375

* **Light Weight Sporter** - .22-250 Rem., .243 Win., .240 Wby. Mag., .25-06 Rem., .270 Win., .280 Rem., .30-06, .308 Win., or 7mm-08 Rem. cal., features raised comb, checkered walnut stock, 54 degree bolt lift, no sights, 24 in. barrel, approx. 6½ lbs. New 1997.

MSR	$1,091		$900	$715	$610	$525	$450	$400	$375

ULTRA LIGHT WEIGHT - .243 Win., .240 Wby. Mag., .257 Wby. Mag. (new 1999), .25-06 Rem., .270 Win., .270 Wby. Mag. (new 1999), .280 Rem., .300 Wby. Mag. (new 1999), .300 Win. Mag. (new 1999), 7mm-08 Rem., 7mm Rem. Mag. (new 1999), 7mm Wby. Mag. (new 1999), .30-06, .308 Win., or .338-06 A-Square (new 2001) cal., features 24 in. barrel and lightweight synthetic stock. New 1998.

MSR	$1,459	$1,235	$1,025	$875	$750	$650	$600	$550

Add $57 for long action Mag. cals. (new 1999).

Add $100 for left hand action (.257 Wby. Mag., .270 Wby. Mag., .300 Wby. Mag., .300 Win. Mag., 7mm Rem. Mag. and 7mm Wby. Mag., new 2000).

WHITETAIL - .257 Sav. cal., limited edition features deluxe high grade Claro walnut, hand checkered bolt knob and engraved floorplate, 22 in. #1 contoured barrel, 6 lbs. Mfg. 1993 only.

	$1,150	$925	$775

Last MSR was $1,366.

SPM (SUPER PREDATORMASTER) - .22-250 Rem., .223 Rem., .243 Win., .308 Win., or 7mm-08 Rem. cal., features 24 in. Criterion button rifled barrel with flutes, black spider webbing on tan Accumark type stock with slim foreend and CNC aluminum bedding block, Pachmayr Decelerator pad, 6½ lbs. New 2001.

MSR	$1,459		$1,225	$1,025	$875	$750	$650	$600	$550

SVM (SUPER VARMINTMASTER) - .220 Swift (single shot only), .22-250 Rem., .223 Rem., .243 Win., .308 Win., or 7mm-08 Rem. cal., features 26 in. Criterion button rifled fluted barrel with crown, available as repeater or single shot, black spider webbing on tan Accumark type stock with beavertail foreend and CNC aluminum bedding block, Pachmayr Decelerator pad, approx. 8½ lbs. New 2000.

MSR	$1,517		$1,275	$1,050	$895	$765	$650	$600	$550

Grading	100%	98%	95%	90%	80%	70%	60%

SBGM (SUPER BIG GAME MASTER) - 12 cals. between .25-06 Rem. - .338-06 A-Square, 24 or 26 (Mag. cals. only) in. Criterion hand-lapped fluted Krieger barrel, barreled action is bed to a specially-designed, hand-laminated, raised comb, Monte Carlo composite stock (a combination of Aramid, graphite and unidirectional fibers and fiberglass) with black spiderweb patterning, Pachmayr Decelerator pad, 6¾ lbs. New 2002.

	MSR	$1,459	$1,225	$1,000	$895	$765	$650	$600	$550

TRR (THREAT RESPONSE RIFLE) - .223 Rem., .308 Win., .300 Win. Mag., .300 Wby. Mag., .30-378 Wby. Mag., or .338-.378 Wby. Mag. cal., Mark V action with black finished metal and black hybrid composite stock, various barrel lengths, optional Picatinney style ring and bass system, 10½ lbs. New 2002.

	MSR	$1,517	$1,255	$1,050	$875	$750	$650	$600	$550

Add $52 for .300 Win. Mag. or .300 Wby. Mag. cals.
Add $208 for .30-378 Wby. Mag. or .338-378 Wby. Mag. cals.

VARMINTMASTER - .22-250 Rem. or .224 Varmintmaster (disc. 1994) cal., 24 (disc. 1991) or 26 in. barrel, 6½ lbs. Disc. 1995.

			$1,075	$775	$625	$525	$475	$450	$410

Last MSR was $1,297.

Not available in left-hand action.

1976 BICENTENNIAL MARK V - .257 Wby. Mag., .270 Wby. Mag., 7mm Wby. Mag., or .300 Wby Mag. cal., 1,000 mfg. in 1976 only.

			$1,495	$1,150	$895				

Last MSR was $2,000.

1984 MARK V OLYMPIC COMMEMORATIVE - .257 Wby. Mag., .270 Wby. Mag., 7mm Wby. Mag., or .300 Wby. Mag. cal., special gold accenting, extra-fancy walnut stock with "star in motion" inlay. Mfg. 1,000 1984 only at $2,000 retail.

			$1,000	$895	$700				

MARK V 35TH ANNIVERSARY COMMEMORATIVE - .257 Wby. Mag., .270 Wby. Mag., 7mm Wby. Mag., or .300 Wby. Mag. cal., limited mfg. 1980, 1,000 produced total.

			$1,000	$895	$700				

RIFLES: BOLT ACTION, CUSTOM SHOP

OUTFITTER CUSTOM - various cals. between .243 Win. - .300 Wby. Mag., , 24 or 26 in. barrel, features ultra lightweight bolt action with titanium nitride hardcoating and a desert camo stock. New 2001.

	MSR	$2,235	$1,850	$1,550	$1,275	$1,000	$800	$650	$575

Add $52 for Mag. cals.

OUTFITTER KREIGER CUSTOM - same cals. as Outfitter Custom, 24 or 26 in. barrel, ultra lightweight action with Kreiger ultra lightweight contoured barrel with cut rifling, trued receiver and bolt face, lapping locking lugs, titanium nitride coating, desert camo stock. New 2001.

	MSR	$3,499	$2,995	$2,550	$2,175	$1,800	$1,500	$1,250	$995

Add $50 for Mag. cals.

DANGEROUS GAME RIFLE (CUSTOM) - .300 Win. Mag. (new 2002), .300 Wby. Mag. (new 2002), .338 Win. Mag. (new 2002), .340 Wby. Mag. (new 2002), .375 H&H, .375 Wby. Mag., .378 Wby. Mag., .416 Rem. Mag., .416 Wby. Mag., .458 Win. Mag., or .460 Wby. Mag. cal., 24 or 26 in. barrel with express sights (rear is adj.), black Kevlar and fiberglass stock with CNC machined aluminum bedding block and Pachmayr Decelerator pad, black oxide metal finish, 8¾ or 9 ½ (.460 Wby. Mag.) lbs. New 2001.

	MSR	$2,703	$2,250	$1,850	$1,525	$1,250	$995	$800	$650

Add $150 for .378 Wby. Mag. or .416 Wby. Mag., and $232 for .460 Wby. Mag. cal.

W

Grading	100%	98%	95%	90%	80%	70%	60%

CUSTOM GRADE - various cals. from .240 Wby. Mag. to .340 Wby. Mag., 24 or 26 in. barrel, super fancy walnut stock featuring No. 7 style inlays, floorplate is engraved "Weatherby Custom", 6-8 months delivery time. Disc. 2001.

	$4,250	$2,750	$2,050	$1,650	$1,450	$1,300	$1,175

Last MSR was $5,099.

TRCM (THREAT RESPONSE CUSTOM MAGNUM) - .300 Win. Mag., .300 Wby. Mag., .30-378 Wby. Mag., or .338-.378 Wby. Mag. cal., Mark V action with ergonomic, fully adjustable composite stock, black finished metal, various barrel lengths, optional Picatinney style ring and bass system. New 2002.

MSR	$2,499	$2,000	$1,450	$1,025	$825	$650	$575	$525

Add $150 for .30-378 Wby. Mag. or .338-378 Wby. Mag. cals.

SAFARI GRADE CUSTOM - .257 Wby. Mag. (new 2000), .270 Wby. Mag. (new 2000), .300 Wby. Mag., .340 Wby. Mag., .375 H&H (new 2000), .378 Wby. Mag., .416 Wby Mag., .460 Wby. Mag., or 7mm Wby. Mag. (new 2000) cal., custom order only, various options available, 12-18 month delivery.

MSR	$5,235	$4,100	$3,000	$2,000	$1,650	$1,425	$1,275	$1,150

Add $207 for .378 Wby. Mag. or .416 Wby. Mag. cal.

Add $615 for .460 Wby. Mag. cal.

ROYAL CUSTOM - same cals. as Crown Custom, custom order only, features high grade fancy Claro walnut with checkering with rosewood pistol grip cap and forend, damascene bolt and follower, engraved receiver and floorplate, select 24 Kt. gold and nickel plating. New 2002.

MSR	$5,399	$4,225	$3,050	$2,025	$1,675	$1,450	$1,300	$1,175

CROWN CUSTOM MODEL - .257 Wby. Mag., .270 Wby. Mag., .300 Wby. Mag., .340 Wby. Mag., or 7mm Wby. Mag. cal., custom order only, engraved barrel, receiver, and scope mount, top-of-the-line model.

MSR	$6,775	$5,700	$3,875	$3,025	$2,475	$1,900	$1,550	$1,350

RIFLES: BOLT ACTION, VANGUARD SERIES

VANGUARD - .243 Win., .25-06 Rem., .270 Win., .30-06, .308 Win., 7mm Rem. Mag., .264 Win. Mag., or .300 Win. Mag. cal., mfg. circa late 1960s-early 1970s.

	$450	$375	$325	$295	$260	$230	$200

Add 10% for .264 Win. Mag. cal.

VANGUARD CLASSIC I - .223 Rem., .243 Win., .270 Win., 7mm/08 Rem., 7mm Rem. Mag., .30-06, or .308 Win. cal., checkered walnut stock with satin finish, black butt pad, 24 in. barrel, 3 (7mm Rem. Mag.) or 5 shot mag., No. 1 barrel contour, approx. 7 lbs. 5 oz. Mfg. 1989-1993.

	$480	$375	$325	$295	$260	$230	$200

Last MSR was $549.

This model was the replacement for the Vanguard VGS and VGL.

VANGUARD CLASSIC II - .22-250 Rem., .243 Win., .270 Wby. Mag., .270 Win., 7mm Rem. Mag., .30-06, .300 Win. Mag., .300 Wby. Mag., or .338 Win. Mag. cal., 24 in. No. 2 barrel contour, 3 or 5 shot mag., custom checkered deluxe walnut stock with pistol grip cap and black forend cap, solid black recoil pad, matte finished metal, approx. 7¾ lbs. Mfg. 1989-92.

	$675	$550	$475	$425	$395	$360	$330

Last MSR was $750.

This model was also available in a No. 3 barrel contour in .22-250 Rem. cal. only.

Grading	100%	98%	95%	90%	80%	70%	60%

VANGUARD VGD - .22-250 Rem., .243 Win., .25-06 Rem., .270 Win., 7mm Rem. Mag., .30-06, or .300 Win. Mag. cal., bolt action, checkered deluxe walnut stock with rosewood tip forearm and pistol grip, 24 in. barrel, no sights, 5 shot mag.(except 3 shot for .300 Win. Mag.), high luster bluing, about 8 lbs. Disc. 1988.

	$525	$425	$365	$330	$300	$275	$255

Last MSR was $600.

Not available in left-hand action.

VANGUARD VGX DELUXE - .22-250 Rem., .243 Win., .270 Win., .270 Wby. Mag., .300 Win. Mag., .300 Wby. Mag., .30-06, .338 Win. Mag., or 7mm Rem. Mag. cal., 24 in. barrel, Monte Carlo stock with skipline checkering, high gloss wood and metal, rosewood forend cap. Mfg. 1989-1993.

	$625	$550	$475	$425	$395	$360	$330

Last MSR was $699.

VANGUARD VGS - same cals. as Vanguard VGX, bolt action, checkered satin finished walnut stock, 24 in. barrel, no sights, approx. 8 lbs. Disc. 1988.

	$415	$355	$295	$265	$245	$220	$200

Last MSR was $467.

Not available in left-hand action.

VANGUARD VGL - .223 Rem., .243 Win., .270 Win., 7mm Rem. Mag., .30-06, or .308 Win. cal., lightweight bolt action, checkered walnut stock, 5 shot mag.(6 on .223 Rem.), 20 in. barrel, no sights, 6½ lbs. Disc. 1988.

	$415	$355	$295	$265	$245	$220	$200

Last MSR was $467.

Not available in left-hand action.

VANGUARD WEATHERGUARD - same cals. as Classic I, replacement for Fiberguard, wrinkle black finished synthetic stock, entry level Weatherby, similar specs. as Classic I, approx. 8 lbs. Mfg. 1989-1993.

	$440	$350	$320	$290	$260	$230	$200

Last MSR was $499.

VANGUARD ALASKAN - same cals. as Classic I, features electroless nickel metal plating, no sights. Mfg. 1993-1994.

	$625	$550	$475	$425	$395	$360	$330

Last MSR was $699.

VANGUARD FIBERGUARD - .223 Rem., .243 Win., .270 Win., 7mm Rem. Mag., .30-06, or .308 Win. cal., 20 in. barrel, green fiberglass stock, 3 to 6 shot mags., no sights, blue metal parts, approx. 6½ lbs. Disc. 1988.

	$500	$450	$395	$355	$285	$255	$220

Last MSR was $560.

Not available in left-hand action.

SHOTGUNS: O/U

Weatherby shotguns are currently mfg. by SKB located in Tokyo, Japan. Current manufacture utilizes the IMC choke system (integral multi-choke), which allows interchangeability with Briley choke tubes.

REGENCY FIELD GRADE - 20 ga. Mag. (new 1968) or 12 ga., checkered stock, VR, engraved side plates, SST, early importation beginning in 1967 was from Italy, later mfg. was switched to Japan.

	$1,250	$895	$800	$700	$600	$550	$500

Add 10-15% for early Italian mfg. (note proof marks).

REGENCY TRAP GRADE - 12 ga., checkered trap stock, engraved, VR, SST. Imported from Italy.

	$900	$800	$700	$600	$550	$500	$475

Grading	100%	98%	95%	90%	80%	70%	60%

OLYMPIAN STANDARD - 12 and 20 ga., lightly engraved sideplates. Disc. 1980.

	$850	$775	$725	$625	$525	$450	$400

OLYMPIAN SKEET - 26 or 28 in. barrel.

	$885	$775	$725	$625	$525	$450	$400

OLYMPIAN TRAP - 30 or 32 in. barrel, VR.

	$850	$775	$725	$625	$525	$440	$400

ATHENA GRADE III CLASSIC FIELD - 12, 20, or 28 (new 2001) ga., 2¾ (28 ga. only) or 3 in. chambers, 26 or 28 in. barrels, features oil finished clear walnut stock with rounded pistol grip and slender forearm, gold SST, silver grey nitride sideplates with rose and scroll engraved gold pheasant and quail hunting scenes, 6½ - 8 lbs. New 1999.

MSR $2,130	$1,875	$1,525	$1,275	$1,050	$875	$750	$625

ATHENA GRADE IV FIELD - 12, 20, 28 (mfg. 1989-1993) ga., or .410 (mfg. 1989-1993) bore, 3 in. chambers, 26 or 28 in. VR barrels with or without choke tubes, boxlock with Greener Cross-bolt, SST, ejectors, high luster finish on hand checkered claro walnut stock (full pistol grip with rosewood cap) and forearm, recoil pad, engraved sideplates with satin nickel finish, vent. barrels and rib, multi-chokes became standard (except .410 bore) 1986 and 1992 (28 ga.), 6½-8 lbs. Introduced 1982.

MSR $2,549	$2,085	$1,525	$1,150	$925	$750	$600	$525

Subtract 10% if without choke tubes.

This model was redesignated the Grade IV in 1989.

✳ ***Skeet & Trap Models*** - 12 (Trap only) or 20 ga., special stock dimensions, target sights. Disc. 1992.

	$1,675	$1,275	$1,000	$875	$725	$600	$525

Last MSR was $1,965.

Skeet models are available in fixed choke only.

✳ ***Single Trap Model*** - 12 ga., 32 or 34 in. barrel with multi-choke feature. Disc. 1992.

	$1,675	$1,275	$1,000	$875	$725	$600	$525

Last MSR was $1,975.

✳ ***Trap Combo*** - 12 ga., includes a set of O/U barrels and oversingle barrel with multi- choke feature. Disc. 1992.

	$2,300	$1,900	$1,605	$1,300	$995	$800	$675

Last MSR was $2,616.

✳ ***Master Skeet Set*** - 12 ga., includes 6 fitted full length Briley tubes with integral extractors (20, 28 ga., and .410 bore), cased. Imported 1988-91.

	$3,100	$2,650	$2,150	$1,900	$1,775	$1,625	$1,525

ATHENA GRADE V CLASSIC FIELD - 12 or 20 ga., 3 in. chambers, similar to Grade IV, except has more elaborate engraving, gold SST, and better walnut. New 1989.

MSR $2,977	$2,465	$1,975	$1,500	$1,225	$950	$775	$675

In 1993, Weatherby changed the styling of this gun to incorporate European shooting features including an oil finished, round knob stock and slim forearm, tight rose-and-scroll engraving, and matted VR.

ORION UPLAND CLASSIC FIELD - 12 or 20 ga., 3 in. chambers, features high luster checkered Claro walnut stock and forearm, blue frame, gold Weatherby flying W on triggerguard, rounded checkered pistol grip stock and slender forearm, 26 or 28 in. VR barrels with choke tubes, 6½ - 8 lbs. New 1999.

MSR $1,274	$1,080	$950	$795	$625	$550	$500	$450

ORION I FIELD - 12 or 20 ga., 3 in. chambers, 26, 28, or 30 (12 ga. only) in. VR barrels with multi-chokes, SST, ejectors, checkered walnut full pistol grip stock and forearm, recoil pad, blue receiver with engraved upland and waterfowl scenes, 6½ - 8 lbs. New 1989.

MSR $1,539	$1,240	$1,040	$860	$675	$575	$525	$475

Grading	100%	98%	95%	90%	80%	70%	60%

✳ Ducks Unlimited Orion - 12 ga. (sponsor gun in 1986) or 20 ga. (sponsor gun in 1987), deluxe walnut with gold duck scenes, blue frame, multi-chokes, includes presentation case.

	$1,395	$1,100	$875				

ORION II FIELD - 12, 20, 28 ga., or .410 bore, 3 in. chambers (except 28 ga.), boxlock with Greener Crossbolt, SST, ejectors, walnut with high-gloss finish, silver nitride receiver with light engraving. Multi- chokes became standard 1986. Field Grade disc. 1993.

	$1,075	$875	$750	$625	$550	$500	$450

Last MSR was $1,207.

Subtract 10% without choke tubes on older models.
Subtract $14 for Skeet grade (12 and 20 ga., fixed chokes only).
This model was redesignated Grade II in 1989. In 1993, the Standard Field Models in this variation were discontinued (Classic Grade took its place) - only Field and Sporting Clays variations are now available.

✳ Orion II Classic Field - 12, 20, or 28 ga., multi-choked barrels, features rounded pistol grip stock and oil finished Claro walnut stock and forearm, waterfowl scene on silver grey nitride finish, matted VR. New 1993.

MSR	$1,590	$1,275	$1,075	$875	$700	$600	$550	$495

ORION II FIELD/CLASSIC SPORTING - 12 ga. only, Sporting Clays configuration, early mfg. was blue finish, current mfg. is silver nitride finish, choice of Field Sporting (with rosewood pistol grip cap and grooved upper forearm) or Classic Field Sporting (rounded pistol grip and smaller forearm), acid etched engraving, rounded recoil pad, matte finish VR, lengthened forcing cones. New 1991.

MSR	$1,753	$1,400	$1,115	$925	$725	$625	$565	$515

SUPER SPORTING CLAYS (SSC) - 12 ga. only, 3 in. chambers, 28, 30, or 32 in. vented barrels with 12mm VR and gas ports, choke tubes, satin oil finished sporter style pistol grip stock with Schnabel forearm, Pachmayr Decelerator pad, approx. 8 lbs. New 1999.

MSR	$2,019	$1,615	$1,325	$1,100	$875	$735	$650	$575

ORION III FIELD - 12 or 20 ga. only, similar to Grade II, except has silver grey receiver with custom engraving including mallard and pheasant game scenes, multi-chokes standard. New 1989.

MSR	$1,917	$1,545	$1,225	$965	$795	$675	$600	$525

✳ Orion III Classic Field - 12 or 20 ga., multi-choked barrels, features rounded pistol grip stock and oil finished Claro walnut stock and forearm, extensive engraving on silver grey nitride finish, matted VR. New 1993.

MSR	$1,917	$1,545	$1,225	$965	$795	$675	$600	$525

✳ Orion III English Field - 12 or 20 ga., 3 in. chambers, features straight grip stock and silver grey nitride receiver with engraving and gold inlays, approx. 6½ lbs. New 1997.

MSR	$1,998	$1,595	$1,300	$1,075	$875	$700	$625	$550

SHOTGUNS: SxS

Current manufacture utilizes the IMC choke system (integral multi-choke), which allows interchangeability with Briley choke tubes.

ORION - 12, 20, 28 ga. or .410 bore, 3 in. chambers standard except for 28 ga., ejectors, case colored boxlock action, gold SST, 18 LPI checkered half-round pistol grip Turkish walnut stock and semi-beavertail forearm, 26 or 28 in. barrels, solid pad, 6¾ - 7 lbs., mfg. in Spain. New 2002.

MSR	$1,099		$925	$825	$725	$625	$525	$450	$395

ATHENA - 12 or 20 ga. 3 in. chambers, ejectors, case colored engraved boxlock action with side-plates, gold SST, 22 LPI checkered straight grip select Turkish walnut stock and splinter fore-arm, 26 or 28 in. barrels with IMC choke system (interchangeable with Briley), solid pad, 6¾ - 7 lbs., mfg. in Spain. New 2002.

	MSR $1,549		$1,250	$1,000	$850	$750	$650	$550	$475

SHOTGUNS: SEMI-AUTO

Current manufacture utilizes the IMC choke system (integral multi-choke), which allows inter-changeability with Briley choke tubes.

CENTURION FIELD GRADE - 12 ga., VR, checkered stock, gas operation, walnut full pistol grip stock. Mfg. 1972-1981.

		$300	$280	$250	$240	$230	$210	$190

CENTURION TRAP GRADE - 12 ga., checkered stock, VR.

		$335	$300	$250	$240	$230	$210	$190

CENTURION DE LUXE - 12 ga., VR, checkered stock, lightly engraved.

	$375	$350	$310	$275	$250	$235	$210

> Add 20% for deluxe wood.

* **Centurion DU** - mfg. 1980 for DU chapters.

	$550	$375	$325

MODEL 82 - 12 ga. only, 2¾ or 3 in. chamber, gas operation, alloy receiver, VR, deluxe walnut, multi-chokes became standard in 1985, Trap Grade was disc. 1984. Mfg. 1983- 89.

	$395	$350	$315	$280	$250	$235	$210

Last MSR was $500.

> Subtract $30 without multi-chokes.
> Subtract $35 for Trap Grade (disc. 1984).

* **Model 82 Buckmaster** - 22 in. barrel choked skeet, rifle sights, 7½ lbs. Disc. 1989.

	$395	$350	$315	$280	$250	$235	$210

Last MSR was $500.

SAS FIELD - 12 or 20 (disc. 2000) ga., 3 in. chamber, self compensating gas operated mecha-nism, high grade satin oil finished checkered Claro walnut stock and forearm, includes stock shim system, 26, 28 (disc. 2001), or 30 (12 ga. only. disc. 2001) in. VR barrel with Briley choke tubes, 6¾ - 7¾ lbs., mfg. in Italy. New 1999.

	MSR $799		$675	$550	$495	$450	$400	$350	$300

* **Model SAS Sporting Clays** - similar to SAS Field, except has choice of 26 or 28 in. ported VR barrel, includes molded plastic case. New 2002.

	MSR $899		$750	$600	$550	$500	$425	$375	$325

* **Model SAS Synthetic** - similar to Model SAS, except has black synthetic stock and forearm. New late 2000.

	MSR $749		$625	$495	$450	$400	$375	$350	$325

* **Model SAS Shadow Grass/Mossy Oak Breakup** - 12 ga. only, 24 (Mossy Oak Breakup only, new 2001) 26, or 28 (Shadow Grass only) in. VR barrel with 5 Briley choke tubes, 100% camo coverage, 7¼ - 7¾ lbs. New late 2000.

	MSR $849		$725	$600	$550	$495	$450	$375	$335

SHOTGUNS: SLIDE ACTION

PATRICIAN FIELD GRADE - 12 ga., checkered stock, VR. Mfg. 1972-1981.

	$275	$230	$210	$190	$180	$160	$140

PATRICIAN TRAP GRADE - 12 ga., checkered stock, VR.

	$295	$250	$225	$200	$185	$175	$165

Grading	100%	98%	95%	90%	80%	70%	60%

PATRICIAN DE LUXE - 12 ga., checkered stock, lightly engraved, fancy wood, VR.

| | $325 | $275 | $250 | $215 | $195 | $175 | $165 |

MODEL 92 - 12 ga. only, 2¾ and 3 in. chambers, ultra-short slide action w/twin rails, 26-30 in. VR barrels, engraved black alloy receiver, checkered pistol grip walnut stock and forearm. New 1983. Subtract $30 for Trap grade (disc. 1984), $20 if fixed choke (multi-chokes became standard 1985) barrel. Disc. 1987.

| | $325 | $275 | $250 | $225 | $200 | $185 | $175 |

Last MSR was $400.

* ✳ *Model 92 Buckmaster* - 22 in. skeet bore barrel, rifle sights, 7½ lbs. Disc. 1987.

| | $345 | $285 | $260 | $240 | $220 | $200 | $185 |

Last MSR was $400.

WEAVER ARMS CORPORATION
Previous manufacturer located in Escondido, CA circa 1984-1990.

CARBINES

NIGHTHAWK CARBINE - 9mm Para. cal., closed bolt semi-auto paramilitary design carbine, fires from closed bolt, 16.1 in. barrel, retractable shoulder stock, 25, 32, 40, or 50 shot mag. (interchangeable with Uzi), ambidextrous safety, parkerized finish, 6½ lbs. Mfg. 1987-1990.

| | $525 | $450 | $375 | $325 | $300 | $275 | $250 |

Last MSR was $575.

PISTOLS: SEMI-AUTO

NIGHTHAWK PISTOL - 9mm Para. cal., closed bolt semi-auto, 10 or 12 in. barrel, alloy upper receiver, ambidextrous safety, black finish, 5 lbs. Mfg. 1987-1990.

| | $650 | $575 | $500 | $450 | $400 | $360 | $330 |

Last MSR was $475.

WEBLEY & SCOTT, LIMITED
Previous firearms manufacturer located in Birmingham, England circa 1898 to 1979. Beginning 1980, Webley & Scott, Ltd. began manufacturing high quality weapons only. Currently, Webley & Scott manufactures airguns only.

Webley & Scott, Ltd. had the shotgun business re-established as a separate company named W & C Scott (Gunmakers) Ltd. in 1979. Shortly after being acquired by Holland & Holland, firearms manufacture was discontinued while airgun production resumed.

For more information and current pricing on both new and used Webley & Scott airguns, please refer to the *Blue Book of Modern Airguns* by Dr. Robert Beeman & John Allen (now online also).

PISTOLS: SEMI-AUTO & SINGLE SHOT

HAMMER MODEL .25 - .25 ACP cal., 6 shot mag., 2 in. barrel, no sights, blue, composition grips. Mfg. 1906-1940.

| | $325 | $250 | $175 | $150 | $135 | $125 | $115 |

HAMMERLESS MODEL .25 - .25 ACP cal., similar to Hammer Model .25, except rare, no exposed hammer and fixed sights. Mfg. 1909-1940.

| | $375 | $225 | $175 | $150 | $135 | $125 | $115 |

SINGLE SHOT TARGET PISTOL - .22 LR, .32 (special order), or .38 (special order) cal., 10 in. barrel, top break, blue, fixed sights on early models. Mfg. 1909-1964.

| | $375 | $250 | $120 | $110 | $100 | $90 | $75 |

Grading	100%	98%	95%	90%	80%	70%	60%

METROPOLITAN POLICE AUTOMATIC - .32 ACP or .380 ACP cal., 7 or 8 shot, 3½ in. barrel, blue, fixed sights, composition grips. Mfg. 1906-1940.

	$450	$300	$165	$120	$110	$100	$85

SEMI-AUTO SINGLE SHOT - .22 Long cal., 4¼ and 9 in. barrel, adj. sights, blue, composition grips, empty case is ejected and hammer cocked as in a semi-auto, then it is loaded singly and slide closed. Mfg. 1911-1927.

	$950	$750	$650	$600	$550	$475	$400

9MM M&P AUTOMATIC - 9mm Browning Long, 8 shot, 5 in. barrel, blue, fixed sights. Mfg. 1909-1930.

	$950	$850	$750	$650	$550	$475	$400

HAMMERLESS MODEL 1913 - .38 cal., high velocity, two variations, fewer than 1,000 mfg.

	$2,200	$1,700	$1,200	$800	$700	$600	$500

MARK I .455 AUTO PISTOL - .455 Webley cal., 7 shot, 5 in. barrel, blue, fixed sights. Mfg. 1912-1945.

	$1,750	$1,300	$1,000	$750	$600	$500	$400

MARK I NO. 2 - similar to Mark I, except adj. sights, modified safety, and cut for shoulder stock.

	$5,000	$4,000	$3,000	$2,500	$2,000	$1,500	$1,000

The shoulder stock is an extremely rare accessory for this variation.

REVOLVERS

MARK III M&P - .32 S&W, .320 S&W, or .38 S&W cal., single/double action, 6 shot, 3 in. and 4 in. barrel, hinged top break, blue, fixed sights, wood service or competition grips. Mfg. 1896-1939.

	$350	$295	$255	$220	$195	$165	$140

Some Mark III revolvers were fitted with a manual safety.

✳ ***Mark III Target Model*** - .38 S&W cal., similar to Mark III M&P, except was also available with 6 - 10 in. barrel with adj. sights.

	$450	$375	$325	$275	$250	$225	$200

MARK IV M&P - similar to Mark III, except 3 in., 4 in., or 5 in. barrel, improved hammer and grip design. Mfg. 1929-1979.

	$350	$295	$255	$220	$195	$165	$140

This was the last of the Webley series of revolvers.

MARK IV .22 TARGET - similar to Mark IV, except .22 LR cal., 6 in. barrel, target sights, mfg. 1931-1967.

	$675	$550	$475	$375	$275	$200	$175

MARK IV SERVICE - .455 Webley cal., single/double action, 4 or 6 in. barrel, top break, blue, fixed sights, known as the Boer War Model and is not to be confused with the smaller, later Mark IV introduced in 1929. Mfg. 1899-1914.

	$550	$400	$325	$275	$225	$175	$150

NO. 1 MARK VI BRITISH SERVICE - .45 LC, .45 ACP, or .455 Webley cal., single/ double action, 4, 6, or 7½ in. barrel, top break, blue, fixed sights, wood service or competition grips. Mfg. 1914-1939.

	$300	$250	$225	$195	$165	$135	$110

MARK VI .22 TARGET - similar to Mark VI, except .22 LR cal., target sights, mfg. until 1945.

	$450	$375	$300	$250	$200	$165	$135

Bayonet and shoulder stock attachments were also available for this model. These accessories are rare and command considerable premiums over values listed.

Grading	100%	98%	95%	90%	80%	70%	60%

MARK V - .455 cal., single/double action. Many were military-modified for .45 Colt or .45 ACP, many were civilian-modified, round butt, top break. Mfg. 1914-1915 only.

	$375	$325	$275	$225	$175	$150	$125

BULLDOG OR RIC MODEL - available in .320 - .476 cals. (.455 Webley most common), 5 shot, 2 1/8 - 4½ in. barrel, solid frame, blue, fixed sights. Mfg. 1867-1939 for Royal Irish Constabulary.

	$295	$250	$225	$175	$140	$110	$90

WEBLEY-FOSBERY AUTOMATIC REVOLVER - .455 Webley cal., 6 shot, top break, recoil revolves cylinder and cocks hammer, walnut or hard rubber grips. Mfg. 1901- 1939.

Add $1,000 for .38 cal.

A small number of Webley-Fosbery pistols were chambered for .38 Colt Auto Cartridge, usually found in 13xx range, features 8 shot cylinder.

✳ *1901 Model* - large frame, early features.

	$6,000	$5,500	$4,800	$4,250	$3,500	$3,000	$2,500

Add 20% for Target Model (adj. rear sight).

✳ *1902 Model* - large frame, late features.

	$5,500	$4,000	$3,000	$2,500	$2,000	$1,500	$1,300

Add 20% for Target Model (adj. rear sight).

✳ *1904 Model* - small frame, late features.

	$5,500	$4,000	$3,000	$2,500	$2,000	$1,500	$1,300

Add 100% for .38 cal.
Add 20% for Target Model (adj. rear sight).

SHOTGUNS: SxS

MODEL 700 - 12 or 20 ga., boxlock, case hardened receiver, minimum engraving, single trigger. Mfg. 1949-1980.

	$1,700	$1,625	$1,500	$1,250	$1,000	$750	$600

Subtract $50 for double trigger.

MODEL 701 - similar to Model 700 but fanciest walnut, most engraving. Mfg. 1949- 1980.

	$3,150	$2,500	$2,100	$1,800	$1,400	$1,150	$925

Subtract $100 for double trigger.

MODEL 702 - similar to Model 700 but middle grade. Mfg. 1949-1980.

	$2,650	$2,200	$1,800	$1,500	$1,250	$950	$750

Subtract $75 for double trigger.

MODEL 712 - 12 ga., specifically designed for the American market.

	$1,700	$1,625	$1,500	$1,250	$1,000	$750	$600

MODEL 720 - 20 ga.

	$2,325	$1,875	$1,750	$1,650	$1,375	$1,100	$825

MODEL 728 - same action as the Model 700, except is 28 ga. and designed specifically for the American market, only 40 were mfg. 1966-1968.

	$3,000	$2,600	$2,175	$1,850	$1,650	$1,375	$1,150

WEIHRAUCH, HANS-HERMANN

Current manufacturer located in Mellrichstadt, Germany. Exclusive factory authorized U.S. distributor is European American Armory, located in Sharpes, FL.

Weihrauch also manufactures a compete line of single and double action revolvers, including target models. To date, they have had little importation into the U.S.

For more information and current pricing on both new and used Weihrauch airguns, please refer to the *Blue Book of Modern Airguns* by Dr. Robert Beeman & John Allen (now online also).

Grading	100%	98%	95%	90%	80%	70%	60%

REVOLVERS: ARMINIUS

Currently manufactured Arminius revolvers are not individually listed, since they are not currently imported into the U.S. There are however, many models, including combat, sport, and target variations. Calibers include .22 LR. .22 Mag., .32 S&W Wadcutter, .357 Mag., and .38 Spl. Please refer to Arminius listing for older models, or contact the company directly regarding U.S. availability and pricing (see Trademark Index).

RIFLES: BOLT ACTION

MODEL HW 60 TARGET - .22 LR cal., target rifle featuring adj. sights, 26¾ in. barrel, single shot, match walnut stock, and other match features, aperture sights, 10.8 lbs. Importation disc. 1995.

	$625	$550	$450	$395	$350	$295	$275

Last MSR was $705.

Add $220 for left-hand action (disc.).

MODEL HW 60J - .22 LR or .222 Rem. cal., sporter model with checkered walnut stock. Importation disc. 1992.

	$525	$465	$435	$395	$345	$300	$260

Last MSR was $585.

Add $304 for .222 Rem. cal.

MODEL HW 66 RIFLE - .22 Hornet or .222 Rem. cal., match grade bolt action rifle. Imported 1989-90 only.

	$575	$495	$395	$325	$285	$250	$215

Last MSR was $688.

Add $78 for double set triggers.
Add $55 for stainless steel barrel (.22 Hornet).

MODEL HW 660 MATCH - .22 LR cal., match rifle variation featuring adj. stock comb with vent. forend, with or w/o aperture sights, 10.8 lbs. Importation began 1991.

MSR	$999	$850	$725	$600	$500	$400	$350	$300

Add $160 for laminate stock (new 1998).
Subtract $160 if w/o Anschütz aperture sights.

WELLS

Current custom rifle manufacturer located in Prescott, AZ. Consumer direct sales.

RIFLES: BOLT ACTION

Fred Wells manufactures a custom rifle based on a Mauser double square bridge action, using the finest materials available. Action prices start at $5,500, and stocks are priced from $5,500 on up. Please contact the company directly for more information regarding complete rifle model and pricing (see Trademark Index).

WERNER BARTOLOT

Current custom gun manufacturer located in Hermagor, Austria. Direct sales only.

Werner Bartolot manufactures very high quality SxS and O/U double rifles, drillings, and single shot rifles. Please contact the company for more information, including availability and an individual price quotation (see Trademark Index).

WESSON, FRANK

Previous manufacturer located in Worcester, MA 1854 to 1865, and Springfield, MA circa 1865-1875.

100%	98%	95%	90%	80%	70%	60%	50%	40%	30%	20%	10%

PISTOLS: SINGLE SHOT

SMALL FRAME FIRST MODEL - .22 cal., tip up action, 3½ in. ½ octagon barrel, brass frame, spur trigger, rosewood grips, round frame, irregular sideplate. Mfg. 2500, 1859-1862.

$605	$550	$495	$440	$385	$330	$275	$220	$195	$165	$140	$110

SMALL FRAME SECOND MODEL - similar to First Model, with flat sided frame and circular sideplate. Mfg. 12,000, 1862-1880.

$550	$495	$440	$385	$330	$305	$250	$195	$165	$110	$105	$85

MEDIUM FRAME FIRST MODEL - .30 S or L, .32 S rimfire cal., 4 in. ½ octagon barrel, iron frame, same as Small Frame in other respects, narrow hinge and short trigger. Mfg. 1000, 1859-1862.

$525	$470	$415	$360	$305	$275	$220	$195	$165	$110	$105	$85

MEDIUM FRAME SECOND MODEL - similar to First Model Medium Frame, with wider hinge and longer trigger. Mfg. 1000, 1862-1870.

$495	$440	$385	$330	$275	$250	$220	$195	$165	$110	$105	$85

RIFLES: SINGLE SHOT

NO. 1 LONG RANGE - .44-100 and .45-100 standard cal., side hammer, falling block lever actuated, 34 in. octagon barrel, tang. sight, select checkered pistol grip stock. Less than 50 mfg., circa 1870-1880.

$4,950	$4,675	$4,400	$3,850	$3,575	$3,080	$2,860	$2,475	$2,200	$2,035	$1,760	$1,540

NO. 2 HUNTING RIFLE - similar to No. 1, with finger loop lever. Less than 100 mfg.

$4,400	$4,180	$3,850	$3,520	$3,025	$2,750	$2,420	$2,255	$2,035	$1,925	$1,760	$1,540

NO. 1 SPORTING RIFLE - .38-100, .40-100, .45-100 standard cal., similar to No. 2, with center hammer, Less than 25 mfg.

$4,400	$4,180	$3,850	$3,520	$3,025	$2,750	$2,420	$2,255	$2,035	$1,925	$1,760	$1,540

RIFLES: SINGLE SHOT, TIP UP

SMALL FRAME TIP UP - .22 Rimfire cal., 6 in. ½ octagon barrel, brass frame, spur trigger, rosewood grips. Approx. 500 mfg., 1865-1875.

$605	$550	$525	$495	$470	$440	$415	$360	$330	$275	$220	$165

If without stock - subtract 25%.

MEDIUM FRAME TIP UP - .22, .30, or .32 rimfire cals, 10 or 12 in. barrel, same as small frame, with exceptions noted and larger frame. Approx. 1,000 mfg., 1862-1870.

$605	$550	$525	$495	$470	$440	$415	$360	$330	$275	$220	$165

If without stock - subtract 25%.

MODEL 1870 SMALL FRAME FIRST TYPE - similar to Small Frame Tip Up, except barrel rotates on its axis to load, detachable stock. Approx. 3,000 mfg., 1870-1890.

$550	$495	$470	$440	$415	$385	$360	$305	$275	$220	$195	$165

If without stock - subtract 25%.

MODEL 1870 SMALL FRAME SECOND TYPE - full octagon barrel.

$525	$470	$440	$415	$385	$360	$330	$275	$250	$195	$165	$140

MODEL 1870 SMALL FRAME THIRD TYPE - iron frame, push button ½ cock.

$495	$440	$415	$385	$360	$330	$305	$250	$220	$165	$140	$110

MODEL 1870 MEDIUM FRAME FIRST TYPE - similar to Small Frame, except in size and availability of .32 cal. Approx. 5,000 mfg., 1870-1893.

$525	$495	$470	$440	$415	$385	$360	$305	$275	$250	$195	$165

Subtract 25% if without stock.

100%	98%	95%	90%	80%	70%	60%	50%	40%	30%	20%	10%

MODEL 1870 MEDIUM FRAME SECOND TYPE - external push-button half cock and iron frame.

$440	$415	$385	$330	$305	$275	$220	$195	$165	$140	$110	$90

Subtract 25% if without stock.

MODEL 1870 MEDIUM FRAME THIRD TYPE - has three screws in frame, iron frame.

$440	$415	$385	$330	$305	$275	$220	$195	$165	$140	$110	$90

Subtract 25% if without stock.

MODEL 1870 LARGE FRAME FIRST TYPE - .32, .38, .42, or .44 rimfire cal., 15-24 in. barrels, similar to smaller frame models, auto extractor. Approx. 500 mfg., 1870- 1880.

$825	$770	$715	$660	$605	$550	$525	$495	$440	$385	$305	$275

Subtract 25% if without stock.

MODEL 1870 LARGE FRAME SECOND TYPE - similar to First Type, with standard sliding extractor.

$825	$770	$715	$660	$605	$550	$525	$495	$440	$385	$305	$275

Subtract 25% if without stock.

WESSON & HARRINGTON

Previous trademark of special/limited editions manufactured by H&R 1871, LLC 1995-2001. During 2000, Marlin Firearms Co. purchased the assets of H&R 1871, Inc., and the name was changed to H&R 1871, LLC. Production of Wesson & Harrington products was at the factory located in Gardner, MA.

RIFLES: SINGLE SHOT

Please refer to the H & R 1871 section for earlier Wesson & Harrington Buffalo Classic & Target Models.

Grading	100%	98%	95%	90%	80%	70%	60%

SHOTGUNS: SINGLE SHOT

WESSON & HARRINGTON NWTF LONG TOM CLASSIC - 12 ga., top lever break open action, 32 in. FC barrel, case hardened frame, checkered straight grip walnut stock and forearm, 7½ lbs. Mfg. 1995-2001.

	$300	$240	$195

Last MSR was $350.

DAN WESSON FIREARMS

Currently manufactured by New York International Corp. (NYI) located in Norwich, NY beginning 1997. Distributor and dealer sales.

Please contact the factory directly for more information, including model availability and current pricing.

PISTOLS: SEMI-AUTO

Dan Wesson currently manufactures a complete line of .45 ACP 1911 style semi-auto pistols. The Pointman Series (full length and Commander size) includes Models Minor (MSR $599), Major (MSR $799), Major Aussie (new 2002, MSR $TBA), Seven (disc., last MSR was $999), Seven Stainless (disc., last MSR was $1,099), Guardian (MSR $799), the Guardian Deuce (MSR $799)., and the Patriot Series (MSR $879-$1,295). The Dave Pruit Signature Series is $899, and the Hi-Cap is $689.

REVOLVERS: DOUBLE ACTION

Dan Wesson currently has a variety of revolver packages available. They include the small frame

Grading	100%	98%	95%	90%	80%	70%	60%

models (blue or stainless) in .22 LR, .22 Mag., .32 H&R Mag., .32-20 WCF, and .357 Mag. 2½, 4, 6, 8, or a 10 in. barrel is available. The base price is $599 (2½ in. barrel, blue or stainless). Barrel lengths over 2½ in. are extra cost, typically priced at approx. $30-$40 for each additional barrel length after 2½ in. Large frame calibers include .357 Mag++, .360 DW, .41 Mag., .44 Mag., .45 LC, .45 ACP - these are available in either blue or stainless. Base prices start at $769 (blue or stainless). A Super Mag. model is also available in .357 Super, .414 Super, and .445 Super - base price is $929 (blue or stainless). Compensated models are also available in small frame, large frame, and Super Mag. - prices range from $674-$1,149. Complete pistol packages (including all interchangeable barrels within a model) are priced at $1,369 (.22 LR cal.) to $1,999 (.455 Super Mag.). The Alaskan Guide Series was released in 2002 - MSR is $TBA. The hunter package (two 8 in. interchangeable barrel assemblies, one with scope base) is priced at $1,349 (.22 LR cal.) to $1,849 (.455 Super Mag.). Standard and Super Ram Silhouette packages are also available – Standard Silhouette is $899, and the Super Ram is $1,109-$1,399. Interchangeable barrels assemblies vary in price from $87 to $400, depending on caliber and barrel length. As in the past, many barrel assembly configurations are optional. Please contact the company directly for current model information and pricing.

RIFLES: BOLT ACTION

COYOTE CLASSIC - .22 LR or .22 Mag. cal., 22 3/4 in. tapered barrel, 6 or 10 shot mag., checkered hardwood stock and forend, adj. rear sight. New 2002.

	MSR	$239	$200	$180	$160	$145	$130	$115	$100

COYOTE TARGET - .22 LR or .22 Mag. cal., 18 3/8 in. heavy bull barrel, 6 or 10 shot mag., uncheckered target hardwood stock with high cheekpiece, w/o sights. New 2002.

	MSR	$279	$230	$200	$175	$155	$145	$135	$125

WESSON FIREARMS CO. INC.

Previous manufacturer located in Palmer, MA until 1995. In late 1990, ownership of Dan Wesson Arms changed (within the family), and the new company was renamed Wesson Firearms Co., Inc.

REVOLVERS: DOUBLE ACTION

As a guideline, the following information is provided on Wesson Firearms frames. The smallest frames are Models 738P and 38P. Small frame models include 22, 722, 22M, 722M, 32, 732, 322, 7322, 8-2, 708, 9-2, 709, 14-2, 714, 15-2, and 715-2. Large frames include 41, 741, 44, 744, 45, and 745. SuperMag frame models include 40, 740, 375 (disc.), 414 (new 1995), 7414 (new 1995), 445, and 7445. Small frames are sideplate design, while large frames are solid frame construction.

Dan Wesson revolvers were mfg. with solid rib barrels as standard equipment.

MODEL 11 - .357 Mag. cal., 6 shot, 2 ½, 4, or 6 in. interchangeable barrels, fixed sights, blue, interchangeable grips, exposed barrel nut. Mfg. 1970-1971.

		$200	$175	$160	$150	$140	$130	$120

Add $60 per extra barrel.

MODEL 12 - similar to Model 11, with adj. sights. Mfg. 1970-1971.

	$245	$200	$175	$160	$150	$140	$130

MODEL 14 - similar to Model 11, with recessed barrel nut. Mfg. 1971-1975.

	$225	$185	$170	$160	$150	$140	$130

MODEL 8 - similar to Model 14, except .38 Spl. cal.

	$200	$170	$155	$145	$135	$125	$115

MODEL 15 - similar to Model 14, with adj. sights. Mfg. 1971-1975.

	$245	$200	$155	$145	$135	$125	$115

MODEL 9 - similar to Model 15, except .38 Spl. cal. Mfg. 1971-1975.

	$245	$200	$155	$145	$135	$125	$115

Grading	100%	98%	95%	90%	80%	70%	60%

MODEL 22 - .22 LR cal., double action, 6 shot, adj. sights, 2 ½, 4, 6, 8, or 10 in. (disc. 1987) barrel, disc. 1995.

	$285	$225	$200	$190	$180	$170	$160

Last MSR was $357.

Add approx. $9 for each additional barrel length, $21 for VR, $57 for vent. heavy rib shroud.

✳ *Model 22 Pistol Pac* - includes 2 ½, 4, 6, and 8 in. barrel assemblies, extra grip, 4 additional front sight blades, and aluminum case. Disc. 1995.

	$520	$400	$360	$330	$300	$275	$260

Last MSR was $653.

Add $103 for full shroud VR barrels.
Add $227 for heavy full shroud VR barrels.

✳ *Model 22 Silhouette* - .22 LR cal., choice of 10 in. vent. or heavy vent. barrel, single action only, combat style grip, narrow rear sight blade and patridge front. Mfg. 1992-95.

	$395	$325	$295	$275	$260	$245	$230

Last MSR was $474.

Add $18 for vent. heavy barrel.

MODEL 22M - .22 Mag. cal., otherwise similar to Model 22. Disc. 1994.

	$290	$230	$200	$190	$180	$170	$160

Last MSR was $349.

✳ *Model 22M Pistol Pac* - includes 2½, 4, 6, and 8 in. barrel assemblies, extra grip, 4 additional front sight blades, and aluminum case. Disc. 1994.

	$500	$400	$360	$330	$300	$275	$260

Last MSR was $637.

Add $101 for full shroud VR barrels.
Add $191 for heavy full shroud VR barrels.

MODEL 32 - .32 H&R Mag. cal., 2 ½, 4, 6, or 8 in. barrel, adj. rear sight, interchangeable colored front sight blades, blue finish, checkered target grips. Mfg. 1986-95.

	$285	$225	$200	$190	$180	$170	$160

Last MSR was $357.

Add $21 for VR barrel shroud (Model 32-V), $57 for VR heavy barrel shroud (Model 32-VH), approx. $9 for each additional barrel length over 2 ½ in.

✳ *Model 32 Pistol Pac* - includes 2 ½, 4, 6, and 8 in. barrel assemblies, extra grip, 4 additional front sight blades, and aluminum case. Disc. 1995.

	$520	$400	$360	$330	$300	$275	$260

Last MSR was $653.

Add $103 for full shroud VR barrels.
Add $227 for heavy full shroud VR barrels.

MODEL 38P - .38+P cal., 5 shot, 6 ½ in. barrel, fixed sights, wood or rubber grips, 24.6 oz. Mfg. 1992-93.

	$230	$190	$170	$150	$135	$120	$110

Last MSR was $285.

MODEL 322 - .32-20 WCF cal., 2 ½, 4, 6, or 8 in. barrel, adj. rear sight, interchangeable colored front sight blades, blue finish, checkered target grips. Mfg. 1991-95.

	$285	$225	$200	$190	$180	$170	$160

Last MSR was $357.

Add $21 for VR barrel shroud (Model 322-V), $57 for VR heavy barrel shroud (Model 322-VH), approx. $9-$30 for each additional barrel length over 2 ½ in.

Grading	100%	98%	95%	90%	80%	70%	60%

✴ **Model 322 Pistol Pac** - includes 2 ½, 4, 6, and 8 in. barrel assemblies, extra grip, 4 additional front sight blades, and aluminum case. Disc. 1995.

	$520	$400	$360	$330	$300	$275	$260

Last MSR was $653.

Add $103 for full shroud VR barrels.
Add $227 for heavy full shroud VR barrels.

MODEL 14 - .357 Mag. cal., 2 ½, 4, 6, or 8 (disc. 1994) in. interchangeable barrels, fixed sights, blue. Mfg. 1975-1995.

	$215	$170	$150	$140	$130	$120	$110

Last MSR was $274.

Add approx. $7 for each additional barrel length.

✴ **Model 14 Fixed Barrel** - .357 Mag. cal., 2 ½ or 4 in. (fixed sight Service Model) barrel, satin blue finish. Mfg. 1993-95.

	$225	$175	$150	$140	$130	$120	$110

Last MSR was $289.

Add $7 for 4 in. barrel.

✴ **Model 14 PPC** - .357 Mag. cal., extra heavy 6 in. bull shroud barrel with removable underweight, Hogue Gripper grips, Aristocrat sights. Mfg. 1992 only.

	$675	$550	$450	$375	$330	$300	$275

Last MSR was $780.

✴ **Model 14 Pistol Pac** - includes 2½, 4, and 6 in. barrel assemblies, extra grip and aluminum case. Disc. 1994.

	$390	$325	$300	$275	$260	$245	$230

Last MSR was $463.

MODEL 8 - similar to Model 14, except .38 Spl. cal. Disc. 1995.

	$220	$170	$150	$140	$130	$120	$110

Last MSR was $274.

Add approx. $6 for each additional barrel length.

✴ **Model 8 PPC** - .38 Spl. cal., extra heavy 6 in. bull shroud barrel with removable underweight, Hogue Gripper grips, Aristocrat sights. Mfg. 1992 only.

	$675	$550	$450	$375	$330	$300	$275

Last MSR was $780.

MODEL 15 - similar to Model 14, except adj. sights, available with 2, 4, 6, 8, 10, 12, or 15 in. barrels. Disc. 1995.

✴ **2 in. barrel**

	$285	$225	$200	$190	$180	$170	$160

Last MSR was $346.

Add approx. $8-$13 for each additional barrel length over 2 inches, $22 for VR barrel (Model 15V), or $60 for VR heavy barrel shroud (Model 15HV).

✴ **Model 15 Target Fixed Barrel** - .357 Mag. cal., 3, 4, 5, or 6 in. barrel, high bright blue finish. Mfg. 1993-95.

	$270	$220	$190	$175	$150	$125	$110

Last MSR was $322.

Add approx. $9 for each barrel length over 3 in.
Add approx. $80 for compensated barrel (4, 5, or 6 in. - new 1994).

MODEL 15 GOLD SERIES - .357 Mag. cal., 6 or 8 in. VR heavy slotted barrel, "Gold" stamped shroud with Dan Wesson signature, smoother action (8 lb. double action pull), 18 kt. gold-plated trigger, white triangle rear sight with orange dot partridge front sight, exotic hardwood grips. Mfg. 1989-94.

	$425	$380	$340	$300	$260	$225	$185

Last MSR was $544.

Grading	100%	98%	95%	90%	80%	70%	60%

✴ ***Model 15 Pistol Pac*** - includes 2½, 4, 6, and 8 in. barrel assemblies, extra grip, 4 additional front sight blades, and aluminum case. Disc. 1995.

| | $500 | $395 | $360 | $330 | $300 | $275 | $260 |

Last MSR was $629.

Add $104 for full shroud VR barrels.
Add $214 for heavy full shroud VR barrels.

MODEL 9 - similar to Model 15, except .38 Spl. cal. Use same add-ons as in Model 15. Disc. 1995.

| | $346 | $285 | $225 | $200 | $190 | $180 | $170 |

Last MSR was $346.

This model was also available in a Pistol Pac - same specifications and values as the Model 15 Pistol Pac.

MODEL 375 SUPERMAG - .375 Super Mag. cal., 4, 6, 8, or 10 in. VR barrel, adj. rear sight, interchangeable front and rear sight blades, bright blue finish, smooth target grips. Mfg. 1986-94.

| | $410 | $335 | $285 | $260 | $240 | $230 | $225 |

Last MSR was $498.

Add approx. $15 for each barrel length after 6 in., $39 for slotted shroud (Model 375-V8S, 8 in. barrel only), $10-$12 for VR heavy shroud (Model 375-VH).

MODEL 40 (.357 SUPERMAG) - .357 Super Mag. cal. (.357 Max.), double action, 6 shot, 4, 6, 8, or 10 in. barrel VR. Disc. 1995.

| | $410 | $340 | $285 | $260 | $240 | $230 | $225 |

Last MSR was $502.

Add $87 for slotted barrel shroud (8 in. barrel only), $22-$129 for heavy VR barrel, approx. $33 for each additional barrel length.

MODEL 41 - .41 Mag. cal., double action, 6 shot, 4, 6, 8, or 10 in. barrel VR. Disc. 1995.

| | $375 | $305 | $265 | $250 | $230 | $215 | $200 |

Last MSR was $447.

Add approx. $20 for heavy barrel shroud, approx. $15 for each additional barrel length.

✴ ***Model 41 Pistol Pac*** - includes 6 and 8 in. VR barrel assemblies, extra grip, 2 additional front sight blades, and aluminum case. Disc. 1995.

| | $555 | $430 | $380 | $330 | $300 | $275 | $260 |

Last MSR was $678.

Add $53 for full shroud VR barrels.

MODEL .414 SUPERMAG - .414 Super Mag. cal., 4, 6, 8, or 10 in. VR barrel, adj. rear sight, interchangeable front and rear sight blades (optional), bright blue finish, smooth target grips. Mfg. 1995 only.

| | $425 | $335 | $290 | $275 | $250 | $230 | $225 |

Last MSR was $519.

Add approx. $14 for each barrel length after 4 in., $58 for slotted shroud (Model 414-V8S, 8 in. barrel only), approx. $23 for VR heavy rib shroud.

MODEL 44 - .44 Mag. cal., double action, similar to Model 41, adj. sights. Disc. 1995.

| | $375 | $305 | $265 | $250 | $230 | $215 | $200 |

Last MSR was $447.

Add approx. $20 for heavy barrel shroud, approx. $15 for each additional barrel length.

✴ ***Model 44 Target Fixed Barrel*** - .44 Mag. cal., 4, 5, 6, or 8 in. barrel, high bright blue finish. Mfg. 1994-95.

| | $375 | $305 | $265 | $250 | $230 | $215 | $200 |

Last MSR was $447.

Add approx. $4 for each barrel length over 3 in.

✴ ***Model 44 Pistol Pac*** - includes 6 and 8 in. VR barrel assemblies, extra grip, 4 additional front sight blades, and aluminum case. Disc. 1995.

| | $555 | $430 | $380 | $330 | $300 | $275 | $260 |

Last MSR was $678.

Add $53 for full shroud VR barrels.

Grading	100%	98%	95%	90%	80%	70%	60%

MODEL 45 - .45 LC cal., 4, 6, 8, or 10 in. VR barrel, same frame as Model 44V, blue finish. Mfg. 1988-95.

| | $375 | $305 | $265 | $250 | $230 | $215 | $200 |

Last MSR was $447.

Add $20 for VR heavy barrel shroud, approx. $15 for each additional barrel length.

⁕ *Model 45 Pistol Pac* - includes 6 and 8 in. VR barrel assemblies, extra grip, 2 additional front sight blades, and aluminum case. Disc. 1995.

| | $555 | $430 | $380 | $330 | $300 | $275 | $260 |

Last MSR was $678.

Add $53 for full shroud VR barrels.

MODEL .45 PIN GUN - .45 ACP cal., competition pin gun model with 5 in. vent. or heavy vent barrel configuration, blue steel, two stage Taylor forcing cone, 54 oz. Mfg. 1993-95.

| | $575 | $495 | $440 | $395 | $350 | $300 | $250 |

Last MSR was $654.

Add $9 for VR heavy shroud barrel.

MODEL .445 SUPERMAG - .445 Super Mag. cal., 4, 6, 8, or 10 in. VR barrel, adj. rear sight, interchangeable front and rear sight blades (optional), bright blue finish, smooth target grips. Mfg. 1991-95.

| | $425 | $335 | $290 | $275 | $250 | $230 | $225 |

Last MSR was $519.

Add approx. $14 for each barrel length after 4 in., $58 for slotted shroud (Model 445-V8S, 8 in. barrel only), approx. $23 for VR heavy rib shroud.

HUNTER SERIES - .357 Super Mag., .41 Mag., .44 Mag., or .445 Super Mag. cal., 7 ½ in. barrel with heavy shroud, Hogue rubber finger grooved and wood presentation grips, choice of Gunworks iron sights or w/o sights with Burris base and rings, non-fluted cylinder, with or w/o compensator, approx. 4 lbs. Mfg. 1994-95.

| | $750 | $575 | $475 | $400 | $360 | $330 | $300 |

Last MSR was $805.

Add $32 for compensated barrel.
Add $33 for scope mounts (w/o sights).

REVOLVERS: STAINLESS STEEL - Models 722, 722M, 709, 715, 732, 7322, 741V, 744V, and 745V were available in a pistol pack including 2½, 4, 6, and 8 in. solid rib barrel assemblies, extra grip, 4 additional sight blades, and fitted carrying case. Last published retail prices were $712 and $785 for the standard and stainless steel models, respectively. VR or full shroud barrels were optional and were approx. priced $103 and $210, respectively.

MODEL 722 - stainless version of Model 22, use same add-ons for various barrel options. Disc. 1995.

| | $335 | $255 | $205 | | | | |

Last MSR was $400.

⁕ *Model 722 Silhouette* - .22 LR cal., choice of 10 in. vent. or heavy vent. barrel, single action only, combat style grip, narrow rear sight blade and patridge front. Mfg. 1992-95.

| | $410 | $340 | $295 | | | | |

Last MSR was $504.

Add $28 for heavy vent. barrel.

MODEL 722M - .22 Mag cal., otherwise similar to Model 722, use same add-ons for various barrel options. Disc. 1994.

| | $320 | $270 | $230 | | | | |

Last MSR was $391.

MODEL 708 - .38 Spl. cal., similar to Model 8. Add approx. $6 for each additional barrel length. Disc. 1995.

| | $265 | $200 | $170 | | | | |

Last MSR was $319.

Grading	100%	98%	95%	90%	80%	70%	60%

✴ ***Model 708 Action Cup/PPC*** - .38 Spl. cal., extra heavy 6 in. bull shroud barrel with removable underweight, Hogue Gripper grips, mounted Tasco Pro Point II on Action Cup, Aristocrat sights on PPC. Mfg. 1992 only.

| | **$725** | **$650** | **$550** | | | | |

Last MSR was $857.

Add $56 for Action Cup Model with Tasco Scope.

MODEL 709 - .38 Spl. cal., target revolver, adj. sights. Also available in special order 10, 12 (disc.), or 15 (disc.) in. barrel lengths. Disc. 1995.

| | **$310** | **$255** | **$205** | | | | |

Last MSR was $376.

Add approx. $10 for each additional longer barrel length, approx. $19 for VR, approx. $56 for heavy VR.

MODEL 714 (INTERCHANGEABLE OR FIXED) - .357 Mag. cal., fixed sight Service Model with 2 ½, 4, or 6 in. barrel, brushed stainless steel. Mfg. 1993-95.

| | **$260** | **$200** | **$160** | | | | |

Last MSR was $319.

Add approx. $6 for 4 or 6 in. barrel.
Subtract $6 for fixed barrel (2 ½ or 4 in. barrel only).

✴ ***Model 714 Action Cup/PPC*** - .357 Mag. cal., extra heavy 6 in. bull shroud barrel with removable underweight, Hogue Gripper grips, mounted Tasco Pro Point II on Action Cup, Aristocrat sights on PPC. Mfg. 1992 only.

| | **$725** | **$650** | **$550** | | | | |

Last MSR was $857.

Add $56 for Action Cup Model with Tasco Scope.

MODEL 715 INTERCHANGEABLE - .357 Mag. cal., 2 ½, 4, 6, 8, or 10 in. with adj. rear sight, brushed stainless steel. Mfg. 1993-95.

| | **$310** | **$255** | **$205** | | | | |

Last MSR was $376.

Add approx. $10 for each additional longer barrel length, approx. $19 for VR, approx. $56 for heavy VR.

✴ ***Model 715 Fixed Target*** - .357 Mag. cal., 3, 4, 5, or 6 in. fixed barrel, adj. rear sight. Mfg. 1993-95.

| | **$280** | **$210** | **$170** | | | | |

Last MSR was $345.

Add approx. $70 for compensated barrel (4, 5, or 6 in. - new 1994).

MODEL 732 - .32 H&R Mag. cal., similar to Model 32, except is stainless steel. Mfg. 1986-95.

| | **$335** | **$255** | **$205** | | | | |

Last MSR was $400.

Add $22 for VR barrel shroud (Model 732-V), $53 for VR heavy barrel shroud (Model 732-VH), approx. $9 for each additional barrel length over 2 ½ in.

MODEL 738P - .38+P cal., 5 shot, 6 ½ in. barrel, fixed sights, wood or rubber grips, 24.6 oz. Mfg. 1992-95.

| | **$275** | **$210** | **$175** | | | | |

Last MSR was $340.

MODEL 7322 - .32-20 WCF cal., similar to Model 322, except is stainless steel. Mfg. 1991-95.

| | **$335** | **$255** | **$205** | | | | |

Last MSR was $400.

Add $22 for VR barrel shroud (Model 7322-V), $53 for VR heavy barrel shroud (Model 7322-VH), approx. $9 for each additional barrel length over 2 ½ in.

Grading	100%	98%	95%	90%	80%	70%	60%

MODEL 740V - .357 SUPERMAG - .357 Max. cal., 4, 6, 8, or 10 in. barrel, adj. rear sight with interchangeable front and rear blades, high polished finish, smooth target grips. Mfg. 1986-95.

$460 $350 $315

Last MSR was $567.

Add approx. $20 for each additional barrel length after 4 in., $78 with vent. slotted shroud (only avail. with 8 in. barrel), $20 for VR heavy barrel shroud (Model 740-VH).

MODEL 741V - .41 Mag. cal., similar to Model 41V. Disc. 1995.

$420 $325 $270

Last MSR was $524.

Add approx. $20 for heavy VR, approx. $13 for each barrel length over 4 in.

MODEL 744V - .44 Mag. cal., similar to Model 44V. Disc. 1995.

$430 $345 $285

Last MSR was $524.

Add approx. $20 for heavy VR, $13 for each barrel length over 4 in.

✱ *Model 744V Target Fixed Barrel* - .44 Mag. cal., 4, 5, 6, or 8 in. barrel, brushed stainless steel. Mfg. 1994-95.

$395 $315 $265

Last MSR was $493.

Add approx. $4 for each barrel length over 3 in.

✱ *Model 744 Commemorative* - limited mfg.

$595 $475 $325

MODEL 745V - .45 LC cal., similar to Model 45, except in stainless steel. Disc. 1995.

$430 $345 $285

Last MSR was $524.

Add $20 for heavy full shroud VR barrels, $13 for each additional barrel length.

MODEL .45 PIN GUN - .45 ACP cal., similar to Model .45 Pin Gun, except is stainless steel. Mfg. 1993-95.

$625 $525 $425

Last MSR was $713.

Add $49 for VR heavy rib shroud.

MODEL 7414 SUPERMAG - .414 Super Mag. cal., 4, 6, 8, or 10 in. VR barrel, adj. rear sight, interchangeable front and rear sight blades (optional), bright blue finish, smooth target grips. Mfg. 1995 only.

$475 $350 $295

Last MSR was $596.

Add approx. $14 for each barrel length after 4 in., $74 for slotted shroud (Model 7414-V8S, 8 in. barrel only), approx. $25 for VR heavy rib shroud.

MODEL 7445 SUPERMAG - .445 Super Mag. cal., 4, 6, 8, or 10 in. VR barrel, adj. rear sight, interchangeable front and rear sight blades (optional), high polished finish, smooth target grips. Mfg. 1991-95.

$475 $350 $295

Last MSR was $596.

Add approx. $17 for each barrel length after 6 in., $74 for slotted shroud (Model 7445-VH8S, 8 in. barrel only), approx. $25 for VR heavy rib shroud, approx. $40 for VR heavy shroud and interchangeable sights (Model 7445-VH).

SUPER RAM SILHOUETTE - .357 Max., .414 Super Mag., or .44 Mag. cal., silhouette variation featuring modified Iron Sight Gun Works rear sight, Allen Taylor throated barrel, factory trigger job, 4 lbs. Mfg. 1995 only.

$695 $550 $375

Last MSR was $807.

Add $43 for .414 Super Mag. cal.

Grading	100%	98%	95%	90%	80%	70%	60%

HUNTER SERIES - .357 Super Mag., .41 Mag., .44 Mag., or .445 Super Mag. cal., 7 ½ in. barrel with heavy shroud, Hogue rubber finger grooved and wood presentation grips, choice of Gunworks iron sights or w/o sights with Burris base and rings, non-fluted cylinder, with or w/o compensator, approx. 4 lbs. Mfg. 1994-95.

$780   **$595**   **$475**

Last MSR was $849.

    Add $32 for compensated barrel.
    Add $32 for scope mounts (w/o sights).

WESTERN ARMS COMPANY

Previous manufacturer located in Ithaca, NY.

SHOTGUNS: SxS

WESTERN LONG RANGE - 12, 16, 20 ga., or .410 bore, 26-32 in. barrels, mod. and full choke, boxlock, extractors, double or single trigger, plain pistol grip stock, Western Arms Co. was a division of Ithaca Gun. Mfg. 1929-1946.

	$275	$225	$200	$175	$150	$125	$100

＊ *Single trigger*

	$325	$275	$250	$225	$200	$150	$125

WESTERN FIELD

Previous trademark used on Montgomery Ward rifles and shotguns.

The Western Field trademark has appeared literally on hundreds of various models (shotguns and rifles) sold through the Montgomery Ward retail network. Most of these models were manufactured through subcontracts with both domestic and international firearms manufacturers. Typically, they were "spec." guns made to sell at a specific price to undersell the competition. Most of these models were derivatives of existing factory models with less expensive wood and perhaps missing the features found on those models from which they were derived. To date, there has been very little interest in collecting Western Field guns, regardless of rarity. Rather than list Western Field models, a general guideline is that values generally are under those of their "1st generation relatives". As a result, prices are ascertained by the shooting value of the gun, rather than its collector value. See Store Brand Crossover List located in the back of this text.

WESTLEY RICHARDS & CO. LTD.

Currently manufactured by Westley Richards and Co., Ltd., Birmingham, England 1812 to date. In 1995, Westley Richards opened their own agency in the US located in Springfield, MO. Originally William Westley Richards was located in Birmingham, England.

There seems to be a lot of confusion regarding W. Richards, W. R. Richards, William Richards, and other generic derivatives of the famous English gunmaker, Westley Richards. Part of the problem is that there are seventeen registered firms in England, including several in London, who have made guns by the name of Richards. A genuine Westley Richards gun never has the first name abbreviated, and the London address is usually found on the rib panel. Further compounding the problem, a previous Belgian gunmaker identifiable by W. Richards on the locks or rib, had many shotguns exported into the United States, which are commonly confused with the real London maker. These Belgian guns are commonly hammer guns with damascus twist barrels most frequently encountered in either 10, 12, or 16 ga. The easiest way to determine this maker is to recognize the Liege proofmarks on the barrel flats and chamber length given in millimeters. Most of these Belgian guns sell in the $100-$400 range, depending on condition and configuration.

Note: Westley Richards guns are essentially custom ordered - only 25-30 guns are made annually. They make many weapons that are impossible to list and evaluate, except on an individual basis. Professional appraisal is necessary upon purchase or sale.

To obtain a quotation for a new Westley Richards shotgun, an inquiry should be submitted to the manufacturer or importer (see Trademark Index for addresses).

Grading	100%	98%	95%	90%	80%	70%	60%

RIFLES

BEST QUALITY BOXLOCK DOUBLE RIFLE - .300 Win. Mag., .375 H&H, .470 NE, .577 NE, or .600 NE cal., auto ejectors, boxlock, hammerless, folding leaf rear sight, hooded front sight, engraved with quality French walnut stock, horn forend tip.

	100%	98%	95%	90%	80%	70%	60%
MSR $25,000	$25,000	$21,000	$18,750	$16,000	$13,750	$10,500	$9,250

Values will vary greatly on this model, depending on caliber.

DETACHABLE DROPLOCK DOUBLE RIFLE - available in most cals., boxlock with detachable locks and hinged cover-plate, ejectors, colored case hardened frame, cased.

	100%	98%	95%	90%	80%	70%	60%
MSR $36,000	$36,000	$30,000	$25,000	$21,000	$18,750	$16,000	$13,000

STALKER MAGAZINE RIFLE - .243 Win., .270 Win., .30-06, .300 H&H, .375 H&H, or .458 Win. Mag. cal., bolt action, Mauser action, 22, 24, or 25 in. barrel, leaf rear and hooded front sight, engraved with French walnut stock, horn forend tip. Current mfg.

	100%	98%	95%	90%	80%	70%	60%
MSR $9,000	$9,000	$7,850	$6,950	$5,750	$4,750	$4,000	$3,300

Add approx. $3,000 for Magnum Mauser action.

SHOTGUNS: PRE-WWII PRODUCTION

Add 20% for 20 ga.
Add 30% for 28 ga.
Add $1,500 for cased extra set of locks.

OVUNDO O/U - detachable lock boxlock, optional sideplates. Disc.

		95%	90%	80%	70%	60%
	$18,000	$15,000	$12,500	$9,750	$8,500	$7,250	$6,000

MODELE DE GRANDE LUXE - SxS - scalloped receiver, detachable locks, profuse scroll & game scene engraving. Disc.

	$15,000	$13,000	$11,000	$9,750	$8,500	$7,250	$6,000

MODEL DE LUXE - SxS - scalloped receiver, detachable locks, fine scroll & game scene engraving. Disc.

	$11,000	$9,500	$8,500	$7,500	$6,000	$5,500	$5,000

HAMMERLESS EJECTOR PLAIN QUALITY - SxS - scalloped receiver, Anson & Deeley fixed locks.

	$6,000	$5,000	$4,000	$3,500	$3,000	$2,500	$2,000

"B" QUALITY EJECTOR - SxS - boxlock with plain (unscalloped) receiver, light scroll engraving. Disc.

	$5,000	$4,000	$3,500	$3,000	$2,500	$2,250	$2,000

SHOTGUNS: SxS, CURRENT PRODUCTION

CONNAUGHT MODEL - 12, 20, or 28 ga., Anson & Deeley scalloped boxlock action, scroll engraving, 26 or 28 in. barrels, ejectors, about 6½ lbs. Disc.

	$9,250	$8,000	$6,600	$5,600	$4,800	$4,000	$3,400

Last MSR was $10,900.

BEST QUALITY DROPLOCK - 12, 16, 20, 28 ga., or .410 bore, boxlock action, barrel lengths and chokes to order, detachable locks with hinged cover-plate, checkered straight or pistol grip stock, auto ejectors.

	100%	98%	95%	90%	80%	70%	60%
MSR $27,000	$27,000	$19,450	$14,000	$10,750	$8,750	$7,600	$6,400

Add $1,000 for SST.

Only six .410 Best Quality Boxlocks have been mfg. to date.

Grading	100%	98%	95%	90%	80%	70%	60%

BEST QUALITY SIDELOCK - 12, 16, 20, 28 ga., or .410 bore, barrel length and choke to order, hand detachable sidelocks, auto ejectors, checkered straight or pistol grip stock.

MSR	$25,000		$25,000	$18,950	$14,000	$10,750	$8,750	$7,600	$6,400

Add 20% for 20 ga.
Add 40% for 28 ga.
Add 60% for .410 bore.
Add $1,000 for SST.

Most specimens in this model were custom ordered, and as a result, each gun has to be evaluated individually.

WILLIAM BISHOP SIDELOCK MODEL - current mfg., best quality sidelock, made to individual customer specifications.

MSR	$29,000		$29,000	$23,500	$18,500	$15,000	$11,750	$9,500	$8,250

CARLTON DETACHABLE LOCK - 12 or 20 ga., current mfg., detachable sidelocks, top-of-the-line shotgun custom made per customer specifications, elaborate game scene engraving. Many options upon request - values listed are for base gun only.

MSR	$34,075		$34,075	$26,500	$21,750	$17,250	$13,750	$10,500	$9,000

WHITNEY ARMS COMPANY

Previous manufacturer located in New Haven, CT, 1798-1886.

Whitney Arms Company began firearms production in 1798. Eli Whitney Sr. & Eli Whitney Jr. were prominent and prolific figures in the arms manufacturing world for a great many decades, and their production plant in New Haven is credited as being the first major manufacturer of commercial firearms in America. The Whitneys produced a tremendous variety of firearms under family ownership for approximately 90 years before selling the company to Winchester in 1888. Numerous long arms, starting with the Whitney 1798 U.S. Contract Musket, and moving forward through various other flintlock, percussion, rimfire, and centerfire rifles, handguns, and shotguns contributed to the vast broadness of the Whitney line. The Whitney name saw collaboration with Burgess, Kennedy, Morse, Tiesing, Howard, Cochran, Scharf, and many others. Many of the early Whitney rifles such as the historic 1798 Flintlock muskets, are rare and highly collectible, commanding substantial premiums when found in original configuration, and not converted to percussion. The Whitney lever action repeaters are also quite popular among collectors. A fair number remain in circulation.

The author wishes to express his thanks to Mr. Steve Engleson for providing the following information on Whitney Arms Company.

100%	98%	95%	90%	80%	70%	60%	50%	40%	30%	20%	10%

RIFLES: LEVER ACTION

WHITNEY-KENNEDY LEVER ACTION MAGAZINE RIFLES - a repeating rifle with loading port on right side, top ejection, approx. 15,000 mfg. between 1879-1886, barrels are typically marked Whitney Arms Co. or Whitneyville Armory, with some variations having the Kennedy name included, often referred to as the Kennedy rifle, 2 basic frame sizes were made, (large & small), both frame sizes were also available in carbines and muskets, 2 other basic variations were the standard loop lever, a serpentine or "S" shaped finger lever, ser. nos. were sequential from 1-5,000, and from there a letter prefix was added, these appeared from A through S, with numbers 1-999 following.

✱ **Large Frame** - .40-60 WCF, .45-60 WCF, .45-75 WCF, and .50-95 Express cal., 26 or 28 in. round or octagon barrels, walnut stocks, crescent steel buttplate, full magazine capacity of 9 rounds in standard rifle.

N/A	N/A	$2,500	$2,125	$1,900	$1,700	$1,475	$1,325	$1,100	$975	$850	$725

Add 300% for .50-95 Express cal. (extremely rare).
Add 50% for carbine or musket.
Add 30% for half-round, half-octagon barrel.
Add 20% for nonprefix (early) serial numbers.
Add 10% for serpentine lever.

100%	98%	95%	90%	80%	70%	60%	50%	40%	30%	20%	10%

✱ Small Frame - .44-40 WCF, .38-40 WCF, and .32-20 WCF cal., 24 in. round or octagon barrel, walnut stock and crescent buttplate, full magazine capacity of 13 rounds in standard rifle.

N/A	N/A	$1,950	$1,675	$1,450	$1,225	$1,075	$950	$825	$700	$600	$500

Add 300% for carbine or musket (extremely rare).
Add 100% for half-round, half-octagon barrel.
Add 20% for half-magazine.
Add 20% for 26 or 28 in. barrel.

1878 BURGESS REPEATING RIFLE - .45-70 Govt. cal., standard sporting rifle, 28 in. octagon or round barrel, loading port on right side, serpentine shaped lever, walnut stock, blue receiver and full magazine capacity of 9 rounds, typically w/o Whitney markings, barrels marked "G.W. Morse Patented Oct. 28th 1856", and tangs are marked "A. Burgess Patented Jan. 7th 1873", several variations, including the first, second, and third models, as well as military carbines and muskets.

N/A	N/A	$3,300	$3,000	$2,700	$2,400	$2,100	$1,850	$1,600	$1,400	$1,250	$1,100

Add 300% for the first model top loader (few made and most converted by the factory to sideloader).
Add 100% for military carbine or musket (certain variations will command a higher premium).
Add 30% for first or second model.
Values shown are for the most typically encountered variation, the third model sporting rifle.
This model was also known as the Whitney-Burgess-Morse lever action repeating rifle, mfg. through a license agreement with Andrew Burgess, total production of approx. 2,000 were made between 1878-1882.

WHITNEY FIREARMS COMPANY

Previous manufacturer from 1956-1959 located in Hartford, CT.

Grading	100%	98%	95%	90%	80%	70%	60%

PISTOLS: SEMI-AUTO

WOLVERINE OR LIGHTNING - .22 Auto cal., unique futuristic Jetsons appearance, 10 shot, 4 5/8 in. barrel, plastic grips, aluminum alloy frame and barrel shroud, blue model is more common (approx. 13,000 mfg.), nickel is rare (approx. 900 mfg.). Mfg. 1955- 1962.

	100%	98%	95%	90%	80%	70%	60%
Blue finish	$425	$350	$300	$260	$230	$200	$175
Nickel finish	$600	$475	$375	$300	$260	$230	$200

WHITWORTH

This trademark can be found in the Interarms section of this text.

WICHITA ARMS, INC.

Current manufacturer located in Wichita, KS. Distributor, dealer, and consumer direct sales.

PISTOLS

WICHITA INTERNATIONAL PISTOL (WIP) - available in 8 cals. between .22 LR and .357 Mag., single shot, break open action, stainless steel, adj. sights, 10 or 14 in. barrel, adj. sights or scope mounts, smooth walnut stocks and forearm. Disc. 1994.

	$680	$465	$350	

Last MSR was $775.

Add $100 for 14 in. barrel.

Grading	100%	98%	95%	90%	80%	70%	60%

WICHITA CLASSIC PISTOL - assorted cals. to .308 Win., 11¼ in. barrel, action has left- hand bolt for shooting with right-hand, deluxe walnut, custom made, 3 lbs. 15 oz. Disc. 1997.

$3,280 $2,550 $2,150

Last MSR was $3,495.

* **Wichita Classic Engraved** - similar to Wichita Classic, except is extensively engraved.

MSR $5,250 $5,250 $3,750 $2,750

WICHITA SILHOUETTE PISTOL (WSP) - .308 Win. or 7mm/IHMSA cal., adj. trigger and sights, 14 15/16 in. barrel, center grip walnut stock, rear grip, 4½ lbs. Left-hand action for shooting with right-hand. Disc. 1994.

$1,520 $1,050 $850

Last MSR was $1,800.

WICHITA MAGAZINE PISTOL - .308 Win. or 7mm/IHMSA cal., fiberthane (disc. 1987) or walnut (new 1988) stock, choice of MK-40, Silhouette, or Classic configuration, 13 in. barrel, adj. trigger, multi-range sights, 4½ lbs. Disc. 1994.

$1,250 $875 $700

Last MSR was $1,550.

* **Wichita Classic Pistol** - features octagon barrel, AAA walnut stock, 11¼ in. barrel, 3 lbs. 15 oz. Disc. 1994.

$2,975 $2,450 $2,000

Last MSR was $3,400

WICHITA BENCH PISTOL - .222 Rem., 6 PPC, or .22 Cheetah cal., uses WBR 1200 action, rear grip, 18 in. stainless steel Douglas barrel. Mfg. 1994-98.

$1,875 $1,500 $1,250

Last MSR was $1,875.

RIFLES: BOLT ACTION

WICHITA CLASSIC RIFLE (WCR) - .17-222, .17-222 Mag., .222 Rem., .222 Mag., 223 Rem., 6x47mm, and other cals. up to and including .308 Win. cal., bolt action, single shot, select walnut, 21 in. octagon barrel, Canjar trigger, no sights, 7 lbs. Disc. 1997.

$3,275 $2,500 $2,150

Last MSR was $3,495.

Add $175 for left-hand action.

* **Wichita Varmint Rifle (WVR)** - similar to WCR, except available only in Varmint cals. (up to and including .308 Win.) and round barrel. Disc. 1997.

$2,500 $1,795 $1,375

Last MSR was $2,695.

Add $175 for left-hand action.

* **Wichita Silhouette Rifle (WSR)** - available in most cals., grey fiberthane stock, 24 in. match grade barrel, 2 oz. Canjar trigger, no sights, 9 lbs. Disc. 1995.

$2,475 $1,775 $1,375

Last MSR was $2,650.

Add $175 for left-hand action.

* **Wichita Magnum** - Mag. cals., stainless steel only. Disc. 1984.

$1,725 $1,300 $1,175

WICKLIFFE RIFLES

Previously manufactured by Triple S Development located in Wickliffe, OH.

Grading	100%	98%	95%	90%	80%	70%	60%

RIFLES: SINGLE SHOT

MODEL 76 STANDARD - falling block action, most popular cals., 22 or 26 in. barrel, no sights, select walnut pistol grip, 2 piece stock. Mfg. 1976-disc.

| | $395 | $350 | $325 | $300 | $275 | $250 | $225 |

MODEL 76 DELUXE GRADE - similar to Standard, in .30-06 cal. only, 22 in. barrel, fancy wood, silver pistol grip cap.

| | $460 | $415 | $385 | $360 | $320 | $290 | $250 |

MODEL 76 COMMEMORATIVE - similar to Deluxe, except etched receiver, U.S. silver dollar inlaid in stock, presentation case. Mfg. 100, 1976.

| | $1,100 | $825 | $550 | $495 | $440 | $330 | $305 |

STINGER - similar to Model 76 Standard, in .22 Hornet or .223 Rem. cal., lightweight 22 in. barrel.

| | $395 | $350 | $325 | $300 | $275 | $250 | $225 |

STINGER DELUXE - similar to 76 Deluxe, in .22 Hornet or .223 Rem. cal., lightweight 22 in. barrel.

| | $460 | $415 | $385 | $360 | $325 | $290 | $250 |

TRADITIONALIST - similar to Standard 76, in .30-06 or .45-70 Govt. cal., 24 in. barrel.

| | $395 | $350 | $325 | $300 | $275 | $250 | $225 |

KODIAK COMMEMORATIVE - similar to Model 76 Deluxe, .338 Win. Mag. cal., 26 in. barrel, etched receiver.

| | $650 | $550 | $475 | $425 | $375 | $325 | $275 |

WIFRA

Please refer to W.R. Saleri listing in the S section.

WILD WEST GUNS

Current custom gunsmith and manufacturer located in Anchorage, AK. Dealer and consumer direct sales.

Wild West Guns also offers a bolt action Summit Rifle Series utilizing a Rem. M-700 stainless action and premium stainless steel match grade barrel - the current package price is $3,150. An additional bolt action ProGuide Model is available in .375 H&H - .458 Lott cal. - the package price is $3,150. Please contact the company directly for more information on these bolt action models.

PISTOLS: SEMI-AUTO

Wild West Guns previously manufactured a customized M1911 style semi-auto model called the ShadowLite package - 1997 retail was $2,495.

RIFLES: LEVER ACTION

ALASKAN COPILOT RIFLE - .30-30 Win. (disc. 1999), .357 Mag. (disc. 1999), .44 Mag. (disc. 1999), .444 Marlin (disc. 1999), .45-70 Govt., .457 Mag. (new 2000), or .50 Alaskan (new 2000) cal., features customized Marlin lever action with takedown conversion, various finishes, ported barrel, matte blue or parkerized finish, includes soft case. New 1996.

| MSR | $1,799 | | $1,625 | $1,325 | $1,075 | $875 | $675 | $625 | $575 |

Add $200 for .50 Alaskan cal. package.
Subtract approx. 20% for older disc. cals.

✱ *Alaskan CoPilot Limited* - .457 Mag. or .45-70 Govt. cal., take down action, features most of Wild West Guns custom shop options, includes hard case. Only 150 to be mfg. beginning 2001 with custom ser. nos.

| MSR | $2,995 | | $2,995 | $2,650 | $2,150 | $1,750 | $1,500 | $1,300 | $1,100 |

Grading	100%	98%	95%	90%	80%	70%	60%

ALASKAN GUIDE - similar to Alaskan Co-Pilot, except has 18½ in. barrel, ghost ring rear sight, straight style stock and recoil control porting. New 1997.

MSR $1,199	$1,075	$950	$850	$775	$675	$575	$495

Add $200 for .50 Alaskan cal. package.
Add $100 for stainless steel.
Add $500 for take-down conversion (Master Guide Model).

WILDEY, INC.

Current manufacturer located in Warren, CT. Previously located in New Milford, CT until 1999. Originally, the company was named Wildey Firearms Co., Inc. located in Cheshire, CT. At that time, serialization of pistols was 45-0000. When Wildey Inc. bought the company out of bankruptcy from the old shareholders, there had been approximately 800 pistols mfg. To distinguish the old company from the present company, the serial range was changed to 09-0000 (only 633 pistols with the 09 prefix were produced). These guns had the Cheshire, CT address. Pistols produced by Wildey Inc., New Milford, CT are serial numbered with 4 digits being used (no numerical prefix).

PISTOLS: SEMI-AUTO

Wildey has plans to introduce 4 new proprietary cartridges. They are the .30 WM, .357 WM, 10mm WM, and 11mm WM based on the .475 Wildey Mag. necked down to respective cartridge dimensions. Norma, located in Sweden, continues to produce the .475 WM brass.

WILDEY AUTO PISTOL - .45 Win. Mag., .45 Wildey Mag., or .475 Wildey Mag., gas operated, 5, 6, 7, 8, 10, or 14 in. VR barrel, selective single shot or semi-auto, 3 lug rotary bolt, fixed barrel (interchangeable), polished stainless steel construction, 7 shot, double action, adj. sights, smooth or checkered wood grips, designed to fire proprietary new cartridges specifically for this gun including the .45 Win. Mag. cal., 64 oz. with 5 in. barrel.

Add $560-$1,148 per interchangeable barrel.

* ***Survivor Model*** - .45 Win. Mag., 45 Wildey Mag., or .475 Wildey Mag. cal., 5, 6, 7, 8, 10, 12 or 14 (new 2000) in. barrel. New 1990.

MSR $1,408	$1,225	$925	$750

Add $107 for 12 in. barrel.
Add $510 for 14 in. barrel.
Add $23 for 8 or 10 in. barrel.
The .475 Wildey cal. is derived from a factory case. This cal. is available in 8 or 10 in. barrel only.

* ***Survivor Guardsman*** - similar to Survivor Model, except has squared off trigger guard. New 1990.

MSR $1,408	$1,225	$925	$750

Add $23 for 8 or 10 in. barrel.

* ***Hunter Model*** - .45 Win. Mag., .45 Wildey Mag., or .475 Wildey Mag. cal., 5, 6, 7, 8, 10, 12 or 14 (new 2000) in. barrel, matte finish on all metal parts, adj. sights. New 1990.

MSR $1,642	$1,375	$1,075	$900

Add $110 for 12 in. barrel.
Add $496 for 14 in. barrel.
Add $24 for 8 or 10 in. barrel.
.475 Wildey Mag. is available in 8, 10, or 12 in. barrel only.

* ***Hunter Guardsman*** - similar to Hunter Model, except has squared off trigger guard. New 1990.

MSR $1,642	$1,375	$1,075	$900

Add $110 for 12 in. barrel.
Add $496 for 14 in. barrel.
Add $24 for 8 or 10 in. barrel.

Grading	100%	98%	95%	90%	80%	70%	60%

* **Presentation Model** - same specifications as Hunter Guardsman model, except is engraved with hand checkered or smooth stocks.

	$2,500	**$2,000**	**$1,600**

Last MSR was $2,000.

* **Older Wildey Mfg.**
  .475 Wildey Mag. cal. was available in 8 or 10 in. barrel only.

◇**SERIAL NOS. 1-200.**

	$1,900	**$1,700**	**$1,550**

Last MSR was $2,180.

Add $20 for 8 or 10 in. barrel.

◇**SERIAL NOS. 201-400.**

	$1,750	**$1,550**	**$1,400**

Last MSR was $1,980.

Add $20 for 8 or 10 in. barrel.

◇**SERIAL NOS. 401-600.**

	$1,650	**$1,375**	**$1,250**

Last MSR was $1,780.

Add $20 for 8 or 10 in. barrel.

◇**SERIAL NOS. 601-800.**

	$1,450	**$1,200**	**$1,000**

Last MSR was $1,580.

Add $20 for 8 or 10 in. barrel.

◇**SERIAL NOS. 801-1,000.**

	$1,100	**$925**	**$800**

Last MSR was $1,275.

Add $25 for 8 or 10 in. barrel.

◇**SERIAL NOS. 1,001-2,489.**

	$1,025	**$850**	**$750**

Last MSR was $1,175.

Add $20 for 8 or 10 in. barrel.

WILKES, JOHN GUNMAKERS LTD.

Current manufacturer established in 1833, and located in London, England. Currently imported and distributed beginning 2001 by First National Gun Banque, located in Colorado Springs, CO.

John Wilkes Gunmakers Ltd. has been manufacturing best quality guns for over 150 years. This trademark was reintroduced with the release of the new O/U sidelock ejector model. Please contact the importer directly for more information, including available options, delivery times, and an individual price quotation.

SHOTGUNS: O/U, SIDELOCK

O/U SIDELOCK BEST MODEL CLASSIC - 20 ga. only initially, unique sideplate locks w/o "V" springs (plungers instead), ST or DT, best quality wood and workmanship, monobloc or chopper lump barrels, lifetime warranty, special order only. Importation began 2001.

MSR	**$19,950**	**$19,950**	**$15,500**	**$13,525**	**$12,000**	**$11,000**	**$10,000**	**$9,250**

Add $2,000 for chopper lump barrels.
Add $2,000 per pair of additional locks.

* **O/U Sidelock Special Series**
  Prices for the Special Series start at $28,950.

Grading	100%	98%	95%	90%	80%	70%	60%

SHOTGUNS: SxS

John Wilkes manufactures a sidelock model in all gauges - MSR is currently $40,700. Boxlock models are also available, with prices ranging from $2,760 - $6,000, depending on special orders/features.

WILKINSON ARMS

Current trademark manufactured by Northwest Arms, located in Parma, ID. Dealer direct sales.

CARBINES

LINDA CARBINE - 9mm Para cal., 16 3/16 in. barrel, aluminum receiver, pre-ban configuration (limited supplies), fixed tubular stock with wood pad, vent. barrel shroud, aperture rear sight, small wooden forearm, 18 or 31 shot mag., beginning 2002, this model came standard with many accessories, 7 lbs. New 2000.

	MSR	$1,800			$1,495	$750	$625	$550	$450	$395	$360

Only 2,200 Linda Carbines were marked "Luger Carbine" on the receiver. The last 1,500 distributed by Northwest Arms include a longer stock, and matched bolt and barrel (Rockwell 57).

✳ *Linda L2 Limited Edition* - mfg. from the last 600 of the original 2,200 pre-ban Linda Carbines, includes many upgrades and accessories. New 2002.

	MSR	$4,800			$4,350	$2,750	$1,900

TERRY CARBINE - 9mm Para. cal., blowback semi-auto action, 31 shot mag., 16 3/16 in. barrel, closed breech, adj. sights, 7 lbs. Disc.

					100%	98%	95%	90%	80%	70%	60%
With black P.V.C. stock					$475	$395	$325	$295	$260	$230	$200
With maple stock					$625	$525	$400	$350	$340	$325	$300

PISTOLS: SEMI-AUTO

SHERRY MODEL - .22 LR cal., 2½ in. barrel, aluminum frame, fully machined steel slide, trigger group, and bolt insert, available in various colors, 9¼ oz. New 2000.

	MSR	$280			$245	$200	$160	$140	$125	$110	$100

Add $25 for gold anodized frame.
Add $20 for collector's edition.
Add $100 for Robar coating.

DIANE MODEL - .25 ACP cal., 6 shot, 2 1/8 in. barrel, fixed sight, matte blue, plastic grips. Disc.

					$150	$125	$95	$80	$65	$55	$50

LINDA MODEL - 9mm Para. cal., blowback action firing from closed bolt, 8.3 in. barrel, 31 shot mag., PVC pistol grip, maple forearm, Williams adj. rear sight. Disc.

					$675	$625	$550	$475	$425	$350	$295

WILLIAM DOUGLAS & SONS

Current manufacturer located in Staffordshire, England. No current U.S. importation. Previously imported and distributed by Cape Outfitters located in Cape Girardeau, MO.

Prices and MSRs listed reflect most recent U.S. importation.

RIFLES: SxS

EXPRESS RIFLE - .375 H&H cal., H&H type back action sidelock with bolster fences, DTs, ejectors, 24 in. regulated barrels, folding leaf rear sight, oil finished European walnut stock with 20 LPI checkering, light engraving, case hardened action.

	MSR	$21,950			$19,750	$15,250	$11,000	$8,750	$7,400	$6,200	$5,300

Grading	100%	98%	95%	90%	80%	70%	60%

BOXLOCK EXPRESS RIFLE - .470 NE or .500 NE (new 1998) cal., Anson & Deeley action with DT (front trigger is articulated), case colored action with deep blue small parts, 24 in. regulated barrels, checkered European walnut stock and forearm with oil finish, light border engraving.

MSR $14,950	$12,975	$9,950	$9,000	$8,250	$7,500	$6,750	$6,000

Add $1,000 for .500 NE cal.

✳ *Deluxe Boxlock Express Rifle* - includes better walnut and fully engraved receiver.

MSR $17,950	$15,650	$12,750	$10,750	$9,500	$8,750	$7,500	$6,750

SHOTGUNS: SxS

WILLIAM DOUGLAS BOXLOCK - 16, 20, or 28 ga., 2¾ in. chambers, case colored receiver, chopper lump barrels, DT, 26 or 28 in. barrels. Importation began 2000.

MSR $4,995	$4,650	$4,200	$3,750	$3,250	$2,750	$2,250	$1,750

Add $800 for ST.

WILLIAM EVANS LIMITED

Current manufacturer of long arms established during 1883, and located in London, England.

William Evans, Gun & Rifle Makers, have been manufacturing high quality shotguns and rifles for over 100 years. Most William Evans shotguns and double rifles must be appraised individually since they were all custom ordered initially. All new guns must be ordered from the factory directly. Currently, the sidelock SxS shotgun starts at £32,000 w/o V.A.T. (add £2,000 for 28 ga. or .410 bore), the sidelock O/U shotgun starts at £41,000 w/o V.A.T., (add £3,000 for 28 ga. or .410 bore), the SxS double rifle starts at £50,000 (add £8,000 for cals. .500 and greater), and the bolt action rifle starts at £8,500, with Mag. cals. starting at £15,000. All prices are FOB England. Please contact William Evans (refer to the Trademark Index) for more information, including any special orders.

WILLIAM POWELL & SON (GUNMAKERS) LTD.

Current manufacturer established in 1802, and located in Birmingham, England. The company is still controlled by the descendants of William Powell I. Currently imported beginning 1999 by John Higgins, located in Richmond Hill, GA. Previously imported by Bells Legendary Countrywear located in New York, NY until 1999. The Heritage Series was introduced into the U.S. in 1984.

William Powell & Sons will be celebrating their 200th anniversary during 2002, and are one of England's oldest premier gun makers. Please contact the factory directly for more information (they have a fine catalog), including their lineup of accessories and clothing.

SHOTGUNS: SxS

Values listed are shown in pounds £, and do not include VAT.

Add 10% for 20, 28 ga. or .410 bore on models listed.

NO. 1 SIDELOCK EJECTOR - 12, 16, 20 ga., or .410 (disc.) bore, chopper lump barrels, extra choice French walnut, DTs, many special orders available. Gold inlays, deep relief carved action fences, can be obtained in self opener.

MSR £32,000	£32,000	$39,500	$34,000	$28,750	$23,250	$17,500	$14,750

Add £3,000 for assisted opening action.
Add £2,500 for SNT.

NO. 3 BOXLOCK EJECTOR - 12, 16, 20 ga., or .410 (disc.) bore, chopper lump barrels, scalloped boxlock action, extra choice French walnut, many special orders available.

MSR £19,063	£19,063	$27,000	$21,000	$16,000	$9,900	$7,500	$6,250

Grading	100%	98%	95%	90%	80%	70%	60%

✳ **Model 4 Boxlock Ejector** - similar to Number 3, but has dovetail lump barrels and less engraving.

MSR £16,583	£16,583	$23,000	$16,500	$10,250	$7,950	$6,600	$5,400

Add £1,754 for SNT.

✳ **Model 6 Boxlock Ejector** - disc. 1988.

	$2,750	$2,450	$2,050	$1,700	$1,400	$1,150	$900

HERITAGE NO. 1 SIDELOCK EJECTOR MKII - 12 or 20 ga., 2¾ in. chambers, chopper lump barrels, choice of game scene or bouquet and scroll engraving, DTs. Mfg. 1984-2000.

$8,710	$12,750	$10,750	$9,000	$7,800	$6,700	$5,500

Last MSR was £8,710.

HERITAGE NO. 2 SIDELOCK MKII - similar to Heritage No. 1, except has less engraving and lesser grade walnut, easy opening action.

MSR £3,875	£3,875	$5,900	$5,200	$4,750	$4,375	$3,675	$3,100

Add £1,250 for traditional scroll engraving.

HERITAGE "CONSORT" SIDELOCK EJECTOR - 12, 20, or 28 ga., 2¾ in. chambers chopper lump barrels, round body action, full bouquet and scroll engraving. New 1998.

MSR £6,695	£6,695	$8,200	$6,850	$6,000	$5,000	$4,250	$3,500

HERITAGE DE LUXE BOXLOCK DETACHABLE LOCK - features detachable locks, choice of traditional scroll or game scene engraving, ejectors. Disc. 1999.

$21,485	$16,750	$13,750	$11,000	$8,500	$7,250	$5,950

Last MSR was $21,485.

HERITAGE ROUND ACTION EJECTOR - features unscalloped, rounded boxlock action with fine English scroll work throughout, DTs. Disc. 1999.

$15,785	$12,000	$9,600	$7,800	$6,600	$5,400	$4,500

Last MSR was $15,785.

WILSON COMBAT

Current firearm manufacturer, customizer, and supplier of custom rifles, shotguns, handguns, and custom firearms accessories located in Berryville, AR since 1978.

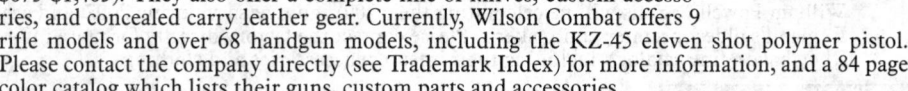

Wilson Combat has extensive line of "high-end" custom AR-15 style rifles (MSR starts at $1,599), tactical shotguns (see Scattergun Technologies listing), and a wide variety of M1911 style pistols (MSRs range from $675-$1,465). They also offer a complete line of knives, custom accessories, and concealed carry leather gear. Currently, Wilson Combat offers 9 rifle models and over 68 handgun models, including the KZ-45 eleven shot polymer pistol. Please contact the company directly (see Trademark Index) for more information, and a 84 page color catalog which lists their guns, custom parts and accessories.

WINCHESTER

Current manufacturer located in New Haven, CT from 1866 to date and by Miroku of Japan since circa 1992. Also includes U.S. Repeating Arms, formed in 1981, with licensing agreement from Olin Corp. to manufacture shotguns and rifles domestically using the Winchester Trademark. Corporate offices are now located in Morgan, UT.

Olin Corp. previously mfg. shotguns and rifles bearing the Winchester Hallmark at the Olin Kodensha Plant (closed 1989) located in Tochigi, Japan and also in European countries. In 1992, U.S. Repeating Arms was acquired by GIAT located in France. In late 1997, the Walloon region of Belgium acquired controlling interest of both Browning and U.S. Repeating Arms.

For more information and current pricing on both new and used Winchester airguns, please refer to the *Blue Book of Modern Airguns* by Dr. Robert Beeman & John Allen (now online also).

WINCHESTER OVERVIEW

Note: Winchester Rifles are a field in themselves. Models Henry, 1866, 1873, 1876, 1885, 1886, 1892, 1894, and 1895 all were produced with a multitude of special order options. Special orders included front and rear special sights, half or 2/3 magazines, takedown, various barrel lengths, configurations, and weights, special metal finishes, deluxe wood (either checkered or carved) in a variety of finishes, an impressive range of engraving options, different butt plates, etc. All of these special orders act independently and interdependently to determine the correct value of a particular Winchester. Some of the finest rifles ever made are special order Winchesters engraved by the Ulrichs, G. Young, L.D. Nimschke, and others. For these reasons a Model 92 Winchester can range in price from $200 to over $500,000 - quite a price range for one model alone! When contemplating a purchase on the higher dollar range, qualified and professional opinions should be secured, preferably from at least 2 sources. Unfortunately many fakes and upgraded (non-original) guns have surfaced in the last 10 years with the sudden increase in prices. Winchesters shown in this section are priced assuming a standard model with no special orders. Any special orders will further add to the prices shown. Caliber rarities must also be considered. Many of the early Winchesters are broken down by year of manufacture. Refer to the "Model Serialization" section in this book.

A factory letter specifying original shipping information by serial number will certainly help solidify values shown on older out of production Winchester rifles and shotguns. A listing has been provided by model number with serialization range which can be historically researched by the Winchester Museum now located in Cody, WY. To use this outstanding service, make sure the model and its serial number fall within the ranges listed. Simply mail in your informational request with serial number, model, and caliber to the Cody Firearms Museum, 720 Sheridan Ave. in Cody, WY, 82414. There is a $45 charge for this service, so please contact them directly for the fee regarding researching your particular firearm(s). Research results will include (if available) specimen caliber, barrel length, any special orders or finishes, return(s) to the factory, as well as any additional provenance contained by interpolating existing factory shipping ledgers. I would recommend a trip to the Buffalo Bill Historical Center as it contains the most comprehensive collection of projectile arms (including Chinese specimens that date back 2,000 years) and Americana housed under one roof in this country.

With the recent price appreciation on most upper condition Winchester rifles, excellent original condition has become so expensive that the many special order features Winchester offered do not cost that much more currently. However, on lesser condition guns that are much less expensive, these same special order features will cost more percentage-wise since the condition factor did not cost a premium.

Model 1866 Lever Action Rifle - ser. no. range 125,000-170,101.
Approx. 33 specimens have been researched outside of this ser. no. range.
Model 1873 Lever Action Rifle - ser. no. range 1-720,496.
Approx. 160 specimens have been researched outside of this ser. no. range.
Model 1876 Lever Action Rifle - ser. no. range 1-63,871.
Model 1883 Bolt Action Rifle (Hotchkiss Repeater) - ser. no. range 1-84,555.
May be referred to as Model 1879, 1880, or 1883.
Model 1885 Single Shot Rifle or Shotgun - ser. no. range 1-109,999.
Not available in ser. nos. 74,459-74,556. Also known as High and Low Wall.
Model 1886 Lever Action Rifle - ser. no. range 1-156,599.
Not available in ser. nos. 135,125-135,144 and 146,000-150,799.
Model 1887 & 1901 Lever Action Shotguns - ser. no. range 1-72,999.
Model 1890 Slide Action Rifle - ser. no. range 1-329,999.
Not available in ser. nos. 10,809-10,884, 20,000-29,999, 32,629-32,698, 37,599-37,627, 234,061-234,140, and 234,142-234,160.
Model 1892 Lever Action Rifle - ser. no. range 1-379,999.
Not available in ser. nos. 374,851-376,100.
Model 1893 Slide Action Shotgun - ser. no. range 1-34,050.
Model 1894 Lever Action Rifle - ser. no. range 1-353,999.
Model 1895 Lever Action Rifle - ser. no. range 1-59,999.
Model "Lee" Bolt Action Rifle - ser. no. range 1-19,999.

Model 1897 Slide Action Shotgun - ser. no. range 34,051-377,999.
Model 1903 Semi-Auto .22 Cal. Rifle - ser. no. range 1-39,999.
Model 1905 Semi-Auto Rifle - ser. no. range 1-29,078.
Model 1906 Semi-Auto Rifle - ser. no. range 1-79,999.
Model 1907 Semi-Auto Rifle - ser. no. range 1-9,999.

Winchester factory data on models produced between approx. 1907-1961 is almost non- existent (except Custom Shop mfg.) since there was a fire at the Winchester factory in 1961.

A NOTE ON WINCHESTER FINISHES: It is very important to understand that there is a big value difference between a Model 1873 with 90% bright blue as opposed to a gun that has patina finish (turning brown). A bright blue specimen might bring several times more, because it is closer to the way it originally left the factory - with bright bluing. "Brown" guns are simply not as desirable as guns that show little or no use and retain bright blue finish.

GRADING EXPLANATION FOR WINCHESTER LEVER ACTIONS

A combination of grading systems is being used exclusively for this section to assist the reader in ascertaining the value of a particular specimen more accurately. They work as follows - the top line contains three value ranges (Above Average, Average, or Below Average) which have been created to encompass most of the specimens commonly encountered within this model.

Since there is a drastic value difference between 95% - 50% bright blue and 30% dull patina/fading finish on older Winchesters, another grading/pricing line has been included to give you an example of the top end of the marketplace. Individual percentages of condition with corresponding values are listed here to give you a complete price range on older Winchester lever actions. While no grading system is perfect, it is hoped that this combination of pricing systems will be an advantage over previous attempts.

The three groupings include "Below Average Price Range", "Average Price Range", and "Above Average Price Range" (note the new grading line underneath specifying these condition factors). These ranges indicate the following:

BELOW AVERAGE PRICE RANGE - a specimen with no finish remaining, perhaps some parts have been replaced, deteriorated metal may be lightly pitted with faint barrel/frame markings, rounded edges of wood and metal, wood showing much wear with possible repairs or cracks, must be in working order.

AVERAGE PRICE RANGE - a specimen with all original parts, exhibits gun metal patina finish, metal mostly smooth (perhaps lightly pitted), principal lettering and markings legible throughout, wood showing honest wear with little finish remaining (may have small cracks and other imperfections), good working order.

ABOVE AVERAGE PRICE RANGE - a specimen featuring unpolished brass (on Henrys and Model 1866s) or plum brown patina with traces of bluing in protected areas (on all steel frame models), sharp corners, crisp barrel markings, traces of original finish remaining, metal should exhibit nice patina or older flaking finish, wood should have some original stock varnish remaining and minor handling marks and dings, good bore, perfect working order with no replacement parts.

VALUES FOR ABOVE AVERAGE CONDITION RANGE - this includes those specimens which are 50% bright blue or better condition - When this type of condition is encountered, refer to the grading/price line listing individual percentage of condition prices located underneath the Above Average, Average, or Below Average pricing line. You may notice a gap in prices between the Above Average high price and 50% price. This is normal, because in some cases, a rare 50% bright blue/bright brass specimen will be worth considerably more than one in Above Average condition.

RIFLES: LEVER ACTIONS - 1860-1964

HENRY RIFLE - .44 rimfire, 15 shot, 24 in. barrel with integral slotted tube mag. and loading lever, blue barrel, brass or iron frame. Approx. 13,000 total production, mfg. 1860-1866.

Because almost all Henrys have little or no original finish left, values below are in ranges rather than in separate condition factors.

Add 25%+ for engraving, depending on amount and condition (these specimens should have fancy wood).

	Above Average	Average	Below Average

* ***Iron Frame Model*** - frame made of iron, round type butt plate, without lever latch, adj. sporting type rear leaf sight, serial numbers are in three digits only. Total production is believed to be less than 300.

	$35,000 - $45,000	$25,000 - $35,000	$15,000 - $25,000

* ***First Model*** - approx. 3,500 mfg., generally serialized below 3,500, with or without lever latch, perch belly stock and slotted receiver for rear sight.

	$16,000 - $20,000	$12,000 - $16,000	$8,000 - $12,000

* ***Martial Marked*** - contracted by U.S. military for Civil War use, denoted by "C.G.C." inspector markings on upper barrel breech and stock, approx. 1,900 with serialization scattered.

	$20,000 - $25,000	$14,000 - $20,000	$10,000 - $14,000

This rifle was the most revolutionary shoulder weapon introduced in the Civil War.

* ***Late Model*** - similar to first model, except butt plate heel has pointed profile, lever latch became standard and receiver is not slotted for rear sight, serial numbers over approx. 3,500, most commonly encountered Henry with approx. 8,000 mfg.

	$12,000 - $16,000	$8,000 - $12,000	$6,500 - $8,000

MODEL 1866 LEVER ACTION

- .44 rimfire or centerfire (4th Model only), 24 in. barrel, blue barrel with brass frame, differs from Henry in that it has a wood forearm, frame cartridge loading port, and separate tube mag. Total production reached 170,101 for all models, mfg. 1866-1898.

* ***Model 1866 First Model Rifle*** - "Improved Henry" action, .44 cal. rimfire, without forend cap, serialization is concealed on lower tang inside butt stock, serial range is from mid 12,000 to mid 15,000 (in Henry serial range sequence).

	$11,000 - $14,000	$8,000 - $14,000	$6,000 - $8,000
	95% = $25,000	75% = $20,000	50% = $16,000

Buyer beware - watch for fakes!

* ***Model 1866 Carbine First Model*** - same action as Rifle, only with 20 in. barrel, 2 barrel bands and saddle ring.

	$5,000 - $7,000	$3,000 - $5,000	$2,500 - $3,000
	95% = $16,000	75% = $12,000	50% = $8,000

* ***Model 1866 Rifle Second Model*** - "New Model" with redesigned frame, with Henry barrel markings, serial number inside on the earlier guns after ser. no. 19,000, outside lower tang beneath lever (approx. after ser. no. 20,000).

	$4,400 - $6,500	$3,000 - $4,500	$2,000 - $3,000
	95% = $15,000	75% = $10,000	50% = $8,000

* ***Model 1866 Carbine Second Model*** - frame and other changes similar to Second Model Rifle.

	$3,000 - $4,500	$2,000 - $3,000	$1,250 - $2,000
	95% = $9,500	75% = $7,500	50% = $5,500

* ***Model 1866 Rifle Third Model*** - block style serial numbers usually located behind trigger, improved frame. Serial numbered approx. 25,000-149,000.

	$3,500 - $4,750	$2,500 - $3,500	$1,500 - $2,500
	95% = $10,000	75% = $8,000	50% = $6,500

* ***Model 1866 Carbine Third Model*** - same changes as Model 1866 Third Model Rifle, 20 in. barrel with 2 bands.

	$2,500 - $3,750	$1,750 - $2,500	$1,250 - $1,750
	95% = $8,250	75% = $6,750	50% = $5,000

* ***Model 1866 Musket Third Model*** - 27 in. round barrel, 24 in. magazine, 3 barrel bands.

	$2,500 - $3,500	$1,750 - $2,500	$1,250 - $1,750
	95% = $8,000	75% = $6,000	50% = $4,600

❋ *Model 1866 Rifle/Carbine/Musket Fourth Model* - .44 cal., twin rimfire and centerfire, script style serial number on lower tang near lever latch, improved frame, serial range approx. 149,000-170,101.

Values for these models are the same as for equivalent Third Model 1866s.
Subtract 20% for steel buttplate and forend cap on rifle.
This rifle is usually found with steel buttplate and forend cap.

MODEL 1873 LEVER ACTION

- .32-20 WCF, .38-40 WCF, or .44-40 WCF cal., iron frame with sideplates, frame loading port, 20 or 24 in. round or octagon barrel, rifles have forearm caps and carbines have forearm bands, tube mag., blue finish with case hardened parts, oil finished stock, serial numbered on lower tang, 720,610 mfg. between 1873-1919.

Since early Model 1873s were only made in .44 cal., no caliber markings are present. After the introduction of additional calibers, the barrels were stamped just in front of the receiver and on the brass elevator with the caliber.

Model 1873s are serial numbered sequentially on the lower tang. On guns serial numbered above 80,000 to 170,000, an "A" followed the number. From 170,000 to 190,000, either "A" or "B" may be found, while after 200,000, usually "B" was used. The letter does not seem to have any definite meaning. The earliest guns had no marking on the upper tang, but were marked "Model 1873" on the lower tang next to the ser. no. up to number 350, after which "Model 1873" is marked on the upper tang, where it remained through the model run.

Add 50% for Deluxe Model 1873 with color case hardened framed.

❋ *Model 1873 First Model Rifle* - serial numbers approx. 1 - 30,000, sliding thumbprint dust cover on 2 guides that are integral part of upper frame, absence of any cal. marking.

$1,400 - $2,000	$1,000 - $1,400	$700 - $1,000
95% = $7,250	75% = $4,500	50% = $2,500

❋ *Model 1873 Carbine First Model* - 20 in. round barrel with carbine style forearm band. Distinctive curved butt plate, with saddle ring.

$1,500 - $2,000	$1,100 - $1,500	$800 - $1,100
95% = $7,500	75% = $4,500	50% = $3,000

❋ *Model 1873 Musket First Model* - 30 in. round barrel, 27 in. mag. with 3 barrel bands, approx. 500 mfg.

$1,750 - $2,250	$1,250 - $1,750	$900 - $1,250
95% = $6,500	75% = $4,500	50% = $3,000

❋ *Model 1873 Rifle Second Model* - improved dust cover featuring slides on center rail on rear section of frame top which is held in place by two screws, serial range 31,000 - 90,000.

$800 - $1,200	$600 - $800	$300 - $600
95% = $3,750	75% = $2,500	50% = $1,500

❋ *Model 1873 Carbine Second Model* - changes similar to 1873 Second Model Rifle, with 20 in. round barrel and 2 barrel bands.

$1,000 - $1,500	$700 - $1,000	$300 - $700
95% = $5,750	75% = $4,250	50% = $3,100

❋ *Model 1873 Musket Second Model* - changes similar to 1873 Second Model Rifle, with 30 in. barrel and 3 barrel bands.

$1,200 - $1,500	$800 - $1,200	$500 - $800
95% = $3,650	75% = $2,750	50% = $1,875

❋ *Model 1873 Rifle Third Model* - dust cover rail integral with frame, serial 90,000- end of production.

$500 - $750	$400 - $500	$300 - $400
95% = $3,350	75% = $2,400	50% = $1,250

Add 20% for .44-40 WCF cal.
Add 30% for octagon barrel for .44-40 WCF cal. only.

	Above Average	Average	Below Average

* *Model 1873 Carbine Third Model* - changes similar to 1873 Rifle Third Model, with 20 in. barrel and 2 barrel bands.

	$800 - $1,250	$600 - $800	$400 - $600
	95% = $4,400	75% = $3,500	50% = $2,000

Add 30% for .32-20 WCF cal.

* *Model 1873 Musket Third Model* - 30 in. round barrel and 3 barrel bands.

	$800 - $1,000	$600 - $800	$400 - $600
	95% = $3,400	75% = $2,500	50% = $1,925

* *Model 1873 .22 Rimfire Rifle* - .22 S, L, or Extra L (very rare) cal., 24 in. barrel, no loading gate, the first .22 caliber repeater, 19,552 produced, mfg. 1884-1904. Made in rifle configuration only.

	$900 - $1,200	$700 - $900	$500 - $700
	95% = $3,250	75% = $2,000	50% = $1,350

Add 30% for takedown model.

* *Model 1873 "One of One Thousand "* - special care taken in manufacture to guarantee better accuracy, markings on top of breech designate model, deluxe walnut, extremely rare, barrel marked "One of One Thousand " in most cases, 136 mfg. Original cost was $100.
Values can range from $30,000 - $200,000, depending on condition. A factory letter is a must for any "One of One Thousand" Winchester. Believe it or not, watch for fake letters.
Note: Rarity of the "One of One Thousand" and the "One of One Hundred" models makes upgrading to this model fairly common. Use extreme caution in purchasing.

* *Model 1873 "One of One Hundred "* - similar to "One of One Thousand" only rarer, 8 mfg. Sold new for $20 over the list price of a similarly equipped Model 1873.
Values can range from $40,000 - $225,000, depending on condition. A factory letter is a must for any "One of One Hundred" Winchester. Believe it or not, watch for fake letters.

MODEL 1876 LEVER ACTION - .40-60 WCF, .45-60 WCF, .45-75 WCF(first caliber offered), or .50-95 Express cal., 22, 26, or 28 in. round or octagon barrel, similar but larger frame than Model 1873, tube mag., rifles have forearm caps while carbines have forearm bands, crescent butt, blue finish, straight grip stock, 63,871 mfg. between 1876-1897.
The Model 1876 was also called the Centennial Model since its introduction coincided with the U.S. Centennial Exposition held in Philadelphia, PA in 1876. Popularity for this model decreased ten years later when the more powerful and advanced Model 1886 was introduced.
Add 50% for Deluxe Model 1876s with color case hardened frames to the values listed.
Deluxe Models 1876 with 90%+ original case colors are rare.

* *Model 1876 Rifle First Model* - serial numbered approx. 1-5,000, distinguishable by no dust cover on frame top.

	$1,800 - $2,200	$1,400 - $1,800	$1,000 - $1,400
	95% = $7,500	75% = $5,500	50% = $4,000

* *Model 1876 Carbine First Model* - 22 in. round barrel, one barrel band, saddle ring, full length forearm giving a musket appearance.

	$2,500 - $3,500	$1,500 - $2,500	$1,000 - $1,500
	95% = $9,000	75% = $7,000	50% = $5,000

* *Model 1876 Musket First Model* - 32 in. round barrel with 1 band, scarce model because no foreign military contracts.

	$4,500 - $6,000	$3,000 - $4,500	$2,000 - $3,000
	95% = $15,000	75% = $10,000	50% = $7,000

* *Model 1876 Rifle Second Model* - "Thumbprint" dust cover rail held on by screw, serial range 5,000-30,000.

	$1,500 - $2,000	$1,200 - $1,500	$800 - $1,200
	95% = $5,500	75% = $4,000	50% = $2,750

Add 25% for .50-95 WCF cal.

	Above Average	Average	Below Average

Model 1876 Carbine Second Model - changes similar to Model 1876 Rifle Early Second Model, with 22 in. round barrel and full length forearm giving a musket appearance.

$1,800 - $2,950 $1,200 - $1,800 $900 - $1,200
95% = $8,000   75% = $5,150   50% = $3,675

Model 1876 Musket Second Model - changes similar to Model 1876 Rifle Early Second Model, with 32 in. round barrel and carbine forend tip.

$3,500 - $5,500 $2,500 - $3,500 $1,500 - $2,500
95% = $13,000   75% = $9,000   50% = $7,500

Model 1876 Rifle Third Model - dust cover rail integral with frame, serial range 30,000-end of production.

$1,500 - $2,000 $1,000 - $1,500 $700 - $1,000
95% = $6,500   75% = $4,000   50% = $2,500

Add 25% for .50-95 WCF cal.

Model 1876 Carbine Third Model - frame similar to Model 1876 Rifle Third Model, with 22 in. round barrel and full length forearm giving a musket appearance.

$1,500 - $2,500 $1,100 - $1,500 $800 - $1,100
95% = $7,500   75% = $5,000   50% = $3,000

Model 1876 Musket Third Model - frame similar to Model 1876 Rifle Third Model, with 32 in. round barrel.

$3,250 - $5,000 $2,250 - $3,250 $1,500 - $2,250
95% = $13,000   75% = $9,000   50% = $7,500

Model 1876 "One of One Thousand" - special care taken in manufacture to guarantee better accuracy, markings on top of breech designate model, deluxe walnut, extremely rare, 54 mfg. Original cost was $100.

Values can range from $35,000 - $250,000, depending on condition. A factory letter is a must for any "One of One Thousand" Winchester. Believe it or not, watch for fake letters.

Values are not listed because too few original specimens are bought or sold to accurately establish pricing. A factory letter is a must for any "One of One Thousand" Winchester.

Note: Rarity of the "One of One Thousand" and the "One of One Hundred" models makes unethical upgrading to this model fairly common. Use extreme caution in purchasing.

Model 1876 "One of One Hundred" - similar to "One of One Thousand" only rarer, 8 mfg. Sold new for $20 over the list price of a similarly equipped Model 1876.

Values can range from $45,000 - $500,000, depending on condition. A factory letter is a must for any "One of One Hundred" Winchester. Believe it or not, watch for fake letters.

Values are not listed because too few original specimens are bought or sold to accurately establish pricing. A factory letter is a must for any "One of One Hundred" Winchester.

Model 1876 Northwest Mounted Police Carbine - .45-75 WCF cal. only, 22 in. barrel, "NWMP" or "MP" marking may appear on stock (with wear, this cartouche may not be visible - the majority were not marked) approx. 1,600 mfg., factory records can only verify 150.

$3,000 - $4,000 $2,250 - $3,000 $1,500 - $2,250
95% = $9,500   75% = $7,750   50% = $5,275

Above average specimens in this model should have traces of blue. Be very wary of the stock cartouche since these butt stocks were sold as surplus back in the 1920s. A letter of authenticity is a good idea on this model.

MODEL 1886 LEVER ACTION - .33 WCF, .38-56 WCF, .38-70 WCF (830 mfg.), .40-65 WCF, .40-70 WCF (629 mfg.), .40-82 WCF, .45-70 Govt., .45-90, .50-110 Express, or .50-100-450 (234 mfg.) cal. available, Browning's first high power lever action design distinguishable by vertical locking bars, .45-70 Govt. most popular cal., 26 in. round or octagon barrel, tube mag., steel forend cap, straight grip stock. Approx. 159,990 mfg. between 1886-1935.

The Model 1886 had case hardening standard on the frame, butt plate, and forend cap until 1901

	Above Average	Average	Below Average

(approx. 122,000 serial range) when the standard finish became blue.

On the Model 1886 variations listed, add the following percentages for special order features.

Add 10% for octagon barrel.

Add 20% premium for Takedown Model.

Add 30% for .45-70 Govt. or .45-90 cal.

Add 100% for .50-110 or 125% for .50-100-450 cal.

Add 100% for Deluxe Model (pistol grip checkered walnut stock).

✳ *Model 1886 Rifle*

	$1,200 - $1,600	$900 - $1,200	$600 - $900
	95% = $4,000	75% = $3,000	50% = $1,600

✳ *Model 1886 Carbine* - same general specifications as Rifle, except 22 in. round barrel and saddle ring, solid frame only.

	$1,800 - $2,500	$1,400 - $1,800	$1,000 - $1,400
	95% = $11,000	75% = $7,500	50% = $4,000

Add 35% for full stock carbine (very rare).

✳ *Model 1886 Musket* - 30 in. round barrel, full length military style forearm, military sights, only 350 mfg., very rare.

	$4,450 - $6,000	$3,000 - $4,450	$2,250 - $3,000
	95% = $13,750	75% = $9,000	50% = $7,000

Most specimens encountered in this variation are in very good condition - a pitted musket is almost never encountered.

✳ *Model 1886 Lightweight Rifle* - .45-70 Govt. or .33 WCF cal. only, 22 (.45-70 Govt. cal.) or 24 (.33 WCF cal.) in. round nickel steel tapered barrel, half mag., rubber shotgun butt plate.

✳ *.33 caliber*

	$800 - $1,000	$600 - $800	$450 - $600
	95% = $2,250	75% = $1,500	50% = $1,100

✳ *.45-70 Govt. caliber*

	$1,400 - $1,850	$1,100 - $1,400	$750 - $1,100
	95% = $3,750	75% = $2,750	50% = $2,000

Since lightweight rifles were fairly late production, all specimens are blue and in very good condition usually.

100%	98%	95%	90%	80%	70%	60%	50%	40%	30%	20%	10%

MODEL 1892 RIFLE - .218 Bee (rare, if original), .25-20 WCF, .32-20 WCF, .38-40 WCF, or .44-40 WCF cal., 24 in. round or octagon barrel, blue, tube mag., forend cap, crescent butt. Mfg. 1,004,067 between 1892-1941.

N/A	N/A	$1,600	$1,275	$1,100	$995	$875	$775	$675	$550	$450	$350

Add 25% for .44-40 WCF cal.

Add 15% for .38-40 WCF cal.

Add 25% for Takedown Model.

Add 50% for fancy pistol grip checkered wood (Deluxe Model).

Add 20% for early antique ser. no. range under 168,000.

MODEL 1892 CARBINE - 20 in. round barrel, 2 barrel bands and saddle ring.

N/A	N/A	$2,275	$1,775	$1,300	$1,100	$995	$875	$775	$675	$550	$450

Add 25% for .44-40 WCF.

	Above Average	Average	Below Average

MODEL 1892 TRAPPER'S CARBINE - all features similar to standard SRC, except has a 14, 15, or 16 in. barrel, so called Trapper's Model because it was handy for trappers who had to carry a powerful but lightweight repeating rifle.

$1,250	$1,000	$750
95% = $5,500	75% = $4,000	50% = $3,000

Most 1892 Trapper's Carbines are in the 15 in., .44-40 WCF cal. configuration. Most of the 1892 Trapper's Carbine were shipped to South America or Australia. This variation is almost never encountered over 30% condition - most are brown guns. Check federal laws regarding 14 and 15 inch barrels.

MODEL 1892 MUSKET - 30 in. round barrel, full length military style forearm with military style rear sight.

$2,500	$2,000	$1,500
95% = $12,000	75% = $7,500	50% = $4,500

100%	98%	95%	90%	80%	70%	60%	50%	40%	30%	20%	10%

MODEL 1894 RIFLE - .25-35 WCF, .30-30 Win. (.30 WCF), .32-40 WCF, .32 Spl., or .38-55 WCF cal., most common (and popular) is .30-30 Win. cal., tube mag., 24 in. round or octagon barrel was standard, blue, straight grip stock. Over 5,000,000 produced to date, mfg. 1894-1929, newer Model 94 mfg. may be found in the RIFLES: MODEL 94 LEVER ACTION - POST 1964 PRODUCTION section.

✳ *1894-1929 Mfg.* - model 94s built post 1894-1929.

N/A	$1,550	$1,325	$1,125	$925	$850	$725	$650	$575	$500	$425	$350

Add 20% for takedown variation.
Add 20%+ for deluxe models.
Add 20% for 1894-1898 mfg. (pre-148,000 ser. no.).
Add approx. 15% for cals. other than .30-30 Win. or .32 Spl.

The Model 1894 Winchester has the distinction of being the world's most popular rifle. Deluxe models will command substantial premiums on models listed

	Above Average	Average	Below Average

MODEL 1894 TRAPPER'S CARBINE - all features similar to the standard SRC, except with a 14, 15, or 16 in. barrel.

$1,250	$1,000	$750
95% = $5,000	75% = $3,750	50% = $2,500

The large majority of this variation are encountered in .30-30 Win. cal. with 15 in. barrel. Any other caliber or barrel length will constitute a premium. Most of these carbines are brown and rusty. Rarely, if ever, encountered with very much finish remaining.
Note: Check federal laws on legality of 14 and 15 in. barrels.

100%	98%	95%	90%	80%	70%	60%	50%	40%	30%	20%	10%

MODEL 1894 SADDLE RING CARBINE - 20 in. round barrel.

N/A	N/A	$1,450	$1,250	$995	$875	$775	$675	$550	$450	$350	$295

Add 30% for Antique Model.
Add 35% for any cal. other than .30-30 Win. or .32 Spl.
Carbines with special order features such as pistol grip, deluxe wood, checkering, etc. can bring even greater premiums than the rifle.

✳ *Eastern Carbine* - features long forearm, early stock design, early style carbine post front sight, and without saddle ring, mfg. late '20s - early '30s.

N/A	N/A	$1,000	$900	$800	$700	$625	$550	$495	$450	$395	$350

100%	98%	95%	90%	80%	70%	60%	50%	40%	30%	20%	10%

MODEL 1894 1940-1964 PRODUCTION CARBINE - 1940-1964 mfg. without saddle ring, barrel is marked Model 94.

$395	$375	$350	$325	$300	$275	$250	$220	$195	$180	$165	$150

Add 40% for .25-35 WCF cal.

Some WWII carbines with special U.S. markings will bring a premium over prices listed.

Above Average	Average	Below Average

MODEL 1895 RIFLE FLATSIDE - .30 US (most common), .38-72, or .40-72 cal., early model, distinguishable in that frame does not have fluting or ridge contouring, serial range approx. 1-5000.

$700	$500	$300
95% = $2,750	75% = $1,750	50% = $1,250

Add 25% for octagon barrel on cals. .38-72 or .40-72.

MODEL 1895 RIFLE - .30-03, .30-06, .30-40 Krag, .303 Brit., .35 Win., .38-72, .40-72, .405 Win., or 7.62mm Russian cal., 24-28 in. barrel, blue action, box mag., straight grip stock, 425,881 mfg. from 1896-1931.

$600	$400	$250
95% = $3,000	75% = $1,750	50% = $1,250

Add 50% for Deluxe Models.
Add 25% for octagon barrel.
Add 50% for .405 Win. cal.
Add 15% for takedown model.

The Model 1895 was a Browning design incorporating the first box type mag. in a lever action repeating rifle. .30 US is the most commonly encountered cal. in this model. A large Russian military contract was secured in 1915 with chambering for the 7.62mm Russian cartridge (over 293,000 mfg. or over 66% of total production).

MODEL 1895 CARBINE - .30 US (.30/40 Krag Army - most common cal.), .30-03, .30-06, or .303 Brit. cal., 22 in. round barrel, military style top handguard wood and military sights, with or without saddle ring.

$650	$450	$300
95% = $2,750	75% = $1,750	50% = $1,250

Add 20% for caliber other than .30 U.S.
Add 50% for U.S. government marked.

MODEL 1895 FLATSIDE MUSKET - early models have serial range under 5,000, no flutes on frame, .30-40 Krag only.

Rarity on this model means only a few specimens in several museums.

MODEL 1895 MUSKET - .30-03, .30-06, or .30-40 Krag cal., 28 in. round barrel with hand guard over barrel, military sights.

$800	$600	$400
95% = $2,500	75% = $1,750	50% = $1,250

Add 10%-15% if U.S. Govt. marked.

MODEL 1895 NRA MUSKET - .30-03, .30-06, or .30-40 Krag cal., similar to Standard Musket grade with 24 or 30 in. barrel, 1901 Krag style rear sight. NRA approved for official NRA competition.

$1,000	$800	$600
95% = $3,000	75% = $2,100	50% = $1,500

Add 30% if U.S. government marked.

MODEL 1895 RUSSIAN MUSKET - 7.62mm Russian cal., over 293,000 mfg. for Imperial Russian Govt., mfg. 1915-1916, various Russian Ordnance stamps should be present.

$800	$600	$400
95% = $2,750	75% = $1,750	50% = $1,250

	Above Average	Average	Below Average

MODEL 53 RIFLE - .25-20 WCF, .32-20 WCF, or .44-40 WCF cal., 22 in. round barrel, ½ tube mag. holding 6 cartridges, solid frame or takedown, blue finish, pistol grip or straight grip stock, serial numbered both separately and within the Model 92 range. Mfg. 24,916 between 1924-1932.

$500	$325	$250
95% = $1,500	75% = $900	50% = $650

Add 40% for .44-40 WCF cal.
Add 15% for Takedown Model.

MODEL 55 RIFLE - .25-35 WCF, .30-30 Win., or .32 Win. Spl. cal., lever action design, solid frame and takedown, 24 in. round barrel, shotgun style butt stock with serrated steel butt plate, tube mag., holds 3 cartridges. Approx. 20,500 mfg. between 1924- 1932. Serial numbered independently to approx. 2,865, then serialized with Model 1894 production on underside of receiver. Simply could not compete with the Model 1894.

$450	$325	$250
95% = $1,200	75% = $700	50% = $500

Add 50% for .25-35 WCF cal.
Add 100% for Deluxe Model.
Add 15% for takedown model.

MODEL 64 RIFLE - .219 Zipper, .25-35 WCF, .30-30 Win., or .32 Win. Spl. cal., 20 or 24 in. round barrel, with standard 26 in. on the .219 Zipper, blue metal, pistol grip stock, revamped Model 55 action with increased mag. capacity, 66,783 mfg. between 1933-1957 and 1972-1973 (over 8,250 mfg. in .30-30 Win. cal. only - these last two years with minor changes).

$400	$300	$250
95% = $700	75% = $600	50% = $500

Add 30% for Deluxe Model.
Add 50% for 20 in. barrel (sometime referred to as Carbine).
Add 100% for .25-35 WCF cal.
Add 200% for .219 Zipper cal.

Many of this variation now have extra holes drilled on the top of the receiver to accept scope mounts - subtract 50% for this alteration. The Model 64 is usually found in excellent condition. Model 64 1972-1973 mfg. may be found in the post-'64 section.

MODEL 65 RIFLE - .218 Bee (introduced 1939), .25-20 WCF, or .32-20 WCF cal., 22 in. round barrel (except .218 Bee - 24 in.), ½ tube mag. holding 7 cartridges, blue with pistol grip stock. Mfg. 5704 between 1933-1947.

$1,000	$700	$500
95% = $2,500	75% = $1,800	50% = $1,250

While the .25-20 WCF cal. is the rarest, the .218 Bee has the most demand.
The Model 65 was a design evolved from the Model 53. The Model 65 was not tapped on receiver side for scope mounts. As a rule, most specimens are in either pretty nice or refinished condition.

100%	98%	95%	90%	80%	70%	60%	50%	40%	30%	20%	10%

MODEL 71 RIFLE STANDARD - .348 Win. cal., 2/3 tube mag. holding 4 cartridges, improved Model 1886 frame, blue metal with pistol grip stock, 20 or 24 in. barrel, short or long tang. Mfg. 47,254 between 1935-1957.

$950	$875	$795	$750	$700	$650	$600	$600	$600	$600	$600	$600

Add 30% for early variation long tang.
Add 100% for 20 in. carbine barrel.
Add 50% for Deluxe Model.

MODEL 88 RIFLE AND CARBINE - see listing under RIFLES: LEVER ACTION - POST-1964 PRODUCTION section.

	Above Average	Average	Below Average

W

RIFLES: SINGLE SHOT

MODEL 1885 - available in most popular cals. between .22-.50, falling block trigger guard activated action, John Browning's first high power single shot rifle design, many variations were made and we will list the standard types. Over 139,725 mfg. between 1885-1920.

This design was originally mfg. as the Model 1878 by the Browning Brothers in Ogden, UT in the early 1880s. Fewer than 600 were mfg. - see the Browning section for values.

✳ *Sporting Rifle Low Wall* - 24 or 26 in. round or octagon barrel was standard, open sights, solid frame, standard trigger.

$300	$225	$150
95% = $1,100	75% = $750	50% = $550

Add 20% for centerfire cal.
Add 50% for case colored frames, if in 95%+ original condition.

✳ *Sporting Rifle High Wall* - 30 in. barrel, standard trigger, open sights, solid frame. Available in various size and weight barrels numbered (in front of forearm) from numeric 1, 2, 3, 3½ (introduced 1910), 4, and 5, lightest to heaviest. Case hardened frames standard until 1901 when bluing became standard, three different frames depending on caliber. Heavier barrels in rare calibers will bring a premium.

$1,000	$800	$600
95% = $2,500	75% = $2,000	50% = $1,500

Add 25% for 20 ga. shotgun.
Add 30% for Takedown Model.
Add 25% for No. 5 barrel.
Add 25% for .45-70 Govt. or .50 cal.
Add 40% for Deluxe Model.
Add 20% for set trigger.
Add 40% for case colored receiver, if in 95%+ original condition.

✳ *Schuetzen Rifle* - high wall, 30 in. octagon barrel, double set triggers, spur lever, aperture sight, Schuetzen style stock, adj. palm rest and butt plate.

$2,500	$1,750	$1,250
95% = $4,500	75% = $3,750	50% = $3,000

Add 20% for Takedown frame.
Add 30% for case colored frame, if in 95%+ original condition.

Prices are for factory original guns only. Since this model had many shooting alterations performed by various aftermarket suppliers of its time, perhaps only 10% of remaining specimens are unaltered (or 100% factory).

✳ *High Wall Musket* - usually found in .22 LR cal.

$600	$500	$400
95% = $1,400	75% = $1,100	50% = $800

Add 50% for .45-70 Govt. or .45-90 cal.

✳ *Low Wall Musket (Winder Musket)* - low wall, 3rd model, .22 Short or LR (most common), 28 in. barrel, standard trigger and lever, military style stock and sights, grooved forearm, one barrel band.

$400	$300	$200
95% = $800	75% = $600	50% = $500

Grading	100%	98%	95%	90%	80%	70%	60%

MODEL 1885 LOW WALL GRADE I (CURRENT PRODUCTION) - .22 LR cal., features 24½ in. half-round, half-octagon barrel with buckhorn rear sights, uncheckered straight grip walnut stock and forearm, crescent buttplate, blue finish only, 8 lbs. 2,400 mfg. late 1999-2001.

$735	$625	$525

Last MSR was $828.

Grading			100%	98%	95%	90%	80%	70%	60%

✳ *Model 1885 Low Wall High Grade* - similar to Model 1885 Low Wall Grade I, except features frame engraving, 24 Kt. squirrel/cottontail scenes, fancy walnut stock and forearm with cut checkering. 1,100 mfg. late 1999-2001.

			$1,050	$875	$750				

Last MSR was $1,180.

100%	98%	95%	90%	80%	70%	60%	50%	40%	30%	20%	10%

MODEL 1900 SINGLE SHOT - .22 S and L cal., 18 in. round barrel, blue metal, open sights, one-piece straight grip gumwood stock without fitted butt plate, takedown, not serial numbered. Approx. 105,000 mfg. between 1899-1902.

N/A	N/A	$500	$400	$300	$250	$200	$175	$150	$140	$125	$110

This model is usually encountered with flaked frames.

MODEL 1902 SINGLE SHOT - similar to 1900, with minor improvements. Distinguishable by special shaped extended trigger guard. Not serial numbered. Approx. 640,299 mfg. between 1902-1931.

N/A		$400	$250	$200	$150	$120	$100	$90	$80	$75	$65 $60

Chambering included .22 cal. Extra Long in 1914 (interchangeable with S&L).

THUMB TRIGGER MODEL 99 - similar to 1902, with button behind cocking piece used to fire with thumb instead of trigger, not serial numbered. Approx. 75,433 were mfg. between 1904-1923.

N/A	$1,800	$1,500	$1,250	$1,000	$750	$600	$400	$350	$300	$250	$200

MODEL 1904 SINGLE SHOT - improved version of 1902, 21 in. round barrel, chambering included .22 Extra Long in 1914, not serial numbered. Approx. 302,859 mfg. between 1904-1931.

N/A	$400	$350	$300	$200	$175	$160	$150	$125	$100	$90	$80

✳ *Model 1904-A* - introduced 1927 with new sear bar and chambered for .22 LR.

N/A	$400	$275	$225	$200	$175	$160	$150	$125	$100	$90	$80

MODEL 47 - .22 S, L, or LR cal., single shot bolt action, 25 in. round barrel, unique bolt design, uncheckered walnut stock, 5¼ lbs., approx. 43,000 (not serial numbered) mfg. during 1948-1954.

$300	$250	$200	$180	$150	$140	$130	$125	$120	$115	$110	$100

MODEL 52 - please refer to listings in the Rifles: Bolt Action section.

MODEL 55 - .22 cal. only, top loading single shot, bottom ejection, 22 in. round barrel, open sporting sights, not serial numbered. Over 45,000 mfg. between 1958-1961.

$175	$135	$125	$115	$105	$95	$85	$75	$70	$65	$60	$60

Grading			100%	98%	95%	90%	80%	70%	60%

MODEL 58 SINGLE SHOT - similar to Models 1902 and 1904, .22 LR cal., 18 in. round barrel, open sights, takedown. Approx. 38,992 mfg. between 1928-1931.

			$600	$500	$300	$250	$200	$130	$120

MODEL 59 SINGLE SHOT - improved Model 58 with 23 in. round barrel and pistol grip stock with butt plate. Approx. 9,200 mfg. between 1930-1931.

			$500	$450	$400	$350	$300	$250	$200

This model was disc. due to lack of sales.

MODEL 60 - .22 S, L, or LR cal., improved Model 59, 23 in. round barrel increased to 27 in. 1933. Approx. 160,754 mfg. between 1930-1934.

			$315	$295	$225	$185	$160	$135	$110

Add 20% for 23 in. barrel.

Grading	100%	98%	95%	90%	80%	70%	60%

MODEL 60A SPORTER - .22 S, L, or LR cal., sporter variation of Model 60, pistol grip walnut stock. Disc.

	100%	98%	95%	90%	80%	70%	60%
	$350	$295	$250	$200	$180	$160	$135

MODEL 60A TARGET - similar to Model 60 with Lyman 55W aperture rear sight, heavier target stock, and 27 in. round tapered barrel. Approx. 6,118 mfg. between 1932- 1939.

	$400	$375	$350	$325	$275	$235	$200

MODEL 67/67A - .22 S, L, LR or .22 WRF (authorized 1935) cal., 20 in. (Boys Rifle), 24 (miniature target boring), and 27 in. (sporting or smooth bore) round barrels, same basic action as the Model 60, not serial numbered. Approx. 383,000 mfg. between 1934- 1963.

	$250	$200	$130	$100	$70	$60	$50

Add 25% for Boys rifle.
Add 100% for .22 WRF cal.
Add 100%-150% for smooth bore, depending on condition.

MODEL 677 - same basic specifications as Model 67, except no iron sights or sight cuts in barrel, not serial numbered, supplied with Win. 5-A scope, .22 WRF is scarce. Approx. 2,240 mfg. between 1937-1939.

	$1,500	$1,200	$1,000	$750	$600	$500	$350

MODEL 68 - .22 LR or .22 WRF cal., bolt action single shot, similar to Model 67, walnut stock, supplied with aperture sight (no rear sight), not serial numbered. Approx. 100,000 mfg. between 1934- 1946.

	$275	$225	$165	$125	$100	$65	$50

Add 200% for .22 WRF cal.

MODEL 121 SINGLE SHOT RIFLE - .22 LR cal., bolt action, 20¾ in. barrel, open sights, plain pistol grip stock. Mfg. 1967-1973.

	$115	$85	$70	$55	$45	$35	$30

MODEL 121Y SINGLE SHOT RIFLE - similar to 121, with shorter stock.

	$115	$85	$70	$55	$45	$35	$30

MODEL 121 DELUXE - similar to 121, with ramp front sight and sling swivels.

	$125	$90	$75	$60	$50	$40	$35

MODEL 310 SINGLE SHOT - .22 LR cal., bolt action, 22 in. barrel, open sights, checkered pistol grip stock, swivels. Mfg. 1972-1975.

	$200	$175	$140	$100	$80	$70	$60

100%	98%	95%	90%	80%	70%	60%	50%	40%	30%	20%	10%

RIFLES: BOLT ACTION

MODEL 1883 (HOTCHKISS REPEATER) - .45-70 Govt. cal., designed by Benjamin D. Hotchkiss, unique tube mag. located in butt stock attached to receiver, up-turn/pull- back bolt action, 26 in. round or octagon barrel standard on rifle. Over 84,000 mfg. between 1879-1889. Also available in carbine configuration (24 in. round barrel with one band), and musket (32 in. round barrel with cleaning rod and two barrel bands) - subtract 25%. Carbine extremely rare in Third Model (20 in. barrel).

※ *First Style* - approx. 6,419 mfg. with magazine cut off and safety control incorporated into one unit.

100%	98%	95%	90%	80%	70%	60%	50%	40%	30%	20%	10%
$2,150	$1,750	$1,500	$1,325	$1,200	$1,100	$1,000	$900	$850	$800	$750	$725

※ *Second Style* - approx. 16,102 mfg., magazine cut off on right receiver top, safety on left side.

100%	98%	95%	90%	80%	70%	60%	50%	40%	30%	20%	10%
$1,950	$1,750	$1,500	$1,300	$1,150	$1,050	$950	$850	$750	$650	$625	$600

100%	98%	95%	90%	80%	70%	60%	50%	40%	30%	20%	10%

✴ *Third Style* - most commonly encountered Hotchkiss, 2-piece stock, approx. 62,034 mfg. 1883- 1899.

$1,650	$1,425	$1,250	$1,100	$900	$825	$750	$675	$625	$565	$525	$480

The Model 1883 Hotchkiss was the first bolt action designed for the U.S. military .45-70 Govt. cartridge. On the First and Second models inspect wood directly below bolt and left frame side for cracks, breaks or older repairs as it is frequently encountered on these early models with thin wrists.

LEE STRAIGHT PULL RIFLE - 6mm Lee (.236 U.S.N. cal.), 5 shot non-detachable box mag., 24 (Sporting Rifle) or 28 (Musket) in. barrel, folding leaf sight, blue metal, military style full stock, mfg. 1897-1902, Navy Issue Model is the Musket with "236 U.S.N." on barrels. Approx. 20,000 mfg. (including 15,000 Muskets for the U.S. Navy military contract)between 1895-1902 with parts clean up occurring in 1916.

✴ *U.S.N. Military Musket*

$1,750	$1,500	$1,350	$1,200	$1,100	$1,000	$900	$800	$700	$650	$600	$550

✴ *Lee Sporting Rifle* - similar to Musket, with 24 in, barrel, sporter style stock. Approx. 1,700 mfg. 1897-1902.

$1,850	$1,625	$1,425	$1,300	$1,200	$1,100	$1,000	$900	$800	$700	$650	$600

This design was originally patented by James Paris Lee and assigned to the Lee Arms Company. Winchester obtained manufacturing rights to produce this model for the U.S Navy military contract 1895-1902.

MODEL 43 - .218 Bee, .22 Hornet, .25-20 WCF, or .32-20 WCF cal., dubbed "Poor Man's Model 70", 24 in. round tapered barrel, box type mag. Approx. 62,617 mfg. between 1949-1957.

$725	$600	$525	$450	$400	$350	$300	$250	$200	$175	$150	$125

Add 30% for Deluxe Model.

Add $50 for Special Grade.

Premiums exist (in order of rarity) for .32-20 WCF, .25-20 WCF, or .218 Bee cals.

Subtract 60% if non-factory drilled and tapped (early models).

On Models 52, 54, 56, 57, 58, 59, 60, 60A, 67, 677, 68, 69, 69A, 697, and 70 values in 50% or less original condition have been omitted since values in those conditions will approximate the 60% price. This reflects the fact that while these lower condition specimens are not as desirable to collectors, they are still sought after as shooters.

Grading	100%	98%	95%	90%	80%	70%	60%

MODEL 52 TARGET - .22 S (rare) or LR cal., 5 shot mag., 28 in. standard or heavy barrel (1st cataloged 1933), target sights and target style stock, speedlock trigger feature was introduced in 1929. Approx. 125,233 Model 52s in all variations were mfg. between 1919-1979.

	100%	98%	95%	90%	80%	70%	60%
	$500	$450	$395	$345	$315	$290	$265
With speedlock	$575	$525	$475	$425	$350	$310	$290

Barrel drilling and tapping for scope blocks was not standard on the first Model 52s, but became more apparent approx. 1926.

✴ *Model 52A Target* - similar to Model 52, except all A-suffix Model 52s have a speedlock action. Values are similar to Model 52 Target. In scarcity, it seems the E suffix is probably the scarcest (also the most poorly mfg.), followed by the A suffix variation.

MODEL 52A HEAVY BARREL - similar to Standard Target, with heavy barrel.

	$700	$750	$650	$550	$450	$400	$350

MODEL 52-B TARGET - extensively redesigned action, improved stock design, offered with a variety of sights. Approx. mfg. 1940-1947.

	$800	$700	$600	$500	$415	$360	$305

MODEL 52-B HEAVY BARREL - similar to 52-B, with heavy barrel, with adj. sling swivel as to position of front swivel, and single shot adapter.

	$850	$750	$650	$550	$500	$400	$350

Grading	100%	98%	95%	90%	80%	70%	60%

MODEL 52-B BULL GUN - extra heavy weight barrel.
| | $1,000 | $800 | $700 | $600 | $500 | $450 | $400 |

MODEL 52 SPORTER (SPORTING RIFLE) - 24 in. round lightweight barrel with front sight cover, sporting type select walnut stock with cheekpiece, hard rubber pistol grip cap, black plastic tipped forearm, checkered steel butt plate, about 7¼ lbs. Mfg. 1934-1958. There is some controversy whether any of the Model 52 Sporters were drilled and tapped per factory worksmanship. Be cautious of "factory" drilled and tapped receivers on all model 52s, as there are many "gunsmith" Sporters that have been made with turned down, shortened target barrels.

* ***Model 52*** - advertised approx. 1936.
| | $3,200 | $2,900 | $2,500 | $2,000 | $1,500 | $1,300 | $1,100 |

* ***Model 52A*** - introduced approx. 1937, receiver and locking lug were strengthened. Very rare.
| | $3,700 | $3,400 | $3,000 | $2,200 | $1,700 | $1,500 | $1,150 |

* ***Model 52B*** - introduced approx. 1940, 5 shot detachable mag.
| | $3,350 | $2,850 | $2,600 | $1,750 | $1,550 | $1,300 | $1,200 |

* ***Model 52B (1993 Re-issue)*** - .22 LR cal., patterned after the original Model 52B and includes steel buttplate, 24 in. barrel w/o sights, Micro Motion trigger with adjustment screw on forend, high-polish blue, 5 shot mag., checkered 52B style stock with ebony forend tip, 7 lbs. Mfg. by Miroku in Japan beginning 1993.
| MSR $662 | $500 | $460 | $430 | $395 | $360 | $330 | $300 |

* ***Model 52C*** - introduced 1947 with adj. Micro Motion trigger, approx. 500-1,000 mfg., 2 screws in trigger guard.
| | $3,500 | $3,200 | $3,000 | $2,500 | $1,650 | $1,275 | $1,150 |

A few Model 52 Sporters & Targets were mfg. with stainless steel barrels (17,XXX-27,XXX serial range) - these guns will command a premium over values shown.

MODEL 52-C STANDARD TARGET - "Micro Motion" trigger and "Marksman" stock, single shot adaptor, 5 or 10 shot mag. was avail., standard barrel, otherwise similar to 52- B. Mfg. 1947-1961.
| | $900 | $800 | $700 | $600 | $500 | $400 | $375 |

MODEL 52-C HEAVY TARGET - similar to Standard Target, with heavy barrel.
| | $950 | $850 | $750 | $600 | $500 | $425 | $350 |

MODEL 52-C BULL TARGET - extra heavy (bull) barrel model of Heavy Target 52-C. Mfg. approx. 1947-1961.
| | $1,200 | $995 | $875 | $625 | $600 | $500 | $400 |

MODEL 52-D TARGET - improved version of 52-C with free floating standard or heavy barrel and adj. bedding device, all 52-Ds were single shot.
| | $800 | $700 | $600 | $500 | $400 | $350 | $300 |

MODEL 52-D INTERNATIONAL MATCH - similar to 52-D, with free rifle stock, accessory rail. Mfg. 1969-1975.
| | $1,000 | $850 | $750 | $625 | $550 | $495 | $470 |

Previous Model 52s had ser. no. suffixes - either A, B, C, or D. After approx. 1975, rifles started appearing with an E serial prefix. Both Model 52 International and Prone could have factory stocks that were not Winchester mfg.

MODEL 52-D PRONE - similar to International Match, with prone style stock. Mfg. 1960-1975.
| | $825 | $725 | $650 | $575 | $500 | $470 | $385 |

MODEL 52-E INTERNATIONAL PRONE - similar to 52-D, with prone stock, removable roll over cheekpiece. Mfg. 1975-1980.
| | $600 | $500 | $450 | $425 | $350 | $325 | $300 |

Grading	100%	98%	95%	90%	80%	70%	60%

MODEL 54 HIGH POWER SPORTER - .270 Win., 7x57mm, 7.65x57mm Mauser(rare), .30-30 Win., .30-06, 9x57mm Mauser (rare) cal., 5 shot mag., 24 in. barrel, open sights, checkered pistol grip stock. Mfg. 1925-1930. Approx. 50,145 Model 54s were mfg. in all variations between 1925-1936.

| | $900 | $800 | $650 | $550 | $450 | $350 | $300 |

Rare cals. will add premiums to the values listed. This model was also mfg. with a stainless steel barrel during the late 1920s - early '30s with premiums also being asked.

MODEL 54 CARBINE - introduced 1927, similar to Rifle, with 20 in. barrel, plain stock.

| | $1,000 | $800 | $750 | $650 | $500 | $400 | $360 |

MODEL 54 IMPROVED SPORTER - .22 Hornet, .220 Swift, .250-3000, .257 Robts., .270, 7x57mm, or .30-06 cal., 5 shot mag., 24 or 26 in. barrel, one piece firing pin, checkered pistol grip stock. Mfg. 1930-1936.

| | $900 | $800 | $700 | $600 | $500 | $400 | $350 |

Rare cals. will add premiums to the values listedlisted.

MODEL 54 CARBINE IMPROVED - similar to Rifle, with 20 in. barrel.

| | $1,000 | $850 | $800 | $750 | $700 | $600 | $500 |

MODEL 54 SUPER GRADE - introduced 1934, similar to Sporter, with better wood and black forend tip and pistol grip cap.

| | $1,500 | $1,250 | $1,100 | $900 | $800 | $700 | $600 |

Rare calibers will command considerable premiums (i.e. this variation in 7x57mm cal. will sell for $2,500 in mint condition).

MODEL 54 SPORTING SNIPER'S RIFLE - introduced 1929, similar to Sporter, with 26 in. heavy barrel, .30-06 only, aperture sight.

| | $1,500 | $1,250 | $1,100 | $1,000 | $850 | $750 | $650 |

MODEL 54 NATIONAL MATCH - introduced 1935, similar to Standard, with Lyman sights and Marksman stock.

| | $1,000 | $875 | $775 | $695 | $625 | $550 | $525 |

MODEL 56 SPORTER - .22 S or LR cal., 5 or 10 shot box mag., 22 in. round barrel, open sights, plain pistol grip stock. Approx. 8,297 mfg. between 1926-1929.

| | $1,250 | $1,000 | $750 | $600 | $500 | $400 | $300 |

The .22 cal. Short was disc. 1929.

MODEL 57 - .22 S or LR cal., 22 in. barrel, open sights, stock cutaway for aperture sight on left side, drilled and tapped receiver, pistol grip walnut stock with barrel band, 5 or 10 shot mag., left side push-button mag. release, approx. 5½ lbs.

| | $575 | $495 | $450 | $395 | $350 | $300 | $250 |

Add 20% for .22 Short cal.

✳ *Model 57 Target* - similar to Model 56, except with aperture sight and heavier target stock. Approx. 18,600 were mfg. between 1926-1936.

| | $595 | $525 | $450 | $375 | $300 | $260 | $220 |

MODEL 69 & 69A - .22 S, LR, or RF cal., 5 or 10 shot repeater, 25 in. barrel, aperture or open rear sight, not serial numbered. Approx. 355,000 mfg. between 1935-1963.

| | $425 | $365 | $300 | $235 | $150 | $100 | $85 |

Add 40% for Target Model.
Add 20% for grooved receiver (Model 69A only).
Add 5% for chrome plated bolt handle and trigger guard.

The Model 69 was cocked by the closing motion of the bolt and had a non-swept back bolt handle, whereas the 69A was cocked by the opening motion of the bolt and had a swept back bolt handle. Number 97B rear aperture sight and 80A hooded front target sights and standard open sights were offered on both the Model 69 and 69A.

Grading	100%	98%	95%	90%	80%	70%	60%

MODEL 72/72A - .22 LR and Gallery Model (.22 short only), tube mag., bolt action, 25 in. round, tapered barrel, aperture or open rear sight, not serial numbered. Over 161,000 mfg. between 1938-1959.

| | $450 | $375 | $300 | $250 | $115 | $100 | $85 |

> **Add 30% for Target Model.**
> **Add 100% for Gallery Model (mfg. 1939-1942) - rare.**
> **Add 20% for grooved receiver (Model 72A only).**
> **Add 5% for chrome plated bolt handle and trigger guard.**
> The Model 72 and 72A both cocked on opening. The Model 72A has a swept back bolt handle and some minor internal mechanical improvements. Same open sight options as Models 69/ 69A.

MODEL 75 TARGET - .22 LR, 5 or 10 shot mag., 28 in. barrel, target sights, slight variation used by Government in WWII. Approx. 88,715 Model 75 Target and Model 75s were mfg. between 1938- 1958.

| | $550 | $475 | $425 | $350 | $300 | $275 | $250 |

> **Add 25% for Olympic sights.**
> **Add 20% for original Winchester leather sling.**

MODEL 75 SPORTER - similar to Target, except 24 in. tapered barrel, detachable mag., non-target sights and select checkered walnut.

| | $795 | $700 | $575 | $475 | $425 | $350 | $275 |

> **Add 20%-25% for "grooved" receiver allowing "tip-off" scope mounts.**

MODEL 131 BOLT ACTION - .22 S, L, and LR, 7 shot mag.

| | $225 | $200 | $175 | $150 | $125 | $95 | $75 |

MODEL 141 BOLT ACTION - .22 S, L, and LR, butt loading tube mage.

| | $225 | $200 | $175 | $150 | $125 | $95 | $75 |

MODEL 320 RIFLE - .22 LR cal., similar to Single Shot 310, with 5 shot mag. Mfg. 1972- 1974.

| | $325 | $325 | $300 | $265 | $235 | $185 | $150 |

MODEL 325 RIFLE - .22 Mag. cal., otherwise similar to Model 320, limited mfg. 1972- 74.

| | $375 | $350 | $325 | $300 | $250 | $200 | $100 |

MODEL 670 BOLT ACTION RIFLE - another economy version of the model 70, .225 Win., .243 Win., .270 Win, .308 Win., or .30-06 cal., 22 in. barrel, open sights, no hinged floorplate, pistol grip stock. Mfg. 1967-1973.

| | $300 | $250 | $220 | $195 | $175 | $165 | $140 |

MODEL 670 CARBINE - similar to 670, with 19 in. barrel, not available in .308 Win. Mfg. 1967-1970.

| | $300 | $250 | $220 | $195 | $175 | $165 | $140 |

MODEL 670 MAGNUM - similar to 670, with reinforced stock, .264 Mag., 7mm Mag., or .300 Win. Mag. cal. Mfg. 1967-1970.

| | $330 | $275 | $255 | $220 | $205 | $195 | $165 |

MODEL 697 - .22 WRF cal., same general specifications as the Model 69, except no iron sights or sight cuts in barrel and no ramp or sight cover. Telescope bases attached to barrel were standard.

| | $1,500 | $1,200 | $1,000 | $750 | $600 | $500 | $400 |

MODEL 770 BOLT ACTION - .22-250 Rem., .222 Rem., .243 Win., .270 Win., .30- 06, or .308 Win. cal., 22 in. barrel, open sights, no floorplate or forend tip. Mfg. 1969- 1971.

| | $325 | $285 | $275 | $260 | $250 | $220 | $195 |

MODEL 770 MAGNUM - similar to Standard, in .264 Mag., 7mm Mag., or .300 Win. Mag. cal., recoil pad. Mfg. 1969-1971.

| | $350 | $310 | $285 | $275 | $265 | $250 | $220 |

W

MODEL 777 - .30-06 cal., bolt action, 4 shot mag., mfg. by Nikko in Japan during 1979-80 for sale to Winchester subsidiaries in Australia, Germany, Italy, and Scandinavia, only 3 were shipped to the U.S., checkered Monte Carlo stock with Wundhammer swell grip, lightweight barrel, engraved action, "Winchester" is cast on the left side of the receiver near the top, approx. 1,000 mfg. with 250 in .30-06 cal. - 750 mfg. in different cal. and sold elsewhere, 8½ lbs.

Extreme rarity factor precludes accurate price evaluation. Some specimens have been reported as sold in the $1,850+ range.

100%	98%	95%	90%	80%	70%	60%	50%	40%	30%	20%	10%

RIFLES: SEMI-AUTO

MODEL 1903 - .22 Win. Auto rimfire cal., 10 shot tube mag., 20 in. round barrel, open sights, straight grip stock cut out for partial magazine filling. Approx. 126,000 mfg. between 1903-1932.

$695	$600	$550	$500	$450	$400	$350	$300	$275	$250	$200	$150

First U.S. semi-auto rifle designed for a special .22 cal. rimfire cartridge. Regular .22 cal. rimfire will not function or chamber properly in this model. The earliest models up to around ser. no. 5,000 were mfg. w/o a safety.

MODEL 1905 - .32 Win. or .35 Win. cal., 5 or 10 shot box mag., 22 in. round barrel, open sights, straight or plain pistol grip stock. Approx. 29,113 mfg. between 1905-1920.

$650	$575	$525	$465	$400	$365	$330	$300	$275	$250	$225	$195

MODEL 1907 - .351 Win. cal., 5 or 10 shot box mag., 20 in. round barrel, open sights, plain pistol grip stock, an improved version of the Model 1905. Approx. 58,490 mfg. between 1907-1957.

$595	$525	$450	$375	$325	$295	$265	$230	$195	$175	$160	$145

MODEL 1910 - .401 Win. cal., 4 shot box mag., 20 in. barrel, open sight, plain pistol grip stock. Mfg. 20,786 between 1910-1936.

$750	$625	$550	$500	$450	$400	$365	$330	$300	$275	$250	$225

Add 25% for Fancy Sporting Rifle (special checkered walnut).

MODEL 55 - please refer to listing in Rifles: Single Shot.

MODEL 63 - .22 LR cal., styling similar to Model 1903, take-down, 10 shot tube mag., 20 (disc. 1936) or 23 in. barrel, open sights, plain pistol grip stock. Approx. 174,692 mfg. between 1933-1958.

$850	$750	$675	$550	$425	$350	$300	$265	$235	$215	$190	$175

Add 20% for grooved receiver variation (WFF)
Add 50%-100% for 20 in. barrel (carbine) depending on condition.

The Model 63 was introduced to take advantage of the new .22 LR cartridge, which the older Model 1903 couldn't chamber.

Grading	100%	98%	95%	90%	80%	70%	60%

MODEL 63 GRADE I - RECENT PRODUCTION - .22 LR cal., similar to original Model 63, 10 shot mag., 23 in. barrel, checkered walnut stock and forearm, blue finish with engraved receiver, 6¼ lbs. Mfg. 1997-98.

	$610	$550	$500				

Last MSR was $678.

* **Model 63 High Grade - Recent Mfg.** - .22 LR cal., similar to original Model 63, 10 shot mag., deluxe checkered walnut stock and forearm, blue finish with engraved gold animals and accents on receiver, 6¼ lbs. 1,000 mfg. 1997 only.

	$950	$825	$700				

Last MSR was $1,083.

100%	98%	95%	90%	80%	70%	60%	50%	40%	30%	20%	10%

MODEL 74 - .22 S or LR cal., tubular mag. in stock, pop-out bolt assembly. Approx. 406,574 mfg. between 1939-1955. Distinguishable by squared off rear receiver.

100%	98%	95%	90%	80%	70%	60%	50%	40%	30%	20%	10%
$295	$250	$215	$175	$150	$125	$95	$90	$85	$80	$75	$70

    Add 25% for .22 Short.
    Add 25% for pre-WWII mfg.

MODEL 77 - .22 LR cal., detachable box mag. or tubular mag. under barrel. Over 217,000 mfg. between 1955-1962.

100%	98%	95%	90%	80%	70%	60%	50%	40%	30%	20%	10%
$250	$225	$200	$175	$110	$100	$95	$90	$85	$80	$75	$70

    Add $50 for tube mag.

Grading	100%	98%	95%	90%	80%	70%	60%

MODEL 100 RIFLE - .243 Win., .284 Win., or .308 Win. cal., 4 shot detachable mag., 22 in. round barrel with open sights, gas operated, basket weave pattern impressed on stock, pistol grip cap. Over 262,000 mfg. 1961-1973 with some production occurring in Japan.

	100%	98%	95%	90%	80%	70%	60%
	$500	$450	$400	$300	$250	$230	$215

The pre-1964 .284 Win. cal. with cut checkering was made for less than one year (WFF, ser. range 72,xxx with no letter suffix or prefix).

✳ *Pre-1964 production*
    Add $25 for .243 Win. cal.
    Add $150 for .284 Win. cal.

MODEL 100 CARBINE - similar to rifle, with 19 in. barrel, plain pistol grip stock, barrel band. Mfg. 1967-1973.

	100%	98%	95%	90%	80%	70%	60%
	$600	$500	$400	$350	$300	$250	$200

    Add $25 for .243 Win. cal.
    Add $150 for .284 Win. cal.

MODEL 190 RIFLE - .22 S, L, or LR cal., semi-auto, 15 shot LR tube mag., alloy receiver, uncheckered walnut finished hardwood stock, 20½ (Carbine Model) or 24 (Rifle Model) in. barrel, approx. 2,150,000 (including the Model 290 listed also) during 1967-1980.

	100%	98%	95%	90%	80%	70%	60%
	$150	$125	$100	$85	$75	$65	$55

MODEL 290 DELUXE RIFLE - similar to 190, with select Monte Carlo stock. Mfg. 1965-1973.

	100%	98%	95%	90%	80%	70%	60%
	$200	$175	$150	$115	$100	$90	$80

MODEL 490 RIFLE - .22 LR cal., 5 shot mag., 22 in. barrel, folding sight, checkered one piece stock. Mfg. 1975-1980.

	100%	98%	95%	90%	80%	70%	60%
	$250	$215	$185	$155	$145	$130	$110

100%	98%	95%	90%	80%	70%	60%	50%	40%	30%	20%	10%

RIFLES: SLIDE ACTION, DISC.

MODEL 1890 SLIDE ACTION - .22 S, L, LR, or WRF rimfire, cals. are non-interchangeable (don't shoot a .22 S in a gun chambered for .22 L) and the barrel is marked for single cal. only, visible hammer, solid-frame (first 15,000) or takedown, 24 in. octagonal barrel, case hardened receivers until 1901. Approx. 849,000 mfg. between 1890-1932.

✳ *Model 1890 First Model Solid Frame* - color case hardened receiver, mfg. 1890-1892.

100%	98%	95%	90%	80%	70%	60%	50%	40%	30%	20%	10%
N/A	$10,000	$8,000	$7,000	$6,000	$4,500	$4,000	$3,500	$3,000	$2,500	$2,000	$1,250

✳ *Model 1890 Second Model Takedown Frame* - color case hardened receiver, takedown feature was added in 1892 after over 15,000 solid frames had been made. Mfg. 1892-1901.

100%	98%	95%	90%	80%	70%	60%	50%	40%	30%	20%	10%
N/A	$4,250	$3,750	$3,000	$2,750	$2,250	$1,750	$1,500	$1,000	$800	$500	$350

100%	98%	95%	90%	80%	70%	60%	50%	40%	30%	20%	10%

❋ *Model 1890 Takedown w/Blue Finish* - most commonly encountered Model 1890, post-1901 manufacture.

N/A	$1,000	$900	$800	$700	$600	$500	$400	$350	$300	$275	$235

Add 50% for .22 LR cal. (mfg circa 1922-1932).

.22 LR cal. accounted for approx. 10% of the total production on this model.

Deluxe model will bring premiums over values listed. There were also a limited amount of guns mfg. with stainless steel barrels which will add to values of post-1901 mfg.

The Model 1890 was Winchester's first slide action repeating rifle. It replaced the Model 1873 .22 cal. It was an excellent and inexpensive .22 rifle that rapidly became the universal firearm used in shooting galleries. Even though production reached approx. 849,000 units, most guns were heavily used and specimens existing today in 98%+ condition are rare. Check carefully for rebarreling (notice proofmarks on barrel).

MODEL 1906 - .22 S, L, or LR, 20 in. round barrel, tube mag., visible hammer, open sights, straight stock with shotgun butt plate. Approx. 848,000 mfg. between 1906- 1932.

N/A	$800	$700	$500	$400	$325	$250	$225	$175	$150	$125	$100

This model is seldom encountered in over 90% original condition.

❋ *Model 1906 Expert* - similar to Model 1906, except has a pistol grip stock and different shaped slide handle, finish choices included blue, nickel trimmed receiver, guard, and bolt, or full nickel trimmed, mfg. 1917-1925.

N/A	$1,200	$1,000	$800	$625	$425	$400	$300	$275	$250	$225	$200

MODEL 61 HAMMERLESS - .22 S, L, LR, or WRF cal., 24 in. round or octagonal barrel (with rifling or smooth bore, i.e. Routledge), tube mag., open sights, plain grip stock. Approx. 343,XXX mfg. between 1932-1963.

$700	$600	$500	$400	$325	$300	$275	$225	$200	$185	$170	$150

Add 50% for single cal. barrel marking.
Add 30% for grooved receiver.
Add 200% for Routledge bore (WFF).

Pre-war manufacture has small forearm. Pre-war octagon barrel in S or L cals. will command a 100% premium. "WRF" marked round barrel is rare - front of receiver must be marked "W.R.F.".

❋ *Model 61 Octagon* - .22 S, LR, or WRF cal., octagon barrel variation of the Model 61. Disc. approx. 1943.

N/A	$1,800	$1,700	$1,500	$1,200	$900	$700	$615	$550	$500	$450	$395

Add 30% for .22 Short cal.

❋ *Model 61 Magnum* - similar to Standard 61, but chambered for .22 Win. Mag. Mfg. 1960-1963.

N/A	$900	$800	$700	$600	$500	$400	$350	$300	$275	$250	$225

MODEL 62/62A VISIBLE HAMMER - modern version of 1890, will shoot calibers interchangably, 23 in. round tapered barrel. Over 409,000 mfg. between 1932-1958.

$650	$600	$500	$400	$350	$300	$250	$200	$185	$170	$155	$130

Add 50% for Gallery model.

Pre-war model is 62, distinguishable by small forearm. The Model 62-A was introduced 1940 at serial number 99,200 with minor changes. Model 62A single cal. barrel markings do not add premiums. .22 Short only models without the Winchester roll die receiver marking are more scarce than the so-called "Gallery Rifle" - mint specimens without the roll die marking are approx. $1,000. Gallery variations of these models will also command sizable premium.

Grading	100%	98%	95%	90%	80%	70%	60%

MODEL 270 SLIDE ACTION - .22 rimfire, tube mag., 20½ in. barrel, checkered walnut pistol grip stock. Mfg. 1963-1973.

	$150	$135	$120	$100	$80	$70	$60

❋ *Plastic forearm variation*

	$150	$135	$120	$100	$80	$70	$60

Grading	100%	98%	95%	90%	80%	70%	60%

* Model 270 Deluxe - similar to 270, with select wood, Monte Carlo stock. Mfg. 1965-1973.

| | $195 | $150 | $110 | $80 | $70 | $60 | $50 |

MODEL 275 - similar to 270, in .22 Mag.

| | $165 | $150 | $135 | $100 | $80 | $70 | $65 |

* Model 275 Deluxe - similar to 270 Deluxe, in .22 Mag.

| | $210 | $160 | $140 | $110 | $80 | $70 | $60 |

RIFLES: LEVER ACTION - POST 1964 PRODUCTION

Beginning in 1992, all Model 94s and variations (not including the 9422 models) received an engineering change utilizing a cross-bolt in the upper rear of the receiver that prevents the hammer from contacting the firing pin.

MODEL 64 1972-1974 MODEL - .30-30 Win. cal., lever action, 5 shot, 2/3 tube mag., 24 in. barrel, open sight, plain pistol grip stock. Mfg. 1972-1974.

| | $400 | $350 | $300 | $250 | $200 | $150 | $125 |

MODEL 88 LEVER ACTION RIFLE - pre-'64 version with diamond cut checkering, no barrel band, 22 in. barrel. Mfg. 1955-1963. Total production for all varieties of the Model 88 Lever Action was approx. 284,000 units.

.308 Win. (1955-1963)	$850	$550	$450	$400	$340	$275	$200
.243 Win. (1956-1963)	$900	$600	$550	$450	$400	$350	$325
.358 Win. (1956-1962)	$1,995	$1,400	$1,200	$1,000	$850	$750	$700
.284 Win. (Intro-1963)	$1,495	$1,200	$1,000	$900	$800	$700	$550

MODEL 88 LEVER ACTION RIFLE - 1964 model with impressed basket weave checkering, no barrel band, 22 in. barrel. Mfg. 1964-1973.

.308 Win. (1964-N/A)	$575	$475	$400	$350	$300	$250	$200
.243 Win. (1964-N/A)	$650	$525	$450	$400	$350	$300	$250
.284 Win. (1964-N/A)	$950	$775	$700	$650	$600	$450	$400

MODEL 88 LEVER ACTION CARBINE - introduced 1968, no checkering, one-piece stock, barrel band, 19 in. barrel. Mfg. 1968-1973.

.308 Win. (1968-1973)	$795	$600	$500	$450	$350	$300	$250
.243 Win. (1968-N/A)	$875	$625	$500	$450	$350	$300	$250
.284 Win. (1968-N/A)	$1,375	$1,200	$900	$650	$575	$475	$350

MODEL 150 LEVER ACTION - .22 rimfire, 20½ in. barrel, tube mag., hammerless, uncheckered hardwood stock and forearm, sling swivels, approx. 47,400 mfg. 1967-1974.

| | $125 | $110 | $95 | $70 | $60 | $50 | $40 |

MODEL 250 LEVER ACTION - .22 rimfire, 20½ in. barrel, tube mag., hammerless, checkered pistol grip stock. Mfg. 1963-1973.

| | $150 | $125 | $110 | $95 | $70 | $60 | $50 |

* Model 250 Deluxe - similar to Model 250, with select wood and sling swivels. Mfg. 1965-1971.

| | $195 | $155 | $110 | $95 | $70 | $60 | $50 |

MODEL 255 - .22 Mag., otherwise similar to Model 250. Mfg. 1964-1970.

| | $195 | $175 | $150 | $135 | $110 | $85 | $70 |

* Model 255 Deluxe - .22 Mag., with select wood and swivels. Mfg. 1965-1973.

| | $260 | $210 | $165 | $150 | $135 | $100 | $75 |

MODEL 1886 GRADE I - .45-70 Govt. cal., 26 in. octagon barrel. Mfg. 1997-98.

| | $900 | $850 | $750 | $650 | $600 | $500 | $450 |

Last MSR was $996.

Grading	100%	98%	95%	90%	80%	70%	60%

✱ *Model 1886 High Grade* - .45-70 Govt. cal., features gold-line receiver engraving with multiple gold animals, polished blue, deluxe checkered walnut stock and forearm with metal cap, 1,000 mfg. 1997 only.

	$1,475	$1,200	$995

Last MSR was $1,588.

MODEL 1886 TAKEDOWN - .45-70 Govt. cal., features original takedown action design, uncheckered semi-pistol grip walnut stock with crescent buttplate, 26 in. octagon barrel with buckhorn rear sight, forend has ebony cap, 9¼ lbs. Mfg. 1999 only.

$995	$875	$750	$625	$600	$500	$400

Last MSR was $1,140.

MODEL 1886 EXTRA LIGHT GRADE I - .45-70 Govt. cal., 22 in. round tapered barrel, shotgun buttplate, half magazine, high polish receiver and barel bluing, open sights, uncheckered walnut stock and forearm, 7¼ lbs. 3,500 mfg. 2000-2001.

$1,025	$875	$750

Last MSR was $1,152.

✱ *Model 1886 Extra Light High Grade* - similar to Model 1886 Extra Light Grade I, except features engraved elk and whitetail deer and game scenes on blue receiver, extra fancy checkered walnut stock and forearm, 7¼ lbs. 1,000 mfg. 2000-2001.

$1,225	$915	$800

Last MSR was $1,440.

MODEL 1892 GRADE I - .357 Mag. (new 1998), .44-40 WCF (new 1998), or .45 LC cal., similar to original Model 1892 Winchester, 24 in. round barrel, top tang mounted manual hammer stop, blue finish with etched receiver engraving, gold trigger, satin finished walnut straight grip stock and forend with metal cap, 6¼ lbs. Mfg. 1997-99.

$665	$560	$430

Last MSR was $744.

✱ *Model 1892 Short Rifle* - .44 Mag. cal., features 20 in. round barrel with full mag., uncheckered staight grip walnut stock with crescent buttplate, buckhorn rear sight, high polish blue finish only, 6 lbs. Mfg. 1999-2000.

$670	$560	$430	$400	$360	$330	$300

Last MSR was $752.

✱ *Model 1892 High Grade* - .45 LC cal., features gold accents and receiver game scene, 1,000 mfg. 1997 only.

$1,125	$995	$750

Last MSR was $1,285.

MODEL 1895 GRADE I - .270 Win. (disc. 1999), .30-06 (mfg. 1998-99), or .405 Win. (new 2000) cal., similar to original Model 1895 Winchester, checkered straight grip stock and Schnabel forearm, 24 in. round barrel, 4 shot mag., top tang safety, blue finish, 8 lbs. New 1997.

MSR	$1,045	$915	$750	$650	$550	$500	$450	$395

Subtract 5% for .270 Win. or .30-06 cal.

MODEL 1895 LIMITED EDITION - .30-06, similar to original Model 1895 Winchester, blue receiver, 24 in. round barrel, 4 shot mag. (box mag.), uncheckered woodstock and forearm, rear buckhorn sight, 2 piece cocking lever, 8 lbs. 4,000 mfg. 1995-97.

$725	$550	$425

Last MSR was $853.

✱ *Model 1895 High Grade* - .30-06 (mfg. 1995-99) or .405 Win. (new 2000) cal., same general specifications as the Model 1895 Limited Edition, features older No. 3 engraving pattern with double scenes, gold borders with multiple gold inlays, deluxe checkered walnut stock and forearm. 4,000 mfg. beginning 1995.

MSR	$1,532	$1,295	$950	$825

Subtract 5% for .30-06 cal.

Grading	100%	98%	95%	90%	80%	70%	60%

RIFLES: MODEL 94 LEVER ACTION - POST 1964 PRODUCTION

100th Anniversary Model 1894s (mfg. 1994) are marked "1894-1994" on the receiver.

Add 20% for Model 94s w/o the cross bolt safety (pre 1992 mfg.) if original condition is 95%+.

MODEL 94 STANDARD RIFLE - .30-30 Win., .32 Win. Spl. (new 1992), 7-30 Waters (new 1989), or .44 Mag. (mfg. circa late 1960s-1970s) cal., lever action, 6 or 7 (24 in. barrel only) shot tube mag., 20 or 24 (mfg. 1987-88 only) in. round barrel, open sights, straight walnut stock, barrel band on forearm. Angled ejection became standard 1982, 6½ lbs. Mfg. 1964-1997.

$275	$215	$180	$165	$150	$140	$135

Last MSR was $363.

Add $15 for 24 in. barrel (disc. 1990).
Add $16 for .44 Mag. cal. (disc. 1986).
Add 15% for 7-32 Waters cal.

MODEL 94 TRADITIONAL (DELUXE WALNUT) - .30-30 Win., .44 Mag. (new 1999), or .480 Ruger Big Bore (new 2002) cal., similar to Standard Rifle, except has plain (new 1998, not available in .44 Mag. cal.) or checkered walnut stock and forearm, 6¼ lbs. New 1988.

MSR	$416		$315	$240	$190	$165	$150	$140	$135

Add $33 for Traditional–CW Model (w/checkered stock and forearm).
Add $55 for .44 Mag. cal. (new 1999, checkered stock only).
Add $102 for .480 Ruger Big Bore cal (new 2002).
Add $55 for 1.5 - 4.5X scope with low mounts (disc.).

MODEL 94 LEGACY - .30-30 Win., .357 Mag. (new 1997), .44 Mag. (new 1997), or .45 LC (new 1997) cal., features pistol grip checkered walnut stock and forearm, 20 (disc. 1999) or 24 (new 1997) in. barrel, 6¾ lbs. New 1995.

MSR	$465		$340	$255	$200	$165	$150	$140	$135

Subtract $15 for 20 in. barrel.

MODEL 94 RANGER - .30-30 Win. only, 20 in. barrel, uncheckered hardwood stock and forearm, 6 shot mag., 6¼ lbs. New 1985.

MSR	$363		$280	$220	$165	$150	$140	$130	$120

Add $56 for 4x32 scope with see-through mounts (disc. 1999).

✳ *Model 94 Ranger Compact* - .30-30 Win. or .357 Mag. cal., 16 in. barrel, uncheckered hardwood stock with 12½ LOP with recoil pad, post-style front sight, 5 (.30-30 Win. cal.) or 9 shot mag., 5 7/8 lbs. New 1998.

MSR	$363		$280	$220	$165	$150	$140	$130	$120

Add $19 for .357 Mag. cal.

MODEL 94 TRAILS END - .357 Mag., .44-40 WCF (mfg. 1998-99), .44 Mag., or .45 LC cal., similar to standard rifle, except has 11 shot tube mag., 20 in. barrel, choice of standard or large loop lever (disc. 1998), cross bolt safety, 6½ lbs. New 1997.

MSR	$453		$345	$260	$210	$165	$150	$140	$135

Add approx. $20 for large loop lever (disc. 1998).

MODEL 94 PACK RIFLE - .30-30 Win. or .44 Mag. cal., 18 in. barrel, 4 or 5 shot ¾ mag., over-dimension walnut stock and forearm cap w/o checkering, removable hood sight, 6¼ lbs. Mfg. 2000-2001.

$380	$280	$220	$180	$165	$150	$140

Last MSR was $496.

Add $10 for .44 Mag. cal.

MODEL 94 TIMBER CARBINE - .444 Marlin cal., 18 in. ported barrel with 5 shot 2/3 mag., checkered semi-pistol grip stock and forearm, blue finish only, hooded front sight, 6 lbs. Mfg. 1999-2001.

$435	$335	$280	$230	$200	$180	$165

Last MSR was $573.

Grading	100%	98%	95%	90%	80%	70%	60%

MODEL 94 WRANGLER LARGE LOOP - .30-30 Win., .44 Mag., or .45 LC (new 1999) cal., 16 in. barrel, has large loop lever, uncheckered walnut stock and forearm, blue finish, open sights, 6 lbs. Mfg. 1992-99.

	$300	$225	$180	$165	$150	$140	$135

Last MSR was $400.

Add $21 for .44 Mag. or .45 LC cal.

WIN-TUFF RIFLE - .30-30 Win. cal., similar to Model 94 Rifle, except has laminated hardwood stock and forearm with checkering. Drilled and tapped for scope mounts. Mfg. 1987 - disc.

	$300	$230	$180	$165	$150	$140	$135

Last MSR was $404.

MODEL 94 BLACK SHADOW - .30-30 Win. or .44 Mag./.44 Spl. cal., 20 or 24 (.30-30 Win. cal. only) in. barrel, 4 or 5 shot mag., non-glare finish, features black composite synthetic stock with recoil pad and Fuller forearm, approx. 6¼ lbs. Mfg. 1998-2000.

	$300	$230	$190	$160	$150	$140	$130

Last MSR was $381.

Add $13 for .44 Mag./.44 Spl. cal.

✱ *Model 94 Black Shadow Big Bore* - .444 Marlin cal., 20 in. barrel only, otherwise similar to Model 94 Black Shadow, 6½ lbs. Mfg. 1998-2000.

	$325	$240	$190	$160	$150	$140	$130

Last MSR was $394.

MODEL 94 TRAPPER - .30-30 Win., .357 Mag. (mfg. beginning 1992), .44 Mag./.44 Spl., or .45 LC (new 1985) cal., 16 in. barrel, side ejection, walnut stock, 5 (.30-30 Win. cal.) or 9 shot tube mag., blue finish, dovetailed front sight, 6 lbs.

MSR	$416		$325	$250	$195	$160	$150	$140	$130

Add $25 for .357 Mag., .44 Mag. or .45 LC cal.
The .44 Mag. cal. was introduced 1985.

MODEL 94 BIG BORE - .307 Win. (disc. 1998), .356 Win. (disc. 1998), or .375 Win. (disc. 1987), or .444 Marlin (new 1998) cal., angled ejection port provides scope mounting, checkered walnut Monte Carlo stock with recoil pad, 20 in. barrel, 6 shot mag., sling swivels, 6½ lbs. New 1983.

	$355	$255	$210	$175	$160	$150	$140

Last MSR was $465.

Add 25% for .356 Win. or .375 Win. cal.
Also mfg. in a top eject (pre-USRA). This model had an "XTR" suffix until 1989.

MODEL 94 HERITAGE CUSTOM 1 OF 100 - .38-55 WCF cal., special edition for the NSSF Heritage Fund, features Winchester's historic No. 2 pattern hand engraved with 24 Kt. gold inlays and individually signed by the engraver, deluxe spade checkered straight grip stock and forearm with metal cap, ½ round, ½ octagon 26 in. barrel, 6¾ lbs. New 2002.

As this edition went to press, prices had yet to be established on this model.

MODEL 94 HERITAGE CUSTOM 1 OF 1000 - .38-55 WCF cal., special edition for the NSSF Heritage Fund, features Winchester's historic No. 3 engraving pattern with 24 Kt. gold inlays, deluxe spade checkered straight grip stock and forearm with metal cap, ½ round, ½ octagon 26 in. barrel, 6¾ lbs. New 2002.

As this edition went to press, prices had yet to be established on this model.

MODEL 94 CUSTOM LIMITED EDITION - .44-40 WCF (mfg. 2000 only) or .38-55 WCF (new 2001) cal., features case colored receiver and 24 in. octagon match (.44-40 WCF cal. only) or ½ round, ½ octagon (.38-55 WCF cal. only) barrel with satin bluing, full (.44-40 WCF only) or ¾ mag. tube, spade checkered straight grip walnut stock and forearm with metal cap, 7¼ (.38-55 WCF cal.) or 7¾ lbs. Only 75 mfg. in .44-40 WCF cal. beginning 2000.

MSR	$2,393		$2,100	$1,775	$1,650

Grading	100%	98%	95%	90%	80%	70%	60%

MODEL 94 LIMITED EDITION CENTENNIAL - .30-30 Win. cal., cross-bolt safety, manufactured to commemorate the 100th anniversary of the Model 94 in 1994.

* ***Grade I Limited Edition*** - features No. 9 style Winchester engraving pattern (rolled) on both sides of receiver, 26 in. half-round half-octagonal barrel, pistol grip stock and forearm with cut checkering, half mag., open sights, crescent butt plate, 12,000 mfg. 1994.

    $725 **$550** **$425**

    Last MSR was $811.

* ***High Grade Limited Edition*** - features No. 6 style Winchester engraving pattern (rolled) on both sides of receiver with gold outlines and 2 gold animals (mountain sheep and deer), Lyman No. 2 tang mounted rear sight, F-style checkering and carving, deluxe walnut, 26 in. half-round half-octagonal barrel, half-mag., crescent butt plate, 3,000 mfg. 1994.

    $1,200 **$875** **$625**

    Last MSR was $1,272.

* ***Custom High Grade Limited Edition*** - .30 WCF cal., features No. 5 style Winchester engraving pattern (hand-executed) on both sides of greyed receiver, gold outline panel scenes featuring caribou and pronghorns, Lyman No. 2 upper tang sight, F- style checkering and carving, 26 in. half-round half-octagonal barrel, half-mag., crescent butt plate, 94 mfg. in 1994.

    $8,700 **$7,750** **$6,800**

    Last MSR was $4,684.

    Currently, a complete set of Model 94 Limited Edition Centennial rifles with the same serial number is selling in the $10,000+ range. Since there were only 94 Custom High Grade Limited Editions mfg., demand has escalated prices radically for this model.

MODEL 94 XTR - .30-30 Win. or 7-30 Waters (new 1985) cal., 20 or 24 (7-30 Waters only) in. barrel, checkered select walnut, hooded front sight (except 7-30 Waters which has dovetailed front blade), 6½ lbs. Disc. 1988.

	$260	$225	$205	$185	$160	$150	$140

Last MSR was $285.

Add $100 for 7-30 Waters cal. rifle.

* ***Model 94 XTR Deluxe*** - .30-30 Win. cal. only, deluxe American walnut stock and lengthened forearm with fancy checkering, 20 in. barrel with deluxe script, rubber butt pad. Mfg. 1987-1988 only.

	$370	$310	$270	$235	$210	$190	$160

Last MSR was $426.

MODEL 94 .44 MAG. S.R.C. - .44 Mag., top eject, 20 in. barrel, SRC. Mfg. 1967-72.

	$325	$275	$250	$225	$200	$175	$150

MODEL 94 CLASSIC SERIES - .30-30 Win. Win. cal., 20 or 26 in. octagon barrel. Approx. 47,000 mfg. 1967-70.

	$325	$285	$235	$200	$185	$160	$150

MODEL 94 ANTIQUE CARBINE - similar to Standard, with scroll on receiver, case hardened, gold-plated saddle ring. Mfg. 1964-1983.

	$250	$225	$200	$175	$160	$150	$140

MODEL 94 WRANGLER - .32 Win. Special, top ejection, only 7,947 mfg. Disc.

	$350	$310	$270	$235	$210	$190	$160

MODEL 94 WRANGLER II - .32 Win. Special (disc. 1984) or .38-55 WCF cal., angle ejection, 16 in. barrel, oversized hoop-shaped lever, roll-engraved receiver, 5 shot mag., 6 1/8 lbs. Made 1983-1985 only.

	$245	$220	$200	$185	$165	$150	$140

Last MSR was $275.

Grading	100%	98%	95%	90%	80%	70%	60%

MODEL 9422 XTR CLASSIC

same general specifications as Model 9422 XTR Standard, except has 22½ in. barrel and non-checkered, satin finished, pistol grip walnut stock and extended forearm, stock also has fluted comb with crescent steel butt plate, curved finger lever, 6½ lbs. Mfg. 1985-1987.

	100%	98%	95%	90%	80%	70%	60%
	$450	$425	$400	$325	$250	$200	$175

Last MSR was $301.

MODEL 9422 TRADITIONAL (STANDARD WALNUT)

.22 LR or .22 Mag. cal., takedown, 20½ in. round barrel, 15 shot (LR) or 11 shot (Mag. cal.) mag., grooved forged steel receiver, checkered straight grip, checkered high gloss (disc.) or satin weather resistant finish (new 1988) walnut stock and forearm, sights, 6 lbs. Mfg. 1972-present.

MSR	$452	$345	$275	$220	$190	$175	$160	$145

Add $25 for large loop lever (disc. 1999).

This model had an "XTR" suffix until 1989. Earlier mfg. including pre-XTR and early XTR rifles had no checkering - these guns will command slight premiums over values listed.

✳ **.22 Mag. cal.** - 11 shot mag., regular or large loop (mfg. 1998-99) lever, 6 lbs.

MSR	$472	$365	$290	$235	$200	$185	$175	$165

MODEL 9422 LEGACY

.22 LR or .22 Mag. (new 1999) cal., features 22½ in. barrel with deluxe checkered semi-pistol grip stock, 11 (.22 Mag.) or 15 shot non-full length mag., 6 lbs. New 1998.

MSR	$484	$380	$310	$250	$200	$185	$175	$165

Add $21 for .22 Mag. cal.

MODEL 9422 TRAPPER

.22 LR or .22 Mag. (new 1998), 16½ in. barrel, checkered walnut stock and forearm, 11 (.22 LR) or 8 (.22 Mag.) shot tube mag., 5¾ lbs. Mfg. 1996-2000.

	100%	98%	95%	90%	80%	70%	60%
	$335	$265	$215	$190	$175	$160	$145

Last MSR was $437.

Add $20 for .22 Mag. cal.

MODEL 9422 WIN-CAM

.22 Win. Mag. only, similar to 9422 XTR Standard, except has checkered greenish laminated hardwood stock and forearm. Mfg. 1987-1997.

	100%	98%	95%	90%	80%	70%	60%
	$330	$270	$225	$200	$185	$175	$165

Last MSR was $424.

MODEL 9422 WINTUFF

.22 LR or .22 Mag., 20½ in. barrel, checkered laminated brown hardwood stock and forearm, 6¼ lbs. Mfg. 1988-1999.

	100%	98%	95%	90%	80%	70%	60%
	$325	$260	$215	$190	$175	$160	$145

Last MSR was $423.

Add $21 for .22 Mag. cal.

MODEL 9422 HIGH-GRADE

.22 LR cal., features engraved receiver with raccoon and coonhound, deluxe checkered walnut stock and forearm. Mfg. 1995-96 only.

	100%	98%	95%
	$415	$340	$265

Last MSR was $489.

MODEL 9422 HIGH GRADE SERIES II

.22 LR cal., 20½ in. barrel, features high grade walnut stock and forearm with cut checkering, engraved receiver includes dog and squirrels, 6 lbs. Mfg. 1998-99.

	100%	98%	95%
	$430	$325	$250

Last MSR was $504.

MODEL 9422 25TH ANNIVERSARY GRADE I

.22 LR cal., features deluxe checkered walnut stock and forearm, engraved receiver with Winchester Horse and Rider, 2,500 mfg. 1997 only, inventory remained through 1999.

	100%	98%	95%
	$535	$425	$325

Last MSR was $606.

Grading	100%	98%	95%	90%	80%	70%	60%

MODEL 9422 25TH ANNIVERSARY HIGH GRADE

- .22 LR cal., features extra- deluxe checkered walnut stock and forearm, high gloss blue and engraved receiver with Winchester Horse and Rider, featuring silver borders and lever accents, 250 mfg. 1997 only.

     $1,175   **$995**   **$850**

Last MSR was $1,348.

RIFLES: BOLT ACTION - PRE-1964 MODEL 70

The Pre-'64 Model 70 Bolt Action Rifle (advertised by Winchester throughout much of its production history as "The Rifleman's Rifle")was produced from 1936 through 1963. Collectors recognize three major manufacturing periods: "Pre-War" (1936- 1941); "Transition" (1946-1948); and "Latter" (1949-1963). There were only eighteen(18) original chamberings, these are: .22 Hornet, .220 Swift, .243 Win., .250 Savage (.250-3000), .257 Roberts, .264 Win. Mag., .270 Win., 7x57mm Mauser, .300 Savage, .300 H&H, .300 Win. Mag., .30-06 (.30 Govt. '06 Springfield - approx. 80% of total mfg. by cal.,), .308 Win. (standard in Featherweight Style only), .338 Win. Mag., .35 Rem., .358 Win. (in Featherweight Style only), .375 H&H, and .458 Win. Mag. (in Super Grade AFRICAN Style only). It is important to note that every caliber was not available during each manufacturing period. Any other caliber encountered (including 7.65mm Argentine and 9mm Mauser) may be regarded as either special ordered or non-original. Magazine capacities are as follows: "Standard Calibers" (including .22 Hornet) five (5) rounds; "H&H Magnums" (.300 & .375) four (4) rounds; and "Winchester Short Magnums" (.264, .300, .338, .458) three (3) rounds. The rifle was produced in a myriad of styles and variations - most of which are covered individually. Unfortunately, a veritable "cottage industry" has developed involving the alteration, "upgrading", and/or outright faking of these guns. Be careful when contemplating a purchase of any rare Model 70 (and get a receipt describing the purchase accurately).

MODEL 70 PRE-WWII PRODUCTION STANDARD GRADE

- 12 standard cals., 5 shot mag., 4 shot mag. on Magnums, 24, 25, or 26 in. barrel, open sights, checkered walnut pistol grip stock, ser. range is 1-31,675. Mfg. 1937-1941.

Values listed assume original, unaltered specimens - modifications/alterations to either the metal or wood surfaces can reduce prices by large amounts. All pre-war Model 70s have only 2 holes drilled in the front of the receiver (none in the back). An extra set of "holes" can decrease value as much as 50%. Some pre-WWII Model 70s have a "D" suffix indicating a doubled up serial number - this variation will command a premium because of its rarity. The Model 70 is one gun that caliber ranks before condition in terms of desirability. Specimens encountered in under 60% condition will not decrease in price substantially since almost any shooter is worth $350-$500.

	100%	98%	95%	90%	80%	70%	60%
Standard Cals.	$995	$875	$750	$625	$550	$475	$350
.22 Hornet	$1,950	$1,700	$1,350	$1,100	$900	$725	$650
.220 Swift	$1,300	$1,000	$825	$700	$595	$500	$450
.257 Roberts	$1,625	$1,525	$1,300	$1,050	$800	$600	$500
.270 Win.	$1,150	$925	$850	$750	$625	$500	$450
.300 H&H	$1,475	$1,275	$995	$850	$700	$550	$500
.375 H&H	$2,000	$1,725	$1,550	$1,250	$1,000	$900	$850
7x57mm Mauser	$2,750	$2,400	$2,000	$1,550	$1,300	$1,125	$895
.250-3000 Savage	$2,450	$2,200	$1,850	$1,400	$1,200	$1,100	$875

Add approx. 80% for Super Grades in common cals.

There are more fakes than legitimate specimens in cals. 7x57mm and .250-3000 Savage! Rare cals. such as the .300 Savage, .35 Rem., 7.65mm, and 9mm Para. are seldomly encountered and their scarcity precludes accurate price evaluation. Cals. 7.65mm and 9mm Para. were special order only and made up from left-over Model 54 barrels. Also, the original factory box, papers, and hanging tag will add 25%-30% to the values listed. Believe it or not, there are getting to be a lot of fake Model 70 boxes that have been intentionally aged. Carefully screen NIB (watch the hanging tag also) specimens in this model.

MODEL 70 CARBINE (MFG. 1936-1946) - available in most cals. during its period, 20 in. barrel, short rifle variation of the Pre-'64 Model 70 (Winchester never officially used the "Carbine" terminology). If original, front sight base will be an integral part of the barrel. All carbines were disc. shortly after WWII. Beware of fakes.

Add 100% for carbine variations mfg. 1936-1946 with 20 in. barrel in .22 Hornet (watch for fakes, examine the front sight carefully), .250-3000 Savage, .257 Roberts, .270 Win., 7mm, or .30-06 (most common) cal.

MODEL 70 TRANSITION (MFG. 1946-1948) - several of the post-war Model 70s mfg. between 1946-1948 exhibit the pre-war receiver characteristics and have a transition safety. This variation is more rare than normal models, with asking prices 25%-35% higher.

On this Transitional Model, the receiver bridge may or may not be factory drilled.

MODEL 70 STANDARD GRADE (1946-1963 PRODUCTION) - 18 standard cals. including .22 Hornet, .220 Swift, .243 Win., .250 Savage (.250-3000), .257 Roberts, .264 Win. Mag., .270 Win., 7x57mm Mauser, .300 Savage, .300 H&H, .300 Win. Mag., .30-06, .308 Win., .338 Win. Mag., .35 Rem., .358 Win., and .375 H&H, 5 shot mag., 4 shot mag. on Magnums, 24, 25, or 26 in. barrel, open sights, checkered walnut pistol grip stock, ser. range is 52,549-581,471. Mfg. 1946- 1963.

Values listed assume original, unaltered specimens - modifications/alterations to either the metal or wood surfaces can reduce prices by large amounts. Most post-war Model 70s are drilled on top of the receiver (2 holes in front and 2 holes in back) to accept scope mounts (except early .300 and .375 H&H cals.). Pre-1952 mfg. Model 70s are desirable since Winchester implemented manufacturing techniques that lowered the quality in 1953.

	100%	98%	95%	90%	80%	70%	60%
.22 Hornet	$1,600	$1,425	$1,300	$1,250	$995	$795	$695
.220 Swift	$1,200	$995	$825	$750	$700	$550	$500
.243 Win.	$1,150	$995	$800	$725	$625	$550	$500
.257 Roberts	$1,450	$1,275	$1,100	$1,000	$850	$600	$500
.264 Win. Mag.	$1,200	$1,050	$895	$795	$695	$550	$500
.270 Win.	$950	$825	$650	$575	$500	$475	$450
.30-06 cal.	$775	$650	$550	$500	$450	$415	$375
.300 H&H	$1,500	$1,250	$1,050	$925	$750	$575	$525
.300 Win. Mag.	$1,600	$1,350	$1,050	$900	$800	$700	$625
.338 Win. Mag.	$1,800	$1,575	$1,375	$1,100	$875	$750	$650
.375 H&H	$1,900	$1,700	$1,425	$1,300	$1,200	$800	$650

Add 30% for .300 H&H or .375 H&H if rear receiver is not drilled and tapped.
Add 30% for stainless steel barrel in .300 H&H cal.
Rare cals. such as the .250-3000, .300 Savage, .308 Win. (extremely rare and watch for fakes), .35 Rem., and 7x57mm Mauser are seldomly seen or sold. Premiums depend on the rarity of the caliber and original condition.

Believe it or not, there are getting to be a lot of fake Model 70 boxes that have been intentionally aged. Carefully screen NIB (watch the hanging tag also) specimens in this model.

MODEL 70 FEATHERWEIGHT - lightened version of Standard, .243 Win., .264 Win. Mag. (Westerner), .270 Win., .308 Win., .30-06, or .358 Win. cal., 22 in. barrel, aluminum trigger guard and floorplate, ser. range is 206,626-581,471. Mfg. 1952-1963.

	100%	98%	95%	90%	80%	70%	60%
.243 Win., .30-06	$825	$750	$675	$600	$550	$500	$450
.264 Win. Mag.	$1,200	$1,100	$1,000	$900	$800	$700	$600
.270 Win.	$1,100	$950	$825	$750	$650	$600	$550
.308 Win.	$825	$750	$575	$475	$450	$425	$400
.358 Win.	$1,950	$1,725	$1,500	$1,175	$1,025	$900	$800

Add 400% for Super Grade Models.

The .358 Win. cal. is rare because Winchester had problems with this cal. Many of them were exchanged for other calibers, and the result is that original guns are rare in this cal.

Grading	100%	98%	95%	90%	80%	70%	60%

MODEL 70 SUPER GRADE - similar to Standard Model, except has deluxe wood, black pistol grip cap and forend tip, all Super Grades have a raised cheekpiece with deluxe wraparound checkering, and Super Grade marked floorplate. Disc. 1960.

A general rule for Super Grades is that if you add 100% to the standard grade in similar cals., values should be rather close. For .375 H&H cal., values are listed.

.375 H&H	$2,995	$2,500	$2,050	$1,775	$1,375	$950	$800

Later Model 70 Super Grades have jeweled action components.

MODEL 70 SUPER GRADE FEATHERWEIGHT - .243 Win., .270 Win., .30- 06, or .308 Win. cal. only, because of inconsistencies of Super Grade action component jeweling (i.e., engine turning), a simple stock and hinged floorplate change can create an "instant" Super Grade Featherweight (check stock carefully for wood filling near area of Standard Super Grade rear sight "boss" in barrel channel), all Super Grade Featherweights have a raised cheekpiece with wraparound "fish tail" checkering, less than 1,000 mfg.

Original S.G. Featherweights will command 4 times the value of a Standard Featherweight Model.

This is perhaps the rarest variation of the Pre-'64 Model 70 - beware of fakes.

MODEL 70 SUPER GRADE AFRICAN - .458 Win. Mag. only, front swivel base relocated and attached to bottom of barrel, nearly all possess one or two visible stock crossbolts (usually covered with Bakelite). Most have all action components (bolt body, extractor, extractor ring and magazine follower) jeweled (i.e., engine turned). 1,226 mfg. 1956-1963.

	$3,995	$3,650	$3,325	$3,050	$2,750	$2,250	$2,000

While other Super Grades were disc. approx. 1960, the "AFRICAN" continued in that style until the end of all production. Normal attrition and collectors owning more than one contribute to extreme rarity. Retains considerable "shooter" value in lesser external conditions. Watch for cracked and/or repaired stocks.

MODEL 70 NATIONAL MATCH - similar to Standard, with target stock and scope bases, .30-06 only. Disc. 1960.

	$1,850	$1,650	$1,500	$1,300	$900	$800	$700

MODEL 70 TARGET - similar to Model 70 Standard, in .243 Win. or .30-06 cal. (mfg. 1955-1963), earlier pre-'51 Target guns were available in virtually any cal. (i.e., .22 Hornet, .220 Swift, etc.), 24 in. medium weight barrel and target stock. Disc. 1963.

Add 50%-75% over standard values if condition is over 90%. 60% condition will be priced the same.

MODEL 70 BULL GUN - similar to Standard Model 70, with 28 in. heavy barrel, .300 H&H or .30-06 cal. only.

Add 150% to Standard Model values.

MODEL 70 VARMINT - similar to Standard Model 70, in .220 Swift or .243 Win. cal., 26 in. heavy barrel, scope bases, varmint style stock. Mfg. 1956-1963.

	$1,200	$1,050	$975	$850	$775	$675	$600

Add 30% for .220 Swift cal.

Less than 900 were mfg. in .220 Swift cal. Stainless steel barrels are also encountered in this model with 3 different types of finishes.

MODEL 70 ALASKAN - similar to Standard Model 70, in .300 Win. Mag. (mfg. 1963 only with 24 in. barrel - known as Westerner-Alaskan), .338 Win. Mag., or .375 H&H cal., 25 in. barrel, recoil pad. Mfg. 1960-1963.

	$1,600	$1,475	$1,300	$1,000	$950	$825	$675

RIFLES: BOLT ACTION - MODEL 70, 1964 - CURRENT PRODUCTION

Beginning 1994, Winchester began using the Classic nomenclature to indicate those models featuring a pre-1964 style action with controlled round feeding.

Grading	100%	98%	95%	90%	80%	70%	60%

MODEL 70 STANDARD - .22-250 Rem., .222 Rem., .225 Win., .243 Win., .270 Win., .308 Win., or .30-06 cal., 5 shot, 22 in. heavy barrel, open sight, Monte Carlo stock, swivels. Mfg. 1964-1980.

	$400	$350	$300	$275	$250	$200	$175

Add 25% for .225 Win. cal.

MODEL 70 MAGNUM - .264 Win. Mag., 7mm Rem. Mag., .300 H&H Mag., .300 Win. Mag., .338 Win. Mag., .375 H&H, or .458 Win. Mag. cal., 24 in. barrel.

	$450	$400	$350	$325	$300	$250	$225

Add 25-35% for .375 H&H or .458 Win. Mag. (African Model) cal.

MODEL 70 SUPER GRADE - various cals., deluxe wood with ebony forend cap, Super Grade appears on the floorplate. Disc.

	$575	$525	$475	$425	$400	$375	$350

MODEL 70 DELUXE - .243 Win., .270 Win., .30-06, or .300 Win. Mag. cal., 22 in. barrel, open sight, hand checkered, black forend tip. Mfg. 1964-1971.

	$475	$415	$360	$320	$285	$220	$180

The Model 70 Deluxe was redesignated the Standard Model 70 in 1972.

MODEL 70 TARGET RIFLE 1964-1971 - .308 Win. or .30-06 cal., 24 in. heavy barrel, no sights, target bases, heavy target style stock with hand stop. Disc. 1971.

	$630	$550	$495	$440	$360	$330	$275

MODEL 70 INTERNATIONAL ARMY MATCH 1971 - .308 Win. cal., 5 shot, 24 in. heavy barrel, no sights, adj. trigger, ISU stock with forearm, accessory rail, adj. butt. Disc. 1971.

	$715	$660	$605	$550	$470	$440	$385

MODEL 70 MANNLICHER 1969-1971 - .243 Win., .270 Win., .30-06, or .308 Win. cal., 19 in. barrel, open sight, full length Monte Carlo stock with steel forend cap. Disc. 1971.

	$700	$600	$550	$500	$450	$400	$350

MODEL 70A - economy version of 1972 type Model 70, same cals., no hinged floorplate or forend tip. Mfg. 1972-1978.

	$325	$285	$265	$230	$200	$165	$140

MODEL 70A MAGNUM - similar to Model 70A, except in Mag. cals. but not .375 H&H or .458. Mfg. 1972-1978.

	$340	$310	$275	$250	$220	$195	$165

MODEL 70 FEATHERWEIGHT - .22-250 Rem., .223 Rem., .243 Win., .25-06 Rem. (disc. 1993), .257 Robts. (disc.), .270 Win., .280 Rem., 6.5x55mm Swedish (new 1991), 7x57mm Mauser (disc.), .30- 06, .308 Win., 7mm-08 Rem. (new 1992), 7mm Rem. Mag. (mfg. 1991-92 only), or .300 Win. Mag. (mfg. 1991-92 only) cal., bolt action, both short and medium action, 5 shot mag., 22 in. barrel (24 in. with .300 Win. Mag.), checkered walnut stock, no sights, approx. 6½ lbs. Mfg. 1981-94.

	$435	$380	$325	$300	$280	$260	$240

Last MSR was $562.

In 1981, during U.S.R.A. takeover transition, guns were distinguishable by the U.S.R.A. trademark on the recoil pad. Some collectors will pay a premium for Win. marked pads. Cals. .257 Robts. and 7x57mm Mauser were disc. 1985.

This model had an "XTR" suffix until 1989.

MODEL 70 CLASSIC FEATHERWEIGHT - .22-250 Rem. (new 1994), .223 Rem. (mfg. 1994 only), .243 Win. (new 1994), .270 Win., .280 Rem. (disc. 2000), .30-06, .308 Win. (new 1994), 6.5x55mm Swedish (new 1997), or 7mm-08 Rem. (new 1994) cal., 22 in. barrel, 5 shot mag., blue action, features claw-controlled round feeding action bedded into standard grade walnut stock, jewelled bolt, knurled bolt handle, includes rings and bases, approx. 7 lbs. New 1992.

MSR	$726	$545	$440	$350	$300	$280	$260	$240

Grading	100%	98%	95%	90%	80%	70%	60%

Model 70 Classic Featherweight BOSS - similar to Model 70 Classic Featherweight, except has 22 in. barrel with BOSS. Mfg. 1996 only.

| | $600 | $500 | $395 | $350 | $325 | $295 | $275 |

Last MSR was $735.

Model 70 Classic Featherweight Stainless - .22-250 Rem., .243 Win., .270 Win., .30-06, .308 Win., .300 Win. Mag. (disc. 1998), or 7mm Rem. Mag. cal., 22 or 24 (Mag. cals. only) in. stainless barrel, checkered walnut stock, 3 or 5 shot mag., approx. 7-7½ lbs. Mfg. 1997-99.

| | $615 | $510 | $390 |

Last MSR was $746.

Model 70 Classic Featherweight All-Terrain - .270 Win., .30-06, .300 Win. Mag., or 7mm Rem. Mag. cal., 22 or 24 in. matte finish stainless steel barrel/receiver, black fiberglass/graphite stock with checkering, with (1996-1997 only) or without BOSS, 3 or 5 shot mag., 7¼ lbs. Mfg. 1996-98.

| | $565 | $475 | $375 |

Last MSR was $672.

Add $100 for BOSS (disc. 1997).

Model 70 Win-Tuff Featherweight Rifle - .22-250 Rem., .223 Rem., .243 Win., .270 Win., .30-06, or .308 Win. cal., features brown laminated, checkered stock with Schnabel forend, includes base and rings, pistol grip cap, 7 lbs., mfg. 1988-1990 - reintroduced 1992-1993.

| | $445 | $385 | $325 | $300 | $280 | $260 | $240 |

Last MSR was $572.

Model 70 Featherweight Special - .243 Win. cal., features custom fitted stock, hand-honed action, barrel, and bolt/follower, custom shop proofstamp, select American walnut with rounded pistol grips, no sights, only 50 mfg.

| | $600 | $525 | $475 | $425 | $380 | $340 | $300 |

This model is distinguishable by the Super Grade floorplate marking.

MODEL 70 XTR EUROPEAN FEATHERWEIGHT - 6.5x55 Swedish Mauser cal., 22 in. barrel, 5 shot mag., rifle sights, 6¾ lbs. Made 1986 only.

| | $390 | $365 | $330 | $305 | $280 | $260 | $240 |

Last MSR was $460.

MODEL 70 LIGHTWEIGHT RIFLE - .22-250 Rem. (disc. 1992), .223 Rem., .243 Win., .270 Win., .280 Rem. (mfg. 1988-92), .30-06, or .308 Win. cal., 22 in. barrel, checkered walnut stock, no sights, 6½ lbs. Mfg. 1987-95.

| | $420 | $335 | $290 | $255 | $230 | $210 | $190 |

Last MSR was $513.

Model 70 Lightweight Carbine - .22-250 Rem., .222 Rem. (scarce), .223 Rem., .243 Win., .250 Savage (new 1986), .308 Win., .270 Win., or .30-06 cal., bolt action, 5 shot mag., both short and medium action, 20 in. barrel, checkered walnut stock, no sights, approx. 6 lbs. Mfg. 1984-87.

| | $355 | $320 | $285 | $255 | $230 | $210 | $190 |

Last MSR was $395.

Add $15 for open sights.

Model 70 Win-Tuff Lightweight Rifle - .22-250 Rem. (mfg. 1988-89), .223 Rem. (new 1989), .243 Win. (new 1988), .270 Win. .30-06 or .308 Win. (new 1989) cal., similar to Model 70 Lightweight Rifle, except has laminated brown hardwood stock with checkering. Mfg. 1987-92.

| | $395 | $330 | $290 | $255 | $230 | $210 | $190 |

Last MSR was $471.

Grading	100%	98%	95%	90%	80%	70%	60%

✳ *Model 70 Win-Cam Lightweight Rifle* - .270 Win. or .30-06 cal., greenish laminated hardwood stock with checkering, 22 in. barrel. New 1987.

	$395	$330	$290	$255	$230	$210	$190

Last MSR was $471.

This model was previously designated Featherweight before 1989.

MODEL 70 SPORTER - .22-250 Rem. (mfg. 1989-1993), .223 Rem. (mfg. 1989- 1993), .243 Win. (mfg. 1989-1993), .25-06 Rem. (mfg. 1985-87 and reintroduced 1990), .264 Win. Mag., .270 Win., .270 Wby. Mag. (new 1988), .30-06, .300 Win. Mag., .300 Wby. Mag. (new 1989), .300 H&H (mfg. 1989- 1992), .308 Win. (mfg. 1986-89), .338 Win. Mag., or 7mm Rem. Mag. cal., 24 in. barrel, 3 or 5 shot mag., custom Sporter styling, Monte Carlo cheek piece, detachable sling swivels, 7¾ lbs. Disc. 1994.

	$435	$375	$325	$300	$280	$260	$240

Last MSR was $556.

Add $34 for iron sights (.270 Win., .30-06, .300 Win. Mag., or 7mm Rem. Mag. only).
This model had an "XTR" suffix until 1989.

✳ *Sporter Win-Tuff* - .270 Win., .30-06, 7mm Rem. Mag., .300 Win. Mag., .300 Wby. Mag., or .338 Win. Mag., similar to Model 70 Sporter, except has checkered brown laminate stock with sling swivels, solid recoil pad, 24 in. barrel, approx. 7¾ lbs. Mfg. 1992 only.

	$445	$380	$325	$300	$280	$260	$240

Last MSR was $572.

MODEL 70 CLASSIC SPORTER LT - .25-06 Rem., .264 Win. Mag. (disc. 2000), .270 Win., .270 Wby. Mag. (disc. 1998), .30-06, .300 Win. Mag., .300 Wby. Mag. (disc. 2000), .338 Win. Mag., 7mm STW (new 1997), or 7mm Rem. Mag. cal., similar to Model 70 Sporter, except features controlled round feeding, 3 (Mag. cals. only) or 5 shot internal mag., 24 or 26 in. barrel, checkered walnut stock, blue finish, stock was redesigned by David Miller in 1999 (denoted by LT Model suffix), approx. 7¾ -8 lbs. New 1994.

MSR	$713	$545	$435	$350	$300	$280	$260	$240

Add $28 for Mag. cals.
Add $44 for left-hand action (new 1997).
Add $38 for iron sights - disc. 1998 (available in .270 Win., .30-06, .300 Win. Mag., .338 Win. Mag., or 7mm Rem. Mag.).
Left-hand action is available in .270 Win., .30-06, .300 Win. Mag., .338 Win. Mag. (disc. 2000), 7mm STW (disc. 2000), or 7mm Rem. Mag.

✳ *Model 70 Classic Sporter BOSS* - .25-06 Rem. (disc. 1996), .270 Win., .30- 06, .264 Win. Mag. (disc. 1996), 7mm STW (new 1997), 7mm Rem. Mag., .270 Wby. Mag. (mfg. 1996 only), .300 Win. Mag. , .300 Wby Mag. (mfg. 1996 only), or .338 Win. Mag. cal., 24 or 26 in. barrel with BOSS, 3 or 5 shot mag., checkered walnut stock, approx. 7¾ lbs. Mfg. 1995-98.

	$620	$535	$440	$350	$295	$275	$250

Last MSR was $728.

Add $28 for left-hand action (new 1997).

✳ *Model 70 Classic Sporter Stainless* - .270 Win., .30-06, .300 Win. Mag., .338 Win. Mag., or 7mm Rem. Mag. cal., 24 or 26 in. barrel with (1997 only) or without BOSS, checkered walnut stock, controlled round feeding, 3 or 5 shot mag., right- or left-hand action, approx. 7¾ lbs. Mfg. 1997-98.

	$615	$530	$440				

Last MSR was $716.

Add $80 for BOSS.
Add $29 for left-hand action.

Grading	100%	98%	95%	90%	80%	70%	60%

✳ *Model 70 Classic Laredo* - .300 Win Mag., 7mm STW (mfg. 1997-98), or 7mm Rem. Mag. cal., features claw extraction and controlled round feeding, 26 in. round or fluted (new 1998) barrel with (.300 Win. Mag and 7mm Rem. Mag. disc. 1997) or without BOSS. Mfg. 1996-99.

	$665	$560	$450	$350	$295	$275	$250

Last MSR was $794.

Add $95 for BOSS on barrel (disc. 1998).
Add $130 for fluted barrel.

✳ *Model 70 Classic Safari Express* - .375 H&H, .416 Rem. Mag., or .458 Win. Mag. cal., features Express style rear sight with standing blade, redesigned stock with negative drop and Pachmayr decelerator recoil pad, trigger guard and floorplate are one assembly, 3 shot mag., 24 in. barrel with barrel band swivel attachment, checkered walnut stock and forearm, 8½ lbs. New 1999.

MSR	$1,103	$895	$760	$650	$585	$525	$475	$430

Add $37 for left-hand action (.375 H&H cal. only).

✳ *Model 70 Classic Super Express Mag.* - .375 H&H, .416 Rem. Mag. (new 1994), or .458 Win. Mag. cal., 3 shot mag., claw extractor controlled round feeding (new 1993), open sights, 22 or 24 in. (.375 H&H or .416 Rem. Mag.) barrel, 8½ lbs. Disc. 1998.

	$730	$585	$525	$495	$460	$430	$400

Last MSR was $865.

Add $29 for left-hand action (new 1997), .375 H&H cal. only.
This model had an "XTR" suffix until 1989.

MODEL 70 CLASSIC WSM - .270 WSM (new 2002), .300 WSM, or 7mm WSM (new 2002) cal., controlled round feeding, 24 in. round barrel, 3 shot internal mag., choice of Featherweight (traditional stock and blue metal finish), Stainless (stainless steel action/barrel with black composite stock), or Laminated (brown laminate stock with blue metal finish) configuration, approx. 7¼ – 7¾ lbs. New 2001.

MSR	$754	$575	$440	$360	$300	$280	$260	$240

Add $23 for laminated wood stock.
Add $59 for stainless steel.

MODEL 70 DBM (DETACHABLE BOX MAGAZINE) - .22-250 Rem. (mfg. 1993 only), .223 Rem. (mfg. 1993 only), .243 Win. (new 1993), .270 Win., .30-06, .308 Win. (mfg. 1993 only), 7mm Rem. Mag., or .300 Win. Mag. cal., checkered walnut stock and forend, features 3 shot detachable box mag., 24 or 26 in. barrel with or without sights, includes bases and rings or iron sights (new 1993, optional) in .30-06, .300 Win. Mag., or 7mm Rem. Mag., 7¾ lbs. Mfg. 1992-94.

	$465	$390	$330	$300	$280	$260	$240

Last MSR was $598.

Add $36 for iron sights.

MODEL 70 CLASSIC DBM - .22-250 Rem., .243 Win., .270 Win., .284 Win., .30-06, .308 Win., .300 Win. Mag., or 7mm Rem. Mag. cal., similar to Model 70 DBM, except has controlled round feeding, 24 or 26 in. barrel. Mfg. 1994 only.

Most cals.	$475	$395	$330	$300	$280	$260	$240
.284 Win. (less than 200 mfg.)	$695	$650	$550	$495	$395	$350	$295

Last MSR was $619.

Add $52 for iron sights (.270 Win., .30-06, .300 Win. Mag., or 7mm Rem. Mag.).

✳ *Model 70 Classic DBM-S* - .270 Win., .30-06, .300 Win. Mag., or 7mm Rem. Mag. cal., similar to Model 70 DBM, except has black synthetic stock, this model became a Classic series in 1994 (featuring controlled round feeding). Mfg. 1993-94.

	$475	$395	$330	$300	$280	$260	$240

Last MSR was $619.

Grading	100%	98%	95%	90%	80%	70%	60%

MODEL 70 STAINLESS - .270 Win., .30-06, 7mm Rem. Mag., .300 Win. Mag., or .338 Win. Mag., features matte finished stainless steel receiver barrel and bolt, black synthetic composite stock, 22 (.270 Win. or .30-06 only, disc. 1992) or 24 in. barrel, approx. 6¾ lbs. Mfg. 1992-94.

$475	**$390**	**$330**					

Last MSR was $616.

MODEL 70 CLASSIC STAINLESS - .22-250 Rem. (disc. 1999), .223 Rem. (disc. 1994), .243 Win. (disc. 1998), .270 Win., .270 WSM (new 2002), .30-06, .308 Win. (disc. 1998), .270 Wby. Mag. (mfg. 1997 only), .300 Win. Mag., .300 Wby. Mag. (disc. 2000), .300 Rem. Ultra Mag., .300 WSM (new 2001), .338 Win. Mag., .375 H&H, 7mm STW (new 2001), 7mm WSM (new 2002) or 7mm Rem. Mag. cal., features controlled round feeding, 22 (disc. 2001), 24, or 26 in. barrel, black synthetic composite stock, 3, 5, or 6 shot mag., without sights except for .375 H&H cal., 6¾-7½ lbs. New 1994.

MSR	**$785**		**$590**	**$450**	**$355**		

Add $121 for .375 H&H cal.

✱ *Model 70 Classic Stainless BOSS* - .22-250 Rem. (disc. 1996), .243 Win. (disc. 1996), .270 Win., .30-06, .308 Win. (disc. 1996), .270 Wby. Mag. (mfg. 1997 only), .300 Win. Mag., .300 Wby. Mag. (mfg. 1996-97), .338 Win. Mag., or 7mm Rem. Mag. cal., 22, 24, or 26 in. barrel with BOSS, black synthetic stock, 6¾-7½ lbs. Mfg. 1995-98.

	$645	**$535**	**$430**				

Last MSR was $788.

MODEL 70 CLASSIC LAMINATED STAINLESS - .270 Win., .30-06, .300 Win. Mag., .338 Win. Mag., or 7mm Rem. Mag. cal., 24 or 26 (Mag. cals. only) in. barrel without sights, checkered grey/black laminate stock with sporter style dimensions, stainless action and barrel, 3 or 5 shot mag., approx. 8 lbs. Mfg. 1998-99.

	$640	**$545**	**$440**				

Last MSR was $753.

✱ *Model 70 Classic Camo Stainless* - similiar to Model 70 Classic Stainless, except has Mossy Oak Treestand stock finish composite stock, not available in .338 Win. Mag. cal. approx. 7¼ lbs. Mfg. 1998 only.

	$630	**$540**	**$445**				

Last MSR was $745.

MODEL 70 COYOTE - .22-250 Rem., .223 Rem., .243 Win., .270 WSM (new 2002), .300 WSM (new 2002), .308 Win. (new 2002), or 7mm WSM (new 2002) cal., push feed action, 24 in. medium heavy stainless steel sporter barrel, uncheckered brown laminate stock with reverse taper on forend, 5 or 6 (.223 Rem. only) shot mag., 9 lbs. New 2000.

MSR	**$691**		**$545**	**$440**	**$345**	**$300**	**$280**	**$260**	**$240**

Add $29 for WSM cals.

MODEL 70 CLASSIC SM (SYNTHETIC MATTE) - .22-250 Rem. (mfg. 1993 only), .223 Rem. (mfg. 1993 only), .243 Win. (mfg. 1993 only), .270 Win., .30-06, .308 Win. (mfg. 1993 only), 7mm Rem. Mag., .300 Win. Mag., .338 Win. Mag., or .375 H&H (new 1993) cal., features black composite stock with checkering and sling swivels, 22 (.22-250 Rem., .223 Rem., .243 Win., or .308 Win. - mfg. 1993 only), 24, or 26 in. barrel with matte metal finish, 3 or 5 shot, approx. 7½ lbs. Mfg. 1992-96.

	$465	**$395**	**$330**	**$300**	**$280**	**$260**	**$240**

Last MSR was $620.

Add $52 for .375 H&H cal. (open sights only).

Until 1993, this model was called the Model 70 SSM. In 1994, this model became the Model 70 Classic SM featuring controlled round feeding.

MODEL 70 CLASSIC SM BOSS - .270 Win., .30-06, 7mm Rem. Mag., .300 Win. Mag., or .338 Win. Mag. cal., 24 or 26 in. barrel with BOSS, 3 or 5 shot, approx. 7¼ lbs. Mfg. 1995-96 only.

	$625	**$525**	**$430**	**$350**	**$295**	**$275**	**$250**

Last MSR was $735.

Grading	100%	98%	95%	90%	80%	70%	60%

MODEL 70 CLASSIC COMPACT - .243 Win., .308 Win., or 7mm-08 Rem. cal., features 12½ in. LOP, 20 in. barrel and shallow profile, pre-64 type action, 4 shot mag., checkered walnut stock and forearm, blue action and barrel, 6-6½ lbs. New 1998.

	MSR	$726		$565	$440	$350	$310	$280	$260	$240

MODEL 70 VARMINT - same general specifications as standard Sporter, .22-250 Rem., .223 Rem., .225 Win., .243 Win., or .308 Win. cal., 26 in. heavy barrel with cold hammer forged rifling and counter-bored at muzzle, no sights, 5 shot mag., target scope bases, 7¾ lbs. Mfg. 1964-1993.

		$470	$375	$325	$295	$280	$260	$240

Last MSR was $720.

> **Add 25% for .225 Win. cal.**
> This model had an "XTR" suffix 1978-89.

＊ *Model 70 Heavy Varmint (HBV)* - .220 Swift (mfg. 1994-98), .22-250 Rem., .222 Rem. (mfg. 1997-98), .223 Rem., .243 Win., or .308 Win. cal., push-feed style action, 26 in. heavy stainless fluted (new 1997) or plain barrel (countersunk muzzle) without sights, features black synthetic beavertail H&S Precision stock with aluminum bedding block, 10¾ lbs. Mfg. 1993-99.

	$645	$515	$410

Last MSR was $795.

> **Add $137 for fluted barrel.**

MODEL 70 SHB (SYNTHETIC HEAVY BARREL) - .308 Win. cal., features checkered black composite stock, 26 in. barrel with matte metal finish, jeweled bolt, 9 lbs. Mfg. 1992 only.

		$460	$375	$325	$300	$280	$260	$240

Last MSR was $563.

MODEL 70 WINLIGHT - .25-06 Rem., .270 Win., .280 Rem. (new 1987), .30-06, 7mm Rem. Mag., .300 Win. Mag., .300 Wby. Mag., or .338 Win. Mag. cal., McMillan fiberglass stock, thermoplastic receiver bedding, blue metal parts, 22 or 24 (Mag. cals. only) in. barrel, 3 or 4 shot mag., no sights, approx. 6½ lbs. Mfg. 1986-90.

		$555	$490	$440	$395	$350	$310	$280

Last MSR was $637.

MODEL 70 RANGER RIFLE - .22-250 Rem. (new 1999), .223 Rem. (new 1992), .243 Win. (new 1991), .270 Win., .30-06, or 7mm Rem. Mag. cal., push-feed action, 22 or 24 in. barrel, 3 (7mm Rem. Mag.), 5 or 6 shot mag., plain hardwood stock without checkering, open sights, approx. 7 lbs. Disc. 1999.

		$375	$285	$220	$200	$180	$165	$155

Last MSR was $503.

＊ *Model 70 Ranger Compact* - .22-250 Rem. (mfg. 1999 only), .223 Rem. (disc. 1989, re-introduced 1997, disc. 1998), .243 Win., .308 Win. (new 1991), or 7mm- 08 Rem. (mfg. 1997-98, reintroduced 2000) cal., push-feed action, 20 (disc. 1992) or 22 (new 1993) in. barrel, 5 or 6 shot mag., shorter hardwood stock dimensions, open sights, 6½ lbs. Disc. 2000.

		$390	$295	$230	$200	$180	$165	$155

Last MSR was $528.

MODEL 70 STEALTH - .22-250 Rem., .223 Rem., .308 Win. cal., push-feed style action, 26 in. heavy barrel w/o sights, Accu Block black synthetic stock with full length aluminum beeding block, 5 or 6 shot mag., 10¾ lbs. New 1999.

	MSR	$785		$675	$585	$475	$415	$360	$330	$300

MODEL 70 BLACK SHADOW - .270 Win., .30-06, .300 Win. Mag., or 7mm Rem. Mag cal., push-feed action, 3 (Mag. cals.) or 5 shot internal mag., 24 or 26 (Mag. cals.) in. barrel w/o sights, matte receiver and barrel finish, black composite stock with conventional floorplate mag., 7¼ lbs. New 1998.

	MSR	$512		$385	$300	$230	$200	$180	$165	$155

> **Add $29 for Mag. cals.**

Grading	100%	98%	95%	90%	80%	70%	60%

MODEL 70 CLASSIC SUPER GRADE - .25-06 Win. (new 2001), .270 Win. (new 1991), .30-06 (new 1991), 7mm STW (230 mfg. 1999 only), 7mm Rem. Mag. (disc. 1998, reintroduced 2000), .264 Win. Mag. (limited mfg. 2000 only), .300 Win. Mag., or .338 Win. Mag. cal., 24 or 26 in. barrel, 3 (Mag. cals.) or 5 shot mag., jewelled bolt, stainless steel extractor for true claw controlled round feeding and ejecting, three-position safety, checkered satin finish walnut stock with wood cheekpiece, black forend tip, bases and rings included, approx. 7¾ - 8 lbs. New 1990.

	MSR	$995		$790	$575	$465	$395	$340	$300	$280

Add $29 for Mag. cals.

This model was designated the Model 70 Super Grade until 1995. During 1999, this model was redesigned to include a new Express style rear sight with standing blade, negative stock drop, Pachmayr Decelerator pad, one-piece floorplate and full barrel band swivel attachment.

✻ *Model 70 Classic Super Grade BOSS* - similar to Model 70 Classic Super Grade, except has BOSS. Mfg. 1995-97.

	$810	$685	$555	$450	$375	$335	$300

Last MSR was $956.

MODEL 70 50TH ANNIVERSARY MODEL - .300 Win. Mag., 24 in. barrel, deluxe walnut stock, engraving and special motifs on metal surfaces, serial numbered 50 ANV 1 - 50 ANV 500, 7¾ lbs. 500 mfg. 1987 only.

	$1,100	$975	$850

Last MSR was $939.

RIFLES: BOLT ACTION - POST 1964 MODEL 70 CUSTOM GRADES

MODEL 70 CUSTOM GRADE - various cals., old style Model 70 action, semi-fancy American walnut checkered stock, engine turned bolt and follower, hand honed internal parts. Mfg. 1988-89 only.

	$1,100	$875	$700	$600	$525	$475	$425

Last MSR was $1,172.

MODEL 70 XTR FEATHERWEIGHT ULTRA GRADE "1 OF 1,000" - .270 Win., bolt action, extensively engraved, finely checkered deluxe French walnut, with mahogany presentation case.

	$1,800	$1,450	$950

Last MSR was $5,000.

MODEL 70 CLASSIC CUSTOM GRADE - .264 Win. Mag. (new 1994), .270 Win., .30-06, 7mm Rem. Mag., .300 Win. Mag., .300 Wby. Mag. (new 1994) or .338 Win. Mag. cal., 24 or 26 in. barrel, similar to Model 70 Super Grade, but must be special ordered through the Custom Gun Shop and includes many custom features including semi-fancy walnut with satin finish and hand-honed internal parts. Mfg. 1990-94.

	$1,625	$1,250	$995	$875	$800	$725	$650

Last MSR was $1,757.

A Model 70 Collector Grade is also a variation of this model that is mfg. in the Custom Gun Shop - this model is priced on request only.

✻ *Model 70 Classic Custom Grade Featherweight* - .22-250 Rem. (new 1994), .223 Rem. (new 1994), .243 Win. (new 1994), .270 Win., .280 Rem., .30-06, .308 Win. (new 1994), 7mm-08 Rem. (new 1994) cal., 22 in. barrel, includes Featherweight features, controlled round feeding, higher grade wood. Mfg. 1992-94.

	$1,625	$1,250	$995	$875	$800	$725	$650

Last MSR was $1,757.

Grading	100%	98%	95%	90%	80%	70%	60%

* **Model 70 Classic/Custom Sharpshooter I/II** - .22-250 Rem. (new 1993), .223 Rem. (mfg. 1993-94), .30-06, .308 Win., or .300 Win. Mag. cal., includes specially designed McMillan A-2 (disc. 1995) or H-S Precision heavy target stock, Schneider (disc. 1995) or H-S Precision (new 1996) 24 (.308 Win. cal. only) or 26 in. stainless steel barrel, choice of blue or grey finish starting 1996. Mfg. 1992-98.

	$1,795	$1,375	$1,000	$875	$800	$725	$650

Last MSR was $1,994.

Subtract $100 if without stainless barrel (pre-1995).

This model was designated the Sharpshooter II in 1996 (features H-S Precision stock and stainless steel barrel).

This model is also available in left-hand action beginning 1998 (.30-06 and .330 Win. Mag. cals. only).

* **Model 70 Classic/Custom Sporting Sharpshooter I/II** - .270 Win. (disc. 1994), 7mm STW, or .300 Win. Mag. cal., ½-minute of angle sporting version of the Custom Sharpshooter, custom shop only, Sharpshooter II became standard in 1996. Mfg. 1993-98.

	$1,725	$1,295	$975	$850	$775	$700	$625

Last MSR was $1,875.

This model was also available in left-hand action in 1998.

* **Model 70 Custom/Sporting Sharpshooter** - .220 Swift cal., 26 in. Schneider barrel, controlled round feeding, available with either McMillan A-2 or Sporting synthetic (disc. 1994) stock. Mfg. 1994-95 only.

	$1,650	$1,250	$975	$850	$775	$700	$625

Last MSR was $1,814.

* **Model 70 Classic Custom Express** - .300 Petersen (mfg. 1995 only), .375 H&H, .375 JRS (mfg. 1992-96), 7mm STW (mfg. 1993-94), .416 Rem. Mag., .458 Win. Mag., or .470 Capstick (disc. 1995) cal., 24 in. (22 in. on .458 Win. Mag.) barrel, features claw controlled round feeding, deluxe walnut with satin finish and checkering, 3-leaf express (disc. 1995) or pre-64 style adj. rear sight (new 1996), high luster metal finish, bolt and follower are engine turned, available by special order through the custom gun shop only. Mfg. 1990-98.

	$2,300	$1,825	$1,550	$1,300	$1,125	$1,000	$895

Last MSR was $2,512.

Subtract $200 for 7mm STW cal.

In 1994, the model nomenclature was changed from Model 70 Custom Grade Express, and in 1996 it was changed from Model 70 Classic Express.

MODEL 70 ULTIMATE CLASSIC (CLASSIC CUSTOM) - .25-06 Rem., 6.5x55mm Swedish (new 2001), .270 Win., .280 Rem. (mfg. 1996, reintroduced 1999), .30-06, 7mm STW, .264 Win. Mag., .270 Wby. Mag. (disc. 1996), .35 Whelen (new 1998), 7mm Rem. Mag., 7mm Rem. Ultra Mag., .300 Win. Mag., .300 Wby. Mag., .300 H&H (mfg. 1996-99), .300 Rem. Ultra (new 2000), .338 Win. Mag., .338-06 (mfg. 1999-2001), .338 Rem. Rem. Ultra Mag. (new 2001), .340 Wby. Mag. (mfg. 1998), .375 H&H (1995 only), .416 Rem. Mag. (1995 only), or .458 Win. Mag. (1995 only) cal., controlled round feeding, checkered fancy walnut stock, choice of 22 (.458 Win. Mag. only), 24 or 26 in. tapered round full-fluted, ½ round, ½ octagonal, or full octagonal tapered stainless barrel, one inch black decelerator recoil pad, choice blue or stainless barreled action, 3 or 5 shot mag., includes bases/rings except on some Mag. cals., approx. 7¾ lbs., except for large disc. cals., includes hard case. New 1995.

MSR	$2,688		$2,320	$1,850	$1,430	$1,200	$950	$800	$700

Add $100 for stainless steel barrel, $110 for fluted round barrel, or $235 for full or half octagon barrel.

Add approx. 15% for .375 H&H and larger Mag. cals (disc. 1995).

This model was previously designated the Model 70 Ultimate Classic until 2000.

Left-hand action (new 1997) available in all current cals.

Grading	100%	98%	95%	90%	80%	70%	60%

MODEL 70 CLASSIC CUSTOM SHORT ACTION - .243 Win. (disc. 2000, reintroduced 2002), .257 Roberts, .260 Rem., .270 WSM (new 2002), .308 Win., .358 Win., .300 WSM (new 2001), 7mm-08 Rem., 7mm WSM (new 2002), or .450 Marlin (new 2001) cal., 22 in. match grade tapered stainless or chrome- moly barrel with cut rifling, controlled round feed, no sights, deluxe high gloss checkered walnut stock and forend, one inch black decelerator recoil pad, high polish blue on action and barrel, 3-5 shot mag., approx. 7½ lbs. New 2000.

	MSR	$2,433		$2,035	$1,635	$1,375	$1,150	$995	$825	$700

MODEL 70 CLASSIC EXTREME WEATHER - .25-06 Rem. (disc. 2001), .270 Win. (disc. 2000), .30-06, .300 Win. Mag., .300 Rem. Rem. Ultra Mag. (new 2001), .338 Win. Mag., 7mm Rem. Mag., or .375 H&H (new 2001) cal., controlled round feed, matte finished stainless action and match grade 22 lightweight (.375 H&H only), 24, or 26 in. fluted stainless barrel w/o sights, black McMillian fiberglass stock with cheekpiece and 1 in. decelerator pad, 3 or 5 shot mag., available in either right or left hand action, approx. 7½ lbs. New 2000.

	MSR	$2,183		$1,855	$1,525	$1,300

MODEL 70 CLASSIC CUSTOM MANNLICHER - .260 Rem., .308 Win., or 7mm- 08 Rem. cal., features full length checkered walnut stock, smooth tapered barrel and blue action, 19 in. barrel w/o sights (sights optional), 4 shot internal mag., approx. 6¾ lbs. Mfg. 1999-2000.

	$2,250	$1,800	$1,400	$1,200	$950	$800	$700

Last MSR was $2,595.

This model was designated the Model 70 Custom Mannlicher until 2000.

MODEL 70 CLASSIC CUSTOM SAFARI EXPRESS - .340 Wby. Mag. (disc. 1999), .358 STA (disc. 2000), .375 H&H, .375 Rem. Rem. Ultra Mag. (new 2001), .416 Rem. Mag., .416 Rigby (mfg. 2001), .458 Win. Mag., .458 Lott, or .470 Capstick (new 2002) cal., features honed internal parts, engine turned bolt and follower, adj. Dietrich Apel Express rear and front sights, deluxe checkered walnut stock and forend, 22 (.458 Win. Mag. & .458 Lott) or 24 in. barrel with sling stud, 3 shot mag., approx. 9¼ lbs. New 1999.

	MSR	$2,846		$2,465	$1,950	$1,465	$1,225	$950	$800	$700

Add $490 for .416 Rigby cal. (mfg. 2001 only).

Beginning in 2000, this model is available in left-hand action in all cals.

This model was designated the Model 70 Custom Safari Express until 2000.

MODEL 70 CLASSIC CUSTOM AFRICAN EXPRESS - .340 Wby. Mag. (disc. 1999), .358 STA (disc. 2000), .375 H&H, .416 Rem. Mag., .416 Rigby (mfg. 2001 only), .458 Win. Mag., .458 Lott, or .470 Capstick (mfg. 2001 only) cal., features drop down floorplate, increasing mag. capacity to 4, checkered fancy English walnut stock with black decelerator pad and ebony pistol grip and forend caps, adj. Dietrich Apel Express rear and front sights, 22 (.458 Win. Mag. only) or 24 in. barrel with sling stud, approx. 9½ lbs. New 1999.

	MSR	$4,078		$3,595	$3,025	$2,675	$2,275	$1,825	$1,400	$1,200

Add $437 for .416 Rigby cal. (disc. 2001).

Beginning in 2000, this model is available in left-hand action in all cals.

This model was designated the Model 70 Custom African Express until 2000.

MODEL 70 CLASSIC CUSTOM TAKE-DOWN - .300 Rem. Rem. Ultra Mag., .300 Win. Mag. (new 2002), .375 H&H, .416 Rem. Mag., or 7mm Rem. Mag. cal., all stainless construction with blue Teflon finish, take-down receiver/barrel assembly, brown synthetic stock and forearm, .75 MOA guaranteed for take-down action assembly/reassembly, 24 (.375 H&H or .416 Rem. Mag. cal. only) or 26 (fluted only) in. barrel, 3 shot internal mag., 8½ - 9 lbs. New 2001.

	MSR	$3,667		$3,150	$2,675	$2,300

While advertised beginning in 1998 with a MSR of $2,495, this model finally got into production during 2001.

MODEL 70 COLLECTOR GRADE - various cals., this variation must be special ordered through the Winchester Custom Shop and prices vary individually per quotation.

Grading	100%	98%	95%	90%	80%	70%	60%

MODEL 70 CUSTOM BUILT - various cals., this variation must be special ordered through the Winchester Custom Shop and prices vary individually per quotation.

MODEL 70 EXHIBITION GRADE - various cals., fancy checkered American walnut stock with hardwood forend tip. Mfg. 1988-89 only.

$1,995	$1,575	$1,000

Last MSR was $2,192.

RIFLES: O/U

DOUBLE EXPRESS RIFLE - .30-06, .257 Roberts, .270 Win., 7x57M, 7x57R, 7x65R, or 9.3x74R cal., 23½ in. O/U barrels, iron sights with claw scope mounts, ejectors, fully engraved satin finish receiver with game scene engraving, walnut specially hand checkered, sling swivels, 8½ lbs. Mfg. 1984-1985 only.

$2,500	$2,150	$1,850	$1,650	$1,450	$1,300	$1,200

Last MSR was $2,995.

In 1984, Aero Marine located in Birmingham, AL special ordered 200 deluxe double rifles in 7x57mm Mauser cal. They featured better engraving and game scenes with bottom of receiver marked Jaeger. Of the 200, 100 were rifles with 90 being standard grade and 10 being deluxe. The other 100 were supplied with an extra set of O/U shotgun barrels. Sales were slow on these special guns and eventually they were liquidated to another wholesaler. Recently, prices are in the $2,250-$3,000 range for the rifle alone and $3,000-$3,750 for the Combo.

100%	98%	95%	90%	80%	70%	60%	50%	40%	30%	20%	10%

SHOTGUNS: 1879-1963

BREECH LOADING SxS - 10 or 12 ga., imported from England for sales through the Winchester New York City office only, exposed hammers, available in 5 grades ranging from Class D - Class A and Match gun (lowest to highest). Higher grades were mfg. by W.C. Scott & Sons, C.G. Bonehill, W.C. McEntree, Richard Redmond, and H. & E. Hammond Gun Mfg.'s. Approx. 10,000 were imported between 1879-1884. Prices vary greatly due to condition and grade. Prices can range from $300 (poor condition Class D) to over $4,000 (95%+ condition specimen in Class A or Match gun).

This side by side model was the first shotgun bearing the Winchester name sold in the U.S. Identifiable by "Winchester Repeating Arms Co., New Haven, Connecticut, U.S.A." marking on barrel rib top.

MODEL 1887 LEVER ACTION - 10 or 12 ga., 4 shot tube mag., 30 or 32 in. full choke fluid steel barrels, plain pistol grip stock, first Browning patent shotgun mfg. by Winchester, first lever action repeating shotgun mfg. domestically. Mfg. 1887-1901. Approx. 64,855 mfg.

$2,750	$2,300	$1,925	$1,600	$1,250	$1,025	$850	$750	$600	$525	$450	$350

Standard frame finish on this model was color case hardening. Premiums exist for original bright case colored specimens. 10 ga. began production with serial number 22148. Also mfg. in Riot configuration (20 in. cylinder bore barrel). Gauges were chambered for 2 5/8 in. (12 ga.) and 2 7/8 in. (10 ga.). A very small amount was also made up in .70-150 cal. - add a significant premium.

✱ *Model 1887 Deluxe* - damascus barrel, checkered stock, and other special order features.

$5,000	$4,000	$3,500	$3,000	$1,750	$1,500	$1,275	$1,100	$950	$795	$650	$525

MODEL 1893 SLIDE ACTION - 12 ga., 30 (standard) and 32 in. barrel, black powder only. First Winchester shotgun with sliding forearm action, first Browning slide action patent, disc. 1897 after run of some 34,050. Note: chambered for 2 5/8 shells only, damascus barrels were available at extra cost, as were fancy stocks.

$950	$850	$750	$675	$600	$525	$485	$425	$375	$325	$275	$225

This gun had limited sales because mechanical weaknesses developed when shooting smokeless powder. Winchester offered a brand new shotgun of the customer's choice when they returned their Model 1893.

	100%	98%	95%	90%	80%	70%	60%	50%	40%	30%	20%	10%

MODEL 1897 SLIDE ACTION - 12 or 16 ga. (introduced 1900), improved Model 1893 action, 26-32 in. barrels, visible hammer, various chokes, takedown or solid frame, plain pistol grip stock. Over 1,024,700 mfg. between 1897-1957.

| $850 | $725 | $575 | $500 | $450 | $350 | $250 | $225 | $195 | $175 | $150 | $125 |

Add 25% for 16 ga.

Early 16 ga. Model 1897s were chambered for 2 9/16 in. shotshells, and are not as valuable because of the 2¾ in. shell length currently manufactured. The Model 1897 was the first Winchester shotgun chambered for 2¾ in. smokeless ammunition. This model was also manufactured with a damascus barrel for a short period of time, and is rare.

MODEL 1897 RIOT GUNS - see the "Trench/Riot Shotgun" category in the T section for more information and prices.

MODEL 1897 TRENCH GUNS - see the "Trench/Riot Shotgun" category in the T section for more information and prices.

This model changed its stock configuration after WWI.

MODEL 1897 TRAP - higher grade version of Standard, checkered stock, could have black diamond inlay in stock until 1919 (Black Diamond Trap), breech block marked Trap until approx. 1926. Mfg. 1897-1931.

| $1,650 | $1,375 | $1,200 | $975 | $700 | $550 | $450 | $325 | $275 | $250 | $225 | $200 |

✱ *Model 1897 Black Diamond Trap* - distinguishable by diamond ebony inlays in stock pistol grip.

| $2,000 | $1,800 | $1,600 | $1,400 | $1,200 | $1,000 | $900 | $750 | $600 | $500 | $400 | $300 |

MODEL 1897 PIGEON - higher grade version of Standard 97, should have engraved pigeon behind hammer on frame, breech block marked "Pigeon", most exhibit black diamond stock inlays until 1919. Mfg. 1897-1939.

| $7,500 | $6,500 | $4,950 | $3,350 | $3,000 | $2,500 | $2,000 | $1,250 | $950 | $775 | $600 | $525 |

MODEL 1901 - 10 ga. only, strengthened Model 1887 action to accept smokeless powder, lever action, standard barrel 32 in., blueblue barrel and frame, 5 shot mag. 13,500 mfg. between 1901-1920, starting with serial number 64,856.

| $2,750 | $2,300 | $1,925 | $1,600 | $1,250 | $1,025 | $850 | $750 | $600 | $525 | $450 | $350 |

Add 25% for Deluxe Grade (checkered wood).

This shotgun was chambered for 2 7/8 in. smokeless powder ammunition.

MODEL 1911 SL AUTOLOADER - 12 ga., recoil operated, 26 or 28 in. barrel, various chokes, pistol grip laminated birch stock. Mfg. 1911-1925, 82,774 produced, action had design problems.

| $550 | $495 | $450 | $300 | $250 | $200 | $175 | $150 | $140 | $130 | $120 | $110 |

Values assume original wood without splitting, repair, or replacement. The Model 1911 was Winchester's first semi-auto shotgun. It did not prove to be satisfactory partly because the design had to be exclusive of the patents for Browning's famous A-5 model, interestingly enough a design which Winchester originally had helped Browning patent.

MODEL 36 SINGLE SHOT - 9mm Rimfire cal., long shot, short shot, and ball, 18 in. round barrel, single shot bolt action, guns were not serial numbered, one-piece plain stock and forearm, special shaped trigger guard, 2¾ lbs. Approx. 20,000 mfg. between 1920-1927.

| $600 | $500 | $450 | $400 | $300 | $250 | $200 | $175 | $150 | $140 | $120 | $100 |

MODEL 12 SLIDE ACTION - 12 (introduced 1914), 16 (introduced 1914), 20 (initial ga., mfg. 1912, 2½ in. chamber mfg. until 1927), or 28 (introduced 1937) ga., 25 (20 ga. only, mfg. 1912-14), 26, 28, 30, or 32 in. standard, nickel, or stainless steel (scarce) barrel with or without rib (matted, solid, or VR), 2 9/16 (early 16 ga. only), 2¾ or 3 in. chamber, 6 shot, blue metal, various chokes, hammerless, plain pistol grip or straight walnut stock and forearm, marked Model 1912 from 1912-1919, approx. ser. no. 172,000. Mfg. 1912-1976.

Special order features on field guns have captured much collector interest in recent years. Combinations of these features can add a considerable percentage to the base values listed. Rare special orders on rare variations are very desirable and prices can double and more if the

Grading	100%	98%	95%	90%	80%	70%	60%

combination is right. As is the case with most other collectible shotguns at this time, Model 12s with open choked barrels in shorter lengths are A LOT more desirable (and expensive) than a specimen with a 30 in. full choke barrel (most common). Values listed are for standard configuration (28 or 30 in. full choke barrel with no rib). For most Model 12s, values for condition factors less than 60% will approximate the 60% price, because of shooter demand. Premiums must be added for the rarer open choked barrels in shorter length on all gauges.

Original gauge can be determined by removing the butt stock and observing the gauge marking on the stock screw boss.

The following add-ons DO NOT apply to 28 ga. values.
Add 30%-40% for Win. solid rib.
Add 40%-50% for Win. milled VR.
Add 50% for each extra barrel(s).
Add 20%-30% for Win. special VR (offset barrel proofmark).

"Donut" post Winchester VRs are more desirable than the rectangular post.

	100%	98%	95%	90%	80%	70%	60%
12 ga.	$525	$395	$325	$295	$225	$175	$150
16 ga.	$575	$450	$325	$295	$225	$175	$150
20 ga.	$800	$650	$550	$495	$450	$395	$375
28 ga.	$3,750	$3,500	$3,000	$2,750	$2,500	$2,000	$1,750

Subtract 50% if with factory Cutts compensator.

Recently, some non-original, re-stamped 28 ga. barrels have been added to 16 or 20 ga. frames "creating" a more desirable (and expensive) gun to unsuspecting buyers. Roll die markings are getting better and better so be very cautious when considering a non-Cutts 28 ga. (as in get a receipt specifying originality). 28 ga. ser. no. range is approx. 720,XXX to 1,857,XXX. 28 ga. Model 12s were available with both 2¾ (common) or 2 7/8 (infrequent) in. chamber. Believe it or not, there are getting to be a lot of fake Model 12 boxes that have been intentionally aged. Carefully screen NIB (watch the hanging tag also) specimens in this model.

Editor's Note: The Model 12 Winchester was produced continuously from 1912-1980. Over 2,027,500 were produced both in standard and deluxe (Pigeon) grades. Pigeon grades were first listed in 1914 and disc. during the war (1941). Reintroduced in 1948, they were disc. permanently in 1964, after which the Super Pigeon Grade became available only on a custom order basis from Winchester's Custom Gun Shop. These guns are worth 50-300% premiums depending on gauge, barrel lengths, stock options, engraving patterns, etc.

With an attrition rate of 33%, Model 12s with rare features 50 years ago will only be much rarer today (and expensive). 28 ga. guns were built between 1934 and 1960. Gauge rarity in increasing order is 12 ga., 16 ga., 20 ga., .410 bore (Model 42), and 28 ga. Serialization breakdown by year of manufacture is provided under the "Model Serialization" section of this book. When collecting Model 12s, ser. numbers on the underside of receiver (forward end), should match ser. no. on bottom rear of Mag. tube. Stainless steel barrel Model 12s were mostly mfg. in the late 1920s - early 1930s (65X,XXX serial range). Values typically range between $1,000-$2,500.

"Y" prefix appears on Model 12s built 1964-1980 - see listing under Post-64 Models.

MODEL 12 FEATHERWEIGHT - similar to Standard, except with alloy guard and different takedown system. Mfg. 1959-1962. "F" suffix after ser. no.

$425	$365	$325	$275	$250	$220	$190

MODEL 12 RIOT GUNS - see the "Trench/Riot Shotgun" category in the T section for more information and prices.

MODEL 12 MILITARY TRENCH GUNS - see the "Trench/Riot Shotgun" category in the T section for more information and prices.

MODEL 12 HEAVY DUCK GUN - 12 ga., 3 in. chamber, 30 or 32 in. barrel, solid rubber recoil pad, ½ in. shorter pull than regular Model 12. Mfg. 1935-1963.

$800	$700	$600	$500	$400	$350	$325

Add 50% for solid rib.
Add 25% for 32 in. barrel.

* ***Vent. rib*** - factory Winchester or 2 different styles mfg. by Simmons, notice barrel proof marking - rare.

Win. VR	$1,900	$1,600	$1,450	$1,200	$950	$800	$700

Grading	100%	98%	95%	90%	80%	70%	60%

MODEL 12 SKEET GUN - 12, 16, 20, or 28 ga., 26 in. barrel, skeet choke, checkered pistol grip stock, pre-WWII. Mfg. 1933-1976.

	100%	98%	95%	90%	80%	70%	60%
	$800	$700	$500	$450	$400	$350	$300

Add 25% for solid rib.
Add 60% for Win. Special VR.
Add 75% for Win. milled VR.
Subtract 50% for Factory-Cutts compensator.
16 gauge - rarity will command a premium.
Add 100% for 20 ga.
Add 500% for 28 ga.
Add approx. 20%-25% for brown plastic Hydrocoil stock.
Add approx. 65%-75% for white plastic Hydrocoil stock (approx. 50 mfg).

MODEL 12 TRAP GUN - various ga.'s, full choke barrel, deluxe straight or pistol grip stock, solid recoil pad. Mfg. 1938-1964.

	$1,100	$850	$750	$650	$500	$435	$400

Add 50% for milled VR.
Add approx. 20%-25% for brown plastic Hydrocoil stock.
Add approx. 65%-75% for white plastic Hydrocoil stock (approx. 50 mfg).
While plain barreled variation is rare, it is not as desirable.

MODEL 12 SUPER FIELD GRADE - 12 or 20 ga. only, features 26, 28, or 30 in. matted rib barrel, deluxe walnut with checkered pistol grip stock and forearm, mfg. 1955- 59.

	$1,250	$1,000	$850	$700	$550	$435	$400

Add 40% for 20 ga.
Add 20% for 16 ga.

MODEL 12 "BLACK DIAMOND" TRAP - various configurations, straight or pistol grip stock, features a small ebony diamond inlaid on each side of the pistol grip, solid rib.

	$1,850	$1,550	$1,250	$1,005	$800	$675	$500

Add 20% for milled VR.

MODEL 12 PIGEON GRADE - finer and more deluxe version of Model 12, many variations. Mfg. 1914-1941 and 1948-1964, engine turned breech block and shell follower, usually with engraved pigeon on bottom rear of mag. tube.

	$2,000	$1,650	$1,300	$1,000	$900	$800	$700
28 ga.	$5,000	$4,500	$4,000	$3,750	$3,500	$3,000	$2,700

Add 25% for VR.
Add 100% for 20 ga.

MODEL 20 - .410 bore, single shot, hammer, boxlock, 26 in. full choke (a few guns have been observed with cylinder choking), 6 pounds. Mfg. 23,616 between 1919-1924.

	$675	$650	$600	$400	$275	$225	$175

While most Model 20s have 2½ in. chambers, late parts cleanup guns could be chambered for 3 in. also.

* ***Winchester Model 20 Junior Trap Shooting Outfit*** - includes shotgun, midget hand trap, 150 .410 bore shells, 100 clay targets and accessories, cased.

	$3,200	$3,000	$2,750	$2,600	$2,500	$2,200	$2,000

Prices for this model assume all accessories are included - if not, subtract substantially. Just the shotshell boxes and accessories from this outfit are worth $2,500+ in nice condition.

MODEL 21 - 12, 16, 20, 28 ga., or .410 bore, boxlock action, after years in the design stage, production began in 1929 with guns being shipped to the warehouse in 1930 and first offered in Winchester's 1931 price list. Regular production continued for thirty years, through 1959. Approx. 32,500 mfg. 1931-1988. Approx. 2,000 were mfg. in Custom Grade. Factory records for this model (early mfg. is sketchy) are available by contacting the Cody Firearms Museum located in Cody, WY.

The early guns were plain, standard 12 gauge models with double triggers and extractors. Later in

Grading	100%	98%	95%	90%	80%	70%	60%

1931, 16 and 20 gauge chamberings became available as did selective single triggers and automatic ejectors.

By the end of 1933 the Model 21 skeet gun had been introduced as had Tournament, Trap and Custom Built grades. By about this time options included fancier wood, beavertail or semi-beavertail fore-ends, checkered butts (standard on skeet guns) or skeleton steel butt plates, recoil pads and almost any variation the customers might desire. Metal finishes on a Model 21 are unusual in that they have salt blue frames and rust blue barrels - this explains the difference in coloration between these metal surfaces.

The Tournament Grade was dropped in 1936 and the Trap Grade in 1940. A Standard Grade Trap Gun was added in 1941. The early Custom Built Grade was dropped in 1942 and the Deluxe Grade was added. This grade included as standard many of the previously available extra cost options.

Relatively few guns were produced in chamberings smaller than 20 gauge. 28 gauge first appeared in the 1936 catalog, although a few were probably produced before that. Winchester records are unclear as to the total but it is generally believed that fewer than 100 original factory guns were made. In addition, a number of original 20 gauge guns have been modified at the factory or elsewhere with factory 28 gauge barrels. These latter guns are just as valuable if the conversion was done at the Winchester Custom Gun Shop. Authenticity of the original guns should be established by factory letter.

.410 bore guns were first listed in 1955 but again some had been produced earlier, one having been built for John Olin in 1950. Throughout Winchester history all the rules seem to have had exceptions and nowhere is this more apparent than with respect to the Model 21 which, after all, has been pretty much a custom gun from the very beginning. Factory records and tallies among dealers indicate the existence of from 40 to 50 original factory guns. As in the case of the 28 gauge, extra barrels were available and at least some of those have been added to original 20 gauge guns.

The 3 inch Magnum 12 gauge Duck gun (stamped "Duck" on floor plate) was offered in Winchester catalogs from 1940 through 1952. Selective single triggers and automatic ejectors were standard as were the solid red Winchester recoil pads and 30 in. or 32 in. barrels. Some cases of non-factory upgrading of 2¾ or 3 inch Magnum guns have been reported. If authenticity is important to the buyer, a factory letter should be requested.

With respect to such letters, in cases where records may be missing or incomplete, the resultant letters may be less conclusive than desired. In some instances, consultation with, or a written appraisal from an authoritative collector arms dealer might be helpful.

Six standard patterns of engraving and several stock checkering and carving styles evolved during the production years. Values added by these and other embellishments such as precious metal inlays are beyond the scope of this work.

The following retail prices are for a standard field gun with average wood, beavertail forearm, ejectors, and single selective trigger with no alterations.

	100%	98%	95%	90%	80%	70%	60%
12 ga.	$4,600	$4,300	$4,000	$3,750	$3,500	$3,100	$2,800
16 ga.	$6,000	$5,700	$5,500	$5,250	$4,950	$4,500	$4,000
20 ga.	$6,500	$6,300	$6,000	$5,600	$5,400	$4,950	$4,500

Add $1,000 for VR.
Add $10%-15% for 3 in. chambers (Duck Gun, 12 ga. only).
Subtract approx. 50% for double triggers w/extractors.
Subtract 20% for double triggers with ejectors (normally encountered with splinter forearm).

✳ **Skeet Gun** - available in Standard, Tournament, and Trap grades. Introduced 1933.
Add 10% depending on grade.

✳ **Trap Gun** - introduced 1940, Trap Grade disc. same year, unaltered specimens will bring premium - add 10-25%.

✳ **3 Inch Duck Gun** - introduced 1940, must be so stamped (observe the 3 in. marking very carefully).

As can be seen, values are partly based on a certain interdependence between options. Higher grade guns, of course, will bring somewhat higher prices although much of their increased value results from many "options" being included as standard features.

Buyers or sellers with limited experience should always seek expert advice or appraisals in dealing

Grading	100%	98%	95%	90%	80%	70%	60%

with a Model 21. This is especially true with regard to higher grade guns and those with extra ornamentation.

* **Model 21 .410 Bore** - retail prices for original guns may be expected to range between $25,000 and $45,000 for mechanically sound guns depending on quality of finish. These prices take into consideration the reported sale of a plain standard gun in recent years for $37,000. Non-original guns with add-on factory barrels would probably be reduced by one-third.

* **Model 21 28 Ga.** - factory original guns will probably bring from $15,000 to $25,000 and, as with the 410s, 20 gauge guns modified to 28 gauge with factory barrels would be worth approx. the same if done at the factory.

Refinishing or Restoration: There is disagreement as to the effects of refinishing a Model 21. Many shooters and at least some collectors prefer a well refinished gun to a badly worn one. Higher grade guns restored by a master craftsman may approach factory original guns in value.

MODEL 21: RECENT PRODUCTION - refer to listing under SHOTGUNS: RECENT PRODUCTION SxS.

MODEL 24 SxS - 12, 16, or 20 ga., boxlock, hammerless, double triggers, approx. 8,000 were mfg. with pistol or straight grip stock. Introduced 1940, disc. 1957 after approx. 116,280 mfg.

	100%	98%	95%	90%	80%	70%	60%
	$650	$575	$425	$300	$225	$175	$150

Add 10% for 16 ga.
Add 40% for 20 ga.

MODEL 25 SLIDE ACTION - 12 ga. only, non-takedown version of the Model 12, 26 or 28 in. barrel. 87,937 mfg. between 1949-1954.

	100%	98%	95%	90%	80%	70%	60%
	$400	$325	$275	$225	$200	$175	$150

MODEL 37 SINGLE SHOT - 12, 16, 20, 28 ga., or .410 bore, top-lever break-open action, all barrels are full choke. Note on pricing that there is a big difference between a 100% gun without a box and NIB condition. Not serial-numbered. Over 1,015,000 mfg. between 1936-1963.

	100%	98%	95%	90%	80%	70%	60%
12 gauge	$295	$250	$200	$125	$100	$90	$75
16 gauge	$250	$200	$175	$115	$100	$90	$75
20 gauge	$325	$275	$225	$140	$110	$90	$75
28 gauge	$1,650	$1,200	$900	$650	$525	$400	$350
.410 bore	$375	$325	$295	$250	$150	$100	$90

If models are truly NIB, add $125-$175 to 100% condition values only, depending on gauge.
Add 20% for "Red Letter" models.
Add 15% for 32 in. barrel (12, 16, or 20 ga. only).
Most 28 ga. Model 37s have the "Red Letter".

* **Model 37 Youth/Boys/Red Dot** - 20 ga. only, 26 in. barrel marked Mod. Choke on barrel, solid red factory pad, identifiable by red dot inset into metal that is visible when hammer is cocked.

	100%	98%	95%	90%	80%	70%	60%
	N/A	$350	$275	$225	$175	$130	$100

MODEL 40 SEMI-AUTO - 12 ga. only, long recoil action, 28 or 30 in. barrel, walnut stock, skeet model also, poorly designed, many recalled by Winchester. Approx. 12,000 mfg. 1940-1941.

	100%	98%	95%	90%	80%	70%	60%
	$750	$600	$525	$450	$400	$300	$225

MODEL 41 BOLT ACTION - .410 bore, 2½ in. chamber until 1933 when it changed to 3 in., bolt action, single shot, 24 in. round barrel bored F, one-piece plain walnut stock and forearm, not serialized, approx. 22,145 were mfg. 1920-1934.

	100%	98%	95%	90%	80%	70%	60%
	$575	$500	$450	$375	$300	$250	$200

This model is rarely encountered with over 80% original condition.

MODEL 42 SLIDE ACTION - first pump specifically designed for the .410 bore, hammerless, 2½ (introduced 1935) or 3 in. chamber, 26 or 28 in. barrel, plain walnut pistol grip stock with circular grooved forearm (modified 1947), invented by William Roemer, approx. 6½ - 7 lbs.

Grading	100%	98%	95%	90%	80%	70%	60%

Approx. 164,800 mfg. in 4 grades between 1933-1963.

Special order features on field guns have captured much collector interest in recent years. Combinations of these features can add a considerable percentage to the base values listed. Rare special orders on rare variations are very desirable and prices can double and more if the combination is right.

Add 25% to any Model 42 chambered for 2½ in. shells.

✳ *Standard Grade* - 26 or 28 in. plain, solid rib or vent. rib barrel, plain walnut straight or pistol grip stock, walnut grooved forearm. Mfg. 1933-1963.

	$1,200	$1,100	$1,000	$900	$800	$700	$600

Add 60% for solid rib.
Add 100% for factory vent. rib.

✳ *Skeet Grade* - 26 or 28 in. plain, solid rib or vent. rib barrel, select checkered walnut straight grip or pistol grip stock and checkered forearm extension, 4 different chokes (full, modified, skeet, or cylinder) during pre-war (approx. ser. no. 1-52,000), post-war (approx. ser. no. 164,000) had same chokes available through 1953, when cylinder choke was dropped.

	$2,500	$2,250	$2,000	$1,800	$1,700	$1,500	$1,350

Add 50% for vent. rib.
Values are for solid rib.

✳ *Trap Grade* - first variation had small checkered forearm with one diamond in center, field choke (full, modified, or cylinder), second variation has large checkered forearm with 2 diamonds in center, both variations had 26 or 28 in. plain or solid rib barrel, select checkered walnut straight grip (one closed diamond on underside of grip) or pistol grip (one closed diamond on each side of grip) stock, usually choked skeet, stamped "TRAP" at bottom of receiver under the ser. no. Only 231 mfg.

	$8,500	$7,000	$6,000	$5,500	$4,500	$3,500	$3,000

✳ *Deluxe Grade* - same configurations as Trap Grade, 20 LPI checkering, most are fitted with special vent. rib after 1954 in 3 styles: round post-donut base, round post, and rectangle post, pre-1954 mfg. had plain or solid rib barrel, 1946-1950 mfg. may have "DELUXE" stamp under ser. no. on receiver. Mfg. 1946-1963.

◇**Solid Rib.**

	$5,500	$4,500	$3,500	$3,000	$2,500	$2,000	$1,500

◇**Vent. Rib (factory).**

	$6,500	$5,000	$4,000	$3,500	$2,750	$2,250	$2,000

✳ *Pigeon Grade* - same configurations as Deluxe Grade, except has pigeon engraved on underside of mag. tube, most were factory engraved, very few mfg.
Must be appraised individually. Before purchasing any factory engraved Model 42, it is advised to consult a reputable dealer/collector.

MODEL 50 SEMI-AUTO - 12 or 20 ga., 3 shot, recoil-operated (non-recoiling barrel), 26- 30 in. barrels, VR optional, steel frame or Feather Weight Model (aluminum receiver, FTW) introduced 1958. Over 196,000 mfg. between 1954-1961, starting with serial number 1,000.

	$500	$425	$400	$350	$300	$250	$200

Add $50 for VR (Simmons installed).
Add $50 for Feather Weight Model.
Add $150 for 20 ga.
Add 50% for Trap & Skeet Model.
Add 200%-350% for Pigeon Grade (denoted by A suffix in ser. no.).

Grading	100%	98%	95%	90%	80%	70%	60%

MODEL 59 SEMI-AUTO - 12 ga. only, 3 shot, short recoil operation, Win-lite (steel and fiberglass) ribless barrels, 26-30 in. barrel lengths, alloy receiver inscribed with hunting scenes, Versalite (first interchangeable choke tubes) option introduced 1961, 6½ lbs. 82,085 mfg. between 1960-1965.

	$600	$500	$400	$350	$300	$250	$200

Add 30% for barrel with all three choke tubes.

Inspect carefully for either cracked receiver (by bolt handle cutout and over serial numbers), or separating fiberglass on end of barrel.

* ✴ *Pigeon Grade* - mfg. 1962-1965, add 200-350% (rare).
  Winchester also mfg. 20 and 14 ga.'s experimentally in this model, extremely rare and expensive.

SHOTGUNS: POST-1964

Shotguns: Post-1964, Lever Action

MODEL 9410 TRADITIONAL/PACKER - .410 bore, 2½ in. chamber, lever action based on the Model 94 rifle, 20 (Packer Model, new 2002) or 24 in. round barrel with cylinder bore, 4 (Packer, 2/3 mag.) or 10 (Traditional, full mag.) shot tube mag., iron sights with TruGlo front and modified V adj. rear, checkered straight or semi-pistol (Packer only) grip walnut stock and forearm, with (Packer) or w/o (Traditional) sling swivel studs, approx. 6¾ lbs. New 2001.

MSR	$553	$455	$375	$310	$270	$235	$215	$195

Add $21 for Packer Model.

Shotguns: Post-1964, Semi-Auto

MODEL 140 RANGER SEMI-AUTO - 12, 16, or 20 ga., entry level model. Disc.

	$275	$250	$220	$200	$175	$155	$140

MODEL 1400 SEMI-AUTO - 12, 16, or 20 ga., 26, 28, or 30 in. barrel, 2¾ in. chamber, alloy receiver, various chokes, gas operated, 2 shot mag., checkered pistol grip stock. Mfg. 1964-1981.

	$275	$250	$220	$200	$175	$155	$140
Vent. rib	$315	$265	$240	$220	$195	$165	$150

Add 33% for Hydro-coil recoil system.

Note: In 1968 the model 1400 series was modified. The action release was improved and the checkering redesigned. From 1968-1972, they were designated MKII, which was then dropped. The values for the later guns mfg. from 1968-1973 may run approx. 10% higher - values shown are for guns mfg. from 1965-1968.

NEW MODEL 1400 WALNUT - 12 or 20 ga., 2 ¾ in. chamber, 22 (disc.), 26 (mfg. 1991-1993), or 28 in. VR barrel, checkered walnut stock and forearm, Winchokes standard, 3 shot mag., rotary bolt system, 7-7½ lbs. Mfg. 1989-94.

	$350	$290	$260	$240	$220	$190	$165

Last MSR was $419.

Add $15 for limited mfg. 1993 Quail Unlimited Model (2,500 mfg. 1993).

MODEL 1400 CUSTOM HIGH GRADE - 12 ga. only, 28 in. VR Winchoke barrel, special order only through the Custom Gun Shop, features deluxe hand checkered walnut and special engraving. Mfg. 1991-1992.

	$1,295	$995	$750

Last MSR was $1,695.

MODEL 1400 SKEET GRADE - similar to 1400, 12 or 20 ga., with 26 in. VR barrel, skeet bore, select skeet style stock. Mfg. 1965-1973.

	$425	$350	$300	$275	$220	$195	$165

Grading	100%	98%	95%	90%	80%	70%	60%

MODEL 1400 TRAP GRADE - similar to 1400, with 30 in. full choke VR barrel, select trap style stock. Mfg. 1965-1973.

	$360	$330	$305	$275	$220	$195	$165

MODEL 1400 DEER GUN - similar to 1400, with 22 in. barrel, rifle sights, 12 ga. only. Mfg. 1965-1974.

	$265	$240	$220	$200	$175	$165	$140

MODEL 1400 SLUG HUNTER - 12 ga. only, 22 in. smooth bore cyl. or rifled Sabot choke-tubed barrel, drilled and tapped for scope, includes bases or iron sights, 7¼ lbs. Mfg. 1990-92.

	$355	$310	$270	$250	$225	$195	$165

Last MSR was $420.

MODEL 1400 RANGER - 12 or 20 ga., gas operation, alloy receiver, 22 cyl. deer, 26 (mfg. 1991-1993), or 28 in. Winchoke barrel, checkered walnut finished hardwood stock and forearm, VR became standard 1985, 7¼ lbs. Disc. 1994.

	$285	$235	$200	$180	$160	$140	$120

Last MSR was $377.

Add $53 for deer combo. (includes extra 22 in. cyl. bore barrel).
Subtract $40 without VR.

MODEL 1500 XTR - 12 or 20 ga., 2¾ inch only, 28 inch barrel, plain or VR, Winchoke tubes, gas operation. Mfg. 1978-1982.

	$300	$260	$240	$220	$200	$180	$160

SUPER X MODEL 1 - 12 ga., 26, 28, or 30 in. VR barrel, various chokes, steel receiver, gas operated - self compensating, checkered pistol grip stock and forearm. Mfg. 1974-1981.

	$500	$450	$400	$350	$300	$250	$225

SUPER X MODEL 1 SKEET - similar to Standard, with 26 in. skeet bore barrel, select skeet style stock. Mfg. 1974-1981.

	$695	$595	$500	$475	$450	$425	$400

Add 20% if NIB condition.

SUPER X MODEL 1 TRAP - similar to Standard, with 30 in. barrel, imp. mod. or full choke, select trap style stock.

	$595	$550	$475	$425	$415	$395	$350

Add 20% if NIB condition.

SUPER X MODEL 1 CUSTOM TRAP OR SKEET - 12 ga. only, limited production from the Custom Shop, deluxe checkered walnut stock and forearm, extensive scroll engraving on receiver, built to custom order. Limited mfg. 1987-1992.

	$1,295	$925	$725

❋ *Super X Model 1 Custom Engraved* - features number 5 engraving pattern with 7 gold inlays. Disc.

	$2,395	$1,900	$1,350

Last MSR was $1,295.

Add $700 for factory gold inlays (8 flying ducks).

SUPER X2 3 IN. MAGNUM FIELD - 12 ga. only, 3 in. chamber, self-adjusting gas operation, 26 or 28 in. VR back-bored barrel with Invector chokes, 5 shot mag., choice of checkered walnut or black synthetic stock and forearm with recoil pad, high gloss blue or matte metal finish, approx. 7¼ - 8 lbs. New 1999.

MSR	$819	$710	$635	$555	$500	$450	$395	$325

❋ *Super X2 Sporting Clays* - 12 ga. only, 28 or 30 in. VR back-bored barrel with Invector chokes, adj. stock using spacers, includes 2 pistons, checkered walnut stock and forearm, approx. 8 lbs. New 2001.

MSR	$921	$815	$695	$595	$550	$495	$450	$375

Grading	100%	98%	95%	90%	80%	70%	60%

✳ Super X2 Practical MK II - 12 ga. only, home defense configuration featuring black composite stock and forearm, black metal finish, 22 in. barrel with cyl. bore Win Choke and ghost ring sights, 8 shot extended mag., includes sling swivels, 8 lbs. New 2002.

MSR $1,065	$925	$775	$650	$575	$500	$465	$395

✳ Super X2 Rifled Deer - 12 ga. only, 22 in. rifled barrel with cantilever scope base and Tru-Glo sights (rear sight folds down), black synthetic stock and forearm, 7¼ lbs. New 2002.

MSR $862	$740	$650	$565	$510	$450	$395	$325

SUPER X2 3½ IN. MAG. - 12 ga. only, 3½ in. chamber, similar to Super X2, black synthetic stock and forearm with vent. recoil pad, 24 (disc. 2000), 26, or 28 in. VR back-bored barrel with Invector chokes, 7½ - 8 lbs. New 1999.

MSR $936	$825	$695	$595	$550	$495	$450	$375

✳ Super X2 3½ In. Mag. Universal Hunter - similar to Super X2 3½ In. Mag., except has full coverage Mossy Oak Break-Up camo ccomposite stock and forearm, 26 in. VR barrel with 3 Invector Plus chokes, including optional extended extra full, TruGlo sights, 7¾ lbs. New 2002.

MSR $1,080	$925	$775	$650	$575	$500	$450	$375

Add $36 for extended extra full choke.

✳ Super X2 3½ In. Mag. Greenhead - similar to Super X2 3½ In. Mag., except has green Dura-Touch stock and forearm for enhanced durability and feel during cold/wet conditions, 28 in. VR barrel, matte metal finish, 8 lbs. New 2002.

MSR $1,116	$945	$785	$660	$580	$500	$450	$375

✳ Super X2 3½ In. Mag. Turkey (NWTF) - similar to Super X2 3½ In. Mag., except has 24 in. VR barrel with TruGlo sights and extra full turkey choke tube, matte finish only, 7½ lbs. New 1999.

MSR $1,018	$880	$730	$615	$555	$495	$450	$375

Beginning in 2001, this model incorporates a "Team NWTF" logo on the stock.

✳ Super X2 3½ In. Mag. Camo Turkey (NWTF) - similar configuration as regular Turkey, except has 100% Mossy Oak Break-Up camo treatment and TruGlo sights. New 2000.

MSR $1,101	$945	$800	$670	$550	$485	$425	$375

Beginning in 2001, this model incorporates a "Team NWTF" logo on the stock.

✳ Super X2 3½ In. Mag. Camo Waterfowl - similar to Super X2 3½ In. Mag., except has 100% Mossy Oak Shadow Grass treatment, 28 in. VR back-bored barrel with Invector chokes, 8 lbs. New 1999.

MSR $1,080	$930	$795	$665	$550	$485	$425	$375

SHOTGUNS: SINGLE BARREL

MODEL 370 - 12, 16, 20, 28 ga., or .410 bore, 28-32 in. full choke plain barrel, replaced the Model 37, top lever break open, exposed hammer, plain pistol grip stock. Approx. 221,578 mfg. between 1968-1973.

	$120	$100	$90	$85	$80	$75	$70

Add 20-60%+ for 28 ga. and .410 bore.

The Model 370 was mfg. in Winchester's Canadian plant in Cobourg, Ontario.

MODEL 370 YOUTH - similar to 370, with 26 in. barrel, 12½ in. stock, with recoil pad.

	$145	$110	$95	$85	$80	$75	$70

MODEL 37A - replaced the Model 370, roll engraved receiver, gold trigger. Approx. 391,168 mfg. between 1973-1980 in the Winchester plant in Cobourg, Ontario.

	$140	$110	$95	$85	$75	$65	$55

Add 10% for 36 in. goose barrel.
Add 50% for 28 ga. and 75% for .410 bore.

Grading	100%	98%	95%	90%	80%	70%	60%

MODEL 37A YOUTH - similar to 37A, except 20 ga. or .410 bore with 12½ in. pull stock.

	$175	$145	$100	$85	$70	$55	$40

MODEL 1370 SLAGBLASTER - 12 ga., 26 in. heavy barrel, commercial sale only - used to clean slag from steel kilns, 9 lbs. Disc.

	$275	$225	$200	$175	$155	$125	$100

Shotguns: Slide Action

MODEL 12 SLIDE ACTION SUPER PIGEON GRADE - 12 ga., slide action, 26, 28, or 30 in. barrel, VR, any choke, hand honed action, engine turned breech block and loading flap, "B" checkering and No. 5 engraving, custom order grade walnut stock. Limited production between 1964-1972.

	$2,995	$2,500	$2,250	$2,100	$1,750	$1,500	$1,300

Subtract 20% for Super Pigeon Grades mfg. 1984-85 (480 total).

MODEL 12 FIELD GRADE - 12 ga., slide action, 26, 28, or 30 in. VR barrel, various chokes, jeweled bolt, hand checkered, checkered select walnut stock. Mfg. 1972-1975, "Y" Serial No. Prefix.

	$750	$650	$600	$550	$500	$450	$400

In 1984, Y series Model 12s were once again available through a private contract with U.S.R.A. Co. which included engraving on Grades 1A-1C, and 2-5. These guns were available in either Field, Trap, or Skeet configurations. Since there was no manufacturer's suggested retail, Model 12 values shown are established by analyzing the sales of the two private contractors - no more of these variations are available.

✳ **Grades 1-A, 1-B, & 1-C** - light engraving depicting dogs or ducks. Disc.

	$1,300	$1,195	$1,000	$875	$785	$695	$600

Last MSR was $1,375.

✳ **Grades 2 & 3** - engraving features large duck and dog game scenes on receiver flats. Disc.

	$1,600	$1,495	$1,295	$1,075	$950	$830	$725

Last MSR was $1,695.

✳ **Grade 4** - more elaborate game scene engraving than Grades 2 & 3. Disc.

	$1,850	$1,695	$1,450	$1,225	$1,075	$950	$850

Last MSR was $1,995.

✳ **Grade 5** - elaborate game scene engraving with style B checkering. Disc.

	$2,195	$1,995	$1,725	$1,500	$1,225	$1,095	$950

Last MSR was $2,450.

Also available with gold inlays - add $1,000 to values.

✳ **3 Barrel Set** - grade 5 engraving with gold inlays and two extra barrels. Disc.

	$5,500	$4,995	$4,350	$3,750	$3,325	$2,750	$2,300

Last MSR was $6,000.

MODEL 12 SKEET GRADE - similar to Field Grade, with 26 in. VR skeet bore barrel, skeet style stock, with recoil pad. Mfg. 1972-1975.

	$950	$800	$625	$550	$495	$450	$425

See listings under Model 12 Field Grade for engraved values.

MODEL 12 TRAP GRADE - similar to Field grade, with 30 in. VR full choke barrel, trap style stock, straight or Monte Carlo, recoil pad. Mfg. 1972-1980.

	$750	$675	$575	$525	$495	$450	$425

See listings under Model 12 Field Grade for engraved values.

MODEL 12 DU - limited mfg. for Ducks Unlimited Chapters.

	$1,500	$1,250	$1,000

Grading	100%	98%	95%	90%	80%	70%	60%

MODEL 12 LIMITED EDITION

✳ Grade I 20 Ga. - 20 ga. only, 2¾ in. chamber only, reproduction of the famous Winchester Model 12 with slight design improvements, 26 in. VR barrel bored modified, 5 shot mag., high post floating rib, walnut stock and forearm with semi-gloss finish, take down, 7 lbs. 4,000 mfg. by Miroku 1993-95.

	$795	$625	$450				

Last MSR was $879

✳ Model 12 Grade V 20 Ga. - similar specifications to Grade I, except has select walnut checkered 22 lines per inch with high gloss finish, extensive game scene engraving including multiple gold inlays. 1,000 mfg. 1993-95.

	$1,175	$850	$650				

Last MSR was $1,431.

MODEL 42 HIGH GRADE LIMITED EDITION - .410 bore, 26 in. full choke VR barrel, features
Grade V-VI wood with special scroll and gold border engraving, 850 mfg. 1993 only.

	$1,400	$1,100	$895				

Last MSR was $1,617.

MODEL 120 RANGER - 12, 16, or 20 ga., entry level model. Disc.

	$200	$180	$165	$140	$110	$100	$90

MODEL 1200 SLIDE ACTION FIELD GRADE - 12, 16, or 20 ga., 26, 28, or 30 in. barrel, alloy
receiver, various chokes, checkered pistol grip stock, pad. Mfg. 1964-1981.

	100%	98%	95%	90%	80%	70%	60%
	$200	$180	$165	$140	$110	$100	$90
Vent. rib	$220	$205	$195	$165	$140	$110	$100
Winchoke	$240	$215	$200	$190	$180	$160	$140

Add 33% for Hydro-coil recoil system.

MODEL 1200 MAGNUM - similar to 1200, chambered for 12 or 20 ga., 3 in. magnum shells. Mfg.
1964-1980.

	$210	$190	$175	$165	$140	$110	$100
Vent. rib	$240	$215	$200	$185	$150	$140	$110

MODEL 1200 SKEET GUN - similar to 1200, 12 or 20 ga., 26 in. VR barrel, skeet bore, 2 shot
mag. and select style stock. Mfg. 1965-1974.

	$325	$275	$235	$200	$165	$140	$120

MODEL 1200 TRAP GUN - similar to 1200, with 12 ga., VR, 30 in. full choke barrel, select trap
style stock. Mfg. 1965-1974.

	$295	$275	$300	$195	$165	$140	$120
Winchoke	$330	$305	$275	$250	$220	$165	$140

MODEL 1200 DEER GUN - similar to 1200, with 22 in. barrel, rifle sights, 12 ga. only. Mfg. 1965-1974.

	$250	$200	$165	$110	$100	$85	$75

MODEL 1200 POLICE STAINLESS - 12 ga. only, 18 in. barrel, 7 shot mag. Disc.

	$250	$195	$165				

MODEL 1200 DEFENDER - 12 ga. only, 18 in. cylinder bore barrel, 7 shot mag., 6 lbs. Disc.

	$250	$200	$180	$155	$140	$125	$110

MODEL 1300 FEATHERWEIGHT SLIDE ACTION - 12 or 20 ga., 3 in. chamber, takedown, 26 (new
1991) or 28 in. barrel, 5 shot, plain or VR (became standard 1990), WinChoke tubes, checkered walnut stock and grooved forearm, alloy frame, recoil pad, 6¾ - 7 1/8 lbs. Mfg. 1978-1993.

	$300	$260	$230	$195	$175	$160	$145

Last MSR was $374.

Subtract $30 without VR.

This model had an "XTR" suffix until 1989. Older Model 1300 Featherweights had roll-engraving but no premiums are being asked at this time.

Grading	100%	98%	95%	90%	80%	70%	60%

MODEL 1300 WALNUT FIELD - 12 or 20 (disc. 1994) ga., 3 in. chamber, 26 or 28 in. VR barrel with WinChoke, checkered walnut stock and forearm, approx. 7¼ lbs. New 1994.

MSR	$405		$320	$235	$195	$155	$135	$120	$110

* **Model 1300 Black Shadow Field** - 12 or 20 (new 1996) ga., 3 in. chamber, 26 or 28 in. (12 ga. only) VR WinChoke barrel, black composite stock and forearm, approx. 7 lbs. New 1995.

MSR	$343		$265	$200	$160	$135	$120	$110	$95

* **Model 1300 Sporting/Field** - 12 ga., 3 in. chamber, 28 in. VR barrel, satin finished checkered walnut full length or compact (13 LOP) stock and forearm with radiused recoil pad, Tru-Glo front sight, matte metal finish, 7½ lbs. New 2002.

MSR	$426		$335	$245	$200	$160	$135	$120	$110

* **Model 1300 Advantage Camo** - 12 ga. only, 28 in. barrel with choke tubes, full coverage. Advantage Camo. Mfg. 1997.

	$340	$265	$235	$195	$165	$145	$125

Last MSR was $432.

MODEL 1300 UPLAND SPECIAL FIELD - 12 or 20 (new 2000) ga., 3 in. chamber, features checkered straight grip walnut stock and forearm, solid recoil pad, 24 in. VR barrel with choke tube, blue only, 6¾ lbs. New 1999.

MSR	$405		$320	$235	$190	$155	$135	$120	$110

MODEL 1300 CUSTOM HIGH GRADE - while advertised, this model was never mfg. Advertised retail was $1,395.

MODEL 1300 WATERFOWL - 12 ga. only, 3 in. chamber, 28 or 30 (disc.) in. VR barrel, matte finished metal, choice of low luster walnut finish or brown Win-Tuff wood, recoil pad, includes camo sling and swivels, Winchokes standard, 7 lbs. Mfg. 1984-91.

	$295	$260	$235	$200	$180	$165	$150

Last MSR was $367.

MODEL 1300 TURKEY GUN - 12 ga. only, 3 in. chamber, 22 in. VR barrel, Winchoked, walnut stock and forearm with low luster finish, metal surfaces have matte finish, supplied with camouflaged fabric sling, 6 3/8 lbs. Mfg. 1985-1988 only.

	$290	$265	$235	$200	$180	$165	$150

Last MSR was $348.

* **Model 1300 Win-Cam Turkey Gun** - similar to Model 1300 Turkey Gun, except has greenish laminated hardwood stock and forearm. Mfg. 1987-1993.

	$350	$295	$250	$200	$180	$165	$150

Last MSR was $435.

* **Model 1300 Win-Cam Combo Pack** - 12 ga., supplied with 22 and 30 in. VR non-glare finished barrels, greenish laminated hardwood stock and forearm, camo sling, matte finished metal. Mfg. 1987-1988 only.

	$375	$330	$290	$260	$230	$200	$185

Last MSR was $425.

* **Model 1300 Ladies-Youth Win-Cam Turkey Gun** - 20 ga. only, 3 in. chamber, 22 in. VR barrel, green camo laminate shortened stock and forearm, includes sling and National Wild Turkey Federation engraving, 6 lbs. Mfg. 1992 only.

	$340	$295	$250	$200	$180	$165	$150

Last MSR was $411.

* **Model 1300 Win-Cam NWTF Series I-IV** - 12 or 20 ga., Series I was released 1989 (12 ga. only) and included special receiver engraving featuring National Wild Turkey Federation motifs, Series II was released 1990 with a choice of either 12 (disc.) or 20 ga. Ladies/Youth model, Series III was released 1991-92, Series IV was released 1993. Disc. 1994.

	$365	$300	$250	$200	$180	$165	$150

Last MSR was $458.

W

Grading	100%	98%	95%	90%	80%	70%	60%

MODEL 1300 TURKEY - SYNTHETIC STOCK

- 12 or 20 (mfg. 1996-99, Black Shadow only) ga., 3 in. chamber, 22 in. VR barrel with choke tube, choice of 2 color Realtree camo patterns on synthetic stock and forearm, full camo coverage available in Realtree or Advantage (new 1996), or non-glare black (Black Shadow) finish on all surfaces, approx. 6¾ lbs. Mfg. 1994-2000.

✳ *Model 1300 Black Shadow Finish* - disc. 2000.

	$260	$195	$160	$135	$120	$110	$95

Last MSR was $328.

✳ *Model 1300 Mossy Oak Break-Up Turkey* - 12 ga. only, 3 in. chamber, 22 in. VR barrel with TruGlo sights, high density X-full turkey tube, 100% Mossy Oak coverage on wood and metal, 6¾ lbs. Mfg. 2000 only.

	$375	$295	$260	$225	$200	$185	$170

Last MSR was $459.

This model was also available with iron sights and rifled sabot choke tube for deer hunting - add approx. $30.

✳ *Model 1300 RealTree/Advantage Camo Finish* - available with stock and forearm, RealTree only or full coverage camo. Disc. 1998.

	$290	$240	$180	$150	$130	$115	$100

Last MSR was $370.

Add $62 for full coverage camo.
Add $40 for full coverage without sling (disc. 1997).
Add $40 for smoothbore barrel (Advantage full camo only).

MODEL 1300 UNIVERSAL HUNTER

- 12 ga. only, 3 in. chamber, 26 in. VR barrel with 3 Win. Chokes, full coverage Mossy Oak Break-Up camo, Tru-Glo 3-dot sights, composite stock and forearm, 7 lbs. New 2002.

MSR	$550	$445	$360	$265	$225	$180	$155	$130

MODEL 1300 NWTF TURKEY MODELS

- 12 ga. only, 3 in. chamber, 18 (Short Turkey, new 2002) or 22 in. barrel, choice of Black Shadow (black synthetic stock and forearm with non-glare metal finish and extra full choke tube, mfg. 2001 only), Turkey Superflauge with full coverage TreBark Superflauge (mfg. 2001) or Mossy Oak Break-Up camo with TruGlo sights, Buck & Tom Superflauge with full coverage TreBark Superflauge (mfg. 2001) or Mossy Oak Break-Up (new 2002) camo with 2 chokes tubes including rifled sabot, or Short Turkey (18 in. barrel with rifled sights and full coverage Mossy Oak Break-Up camo) configurations, "Team NWTF" logo printed on stock, 6¾ lbs. New 2001.

MSR	$489	$400	$340	$250	$215	$175	$150	$125

Subtract approx. $160 for Black Shadow configuration.
Add $36 for Buck & Tom Superflauge configuration.

MODEL 1300 LADIES-YOUTH

- 20 ga. only, 3 in. chamber, 22 in. VR barrel, shortened stock dimensions, walnut stock with recoil pad and rear positioned, grooved forearm, 6¼ lbs. Mfg. 1992 only.

	$315	$260	$220	$180	$165	$150	$135

Last MSR was $355.

MODEL 1300 SLUG HUNTER

- 12 ga. only, 3 in. chamber, 22 in. rifled or smooth bore barrel with iron sights, checkered stock and forearm, satin walnut finish or brown laminate stock (Win-Tuff). Supplied with camo fabric sling and rings and bases. Mfg. 1988 - Disc.

	$360	$300	$250	$200	$180	$165	$150

Last MSR was $445.

Add $10 for smooth bore barrel with Sabot rifled tubes (disc. 1992).
Add $4 for "Whitetails Unlimited" Model (new 1991).

Grading	100%	98%	95%	90%	80%	70%	60%

MODEL 1300 WALNUT DEER - 12 ga. only, 3 in. chamber, 22 in. rifled barrel, non- glare metal surfaces, rifle sights, checkered walnut stock with recoil pad and forearm, 7¼ lbs. Mfg. 1994-99.

	$350	$285	$255	$225	$200	$185	$170

Last MSR was $429.

✸ *Model 1300 Black Shadow Deer* - 12 or 20 (mfg. 1996-97, reintroduced 2000) ga., 3 in. chamber, 22 in. smoothbore (12 ga. only) or rifled (new 1996) barrel with IC Winchoke matte black stock, forearm, and metal parts, rifle sights, drilled and tapped receiver, approx. 6¾ lbs. New 1994.

MSR	$341		$270	$205	$160	$135	$120	$110	$95

Add $25 for rifled barrel (new 1996).
Add $66 for Cantilever scope mount, available in 12 ga. only (new 2000).
Add $102 for deer combo package that includes 22 in. cyl. bore (disc. 1998) or rifled (new 2000) barrel and 28 in. VR WinChoke barrels.

✸ *Model 1300 Deer Ranger Compact* - 20 ga. only, 3 in. chamber, 22 in. rifled barrel with rifle sights, smaller dimensions (13 in. LOP), brown composite stock and forearm, non-glare finish, 6 5/8 lbs. New 2000.

MSR	$377		$295	$225	$165	$145	$125	$110	$100

✸ *Model 1300 Full Advantage Camo* - 12 ga. only, 3 in. chamber, choice of 22 in. rifled or smoothbore barrel, entire gun is in Full Advantage camo pattern, drilled and tapped receiver, iron sights, 7 lbs. Mfg. 1995-98.

	$350	$295	$260	$225	$200	$185	$170

Last MSR was $432.

Subtract $22 for smoothbore barrel.

MODEL 1300 RANGER SLIDE ACTION - 12 or 20 ga., 3 in. chamber, 22 cyl. or rifled (deer only disc.), 24 1/8 cyl. (disc. deer barrel), 26 (mfg. 1991-98), 28, or 30 (disc. 1992) in. plain or VR barrel, walnut finished hardwood stock, alloy receiver, approx. 7¼ lbs. New 1983.

MSR	$357		$280	$210	$165	$135	$120	$110	$95

Subtract $40 without VR or WinChokes.
This model was also available in a deer combination package which included either a 22 in. rifled or smoothbore deer barrel and a 28 in. VR WinChoke barrel in either 12 or 20 ga. (disc.). - add approx. 25% to values listed.

✸ *Ranger Ladies/Youth Model* - 20 ga. only, 3 in. chamber, 22 in. VR barrel, shorter stock dimensions - 13 in. LOP and rearward positioned forearm. Disc. 1998.

	$285	$235	$200	$170	$150	$125	$110

Last MSR was $309.

Subtract $40 if without WinChoke and VR.

✸ *Ranger Compact* - 12 or 20 ga., 3 in. chamber, features shorter dimensions (13 LOP), 22 (20 ga. only) or 24 (12 ga. only) in. VR barrel with WinChoke and TruGlo sights uncheckered hardwood stock and grooved forearm, blue only, approx. 6¾ lbs. New 1999.

MSR	$356		$280	$210	$165	$135	$120	$110	$95

MODEL 1300 CAMP DEFENDER - 12 ga. only, 3 in. chamber, 8 shot mag., 22 in. barrel with rifle sights and WinChoke, choice of black synthetic (disc. 2000) or hardwood (new 2001) stock and forearm, matte metal finish, 6 7/8 lbs. New 1999.

MSR	$380		$295	$225	$175	$145	$125	$110	$100

MODEL 1300 DEFENDER - 12 or 20 (disc. 1996, reintroduced 2001) ga., 3 in. chamber, available in Police (disc. 1989), Marine, and Defender variations, 18 or 24 (mfg. 1994-98) in. cyl. bore barrel, 5 (disc. 1998), 7 (disc. 1998), or 8 shot mag., matte metal finish, choice of hardwood (disc. 2001), composite (matte finish), or pistol grip (matte finish, 12 ga. only) stock, TruGlo sights became standard 1999, 5¾ - 7 lbs.

MSR	$333		$265	$205	$160				

Add $13 for short pistol grip and full stocks.
Add approx. $100 for Combo Package (includes extra 28 in. VR barrel - disc. 1998).

W

Grading	100%	98%	95%	90%	80%	70%	60%

* **Stainless Coastal Marine Defender** - 12 ga. only, 18 in. cyl. bore barrel, a Sandstrom 9A phosphate coating was released late 1989 to give long lasting corrosion protection to all receiver and internal working parts, 6 shot mag., synthetic pistol grip (disc. 2001) or full black stock configuration, approx. 6 3/8 lbs.

MSR	$518	$430	$355	$260

* **Model 1300 Lady Defender** - 20 ga. only, 3 in. chamber, choice of synthetic regular or pistol grip stock, 4 (disc. 1996) or 7 shot mag., 18 in. cyl. bore barrel (new 1996), 5 3/8 lbs. Disc. 1998.

	$235	$190	$150

Last MSR was $290.

SHOTGUNS: O/U - RECENT PRODUCTION

Model 101 dates of manufacture and serialization data can be found in the SERIALIZATION section in the back of this text.

In November of 1987 Olin/Winchester disc. the Model 101. Classic Doubles (listed separately in this text) imported this model under their own trademark until approx. 1990. With the discontinuance of the Model 101 and its many variations, both dealers and collectors have created a lot more demand for this model recently. As a result, prices have escalated and the scramble is on to try and pick off those rare and desirable variations. Since there have been a lot of limited editions and production changes in the 101 O/U series, it could very well be that this model might become very collectible in upcoming years (as in look what happened to the Model 12).

Note: Model 101 and Model 96 Xpert guns were made by Olin Kodensha located in Tochigi, Japan.

Values listed for 100% condition Model 101s assume NIB - subtract 10%-15% if without box, warranty card, and original shipping container (with packing materials).

MODEL 91 - 12 ga. only, mfg. by Laurona in Spain for international sales including Europe, SST, ejectors optional, VR, distinguishable by black chrome finish on metal parts. Disc.

Prices hard to evaluate because of limited importation domestically. In some regions they are bought as medium priced field guns ($550-$650), while in others they are sold as a rare Winchester O&U ($900-$1,100).

MODEL 96 XPERT FIELD GRADE - 3 in. chambers, similar action to Model 101, 12 or 20 ga., auto ejectors, SST, various barrel lengths and chokes, action similar to 101, no engraving, checkered pistol grip stock and forearm. Mfg. 1976-1982.

	$875	$775	$650	$550	$475	$425	$375

Add 10% for 20 ga.

This model has become known as the "Poor Man's 101".

MODEL 96 XPERT SKEET GRADE - 2¾ in. chambers, similar to Field Grade, with 27 in. skeet barrels, skeet style stock. Mfg. 1976-1982.

	$925	$850	$725	$600	$500	$450	$410

Add 10% for 20 ga.

MODEL 96 XPERT TRAP GRADE - 2¾ in. chambers, similar to Field, 12 ga. only, 30 in. imp. mod. and full or full and full choke, trap style stock. Mfg. 1976-1982.

	$875	$775	$650	$550	$475	$425	$375

MODEL 99 - 12 ga., DT, no engraving. Disc.

	$700	$575	$525	$470	$430	$395	$360

MODEL 101 FIELD GRADE - 12, 20 ga., or .410 bore, 26, 28, or 30 in. barrels, various chokes, boxlock, auto ejectors, SST, engraved receiver, checkered American walnut pistol grip stock. Mfg. 1963-1987. Values assume Winchokes (standard since 1983) - subtract $60 if without.

* **Older production** - checkered walnut stock and forearm, ejectors, SST, blue metal with light engraving on receiver, various barrel lengths, w/o choke tubes.

	$995	$850	$725	$625	$585	$550	$500

Add 20% for 28 ga. or .410 bore.
Add 10% for 20 ga.

Grading	100%	98%	95%	90%	80%	70%	60%

✳ **Field Special** - 12 or 20 ga., 3 in. chambers, VR, 27 in. barrels with Winchokes, blue receiver with scroll engraving ejectors, 7 lbs. Disc. 1987.

| | $1,225 | $995 | $875 | $775 | $695 | $600 | $500 |

Last MSR was $1,185.

Add 10% for 20 ga.

✳ **Lightweight Field** - 12 or 20 ga., similar to regular Field Grade, except has coin finished receiver, vent. barrels, and solid rubber recoil pad, 6½ - 7 lbs. Disc. 1987.

| | $1,325 | $1,075 | $950 | $825 | $725 | $625 | $525 |

Last MSR was $1,425.

Add 10% for 20 ga.

✳ **Waterfowl Model** - 12 ga. only, 3 in. chambers, 30 or 32(disc.) in. Winchoked barrels, VR, matte blue receiver with moderate engraving, low gloss walnut stock with vent. recoil pad, 7¾ lbs. Disc. 1987.

| | $1,695 | $1,400 | $1,250 | $1,000 | $900 | $800 | $700 |

Last MSR was $1,570.

✳ **Model 101 Field Grade 2 Barrel Hunting Set** - 12 or 20 ga. barrels, both with Winchokes, 26 in. barrels - 20 ga., 28 in. barrels - 12 ga., scroll engraved, blue receiver with game scene engraving and borders, cased. Mfg. 1984-1987.

| | $2,500 | $2,050 | $1,575 | $1,375 | $1,220 | $1,050 | $975 |

Last MSR was $2,345.

✳ **Quail Special** - 12, 20 (disc.1984), 28 (new 1987) ga., or .410 bore (new 1987), 25½ in. Winchoke barrels, 6¾ lbs. - 12 ga., straight grip stock, vent. barrels and rib, coin finished receiver with game scene engraving, 500 of each ga. were mfg. Imported 1984-1986.

	100%	98%	95%	90%	80%	70%	60%
12 ga.	$2,200	$1,995	$1,800	$1,600	$1,200	$975	$875
20 ga.	$2,600	$2,175	$1,775	$1,500	$1,275	$1,100	$925
28 ga.	$3,950	$3,600	$3,250	$2,500	$1,850	$1,475	$1,200
.410 bore	$3,250	$2,850	$2,350	$1,800	$1,500	$1,250	$975

Last MSR was $1,950.

All 28 ga. models are baby frames.

✳ **National Wild Turkey Federation Commemorative** - features golden turkeys on receiver sides, 27 in. VR barrels with choke tubes, only 300 mfg.

| | $2,295 | $1,775 | $1,200 |

Original issue price was $1,950.

✳ **American Flyer Live Bird** - 12 ga. only, 28 or 29½ (new 1988) in. separated barrels with special competition VR, blue frame with gold wire borders and pigeon inlay, 8 - 8½ lbs. Imported 1987 only.

| | $2,595 | $2,275 | $1,950 | $1,775 | $1,600 | $1,425 | $1,300 |

Last MSR was $2,910.

Add $925 for Combo Model (extra set of 29½ in. barrels - 45 mfg.).
Add $265 for 29½ in. barrel with WT4 choke tubes.
Approx. 200 of this model were mfg.

MODEL 101 MAGNUM - similar to 101 Field, 12 or 20 ga., 3 in. Mag. chambering, recoil pad, 30 in. barrels, full and mod., or full and full choke. Mfg. 1966-1981.

| | $975 | $850 | $725 | $650 | $575 | $500 | $460 |

Add 10% for 20 ga.

MODEL 101 SKEET GRADE - similar to 101 Field, with 26½ (12 or 20 ga.) or 28 (28 ga. or .410 bore) in. skeet bored barrels, skeet style stock. Mfg. 1966-1984.

| | $1,000 | $825 | $770 | $700 | $650 | $595 | $540 |

Add 40% for 28 ga. or .410 bore.
Add 20% for 20 ga.

W

Grading	100%	98%	95%	90%	80%	70%	60%

MODEL 101 THREE GAUGE SKEET SET - similar to Skeet 101, with 20, 28 ga., and .410 bore barrels, cased. Mfg. 1974-1984.

	100%	98%	95%	90%	80%	70%	60%
	$2,975	$2,600	$2,275	$1,975	$1,650	$1,300	$1,100

MODEL 101 TRAP GRADE - 12 ga. only, 30 or 32 in. barrels with normal or wide VR, imp. mod. and full or full and full chokes, trap style stock. Mfg. 1966-1984.

	$1,320	$1,100	$935	$825	$715	$660	$605

MODEL 101 SINGLE BARREL TRAP - similar to O/U Trap, with 32 or 34 in. F or IM choke barrel, Monte Carlo trap style stock. Mfg. 1967-1971.

	$880	$660	$550	$495	$385	$360	$330

Add 100% for an extra O/U barrel (Trap Set).

MODEL 101 PIGEON GRADE (XTR) - 12, 20, 28 ga. or .410 bore(disc. 1986), vent. O/U barrels, deluxe engraved silver receiver version of 101, select checkered wood. Mfg. 1974-1987.

* **Lightweight Field Model** - lightweight variation, Winchokes standard, 28 ga. baby frame has 27 in . barrels, 6½ - 7 lbs. Disc. 1987.

	100%	98%	95%	90%	80%	70%	60%
12 ga.	$1,995	$1,650	$1,475	$1,245	$1,050	$900	$775
20 ga.	$2,295	$1,995	$1,750	$1,500	$1,250	$975	$895
28 ga. standard	$2,650	$2,350	$1,950	$1,595	$1,350	$1,150	$1,050
28 ga. baby frame	$3,950	$3,600	$3,250	$2,500	$1,850	$1,475	$1,200

Last MSR was $1,950.

Subtract 5% if without Winchokes (available in all gauges).

* **Lightweight recent mfg.** - 20 ga. only, 27 in. barrels only with Winchokes, previously manufactured guns that have been photo-chemically engraved and gold-plated, 101 (total mfg.) shotguns were sold by Guns Unlimited Inc. located in Omaha, NE 1995-1996.

Lightweight mfg. 1995-1996)

	$1,995	$1,795	$1,500	$1,250	$1,050	$950	$750

Last MSR was $1,795.

* **Lightweight two barrel set** - includes either 12/20 ga. with Winchokes (28 in. barrels on 12 ga. and 27 in. on 20 ga.) or 28 ga./.410 bore (27 in. barrels, 28 ga. has Winchokes; .410 bore has fixed M/F chokes), 250 sets mfg. serial numbered HS1- HS250. Disc. 1986.

	$3,500	$3,150	$2,700	$2,350	$2,025	$1,800	$1,575

Last MSR was $2,500.

Add 10% for 28 ga./.410 bore combo.

* **Pigeon Grade 3 barrel set** - coin finished Pigeon Grade frame, approx. 250 mfg.

	$3,950	$3,375	$2,850	$2,300	$2,000	$1,850	$1,700

* **Featherweight** - 12 or 20 ga., English straight stock, 25½ in. barrels bored IC/ IM, 6½ - 6¾ lbs. Disc. 1987.

	$1,950	$1,750	$1,450	$1,275	$950	$850	$750

Last MSR was $1,580.

Add 20% for Winchokes.

* **Skeet Grade** - 12, 20, 28 ga., or .410 bore.

	$1,275	$1,100	$995	$880	$770	$715	$660

Add 20% for 20 ga.
Add 40% for 28 ga. or .410 bore.

* **Trap Grade** - 12 ga. only, vent. barrels and rib, coin finish receiver with fine scroll engraving, engraved pigeon on floorplate, Winchoke standard, 8¼ lbs. Disc. 1985.

	$1,300	$1,180	$990	$880	$770	$715	$660

Last MSR was $1,475.

Subtract 15% if w/o Winchokes.

Grading	100%	98%	95%	90%	80%	70%	60%

✳ **Super Pigeon Grade** - 12 ga. only, blue receiver with elaborate engraving including multiple gold inlays, extra select walnut with fleur-de-lis checkering on stock and forearm, Winchoke standard, 7½ lbs. Imported 1985-1987 only.

	$4,025	$3,625	$3,225	$2,835	$2,500	$2,150	$1,920

Last MSR was $4,590.

101 DIAMOND GRADE - Trap or Skeet O/U, 12 (Trap only), 20, 28 ga., or .410 bore, vent. barrels and rib, Winchoke standard on Trap - add $75 on Skeet model (disc.1986), select hand checkered walnut, engraved satin-finish receiver. Trap model has extra high VR. Skeet model has raised rib and muzzle vents.

✳ **Standard Trap** - 12 ga. only, 30 or 32 in. vent. barrels, 8¾ - 9 lbs. Disc. 1987.

	$1,620	$1,440	$1,230	$1,075	$900	$780	$640

Last MSR was $1,860.

✳ **Unsingle Trap** - 12 ga. only, lower single barrel, 32 or 34 in. barrel, extended rib. Add $60 for Winchoke. Disc. 1986.

	$1,700	$1,525	$1,250	$995	$895	$830	$740

Last MSR was $1,760.

✳ **Oversingle Trap** - 12 ga. only, Winchokes, 34 in. upper barrel only, 8½ lbs. Imported 1986-1987 only.

	$1,985	$1,695	$1,545	$1,395	$1,200	$995	$895

Last MSR was $2,145.

✳ **Oversingle Combo** - includes one set of O/U barrels and an oversingle barrel, cased. Imported 1987 only.

	$3,075	$2,750	$2,525	$2,300	$2,000	$1,750	$1,625

Last MSR was $3,550.

✳ **Trap Combo** - 12 ga. only, includes a set of 30 or 32 in. vent. O/U barrels and a 32 or 34 in. high ribbed unsingle (lower) barrel, standard or Monte Carlo stock, approx. 9 lbs. Disc. 1987.

	$2,570	$2,320	$1,975	$1,800	$1,600	$1,400	$1,200

Last MSR was $2,940.

Add $275 for ATA Trap set.

✳ **Standard Skeet** - 12, 20, 28 ga., or .410 bore, 27½ in. vent. barrels and competition rib, 6½ - 7¼ lbs. Disc. 1987.

	$1,650	$1,465	$1,240	$1,075	$900	$780	$640

Last MSR was $1,950.

Add 20% for 28 ga. or .410 bore.
Add 10% for 20 ga.
Certain design features may increase/decrease the values of this model.

✳ **Four Gauge Skeet Set** - includes 12, 20, 28 ga., and .410 bore 27½ in. separated barrel assemblies, cased. Imported 1985-1987 only.

	$4,850	$4,025	$3,650	$3,200	$2,800	$2,500	$2,150

Last MSR was $5,025.

✳ **Sporting Clays Grade** - 12 ga. only, marked Diamond Sporter, 28 in. barrels with Winchokes, designed for Sporting Clay competition. Disc. 1987.

	$1,950	$1,625	$1,350	$1,100	$925	$795	$650

Last MSR was $1,965.

501 GRAND EUROPEAN - Trap or Skeet, 12 or 20 (Skeet only) ga., 27, 30, or 32 in. barrels, extra select hand checkered walnut with oil finish, Schnabel forearm, entensive scroll engraving on satin-finished receiver, vent. barrels and rib. Mfg. 1981-86.

	$1,650	$1,450	$1,225	$1,050	$900	$780	$640

Last MSR was $1,720.

Add 20% for 20 ga. Skeet.

Grading	100%	98%	95%	90%	80%	70%	60%

✴ *Grand European Featherweight* - 20 ga. only, straight grip stock, 25½ in. VR barrels, 5¾ lbs. Disc. 1986.

| | $2,495 | $2,250 | $1,875 | $1,550 | $1,200 | $975 | $800 |

Last MSR was $1,720.

PRESENTATION GRADE - 12 ga. only, available in both Trap and Skeet models, blue action-extensively engraved with gold inlays, special crotch walnut, 27 (Skeet) or 30 in. vent. barrels, hand checkered, silver wire borders on perimeter of receiver. Imported 1984-1987 only.

| | $3,950 | $3,395 | $3,075 | $2,400 | $2,000 | $1,800 | $1,600 |

Last MSR was $3,840.

Subtract 10% for Trap Model.

SHOTGUN/RIFLE COMBINATION - combination 12 ga. under .222 Rem., .223 Rem., .243 Win., .270 Win., .30-06, .308 Win., .300 Win. Mag., 5.6x57R, 7x65R, 7x57 Mauser, or 9.3x74R cal. rifle, O/U, 25 in. barrels, top barrel is Winchoked, Grand European engraving and finish, 8½ lbs. Mfg. 1983-1985.

| | $2,150 | $1,950 | $1,650 | $1,350 | $1,175 | $875 | $750 |

Last MSR was $2,550.

This model was advertised in .222 Rem., .223 Rem., 6.5x55mm, or .300 Win. Mag. cal., but very few 6.5x55mm or .300 Win. Mag. cals. have been encountered to date.

MODEL 1001 FIELD GRADE - 12 ga. only, 3 in. chambers, boxlock action, 28 in. VR (8mm) barrel with WinPlus chokes, blue metal featuring 40% engraving coverage, Grade I stock and forearm, high luster finish, mfg. in Italy by Marocchi 1993, disc. 1998.

| | $975 | $795 | $725 | $650 | $595 | $550 | $495 |

Last MSR was $1,099.

✴ *Model 1001 Sporting Clays* - 12 ga. only, 2¾ in. chambers, 28 or 30 in. VR (10mm) vent. barrels with WinPlus chokes, full engraving (includes scroll and flying W with clay bird), silver nitrate receiver with remaining parts blue, Grade II-III stock and forearm, satin finish, mfg. in Italy by Marocchi 1993, disc. 1998.

| | $1,075 | $925 | $795 | $725 | $650 | $595 | $550 |

Last MSR was $1,253.

✴ *Model 1001 Sporting Clays Lite* - 12 ga. only, 3 in. chambers, blue finish, 28 in. VR barrels with WinPlus chokes, checkered walnut stock and forearm, gold SST, 7 lbs. Mfg. 1995-98.

| | $1,000 | $795 | $725 | $650 | $595 | $550 | $495 |

Last MSR was $1,153.

MODEL G5500 SPORTER - 12 ga. only, marked Sporter, 28 or 30 in. barrels with fixed chokes (bored IC/M, IM/F, or XF/F) or Winchokes.

| | $1,795 | $1,475 | $1,275 | $1,075 | $900 | $780 | $640 |

Add 20% for Winchokes.

MODEL G6500 SPORTER - 12 ga. only, marked Sporter, barrels and chokes same as G5500.

| | $2,295 | $1,925 | $1,625 | $1,400 | $1,225 | $1,050 | $900 |

Add 20% for Winchokes.

SUPREME FIELD - 12 ga. only, 3 in. chambers, low profile boxlock action with dual tapered locking lugs positioned between the barrels, SST, ejectors, game scene engraved receiver, 26 (new 2001) or 28 in. 6mm VR back-bored barrels with Invector Plus choking, checkered walnut stock and forearm, blue action and barrels, barrel selector on safety switch, approx. 7¼ lbs. New 2000.

| MSR | $1,383 | $1,195 | $950 | $840 | $735 | $655 | $575 | $475 |

SUPREME SPORTING - 12 ga. only, 2¾ in. chambers, features satin finished receiver w/o engraving, 28 or 30 in. 10mm VR back-bored barrels with porting, SST with adj. trigger shoe system, sharply checkered walnut stock and Schnabel style forearm, approx. 7 lbs., 10 oz. New 2000.

| MSR | $1,550 | | $1,325 | $1,050 | $940 | $835 | $725 | $650 | $575 |

Grading	100%	98%	95%	90%	80%	70%	60%

SHOTGUNS: RECENT PRODUCTION SxS

Values for recently manufactured side-by-sides (including Models 96 and 101 with variations) assume NIB condition - subtract 10%-15% if without box, warranty card, and original shipping container (with packing materials).

MODEL 21: RECENT/CURRENT MFG. - Model 21 production was limited to high grade, built to special order only from 1960-1988, the last year Winchester carried Model 21 pricing in its catalog, on custom shop guns mfg. 1960-1969, there is no Winchester name on the barrels, but the Winchester proofmark is on the water table, along with a designation "Model 21" or "New Haven, CT", plus ser. no. On Model 21s produced from 1969-1988, the water tables are stamped as already noted, and the designation "Model 21 - Winchester" is stamped on the top of the left barrel adjacent to the rib, next to the receiver. Connecticut Shotgun Manufacturing Company is currently fufilling a contract with U.S.R.A. to produce a limited amount of very high grade, multi-barrel, multi-gauges sets. These guns are not marked "Winchester" or "Model 21", are not finished in the Winchester custom shop, and will not letter from the Cody Firearms Museum. Plans are under way for the Connecticut Shotgun Manufacturing Company to release a Model 21 shortly, with no connection to Winchester.

   Add 10% for 20 ga.

✳ ***Custom Built*** - standard model with no engraving.

      $7,500   **$6,500**   **$4,500**

                                   Last MSR was $8,100.

✳ ***Custom Grade*** - includes No. 6 engraved receiver and VR.

      $11,000   **$9,500**   **$8,000**

                                   Last MSR was $11,080.

✳ ***Grand American Grade*** - includes 2 sets of barrels with forearms, No. 6 engraved with gold inlays, cased.

      $22,750   **$18,250**   **$15,500**

                                   Last MSR was $22,745.

✳ ***Grand American Small Gauge*** - 28 ga. or .410 bore.

      $37,500   **$29,500**   **$23,000**

                                   Last MSR was $34,460.

   Add 25% for 28 ga./.410 bore combo.

✳ ***Grand American "1 of 8" set*** - includes 20, 28 ga., and .410 bore VR barrels. Only 4 sets mfg.

      N/A   **$52,000**   **$39,500**

                                   Last MSR was $55,000.

MODEL 22 - 12 ga. only, subcontracted by Winchester and manufactured in Spain by Laurona circa 1975 for international sales including Europe, field configuration only with 28 in. barrels, DT, oil finished checkered walnut stock and semi-beavertail forearm, matted rib, black-chrome finish on metal parts, hand engraved receiver, limited mfg.

      $1,200   **$995**   **$825**   **$700**   **$600**   **$525**   **$475**

MODEL 23 XTR - 12 or 20 ga., 3 in. chambers, 25½, 26, 28, or 30 in. barrels, various chokes, single trigger, VR, auto ejectors, scroll engraved, silver grey satin finish, blue barrel, checkered select walnut stock and forearm, first commercial gun to employ interchangeable chokes. Mfg. 1978-disc.

   Grade 1 (disc.)   **$1,650**   **$1,450**   **$1,295**   **$1,095**   **$850**   **$750**   **$650**

   Add 15% for 20 ga.

   Subtract 10% for fixed chokes.

Grading	100%	98%	95%	90%	80%	70%	60%

* ***Pigeon Grade*** - standard weight model, 6½ - 7 lbs, coin finished receiver with scroll engraving. Winchoke option became standard in 1986. Disc. 1986.

	$1,875	$1,675	$1,350	$1,150	$925	$775	$700

Last MSR was $1,460.

Add 15% for 20 ga.
Subtract $200 if w/o Winchokes.

* ***Pigeon Grade Lightweight*** - 25½ in. barrels only bored IM/IC (12 ga.) or IC/M (20 ga.) or with Winchokes, 6¼ - 6¾ lbs., coin finished receiver with scroll engraving. English stock. Disc. 1986.

	$1,895	$1,675	$1,475	$1,175	$950	$850	$750

Last MSR was $1,420.

Add 15% for 20 ga.
Add 20% for Winchokes.

* ***Pigeon Grade Ducks Unlimited*** - only 500 mfg. 1981, "SPO" serial no. suffix, cased.

	$1,795	$1,550	$1,300	$975	$875	$795	$695

* ***Golden Quail Model Series*** - 12 ga. (1986), 20 ga. (1984), 28 ga. (1985), or .410 bore (1987), 25½ in. solid rib barrels bored IC/M, mono-blocks are marked IC/ M but the barrels are marked Q1/ Q2, coin finished receiver with one gold inlay on floorplate, beavertail forearm, straight grip English stock with recoil pad, Only 500 mfg. each year per gauge. Disc. 1987.

	100%	98%	95%	90%	80%	70%	60%
12 ga.	$2,195	$1,950	$1,750	$1,500	$1,350	$1,150	$1,075
20 ga.	$2,395	$2,195	$1,895	$1,650	$1,450	$1,250	$1,150
28 ga.(20 ga. frame)	$3,250	$2,950	$2,695	$2,100	$1,650	$1,450	$1,200
410 bore (small frame)	$3,250	$2,950	$2,695	$2,100	$1,650	$1,450	$1,200

Last MSR was $1,950.

* ***Model 23 Light Duck*** - limited edition, 500 mfg., introduced 1985, blue receiver and barrels, select walnut, 20 ga., 28 in.- F&F, 8½ lbs.

	$2,150	$1,850	$1,575	$1,200	$975	$875	$725

Last MSR was $1,660.

* ***Model 23 Heavy Duck*** - limited edition, 500 mfg. 1984 only, blue receiver and barrels, select walnut, 12 ga., 30 in.- F&F, 8½ lbs.

	$1,950	$1,750	$1,450	$1,195	$950	$850	$795

* ***Custom 2 Barrel Set*** - interchangeable 20 and 28 ga. 26 in. barrels, blue engraved receiver with gold inlays, "B" checkering on stock and forearm, leather cased with accessories, only 500 sets mfg. 1986. Disc. 1987.

	$4,650	$4,150	$3,550	$3,050	$2,800	$2,500	$2,150

Last MSR was $4,625.

MODEL 23 GRANDE CANADIAN - 12 or 20 ga., 25½ in. barrels with fixed chokes, coin finished receiver with oak leaf engraving and one gold leaf inlay on receiver bottom, English AAA select walnut stock with beavertail forearm, 51 mfg. in 12 ga., 450 mfg. in 20 ga., approx. 50 two-gun sets were also offered with cases (approx. ser. numbers 1-51).

	$2,650	$2,200	$1,750	$1,500	$1,300	$1,050	$925
Cased set	$6,500	$5,800	$4,900	$4,200	$3,750	$3,200	$2,750

MODEL 23 CUSTOM - 12 ga. only, 27 in. Winchoke barrels, high luster bluing, no engraving, SST, ejectors, solid red rubber recoil pad, 7 lbs. Imported 1987 only.

	$2,250	$1,775	$1,275	$1,050	$900	$775	$650

Last MSR was $1,975.

Grading	100%	98%	95%	90%	80%	70%	60%

MODEL 23 CLASSIC - 12, 20, 28 ga., or .410 bore, 26 in. VR barrels, single trigger, deluxe hand checkered walnut stock and beavertail forearm, solid recoil pad, brass name plate, gold inlay on bottom of receiver, ebony inlay in forearm, 5¾ - 7 lbs. Imported 1986-1987 only.

12 ga.	$2,195	$1,995	$1,750	$1,400	$1,250	$1,150	$1,050
20 ga.	$2,395	$2,150	$1,850	$1,650	$1,395	$1,295	$1,195
28 ga. (small frame)	$3,250	$2,950	$2,595	$2,250	$1,695	$1,450	$1,350
.410 bore (small frame)	$2,950	$2,650	$2,250	$1,775	$1,495	$1,350	$1,250

Last MSR was $1,975.

100% values assume NIB for this model.
The 28 ga. on this model features a smaller frame, and was the only 28 ga. small frame produced in the Model 23 Series.

WINCHESTER COMMEMORATIVES: U.S. PRODUCTION

During the course of a year, I receive many phone calls and letters on Winchester special editions and limited editions that do not appear in this section. It should be noted that a factory commemorative issue is a gun that has been manufactured, marketed, and sold through the auspices of the specific trademark. There have literally been hundreds of special and limited editions which, although mostly made by Winchester (some were subcontracted), were not marketed or retailed by Winchester. These guns are NOT Winchester commemoratives and for the most part, do not have the desirability factor that the factory commemoratives have. Special/limited editions are not listed in this text, because there is minimal collector interest. Remember, the least your special/limited edition can be worth is a little more than the standard edition value. Don't concentrate on the rarity, you'll be disappointed.

Typically, special and limited editions are made for distributors (these sub-contracts are the most common), an organization, state, special event, personality, etc. and are typically sold and marketed through a distributor to dealers, or a company/individual to those people who want to purchase them. These special editions may or may not have a retail price and often times, since demand is regional, values decrease rapidly in other areas of the country. Desirability is the key to determining values on these editions.

Until recently, the over-production of many factory commemoratives had created a "softness" in the commemorative marketplace. Commemorative production in some trademarks has totalled well over 250,000 units, and some collectors have weighed the "limited production" factor on each model before paying a premium over the standard production model of that particular commemorative. Approximately 10 years ago, Winchester decided to cut down on commemorative manufacture after perhaps too many years of over-production. Many commemorative consumers were starting to think that these "limited manufacture" guns had become more of a company marketing tool and sales gimmick rather than a legitimate vehicle for investment potential and collector support. During this 8 year period, both distributors and retailers saw their commemorative inventory levels gradually reach near zero - perhaps the first time in over two decades that they sold out of factory commemoratives. In other words, the commemorative "blow-out" sales were over. As this transition from distributor/dealer inventory to consumer purchases occurred, the commemorative marketplace became stronger and prices began to rise. Because the commemorative consumer is now more in charge (consumers now own most of the guns since distributor/dealer inventories are depleted) than during the 1980s, commemorative firearms are possibly as strong as they have ever been. When the supply side of commemorative economics has to be purchased from knowledgable collectors or savvy dealers and demand stays the same or increases slightly, prices have no choice but to go up. If and when the manufacturers crank up the commemorative production runs again (and it won't be like the good old days), then the old marketplace characteristics may reappear. Until then, however, the commemorative marketplace remains strong with values becoming more predictable.

As a reminder on commemoratives, especially for the beginning collector, here are a few facts applicable to all manufacturers of commemoratives. Commemoratives are current production guns designed as a reproduction of an historically famous gun model, or as a tie-in with historically famous persons or events. They are generally of very excellent quality and often embellished with select woods and finishes such as silver, nickel, or gold plating. Obviously, they are manufactured to be instant collectibles and to be pleasing to the eye. As with firearms in general, not all commemorative models have achieved collector status, although most enjoy an active market - especially during the past three years. Consecutive-numbered pairs as well as collections based on the same serial number will bring a premium. Remember that handguns usually are in some type of wood presentation case, and that rifles may be cased or in packaging with graphics styled to the particular theme of the collectible. The original factory packaging and papers should always accompany the firearm as they are necessary to realize full value at the time of sale. All commemorative firearms should be absolutely new, unfired, and as issued since any obvious use or wear removes it from collector status and lowers its value significantly. Many owners have allowed their commemoratives to sit in their boxes and plastic bags (could be serious if there's moisture where storage occurs) for years without inspecting them for corrosion or oxidation damage. Periodic inspection should be implemented to insure no damage occurs - this is important, since even light "freckling" created from touching the metal surfaces can reduce values significantly. A fired gun with obvious wear or without its original packaging can lose as much as 50% of its normal value - many used commemoratives get sold as "fancy shooters" with little, if any, premiums being asked.

The values listed reflect actual prices paid recently in various areas of the U.S. In some regions it is possible to purchase a Winchester 94 commemorative made in substantial quantity for almost no premium over a standard production Winchester 94. Because of this, prices could fluctuate over 25% depending on the geographic location of purchase or sale.

A final note on commemoratives: One of the characteristics of commemoratives/ special editions is that over the years of ownership, most of the original amount manufactured stays in the same NIB condition. Thus, if supply always is constant and in one condition, demand has to increase before price appreciation can occur. Many commemorative dealers have told me that recent changes in overseas currency rates have made domestic guns less expensive to own - for Europeans especially. For this reason, more commemoratives are being sold overseas resulting in less supply for the domestic market. Coupled with this increased foreign demand is the recent increase of domestic support and sales. After 38 years of commemorative/special edition production, many models' performance records can be accurately analyzed and the appreciation (or depreciation) can be compared against other purchases of equal vintage. You be the judge.

U.S. Repeating Arms had announced in 1990 that they would once again resume the production of factory commemorative firearms.

Grading	100%	Issue Price	Qty. Made
1964 WYOMING DIAMOND JUBILEE 94 CARBINE			
	$1,295	$100	1,501
1966 CENTENNIAL '66 RIFLE			
	$450	$125	-
1966 CENTENNIAL '66 CARBINE - total mfg. of both the rifle and carbine was 102,309.			
	$425	$125	102,309
Add $50-$75 over individual prices for consecutively serial numbered rifle and carbine set.			
1966 NEBRASKA CENTENNIAL 94 RIFLE			
	$1,195	$100	2,500
1967 CANADIAN '67 CENTENNIAL RIFLE			
	$450	$125	-
1967 CANADIAN '67 CENTENNIAL CARBINE - total mfg. of both the rifle and carbine was 90,301.			
	$425	$125	90,301
Add $50-$75 over individual prices for consecutively serial numbered rifle and carbine set.			
1967 ALASKAN PURCHASE CENTENNIAL CARBINE			
	$1,495	$125	1,501

Grading	100%	Issue Price	Qty. Made
1968 ILLINOIS SESQUICENTENNIAL 94 CARBINE			
	$395	$110	37,468
1968 BUFFALO BILL RIFLE "1 OF 300" PRES.			
	$2,650	$1,000	300
1968 BUFFALO BILL RIFLE			
	$450	$130	-
1968 BUFFALO BILL CARBINE - total mfg. of both the rifle and carbine was 112,923.			
	$425	$130	112,923

Add $50-$75 over individual prices for consecutively serial numbered rifle and carbine set.

Grading	100%	Issue Price	Qty. Made
1969 GOLDEN SPIKE CARBINE			
	$495	$120	69,996
1969 THEO. ROOSEVELT RIFLE			
	$450	$135	-
1969 THEO. ROOSEVELT CARBINE - total mfg. of both the rifle and carbine was 52,386.			
	$425	$135	52,386
1970 COWBOY COMMEMORATIVE CARBINE			
	$450	$125	27,549
1970 COWBOY CARBINE "1 OF 300"			
	$2,650	$1,000	300
1970 LONE STAR RIFLE			
	$450	$140	-
1970 LONE STAR CARBINE - total mfg. of both the rifle and carbine was 38,385.			
	$425	$140	38,385
1971 NRA CENTENNIAL MUSKET			
	$425	$150	23,400
1971 NRA CENTENNIAL RIFLE			
	$425	$150	21,000
1974 TEXAS RANGER CARBINE			
	$695	$135	4,850
1974 TEXAS RANGER PRESENTATION			
	$2,650	$1,000	150
1976 U.S. BICENTENNIAL CARBINE			
	$595	$325	19,999
1977 WELLS FARGO			
	$495	$350	19,999
1977 "LIMITED EDITION I"			
	$1,395	$1,500	1,500
1977 LEGENDARY LAWMEN			
	$495	$375	19,999
1978 ANTLERED GAME CARBINE			
	$550	$375	19,999

Grading	100%	Issue Price	Qty. Made
1979 LEGENDARY FRONTIERSMAN RIFLE			
	$550	$425	19,999
1979 "LIMITED EDITION II"			
	$1,395	$1,750	1,500
1979 MATCHED SET OF 1000			
	$2,250	$3,000	1,000
1980 BAT MASTERSON CARBINE			
	$795	$650	8,000
1980 "OLIVER WINCHESTER"			
	$695	$375	19,999
1981 U.S. BORDER PATROL			
	$595	$1,195	1,000
1981 U.S. BORDER PATROL - MEMBERS MODEL			
	$595	$695	800
1981 JOHN WAYNE			
	$995	$600	49,000

Optional accessories were also available for this model: the gun rack with leather insert is currently selling for approx. $40 and the leather scabbard is trading for $60.

1981 "DUKE"			
	$2,950	$2,250	1,000
1981 JOHN WAYNE "1 OF 300" SET			
	$6,500	$10,000	300
1982 GREAT WESTERN ARTIST I			
	$1,195	$2,200	999
1982 GREAT WESTERN ARTIST II			
	$1,195	$2,200	999
1982 ANNIE OAKLEY			
	$695	$699	6,000
1982 OKLAHOMA DIAMOND JUBILEE			
	$1,395	$2,250	1,001
1982 AMERICAN BALD EAGLE - SILVER			
	$595	$895	2,800
1982 AMERICAN BALD EAGLE - GOLD			
	$3,000	$2,950	200
1983 CHIEF CRAZY HORSE			
	$595	$600	19,999

1984 WINCHESTER-COLT COMMEMORATIVE SET - 1 each of the Model 1894 Carbine and Colt Peacemaker, serial numbered 1 WC-4440 WC., .44-40 WCF cal., elaborate gold etching, cased.

	$2,250	$3,995	2,300

Approx. 2,300 sets were actually put together in this combination. These sets have been split up with individual prices being discounted (Colt SAAs have been trading in the $700- $800 range).

Grading	100%	Issue Price	Qty. Made

1985 BOY SCOUTS 75TH ANNIVERSARY - Model 9422 action, .22 cal., rifle configuration, 6¼ lbs.

* **Boy Scout** - 15,000 mfg., serial numbered BSA 1 - BSA 15,000, roll engraved, antique pewter receiver, hooded front sight.

	$595	$495	15,000

* **Eagle Scout** - 1,000 mfg., serial numbered Eagle 1 - Eagle 1,000, receiver has triple level gold etching, select American walnut stock and forearm, gold-plated lever, hammer, and forearm cap.

	$3,000	$1,710	1,000

1985 MODEL 94 TEXAS SESQUICENTENNIAL - .38-55 WCF cal., available in carbine or rifle.

* **Model 94 Rifle** - 24 in. round barrel, elaborate gold etching, includes Bowie knife, oak cased, 586 mfg.

	$2,400	$2,995	1,500

* **Model 94 Carbine** - 18½ in. round barrel, gold finished receiver and barrel bands, roll engraved receiver, 2,600 mfg., serial numbered TEX 1 and up.

	$695	$695	15,000

* **Rifle/Carbine Set** - includes one each of the Model 94 rifle and carbine, Bowie knife, 150 mfg.

	$6,250	$7,995	150

1986 120TH ANNIVERSARY MODEL 94 CARBINE - .44-40 WCF cal. only, 20 in. barrel, hoop-type finger lever, crescent butt plate, deluxe checkered walnut stock and forearm, extensive gold etching on barrel and framesides, 1,000 mfg. ser. no. WRA001- WRA1000.

	$895	$995	1,000

1986 STATUE OF LIBERTY MODEL 94 - Model 94 rifle in .30-30 Win. cal. with octagon barrel, extensive C. Giovanelli scroll engraving with multiple 22Kt. gold inlays, deluxe walnut with fine checkering, also includes 29 in. hand carved wooden statue of the Statue of Liberty, serial numbered SL1-SL62. This model is a USRAC factory commemorative.

	$7,000	$6,500	62

1986 MODEL 94 DU - .30-30 Win. cal., approx. 2,800 rifles were mfg. in the U.S. Since each Model 94 DU was bid on for ownership, prices will vary from points of origin. An average bid price seems to be in the $700-$995 range with lower and completing set ser. numbers selling at premiums. Serial numbered DU-86 0001 on up.

This model is not a factory commemorative, but rather a trade gun commissioned by Ducks Unlimited.

1987 U.S. CONSTITUTION 200TH ANNIVERSARY

	$13,000	$12,000	17

This model was distributed exclusively by Cherry's, located in Greensboro, NC.

1988 WINCHESTER ARMS COLLECTOR'S ASSOCIATION CASED SET - includes Colt SAA and Winchester Model 1894 in cased set, features special embellishments and W.A.C.A. emblems and medallions. 100 sets were advertised, but only 22 were sold. This is not a USRAC factory commemorative.

	$2,995	$2,695	22 sets

1990 WYOMING CENTENNIAL .30-30

	$1,195	$895	500

This model was distributed exclusively by Cherry's, located in Greensboro, NC.

Grading	100%	Issue Price	Qty. Made

1991 125TH ANNIVERSARY .30-30

	$5,500	$4,995	61

This model was distributed exclusively by Cherry's, located in Greensboro, NC.

1992 KENTUCKY BICENTENNIAL .30-30 - Winchester Model 94 with true charcoal case coloring, engraving depicts important KY graphics, serial numbered KY001- KY500.

	$1,195	$995	500

This model was distributed exclusively by Cherry's, located in Greensboro, NC.

1992 ARAPAHO .30-30 - features gold-plated receiver with etched Indian scenes on both sides, checkered semi-fancy American walnut stock.

	$1,195	$895	500

This model is distributed exclusively by Cherry's, located in Greensboro, NC.

1993 NEZ PERCE MODEL 94 CARBINE - features nickel finished receiver and barrel bands, extensively etched receiver, checkered semi-fancy American walnut stock and forearm, serial numbered NEZ 001 - NEZ 600.

	$1,195	$950	600

This model is distributed exclusively by Cherry's, located in Greensboro, NC.

1995 FLORIDA SESQUICENTENNIAL 94 CARBINE - features motifs from Florida including alligator scene and space shuttle launch, 24 kt. gold-plated receiver, 500 mfg. ser. numbered FL001-FL500 during 1995 only.

	$1,195	$1,195	500

This model is distributed exclusively by Cherry's, located in Greensboro, NC.

1997 EARP BROTHERS MODEL 94 CARBINE - features engraving motifs with multi-colored cameos of the characters involved in the Tombstone OK Corral gunfight, gold plated hammer, trigger, and barrel bands, crossbolt safety. 250 Mfg. 1997 only.

	$1,195	$1,195	250

This model is distributed exclusively by Cherry's, located in Greensboro, NC.

WINCHESTER COMMEMORATIVES: NON-DOMESTIC - 1970 TO DATE

1970 NORTH WEST TERRITORIES (CANADIAN)

	$850	$150	2,500

1970 NORTHWEST TERRITORIES DELUXE (CANADIAN)

	$1,100	$250	500

1973 YELLOW BOY (SOLD IN EUROPE ONLY)

	$1,150	$150	4,903

1973 M.P.X. (MADE ESPECIALLY FOR A MOVIE)

	$4,995	$78	32

1973 R.C.M.P. (CANADIAN)

	$795	$190	9,500

1973 R.C.M.P. MEMBERS ISSUE (CANADIAN)

	$795	$190	4,850

1973 R.C.M.P. PRESENTATION - (CANADIAN)

	$9,995	N/A	100

1974 APACHE (CANADIAN)

	$795	$150	8,600

Grading	100%	Issue Price	Qty. Made
1975 KLONDIKE GOLD RUSH (CANADIAN)	$795	$230	10,200
1975 K.G.R. (DAWSON CITY ISSUE) - (CANADIAN)	$8,500	N/A	25
1975 COMANCHE (CANADIAN)	$795	$230	11,511
1976 SIOUX (CANADIAN)	$795	$280	10,000
1976 LITTLE BIG HORN (CANADIAN)	$795	$230	11,000
1977 CHEYENNE (CANADIAN) - .44-40 WCF Cal.	$795	$300	11,225
1977 CHEYENNE (CANADIAN) - .22 LR Cal.	$695	$320	5,000
1978 CHEROKEE (CANADIAN) - .30-30 Win. Cal.	$795	$385	9,000
1978 CHEROKEE (CANADIAN) - .22 LR Cal.	$695	$385	3,950
1978 ONE OF ONE THOUSAND (SOLD IN EUROPE ONLY)	$7,995	$5,000	250
This model was not advertised in the U.S.			
1980 ALBERTA DIAMOND JUBILEE (CANADIAN)	$795	$650	2,700
1980 A.D.J. DELUXE PRESENTATION (CANADIAN)	$1,495	$1,900	300
1980 SASKATCHEWAN DIAMOND JUBILEE (CANADIAN)	$795	$695	2,700
1980 S.D.J. DELUXE PRESENTATION (CANADIAN)	$1,495	$1,995	300
1981 CALGARY STAMPEDE (CANADIAN)	$1,250	$2,200	1,000
1981 CANADIAN PACIFIC CENTENNIAL (CANADIAN)	$550	$800	2,700
1981 CANADIAN PACIFIC CENTENNIAL PRESENTATION (CANADIAN)	$1,100	$2,200	300
1981 CANADIAN PACIFIC (EMPL.) - (CANADIAN)	$550	$800	2,000
1981 JOHN WAYNE (CANADIAN)	$1,095	$995	1,000
1986 SECOND SERIES EUROPEAN 1 OF 1,000 - mfg. for European sales only 1986.	$6,500	$6,000	150

Grading	100%	Issue Price	Qty. Made

1992 ONTARIO CONSERVATION - this model was marketed in Canada only.

	$1,195	$1,195	400

WINSLOW ARMS COMPANY
Previous manufacturer located in Camden, SC.

Grading	100%	98%	95%	90%	80%	70%	60%

RIFLES: BOLT ACTION

WINSLOW BOLT ACTION SPORTING RIFLE - offered with various actions, FN Supreme, Mark X Mauser, Rem. 700 and 788, Sako, and Win. 70, offered in all popular calibers from .17 Rem. to .458 Mag., standard calibers have 24 in. barrels and 3 shot magazines, magnum calibers have 26 in. barrels and 2 shot magazines, two style stocks, "Bushmaster Conventional", slender pistol grip and beavertail forearm, "Plainsmaster", full curl, hooked pistol grip and flat wide forearm, both are Monte Carlo with cheekpieces, recoil pads and swivels, walnut, maple, and myrtle are used with rosewood forend tip and pistol grip cap, rifle comes in 8 basic grades, custom embellishments can increase values greatly, discretion must be used, values are for basic models.

Grade	100%	98%	95%	90%	80%	70%	60%
COMMANDER GRADE	$495	$475	$440	$385	$360	$330	$305
REGAL GRADE	$605	$590	$560	$525	$470	$440	$415
REGENT GRADE	$725	$700	$670	$640	$605	$550	$495
REGIMENTAL GRADE	$935	$890	$855	$800	$745	$660	$605
CROWN GRADE	$1,375	$1,265	$1,155	$990	$910	$825	$715
ROYAL GRADE	$1,540	$1,375	$1,210	$1,100	$1,020	$965	$825
IMPERIAL GRADE	$3,520	$3,080	$2,860	$2,475	$2,200	$1,925	$1,320
EMPEROR GRADE	$6,215	$5,500	$4,950	$4,400	$3,300	$2,750	$2,200

WISCHO JAGD-UND SPORTWAFFEN GmbH & CO. KG
Current firearms manufacturer located in Erlangen, Germany.

Wischo makes a complete line of shotguns, rifles, pistols, and revolvers. No current U.S. importation. Please contact the factory directly for more information regarding model lineup, availability, and pricing (see Trademark Index).

WISEMAN, BILL AND CO.
Current custom rifle and pistol manufacturer located in College Station, TX.

Wiseman/McMillan also manufactures rifle barrels and custom stocks.

Grading	100%	98%	95%	90%	80%	70%	60%

PISTOLS

SILHOUETTE PISTOL - various cals., Sako action, 14 in. Wiseman/McMillan fluted stainless barrel, 5 or 7 shot magazine, laminate or fiberglass (new 1999) pistol grip stock, no sights, 4½-5½ lbs. Limited mfg. beginning 1989.

	MSR	$1,295		$1,295	$1,000	$900	$800	$750	$700	$650

Subtract $200 for fiberglass stock.

RIFLES: BOLT ACTION

Add 11% excise tax to prices shown for new manufacture. Some models listed have very limited production.

HUNTER MODEL - available in various cals., Sako action, stainless steel barrel by Wiseman/McMillan, laminate stock, teflon finished metal parts, Pachmayr Decelerator pad, sling swivels, glass bedded action.

	MSR	$2,895		$2,895	$2,350	$1,825	$1,400	$1,150	$925	$775

HUNTER DELUXE - similar to Hunter Model except has custom checkering.

	MSR	$3,395		$3,395	$2,775	$2,350	$1,850	$1,400	$1,075	$925

Add $500 for detachable mag.

MAVERICK - similar to Hunter but with black fiberglass stock.

	MSR	$1,995		$1,995	$1,575	$1,200	$1,050	$900	$775	$675

VARMENTER - similar to Hunter but with thumbhole stock.

	MSR	$2,395		$2,395	$1,925	$1,500	$1,250	$1,025	$875	$775

TEXAS SAFARI RIFLE - various cals., choice of hidden mag. (no floorplate), standard floorplate or 4 shot detachable mag., 2 or 3 position tang safety, stainless steel fluted barrel with integral muzzle brake, synthetic stock. New 1996.

	MSR	$1,995		$1,995	$1,500	$1,100

Add $300 for 4 shot detachable mag. (TSR-I).
Add $345 for extra magazine concealed in stock.
Add $195 for 3 position tang safety.

TSR TACTICAL - .300 Win. mag., .308 Win., or .338 Lapua Mag., 5 shot inline, detachable mag., or standard floorplate, synthetic stock with adj. cheekpiece, stainless steel fluted barrel with integral muzzle brake, guaranteed ½ minute of angle. New 1996.

	MSR	$2,795		$2,795	$2,200	$1,700

Add $195 for fluted barrel.
Add $195 for muzzle brake.
Add $150 for 3 position safety.

WOLF SPORTING PISTOLS

Previous trademark of pistols manufactured in Vienna, Austria. Previously imported and distributed by J R Distributing, located in Moorpark, CA until 1999.

Wolf pistols were noted for their features, quality construction, and were based on the M 1911 type action.

WOODWARD, JAMES AND SONS

Previously mfg. in London, England. Acquired by James Purdey & Sons approx. 1935. In 1996, James Purdey & Sons once again started manufacturing a best quality Woodward SxS shotgun.

SHOTGUNS: DOUBLE AND SINGLE BARREL

Woodward made one of the world's finest shotguns. Prior to WWII, they were acquired by Purdey and Sons. Many of the weapons they made were custom built and grading and pricing should be done individually. We will list some of the general models with approximate values as a guideline,

Grading	100%	98%	95%	90%	80%	70%	60%

but strongly urge competent professional appraisal when contemplating purchase or sale.

Prices indicated are for manufacturer's suggested retail and 100% condition factors are listed in English pounds. All new prices do not include VAT. Values for used guns in 98%-60% condition factors are priced in U.S. dollars.

BEST QUALITY SxS SHOTGUN - custom built in all gauges, barrel lengths and chokes, sidelock, auto ejectors, stocked to specifications, pre-WWII and new mfg. beginning 1996.

	100%	98%	95%	90%	80%	70%	60%
	$26,000	$23,000	$19,950	$17,000	$14,250	$12,000	$10,000

Add 20% for 20 ga.
Add 40% for 28 ga.
Add 60% for .410 bore.
Add $1,000 for SST

❋ **New Mfg.** - 20 ga. only beginning 1996.

MSR	£40,100						
	£40,100	$43,000	$35,000	$30,500	$22,000	$17,500	$14,250

BEST QUALITY O/U SHOTGUN - custom built in all gauges, barrel lengths, and chokes, VR, sidelock, auto ejectors, stocked to customer specifications, pre-WWII and new mfg. beginning 1996.

	$29,500	$25,500	$21,500	$18,500	$15,750	$13,800	$12,000

Add 35% for 20 ga.
Add 75% for 28 ga.
.410 bore - too rare to accurately predict.
Add $1,000 for ST.

❋ **New Mfg.** - 12, 16, 20, 28 ga., or .410 bore.

MSR £40,100	£40,100	$43,000	$35,000	$30,500	$22,000	$17,500	$14,250

BEST QUALITY SINGLE BARREL TRAP GUN - 12 ga. only, limited mfg. - pre-WWII only.

	$12,750	$10,000	$8,950	$7,725	$6,500	$5,750	$4,900

WYOMING ARMS MFG. CORP.

Previous manufacturer located in Thermopolis, WY. Very small quantities of Parker pistols were mfg.

PARKER PISTOLS: STAINLESS STEEL

STANDARD PISTOL - 9mm Para., 10mm, .40 S&W, or .45 ACP cal., 3 3/8, 5, or 7 in. barrel, 7 (.45 ACP), 8 (10mm & .40 S&W), or 9 (9mm Para.) shot mag., Millett adj. sights, grooved synthetic grips, 29-39 oz. Disc. 1992.

$350	$300	$250

Add $50 for 7 in. barrel.

Last MSR was $399.

.357 MAG. - .357 Mag. cal., single action semi-auto, 7 in. barrel, adj. sights, 8 shot mag., lifetime warranty, 44 oz. Disc. 1992.

$425	$350	$300

Last MSR was $479.

Z Section

Z-B RIFLE

Previous trademark of rifles manufactured by Brno & Uhersky Brod, located in Czechoslovakia.

Grading	100%	98%	95%	90%	80%	70%	60%

RIFLES: BOLT ACTION

Z-B MAUSER VARMINT RIFLE - .22 Hornet cal., short Mauser bolt action, 23 in. barrel, double set triggers, 3 leaf sight, checkered pistol grip stock, (also known as Brno Hornet).

	$825	$745	$690	$605	$550	$470	$415

ZDF IMPORT EXPORT INC.

Current importer located in Salt Lake City, UT since 1995.

RIFLES: SEMI-AUTO

Please refer to Robinson Armament listing.

Z-M WEAPONS

Current rifle manufacturer and pistol components maker located in Bernardston, MA. Dealer and consumer direct sales.

PISTOLS: SEMI-AUTO

STRIKE PISTOL - .38 Super, .40 S&W, or .45 ACP cal., several configurations available, with or without compensator. Limited mfg. 1997-2000.

	$2,375	$1,825	$1,700	$1,400	$1,150	$995	$750

Last MSR was $2,695.

RIFLES: SEMI-AUTO

LR 300 & VARIATIONS - .223 Rem. cal., modified gas system using AR-15 style action, features pivoting skeletal metal stock, 16¼ in. barrel, flat-top receiever, matte finish, 7.2 lbs. New 1997.

MSR	$1,995		$1,775	$1,575	$1,350	$1,125	$900	$775	$650

Subtract $510 for LR 300 SR kit.

ZABALA HERMANOS, S.A.

Current manufacturer located in Eibar, Spain. Z. Hermanos is currently private labeling shotguns for KBI, Inc. (Charles Daly SxSs only), and Tristar, located in N. Kansas City. Previously imported and distributed by American Arms located in Kansas City, MO until 2000.

Zabala Hermanos manufactures good quality boxlock SxS or O/U shotguns and sidelock SxSs. For more information regarding this trademark, (including current models and prices) please contact the manufacturer directly (see Trademark Index).

ZANARDINI

Current manufacturer established in 1946, and located in Brescia, Italy. Currently imported by S.O.G. Arms, located in Hacienda Heights, CA. Several U.S. firms have stocked a few Zanardini models in the past, but not the complete line.

All rifles and shotguns are custom built. For current information and up-to-date pricing, please contact the importer directly (see Trademark Index).

The values listed represent older importation.

Grading	100%	98%	95%	90%	80%	70%	60%

Z

COMBINATION GUNS: O/U

Zanardini is currently offering the Model 2000 Deluxe Super Light (with or w/o new loading system), and the Boxer Model with H&H style sidelocks.

PRINCESS - super light variation.

	$2,200	$1,925	$1,675	$1,400	$1,200	$1,000	$800

Last MSR was $2,542.

BOXER MODEL - H&H styled sidelocks, top-quality engraving.

	$5,750	$5,150	$4,600	$4,000	$3,550	$3,000	$2,650

Last MSR was $6,246.

BOXER 4-LOCKS MODEL

	$3,900	$3,400	$2,975	$2,625	$2,300	$2,050	$1,750

Last MSR was $4,562.

402 STRAUSS - top-of-the-line combination gun with best quality engraving and wood.

	$9,000	$8,000	$7,000	$6,000	$5,000	$4,000	$3,000

Last MSR was $10,548.

RIFLES

FUCHS A FOLDING RIFLE - double lock system.

MSR	$2,495	$2,275	$1,850	$1,500	$1,250	$1,200	$800	$600

PRINZ A 401 SUPER DELUXE SINGLE SHOT - internal and external hammers.

MSR	$16,995	$15,250	$12,500	$9,950	$8,750	$7,500	$6,250	$5,000

✽ *Prinz B Deluxe*

MSR	$9,995	$8,950	$7,750	$6,500	$5,200	$4,200	$3,200	$2,200

✽ *Prinz C Deluxe Standard*

MSR	$3,595	$3,200	$2,800	$2,400	$2,000	$1,800	$1,600	$1,400

403 OXFORD SxS - 9.3x74R and smaller cals.

	$3,400	$3,000	$2,700	$2,425	$2,150	$1,875	$1,575

Last MSR was $3,835.

✽ *Larger cals.* - .375 H&H Mag., .458 Win. Mag., or .470 Nitro cal.

	$6,700	$6,000	$5,500	$5,000	$4,500	$3,950	$3,450

Last MSR was $7,555.

Add approx. 135% for .470 Nitro cal.

EXPRESS RIFLE SxS - .470 NE cal., boxlock action, ST, checkered walnut stock (with cheekpiece), express sights. Other cals. available upon special order.

	$8,400	$8,100	$7,450	$6,750	$6,000	$5,500	$5,000

Last MSR was $8,995.

409 BRISTOL SxS - H & H style sidelock, ejectors, ST or DT.
Prices on this model start at $26,995.

407 OXFORD SL SxS - Anson & Deeley scalloped reinforced boxlock action, ejectors, ST or DT.
Prices on this model start at $14,995.

KONIG SIDELOCK O/U - 7.65R or 9.3x74R cal., H &H style sidelock, ejectors.

MSR	$26,995	$23,000	$20,000	$17,000	$13,500	$11,000	$9,950	$8,600

KONIG BOXLOCK O/U - Anson & Deely boxlock.

MSR	$14,995	$13,500	$11,000	$9,000	$7,500	$6,250	$5,000	$4,000

Grading	100%	98%	95%	90%	80%	70%	60%

SHOTGUNS: SxS

Models listed are available in 12, 16, 20, 28 ga. or .410 bore, magnum chambers in 20 and 12 ga.

HAMMER LONDON MODEL SxS - features external hammers.

	$9,150	$8,125	$7,100	$6,100	$5,050	$4,000	$3,050

Last MSR was $10,735.

HAMMERLESS LONDON MODEL SxS - 12 or 20 ga., external hammers.
Prices on this model range from $11,000 - $15,000, depending on engraving.

DONAU STANDARD MODEL SxS - boxlock action.

	$9,000	$8,000	$7,000	$6,000	$5,000	$4,000	$3,000

Last MSR was $10,548.

DONAU SIDELOCK SxS - H&H style sidelock action.
Prices on this model range from $17,000 - $23,000, depending on engraving.

PRESTIGE TRAP AND SKEET SxS

	$2,250	$1,950	$1,675	$1,400	$1,200	$1,000	$800

Last MSR was $2,598.

HASE CACCIA MONTECATINI SxS - boxlock action, double set triggers, extractors.

	$900	$800	$700	$600	$550	$495	$450

Last MSR was $1,027.

Add 30% for ejectors.

HORN MODEL SxS - boxlock action, double set triggers, extractors.

	$950	$850	$750	$625	$550	$495	$450

Last MSR was $1,102.

Add 40% for ejectors.

ZANOTTI, FABIO

Current manufacturer established during 1625, and located in Brescia, Italy. Previously imported and distributed by New England Arms Corp. located in Kittery Point, ME until 1999. Fabio Zanotti became part of the Renato Gamba Group in 1985.

Fabio Zanotti is one of the world's oldest quality shotgun manufacturers. Current domestic importation is often times done on a custom order only basis. For more information on current Zanotti models, please contact the factory directly. Values listed are for most recent importation.

SHOTGUNS: O/U

MODEL 725 - 28 ga. or .410 bore only, scalloped case hardened shallow frame, DT or ST, ejectors, game scene and scroll engraving, custom built to individual specifications.

MSR	$7,000		$6,000	$4,500	$3,650	$3,000	$2,450	$2,000	$1,875

CASSIANO - 12, 20, 28 ga., or .410 bore, Boss style shallow action, best quality gun built to individual specifications. Prices start at $27,500 and go up accordingly.

SHOTGUNS: SxS

Add $500 for ST.
Add $250 for beavertail forearm.
Add $650 for leather case.

MODEL 625 BOXLOCK

MSR	$6,995		$6,275	$5,500	$4,250	$3,150	$2,500	$2,000	$1,750

MODEL 626 BOXLOCK - scroll, game scene, or combination engraving.

MSR	$7,995		$7,000	$6,000	$4,450	$3,375	$2,750	$2,175	$1,900

Grading	100%	98%	95%	90%	80%	70%	60%

Z

MODEL GIACINTO - hammer gun.

MSR $6,500 $5,875 $5,300 $4,000 $2,950 $2,400 $1,900 $1,650

MODEL MAXIM SIDELOCK

MSR $12,000 $10,750 $8,600 $7,450 $6,200 $5,200 $4,600 $3,850

MODEL EDWARD SIDELOCK

MSR $15,000 $13,000 $9,900 $8,700 $7,000 $5,875 $5,000 $4,000

MODEL CASSIANO I SIDELOCK

MSR $17,500 $15,500 $13,250 $9,900 $8,700 $7,000 $5,875 $5,000

MODEL CASSIANO II

MSR $20,000 $17,750 $15,500 $13,250 $9,900 $8,700 $7,000 $5,875

CASSIANO EXECUTIVE - prices vary per individual order, top-of-the-line model. Prices start at $20,000 and go up.

ZASTAVA ARMS

Current trademark manufactured by Advanced Weapons Technologies, located in Athens, Greece. KBI currently imports certain models and actions. Previous manufacture was in Yugoslavia until circa 1996. Previously imported by T.D. Arms, followed by Brno U.S.A., circa 1990. Previously distributed by Nationwide Sports Distributors located in Southampton, PA.

Zastava Arms makes a wide variety of quality pistols, rifles, and sporting shotguns. Please contact KBI or the company directly for more information regarding model availability and prices (see Trademark Index).

HANDGUNS: SEMI-AUTO

MODEL CZ99 - 9mm Para. cal., double action, 15 shot, 4¼ in. barrel, short recoil, choice of various finishes, SIG locking system, hammer drop safety, ambidextrous controls, 3-dot Tritium sighting system, alloy frame, firing pin block, chamber indicator, squared-off trigger guard, checkered dark grey polymer grips, 32 oz.

    $450 $395 $365 $330 $300 $285 $265

Last MSR was $495.

While a latter Z9 was advertised, it was never commercially imported. All guns were CZ99 or CZ40. Zastava CZ99 configurations (with finishes) included matte blue with synthetic grips (500 imported), commercial blue with synthetic grips (750 imported), military "painted finish" with synthetic grips (1,000 imported), matte blue finish with checkered wood grips (115 imported), high polish blue with checkered grips (115 imported), and military "painted finish" with wood grips (2 prototypes only).

MODEL CZ40 - .40 S&W cal., 55 prototypes were imported for testing, but most had a feeding problem due to improper magazine design, mag. design changes were planned, but were cancelled due to the Serbian/Croatian war. Suggested retail was $495.

    $450 $395 $365 $330 $300 $285 $265

RIFLES: BOLT ACTION

MODEL CZ22 - .22 LR, .22 Mag. or .22 Hornet cal., 35 of each cal. imported circa 1990. Suggested retail was $275.

    $225 $195 $175 $150 $135 $120 $110

Add 15% for .22 Mag. or .22 Hornet cal.

ZIEGENHAHN & SOHN OHG

Current custom gun manufacturer located in Zella-Mehlis, Germany. Currently imported by New England Custom Gun Service, Ltd., located in Plainfield, NH.

Ziegenhahn & Sohn manufactures high quality, classic Anson & Deeley boxlock "Big Five" double rifles with Holland & Holland pattern sidelocks and ejectors, and sidelocks in calibers

Grading	100%	98%	95%	90%	80%	70%	60%

up to .500 NE. Ziegenhahn & Sohn also manufactures high quality shotguns, drillings, and combination guns with a variety of custom order options. Please contact the importer directly for current pricing, availability, and delivery time.

ZEPHYR

Previous Stoeger trademark of guns manufactured in Spain, and imported by Stoegers circa 1930s-1972.

RIFLES

Stoeger's has imported a wide variety of bolt action rifles during the past 60 years. Rather than list the many models individually, each Zephyr rifle should be compared to a gun of equal caliber, quality, and features to ascertain an approximate value range.

SHOTGUNS: SxS

WOODLANDER II - 12 or 20 ga., various chokes, boxlock, double triggers, extractors, engraved, checkered pistol grip stock.

	100%	98%	95%	90%	80%	70%	60%
	$495	$440	$385	$360	$305	$275	$250

UPLANDER (4E) - 12, 16, 20, 28 ga., or .410 bore, sidelock action, double triggers, ejectors, engraved.

	100%	98%	95%	90%	80%	70%	60%
	$775	$695	$640	$585	$570	$480	$440

STERLINGWORTH II - similar to Woodlander, with sidelock action.

	100%	98%	95%	90%	80%	70%	60%
	$825	$725	$660	$605	$580	$525	$495

VICTOR SPECIAL - 12 ga., 25, 28, or 30 in. barrels, various chokes, double triggers, extractors, checkered pistol grip stock.

	100%	98%	95%	90%	80%	70%	60%
	$440	$385	$330	$305	$250	$220	$195

UPLAND KING - 12 or 16 ga., sidelock, single trigger, VR, ejectors, fully engraved.

	100%	98%	95%	90%	80%	70%	60%
	$1,000	$900	$800	$725	$650	$600	$550

THUNDERBIRD - 10 ga. Mag, 32 in. barrels, double triggers, French walnut, engraved.

	100%	98%	95%	90%	80%	70%	60%
	$850	$750	$625	$550	$510	$490	$475

Add $175 for ejectors.

SHOTGUNS: SINGLE SHOT

HONKER - 10 ga. Mag., 36 in. VR barrel, lightly engraved.

	100%	98%	95%	90%	80%	70%	60%
	$500	$460	$420	$350	$310	$290	$270

VANDALIA TRAP - 12 ga. Trap Model, 32 in. barrel, engraved.

	100%	98%	95%	90%	80%	70%	60%
	$700	$620	$575	$525	$475	$425	$390

ZOLI, ANGELO

Previous manufacturer located in Brescia, Italy. Previously imported and distributed exclusively by Angelo Zoli USA located in Addison, IL. Mfg. 1985-87.

Angelo Zoli went out of business in December, 1987 and was taken over by the Italian Bank of Brescia in 1989. Many people tend to confuse the shotguns of Angelo and Antonio Zoli (it is hard to determine which manufacturer made a gun marked "A. Zoli"). There is no correlation between these trademarks and Antonio Zoli DOES NOT have parts for these earlier Angelo Zoli long arms. Even though both trademarks may indicate "A. ZOLI" for a barrel address, they are mostly discernable by the model listings under both headings in this section.

COMBINATION GUNS

AIRONE - 12 ga./.30-06 or .308 Win. cal., boxlock with false sideplates, double triggers, checkered walnut stock and forearm, swivels. Disc. 1987.

	100%	98%	95%	90%	80%	70%	60%
	$1,450	$1,275	$1,050	$900	$800	$700	$600

Grading	100%	98%	95%	90%	80%	70%	60%

Z **CONDOR** - similar to Airone, except does not have false sideplates. Disc. 1987.

	$1,295	$1,050	$900	$800	$700	$600	$500

RIFLES: SxS

LEOPARD EXPRESS - .30-06, .308 Win., .375 H&H Mag., or 7x65R cal., boxlock action, double triggers, checkered walnut stock and forearm. Disc. 1987.

	$1,325	$1,150	$975	$900	$840	$775	$725

Last MSR was $1,529.

SHOTGUNS: O/U

SNIPE - .410 bore, 3 in. chambers, 26 or 28 in. barrels, single trigger. Disc. 1987.

	$230	$200	$185	$170	$155	$145	$135

Last MSR was $265.

TEXAS - all ga.'s, 26 or 28 in. barrels, double triggers, folding design, lever action. Disc. 1987.

	$250	$220	$200	$185	$170	$155	$145

Last MSR was $291.

DOVE - .410 bore only, 3 in. chambers, 26 or 28 in. barrels, single trigger. Disc. 1987.

	$260	$230	$200	$185	$170	$155	$145

Last MSR was $306.

FIELD SPECIAL - 12, 20, or 28 ga., 3 in. chambers, various barrel lengths and chokings, single trigger. Disc. 1987.

	$450	$400	$360	$330	$300	$270	$240

Last MSR was $699.

PIGEON MODEL - 12 or 20 ga., 3 in. chambers, various barrel lengths, single trigger. Disc. 1987.

	$350	$295	$270	$250	$220	$195	$175

Last MSR was $394.

Add $60 for 20 ga.

STANDARD MODEL - 12 or 20 ga., 3 in. chambers, various barrel lengths and chokings, single trigger. Disc. 1987.

	$395	$345	$320	$300	$280	$260	$245

Last MSR was $459.

SILVER SNIPE - 12 or 20 ga., 3 in. chambers on the 20 ga., single trigger, ejectors, light engraving. Disc. 1987.

	$675	$585	$530	$485	$440	$400	$375

Last MSR was $739.

Add $50 for multi-chokes (12 ga. only).

This model was distributed by Euroarms of America, Inc.

CONDOR MODEL - 12 ga. skeet model, 28 in. barrels, SST, ejectors, wide VR, engraved silver finished receiver, recoil pad. Disc. 1987.

	$795	$700	$640	$585	$530	$485	$440

Last MSR was $895.

This model was distributed by Mandall Shooting Supplies, Inc.

TARGET MODEL 208 - 12 ga. only, available in either Trap, Skeet, or Monotrap configuration. Disc. 1987.

	$895	$775	$695	$620	$575	$500	$450

Last MSR was $996.

Add $494 for Monotrap II 208 Model.

Grading	100%	98%	95%	90%	80%	70%	60%

TARGET MODEL 308 - 12 ga. only, available in either Trap, Skeet, or Monotrap configuration. Disc. 1987.

	$1,375	$1,125	$950	$875	$795	$725	$650

Last MSR was $1,581.

Add $76 for multi-chokes.
Add $824 for Monotrap II 308 Model.

SPECIAL MODEL - 12 ga. only, 3 in. chambers, various barrel lengths and chokings, SST. Disc. 1987.

	$465	$395	$355	$325	$290	$270	$250

Last MSR was $528.

Add $120 for multi-chokes.

DELUXE MODEL - similar to Special Model, except better wood and engraving. Disc. 1987.

	$645	$550	$495	$450	$400	$360	$320

Last MSR was $730.

Add $80 for multi-chokes.

PRESENTATION MODEL - 12 ga. only, includes sideplates. Disc. 1987.

	$740	$630	$575	$495	$450	$395	$350

Last MSR was $842.

Add $42 for multi-chokes.

ANGEL MODEL - 12 ga. only, field grade, SST, ejectors, wide VR, engraved receiver, recoil pad. Disc. 1987.

	$850	$775	$700	$640	$585	$530	$485

This model was distributed by Mandall Shooting Supplies, Inc.

ST. GEORGE'S TARGET - 12 ga. only, trap or skeet gun, SST, fixed choke. Disc. 1987.

	$900	$730	$645	$550	$495	$450	$400

Last MSR was $1,024.

✳ *St. George's Competition* - 12 ga. only, includes 30 in. O/U barrels and single barrel multi-choke. Disc. 1987.

	$1,995	$1,750	$1,550	$1,250	$995	$875	$775

Last MSR was $1,627.

PATRICIA MODEL - .410 bore only, 3 in. chambers, 28 in. barrels, SST. Disc. 1987.

	$1,175	$1,010	$900	$895	$820	$740	$650

Last MSR was $1,345.

Add $121 for case.

SHOTGUNS: SxS

QUAIL SPECIAL - .410 bore, 3 in. chambers, single trigger, 28 in. barrels. Disc. 1987.

	$205	$185	$170	$150	$125	$110	$100

Last MSR was $243.

FALCON II - .410 bore, 3 in. chambers, 26 or 28 in. barrels, double triggers. Disc. 1987.

	$205	$185	$170	$150	$125	$110	$100

Last MSR was $246.

SILVER HAWK - 12 or 20 ga., double trigger, engraved.

	$420	$395	$360	$330	$300	$280	$260

SILVER SNIPE - 12 or 20 ga., various barrel lengths, VR, single trigger, engraved.

	$485	$440	$400	$360	$330	$300	$280

PHEASANT - 12 ga. only, 3 in. chambers, 28 in. barrels only, single trigger. Disc. 1987.

	$370	$320	$300	$280	$260	$240	$220

Last MSR was $428.

Grading	100%	98%	95%	90%	80%	70%	60%

Z ALLEY CLEANER - 12 or 20 ga., 3 in. chambers, 20 in. barrels, riot configuration, SST. Disc. 1987.

	$575	$495	$460	$420	$390	$350	$310

Last MSR was $649.

Add $65 for multi-chokes.

CLASSIC - 12 or 20 ga., 3 in. chambers, 26-30 in. barrels, ST. Disc. 1989.

	$995	$875	$750	$650	$550	$475	$400

Last MSR was $706.

Add $80 for multi-chokes.

SHOTGUNS: LEVER ACTION

APACHE - 12 ga. only, 3 in. chambers, 20 in. barrel, SST. Disc. 1987.

	$410	$355	$325	$300	$280	$260	$245

Last MSR was $473.

Add $80 for multi-chokes.

SHOTGUNS: SINGLE BARREL

DIANO I - 12, 20 ga., or .410 bore, 3 in. chambers, top lever single barrel action, folding configuration, VR. Disc. 1987.

	$115	$95	$85	$80	$75	$70	$65

Last MSR was $129.

DIANO II - similar to Diano I, except has bottom lever opening. Disc. 1987.

	$115	$95	$85	$80	$75	$70	$65

Last MSR was $129.

LONER I - similar to Diano I. Disc. 1987.

	$95	$80	$75	$65	$55	$45	$35

Last MSR was $109.

LONER II - similar to Diano II. Disc. 1987.

	$95	$80	$75	$65	$55	$45	$35

Last MSR was $109.

SHOTGUNS: SLIDE ACTION

PUMP ACTION - 12 ga. only, available in riot, field, or deer (slug) barrel configurations, 3 in. chamber, hunter model has multi-chokes standard. Disc. 1987.

	$290	$245	$205	$185	$170	$150	$125

Last MSR was $329.

ZOLI, ANTONIO

Current manufacturer located in Brescia, Italy. O/U rifles were imported by Cape Outfitters, located in Cape Girardeau, MO. Previously imported and distributed (1990-91 only) by European American Armory Corp. located in Hialeah, FL. Prior to 1990, A. Zoli was imported and distributed exclusively by Antonio Zoli U.S.A., Inc. located in Fort Wayne, IN.

Antonio Zoli firearms are totally unrelated to those guns of Angelo Zoli (guns marked "A. Zoli" make it hard to determine the correct manufacturer). Parts are not interchangeable and warranties from Antonio Zoli firearms DO NOT apply to Angelo Zoli guns.

Cape Outfitters (see Trademark Index) has parts for some Antonio Zoli guns and should be contacted directly for availability and prices. All repairs are strictly non-warranty.

Grading	100%	98%	95%	90%	80%	70%	60%

COMBINATION GUNS

COMBINATO - 12 or 20 ga. over .243 Win. or .222 Rem. cal., boxlock action, game scene engraved receiver with silver finish, double triggers, folding rear sight, skipline checkering, with sling swivels. Importation disc. 1993.

	100%	98%	95%	90%	80%	70%	60%
	$1,750	$1,500	$1,300	$1,100	$950	$775	$600

Last MSR was $1,995.

✴ *Combinato Set* - includes one set of either 20 or 12 ga. barrels and an additional rifle/shotgun barrel set, same cals. as Combinato, cased. Importation disc. 1993.

	100%	98%	95%	90%	80%	70%	60%
	$2,400	$2,150	$1,850	$1,600	$1,400	$1,200	$995

Last MSR was $2,700.

SAFARI DELUXE - similar to Combinato, except has sideplates with elaborate game scene engraving. Importation disc. 1993.

	100%	98%	95%	90%	80%	70%	60%
	$4,850	$4,400	$3,950	$3,550	$3,175	$2,800	$2,400

Last MSR was $5,200.

Add approx. 50% for Safari Deluxe 2 (includes 2 sets of shotgun barrels).

EXPRESS E3 SET - includes one set of .30-06 cal. O/U barrels, one set of 20 ga./.243 Win. cal. barrels, one set of 20 ga./20 ga. barrels, special order, elaborate game scene engraving, includes German claw mount 4X scope and case. Disc.

	100%	98%	95%	90%	80%	70%	60%
	$2,750	$2,400	$2,100	$1,850	$1,650	$1,500	$1,375

RIFLES: BOLT ACTION

AZ 1900C - .243 Win., .270 Win., 6.5x55mm, .30-06, .308 Win., 7mm Rem. Mag., or .300 Win. Mag. cal., 21 or 24 (Mag. cals.) in. barrel, checkered walnut stock with weatherproof stock finish, sling swivels, iron sights, 7.4 lbs. Importation disc. 1993.

	100%	98%	95%	90%	80%	70%	60%
	$1,100	$850	$740	$660	$585	$500	$450

Last MSR was $1,295.

Add approx. 10% for AZ 1900 Deluxe (better walnut).
Add 60% for AZ 1900 Super Deluxe (select walnut and moderate engraving).
Add approx. 10% for Model AZ 1900 DL (photo engraved receiver and floorplate).

MODEL AZ 1900M - .243 Win., 6.5x55mm, .270 Win., .30-06, or .308 Win. cal., 21 in. barrel, composite stock is composed of fiberglass, Kevlar, and graphite and features baked on walnut wood grain finish with checkering, drilled and tapped receiver. Imported 1991 only.

	100%	98%	95%	90%	80%	70%	60%
	$725	$625	$550	$495	$450	$415	$375

Last MSR was $840.

Add approx. 10% for Model AZ 1900M DL (photo engraved receiver and floorplate).

RIFLES: O/U

Please contact Cape Outfitters (see Trademark Index) for more information and current domestic pricing on the models listed.

EXPRESS - 7x65R, 7x57mm, .30-06, .308 Win., or 9.3x74R cal., 25.6 in. barrels, hand checkered walnut stock with cheekpiece, set trigger for bottom barrel, extractors. Importation disc. 1993.

	100%	98%	95%	90%	80%	70%	60%
	$3,875	$3,250	$2,900	$2,600	$2,200	$1,950	$1,650

Last MSR was $4,400.

Add $600 for E Model (with ejectors).

Grading	100%	98%	95%	90%	80%	70%	60%

Z EXPRESS EM - 7x65R, .30-06, .308 Win., or 9.3x74R cal., mechanical single trigger, ejectors. Importation disc. 1990, reintroduced 1992 only.

	$4,850	$3,975	$3,300	$2,900	$2,600	$2,200	$1,900

Last MSR was $5,300.

Add $2,395 for De Luxe Model (disc.).
Add $7,200 for E3 De Luxe Model (disc.).
The Express E3 De Luxe Model includes 2 extra sets of barrels - 1 set is shotgun (20 ga. - 2¾ or 3 in. chambers).

RIFLES: SxS

SAVANA E - 7x65R, .30-06, .308 Win., or 9.3x74R cal., boxlock action, ejectors. Importation disc. 1990.

	$5,850	$4,850	$3,975	$3,300	$2,800	$2,350	$2,000

Last MSR was $6,600.

Add $400 for Savana EM Model (single trigger).

* **Savana Deluxe** - similar to Savana E, except has elaborate game scene engraving. Importation disc. 1990.

	$7,750	$7,100	$6,500	$6,000	$5,500	$5,000	$4,600

Last MSR was $8,295.

SHOTGUNS: O/U, RECENT PRODUCTION

GOLDEN SNIPE - 12 or 20 ga, various barrel lengths, VR, single trigger, ejectors, engraved.

	$560	$520	$475	$430	$395	$360	$330

DELFINO - 12 or 20 ga., 3 in. chambers, 26 or 28 in. barrels, ejectors, VR, single non- selective trigger, blue frame with delicate engraving, walnut pistol grip stock and forearm. Disc.

	$500	$425	$375	$325	$295	$280	$265

RITMO HUNTING - 12 ga. only, 3 in. chambers, 26 or 28 in. vent. barrels and rib, SST, ejectors, select checkered walnut, blue frame and barrels with moderate engraving, recoil pad, 7¼ lbs. Disc.

	$575	$510	$465	$410	$370	$350	$335

RITMO PIGEON GRADE IV - 12 ga. only, live pigeon gun, 28 in. barrels, SST, ejectors, superbly engraved silver finished receiver, extra fine checkering on deluxe walnut, vent. barrels and rib, cased, 7½ lbs. Disc.

	$1,600	$1,450	$1,200	$1,000	$875	$795	$725

M85 RITMO TRAP OR SKEET - 12 ga. only, 28 in. (Skeet only), 30, or 32 in. barrels, ejectors, SST, special stock dimensions, engraved blue receiver, select checkered walnut stock and forearm, cased, 7¾ lbs. Disc.

	$595	$500	$465	$440	$415	$395	$370

This model was also available in a single barrel trap model at no extra charge.

* **M85 Ritmo Trap Combination** - 12 ga. only, supplied with O/U and single barrel sets, various barrel lengths, cased. Disc.

	$995	$895	$800	$700	$620	$575	$500

SILVER FALCON - 12 or 20 ga., 3 in. chambers, boxlock action, SST, ejectors, 26 or 28 in. barrels with multi-chokes, coin finished receiver with engraving, checkered Turkish walnut stock and forearm with weatherproof finish. Importation disc. 1991.

	$1,450	$700	$575	$500	$450	$400	$365

Last MSR was $1,695.

Grading	100%	98%	95%	90%	80%	70%	60%

WOODSMAN - 12 ga. only, 3 in. chambers, 23 in. vent. barrels are designed to shoot rifle slugs at 55 yards and to accept 5 interchangeable choke tubes, SST, ejectors, quarter rib on barrels with pop- up rifle sights, checkered Circassian walnut stock and forearm with swivels (waterproof finish).

	$1,650	$1,150	$950	$800	$700	$600	$500

Last MSR was $1,895.

* **Woodsman Combo** - includes 2 sets of barrels (3 in. chambers) with Zoli interchangeable choke system.

	$2,050	$1,700	$1,475	$1,200	$1,050	$925	$800

Last MSR was $2,320.

MODEL Z-90 TARGET MODEL - 12 ga. only, boxlock action, adj. SST, black competition receiver, deluxe checkered Turkish walnut stock with recoil pad and forearm, vent. barrels and rib, SST, ejectors.

* **Trap Gun** - 29½ or 32 in. barrels with screw-in chokes and raised VR, Monte Carlo stock, blue finish. Importation disc. 1993.

	$2,150	$1,450	$1,200	$995	$850	$700	$600

Last MSR was $2,495.

* **Mono Trap Gun** - 32 or 34 in. barrel with screw-in chokes and raised VR, Monte Carlo stock. Importation disc. 1993.

	$2,150	$1,450	$1,200	$995	$850	$700	$600

Last MSR was $2,495.

* **Z-90 Combo Trap Set** - includes O/U trap barrels as well as Mono trap barrel on same receiver, available as 30/32 in. sets or 32/34 in. sets. Imported 1991-92.

	$2,350	$1,900	$1,650	$1,400	$1,150	$950	$825

Last MSR was $2,700.

* **Skeet Gun** - 28 in. barrels only with screw-in chokes. Importation disc. 1993.

	$2,150	$1,450	$1,200	$995	$850	$700	$600

Last MSR was $2,495.

* **Sporting Clays Gun** - 28 in. barrels with screw-in chokes, coin finished receiver with engraved sideplates, separated barrels, Schnabel forend, solid recoil pad. Importation disc. 1990.

	$2,150	$1,450	$1,200	$995	$850	$700	$600

Last MSR was $2,495.

SHOTGUNS: SxS, RECENT PRODUCTION

UPLANDER - 12 or 20 ga., 3 in. chambers, 25 in. barrels with fixed chokes (IC/M), ST, ejectors, color case hardened receiver, English style checkered Circassian walnut stock and forearm with oil or polyurethane finish. Importation disc. 1990.

	$750	$625	$560	$520	$485	$450	$425

Last MSR was $1,295.

SILVER FOX - 12 or 20 ga., 3 in. chambers, 26 or 28 (12 ga. only) in. barrels with fixed chokes, ST, ejectors, hand engraved silver finished receiver with "AZ" in gold, straight grip checkered Circassian walnut stock and forearm. Importation disc. 1990.

	$1,650	$1,425	$1,200	$995	$875	$750	$625

Last MSR was $2,995.

ARIETE M3 - 12 ga. only, 26 or 28 in. barrels, matted rib, single non-selective trigger, ejectors, blue receiver with fine scroll engraving, cased. Disc.

	$550	$475	$400	$360	$330	$310	$285

Grading	100%	98%	95%	90%	80%	70%	60%

EMPIRE - 12 or 20 ga. Mag., 27 or 28 in. barrels, moderate engraving, coin finished receiver. Disc.

	$1,425	$1,175	$975	$875	$795	$725	$650

Add $100 for 3 in. Mag. chambers.

This model was distributed by Euroarms of America, Inc.

VOLCANO RECORD - 12 ga. only, 28 in. barrels, H&H type sidelocks, ejectors, SST, treble Purdey locks, silver finished receiver with elaborate engraving, best quality fine checkered walnut, special order only. Disc.

	$5,300	$4,475	$3,950	$3,400	$2,950	$2,650	$2,300

* ***Volcano Record ELM*** - 12 ga. only, built to individual customer specifications, best quality H&H style sidelock. Disc.

	$13,250	$11,000	$9,750	$8,600	$7,400	$6,300	$5,450

This model was distributed by Euroarms of America, Inc.

CUSTOM SERIES - SxS, individual custom order only, every refinement is used in the construction of these extremely rare and expensive shotguns. The Volcano Extra Lusso shotgun is probably the most elaborate Antonio Zoli shotgun with the list price being $58,850. Also, the Tornado Extra begins at $45,000 with a mint 12 ga. currently bringing approx. $25,000.

Z is for zany, and it doesn't get any zanier than hanging out with John Risdall (l) of Magnum Research and Risdall-Linnehan Advertising, and long time manufacturer's representative Owen Brown (the straight guy) of Owen Brown & Associates. Got humour, and what's for dessert?

TRADEMARK INDEX

The following listings represent the most up-to-date information we have regarding firearms Manufacturers, Trademarks, Importers, Distributors, Service Centers, Auction Houses, Airguns, and Black Powder (both domestic and international) to assist you in obtaining additional information from these companies/individuals. Even more so than last year, you will note the addition of web site and email listings whenever possible - this may be your best way of obtaining up-to-date model and pricing information directly from the manufacturers, importers, and/or distributors. More and more companies are offering online access on their products/services, and finding their information on their web site is sometimes the fastest and easiest way.

If parts are needed for older, discontinued makes and models (even though the manufacturer/trademark is current), it is recommended you contact either Numrich Gun Parts Corp. located in West Hurley, NY, or Jack First, Inc. located in Rapid City, SD for domestic availability and prices. For current manufacturers, it is recommended that you contact an authorized warranty repair center or stocking gun shop - unless a company/trademark has an additional service/parts listing. In Canada, please refer to the Bowmac Gunpar Inc. listing. Remember, most of the people you come in contact with requesting customer service questions or parts/service will probably be busy - have patience and respect their time.

As the 23rd Edition goes to press, we feel confident that the information listed below is the most up-to-date and accurate we can provide, especially the ever-changing email, web site addresses, and area codes. International Fax/phone numbers may require additional overseas and country/city coding. If you should require additional assistance in "tracking" any of the current companies listed in this publication, please contact us and we will try to help you regarding these specific requests.

A.A. ARMS INC.
(Parts only)
4811 Persimmon Court
Monroe, NC 28110
Phone No.: 704-289-5356
Fax No.: 704-289-5859

ADC
Armi Dallera Custom
Via Michelangelo, 64
I-25063 Gardone, VT (BS) ITALY
Fax: 011-39-0308911562
Web site: www.intred.com/adc

AMOSKEAG AUCTION COMPANY, INC.
250 Commercial Street, Unit 3011
Manchester, NH 03101
Phone No.: 603-627-7383
Fax No.: 603-627-7384
Web site: www.amoskeag-auction.com

AMP TECHNICAL SERVICE
Importer – CQB Products
13681 Newport Ave.
Ste. 8330
Tustin, CA 92780
Phone/Fax No.: 714-731-9706
Web site: www.cqbproducts.com
Email: cqb@cqbproducts.com
Factory – AMP Technical Service GmbH
Postfach 12 35
Puchheim-Bhf. D-82168 GERMANY
Fax No.: 011-49-089-89025248
Web site: www.amp-ts.com
Email: g.kst@amp-ts.com

ARMI SPORT DI CHIAPPA SILVIA & C. SNC
Factory - Black Powder
Via Fornaci 66
25131 Brescia ITALY
Fax No.: 011-39-30-358-0109

AR-7 INDUSTRIES L.L.C.
998 N. Colony Rd.
Meriden, CT 06450
Phone No.: 203-630-3536
Fax No.: 203-630-3637
Web site: www.ar-7.com
Email: sales@ar-7.com

ASAI AG
Factory
Wengihof P.O. Box 260
CH-4503 Solothurn, Switzerland
Phone No.: 011-41-32-622-8618
Fax No.: 011-41-32-622-8317

ARS/FARCO (Airguns)
Importer - See Air Rifle Specialists listing.

A-SQUARE COMPANY
One Industrial Park
Bedford, KY 40006
Phone No.: 502-255-3021
Fax No.: 502-255-9149
Web site: www.a-squarecompany.com

AYA
Importer/Distributor – see New England Custom Gun Service, Ltd. listing
Importer/Distributor - Fieldsport
3313 W. South Airport Road
Traverse City, MI 49684
Phone No.: 616-933-0767
Phone No.: 616-933-0768
Importer/Distributor and AYA Warranty Service & Repairs
John F. Rowe
4213 Oakcrest Ave.
Enid, OK 73702
Phone No.: 405-233-5942
Phone No.: 405-233-4038
Retailer - Bill Hanus Birdguns LLC
Bill Hanus models only
P.O. Box 533
Newport, OR 97365
Phone No.: 541-265-7400
Fax No.: 541-265-7433
Web site: www.billhanusbirdguns.com
U.K. Importer/Distributor - A.S.I.
Alliance House, Snape, Saxmundham
Suffolk, ENGLAND IP17 1SW
Fax No.: 011-44-1728-688950
Factory - AYA – Aguirre Y Aranzabal, S.A.L.
Avda. Otaol, 25-3
P.O. Box 45
20600 EIBAR (Guipuzcoa) SPAIN
Fax No.: 011-34-943100133
Web site: www.aya-fineguns.com
Email: aya@aya-fineguns.com

ABBIATICO & SALVINELLI (FAMARS)
see Famars di Abbiatico & Salvinelli listing.

ACCURACY INTERNATIONAL LTD.
Importer and Distributor - Accuracy International North America Inc.
P.O. Box 5267
Oak Ridge, TN 37831
Phone No.: 423-482-0330
Fax No.: 423-482-0336
Web site: www.accuracyinternational.com
Email: neatguns@aol.com
Factory - Accuracy International Ltd.
P.O. Box 81, Portsmouth
Hampshire, ENGLAND PO3 5SJ
Fax No.: 011-44-23-9269-1852

ACCU-TEK
4510 Carter Court
Chino, CA 91710
Fax No.: 909-627-7817
Web site: www.accu-tekfirearms.com
Email: accutek1@earthlink.net

ADAMY, GEBR. JADGWAFFEN
Importer - see New England Custom Gun Service, Ltd. listing.
Factory - Adamy-Jadgwaffen
Bchsenmacher-Handwerksbetrieb
Windeweg 3, Suhl
D-98527 GERMANY
Fax No.: 011-49-3681-709076
Web site: www.gunmaker,org
Email: adamy.jadgwaffen@t-online.de

ADCO SALES INC.
4 Draper Street
Woburn, MA 01801-4522
Phone: 781-935-1799
Fax: 781-935-1011
Web site: www.adcosales.com
Email: questions@adcosales.com

ALFA PROJ. spol. s.r.o.
Zabrdovicka 11
615 00 Brno CZECH REPUBLIC
Fax: 011-420-54521-4497
Web site: www.alfa-proj.cz
Email: prodej@alfa-proj.cz

AIR FORCE TALON (Airguns)
P.O. Box 2478
Ft. Worth, TX 76113
Phone No.: 817-451-8966
Fax No.: 817-451-1613

AIR GUNS OF ARIZONA (Airguns)
Importer for Daystate Airguns
Retailer for Air Arms
251 East Broadway
Mesa, AZ 85201
Phone No.: 480-461-1116

AIR LOGIC LIMITED (Airguns)
3 Medway Bldgs., Lower Road Forest Row
East Sussex, RH18 5HE, ENGLAND

AIR RIFLE SPECIALISTS (Airguns)
P.O. Box 138
130 Holden Road
Pine City, NY 14871
Fax No.: 607-733-3261

ALCHEMY ARMS CO.
3202 C Street NE
Auburn, WA 98002
Phone No.: 800-282-4664
Fax No.: 253-939-4114
Web site: www.alchemyltd.com
Email: armsco@alchemyltd.com

AMERICA REMEMBERS
10226 Timber Ridge Dr.
Ashland, VA 23005
Phone No.: 804-550-9616
Fax No.: 804-550-9603
Web site: www.americaremembers.com
Email: americaremembers@erols.com

AMERICAN DERRINGER CORPORATION

127 N. Lacy Dr.
Waco, TX 76705
Phone No.: 254-799-9111
Fax No.: 254-799-7935
Web site: www.amderringer.com
Web site: www.ladyderringer.com
Email: amderr@aol.com

AMERICAN HISTORICAL FOUNDATION, THE

1142 W. Grace St.
Richmond, VA 23220
Phone No.: 804-353-1812
Fax No.: 804-359-4895
Web site: www.ahfrichmond.com
Email: ahf@richmond.infi.net

AMERICAN HUNTING RIFLES, INC.

P.O. Box 300
Hamilton, MT 59840
Phone No.: 800-716-4445
Phone No.: 406-961-4944
Fax No.: 406-961-1430
Web site: www.hunting-rifles.com
Email: info@hunting-rifles.com

AMERICAN SPIRIT ARMS CORP.

15001 North Hayden Road, Ste. 112
Scottsdale, AZ 85260
Phone No.: 888-486-5487
Fax No.: 480-483-5301
Web site: www.gunkits.com
Email: gunkits@gunkits.com

AWA INTERNATIONAL, INC.

American Western Arms, Inc.
1450 Southwest 10th St., 3B
Delray Beach, FL 33444
Phone: 877-292-4867
Fax: 561-330-0881
Web site: www.awaguns.com
Email: info@awaguns.com
American Western Arms, Inc. Italy – srl
Branch Office
Via De Gusperi
I-25013 Carpenedolo (BS) ITALY
Fax No.: 011-390-30-9966322

ANICS CORP. (Airguns)

Importer – Air Rifle Specialists
P.O. Box 138
130 Holden Rd.
Pine City, NY 14871
Factory
7 Vorontsovo Pole St.
Moscow, RUSSIA 103062
Web site: www.anics.com

ANSCHÜTZ

Distributors - Sporting Rifles & Pistols
AcuSport Corporation (Headquarters)
1535 Industrial Ave.
Billings, MT 53603
Phone No.: 800-238-4665
Fax No.: 406-248-7767
Web site: www.acusport.com

ANSCHÜTZ, cont.
Zanders Sporting Goods, Inc.
7525 Hwy. 154 W.
Baldwin, IL 62217-9706
Phone No.: 618-785-2235
Fax No.: 618-785-2320
Web site: www.gzanders.com
Email: jbe@egyptian.net
Ellett Brothers
267 Columbia Ave.
Chapin, SC 29036
Phone: 803-345-3751
Fax: 803-345-1820
Web site: www.ellettbrothers.com
Distributors - Target Rifles
International Shooters Service (Airguns also)
P.O. Box 185 234
Fort Worth, TX 76181-0234
Phone/Fax No.: 817-595-2090
Champion's Choice Inc. - see separate listing.
Champions Shooter's Supply (Airguns also)
P.O. Box 303
New Albany, OH 43054
Phone No.: 614-855-1603
Fax No.: 614-855-1209
Web site: www.championshooters.com
Gunsmithing Inc. (Airguns also)
30 West Buchanan Street
Colorado Springs, CO 80907
Phone No.: 800-284-8671
Fax No.: 719-632-3493
Web site: www.nealjguns.com
Email: neal@nealjguns.com
Repair/Gunsmithing Services
10-Ring-Service, Inc.
2227 West Lou Drive
Jacksonville, FL 32216
Phone No.: 904-724-7419
Fax No.: 904-724-7149
Factory - ANSCHÜTZ, J.G. GmbH & Co. KG
Daimlerstrasse 12
D-89079 Ulm, GERMANY
Fax No.: 011-49-731-4012-2700
Web site: www.anschuetz-sport.com
Email: JGA-Info@anschuetz-sport.com

ANZIO IRONWORKS

1905 16th Street North
St. Petersburg, FL 33704
Phone No.: 727-895-2019
Fax No.: 727-827-4728
Web site: www.anzioironworks.com
Email: anzioshop@hotmail.com

ARMALITE, INC.

P.O. Box 299
Geneseo, IL 61254
Phone No.: 309-944-6939
Fax No.: 309-944-6949
Web site: www.armalite.com
Email: info@armalite.com

ARMALITE, INC., cont.
Law Enforcement Support Only
P.O. Box 340
Campbellsburg, KY 40011
Phone No.: 502-532-0300
Fax No.: 502-532-0775
Email: toppc@armalite.com

ARMAMENT TECHNOLOGY
3045 Robie St., Suite 113
Halifax, N.S. CANADA B3K 4P6
Phone No.: 902-454-6384
Fax No.: 902-454-4641
Web site: www.armament.com
Email: info@armament.com

ARMES DE CHASSE LLC
P.O. Box 86
Hertford, NC 27944
Phone No.: 252-426-2245
Fax No.: 252-426-1557

ARMES PIERRE ARTISAN
Le Mont Mille B.P. 12
F-42380 Saint Bonnett Le Chateau FRANCE
Fax: 011-33-04-77-50702

ARMI SAN PAOLO (Black Powder)
3590 NW 49th Street
Miami, FL 33142
Fax No.: 305-633-2877

ARMINIUS
Herman Weihrauch Revolver GmbH
Please refer to Weihrauch listing.

ARMS MORAVIA LTD.
Factory
Nadrazni 22
Ostrava 2, CZ-70200
CZECH REPUBLIC
Web site: www.arms.elite.cz

ARMSCOR (ARMS CORPORATION OF THE PHILIP-PINES)
Importer (paramilitary style rifles only) – see the K.B.I., Inc. listing
Importer & Distributor Armscor Precision International
5329 S. Cameron St., Ste. 110
Las Vegas, NV 89118
Phone No.: 702-362-7750
Fax No.: 702-362-5019
Email: apiusa@earthlink.com
Factory office - Arms Corp. of the Philippines
Parang Marikina 1800
Metro Manilla, PHILIPPINES
Phone No.: 632-942-5936
Fax No.: 632-942-0862
Web site: www.armscor.com.ph
Email: armscor@info.com.ph
Executive office - Arms Corp. of the Philippines
Fax No.: 632-634-3906
Email: squires@cnl.net

ARMSCORP USA, INC.
4424 John Avenue
Baltimore, MD 21227-1506
Phone No. 410-247-6200
Fax No.: 410-247-6205
Web site: www.armscorpusa.com
Email: info@armscorpusa.com

ARRIETA, S.L.
Importer & Distributor - See New England Arms, Corp. listing.
Importer & Distributor - See Quality Arms listing.
Importer - See Griffin & Howe listing.
Importer - See Orvis listing.
Importer - Wingshooting Adventures
O-1845 West Leonard
Grand Rapids, MI 49544-9510
Phone No.: 616-677-1980
Fax No.: 616-677-1986
Factory - Arrieta, Manufacturas, S.L.
C/.Morkaiko, 5 Barrio Urasandi
E-20870 Elgoibar (Guipuzcoa) SPAIN
Fax No.: 011-34-43-74-3154

ARRIZABALAGA, PEDRO
Importer - See Harry Marx Hi-Grade Imports listing.
Importer - See New England Arms Corp. listing.
Factory - Arrizabalaga, Pedro, S.A.
Errekatxu, 5
E-20600 Eibar (Guipuzcoa) SPAIN
Fax No.: 011-34-943-11-1743

ARSENAL INC.
5015 West Sahara Ave., Ste. 125
Las Vegas, NV 89146-3407
Phone No.: 888-539-2220
Fax No.: 702-643-2088

ARSENAL USA, LLC
7311 Galveston Road, Ste. 260
Houston, TX 77034
Phone/Fax No.: 713-378-0226

ART MANIFATTURA ARMI
Via Madonnina 89
Gardone, VT
I-25063 ITALY
Fax No.: 011-030-861591
Email: armi.art@intred.it

ASPEN OUTFITTING CO.
315 East Dean St.
Aspen, CO 81611
Phone no.: 970-925-3406
Fax no.: 970-920-3706

WILLIAM R. ASPREY, ESQ.
10 Mount Street
London, ENGLAND W1K 2TY
Fax: 011-44-020-7493-8386
Web site: www.williamandson.com
Email: info@williamandson.com

ATKIN, GRANT & LANG
Broomhill Leys, Windmill Road, Markyate
St. Albans, Hertfordshire AL3 8LP ENGLAND
Fax No.: 011-44-1582-842318
Web site: www.broomhills.co.uk
Email: AtkinGrant.Lang@btinternet.com

ATKIN, HENRY
Factory - see Atkin, Grant & Lang listing.

AUSTIN & HALLECK (Black Powder)
1099 Welt
Weston, MO 64098
Phone No.: 816-386-2176
Fax No.: 816-386-2177

AUSTRALIAN INTERNATIONAL ARMS
Importer - see Tristar listing.
Brisbane, AUSTRALIA

AUTAUGA RIFLES, INC.
740 East Main, Suite 13
Prattville, AL 36067
Phone No.: 334-361-2950
Fax No.: 334-358-0962
Web site: www.autaugarifles.com
Email: hardrock308@mindspring.com

AUTO-ORDNANCE CORP.
See the Kahr Arms listing.
Web site: www.tommygun.com

AXTELL RIFLE COMPANY
Distributor - The Riflesmith Inc.
353 Mill Creek Road
Sheridan, MT 59749
Phone/Fax No.: 406-842-5814
Web site: www.riflesmith.com
Email: sharps77@3rivers.net

BSA GUNS (UK) LTD. (Airguns)
Importer - see Precision Sales listing.
BSA Factory
Armoury Rd., Small Heath
Birmingham, W. Mids, B11 2PX, ENGLAND
Fax No.: 011-44-21-773-0845

BAER, LES
See the Les Baer Custom listing.

BAIKAL
Importer – see European American Armory Corp listing.
Baikal Factory
Izhevsky Mekhanichesky Zavod
8, Promyshlennaya str.
Izhevsk, 426063 RUSSIA
Fax No.: 011-95-007-341-2765830
Web site: www.baikalinc.ru
Email: worldlinks@baikalinc.ru

BAILONS GUNMAKERS LTD.
Correspondence and Repair - Guthrie Consulting
Attn: Sir Malcolm Guthrie
P.O. Box 134
Stourbridge, West Midlands, ENGLAND DY9 0YS
Phone/Fax No.: 011-44-562-730711

BALLARD RIFLE, LLC
113 West Yellowstone Avenue
Cody, Wyoming 82414
Phone No.: 307-587-4914
Fax No.: 307-527-6097
Web site: www.ballardrifles.com
E-mail: ballard@wyoming.com

BANSNER'S ULTIMATE RIFLES L.L.C.
P.O. Box 839
261 East Main Street
Adamstown, PA 19501
Phone No.: 717-484-2370
Fax No.: 717-484-0523
Web site: www.bansnersrifle.com
Email: bansner@aol.com

BARRETT FIREARMS MANUFACTURING, INC.
P.O. Box 1077
Murfreesboro, TN 37133
Phone No.: 615-896-2938
Fax No.: 615-896-7313
Web site: www.barrettrifles.com
Email: mail@barrettrifles.com

BATTAGLIA, MAURO
Via Dismano, 181
S. Stefano, Ravenna ITALY
Fax: 011-39-0544-497879
Web site: www.maurobattaglia.armifini.com
Email: maurobattaglia@armifini.com

BEAUCHAMP & SONS (dba FLINTLOCKS, ETC.)
160 Rossiter Rd.
Richmond, MA 01254

BEEMAN PRECISION AIRGUNS (Airguns)
Division of S/R Industries (Maryland Corp.)
5454 Argosy Dr.
Huntington Beach, CA 92649-1039
Phone No.: 714-890-4800
Phone No.: 800-227-2744
Fax No.: 714-890-4808
Web site: www.beeman.com

BENELLI
Importer - Benelli USA
17603 Indian Head Highway
Accokeek, MD 20607-2501
Phone No.: 301-283-6981
Fax No.: 301-283-6988
Web site: www.benelliusa.com
Email: benusa1@aol.com
Warranty Repair Address – Benelli USA Corp.
901 Eight Street
Pocomoke, MD 21851
Factory - Benelli Armi S.p.A.
Via della Stazione, 50
I-61029 Urbino (PS) ITALY
Fax No.: 011-39-722-30-72-07-227
Web site: www.benelli.it

BENJAMIN AIR RIFLE COMPANY (Airguns)
Routes 5 & 20
East Bloomfield, NY 14443
Fax No.: 716-657-5405

BERETTA, PIETRO
Importer - Beretta U.S.A. Corp
17601 Beretta Drive
Accokeek, MD 20607
Fax No.: 301-283-0435
Web site: www.berettausa.com

BERETTA, PIETRO, cont.
Beretta Premium Grades
c/o Beretta Gallery
41 Highland Park Village
Dallas, TX 75205
Phone No.: 214-559-9800
Fax No.: 214-559-9805
c/o Beretta Gallery
718 Madison Avenue
New York, NY 10021
Phone No.: 212-319-3235
Fax No.: 212-207-8219
c/o Beretta Gallery
1061 Capital Federal
Arendales 1654/56
Buenos Aires, ARGENTINA
Phone No.: 011-54-813.92558
Factory - Fabbrica d'Armi Pietro Beretta S.p.A
Via Pietro Beretta 18
25063 Gardone Val Trompia
Brescia, ITALY
Phone No.: 011-39-30-8341-1
Fax No.: 011-39-30-8341-421
Web site: www.beretta.it

WAYNE BERGQUIST CUSTOM PISTOLS
5760 Shirley St., Suite #21
Naples, FL 34109
Phone No.: 941-594-1573
Fax No.: 941-597-8259

BERNARDELLI, VINCENZO
Via Grandi, 10
Sede Legale Torbole Casaglia
I-25030 Brescia, ITALY
Fax: 011-39-030-2150963
Web site: www.bernardelli.com
Email: bernardelli@bernardelli.com

BERSA
Importer – Eagle Imports, Inc.
1750 Brielle Ave., Unit B-1
Wanamassa, NJ 07712
Phone No.: 732-493-0333
Fax No.: 732-493-0301
Web Site: www.bersa-llama.com
Email: gsodini@aol.com
Factory - Bersa S.A.
Castillo 312
(1704) Ramos Mejia, ARGENTINA
Fax No.: 011-54-1-656-2093

BERTUZZI
Importer - See New England Arms Corp. listing.
Factory - Bertuzzi, F.lli
Via Alessandro Volta, 65
I-25063 Gardone V.T. (BS) ITALY
Fax No.: 011-39-30-8912188

BETTINSOLI, TARCISIO Srl
Via I Maggio, 116
Sarezzo, Brescia, I-25068 ITALY
Fax: 011-39-030-890-0240

BLAND, THOMAS & SONS GUNMAKERS LTD.
Woodcock Hill, Inc.
P.O. Box 363
192 Spencers Road
Benton, PA 17814
Phone No.: 570-864-3242
Fax No.: 570-864-3232
Web site: www.woodcockhill.com
Email: bland@epix.net

BLASER
Importer & Distributor - see SIG Arms listing.
Factory - Blaser Jagdwaffen GmbH
Ziegelstadel 1
D-88316 Isny im Allgu, GERMANY
Fax No.: 011-49-75-62702-43
Web site: www.blaserrifles.com

H. BLEIKER FEINMECHANIK/SPORTWAFFEN
Ausserfeld 8
CH – 9606 Bütschwil, SWITZERLAND
Phone No.: 011.41.71.982.8210
Fax No.: 011.41.71.982.8219
Web site: www.bleiker.ch
Email: hbleiker@bleiker.ch

BOHEMIA ARMS
17101 Los Modelos
Fountain Valley, CA 92708
Phone/Fax No.: 619-442-7005
Phone/Fax No.: 714-963-0809

BOWEN, BRUCE & COMPANY
3541 Mayer Ave.
Sturgis, SD 57785
Phone: 402-203-5575
Email: Bbowen999@aol.com

BOWMAC GUNPAR INC.
Canadian Parts Supplier
69 Iber Rd., Unit 101
Stittsville, Ontario CANADA K2S 1E7
Phone No.: 800-668-2509
Phone No.: 613-831-8548
Fax No.: 613-831-0530

BOND ARMS, INC.
P.O. Box 1296
204 Alpha Lane
Granbury, Texas 76048
Phone No.: 817-573-4445
Fax No.: 817-573-5636
Web site: www.bondarms.com
Email: bondarms@shooters.com

BOSIS, LUCIANO
Importer – see New England Arms Corp. listing.
Factory
via Marconi 30
25039 Travagliato
Brescia, ITALY
Phone/Fax No.: 011-39-30-660413
Web site: www.bosis.com
Email: bosis@info.com

BOSS & CO., LTD.
16 Mount Street
London, ENGLAND W1K 2RH
Phone No.: 011-44-020-7493-1127
Fax No.: 011-44-020-7493-0711
Web site: www.bossguns.com
Email: mail@bossguns.com

BREDA MECCANICA BRESCIANA
Importer – see Tristar listing.
Factory
Via Lunga, 2
I-25126 Brescia ITALY
Fax No.: 011-39-030-3791330-322115

BRETTON
Factory
19, Rue Victore
Grignard Z1
Montreynaud St. Etienne, Cedex
F-42026 FRANCE
Fax No.: 011-33-77-790653

BRILEY MANUFACTURING INC.
1230 Lumpkin Rd.
Houston, TX 77043
Phone No.: 713-932-6995 (Technical)
Phone No.: 800-331-5718 (Orders only)
Fax No.: 713-932-1043
Web site: www.briley.com

BRNO AERON (Airguns)
Also see RWS under Dianawerk, Mayer & Grammel-spacher
PO Box 714
St. Albans, VT 05478
Fax No.: 802-527-0470

BRNO ARMS
Importer – see EAA Corp listing.
Factory - ZBROJOVKA BRNO, a.s.
Lazaretni 7
656 17 BRNO
CZECH REPUBLIC
Fax No.: 011-42-545-152772
Email: arms.sales@zbrojovka.com

BROCKMAN'S CUSTOM GUNSMITHING
445 Idaho St.
Gooding, Idaho 83330
Phone No.: 208-934-5050
Fax No.: 208-934-5284
Web site: www.brockmansrifles.com
Email: Brockman@brockmansrifles.com

DAVID MCKAY BROWN GUNMAKERS, LTD.
32 Hamilton Road, Bothwell
Glasgow, SCOTLAND (U.K.) G71 8NA
Fax No.: 011-44-141-1698-854207
Web site: www.mckaybrown.com
Email: info@mckaybrown.com

ED BROWN CUSTOM, INC.
(Rifles Only)
P.O. Box 492
43825 Muldrow Trail
Perry, MO 63462
Phone No.: 573-565-3261
Fax No.: 573-565-2791
Web site: www.edbrown.com
Email: rifles@edbrown.com

ED BROWN PRODUCTS, INC.
(Pistols only)
P.O. Box 492
43825 Muldrow Trail
Perry, MO 63462
Phone No.: 573-565-3261
Fax No.: 573-565-2791
Web site: www.edbrown.com
Email: 1911@edbrown.com

BROWN PRECISION, INC.
P.O. Box 270 W
7786 Molinos Avenue
Los Molinos, CA 96055
Phone No.: 530-384-2506
Fax No.: 530-384-1638
Web site: www.brownprecision.com

BROWNING
Administrative Headquarters
One Browning Place
Morgan, UT 84050-9326
Phone No.: 801-876-2711
Sales Information: 800-234-2045
Product Service: 800-322-4626
Fax No.: 801-876-3331
Web site: www.browning.com
International Web site (including Custom Shop):
www.browningint.com
Browning Parts and Service
3005 Arnold Tenbrook Rd.
Arnold, MO 63010
Phone No.: 314-287-6800
Fax No.: 800-817-4755 (Parts only)

BRUCHET
see Darne listing.

BRYCO ARMS
Distributor - Jennings Firearms, Inc.
P.O. Box 20135
3680 Research Way
Carson City, NV 89721
Phone No.: 800-518-1666
Fax No.: 702-882-3129

BUL TRANSMARK LTD.
Importer – EAA Corp.
Factory - Bul Transmark Ltd.
10 Rival Street
Tel-Aviv 67778, ISRAEL
Fax No.: 011-972-3-687-4853
Web site: www.bultransmark.com
Email: info@bultransmark.com

BUTTERFIELD & BUTTERFIELD (Auctions)
Main Gallery & Corporate Office
220 San Bruno Ave.
San Francisco, CA 94103
Phone No.: 415-861-7500
Fax No.: 415-861-8951
Web site: www.butterfields.com

BUSHMASTER FIREARMS
P.O. Box 1479
999 Roosevelt Trail
Windham, ME 04062
Phone No.: 800-883-6229
Fax No.: 207-892-8068
Web site: www.bushmaster.com
Email: info@bushmaster.com

C Z (CESKA ZBROJOVKA)
Firearms & Airguns Importer - CZ-USA
P.O. Box 171073
Kansas City, KS 66117-0073
Phone No.: 913-321-1811
Toll Free No.: 800-955-4486
Fax No.: 913-321-2251
Web site: www.cz-usa.com
Email: info@cz-usa.com
Administration Offices - Ceska Zbrojovka
Svatopluka Cecha 1283
CZ-68827 Uhersky Brod
CZECH REPUBLIC
Fax No.: 011-420-63363-3811
Web site: www.czub.cz
Email: info@czub.cz

CBC
Av. Humberto de Campos 3220
09400 000 Ribeiro Pires SP BRAZIL
Fax No.: 011-55-11-4822-8323
Web site: www.cbc.com.br

CABELAS INC.
One Cabela Dr.
Sidney, NE 69160
Phone No.: 800-237-4444
Fax No.: 800-496-6329
Web Site: www.cabelas.com

RENATO CAEM
U.S. Agents - S.R. Lamboy & Co., Inc.
The Old Station
5 Railroad Street
Victor, NY 14564
Phone No.: 716-924-2710
Fax No.: 716-924-2737
Web site: www.gunshop.com

CAESAR GUERINI, s.r.l.
Via Parte, 33
I-25060 Marcheno VT Brescia, ITALY
Fax: 011-39-030-8966147
Web site: www.caesarguerini.it
Email: info@caesarguerini.it

CAPE OUTFITTERS, INC.
599 County Rd. #206
Cape Girardeau, MO 63701
Phone No.: 573-335-4103
Fax No.: 573-335-1555
Web site: www.capeoutfitters.com
Email: jmayfield@capeoutfitters.com

CASPIAN ARMS, LTD.
P.O. Box 465
Hardwick, VT 05843-0465
Phone No.: 802-472-6454
Fax No.: 802-472-6709
Web site: www.caspianarms.com
Email: caspianarm@aol.com

CASULL ARMS CORPORATION
P.O. Box 1629
Afton, WY 83110
Phone No.: 307-886-0200
Fax No.: 307-886-0300
Web site: www.casullarms.com
Email: email@casullarms.com

CENTURION ORDNANCE, INC.
11614 Rainbow Ridge
Helotes, TX 78023
Phone No.: 210-695-4602
Fax No.: 210-695-4603
Web site: www.aguilaammo.com
Email: info@aguilaammo.com

CENTURY INTERNATIONAL ARMS, INC.
1161 Holland Dr.
Boca Raton, FL 33487
Phone No.: 561-998-1997
Fax No.: 561-998-1993
Web site: www.centuryarms.com
Email: support@centuryarms.com

CENTURY MFG., INC.
32 E. Main St.
Knightstown, IN 46148
Phone No.: 765-345-5670
Web site: www.centurymfg2002.com
Email: email@centurymfg2002.com

CHAMPIONS CHOICE, INC.
201 International Blvd.
LaVergne, TN 37086
Phone No.: (Orders Only) 800-345-7179
Phone no.: 615-793-4066
Fax no.: 615-793-4070
Email: champchoice@nashville.com

CHAMPLIN FIREARMS, INC.
P.O. Box 3191
Enid, OK 73702
Phone No.: 580-237-7388
Fax No.: 580-242-6922
Web site: www.champlinarms.com
Email: info@champlinarms.com

CHAPUIS ARMES

Importer - Chadick's, Ltd.
P.O. Box 100
119 Moore Ave.
Terrell, TX 75160
Phone No.: 972-563-7577
Fax No.: 972-563-1265
Web site: www.doubleguns.com
Email: chadicksltd@aol.com
Factory - Chapuis Armes
Z.I. La Gravoux, BP 15
F-42380 St. Bonnet le Chateau, FRANCE
Fax No.: 011-33-4-77/501070
Web site: www.chapuis-armes.com
Email: info@chapuis-armes.com

CHAPUIS, P. ARMES ET FILS

Le Mont Mille, BP 12
F-42380 St. Bonnet le Chateau FRANCE
Fax No.: 011-33-47750-7027

CHARTER 2000, INC.

273 Canal St.
Shelton, CT 06484
Phone No.: 203-922-1652
Fax No.: 203-922-1469
Web site: www.charterfirearms.com

CHATTAHOOCHEE BLACK POWDER ARMS

4153 Drew Road
Cummings, GA 30040
Phone No.: 770-889-3711
Fax No.: 770-889-8134

CHENEY RIFLE WORKS/LEMAN RIFLES (Black Powder)

Distributor - See Mountain States Muzzleloading Supplies, Inc.

CHERRY'S FINE GUNS & AUCTION SERVICE

3402-A West Wendover Avenue
Greensboro, NC 27407
Phone No.: 336-854-4182
Fax No.: 336-854-4184
Web site: www.cherrys.com

CHIPMUNK RIFLES

Factory - Rogue Rifle Co., Inc.
1140 36th St. N Ste. B
Lewiston, ID 83501
Phone No.: 208-743-4355
Fax No.: 208-743-4163
Web site: www.chipmunkrifle.com
Email: roguerifle@earthlink.net

CHRISTENSEN ARMS

192 East 100 North
Fayette, UT 84630
Phone No.: 435-528-7999
Fax No.: 435-528-7494
Web site: www.christensenarms.com
Email: christensenarms@yahoo.com

CHRISTIE'S (Auctions)

Rockefeller Center
20 Rockefeller Plaza
New York, NY 10020
Phone No.: 212-636-2000
Fax No.: 212-636-2399
Web site: www.christies.com

CHURCHILL GUNMAKERS

West Wycombe Gunmakers Ltd.
Park Lane, Lane End, High Wycombe
Buckinghamshire, HP14 3NS ENGLAND
Phone No.: 011-44-1494-883066
Fax. No.: 011-44-1494-883215
Web site: www.churchillguns.demon.co.uk
Email: info@churchillguns.demon.co.uk

CIMARRON, F.A. CO., INC.

105 Winding Oaks
Fredericksburg, TX 78624-0906
Phone No.: 830-997-9090
Fax No.: 830-997-0802
Web site: www.cimarron-firearms.com
Email: cimarron@fbg.net

CLARK CUSTOM GUNS, INC.

336 Shootout Lane
Princeton, LA 71067
Phone No.: 318-949-9884
Toll Free Order No.: 888-458-4126
Fax No.: 318-949-9829
Web Site: www.clarkcustomguns.com
Email: clarkguns@prysm.net

COBRA ENTERPRISES

1960 S. Milestone Drive, Ste. F
Salt Lake City, UT 84104
Phone No.: 801-908-8300
Fax No.: 801-908-8301
Web site: www.cobrapistols.com
Email: cobrapistols@networld.com

COGSWELL & HARRISON

UK Office
Thatcham House
95 Sussex Place
Slough Berks SL1 1NN, U.K.
Phone No.: 011-44-1753/520866
Fax No.: 011-44-1753/575770
Web site: www.cogswell.co.uk
Email: info@cogswell.co.uk

COLT BLACKPOWDER ARMS (Black Powder)

110 8th Street
Brooklyn, NY 11215
Phone No.: 718-499-4678
Fax No.: 718-768-8056
Web site: www.coltblackpowder.com

COLT'S MANUFACTURING CO., INC.

P.O. Box 1868
Hartford, CT 06144-1868
Phone No.: 800-962-COLT
Fax No.: 860-244-1449
Web site: www.colt.com

If research is needed, make sure the proper research fee is enclosed (see appropriate Colt section for current fee listings) and address the correspondence Attn: Historical Dept.

COMANCHE
Importer – SGS Imports Int'l, Inc.
1750 Brielle Ave., Unit B-1
Wanamassa, NJ 07712
Phone No.: 732-493-0302
Fax No.: 732-493-0301
Email: gsodini@aol.com

COMPASSECO, INC. (Airguns)
151 Atkinson Hill
Bardstown, KY 40004
Phone No.: 800-726-1696
Fax No.: 502-349-9596
Web site: www.compasseco.com

COMPETITOR CORPORATION
26 Knight Street, Unit 3
P.O. Box 352
Jaffrey, NH 03452
Phone: 603-532-9483
Fax No.: 603-532-8209
Web site: www.competitor-pistol.com
Email: Competitorcorp@aol.com

CONNECTICUT SHOTGUN MANUFACTURING COMPANY
P.O. Box 1692
35 Woodland St.
New Britain, CT 06501-1692
Phone No.: 860-225-6581
Fax No.: 860-832-8707
Web site: www.connecticutshotgun.com
Email: Galazan@msn.com

CONQUEST
MK Vertriebs-Gesellschaft
Am Tairnbacher Weg 14
Dielheim D-69234 GERMANY
Fax No.: 011-49-06222-7721-35
Web site: www.mk-v.de
Email: conquest@mk-v.de

COOPER FIREARMS OF MONTANA, INC.
P.O. Box 114
4004 Hwy. 93 North
Stevensville, MT 59870
Phone No.: 406-777-0373
Fax No.: 406-777-5228
Web site: www.cooperfirearms.com
Email: cooper@bigsky.net

COSMI, AMERICO & FIGLIO s.n.c.
Importer – Autumn Sales, Inc.
1320 Lake Street
Fort Worth, TX 76102
Phone No.: 817-335-1634
Fax No.: 817-338-0119
Factory - Via Flaminia 307
I-60020 Torrette di Ancona, ITALY
Fax No.: 011-39-71-887008
Web site: www.cosmi.net
Email: cosmi@cosmi.net

CRICKETT RIFLE
Keystone Sporting Arms
RD2 Box 20
Milton, PA 17847
Phone No.: 570-742-2777
Fax No.: 570-742-1455
Web site: www.crickett.com

CROSMAN AIR GUNS (Airguns)
P.O. Box 308
East Bloomfield, NY 14443
Phone No.: 800-7-AIRGUN
Fax No.: 716-657-5405
Web site: www.crosman.com

DGS, INC.
404 N. Jackson
Casper, WY 82601
Phone No.: 307-237-2414
Web site: www.dgsrifle.com
Email: dalest@trib.com

DPMS, INC.
13983 Industry Avenue
Becker, MN 55308
Phone No.: 763-261-5600
Fax No.: 763-261-5599
Web site: www.dpmsinc.com
Email: dpmsinc@aol.com

DSA, INC.
P.O. Box 370
Barrington, IL 60011
Phone No.: 847-277-7258
Fax No.: 847-227-7259
Web site: www.dsarms.com
Email: dsarms@earthlink.net

DAISY MANUFACTURING CO. (Airguns)
400 W. Stribling Dr.
P.O. Box 220
Rogers, AR 72757-0220
Phone No.: 501-636-1200
Fax No.: 501-636-1601
Web site: www.daisy.com
Email: info@daisy.com

DAKOTA ARMS, INC.
HC 55 Box 326
Sturgis, SD 57785
Phone No.: 605-347-4686
Fax No.: 605-347-4459
Web site: www.dakotaarms.com
Email: dakarms@sturgis.com

DAKOTA SINGLE ACTION REVOLVERS
Importer - See E.M.F. Company listing.

DALVAR OF U.S.A.
See the Radom listing.

DALY, CHARLES: CURRENT MFG.
Importer - See K.B.I., Inc. listing.
Web site: www.charlesdaly.com

DARNE S.A.
Importer - The Drumming Stump, Inc.
P.O. Box 151
Circle Pines, MN 55014
Phone: 763-785-7083
Fax: 763-434-4897
Email: tedJS@usfamily.net
Factory
4 ter, rue de la Convention
F-42100 Saint Etienne, FRANCE

DAVID MILLER CO.
3131 E. Greenlee Rd.
Tucson, AZ 85716
Phone No.: 520-323-3117
Fax No.: 520-327-7672

DEER CREEK RIFLE WORKS (Black Powder)
Distributor - See Mountain States Muzzleloading Supply listing.

DEFOURNEY
No current information available.

DEMAS, Ets
Importer - The Drumming Stump, Inc.
P.O. Box 151
Circle Pines, MN 55014
Phone: 763-785-7083
Fax: 763-434-4897
Email: tedJS@usfamily.net
Factory - Demas, Ets
5 Bis, rue Xavier Privas
F-42000 St. Etienne, FRANCE
Fax No.: 011-33-04-77-25-4198

J.C. DEVINE, INC. (Auctions)
P.O. Box 413
20 South Street
Milford, NH 03055
Phone No.:603-673-4967
Fax No.: 603-672-0328
Web site: www.jcdevine.com
Email: jcdevine@empire.net

DIANAWERK, MAYER AND GRAMMELSPACHER (Airguns)
See Dynamit Nobel - RWS listing.

DICKSON & MACNAUGHTON
21 Frederick Street
Edinburgh, Scotland UK EH2 2NE
Fax: 011-44-131-225-3658

JOHN DICKSON & SON
See the Dickson & MacNaughton listing.

DLASK ARMS CORP.
U.S. Office
P.O. Box 607
683 Peace Portal Dr.
Blaine, WA 98231-0607
Factory
202B 1546 Derwent Way
Delta, British Columbia, V3M 6M4 CANADA
Phone No.: 604-527-9942
Fax No.: 604-527-9982
Web site: www.dlask.com
Email: dlask@attglobal.net

DIXIE GUN WORKS (Black Powder)
Hwy. 51 South
Union City, TN 38261
Fax No.: 901-885-0440

DOWNSIZER CORPORATION
P.O. Box 710316
Santee, CA 92072-0316
Phone No.: 619-448-5510
Fax No.: 619-448-5780
Web site: www.downsizer.com

DUCKS UNLIMITED, INC.
One Waterfowl Way
Memphis, TN 38120-2351
Phone No.: 901-758-3825
Fax No.: 901-758-3850
Web Site: www.ducks.org

DUMOULIN, ERNEST S.P.R.L.
Factory
Rue du Bouxthay 41
B-4041 Vottem-Herstal, BELGIUM
Fax No.: 011-32-41-228-89-69
Web site: www.dumoulin-herstal.com
Email: contact@dumoulin-herstal.be

DUMOULIN, HENRI & FILS
Importer - See New England Arms Corp. listing.
Factory - Dumoulin, Henri & Fils
P.O. Box 30
Herstal 4400, BELGIUM
Fax No.: 011-32-49-3013255
Email: dumoulinrifles@cs.com

DUMOULIN HERSTAL S.A.
Factory
Rue du Bouxthay 41
B-4041 Vottem-Herstal, BELGIUM
Fax No.: 011-32-41-228-89-69
Web site: www.dumoulin-herstal.com
Email: contact@dumoulin-herstal.be

DYNAMIT NOBEL (Airguns & Rottweil)
81 Ruckman Road
Closter, NJ 07624
Phone No.: 201-767-1995
Fax No.: 201-767-1589
Web Site: www.shooters.com
Email: fturner@cybernex.net
Factory
Dynamit Nobel GmbH
Postfach 12 61
Troisdorf D-53839 GERMANY
Email: RWS@dynamit-nobel.com

E.D.M. ARMS
1653 Plum Lane
Redlands, CA 92374
Toll-free Phone No.: 877-884-4EDM
Phone No.: 909-307-8877
Fax No.: 909-307-8866
Web site: www.edmarms.com

E.D.M. ARMS, cont.
Intervention Tactical Models only - THEIS, LLC
1147 Hawthorne Road
Grosse Pointe Woods, MI 48236
Phone: 877-251-7711
Fax: 281-251-7741
Web site: www.THEIS408.com
Email: info@THEIS408.com

E.M.F. COMPANY
1900 E. Warner Ave., Suite 1-D
Santa Ana, CA 92705
Phone No.: 714-261-6611
Fax No.: 714-756-0133
Web site: www.emf-company.com
Email: sales@emf-company.com

EAGLE ARMS INC.
Division of ArmaLite, Inc. - refer to ArmaLite, Inc. listing.

EFFEBI snc
Factory
Via Rossa, 4
I-25062 Concesio (BS) ITALY
Fax. No.: 011-39-30-2180414
Web site: www.effebi.org
Email: info@effebi.org

EGO ARMAS, S.A.
Victor Sarasqueta, 1
E-20600 Eibar (Guipuzcoa) SPAIN
Fax No.: 011-34-43-120463

ENTRÉPRISE ARMS INC.
15861 Business Center Dr.
Irwindale, CA 91706
Phone No.: 626-962-8712
Fax No.: 626-962-4692
Web sites: www.entreprise.com

ERMA SUHL, GmbH
Schtzenstrasse 26
D-98527 Suhl, GERMANY
Fax no.: 011-49-3681-854-203

ESCORT
Importer – see Legacy Sports International listing.
Factory
Hatsan Arms Company
1. Sanayi Sitsei 2835 No. 3
Izmir, TURKEY
Fax no.: 011-09232-458-1999
Web site: www.hatsan.com
Email: info@hatsan.com

ESSEX ARMS (Parts)
Box 345
Island Pond, VT 05846
Phone No.: 802-723-4313
Fax No.: 802-723-6203

EUROARMS OF AMERICA (Black Powder)
208 East Piccadilly Street
P.O. Box 3277
Winchester, VA 22604
Phone No.: 540-662-1863
Fax No.: 540-662-4464
Web site: www.euroarms.net
Email: mail@euroarms.net

EUROARMS OF AMERICA (Black Powder), cont.
Factory - Euroarms - Armi San Paolo
P.O. Box 64
I-25060 Concesio, ITALY
Fax No.: 011-39-30-218-0365

EUROPEAN AIR PISTOLS
see Top Gun Air Guns listing.

EUROPEAN AMERICAN ARMORY CORP.
P.O. Box 1299
Sharpes, FL 32953
Phone No.: 321-639-4842
Fax No.: 321-639-7006
Web site: www.eaacorp.com
Email: eaacorp@bv.net

EVOLUTION USA
P.O. Box 154
White Bird, ID 83554
Phone No.: 208-983-9208
Fax. No. 208-983-0944
Web site: www.evo-rifles.com
Email: lwoslum@camasnet.com

F.A.I.R. TECNI-MEC
Importer - See New England Arms Corp. listing.
Factory - F.A.I.R. Tecni-Mec Snc di Isidoro Rizzini & C.
Via Gitti, 41
I-25060 Marcheno (BS) ITALY
Fax No.: 011-39-30-861-0179
Web site: www.fair.it
Email: info@fair.it

F.A.V.S.
Factory – Fabbrica Armi Valle Susa
Via Nazionale Moncenisio 35
10050 Villar Focchiardo (To) ITALY
Fax No.: 011-39-9645496

FAS
No current U.S. importation - Milano, ITALY

FEG
Importer - See K.B.I., Inc. listing.
Importer - See Century International Arms, Inc. listing.
Web site: www.fegarms.com
Factory - FEGARMY
1095 Budapest, Soroksari ut 158
Levelcim: H-1440 Budapest Pf. 6 HUNGARY
Fax: 011-361-280-6669

FIAS
Fabrica Italiana Armi Sabatti
Via Volta 90
Gardone Val Trompia I-25063 ITALY
Fax No.: 011-39-30-831312

F.I.E. FIREARMS CORP. (parts/repairs only)
See the Heritage Manufacturing, Inc. and the Numrich Gun Parts Corp. listings.

FABARM S.p.A.
Importer - see Heckler & Koch listing.
Factory - Fabbrica Breciana Armi

Via Averolda 31
I-25039 Travagliato, Brescia ITALY
Fax No.: 011-39-30-6863684
Web site: www.fabarm.com

FABBRI s.n.c.
Factory

Via Dante Alighieri, 29
I-25062 Concesio (BS) ITALY
Fax No.: 011-39-030-218-7301
Web site: www.fabbri.it
Email: tullio@fabbri.it
Email: fabbri@fabbri.it

FABRIQUE NATIONALE
Factory - Browning S.A.
Fabrique Nationale Herstal SA

Parc Industriel des Hauts Sarts
3me Ave. 25
B-4040 Herstal, BELGIUM
Fax No.: 011-32-42-40-5212

FALCO, s.r.l.
Importer (select models) – see K.B.I. listing.
Factory

via Gitti, 37
I-25060 Marcheno (Brescia) ITALY
Fax No.: 011-39-30-861-267
Web site: www.intred.com/falco
Email: falco@intred.com

FAMARS di ABBIATICO & SALVINELLI srl
Distributor – Robin Hollow Outfitters

Addieville East Farm
200 B Pheasant Dr.
Mapleville, RI 02839
Phone No.: 401-568-0331
Fax No.: 401-568-0264
Web site: www.robinhollow.com
Email: RHOAddieville@aol.com
Factory

Via Valtrompia 16/18
25063 Gardone, V.T. Brescia ITALY
Fax No.: 011-39-030-8912894
Web site: www.famars.com
Email: info@famars.com

FANZOJ, JOHANN
Factory - Fanzoj GesmbH

Greisgasse 1
9170 Ferlach, AUSTRIA
Fax No.: 011-43-4227-2867
Email: jfanzoj@netway.at

FAUSTI, STEFANO SRL
Importer - See Traditions Performance Firearms listing.
Factory

Via Martiri Dell'Indipendenza, 70
I-25060 Marcheno (Brescia) ITALY
Fax No.: 011-39-30-861-0155
Web site: www.faustistefanoarms.com
Email: info@faustistefanoarms.com

FEINWERKBAU
Airguns & Firearms Importer - see Beeman Precision Airgun listing.
Factory - Westinger & Altenburger GmbH

Neckarstrasse 43
D-78727 Oberndorf/Neckar GERMANY
Fax No.: 011-49-7423/814-89
Web site: www.feinwerkbau.de

FERLACH GUNS
Ferlach Genossenschaft

Attn: Customer Service
Waagplatz 6
A-9170 Ferlach, AUSTRIA
Fax No.: 011-43-4227/3714
Email: Josef.Krainer@aon.at

FERLIB
Importer - see Dakota Arms listing.
Factory - Ferlib

Via Costa 46, Gardone 1-25063
ITALY
Fax No. 011-39-3089-12586
Web site: www.ferlib.com
Email: info@ferlib.com

FIREARMS INTERNATIONAL INC.
5200 Mitchelldale, Suite E-17
Houston, TX 77092
Phone No.: 713-462-4200
Fax No.: 713-681-5665
Web site: www.highstandard.com
Email: info@highstandard.com

FIRESTORM
Importer – SGS Imports Int'l, Inc.

1750 Brielle Ave., Unit B-1
Wanamassa, NJ 07712
Phone No.: 732-493-0302
Fax No.: 732-493-0301
Web site: www.firestorm-sgs.com
Email: firestormsgs@aol.com

FIOCCHI OF AMERICA, INC. (Ammunition & Components)
5030 Fremont Rd.
Ozark, MO 65721
Phone No.: 417-725-4118
Fax No.: 417-725-1039
Factory - Fiocchi Munizioni S.P.A.

Via Santa Barbara, 4
I-22053 Lecco ITALY
Fax No.: 011-39-341/281-171

FLODMAN GUNS SWEDEN
Skullman Enterprise AB
640 60 kers styckebruk
Jrsta SWEDEN
Fax No.: 011-46-159-30061
Web site: www.flodman.com
Email: virve@flodman.com

A.H. FOX (Current mfg. only)
Manufacturer – see Connecticut Shotgun Manufacturing Co. listing.
Older A.H. Fox Historical Research
Mr. John Callahan
53 Old Quarry Rd.
Westfield, MA 01085
$25.00 - $30.00 gun research fee.

FRANCHI, LUIGI
Importer – See Benelli USA listing.
Web site: www.franchiusa.com
Factory - Franchi, Luigi, S.p.A.
Via del Serpente, 12
I-25131 Fornaci (Brescia) ITALY
Fax No.: 011-39-30-3581554
Web site: www.franchi.com

FRANCOTTE, AUGUSTE & CIE. S.A.
Factory
Rue due 3 Juin 109
B - 4040 Herstal BELGIUM
Fax No.: 011-32-42-40-4630
Email: francotte@cybernet.Be

FRASER, DANL. & CO.
See the Dickson & MacNaughton listing.

FREEDOM ARMS
P.O. Box 150
314 Hwy. 239
Freedom, WY 83120
Phone No.: 307-883-2468
Fax No.: 307-883-2005
Web site: www.freedomarms.com
Email: freedom@freedomarms.com

GALAZAN
See Connecticut Shotgun Manufacturing Co. listing.

GALIL
No current U.S. importation.
Semi-auto configuration was banned April, 1998.

GAMBA, RENATO
Exclusive Importer and Distributor – Renato Gamba U.S.A. Corp.
Seagram Building
375 Park Ave., Ste. 208
New York, NY 10152
Phone No.: 212-980-6687
Fax No.: 212-980-3378
U.S. Service Center
33 Claremont Road
Bernardsville, NJ 07924
Phone No.: 908-766-2287
Fax No: 908-766-1068
Factory - S.A.B. s.r.l. - Renato Gamba
Via Artigiani, 91/93
I-25063 Gardone V.T. (Brescia), ITALY
Fax No.: 011-39-30-8912-180
Web site: www.renatogamba.it
Email: infocomm@renatogamba.it

GAMO USA Corp. (Airguns)
3911 S.W. 47th Avenue, Suite 914
Ft. Lauderdale, FL 33314
Phone No.: 954-581-5822
Fax No.: 954-581-3165
Email: gamousa@gate.net

GARBI
Importer - See W. L. Moore & Co. listing.
Factory - Armas Garbi
Urki, 12-14
E-20600 Eibar, SPAIN

GASTINNE RENETTE
39 Avenue Franklin D. Roosevelt
F-75008 Paris, FRANCE
Fax No.: 011-33-1-4256-2111
Email: gastinne.renette@guene.com

GATLING GUN COMPANY
Manufacturer and distributor - Furr Arms
485 South Commerce Road
Orem, UT 84058
Phone No.: 801-226-3877

GAZELLE ARMS
Hisar Avcilik & Doga Sporlasi San Ve Tic. Ltd. Sti.
Sokak No. 48
Konak/Izmir, 861
TR-35250 TURKEY
Fax No.: 011-90-0232-441-6667
Web site: www.hisarexport.com
Email: hisaras@ixir.com

GAUCHER
Factory - Armes S.A.
46, rue Desjoyaux
F-42000 Saint-Etienne, FRANCE
Fax No.: 011-33-477419572

GENTRY, DAVID - CUSTOM GUNMAKER
314 N. Hoffman
Belgrade, MT 59714
Phone No.: 406-388-GUNS

GIBBS RIFLE COMPANY, INC. (G.R.C., INC.)
211 Lawn St.
Martinsburg, WV 25401
Phone No.: 304-262-1651
Fax No.: 304-262-1658
Web site: www.gibbsrifle.com
Email: support@gibbsrifle.com

GIL, ANTONIO & CO.
Importer – See the New England Arms Corp. listing.

GLOCK, INC.
6000 Highlands Pkwy.
Smyrna, GA 30082
Fax No.: 770-433-8719
Web site: www.glock.com

GONIC ARMS INC. (Black Powder)
134 Flagg Rd
Gonic, NH 03839
Phone No.: 603-332-8456

GRANGER, G.

U.S. Agent - Jean-Jacques Perodeau

P.O. Box 3191
Woodring Municipal Airport
Enid, OK 73702
Phone No.: 580-237-7388
Fax No.: 580-242-6922

Factory

66 Cours Fauriel, 66
F-42100 St. Etienne FRANCE
Fax No.: 011-33-0477-38-66-99

GRANT, STEPHEN

Factory - see Atkin, Grant & Lang listing.

GREG MARTIN AUCTIONS

298 San Bruno Ave.
San Francisco, CA 94103
Phone No.: 800-509-1988
Phone No.: 415-522-5708
Fax No.: 415-522-5706
Web site: www.colt-auctions.com
Email: info@gmartin-auctions.com

GREENER, W. W.

Factory

One Belmont Row
GB-Birmingham, ENGLAND B4 7RE
Fax No.: 011-44-21-359-4300

GRIFFIN & HOWE

36 West 44th Street, Suite 1011
New York, NY 10036
Phone No.: 212-921-0980
Fax No.: 212-921-2327

Griffin & Howe

33 Claremont Road
Bernardsville, NJ 07924
Phone No.: 908-766-2287
Fax No.: 908-766-1068
Web site: www.griffinhowe.com
Email: prather@griffinhowe.com

GRIFFON

Importer - Griffon USA, Inc.

2513 East Loop 820 N
Ft. Worth, TX 76118
Phone No.: 817-284-7474
Fax No.: 817-284-7528
Email: griffonusa@aol.com

European Distributor

Kung GmbH
Amtshausgasse 2
Liestal, Switzerland CH-4410
Fax: 011-41-061-922-1245

Manufacturer - Continental Weapons (Pty) Ltd.

322 15th St. Randjespark
Midrand 1685, Johannesburg, South Africa
Phone No.: 011-27-11-314-5088
Fax No.: 011-27-11-314-5050

GRULLA ARMAS, S.L.

Importer - see Harry Marx Hi-Grade Import listing.
Importer & Distributor - see Lion Country Supply listing.
Importer - Kevin's - Tallahassee, FL. (double rifles only)
Importer - Dale Decoys Service - Nelsonville, OH.

GRULLA ARMAS, S.L., cont.

Factory - Grulla Armas

P.O. Box 453
Avda. de Otaola, 12
E-20600 Eibar (Guipuzcoa) SPAIN
Fax No.: 011-34-9-43-702133
Web site: www.grullarmas.com
Email: usobiaga@grullaarmas.com

GRÜNIG & ELMIGER AG

Industriestr. 22
CH-6102 Malters SWITZERLAND
Fax No.: 011-041-499-9049
Web site: www.gruenel.ch
Email: gruenel@gruenel.ch

GUN POWER (Airguns)

P.O. Box 567
Ashford, Kent, TN23 5FP ENGLAND
Phone No.: 011-44-1233-624-357

GUN SOUTH, INC. (GSI)

P.O. Box 129
7661 Commerce Lane
Trussville, AL 35173
Phone No.: 205-655-8299
Fax No.: 205-655-7078
Web site: www.GSIfirearms.com
Email: info@GSIfirearms.com

G.U. INC.

See SKB Shotguns listing.

GUSTAF, CARL

See Carl Gustaf listing.

HHF

Importer – Armsco

2250 East Devon Ave., Ste. 213
Des Plaines, IL 60018-4509
Phone No.: 847-768-1000
Fax No.: 847-768-1001
Web site: www.armsco.net
Email: info@armsco.net

Factory - Huglu Tfekleri Kooperatifi AV

Antalya Caddesi no 58
TR-42710 Huglu/Besehir/Konya TURKEY
Fax No.: 011-90-332-516-1032

HJS ARMS, INC.

P.O. Box 3711
Brownsville, TX 78523-3711
Phone No.: 800-453-2767

H & R 1871, LLC

Harrington & Richardson (post-1991 mfg. only)

60 Industrial Rowe
Gardner, MA 01440
Phone No.: 978-632-9393
Fax No.: 978-632-2300
Web site: www.hr1871.com
Email: hr1871@hr1871.com

H-S PRECISION, INC.

1301 Turbine Dr.
Rapid City, SD 57703
Phone No.: 605-341-3006
Fax No.: 605-342-8964
Web site: www.hsprecision.com

HASBSBURG, LINIE
Griegasse 3
A-9170 Ferlach Austria
Email: jfanzoj@netway.at
Email: peterhofer@hoferwaffen.com

HAENEL (Airguns)
Importer - See Gun South, Inc. listing.

HAMBRUSCH JAGDWAFFEN GmbH
Importer - CONCO Arms International
P.O. Box 159
Emmaus, PA 18049
Fax No.: 610-967-5477
Factory - Hambrusch Jagdwaffen Gesellschaft
Gartengasse 4
A-9170 Ferlach, AUSTRIA
Fax No.: 011-43-4227/4106
Web site: www.ferlachguns.com
Email: hambrush@ferlachguns.com

HÄMMERLI AG
Importer – see SIG Arms Inc. listing
Web site: www.sigarms.com
Importer – see Champion's Choice listing.
Importer, Sales & Service – Larry's Guns Inc.
49 Hawthorne Street
Portland, ME 04103
Phone No.: 207-772-0998
Fax No.: 207-772-0628
Web site: www.larrysguns.com
Importer - Gunsmithing Inc.
30 West Buchanan Street
Colorado Springs, CO 80907
Phone No.: 800-284-8671
Fax No.: 719-632-3493
Web site: www.nealjguns.com
Email: neal@nealjguns.com
Factory - Hämmerli AG
37 Seoner Strasse
CH-5600 Lenzburg SWITZERLAND
Fax No.: 011-41-62-888-2200
Web site: www.haemmerli.ch
Email: info@haemmerli.ch

HARRY MARX HI-GRADE IMPORTS
8707 Monterey Road
P.O. Box 519
6720 Bearcat Road
Gilroy, CA 95020
Phone No.: 408-842-9301
Phone No.: 408-842-7270
Fax No.: 408-842-9323
Fax No.: 408-842-7270
Web site: www.hi-gradeimports.com
Email: Hi-gradeimports@mindspring.com

HARTMANN & WEISS GmbH
Rahlstedter Bahnhofstr. 47
22143 Hamburg, GERMANY
Phone No.: 011-49-40-677-5585
Fax No.: 011-49-40-677-5592

KARL HAUPTMANN JAGDWAFFEN
Bahnhofstrasse 5
A-9170 Ferlach, AUSTRIA
Fax: 011-43-4227-3435
Web site: www.hauptmann-rifles.com
Email: office@hauptmann-rifles.com

HASKELL MFG. INC.
See Hi-Point listing.

HECKLER & KOCH, INC.
U.S. Headquarters
21480 Pacific Blvd.
Sterling, VA 20166-8903
Phone No.: 703-450-1900
Fax No.: 703-450-8160
Web site: www.hecklerkoch-usa.com
Factory - Heckler & Koch GmbH
Alte Steige 7
P.O. Box 1329
D-78727 Oberndorf Neckar GERMANY
Fax No.: 011-49-7423-7922-80
Web site: www.heckler-koch.de

HEINIE SPECIALTY PRODUCTS
301 Oak Street
Quincy, IL 62301
Phone No.: 217-228-952
Fax No.: 217-228-9502
Web site: www.heinie.com
Email: rheinie@heinie.com

HENDRY, RAMSAY & WILCOX
55/57 North Methven Street
Perth PH1 5PX, SCOTLAND
Phone No.: 01-738-623679
Fax No.: 01-738-443327

HENRY, ALEX
See the Dickson & MacNaughton listing.

HENRY REPEATING ARMS
110 8th St.
Brooklyn, NY 11215
Phone No.: 718-499-5600
Fax No.: 718-768-8056
Web site: www.henryrepeating.com

HERITAGE MANUFACTURING, INC.
4600 NW 135th St.
Opa Locka, FL 33054
Phone No.: 305-685-5966
Fax No.: 305-687-6721
Web site: www.heritagemfg.com
Email: infohmi@heritagemfg.com

HESSE ARMS
9487 Inver Grove Trail
Inver Grove Heights, MN 55076-3718
Phone No: 651-455-5760
Web site: www.hessearms.com
Email: HesseArms@Juno.com

HEYM Waffenfabrik GmbH

Importer - see New England Custom Gun Service Ltd. listing.

Factory

Am Aschenbach 2
D-98646 Gleichamberg GERMANY
Fax No.: 011-49-368-75-63222
Web site: www.heym-waffenfabrik.de
Email: heym-waffenfabrik@t-online.de

HI-POINT FIREARMS

U.S. Marketer - MKS Supply, Inc.

8611-A North Dixie Drive
Dayton, OH 45414
Phone No.: 937-454-0363
Fax No.: 937-454-0503
Web site: www.hi-pointFirearms.com
Email: mkshpoint@aol.com

HIGH STANDARD MANUFACTURING CO.

5200 Mitchelldale, Ste. E17
Houston, TX 77092
Phone No.: 713-462-4200
Fax No.: 713-681-5665
Web site: www.highstandard.com
Email: info@highstandard.com

HIGH-TECH CUSTOM RIFLES

3102 Beacon Street
Colorado Spings, CO 80907
Phone/Fax No.: 719-634-4309
Email: htcustoms@pcisys.net

HILL COUNTRY RIFLE COMPANY

5726 Morningside Dr.
New Braunfels, TX 78132
Phone No.: 830-609-3139
Fax No.: 830-625-4020
Web site: www.hillcountryrifle.com
Email: matt@hillcountryrifle.com

GEORGE HOENIG INC.

6521 Morton Dr.
Boise, ID 83704
Phone No.: 208-375-1116

HOFER-JAGDWAFFEN, PETER

Kirchgasse 24
A-9170 Ferlach, AUSTRIA
Phone No.: 011-43-4227-3683
Fax No.: 011-43-4227-3683-30
Web site: www.hoferwaffen.com
Email: peterhofer@hoferwaffen.com

P.L. HOLEHAN, INC.

5758 E. 34th St.
Tucson, AZ 85711
Phone No.: 520-745-0622
Fax No.: 520-745-2248
Email: plholehan@juno.com

HOLLAND & HOLLAND LTD.

H&H – U.S.

50 East 57th Street
New York, NY 10022
Phone No.: 212-752-7755
Fax No.: 212-752-6805
Web site: www.hollandandholland.com
Email: nygunroom@aol.com

HOLLAND & HOLLAND LTD., cont.

H&H - France

29 Avenue Victo Hugo
F-75116 Paris FRANCE
Phone No.: 011-133-450-22200

Factory

Attn: Customer Service-BB
31-33 Bruton Street
London, ENGLAND W1X 8JS
Phone No.: 011-44-71-499 4411
Fax No.: 011-44-71-499 4544
Email: gunroom@holland-holland.co.uk

HOLLOWAY & NAUGHTON

See Premier English Shotguns, Ltd. listing.

HORTON, LEW, DIST. CO.

See Lew Horton Dist. Co. listing.

HOWA

Importer – see Legacy Sports International, LLC listing.

HUGLU

Importer – Huglu USA

P.O. Box 141
Rigby, ID 83442
Phone No.: 208-538-6744
Web site: www.huglushotgunsusa.com
Email: HugluUSA@srv.net

Factory – Huglu Shotguns, Inc.

Cumhuriyet Mh. Tepebasi Sk. No.: 22
Huglu-Beysehir-Konya TR-42710 TURKEY
Phone No.: 011-90-332-516-1703
Fax No.: 011-90-332-516-1074
Web site: www.huglushotguns.com
Email: contact@huglushotguns.com

HUG-SAN

Tfekleri San. Tic. A.S.

Huglu Beysehir Konya TURKEY
Fax No.: 011-90-331-516-15-06

I.A.B.

Factory - Industria Armi Bresciane

Via 1 Maggio, 39
Sarezzo Brescia 1-25068 ITALY
Phone/Fax No.: 011-39-3080-0313
Web site: www.iabarms.com
Email: info@iabarms.com

IAI

Please refer to Intrac Arms International LLC listing.

IAI - ISRAEL ARMS INTERNATIONAL, INC.

American Legends

1085 Gessner Road #F
Houston, TX 77036
Phone No.: 713-789-0745
Fax No.: 713-789-7513
Web site: www.israelarms.com
Email: iaipro@wt.net

IAR, INC.

33171 Camino Capistrano
San Juan Capistrano, CA 92675
Phone No.: 949-443-3642
Fax No.: 949-443-3647
Web site: www.iar-arms.com
Email: sales@iar-arms.com

IGA SHOTGUNS
Importer - See Stoeger Industries, Inc. listing.

IBERIA FIREARMS
See Hi-Point listing.

INFINITY FIREARMS
Manufacturer - Strayer Voight, Inc.
3435 Roy Orr Blvd., Ste. 200
Grand Prairie, TX 75050
Phone No.: 972-513-1911
Fax No.: 972-513-0575
Web site: www.sviguns.com
Factory - INTERTEX-Maschinenbau GmbH & Co.
Ludwigstrasse 24-28
D-73054 Eislingen GERMANY
Fax no.: 011-49-7161-98-40-5-50
Email: intertex@t-online.de

INTRAC ARMS INTERNATIONAL L.L.C.
Importation & Distribution only - U.S. Headquarters
HS America
5005 Chapman Highway
Knoxville, TN 37920
Phone No.: 865-573-0065
Fax No.: 865-579-0937
Web site: www.hsarms.com
Email: Defence@TDS.net
European Headquarters
Schlossgasse 12
A-2540 Bad Vuslau, AUSTRIA
Fax No. 011-43-2252-78897

INVESTARM, s.p.a.
Factory - Fabbrica D'Armi
25060 Marcheno, via Zanardelli, 210
Brescia ITALY
Fax No.: 011-39-30-861-285
Web site: www.investarm.com
Email: info@investarm.com

INVESTMENT ARMS INC.
4631 South Mason, Ste. B3
Fort Collins, CO 80525
Phone No.: 888-708-4867
Phone No.: 800-809-4867

ISRAELI MILITARY INDUSTRIES
No current information available.

ITHACA CLASSIC DOUBLES
The Old Station
No. 5 Railroad St.
Victor, NY 14564
Phone No.: 716-924-2710
Fax No.: 716-924-2737
Web site: www.gunshop.com/ithaca_classic.htm
Email: ithacadoubles@gunshop.com

ITHACA GUN COMPANY, LLC
901 Route 34B
King Ferry, NY 13081
Phone No.: 888-9-ITHACA
Phone No.: 315-364-7171
Fax No.: 315-364-5134
Web site: www.ithacagun.com

IZHMASH
Importer & Distributor – European American Armory listing.
Distributor - L.A. Austin International, Inc.
14416 W. Powderhorn Dr.
Surprise, AZ 85374-3811
Phone No.: 623-584-5016
Email: laaustininter@email.msn.com
Distributor - Interstate Arms Corp.
6G Dunham Road
Billerica, MA 01821
Phone No.: 800-243-3006
Importer - Kalashnikov USA, Ltd.
1053 SE Holbrook Ct. #D-1
Port St. Lucie, FL 34952-3431
Web site: www.weapons-russian.com
Email: weapons@weapons-russian.com
Factory
Izhmash, Concern OJSC
R-426006. 3, proezd, Deryabina
Izhevsk, RUSSIA
Web site: www.izhmash.ru
Email: itc@izhmash.ru

JMC FABRICATION & MACHINE, INC.
Firearms Division
396 Gus Hipp Blvd.
Rockledge, FL 32955
Phone No.: 407-636-1943
Fax No.: 407-632-1040
Web site: www.safefuel.com/bfg

JP ENTERPRISES, INC.
7605 N. 128th Street
White Bear Lake, MN 55110
Phone No.: 651-426-9196
Fax No.: 651-426-2472
Website: www.jpar15.com
Email: jpar15@aol.com

J R DISTRIBUTING
15634 Tierra Rejada Rd.
Moorpark, CA 93021
Fax No.: 805-529-2368

JAGD–UND SPORTWAFFEN SUHL GmbH (MERKEL)
Importer - See Gun South, Inc. listing.
Factory - See Merkel listing.

JACK FIRST, INC.
Gun Parts/Accessories/Service
1201 Turbine Dr.
Rapid City, SD 57701
Phone No.: 605-343-8481

JAMES D. JULIA, INC. (Auctions)
P.O. Box 830, Rte. 201
Skowhegan Rd.
Fairfield, ME 04937
Phone No.: 207-453-7125
Fax No.: 207-453-2502
Web site: www.juliaauctions.com
Email: juliagun@juliaauctions.com

JANZ GmbH
Factory - JANZ-Labortechnik GmbH

Ltjenburger Str. 84
D-23714 Malente/Holst. GERMANY
Fax: 011-49-045-23-6968
Web site: www.jrl.de
Email: info@jrl.de

JARRETT RIFLES, INC.
383 Brown Road
Jackson, SC 29831
Phone No.: 803-471-3616
Fax No.: 803-471-9246
Web site: www.jarrettrifles.com
Email: jarrett@groupz.net

JENNINGS, B.L., INC.
See Bryco Arms listing.

JOHANNSEN RIFLES
Importer - Johannsen, Inc.

438 Willow Brook Road
Plainfield, NH 03781
Phone No.: 603-469-3450
Fax No.: 603-469-3471
Email: bestguns@cyberportal.net
Factory – Reimer Johannsen GmbH

Haart 49
D-24534 Neumnster GERMANY
Fax: 011-39-043-21-29325
Web site: www.johannsen-jagd.de
Email: info@johannsen-jagd.de

JUST, JOSEF
Hauptplatz 18
A-9170, Ferlach, AUSTRIA
Fax: 011-41-04227-4284
Web site: www.ferlacherjagdwaffen.at/just

K.B.I., INC.
P.O. Box 6625
5480 Linglestown Road
Harrisburg, PA 17112-0625
Phone No.: 717-540-8518
Fax No.: 717-540-8567
Web site: www.kbi-inc.com
Email: sales@kbi-inc.com

KDF, INC.
2485 Highway 46 North
Seguin, TX 78155
Phone No.: 830-379-8141
Fax No.: 830-379-5420

KAHNKE GUNWORKS (Black Powder)
206 West 11th
Redwood Falls, MN 56283
Fax No.: 507-637-2971

KAHR ARMS
d/b/a of Saelio, Inc.

P.O. Box 220
Blauvelt, NY 10913
Customer Service phone no.: 508-795-3919
Sales phone No.: 845-353-7770
Fax No.: 845-353-7833
Web site: www.kahr.com
Email: kahrhq@compuserve.com

KEL-TEC CNC INDUSTRIES, INC.
1485 Cox Road
Cocoa, FL 32926
Phone No.: 407-631-0068
Fax No.: 407-631-1169
Web site: www.kel-tec.com
Email: aimkeltec@aol.com

KEMEN
Importer – See New England Custom Gun Service listing.
Importer - Fieldsport

3313 W. South Airport Road
Traverse City, MI 49684
Phone No.: 616-933-0767
Phone No.: 616-933-0768
Factory - Armas Kemen, S.L.

Ermuraranbide, 14 - Apartado n. 60
20870 Elgoibar (Guipuzcoa), SPAIN
Fax No.: 011-34-43-74-4401
Web site: www.sport-kemen.com
Email: kemen@sport-kemen.com

KEPPELER TECHNISCHE ENTWICKLUNG GmbH
Friedrich-Reinhardt Strasse 4
D-74427 Fichtenberg, GERMANY
Fax No.: 011-49-7971-91-1243
Email: Keppeler.TE@t-online.de

KIMAR SRL
Via Fornaci, 66/A
25131 Brescia - Italy
Phone No.: 011.39.030.3581174
Fax No.: 011.39.030.3580109
Web site: www.kimar.com
Email: info@kimar.com

KIMBER
Corporate Offices - Kimber Mfg., Inc.

1 Lawton St.
Yonkers, NY 10705
Phone No.: 800-880-2418
Fax No.: 406-758-2223
Custom Shop Phone No.: 914-964-0742
Web site: www.kimberamerica.com
Email: info@kimberamerica.com

KING'S GUN WORKS INC.
1837 West Glenoaks Blvd.
Glendale, CA 91201
Phone No.: 818-956-6010
Fax No.: 818-548-8606
Web site: www.kingsgunworks.com
Email: kngswks@earthlink.net

KNIGHTS MANUFACTURING CO. (KMC)
7750 9th St. S.W.
Vero Beach, FL 32968
Phone No.: 561-562-5697
Fax No. 561-569-2955
Email: kacsr25@aol.com

KNIGHTS RIFLES (Black Powder)
P.O. Box 130, 21852 Hwy. J46
Centerville, IA 52544
Phone No.: 515-856-2626
Fax No.: 515-856-2628
Web site: www.knightrifles.com

KORA BRNO

Factory - Kroko a.s.

Hybesova 46
CZ-60200 Brno, Czech Republic
Fax no.: 011-42-0543244346
Web site: www.korabrno.cz
Email: kroko@korabrno.cz

KORRIPHILA

Importer – Korriphila, Inc.

1100 Culp Road
Pineville, NC 28134
Phone No.: 704-587-0068
Fax No.: 704-587-0079
Email: info@korriphila.com

Factory - INTERTEX-Maschinenbau GmbH & Co.

Ludwigstrasse 24-28
D-73054 Eislingen GERMANY
Fax no.: 011-49-7161-98-40-5-50
Email: intertex@t-online.de

KORTH

Importer – Korth USA (division of Earl's Repair Service, Inc.)

437 Chandler Street (rear)
Tewksbury, MA 01876
Phone No.: 978-851-2656
Fax No.: 978-851-9462
Web site: www.korthusa.com

Factory - Korth Vertriebsgesellschaft GmbH

Robert Bosch Strasse 4
D-23909 Ratzeburg, GERMANY
Fax No.: 011-49-45-4182479

KRICO

Distributor - see Precision Sales Int'l listing.
Factory - Krico Jagd-und Sportwaffen GmbH

Nrnberger Strasse 6
Pyrbaum, D-90602 GERMANY
Fax No.: 011-49-091-80-2661
Web site: www.krico.de
Email: omlon@krico.de

KRIEGHOFF, H., GUN CO.

Importer - Krieghoff Intl., Inc.

P.O. Box 549
7528 Easton Rd.
Ottsville, PA 18942
Phone No.: 610-847-5173
Fax No.: 610-847-8691
Web site: www.krieghoff.com
Email: info@krieghoff.com

Factory - H. Krieghoff GmbH

Boschstrasse 22
D-89079 Ulm, GERMANY
Fax No.: 011-49-731-40-18270
Web site: www.krieghoff.de

KUFSTEINER WAFFENSTUBE

Ing. Hannes Kepplinger
Carl-Wagner-Strasse 1
A-6330 Kufstein, AUSTRIA
Fax No.: 011-43-5372-61887

L.A.R. MANUFACTURING, INC.

4133 West Farm Road
West Jordan, UT 84088-4997
Phone No.: 801-280-3505
Fax No.: 801-280-1972
Web site: www.largrizzly.com
Email: guns@largrizzly.com

S.R. LAMBOY & CO., INC.

The Old Station
5 Railroad Street
Victor, NY 14564
Phone No.: 716-924-2710
Fax No.: 716-924-2737
Web site: www.gunshop.com

LANBER ARMAS S.A.

Importer - Wingshooting Adventures

O-1845 West Leonard
Grand Rapids, MI 49544-9510
Phone No.: 616-677-1980
Fax No.: 616-677-1986

Factory - ComLanber, S.A.

Attn: Customer Service-BB
Zubiaurre, 5 - Apdo. 3
E-42850 Zaldibar SPAIN
Fax No.: 011-34-4-6827999

LANG, JOSEPH

See the Atkin, Grant & Lang listing.

LAURONA

Factory - Armas Laurona S.A.L.

P.O. Box 260, Avda de Otaola, 25
E-20600 Eibar (Guipuzcoa) SPAIN
Fax No.: 011-34-43-700616

HARRY LAWSON

3328 N. Richey Blvd.
Tucson, AZ 85716
Phone no.: 520-326-1117

LAZZERONI ARMS COMPANY

P.O. Box 26696
Tucson, AZ 85726-6696
Phone No.: 888-492-7247
Fax No.: 520-624-4250
Web site: www.lazzeroni.com
Email: arms@lazzeroni.com

LEBEAU-COURALLY

Importer - see William Larkin Moore & Co. listing.
Factory - Aug. Lebeau-Courally

386, rue Saint-Gilles
B-4000 Liege, BELGIUM
Fax No.: 011-32-41-52-2008

LEGACY SPORTS INTERNATIONAL LLC

206 South Union Street
Alexandria, VA 22314
Phone No.: 703-548-4837
Fax No.: 703-549-7826
Web Site: www.legacysports.com

LEITNER-WISE RIFLE CO.

1033 North Fairfax St., Ste. 402
Alexandria, VA 22314
Phone No.: 703-837-9390
Fax No.: 703-837-9686
Web site: www.leitner-wise.com
Email: info@leitner-wise.com

LES BAER CUSTOM, INC.

29601 34th Avenue N.
Hillsdale, IL 61257
Phone No.: 309-658-2716
Fax No.: 309-658-2610
Web site: www.lesbaer.com
Email: lesbaer@netexpress.net

LEW HORTON DISTRIBUTING CO.

Distributor Only
15 Walkup Dr., P.O. Box 5023
Westboro, MA 01581
Phone No.: 508-366-7400
Fax No.: 508-366-5332
Web site: www.lewhorton.com
Email: 1horton@tiac.net

LIBERTY

Importer and Distributor - see K.B.I. listing.
Web site: www.libertyarms.com

LION COUNTRY SUPPLY

P.O. Box 480
Port Matilda, PA 16870
Phone No.: 800-662-5202
Fax No.: 814-684-5900
Web site: www.ugartechea.com

LITTLE JOHN'S AUCTION SERVICE

1740 W. LaVeta Ave.
Orange, CA 92868
Phone No.: 714-939-1170
Fax No.: 714-939-7955
Web site: www.littlejohnsauctionservice.com
Email: Ltljohns@aol.com

LITTLE SHARPS RIFLE MFG.

Mr. Aaron Pursley
HC 76 Box 1037
Big Sandy, MT 59520
Phone No.: 406-378-3200
Mr. Ronald Otto
P.O. Box 336
Big Sandy, MT 59520
Phone No.: 406-378-3855

LJUTIC INDUSTRIES, INC.

732 North 16th Ave., Ste. 22
Yakima, WA 98902
Phone No.: 509-248-0476
Fax No.: 509-576-8233
Web site: www.ljuticgun.com
Email: ljuticgun@earthlink.net

LLAMA

Master Distributor - Import Sports, Inc.
1750 Brielle Ave., Unit B-1
Wanamassa, NJ 07712
Phone No.: 732-493-0302
Fax No.: 732-493-0301
Web site: www.bersa-llama.com
Email: gsodini@aol.com
Factory - Llama Gabilondo Y Cia, S.A.
P.O. Box 290
E-01013 Vitoria (Alava) SPAIN
Fax no.: 011-34-45-26-2444

LONE STAR RIFLE CO., INC.

11231 Rose Road
Conroe, TX 77303
Phone/Fax No.: 936-856-3363
Web site: www.lonestarrifle.com
Email: dave@lonestarrifle.com

LUCCHINI, SANDRO

North American Sales – Springbrook Manufacturing Ltd.
3809 Ninth St. SE
Calgary, AB T2G 3C7 CANADA
Phone No.: 403-243-3308
Fax No.: 403-243-3762
Web site: www.sbm-mangrove.com
Email: sbm-info@sbm-mangrove.com
Factory - Lucchini, Sandro
25060 Ponte Zanano V.T.
Via Petrarca, 47
Sarezzo (Brescia), ITALY
Fax no.: 011-39-30-89-11573

LU-MAR S.R.L.

Factory - Lu-Mar s.rl. ARMI
Via Artigiani 11
I-25063 Gardone, (BS) ITALY
Fax No.: 011-39-30-891-1185
Web site: www.lu-mar.it
Email: info@lu-mar.it

M-K SPECIALTIES

Rt. 3, Box 470
Grafton, WV 26354
Phone No.: 304-265-3675
Fax No.: 304-265-0373
Web site: www.m-kspecialties.com
Email: mkspecialties@mindspring.com

M.O.A. CORPORATION

2451 Old Camden Pike
Eaton, OH 45320
Phone No.: 937-456-3669
Fax No.: 937-456-9331
Web site: www.moaguns.com

MTs ARMS

Factory
Sporting & Hunting Guns Central Design & Research Bureau
17 Krasnoarmeysky Prospekt
R-300041 Tula, RUSSIA
Fax No. : 011-7-0872-31-5959
Web site: www.home.tula.net/tularms
Email: tularms@tulsa.net

MAADI-GRIFFIN CO.
2812 N. 34th Place
Mesa, AZ 85213-5625
Phone No.: 480-325-5623
Fax No.: 480-325-5625
Web site: www.maadigriffin.com
Email: griffin@doitnow.com

JAMES MacNAUGHTON & SONS
See the Dickson & MacNaughton listing.

MAGNUM RESEARCH, INC.
7110 University Ave. NE
Minneapolis, MN 55432
Phone No.: 763-574-1868
Fax No.: 763-574-0109
Web site: www.magnumresearch.com

MAGTECH AMMUNITION CO., INC.
6845 20th Ave. S., Ste. 120
Centerville, MN 55038
Phone No.: 651-762-8500
Fax No.: 651-429-9485
Web site: www.magtechammunition.com

MAJESTIC ARMS, LTD.
101A Ellis St.
Staten Island, NY 10307
Phone No.: 718-356-6765
Fax No.: 718-356-6835
Web site: www.majesticarms.com
Email: majesticarms@juno.com

MAKAROV
Importer - See Century International Arms listing.

MANDALL SHOOTING SUPPLIES
3616 N. Scottsdale Rd.
Scottsdale, AZ 85252
Phone No.: 480-945-2553
Fax No.: 480-949-0734

MANU-ARM
B.P. 8 – 43, avenue de la liberation
F-42340, Veauche, FRANCE
Fax No.: 011-33-0477-947936
Web site: www.manuarm.fr
Email: manuarm@manuarm.fr

MANUFRANCE
6, Rue de Lodi
F-42000 St. Etienne 1 FRANCE
Fax No.: 011-33-0477-418830
Email: manufrance@wanadoo.fr

MANURHIN REVOLVERS
Factory – Manufacture d. Armes de tir Chapuis –
M.A.T.C.H.
Z.I. La Gravoux, BP 15
F-42380 St. Bonnet le Chateau, FRANCE
Fax No.: 011-33-4-77/501070
Web site: www.chapuis-armes.com
Email: info@chapuis-armes.com

MARCEL THYS & SONS
U.S. Agent - Jean-Jacques Perodeau
P.O. Box 3191
Woodring Municipal Airport
Enid, OK 73702
Phone No.: 580-237-7388
Fax No.: 580-242-6922
Factory
Rue de Villers, 8
B-4367 Crisne BELGIUM
Fax No.: 011-32-4-240-1718
Web site: www.marcelthys.com
Email: info@marcelthys.com

MARKSMAN (Airguns)
5482 Argosy Drive
Huntington Beach, CA 92649
Fax No.: 714-891-0782

MARLIN FIREARMS COMPANY
100 Kenna Drive
P.O. Box 248
North Haven, CT 06473-0905
Phone No.: 203-239-5621
Fax No.: 203-234-7991
Web Site: www.marlinfireams.com

MAROCCHI SHOTGUNS
Distributor - see Precision Sales Int.'l Inc. listing.
Factory - C.D. Europe SRL
Via Galilei, 6
I-25068 Sarezzo (Brescia) ITALY
Fax No.: 011-39-30/890-0370
Web site: www.classicdoubles.com
Email: info@classicdoubles.com

MARTIN, ALEX
See the Dickson & MacNaughton listing.

MASTERPIECE ARMS, INC.
217 Brumbelow Road
Carrollton, GA 30117
Phone No.: 770-832-9430
Fax No.: 770-832-3495
Email: vickyb@pencinc.com

MATCHGUNS srl
Via cartiera 6/d
I-43010 Vigatto, Parma ITALY
Fax No: 011-0524631973

MATCH GRADE ARMS & AMMUNITION
6030 Treaschwig
Spring, TX 77373
Phone No.: 281-821-8282
Fax No.: 281-821-2775
Web site: www.matchgradearms.com
Email: mgarms@swbell.net

MATEBA
Importer – see AWA International listing.
Factory – Mateba srl
Via Villa Serafina, 2B
I-27100 Pavia ITALY
Fax: 011-39-0382-472118
Web site: www.mateba-arms.com

MATHELON ARMES

Rue de l'Artisanat
Zone Industrielle
F-74150 Rumilly FRANCE
Fax No.: 011-33-4-50-016786
Email: induspo@wanadoo.fr

MAUSER

Importer – see SIG Arms listing.
Factory – Mauser Jagdwaffen GmbH

Ziegelstadel 1
D-88316 Isny, GERMANY
Fax No.: 011-490-368-4750794
Web site: www.mauserwaffen.de
Email: postmaster@mauserwaffen.de

MAVERICK ARMS, INC.

See Mossberg listing.

McMILLAN BROS RIFLE CO., INC.

1638 W. Knudsen Dr. #102
Phoenix, AZ 85027
Phone No.: 623-582-3713
Fax No.: 623-582-3930
Email: mcbros@mcmfamily.com
Web site: www.mcmfamily.com

MEDWELL & PERRETT LIMITED

Nicks Lane, Brome
Suffolk, ENGLAND IP23 8AN
Fax No.: 011-44-01379-870777
Email: nicky@medwellandperrett.com

MERKEL

Importer - see Gun South, Inc. listing.
Factory - Suhler Jagd-und Sportwaffen GmbH

Schtzenstrasse 26
D-98527 Suhl, GERMANY
Fax No.: 011-49-3681-854-203
Web site: www.merkel-waffen.de

MIL-SPEC INDUSTRIES CORP.

10 Mineola Avenue
Roslyn Heights, NY 11577
Phone No.: 516-625-5787
Fax No.: 516-625-0988
Web site: www.milspecindustries.com
Email: info@mil-spec-industries.com

MILLER, DAVID

See David Miller Co. listing.

MIROKU FIREARMS MFG. CO.

537-1 Shinohara
Nangoku City
Kochi, JAPAN

MITCHELL ARMS, INC.

P.O. Box 20855
Fountain Valley, CA 92728
Phone No.: 714-751-5258
Fax No.: 714-593-6971
Web site: www.mitchellsales.com
Email: gunfighter@surfside.net

MODERN MUZZLELOADING, INC. (Black Powder)

PO Box 130-CAT
Centerville, IA 52544
Fax No.: 515-856-2628

MOLL, M.F.

Steins Strasse 101
D-41199 Moenchengladbach GERMANY
Fax No.: 01149-2166-997091

MONTANA ARMORY, INC.

See C. Sharps Arms Co. Inc. listing.

MOORE, W.L. & CO.

See William Larkin Moore & Co. listing.

MORAVIA

See Arms Moravia listing.

MORINI

Importer - see Nygord Precision Products listing.
Importer – see Pilkington Competition Equipment LLC listing.
Factory - Morini Competition Arm SA

Casella Postale 92
CH-6930 Bedano SWITZERLAND
Fax No.: 011-41-91-9-45-1502
Web site: www.morini.ch
Email: morini@bluewin.ch

MORTIMER, THOMAS

See the Dickson & MacNaughton listing.

MOSSBERG

O.F. Mossberg & Sons, Inc.

7 Grasso Ave., P.O. Box 497
North Haven, CT 06473-9844
Phone No.: 203-230-5300
Fax No.: 203-230-5420

Factory Service Center - OFM Service Department

Eagle Pass Industrial Park
Industrial Blvd.
Eagle Pass, TX 78853
Phone No.: 800-989-4867
Web site: www.mossberg.com
Email: service@mossberg.com

MOUNTAIN RIFLERY

1775 North Elk Road
Pocatello, ID 83204
Phone No.: 208-234-7142

MOUNTAIN STATES MUZZLELOADING SUPPLY (Black Powder)

P.O. Box 324
Williamstown, WV 26187
Phone No.: 304-295-6959
Fax No.: 304-295-8166
Web site: www.msmfg.com
Email: msminc@msmfg.com

MOWREY GUN WORKS (Black Powder)

See Cheney Rifle Works/Lehman Rifles
Distributor - See Mountain States Muzzleloading Supply listing.

MUSGRAVE

No current information available.

NATIONAL WILD TURKEY FEDERATION

P.O. Box 530
Edgefield, SC 29824
Phone No.: 803-637-3106
Fax No.: 803-637-0034
Email: NWTF@nwtf.net

NAVY ARMS CO.
815 22nd St.
Union City, NJ 07087
Phone No.: 201-863-7100
Fax No.: 201-863-8770
Web site: www.navyarms.com
Email: info@navyarms.com

NELSON, P.V., (GUNMAKERS)
Folly Meadow, Hammersley Lane
Penn, Bucks
HP10 8HF, ENGLAND
Phone/Fax No.: 011-44-49-4812836

NESIKA
Nesika Bay Precision, Inc.
5809 NE Minder Rd. #8
Poulsbo, WA 98370
Phone No.: 360-297-5555
Fax No.: 360-297-3973

NEW ENGLAND ARMS, CORP.
P.O. Box 278, #6 Lawrence Lane
Kittery Point, ME 03905-0278
Phone No.: 207-439-0593
Fax No.: 207-439-6726
Web site: www.newenglandarms.com
Email: info@newenglandarms.com

NEW ENGLAND CUSTOM GUN SERVICE LTD. (NECG)
438 Willow Brook Rd.
Plainfield, NH 03781
Phone No.: 603-469-3450
Fax No.: 603-469-3471
Web site: www.newenglandcustomgun.com
Email: bestguns@cyberportal.net

NEW ENGLAND FIREARMS
60 Industrial Rowe
Gardner, MA 01440
Phone No.: 978-632-9393
Fax No.: 978-632-2300
Web site: www.newenglandfirearms.com
Email: hr1871@tiac.net

NEW ULTRA LIGHT ARMS LLC
1024 Grafton Road
Morgantown, WV 26508
Phone No.: 304-292-0600
Fax No.: 304-292-9662

NORICA-FARMI S.L.A. (Airguns)
Avda. Otaola, 16
Eibar, Guipuzcoa, SPAIN 26000
Fax No.: 011-34-943-207-449

NORINCO
Importer - Norinco Sports U.S.A.
P.O. Box 5575
Diamond Bar, CA 91765
Phone: 888-887-7381
Fax No.: 909-598-8819

NORSMAN SPORTING ARMS
1919 5th Ave.
P.O. Box 500
Havre, MT 59501
Phone No.: 406-262-2403
Web site: www.norsmansportingarms.com
Email: norsman@ttc-cmc.net

NORTHWEST ARMS
Please refer to Wilkinson Arms listing.

NORTH AMERICAN ARMS, INC.
2150 South, 950 East
Provo, UT 84606-6285
Phone No.: 801-374-9990
Fax No.: 801-374-9998
Customer Service and Custom Shop: 800-821-5783
Web site: www.naaminis.com

NOWLIN MFG. INC.
20622 4092 Rd., Unit B
Claremore, OK 74017
Phone No.: 918-342-0689
Fax No.: 918-342-0624
Web site: www.nowlinguns.com
Email: nowlinguns@msn.com

NUMRICH GUN PARTS CORP.
Parts supplier only
226 Williams Lane
P.O. Box 299
W. Hurley, NY 12491
Phone No.: 845-679-2417
Fax No.: 877-486-7278
Web site: www.e-gunparts.com
Email: info@gunpartscorp.com

NYGORD PRECISION PRODUCTS, INC.
P.O. Box 12578
Prescott, AZ 86304
Phone No.: 928-717-2315
Fax No.: 928-717-2198
Web site: www.nygord-precision.com
Email: nygords@northlink.com

O.D.I.
Essex Arms (Parts only)
Box 345
Island Pond, VT 05846
Phone No.: 802-723-4313

OCTOBER COUNTRY
P.O. Box 969
Hayden, ID 83835-0969
Phone No.: 208-772-2068
Fax No.: 208-772-9230

OHIO ORDNANCE WORKS, INC.
P.O. Box 687
Chardon, OH 44024
Phone No.: 440-285-3481
Fax No.: 440-286-8571
Web site: www.ohioordnanceworks.com

OLD TOWN STATION LTD. (Online Auctions)

P.O.B. 14040
Lenexa, KS 66285
Phone No.: 913-492-3000
Fax No.: 913-492-3022
Web site: www.armsbid.com
Email: armsbid@aol.com

OLYMPIC ARMS, INC.

624 Old Pacific Hwy. S.E.
Olympia, WA 98513
Phone No.: 360-459-7940
Fax No.: 360-491-3447
Web site: www.olyarms.com
Email: info@olyarms.com

OMEGA WEAPONS SYSTEMS, INC.

Distributor - Defense Technology, Inc.
P.O. Box 482
Lake Forest, CA 92630
Phone No.: 949-830-8540
Fax No.: 949-830-1103
Factory
2918 E. Ginter
Tucson, AZ 85706
Phone No.: 520-889-8895
Fax No.: 520-741-9466

OMNI

See E.D.M. Arms listing.

ORVIS (Custom shotgun information only)

Historic Route 7A
Manchester, VT 05254
Phone No.: 802-362-2580
Fax No.: 802-362-3525
Web site: www.orvis.com

P.A.W.S., INC.

Factory
8175 River Road N.E.
Salem, OR 97303
Phone No.: 503-393-0838
Fax No.: 503-390-6075

PARA-ORDNANCE MANUFACTURING INC.

980 Tapscott Rd.
Scarborough, Ontario
M1X 1C3 CANADA
Phone No.: 416-297-7855
Fax No.: 416-297-1289
Web Site: www.paraord.com
Email: info@paraord.com

PARDINI, ARMI S.r.l.

Importer - See Nygord Precision Products listing.
Factory
154/A via Italica
I-55043 Lido di Camaiore, ITALY
Fax No.: 011-39-584-90122
Web site: www.pardini.it
Email: info@pardini.it

PARKER REPRODUCTIONS

Parker Reproduction Div.
115 U.S. Hwy 202
Ringoes, NJ 08551
Phone No.: 908-284-2800
Fax No.: 908-284-2113

PEDERSOLI, DAVIDE & C. Snc

Distributor - please refer to Cherry's listing.
Distributor - please refer to Dixie Gun Works listing.
Importer - please refer to Cabela's listing.
Importer - please refer to Cape Outfitters listing.
Importer - please refer to Cimarron, F.A. & Co listing.
Importer - please refer to E.M.F. Co. Inc. listing.
Importer - please refer to Navy Arms listing.
Distributor – Flintlocks, Etc.
160 Rossiter Rd.
Richmond, MA 01254
Fax No.: 413-698-3866
Factory
Via Artigiani 57
I-25063 Gardone V.T. (BS), ITALY
Fax No.: 011-39-30-8911019
Web site: www.davide-pedersoli.com

PEIFER RIFLE CO. (Black Powder)

P.O. Box 192
Nokomis, IL 62075
Fax No.: 217-563-7060

PENTHENY de PENTHENY, INC.

2352 Baggett Ct.
Santa Rosa, CA 95401
Phone/Fax No.: 707-573-1390

PERAZZI

Importer - Perazzi USA, Inc.
1010 W. Tenth St.
Azusa, CA 91702
Phone No.: 626-334-1234
Fax No.: 626-334-0344
Email: perazziusa@aol.com
Factory - Armi Perazzi S.p.A.
Via Fontanelle, 1/3
I-25080 Botticino Mattina Brescia ITALY
Fax No.: 011-39-30-269-2594
Web site: www.perazzi.it

PERUGINI & VISINI

Factory
Via Camprelle 126
Nuvolera, Brescia
I-25080 ITALY
Fax No.: 011-39-30-689-7821
Web site: www.intred.it/perugini-visini
Email: pervis@intred.it

PETERS STAHL GmbH

Factory
Stettiner Strasse 42
D-33106 Paderborn, GERMANY
Fax No.: 011-49-5251-75611
Web site: www.peters-stahl.com

PHILLIPS & ROGERS, INC.
852 FM 980
Huntsville, TX 77340
Phone No.: 409-435-0011
Fax No.: 409-435-0022
Web site: www.phillipsrodgers.com

PHOENIX ARMS
1420 S. Archibald Ave.
Ontario, CA 91761
Phone No.: 909-937-6900
Fax No.: 909-937-0060

PIETTA, F.A.P. F.lli e C. Snc.
Various U.S. distributors and importers
Factory
Via Mandolossa 102
I-25064 Gussago (Brescia) ITALY
Fax No.: 011-39-030-3737100
Web site: www.pietta.it
Email: fap@spidernet.it

PILKINGTON COMPETITION EQUIPMENT LLC
P.O. Box 97
#2 Little Tree's Ramble
Monteagle, TN 37356
Phone No.: 931-924-3400
Fax No.: 931-924-3489
Web site: www.pilkguns.com
Email: info@pilkguns.com

PIOTTI
Importer - see William Larkin Moore & Co. listing.
Factory - Piotti, F.lli, S.n.c.
Via Cinelli, 10-12
I-25063 Gardone V.T. Brescia, ITALY
Fax No.: 011-39-30-891-2578

PRAIRIE GUN WORKS
1-761 Mairon St.
Winnipeg, Manitoba
R2J 0K6 CANADA
Phone No.: 204-231-2976
Fax No.: 204-231-8566
Web site: www.prairiegunworks.com
Email: rifles@prairiegunworks.com

PRAIRIE RIVER ARMS (Black Powder)
1220 North 6th St.
Princeton, IL 61356
Fax No.: 815-875-1402

PRECISION SALES INT'L, INC.
P.O. Box 1776
14 Coleman Avenue
Westfield, MA 01086
Phone No.: 413-562-5055
Fax No.: 413-562-5056
Web site: www.precision-sales.com

PRECISION SMALL ARMS, INC. (PSA)
9272 Jeronimo Rd., Ste. 121
Irvine, CA 92618
Phone No.: 949-768-3530
Fax No.: 949-768-4808
Web site: www.lebebe.com
Email: zebraops@att.com

PREMIER ENGLISH SHOTGUNS LTD.
Turners Barn Farm - Kibworth Road, Three Gates
Illston-on-the-Hill, Leicestershire
LE7 9ER ENGLAND
Fax No.: 011-44-116-2596-574

PROFESSIONAL ORDNANCE, INC.
1070 Metric Dr.
Lake Havasu City, AZ 86403
Phone No.: 520-505-2420
Fax No.: 520-505-2141
Web site: www.professional-ordnance.com
Email: proord2@ctaz.com

PUMA RIFLES
Importer – see Legacy Sports International, LLC listing.

PURDEY, JAMES, & SONS, LTD.
Factory
57-58 South Audley Street
London, W1Y 6ED ENGLAND
Phone No.: 011-44-20-7499-1801
Fax No.: 011-44-20-7355-3297
Web site: www.purdey.com
Email: james.purdey@btinternet.com

QUAIL UNLIMITED, INC.
31 Quail Run
PO Box 610
Edgefield, SC 29824
Phone No.: 803-637-5731
Fax No.: 803-637-0037
Web site: www.qu.org
Email: National@qu.org

QUALITY ARMS, INC.
P.O. Box 19477
Houston, TX 77224
Phone No.: 281-870-8377
Fax No.: 281-870-8524
Web site: www.arrieta.com
Email: Arrieta2@excite.com

QUALITY PARTS CO.
See Bushmaster Firearms, Inc. listing.

R.F.M.
Factory - R.F.M. di Rota Luciano
via Patrioti, 26
I-25068 Noboli di Sarezzo
V.T. (Brescia) ITALY
Fax No.: 011-49-30-800442

RND MANUFACTURING
14311 Mead Street
Longmont, CO 80501
Phone/Fax No.: 303-623-2012
Email: rndedge@bwn.net

RPB INDUSTRIES
P.O. Box 367
Avondale, GA 30002
Phone No.: 800-858-0809
Fax No.: 404-297-0917

RPM PISTOLS

15481 N. Twin Lakes Dr.
Tuscon, AZ. 85739
Phone No.: 520-825-1233
Fax No.: 520-825-3333
Web site: www.RPMXL.com
Email: rpmXL1@theriver.com

RWS

(Airguns and older disc. firearms only) - see Dynamit Nobel listing.

RADOM

Importer (Current mfg.) - Dalvar of U.S.A.

740 East Warm Springs Rd., Ste. 122
Henderson, NV 89015
Phone/Fax: 702-558-6707
Web site: www.geocities.com/Pentagon/4050/
Email: dalvar_usa@juno.com

RAMO DEFENSE SYSTEMS

450 Allied Drive
Nashville, TN 37211
Phone No.: 615-333-0077
Fax No.: 615-333-6229
Web site: www.ramo.com

RANDALL FIREARMS COMPANY

Historian - Mr. Rick Kennerknecht

P.O. Box 1180
Mills, WY 82644-1180
Phone No.: 877-464-0180, ext. 319
U.S. Fax: 419-464-0180
International Fax: 011-44-0870-131-2598
Web site: www.Randall45.com
Email: Admin@Randall45.com
Factory Research Letters: $30 (Randall Pistols Only)

GARY REEDER CUSTOM GUNS

2601 E. 7th Ave.
Flagstaff, AZ 86004
Phone No.: 928-527-4100
Fax No.: 928-527-0840
Web Site: www.reedercustomguns.com
Email: gary@reedercustomguns.com

REMINGTON ARMS CO., INC.

Attn: Consumer Services
870 Remington Drive
P.O. Box 700
Madison, NC 27025-0700
Phone No.: 800-243-9700
Fax No.: 336-548-7801
Web site: www.remington.com
Email: info@remington.com

Repairs

14 Hoefler Ave.
Ilion, NY 13357
Phone No.: 800-243-9700
Fax No.: 336-548-7801
Email: info@remington.com

REPUBLIC ARMS OF SOUTH AFRICA

Importer/Distributor – Century Arms, Inc.

236 Bryce Blvd.
Fairfax, VA 05454
Phone No.: 802-527-1258
Fax No.: 802-752-1260

REPUBLIC ARMS OF SOUTH AFRICA, cont.

Factory

74 Auret St. Jeppe
Jeppestown, South Africa 2043
Phone No.: 011-27-11-614-8137

REXIO

VAM Distribution Company LLC

1141-B Mechanicsburg Rd.
Wooster, OH 44691
Phone No.: 330-262-0622
Fax No.: 330-262-0623
Web site: www.rexio.com
Web site: www.vamdist.com

RIFLES, INC.

3580 Leal Rd.
Pleasanton, TX 78064
Phone No.: 830-569-2055
Fax No.: 830-569-2297
Web site: www.riflesinc.com
Email: rifles@ev1.net

RIGANIAN, RAY (RIFLEMAKER)

324 N. Central Ave., Unit B
Glendale, CA 91203
Phone No.: 818-502-2678

RIGBY, JOHN & CO. (GUNMAKERS), INC.

500 Linne Rd., Ste. D
Paso Robles, CA 93446
Phone No.: 805-227-4236
Fax No.: 805-227-4723
Web site: www.johnrigbyandco.com
Email: jrigby@calinet.com

RIZZINI, BATTISTA

Importer - see New England Arms Corp. listing.
Importer - see W.L. Moore listing.

Factory

Via 2 Giugno, 7/7 bis
I-25060 Marcheno (Brescia), ITALY
Fax No.: 011-39-30/861319
Web site: www.rizzini.it

RIZZINI, EMILIO, s.n.c.

Importer - see Tristar listing.

Factory

Via M dell' Independanza 70
I-25060 Marcheno (BS) ITALY
Fax No.: 011-39-30-861-367
Web site: www.emiliorizzini.com
Email: info@emiliorizzini.com

RIZZINI, F.LLI

Importer - See William Larkin Moore & Co. listing.
Importer - See New England Arms Corp. listing.

ROBAR COMPANIES, INC., THE

21438 N. 7th Avenue
Phoenix, AZ 85027
Phone No.: 623-581-2648
Fax No.: 623-582-0059
Web site: www.robarguns.com
Email: info@robarguns.com

ROBERTS, J. & SON (GUNMAKERS) LTD.

22 Wyvil Road
London SW8 2TG ENGLAND
Phone No.: 011-44-207-622-1131
Fax No.: 011-44-207-627-4442
Web site: www.jroberts-gunmakers.co.uk
Email: shop@jroberts-gunmakers.co.uk

ROBINSON ARMAMENT CO.

See ZDF Import/Export listing.
Factory
P.O. Box 16776
Salt Lake City, UT 84116-0776
Phone No.: 801-355-0401
Fax No.: 801-355-0402
Web site: www.robarm.com
Email: ZDF@robarm.com

ROCHE, CHRISTIAN

12 Lotissement les Eglantiers
42 340 Veauche, France
Phone No.: 011-33-77-93-35-33
Fax No.: 011-33-77-94-35-33

ROCK ISLAND AUCTION COMPANY (Auctions)

1050 35th Ave.
Moline, IL 61265
Phone No.: 309-797-1500
Fax No.: 309-797-1655
Web site: www.mgnteam.com
Email: riauction@aol.com

ROCK RIVER ARMS, INC.

101 Noble St.
Cleveland, IL 61241
Phone No.: 309-792-5780
Fax No.: 309-792-5781
Web site: www.rockriverarms.com
Email: rockriverarms@revealed.net

ROCKY MOUNTAIN ARMS, INC.

1813 Sunset Place, Unit D
Longmont, CO 80501
Phone No: 303-678-8522
Fax No.: 303-678-8766
Web site: www.bearcoat.com
Email: gunmkr@aol.com

ROCKY MOUNTAIN ELK FOUNDATION

2291 W. Broadway
Missoula, MT 59802
Phone No.: 406-523-4500
Fax No.: 406-523-4581
Web site: www.rmef.org

ROGUE RIVER RIFLEWORKS

1317 Spring St.
Paso Robles, CA 93446
Phone No.: 805-227-4706
Fax No.: 805-227-4723

ROHRBAUGH FIREARMS

API
P.O. Box 785
Bayport, NY 11705
Phone No.: 631-363-2843
Fax No.: 631-363-2681
Email: api380@aol.com

ROSSI

Importer – BrazTech International L.C.
16175 N.W. 49th Ave.
Miami, FL 33014
Phone No.: 305-474-0401
Fax No.: 305-624-3180
Web site: www.rossiusa.com
Factory
Amadeo Rossi, S.A.
Rua Amadeo Rossi, 143
B-93030-220 Sao Leopoldo-RS BRAZIL
Email: rossi.firearms@pnet.com.br

ROTA, LUCIANO

Importer - see New England Arms Corp. listing

ROTTWEIL

See Dynamit Nobel/RWS listing.

RUTTEN HERSTAL (Airguns)

Factory - Rutten Herstal
Parc Industriel des Hauts-Sarts
Premiere Avenue, 7-9
B-4040 Herstal, BELGIUM
Fax No.: 011-32-41/648589

S.I.A.C.E.

Importer - see New England Arms Corp. listing.

SKB SHOTGUNS

Importer - Guns Unlimited, Inc.
4325 S 120th Street
Omaha, NE 68137
Phone No.: 402-330-4492
Fax No.: 402-330-8040
Web site: www.skbshotguns.com
Email: SKB@radiks.net
Factory – SKB (New) Arms Co.
J-Nishi-Ibaraki-Gun/Tokyo
C.P.O. Box 14 01
Fax No.: 011-81-0339-430695
Web site: www.shirstone.com/skb
Email: mailskb@shirstone.com

SSK INDUSTRIES

590 Woodvue Lane
Wintersville, OH 43953
Phone No.: 740-264-0176
Fax No.: 740-264-2257
Web site: www.sskindustries.com
Email: info@sskindustries.com

STI INTERNATIONAL

114 Halmar Cove
Georgetown, TX 78628
Phone: 800-959-8201
Fax No.: 512-819-0465
Web site: www.stiguns.com
Email: sales@sti-guns.com

SABATTI s.p.a.

Importer - See European American Armory listing.
Factory - Sabatti S.P.A.
Via Alessandro Voltra No. 90
I-25063 Gardone Valtrompia, (BS) ITALY
Fax No.: 011-39-30-89-12059
Web site: www.sabatti.com
Email: info@sabatti.it

SAFARI ARMS
See Olympic Arms listing.

SAFARI CLUB INTERNATIONAL
4800 West Gates Pass Road
Tucson, AZ 85745
Phone No.: 602-620-1220
Fax No.: 602-622-1205

SAIGA
Importer – see European American Armory listing.

SAKO LTD.
Importer (USA) - See Beretta USA listing.
Importer (CANADA) – Stoeger Canada Ltd.
1801 Wentworth St., Unit 16
Whitby, Ontario, L1N 8R6 CANADA
Phone No.: 905-436-9077
Fax No.: 905-436-9079
Email: stoeger@idirect.com
Factory - Sako, Limited
P.O. Box 149
FIN-11101 Riihimki, FINLAND
Fax No.: 011-358-19-720446
Web site: www.sako.fi
Email: export@sako.fi

SALERI, W.R. di WILLIAM & C. snc
Via Filipinni, 2
I-25063 Gardone, VT Brescia ITALY
Fax No.: 011-39-030-8916-168

SAMCO GLOBAL ARMS, INC.
6995 N.W. 43rd St.
Miami, FL 33166
Phone No.: 305-593-9782
Fax No.: 305-593-1014
Web site: www.samcoglobal.com
Email: samco@samcoglobal.com

SAN SWISS ARMS AG
Industrieplatz
CH-8212 Neuhausen am Rheinfall
SWITZERLAND
Fax No.: 011-41-052-674-6418
Web site: www.swissarms.ch
Email: info@swissarms.ch

SARSILMAZ
Distributor – PMC
P.O. Box 62508
Boulder City, NV 89005
Phone No.: 702-294-0025
Fax No.: 702-294-0121
Web site: www.pmcammo.com
Email: pmcecc@aol.com
Factory
Mercan Uzuncarsi Cad. No. 69
34450 Istanbul/TURKEY
Phone No.: 011900-2125133507
Fax No.: 011-90212-51119-99
Web site: www.sarsilmaz.com.tr
Email: sarsilmaz@sarsilmaz.com.tr

SAUER, J.P. & SOHN
Importer - See SIG Arms listing.
Factory – J.P. Sauer & Sohn GmbH
Sauerstrasse 2-6
D-24340 Eckernfrde, GERMANY
Fax No.: 011-49-43-51-471-160
Web site: www.sauer-waffen.de

SAVAGE ARMS, INC.
100 Springdale Road
Westfield, MA 01085
Phone No.: 413-568-7001
Fax No.: 413-562-7764
Web site: www.savagearms.com
Older Savage Arms Historical Research
Mr. John Callahan
53 Old Quarry Rd.
Westfield, MA 01085
$15.00/gun research fee, $20.00 per gun for Models 1895,
1899, and 99 rifles.

SAVIN, J.C.
11 Place de la Cite
F-42220 Bourg Argental, FRANCE
Fax No.: 011-33-4-77-39-1855

SAXONIA GbR – Spezialwaffentechnik GbR
Am Schwarzwasser 1
D-08340 Schwarzenberg GERMANY
Fax No.: 011-49-3774-1807424
Web site: www.saxonia-waffen.de

SCATTERGUN TECHNOLOGIES INC.
See Wilson Combat listing.

SCHEIRING GES. m.b.H.
Klagenfurter Strasse 19
A-9170 Ferlach AUSTRIA
Fax No.: 011-43-4227-287620
Web site: www.ferlacherjadgwaffen.at/scheiring

FA. ALFRED SCHILLING
Peter-Haseney Strasse 32
D-98544 Zella-Mehlis, GERMANY
Fax No.: 011-49-0362-486706
Web site: www.Alfred-Schilling.de
Email: joergschilling@gmx.de

SCHUERMAN ARMS, LTD.
9301 E. Adobe Dr.
Scottsdale, AZ 85255
Phone No.: 480-473-2980
Web site: www.schuermanarms.com
Email: info@schuermanarms.com

SCHUETZEN PISTOL WORKS, INC.
See Olympic Arms listing.

SCHUTZEN BOHME GmbH
Muhlenstrasse 6-8
31737 Rintein, GERMANY
Phone No.: 011-49-5751-44770
Fax No.: 011-49-5751-42490

SCOTT, W. C., LTD.
Holland & Holland, Ltd. (Repairs)
Attn: Mr. P. C. Chismon
31-33 Bruton St.
London WiJ 6HH ENGLAND
Phone No.: 011-44-020-7499-4411
Fax No.: 011-44-020-7409-3283
Web site: www.hollandandholland.com
Email: peter.chismon@holland-holland.co.uk

SEARCY, B. & CO.
26293 Twenty Mule Team Rd.
P.O. Box 584
Boron, CA 93516
Phone No.: 760-762-6313
Fax No.: 760-762-0191
Web site: www.searcyent.com
Email: searcy@ccis.com

SEECAMP, L.W. CO., INC.
301 Brewster Road
Milford, CT 06460
Phone No.: 203-877-7926

SEMMERLING
Manufacturer - see American Derringer Corp. listing.

C. SHARPS ARMS CO. INC.
Distributor - Montana Armory, Inc.
100 Centennial
P.O. Box 885
Big Timber, MT 59011
Phone No.: 406-932-4353
Fax No.: 406-932-4443
Web site: www.csharpsarms.com
Email: csharps@ttc-cmc.net

SHILOH RIFLE MFG. CO.
P.O. Box 279
Big Timber, MT 59011
Phone No.: 406-932-4454
Fax No.: 406-932-5627
Email: shilohrifle@mcn.net

SHOOTERS ARMS MANUFACTURING INCOR-PORATED
National Highway, Wireless
Mandaue City, Cebu, Phillipines
Phone No.: 011-6032-346-2331
Fax No.: 011-6032-346-2331
Web site: www.shootersarms.com.ph
Email: rhonedeleon@yahoo.com

SIG ARMS, INC.
18 Industrial Park Drive
Exeter, NH 03833
Phone No.: 603-772-2302
Fax No.: 603-772-9082
Customer Service Fax No.: 603-772-4795
Web Site: www.sigarms.com

SIG SAUER
Importer - see SIG Arms, Inc. listing.
Factory - SIG - Schweizerische Industrie-Gesellschaft
Industrielplatz
CH-8212 Neuhausen am Rheinfall, SWITZERLAND
Fax No.: 011-41-153-216-601

SILMA s.r.l.
Distributor & Importer – see Legacy Sports International, LLC listing.
Factory
Via I Maggio, 74
I-25060 Zanano di Sarezzo, (BS) ITALY
Fax No.: 011-39-30-8900712
Web site: www.silma.net
Email: info@silma.net

GENE SIMILLION GUNMAKER
220 S. Wisconsin
Gunnison, CO 81230
Phone No.: 970-641-1126

SIMSEK
Factory
TR-Duze, Mergic Yolu F-5 Uzer No. 3 TURKEY
Fax No.: 011-90-0216-338-6370

SMITH & WESSON
2100 Roosevelt Avenue
P.O. Box 2208
Springfield, MA 01102-2208
Phone No.: 800-331-0852
Fax No.: 413-747-3317
Web site: www.smith-wesson.com
Smith & Wesson Research
Attn: Mr. Roy Jinks, S&W Historian
P.O. Box 2208
Springfield, MA 01102-2208
Phone No.: 413-781-8300
Fax No.: 413-731-8980

SNAKE CHARMER
Verney-Carron USA, Inc.
320 Court Street
Clay Center, KS 67432
Phone No.: 785-632-3169
Fax No.: 785-632-6554
Web site: www.snake-charmer.net
Email: email@snake-charmer.net

SOLD USA (Auctions)
6415 Idlewild Rd., Ste. 207
Charlotte, NC 28212
Phone No.: 877-SOLDUSA
Web site: www.soldusa.com

SOMMER + OCKENFUSS GmbH
Importer – Lothar Walther Precision Tool
3425 Hutchinson Road
Cumming, GA 30040
Phone No.: 770-889-9998
Fax No.: 770-889-4919
Factory
Bhlerweg 4
D-72270 Baiersbronn GERMANY
Fax No.: 011-49-7447-94-74-20
Web site: www.sommer-ockenfuss.de
Email: weapons@sommer-ockenfuss.de

SOTHEBY'S (AUCTIONS)

U.S. Office

1334 York Ave. at 72nd St.
New York, NY 10021
Phone: 212-606-7000
Fax: 212-606-7107

U.K. Office

34-35 New Bond Street at Bloomfield Place
London, WIA 2AA ENGLAND
Phone: 011-44-20-7293-5000
Fax: 011-44-20-7293-5989
Web site: www.sothebys.com

SPECIAL WEAPONS LLC

P.O Box 22139
Mesa, AZ 85277-2139
Phone No.: 480-325-7885
Fax No.: 520-396-1538
Web site: www.specialweaponsllc.com
Email: SpecialWP@aol.com

SPHINX SYSTEMS LTD.

Gsteigstrasse 12
CH-3800 Maten b.I. Interlaken SWITZERLAND
Fax No.: 011-41-033-821-1006
Web site: www.sphinxarms.com
Email: info@sphinxarms.com

SPRINGFIELD ARMORY

Springfield Inc.

420 W. Main St.
Geneseo, IL 61254
Phone No.: 309-944-5631
Phone No.: 800-680-6866
Fax No.: 309-944-3676
Web site: www.springfieldarmory.com
Email: sales@springfield-armory.com

STALLARD ARMS

See Hi-Point listing.

STEVENS, J., ARMS COMPANY

Older Stevens Historical Research

Mr. John Callahan
53 Old Quarry Rd.
Westfield, MA 01085
$15.00/gun research fee.

STEYR AIRGUNS

Importer – see Pilkington Competition Equipment LLC listing.

STEYR MANNLICHER

Factory - Steyr Mannlicher A.G. & Co. KG

Box 1000, Mannlicher Str. 1
Steyr A-4400 AUSTRIA
Fax No.: 01143-7252-78621
Web site: www.steyr-mannlicher.com
Email: office@steyr-mannlicher.com

STOCKWORKS

183A S. Los Alamos
Mesa, AZ 85204
Phone No.: 480-545-2994
Fax No.: 480-507-7560
Web site: www.robertthisserichco.com
Email: bhisserich@earthlink.net

STOEGER INDUSTRIES

17601 Indian Head Hwy.
Accokeek, MD 20607-2501
Fax No.: 301-283-6300
Web site: www.stoegerindustries.com

STONE MOUNTAIN ARMS, INC. (Black Powder)

5988 Peachtree Corners East
Norcross, GA 30071
Fax No.: 404-242-8546

STONER RIFLE

Factory – see Knight's Manufacturing Co. listing.

STRAYER TRIPP INTERNATIONAL

See the STI Internation listing.

STURM, RUGER & CO., INC.

Headquarters

1 Lacey Place
Southport, CT 06490
Phone: 203-259-7843
Fax: 203-256-3367
www.ruger.com

Service Center for Pistols, PC4 & PC9 Carbines

200 Ruger Road
Prescott, AZ 86301-6181
Phone: 928-778-6555
Fax: 928-778-6633
Web site: www.ruger-firearms.com

Ruger Date of Information & Service Center for Revolvers & Long Guns

411 Sunapee Street
Newport, NH 03773
Phone: 603-865-2442
Fax: 603-863-6165

SUNDANCE INDUSTRIES

25163 W. Ave. Stanford
Valencia, CA 91355
Phone No.: 805-257-4807
Fax No.: 805-257-4891

SUPERIOR AMMUNITION, INC.

1320 Cedar Street
Sturgis, SD 57785
Phone No.: 605-347-9192
Fax No.: 605-347-9392
Web site: www.superiorammo.com
Email: superiorammo@dtgnet.com

SUPER SIX LLC

3806 W. Lisbon Ave.
Milwaukee, WI 53208
Phone No.: 414-344-3343
Fax No.: 414-344-0304

SZECSEI Et. FUCHS FINE GUNS GmbH

North America Office

450 Charles St.
Windsor, Ontario N8X 3Z1 CANADA
Phone No.: 519-966-1234

SZECSEI Et. FUCHS FINE GUNS GmbH, cont.
Factory
Bozner Platz 1
corner Wilhelm-Greil-Strasse
A-6020 Innsbruck AUSTRIA
Phone/Fax No.: 011-43-512-5872-67
Web site: www.jagdwaffe.com
Email: fuchs@jagdwaffe.com

TNW INC.
P.O. Box 311
Vernonia, OR 97064
Phone No.: 503-429-5001
Fax No.: 503-429-3505
Email: tnwcorp@aol.com

TACONIC FIREARMS, LTD.
Perry Lane, P.O. Box 553
Cambridge, NY 12816
Phone No.: 518-677-2704
Fax No.: 518-677-5974

TANFOGLIO, FRATELLI, S.r.l.
Importer - See European American Armory listing.
Factory
Via Vaitrompia 39/41
I-25063 Gardone V.T. (BS) ITALY
Fax No.: 011-39-30-8910183
Web site: www.tanfoglio.it
Email: info@tanfoglio.it

TANNER, ANDRE
No current information available.

TAR-HUNT CUSTOM RIFLES, INC.
101 Dogtown Rd.
Bloomsburg, PA 17815-7544
Phone/Fax No.: 570-784-6368
Web site: www.tar-hunt.com

TAURUS INTERNATIONAL
16175 NW 49th Ave.
Miami, FL 33014-6314
Phone No.: 305-624-1115
Fax No.: 305-624-3180
Web site: www.taurususa.com

TAYLOR'S & CO. (Black Powder & Reproductions)
304 Lenoir Dr.
Winchester, VA 22603
Phone No.: 540-722-2017
Fax No.: 540-722-2018
Web Site: www.taylorsfirearms.com
Email: info@taylorsfirearms.com

THOMPSON & CAMPBELL
Cromarty the Black Isle
Ross-shire IV11 8YB SCOTLAND
Fax No.: 011-44-01381-600767
Web site: www.rifle.co.uk
Email: info@rifle.co.uk

THOMPSON/CENTER ARMS CO., INC.
P.O. Box 5002
Rochester, NH 03866
Customer Service Phone No.: 603-332-2333
Fax no.: 603-332-5133
Web site: www.tcarms.com

TIKKA
Importer - See Beretta U.S.A. Corp. listing.
Factory - see Sako listing.
Web site: www.tikka.fi

TIME PRECISION ARMS
640 Federal Rd.
Brookfield, CT 06804
Phone No.: 203-775-8343
Fax No.: 203-775-6343
Web site: www.timeprecision.com
Email: timprecision@aol.com

TOLLEY, J & W
See Premier English Shotguns Ltd. listing.

TOP GUN AIR GUNS (Airguns)
8442 East Hackamore Dr.
Scottsdale, AZ 85255
Phone No.: 480-585-9564

TORNADO
Factory - AseTekno OY
P.O. Box 94 Plkneentie 18
FIN-00511 Helsinki, Finland
Fax No.: 011-358-9-753-6463
Web site: www.asetekno.fi
Email: jaakko.vottonen@asetekno.fi

TOZ
Importer (TOZ 35 only) – see Nygord listing.
Factory
Fax: 011-0872-27-3439
Web site: www.toz.vpk.ru
Email: toz@tula.net

TRADITIONS PERFORMANCE FIREARMS
1375 Boston Post Road
P.O. Box 776
Old Saybrook, CT 06475
Phone No.: 860-388-4656
Fax No.: 860-388-4657
Web site: www.traditionsfirearms.com
Web site: www.traditionsmuzzle.com
Email: info@traditionsfirearms.com

TRAIL GUN ARMORY (Black Powder)
Route 22, Box 760
Conroe, TX 77303

TRISTAR SPORTING ARMS LTD.
P.O. Box 7496
1814 - 16 Linn St.
N. Kansas City, MO 64116
Phone No.: 816-421-1400
Fax No.: 816-421-4182
Web site: www.tristarsportingarms.com
Email: tristar@blitz-it.net

TRUVELO MANUFACTURERS (PTY) LTD.
Factory – Truvelo Armoury
107 Packard Street
Randjespark, Ext. 22
Midrand SOUTH AFRICA
Fax No.: 011-27-11-314-1409
Web site: www.truvelo.co.za
Email: armoury@truvelo.co.za

TULA ARMS PLANT
Factory
Fax: 011-0872-27-3439
Web site: www.toz.vpk.ru
Email: tozmarketing@tula.net

DOUG TURNBULL RESTORATION, INC.
6680 Rts. 5 & 20, Box 471
Bloomfield, NY 14469
Phone/Fax No.: 585-657-6338
Web site: www.turnbullrestoration.com

U.S.R.A. PISTOLS (Information Only)
Mr. L. Richard Littlefield
P.O. Box 9
Jaffrey, NH 0342
Phone No.: 603-532-8004

U.S. ORDNANCE
P.O. Box 70425
Reno, NV 89570-0443
Phone No.: 775-356-1303
Fax No.: 775-356-1313
Web site: www.usord.com

UBERTI, A. & C., S.r.l.
Importer - Uberti USA, Inc.
P.O. Box 509
362 Limerock Road
Lakeville, CT 06039
Fax No.: 860-435-8146
Web site: www.uberti.com
Email: mail@uberti.com
Factory - A. Uberti & C., S.r.l.
Via G. Carducci, 41
I-25060 Ponte Zanano Sarezzo (BS) ITALY
Fax No.: 011-39-30-891-1061
Web site: www.ubertireplicas.com
Email: info@ubertireplicas.it

UGARTECHEA, ARMAS
Importer - see Lion Country Supply listing.
Importer - see Aspen Outfitting Co. listing.
Factory - Ugartechea, Ignacio
P.O. Box 21
E-20600, Eibar, SPAIN
Fax No.: 011-3443-121669

UMAREX SPORTWAFFEN GmbH & CO. KG
Donnerfeld 2
D-59757 Arnsberg GERMANY
Fax No.: 011-49-2932-638-222

UNIQUE
Importer - see Nygord Precision Products listing.
Factory - Unique Manufacture d'Armes
10, rue des Allees
F-64704 Hendaye, FRANCE
Fax No.: 011-33-5920/5085

U.S. HISTORICAL SOCIETY
See America Remembers listing.

UNITED STATES FIRE ARMS MANUFACTURING COMPANY, INC.
55 Van Dyke Ave.
Hartford, CT 06106
Phone No.: 877-277-6901
Fax No.: 860-724-6809
Web site: www.usfirearms.com
Email: Sales@usfirearms.com

UZI
No commercial importation.

VALKYRIE ARMS LTD.
120 State Ave. NE, No. 381
Olympia, WA 98501
Phone No.: 360-482-4036
Fax No.: 360-482-4036
Web site: www.valkyriearms.com

VALTRO
Importer - Valtro USA Inc.
1281 Andersen Dr.
San Rafael, Ca 94901
Phone No.: 415-256-2575
Fax No.: 415-256-2576
Factory - Valtro Stocchetta s.r.l.
Via Italia, 76
I-25060 Villa Carcina Brescia, ITALY
Fax No.: 011-39-030-8988252
Email: valtro@itigroup.it

VARBERGER
No current U.S. importation.

VEKTOR
P.O. Box 5445
Pretoria 0001 South Africa
Fax No.: 011-27-12-620-2407

VEPR. RIFLES
Importer – See ZDF Import Export listing.
Factory – MOLOT JSC
Vyatskie Polyany Machine Building Plant
135 Lenin St.
Vyatskie Polyany, Kirov Region, 612960 RUSSIA
Fax No.: 011-007-83334-61462
Email: gusakov@ezmail.ru
Email: admir@molot.kirov.ru

VERNEY-CARRON
Distributor - Verney-Carron U.S.A., Inc.
320 Court Street
Clay Center, KS 67432-3169
Phone No.: 785-632-2184
Fax No.: 785-632-6554
Importer – The Graystone Group
3627 N. Wilton Ave.
Chicago, IL 60613-4312
Fax No.: 773-913-2832
Web site: www.TheGraystoneGroup.com
Email: GraystoneGroup@iname.com

VERNEY-CARRON, cont.
Factory - Verney-Carron S.A.
54, Boulevard Thiers
Boite Postale 72
F-42002 St. Etienne Cedex 1 FRANCE
Phone No.: 011-33-477-791500
Fax No.: 011-33-477-790702
Web site: www.verney-carron.com
Email: email@verney-carron.com

VERONA
Importer - B.C. Outdoors
P.O. Box 61497
Boulder City, NV 89006
Phone No.: 702-294-3056
Email: verona@pmcammo.com

VIRGIN VALLEY CUSTOM GUNS
2410 West 350 North
Hurricane, UT 84737
Phone No.: 702-528-8801
Fax No.: 435-635-8943
Web site: www.virginvalleyguns.com

VOERE
Factory - Voere Austria
Untere Spaerchen 56
A-6330 Kufstein, AUSTRIA
Fax No.: 011-43-5372-65752
Web site : www.voere.de
Email: voere@aon.at

VOLQUARTSEN CUSTOM LTD.
P.O. Box 397
24276 240th St.
Carroll, IA 51401
Phone No.: 712-792-4238
Fax No.: 712-792-2542
Web site: www.volquartsen.com
Email: VCL@netins.net

WAFFENSTUBE GUGGI
Wienerstrasse 9
8020 Graz AUSTRIA
Fax No.: 011-43-316-711878
Web site: www.guggi-arms.com
Email: office@guggi-arms.com

WAFFEN JUNG GMBH
Am Alten Garten 7
53797 Lohmar, GERMANY
Fax No.: 011-0224618491

WAFFEN VERATSHNIG
Factory
Gablenzgasse 42/7
A-1160 Vienna, AUSTRIA
Fax No.: 011-43-664-342-5609

WALTHER
Importer – see Smith & Wesson listing.
Target pistol importer - see Champion's Choice Inc. listing.
GSP/rifle conversion kit importer and factory repair station

WALTHER, cont.
Earl's Repair Service, Inc.
437 Chandler Street (rear)
Tewksbury, MA 01876
Phone No.: 978-851-2656
Fax No.: 978-851-9462
Web site: www.carlwalther.com
Email: info@carlwalther.com
German Company Headquarters
Carl Walther Sportwaffen GmbH
Donnerfeld 2
D-59757 Arnsberg GERMANY
Fax No.: 011-49-29-32-638149
Factory - Carl Walther, GmbH
Sportwaffenfabrik
Postfach 4325
D-89033 Ulm/Donau, GERMANY
Fax No.: 011-49-731-1539170

WATSON BROS.
39 Redcross Way
London Bridge
SE1 1HG ENGLAND
Phone/Fax No.: 011-44-171-4033367

WEATHERBY
3100 El Camino Real
Atascadero, CA 93422
Phone No.: 805-466-1767
Fax No.: 805-466-2527
Web site: www.weatherby.com

WEBLEY & SCOTT (Airguns)
Importer - Pyramyd Air, Inc.
2447 Suffolk Lane
Pepper Pike, OH 44124
Phone No.: 888-262-4867
Fax No.: 440-605-1936
Web site: www.pyramydair.com
Factory
Frankley Industrial Park
Tay Road, Rubery, Rednal
GB-Birmingham ENGLAND B45 0PA
Phone No.: 011-21-453-1864
Fax No.: 011-21-457-7846

WEIHRAUCH, HANS-HERMANN
Airgun Importer - See Beeman Precision Airguns listing.
Airgun Importer - See Pyramyd Air, Inc. listing.
Firearms Importer - See European American Armory listing.
Factory - H. Weihrauch, Sportwaffenfabrik
Postfach 25
D-97638 Mellrichstadt, GERMANY
Fax No.: 011-49-97-76-707679

WELLS CUSTOM RIFLES
110 North Summit Street
Prescott, AZ 86301
Phone No.: 520-445-3655
Web site: www.cutrifle.com
Email: dan@cutrifle.com

WERNER BARTOLOT
Haupstrasse 11
A-9620 Hermagor, AUSTRIA
Fax No.: 011-43-0428225205
Web site: www.jagdwaffe.at
Email: w.bartolot@utanet.at

DAN WESSON FIREARMS
New York International Corp.
119 Kemper Ln.
Norwich, NY 13815
Phone No.: 607-336-1174
Fax No.: 607-336-2730
Web site: www.danwessonfirearms.com
Email: danwessonfirearms@citlink.net

WESTLEY RICHARDS & CO., Ltd.
Importer - Westley Richards Agency USA
Chesnut Hall, 4319 Chesnut Expressway
Springfield, MO
Phone No.: 417-869-8447
Fax No.: 417-831-0089
Factory - Westley Richards & Co., Ltd.
40 Grange Road
Bournbrook, Birmingham, ENGLAND B29 6AR
Fax No.: 011-44-121-414-1138

WHITE MUZZLE LOADING SYSTEMS, INC. (Black Powder)
25 E. Hwy 40
Roosevelt, UT 84066
Fax No.: 801-722-3054

WICHITA ARMS, INC.
923 E. Gilbert
Wichita, KS 67211
Phone No.: 316-265-0661
Fax No.: 316-265-0760

WIFRA
Please refer to W.R. Saleri listing.

WILD WEST GUNS, INC.
7521 Old Seward Hwy., Unit A
Anchorage, AK 99518
Phone No.: 907-344-4500
Fax No.: 907-344-4005
Web site: www.wildwestguns.com
Email: wwguns@ak.net

WILDERNESS RIFLE WORKS (Black Powder)
Distributor - See Mountain States Muzzleloading Supplies listing.

WILDEY F.A. INC.
45 Angevine Road
Warren, CT 06754
Phone No.: 860-355-9000
Fax No.: 860-354-7759
Web site: www.wildeyguns.com

WILKES, JOHN GUNMAKERS LTD.
Distributor & Importer - The First National Gun Banque
P.O. Box 60719
Colorado Springs, CO 80960
Phone No.: 719-444-0786
Fax No.: 719-444-0731
Web site: www.fngbcorp.com
Email: karl@fngbcorp.com

WILKINSON ARMS
Factory - Northwest Arms
26884 Pearl Rd.
Parma, ID 83660
Phone No.: 208-722-6771
Fax No.: 208-722-1062

WILLIAM LARKIN MOORE & CO.
8340 East Raintree Dr., Suite B-7
Scottsdale, AZ 85260
Phone No.: 480-951-8913
Fax No.: 480-951-3677
Web site: www.williamlarkinmoore.com
Email: info@williamlarkinmoore.com

WILLIAM DOUGLAS & SONS
No current U.S. importation.

WILLIAM EVANS LIMITED
67 St. James's Street
London SW1A 1PH
ENGLAND
Fax No.: 011-44-171-499-1912
Email: sales@williamevans.com

WILLIAM POWELL & SON (GUNMAKERS), Ltd.
Importer - John Higgins
The Ford Plantation
12511 Ford Ave.
Richmond Hill, GA 31324
Factory & Store
35-37 Carrs Lane
Birmingham B47SX ENGLAND
Phone No.: 011-44-121-643-8362
Fax No.: 011-44-121-631-3504
Web site: www.william-powell.co.uk
Email: sales@william-powell.co.uk

WILSON COMBAT
2234 CR 719
P.O. Box 578
Berryville, AR 72616-0578
Phone No.: 800-955-4856
Fax No.: 870-545-3310
Web site: www.wilsoncombat.com
Email: info@wilsoncombat.com

WINCHESTER - U.S.REPEATING ARMS
Administrative Offices
275 Winchester Avenue
Morgan, UT 84050-9333
Customer Service Phone No.: 800-945-1392
Fax No.: 801-876-3737
Web site: www.winchester-guns.com
Factory - U.S. Repeating Arms Company, Inc.
275 Winchester Ave., P.O. Box 30-300
New Haven, CT 06511-1970
Winchester Custom Shop
344 Winchester Ave.
New Haven, CT 06511-1970
Phone No.: 203-789-5503
Fax No.: 203-789-5853

WINCHESTER/OLIN

Models 101 & 23 only (Disc.)

Attn: Shotgun Customer Service
427 N. Shamrock Street
East Alton, IL 62024
Fax No.: 618-258-3393
Web site: www.winchester.com

WISCHO JAGD-UND SPORTWAFFEN

Dresdener Strasse 30,
D-91058 Erlangen, GERMANY
Fax No.: 011-91-31-300930
Web site: www.wischo.com
Email: info@wischo.com

WISEMAN, BILL & CO.

P.O. Box 3427
Bryan, TX 77805
Phone No.: 979-690-3456
Fax No.: 979-690-0156

WM. PETE HARVEY AUCTIONS

P.O. Box 280
Cataumet, MA 02534
Phone No.: 508-548-0660
Fax No.: 508-457-0660
Web site: www.firearmsauctions.com

WOODWARD, JAMES AND SONS

Factory - Purdey, James, & Sons, Ltd.

57-58 S Audley Street
London, W1Y 6ED ENGLAND
Phone No.: 011-44-71 499 1801
Fax No.: 011-44-71 355 3297

YILDIZ SILAH SANAYI

Factory

Organize Sanayi Blgesi 40 Sokak No. 13
Burdur TURKEY
Fax No.: 01190-0248-252-9569

ZDF IMPORT EXPORT INC.

2975 South 300 West
Salt Lake City, UT 84115
Phone No.: 801-485-1012
Fax No.: 801-484-4363
Web site: www.robarm.com
Email: zdf@robarm.com

Z-M WEAPONS

203 South St.
Bernardston, MA 01337
Phone No.: 413-648-9501
Fax No.: 413-648-0219
Web site: www.zmweapons.com
Email: zm@zmweapons.com

ZABALA HERMANOS, S.A.

Lasao, 6
20690 Elgueta (Guipuzcoa), SPAIN
Fax No.: 011-34-943-768201
Web site: www.zabalahermanos.com
Email: imanol@zabalahermanos.com

ZANARDINI

Importer - S.O.G. Arms

15902A Halliburton Road #267
Hacienda Heights, CA 91745
Phone No.: 626-968-3208
Fax: No.: 626-961-7719
Email: SOGARMS@earthlink.net

Factory - Zanardini, P. & C., S.n.c.

Via C. Goldoni, 34
I-25063 Gardone V.T. (Brescia), ITALY
Fax No.: 011-39-30-8910590
Web site: www.zanardini.com
Email: info@zanardini.com

ZANOTTI, FABIO

Factory - R. Gamba c/o Zanotti

Via Artigiani, 93
I0-25063 Gardone Val Trompia
Brescia, ITALY
Fax No.: 011-39-30-837180

ZASTAVA ARMS

Importer – see KBI listing (certain models only).
Factory - Advanced Weapons Technologies

2A, Andrea Papandreou St.
GR-151 27 Melissia, Athens, GREECE
Fax No.: 011-30-161-37-676
Web site: www.awt-zastava.com
Email: europe@zastava.com

ZIEGENHAHN & SOHN OHG

Importer - see New England Custom Gun, Ltd. listing.
Factory

Suhler Str. 9 A
D-98544 Zella-Mehlis GERMANY
Fax No.: 011-49-36-82-896-28
Web site: www.ziegenhahn.de
Email: info@ ziegenhahn.de

ZOLI, ANTONIO

Not affiliated with Angelo Zoli.
Factory - Zoli Antonio S.p.A.

Via Zanardelli, 39
I-25063 Gardone V.T. (BS) ITALY
Fax No.: 011-39-30-891-1165

ABBREVIATIONS

	Banned due to 1994 Crime Bill
	Standard Grade Walnut
	Extra Grade Walnut
	Best Quality Walnut
	Automatic Colt Pistol
	Adjustable
	Automatic Ejectors or Action Express
ots.	appointments
	Blue
C	Browning Arms Company
L	Barrel
G	Browning Machine Gun
SS	Ballistic Optimizing Shooting System
	Butt Plate or Black Powder
E	Black Power Express
	Bench Rest
	Beavertail
B 1994	Introduced because of 1994 Crime
	Caliber
	Crescent Buttplate
	Case Colors
A	Colt Collectors Association
	Centerfire
	Cross Hair
OMP	Compensated/Competition
Y/C	Cylinder
	Double Action
AO	Double Action Only
B	Double Barrel
ISC	Discontinued
SL	Detachable Side Locks
ST	Double Set Triggers
T	Double Triggers
WM	DeutscheWaffen and Munitions
	Fabrik
JT	Ejectors
XC	Excellent
XT	Extractors
	Full Choke
&M	Full & Modified
A	Forearm
BT	Full Beavertail Forearm
E	Fore End
FL	Federal Firearms License
K	Flat Knob
KLT	Flat Knob Long Tang
FM	Full Mag
MJ	Full Metal Jacket
FN	Fabrique Nationale
PS	Feet Per Second
TPOS	For that piece of s...
ga.	gauge
GCA	Gun Control Act
GOVT	Government
H&H	Holland & Holland
HB	Heavy Barrel
HC	Hard Case

HMR	Hornady Magnum Rimfire
HP	Hollow Point
I	Improved
IC	Improved Cylinder
IM	Improved Modified
intro.	Introduced
IPSC	International Practical Shooting Confederation
L	Long
LC	Long Colt
LOP	Length of Pull
LPI	Lines Per Inch
LR	Long Rifle
LT	Long Tang or Light
LTRK	Long Tang Round Knob
M	Modified Choke
M&P	Military & Police
Mag.	Magnum Caliber
mag.	Magazine or Clip
MC	Monte Carlo
MFG	Manufactured/manufacture
MIL SPEC	Mfg. to Military Specifications
MK	Mark
MOA	Minute of Angle
MR	Matted Rib
MSR	Manufacturer's Suggested Retail
N	Nickel
N/A	Not Applicable or Not Available
NE	Nitro Express
NIB	New in Box
NM	National Match
no.	Number
NSST	Non Selective Single Trigger
O/U	Over and Under
OA	Overall
OAL	Overall Length
OB	Octagon Barrel
OBFM	Octagon Barrel w/full mag.
OBO	Or Best Offer
OCT	Octagon
ODB	Or Don't Bother
Para.	Parabellum
PG	Pistol Grip
POR/P.O.R.	Price on Request
POST-'89	Paramilitary mfg. after Federal legislation in Nov. 1989
POST-BAN	Mfg. after September 13, 1994 per C/B
PPD	Post Paid
PRE-'89	Paramilitary mfg. before Federal legislation in Nov. 1989
PRE-BAN	Mfg. before September 13, 1994 per C/B
QD	Quick Detachable
RB	Round Barrel/Round Butt
REC	Receiver
REM	Remington
REM. MAG.	Remington Magnum

RF	Rimfire
RFM	Rim Fire Magnum
RK	Round Knob
RKLT	Round Knob Long Tang
RKST	Round Knob Short Tang
RR	Red Ramp
RSM	Remington Short Magnum
S	Short
S&W	Smith & Wesson
S/N	Serial Number
SA	Single Action
SAA	Single Action Army
SAE	Selective Automatic Ejectors
SB	Shotgun Butt
ser.	serial
SG	Straight Grip
SK	Skeet
SMG	Sub Machine Gun
SML	Short Magazine Lee Enfield Rifle
SNT	Single Non-Selective Trigger
SPEC	Special
SPG	Semi-Pistol Grip
Spl.	Special
SR	Solid Rib
SRC	Saddle Ring Carbine
SS	Single Shot or Stainless Steel
SST	Single Selective Trigger
ST	Single Trigger
SxS	Side by Side
TBA	To be Announced
TD	Take Down
TGT	Target
TH	Target Hammer
TT	Target Trigger
UMC	Union Metallic Cartridge Co.
VG	Very Good
VR	Ventilated Rib
w/o	without
WBY	Weatherby
WC	Wad Cutter
WCF	Winchester Center Fire
WD	Wood
WFF	Watch For Fakes
WIN	Winchester
WO	White Outline
WRA	Winchester Repeating Arms Co.
WRF	Winchester Rim Fire
WRM	Winchester Rimfire Magnum
WSM	Winchester Short Magnum
WW	World War
WYTL	Would You Take less?
X (1X)	1X Wood Upgrade or Extra Full Choke Tube
XX (2X)	2X Wood Upgrade or Extra Extra Full Choke Tube
XXX (3x)	3X Wood Upgrade (on film, a full woody)

GLOSSARY

ACCOUTERMENT

All equipment carried by a soldier on outside of uniform, such as buckles, belts, or canteens, but not including weapons.

ACTION

The heart of the gun, receiver, bolt or breechblock feeding and firearm mechanism - see Boxlock, Rolling Block, or Sidelock.

ADJUSTABLE CHOKE

A device built into the muzzle of a shotgun enabling changes from one choke to another.

AIR GUN

A gun that utilizes compressed air or gas to launch the projectile.

APERTURE SIGHT

A rear sight assembly consisting of a hole or aperture located in an adj. rear sight through which the front sight and target are aligned.

AUTO LOADING

See semi-automatic.

BACKSTRAP

That parts of the revolver or pistol frame that are exposed at the rear of the grip.

BARREL

The steel tube (may be a sleeve wrapped in a synthetic material) that a projectile travels through.

BARREL BAND

A metal band, either fixed or adjustable, around the forend of a gun that holds the barrel to the stock.

BARREL THROAT

The breech end of a barrel that is chambered and somewhat funneled for passage of bullet from cartridge case mouth into barrel, also known as forcing cone.

BEAVERTAIL FOREND

A wider than normal forend.

BLUING

The chemical process of artificial oxidation (rusting) applied to gun parts so that the metal attains a dark blue or nearly black appearance.

BORE

Internal dimensions of a barrel (smooth or rifled) that can be measured using the Metric system (ie. Millimeters), English system (ie. Inches), or by the Gauge system (see Gauge). On a rifled barrel the bore is measured across the lands. Also, traditional English term used when referring to diameter of a shotgun muzzle (ga. in U.S. measure).

BOXLOCK ACTION

Typified by Parker shotgun in U.S. and Westley Richards in England. Generally considered not being as strong as the sidelock. Developed by Anson & Deeley, the boxlock is hammerless. It has two disadvantages: Hammer pin must be placed directly below knee of action, which is its weakest spot, and action walls must be thinned out to receive locks. These are inserted from below into large slots in action body, which is then closed with a plate. Greener crossbolt, when made correctly, overcomes many of the boxlock weaknesses.

BREECH

That portion of a gun which contains the rear chamber portion of the barrel(s), action, the trigger or firing mechanism, and the magazine.

BUCKHORN SIGHT

Open metallic rear sight with sides that curl upward and inward.

BULL BARREL

A heavier, thicker than normal barrel with little or no taper.

BUTTPLATE

A protective plate (usually steel) attached to the butt.

CALIBER

The diameter of the bore (measured from land to land). It does not designate bullet diameter.

CENTERFIRE

Self contained cartridge where the detonating primer is located in the center of the case head.

CHAMBER

Rear part of the barrel that has been reamed out so that it will contain a cartridge. When the breech is closed, the cartridge is supported in the chamber, and the chamber must align the primer with the firing pin, the bullet with the bore.

GLOSSARY

CHAMBER THROAT
Also called THROAT, is that area in the barrel that is directly forward of the chamber and that tapers to bore diameter.

CHECKERING
A functional decoration consisting of pointed pyramids cut into the wood generally applied to the pistol grip and forend/forearm areas affording better handling and control.

CHOKE
The muzzle constriction on a shotgun to control spread of the shot.

COCKING INDICATOR
Any device, which the act of cocking a gun moves into a position where it may be seen or felt in, orders to notify the shooter that the gun is cocked. Typical examples are the pins found on some high-grade hammer-less shotguns, which protrude slightly when they are cocked, and also the exposed cocking knobs on bolt-action rifles. Exposed hammers found on some rifles and pistols are also considered cocking indicators.

COLOR CASE HARDENING
A method of hardening steel and iron while imparting colorful swirls as well as surfaces figure. Normally, the desired metal parts are put in a crucible packed with a mixture of charcoal and finely ground animal bone to temperatures in the 800 degree C - 900 degree C range, after which they are slowly cooled, and then submerged into cold water.

COMB
The portion of the stock on which the shooter's cheek rests.

COMBINATION GUN
Generally a break-open shotgun type configuration fitted with at least one shotgun barrel and one rifle barrel. Such guns may be encountered with either two or three barrels, and less frequently with as many as four or five, and have been known to chamber for as many as four different calibers.

COMPENSATOR
A recoil-reducing device that mounts on the muzzle of a gun to deflect part of the powder gases up and rearward. Also called a "muzzle brake"

CRANE
In a modern solid-frame, swing-out cylinder revolver, the U-shaped yoke on which the cylinder rotates, and which holds the cylinder in the frame.

CROWNING
The rounding or chambering normally done to a barrel muzzle to insure that the mouth of the bore is square with the bore axis and that the edge is countersunk below the surface to protect it from impact damage. Traditionally, crowning was accomplished by spinning an abrasive-coated brass ball against the muzzle while moving it in a figure-eight pattern, until the abrasive had cut away any irregularities and produced a uniform and square mouth.

CRYOGENIC TEMPERING
Computer controlled cooling process that relieves barrel stress by subjecting the barrel to a temperature of -310 degree F for 22 hours.

CYLINDER
A rotating cartridge holder in a revolver. The cartridges are held in chambers and the cylinder turns, either to the left or the right, depending on the gun maker's design, as the hammer is cocked.

CYLINDER ARM
See Crane.

DAMASCENE
The decorating of metal with another metal, either by inlaying or attaching in some fashion.

DAMASCUS BARREL
A barrel made by twisting, forming and welding thin strips of steel around a mandrel.

DERRINGER
Usually refers to a small, concealable pistol with one or two short barrels.

DOUBLE ACTION
The principle in a revolver or auto-loading pistol wherein the hammer can be cocked and dropped by a single pull of the trigger. Most of these actions also provide capability for single action fire. In auto-loading pistols, double action normally applies only to the first shot of any series, the hammer being cocked by the slide for subsequent shots.

DOUBLE ACTION ONLY
Hammer no longer cocks in single action stage (many new DAO models are hammerless).

GLOSSARY

DOUBLE-BARRELED

A gun consisting of two barrels joined either side-by-side or one over the other.

DOUBLE-SET TRIGGER

A device that consists of two triggers one to cock the mechanism that spring-assists the other trigger, substantially lightening trigger pull.

DOVETAIL

A flaring machined or hand-cut slot that is also slightly tapered toward one end. Cut into the upper surface of barrels and sometimes actions, the dovetail accepts a corresponding part on which a sight is mounted. Dovetail slot blanks are used to cover the dovetail when the original sight has been removed or lost; this gives the barrel a more pleasing appearance and configuration.

DRILLING

German for "triple", which is their designation for a three-barrel gun.

EJECTOR

Mechanical device used to eject empty cartridges from chamber(s).

ENGINE TURNING

Overlapped spots of circular polishing.

ENGLISH STOCK

A straight, slender-gripped stock.

ENGRAVING

The art of engraving metal in decorative patterns. Scroll engraving is the most common type of hand engraving encountered. Much of today's factory engraving is rolled on which is done mechanically. Hand engraving requires artistry and knowledge of metals and related materials.

ETCHING

A method of decorating metal gun parts, usually done by acid etching or photo engraving.

EXTRACTOR

A device which partially lifts the spent casing(s) from the breech area, allowing the empty shell(s) to be removed manually.

FALLING BLOCK

A single-shot action where the breechblock drops straight down when the lever is actuated.

FIT AND FINISH

Terms used to describe over-all firearm workmanship.

FLOATING BARREL

A barrel bedded to avoid contact with any point on the stock.

FLOOR PLATE

Usually, a removable/hinged plate at the bottom of the receiver covering the magazine well.

FORCING CONE

Forward part of the chamber in a shotgun where the chamber diameter is reduced to bore diameter. The forcing cone aids the passage of shot into the barrel.

FOREARM

Usually a separate piece of wood in front of the receiver and under the barrel used for hand placement when shooting.

FOREND

Usually the forward portion of a one-piece rifle or shotgun stock, but can also refer to a separate piece of wood.

FRAME

The part of a firearm that the action (lock work), barrel, and stock/grip are connected to. Most of the time used when referring to a handgun or hinged frame long gun.

FREE RIFLE

A rifle designed for international-type target shooting. The only restriction on design is weight maximum 8 kilograms (17.6 lbs.).

FRONT STRAP

That part of the revolver or pistol grip frame that faces forward and often joins with the trigger guard. In target guns, notably the .45 ACP, the front strap is often stippled to give shooter's hand a slip-proof surface.

GAUGE/GA.

A unit of measure used to determine a shotgun's bore. Determined by the amount of pure lead balls equaling the bore diameter needed to equal one pound (i.e., a 12 ga. means that 12 lead balls exactly the diameter of the bore weigh one pound). In this text, .410 is referenced as a bore (if it was a gauge, it would be a 68 ga.).

GLOSSARY

GAUGE VS. BORE DIAMETER
> 10-Gauge = Bore Diameter of .775 inches or 19.3mm
> 12-Gauge = Bore Diameter of .729 inches or 18.2mm
> 16-Gauge = Bore Diameter of .662 inches or 16.8mm
> 20-Gauge = Bore Diameter of .615 inches or 15.7mm
> 28-Gauge = Bore Diameter of .550 inches or 13.8mm
> 68-Gauge = Bore Diameter of .410 inches or 12.6mm

GRIP
> The handle used to hold a handgun, or the area of a stock directly behind and attached to the frame/receiver of a long gun.

GRIPS
> Can be part of the frame or components attached to the frame used to assist in accuracy, handling, control, and safety of a handgun. Many currently manufactured semi-auto handguns have grips that are molded w/checkering as part of the synthetic frame.

GROOVES
> The spiral cuts in the bore of a rifle or handgun barrel that give the bullet its spin or rotation as it moves down the barrel.

HAMMERLESS
> Some "hammerless" firearms do in fact have hidden hammers, which are located in the action housing. Truly hammerless guns, such as the Savage M99, have a firing mechanism that is based on a spring-activated firing pin.

HEEL
> Back end of the upper edge of the butt-stock at the upper edge of the butt-plate or recoil pad.

JUXAPOSED
> See Side-by-Side listing.

LAMINATED STOCK
> A gunstock made of many layers of wood glued together under pressure. Together, the laminations become very strong, preventing damages from moisture, heat, and warping.

LANDS
> Portions of the bore left between the grooves of the rifling in the bore of a firearm. In rifling, the grooves are usually twice the width of the land. Land diameter is measured across the bore, from land to land.

MAGAZINE (mag.)
> The container which holds cartridges under spring pressure to be fed into the gun's chamber.

MAGNUM (Mag.)
> A modern cartridge with a higher-velocity load or heavier projectile than standard.

MAINSPRING
> The spring that delivers energy to the hammer or striker.

MANNLICHER STOCK
> A full-length slender stock with slender forend extending to the muzzle (full stock) affording better barrel protection.

MICROMETER SIGHT
> A finely adjustable target sight.

MONTE CARLO STOCK
> A stock with an elevated comb used primarily for scoped rifles.

MUZZLE
> The forward end of the barrel where the projectile exits.

MUZZLE BRAKE
> A recoil-reducing device attached to the muzzle.

NEEDLE GUN
> Ignition system invented by Johan Nikolas v. Dreyse in 1929. This ignition system using a paper cartridge became obsolete with the invention of the metallic cartridge.

OVER-UNDER (Superposed)
> A two-barrel gun in which the barrels are stacked one on top of the other.

PARALLAX
> Occurs in telescopic sights when the primary image of the objective lens does not coincide with the reticle. In practice, parallax is detected in the scope when, as the viewing eye is moved laterally, the image and the reticle appear to move in relation to each other.

GLOSSARY

PARKERIZING

Matted rust-resistant oxides finish, usually matte or dull gray, or black in color, found on military guns.

PEEP SIGHT

Rear sights consisting of a hole or aperture through which the front sight and target are aligned.

PEPPERBOX

An early form of revolving repeating pistol, in which a number of barrels were bored in a circle in a single piece of metal resembling the cylinder of a modern revolver. Functioning was the same as a revolver, the entire cylinder being revolved to bring successive barrels under the hammer for firing. Though occurring as far back as the 16th century, the pepperbox did not become practical until the advent of the percussion cap in the early 1800s. Pepperboxes were made in a wide variety of sizes and styles, and reached their popularity peak during the percussion period. Few were made after the advent of practical metallic cartridges. Both single- and double-action pepperboxes were made. Single-barreled revolvers after the 1840s were more accurate and easier to handle and soon displaced the rather clumsy and muzzle-heavy pepperbox.

PINFIRE

Self contained cartridge which is detonated by striking a small pin sticking through the side wall of the cartridge casing.

PICATINNY

Refers to a flat rail on top of the frame/slide, allowing different optics/sights to be used on the gun.

POLYGONAL

Circular rifling w/o hard edged lands and grooves.

POPE RIB

A rib integral with the barrel. Designed by Harry M. Pope, famed barrel maker and shooter, the rib made it possible to mount a target scope low over the barrel.

PROOFMARK

Proofmarks are usually applied to all parts actually tested, but normally appear on the barrel (and possibly frame), usually indicating the country of origin and circa of proof (especially on European firearms). In the U.S., there is no federalized or government proof house, only the manufacturer's in-house proofmark indicating that a firearm has passed its internal quality control standards per government specifications.

RECEIVER

That part of a rifle or shotgun (excluding hinged frame guns) that houses the bolt, firing pin, mainspring, trigger group, and magazine or ammunition feed system. The barrel is threaded into the somewhat enlarged forward part of the receiver, called the receiver ring. At the rear of the receiver, the butt or stock is fastened. In semi-automatic pistols, the frame or housing is sometimes referred to as the receiver.

RELEASE TRIGGER

A trap shooting trigger that fires the gun when the trigger is released.

RIB

A raised sighting plane affixed to the top of a barrel.

RIFLING

The spirally cut grooves in the bore of a rifle or handgun. The rifling stabilizes the bullet in flight. Rifling may rotate to the left or the right, the higher parts of the bore being called lands, the cuts or lower parts being called the grooves. Many types exist, such as oval, polygonal, button, Newton, Newton-Pope, parabolic, Haddan, Enfield, segmental rifling, etc. Most U.S.-made barrels have a right-hand twist, while British gun makers prefer a left-hand twist. In practice, there seems to be little difference in accuracy or barrel longevity.

RIMFIRE

Self contained metallic cartridge where the priming compound is contained inside the rim of the cartridge case. Detonated by the firing pin(s) striking the bottom edge of the outside rim.

ROLLING BLOCK ACTION

Single shot action, designed in the U.S. and widely used in early Remington arms. Also known as the REMINGTON-RIDER action, the breechblock, actuated by a lever, rotates down and back from the chamber. Firing pin is contained in block and is activated by hammer fall.

SCHNABEL FOREND

The curved/carved flared end of the forend that resembles the beak of a bird (Schnabel in German). This type of forend is common on Austrian and German guns; was popular in the U.S., but the popularity of the Schnabel forend/forearm comes and goes with the seasons. A schnozzle forend is often seen on custom stocks and rifles.

SHORT ACTION

A rifle action designed for shorter cartridges.

GLOSSARY

SHOTSHELL

Self contained round of ammunition used in shotguns, generally either brass and paper (older mfg.) or brass/steel and plastic (newer mfg.).

SIDE-BY-SIDE (JUXTAPOSED)

A two-barrel shotgun where the barrels are arranged side-by-side.

SIDELOCK

A type of action, usually long gun, where the moving parts are located on side of the lock plates, which in turn are inlet in the stock. Usually found only on better quality shotguns and rifles.

SIDEPLATES

Ornamental steel panels normally attached to a boxlock action to simulate a sidelock.

SINGLE ACTION

A firearms design which requires the hammer to be manually cocked for each shot. Also an auto-loading pistol design which requires manual cocking of the hammer for the first shot only.

SINGLE TRIGGER

One trigger on a double-barrel gun. It fires both barrels singly by successive pulls.

SLING SWIVELS

Metal loops affixed to the gun on which a carrying strap is attached.

SPUR TRIGGER

A trigger mounting system that housed the trigger in an extension of the frame in some old guns. The trigger projected only slightly from the front of the extension or spur, and no trigger guard was used on these guns.

STOCKS

See grips.

SUICIDE SPECIAL

A mass-produced variety of inexpensive single action revolvers and derringers, usually with a spur trigger. Produced under a variety of trade names, these guns earned their nickname by being almost as dangerous to shoot as to be shot at.

SUPERPOSED

Refers to an O/U barrel configuration.

TAKE DOWN

A gun which can be easily taken apart in two sections for carrying or shipping.

TANG (S)

The extension straps of the receiver/frame to which the stock/grips are attached.

TOP STRAP

The upper part of a revolver frame, which often is either slightly grooved - the groove serving as rear sight - or which carries at its rearward end a sight that may be adjustable.

TRAP STOCK

A shotgun stock with greater length and less comb drop (Monte Carlo, in many cases) used for trap shooting, enabling a built in height lead when shooting.

TRIGGERGUARD

Usually a circular or oval band of metal, horn, or plastic that goes around the trigger to provide both protection and safety in shooting circumstances.

TWIST BARRELS

A process in which a steel rod (called a mandrel) was wrapped with "skelps" - ribbons of iron. The skelps were then welded in a charcoal fire to form one piece of metal, after which the rod was driven out to be used again. The interior of the resulting tube then had to be laboriously bored out by hand to remove the roughness. Once polished, the outside was smoothed on big grinding wheels, usually turned by waterpower.

UNDER-LEVER

Action opening lever that is usually located below or in triggerguard, can also be side pivoting from forearm.

VENTILATED RIB

A sighting plane affixed along the length of a shotgun barrel with gaps or slots milled for cooling and lightweight handling.

VERNIER

Typically used in reference to a rear aperture (peep) sight. Usually upper tang mounted, and is adj. for elevation by means of a highly accurate vernier.

VIERLING

A German word designating a four barrel gun.

YOUTH DIMENSIONS

Usually refers to shorter stock dimensions and/or lighter weight enabling youth/women to shoot and carry a lighter, shorter firearm.

Listed below are the names and addresses of various firearms organizations/associations throughout the U.S. You are encouraged to join those organizations that pertain to your region and area(s) of interest. As thorough as we try to be, every year we get back quite a bit of mail for individual firearms associations that unfortunately, is undeliverable. If your club does not appear on the following pages or doesn't have a current address, please forward the correct information to us for inclusion in the next edition.

Academics for the Second Amendment (A2A)
Prof. J.E. Olson, President
Hamline University
P.O. Box 131254
St. Paul, MN 55113
Web site: www.2nd-scholars.org
Email: jolson@gw.hamline.edu

Alabama Gun Collectors
P.O. Box 70965
Tuscaloosa, AL 35407

Alamo Arms Collectors' Association, Inc.
PO Box 680642
San Antonio, TX 78268-0642
$20 yearly membership, meetings first Tuesday of each month
Leslie W. Moch, Secretary
Phone: 830-980-4746
George O. Stenzel, Treasurer
Phone: 210-523-5540

Alaska Gun Collectors Association
P.O. Box 242233
Anchorage, Alaska 99524
Web site: www.agca.net

American Custom Gunmakers Guild
Jan Billeb, Executive Director
22 Vista View
Cody, WY 82414-9606
Phone: 307-587-4297
$60 Associate Membership Fee
$100 Commercial Associate Membership Fee

American Self-Defense Institute
PO Box 430
Whitefish, MT 59937
Phone: 406-862-9530
Fax: 406-863-4009
Web site: www.americanselfdefense.com
E-mail: webmaster@americanselfdefense.com
Membership dues $49.95

Ark - La - Tex - Gun Collectors
Thomas L. Baird, President
9601 Blom Blvd.
Shreveport, LA 71118

Bay Colony Weapons Collectors, Inc.
Mr. Paul Livoli
53 Berkeley Street
Somerville, MA 02143

Boardman Valley Collectors Guild
Jack Johnson, Secretary
County Road 600
Manton, MI 49663

Browning Collectors Assn.
Anthony Vanderlinden, Secretary
5603-B West Friendly Ave., Ste. 166
Greensboro, NC 27410
Phone: 336-349-5427
Web site: www.browningcollectors.com

Buffalo Bill Historical Center
Cody Firearms Museum
720 Sheridan Ave.
Cody, WY 82414
Phone: 307-587-4771
Web site: www.bbhc.org

C.A.D.A. (Collector Arms Dealer Association)
P.O. Box 427
Thomson, IL 61285

California Rifle & Pistol Association, Inc.
271 E. Imperial Highway, Suite #620
Fullerton, CA 92835
Phone: 714-992-2772

Central Illinois Gun Collectors Assn. Inc.
Russ Gardner, Sec./Treas.
P.O. Box 875
Jacksonville, IL 62651-0875

Central Penn Antique Arms Association
John E. Holman Jr.
978 Thistle Road
Elizabethtown, PA 17022

Chisholm Trail Antique Gun Association
E.D. Stone
1906 Richmond
Wichita, KS 67203

Civil War Round Table of
North New Jersey
James F. Elliott
124 Conover Lane
Red Bank, NJ 07701

Colorado Gun Collectors Assoc.
Mr. William E. Pittman, Secretary/Treasurer
8075 S. Harrison Way
Littleton, CO 80122
Phone: 303-771-6830
Web site: www.cgca.com

Email: Tribune@uswest.net
$25 Annual Membership Fee

Colt Collectors Association
Karen Green, Secretary
25000 Highland Way
Los Gatos, CA 95033
Web site: www.coltcollectorsassoc.com
$35 Annual Membership Fee
$60 - Annual Membership Fee - Outside U.S.

Contemporary Longrifle Association
P.O. Box 2097
Staiton, VA 24402
Phone: 540-886-6189
Web site: www.longrifle.ws

Dallas Arms Collectors Association, Inc.
Richard Shea
PO Box 704
DeSoto, TX 75123
Phone: 972-223-3066
Fax: 972-223-3277
Web site: www.dallasarms.com

The Firearms Coalition of Colorado
Len Horner, Chairman
P.O. Box 1454
Englewood, CO 80150-1454
Phone: 303-296-4867
Fax: 303-295-6587
Web site: www.firearmscoalition-co.org
Email: firearmscoalition@juno.com
$20 Annual Membership Fee

Forks of the Delaware Historical Arms Society, Inc.
Mr. Howard A. Hoffman
3491 Linden St.
Bethlehem, PA 18017
Phone: 610-997-8613
Fax: 610-997-8614
$20 Annual Membership Fee

German Gun Collectors Association
Dietrich Apel
438 Willow Brook Rd
P.O. Box 385
Plainfield, NH 03781
Phone: 603-469-3450
Fax: 603-469-3471
Web site: www.germanguns.com
Email: jaeger@valley.net

Gibbs Military Collector's Club
211 Lawn St.
Martinsburg, WV 25401
Phone: 304-262-1651
Fax: 304-262-1658
Web site: www.gibbsrifle.com
Email: support@gibbsrifle.com

Glock Collectors Association
P.O. Box 1063
Maryland Heights, MO 63043
Phone/Fax: 314-878-2061

Golden Eagle Collectors Association
Chris Showler, Secretary
11144 Slate Creek Rd.
Grass Valley, CA 95945

Great Lakes Military Collectors Association
P.O. Box 401
Maumee, OH 43537

Gun Owners Civil Rights Alliance/Concealed Carry Reform Now!
Joseph E. Olson, President
P.O. Box 131254
St. Paul, MN 55113
Phone: 651-636-4465
Web site: www.mnccrn.org
$30 Annual Membership Fee

Gun Owners of America
Larry Pratt, Executive Director
8001 Forbes Pl., Suite 102
Springfield, VA 22151
Fax: 703-321-8408
Email: goamail@gunowners.org
$20 Annual Membership Fee

Hawaii Historic Arms Association
Box 1733
Honolulu, HI 96806

High Standard Collectors Association
540 W. 92nd St.
Indianapolis, IN 46260
$15 Annual Membership Fee

Hopkins & Allen Arms & Memorabilia Society
P.O. Box 187
Delphos, OH 45833
$6.00 Annual Donation for 6 Issues

Houston Gun Collectors Association
P.O. Box 741429
Houston, TX 77274-1429

Indianhead Firearms Assn.
13810 25th Ave.
Chippewa Falls, WI 54729
Phone: 715-723-0860

Indian Territory Gun Collectors Association
Mr. Joe Wanenmacher, Secretary - Treasurer
P.O. Box 33201
Tulsa, OK 74153-1201

Iroquois Arms Collectors Association
Kenneth Keller, Secretary
Susann Keller, Show Secretary
214 70th St.
Niagara Falls, NY 14304

Jersey Shore Antique Arms Collectors
Joe Sisia
P.O. Box 100
Bayville, NJ 08721-0100
$20 Annual Membership Fee

Kansas Cartridge Collectors Association
Vic Suetter
Route 1
Lincoln, KS 67455

Kentuckiana Arms Collectors Assoc.
Sally Harper, Secretary
P.O. Box 1776
Louisville, KY 40201
$20 Annual Membership Fee
Phone: 502-425-2460

Kentucky Rifle Association
Attn: Ruth Collis
2319 Sue Ann Dr.
Lancaster, PA, 17602.

Lancaster Muzzle Loading Rifle Association
James H. Frederick, Jr.
700 Prospect Road
Columbia, PA 17512

Lee County Gun Collectors Association
PO Box 6168
Fort Myers Beach, FL 33932
Phone: 941-463-2840

Long Island Antique Gun Collectors Assoc.
Frederick R. Wilkens
35 Beach Street
Farmingdale, L.I., NY 11735
$30 Annual Membership Fee

Mannlicher Collectors Association
P.O. Box 1249
The Dalles, OR 97058

Marlin Firearms Collectors Association, Ltd.
P.O. Box 491
Clay Center, KS 67432-0491
$5 Initiation Fee
$15 Annual Membership Fee
$17 Canadian (U.S. funds)
$24 International (U.S. Funds)

Maryland Arms Collectors Assoc. (MACA)
Del Kuzemchak, Secretary
33 S. Main Street P.O. Box 206
Loganville, PA 17342-0206
$25 Annual Membership Fee

Maryland Licensed Firearms Dealers Assoc., Inc.
P.O. Box 10237
Baltimore, MD 21234-9998
Phone: 410-356-9485
Fax: 410-356-9486

Maumee Valley Gun Collectors Association
P.O. Box 492
Maumee, OH 43537

Memphis Antique Weapons Association
Lonnie Griffin 108 Clark Place
Memphis, TN 38104

Minnesota Rifle and Revolver Association
Cliff Secord
5344 Morgan Ave. N.
Brooklyn Center, MN 55430

Minnesota Weapons Collectors Association
Gail Foster, Executive Director
P.O. Box 662
Hopkins, MN 55343
www.mwca.org
$25 Annual Dues
$5 Admission - 8 shows/year

Miniature Arms Collectors/Makers Society, Ltd.
Bill Adrian, Membership Chairman
2502 Fresno Ln.
Plainfield, IL 60544-8470

Missouri Valley Arms Collectors Association, Inc. (MVACA)
L.P. Brammer, Membership Secretary
P.O. Box 33033
Kansas City, MO 64114
Phone: 816-333-6509
Annual Membership $20.00 - ages 21+;
$10.00 - under 21

Montana Arms Collectors Association
Dean E. Yearout
1516 - 21st Ave. S.
Great Falls, MT 59405
Phone: 406-761-7280
$20 Annual Membership Fee

Nat'l Automatic Pistol Collectors Assoc. (N.A.P.C.A.)
Thompson D. Knox
Box 15738
St. Louis, MO 63163
Phone: 314-481-4344
$40 Annual Membership Fee - U.S. & Canada
$50 Elsewhere

National Mossberg Collectors Association
Victor Havlin
P.O. Box 487
Festus, MO 63028
$10 Annual Membership Fee
Phone: 636-937-6401

National Rifle Association (NRA)
11250 Waples Mill Rd.
Fairfax, VA 22030
Phone: 888-JOIN-NRA/800-NRA-3888
Fax: 703-267-3970
Web site: www.nra.org
Email: membership@nrahq.org
$35 Regular Annual Membership Dues
$30 Annual Senior Membership
 (65+, also disabled vets)
$60 for 2 years
$85 for 3 years
$125 for 5 years
$750 Life Membership Dues
$375 Senior Life Membership (also disabled vets)
$15 Annual Junior Membership (18 years and younger)
$10 Annual Liberty Associate Membership (w/o magazine)

New East-Coast Arms Collectors Associates, Inc.
www.NEACA.com

New Hampshire Arms Collectors, Inc.
Warren Thayer
P.O. Box 6
Harrisville, N.H. 03450

North Eastern Arms Collectors Assoc., Inc.
Thomas J. Mulligan
P.O. Box 306
Island Park, NY 11558
Email: Mulligun@aol.com
$20 Annual Membership Fee

Northwest Montana Arms Collectors
Association (NWMACA)
Paul Willis, Treasurer
P.O. Box 653
Kalispell, MT 59903-0653
Phone: 406-755-3980
Email: pswillis@centurytel.net

Ohio Gun Collectors Association
Laura Knotts - Business Manager
P.O. Box 406
Sagamore Hills, OH 44067-0406
Phone: 330-467-5733
Fax: 330-467-5793
Web site: www.ogca.com
Email: ogca@ogca.com
$25.00 Annual Membership Fee
$10.00 Application Fee
Members and guests of members only.

Oregon Arms Collectors, Inc.
P.O. Box 8986
Portland, OR 97207-8986
Web site: members.tripod.com/~oregon-armscollectors/index.html
$15 Annual Membership Fee

Parker Gun Collectors Association
Ron Kirby, Executive Director
8825 Bud Smith Road
Wake Forest, NC 27587
Phone: 919-554-4556
Fax: 919-554-8120
Web site: www.parkergun.org

Peoples Rights Organization
3953 Indianola Ave.
Columbus, OH 43214
Phone: 614-268-0122
Fax: 614-261-9100
Firearms Classes: 614-846-0597
Refuse to be a Victim Classes: 614-323-3102
Web site: www.peoplesrights.org
Email: d-walker@juno.com
$25 Annual Membership Fee
$37.50 Family Membership Fee
$300 Lifetime Membership Fee

Potomac Arms Collectors Association
Attn: Secretary
P.O. Box 1812
Wheaton, MD 20915
$25 Annual Membership Fee

Randall Firearms/Pistol Collectors
Association
Mr. Rick Kennerknecht, Historian
P.O. Box 4957
Casper, WY 82604-4957
Phone: 866-422-4578
Fax: 413-521-7027
Web site: www.Randall45.com
E-Mail: Collectors@Randall45.com
Membership: Free
Online Research: Free
$30 Factory Research letter (Randall Pistols Only)

Remington Society of America
Gordon W. Fosburg, Membership
11900 N. Brinton Road
Lake, MI 48632
Phone: 313-659-5427
Web site: www.remingtonsociety.com
Annual Membership $30 + $5 application fee
Life Membership $300 + $5 application fee

Ruger Collectors Association, Inc.
P.O. Box 240
Green Farms, CT 06436
Phone: 203-259-6222, Ext. 124
$25 Annual Membership Fee

SAAMI
Sporting Arms & Ammunition Manufacturers' Institute
11 Mile Hill Road
Newtown, CT 06470
www.saami.org

SASS
Single Action Shooting Society
www.sass.com

Sako Collectors Association
Konie Wheeler, President
57330 Walker Road
Scappoose, OR 97056
Phone: 503-543-4410

Santa Barbara Historical Arms Coll. Assoc.
P.O. Box 6291
Santa Barbara, CA 93160-6291
$35 Initiation
$20 Annual Membership Fee

San Bernardino Valley Arms Collectors
Robert Walter
18710 Cajon Blvd.
San Bernardino, CA 92407
Los Alamos, NM 87544

San Gabriel Valley Arms Collectors
Gerald C. Knight, Secretary/Treasurer
1140 Daveric Drive
Pasadena, CA 91107-1740
Phone: 818-351-9368
$20 Annual Dues

Second Amendment Foundation
The New Gun Week
Womens & Guns Magazine
Gun News Digest
Gottlieb-Tartaro Report
Second Amendment Reporter
Alan Gottlieb, Founder
James Madison Building
12500 NE Tenth Place
Bellevue, WA 98005
Phone: 425-454-7012
Fax: 425-451-3959
Member Services (800)426-4302
web site: www.SAF.org
E-mail: info@saf.org
Tax Deductible membership dues $15.00
Tax Deductible Life membership dues $150

Smith & Wesson Collectors Association
S. Cheely, Administrative Assistant
P.O. Box 32
Great Bend, KS 67530
Fax: 620-792-2481
Email: s&w@greatbend.com

Southern California Arms Collectors Association, Inc.
Dr. Matthew Schneiderman
P.O. Box 7432
Thousand Oaks, CA 91359-7432
$30 Annual Membership Fee
Phone: 818-995-3781

Tampa Bay Arms Collectors Association, Inc.
H. Allen Bounds, Secretary/Treasurer
P.O. Box 41666
St. Petersburg, FL 33743-1666
$15 Annual Membership Fee

Texas Gun Collectors Association (TGCA)
Carolyn Mims
P.O. Box 701314
San Antonio, TX 78270

The Thompson Center Association
P.O. Box 792
Northboro, MA 01532
Email: TCA@aol.com
$30 Annual Membership Fee

Tri-State Gun Collectors, Inc.
Manette Sneary - Business Manager
P.O. Box 1201
Lima, OH 45802
Phone: 419-647-0067

United Sportshooting Association
P.O. Box 610
Laurel, MD 20725-0610
Phone: 301-953-3301
Fax: 301-490-8904

Washington Arms Collectors, Inc.
Susan Elings Director of Office Operations
P.O. Box 389
Renton, WA 98057-0389

Phone: 425-255-8410
Fax: 425-255-8946
Web site: www.halcyon.com/wac/
E-mail: wac@halcyon.com
Membership dues $20
Life membership dues $400

Weatherby Collectors Association, Inc.
P.O. Box 478
Pacific, MO 63069
$30 - Membership Fee
$500 Lifetime Membership Fee
Phone: 636.271.3336
Web site: www.weatherbycollectors.com
Email: WCAsecretary@aol.com

Williamette Valley Arms Collectors Association, Inc.
James Crudele, Executive Secretary
P.O. Box 5191
Eugene, OR 97405
Phone: 541-747-5271
$15 Membership Fee

Winchester Arms Collectors Association
David P. Bichrest Executive Secretary
P.O. Box 367

Silsbee, TX 77656-0367
Phone: 409-385-5768
Fax: 409-385-5726
Web site: www.winchestercollector.org
Email: davidwaca@msn.com
$45 to join (includes $35 annual dues)
U.S.A.
$55 to join (includes $45 annual dues)
Canada
$65 to join (includes $55 annual dues)
Foreign
$500 Lifetime Membership Fee

Winchester Club of America
Karen Sellers
Box 151B Crane Brook Rd
Alstead, NH 03602
$35 U.S. Annual membership
$50 Foreign membership
$350 Life U.S. membership
$500 Life Foreign membership

Zumbro Valley Arms Collectors, Inc.
Box 6621
Rochester, MN 55901

CONSERVATION ORGANIZATIONS

The following are not firearms associations, but are conservation organizations that may or may not have links to hunting/shooting sports. These organizations are dedicated to preserving wildlife and natural habitat. You are encouraged to contact these organizations to learn more.

Ducks Unlimited
One Waterfowl Way
Memphis, TN 38120
Phone No.: 901-758-3825
Fax No.: 901-758-3850

Foundation for North American Wild Sheep
Raymond Lee, Executive Director
720 Allen Ave.
Cody, WY 82414-9981
Phone No.: 307-527-6261
1 Yr. Membership $45; 3 Yrs.
$120

The Mule Deer Foundation
1005 Terminal Way, Ste. 170
Reno, NV 89502
$25 Annual Membership Fee

The National Wild Turkey Federation
P.O. Box 530
Edgefield, SC 29824
Phone No.: 1-800-843-6983
Call for membership details

North American Wild Sheep
Foundation
Minnesota-Wisconsin Chapter

PO Box 892
Hudson, WI 54016

Pheasants Forever
1783 Buerkle Circle
White Bear Lake, MN 55110
Phone No.: 651-773-2000
Fax No.: 651-773-5500
Web site:
www.pheasantsforever.org
Email: pf@pheasantsforever.org
$25 Annual Membership Fee
includes 5 issues of Pheasants
Forever magazine

Quail Unlimited
31 Quail Run
P.O. Box 610
Edgefield, SC 29824
Phone No.: 803-637-5731
Fax No.:803-637-0037
Email: Quaill@jetbn.net
$25 Annual Membership includes
bimonthly subscription to Quail
Unlimited

Rocky Mountain Elk Foundation
2291 W. Broadway
Missoula, MT 59802
Phone No.: 406-523-4500
Fax No.: 406-523-4581

$30 Membership Fee (includes 6
issues of Bugle magazine)

The Ruffed Grouse Society
Ronald P. Burkert
451 McCormick Rd.
Coraopolis, PA 15108
Phone No.: 888-564-6747
Web site: www.ruffedgrousesociety.org
Email: rgs@ruffedgrousesociety.org
$20 Annual Membership Fee
$30 Conservation Membership
Fee
$100 Sustaining Membership Fee
$200+ Various Sponsor
Membership Fee
(all memberships includes subscription to Ruffed Grouse Society
magazine)

Safari Club International
4800 W. Gates Pass Rd.
Tucson, AZ 85745
Phone No.: 602-620-1220
$55 Annual Membership Fee
USA/CAN/MEX

REFERENCE SOURCES

Adler, Dennis, *The 1st Edition Blue Book of Airguns.* Minneapolis, MN: Blue Book Publications, 2001.

Adler, Dennis, *The 1st Edition Blue Book of Modern Black Powder Values.* Minneapolis, MN: Blue Book Publications, 2000.

Adler, Dennis, *The 2nd Edition Blue Book of Modern Black Powder Values.* Minneapolis, MN: Blue Book Publications, 2002.

Adler, Dennis, *Colt Blackpowder Reproductions & Replicas.* Minneapolis, MN: Blue Book Publications, 1998

Allen, John, *The 2nd Edition Blue Book of Airguns,* Minneapolis, MN: Blue Book Publications, Inc., 2002.

Antaris, Leonardo, Dr., *Astra Automatic Pistols.* Sterling, CO: FIRAC Publishing Co., 1988.

Antaris, Leonardo, Dr. *Star Firearms,* Davenport, IA, Firac Publishing, 2002.

Bady, Donald B., *Colt Automatic Pistols.* Los Angeles, CA: Borden Publishing Co., 1973.

Baer, Larry L., *The Parker Book* North Hollywood, CA: Beinfeld Publishing Co., 1974.

Ball, Robert., *Mauser Military Rifles of the World,* Iola, WI: Krause Publications, 1996.

Ball, Robert., *Remington Firearms: The Golden Age of Collecting,* WI: Krause Publications, 1995.

Barns, Frank C., *Cartridges of the World.* Northbrook, IL: DBI Books, Inc., 1989.

Beeman, Robert, Dr., & John Allen, *The 2nd Edition Blue Book of Airguns,* Minneapolis, MN: Blue Book Publications, Inc., 2002

Belford, James N. and Dunlap, Jack, *Mauser Self Loading Pistol.* Alhambra, CA: Borden Publishing Co., 1969.

Bender, Roy G. III, *Mauser.* Houston, TX: Collector's Press, 1971.

Boothroyd, Geoffry & Susan M., *Boothroyd's Directory of British Gunmakers.* Amity, OR: Sand Lake Press, 1994.

Breathed and Schroeder, *System Mauser.* Chicago, IL: Handgun Press, 1967.

Brophy, William S., *L.C. Smith Shotguns.* North Hollywood, CA: Beinfeld Publishing Co., 1977.

Brophy, William S., *Marlin Firearms.* Harrisburg, PA: Stackpole Books, 1989.

Butzer, David F., *The American Shotgun.* Middlefield, CT: Lyman Publications, 1973.

Buxton, Warren H., *The P-38 Pistol: Volumes I, II & III.* Los Alamos, NM: U.C. Ross Books.

Byron, David, *Gunmarks, Tradenames, Codemarks, and Proofs from 1870 to the Present.* New York, NY: Crown Publishers, 1979.

Carder, Charles, *Side by Sides of the World.* Delphos, OH: AVIL ONZE Publishing.

Carder, Charles, *Side by Sides of the World Y2K.* Delphos, OH: AVIL ONZE Publishing, 2000.

Condry, Ken, & Jones, Larry, *The Colt Commemoratives, 1961-1986.* Dallas, TX: Taylor Publishing Co., 1989.

Costanza, Sam, *World of Lugers: Volume I.* Mayfield Heights, OH: World of Lugers, 1977.

Eastman, Matt, *Browning, Sporting Arms of Distinction.* Fitzgerald, GA: Published by Author, 1994.

Ezell, Edward Clinton, *Handguns of the World.* Harrisburg, PA: Stackpole Books, 1981.

Ezell, Edward Clinton, *Small Arms of the World (12th Ed).* Harrisburg, PA: Stackpole Books, 1983.

Dance, Tom, *High Standard; A Collector's Guide to the Hamden & Hartford Target Pistols.* Lincoln, RI: Andrew Mobray Publishers, 1991.

Flayderman, Norm, *Flayderman's Guide (7th ed.).* Northbrook, IL: DBI Books, Inc., 1998.

Gardner, Col. Robert, *Small Arms Makers.* New York, NY: Bonanza Books, 1963.

Grant, James. J., *Boys' Single Shot Rifles.* Prescott, AZ: Wolfe Publishing Company, 1991.

Groenewold, John, *Quackenbush Guns.* Mundelein, IL, published by author, 2000.

Gunther, Mullins, Price, and Cote', *The Parker Story, Vol. I.* Knoxville, TN: Parker Story Joint Venture Group, 1998.

Gunther, Mullins, Price, and Cote', *The Parker Story, Vol. II.* Knoxville, TN: Parker Story Joint Venture Group, 2000.

Hill and Anthony, *Confederate Long Arms and Pistols.* Charlotte, NC: Confederate Arms, 1978.

Jinks, Roy G., *History of Smith & Wesson.* North Hollywood, CA: Beinfeld Publishing Co., 1977.

Karr and Karr, Jr., *Remington Handgun.* Stackpole Co., Second Edition, 1951.

Kenyon, Charles Jr., *Lugers at Random.* Chicago, IL: Handgun Press, 1969.

Kersten, Manfred, *Walther: A German Legend,* Long Beach, CA: Safari Press, Inc., 2001.

Kimmel, J., *Savage & Stevens Arms.* Portland, OR: Corey/Stevens Pub., Inc., 1990.

Kopel, Graham, and Moore, *A Study of the Colt Single Action Army Revolver.* La Puente, CA: Kopel, Graham, and Moore Publishers, 1978.

Krasne, Jerry A., *Enyclopedia and Reference Catalog for Auto Loading Guns.* San Diego, CA: Triple K Manufacturing, 1989.

Leithe, Frederick, *Japanese Handguns.* California: Borden Publishing Co., 1968.

Madis, George, *The Model 12.* Lancaster, TX: Published by Author, 1981.

Madis, George, *The Winchester Book.* Lancaster, TX: Privately Published by Author, 1975.

Marcot, Roy, *Remington, America's Oldest Gunmaker.* Peoria, IL: Primedia Special Interest Publications, 1998.

Maxwell, Samuel L., Sr., *Lever Action Magazine Rifles.* Published by Author, 1978.

Muderlak, Ed, Parker Guns, *The Old Reliable.* Long Beach, CA: Safari Press, 1997.

Murray, Douglas, *The Ninety-Nine.* Published by Author, 1985.

Nonte, Jr., George C., *Firearms Encyclopedia.* Outdoor Life: New York, NY, 1973.

Olson, Ludwig, *Mauser Bolt Action Rifles.* Montezuma, IA: F. Brownell & Son Publishers, Inc., 1976.

Rankin, James L., *Walther, Vols. I, II, III.* Coral Gables, FL: Published by Author, 1976.

Rule, Roger C., *The Rifleman's Rifle.* Northridge, CA: Alliance Books, Inc., 1982.

Sellers, Frank, *American Gunsmiths.* Highland Park, NJ: The Gun Room Press, 1983.

Sellers, Frank, *Sharp's Firearms.* North Hollywood, Ca: Beinfeld Publishing Co., 1978.

Serven, editor, *The Collecting of Guns.* Bonanza Books, 1964.

Sharpe, Phillip B., *The Rifle in America.* Funk and Wagnalls, 1947.

Shooter's Bible. S. Hackensack, NJ: Published annually by Stoeger Industries.

Steindler, *Steindler's New Firearms Dictionary.* Phoenix, AZ: Stackpole Books, 1985.

Still, Jan C., *Axis Pistols.* Marceline, MO: Walsworth Publishing Co., 1986.

Still, Jan C., *Imperial Lugers.* Marceline, MO: Walsworth Publishing Co., 1991.

Still, Jan C., *Third Reich Lugers.* Marceline, MO: Walsworth Publishing Co., 1988.

Supica, Jim and Nahas, Richard, *Standard Catalog of Smith & Wesson.* Iola, WI: Krause Publications, 1996.

Supica, Jim, *Standard Catalog of Smith & Wesson Vol. II,* Iola, WI: Krause Publications, 2001.

Tanner, Hans, *Guns of the World.* Bonanza Books, 1972, 1977.

Vanderlinden, Anthony, *Belgian Browning Pistols 1889-1949,* Greensboro, NC, Wet Dog Publications, 2001.

Webster, Donald B. Jr., *Suicide Specials.* Harrisburg, PA: Stackpole, Co., 1958.

West, Bill, *Browning Arms & History.* Santa Fe Springs, CA: Stockton Trade Press, Inc., 1972.

West, Bill, *Marlin and Ballard Firearms & History.* Norwalk, CA: Stockton Trade Press, Inc., 1977.

West, Bill, *Remington Arms & History.* Whittier, CA: Stockton Trade Press, Inc., 1970.

West, Bill, *Savage and Stevens Arms & History.* Whittier, CA: Stockton Trade Press, Inc., 1971.

Whitaker, Dean H., *Model 70 Winchester 1937-1964.* Dallas, TX: Taylor Publishing Co., 1978.

Wilkerson, Don, *Post War Colt Single Action Army.* Published by Author, 1978.

Wilkerson, Don, *Post-War Colt Single-Action Revolver, 1976-1986.* Dallas, TX: Taylor Publishing, 1986.

Wilkerson, Don, *Colt Scouts, Peacemakers, and New Frontiers in .22 Caliber,* Marceline, MO, Walsworth Publishing Co., 1993.

Wilkerson, Don, *Colt Single Action Army Revolver, Pre-War/Post-War Model,* Minneapolis, MN, Broughton Printing Inc., 1991.

Wilson, R.L., *The Colt Engraving Book, Vols. I & II.* New York, NY: Bannerman's Limited Edition, 2001.

Wilson, R.L., *The Book of Colt Firearms.* Minneapolis, MN: Blue Book Publications, Inc., 1993.

Wilson, R.L., *Colt, An American Legend.* New York, NY: Abbeville Press.

Wilson, R.L., *Colt Commemorative Firearms.* Geneseo, IL: Robert E.P. Cherry Publishing Co., 1973.

Wilson, R.L., *The Colt Heritage.* New York, NY: Simon and Schuster.

Wilson, R.L., *Winchester: An American Legend,* New York: Random House. 1991.

Wilson, R.L., *The World of Beretta: An International Legend,* New York: Random House. 2000.

Wilson, R.L., *Ruger & His Guns.* New York: Simon and Schuster. 1996.

Wirnsberger, Gerhard, *The Standard Directory of Proofmarks.* Jolex, Inc.

Wood, J.B., *Beretta Auotmatic Pistols, The Collector's & Shooter's Comprehensive Guide.* Harrisburg, PA: Stackpole Books, 1985.

Zhuk, A.B., *The Illustrated Encyclopedia of Handguns.* London: Greenhill Books. 1995.

PERIODICALS

American Firearms Industry - 1525 So. Andrews Ave. Suite #214, Ft. Lauderdale, FL 33316. Phone No.: 954-467-9994. Membership is $55 per year. Trade publications and related material.

American Gunsmith - P.O. Box 540638, Merrit Island, FL 32954. Phone No.: 321-459-1558. Published monthly. Subscription is $47 per year.

American Handgunner - Published by Publisher's Development. 591 Camino de la Reina, Suite 200, San Diego, CA 92108. Phone No.: 800-537-3006. Published bi-monthly. Subscription is $16.95 per year.

American Hunter - Published by the NRA, 11250 Waples Mill Rd., Fairfax, VA 22030. Phone No.: 800-672-3888. Subscription included in price of NRA Membership ($35). Published monthly.

American Rifleman - Published by the NRA, 11250 Waples Mill Rd., Fairfax, VA 22030. Phone No.: 800-672-3888. Subscription included in price of NRA Membership ($35). Published monthly.

Australian Shooter's Journal - Published by the Sporting Shooters Association of Australia, Inc., P.O. Box 2066, Kent Town, SA 5071 AUSTRALIA. Phone No.: 011-61-8-8272-7622, Fax No.: 011-61-8-8272-2945. Subscription is $50 per year in Australia, $60 per year elsewhere, published monthly.

Black's Buyer Directories - Published by Black's Directories, P.O. Box 2029, 43 West Front St., Ste. 11, Red Bank, NJ 07701. Phone No.: 732-224-8700 or 800-224-9464, Fax No.: 732-741-2827. Published annually, $14.95 (+ S&H).

The Clay Pigeon - P.O. Box 1022, Milford, PA 18337. Phone No.: 570-296-5768, Fax No.: 570-296-9298. Subscription is $18 per year (11 issues).

Combat Handguns - Published by Harris Publications, 1115 Broadway, Fifth Floor, New York, NY 10010. Phone No.: 212-807-7100, Fax No.: 212-627-4678. Subscription rate: $19.97 for 1 year (8 issues).

Deutsches Waffen Journal - Journal-Verlag Scwend GmbH, Schmollerstrasse 31, D-74523, Schwabish Hall, GERMANY. Phone No.: 011-49-791-404-511, Fax No.: 011-49-791-404-505

The Double Gun Journal - P.O. Box 550, East Jordan, MI 49727-9636. Phone No.: 231-536-7439, Fax No.: 231-536-7450. Published quarterly.

Ducks Unlimited - One Waterfowl Way, Memphis, TN 38120. Phone No.: 901-758-3825, Fax No.: 901-758-3850. Membership rate: $25 per year, includes 6 issues.

Euro Shot Business - Published by Emap USA, 6420 Wilshire Blvd., Los Angeles, CA 90048-5515. Phone No.: 323-782-2000.

Field & Stream Magazine - P.O. Box 55652, Boulder, CO 80322. Phone No.: 800-289-0639 or 212-779-5000. Subscription rate $15.94 annually. Published monthly (12 issues).

Firearms Industry Showcase - Published by the United Sportshooting Association, P.O. Box 610, Laurel, MD 20725-0610. Phone No.: 301-953-3301, Fax: 301-490-8904.

Game & Gun - P.O. Box 968, Traverse City, MI 49685. Published bimonthly.

Gray's Sporting Journal - Published by North American Publications, Inc., 735 Broad Street, Augusta, GA 30901. Phone No.: 706-722-6060. Subscription is $36.95 for 7 issues.

Gun Dog - Published by Emap USA, 6420 Wilshire Blvd., Los Angeles, CA 90048-5515. Phone No.: 323-782-2000.

Gun Report - P.O. Box 38, Aledo, IL 61231, Phone No.: 309-582-5311. $33.00 per year (USA), published monthly.

Gun Runner - Box 565, Lethbridge, Alberta T1J3Z4, CANADA. Phone No.: 905-372-2269.

Guns and Ammo - Published by Emap USA. PO Box 58505 Boulder, CO 80323. Phone No.: 800-800-2666. $17.94 per year (USA), published monthly.

Guns & Gear - Published by B.A.S.S., Inc., 5845 Carmichel Rd., Montgomery, AL 36117. Phone No.: 334-277-3940. Subscription is $18 per year, published monthly.

Gun List - Published by Krause Publications, 700 E. State St., Iola, WI 54990. Phone No.: 715-445-2214. $36.98 per year, published bi-weekly.

Gun Week - P.O. Box 488, Buffalo, NY 14209. Annual Subscription - $35. Published 3 times a month. Phone No.: 716-885-6408

Guns Magazine - Published by Publisher's Development. 591 Camino de la Reina, Suite 200, San Diego, CA 92108. Phone No.: 800-537-3006. Subscription is $19.95 per year (12 issues).

Handguns Magazine - Published by Emap USA., PO Box 56195 Boulder, CO 80322. Phone No.: 800-800-4486. Subscription is $17.94 (12 issues).

Hunting - Published by Emap USA., PO Box 56295 Boulder, CO 80322. Phone No.: 800-800-4246. Subscription is $17.94 (12 issues).

Man at Arms - P.O. Box 460, Lincoln, RI 02865. Published bimonthly ($32 yearly). Phone No.: 401-726-8011.

Michigan Hunting & Fishing - P.O. Box 1000, Sault Ste. Marie, MI 49783.

Muzzle Blasts - Published by the National Muzzle Loading Rifle Association, P.O. Box 67, Friendship, IN 47021. Phone No.: 812-667-5131. Subscription is $35 per year, published monthly.

PERIODICALS

North American Hunter - 12301 Whitewater Dr., Minnetonka, MN 55343. Phone No.: 952-936-9333. Published 8 times per year (subscription included in membership).

Outdoor Guide Magazine - 505 S. Ewing, St. Louis, MO 63103, Phone No.: 314-535-9786. Subscription is $12 for 6 issues.

Outdoor Life Magazine - Two Park Ave., New York, NY 10016. Phone No.: 800-365-1580 or 212-779-5000. Subscription is $15.97 for 9 issues.

Pennsylvania Sportsman - P.O. Box 223, Farmington, PA 15437

Pheasants Forever - 1783 Buerkle Circle, White Bear Lake, MN 55110. Phone No.: 651-773-2000, Fax No.: 651-773-5500. Membership is $25 per year, includes 5 issues.

Pointing Dog Journal/Retriever Journal - Published by the Village Press, 2779 Aero Park Dr., Traverse City, MI 49686. Phone No.: 231-946-3712, Fax No.: 231-946-3289. Subscription is $25.95 for 8 issues.

Quail Unlimited - P.O. Box 610 Edgefield, SC 29824. Phone No.: 803-637-5731, Fax No.: 803-637-0037. Membership is $25 per year, published bimonthly.

Rifle Shooter - Published by Emap USA. Rifle Shooter c/o Customer Service, PO Box 53366, Boulder, CO 80322. Phone No.: 800-627-7975. Subscription is $19.94 for 6 issues.

Safari Club International - 4800 W. Gates Pass Rd., Tucson, AZ 85745. Phone No.: 602-620-1220. Publications: Safari magazine, Safari Africa, Deer of the World, Sheep of the World, International Record Book of Trophy Animals, Record Book Field Edition.

SHOT Business - Published monthly by Petersen Publishing.

Shooting Industry - 591 Camino de la Reina #200, San Diego, CA 92108. Phone No.: 800-537-3006, $25 per year (USA). Published monthly.

Shooting Sportsman - Published by Down East Enterprise, Inc., P.O. Box 1357, Camden, ME, 04843. Phone No.: 207-594-9544, Fax No.: 207-594-5144. Subscription is $30 for 6 issues.

Shooting Sports Retailer - 130 W. 42nd St., New York, NY 10036. Phone No.: 212-840-0660. Free to retailers. Published 6 times per year.

Shooting Times - Published by Primedia, Inc. 2 News Plaza, Peoria, Il 61614. Phone No.: 800-495-8362. Subscription is $19.95 for 18 issues.

Shotgun News - Published by Primedia, Inc. 2 News Plaza, Peoria, Il 61614. Phone No.: 800-495-8362. Subscription is $29 yearly (36 issues), but offer fewer issues per year for a reduced price.

Shotgun Sports - P.O. 669, Hastings, NE 68902. Subscription is $20 yearly (36 issues). Phone No.: 402-463-4589.

Skeet - 5931 Roft Road, San Antonio, TX 78253. Phone No.: 210-688-3371. $20 per year. Published monthly.

Sporting Classics - 9330A Two Notch Road, Columbia, SC 29223. Phone No.: 803-736-2424. Subscription is $28.95 for 6 issues.

Sporting Clays Magazine - 5211 S. Washington Ave., Titusville, FL 32780. Phone No.: 800-376-2237. $29.95 per year (USA). Published monthly.

Sporting Goods Business - 1 Penn Plaza, New York, NY 10119. $65 per year.

The Sporting Goods Dealer - 1212 N. Lindbergh Blvd., St. Louis, MO 63132. Phone No.: 314-997-7111.

Sports Afield Magazine - PO Box 7166, Red Oak, IA 51591. Phone No.: 818-763-9221 or 800-234-3537. (12 issues) $13.97.

Trap & Field - Published by Curtis Magazine Group. 1000 Waterway Blvd., Indianapolis, IN 46202. Phone No.: 317-633-8802. Subscription is $25 (12 issues).

Turkey & Turkey Hunting - Published by Krause Publications, Inc. 700 E. State St., Iola, WI 54990. Phone No.: 715-445-2214. Published bimonthly for $14.95 (6 issues)

Varmint Hunter Magazine - Published by the Varmint Hunter's Association. 436 S. Pierre St., Pierre, SD, 57501. Phone No.: 605-224-6665, Fax No.: 605-224-6544. Subscription is $24 per year (4 issues).

Varmint Master Magazine - Published by the Vulcan Outdoor Group. 1 Chase Corp. Dr., Ste. 300, Birmingham, AL 35244.

Visier - International Waffen Magazine - Erich-Kastner-Strasse 2, D-56379, Singhofen, GERMANY. Phone No.: 011-49-2604-9780, Fax No.: 011-49-2604-978-703

Waterfowl Magazine - P.O. Box 50, Edgefield, SC 29824. Phone No.: 803-637-5767. 6 issues per year.

Western Outdoors - 3197-E East Airport Dr., Costa Mesa, CA 92626. Phone No: 714-546-4370. Published 9 times per year for $14.95

Wildfowl - Published by Primedia. 6420 Wilshire Blvd., Los Angelos, CA 90048. Phone No: 323-782-2000. Published bimonthly.

Wing & Shot - Published by Emap USA, 6420 Wilshire Blvd., Los Angeles, CA 90048-5515. Phone No.: 323-782-2000.

Women & Guns - Published by Second Amendment Foundation, P.O. Box 488, Station C, Buffalo, NY 14209. $18 annual subscription. Published bimonthly.

STORE BRAND CROSS-OVER LIST

The following listing is provided as a cross reference of (c)Store Brands[a] to original manufacturer and model number. Although not exhaustive, this list covers most major stores and chains that have had their name put on guns by other manufacturers. The values for the firearms listed on these pages are approximately 15% - 40% less than the original manufacturers model(s).

Our thanks goes out to Numrich Gun Parts Corp., West Hurley, NY. They can be reached (914) 679-4867.

House Brand	Model No.	Orig. Mfgr.	Orig. Model		House Brand	Model No.	Orig. Mfgr.	Orig. Model
Aldens	670	Springfield	67		Cotter & Co	949Y	Savage	944Y
Aldens	670	Savage	67					
					C.I.L.	125	Anschutz	184
Belknap	964A	Stevens	87N		C.I.L.	212	Savage	7J
Belknap	B63	Springfield	947		C.I.L.	221	Savage	7J
Belknap	B63	Savage	947B		C.I.L.	227	Savage	871
Belknap	B63E	Savage	940E		C.I.L.	233	Savage	85N
Belknap	B64	Savage	67		C.I.L.	266	Savage	187
Belknap	B65C	Springfield	745		C.I.L.	470	Anschutz	520/61
Belknap	865C	Savage	745		C.I.L.	607	Savage	67
Belknap	B68	Savage	94C		C.I.L.	607 TD	Savage	30 FLD GR.
Belknap	B68D	Savage	94D		C.I.L.	621	Savage	30
Belknap	B963	Springfield	120		C.I.L.	621 TD	Savage	30D
Belknap	B963	Savage	120		C.I.L.	710	Savage	311
Belknap	B964	Savage	87J		C.I.L.	725	Savage	FOX BDE
Belknap	B967	Savage	87N		C.I.L.	830	Savage	340
					C.I.L.	871	Savage	170
Coast to Coast	180	Savage	58		C.I.L.	950C.D	Savage	110C.D
Coast to Coast	1800	Savage	18D		C.I.L.	MKVII	H & R	865
Coast to Coast	182	Savage	18S					
Coast to Coast	184	Savage	951		Eastern Arms	101.1	Stevens	94B
Coast to Coast	267	Savage	77		Eastern Arms	I0I.23	Savage	416
Coast to Coast	285	Savage	7J					
Coast to Coast	286	Savage	46		Foremost See J.C.Penney			
Coast to Coast	288	Savage	87J					
Coast to Coast	320	Savage	120		Gamble Skogkmo, Hiawatha			
Coast to Coast	367	Savage	30					
Coast to Coast	40	Marlin	99C		Gamble Skogkmo	130	Savage	30
Coast to Coast	42	Marlin	70		Gamble Skogkmo	1300-567 VR	Savage	67-VR
Coast to Coast	650	Marlin	55		Gamble Skogkmo	180N	Savage	87N
Coast to Coast	779	Mossberg	479		Gamble Skogkmo	1 89J	Savage	87J
Coast to Coast	843	Savage	340		Gamble Skogkmo	189N	Stevens	87N
Coast to Coast	843	Springfield	840		Gamble Skogkmo	521	Savage	120
Coast to Coast	843V2DS	Savage	340(.222)		Gamble Skogkmo	567	Savage	67
Coast to Coast	843V3DS	Savage	340(.30/30)		Gamble Skogkmo	S87	Savage	187
Coast to Coast	946	Stevens	940		Gamble Skogkmo	594	Savage	944
Coast to Coast	946	Springfield	947		Gamble Skogkmo	594Y	Savage	944Y
Coast to Coast	946E	Stevens	940E		Gamble Skogkmo	GU12-5517A	J.C.Higgins	60 & 66
Coast to Coast	946Y	Stevens	940Y		Glenfield	10	Marlin	101
					Glenfield	20	Marlin	80
Cotter & Co	10-40	Glenfield	10		Glenfield	25	Marlin	80 W/swivels
Cotter & Co	10-40	Marlin	101		Glenfield	30A	Marlin	336
Cotter & Co	121	Stevens	120-15		Glenfield	35	Marlin	336 .35 cal
Cotter & Co	167	Springfield	67		Glenfield	50	Marlin	55
Cotter & Co	167T	Savage	30		Glenfield	60	Marlin	5
Cotter & Co	168	Savage	30		Glenfield	60	Marlin	99C
Cotter & Co	168	Springfield	67VR		Glenfield	65	Marlin	99M1
Cotter & Co	287	Springfield	87J		Glenfield	70	Marlin	989M2
Cotter & Co	33	Marlin	336C		Glenfield	75	Marlin	989MI
Cotter & Co	410	Savage	110E					
Cotter & Co	424	Savage	24F		Globco	Mohawk	Russian	Tokarev
Cotter & Co	434	Savage	34					
Cotter & Co	474	Savage	170		Hawthorn See Wards			
Cotter & Co	474	Springfield	174					
Cotter & Co	487T	Springfield	187		Hercules	50	Stevens	5100
Cotter & Co	489	Savage	89					
Cotter & Co	60-50	Glenfield	60		Hiawatha See Gambles			
Cotter & Co	60-50	Marlin	99C					
Cotter & Co	645	Savage	745		J.C. Higgins See Sears			
Cotter & Co	645C	Savage	745C					
Cotter & Co	75-46	Marlin	99M1		J.C. Penney common name, F - Foremost			
House Brand	**Model No.**	**Orig. Mfgr.**	**Orig. Model**					
					J.C.Penney	2025	Marlin	80C
Cotter & Co	75-45	Glenfield	75		J.C.Penney	2035	Marlin	80
Cotter & Co	842	Springfield	840		J.C.Penney	2035	Glenfield	20
Cotter & Co	911	Springfield	511		J.C.Penney	2066	Marlin	49DL
Cotter & Co	918	Springfield	18		J.C.Penney	2935	Marlin	336
Cotter & Co	948	Stevens	940		J.C.Penney	3040	Marlin	336
Cotter & Co	948E	Savage	948E		J.C.Penney	3040	Glenfield	30A
Cotter & Co	949	Springfield	944		J.C.Penney	4011	High Standard	FLIGHT KING
Cotter & Co	949C	Savage	940		J.C.Penney	6400	Savage	340
					J.C.Penney	6610	Savage	120

House Brand	Model No.	Orig. Mfgr.	Orig. Model	House Brand	Model No.	Orig. Mfgr.	Orig. Model
J.C.Penney	6630	Glenfield	50	Sears	101.1120	Savage	51 and 951
J.C.Penney	6630	Marlin	66	Sears	101.12	Stevens	39
J.C.Penney	6647	Savage	944	Sears	101.13	Stevens	86-7
J.C.Penney	6647	Springfield	944	Sears	101.138	Savage	38A and 58A
J.C.Penney	6660	Glenfield	60	Sears	101.138	Springfield	18.410
J.C.Penney	6660	Marlin	99C	Sears	101.1380	Springfield	18,18C
J.C.Penney	6670	Springfield	67H	Sears	101.1380	Stevens	58,C
J.C.Penney	6670	Savage	67	Sears	101.1381	Springfield	18,951 E,F
J.C.Penney	6870	Savage	30	Sears	101.1381	Stevens	58,51, E,F
J.C.Penney	6870H	Savage	30H	Sears	101.16	Savage	6,87
				Sears	101.1610	Savage	540 DL
Katz	F-1282	Marlin	989M2	Sears	101.1610	Savage	FOX BDL
Katz	F-1282	Glenfield	70	Sears	101.1610	Fox BST	EC,BD,BE,B-F
Katz	F-1287	Marlin	55	Sears	101.1620-1670	Stevens	530,A;311,A,C
Katz	F-1287	Glenfield	50	Sears	101.1700	Savage	94
				Sears	101.1701	Fox BSE	C,D,Ser F,H
Kresge	151	Boito	CBC	Sears	101.1701-C	Savage	BSE
				Sears	101.1710	Savage	FOX BDE
K-Mart	151	Boito	CBC	Sears	101.1710	Savage	540 BDE
				Sears	101.1750	Savage	94
Marlin/new	780	Marlin/old	80	Sears	101.1760	Savage	94
Marlin/new	781	Marlin/old	81	Sears	101.19	Stevens	827-7
Marlin/new	782	Marlin/old	980	Sears	101.20	Stevens	15
				Sears	101.22	Stevens	87M(MUSKET)
New Haven	220K	Mossberg	320K-A	Sears	101.25	Stevens	39A,59A,BandC
New Haven	240K	Mossberg	340K	Sears	101.2830	Savage	63-73
New Haven	246K	Mossberg	346K-A	Sears	101.2830	Savage	73
New Haven	250K	Mossberg	152K	Sears	101.3	Stevens	237
New Haven	250K8	Mossberg	350K-A	Sears	101.3538830	Stevens	89
New Haven	273	Mossberg	173	Sears	101.4	Stevens	38
New Haven	273A	Mossberg	173A	Sears	101.40	Springfield	947,D,Y
New Haven	283.D	Mossberg	183D	Sears	101.40	Stevens	940,D,Y,DY
New Haven	284	Mossberg	173	Sears	101.451	Marlin	336
New Haven	285	Mossberg	185D-C	Sears	101.5	Stevens	37
New Haven	290	Mossberg	190D-A	Sears	101.51004	Savage	94
New Haven	453	Mossberg	353	Sears	101.510070	Savage	94
New Haven	600AT	Mossberg	500A	Sears	101.51009	Springfield	944,Yseries A
New Haven	600C	Mossberg	500C	Sears	101.51013	Springfield	944,Yseries A
New Haven	600E	Mossberg	500E	Sears	101.51024	Savage	94
New Haven	679	Mossberg	472	Sears	101.510270	Savage	94
New Haven	740	Mossberg	640	Sears	101.51044	Savage	94
				Sears	101.510660	Stevens	9478
Otasco	30	Marlin	336	Sears	101.510660	Springfield	944,Y series A
Otasco	30	Glenfield	30A	Sears	101.510670	Stevens	9478
Otasco	65	Glenfield	60	Sears	101.510680	Stevens	9478
Otasco	65	Marlin	99C	Sears	101.512220	Stevens	5100,530,311
				Sears	101.512230	Stevens	5100,530,311
Palmetto	11	Stevens	85,89	Sears	101.51451	Springfield	67
				Sears	101.51452	Springfield	67
Premier	Trail Blazer	Stevens	29A	Sears	101.51454	Springfield	67
				Sears	101.51472	Springfield	67 Series B
Revelation, see Western Auto				Sears	101.52701	Stevens	71,74 S/S
				Sears	101.52772	Savage	34,65,34M.65M
Sears. Ranger. J.C. Higgins				Sears	101.52773	Savage	34,65,34M,65M
				Sears	101.5350	Springfield	18.58
J.C.Higgins	30	High Standard	30	Sears	101.5350-D	Stevens	18D
J.C.Higgins	101.1	Savage	94	Sears	101.53521	Savage	340
J.C.Higgins	101.24	Savage	15-120	Sears	101.53527	Savage	340
J.C.Higgins	20	High Standard	200	Sears	101.5380	Savage	18/18AC.58
J.C.Higgins	42 DL	Marlin	80	Sears	101.5380	Springfield	18,12,16,20ga.
J.C.Higgins	52	Sako	L46	Sears	101.5380D	Stevens	18ADC
J.C.Higgins	S4	Browning	FN-300	Sears	101.538840	Savage	34,65,34M,65M
J.C.Higgins	583.13 to.23	High Standard	10	Sears	101.540	FOX	B-BST,BDL
J.C.Higgins	583.2078-79	High Standard	20ga pump	Sears	101.5410	Springfield	18,58
J.C.Higgins	583.514-730	High Standard	20ga pump	Sears	101.5410D	Savage	18D
J.C.Higgins	6670H	Stevens	67H	Sears	101.5410D	Springfield	18DS
J.C.Higgins	80	High Standard	101	Sears	101.54880	Stevens	80 Series A
				Sears	101.54880	Springfield	187 Series A
Ranger	101.2	Savage	238	Seem	101.64881	Marlin	980 DL,987
Ranger	101.8	Stevens	83	Sears	101.600	Stevens	39A,59A,B,C
Ranger	104.7	H&R	120	Sears	101.7	Stevens	311
Ranger	105.20	H&R	120	Sears	101.750	SpringField	18.410
Ranger	120	Winchester	1200	Sears	101.750	Savage	38A and 58A
Ranger	30	Stevens	520A	Sears	101.7C	Stevens	311-C
Ranger	34A	Marlin	80.C,780	Sears	101.8	Stevens	83
Ranger	34A	Marlin	50-50E	Sears	102	Stevens	240
Ranger	35A	Stevens	66A	Sears	102.25	Stevens	520A
Ranger	36	Marlin	80 Adj. Trigger	Sears	102.35	Savage	M521
Ranger	400	Stevens	311	Sears	102.35	Savage	M29-D2
				Sears	103.13	Marlin	81
Sears	101.1	Savage	94	Sears	103.16	Marlin	80
Sears	101.100	Savage	96/96Y	Sears	103.18	Marlin	100
Sears	101.10040	Savage	94	Sears	103.181	Marlin	101
Sears	101.10041	Savage	94	Sears	103.1977	Marlin	101
Sears	101.10080	Stevens	940	Sears	103.19770	Marlin	101

House Brand	Model No.	Orig. Mfgr.	Orig. Model
Sears	103.19771	Marlin	101
Sears	103.19780	Marlin	101
Sears	103.19790	Marlin	80
Sears	103.19791	Marlin	80
Sears	103.19800	Marlin	80
Sears	103.19801	Marlin	80
Sears	103.1981	Marlin	81
Sears	103.19810	Marlin	81
Sears	103.19811	Marlin	81
Sears	103.1982	Marlin	81DL
Sears	103.19820	Marlin	81
Sears	103.19821	Marlin	81
Sears	103.19840	Marlin	56
Sears	103.19880	Marlin	57 LR-MAG.
Sears	103.19881	Marlin	57 LR-MAG.
Sears	103.19890	Marlin	57 LR-MAG.
Sears	103.2	Marlin	80
Sears	103.228	Marlin	80
Sears	103.229	Marlin	81
Sears	103.273	Marlin	782
Sears	103.273	Marlin	980
Sears	103.274	Marlin	122
Sears	103.275	Marlin	122
Sears	103.2751	Marlin	122
Sears	103.2840	Marlin	80
Sears	103.2850	Marlin	81
Sears	103.2870	Marlin	56
Sears	103.350	Marlin	M90
Sears	103.360	Marlin	90
Sears	103.4	Marlin	A1
Sears	103.450	Marlin	336
Sears	103.451	Marlin	336
Sears	103.720	Marlin	59
Sears	103.740	Marlin	59
Sears	103.8	Marlin	100
Sears	10.19790	Marlin	80
Sears	11.2	Stevens	238
Sears	153.512350	Laurona	S/S
Sears	153.512351	Laurona	S/S
Sears	153.512360	Laurona	S/S
Sears	153.512361	Laurona	S/S
Sears	153.512740	Laurona	71 O/U
Sears	18	Mossberg	183K
Sears	18AC	Savage	18C
Sears	2C	Winchester	131
Sears	20	High Standard	? PUMP
Sears	200	Winchester	1200
Sears	200	Mossberg	G4
Sears	201	Mossberg	80
Sears	202	Mossberg	80
Sears	203	Mossberg	85
Sears	204	Mossberg	83
Sears	205	Mossberg	73
Sears	206	Mossberg	70
Sears	207	Mossberg	75
Sears	209	Stevens	84-7
Sears	21	High Standard	K2011
Sears	210	Mossberg	85B
Sears	211	Mossberg	83B
Sears	211	Stevens	86-7
Sears	212	Mossberg	73B
Sears	213	Mossberg	75B
Sears	215	Mossberg	85C
Sears	216	Mossberg	83C
Sears	217	Mossberg	75C
Sears	217	Stevens	87M (MUSKET)
Sears	218	Mossberg	73C
Sears	218	Stevens	22/410
Sears	231	Stevens	83
Sears	232	Stevens	87-7
Sears	233	Stevens	87-7
Sears	234	Savage	234
Sears	238	Stevens	827-7
Sears	25	High Standard	A1041 .22 auto
Sears	273.2400	Winchester	190
Sears	273.27S10(2C)	Winchester	131
Sears	273.27520(2M)	Winchester	131
Sears	273.510770	Winchester	37A
Sears	273.510780	Winchester	37A
Sears	273.510790	Winchester	37A
Sears	273.53421	Winchester	100
Sears	277	Stevens	1S
Sears	278.28180	Cooey	64
Sears	281.512650	Antonio Zoli	O/U
Sears	281.512651	Antonio Zoli	O/U
Sears	281.512660	Antonio Zoli	O/U
Sears	281.512661	Antonio Zoli	O/U
Sears	281.512750	Antonio Zoli	O/U
Sears	282.510821	Boito	ERA Single Bbl
Sears	282.510831	Boito	ERA Single Bbl
Sears	282.510841	Boito	ERA Single Bbi
Sears	282.5227740	CBC	122
Sears	282.527740	FIE	122
Sears	2C	Winchester	131
Sears	2T	Winchester	121,131,141
Sears	2/57	Stevens	66
Sears	2/58	Stevens	66
Sears	30	High Standard	22 PUMP
Sears	300	Winchester	1400
Sears	31	J.C. Higgins	31
Sears	33	J.C. Higgins	33
Sears	34	J.C. Higgins	34
Sears	340.530430	Ithaca	49SS
Sears	35A	Stevens	66A
Sears	36	Marlin	80
Sears	375	Mossberg	45B
Sears	377	Mossberg	42C
Sears	381	Mossberg	46B
Sears	382	Mossberg	46B
Sears	384	Mossberg	45A
Sears	385	Mossberg	45B
Sears	387	Mossberg	42C
Sears	388	Mossberg	42C
Sears	389	Mossberg	42A OR 26C
Sears	390	Mossberg	26C
Sears	3T	Winchester	190
Sears	41	Marlin	101
Sears	41 DLA	Marlin	122
Sears	42	Marlin	80
Sears	42DL	Marlin	80
Sears	42DLM	Marlin	980
Sears	43	Marlin	81
Sears	43DL	Marlin	81
Sears	44DL	Marlin	57
Sears	44DLM	Marlin	57M
Sears	45	Marlin	336C
Sears	46	Marlin	56
Sears	46DL	Marlin	56
Sears	4980	Stevens	94-2 W/PAD
Sears	49.11830/30	Savage	99 A
Sears	53	Winchester	70
Sears	54	Winchester	94
Sears	583.1	High Standard	?
Sears	583.126	Sako	L46
Sears	583.13	High Standard	?
Sears	583.14	H & R	120
Sears	583.15	H&R	121
Sears	583.16	High Standard	10
Sears	583.17	High Standard	?
Sears	583.18	H & R	120
Sears	583.2	H & R	M120
Sears	583.20	High Standard	Flight King
Sears	583.2085-87	High Standard	20ga pump
Sears	583.21	H&R	M120
Sears	583.25	H&R	M121
Sears	583.3	H&R	M121
House	583.4	High Standard	10
Sears	583.7	High Standard	10
Sears	583.91	H & R	121
Sears	6C (Canada)	Winchester	Cooy 64,64B
Sears	6C(American)	Winchester	490
Sears	66	High Standard	66
Sears	73	Savage	73
Sears	870.528140	Voere	Clip .22
Sears	92	Stevens	39
Sears	93	Stevens	38
Sears	94	Stevens	237
Sears	95	Stevens	238
Sears	97	Savage	94
Sears	97AC	Savage	94AC
Sears	98	Stevens	37
Sears	98	Springfield	944
Sears	M30	Stevens	M520
Sears	mzm	Savage	34
Sears 100	273.532141	Winchester	NM 94
Sears 200	2732.5320	Winchester	1200
Sears 200	273.2011	Winchester	1200
Sears 200	273.21010	Winchester	1200
Sears 200	273.2160	Winchester	1200
Sears 200	273.2250	Winchester	1200

House Brand	Model No.	Orig. Mfgr.	Orig. Model	House Brand	Model No.	Orig. Mfgr.	Orig. Model
Sears 200	273.2251	Winchester	1200	Sears MI	273.27010	Winchester	121
Sears 200	273.2280	Winchester	1200	Sears M5,M-5T	273.2340	Winchester	150-250
Sears 200	273.4310	Winchester	1200	Sears M5,M-5T	273.2341	Winchester	150-250
Sears 200	273.4320	Winchester	1200	Sears M5,M-5T	273.2350	Winchester	150-250
Sears 200	273.4340	Winchester	1200	Sears M5,M-5T	273.2351	Winchester	150-250
Sears 200	273.4350	Winchester	1200	Sears T.W. 73	273.532730	Winchester	670 Mag.
Sears 200	273.4410	Winchester	1200	Sears T.W. 73	23.31020	Winchester	New Mod 70
Sears 200	273.4420	Winchester	1200	Sears T.W. 73	273.1390	Winchester	MN 30-06
Sears 200	273.4450	Winchester	1200	Sears T.W. 73	273.1400	Winchester	MN 70 (.270)
Seem 200	273.514010	Winchester	1200	Sears T.W. 73	273.1830	Winchester	New Mod 70
Sears 200	273.614010	Winchester	1200	Sears T.W. 73	273.1840	Winchester	New Mod 70
Sears 200	273.514011	Winchester	1200	Sears T.W. 73	273.1850	Winchester	New Mod 70
Sears 200	273.514020	Winchester	1200	Sears T.W. 73	273.1860	Winchester	New Mod 70
Seem 200	273.514040	Winchester	1200	Sears T.W. 73	273.1870	Winchester	New Mod 70
Sears 200	273.514050	Winchester	1200	Sears T.W. 73	273.31010	Winchester	New Mod 70
Sears 200	273.514051	Winchester	1200	Sears T.W. 73	273.31060	Winchester	New Mod 70
Sears 200	273.514210	Winchester	1200	Sears T.W. 73	273.32020	Winchester	New Mod 70
Sears 200	273.514220	Winchester	1200	Sears T.W. 73	273.32030	Winchester	New Mod 70
Sears 200	273.514250	Winchester	1200	Sears T.W. 73	273.32040	Winchester	New Mod 70
Sears 200	273.514251	Winchester	1200	Sears T.W. 73	273.532061	Winchester	New Mod 70
Sears 200	273.514810	Winchester	1200	Sears T.W. 73	273.532071	Winchester	New Mod 70
Sears 200	273.614820	Winchester	1200	Sears T.W. 73	273.532081	Winchester	New Mod 70
Sears 200	273.514830	Winchester	1200	Sears T.W. 73	273.53403	Winchester	New Mod 70
Sears 200	273.514840	Winchester	1200	Sears T.W. 73	273.53406	Winchester	New Mod 70
Sears 200	273.515010	Winchester	1200	Sears T.W. 73	273.53409	Winchester	New Mod 70
Sears 200	273.515020	Winchester	1200	Sears T.W. 73	273.32010	Winchester	Now Mod 70
Sears 200	273.515050	Winchester	1200				
Sears 200	273.515051	Winchester	1200	Ted Williams	340.530430	Ithaca	49SS
Sears 200	273.515080	Winchester	1200				
Sears 200	273.515090	Winchester	1200	Shapleigh's	KING NITRO	Savage	15
Sears 200	273.515220	Winchester	1200				
Sears 200	273.515221	Winchester	1200	Simmons	411	Savage	540DL
Sears 200	273.515250	Winchester	1200	Simmons	411	Savage	Fox BDE 20ga
Sears 200	273.515251	Winchester	1200				
Sears 200	273.515280	Winchester	1200	Simmons	411E	Savage	540 BDE
Sears 200	273.515290	Winchester	1200	Simmons	411E	Savage	Fox BDE 20ga
Sears 200	273.515410	Winchester	1200				
Sears 200	273.515420	Winchester	1200	Talo	12DL	Stevens	120
Sears 200	273.515470	Winchester	1200	Talo	176 VR	Springfield	67 VR
Sears 200	273.515710	Winchester	1200	Talo	176DL	Springfield	67
Sears 200	273.515720	Winchester	1200				
Sears 200	273.515920	Winchester	1200	Western Auto,Revelation			
Sears 200	273.5310	Winchester	1200				
Sears 200	273.5350	Winchester	1200	Revelation	300	Savage	30 D,E,F
Sears 2T	273.27530	Winchester	141	Revelation	394 Series P	Stevens	94P
Sears 300	273.1310	Winchester	1400	Revelation	76	High Standard	Double Nine
Sears 300	273.1320	Winchester	1400	Revelation	R310	Mossberg	500AB
Sears 300	273.1350	Winchester	1400				
Sears 300	273.21550	Winchester	1400	Western Auto	100	Mossberg	321
Sears 300	273.2500	Winchester	1400	Western Auto	101Y	Savage	73Y
Sears 300	273.2540	Winchester	1400	Western Auto	101.1701	Savage	540BS
Sears 300	273.32060	Winchester	1400	Western Auto	101.171	Savage	540BD
Sears 300	273.32070	Winchester	1400	Western Auto	101.2830	Savage	73
Sears 300	273.521050	Winchester	1400	Western Auto	101.52772	Savage	65M
Sears 300	273.521051	Winchester	1400	Western Auto	101.535D	Savage	18
Sears 300	273.521080	Winchester	1400	Western Auto	101.53500	Savage	18D
Sears 300	273.521090	Winchester	1400	Western Auto	101.53521	Savage	340
Sears 300	273.521160	Winchester	1400	Western Auto	101.5380	Savage	18AC
Sears 300	273.521161	Winchester	1400	Western Auto	101.5380D	Savage	18DAC
Sears 300	273.521250	Winchester	1400	Western Auto	101.5410	Savage	18DS,S
Sears 300	273.521251	Winchester	1400	Western Auto	103	Savage	89
Sears 300	273.521260	Winchester	1400	Western Auto	103.13	Marlin	81
Sears 300	273.521280	Winchester	1400	Western Auto	103.16	Marlin	80
Sears 300	273.521290	Winchester	1400	Western Auto	103.18	Marlin	80
Sears 300	273.521580	Winchester	1400	Western Auto	103.181	Marlin	101
Sears 300	273.521680	Winchester	1400	Western Auto	103.19780	Marlin	101
Sears 300	273.521710	Winchester	1400	Western Auto	103.19790	Marlin	80
Sears 300	273.521770	Winchester	1400	Western Auto	103.19800	Marlin	80
Sears 300	273.521780	Winchester	1400	Western Auto	103.1981	Marlin	81
Sears 300	273.523251	Winchester	1400	Western Auto	103.1982	Marlin	81DL
Sears 300	273.52151	Winchester	1400	Western Auto	103.19820	Marlin	81
Sears 3T-A	273.2390	Winchester	190-290	Western Auto	103.19840	Marlin	56
Sears 3T-A	273.2400	Winchester	190-290	Western Auto	103.19880	Marlin	57
Sears 3T-A	273.528110	Winchester	190-290	Western Auto	103.19890	Marlin	57M
Sears 3T-A	273.528111	Winchester	190-290	Western Auto	103.1997	Marlin	101
Sears 4T	273.2360	Winchester	270	Western Auto	103.2	Marlin	80
Sears 53A	273.532780	Winchester	70A	Western Auto	103.228	Marlin	80
Sears 54	273.2120	Winchester	NM 94	Western Auto	103.229	Marlin	81
Sears 54	273.532140	Winchester	NM 94	Western Auto	103.273	Marlin	980
Sears 54	273.53419	Winchester	NM 94	Western Auto	103.274	Marlin	122
Sears 54	273.810	Winchester	NM 94	Western Auto	103.2751	Marlin	122
Sears 54	273.811	Winchester	NM 94	Western Auto	103.2840	Marlin	80
Sears 6C	273.28130	Winchester	490	Western Auto	103.2850	Marlin	81
Sears 6C	273.528131	Winchester	490	Western Auto	103.2870	Marlin	56
Sears 6C	273.528132	Winchester	490	Western Auto	103.360	Marlin	90

House Brand	Model No.	Orig. Mfgr.	Orig. Model
Western Auto	103.450	Marlin	336
Western Auto	103.451	Marlin	336
Western Auto	103.720	Marlin	59
Western Auto	103.740	Marlin	59
Western Auto	105-2060	Marlin	780
Western Auto	105-2060	Marlin	80
Western Auto	107	Mossberg	640K
Western Auto	107A	Mossberg	640
Western Auto	110-2140	Marlin	81
Western Auto	110-2140	Marlin	781
Western Auto	115	Savage	46
Western Auto	115-2277	Marlin	57
Western Auto	116-2276	Marlin	57M
Western Auto	117	Mossberg	402
Western Auto	120-2220	Marlin	99
Western Auto	125	Mossberg	353
Western Auto	135	Savage	187
Western Auto	135	Springfield	187A
Western Auto	150m	Marlin	49
Western Auto	150-2225	Marlin	49
Western Auto	160	Springfield	187A
Western Auto	160	Savage	80
Western Auto	200-2280	Marlin	39A
Western Auto	200-2282	Marlin	39A
Western Auto	200-2550	Marlin	336
Western Auto	200-2554	Marlin	336(.44MAG)
Western Auto	205	Mossberg	472PCA
Western Auto	210A	Mossberg	810AH
Western Auto	220A	Mossberg	800A
Western Auto	220AD	Mossberg	800AD
Western Auto	220B	Mossberg	800B
Western Auto	220BD	Mossberg	800BD
Western Auto	220C	Mossberg	800C
Western Auto	220CD	Mossberg	800CD
Western Auto	225	Savage	340
Western Auto	2280	Marlin	39A
Western Auto	2282	Marlin	39A Mountie
Western Auto	230	Savage	340
Western Auto	250	Savage	110E
Western Auto	250A	Savage	110D
Western Auto	250D	Savage	110
Western Auto	260	Savage	170
Western Auto	260	Springfield	174
Western Auto	300	Springfield	67
Western Auto	300	Stevens	30
Western Auto	300A	Savage	30AC
Western Auto	300F	Stevens	77C
Western Auto	300H	Savage	30,HAC
Western Auto	300-300AC	Springfield	67
Western Auto	310	Mossberg	500
Western Auto	310A	Mossberg	500A
Western Auto	310AB	Mossberg	500AB
Western Auto	310B	Mossberg	500B
Western Auto	310C	Mossberg	500C
Western Auto	310E	Mossberg	500E
Western Auto	312	Mossberg	395
Western Auto	312AK	Mossberg	395K
Western Auto	312SB	Mossberg	395T
Western Auto	316	Mossberg	390
Western Auto	316BB	Mossberg	390T
Western Auto	316BK	Mossberg	390K
Western Auto	325B	Mossberg	385T
Western Auto	325BK	Mossberg	385K
Western Auto	330	Mossberg	183 & 183K
Western Auto	330B	Mossberg	183T
Western Auto	335-3725	Marlin	59
Western Auto	336	Springfield	951
Western Auto	350	Stevens	94
Western Auto	350A	Savage	94D
Western Auto	350M	Stevens	94
Western Auto	355	Stevens	947
Western Auto	355Y	Savage	94Y
Western Auto	355YE	Springfield	947YE
Western Auto	356Y	Springfield	944Y
Western Auto	360	Savage	540
Western Auto	360	Savage	FOX mod B
Western Auto	360C	Savage	540C
Western Auto	400	Stevens	745
Western Auto	400C	Savage	745C
Western Auto	420	High Standard	Supmatic C-011
Western Auto	425	High Standard	Supmatic C-120
Western Auto	460	Springfield	511
Western Auto	SD52A	Stevens	311

House Brand	Model No.	Orig. Mfgr.	Orig. Model
West Point	45	Marlin	60
Wards, Western Field, and Hawthorn			
Hawthorn	110	Unknown	S shot SG
Hawthorn	580 EJN	Colt	Colteer/bolt
Hawthorn	814 EJN	Colt	Colteer/SS
Hawthorn	820B	Mossberg	340
Hawthorn	880	Colt	Colteer/semi
Hawthorn	880 EJN	Colt	Colteer/bolt
Wards	24M 419A	Mossberg	9
Wards	472	Noble	50
Wards	850	Mossberg	353
Wards Triumph	52	Stevens	315
Western Field	04M-489A	Mossberg	50
Western Field	04M-218A	Mossberg	73C
Western Field	04M-2117A	Mossberg	9
Western Field	04M-217A	Mossberg	75C
Western Field	04M-214A	Mossberg	85C
Western Field	04M-216A	Mossberg	83C
Western Field	I	Mossberg	RF-1
Western Field	10-SD247A	Stevens	94B (Tenite)
Western Field	14	Savage	39A
Western Field	14	Savage	59A
Western Field	14M-215A	Mossberg	85
Western Field	14M-497B	Mossberg	M42
Western Field	14M-488A	Mossberg	50
Western Field	15	Mossberg	80
Western Field	150	Mossberg	183K
Western Field	151X	Kessler	?
Western Field	155	Mossberg	173
Western Field	15A	Mossberg	83
Western Field	16	Mossberg	85
Western Field	160	Mossberg	385K
Western Field	16A	Mossberg	85
Western Field	17	Mossberg	73
Western Field	170	Mossberg	395K
Western Field	172	Mossberg	395K
Western Field	173	Mosaberg	395
Western Field	175	Mossberg	385K
Western Field	17A	Mossberg	73
Western Field	I8	Mossberg	75
Western Field	20	Mossberg	9R
Western Field	215A	Mossberg	85
Western Field	24M,488A	Mossberg	51
Western Field	30	Stevens	520
Western Field	31A	Mossberg	44
Western Field	31A	Mossberg	40
Western Field	32	Mossberg	21
Western Field	32	Mossberg	20
Western Field	33	Marlin	336
Western Field	35A	Mossberg	30
Western Field	36	Stevens	521
Western Field	36	Mossberg	10
Western Field	36B	Mossberg	25A
Western Field	36B	Mossberg	10
Western Field	36C	Mossberg	25A
Western Field	360	Mossberg	26C
Western Field	37	Mossberg	30
House Field	39	Mossberg	25
Western Field	390A	Mossberg	26C
Western Field	40,D	Mossberg	44
Western Field	40	Marlin	101
Western Field	40N	Noble	40NA
Western Field	40M-215A	Mossberg	185
Western Field	41	Mossberg	45
Western Field	45	Marlin	989M2
Western Field	45	Mossberg	42
Western Field	45B	Mossberg	26C
Western Field	45C	Mossberg	25A
Western Field	46	Mossberg	42
Western Field	466	Mossberg	RA1
Western Field	469	Mossberg	RA1-Kit
Western Field	46A	Mossberg	42
Western Field	46C	Mosoberg	42A
Western Field	46D	Mossberg	42C
Western Field	47	Mossberg	45A
Western Field	472	Noble	50
Western Field	47A,L	Mossberg	45A
Western Field	48	Mossberg	45A
Western Field	488A	Mossberg	51
Western Field	48A	Mossberg	45B
Western Field	48A	Mossberg	46MLB

House Brand	Model No.	Orig. Mfgr.	Orig. Model	House Brand	Model No.	Orig. Mfgr.	Orig. Model
Western Field	5-4	Mossberg	8-M4	Western Field	93M-210A	Mossberg	85B
Western Field	50	Glenfield	60	Western Field	93M-497A	Mossberg	42C
Western Field	502-26FR	Mossberg	500	Western Field	93M-491A	Mossberg	465
Western Field	505	Mossberg	500	Western Field	93M-495A	Mossberg	45B
Western Field	509	Mossberg	500	Western Field	EMN 171	Marlin	50
Western Field	524	Mossberg	500	Western Field	EMN 176	Marlin	55
Western Field	534	Mossberg	500	Western Field	M-SD57	Stevens	M87
Western Field	536	Mossberg	500	Western Field	M025	Savage	520A
Western Field	539	Mossberg	500	Western Field	M040 O/U	Marlin	90
Western Field	550A	Mossberg	500A	Western Field	M040N	Stevens	820
Western Field	550AS	Mossberg	500AB	Western Field	M051	Stevens	515
Western Field	550B	Mossberg	500B	Western Field	M059	Stevens	M87
Western Field	550C	Mossberg	500B	Western Field	M060	Stevens	620
Western Field	550E	Mossberg	500E	Western Field	M080	Savage	29 & 75
Western Field	550E	Mossberg	500E	Western Field	M087	Stevens	M87
Western Field	60	Savage	620A	Western Field	M10	Stevens	9.4
Western Field	600ERI 12 GA	Remington	SPT 58				Short tang
Western Field	60SB	Savage	620A	Western Field	M150	Mossberg	183T
Western Field	679	Mossberg	472	Western Field	M155	Mosaberg	183D
Western Field	710	Savage	110	Western Field	M160	Mossberg	385T
Western Field	72	Noble	50	Western Field	M170	Mossberg	395S
Western Field	72C	Mossberg	472	Western Field	M172	Mossberg	395K
Western Field	730	Mossberg	8I0AH	Western Field	M175	Mossberg	385K
Western Field	732	Mossberg	810AH	Western Field			
Western Field	734	Mossberg	810A		KC3 NH402A	Stevens	820
Western Field	740	Marlin	336	Western Field	M35	Savage	520 POLY
Western Field	765	Mossberg	810A	Western Field	M36	Savage	521
Western Field	766	Mossberg	810B	Western Field	M60	Savage	620 DELUX
Western Field	767	Mossberg	800A	Western Field	M61	Savage	621 DELUX
Western Field	768	Mossberg	800A	Western Field	M72	Mossberg	472 PRA
Western Field	771	Mossberg	472BA	Western Field	M734	Mossberg	810BH
Western Field	772	Mossberg	472PCA	Western Field	M771	Moseberg	472SBA
Western Field	775	Mossberg	800AD	Western Field	M772	Mossberg	472PCA
Western Field	776	Mossberg	800BD	Western Field	M7 75	Mossberg	800AD
Western Field	778	Mossberg	472BAS	Western Field	M776	Mossberg	800BD
Western Field	780	Mossberg	800A	Western Field	M778	Mossberg	472BAS
Western Field	782	Mossberg	800B	Western Field	M780	Mossberg	800A
Western Field	79	Mossberg	472 PRA	Western Field	M782	Mossberg	800B
Western Field	50	Savage	29	Western Field	M808.C	Stevens	87,C,J
Western Field	807A ECH	Colt	Colteer S.S.	Western Field	M808N	Stevens	87N
				Western Field	M80A	Savage	M29-D1
Western Field	808	Savage	87	Western Field	M815	Mossberg	320
Western Field	808C	Savage	87J	Western Field	M822	Mossberg	640K
Western Field	815	Mossberg	321	Western Field	M85	Stevens	85
Western Field	820B	Mossberg	340	Western Field	M-SD57	Stevens	87
Western Field	822	Mossberg	640K	Western Field	SS 94B	Stevens	94C
Western Field	828	Mossberg	353	Western Field	SB033	Savage	520 W/POLY
Western Field	830	Mossberg	340K	Western Field	SB066	Savage	621 DELX POLY
Western Field	832	Mossberg	341	Western Field	SB067	Savage	621 DELX COMP
Western Field	836	Savage	187N	Western Field	S5112C	Savage	540C
Western Field	840	Mossberg	640	Western Field	SB115	Savage	115
Western Field	842	Mossberg	346K	Western Field	SB300,C	Stevens	311,C
Western Field	846	Mossberg	351C	Western Field	SB30A	Savage	520
Western Field	850 855	Mossberg	353	Western Field	SB311C	Savage	311C
				Western Field	SB312	Savage	540D
Western Field	852	Mossberg	341	Western Field	SB312	Savage-Fox	BDL
Western Field	865	Mossberg	402	Western Field	SB33	Savage	520 POLY
Western Field	880	Colt	Colteer Semi.	Western Field	SB60A	Savage	620 DELUX
Western Field	894	Mossberg	430-432	Western Field	SB61A	Savage	621 DELUX
Western Field	895	Mossberg	402	Western Field	SB620A	Stevens	620A
Western Field	9-2 3/4	Mossberg	9-2 1/2	Western Field	SB66	Savage	621 DELX POLY
Western Field	93M	Mossberg	26C	Western Field	SB712	Savage	840
Western Field	93M-213A	Mossberg	75B	Western Field	SB80A	Savage	29-DI
Western Field	93M-2116A	Mossberg	9	Western Field	SB85TA	Stevens	85
Western Field	93M-212A	Mossberg	738	Western Field	SB87,TA	Stevens	M87
Western Field	93M-211A	Mossberg	83B	Western Field	XNH 175	Marlin	55
				Western Field	XNH 565	Noble	60-66
				Widgeon	SA 650	Marlin	55 12 GA

SERIALIZATION

This section is included to identify year of manufacture dates on Brownings, Colts (including 3rd generation Colt S.A. model numbers), High Standard, Mauser broomhandles, Parker shotguns, Remington (manufacture dates), Savage/Stevens model information, Savage M-1899, selected Winchesters, and others. To use these tables, simply locate the Ser. no. of the above mentioned trademarks, locate the proper bracket it falls into by model, and refer to the adjacent year to determine the year of manufacture. In several cases, caliber rarity can also be determined.

BROWNING BELGIUM PRODUCTION

A-5 (AUTOMATIC 5) SHOTGUN -12 ga.

Year	Ser. # Start	Ser. # End
1924	1	3000
1925	3001	18000
1926	18001	33000
1927	33001	48000
1928	48001	63000
1929	63001	78000
1930	78001	93000
1931	93001	108000
1932	108001	123000
1933	123001	138000
1934	138001	153000
1935	153001	168000
1936	168001	183000
1937	183001	198000
1938	198001	213000
1939	213001	229000
1940 -1945	NO PRODUCTION	
1946	229001	237000
1947	237001	249000
1948	249001	270000
1949	270001	285000
1950	285001	315000
1951	315001	346000
1952	346001	387000
1953	387001	438000

In 1954 Browning added an alpha prefix to the serial number to differentiate between Light-weight and Standard weight guns.

Year	Std. 12	Lt. Wt. 12
1954	H1-H39000	L1-L42000
1955	H39001-H83000	L42001-L83000
1956	H83001-H99000	L83001-L99000
1956	M1-M22000	G1-G23000
1957	M22001-M85000	G23001-G85000
1958	M85001-M99000	G85001-G99000

1958-1976 Ser. No. sequence changed to include a one or two digit numeral followed by an alpha character.

Year	Std. Wt.	Lt. Wt.	Magnum
1958	8M	8G	8V
1959	9M	9G	9V
1960	0M	0G	0V
1961	1M	1G	1V
1962	2M	2G	2V
1963	3M	3G	3V
1965	5M	5G	5V
1966	6M	6G	6V
1964	4M	4G	4V
1967	7M	7G	7V
1968	8M	8G	8V
1969	69M	69G	69V
1970	Disc.	70G	70V
1971	Disc.	71G	71V
1972	Disc.	72G	72V
1973	Disc.	73G	73V
1974	Disc.	74G	74V
1975	Disc.	75G	75V
1976	Disc.	76G	76V

A-5 (AUTOMATIC 5) SHOTGUN -16 ga.

Year	Ser. # Start	Ser. # End
1925	1	1000
1926	1001	10000
1927	10001	19000
1928	19001	28000
1929	28001	37000
1930	37001	46000
1931	46001	55000
1932	55001	64000
1933	64001	73000
1934	73001	82000
1935	82001	91000
1936	91001	100000
1937	100001	109000
1938	109001	118000
1939	118001	127000
1940 -1946	NO PRODUCTION	
1947	127001	128500
1947	X1000	X13700
1948	X13701	X22600
1949	X26001	X31500
1950	X31501	X42500
1951	X42501	X58300
1952	X58301	X74000
1953	X74001	X99000

In 1953 Browning changed the Ser. No. alpha-betic character to differentiate between Light-weight & Standard weight guns.

Year	Std. 16	Sweet 16
1953	R1-R1400	S1-S2500
1954	R1401-R19400	S2501-S24000
1955	R19401-R40000	S24001-S41000
1956	R40001-R68000	S41001-S62000
1957	R68001-R99000	S62001-S99000
1957		A1-A1000
1958	T1400-T10000	A1001-A10000

1958-1976 Ser. No. sequence changed to include a one or two digit numeral followed by an alpha character.

Year	Std. 16	Sweet 16
1958	8R	8S
1959	9R	9S
1960	0R	0S
1961	1R	1S
1962	2R	2S

Year	Std. 16	Sweet 16
1963	3R	3S
1964	4R	4S
1965	5R	5S
1966	Disc.	6S
1967	Disc.	7S
1968	Disc.	8S
1969	Disc.	69S
1970	Disc.	70S
1971	Disc.	71S
1972	Disc.	72S
1973	Disc.	73S
1974	Disc.	74S
1975	Disc.	75S
1976	Disc.	76S

A-5 (AUTOMATIC 5) SHOTGUN - 20 ga.

Year	Lt. Wt. 20	Magnum 20
1958	8Z	Introduced in
1959	9Z	1967
1960	0Z	
1961	1Z	
1962	2Z	
1963	3Z	
1964	4Z	
1965	5Z	
1966	6Z	
1967	7Z	67X
1968	68Z	68X
1969	69Z	69X
1970	70Z	70X
1971	71Z	71X
1972	72Z	72X
1973	73Z	73X
1974	74Z	74X
1975	75Z	75X
1976	76Z	76X

SUPERPOSED MODEL - O & U - 12 ga.

Year	Ser. # Start	Ser. # End
1931	1	2000
1932	2001	4000
1933	4001	6000
1934	6001	8000
1935	8001	10000
1936	10001	12000
1937	12001	14000
1938	14001	16000
1939	16001	17000
1939-1947	NO PRODUCTION	
1948	17001	17200
1949	17201	20000
1950	20001	21000
1951	21001	27000
1952	27001	33000
1953	33001	37000
1954	37001	43000
1955	43001	48000
1956	48001	54000
1957	54001	59000
1958	59001	68500
1959	68501	76500
1960	76501	86500
1961	86501	96500
1962	96501	99999
1962	1	6500
1962	S2 suffix after Ser. No.	
1963	S3 suffix after Ser. No.	
1964	S4 suffix after Ser. No.	
1965	S5 suffix after Ser. No.	
1966	S6 suffix after Ser. No.	
1967	S7 suffix after Ser. No.	
1968	S8 suffix after Ser. No.	

Year	Ser. # Start	Ser. # End
1969	S69 suffix after Ser. No.	
1970	S70 suffix after Ser. No.	
1971	S71 suffix after Ser. No.	
1972	S72 suffix after Ser. No.	
1973	S73 suffix after Ser. No.	
1974	S74 suffix after Ser. No.	
1975	S75 suffix after Ser. No.	
1976	S76 suffix after Ser. No.	
1976 to 1984	"P" or Presentation Models only	

SUPERPOSED MODEL - O & U - 20 ga.

Year	Ser. # Start	Ser. # End
1949	201	1700
1950	1701	2800
1951	2801	3200
1952	3201	5300
1953	5301	6700
1954	7601	8400
1955	8401	9400
1956	9401	10500
1957	10501	11500
1958	11501	14180
1959	14181	17060
1960	17061	20640
1961	20641	23820
1962	23821	27300
1963	V3 suffix after Ser. No.	
1964	V4 suffix after Ser. No.	
1965	V5 suffix after Ser. No.	
1966	V6 suffix after Ser. No.	
1967	V7 suffix after Ser. No.	
1968	V8 suffix after Ser. No.	
1969	V69 suffix after Ser. No.	
1970	V70 suffix after Ser. No.	
1971	V71 suffix after Ser. No.	
1972	V72 suffix after Ser. No.	
1973	V73 suffix after Ser. No.	
1974	V74 suffix after Ser. No.	
1975	V75 suffix after Ser. No.	
1976	V76 suffix after Ser. No.	

SUPERPOSED MODEL - O & U - 28 ga. &.410 bore

Year	28 ga.	.410 bore
1960-1962	NOT AVAILABLE	
1963	F3	J3
1964	F4	J4
1965	F5	J5
1966	F6	J6
1967	F7	J7
1968	F8	J8
1969	F69	J69
1970	F70	J70
1971	F71	J71
1972	F72	J72
1973	F73	J73
1974	F74	J74
1975	F75	J75
1976	F76	J76

LIEGE O & U - Approximately 10,000 produced

1973	73J prefix before Ser. No.
1974	74J prefix before Ser. No.
1975	75J prefix before Ser. No.

DOUBLE AUTOMATIC SHOTGUN

Year	Ser. # Start	Ser. # End
1952 -		
1959	N/A	
1960 -		
1971		

1st or both digits indicate last 2 digits in year of manufacture (i.e. - OA1947 - 1960 mfg., 70A245671 - 1970 mfg.)

HI-POWER (9mm) PISTOL

Year	Ser. # Start	Ser. # End
1955	72251	75000
1956	75001	77250
1957	77251	80000
1958	80001	85267
1959	85268	89687
1960	89688	93027
1961	93028	109145
1962	109146	113548
1963	113549	115822
1964	115823	T136538
1965	T136569	T146372
1966	T146373	T173285
1967	T173286	T213999
1968	T214000	T258000
1969	T258001	T261000+
	and 69C prefix before Ser. No.	
1970	70C prefix before Ser. No.	
1971	71C prefix before Ser. No.	
1972	72C prefix before Ser. No.	
1973	73C prefix before Ser. No.	
1974	74C prefix before Ser. No.	
1975	75C prefix before Ser. No.	
1976	76C prefix before Ser. No.	
1977 to date	New style serialization	

BROWNING .380

Year	Ser. # Start	Ser. # End
1955 -		
1964		No records exist
1965	500000	598804
1966	598805	603890
1967	603891	619474
1968	619475	N/A
1969 -		

1970 Discontinued due to GCA of 1968. New model has longer barrel, adj. rear sight, modified grip.

1971	71N prefix before Ser. No.	
1972	72N prefix before Ser. No.	
1973	73N prefix before Ser. No.	
1974	74N prefix before Ser. No.	
1975	75N prefix before Ser. No.	

.25 CAL. BABY BROWNING PISTOL

Year	Ser. # Start	Ser. # End
1955 -1958		Records not available
1959	181000	206349
1960	206350	230999
1961	231000	250999
1962	251000	278999
1963	279000	286099
1964	286100	308499
1965	308500	329999
1966	333000	367443
1967	367444	412999
1968	413000	479000
1969	Discontinued because of GCA of 1968	

.22 CAL. PISTOLS (Nomad-Challenger-Medalist)

Year	Nomad	Challenger	Medalist
1959	P9	U9	T9
1960	P0	U0	T0
1961	P1	U1	T1
1962	P2	U2	T2
1963	P3	U3	T3
1965	P5	U5	T5
1966	P6	U6	T6

Year	Nomad	Challenger	Medalist
1967	P7	U7	T7
1968	P8	U8	T8
1969	P69	U69	T69
1970	P70	U70	T70
1971	P71	U71	T71
1972	P72	U72	T72
1973	P73	U73	T73
1974	Disc.	U74	T74
1975	Disc.	Disc.	Disc.

BOLT ACTION RIFLES
(Safari, Medallion, & Olympian Models)

Year	
1959 -	
1962	No prefix (numeral-letter) before Ser. No. (i.e., only digits)
1963	3-single letter prefix or suffix by Ser. No.
1964	4-single letter prefix or suffix by Ser. No.
1965	5-single letter prefix or suffix by Ser. No.
1966	6-single letter prefix or suffix by Ser. No.
1967	7-single letter prefix or suffix by Ser. No.
1968	8-single letter prefix or suffix by Ser. No.
1969	Single letter (Y, Z, or L) followed by last 2 digits of year of mfg. Prefix only.
1970	"Y70" prefix
1971	"L71" prefix
1972	"Z72" prefix
1973	"Y73" prefix
1974	"Z74" prefix
1975	"L75" prefix

B.A.R.

Year	
1967	"M7" suffix after Ser. No.
1968	"M8" suffix after Ser. No.
1969	"M69" suffix after Ser. No.
1970	"M70" suffix after Ser. No.
1971	"M71" suffix after Ser. No.
1972	"M72" suffix after Ser. No.
1973	"M73" suffix after Ser. No.
1974	"M74" suffix after Ser. No.
1975	"M75" suffix after Ser. No.
1976	"M76" suffix after Ser. No.
1976 to date	New sequence with "RT" appearing in middle of Ser. No.

.22 AUTO RIFLE (Grades I, II, and III)

Year	
1956 -	
1964	Numeric only - 5 digits or less
1965	"5T" or "5E" prefix before Ser. No.
1966	"6T" or "6E" prefix before Ser. No.
1967	"7T" or "7E" prefix before Ser. No.
1968	"8T" or "8E" prefix before Ser. No.
1969	"69T" or "69E" prefix before Ser. No.
1970	"70T" or "70E" prefix before Ser. No.
1971	"71T" or "71E" prefix before Ser. No.
1972	"72T" or "72E" prefix before Ser. No.
1973	Japan production

T-BOLT RIFLE (T1 and T2)

Year	
1965	"X5" suffix after Ser. No.
1966	"X6" suffix after Ser. No.
1967	"X7" suffix after Ser. No.
1968	"X8" suffix after Ser. No.
1969	"X69" suffix after Ser. No.
1970	"X70" suffix after Ser. No.
1971	"X71" suffix after Ser. No.
1972	"X72" suffix after Ser. No.
1973	"X73" suffix after Ser. No.

Year	
1974	"X74" suffix after Ser. No.
1975	"X75" suffix after Ser. No.

COLT'S FIREARMS

YearSerial Number Beginning of Year Serial Number at End of Year Total Guns Produced in Year

MODEL 1849 POCKET REVOLVER

Year	*Ser. # Start*	*Ser. # End*
1849	1	11999
1850	12000	15999
1851	16000	24999
1852	25000	54999
1853	55000	84999
1854	85000	99999
1855	100000	109999
1856	110000	129999
1857	130000	139999
1858	140000	149999
1859	150000	159999
1860	160000	183999
1861	184000	196999
1862	197000	222999
1863	223000	249999
1864	250000	269999
1865	270000	279999
1866	280000	289999
1867	290000	299999
1868	300000	309999
1869	310000	319999
1870	320000	324999
1871	325000	329999
1872	330000	330999
1873	331000	340000

MODEL 1849 POCKET REVOLVER -LONDON BARREL ADDRESS

Year	*Ser. # Start*	*Ser. # End*
1853	1	999
1854	1000	4999
1855	5000	8999
1856	9000	11000

MODEL 1851 NAVY

Year	*Ser. # Start*	*Ser. # End*
1850	1	2499
1851	2500	9999
1852	10000	19999
1853	20000	34999
1854	35000	39999
1855	40000	44999
1856	45000	64999
1857	65000	84999
1858	85000	89999
1859	90000	92999
1860	93000	97999
1861	98000	117999
1862	118000	131999
1863	132000	174999
1864	175000	179999
1865	180000	184999
1866	185000	199999
1867	200000	203999
1868	204000	206999
1869	207000	209999
1870	210000	211999
1871	212000	213999
1872	214000	214999
1873	215000	215348

MODEL 1851 NAVY - LONDON BARREL ADDRESS

Year	*Ser. # Start*	*Ser. # End*
1853	1	3999
1854	4000	14999
1855	15000	40999
1856	41000	42000

MODEL 1860 ARMY

Year	*Ser. # Start*	*Ser. # End*
1860	1	1999
1861	2000	24999
1862	25000	84999
1863	85000	149999
1864	150000	152999
1865	153000	155999
1866	156000	161999
1867	162000	169999
1868	170000	176999
1869	177000	184999
1870	185000	189999
1871	190000	197999
1872	198000	198999
1873	199000	200500

MODEL 1861 NAVY

Year	*Ser. # Start*	*Ser. # End*
1861	1	4599
1862	4600	9999
1863	10000	16999
1864	17000	24999
1865	25000	27999
1866	28000	29999
1867	30000	30999
1868	31000	32999
1869	33000	33999
1870	34000	34999
1871	35000	35999
1872	36000	36999
1873	37000	38843

MODEL 1862 POLICE

Year	*Ser. # Start*	*Ser. # End*
1861	1	8499
1862	8500	14999
1863	15000	25999
1864	26000	28999
1865	29000	31999
1866	32000	34999
1867	35000	36999
1868	37000	39999
1869	40000	41999
1870	42000	43999
1871	44000	44999
1872	45000	45999
1873	46000	47000

MODEL 1873 - SINGLE ACTION ARMY (SAA) - PRE-WAR

Year	*Caliber*	*Ser. # Start*
1873	.45 Colt Caliber, Standard	1
1874	.450 Boxer	200
1875	.44 Rimfire series (own serials, 1-1863 made through 1880)	15000
1876	.476 Eley introduced	22000
1877		33000
1878	.44-40 introduced in quantity	41000
1879		49000
1880		53000
1881		62000
1882	Sheriff's model introduced	73000
1883	.22 rimfire introduced	85000

Year	Caliber	Ser. # Start
1884	.32-20 and .38-40 introduced	102000
1885	.41 Colt introduced	114000
1886	.38 Colt introduced	117000
1887	.32 Colt and .32 S&W introduced	119000
1888	Flattop Target	125000
	S.A.A. began; no.	126530
1889	.32 rimfire; .32-44 S&W, .38 S&W; and .44 Russian introduced	128000
1890	.44 Smoothbore; .380 and .450 Eley; and .44 S&W introduced	130000
1891	.38-44 introduced	136000
1892	Transverse cylinder latch introduced, screw lock at front of frame dropped	144000
1893		149000
1894	Beginning of Bisley models	154000
1895		159000
1896		163000
1897		168000
1898		175000
1899		182000
1900	Revolvers built to handle smokeless powder	192000
1901		203000
1902		220000
1903		238000
1904		250000
1905		261000
1906		273000
1907		288000
1908		304000
1909		308000
1910		312000
1911		316000
1912	Discontinue Bisley model	321000
1913	S&W Special introduced	325000
1914		328000
1915	Long flute cylinders; range no. 330001 to 331480	329500
1916		332000
1917		335000
1918		337000
1919		337200
1920		338000
1921		341000
1922		343000
1923		344500
1924	.45 ACP introduced, requiring special cylinders	346400
1925		347300
1926		348200
1927		349800
1928		351300
1929		352400
1930	.38 Special introduced	353800
1931		354100
1932		354500
1933		354800
1934		355000
1935	.357 Magnum introduced	355200
1936		355300
1937		355400
1938		356100
1939		356600
1940	A few S.A.A. during and just after the war	357000 thru 357859

COLT SINGLE ACTION ARMY – POST-WAR PRODUCTION

"SA" suffix from 1956 to 1978, "SA" prefix 1978 to 1981

Year	Ser. # Start	Ser. # End
1956	0001SA	8799SA
1957	8800SA	18499SA
1958	18500SA	23399SA
1959	23400SA	28499SA
1960	28500SA	33599SA
1961	33600SA	35649SA
1962	35650SA	37299SA
1963	37300SA	38499SA
1964	38500SA	39999SA
1965	40000SA	41499SA
1966	41500SA	43799SA
1967	43800SA	46299SA
1968	46300SA	48999SA
1969	49000SA	52599SA
1970	52600SA	59399SA
1971	59400SA	61699SA
1972	61700SA	64399SA
1973	64400SA	69399SA
1974	69400SA	73319SA
1975		NONE PRODUCED
1976 (start of 3rd generation of production)	80000SA	82000SA
1977	82001SA	95999SA
1978	96000SA	99999SA
1978	Start of "SA" prefix on front of Ser. No.	
Mid - 1978	SA01000	SA14808
1979	SA14809	SA30254
1980	SA30255	SA46919
1981	SA46920	SA58627
1982	SA58628	SA65255
1983	SA65256	SA66495
1984	SA66496	C.S. PROD.

NEW FRONTIER SINGLE ACTION ARMY

Year	Ser. # Start	Ser. # End
1961	3000NF	3005NF
1962	3006NF	3849NF
1963	4325NF	4699NF
1964	4700NF	4974NF
1965	4975NF	5399NF
1966	5400NF	5674NF
1967	5675NF	5699NF
1968	5700NF	
1969	5701NF	5924NF
1970	5925NF	6874NF
1971	6875NF	7049NF
1972	7050NF	7074NF
1973	7075NF	7174NF
1974	7175NF	7264NF
1975	7265NF	7288NF
1978	7501NF	
	REINTRODUCED IN SEPTEMBER	
1978	01001NF	04424NF
1979	04425NF	06274NF
1980	06275NF	11374NF
1981	11375NF	16584NF
1982	16584NF	DISC. 1982

COLT SINGLE ACTION ARMY - CALIBER BREAKDOWN

Caliber	S.A.A	Flattop Target	Bisley	Bisley Target
.22 Rimfire	107	93	0	0
.32 Rimfire	1	0	0	0
.32 Colt	192	24	160	44

Caliber	S.A.A	Flattop Target	Bisley	Bisley Target
.32 S&W	32	30	18	17
.32-44	2	9	14	17
.32-20	29,812	30	13,291	131
.38 Colt (through 1914)	1,011	122	412	96
.38 Colt (post-1922)	1,365	0	0	0
.38 S&W	9	39	10	5
.38 Colt Special	82	7	0	0
.38 S&W Special	25	0	2	0
.38-44	2	11	6	47
.357 Magnum	525	0	0	0
.380 Eley	1	3	0	0
.38-40	38,240	19	12,163	98
.41	16,402	91	3,159	24
.44 Smoothbore	15	0	1	0
.44 Rimfire	1,863	0	0	0
.44 German	59	0	0	0
.44 Russian	154	51	90	62
.44 S&W	24	51	29	64
.44 S&W Special	506	1	0	0
.44-40	64,489	21	6,803	78
.45	150,683	100	8,005	97
.45 Smoothbore	4	0	2	0
.45 ACP	44	0	0	0
.450 Boxer	729	89	0	0
.450 Eley	2,697	84	5	0
.455 Eley	1,150	37	180	196
.476 Eley	161	2	0	0
Total Quantities	310,386	914	44,350	976

MODEL 1911 AND 1911A1 – Commercial production – Capital "C" prefix - .45 cal.

Year	Ser. # Start	Ser. # End
1912	C1	C1899
1913	C1900	C5399
1914	C5400	C16599
1915	C16600	C27599
1916	C27600	C74999
1917	C75000	C98999
1918	C99000	C105999
1919	C106000	C120999
1920	C120000	C126999
1921	C127000	C128999
1922	C129000	C133999
1923	C134000	C134999
1924	C135000	C139999
1925	C140000	C144999
1926	C145000	C150999
1927	C151000	C151999
1928	C152000	C154999
1929	C155000	C155999
1930	C156000	C158999
1931	C159000	C160999
1932	C161000	C164799
1933	C164800	C174599
1934	C174600	C177999
1935	C178000	C179799
1936	C179800	C183199
1937	C183200	C188699
1938	C188700	C189599
1939	C189600	C198899

Year	Ser. # Start	Ser. # End
1940	C198900	C199299
1941	C199300	C208799
1942	C208800	C215018
1943-1945: Commercial production interrupted by WWII		
1946	C221001	C222000
1947	C222001	C231999
1948	C232000	C238500
1949	C238501	C240000
1950	C240000	247701C
	"C" SUFFIX STARTED WITH SER. NO. 240228	
1951	247701C	253179C
1952	253180C	259549C
1953	259550C	266349C
1954	266350C	270549C
1955	270550C	272549C
1956	272550C	276699C
1957	276700C	281999C
1958	282000C	283799C
1959	283800C	285799C
1960	285800C	287999C
1961	288000C	289849C
1962	289850C	291299C
1963	291300C	293799C
1964	293800C	295999C
1965	296000C	300299C
1966	300300C	308499C
1967	308500C	315599C
1968	315600C	324499C
1969	324500C	332649C
1970	332650C	336169C
New Range	70G01001	70G05550
1971	70G05551	70G18000
1972	70G18001	70G34400
1973	70G34401	70G43000
1974	70G43001	70G73000
1975	70G73001	70G88900
1976	70G88901	70G99999
New Range	01001G70	13900G70
1977	13901G70	45199G70
1978		
TO DATE	45200G70	

MODEL 1911 AND 1911A1 MILITARY PRODUCTION

Year	Ser. # Start	Ser. # End	Manufacturer
1912	1	500	COLT
	501	000	COLT USN
	1001	1500	COLT
	1501	2000	COLT USN
	2001	2500	COLT
	2501	3500	COLT USN
	3501	3800	COLT USMC
	3801	4500	COLT
	4501	5500	COLT USN
	5501	6500	COLT
	6501	7500	COLT USN
	7501	8500	COLT
	8501	9500	COLT USN
	9501	10500	COLT
	10501	11500	COLT USN
	11501	12500	COLT
	12501	13500	COLT USN
	13501	17250	COLT USN
1913	17251	36400	COLT
	36401	37650	COLT USMC
	37651	38000	COLT
	38001	44000	COLT USN
	44001	60400	COLT
1914	60401	72570	COLT
	72571	83855	SPRINGFIELD-
(THESE NUMBERS RESERVED SPRINGFIELD)			

Year	Ser. # Start	Ser. # End	Manufacturer
83856	83900		COLT
	83901	84400	COLT USMC
	84401	96000	COLT
	96001	97537	COLT USN
	97538	102596	COLT
	102597	107596	
SPRINGFIELD(RESERVED NO. RANGE)			
1915	107597	109500	COLT
	109501	110000	COLT USN
	110001	113496	COLT
	113497	120566	SPRINGFIELD-
(RESERVED FORSPRINGFIELD)			
	120567	125566	COLT
	125567	133186	SPRINGFIELD-
(RESERVED FORSPRINGFIELD)			
1916	133187	137400	COLT
1917	137401	151186	COLT
	151187	151986	COLT USMC
	151987	185800	COLT
	185801	186200	COLT USMC
	186201	209586	COLT
	209587	210386	COLT USMC
	210387	215386	COLT
FRAMES(RESERVED FOR RECEIVERS)			
	215387	216186	COLT USMC
	216187	216586	COLT
	216587	216986	COLT USMC
1918	216987	217386	COLT USMC
	217387	223952	COLT
	223953	223990	COLT USN
	223991	232000	COLT
	232001	233600	COLT USN
	233601	580600	COLT
	1	13152	REM. UMC
1919	13153	21676	REM. UMC
	580601	629500	COLT
	629501	717386	COLT
1924	700001	710000	COLT
1937	710001	712349	COLT USN
1938	712350	713645	COLT
1939	713646	717281	COLT USN
1940	717282	721977	COLT
1941	721978	756733	COLT
1942	756734	793657	COLT
	793658	797639	COLT USN
	797640	800000	COLT
	S800001	S800500	SINGER
	800501	801000	H&R
	801001	856100	COLT
1943	856101	958100	COLT
** 856101	856404		Replacement No
** 856405	916404		ITHACA
** 916405	1041404		REM. RAND
	1041405	1096404	US&S
	1088726	1208673	COLT
	1208674	1279673	ITHACA
	1279674	1279698	RE NO AA
	1279699	1441404	REM. RAND
	1441431	1471430	ITHACA
	1471431	1609528	REM. RAND
1944	1609529	1743846	COLT
	1743847	1816641	REM. RAND
	1816642	1890503	ITHACA
	1890504	2075103	REM. RAND
1945	2075104	2134403	ITHACA
	2134404	2244803	REM. RAND
	2244804	2380013	COLT
	2380014	2619013	REM. RAND
	2619014	2693613	ITHACA

* Denotes double issue ranges.

COLT SINGLE-ACTION MODEL NUMBERS

The author wishes to express thanks to Mr. Don Wilkerson for allowing the edited information published below from his 1986 **Post-War Single-Action Revolver, 1976-1986** publication.

A working knowledge of model numbers for the various Colt single-action revolvers is a must for even a novice collector. Since the mid-1970s Colt has placed the model number on the end label of the shipping cartons of virtually all their firearms. Many collectors and publications regularly use the model number to describe or differentiate between revolvers. Using the model number is an accurate and efficient method to delineate a particular variation. Example: .45 caliber revolver with a 4 3/4 in. barrel, blue and casehardened finish and eagle stocks can be described as a simple "P-1840".

Each Colt model is specified by an alphabetical letter and 4 numerical digits. The basic model number as it pertains to single-action revolvers can be broken down as follows:

MODEL P - basic type of frame. The letter "P" is used to delineate the single-action type of frame.

FIRST NUMERAL - "1" is the first model built on a particular type of frame. Numerals 2, 3, 4, etc. indicate later versions. These versions are not always numbered in numerical order and the same number has been used for different models at different times. A "1" denotes the basic standard single-action frame. A "2" denotes the new black powder frame available through the Colt Custom Gun Shop. A "3" has been used at various times to denote a non-standard frame or cylinder. The "4" is used to specify the New Frontier style of frame. Numbers such as "7" and "8" are frequently used to specify commemorative or special editions.

SECOND NUMERAL - specifies caliber. A "4" denotes .32-20, a "6" denotes .357 Magnum, a "7" denotes .44 Special, an "8" denotes .45 caliber, and a "9" specifies .44-40 caliber.*

THIRD NUMERAL - denotes barrel length. "3" is used to denote both a 3 inch and a 4 inch barrel. "4" is 4 3/4 inch or 5 inch, "5" is 5 1/2 inch, "7" is 7 1/2 inch, and "1" is 12 inch.*

FOURTH NUMERAL - is used to denote several different variations of the standard model. Some of the most common examples are: "1", "2", or "6" for nickel finish, "1" for full blue finish in the case of P-1871, and "2", "3", and "4" as used for the Sheriff's Model series to denote blue and casehardened finish, nickel finish, and Royal Blue and casehardened finish, respectively. The fourth numeral can also denote the type of stocks as in P-1673. The fourth numeral in the basic model designation must be used in conjunction with the preceding three numerals to determine its exact meaning. The fourth numeral is kind of a "catch-all" number. Many times this number serves only to differentiate a later model from a similar model assembled years earlier.

The .32-20 caliber and the 5 inch barrel length are listed in the 1984 Colt Buyer's Guide, but as of this date neither have been produced.

STANDARD MODEL P REVOLVER

The primary model numbers used by Colt for Model P revolvers produced since 1976 are as follows:

P-1640 - .357 Magnum, 4 3/4 in. barrel, blue finish, eagle stocks.

P-1641 - .357 Magnum, 4 3/4 in. barrel, nickel finish, wood stocks.

P-1650 - .357 Magnum, 5 1/2 in. barrel, blue finish, eagle stocks.

P-1656 - .357 Magnum, 5 1/2 in. barrel, nickel finish, wood stocks.

P-1670 - .357 Magnum, 7 1/2 in. barrel, blue finish, eagle stocks.

P-1673 - .357 Magnum, 7 1/2 in. barrel, blue finish, wood stocks.

P-1676 - .357 Magnum, 7 1/2 in. barrel, nickel finish, wood stocks.

P-1740 - .44 Special, 4 3/4 in. barrel, blue finish, eagle stocks.

P-1746 - .44 Special, 4 3/4 in. barrel, nickel finish, wood stocks.

P-1750 - .44 Special, 5 1/2 in. barrel, blue finish, eagle stocks.

P-1756 - .44 Special, 5 1/2 in. barrel, nickel finish, wood stocks.

P-1770 - .44 Special, 7 1/2 in. barrel, blue finish, eagle stocks.

P-1776 - .44 Special, 7 1/2 in. barrel, nickel finish, wood stocks.

P-1716 - .44 Special, 12 in. barrel, nickel finish, wood stocks.

P-1840 - .45 Colt, 4 3/4 in. barrel, blue finish, eagle stocks.

P-1841 - .45 Colt, 4 3/4 in. barrel, nickel finish, wood stocks.

P-1850 - .45 Colt, 5 1/2 in. barrel, blue finish, eagle stocks.

P-1856 - .45 Colt, 5 1/2 in. barrel, nickel finish, wood stocks.

P-1870 - .45 Colt, 7 1/2 in. barrel, blue finish, eagle stocks.

P-1876 - .45 Colt, 7 1/2 in. barrel, nickel finish, wood stocks.

P-1813 - .45 Colt, 12 in. barrel, blue finish, eagle stocks.

P-1816 - .45 Colt, 12 in. barrel, nickel finish, wood stocks.

P-1940 - .44-40 caliber, 4 3/4 in. barrel, blue finish, eagle stocks.

P-1941* - .44-40 caliber, 4 3/4 in. barrel, nickel finish, wood stocks.

P-1950 - .44-40 caliber, 5 1/2 in. barrel, blue finish, eagle stocks.

P-1970 - .44-40 caliber, 7 1/2 in. barrel, blue finish, eagle stocks.

P-1976* - .44-40 caliber, 7 1/2 in. barrel, nickel finish, wood stocks.

P-1911 - .44-40 caliber, 12 in. barrel, nickel finish, wood stocks.

*These model numbers were used primarily for engraved or special ordered revolvers as the two models indicated were never produced as a regular model. "Blue finish" in the above chart denotes the standard blue finish, i.e., blue with case-hardened frame.

NEW FRONTIER MODEL

P-4671 - .357 Magnum, 7 1/2 in. barrel, nickel finish, wood stocks.

P-4750 - .44 Special, 5 1/2 in. barrel, Royal Blue finish, wood stocks.

P-4770 - .44 Special , 7 1/2 in. barrel, Royal Blue finish, wood stocks.

P-4840 - .45 Colt, 4 3/4 in. barrel, Royal Blue finish, wood stocks.

P-4850 - .45 Colt, 5 1/2 in. barrel, Royal Blue finish, wood stocks.

P-4870 - .45 Colt, 7 1/2 in. barrel, Royal Blue finish, wood stocks.

P-4940 - .44-40 caliber, 4 3/4 in. barrel, Royal Blue finish, wood stocks.

P-4970 - .44-40 caliber, 7 1/2 in. barrel, Royal Blue finish, wood stocks.

Note: The term "Royal Blue" in the New Frontier chart denotes a revolver with a casehardened frame and a Royal (high polish) Blue finish on the other major components.

SHERIFF'S MODELS

P-1932 - .44-40 caliber, 3 in. barrel, blue finish, eagle stocks.

P-1933* - .44-40/.44 Special, 3 in. barrel, nickel finish, wood stocks.

P-1934* - .44-40/.44 Special, 3 in. barrel, Royal Blue finish, wood stocks.

*Circa 1984 all Sheriff's Models are listed as single calibers: .44-40 or .45 caliber.

REVOLVERS WITH FULL BLUE FRAMES

Some of the "full blue" models have had more than one model number assigned to the same variation. As a result, a particular model may have been identified by different model numbers at different times. Following the model numbers and descriptions in this chart will be an approximate time frame during which that particular model was in use. No date following the description indicates that only one model number for that particular variation is known to the author (Don Wilkerson).

P-1640 - FB - .357 Magnum, 4 3/4 in. barrel, fluted cylinder, eagle stocks.

P-1650 - FB - .357 Magnum, 5 1/2 in. barrel, fluted cylinder, eagle stocks.

P-1740 - FB - .44 Special, 4 3/4 in. barrel, fluted cylinder, eagle stocks.

P-1750 - FB - .44 Special, 5 1/2 in. barrel, fluted cylinder, eagle stocks.

P-1770 - FB - .44 Special, 7 1/2 in. barrel, fluted cylinder, eagle stocks.

P-1770 - UB - .44 Special, 7 1/2 in. barrel, unfluted cylinder, eagle stocks.

P-3840 - .45 Colt, 4 3/4 in. barrel, both fluted and unfluted cylinders, eagle stocks (early to mid-1982).

P-1840 - FB - .45 Colt, 4 3/4 in. barrel, fluted cylinder, eagle stocks (mid to late 1982 to date).

P-1840 - UB - .45 Colt, 4 3/4 in. barrel, unfluted cylinder, eagle stocks (mid to late 1982 to date).

P-1850 - FB - .45 Colt, 5 1/2 in. barrel, fluted cylinder, eagle stocks.

P-1850 - UB - .45 Colt, 5 1/2 in. barrel, unfluted cylinder, eagle stocks.

P-1871 - .45 Colt, 7 1/2 in. barrel, fluted cylinder, wood stocks (1977 to 1979).

P-1870 - FB - .45 Colt, 7 1/2 in. barrel, fluted cylinder, wood stocks (1982 to date).

P-1870 - UB - .45 Colt, 7 1/2 in. barrel, unfluted cylinder, wood stocks (1982 to date).

P-1871 - FB - .45 Colt, 12 in. barrel, fluted cylinder, eagle stocks.

FULL BLUE NEW FRONTIERS

P-4770 - FB - .44 Special, 7 1/2 in. barrel, fluted cylinder, wood stocks.

P-4870 - FB - .45 Colt, 7 1/2 in. barrel, fluted cylinder, wood stocks.

P-4870 - UB - .45 Colt, 7 1/2 in. barrel, unfluted cylinder, wood stocks.

MISCELLANEOUS MODEL NUMBERS

1750 - AA - .44 Special, 5 1/2 in. barrel, blue finish
with nickel cylinder, eagle stocks.

1750 - AB - .44 Special, 5 1/2 in. barrel, blue finish
with nickel cylinder with blue flutes, eagle stocks.

1840 - UC - .45 Colt, 4 3/4 in. barrel, blue finish,
unfluted cylinder, eagle stocks.

1850 - UC - .45 Colt, 5 1/2 in. barrel, blue finish,
unfluted cylinder, eagle stocks.

1870 - UC - .45 Colt, 7 1/2 in. barrel, blue finish,
unfluted cylinder, eagle stocks.

Note: The term "blue finish" in this chart is the standard blue finish with a casehardened frame.

BLACK POWDER MODEL P REVOLVERS

P-2830 - .45 Colt, 3 in. barrel, blue finish.
P-2833 - .45 Colt, 3 in. barrel, nickel finish.
P-2834* - .45 Colt, 3 in. barrel, Royal Blue finish.
P-2836 - .45 Colt, 4 in. barrel, Royal Blue finish.
P-2837 - .45 Colt, 4 in. barrel, nickel finish.
P-2840 - .45 Colt, 4 3/4 in. barrel, blue finish.
P-2841 - .45 Colt, 4 3/4 in. barrel, nickel finish.
P-2847* - .45 Colt, 5 in. barrel, nickel finish.
P-2870 - .45 Colt, 7 1/2 in. barrel, blue finish.
P-2871 - .45 Colt, 7 1/2 in. barrel, nickel finish.
P-2940 - .44-40 caliber, 4 3/4 in. barrel, blue finish.
P-2941 - .44-40 caliber, 4 3/4 in. barrel, nickel finish.
P-2970 - .44-40 caliber, 7 1/2 in. barrel, blue finish.
P-2971 - .44-40 caliber, 7 1/2 in. barrel, nickel finish.
P-2437* - .32-20 caliber, 4 in. barrel, nickel finish.
P-2474* - .32-20 caliber, 7 1/2 in. barrel, Royal Blue finish.

As of this writing these calibers have not been produced. The terms "blue finish" and "Royal" in this chart refer to Colt's standard single- action finish, i.e., casehardened frame with all components finished in either standard blue or Royal Blue.

COLT BLACKPOWDER 2ND GENERATION SERIALIZATION

Model No.	Ser. # Range		Total Prod.	Prod. Began	Prod. Ended
MODEL 1851 NAVY					
C-1121	4201	25100	20900	1971	1978
C-1122					
As above but at higher range of numbers Unk'n - 1978					
MODEL 1851 NAVY, R. E. LEE					
C-9001251 REL	5000 REL	4750		-	1971
MODEL 1851 NAVY, U. S. GRANT					
C-9002251 USG	5000 USG	4750		-	1971
MODEL 1851 GRANT-LEE PAIR					
C-9003 01 GLP	250 GLP		250		1971
3rd MODEL DRAGOON					
C-1770	20801	208	25	1974	1978
Prototype					
	20901	24501	3601		
C-1770MN					
S/N As Above			20	1984	1984
MODEL 1851 NAVY					
F-1100	24900	29150	4250	5/80	10/81
F-1101					
S/N As Above			300	10/81	11/81
W/Blank Cylinders					
F-1110	29151 S	29640 S	489	6/82	10/82
Stainless Steel					
MODEL 1860 ARMY					
F-1200	201000	212835	7593	11/78	11/82
Rebated Cylinder					
F-1200 EBO					

Model No.	Ser. # Range		Total Prod.	Prod. Began	Prod. Ended
S/N As Above			500	1979	1979
Butterfield					
F-1200 LNK					
S/N As Above			Unk'n	Unk'n	Unk'n
Electroless Nickel					
F-1200 MN					
S/N As Above			12	1984	1984
Nickel/Ivory					
F-1202					
S/N As Above			500	1979	1979
Limited Edition					
F-1203	207330	211250	2670	7/80	10/81
Fluted Cylinder					
F-1210	211263 S	212540 S	1278	1/82	4/82
Stainless Steel					
1861 NAVY					
F-1300	40000	43165	3166	9/80	10/81
1862 POCKET NAVY					
F-1400	48000	58850	5765	12/79	11/81
and skip odd no.					
F-1400MN					
S/N As Above			25	1984	1984
Nickel/Ivory					
F-1401					
S/N As Above			500	1979	1980
Limited Edition					
1862 POCKET POLICE					
F-1500	49000	57300	4801	1/80	9/81
and skip even no.					
F-1500 MN					
S/N As Above			25	1984	1984
Nickel/Ivory					
F-1501					
S/N As Above			500	1979	1980
Limited Edition					
1847 WALKER					
F-1600	1200	4120	2573	6/80	4/82
	32256	32500	245	5/81	9/81
1st MODEL DRAGOON					
F-1700	25100	34500	3878	1/80	2/82
2nd MODEL DRAGOON					
F-172 S/N As Above and Mix at Random for					
1st, 2nd & 3rd			2676	1/80	2/82
3rd MODEL DRAGOON					
F-140 S/N As Above and Mix at Random for					
1st, 2nd & 3rd			2856	1/80	2/82
	31401	31450	50	10/81	11/81
F-1740EGA	Unk'n	Unk'n	200	1982	1982
(Garabaldi Model<- "GCA" prefix)					
BABY DRAGOON					
F-1760	16000	17851	1852	2/81	4/81
F-1761 S/N As Above			500	1979	1980
Limited Edition					
1860 ARMY					
F-9005 US 001/001 US to					
US 3025/3025 US			3025	9/77	1/80
Cavalry Commemorative (Two Gun Set)					
HERITAGE WALKER					
F-9006	01	1853	1853	6/80	6/81

HARRINGTON & RICHARDSON SERIALIZATION 1940 - 1982

The following serial numbered prefixes are related to the corresponding year of manufacture:

Year Starting	S.N. Prefix
1940	A
1941	B
1942	C
1943	D
1944	E
1945	F
1946	G
1947	H
1948	I
1949	J
1950	K
1951	L
1952	M
1953	N
1954	P
1955	R
1956	S
1957	T
1958	U
1959	V
1960	W
1961	X
1962	Y
1963	Z
1964	AA
1965	AB
1966	AC
1967	AD
1968	AE
1969	AF
1970	AG
1971	AH(Snap on forecap)
1972	AJ
1973	AL
1974	AM
1975	AN
1976	AP
1977	AR(Striker Mech. Intr.)
1978	AS
1979	AT
1980	AU
1981	AX
1982	AY

HIGH STANDARD SERIAL NUMBERS 1932 - 1957

Year Starting	Serial Number
1932	5,000
1933	5,050
1934	6,500
1935	8,300
1936	11,500
1937	18,500
1938	29,600
1939	39,200
1940	50,500
1941	70,600
1942	92,600
1943	103,600
1944	115,000
1945	134,700

Year Starting	Serial Number
1946	145,800
1947	174,200
1948	235,000
1949	299,000
1950	325,000
1951	330,000
1952	355,000
1953	400,000
1954	440,000
1955	480,000
1956	550,000
1957	640,000
1958	8192XX
1959	9854XX
1962	12606XX
1963	12954XX
1965	14204XX
1965	15709XX
1966	16078XX
1967	17509XX
1967	18141XX
1968	18891XX
1968	19909XX
1969	20485XX
1969	21609XX
1970	21971XX
1971	22662XX
1972	22874XX
1972	23337XX
1973	23639XX
1973	24140XX
1974	24337XX
1975	ML15XXX
1976	ML19XXX
1977	ML23XXX
Feb.1981	ML71000
Apr.1981	ML84000
May 1981	ML85000
June 1981	ML86000
June 1981	SH10000
Sept.1982	SH14000
Oct. 1982	SH15000
Nov. 1982	SH16000
Dec. 1982	SH17000
Jan. 1983	SH18000
Feb. 1983	SH19000
Apr. 1983	SH21000
May 1983	SH23000
Oct. 1983	SH24000
Feb. 1984	SH25000
Apr. 1984	SH26000
May 1984	SH27000
June 1984	SH29000
Sept. 1984	SH34000

HOLLAND & HOLAND
PARADOX SERIES

Year Starting	Serial Number
1885	11500
1886	
1887	
1888	11691
1889	11788
1890	11865
1891	11948
1895	15036
1892	15075
1895	15347
1900	15558
1903	15655
1905	15750

Year Starting	*Serial Number*
1906	15825
1907	15860
1911	15900
1914	15950
1919	19560
1922	15970
1930	15980
1956	15979

RECORDED DATES

Year Starting	*Serial Number*
March 1856	565 (First Recorded Date)
October 1868	580
February 1857	584
August 1859	700
A gap in records	728-1059
1864	1060
1865	1101
1868	1352
1869	1439
1870	1578
1871	1769
1872	2002
1873	2401
1874	2759
1875	3174
1876	3649
1877	4179
1878	4774
1879	5274
1880	5819
1881	6382
1882	7009
1883	7473
1884	7904
1885	8406
1886	8809
1887	8999
Unused	9000-10000
Missing	10000-10849
Rook Rifles	10850-10999
Normal Series	11000-11499
Paradox Guns	11500-11999
Normal Series	12000-12999
Rook Rifles	13000-13999
Normal Series	14000-14999
Paradox Guns	15000-15999
Normal Series	16000-16999
Normal Series	17000-17399
Rifles and Rook Rifles	17400-17999
Believed Unused Rifles	18000-18999
Rifles	19000-19999
Misc. Guns and Rifles	20000-21999
See separate lists	22000+

ROOK RIFLES

Year Starting	*Serial Number*
1887	10850-10999
Assumed 1888 records missing	11000-11499
1889	13106
1890	13465
1891	13566
1892	13674
1893	13885-13999
1894 Some rook rifles among others	17401
1899	17999

MAGAZINE RIFLES

Year Starting	*Serial Number*
1910	28000
1911	28100
1913	28199
1913	28300
1919	28399
1920-29	1-581
1930-33	582-880
1920-32	881-1181
1935-49	1182-1782
1949-60	1783-2179
1951-58	2180-2577
1952-62	2578-2977
1958-65	2978-3377
1964-74	3378-3783
1975-80	3784-4000
1981-87	4001-4250
1988-92	4251-4330

PLAIN GUNS

Year Starting	*Serial Number*
1907	26200
1908	26300
1909	26400
1909	26500
1910	26600
1911	26700
1912	26800
1913	26900
1913	26999
1913	28600
1914	28700
1914	28800
1915	28900
1915	28999
1915	29500
1915	29600
1916	29700
1919	29800
1919	29900
1919	30000
1920	30100
1922	30200
1924	30300
1925	30334
1925	31100
1926	31200
1928	31300
1929	31399
1929	32200
1931	32300
1933	32400
1935	32499
1935	34000
1936	34100
1937	34200
1939	34300
1949	34400
1953	34500
1956	34600
1961	34700
1975	34800

ROYAL GUNS

Year Starting	*Serial Number*
1899	22000
1900	22500
1902	23000
1903	23500
1906	25000
1907	25500

Year Starting	Serial Number
1910	25599
1910	27000
1911	27250
1912	27500
1913	27750
1914	27999
1914	29000
1915	29100
1919	29200
1920	29300
1920	29400
1921	29499
1921	30500
1922	30600
1922	30700
1924	30800
1925	30900
1926	30999
1926	31500
1927	31600
1927	31700
1928	31800
1929	31900
1929	32900
1934	32999
1934	33000
1935	33100
1936	33200
1937	33300
1937	33400
1939	33500
1946	33600
1948	33700
1950	33800
1952	33900
1954	33999
1954	36251
1956	36300
1958	36400
1959	36500
1962	36600
1964	36700
1965	36800
1970	36900
1970	40006
1972	40100
1974	40200
1979	40300
1980	40400
1981	40500
1982	40530
1983	40560
1984	40590
1985	40650
1986	40770
1987	40820
1988	40880
1989	40920
1990	41000
1991	41075
1992	41150
1993	41210

ROYAL OVER & UNDER GUNS

Year Starting	Serial Number
1950	36000
1952	36010
1954	36020
1958	36029
1993	51001

SPORTING OVER & UNDER GUNS

Year Starting	Serial Number
1993	50500

CAVALIER GUNS

Year Starting	Serial Number
1986	50001
1989	50150
1992	50250

ROYAL DOUBLE RIFLES - .450 & .465

Year Starting	Serial Number
1910	28200
1914	28299
1914	28500
1919	28535
1921	30335
1921	30415
1925	31042
1925	31049
1927	32000
1941	32099

ROYAL DOUBLE RIFLES - .375

Year Starting	Serial Number
1911	28400
1920	28499
1920	30416
1925	30499
1925	31050
1927	31099
1927	32100
1933	32199

ROYAL DOUBLE RIFLES - .240 & Small Bores

Year Starting	Serial Number
1920	28566
1923	28599
1923	31000
1926	31041
1926	31400
1931	31450
1955	31499

ALL CALIBRES

Year Starting	Serial Number
1933	35000
1939	35100
1950	35200
1953	35250
1956	35300
1963	35350
1968	35450
1975	35495
1977	35498
1980	35500
1981	35505
1984	35524
1985	35527
1988	35540
1989	35542
1990	35552
1991	35590

ITALIAN YEAR OF MFG. DATE CODES

All Dates Prior to 1943 Have Month and Year (i.e. IXXII = January 1922.) 1944 -1953 = I - IX

X =	1954
XI =	1955
XII =	1956

XIII =	1957
XIV =	1958
XV =	1959
XVI =	1960
XVII =	1961
XVIII =	1962
XIX =	1963
XX =	1964
XXI =	1965
XXII =	1966
XXIII =	1967
XXIV =	1968
XXV =	1969
XVI =	1970
XXVII =	1971
XXVIII =	1972
XXIX =	1973
XXX =	1974
AA =	1975
AB =	1976
AC =	1977
AD =	1978
AE =	1979
AF =	1980
AH =	1981
AI =	1982
AL =	1983
AM =	1984
AN =	1985
AP =	1986
AS =	1987
AT =	1988
AW =	1989
AZ =	1990
BA =	1991
BB =	1992
BC =	1993
BD =	1994
BF =	1995
BH =	1996
BI =	1997
BL =	1998
BM =	1999
BN =	2000

MARLIN

Approximate serialization for Marlin rifles from 1883 to 1906 including Models 1881, 1888, 1889, 1891, 1892, 1893, 1894, and 1897. Marlin did not assign a specific block of Ser. No. to these models, rather the models being produced that time were mixed. Using this list will place the year of manufacture plus or minus one year.

For a factor letter on an older Marlin firearm, contact the Buffalo Bill Historical center, Cody Firearms Museum, 720 Sheridan Ave., Cody, WY 82414. Web site www.bbhc.org or phone 307-587-4771. There is a $45 fee per serial number search.

Older Rifles Mfg.

Year	From #	To #
1883	4001	6700
1884	6700	8850
1885	8850	11300
1886	11300	15000
1887	15000	17800
1888	17800	21500
1889	21500	30000
1890	30000	45000
1891	45000	63250
1892	63250	80250

Year	From #	To #
1893	80250	95750
1894	95750	115000
1895	115000	133000
1896	133000	144400
1897	144400	161200
1898	161200	175500
1899	175500	196000
1900	196000	213000
1901	213000	233300
1902	233300	262500
1903	262500	287300
1904	287300	310500
1905	310500	329000
1906	329000	355300

1948-1968 Mfg.

Year	Serial No. Prefix
1948	E
1949	F
1950	G
1951	H
1952	J
1953	K
1954	L
1955	M
1956	N
1957	P
1957-1958	R
1958-1959	S
1960	T
1960-Aug. 1961	U
1961-Aug. 1962	V
1963	W
1964	Y & Z
1965	AA

1948-1968 Mfg.

Year	Serial No. Prefix
1966	AB
1967	AC
1968	AD

MAUSER BROOMHANDLES 1896 - late 1930

Serial # Range	Date	Nature of Changes
before	1896	-The cone hammer used in place of spur hammer.
#25-#50	1896	- "SYSTEM MAUSER" marked on top of the chamber.
before	1897	- The locking system changed from one to two lugs.
#200		- The barrel contour at the chamber is tapered instead of stepped.
#390	1897	- "WAFFENFABRIK MAUSER OBERNDORF A/N" marked on top of the chamber.
#975	1897	- The center section of the rear panel on the left side of the frame is not milled out (this feature appears earlier on a few 20-shot pistols). This area is sometimes used for special markings on contract pieces such as the Turkish and Persian.
#12,200 to #14,999		
	1898	- The large ring hammer replaces the cone hammer.
#21,000	1899	- There is no panel milling on either side of the frame.

Serial #
Range   Date   Nature of Changes

- A single lug bayonet type mount adopted for retaining the firing pin instead of the dovetail plate.
- The trigger is mounted directly to the frame by two integral lugs rather than attached to a removable block.
- The position of the serial number moved from the rear of the frame above the stock slot to the left side of the chamber.

#22,000   1900   - Two integral lugs used to mount the rear sight instead of a pin.

#29,000   1902   - Very shallow panels milled into the frame on both sides.*

#31,200   1903   - "WAFFENFABRIK MAUSER OBERNDORF A NECKAR" added to the right rear frame panel.*

#34,000   1904   - The depth of the frame panel milling increased.*

#35,000   1904   - The barrel extension side rails lengthened about a half inch.*

- An additional lug for mounting added to the firing pin.*
- The hammer changed to the small ring pattern.*
- The safety mechanism altered to require that the lever be pushed up to engaged it instead of down.*
- The center of the safety lever knob is no longer milled out.*

#38,000   1905   - The short extractor with two ribs replaces the long thin extractor.*

#100,000   1910   - The rifling changed from four groove to six groove.
to
#130,000   1911

#270,000   1915   - "NS" (Neues Sicherung or New Safety) appears on the back of the hammer. The hammer must be moved back beyond the cocked position to engage the safety.

#440,000   1921   - The lanyard ring stud is rotated 90 degrees.

#501,000   1923   - The Mauser "banner" appears on the left rear frame panel.

#800,000   1930   - The Mauser banner is enlarged.
- A step is added to the barrel contour just ahead of the chamber.
- The safety is changed to allow the hammer to be dropped from a cocked position, without danger, by pulling the trigger (called Universal Safety).
- The front of the grip frame widened to equal the rear part where the stock slot is.

#850,000   1932   - "D.R.P.u.A.P." (Deutsches Reich Patenten und Anderes Patenten) added below the inscription on the right rear frame panel.

#860,000   1932   - The lettering in the frame inscription is slanted forward.

#900,000   1934   - The serial number is moved to the rear of the barrel extension behind the sight.
- The two grooves in each side of the barrel extension side rails are eliminated.

These nine changes appear out of sequence (either early or late) on three small batches of guns (29,000 to 29,900, 40,000 to 41,000, and 42,600 to 43,900). Most of these pistols are of the "bolo" style, that is they have 3.9 inch barrels, small grips, six or 10-shot magazines and fixed or adjustable rear sights. A few of these pistols show non-standard barrel contours, barrel extension milling and hammer safety devices. Apparently the factory withheld these numbers from the regular production series and reissued them at later dates.

PARKER SHOTGUNS 1866 - 1942

Number	Date Serial
1866-1868	0-6,800
1868-1877	9,700
1877-1879	15,700
1880	17,600
1881	22,700
1882	27,300
1883	34,900
1884	36,000
1885	46,450
1886	48,125
1887	56,650
1889	59,500
1890	61,350
1891	66,800
1892	71,600
1893	77,000
1894	80,300
1895	82,400
1896	85,200
1897	86,450
1898	89,350
1899	92,450
1900	97,300
1901	105,750
1902	113,100
1903	121,900
1904	129,200
1905	132,000
1906	138,300
1907	144,250
1908	148,250
1910	153,000
1911	157,050
1912	157,800
1913	165,000
1914	168,200
1915	171,500
first year of Trojan grade	
1916	173,450
1917	175,650
first single barrel trap gun	
1918	180,250
1919	184,900
1920	190,100
1921	195,000
1922	200,500
first Parker single trigger	
1923	205,150
1924	207,150
first beaver tail forend	
1925	214,400
1926	218,050
first ventilated rib, first .410	
1927	222,650
1928	228,200
PH grade dropped	
1929	230,700
1930	234,200
1931	235,950
1932	236,100
1933	236,300
1934	236,650
first skeet guns, takeover of factory by Remington	
1935	237,000
1936	239,900
last regular catalog	
1937	240,300
1938-1942	242,385

REMINGTON

Firearms Serial Number Identification (Code located on barrel, left side at frame) Month of Manufacture (Code letter corresponds to numeral underneath)

B	L	A	C	K	P	O	W	D	E	R	X
1	2	3	4	5	6	7	8	9	10	11	12

Year of Manufacture and letter code

1921	M
1922	N
1923	P
1924	R
1925	S
1926	T
1927	U
1928	W
1929	X
1930	Y
1931	Z
1932	A
1933	B
1934	C
1935	D
1936	E
1937	F
1938	G
1939	H
1940	J
1941	K
1942	L
1943	MM
1944	NN
1945	PP
1946	RR
1947	SS
1948	TT
1949	UU
1950	WW
1951	XX
1952	YY
1953	ZZ
1954	A
1955	B
1956	C
1957	D
1958	E
1959	F
1960	G
1961	H
1962	J
1963	K
1964	L
1965	M
1966	N
1967	P
1968	R
1969	S
1970	T
1971	U
1972	W
1973	X
1974	Y
1975	Z
1976	I
1977	O
1978	Q
1979	V
1980	A
1981	B
1982	C
1983	D
1984	E
1985	F

Year of Manufacture and letter code

1986	G
1987	H
1988	I
1989	J
1990	K
1991	L
1992	M
1993	N
1994	0
1995	P
1996	Q
1997	R
1998	S
1999	T
2000	U
2001	W
2002	X

SAVAGE/STEVENS PRODUCTION DATA

The information below represents a listing of most Savage/Stevens rifles and shotguns mfg. in the past (some data has been approximated). Rather than list these models separately, they have been provided in this section for quick reference. Values on many of the models listed below typically range between $50 - $175, depending on rarity and condition.

SAVAGE

MODEL	DATES	APPROX. GUNS
1903	1912-20	13,000
1904	1912-32	62,000
1905	1912-15	6,500
1909	1912-15	3,500
1911	1912-15	22,500
1912	1913-15	12,000
1914	1914-26	49,500
19	1933-45	16,000
1920	1920-32	12,000
1922	1922-25	16,000
'23A	1924-45	88,000
'23B	1924-45	16,500
'23C	1924-42	14,500
'23D	1932-45	15,000
3	1931-45	121,000
4	1933-45	38,000
5	1936-45	22,000
6	1938-45	45,500
7	1939-45	6,000
40	1928-42	16,000
45	1928-42	6,000
1925	1925-32	36,000
29	1933-45	23,500
CS22	1926-45	87,500
219	1938-45	12,500
220	1937-45	50,000
420	1937-42	13,500
430	1937-42	11.000
1921	1921-32	13,000
1928	1928-32	6,500
721	1930-32	12,000
FOX	1933-45	31,000
FX B	1940-45	20,000

STEVENS

MODEL	DATES	APPROX. GUNS
No. 12	1912-35	166,500
14-1/2	1912-41	592,500
Fav.	1912-42	462,000
No. 26	1912-45	501,500
44+414	1912-35	23,000
No. 70	1912-31	295,500

MODEL	DATES	APPROX.GUNS
No. 71	1930-34	10,000
No. 75	1928-34	19,000
15+425	1912-17	11,500
No. 35	1912-19	12,500
No. 35	1923-42	43,000
41-43	1912-18	18,500
No. 10	1919-34	9,500
85-89	1912-42	38,500
No. 93	1912-19	12,500
No. 97	1912-19	16,000
No. 101	1914-20	5,000
No. 105	1912-45	221,500
No. 107	1912-45	443,500
106-08	1916-35	56,500
No. 115	1912-31	23,000
No. 124	1949-55	----
No. 125	1912-23	5,000
180-85	1912-23	16,000
No. 958	1925-33	5,000
116-17	1926-35	5,000
946-48	1928-34	7,000
No. 215	1913-32	61,000
No. 235	1912-32	61,500
No. 315	1914-36	192,000
No. 335	1912-31	67,500
No. 345	1916-31	3,500
No. 311	1926-45	145,500
No. 330	1926-35	33,500
No. 335	1926-35	2,000
No. 520	1912-32	191,000
No. 521	1930-32	5,000
60&61	1930-34	6,500
620-21	1926-45	66,500
Mod. 30	1933-34	26,000
Mod. 31	1933-34	2,000
No. 15	1936-45	224,000
No. 11	1923-33	141,500
No. 95	1926-35	55,000
No. 52	1933-37	88,000
No. 55	1935-36	3,500
No. 54	1933-42	23,500
No. 56	1933-45	97,500
No. 57	1939-42	500
No. 58	1933-45	29,500
No. 37	1936-42	29,000
No. 38	1936-45	33,500
No. 39	1938-45	64,000
No. 59	1938-45	21,000
No. 76	1938-45	6,000
65-66	1929-45	174,000
No. 82	1936-37	35,500
No. 83	1936-42	159,000
No. 84	1936-45	99,500
No. 85	1939-43	14,000
No. 86	1936-43	82,500
No. 87	1938-45	200,000
No. 872	1940-42	3,500
NO. 89	1926-37	12,000
No. 94	1926-45	934,000
No. 96	1926-33	3,500
No. 416	1937-42	2,000
No. 417	1932-42	1,000
No. 418	1932-42	1,500
No. 419	1932-36	1,000
No. 237	1936-43	16,000
No. 254	1936-42	1,000
No. 238	1936-45	40,000
No. 258	1936-45	11,000
102-04	1936-42	500
No. 116	1936-42	1,000
No. 944	1936-42	1,500
No. 600	1936-42	5,500
No. 900	1936-42	2,000

MODEL	DATES	APPROX.GUNS
No. 515	1936-42	500
No. 5151	1936-42	95,000
No. 530	1936-42	8,000
No. 500	1936-42	500
22-410	1939-45	105,000
M.240	1940-45	20,500

THE NINETY-NINE

Serial Numbers At Year End:

10,000	1899
13,400	1900
19,500	1901
25,000	1902
35,000	1903
45,000	1904
53,000	1905
67,500	1906
73,500	1907
81,000	1908
95,000	1909
110,000	1910
119,000	1911
131,000	1912
146,500	1913
162,000	1914
175,500	1915
187,500	1916
193,000	1917
-	1918
212,500	1919
229,000	1920
237,500	1921
244,500	1922
256,000	1923
270,000	1924
280,000	1925
292,500	1926
305,000	1927
317,000	1928
324,500	1929
334,500	1930
338,500	1931
341,000	1932
344,500	1933
345,800	1934
350,800	1935
359,800	1936
-	1937
381,351	1938
388,640	1939
398,400	1940
416,000	1941
438,000	1946
464,000	1947
494,000	1948
528,000	1949
566,000	1950

L.C. SMITH
SERIAL NUMBER RECORDS

Existing L.C. Smith shotgun records include:
Hunter Arms Company factory records circa 1890-1919,
Hunter Arms Company shipping records circa 1918-1946,
L.C. Smith Gun Company, 1946-1950 (FWS prefix), Marlin
Firearms Company, 1969-71 (FWS prefix).
For a factor letter on an older Marlin firearm, contact the
Buffalo Bill Historical center, Cody Firearms Museum, 720
Sheridan Ave. Cody, WY 82414. Web site www.bbhc.org
or phone 307-587-4771. There is a $45 fee per serial
number search.

WINCHESTER RIFLES

The following Winchester serial numbers appear courtesy of U.S. Repeating Arms, New Haven, CT. I would like to thank U.S. Repeating Arms and Mr. Pardee for making these production figures available.

Records at the factory indicate the following serial numbers were assigned to guns at the end of the calendar year

MODEL 1866

1866 -	12476 to 14813
67 -	15578
68 -	19768
69 -	29516
70 -	52527
71 -	88184
72 -	109784
73 -	118401
74 -	125038
75 -	125965
76 -	131907
77 -	148207
78 -	150493
79 -	152201
80 -	154379
81 -	156107
82 -	159513
1883 -	162376
84 -	163649
85 -	163664
86 -	165071
87 -	165912
88 -	167155
89 -	167401
90 -	167702
91 -	169003
92 -	NONE
93 -	169007
94 -	169011
95 -	NONE
96 -	NONE
97 -	169015
98 -	170100
99 -	DISCONTINUED

MODEL 1873

Year	Serial
1873 -	1 to 126
74 -	2726
75 -	11325
76 -	23151
77 -	23628
78 -	27501
79 -	41525
80 -	63537
81 -	81620
82 -	109507
83 -	145503
84 -	175126
85 -	196221
86 -	222937
87 -	225922
88 -	284529
89 -	323220
90 -	363220
91 -	405026
92 -	441625
93 -	466641
94 -	481826
95 -	499308
96 -	507545
97 -	513421
98 -	525922
99 -	541328

Year	Serial
1900 -	554128
01 -	557236
02 -	564557
03 -	573957
04 -	588953
05 -	602557
06 -	613780
07 -	NONE
08 -	NONE
09 -	630385
10 -	656101
11 -	669324
12 -	678527
13 -	684419
14 -	686510
15 -	688431
16 -	694020
17 -	698617
18 -	700734
19 -	702042
No last # available	
20, 21, 22, 23,	720609

MODEL 1876

Year	Serial
1876 -	1 to 1429
77 -	3579
78 -	7967
79 -	8971
80 -	14700
81 -	21759
82 -	32407
83 -	42410
1884 -	54666
85 -	58714
86 -	60397
87 -	62420
88 -	63539
89 -	NONE
90 -	NONE
91 -	NONE
92 -	63561
93 -	63670
94 -	63678
95 -	NONE
96 -	63702
97 -	63869
98 -	63871

MODEL 1885 SINGLE SHOT

1885 -	1 to 375
86 -	6841
87 -	18328
88 -	30571
89 -	45019
90 -	NONE
91 -	53700
92 -	60371
93 -	69534
94 -	NONE
95 -	73771
96 -	78253
97 -	78815
98 -	84700
99 -	85086
1900 -	88501
01 -	90424
02 -	92031
03 -	92359
04 -	92785
05 -	93611
06 -	94208
07 -	95743
08 -	96819

09 -	98097
10 -	98506
11 -	99012
12 -	NONE
13 -	100352

No further serial numbers were recorded until the end of 1923. Last No. known was: 139700

MODEL 1886

1886 -	1 to 3211
87 -	14728
88 -	28577
89 -	38401
90 -	49723
91 -	63601
92 -	73816
93 -	83261
94 -	94543
95 -	103708
96 -	109670
97 -	113997
98 -	119192
99 -	120571
1900 -	122834
01 -	125630
02 -	128942
03 -	132213
04 -	135524
05 -	138838
06 -	142249
07 -	145119
1908 -	147322
09 -	148237
10 -	150129
11 -	151622
12 -	152943
13 -	152947
14 -	153859
15 -	154452
16 -	154979
17 -	155387
18 -	156219
19 -	156930
20 -	158716
21 -	159108
22 -	159337

No further serial numbers were recorded until the discontinuance of the model which was in

1935 - at -	159994

MODEL 1887

1887 -	1 to 7431
88 -	22408
89 -	25673
90 -	29105
91 -	38541
92 -	49763
93 -	54367
94 -	56849
95 -	58289
96 -	60175
97 -	63952
98 -	64855

According to these records no guns were produced during the last few years of this model and it was therefore discontinued in 1901.

MODEL 1890

Records on the Model 1890 are somewhat incomplete. Our records indicate the following serial numbers were assigned to guns at the end of the calendar year beginning with 1908. Actual records on the firearms which were manufactured between 1890 and 1907 will be available from the

"Cody Firearms Museum", located at the "Buffalo Bill Historical Center"
Attn: Cody Firearms Museum
P.O. Box 1000,
Cody, WY 82414

1908 -	330000 to 363850
09 -	393427
10 -	423567
11 -	451264
12 -	478595
13 -	506936
14 -	531019
15 -	551290
16 -	570497
17 -	589204
18 -	603438
19 -	630801
20 -	NONE
21 -	634783
22 -	643304
23 -	654837
24 -	664613
25 -	675774
26 -	687049
27 -	698987
28 -	711354
29 -	722125
30 -	729015
31 -	733178
32 -	734454

The Model 1890 was discontinued in 1932, however, a clean up of the production run lasted another 8+ years and included another 14 to 15000 guns. Our figures indicate approximately 749,000 guns were made.

MODEL 1892

1892 -	1 to 23701
93 -	35987
94 -	73508
95 -	106721
96 -	144935
97 -	159312
98 -	165431
99 -	171820
1900 -	183411
01 -	191787
02 -	208871
03 -	253935
04 -	278546
05 -	315425
06 -	376496
07 -	437919
08 -	476540
09 -	522162
10 -	586996
11 -	643483
12 -	694752
13 -	742675
14 -	771444
15 -	804622
16 -	830031
17 -	853819
18 -	870942
19 -	903649
20 -	906754
21 -	910476
22 -	917300
23 -	926329
24 -	938641
25 -	954997
26 -	973896
27 -	990883

28 -	996517
29 -	999238
30 -	999730
31 -	1000727
32 -	1001324

MODEL 1894

Records at the factory, and in some years, estimates, indicate the following serial numbers were assigned to guns at the end of the calendar year.

1894 -	1 to 14579
95 -	44359
96 -	76464
97 -	111453
98 -	147684
99 -	183371
1900 -	204427
01 -	233975
02 -	273854
03 -	291506
04 -	311363
05 -	337557
06 -	378878
07 -	430985
08 -	474241
1909 -	505831
10 -	553062
11 -	599263
12 -	646114
13 -	703701
14 -	756066
15 -	784052
16 -	807741
17 -	821972
18 -	838175
19 -	870762
20 -	880627
21 -	908318
22 -	919583
23 -	938539
24 -	953198
25 -	978523
26 -	997603
27 -	1027571
28 -	1054465
29 -	1077097
30 -	1081755
31 -	1084156
32 -	1087836
33 -	1089270
34 -	1091190
35 -	1099605
36 -	1100065
37 -	1100679
38 -	1100915
39 -	1101051
40 -	1142423
41 -	1191307
42 -	1221289
43 -	No Record Available
44 -	No Record Available
45 -	No Record Available
46 -	No Record Available
47 -	No Record Available
48 -	1500000
49 -	1626100
50 -	1724295
51 -	1724295
52 -	1910000
53 -	2000000
54 -	2071100
55 -	2145296
56 -	2225000
57 -	2290296

58 -	2365887
59 -	2410555
60 -	2469821
61 -	2500000
62 -	2551921
63 -	2586000
*1964	2700000 - 2797428
65 -	2894428
66 -	2991927
67 -	3088458
68 -	3185691
69 -	3284570
70 -	3381299
71 -	3557385
72 -	3806499
73 -	3929364
74 -	4111426
75 -	4277926
75 -	4463553
76 -	4463553
77 -	4565925
78 -	4662210
1979 -	4826596
80 -	4892951
81 -	5024957
82 -	5103248

The post-64 Model 94 began with serial number 2,700,000.

Serial number 1,000,000 was presented to President Calvin Coolidge in 1927.

Serial number 1,500,000 was presented to President Harry S. Truman in 1948.

Serial number 2,500,000 and 3,000,000 were presented to the Winchester Gun Museum, now located in Cody, Wyoming.

Serial number 3,500,000 was not constructed until 1979 and was sold as auction in Las Vegas, Nevada.

Serial number 4,000,000 - whereabouts unknown at this time.

Serial number 4,500,000 - shipped to Italy by Olin in 1978. Whereabouts unknown.

Serial number 5,000,000 - in New Haven, not constructed as of March 1983.

Records at the factory indicate the following serial numbers were assigned to guns at the end of the calendar year.

MODEL 1895

1895 -	1 to 287
96 -	5715
97 -	7814
98 -	19871
99 -	26434
1900 -	29817
01 -	31584
02 -	35601
03 -	42514
04 -	47805
05 -	54783
06 -	55011
07 -	57351
08 -	60002
09 -	60951
10 -	63771
11 -	65017
12 -	67331
13 -	70823
14 -	72082
15 -	174233
16 -	377411
17 -	389106

18 -	392731
19 -	397250
20 -	400463
21 -	404075
22 -	407200
23 -	410289
24 -	413276
25 -	417402
26 -	419533
27 -	421584
28 -	422676
29 -	423680
30 -	424181
31 -	425132
32 -	425825

MODEL 1903

1903 -	# Not Available
04 -	6944
05 -	14865
1906 -	23097
07 -	31852
08 -	39105
09 -	46496
10 -	54298
11 -	61679
12 -	69586
13 -	76732
14 -	81776
15 -	84563
16 -	87148
17 -	89501
18 -	92617
19 -	96565
20 -	# Not Available
21 -	97650
22 -	99011
23 -	100452
24 -	101688
25 -	103075
26 -	104230
27 -	105537
28 -	107157
29 -	109414
30 -	111276
31 -	112533
32 -	112992

This model was discontinued in 1932, however, a clean up of parts was used for further production of approximately 2000 guns. Total production was stopped at serial number 114962... in 1936.

MODEL 1905

1905 -	1 to 5659
06 -	15288
07 -	19194
08 -	20385
09 -	21280
10 -	22423
11 -	23503
12 -	24602
13 -	25559
14 -	26110
15 -	26561
16 -	26910
17 -	27297
18 -	27585
19 -	28287
20 -	29113

MODEL 1906

1906 -	1 to 52278
07 -	89147

08 -	114138
09 -	165068
10 -	221189
11 -	273355
12 -	327955
13 -	381922
14 -	422734
15 -	453880
16 -	483805
17 -	517743
18 -	535540
19 -	593917
20 -	NONE
21 -	598691
22 -	608011
23 -	622601
24 -	636163
25 -	649952
26 -	665484
1927 -	679892
28 -	695915
29 -	711202
30 -	720116
31 -	725978
32 -	727353

A clean up of production took place for the next few years with a record of production reaching approximately 729305.

MODEL 1907

1907 -	1 to 8657
08 -	14486
09 -	19707
10 -	23230
11 -	25523
12 -	27724
13 -	29607
14 -	30872
15 -	32272
16 -	36215
17 -	38235
18 -	39172
19 -	40448
20 -	No # Available
21 -	40784
22 -	41289
23 -	41658
24 -	42029
25 -	42360
26 -	42688
27 -	43226
28 -	43685
29 -	44046
30 -	44357
31 -	44572
32 -	44683
33 -	44806
34 -	44990
35 -	45203
36 -	45482
37 -	45920
38 -	46419
39 -	46758
40 -	47296
41 -	47957
42 -	48275
43 -	NONE
44 -	NONE
45 -	48281
46 -	48395
47 -	48996
48 -	49684
**49 -	50662
**50 -	51640

**51 -	52618
**52 -	53596
**53 -	54574
**54 -	55552
**55 -	56530
**56 -	57508
**57 -	58486

** Actual records on serial numbers stops in 1948. The serial numbers ending each year from 1948 to 1957 were derived at by taking the last serial number recorded (58486) and the last number from 1948, (49684) and dividing the years of production (9), which relates to 978 guns each year for the nine year period.

MODEL 1910

1910 -	1 to 4766
11 -	7695
12 -	9712
13 -	11487
14 -	12311
15 -	13233
16 -	13788
17 -	14255
18 -	14625
19 -	15665
20 -	No # Available
21 -	15845
22 -	16347
23 -	16637
24 -	17030
25 -	17281
26 -	17696
27 -	18182
28 -	18469
29 -	18893
30 -	19065
31 -	19172
32 -	19232
33 -	19281
34 -	19338
35 -	19388
36 -	19445

A cleanup of production continued into 1937 when the total of the guns was completed at approximately 20786

MODEL 1911 S.L.

1911 -	1 to 3819
12 -	27659
13 -	36677
14 -	40105
15 -	43284
16 -	45391
17 -	49893
18 -	52895
19 -	57337
20 -	60719
21 -	64109
22 -	69132
23 -	73186
24 -	76199
25 -	78611

The Model 1911 was discontinued in 1925. However, guns were produced for three years after that date to clean up production and excess parts. When this practice ceased there were approximately 82774 guns produced.

MODEL 52

1920 -	None indicated
21 -	397
22 -	745

23 -	1394
24 -	2361
25 -	3513
26 -	6383
27 -	9436
28 -	12082
29 -	14594
30 -	17253
31 -	21954
32 -	24951
33 -	26725
34 -	29030
35 -	32448
1936 -	36632
37 -	40419
38 -	43632
39 -	45460
40 -	47519
41 -	50317
42 -	52129
43 -	52553
44 -	52560
45 -	52718
46 -	56080
47 -	60158
48 -	64265
49 -	68149
50 -	70766
51 -	73385
52 -	76000
53 -	79500
54 -	80693
55 -	81831
56 -	96869
57 -	97869
58 -	98599
59 -	98899
60 -	102200
61 -	106986
62 -	108718
63 -	113583
64 -	118447
65 -	120992
66 -	123537
67 -	123727
68 -	123917
69 -	E 124107
70 -	E 124297
71 -	E 124489
72 -	E 124574
73 -	E 124659
74 -	E 124744
75 -	E 124828
76 -	E 125019
77 -	E 125211
78 -	E 125315

This Model was discontinued in 1978. A small clean up of production was completed in 1979 with a total of - 125419.

MODEL 53

The Model 53 was serial numbered in both its' own series (1 to slightly over 15,000) as well as within the Model 1892 series. Early guns predominate the Model 53 serial number series with Model 1892 series serial numbers appearing more frequently mid to late production.

This Model was discontinued in 1932, however, a clean up of production continued for 9 more years.

1924 -	1 to 1488
25-	4350
26-	6882
27-	9180
28-	11139

29-	12873
30-	13794
31-	14416
32-	14623
33-	14727
34-	14817
35-	14976
36-	15047
37-	15078
38-	15092
39-	15099
1940-	15109
41-	15118

Total Production
Approximately - 24,916
Records at the factory indicate the following serial numbers were assigned to guns at the end of the calendar year.

MODEL 54

1925 -	1 to 3140
26 -	8051
27 -	14176
28 -	19587
29 -	29104
30 -	32499
31 -	36731
32 -	38543
33 -	40722
34 -	43466
35 -	47125
36 -	50145

MODEL 55 CENTERFIRE

1924 -	1 to 836
25 -	2783
26 -	4957
27 -	8021
28 -	10467
29 -	12258
30 -	17393
31 -	18198
32 -	19204
33 -	Clean up 20580

MODEL 61

1932 -	1 to 3532
33 -	6008
34 -	8554
35 -	12379
36 -	20615
37 -	30334
38 -	36326
39 -	42610
40 -	49270
41 -	57493
42 -	59871
43 -	59872
44 -	59879
45 -	60512
46 -	71629
47 -	92297
48 -	115281
49 -	125461
50 -	135461
51 -	145821
52 -	156000
53 -	171000
54 -	186000
55 -	200962
56 -	216923
57 -	229457
58 -	242992

59 -	262793
60 -	282594
61 -	302395
62 -	322196
63 -	342001

This Model was discontinued in 1963. For some unknown reason there are no actual records available from 1949 through 1963. The serial number figures for these years are arrived at by taking the total production figure of 342001, subtracting the last known # of 115281, and dividing the difference equally by the amount of remaining years available, (15).

MODEL 62

1932 -	1 to 7643
33 -	10695
34 -	14090
35 -	23924
36 -	42759
37 -	66059
38 -	80205
39 -	96534
40 -	116393
41 -	137379
42 -	155152
43 -	155422
44 -	155425
45 -	156073
46 -	183756
47 -	219085
48 -	252298
49 -	262473
50 -	272648
51 -	282823
52 -	293000
53 -	310500
54 -	328000
55 -	342776
56 -	357551
57 -	383513
58 -	409475

MODEL 63

1933 -	1 to 2667
34 -	5361
35 -	9830
36 -	16781
37 -	25435
38 -	30934
39 -	36055
40 -	41456
41 -	47708
42 -	51258
43 -	51631
44 -	51656
45 -	53853
46 -	61607
47 -	71714
48 -	80519
49 -	88889
50 -	97259
51 -	105629
52 -	114000
53 -	120500
54 -	127000
55 -	138000
56 -	150000
57 -	162345
58 -	174692

MODEL 70

1935 -	1 to 19

36 -	2238
37 -	11573
38 -	17844
39 -	23991
40 -	31675
41 -	41753
42 -	49206
43 -	49983
1944 -	49997
45 -	50921
46 -	58382
47 -	75675
48 -	101680
49 -	131580
50 -	173150
51 -	206625
52 -	238820
53 -	282735
54 -	323530
55 -	361025
56 -	393595
57 -	425283
58 -	440792
59 -	465040
60 -	504257
61 -	545446
62 -	565592
63 -	581471

All post 64 Model 70s began with the serial number 700,000.

1964 -	740599
65 -	809177
66 -	833795
67 -	869000
68 -	925908
69 -	G941900
70 -	G957995
71 -	G1018991
72 -	G1099257
73 -	G1128731
74 -	G1175000
75 -	G1218700
76 -	G1266000
77 -	G1350000
78 -	G1410000
79 -	G1447000
80 -	G1490709
81 -	G1537134

MODEL 71

1935 -	1 to 4
36 -	7821
37 -	12988
38 -	14690
39 -	16155
40 -	18267
41 -	20810
42 -	21959
43 -	22048
44 -	22051
45 -	22224
46 -	23534
47 -	25728
48 -	27900
49 -	29675
50 -	31450
51 -	33225
52 -	35000
53 -	37500
54 -	40770
55 -	43306
56 -	45843
57 -	47254

MODEL 74

1939 -	1 to 30890
40 -	67085
41 -	114355
42 -	128293
1943 -	NONE
44 -	128295
45 -	128878
46 -	145168
47 -	173524
48 -	223788
49 -	249900
50 -	276012
51 -	302124
52 -	328236
53 -	354348
54 -	380460
55 -	406574

MODEL 88

1955 -	1 to 18378
56 -	36756
57 -	55134
58 -	73512
59 -	91890
60 -	110268
61 -	128651
62 -	139838
63 -	148858
64 -	160307
65 -	162699
66 -	192595
67 -	212416
68 -	230199
69 -	H239899
70 -	H258229
71 -	H266784
72 -	H279014
73 -	H283718

MODEL 100

1961 -	1 to 32189
62 -	60760
63 -	78863
64 -	92016
65 -	135388
66 -	145239
67 -	209498
68 -	210053
69 -	A210999
70 -	A229995
71 -	A242999
72 -	A258001
73 -	A262833

WINCHESTER SHOTGUNS

Records at the factory indicate the following serial numbers were assigned to guns at the end of the calendar year.

MODEL 1897

1897 -	1 to 32335
98 -	64668
99 -	96999
1900 -	129332
01 -	161665
02 -	193998
03 -	226331
04 -	258664

Year	Ser. No.
05 -	296037
06 -	334059
07 -	377999
08 -	413618
09 -	446888
1910 -	481062
11 -	512632
12 -	544313
13 -	575213
14 -	592732
15 -	607673
16 -	624537
17 -	646124
18 -	668383
19 -	691943
20 -	696183
21 -	700428
22 -	715902
23 -	732060
24 -	744942
25 -	757629
26 -	770527
27 -	783574
28 -	769806
29 -	807321
30 -	812729
31 -	830721
32 -	833926
33 -	835637
34 -	837364
35 -	839728
36 -	848684
37 -	856729
38 -	860725
39 -	866938
40 -	875945
41 -	891190
42 -	910072
43 -	912265
44 -	912327
45 -	916472
46 -	926409
47 -	936682
48 -	944085
49 -	953042
50 -	961999
51 -	970956
52 -	979913
53 -	988860
54 -	997827
55 -	1006784
56 -	1015741
57 -	1024700

Records on this Model are incomplete. The above serial numbers are estimated from 1897 thru 1903 and again from 1949 thru 1957. The actual records are in existence from 1904 through 1949.

MODEL 1897 TRENCH/RIOT SHOTGUN

This information is provided by Mr. Pat Redmond, after many years of research and collecting. Reference a Winchester Repeating Arms Co. Memorandum dated September 1945. Trench, Riot, and Long Barrel Contract Dates 1/31/42 - 3/23/43, Contract Shipments 24829 shotguns.

Year	Ser. No's.	Type	Configuration
1937	902117-903762	Mil.	Long Barrel
1939	911788-911813	Mil.	Trench Gun
1940	914087	Com.	Trench Gun
1940	924312	Com.	Trench Gun
1941	920235-956126	Mil.	Trench Gun
1942	930537-956216	Mil.	Trench Gun
1943	956628	Mil.	Trench Gun

Year	Ser. No's.	Type	Configuration
1944	965482	Com.	Trench Gun
1944	966144	Com.	Trench Gun
1944	967371	Com.	Riot Gun
1949	993750	Com.	Riot Gun

MODEL 1901 SHOTGUN

Year	Ser. No.
1904 -	64,856 to 64,860
05 -	66453
06 -	67486
07 -	68424
08 -	69197
09 -	70009
10 -	70753
11 -	71441
12 -	72167
13 -	72764
14 -	73202
15 -	73509
1916 -	73770
17 -	74027
18 -	74311
19 -	74872
20 -	77000

MODEL 12

Year	Ser. No.
1912 -	5308
13 -	32418
14 -	79765
15 -	109515
16 -	136412
17 -	159391
18 -	183461
19 -	219457
20 -	247458
21 -	267253
22 -	304314
23 -	346319
24 -	385196
25 -	423056
26 -	464564
27 -	510693
28 -	557850
29 -	600834
30 -	626996
31 -	651255
32 -	660110
33 -	664544
34 -	673994
35 -	686978
36 -	720316
37 -	754250
38 -	779455
39 -	814121
40 -	856499
41 -	907431
42 -	958303
43 -	975640
44 -	975727
45 -	990004
46 -	1029152
47 -	1102371
48 -	1176055
49 -	1214041
50 -	1252028
51 -	1290015
52 -	1328002
53 -	1399996
54 -	1471990
55 -	1541929
56 -	1611868
57 -	1651435
58 -	1690999

59 -	1795500
60 -	1800000
61 -	1930999
62 -	1956990
63 -	1962001

A clean up of production took place from 64 through 66 with the ending serial # 1970875.

MODEL 12 TRENCH/RIOT SHOTGUN

This information is provided by Mr. Pat Redmond after many years of research and collecting. Reference a Winchester Repeating Arms Co. Memorandum dated September 1945. Trench/Riot and long barrel Contract Dates 4/1/42 - 3/21/44, Contract Shipments 61014 shotguns.

Blue Finish

Year	Ser. No's.	Type	Configuration
1941	926558--956504	Mil.	Riot & Long Barrel
1942	961934-1001014	Mil.	Trench/Riot/Long
1943	996899-1028856	Mil.	Trench & Riot

Parkerized Finish

1943	1030000-1035214	Mil.	Trench Gun
1944	1035458	Mil.	Trench Gun
1944	1035525	Mil.	Trench Gun
1946	1071586	Com.	Riot Gun
1949	1740610	Com.	Riot Gun

NEW STYLE M/12

1972 -	Y200 011-Y2006396
73 -	Y2015662
74 -	Y2022061
75 -	Y2024478
76 -	Y2025482
77 -	Y2025874
78 -	Y2026156
79 -	Y2026399

MODEL 24

1939 -	1 to 8118
40 -	21382
41 -	27045
42 -	33670
43 -	NONE RECORDED
44 -	33683
45 -	34965
46 -	45250
47 -	58940
48 -	64417

There were no records kept on this model from 1949 until its discontinuance in 1958. The total production was approximately 116280.

MODEL 42

1933 -	1 to 9398
34 -	13963
35 -	17728
36 -	24849
37 -	30900
38 -	34659
39 -	38967
40 -	43348
41 -	48203
42 -	50818
43 -	50822
44 -	50828
45 -	51168
46 -	54256
47 -	64853
48 -	75142
49 -	81107
50 -	87071
51 -	93038
52 -	99000
53 -	108201

54 -	117200
55 -	121883
56 -	126566
57 -	131249
58 -	135932
59 -	140615
60 -	145298
61 -	149981
62 -	154664
63 -	159353

MODEL 50

1954 -	1 to 24550
55 -	49100
56 -	73650
57 -	98200
58 -	122750
59 -	147300
60 -	171850
61 -	196400

WINCHESTER MODEL 101 SERIALIZATION

12 gauge

Ser. No.	Mfg. Mo.	Year
50,000	10	1959
50,500	3	1960
51,000	5	1960
51,500	6	1960
52,000	9	1961
52,500	3	1962
53,000	4	1962
53,500	5	1962
54,000	8	1962
54,500	9	1962
55,000	10	1962
55,500	12	1962
56,000	1	1963
56,500	2	1963
57,000	3	1963
57,500	3	1963
58,000	4	1963
58,500	5	1963
59,000	6	1963
59,500	6	1963
60,000	7	1963
60,500	8	1963
61,000	8	1963
61,500	11	1963
62,000	11	1963
62,500	11	1963
63,000	12	1963
63,500	1	1964
64,000	1	1964
64,500	2	1964
65,000	3	1964
65,500	3	1964
66,500	3	1964
67,000	5	1964
67,500	5	1964
68,000	5	1964
68,500	5	1964
69,000	6	1964
69,500	6	1964
70,000	7	1964
70,500	7	1964
71,000	8	1964
71,500	9	1964
72,000	9	1964
72,500	10	1964
73,000	10	1964
73,500	11	1964

Ser. No.	Mfg.Mo.	Year	Ser. No.	Mfg. Mo.	Year
74,000	11	1964	111,000	2	1968
74,500	12	1964	111,500	3	1968
75,000	12	1964	112,000	3	1968
75,500	1	1965	112,500	3	1968
76,000	2	1965	113,000	3	1968
76,500	2	1965	113,500	4	1968
77,000	3	1965	114,000	5	1968
77,500	4	1965	114,500	5	1968
78,000	4	1965	115,000	6	1968
78,500	4	1965	115,500	6	1968
79,000	4	1965	116,000	7	1968
79,500	4	1965	116,500	7	1968
80,000	5	1965	117,000	9	1968
80,500	6	1965	117,500	10	1968
81,000	6	1965	118,000	1	1969
81,500	6	1965	118,500	1	1969
82,000	6	1965	119,000	2	1969
82,500	8	1965	119,500	3	1969
83,000	8	1965	120,000	4	1969
83,500	8	1965	120,500	4	1969
84,000	9	1965	121,000	4	1969
84,500	9	1965	121,500	4	1969
85,000	10	1965	122,000	5	1969
85,500	10	1965	122,500	6	1969
86,000	10	1965	123,000	6	1969
86,500	10	1965	123,500	6	1969
87,000	10	1965	124,000	7	1969
87,500	10	1965	124,500	7	1969
88,000	11	1965	125,000	7	1969
88,500	11	1965	125,500	8	1969
89,000	11	1965	126,000	8	1969
90,000	12	1965	126,500	9	1969
90,500	12	1965	127,000	9	1969
91,000	12	1965	127,500	10	1969
91,500	1	1966	128,000	11	1969
92,000	1	1966	128,500	11	1969
92,500	2	1966	129,000	11	1969
93,000	2	1966	129,500	2	1970
93,500	2	1966	130,000	2	1970
94,000	3	1966	130,500	3	1970
94,500	3	1966	131,000	3	1970
95,000	5	1966	131,500	4	1970
95,500	5	1966	132,000	4	1970
96,000	6	1966	132,500	4	1970
96,500	7	1966	133,000	4	1970
97,000	7	1966	133,500	5	1970
97,500	7	1966	134,000	5	1970
98,000	8	1966	134,500	5	1970
98,500	8	1966	135,000	6	1970
99,000	9	1966	135,500	6	1970
99,500	9	1966	136,000	6	1970
100,000	10	1966	136,500	8	1970
100,500	10	1966	137,000	8	1970
101,000	10	1966	137,500	8	1970
101,500	11	1966	138,000	8	1970
102,000	11	1966	138,500	11	1970
102,500	12	1966	139,000	12	1970
103,000	1	1967	139,500	12	1970
103,500	1	1967	140,000	12	1970
104,000	2	1967	140,500	1	1971
104,500	3	1967	141,000	2	1971
105,000	4	1967	141,500	2	1971
105,500	5	1967	142,000	2	1971
106,000	5	1967	142,500	3	1971
106,500	5	1967	143,000	3	1971
107,000	9	1967	143,500	4	1971
107,500	10	1967	144,000	4	1971
108,000	10	1967	144,500	4	1971
108,500	11	1967	145,000	4	1971
109,000	11	1967	145,500	5	1971
109,500	11	1967			
110,000	12	1967			
110,500	1	1968			

20 gauge

Ser. No.	Mfg. Mo.	Year	Ser. No.	Mfg. Mo.	Year
200,000	3	1966	214,500	12	1968
200,500	3	1966	215,000	1	1969
201,000	3	1966	215,500	2	1969
201,500	3	1966	216,000	5	1969
202,000	4	1966	216,500	6	1969
202,500	4	1966	217,000	9	1969
203,000	4	1966	217,500	10	1969
203,500	5	1966	218,000	11	1969
204,000	6	1966	218,500	12	1969
204,500	6	1966	219,000	12	1969
205,000	7	1966	219,500	12	1969
205,500	8	1966	220,000	12	1969
206,000	8	1966	220,500	1	1970
206,500	8	1966	221,000	1	1970
207,000	9	1966	221,500	2	1970
207,500	9	1966	222,000	3	1970
208,000	9	1966	222,500	7	1970
208,500	12	1966	223,000	9	1970
209,000	2	1967	223,500	9	1970
209,500	7	1967	224,000	9	1970
210,000	10	1967	224,500	9	1970
210,500	12	1967	225,000	10	1970
			225,500	10	1970
			226,000	11	1970

28 ga. & .410 ga. added

Ser. No.	Mfg. Mo.	Year	Ser. No.	Mfg. Mo.	Year
211,000	1	1968	226,500	11	1970
211,500	1	1968	227,000	11	1970
212,000	10	1968	227,500	12	1970
212,500	10	1968	228,000	12	1970
213,000	10	1968	228,500	4	1971
213,500	11	1968	229,000	4	1971
214,000	12	1968	229,500	4	1971

PROOF MARKS

The proof marks shown below will assist in determining nationality of manufacturers when no other markings are evident. Since the U.S. has no proofing houses (as in England, France, Germany and other European countries), most U.S. manufacturers voluntarily proof their firearms with a specified style of proofmark (i.e. the interlocked WP[a] synonymous with the Winchester trademark can be fired using modern smokeless powder) shells. Pre-1850 European firearms oftentimes do not exhibit any commercial proof marks and with the exception of an occasional barrel address, they represent the single hardest bracket of firearms one can research properly. Captured weapons from major wars occasionally show 2 different nationalities of proofmarks. This is acceptable since the gun was proofed in a national proof house after original manufacture and again when the gun was exported[4] to a different country as a military acquisition. Please refer to the References section in this text for proofmark source information.

AUSTRIAN PROOF MARKS

PROOF MARK	CIRCA	PROOF HOUSE	TYPE OF PROOF and GUN
	since 1891	Vienna	provisional proof for multi barrel guns
	since 1891	Ferlach	provisional proof for multi barrel guns
	1829-1958	Vienna	black powder proof for multi barrel guns
	1829-1958	Ferlach	black powder proof for multi barrel guns
BH	since 1891	Bundesheer	preliminary proof for multi barrel guns
NB	1891-1928	Budapest	smokeless powder proof for parabellum pistols
NF	1891 to date	Ferlach	smokeless powder proof for parabellum pistols
NP	1891-1931	Ferlach	smokeless powder proof for parabellum pistols
NB	since 1891	Vienna	smokeless powder proof for parabellum pistols
NW	1891-1931	Weipert	smokeless powder proof for parabellum pistols

BELGIAN PROOF MARKS

PROOF MARK	CIRCA	PROOF HOUSE	TYPE OF PROOF and GUN
	since 1852	Belgium	provisional black powder proof for breech loading guns & rifled barrels
	-		double proof marking for unfurnished barrels
	-		triple proof provisional marking for unfurnished barrels
	since 1893	-	definitive black powder proof for breech loading guns, small bore guns & handguns
	since 1853	Perron	View stamp & inspectors mark for parabellum pistols
P.V	since 1924	-	Nitro proof for rifled barrel & parabellum pistols
R	since 1852	-	rifled arms defense for smokeless proof parabellum pistols
PV	-	-	Superior nitro proof

BRITISH PROOF MARKS - ENGLAND

PROOF MARK	CIRCA	PROOF HOUSE	TYPE OF PROOF and GUN
	since 1856	London	provisional proof for barrels
	since 1856	Birmingham	provisional proof for barrels
	since 1637	London	definitive black powder proof for shotguns, muzzle loader barrels
NP	since 1904	London	definitive nitro proof for all guns - parabellum pistols
BNP	since 1954	Birmingham	definitive nitro proof for barrel & action
BP	since 1904	Birmingham	black powder proof only for parabellum pistols

PROOF MARK	CIRCA	PROOF HOUSE	TYPE OF PROOF and GUN
GP	1868-1925	London	definitive special super power proof for parabellum pistols
SP	1868-1925	Birmingham	voluntary special black powder proof
R	1868-1925	London	reproof marking for black powder rifles
R	1868-1925	Birmingham	reproof marking for black powder rifles
BPC	1868-1925	Birmingham	definitive black powder proof for shotguns
NP	since 1904	Birmingham	definitive nitro proof for all guns
V	since 1670	London	view mark
BV	since 1904	Birmingham	view mark

FRENCH PROOF MARKS

PARIS HOUSE	ST ETIENNE HOUSE	CIRCA	TYPE OF PROOF and GUN
		since 1897	provisional proof unfinished short barreled guns
	ST ETIENNE	1897	standard proof for finished guns
	ST ETIENNE	1897	double proof finished & joined barrels
N.A.	N.A. ST ETIENNE	1897	single barrel proof for non-assembled guns
	F	1897	finished black powder guns
	S	1897	special proof for finished guns
	✕	1897	ordinary smokeless powder proof
	AR ST. ETIENNE	1897	superior smokeless powder proof

GERMAN PROOF MARKS

PROOF MARK	CIRCA	PROOF HOUSE	TYPE OF PROOF and GUN
	since 1952	Ulm	
	since 1968	Hannover	
	since 1968	Kiel (W. German)	
	since 1968	Munich	
	since 1968	Cologne (W. German)	
	since 1968	Berlin (W. German)	
FB	since 1952	W. German	voluntary proof for Flobert rifle
J	since 1952	W. German	repair proof for major gun parts
M	since 1952	W. German	provisional black powder for shotgun & multi barreled rifles
N	since 1952	W. German	definitive nitro proof for all guns
SP	since 1952	W. German	definitive black powder for smokeless ammo guns
	since 1952	W. German	Flobert for special purpose guns signal, flare, gas, & stun guns
N	since 1945	E. German, Suhl	smokeless powder proof
G	since 1950	E. German, Suhl	1st black powder proof for rifled barrels
N	since 1950	E. German, Suhl	nitro powder proof
R	since 1950	E. German, Suhl	repair proof
S	since 1950	E. German, Suhl	1st black powder proof for smooth bored barrels

PROOF MARK	CIRCA	PROOF HOUSE	TYPE OF PROOF and GUN
	since 1950	E. German, Suhl	inspection mark
	since 1950	E. German, Suhl	choke-bore barrel mark

ITALIAN PROOF MARKS

PROOF MARK	CIRCA	PROOF HOUSE	TYPE OF PROOF and GUN
	since 1951	Brescia	provisional proof for all guns
	since 1951	Gardone	provisional proof for all guns
	since 1951	Gardone & Brescia	definitive proof for guns with smokeless powder
	since 1951	Gardone & Brescia	finish proof for firearms ready for sale.
	since 1951	Gardone & Brescia	1st black powder proof

SPANISH PROOF MARKS

PROOF MARK	CIRCA	PROOF HOUSE	TYPE OF PROOF and GUN
	since 1910	Eibar	provisional black powder proof for shotguns
	since 1910	Eibar	temporary black powder proof for shotguns
	since 1910	Eibar	final black powder proof for breech loading shotguns
	since 1910	Eibar	final smokeless powder proof for breech loading shotguns
	since 1910	Eibar	re-enforced smokeless powder proof for breech loading shotguns
	since 1910	Eibar	provisional proof for shotguns
	since 1910	Eibar	final black powder proof for breech loading shotgun

PROOF MARK	CIRCA	PROOF HOUSE	TYPE OF PROOF and GUN
	since 1923	Eibar	final & single black powder proof for double barreled muzzle loading shotun
	since 1923	Eibar	final & single black powder proof for single barrel smooth bored breechloading guns
	since 1923	Eibar	final black powder proof for double barreled breechloading rifles
	since 1923	Eibar	final black powder proof for single barrel breechloading rifles
	since 1923	Eibar	re-enforced voluntary proof for single proof for single & double barrel shotguns
	since 1923	Eibar	Final proof of military-style rifle
	since 1923	Eibar	single & final proof of non-self loading pistols
	since 1923	Eibar	single & final proof for self loading pistols & revolvers
	since 1929	Eibar	admission proof for guns with old marks
	since 1929	Eibar	proof used in Barcelona for guns with old marks
	since 1929	Eibar	final proof for revolver
	since 1929	Eibar	proof for semi-automatic pistols
	since 1929	Eibar	special manufacturer's mark for guns made for foreign sales
	since 1929	Eibar	smokeless proof for shotgun barrels
	since 1929	Eibar	re-inforced smokeless proof for shotgun barrels

ATF GUIDE

A listing has been provided below of Field Division offices for the ATF. You are encouraged to contact them if you have any question(s) regarding the legality of any weapon(s) or their interpretation of existing laws and regulations. Remember, ignorance is no excuse when it involves Federal Firearms Regulations and Laws. Although these various offices may not be able to help you with state, city, county, or local firearms regulations and laws, their job is to assist you on a Federal level.

Atlanta Field Division
2600 Century Parkway,
Room 300
Atlanta, GA 30345
Phone No.: 404-417-2600

Baltimore Field Division
G.H. Fallon Bldg.
31 Hopkins Plaza, 5th Floor
Baltimore, MD 21201-2825
Phone No.: 410-779-1700

Boston Field Division
The Boston Federal Building
10 Causeway Street,
Room 253
Boston, MA 02222-1047
Phone No.: 617-557-1200

Charlotte Field Division
6701 Carmel Rd. #200
Charlotte, NC 28226
Phone No.: 704-716-1800

Chicago Field Division
300 S. Riverside Plaza,
Suite 350 S.
Chicago, IL 60606
Phone No.: 312-353-6935

Columbus Field Division
37 W. Broad St.
Suite 200
Columbus, OH 43215
Phone No.: 614-469-5303

Dallas Field Division
1114 Commerce St.
Room 303
Dallas, TX 75242
Phone No.: 469-227-4300

Detroit Field Division
1155 Brewery Park
Boulevard, Suite 300
Detroit, MI 48207-2602
Phone No.: 313-393-6000

Houston Field Division
15355 Ventage Parkway West,
Suite 200
Houston, TX 77032
Phone No.: 281-372-2900

Kansas Field Division
2600 Grand Avenue,
Suite 200
Kansas City, MO 64108
Phone No.: 816-559-0700

Los Angeles Field Division
350 S. Figueroa Street,
Suite 800
Los Angeles, CA 90071
Phone No.: 213-534-2450

Louisville Field Division
600 Martin Luther King Jr.
Place, Suite 322
Louisville, KY 40202
Phone No.: 502-753-3400

Miami Field Division
5225 NW 87th Avenue,
Suite 300
Miami, FL 33178
Phone No.: 305-597-4800

Nashville Field Division
5300 Maryland Way #200
Brentwood, TN 37027
Phone No.: 615-565-1400

National Licensing Center
P.O. Box 2994
Atlanta, GA 30301-2994
Phone No.: 404-417-2750

National Revenue Center
550 Main Street, Room 8002
Cincinnati, OH 45202-3263
Phone No: 800-398-2282

New Orleans Field Division
Heritage Plaza, Suite 1050
111 Veterans Boulevard
Metarie, LA 70005
Phone No.: 504-841-7000

Philadelphia Field Division
US Custom House,
Room 607
Philadelphia, PA 19016
Phone No.: 215-597-7266

Phoenix Field Division
3003 North Central Avenue
Suite 1010
Phoenix, AZ 85012
Phone No.: 602-776-5400

San Francisco Field Division
221 Main St, Suite 1130
San Francisco, CA 94105
Phone No.: 415-947-5100

2002 - SHOW TIME - 2003

During the course of a year, we get many requests about which upcoming trade/gun shows we'll be attending. If you want to hook up with Steve, John and related troops through 2002, here's where we'll be. At these shows we will be displaying all of our publications, in addition to using our state-of-the-art interactive display to actively demonstrate our critically acclaimed e-commerce solution providing anyone with access to the world wide web to download sections of the Blue Book of Gun Values database.

GOOD INFORMATION NEVER SLEEPS!

April 11-13, 2002
EXA
Brescia, Italy
Attending Only

April 26-28, 2002
The 131st NRA
Annual Meetings & Exhibits Show
Reno-Sparks Convention Center
Contact: NRA
Ph.800-694-9300
www.nra.org

June 29-30, 2002
Duluth Gun Show
Duluth Entertainment Convention Center
South Pioneer Hall
Sat. 9-5pm. Sun. 9-3pm.
$5.00 admission
Contact: Bob White
1920 Greysolon Rd
Duluth, MN 55812
Ph.218-724-8387
Fax:218-724-8740

July 26-28, 2002
32nd Annual Kansas City National Summer Arms
Show & 7th NRA Gun Collectors Show
K.C.I. Expo-Center
Kansas City, MO
Contact: MVACA Show Committee
P.O. Box 33033
Kansas City, MO 64114
Ph. 913-642-2863

October 3-6, 2002
23rd Annual Colt Collectors Association, Inc.
(All Colt only Show)
Radisson Austin Hotel
Austin, TX
Contact: Dick Burdick
Ph.805-644-8731
www.coltcollectorsassoc.com

October 19-20, 2002
Tulsa Gun & Knife Show
at Expo Center - Expo Square
Tulsa Fairgrounds
Sat. 8-7pm, Sun. 8-5pm

Contact: Tulsa Gun Show, Inc.
P.O. Box 33201
Tulsa, OK 74153-1201
Ph.918-492-0401
www.tulsagunshow.com
mail@tulsagunshow.com

November 21-23, 2002
NASGW
Fort Worth Convention Center
Fort Worth, TX
Attending Only

March 14-17, 2003
IWA
Exhibition Centre Nuremberg (NurnbergMesse)
Nuremberg, Germany
Attending Only

January 16-18, 2003
Antique Arms Show & International Sporting Arms
Show
Riviera Hotel
Las Vegas, NV
Contact: Wallace Beinfeld Productions, L.L.C.
P.O. Box 2231
Palm Springs, CA 92263
Wallace Beinfeld - Show Director
Ph. 760-320-5389 FAX 760-320-5231
www.antiquearmsshow.com
gunshowpro@aol.com

February 13-16, 2003
SHOT Show 25th Annual
Trade Show only-no consumers
Orange County Convention Center
Orlando, FL

April 5-6, 2003
Tulsa Gun & Knife Show
at Expo Center - Expo Square
Tulsa Fairgrounds
Sat. 8-7pm, Sun. 8-5pm
Contact: Tulsa Gun Show, Inc.
P.O. Box 33201
Tulsa, OK 74153-1201
Ph.918-492-0401
www.tulsagunshow.com
mail@tulsagunshow.com

INDEX

INDEX

INDEX

INDEX

INDEX

INDEX

INDEX

INDEX

INDEX

INDEX

P.S.

So you know where there are a few dinosaurs left, were lucky enough to draw a hunting tag from the DNR, and have already purchased your T-rex, no scent camo hunting outfit. Don't be under calibered - this is the gun for you! Szecsei & Fuchs Fine Guns GmbH, well known for its high quality SxS double barrel repeaters, rifles and shotguns, also produced this giant dino slayer. Austrian Gerhard Fuchs is holding a prototype bolt action O/U Model SSS (Szecsei Sevenhundred Safari) double rifle in .700 NE cal. (1,000 grain bullet). The jumbo titanium double bolt quickly opens up both chambers, and the side magazine (on left of receiver) makes sure that if 4 shots are needed (and you're still standing), it's possible. Don't be embarrassed of flinching big time if you need a fifth. $100+ a round, and the kicks are for free!